MR '87

FOR REFERENCE

Do Not Take From This Room

The New Grove Dictionary of

American Music

Volume One

The New Grove Dictionary of
American Music

Volume One

A-D

Edited by

H. Wiley Hitchcock

and

Stanley Sadie

Editorial Coordinator

Susan Feder

MACMILLAN PRESS LIMITED, LONDON
GROVE'S DICTIONARIES OF MUSIC INC., NEW YORK, NY

© Macmillan Press Limited 1986

All rights reserved.
No part of this publication may be reproduced or transmitted,
in any form or by any means,
without permission.

The New Grove Dictionary of American Music
edited by H. Wiley Hitchcock and Stanley Sadie, in four volumes, 1986

First published 1986 by the Macmillan Press Limited, London.
In the United States of America and Canada, the Macmillan Press has appointed
Grove's Dictionaries of Music Inc., New York, NY, as sole distributor.

Parts of this dictionary were first published in
The New Grove Dictionary of Music and Musicians ®
edited by Stanley Sadie, in twenty volumes, 1980
© Macmillan Publishers Limited 1980
and
The New Grove Dictionary of Musical Instruments
edited by Stanley Sadie, in three volumes, 1984
© Macmillan Press Limited 1984

The New Grove and *The New Grove Dictionary of Music and Musicians*
are registered trademarks of Macmillan Publishers Limited, London

Library of Congress Cataloging in Publication Data

The New Grove dictionary of American music.
Includes bibliographies
1. Music—United States—Dictionaries.
2. Music—United States—Bio-bibliography.
I. Hitchcock, H. Wiley (Hugh Wiley), 1923–
II. Sadie, Stanley
ML101.U6N48 1986 781.773'03'21 86-404
ISBN 0-943818-36-2 (set)

British Library Cataloguing in Publication Data

The New Grove dictionary of American music.
1. Music—United States—Dictionaries
I. Hitchcock, H. Wiley II. Sadie, Stanley
781.773'03'21 ML100
ISBN 0-333-37879-2

Typeset by Edwards Brothers Inc., Ann Arbor, MI, USA
Music examples processed by Halstan & Co. Ltd, Amersham, England

Printed and bound in Hong Kong

Contents

Editors
H. Wiley Hitchcock
Stanley Sadie

Editorial Coordinator
Susan Feder

Principal Advisers
Edward A. Berlin
Horace Clarence Boyer
William Brooks
Raoul Camus
Richard Crawford
Vernon Gotwals
George N. Heller
Cynthia Adams Hoover
Michael Hovland
Bill C. Malone
Paula Morgan
Helen Myers
Pauline Norton
Carol J. Oja
Paul Oliver
William Osborne
J. Bradford Robinson
John Rockwell
Deane L. Root
Patrick J. Smith
Susan Thiemann Sommer
Eileen Southern
Judith Tick

Preface

GROVE AND AMERICA. The idea of a specifically American *Grove* is not new. In 1920 the Macmillan Company of America, seeking to repair the relative neglect of the music and musicians of the United States in the existing editions of *Grove's Dictionary of Music and Musicians*, published an American Supplement to the second (1904–10). In this, under the editorship of Waldo Selden Pratt, an account was given of the musical traditions of the United States – mainly those of concert and church music – in chronological and lexicographical form. This supplement was revised in 1928 and many times reprinted into the 1950s.

The New Grove Dictionary of Music and Musicians (1980) does not by any means overlook American traditions. Yet, even as a fully international dictionary, it retains a firm base in European musical and cultural traditions. Indeed, one percipient reviewer of *The New Grove* noted that, despite the very large contribution made by American scholarship to that dictionary, and its significantly higher content on American topics than its predecessors, it nevertheless did not reflect "the essence of American music." It was partly in recognition of this that from the earliest days of work on *The New Grove*, at the beginning of the 1970s, the possibility was contemplated of following it with a dictionary of American music that would be based on a different cultural model, of a more pluralistic character than that of Europe, and without the same foundation in ecclesiastical, aristocratic, and state patronage.

This idea was all the more attractive since there exists no other reference work on the music of the United States that is comprehensive in approach, academically sound, and written by a team of specialists. It is this lacuna that the present work aims to fill. It strives to cover the music of the United States not only in greater detail than has been done in the past but, more particularly, in greater cultural depth. By this we mean that, in addition to the acknowledged (and, in the past, relatively well-served) traditions of American music that correspond to those of European art music, we aim to treat others of special significance in American life – for example, jazz, popular music of all kinds (including musical theater and popular song, rock, camp-meeting and gospel hymnody, country and dance music), the music of many of the religious denominations active in the United States, and the music of American Indian tribes.

When we began giving serious consideration to these issues, and drawing together a team of specialist advisers to help us deal with them properly, it quickly became clear that our initial plan for the dictionary – as a one-volume work expanding and supplementing material already included in *The New Grove* – was inadequate to the purpose of a comprehensive dictionary of American music. Our intention of updating *New Grove* material and adding to it about as much again gave way to plans for revision of that material in terms of a different context, for recommissioning a great deal of it, and for supplementing it not by an equal number of new articles but by approximately three times as many – not only on individuals but on many other topics germane to the specific character of American musical traditions.

It may be helpful to spell out, with a little exemplification, some aspects of the relationship between the present work and *The New Grove*. Let us take, for example, the field of popular music. *The New Grove* includes a substantial article of international scope under the heading "Popular music" and a modest number of entries on individual musicians in that field. The present work has not only an extensive article "Popular music" (by one of the authors of the *New Grove* entry) but also many other separate subject articles concerned with subspecies of popular music and, further, a large number of entries on a wide range of popular musicians. Analogously, while *The New Grove* includes a substantial article on the music of North American Indians, the present work includes not only an updated version of that article but also a series of individual articles treating the distinct traditions of close to 40 North American tribes or tribal groups. Our entries on American cities (more than twice as many as in *The New Grove*) deal not only with the development within them of music of the cultivated tradition but also with significant traditions of vernacular music. In a rather different way, the American approach will be seen in our entries on musical scholars, whose smaller-scale studies, or writings on non-American music, though often referred to in the texts of entries, do not have the claim here for detailed itemization that they do in a work of the international scholarly scope of *The New Grove*.

CONTENT, SCOPE. What is "American music"? In the sense we use it here, it comprehends first of all the music made in the United States, by Americans; more ambiguous is the situation regarding music written by foreign composers who retain their national identity while living in the USA. Analogous to them are conductors, singers, and instrumentalists who settle in the United States or pay it prolonged visits. The other side of that coin is the American musician who makes his or her career abroad, and often settles there. In the former cases, we have had to weigh the importance of such visitors to the United States in terms of their contributions to the musical life of the country and include them (or not) in the dictionary accordingly. Americans abroad remain Americans, and likewise have a claim to consideration in our pages. If we have erred, we hope it is on the side of inclusiveness.

This is not a general dictionary of music; it is a dictionary of American music. It does not, for example, include entries on a complete range of musical terminology or of instruments, such as might be found in a comprehensive music dictionary; it does, however, include such terminology and such instruments as have a particular meaning or occupy a particular place in American music. Our entry "Banjo" concerns an instrument that is specifically an American creation; our entry "Bass viol" treats an instrument quite different from the European bass viol; and our entry "Organ" deals with specifically American traditions of constructing that instrument, which has of course a direct European counterpart.

Attention may usefully be drawn to groups of articles on topics that a reader may not take for granted in a dictionary of music (as opposed, for instance, to articles on composers, performers, and so on). There are, for example, entries on patriotic and political music; there are entries on special aspects of the "patronage" of music (awards, festivals, etc.) in addition to individual patrons; there are entries relating to the music industry (copyright, trade unions, etc.); there are entries on the bibliography of American music and on its discography, as well as on the impact of sound recordings in general; and there are entries on aspects of American musical life with significant traditions of their own (we are referring to matters as diverse as the history of orchestras, tuning systems, and music criticism in the United States). Repertories of American music are considered under such headings as "Chamber music" and "Choral music"; where appropriate these also take account of the institutions that have cultivated the genre. Entries will also be found on people who, not themselves musicians, have made contributions that bear on American music: literary figures, impresarios and stage directors, lyricists, and administrators of various kinds; and there are entries on music publishers and makers of musical instruments.

Numerous musical institutions – societies, college and university departments, conservatories, etc. – have individual entries; those within cities that are entered in the dictionary in their own right, especially orchestras, choirs, opera companies, and bands, are normally discussed within the appropriate city entry (indicated by a cross-reference if necessary), since they represent a part of that city's musical life.

Even as regards composers and performers, the dictionary does not, and could not, aim at completeness – it does not attempt to include every known American composer of the past and present. In accordance with *Grove* traditions, it is a critically organized repository of historically significant information, not a directory; that is a role served by other kinds of reference work. We have however tried particularly hard to give generous representation to the music of the present day, covering the widest possible spectrum from avant-garde and experimental music, including the work of performance artists, to the latest developments in jazz and rock. Theoretical aspects of contemporary music, including electroacoustic and computer music, are of course included.

It is appropriate to mention at this point that the two editors of this dictionary, while happily collaborating – at a distance of 3000 miles – have filled somewhat distinct roles: the first-named has been concerned chiefly with the detailed content of the dictionary, the second with applying to the present work many aspects of the lexicographical experience gained with *The New Grove.*

ACKNOWLEDGMENTS. The preparation of a reference work of this kind involves, in accordance with the traditions of *Grove* dictionaries, a large-scale and extended collaboration among many authors, most of them the leading authorities on the topics they are treating, numerous advisers, and a team of editors, as well as administrative, clerical, publishing, and printing staff. It is not possible in these pages to acknowledge everyone who contributed to the dictionary, and we can only apologize to those who are not mentioned individually. Our first thanks, however, must go to the people who wrote the dictionary: the contributors, close to a thousand in number, whose names, together with the titles of the articles they wrote, are listed at the end of Volume 4. Many of them have provided help well beyond the normal obligations of scholarly cooperation by assisting us in numerous ways, for example by drawing our attention to additional material worthy of inclusion, by warning us of sources of error, and by helping us keep our entries up to date. And there are others besides contributors who have generously provided such assistance.

Advisers. In the early stages of the planning of this dictionary, help was enlisted from a number of specialists as advisers on particular subject areas. American composers of the cultivated tradition were the concern of the first-named of the editors, whose general planning was rounded out by Richard Crawford (the Colonial and Federal eras), William Brooks (the 19th century), and John Rockwell (20th-century experimental music). For the various vernacular traditions, besides William Brooks and John Rockwell (who helped us on figures of, respectively, the 19th century and the rock era), our advisers included Edward A. Berlin (ragtime), Horace Clarence Boyer (black gospel music), Raoul Camus (band music), Bill C. Malone (country music), Paul Oliver (blues), J. Bradford Robinson (jazz), and Deane L. Root (popular genres). Susan Thiemann Sommer was our principal adviser on the coverage of cities, musical institutions, and bibliographical topics. On musical instruments and their makers we were assisted by Cynthia Adams Hoover. Helen Myers was our adviser on native American and other ethnic traditions. Patrick J. Smith helped us in the preparation of our coverage of 20th-century performers, with additional advice from Vernon Gotwals and William Osborne on organists (historical as well as present-day); he also, with John Rockwell, assisted Paula Morgan on writers about music. Michael Hovland advised on literary figures important to American music and George N. Heller on music educators. Pauline Norton helped plan the material on dance. To ensure proper representation for two categories of person whose contributions have been especially important in American musical culture, we sought advice from Eileen Southern (on Blacks) and Judith Tick and Carol J. Oja (on women).

In many specialized areas, additional counsel was needed; we are particularly grateful for the help given by Charlotte J. Frisbie and Bruno Nettl on ethnic traditions, by Barry Kernfeld and James Patrick on jazz, and by Leonard Burkat, J. Bunker Clark, Robert Commanday, Elizabeth Forbes, the late Irving Lowens, Philip Lieson Miller, Andrew Porter, and the late Boris Schwarz on performers. Among the numerous others – some of them contributors, some not – whose assistance invites, for one reason or another, particular acknowledgment, we would name the following: Dee Baily, Mary Wallace Davidson, Charles Dodge, Paul C. Echols, Gary-Gabriel Gisondi, D. W. Krummel, Dennis K. McIntire, Barbara A. Petersen, Katherine K. Preston, Emile H. Serposs, John Shepard, and James Wierzbicki.

Editors. The huge task of coordinating the editorial preparation of this dictionary was undertaken by Susan Feder, whose achievement in mastering and controlling its editorial and administrative systems, in maintaining happy and productive relations between contributors and staff, and in nursing the dictionary at all stages from the initial gleam in its editors' eyes into four large volumes, cannot be too highly praised or too extravagantly acknowledged. Without her at the heart of its organization, the dictionary could never have come into being, and we are deeply and gratefully conscious of the intellectual energy, the professional skills, and the personal commitment which she brought to this often trying and sometimes ungrateful role.

The office editorial staff was headed by Rosemary Roberts and Jane Aspden, both of whom also contributed generously to editorial planning and were invaluable in the shaping of many complex articles; Jane Aspden in addition played a critical role in the dictionary's production. Other senior editors were Caroline Richmond, Ruth Thackeray, Julie Halitsky, Laura McCann, Fred Kameny, J. Bradford Robinson, and Helen Myers. Others involved in the editorial preparation of the dictionary included Anthony Marks (who had responsibility for music examples), Carl Skoggard, Louise Bloomfield, Nancy Toff, Sarina Turner, and Adele Poindexter Evidon. Helen Ottaway was illustrations editor. Our team of research assistants, headed by R. Allen Lott and Emily Good, included Elizabeth Wright, Mark Stevens, and Stephen Davison; in this sphere we are also indebted to the staff of the Institute for Studies in American Music at Brooklyn College, City University of New York. Administrative support was provided by Linda Powell and Nancy Shavick, along with Nancy Pardo of the Institute for Studies in American Music. The dictionary's computer management system was devised and maintained by Doug Bruce, Jr., of the William Byrd Press, Richmond, Virginia.

Many institutions in American musical life provided assistance; we are particularly grateful for the contributions of the Performing Arts Research Center (especially the Music Division) of the New York Public Library, the Music Division of the Library of Congress, the American Music Center, and ASCAP, as we are to the many individual librarians who responded to our calls for help. Acknowledgments to the copyright holders of illustrations and music examples are to be found at the end of each volume.

Finally, we should like to acknowledge the role of the publishers, the Macmillan Press Ltd. of London, who have retained their faith throughout in our ability to see this project through, even when it grew, as such dictionaries do, well beyond the boundaries initially conceived for it; and above all the contribution of Alyn Shipton (Music Publisher), without whose energy and commitment the dictionary could never have reached publication.

H. Wiley Hitchcock (New York)

Stanley Sadie (London)

March 1986

Introduction

1. Alphabetization. 2. Usages. 3. Authors. 4. Article headings. 5. Article definitions. 6. Article structure. 7. Cross-references. 8. Transliteration. 9. Work-lists. 10. Recording-lists, discographies. 11. Bibliographies.

1. ALPHABETIZATION. Entries are ordered alphabetically according to their headings – fully explained in §4 below – which are read as if continuous, ignoring spaces, hyphens, ampersands, apostrophes, accents, modifications, and diacritical marks; German *ä*, *ö*, and *ü* are read as *a*, *o*, and *u*, not as *ae*, *oe*, and *ue*. These rules apply up to the comma, then again thereafter (except in the case of composite names of companies, where the comma is ignored). Where two entire headings are identical but for an accent or the like, the unmodified heading is placed first. Parenthesized letters and words, and square-bracketed matter, are ignored in alphabetization. "St." is alphabetized as "Saint" and the prefixes "Mac" and "Mc" as "Mac"; "Dr." is alphabetized as "Doctor," "Mr." as "Mister." Headings containing numerals are ordered as though the numerals were spelled out. Some of these points are illustrated by the following (partly hypothetical) sequence of headings:

Sahm, Doug
Sainte-Marie, Buffy
St. Louis
Salchow, William
S. Allman & Sons
San Antonio
Sandburg, Carl
Sanders, Pharoah
Sanders, Samuel
Sanderson, Sibyl
Sanderson, MacKenzie & Co.
San Diego
San [Saint] Difuso
Sándor, Arpad
Sandor, György
Sándor, György
Sanford, Sam(uel)
Sanford, Samantha
San Francisco
Sankey, Ira

As a very general principle, we have tried to place each entry where the majority of users of the dictionary will expect to find it. Common sense and established usage are important factors.

2. USAGES. In the editing of this dictionary every effort has been made to achieve consistency in presentation. Usages in such matters as italicization and capitalization will become evident (as far as that is necessary) to readers of the dictionary and do not need explanation here. It should however be said that orthography and terminology follow American practices; the editorial style largely follows that of *The New Grove* (*Grove* 6) and *The New Grove Dictionary of Musical Instruments* (*GroveI*). Abbreviations are confined to those listed on pp.xviii–xxix (pp.vii–xviii in later volumes).

Some of the editorial usages in the dictionary are explained below:

Dates. Methods of citing dates that are approximate or conjectural are outlined in §4 below. Here it should be mentioned that when a period is expressed in the form "*c*1830–48" the dates

1830 and 1848 are both approximate, whereas the form "*c*1830–1848" means that only the first is.

Pitch notation. The system used is a modified version of Helmholtz's: middle C is *c'*, with octaves above as *c''*, *c'''*, etc., and octaves below as *c*, *C*, *C'*, *C''*, etc. Octaves are reckoned from C upwards. Italic type is used for specific pitches; pitch-classes are given in roman capital letters.

Place names. In article texts, names of states (USA) and provinces (Canada) are given if there is a risk of confusion between two places with the same name; for places outside the USA and Canada country names are given where this may be helpful. For present-day cities, the usage of *The Times Atlas of the World* (New York, 1983 edn) is followed, except for those cities where there is a traditional and universally applied English name that differs from the local one (e.g., Vienna, Rome, Munich). Where a city's name has changed in the course of history, an attempt has been made to call it by the name current at the time under discussion; on its initial appearance in an entry its present-day name is given as well if that seems to be necessary or helpful (e.g., "Pressburg [now Bratislava]"). Occasionally common sense demands a little flexibility in the application of this rule (e.g., in the case of "Puerto Rico," at one time "Porto Rico," we consistently use the modern form). (For practices followed in article headings see §4.)

Institutional names. These are given according to the correct title at the time under discussion; for example, references before 1946 to what is now the Juilliard School are to the Institute of Musical Art or the Juilliard Graduate School.

Titles. In article texts, titles of works are italicized unless they are descriptive or generic (e.g., Nocturne, Symphony no. 1); excerpts from larger works, when discussed as such, are printed in roman type in quotation marks (e.g., "Maria" from *West Side Story*).

Weights and measures. To conform with international practice and with the declared policy of the United States government, metric units are used in this dictionary (except for conventional usage and in quoted matter). Metricization has in fact proceeded slowly, and we ask the indulgence of readers who are surprised to read that (say) Memphis is 620 km from Louisville.

Population figures. These are taken from the 1980 Census of Population of the US Bureau of the Census.

Charts. References to "charts" are to the popularity charts published in *Billboard*.

3. AUTHORS. The names of authors appear, in the form each has chosen, at the ends of the articles to which they apply. Where authorship is joint or multiple, this is indicated, and the contribution of each author is shown by reference to the numbered sections of the article. Where two or more names appear, separated only by a comma, the entire authorship is joint or the contributions are fused to a degree where it would be impractical to show how responsibility was divided. A signature of the form

JOHN DOE/MARY BROWN

indicates that an article originally by John Doe (normally it will be an article from *Grove* 6 or *GroveI*) has been revised and updated by Mary Brown;

JOHN DOE/R

signifies editorial revision and updating of such an article, or the deletion of material irrelevant to this dictionary. A signature of the form

JOHN DOE (with MARY BROWN)

means that John Doe is the principal author but Mary Brown contributed material that the author or the editors of the dictionary felt was appropriate for acknowledgment. A signature of the form

JOHN DOE (after *Grove* 6)

means that John Doe has substantially modified material from the *Grove* 6 article to suit the needs of this dictionary.

Unsigned articles are of two main kinds: those that are too short for acknowledgment to be appropriate, and those that are contributed by a group of editors working collectively. In a few cases an article is left unsigned at the request of the author.

4. ARTICLE HEADINGS. Articles on persons begin with their name and place and date of birth and death:

Doe, John (*b* Boston, MA, 1 Jan 1800; *d* St. Louis, MO, 31 Dec 1870).

Parentheses and brackets in name headings have specific meanings:

Doe, John (Robert) – full name "John Robert Doe"; "Robert" not normally used
Doe, John R(obert) – full name "John Robert Doe," normally used in the form "John R. Doe"
Doe [Dowe], **John** – the name "Doe" sometimes takes the form "Dowe"; or "Dowe" is an earlier family spelling of the name "Doe"
Doe, John [Jack] – John Doe is sometimes known as "Jack"
Doe, John [Dowe, Johann] – the entire name sometimes takes the form "Johann Dowe"; or "Johann Dowe" is an earlier family spelling of the name "John Doe"
Doe, John [Brown, Thomas] – "John Doe" is the pseudonym or stage name under which Thomas Brown is generally known; or John Doe used the pseudonym or stage name "Thomas Brown" (this is made clear in the text)
Doe, Bobbie [John Andrew] – "Bobbie Doe" is the name under which John Andrew Doe is generally known
Doe [née Brown], **Mary** – "Doe" is Mary Brown's married name, under which she is generally known
Doe [Brown], **Mary** – Mary Doe has the married name or pseudonym "Brown"; or Mary Brown is generally known under the name "Doe" (this is made clear in the text)
Brown, Mrs. [Mary] – Mary Brown was known professionally as "Mrs. Brown."

Figures known by a sobriquet that cannot be interpreted as consisting of a surrogate forename and surname are entered under the first element of the name (e.g., Dr. John, Muddy Waters, Taj Mahal).

When three or more members of a family merit entries, they are grouped in a "family" article, entered under the family surname. Each member is numbered, thus:

Doe. Family of composers.
(1) **John Doe** (*b* . . . [etc.]
(2) **Robert Doe** (*b* . . . [etc.]
(3) **Mary Doe** (*b* . . . [etc.]

If two people bear the same name (which for this purpose means the same name in bold type, excluding parenthesized matter), that name is always followed by a parenthesized lower-case roman numeral, chronologically determined (e.g., John Doe (i)), and is normally used in this form throughout the dictionary. Generally persons entered in the dictionary are referred to only by their last names unless this leads to ambiguity.

Articles dealing with groups of people (such as performing ensembles and families of publishers) are normally found under their corporate name. Where a single member of a group or family has an important independent career, this may be dealt with in a separate article on the member.

Places and dates of birth and death are given where they are known; where nothing is known nothing is stated. For places in the USA, except for the city of New York, state names are given, in abbreviated form, and for places in Canada provinces are given, in abbreviated form (see pp.xviii–xxii for these abbreviations). For places outside the USA and Canada, country names are given. Where dates of baptism and burial are given, dates of birth and death are unknown. If the year but not the month or day of birth is known, that is indicated in the form

(*b* Boston, MA, 1800; *d* St. Louis, MO, 31 Dec 1870).

According to the state of knowledge, the date of birth may be given with less precision: for example, "1800–05" (at some time between those years), "*c*1800" (around that year), or "?1800" (to signify conjecture). The question mark is placed close to the statement it qualifies; where it is spaced, it qualifies the series of statements that follows:

(*b* ?Boston, MA, 1 Jan 1800 . . .) – born, conjecturally in Boston
(*b* Boston, MA, ?Jan 1800 . . .) – born in Boston in 1800, conjecturally in January
(*b* Boston, MA, ?1800 . . .) – born in Boston, conjecturally in 1800
(*b* ? Boston, MA, 1800 . . .) – born, conjecturally in Boston, conjecturally in 1800
(*b* Boston, MA, 1 Jan ?1800 . . .) – born in Boston, on 1 January, conjecturally in 1800
(*b* Boston, MA, 1 ?Jan 1800 . . .) – born in Boston, on the first day of a month, conjecturally January, in 1800.

Where a birthdate cannot be conjectured, *fl* (*floruit*: "he or she flourished") dates may be given, e.g., "*fl* 1825," "*fl* 1820–35," "*fl* early 19th century," etc. Any other forms used in such contexts are self-explanatory.

5. ARTICLE DEFINITIONS. All articles begin with a statement defining or describing the subject. Articles on people begin with a statement of nationality, if other than American, and a description. A person is regarded as American if he or she at any time took American citizenship or was naturalized; reference to a person's immigration, taking of citizenship, or naturalization is normally made in the text. Sometimes, where non-American affiliation seems of special importance, it is noted: "Conductor of Russian descent." The word or words of description outline the subject's musical significance – essentially the reason for his or her being entered in the dictionary. Someone who is noted as a composer but engages in other activities is not normally described as (for example) "composer, conductor, writer on music, teacher, and pianist": supplementary activities may be referred to in the text. Articles on genres, terms, instruments, etc., normally begin with a definition of the subject and may continue with a statement of the terms of reference of the article, in which attention is drawn to its specifically American subject matter; where no such statement is included (in articles on genres of American origin, for example) it should be understood.

6. ARTICLE STRUCTURE. The longer article texts in the dictionary are divided into sections for ease of reference. The most usual division is into sections numbered with arabic numerals and having headings in large and small capitals (e.g., 1. LIFE, 2. WORKS); this method is used in many entries on composers. Sections of this kind may be subdivided into smaller ones, numbered with parenthesized lower-case roman numerals and having headings in italics. Occasionally other forms of subdivision are needed. Where a long entry consists of two or more substantial sections, these sections are numbered with capital roman numerals and the headings are printed in bold italic type. The following illustrates all three levels of the hierarchy, as well as the lists of "contents" which are designed to guide the reader to the material he is seeking:

Gospel music. [general definition]

I. White gospel music. II. Black gospel music.

I. White gospel music

1. Gospel hymnody and American revivalism: (i) General (ii) The Sunday-school era, 1840–75 (iii) The Moody–Sankey era, 1875–1910 (iv) The Sunday–Rodeheaver era, 1910–30 (v) Modern urban revivalism, 1930–80. 2. Gospel music and the popular commercial tradition. 3. Performance styles.

1. GOSPEL HYMNODY AND AMERICAN REVIVALISM

(i) General. Although gospel hymnody has developed stylistic diversity . . .

7. CROSS-REFERENCES. Cross-references in the dictionary are distinguished by the use of small capitals, with a large capital for the initial letter of the entry referred to, for example:

see CAGE, JOHN.

If the reference is in running prose it takes the form

> he was a pupil of JOHN CAGE.

All cross-references give the title of the article referred to in exactly the wording in which it appears, in bold type (but excluding parenthesized matter), at the head of the entry. The word "see" is always italicized in a cross-reference to another entry in the dictionary; where it is printed in roman type the reference is to a different part of the same entry, or to another publication.

Cross-references are of two basic kinds. First, there are those cross-reference entries that direct the reader to where he can find the entry he is seeking, thus:

> **Tomlinson, Arthur.** Pseudonym of CHARLES T. GRIFFES.

Simple cross-references have been included in abundance to help the reader who first looks under a different orthography or formulation:

> **Chatianov, Samuel.** *See* CHOTZINOFF, SAMUEL.

Many cross-reference entries include, for the benefit of the reader who does not require fuller information (or to distinguish usages of a term), a brief definition, thus:

> **Abenaki** [Abnaki]. American Indian tribe of the WABANAKI confederacy.
>
> **Rice University.** Institution of higher education founded in Houston in 1892. Its music department, the Shepherd School of Music, sponsors many musical activities in the city. *See* HOUSTON, §2(i).

Such a cross-reference may lead to two or more other entries.

The other type of cross-reference is that within articles. Some are placed at the ends of short articles, or at the ends of sections, directing the reader to another entry where further information relevant to the subject may be found; these may, as appropriate, embody such formulae as "*see also*" or "for a fuller discussion *see*." Many further cross-references are found in running text; but none is provided to an entry (name, place, genre, etc.) that would be expected to appear in this dictionary unless there is particular material to which attention needs to be drawn. The intention is to direct the reader to places where he or she can, but might not have expected to, find further information on the topic which is first looked up. Thus the article "Musical theater" need not contain cross-references to the entries on Victor Herbert or Stephen Sondheim, although those of course contain material relevant to the history of musical theater; it does however carry cross-references to entries on related forms or subgenres (for example "Minstrelsy" and "Ballad opera") which are separately considered.

Where an illustration, table, or music example is relevant to more than one entry, that is indicated by a cross-reference.

8. TRANSLITERATION. The transliteration of Cyrillic script in this dictionary follows the system used in *Grove* 6, with certain exceptions that arise from standard American practice: for example, Balanchine, Chaliapin, Fokine, Glière, Mussorgsky, Piatigorsky, Rachmaninoff, and Scriabin.

9. WORK-LISTS. Work-lists are designed to show a composer's output and to serve as a starting-point for its study. The aim has always been to supply complete lists of works, even if in summarized form; where a list is selective, this is noted. Every effort has been made to include works composed up to 1984. Withdrawn works and juvenilia are not normally cited except in lists for major composers. An attempt has been made to include basic publication information and, in the case of manuscript material, locations: for music of the 17th to 19th centuries, place and date of first publication are given (later printings are referred to only if of particular significance), and, for 20th-century music, the names of a composer's principal publishers. Any parenthesized date in a work-list is a date of publication. Locations of manuscript material are normally given by means of abbreviations (always printed here in italics) taken from *Symbols of American Libraries* (Washington, DC, rev. 12/1980); those used in the dictionary are listed on pp.xxvi–xxix in this

volume, pp.xv–xviii in later volumes. Manuscript locations are not generally supplied when material is published.

Work-lists are normally categorized, by genre, function, or medium, and items listed chronologically within categories. Numbers from established listings are normally given. Titles may be given in short form; alternative titles are parenthesized. A statement of the genre may be given, often (especially in the case of experimental music) in the wording used by the composer. For dramatic works, a parenthesized arabic numeral following the title denotes the number of acts. Names in parentheses are those of text authors (or sources), librettists, book authors, or lyricists for vocal works, of choreographers for dance music. Where a key is named, it precedes the details of instrumentation; capital letters denote major keys, lower-case minor. Alternative instrumentation is denoted by a slash (/) or, in complex cases, by a slash and parentheses: "Qt, A, (pf, fl/ob, cl, bn)/(pf, str trio)." Instrumental doubling is denoted by a plus sign: "fl + a fl + pic." For voices, abbreviations separated by commas denote soloists, and those printed continuously represent a choral group; thus "S, A, Bar, SATB" stands for soprano, alto, and baritone soloists with a chorus of soprano, alto, tenor, and bass. Information may be given in less specific form: "3 solo vv, 4vv" means that the work is for three soloists and four-part chorus. Unless they are parenthesized (when they constitute information on publication), places and dates following dates of composition are those of first performance.

Editions that include a substantial number of works are cited at the heads of work-lists (or sections of them); often they are assigned abbreviations, appended in square brackets, which are noted, with volume and page numbers if appropriate, against the relevant items in the list. Smaller editions, and editions of individual works or groups of works in modern anthologies or collections, are cited alongside particular entries (such citations may refer to a work listed in the bibliography of the article, e.g., "ed. in Doe (1950)"). Individual items in a work-list may be referred, by abbreviation, to a list of publications above. Any abbreviation found in a work-list and not in the abbreviations list at the beginning of each volume is explained at the head of the list (or section of the list) concerned.

10. RECORDING-LISTS, DISCOGRAPHIES. Selective lists of recordings are provided for composers whose music is preserved chiefly in recorded media; they aim to give a representative survey of the subject's output. This applies especially to jazz and popular music. A recording-list as well as a work-list is provided only in exceptional cases (e.g., Duke Ellington, Jelly Roll Morton, Robert Ashley). A recording-list is not normally provided for a performer or group who recorded only material composed by others, though certain exceptions are made for prominent figures such as Elvis Presley and Frank Sinatra.

Original issues are cited in preference to reissues and collections of hits. Citations normally consist of the following information: title of album, single, or EP, and details of recording and/or issue, given in parentheses (abbreviations used for the names of record labels are explained on p.xxiii in this volume, p.xii in later volumes). Italic type denotes an album title, roman type a single or EP title (the latter is noted as such). Where an album contains a single track to which attention should be drawn, it is noted thus:

Thriller (Epic 38112, 1982), incl. Human Nature

A date that precedes citation of record label and issue number is a date of recording (such dates are normally given for jazz recordings); one that follows is a date of issue. Lists using recording dates are ordered chronologically, both from year to year and within each year; lists using issue dates are ordered chronologically by year and alphabetically within each year. (These procedures are determined by the state of research on popular music: recordings by popular, rock, and country-music performers are less well documented than jazz recordings, and the precise chronology of recording and issue is often not established.) Prefixes and suffixes to issue numbers are omitted unless required to identify recordings uniquely.

Recording-lists may be categorized by function (e.g., "As leader," "As sideman," "As soloist"), recording format ("LPs," "Singles"), type of ensemble ("Big band," "Combo"), genre, or period. In the sideman category the name of the bandleader precedes the title of the recording on which the subject appears as sideman, thus:

As sideman: O. Coleman: *Free Jazz* (1960, Atl. 1477)

Any one leader's name stands until canceled by the next.

Selective discographies are normally provided for articles on American Indian peoples. They consist of commercially issued recordings; other important collections of recorded material are cited in the texts of articles, not in discographies.

11. BIBLIOGRAPHIES. Many articles in the dictionary are followed by bibliographies, which in general have been supplied by authors. They normally include studies on which authors have drawn as well as recommended reading. Bibliographies are not intended to represent complete lists of the literature on the topic. General histories of music or of American music (or of specific periods, etc.) are not normally cited unless they contain material of special importance or are a principal source of information on the topic or person in question. For figures on whom little or nothing has been published in scholarly literature, ephemeral items such as magazine and newspaper articles are often cited. English-language sources are normally favored over those in foreign languages.

Bibliographies are chronologically arranged; items are listed in order of first publication (chronologically within categories for a bibliography that is categorized, as most longer ones are). Items published in the same year are listed alphabetically by author, or, for the same author, by title. At the head, however, certain standard works of reference may be listed in abbreviated form, in alphabetical order of abbreviation.

The procedures of citation are broadly speaking self-evident, but it may nevertheless be helpful to outline here the main principles (the reader is also referred to the list of bibliographical abbreviations on pp.xxiv–xxv in this volume, pp.xiii–xiv in later volumes, and especially its prefatory note). The place and date of first American publication are normally given where the date does not differ significantly from that of a first edition published elsewhere. For books that have appeared in several editions, only the first and the most recent are cited, unless there is particular reason to note intermediate editions – for example, because one was revised or translated, or one has been photographically reprinted (which is denoted by *R*). Thus, while "1950, 4/1958" is a common form of citation, "1950, 2/1951/*R*1978, rev. 3/1955, 4/1958" is also possible, to signify that the second edition was reprinted and the third substantially revised. Places of publication are normally given only for first publication. Title-page breaks and punctuation (other than commas) may be represented by a colon. Multi-volume books are not noted as such, but (unless they are through-paginated) specific references within them include the volume number, in lower-case roman numerals. Lower-case roman numerals always, in bibliographical contexts, denote volume numbers, as for periodicals: "xiv (1950), 123" indicates that the cited article begins on page 123 of volume xiv, published in 1950. When periodicals are reckoned by issue rather than volume, arabic numerals are used. For periodicals not through-paginated by volume, the fascicle number within the volume is indicated after a slash (e.g., "xiv/3"). For long articles, of 30 or more pages, a terminal page number is given. Doctoral dissertations are noted as "diss." and the institution is named, with the date of acceptance. If the dissertation is published, the citation may refer only to the published volume; in a full citation, the place and date of publication follow, thus: "(diss., Ohio State U., 1975; Ann Arbor, MI, 1979)." Other unpublished works are dated, where possible, and provided with an abbreviation identifying the library where they may be found (for the use of abbreviations see §9 above). Liner notes are identified as such, and the discographical citations conform with the principles outlined in §10 above.

Lists of writings (and of editions) found in entries on scholars, critics, composers, and others are organized according to the same principles. Such lists are as a rule selective and limited to publications in book form. Items listed as "ed.:" are edited by the subject; items listed as "ed. J. Doe:" are works by the subject edited, usually posthumously, by J. Doe. Fuller lists of the subject's writings may be noted in the bibliography.

General Abbreviations

A — alto, contralto [voice]
a — alto [instrument]
AA — Associate of the Arts
AB — Bachelor of Arts
ABC — American Broadcasting Company
ABI — Alexander Broude, Inc.
ACA — American Composers Alliance
acc. — accompaniment, accompanied (by)
AD — anno Domini (Lat.: in the year of our Lord)
addl — additional
addn — addition
ad lib — ad libitum (Lat.: at pleasure)
AK — Alaska
AL — Alabama
Alb. — Alberta (Canada)
a.m. — ante meridiem (Lat.: before noon)
amp — amplified
AMS — American Musicological Society
anon. — anonymous(ly)
appx — appendix
AR — Arkansas
arr. — arrangement, arranged (by/for)
ARSC — Association for Recorded Sound Collections
AS — American Samoa
ASCAP — American Society of Composers, Authors and Publishers
attrib. — attribution, attributed (to)
Aug — August
aut. — autumn
AZ — Arizona

B — bass [voice]
B — Brainard catalogue [of G. Tartini's works]
b — bass [instrument]
b — born
BA — Bachelor of Arts
Bar — baritone [voice]
bar — baritone [instrument]
BBC — British Broadcasting Corporation
BC — British Columbia (Canada)
BC — before Christ
bc — basso continuo
BEd — Bachelor of Education
BFA — Bachelor of Fine Arts
BLitt — Bachelor of Letters; Bachelor of Literature
BM — Bachelor of Music
BME; BMEd — Bachelor of Music Education
BMI — Broadcast Music, Inc.
BMus — Bachelor of Music
bn — bassoon
Bros. — Brothers
BS — Bachelor of Science
BSM — Bachelor of Sacred Music
BWV — Bach-Werke-Verzeichnis [Schmieder, catalogue of J. S. Bach's works]

c — circa (Lat.: about)
¢ — cent(s)
CA — California
cb — contrabass [instrument]
CBC — Canadian Broadcasting Corporation
CBE — Commander of the Order of the British Empire
cbn — contrabassoon
CBS — Columbia Broadcasting System; CBS, Inc.
cel — celesta
cf — confer (Lat.: compare)
CFE — Composers Facsimile Edition
chap. — chapter
Chin. — Chinese
chit — chitarrone
Cie — Compagnie (Fr.: Company)
cimb — cimbalom
cl — clarinet
clvd — clavichord
CM — Northern Mariana Islands (US Trust Territory of the Pacific Islands)
cm — centimeter(s)
CNRS — Centre National de la Recherche Scientifique (France)
CO — Colorado

Co.	Company; County
col.	column
coll.	collection, collected (by)
collab.	(in) collaboration (with)
comp.	compiler, compiled (by)
conc.	concerto
cond.	conductor, conducted (by)
cont	continuo
Corp.	Corporation
CPE	Composer/Performer Edition
c.p.s.	cycle(s) per second
cptr	computer
CRI	Composers Recordings, Inc.
CT	Connecticut
Ct	countertenor
CUNY	City University of New York
Cz	Czech
D	Deutsch catalogue [of F. Schubert's works]; Dounias catalogue [of G. Tartini's works]
d	died
d.	denarius, denarii (Lat.: penny, pence [sterling])
DA	Doctor of Arts
Dan.	Danish
db	double bass
DBE	Dame Commander of the Order of the British Empire
DC	District of Columbia
DE	Delaware
Dec	December
ded.	dedication, dedicated (to)
Dept	Department
DFA	Doctor of Fine Arts
dir.	director, directed (by)
diss.	dissertation
DLitt	Doctor of Letters; Doctor of Literature
DM	Doctor of Music
DMA	Doctor of Musical Arts
DME; DMEd	Doctor of Music Education
DMus	Doctor of Music
DMusEd	Doctor of Music Education
DPhil	Doctor of Philosophy
Dr.	Doctor
DSc	Doctor of Science; Doctor of Historical Sciences
DSM	Doctor of Sacred Music
ed.	editor, edited (by)
EdD	Doctor of Education
edn	edition
EdS	Education Specialist
e.g.	exempli gratia (Lat.: for example)
elec	electric, electronic
EMI	Electrical and Musical Industries
Eng.	English
eng hn	english horn
ens	ensemble
EP	extended-play (record)
esp.	especially
etc.	et cetera (Lat.: and so on)
ex., exx.	example, examples
f	following (page)
f	forte
f.	folio
facs.	facsimile
fasc.	fascicle
Feb	February
ff	following (pages)
ff	fortissimo
ff.	folios
fff	fortississimo
fig.	figure [illustration]
FL	Florida
fl	flute
fl	floruit (Lat.: he/she flourished)
fp	fortepiano
Fr.	French
frag.	fragment
GA	Georgia
Ger.	German
Gk.	Greek
glock	glockenspiel
GU	Guam
gui	guitar
H	Hoboken catalogue [of J. Haydn's works]
Heb.	Hebrew
HI	Hawaii
HMV	His Master's Voice
hn	horn
Hon.	Honorary
hpd	harpsichord
Hung.	Hungarian
Hz	Hertz [cycle(s) per second]
IA	Iowa
ibid.	ibidem (Lat.: in the same place)
ID	Idaho
i.e.	id est (Lat.: that is)
IFMC	International Folk Music Council
IL	Illinois
IN	Indiana
Inc.	Incorporated
inc.	incomplete
incl.	includes, including
inst	instrument, instrumental
IRCAM	Institut de Recherche et de Coordination Acoustique/Musique (France)
ISAM	Institute for Studies in American Music
ISCM	International Society for Contemporary Music
It.	Italian
Jan	January
Jap.	Japanese
Jb	Jahrbuch (Ger.: yearbook)
JD	Doctor of Jurisprudence
Jg.	Jahrgang (Ger.: year of publication, volume)
Jr.	Junior

K	Köchel catalogue [of W. A. Mozart's works; number following a / is from the 6th edn]
kbd	keyboard
KBE	Knight of the Order of the British Empire
kHz	kilohertz [1000 cycles per second]
km	kilometer(s)
KS	Kansas
KY	Kentucky
L	Longo catalogue [of D. Scarlatti's works]
£	libra, librae (Lat.: pound, pounds [sterling])
LA	Louisiana
Lat.	Latin
lb	libra (Lat.: pound [weight])
lib.	libretto
LLB	Bachelor of Laws
LLD	Doctor of Laws
LP	long-play (record)
Ltd.	Limited
M.	Monsieur
MA	Massachusetts; Master of Arts
MALS	Master of Arts in Library Science
Man.	Manitoba (Canada)
mand	mandolin
mar	marimba
MAT	Master of Arts and Teaching
MB	Bachelor of Music
MD	Maryland; Doctor of Medicine
ME	Maine
MEd	Master of Education
Mez	mezzo-soprano
mf	mezzo-forte
MFA	Master of Fine Arts
MGM	Metro-Goldwyn-Mayer
MI	Michigan
mic	microphone
MIT	Massachusetts Institute of Technology
MLA	Music Library Association
MLitt	Master of Letters; Master of Literature
Mlle.	Mademoiselle
MLS	Master of Library Science
MM	Master of Music
M.M.	Metronom Maelzel (Ger.: Maelzel's metronome) [tempo indication showing number of notes of a given value per minute]
mm	millimeter(s)
MMA	Master of Musical Arts
MME	Master of Music Education
Mme.	Madame
MMEd	Master of Music Education
MMT	Master of Music in Teaching
MMus	Master of Music
MN	Minnesota
MO	Missouri
mod	modulator
movt	movement
mp	mezzo-piano
MPhil	Master of Philosophy
MS	Mississippi; manuscript; Master of Science(s)
Msgr.	Monsignor
MSLS	Master of Science in Library and Information Science
MSM	Master of Sacred Music
MSS	manuscripts
MT	Montana
MusB; MusBac	Bachelor of Music
MusD; MusDoc	Doctor of Music
MusM	Master of Music
nar	narrator
NB	New Brunswick (Canada)
NBC	National Broadcasting Company
NC	North Carolina
ND	North Dakota
n.d.	no date (of publication)
NE	Nebraska
NEA	National Endowment for the Arts
NEH	National Endowment for the Humanities
Nfld	Newfoundland (Canada)
NH	New Hampshire
NJ	New Jersey
NM	New Mexico
no.	number
Nor.	Norwegian
Nov	November
n.p.	no place (of publication)
n.pub.	no publisher
nr	near
NS	Nova Scotia (Canada)
NV	Nevada
NWT	North West Territories (Canada)
NY	New York (state)
ob	oboe
obbl	obbligato
Oct	October
OH	Ohio
OK	Oklahoma
Ont.	Ontario (Canada)
op.	opus (Lat.: work)
op. cit.	opere citato (Lat.: in the work cited)
opp.	opera (Lat.: works)
opt.	optional
OR	Oregon
orch	orchestra, orchestral
orchd	orchestrated (by)
org	organ
orig.	original(ly)
ORTF	Office de Radiodiffusion-Télévision Française (France)
OUP	Oxford University Press
ov.	overture
P	Pincherle catalogue [of A. Vivaldi's works]
p	piano
p.	page
PA	Pennsylvania

p.a.	per annum (Lat.: by the year, annually)
PBS	Public Broadcasting System
PEI	Prince Edward Island (Canada)
perc	percussion
perf.	performance, performed (by)
pf	piano(forte)
pfmr	performer
PhB	Bachelor of Philosophy
PhD	Doctor of Philosophy
PhDEd	Doctor of Philosophy in Education
pic	piccolo
pl.	plate; plural
p.m.	post meridiem (Lat.: after noon)
PO	Philharmonic Orchestra
Pol.	Polish
pop.	population
Port.	Portuguese
posth.	posthumous(ly)
POW	prisoner of war
pp	pianissimo
pp.	pages
ppp	pianississimo
PR	Puerto Rico
pr.	printed
prol.	prologue
Ps.	Psalm
pseud.	pseudonym
Pss.	Psalms
pt.	part
ptbk	partbook
pubd	published (by)
pubn	publication
Que.	Quebec (Canada)
qnt	quintet
qt	quartet
R	(editorial) revision [in signature]
R	Ryom catalogue [of A. Vivaldi's works]
R	photographic reprint
r	recto
RAI	Radio Audizioni Italiane (Italy)
RCA	Radio Corporation of America; RCA Corporation
rec	recorder
rec.	recorded
recit	recitative
red.	reduction, reduced (for)
repr.	reprinted
Rev.	Reverend
rev.	revision, revised (by)
RI	Rhode Island
RILM	Répertoire International de Littérature Musicale
RISM	Répertoire International des Sources Musicales (Germany)
RKO	Radio-Keith-Orpheum
RO	Radio Orchestra
Rom.	Romanian
r.p.m.	revolution(s) per minute
Rt Hon.	Right Honourable
Russ.	Russian
S	soprano [voice]
S.	San, Santa
$	dollar(s)
s	soprano [instrument]
s.	solidus, solidi (Lat.: shilling, shillings [sterling])
Sask.	Saskatchewan (Canada)
sax	saxophone
SC	South Carolina
SD	South Dakota
Sept	September
ser.	series
sf, *sfz*	sforzando, sforzato
sing.	singular
SO	Symphony Orchestra
Sp.	Spanish
spr.	spring
sq.	square
Sr.	Senior
SSR	Soviet Socialist Republic
St.	Saint
STB	Bachelor of Sacred Theology
str	string(s)
sum.	summer
SUNY	State University of New York
suppl.	supplement, supplementary
Swed.	Swedish
sym.	symphony, symphonic
synth	synthesizer, synthesized
T	tenor [voice]
t	tenor [instrument]
ThM	Master of Theology
timp	timpani
TN	Tennessee
tpt	trumpet
Tr	treble [voice]
tr	treble [instrument]
trad.	traditional
trans.	translation, translated (by)
transcr.	transcription, transcribed (by/for)
trbn	trombone
TT	Trust Territory
TX	Texas
U.	University
UCLA	University of California, Los Angeles
UHF	ultra-high frequency
UK	United Kingdom of Great Britain and Northern Ireland
unacc.	unaccompanied
unattrib.	unattributed
UNESCO	United Nations Educational, Scientific and Cultural Organization
unorchd	unorchestrated
unperf.	unperformed
unpubd	unpublished
UP	University Press
US	United States [adjective]
USA	United States of America
USO	United Service Organizations

USSR	Union of Soviet Socialist Republics
UT	Utah
v	voice
v	verso
v.	verse
VA	Virginia
va	viola
vc	(violon)cello
VHF	very high frequency
VI	Virgin Islands
vib	vibraphone
viz.	videlicet (Lat.: namely)
vle	violone
vn	violin
vol.	volume
vs	vocal score, piano-vocal score
VT	Vermont
vv	voices
vv.	verses
WA	Washington
WI	Wisconsin
win.	winter
WoO	Werk(e) ohne Opuszahl (Ger.: work(s) without opus number)
WPA	Works Progress Administration
WQ	Wotquenne catalogue [of C. P. E. Bach's works]
WV	West Virginia
ww	woodwind
WY	Wyoming
xyl	xylophone
YT	Yukon Territory (Canada)

Discographical Abbreviations

The abbreviations used in this dictionary for the names of record labels are listed below. In recording-lists the label on which each recording was originally issued is cited, and no attempt is made here to indicate the affiliations of labels to companies. The names of a number of record labels consist of series of capital letters; although these may be abbreviated forms of company names they are not generally listed here as they constitute the full names of the labels concerned.

AAFS	Archive of American Folksong (Library of Congress)
Ari.	Arista
Asy.	Asylum
Atl.	Atlantic
BN	Blue Note
Bruns.	Brunswick
Cad.	Cadence
Can.	Canyon
Cap.	Capitol
Cas.	Casablanca
Col.	Columbia
Com.	Commodore
Conc.	Concord
Cont.	Contemporary
Cot.	Cotillion
Elek.	Elektra
Fan.	Fantasy
FW	Folkways
Gal.	Galaxy
Hick.	Hickory
Hor.	Horizon
IH	Indian House
Imp.	Impulse
Imper.	Imperial
Isl.	Island
Lml.	Limelight
Mer.	Mercury
Mlst.	Milestone
NW	New World
OK	Okeh
Para.	Paramount
Per.	Perfect
Phi.	Philips
Pol.	Polydor
Prst.	Prestige
Rep.	Reprise
Riv.	Riverside
Roul.	Roulette
Tak.	Takoma
TL	Time-Life
UA	United Artists
Van.	Vanguard
Vic.	Victor
Voc.	Vocalion
WB	Warner Bros.

Bibliographical Abbreviations

The bibliographical abbreviations used in this dictionary are listed below. Full bibliographical information is not normally supplied for nonmusical sources (national biographical dictionaries) or if it may be found elsewhere in this dictionary (in the lists following the articles "Dictionaries," "Histories," and "Periodicals") or in *The New Grove Dictionary of Music and Musicians* (in the lists that form parts of the articles "Dictionaries and encyclopedias of music," "Editions, historical," and "Periodicals"). The serial numbers of entries in the two articles "Periodicals" are given here in brackets; an asterisk denotes the appearance of an item in the article in this dictionary. The typographical conventions used throughout the dictionary are followed here: broadly, italic type is used for periodicals and reference works, and roman type for anthologies, series, etc. (titles of individual volumes are italicized).

ACAB — *American Composers Alliance Bulletin* [*US557]
AcM — *Acta musicologica* (1928/9–) [Intl 5]
AMw — *Archiv für Musikwissenschaft* (1918/19–) [Germany 552]
AMZ — *Allgemeine musikalische Zeitung* (1798/9–1882) [Germany 32, 154, 170]
AMz — *Allgemeine Musik-Zeitung* (1874–1943) [Germany 203]
Anderson 2 — E. R. Anderson: *Contemporary American Composers: a Biographical Dictionary* (Boston, 2/1982)
AnM — *Anuario musical* (1946–) [Spain 91]
AnMc — *Analecta musicologica* (some vols. in series Studien zur italienisch-deutschen Musikgeschichte), Veröffentlichungen der Musikabteilung des Deutschen historischen Instituts in Rom (Cologne, Germany, 1963–)
AnnM — *Annales musicologiques* (1953–) [France 638]
Baker 5(–7) — *Baker's Biographical Dictionary of Musicians*, rev. N. Slonimsky (New York, 5/1958/*R*1965, 6/1978, 7/1984; suppls., 1965, 1971)
BAMS — *Bulletin of the American Musicological Society* [*US550]
BMB — Biblioteca musica bononiensis (Bologna, Italy, 1959–)
BMw — *Beiträge zur Musikwissenschaft* [Germany 1013]
BPiM — *The Black Perspective in Music* [*US941]
BWQ — *Brass and Woodwind Quarterly* [*US811]
CBY — *Current Biography Yearbook* (New York, 1940–)
CEKM — Corpus of Early Keyboard Music (Rome, 1963–)
CMc — *Current Musicology* [*US800]
CMM — Corpus mensurabilis musicae (Rome, 1947–)
DAB — *Dictionary of American Biography* (New York, 1928–36; 7 suppls., 1944–81)
DBL — *Dansk biografisk leksikon* (Copenhagen, 1887–1905, 2/1933–)
DBY — *Down Beat Yearbook* [*US709]
DJbM — *Deutsches Jahrbuch der Musikwissenschaft* (1957–) [Germany 980]
DNB — *Dictionary of National Biography* (London, 1885–1901, suppls.)
EDM — Das Erbe deutscher Musik (Berlin and elsewhere, 1935–)
EitnerQ — R. Eitner: *Biographisch-bibliographisches Quellen-Lexikon* (Leipzig, Germany, 1900–04, rev. 2/1959–60)
EM — *Ethnomusicology* [*US692]
ES — F. D'Amico: *Enciclopedia dello spettacolo* (Rome and Florence, 1954–62; suppl., 1966)
EwenD — D. Ewen: *American Composers: a Biographical Dictionary* (New York, 1982)
FAM — *Fontes artis musicae* (1954–) [Intl 16]
FétisB (FétisBS) — F.-J. Fétis: *Biographie universelle des musiciens* (Brussels, 2/1860–65/*R*1972; suppl., 1878–80/*R*1972)
Grove 1(–5) — G. Grove, ed.: *A Dictionary of Music and Musicians* (London, 1878–90; 2/1904–10 ed. J. A. Fuller Maitland, 3/1927–8 and 4/1940 ed. H. C. Colles, 5/1954 ed. E. Blom with suppl. 1961, all as *Grove's Dictionary of Music and Musicians*)
Grove 6 — S. Sadie, ed.: *The New Grove Dictionary of Music and Musicians* (London, 1980)
GroveAS — W. S. Pratt, ed.: *Grove's Dictionary of Music and Musicians: American Supplement* (New York, 1920, 2/1928, many reprs.)

GroveI	S. Sadie, ed.: *The New Grove Dictionary of Musical Instruments* (London, 1984)
GSJ	*The Galpin Society Journal* (1948–) [Great Britain 415]
HiFi	*High Fidelity* [*US681]
HiFi/ MusAm	*High Fidelity/Musical America* [*US681]
HMYB	*Hinrichsen's Musical Year Book* (1944–61) [Great Britain 381]
IAJRCJ	*International Association of Jazz Record Collectors Journal* [*Intl 10]
IMSCR	*International Musicological Society Congress Report* (1930–)
IRASM	*International Review of the Aesthetics and Sociology of Music* (1970–) [Intl 32]
ISAMm	Institute for Studies in American Music, monograph [see entry on the institute]
ITO	*In Theory Only* [*US974]
JAMIS	*Journal of the American Musical Instrument Society* [*US983]
JAMS	*Journal of the American Musicological Society* [*US633]
JbMP	*Jahrbuch der Musikbibliothek Peters* (1895–1941) [Germany 336]
JEFDSS	*The Journal of the English Folk Dance and Song Society* (1932–64) [Great Britain 341]
JEMF Quarterly	*J[ohn] E[dwards] M[emorial] F[oundation] Quarterly* [*US802]
JFSS	*The Journal of the Folk-song Society* (1899–1904; 1927–31) [Great Britain 183]
JIFMC	*Journal of the International Folk Music Council* (1949–68) [Intl 10]
JMT	*Journal of Music Theory* [*US716]
JRBM	*Journal of Renaissance and Baroque Music* [*US609]
JRME	*Journal of Research in Music Education* [*US693]
JVdGSA	*Journal of the Viola da Gamba Society of America* [*US791]
LaMusicaD	G. M. Gatti and A. Basso: *La musica: dizionario* (Turin, Italy, 1968–71)
MB	Musica britannica (London, 1951–)
MD	*Musica disciplina* [*US609]
MEJ	*Music Educators Journal* [*US435]
Mf	*Die Musikforschung* (1948–) [Germany 839]
MGG	F. Blume, ed.: *Die Musik in Geschichte und Gegenwart* (Kassel, Germany, and Basle, Switzerland, 1949–68; suppl., 1973–9)
MJ	*Music Journal* [*US592]
ML	*Music and Letters* (1920–) [Great Britain 280]
MM	*Modern Music* [*US493]
MMR	*The Monthly Musical Record* (1871–1960) [Great Britain 75]
MO	*Musical Opinion* (1877/8–) [Great Britain 90]
MQ	*The Musical Quarterly* [*US451]
MR	*The Music Review* (1940–) [Great Britain 376]
MSD	Musicological Studies and Documents (Rome, 1951–)
MT	*The Musical Times* (1844/5–) [Great Britain 33]
MTNAP	*Music Teachers National Association: Proceedings* [*US119, 370]
MusAm	*Musical America* [*US302, 681]
NAW	E. T. James, J. W. James, and P. S. Boyer, eds.: *Notable American Women* (Cambridge, MA, 1971; suppl., 1980)
NOHM	*The New Oxford History of Music*, ed. E. Wellesz, J. A. Westrup, and G. Abraham (London, 1954–)
NRMI	*Nuova rivista musicale italiana* (1967–) [Italy 282]
NZM	*Neue Zeitschrift für Musik* (1834–) [Germany 75, 1088] [retitled 1920, see *ZfM*]
ÖMz	*Österreichische Musikzeitschrift* (1946–) [Austria 233]
PAMS	*Papers of the American Musicological Society* [*US553]
PASUC	*Proceedings of the American Society of University Composers* [*US809]
PMA	*Proceedings of the Musical Association* (1874/5–) [Great Britain 80] [retitled 1944, see *PRMA*]
PMFC	Polyphonic Music of the Fourteenth Century, ed. L. Schrade and F. Ll. Harrison (Monaco, 1956–)
PNM	*Perspectives of New Music* [*US771]
PRMA	*Proceedings of the Royal Musical Association* [see *PMA*]
RaM	*La rassegna musicale* (1928–72) [Italy 197, 272]
RBM	*Revue belge de musicologie* (1946–) [Belgium 126]
RdM	*Revue de musicologie* (1917–) [France 462]
ReM	*La revue musicale* (1920–) [France 475]
RiemannL 12	*Riemann Musik Lexikon*, rev. W. Gurlitt (Mainz, Germany, 12/1959–75)
RISM	*Répertoire international des sources musicales* (Munich, Duisburg, and Kassel, Germany, 1971–)
RN	*Renaissance News* [*US609]
RRAM	Recent Researches in American Music (Madison, WI, 1977–)
SH	*Slovenská hudba* (1957–71) [Czechoslovakia 192]
SIMG	*Sammelbände der Internationalen Musik-Gesellschaft* (1899/1900–1913/14) [Intl 2]
SM	*Studia musicologica Academiae scientiarum hungaricae* (1961–) [Hungary 89]
SMA	*Studies in Music* (1967–) [Australia 20]
SMz	*Schweizerische Musikzeitung/Revue musicale suisse* (1861–) [Switzerland 4]
SouthernB	E. Southern: *Biographical Dictionary of Afro-American and African Musicians* (Westport, CT, 1982)
Thompson 1(–10)	O. Thompson: *The International Cyclopedia of Music and Musicians* (New York, 1939, 2/1943 and 3/1944 ed. O. Thompson and G. W. Harris, 4/1946–8/1958 ed. N. Slonimsky, 9/1964 ed. R. Sabin, 10/1974 ed. B. Bohle)
VintonD	J. Vinton, ed.: *Dictionary of Contemporary Music* (New York, 1974)
VMw	*Vierteljahrsschrift für Musikwissenschaft* (1885–94) [Germany 282]
YIFMC	*Yearbook of the International Folk Music Council* [*Intl 11]
ZfM	*Zeitschrift für Musik* [see *NZM*]
ZIMG	*Zeitschrift der Internationalen Musik-Gesellschaft* (1899/1900–1913/14) [Intl 3]

Library Abbreviations

The abbreviations used in this dictionary for the names of libraries are those established by the Catalog Publication Division of the Library of Congress and published in *Symbols of American Libraries* (Washington, DC, rev. 12/1980). Only those abbreviations that appear in the dictionary (where they are always printed in italic type) are listed here.

A-Ar	Alabama Department of Archives and History, Montgomery, AL
AB	Birmingham Public and Jefferson County Free Library, Birmingham, AL
ABH	Samford University, Birmingham, AL
AkU	University of Alaska, Fairbanks, AK
ArU	University of Arkansas, Fayetteville, AR
ATrT	Troy State University, Troy, AL
AU	University of Alabama, University, AL
AzTeS	Arizona State University, Tempe, AZ
AzTP	Arizona Historical Society, Tucson, AZ
AzU	University of Arizona, Tucson, AZ
CBGTU	Graduate Theological Union, Berkeley, CA
CBbWD	Walt Disney Productions, Burbank, CA
CCC	Honnold Library, Claremont, CA
CHi	California Historical Society, San Francisco, CA
CL	Los Angeles Public Library, Los Angeles, CA
CLAS	Arnold Schoenberg Institute, University of Southern California, Los Angeles, CA
CLobS	California State University, Long Beach, Long Beach, CA
CLS	California State University, Los Angeles, Los Angeles, CA
CLSU-Music	University of Southern California, Music Library, Los Angeles, CA
CLU-MUS	University of California, Los Angeles, Music Library, Los Angeles, CA
CO	Oakland Public Library, Oakland, CA
CoD	Denver Public Library, Denver, CO
CoHi	Colorado State Historical Society, Denver, CO
COMC	Mills College, Oakland, CA
COMus	Oakland Museum, Oakland, CA
CoU	University of Colorado, Boulder, CO
CSd	San Diego Public Library, San Diego, CA
CSf	San Francisco Public Library, San Francisco, CA
CSfCP	Society of California Pioneers, San Francisco, CA
CSfSt	San Francisco State University, San Francisco, CA
CSmH	Henry E. Huntington Library, San Marino, CA
CSt-H	Stanford University, Hoover Institution on War, Revolution, and Peace, Stanford, CA
Ct	Connecticut State Library, Hartford, CT
CtHi	Connecticut Historical Society, Hartford, CT
CtHT	Trinity College, Hartford, CT
CtHT-W	Trinity College, Watkinson Library, Hartford, CT
CtNhHi	New Haven Colony Historical Society, New Haven, CT
CtW	Wesleyan University, Middletown, CT
CtWeharU	University of Hartford, West Hartford, CT
CtY	Yale University, New Haven, CT
CtY-Mus	Yale University, School of Music, New Haven, CT
CU-MUSI	University of California, Berkeley, Music Library, Berkeley, CA
CU-Riv	University of California, Riverside, Main Library, Riverside, CA
CU-S	University of California, San Diego, Main Library, La Jolla, CA
CU-SB	University of California, Santa Barbara, Main Library, Santa Barbara, CA
DCU	Catholic University of America, Washington, DC
DeHi	Historical Society of Delaware, Wilmington, DE
DeU	University of Delaware, Newark, DE
DeWint-M	Henry Frances DuPont Winterthur Museum, Joseph Downs Manuscript and Microfilm Collection, Winterthur, DE
DFo	Folger Shakespeare Library, Washington, DC
DHU	Howard University, Washington, DC
DLC	United States Library of Congress, Washington, DC
DMaM	United States Marine Corps Museum, Washington, DC
DNA	United States National Archives and Records Service, National Archives Library, Washington, DC
DNC	Washington Cathedral, Washington, DC
DOAS	Organization of American States, Washington, DC
DSI	Smithsonian Institution, Washington, DC
FMU	University of Miami, Coral Gables, FL
FTaSU	Florida State University, Tallahassee, FL

GAHi	Atlanta Historical Society, Atlanta, GA
G-Ar	Georgia State Department of Archives and History, Atlanta, GA
GASU	Georgia State University, Atlanta, GA
GAU	Atlanta University, Atlanta, GA
GEU	Emory University, Atlanta, GA
GEU-T	Emory University, Candler School of Theology, Atlanta, GA
GU	University of Georgia, Athens, GA
H-Ar	Public Archives, Honolulu, HI
HHB	Bernice P. Bishop Museum, Honolulu, HI
HHMC	Hawaiian Mission Children's Society, Honolulu, HI
HU	University of Hawaii, Honolulu, HI
IaDm	Des Moines Public Library, Des Moines, IA
IaHi	State Historical Society of Iowa, Iowa City, IA
IaU	University of Iowa, Iowa City, IA
IBloHi	McLean County Historical Society, Bloomington, IL
IBloW	Illinois Wesleyan University, Bloomington, IL
IC	Chicago Public Library, Chicago, IL
ICarbS	Southern Illinois University, Carbondale, IL
ICD	De Paul University, Chicago, IL
ICHi	Chicago Historical Society, Chicago, IL
ICIU	University of Illinois, Chicago Circle, Chicago, IL
ICN	Newberry Library, Chicago, IL
ICU	University of Chicago, Chicago, IL
IdCaC	College of Idaho, Caldwell, ID
IE	Evanston Public Library, Evanston, IL
IEdS	Southern Illinois University, Edwardsville Campus, Edwardsville, IL
IEN	Northwestern University, Evanston, IL
IEWT	National Women's Christian Temperance Union, Evanston, IL
IHi	Illinois State Historical Library, Springfield, IL
InGo	Goshen College, Goshen, IN
InHi	Indiana Historical Society, Indianapolis, IN
InI	Indianapolis–Marion County Public Library, Indianapolis, IN
InMuB	Ball State University, Muncie, IN
InNd	University of Notre Dame, Notre Dame, IN
INS	Illinois State University, Normal, IL
InU	Indiana University, Bloomington, IN
IU-Mu	University of Illinois, Music Library, Urbana, IL
IWW	Wheaton College, Wheaton, IL
KHi	Kansas State Historical Society, Topeka, KS
KNnB	Bethel College, North Newton, KS
KU	University of Kansas, Lawrence, KS
KU-S	University of Kansas, Kenneth Spencer Research Library, Lawrence, KS
KWiU	Wichita State University, Wichita, KS
KyBB	Berea College, Berea, KY
KyBgW	Western Kentucky University, Bowling Green, KY
KyBgW-K	Western Kentucky University, Kentucky Library, Bowling Green, KY
KyLo	Louisville Free Public Library, Louisville, KY
KyLoF	Filson Club, Louisville, KY
KyLoS	Southern Baptist Theological Seminary, Louisville, KY
KyLoU	University of Louisville, Louisville, KY
KyLoU-Ar	University of Louisville, University Archives and Records Center, Louisville, KY
KyU	University of Kentucky, Lexington, KY
LLafS	University of Southwestern Louisiana, Lafayette, LA
L-M	Louisiana State Museum, New Orleans, LA
LN	New Orleans Public Library, New Orleans, LA
LNB	New Orleans Baptist Theological Seminary, New Orleans, LA
LNT	Tulane University, New Orleans, LA
LU	Louisiana State University, Baton Rouge, LA
MB	Boston Public Library and Eastern Massachusetts Regional Public Library System, Boston, MA
MBAt	Boston Athenaeum, Boston, MA
MBBS	Bostonian Society, Boston, MA
MBCM	New England Conservatory of Music, Boston, MA
MBG	Isabella Stewart Gardner Museum, Boston, MA
MBHM	Harvard Musical Association, Boston, MA
MBU	Boston University, Boston, MA
MBU-T	Boston University, School of Theology, Boston, MA
MCM	Massachusetts Institute of Technology, Cambridge, MA
MCR-S	Radcliffe College, Schlesinger Library on the History of Women in America, Cambridge, MA
MdBE	Enoch Pratt Free Library, Baltimore, MD
MdBJ	Johns Hopkins University, Baltimore, MD
MdBMC	Morgan State College, Baltimore, MD
MdBP	Enoch Pratt Free Library, George Peabody Branch, Baltimore, MD
MdBPC	Peabody Conservatory of Music, Baltimore, MD
MdHi	Maryland Historical Society, Baltimore, MD
MdU	University of Maryland, College Park, MD
Me	Maine State Library, Augusta, ME
MeHi	Maine Historical Society, Portland, ME
MeP	Portland Public Library, Portland, ME
MeU	University of Maine, Orono, ME
MH	Harvard University, Cambridge, MA
MH-AH	Harvard University, Andover-Harvard Theological Library, Cambridge, MA
MH-BA	Harvard University, Graduate School of Business Administration, Boston, MA
MH-Ed	Harvard University, Graduate School of Education, Cambridge, MA
MH-H	Harvard University, Houghton Library, Cambridge, MA
MHi	Massachusetts Historical Society, Boston, MA
MH-Mu	Harvard University, Music Library, Cambridge, MA
MH-P	Harvard University, Peabody Museum, Cambridge, MA
MiD	Detroit Public Library, Detroit, MI
MiDbEI	Edison Institute, Henry Ford Museum, and Greenfield Village Library, Dearborn, MI
MiDW	Wayne State University, Detroit, MI
MiGrC	Calvin College and Seminary, Grand Rapids, MI
MiKW	Western Michigan University, Kalamazoo, MI
MiU-C	University of Michigan, William L. Clements Library, Ann Arbor, MI
MiU-H	University of Michigan, Michigan Historical Collection, Ann Arbor, MI
MMeT	Tufts University, Medford, MA
MMHi	Milton Historical Society, Milton, MA
MnCS	St. John's University, Collegeville, MN
MNe	Newburyport Public Library, Newburyport, MA
MnHi	Minnesota Historical Society, St. Paul, MN
MnM	Minneapolis Public Library, Minneapolis, MN
MnNHi	Norwegian-American Historical Association, c/o St. Olaf College, Northfield, MN
MnNS	St. Olaf College, Northfield, MN
MNS	Smith College, Northampton, MA
MnU	University of Minnesota, Minneapolis, MN
MnU-IA	University of Minnesota, Immigration History Research Center, St. Paul, MN
MnU-SW	University of Minnesota, Social Welfare History Archives Center, St. Paul, MN

MoHi	Missouri State Historical Society, Columbia, MO
MoK	Kansas City Public Library, Kansas City, MO
MoKB	Bar Library Association of Kansas City, Kansas City, MO
MoKU	University of Missouri at Kansas City, Kansas City, MO
MoKU-Mus	University of Missouri at Kansas City, Music Conservatory, Kansas City, MO
MoS	St. Louis Public Library, St. Louis, MO
MoSHi	Missouri Historical Society, St. Louis, MO
MoSW	Washington University, St. Louis, MO
MoU	University of Missouri, Columbia, MO
MPB	Berkshire Athenaeum, Pittsfield, MA
MSaE	Essex Institute, Salem, MA
Ms-Ar	Mississippi Department of Archives and History, Jackson, MS
MsHaW	William Carey College, Hattiesburg, MS
MsJMC	Millsaps College, Jackson, MS
MStuO	Old Sturbridge Village Library, Sturbridge, MA
MU	University of Massachusetts, Amherst, MA
MWA	American Antiquarian Society, Worcester, MA
MWalB	Brandeis University, Waltham, MA
MWelC	Wellesley College, Wellesley, MA
MWiW	Williams College, Williamstown, MA
NB	Brooklyn Public Library, Brooklyn, NY
NBC	Brooklyn College, City University of New York, Brooklyn, NY
NbHi	Nebraska State Historical Society, Lincoln, NE
NbL	Lincoln City Libraries, Lincoln, NE
NbRcW	Willa Cather Pioneer Memorial, Red Cloud, NE
NbU	University of Nebraska, Lincoln, NE
NBuU-AR	State University of New York, Buffalo, Archives, Buffalo, NY
NBuU-Mu	State University of New York, Buffalo, Music Library, Buffalo, NY
NbWi	Dvoracek Memorial Library, Wilber, NE
Nc-Ar	North Carolina State Department of Archives and History, Raleigh, NC
NcBoA	Appalachian State University, Boone, NC
NcD	Duke University, Durham, NC
NcGU	University of North Carolina, Greensboro, Greensboro, NC
NcU	University of North Carolina, Chapel Hill, NC
NcWsMM	Moravian Music Foundation, Inc., Winston-Salem, NC
NdU	University of North Dakota, Grand Forks, ND
Nh	New Hampshire State Library, Concord, NH
NhD	Dartmouth College, Hanover, NH
NhHi	New Hampshire Historical Society, Concord, NH
NHi	New-York Historical Society, New York, NY
NhM	Manchester City Library, Manchester, NH
NhU	University of New Hampshire, Durham, NH
NIC	Cornell University, Ithaca, NY
NIHi	DeWitt Historical Society of Tompkins County, Ithaca, NY
NjHi	New Jersey Historical Society, Newark, NJ
NjMD	Drew University, Madison, NJ
NjP	Princeton University, Princeton, NJ
NjR	Rutgers, the State University of New Jersey, New Brunswick, NJ
NmLvH	NewMexico Highlands University, Las Vegas, NM
NN	New York Public Library, New York, NY
NNAL	American Academy of Arts and Letters, New York, NY
NNC	Columbia University, New York, NY
NNCU-G	City University of New York, Graduate Center, New York, NY
NNH	Hispanic Society of America, New York, NY
NNJu	Juilliard School of Music, New York, NY
NNL	Herbert H. Lehman College, City University of New York, New York, NY
NN-L	New York Public Library, Research Library for the Performing Arts at Lincoln Center, New York, NY
NNLBI	Leo Baeck Institute, New York, NY
NNMMA	Museum of Modern Art, New York, NY
NNPM	Pierpont Morgan Library, New York, NY
NNR	City College, City University of New York, New York, NY
NN-Sc	New York Public Library, Schomburg Collection, New York, NY
NNU	New York University, New York, NY
NNUT	Union Theological Seminary, New York, NY
NNYI	Yivo Institute for Jewish Research, New York, NY
NPotU	State University of New York, College at Potsdam, Potsdam, NY
NPurU	State University of New York, College at Purchase, Purchase, NY
NPV	Vassar College, Poughkeepsie, NY
NRU-Mus	University of Rochester, Eastman School of Music, Rochester, NY
NSbSU	State University of New York, Stony Brook, Stony Brook, NY
NSyU	Syracuse University, Syracuse, NY
NvHi	Nevada State Historical Society, Reno, NV
OBerB	Baldwin-Wallace College, Berea, OH
OBgU	Bowling Green State University, Bowling Green, OH
OC	Public Library of Cincinnati and Hamilton County, Cincinnati, OH
OCH	Hebrew Union College–Jewish Institute of Religion, Cincinnati, OH
OCHP	Cincinnati Historical Society, Cincinnati, OH
OCl	Cleveland Public Library, Cleveland, OH
OClCIM	Cleveland Institute of Music, Cleveland, OH
OClU	Cleveland State University, Cleveland, OH
OClWHi	Western Reserve Historical Society, Cleveland, OH
OClW-S	Case Western Reserve University, Sears Library, Cleveland, OH
OCU-Mu	University of Cincinnati, College Conservatory of Music, Cincinnati, OH
ODW	Ohio Wesleyan University, Delaware, OH
OHi	Ohio Historical Society, Columbus, OH
OkU	University of Oklahoma, Norman, OK
OOC	Oberlin College Conservatory of Music, Oberlin, OH
OOxM	Miami University, Oxford, OH
OrCs	Oregon State University, Corvallis, OR
OrHi	Oregon Historical Society, Portland, OR
OrP	Library Association of Portland (Public Library for Portland and Multnomah County), Portland, OR
OrU	University of Oregon, Eugene, OR
OSW	Wittenberg University, Springfield, OH
OU	Ohio State University, Columbus, OH
OYU	Youngstown State University, Youngstown, OH
P	Pennsylvania State Library, Harrisburg, PA
PBMCA	Archives of the Moravian Church, Bethlehem, PA
PHarH	Pennsylvania Historical and Museum Commission, Harrisburg, PA
PHi	Historical Society of Pennsylvania, Philadelphia, PA
PLatS	St. Vincent College and Archabbey, Latrobe, PA
PP	Free Library of Philadelphia, Philadelphia, PA
PPAmP	American Philosophical Society, Philadelphia, PA
PPCI	Curtis Institute of Music, Philadelphia, PA
PPi	Carnegie Library of Pittsburgh, Pittsburgh, PA

PPiHi	Historical Society of Western Pennsylvania, Pittsburgh, PA
PPiPT	Pittsburgh Theological Seminary, Pittsburgh, PA
PPiU	University of Pittsburgh, Pittsburgh, PA
PPL	Library Company of Philadelphia, Philadelphia, PA
PPPCity	Philadelphia City Institute Branch Free Library, Philadelphia, PA [collection no longer available]
PPT	Temple University, Philadelphia, PA
PrU	University of Puerto Rico, Rio Piedras, PR
PSt	Pennsylvania State University, University Park, PA
PU	University of Pennsylvania, Philadelphia, PA
PU-Music	University of Pennsylvania, School of Music, Philadelphia, PA
RHi	Rhode Island Historical Society, Providence, RI
RP	Providence Public Library, Providence, RI
RPB	Brown University, Providence, RI
RPB-JH	Brown University, John Hay Library of Rare Books and Special Collections, Providence, RI
ScHi	South Carolina Historical Society, Charleston, SC
ScSpC	Converse College, Spartanburg, SC
ScU	University of South Carolina, Columbia, SC
SdU	University of South Dakota, Vermillion, SD
TMM	Memphis State University, Memphis, TN
TNC	Country Music Foundation Library and Media Center, Nashville, TN
TNJ	Joint University Libraries, Nashville, TN
TNSB	Southern Baptist Convention Historical Commission, Nashville, TN
TU	University of Tennessee, Knoxville, TN
TxAm	Amarillo Public Library, Amarillo, TX
TxDa	Dallas Public Library, Dallas, TX
TxDaM	Southern Methodist University, Dallas, TX
TxDN	North Texas State University, Denton, TX
TxFS	Southwestern Baptist Theological Seminary, Fort Worth, TX
TxHR	Rice University, Houston, TX
TxLT	Texas Tech University, Lubbock, TX
TxSa	San Antonio Public Library, San Antonio, TX
TxU	University of Texas, Austin, TX
TxWB	Baylor University, Waco, TX
UCS	Southern Utah State College, Cedar City, UT
UHi	Utah State Historical Society, Salt Lake City, UT
Uk	British Library, London, England
UPB	Brigham Young University, Provo, UT
USIC	Church of Jesus Christ of Latter-day Saints, Historian's Office, Salt Lake City, UT
UU	University of Utah, Salt Lake City, UT
ViFGM	George Mason University, Fairfax, VA
ViHal	Hampton Institute, Hampton, VA
ViHi	Virginia Historical Society, Richmond, VA
ViR	Richmond Public Library, Richmond, VA
ViSwC	Sweet Briar College, Sweet Briar, VA
ViU	University of Virginia, Charlottesville, VA
ViU-Mu	University of Virginia, Music Library, Charlottesville, VA
ViWC	Colonial Williamsburg, Inc., Williamsburg, VA
VtHi	Vermont Historical Society, Montpelier, VT
VtMiM	Middlebury College, Middlebury, VT
VtU	University of Vermont and State Agricultural College, Burlington, VT
WaPS	Washington State University, Pullman, WA
WaS	Seattle Public Library, Seattle, WA
WaU	University of Washington, Seattle, WA
WBaraC	Circus World Museum, Baraboo, WI
WHi	State Historical Society of Wisconsin, Madison, WI
WKenOS	Old Songs Library, Kenosha, WI
WM	Milwaukee Public Library, Milwaukee, WI
WMUW	University of Wisconsin-Milwaukee, Milwaukee, WI
WU	University of Wisconsin, Madison, WI
WvU	West Virginia University, Morgantown, WV
Wy-Ar	Wyoming State Archives and Historical Department, Cheyenne, WY
WyU	University of Wyoming, Laramie, WY

Volume One

A–D

A Note on the Use of the Dictionary

This note is intended as a short guide to the basic procedures and organization of the dictionary. A fuller account will be found in the Introduction, pp.xi–xvii.

Alphabetization of headings is based on the principle that words are read continuously, ignoring spaces, hyphens, accents, parenthesized and bracketed matter, etc., up to the first comma; the same principle applies thereafter. "Mc" and "Mac" are alphabetized as "Mac," "St." as "Saint."

Cross-references are shown in small capitals, with a large capital at the beginning of the first word of the entry referred to. Thus "The UNIVERSITY OF CALIFORNIA established a campus at Berkeley in 1868" means that the entry referred to is not "**University of California**" but "**California, University of.**"

Abbreviations used in the dictionary are listed on pp.xviii–xxix, in the order General (beginning on p.xviii), Discographical (p.xxiii), Bibliographical (p.xxiv), and Library (p.xxvi).

Work-lists are normally arranged chronologically (within section, where divided), in order of year of composition or first publication (in the latter case dates are given in parentheses). Italicized abbreviations (such as *DLC* and *NN-L*) stand for libraries holding sources and are explained on pp.xxvi–xxix.

Recording-lists are arranged chronologically (within section, where divided), in order of date of recording for jazz musicians and date of issue for others (dates respectively precede and follow issue information). Abbreviations standing for record labels are explained on p.xxiii.

Bibliographies are arranged chronologically (within section, where divided), in order of year of first publication, and alphabetically by author within years. Abbreviations standing for periodicals and reference works are explained on pp.xxiv–xxv.

AACM. *See* ASSOCIATION FOR THE ADVANCEMENT OF CREATIVE MUSICIANS.

Abbott, Emma (*b* Chicago, IL, 9 Dec 1850; *d* Salt Lake City, UT, 5 Jan 1891). Soprano and impresario. She studied first with her father, a singer and music teacher, and later in New York with Achille Errani. In 1872 she went to Europe, studying further with Antonio Sangiovanni in Milan and Mathilde Marchesi, P. F. Wartel, and Enrico delle Sedie in Paris. She made her operatic début in London on 2 May 1876, but her contract was canceled when she declined to appear in *La traviata* (on the grounds that it was immoral). Her New York début in February 1877 was well received, but American critics never approved of the licenses she took with scores, such as interpolating hymns by Lowell Mason into operas by Donizetti or Bellini. Her favorite role was said to be Marguerite in Gounod's *Faust*.

Abbott was important for the role she played in popularizing opera and operetta in the USA. In 1878 she formed her own small company under the management of her husband, Eugene Wetherell. It toured, chiefly in the West, with a repertory that included such works as Massé's *Paul and Virginia*, Planquette's *The Chimes of Normandy*, Balfe's *The Bohemian Girl*, *Romeo and Juliet*, *The Mikado*, and *Norma* – a mixture of opera (always sung in English) and operetta. Abbott's company is said to have opened some 35 new opera houses between 1878 (Waterloo, Iowa) and December 1890 (Ogden, Utah). She herself amassed a large estate and made large contributions to charities and churches in her will.

BIBLIOGRAPHY

S. E. Martin: *The Life and Professional Career of Emma Abbott* (Minneapolis, 1891)
H. E. Johnson: "Abbott, Emma," *NAW*
O. Thompson: *The American Singer* (New York, 1937/*R*1969), 127

H. WILEY HITCHCOCK

Abenaki [Abnaki]. American Indian tribe of the WABANAKI confederacy.

Abercrombie, John (*b* Portchester, NY, 16 Dec 1944). Jazz guitarist. He attended the Berklee Music School in Boston from 1962 to 1966, during which time he also toured with organist Johnny "Hammond" Smith. After moving to New York in 1969 he played first in Chico Hamilton's group and later with Billy Cobham's jazz-rock group Spectrum, where he attracted widespread attention. Since 1974, when his highly regarded trio recording *Timeless* was issued, he has preferred a subdued, "chamber" jazz style, either in his own small groups or as a much sought-after sideman, notably with Jack DeJohnette's combos. Though not primarily an innovator, Abercrombie makes imaginative use of distorting devices such as the phase shifter and volume pedal with the electric guitar (and occasionally electric mandolin), playing in a distinctive personal style that combines elements from bop to free jazz. His sensitive control of tone-color is particularly apparent in his duo performances with the acoustic guitarist Ralph Towner.

RECORDINGS
(selective list)

As leader: *Timeless* (1974, ECM 1047); *Gateway* (1975, ECM 1061); *Gateway 2* (1977, ECM 1105); *Characters* (1977, ECM 1117); *M* (1980, ECM 1191)
Duos with R. Towner: *Sargasso Sea* (1976, ECM 1080); *Five Years Later* (1981, ECM 1207)
As sideman: B. Cobham: *Crosswinds* (1974, Atl. 7300); J. DeJohnette: *Sorcery* (1974, Prst. 10081), *Untitled* (1976, ECM 1074), *New Directions* (1978, ECM 1128)

BIBLIOGRAPHY

C. Berg: "John Abercrombie's Six-string Stylistic Summit," *Down Beat*, xlii/4 (1976), 16
T. Schneckloth: "John Abercrombie: a Direction of his Own," *Down Beat*, xliv/4 (1979), 16

J. BRADFORD ROBINSON

Abrams, Muhal Richard (*b* Chicago, IL, 19 Sept 1930). Jazz pianist, composer, and organizer. He studied piano from the age of 17, spending four years at Chicago Musical College. In 1950 he began writing arrangements for the King Fleming Band, and in the middle of the decade he played in a hard-bop band, the Modern Jazz Two + Three. For years his versatile talents as a pianist were used by many jazz soloists visiting Chicago, but he made his greatest impact as the founder of the Experimental Band (1961), which later gave way to the influential ASSOCIATION FOR THE ADVANCEMENT OF CREATIVE MUSICIANS. As president of this musicians' cooperative, Abrams emphasized the entire history of jazz while encouraging young musicians to experiment with avant-garde forms. His influence on an entire generation of Chicago jazz musicians has been immeasurable. Since moving to New York in the early 1970s Abrams has performed and recorded in a number of contexts – from solo piano to his own big band – always with his unique, eclectic jazz compositions.

RECORDINGS
(selective list)

Levels and Degrees of Light (1967, Delmark 413); *Young at Heart, Wise in Time* (1969, Delmark 423); *Sightsong* (1975, Black Saint 0003); *1 – OQA + 19* (1977, Black Saint 0017); *Lifea Blinec* (1978, Arista Novus 3000); *Spihumonesty* (1979, Black Saint 0032); *Rejoicing with the Light* (1983, Black Saint 0071)

BIBLIOGRAPHY

T. Martin: "The Chicago Avant-garde," *Jazz Monthly*, no.157 (1968), 12
E. Jost: *Free Jazz* (Graz, Austria, 1974/R1981)
R. Townley: "Profile: Muhal Richard Abrams," *Down Beat*, xli/14 (1974), 34
V. Wilmer: *As Serious as your Life* (London, 1977)
J.-E. Berendt: *Jazz: a Photo History* (New York, 1978)

LEE JESKE

Abravanel, Maurice (de) (*b* Thessaloniki, Greece, 6 Jan 1903). Conductor of Spanish-Portuguese Sephardic descent. He worked towards a medical degree at the University of Lausanne but, on Busoni's recommendation, went to Berlin to study with Weill. He began his conducting career in Berlin, appearing at theaters there and in various other German cities until Hitler came to power in 1933. He then went to Paris, where he conducted the Balanchine ballet company, and toured Australia with the British National Opera Company. In 1936, on the recommendation of Walter and Furtwängler, he was engaged by the Metropolitan Opera, taking charge during the next two years of repertory as diverse as *Lohengrin* and *Lakmé*, *Tannhäuser* and *Les contes d'Hoffmann*. A victim of internal politics, he moved to Broadway, conducting Weill's *Knickerbocker Holiday*, and becoming known during the next decade as a specialist in the work of his former teacher, some of whose premières he had conducted during his Paris days. He also conducted at the Chicago Grand Opera Company during the 1940–41 season.

In 1947 the opportunity came to return full time to serious music. The year before, the Utah SO had been organized on a permanent and professional basis. Again on Walter's recommendation, Abravanel was engaged as conductor. His achievement and that of the Utah SO were musically valuable, and they made many recordings of special interest. The situation is even more notable sociologically: Utah is one of the poorest states, with no tradition of philanthropy towards the arts, yet under Abravanel's leadership it became the state with the highest rate of concert attendance. Abravanel conducted the local premières of such works as Mozart's "Jupiter" Symphony, Bach's *St. Matthew Passion*, and several of the Beethoven and Brahms symphonies. His recordings range from Handel and Scarlatti to the complete Mahler symphonies and symphonies by Gould, Rorem, and Schuman. After his retirement in 1979 he was named conductor emeritus.

Abravanel also served as artistic director of the Music Academy of the West, Santa Barbara (1954–80). In 1981 he was honored with the Gold Baton of the American Symphony Orchestra League. If not the most authoritative or imaginative of interpreters, he was always a highly competent and committed conductor.

BIBLIOGRAPHY

H. Stoddard: "Maurice Abravanel," *Symphony Conductors of the U.S.A.* (New York, 1957)
P. Hart: *Orpheus in the New World: the Symphony Orchestra as an American Cultural Institution* (New York, 1973), 171
L. M. Durham: *Abravanel* (in preparation)

MICHAEL STEINBERG/DENNIS K. McINTIRE

Maurice Abravanel conducting the Utah SO

Absaroke. *See* CROW.

ACA. *See* AMERICAN COMPOSERS ALLIANCE.

Academy of Music. Later name of the American Academy of Music, one of the finest opera houses built in the USA in the 19th century; *see* PHILADELPHIA, §2.

Ace, Johnny [Alexander, John Marshall, Jr.] (*b* Memphis, TN, 9 June 1929; *d* Houston, TX, 25 Dec 1954). Rhythm-and-blues singer and songwriter. He served in the US Navy in World War II, then played piano with the Beale Streeters from Memphis, whose other members included Bobby Bland, Junior Parker, Roscoe Gordon, and B. B. King; they played "electric" blues in the style of Sonny Boy Williamson, and in the early 1950s recorded for Ike Turner and Sam Phillips. Ace then signed a contract as a solo artist with Don Robey's Duke recording company; his recording of *My Song* reached no. 1 on the rhythm-and-blues chart in 1952, as did his song *The Clock* the following year. Developing a smoother style, he made a series of successful recordings in 1953–4 and became a popular live performer. After his death, incurred during a game of Russian roulette, his song *Pledging my love* became his greatest hit; it was later recorded by Presley and others. Ace evolved a sophisticated type of rhythm-and-blues, which brought him more success as a performer of emotional ballads than as a bluesman; his earnest, suppliant style became a model for later romantic singers.

RECORDINGS

(selective list; all recorded for Duke)

My Song (102, 1952); The Clock (112, 1953); Cross my heart (107, 1953); Please forgive me (128, 1954); Saving my love for you (118, 1954); Anymore (144, 1955); Pledging my love (136, 1955)

BIBLIOGRAPHY

SouthernB

JOHN PICCARELLA

Achron, Isidor (*b* Warsaw, Poland, 24 Nov 1892; *d* New York, 12 May 1948). Pianist and composer of Lithuanian descent, brother of Joseph Achron. He studied the piano with Anna Esipova, composition with Anatol Liadov, and orchestration with Maximilian Shteynberg at the St. Petersburg Conservatory. In 1922 he came to the USA and in 1928 became an American citizen. Until 1933 he was accompanist to Heifetz, with whom he had first performed in Russia in 1909. Achron then began a successful solo career and gave joint recitals occasionally with his brother, Joseph, and with his wife, Lea Karina, a Finnish-born mezzo-soprano. His works include two piano concertos (1937, 1942), the first given its première by the composer with the New York PO (9 December 1937); the *Suite grotesque* (1941), first performed by the St. Louis SO (30 January 1942); and several pieces for piano and violin.

R. ALLEN LOTT

Achron, Joseph (*b* Lozdzieje, Poland, 13 May 1886; *d* Hollywood, CA, 29 April 1943). Violinist and composer of Lithuanian descent, brother of Isidor Achron. At the St. Petersburg Conservatory, from which he graduated in 1904, Joseph studied violin with Leopold Auer and composition with Anatol Liadov. He went to the Ukraine in 1913 to teach at the Khar'kov Musical Institute. After touring as a concert artist and teaching at the Leningrad Artists' Union in the years following World War I, he immigrated to the USA in 1925 and settled in New York, where he taught at the Westchester Conservatory. He performed his Violin Concerto no. 1 with the Boston SO in 1927. His Golem Suite, also of this period, was chosen by the ISCM for performance in Venice in 1932; its opening section is recapitulated in exact retrograde to symbolize the downfall of the monster. In 1934 Achron moved to Hollywood, where he composed music for films and continued his career as a concert violinist, performing his Second Violin Concerto with the Los Angeles PO in 1936 and his third (commissioned by Heifetz) with the same orchestra in 1939. His early works, Romantic in style, show the influence of his Russian training; later he employed atonal and polytonal techniques.

WORKS

(only those composed in the USA; selective list)

Orch: 3 vn concs., no. 1, op.60, 1925, no. 2, op.68, 1933, no. 3, op.72, 1937; Konzertanten-Kapelle, vn, orch, op.64, 1928; Dance Ov., 1932; Golem Suite, chamber orch, 1932; Little Dance Fantasy, 1933

Choral: Salome's Dance, mixed vv, pf, perc, op.61, 1925; Evening Service of the Sabbath, Bar, 4vv, org, op.67, 1932

Chamber and inst: Elegy, str qt, op.62, 1927; 4 Improvisations, str qt, op.65, 1927; Statuettes, pf, 1929; Golem, vc, tpt, hn, pf, 1931; Sinfonietta, str qt, op.71, 1935

Film music, incl. Spring Night (ballet), 1935

Principal publishers: C. Fischer, Boosey & Hawkes, Bloch, Israeli Music

BIBLIOGRAPHY

P. Moddel: *Joseph Achron* (Tel-Aviv, 1966)

PEGGY GLANVILLE-HICKS/R

Acid rock. *See* PSYCHEDELIC ROCK.

Ackley, Alfred H(enry) (*b* Spring Hill, PA, 21 Jan 1887; *d* Whittier, CA, 3 July 1960). Composer and hymnwriter. He studied harmony and composition in New York and London, and later became an accomplished cellist. He was ordained by the Presbyterian Church in 1914 and served as pastor of churches in Pennsylvania and California. He was active with his brother Bentley DeForest Ackley as an editor for Homer A. Rodeheaver's publishing company, and many of his approximately 1500 hymns, gospel songs, children's songs, secular songs, and glees were used in the firm's publications. His most popular composition is the gospel song *He Lives* ("I serve a risen Saviour"), for which he wrote both text and tune.

BIBLIOGRAPHY

T. H. Porter: *Homer Alvan Rodeheaver (1880–1955): Evangelistic Musician and Publisher* (diss., New Orleans Baptist Theological Seminary, 1981)

THOMAS HENRY PORTER

Ackley, Bentley DeForest (*b* Spring Hill, PA, 27 Sept 1872; *d* Winona Lake, IN, 3 Sept 1958). Writer and editor of gospel hymns. He learned to play several instruments, including melodeon, piano, reed organ, alto horn, cornet, piccolo, and clarinet. He studied shorthand and typing and then worked as a stenographer in New York and Philadelphia. Several of his secular songs were published in the 1890s. From 1908 to 1915 he was pianist and private secretary to the evangelist Billy Sunday, and during this period began to compose gospel songs. In 1910 he and Homer A. Rodeheaver founded the Rodeheaver–Ackley publishing company in Chicago; with his brother Alfred H. Ackley and Charles H. Gabriel, Ackley provided a major portion of the copyrighted publications of the firm. He worked for Rodeheaver's company as music writer and editor until his death. More than 2000 of Ackley's gospel songs were published, including *If your heart keeps right* (1912), *I walk with the King* (1913), and *Sunrise* (1924).

BIBLIOGRAPHY

W. G. McLoughlin, Jr.: *Billy Sunday was his Real Name* (Chicago, 1955)

T. H. Porter: *Homer Alvan Rodeheaver (1880–1955): Evangelistic Musician and Publisher* (diss., New Orleans Baptist Theological Seminary, 1981)

HARRY ESKEW

Acuff, Roy (Claxton) (*b* Maynardville, TN, 15 Sept 1903). Country-music singer, fiddler, songwriter, and publisher. He became a medicine-show performer in 1932, and by 1933 had organized his first band. By the time he made his first recordings in 1936, he had appeared on radio stations in Knoxville with two bands, the Tennessee Crackerjacks and the Crazy Tennesseans. He joined the "Grand Ole Opry" in 1938, performing with a band named the Smoky Mountain Boys, which included some of the musicians from the earlier groups; among its best-known members were Jess Easterday (who played mandolin, double bass, and guitar), Pete Kirby, better known as Bashful Brother Oswald (who sang tenor and played dobro, guitar, and banjo), and Jimmie Riddle (who played harmonica, accordion, and piano). Through such songs as *Wabash Cannon Ball* and *The Great Speckled Bird*, and appearances in eight western films, including *Grand Ole Opry* (1940), *My Darling Clementine* (1943), and *Night Train to Memphis* (1946), Acuff became the best-known country singer of the World War II era. His personal popularity did much to make the "Grand Ole Opry" the leading country-music radio and stage show. His intense, wailing style, suggestive of southern fundamentalist country churches, was atypical at a time when jazzy, swing styles were gaining ground in country music. Until the 1950s Acuff's group was a traditional mountain string band, its hallmark the prominent dobro; though he resisted the use of electric instruments, he introduced them towards the end of the decade.

In 1942 Acuff and his wife, Mildred, and Fred Rose founded a publishing firm, Acuff–Rose Publications, which helped to establish Nashville as the center of country music; among the famous titles it issued were *Tennessee Waltz*, *Jambalaya*, and *Your cheatin' heart*. In 1953 they founded Hickory Records. Acuff was elected to the Country Music Hall of Fame in 1966, the first living performer to be honored in this way.

BIBLIOGRAPHY

E. Schlappi: *Roy Acuff and his Smoky Mountain Boys – Discography* (Denton, MD, 1966)

B. C. Malone: *Country Music U.S.A.: a Fifty-year History* (Austin, 1968, 2/1985)

E. Schlappi: "Roy Acuff," *Stars of Country Music*, ed. B. C. Malone and J. McCulloh (Urbana, IL, 1975), 179

"Acuff, Roy," *CBY 1976*

E. Schlappi: *Roy Acuff, the Smoky Mountain Boy* (Gretna, LA, 1978)

D. Rhodes: "Roy Acuff, the Real Speckled Bird," *Bluegrass Unlimited*, xiii/11 (1979), 14

B. Allen: "Roy Acuff: the Grand Old Man of the Grand Ole Opry," *Country Music*, no.110 (1984), 18

BILL C. MALONE

Adam, Claus (*b* Sumatra, Indonesia, 5 Nov 1917; *d* New York, 4 July 1983). Cellist and composer. He spent the first six years of his life in Indonesia, where his father, Tassilo Adam, worked as an ethnologist; after the family returned to Europe he studied at the Salzburg Mozarteum. In 1929 the family moved to New York, where Adam studied cello with E. Stoffnegen, D. C. Dounis, and (from 1938 to 1940) Feuermann; he also studied conducting with Barzin and composition with Blatt, and was a member of the National Orchestral Association, a training group for young instrumentalists (1935–40). From 1940 to 1943 he was principal cellist of the Minneapolis SO. After serving in the US Air Force during World War II, he studied composition in New York with Wolpe. In 1948 he formed the New Music Quartet, with which he performed until 1955, when he joined the JUILLIARD STRING QUARTET; he left the group in 1974 to devote his full energies to composition. Adam also had an active teaching career, with positions at the Aspen Music Festival (from 1953), the Juilliard School (from 1955), and the Mannes College (from 1974). His compositions include a Piano Sonata (1948), String Trio (1967), String Quartet (1975), Cello Concerto (1973), and Concerto-variations for orchestra (1976). Like his cello playing, they are characterized by robust expressiveness and infectious rhythmic energy. Adam's honors include an NEA grant (1974), a Guggenheim Fellowship (1975), residency at the American Academy in Rome (1976), and the Friedheim Chamber Music Award (1980), as well as commissions from the Naumburg (1974) and Paderewski (1976) foundations, among others.

JAMES WIERZBICKI

Adamowski, Timothée [Timoteusz] (*b* Warsaw, Poland, 24 March 1858; *d* Boston, MA, 18 April 1943). Violinist. He began violin studies at the age of seven, and later studied under Apolinary Katski and Gustaw Roguski at the Warsaw Conservatory, where he graduated with honors in 1874. He made his first American tour in 1879, and played with the Boston SO from 1884 until 1907 (except in 1887–8 when he made a European tour). He appeared 82 times as soloist, and after 1890 occasionally appeared as conductor of the summer "pops" concerts. He also appeared with orchestras in London, Paris, and Warsaw. In 1888 he formed the Adamowski Quartet with the violinist E. Fiedler, the violist D. Kuntz, and the cellist G. Campanari; the group was reconstituted the following year with A. Moldauer, Max Zach, and Adamowski's brother Joseph, and gave several series of subscription concerts each year. According to Zach's son, Leon Henry Zach (the source of information regarding the quartet in the article on his father in *DAB*), the group was active until 1906. In 1896 Adamowski formed the Adamowski Trio with his brother Joseph and Joseph's wife Antoinette, a pianist. While continuing to perform chamber music, he taught violin at the New England Conservatory from 1908 until 1933. He was known for his fluent and masterly technique and musical tone. He also composed pieces for violin and piano.

BIBLIOGRAPHY

GroveAS

W. S. B. Mathews: *A Hundred Years of Music in America* (Chicago, 1889/*R*1970)

M. A. D. Howe: *The Boston Symphony Orchestra: an Historical Sketch* (Boston, 1914, rev. and enlarged 2/1931/*R*1978)

H. C. Lahee: *Annals of Music in America* (Boston, 1922)

Obituary, *New York Times* (19 April 1943)

JEFFREY R. REHBACH

Adams, Alton A(ugustus) (*b* St. Thomas, VI, 4 Nov 1889). Bandmaster, composer, and educator. He took correspondence courses from several universities, and received a BMus degree from the University Extension Conservatory of Music, Chicago. In 1910 he formed Adams' Juvenile Band, which was incorporated into the US Navy when the navy assumed the administrative duties of the US Virgin Islands in 1917. He was editor of the band department of *Jacobs' Band Monthly* from 1913 to 1917, the Virgin Islands correspondent for the Associated Press, and the author of articles for various music journals, newspapers, and magazines. From 1918 to 1931 he supervised the music program for the Virgin Islands public schools, which he modeled after similar programs on the mainland. After retiring from the navy in 1947 he produced musical radio programs for 16 years. He wrote many compositions for band, most of which were destroyed by fire in 1933. His works include the *Virgin Islands March*, the islands' national anthem.

BIBLIOGRAPHY

K. R. Farr: "Adams, Alton August," *Historical Dictionary of Puerto Rico and the U.S. Virgin Islands*, Latin American Historical Dictionaries, no.9 (Metuchen, NJ, 1973)

S. A. Floyd, Jr.: "Alton Augustus Adams," *BPiM*, v (1977), 173

T. Schlesinger: "Alton Adams: a Point of View," *All-Ah-Wee*, i/3 (1977), 28

M. L. Philipp: *Die Musikkultur der Jungferninseln* (diss., U. of Cologne, Germany, in preparation)

MARGOT LIETH PHILIPP

Adams, Charles R. (*b* Charlestown, MA, 9 Feb 1834; *d* West Harwich, MA, 4 July 1900). Tenor. He studied singing in Boston and in 1856 was soloist in the Handel and Haydn Society's performance of *The Creation*. In 1861 he made concert and opera appearances in the West Indies and Holland. He studied in Vienna with Carlo Barbieri, was engaged for three years by the Royal Opera, Berlin, then for eight seasons in the period 1867–76 as principal tenor of the Vienna Hofoper. He also sang at La

Scala and Covent Garden. In 1877 he returned to the USA and in March 1878 sang the title role in the first American production of Wagner's *Rienzi*. The next season, 1878–9, he attempted with Eugenie Pappenheim to mount a series of four Wagner operas but met with little success. His greatest roles were thought to be Tannhäuser and Lohengrin. From 1879 he lived in Boston as a successful singing teacher; Nellie Melba and Emma Eames were among his pupils.

BIBLIOGRAPHY

F. L. Gwinner Cole: "Adams, Charles R.," *DAB*
O. Thompson: *The American Singer* (New York, 1937/*R*1969), 85

H. WILEY HITCHCOCK

Adams, John (Coolidge) (*b* Worcester, MA, 15 Feb 1947). Composer and conductor. After learning clarinet at first with his father and then with Felix Viscuglia (of the Boston SO) he studied composition with Kirchner at Harvard University (BA 1969, MA 1971); he also studied conducting with Mario di Bonaventura at Dartmouth College (summer 1965). While at Harvard, he worked as a freelance performer, occasionally substituting with the Boston SO; he also gave the first performances in Boston, New York, and Washington of Piston's Clarinet Concerto. He served as composer-in-residence at the Marlboro Festival (1970) and from 1972 to 1982 he taught at the San Francisco Conservatory and directed the New Music Ensemble there. During his tenure with that group he commissioned and introduced many works by leading and emerging experimental composers. In 1978 he became new-music adviser to the San Francisco SO, where with De Waart he created the New and Unusual Music series, which served as the model for the Meet the Composer residency program; through this program he was appointed composer-in-residence of the San Francisco SO (1982–5). In 1982 he was awarded a Guggenheim Fellowship.

Early in his career, Adams became interested in electronics, jazz, and such experimental American composers as John Cage, Christian Wolff, Morton Feldman, and Robert Ashley, and this, along with his move to California in 1971, led him away from the academic structuralism of, for example, the Piano Quintet, to the freer, somewhat aleatory style of *American Standard*, in which elements of gospel, jazz, march music, and "found" texts are juxtaposed. Although *Onyx* leans towards a quiet expressiveness, Adams's latent lyricism did not emerge until *Phrygian Gates* (1977). With it his driving, pulsating harmonic style came to the fore; the work is repetitive but continually modulates to different modes through a "gating" principle derived from electronic music. *Shaker Loops*, written a year later, has become known for the distinctive personality it projects within a repetitive structure (for excerpt from score *see* NOTATION, fig.24). Adams differs from many of the minimalist school in that he writes detailed, through-composed, formalized music that is also quite accessible. With *Harmonium*, commissioned by the San Francisco SO in 1980, he established a reputation as a composer for traditional forces. The three-movement *Harmonielehre* (*see* ORCHESTRAL MUSIC, fig.3) owes much of its inspiration to Schoenberg's *Gurrelieder* and the symphonies of Sibelius. Its style is more chromatic, with faster harmonic motion, than Adams's previous works. Both it and *Harmonium* possess a striking orchestral resonance. In 1985 Adams was collaborating with Peter Sellars and the poet Alice Goodman on an opera entitled *Nixon in China*. Adams's recorded works include *Harmonium*, *Grand Pianola Music*, the orchestral version of *Shaker Loops*, *Light over Water*, and *Harmonielehre*.

John Adams, 1981

See also NOTATION, §2.

WORKS

Pf Qnt, 1970; American Standard, unspecified ens, 1973; Grounding, 3 solo vv, insts, elec, 1975; Onyx, tape, 1976; Saxophone, videotape, 1976, collab. M. Fisher; China Gates, pf, 1977; Phrygian Gates, pf, 1977; Shaker Loops, str septet, 1978, arr. str orch, 1983; Common Tones in Simple Time, orch, 1979; Harmonium (Donne, Dickinson), SATB, orch, 1980; Grand Pianola Music, 2 S, 2 pf, small orch, 1981–2; Matter of Heart, film score, 1982; Available Light (dance music, L. Childs, F. Gehry), 1983, incl. Light over Water, brass, synth; Harmonielehre, orch, 1984–5

Principal publisher: Associated

BIBLIOGRAPHY

A. Porter: "Bay Laurels," *New Yorker*, lvii (10 Aug 1981), 76
T. Page: "Framing the River: a Minimalist Picture," *HiFi*, xxxi/11 (1981), 64
M. Walsh: "The Heart is Back in the Game," *Time* (20 Sept 1982), 60
G. Sandow: "Tasting the New Era," *Village Voice* (29 Jan 1985), 72

INGRAM D. MARSHALL

Adams, Lee (*b* 1924). Lyricist who collaborated on several Broadway shows with CHARLES STROUSE.

Adams, Nathan (*b* Dunstable, NH, 21 Aug 1783; *d* Milford, NH, 16 March 1864). Brass instrument maker. He is listed as a musical instrument maker in the New York City Directory for 1824. For the next four years he was bandmaster on the *USS Constitution*. In about 1828 he settled in Lowell, Massachusetts, continuing there as a music instrument maker until 1835. He invented a valve with movable tongues or flaps within the windway. One of his trumpets with three such valves is displayed on board the *USS Constitution*; it dates from about 1830. A similar instrument, unsigned, with three primitive rotary valves, is in the Essig Collection, Warrensburg, Missouri. The latter part of Adams's life was spent as a machinist and repairman in Provincetown, Massachusetts. He was the composer of at least one published song, *The Ruins of Troy*, written while on board the *Constitution*.

BIBLIOGRAPHY

Contributions of the Old Residents' Historical Association, Lowell, Massachusetts, v (Lowell, 1894)

R. E. Eliason: "Early American Valves for Brass Instruments," *GSJ*, xxiii (1970), 86

ROBERT E. ELIASON

Adams, Pepper [Park] (*b* Highland Park, MI, 8 Oct 1930). Jazz baritone saxophonist. After playing various reed instruments in school, he was inspired by Harry Carney of Duke Ellington's band to concentrate solely on the baritone saxophone. He began his professional career in 1947 in Detroit, where he worked with Lucky Thompson, Tommy Flanagan, Kenny Burrell, and others. In 1956 he moved to New York; during the next decade he worked in the big bands of Stan Kenton, Benny Goodman, Maynard Ferguson, and Lionel Hampton, with Charles Mingus, and as leader of a quintet with the trumpeter Donald Byrd (1958–61). In 1965 he began an important affiliation with the highly influential Thad Jones–Mel Lewis Orchestra. He left this group in 1976, and has continued to appear mainly as a leader, playing with local rhythm sections throughout the USA and Europe, where his gruff, authoritative sound continues to grow as an influence.

RECORDINGS
(selective list)

10-4 at the 5-Spot (1958, Riv. 265); *Plays Charlie Mingus* (1963, Jazz Workshop 219); *Encounter* (1968, Prst. 7677); *Ephemera* (1974, Spotlite 6); *Julian* (1975, Enja 2060); *Reflectory* (1979, Muse 5182); *The Master* (1981, Muse 5213); *Urban Dreams* (1981, Palo Alto 8009)

BIBLIOGRAPHY

A. J. Smith: "The Essence of Spice," *Down Beat*, xliv/18 (1977), 18

L. Jeske: "Pepper Adams," *Down Beat*, xlix/8 (1982), 28

LEE JESKE

Adams, Suzanne (*b* Cambridge, MA, 28 Nov 1872; *d* London, England, 5 Feb 1953). Soprano. She studied with Mathilde Marchesi and Jacques Bouhy in Paris and made her début at the Paris Opéra in 1895 as Juliet, a role which, together with Marguerite in *Faust*, she seems to have studied with Gounod, who greatly admired her brilliant yet flexible tone and fine vocal method. She sang at Covent Garden (1898–1904), where she created Hero in C. V. Stanford's *Much Ado About Nothing*; during the same period (1899–1903) she was a member of the Metropolitan Opera. Her repertory included Gluck's Eurydice, Donna Elvira, Micaela, and Marguerite de Valois. As an oratorio singer she earned distinction in England and the USA, and her singing of the soprano in *Messiah* at Carnegie Hall in 1904 was described as the finest heard in New York since Therese Tietjens sang it there. She married the cellist Leo Stein, whose death in 1904 led to her early retirement from the stage. She then taught singing in London.

BIBLIOGRAPHY

O. Thompson: *The American Singer* (New York, 1937/*R*1969), 199

J. Freestone: "Suzanne Adams," *Gramophone*, xxxi (1953–4), 37 [with discography]

HERMAN KLEIN/HAROLD ROSENTHAL/R

Adderley, Cannonball [Julian Edwin] (*b* Tampa, FL, 15 Sept 1928; *d* Gary, IN, 8 Aug 1975). Jazz alto saxophonist and teacher. The nickname "Cannonball" was a childhood corruption of "cannibal," describing his large appetite. He played alto saxophone in Florida bands from around 1942 and directed a high school band in Fort Lauderdale for over two years from September 1948. After serving in army bands from 1950 to 1953 he resumed teaching until 1955. He then moved to New York, intending to play with his brother Nat, a jazz cornetist, and to begin graduate studies at New York University. Instead, a chance jam session led to his joining the Oscar Pettiford band and signing a recording contract.

The Adderley brothers formed a promising quintet in January 1956, but in September 1957 the group was forced to disband because of financial difficulties. Adderley then replaced Sonny Rollins in the Miles Davis Quintet in October 1957. He stayed in Davis's famous sextets, playing with John Coltrane, until September 1959, when he formed a second quintet with his brother. This group, which played soul jazz and bop, remained intact until 1975, achieving considerable success. At various times the members included the pianists George Duke, Victor Feldman, and Joe Zawinul (who composed their hit tune *Mercy, mercy, mercy*) and drummers Louis Hayes and Roy McCurdy. From January 1962 to July 1965 the group expanded to form a sextet with the addition of Yusef Lateef and later Charles Lloyd on reeds. Articulate and effective as a teacher, Adderley led the quintet at college workshops in the late 1960s and early 1970s, speaking on the musical and sociological aspects of jazz.

A masterful, confident improviser, Adderley was called "the new Bird" because his début in 1955 occurred shortly after Charlie Parker's death. This unfortunate label caused resentment among the press and public, and set him unattainable standards. Though he at times imitated Parker (as did all bop alto saxophonists), his first bop recordings reveal more chromatic and continuous lines and a more cutting tone than Parker's; on other early recordings he played and composed in a simple blues- and gospel-oriented style. His approach to improvisation changed significantly while he was with Davis, who taught him to use silence effectively, and again during the mid-1960s when he incorporated elements of free jazz. From 1969 he also performed on soprano saxophone.

RECORDINGS
(selective list)

As leader: *Presenting Cannonball Adderley* (1955, Savoy 12018); *Somethin' Else* (1958, BN 1595); *Portrait of Cannonball Adderley* (1958, Riv. 269); *Things are Getting Better* (1958, Riv. 286); *The Cannonball Adderley Quintet in San Francisco* (1959, Riv. 311); *Them Dirty Blues* (1960, Riv. 322); *African Waltz* (1961, Riv. 377); *Nippon Soul* (1963, Riv. 477); *Live!* (1964, Cap. 2399); *Mercy, Mercy, Mercy!* (1966, Cap. 2663); *Country Preacher* (1969, Cap. 0414); *Inside Straight* (1973, Fan. 9435)

As sideman with M. Davis: *Milestones* (1958, Col. CL1193); *Jazz Track* (1957–8, Col. CL1268); *Miles and Monk at Newport* (1958, Col. CL2178); *Jazz at the Plaza*, i (1958, Col. C32470); *Kind of Blue* (1959, Col. CL1355)

BIBLIOGRAPHY

I. Gitler: "Julian 'Cannonball' Adderley," *Jazz* (1959), no.3, p.197; no.4, p.289

J. Adderley: "Paying Dues: the Education of a Combo Leader," *Jazz Review*, iii/4 (1960), 12

"Adderley, Julian E(dwin)," *CBY 1961*

D. DeMichael: "The Responsibilities of Success: Cannonball," *Down Beat*, xxix/13 (1962), 13

F. Postif: "Julian 'Cannonball' Adderley," *Jazz hot*, no.184 (1963), 17

J. Ginibre: "Les frères amis à la question," *Jazz magazine*, no.131 (1966), 18

B. Quinn: "The Well Rounded 'Ball'," *Down Beat*, xxxiv/23 (1967), 17

C. Albertson: "Cannonball the Communicator," *Down Beat*, xxxvii/1 (1970), 12

P. Wilson: "Conversing with Cannonball," *Down Beat*, xxxix/12 (1972), 12

B. Priestley: "Cannonball: from the Soul," *Melody Maker*, xlvii (4 Nov 1972), 48

"Farewell Cannonball," *Swing Journal*, xxix/12 (1975), 248 [discography]

W. van Eyle: "Cannonball Adderley discografie," *Jazz Press*, no.37 (1977), 14; no.38 (1977), 7; no.40 (1977), 19; no.43 (1977), 6 [addns and corrections]
D. Baker: *The Jazz Style of Cannonball Adderley* (Lebanon, IN, 1980)
B. Kernfeld: *Adderley, Coltrane, and Davis at the Twilight of Bebop: the Search for Melodic Coherence (1958–59)* (diss., Cornell U., 1981)
J. Winter: "Julian Cannonball Adderley," *Coda*, no.186 (1982), 4

BARRY KERNFELD

Addison, Adele (*b* New York, 24 July 1925). Soprano. Her vocal and musical abilities won her scholarships to Westminster Choir College, Princeton (BM 1946), and the Berkshire Music Center, where she studied with Goldovsky. She made her recital début at Boston in April 1948 and, after further coaching with Povla Frijsh in New York, appeared at Town Hall on 27 January 1952. This established her reputation as an intelligent musician and led to engagements with most American orchestras and the New England and New York City Opera companies. On 23 September 1962 she sang in the inaugural concert at Lincoln Center; she toured the USSR in 1963. The silvery timbre of her voice, her agility, and distinguished musicianship all made her an ideal performer of Baroque music, as her recordings of Bach (*St. Matthew Passion*) and Handel (*Ode for St. Cecilia's Day*) attest. These qualities also made her an admired exponent of contemporary music – she gave the first performances of Foss's *Time Cycle* (1960) and Poulenc's *Gloria* (1961), among many other works. She has taught at the Eastman School, Philadelphia College of the Performing Arts, Aspen Music School, and SUNY, Stony Brook.

BIBLIOGRAPHY

SouthernB

RICHARD BERNAS/R

Adgate, Andrew (*b* Norwich, CT, 22 March 1762; *d* Philadelphia, PA, 30 Sept 1793). Singing teacher, conductor, and tunebook compiler. He assisted Andrew Law at a singing-school in Philadelphia in April 1783, and by 1784 had set up an Institution for the Encouragement of Church Music. This was superseded the next year by his "Free School. . . for diffusing more generally the knowledge of vocal music," which came to be called the Uranian Society, and was finally reorganized in 1787 as the Uranian Academy. Unlike traditional singing-schools, which were private institutions with each scholar paying his or her own way, Adgate's schools were supported by subscription and charged no fees – an early instance of educational democracy. Subscribers received tickets for concerts devoted chiefly to sacred music, given by the singing scholars and their associates under Adgate's direction. These concerts, which took place between 1785 and 1790, were probably the first of their kind in Philadelphia, and perhaps the first anywhere in the USA. A "Grand Concert" on 4 May 1786, which included works by Handel, Lyon, Billings, and Tuckey, performed by 230 choristers and an orchestra of 50, was a benefit held for the Pennsylvania Hospital, the Philadelphia Dispensary, and "the Poor."

Adgate's first compilation was an anthology of sacred texts: *Select Psalms and Hymns for the Use of Mr. Adgate's Pupils* (Philadelphia, 1787). In 1788 he brought out *The Rudiments of Music*, an instructional manual proposing an original method of solmization, and the next year he issued *The Philadelphia Harmony*, a tunebook containing the most popular American and European sacred pieces; combined in one volume, these two items ran through nine editions in Philadelphia by 1807. Some authorities have claimed that Adgate was "Absalom Aimwell," the compiler of *The Philadelphia Songster* (Philadelphia, 1789).

BIBLIOGRAPHY

O. G. T. Sonneck: *Early Concert-life in America (1731–1800)* (Leipzig, 1907/*R*1978), 103
W. S. Pratt: "Adgate, Andrew," *DAB*
C. Rourke: *The Roots of American Culture* (New York, 1942), 170
R. Crawford: *Andrew Law, American Psalmodist* (Evanston, IL, 1968/*R*1981), 62
H. D. Cummings: *Andrew Adgate: Philadelphia Psalmodist and Music Educator* (diss., U. of Rochester, 1975)
I. Lowens: *A Bibliography of Songsters Printed in America before 1821* (Worcester, MA, 1976), 20

RICHARD CRAWFORD

Adler, Kurt Herbert (*b* Vienna, Austria, 2 April 1905). Conductor and opera director. He was educated at the academy and university in Vienna, and made his début in 1925 as a conductor for the Max Reinhardt theater, then conducted at the Volksoper and at opera houses in Germany, Italy, and Czechoslovakia. He assisted Toscanini in Salzburg (1936) and went to the USA in 1938 for an engagement with the Chicago Opera. He joined the staff of the San Francisco Opera in 1943, initially as chorus master, becoming artistic director in 1953 and general director in 1956; he retained the last post with much distinction until his retirement on 31 December 1981 and was then named general director emeritus. Although he occasionally conducted, most of his time was devoted to administrative duties. During his regime the San Francisco Opera became increasingly adventurous in repertory; it also became noted for the engagement of unproven talent, and the implementation of modern staging techniques. Adler organized subsidiary groups in San Francisco to stage experimental works, to perform in schools and other unconventional locales, and to train young singers. Besides his work in the USA, he has continued to conduct in Europe, Australia, and China, and has received citations from a number of European governments.

See also SAN FRANCISCO, §I, 3, and fig.3.

BIBLIOGRAPHY

S. Jenkins: "The Maestro: Kurt Herbert Adler Talks to Speight Jenkins," *Opera News*, xxxviii/4 (1973), 14
"Adler, Kurt Herbert," *CBY1979*
K. Lockhart, ed.: *The Adler Years* (San Francisco, 1981)

MARTIN BERNHEIMER/R

Adler, Larry [Lawrence] (*b* Baltimore, MD, 10 Feb 1914). Harmonica player. He is acknowledged as the first harmonica player to achieve recognition and acceptance in classical musical circles and to have elevated the instrument to concert status. His ability has been recognized by such composers as Vaughan Williams, Milhaud, Gordon Jacob, Malcolm Arnold, Arthur Benjamin, and Joaquín Rodrigo, all of whom have written orchestral works with Adler as soloist. From the 1940s he performed with the dancer Paul Draper. In 1949 the two were accused of being Communist sympathizers; after they sued their attacker unsuccessfully for libel, Adler settled in London, returning to the USA first in 1959. His concerts in 1967 with Kostelanetz at Lincoln Center, where among other works he played Francis Chagrin's *Roumanian Fantasies* for harmonica and orchestra (a piece written for him in 1956), were highly acclaimed. His more recent New York appearances have been mostly at nightclubs.

He has toured extensively and broadcast frequently on radio and television in many countries throughout his career, and has

Larry Adler, 1950

taken a keen interest in all aspects of teaching his instrument. Adler has written scores for a number of films, including *Genevieve* (for which he received an Academy nomination), *King and Country*, and *A High Wind in Jamaica*. Among his recordings is a collection of little-known works by Gershwin, Kern, Porter, Rodgers, and others.

BIBLIOGRAPHY

"Seeking a Mark," *Time*, lxxxix (30 June 1967), 48

L. Adler: "Larry Adler – my Life on the Blacklist," *New York Times* (15 June 1975)

G. Giddins: "Larry Adler's Ghost Stories," *Village Voice* (20 Aug 1979), 70

L. Adler: *It ain't Necessarily So* (London, 1984)

IVOR BEYNON/R

Adler, Peter Herman (*b* Jablonec [now in Czechoslovakia], 2 Dec 1899). Conductor. After studying composition and conducting with Zemlinsky at the Prague Conservatory, he became music director of the Bremen Staatsoper (1929–32) and the State Philharmonia of Kiev (1933–6), and also appeared as a guest conductor throughout Europe. He left for the USA in 1939 and made his début with the New York PO in 1940, after which he toured in the USA. From 1949 to 1959 he was music and artistic director of the NBC Opera Company, sharing artistic responsibility with Toscanini, who was then conductor of the NBC SO. After Toscanini's death Adler became music director of the Baltimore SO (1959–68) and in 1969 music and artistic director of WNET (National Educational Television). His Metropolitan Opera début was in 1972. He was director of the American Opera Center at the Juilliard School from 1973 to 1981, and continued to be associated with it after his retirement. Adler was a pioneer director of television opera in the USA and commissioned many works for television, among them Menotti's *Amahl and the Night Visitors* and *Maria Golovin* (of which he conducted the première at the 1958 Brussels World's Fair), Dello Joio's *St. Joan* and Martinů's *The Marriage* (all at NBC); and Beeson's *My Heart's in the Highlands*, Pasatieri's *The Trial of Mary Lincoln*, and Henze's *La cubana* (at WNET).

ELLIOTT W. GALKIN/R

Adler, Richard (*b* New York, 3 Aug 1921). Composer and lyricist. He was the son of the concert pianist Clarence Adler and was largely self-taught in music; after studying at the University of North Carolina (BA 1943) and serving in the navy (1943–6) he began writing songs. From 1950 he collaborated with Jerry Ross (*b* New York, 9 March 1926; *d* New York, 11 Nov 1955); their first success was *Rags to Riches* (1953) and their first work for Broadway was six songs in the revue *John Murray Anderson's Almanac* (1953). The wit both of their music and their lyrics impressed Frank Loesser, who helped to promote their early work. In 1954 they were acclaimed for their first musical *The Pajama Game*; its songs (e.g., "Hey there" and "Hernando's Hideaway") were mostly well integrated with the plot and used American speech idioms. Adler and Ross followed this with *Damn Yankees* (1955), from which the songs "Heart" and "Whatever Lola wants" became famous. After Ross's death Adler began to compose television musicals and advertising jingles; he also wrote three further musicals – *Kwamina* (1961), *A Mother's Kisses* (1968), and *Music Is* (1976) – though these were not successful. During the late 1970s and early 1980s he wrote works for orchestra. He was arts consultant to the White House (1965–9) and has produced several Broadway shows. As a songwriting team (each man contributed both music and lyrics), Adler and Ross were adept at blending a wide range of musical styles and rhythms within a single score; the best of their theater music is original, imaginative, and wittily colloquial. Adler's son, the lyricist Christopher Adler, died in 1984 at the age of 30.

WORKS
(selective list)

STAGE

All musicals; unless otherwise indicated, dates are those of first New York performance.

The Pajama Game (G. Abbott, R. Bissell, after Bissell: $7\frac{1}{2}$ Cents), collab. J. Ross, 13 May 1954 [incl. Hey there, Hernando's Hideaway]; film, 1957

Damn Yankees (Abbott, D. Wallop), collab. Ross, 5 May 1955 [incl. Heart, Whatever Lola wants]; film, 1958

Kwamina (R. A. Arthur), 23 Oct 1961

A Mother's Kisses, New Haven, CT, 1968

Music Is (Abbott, W. Holt, after Shakespeare: Twelfth Night), 20 Dec 1976

SONGS
(all written with J. Ross)

Rags to Riches (1953); Harlequinade, Queen for a Day, You're so much a part of me, Hope you come back, Acorn in the Meadow, When am I going to meet your mother?, in John Murray Anderson's Almanac, 1953

OTHER WORKS

Television musicals: Little Women, 1957; The Gift of the Magi, 1958; Olympus 7-0000, 1966

Orch: Memory of a Childhood, 1978; Retrospection, 1979; Yellowstone, ov., 1980; Wilderness Suite, 1982

BIBLIOGRAPHY

S. Green: *The World of Musical Comedy* (New York, 1960, rev. and enlarged 4/1980)

D. Ewen: *Popular American Composers* (New York, 1962; suppl. 1972)

Adler, Samuel (Hans) (*b* Mannheim, Germany, 4 March 1928). Composer, conductor, and teacher. Both of his parents were musical, his father being a cantor and composer of Jewish liturgical music. The family came to the USA in 1939 and Samuel attended Boston University (BM 1948) and Harvard University (MA 1950). He studied composition with Copland, Fromm, Hindemith, Hugo Norden, Piston, and Randall Thompson; musicology with Geiringer, A. T. Davison, and Pisk; and conducting with Koussevitzky at the Berkshire Music Center. In 1950 he joined the US Army and organized the Seventh Army SO, which he conducted in more than 75 concerts in Germany and Austria; he was awarded the Army Medal of Honor for his musical services. Subsequently he conducted concerts and operas and lectured extensively throughout Europe and the USA. In 1957 he was appointed professor of composition at North Texas State University and in 1966 he joined the faculty of the Eastman School, where he has served as chairman of the composition department from 1974. He has received numerous commissions and awards, including grants from the Rockefeller (1965) and Ford (1966–71) foundations and the NEA (1977, 1980), a Koussevitzky Foundation commission for a symphonic work (1983), and a Guggenheim Fellowship (1984–5). He has been an active member of ASCAP and other musical societies. His book *A Study of Orchestration* received the ASCAP-Deems Taylor award in 1983.

Adler is a prolific composer whose music embraces a wide variety of contemporary styles. His works exhibit great rhythmic vitality, with a predilection for asymmetrical rhythms and meters, and a keen sensitivity to counterpoint. His harmonic materials vary from diatonicism and pan-diatonicism (in the works before 1969) to serial techniques (substantial use beginning with Symphony no.4, 1967) and occasional improvisatory and aleatory elements (e.g., in the Concerto for wind, brass, and percussion, 1968, and Symphony no.5, 1975). Clustered effects and a colorful orchestral palette typify works such as the Concerto for flute and orchestra (1977). Adler's vocal compositions range from large-scale pieces reflecting a strong liturgical background to secular miniatures that are often lighthearted and humorous in nature. A number of his works have been recorded, and more than 200 have been published.

WORKS

STAGE

The Outcast of Poker Flat (opera, 1, J. Stampfer), 1959; The Wrestler (opera, 1, Stampfer), 1971; The Lodge of Shadows (music-drama, J. Ramsey), Bar, dancers, orch, 1973; The Disappointment (opera, A. Barton), 1974 [reconstruction of an early ballad opera]; The Waking (ballet, T. Roethke, others), chorus, orch, 1978

ORCHESTRAL

Sym. no.1, 1953; Sym. no.2, 1957; Southwestern Sketches, 1960; Sym. no.3 "Diptych," 1960, rev. 1980; Requiescat in pace, 1963; Sym. no.4 "Geometrics," 1967; Conc., wind, brass, perc, 1968; Org Conc., 1970; Conc. for Orch, 1971; Sym. no.5 "We are the Echoes" (C. Adler, Heschel, Oppenheimer, Rukeyser, Wolfkehl), Mez, orch, 1975; Concertino no.2, orch, 1976; Fl Conc., 1977; Pf Conc., 1983; Sym. no.6, 1985; *c*25 other works incl. *c*12 for wind ens/brass

CHAMBER AND INSTRUMENTAL

Hn Sonata, 1948; Str Qts nos.3–7, 1953–81, incl. no.6 (Whitman), Mez/Bar, str qt, 1975; Vn Sonata no.2, 1956; Toccata, Recitation and Postlude, org, 1959; Sonata breve, pf, 1963; Introduction and Capriccio, harp, 1964; 2 pf trios, 1964, 1978; Vn Sonata no.3, 1965; Vc Sonata, 1966; Cantos I–XI, various insts, 1968–83

4 Dialogues, euphonium, mar, 1974; Aeolus, God of the Winds, cl, vn, vc, pf, 1977; Of Musique, Poetrie, Nature, and Love (Herrick), Mez, fl, pf, 1978; Pf Sonatina, 1979; Fl Sonata, 1981; Gottschalkiana, brass qnt, 1982; Hpd Sonata, 1982; Duo Sonata, 2 pf, 1983; Va Sonata, 1984; Gui Sonata, 1985; Ob Sonata, 1985; *c*15 other inst works, *c*20 ens works

VOCAL

Shir chadash (Sabbath service), B, SAB, org, 1960; The Vision of Isaiah (Bible), B, SATB, orch, 1962; B'Shaaray tefilah (Sabbath service), B, SATB, org/orch, 1963; Shiru Ladonay (Sabbath service), solo/unison vv, org, 1965; Behold your God (Bible), cantata, 1966; The Binding (Friedlander), oratorio, 1967; From out of Bondage (Bible), S, A, T, B, SATB, brass qnt, perc, org, 1968; A Whole Bunch of Fun (Catullus, Finjan, Moore, Nash, Roethke, Seuss), cantata, vv, orch, 1969

We Believe (liturgical), mixed vv, 8 insts, 1974; Of Saints and Sinners (Feldman, Kauffman, others), medium v, pf, 1976; A Falling of Saints (Rosenbaum), T, B, chorus, orch, 1977; It is to God I shall Sing (Psalms), chorus, org, 1977; Snow Tracks (American poets), high v, wind, 1981; 7 other large choral works; numerous smaller sacred and many secular choral works; 12 works for solo vv, acc. and unacc.; works for children; arrs.

Principal publishers: Boosey & Hawkes, C. Fischer, Ludwig, Oxford UP, Peters, Presser, G. Schirmer, Southern

WRITINGS

Anthology for the Teaching of Choral Conducting (New York, 1971)
Sightsinging, Pitch, Interval, Rhythm (New York, 1979)
A Study of Orchestration (New York, 1982)

BIBLIOGRAPHY

EwenD

A. M. Rothmüller: *The Music of the Jews: an Historical Appreciation* (South Brunswick, NJ, rev. 2/1967)

J. D. Lucas: *The Operas of Samuel Adler: an Analytical Study* (diss., Louisiana State U., 1978)

MARIE ROLF

Advertising, music in. The practice of employing music to convey a commercial message began in America in colonial times, when street vendors in the seaports hawked their goods to the accompaniment of a melodic cry or chant. Besides its direct use to advertise merchandise, music has also been the means of fixing certain commodities in the minds of the public: music written in celebration of particular products or services, but not commissioned by the companies that provide them, has sometimes benefited whole industries. Much of the early history of the link between music and commerce concerns advertising in this indirect sense. Tobacco was immortalized by James Hewitt's *Pipe de tabac* in the early 1800s, and in 1836 John Ashton of Boston published a song by Joseph Gear called *Think & smoke tobacco*, introducing it as "A Favorite Old Song on Mortality," which was "Made agreeable & pleasing to all Classes, from the King to the Beggar." Advances in the transportation industry were praised in such pieces as the *Rail Road March* (published for Independence Day 1828 by George Willig and dedicated to the directors of the Baltimore & Ohio Rail Road), *The Alsacian Rail Road Gallops* (published by A. Fiot in 1845), and *The Iron Horse* (published by Lee & Walker in 1870 and dedicated to the Brotherhood of Locomotive Engineers). Other song tributes to commercial enterprise include the *Telephone March* (published in 1877 by White, Smith & Co. of Boston) and *Since my daughter plays on the typewriter* (published in 1889 by Thomas P. Getz). *The American Stamp Polka* and *Postal Card Galop* (published in 1864 and 1875 respectively by William A. Pond; see illustration, p.10) commemorated the postal service, and *The Baseball Quadrille* (1867, a predecessor of *Take me out to the ball game*) praised the nation's newest professional sport.

Before the advent of radio, music and lyrics were incorporated into printed advertisements in a number of different ways. A trade card circulated in 1883 contained the musical notation and words for a catchy four-line jingle about Vegetable Compound:

> Mrs. Brown had female weakness,
> She could have no children, dear,
> Till she took two bottles of Compound,
> Now she has one every year.

Other examples of trade-card songs include *The American Mechanics March* (1890), the banking theme song *March of the 1/8 Brigade* (1903), *The Drake's Cake Walk* (1909), and *The Uncle Sam Shoe* (1913). Advertisements that incorporated music, such as the setting of the slogan for Pears soap (for illustration *see* PATTI, ADELINA), also appeared in newspapers and other kinds of printed matter. The firm of Warner Lambert took advantage of the interest in parlor music by printing advertisements for its product Bromo Seltzer on the covers of organ transcriptions of such popular songs as *Annie Laurie* and *Ben Bolt* and distributing them

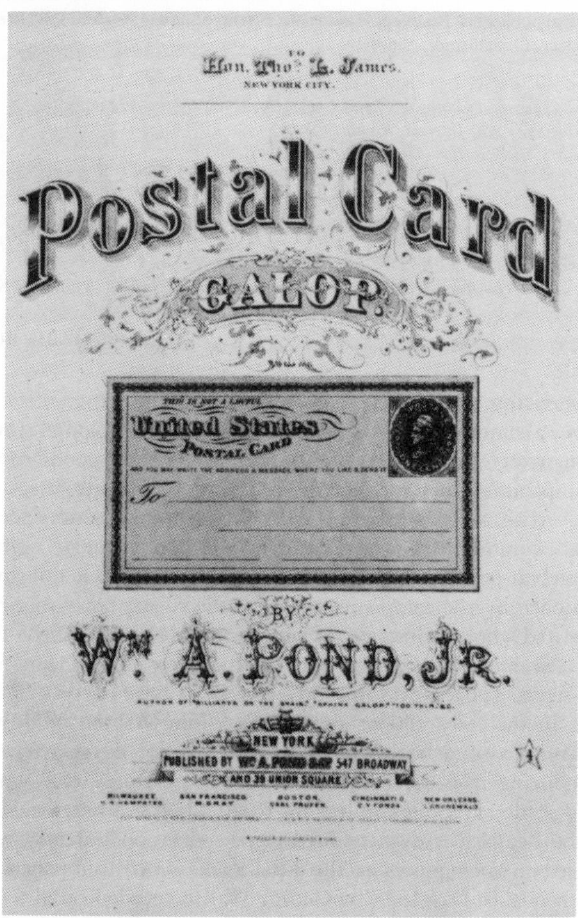

Sheet-music cover of the "Postal Card Galop" by William A. Pond, published by his firm in New York in 1875

free of charge. Some American companies published commercial songs in the form of sheet music, such as *American Petroleum* (published in 1864 by William Hall), *My Kola Girl* (1895, with the lyrics "She chews good Kola gum/The best that's made, they say"), and *Oh you spearmint kiddo with the Wrigley eyes*, which declared that a certain lady's "Every kiss is loaded with bliss peptonized." An early example of a sung advertisement was an adaptation by the Lion Coffee Company of *Rally 'round the Flag*. Other songs exploited well-known manufacturers' or popular brand names (thus advertising products indirectly), such as two songs with music by Harry Von Tilzer that celebrated beer drinking, *Down where the Wurzburger flows* (1902) and *Under the Anheuser Bush* (1903), the latter playing on the name of the brewers of Budweiser beer.

In 1925, the composer and writer on music Nicolas Slonimsky took whole passages of advertising copy from the *Saturday Evening Post* and set them to music, choosing a melodramatic idiom suitable to such phrases as "Mother, relieve your constipated child!", which he worked into a song for Fletcher's Castoria. He attempted to sell his settings to the manufacturers but met with only limited success: he secured permission to publish the advertising copy for Castoria and was offered a phonograph horn from the Utica Sheets Company by way of payment, but Pepsodent threatened to sue him for infringement of copyright (Slonimsky eventually changed the name of the product from Pepsodent to Plurodent when he recorded the songs in 1972).

As soon as radio became a feature of a large number of homes (in the late 1920s and 1930s) manufacturers began to exploit its potential as an advertising medium, and radio commercials, consisting of rhymed lyrics set to music, became a principal element in marketing strategies. Notable examples of such jingles include those for the breakfast cereal Wheaties and the soft drink Pepsi Cola ("Pepsi Cola hits the spot/12 full ounces, that's a lot/Twice as much for a nickel, too/Pepsi Cola is the drink for you."), both from the 1950s.

The invention of television extended the opportunities for advertisers to reach the public through broadcasting, not only by providing another medium but by adding a visual element to support the effect made by the lyrics and music of the jingles. Advertising agencies began to create television programs in order to sell their products, and jingle singers went from show to show to perform live. As technical skills became more refined, commercial music grew more sophisticated. Proof of a new professionalism and the high value set on skillful production was provided by the founding in 1959 of the Clio awards for excellence in advertising; in 1983 over 8000 entries were received for awards in the nonprint categories, which included new arrangements of commercial themes, original music and lyrics, original music scoring, and the use of sound. Outstanding musicians such as Richard Rodney Bennett, Robert Russell Bennett, and John Barry have written a number of commercial underscores (the background music for spoken sections of a commercial). Technological advances have enabled composers to avail themselves of electronically produced sound effects ranging from liquids being poured into glasses to trees falling in a forest.

The commercial industry is now a highly competitive and potentially lucrative business. According to Hunter Murtaugh, vice-president and music director of an advertising agency in New York, six or eight recording studios in the city operate 16 hours a day, seven days a week, in the production of recordings of commercials. Studio musicians, who are expert in all popular styles, earn more than $60 an hour and receive additional payments if their recorded performances are used beyond an initial 13-week period. Advertisers spend between $50,000 and $2 million for the production of a single 60-second commercial and an additional $150,000–$200,000 each time it is used on national television (which enables them to reach 20 million people). As much as $75,000 has been paid for the exclusive use of a well-known copyrighted tune in a commercial.

Musical marketing has become a science of precise demographics, and a well-made commercial of 20 to 30 seconds is a synthesis of brilliantly compressed artistic elements. According to the advertisers, the perfect jingle attracts attention, sets a mood, creates the image of the product, entertains, is simple yet memorable, and appeals to the largest possible audience. Unlike radio spots, which because they are less expensive can be geared to a relatively small target audience, television commercials must, if they are to be cost-effective, stimulate large numbers of people. Different musical styles are employed to attract the attention of specific sectors of the public: hard rock, for example, appeals to viewers aged between ten and 25. Within such a stylistic framework, the aim of the jingle writer (who usually produces both the lyric and the music for a jingle) is to create as simple and catchy a phrase, or "hook," as possible. The most successful jingle writer in the USA is Steve Karmen, whose musical hooks have included "I love New York," "You can take Salem out of the country, but . . . " (Salem cigarettes), "Sooner or later, you'll own Generals" (General Tire), and "When you've said Budweiser, you've said it all" (Budweiser beer). (A collection of Karmen's jingles was published in 1980 as *The Jingle Man*. Other, similar collections include B. C. Landauer, ed., *Striking the Right Note in Advertising*, 1951; and P. Norback and C. Norback, eds., *Great Songs of Madison Avenue*, 1976.)

In 1976 a group of composers and producers in advertising established the Society of Advertising Music Producers, Arrangers, and Composers (SAMPAC), which is open to anyone who has achieved some success in the field. The society, which has its headquarters in New York and chapters in Los Angeles, Dallas, and Chicago, promotes the welfare and interests of its members, provides a forum for the exchange of technical and creative ideas, and honors excellence and artistic merit in the industry; in 1983 it instituted the Sammy awards for special merit in advertising. Members receive a *Guide to Negotiation in the Jingle Industry* and participate in a project to compile data about business practices. SAMPAC counts among its achievements BMI's agreement to pay performance fees for music used in advertising; ASCAP, the other large national performing rights organization, makes a payment to its members of a hundredth of an ASCAP credit for advertising music broadcast within any one-hour period.

BIBLIOGRAPHY

B. C. Landauer: *Some Music Sheets from the Bella C. Landauer Tradecard Collection at the New York Historical Society* (MS, 1940, *NHi*)

H. Dichter and E. Shapiro: *Early American Sheet Music* (New York, 1941/*R*1977)

D. Martin: "The Old-fashioned Singing Commercial," *MJ*, xx/7 (1962), 16; repr. in *Musigram*, ii/10 (1965), 112

S. Shemel and M. W. Krasilovsky: *This Business of Music* (New York, 1964, rev. and enlarged 4/1979), 268ff

R. Lockhart and D. Weissman: *Audio in Advertising* (New York, 1982)

H. Rosing: "Music in Advertising," *Popular Music Perspectives*, ed. D. Horn and P. Tagg (Göteborg, Sweden, and Exeter, England, 1982), 41

W. Woodward: *An Insider's Guide to Advertising Music* (New York, 1982)

N. Slonimsky: "The Strange History of the Singing Commercial," *Keyboard Classics*, iii/3 (1983), 10

STUART ISACOFF

AEC. *See* ART ENSEMBLE OF CHICAGO.

Aeolian American Corporation. American firm of instrument makers. It was formed in 1932 when the American Piano Corporation (the successor of the AMERICAN PIANO CO.) merged with the AEOLIAN CO. The name of the parent company was changed to AEOLIAN CORPORATION in 1964.

Aeolian Chamber Players. Quartet. Formed in New York in 1961 by the violinist Lewis Kaplan, the Aeolian Chamber Players were the first American ensemble of mixed instruments to perform together on a permanent basis. The group, which first played at Mount Holyoke College, Massachusetts, in October 1961 and made its New York début shortly thereafter (Town Hall, January 1962), originally consisted of Kaplan, flutist Harold Jones, clarinetist Robert Listokin, and pianist Gilbert Kalish; a cello was added in 1966, and the flute has been used only rarely since 1977. Present members are Kaplan, Jennifer Langbaum (cello), Charles Neidrich (clarinet), and Peter Basquin (piano). Since its début, when the ensemble played Shapey's *Discourse*, written specially for the occasion, it has given first performances of works by more than three dozen composers, including Berio, Bolcom, Rochberg, Pleskow, and Subotnick (some commissioned on its behalf by Bowdoin College, Maine, where the Bowdoin Summer Music Festival, co-founded and directed by Kaplan, takes place). It has made a number of recordings, the best-known of which is Crumb's *Vox balaenae*.

KAREN MONSON

Aeolian Co. Firm of player piano makers. It was founded by William B(urton) Tremaine (*b* New York, 1840; *d* New York, 1907), who had begun as a piano builder with Tremaine Brothers; he formed the Mechanical Orguinette Co. in New York in 1878. By 1888 he had started the Aeolian Organ & Music Co. (from 1895 the Aeolian Co.) to manufacture automatic organs and perforated music rolls. His son Henry B(arnes) Tremaine (*b* Brooklyn, NY, 20 July 1866; *d* Washington, DC, 13 May 1932) sensed the possibility of a larger market and directed the company in an extensive advertising campaign that resulted in the sale of millions of player pianos during the first three decades of the 20th century. In 1913 the company introduced the Duo-Art Reproducing Piano, a sophisticated mechanism that made it possible to record and reproduce through paper rolls the slightest nuances of a performer's dynamics, tempo, and phrasing; this was used to record a number of leading pianists of the time.

In 1903 Tremaine formed the Aeolian Weber Piano & Pianola Co. with $10 million of capital; the Aeolian Co. was a significant part of the new firm, which became the first successful American piano trust. The parent company eventually controlled such firms as the Chilton Piano Co., the Choralian Co. of Germany and Austria, Mason & Hamlin, the Orchestrelle Co. of England, the Pianola Company Proprietary of Australia, George Steck & Co.,

Advertisement (1900) for the pianola manufactured by the Aeolian Co. and marketed in England by its subsidiary the Orchestrelle Co.

the Stroud Piano Co., the Stuyvesant Piano Co., Technola, the Universal Music Co., the Vocalion Organ Co., the Votey Organ Co., the Weber Piano Co., and the Wheelock Piano Co. Noted for its development and aggressive marketing of various mechanical instruments, the Aeolian Co. manufactured the Aeriole, the Aeolian Orchestrelle Pianola, the Metrostyle Pianola, and Aeolian pipe organs. The firm's offices were in New York where it maintained the Aeolian Concert Hall. In 1931 the company's organ department merged with the Ernest M. Skinner Co. to form the Aeolian-Skinner Organ Co. In 1932 the company merged with the American Piano Corporation (formerly the AMERICAN PIANO CO.) to form the Aeolian American Corporation.

CYNTHIA ADAMS HOOVER

Aeolian Corporation. Firm of piano makers. It was formed as the result of two transactions; the first of these, a merger of the AEOLIAN CO. and the American Piano Corporation (formerly the AMERICAN PIANO CO.) on 1 September 1932, created the Aeolian American Corporation. In May 1959 the assets of Aeolian American were purchased by Winter & Co. The parent company changed its name to the Aeolian Corporation on 12 June 1964; the name Aeolian American Corporation was retained by the firm's East Rochester, New York, division until 1971, when it became the Aeolian American Division of the Aeolian Corporation.

The corporation acquired the assets (including trademarks, plans, and factories) of many formerly independent American piano companies. Its instruments are made in three cities under the following trade names: Mason & Risch (Toronto); Mason & Hamlin; Chickering; Wm. Knabe & Co. (East Rochester); Cable; Winter; Hardman, Peck; Kranich & Bach; J. & C. Fischer; George Steck; Vose & Sons; Henry F. Miller; Ivers & Pond; Melodigrand; Duo-Art; Musette; and Pianola Player Piano (Memphis). In 1980 the name of the corporation was changed to Aeolian Piano, Inc.; it was purchased in 1983 by Peter Perez, a former president of Steinway & Sons, but was declared bankrupt in 1985.

CYNTHIA ADAMS HOOVER

Aeolian-Skinner Organ Co. Firm of organ builders. Ernest M(artin) Skinner (*b* Clarion, PA, 15 Jan 1866; *d* Duxbury, MA, 27 Oct 1961) started an organ company in 1901. He had begun as an apprentice with George H. Ryder of Reading, Massachusetts, and was then employed by Hutchings of Boston as a draftsman and, later, a foreman. Soon after beginning his own business in South Boston, he began to obtain important contracts, one of the earliest of which was for an organ for the Cathedral of St. John the Divine, New York (1910). While still with Hutchings, Skinner developed his version of the "Pitman" windchest, which is still used extensively in electropneumatic action organs. Much of his reputation derived from his success in developing organ stops imitating orchestral instruments during the period when orchestrally oriented organ literature was in vogue. By 1920 the firm's rapid growth led to its acquisition of the Steere Organ Co. of Springfield, Massachusetts.

In 1927 G. Donald Harrison (*b* Huddersfield, England, 21 April 1889; *d* New York, 14 June 1956) entered the firm. He was a graduate of Dulwich College who had previously worked as a patent attorney and as an engineer with the Willis Organ Co., of which he ultimately became a director.

In 1931 the Skinner firm merged with the organ department of the Aeolian Co., which had made its reputation building self-playing mechanisms and organs for private houses. In 1933 a reorganization occurred in which Harrison became technical director and Skinner's activities were curtailed. In 1932 Skinner, after increasing disagreement with Harrison over tonal matters, began a new company in Methuen, Massachusetts, managed by his son, Richmond, although he appears to have maintained a contractual connection with Aeolian-Skinner until 1936. Skinner's new venture was undistinguished and small in scope, and after World War II it was sold to Carl Bassett, who subsequently moved it to Florida, still under the Skinner name. In 1970 the company was purchased by John Bolten and Roy E. H. Carlson and moved first to Newburyport, Massachusetts, and then to East Kingston, New Hampshire, where it now operates as a supplier of Pitman chests to the trade.

During the 1930s the Aeolian-Skinner Co. continued to rise in popularity, and in 1940 Harrison became president, succeeding Arthur Hudson Marks (1874–1939), a wealthy businessman who had held a financial interest in the company since 1916, and later became the principal owner. Under Harrison the firm became a leader in the trend away from orchestral tonal practices and towards a more classical sound. On Harrison's death, Joseph S. Whiteford, a lawyer and majority stockholder, became president. Although he had some experience of organ building, he did not possess Skinner's or Harrison's technical background, and under him the company slowly began to decline. In the early 1960s he withdrew his interest, and Donald M. Gillett, the head voicer, became president. In 1968 Robert L. Sipe, who for ten years had been building organs in Dallas, joined the company and in 1970 became vice-president and tonal director. A year earlier the firm had moved to new premises in Randolph, Massachusetts. In 1970 Aeolian-Skinner built its first mechanical-action organ for Zumbro Lutheran Church, Rochester, Minnesota. However, by 1972 the firm's financial position had worsened, and it was forced to leave its new quarters and reorganize. Gillett left to become tonal director for M. P. Möller, Sipe returned to Texas and his own business, and Emil David Knutson, chairman of the board, became president. Less than a year later the firm's few remaining assets were sold and it ceased to exist.

At the peak of its activity Aeolian-Skinner built many organs for notable churches, halls, and colleges, including Grace Cathedral, San Francisco (1934), Symphony Hall, Boston (1950), the Christian Science Mother Church, Boston (1952), Riverside Church, New York (1955), Lincoln Center (1962, moved to the Garden Grove (California) Community Church in 1976), and Kennedy Center (1969).

BIBLIOGRAPHY

E. M. Skinner: *The Modern Organ* (New York, 1917)
W. K. Covell: "G. Donald Harrison," *MO*, lxxix (1955–6), 671
"Ernest M. Skinner will be 90 Years Old," *The Diapason*, xlvii/2 (1956), 1
J. Fesperman: *Two Essays on Organ Design* (Raleigh, 1975)
O. Ochse: *The History of the Organ in the United States* (Bloomington, IN, 1975)
D. J. Holden: *The Life & Work of Ernest M. Skinner* (Richmond, VA, 1985)

BARBARA OWEN

Aeolian Vocalists. Vocal trio, nucleus of the group later known as the Hutchinson Family; *see* HUTCHINSON.

Aerosmith. Rock group. Formed in 1970, its original members were Steven Tyler (*b* New York, 26 March 1948), lead singer; Joe Perry (*b* Boston, MA, 10 Sept 1950), guitarist; Brad Whitford (*b* Winchester, MA, 23 Feb 1952), guitarist; Tom Hamilton (*b*

Colorado Springs, CO, 31 Dec 1951), bass guitarist; and Joey Kramer (*b* New York, 21 June 1950), drummer. They performed and recorded in relative obscurity until 1976, when their song *Dream on* reached no.6 on the chart. This was followed by *Walk this Way* (no.10, 1976), *Last Child* (no.21, 1976), *Back in the Saddle* (no.38, 1977), and their version of the Beatles' *Come Together* (no.23, 1978) from the soundtrack of Robert Stigwood's film *Sgt. Pepper's Lonely Hearts Club Band*, in which they appeared. Perry left the group in 1979, and Whitford did so in 1980; they were replaced by Jimmy Crespo and Rick Dufay. In 1982 Aerosmith issued *Rock in a Hard Place*, its first recording in three years. The group's songs have the loud, aggressive sound of heavy-metal rock, and Tyler's ragged, petulant, but passionate vocal style has led critics to compare him with Mick Jagger of the Rolling Stones; but their best work also has a parodistic element and a good humor that are rare in this area of rock music.

RECORDINGS

(selective list; all recorded for Columbia)

Aerosmith (32005, 1973), incl. Dream on; *Get your Wings* (32847, 1974); *Toys in the Attic* (33479, 1975), incl. Walk this Way; *Rocks* (34165, 1976), incl. Last Child, Back in the Saddle; *Draw the Line* (34865, 1977); *Live! Bootleg* (35564, 1979); *Night in the Ruts* (36050, 1979); *Rock in a Hard Place* (38061, 1982)

KEN TUCKER

AFM. *See* AMERICAN FEDERATION OF MUSICIANS.

Afro-American music. A term applied to the music of black Americans, which is characterized by a style that fuses African and European musical elements; this fusion has resulted in certain unique stylistic features, though it is primarily African in tone and conception. No basic dichotomy exists between Afro-American folk music and art music, since the black composer draws freely upon folk elements; indeed, a large body of Afro-American music, including that for theater and dance as well as popular music and religious concert music, falls between the two poles of art and folk music. Since the mid-19th century there has been a continuous absorption of Afro-American music into the mainstream of American music, so that in many instances, for example, jazz, the two have become indistinguishable. Thus it is important to focus on the identifiable origins of the various genres of Afro-American music and on its role as a catalyst in the history of American music.

1. From colonial times to the Emancipation Proclamation, 1863. 2. The post-slavery era, 1863–1920. 3. The modern era, 1920–68. 4. After 1968. 5. Folk music: structures, instruments, and performance practices.

1. FROM COLONIAL TIMES TO THE EMANCIPATION PROCLAMATION, 1863. The 15 million and more Africans who were taken as slaves to the New World from the 16th century to the 19th were cut off precipitately and harshly from their own cultures. But they retained memories of their rich religious and artistic traditions and followed the ways of their ancestors well into the 20th century. Despite the dispersal of the Africans throughout the country, music united the slaves in a way that transcended barriers of language and custom. Early music historians overlooked the importance of the African heritage in the development of Afro-American music; some even denied the existence of Africanisms in America. But modern research has uncovered much data that proves the persistence and vitality of African traditions among the slaves – most dramatically in the 'Lection Day festivities of New England, the Pinkster celebrations of New York state, the annual fairs in urban communities such

1. "The Old Plantation" depicting dancing slaves accompanied by banjo and bones: watercolor, late 18th century (Abby Aldrich Rockefeller Folk Art Center, Williamsburg, Virginia)

2. *Richard Allen: engraving by John Sartain*

as Philadelphia, the John Conny festivals on the southeastern seaboard, and the dancing in Place Congo, New Orleans. The strength of the African heritage was also manifested in the development of functional song repertories (*see* WORK SONGS, §3, and FIELD HOLLER), the preference for certain musical instruments, the practice of certain performance styles, and the adherence to certain musical habits (*see also* JAZZ, §II, 1).

As they became naturalized, the Afro-Americans gradually developed new traditions that were shaped by the isolation of slavery (and later of segregation) but at the same time influenced by the traditions of the Anglo-Saxon Protestant society in which most of them lived. The new Afro-American music had certainly emerged by the beginning of the 19th century. It was primarily African in concept: a functional, social, and communal music, much of which reflected the dominant role played by religion in the lives of the people.

During the colonial period Blacks worshiped in the meetinghouses of the Whites (although they remained in segregated pews) and sang Protestant psalms and hymns. The Revolutionary War that brought freedom to the colonists also brought measures of freedom to the slaves: some earned release by fighting in the war, others seized the opportunity to escape; most important, in 1778 the northern states began to pass laws that provided for the immediate or gradual abolition of slavery, and by 1827 there were few slaves living north of the Mason–Dixon line. Freedom also offered Blacks the opportunity to form their own societies and organizations away from the control and supervision of Whites. The first permanent black religious groups were Baptist churches founded in the South at Silver Bluff, South Carolina (about 1774), and at Savannah, Georgia, in 1788. The southern black churches, however, were unable to retain their independence as slavery became more oppressive during the 19th century, and they eventually came under the general control of Whites.

Blacks in the North began to form such organizations as the Free African societies as early as the 1770s (one of the earliest was in Newport, Rhode Island), and soon afterwards the first black congregations were established in Philadelphia. The world's first black sect, the African Methodist Episcopal Church (AME), developed in 1794 from a group formed in 1792 by the former slave Richard Allen. The church received its charter of incorporation in 1816, and Allen was elected its first bishop. A second sect, the AME Zion Church in New York, obtained its charter in 1821. Generally black congregations retained ties with the white mother churches but maintained their own meetinghouses and controlled their services of worship; they generally adopted the doctrines and liturgies of the mother churches but allowed changes to fit their special needs. Some churches, to the consternation of contemporary white (and some black) clergymen, won notoriety for their musical performance practices. But the Europeans who traveled to the USA during the early 19th century made a point of visiting black churches and camp meetings in order to hear the exotic singing and watch the religious dancing.

Contemporary references to the religious songs of the Blacks indicate that texts were improvised by stringing together scraps of pledges and prayers, verses from the Scriptures, or psalms and hymns with fresh lines; melodies were improvised or adapted from existing tunes (*see* SPIRITUAL, §II). The new song thus had a distinctive identity, which was far removed from the hymn or Bible verse that served as a source. The process can be reconstructed, as in the following example which compares the text of a Protestant hymn with texts of related spirituals:

Hymn

Behold the awful trumpet sounds,
The sleeping dead to raise,
And calls the nations underground:
O how the saints will praise!

Behold the Saviour how he comes
Descending from his throne
To burst asunder all our tombs
And lead his children home.

But who can bear that dreadful day,
To see the world in flames:
The burning mountains melt away,
While rocks run down in streams.

The falling stars their orbits leave,
The sun in darkness hide:
The elements asunder cleave,
The moon turn'd into blood!

Spiritual 1

My Lord, what a morning
My Lord, what a morning
My Lord, what a morning
When the stars begin to fall.

You'll hear the trumpet sound
To wake the nations underground
Looking to my God's right hand
When the stars begin to fall.

Spiritual 2

There's no hiding-place down there
There's no hiding-place down there
Went to the rocks to hide my face
The rocks cried out, no hiding-place
No hiding-place down there.

Spiritual 3

And the moon will turn to blood
And the moon will turn to blood
And the moon will turn to blood in that day.
Oh, joy, my soul!
And the moon will turn to blood in that day.

Depending on the whim of the improvising singer, one or two scriptural verses might also serve as the basis for a long and lively spiritual, such as *Joshua fit de battle of Jericho*. "Song families" of considerable size, consisting of spirituals that share textual sources, can be identified, though such groupings have nothing to do with the melodies of the songs, which often differ markedly in character within one family. Finally, there are the texts that resulted from individual inspiration, such as the homiletic spirituals of preachers and deacons.

Music for formal worship consisted of psalms and hymns. Although some black clergymen allowed informal spirituals to be sung in church, they were generally performed during special services held after the regular worship periods or during midweek services. Together with the singing went a form of religious dancing, called a "shout." The benches were pushed back against the walls, and worshipers of all ages formed a circle, moving first slowly, then faster and faster in shuffling steps around the room to the accompaniment of hand-clapping, foot-stomping, and the singing of spirituals by the onlookers. Often the "shouters" (i.e., dancers) joined in the singing of the special "running spirituals" or "ring-shout spirituals." This singing and dancing exemplifies the persistence of African traditions among black Christians, despite vigorous efforts by the church authorities to abolish such "heathen practices."

A large amount of 19th-century black folksong was undoubtedly lost in the course of its oral transmission, but there are several documents that illustrate its development. In 1801 Richard Allen published *A Collection of Hymns and Spiritual Songs* for the use of his congregation – important as the first publication by a black hymn compiler and also as an anthology of the hymns that were then popular among Blacks. Significantly, several verses and some of the "wandering" choruses from these hymns reappear in spirituals, supplying evidence of the techniques of folk composers outlined above. From the early 19th century contemporary writers have described the singing of the Blacks, quoting from the texts of the songs improvised by the singers and attempting, in some instances, to identify the tunes (see Watson, 28; Faux, 420). Since this improvisational practice continued throughout the antebellum period, there exists a slave song-text repertory of considerable size that predates Emancipation, although the texts are widely scattered in the literature. At least five notated songs were published before the Civil War, but it was not until after Emancipation that the first collection, *Slave Songs of the United States* (1867), was published.

The first black musician known to have written in the European tradition was the former slave Newport Gardner (1746–1826), a native of Africa who was sold to a merchant in Newport, Rhode Island. As a youth Gardner was allowed to study music briefly with Andrew Law; after obtaining his freedom he became a singing-school teacher and attracted wide attention for his songs, particularly the *Promise Anthem*. The first "school" of black composers began to evolve in the second decade of the 19th century, led by the composer and bandmaster Frank Johnson in Philadelphia. Later the circle widened to include composers in New York, Boston, Baltimore, and other urban centers, but most of those who published music during the first half of the 19th century came under the influence of Johnson. They included James Hemmenway, Aaron J. R. Connor (*d*1850), William Appo, and Henry F. Williams; later Justin Holland won critical acclaim for his guitar compositions and method books, the bandmaster Joseph Postelwaite (1837–89), a native of St. Louis, published instrumental and vocal music that became very popular, and Thomas Bethune gained an international reputation as a concert pianist and also composed prolifically. Bandsmen and instrumentalists by profession, these men responded to the enormous demand for sheet music by producing art songs, sentimental ballads, and piano arrangements of the overtures, marches, and cotillions they played in the ballroom and on the concert stage. They also published piano arrangements of operatic arias, particularly from the works of Bellini and Donizetti. Stylistically, there is little to distinguish the music of these black composers from that of their white contemporaries, except for an occasional reference to a racial theme, such as Johnson's *Recognition March of the Independence of Hayti* (1825). Much of the music remained popular throughout the 19th century.

See also POLITICAL MUSIC, §1.

2. THE POST-SLAVERY ERA, 1863–1920. After the Civil War had brought freedom to almost four million slaves, Afro-American music began to spread. From 1872 amateur student groups, such as the Fisk JUBILEE SINGERS and the Hampton Institute Singers, toured abroad, singing their plantation songs in Great Britain, Germany, Spain, and other European countries. They were soon followed by professional groups, often calling themselves Jubilee Singers, who toured as far afield as Australia, New Zealand, South Africa, and the Far East. The best-known of these "concert companies" were those directed by Frederick Loudin, Orpheus McAfee, and Charles Williams; the worldwide tours of the Williams Jubilee Singers (also known as the Williams Colored Singers) continued into the 1920s.

Black choral groups that sang "genuine" plantation songs were widely used in white stage shows of the late 19th century, particularly *Uncle Tom's Cabin*, *In Old Kentucky*, and *The South before the War*, as well as in the productions of such black troupes as that run by the Hyers Sisters. Some of these groups published collections of the songs they performed: the Fisk Jubilee collections ran to 18 editions between 1875 and 1903, and the Hampton collections to more than a dozen. Early transcribers made special efforts to preserve the originality of the slave music; they pointed out in the prefaces to their collections that they had taken down the songs from the lips of the singers without altering the notes or attempting to "improve" the songs, despite the difficulties involved in trying to capture in notation the weird melodies and complex rhythms. But by the 1890s the published and performed versions of the plantation songs were becoming more and more sophisticated, and it seemed that the compilers were "arranging" them to meet the demands of the concert and show-music stages.

Lightly disguised, plantation songs also appeared on the minstrel stage, introduced by black entertainers who began to invade MINSTRELSY after Emancipation. Celebrated minstrel–songwriters, including Horace Weston, Sam Lucas, James Bland, and Gussie Lord Davis, contributed their arrangements of slave songs (both vocal and instrumental), as well as comic songs and character songs, and ballads that "jerked the tears." Many of the newly composed songs made explicit reference to slave songs in text or style, as do Bland's *Oh, dem golden slippers* and Lucas's *Carve dat possum*. Davis won distinction as the first black songwriter to succeed in Tin Pan Alley. His lachrymose ballads made his name a household word in the 1890s, and one of his songs, *In the Baggage Coach Ahead* (1896; fig.3, p.16), sold more than a million copies.

As the minstrel show was succeeded by the stage musical at the turn of the century, a new type of black composer appeared who had generally had some kind of musical training. The first

3. Sheet-music cover of "In the Baggage Coach Ahead" by Gussie Lord Davis, published in New York in 1896

full-length musical written and produced by Blacks to be presented at a New York theater (though it was given off-Broadway) was Bob Cole's and Billy Johnson's *A Trip to Coontown* (1898); the first to appear on Broadway, *Clorindy, or The Origin of the Cakewalk* (1898), was written and produced by Will Marion Cook with Paul Laurence Dunbar providing the lyrics. From 1899 to 1908 the shows produced by Bert Williams and George Walker – particularly *In Dahomey*, *In Abyssinia*, and *In Bandanna Land* – provided a haven for talented writers and performers, as did the musicals written and produced by Cole and the brothers J. Rosamond Johnson and James Weldon Johnson, the Smart Set companies, the Pekin Theatre Company, and similar organizations. Other composers associated with show music included J. Leubrie Hill (*c*1869–1916), who produced his own musicals, James Reese Europe, Ford Dabney (1883–1958), and Will Vodery. They also wrote for white Broadway musicals – Vodery, for example, contributed to Ziegfeld's *Follies* from 1913 to 1933 – and wrote for Tin Pan Alley, where the Cole–Johnson trio, Europe, and Dabney were particularly successful.

At the same time as some of the most talented Blacks were contributing to show music, others were laying the foundations of a black musical nationalism. Selfconsciously, they set about establishing traditions for black-American writers of cultivated music in the same way as some European composers had done for their countries in the 19th century. They collected and published black folksong, drew on black folk idioms, turned to racial themes in their program music and dramatic works, used the poems of black writers in their vocal composition, published manifestos, and sponsored "all Negro-composer" concerts. Acknowledging their indebtedness to Dvořák, they regarded as appropriate models his so-called American works – the Symphony "From the New World," the Quartet op.96, and the Quintet op.97. They were also inspired by the English composer Samuel Coleridge-Taylor, particularly his piano works *African Suite* (1898) and *24 Negro Melodies* (1905).

While Dvořák was director of the National Conservatory of Music in New York (1892–5), a pioneer of black musical nationalism, Harry T. Burleigh, was a student there. The first black composer since Frank Johnson to win wide critical acclaim, Burleigh began to experiment with making arrangements of spirituals for solo voice in the style of art songs, and in 1916 published his *Jubilee Songs of the United States of America*. For the first time concert singers had access to spirituals in a form that could be used in recitals, and it became customary for black artists to conclude their recitals with a group of arranged spirituals.

Burleigh and his contemporaries adopted a neoromantic style and mostly small forms for their nationalistic compositions, producing vocal and instrumental solos, chamber music, and suites, in which black idioms were fused with European structures and procedures. They gave their attention chiefly to the arrangement of spirituals for the pragmatic reason that this music most easily found publishers and performers. But Cook, R. Nathaniel Dett, and J. Rosamond Johnson also wrote effective choral works, Dett published a quantity of piano music (of which the best-known piece was the suite *In the Bottoms*, 1913), and Clarence Cameron White wrote for violin and string ensembles, and, later, for orchestra; Harry Lawrence Freeman attracted attention as the first black composer of opera in 1893 (*The Martyr*), though the earliest of his works to employ black folk idioms was *Voodoo*, 1914. During the 1920s the nationalistic composers made important contributions to the so-called Harlem Renaissance.

As a counterpart to the developments in the areas of stage and concert music, new folk styles emerged in black communities during the late 19th century. The piano rag, originally played in black honky-tonks, cafés, and gambling saloons across the nation, reflected the coalescence of European marches and quadrilles with the elements of plantation dance music (*see* RAGTIME). Long before the first rags were published, in 1897, however, ragtime had established its own traditions, including local and national competitions; its own state, Missouri; its own capital cities, Sedalia and St. Louis; and its own "king," Scott Joplin. Joplin wrote numerous piano rags, a ragtime ballet, and two operas, of which *Treemonisha* (completed in 1909) is the first folk opera written by an American. Piano rags belonged largely to the oral tradition and many of them were never published, though a number of established composers, including Blind John Boone, James Scott, Joe Jordan, Jelly Roll Morton, and Eubie Blake wrote in the style. The influence of the rag was strong for almost 30 years, particularly in the coon song and in jazz, but ragtime then disappeared as an individual genre until the 1960s, when Blake brought about a revival which was maintained by a host of young Whites in the 1970s and 1980s.

A second folk style, the vocal BLUES, had an obscure origin. Although folksong collectors seem not to have noticed it until about 1901, black musicians remembered it as an earthy music of their childhood years, dating back as far as the 1880s and earlier. The minstrel bandleader W. C. Handy was the first to popularize the blues with his publications of *Memphis Blues* (1912) and *St. Louis Blues* (1914). But like the arrangements of spirituals, the published blues were sophisticated in comparison with the earthy folk forms.

During the early 20th century the various types of Afro-American music – spirituals, shouts, rags, blues, and syncopated music played by brass bands and dance orchestras – began to fuse into what later became known as JAZZ. Morton is credited with being the first to notate a jazz arrangement, his *Jelly Roll Blues* (published 1915). Jazz brought to the fore a new kind of composer, one who improvised upon existing music as he performed, thus creating a new music. Early jazzmen drew upon the easily available stock of Afro-American traditional tunes, such as the spiritual *When the saints go marching in*, or a blues or rag; they also wrote their own tunes.

3. THE MODERN ERA, 1920–68. Black musical nationalism reached its peak in the works of William Grant Still, the first composer to employ in symphonic music all the folk idioms known to his generation, from the lofty spiritual to the lowly blues. His *Afro-American Symphony* (1930), with its invented blues theme and use of the banjo, is representative, as is William Dawson's *Negro Folk Symphony* (1934). Still and Dawson and their contemporaries – Florence Price, Hall Johnson, Edward Boatner (1898–1981), Frederick Hall, and John Wesley Work – wrote symphonic and large-scale choral music after serving an apprenticeship in the writing of spiritual arrangements and small forms. The most successful of their works include Price's Symphony in E Minor (1932), White's opera *Ouanga* (1932), Johnson's folk opera *Run Little Chillun* (1933), Dett's oratorio *The Ordering of Moses* (1937; see fig.4), Still's opera *Troubled Island* (1941), and Work's cantata *The Singers* (1941).

Nationalist feeling was also evident in the musical comedies produced by Blacks from the 1920s. *Shuffle Along* (1921), written and produced by Blake with the lyricist Noble Sissle and librettists Flournoy Miller and Aubrey Lyles, was the first black musical on Broadway for more than a decade, and was followed by similar works by Blake, Dabney, James P. Johnson, Jordan, J. Turner Layton, Luckey Roberts, and Fats Waller. All these musicals drew on black folk music, offering Broadway audiences traditional songs and dances, some of which, such as the charleston, reappeared in the nation's ballrooms. Blake's *Swing It* (1937) represented the end of an era: except for one or two individuals, black composers displayed no further serious interest in the musical theater until the 1950s.

The term "jazz" was used as early as 1916 to refer to the syncopated music played by black orchestras and bands; in 1918 Handy staged a "jass and blues" concert in New York, and the press lauded Europe for carrying jazz to France. It was not until the 1920s, however, that genuine jazz groups began to attract wide public attention – primarily through recordings, for the groups performed in black communities. New Orleans early became established as the capital of jazz; but jazzmen soon carried the music to Chicago, where the first recordings were made of the groups led by King Oliver, Louis Armstrong, and Morton. Thereafter Chicago became a mecca for jazzmen. New York was the major center for the big bands, one of the first of which was organized in 1923 by Fletcher Henderson (who, along with Don Redman, was one of the first important jazz arrangers). The big-band tradition was continued by the ensembles of Duke Ellington, Count Basie, Cab Calloway, Chick Webb, and Lionel Hampton, among many others. These bands worked out the basic principles and procedures of collective improvisation, which, because of the larger numbers of sidemen involved, was more complicated than among the Chicago bands.

Among important jazz figures of the 1930s who "created" music as they improvised were Teddy Wilson, Fats Waller, and Art Tatum. Some jazzmen, for example Armstrong, also wrote tunes that served as the basis for improvisation. And some composed in the traditional sense of the word: Ellington wrote dozens of symphonic works in large forms, including three sacred pieces; other jazz composers were James P. Johnson, Willie "the Lion" Smith, Luckey Roberts, Mary Lou Williams, and John Lewis.

During the 1920s and 1930s a new kind of religious music (later called gospel) appeared in black churches of various denominations (*see* GOSPEL MUSIC, §II). Originally associated with the new sects that emerged in the late 19th century – generally known as Holiness, Pentecostal, Sanctified, or Spiritualist churches – the music was a direct heir to the shouts, jubilee songs, and other African-rooted practices of the plantation "praise cabins." It was brought to public attention by Baptists and Methodists, and by the publication of hymns by such writers as Charles A. Tindley and Lucie Campbell. Thomas A. Dorsey, the "father of gospel music," laid the foundation for modern gospel with his gospel songs (as distinct from gospel hymns) in the 1930s. Dorsey

4. The National Negro Opera Company in a staged performance of R. Nathaniel Dett's oratorio "The Ordering of Moses," Griffith Stadium, Washington, DC, 1951

brought a heavy infusion of jazz and blues into the music; he also organized in Chicago the first gospel chorus (1931, with Theodore Frye, Magnolia Butts, and Sallie Martin), the first national organization, the National Convention of Gospel Choirs and Choruses (1932), and the first gospel publishing house.

Despite the amount of published music, gospel was essentially a folk-music genre disseminated largely through oral tradition, notably by means of such gatherings as the annual meetings of the National Baptist Convention, USA (several early gospel figures, including Dorsey, Roberta Martin, Mahalia Jackson, and the Clara Ward Singers, first attracted attention at these meetings). During the late 1930s gospel began to be performed in the concert hall, and soon became part of the repertories of nightclub and jazz performers; it was also incorporated into works for the musical theater. Its influence was widespread, and was felt in all types of black music. Leading composers and performers included James Cleveland, Alex Bradford, Andrae Crouch, and Edwin Hawkins. An important contemporary gospel publication is *Songs of Zion* (1981), issued by the United Methodist Church, which includes a wide variety of gospel music from the hymns of the pioneers to the elaborate improvisatory works of contemporary writers.

In the 1940s, in response to the availability of employment in wartime industries, many hundreds of thousands of Blacks left the rural South for the cities. Within a short period Afro-Americans were transformed from a rural people to an urban people, and they adapted their music to the new environment. The country blues gave way to city blues with its use of electric instruments; this in turn gave rise to rhythm-and-blues, out of which came rock-and-roll, soul, funk, and other types of black popular music. All these styles felt the impact of gospel, not only through their absorption of gospel elements, but because gospel singers such as Aretha Franklin and Sam Cooke also performed secular music.

Jazzmen of the 1940s turned away from the traditional in their experimentation with new ideas, resulting in a new style called bebop, then simply bop. Bop was born in New York's Harlem, where jazzmen developed the habit of dropping into Minton's Playhouse and Monroe's Uptown House after their working hours to "jam" (improvise) together; its chief architects were Kenny Clarke, Charlie Christian, Thelonious Monk, Dizzy Gillespie, and Charlie Parker. In 1944 Billy Eckstine organized a big band expressly to feature the new music; it included some of the most talented jazzmen of the time (several of whom came from Earl Hines's big band of 1943), and bop's first important singer, Sarah Vaughan. Boppers explored new tonal areas and procedures, rhythmic possibilities, ranges, sounds, and performance practices. Predictably, bop generated new styles – cool jazz, hard bop, and eventually free jazz – and new leaders, chief among them Miles Davis, John Coltrane, and Ornette Coleman.

In the area of classical music, racism and discrimination proved lesser obstacles than in previous eras: talented individuals found it possible to obtain musical training at the institutions of their choice and fellowships that enabled them to study with eminent teachers at home and abroad, as well as to have their symphonic works performed. The composers active during the mid-20th century whose music received first performances during the 1940s and early 1950s generally employed neoclassical techniques and forms: among them were Howard Swanson, Ulysses Kay, George Walker, and Julia Perry. Kay's overture *Of New Horizons* (1944) was the first work by one of this group to attract wide attention; in 1948 Swanson's Short Symphony won the New York Music Critics' Circle Award; and in 1951 Perry's *Stabat mater* won critical acclaim on both sides of the Atlantic.

Another group of composers who came to maturity during the 1950s and 1960s were more eclectic in their interests and employment of musical styles and forms. Although they were intimate with all types of black music, they were not restrained by race consciousness and insisted on the right to be identified as American, rather than black, composers. They used 12-tone methods, neoclassical procedures, aleatory techniques, electronic forces, and other avant-garde practices. Having earned degrees from music schools in the USA, many studied abroad with composers such as Boulanger and Dallapiccola. The Society of Black Composers had 30 active members when it was organized in 1968. Representative of the group are Hale Smith, T. J. Anderson, Noel Da Costa, Frederick Tillis, Roger Dickerson, Carman Moore, Olly Wilson, Wendell Logan, and Dorothy Rudd Moore. The titles of their works, for example Anderson's *Essay* for orchestra (1965) and Logan's *Proportions for Nine Players* (1969), suggest how far they strayed from the paths of their neoromantic, nationalistic predecessors.

4. After 1968. In the 1960s black composers were active against a background of social upheaval as more people became involved in the struggle to secure civil rights that had begun after World War II, when servicemen returning home began to demand for themselves the "four freedoms" embodied in the Constitution and for which they had fought abroad. As it became evident that government legislation was powerless against the entrenched racism in the nation, people took to the streets in massive marches for freedom. As they marched, they sang the plantation songs of the slavery period and the later gospel songs, adapting texts to fit their new circumstances. Despite the efforts of the leaders to maintain an attitude of peaceful protest, there were violent reactions, and in 1968 the murder of Martin Luther King, Jr., nonviolent leader of the civil rights movement, left black Americans numb. Composers poured out their feelings of desolation in a flood of memorial works, drawing on black musical elements and using texts of black poets and writers: for example, Olly Wilson's *In memoriam Martin Luther King Jr.*, Carman Moore's *Drum Major*, and David Baker's Jazz Cantata (which includes a movement entitled "Martyrs: Malcolm, Medgar, and Martin").

King's murder stirred all black Americans into a renewed sense of purpose and resolve. In the musical world it seemed to shake composers loose from their European moorings, for by consciously employing elements of black music in their writing, they inaugurated a new era of "neoclassical" and avant-garde black musical nationalism. Wilson, for example, wrote *SpiritSong* (1974) for soprano, women's chorus, gospel chorus, and orchestra; his *Sometimes* (1976) for tenor and tape refers to the spiritual *Sometimes I feel like a motherless child* in abstract terms only. Some works harked back to the slavery era, for example Kay's opera *Jubilee* (1976, based on the novel by Margaret Walker) and Tillis's *Ring Shout Concerto* (1973). The omnipresent interest in the past occasioned the première of Joplin's opera *Treemonisha* in 1972. Ballets and symphonic works that celebrated the spiritual and gospel music began to appear, and on Broadway a succession of black musicals recalled the 1920s.

Composers also looked to Africa and India in search of new ideas and exotic instruments and performance practices. Jazz and classical composers were brought closer together through the

5. *The Roy Haynes Hip Ensemble performing at a free concert sponsored by Jazzmobile at Grant's Tomb, New York, in the mid-1970s*

employment of black-music elements alongside avant-garde techniques; jazzmen such as Anthony Braxton and Leo Smith preferred to be called "improvisers" rather than composers. Both groups of composers, among them J. J. Johnson, Oliver Nelson (1932–75), Quincy Jones, and Curtis Mayfield, were drawn to Hollywood, where they wrote scores for commercial and documentary films and for television.

During these years composers began to band together in organizations such as the Society of Black Composers to protect their interests and provide a forum for the performance of their music. In New York Billy Taylor and others founded Jazzmobile (1965), which aimed to develop an appreciation for jazz by offering free concerts and workshops to the public (see fig.5). In Chicago Muhal Richard Abrams founded the Association for the Advancement of Creative Musicians (1965), and in St. Louis Oliver Lake set up the Black Artist Group (1972). Another phenomenon was the Black Music Symposium (or Festival) sponsored by various institutions, which periodically brought together composers from all over the USA to listen to performances of their music and to talk to audiences; a corollary was the Black Composers Series of Columbia Records (1974–8), comprising nine albums of classical music. Blacks began to establish blues and gospel festivals in the 1960s and participated widely in the jazz festivals staged by white sponsors throughout the world. Newly founded scholarly journals, such as *Black Perspective in Music* (1973) and *Black Music Research Journal* (1980, issued by the Institute for Research in Black American Music, Fisk University), published interviews with composers and performers, analyses of their music, and lists of new works and recordings.

5. FOLK MUSIC: STRUCTURES, INSTRUMENTS, AND PERFORMANCE PRACTICES. Many of the fundamental characteristics of Afro-American music – its distinctive rhythms and scales, and its modes of performance – are common to genres as far removed from each other historically as plantation songs and modern black popular musics. They arise from the forms and musical practices of black folk music, which derive ultimately from those of Africa and about which certain general observations may be made. The most distinctive trait of Afro-American music is its rhythms. The early music generally has duple meters and syncopation; modern blues and gospel in slow tempos typically employ triplets overlaying the basic pulse, and dotted rhythms are frequent. The music is always polyrhythmic, with strong cross-accents, and occasionally may be polymetric, as in piano rag. The solo singer provides his own rhythmic context by drumming with his fingertips and tapping his foot as he sings. Group singers generally convey four rhythms simultaneously through the melody, foot stamping, and hand clapping, both on and off the beat. The range of patterns increases with the number of instruments used.

Strict unison singing is rare, but polyphonic textures are more often heterophonic (i.e., elaborations on the melody) than truly harmonic in nature; the "barbershop" triadic harmonies often attributed to black music belong to popular rather than folk music. Pieces generally consist of small units (e.g., the 12-bar blues *AAB* – *see* BLUES PROGRESSION – and the 16-bar spiritual *AAAB* or *ABCB*) repeated many times. Improvisation prevents monotony, ensuring that no unit is identical with another.

Modes and pentatonic scales are common in the early music and in present-day rural music, while the more sophisticated urban 20th-century musicians generally prefer the blues scale (though this also occurs in early spirituals). The only stable notes of the blues scale are the first, second, and fourth (using the major scale as a pattern); the rest of the scale is handled freely, and a single melody can include lowered and natural thirds, fifths, sixths, or sevenths, or any combination of these. The altered notes do not fit the European chromatic scale but sound slightly below the pitch: for example, one of the oldest spirituals, *Roll, Jordan, Roll*, uses both the natural and lowered seventh, an effect the blues pianist achieves by striking lowered and natural tones simultaneously. (For a different interpretation, *see* BLUE NOTE.)

Early Afro-American music used both folk and conventional instruments, each genre having its preferred sound: for example, the guitar for the blues, or the tambourine for gospel. Mixed ensembles of homemade and commercially manufactured instruments were common: for example, washboards, jugs, washtub basses, and toy kazoos were combined with banjos, guitars, mandolins, fiddles, drums, trumpets, etc. Electronic instruments are now often preferred by folk musicians, whether performing blues or gospel. Accompaniment forces for the latter may range in size from the piano and organ or small ensembles to full-size orchestras (similar in makeup to the jazz big band) or groups that include several synthesizers along with electronic and acoustic instruments.

Certain characteristics of performing practice unify and define black music's multiple forms. For the black musician a piece of music is a pliable, ambiguous idea to be given distinct shape during performance through improvisation, which is more than mere embellishment: the performer actually re-creates the music, altering tones, rhythms, voice quality, instrumental timbre, and sometimes even structure. The measure of his success is his ability to create anew in each performance; his listeners assist with encouraging exclamations ("Amen," "Sing, brother!," "Right on!") and often the performer encourages himself or his instrument in the same way. This "call and response" may be informal, as in the blues where the singer allows his guitar the two-bar "break" at the end of each line, or a structural element, as in spirituals that have refrains in alternate lines sung antiphonally:

I looked over Jordan and what did I see,
Coming for to carry me home.
A band of angels coming after me,
Coming for to carry me home.

Performers are fond of distinctive timbres, preferring the strident, throaty, rough, high-pitched, or falsetto to the clear, bright, and sweet. This preference is evident not only in vocal style but in instrumental style as well. Performances must appeal to the eye as well as the ear. The singer's clothes, stance, facial expression, gestures, and body movements are as important as the musical sound. Above all, he must touch his listeners' souls, and to do this he must perform with "soul." When "filled with the spirit," he can moan, hum, scream, wail, grunt, whisper, growl, caress, and seduce with his voice or instrument; he may pace back and forth, jump up and down, fall to the floor, or spin round; he may repeat a syllable endlessly or use nonsense words. The performer becomes "possessed" and shares his ecstasy with his listeners (*see also* GOSPEL MUSIC, §II, 2).

Black music is remarkable for its density: the framework is filled with a profusion of musical events, both melodic and rhythmic, producing the characteristic surging and sliding melodic style and the overlapping solo and chorus entries in antiphonal performance. Tremendous energy is expended in its performance; when the music ends, performer and listeners are physically and emotionally exhausted.

See also POPULAR MUSIC, §§II, 3, III, 1, 2, 4, IV, 6; RHYTHM-AND-BLUES; SOUL MUSIC.

BIBLIOGRAPHY

SouthernB

J. Watson: *Methodist Error, or Friendly Christian Advice, to Those Methodists who Indulge in Extravagant Religious Emotions and Bodily Exercises* (Trenton, NJ, 1819); excerpts repr. in *Readings in Black American Music*, ed. E. Southern (New York, 1971, rev. 2/1983)

W. Faux: *Memorable Days in America* (London, 1823)

J. Hungerford: *The Old Plantation, and What I Gathered There in an Autumn Month* (New York, 1859)

W. Allen: Introduction to *Slave Songs of the United States* (New York, 1867)

J. B. T. Marsh: *The Story of the Jubilee Singers, with their Songs* (London, 1875, rev. 3/1892 with suppl.) [with music]

D. Payne: *Recollections of Seventy Years* (Nashville, 1888)

——: *History of the African Methodist Episcopal Church* (Nashville, 1891)

W. E. Barton: *Old Plantation Hymns* (Boston, 1899); repr. in *The Social Implications of Early Negro Music in the United States*, ed. B. Katz (New York, 1969), 75–118

R. Hughes: "A Eulogy of Ragtime," *Musical Record*, no.447 (1899), 157

E. L. Rice: *Monarchs of Minstrelsy* (New York, 1911)

H. E. Krehbiel: *Afro-American Folksongs* (New York, 1914/*R*1976)

R. W. Gordon: "Negro Shouts from Georgia," *New York Times Magazine* (24 April 1927)

E. E. Hipsher: *American Opera and its Composers* (Philadelphia, 1927, rev. 2/1934/*R*1978)

G. B. Johnson: *Folk Culture on St. Helena Island, South Carolina* (Chapel Hill, 1930)

J. W. Johnson: *Black Manhattan* (New York, 1930)

E. Marks: *They All Sang: from Tony Pastor to Rudy Vallée* (New York, 1934)

M. C. Hare: *Negro Musicians and their Music* (Washington, DC, 1936)

W. C. Handy: *Father of the Blues: an Autobiography* (New York, 1941/*R*1957)

M. Herskovits: *The Myth of the Negro Past* (New York, 1941)

G. P. Jackson: *White and Negro Spirituals* (New York, 1943)

R. A. Waterman: "'Hot' Rhythm in Negro Music," *JAMS*, i (1948), 24

J. W. Work: "Changing Patterns in Negro Folk Songs," *Journal of American Folklore*, lxii (1949), 136

R. Blesh and H. Janis: *They All Played Ragtime* (New York, 1950, rev. 4/1971)

J. Burton: *The Blue Book of Tin Pan Alley* (Watkins Glen, NY, 1950, enlarged 2/1962)

J.-E. Berendt: *Das Jazzbuch: Entwicklung und Bedeutung der Jazzmusik* (Frankfurt am Main, Germany, 1953; Eng. trans. as *The New Jazz Book: a History and Guide*, New York, 1962, rev. and enlarged as *The Jazz Book: from New Orleans to Jazz Rock and Beyond*, 1982)

T. Fletcher: *100 Years of the Negro in Show Business* (New York, 1954)

C. Keil: *Urban Blues* (Chicago, 1966)

B. Jackson, ed.: *The Negro and his Folklore in Nineteenth-century Periodicals* (Austin, 1967)

G. Schuller: *Early Jazz: its Roots and Musical Development* (New York, 1968)

P. Garland: *The Sound of Soul* (Chicago, 1969)

B. Katz, ed.: *The Social Implications of Early Negro Music in the United States* (New York, 1969)

P. H. Oliver: *The Story of the Blues* (London, 1969)

D.-R. de Lerma, ed.: *Black Music in our Culture* (Kent, OH, 1970)

T. Heilbut: *The Gospel Sound: Good News and Bad Times* (New York, 1971/*R*1975)

E. Southern: *The Music of Black Americans: a History* (New York, 1971, rev. 2/1983)

E. Southern, ed.: *Readings in Black American Music* (New York, 1971, rev. 2/1983)

J. Tinney: "Black Origins of the Pentecostal Movement," *Christianity Today*, xvi (1971), 4

J. H. Cone: *The Spirituals and the Blues: an Interpretation* (New York, 1972)

L. F. Emery: *Black Dance in the United States from 1619 to 1970* (Palo Alto, CA, 1972)

J. Lovell: *Black Song: the Forge and the Flame* (New York, 1972)

J. Washington: *Black Sects and Cults* (New York, 1972)

D.-R. de Lerma, ed.: *Reflections on Afro-American Music* (Kent, OH, 1973)

H. Roach: *Black American Music: Past and Present*, i (Malabar, FL, 1973, rev. 2/1985)

L. Ekwueme: "African Music Retentions in the New World," *BPiM*, ii (1974), 128

C. E. Lincoln, ed.: *The Black Experience in Religion* (New York, 1974)

R. C. Toll: *Blacking Up: the Minstrel Show in Nineteenth-century America* (New York, 1974)

O. Wilson: "The Significance of the Relationship between Afro-American and West-African Music," *BPiM*, ii (1974), 3
P. Maultsby: *Afro-American Religious Music, 1619–1861* (diss., U. of Wisconsin, 1975)
H. Courlander: *A Treasury of Afro-American Folklore* (New York, 1976)
D. Epstein: *Sinful Tunes and Spirituals: Black Folk Music to the Civil War* (Urbana, IL, 1977)
G. Ricks: *Some Aspects of the Religious Music of the United States Negro* (New York, 1977)
F. Tirro: *Jazz: a History* (New York, 1977)
D. N. Baker, L. M. Belt, and H. C. Hudson: *The Black Composer Speaks* (Metuchen, NJ, 1978)
S. Floyd: "J. W. Postlewaite of St. Louis," *BPiM*, vi (1978), 151
D. Jasen and T. Tichenor: *Rags and Ragtime: a Musical History* (New York, 1978)
A. Raboteau: *Slave Religion: the "Invisible Institution" in the Antebellum South* (New York, 1978)
H. C. Boyer: "Contemporary Gospel," *BPiM*, vii (1979), 5
E. Berlin: *Ragtime: a Musical and Cultural History* (Berkeley, CA, 1980/*R*1984 with addns)
H. Sampson: *Blacks in Blackface* (Metuchen, NJ, 1980)
D. A. Handy: *Black Women in American Bands and Orchestras* (Metuchen, NJ, 1981)
R. Palmer: *Deep Blues* (New York, 1981)
D.-R. de Lerma: *Bibliography of Black Music* (Westport, CT, 1981–) [i: *Reference Materials*; ii: *Afro-American Idioms*; iii: *Geographical Studies*; iv: *Theory, Education, and Related Studies*]
J. Skowronski: *Black Music in America: a Bibliography* (Metuchen, NJ, 1981)
A. Tischler: *Fifteen Black American Composers: a Bibliography of their Works* (Detroit, 1981)
E. D. White: *Choral Music by Afro-American Composers: a Selected, Annotated Bibliography* (Metuchen, NJ, 1981)
D. Evans: *Big Road Blues* (Berkeley, CA, 1982)
S. A. Floyd and M. J. Reisser: *Black Music in the United States: an Annotated Bibliography of Selected Reference and Research Materials* (Millwood, NY, 1983)
M. Green: *Black Women Composers: a Genesis* (Boston, 1983)
A. Woll: *Dictionary of the Black Theatre* (Westport, CT, 1983)
T. Brooks: *America's Black Musical Heritage* (Englewood Cliffs, NJ, 1984)
P. Oliver: *Songsters and Saints: Vocal Traditions on Race Records* (Cambridge, England, 1984)
T. B. Yizar: *Afro-American Music in North America before 1865: a Study of "The First of August Celebration" in the United States* (diss., U. of California, 1984)
K. Bloom: *American Song: the Complete Musical Theatre Companion, 1900–1984* (New York, 1985)
I. V. Jackson, ed.: *More than Dancing: Essays on Afro-American Music and Musicians* (Westport, CT, 1985)
H. Roach: *Black American Music*, ii (Malabar, FL, 1985)

EILEEN SOUTHERN

Afro-Cuban jazz. A jazz style, created from a fusion of bop with Latin American elements, that arose in the late 1940s, primarily in the work of the trumpeter and bandleader Dizzy Gillespie. Although a Latin American influence is discernible in jazz from its earliest beginnings and in the 1930s appeared openly in the work of Mario Bauza (trumpeter with Cab Calloway) and Juan Tizol (trombonist with Duke Ellington), Afro-Cuban jazz became a clearly defined style and acquired an international following only when Gillespie (who was at first influenced by Bauza) began to collaborate with the outstanding Cuban percussionist and composer Chano Pozo from 1946. The next year Gillespie with his big band recorded several notable examples – *Manteca*, *Algo bueno (Woody 'n' you)*, and George Russell's *Cubana Be/Cubana Bop* – all of which featured Pozo's playing of the conga drum and combined Latin American rhythms with the bop idiom. Other examples have appeared in the work of Gillespie and many other jazz musicians, as well as such Latin bands and performers as Perez Prado, Tito Puente, Candido, and Machito, though not sufficiently often to establish Afro-Cuban jazz as an independent genre.

BIBLIOGRAPHY

J. S. Roberts: *Black Music of Two Worlds* (New York, 1972), chap.8
——: *The Latin Tinge* (New York, 1979), chap.5

See also LATIN JAZZ and SALSA.

GUNTHER SCHULLER

Ager, Milton (*b* Chicago, IL, 6 Oct 1893; *d* Los Angeles, CA, 6 May 1979). Composer. He began his career as a song plugger and arranger for the publishing companies of George M. Cohan and Irving Berlin, and had his first success as a songwriter (in collaboration with the composer George W. Meyer) with *Everything's peaches down in Georgia* (G. Clarke, 1918), introduced by Al Jolson. He wrote many songs to lyrics by Jack Yellen (with whom he founded the publishing firm Ager, Yellen & Bornstein in 1922), including *I wonder what's become of Sally* (1924), *Ain't she sweet?* (1927), and *Happy days are here again* (1930); the last became closely associated with the presidential campaigns of Franklin D. Roosevelt. Other well-known songs by Ager are *I'm nobody's baby* (lyrics by B. Davis; 1921), *Auf Wiedersehen, my dear* (A. Hoffman, E. G. Nelson, A. Goodhart; 1932), and, in collaboration with Jean Schwartz, *Trust in me* (N. Wever; 1936). His contributions to stage scores include songs for *What's in a Name?* (1920, with "A Young Man's Fancy"), *Rain or Shine* (1928), and *John Murray Anderson's Almanac* (1929). He also wrote music for the films *Honky Tonk* (1929), *Chasing Rainbows* (1930), and *King of Jazz* (1930).

BIBLIOGRAPHY

J. Burton: *Blue Book of Tin Pan Alley* (Watkins Glen, NY, 1950, rev. 2/1965)
Obituary, *New York Times* (8 May 1979)

SAMUEL S. BRYLAWSKI

AGMA. *See* AMERICAN GUILD OF MUSICAL ARTISTS.

Aiken, Conrad (Potter) (*b* Savannah, GA, 5 Aug 1889; *d* Savannah, 17 Aug 1973). Poet. A prolific writer throughout most of his long career, he produced 33 volumes of poetry, five novels, five short story collections, two books of criticism, and a play. He greatly admired Freud, and his works often stress psychological themes. In many of his early poems Aiken experimented with quasi-musical forms. Most notable among these are the six poetic sequences that he called "symphonies": *The Charnel Rose* (1918), *The Jig of Forslin* (1916), *The House of Dust* (1920), *Senlin* (1918), *The Pilgrimage of Festus* (1923), and *Changing Mind* (written in 1925). These works were revised, rearranged in the above order, and presented together in 1949 as *The Divine Pilgrim.* Aiken admitted that he used the word symphony "with considerable license," as he did not attempt to imitate symphonic forms. Instead he achieved a "symphonic" effect through the use of many recurring lyric motives and highly connotative or suggestive language. He described it as poetry that "will not so much present an idea as use its resonance." He also used a great deal of musical imagery, both in these works and in works not specifically related to musical forms.

One of Aiken's lyrics has proved particularly popular with composers – "Discordants," which was first published in *Turns and Movies and other Tales in Verse* (1916). Its first 12 lines have been extracted for use in several anthologies and variously retitled "Bread and Music," "Music I heard," or "Music I heard with you." No fewer than 12 musical settings of this excerpt have been published, including versions by Bernstein (in *Songfest*), Nordoff, and Hageman. Nordoff, Persichetti, and Crist have set other Aiken excerpts. Although many critics prefer the greater clarity and precision of his later poetry (especially the *Preludes* of the 1930s), composers have clearly concentrated on the more elusive, lyrical expressiveness found in the earlier poems.

BIBLIOGRAPHY

C. S. Lenhart: *Musical Influence on American Poetry* (Athens, GA, 1956)
J. Martin: *Conrad Aiken: a Life of his Art* (Princeton, NJ, 1962)
V. Mizelle: "Conrad Aiken's 'Music Strangely Subtle'," *Georgia Review*, xix (1965), 81
R. E. Carlile: "Great Circle: Conrad Aiken's Musico-literary Technique," *Georgia Review*, xxii (1968), 27
——: *Conrad Aiken's Prose: the Musico-literary Perspective* (diss., U. of Georgia, 1971)
H. Hagenbuechle: "Epistemology and Musical Form in Conrad Aiken's Poetry," *Studies in the Literary Imagination*, xiii (1980), 7
R. J. Nicolosi: "T. S. Eliot and Music: an Introduction," *MQ*, lxvi (1980), 192
M. Hovland: *Musical Settings of American Poetry: a Bibliography* (in preparation) [incl. list of settings]

HOWARD NIBLOCK

Aikin, Jesse B(owman) (*b* Chester Co., PA, 5 March 1808; *d* Montgomery Co., PA, 1900). Tunebook compiler. He invented his own system of seven-shape notation, which first appeared in *The Christian Minstrel* (Philadelphia, 1846; for illustration *see* NOTATION, fig.4*a*), a tunebook containing many pieces found in the publications of Lowell Mason. It appeared in at least 171 reprintings (not actual editions) by 1873, and reportedly sold more than 180,000 copies. Aikin's notation found widespread acceptance, particularly in the South; it eventually supplanted all other forms of shape-notation, and continues to be used in the 20th century in denominational hymnals and books of the southern gospel-music tradition. His other publications include *The Juvenile Minstrel* (Philadelphia, 1847); *Harmonia ecclesiae, or Companion to the Christian Minstrel* (Philadelphia, 1853); *The Sabbath-school Minstrel* (Philadelphia, 1859); *The Imperial Harmony* (with Chester G. Allen and Hubert P. Main, New York, 1876); and *The True Principles of the Science of Music* (Philadelphia, 1891, rev. 2/1893; round notation). Aikin was also a singing-school teacher, and sold organs in association with his son-in-law, Isaac R. Hunsberger.

See also SHAPE-NOTE HYMNODY, §3.

BIBLIOGRAPHY

G. P. Jackson: *White Spirituals in the Southern Uplands* (Chapel Hill, 1933/*R* 1965)
P. G. Hammond: *A Study of "The Christian Minstrel" (1846) by Jesse B. Aikin* (thesis, Southern Baptist Theological Seminary, 1969)

PAUL HAMMOND

Ailey, Alvin (*b* Rogers, TX, 5 Jan 1931). Choreographer. After studying dance with Lester Horton, Hanya Holm, and Martha Graham, he founded the Alvin Ailey American Dance Theater in New York in 1958. Initially Ailey included only black dancers in his company, and he strove to represent black American culture and experiences in many of his ballets, such as *Revelations* (1960), danced to Negro spirituals. In 1962, however, the company was racially integrated and Ailey broadened his artistic vision to include more universal experiences. He often creates works from popular music or jazz, especially the music of Duke Ellington, most notably in *The River* (1970), and he has selected music for his ballets by such American composers as Glenn Branca, Alice Coltrane, Keith Jarrett, Charles Mingus, Laura Nyro, Leon Russell, Carlos Surinach, and Mary Lou Williams. Ailey has also choreographed for musical comedies, television programs, films, operas (including Barber's *Antony and Cleopatra*), and other stage works, such as Bernstein's *Mass*. In 1985 he joined the faculty of the Borough of Manhattan Community College, becoming the first choreographer to be awarded a distinguished professorship at CUNY.

BIBLIOGRAPHY

S. Cook and J. H. Mazo: *The Alvin Ailey American Dance Theater* (New York, 1978)

SUSAN AU

Ainsworth, Henry (*b* Swanton Morley, Norfolk, England, 1570; *d* Amsterdam, Netherlands, ?1622–3). English minister and biblical scholar. He was expatriated as a "Brownist" in 1593 and settled in Amsterdam. He was the author of a number of religious tracts and translations, including *The Book of Psalmes: Englished both in Prose and Metre. With Annotations* (1612, 5/1644). This psalter, which includes 39 monophonic psalm tunes, "most taken from our former Englished psalms [and also] the gravest and easiest tunes of the French and Dutch psalms," was used by the Pilgrim settlers of the Plymouth Colony in 1620, thereby beginning the tradition of PSALMODY in New England. By the late 17th century, however, it was no longer in use there, having been replaced by the Bay Psalm Book and other psalters.

See also PSALMS, METRICAL, §1 (ii).

BIBLIOGRAPHY

W. E. A. Axon: "Ainsworth, Henry," *DNB*
W. S. Pratt: *The Music of the Pilgrims* (Boston, 1921/*R* 1971 and 1980)
M. Frost: *English and Scottish Hymn Tunes* (London, 1953)
L. Inserra and H. W. Hitchcock: *The Music of Henry Ainsworth's Psalter*, ISAMm, xv (Brooklyn, NY, 1981) [incl. facs. and transcrs. of all 39 tunes]

H. WILEY HITCHCOCK

Airto. *See* MOREIRA, AIRTO.

Aitken, Hugh (*b* New York, 7 Sept 1924). Composer. His early musical training was with his father (violin lessons) and his paternal grandmother (piano lessons). After service in the US Air Force during World War II, he entered the Juilliard School, where he studied composition with Persichetti, Wagenaar, and Ward (MS 1950). Between 1950 and 1960 he taught privately and in the Juilliard Preparatory Division; he then joined the main Juilliard faculty. In 1970 he was appointed chairman of the music department at William Paterson College, Wayne, New Jersey, where he became professor of music in 1973. He has received commissions from the NEA, Elizabeth Sprague Coolidge Foundation, Naumburg Foundation, Juilliard School, Jose Limon Dance Company, and the Concord String Quartet, among others.

A strong sense of the past permeates much of Aitken's work. Such conservative if eclectic compositions as those after Rameau and Cervantes or his Cantata no.1 on Elizabethan texts seem influenced stylistically by their literary sources, and even his more dissonant music incorporates gestures to earlier styles or stylistic principles. Structurally his work is concise and displays a good command of instrumental techniques and resources, particularly in his pieces for various unaccompanied solo instruments.

WORKS

Stage: Fables (chamber opera, L. Tapia, after La Fontaine), 1975; Felipe (opera, 3, Aitken, after Cervantes), 1981; 4 dance scores, 1949–63

Large ens: Chamber Conc., pf, 13 insts, 1949, rev. 1977; Toccata, orch, 1950; Pf Conc., 1953; Short Suite, str, 1954; 7 Pieces, chamber orch, 1957; Partitas

I–IV, orch, 1957, 1959, 1964, 1964; Serenade, chamber orch, 1958; 15 Short Pieces, pf, str, 1960; Suite in Six, band, 1961; 4 Quiet Pieces, band, 1962; Partita, str qt, orch, 1964; Partita, band, 1967; Variations on a Toccata, band, 1968; Rameau Remembered, fl, chamber orch, 1980; In Praise of Ockeghem, str, 1981, arr. org, 1981; Vn Conc., 1984

Choral: 2 masses, 1950, 1964; 6 cantatas, 1v, insts, no.1 (Elizabethan texts), 1958, no.2 (Rilke), 1959, no.3 (W. Barnstone), 1960, no.4 (A. Machado), 1961, no.5 (Rilke), 1962, no.6 (Rilke), 1981; The Revelation of St. John the Divine, pt.1, 1965; 3 other choral works

Inst: Short Suite, wind qnt, pf, 1948; Str Trio, 1951; Short Fantasy, vn, pf, 1954, rev. 1980; Cl Suite, 1955; Partita, 6 insts, 1956; Qnt, ob, str qt, 1957; 8 Studies, wind qnt, 1958; Vn Partita, 1958; Trbn Music, 1961; Db Suite, 1961; Montages, bn, 1962; Trios, 11 performers, 1970; Ob Music, 1975; Johannes: an Hommage to Ockeghem, 5 insts, 1977; For the Va, 1978; Opus 95, Revisited, str qt, 1980; Pastiche, pic, pf, 1980; 5 Short Pieces, 3 cl, 1982; other works

Kbd: Pf Sonatina, 1947; 3 choral preludes, org, 1952, rev. 1980; 4 Pieces, pf 4 hands, 1952; 3 Short Pieces, pf, 1952; 7 Bagatelles, pf, 1957; Pf Fantasy, 1966; 3 Connected Pieces, pf, 1967

Principal publishers: Oxford UP, Presser

BIBLIOGRAPHY

EwenD

ROBERT SKINNER

Aitken, John (*b* Dalkeith, Scotland, ?1745; *d* Philadelphia, PA, 8 Sept 1831). Metalsmith, music engraver, compiler, publisher, and dealer. He had arrived in Philadelphia by 1785 and began his career as a music publisher in 1787, when he brought out three large works: Reinagle's *A Selection of the most Favorite Scots Tunes*, William Brown's *Three Rondos for the Piano Forte*, and his own *A Compilation of the Litanies and Vespers, Hymns and Anthems* (2/1791), the only 18th-century American collection of music for the Roman Catholic Church. In 1788 he issued another anthology by Reinagle and may also have printed Hopkinson's *Seven Songs*; a few pieces of sheet music and more of Reinagle's song collections followed in 1789. By 1793 he had brought out at least 20 titles, but between then and 1806 he published only the compendious *Scots Musical Museum* (1797) and one of his own songs, *The Goldsmith's Rant* (1802). He continued to work as a silversmith, but by 1806 he had reestablished himself in the music business. As one of Philadelphia's busiest music publishers during the years 1806–11, he brought out many secular songs and several secular collections as well as more sacred music – a total of perhaps 200 titles. Aitken's musical activity seems to have ceased after 1811, though he continued in the metalworking and printing trades in Philadelphia until at least 1825.

Aitken has been identified by Wolfe as the first professional publisher of secular music in the USA. His publications of the 1780s mark the earliest sustained commitment to the printing and sale of music of this type, and were also the first known American publications to have been produced using the intaglio method of engraving metal plates with steel punches rather than by hand.

BIBLIOGRAPHY

F. J. Metcalf: *American Writers and Compilers of Sacred Music* (New York, 1925/*R*1967)

D. W. Krummel: *Philadelphia Music Engraving and Publishing* (diss., U. of Michigan, 1958), 116

R. J. Wolfe: *Secular Music in America, 1801–1825: a Bibliography* (New York, 1964)

——: *Early American Music Engraving and Printing* (Urbana, IL, 1980), 41, 108

RICHARD CRAWFORD

Aitken, Webster (*b* Los Angeles, CA, 17 June 1908). Pianist. After studying in California under Alexis Kall and Alfred Mirovitch, he studied with three pupils of Liszt – Arthur Friedheim, Moriz Rosenthal, and Emil Sauer – as well as with Schnabel and Marie Prentner (Theodor Leschetizky's principal assistant). He made his professional début in Vienna in 1929 and his New York début at Town Hall on 17 November 1935. In 1938 he played the complete cycle of Schubert's piano sonatas both in London and in New York. During the 1940s Aitken commanded the esteem of Virgil Thomson and of the intellectual public as Schnabel had in the previous generation; his wide-ranging repertory included contemporary works such as Elliott Carter's Piano Sonata, of which Aitken gave the first performance in a radio broadcast in 1947. He gave performances of Beethoven's late piano music in New York and at Harvard University in 1950, and through the next decade appeared often in concert, although chiefly in academic settings; after 1960 he gradually withdrew from public performance but continued to play privately, expanding his repertory to include works by Boulez and Stockhausen. Aitken's recordings of familiar works by Handel, Beethoven, Schubert, and Webern are remarkable for the disturbing intensity of their unconventional interpretations.

RICHARD DYER

Akers, Doris (Mae) (*b* Kirksville, MO, 1922). Gospel singer, pianist, and composer. She began piano lessons when she was five and by the age of ten was playing for her church choir. She started to compose while still in her teens. Later she moved to California and formed the Simmons–Akers Singers, with whom she remained until the mid-1950s. Thereafter she served as music director for various white congregations, composing and performing in a style more closely associated with white gospel. She has therefore been only modestly successful in black gospel circles, although many of her compositions are standards among black singers, including *Lead me, guide me* (1953), *You can't beat God giving* (1957), *Sweet, sweet spirit* (1972), and *Lord, don't move the mountain* (1972). Her songs have been recorded by George Beverly Shea and Mahalia Jackson and sung by the Stamps Quartet in the documentary film about Elvis Presley, *Elvis on Tour* (1972).

BIBLIOGRAPHY

H. C. Boyer: "An Overview: Gospel Music Comes of Age," *Black World*, xxiii/1 (1973), 42, 79

I. V. Jackson: *Afro-American Religious Music: a Bibliography and Catalogue of Gospel Music* (Westport, CT, 1979)

HORACE CLARENCE BOYER

Akiyoshi, Toshiko (*b* Dairen, China, 12 Dec 1929). Jazz composer, pianist, and bandleader. She studied classical music and turned to jazz only in 1947 after moving to Japan. There she was discovered by visiting American jazz musicians, among them Oscar Peterson, who urged her to take up a career in the USA. After studying at the Berklee School in Boston (1956–9) she became an active and highly regarded bop pianist, especially in groups with the alto saxophonist Charlie Mariano (who was at that time her husband), and with Charles Mingus (1962). In 1973 she founded a large rehearsal band in Los Angeles with the tenor saxophonist and flutist Lew Tabackin, whom she married. Their first album, *Kogun*, was commercially successful in Japan, and the group attracted increasing popularity and critical acclaim until, by 1980, it was generally regarded as the leading big band in jazz. Here Akiyoshi cultivated her gifts as a composer, writing rich, subtle scores in the modern big-band tradition of Gil Evans and Thad Jones–Mel Lewis, often incorporating elements from Japanese music. She has also continued to develop as a pianist, playing in a delicate, accurate bop style. A number of her scores have been published by Toba Music, Hollywood.

RECORDINGS
(selective list)

Combo: *Toshiko's Blues* (1954, Norgran EPN47); *Mariano-Toshiko Quartet* (1963, Takt Jazz 12); *Finesse* (1978, Concord 69)

Big band: *Kogun* (1974, RCA JPL1-0236); *Long Yellow Road* (1974–5, RCA JPL1-1350); *Tales of a Courtesan* (1975, RCA JPL1-0723); *Road Time* (1976, RCA CLP2-2242); *Insights* (1976, RCA AFL1-2678); *Sumi-e* (1979, RCA PL37537); *Tanuki's Night Out* (1981, JAM 006)

BIBLIOGRAPHY

"Toshiko Akiyoshi Discography," *Swing Journal*, xxviii/12 (1974), 76

L. Feather: "East Meets West or Never the Twain Shall Cease," *Down Beat*, xliii/11 (1976), 16

——: "Toshiko Akiyoshi: Contemporary Sculptress of Sound," *Down Beat*, xliv/17 (1977), 13

——: "Toshiko Akiyoshi," *Contemporary Keyboard*, vii/9 (1980), 58

J. BRADFORD ROBINSON

Alabama Symphony Orchestra. Symphony orchestra founded as the Birmingham Symphony Orchestra in 1933 and based in BIRMINGHAM.

Alaskan Eskimo. *See* INUIT.

Albanese, Licia (*b* Bari, Italy, 22 July 1913). Soprano. After study with Emanuel de Rosa and Giuseppina Baldassare-Tedeschi, her career began at the Teatro Lirico, Milan, where in 1934 she was an emergency replacement for an indisposed Butterfly in *Madama Butterfly*. The same opera, always closely identified with her, occasioned her formal début at Parma (10 December 1935) and her début at the Metropolitan Opera (9 February 1940). During her career she made more than 1000 appearances in 48 roles, in the lyric or *lirico spinto* repertory, including Mozart (Donna Anna, Zerlina, Susanna) and French opera (Micaela, Manon, Gounod's Marguerite), as well as the obvious Italian challenges; her specialty was the Puccini heroines. A singer of extraordinary technical skill and emotional intensity, she was the Violetta and Mimì in Toscanini's recorded NBC broadcasts. Active in the movement to save the old Metropolitan Opera House, she sang Manon as her last role there on 20 January 1966, and took part in the gala farewell to the old house on 16 April of that year singing "Un bel dì" from *Madama Butterfly*; she never rejoined the company at Lincoln Center. In later years she taught, and sang sporadically in concert and in roles the Metropolitan had, perhaps wisely, denied her, such as Aida and Mascagni's Santuzza. She became an American citizen in 1945.

BIBLIOGRAPHY

E. Gara and R. Celletti: "Albanese, Licia," *Le grandi voci*, ed. R. Celletti (Rome, 1964) [with opera discography by R. Vegeto]

J. Hines: *Great Singers on Great Singing* (Garden City, NY, 1982)

MARTIN BERNHEIMER/R

Albanian-American music. *See* EUROPEAN-AMERICAN MUSIC, §III, 1.

Albersheim, Gerhard (Ludwig) (*b* Cologne, Germany, 17 Nov 1902). Musicologist and pianist. After schooling in Cologne he was awarded a music teacher's diploma in 1930. He studied musicology at the University of Vienna (1933–8) and obtained his doctorate in 1938 with a dissertation on acoustical psychology. He also studied privately with Heinrich Schenker. In 1940 he immigrated to the USA, later becoming an American citizen, and was active as a conductor, teacher, accompanist, and opera coach. He held teaching posts at the Los Angeles Conservatory of Music and Art (1947–53) and at UCLA (1953–6), before his appointment in 1956 as professor of music at the California State University, Los Angeles, where he taught until his retirement in 1970. He frequently accompanied distinguished singers such as Elisabeth Schumann, Ezio Pinza and Dietrich Fischer-Dieskau. Albersheim was one of the first to write on the importance of Schenker's theories. His main studies have been in the areas of acoustics and the psychology of hearing, and their relationships to musical aesthetics.

SAUL NOVACK/R

Albert. Family of violin makers and dealers. John Albert (*d* 1887) came to the USA from Freiburg, Germany, as a refugee of the 1848 revolution. He settled first in New York and about 1859 established a shop in Philadelphia. He retired in the early 1880s and was succeeded by his son Eugene John Albert (*b* New York, 1852; *d* Philadelphia, PA, 1920). John's eldest son, Charles Francis Albert (*b* Freiburg, 1842; *d* Philadelphia, 1901), established his own shop in Philadelphia about 1868. Although the Alberts were not the first violin makers to establish themselves in Philadelphia, they were the finest of their period; their violins were modeled on the Saxon type of instrument. Charles Francis Albert, considered the best maker in the family, received highest honors in the Philadelphia Centennial Exposition of 1876. He was noted as an excellent repairer and connoisseur and also introduced numerous advancements in violin accessories; his wound strings and chin rests, for example, were very popular. His son Charles Francis Albert, Jr. (1869–1916) was his successor.

BIBLIOGRAPHY

N. Groce: *Musical Instrument Making in New York City during the Eighteenth and Nineteenth Centuries* (diss., U. of Michigan, 1982)

PHILIP J. KASS

Albert, Stephen (Joel) (*b* New York, 6 Feb 1941). Composer. He began his composition study with Siegmeister (1956–8) and Milhaud (summer 1958). He also studied with Bernard Rogers at the Eastman School (1958–60), Castaldo at the Philadelphia Academy of Music (BM 1962), and Rochberg at the University of Pennsylvania (autumn 1963). For the 1967–8 academic year Albert received a Ford Foundation grant to serve as composer-in-residence for the Lima (Ohio) public schools and community orchestra; positions followed at the Philadelphia Musical Academy (1968–70), Stanford University (1970–71), and Smith College (1974–6). His honors include MacDowell Colony fellowships (1964, 1969), a Huntington Hartford Fellowship (1964–5), Guggenheim fellowships (1967–8, 1978–9), two Rome Prizes (1965, 1966), and grants from the Martha Baird Rockefeller Fund (1967, 1970, 1979), the NEA (1977–8), and the Alice M. Ditson foundation (1979). He has received a joint commission from the Fromm Foundation and the Berkshire Music Festival (1975) and two commissions from the Chicago SO. Albert composes for both electronic and traditional instruments and has combined the two in works such as *Cathedral Music*. Like others who have experimented with sound production in search of a synthesis of electronic and traditional sounds, Albert has looked to neoclassical and neoromantic melodic and harmonic ideas as vehicles of expression. In 1985 he was awarded a Pulitzer Prize for his symphony *RiverRun*, and began a two-year period as composer-in-residence with the Seattle SO.

WORKS

Orch: Illuminations, brass, perc, pfs, harps, 1962; Winter Songs (W. C. Williams, W. D. Snodgrass, R. Frost), T, orch, 1965; Leaves from the Golden Notebook, 1970; Bacchae (Euripides, trans. W. Arrowsmith), solo vv, mixed chorus, nar, elec guis, saxs, orch, 1970; Voices Within, pic, pic cl, cl, sax, cornet, trbn, harp, pf, vn, db, orch, 1975; RiverRun, sym., 1983–4

Chamber: 2 Toccatas, pf, 1958–9; Imitations, str qt, 1964; Supernatural Songs (Yeats), S, chamber orch, 1964; Canons, str qt, 1964; Wolf Time (10th-century Icelandic), S, amp chamber orch, 1969; Cathedral Music (Conc. for 4 Qts), 2 amp fl, 2 amp vc, tpt + pic tpt, 2 hn, trbn, perc, amp harp, elec org, elec pf, 2 pf, 1971; To Wake the Dead (from Joyce: Finnegans Wake), S, fl, cl, vn, vc, 1977; Music from the Stone Harp, 7 players, 1979–80, withdrawn; Into Eclipse (after T. Hughes, after Seneca: Oedipus), T, 12 insts, 1983–4; TreeStone (from Joyce: Finnegans Wake), 1983–4

Principal publisher: C. Fischer

BIBLIOGRAPHY

EwenD

BARBARA L. TISCHLER

Alberti, Solon (*b* Mt. Clemens, MI, 6 Dec 1889; *d* Chicago, IL, 16 Oct 1981). Pianist and accompanist. He was one of 11 children, all musical. His early years were spent in Chicago where he studied cello and piano. He graduated from the Chicago Musical College at 18 and taught there from 1910 to 1914. He conducted the college orchestra, directed its opera workshop, and began his career as accompanist. At the age of 24 he moved to Kansas City to head the piano, theory, and music history departments at the Conservatory of Music (1914–19); he was also conductor of the Kansas City Opera Association. In 1920 he went to New York, where he lived for the rest of his professional life. His summers were spent conducting opera workshops in various universities and conservatories. He toured extensively with such artists as Melchior, Schumann-Heink, Ruffo, Kullman, Bonelli, Teyte, Meisle, and De Luca. First working as a coach, he became well known as a singing teacher. He was organist and choir director at the Park Avenue Christian Church, 1932–67. In 1978 he retired and moved to Chicago. He composed a number of piano pieces and songs.

PHILIP LIESON MILLER

Albrecht [Albright], **Charles** (*b* Germany, 1759/60; *d* Philadelphia, PA, 28 June 1848). Piano maker. He was active in Philadelphia as a piano maker by the 1790s. He is not listed in the 1785 city directory, but his name appears in tax records, census entries, and city directories from 1788 onwards. Described as a "joiner" until 1793, he had already begun to make pianos in Philadelphia (a square piano dated 1789 is now owned by the Historical Society of Pennsylvania). From 1793 to 1824 he made instruments at 95 Vine Street, after which he retired. Albrecht made some of the earliest surviving American pianos; his square pianos (four are at the Smithsonian Institution) have handsome cabinet work and a range of five to five and a half octaves (*F'* to *c''''*). No relationship between Charles Albrecht, C. F. L. Albrecht, and Albrecht & Co. has yet been established.

CYNTHIA ADAMS HOOVER

Albrecht, Christian Frederick Ludwig (*b* Hanover, Germany, 6 Jan 1788; *d* Philadelphia, PA, March 1843). Piano maker. He immigrated to the USA, arriving in Philadelphia on 17 October 1822, and from 1823 to 1824 ran a business there at 106 St. John Street; from 1830 to 1843 his address was 144 South 3rd Street. On his death his small business was bequeathed to his wife Maria. His pianos exhibit excellent craftsmanship; pianos by him (one upright and one square) at the Smithsonian Institution are in empire style and have six octaves. No relationship between Christian Albrecht, Charles Albrecht, and Albrecht & Co. has yet been established.

CYNTHIA ADAMS HOOVER

Albrecht, Otto E(dwin) (*b* Philadelphia, PA, 8 July 1899; *d* Newtown, PA, 6 July 1984). Musicologist and music librarian. He studied Romance languages and literature at the University of Pennsylvania (BA 1921, MA 1925, PhD 1931) and at the University of Copenhagen (1922–3). He taught French and music at the University of Pennsylvania from 1923 until 1970, when he retired. From 1937 he was curator of the university's music library, which was named the Otto E. Albrecht Music Library on his retirement. He held several government positions in post-war Germany and visited Russia as specialist in musicology for the Department of State (1961). Albrecht's historical interests included German lieder and music in America to 1860. He compiled several important bibliographies, including *A Census of Autograph Music Manuscripts* (1953), an indispensable guide to European manuscripts in the USA, and the catalogue and manuscript descriptions of the Mary Flagler Cary Music Collection of the Pierpont Morgan Library, New York (of which he was elected honorary fellow in 1971). He twice served as vice-president of the Music Library Association, and was treasurer of the American Musicological Society, 1954–70. A Festschrift in his honor, *Studies in Musicology* (ed. J. Hill), was published in 1977.

PAULA MORGAN

Albrecht & Co. Firm of piano makers. Charles Albright (Albrecht by 1864) is listed in Philadelphia city directories from 1863. He was in partnership with Frederick Riekes (as Albrecht & Riekes, 1864–5), with Riekes and Richard T. Schmidt (as Albrecht, Riekes & Schmidt, 1866–74), and with Riekes and Edmund Wolsieffer (as Albrecht & Co., 1875–86). From 1887 to 1916 the firm was owned by Blasius & Sons, which in turn was owned by Rice-Wuerst & Co., a manufacturer based in Woodbury, New Jersey, from around 1916; Albrecht pianos were listed by Rice-Wuerst until 1920. Although some advertisements for Albrecht & Co. stated that the firm was established in 1789, there is no evidence to support this claim; no relationship between Albrecht & Co., Charles Albrecht, and Christian Albrecht, all piano makers active in Philadelphia, has been established.

CYNTHIA ADAMS HOOVER

Albright, Charles. *See* ALBRECHT, CHARLES.

Albright, William Hugh (*b* Gary, IN, 20 Oct 1944). Composer, organist, and pianist. He attended the Juilliard Preparatory Department (1959–62), the University of Michigan (1963–70), and the Paris Conservatoire (1968–9); his teachers included Finney, Rochberg, and Olivier Messiaen for composition, and Marilyn Mason for organ. Albright has received many commissions and honors, including two awards from the Koussevitzky Foundation, the Queen Marie-José Prize (for his *Organbook I*), and an award from the American Academy of Arts and Letters. He was selected to represent the USA in UNESCO's International Rostrum of Composers (1979). In 1970 he joined the faculty of the University of Michigan where, as associate director of the electronic music studio, he has pursued research into live and electronic modification of acoustic instruments. In 1982 he became professor of music there. Through his own modern rag compositions and his performances and recordings of classical ragtime, stride piano, and boogie-woogie, Albright has been a principal figure in the revival of interest in Joplin and other ragtime and stride masters. He has given many first performances of organ and piano works by American and European composers; and the series of organ works he has commissioned independently from 1970 has substantially enriched the repertory for that instrument.

Although Albright's early organ works reflect the influence of Messiaen in their colorful registration and chromaticism, his later works, in a variety of mediums, combine a complex rhythmic and atonal style with elements of American popular music. Albright stresses the value of music as communication and the supremacy of intuition, imagination, and beauty of sound. Much of his music displays exuberant humor and a fresh improvisatory spirit. A section of *Organbook III* (1978) briefly evokes "a wandering improvisation by an inebriated Sunday School organist"; *The King of Instruments* (1978) affectionately parodies the composer's own world of the pipe organ, with admonitions to the organist to add "the funniest sounding stop," to perform "in Chicago Blues style," and, with samba rhythms, to "keep repeating ad nauseam." *Seven Deadly Sins* (1974) subtly satirizes contemporary musical styles, and concludes with a *grand galop* finale. Albright's seeming spontaneity and his shifts from romantic ebullience to nostalgic lyricism are held firmly in balance by rigorous formal concision and control. In the virtuoso *Five Chromatic Dances* for piano (1976), for example, opening pitches outline the tonal centers and direction for a large-scale structure filled with contrasting textures, colors, and moods. An opera, *The Magic City*, was commissioned from him by the University of Michigan in 1978.

WORKS

Inst: Foils, wind, perc, 1963–4; Frescos, ww qt, 1964; 2 Pieces for Nine Insts, 1965–6; Caroms, 8 players, 1966; Marginal Worlds, 12 players, 1969–70; Danse Macabre, vn, vc, fl, cl, pf, 1971; Take That, 4 drummers, 1972; Night Procession, chamber orch, 1972; Gothic Suite, org, str, perc, 1973; Introduction, Passacaglia, and Rondo capriccioso, solo tack pf, 8 players, 1974; Doo-dah, 3 a sax, 1975; Jericho, tpt, org, 1976; Peace Pipe, 2 bn, 1976; Saints Preserve Us, cl, 1976; Heater, a sax, band, 1977; Shadows, gui, 1977; Romance, hn, org, 1981; The Enigma Syncopations, fl, db, perc, org, 1982; Canon in D, db, hpd, 1984; Sonata, a sax, pf, 1984

Kbd: Juba, org, 1965; Pianoàgogo, pf, 1965–6; Pneuma, org, 1966; Organbook I, org, 1967; 3 Original Rags, pf, 1967–8; Grand Sonata in Rag, pf, 1968; 3 Novelty Rags, pf, 1968; The Dream Rags, pf, 1970; Organbook II, org, tape, 1971; Stipendium peccati, org, pf, perc, 1973; Dream and Dance, org, perc, 1974; Sweet Sixteenths, pf, 1975; 5 Chromatic Dances, pf, 1976; Organbook III, org, 1977–8; The King of Instruments, org, nar, 1978; Halo, org, metal insts, 1978; 4 Fancies, hpd, 1979; De spiritum, org, 2 assistants, 1980–81; Bacchanal, org, orch, 1981; That Sinking Feeling, org, 1982; In memoriam, org, 1983; 1732: In memoriam Johannes Albrecht, org, 1984; Sphaera, pf, 4-track tape, 1985

Theater and mixed-media: Tic, soloist, 2 ens, tape, films, 1967; Beulahland Rag, nar, jazz qt, improvisation ens, tape, films, slides, 1967–9; Alliance, 3 pts, orch, 1967–70; 7 Deadly Sins, 7 players, opt. nar, 1974; Cross of Gold, actors, chorus, insts, 1975; Full Moon in March (incidental music, Yeats), 1978; The Magic City (opera, G. Garrett), 1978–

Vocal: An Alleluia Super-round, 8 or more vv, 1973; Mass in D, chorus, congregation, org, perc, 1974; Chichester Mass, chorus, 1974; Pax in terra, A, T, chorus, 1981; David's Songs (Psalms), S, A, T, B/SATB, 1982; 6 New Hymns, unison vv, kbd, 1974–83; A Song to David (C. Smart), 2 choruses, solo vv, org, 1983

Principal publishers: Elkan-Vogel, Jobert, Marks, Peters

BIBLIOGRAPHY

A. G. Fried: "New York Premieres of Two Works on Albright Program," *Music: the AGO and RCCO Magazine*, vi/3 (1972), 30

W. Salisbury: "William Albright: a Review," *Diapason*, lxiii/4 (1972), 17

E Hantz: "An Introduction to the Organ Music of William Albright," *Diapason*, lxiv/6 (1973), 1

D. Reed: *The Organ Music of William Albright* (diss., U. of Rochester, 1976)

D. Burge: "An Interview with William Albright," *Contemporary Keyboard*, iii/3 (1977), 52

A. Parks: "William Albright's *Organbook I*: a Master Lesson," *Diapason*, lxix/6 (1978), 1

D. Burge: "Albright's *Five Chromatic Dances*," *Contemporary Keyboard*, vii/3 (1981), 56

L. Raver: "William Albright's *Organbook III*," *American Organist*, xv/10 (1981), 48

J. Ferguson: "Albright Première in Minneapolis," *American Organist*, xviii/2 (1984), 30 [on A Song to David]

DON C. GILLESPIE

Albuquerque. City in New Mexico (pop. 331,767; metropolitan area 454,499), founded in 1706. Western art music was first cultivated in Albuquerque as a result of the stimulus supplied by musical activities at the University of New Mexico. Among its earliest full-time music faculty members were Grace Edminster Thompson, founder (in 1931) and first conductor of the Albuquerque Civic SO; John Donald Robb, a composer and collector of southwestern Indian and Hispanic folk music; and Kurt Frederick, a Viennese violist who joined the faculty in 1941 to teach viola and conducting. The university has been a major force in training teachers and performers active throughout the state; it offers bachelor's and master's degrees in music and music education.

The university's Fine Arts Library and its historical collections in the Zimmerman Library contain manuscript materials and field recordings of Hispanic and Indian folk music of the American Southwest, collected by Robb and others. The archive of recorded sound in the Fine Arts Library, under the direction of Charlemaude Curtis, has assembled extensive oral history materials on musicians and musical activity in New Mexico. (*See* LIBRARIES AND COLLECTIONS, §3.)

The Albuquerque Civic SO has continued without interruption for over 50 years; its name was changed first to the Albuquerque SO, and then, in 1976, to the New Mexico SO. Its conductors have included Mrs. Thompson, Kurt Frederick (under whom it gave the world première of Schoenberg's *A Survivor from Warsaw* in 1948), Hans Lange, Maurice Bonney, and José Iturbi. In the 1970s the orchestra gradually became fully professional under the direction of Yoshimi Takeda (1970–84); Takeda was succeeded by Neal Stulberg in 1985. In addition to a subscription series in the university's Popejoy Hall, it offers popular, youth, and small-ensemble concerts throughout New Mexico and has toured to Mexico. The June Music Festival, founded in 1940 by Albert Simms and his wife, offers a summer series of chamber music concerts given on the university campus by such well-known ensembles as the Fine Arts and Guarneri quartets. The long-established Community Concerts series has given way to concerts by visiting performers, sponsored by the university and the New Mexico SO and presented in Popejoy Hall. In 1982 the city authorities restored to use the Kimo Theater, built in 1927 and formerly a movie theater, where such semi-professional groups as the Albuquerque Opera Theater (founded 1973) and Albuquerque Civic Light Opera (founded 1967) now perform.

BIBLIOGRAPHY

P. Hart: "Albuquerque Symphony Orchestra," *Orpheus in the New World: the Symphony Orchestra as an American Cultural Institution* (New York, 1973), 239

PHILIP HART

Alda [Davies], Frances (Jeanne) (*b* Christchurch, New Zealand, 31 May 1883; *d* Venice, Italy, 18 Sept 1952). New Zealand soprano. Brought up by her maternal grandparents in Australia, her first engagements were in light opera in Melbourne. She then went to Paris and studied with Marchesi, who suggested that she adopt the name Alda and arranged her début as Manon at the Opéra-Comique in 1904. After successful appearances in Brussels (1905), Covent Garden (1906), and La Scala (1908), where she met Toscanini and Gatti-Casazza, she was engaged by the Metropolitan Opera, where she sang from December 1908 until December 1929. In 1910 she married Gatti-Casazza, who had left La Scala to become director of the Metropolitan two years earlier. Alda's pure, lyrical voice, technically almost faultless, was ideally suited to such roles as Gilda, Violetta, Desdemona, Manon (Massenet), Louise, Mimì, and Butterfly. She created the leading soprano roles in Damrosch's *Cyrano de Bergerac*, Herbert's *Madeleine*, and Hadley's *Cleopatra's Night*. She is well represented on recordings.

BIBLIOGRAPHY

F. Alda: *Men, Women and Tenors* (Boston, 1937)
A. Favia-Artsay: "Frances Alda," *Record Collector*, vi (1951), 221 [with discography]
B. and F. MacKenzie: *Singers of Australia* (Melbourne, 1967), 97

ALAN BLYTH/R

Aldrich, Putnam C(alder) (*b* Swansea, MA, 14 July 1904; *d* Cannes, France, 18 April 1975). Musicologist and harpsichordist. After schooling at Yale University (BA 1926), Aldrich went to Europe, where he studied piano with Tobias Matthay in London and harpsichord with Landowska in France. He returned to the USA to work at Harvard (MA 1936, PhD 1942). From 1936 to 1944 he was director of the Boston Society of Ancient Instruments. He began his teaching career at the University of Texas (1942–4), and was on the faculty of Western Reserve University (1946–8) and Mills College, Oakland (1948–50). In 1950 he was appointed professor of music at Stanford University, where he taught until his retirement in 1969.

Aldrich combined his scholarly interests with an active career as a harpsichordist. In particular he wrote on the performance practice of early music and the musical ornamentation of the 17th and 18th centuries, notably *Ornamentation in J. S. Bach's Organ Works* (1950, 2/1969). His study *Rhythm in Seventeenth-century Italian Monody* (1966) examines notational problems encountered by present-day performers and editors of this music and furnishes provocative, sometimes controversial solutions.

PAULA MORGAN

Aldrich, Richard (*b* Providence, RI, 31 July 1863; *d* Rome, Italy, 2 June 1937). Critic. He was educated at Harvard University, where he studied music under Paine, graduating in 1885. In the same year he became music critic of the *Providence Journal*, after serving his apprenticeship in general journalism. In 1889 he became private secretary to US Senator Dixon and at the same time was music critic of the *Evening Star*, Washington. In 1891 he relinquished both posts to join the staff of the *New York Tribune*, on which paper he held various editorial posts, particularly that of assistant critic to H. E. Krehbiel, until 1902, when he became music editor of the *New York Times*; he retired in 1923 but remained on the editorial staff in an advisory capacity.

Throughout his career Aldrich was notable for the breadth of his musical knowledge and the soundness of his judgment; in general he was sympathetic to modern music, though vehemently opposed to extreme trends. As one might expect from a member of the National Institute of Arts and Letters he was distinguished for the excellence of his style and for the wit and urbanity of his writing. His personal library of books on music, an important collection that he catalogued during the leisure of his later years, was donated to the Eda Kuhn Loeb Music Library and the Houghton Library at Harvard in 1955.

See also CRITICISM, §3.

WRITINGS

A Guide to Parsifal (Boston, 1904)
A Guide to the Ring of the Nibelung (Boston, 1905)
Musical Discourse: from the New York Times (Oxford, England, 1928)
A Catalogue of Books relating to Music in the Library of Richard Aldrich (New York, 1931)
Concert Life in New York, 1902–1923 (New York, 1941/*R*1971)

BIBLIOGRAPHY

O. Thompson: "An American School of Criticism," *MQ*, xxiii (1937), 428
M. Sherwin: *The Classical Age of New York Musical Criticism, 1880–1920: a Study of Henry T. Finck, James G. Huneker, W. J. Henderson, Henry E. Krehbiel, and Richard Aldrich* (thesis, City College, CUNY, 1972)

H. C. COLLES/MALCOLM TURNER

Aldrich, Thomas Bailey (*b* Portsmouth, NH, 11 Nov 1836; *d* Boston, MA, 19 March 1907). Poet. He held various editorial positions in New York and Boston from 1855 to 1890 and produced four novels as well as several volumes of poetry, short stories, and essays. With the publication in 1855 of his poem *The Ballad of Babie Bell*, Aldrich achieved almost instant success. He went on to become one of the leading poets and writers of his age. He exerted perhaps his greatest influence on American literature during his years as editor of the *Atlantic Monthly*, succeeding William Dean Howells in that position in 1881. Along with E. C. Stedman, Bayard Taylor, R. H. Stoddard, and other writers of the genteel tradition, Aldrich faded into obscurity in the early 20th century.

In his poetry and prose Aldrich was at his best in shorter forms. His carefully crafted poems are noted for their neatness, precision, and delicacy. Like Oliver Wendell Holmes, he excelled in the type of poetry commonly called "vers de société" or "familiar verse." His light, bright, and easy lyrics were very popular as song and choral texts, especially in the years 1875–1900. The poems most often set were *Nocturne*, *Cradle Song*, *Forever and a Day*, and the song "Sweetheart, sigh no more" from the longer narrative poem *Wyndham Towers*. C. Henshaw Dana, Sebastian Schlesinger, and William H. Pommer set the most poems; other composers of Aldrich settings include Arthur Foote and Alfred Pease. Comparatively few settings appeared after 1910.

BIBLIOGRAPHY

C. E. Samuels: *Thomas Bailey Aldrich* (New York, 1965)
R. C. Friedberg: *American Art Song and American Poetry* (Metuchen, NJ, 1981)
M. A. Hovland: *Musical Settings of American Poetry: a Bibliography* (in preparation) [incl. list of settings]

MICHAEL HOVLAND

Aler, John (*b* Baltimore, MD, 4 Oct 1949). Tenor. He was trained by Rilla Mervine and Raymond McGuire at Catholic

University, Washington, DC (1969–72), by Oren Brown at the American Opera Center at the Juilliard School (1972–6), and by Marlene Malas. While at the American Opera Center he made his début as Ernesto (in Donizetti's *Don Pasquale*). In 1977 he won two first prizes at the Concours International de Chant de Paris; his European début, two years later, was as Belmonte (*Die Entführung aus dem Serail*) at the Théâtre Royal de la Monnaie, Brussels. He first sang at the Santa Fe Opera in 1978, and has subsequently appeared at Glyndebourne, the New York City Opera, the San Diego Opera, and with the leading American orchestras. Aler's light, clear, and appealing tenor is best suited to the operas of Mozart, Rossini, Donizetti, and Bellini, in which he can demonstrate his tone and vocal agility. He has sung less familiar music, including the role of Hippolyte in Rameau's *Hippolyte et Aricie* at Aix-en-Provence. Much in demand for oratorio performances, he is especially persuasive in Handel's *Messiah*, which he sang in Mozart's arrangement at the 1983 Mostly Mozart Festival in New York.

MICHAEL WALSH

Alessandro, Victor (Nicholas) (*b* Waco, TX, 27 Nov 1915; *d* San Antonio, TX, 27 Nov 1976). Conductor. He studied horn with his father, Victor Alessandro, who was one of the founders of the Houston SO. He was a pupil of Howard Hanson and Bernard Rogers at the Eastman School (MusB 1937), and then studied at the Mozarteum in Salzburg (1937), and with Pizzetti at the Accademia di S. Cecilia in Rome (1938). From 1938 to 1951 he was the music director of the Oklahoma City SO, and from 1951 to his death of the San Antonio SO. He made several recordings with both ensembles. During this period he was also associated with the San Antonio Grand Opera and Rio Grande Valley music festivals, and the Mastersingers choral group. The successes he achieved with these ensembles played an important part in making San Antonio a leading musical center in the Southwest. Alessandro made his European conducting début with the Oslo PO in 1968, and was guest conductor of a number of orchestras and opera companies, including the Helsinki SO in 1971. For his services to American music he received the Alice M. Ditson Award in 1956 and 1963, and he was granted honorary doctorates by the University of Rochester and Southern Methodist University.

BIBLIOGRAPHY

H. Stoddard: "Victor Alessandro," *Symphony Conductors of the U.S.A.* (New York, 1957), 17

V. Alessandro: "The Operatic Symphony of St. Anthony's Town," *MJ*, xxiii/3 (1965), 34

ROBERT SKINNER

Alexander, Alger(non) Texas (*b* Jewett, TX, 12 Sept 1900; *d* Richards, TX, 18 April 1954). Blues singer. He spent most of his life in east Texas, where he worked as a farmhand in Leon and Grimes Counties and as a storeman in Dallas. There he was heard by the record salesman and blues pianist Sam Price, who arranged his first recording session. Alexander became one of the most popular recording blues singers of the 1920s. He was imprisoned for at least two offenses in the course of his career, and his earliest recordings, including *Levee Camp Moan* (1927, OK 8498), are strongly influenced by work song. Unlike most male folk blues singers, he did not accompany himself; on this and the well-known *West Texas Blues* (1928, OK 8603) among others, he was supported by the guitarist Lonnie Johnson, who was able to complement his irregular timing and verse structure. Alexander had a low, moaning singing style, and used hummed choruses to good effect, as on *St. Louis Fair Blues* (1928, OK 8688) and *Awful Moaning Blues* (1929, OK 8731), with Dennis "Little Hat" Jones on guitar. His lyrics were often unusual and poetic, but he favored a limited number of tunes and sang almost exclusively in the three-line blues form. A variety of accompanists saved his recordings from the monotony that might have ensued, an example being the sympathetic violin playing of Bo Carter on *Days is Lonesome* (1934, OK 8835). After 1934 Alexander made only one more recording, *Bottom's Blues* (1950, Freedom 1538), but his singing is poorly integrated with the accompaniment. Although he continued for some time to sing in the streets, his health deteriorated and he died of syphilis.

BIBLIOGRAPHY

G. Van Rijn and H. Vergeer: Liner notes, *Texas Troublesome Blues: Alger "Texas" Alexander* (Agram 2009, 1982)

PAUL OLIVER

Alexander, Charles M(cCallom) (*b* Meadow, TN, 24 Oct 1867; *d* Birmingham, England, 13 Oct 1920). Evangelistic musician. He attended Maryville College, Tennessee, and the Moody Bible Institute, Chicago, where for a time he was music director of the Moody Church. In 1893 he assisted Moody in his revival at the World's Columbian Exposition in Chicago. For seven years he was the musical associate of the evangelist Milan B. Williams at revivals in small towns and cities of the Midwest. From 1901 to 1908 he worked with Reuben A. Torrey and from 1908 with J. Wilbur Chapman, with whom he toured the USA, Great Britain, Australia, and missionary areas of the Far East. Alexander was noted for his skill in inspiring a congregation to sing enthusiastically and in conducting large choirs; the 4000-voice choir that he conducted daily for two months at London's Royal Albert Hall was reportedly the largest choir ever organized for a revival meeting. He published a number of revival songbooks and owned the copyrights of several popular gospel hymns, such as Charles H. Gabriel's *His eye is on the sparrow* (1905); he also popularized Gabriel's *Glory Song* (1900) in countries where he toured. *Alexander's Hymns No. 3* (1915) was still in print in England in the 1980s. Alexander married Helen Cadbury in 1904 and moved to Birmingham, England. (*See also* GOSPEL MUSIC, §I, 1(iv).)

BIBLIOGRAPHY

H. C. Alexander and J. K. Maclean: *Charles M. Alexander: a Romance of Song and Soul-winning* (London, n.d. [*c*1920])

HARRY ESKEW

Alexander, James Woodie (*b* Texas, 21 Jan 1916). Gospel singer. He moved to Los Angeles in the early 1940s to become a member of the Southern Gospel Singers, an all-male quartet. In 1946 he joined the Pilgrim Travelers, another male quartet, of which he soon became the guiding force. During its period of greatest popularity in the 1950s and 1960s the group became known for its close and smooth harmonies. Its members have included Kylo Turner and Keith Barber (leads), Jesse Whitaker (baritone), and Raphael Taylor (bass); jazz singer Lou Rawls (*b* 1936) also sang with the group in the late 1950s. Among their popular recordings were *Mother bowed* (Specialty 315, 1950) and *I was there when the spirit came* (Specialty 382, 1952). The group performed in concert throughout the USA and won acclaim for their appearances at the Apollo Theater in New York. Alexander was instrumental in securing a recording contract for Dorothy

Love Coates and the Original Gospel Harmonettes, and recommended the singer Jessy Dixon to Brother Joe May.

BIBLIOGRAPHY

T. Heilbut: *The Gospel Sound: Good News and Bad Times* (New York, 1971/*R*1975)

M. Warrick and others: *The Progress of Gospel Music* (New York, 1977)

HORACE CLARENCE BOYER

Alexander, John (*b* Meridian, MS, 21 Oct 1923). Tenor. After pre-medical studies at Duke University and service with the US Air Force he trained at the Cincinnati Conservatory; his most influential teacher was the baritone Robert Weede. He made his début as Faust with the Cincinnati Opera in 1952 and joined the New York City Opera five years later (his first role was Alfredo). His Metropolitan Opera début, as Ferrando, was on 19 December 1961. Important European engagements found him singing in Korngold's *Die tote Stadt* at the Vienna Volksoper (1967), *La bohème* at the Vienna Staatsoper (1968), and Pollione in *Norma* at Covent Garden (1970). The last-named became one of his specialties, and he has sung the part in a single season opposite the three most celebrated Normas of the time: Caballé, Sills, and Sutherland, with whom he recorded the opera. In May 1973 he undertook the title role in the first American performance of the original French version of *Don Carlos*, staged by the Boston Opera. He has appeared widely as an oratorio and concert singer. In 1974 he joined the faculty of the Cincinnati Conservatory. Alexander's value to leading American opera companies rests partly on his remarkable versatility and reliability in an enormous repertory, spanning bel canto at one extreme and such Germanic roles as Bacchus (in Strauss's *Ariadne auf Naxos*) and Walther von Stolzing (in Wagner's *Die Meistersinger von Nürnberg*) at the other. Although his acting sometimes lacks ardor and his singing is not invariably noted for dynamic finesse, he makes the most of taste, fervor, stamina, and a voice that commands an exceptionally brilliant ring at the top.

BIBLIOGRAPHY

J. Hines: *Great Singers on Great Singing* (Garden City, NY, 1982)

MARTIN BERNHEIMER/R

Alexander, Josef (*b* Boston, MA, 15 May 1907). Composer. He graduated from the New England Conservatory in 1925 and the following year received a postgraduate diploma. At Harvard University (BA 1938, MA 1939) he was a composition pupil of Piston; his other teachers there included Hill and Leichtentritt (orchestration) and Apel (musicology). Alexander also studied with Boulanger in Paris and with Copland at the Berkshire Music Center. He taught at the St. Rosa Convent, Boston College, and at Harvard. In 1943 he became a faculty member at Brooklyn College, CUNY, from which he retired as professor emeritus in 1977. His honors include an International Humanities Award (1960), an NEA grant (1969), and Naumburg and Fulbright fellowships. A spokesman for American composers, he has served as president of the New York chapter of the National Association of Composers/USA and is active in other contemporary music organizations.

Although he has written in nearly every instrumental and nondramatic vocal medium, Alexander has concentrated on works for solo piano, mixed chamber ensembles, and large orchestra. He takes a middle ground stylistically between staunch conservatism and unrelenting modernity or complexity, refusing to be influenced by any particular school or current trend of composition. Many of his works are programmatic – but they are never too literally explicit. With the musical portraits in *Epitaphs* (1947) he sought "to capture an essence and cross section of humanity." He often chooses colorful and unusual combinations of instruments, as in *Triptych* for cornet, marimba, and guitar, and *Dyad* for four tubas.

WORKS

Orch: Pf Conc., 1938; The Ancient Mariner, sym. poem, 1938; Doina, 1940; Dialogues spirituels (Bible), chorus, orch, 1945; Dithyrambe, 1947; Epitaphs, 1947; 4 syms., 1948, 1954, 1961, 1968; Campus Suite, band, 1950; Canticle of Night (Tagore), low v, orch, 1955; Concertino, tpt, str, 1959; Quiet Music, str orch, 1965; Duo concertante, trbn, perc, str orch, 1965; Salute to the Whole World (Whitman), nar, orch, 1976; Trinity, brass, perc, 1979; a few shorter works

Inst: 3 Pieces for 8, 1965; Requiem and Coda, Bar/tuba, hn, pf, 1974; 3 Diversions, timp, pf, 1975; Hexagon, wind qnt, pf, 1980; 3 Conversation Pieces, cl, b cl, 1982; Of Masks and Mirrors, s sax/cl, vc, pf, perc, 1983; 5 qnts, incl. Festivities, 4 brass, org, 1968, 2 for brass; 4 qts, incl. Interplay, 4 hn, 1975, Dyad, 4 tubas, 1979; 4 trios, incl. Triptych, cornet, mar, org, 1969, 5 Fables, ob, bn, pf, 1981; sonatas for vn, fl, vc, cl, va, trbn, tuba, hn; over 10 other works

Pf: 2 sonatas, 1936, 1943; 4 Incantations, 1964; 10 Bagatelles, 1967; 12 Pieces in the Attic, 1972; 12 Signs of the Zodiac (Astral Preludes), 1974; Games Children Play, 1976; 9 Etudes, 1979; Of Chinese New Years, 1980; many other works

Vocal: Songs for Eve (MacLeish), S, eng hn, vn, vc, harp, 1957; 4 Preludes on Playthings of the Wind (Sandburg), high v, chorus, 7 brass, pf, 1969; Gitanjali: Song Offerings (Tagore), S, hpd, perc ens, 1973; Aspects of Love, 9 songs, S, fl/pic, cl/b cl, vn/va, vc, pf, 1974; Adventures of Alice (L. Carroll), female vv, pf, 1976; Rossettiana (C. Rossetti), S, str qt, 1982; Contrasts (Sandburg), SATB, 1984; over 20 other choruses; other songs

Principal publishers: General, Lawson-Gould, Peer-Southern

BIBLIOGRAPHY

EwenD

BARBARA A. PETERSEN

Alexander, Russell (*b* Nevada, MO, 26 Feb 1877; *d* Liberty, NY, 2 Oct 1915). Composer. Little is known of his early life, although he seems to have been involved in the circus. He toured Europe with the Barnum & Bailey Circus Band as a euphonium player in 1897–1902; he also arranged all the music for the tour, producing some of his finest works. He returned to the USA, and in 1903 joined the Exposition Four, which included his brothers Newton and Woodruff, and James Brady. He is considered by many to be one of America's finest march composers; his best-known marches include *Colossus of Columbia*, *From Tropic to Tropic*, and *Olympia Hippodrome*. A number of his compositions are recorded in the Heritage of the March series (compiled by ROBERT HOE, JR.), subseries 7, U, AA, ZZ, CCC, and RRR.

WORKS

(selective list; all marches and galops for band)

The Crimson Flush (1896); The Darlington (1896); Belford's Carnival (1897); Burr's Triumphal (1897); International Vaudeville (1897); From Tropic to Tropic (1898); Olympia Hippodrome (1898); Across the Atlantic (1899); Rival Rovers (1899); Memphis, the Majestic (1900); The Steeplechase (1900); Colossus of Columbia (1901); Shoot the Chutes (1901); Embossing the Emblem (1902); The Exposition Four (1903); Storming El Caney Galop (1903); Paramour of Panama (1904); Salute to Seattle (1905); Song of the South (1905); The Comedy Club (1907); La Reine (1907); Baltimore's Boast (1908); Bastinado Galop (1908); The Cantonians (1908); The Southerner (1908); Hampton Roads (1909); Pall Mall Famous (1909); The Conquest (1913); Patriots of the Potomac (1913); Round-up (1916)

Principal publisher: Barnhouse

BIBLIOGRAPHY

R. Hoe, Jr.: "Brief Biographies of Famous March Composers," *Journal of Band Research*, xiv/1 (1978), 54

LOREN D. GEIGER

Algonquian. American Indian language family; *see* ARAPAHO, BLACKFOOT (i), OJIBWE, and WABANAKI.

Ali, Rashied [Patterson, Robert] (*b* Philadelphia, PA, 1 July 1935). Jazz drummer. He studied at the Granoff School in Philadelphia, where he worked with various rhythm-and-blues bands and occasionally with jazz groups. After moving to New York in 1963, he worked with Pharoah Sanders and others until he began an important association with John Coltrane in 1965. Following Coltrane's death in 1967, Ali worked with Alice Coltrane, then began leading his own groups. He helped organize the New York Jazz Musicians' Festival in summer 1972, thus taking a leading part in the movement among jazz musicians to exercise economic control over their music. In 1973 he founded Survival Records to issue his own music, and in about 1974 he opened a "loft" club, Ali's Alley. A propulsive drummer influenced by Elvin Jones, Ali is still best known for his playing with Coltrane, who praised him for his ability to lay down "multidirectional rhythms" which allow the soloist maximum freedom.

RECORDINGS
(*selective list*)

As leader: with F. Lowe: *Duo Exchange* (1973, Survival 101); *Moon Flight* (1975, Survival 109); *New Directions in Modern Music* (1973, Survival 103)

As sideman with J. Coltrane: *Meditations* (1965, Imp. 9110); *Cosmic Music* (1966, Coast Recorders 4950); *Live at the Village Vanguard Again* (1966, Imp. 9124); *Concert in Japan* (1966, Imp. 9246-2); *Interstellar Space* (1967, Imp. 9277); *Jupiter Variations* (1967, Imp. 9360)

As sideman with others: A. Shepp: *On this Night* (1965, Imp. 97); J. McLean: *'Bout Soul* (1967, BN 84284)

BIBLIOGRAPHY

V. Wilmer: *As Serious as your Life: the Story of the New Jazz* (London, 1977)

MICHAEL ULLMAN

Alleghanians. Mixed vocal quartet. It was established around 1845. The group's repertory of glees and sentimental ballads and their wholesome public image were typical of the popular singing families of the day. By 1846 they were filling halls all over the eastern USA. In December 1851, Jesse Hutchinson left his family troupe to manage the Alleghanians (at that time including James M. Boulard, bass; Richard Dunning, tenor; William H. Oakley, alto; and Miriam G. Goodenow, soprano), and organized a tour to California in 1852; at the same time the Alleghanians began to include pieces from the Hutchinsons' repertory in their programs. The Alleghanians went on a world tour from 1857 to 1860. By 1861, however, the group had undergone significant changes, and of the original Alleghanians the personnel included only the bass; their programs had also moved beyond the early repertory to include English and German songs, Italian and French arias, and "Swiss bellringing." The Alleghanians continued to tour for the next ten years, but public interest in such groups began to wane, and their last concert seems to have taken place in the mid-1870s.

BIBLIOGRAPHY

P. D. Jordan: *Singin' Yankees* (Minneapolis, 1946), 173

DALE COCKRELL

Allen [Lee], **Betty** (*b* Campbell, OH, 17 March 1930). Mezzo-soprano. Financial hardships resulted in several interruptions of her early studies, but in 1950 she was awarded a private scholarship to the Hartford School of Music. She studied with Sarah Peck More, later with Zinka Milanov. Winning a contest resulted in a scholarship to the Berkshire Music Center, where she was chosen by Bernstein to sing the solo in his "Jeremiah" Symphony. In 1952 she sang in the New York revival of Thomson's *Four Saints in Three Acts* and on 28 October 1954 made her first New York City Opera appearance as Queenie in *Showboat*. In 1955 she undertook a European tour sponsored by the US State Department. She has sung with the opera companies of Boston, San Francisco, Houston, and Santa Fe, and was on the roster of the New York City Opera (1972–5). She has earned a considerable reputation as soloist in concerts (notably in Mahler) and recitals, to which the richness and wide emotional range of her large voice are particularly suited. In the 1970s her tone acquired a contralto-like deepening (and a degree of hardening), which can be heard on her recording of Prokofiev's *Alexander Nevsky* under Ormandy. She has taught at the Manhattan School of Music and the North Carolina School of the Arts. In 1979 she became executive director of the Harlem School of the Arts.

BIBLIOGRAPHY

SouthernB

RICHARD BERNAS/DENNIS K. McINTIRE

Allen, Henry "Red" [Allen, Henry James, Jr.] (*b* Algiers, LA, 7 Jan 1908; *d* New York, 17 April 1967). Jazz trumpeter. He learned trumpet in New Orleans in the brass band of his father, Henry Allen, Sr. (1877–1952). After playing in various New Orleans groups, including George Lewis's, he went to St. Louis in 1927 to join King Oliver, with whom he traveled to New York and made his first recording (never issued). In 1928–9 he played in Fate Marable's Mississippi riverboat bands, where he was discovered by Victor representatives searching for a jazz trumpeter to offset the tremendous success of Louis Armstrong on the Okeh label. Brought to New York, Allen immediately recorded four sides in July 1929 for Victor with members of the Luis Russell band. These performances, Allen's recording début, were sensationally received among jazz musicians, and Allen immediately began a long engagement as lead trumpeter in the Luis Russell band (1929–32), followed by similar terms with Fletcher Henderson (1933–4) and the Mills Blue Rhythm Band (1934–7). Here, and in many small-group studio recordings under his leadership, Allen established himself as a leading soloist in the early swing period, setting standards for big-band trumpet playing.

In 1937 Allen returned to Luis Russell's band, which was then being used to accompany Louis Armstrong. Removed from his role as a soloist, and perhaps troubled by the new swing style of Roy Eldridge and others, he lost some of his power and direction. After leaving Armstrong in 1940 he took part in the burgeoning traditional jazz movement, recording in New Orleans formats with Jelly Roll Morton, Sidney Bechet, and his own sextets. In the late 1940s and 1950s he regained his momentum and became a leading figure in the mainstream jazz movement, leading his own combos and recording prolifically with musicians such as Coleman Hawkins, Buster Bailey, Kid Ory, PeeWee Russell, and J. C. Higginbotham. He held a long residency at the Café Metropole, New York, from 1954 to 1965, and undertook several tours of Europe in the 1960s.

Like that of many swing trumpeters, Allen's early style was very similar to Louis Armstrong's; he had heard Armstrong in his father's band in New Orleans and mastered to perfection the same technical prowess and rhythmic freedom (the two musicians are indistinguishable in their joint solo on *I Ain't Got Nobody* of 1929). Later, with the Luis Russell band and especially with

Henry "Red" Allen, c1960

Henderson, Allen developed a personal manner with a fluid, legato articulation, a remarkably free rhythmic conception which seemed to stand outside the fixed pulse, a wide dynamic range, and above all a large arsenal of timbral effects (lip trills, smears, rips, glissandos, spattered notes, and growls). In later years he further explored these effects to such an extent that, in the 1960s, he drew the attention of free-jazz players looking for alternatives to the uniform sonority of bop trumpet playing. Though famous in the 1930s for his flamboyant middle- and high-register solos, in the 1950s he cultivated an expressive, quasi-vocal manner in the low register as a complement to his jazz singing. Gradually he came to reject his swing legacy and concentrate on the New Orleans ensemble format and repertory, particularly the blues, of which he was an outstanding interpreter.

RECORDINGS
(selective list)

As leader: It Should Be You/Biff'ly Blues (1929, Vic. 38073); Feeling Drowsy/Swing Out (1929, Vic. 38080); Sugar Hill Function (1930, Vic. 38140); Body and Soul (1935, Voc. 2965); Get the Mop (1946, Vic. 201808); *Ride, Red, Ride in Hi-fi* (1957, RCA LPM1509); *Stormy Weather* (1957–8, Jazz Groove 002); *Feeling Good* (1965, Col. CS9247)

As sideman: L. Armstrong: I Ain't Got Nobody (1929, OK 8756); L. Russell: Song of the Swanee (1930, OK 8780); K. Oliver: Stingaree Blues (1930, Vic. 23009); S. Hughes: Sweet Sorrow Blues (1933, Decca 5101); F. Henderson: Wrappin' it up (1934, Decca 157); Mills Blue Rhythm Band: Ride, Red, Ride (1935, Col. 3087D); T. Wilson: Sentimental and Melancholy (1937, Bruns. 7844); S. Bechet: Egyptian Fantasy (1941, Vic. 27337)

BIBLIOGRAPHY

D. Ellis: "Henry (Red) Allen is the most Avant-garde Trumpet Player in New York City," *Down Beat*, xxxii/2 (1965), 13

W. Balliett: "The Blues is a Slow Story," *Such Sweet Thunder* (Indianapolis, 1966); repr. in *Improvising* (New York, 1977)

M. Williams: "Henry Red," *Jazz Masters of New Orleans* (New York, 1967)

H. Allen and A. J. McCarthy: "The Early Years," *Jazz Monthly*, no. 180 (1970), 2

J. Evensmo and P. Borthen: *The Trumpet and Vocal of Henry Red Allen, 1927–1942* (Hosle, Norway, 1977)

F. Hoffman: *Henry "Red" Allen/J. C. Higginbotham Discography* (Berlin, 1982)

J. BRADFORD ROBINSON

Allen, J(oseph) Lathrop (*b* Holland, MA, 24 Sept 1815; *d* *c*1905). Brass instrument maker. He began making brass instruments about 1838 in Sturbridge, Massachusetts, a short distance from his birthplace. In 1842 he moved to Boston, where his experiments with valved instruments began. From 1846 to 1849 he is known to have worked in Norwich, Connecticut; and in 1852 he returned to Boston. About 1850 he designed a very efficient rotary valve, featuring flattened windways, string linkage, and enclosed stops. During the 1850s in Boston this valve won respect among leading musicians and his instruments received favorable comment at mechanics' exhibitions.

From 1846 to 1870 Allen also worked in New York City, but after that little is known about him even though he is thought to have lived for at least another 30 years. His valve continued to be quite successful in the USA during the second half of the 19th century. Other makers who adopted the Allen valve included B. F. Richardson, D. C. Hall, and B. F. Quinby, all of whom had at one time worked with Allen. There are many instruments with Allen valves in American collections of 19th-century brass instruments. Several instruments signed by Allen are found in the collections of Fred Benkovic, Milwaukee, and the Henry Ford Museum, Dearborn, Michigan.

BIBLIOGRAPHY

R. E. Eliason: "Early American Valves for Brass Instruments," *GSJ*, xxiii (1970), 86

——: *Early American Brass Makers* (Nashville, 1979)

N. Groce: *Musical Instrument Making in New York City during the Eighteenth and Nineteenth Centuries* (diss., U. of Michigan, 1982)

ROBERT E. ELIASON

Allen, Paul Hastings (*b* Hyde Park, MA, 28 Nov 1883; *d* Boston, MA, 28 Sept 1952). Composer. After graduating from Harvard University (BA 1903), he moved to Florence, serving in the US diplomatic service in Italy during World War I. He returned to the USA in 1920 and settled in Boston. He was a prolific composer, particularly of operas and chamber music. His *Pilgrim Symphony* (1910) won the Paderewski Prize.

WORKS

12 operas, incl. O munasterio, 1911; Il filtro, 1912; Milda, 1913; L'ultimo dei Moicani (after Cooper), 1916; Cleopatra, 1921; La piccola Figaro, 1931

Orch: 8 syms., "Al mare," g, "Cosmopolitan," C, "Liberty," E, "Lyra," A, "Phoebus," E, "Pilgrim," D, "Somerset," E♭, "Utopia," D; 9 other orch works incl. Serenade (1928), suite

Chamber: Over 100 works for str qt/str qnt/str orch; *c*50 sonatas, incl. 15 pf sonatas, 8 vn sonatas, 2 solo vn sonatas, vc sonata; pf trio; Heaven's Gifts, 2 cl, a cl/basset hn, b cl; The Muses, wind ens; ww trio; suite, chamber orch; short works for vn, pf; other pf pieces

Over 150 songs; choral works

Principal publishers: Whitney Blake; G. Mignani; Riker, Brown & Wellington; L. Sonzogno

H. WILEY HITCHCOCK

Allen, Rex (Elvey) (*b* Willcox, AZ, 31 Dec 1924). Country-music singer and songwriter. After completing high school in 1938, he performed as "Cactus Rex" at rodeos, where he participated in the competitions and sang between events, accompanying himself on the guitar; subsequently he worked as an announcer on radio station WTTM in Trenton, New Jersey. In 1945 he joined the "National Barn Dance" on WLS radio in Chicago, where he appeared until 1950; during this time he made his first recordings for the Mercury label. Between 1950 and 1953 Allen appeared in 18 musical western films for Republic as "The Arizona Cowboy" and in 1958 starred in the "Frontier

Doctor" television series. He is well known as a warm and engaging narrator in a number of Walt Disney films.

RECORDINGS

(selective list)

Chime Bells/Miranda Doaks (Mer. 6122, 1948); Slap her down again, Paw/Teardrops in my Heart (Mer. 6095, 1948); Foggy River/Afraid (Mer. 6271, 1950); Crying in the Chapel/I thank the Lord (Decca 28758, 1953); Nothin' to do/The Trail of the Lonesome Pine (Decca 30066, 1956); Don't go near the indians/Touched So Deeply (Mer. 71997, 1962)

RONNIE PUGH

Allen, Richard (*b* Philadelphia, PA, 14 Feb 1760; *d* Philadelphia, 26 March 1831). Tunebook compiler. A former slave, he founded the African Methodist Episcopal Church in Philadelphia in 1794 and was elected its first bishop on the incorporation of the church in 1816. He compiled a hymnbook of 54 hymns, *A Collection of Spiritual Songs and Hymns*, for use by his congregation, the Bethel AME Church, in 1801. Later that year an enlarged version was published as *A Collection of Hymns and Spiritual Songs*. It was the first hymnbook published by a Black for use by Blacks, and many of the hymns later became sources for black spirituals. With Daniel Coker and James Champion, Allen also compiled the first official hymnbook of the AME Church in 1818. (*See also* AFRO-AMERICAN MUSIC, §1; GOSPEL MUSIC, §II, 1(i); and METHODIST CHURCH, MUSIC OF THE, §4(i).)

BIBLIOGRAPHY

SouthernB

R. Allen: *The Life Experience and Gospel Labours of the Right Reverend Richard Allen* (Philadelphia, 1887/*R*1960)

C. Wesley: *Richard Allen, Apostle of Freedom* (Washington, DC, 1935)

C. V. R. George: *Segregated Sabbaths* (New York, 1973)

Allen, Ross (Clearman) (*b* Kirksville, MO, 10 March 1921). Opera director and teacher. He was educated at Indiana University, where he staged the choral episodes of Britten's *Billy Budd* for the first American production (1952). He joined the faculty there in 1953 and has directed more than 130 works, including the first presentation outside New York of Bernstein's *Candide* (1958), American premières of Rimsky-Korsakov's *Christmas Eve* and Martinů's *The Greek Passion*, and world premières of John Eaton's *Myshkin* (1973) and (for children) *The Lion and Androcles* (1974). In Houston he staged the *Aida* that opened Jones Hall (1966); he has also been involved in modern re-creations of liturgical drama and Renaissance entertainments. In 1969 he won a Peabody Award for his television production of Henze's *Elegy for Young Lovers*.

FRANK MERKLING

Allen, Steve [Stephen Valentine Patrick William] (*b* New York, 16 Dec 1921). Composer, pianist, singer, and comedian. The son of parents in vaudeville, Belle Montrose and Billy Allen, he moved from place to place, attending many schools for short periods of time. He played piano from an early age, though his musical training was mainly informal. He began a professional career in Los Angeles as a disc jockey on radio during the 1940s, then turned to television in the 1950s; he established himself as a comedian, though often played the piano on his shows, improvising jazz and singing his own songs. Among the musicians who appeared with him regularly was the vibraphonist Terry Gibbs. His most popular television program was "The Tonight Show," which became a nationwide success. Allen performed the title role in the film *The Benny Goodman Story* (1955) and in 1957 produced a jazz television series, "Jazz Scene USA." In the late 1950s he combined his musical and comic talents in making an album of boogie-woogie piano music under the name Buck Hammer and an album of "modern" jazz as Miss Maryanne Jackson. He has composed a musical, *Sophie* (1963), on the life of Sophie Tucker, and music for television and films, such as *A Man Called Dagger*, and is said to have written over 4000 songs, some of which, including *Let's go to church next Sunday*, *Cotton candy and a toy balloon*, and *This could be the start of something big*, have been modest hits. Allen has also appeared on the Broadway stage, notably in *The Pink Elephant*, and has published several novels, as well as autobiographical works, poems, plays, and humorous books.

BIBLIOGRAPHY

"Steve Allen: Man in Motion," *Down Beat*, xxv/23 (1958), 16

S. Allen: *Mark it and Strike it* (New York, 1960)

——: *Bigger than a Breadbox* (New York, 1967)

"Allen, Steve," *CBY 1982*

MARK TUCKER

Allen Organ Company. Firm of electronic instrument makers. It was founded in Allentown, Pennsylvania, in 1939 by Jerome Markowitz (*b* New York, 14 May 1917) to produce a patented, fully electronic organ; the first such instrument made by the firm, since replaced by another Allen organ, was installed in St. Catherine's Church, Allentown. In 1953 the expanding company moved its factory to Macungie, Pennsylvania, and, in keeping with the rapid changes in electronic technology, began in 1959 to use transistors instead of vacuum tubes in its instruments. Further developments resulted in the adoption of digital computer technology in 1971; electronic analysis of the sounds of pipe organs permits accurate simulation of organ tone-colors. Standard playing aids on most models of the Allen organ (which range from instruments for churches to small domestic organs) include a transposing knob, "double memory capture" combination action, and a computer card system for changing the sounds of certain stops. In 1982 Lawrence I. Phelps became the firm's tonal director; Markowitz continues as its president. Allen instruments are installed in churches throughout the USA as well as in several foreign countries, and are sometimes rented for use with orchestras and choral groups. Allen is one of the largest firms of its kind, and in the mid-1980s its annual sales totaled $20 million.

BIBLIOGRAPHY

L. I. Phelps: "The Third Kind of Organ: its Evolution and Promise," *The Diapason*, lxxiv/3 (1983), 14

BARBARA OWEN

Allison, Margaret (*b* McCormick, SC, 1920). Gospel singer, pianist, and composer. She moved to Philadelphia at an early age and sang and played at a local Church of God in Christ. In 1942 she joined a female quartet, the Spiritual Echoes, and served as their pianist for two years, leaving the group in 1944 to organize the Angelic Gospel Singers with her sister Josephine McDowell and two friends, Lucille Shird and Ella Mae Norris. Their first recording, *Touch Me, Lord Jesus* (1950), sold 500,000 copies in less than six months and is still popular, as is her most famous composition, *My Sweet Home* (1960). The incidental harmony of their rural singing style and Allison's sliding technique appealed to a large number of supporters who otherwise found the gospel music of the period controlled and calculated. The group traveled and recorded with the Dixie Hummingbirds during the 1950s. Since the 1980s Allison has performed in a trio with her sister and Bernice Cole, appearing mostly in the deep South.

BIBLIOGRAPHY

T. Heilbut: *The Gospel Sound: Good News and Bad Times* (New York, 1971/*R*1975)

H. C. Boyer: "Gospel Music," *MEJ*, lxiv/9 (1978), 34

HORACE CLARENCE BOYER

Allman Brothers Band. Rock group. Its original members were (Howard) Duane Allman (*b* Nashville, TN, 20 Nov 1946; *d* Macon, GA, 29 Oct 1971), guitarist; Gregg (Gregory Lenoir) Allman (*b* Nashville, TN, 8 Dec 1947), guitarist, keyboardist, and singer; Dickey (Richard) Betts (*b* West Palm Beach, FL, 12 Dec 1943), guitarist and singer; Jai Johanny (Jaimoe) Johanson (John Lee Johnson, *b* Ocean Springs, MS, 8 July 1944), percussionist; Berry Oakley (*b* Chicago, IL, 4 April 1948; *d* Macon, GA, 11 Nov 1972), bass guitarist; and Butch Trucks (*b* Jacksonville, FL), percussionist. The two Allman brothers grew up in Florida, and formed the Kings in Daytona Beach in 1960; during the next eight years they worked in several short-lived groups. Using the name the Hourglass, they and two other musicians recorded two albums for Liberty Records in Los Angeles; they then moved to Fame Studios in Muscle Shoals, Alabama. Although the Hourglass recordings were not released, Fame engaged Duane Allman as a studio guitarist in 1968; he participated in sessions with Wilson Pickett, Clarence Carter, Percy Sledge, King Curtis, Arthur Conley, and Aretha Franklin. Having signed a recording contract with Atlantic Records through its vice-president Jerry Wexler, Duane Allman with his brother Gregg formed the Allman Brothers Band, though even after the release of its first album and during its early tours he continued his session work, recording with Delaney and Bonnie, Otis Rush, Laura Nyro, Boz Scaggs, Ronnie Hawkins, and, most significantly, with Eric Clapton on Derek and the Dominos' single *Layla* (1971). The group's second album, *Idlewild South* (1970), and constant touring strengthened its national reputation.

By 1971 the Allman Brothers Band had developed a consistent sound that amalgamated various southern musical styles: Muscle Shoals soul, blues and country music, and improvisatory hard rock. Whereas other blues-influenced rock groups tended to lapse into meandering 12-bar improvisations the Allmans kept their rhythms and song structures tight; Gregg Allman used a gruff tenor voice effectively, while Betts and Duane Allman often executed harmonized guitar runs on memorable melodic lines, as in Betts's *In Memory of Elizabeth Reed* (1970). Capable of fiercely eloquent solos, Duane Allman was also an articulate slide guitarist, using a glass slide. *At Fillmore East* (1971) placed the group in the commercial and artistic forefront of American rock. After Duane Allman's death in a motorcycle accident, the group did not replace him, but its album *Eat a Peach* (1972), which included studio and concert material recorded before Allman's death, reached the Top Ten. A year later, Oakley, too, died in a motorcycle crash; Lamar Williams replaced him. The 1973 album *Brothers and Sisters* contained recapitulations of the group's old style but broke new ground with the song *Ramblin' Man*, a country-rock tune sung by Betts that became a hit single, and *Pony Boy*, a country blues, also by Betts. After Allman and Betts undertook solo projects, the group made *Win, Lose or Draw* (1975), which revealed a lack of direction; internal dissension led to the departure of several members (including Betts, who formed Dickey Betts and Great Southern and Sea Level), but the group reunited (without Williams, who died in 1979, but with two new members) to make *Enlightened Rogues* (1979), which marked a partial return to form. More recordings and tours followed in the early 1980s, but by then the southern rock movement that the Allman Brothers Band had inspired a decade earlier had all but played itself out.

RECORDINGS

(selective list; recorded for Capricorn unless otherwise stated)

The Allman Brothers Band (Atco 308, 1969); *Idlewild South* (Atco 342, 1970), incl. In Memory of Elizabeth Reed; *At Fillmore East* (2-0802, 1971); *Eat a Peach* (2-0102, 1972); *Brothers and Sisters* (0111, 1973); *Win, Lose or Draw* (0156, 1975); *Enlightened Rogues* (0218, 1979)

BIBLIOGRAPHY

C. Crowe: "The Allman Brothers Story," *Rolling Stone*, no. 149 (6 Dec 1973), 46

H. Barnes: "The Allman Brothers Band," *The Rolling Stone Illustrated History of Rock & Roll*, ed. J. Miller (New York, 1976)

CHRIS WALTERS

The Allman Brothers Band, 1971

Almanac Singers. Group of folksingers and songwriters. It was formed in 1941 by Pete Seeger, Lee Hays, Millard Lampell, and Woody Guthrie for the purpose of raising social consciousness through song; other musicians who performed and recorded with the regular members included Cisco Houston, Burl Ives, Bess Lomax, and Earl Robinson. The group performed most frequently at left-wing functions in New York, and also held weekly musical gatherings at Almanac House, its headquarters and cooperative residence in Greenwich Village, which helped to inspire the hootenanny fad of the 1950s and early 1960s. The repertory of the Almanac Singers consisted chiefly of songs concerned with current topics, such as labor unions, peace, and war; many of the best-known, including *Union Maid* (1941), *Reuben James* (1941), and *'Round and 'round Hitler's grave* (1942), were written by members of the group and are set to American folk tunes. The Almanac Singers disbanded in 1942.

BIBLIOGRAPHY

L. Hays: "History of Almanac Singers," *People's Songs Bulletin*, iii (1948), no.8, p.9; no.10, p.9; no.11, p.9

R. S. Denisoff: *Great Day Coming: Folk Music and the American Left* (Urbana, IL, 1971)

J. Klein: *Woody Guthrie: a Life* (New York, 1980)

CHERYL A. BRAUNER

Alpert, Herb (*b* Los Angeles, CA, 31 March 1935). Trumpeter, bandleader, composer, and record company executive. He studied jazz and classical trumpet as a child, and spent two years in the army as a trumpeter and bugler. He then set himself up as an independent record producer, having his first success in 1959. In 1962, in association with Jerry Moss, he launched the company A&M Records with his own first recording as a trumpeter and bandleader, *The Lonely Bull*; because band sounds and crowd noise from the bullring at Tijuana, Mexico, were dubbed on to the record, Alpert's band became known as the Tijuana Brass. This piece, a *mariachi*-style trumpet duet over guitar and drum accompaniment, set the pattern for a number of hits, including *Mexican Shuffle* and *A Taste of Honey*, that exploited a distinctive combination of Mexican brass sound and jazz rhythms. In 1968 the band's recording of *This guy's in love with you* (by Bacharach and David), on which Alpert appeared as both vocalist and trumpeter, reached no.1 on the chart. Alpert's style influenced the instrumental accompaniments of a number of other groups, such as Diana Ross and the Supremes, and the Beatles. A&M Records became a highly successful company (it was taken over by RCA in 1979) and in the late 1960s Alpert devoted much of his time to his business activities. He disbanded his group in 1970, but by 1974 he had begun to perform again and in 1979 he made another hit recording, *Rise*, a jazz-rock instrumental influenced by disco music.

BIBLIOGRAPHY

E. Tiegel: "Tijuana Sound Pacesetter for New Pop Style," *Billboard*, lxxvii (25 Dec 1965), 1

"Small Band, Big Sound: the Tijuana Brass," *Look*, xxx (14 June 1966), 104

L. Feather: "Herb Alpert: the Brass Ring that Turned to Gold," *International Musician*, lxvi/3 (1967), 5

"Alpert, Herb," *CBY 1967*

J. Sims: "Two Lonely Bulls and How they Grew," *Rolling Stone*, no.119 (12 Oct 1972), 14

R. Coleman: "Tijuana Taxi to South Africa: Trumpeters Herb Alpert and Hugh Masekela," *Melody Maker*, liii (25 March 1978), 10

S. Pond: "Herb Alpert: the 'Rise' of a Vice-chairman," *Rolling Stone*, no.306 (13 Dec 1979), 24

TERENCE J. O'GRADY

Althouse, Monroe A. (*b* Centre Township, nr Reading, PA, 26 May 1853; *d* Reading, 12 Oct 1924). Conductor and composer. After playing violin and, later, trombone in local organizations, he decided on a musical career and left Reading, touring with various bands, one of which accompanied Buffalo Bill's Wild West Show. In 1872 he returned to Reading, worked in a hat factory, and played with local bands and orchestras. In 1886 he organized a ten-piece pit orchestra at the Reading Academy of Music, later renamed the Rajah Theater; for the next 20 years this ensemble accompanied all the legitimate theatrical productions there. He revived the Germania Orchestra, and in 1887 organized the Germania Band, which achieved some popularity and an excellent reputation. He also assumed leadership of the Ringgold Band of Reading on the death of its bandmaster. The Germania Band was then effectively dissolved, its members joining the Ringgold Band; under Althouse's direction (until 1922) the band expanded its activities, giving regular summer concerts in Reading, as well as performances across the country. Althouse was associated with many of the important performers of his time, including Sousa, who became his close friend.

Althouse composed about 150 works, of which the best-known are his marches; they are effective, inspiring "street" marches, somewhat simple in structure. A number of his works are recorded in the Heritage of the March series (compiled by ROBERT HOE, JR.). In 1961 his *Tall Cedars* was made the official march of the Tall Cedars of Lebanon of North America, a Masonic organization.

BIBLIOGRAPHY

R. Hoe, Jr., ed.: "Brief Biographies of Famous March Composers," *Journal of Band Research*, xv/2 (1980), 53

G. M. Meiser: "Monroe Althouse: Reading's 'March King'," *Reading Eagle* (3 Nov 1982), 15

RAOUL CAMUS

Althouse, Paul (Shearer) (*b* Reading, PA, 2 Dec 1899; *d* New York, 6 Feb 1954). Tenor. Educated at Bucknell University, he studied with P. D. Aldrich in Philadelphia and later with Oscar Saenger and P. R. Stevens in New York. The first American tenor without European training or experience to sing at the Metropolitan Opera, he made his début there as the Pretender Dimitri in the American première of *Boris Godunov* under Toscanini (13 March 1913); between then and 1920, when he left the company for a period, he participated in its first productions of Giordano's *Madame Sans-Gêne*, Herbert's *Madeleine*, De Koven's *Canterbury Pilgrims*, Cadman's *Shanewis*, and Breil's *The Legend*. His voice at that time was described as a "lyric tenor of the more robust Italian type." In addition to opera, Althouse also performed in oratorio and concerts, singing at the principal festivals and touring with the New York SO; in fact, during part of the 1920s he devoted himself exclusively to concerts, making tours of Europe, Australia, and New Zealand. After a visit to Bayreuth, he decided to retrain his voice as a *Heldentenor*. Returning to the USA, he took part in the American première of Schoenberg's *Gurrelieder* under Stokowski (which was recorded) and in performances of the New York Philharmonic-Symphony Society under Toscanini, both in 1932. The following year he sang Tristan in San Francisco, and returned to the Metropolitan as Siegmund, which he repeated in 1935 at Flagstad's début. Until the 1939–40 season he shared the principal Wagnerian roles at the Metropolitan with Melchior; he was the first American to sing Tristan with the company. After a final appearance as Loge in 1941, he devoted himself to teaching; among his pupils were Tucker, Steber, Simoneau, and Dalis.

BIBLIOGRAPHY

O. Thompson: *The American Singer* (New York, 1937/*R*1969), 280

PHILIP LIESON MILLER

Altmeyer, Jeannine (Theresa) (*b* La Habra, CA, 2 May 1948). Soprano. She studied with Martial Singher and Lotte Lehmann in Santa Barbara and later at the Salzburg Mozarteum. After winning the Illinois Opera Guild Auditions in 1971, she made her début at the Metropolitan Opera (as the Heavenly Voice in Verdi's *Don Carlos*, 25 September 1971) and sang the First Lady in Mozart's *Die Zauberflöte* the following season. As Freia in Wagner's *Das Rheingold* she sang for the first time with three companies: the Chicago Lyric Opera (1972), Salzburg (1973), and Covent Garden (1975). After several seasons at Stuttgart (1975–9), during which time she performed in many other leading European houses, she sang Sieglinde in Patrice Chéreau's production of *Der Ring* (1979) at Bayreuth. Apart from her many Wagnerian roles (which also include Elsa, Eva, Elisabeth, Gutrune, and Brünnhilde in *Siegfried*), Altmeyer sings Agathe (in Weber's *Der Freischütz*), Strauss's Salome and Chrysothemis (*Elektra*), and Tchaikovsky's Liza (*The Queen of Spades*). The radiant tone of her voice and the intensity of her expression make her a particularly fine interpreter of Wagner.

ELIZABETH FORBES

Amacher, Maryanne (*b* Kates, PA, 25 Feb 1943). Composer, performer, and mixed-media artist. She studied composition with Rochberg at the University of Pennsylvania (BFA 1964) and with Stockhausen. She later studied computer science at the universities of Pennsylvania and Illinois. Her music has been greatly influenced by science and has been devoted to exploring the psychoacoustical effects of sound. In 1967 Amacher began creating a series of projects called *City-Links* for which microphones were installed at distant locations (cities, or places within a city); the live sounds were then transmitted to mixing facilities at her studio or at a performance space. The effect was to "displace" the listener by setting up an unaccustomed sound environment. Amacher continued this work as a Fellow at the Massachusetts Institute of Technology (1972–6) and at Radcliffe College, Harvard University (1978–9). While at MIT, Amacher set up a system for the transmission of sounds directly to her office and home from a nearby pier in Boston for an extended period of time. Her observations showed that living in the sound environment of a distant site (in this case the pier) could have a great effect on everyday patterns of working, talking, sleeping, and dreaming, thus proving that people's lives are greatly determined by the sounds around them. Amacher has also used the results of her sound experiments in collaborations with Cage and with the choreographer Merce Cunningham. In the series *Music for Sound-joined Rooms* (1980–82) she has created a unique form of avant-garde theater music by using the rooms of a building to tell a story.

WORKS

(selective list)

City-Links, perf. New York, Buffalo, Chicago, Paris, and elsewhere, mixed media, 1967–79; Lecture on the Weather, collab. Cage, mixed media, 1975; Remainder (dance music, for M. Cunningham: Torse), tape, elec, 1976; Close Up, acc. to Cage: Empty Words, tape, elec, 1979; Music for Sound-joined Rooms, mixed media, 1980–82; other elec and mixed-media works

BIBLIOGRAPHY

T. Johnson: "Maryanne Amacher: Acoustics joins Electronics," *Village Voice* (15 Dec 1975)
T. Hight: "The Arts: Music," *Omni*, iv/2 (1981), 32, 142

CHARLES PASSY

Amadé Trio. A fortepiano trio formed in 1974 by MALCOLM BILSON (fortepiano), SONYA MONOSOFF (violin), and JOHN HSU (cello).

Amara [Armaganian], **Lucine** (*b* Hartford, CT, 1 March 1927). Soprano. She studied with Stella Eisner-Eyn in San Francisco, sang for a short time in the opera chorus, and made her concert début at the San Francisco Memorial Auditorium in 1946. Two years later she won a contest leading to an appearance at the Hollywood Bowl. She made her début at the Metropolitan Opera in November 1950 as the Heavenly Voice in *Don Carlos*. By her 25th anniversary performance with the company she had sung 41 roles, both lyric and dramatic, in 35 operas, with regular appearances as Leonora (*Il trovatore*), Aida, Butterfly, Mimì, Donna Anna, Pamina, Tatyana (*Eugene Onegin*), Gluck's Eurydice, Nedda (*Pagliacci*), and Ellen (*Peter Grimes*). She has also sung at Glyndebourne (Ariadne and Donna Elvira in the 1950s), the Vienna Staatsoper, and other leading houses. Her recorded roles include Nedda (twice), Musetta (under Beecham), and Elsa. Amara's voice is clear, cool, refined in timbre and production, and used with sure musicianship; a want of dramatic projection has sometimes robbed her portrayals of full impact.

BIBLIOGRAPHY

H. Rosenthal: "Lucine Amara," *Great Singers of Today* (London, 1966), 18
R. D. Daniels: "Lucine Reflects," *Opera News*, xxxviii/15 (1974), 22

ALAN BLYTH/R

Amateur Chamber Music Players. Association founded in 1947 by Leonard A. Strauss of Indianapolis as an information center for those who play chamber music at home. A biennial directory (begun in 1949) and its successors, the *North American Directory* and the *Overseas Directory*, facilitate the meeting of compatible ensemble participants, who rate their performing proficiency by responding to a detailed questionnaire; since 1974 listings for vocalists and piano-duet players have also been included. Under the initial guidance of the founding member and secretary Helen Rice (to 1980), the association's membership had grown to 6000 by the mid-1980s; 1000 of the members lived in 50 foreign countries. Occasional newsletters provide members with lists of graded chamber works in particular areas (such as contemporary American music). The association's headquarters are in Washington, DC.

JOHN SHEPARD

Amato, Pasquale (*b* Naples, Italy, 21 March 1878; *d* Jackson Heights, NY, 12 Aug 1942). Italian baritone. He studied in Naples and made his début there in 1900. Soon in much demand, he sang at Covent Garden (1904) and at La Scala under Toscanini (1907–8) before making his début at the Metropolitan Opera as Germont in *La traviata* on 20 November 1908. He established himself quickly as an indispensable member of the New York company, and was on its roster for all but one season until 1921. He sang there all the principal roles of the Italian repertory, as well as Valentin (Gounod's *Faust*), Escamillo (*Carmen*), and many other parts in French, and Wagner's Kurwenal (*Tristan und Isolde*) and Amfortas (*Parsifal*) in German. Amato often sang with Caruso, notably in the role of Jack Rance in the première of Puccini's *La fanciulla del West* (1910). After his retirement from the Metropolitan, he made sporadic appearances with smaller opera companies elsewhere in the USA, then settled in New York as a singing teacher. On the 25th anniversary of his Metropolitan début he emerged from retirement to sing the same role (Germont) to an audience of 5000 at the New York Hippodrome.

Amato's voice was of splendid quality and extensive range, with brilliant resonance in the upper register. During his New York years he became an exceptionally reliable and complete artist, with impeccable enunciation, classical purity of style, and strong dramatic powers. These and other qualities, including pathos and humor, are best shown in a long series of admirable recordings made for Victor (1911–15), among which the *Pagliacci* Prologue, Figaro's "Largo al factotum," and several duets with Caruso, Gadski, and Hempel may be called exemplary.

BIBLIOGRAPHY

R. Celletti: "Amato, Pasquale," *Le grandi voci* (Rome, 1964) [with discography by R. Vegeto]

P. Kenyon and C. Williams: "Pasquale Amato," *Record Collector*, xxi (1973–4), 3–47 [with discography]

D. Ewen: *Musicians since 1900* (New York, 1978), 12

DESMOND SHAWE-TAYLOR/R

Amber, Lenny. Pseudonym of LEONARD BERNSTEIN.

Ambient music. Term used by BRIAN ENO to describe his own type of ENVIRONMENTAL MUSIC.

America. A national song of the USA, also known by the words of its first line, "My country, 'tis of thee"; *see* PATRIOTIC MUSIC, §1.

American Academy and Institute of Arts and Letters. Organization of American writers, artists, and composers. The National Institute of Arts and Letters, founded in 1898 by the American Social Sciences Association, formed the American Academy of Arts and Letters in 1904 to confer further distinction on 50 of its 250 members. In 1976 the two organizations merged under a single board of directors, although they continue to function as separate bodies; their headquarters are in New York. The institute's department of music, comprising roughly a fifth of the total membership, has encouraged the advancement of American music by presenting concerts of American works and by giving financial assistance to composers. Among the musicians elected to the academy have been Barber, Bernstein, Carter, Copland, Piston, Schuman, Sessions, Stravinsky, and Thomson. At an annual ceremonial, new members are inducted, honorary membership is bestowed on foreign artists (such as Britten and Boulez), and various awards are presented (*see* AWARDS, §1). The institute's *Proceedings* (1909–) are published annually.

BIBLIOGRAPHY

G. T. Hellman: "Some Splendid and Admirable People," *New Yorker*, lii (23 Feb 1976), 43

JOHN SHEPARD

American Academy of Music. One of the finest opera houses built in the USA in the 19th century; *see* PHILADELPHIA, §2.

American Bandmasters Association (ABA). Professional organization founded in 1929 in New York by Edwin Franko Goldman (who also became its first president) and a group of eminent bandmasters from the USA and Canada. John Philip Sousa served as its first honorary life president. The objectives of the ABA are to honor (by invitation to membership) outstanding achievement in the area of the concert band and its music; to work for progress toward a standardized international band instrumentation; to encourage prominent composers of all countries to write for the concert band; and by example and leadership to enhance the cultural standing of bands. The association cosponsors and administers the ABA–NABIM (National Association of Band Instrument Manufacturers) Band Composition Contest, formerly known as the ABA–Ostwald Band Composition Award, and maintains the ABA Research Center at the University of Maryland; it has also published since 1964 the *Journal of Band Research* (now biannual) in conjunction with other band associations. Its headquarters are in Arlington, Texas.

RAOUL CAMUS

American Brass Quintet. Brass quintet, formed by trombonists Arnold Fromme and Gilbert Cohen in 1960; its present members are Chris Gekker and Raymond Mase, trumpets; David Wakefield, horn; Michael Powell, tenor trombone; and Robert Biddlecome, bass trombone. The group gave its first public performance at the 92nd Street "Y" and made its official New York début at Carnegie Recital Hall in 1962. At that time the brass quintet was little heard in the concert hall, and the ensemble played a major part in introducing audiences to brass instruments in the chamber context. Its commitment to the expansion of the brass chamber literature and its renowned virtuosity, precision, and stylistic accuracy have resulted in the composition of more than 100 new works by such composers as Carter (1974), Thomson (1975), Druckman (1976), and Schuman (1980). The group gives an annual series of concerts in New York, which usually includes premières and the performance of "rediscovered" older pieces. The quintet has also explored performance practice on older instruments, and its many recordings include two of 19th-century American brass music played on period instruments. The ensemble is in residence each summer at the Aspen Music Festival and at Brooklyn College, CUNY, during the academic year.

ELLEN HIGHSTEIN

American Choral Directors Association. Association founded in 1959; its headquarters are in Lawton, Oklahoma. *See* CHORAL MUSIC, §I, 3.

American Composers Alliance (ACA). Organization owned and operated by composers, founded in 1938 by Copland, Thomson, Riegger, and others to promote the interests of American composers. Because of the delay between the composition of a work and the time it is published, a special service, the Composers Facsimile Edition (known as the American Composers Edition from 1972) was established in 1952 by Goeb to make copies of members' works more accessible in the interim; in 1967 the service was extended to nonmembers as well. The reproductions are made from fair masters or transparencies and offered at cost. The ACA also sponsors concerts and radio broadcasts and produces recordings of contemporary works through CRI. In 1972 it became affiliated with BMI, which collects performance royalties for its members and pays salaries and rent in return. As a 40th anniversary celebration in 1977, the ACA sponsored the initial concert of the American Composers Orchestra, an independent organization. A bulletin was published in 1938 and again between 1952 and 1965. There were over 250 members in the mid-1980s.

BIBLIOGRAPHY
F. Thorne: "The ACA Story," *BMI: The Many Worlds of Music*, no.1 (1984), 32

RITA H. MEAD, FRANCES BARULICH

American Conservatory of Music. Conservatory founded in Chicago in 1886. *See* CHICAGO (i), §4.

American Federation of Musicians (AFM). A trade union founded in 1896 for professional musicians. Membership was extended to include Canadian musicians in 1900, when "of the US and Canada" was added to its title. Affiliated with the AFL-CIO in the USA and with the Central Labor Council in Canada, in 1982 it had 280,000 members in 596 local affiliates, making it the largest entertainment union in the world. Local unions have jurisdiction over local areas of employment, but the international union has exclusive jurisdiction over recordings, film, and network broadcasting. International agreements negotiated by the federation contain pension, health, and welfare benefits, and its recording agreement provides for employer contributions to the Music Performance Trust and Special Payments funds. It publishes the *International Musician* (1901–), which appears monthly.

See also UNIONS, MUSICIANS'.

BIBLIOGRAPHY
P. Hart: *Orpheus in the New World* (New York, 1973), 96

RITA H. MEAD

American Guild of Musical Artists (AGMA). Labor union for artists who perform in opera, oratorio, ballet, and concerts. It was founded in 1936 by Lawrence Tibbett and a group of internationally known artists and music professionals, including Heifetz and Deems Taylor, and seeks to protect its members in their contractual arrangements with impresarios and concert managers. In 1937 it became a branch of the Associated Actors and Artistes of America, a union affiliated with the AFL-CIO that has exclusive jurisdiction over actors and other performers. A year later AGMA signed its first agreement with the Metropolitan Opera and was recognized as the exclusive bargaining agent for all artists engaged by the company. Preliminary meetings were held in 1938 with the Columbia Concerts Corporation and the NBC Artists' Service (later the National Concert and Artist Corporation) to establish the basic rights of concert artists and their managers. The guild's headquarters are in New York, and it has jurisdiction in the USA, Canada, and Central America; its official publication is *AGMAzine*, issued quarterly since 1949.

See also UNIONS, MUSICIANS', §2.

RITA H. MEAD

American Guild of Organists. An educational and service organization for organists and choral conductors, founded in 1896 by John Knowles Paine and George Chadwick and chartered by the New State Board of Regents. Its goals are to foster an interest in organ and choral music and to set and maintain standards of artistic excellence among its members. In order to encourage consistently high standards, the guild conducts examinations in organ playing, choir training, and the theory and general knowledge of music, awarding successful candidates certificates and designating them as fellows, associates, or choirmasters. It has published the *American Organist* monthly since 1967. With some 20,000 members in 325 chapters and 80 student groups in all 50 states, Panama, and Europe, the guild is one of the world's largest organizations of musicians specializing in a single instrument.

RITA H. MEAD

American Harp Society. Organization founded in New York in 1962. Its forerunner was the National Association of Harpists, which was active between 1920 and 1933. Under the guidance of Marcel Grandjany, chairman of the founding committee, the society was established to serve as a clearinghouse for information related to the harp, to foster high standards of harp performance, and to stimulate interest in the harp among composers and the general public. The membership (about 3000 in 1983) elects a board of trustees to oversee its activities; these include an annual national conference (since 1963), which combines concerts and workshops with a general meeting, the administration of the Young Artists Fund and the Close Scholarship (awarded annually), and a triennial national performance competition. In addition to a tape library, the society has since 1980 maintained a harp repository at the Library of Congress in which a wide range of scores, recordings, and memorabilia are preserved. It has published the *American Harp Journal* biannually since 1967.

JOANNE SHEEHY HOOVER

American Indians. *See* INDIANS, AMERICAN.

American Institute of Musicology. Organization founded in Cambridge, Massachusetts, by Armen Carapetyan in 1945 as the Institute of Renaissance and Baroque Music. The primary activity of the institute is to publish scholarly editions of compositions and theoretical works, primarily those of the Middle Ages and the Renaissance, and thus to promote the study of these sources in the humanistic disciplines in institutions of higher education. In 1946 the new name was adopted, and headquarters were moved to Rome (though offices were maintained in Cambridge and in Dallas, the latter's circulation office moving to Stuttgart, Germany, in 1974). A group of eminent scholars served as an advisory board until 1949, when Carapetyan became the sole director. A choir was established in 1947, and summer sessions featuring advanced studies in medieval and Renaissance music history were held in 1947 and 1948; both were soon discontinued.

The institute's publications aim at high standards of scholarship and book production. It issues several series: Corpus Mensurabilis Musicae (CMM), covering the principal musical sources of the Middle Ages and Renaissance, including collected works and transcriptions of manuscript sources; Corpus Scriptorum de Musica (CSM), editions of theoretical treatises published in the original languages; Musicological Studies and Documents (MSD), consisting of monographs on various topics of medieval and Renaissance music history as well as source materials not covered by CMM or CSM; Corpus of Early Keyboard Music (CEKM), consisting of keyboard works in modern notation; Renaissance Manuscript Studies; and Miscellanea, covering other studies and sources. The institute's yearbook, *Musica disciplina* (founded in 1946 as the *Journal of Renaissance and Baroque Music* and renamed the following year), is devoted to research studies and inventories of primary sources.

BIBLIOGRAPHY

Ten Years of the American Institute of Musicology, 1945–1955 (Nijmegen, Netherlands, 1955)

PAULA MORGAN

American Musical Fund Society. Benevolent organization for musicians, founded in Philadelphia in 1849; *see* UNIONS, MUSICIANS', §1.

American Musical Instrument Society. Organization founded in New York in 1971 "to promote study of the history, design, and use of musical instruments in all cultures and from all periods." Its 640 members include museum curators, collectors, performers, and amateurs in the USA and abroad. Annual meetings, devoted to symposia, performances, and the presentation of papers, have been held at the Smithsonian Institution, the Boston Museum of Fine Arts, the Metropolitan Museum of Art, and major American universities. The society's *Journal* (published annually since 1974) and *Newsletter* (triannually since 1971) contain articles, bibliographies, and news of worldwide activities of interest to members. The research for S. C. Farrell's *Directory of Contemporary American Musical Instrument Makers* (1981) was performed under its auspices. The society's headquarters are in Vermillion, South Dakota.

JOHN SHEPARD

American Music Center. Organization founded in 1940 by composers Marion Bauer, Aaron Copland, Howard Hanson, Otto Luening, and Quincy Porter to encourage the creation, performance, publication, and distribution of American music. In 1947 it was named the official American music information center by the National Music Council, and it is a member of the Music Information Centers Group of the International Association of Music Libraries of UNESCO. Having some 1200 members, it is governed by a large, elected board of composers and other professionals in the field of music. Its offices are in New York. It has published and recorded American music, it develops programs to bring audiences and composers together, and it provides technical assistance to composers and performing ensembles; it also publishes a multivolume listing (the *AMC Library Catalog*, 1975–) of its circulating library of scores, tapes, and discs, the Contemporary Music Performance Directory (1975), and its own newsletter (since 1958, now quarterly). It maintains files on composers and their works, as well as on publishers, recording companies, and performing ensembles, and administers a collection of works written by American composers under NEA fellowships (catalogue published 1977). The organization awards a Letter of Distinction annually to a person or organization that has made a significant contribution to American music and administers several grant programs of benefit to composers. Donald Erb was elected president in 1982 and among his predecessors were Charles Dodge, Leo Kraft, Ezra Laderman, and Hugo Weisgall.

MARGARET F. JORY

American Music Guild. Organization formed in New York in 1921 to encourage serious efforts in composition by American composers. Its founding members, Marion Bauer, Louis Gruenberg, Sandor Harmati, Charles Haubiel, Frederick Jacobi, A. Walter Kramer, Harold Morris, Albert Stoessel, and Deems Taylor, first met informally to listen to each other's works and offer criticism. From 1922 until 1924 they presented public and private concerts, performing their own works as well as those of Carpenter, Griffes, Loeffler, Daniel Gregory Mason, John Powell, Sowerby, and others.

BIBLIOGRAPHY

C. D. McNaughton: *Albert Stoessel, American Musician* (diss., New York U., 1957) [contains list of programs given by the guild]

R. ALLEN LOTT

American Musicological Society (AMS). An organization founded in Philadelphia in 1934 to advance scholarly research in the various fields of music. First named the American Musicological Association, it grew out of the New York Musicological Society (1930–34). Its founders were George Dickinson, Carl Engel, Gustave Reese, Helen Heffron Roberts, Joseph Schillinger, Charles Seeger, Harold Spivacke, Oliver Strunk, and Joseph Yasser; the first president was Otto Kinkeldey. In 1983 the society had 3400 members and 1200 institutional subscribers. It holds annual meetings where papers, symposia, and concerts are given; members also read papers at meetings of the 15 regional chapters. In addition the society gives awards and coordinates activities with other music societies and councils. It is a constituent member of the American Council of Learned Societies and has a joint committee with the Music Library Association to serve RISM.

Major efforts are directed to publications. Earlier, annual bulletins (1936–47) and papers read at annual meetings (1936–41) were issued; members now receive abstracts of papers, the *Journal of the American Musicological Society* (published three times yearly; 1948–), and the *AMS Newsletter* (chiefly biannually; 1971–). Other studies and documents published by the society include Ockeghem's collected works (1966), edited by Plamenac; Dunstable's complete works (published jointly with Musica britannica, 2/1970), edited by Bukofzer; Kerman's *The Elizabethan Madrigal* (1962); E. R. Reilly's *Quantz and his Versuch* (1971); E. H. Sparks's *The Music of Noel Bauldeweyn* (1972); *Doctoral Dissertations in Musicology*, edited by Cecil Adkins in succession to Helen Hewitt (seven editions, 1952–84); *A Selective List of Masters' Theses in Musicology*, compiled by D. R. de Lerma (1970); and an *International Index of Dissertations* (1977). Three awards are given annually: the Alfred Einstein Award for an article on a musicological subject; the Otto Kinkeldey Award for a major book, edition, or other piece of scholarship; and the Noah Greenberg Award for a contribution to the study and performance of early music. (*See also* MUSICOLOGY, §3.)

BIBLIOGRAPHY

The American Musicological Society 1934–1984 (Philadelphia, 1984) [incl. R. Crawford: "American Musicology Comes of Age: the Founding of the AMS"]

RITA H. MEAD

American Opera Company. Opera company founded in 1885 by Jeannette Thurber, whose policy was to engage competent but unknown American singers for productions of grand opera sung in English. Thurber appointed a board of eminent directors with Andrew Carnegie as president, and engaged Theodore Thomas, who had his own touring orchestra, as music director. Among the fully staged operas presented by the troupe were Mozart's *The Magic Flute*, Gluck's *Orpheus and Euridice*, Wagner's *Lohengrin* and *The Flying Dutchman*, Victor Massé's *Galatea*, Verdi's *Aida*, Karl Goldmark's *Queen of Sheba*, and the American première of

Anton Rubinstein's *Nero*; the repertory also included the ballets *Sylvia* and *Coppélia* by Léo Delibes. The first season opened on 4 January 1886 at the Brooklyn Academy of Music, and the company's ensuing six-month tour of the USA (mainly the Northeast) was hailed as an artistic success and a commendable effort in spite of poor management. After the first season, the company was reincorporated: Thomas became president, and it began its second season in November 1886 as the National Opera Company, with performances at the Metropolitan Opera House and the Brooklyn Academy of Music. Lacking adequate financial support, the enterprise eventually failed when the company was performing on tour in Buffalo in June 1887, and Thomas left the group. After a few performances during the 1887–8 season under different directors, it soon collapsed altogether. Programs for the years 1886–8 are preserved in the New York Public Library.

BIBLIOGRAPHY

T. Thomas: *A Musical Autobiography*, ed. G. P. Upton (Chicago, 1905/R1964)

DEE BAILY

American Piano Co. Firm of piano makers. Its incorporation in June 1908 consolidated such older American piano firms as Chickering & Sons and Wm. Knabe & Co. with the firms owned by the Foster–Armstrong Co. Founded in Rochester by George G. Foster and W. B. Armstrong in 1894, Foster–Armstrong had bought the Marshall & Wendell Piano Co. of Albany, New York, in 1899; after the construction of a new plant in 1906 in East Rochester, it acquired other firms and incorporated with a capital of $12 million.

Formed to market pianos that ranged from concert instruments to mass-produced commercial ones, the American Piano Co. also established a player-piano department in 1909 and developed a reproducing player mechanism under the name of Ampico; this, along with its competitors, the Welte Mignon and the Duo-Art, dominated the American market for sophisticated automatic piano mechanisms. In 1922 the Mason & Hamlin Piano Co. became part of the firm, but was sold to the Aeolian Co. in the early 1930s. The American Piano Corporation succeeded the American Piano Co. in 1930, at which time numerous lease commitments on company-owned retail operations were terminated. On 1 September 1932 the American Piano Corporation merged with its competitor the AEOLIAN CO. to form the Aeolian American Corporation, in an attempt to create a firm that would withstand the effects on the piano trade of the Depression, the radio, and the phonograph.

CYNTHIA ADAMS HOOVER

American Recorder Society. Amateur early-music society founded in 1939. *See* EARLY-MUSIC REVIVAL, §2.

American Samoa. *See* SAMOA, AMERICAN.

American School Band Directors' Association. Professional association of band directors teaching at the elementary- or secondary-school level. It was established at a convention in Cedar Rapids, Iowa, in 1953. The objectives of the association are to represent school band directors in the academic and business communities; to foster not only the exchange of ideas and methods that will advance the standards of musical and educational achievement but also a spirit of friendliness, fellowship, and cooperation; to stress the importance of the school band in the educational process and establish band playing as a basic course in the school curriculum; to maintain a program for the improvement of school bands through research and experimentation; and to cooperate with existing associations that share the aim of promoting the band as a worthwhile medium of musical expression. Membership (which exceeded 1000 in 1982) is open to established and active school band directors with a minimum of seven years' teaching experience who command the respect of their colleagues for the standard of performance and musicianship achieved by their bands. The headquarters of the association are in Otsego, Michigan.

RAOUL CAMUS

American Society for Jewish Music. Organization founded in New York in 1974, a successor to the Mailamm (active 1931–9), the Jewish Music Forum (1939–63), and the Jewish Liturgical Music Society of America (1963–74). Membership includes cantors, composers, educators, musicologists, performers, and laymen who are active or interested in Jewish liturgical and secular music. The society maintains relationships with similar organizations throughout the world. It presents a variety of public programs each season and publishes scholarly works relevant to Jewish music, notably the multilingual journal *Musica judaica* (annually since 1975). It also sponsors seminars and workshops at which scholars and composers discuss and analyze works in progress. Albert Weisser served as its first president, followed by Paul Kavon (from 1983).

ISRAEL J. KATZ

American Society of Ancient Instruments. Chamber ensemble formed in Philadelphia in 1925 by Ben Stad. *See* EARLY-MUSIC REVIVAL, §2.

American Society of Composers, Authors and Publishers (ASCAP). The oldest performing rights organization in the USA (founded 1914), and the largest in terms of revenue and distribution of royalties to its membership, which comprises more than 35,000 composers, lyricists, and music publishers. The society licenses virtually every kind of composition (with the exclusion of nondramatic works) to more than 10,000 radio stations, 800 television stations, and 150,000 other music users (*see* PERFORMING RIGHTS SOCIETIES, §2), and, in addition to the royalties it distributes from such uses, makes financial awards in popular music and other fields to composers whose works are performed in the media outside its traditional domain. ASCAP has a number of awards and programs to help new composers and encourage the growth of music in the USA; these include the Rudolph Nissim Competition (grants to composers for new or previously unperformed orchestral works), the ASCAP Foundation Grants to Young Composers, the Raymond Hubbell Scholarships for music students, the Nathan Burkan Memorial Competition for outstanding essays on copyright law by law students, orchestra awards for adventurous programming of contemporary music, the Deems Taylor Award for excellence in writing about music (*see also* AWARDS), songwriter workshops, and educational music programs for inner-city youth. ASCAP publishes *ASCAP in Action* (1979–), *The ASCAP Biographical Dictionary of Composers, Authors and Publishers* (1948, 4/1980), the *ASCAP Symphonic Catalog* (1959, 3/1977), and various other catalogues and surveys relating to songs and the publication of music. With headquarters in New York, the society has membership offices in Los Angeles, Nashville, Puerto Rico, and London, as well as 22 licensing offices in metropolitan areas throughout the USA. (*See also* BROADCASTING, §3.)

BIBLIOGRAPHY

R. Hubbell: *The Story of ASCAP by a Founder* (MS, *c*1937, *NN*)

B. L. DeWhitt: *The American Society of Composers, Authors and Publishers, 1914–1938* (diss., Emory U., 1977)

For further bibliography *see* COPYRIGHT; PERFORMING RIGHTS SOCIETIES.

KAREN SHERRY

American Society of University Composers (ASUC). Organization serving composers in American universities founded in New York in 1966 by Donald Martino, J. K. Randall, Claudio Spies, Henry Weinberg, Peter Westergaard, Charles Wuorinen, and Benjamin Boretz. The ASUC works to establish standards for teaching composition, improve communication within the profession, disseminate information about composition in institutes of higher learning, represent its members' interests to the public, and provide services helpful to composers developing their careers. In addition to the proceedings of its annual conference (published since 1966), a triannual *Newsletter* (since 1967), and news bulletin, the society publishes facsimile editions of contemporary music in a series entitled ASUC Journal of Music Scores. It also produces one or two recordings each year in the ASUC Record Series (on the Advance label) and prepares radio programs of American contemporary music (Radiofests) for distribution to American and European stations. In conjunction with SESAC, Inc., the society sponsors the ASUC-SESAC Student Composition Contest for unpublished works. In 1984 ASUC had about 900 members (mostly composers) in nine regions; the chairperson of the executive committee was Reynold Weidenaar and of the national council Elliott Schwartz.

RITA H. MEAD

American String Quartet. Chamber ensemble formed in 1974 by students at the Juilliard School. Its members are Mitchell Stern (*b* Cleveland, OH, 26 July 1955) and Laurie Carney (*b* Englewood, NJ, 28 Sept 1956), violins; Daniel Avshalomov (*b* Portland, OR, 23 May 1953), son of the composer Jacob Avshalomov, viola; and David Geber (*b* Los Angeles, CA, 2 Feb 1951), cello. Stern replaced the original first violinist, Martin Foster, in 1980, and Avshalomov replaced Robert Becker, the original violist, in 1976. After performing at the Aspen Music Festival in 1974, the quartet made its New York début at Alice Tully Hall in 1975 and won the Coleman Competition and the Naumburg Award the same year. It has toured throughout the USA and has performed at the Spoleto Festival (1976), the Mostly Mozart Festival (from 1982), and the Music Academy of the West. Regular tours to Europe followed the ensemble's début there in 1980. The quartet has often appeared with other artists, including the pianists Emanuel Ax, Claude Frank, Richard Goode, Lorin Hollander, and Lilian Kallir, the singers Maureen Forrester and Frederica von Stade, the oboist Heinz Holliger, the flutist Paula Robison, and the Cleveland and Tokyo quartets.

With a sound that is polished and exceptionally well balanced, and a style at once authoritative and unmannered, the American String Quartet performs a wide-ranging repertory, including works by Prokofiev, Shostakovich, and Schoenberg. It has given the premières of Claus Adam's String Quartet no.2 (1979) and Trimble's Third Quartet (1980), and has recorded both of Prokofiev's quartets and those of Adam, Barkin, and Corigliano. Equally committed to teaching, the ensemble has taught and performed at Mannes College (1975–80), the Taos School of Music (from 1979), the Peabody Conservatory (where it initiated the chamber music department in 1980), and the Manhattan School (from 1984). In recognition of the quartet's teaching activities, it was awarded an NEA grant in 1978.

SUSAN FEDER

American String Teachers Association. Organization founded in 1946 to encourage student performance of bowed instruments and foster study, research, and pedagogy of string playing, and the continuing education of string teachers; it was set up partly in reaction to the proliferation of wind bands in the public schools. In addition to the string instrument repair sessions it conducts on a regular basis, the association's activities have included a special study of violin pedagogy (1966), workshops for school orchestra directors who are not string players (1971), and an international workshop (with the European String Teachers Association) in Exeter, England (1975). It also makes annual awards to an artist–teacher and for distinguished service. In addition to various monographs and bulletins, the association has published the *American String Teacher* since 1951 (now quarterly). Its 5000 members are public school and college teachers in 47 states; its headquarters (1985) are in Athens, Georgia.

BIBLIOGRAPHY

R. A. Ritsema: *History of the American String Teachers Association* (Bryn Mawr, PA, 1972)

JOHN SHEPARD

American Symphony Orchestra League (ASOL). Organization founded in 1942 by Leta G. Snow and Theresa Shier and guided in its formative years by HELEN M. THOMPSON; it serves as a coordinating, research, and educational agency for symphony orchestras, assists in the formation of new orchestras, and encourages the work of American musicians, conductors, and composers. Symphony orchestras (which the league classifies according to the size of their budgets) are voting members; individual firms and institutions are associate members and have no vote. In addition to offering training sessions for orchestra managers, ASOL works actively for financial and legislative support for the performing arts. The Volunteer Council, an affiliated body established in 1964, raises funds and organizes community activities for symphony orchestras. The league has published a large number of studies, including more than 600 monographs, and, since 1948, the bimonthly *Symphony Magazine* (originally a newsletter). Individual and corporate Gold Baton Awards are presented for significant contributions to music. In 1984 the league's president was Peter R. Kermani and the chairman of the board was Schuyler Chapin; its national headquarters are in Washington, DC.

In 1975 ASOL formed the Conductors' Guild under the leadership of Harold Farberman to lobby the managers and board members of the 1500 member orchestras in the USA to give fair consideration to American conductors, who have often been overlooked when openings have occurred. The guild publishes its own *Journal* (founded 1980) and conducts seminars and symposia throughout the country at which composers and musicologists join with conductors in discussions of current issues. It has also established a Summer Institute for conductors at West Virginia University. Donald Portnoy was the president in 1984, and the guild's headquarters are at the ASOL offices in Washington.

BIBLIOGRAPHY

P. Hart: *Orpheus in the New World: the Symphony Orchestra as an American Cultural Institution* (New York, 1973), 120

RITA H. MEAD

American Tract Society. An interdenominational Protestant organization devoted to the publication and distribution of religious literature. It was founded in Massachusetts in 1814 by Ebenezer Porter, a Congregational minister, and adopted the name American Tract Society in 1823. In 1825 it merged with a similar group, the New York Religious Tract Society, and the resulting national organization operated from headquarters in New York. The society was most active during the 30 years before the Civil War, after which it was largely superseded by newer religious agencies. In addition to publishing millions of copies of tracts, the society issued a number of hymn and tune collections, aiming for the broadest possible circulation among middle- and working-class families. These collections became progressively less Calvinist and more evangelical in outlook, and they provide an interesting and useful record of changing tastes in American hymnody, their contents ranging from traditional 18th-century melodies through hymn tunes of the Mason–Hastings reform movement and popular sacred songs in the style of Bradbury and the Methodist revivalists to early gospel hymns. The society's most important publications were *The Family Choir*, edited by S. S. Arnold and E. Colman (1837), Hastings's *Sacred Songs for Family and Social Worship* (1842, rev. and enlarged with Lowell Mason 2/1855) and *Songs of Zion* (1851, enlarged 2/1864), and three anonymously compiled collections – *Hymns and Tunes for the Army and Navy* (n.d. [*c*1861]), *Happy Voices* (1865), and *Gems for the Prayer-meeting* (n.d. [*c*1868]).

BIBLIOGRAPHY

Brief History of the American Tract Society (New York, 1855)

C. Bode: *The Anatomy of American Popular Culture, 1840–1861* (Berkeley, CA, 1959/*R*1970 as *Antebellum Culture*), 132

PAUL C. ECHOLS

American University. University founded in Washington, DC, in 1893; *see* WASHINGTON, §6.

American Women Composers. Organization founded in 1976 (originally as the Female Composers of America) by Tommie Ewert Carl, for the purpose of "alleviating the gross inequities" experienced by American women composers "in all areas of musical life." Almost immediately membership was expanded to include performers, conductors, and musicologists, and at present there are more than 200 members in the USA. The organization serves as a vehicle to obtain status and recognition for women composers. It holds workshops and symposia, sponsors festivals of music composed by women, and maintains a library of scores. It has published the quarterly *AWC News* since 1977; its headquarters are in McLean, Virginia.

RITA H. MEAD

America the Beautiful. A national song, first published in 1910; *see* PATRIOTIC MUSIC, §2.

Amerindian. *See* INDIANS, AMERICAN.

Ames Brothers. Vocal quartet. The Urick brothers, Joe (*b* Malden, MA, 3 May 1924), Gene (*b* Malden, 13 Feb 1925), Vic (*b* Malden, 20 May 1926; *d* Nashville, TN, 23 Jan 1978), and Ed (*b* Malden, 9 July 1927), sang together from childhood, and first appeared professionally as the Ames Brothers in Boston in the late 1940s. During the following decade they enjoyed considerable success in nightclubs and theaters and on television (they had their own show in 1955). Their performances were highly regarded for their display of excellent musicianship, straightforward yet polished ballad singing, humor, and showmanship. The Ames Brothers made several recordings, including *Rag Mop* (1950), *You, you, you* (1953), *Naughty Lady of Shady Lane* (1954), and *Mélodie d'amour* (1957). When the ensemble disbanded in the late 1950s the youngest brother, Ed, continued an independent career in musical theater and television.

MICHAEL J. BUDDS

Amfiteatrov, Daniele (*b* St. Petersburg [now Leningrad], Russia, 29 Oct 1901; *d* Rome, Italy, 7 June 1983). Composer and conductor. He studied composition at the St. Petersburg Conservatory under Joseph Withol and V. V. Shcherbachov, in Prague with Jaroslav Křička, and in Rome with Ottorino Respighi. He was appointed assistant conductor of the Augusteo Orchestra and conducted in several European cities before coming to the USA in 1937 as assistant conductor of the Minneapolis SO. He became an American citizen in 1944. From 1941 to 1965 he worked in Hollywood, where he wrote more than 50 film scores as well as music for television (he had composed a number of orchestral, choral, and chamber works while in Italy). Amfiteatrov's music reveals the influence of Respighi in its lush romanticism and vivid orchestral coloring.

WORKS

(selective list)

Film scores: more than 50, incl. Lassie Come Home, 1943; Days of Glory, 1944; Guest Wife, 1945; Song of the South, 1946; The Beginning or the End, 1947; The Lost Moment, 1947; Letter from an Unknown Woman, 1948; Rogues' Regiment, 1948; The Fan, 1949; House of Strangers, 1949; The Damned Don't Cry, 1950; The Desert Fox, 1951; Devil's Canyon, 1953; Human Desire, 1954; Naked Jungle, 1954; The Mountain, 1956; The Unholy Wife, 1957; From Hell to Texas, 1958; Major Dundee, 1965

BIBLIOGRAPHY

C. McCarty: *Film Composers in America: Checklist of their Works* (Glendale, CA, 1953/*R*1972)

J. L. Limbacher, ed.: *Film Music* (Metuchen, NJ, 1974)

SORAB MODI

Amirkhanian, Charles (Benjamin) (*b* Fresno, CA, 19 Jan 1945). Composer. He was educated at California State University, Fresno (BA in English literature, 1967), San Francisco State University (MA in interdisciplinary creative arts, 1969), and Mills College, where he studied electronic music and sound recording techniques with David Behrman, Robert Ashley, and Paul de Marinis (MFA 1980). He was composer-in-residence for Ann Halprin's Dancers Workshop Company, 1968–9, and lecturer at San Francisco State University from 1977 to 1980; from 1969 he has acted as music director at the radio station KPFA in Berkeley, introducing audiences to much new music. He has also written articles on contemporary composition, in particular on Antheil and Nancarrow, and produced a set of recordings of the latter's Studies for Player Piano. Amirkhanian received commissions from the Fylkingen Society for works realized in the studios of Swedish Radio for the fifth Festival of Sound-Text Composition (Stockholm, 1972) and wrote works for the Arch Ensemble, Berkeley, and the 1984 Summer Olympics Arts Festival.

Most of Amirkhanian's early music was for percussion ensem-

Charles Amirkhanian, 1984

bles (he studied piano and percussion), and was written under the influence of Cage and Harrison; he used speaking voices and his own experimental texts for the first time in 1965. From 1970 he devoted himself chiefly to tape composition. His mature works are characterized by brisk, tightly articulated enunciation of words usually grouped in iterative sequences. The influence of Reich's tape-loop style and the nonsyntactic texts of Gertrude Stein and Clark Coolidge, apparent in works from the early 1970s, culminated in *Seatbelt Seatbelt* (1973), a 15-minute piece for 24 tape loops juxtaposed to create complex polyrhythms. Such music is not unlike percussion music, although its materials are of purely vocal origin. In more recent works he has not adhered to strict text-sound procedures; *Mahogany Ballpark* (1976) incorporates recordings of ambient sound with characteristically nonlinear texts that function as percussive events in an ever-changing soundscape (the effect is of simultaneous poetry readings in several locations), while *Gold and Spirit* (1984) combines football cheers and pep-band drum cadences with recorded ambient sounds of many sports events, from racquet ball to lawn bowling. Beginning in 1974 performances of Amirkhanian's tape works have often included slides and films by Carol Law as well as live interpolations of his own voice.

WORKS

LIVE-PERFORMANCE

Canticle no.1, perc qt, 1963, no.2, fl, timp, 1963, no.3, perc trio, 1966, no.4, perc qt, 1966; Trio no.1, perc, 1963, no.2, perc, 1964; Composition nos. 1–5, 1965–7; Genesis 28 Four Speakers, 4 speakers, 1965; Sym. I, 2 solo perc, perc duo, amp perc, tpt trio, trbn, pf/cl, va, 1965; Demonstration IV, graphic score, any medium, 1967; Mooga Pook, graphic score, any medium, 1967

Ode to Gravity, theater piece, graphic score, any medium, 1967; Serenade II Jance Wentworth, graphic score, any medium, collab. T. Greer, 1967; Spoilt Music, theater piece, tape, 1v, collab. C. Law, 1979; Egusquiza to Falsetto, theater piece, chamber orch, tape, collab. M. Fisher, 1979; many other works, 1961–8

TEXT-SOUND (TAPE)

Oratora Konkurso Rezulto: Autoro de la Jaro (Portrait of Lou Harrison), 1970; Radii, 1970, rev. 1972; Each'll, 1971; If In Is, 1971; Spoffy Nene, 1971; Dzarin Bess Ga Khorim, 1972; Just, 1972; Sound Nutrition, 1972, rev. 1972; Awe, 1973; Haveevery, 1973; Heavy Aspirations (Portrait of Nicolas Slonimsky), 1973; Jump, 1973; Making Opera, 1973; Mugic, 1973; Roussier (not Rouffier), 1973; Seatbelt Seatbelt, 1973; Double Agent, 1974; Muchrooms, 1974; Ray Man Ray, 1974; She she and she, 1974; Beemsterboer, 1975

Mahogany Ballpark, 1976; Dutiful Ducks, 1977; Audience, 1978; Dreams Freud Dreamed, 1979; Lower East Seagull, 1979; The Type without Time, 1979; Church Car, 1980, 2 other versions 1981; Dot Bunch, 1981; History of Collage, 1981; Hypothetical Moments (in the Intellectual Life of Southern California), 1981; Maroa, 1981; The Putts, 1981; Andas, 1982; Dog of Stravinsky, 1982; Too True, 1982; Gold and Spirit, 1984; Martinique and the Course of Abstractionism, 1984; The Real Perpetuum Mobile, 1984; many other works, 1969–84

Principal publisher: Arts Plural Publishing

BIBLIOGRAPHY

R. Kostelanetz: "Text-sound Art," *New York Times* (24 July 1977)

T. Johnson: "Getting Looped," *Village Voice* (22 Oct 1978)

P. Kresh: "An Art between Speech & Music," *New York Times* (3 April 1983)

JOHN ADAMS

Amish and Mennonite music. The Protestant denominations of the Amish (100,000 in the USA in the 1980s) and Mennonites (180,000) have a common source in the Anabaptist movement of 16th-century Europe. In the 1520s the first group, the Swiss Brethren, separated from the early Reformers and the Roman Catholics for reasons more radical than those of Luther or Zwingli: believers' baptism (thus Anabaptists, Rebaptizers), separation of church and state, and the commitment to discipleship of Christ to the point of rejecting participation in war. Anabaptists emerged in Bohemia, south Germany, and the Netherlands within the next decade.

Although a few Anabaptist leaders followed Zwingli's example in advocating the complete elimination of music from church services, Anabaptists who were persecuted for their faith soon produced a distinctive hymnody. The first publication, *Etlicher schöner christlicher Geseng* (1564), was a collection of 53 hymns composed by prisoners at Passau between 1535 and 1540. It was followed by *Ausbund, das ist etliche schöne christliche Lieder* (1583), its first part consisting of 80 Anabaptist hymns from as early as 1524 onwards and the second of all but one of the 53 hymns from the 1564 collection. Up to 1838 the *Ausbund* appeared in 11 known European editions.

Mennonites, as 17th-century Anabaptists were called – after Menno Simons (*d* 1561) – brought the *Ausbund* to America in 1683, when they began a long succession of immigrations. The Amish, following the Swiss bishop Jacob Ammann, broke away from the Mennonites in Europe in 1693 over matters relating to stricter discipline and adherence to uniformity of dress. They first immigrated to America about 1720 and also brought the *Ausbund* with them. It was printed at Germantown, Pennsylvania, in 1742, and there were at least 32 further editions and reprints up to 1980. The *Ausbund*, still the most used hymnal of the Old Order Amish, is thus unique in Protestant hymnody in having been in continuous use for over 400 years.

The retention of past traditions is essential to the Amish, who still speak in a German dialect, dress in 17th-century fashions, and reject many aspects of a technological age. Their church singing is unique: always monophonic, melismatic, unaccompanied, non-metrical, and extremely slow. Because they do not record their worship on principle, few recordings exist. The *Ausbund* had no printed tunes. However, a heading to each hymn indicated its association with a secular or sacred folktune, a Latin hymn, or a melody from other Reformers; a few hymns named their own tunes. Jackson (1945), the first to trace relationships between the ornamented versions the Amish now sing and the 16th-century forms of the specified tunes, speculated that oral transmission of the melodies at a slow tempo gradually resulted in group alterations and embellishments of the original. (For transcriptions of Amish melodies, see Burkhart, 1953, and Hohmann, 1959.)

In contrast to the Amish, the Mennonites have, slowly but continuously, assimilated the culture around them. They moved beyond the *Ausbund* in the early 19th century with two German hymnals: *Die kleine geistliche Harfe der Kinder Zions* (1803), published by the descendants of the Germantown settlers, and *Ein unpartheyisches Gesang-Buch* (1804). Both books consist of selected German hymns, and French Calvinist psalms in Ambrosius Lobwasser's translation; the 1804 book borrowed 64 *Ausbund* songs as well.

The most important Mennonite tunebook is Joseph Funk's *A Compilation of Genuine Church Music* (1832, rev. 5/1851 as *Harmonia sacra*, rev. 12/1876 as *New Harmonia sacra*). Funk had published a German tunebook in 1816, but *Genuine Church Music* reflected the Mennonites' appropriation of English. Its oblong format, characteristic of singing-school books, and its didactic function paralleled similar American books, such as Ananias Davisson's *Kentucky Harmony* (1816). Funk began with the rudiments of music and music-reading in the four shapes (*mi*, *fa*, *sol*, *la*) of W. Little and W. Smith's *The Easy Instructor* (1801; *see also* SHAPE-NOTE HYMNODY). Part II consists of "the most appropriate tunes of the different meters, for public worship"; English psalm tunes, American hymn tunes, and revival melodies of the early 19th century thus entered the Mennonite repertory. Funk notated some of the oral folktunes, possibly for the first time. He incorporated early American anthems, which are still used in Mennonite congregations. Part-singing – three parts, with the melody in the middle, expanding to four parts in the 12th edition – probably entered Mennonite worship through Funk's influence. *Genuine Church Music* continues to be published under the title *New Harmonia sacra*.

The first Mennonite hymnal in English was *A Selection of Psalms, Hymns, and Spiritual Songs* (1847, 7/1877/*R*1972; title from 2nd edn, *A Collection . . .*). It consists only of texts, and the editors specified that *Genuine Church Music* be used as the companion tunebook, recommending specific combinations of text and tune. *Hymns and Tunes for Public and Private Worship, and Sunday School Songs Compiled by a Committee* (1890) borrowed heavily from it. A number of the very simple texts and tunes were ascribed to the compiling committee rather than to an individual; the preface indicates that "no intricate pieces were allowed" in the book.

The General Conference Mennonite Church, organized at Donnelson, Iowa, in 1860, chose and republished a hymnal from south Germany. Successive immigrations from Prussia and Russia greatly enlarged the group. Through these German-speaking immigrants the chorale and hymn traditions of the German Lutherans and Pietists were revived and strengthened. They brought their hymnal, *Gesangbuch in welchem eine Sammlung geistreicher*, published in Russia in 1844 but harking back to the Prussian *Geistreiches Gesangbuch* of 1767. Its roots probably extended back to the Dutch Anabaptist martyr hymns of *Veelderhande Liedekens* (1556). The Old Colony Mennonites of Mexico still use it. In 1890 the General Conference Mennonites published a hymnal, *Gesangbuch mit Noten* (16/1936), which combined their German traditions. They turned to a mainline Protestant book, *Many Voices*, when in 1894 they also needed an English hymnal.

In 1969 the Mennonite Church and the General Conference Mennonite Church published *The Mennonite Hymnal* (in both round- and shape-note editions), which drew together these historical strands and incorporated songs from the Moody–Sankey revival as well. Mennonites today tend to sing in four parts, often with instrumental accompaniment, although until the mid-1960s the Mennonite Church vigorously rejected the use of instruments in worship; the first organ appeared in the General Conference Mennonite Church in 1874.

Other, smaller groups of Mennonites have unique musical traditions that reveal their religious, geographic, or ethnic situations. Two examples will suffice: the Mennonite Brethren, who started to immigrate to the USA from Russia in 1874, were influenced by German Pietism, and their hymns tend to be evangelical and folklike in character; and in 1982 the Mennonite Indian Leaders' Council published a book of Cheyenne spiritual songs based on traditional Cheyenne music, *Tsese-ma'heone-nemeotôtse*.

BIBLIOGRAPHY

R. Wolkan: *Die Lieder der Wiedertäufer* (Berlin, 1903/*R*1965)

"The Mennonites and Dunkers, their Emigration and Hymnody," *Church Music and Musical Life in Pennsylvania*, ed. Committee on Historical Research of the Colonial Dames of America, ii (Philadelphia, 1927)

H. S. Bender: "The First Edition of the Ausbund," *Mennonite Quarterly Review*, iii (1929), 147

J. Umble: "The Old Order Amish, their Hymns and Hymn Tunes," *Journal of American Folklore*, lii (1939), 82

——: "Amish Service Manuals," *Mennonite Quarterly Review*, xv (1941), 26

G. P. Jackson: "The Strange Music of the Old Order Amish," *MQ*, xxxi (1945), 275

L. Hostetler: *Handbook to the Mennonite Hymnary* [1940] (Newton, KS, 1949)

C. Burkhart: "The Music of the Old Order Amish and the Old Colony Mennonites: a Contemporary Monodic Practice," *Mennonite Quarterly Review*, xxvii (1953), 34

"Amish Division," "Ausbund," "Hymnology of the American Mennonites," "Hymnology of the Mennonites of West and East Prussia, Danzig, and Russia," "Music, Church," "Old Order Amish," *Mennonite Encyclopedia* (Scottdale, PA, 1955–9)

R. R. Duerksen: *Anabaptist Hymnody of the Sixteenth Century: a Study of its Marked Individuality Coupled with a Dependence upon Contemporary Secular and Sacred Music, Style and Form* (diss., Union Theological Seminary, New York, 1956)

P. Wohlgemuth: *Mennonite Hymnals Published in the English Language* (diss., U. of Southern California, Los Angeles, 1956)

R. R. Duerksen: "The Ausbund," *The Hymn*, viii (1957), 82

H. A. Brunk: *History of the Mennonites in Virginia* (Staunton, VA, 1959)

R. K. Hohmann: *The Church Music of the Old Order Amish of the United States* (diss., Northwestern U., 1959)

P. M. Yoder: *Nineteenth Century Sacred Music of the Mennonite Church in the United States* (diss., Florida State U., 1961)

J. A. Hostetler: *Amish Society* (Baltimore, 1963, 3/1980)

P. M. Yoder and others: *Four Hundred Years with the Ausbund* (Scottdale, PA, 1964)

W. Jost: *The Hymn Tune Tradition of the General Conference Mennonite Church* (diss., U. of Southern California, Los Angeles, 1966)

A. Kadelbach: *Die Hymnodie der Mennoniten in Nordamerika (1742–1860): eine Studie zur Verpflanzung, Bewahrung und Umformung europäischer Kirchenliedtradition* (Mainz, 1971)

M. E. Ressler: *A Bibliography of Mennonite Hymnals and Songsbooks 1742–1972* (Quarryville, PA, 1973)

A. Kadelbach: "Hymns written by American Mennonites," *Mennonite Quarterly Review*, xlviii (1974), 343

M. E. Ressler: "A History of Mennonite Hymnody," *Journal of Church Music*, xxiii (1976), 2

——: "Hymnbooks Used by the Old Order Amish," *The Hymn*, xxviii (1977), 11

N. Springer: *Mennonite Bibliography, 1631–1961* (Scottdale, PA, 1977)

M. Oyer: *Exploring the Mennonite Hymnal: Essays* (Newton, KS, 1981)
O. Schmidt: *Church Music and Worship among the Mennonites* (Newton, KS, 1981)
A. Loewen and others: *Exploring the Mennonite Hymnal: Handbook* (Newton, KS, 1983)

MARY OYER

Ammons, Albert (C.) (*b* Chicago, IL, 23 Sept 1907; *d* Chicago, 2 Dec 1949). Jazz pianist. After playing as a soloist and with various bands in Chicago, he formed his own Rhythm Kings sextet in 1934, and with them recorded his version of Pine Top Smith's *Boogie Woogie*, which he called *Boogie Woogie Stomp* (1936). He later became identified with that piano blues style. From 1938 he was active in New York, first in piano trios with Meade "Lux" Lewis and Pete Johnson, later in a duo with Johnson, with whom he made a series of recordings (1941). Ammons's early solos *Boogie Woogie Stomp*, *Bass Gone Crazy*, and *Suitcase Blues* were frequently based on the styles of his predecessors, but his later work was quite individual.

RECORDINGS
(selective list)

As leader: Boogie Woogie Stomp (1936, Decca 749); Shout for Joy (1939, Voc. 4608); Boogie Woogie Stomp/Boogie Woogie Blues (1939, BN 2); Bass Gone Crazy/Monday Struggle (1939, Solo Art 12000); Albert's Special Boogie/The Boogie Rocks (1944, Com. 617)

Duos with P. Johnson: Boogie Woogie Man/Walkin' the Boogie (1941, Vic. 27505); Suitcase Blues/Bass Goin' Crazy (1942, BN 21)

BIBLIOGRAPHY

W. Russell: "Boogie Woogie," *Jazzmen*, ed. F. Ramsey, Jr., and C. E. Smith (New York, 1939), 183
M. Harrison: "Boogie Woogie," *Jazz*, ed. N. Hentoff and A. J. McCarthy (New York, 1959), 105–37
Y. Bruynoghe: "Albert Ammons," *Jazz Era: the 'Forties*, ed. S. Dance (London, 1961), 48
J. Hopes: "Boogie Woogie Man: a Bio-Discography of Albert Ammons," *Jazz & Blues*, i/6 (1971), 5

MARTIN WILLIAMS/R

Ammons, Gene [Eugene; Jug] (*b* Chicago, IL, 14 April 1925; *d* Chicago, 6 Aug 1974). Jazz tenor saxophonist, son of Albert Ammons. At 18 he left Chicago with the King Kolax band. He then became the soloist in Billy Eckstine's innovative big band (1944–7), and played briefly with Woody Herman (mid-1949). Thereafter he led small combos, initially in partnership with Sonny Stitt (1950–52). He became a leading exponent of the impassioned blend of bop and black gospel preaching called "soul jazz." Problems with drugs disrupted his career, although he was allowed to continue playing in prison (1958–60, 1962–9). His term in prison coincided with the rise of soul music as a commercial genre, and after his release his improvisations, now accompanied by electric instruments, were more popular than ever before.

RECORDINGS
(selective list)

As leader with S. Stitt: Blues Up and Down (1950, Birdland 6005); Woofin' and Tweetin' (1955, Prst. 45–166); *Boss Tenor* (1961, Verve 68426)

As leader: *The Happy Blues* (1956, Prst. 7039); *Boss Tenor* (1960, Prst. 7180); *Soul Summit* (1962, Prst. 7234); *The Boss is Back* (1969, Prst. 7739); *Together again for the Last Time* (1973, Prst. 10100)

As sideman: B. Eckstine: Blowin' the Blues Away (1944, De Luxe 2001); W. Herman: More Moon (1949, Cap. 682)

BIBLIOGRAPHY

M. Crawford: "Jug ain't Changed," *Down Beat*, xxviii/17 (1961), 24
L. Feather: "The Rebirth of Gene Ammons," *Down Beat*, xxxvii/12 (1970), 12
Obituary, *Down Beat*, xli/16 (1974), 11

BARRY KERNFELD

Amram, David (Werner) (*b* Philadelphia, PA, 17 Nov 1930). Composer, horn player, and conductor. As a youth he played the piano, trumpet, and horn, developing a strong interest in jazz as well as classical music. After a year at Oberlin Conservatory (1948), where he studied horn, he attended George Washington University (BA in history, 1952). He was engaged as a horn player with the National SO, Washington, DC (1951–2), and then played with the Seventh Army SO in Europe; during his three years there he also toured as a soloist, performed with chamber ensembles, and in Paris took part in jazz sessions. He returned to the USA in 1955 and enrolled in the Manhattan School, where he studied with Mitropoulos, Giannini and Schuller; he was also a member of the Manhattan Woodwind Quintet. In 1979 he was awarded an honorary degree from Moravian College, Bethlehem, Pennsylvania.

In 1956 Amram began a long association with Joseph Papp, producer for the New York Shakespeare Festival, who commissioned incidental music for *Titus Andronicus*; during the period 1956–67 Amram composed scores for 25 Shakespeare productions at the festival. Among his many subsequent commissions for television, jazz bands, films, and the theater is the incidental music for Archibald MacLeish's *J.B.*, which won a Pulitzer Prize in 1959. Amram was the first composer-in-residence with the New York PO (1966–7), and in 1972 he was appointed conductor of the Brooklyn Philharmonia's youth concerts. He has also undertaken several State Department tours: he visited Brazil in 1969 (an experience that was to affect his compositional style), Kenya in 1975 (with the World Council of Churches), and Cuba in 1977 with Dizzy Gillespie, Stan Getz, and Earl Hines; he also made successful State Department tours to Central America in 1977 and the Middle East in 1978. Amram's works reflect his love of music of all cultures; they are romantic, dramatic, and colorful, and are marked by rhythmic and improvisatory characteristics of jazz.

WORKS

Dramatic: The Final Ingredient (television opera, A. Weinstein after R. Rose), 1965; Twelfth Night (opera, J. Papp, after Shakespeare), 1965–8; incidental music, incl. The Beaux Strategem, J.B., The Family Reunion, Caligula, Peer Gynt, Lysistrata, The Passion of Josef D., 25 Shakespeare scores; numerous film scores

Orch: Autobiography, str, 1959; Shakespearean Conc., ob, hn, str, 1959; The American Bell, narrator, orch, 1962; King Lear Variations, wind band, 1965; Hn Conc., wind ens/orch/pf, 1965; Triple Conc., ww qnt, brass qnt, jazz qnt, orch, 1970; Elegy, vn, orch, 1970; Bn Conc., 1971; Vn Conc., 1972; Brazilian Memories, 1973; Fanfare, brass, perc, 1974; En memoria de Chano Pozo, fl, elec b gui, pf, orch/wind band, 1977; Ov., brass, perc, 1977; Ode to Lord Buckley, a sax, orch, 1980; Honor Song, vc, orch, 1983; Across the Wide Missouri, a Musical Tribute to Harry S. Truman, 1984; Andante and Variations on a Theme for Macbeth, band, 1984; Fox Hunt, 1984; Travels, tpt, orch, 1985; jazz ens/(jazz qnt, orch) works

Inst: over 20 chamber works for 1–5 insts, incl. Trio, t sax, bn, hn, 1958; Pf Sonata, 1960; Str Qt, 1961; 3 Songs for Marlboro, hn, vc, 1962; Dirge and Variations, vn, vc, pf, 1962; The Wind and the Rain, vn, pf, 1963; Vn Sonata, 1964; Fanfare and Processional, brass qnt, 1966; Wind Qnt, 1968; Zohar, fl/a rec, 1974; Native American Portraits, vn, perc, pf, 1977; Landscapes, perc qt, 1980; jazz ens works

Vocal: Friday Evening Service, T, SATB, org, 1960; A Year in our Land (cantata, J. Baldwin, J. Dos Passos, J. Kerouac, J. Steinbeck, T. Wolfe, W. Whitman), S, A, T, B, SATB, orch/pf, 1964; Let us Remember (cantata, L. Hughes), solo vv, SATB, orch, 1965; The Trail of Beauty (Indian texts), Mez, ob, orch,

1976; other sacred choral works; songs, incl. 3 Songs for America, B, wind qnt, str qnt, 1969

Principal publishers: C. F. Peters, New Chamber Music, Remsen

BIBLIOGRAPHY

EwenD

D. Amram: *Vibrations: the Adventures and Musical Times of David Amram* (New York, 1968)

"Amram, David (Werner)," *CBY 1969*

BARBARA A. PETERSEN

AMS. *See* AMERICAN MUSICOLOGICAL SOCIETY.

Analysis. The resolution of a musical structure into relatively simpler elements, and the investigation of the functions of those elements within the structure. For a discussion of the principal analytical theories developed by American writers on music *see* THEORY.

Anchorage. City in Alaska (pop. 174,431). It had its beginnings in 1917 as a construction camp and port for the Alaska Railroad. Few records exist of the frontier town's musical life before 1928, when the local high school engaged Lorene Harrison, a young college graduate from Kansas, to teach music and home economics; she also sang, produced shows, founded groups, and directed the choir at the local Presbyterian church. For many years she guided virtually all of the city's musical activities; during World War II, when most civilians were evacuated from Alaska, she stayed on as director of the United Service Organizations, and arranged and conducted concerts at which military personnel and local residents performed. In 1946 the members of the orchestra of the Anchorage Little Theatre formed the Anchorage SO; this began as a small group but by the 1960s was a full symphony orchestra with a schedule of six subscription concerts a year. In 1947 the Little Theatre produced Handel's *Messiah*, and the chorus members formed the Anchorage Community Chorus under Harrison's direction. One of the first guest artists to appear with the Anchorage SO was the Russian-born pianist Maxim Shapiro, who began organizing Alaskan tours for other performers; these were sponsored by an informal organization known as the Alaska Music Trail. The tours were at first confined to Alaska's larger cities – Ketchikan, Juneau, Anchorage, and Fairbanks – but eventually included as many as 18 communities in Alaska and western Canada; in Anchorage they led to the formation of the Anchorage Concert Association, which continues to present performances by well-known musicians. In 1955 the Anchorage Community Chorus invited Robert Shaw to conduct a summer festival; soon after, the Alaska Festival of Music, now held annually in September, was begun, and Shaw continued as its director for a number of years.

In the late 1940s and 1950s there were no regular presentations of musical theater in Anchorage, though occasional productions of light opera were mounted. In 1955 the Anchorage Civic Opera was formed under the direction of the opera singer Marita Ferall; this produced several operas, then became inactive. In the mid-1960s the Lyric Opera Theatre mounted a number of productions, but it was not until 1975 that a revitalized Anchorage Civic Opera, under the direction of Elvera Voth, began regularly to present the standard operatic repertory. Voth also conducted the Community Chorus and founded and directed the Anchorage Boys Choir and the Basically Bach Festival, a series of concerts devoted to the works of Bach and other Baroque composers that takes place annually in June.

Voth had gone to Alaska in 1961 to assist with the music festival, and remained to organize and direct the music department at Anchorage Community College. Ten years later she organized the music department at the newly formed University of Alaska, Anchorage; the university now sponsors a choral group (the University Singers, originally the University Chorale) and the Museum Recital Series (both founded and directed by Voth), and a wind ensemble. The university offers bachelor's degrees in music with majors in performance, elementary education, and secondary education; the music department has four full-time and several part-time faculty members. Alaska Methodist University (later Alaska Pacific University) was founded in Anchorage in 1960; for several years its music department was directed by Murray North, who also conducted a university/civic orchestra that for a short time competed with the Anchorage SO. In 1965 Frank Pinkerton became the Anchorage public schools' first full-time music teacher and administrator; under his direction an extensive string program was developed. He founded and conducted the Anchorage Youth SO, directed for several years the Anchorage SO, and organized the Anchorage school district's fine-arts summer camp. In 1982 the Alaska Conservatory of Music was formed to provide private instrumental instruction to secondary school students.

Among those who have figured prominently in the development of Anchorage's musical life are Mary Hale, who was a conductor of the Community Chorus and a founder of the Alaska Festival of Music; Dewey Ehling, who administered the Anchorage Community College music department and the Anchorage school district's music program, and who now directs the Community Chorus and Youth SO; Jean-Paul Billaud, a pianist who was chairman of the department of music at the University of Alaska; and Paul Rosenthal, a violinist who directs the Sitka Summer Music Festival, a chamber music festival that sponsors concerts in Sitka and Anchorage.

For some time Anchorage has faced a shortage of suitable venues for the performing arts; to answer this need a performing arts center is planned (scheduled for completion in 1987). The city's Sydney Laurence Auditorium will be remodeled as part of the center; at present it seats 600 and is used for operas, musicals, and small concerts. Anchorage also has two larger auditoriums: the West High School Auditorium (seating 2000), which for years has served the local concert association, the Alaska Festival of Music, and the Community Chorus; and the 900-seat Performing Arts Center Theater at the Community College, which serves the Anchorage SO and university performing groups. Grant Hall, a 200-seat theater at Alaska Pacific University, is used for recitals and chamber music programs. The George M. Sullivan Arena (seating 8000), opened in 1982, is used for popular-, rock-, and country-music concerts. In 1984 a 231-seat recital hall was completed at the Anchorage Museum of History and Art. A building for the arts, currently under construction at the University of Alaska, Anchorage, will house a 200-seat recital hall (scheduled for completion in 1986).

In 1980 Alice Countryman, George R. Belden (a member of the faculty at the University of Alaska), and other composers living in Anchorage established the Alaska New Music Forum to present their works in recital and further the cause of contemporary music. Among the other musical organizations active in the city are the Alaska Jazz Society, the American Guild of Organists, the Anchorage Community Concert Band, the Anchorage Jazz Ensemble, the Anchorage Music Teachers Association, Arioso, the Renaissance Singers, the Sweet Adelines, and a chapter of the Society for the Preservation and Encouragement of Barber Shop Quartet Singing in America. Each of two local military installations, Fort Richardson and Elmendorf Air Force Base, maintains a wind band, and a number of military personnel have performed with the Anchorage SO and other organizations.

GEORGE R. BELDEN

Anderson, Beth [Barbara Elizabeth] (*b* Lexington, KY, 3 Jan 1950). Composer. She studied piano at the University of Kentucky, and piano and composition at the University of California, Davis (BA 1971), where she was a pupil of Austin, Cage, and Swift; she also studied at Mills College, Oakland (MFA 1973, MA 1974), with Ashley and Riley. For her master's thesis (1973) she presented an opera using pageantry, popular music, tape collage, and live performance (*Queen Christina*), and in 1974 completed the oratorio *Joan* as a commission for the Cabrillo Music Festival. Among her awards have been an NEA grant (1975) and two grants from the New York State Council of the Arts (1976, 1977). Active as a writer and editor, Anderson was co-editor of *Ear*, 1973–9, as well as one of its principal contributors, and after moving to New York in 1975 founded *Ear Magazine – New York*; her criticism has also appeared in the *Soho Weekly News*, *Heresies*, and *Intermedia*. She has devoted herself increasingly to solo performance (piano, voice), and to support herself she teaches college music courses and accompanies dancers (she has been associated with the Martha Graham School of Dance, the American Dance Studio, and Ballet Hispanico, among others).

By the early 1970s Anderson had composed graphic scores (*Music for Charlemagne Palestine*), text-sound pieces (*Torero Piece*), and tape works (*Tulip Clause*). In the late 1970s, partly influenced by dance and in keeping with a widespread trend, her music became more regular in rhythm, more popular in orientation, and overtly "romantic." As a composer she often adopts a principled arbitrariness in determining pitches by code transfer from letters of texts or from numbers (Anderson is a practicing astrologist); she has also shown consistent interest in feminist imagery and history and a fondness for music as theatrical entertainment.

WORKS

Dramatic: Queen Christina (opera, Anderson), 1973; Soap Tuning (theater piece, Anderson), 1976; Zen Piece (theater piece, Anderson), 1976; Nirvana Manor (musical, J. Morely), 1981; Elizabeth Rex: or the Well-bred Mother Goes to Camp (musical, Jo-Ann Kreston), 1983

Orch: Ov., band, 1981; Revelation, 1981, rev. chamber orch as Revel, 1984; Suite, wind, perc, 1981

Inst: Lullaby of the Eighth Ancestor, fl, pf, 1979–80, arr. pf; Preparation for the Dominant: Outrunning the Inevitable, fl/vn/ocarina, 1979; Dream (Trio: Dream), pf, fl, vc, 1980; Skater's Suite, 4 insts, 1980, arr. pf as Skate Suite; 3 other works

Pf: Quilt Music, 1982; Taking Sides, 1983; Belgian Tango, 1984

Tape: Tulip Clause, chamber ens, tape, 1973; Tower of Power, org, tape, 1973; Good-bye Bridget Bardot or Hello Charlotte Moorman, vc, tape, 1974; They Did It, pf, tape, 1975–6; Ode, 1976; Joan, 1977; several other works

Mixed-media: Music for Charlemagne Palestine, graphic score, 2 str insts, 2 lighting technicians, 1973; Peachy Keen-O, org, elec gui, vib, perc, vv, dancers, light, tape, 1973; Morning view & Maiden Spring, speaker, slides, light, tape, 1978; 1 other work

Vocal, all texts by Anderson unless otherwise stated: Joan, oratorio, 1974; Incline Thine Ear to Me, chant, 1975; Black/White, chant, 1976; text-sound pieces, incl. Torero Piece, 2 vv, 1973, The People Rumble Louder, 1v, 1975, I Can't Stand It, v, perc, 1976; Yes Sir Ree, 1v, 1978; many songs, incl. A Day, 1967, WomanRite, 1972, Music for Myself, 1973, Beauty Runs Faster, 1978, In Six, 1979, Knots (R. D. Laing), 1981

Other: Hallophone, musical environment, 1973; 1 film score, 1980

Principal publisher: ACA

CHARLES SHERE

Anderson, Cat [William Alonzo] (*b* Greenville, SC, 12 Sept 1916; *d* Norwalk, CA, 29 April 1981). Jazz trumpeter. He grew up in the Jenkins Orphanage in Charleston, playing in its famous student band and receiving a thorough training in the rudiments of music. In the early 1930s, while still a teenager, he formed the Carolina Cotton Pickers, a touring band consisting of orphanage students like himself. When the Cotton Pickers disbanded in 1937 he played in the big bands of Claude Hopkins, Lionel Hampton, and others before attracting the attention of Duke Ellington, who immediately engaged him for his band as a high-note specialist (1944–7). After leading his own band from 1947 to 1950 Anderson rejoined Ellington until 1959, taking a prominent part in many of Ellington's "suites" of that period. He rejoined Ellington in 1961, playing intermittently until 1971, but thereafter worked freelance on the West Coast, joining Ellington only for special occasions. Anderson's celebrated high-note forays (he could effortlessly strike *c''''*) tended to overshadow his outstanding abilities as a section leader, and as a jazz soloist with an uninhibited, good-humored style and remarkable precision of execution.

RECORDINGS

(selective list)

As leader: Swingin' the Cat (1947, Apollo 771); Cat's Boogie/For Jumpers Only (1947, Apollo 774); Cat's in the Alley (1949, Gotham 174); *Cat on a Hot Tin Horn* (1958, EmArcy 36142)

As sideman with Duke Ellington: A Gatherin' in a Clearin' (1946, Vic. 474281); Trumpet No End (1946, Musicraft 484); Madness in Great Ones, on *Such Sweet Thunder* (1957, Col. CL1033); The Eighth Veil, on *Afro-Bossa* (1962–3, Rep. 6069); Jungle Kitty, on *Concert in the Virgin Isles* (1965, Rep. 6185)

BIBLIOGRAPHY

S. Dance: *The World of Duke Ellington* (New York, 1970), 144ff

W. Anderson: *The Cat Anderson Trumpet Method: Dealing with Playing in the Upper Register* (Los Angeles, 1973)

J. Chilton: *A Jazz Nursery: the Story of the Jenkins' Orphanage Bands* (London, 1980)

E. Lambert: "Cat Anderson: a Resumé of his Recorded Work," *Jazz Journal International*, xxxv/6 (1982), 16

J. BRADFORD ROBINSON

Anderson, John (*b* Apopka, FL, 13 Dec 1955). Country-music and rock singer and songwriter. He began playing guitar at the age of seven and formed a rock-and-roll band while in high school. He was influenced particularly by Jimi Hendrix and the Rolling Stones. For three years (1972–5) he performed in Nashville clubs with his sister Donna, a singer, and in 1975 recorded his song *Swoop down, sweet Jesus*, for the Ace of Hearts label. Al Gallico then signed Anderson to his publishing company and introduced him to Norro Wilson at Warner Bros. Records, with which he signed a contract in 1978. His Warner singles, many of them in the honky-tonk genre, included *The girl at the end of the bar* (1978), *She just started liking cheatin' songs* (1980), and *I'm just an old chunk of coal* (1981). His 1983 album *All the People are Talkin'* combined traditional country with hard rock. *Eye of a Hurricane* (1984) reflects the influence of Memphis rhythm-and-blues, the late recordings of Elvis Presley, and the western swing-rock of Marshall Tucker. Throughout his career Anderson's sound has been a combination of traditional country, redneck rock, rock-

and-roll, and rhythm-and-blues, combining the beat of rock with the incisive lyrics of country music.

RECORDINGS

(selective list; recorded for Warner Bros. unless otherwise stated)

Swoop down, sweet Jesus (Ace of Hearts 500, 1975); The girl at the end of the bar (8705, 1978); My pledge of love (8770, 1979); She just started liking cheatin' songs (49191, 1980); I'm just an old chunk of coal (49699, 1981); *All the People are Talkin'* (23912, 1983); *Eye of a Hurricane* (25099, 1984)

BIBLIOGRAPHY

B. Allen: "John Anderson," *Country Music*, ix/5 (1981), 60

DON CUSIC

Anderson, Laurie (*b* Chicago, IL, 5 June 1947). Performance artist and composer. She was trained as a violinist and, after moving to New York in 1966, as a painter and sculptor at Barnard College and Columbia University; later she studied privately with the minimalist painter Sol LeWitt, and in the early 1970s taught art history and wrote art criticism. Her first performance piece dates from 1972. In 1974 she began making her own instruments (the first was a violin with an internal speaker).

Laurie Anderson

Anderson's work reached maturity in 1979 with *Americans on the Move*; this piece eventually became incorporated into her two-evening performance-art work, *United States*, given its première in its complete four-part form in 1983 at the Brooklyn Academy of Music and issued on record as *United States Live* (WB 25192-1, 1985). By this time she had made many tours of Europe and her performances, conceived for intimate gallery spaces, were staged in opera houses and rock-concert theaters. This was the result of the unexpected commercial success of her "song" from *United States*, *O Superman (for Massenet)*, which in 1981 reached no.2 on the British pop chart. After signing a contract with Warner Bros., she released *Big Science* (WB 3674, 1982) and *Mister Heartbreak* (WB 25077-1, 1984), two LPs that won her a progressive-rock audience. Her emphasis on the visual coincided exactly with a fad in rock for video vignettes. In the early 1980s she had become the best-known American performance artist, but apart from bringing about a welcome adjustment of scale and an enrichment of musical resources, her popular success did not deflect her artistic direction significantly.

Anderson's pieces are mixed-media collages, solo operas built up from a sequence of "songs" that alternate recitation and child-like singing and employ deft, sophisticated art-rock accompaniments and numerous sound effects. Perhaps the most significant of her innovations in instrument design is the tape-bow violin, created in 1977, which consists of a violin with a tape playback head mounted on the bridge and a bow that has prerecorded lengths of audio tape instead of hair; drawing the bow across the head, the performer activates the tape, controlling the speed, intensity, and direction of the playback. Anderson often modifies her voice – for example, transposing it into a male range – by means of a voice-activated synthesizer, the Vocoder, and with contact microphones she has turned her body into a booming percussion set. A poet as well as a musician (William Burroughs is an honored influence), she illustrates her performances with sophisticated lighting effects, films, slides, and props. If her art seems naive to the unsympathetic, for her admirers Anderson creates an original world expressive of bemusement, alienation, and a futuristic romanticism.

BIBLIOGRAPHY

"Anderson, Laurie," *CBY 1983*

J. Kardon, ed.: *Laurie Anderson: Works from 1969 to 1983* (Philadelphia, 1983)

J. Rockwell: "Women Composers, Performance Art & the Perils of Fashion: Laurie Anderson," *All American Music: Composition in the Late Twentieth Century* (New York, 1983), 123

L. Anderson: *United States* (New York, 1984)

JOHN ROCKWELL

Anderson, Leroy (*b* Cambridge, MA, 29 June 1908; *d* Woodbury, CT, 18 May 1975). Composer, arranger, and conductor. He studied with Spalding (theory), Ballantine (counterpoint), Heilman (fugue), and Enesco and Piston (composition) at Harvard (BA 1929, MA 1930), where from 1930 to 1934 he pursued studies in German and Scandinavian languages. During these latter years he became involved in numerous musical activities, serving as a tutor at Radcliffe College (1930–32), director of the Harvard University Band (1931–5), and organist, instrumentalist, and conductor in Boston (1931–5). He then worked as an arranger and orchestrator in Boston and New York from 1935 to 1942; during the war he acted as a translator and interpreter for the US Army in Iceland and the USA. A member of various organizations, he was chairman of the board of review of ASCAP, and a member of the boards of directors of the New Haven SO and Hartford (Connecticut) SO. As a composer he specialized in light music for the standard orchestra, work which brought him renown in art- and popular-music circles. His works obtain their appeal by means of infectious melody, popular dance rhythms (*Belle of the Ball* and *Blue Tango*), and novel orchestral effects that often relate to the titles (e.g., pizzicato strings in *Plink, Plank, Plunk!*, percussion in *Sleigh Ride* and *The Syncopated Clock*, and unconventional instruments in *The Typewriter* and *Sandpaper Ballet*). He arranged his orchestral works for other instrumental combinations in order to make them accessible to amateur groups and soloists.

WORKS

Musical: Goldilocks (J. and W. Kerr), 1958, New York, 11 Oct 1958

Orch: Harvard Fantasy, 1936, rev. as A Harvard Festival, 1969; Jazz Legato, str orch, 1938; Jazz Pizzicato, str orch, 1938; Promenade, 1945; The Syncopated Clock, 1945; Chicken Reel, 1946; Fiddle-Faddle, str orch, 1947; Irish Suite, 1947; Serenata, 1947; Sleigh Ride, 1948; A Trumpeter's Lullaby, 1949; The Typewriter, 1950; The Waltzing Cat, 1950; Belle of the Ball, 1951; Blue Tango, 1951; Horse and Buggy, 1951; The Penny-Whistle Song, 1951; Plink, Plank, Plunk!, str orch, 1951; Forgotten Dreams, 1954; Sandpaper Ballet, 1954; Suite of Carols, str orch, 1955; Lady in Waiting, ballet, 1959; Arietta, 1962; Balladette, 1962; The Captains and the Kings, 1962; Home Stretch, 1962; many other works

Principal publishers: Belwin-Mills, Woodbury Music

BIBLIOGRAPHY

"Leroy Anderson," *Pan Pipes*, xlv/2 (1953), 38

L. W. Grant: "Salute to a 'Popular' Master," *MJ*, xii/11 (1954), 25

"The *Syncopated Clock* Still Ticks," *MJ*, xxvi/7 (1968), 30

G. W. Briggs, Jr.: "Leroy Anderson on Broadway: Behind-the-scene Accounts of the Musical *Goldilocks*," *American Music*, iii (1985), 329

DAVID E. CAMPBELL

Anderson, Marian (*b* Philadelphia, PA, 17 Feb 1902). Contralto. After graduating from South Philadelphia High School, she studied in her native city with Giuseppe Boghetti. Having won first prize in a competition sponsored by the New York PO, she appeared as a soloist with the orchestra at Lewisohn Stadium on 27 August 1925. After further study with Frank La Forge, she made a number of concert appearances in the USA, and her European début took place at the Wigmore Hall, London, in 1930. She subsequently made tours of Germany and Scandinavia, winning from Toscanini the reported tribute: "A voice like yours is heard only once in a hundred years." By then a mature artist, Anderson gained high critical acclaim for her first appearance at Town Hall in New York (1935) and then undertook further tours, across the USA and in Europe. In 1939 she became the center of national interest when, on account of her race, she was denied the use of Constitution Hall in Washington, DC, for a concert; with the support of Eleanor Roosevelt and other prominent Americans, she gave a concert at the Lincoln Memorial (9 April 1939), which drew an audience of some 75,000 people.

Marian Anderson as Ulrica in Verdi's "Un ballo in maschera"

At the invitation of Rudolf Bing, she made a belated début in opera at the Metropolitan Opera in New York as Ulrica in *Un ballo in maschera* (7 January 1955; see illustration). Although her voice was no longer at its best, as the first black singer on the company's roster she paved the way for others.

After leaving the Metropolitan in 1956, Anderson continued her concert career, making a farewell tour in 1965, which concluded with a recital at Carnegie Hall (19 April 1965). She has received numerous honorary doctorates and awards, among them the Presidential Medal of Freedom (1963), a Congressional Gold Medal (1978), and the first Eleanor Roosevelt Human Rights Award of the City of New York (1984). With a $10,000 award from the Bok Foundation, she established the Marian Anderson Fellowship for young artists in 1972. Her 75th birthday was celebrated with a concert tribute at Carnegie Hall, New York, in which many renowned artists participated. Anderson's voice was large and striking, and although it was not exceptionally even throughout the range, she could adapt it admirably to lieder. Artistic integrity was the hallmark of this pioneering artist, and in spirituals she was compelling.

BIBLIOGRAPHY

SouthernB

K. Vehanen: *Marian Anderson: a Portrait* (New York, 1941/*R*1970)

M. Anderson: *My Lord, What a Morning: an Autobiography* (New York, 1956)

J. L. Sims: *Marian Anderson: an Annotated Bibliography and Discography* (Westport, CT, 1981)

N. M. Westlake and O. E. Albrecht: *Marian Anderson: a Catalogue of the Collection at the University of Pennsylvania* (Philadelphia, 1982)

MAX DE SCHAUENSEE/DENNIS K. McINTIRE

Anderson, Maxwell (*b* Atlantic, PA, 15 Dec 1888; *d* Stamford, CT, 28 Feb 1959). Playwright. After studies at the University of North Dakota and at Stanford University he taught in North Dakota and California. In 1918 he moved to New York, where he worked for several years as a journalist before establishing himself as a playwright. His writings include several verse dramas, radio plays, film scripts, music dramas, essays, and one volume of poetry.

Anderson had a lifelong interest in the musical stage. For many years he was associated closely with Kurt Weill, with whom he collaborated on *Knickerbocker Holiday* and *Lost in the Stars*, a dramatization of Alan Paton's novel *Cry, the Beloved Country*. Uncompleted works with Weill include *Ulysses Africanus* (whose leading role was intended for Paul Robeson) and *Raft on the River*, a musical adaptation of Twain's *Adventures of Huckleberry Finn*. Weill and Anderson also collaborated on a scenic cantata, *The Ballad of Magna Carta*, and Anderson translated Brecht's *Der Jasager* for Weill's school opera.

Other uncompleted music dramas are *Hell On Wheels* (with John Jacob Niles and Douglas S. Moore), and *Devil's Hornpipe* (with Allie Wrubel), and *Art of Love*, for which Anderson found no collaborator. One of the few Anderson poems set to music is *St. Agnes' Morning* by Henry Cowell, a friend of the author. Other adaptations include *A Christmas Carol*, a version of Dickens's story with music by Bernard Herrmann, and a musical adaptation for television of Anderson's play *High Tor*, with music by Arthur Schwartz.

See also IRVING, WASHINGTON.

BIBLIOGRAPHY

M. Anderson: "Assembling the Parts for a Musical Play," *New York Herald Tribune* (30 Oct 1949)

——: "Kurt Weill," *Theatre Arts*, xxxiv (1950), 58–88

——: "Inside Story of a Musical: from Book to Broadway," *New York Herald Tribune* (29 Oct 1951)
L. G. Avery: *A Catalogue of the Maxwell Anderson Collection at the University of Texas* (Austin, 1968)
——: "Maxwell Anderson and *Both your Houses*," *North Dakota Quarterly*, xxxviii (1970), 5
M. Matlaw: "Alan Paton's *Cry, the Beloved Country* and Maxwell Anderson's/Kurt Weill's *Lost in the Stars*: a Consideration of Genres," *Arcadia*, x (1975), 262
L. G. Avery, ed.: *Dramatist in America: Letters of Maxwell Anderson, 1912–1958* (Chapel Hill, 1977)
R. Sanders: *The Days Grow Short: the Life and Music of Kurt Weill* (New York, 1980)
M. A. Hovland: *Musical Settings of American Poetry: a Bibliography* (in preparation) [incl. list of settings]

MICHAEL HOVLAND

Anderson, (Evelyn) Ruth (*b* Kalispell, MT, 21 March 1928). Composer and flutist. She received the BA in flute (1949) and MA in composition (1951) from the University of Washington. She took further studies at Columbia and Princeton universities with Ussachevsky and Kim (electronic music and composition), and also had private lessons with Boulanger and Milhaud (composition), and John Wummer and Jean-Pierre Rampal (flute). She has won several awards including five MacDowell Colony Fellowships (1957–73), two Fulbright scholarships (1958, 1959), and grants from the NEA, the Martha Baird Rockefeller Fund, and the Alice M. Ditson Fund. In the 1950s she was active as a flutist with the Totenberg Instrumental Ensemble, the Seattle and Portland symphony orchestras, and for a season with the Boston Pops Orchestra. She worked during the 1960s as an orchestrator (for NBC television and for Broadway shows, including work for Robert Russell Bennett and Robert Cobert), and from 1966 as a composer and teacher of composition, theory, and electronic music at Hunter College, CUNY; she has been director of the electronic music studio there since designing and installing it in 1968–70.

Anderson's text pieces, sound sculptures, collages, and tape music reflect her research in electronics, acoustic design, and psychoacoustics. Her music is derived from holistic concepts of stress reduction and interactive participation designed to make performers aware of the wholeness of the self and of unity with others. *Centering* (1979), for four musicians and a dancer, integrates biofeedback techniques with live electronics: changes in bioelectrical currents created by the musicians' responses to watching the dancer generate rising and falling pitches by means of a GSR ("galvanic skin resistance" oscillator), with which the musicians have contact through their fingers. The dancer, in turn, reacts spontaneously to the changing pitch patterns.

WORKS

Many early works for vv, pf, str, chamber ens with fl, withdrawn; numerous orchestrations, arrs., for television, theater groups, etc.
Tape: The Pregnant Dream (Swenson), 1968; ES II, 1969; DUMP, collage, 1970; 3 Studies, 1970; 3 Pieces, 1970–71; So What nos. 1–2, 1971; SUM (State of the Union Message), collage, 1973; Conversations, 1974; Points, 1974; Dress Rehearsal, 1976; I Come out of your Sleep, 1979; several others
Text pieces: Naming, 1975; A Long Sound, 1976; Sound Portraits I–II, 1977; Silent Sound, 1978; Greetings from the Right Hemisphere, 1979; Communications, 1980
Mixed media: Centering, dance, 4 pfmrs, live elec, 1979
Sound sculptures: Sound Environment, 1975; Time and Tempo, 1984
Other: Fugue, pf/str, 1948; The Merchant's Song (Coombs), A, pf, 1951; 2 Pieces, str, 1957; 2 Movts, str, 1958

Principal publisher: American Composers Edition

BARBARA A. PETERSEN

Anderson, T(homas) J(efferson) (*b* Coatesville, PA, 17 Aug 1928). Composer. He was born into a musical family and studied piano as a child. After touring with a jazz orchestra as a youth, he studied at West Virginia State College (BMus 1950), Pennsylvania State University (MMEd 1951), and the University of Iowa (PhD 1958), where his teachers included Bezanson and Hervig; he also studied with Milhaud at the Aspen School (summer 1964). He taught in the High Point, North Carolina, public schools (1951–4) and at West Virginia State College (1955–6), Langston University (1958–63), and Tennessee State University (1963–9) before being appointed chairman of the music department at Tufts University in 1972. His honors include appointment as the first black composer-in-residence of the Atlanta SO (1969–71), MacDowell Colony Fellowships, Fromm Foundation awards, honorary doctorates (College of the Holy Cross, 1983; West Virginia State University, 1984), lecture tours abroad for the US Department of State, and numerous commissions. In 1972 he played an important part in staging the première of Scott Joplin's opera *Treemonisha* at Atlanta and orchestrated the score for the performance. His music reflects the influence of both jazz and post-Webern styles, and his predilection for rhythmic complexities and his imaginative use of instrumental color are particularly noteworthy. The recordings of the Chamber Symphony, *Squares*, and Variations on a Theme by M. B. Tolson illustrate his mature style.

WORKS

Stage: The Shell Fairy (operetta, S. Beattie, after C. M. Pierce), 4 solo vv, chorus, dancers, chamber orch, 1976–7; Re-creation (L. Forrest), 3 speakers, dancer, tpt, a sax, drums, vn, vc, pf, 1978; Soldier Boy, Soldier (opera, Forrest), 5 solo vv, chorus, jazz combo, orch, 1982
Orch: Pyknon Ov., 1958; Introduction and Allegro, 1959; New Dances, chamber orch, 1960; Classical Sym., 1961; 6 Pieces, cl, chamber orch, 1962; Sym. in 3 Movts, 1964; Squares, essay, orch, 1965; Chamber Sym., 1968; Intervals, 1970–71; Messages, a Creole Fantasy, 1979; early works
Chamber: Str Qt no. 1, 1958; 5 Bagatelles, ob, vn, hpd, 1963; 5 Etudes and a Fancy, ww qnt, 1964; 5 Portraitures of 2 People, pf 4 hands, 1965; Connections, 2 vn, 2 va, vc, 1966; Transitions, fantasy, 10 insts, 1971; Watermelon, pf, 1971; Swing Set, cl, pf, 1972; 5 Easy Pieces, vn, pf, jew's harp, 1974; Minstrel Man, b trbn, perc, 1977; Street Song, pf, 1977; Variations on a Theme by Alban Berg, va, pf, 1977; Play me Something, pf, 1979; Vocalise, vn, harp, 1980; Call and Response, pf, 1982; Inaugural Piece, 3 tpt, 3 t trbn, 1982; Intermezzi, cl, a sax, pf, 1983; other works
Vocal: Personals (A. Bontemps), cantata, nar, chorus, brass septet, 1966; Variations on a Theme by M. B. Tolson, cantata, S, a sax, tpt, trbn, vn, vc, pf (1969); This House, male vv, 4 pitch pipes, 1971; Block Songs (P. C. Lomax), S, pitch pipe, jack-in-the-box, musical busy box, 1972; Beyond Silence (P. Hanson), T, cl, trbn, va, vc, pf, 1973; In Memoriam Malcolm X (R. Hayden), S, orch, 1974; Horizons '76 (M. Kessler), S, orch, 1975; Spirituals (Hayden), T, nar, children's vv, chorus, jazz qt, orch, 1979; Jonestown, children's chorus, pf, 1982; Thomas Jefferson's Minstrels (T. J. Anderson), Bar, male chorus, jazz band, 1982; other choral and solo vocal works
Band: Trio Concertante, cl, tpt, trbn, band, 1960; Rotations, 1967; In Memoriam Zach Walker, 1968; Fanfare, tpt, 4 small bands, 1976
Orchd Joplin: Treemonisha, 1972

Principal publishers: ACA, Bote & Bock, C. Fischer, Peters

BIBLIOGRAPHY

EwenD; *SouthernB*
D. de Lerma, ed.: *Black Music in our Culture* (Kent, OH, 1970)
E. Southern: *The Music of Black Americans: a History* (New York, 1971, rev. 1983)
——, ed.: *Readings in Black American Music* (New York, 1971, rev. 1983)
J. Hunt: "Blacks and the Classics," *BPiM*, i (1973), 157
D. de Lerma, ed.: *Reflections on Afro-American Music* (Kent, OH, 1973)
H. Roach: *Black American Music: Past and Present*, i (Malabar, FL, 1973, rev. 1985)
E. Southern: "America's Black Composers of Classical Music," *MEJ*, lvii (1975), 46
D. Baker, L. Belt, H. Hudson, eds., *The Black Composer Speaks* (Metuchen, NJ, 1978)

C. Oliver: *Selected Orchestral Works of Thomas J. Anderson, Arthur Cunningham, Talib Rasul and Olly Wilson* (diss., Florida State U., 1978)
B. A. Thompson: *Musical Style and Compositional Techniques in Selected Works of T. J. Anderson* (diss., Indiana U., 1978)
H. Roach: *Black American Music: Past and Present*, ii (Malabar, FL, 1985)

EILEEN SOUTHERN

Andrews, Julie (*b* Walton-on-Thames, England, 1 Oct 1935). Actress and singer. She received singing lessons as a child and made her professional début in the show *Starlight Roof* in London in 1947. After her performance in the pantomime *Cinderella* at the London Palladium she was engaged to play the leading role in *The Boy Friend* on Broadway (1954), and subsequently starred in *My Fair Lady* (1956) and *Camelot* (1960). These successes led to work in Hollywood; she won an Academy Award for *Mary Poppins* (1964) and was nominated for another for *The Sound of Music* (1965). Her career then suffered a decline, owing in part to the purity and wholesomeness of her image; after she married the director Blake Edwards, however, she regained her former prominence, playing leading roles in the films *10* and *S.O.B.*, and received another Oscar nomination for *Victor/Victoria* in 1982. She has also appeared frequently on television and presented her own series in 1972–3.

Her trained voice, with its unusual range and clear diction, is only one aspect of Andrews's talent; she is also an accomplished dancer, comedian, and actress of great warmth and charm. At the peak of her career she was one of the most successful singing actresses in the world. She is also known for her interest in and work on behalf of orphans in Southeast Asia.

BIBLIOGRAPHY

J. Cottrell: *Julie Andrews* (London, 1970)
R. Windeler: *Julie Andrews* (New York, 1983)

RICHARD C. LYNCH

Andrews Sisters. Vocal trio. It was formed in 1932 by the sisters LaVerne (*b* Minneapolis, MN, 6 July 1915; *d* Brentwood, CA, 8 May 1967), Maxene (Maxine) (*b* Minneapolis, 3 Jan 1918), and Patti (Patricia) (*b* Minneapolis, 16 Feb 1920) Andrews. They began performing in vaudeville houses in the Midwest with the Larry Rich Orchestra in 1932, and first achieved national prominence with a version of *Bei mir bist du schön* in 1937. They made frequent radio appearances in the late 1930s and 1940s, including regular performances with the Glenn Miller Orchestra; they acted in 16 films (1940–48), often cast as themselves; they made nationwide tours; and they produced a steady stream of popular song recordings, some with Bing Crosby and Guy Lombardo. Among the most popular of their recordings were *Beer Barrel Polka* (1939), *In apple blossom time* (1940), *Boogie Woogie Bugle Boy* (1941), *Don't sit under the apple tree* (1942), and *Rum and Coca-cola* (1944).

The Andrews Sisters began by emulating their idols the Boswell Sisters of New Orleans, and first achieved success with settings in close harmony that had a dixieland flavor; Patti sang lead soprano, Maxene second soprano, and LaVerne alto. They went on to embrace all the current strains of popular song – the ballad of the swing era, boogie woogie, South American dance songs, and novelty songs. Their singing presented a generally sweet and optimistic mood and exhibited a strong sense of ensemble and swing; improvisation played only a small role and was usually confined to Patti's solos.

The retirement of the Andrews Sisters in the mid-1950s, caused by the changing temper of popular music and Patti's attempt at a solo career, was short-lived, and from the late 1950s until LaVerne's death in 1967 they performed in nightclubs. Bette Midler's unabashed imitation of *Boogie Woogie Bugle Boy* in 1973 sparked a renewal of interest in their recordings, and Patti and Maxene, with a substitute for LaVerne, starred in the nostalgic Broadway musical *Over There* (1974).

BIBLIOGRAPHY

D. Ewen: *All the Years of American Popular Music* (Englewood Cliffs, NJ, 1977)
C. Hamm: *Yesterdays: Popular Song in America* (New York, 1979)

MICHAEL J. BUDDS

Anievas, Agustin (*b* New York, 11 June 1934). Pianist. He was taught piano by his mother from the age of four. After some appearances as a child, he entered the Juilliard School where he studied with Edward Steuermann, Samaroff, and Marcus. He made his début as a soloist with the Little Orchestra Society in New York at the age of 18. In 1959 he won the Concert Artists Guild Award, followed by first prizes in a number of other important competitions in Europe and the USA including the Dimitri Mitropoulos Competition in 1961. Since then he has toured widely in the USA, South America, Europe, South Africa, Australia, and the Far East. Anievas settled in Belgium for ten years but in 1974 returned to New York where he became a piano professor at Brooklyn College. His repertory is principally of 19th- and early 20th-century music and includes the concertos of Bartók and Prokofiev. He has recorded all of Rachmaninoff's concertos, the complete impromptus of Schubert, and the complete waltzes, studies, ballades, and impromptus of Chopin, as well as works by Liszt and Brahms.

RONALD KINLOCH ANDERSON/R

Animal dances. Popular name for a large number of dances associated with the music of ragtime in the 1910s. These include the bull-frog hop, bunny hop (CONGA), buzz, buzzard lope, camel walk, chicken scratch, crab walk, EAGLE ROCK, fanny bump, fish tail, FOXTROT, funky butt, grind, GRIZZLY BEAR, horse trot, itch (heebie-jeebies), kangaroo dip, maxixe, monkey glide, mooch, ONE-STEP, possum trot, scratchin' the gravel, SLOW DRAG, squat, TANGO, TEXAS TOMMY, TURKEY TROT, veleta and walkin' the dog.

Annapolis Brass Quintet. Brass quintet formed in 1971; its present members are David Cran, trumpet (from 1971), Robert Suggs, trumpet (from 1974), Marc Guy, horn (from 1979), Wayne Wells, trombone (from 1980) and Robert Posten, bass trombone and tuba (from 1971). It was the first American brass quintet to serve as the full-time and exclusive professional occupation of its members. The group has toured extensively in the USA (New York début, 21 January 1984), Europe, and the Far East, and has held summer residencies at the International Music Camp in North Dakota (1971–6) and Artpark in Lewiston, New York (from 1975). Festivals at which the ensemble has appeared include the Festival Casals, Festival of American Music (Portugal), and the Chautauqua and Rockport Chamber Music festivals. The group has played a major role in developing brass quintet literature through editions of Renaissance and Baroque music and an active commissioning program; it has given over 40 premières of works by European and American composers, including George Walker, Robert Starer, Lawrence Moss, and Jiri LaBurda. In 1979 the ensemble organized the Brass Chamber Music Society of Annapolis, and in 1980 it established the International Brass

Quintet Festival in Baltimore, to bring together professionals from both Europe and the USA as well as student ensembles for four weeks of performance and study.

JOANNE SHEEHY HOOVER

Antes, John [Johann] (*b* Frederick, nr Bethlehem, PA, 24 March 1740; *d* Bristol, England, 17 Dec 1811). Moravian composer. He was educated in the Moravian boys' school at Bethlehem; among his early teachers was Johann Christoph Pyrlaeus (1713–85). For several years during the early 1760s Antes manufactured musical instruments in Bethlehem, and is known to have made at least seven string instruments (five violins, a viola, and a cello) of which a violin and viola are in museums in Nazareth and Lititz, Pennsylvania, respectively. He is thought to have also made several keyboard instruments, although none bearing his name is known. In 1764 he went to Herrnhut, Saxony, for further training and in 1765 to Neuwied to learn watchmaking. He was ordained a Moravian minister in 1769, and accepted missionary service in Egypt from 1770 to 1781. In 1779 he was captured by the henchmen of Osman Bey, whose intention was to extort money from him, and received a severe beating, which impaired his health for the rest of his stay. In 1781 he returned to Herrnhut, and in 1783 he was again living in Neuwied. In 1785 he became warder (business manager) of the Fulneck Moravian community in England, a position he occupied for most of the rest of his life.

Antes's extant music consists of three trios for two violins and cello op.3 (*c*1790), 31 concerted anthems and solo songs, and 59 hymn tunes. A letter from Antes to Benjamin Franklin, dated 10 July 1779, clearly indicates that Antes had composed "Six Quartettos," presumably for strings. Besides the trios, only one solo song and several hymn tunes appeared in print during his lifetime. Manuscripts of his anthems are in the archives of the Moravian Church in Bethlehem and Winston-Salem, North Carolina, and in the Archiv der Brüder-Unität at Herrnhut. The London Moravian Archives have two manuscript books of hymn tunes. The music is close to Haydn's in technique and spirit. The three trios composed while Antes was in Egypt, the earliest known chamber music by a native American composer, show him as a composer of real talent with a good command of technique and a lively imagination. The anthems and solo songs are finely wrought works with instrumental accompaniment for strings and occasional wind: the solo and chorus *Go, congregation, go – Surely he has borne our griefs* is one of the most moving works in the Moravian repertory.

Antes was modest about his musical accomplishments, and referred to himself as a musical dilettante on several occasions. His long memoir, written shortly before his death, does not even mention his musical activities. He published a summary of his experiments for improving piano hammers, the violin tuning mechanism, and violin bows (*AMZ*, viii, 1806, 657), and invented a music stand, using which a player could turn pages automatically.

See also MORAVIAN CHURCH, MUSIC OF THE.

BIBLIOGRAPHY

"Lebenslauf des Bruders John Antes," *Nachrichten aus der Brüder-Gemeine* (1845), no.2, p.249 [autobiography]

D. M. McCorkle: "John Antes, 'American Dilettante'," *MQ*, xlii (1956), 486; repr. (Winston-Salem, NC, 1956/*R*1980) [with list of works]

F. M. Blandford: "John Antes: an American Hero," *The Moravian*, cvii/4 (1962), 6

W. J. Smith: *A Style Critical Study of John Antes' String Trios in Relation to Contemporary Stylistic Trends* (thesis, SUNY, Binghamton, 1974)

R. D. Claypool: "Mr John Antes, Instrumentmaker," *Moravian Music Foundation Bulletin*, xxiii/2 (1978), 10

K. M. Stolba: "From John Antes to Benjamin Franklin: a Musical Connection," *Moravian Music Foundation Bulletin*, xxv/2 (1980), 5

——: "Evidence for Quartets by John Antes, American-born Moravian Composer," *JAMS*, xxxiii (1980), 565

K. Kroeger: "John Antes at Fulneck," *Moravian Music Journal*, xxx/1 (1985), 12

KARL KROEGER

Antheil, George [Georg] **(Carl Johann)** (*b* Trenton, NJ, 8 July 1900; *d* New York, 12 Feb 1959). Composer and pianist of German descent.

1. Revolution: up to 1925. 2. Reaction: 1925–59.

1. REVOLUTION: UP TO 1925. Antheil began piano lessons when he was six and from the age of 16 traveled regularly to Philadelphia for theory and composition lessons with Constantin von Sternberg. On the advice of Sternberg, Antheil went to New York in 1919 to study composition with Ernest Bloch, who had accepted him as a pupil on the basis of his Five Songs, his first mature compositions. In 1920 while studying with Bloch, Antheil began his first major work, the *Symphonie no.1* "Zingareska"; it is interesting for the jazz rhythms in the last movement. After leaving Bloch's tutelage in 1921, Antheil returned to Philadelphia, where financial problems forced him to look for a patron. With Sternberg's help he sought the support of Mary Louise Curtis Bok; although she soon disapproved of Antheil's music, she continued to give him financial assistance for the next 19 years.

Antheil went to Europe on 30 May 1922 to pursue a career as a concert pianist. After presenting his first recital on 22 June 1922 at Wigmore Hall in London, he settled in Berlin and from there made a successful tour of central Europe, often with recitals of his own music. In Berlin Antheil met Stravinsky, who exercised the single most important influence on his compositional style during the 1920s. The American's admiration of the Russian's anti-Romantic, machine-like, rhythmically propulsive style is reflected in the piano compositions *Airplane Sonata*, *Mechanisms*, *Sonata Sauvage*, *Death of Machines*, and *Jazz Sonata*. The *Airplane Sonata* exemplifies Antheil's preoccupation with machines and time-space theories in the early 1920s. It is constructed out of the addition and manipulation of rhythmically activated blocks, each delineated by a different ostinato pattern. These blocks, Antheil's "time-space" components, derive their energy from the rhythmic momentum of repeated musical fragments and the changing metrical structure. Antheil's chromatic chordal vocabulary, which includes clusters (usually gapped and not entirely black- or white-note), is regulated by ostinato patterns and pedals that establish a tonal center (sometimes a different one in each hand); he favored chords built of perfect, diminished, or augmented 4ths and 5ths contained within the interval of a 7th or 9th. Stuckenschmidt (1923) summarized the style of Antheil's Berlin piano pieces as "a most lively polyrhythmical homophony."

Antheil moved from Berlin to Paris in June 1923. His notoriety was ensured by the riotous reception of his performance of his piano pieces at the Théâtre des Champs-Elysées on 4 October 1923, and he was championed and befriended by Joyce, Pound, Yeats, Satie, Picasso, and other artists, including the violinist

Olga Rudge (see fig.1). Applauded as a genius by the Parisian literary community, he became the musical spokesman for their "modernist" ideas. Pound wrote a book and numerous articles in praise of Antheil's music, and, together with Rudge, he commissioned two violin sonatas which were first performed on 11 December 1923 at the Salle du Conservatoire with Antheil accompanying Rudge; they performed them throughout Europe in the next few years. These sonatas, together with a third violin sonata (1924) and a string quartet (1924), illustrate Antheil's musical discourse of this period: an abstract juxtaposition of musical blocks on a time canvas, similar to the arrangements of objects in a Cubist painting. Summarizing the formal procedures of these chamber pieces is the massive *Ballet mécanique*, dating from the same period; it is a comprehensive statement of the composer's mechanistic outlook and time-space formulas modeled after Stravinsky's *Les noces*. (Antheil sought to accompany this large-scale synthesis of his formal ideas with a motion picture. The problems of coordinating the film with the music, scored for 16 pianolas, xylophones, drums, and other percussion, proved, however, insurmountable and both works became autonomous.) *Ballet mécanique* was first performed publicly on 19 June 1926 in a reduced version for one pianola with amplifier, two pianos, three xylophones, electric bells, small wood propeller, large wood propeller, metal propeller, tam-tam, four bass drums, and siren.

The *Ballet mécanique*, a milestone in the literature for percussion ensemble, is more tightly unified than Antheil's other Paris works. The fabric is melody and accompaniment, a melody organized on repeated, small-range motifs treated in a multimetric continuum with an accompaniment of rhythmic chordal pedals supported by pitched (including piano) and nonpitched percussion instruments. Within a dissonant harmonic idiom, changes in tension in the melodic-rhythmic musical blocks replace the harmonic tension and resolution of a tonal language, and stability is established by ostinato patterns, pedal chords, and rhythmic pedal tones.

2. REACTION: 1925–59. With the enthusiastic reception of the *Ballet mécanique*, Antheil felt that he had become the leading young composer in Paris. He also believed that the *Ballet* had been a summary, and he consciously chose to change his compositional style in the *Symphonie en fa* (1925–6) and the Piano Concerto (1926), compositions which in 1936 he labeled neoclassic. Antheil continued to eschew developmental processes in favor of additive block construction but replaced the rhythmically charged homophony of each block with units characterized by rhythmic consistency, repetitious and triadic melodies, and harmonies built on 3rds. The momentum provided by an erratic rhythmic continuum disappeared, and was not replaced except by an occasional chromatic chord or bitonal melody.

The *Symphonie en fa* was well received when first performed with the *Ballet mécanique* (19 June 1926), but the Piano Concerto, given its première on 12 March 1927, was criticized as being a mere imitation of Stravinsky's neoclassicism and an abandonment of the earlier iconoclastic mechanistic style. Antheil's prominent position in Parisian musical life began to erode. The decline was cemented on the other side of the Atlantic by the disastrous American première of the *Ballet mécanique* on 10 April 1927 in Carnegie Hall, a carnival presentation by the over-eager promoter Donald Friede that alienated many.

Antheil's rejection in Paris and then New York in 1927 caused him to approach a new musical genre; attracted by the operatic

1. George Antheil with Olga Rudge, Paris, c1924

"renaissance" in Germany, he moved to Vienna in 1928 to complete *Transatlantic*, an opera whose plot centers on an American presidential election and presents a wild caricature of American life. Its première in Frankfurt am Main on 25 May 1930 was a modest success, as was its American première more than 50 years later (Trenton, New Jersey, 1981). Antheil electrifies the drama with fast cinematographic staging: the final act is played on an arrangement of four stages and a screen that allow quick cuts between scenes (see fig.2). Musically, the modular structure, jazz-inspired rhythms, and parody of popular tunes reinforce the pace of the plot and underline the satirical tone of the opera. Within a stable harmonic framework, declamatory recitatives with ostinato contours are accompanied by chromatically inflected (sometimes polytonal) chordal pedals.

While Antheil was preparing for the production of this opera, he also worked on his second large-scale opera *Helen Retires*, which proved to be critically unsuccessful, and several smaller dramatic compositions. From 1929 to 1933 he divided his time between Europe and America. In the two nondramatic orchestral works *Capriccio* and *Morceau for Orchestra* Antheil solidified what he called "a fundamentally American style," one that had appeared in embryo form in *Transatlantic* and would be strengthened by his study of symphonic form in the late 1930s and 1940s, culminating in the Fourth Symphony. Structures are still additive, and relationships between the blocks continue to be nonfunctional; but changes begun in his neoclassical works in the content of the blocks are completely integrated. Musical units are not only considerably longer, but they become thematic sections rather than rhythmically homophonic motivic cells and are characterized either by short, rhythmically snappy themes that are developed motivically through imitation, or by slow, chordal, harmonically expressive melodies; sections recur regularly to integrate the structure. In both these works Antheil made a conscious effort to be "popular," using a synthesis of American folk-like material that appears in almost all of his later compositions.

Melodies still exhibit a small range but now possess a memorable rhythmic identity (unlike those of the neoclassical works) and are no longer the nonmelodic multimetric ostinato patterns of the mechanistic compositions. Harmonic orientation emerges as an important controlling factor: although bass figures are still repetitive ostinatos or pedal points, they are tonally conceived, with a single chordal sonority supporting an entire section.

Before returning permanently to the USA in August 1933, Antheil completed *La femme 100 têtes*, a collection of 44 preludes and a concluding "Percussion Dance" for piano after the surrealist collage novel of etchings by the painter Max Ernst; it presents the mechanistic style of Antheil's early Paris years within a controlled framework. Once home, Antheil continued to write works for musical theater, a genre he believed could broaden the public's support for modern music. In New York he became a part of what he identified as "a new theater movement – musical ballet-opera theater," and wrote ballet scores for Balanchine and Martha Graham. He also began composing background music for films.

After leaving New York in May 1936 and traveling in the South seeking inspiration and material for his *American Symphony*, Antheil settled in Hollywood in August 1936. He viewed Hollywood as "the Mecca of young American composers," a place that offered him the opportunity of becoming financially independent. To support himself and his family he not only composed film scores but became involved in numerous other activities: a tablature notation for piano, called "SEE-Note," to simplify learning; articles for *Esquire* on romance, endocriminology, and the war; a syndicated lonely-hearts column; an anonymously published book, *The Shape of War to Come* (1940); radio analysis on the war; and a radio-directed torpedo invented in collaboration with the actress Hedy Lamarr. By 1941 all of these ventures had evaporated, and he felt he had reached the low point of his career.

In 1942, however, with the acceptance by Boosey & Hawkes of his Fourth Symphony Antheil recovered momentum and embarked on the most creative period of his life. Although he continued to earn a living writing film music, he no longer let this consume all of his energies. The Fourth Symphony marks Antheil's turn to a Romantic spirit in music, embodies the preoccupation with symphonic form that had governed his musical philosophy for two decades, and reflects his admiration of Shostakovich's music. Its four programmatic movements are cast in traditional forms, and the entire cycle is unified through the transformation of thematic contours and intervallic patterns. Motivic unity results from an extensive use of developmental techniques, used infrequently in earlier works. By placing fragmented and altered themes in contrapuntal textures he creates a fabric that is more polyphonic than in previous works, but the basic architecture is still block-like, giving the music a mosaic rather than an organic quality. Written to appeal to the public, the work's success is due to the infectious and "schmaltzy" melodies, similar in character to those of *Capriccio* and *Morceau*. After the première by the NBC SO under Stokowski on 13 February

2. Scene from the final act of Antheil's "Transatlantic," Frankfurt am Main, Germany, May 1930; the set, divided into four stages and a projection screen, was designed by Ludwig Sievert

1944, the symphony was described in *Time* magazine as "the loudest and liveliest symphonic composition to turn up in years" (xliii/9, 1944).

Antheil's embrace of a new Romanticism is most evident in his Symphony no.5 "Joyous" (this work is not the "Tragic" Fifth Symphony discussed in his autobiography). It crystallizes the formal, stylistic, and emotional principles of the Symphony no.4 and epitomizes his preoccupation with Beethoven and obsession with form dating from the mid-1920s. Evoking in its melodic and rhythmic motifs an American nationalist sound and using the same structures and developmental techniques as the previous piece, the Symphony no.5 was regarded by Virgil Thomson as Antheil's most skillfully crafted work. After 1942 Antheil wrote other compositions of a similar expressive intent with varying degrees of success; when weaknesses do occur, they are to be found in the music's occasional ponderous and pompous nature and static block construction. Their strengths lie in the ironic wit and American popular spirit of forceful, often "jazzy" ostinato rhythms, clashing dissonances, invigorating American-flavored tunes, soulful lyricism, and pounding chords. The best of the later works include the Serenade for String Orchestra, Violin Sonatina, Violin Sonata no.4, Piano Sonata no.4, *Songs of Experience*, and *Eight Fragments from Shelley*.

In 1949 Antheil revived his interest in music drama with the opera *Volpone*, the most successful of a set of four operas completed in the early 1950s. The libretto is farcical, fast-moving, and singable, and the music not only supports but, in the manner of Antheil's film music, expertly enhances the comedy. The heterogeneous harmonic language, the thematic versatility, the rhythmic continuum, the mosaic construction, and the colorfully programmatic timbres all combine to reinforce the plot dramatically. Antheil's talent for satire and caricature also promotes the spirit of his last ballet *Capital of the World*. It attracts, as does the best in all Antheil's music, because of its rhythmic vitality, harmonic pungency, and melodic vigor.

3. George Antheil, California, c1952

WORKS

Projected and incomplete works not listed; for a fuller list see Whitesitt (1983).

STAGE

Transatlantic (opera, Antheil), 1927–8; Frankfurt am Main, Germany, 25 May 1930

Oedipus Rex (incidental music, Sophocles), 1928, lost; Berlin, 4 Jan 1929

U.S.A. with Music (incidental music, W. Lowenfels), 1928, lost

Fighting the Waves (incidental music, Yeats), female v, chorus, small orch, 1929; Dublin, Ireland, 13 Aug 1929

Flight (Ivan the Terrible) (opera-ballet, 1, G. and B. Antheil), 1927–30; arr. str orch as Crucifixion Juan Miro, 1927, lost

Helen Retires (opera, 3, J. Erskine), 1930–31; New York, 28 Feb 1934

Dance in Four Parts (ballet, M. Graham), based on La femme 100 têtes [see under PIANO], *c*1933–4, lost; New York, 11 Nov 1934

Eyes of Gutne (ballet, Balanchine), *c*1934, lost

The Seasons (ballet, Balanchine), *c*1934, lost

Dreams (ballet, Balanchine), 1934–5; New York, 5 March 1935

Serenade (ballet), orchd from Tchaikovsky, 1935, lost; New York, 9 June 1934

Transcendence (ballet), arr., orchd from Liszt, 1935, lost; Bryn Mawr, PA, 7 Feb 1935

Course (ballet, Graham), 5 insts, 1935, lost

The Cave Within (ballet), arr. of pf pieces, *c*1948, lost

Capital of the World (ballet, after Hemingway), 1952, arr. orch suite, *c*1955; television broadcast, 6 Dec 1953

Volpone (opera, 3, A. Perry, after Jonson), 1949–52; Los Angeles, 9 Jan 1953

The Brothers (opera, 1, Antheil), 1954; Denver, 28 July 1954

Venus in Africa (opera, 1, M. Dyne), 1954; Denver, 24 May 1957

The Wish (opera, 4 scenes, Antheil), 1954; Louisville, 2 April 1955

Tongue of Silver (incidental music, M. Dyne), *c*1955–9, lost

ORCHESTRAL

Conc. for Pf (Conc. no. 1), 1922; Symphonie no. 1 "Zingareska," 1920–22, rev. 1923; Ballet mécanique, large perc ens, 1923–5, rev. 1952–3, Paris, 19 June 1926; A Jazz Sym., 1925, rev. 1955; Symphonie en fa, 1925–6; Pf Conc., 1926; Suite for Orch, 1926; Capriccio, 1930; Sym. no.2, 1931–8, rev. 1943; Morceau (The Creole), 1932; Archipelago "Rhumba" [= 3rd movt of Sym. no.2], 1935; Sym. no.3 "American," 1936–9, rev. 1946; The Golden Spike [= 2nd movt of Sym. no.3], 1939; Sym. no.4 "1942," 1942; Water-Music for 4th-of-July Evening, str, 1942–3; Decatur at Algiers, 1943

Heroes of Today [= 1st movt of Sym. no.6], 1945; Over the Plains, 1945; Sym. no.5 "Tragic," 1945–6; Vn Conc., 1946; Spectre of the Rose Waltz [arr. from film], 1946–7; Autumn Song "An Andante for Orch," 1947; Sym. no.5 "Joyous," 1947–8; Sym. no.6 "after Delacroix," 1947–8, rev. 1949–50; American Dance Suite no. 1, 1948; McKonkeys Ferry Ov., 1948; Serenade, str, 1948; Serenade II, chamber orch, 1949; Tom Sawyer, 1949; Accordion Dance, 1951; Nocturne in Skyrockets, 1951

VOCAL

(choral)

Election (Antheil) [from opera Transatlantic], *c*1927, lost; Merry-go-round from "Candide" [from inc. musical play after Voltaire], 1v, unison chorus, pf, 1932; 8 Fragments from Shelley, chorus, pf, 1951, 3 movts orchd 1951; Cabeza de vaca (A. Dowling, after A. Nuñez), cantata, mixed chorus, 1955–6, orchd E. Gold, 1959

(songs, 1v, pf, unless otherwise stated)

5 Songs (A. Crapsey): November Night, Triad, Suzanna and the Elders, Fate Defied, The Warning, 1919–20; 5 Lieder, 1922; You are Old Father William (L. Carroll), 1924; Turtle Soup (Carroll), 1924; Nightpiece (Joyce), 1930; 6 Songs: The Vision of Love (G. Russell), Down by the Sally Gardens (Yeats), The Sorrow of Love (Yeats), Lightning (D. H. Lawrence), I Hear an Army (Joyce), An End Piece (F. M. Ford), 1933; Frankie and Johnny [arr.], 1936

Songs of Experience (Blake): The Garden of Love, A Poison Tree, The School Boy, The Sick Rose, The Little Vagabond, I Told my Love, I Laid me Down upon a Bank, Infant Sorrow, The Tyger, 1948; 2 Odes (Keats): Ode to a Nightingale, Ode on a Grecian Urn, speaker, pf, 1950; Sighs and Grones (Herbert), 1956; The Ballade of Jessie James, n.d.; Bequest (M. Shelton), n.d.; Madonna of the Evening Flowers (A. Lowell), n.d.; Song of Spring, n.d.; In Time of Death (Lowell), n.d.

CHAMBER

Sym. for 5 Insts, fl, bn, tpt, trbn, va, 1st version, 1922–3, 2nd version, 1923; Vn Sonata no. 1, 1923; Vn Sonata no.2, vn, pf, drums, 1923; Vn Sonata no.3, 1924; Str Qt, 1st version, 1924, 2nd version, 1925; Str Qt no.2, 1927, rev. 1943; Concertino, fl, bn, pf, 1930

6 Little Pieces, str qt, 1931; Concert, chamber orch, wind qnt, cbn/db, tpt, trbn, 1932; Sonatina, vn, vc/pf, 1932; Vn Sonatina, 1945; Vn Sonata no.4 (no.2), vn, pf, 1947–8; Str Qt no.3, 1948; Fl Sonata, 1951; Tpt Sonata, 1951; Bohemian Grove at Night, fl, ob/eng hn, cl, b cl, bn, 1952

PIANO

Fireworks and the Profane Waltzers, 1919, part lost; Golden Bird, 1921, orchd *c*1921; 4-hand Suite, 1922, rev. 1939; Airplane Sonata (Sonata no.2), 1921; Sonata Sauvage (Sonata no.1), 1922 or 1923; Death of Machines (Sonata no.3), 1923; Jazz Sonata (Sonata no.4), 1922 or 1923; Sonata no.5, 1923, part lost; Sonata, 1923; Woman Sonata (Sonata no.6), *c*1923, lost; The Perfect Modernist, *c*1923, lost; Mechanisms, pianola, 1923 or 1924, lost

Habañera, Tarantelle, Serenata, 2 pf, 1924; Sonatina für Radio, 1929; Tango [from opera Transatlantic], arr. A. Steinbrecher, *c*1930; La femme 100 têtes, 44 preludes and Perc Dance, 1933; La vie Parisienne, 1939; Suite, pedagogical, 1941; The Ben Hecht Valses, 1943; Musical Picture of a Friend, 1946; Sonata no.3, 1947; Prelude, d, *c*1948; Sonata no.4, 1948; 2 Toccatas, 1948; Valentine Waltzes, 1949; Sonata no.5, 1950; Waltzes from Volpone [arr. from opera], 1955; Piano Pastels, pedagogical, 1956

FILM, TELEVISION, AND RADIO SCORES

Ballet mécanique [music never synchronized with film; see under ORCHESTRAL]; Harlem Picture, 1934 or 1935; Once in a Blue Moon, 1935; The Scoundrel, 1935, lost; The Plainsman, 1936; Make Way for Tomorrow, 1937, lost; The Buccaneer, 1938, lost; Music to a World's Fair Film for World's Communications Building, 1939, lost; Angels Over Broadway, 1940; Orchids for Charlie, 1941; The Plainsman and the Lady, 1946; Spectre of the Rose, 1946; That Brennan Girl, 1946; Repeat Performance, 1947; The Fighting Kentuckian, 1949; Knock on Any Door, 1949; Tokyo Joe, 1949

We Were Strangers, 1949, lost; House by the River, 1950; In a Lonely Place, 1950, lost; Sirocco, 1951; Actors and Sin, 1952, lost; The Juggler, 1952; The Sniper, 1952; Conquest of the Air (television), 1955, lost; Dementia, 1955; Hunters of the Deep, 1955; Not as a Stranger, 1955; Target Ploesti (television), 1955, lost; The Pride and the Passion, 1957; The Young Don't Cry, 1957, only 2 songs extant; Woman Without Shadow (CBS television), 1957; The Twentieth Century Series, 10 CBS television documentaries, 1957–8; 2 Edward R. Murrow programs, 1959, lost; Rough Sketch, n.d.; Airpower (television), n.d.; The Path and the Door (radio), n.d.

MSS in *CLU-MUS, DLC, GU, KyLoU-Ar, NRU-Mus, PPCI*

Principal publishers: Antheil Press, Boosey & Hawkes, Leeds, Schirmer, Universal, Weintraub

BIBLIOGRAPHY

EwenD

H. Stuckenschmidt: "Umschau: Ausblick in die Musik," *Das Kunstblatt*, vii (1923), 221

M. Lee: "George Antheil: Europe's American Composer," *The Reviewer*, iv/4 (1924), 267

E. Pound: *Antheil and the Treatise on Harmony with Supplementary Notes* (Paris, 1924, 2/1927/*R*1968)

——: "George Antheil," *Criterion: a Quarterly Review*, ii/7 (1924), 321

W. Atheling [E. Pound]: "Notes for Performers," *Transatlantic Review*, i/2 (1924), 111, i/5 (1924), 370, ii/2 (1924), 222[with marginalia by Antheil]

E. Pound: "Treatise on Harmony," *Transatlantic Review*, i/3 (1924), 77

A. Copland: "George Antheil," *League of Composers Review*, ii/1 (1925), 26

E. Walsh, ed.: Antheil suppl. to *This Quarter*, i/2 (1925)

A. Copland: "America's Young Men of Promise," *MM*, iii/3 (1926), 13

E. Pound: "Antheil, 1924–1926," *New Criterion*, iv (1926), 695

E. Cushing: "The Antheil Episode," *The Arts*, xi/5 (1927), 271

R. Hammond: "Ballyhoo," *MM*, iv/4 (1927), 30

A. Lincoln Gillespie, Jr.: "Antheil & Stravinski," *Transition*, xiii (1928), 142

S. Salt: "Antheil and America," *Transition*, xii (1928), 176

L. Zukofsky: "Critique of Antheil," *The Exile*, iv (1928), 81

[L. Liebling]: "Variations," *Musical Courier*, c (22 Feb 1930), 37

T. Wiesengrund-Adorno: "Transatlantic," *MM*, vii/4 (1930), 38

R. Thompson: "American Composers: V George Antheil," *MM*, viii/4 (1931), 17

A. Copland: "Our Younger Generation Ten Years Later," *MM*, xiii/4 (1936), 3

"Antheil, 1945," *New Yorker*, xxi/15 (26 May 1945), 17

G. Antheil: *Bad Boy of Music* (Garden City, NJ, 1945/*R*1981)[autobiography]

D. Friede: *The Mechanical Angel: his Adventures and Enterprises in the Glittering 1920's* (New York, 1948)

L. Morton: "An Interview with George Antheil," *Film Music Notes*, x/11 (1950), 4

H. Stoddard: "Stop Looking – and Listen! An Interview with George Antheil," *International Musician*, xliv/5 (1950), 24, 33

P. Lesser and F. Moore: "George Antheil: *8 Fragments from Shelley*," *Notes*, ix (1951–2), 494

"Antheil, George," *CBY 1954*

R. Sabin: "George Antheil: Sixth Symphony," *Notes*, xiii (1955–6), 145

W. Hoffa: "Ezra Pound and George Antheil: Vorticist Music and the *Cantos*," *American Literature*, xliv/1 (1972), 52

C. Amirkhanian: "An Introduction to George Antheil," *Soundings*, vii–viii (1973), 176

G. Freedman: "George Antheil: Ballet Mécanique," *MJ*, xxxiv/3 (1976), 10

E. Schönberger: "The Nightmare of George 'Bad Boy of Music' Antheil," trans. K. Freeman, *Key Notes*, iv/2 (1976), 48

D. Albee: *George Antheil's "La femme 100 têtes": a Study of the Piano Preludes* (diss., U. of Texas, Austin, 1977)

W. Shirley: "Another American in Paris: George Antheil's Correspondence with Mary Curtis Bok," *Quarterly Journal of the Library of Congress*, xxxiv/1 (1977), 2

A. Henderson: *Pound and Music: the Paris and Early Rapallo Years* (diss., UCLA, 1983) [incl. bibliography of Antheil's writings]

L. Whitesitt: *The Life and Music of George Antheil, 1900–1959* (Ann Arbor, MI, 1983) [incl. complete catalogue of works, discography, and full bibliography]

H. Ford: *Paris Portraits: Six Americans in Paris* (in preparation)

LINDA WHITESITT, CHARLES AMIRKHANIAN

Anthem. A sacred choral composition, of 16th-century English origin, usually a setting of English prose text taken or adapted from scripture. It was adopted by 18th-century American composers and tunebook compilers and became the principal non-congregational form of American Protestant vocal church music (*see also* PSALMODY).

1. To 1800. 2. The 19th century. 3. After 1900.

1. TO 1800. The models for the American anthem were the English anthems in the collections of church music brought by immigrants or imported from England; such works began to appear in American publications about the middle of the 18th century. The most important of the English collections were William Tans'ur's *The Royal Melody Compleat* (1754–5) and Aaron Williams's *The Universal Psalmodist* (1763); the first American publication to include a significant number of English anthems was James Lyon's *Urania* (1761), but two other Americans, Josiah Flagg of Boston and Daniel Bayley of Newburyport, Massachusetts, were more influential in the introduction of the anthem to the New World. Flagg issued 16 works in *A Collection of Tans'ur's and a Number of Other Anthems* (1766), and Bayley was responsible for printing and distributing Tans'ur's collection as well as his own *New Universal Harmony* (1773), which contained 20 anthems by seven English composers, including John Arnold, William Knapp, Joseph Stephenson, and Aaron Williams. Bayley also published John Stickney's *The Gentleman and Lady's Musical Companion* (1774), the largest collection of English anthems compiled in America during the 18th century. Among the most popular anthems taken from English sources were Tans'ur's *O clap your hands* and *O give ye thanks unto the Lord*, Knapp's *The beauty of Israel is slain* and *Give the king thy judgments*, Williams's *Arise, shine, o Zion* and *O Lord God of Israel*, and Arnold's *The beauty of Israel*. English composers and musicians such as William Tuckey and William Selby were also influential when they immigrated to the colonies and established themselves as leaders of the musical communities in New York and Boston.

These English anthems were generally composed for rural Anglican parishes or nonconformist congregations; they were a little longer than the more numerous psalm tunes and hymns of the period, and were typically unaccompanied works for four-part mixed chorus with occasional brief solos. Each line of the text, usually a prose paraphrase of verses from the book of *Psalms*, served as the basis of an independent section; most sections were chordal with only short imitative passages.

After Independence, works by native composers quickly outnumbered English ones in American publications. Of about 7000 sacred compositions published in the USA up to 1810, about 200 are anthems by Americans. Most were printed, alongside the simpler and slighter plain tunes, fuging-tunes, and set-pieces, in the tunebooks of singing-school masters; they were performed in singing-school "assemblies" (concerts), as well as in services of worship, where they were most often sung during collection of the offering, thus functioning both as concert pieces and as part of the service.

The center of anthem composition during the 18th century was New England, where the pioneer was William Billings. Among the best-known of his 47 anthems are *Lamentation over Boston* (the first line of which parodies Psalm cxxxvii), *Retrospect*, and *David's Lamentation* (all three from *The Singing Master's Assistant*, 1778), and *Be glad then, America* (from *The Continental Harmony*, 1794). Other prolific composers of anthems were Oliver Holden, Jacob French, Amos Bull, and Samuel Holyoke. Holden, who composed 25 anthems, leaned heavily on Martin Madan's "Lock Collection" (London, 1769) as a model for his style and a source of materials to borrow; his own collections, such as the *Charlestown Collection* (1803), reflect the English veneration of Handel and other continental composers. Another New England composer of anthems was Justin Morgan; his *Judgment Anthem* ("Hark, ye mortals, hear the trumpet") is an especially lengthy example of the genre (lasting about seven minutes), with vivid pictorialism, contrasting textures, and startling shifts back and forth between the keys of E minor and E♭ major.

Outside the mainstream were the German-speaking immigrants, most notably the Moravians, who settled in Pennsylvania and North Carolina (*see* MORAVIAN CHURCH, MUSIC OF THE). Chief among them were Christian Gregor, Johannes Herbst, John Antes, and J. F. Peter. Herbst composed more than 115 anthems during the 15 years of his residence in the USA (1787–1812), among them the moving chorale-anthem for chorus and orchestra *O Haupt voll Blut und Wunden*. Antes's best-known anthem is the solo and chorus *Go, congregation, go! – Surely he has borne our griefs* (1795). A few Moravian anthems were printed in 19th-century American collections, but most were not known outside the sect's isolated communities. Many, unlike the English imports or the New England examples, call for organ accompaniment and some require obbligato instruments. By the turn of the century instrumental participation in anthems was gaining ground generally. Daniel Read included an optional instrumental bass part in his *O be joyful in the Lord* (*Columbian Harmonist no.3*, 1795), and Benjamin Carr prescribed an organ accompaniment for the *Anthem for Christmas* in his collection of *Masses, Vespers, Litanies, Hymns, Psalms, Anthems & Motets* (1805). Most later anthems included at least an accompanying keyboard part.

2. THE 19TH CENTURY. During the 19th century the nationalistic fervor of the late 18th century abated, and the English anthem remained for a time the model for American composers. Immigrants, such as George K. Jackson, Benjamin Carr (in his *Miserere or the 51st Psalm*, "as chaunted in the Churches during the season of Lent"), and Edward Hodges, continued to set the standard for the new generation of native composers, the most significant of whom was Lowell Mason. Beginning with *The Boston Handel and Haydn Society Collection of Church Music* (1822), which included about a dozen anthems to music by Mozart, Madan, Arnold, Jackson, and other lesser figures, Mason established a formula adopted by many of his contemporaries and successors – the adaptation of European works, both vocal and instrumental, to English words for publication as anthems. George Webb, Nathaniel Gould, Thomas Hastings, William Bradbury, and Isaac Woodbury, among others, followed Mason's example in publishing collections of church music that included such anthems alongside original works.

During the second half of the 19th century the European influence on American anthems intensified because a large number of American composers studied in Europe, especially in Germany. At the same time numerous anthems by native composers were published, either singly or in collections in periodicals; they appeared in such numbers because the genre was functional and not too difficult to compose, and the market was great. Edmund Lorenz, following the example of Novello's *Musical Times* in England, began in 1894 to issue the *Choir Leader*, a monthly publication containing anthems suitable for choirs of modest abilities. The Lorenz firm helped to popularize the octavo format for church music publications and also provided outlets for many anthem composers; among these were a number of women, including Mrs. E. L. Ashford, who published a steady stream of anthems in the Lorenz periodicals. Most of these works were as undistinguished and undemanding as their English counterparts, although some anthems by Americans trained in Europe were musically admirable.

Most influential among the European-trained Americans were Dudley Buck and Horatio Parker. Buck spent four years in Leipzig and Paris before returning to serve as organist and choirmaster in several American cities; he composed 55 anthems, a number of them for the "quartet choir" of professionally trained soloists that had become increasingly fashionable in city churches as a replacement for volunteer choirs. His *Rock of Ages* and the highly chromatic *Sing, alleluia forth* (both *c*1873) are notable. Parker, who served churches in New York and Boston before becoming Yale University's first professor of music (1894), composed numerous anthems, among which *The Lord is my light* (1890), a well-crafted, three-part structure, is especially effective.

Buck's pupils, especially Harry Rowe Shelley and William H. Neidlinger, also developed a large following among church musicians: Shelley's *The king of love my shepherd is* (1886) and Neidlinger's *The Silent Sea* (1908) and *The Birthday of a King* (1890) remained popular for more than half a century. The rise of the hymn-anthem, a straightforward choral piece based on a familiar text and melody, dates from this period; many representative examples of the genre were composed by P. A. Schnecker (*My faith looks up to thee*) and George B. Nevin (*Jesus, my Saviour! look on me*, 1899). Charles Ives also contributed to it, with *Crossing the Bar* (?1891); other sacred choral works by him that have been used as anthems include *Easter Carol* (1892) and the remarkable series of psalm settings (?summer 1894) that are the major achievement of his early years.

3. AFTER 1900. The publication of immense numbers of American anthems continued in the 20th century. Some of the most prolific composers have produced music lacking in taste, originality, and artistic merit. But others have enjoyed deserved success, among them Carl F. Mueller (*We come unto our father's God,*

1946, and *Come, Christians, join to sing*, 1948), Everett Titcomb (*Ride on, ride on in majesty*, 1949), Leo Sowerby (*Love came down at Christmas*, 1935, among almost 100 anthems), Clarence Dickinson, and F. Melius Christiansen. Dickinson based some of his anthems on folksongs; *What a wonder*, for example, is a setting with instruments and organ of a Lithuanian tune. Christiansen used German and Scandinavian chorales as the basis for many unaccompanied but full-textured works, among which *Beautiful Savior* (1919) and *Wake, awake, for night is flying* (1925) became especially popular. One development, dating from about 1910 and lasting past the mid-century, was the adaptation to English texts of anthem-like compositions originally written for the Russian Orthodox liturgy – majestic, chordal works for unaccompanied choir, with rich, resonant textures that compensated for the lack of instruments in the Russian service. Pieces by such composers as Alexandr Kastal'sky, Dmitry Bortnyansky, and Rachmaninoff, and by their American imitators, served many different churches until this style fell out of favor.

Many major 20th-century American composers have occasionally composed works to religious texts, which, in parishes where liturgical niceties are not too rigidly observed, can serve as anthems: Stevenson (1966) comments on works by Barber, Copland, Ross Lee Finney, Foss, Hanson, Hovhaness, Dello Joio, Normand Lockwood, Mennin, Persichetti, and Sowerby on texts ranging "from the creation poem in Genesis, psalms in both scriptural prose and rough-hewn Bay Psalm Book meter, selections from such other books of the Bible as Isaiah, Ecclesiastes, and Luke's gospel, to John Chrysostom's Greek liturgy and selected prayers from Kierkegaard." Other composers especially associated with church composition who have found wide acceptance for their anthems include Pinkham (*Thou hast loved righteousness*, 1964), Austin C. Lovelace (*The beauty of the Lord*, 1946), Dale Wood (*God is made the sure foundation*, 1959), and Jane M. Marshall (*Blessed is the man*, 1960 and *My eternal King*, 1959).

BIBLIOGRAPHY

L. Ellinwood: *The History of American Church Music* (New York, 1953/*R*1970)

E. A. Wienandt: *Choral Music of the Church* (New York, 1965/*R*1980)

R. T. Daniel: *The Anthem in New England before 1800* (Evanston, IL, 1966/*R*1979)

R. Stevenson: *Protestant Church Music in America* (New York, 1966)

E. A. Wienandt and R. H. Young: *The Anthem in England and America* (New York, 1970)

R. Crawford and D. P. McKay: *William Billings of Boston* (Princeton, NJ, 1975)

N. Temperley: *The Music of the English Parish Church* (Cambridge, England, 1979)

RALPH T. DANIEL/ELWYN A. WIENANDT

Anthony, Jacob (*b* Germany, 1736; *d* Philadelphia, PA, 29 Dec 1804). Woodwind instrument maker. Jacob Anthony was one of the earliest woodwind makers to bring his skills to America. He arrived in Philadelphia about 1764 and continued in business as a turner and musical instrument maker until his death in 1804. Two of his instruments are in the Dayton C. Miller collection at the Library of Congress. One of these is an excellent ebony flute with three graduated upper joints, a foot extension to *c'*, and five silver keys. Although this instrument has a *c'* key there is no key for *c♯'*. Anthony's business was continued by his son Jacob Anthony, Jr., until 1811.

ROBERT E. ELIASON

Anthony, Lamont. Pseudonym under which Lamont Dozier made recordings before he became a member of the HOLLAND–DOZIER–HOLLAND songwriting and record-producing team.

Antoniou, Theodore (*b* Athens, Greece, 10 Feb 1935). Greek composer. In Athens he studied violin, singing, and composition at the National Conservatory (1947–58) and composition under Yannis Andreou Papaioannou at the Hellenic Conservatory (1956–61); he also studied composition and conducting with Günter Bialas at the Munich Musikhochschule, where he gained his first experience in electronic music (1961–5). During 1966 he toured the USA at the invitation of the State Department, and a grant from the Deutscher Akademischer Austauschdienst and the city of Berlin enabled him to spend 1968 in Berlin. In 1967 he founded a contemporary music group in Athens; he has also founded other such ensembles, including Alea II (Stanford), Alea III (Boston), and the Philadelphia New Music Group. He has taught composition and orchestration at Stanford University (1969–70), the University of Utah (1970), the Philadelphia Musical Academy (1970–77), the Berkshire Music Center (1975), and the University of Pennsylvania (1978); in 1979 he joined the faculty of Boston University. He has been active as a conductor and has made several recordings for Columbia, conducting his own works and those of other composers; in 1974 he was appointed assistant director of contemporary activities for the Berkshire Music Center Orchestra. Besides several European awards he has received two NEA grants (1975, 1977) and many commissions, including those from the Koussevitzky Foundation for *Fluxus I* (1972) and from the Fromm Foundation for *Epigrams* (1981). Antoniou is a prolific composer; his music hesitated at first between a somewhat naive atonality (Violin Sonatina, 1959) and an engaging Bartókian folklorism (Trio, 1961). Later he turned to modified serial procedures in works with elegantly designed small forms. The influences of Jani Christou, Bernd Alois Zimmermann, and Krzysztof Penderecki became evident in the large-scale works of the early 1970s.

WORKS

STAGE

Noh-Musik (music theater), 4 pfmrs, 1964; Clytemnestra (sound-action, T. Roussos), actresses, dancers, orch, tape, 1967; Cassandra (sound-action for television), dancers, actors, chorus, lights, projections, 1969; Protest I, actors, tape, 1970; Protest II, medium v, actors, tape, synth, 1971; Aftosyngentrossipetrama [Meditation-experiment], mixed media, 1972

Chorochronos I, Bar, nar, insts, film, slides, lighting, 1973; Periander (opera, Y. Christodoulakis, Ger. trans. P. Kertz), 1977–9; Bacchae (ballet), chamber orch, tape, 1980; The Magic World (ballet, S. Lambert), 1984; incidental music to over 30 plays; several film scores

ORCHESTRAL

Conc., cl, tpt, vn, orch, 1959; Ov., 1961; Antitheses, 1962; Pf Concertino, 1962; Jeux, vc, str, 1963; Micrographies, 1964; Vn Conc., 1965; Kinesis ABCD, 2 str orch, 1966; Op Ov., orch, tape, 1966; Events 1, vn, pf, orch, 1967–8, II, 1969, III, small orch, tape, slides, 1969; Threnos, wind ens, pf, perc, db, 1972; Fluxus I, 1974–5; Fluxus II, pf, chamber orch, 1975; Double Conc., perc, orch, 1977; The GBYSO Music, 1982

CHORAL

Greek Folk Songs I–V, VI–X, SATB, 1961; Epirus [after folksongs], 1962; Kontakion (Romanos the Melode), S, Mez, T, B, chorus, str, 1965; 10 School Songs, 1965–6; Nenikíkamen [We are victorious] (T. S. Tolia), Mez, Bar, nar, chorus, 1971; Verleih uns Frieden [after Schütz], 3 choruses, 1971–2; Die weisse Rose (Tolia, others), Bar, 3 nar, children's chorus, chorus, orch, 1974–5; Circle of Thanatos and Genesis (T. Antoniou), cantata, T, nar, chorus, orch, 1977–8; Die Revolution der Toten: Antiliturgy, S, A, T, B, SATB, orch, 1981; Prometheus (Aeschylus), cantata, Bar, nar, mixed chorus, orch, 1983; smaller works

SOLO VOCAL

8 Musical Pictures, 1v, pf, 1953; Melos (Sappho), Mez, Bar, orch, 1962; Epilogue (Odyssey), Mez, nar, 6 insts, 1963; Klima tis apoussias [Climate of Absence] (O. Elytis), Bar, chamber orch, 1968; Moirologia for Jani Christou, medium v, 6 insts/pf, 1970; Parodies (H. Ball), 1v, pf, 1970; Chorochronos II (sacred

texts, Eliot), 1v, orch, 1973; Chorochronos III (sacred texts), Bar, pf, perc, tape, 1975

Epigrams (from Gk., Lat. trans. Antoniou), S, chamber orch, 1981; 11 Aphighisis (Kavafis), medium v, pf, 1983, arr. medium v, chamber orch, 1984; Oneiro Mega (D. Kakavelakis), S, T, nar, chamber orch, 1984

INSTRUMENTAL AND TAPE

Large ens: Suite, 8 insts, 1960; Concertino, pf, 9 wind, perc, 1963; Katharsis, fl, ens, tape, lights, 1968; Cheironomiai [Gestures], at least 8 pfmrs, 1971; Synthesis, ob, elec org, perc, db, 4 synth, 1971; Circle of Accusation, 16 insts, 1975; Parastasis II, perc, chamber ens, tape, 1977; DO Qnt, 2 tpt, hn, tuba, perc, tape, 1978

Small ens: Sonatina, vn, pf, 1959; Str Qt, 1960; Trio, fl, va, vc, 1961; Dialogues, fl, gui, 1962; Quartetto giocoso, ob, pf trio, 1965; Lyrics, vn, pf, 1967; Stichomythia, fl, gui, 1976; Parastasis, perc, tape, 1977

Solo inst: Aquarelles, pf, 1958; Pf Sonata, 1959; Vn Sonata, 1961; Music, harp, 1965; Sil-ben, pf, 1965; 6 Likes, tuba, 1967; 5 Likes, ob, 1969; 4 Likes, vn, bells, 1972; 3 Likes, cl, 1973; 2 Likes, db, 1976; Stichomythia II, gui, 1977; Prelude and Toccata, pf, 1982; Entrata, pf, 1983

Tape: Gravity, video, 1966; Heterophony, 1966; Telecommunications, 1970; early works

Principal publishers: Antoniou, Bärenreiter, Modern, G. Schirmer

BIBLIOGRAPHY

VintonD

K. Hashagen: "Theodor Antoniou," *Musica*, xxii (1968), 276

N. Skalottas: "T. Antoniou," *SMz*, cix (1969), 136

K. Kirchberg: "Noten: der Weg zur Klang-Aktion," *Musica*, xxx (1976), 62

D. Rosenberg and B. Rosenberg: *The Music Makers* (New York, 1979), 71

GEORGE LEOTSAKOS/R

Apache. American Indians of northwestern, north-central, and southeastern New Mexico, southeastern Arizona, the southern Plains, and northern Mexico (*see* INDIANS, AMERICAN, fig.1). Numbering about 14,000, they are divided into six tribes, all southern Athapaskan: Jicarilla, Lipan, Kiowa-Apache, Mescalero, Chiricahua, and Western Apache (of whom four internal subdivisions are recognized: White Mountain, San Carlos, Cibecue, and Tonto groups). All speak Apachean dialects closely related to that of the NAVAJO, and in many respects their culture is a conservative form of the way of life of their Navajo neighbors. This similarity extends to their music.

Like that of all American Indians, the traditional music of the Apache is almost entirely vocal. A chorus–verse–chorus alternation, an old Athapaskan musical form, is found in most Apache traditional music, both popular and sacred, in contrast to the multiplicity of musical forms used by the Navajo. The Apache vocal style is strikingly nasal and rises to falsetto in some of the (highly melodic) choruses. The verses, more like chants, are sung with a choppy, almost parlando delivery. Some syllables are sharply emphasized and others suddenly muffled or swallowed. The tonal system very often incorporates major or minor triads.

A focal point in traditional Apache culture is the girls' puberty rite (see illustration), which is considered to support the life of the whole tribe. Long song cycles celebrate the life story of Changing Woman, or White Painted Woman, the principal deity, in her role as creator and source of fertility. There may be one or several young girls honored in the ceremony, where they are identified with Changing Woman. Curing ceremonies reenact other aspects of the Apache creation story. Deities such as Monster Slayer, White God, and Black God, and various forces of nature such as wind, lightning, and prototypical birds and animals, are invoked in song and prayer for help in curing those for whom the ceremonies are performed. Designs in colored pigments may be laid out on the floor of the ceremonial shelter to depict the powers being appealed to. At curing or puberty rites a special feature may be included – an appearance of mountain gods represented by masked dancers wearing headdresses of crown-like wooden slats in carved and painted designs. The dancers' strong,

Apache puberty ceremony, Western Apache, San Carlos reservation, Arizona, March 1981

straddling steps and repetitive calls are thought to bring mountain power to the occasion.

Besides the ritual music, the traditional Apache repertory includes social dance-songs, songs honoring great warriors of the past, and joking songs to accompany small drinking parties. Moccasin Game songs accompany a form of gambling in which tokens are concealed by one side and their location is guessed by the other. The songs mention humorous incidents from the creation story to confuse the guessers.

The Apache fiddle, which has one or two strings stretched on a length of century-plant stalk, is one of the few string instruments among North American Indians (for further details, *see* KÍZH KÍZH DÍHÍ and INDIANS, AMERICAN, §6(i)). Most fiddle tunes derive from the drinking-song repertory. Another Apache musical instrument is a flageolet made of river cane with three stops tuned approximately to the first, third, fourth, and fifth degrees of a diatonic major scale. Short repetitive melodies are played with a breathy overblowing technique and a wide vibrato. The drum, used in most ceremonial music, is made of a large iron pot with water inside and a wet buckskin stretched over the mouth. Two or three drummers play in unison on the same instrument, producing a deep, booming accompaniment for the voice.

New musics of the Apache include the songs of the Native American Church (Peyote religion) and of other recent movements such as the Silas John religion and the various Christian denominations on the reservations. Records and tapes of powwow music in Plains Indian style are prized, and country and rock music are favorites in radio entertainment. Ritual music, somewhat revised, and traditional popular songs, such as social songs and love-songs, have been recorded by Philip Cassadore and his sister Patsy. A. Paul Ortega has invented a hybrid music with his own unique vocables and instrumental accompaniments; his lyrics stress Apache values, such as friendship and an understanding of nature.

Recordings of Apache music are in the holdings of the Wesleyan University Archive of World Music, Middletown, Connecticut; the Indiana University Archives of Traditional Music, Bloomington, Indiana; and the Archive of Folk Culture, Library of Congress, Washington, DC.

See also INDIANS, AMERICAN, esp. §I, 4(ii)(c), and COURTING FLUTE, fig. 1.

DISCOGRAPHY

Music of the Pueblos, Apache, and Navaho (Taylor Museum, Colorado Springs, R61-1317, 1961)

Apache: Songs by Philip and Patsy Cassadore of the San Carlos Apache Tribe (Can. ARP6053, 1966)

Philip Cassadore: *Apache Songs in the Authentic Rhythms and Language* (Can. ARP6056, 1968)

The Three Worlds of A. Paul Ortega (Waltiska, *c*1974)

BIBLIOGRAPHY

D. Nicholas: "Mescalero Apache Girl's Puberty Ceremony," *El palacio*, xlvi (1939), 193

M. E. Opler: *An Apache Life Way* (Chicago, 1941/*R*1965)

——: *The Character and Derivation of the Jicarilla Holiness Rites* (Albuquerque, 1943)

C. L. Sonnichsen: *The Mescalero Apaches* (Norman, OK, 1958)

D. P. McAllester: "The Role of Music in Western Apache Culture," *Men and Cultures: Selected Papers of the Fifth International Congress of Anthropological and Ethnological Sciences: Philadelphia, 1956*, ed. A. F. C. Wallace (Philadelphia, 1960)

D. P. McAllester: *Indian Music of the Southwest* (Colorado Springs, 1961)

M. E. Opler: *An Apache Odyssey: a Journey Between Two Worlds* (New York, 1969)

K. H. Basso: *The Cibecue Apache* (New York, 1970)

D. A. Gunnerson: *The Jicarilla Apaches: a Study in Survival* (DeKalb, IL, 1974)

C. R. Farrer: "Singing for Life: the Mescalero Apache Girls Puberty Ceremony," *Southwestern Indian Ritual Drama*, ed. C. J. Frisbie (Albuquerque, 1980), 125–59

DAVID P. MCALLESTER

Apel, Willi (*b* Konitz [now Chojnice, Poland], 10 Oct 1893). Musicologist. He studied mathematics at the universities of Bonn and Munich (1912–14) and the University of Berlin (1918–22). His interests turned to musicology in the 1920s, in which field he was largely self-taught; in 1936 he was awarded the doctorate in Berlin and came to the USA. He taught at Harvard University (1938–42) and Indiana University, Bloomington (1950–70). Apel's first large books in English were remarkable for their timeliness and durability. *The Notation of Polyphonic Music: 900–1600* (1942) is still an essential tool for young scholars. The *Harvard Dictionary of Music* (1944, enlarged 2/1969) and *Historical Anthology of Music* (with A. T. Davison, 1946; rev. 2/1950) show an attitude of "historical equality" in according earlier and exotic musics as much attention as the familiar ground. These three works were major agents in changing the climate of higher music education in the USA. Apel then turned to his favorite studies, on which he has published numerous articles: the notation of 14th-century music, Latin chant, and the history of instrumental music. His work on the problems of transcribing late 14th-century music culminated in *French Secular Compositions of the Fourteenth Century* (1970–71). In *Gregorian Chant* (1958) Apel provided, for the first time in English, a reliable guide to the entire field of plainsong. In his *Geschichte der Orgel- und Klaviermusik* (1967; Eng. trans., rev., 1972) and *Die italienische Violinmusik im 17. Jahrhundert* (1983; a collection of articles first published in *AMw*, xxx–xxxv, 1973–8) he exhaustively reviewed two important repertories. He was the founding editor of the Corpus of Early Keyboard Music, to which he has contributed ten volumes and his pupils many more.

See also DICTIONARIES, §1.

JOHN REEVES WHITE/JOHN CALDWELL/R

Apollo Club. Choral society founded in Chicago in 1872. *See* CHICAGO (i), §1.

Aponte-Ledée, Rafael (*b* Guayama, Puerto Rico, 15 Oct 1938). Composer. After studying harmony, counterpoint, composition, and piano at the Madrid Conservatory with Cristóbal Halffter and others (1957–64), he attended the Latin American Institute of Higher Musical Studies, Di Tella Institute, in Buenos Aires (diploma 1966). In 1966 he returned to Puerto Rico, where with the composer Francis Schwartz he was instrumental in promoting avant-garde music through the organization of the festivals, the Puerto Rico Biennials of 20th-century Music I (1978), II (1980), III (1982), and IV (1984); he has also taught music theory and composition at the University of Puerto Rico (1968–73) and at the Puerto Rico Conservatory (from 1968), where he is an associate professor. In his compositions Aponte-Ledée has explored many facets of modern expression ranging from electronic music (*Presagio de pájaros muertos*, *Estravagario*) to experiments in the playing techniques of traditional instruments such as percussive pizzicato and bowing below the bridge on string instruments, blowing through woodwind instruments in manners that create pitchless sounds, and striking the mouthpieces of brass instruments with the palm of the hand (*Elejía*, *Impulsos*).

WORKS

Orch: Elejía, 1965, rev. 1967; Impulsos, in memoriam Julia de Burgos, 1967; Estravagario, in memoriam Salvador Allende, orch, tape, 1973; El palacio en sombras, 1977

Chamber: Dialogantes 1, fl, va, 1965; Dialogantes 2, 3 fl, 3 cl, 3 trbn, 1968; Epíthasis, 3 ob, 2 trbn, db, 3 perc, 1968; Tentativas, vn, ens, tape, 1969; ¡Aquí, presente!, 5 tpt, 1969; $SSSSSS_2$, db, 3 fl, tpt, perc, 1971

Pf: Tema y 6 diferencias, 1963; Volúmenes, 1971

Vocal (wordless): Presagio de pájaros muertos, nar, tape, 1966; La ventana abierta, 3 Mez, chamber ens, 1968, rev. 1969; Streptomicyne, S, chamber ens, 1970, version for chamber ens only, 1971

Numerous other works for various combinations of insts; other vocal works; other tape pieces

BIBLIOGRAPHY

Compositores de América/Composers of the Americas, ed. Pan American Union, xvii (Washington, DC, 1971), 23

DONALD THOMPSON

Appalachian dulcimer [lap dulcimer, mountain dulcimer, Kentucky dulcimer, plucked dulcimer]. A fretted zither developed in the southern Appalachian mountains of the eastern USA from a zither found among German immigrant communities in Pennsylvania. Variant names in the area include "delcimer," "dulcymore," "harmonium," "hog fiddle," "music box," and "harmony box." The instrument (unrelated to the HAMMERED DULCIMER) consists of a narrow fingerboard attached to a larger soundbox underneath. It is usually about 75 to 90 cm long, its width varying according to the shape of the soundbox, commonly hourglass or oval, though diamond, rectangular, and other shapes are found. Instruments made before 1940 had three, four, or sometimes six metal strings stretched over a fingerboard divided by frets into two and a half to three octaves of a diatonic scale. Whereas frets on these instruments were under only the first two strings, most dulcimers made since 1940 have frets extending over the full width of the fingerboard. The instrument was traditionally tuned to the Ionian (major) mode. A standard tuning had the first (treble) and middle strings at the same pitch, a 5th or an octave above the third (bass) string. Other tunings accommodated other modes. Melodies were usually played on the first string only; the other strings functioned as drones.

Although the earliest known dulcimers date from the early 1800s, the instrument was in transition until at least the mid-19th century; the modern form became established during the early 1900s. There are many local variations in design and construction. European prototypes include the German *Scheitholt* and possibly the Swedish *hummel* and Norwegian *langeleik*. Dulcimers were never widespread in Appalachia, but appeared in isolated pockets of families or small communities. Settlement schools and craft cooperatives in the early 1900s helped disseminate them, and national magazines made them a popular symbol of the romanticized "Elizabethan" culture of Appalachia. The folk-music revivals of the 1940s and 1950s and such musicians as John Jacob Niles (see illustration), Jean Ritchie, Richard Fariña, Paul Clayton, and Howie Mitchell introduced the dulcimer to national and international audiences, as have recordings and public appearances by such traditional players as Frank Proffitt, I. D. Stamper, and the Russell, Hicks, and Ritchie families. Numerous dulcimer clubs have been formed in the USA, and a quarterly dulcimer magazine, *Dulcimer Players News*, began publication in Winchester, Virginia, in 1975.

The dulcimer was traditionally plucked, though sometimes bowed. Chicken quills and twigs were used as picks, although some players may have strummed with their thumb or fingers.

Appalachian dulcimer, played by John Jacob Niles

Players now use manufactured as well as traditional guitar and dulcimer picks. Many also fingerpick, adapting guitar and banjo techniques. The dulcimer was traditionally placed across the seated player's lap. Some players now hold it in a guitar position.

The dulcimer's repertory came from Anglo-American traditions of religious songs and hymns, instrumental dance tunes, and ballads – broadside and American ballads more frequently than earlier British ones. The dulcimer was often played for dances and to accompany singing. Players of the modern revival have expanded the traditional repertory enormously and have experimented with the dulcimer's musical possibilities by adding chromatic frets and capos, by having equidistant strings, by enlarging the body and lengthening the fingerboard to increase the volume and brilliance of the sound, and by developing playing techniques such as fingerpicking and chording. Electric dulcimers are now being made commercially.

BIBLIOGRAPHY

C. Seeger: "The Appalachian Dulcimer," *Journal of American Folklore*, lxxi (1958), 40

J. Ritchie: *The Dulcimer Book* (New York, 1963)

D. Kimball: *Constructing the Mountain Dulcimer* (New York, 1974)

Dulcimer Players News (Winchester, VA, 1975–)

J. Ritchie: *Jean Ritchie's Dulcimer People* (New York, [1975])

M. Murphy: *The Appalachian Dulcimer Book* (St. Clairsville, OH, 1976)

L. A. Smith: "Toward a Reconstruction of the Development of the Appalachian Dulcimer: What the Instruments Suggest," *Journal of American Folklore*, xciii (1980), 385

H. Rasof: *The Folk, Country, and Bluegrass Musician's Catalogue* (New York, 1982)

L. A. Smith: *A Catalogue of Pre-revival Appalachian Dulcimers* (Columbia, MO, 1983)

LUCY M. LONG

Appel, Toby (*b* Elmer, NJ, 22 Nov 1952). Violist and violinist. Born into a family of amateur musicians, he began viola studies with Max Aronoff, first at the New School of Music in Philadelphia, and then at the Curtis Institute. His professional musical life began at an early age, and by 15 he was playing engagements ranging from popular music and church concerts to performances with the Philadelphia Orchestra. He became assistant principal violist with the St. Louis SO in 1970 and the following year made his Carnegie Hall début. From 1975 to 1977 he was a member of the Lenox Quartet and he was on the music faculty of SUNY, Binghamton, from 1972 to 1979.

Appel has given recitals at Alice Tully Hall and the Metropolitan Museum of Art and has appeared at the Marlboro Festival. In demand as a chamber music player, he is a regular guest artist with Tashi. He has an interest in many different areas of music and gave the world première of Laderman's *Other Voices* for three violas in 1977 on a CBS television special, playing all three parts himself (live and on tape). Having taken up the violin, in part for the sake of its larger repertory, he served briefly as first violinist of the Audubon Quartet (1983–4). He has given recitals on both his instruments and in 1983–4 toured Europe and Japan with Chick Corea. In 1984 he was appointed to the faculty of the University of New Mexico, Albuquerque.

ELLEN HIGHSTEIN

Appleton, Jon (Howard) (*b* Los Angeles, CA, 4 Jan 1939). Composer. Born to a family of musicians, he studied piano and began composing as a child. He attended Reed College (BA 1961), studied privately in Berkeley, California, with Imbrie (1961–2), and then taught music at a private school in Arizona (1962–3). While at the University of Oregon (MA 1965) he studied under Homer Keller and began composing electronic music, an interest that led to further study at the Columbia-Princeton Center for Electronic Music (1965–6), principally under Ussachevsky, Davidovsky, and William J. Mitchell. He taught for a year at Oakland University, Rochester, Michigan, before joining the faculty of Dartmouth College in 1967, where he founded and directed the Bregman Electronic Music Studio and in 1979 received an endowed chair. Since 1968 Appleton has worked periodically in Sweden and in 1976 he directed the Stiftelsen Elektronmusikstudion, Stockholm (EMS). In 1973 in Tonga and in 1979 in Ponape and Truk he took part in projects to record and broadcast traditional Polynesian and Micronesian musics. He received Guggenheim and Fulbright fellowships (1970) and two NEA awards (1976). In writings for popular and scholarly publications he has dealt with the social role, aesthetics, theory, and technology of electronic music, and with Perera has edited *The Development and Practice of Electronic Music* (1975).

Appleton's electronic compositions are tonally based and his compositional techniques remain those traditional to Western music, but they are worked out using 20th-century technology – for example, musical ideas, including those based on timbre, are developed by electronic manipulation. Although much of his electronic music is synthesized, between 1967 and 1973 Appleton extended the earlier technique of *musique concrète*, often combining *concrète* and synthesized sounds. In some of his *concrète* works he exploits the tension between extramusical allusions of *concrète* sounds and their purely musical development.

In the 1970s, concerned that electronic music was functioning primarily as a "studio" rather than a "performing" art, Appleton collaborated with the engineer Sydney Alonso and the software specialist Cameron Jones to develop the Synclavier, a polyphonic digital synthesizer that can be used for live performance. Based on the Dartmouth Digital Synthesizer designed by the same team between 1972 and 1974 for use at the Bregman Electronic Music Studio, the Synclavier was the first such instrument to utilize microcomputers and the first to be manufactured commercially. In 1980 it was updated as the Synclavier II, and further developments were incorporated in 1981–2 (*see* ELECTROACOUSTIC MUSIC, §4).

WORKS

Orch: After "Nude Descending a Staircase," 1965; The American Songs (Dickinson, H. Crane), T, orch, 1966, arr. T, pf, 1966

Inst: 3 Lyrics, pf, 1963; 2 Movts, ww qnt, 1963; 6 Movts, ww qnt, 1964; 4 Explorations, vn, pf, 1964; 4 Inventions, 2 fl, 1965; Pf Sonata no.2, 1968; Winesburg, Ohio, fl, cl, vn, vc, pf, 1972; Str Qt, 1976

Vocal: 2 Songs (Brecht, J. B. Friedman), 1v, pf, 1964; The Green Wave (E. Baker), SATB, 1964; The Dying Christian to His Soul (Pope), 1v, pf, 1965; Ballad of the Soldier (Brecht), TTBB, 1974; This is America (C. Watson), SATB, 1976; Sonaria (Appleton), 4vv, live elec, 1978; The Lament of Kamuela (Appleton), 4vv, live elec, rock band, str qt, shamisen, slides, film, video, 1983

Elec: Georganna's Fancy, 1966; Chef d'oeuvre, 1967; Times Square Times Ten, 1969; Apolliana, 1970; Kungsgatan 8, 1971; Stereopticon, 1972; 'Otahiti, 1973; Ciona, dance score, 1974; Zoetrope, 1974; Georganna's Farewell, 1975; Mussems Song, 1976; In deserto, 1977; In medias res, 1978; Kapingsamarangi, live elec, 1979; Nukuoro, live elec, 1979; Sashasonjon, 1981; The Snow Queen, nar, live elec, 1981; The Sweet Dreams of Miss Pamela Beach, 1981; many other works, incl. 6 dance scores, 5 film scores

Other: Scenes Unobserved, wind, str, perc, pf, tape, film, 1969; The Bremen Town Musicians, toy pf, 12 toy insts, 1971; Dbl Structure, mixed media, collab. C. Wolff; 2 film scores, small ens; incidental music for 2 plays

Numerous works now withdrawn

BIBLIOGRAPHY

D. Walley and P. Kennely: "Electronic Composers," *Jazz & Pop*, viii/12 (1969), 26

P. Wienecke: "Music for Synclavier and other Digital Systems," *Computer Music Journal*, iii/1 (1979), 7

H. Davies: "Synclavier," *GroveI*

GENEVIEVE VAUGHN

Appleton, Thomas (*b* Boston, MA, 26 Dec 1785; *d* Reading, MA, 11 July 1872). Organ builder. After serving an apprenticeship with a Boston cabinetmaker, Appleton entered the workshop of William Goodrich in 1805. In 1811 he became a partner in the firm of Hayts, Babcock & Appleton, whose retail store was called the Franklin Musical Warehouse; Goodrich was occasionally associated with the firm, which built church and chamber organs, pianos, and claviorgans. Appleton was also a partner in the firm of Babcock, Appleton & Babcock (1813–15). In 1820 Hayts, Babcock & Appleton was dissolved, and Appleton became an independent builder, quickly gaining a reputation and securing important commissions. Between 1847 and 1850 Thomas D. Warren (whose brother, Samuel R. Warren (1809–82) was also an organ builder) was his partner; in the latter year Appleton moved his workshop from Boston to Reading, where he worked until his retirement in 1868. Appleton's most important work was carried out between 1825 and about 1845, and includes instruments made for the Bowdoin Street Church, Boston (1831), where Lowell Mason was organist; for the Handel and Haydn Society, Boston (1832); for Center Church, Hartford (1835); and for the Church of the Pilgrims, Brooklyn (1846). His work is characterized by its meticulous craftsmanship, refined tone, and, during his most active period, strikingly handsome casework, often executed in mahogany in the Greek revival style.

BIBLIOGRAPHY

W. H. Clarke: "Thomas Appleton," *The Organ*, i/2 (1892), 29

B. Owen: "The Goodriches and Thomas Appleton," *The Tracker*, iv/1 (1959), 2

O. Ochse: *The History of the Organ in the United States* (Bloomington, IN, 1975)
B. Owen: *The Organ in New England* (Raleigh, 1979)
L. Libin: "Thomas Appleton and his Organ at the Metropolitan Museum of Art," *The Tracker*, xxvii/4 (1983), 12
B. Owen: "An Early New England Organ on the West Coast," *The Tracker*, xxvii/4 (1983), 16

BARBARA OWEN

Appo, William (*b* Philadelphia, PA, *c*1808; *d* NY, after 1877). Composer, horn player, and conductor. One of the earliest black American composers, Appo worked in New York, where he performed and taught music, and Philadelphia, where he was a member of the Frank Johnson Band (1830s); he was with the band during its celebrated tour of England in 1837. Appo was also active as a singer and well known as a conductor; Daniel Alexander Payne, Bishop of the African Methodist Episcopal Church, considered him "the most learned musician of the race." His best-known compositions are an anthem, *Sing unto God*, and a composition for male voices, *John Tyler's Lamentation*, commissioned by the Utica (New York) Glee Club, probably with reference to the presidential election campaign of 1844.

BIBLIOGRAPHY

SouthernB
J. Trotter: *Music and Some Highly Musical People* (Boston, 1881/*R*1968)
D. A. Payne: *Recollections of Seventy Years* (Nashville, 1888)
E. Southern: "A Portfolio of Music: the Philadelphia Afro-American School," *BPiM*, iv (1976), 238

DORIS EVANS McGINTY

Apthorp, William Foster (*b* Boston, MA, 24 Oct 1848; *d* Vevey, Switzerland, 19 Feb 1913). Critic and writer on music. In 1869 he graduated from Harvard College, where he studied music theory under Paine. After brief service on the staff of other newspapers he became music critic of the *Boston Evening Transcript*, in which capacity he exercised much influence. He retained this post until 1903, when he retired and went to live in Switzerland. From 1892 to 1901 he edited the program books of the Boston SO, giving them a value and individual character that were afterwards maintained by Philip Hale. He published *Musicians and Music-Lovers* (1894), *By the Way, being a Collection of Short Essays about Music and Art in General* (1898, reprinted from the Boston SO program books), *The Opera, Past and Present* (1901), and several translations. He was editor, with John Denison Champlin, of Scribner's *Cyclopedia of Music and Musicians* (1888–90). *See also* CRITICISM, §3, and DICTIONARIES, §2.

RICHARD ALDRICH

Arapaho. American Indian tribe of the central part of the western Plains. They speak an Algonquian language closely related to Cheyenne and Blackfoot and more distantly to many of the Indian languages of eastern North America. In late prehistoric times they were probably agriculturalists in the area that is now Minnesota, but by the 19th century they had moved westward and established the nomadic, buffalo-hunting culture typical of Plains peoples. Although they were among the smaller tribes of the area (in the 19th century the population was estimated at *c*2000), the Arapaho were central in developing the Plains culture type. After 1850 they suffered great deprivation and were eventually divided into three groups. The Gros Ventres or Atsina moved to Canada and gained independent status in association with the Blackfoot; a group of Arapaho were assigned in 1867 to Oklahoma, where they shared land and eventually culture traits with the Cheyenne; and in 1876 the remainder were placed on the Wind River Reservation in Wyoming, which they share with Shoshone people. (*See* INDIANS, AMERICAN, fig. 1.)

The traditional characteristics of Arapaho musical life are typical of Plains culture. The music is largely vocal. Religious music dominates and includes songs of the main public ceremony, the Sun Dance, which is thought to have become most complex among the Arapaho and possibly to have originated with them. Also important in religion is music for the ceremony of the "flat pipe," the tribe's chief ritual object, as well as ceremonial songs of age-grade societies, songs preceding and following war parties, personal songs received by individuals from guardian spirits in visions, and curing songs. Social dances include the Owl, Rabbit, Snake, Wolf, Round, and Grass dances, all introduced after 1850 by neighboring tribes. There are also hunting songs, love-songs, and many songs to accompany gambling in a hiding game still widely played. Instruments include duct flutes, many types of container and strung rattles, frame drums, large drums played by several singers at a time, bullroarers, and bone buzzers.

Drummer of the Dog Soldier Society; Arapaho Sun Dance, 1902

The style of the Arapaho repertory is typical of the Plains. Songs have sharply descending melodic contours, complex but strictly maintained rhythmic divisions, drumming off the melodic beat, an ambitus of an octave or a 9th, and pentatonic and tetratonic scales. The form usually consists of a short section sung by a soloist and repeated by a second singer, followed by several phrases sung by the group and then repeated by the group (*AA BCD BCD*). The manner of singing is harsh and tense with pulsation on the longer tones. Song texts are short, taking up only part of a melody, and are surrounded and sometimes interrupted by nonlexical vocables.

The Arapaho were among the most prominent participants in the Ghost Dance religion of the 1880s and had many dozens of songs of this cult with a characteristic small ambitus and paired-phrase form. In the 20th century the Peyote religion (Native American Church) was introduced, and a large repertory of these musically distinctive songs developed through borrowing and indigenous composition. In this century also the Arapaho began to participate in the pan-Indian musical culture of the Plains, in which many songs with texts consisting only of vocables and some with words in English were used. By the 1950s the total repertory had great diversity. In the 1970s, tribal authorities in Oklahoma established an archive for collecting recordings and other documents for preservation and study of the musical culture.

See also INDIANS, AMERICAN, esp. §§I, 4(ii)(a), 6.

BIBLIOGRAPHY

J. Mooney: *The Ghost-dance Religion and the Sioux Outbreak of 1890* (Washington, DC, 1896, rev. 2/1965)
A. L. Kroeber: *The Arapaho* (New York, 1902)
F. Densmore: *Cheyenne and Arapaho Music* (Los Angeles, 1936)
B. Nettl: "Musical Culture of the Arapaho," *MQ*, xli (1955), 325

BRUNO NETTL

Arbuckle, Matthew (*b* Lochside, ?Kincardine, Scotland, 1828; *d* New York, 23 May 1883). Bandmaster and cornetist. He joined the 26th Regiment of the British Army, known as the Cameronians, at 13; he served in India and China, returned to Britain, then went to Canada with a military band. He reportedly deserted his regiment to assume the leadership of a band in Troy, New York, where he remained for six months before accepting a similar position in Worcester, Massachusetts. Three years later, in 1860, he joined the Gilmore Band, which in 1861 became attached to the 24th Massachusetts Infantry Regiment; he served with the band during the Civil War. Arbuckle was an outstanding cornet soloist, who was admired for his beautiful, cantabile style of playing. He was a soloist at the National Peace Jubilee of 1869 and the World Peace Jubilee of 1872, both of which were organized by Gilmore. In 1873, when Gilmore was appointed leader of the 22nd Regiment Band in New York, Arbuckle went with him and became the cornet soloist with the band, which acquired a national reputation and toured throughout the USA. In New York, where he settled, he also performed under such well-known bandmasters as Cappa and David L. Downing. In 1880 he became bandmaster of the Ninth Regiment of the New York Militia and in 1883 organized a band under his own name; he died shortly before embarking on a tour with the new ensemble.

BIBLIOGRAPHY

Obituaries: *Musical Herald*, iv (1883), 157; *New York Times* (24 May 1883)
F. O. Jones, ed.: *A Handbook of American Music and Musicians* (Canaseraga, NY, 1886/*R*1971)
A. Roe: *The Twenty-fourth Massachusetts Volunteers 1861–66, "New England Guard Regiment"* (Worcester, MA, 1907)
G. Bridges: *Pioneers in Brass* (Detroit, 1965)

FRANK J. CIPOLLA

Archer, Frederick [Frederic] (*b* Oxford, England, 16 June 1838; *d* Pittsburgh, PA, 22 Oct 1901). Organist, conductor, and composer. He became organist of Merton College, Oxford, and in 1873 was appointed to Alexandra Palace in London, where he afterwards became conductor, a post he held until 1880. In 1881 he visited the USA, giving organ recitals in several cities, and later the same year returned to become organist first at Henry Ward Beecher's church in Brooklyn and then at the Church of the Incarnation in New York. In 1883 he founded the illustrated weekly *The Keynote*, which he edited for a year. He moved to Boston in 1887 to become conductor of the Boston Oratorio Society, and subsequently to Chicago where he was organist of St. James's Church.

When Andrew Carnegie established the Carnegie Institute and Library in Pittsburgh, he instituted weekly free organ recitals there; Archer was engaged as organist and inaugurated the series on 7 November 1895. The institute's music hall also served the new Pittsburgh Orchestra, which Archer conducted from its first concert on 27 February 1896 until 28 January 1898, when he was succeeded by Victor Herbert. He continued as organist until his death, however, and also worked as organist of the Church of the Ascension. Archer composed many works for the organ, piano pieces, songs, and a cantata, *King Witlaf's Drinking-Horn*. He wrote several instructional manuals and also compiled anthologies of organ pieces.

BIBLIOGRAPHY

"Archer, Frederic," *The Cyclopedia of Music and Musicians*, ed. J. D. Champlin, Jr., and W. F. Apthorp (New York, 1888) [autobiographical article]
Obituary, *MT*, xlii (1901), 827
H. C. Lahee: *The Organ and its Masters* (Boston, 1903/*R*1976, rev. 2/1927)
C. N. Boyd: "Archer, Frederic," *DAB*
R. Wolfe: *A Short History of the Pittsburgh Orchestra* (diss., Carnegie Library School, Carnegie Institute of Technology, 1954)

ALEXIS CHITTY/BRUCE CARR

Arden, Victor [Fuiks, Lewis J.]. Duo-piano partner of PHIL OHMAN.

Arditi, Luigi (*b* Crescentino, Italy, 16 July 1822; *d* Hove, England, 1 May 1903). Italian conductor, composer, and violinist. After studying and working in Milan until 1846, he went with Giovanni Bottesini, a lifelong friend, to Havana, where he conducted the Havana Italian Opera Company and produced his own one-act opera, *Il corsaro*. In the summer months he performed in the USA and conducted the Havana company in New York in 1847 and 1850. From 1851 to 1856 he was the conductor for various opera troupes in New York, including Maretzek's company (1851), and toured with Marietta Alboni. He conducted the concert for the opening of the Academy of Music (2 October 1854), where his opera *La spia*, based on James Fenimore Cooper's novel, was given its first performance on 24 March 1856.

After leaving New York, Arditi settled in London in 1858 as conductor at Her Majesty's Theatre, where he remained for 11 years. He continued to compose, mostly occasional orchestral music, popular songs, and ballads; the vocal waltz *Il bacio* was renowned. He also conducted operas and promenade concerts at Covent Garden and made many tours in the provinces and Europe, chiefly with Italian opera companies. From 1878 to 1886 he conducted Mapleson's annual opera tours of the USA. Several of these were with Patti, as were all his remaining American tours, the last of which took place in 1893–4.

BIBLIOGRAPHY

The Mapleson Memoirs (London, 1888, rev. 2/1966, ed. H. Rosenthal)
L. Arditi: *My Reminiscences* (New York, 1896/*R*1977)
J. F. Cone: *First Rival of the Metropolitan Opera* (New York, 1983)

KEITH HORNER/R. ALLEN LOTT

A-R Editions. Firm of music publishers. It was founded in New Haven in 1962 by Gary J. N. Aamodt and Clyde Rykken to provide modern critical editions of music of historical interest and artistic integrity for scholars, students, and performers of Western art music. The "Recent Researches" series were launched in 1964 with volumes of music from the Renaissance and Baroque periods and expanded to include music of the Middle Ages and early Renaissance, the Classical era, and the 19th century. The series Recent Researches in American Music was initiated in 1977 in collaboration with the Institute for Studies in American Music. In 1968 the firm moved to Madison, Wisconsin, and the same year took over the production and distribution of the Yale University Collegium Musicum series of historical editions. Rykken left the firm in 1971 and was replaced the following year by Lila Aamodt. A-R executes its own music engraving: Lewis Lockwood's edition of the masses of Vincenzo Ruffo (1979) was the first music publication to have been produced entirely by computerized photocomposition. The company also undertakes engraving for other publishers.

BIBLIOGRAPHY

G. J. N. Aamodt: "Music Publishing Today: a Symposium," *Notes*, xxxii (1975–6), 235

JEAN M. BONIN

Arel, Bülent (*b* Istanbul, Turkey, 23 May 1919). Composer. He studied composition under Necil Kâzım Akses and Edward Zuckmayer at the Ankara Conservatory (1941–7) and sound engineering in Paris (1951). Active as a teacher and conductor, he held positions with Radio Ankara during the years 1951–9 and 1963–5. In 1959 he came to the USA (of which he became a citizen in 1973), where he worked as a technician at the Columbia–Princeton Electronic Music Center (1959–63) and taught at Yale University (1961–2, 1965–70). He was appointed professor of music at SUNY, Stony Brook, in 1971. His music is rich and spontaneous yet carefully controlled. Among his electronic works are pieces that are pioneering in their combination of tape and instruments, in electronic music notation (*Stereo Electronic Music no.2*), and in their joint use of video- and audio tape (*Capriccio for TV*, 1969). He has received two NEA grants and a Rockefeller Foundation award. Several of his works have been recorded.

WORKS

(selective list)

Masques, wind, str, 1949; Music for Str Qt and Tape, 1957, rev. 1962; Elec Music no.1, tape, 1960; Stereo Elec Music no.1, tape, 1961; For Vn and Pf, 1966; Mimiana I–III, dance series, tape, 1968, 1969, 1973; Capriccio for TV, tape, 1969, collab. J. Seawright; Stereo Elec Music no.2, tape, 1970; Fantasy and Dance, 5 viols, tape, 1974

Principal publisher: ACA

BIBLIOGRAPHY

R. Teitelbaum: "Son-Nova 1988: Electronic Music by Bülent Arel, Mario Davidovsky and Vladimir Ussachevsky," *PNM*, iii/1 (1964), 127

BRIAN FENNELLY

Argento, Dominick (*b* York, PA, 27 Oct 1927). Composer. The son of Italian immigrants, he taught himself music theory and harmony, and to play the piano. After military service (as a cryptographer in North Africa) he enrolled at the Peabody Conservatory, Baltimore (BM 1951), where his harmony teacher Nabokov interested him in composing; at the same time he was influenced in the direction of opera by Hugo Weisgall. A Fulbright grant (1951–2) enabled him to study in Florence – a city that was to become his second home – with Pietro Scarpini (piano) at the Conservatorio Cherubini and with Dallapiccola, whose serial approach Argento absorbed in a characteristically discreet and unforced way. He returned to Peabody (MM 1954) and then attended the Eastman School (PhD 1957); his major teachers in Rochester were Hanson, Rogers, and Hovhaness. In 1958, following a second sojourn in Italy, this time as a Guggenheim Fellow, he became a theory and composition teacher at the University of Minnesota, Minneapolis, where he was named Regents Professor in 1979. A co-founder of the Center Opera, Minneapolis, he composed *The Masque of Angels* for its inaugural production (1964) and wrote other works for the Minnesota Opera, its successor-company. In the 1960s he wrote incidental music for productions at the Guthrie Theatre (*Volpone*, 1964, and *The Oresteia*, 1967) and composed works for the St. Paul Philharmonic Society (later St. Paul Chamber Orchestra) and Minneapolis Civic Orchestra; subsequent commissions came to him from the Minnesota Orchestra (*A Ring of Time*, 1972) and the New York City Opera (*Miss Havisham's Fire*, 1977–8), among others. His song cycle *From the Diary of Virginia Woolf*, first performed by Janet Baker, won the Pulitzer Prize in 1975. Argento has been awarded honorary degrees from York (Pennsylvania) College and Valparaiso (Indiana) University, and in 1980 was elected to the Institute of the American Academy and Institute of Arts and Letters.

Argento is especially distinguished as a composer for the voice, having won recognition for his operas, song cycles, and choral music. His inherent lyricism extends also to the orchestra, for which he has written brilliant and inventive works, sometimes influenced by extra-musical sources; their quiet endings are a hallmark of his style. Although he came of age with the postwar avant garde, Argento remained aloof from its preoccupation with abstraction, choosing to work in relative isolation in the upper Midwest, where his penchant for melody and color won him the allegiance of performers and public alike. When the so-called new romanticism emerged in the early 1970s, he had already matured as an original voice whose works assuaged the yearnings of a new aesthetic sensibility and quickly earned him an international reputation.

His early one-act *opera buffa The Boor* (1957) embodies the essence of his musical style, namely, a vocalism that ranges from flexible arioso to full-fledged aria, skillful writing for ensembles, theatrical verve, and marked affinities with operatic tradition. Argento has, moreover, always shown a distinct literary sensitivity – a trait he shares with Benjamin Britten; in Variations for Orchestra (*The Mask of Night*, 1965) he drew on Shakespearean allusions to night, while *Letters from Composers* (1968), based on the words of Chopin, Mozart, and Bach, offers in seven songs a series of condensed operatic scenas in which the texts are perfectly mirrored by the music.

Argento's fondness for intimate vocal forms, in him paradoxically coupled with a keen sense of theater, produced characteristic works of the 1970s. *Postcard from Morocco* (1971), a full-length opera in one act, explores the theme of self-discovery (one central to Argento); the apparently lighthearted story, surreal and ample in incident, deals with travelers stranded in a North African railroad station, one of whom is finally tricked into opening his suitcase, to reveal the emptiness of his life. *Jonah and the Whale* (1973) shows more fully Argento's mastery of large-scale form and diverse idioms; the oratorio is set to a hybrid text drawing on medieval English poetry, a hymnal, and sea chanteys. Its eclectic score uses borrowed tunes as well as a dodecaphonic theme (Jonah's music), and is fabricated from patterns of threes (three kinds of triads, an orchestra comprising three trios, etc.). *From the Diary of Virginia Woolf* (1974), elaborated on a single tone-row, accommodates plainsong, café tunes, and a virtual operatic scena in the course of eight songs that trace a woman's life to the brink of suicide.

Of his more recent stage works, perhaps the most convincing is *A Water Bird Talk* (1974); the composer improbably based its libretto on Chekhov's medical treatise *On the Harmful Effects of Smoking Tobacco*. During this 45-minute monodrama, a professor gives a lecture, illustrated with lantern slides, on water birds whose mating habits increasingly remind him of his own henpecked and humiliating life. The miniature opera is structured as a theme and six variations with coda, with each section describing a different fowl. Delicately scored for a dozen players (the puffin is depicted in a march for horn and timpani, the grebe in an elegy for oboe and chimes), the score germinates pungent yet luscious harmonies. A small masterpiece in which wry comedy is succeeded by an anguished moment of self-recognition, the work reflects Argento's exceptional skill as a librettist as well as his musical versatility.

In 1981 Argento completed *Fire Variations*, eight transformations, with finale, of a blacksmith's song that he had first used in his opera *Miss Havisham's Fire*. Structurally the score follows closely Brahms's Haydn Variations – another instance of Argento's tendency to impose explicit formal restraints on his creative impulse. His major project of the early 1980s was the opera *Casanova's Homecoming* (1980–84). Written to his own libretto, it is a large and impressive modern-day *opera buffa* replete with elaborate ensembles, striking choruses, and episodes of great theatricality. Act 1 incorporates an *opera seria* which Casanova himself might have heard, thereby allowing for a juxtaposition of Argento's own style with an 18th-century idiom.

For all their wide-ranging eclecticism, Argento's works impress on the listener a strong musical personality, a result of his being drawn perpetually to the human voice. "The voice is our representation of humanity," he has observed, and the vocalism that informs all his writing corresponds to his belief that instruments are essentially imitators of the voice.

WORKS

STAGE WORKS

The Resurrection of Don Juan (ballet, 1), 1956, Karlsruhe, Germany, 24 May 1959, arr. orch suite, 1956

The Boor (opera buffa, 1, J. Olon-Scrymgeour, after Chekhov), 1957, Rochester, 6 May 1957

Colonel Jonathan the Saint (comic opera, 4, Olon-Scrymgeour), 1958–61, Denver, 31 Dec 1971

Christopher Sly (comic opera, 2, J. Manlove, after Shakespeare: The Taming of the Shrew), 1962–3, Minneapolis, 31 May 1963

The Masque of Angels (opera, 1, Olon-Scrymgeour), 1963, Minneapolis, 9 Jan 1964

Royal Invitation, or Homage to the Queen of Tonga (ballet, 5 parts), 1964, St. Paul, 22 March 1964, arr. orch suite, 1964

St. Joan (incidental music, Shaw), 1964

Volpone (incidental music, Molière), 1964

S. S. Glencairn (incidental music, O'Neill), 1966

Oresteia (incidental music, Aeschylus), 1967

The Shoemaker's Holiday (ballad opera, 2, Olon-Scrymgeour, after T. Dekker), 1967, Minneapolis, 1 June 1967

Postcard from Morocco (opera, 1, J. Donahue), 1971, Minneapolis, 14 Oct 1971

A Water Bird Talk (monodrama, 1, Argento, after Chekhov: On the Harmful Effects of Tobacco), 1974, Minneapolis, 1 May 1981

The Voyage of Edgar Allan Poe (opera, 2, C. Nolte), 1975–6, Minneapolis, 24 April 1976

Miss Havisham's Fire (opera, 2, Olon-Scrymgeour, after Dickens: Great Expectations), 1977–8, New York, 22 March 1979

Miss Havisham's Wedding Night (monodrama, Olon-Scrymgeour, after Dickens), 1980, Minneapolis, 1 May 1981

Casanova's Homecoming (opera buffa, 3, Argento), 1980–84, St. Paul, 12 April 1985

INSTRUMENTAL

Orch: Ode to the West Wind (Shelley), conc., S, large orch, 1956; Ov., The Boor, 1957; Variations for Orch: The Mask of Night, 1965; Bravo Mozart!: an Imaginary Biography, vn, ob, hn, orch, 1969; A Ring of Time, Preludes and Pageants for Orch and Bells, 1972; In Praise of Music, 7 songs, 1977; Fire Variations, 8 variations and finale, 1981; Casa Guidi (E. B. Browning), 5 songs, Mez, orch, 1983

Chamber: Divertimento, pf, str, 1954; Str Qt, 1956; From the Album of Allegra Harper, 2 pf, 1962 [arr. of dance suite from Colonel Jonathan the Saint]

VOCAL

Songs about Spring (E. E. Cummings), 5 songs, S, pf, 1954, arr. S, chamber orch; 6 Elizabethan Songs, high v, pf, 1958, arr. Baroque ens; The Revelation of St. John the Divine, rhapsody, T, male vv, brass, perc, 1966; A Nation of Cowslips (Keats), 7 bagatelles, SATB, 1968; Letters from Composers (Chopin, Mozart, Bach), 7 songs, T, gui, 1968; Tria carmina paschalia, Easter cantata, female vv, harp, gui, 1970

To be Sung upon the Water (Wordsworth), song cycle, high v, cl, pf, 1972; Jonah and the Whale (medieval Eng.), oratorio, T, B, nar, SATB, small ens, 1973; From the Diary of Virginia Woolf, song cycle, Mez, pf, 1974; Peter Quince at the Clavier (W. Stevens), sonatina, SATB, pf, 1979; I Hate and I Love (Catullus), song cycle, SATB, perc, 1981; The André Expedition (explorers' notebooks), song cycle, Bar, pf, 1982

Principal publisher: Boosey & Hawkes

BIBLIOGRAPHY

EwenD

W. Sargent: "A Glimpse Ahead," *New Yorker*, xxxiv (29 March 1958), 100 [*The Boor*]

R. Ericson: "Minnesota Opera Begins Strongly," *New York Times* (16 Oct 1971) [*Postcard from Morocco*]

M. Steele: "Dominick Argento," *HiFi/MusAm*, xxv/9 (1975), 8

P. Altman: "The Voyage of Dominick Argento," *Opera News*, xl/21 (1976), 12

A. Porter: "Song from the Twin Cities," *New Yorker*, li (9 Feb 1976), 99 [*From the Diary of Virginia Woolf*]

——: "By a Route Obscure," *New Yorker*, lii (17 May 1976), 159 [*The Voyage of Edgar Allan Poe*]

G. Schuller: "Amerikas Avantgarde – zwischen Tradition und Experiment," *ÖMz*, xxxi (1976), 482

D. J. Speer, ed.: *Commemorating the World Premiere of "The Voyage of Edgar Allan Poe"* (St. Paul, MN, 1976)

M. Steele: "Dominick Argento," *ASCAP Today*, viii/1 (1976), 16

"Argento, Dominick," *CBY 1977*

A. K. Gebuhr: "Structure and Coherence in *The Diary*; from Dominick Argento's Cycle *From the Diary of Virginia Woolf*," *Indiana Theory Review*, i/3 (1978), 12

A. Porter: "Fire in April," *New Yorker*, lv (9 April 1979), 125 [*Miss Havisham's Fire*]

T. M. Sabatino: *A Performer's Commentary on "To Be Sung upon the Water" by Dominick Argento* (diss., Ohio State U., 1980)

A. T. Brewer: *Characterization in Dominick Argento's Opera "The Boor"* (diss., U. of Texas, Austin, 1981)

L. E. Swales: *Characterization in Dominick Argento's Opera, "Postcard from Morocco": a Director's Guide* (diss., U. of Iowa, 1983)

MARY ANN FELDMAN

Arizona, University of. A state university founded in TUCSON, Arizona, in 1891; *see also* LIBRARIES AND COLLECTIONS, §3.

Arizona State University. State university in Tempe, Arizona. It dates back to the founding in 1885 of the Arizona Territorial Normal School; this later became Arizona State College and, in 1958, was renamed Arizona State University. The school of music, within the College of Fine Arts, was established in 1885. In 1980 it enrolled approximately 450 students and employed a full-time faculty of about 57 under director George Umberson. It offers BA, BM, MA, MM, DMA, EdD, and PhD degrees in performance, composition, theory, and education, and maintains active choral and music theater programs. The music library includes the Wayne King collection of orchestral and band materials, the International Percussion Reference Library, and the Pablo Casals International Cello Library (*see* LIBRARIES AND COLLECTIONS, §3); the research facility houses the Laura Boulton collection of more than 300 ethnic instruments and other items, and the Hugh Long collection of string instruments. The campus is also the home of the Gammage Center for the Performing Arts (*see* PHOENIX).

GRAYDON BEEKS

Arlen, Harold [Arluck, Hyman](*b* Buffalo, NY, 15 Feb 1905). Composer. The son of a cantor, he sang in the choir at his father's synagogue as a child, and at the age of 15 played piano in local movie houses and on excursion boats on Lake Erie. He organized his own band, the Snappy Trio, and later joined another, the Yankee Six, which, as the expanded dance orchestra the Buffalodians, went to New York in the mid-1920s. He made some band arrangements for Fletcher Henderson but worked mostly as a pianist and singer on radio, in theater pit orchestras, and in dance bands; he recorded as a singer with Benny Goodman, Red Nichols, and Joe Venuti. In 1929 he began a songwriting collaboration with lyricist Ted Koehler and achieved his first success with the song *Get Happy*, which appeared in the *9:15 Revue* (1930). The two men went on to produce several memorable revue songs for the Cotton Club in Harlem (1930–34), including *Between the devil and the deep blue sea*, *I've got the world on a string*, *I love a parade*, *Ill Wind*, and *Stormy Weather*. These songs blended the forms and idioms of Tin Pan Alley with blues inflections and they helped to popularize the sounds of black music with a wider audience.

In 1934 Arlen composed his last important revue, *Life Begins at 8:40*, and began to write for Hollywood films. During the next two decades he created several notable songs with the lyricists Ira Gershwin and E. Y. Harburg, including *Over the Rainbow* (Harburg, 1939) and *The man that got away* (Gershwin, 1954), both for the singer Judy Garland. Unlike many Hollywood composers of the period, Arlen managed to preserve a strong musical identity; many of his films place an emphasis on the dramatic function of songs (which is more typical of musical plays) rather than on spectacle and dance (which characterize the songs in musical comedies and revues); *The Wizard of Oz* (1939) is one of the earliest film musicals to attempt to integrate the use of song into the development of character and plot. From 1941 to 1945 Arlen worked closely with the lyricist Johnny Mercer on such jazz-influenced songs as *Blues in the Night*, *That old black magic*, *One for my baby*, and *Ac-cent-tchu-ate the positive*. In the mid-1940s he turned his attention to the theater once again. Of his five subsequent Broadway musicals, *Bloomer Girl* (1944) and *Jamaica* (1957) were written with Harburg, *St. Louis Woman* (1946) and *Saratoga* (1959) with Mercer, and *House of Flowers*, which many consider his most distinguished score, with Truman Capote. While Arlen's contributions remained on a consistently high level, most of these shows were marred by serious weaknesses in their librettos, and this may have prevented several of his most exquisite songs, such as *Right as the Rain* and *I never has seen snow*, from attaining the popularity of his earliest theater works.

Arlen's musical style shows an affinity with black musical expression. Many of his shows were written for all- or predominantly black casts (the Cotton Club revues, *St. Louis Woman* and its later expansion as a blues opera, *Free and Easy*, *House of Flowers*, and *Jamaica*), while others demonstrate a concern with black themes (*Bloomer Girl* and *Saratoga*). Much of his songwriting has been influenced by the blues, often simply in the form of blue melodic inflections applied to a traditional song structure (as in *Stormy Weather*), but also more radically in an attempt to incorporate the entire 12-bar harmonic structure of the blues within a new form of popular song (for example, *Blues in the Night*). Arlen has frequently broken the mold of a 32-bar, *AABA* song form to write melodies both unconventional in length and asymmetrical in their sectional makeup. He has extended the traditional eight-bar opening section of a song to ten bars (*Ill Wind*), 12 bars (*I wonder what became of me*), 13 bars (*For every man there's*

Harold Arlen (right) with E. Y. Harburg

a woman), 14 bars (*Fun to be Fooled*), 16 bars (*Down with love*), 18 bars (*What's good about goodbye?*), and even 20 bars (*Out of this World*). He also had a tendency to vary and develop a melodic idea rather than simply repeat it. *Right as the Rain*, for example, is so continuously developmental as to give the impression of not having been sectionally conceived at all.

WORKS

STAGE

Unless otherwise stated, all are musicals and all dates are those of first New York performance. Librettists and lyricists are listed in that order in parentheses.

You Said It (J. Yellen, S. Silvers; Yellen, T. Koehler), orchd H. Jackson, 19 Jan 1931 [incl. Sweet and Hot, While you are young, It's different with me, Learn to croon, If he really loves me]

Life Begins at 8:40 (revue, D. Freedman, H. I. Phillips, A. Baxter, H. C. Smith, F. Gabrielson; I. Gershwin, E. Y. Harburg), orchd H. Spialek, 27 Aug 1934 [incl. You're a builder-upper, Fun to be Fooled, Let's take a walk around the block, I couldn't hold my man, What can you say in a love song?]

Hooray for What? (H. Lindsay, R. Crouse; Harburg), orchd D. Walker, 1 Dec 1937 [incl. God's Country, Moanin' in the Mornin', Down with love, In the shade of the new apple tree, Buds won't bud, I've gone romantic on you]

Bloomer Girl (F. Saidy, S. Herzig; Harburg), orchd R. R. Bennett, 5 Oct 1944 [incl. The Eagle and me, Right as the Rain, It was good enough for grandma, Evelina, Sunday in Cicero Falls]

St. Louis Woman (A. Bontemps, C. P. Cullen; J. Mercer), orchd T. Royal, A. Small, M. Salta, W. Paul, 30 March 1946; rev. as Free and Easy (addl lyrics, Koehler), orchd Q. Jones, B. Byers, Amsterdam, Holland, 17 Dec 1959 [incl. Come rain or come shine, Any place I hang my hat is home, I had myself a true love, Legalize my name, I wonder what became of me]

House of Flowers (T. Capote; Capote, Arlen), orchd Royal, 30 Dec 1954 [incl. A Sleepin' Bee, Two ladies in de shade of de banana tree, Bamboo Cage, I'm gonna leave off wearin' my shoes, I never has seen snow, Don't like goodbyes]

Jamaica (Harburg, Saidy; Harburg), orchd P. J. Lang, 31 Oct 1957 [incl. Pretty to walk with, Push de button, Cocoanut Sweet, Take it slow Joe, Leave the atom alone]

Saratoga (M. DaCosta; Mercer), orchd Lang, 7 Dec 1959 [incl. Petticoat High, Love held lightly, Goose never be a peacock, You or no one]

FILMS

Let's Fall in Love (Koehler), 1934; Gold Diggers of 1937 (Harburg), 1936; The Singing Kid (Harburg), 1936; Stage Struck (Harburg), 1936; Strike me Pink (L. Brown), 1936; At the Circus (Harburg), 1939; The Wizard of Oz (Harburg), orchd H. Stothart, 1939 [incl. Over the Rainbow]; Blues in the Night (Mercer), 1941 [incl. Blues in the Night]; Star Spangled Rhythm (Mercer), 1942 [incl. That old black magic]; The Sky's the Limit (Mercer), 1943 [incl. One for my baby, My Shining Hour]

Here Come the Waves (Mercer), 1944 [incl. Ac-cent-tchu-ate the positive]; Kismet (Harburg), 1944; Up in Arms (Koehler), 1944; Casbah (L. Robin), 1948 [incl. For every man there's a woman, What's good about goodbye?]; My Blue Heaven (R. Blane, Arlen), 1950; The Petty Girl (Mercer), 1950; Mr. Imperium (D. Fields), 1951; Down Among the Sheltering Palms (Blane, Arlen), 1953; The Farmer Takes a Wife (Fields), 1953; The Country Girl (Gershwin), 1954; A Star is Born (Gershwin), 1954 [incl. The man that got away]; Gay Purr-ee (Harburg), 1962; I Could Go on Singing (Harburg), 1963

SONGS

Selective list; except for films, all dates are those of first New York performance.

The Album of my Dreams (L. Davis), 1929; Get Happy (Koehler), in 9:15 Revue, 1930; Out of a clear blue sky (Koehler), in Earl Carroll Vanities, 1930; Linda, Song of the Gigolo (Koehler), in Brown Sugar, 1930; I love a parade, Between the devil and the deep blue sea (Koehler), in Rhythmania, 1931; I gotta right to sing the blues (Koehler), in Earl Carroll Vanities, 1932; Satan's li'l lamb (Harburg, Mercer), in Americana, 1932; I've got the world on a string (Koehler), in Cotton Club Parade, 1932

Cabin in the Cotton (I. Caesar, G. White), Two feet in two four time (Caesar), in George White's Music Hall Varieties, 1932; It's only a paper moon (B. Rose, Harburg), in The Great Mazoo (film), 1932; Stormy Weather (Koehler), in Cotton Club Parade, 1933; Ill Wind (Koehler), in Cotton Club Parade, 1934; Last night when we were very young (Harburg), 1935; How's by you?, Song of the Woodman (Harburg), in The Show is On, 1936; Happiness is a Thing Called Joe (Harburg), in Cabin in the Sky (film), 1943

INSTRUMENTAL

(selective list)

Minor Gaff, blues fantasy, pf, collab. D. George, 1926; Rhythmic Moments, pf, 1928; Mood in Six Minutes, orchd R. R. Bennett, 1935; American Minuet, orch, 1939; Americanegro Suite (Koehler), vv, pf, 1941

BIBLIOGRAPHY

"Arlen, Harold," *CBY 1955*

E. Jablonski: *Harold Arlen: Happy with the Blues* (Garden City, NY, 1961) [incl. list of works]

A. Wilder: *American Popular Song: the Great Innovators, 1900–1950* (New York, 1972)

A. Harmetz: *The Making of the Wizard of Oz* (New York, 1977)

J. Haskins: *The Cotton Club* (New York, 1977)

LARRY STEMPEL

Armenian-American music. *See* EUROPEAN-AMERICAN MUSIC, §III, 2.

Armonica. An improved form of musical glasses invented by BENJAMIN FRANKLIN in 1761, in which a row of glass bowls, nested within one another concentrically, is mounted on a horizontal axle which is turned with a pedal.

Armstrong, Karan (*b* Havre, MT, 14 Dec 1941). Soprano. As a child she studied piano and clarinet; later she received the BA from Concordia College in Minnesota and studied singing privately with a number of teachers, including Lotte Lehmann in Santa Barbara. She sang Elvira (in Rossini's *L'italiana in Algeri*) for her début with the San Francisco Opera in 1966, and a year later sang for the first time at the Metropolitan Opera, as the Dew Fairy in Engelbert Humperdinck's *Hänsel und Gretel*. She appeared at Santa Fe (1968) and the Caramoor Festival (1974), and was a member of the New York City Opera from 1975 to 1978. Her European career has included a very successful Salome at Strasbourg (1976), a role she repeated in Munich, Vienna, and elsewhere. She made her Bayreuth début as Elsa (*Lohengrin*) in 1979, took the role of Death in the première of Gottfried von Einem's *Jesu Hochzeit* in Vienna (1980), and made her Covent Garden début as Lulu in 1981. Among her numerous appearances in television productions has been a performance as Alice Ford in Verdi's *Falstaff* under Solti's direction. Her repertory also includes Fiordiligi (*Così fan tutte*), Tosca, Violetta, Butterfly, the Marschallin, Mélisande, and Minnie (in Puccini's *La fanciulla del West*); her strong voice, striking appearance, and acting ability are particularly effective in contemporary parts, such as the title role in Giuseppe Sinopoli's *Lou Salome* and Marie in Berg's *Wozzeck*, both of which she sang in 1981. She is married to the director Götz Friedrich.

ELIZABETH FORBES

Armstrong, Louis [Dippermouth, Pops, Satchelmouth, Satchmo] (*b* New Orleans, LA, *c*1898; *d* New York, 6 July 1971). Jazz trumpeter and singer. His musical presence, technical mastery, and imaginative genius so overwhelmed jazz musicians of his day that he became their principal model, leaving an indelible imprint on this music.

1. LIFE. It was long believed that Armstrong was born on 4 July 1900, but there is ample evidence to suggest that his birth took place earlier, probably in 1898, on a date that even he did not know. His father was a laborer named Willie Armstrong, his mother a domestic and probably a part-time prostitute called Mayann. Armstrong was born in a cabin in a dilapidated black

Louis Armstrong

slum in the Back o' Town section of New Orleans. His father abandoned the family around the time of Armstrong's birth, and shortly afterwards his mother moved into a nearby area reserved for black prostitutes. After spending his first few years with his paternal grandmother, Josephine Armstrong, he returned to his mother in "Black Storyville," a tawdry, run-down neighborhood of brothels, cribs, seedy dance halls, and honky-tonks frequented by black laborers and some Whites. Here Armstrong grew up, hearing in the dance halls and clubs around him the blues and the new "hot" music then emerging from ragtime.

He was brought up without a father in deepest poverty, wearing little more than rags and eating the cheapest of food, occasionally even scavenging for refuse in garbage cans. His mother, although warm and loving, was irresponsible, and frequently left Armstrong and his younger sister to the kindness of strangers for days at a time. He grew up deprived both physically and emotionally to an exceptional degree, and the experience left him scarred with a deep-seated, lifelong sense of insecurity.

He began singing in a barbershop quartet, which, over several years, amounted to an excellent course in ear training. Sometime in his early teens he was sentenced to the Home for Colored Waifs – not, as once believed, for firing a pistol on New Year's Eve, but for more general delinquency. While in the home he joined the band and eventually was given a cornet. With this band he played customary band music of the day – marches, rags, and sentimental songs. When he was released from the home about two years later he was determined to become a musician. Using borrowed instruments, he began sitting in at the honky-tonks around his home, playing mainly the blues and the few songs in his slowly expanding repertory.

Throughout his life Armstrong habitually put himself under the wing of a tough, aggressive older man. One of these was the strong-minded King Oliver, then considered to be the best jazz cornetist in New Orleans. Armstrong, a genius who invented his own methods, owed little musically to Oliver or anyone else; but Oliver's sponsorship provided him with opportunities to play in public and so to develop his musical personality. When Oliver left for Chicago in 1918 during the general migration of Blacks to the North, Armstrong took his place in a band led by Kid Ory, then regarded as the leading jazz band in the city. In 1918 he married a prostitute named Daisy, beginning a stormy and short-lived relationship. By 1919 he was working in clubs and also on riverboats, the floating dance halls which traveled from town to town on the Mississippi every summer. This experience in particular contributed towards Armstrong's development as a professional musician who could read and play any music required of him.

In 1922 Oliver invited Armstrong to Chicago to play second cornet in his band, which was then working at a black dance hall called Lincoln Gardens. This Creole Jazz Band had an extraordinary impact on musicians in the Chicago area, and through it Armstrong began to draw their attention. At this time he also made his first recordings with Oliver's group. In 1924 he married the band's pianist, Lillian Hardin. (He subsequently married Alpha Smith and then Lucille Wilson.) Shortly thereafter, at his wife's urging, he left Oliver, and in autumn 1924 he moved to New York to join the Fletcher Henderson Orchestra, one of the leading black dance bands in the city (for illustration *see* HENDERSON, FLETCHER). Through his work as jazz specialist with this band he soon became known to musicians; they quickly recognized in him the pre-eminent player of the new "hot" music, and his influence began to be felt.

Armstrong returned to Chicago in November 1925, and immediately began recording a series of more than 60 performances that were to transform jazz. Issued under a variety of names, they can collectively be called the "Hot Fives," and their effect on musicians and jazz enthusiasts was instantaneous and profound; few performers, either in or outside jazz, entirely escaped their influence. During this period Armstrong changed from cornet to the more brilliant trumpet. One of the series, *Heebie Jeebies*, was his first recording as a scat singer, and its success led to his singing being given greater prominence (*see also* SCAT SINGING).

In 1929 Armstrong's record director, Tommy Rockwell, took him to New York. There he played in the orchestra for the Broadway show *Hot Chocolates* by Andy Razaf and Fats Waller, where he attracted attention singing *Ain't Misbehavin'*. From this point he moved gradually, but inevitably, away from jazz to become a popular entertainer. In part he did this at the urging of Rockwell, and more especially under the influence of another strong figure in his life – Joe Glaser, who managed him from 1935. But in part Armstrong was drawn to show business through an insatiable hunger for applause, rooted in the insecurities formed in his early years. Under Glaser's guidance he became the first Black to appear regularly in feature-length films and to have a sponsored radio show; by the late 1930s he was a nationwide star. Until 1947 he worked with a big band, for many years using the group led by Luis Russell, playing music of an increasingly commercial nature. Then, with the collapse of the big-band movement after World War II, he performed with smaller groups with a New Orleans format, sometimes playing good jazz but more frequently using the band as a showcase for singing popular songs. The public found him a winning and attractive personality and, helped by shrewd management, by the mid-1950s he was one of the best-known entertainers in the world; he appeared in almost 20 popular films (for illustrations *see* KAYE,

DANNY and MUSICAL FILM, fig.3). The American Department of State sponsored him on numerous international tours, earning him the title "Ambassador Satch." He suffered a heart attack in 1959, and from then on recurrent health problems forced him gradually to curtail his trumpet playing and eventually his singing as well. His death produced headlines in newspapers throughout the world.

2. MUSIC. Armstrong's recordings can be divided into three groups: those with New Orleans-style bands (up to 1928), those with big dance bands (from 1928 to 1947), and finally those of his return to the New Orleans format (from 1947 until his death). In his first recorded solo, with Oliver's band on *Chimes Blues* (1923), he merely played a preset melody. However, during the same session he recorded his first important jazz solo on *Froggie Moore*; here Armstrong did not entirely depart from the melody, but already he was producing the "swing" which so delighted his contemporaries. The origins of swing are still obscure, but even if Armstrong did not invent this phenomenon he "swung" more than anyone else of his time – an important quality that attracted other players to his style. Armstrong's swing was created by at least four devices: a terminal vibrato which begins after the note has been struck, making it seem suddenly to leap; a division of a quarter note into two eighth-notes of varying but decidedly unequal duration; a constant displacement of accent, so that the music seems alternately to move towards and away from the listener; and a placement of notes fractionally in front of or behind the beat. This last trait later became increasingly significant in Armstrong's playing.

This sense of swing is also apparent in Armstrong's recordings with Henderson, where in addition he began to abandon fixed melody for pure invention. His improvisations are not simply random, for the parts always combine to form unified wholes: on Henderson's *Go 'long Mule* (1924) he played three parallel figures over the first six bars (ex.1); in *Copenhagen* (1924) he

Ex.1 From *Go 'long Mule* (1924, Col. 228D), transcr. G. Schuller

placed parallel figures over the first two segments of the blues strain and a contrasting one over the last segment. This ability to construct an entire dramatic form, along with his powerful swing, astonished musicians from the start. During his stay with Henderson Armstrong accompanied many blues singers. His recording of *St. Louis Blues* (1925) with Bessie Smith is particularly fine. He also recorded many numbers in the New Orleans style for Clarence Williams. Some of these featured the New Orleans clarinetist and saxophonist Sidney Bechet, including a driving rendition of *Cake Walkin' Babies* (1924) which is considered a classic of the genre, and *Texas Moaner Blues* (1924), the finest extant example of the blues as played in the honky-tonks of Storyville.

All the foregoing recordings, however, must be seen as precursors to the Hot Fives which, because of their profound effect on later music, are one of the most important bodies of recordings in 20th-century music. They provide an astonishing record of Armstrong's musical growth – his quick, electric climb to artistic maturity. Four trends are evident: a steady improvement in his technical skills; a growing confidence in the value of what he had to say; a progressive turning away from paraphrase to fresh invention; and a steady increase in emotional depth.

The Hot Fives may be divided into four groups. The initial group of 26 recordings (made from 12 November 1925 to 27 November 1926, with cornet, clarinet, trombone, piano, and banjo), are basically in the New Orleans style. However, as the series progressed, Armstrong came more to the fore as a soloist and, following the success of his scat singing on *Heebie Jeebies*, as a singer as well. It was not his singing but the sequence of breaks which most impressed musicians on *Cornet Chop Suey*. They are set over 16 bars of stop-time accompaniment. The first eight bars are cut neatly into two-bar segments, each appearing to comment or reflect on the preceding one. In the second eight bars, the figures are cut more unevenly, enhancing the effect of a musical dialogue. Nonetheless Armstrong had not yet reached his musical maturity: he sometimes fumbled notes, and a mood of cheerfulness predominates throughout the series.

A second group of recordings was cut between 7 and 14 May 1927 by the Hot Five, this time augmented by drums and tuba, and issued under the name of Louis Armstrong and his Hot Seven. These performances include more solo playing at the expense of the ensemble, and show Armstrong moving even further away from paraphrase. On *Potato Head Blues*, the most celebrated of this group, he again played a solo over stop-time accompaniment, throwing long figures, at first regular in length but then increasingly varied, over the punctuation of the band. He also created short stretches of counter-melody where the accents fall away from the standard 4/4 pattern, for example at the beginning of the last eight bars of the solo and in the coda. His playing is more confident, and radiates variety and novelty.

The third group in the series returns to the original Hot Five band for nine sides made in September and December of 1927. Armstrong produced many brilliant moments in these performances, including a delicate solo on *Savoy Blues* and a fine bravura solo on *Struttin' with Some Barbecue*. The masterpiece of the set, however, is *Hotter than That*, possibly the most exuberant recorded performance in jazz. The piece opens with a boisterous introduction, and leaps immediately into a fervent trumpet solo. Later in the piece is a chorus of Armstrong's scat singing, the second half of which consists of a string of hemiolas over three-beat groups in the 4/4 accompaniment – an experiment in polymeters that foreshadows jazz performances of 30 years later (ex.2). By this point in his career Armstrong possessed the finest technique of any trumpeter in jazz, a reckless confidence, and an extraordinarily rich melodic imagination.

Ex.2 From *Hotter than That* (1927, OK 8535), transcr. J. B. Robinson

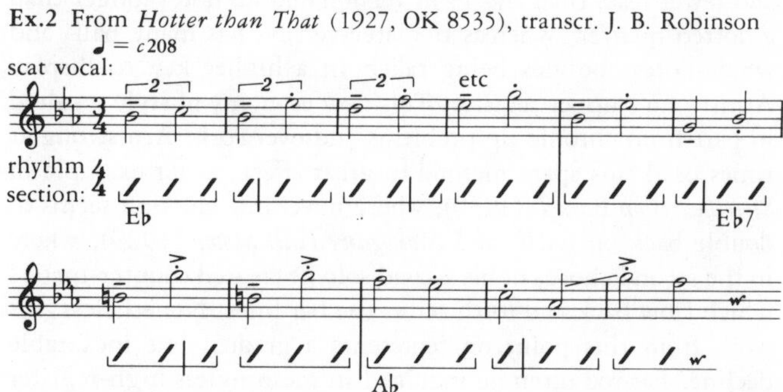

The final group in this seminal series of recordings was issued under several band names as it involved various personnel, the most important of whom was Earl Hines, then the leading jazz pianist. Armstrong had deepened emotionally: there is brooding melancholy in *Tight like This*, playfulness in *Weather Bird*, tragic sadness in *West End Blues*. This last is considered by many critics to be the greatest of Armstrong's recorded performances. It opens with a long rising and falling introduction, containing shifts in tempo and meter. Then follows a simple statement of the theme, which grows denser and rises at the end in a figure that echoes the introduction. There is a poignant vocal exchange with the clarinet, then a final chorus which Armstrong begins by holding a single high B♭ for nearly four bars, creating unbearable tension. This finally breaks into a sequence of desperate descending figures, followed by a long swirl to a quiet completion and resignation in the coda (ex.3). *West End Blues* is built on a series of

Ex.3 From *West End Blues* (1928, OK 8597), transcr. G. Schuller
♩ = c88

climaxes, each higher than its predecessor. It has a unity of form and feeling rare in jazz, and was recognized immediately by the jazz community as a work of genius. It made clear once and for all that jazz was not a simple music meant to accompany drinking and dancing, but harbored expressive possibilities that had hardly been explored.

In 1929 Armstrong developed a much less dense style which involved throwing long, looping, out-of-time figures over the ground beat. There are many pauses, more long notes, and fewer bursts of fast notes. The two versions of *Struttin' with Some Barbecue* (ex.4) show the change clearly: the 1927 version has more notes and fewer rests than the 1938 version and no notes longer than a dotted quarter, whereas the later version has many half- and whole-notes, besides being taken in a higher key to display Armstrong's upper register. This new economy of style resulted in part from chronic lip problems and overwork. Armstrong at times used this spare method to great effect, as for example in *Sweethearts on Parade* (1930), whose novel introduction seems to double back on itself, and *Mahogany Hall Stomp* (1929), where in the second chorus of his second solo he created counter-meters which flow back and forth across the bar lines. Nonetheless, his work from this point on represents a gradual but inexorable decline. Far too often he indulged in meaningless high-register riffs which excited audiences of the time but lacked the passion and musical interest of his performances with the Hot Fives. Yet even here there are gems to be discovered: *Star Dust* (1931), a final example of his spare method; *I Double Dare You* (1938), in which the lines are cut obliquely to the shape of the tune; and the big-band version of *Struttin' with Some Barbecue* (1938), which he turned into a mere skeleton of the song. And whatever his excesses Armstrong always swung, and frequently created more pure jazz from straightforward statements of mediocre tunes than lesser players could produce from much better material.

During these years Armstrong's singing style also changed. On his early recordings with the Hot Five he used his natural gravelly voice, but later he adopted a smoother, lighter tone in the style of the crooners. By the mid-1930s, however, thickening of the vocal chords made it difficult for him to produce a smooth sound, and he reverted to his natural voice.

In 1947 Armstrong returned to a small-band format, the All Stars, which he led until shortly before his death, although he continued to record occasionally with large studio orchestras. His formal recordings tended to be commercialized. However, a great deal of music from informal concerts and broadcasts is available. Although quite uneven and often replete with showy and well-worn phrases, it is nevertheless sometimes filled with Armstrong's former passion. Among the best recordings from this period is a collection of new versions of his classic performances called *Satchmo: a Musical Autobiography of Louis Armstrong* (1947–56, Decca DXM155). At times in these he reaches the heights he attained in the originals, as in *See See Rider* and *King of the Zulus*.

Armstrong's greatest significance lies in his music up to about 1936, after which he became primarily a popular entertainer. His first achievement was his incessant, intense swing, of which he was the consummate master and prime exemplar. Second was the originality and passion of his musical invention, through which the listener seemed directly to sense the artist's personality. Finally, through his example, he turned jazz from an ensemble to a soloist's music. His approach was so remarkable that Armstrong became the model for virtually all jazz musicians of his time.

See also JAZZ, §III, 5.

Ex.4
(a) From *Struttin' with Some Barbecue* (1927, OK 8566), transcr. G. L. Collier

(b) From *Struttin' with Some Barbecue* (1938, Decca 1661), transcr. G. L. Collier

RECORDINGS
(selective list)

As the leader of the Hot Fives, Hot Sevens: Heebie Jeebies (1926, OK 8300); Cornet Chop Suey (1926, OK 8320); Skid-dat-de-dat (1926, OK 8436); Big Butter and Egg Man (1926, OK 8423); Willie the Weeper (1927, OK 8432); Potato Head Blues (1927, OK 8503); S.O.L. Blues (1927, Col. 35661); Gully Low Blues (1927, Col. 8474); Struttin' with Some Barbecue (1927, OK 8566); I'm not Rough (1927, OK 8551); Hotter than That/Savoy Blues (1927, OK 8535); Fireworks (1928, OK 8597); A Monday Date (1928, OK 8609); West End Blues (1928, OK 8597); Save it Pretty Mama (1928, OK 8675); Weather Bird (1928, OK 41454); Muggles (1928, OK 8703); Tight like This (1928, OK 8649)

As big-band leader: Mahogany Hall Stomp (1929, OK 8680); Ain't Misbehavin' (1929, OK 8714); When You're Smiling (1929, OK 8729); Sweethearts on Parade (1930, Col. 2688D); Star Dust (1931, OK 41530); Between the Devil and the Deep Blue Sea (1932, OK 41550); I Gotta Right to Sing the Blues (1933, Vic. 24233); Struttin' with Some Barbecue (1938, Decca 1661); I Double Dare You (1938, Decca 1636)

As leader of the All Stars: Rockin' Chair/Save it Pretty Mama (1947, Vic. 40-4004); I surrender, Dear/Baby, Won't You Please Come Home (1950, Decca 9-27190); Basin Street Blues (1954, Decca 29102); St. Louis Blues/Yellow Dog Blues (1954, Col. B1933); Black and Blue/Honeysuckle Rose (1955, Col. B2187); Hello Dolly (1963, Kapp 573)

As sideman: K. Oliver: Chimes Blues/Froggie Moore (1923, Gennett 5135); F. Henderson: Go 'long Mule (1924, Col. 228D); C. Williams: Texas Moaner Blues (1924, OK 8171); F. Henderson: Copenhagen (1924, Voc. 14926); Mandy Make Up Your Mind (1924, Para. 20367); Red Onion Jazz Babies: Cake Walkin' Babies (1924, Gennett 5627); F. Henderson: Sugar Foot Stomp (1925, Col. 395D)

As accompanist: B. Smith: St. Louis Blues (1925, Col. 14064D), Reckless Blues (1925, Col. 14056D); T. Smith: Railroad Blues (1925, Para. 12262); C. Smith: Shipwrecked Blues (1925, Col. 14077D); C. Hill: Lonesome Weary Blues (1926, OK 8453)

BIBLIOGRAPHY

DISCOGRAPHIES, ETC.

Satchmo: Collector's Copy (Hollywood, CA, 1971) [iconography]

J. G. Jepsen: *A Discography of Louis Armstrong: 1923–1971* (Copenhagen, 1973)

B. Englund: "A Louis Armstrong Filmography," *Coda*, xii/1 (1974), 5; no.145 (1976), 32

K. Strateman: "Louis Armstrong: a Filmo-discography," *IAJRCJ*, x–xi (aut. 1977 – aut. 1978)

H. Westerberg: *Boy from New Orleans: Louis "Satchmo" Armstrong* (Copenhagen, *c*1981) [discography]

TRANSCRIPTIONS

L. Armstrong: Fifty Hot Choruses (New York, 1927)

——: *125 Hot Breaks* (New York, 1927)

——: *A Jazz Master* (New York, 1961) [20 solos]

LIFE AND WORKS STUDIES

L. Armstrong: *Swing that Music* (New York, 1936)

R. Goffin: *Louis Armstrong: le roi du jazz* (Paris, 1947; Eng. trans. 1947/*R*1977 as *Horn of Plenty*)

H. Panassié: *Louis Armstrong* (Paris, 1947; Eng. trans. 1971)

L. Armstrong: *Satchmo: my Life in New Orleans* (New York, 1954)

A. McCarthy: *Louis Armstrong* (London, 1960); repr. in *The Kings of Jazz*, ed. S. Green (New York, 1978)

M. Jones, J. Chilton, and L. Feather: *Salute to Satchmo* (London, 1970)

R. Meryman: *Louis Armstrong: a Self-portrait* (New York, 1971)

M. Jones and J. Chilton: *Louis: the Louis Armstrong Story 1900–1971* (London, 1971)

J. L. Collier: *Louis Armstrong: an American Genius* (New York, 1983)

G. Giddins, ed.: "Armstrong at 85," *Village Voice*, xxx (27 Aug 1985), 65 [special section]

ANALYTICAL AND SPECIALIST STUDIES

F. Ramsey Jr. and C. E. Smith, eds.: *Jazzmen* (New York, 1939/*R*1977)

J. Slawe: *Louis Armstrong: zehn monographische Studien* (Basle, 1953)

A. Hodeir: *Hommes et problèmes du jazz* (Paris, 1955; Eng. trans., 1956/*R*1975 as *Jazz: its Evolution and Essence*), chap.4

M. Edey: "Louis Armstrong," *Jazz Review*, ii/7 (1959), 28

R. Hadlock: *Jazz Masters of the Twenties* (New York, 1965, 2/1974)

W. Austin: *Music in the 20th Century* (New York, 1966)

M. Williams: *Jazz Masters of New Orleans* (New York, 1967)

G. Schuller: *Early Jazz: its Roots and Musical Development* (New York, 1968), 89–133

H. Pleasants: *The Great American Popular Singers* (New York, 1974)

H. D. Caffey: "The Musical Style of Louis Armstrong," *Journal of Jazz Studies*, iii/1 (1975), 72

C. Albertson and J. S. Wilson: Liner notes, *Giants of Jazz* (TL 01, 1978)

JAMES LINCOLN COLLIER

Armstrong, William D(awson) (*b* Alton, IL, 11 Feb 1868; *d* Alton, 9 July 1936). Organist. He was trained in St. Louis and then in Chicago under Clarence Eddy. In 1890 he returned to Alton, becoming organist at the First Baptist Church, then at St. Paul's, and, in 1894, at the Church of the Redeemer, where he remained for four years. Beginning in 1898 he held a decade-long appointment at the Church of the Unity, St. Louis. He began his work as a teacher at the Forest Park University for Women, St. Louis, in 1891; the following year he became music director and chairman of the newly founded music department of Shurtleff College and the Western Military Academy, both in Upper Alton. Although he relinquished his administrative duties in 1908 or 1909, he continued to teach there for several more years, resigning eventually to found the Armstrong School of Music in Alton. He served as organist of the St. Louis Exposition, 1904, as vice-president of the Music Teachers National Association, 1905–6, and in 1914 was offered but refused a position as director of a new school of music at what was then the Illinois State University in Champaign. Armstrong composed an opera, *The Spectre Bridegroom* (1899, after Washington Irving), orchestral and choral works including two masses (1899, 1908) and two complete services, as well as chamber music, keyboard pieces, and songs. He is the author of *Rudiments of Musical Notation* (1900), *The Pianoforte Pedals* (1911), and *The Romantic World of Music* (1922/*R*1969), the last a series of entertaining biographical sketches.

BIBLIOGRAPHY

W. T. Norton: *William Dawson Armstrong, American Composer* (New York, 1916) [incl. complete list of works]

WILLIAM OSBORNE

Arndt, Felix (*b* New York, 20 May 1889; *d* Harmon, NY, 16 Oct 1918). Composer and pianist. After studying piano at the New York Conservatory and taking private lessons with Alexander Lambert, he pursued a varied career in New York, writing material for vaudeville entertainers, serving as staff pianist for various publishers, and recording extensively both on piano rolls (Duo-Art, QRS) and discs (Victor). Arndt's compositions combine salon gentility with occasional ragtime syncopation, foreshadowing the novelty-piano works of the 1920s by such composers as Confrey and Bargy. They include *Clover Club*, *Desecration*, *Love in June*, *Marionette*, and the especially well-known *Nola* (published in 1916).

RONALD RIDDLE

Arnold, Eddy (*b* nr Henderson, TN, 15 May 1918). Country-music and popular singer. He began his career in 1935 as a guitarist in a fiddle and guitar band in Jackson, Tennessee. He performed on radio stations in Memphis, St. Louis, and Louisville in the late 1930s and early 1940s, and began to gain recognition as a vocal soloist with Pee Wee King's Golden West Cowboys. In 1943 he signed a recording contract with RCA Victor, and during the next five years he became the most commercially successful singer in country music. He also performed regularly on the "Grand Ole Opry" and "Checkerboard Square" radio programs. At this stage of his career he sang in a rural style and was known as the "Tennessee Plowboy"; much of the distinctive instrumental flavor of songs by him such as *Cattle Call* and *Bouquet of Roses* was supplied by the melodious steel-guitar playing of Roy Wiggins.

From 1949 Arnold increasingly adopted a more mainstream popular approach: his choice of songs, the character of the accompaniments, and his full, crooning vocal sound were all calculated to give his music a broader appeal; his recording of *I really don't want to know* (1954), with its muted guitars and background voices, epitomizes this new style, which was the one that suited him best. In the 1960s Arnold sought a sophisticated, cosmopolitan image, in striking contrast to that of his early career; he performed in Nevada nightclubs and on most of the major variety shows on national television. He also had his own syndicated television show, "Eddy Arnold Time." Though he was no longer strictly a country singer, in 1966 he was elected to the Country Music Hall of Fame.

BIBLIOGRAPHY

E. Arnold: *It's a Long Way from Chester County* (New York, 1969)

"Arnold, Eddy," *CBY 1970*

BILL C. MALONE

Arnold, Kokomo [James; Gitfiddle Jim] (*b* Lovejoy, GA, 15 Feb 1901; *d* Chicago, IL, 8 Nov 1968). Blues singer and guitarist. He grew up on a Georgia farm, learning to play guitar at the age of ten, and was an accomplished musician by the time he settled in Buffalo at the age of 18. In the 1920s he performed in local clubs and traveled with other singers as far south as Mississippi. Arnold played a steel-bodied guitar laid horizontally across his lap, stroking the strings with a glass flask to produce a wailing sound. Although his natural voice was low, the singing on many of his records is high-pitched; he often employed a buzzing tone as a drone to accompany guitar solos. As Gitfiddle Jim he recorded *Paddlin' Blues* (1930, Vic. 23268), an instrumental tour de force, in Memphis, but despite his dazzling technique, Victor did not record him again. In 1934 his *Old Original Kokomo Blues* (Decca 7026) was an immediate success; he made over 70 titles as Kokomo Arnold in the next four years, and several more with the pianist Peetie Wheatstraw, including *Set Down Gal* (1937, Decca 7361), a fine example of their barrelhouse duets. The solo *Policy Wheel Blues* (1935, Decca 7147) was typical of his lyrically original blues, while *Twelves* (1935, Decca 7083), a version of *The Dirty Dozens*, demonstrated his use of traditional themes as a vehicle for his exciting playing. In 1936 he began working in a steel mill, and eventually gave up music altogether.

BIBLIOGRAPHY

P. Oliver: "Kokomo Arnold," *Jazz Monthly*, viii/3 (1962), 10

J. Parsons: "Kokomo Arnold Discography," *Jazz Monthly*, viii (1962), no.3, p.16; no.4, p.15

PAUL OLIVER

ARP. Company of synthesizer manufacturers. It was founded as ARP Instruments by Alan R. Pearlman (and named from his initials) in Newton Highlands, near Boston, in 1970; a division of Tonus Inc., it later moved to nearby Newton and Lexington. Pearlman had previously founded a company (which he sold in 1967) that marketed operational amplifiers; this experience provided the basis for what was at the time the exceptional stability of the temperature-controlled oscillators in the ARP synthesizers. At various times ARP employed musicians, including David Friend, Roger Powell, and Thomas Piggott, in different roles; besides Pearlman, the designers included Friend, Dennis Colin, Jeremy Hill, and Philip Dodds.

The ARP synthesizer was one of the principal "second-generation" synthesizers, which profited from the greatly increased availability of integrated circuits in the five or six years that had elapsed since the first generation. ARP at first marketed modular synthesizers in several sizes as the 2000 series. The most successful of these instruments was the ARP 2500 (1970). Like all synthesizers up to that time, the ARP 2500 was designed primarily for electronic music studios, but it found some concert applications. In 1971 the 2600 model was introduced, which was followed later that year by the Odyssey, a direct rival to the Minimoog (introduced in 1970 by the R. A. Moog Co.), and about 1973 by the three-octave Pro-Soloist, which could be used in conjunction with an electronic organ.

During the second half of the 1970s ARP's sales became the highest of any synthesizer company – a survey published in 1980 showed that it had taken 39% of the American market. The models produced by the company after 1973 included the Explorer, Pro/DGX (developed from the Pro-Soloist), Solus and Axxe, and the Avatar, a guitar synthesizer, marketed in 1978 and based in part on the Odyssey (it was a comparative failure, from which ARP did not recover). The Quadra, the company's first polyphonic synthesizer (*c*1980), was followed by the digital Chroma (developed though not manufactured by ARP), which includes a microcomputer programmed from a touch panel. From about 1974 ARP also manufactured the Solina string synthesizer, under license from the Dutch Solina company, and subsequently developed its own models, the Omni (1975, the best-seller of the ARP range), and the Quartet (*c*1980, manufactured for ARP in Italy) which included brass, organ, and piano sections. In spite of its success, ARP ceased to operate in 1981, owing to "corporate mismanagement"; after its demise the Chroma and two electronic pianos were taken over by CBS Musical Instruments and marketed by its Rhodes division.

BIBLIOGRAPHY

D. Friend: "The Super-Stable ARP Precision Voltage Controlled Oscillator," *Synthesis*, no.1 (1970), 9

D. Friend, A. R. Pearlman, and E. Maltzman: *Lessons in Electronic Music* (Milwaukee, 1974)

D. Friend, A. R. Pearlman, and T. D. Piggott: *Learning Music with Synthesizers* (Milwaukee, 1974)

B. L. Gardner: *The Development and Testing of a Basic Self-Instructional Program for the ARP 2600 Portable Electronic Synthesizer and Effects on Attitudes toward Electronic Music* (diss., Michigan State U., 1978)

D. T. Horn: *Electronic Music Synthesizers* (Blue Ridge Summit, PA, 1980), 59

Devarahi: *The Complete Guide to Synthesizers* (Englewood Cliffs, NJ, 1982), 177

R. Powell: "ARP: the Early Years," *Keyboard*, viii/5 (1982), 58

C. R. Waters: "Raiders of the Lost ARP," *Inc.* (Nov 1982); rev. as "The Rise & Fall of ARP Instruments," *Keyboard*, ix/4 (1983), 16

HUGH DAVIES

Arpino, Gerald (*b* Staten Island, NY, 14 Jan 1928). Choreographer. He studied ballet with Mary Ann Wells in Seattle and with Margaret Craske, Antony Tudor, Alexandra Fedorova, and Muriel Stuart in New York, where he also studied modern dance with May O'Donnell and Gertrude Shurr. After a career as a leading dancer with the Joffrey Ballet, he became the associate director and resident choreographer of that company. His ballets to American music include *Nightwings* (1966; music by La Montaine), *Trinity* (1970; Alan Raph and Lee Holdridge), *Valentine* and *Jackpot* (1971, 1973; Druckman), *Sacred Grove on Mount Tamalpais* (1972; Raph), *The Relativity of Icarus* (1974; Samuel), and *Light Rain* (1981; Douglas Adams and Russ Gauthier); he also choreographed *Jamboree* (1984; Teo Macero), a tribute to the American Southwest and the first ballet commissioned by an American city (San Antonio). In *Drums, Dreams, and Banjos* (1975) he used songs by Stephen Foster, orchestrated by Peter Link. Arpino has also created dances for musical comedy, television, and opera.

SUSAN AU

Arrau, Claudio (*b* Chillán, Chile, 6 Feb 1903). Pianist. A child prodigy, he gave his first public recital at the age of five in Santiago. After studying with Bindo Paoli for two years, he was sent, with the support of the Chilean government, to study at Stern's Conservatory in Berlin, where he was a pupil of Martin Krause from 1912 to 1918. He gave his first recital in Berlin in 1914, followed by extensive tours of Germany and Scandinavia, and a European tour in 1918, during which he played with many of the leading orchestras. In 1921 he returned for the first time to South America, where he gave successful concerts in Argentina and Chile. He first played in London in 1922 and a year later toured the USA, making his Carnegie Hall début and appearing with the Boston SO, under Pierre Monteux, and the Chicago PO, under Frederick Stock.

In 1924 Arrau joined the faculty of Stern's Conservatory, where he taught until 1940, and in 1927 he further enhanced his international reputation by winning the Grand Prix International des Pianistes in Geneva. Notable among his European concerts before World War II was a series of 12 recitals in Berlin in 1935, in which he played the entire keyboard works of Bach. In 1940 he left Berlin, returning to Chile to found a piano school in Santiago. A year later, following a further tour of the USA (which was greeted with the highest critical acclaim), he and his family settled in New York. He became an American citizen in 1979, after giving up his Chilean nationality the previous year as a protest against the military regime in the country of his birth.

Highlights of Arrau's international career have included complete performances of Beethoven's piano sonatas in London and New York (1952–4), and world tours in 1968 and 1974–5. Reducing the number of concerts he gave annually (from as many as 100 to about 70) as he approached his ninth decade, he toured the USA, Canada, Europe, Brazil, and Japan in 1981–2. After a 17-year absence he made an emotional tour of Chile in May 1984, in part a result of his having been awarded the Chilean National Arts Prize the previous year.

Arrau has acquired a special reputation for his interpretations of Brahms, Schumann, Liszt, Chopin and, above all, Beethoven, a reputation which is reflected by his many recordings. He has the technique of a virtuoso, but is one of the least ostentatious of pianists. His tempos are sometimes unusually slow, and even when they are not he gives the impression of having considered deeply the character and shape of each phrase. He can give a performance that is so thorough in its consideration of detail that it seems lacking in spontaneity and momentum; but at its best his rich-toned and thoughtful playing conveys exceptional intellectual power and depth of feeling. He received the Bülow Medal from the Berlin PO in 1980, to mark the 60th anniversary of his début with the orchestra, and several recording companies issued special editions of his performances in 1983, in honor of his 80th birthday. He completed an Urtext edition of the Beethoven sonatas for Peters in 1978.

BIBLIOGRAPHY

N. Boyle: "Claudio Arrau," *Gramophone Record Review*, lxxvi (1960), 195 [with discography by F. F. Clough and G. J. Cuming]

J. Kaiser: *Grosse Pianisten in unserer Zeit* (Munich, 1965, rev. 2/1972), 110; Eng. trans. (London, 1971), 86 [with enlarged discography]

C. Arrau: "A Performer Looks at Psychoanalysis," *HiFi/MusAm*, xvii/2 (1967), 50

R. Osborne: "Keyboard Oracle: Claudio Arrau in Conversation," *Records and Recording*, xvi/1 (1972), 26

——: "Claudio Arrau at 75," *Gramophone*, lv (1977–8), 1385

B. Morrison: "Arrau at 75," *Music and Musicians*, xxvi/8 (1978), 32

D. and B. Rosenberg: *The Music Makers* (New York, 1979), 217

J. Horowitz: *Conversations with Arrau* (New York, 1983)

ROBERT PHILIP/R

Arrow Music Press. Music publishing firm. It was founded in New York in 1938 by Marc Blitzstein, Aaron Copland, Lehman Engel, and Virgil Thomson to encourage the composition, publication, and distribution of contemporary American music. In addition to leasing the catalogue of the Cos Cob Press, it published works by Carter, Cowell, Diamond, Ray Green, Harris, Ives, Piston, Schuman, and Sessions as well as its founders. Its catalogue was acquired by Boosey & Hawkes in 1956, but with the provision that composers could withdraw their works for placement elsewhere.

BIBLIOGRAPHY

V. Thomson: *Virgil Thomson* (New York, 1966), 278

L. Engel: *This Bright Day: an Autobiography* (New York, 1974), 88

R. ALLEN LOTT

Arroyo, Martina (*b* New York, 2 Feb 1936). Soprano. She studied singing with Josef Turnau, among others, and attended Hunter College in New York (BA 1956). With Grace Bumbry she won the Metropolitan Opera Auditions in 1958, and in the same year sang in the American première of Ildebrando Pizzetti's *Assassinio nella cattedrale* at Carnegie Hall. After taking minor roles at the Metropolitan, she went to Europe and sang leading roles at Vienna, Düsseldorf, Berlin, Frankfurt, and (from 1963 to 1968) Zurich. At the Metropolitan she has sung all the major Verdi roles (which form the core of her repertory) as well as Donna Anna, Butterfly, Liù (*Turandot*), Santuzza (*Cavalleria rusticana*), La Gioconda, and Elsa (*Lohengrin*). She first performed at Covent Garden in 1968 (as Aida) and at the Paris Opéra in 1973. In the USA Arroyo has often sung in oratorio and recitals. She gave the première of Barber's concert scena *Andromache's Farewell* (April 1963), and her many recordings include not only opera, ranging from Handel and Mozart to Verdi, but also the first revised version of Stockhausen's *Momente*, in the first performance of which she took part at the 1965 Donaueschingen Festival. Her rich, powerfully projected voice, heard to greatest advantage in the Verdi *spinto* roles, is yet flexible enough for Mozart; her stage presence is dignified, if somewhat undramatic.

BIBLIOGRAPHY

SouthernB

"Arroyo, Martina," *CBY 1971*

J. B. Steane: *The Grand Tradition* (New York, 1974), 413

S. E. Rubin: "Arroyo," *Opera News*, xli/8 (1976), 22

J. Hines: *Great Singers on Great Singing* (Garden City, NY, 1982), 30

ALAN BLYTH/R

ARSC. *See* ASSOCIATION FOR RECORDED SOUND COLLECTIONS.

Art Ensemble of Chicago (AEC). Avant-garde jazz quintet. Its members are Roscoe Mitchell and Joseph Jarman (reed instruments, vibraphone, marimba, and unusual winds such as whistles, conch shells, etc.), LESTER BOWIE (brass instruments, harmonica, celeste, kelp horn, etc.), Malachi Favors (double bass, zither, melodica, banjo), and Don Moye ("sun percussion"). All vocalize and all play percussion instruments, including drums from several continents (especially Africa), cymbals, gongs, bells, woodblocks, sirens, bicycle horns, etc.

This eclectic and theatrical group evolved gradually from Mitchell's combo and, more generally, from the spirit of cooperative discovery encouraged in Chicago's Experimental Band (formed 1961) and formalized in the ASSOCIATION FOR THE ADVANCEMENT OF CREATIVE MUSICIANS (1965). It officially formed in Paris in 1969 as a "drummer-less" (but not percussion-less) quartet consisting of Mitchell, Jarman, Bowie, and Favors, with Moye joining in 1970. While based in France the ensemble appeared on television and radio, recorded 11 albums and three film scores, and presented hundreds of government-sponsored concerts throughout Western Europe. Upon returning to the USA in 1971 they decided, for financial reasons, to restrict their performances to profitable events such as large concerts, jazz festivals, and university workshops. In 1975 extended club engagements and a tour of the West Coast brought them considerable recognition. Thereafter, they were able to collaborate sporadically and to cultivate individual projects without undermining the group's popularity, which grew in the late 1970s and early 1980s with the release of albums from a major international recording company (ECM) and their own label (AECO).

The Art Ensemble of Chicago developed within the free jazz tradition, their principal instruments being trumpet, alto saxophone, double bass, and drums. Its members are virtuoso, experimental improvisers in this tradition who liberally use dissonance, non-tempered intonation, noise, fast flurries of saxophone melody, dense textures, and irregular rhythms. However, their motto, "Great Black Music – Ancient to Modern," more accurately describes the breadth of their music than the term "free jazz." Their performances combine theatricality – costumes, make-up, dance, pantomime, comedy, parody, absurd dialogue, playlets – with musics from Africa (drum choirs), black America (blues, gospel, pop, jazz), and Europe (waltzes, marches). This diversity is magnified further by an economical, sensitive use of the tone colors of several hundred standard, exotic, or invented instruments, and by an ever-changing mélange of original compositions, individual features, and collective improvisation. These widely varying actions or sounds might appear at any time within a performance, yet years of rehearsal have enabled each member to react immediately to his fellows, the result being spontaneous and yet immanently coherent musical structures.

RECORDINGS
(selective list)

A Jackson in your House (1969, BYG 529302); *People in Sorrow* (1969, Pathé 2C062-10523); *Message to our Folks* (1969, BYG 529328); *Reese and the Smooth Ones* (1969, BYG 529329); *Les stances à Sophie* (1970, Pathé 2C062-11365); *Phase One* (1970, America 6116); *With Fontella Bass* (1970, America 6117); *Live at Mandel Hall* (1972, Trio 6022-3); *Bap-tizum* (1972, Atl. 1639); *Kabalaba* (1974, AECO 004); *Nice Guys* (1978, ECM 1126); *Full Force* (1980, ECM 1167); *Urban Bushmen* (1980, ECM 1211-2)

BIBLIOGRAPHY

E. Jost: *Free Jazz* (Graz, Austria, 1974)

R. Zabor: "Profile: the Art Ensemble," *Musician, Player and Listener*, no.17 (1979), 39

L. Birnbaum: "Art Ensemble of Chicago: 15 Years of Great Black Music," *Down Beat*, xlvi/9 (1979), 15

R. Palmer: "Art Ensemble of Chicago Takes Jazz to the Stage," *Rolling Stone*, no.303 (1 Nov 1979), 9

C. Gans: "Art Ensemble of Chicago: Nice Guys Finish First," *Jazz Forum*, no.68 (1980), 33

P. Kemper: "Zur Funktion des Mythos im Jazz der 70er Jahre: soziokulturelle Aspekte eines musikalischen Phänomens dargestellt an der ästhetischen Konzeption des 'Art Ensemble of Chicago'," *Jazzforschung*, xiii (1981), 45

J. Litweiler: "The Art Ensemble of Chicago: Adventures in the Urban Bush," *Down Beat*, xlix/6 (1982), 19

E. Janssens and H. de Craen: *Art Ensemble of Chicago Discography, Unit and Members* (Brussels, 1983)

J. Rockwell: "Jazz, Group Improvisation, Race and Racism," *All American Music: Composition in the Late Twentieth Century* (New York, 1983), 164

G. Lock: "Windy City Warriors," *The Wire*, no.9 (1984), 26

D. Palmer: "20th Anniversary for an Unusual Jazz Ensemble," *New York Times* (14 April 1985), §H, p.24

BARRY KERNFELD

Art rock. A term applied to rock music that has artistic or aesthetic pretensions. Art rock developed in Britain in the 1960s out of an artistic self-consciousness engendered by the art-school background of many British rock musicians, together with the pervasive populism of the period. The Beatles' *Sgt. Pepper's Lonely Hearts Club Band* (1968) is generally considered the seminal art-rock album. The ponderous British art-rock bands of the early 1970s found imitators in the USA, where their simplistic emulations of the grandeur of classical music declined into the pomposity of "arena rock." A sparer, more dissonant, minimalist style of rock (which better merits the description "art rock") was introduced in New York by the Velvet Underground in the late 1960s and perpetuated in the early 1970s by the New York Dolls, Lou Reed, and Patti Smith. This style blossomed in New York in the mid-1970s in the work of such punk and new-wave bands as the Ramones, Television, Blondie, and Talking Heads. Thereafter, most American noncommercial new-wave rock, with its rejection of conventional popular expectations, took on the aura of art.

BIBLIOGRAPHY

J. Rockwell: "Art Rock," "The Sound of Manhattan," *The Rolling Stone Illustrated History of Rock & Roll*, ed. J. Miller (New York, rev.2/1980), 347, 415

JOHN ROCKWELL

Art song. A short vocal piece of serious artistic purpose. During the 18th century "art song" came to have its predominant modern meaning of secular solo song with an independent keyboard accompaniment; for a discussion of songs for more than one voice (or partsongs) *see* CHORAL MUSIC. The subject of this article is the development of the art song tradition in the USA. Other types of song (discussed elsewhere in this dictionary) include theater songs, popular songs (*see* POPULAR MUSIC), ragtime and jazz songs, folksongs, and work songs.

1. *c*1750–*c*1850. 2. *c*1850 to World War II. 3. After World War II.

1. *c*1750–*c*1850. The earliest extant American art songs, signed "F. H.," are contained (along with some 100 mid-18th-century English songs) in a manuscript copied out by Francis Hopkinson, an amateur musician from Philadelphia. The first of these to appear in the manuscript is *My days have been so wondrous free*, dated 1759 and long regarded as the first American secular song; the others initialed by Hopkinson – *The Garland*, *Oh come to Mason Borough's grave*, and *With pleasure I have past my days* – may

be contemporaneous. Like the songs in Hopkinson's later published collection, *Seven Songs for the Harpsichord or Forte Piano* (1788), dedicated to George Washington and in fact containing eight songs, the pieces in the manuscript are in the style of English songs written by such composers as Thomas Arne, Stephen Storace, William Shield, and James Hook for performance in pleasure gardens or to be inserted in light operas.

English songs provided the models for American songs throughout the colonial and federal periods; indeed, Hopkinson's most notable successors were British immigrants. Benjamin Carr, also of Philadelphia, published many of his 61 songs in two serial anthologies, *Musical Journal for the Piano Forte* (1800–04) and *Carr's Musical Miscellany in Occasional Numbers* (1812–25). Also among Carr's songs are several sets of ballads, including *Six Ballads . . . from The Lady of the Lake* op.7, published in the same year (1810) as the poem by Sir Walter Scott on which they are based; the set contains the *Hymn to the Virgin* ("Ave Maria"), which is especially notable for its harp-like arpeggiated accompaniment. Carr's most popular song was *The Little Sailor Boy* (1798). James Hewitt, who immigrated in 1792, was second only to Carr in his success as a composer of songs: *The Wounded Hussar* (*c*1880) went through 12 printings, as did *Primroses* (or *The Primrose Girl*, *c*1793). Oliver Shaw, the first native American to make a mark as a composer of songs, was best known for his settings of texts by Thomas Moore, such as *Mary's Tears* (1812) and *There's nothing true but heav'n* (1816), both on poems from Moore's *Sacred Melodies*.

In the period between the War of 1812 and the Civil War American art song moved away from the English style and began to reflect the influence of various musical genres and styles in a way that became typical of American artistic expression. John Hill Hewitt, the son of James Hewitt, composed more than 300 songs, beginning with the successful *The Minstrel's Return'd from the War* (?1828), which was written in the manner of his father's songs; later he incorporated elements of Italian opera arias, Alpine yodeling songs (which were performed in the USA by visiting singers from Switzerland and Austria), and minstrel songs. Anthony Philip Heinrich, an immigrant from Bohemia who became known as "the Beethoven of America," began to compose after his arrival in the USA. Heinrich's songs, many of which are occasional pieces (such as the *Visit to Philadelphia*, 1820), are less audacious than his keyboard works; nevertheless, the vocal lines often combine a mellifluous Viennese charm with surprising outbursts of coloratura and are supported by elaborate accompaniments. The cadenza of the *Prologue Song* which opens *The Dawning of Music in Kentucky* op.1 (1820), an extensive collection of songs and instrumental pieces, extends over more than two octaves; his setting of Robert Burns's *From thee Eliza I must go*, has a similar range and exploits abrupt harmonic contrasts between tonic major and minor keys.

The most gifted song composer of the era was Stephen Foster. Foster was well acquainted with the various song styles of his day, and this knowledge is evident in his own songs, of which there are approximately 200. *Open thy lattice, love* (1844), his first published song, is in the English tradition. But echoes of Italian opera arias by Rossini, Bellini, and Donizetti can be heard in *The Voice of By Gone Days* and *Ah! may the red rose live alway* (both 1850) and *Beautiful dreamer* (1864), among others. And Foster, of Irish ancestry himself, readily absorbed the style of Thomas Moore's popular *A Selection of Irish Melodies* (1808–34), as is demonstrated in such songs as *Jeanie with the Light Brown Hair* (1854) and *Gentle Annie* (1856). Some of his songs for minstrel shows – perhaps especially *Nelly was a lady* (1849), *Old Folks at Home* (1851), *My old Kentucky home, good night* (1853), and *Old Black Joe* (1860) – transcend that genre in sensitivity of expression. In the period immediately before, during, and after the Civil War, the songs of George Frederick Root and Henry Clay Work addressed popular causes, and rivaled Foster's songs in public acceptance.

See also POPULAR MUSIC, §II.

2. *c*1850 TO WORLD WAR II. Before the Civil War the aim of both popular and art songs was usually to express common emotions, but thereafter some American composers became artistically more ambitious, and the distinction between the popular song and the "serious" art song became greater. An increasing number of American composers chose to study in Europe, where they found in the German lied and the French *mélodie* new ways of enhancing the relationship between lyric poetry and music. As early as 1846, in *Thine eye hath seen the spot*, George F. Bristow extended the range of modulation, anticipating the sophistication of such composers as Amy Beach, George W. Chadwick, Edward MacDowell, and Ethelbert Nevin, who were a generation younger. Beach passionately embraced the chromatic styles of Chopin and Liszt in songs such as *Ah, love, but a day* (1900). The same skill is evident in *A Flower Cycle* (1892) and *Lyrics from Told in the Gate* (1897), two sets of songs by Chadwick, although the texts of these songs, by Arlo Bates, are less impressive than the music. The 42 songs by MacDowell are equally well crafted, but they too are limited by their texts, which for the most part are MacDowell's own. Many other composers wrote songs in this period, but few are as polished as the early ones by Nevin, and none had the success of his *The Rosary* (1898).

The growing interest of American composers in French songs is apparent in many songs of the first two decades of the 20th century, including several cycles by John Alden Carpenter, such as *Water-colors* (1916) and the widely performed *Gitanjali* (1913). Carpenter's *Serenade* (1920) imitates Debussy in its use of Spanish elements. Early in his career Charles T. Griffes composed settings of both German and French texts; later he reconciled the two strands of influence in such strikingly original works as *Three Poems of Fiona MacLeod* (1918), the orchestral version of which reflects his knowledge of the music of Richard Strauss, and *Sorrow of Mydath* (1917), the second of two settings of poems by John Masefield.

The indigenous influences parodied in minstrel shows early in the century entered the recital hall in the form of folk music arranged for voice and piano. Arthur Farwell was one of many composers who used American Indian melodies. (Farwell also set many texts by Emily Dickinson, the first as early as 1907.) Charles Wakefield Cadman wrote over 300 songs; his adaptations of tribal melodies, especially *From the Land of the Sky-blue Water* (1909) and *At Dawning* (1906), became favorite recital pieces and were extensively recorded. Other composers turned to arrangements of black spirituals for voice and piano. Those by H. T. Burleigh are especially noteworthy; the composer himself sang them for Dvořák, and they have been performed internationally by many singers.

Charles Ives, the first American composer of international stature, made particularly important contributions to the song repertory. His heterogeneous output of about 150 songs includes a wide range of styles and subjects and forms a kind of musical diary of his composing career. Like some of his piano studies and parodies, the songs adumbrate many distinctive Ivesian techniques and effects: interval control in *The Cage* (1906) and *Soliloquy* (1907); Victorian potpourri in *He is There!*, *The Things our Father Loved*, and *In Flanders Fields* (all 1917); rhythmic and harmonic disruption of pre-existing music in the hymns *Watchman* (1913) and *At the River* (?1916), and in *The Side-show* (1921), based on a popular song by Pat Rooney; microtonal sliding in *Like a Sick Eagle* (?1913); rhythmic speech in *Charlie Rutlage* (1920/21; *see* NOTATION, fig. 10); and the capturing of popular culture in *The Circus Band* and *Waltz* (both ?1894).

Some of Ives's songs are reductions of works for larger forces, while others are sketches intended to be incorporated into larger works. Ives wrote no song cycles, though he suggested some groupings of songs for performance without voice as instrumental pieces. He wrote early songs to German and French texts, trivial comedies for the salon, and such intensely dissonant works as *Majority* (1921), the first piece in the collection *114 Songs* which he printed privately in 1922. The tone-clusters of *Majority* are characteristic, as is the use of quotation (from the "Dead March" in Handel's *Saul*) in *Slow March* (?1887) for the funeral of a family pet. Generations of singers have used the ungainly but powerful *General William Booth Enters into Heaven* (1914), on a poem by Vachel Lindsay, almost as a campaign song to gain recognition for the uncompromising – and uncompromisingly American – Ives.

It is difficult to generalize about the nature of American art song between the world wars. The major composers of the period were occupied with work in other genres, and the few songs they wrote exemplify their personal styles rather than any general aesthetic trends. Early and concentrated atonality, for example, appears in *Toys* (1919) by Carl Ruggles. A mellow neoclassicism informs two songs of 1943 by Elliott Carter: *Voyage* (to a text by Hart Crane) and *Warble for Lilac-time* (Walt Whitman). Roger Sessions produced only one song with piano accompaniment, *On the Beach at Fontana* (1930; James Joyce). The prolific Henry Cowell wrote but a handful of songs and no song cycles.

Of the generation of composers born around 1900, Aaron Copland is noteworthy for his *Twelve Poems of Emily Dickinson* (1949–50), which has gained recognition as one of the finest song cycles to an English text, and his two sets of arrangements entitled *Old American Songs* (1950, 1952). The songs of Samuel Barber are of the same high quality. Barber was steeped in the vocal idiom, being a singer himself and the nephew of the opera singer Louise Homer, who was married to the songwriter Sidney Homer. Barber's *Hermit Songs* (1952–3) is a major cycle, and his Three Songs to texts by Joyce (1936) are among the most atmospherically effective settings of the poems concerned, which were also used by Sessions, Citkowitz, Antheil, Persichetti, and Del Tredici, among others.

3. AFTER WORLD WAR II. Three factors began to have an important impact on the composition of art songs after 1945: the development of modern American poetry, which provided composers with a new kind of text; the influence of the expressionistic, serial music of Schoenberg and Webern, a style that came to dominate progressive American music after 1950; and a growing interest in the expressive and structural possibilities of sonority, which led composers to seek alternatives to the traditional piano accompaniment.

By the mid-20th century American composers could benefit from the rich maturity of their country's literature. The personality of the poet, now treated as an equal partner in the creative process, emerges clearly in songs of differing musical styles. Two poets, Gertrude Stein and E. E. Cummings, have been especially influential. It was in response to Stein's poetry that Virgil Thomson developed his distinctive style in the 1930s, characterized by simplicity and a concern for natural wordsetting. His large output includes several cycles, among them *Five Songs to Poems of William Blake* (1951) and *Praises and Prayers* (1963). The influence of Stein is also evident in the works of John Cage, who set her poems in the early Three Songs (1932), and in Gunther Schuller's *Meditations* (1960) and William Brooks's *Medley* (1978), an anthology which makes use of various American song styles. Texts by Cummings have been set by Cage and Copland, as well as Morton Feldman, Salvatore Martirano, Marc Blitzstein, David Diamond, William Bergsma, Celius Dougherty, and John Duke, among many others.

After 1945 there emerged a distinction between composers specializing in songs of a traditional sort and those with wider interests. Eminent among the former is Ned Rorem, whose more than 400 songs cover a range of subjects almost as wide as Ives's. Rorem's cycle *Poems of Love and the Rain* (1963) is especially notable for its ingenious form: each poem is set twice, and the cycle is ordered palindromically. Theodore Chanler and Paul Bowles are two of the many composers of songs who have adopted conservative, tonal styles; Chanler's cycle *The Children* (1945) approaches the diatonic insouciance of Poulenc, and Bowles is fearlessly nostalgic in setting such texts as his own *Once a Lady was Here* (1946).

A large group of postwar composers has written in a more dissonant idiom, using the serial techniques developed by Schoenberg and Webern. This group includes Milton Babbitt, Ruth Crawford, Wallingford Riegger, Ernst Krenek, George Rochberg, and George Perle, whose *13 Dickinson Songs* (1979) were written for the soprano Bethany Beardslee, one of the most important interpreters of this repertory. The most adventurous composers have experimented with new treatments of both text and accompaniments. The piano parts for Cage's early Five Songs (1938) are fully notated, but carry no dynamic markings; the piano is closed in the accompaniment to *The Wonderful Widow of Eighteen Springs* (1942); and in later works such as *Aria* (1958) and the *Song Books* (1970) the voice is unaccompanied. Milton Babbitt's *Sounds and Words* (1960) has an abstract phonetic text, influenced perhaps by the verbal experiments of Cummings. And Babbitt is one of many composers who have combined voice and electronic tape, notably in works such as *Vision and Prayer* (1961), *Philomel* (1964), and *Phonemena* (1975), the last of which was originally conceived for voice and piano. The substitution of tape for piano in these works might be seen as symptomatic of the dissatisfaction of composers with the limitations of the piano.

Indeed, the popularity of the art song in its traditional guise has declined in the later 20th century, at least in more progressive circles. Some composers have turned instead to a different, but related genre, works for solo voice and chamber ensemble.

BIBLIOGRAPHY

O. G. T. Sonneck: *Early Concert-life in America (1731–1800)* (Leipzig, Germany, 1907/*R*1978)

W. T. Upton: *Art-song in America* (Boston, 1930/*R*1969 with suppl. 1938)

H. Nathan: "United States of America," *A History of Song*, ed. D. Stevens (New York, 1960), 408–60

G. D. Yerbury: *Song in America, from Early Times to about 1850* (Metuchen, NJ, 1971)

J. E. Carman, W. K. Gaeddert, and R. M. Resch: *Art-song in the United States, 1801–1976: an Annotated Bibliography* (New York, 1976; suppl., 1978) [incl. G. Myers: "Art-song in the United States 1759–1811"]

P. L. Miller: "The American Art Song, 1900–1940," *When I have Sung my Songs* (NW 247, 1976) [liner notes]

C. Hamm: *Yesterdays: Popular Song in America* (New York, 1979)

K. W. Keller and C. Rabson, eds.: *The National Tune Index: 18th-century Secular Music* (New York, 1980)

R. C. Friedberg: *American Art Song and American Poetry*, i: *America Comes of Age* (Metuchen, NJ, 1981); ii: *Voices of Maturity* (Metuchen, 1984); iii: *The Century Advances* (in preparation)

PETER DICKINSON, H. WILEY HITCHCOCK

Artzt, Alice (Josephine) (*b* Philadelphia, PA, 16 March 1943). Guitarist. As a child she studied piano and flute, and then at the age of 13 the classical guitar, completing her training in France with Ida Presti and Alexandre Lagoya, and in England with Julian Bream. She graduated from Columbia University (BA 1967), where she studied with Paul Henry Lang and Luening; additional coaching in composition was with Milhaud. Her début (London, 1969) was followed by concert tours of Europe and North America. Later tours took her through South and Central America, Africa, Australia, and the Far East. An innovative programmer, she is considered by many to be the leading woman guitarist of the USA. Two of Artzt's albums have been cited by critics as their choice for the year: *Alice Artzt Classic Guitar* (in *Records and Recording*, 1971) and *Guitar Music by Fernando Sor* (in the *Gramophone*, 1978). Author of *The Art of Practicing* (London, 1978), she has contributed many articles and reviews to music magazines. She taught at Mannes College (1966–9) and Trenton State College, New Jersey (1977–80), and was elected to the board of directors of the Guitar Foundation of America in 1978.

THOMAS F. HECK

ASCAP. *See* AMERICAN SOCIETY OF COMPOSERS, AUTHORS AND PUBLISHERS.

Ashbrook, William (Sinclair) (*b* Philadelphia, PA, 28 Jan 1922). Musicologist. He received a BA from the University of Pennsylvania in 1946 and an MA from Harvard University in 1947. He taught humanities at Stephens College (1949–55) and was a member of the English department at Indiana State University (1955–74). From 1974 to 1984 he was professor of opera at the Philadelphia College of the Performing Arts. Ashbrook has a lively interest in Italian opera and has contributed numerous articles on the subject. His books on Italian opera (*Donizetti*, 1965; *The Operas of Puccini*, 1968; and *Donizetti and his Operas*, 1982) are particularly valuable in this field.

PAULA MORGAN

Asheville Mountain Dance and Folk Festival. Annual folk festival founded in 1928 in Asheville, North Carolina. The oldest folk festival in the USA in continuous existence, it began when a local folklorist, Bascom Lamar Lunsford, was asked by the municipal chamber of commerce to organize performances of southern Appalachian mountain music and dance at the local Rhododendron Festival. Directed by Lunsford until the late 1960s, the festival has sought to preserve the cultural heritage of Appalachia, and to this end encourages young performers to enter competitions of traditional forms of music and dance. Held in the Thomas Wolfe Auditorium in the Civic Center in early August, the festival attracts mountain fiddlers, dulcimer sweepers, banjo and mouth-harp players, and dancers.

SARA VELEZ

Ashford and Simpson. Team of soul singers, songwriters, and record producers. Nikolas Ashford (*b* Fairfield, Hilton Head Island, SC, 4 May 1942) and Valerie Simpson (*b* New York, 26 Aug 1948) met in 1964, and began writing songs two years later; their first successful collaboration was *Let's go get stoned* (1966) which, in a recording by Ray Charles, reached no.31 on the pop chart. They became staff writers and producers for Motown, where they worked with such performers as Marvin Gaye and Tammi Terrell (*You're all I need to get by* (no.7, 1968) and *Ain't nothing like the real thing* (no.8, 1968)) and Diana Ross (*Ain't no mountain high enough* (no. 1, 1970)). Ashford produced two albums that Simpson recorded as a soloist (*Exposed!*, 1971, and *Valerie Simpson*, 1972), and in 1973, after they left Motown, they made their first album together, *Gimme Something Real*; they married in 1974. They continued to make recordings through the 1970s and into the 1980s, and produced albums for Diana Ross (*The Boss*, 1979) and Gladys Knight and the Pips (*About Love*, 1980), among others. As songwriters their best work is in a pop-gospel style, distinguished by Simpson's wide-ranging melodies and Ashford's inspirational love lyrics.

RECORDINGS

(selective list; recorded for Warner Bros. unless otherwise stated)

Gimme Something Real (2739, 1973); *Keep it Comin'* (Tamla 7351, 1973); *I Wanna Be Selfish* (2789, 1974); *Come As you Are* (2858, 1976); *Send it* (3088, 1977); *Is it Still Good to ya?* (3219, 1978); *Stay Free* (3357, 1978), incl. Found a Cure; *A Musical Affair* (3458, 1980); *Secret Opera* (Cap. 12207, 1982)

BIBLIOGRAPHY

SouthernB

STEPHEN HOLDEN

Ashforth, Alden (Banning) (*b* New York, 13 May 1933). Composer and teacher. He studied composition with Joseph Wood and Richard Hoffmann at Oberlin (BA 1958, BM 1958) and with Sessions, Kim, and Babbitt at Princeton (MFA 1960, PhD 1971). He began his teaching career at Princeton (1961) and held positions at Oberlin (1961–5) and several other schools before joining the faculty of UCLA in 1967. In 1969 he became coordinator of the UCLA electronic music studio and in 1980 he was made a full professor. Since 1952 he has been active as a producer of New Orleans jazz recordings. His writings include contributions to *Perspectives of New Music* (on Schoenberg) and *Footnote* (on Doc Paulin). Ashforth has received particular notice for his electronic works. *Byzantia: Two Journeys after Yeats* (1971–3) is pointillistic in effect, with mosaic-like juxtapositions of electronic, acoustical (voice, traditional instruments), and natural (flowing water, bird calls) sounds.

WORKS

Stage: The Quintessential Zymurgistic Waffle (musical comedy), elec, 1975, collab. P. Reale

Inst: Pf Sonata, 1955; Sonata, fl, hpd, 1956; 2 Pf Pieces, 1957; Variations, orch, 1958; Fantasy-variations, vn, pf, 1959; Episodes, chamber conc., 8 insts, 1962–8; Big Bang, pf 4 hands, 1970; Pas seul, fl, 1974; The Flowers of Orcus (Intavolatura), gui, 1976; Sentimental Waltz, pf, 1977; St. Bride's Suite, hpd, 1983

Vocal: The Unquiet Heart (Tanka Songs), S, chamber orch/pf, 1959–68; 4 Lyric Songs, high v, pf, 1961; Our Lady's Song, A, va, hpd, 1961; Aspects of Love, T/S, pf, 1978; Christmas Motets, chorus, 1980

Elec: Vocalise, 1965; Cycles, 1965; Mixed Brew, 1968; Byzantia: Two Journeys after Yeats, tape/(org, tape), 1971–3

Principal publishers: E. C. Schirmer, C. F. Peters

KATHERINE K. PRESTON

Ashley, Robert (Reynolds) (*b* Ann Arbor, MI, 28 March 1930). Composer and performer. He studied music theory at the University of Michigan (1948–52) and piano and composition at the Manhattan School (MS 1953), then returned to Ann Arbor to study acoustics and composition (1957–60). His teachers in composition included Riegger, Finney, Bassett, and Roberto Gerhard. As a composer and performer Ashley was active in Milton Cohen's Space Theater (1957–64), the ONCE Festivals and ONCE Group (*c*1958–69), and the Sonic Arts Union (1966–76); with each of these groups he toured the Americas and Europe. From 1969 to 1981 he directed the Center for Contemporary Music at Mills College, Oakland, California, where he organized an important public-access music and media facility.

Ashley was much influenced by his associations with Cohen, a painter and sculptor, and Gordon Mumma, a fellow member of the ONCE Group. He realized his first electroacoustic pieces while working with Cohen's mixed-media group Space Theater. With Mumma he wrote electroacoustic scores and invented electronic devices for live generation, manipulation, and deployment of sounds; their accumulated equipment became known as the Cooperative Studio for Electronic Music and formed the principal resource of the ONCE Group in Ann Arbor from 1958 to 1966. Rather than create specific electroacoustic compositions, they developed assorted sound materials which were then used in combinations in several pieces. Other influences were the film maker George Manupelli, the artist Mary Ashley (Ashley's wife), and "Blue" Gene Tyranny; also important was his early work on psychoacoustics and speech patterns, which reinforced his preoccupation with language and its levels of meaning.

Ashley describes his musical thinking as inherently theatrical. Even in his instrumental pieces, nearly all of which were written during the years 1959–63, his subject matter is frequently conceptual (and even theatrical), as in the portrayal in *Fives* (1962) of the improvisatory freedoms and relationships in jazz. In *Kittyhawk* (1964), an electronic theater piece about male and female interactions, the personalities of the performers themselves are brought out and contribute to the exploration of sexual roles. The *In memoriam* series (1963) discloses parallels between traditional musical forms and the patterns of relationships surrounding four figures in American history.

During the 1960s Ashley became a pioneer in mixed-media performance art. In such pieces as *Night Train* (1965), one of several in which he worked with Mary Ashley, his original ideas are developed and realized in collaboration with others and yet remain tightly controlled (the performances were carefully rehearsed). While working with Manupelli on multiple-projection films – Ashley was often responsible for the scripts as well as the music – he became interested in creating analogous musical simultaneities. In *The Trial of Anne Opie Wehrer and Unknown Accomplices for Crimes Against Humanity* (1968), a taped voice interrogates the protagonist while her two surrogates on stage reply, and all three are questioned by two additional interrogators: the resulting multilevel composition frequently dislocates the listener's sense of time. Manipulation of the perception of time is also a primary focus in *The Wolfman Motorcity Revue* (1968), another theater piece.

Robert Ashley as the speaker in the television opera "Perfect Lives (Private Parts)" (1977–83): still frame showing a fade from Ashley to the video screens that are an important component of the work

In the mid-1970s Ashley's interests coalesced in televised opera. *Music with Roots in the Aether* (1976) and *Perfect Lives (Private Parts)* (1977–83; see illustration) are operatic portraits in television-episode format, highly unconventional in their use of the medium, and alive with levels of meaning that defy selective attention to specific elements. In themselves striking, the spoken texts and visual imagery of Ashley's television works contribute to lyrical and aurally varied compositions and help to reveal the deeper musical structures. While an interest in simultaneity, artistic collaboration, speech patterns, and multiple levels of meaning is scarcely unique to Ashley, it is his achievement to have successfully incorporated these elements into aurally conceived and organized performance art.

WORKS

OPERAS

(for television unless otherwise stated: all with librettos by Ashley)

That Morning Thing (stage opera), 1967, Ann Arbor, 8 Feb 1968

Music with Roots in the Aether, 1976, Paris, 1976

Title Withdrawn, 1976, Paris, 1976

Perfect Lives (Private Parts), 1977–83, Great Britain, 1984

The Lessons, 1981, New York, 1981 [may be perf. as part of Perfect Lives (Private Parts)]

Atalanta (Acts of God), 1982, Paris, 1982

Atalanta Strategy, 1984

ELECTRONIC MUSIC THEATER

+ Heat, pfmr, tape, 1961, Ann Arbor, Dec 1962

Public Opinion Descends upon the Demonstrators (Ashley), 1961, Ann Arbor, 18 Feb 1962

Boxing, sound-producing dance, 1963, Detroit, 9 April 1964

Combination Wedding and Funeral (Ashley), 1964, New York, 9 May 1965

Interludes for the Space Theater, sound-producing dance, 1964, Cleveland, 4 May 1965

Kittyhawk (An Antigravity Piece) (Ashley), 1964, St. Louis, 21 March 1965

The Lecture Series (Ashley), 1964, collab. M. Ashley; New York, 9 May 1965

Morton Feldman Says, sound-producing dance, 1965, Oberlin, OH, April 1965

Night Train (Ashley), 1965, collab. M. Ashley; Brandeis U., Waltham, MA, 7 Jan 1967

Orange Dessert (Ashley), 1965, Ann Arbor, 9 April 1966

Unmarked Interchange (Ashley), 1965, collab. ONCE Group; Ann Arbor, 17 Sept 1965
Purposeful Lady Slow Afternoon, 1968, New York, 1968
The Trial of Anne Opie Wehrer and Unknown Accomplices for Crimes Against Humanity (Ashley), 1968, Sheboygan, WI, 30 April 1968
The Wolfman Motorcity Revue (Ashley), 1968, Newport Beach, CA, 11 Jan 1969
Fancy Free (Ashley), 1970, Ann Arbor, April 1971 [companion piece to It's There]
Illusion Models, hypothetical computer tasks, 1970
It's There (Ashley), 1970, Brussels, April 1970 [companion piece to Fancy Free]
[Night Sport], simultaneous monologues, 1975, L'Aquila, Italy, April 1975
[Over the Telephone], remote/live audio installations, 1975, New York, March 1975

INSTRUMENTAL

Pf Sonata (Christopher Columbus Crosses to the New World in the Niña, the Pinta and the Santa Maria Using Only Dead Reckoning and a Crude Astrolabe), 1959, rev. 1979; Maneuvers for Small Hands, pf, 1961; Fives, 2 pf, 2 perc, str qnt, 1962; Details, 2 pf, 1962; In memoriam . . . Crazy Horse, sym., 20 or more str/wind/other sustaining insts, 1963; In memoriam . . . Esteban Gomez (Quartet), 4 pfmr, 1963; In memoriam . . . John Smith, conc., 3 pfmr, assistants, 1963; In memoriam . . . Kit Carson (opera), 8-part ens, 1963; Trios (White on White), 1963; Waiting Room (Quartet), any wind/str, 1965, rev. 1978; The Entrance, org, 1965; Revised, Finally, for Gordon Mumma, bell-like insts in pairs, 1973

OTHER ELECTRONIC

Tape: The 4th of July, tape, 1960; Something for Clarinet, Pianos and Tape, 1961; Complete with Heat, orch insts, tape, 1962; Detroit Divided, tape, 1962; Big Danger in 5 Parts, tape, 1964; The Wolfman Tape, 1964 [with opt. amp v as The Wolfman]; Untitled Mixes, tape, 1965, collab. Bob Jones Trio; Str Qt Describing the Motions of Large Real Bodies, str qt, elec, 1972; How Can I Tell the Difference, v/va, elec, tape, 1974
Discs: In Sara, Mencken, Christ, and Beethoven there were Men and Women (J. B. Wolgamot), v, elec, 1972 (Cramps 6103, 1974); Automatic Writing, v, elec, 1979 (Vital 1002, 1979)

FILMS AND VIDEOTAPES

Films (collab. G. Manupelli unless otherwise stated): The Image in Time, 1957; Bottleman, 1960; The House, 1961; Jenny and the Poet, 1964; My May, 1965; Overdrive, 1967; Dr. Chicago, 1968–70; Portraits, Self-portraits, and Still Lifes, 1969; Battery Davis, 1970, collab. P. Makanna
Videotapes: The Great Northern Automobile Presence, lighting accompaniments for other people's music, 1975; What she Thinks, 1976

Principal publisher: Visibility

BIBLIOGRAPHY

H. W. Hitchcock: "Current Chronicle," *MQ*, xlviii (1962), 245
U. Kasemets: "Current Chronicle," *MQ*, l (1964), 515
G. Mumma: "The ONCE Festival and how it Happened," *Arts in Society*, iv (1967), 381
R. Ashley: "The ONCE Group," *Arts in Society*, v (1968), 86
——: "The ONCE Group," *Source*, no.3 (1968), 19
T. Johnson: "New Music," *HiFi/MusAm*, xxvi/1 (1976), 2
W. Zimmermann: *Desert Plants: Conversations with 23 American Musicians* (Vancouver, BC, 1976), 121
N. Osterreich: "Music with Roots in the Aether," *PNM*, xvi/1 (1977), 214
J. Howell: "Robert Ashley's *Perfect Lives (Private Parts)*," *Live: Performance Art*, iii (1980), 3
T. DeLio: "Sound, Gesture and Symbol: the Relationship between Notation and Structure in American Experimental Music," *Interface*, x (1981), 199
——: "Structural Pluralism: Open Structures in the Musical and Visual Arts of the Twentieth Century," *MQ*, lxvii (1981), 527
C. Gagne and T. Caras: "Robert Ashley," *Soundpieces: Interviews with American Composers* (Metuchen, NJ, 1982), 15
J. Rockwell: "Post-Cageian Experimentation & New Kinds of Collaboration: Robert Ashley," *All American Music: Composition in the Late Twentieth Century* (New York, 1983), 96
T. DeLio: *Circumscribing the Open Universe: Essays on Cage, Feldman, Wolff, Ashley and Lucier* (Washington, DC, 1984)

RICHARD S. JAMES

Asian-American music. The 3.5 million Asians in the USA include people of Chinese, Japanese, and Korean extraction (approximately half the total number), South Asians (primarily from India and Pakistan), Filipinos, and recent arrivals from mainland Southeast Asia (especially Vietnam, Laos, and Cambodia), most of whom have been given asylum as refugees. The numbers of Asian immigrants rose sharply after the passage of the Immigration and Nationality Act in 1965.

1. Introduction. 2. Chinese. 3. Japanese. 4. Korean. 5. South Asian. 6. Southeast Asian: (i) Mainland (ii) Filipino.

1. INTRODUCTION. In general immigrant populations feel two essential but often conflicting needs: to adapt to their new cultural and physical environment, and to maintain their ethnic heritage and individuality. Each immigrant community appears to balance these two elements according to its own time scale; in some cases immigrants rapidly adopt the culture of the new world and disperse throughout the community, in others they cluster together and form enclaves. Music, together with language, is a vitally important part of both processes, that of the new world functioning as a symbol of assimilation and adaptation, and that of the old as a means of preserving cultural identity.

Many immigrants come from the larger Asian cities, which have a strong international flavor. In many of these urban centers traditional music has mostly been replaced by Western art music and new forms greatly influenced by Western popular music. This is particularly evident in the Far East, especially Korea, where children in the major cities are more likely to receive instruction in Western instrumental music than in any of their native traditions; the same is becoming increasingly true of children in China and Japan. In South Asia, however, although Westernized film music dominates the urban scene, traditional forms such as classical music and dance, devotional music, and folksong continue to be prominent. In mainland Southeast Asia much of the population is rural and, although influenced by the new pan-Asian music, still retains contact with its indigenous musical traditions. Recent immigrants to the USA are less deeply steeped in their native musical traditions than were earlier ones, and the impetus to maintain their ethnic culture often comes from previous generations of immigrants. However, some second- and third-generation Asians in the USA, particularly the Chinese and Japanese, want to revive and perpetuate their cultural heritage, and participate in the musical functions of the community.

In this article the state of music among the larger Asian immigrant populations is examined. Influences and responses vary considerably. Some groups appear to have adopted the Western musical world exclusively; others maintain a dual involvement; and others, like the Filipinos, have created neotraditional forms. It would be premature to predict the future of Asian music in the USA, but presumably the balancing of tradition, acculturation, and innovation will continue.

2. CHINESE. The history of Chinese-American music can be divided into two periods: the flourishing of Cantonese opera from the 1850s to the 1940s and the introduction of diverse musical styles since the 1950s.

In the 1850s Chinese laborers came to California from the Kuangtong province to construct railroads. Living in "Chinatowns," these men attended Cantonese operas performed by troupes from Canton and Hong Kong. From 1870 to 1890 this theatrical tradition enjoyed a golden era. San Francisco supported four theaters with nightly performances, accompanied by local amateur musicians. Male troupes were established in Portland (Oregon), New York, and Boston. Performers and local Chinese enthusiasts organized music clubs to support the Cantonese opera tradition. After the 1890s, however, a series of events contributed to its decline: the Exclusion Acts of the 1880s began to limit Chinese immigration; the San Francisco earthquake of 1906 destroyed the theaters; and competition from new forms of entertainment, chiefly motion pictures and television, became strong. The opera tradition now survives mainly in the private Cantonese music clubs of older Chinese communities; the music is seldom performed in public.

Immigration of Chinese of diverse social backgrounds and from many regions of China resumed in 1949. In contrast to the earlier settlers, who patronized southern Chinese music, the new immigrants favored northern styles, including Peking opera, instrumental music, and choral singing. From the 1970s, the increasing pride and interest of Chinese-Americans in their ethnic roots added a new dimension to their musical subculture. In the 1980s music clubs organized by generations of northern Chinese continue to nurture and promote Peking opera. In all these clubs – four in New York, three in Los Angeles, two in Washington, DC, and others in Chicago, San Francisco, and Seattle – professionals are hired to perform the leading roles and to instruct amateurs. Instruments, stage properties, and costumes are acquired from Hong Kong and Taiwan, though from the late 1970s musical organizations have looked increasingly to mainland China for resources.

Younger Chinese-Americans appear to prefer instrumental ensemble music. San Francisco clubs offer an unusual variety of styles, each group emphasizing a particular repertory: Chinese traditional classical music, Chinese modern classical music, Chinese and Western pop and rock music, Chinese and American dance-band music, Western classical music, and contemporary music. The instruments include the *huqin* (fiddle), *pipa* (pear-shaped lute), *sheng* (mouth organ), *yangqin* (struck zither), *xiao* (end-blown flute), *di* (transverse flute), *luo* (gong), *nao* (bell), *muyu* (woodblock), *gu* (drum), violin, banjo, electric guitar, and organ. In kung fu clubs percussion music is performed to accompany the Lion Dance. The contemplative music for the *qin* (plucked long zither) is appreciated by connoisseurs. The more flamboyant virtuoso display of *pipa* and *zheng* (half-tube plucked zither) reaches a more general audience. A few virtuosos in the USA are preserving these three highly refined solo traditions by means of oral transmission from master to pupil.

Choral singing is also practiced. Chinese Protestant church choirs and congregations sing mainly Western hymns with Chinese texts, but also include a few Chinese songs accompanied by piano or organ. College choral groups aim to promote Chinese culture and often foster community participation; they perform Chinese art songs and folksongs, composed or arranged by musicians trained in the West.

Chinese-Americans have always had their own music, but it has not been publicized outside their own communities. Few musicians can make a living solely through performances of Chinese music, and amateurs join music clubs primarily for social reasons. The traditional restraints of the Chinese community on ostentation, and therefore on performances at informal public locations such as restaurants, limit the promulgation of their music. While it is probable that some traditional forms will be preserved in pockets in the USA, it is evident that the processes of acculturation will dominate, as in mainland China, Hong Kong, and Taiwan.

1. Young Chinese-Americans playing zheng (half-tube plucked zithers) and the di (transverse flute)

3. JAPANESE. From the mid-1970s Japanese-Americans have experienced a renewal of cultural pride. For the younger generations, in particular, this is marked by a return to traditional Japanese performing arts as a creative means for expressing their Japanese-American heritage. Japanese-American music ranges from traditional Japanese genres, performed in new contexts suited to American life, to a fusion of Japanese elements with jazz to form a style that incorporates the koto (13-string zither), shamisen (three-string plucked lute), biwa (four-string plucked lute), *shakuhachi* (end-blown flute), *kotsuzumi* (hourglass drum), and *taiko* (double-headed barrel drum).

The O-Bon Festival is the most popular event at which Japanese music is heard. In this ritual ancestors are honored with celebrations and traditional dancing accompanied by folksongs. In Japan O-Bon music and dancing are traditionally performed at Shinto shrines, and are accompanied by *taiko*, *takebue* (bamboo transverse flute), bell or gong, and shamisen; in American cities the festival is held annually in July or August, usually at Buddhist temples. The festivities are accompanied by amplified recordings of pop arrangements of traditional folksongs, sometimes with the live accompaniment of a single *taiko* reinforcing the rhythmic line. Pop arrangements of traditional folksongs also provide accompaniment to dancing at the Nisei Week Festival. This celebration was initiated in 1934 by *nisei* (second generation Japanese-Americans) in Los Angeles to stimulate business in the "Little Tokyo" area of the city. It is held annually on two consecutive summer weekends, and includes a parade and street dance. The dances are choreographed by teachers of Japanese classical dance, and tend to have more complex movements than dances of the O-Bon Festival. In both the parade and street dance, recorded music is amplified by a public-address system. For *nisei* this festival celebrates their economic and social survival in the USA and reinforces their image as Americans.

Taiko drumming is the most popular Japanese-American genre among *sansei* and *yonsei* (third and fourth generation Japanese-Americans). It is an adaptation of the Japanese folk genre *suwa daiko*, which combines music and dance. A *taiko* ensemble consists of five to 30 or more performers, and includes *taiko* drums of various sizes (most of which are made by the drummers themselves), *atarigane* (small bronze gong), *hōragai* (conch trumpet), and *takebue*. *Taiko* drumming is performed at other events, both sacred and secular, including the Buddhist Horaku Festival, the Cherry Blossom Festivals of San Francisco, New York, and Washington, DC, and the Asian/Pacific American Heritage Festival in New York, during which traditional koto pieces and *sankyoku* (chamber ensemble music) are also played.

Japanese music has also contributed various timbres, tunings, instruments, and vocal techniques to Western jazz. Toshiko Akiyoshi, an American composer and arranger of big-band jazz, has used kabuki vocal techniques and melodic phrasing and harmonies reminiscent of traditional Japanese music. The members of the fusion group Hiroshima, based in Los Angeles, are predominantly *sansei*; they have achieved a unique blend of jazz rhythms and linear movement by exploiting the timbres and techniques of Japanese instruments, including koto, shamisen, *shakuhachi*, and *taiko*. Osamu Kitajima combines the sound of the biwa, *shakuhachi*, shamisen, *kotsuzumi*, and koto into interesting textures by mixing Japanese and jazz elements, and Yutaka Yokokura also merges Japanese melodic ideas and instruments with those of jazz to create a distinctively Japanese-American sound.

4. KOREAN. Music in Korean-American communities reflects the first-generation, urban, and highly Westernized character of this group. While Koreans have immigrated to the American mainland since the late 19th century, it is only since 1965, following reform of the immigration laws, that their numbers have increased substantially; the total Korean population increased from around 70,000 in 1970 to an estimated half a million in 1985. In the cities where the largest numbers of Koreans have settled – Los Angeles, New York, and Chicago – they have formed musical societies and ensembles, most of which are devoted to Western art music. In Los Angeles, the city with the largest Korean population, there are five symphony orchestras organized and directed by Koreans, and numerous choral societies which are similarly oriented to the performance of Western music.

For most Korean-Americans, the focus of musical participation is Western hymnody sung in Korean; the majority of the immigrants are Protestant churchgoers, whose adherence to the church is the result of the vigorous activities of American missionaries in Korea since the late 19th century. The musical education of Korean-American children centers on Western instrumental training, as in Korean cities, and childhood piano lessons are the rule rather than the exception. The results of such study are reflected in widespread participation in amateur and semiprofessional ensembles as well as in rigorously rehearsed church choirs (over 400 in the Los Angeles area).

Interest in music from Korea is maintained through local radio broadcasts in the Korean language, television programs taped in Seoul, and recordings of modern, highly Westernized Korean popular music on recordings. Only perfunctory attention is given to ethnic Korean music and musical instruments, though small groups of devoted traditionalists exert an influence out of proportion to their numbers. The oldest of these is the Korean Classical Music and Dance Company (Los Angeles), organized in 1973, which features the performance of music on the *kayagŭm* (plucked long zither), the *p'iri* (oboe), and other traditional instruments. Native Korean music is rarely presented elsewhere except for occasional arrangements of Korean folksongs played by Korean-American orchestras, such as the Korean PO (founded 1967) and Nasung SO (founded 1976) of Los Angeles.

5. SOUTH ASIAN. Although South Asians began to arrive in the USA as early as 1899, most entered after 1965; they are thus sometimes referred to as the "new ethnics." The majority come from India (360,000 according to the 1980 census). Most of the early migrants were laborers from rural communities, but the later arrivals are generally from middle- and upper-class families with urban backgrounds and professional vocations. Many are from large cosmopolitan cities and reflect the regional, ethnic, linguistic, and religious diversity that characterize them. South Asians are scattered throughout the USA though major concentrations are present in New York, Chicago, Detroit, and parts of California.

The South Asian community is much concerned with keeping alive its cultural, religious, and linguistic heritage. The diverse backgrounds of the community are reflected in the number and variety of organizations that have been established. It is estimated that there are 1000 Indian organizations in the USA. These are often founded on regional or linguistic bases – for instance, Gujarati, Punjabi, Tamil, and Kannada societies – or have a religious or philosophical bias and involve worship, meditation, yoga, and the like. In spite of this diversity, most South Asian immigrants share a sense of community and national identity. The Indians present programs involving local talent on special occasions such as Republic Day and the Divali festival. There are also organizations to promote South Asian cultural activities, particularly music and dance, and to present concerts by leading professional artists, some of whom now live in the USA. The community is also served by temples and mosques, newspapers (e.g., *India Abroad* and *Overseas Times*), regular radio and television programs, neighborhood cinemas that show Indian films, restaurants, and spice shops, which also offer other South Asian products, including recordings of South Asian music and video cassettes of Indian films.

Since recent migrants have come largely from urban backgrounds, it is not surprising that it is mostly urban musical forms that are prominent in the USA. Classical music and dance are the most highly thought of. As a result of the pioneering efforts of musicians such as Ravi Shankar and Ali Akbar Khan, classical music achieved considerable popularity in the USA during the early 1960s. Concerts of classical music continue, now increasingly supported by South Asians and often sponsored by their organizations. Instruction in instrumental music – particularly that for sitar, *sarod* (double-chested plucked lute), and *tablā* (pair of small tuned drums) – and classical dance is available in many American cities, both on a private basis and in institutions. The Ali Akbar College of Music (founded 1967) in the San Francisco Bay area has produced many competent performers. While most South Asians are not involved actively in the performance of classical music, the concerts serve an important social role.

In the USA, as in South Asia, film songs and "light" classical genres such as *ghazal* are extremely popular. In most Indian films the action is interspersed with songs, usually dubbed by "playback" singers on to the mime of the actors. The style is eclectic, drawing on Indian musical traditions as well as Western popular and other musical idioms. Since light classical and popular music does not require the rigorous training and virtuoso skills expected in classical music, there are many amateur singers in the USA who perform on social occasions and at cultural functions. Devotional songs, including *bhajan* and *kirtan*, are performed by congregations in the many Hindu, Sikh, and Jain temples throughout the USA. These organizations also support religious discourses (*katha*) by visiting scholars and priests, many of whom incorporate devotional songs in their presentations. (Parallel Muslim devotional and mystical songs of the Sufis of Pakistan and India, sometimes referred to by the general term *qawwali*, are not sung at public gatherings in the home countries and are seldom heard in the USA.)

South Asian folk-music traditions in the USA are usually associated with social activities such as dancing. The Gujarati *garba* and the Punjabi *bhangra* dances, with their accompanying songs, are regularly performed at social and cultural functions. However, the functional folksong repertory that accompanies life-cycle and agricultural events or work-related activities in South Asia is rarely heard in the USA.

6. Southeast Asian

(i) Mainland. Beginning in 1975, many refugees from Laos, Cambodia, and Vietnam were given asylum in the USA and by 1984 there were nearly 700,000 immigrants from these countries; over a third of them settled in California, and there are large population clusters in several other states. Representing virtually all segments of mainland Southeast Asian society, they continue their traditional musical practices. In addition they are creating innovative as well as imitative cultural forms that reflect the new elements of their ethnic and social identity created by their radically changed environment.

(a) Laotian. Laotians in the USA include both Lao-speaking lowland villagers and urban dwellers, and members of non-Lao-speaking tribal groups from mountain villages. Of their several musical traditions the best-known is the court music, which is Khmer and Thai in origin but has been established in Laos for many centuries. The two major Lao classical-music traditions derived from the court – that of the orchestra and dance ensemble of the royal palace in Luang Prabang, and that of the more Thai-influenced and modernized Lao Natassin (National School of Fine Arts) in Vientiane – both have representatives in the USA. Using imported masks, costumes, and musical instruments, the immigrants continue to perform the most important items of the repertory in concerts and community festivals such as the Lao New Year. These presentations include parts of the *Ramayana* story as well as other tales and dances related to religious themes. Many are accompanied by the *pī phāt* orchestra of xylophones (*rangnāt*), gong-chimes (*khōng wong*), flutes (*khui*), and drums.

Lao Buddhist ritual forms, which include chanting and sermons, are practiced at religious festivals, other rites, and wakes by Lao monks now living in the USA. The musical content of these rituals ranges from near-monotone recitations of Pali texts to highly ornate cantillation of scriptures.

The lowland village traditions featuring the national instrument, the *khāen*, a free-reed bamboo mouth organ, also continue in many American Lao communities. The solo repertory for this instrument includes both metered and unmetered polyphonic compositions; the instrument is also used to accompany the memorized or extemporized verses sung by one *mohlam* ("song expert") or several. Singers and instrumentalists alike may incorporate dance movements in these performances. Since Lao is a tonal language, the melodic contours of the songs are generated, in part, by speech tone. The texts of the songs are usually romantic, but often contain philosophical, poetic, and humorous comments on current events. Social circle-dancing (*lamvong*) may also take place during *mohlam* performances, or may be performed to modernized folksong renditions played by Lao rock bands.

Modern urban forms are particularly prominent among the Lao communities in the USA. Lao rock bands, usually deriving their tunes from the large repertory of Southeast and East Asian popular songs (Lao, Thai, Filipino, Taiwanese, Hong Kong Chinese, and Japanese), commonly perform at the major festivals and provide an occasion for social dancing. Stylistic elements of this music are derived from both Asian and Western popular music.

Laotian tribal groups in the USA include the Hmong (Miao, Meo), Tai Dam, Kmhmu, Mien (Yao), and others. The Hmong are the largest group in the USA and in Laos, and have continued the unique and rich musical traditions of their homeland. These include over 30 genres of sung poetry. Among their instruments, always played individually, are the *geng* (*geej*), a free-reed mouth organ, the *ja* (*raj nplaim*), a side-blown free-reed bamboo aerophone, and the *nja* (*ncas*), a jew's harp. The melodic contours follow speech tones and may function, to some extent, as "speech surrogate" systems. Ritual performances involving music still accompany life-cycle rites, although the same forms are also heard

2. Laotian geng (mouth organ) dance performed by Chia Chu Kue, Blue Hmong, during the Hmong New Year festival, Providence, Rhode Island, 1981

at New Year festivals. The mouth organ is characteristic of funerals, at which the tones and rhythms of its music represent sacred texts, and the player's dance movements are ritually meaningful. Some of the traditional Hmong sung poetry has been incorporated into Catholic masses and pageants. As among other Southeast Asian communities, the rock band (with lyrics in the native language) is a prominent feature at Hmong festivals for social dancing.

(b) Cambodian. Cambodian musical traditions have much in common with those of Laos and Thailand. In the USA the court orchestra (*biṇ bādy*) is sometimes augmented by aerophones and chordophones from the folk orchestra (*mahōrī*). The combined ensemble may include xylophones (*ranāt*), tuned gong-chimes (*gaṅ tūc*), flutes (*khluy*), oboes (*sraḷai*), two-string fiddles (*dra*), struck zithers (*khim*), plucked zithers (*krapeu*), drums (*sgar*), wooden clappers (*krap*), and finger cymbals (*jhiṇṅ*). A chorus (*chamrieng*) sings poetic texts that narrate the classical dance dramas, such as the *Ramayana* story, as well as other dances of religious significance. The wedding orchestra (*bhleṅ khmaer*), considered to be the most characteristically Khmer ensemble, can be heard at Cambodian weddings and festival occasions. It includes a three-string spike fiddle (*dra khmaer*), plucked lute (*cāp̈ī*), small oboe (*p̈ī a*), drums, and voices.

Folkdance and folk music have been popular in Phnom Penh at least since 1960, when the national schools of theater and music were established. Many Cambodian-American communities too have youth groups devoted to folk traditions, whose dances depict the cultural forms of various Khmer village and tribal groups; they perform chiefly at Cambodian New Year. Like the other Southeast Asian groups, Cambodian-American youths also enjoy their own version of contemporary urban rock music.

Cambodian Buddhist forms, such as the chanting of Pali scriptures by Khmer monks, are maintained at Cambodian temples in the USA. Congregational singing of contemporary Khmer devotional poetry, following classical rhyme-tune formulae, can also be heard.

(c) Vietnamese. Vietnamese music is quite distinct from that of Cambodia and Laos. Although many Vietnamese instruments resemble Chinese models, they are used in unmistakably Vietnamese fashion. The most popular classical solo instrument for both study and listening among Vietnamese-Americans is the 16-string board zither (*đàn tranh*), a smaller and more delicate counterpart of the Chinese *zheng*, the metal strings of which are particularly well suited to ornamentation and arpeggiation. The four-string pear-shaped lute (*đàn tỳ bà*), moon-shaped lute (*đàn nguyệt*), and others also have Chinese counterparts. The plucked single-string box zither (*đàn bầu*), however, is uniquely Vietnamese; its delicate tone is produced from harmonics and by manual variations in string tension. Many of these instruments are played in the USA at Tet (Vietnamese New Year); also presented are excerpts from classical theater (*hát bội*), folk theater (*hát chèo*) and "modernized" theater (*hát cải lương*), folkdances, nightclub routines, and at least one performance of the aria *Vong cô*. This aria, sometimes called *Nostalgia for the Past*, is the most widely known item of South Vietnamese music, and can be sung to virtually any suitable text. It allows the singer extensive opportunities to express his feelings, either in the song or in the unmetered prelude (*rao*); a few string instruments supply a freely heterophonic accompaniment, the improvised ornaments and melodic contours of which create new polyphonic strata and textures in each performance.

(ii) Filipino. Filipinos in the USA are predominantly of lowland (Christian) origin. They have settled chiefly in the western states and in Hawaii and Alaska. During the 70 years of their presence, they have maintained the musical traditions of the homeland while being open to innovations from their new environment. Each Filipino-American community responds to its local circumstances rather than to regional or national influences. The responses vary according to language, educational background at the time of immigration, the period of immigration (before World War II, immediately after the war, or the 1970s and 1980s), and location in the USA, whether urban or rural.

Instrumental music was popular in the prewar period, especially in the agricultural centers of the West. *Rondalla* (string ensembles), such as the Black and Tan (Kauai, Hawaii), and *banda* (wind bands), such as the Filipino Federation Band (Stockton, California), were organized early on. However, talented musicians quickly found employment in hotel and nightclub dance bands, playing popular American rather than traditional Filipino repertory. Few wind bands are currently active, though the Honolulu community established a *banda* in 1980. In recent years communities in California, Texas, and Hawaii have formed *rondalla* ensembles. The University of Hawaii provides instruction in *rondalla* and *kulintang* (gong ensembles), as well as in song and dance, and the University of Washington, Seattle, teaches *kulintang* in Maranao and Magindanao styles. The Kalilang Ensemble (San Francisco) studies and presents authentic

3. The Kalilang Ensemble of San Francisco performing kulintang (gong ensemble) music from the repertory of the Maranao culture of the Philippines

performances of repertory from Maranao and Magindanao cultures (see fig.3).

Traditional vocal music, which is generally solo, is performed in both informal and formal settings. It is part of cultural presentations and nationalistic celebrations, such as Rizal Day, when Filipinos celebrate their national hero. Choral groups have gained in popularity among civic organizations since 1946, and touring choirs from the Philippines reinforce this interest; performances include choral arrangements of folksongs, as well as *kundiman* (love-songs) and Tagalog film songs, and contemporary works by Filipino composers are occasionally presented. The principal motivation for the groups is singing in Filipino languages.

Commercial and pop genres from the Philippines (e.g., "Pinoy rock") have found a market in the USA, chiefly among young, recent immigrants, but also to some extent among the American-born. Sound recordings are an important means of dissemination, as are Filipino-language radio and television broadcasts, Tagalog films, and concert tours by singers such as Freddie Aguilar and Jun Polistico.

The development of neotraditional music arises from the concern for a Filipino-American identity among the younger generation, and is part of a larger Asian-American movement. Gong music of upland and Islamic cultures (those least influenced by the West) form the basis for such creativity, as exemplified by the Samahan Percussion Ensemble (San Diego, California) and the Cumbanchero Percussionaires (Seattle, Washington). In addition, neotraditional music of Philippine and American origin provides musical material for folkdance groups inspired by Bayanihan traditions.

The transfer of music from a Philippine to an American setting has caused changes in musical style and in social context. Performances are predominantly presented as entertainment rather than participated in as social or ritual events. An important function for music is to stress ethnic solidarity and identity in contrast to the mainstream of American culture. Many Filipino-Americans, however, choose to concentrate on Western art music and popular music rather than Filipino traditions. This focus and commitment are also a significant part of the Filipino-American experience, and are consistent with patterns of adaptation developed in the Philippines during the Spanish and American colonial periods.

BIBLIOGRAPHY

GENERAL

N. A. Jairazbhoy and S. C. DeVale, eds.: "Asian Music in North America," *Selected Reports in Ethnomusicology*, vi (1985) [complete issue]

CHINESE

F. Lieberman: *Chinese Music: an Annotated Bibliography* (New York, 1970, 2/1979)

N. Yeh: *The Yüeh Chü Style of Cantonese Opera with an Analysis of "The Legend of Lady White Snake"* (thesis, UCLA, 1972)

B. B. Smith: "Chinese Music in Hawaii," *Asian Music*, vi/1–2 (1975), 225

R. Riddle: "The Cantonese Opera: a Chapter in Chinese-American History," *The Life, Influence, and the Role of the Chinese in the United States, 1776–1960*, ed. T. Chinn (San Francisco, 1976), 40

——: *Chinatown's Music: a History and Ethnography of Music and Music-drama in San Francisco's Chinese Community* (diss., U. of Illinois, 1976)

Chun-kin Leung: "Notes on Cantonese Opera in North America," *Chinoperl Papers*, no.7 (1977), 9

R. Riddle: "Music in America's Chinatowns in the Nineteenth Century," *Chinese Historical Society of America Bulletin*, xii/5 (1977), 1

——: "Music Clubs and Ensembles in San Francisco's Chinese Community," *Eight Urban Musical Cultures: Tradition and Change*, ed. B. Nettl (Urbana, IL, 1978), 223–59

Kuo-Huang Han: "The Modern Chinese Orchestra," *Asian Music*, xi/1 (1979), 1–40

R. Riddle: "Recent Trends in the Musical Life of America's Urban Chinese," *Chinese Historical Society of America Bulletin*, xiv/3 (1979), 3

Kuo-Huang Han: "Chinese Music in America," *From East to West: Essays on Chinese Music* (Taipei, Taiwan, 1981), 79
R. Riddle: *Flying Dragons, Flowing Streams: Music in the Life of San Francisco's Chinese* (Westport, CT, 1983)

JAPANESE

K. Onishi: " 'Bon' and 'Bon-odori' in Hawaii," *Social Process in Hawaii*, iv (1938), 49
W. A. Caudill: *Japanese-American Acculturation and Personality* (Chicago, 1950)
——: "Achievement, Culture and Personality: the Case of the Japanese Americans," *American Anthropologist*, no.58 (1956), 1102
M. Kodani, ed.: *Hōraku* (Los Angeles, 1979)
B. B. Smith: "Sociocultural Traditions of Asian Musics in Hawaii," *Asian Cultural Quarterly*, viii/3 (1979), 8
C. Tong: "Taiko," *Bridge*, vii/1 (1979), 43
M. Omi: "Hiroshima Reborn," *Bridge*, vii/3 (1980), 43
——: "Cultural Fusion: an Interview with Dan and June Kuramoto of Hiroshima," *Bridge*, vii/4 (1981–2), 3; viii/1 (1982), 31

KOREAN

Hyung-Chan Kim: "Koreans," *Harvard Encyclopedia of American Ethnic Groups*, ed. S. Thernstrom (Cambridge, MA, 1980), 601
Eui-Young Yu and others, eds.: *Koreans in Los Angeles: Prospects and Promises* (Los Angeles, 1982)
Eui-Young Yu: "Korean Communities in America: Past, Present, and Future," *Amerasia Journal*, x/2 (1983), 23
R. Riddle: "Korean Musical Culture in Los Angeles," *Selected Reports in Ethnomusicology*, vi (1985). 189

SOUTH ASIAN

R. K. Das: *Hindustani Workers on the Pacific Coast* (Berlin, 1923)
R. E. Brown: "Intercultural Exchange and the Future of Traditional Music in India," *Contributions to Asian Studies*, xii (1978), 20
D. M. Neuman: "Journey to the West," *Contributions to Asian Studies*, xii (1978), 40
D. Reck: "The Neon Electric Saraswati," *Contributions to Asian Studies*, xii (1978), 3
B. C. Wade: "Indian Classical Music in North America: Cultural Give and Take," *Contributions to Asian Studies*, xii (1978), 29
M. P. Fisher: *The Indians of New York City: a Study of Immigrants from India* (New Delhi, 1980)
P. Saran and E. Eames, eds.: *The New Ethnics* (New York, 1980)
V. Kaiwar and S. Mazumdar, eds.: "Immigration to North America," *South Asia Bulletin*, ii/1 (1982) [complete issue]

SOUTHEAST ASIAN

J. R. Brandon: *Theatre in Southeast Asia* (Cambridge, MA, 1967)
P. Duy: *Musics of Vietnam* (Carbondale, IL, 1975)
E. Mareschal: *La musique des Hmong* (Paris, 1976)
A. Catlin: *Music of the Hmong: Singing Voices and Talking Reeds* (Providence, 1981)
——: "Speech Surrogate Systems of the Hmong: From Singing Voices to Talking Reeds," *The Hmong in the West: Observations and Reports*, ed. B. T. Downing and D. P. Olney (Minneapolis, 1982), 170

NAZIR A. JAIRAZBHOY (1, 5), NORA YEH (2)
SUSAN MIYO ASAI (3), RONALD RIDDLE (4)
AMY R. CATLIN (6(i)), RICARDO D. TRIMILLOS (6(ii))

Asleep at the Wheel. Western-swing band. It was formed in Paw Paw, West Virginia, in 1970. The personnel has changed frequently, but the best-known combination had as its principal members the singer, guitarist, and songwriter Ray Benson (Seifert); the singer, songwriter, drummer, and guitarist Leroy Preston; the singer and guitarist Chris O'Connell; the steel guitarist Lucky Oceans (Ruben Gosfield); and the pianist Floyd Domino (James Haber). The band has consisted of as many as 13 musicians simultaneously, and more than 60, most of them fiddlers and wind players, have been associated with it at some time; the original members began to leave the group in 1978 until only Benson remained. Asleep at the Wheel began its career in West Virginia performing the traditional rockabilly and country-music repertory; by the time it moved to Berkeley, California, in 1971, it had become a western-swing group in the style of Bob Wills. Preston emerged as a witty songwriter and the group gained a reputation for its diverse repertory, which included country-western and country-boogie standards, as well as original songs. After a second move, to Austin in 1975, it established itself as one of the most important bands in progressive country music. Although the group has had only one hit single, *The letter that Johnny Walker read* (country no. 10, 1975), it has achieved a large audience of rock and country-music listeners through steady touring.

RECORDINGS

(selective list)

Comin' Right at ya (UA 038, 1973); The letter that Johnny Walker read (Cap. 4115, 1975); *Texas Gold* (Cap. 11441, 1975); *The Wheel* (Cap. 11620, 1977); *Collision Course* (Cap. 11726, 1978); *Framed* (MCA 5131, 1980)

BIBLIOGRAPHY

J. Morthland: "Asleep at the Wheel," *Country Music*, v/10 (1977), 28

JOHN MORTHLAND

Aspen Music Festival. A nine-week summer program, comprising concerts and training courses (the Aspen Music School), held in Aspen, Colorado. It grew out of the Goethe Bicentennial Convocation and Music Festival of 1949; concerts have been presented by faculty members, students of the music school, and guest artists since 1950. The festival includes performances by five student orchestras, as well as concerts of chamber, choral, contemporary and electronic music, and jazz. The music school program includes an opera workshop, an audio-recording institute, master classes, and a choral program; the Center for Advanced Quartet Studies, founded by Claus Adam, provides opportunities for students to work with such renowned ensembles as the Cleveland and Emerson quartets, which have been in residence. Under another program, the Conference on Contemporary Music, founded by Darius Milhaud, students attend lectures and seminars given by one or more composers-in-residence. From 1985 Paul Fromm sponsored conferences and concerts of contemporary music at the festival. Concerts are held in the Music Tent and at various locations in and around Aspen, including the Wheeler Opera House (seating 442). In a natural setting of rugged mountains, forested slopes, meadows, and rapid rivers, the festival is attended by more than 80,000 people each year. Among works that have received their premières at Aspen are Milhaud's *Music for New Orleans* (11 August 1968), Wernick's *Visions of Wonder and Terror* (19 July 1976), and Del Tredici's *Child Alice*, part 2 (complete, 1 August 1984).

RITA H. MEAD

Associated Music Publishers. Firm of music publishers. It was founded in 1927 by Paul Heinicke, originally as the sole American agency for leading European music publishing houses, including Bote & Bock, Breitkopf & Härtel, Doblinger, Eschig, Schott, Simrock, Union Musical Español, and Universal Edition. The firm began publishing in its own right and has built up an important catalogue of American composers including Carter, Cowell, Harris, Ives, Piston, and Riegger. In 1964 it was acquired by G. Schirmer, but it has retained an independent publishing program.

ALAN PAGE

Association for Recorded Sound Collections (ARSC). Organization founded in 1966 to communicate with libraries, recording archives, and recording collectors; to encourage cooperation among sound archivists and provide research grants for documentation and preservation projects (*see* DISCOGRAPHIES, §1); and to act as a central information center. Its 750 members include persons in the broadcasting and recording industries, librarians, curators, private collectors, and archivists connected with museums, libraries, and sound archives. Institutional and corporate membership includes libraries and research foundations. The ARSC maintains a Technical Committee, which considers the implications of new technology on sound archives and recommends technical standards for recording and playback equipment, and a Committee on Bibliographic Access to Sound Recordings. Publications of the association include *A Preliminary Directory of Sound Recordings Collections in the United States and Canada* (1967, with the New York Public Library) and *Rules for the Archival Cataloging of Sound Recordings* (1980), in addition to several periodicals (*Journal*, 1967–; *Bulletin*, 1968–; and *Newsletter*, 1977–). The society's headquarters are in Manassas, Virginia.

BIBLIOGRAPHY

D. Hamilton: "For Sound Collectors, ARSC is the Answer," *HiFi/MusAm*, xxviii/6 (1978), 30

T. Brooks: "Association for Recorded Sound Collections: an Unusual Organization," *Goldmine*, no.81 (1983), 22

JOHN SHEPARD

Association for the Advancement of Creative Musicians (AACM). A nonprofit organization devoted to black avant-garde jazz. It is based in Chicago. The AACM grew out of the Experimental Band, a large free-jazz ensemble established by the composer and pianist Muhal Richard Abrams in 1961. Founded on 8 May 1965 (with Abrams as president), the AACM provided a framework for sympathetic rehearsals and public performances of new works. Its members were required to contribute original compositions, to give a solo recital, and to maintain high moral standards. In addition, experienced players trained the younger musicians.

In its early years the AACM sponsored local recording sessions led by Abrams, the saxophonists Roscoe Mitchell, Joseph Jarman, and Anthony Braxton, or the trumpeter Lester Bowie (AACM's second president); it also produced a weekly radio show and presented concerts and jam sessions in the ghetto's Abraham Lincoln Center or at the University of Chicago. In 1969 Braxton, the violinist Leroy Jenkins, the trumpeter Leo Smith, the drummer Steve McCall, and the members of the ART ENSEMBLE OF CHICAGO settled temporarily in Paris, thereby bringing the methods and goals of the AACM to new international affiliations. Later the organization held a festival in New York (1977) and continued to flourish in Chicago: many of its members received grants from the NEA and the Illinois Arts Council, and new talent emerged – notably the saxophonist Chico Freeman, the trombonist George Lewis, and the group Air. In a genre traditionally dominated by individual performers, the AACM has proved to be a lasting, historically significant cooperative venture.

BIBLIOGRAPHY

"Jazz Musicians Group in Chicago Growing," *Down Beat*, xxxiii/15 (1966), 11

T. Martin: "The Chicago Avant-garde," *Jazz Monthly*, no.157 (1968), 12

E. Jost: *Free Jazz* (Graz, Austria, 1974)

"AACM," *Swing Journal*, xxix/8 (1975), 231 [discography]

G. Giddins: "Inside Free Jazz: the AACM in New York," *Village Voice*, xxii (30 May 1977), 46

V. Wilmer: "Chicago's Alternative Society," *As Serious as your Life* (London, 1977), 112

J. DeMuth: "15 Years of the AACM," *Jazz Forum*, no.68 (1980), 28

BARRY KERNFELD

Association of Concert Bands. Professional organization designed to serve the particular interests of adult band musicians, rather than those of school or college groups. Founded by Frederic Fay Swift, Willard Musser, Wendell Margrave, and Edmond DeMattia in 1977 in Allentown, Pennsylvania, as the Association of Concert Bands of America, it dropped the last part of its original name in 1982 when it began to broaden its activities to include foreign bands. The objectives of the association are to foster a high standard of concert band music; to promote cooperation among its members for their mutual benefit and in general to enhance the status of adult concert bands; to stimulate and nurture public interest in and appreciation of concert bands; to afford the public opportunities to hear performances of major works in the repertory; and to publish books, journals, papers, and magazines about bands. The association's headquarters are in Utica, New York.

RAOUL CAMUS

Astaire [Austerlitz], **Fred(erick)** (*b* Omaha, NE, 10 May 1899). Popular dancer, choreographer, and singer. He began his career at the age of seven in a dance-comedy duo with his sister Adele (*b* Omaha, 10 Sept 1897; *d* Phoenix, AZ, 25 Jan 1981). They appeared in vaudeville from 1906 to 1916 and thereafter in revues and musical comedies, such as Gershwin's *Lady be Good!* (1924), Youmans's *Smiles* (1930), and *The Band Wagon* (1931) by Arthur Schwartz; Adele's talent for soubrette roles and whimsical singing and dancing made her the more popular of the pair. After Adele retired from the stage to marry, Fred went to Hollywood. In 1933 he appeared in *Flying Down to Rio* with the dancer Ginger Rogers, with whom he went on to make nine further films; these include *Top Hat* (1935), *Swing Time* (1936), and *Shall we Dance* (1937), which are among the most popular and important musical films ever made. Astaire collaborated with directors, screenwriters, composers, lyricists, and other choreographers (notably Hermes Pan) in the production of these films, where the narrative is carried and the characters express themselves through romantic and intimate dance sequences; these were filmed in long, fluid shots, without close-ups, that transmitted a feeling of the personal chemistry between the dancers. Astaire's seemingly effortless dances – an inventive mixture of tap, ballroom, and ballet – were marked by an appearance of improvisation, though they were always carefully rehearsed. He cultivated a stage persona of debonair charm and nonchalance. In the 1940s and 1950s Astaire continued to develop new dance routines with, among others, Eleanor Powell, Rita Hayworth, Judy Garland, and Bing Crosby; he received a special Academy Award in 1949 for his contributions to films. His singing, characterized by its casual air and retardation of attack, inspired some of the finest songs of Berlin, Kern, Gershwin, Youmans, and Porter. Astaire has also appeared in dramatic roles and on television, and has composed songs, notably *I'm building up to an awful let-down* (1935), with lyrics by Johnny Mercer.

See also DANCE, §III, 3, and GERSHWIN, GEORGE, fig. 1.

BIBLIOGRAPHY

F. Astaire: *Steps in Time* (New York, 1959/*R*1981)

"Astaire, Fred," *CBY 1964*

M. Stearns and J. Stearns: *Jazz Dance: the Story of American Vernacular Dance* (New York, 1968/*R*1979)

A. Croce: *The Fred Astaire and Ginger Rogers Book* (New York, 1972/*R*1977)

S. Green and B. Goldberg: *Starring Fred Astaire* (New York, 1973/*R*1977)

B. Thomas: *Astaire: the Man, the Dancer* (New York, 1984)

SAMUEL S. BRYLAWSKI

Fred Astaire with Ginger Rogers in the film "Swing Time" (1936)

Aston Magna Foundation for Music. Organization founded in New York in 1972 by the harpsichordist Albert Fuller for the study and performance of music from the 17th and 18th centuries. Under Fuller's artistic direction (1972–83), the foundation has presented many concerts, sponsored recordings, and made it possible for performing artists, instrument makers, and scholars to assemble during the summer at its headquarters in Great Barrington, Massachusetts, to share their knowledge and insights. It organizes the only annual festival devoted to music of the Baroque and Classical periods performed on original instruments. The annual Aston Magna Academy of 17th- and 18th-century Culture, a three-week period of intensive study, funded by grants from the NEH and directed by the music historian Raymond Erickson, attracts musicians and scholars in the arts from universities and conservatories in the USA and Europe. The foundation has been awarded a further NEH grant in order to develop lecture series, residencies, and other programs in association with various institutions and organizations to explore the music and culture of the Baroque and Classical periods. Its award-winning recording of Bach's Brandenburg Concertos, the first American recording of the works made on original instruments, was particularly successful commercially and received international critical acclaim. The cellist and gamba player John Hsu assumed the position of artistic director in 1985.

RITA H. MEAD

Astor, John [Johann] **Jacob** (*b* Waldorf, nr Heidelberg, Germany, 1763; *d* New York, 29 March 1848). Instrument maker and importer. He went to London to join his brother George [Georg] Astor (*b* Waldorf, *c*1760), who had gone to England about 1778; together they started business as flute makers, their firm operating as George & John Astor from 1782 to 1797. In 1783 John Jacob came to the USA with a small consignment of flutes, visiting another brother who had settled in Baltimore. The value of his stock of flutes is said to have been only about £5, but on advice given him by a fellow voyager he invested the proceeds of his sales in furs and by selling these in England made a handsome profit. He returned to the USA and quickly profited by fur trading and by the sale of musical instruments sent to him from England. By 1786 he had opened a music shop in his mother-in-law's house at 81 Queen Street, New York. His merchandise, most of which was imported from London, included pianos, spinets, guitars, violins, flutes, clarinets, oboes, fifes, music books, paper, and strings. He relinquished the business to Michael and John Paff in 1802, but continued to import instruments as late as 1807. In 1809 Astor established a fur-trading company, and by this and the purchase of land in the Bowery laid the foundations of the Astor wealth. His brother's firm continued in London as Astor & Co. until 1831.

Some of the instruments which Astor had brought to the USA when visiting Baltimore in 1783 were purchased by Samuel W. Hildebrandt of 19 North Liberty Street, Baltimore, a maker of brass instruments; they remained in the firm's possession well into the 20th century.

See also MUSIC TRADES, §2.

BIBLIOGRAPHY

J. Parton: *Life of John Jacob Astor, to which is Appended a Copy of his Last Will* (New York, 1865)

"Astor: Musical Instrument Maker," *Musical Courier*, xxxix/6 (9 Aug 1899), 15

W. J. Ghent: "Astor: John Jacob," *DAB*

A. D. H. Smith: *John Jacob Astor: Landlord of New York* (Philadelphia, 1929)

K. W. Porters: *John Jacob Astor, Business Man* (Cambridge, MA, 1931)

FRANK KIDSON/H. G. FARMER/R

ASUC. *See* AMERICAN SOCIETY OF UNIVERSITY COMPOSERS.

Athapaskan. American Indian language family; *see* APACHE and NAVAJO.

Atheling, William. Pseudonym of EZRA POUND.

Atherton, James (Peyton, Jr.) (*b* Montgomery, AL, 27 April 1943). Tenor. He studied at the Peabody Conservatory (BM 1965, MM 1967), chiefly with Singher but also with Ponselle; later he served on the faculties of Peabody, Goucher College, Towson State University, and Dickinson College. He made his début with the San Francisco Opera in 1971 as Goro in *Madama Butterfly*, with the Santa Fe Opera in 1973 as Major Wingrave in the American stage première of Britten's *Owen Wingrave*, with the Canadian Opera Company in 1976 as Fritz in Offenbach's *La grande duchesse de Gérolstein*, and with the Metropolitan Opera in 1977 as the Simpleton in *Boris Godunov*; he made his English début at Glyndebourne in 1979 in Haydn's *La fedeltà premiata*. Since 1977 Atherton has been gaining experience as a director of opera. His flexible vocal technique and dramatic abilities have made him highly respected as a *comprimario* performer in operas from all stylistic periods, and since the late 1970s he has been equally successful in major roles with opera companies in Dallas, Miami, Houston, and other cities.

JAMES WIERZBICKI

Atkins, Chet [Chester Burton] (*b* nr Luttrell, TN, 20 June 1924). Country-music guitarist and recording company executive. Although his first professional instrument was the fiddle, he became internationally famous as a guitarist. His style of guitar playing is characterized by the use of the thumb to establish a rhythm on the lower strings while the fingers play melodic or improvisational passages on the higher strings. In the early 1940s Atkins toured with Archie Campbell and Bill Carlisle, playing both fiddle and guitar. He joined Red Foley in 1946, and began his association with the "Grand Ole Opry" and with Nashville, where he settled in 1950; in the late 1940s he participated in numerous recording sessions there, and he also toured as a sideman with the Carter Family. In the early 1950s he began playing the electric guitar, an instrument he was chiefly responsible for popularizing as a solo instrument in country music. He made his first solo recording, *Chet Atkins' Gallopin' Guitar*, for RCA in 1953.

Atkins became assistant to Steve Sholes in RCA's artists and repertory department in 1952 and was later manager of RCA's Nashville studio. In 1960 he became artists and repertory manager and in 1968 vice-president of RCA. He produced best-selling records by such singers as Jim Reeves, Hank Snow, and Waylon Jennings, and played an important role in both the resurgence of country music in the 1950s and 1960s and in the creation of the NASHVILLE SOUND. In the 1960s he toured with saxophonist Boots Randolph and pianist Floyd Cramer and became interested in classical guitar playing, a style that required a technique similar to his own. After he retired from RCA in 1982, he signed a recording contract with CBS Records. He was elected to the Country Music Hall of Fame in 1973.

BIBLIOGRAPHY

C. Atkins and B. Neely: *Country Gentleman* (Chicago, 1974)
W. Ivey: "Chet Atkins," *Stars of Country Music*, ed. B. C. Malone and J. McCulloh (Urbana, IL, 1975), 274
"Atkins, Chet," *CBY 1975*

BILL C. MALONE

Atlanta. Capital city of Georgia (pop. 425,022; metropolitan area 2,029,710). First known in the early 19th century as Terminus because of a decision to build a railway center there, and later for a short while as Marthasville, Atlanta enjoyed a sporadic musical life in the aftermath of the Civil War (1861–5). Most music-making was of local origin, although famous artists such as Victor Herbert, Walter Damrosch, Sousa, Pachmann, and Melba visited later in the century. The Cotton State and International Exposition of 1895 was the scene of many such performances. Probably the city's earliest first-rate musical event was a recital by Paderewski on 22 February 1900.

In 1909 the Atlanta Music Festival Association arranged a series of five concerts over a three-day period, featuring famous opera singers such as Caruso (who was, however, indisposed), Farrar, Fremstad, and Scotti. The concerts included performances by the Dresden PO (with Spalding as violin soloist) and were enormously successful. Special excursions from neighboring cities were provided by the railroads, indicating the degree of interest generated. The venture whetted Atlanta's appetite for opera and, as a result, the New York Metropolitan Opera was engaged in 1910 for six performances, with spectacular success. This marked the beginning of regular spring visits by the company, interrupted only during the two world wars. The "Opera Week," comprising seven performances in six days, has become a highlight of the social season.

The Atlanta Music Club was formed in 1915 for the purpose of enriching the city's musical life through engaging famous artists as well as supporting local endeavor. Primarily a women's organization, the club continues its role of providing vital musical stimulus to the community. It was instrumental in creating the Atlanta SO, the Choral Guild of Atlanta (1940), and the amateur Atlanta Community Orchestra (1958), as well as other musical organizations that have not survived. The club also sponsors a broad and effective music scholarship program for talented young musicians.

Earlier attempts to establish an enduring symphony orchestra for Atlanta had met with little success, but in 1944 the Atlanta Music Club founded the Atlanta Youth SO by the amalgamation of two school orchestras. The Chicago conductor Henry Sopkin was engaged as music director, a post he held, through the transformation of the group three years later into the Atlanta SO, until his retirement in 1966. Sopkin was responsible for building the orchestra into a reasonably proficient body of semi-professional players.

An air crash in Paris on 3 June 1962 took the lives of more than 100 Atlanta art patrons on a chartered European tour, an event which sent a powerful wave of feeling, first of grief and then of determination to honor the victims, through the community. Funds were raised to build the Memorial Arts Center, with four performance halls, the largest of which is Symphony Hall (capacity 1762), the orchestra's first permanent home; the complex, which also houses an art school and an art museum, opened in 1968. The decision was also made to upgrade the orchestra to full professional status and engage a music director of international repute to succeed Sopkin. Robert Shaw, then serving as associate conductor to Szell in Cleveland, was appointed in 1967. Under Shaw's direction the orchestra has become one of the nation's finest. From the two concerts of the 1944–5 season it progressed to giving well over 200, in Atlanta and on tour, during the 1981–2 season. The annual tours, which serve principally the southeastern USA, also extend to New York, Boston, Chicago, Philadelphia, and Washington, DC. The orchestra has a growing discography and has won awards for adventurous programming of contemporary music. In 1974 the Atlanta Symphony Youth Orchestra was created. Section leaders of the main orchestra coach young Atlanta musicians in weekly rehearsals; the orchestra gives several concerts a year and has maintained a high standard.

Atlanta has many churches, predominantly Protestant, in which the sacred-music repertory is regularly performed; many have fine organs, affording ample opportunity for oustanding recitals. Virtually all the universities, colleges, and junior colleges in the area offer some musical instruction. The most important is Georgia State University (20,000 students), with a music teaching staff numbering 40 (in 1982), which offers undergraduate and graduate music degrees in a number of specialized performance areas as well as in piano pedagogy and sacred music. Emory University also contributes to the musical life of the city with its orchestra and chorus, but even more through a series of concerts (sponsored by endowment funds) featuring well-known international performers. Two predominantly black colleges, Spelman and Morehouse, provide advanced music training programs, the former being the only school in Atlanta other than Georgia State University nationally accredited to offer music degrees. The Georgia Academy of Music, a private endeavor, has demonstrated noteworthy success in stimulating interest in music study for children of all ages.

Other prominent features of local musical life include the Atlanta Boy Choir, the Pro-Mozart Society of Atlanta, the Atlanta SO Chorus, a number of amateur performing groups, and recitals presented by the many excellent musicians resident in Atlanta. Several chamber music groups have achieved widespread recognition, notably the Atlanta Chamber Players and the Atlanta Virtuosi. One setback was the failure of Atlanta's most important attempt (1968) to establish local opera as part of the move to commemorate the 1962 tragedy. Mismanagement and unrealistic planning brought the project to financial collapse in its second month of operation, following a series of performances of Purcell's *King Arthur* and of a highly controversial version of Puccini's *La bohème*, set in the Paris of the 1920s. Since then, several short-lived opera companies have been formed. Even with several successful productions behind it, the Atlanta Civic Opera (founded 1979), under the artistic direction of composer Thomas Pasatieri, was in 1982 still seeking a workable solution to its financial problems.

By the early 1980s, a number of recording companies specializing in popular music had been established in Atlanta.

JOHN SCHNEIDER

Atwill, Joseph F(airfield) (*b* Boston, MA, 1811; *d* Oakland, CA, 1891). Music publisher. From 1833 to 1849 he ran a music store and publishing business in New York, where he also used plates of the Thomas Birch company. In 1849 Samuel C. Jollie took over the business. Atwill went to California and established the first music store in San Francisco, at 158 Washington Street. He began publishing in 1852 with the song *The California Pioneers*, the cover of which bears the legend "N. B. The First Piece of Music Pubd. in Cala." A branch of Atwill & Co. was established in Sacramento the following year, but by 1854 it was being run by Dan H. Dougliss. Atwill remained in business until 1860, when he sold his interests to Matthias Gray.

BIBLIOGRAPHY

H. Dichter and E. Shapiro: *Early American Sheet Music* (New York, 1941/*R*1977)
M. K. Duggan: "Music Publishing and Printing in San Francisco before the Earthquake & Fire of 1906," *Kemble Occasional*, no.24 (1980), esp.3f

BARBARA TURCHIN

Auden, W(ystan) H(ugh) (*b* York, England, 21 Feb 1907; *d* Vienna, Austria, 29 Sept 1973). Poet. He immigrated to the USA in 1938 and was naturalized in 1946. Part 3 of his *Collected Poems* (New York, 1945) consists of 38 "songs and other musical pieces," including the five lyrics set in Benjamin Britten's cycle *On this Island* and arias from his opera *Paul Bunyan*, as well as the frequently set poems *Song for St. Cecilia's Day* and "Carry her over the water." Among poets of the mid-20th century, Auden was one of those most actively concerned with music.

Auden's friend Chester Kallman was largely responsible for arousing his interest in opera. Kallman and Auden collaborated on the libretto for Stravinsky's *The Rake's Progress* and the masque *Delia*, written for Stravinsky but not set. Thereafter they produced two librettos for Hans Werner Henze, *Elegy for Young Lovers* and *The Bassarids*, and for Nicolas Nabokov adapted *Love's Labours Lost*. A self-declared "opera addict," despite his preference for opera in the original language Auden also collaborated with Kallman in translating a number of librettos, including several for operas by Mozart and Weill.

Many composers have been attracted by Auden's poetry, among them Berio (*Nones*), Foss (in *Time Cycle*), Marvin David Levy (*For the Time Being*), Persichetti (in *Hymns and Responses for the Church Year*), and Rorem (in *Poems of Love and the Rain*). Auden's poem *The Age of Anxiety* inspired Bernstein's symphony of the same title. With Britten Auden collaborated on films, broadcasts, plays, and numerous songs. Later poems written specifically for musical setting include two translations from Irish texts in Barber's *Hermit Songs* and Stravinsky's *Elegy for J.F.K.* Auden and Kallman were the text editors of *An Elizabethan Song Book* (1955), whose music editor was Noah Greenberg, and in 1957 Auden wrote the narratives for Greenberg's performing edition of the medieval liturgical play *The Play of Daniel*.

BIBLIOGRAPHY

J. Kerman: "Opera à la mode," *Hudson Review*, vi (1954), 560; rev. in *Opera as Drama* (New York, 1956), 234ff
J. W. Beach: *The Making of the Auden Canon* (Minneapolis, 1957), 190ff
J. Kerman: "Auden's Magic Flute," *Hudson Review*, x (1957), 309
I. Stravinsky and R. Craft: *Memories and Commentaries* (New York, 1960), 144ff
M. K. Spears: *The Poetry of W. H. Auden: the Disenchanted Island* (New York, 1963), 105ff, 262ff
I. Stravinsky and R. Craft: *Dialogues and a Diary* (New York, 1963)
B. Wright: "Britten and Documentary," *MT*, civ (1963), 779
H. W. Henze: *Essays* (Mainz, Germany, 1964), 95ff
J. C. Blair: *The Poetic Art of W. H. Auden* (Princeton, NJ, 1965), 163ff
U. W[eisstein]: "Sarastro's Brave New World, or 'Die Zauberflöte' Transmogrified," *Your Musical Cue*, ii (Bloomington, IN, 1965–6), 3
I. Stravinsky and R. Craft: *Themes and Episodes* (New York, 1966), 56ff
E. W. White: *Stravinsky: the Composer and his Works* (London, 2/1966), 412ff
P. H. Salus: "Auden and Opera," *Quest*, ii (New York, 1967), 7
I. Stravinsky and R. Craft: *Retrospectives and Conclusions* (New York, 1969), 145ff, 160ff, 173ff

E. W. White: *Benjamin Britten* (London, 2/1970), 22ff, 95ff
U. Weisstein: "Reflections on a Golden Style: W. H. Auden's Theory of Opera," *Comparative Literature*, xxii (1970), 108
B. C. Bloomfield and E. Mendelson: *W. H. Auden: a Bibliography* (Charlottesville, 2/1972)
B. N. S. Gooch and D. S. Thatcher: *Musical Settings of Late Victorian and Modern British Literature: a Catalogue* (New York, 1976)
W. Spiegelman: "The Rake's Progress: an Operatic Version of Pastoral," *Southwest Review*, lxiii (1978), 28
R. G. Alvey: "Toward an Appreciation of Auden's Use of Folksong," *Southern Folklore Quarterly*, xliii (1979), 71
M. A. Roth: "The Sound of a Poet Singing Loudly: a Look at *Elegy for Young Lovers*," *Comparative Drama*, xiii (1979), 99
A. Porter: "Auden, W(ystan) H(ugh)," *Grove 6*
D. Mitchell: *Britten and Auden in the Thirties* (London, 1981)
W. Spiegelman: "The Rake, the Don, the Flute: W. H. Auden as Librettist," *Parnassus*, x/2 (1982), 171
D. J. Farnan: *Auden in Love* (New York, 1984)

MICHAEL HOVLAND (after *Grove 6*)

Audsley, George Ashdown (*b* Elgin, Scotland, 1838; *d* New York, 1925). Organ designer, architect, and art expert. His consuming interest in the organ resulted in his installing a large chamber organ in his home. He immigrated to the USA in 1892, where he worked as an architect, author, and organ consultant. In addition to books on architecture, oriental art, and religious symbolism, Audsley wrote four influential works on organ design: *The Art of Organ-building* (1905), *The Organ of the 20th Century* (1919), *Organ-stops and their Artistic Registration* (1921), and *The Temple of Tone* (1925). These are lavishly illustrated with prints of organ cases and Audsley's own meticulous drawings of pipes and mechanisms. His approach to organ design was conservative and provided a much-needed balance to the excesses of Robert Hope-Jones and others during the early 20th century. He advocated ornamental organ cases and eclectic tonal designs. He also espoused the prevalent orchestral concepts, which emphasized string tone, and believed that all the divisions of an organ should be enclosed in expression boxes.

BIBLIOGRAPHY

O. Ochse: *The History of the Organ in the United States* (Bloomington, IN, 1975)

BARBARA OWEN

Audubon Quartet. String quartet formed in 1974 by Gregory Fulkerson, Janet Brady, Larry Bradford, and Thomas Shaw. After several changes of membership, it consisted, in 1984, of Laurence Shapiro, Sharon Smith Polifrone, Doris Lederer Horowitz, and Shaw. The group was quartet-in-residence at Marywood College in Scranton, Pennsylvania, between 1974 and 1980, and at the Virginia Polytechnic Institute and State University, Blacksburg, from 1981. It has toured extensively and was the first American string quartet to perform in mainland China (January 1982). In 1977 it won first prizes in the Villa-Lobos International String Quartet Competition in Rio de Janeiro and in the contemporary music category at the Evian Festival. Equally adept at the Classical and contemporary repertories, the Audubon has given several world premières, including those of Laderman's String Quartet no.6 (1981), which is named after it, and Schickele's String Quartet no. 1 (1984), which it commissioned.

DAVID HUNTER

Auer, Leopold (von) (*b* Veszprém, Hungary, 7 June 1845; *d* Loschwitz, nr Dresden, Germany, 15 July 1930). Hungarian violinist and teacher. He began his studies at the Budapest Conservatory with Ridley Kohné, continued them at the Vienna Conservatory with Jacob Dont (1857–8), and, after concert tours in the provinces, completed them with Joachim in Hanover (1863–4). After a successful début at the Leipzig Gewandhaus, he was engaged as concertmaster at Düsseldorf (1864–6) and then at Hamburg, where he also led a string quartet. In 1868 Auer was appointed to succeed Henryk Wieniawski as violin professor at the St. Petersburg Conservatory; he remained there until 1917. He also taught in London during the summers of 1906–11, and in Loschwitz in 1912–14. In June 1917 he left strife-torn Russia for Norway, ostensibly on a holiday, and sailed for New York in February 1918; he settled permanently in the USA, and, despite his age, gave concerts and taught, both at the Institute of Musical Art in New York and at the Curtis Institute.

Auer contributed decisively to the world renown of the Russian violin school. His first students to arouse international attention were Elman in 1905 and Zimbalist in 1907, followed by Heifetz, Milstein, and many others. Among his students in the USA were Dushkin, Rabinof, and Shumsky. Most of his students came to him as finished technicians so that he could develop their taste and interpretive powers. His approach was geared to the temperament of each. It is more appropriate to speak of an Auer style than of a school: virtuosity controlled by fine taste, classical purity without dryness, intensity without sentimentality.

Auer's solo technique lacked a certain virtuoso flair – perhaps because of the poor physical structure of his hand; yet his noble and fine-grained interpretations of the great concertos succeeded in winning him many admirers. Tchaikovsky (*Sérénade mélancolique*), Glazunov, Anton Arensky, and Sergey Taneyev all dedicated works to him. Yet he declined the dedication of Tchaikovsky's Violin Concerto, declaring it technically awkward and too long. His transcriptions, arrangements, and several compositions are tasteful but largely forgotten. His editions of the classical violin repertory are still useful, as are his *Violin Playing as I Teach it* (1921) and *Violin Masterworks and their Interpretation* (1925). He also published *My Long Life in Music* (1923).

BIBLIOGRAPHY

G. Saleski: *Famous Musicians of Jewish Origin* (New York, 1949)
C. Flesch: *Memoirs* (London, 1957/*R*1979)
L. Raaben: *Leopold Semenovich Auer* (Leningrad, 1962)
J. Hartnack: *Grosse Geiger unserer Zeit* (Gütersloh, Germany, 1968)
J. Creighton: *Discopaedia of the Violin, 1889–1971* (Toronto, 1974)
B. Schwarz: "The Russian Violin School Transplanted to America," *Journal of the Violin Society of America*, iii/1 (1977), 27
——: *Great Masters of the Violin* (New York, 1983)

BORIS SCHWARZ

Aufderheide, May (Frances) (*b* Indianapolis, IN, 21 May 1888; *d* Pasadena, CA, 1 Sept 1972). Ragtime composer. She studied piano with her aunt, and composed her first piano rag, *Dusty Rag*, at the age of 19. This piece became a commercial success, encouraging her father, John H. Aufderheide, to purchase the rights and become a music publisher. His firm published all Aufderheide's works, as well as those of other Indiana songwriters, and achieved modest, though brief, national success. Shortly after the publication of *Dusty Rag* Aufderheide moved with her husband to Richmond, Indiana. Late in 1908 her *Richmond Rag* (named for her new home) was issued, and by the following summer she had attracted the attention of a New York music trade magazine. Between 1908 and 1912 she produced 19 published compositions, including *The Thriller Rag* (1909) which, like *Dusty Rag*, achieved popularity in sheet-music, piano-roll, and orchestrated versions, and remained in the rag repertory for decades. By about 1912 Aufderheide apparently ceased composing, spending the remainder of her life as a housewife.

Aufderheide's rags are melodious, catchy, and not difficult to perform. Her brief career was atypical: unlike most ragtime composers she came from a wealthy family and played piano on an amateur rather than a professional basis; furthermore, she made her mark in a male-dominated field, becoming perhaps the leading woman composer of ragtime.

WORKS

(selective list; all printed works published in Indianapolis)

Pf: Dusty Rag (1908); The Richmond Rag (1908); Buzzer Rag (1909); The Thriller Rag (1909); A Totally Different Rag (1910); Blue Ribbon Rag (1910); Novelty Rag (1911); Pompeian Waltzes (1912); Pelham Waltzes (1912)

Songs: A Totally Different Rag (E. C. Jones) (1910); In Bamboo Land (Jones) (1910); You and Me in the Summertime (R. Aufderheide) (1911); Dusty Rag Song (J. W. Callahan) (1912); 6 others

Principal publisher: Aufderheide

BIBLIOGRAPHY

" 'Classic Rags' Composed by May Aufderheide: Talented Indianapolis Girl is Achieving Enviable Reputation," *American Musican and Art Journal*, xxv (13 Aug 1909), 20

J. E. Hasse: *The Creation and Dissemination of Indianapolis Ragtime, 1897–1930* (diss., Indiana U., 1981), 134

J. E. Hasse and F. J. Gillis: Liner notes, *Indiana Ragtime: a Documentary Album* (Indiana Historical Society, 1981)

M. Morath: "May Aufderheide and the Ragtime Women," *Ragtime: its History, Composers, and Music*, ed. J. E. Hasse (New York, 1985), 154

JOHN EDWARD HASSE

Augér, Arleen (Joyce) (*b* Los Angeles, CA, 13 Sept 1939). Soprano. She graduated from California State University, Long Beach (BA in education 1963). From 1965 Ralph Errolle was her teacher and in 1967, after winning a competition to study in Europe, she was engaged by the Vienna Staatsoper as a coloratura; her début was as Queen of Night in Mozart's *Die Zauberflöte*. For the following seven years she remained under contract in Vienna, although she sang extensively in Europe and in 1969 made her début with the New York City Opera. In 1974 she joined the German conductor Helmuth Rilling in a tour of Japan presenting works by Bach and Haydn. She began to concentrate on lyric roles, and at this time made the first of more than 100 recordings (some 50 of them of cantatas by Bach), for many of which she has won awards. Beginning in 1971 she taught singing at Goethe University in Frankfurt am Main, Germany.

Despite her international reputation Augér sang rarely in the USA until the early 1980s. Her début with the Metropolitan Opera was in 1978 as Marcellina in Beethoven's *Fidelio* and she later sang at summer Bach festivals. In 1983 and 1984 her numerous American appearances included the Aspen Music Festival; the New England Bach Festival; with the Philadelphia Orchestra in Carl Orff's *Carmina burana*; a New York recital début at Alice Tully Hall; and as Donna Anna in Mozart's *Don Giovanni* with the Kentucky Opera, Louisville. She has a limpid, pure soprano voice, with an edge of sensuality to the tone, and although her voice is small it is distinguished by innate lyricism and effortless musicianship.

PATRICK J. SMITH

Austin. Capital city of Texas (pop. 345,496; metropolitan area 536,688), situated on the Colorado River in the central area of the state. The area was first settled in 1835, and has a large population of German descent; the city was incorporated in 1839. The Austin Lyceum was established in 1841, and evening concerts were given on the grounds of the state capitol beginning in 1846. Around 1850 a German singing society was formed; this lasted nearly 70 years. By the late 1800s Austin, with a population of about 15,000, had three opera halls and a municipal band which, during the summer, played twice weekly in Hyde Park. The Austin Musical Union, organized in 1886, gave opera and concert performances, chiefly at Scholz Garden; other concerts were held at Tips Hall, Turner Hall, and the Jones Library. The Austin SO was incorporated in 1911 with a concert at the Hancock Opera House conducted by Hans Harthans; the orchestra remained loosely organized until 1938, when it was more formally established under the direction of Henrik J. Buytendorf. Later its conductors included Ezra Rachlin (from 1948 to 1969), Andor Toth (from 1969 to 1970), Maurice Peress (from 1970 to 1972), Lawrence Smith (from 1972 to 1973), Walter Ducloux (from 1973 to 1975), Akira Endo (from 1975 to 1980), and Sung Kwak (from 1982). During the 1983–4 season the orchestra offered a subscription series of 17 concerts. The Austin Civic Orchestra, formed in 1977, has 70 members and schedules nine or ten concerts each season; on occasion it performs operas and oratorios with the Austin Opera Company and the Austin Civic Chorus. Other musical groups active in the city include the Austin Civic Wind Ensemble (formed in 1976), the Austin Symphonic Band (1981), the Austin Baroque Players, and a number of ensembles assembled by local churches. Performances by visiting orchestras are sponsored by the Cultural Entertainment Committee of the University of Texas.

Austin's large German population has given opera a prominent place in the city's musical life since the late 19th century; operas are performed at the University of Texas, where Walter Ducloux was director of the opera theater from 1968 until 1983, when he was succeeded by Robert DeSimone, and in such civic theaters as the Capitol City Playhouse, where the opera director is Jess Walters. The city also has a Gilbert and Sullivan Society, a number of companies that stage musical theater productions, and several choral groups, including the Austin Choral Union and the Austin Saengerrunde.

The music department at the University of Texas presents more than 400 concerts and recitals annually by faculty, students, visiting artists, and 30 faculty and student ensembles. The department is housed in the university's Performing Arts Center; opened in 1980, the center has extensive instrument collections and the largest tracker-action organ built in the USA. The Humanities Research Center houses the largest collection in existence of manuscripts by modern French composers; the University String Project, under the leadership of its founder, Phyllis Young, brings local public-school students to the campus for private and group lessons on string instruments, and is a model for similar programs throughout the country. Huston-Tillotson College offers BA degrees in music and music education; music courses are also given at Concordia Lutheran College, St. Edwards University, and Austin Community College.

Austin has long been associated with country music, progressive country music (a fusion of folk and rock elements), and western swing. Such prominent exponents of these styles as Willie Nelson, Jerry Jeff Walker, and Gary P. Nunn reside in the area, as do members of the groups Asleep at the Wheel and the Lost Gonzo Band. From 1970 to 1980 the Armadillo World Headquarters, an old armory converted into a concert hall and community arts center, was the focus of much popular-music activity. Austin has over 300 nightclubs, many of which offer live performances of country music, jazz, rock, and Mexican, German, and Bohemian folk music.

Among Austin's most important concert halls are the municipal Palmer Auditorium (seating 6000), the Paramount Theater for the Performing Arts (1332), and the City Coliseum (3800). On the campus of the University of Texas are the Jessen Auditorium (330), the Recital Studio (194), Bates Recital Hall (700), the Opera Lab Theater (400), Hogg Memorial Auditorium (1200), the LBJ Library Auditorium (1000), the Grand Concert Hall of the Performing Arts Center (3000), the Frank C. Erwin, Jr., Special Events Center (18,000), and the Texas Union Ballroom (1200). Concerts are also given at Huston-Tillotson College, St. Edwards University, Concordia Lutheran College, Austin Community College, the Presbyterian and Episcopal seminaries, and at local churches; outdoor performances are given in the Zilker Park Hillside Theater and the Symphony Square Amphitheater.

The Music Umbrella of Austin, a nonprofit corporation that receives municipal funds, promotes the appreciation and performance of all types of music in Austin. There are about 50 music study, appreciation, and performance societies in the city, ranging from the Wednesday Morning Music Club to the Austin Friends of Traditional Music.

See also LIBRARIES AND COLLECTIONS, §3.

BIBLIOGRAPHY

L. M. Spell: *Music in Texas* (Austin, 1936)
M. O. James-Reed: *Music in Austin, 1900–1956* (Austin, 1957)
M. S. Barkley: *History of Travis County and Austin, 1839–1899* (Waco, TX, 1963)
B. Brammer: "Austin's Musical History Explored," *Austin Sun* (17–23 October 1974), 18
J. Reid: *The Improbable Rise of Redneck Rock* (Austin, 1974)
T. Holland: *Texas Genesis: a Wild Ride Through Texas Progressive Country Music 1963–78, with Digressions* (Austin, 1978)
B. C. Malone: *Southern Music, American Music* (Lexington, KY, 1979)
H. C. Sparks: *Stylistic Development and Compositional Processes of Selected Solo Singer/Songwriters in Austin, Texas* (diss., U. of Texas, Austin, 1984)

HUGH CULLEN SPARKS

Austin, Elizabeth (*b* Leicester, England, *c*1800; *d* England, after 1835). English singer. She was trained by William Gardiner, Gesualdo Lanza, and Thomas Cooke. Her performances at the Theatre Royal in Dublin in 1821 led to engagements in London at the Theatre Royal, Drury Lane, where she made her début on 23 November 1822, and the English Opera House. After appearing in France, she returned to England to perform at Drury Lane, Vauxhall, and in summer festivals.

In August 1827, advised by the brothers F. H. F. and William Berkeley, Mrs. Austin contracted with F. C. Wemyss to appear at William Warren's Chesnut Street Theatre, Philadelphia. She arrived with F. H. F. Berkeley in late November 1827 and made her début in Thomas Arne's *Love in a Village* on 10 December; she made her first appearance in New York at the Park Theatre on 2 January 1828. Mrs. Austin toured widely with Charles Edward Horn and other singers, and for the next five years was America's reigning *prima donna*. Guided by Berkeley, himself an amateur musician, she did much to popularize English opera adaptations in America. Her repertory ranged from *The Beggar's Opera* to Weber's *Der Freischütz*; she also launched Michael Rophino Lacy's opera *Cinderella* in America, where it was extremely successful. Her voice was high, sweet, and flexible, but since she was only a mediocre actress, her best performances were in oratorio and in coloratura roles such as Cinderella and Mandane in Arne's *Artaxerxes*. After 1834, when Mary Anne Paton Wood arrived in America, Mrs. Austin's prestige began to decline; in May 1835 she and Berkeley returned to England and she retired from the stage.

BIBLIOGRAPHY

"Mrs. Austin," *The Euterpeiad: an Album of Music, Poetry & Prose*, i (1830), 147
F. C. Wemyss: *Twenty-Six Years of the Life of an Actor and Manager* (New York, 1847)

WILLIAM BROOKS

Austin, John Turnell (*b* Podington, Bedfordshire, England, 16 May 1869; *d* Hartford, CT, 17 Sept 1948). Organ builder. The son of a gentleman farmer, Austin immigrated to the USA in 1889. He first worked for Farrand & Votey of Detroit, rapidly advancing to become foreman. Here he first conceived the idea of a radically different system of organ construction called the "universal wind-chest" system; this consisted of an individual-valve chest, the lower portion of which was a walk-in air chamber with regulator. Pipe valves were operated by a thin wooden trace attached to a motor bellows for each note. Stop action was first achieved by sliders; later a pivoting fulcrum affecting the valves was used. Although Farrand & Votey allowed Austin to experiment, they showed no interest in his ideas, and in 1893 he left them for Clough & Warren of Detroit, who in the same year built their first small organ based on Austin's system. In 1898 Clough & Warren were closed by fire, and Austin moved to Boston. A year later he was persuaded by some Hartford businessmen to move to their city, and with their backing he opened a factory there. He obtained patents for an all-electric console in 1913, and for a self-player mechanism in 1914. Austin's mechanical ingenuity was not limited to organ mechanisms; he also designed many labor-saving machines for his factory. In 1937 he retired, and his firm reorganized under the name of Austin Organs, Inc., with his nephew, Frederic B. Austin, as president. Richard J. Piper joined the company in 1949, becoming vice-president and tonal director. Donald Austin became president in 1973. Noteworthy Austin organs include those in City Hall Auditorium, Portland, Maine (1912), the University of Pennsylvania (1926), St. Joseph's Cathedral, Hartford (1962), Trinity College, Hartford (1972), and Holy Family Cathedral, Tulsa (1984).

BIBLIOGRAPHY

"Science Aids Art," *Connecticut Industry*, xxxviii/5 (1960), 6
W. H. Barnes: *The Contemporary American Organ* (Glen Rock, NJ, 8/1964)
O. Ochse: *The History of the Organ in the United States* (Bloomington, IN, 1975)

BARBARA OWEN

Austin, Larry (Don) (*b* Duncan, OK, 12 Sept 1930). Composer. He studied at North Texas State University (BM 1951, MM 1952), then did graduate work at Mills College (summer 1955) and at the University of California, Berkeley (1955–8). His principal teachers were Imbrie, Milhaud, and Shifrin. He has taught at the University of California, Davis (1958–72), the University of South Florida, Tampa (1972–8), and North Texas State University (from 1978). In 1968 he was Creative Associate at the Center for the Creative and Performing Arts of SUNY, Buffalo. He played a leading role in founding the avant-garde music journal *Source* and was its first editor (1966–71). *Improvisations for Orchestra and Jazz Soloists* (1961) was the first of his compositions to gain wide recognition, through a performance on national television and a recording, both by the New York

PO under Bernstein. Subsequent experiments with group improvisation led to a series of works in "open style" (1965–6) in which the performers are given areas of improvisational choice while overall control is maintained by means of analog notation. Later works (for example *Walter*) reflect Austin's interest in electronic and theatrical media as compositional resources. Four of his compositions – the First Fantasy (1975), the Second Fantasy (1976), *Phantasmagoria* (1977), and *Life Pulse Music* (1984) – are based on Ives's sketches towards *Universe Symphony*.

WORKS

Stage: Richard II (incidental music, Shakespeare), 1963; Roma, improvisation ens, tape, 1965; Bass, db player, tape, film, 1966; The Maze, perc, dancers, machines, film, 1966; Amphitryon 38 (incidental music, J. Giraudoux), tape, 1967; The Magicians (children's theater piece), tape, film, slides, 1968; Agape (Bible), actors, dancers, insts, tape, film, sculpture, 1970; Walter, va, va d'amore, tape, film, 1970–71; Euphonia (opera, 2, T. Holliday, after Berlioz), 1982; Beachcombers (dance music, M. Cunningham), elec, 1983

Inst: Pf Variations, 1960; Improvisations for Orch and Jazz Soloists, 1961; A Broken Consort, fl, cl, hn, db, pf, perc, 1962; Pf Set in Open Style, 1964; Open Style for Orch and Pf Soloist, 1965; Heaven Music, multiple fl, 1976; Life Pulse Music, 20 perc, 1984 [realization of Ives's Universe Sym.]; *c*12 others

With tape: Quadrants 1–11, insts, chorus, tape, 1972–7; Tableaux vivants, unspecified insts, unspecified vv, tape, 1973, rev. 1981, collab. C. Rinsness; Fantasies on Ives's Universe Sym.: no. 1, double brass qnt, nar, tape, 1975, no. 2, cl, va, kbds, perc, tape, 1976; *c*12 others

Mixed-media and cptr: Accidents, pf, tape, film, 1967; Prelude, Postlude, and Plastic Surgery, pf, tape, film, 1967–8; Transmission no. 1, video, elec, 1969; Phantasmagoria, fantasy on Ives's Universe Sym., orch, nar, tape, synth, 1977, rev. 1981; Canadian Coastlines, unspecified vv, unspecified insts, tape, synth, 1981; Sonata concertante, pf, cptr, 1983; *c*10 others

15 student works, 1948–58; a few acc. vocal works, incl. Ceremony, 1v, org, 1980

Principal publishers: ACA, Composer Performer (*Source*), MJQ, Peer-Southern

BIBLIOGRAPHY

EwenD; *VintonD*

A. Kennedy: "Sound-script Relations and the New Notation," *Artforum*, xii/1 (1973), 38

D. Ernst: *The Evolution of Electronic Music* (New York, 1976)

W. Zimmermann: *Desert Plants: Conversations with 23 American Musicians* (Vancouver, BC, 1976), 207

JEROME ROSEN

Austin, William W(eaver) (*b* Lawton, OK, 18 Jan 1920). Musicologist. He was educated at Harvard University (BA 1939, MA 1940, PhD 1951). He has taught at Cornell University since 1947, and in 1969 he was appointed Goldwin Smith Professor of Musicology there and elected a Fellow of the American Academy of Arts and Sciences. He was a visiting professor at Princeton University during the academic year 1957–8. Austin specializes in the music of Russia and the USA in the 19th century, and in the history of 20th-century music. With *Music in the 20th Century* (1966) he contributed a broad survey of music from 1900 to 1950, approaching it primarily from the stylistic standpoint. While his evaluations are sometimes debatable (a lengthy chapter is devoted to Debussy's "unique achievement," and the treatment of Schoenberg has been criticized), Austin successfully avoided the use of "isms" and similar labeling, and was the first scholar to elevate jazz to a position of first-rank importance in a serious historical study. *Susanna, Jeanie, and The Old Folks at Home* (1975) is not only a concentrated analysis of Stephen Foster's songs but a highly original and perceptive inquiry into the reasons for their unique durability in American culture from Foster's time to the mid-1970s.

PAULA MORGAN/H. WILEY HITCHCOCK

Austin High School Gang. Name given to an informal group of midwestern jazz musicians, whose principal members had attended Austin High School, Chicago, in the early 1920s. *See* CHICAGO JAZZ and CHICAGO (i), §7.

Autoharp. Chord zither used to teach rudimentary harmony in schools, and as an Appalachian folk instrument. *See* ZIMMERMANN, CHARLES F.

Autry, (Orvon) Gene (*b* Tioga, TX, 29 Sept 1907). Country-music and popular singer and songwriter, and actor. He began his career as a member of the Fields Brothers Marvelous Medicine Show. Encouraged by Will Rogers, in 1929 he left his job as a relief telegraph operator for the railroad in Oklahoma, and went to New York, where he made his first recordings for RCA Victor and several other labels. He sang on radio station KVOO in Tulsa

Gene Autry, 1930s

as "Oklahoma's Singing Cowboy," much in the style of Jimmie Rodgers, which led to a contract with the American Record Company. He received national attention from his broadcasts on the "National Barn Dance" on WLS in Chicago, and in 1931 made his first hit recording, *That silver haired daddy of mine*. On the strength of his radio popularity he went to Hollywood in 1934, where he became the first of the "singing cowboys." He appeared in nearly 100 films, including the first feature-length musical western, *Tumbling Tumbleweeds* (1935), which he made for Republic. From 1939 to 1956 he was the host of a popular CBS radio show, "Melody Ranch." Autry also developed a number of business interests, including a music publishing company, Golden West Melodies; a chain of radio and television stations; and two recording companies, Champion and Republic. By giving country music the image of the singing cowboy to replace the less popular hillbilly stereotype, he did more than any other singer to introduce the genre to a national audience. He was elected to the Country Music Hall of Fame in 1969.

BIBLIOGRAPHY

D. B. Green: "Gene Autry," *Stars of Country Music*, ed. B. C. Malone and J. McCulloh (Urbana, IL, 1975), 142

G. Autry and M. Herskowitz: *Back in the Saddle Again* (Garden City, NY, 1978)

BILL C. MALONE

Avant-garde jazz. A term applied to a broad range of relatively fresh jazz styles during the late 1950s and early 1960s, especially those of John Coltrane, Ornette Coleman, Cecil Taylor, and Albert Ayler. Though applied with little uniformity, sometimes the term was used synonymously with a second term, "the New Thing." FREE JAZZ is a third term that frequently was attached to the work of these players, though little of the music was entirely free of pre-set melody, and almost none of the music was free of pre-set distinctions between roles of soloists and accompanists, nor was it free of tempo, key, or tonality, though improvisations in the performance of some music by Coleman and Taylor did not require chord progressions to be pre-set.

See also JAZZ, §V.

BIBLIOGRAPHY

E. Jost: *Free Jazz* (Graz, Austria, 1974)

M. C. Gridley: *Jazz Styles: History and Analysis* (Englewood Cliffs, NJ, 1978, rev. 2/1985), 226, 243, 268, 279, 301

MARK C. GRIDLEY

Avshalomov, Jacob (David) (*b* Tsingtao, China, 28 March 1919). Composer and conductor, son of the composer Aaron Avshalomov. In 1937 he came to the USA, where he studied with Bernard Rogers at the Eastman School (MA 1942); he became a naturalized American citizen in 1944. From 1946 to 1954 he taught at Columbia University, where he conducted the university chorus and orchestra in the American premières of Bruckner's Mass in D minor, Tippett's *A Child of our Time*, and Handel's *The Triumph of Time and Truth*; since 1954 he has been conductor of the Portland (Oregon) Junior SO. He received a Guggenheim Fellowship in 1951, the New York Music Critics' Circle Award in 1953 for *Tom O'Bedlam*, the Naumburg Recording Award in 1956 for *Sinfonietta*, and the Alice M. Ditson Award in 1965 for his work with the Portland Junior SO. In February 1968 President Johnson appointed him to the National Council on the Humanities, and from 1976 to 1979 he served as co-chairman of the planning section of the NEA. His music encompasses a broad spectrum from an exotic Chinese style to a colorful American folk idiom. He is the author of two volumes entitled *Music is where you Make it* (1959, 1979).

WORKS

Orch: The Taking of T'ung Kuan, *c*1943; Slow Dance, *c*1945; Sinfonietta, *c*1946; Suite from the Plywood Age, unison vv, orch; Phases of the Great Land, *c*1958; Sym. "The Oregon," 1962; The 13 Clocks, 2 nar, orch, 1973; Raptures for Orch on Madrigals of Gesualdo, vv, orch, 1975

Choral: over 15 works, incl. How Long, O Lord, cantata, A, chorus, orch, *c*1948; Tom O'Bedlam (17th-century anon.), SATB, ob, tabor, jingles, *c*1953; Inscriptions at the City of Brass, female nar, chorus, orch without str, *c*1957; Make a Joyful Noise unto the Lord, SATB, (cl, tpt, 2 hn, b trbn, perc)/(org, perc); City upon a Hill (Blake), nar, chorus, liberty bell, orch, *c*1964; Praises from the Corners of the Earth (Donne, Strongwolf, Koran, Cummings), SATB, org, 3 perc, *c*1964, arr. orch

Chamber: 2 Bagatelles, cl, pf; Cues from the Little Clay Cart, chamber ens, arr. orch; Disconsolate Muse, fl, pf; Sonatine, va, pf, *c*1943; Evocations, cl/va, pf, *c*1947, arr. cl, chamber orch; Quodlibet Montagna, tpt, 4hn, trbn; 3 kbd pieces

10 works for 1v, pf, incl. Songs for Alyce (Dickinson, M. Swenson), 1976

The Little Clay Cart, incidental music

Principal publishers: ACA, Galaxy, MCA, E. C. Schirmer

BIBLIOGRAPHY

EwenD

W. Bergsma: "The Music of Jacob Avshalomov," *ACAB*, iii/3 (1956), 3 [with list of works]

C. H. Encell: *Jacob Avshalomov's Works for Chorus and Orchestra: Aspects of Style* (diss., U. of Washington, 1983)

JAMES G. ROY, JR./R

Awards. Prizes for excellence in music can be loosely divided into two categories: honors, for which an individual must be nominated, and competitive awards, for which he or she must apply or in some other way compete. Some awards, such as medals, citations, or membership in certain organizations, are honorary. Others are monetary gifts in the form of grants, fellowships for particular study programs, commissions, promotional funding (management, concert performances, etc.), and similar kinds of subsidy. The following list of honors and competitive awards is selective and with few exceptions includes only those awards that were made on a regular basis in 1985. For various other commissioning projects, *see* COOLIDGE, ELIZABETH SPRAGUE; FROMM, PAUL; KOUSSEVITZKY FOUNDATIONS; LOUISVILLE ORCHESTRA COMMISSIONING PROJECT; and ROCKEFELLER, MARTHA BAIRD.

1. Honors. 2. Competitive awards.

1. HONORS. The honors listed below are ordered alphabetically according to the name of the award or the organization that sponsors it. Date of founding, frequency of presentation, the nature and purpose of the award, and categories in which it is given are listed whenever possible; the names of recipients (and in some cases the compositions for which they have been honored) are also listed for some of the more important prizes.

ACADEMY AWARDS, Academy of Motion Picture Arts and Sciences (annually in various categories; music awards 1934–); for achievements in motion pictures. Categories in music include original song, scoring, and adaptation.

ACADEMY OF COUNTRY MUSIC AWARDS (annually in various categories, 1964–). Categories include entertainer, female vocalist, male vocalist, vocal group, new female vocalist, new male vocalist, vocal duo, album, single, song, and country film.

ALICE M. DITSON FUND OF COLUMBIA UNIVERSITY (1940–): for the "funding of performances, recordings, and publications of works by younger American composers and those older American composers who are not widely known." Programs include support for performances, partial subsidies for recordings (especially to small record companies that would not otherwise be able to produce and market releases of works by contemporary American composers), and grants to individual composers.

AMERICAN ACADEMY AND INSTITUTE OF ARTS AND LETTERS. The American Academy of Arts and Letters, founded in 1904 by the National Institute of Arts and Letters (founded 1898), merged with the parent organization in 1976 to form the American Academy and Institute of Arts and Letters. The two organizations function as separate bodies under a single board of directors, and election to the prestigious Academy is one of the highest honors accorded for artistic achievement. In 1985 seven of the 50 members were composers: L. Bernstein, E. Carter, A. Copland, L. Foss, G. Schuller, W. Schuman, and V. Thomson; 45 of the 250 members of the Institute were also composers. Former composer members of the Academy include S. Barber, E. Bloch, J. A. Carpenter, G. W. Chadwick, F. B. Converse, W. Damrosch, H. Hadley, H. Hanson, R. Harris, C. M. Loeffler, E. MacDowell, D. Moore, H. Parker, W. Piston, R. Sessions, I. Stravinsky, D. Taylor, and F. Van der Stucken. Honorary membership has been granted to 75 foreign artists, writers, and composers, among them G. C. Menotti. Awards relating to music:

Academy-Institute Awards (annually in art, literature, and music, 1941–): to a composer, $4000 and subsidy for a recording

Charles E. Ives Awards, established by Harmony Twichell (Mrs. Charles) Ives: scholarships to young composers (until 1980 grants were also awarded to scholars and organizations, notably the Charles Ives Society, to further the publication and performance of Ives's music)

Goddard Lieberson Fellowships, established by the CBS Foundation (one or more annually, 1979–): to young composers of "extraordinary gifts," $10,000

Gold Medal (two annually in rotating categories: music awards 1919–). Recipients in music: S. Barber, J. A. Carpenter, E. Carter, G. W. Chadwick, A. Copland, W. Damrosch, C. M. Loeffler, W. Schuman, R. Sessions, I. Stravinsky, V. Thomson

Marc Blitzstein Award for the Musical Theatre (irregularly, 1965–): to a composer, librettist, or lyricist, for a music-theater work, $2500

Marjorie Peabody Waite Award: to a mature artist, writer, or composer (in rotation), $1500

Walter Hinrichsen Award, established by the C. F. Peters Corporation (1984–): to an American composer

See also Richard Rodgers Production Award under "Competitive awards, Composers."

AMERICAN COMPOSERS ALLIANCE LAUREL LEAF AWARD (generally one annually, 1951–): parchment scroll to a composer for "distinguished achievement in fostering and encouraging American music"

AMERICAN MUSICOLOGICAL SOCIETY

Alfred Einstein Award (annually, 1967–): to a young scholar resident in the USA or Canada for the "most significant" article on a musicological subject, $400

Otto Kinkeldey Award (annually, 1967–): to a scholar resident in the USA or Canada for a work of musicological scholarship considered to be "the most distinguished of those published in the previous year," $400

See also Noah Greenberg Award under "Competitive awards, Performers."

ASCAP: see Deems Taylor Awards.

AVERY FISHER ARTIST PROGRAM

Avery Fisher Career Grants (three to five annually): including one to a young instrumentalist, $7500

Avery Fisher Prize, established by Avery Fisher (one or two annually, 1975–): to an outstanding American instrumentalist nominated by a recommendation board, "to provide recognition and major career assistance," $10,000, sponsorship of performances with the organizations of Lincoln Center, and a recording

BRANDEIS UNIVERSITY

Brandeis University Creative Arts Awards (annually in four categories, 1957–): medals and cash awards to "established artists in celebration of a lifetime of distinguished achievement"; citations and cash awards to younger artists or to those who have not yet received other honors. Categories: sculpture, painting, and architecture; poetry, fiction, and nonfiction; theater arts and film; and music or dance (1957–71, all in music; 1972–, music and dance rotated annually)

Commission Awards for Notable Achievement in the Arts (annually, 1964–)

COUNTRY MUSIC ASSOCIATION AWARDS (annually, 1967–). Categories include entertainer, single, album, song, female vocalist, male vocalist, vocal group, vocal duo, instrumental group or band, and instrumentalist.

COUNTRY MUSIC HALL OF FAME, founded by the Country Music Association and administered since 1964 by the Country Music Foundation (1961–): to "those all-time greats in the development of country music whose careers have made an indelible impact upon the direction of country performance," plaque and portrait in the Country Music Hall of Fame and Museum (opened in 1967)

DEEMS TAYLOR AWARDS, ASCAP (annually, 1967–): cash awards for excellence in writing about music (popular and serious, for articles and book-length works)

DITSON FUND: see Alice M. Ditson Fund.

EDWARD MacDOWELL MEDAL, established to commemorate the 100th anniversary of MacDowell's birth (annually in rotating categories, 1960–): medal to a composer, visual artist, or writer

GODDARD LIEBERSON FELLOWSHIP, endowed by the CBS Foundation (annually, 1979–): to a young composer "of extraordinary gifts," $10,000

GRAMMY AWARDS: see National Academy of Recording Arts and Sciences.

GRAWEMEYER AWARD FOR MUSIC COMPOSITION, administered by the University of Louisville (annually): for a work in a large genre (e.g., choral, orchestral, chamber, song cycle, dance, opera, musical theater, extended solo), $150,000

JAZZ MASTERS AWARDS, sponsored by the NEA: to "distinguished jazz masters who have significantly altered the language of the art form in the African-American tradition"

KENNEDY CENTER HONORS (annually, 1978–): honorary awards to outstanding artists. Recipients in music include R. Rodgers, M. Anderson, A. Rubinstein (1978); E. Fitzgerald, A. Copland (1979); L. Bernstein, L. Price (1980); Count Basie, R. Serkin (1981); B. Goodman, E. Ormandy (1982); F. Sinatra, V. Thomson (1983); L. Horne, G. C. Menotti, I. Stern (1984).

KINDLER FOUNDATION IN THE LIBRARY OF CONGRESS (at least one every two years, 1952–): a commission for a chamber work and sponsorship of a performance

LAUREL LEAF AWARD: see American Composers Alliance Laurel Leaf Award.

LEVENTRITT AWARD: see Edgar M. Leventritt Foundation International Competition under "Competitive awards, Performers."

LIEBERSON FELLOWSHIP: see Goddard Lieberson Fellowship.

MABEL MERCER FOUNDATION AWARD (annually, 1985–): to a performer who best exemplifies the qualities that made Mabel Mercer an archetypal cabaret performer, $1500

MacARTHUR FELLOWS PROGRAM, John D. and Catherine D. MacArthur Foundation (1981–): to musicians and others "to give personal support over an extended period of time . . . rather than to their projects," *c*$300,000 to cover a period of five years. Recipients in music: C. Nancarrow, R. Shapey

MacDOWELL MEDAL: see Edward MacDowell Medal.

McKIM FUND IN THE LIBRARY OF CONGRESS (irregularly, 1970–): commission to an American composer for a composition scored for violin and piano, and sponsorship of performances

MUSIC LIBRARY ASSOCIATION PUBLICATION PRIZES (annually, 1977–). Categories: book-length bibliography or other research tool in music; article-length bibliography, article on music librarianship, or similar work; and book or music review published in *Notes*

NASHVILLE SONGWRITERS ASSOCIATION AWARDS (annually, 1968–): certificate of achievements, etc., to songwriters

NATIONAL ACADEMY OF RECORDING ARTS AND SCIENCES

Bing Crosby Award: plaque from the Board of Trustees to individuals in the recording industry "who have made creative contributions of outstanding or scientific significance to the field of phonograph records"

Grammy Awards (annually in numerous categories, 1958–). Nominations solicited from Academy members (singers, songwriters, producers, and others active in the recording field) and record companies. Categories include record, album, song, new artist, classical album, and opera recording.

Lifetime Achievement Awards: to performers "whose achievements with the recording field over a period of many years have been deemed exceptionally outstanding"

Recording Hall of Fame Award (1973–): "to recognize recordings of lasting, qualitative or historical significance" released before the inauguration of the Grammy Awards

Trustees Awards: "to recognize outstanding contributions to the recording field that are of such broad scope that they do not fall within the framework of any particular Grammy Awards category"

NEW YORK MUSIC CRITICS' CIRCLE AWARD (annually, 1941–65): to a composer for the most important work or works heard in New York each year

PULITZER PRIZE, Columbia University (annually, 1943–; originally the Pulitzer Prize Music Scholarship, 1917–42, established by Joseph Pulitzer): to an American composer for a "distinguished musical composition . . . in any of the larger forms, including chamber, orchestral, choral, opera, song, dance, or other forms of musical theater, which has had its first performance in the United States during the previous year," $1000. Nominations are evaluated by juries in each field. Recipients: W. Schuman (*A Free Song*, cantata, 1943), H. Hanson (Symphony no.4, 1944), A. Copland (*Appalachian Spring*, orch, 1945), L. Sowerby (*Canticle of the Sun*, cantata, 1946), C. Ives (Symphony no.3, 1947), W. Piston (Symphony no.3, 1948), V. Thomson (*Louisiana Story*, film score, 1949), G. C. Menotti (*The Consul*, musical drama, 1950), D. Moore (*Giants in the Earth*, opera, 1951), G. Kubik (Symphony concertante, pf, va, tpt, orch, 1952), Q. Porter (Concerto concertante, 2 pf, orch, 1954), G. C. Menotti (*The Saint of Bleecker Street*, opera, 1955), E. Toch (Symphony no.3, 1956), N. Dello Joio (*Meditations on Ecclesiastes*, str, 1957), S. Barber (*Vanessa*, opera, 1958), J. La Montaine (Piano Concerto, 1959), E. Carter (String Quartet no.2, 1960), W. Piston (Symphony no.7, 1961), R. Ward (*The Crucible*, opera, 1962), S. Barber (Piano Concerto, 1963), L. Bassett (Variations, orch, 1966), L. Kirchner (String Quartet no.3, 1967), G. Crumb (*Echoes of Time and the River*, orch, 1968), K. Husa (String Quartet no.3, 1969), C. Wuorinen (*Time's Encomium*, tape, 1970), M. Davidovsky (*Synchronisms* no.6, pf, tape, 1971), J. Druckman (*Windows*, orch, 1972),

E. Carter (String Quartet no.3, 1973), D. Martino (*Notturno*, 1974), D. Argento (*From the Diary of Virginia Woolf*, Mez, pf, 1975), N. Rorem (*Air Music*, orch, 1976), R. Wernick (*Visions of Wonder and Terror*, Mez, orch, 1977), M. Colgrass (*Déjà vu*, perc, orch, 1978), J. Schwantner (*Aftertones of Infinity*, orch, 1979), D. Del Tredici (*In Memory of a Summer Day*, amp S, orch, 1980), R. Sessions (Concerto for Orchestra, 1982), E. Zwilich (Three Movements for Orchestra, 1983), B. Rands (*Canti del sole*, T, orch, 1984), S. Albert (*RiverRun*, 1985); special awards and citations to R. Sessions (1974), S. Joplin (1976), M. Babbitt (1982), W. Schuman (1985)

SCHUMAN AWARD: see William Schuman Award.

SOCIETY FOR ETHNOMUSICOLOGY

Jaap Kunst Prize (annually): in recognition of an outstanding paper written and presented by a foreign graduate student

Charles Seeger Prize (annually): in recognition of an outstanding paper written and presented by an American graduate student

WILLIAM SCHUMAN AWARD, Bydale Foundation, administered by the School of the Arts, Columbia University (quadrennially, 1981–): to an American composer "whose works have been widely performed and generally acknowledged to be of lasting significance," $50,000. Recipients: W. Schuman, D. Diamond

2. Competitive awards.

All the cash prizes in the following selective list of awards to composers, performers, and scholars are of $500 or more.

(i) Composers

ABA-NABIM BAND COMPOSITION CONTEST, American Bandmasters Association and the National Association of Band Instrument Manufacturers (annually): cash awards for a new work for band and for a work by an undergraduate student

ALIÉNOR HARPSICHORD COMPOSITION AWARDS, Society for the Publication of American Music (two annually, 1920–): cash awards for a work 15 minutes or longer and a work 8 minutes or less

AMERICAN ACADEMY IN ROME

Residents Program (about ten annually): program under which distinguished artists and scholars are invited to reside at the academy for a year

Rome Prize Fellowships (25–30 annually in various fields including music composition): stipend and expenses to American composers with a BA degree or the equivalent to enable them to study at the academy

ASCAP

ASCAP Foundation Grants to Young Composers (annually, 1978–): cash awards to American citizens or permanent residents 29 years of age or under for an unpublished composition that has not already received an award

Rudolf Nissim Composer Competition (annually, 1982–): cash award to a member of ASCAP for an orchestral work, and sponsorship of the first performance by a major orchestra

ASUC-SESAC STUDENT COMPOSITION CONTEST, American Society of University Composers and SESAC Inc. (annually): cash award to a student composer 28 years of age or under who is a student member of ASUC or is a present or former student of a member of ASUC, for an unpublished composition (maximum of five instruments/voices or four instruments and tape)

BEARNS PRIZE: see Joseph H. Bearns Prize in Music.

BMI AWARDS TO STUDENT COMPOSERS (annually, 1951–): cash awards to American citizens or permanent residents of the Western hemisphere under 26 years of age enrolled in an accredited school or studying with an established teacher, for a musical composition of any instrumentation, style, or length

CONCERT ARTISTS GUILD DÉBUT/PREMIÈRE PROJECT (1951–): commissions for works to be performed for the first time by winning artists in the Annual Auditions (see under "Competitive awards, Performers")

DELIUS COMPOSITION CONTEST, Jacksonville University (annually): cash awards to composers 35 years of age or under for unpublished compositions, and sponsorship of performances. Categories: vocal, keyboard, and instrumental or chamber (ensembles of up to 20 players)

DELTA OMICRON INTERNATIONAL MUSIC FRATERNITY TRIENNIAL COMPOSITION COMPETITION (triennially in rotating categories): cash award to a woman of college age or over for a previously unpublished and unperformed work, and sponsorship of the first performance

EASTMAN–HANSON COMPOSITION PRIZE, established in memory of Howard Hanson by the Institute of American Music of the Eastman School: cash award to an American citizen over the age of 17 for a previously unpublished and unperformed composition, 10–15 minutes long, for chamber orchestra

EASTMAN PRIZE: see George Eastman Prize.

FORD FOUNDATION. In addition to individual grants to composers, scholars, performers, and arts administrators, grant programs in music included:

Opera Commissions (1960–69): 22 commissions issued to American composers and librettists selected by the New York City Opera, the Kansas City Lyric Theatre, the Lyric Opera of Chicago, the Metropolitan Opera, and the San Francisco Opera

See also under "Competitive awards, Performers."

FRIEDHEIM AWARDS: see Kennedy Center Friedheim Awards.

GEORGE EASTMAN PRIZE, Eastman School (1982–): cash award to encourage works for instruments with limited repertories

GEORGE GERSHWIN AWARD, New York Victory Lodge of B'nai Brith (annually, 1945–?): cash award "as encouragement to young composers"

GUGGENHEIM FELLOWSHIPS, John Simon Guggenheim Memorial Foundation (annually, 1925–): grants to composers and scholars 30–45 years of age who propose research into the history or theory of music. Categories: citizens and residents of the USA and Canada, and citizens and residents of other countries in the Western hemisphere

JOSEPH H. BEARNS PRIZE IN MUSIC, Columbia University (two annually, 1928–): cash awards to American composers 18–25 years of age. Categories: a large-scale work and a composition in a smaller form

KENNEDY CENTER FRIEDHEIM AWARDS (annually in alternating categories, 1978–): cash awards and two honorable mentions to American composers for orchestral or chamber works that have received their first performances in the USA within the two preceding years. Categories: orchestral (even-numbered years), chamber (odd-numbered years)

LADO COMPOSITION COMMISSION (biennially, 1948–?75): originally a competition, later a commission and sponsorship of the performance of a work

LEAGUE–ISCM NATIONAL COMPOSERS COMPETITION (annually): performance of a new work in the society's concert series and entry of it in the annual ISCM World Music Days

NATIONAL ENDOWMENT FOR THE ARTS: see NEA.

NATIONAL FEDERATION OF MUSIC CLUBS. Seven broad categories of programs include:

Annual Special Awards (annually): including Orchestra Composition Award

Biennial Awards (annually in alternating categories): various grant programs for singers and instrumentalists (odd-numbered years) and composers (even-numbered years)

See also under "Competitive awards, Performers."

NAUMBURG RECORDING AWARD, Walter W. Naumburg Foundation (1949–): partial subsidy for the recording of a work chosen by a jury. The recording is produced by CRI, which must ensure that it remains available for five years.

See also Walter W. Naumburg Foundation under "Competitive awards, Performers."

NEA. Annual programs relating to music include:

Composer Fellowships Program (1973–): to American composers alone or in collaboration with librettists, video artists, film makers, poets, choreographers, etc.

Jazz Program: grants to composers and performers

See also Jazz Masters Awards under "Honors," and Affiliate Artists Inc., NEA, and Walter F. Naumburg Foundation under "Competitive awards, Performers."

NEW MUSIC COMPETITION, Louisville Orchestra (1984–): cash award for a previously unperformed orchestral work 15–24 minutes long, sponsorship of a performance with the Louisville Orchestra, and a recording. (*See also* LOUISVILLE ORCHESTRA COMMISSIONING PROJECT.)

NEW MUSIC FOR YOUNG ENSEMBLES, Intermediate Ensembles Composers' Competition (annually): cash awards for previously unpublished and unperformed chamber works of medium difficulty, and sponsorship of the first performances

NISSIM COMPETITION: see ASCAP.

NONESUCH COMMISSION AWARDS: see under "Competitive awards, Performers."

RICHARD RODGERS PRODUCTION AWARD, established by Richard Rodgers and administered by the American Academy and Institute of Arts and Letters

(1978–): subsidy to a composer or lyricist for the production in New York by a nonprofit theater organization of a previously unproduced music theater work, "to encourage the development of the musical theatre"

ROME PRIZE FELLOWSHIPS: see American Academy in Rome.

RUDOLF NISSIM COMPOSER COMPETITION: see ASCAP.

ST. PAUL CHAMBER ORCHESTRA ANNUAL COMPOSERS COMPETITION (annually): cash award to a composer for a previously unperformed work for chamber orchestra 10–15 minutes long, and sponsorship of the first performance by the St. Paul Chamber Orchestra

SOCIETY FOR THE PUBLICATION OF AMERICAN MUSIC AWARD (1920–69): cash award, publication, and royalties for a composition

SONGSEARCH CONTEST AND CONCERT, administered by Songwriters Resources and Services (annually): cash awards for unrecorded songs. Categories: rock/new wave, gospel/inspirational, pop/adult contemporary, country/folk, Black-oriented, topical

(ii) Performers

AFFILIATE ARTISTS, INC. (founded 1966)

Affiliate Artists Residencies: salaried positions, lasting a week or more, as leader of informal discussion programs and performances

Affiliate Artists Seaver Conducting Award (biennially, 1985–): cash awards to conductors starting international careers

Exxon/Arts Endowment Conductors Program, Exxon Corporation and the NEA (1973–): full-time residencies for conductors with major orchestras

San Francisco Affiliate Artists Opera Program (five annually): participation in the San Francisco Opera for a season

Xerox Pianists Program, Xerox Corporation and the NEA (six annually, 1982–): performances

AMERICAN MUSIC SCHOLARSHIP ASSOCIATION INTERNATIONAL PIANO COMPETITION (annually, 1956–): cash awards (first prize also includes début in Alice Tully Hall) to pianists 5–30 years of age

AMERICAN NATIONAL CHOPIN COMPETITION, Chopin Foundation of the United States (quinquennially): cash awards (first prize also includes transportation costs to the International Chopin Competition in Warsaw and sponsorship of performances) to American pianists 17–30 years of age

ANDERSON SCHOLARSHIP: see Marian Anderson Scholarship.

ARTISTS INTERNATIONAL

Distinguished Artists Awards Auditions (annually): sponsorship of recitals in New York by artists and chamber groups not yet fully established in their careers

Young Musicians Auditions (annually): sponsorship of New York recital débuts of instrumentalists under the age of 32, singers under 35, and chamber ensembles

BACHAUER INTERNATIONAL PIANO COMPETITION: see Gina Bachauer International Piano Competition.

BALTIMORE SYMPHONY ORCHESTRA'S YOUNG CONDUCTOR'S COMPETITION (biennially): cash awards (first prize also includes performance with the Baltimore SO) to American conductors under 35 years of age

CARNEGIE HALL INTERNATIONAL AMERICAN MUSIC COMPETITIONS: see International American Music Competitions.

CASADESUS INTERNATIONAL PIANO COMPETITION: see Robert Casadesus International Piano Competition.

CLIBURN INTERNATIONAL PIANO COMPETITION: see Van Cliburn International Piano Competition.

CONCERT ARTISTS GUILD ANNUAL AUDITIONS (up to eight annually, 1951–): cash awards to singers, instrumentalists, and chamber ensembles, and sponsorship of Carnegie Recital Hall début and other concert appearances

DALLAS MORNING NEWS G. B. DEALEY AWARDS (annually in alternating categories, 1931–): cash awards to instrumentalists 30 years of age or under and vocalists 32 years of age or under. Categories: strings and piano, voice

DIMITRI MITROPOULOS INTERNATIONAL MUSIC COMPETITION, Federation of Jewish Philanthropies (1961–72): cash awards to conductors and engagements with American orchestras

EAST AND WEST ARTISTS ANNUAL AUDITIONS FOR PERFORMERS (annually in two categories): sponsorship of recitals in Carnegie Recital Hall by instrumentalists, singers, and ensembles. Categories: performers 18–35 years of age who have not yet given a recital in New York, and performers of any age who have given a major recital in New York but are not under management

EDGAR M. LEVENTRITT FOUNDATION INTERNATIONAL COMPETITION (annually, 1940–76; 1981–): cash awards to pianists and violinists (alternating years), RCA recording contracts, and sponsorship of appearances with major American orchestras; Gold Medal Award is given to exceptionally gifted artists. From 1981 the policy has been to make awards on the basis of observation over a period of time rather than by competition.

ELEANOR STEBER MUSIC FOUNDATION VOCAL COMPETITION (annually, 1979–): cash awards to young professional vocalists who are affiliated as apprentices with American opera companies, and sponsorship of a recital in New York

FISCHOFF NATIONAL CHAMBER MUSIC COMPETITION (annually in two divisions): cash awards to chamber ensembles of three to five players with no more than one vocalist. Categories: senior (30 years of age and under), junior (18 years of age and under)

FORD FOUNDATION CONCERT ARTISTS PROGRAM (1959, 1962, 1969): grants to concert artists for the commissioning of a new work from a composer of their choice

G. B. DEALEY AWARDS: see Dallas Morning News G. B. Dealey Awards.

GINA BACHAUER INTERNATIONAL PIANO COMPETITION, sponsored from 1982 by the Utah SO (biennially, 1976–): cash awards (first prize also includes Steinway piano and sponsorship of a New York début) to pianists 19–33 years of age; the six finalists appear in concert with the Utah SO.

GREENBERG AWARD: see Noah Greenberg Award.

INTERNATIONAL AMERICAN MUSIC COMPETITIONS, Carnegie Hall (before 1981, the Kennedy Center) and the Rockefeller Foundation (annually, from 1985 biennially, in rotating categories, 1978–): cash awards (first prize includes sponsorship of a recital at Carnegie Hall and other performances, and a recording contract) to performers to stimulate greater interest in music written by American composers since 1900. Competitors must choose a large portion of their program from a list of works by contemporary American composers and are encouraged to perform published or unpublished works in the same repertory not on the list. Categories: violin, voice, piano

INTERNATIONAL VIOLIN COMPETITION OF INDIANAPOLIS (quadrennially): cash award, and sponsorship of recordings and concert appearances throughout the USA and Europe to a violinist 18–30 years of age

LEOPOLD STOKOWSKI CONDUCTING PRIZE, American SO (1979–): cash awards (first prize also includes sponsorship of a concert with the American SO at Carnegie Hall) to American conductors 35 years of age and under

LEVENTRITT AWARD: see Edgar M. Leventritt Foundation International Competition.

LIEDERKRANZ FOUNDATION SCHOLARSHIP AWARDS (annually): cash awards. Categories: vocalists 17–30 years of age, Wagnerian singers, pianists 17–30 years of age

LUCIANO PAVAROTTI INTERNATIONAL VOICE COMPETITION: see Opera Company of Philadelphia Luciano Pavarotti International Voice Competition.

MARIAN ANDERSON SCHOLARSHIP (annually, 1942–72): cash awards to singers 16–30 years of age

METROPOLITAN OPERA NATIONAL COUNCIL REGIONAL AUDITIONS PROGRAM (annually, 1952–): cash awards and other educational funding to singers; the purpose of the auditions is "to discover new talent for the Metropolitan Opera and to find, assist and encourage young singers in preparation for their careers." Auditions at the district, semifinal, and final levels

MITROPOULOS INTERNATIONAL MUSIC COMPETITION: see Dimitri Mitropoulos International Music Competition.

NATIONAL ASSOCIATION OF COMPOSERS, USA, YOUNG PERFORMERS COMPETITION: cash awards to solo instrumentalists and singers 18–30 years of age, and sponsorship of performances

NATIONAL ENDOWMENT FOR THE ARTS: see NEA.

NATIONAL FEDERATION OF MUSIC CLUBS. Seven broad categories of programs include:

Annual Artist and Advanced Musician Awards (annually): various award programs

Biennial Awards (annually in alternating categories): various grant programs for singers and instrumentalists (odd-numbered years) and composers (even-numbered years)

See also under "Competitive awards, Composers."

NATIONAL OPERA INSTITUTE CAREER AWARDS FOR SINGERS (annually): cash awards to young American singers having previous professional experience in opera or music theater

NAUMBURG FOUNDATION: see Walter W. Naumburg Foundation.

NEA. Programs relating to music include:

Consortium Commissioning Program: funding to a consortium of at least three ensembles or soloists for the commissioning of new works by American composers

Opera-Musical Theater Program: grants to opera or music-theater groups for the commissioning of new works and for the production of new or seldom-produced contemporary American works

See also Affiliate Artists, Inc., and Walter W. Naumburg Foundation, NEA under "Competitive awards, Composers," and Jazz Masters Awards under "Honors."

NOAH GREENBERG AWARD, established by the New York Pro Musica and presented by the American Musicological Society (annually, 1978–): cash awards to performers and scholars "for a distinguished contribution to the study and performance of early music"

NONESUCH COMMISSION AWARDS, American Music Center (four annually, 1982–): cash awards to performing ensembles (and/or alternative performance spaces) for the commissioning of new works by young American composers, "in recognition of the contribution of Nonesuch Records to contemporary American music"; the commissioned work must be performed at least three times during the following two seasons.

OPERA COMPANY OF PHILADELPHIA LUCIANO PAVAROTTI INTERNATIONAL VOICE COMPETITION (irregularly, 1981–): performances with Pavarotti in productions of the Philadelphia Opera granted to male singers 35 years of age or under and female singers 33 years of age or under

ORATORIO SOCIETY OF NEW YORK SOLO COMPETITION FOR SINGERS (annually): cash award and possible performance contract to singers 40 years of age or under who have not yet made a formal New York oratorio début in a reviewed New York concert

PAVAROTTI COMPETITION: see Opera Company of Philadelphia Luciano Pavarotti International Voice Competition.

PEABODY-MASON MUSIC FOUNDATION SPONSORSHIP FOR PIANISTS: financial support for two years and recitals in Boston and New York for an American pianist 23–35 years of age

ROBERT CASADESUS INTERNATIONAL PIANO COMPETITION, Cleveland Institute and the Robert Casadesus Society (biennially): cash awards (first prize also includes sponsorship of an appearance with the Cleveland Orchestra and other groups) to pianists 17–32 years of age

SAN FRANCISCO OPERA CENTER AUDITIONS, MEROLA FUND (ten annually): admission into the summer Merola Opera Program, and eligibility for a contract with the Western Opera Theater and an Adler Fellowship (of which six are given annually, involving a year's stipend and performance opportunities with the San Francisco Opera Center and Opera), for singers

SEVENTEEN MAGAZINE AND GENERAL MOTORS NATIONAL CONCERTO COMPETITION (annually in various categories): cash awards (first prize also includes sponsorship of an appearance with a major symphony orchestra) to performers of high-school age

STEBER MUSIC FOUNDATION: see Eleanor Steber Music Foundation Vocal Competition.

STOKOWSKI CONDUCTING PRIZE: see Leopold Stokowski Conducting Prize.

SULLIVAN FOUNDATION: see William Matheus Sullivan Musical Foundation.

UNIVERSITY OF MARYLAND INTERNATIONAL PIANO FESTIVAL AND COMPETITION (annually): cash awards (first prize also includes sponsorship of performances) to pianists 16–32 years of age

VAN CLIBURN INTERNATIONAL PIANO COMPETITION (quadrennially, 1962–): cash awards (first prize also includes sponsorship of a recital in Carnegie Hall, first appearances with major orchestras, and a European concert tour; other prizes include performances as well) to pianists 19–30 years of age

WALTER W. NAUMBURG FOUNDATION

Naumburg Chamber Music Award, co-sponsored by the NEA (from 1972 one or two annually, 1965–): sponsorship of a recital in Alice Tully Hall for an ensemble, and funds for the commissioning of a new work by a composer chosen in consultation with the foundation

Naumburg International Competition (annually in rotating categories): cash award (first prize also includes sponsorship of two recitals in Alice Tully Hall, other performances, and a recording). Categories: piano, instrumental, voice

See also Naumburg Recording Award under "Competitive awards, Composers." (*See also* NAUMBURG, WALTER W.)

WILLIAM MATHEUS SULLIVAN MUSICAL FOUNDATION (annually): cash awards to young singers who have begun professional careers, and sponsorship of performances with orchestras and other professional ensembles

YOUNG CONCERT ARTISTS INTERNATIONAL AUDITIONS (any number annually, 1961–): sponsorship of a recital in New York and Washington, DC, and membership of Young Concert Artists until the performer or ensemble signs a contract with commercial management

(iii) Scholars

AMERICAN ACADEMY IN ROME: see under "Competitive Awards, Composers."

AMERICAN ASSOCIATION OF UNIVERSITY WOMEN EDUCATIONAL FOUNDATION (1882–): fellowships to American women for scholarly research in all disciplines

AMERICAN COUNCIL OF LEARNED SOCIETIES (1975–): fellowships for humanistic research to scholars whose degrees were awarded in the year of or the two calendar years preceding the competition

INSTITUTE OF INTERNATIONAL EDUCATION: Fulbright and other fellowships to American citizens with BA degrees for graduate study outside the USA

NEH FELLOWSHIPS, Division of Fellowships and Seminars and Division of Research Programs: grants for full-time independent study and research

NOAH GREENBERG AWARD: see under "Competitive Awards, Performers."

SINFONIA FOUNDATION, Phi Mu Alpha Sinfonia Fraternity (annually, 1969–): grants for scholarly research in American music or music education

BIBLIOGRAPHY

Musical America . . . International Directory of the Performing Arts (New York, 1960–) [annual pubn]

L. Harlow: "Twenty-Five Years of the Pulitzer for Music," *Saturday Review*, li (27 April 1968), 67

P. Wasserman and J. McLean: *Awards, Honors, and Prizes* (Detroit, 1969, 5/1982)

J. Hohenberg: *The Pulitzer Prizes: a History of the Award . . . over Six Decades* (New York, 1974)

C. Pavlakis: *The American Music Handbook* (New York, 1974), 419–53

L. Coe: *Cultural Directory: Guide to Federal Funds and Services* (New York, 1975, rev. by the Federal Council on the Arts and Humanities 2/1980 as *Cultural Directory*, ii)

D. Netzer: *The Subsidized Muse: Public Support for the Arts in the United States* (New York, 1978)

C. Walter: *Winners: the Blue Ribbon Encyclopedia of Awards* (New York, 1978, rev. 2/1982)

Sharps & Flats: a Report on Ford Foundation Assistance to American Music (New York, 1980)

M. Kaplan: *Variety: Major U.S. Showbusiness Awards* (New York, 1982)

JANE GOTTLIEB

Ax, Emanuel (*b* L'vov, Ukraine, 8 June 1949). Pianist. His first teacher was his father, a coach at the L'vov Opera. The family immigrated to Canada in 1959, settling in Winnipeg, then moved to New York in 1961. Ax began seven years of study with Mieczysław Munz at the Juilliard School in 1966 and also attended Columbia University (BA 1970). He had already won honors in the Chopin competition, Warsaw, the Vienna da Motta Competition, Lisbon, and the Queen Elisabeth of Belgium Competition, and had made his New York début (Alice Tully Hall, 13 April 1973) when he won the first Artur Rubinstein International Piano Competition in 1974. The next year he received the Young Concert Artists' Michaels Award, and in 1979 he won the Avery Fisher Prize. Ax has performed with the Boston SO, the Philadelphia Orchestra, and the New York PO, and has recorded with the Dallas SO, the Philadelphia Orchestra, and the St. Paul Chamber Orchestra. He has taken part in numerous chamber music and recital series, including performances by the Chamber Music Society of Lincoln Center, the Mostly Mozart Festival, and a three-concert series entitled "Emanuel Ax Invites" at Alice Tully Hall. In 1980 he formed a trio with the violinist Young-Uck Kim and the cellist Yo-Yo Ma; he and Ma also play together as a duo.

Ax is in the front rank of his generation of pianists; his often aggressive, dramatic musical inclinations seem to be increasingly tempered by a maturing musical intelligence and sensibility.

BIBLIOGRAPHY

P. Hertelendy: "Casual Conversation with a Touring Virtuoso," *Contemporary Keyboard*, vi/2 (1980), 22

L. P. Yost: "Time Off With Emanuel Ax," *Clavier*, xix/1 (1980), 12

P. G. Davis: "Emanuel Ax, Epitome of a New Breed of Pianist," *New York Times* (17 July 1981)

"Ax, Emanuel," *CBY 1984*

A. Kozinn: "Emanuel Ax Goes 20th Century," *Keynote*, viii/6 (1984), 18

JAMES CHUTE

Axt, William L. (*b* New York, 19 April 1888; *d* Ukiah, CA, 13 Feb 1959). Composer and conductor. After private music study in Berlin following high school, he conducted for Hammerstein's Grand Opera Company (which closed in 1910), then for other productions on Broadway. By 1921 he had joined the staff of the Capitol Theatre, where spectacular stage shows and silent films were presented with full orchestral accompaniment. He composed many pieces of incidental film music and also collaborated with David Mendoza on complete film scores; several (such as that for *The Big Parade*, 1925) were published and distributed with the films to theatrical syndicates. Axt and Mendoza also worked together on *Don Juan* (Warner Bros., 1926), the first recorded score for a feature film that used the Vitaphone process, in which the playback of music recorded on wax discs was mechanically synchronized with the projection of the film. From 1931 until his retirement in the 1940s Axt worked in Hollywood for the music department of MGM, producing a number of other film scores.

WORKS

(selective list; all film scores)

The Big Parade, 1925, collab. D. Mendoza, *NN*; Ben Hur, 1926, collab. Mendoza, *NN*; Don Juan, 1926, collab. Mendoza, *DLC*; Our Dancing Daughters, 1928, collab. Mendoza; Smilin' Through, 1932; Broadway to Hollywood, 1933; Dinner at Eight, The Thin Man, 1934; Pursuit, 1935; Libeled Lady, 1936; The Last of Mrs. Cheney, 1937

BIBLIOGRAPHY

New York Dramatic News, lxiii (30 Dec 1916), 24

Musical Courier, lxxxvii (27 Dec 1923), 44

D. Mendoza: "The Theme Song," *American Hebrew*, cxxiv (15 March 1929), 664

C. Hofmann: *Sounds for Silents* (New York, 1970)

MARTIN MARKS

Ayler, Albert (*b* Cleveland, OH, 13 July 1936; *d* New York, between 5 and 25 Nov 1970). Jazz tenor saxophonist. At the age of seven he began three years of lessons on alto saxophone with his father, a violinist and tenor saxophonist. He played professionally in rhythm-and-blues bands by his mid-teens, touring with Little Walter and his Jukes at the age of 16. In 1959 he began a three-year term in army concert bands, during which time he changed to tenor saxophone. He occasionally played in Paris clubs while stationed in France in 1960–61. After his discharge he remained in Europe, leading a bop trio for eight months in Sweden (one performance, in 1962, was recorded) and playing with Cecil Taylor in winter 1962–3 in Copenhagen, where he also led a studio recording. He moved to New York in 1963. There he performed infrequently with Taylor and made another obscure LP recording in winter 1963–4. After returning to Cleveland briefly, owing to lack of work, in summer 1964 he formed a quartet in New York with Don Cherry (trumpet), Gary Peacock (double bass), and Sunny Murray (drums). This quartet toured Europe in late 1964.

Albert Ayler, 1966

Ayler was never to find a steady audience for his radical music – his group appeared perhaps only three times in 1965 – and although his albums were well received by the critics he remained poor. He made no effort to clarify his music for his listeners, actively discouraging musical interpretations of his recordings and instead stressing their social and spiritual issues; the inconsistent and confusing titles to his pieces further obscured his work (see Litweiler). Nevertheless, in studios and New York clubs (1965–8), at the Newport Jazz Festival (1966), on a brief European tour (November 1966), and for college concerts he was able to assemble faithful sidemen. His groups included his younger brother Don Ayler (trumpet), one or two double bass players, such as Peacock and Henry Grimes, the drummers Murray, Milford Graves, or Beaver Harris, and Cal Cobbs on piano or harpsichord. Only Cobbs remained in Ayler's new rhythm-and-blues groups of 1969–70. On 5 November 1970, shortly after having returned from a European tour with his quintet, Ayler was reported missing in New York; his body was found in the East River on 25 November.

Ayler's extraordinary music of the mid-1960s was difficult and controversial. Without losing its identity as jazz, it rejected most of the conventions of the prevailing bop and free styles. According to Jost (who alone has surveyed his career analytically),

Ayler often replaced tempered melody with sweeping flourishes; he combined these "sound-spans" (Jost) with sudden low-pitched honks and a wide, sentimental vibrato (ex.1). His 1962–3 recordings in Scandinavia were unsuccessful because of the stylistic gulf

Ex.1 "Ghosts" from *Ghosts* (1964, Debut 144), transcr. B. Kernfeld

between the "in-tune" bop accompanists and the "out-of-tune" saxophone. By contrast, Peacock and Murray provided sympathetic accompaniments to Ayler's highly original playing. Their 1964 recordings juxtapose difficult collective improvisation and Ayler's simple, rhythmically square, frequently tonal themes. Sometimes these two factors are interrelated, as in the gradual deformation of the folk-like melody in several 1964 versions of *Ghosts*. More often, however, the brief themes serve as foils for lengthy, exciting improvisations in which the group, avoiding predictable sounds, achieves remarkably varied textures and rhythms (as in *Spirits* on the album *Spiritual Unity*, or *Ay* and *Itt* on *New York Eye and Ear Control*).

Soon after the performance of *Bells* in May 1965 the balance shifted from improvisation to composition. Three tracks on *Spirits Rejoice* emphasize thematic material: the title track (representative of Ayler's growing preference for marches) includes numerous repetitions of a theme that incorporates bits of the *Marseillaise*; *Holy Family* consists of rhythm-and-blues riffs, and *Angels* is a strange ballad delivered to the accompaniment of harpsichord, bowed double bass, and cymbal rolls. Later, in a new version of *Ghosts* (1967), the players never depart from thematic statements. This striving for simplicity, augmented by pressure from Impulse Records to increase his sales, led Ayler to return to rhythm-and-blues in the late 1960s. Unfortunately, his late rhythm-and-blues songs and his singing were dull, and his last two albums received little attention.

RECORDINGS

(selective list)

My Name is Albert Ayler (1963, Debut 140); *Spirits* (1964, Debut 146); *Spiritual Unity* (1964, ESP 1002); *New York Eye and Ear Control* (1964, ESP 1016); *Ghosts* (1964, Debut 144); *Bells* (1965, ESP 1010); *Spirits Rejoice* (1965, ESP 1020); *Lörrach/Paris* (1966, Hat Hut 3500); *In Greenwich Village* (1966–7, Imp. 9155); *Love Cry* (1967, Imp. 9165); *New Grass* (1968, Imp. 9175); *Music is the Healing Force of the Universe* (1969, Imp. 9191)

BIBLIOGRAPHY

N. Hentoff: "The Truth is Marching In," *Down Beat*, xxxiii/23 (1966), 16
V. Wilmer: "Albert and Don Ayler," *Jazz Monthly*, xii/10 (1966), 11
P. Burke: "Albert Ayler: a Preliminary Checklist of Concert/Club etc. Appearances," *Discographical Forum*, nos.12–15 (1969)
E. Raben: *A Discography of Free Jazz* (Copenhagen, 1969)
Obituary, *Down Beat*, xxxviii/1 (1971), 8
E. Jost: *Free Jazz* (Graz, Austria, 1974/*R*1981)
V. Wilmer: "Spiritual Unity," *As Serious as your Life* (London, 1977), 92
J. Litweiler: "Albert Ayler," *Down Beat*, xlix/2 (1982), 45
M. Hames: *Albert Ayler . . . on Disc and Tape* (Chigwell, England, 1983)
B. Smith and B. Case: "The Truth is Marching In," *The Wire*, no.3 (1983), 12

BARRY KERNFELD

Ayres (Johnson), Frederic (*b* Binghamton, NY, 17 March 1876; *d* Colorado Springs, CO, 23 Nov 1926). Composer. After studying engineering at Cornell University (1892–3) he worked designing electric motors. He studied composition with Edgar S. Kelley (1897–1901) and Arthur Foote (summer 1899) "to perfect . . . what I believed to be my proper work" (Ayres). Because of ill health (tuberculosis) he moved to Las Cruces, New Mexico (1901), and then to Colorado Springs (1902), where he lived for the rest of his life composing and teaching theory privately. The opening theme of the overture *From the Plains* op.14 contains an obvious evocation of Indian themes, but Ayres claimed that he was not consciously influenced in that way. The late compositions (the Trio in D minor, the Violin Sonata in B minor) have an open, sturdy, and often abstract lyricism; the Violin Sonata and the String Quartet op.16 explore an interest in the unconventional arrangement of movements.

WORKS

(printed works published in New York unless otherwise stated)

op.

INSTRUMENTAL

9 2 Fugues, pf (Berlin, 1910)
11 The Open Road, intermezzo, pf (1916)
12 3 Compositions, pf, no.1 (Newton Centre, MA, 1910), ed. V. B. Lawrence (1970), no.2 (1917), no.3, unpubd
13 Pf Trio (Berlin, 1914)
14 From the Plains, ov., orch, unpubd
15 Vn Sonata (Berlin, 1914)
16 Str Qt, rev. 1916, unpubd
– Pf Trio, d (1925)
Elegy, vc, pf; Pf Preludes, b, e♭; Str Qt no.2; The West Wind and the Daughter of Nokomis, pf; Vc Sonata; Vn Sonata, b; all unpubd

VOCAL

2 3 Songs (Browning, M. Fuller) (Berlin, 1906)
3 3 Songs (Shakespeare) (Newton Centre, MA, 1906–7), ed. Lawrence (1970)
4 2 Songs (Shakespeare), no.1 (Berlin, 1907), no.2 (Newton Centre, MA, 1907), ed. Lawrence (1970)
5 2 Songs (anon., Shakespeare) (1918)
6 3 Songs (Shakespeare, H. Van Dyke, M. T. Ritter), no.1 (1915), no.2 (Newton Centre, MA, 1911), ed. Lawrence (1970), no.3 (1923)
7 Mother Goose Melodies (1919)
8 Sunset Wings (Rossetti) (1918)
10 The Seeonee Wolves (Kipling), song cycle, unpubd
– 3 Songs (Kipling, H. C. Bunner, W. V. Moody) (1921)
– My Love in her Attire (anon.) (1924)
– 2 Songs (Kipling, C. Roberts) (1924)
– Christmas Eve at Sea (J. Masefield) (1925)
– Sappho (1927)
19 other unpubd songs

MSS in *DLC*

Principal publishers: G. Schirmer, Stahl (Berlin), Wa-Wan Press

BIBLIOGRAPHY

A. G. Farwell: "Frederic Ayres," *Wa-Wan Press Monthly*, vi (1907), April; repr. in *The Wa-Wan Press, 1901–1911*, iv, ed. V. B. Lawrence (New York, 1970), 44
W. T. Upton: "Frederic Ayres," *MQ*, xviii (1932), 39 [incl. full list of works]
J. R. Perkins: *An Examination of the Solo Piano Music Published by the Wa-Wan Press* (diss., Boston U., 1969)

BARNEY CHILDS

Azpiazú, Don [Justo Angel] (*b* Cienfuegos, Cuba, 20 Jan 1893; *d* Havana, Cuba, 11 Feb 1943). Pianist and bandleader. He led the band at the Havana Casino during the 1920s. His recording of *El manisero (The Peanut Vendor)* for Victor in 1930 introduced both the "rumba" (as American dancers called almost any fast and lively Cuban music during the 1930s) and Cuban percussion instruments to the USA, launching a Cuban influence in American popular music that has been present ever since. In 1931 Azpiazú followed this success with a recording of *Green Eyes (Aquellos ojos verdes)*, with the singer Chick Bullock, possibly the first recording that fused Cuban music and American popular song. For a while Azpiazú enjoyed enormous popularity in the USA, and also made successful tours of Europe in 1931 and 1932; his return to Cuba, however, enabled Cugat and other Latin bandleaders to profit from his success. Although he made several other recordings during the late 1930s and early 1940s, he died in Cuba virtually forgotten by the American public.

BIBLIOGRAPHY

J. S. Roberts: *The Latin Tinge* (New York, 1979)

JOHN STORM ROBERTS

B

Babbitt, Milton (Byron) (*b* Philadelphia, PA, 10 May 1916). Composer. He has contributed extensively to the understanding and extension of 12-tone compositional theory and practice and has been one of the most influential composers and teachers in the USA since World War II.

1. Life. 2. Works.

1. Life. Brought up in Jackson, Mississippi, he started playing the violin at the age of four and several years later also studied clarinet and saxophone. He graduated from high school in 1931, having already demonstrated considerable skills in jazz ensemble performance and the composition of popular songs. His father's professional involvement with mathematics (as an actuary) was influential in shaping Babbitt's intellectual environment. In 1931 Babbitt entered the University of Pennsylvania with the intention of becoming a mathematician, but he soon transferred to New York University, concentrating on music under Marion Bauer and Philip James. In 1935 he received the BA in music. His early attraction to the music of Varèse and Stravinsky soon gave way to an absorption in that of Schoenberg, Berg, and Webern – particularly significant at a time when 12-tone music was unknown to many and viewed with skepticism by others.

After graduation Babbitt studied privately with Sessions, wrote criticism for the *Musical Leader*, and then enrolled for graduate work at Princeton University, where he continued his association with Sessions. In 1938 he joined the Princeton music faculty and in 1942 received one of Princeton's first MFAs in music. His *Composition for String Orchestra*, a straightforward 12-tone work, was completed in 1940.

During World War II Babbitt divided his time between Washington, DC, where he was engaged in mathematical research, and Princeton, as a member of the mathematics faculty (1943–5). Musically, these were years of thought and discovery, rather than of actual composition; they resulted in 1946 in a paper (unpublished), *The Function of Set Structure in the Twelve-tone System*, which was the first formal and systematic investigation of Schoenberg's compositional method. In 1946–8, shuttling between Jackson and New York, he once again directed his energies to composition, writing some film scores and an unsuccessful Broadway musical.

In 1948 Babbitt rejoined the music faculty at Princeton, eventually to become Conant Professor of Music (1960); in 1973 he became a member of the composition faculty of the Juilliard School and he has also taught at the Salzburg Seminar in American Studies, the Berkshire Music Center, the New England Conservatory of Music, and the summer courses in new music at Darmstadt, Germany. He has won the Joseph Bearns Prize (for *Music for the Mass I* in 1942), New York Music Critics' Circle citations (for *Composition for Four Instruments* in 1949 and for *Philomel* in 1964), a National Institute of Arts and Letters Award (1959) for demonstrating a "penetrating grasp of musical order that has influenced younger composers," a Guggenheim Fellowship (1960–61), membership in the National Institute (1965), and a Brandeis University Gold Medal (1970). In 1974 he became a fellow of the American Academy of Arts and Sciences. Throughout his career, he has been actively involved in contemporary music organizations, including the ISCM (he was president of the American section, 1951–52), the American Music Center, *Perspectives of New Music* (as a member of its editorial board), and the Columbia-Princeton Electronic Music Center (as director from 1959). Babbitt has received several honorary doctorates and numerous commissions. In 1982, he received a Pulitzer Prize Special Citation for "his life's work as a distinguished and seminal American composer." Articles, reviews, and interviews by him have appeared in many music publications; he has traveled widely, speaking on issues of current musical thought. Babbitt is a remarkably successful lecturer; perceptive and adept at logical extemporization, he continually stimulates and provokes his audiences. He is also an inveterate follower of popular sports, a raconteur and punster, and an omnivorous reader.

2. Works.

(i) Serial theory and practice to 1970. Babbitt's early fascination with 12-tone practice, particularly in its formal aspects, developed into a total reconsideration of musical relations. Throughout his compositional career he has been occupied with the extension of techniques related to Schoenberg's (and Webern's) "combinatorial" sets; with the investigation of sets that have great flexibility and potential for long-range association; and with an exploration of the structuring of nonpitch components "determined by the operations of the [12-tone] system and uniquely analogous to the specific structuring of the pitch components of

the individual work, and thus, utterly nonseparable" ("Some Aspects of Twelve-tone Composition," 1955). He has been a pioneer in his ways of talking and thinking about music, invoking terms from other disciplines, such as philosophy, linguistics, mathematics, and the physical sciences.

Babbitt revealed and formalized many of the most salient aspects of 12-tone compositional technique in several important essays. In "Some Aspects of Twelve-tone Composition," "Twelve-tone Invariants as Compositional Determinants" (1960), and "Set Structure as a Compositional Determinant" (1961), he systematically investigates the compositional potential of the 12 pitch-class set, introducing such terms (derived from mathematics) as "source set," "combinatoriality," "aggregate," "secondary set," and "derived set." These terms facilitate the classification of the various types of pitch-class set and contribute to the description of diverse procedures for the compositional projection of such sets. A secondary set, for example, results when a "new" set of 12 pitch classes emerges from the linear linking of segments of two forms of a 12-tone series, as shown below:

secondary set

P_0: B♭ E♭ F D C D♭ G B F♯ A A♭ E
P_6: E A B A♭ F♯ G D♭ F C E♭ D B♭

original set: 0, 5, 7, 4, 2, 3, 9, 1, 8, 11, 10, 6
secondary set: 0, 5, 7, 4, 2, 3, 6, 11, 1, 10, 8, 9
(B♭ = 0; adapted from *Three Compositions for Piano* no. 1)

Similarly, an "aggregate can be thought of as a simultaneous statement of . . . parts [of a 12-tone set] . . . it is not a set, inasmuch as it is not totally ordered, because only the elements within the component parts are ordered, but not the relationship between or among the parts themselves" ("Some Aspects of Twelve-tone Composition"). 12-tone sets that yield such aggregate and secondary set formations are called "combinatorial." (Further distinctions between various types of combinatorial sets – that is, semi- and all-combinatorial sets, the first-, second-, third- and fourth-order all-combinatoriality – are discussed in the same essay.) The nomenclature that Babbitt has introduced in his prose writings has become widely adopted and is the basis for much theoretical work and composition. Moreover, in his compositions he has demonstrated the efficacy of his theories. Thus Babbitt has extended the notion of compositional creativity to encompass the development of musical systems themselves, as well as specific compositional achievements within such systems. He has also realized the implications of procedures of set transformation and derivation for large-scale musical structures and has used such procedures to articulate formal boundaries in numerous works.

In "Twelve-tone Rhythmic Structure and the Electronic Medium" (1962) Babbitt demonstrates a number of methods for interpreting the structures of pitch-class sets in the temporal domain. By positing an analogy between the octave (in pitch structure) and the bar (in rhythmic and metrical structure), and by dividing the bar into 12 equal units (each of which can be musically articulated by individual points of attack), Babbitt provides a basis for mapping pitch-class sets onto "time-point sets." Thus an uninterpreted set of integers (for example, 0, 11, 6, 7, 5, 1, 10, 2, 9, 3, 4, 8) may be interpreted as a specific instance of a pitch-class set (ex. 1) or as a specific instance of a

time-point set (ex. 2). (The time-point of a particular point of attack is a measure of its position within the bar. In ex. 2 the metrical unit is a 32nd-note [a 12th of the whole bar]; time-

1. Milton Babbitt programming the Mark II RCA synthesizer (built early 1950s) at the Columbia-Princeton Electronic Music Center, New York

point 0 therefore occurs on the first 32nd-note of the bar, time-point 1 on the next, and so on. In this example the 12 available points of attack within a bar are ordered according to the numerical set given above.) Exx. 1 and 2 are each only one of the possible interpretations of the numerical set given above; pitch classes may be presented in various registers, just as time-points may be displaced to subsequent bars, as long as the same order of presentation (of pitches or points of articulation) is preserved. Furthermore, a time-point set and a pitch-class set determined by the same set of integers may unfold at different speeds: in the first four bars of the second violin part of Babbitt's String Quartet no.3 (1969–70) the first six notes may be understood as a realization in terms of pitch of the first five integers in the set indicated above (ex.3). Also, the three *forte* markings in this

Ex.3

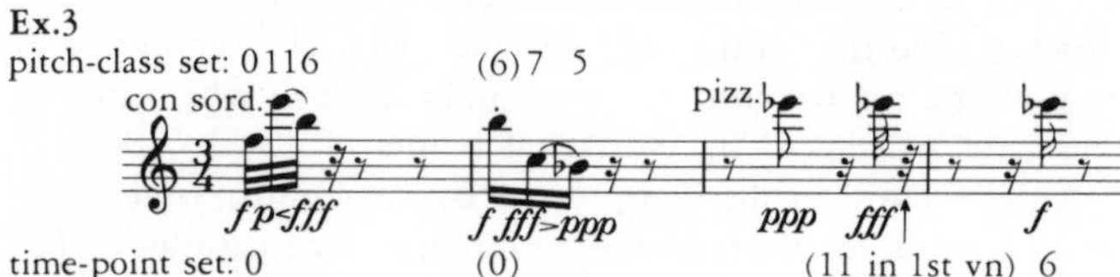

passage articulate the time-points that correspond to the first and third entities of the same numerical set (time-point 0 is reiterated in bar 2 before the third time-point, 6, is articulated in bar 4). The second time-point of this set is presented in a different instrumental line, the last note of violin 1 in bar 3 (ex.4). Each of the eight dynamic gradations from *ppp* to *fff* inclusive is employed in the String Quartet no.3 to articulate a particular layer of the time-point structure, and each of these layers is analogous to one of eight layers of pitch-class sets simultaneously presented in the work; the eight layers of pitch-class sets are differentiated by distinctions of instrumentation, register, and mode of sound production (for example, the use of pizzicato and arco) throughout the work. This brief discussion of a musical fragment may serve as an indication of the extraordinary richness of structural relationships that are projected in Babbitt's music.

An earlier example of Babbitt's approach may be seen in his *Three Compositions for Piano* (1947), one of his first consistent attempts to extend Schoenbergian 12-tone procedures. The surface of the music is, in some respects, reminiscent of Schoenberg: registrally dispersed lines alternate with thickly clustered chordal attacks (in the framework of a quasi-ternary structure), yet the absence of expressive indications and the reliance on metronome markings would seem to reveal a Stravinskian concern for a clear, undistracted projection of the temporal domain. Some of the innovative aspects of the work reside in the conjunction of the structuring of pitch and other domains, resulting in an early example of "totally serialized" music. Points of articulation made by the superimposition of lines and the number of consecutive attacks within a contrapuntal line are determined by a set (whose prime form is 5, 1, 4, 2). In the first four bars of the work, this set is presented twice in its prime form (P), once in retrograde (R), and once in retrograde inversion (RI; ex.5). There is also a correspondence between dynamics and pitch-set forms.

Babbitt's *Composition for Four Instruments* and *Composition for Twelve Instruments* (both of which were written in 1948) go a step further towards a structuring of rhythm isomorphic with 12-tone pitch structuring. In the 12-instrument work a set of 12 durations emerges and operates throughout. It is transformed by "classical" serial operations: transposition (addition of a constant to each duration number of the set), inversion (the complementation of the duration numbers), retrogression (the complementation of the order numbers of the set), and retrograde inversion. The ending of each of the three major sections of the work is articulated by the completion of a rhythmic set. The presentation of the rhythmic sets is often complex – various instruments characteristically participate in the presentation of a single rhythmic set, and more than one rhythmic set may be presented simultaneously. Nonetheless, the surface characteristics of the work delineate a simple process. Beginning with sparsely textured single events (which can be considered an extension of Webern's sound-world) and slowly becoming more compact (with regard to aggregate completions), the work concludes with thicker textures and sustained sonorities, within which notes attacked only once resound in newly shaped but familiar harmonic environments.

Babbitt has been profoundly involved in the clarification and extension of the systematic aspects of 12-tone composition, but his music is in no sense rigidly determined by precompositional schemes. Within the constraints of serial techniques, he uses a great range of expressive possibilities and contextually varied structures. A work such as *Partitions* (1957) demonstrates numerous precompositional constraints (such as the projection of an all-interval set, a polyphonic texture in which distinct transformations of 12-tone pitch sets are unfolded in each line and aggregates formed by various vertical partitionings of segments of these lines). In the first four bars a hexachord is presented in

Ex.4 String Quartet no.3, bars 1–4

Ex.5 Three Compositions for Piano, no.1, bars 1–4

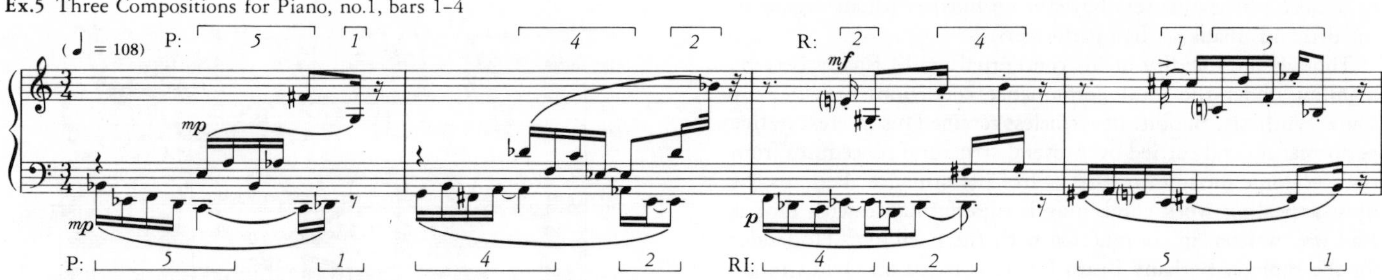

each of four different registers (ex.6). The hexachords in the lower two registers (E♭ A♭ F♯ F C♯ E; C G A B♭ D B) are complementary and are, respectively, the retrogrades of the hexachords presented in the higher two registers. There are 49 different ways in which the pitches presented in these hexachords might be partitioned to form aggregates. (For example, each hexachord might be divided 3 + 3; or the hexachords might be divided alternately 2 + 4 and 4 + 2, etc.) The actual partitioning of pitches (1 + 5 in the highest register, 3 + 3 in the next highest register, 5 + 1 in the next register, and 3 + 3 in the lowest register) contributes to a rich pattern of interval and pitch associations and echoes. Such partitioning establishes a specific rate of movement through the pitch-class sets in each register and also suggests possibilities for hierarchical distinctions among the pitch classes that constitute the sets involved. Each registral line has its own rhythm of movement through its pitch-class sets, and these characteristic rhythms are varied contextually throughout the work.

The commitment to systematic precompositional planning is maintained in works with dramatic, poetic, or other associative aspects. In *Du* (1951), a song cycle for soprano and piano (which represented the USA at the 1953 ISCM Festival), there is continual interplay between the text and the vocal and piano lines. Phoneme, syllable, word, and line are carefully contoured, subtly and imaginatively set to music: the pitch, durational, dynamic, and registral schemata, themselves transformed from poem to poem, are allied with the verbal elements and indeed help to project the many delicate nuances of the text. These lyrical, imagist tendencies were most fully realized in *Philomel* (1964) but are also evident in *All Set* (1957), for small jazz ensemble, with its conjunction of 12-tone structure (based on an all-combinatorial set) and "jazz-like properties . . . the use of percussion, the Chicago jazz-like juxtapositions of solos and ensembles recalling certain characteristics of group improvisation" (Babbitt).

Babbitt took a novel serial approach to handling the sonic resources of a large orchestra in *Relata I* (1965). Here timbral "families" are correlated with set structure and thus articulated as part of the overall network, with woodwind instruments as four trios, brass as three quartets, and string instruments as two sextets (one bowed, the other plucked). The work is insistently polyphonic (with as many as 48 instrumental lines), framed at both ends by massive sonorities and filled with constantly changing and recombined textures and colors. While parts of the work are analogous to other parts, there is no simple repetition: all aspects undergo reinterpretation, rearrangement and "resurfacing." In the more timbrally homogeneous works of the late 1960s (*Sextets*, *Post-partitions*, parts of *Correspondences* (*see* NOTATION, §2 and fig.18), the String Quartets nos.3 and 4), the handling of timbre and tone-color seems even more refined. Sonorously embodied successions of relations are projected in ever varying contexts, producing changes of "atmosphere" from the most rarefied to the most dense, with every conceivable gradation.

(ii) Electronic works. Another continuing concern of Babbitt's has been electronic sound synthesis. At the time of the first instrumental film soundtrack, in the late 1930s, he had already recognized the enormous compositional potential of such synthesis. Two decades later, in the mid-1950s, when he was invited by RCA to be a composer-consultant, he became the first composer to work with its newly improved and developed synthesizer, the Mark II (see fig.1, p.103). *Composition for Synthesizer* (1961) was Babbitt's first totally synthesized work. It was followed soon after by *Vision and Prayer* for soprano and synthesizer (1961) and *Ensembles for Synthesizer* (1962–4). His basic compositional attitudes and approaches underwent little change with the new resource; rather, with the availability and flexibility of the synthesizer's programming control they were now realizable to a degree of precision previously unattainable in live performances of his music. Babbitt's interest in synthesis was not concerned with the invention of new sounds *per se* but with the control of all aspects of events, particularly the timing and rate of change of timbre, texture, and intensity. (His Woodwind Quartet (1953) and String Quartet no.2 (1954) had already given some indication of the rapidity of dynamic change he wished to achieve, on both single and consecutive pitches.) The electronic medium allowed him

Ex.6 *Partitions*, bars 1–4

to project time-point sets however he liked, without regard to the demands made on live performers.

Though the lucidity of his conceptual world finally became manifest under the ideal performance conditions provided by sound synthesis, Babbitt nevertheless retained his interest in live performance, and carried over several structural procedures from the electronic medium to that of live performance. Perhaps the most appealing work combining live performance with tape is *Philomel*, written in conjunction with the poet John Hollander for the soprano Bethany Beardslee. It is based on Ovid's interpretation of the Greek legend of Philomela, the ravished, speechless maiden who is transformed into a nightingale. New ways of combining musical and verbal expressiveness were devised by composer and poet: music is as articulate as language; language (Philomela's thoughts) is transformed into music (the nightingale's song). The work is an almost inexhaustible repertory of speech-song similitudes and differentiations, and resonant word-music puns (unrealizable without the resources of the synthesizer).

(iii) Later serial developments. During the 1970s and early 1980s Babbitt was increasingly prolific. The fecundity of his compositional thought has been revealed in such diverse combinations as saxophone and tape, female chorus, and orchestra and tape. He has continued to explore the potential and refine the procedures of 12-tone compositional technique, always discovering new ways of correlating the various dimensions of his musical universe and of articulating such correlations.

In works such as *Arie da capo* (1973–4), for example, Babbitt incorporates "weighted aggregates" – that is, transformations of pitch arrays which do not contain unique instances of each pitch class. (He demonstrated the derivation of such array transformations in the article "Since Schoenberg," 1974.) Each of the sections of *Arie da capo* may be construed as an "aria" for one of the five instruments; but the conception of the aria is reimagined, so that "the central instrument dominates less quantitatively than relationally, in that its music is the immediate source of, and is complemented and counterpointed by, the music of the 'accompanying' instruments." As in many other works, Babbitt explores a full range of possibilities within a formally constrained context, in this case the possible partitionings of 12-tone sets into as many as six parts. *Da capo* repetitions of set forms recur throughout the arias, both on the musical surface and as nonconsecutive pitches associated by register, articulation, or instrumentation.

A Solo Requiem, for soprano and two pianos (1976–7), is Babbitt's most extended composition for voice. This magisterial work (a memorial to the composer Godfrey Winham) incorporates a wide range of vocal techniques and reveals the extraordinary range and sensitivity of Babbitt's response to a variety of dramatic and lyrical poetic texts. In *My Complements to Roger* (1978), one of several short works of the late 1970s and early 1980s for solo piano, Babbitt demonstrates a number of methods of correlating pitch and rhythmic structures: the partitioning of metrical units in each bar is correlated with the partitioning (in the same bar) of pitch-class sets to form aggregates; and, in numerous instances, a string of pitches extracted from the pitch-class array is projected by its presentation within the same beat and by the articulation of a basic subdivision of this beat into the same number of parts as there are pitches in the string. Among Babbitt's later works is *The Head of the Bed* (1982; fig.2) for soprano and four instruments.

2. Page 68 of the autograph MS of Babbitt's "The Head of the Bed" (1982) for soprano, flute, clarinet, violin, and cello, to a text by John Hollander

The world that Babbitt's music evokes is not simple. He has said "I want a piece of music to be literally as much as possible." While some critics have felt that such an attitude has resulted in a body of inaccessible music, others have praised his pioneering approach, involving as it has a systematic and comprehensive exploration of the 12-tone compositional universe. His emphasis on the relation between practice and theory, his insistence on the composer's assumption of responsibility for every musical event in a work, and his reinterpretation of the constituent elements of the Western musical tradition have had a vital influence on the thinking and music of numerous younger composers.

WORKS

(all published unless otherwise stated)

ORCHESTRAL

Generatrix, 1935, inc., withdrawn
Composition for String Orchestra, 1940, inc., withdrawn
Symphony, 1941, inc., withdrawn
Fabulous Voyage, musical theater, 1946
Into the Good Ground, film score, 1949, inc., withdrawn
Relata I, 1965, Cleveland, 3 March 1966
Relata II, 1968, New York, 16 Jan 1969
Ars combinatoria, small orch, 1981, Bloomington, IN, 16 July 1981
Concerto for Piano and Orchestra, 1985, New York, 19 Jan 1986

CHAMBER AND INSTRUMENTAL

String Trio, 1941, withdrawn
Three Compositions for Piano, 1947
Composition for Four Instruments, fl, cl, vn, vc, 1948

Composition for Twelve Instruments, wind qnt, tpt, harp, cel, str trio, db, 1948, rev. 1954
String Quartet no.1, 1948, withdrawn
Composition for Viola and Piano, 1950
Woodwind Quartet, 1953
String Quartet no.2, 1954
Duet, pf, 1956
Semi-simple Variations, pf, 1956
All Set, a sax, t sax, tpt, trbn, db, pf, vib, perc, 1957
Partitions, pf, 1957
Post-partitions, pf, 1966
Sextets, vn, pf, 1966
String Quartet no.3, 1969–70
String Quartet no.4, 1970
Tableaux, pf, 1972
Arie da capo, fl, cl + b cl, pf, vn, vc, 1973–4
Minute Waltz (3/4 ± 1/8), pf, 1977
Playing for Time, pf, 1977
My Complements to Roger, pf, 1978
My Ends are My Beginnings, cl, 1978
Paraphrases, fl, ob + eng hn, cl, b cl, bn, hn, tpt, trbn, tuba, pf, 1979
Dual, vc, pf, 1980
Don, pf 4 hands, 1981
About Time, pf, 1982
Melismata, vn, 1982
String Quartet no.5, 1982
Canonical Form, pf, 1983
Groupwise, pic + fl + a fl, vn, va, vc, pf, 1983
Playing for Time, pf, 1983
Four Play, cl, vn, vc, pf, 1984
It Takes Twelve to Tango, pf, 1984
Sheer Pluck (Composition for Guitar), 1984
Lagniappe, pf, 1985

VOCAL

Music for the Mass I, SATB, 1940, withdrawn
Music for the Mass II, SATB, 1941, withdrawn
Three Theatrical Songs, 1v, pf: As long as it isn't love (Babbitt), Penelope's Night Song (R. S. Childs), Now you see it (Babbitt, R. H. Koch), 1946 [from Fabulous Voyage (musical)]
The Widow's Lament in Springtime (W. C. Williams), S, pf, 1950
Du (A. Stramm), song cycle, S, pf, 1951
Vision and Prayer, S, pf, 1954, unpubd, unperf.
Two Sonnets (G. M. Hopkins), Bar, cl, va, vc, 1955
Composition for Tenor and Six Instruments, T, fl, ob, vn, va, vc, hpd, 1960
Sounds and Words, S, pf, 1960
Four Canons [after Schoenberg], female chorus, 1968
Phonemena, S, pf, 1969–70
A Solo Requiem (Shakespeare, Hopkins, G. Meredith, Stramm, Dryden), S, 2 pf, 1976–7
More Phonemena, 12vv, 1978
An Elizabethan Sextette, 6 female vv, 1979
The Head of the Bed (J. Hollander), S, fl, cl, vn, vc, 1982

WORKS WITH TAPE

Composition for Synthesizer, 4-track tape, 1961
Vision and Prayer (D. Thomas), S, 4-track tape, 1961
Ensembles for Synthesizer, 4-track tape, 1962–4
Philomel (Hollander), S, 4-track tape, 1964
Correspondences, string orch, tape, 1967
Occasional Variations, 4-track tape, 1971
Concerti, vn, small orch, tape, 1974–6
Phonemena, S, tape, 1975
Reflections, pf, tape, 1975
Images, sax, tape, 1979

Principal publishers: Associated, Boelke-Bomart, Peters

BIBLIOGRAPHY

M. Babbitt: Introduction to M. Bauer: *Twentieth Century Music* (New York, 1933/*R*1978)
——: "Some Aspects of Twelve-tone Composition," *Score and IMA Magazine*, xii (1955), 53
——: "Who Cares if you Listen?," *HiFi*, viii/2 (1958), 38; repr. in *The American Composer Speaks*, ed. G. Chase (Baton Rouge, 1966), 234; repr. in *Contemporary Composers on Contemporary Music*, ed. E. Schwartz and B. Childs (New York, 1967), 243
——: "Twelve-tone Invariants as Compositional Determinants," *MQ*, xlvi (1960), 246; repr. in *Problems of Modern Music*, ed. P. H. Lang (New York, 1962), 108
——: "Set Structure as a Compositional Determinant," *JMT*, v (1961), 72; repr. in *Perspectives on Contemporary Music Theory*, ed. B. Boretz and E. T. Cone (New York, 1972), 129
"Babbitt, Milton," *CBY 1962*
M. Babbitt: "Twelve-tone Rhythmic Structure and the Electronic Medium," *PNM*, i/1 (1962), 49–79; repr. in *Perspectives on Contemporary Music Theory*, ed. B. Boretz and E. T. Cone (New York, 1972), 148–79
G. Perle: *Serial Composition and Atonality* (Berkeley, CA, 1962, 5/1981)
R. French: "Current Chronicle: New York," *MQ*, l (1964), 382
P. Westergaard: "Some Problems Raised by the Rhythmic Procedures in Milton Babbitt's *Composition for Twelve Instruments*," *PNM*, iv/1 (1965), 109
E. Barkin: "A Simple Approach to Milton Babbitt's 'Semi-simple Variations'," *MR*, xxviii (1967), 316
J. Hollander: "Notes on the Text of *Philomel*," *PNM*, vi/1 (1967), 132
R. Kostelanetz: "The Two Extremes of Avant-garde Music," *New York Times Magazine* (15 Jan 1967), 34
E. Salzman: "Babbitt and Serialism," *Twentieth Century Music: an Introduction* (Englewood Cliffs, NJ, 1967)
"An Interview with Milton Babbitt," *MEJ*, lv/3 (1968), 56
S. Arnold and G. Hair: "Milton Babbitt," *Music and Musicians*, xvii/10 (1969), 46
H. W. Hitchcock: "Systematic Serial Composition," *Music in the United States* (Englewood Cliffs, NJ, 1969, rev. 2/1974), 231
M. Babbitt: "On Relata I," *The Orchestral Composer's Point of View*, ed. R. S. Hines (Norman, OK, 1970), 11; repr. in *PNM*, ix/1 (1970), 1
M. Babbitt: "Contemporary Music Composition and Music Theory as Contemporary Intellectual History," *Perspectives in Musicology*, ed. B. S. Brook, E. O. D. Downes and S. J. van Solkema (New York, 1971), 151–84
D. Ewen: "Milton Babbitt," *Composers of Tomorrow's Music* (New York, 1972)
M. Babbitt: "Present Music Theory and Future Practice," *IRCAM Conference: Abbaye de Senanque 1973*, 1
——: "Since Schoenberg," *PNM*, xii/2 (1974), 3
B. Boretz: "Milton Babbitt," *Dictionary of Contemporary Music*, ed. J. Vinton (New York, 1974), 43
P. Lieberson, E. Lundborg, and J. Peel: "Conversation with Milton Babbitt," *Contemporary Music Newsletter*, viii/1 (1974), 2
J. Peel: "Milton Babbitt: String Quartet no.3," *Contemporary Music Newsletter*, viii/1 (1974), 1
PNM, xiv/2–xv/1 (1976) [special issue, incl. list of works and writings; articles with reply by Babbitt: "Responses: a First Approximation," xiv/2, p.3]
B. Benward: "The Widow's Lament in Springtime," *Music in Theory and Practice*, ii (Dubuque, IA, 1977, 2/1981), 483
R. Gauldin: "A Pedagogical Introduction to Set Theory," *Theory and Practice*, iii/2 (1978), 3
J. Machlis: "Four Representative American Composers," *Introduction to Contemporary Music* (New York, 2/1979), 515
D. Rosenberg and B. Rosenberg: "Milton Babbitt," *The Music Makers* (New York, 1979), 39
H. Wilcox and P. Escot: "A Musical Set Theory," *Theory and Practice*, iv/2 (1979), 17
M. Babbitt: "The Next Thirty Years," *HiFi*, xxxi/4 (1981), 62
M. Capalbo: "Charts," *PNM*, xix/1–2 (1981–2), 310
C. Gagne and T. Caras: "Milton Babbitt," *Soundpieces: Interviews with American Composers* (Metuchen, NJ, 1982), 35
A. Mead: "Detail and Array in Milton Babbitt's My Complements to Roger," *Music Theory Spectrum*, v (1983), 89
J. Rockwell: "The Northeastern Academic Establishment & the Romance of Science," *All American Music: Composition in the Late Twentieth Century* (New York, 1983), 25
A. Mead: "Recent Developments in the Music of Milton Babbitt," *MQ*, lxx (1984), 310

ELAINE BARKIN/MARTIN BRODY

Babcock, Alpheus (*b* Dorchester, MA, 11 Sept 1785; *d* Boston, MA, 3 April 1842). Piano maker. He began his career as an apprentice to BENJAMIN CREHORE, as did his brother Lewis (*d* 1817); the brothers had their own firm from 1809 to 1811. Alpheus Babcock worked for or was a partner in the following firms: Babcock, Appleton & Babcock (Boston, 1811–14); Hayts, Babcock & Appleton (Boston, 1814–15); J. A. Dickson (Boston); John and G. D. Mackay (Boston, 1822–9); J. G. Klemm (Philadelphia, 1830–32); William Swift (Philadelphia, 1832–7), and Chickering (Boston, 1837–42). His most significant contribution to the evolution of the piano was his invention of a one-piece cast-iron frame including hitchpin plate, for which he received a patent on 17 December 1825. This invention is regarded as the basis for subsequent piano frame development. His patents for "cross-stringing" (24 May 1830), improved action (31 December 1833), and improvement in the jack or "grasshopper" (31 October 1839) were not of lasting importance. Many historians erroneously credit Babcock with having invented or advocated the overstrung scale. This conclusion undoubtedly results from the equation of overstringing with cross-stringing. Babcock's "cross-stringing" patent concerns itself with unison double-strung piano strings (formed from a single wire which crosses over itself when looped over either hitchpin or hook), not with bass strings running diagonally above the others. Babcock's instruments, acclaimed for their superb craftsmanship, are generally of the square variety, patterned after the double-action pianos of Broadwood, and with either one or two pedals and a range of either five and a half or six octaves (*F'* to *c''''* or *F'* to *f''''*). Representative instruments are at the Smithsonian Institution (*see* PIANO, fig. 1) and Yale University.

BIBLIOGRAPHY

D. Spillane: *History of the American Pianoforte* (New York, 1890/*R*1969)
C. M. Ayars: *Contributions to the Art of Music in America by the Music Industries of Boston, 1640 to 1936* (New York, 1937/*R*1969)
H. E. Johnson: *Musical Interludes in Boston, 1795–1830* (New York, 1943)
K. G. Grafing: *Alpheus Babcock, American Pianoforte Maker (1785–1842): his Life, Instruments, and Patents* (diss., U. of Missouri, Kansas City, 1972)
——: "Alpheus Babcock's Cast-iron Piano Frames," *GSJ*, xxvii (1974), 118

KEITH G. GRAFING

Babin, Victor (*b* Moscow, Russia, 13 Dec 1908; *d* Cleveland, OH, 1 March 1972). Pianist and composer. He studied at Riga (Latvia) in 1928, moving to Berlin to learn composition with Franz Schreker and piano with Schnabel at the Hochschule für Musik. In 1933 he married another of Schnabel's pupils, Vitya (Victoria) Vronsky (*b* Evpatoria, Crimea, 22 Aug 1909), and his career as a player thereafter was chiefly that of a duo-pianist with his wife. Vronsky and Babin quickly established themselves in Europe, then moved to the USA in 1937 (Babin became an American citizen in 1944). On 27 October 1939 they performed Mozart's Concerto K365/316*a* with the New York PO. Their repertory extended from Bach to Babin, and their recordings included works by Copland, Stravinsky, and Vaughan Williams. From 1954 to 1962 Babin was the pianist of the Festival Quartet. He taught at the Aspen Music School (where he was director, 1951–4), at the Berkshire Music Center, at the Cleveland Institute of Music (where he was director from 1961 until his death), and at Case Western Reserve University. His compositions, in a conservative, post-Romantic language, include two concertos for two pianos and orchestra, other compositions for one and two pianos, several works for orchestra, chamber music, and many songs, including a cycle, *Beloved Stranger*, on texts by Witter Bynner.

MICHAEL STEINBERG/R

Baccaloni, Salvatore (*b* Rome, Italy, 14 April 1900; *d* New York, 31 Dec 1969). Bass. He was trained at the choristers' school of the Sistine Chapel. In 1921 he became a pupil of Giuseppe Kaschmann, and in 1922 made his début at the Teatro Adriano in Rome as Dr. Bartolo in *Il barbiere di Siviglia*. He sang regularly at La Scala from 1926 to 1940. His North American début was in Chicago during the 1930–31 season, and he made his Metropolitan Opera début, again as Dr. Bartolo, on 3 December 1940. In his 22 seasons at the Metropolitan he sang 297 performances, mostly in the Italian buffo repertory. He also made numerous tours of the USA and appeared often with the San Francisco Opera. Portly in build and good-humored, Baccaloni was widely regarded as one of the greatest of comic basses. He had a gift for comedy and was noted for his musicianship and for his careful study of roles. In his earlier years at the Metropolitan he displayed a vocal quality rare in buffo singing. He had a particularly large repertory, consisting of some 150 roles in many languages. He also appeared in several films, including *Full of Life* with Judy Holliday (1957) and *Fanny* (1961).

BIBLIOGRAPHY

R. Celletti: "Baccaloni, Salvatore," *Le grandi voci* (Rome, 1964), 33 [with discography by R. Vegeto]

FRANCIS D. PERKINS/HAROLD ROSENTHAL/R

Bach, P. D. Q. Persona invented by PETER SCHICKELE.

Bach [Schrotenbach], **Vincent** (*b* Baden, nr Vienna, Austria, 24 March 1890; *d* New York, 8 Jan 1976). Brass instrument maker. He played violin and bugle as a child and studied trumpet with Josef Weiss and Georg Stellwagen. He also pursued a complete course in mechanical engineering, a training which was later to stand him in good stead. In 1910 he earned a degree from the Maschinenbauschule in Wiener Neustadt. In 1912 he studied the solo trumpet literature in Wiesbaden with Fritz Werner, and then toured until 1914 as a cornet virtuoso through Germany, Denmark, Sweden, Russia, Poland, England, and the USA. While in the USA he was invited to play first trumpet with the Boston SO (1914), with which he remained for a year. He then spent one and a half years as first trumpeter with the Diaghilev Ballet Orchestra at the Metropolitan Opera House. During World War I he was bandmaster of the 306th US Field Artillery Regiment. He became an American citizen in 1923.

On 1 April 1919 Bach set up a shop at 204 East 85th Street in New York, mainly for the purpose of making mouthpieces for his own use. In 1922 he moved to 241 East 41st Street, where he had ten employees; the manufacture of cornets and trumpets was started there in 1924. From 1928 to 1952 he was at 621 East 216th Street, with 50 employees, and began the manufacture of tenor and bass trombones. In 1952 he built a factory at 52 McQuesten Parkway, Mount Vernon, New York. He sold his business to H. & A. Selmer in 1962; two years later the firm moved to Elkhart, Indiana.

In combining his musical proficiency with his engineering training, Bach succeeded in establishing the most exacting standards of brass instrument design and construction. His point of departure, as with Elden Benge, was the French Besson B♭ trumpet; unlike Benge, however, who desired more flexible intonation, Bach strove to give his instruments a secure "feel" for each note in the scale. Bach was also the first to set up a system for duplicating mouthpieces exactly. His instruments, especially trumpets, are employed more widely than any others. They are prized for their full and yet compact tone, with a solid core.

BIBLIOGRAPHY

G. Fladmoe: *The Contributions to Brass Instrument Manufacturing of Vincent Bach, Carl Geyer and Renold Schilke* (diss., U. of Illinois, 1975)

EDWARD H. TARR

Bacharach, Burt (F.) (*b* Kansas City, MO, 12 May 1928). Composer and pianist. He studied music at McGill University, Montreal, the New School of Social Research, the Mannes School of Music, New York, and the Music Academy of the West, Santa Barbara, California; his composition teachers included Milhaud, Martinů, and Cowell. He served in the army, touring as a concert pianist (1950–52), and then became an accompanist for such entertainers as Vic Damone, Polly Bergen, Steve Lawrence, and the Ames Brothers. From 1958 to 1961 he toured internationally with Marlene Dietrich. Bacharach began writing arrangements and composing songs in the mid-1950s. He collaborated with the lyricist Hal David on a large number of popular songs, including *Anyone who had a heart* (1963), *Walk on by* (1964), and *There's always something there to remind me* (1964), many of which were recorded by their protégée Dionne Warwick. These and the Broadway musical score *Promises, Promises* (1968) made them one of the most successful songwriting teams in American music history. Bacharach's style, though eclectic, is well defined and accessible; its heterogeneous elements include variable meter, irregular phrasing, pandiatonic and jazz harmonies, rhythmic ostinatos from various sources, and Afro-American effects. Many of his melodies – for example, *Do you know the way to San Jose?* – exhibit an internal momentum, created by the repetition of short, syncopated rhythmic patterns, which complements David's clever, colloquial lyrics. Bacharach has written a number of film scores, and won two Academy Awards for *Butch Cassidy and the Sundance Kid* (1969, the second for the song "Raindrops keep fallin' on my head"). He has also contributed to other films, including the title songs for *Made in Paris* (1966) and *Alfie* (1966).

WORKS
(selective list)

Collections: *The Bacharach and David Songbook*, ed. N. Monath (New York, 1970) [BS]
Burt Bacharach Anthology (New York, n.d.) [BA]

STAGE

Promises, Promises (musical, N. Simon, H. David), New York, 1 Dec 1968 [incl. Promises, Promises; I'll never fall in love again; Whoever you are I love you]

FILM SCORES
(all lyrics by H. David)

The Man who Shot Liberty Valance, 1962; What's New Pussycat?, 1965 [incl. Anyone who had a heart, Here I am, My Little Red Book]; Casino Royale, 1968 [incl. The Look of Love]; Butch Cassidy and the Sundance Kid, 1969 [incl. Raindrops keep fallin' on my head, Come touch the sun]; Lost Horizon (musical), 1973 [incl. The World in a Circle, Question me an answer, Reflections]

SONGS
(all lyrics by H. David)

*c*120 songs, incl. Magic Moments, 1957, BS; I just don't know what to do with myself, 1962, BS; Make it easy on yourself, 1962, BS; Twenty-four hours from Tulsa, 1963, BS; Wishin' and hopin', 1963, BS; Everyone needs someone to love, 1964, BA; There's always something there to remind me, 1964, BS; Walk on by, 1964, BS; Don't go breaking my heart, 1965, BS; What the world needs now is love, 1965, BS; Alfie, 1966, BS; Made in Paris, 1966, BA; Do you know the way to San Jose? 1967, BS; This guy's in love with you, 1968; BS; The hurtin' kind, 1970, BA

Principal publishers: Blue Seas, Jac, US Songs

BIBLIOGRAPHY

"Bacharach, Burt," *CBY 1970*
D. Ewen: *Popular American Composers* (New York, 1972)
B. A. Lohof: "The Bacharach Phenomenon: a Study in Popular Heroism," *Popular Music and Society*, i (1972), 73

MICHAEL J. BUDDS

Bach Aria Group. Chamber ensemble. It was founded in New York in 1946 by William H. Scheide, who guided it for more than 30 years; its purpose was to perform arias from Bach's cantatas and other works. It originally consisted of five singers (Ellen Osborn and Jean Carlton, sopranos; Margaret Tobias, alto; Robert Harmon, tenor; and Norman Farrow, bass-baritone), and five instrumentalists (Maurice Wilk, violin; Robert Bloom, oboe; Julius Baker, flute; David Soyer, cello; and Sergius Kagen, keyboard). The group made its début at Carnegie Hall in 1948, and from the 1950s made regular tours, appearing with a number of leading orchestras as a solo group in works such as Bach's Passions; it also made a number of recordings. In 1980, by which time its style was out of keeping with current thought concerning Baroque performance practice, Scheide announced his intention of disbanding the ensemble, but the flutist Samuel Baron, who had joined in 1965, assumed its leadership; other changes of membership had occurred, and the group now included Ronald Roseman (oboe), Timothy Eddy (cello), Yehudi Wyner (keyboard), and the singers Susan Davenny Wyner, Janice Taylor, Seth McCoy, and Thomas Paul. In 1981 the new Bach Aria Group took up a summer residence at SUNY, Stony Brook, and in the following year began to tour again.

BIBLIOGRAPHY

V. O'Brien: "From Cantata to Concerto: Bach in Style," *Symphony Magazine*, xxii/6 (1981), 22
B. Holland: "The Reborn Bach Aria Group," *New York Times* (21 March 1982)

MICHAEL FLEMING

Bach Choir of Bethlehem. Vocal ensemble founded in 1898; it presents the BETHLEHEM BACH FESTIVAL.

Background music. *See* ENVIRONMENTAL MUSIC.

Bacon, Ernst (*b* Chicago, IL, 26 May 1898). Composer and pianist. He studied at Northwestern University (1915–18), the University of Chicago (1919–20), and the University of California (MA 1935). Among his teachers were Alexander Raab and G. D. Dunn (piano), Weigl and Bloch (composition), and Goossens (conducting), under whom he was assistant conductor of the Rochester Opera Company. He taught at the Eastman School (1925–8) and the San Francisco Conservatory (1928–30); in 1935 he instituted and conducted the Carmel Bach Festival in California, and the next year he was supervisor of the WPA Federal Music Project in San Francisco and conductor of its orchestra. Subsequent teaching appointments took him to Converse College, Spartanburg, South Carolina, as dean and professor of piano (1938–45), and to Syracuse University, as director of the school of music and professor (1945–63, professor emeritus from 1964). Among his honors are a Pulitzer Award (1932, for the Symphony in D minor) and two Guggenheim Fellowships.

As a composer Bacon is best known for his songs, which show unusual sensitivity to the color and inflection of words and a masterly use of syncopation to give the impression of natural speech. He prefers short poems with "a certain philosophical undercurrent together with a relatively simple and not-too-involved lyricism" and has been most successful with his settings of texts by Emily Dickinson and Walt Whitman. He has also made many arrangements of American folk music. *Our Musical Idiom* (1917), his early study of new harmonies, pointed the direction he was to follow, one close to tradition. Yet his style is individual, finding its basis in nondiatonic scales, American subjects, and a mastery of counterpoint. 22 of his Dickinson songs have been recorded by Helen Boatwright with the composer at the piano. In addition to composing, Bacon performed as a pianist in Europe and the USA, and he has also shown talent as a painter. His published writings include *Words on Music* (1960) and *Notes on the Piano* (1963).

WORKS

Dramatic: Take your Choice, collab. P. Mathias and R. Stoll, San Francisco, 1936; A Tree on the Plains (musical play, P. Horgan), Spartanburg, SC, 1942; A Drumlin Legend (opera, H. Carus), New York, 1949; Dr. Franklin (musical play, C. Lengyel), 1976; ballets

Orch: Fantasy and Fugue, 1926; Sym. Fugue, pf, str, 1932; 2 syms., 1932, 1937; Bearwalla, pf, str, 1936; Country Roads, Unpaved, suite, 1936; Ford's Theater, 1946; From these States, suite, 1951; Fables (E. Bacon, J. Edmunds), nar, orch, 1953; Conc. grosso, 1957; Elegy, ob, str, 1957; Erie Waters, suite, 1961; Pf Conc. no. 1 "Riolama," 1963; Over the Waters, ov., 1976; Pf Conc. no. 2, 1982; band works; a few other orch pieces

Chamber: Qnt, str qt, db, 1950; Peterborough, suite, va, pf, 1961–82; A Life, suite, vc, pf, 1966–81; Tumbleweeds, cycle, vn, pf, 1979; Pf Trio, 1981; Vc Sonata, 1982; Vn Sonata, 1982; pieces for pf, pf 4 hands, and org; other works for various insts

Vocal: On Ecclesiastes, cantata, 1936; From Emily's Diary (Dickinson), women's chorus, pf/small orch, 1947; By Blue Ontario (Whitman), cantata, 1958; Requiem "The Last Invocation" (Dickinson, Whitman), B, chorus, orch, 1968–71; oratorios; songs with orch; choral folksong arrs, hymns, and anthems; *c*250 songs, 1v, pf, to texts by Dickinson and others

Principal publishers: Associated, Birchard, Broude, Chappell, Lawson-Gould, Leeds, E. B. Marks, Mercury, G. Schirmer, Shawnee, Southern, Syracuse UP, Peters, L. Webster

BIBLIOGRAPHY

EwenD; *VintonD*

E. Bacon: *Ernst Bacon* (Orinda, CA, ?1974) [incl. bibliography, discography, and P. Horgan: "A Contemporary Tribute"]

J. St. Edmunds: "The Songs of Ernst Bacon," *Shawnee Review* (Oct 1941)

W. Fleming: "Ernst Bacon," *MusAm*, lxix/36 (1949), 8

PHILIP LIESON MILLER

Bacon, Fred(erick J.) (*b* Holyoke, MA, 17 Jan 1871; *d* Newfane, VT, 18 Nov 1948). Banjoist and banjo maker. He began his career playing with a medicine show and a Wild West show, then from 1890 to 1915 performed in a vaudeville act with his wife. He studied with Alfred A. Farland in the mid-1890s and about 1897 organized the Bacon Banjo Quintette. He toured with the Bacon Trio in 1905–06, and made another very successful tour in 1908 with "The Big Three," consisting of himself, the guitarist William Foden, and the mandolinist Guiseppe Pettine. Bacon continued to play into the 1940s and his few recordings attest to his virtuoso performances; contemporary reviewers praised his tone, his great technique, and the expressiveness of his playing. He taught, published several method books, and wrote many arrangements and compositions for five-string banjo. Bacon also designed banjos, bringing out his first instrument in 1905 and opening his own factory in 1913; the famous "Silver Bell" model, produced with David L. Day, was introduced in 1923. His banjos are still prized for their power and tone.

BIBLIOGRAPHY

N. Howard: *The Banjo and its Players* (MS, 1957, *NN-L*)

E. Kaufman and M. Kaufman: "Fred Bacon," *The 5-stringer*, no. 120 (1975), 1, 10; no. 121 (1976), 1, 3, 9

ROBERT B. WINANS

Bacon, Leonard (*b* Detroit, MI, 19 Feb 1803; *d* New Haven, CT, 23 Dec 1881). Author of hymn texts and hymnbook compiler. The son of a missionary to the Indians, he was educated at Yale University and Andover Theological Seminary. While at Andover he compiled a small pamphlet containing 101 missionary hymns, three of them his own; entitled *Hymns and Sacred Songs; for the Monthly Concert* (Andover, MA, 1823), it was intended for use at missionary prayer meetings and was the first such collection to be published in the USA. In 1825 Bacon was ordained and became pastor of the Center Church, New Haven, where he served until he joined the faculty of the Yale Divinity School in 1866. In 1833 he published in New Haven a revision of Timothy Dwight's edition of Isaac Watts's *Psalms and Hymns*, to which he appended the collection *Additional Hymns, Designed as a Supplement to Dwight's Psalms & Hymns* (2/1837); it included four of his own texts. He also supervised the preparation of a new Connecticut Congregational hymnal, *Psalms and Hymns, for Christian Use and Worship* (1845), which contained five of his texts. He is best known for his hymn "O God, beneath thy guiding hand," written for New Haven's bicentennial celebration in 1833, and since sung generally to John Hatton's tune "Duke Street."

BIBLIOGRAPHY

F. M. Bird: "Bacon, Leonard," *A Dictionary of Hymnology*, ed. J. Julian (New York, 1892, 2/1907/*R*1957), i, 105

T. D. Bacon: *Leonard Bacon, a Statesman in the Church* (New Haven, 1931)

C. W. Hughes: *American Hymns Old and New: Notes on the Hymns* (New York, 1980), 174, 265

PAUL C. ECHOLS

Bacon, Thomas (*b* Isle of Man, *c*1700; *d* Frederick, MD, 24 May 1768). Violinist and composer. He spent his early years in Ireland, where he was ordained a priest. In 1745 he immigrated to America and settled in Oxford, Maryland, where he was appointed rector of St. Peter's Church. By 1750 he had organized the Eastern Shore Triumvirate, a musical club with a membership of local merchants, which regularly presented concerts; Bacon played violin and viola da gamba. His plans for establishing the first charity school in Maryland led to a series of benefit concerts in Maryland and Virginia from 1750 to 1754. Bacon was also an honorary member of the Tuesday Club, a musical organization in Annapolis, Maryland. He wrote an *Anniversary Ode of the Tuesday Club* in 1750, the earliest extant piece of chamber music composed in America, as well as other similar works. In 1758 he moved to Frederick, Maryland, where he was appointed rector of All Saints Church in 1762. He spent his later years working on educational projects, and he published a compilation of the laws of Maryland (1766).

BIBLIOGRAPHY

E. Allen: "Rev. Thomas Bacon," *American Quarterly Church Review*, xvii (1865), 430

W. E. Deibert: "Thomas Bacon, Colonial Clergyman," *Maryland Historical Magazine*, lxxiii (1978), 79

J. B. Talley: *Secular Music in Colonial Annapolis: the Tuesday Club, 1745–1756* (diss., Peabody Conservatory, 1983)

JAMES R. HEINTZE

Badger, Alfred G. (*b* 1815; *d* Brooklyn, NY, 8 Nov 1892). Flute maker. He began to make fifes and recorders at the age of 12, and in 1834 became apprenticed to Ball & Douglass, flute makers, in Utica, New York. In 1838 he went to Buffalo, where he became a partner in the Nickels & Badger music store from 1839 to 1841. He moved to Newark, New Jersey, after 1843, opened his workshop in New York in 1846, and was briefly associated with Theobald Monzani in 1858. Badger, a superb craftsman, stated that he always tried to make each instrument superior to its predecessor; many of his flutes are beautifully engraved. His instruments won silver medals and diplomas at several fairs and exhibitions in Massachusetts and New York. His insistence on excellence, his support of performers, and his widespread publications encouraged the rapid acceptance of the Boehm flute, of which he was the first commercial manufacturer in the USA (1846) and the most important American manufacturer during the mid-19th century. He was also the first musical-instrument manufacturer to use ebonite; he made four flutes in 1851 for Charles Goodyear, who exhibited in London and Paris. Badger apparently made the first American silver Boehm flute in 1866 and was the first to use ebonite heads on silver bodies. He also made piccolos, alto flutes, experimental flutes, and a combination flute-clarinet. Were it not for the excessively high pitch at which most of Badger's flutes were built (some as high as $a'=452$), his instruments might be played by flutists today. The Dayton C. Miller collection at the Library of Congress has 11 of Badger's flutes, four are in the Yale University Collection, and many others are maintained in public and private collections.

BIBLIOGRAPHY

A. G. Badger: *An Illustrated History of the Flute* (New York, 1853, 4/1875)
"India-rubber Flutes," *Scientific American*, new ser., i (1859), 284
C. R. Anderson and A. H. Starke, eds.: *Sidney Lanier, Centennial Editions* (Baltimore, 1943) [vii–x, 1857–77]
N. Groce: *Musical Instrument Making in New York City during the Eighteenth and Nineteenth Centuries* (diss., U. of Michigan, 1982)
M. J. Simpson: *Alfred G. Badger (1815–1892), Nineteenth-century Flute-maker: his Art, Innovations, and Influence on Flute Construction, Performance and Composition, 1845–1895* (diss., U. of Maryland, 1982)

MARY JEAN SIMPSON

Baermann, Carl [Bärmann, Karl] (*b* Munich, Germany, 9 July 1839; *d* Newton, MA, 17 Jan 1913). Pianist, teacher, and composer. His father, Karl Bärmann (1811–85), and his grandfather, Heinrich Joseph Bärmann (1784–1847), were both renowned clarinetists; the latter was an intimate friend of Weber and Mendelssohn, both of whom composed works for him. Baermann studied in Munich with Franz Lachner and Peter Cornelius and later became a pupil and close friend of Liszt. He taught for many years at the Königliche Musikschule in Munich, becoming a professor in 1876, then in 1881 came to the USA. He made a successful début as pianist in Boston (22 December 1881). Having decided to remain, he became prominent there as a performer, and was also highly esteemed as a teacher (Amy Beach and Frederick Converse were among his pupils). Baermann wrote a *Festival March* for orchestra and a number of piano compositions. Among the very few published works are a magnificent set of 12 *Etüden* op.4 (1877) and a stylish *Polonaise pathétique* (1914).

BIBLIOGRAPHY

J. P. Brown: "Carl Baermann," *Musical Record and Review*, no.481 (1902), 40
L. C. Elson: *The History of American Music* (New York, 1904, enlarged 3/1925/*R*1971)
"Carl Baermann," *New England Conservatory Review*, ii/1 (1912), 1

JOHN GILLESPIE

Baez, Joan (Chandos) (*b* Staten Island, NY, 9 Jan 1941). Folksinger and songwriter. She started to play guitar at the age of 12. Although she enrolled in Boston University Fine Arts School of Drama, she left after a few weeks to sing in local coffeehouses. After two strikingly successful appearances at the Newport Folk Festival in 1959 and 1960, she recorded her first album, which was an immediate success; critics noted the evocative purity and mystery of her soprano voice and her straightforward interpretations. Her early repertory consisted almost exclusively of traditional ballads but by 1963 she had begun to include protest songs and works by Bob Dylan, with whom she appeared frequently. Baez led the boycott of the television program "Hootenanny" in 1963 when Pete Seeger was blacklisted for his alleged

Joan Baez, 1982

communist sympathies. Her involvement in political activities increased in the mid-1960s and she gave many benefit concerts for the civil rights and antiwar movements; her commitment to the cause of world peace also led to tours and performances abroad. Although her numerous albums sold well throughout the 1960s and 1970s, her only hit single was a recording of Robbie Robertson's rock-influenced song *The night they drove old Dixie down* (1971); her later albums continue to exhibit a mixture of traditional material and pop ballads. Among her notable original compositions are *A Song for David*, *Honest Lullaby*, and *Diamonds and Rust*.

RECORDINGS
(selective list)

Joan Baez (Van. 2077, 1960); *Farewell Angelina* (Van. 79200, 1965); *One Day at a Time* (Van. 79310, 1970), incl. A Song for David; *Blessed are* (Van. 6570/1, 1971), incl. The night they drove old Dixie down; *Come from the Shadows* (A&M 4339, 1972); *Diamonds and Rust* (A&M 4527, 1975); *Honest Lullaby* (Portrait 35766, 1979)

BIBLIOGRAPHY

"Baez, Joan," *CBY 1963*
J. Cohen: "Joan Baez," *Sing Out*, xiii/3 (1963), 5
J. Baez: "A Personal Statement: I Do not Believe in War," *Sing Out*, xiv/3 (1964), 57
J. Baez: *Daybreak* (New York, 1968) [autobiography]
J. Grissim: "Joan Baez," *Rolling Stone*, no.23 (7 Dec 1968), 12
A. Means: "America's Joan of Arc," *Melody Maker*, xlvi (25 Dec 1971), 16
J. Swanekamp, ed.: *Diamonds and Rust: a Bibliography and Discography on Joan Baez* (Ann Arbor, MI, 1980)

TERENCE J. O'GRADY

Bags. *See* JACKSON, MILT.

Bailes Brothers. Country-music group. Its principal members were four brothers: Kyle (Otis) Bailes (*b* Enoch, WV, 7 May 1915), Johnnie (John Jacob) Bailes (*b* St. Albans, WV, 24 June 1918), Walter (Butler) Bailes (*b* North Charleston, WV, 17 Jan 1920), and Homer (Vernon) Bailes (*b* North Charleston, 8 May 1922); at different times various combinations of the brothers and other musicians made up the group. Brought up by a widowed mother during the Depression, the brothers formed a group called the Hymn Singers to earn their living. Among the performers who influenced their style were Hank and Slim Newman and the Holden Brothers. They worked on many West Virginia radio stations, where their colleagues included Molly O'Day (then known as Dixie Lee) and Little Jimmy Dickens, billed by Johnnie as the "Singing Midget." During World War II, while Homer was in military service, Johnnie and Walter performed as a duo on the "Grand Ole Opry," having secured the booking through their friendship with Roy Acuff. In the mid-1940s the group made its most successful recordings, mostly of songs written by Walter, for Columbia; at that time it was known as the West Virginia Home Folks. In 1946 the brothers moved to Shreveport, Louisiana, to perform on radio station KWKH; with Dean Upson, formerly commercial manager at WSM, Nashville, they founded the "Louisiana Hayride" program in April 1948, which helped to launch the careers of Hank Williams and Webb Pierce. Walter left the group in 1947 to become a minister and it disbanded in 1949, but two pairs of brothers (Walter and Johnnie, and Kyle and Homer) continued to perform and record intermittently as late as the mid-1970s.

The Bailes Brothers were among the most popular performers on the "Grand Ole Opry" and "Louisiana Hayride." Their style was a unique mixture of old-time secular duet singing and gospel intensity, and they sang both secular and sacred repertory. Many of the Bailes Brothers' songs were recorded successfully by other country and bluegrass artists, for example, *Dust on the Bible* by the Blue Sky Boys and *Give mother my crown* by Flatt and Scruggs.

RECORDINGS
(selective list)

As long as I live (Col. 36932, 1945); Dust on the Bible (Col. 37154, 1945); I want to be loved (Col. 37341, 1945); There's tears in my eyes all the time (King 938, 1946); Whiskey is the devil (Col. 37583, 1947)

BIBLIOGRAPHY

I. M. Tribe: "Bailes Brothers Discography," *Bluegrass Unlimited*, ix/8 (1975), 13
——: "West Virginia Home Folks: the Bailes Brothers," *Old Time Music*, no.19 (1975–6), 17

RONNIE PUGH

Bailey, Buster [William C.] (*b* Memphis, TN, 19 July 1902; *d* New York, 12 April 1967). Jazz clarinetist. As a teenager he played in the orchestra led by the blues composer W. C. Handy. In 1919 he settled in Chicago and worked with Erskine Tate and King Oliver before moving to New York in 1924 to join Fletcher Henderson's band (for illustration *see* HENDERSON, FLETCHER). There his considerable technique on clarinet became a feature on many of Henderson's recordings during the years from 1924 to 1937. At first, the ruggedness of Johnny Dodds's and Sidney Bechet's improvisations exerted an effect on Bailey's classically trained approach, but later, with John Kirby's Sextet (1937–46), his playing became smoother. One of the best demonstrations of his exceptionally fast fingering is heard on *Man with a Horn goes Berserk* (1938). Bailey remained a master technician until the end of his life, and although he rarely "swung" in the manner of the great jazz clarinetists, and his playing lacked passion, his solos were always facile and tuneful. The last two years of his life were spent in Louis Armstrong's All Stars.

RECORDINGS
(selective list)

As leader: Afternoon in Africa (1937, Variety 668), Man with a Horn goes Berserk (1938, Voc. 4564), Am I Blue? (1940, Varsity 8333)
As sideman: F. Henderson: Shanghai Shuffle (1934, Decca 158); J. Kirby: 9:20 Special (1945, Asch 3571); Dixie All Stars: *Dixiecats* (1957, Roul. 25015), incl. Tin Roof Blues

BIBLIOGRAPHY

Obituary, *Down Beat*, xxxiv/10 (1967), 13
A. McCarthy, ed.: *Jazz on Record* (London, 1968), 13

JOHN CHILTON

Bailey, Lillian. *See* HENSCHEL, LILLIAN.

Bailey [née Rinker], **Mildred** (*b* Tekoa, WA, 27 Feb 1907; *d* Poughkeepsie, NY, 12 Dec 1951). Jazz singer and pianist. She was educated in Spokane and began her career on the West Coast as a cinema pianist and radio performer. In 1929 she made her first recording, and from then until 1933 sang with the band led by Paul Whiteman, to whom she was introduced by her brother, Al Rinker, a member of Whiteman's Rhythm Boys vocal trio. She sang on the radio shows of George Jessel and Willard Robison (1934–5), in Eddie Sauter's arrangements for Red Norvo's band (1936–9), and on the radio with Benny Goodman (1939). During the 1930s she was known as the "Rockin' Chair Lady" because of her performances of Hoagy Carmichael's song *Rockin' Chair*; from 1933 to 1945 she was married to Norvo and the couple were known as "Mr and Mrs Swing." Despite recurrent illness after 1940, she continued to perform. She had a clear, warm voice, and her jazz interpretations of songs owed much to the styles of Ethel Waters and Bessie Smith.

RECORDINGS
(selective list)

Rockin' Chair (1932, Vic. 24117); Someday Sweetheart/When Day is Done (1935, Voc. 3057); Willow Tree/Honeysuckle Rose (1935, Decca 18108); Arkansas Blues (1939, Voc. 4801); Fools Rush in/From another World (1940, Col. 35463)

BIBLIOGRAPHY

S. Dance: *The World of Swing* (New York, 1974), 391
H. Pleasants: *The Great American Popular Singers* (London, 1974), 143

RAYMONDE S. KRAMLICH/R

Bailey, Pearl (*b* Newport News, VA, 29 March 1918). Jazz and popular singer. She sang with the Noble Sissle Band in the mid-1930s and with Cootie Williams and Count Basie in the early 1940s. Her solo début at the Village Vanguard in Greenwich Village in 1944 led to an association with Cab Calloway and his band. During this period she developed a comical, offhand style of performance, which included a patter of droll asides. She made her Broadway début in Arlen's musical *St. Louis Woman*, for which she won a Donaldson Award. She later starred in Arlen's *House of Flowers* (1954) and in an all-black version of Jerry Herman's *Hello, Dolly!* (1967), which earned her a Special Tony Award in 1968. Of her film roles, she is best-remembered for her appearances in *Carmen Jones* (1954), *That Certain Feeling* (1956, with Bob Hope), *St. Louis Blues* (1958), and *Porgy and Bess* (1959). Her first hit recording was *Tired* (1947), and her most successful the comic *Takes Two to Tango* (1953). Although she announced her retirement in 1976 to serve as a member of the American delegation to the United Nations, she later resumed television and concert appearances, frequently performing with the band led by jazz drummer Louis Bellson, whom she married in 1952.

BIBLIOGRAPHY

SouthernB
P. Bailey: *The Raw Pearl* (New York, 1968)
"Bailey, Pearl," *CBY 1969*

ARNOLD SHAW

Bain, Wilfred Conwell (*b* Shawville, Que., 20 Jan 1908). Music educator and administrator. He was educated at Houghton College (BA 1929), Westminster Choir College (BMus 1931), and New York University (MA 1936, EdD 1938). He was head of the music department at Wesleyan Methodist College, Central, South Carolina (1929–30), head of voice and choral music at Houghton College (1931–8), dean of music at North Texas State University (1938–47), and dean of the school of music at Indiana University (1947–73). After retiring from the post he became artistic director of the Opera Theater at Indiana University. The eminence of the Indiana School of Music, especially its excellent facilities for operatic production, is largely due to his efforts, and he has been instrumental in engaging professional artists, including the mezzo-soprano Margaret Harshaw and the cellist Janos Starker, to teach at the music school. He has also been active in national music education, and was a former chairman of the US Information Agency Music Advisory Panel.

PATRICK J. SMITH

Baird, Martha. *See* ROCKEFELLER, MARTHA BAIRD.

Baker. Family of singers who between 1844 and the 1880s formed various differently constituted groups under the family name. A vocal quartet named the Baker Family was first formed around 1844 by John, George, Sophie, and Henry Baker in Salisbury, New Hampshire. They followed the example of the Hutchinson Family in style, repertory, and presentation, and became one of the most popular ensembles of this type. The group, sometimes with the addition of other family members including Jaspar and Emilie, toured widely in the mid- and late 1840s, especially to smaller cities and towns. In 1851 some of the family moved to Waukegan, Illinois, from where the newly named Baker Vocalists made periodic tours to the West until the 1880s. Although the bass, George (*d c*1879), had the most impressive voice, it was John (1822–1905) who was the leading member of the group. A Baker Family concert often consisted only of his glees, choruses, and ballads; among his 34 published pieces, *Where can the soul find rest?* (1845), *The Burman Lover* (1845), and *My Trundle Bed* (1860) achieved significant popularity. He also wrote a cantata, *Esther*, and an oratorio, *The Great Feast of Babylon*. *The Baker Vocalists: Book of Words* was issued in 1862. Dartmouth College, Hanover, New Hampshire, and the New Hampshire Historical Society, Concord, have collections of music and papers relating to the family.

BIBLIOGRAPHY

J. T. Howard: *Our American Music* (New York, 1931), 182

DALE COCKRELL

Baker, Benjamin Franklin (*b* Wenham, MA, 10 July 1811; *d* Boston, MA, 11 March 1889). Teacher, singer, and composer. He sang, directed choirs, and taught music in Salem, Massachusetts, and in 1833 toured the country with a concert company. He then settled in Bangor, Maine, as a businessman, but moved to Boston in 1837 to study music with John Paddon. He was director of music at W. E. Channing's church for eight years, and succeeded Lowell Mason as superintendent of musical instruction in the Boston public schools in 1841. Also in that year he began holding "musical conventions," which led to many appearances as soloist with the Handel and Haydn Society, of which he later became vice-president. He founded the Boston Music School and served as principal and head of the singing department until 1868, when he retired and the school closed. He was editor of the *Boston Musical Journal* for several years. Baker collaborated in compiling over 25 collections of songs, hymns, anthems, and glees, including *The Boston Musical Education Society's Collection of Church Music* (with Isaac B. Woodbury, 1842) and *Baker's Church Music* (1855). He wrote two harmony textbooks (1847 and 1870), and composed vocal music, including three secular cantatas: *The Storm King* (1856), *The Burning Ship* (1858), and *Camillus, the Roman Conqueror* (1865).

BIBLIOGRAPHY

F. O. Jones, ed.: *A Handbook of American Music and Musicians* (Canaseraga, NY, 1886/*R*1971)
F. L. G. Cole: "Baker, Benjamin Franklin," *DAB*

WILLIAM E. BOSWELL

Baker, Chet [Chesney H.] (*b* Yale, OK, 23 Dec 1929). Jazz trumpeter. He first encountered jazz while playing in army bands, and by the time of his discharge in 1951 his distinctive, reticent style was fully developed. In 1952 he played briefly with Charlie Parker before beginning an important association with the baritone saxophonist Gerry Mulligan in the latter's celebrated "pianoless" quartet. These performances, particularly his ballad rendition of *My Funny Valentine*, brought him instant fame; his clear tone and subdued, lyrical manner, rarely rising above *mezzo-forte* and sometimes not exceeding the span of an octave, immediately became hallmarks of West Coast cool jazz, and were widely imitated. After leaving Mulligan in 1953 Baker rejoined Parker briefly and led his own combos. He continued to dominate domestic and international jazz opinion polls for the next few years. Thereafter, owing largely to the effects of drug addiction, his career became erratic, being interrupted at one point by a prison sentence in Italy for drug-related offenses (1960–61). In the 1970s he resumed playing regularly with some success, particularly in combos without piano or drums.

RECORDINGS

(selective list)

As leader: Maid in Mexico (1953, Pacific Jazz 605); *Chet Baker in New York* (1958, Riv. 281); *Cool Burnin'* (1965, Prst. 7496); *The Touch of your Lips* (1979, SteepleChase 1122)

As sideman with G. Mulligan: Line for Lyons/Carioca (1952, Fan. 522); My Funny Valentine/Bark for Barksdale (1952, Fan. 525)

BIBLIOGRAPHY

I. Gitler: "Chet Baker's Tale of Woe," *Down Beat*, xxxi/20 (1964), 22

M. James: "A Case of Mistaken Identity," *Jazz Monthly*, no.173 (1969), 4

G. Gautherin and A. Tercinet: "Discographie de Chet Baker," *Jazz hot*, no.327 (1976), 12

M. Hawthorn: "Chet Baker," *Down Beat*, xlviii/10 (1981), 24

J. BRADFORD ROBINSON

Baker, David (Nathaniel) (*b* Indianapolis, IN, 21 Dec 1931). Composer and jazz cellist. He received the BMEd (1953) and MMEd (1954) degrees from Indiana University and studied privately with George Russell and John Lewis, among others. In addition to playing jazz cello (from 1948) with such artists as Maynard Ferguson, Quincy Jones, George Russell, John Montgomery, and Lionel Hampton, he has taught at Lincoln University, Jefferson City, Missouri, at Indiana Central University, Indianapolis, and in the Indianapolis public schools. In 1966 he joined the faculty of Indiana University, where he serves as chairman of the jazz department of the School of Music. He has also toured as a lecturer, conducted workshops, and written over 200 articles and books on jazz and black American music, including *Jazz Improvisation: a Comprehensive Method of Study for All Players* (1969), *Techniques of Improvisation* (1971), and *Jazz Styles and Analysis: Trombone* (1973). Baker has served as chairman of the jazz, folk, and ethnic advisory panel to the NEA and of the jazz advisory panel to the Kennedy Center. An extraordinarily prolific composer, Baker has written more than 2000 works, over 500 of which were commissioned. His compositional style blends black American elements with traditional European techniques and forms, drawing on jazz, serial, and electronic techniques, as well as gospel and folk materials.

WORKS

(selective list; for a fuller list see Baker, Belt, and Hudson, 1978)

Dramatic: Psalm xxii, jazz oratorio, nars, SATB, jazz ens, str orch, dancers, 1966; The Beatitudes (Bible), nar, solo vv, SATB, jazz ens, str orch, dancers, 1968; Sangre negro (J. Schenz, S. Rausch), jazz ballet, 1974, arr. jazz ens, arr. jazz trio, orch; television scores; incidental music

Orch: Afro-Cuban Suite, band, 1954; Little Princess Waltz, str orch, 1959; Reflections (My Indianapolis), jazz ens, orch, 1969; 9 str orch pieces, 1970; Kosbro, 1973, rev. 1975; Levels, db, fl qt, hn qt, str qt, jazz band, 1973; 2 Improvisations, jazz ens, orch, 1974; Conc., vc, chamber orch, 1975; Conc., 2 pf, jazz band, chamber orch, perc, 1976; Cl Conc., 1985

Jazz ens: Passion, 1956; Le roi, 1957; Kentucky Oysters, 1958; April B, 1959; Honesty, 1960; Terrible T, 1962; Black Thursday, 1964; The Professor, 1966; A Summer Day in 1945 (Summer 1945), with tape, 1968; Penich, 1970; Calypso-nova, no.1, 1970, no.2, 1971, both arr. str orch; Adumbratio, 1971; Louis Armstrong in memoriam, 1972; Harlem Pipes, 1973, arr. jazz trio, orch; Bebop Revisited, 1974; Le miroir noir, 1974; An Evening Thought, 1977; This One's for 'Trane, 1981; Cahaphi, 1983; Padospe, 1983; Birdsong, 1984; Groovin' for Diz, 1984; 8 concs., solo inst, jazz band, incl. Vc Conc., 1985

Other inst: 10 sonatas, 1966–74; Ballade, hn, a sax, vc, 1967; Fantasy, ww qnt, 1969; 5 Short Pieces, pf, 1970; 6 poèmes noir, fl, pf, 1974; Improvisations nos.1–2, vn, 1975; Stere-opticon, vc, elec insts, 1975; Suite, vn, 1975; Blues Waltz, pf trio, 1976; Contrasts, pf trio, 1976; Ethnic Variations on a Theme of Paganini, vn, pf, 1976; Roots, pf trio, 1976; Fantasy, a sax, 4 vc, perc, 1977; Shapes, perc ens, 1977; Jazz Suite, vn, pf, 1979; Conc. for Fours, fl, vc, tuba, db, 4 tuba, 4 db, 4 perc, 1980; Singers of Songs, Weavers of Dreams, vc, perc, 1980; Sonata, vn, vc, 4 fl, 1980; Dedication, s sax, db, str qt, 1981; Blues, vn ens, pf, 1985; Calypso, vn ens, pf, 1985; En rouge et noir, fl, pf, db, drums, 1985; Suite, hn, tpt, sax, rhythm section, 1985

Vocal: Abyss (C. Wright), S, pf, 1968; Black America: to the Memory of Martin Luther King, Jr. (S. Warren, L. Hughes, P. Murray, C. Hines, C. McKay, and others), cantata, nars, solo vv, SATB, jazz ens, str orch, 1968, rev.; 5 Songs to the Survival of Black Children (Hines, C. K. Rivers, Hughes, McKay), SATB, unacc., 1970; Songs of the Night (Hughes, F. Horne, Evans, A. Bontemps, Rivers, Hines), S, str qt, pf, 1972; The Black Experience (M. Evans), T, pf, 1973; Le chat qui pêche (Baker), S, jazz qt, orch, 1974; 2 masses; other songs and choruses

BIBLIOGRAPHY

SouthernB

D. Baker, L. Belt, and H. C. Hudson, eds.: *The Black Composer Speaks* (Metuchen, NJ, 1978) [incl. list of works, extensive bibliography, list of writings]

A. J. Thomas: *A Study of the Selected Masses of Twentieth-century Black Composers: Magaret Bonds, Robert Ray, George Walker and David Baker* (diss., U. of Illinois, 1983)

CARMAN MOORE

Baker, Israel (*b* Chicago, IL, 11 Feb 1921). Violinist. His early studies were with Adolph Pick at the Chicago Conservatory, and he made his début at Orchestra Hall in Chicago when he was six years old. After further periods of study under Louis Persinger at the Juilliard School and under Jacques Gordon and Bronisław Huberman, he developed a considerable reputation as chamber musician, as concertmaster, and as soloist. Much of this activity has been concentrated in California, where Baker was the regular second violinist in the Heifetz–Piatigorsky Chamber Concerts, and where he was the concertmaster in the long series of recordings by Stravinsky and by Bruno Walter. As a soloist he has had particular success with such works as Schoenberg's Concerto and Phantasy and Berg's Chamber Concerto. His recordings of these three 20th-century classics combine stylistic acumen with the benefits of a thorough grounding in the Viennese Romantic tradition. Both as a soloist and as a member of the Pacific Art Trio, Baker has also performed and recorded works by Antheil, Ives, Vernon Duke, and Gail Kubik. He has served as professor of music at Scripps College in Claremont, California.

BERNARD JACOBSON

Baker, Josephine (*b* St. Louis, MO, 3 June 1906; *d* Paris, France, 12 April 1979). Singer and actress. She became a professional street musician at the age of 13, and toured with the Dixie Steppers vaudeville troupe. Following her success as end-girl in the chorus line on tour with the musical *Shuffle Along* (1921), she was featured in its sequel, *Chocolate Dandies* (1924), and in a New York nightclub revue. In 1925 she moved to Paris to star in *La revue nègre* at the Théâtre des Champs-Elysées, in which she indulged in frenzied dancing and exaggerated mimicry; the show concluded with a nude savage dance duet. Baker then appeared in the Folies-Bergère (1925), where she made her entrance clad in three bracelets and a girdle of rhinestone-studded bananas. Her combination of the erotic and comic made her one of the

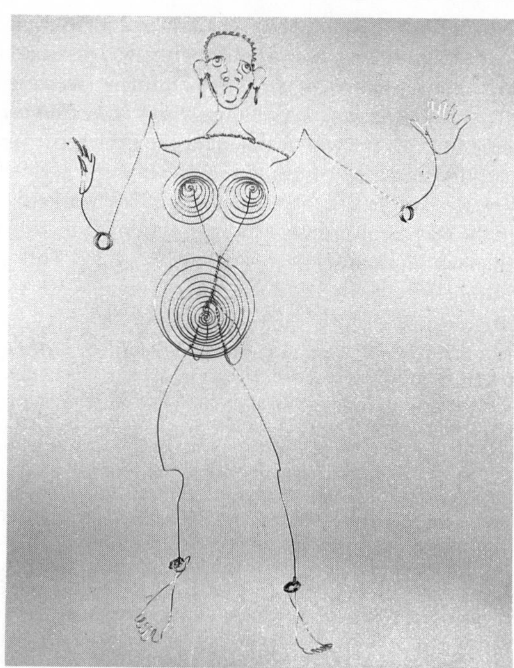

Josephine Baker: iron-wire construction (1927–9) by Alexander Calder (Museum of Modern Art, New York)

most celebrated performers in France: she became a darling of society, portrayed by such artists as Picasso and Calder, and acclaimed as an inspiration to American Blacks. In the 1930s she ran nightclubs, appeared in films, toured, and played the leading role in a production of Offenbach's *La créole* (1934). During this period her image became more cultured and she included more songs in her act; her theme song was Vincent Scotto's *J'ai deux amours*. After World War II, during which she assisted the French Resistance and entertained troops, she devoted much of her time to civil rights struggles and her 12 adopted children of different nationalities, her "Rainbow Tribe." Her popularity fluctuated after the 1940s, as a consequence of civil rights confrontations, controversial political alliances, and fewer successful performances.

BIBLIOGRAPHY

SouthernB
"Baker, Josephine," *CBY 1974*
J. Baker and J. Bouillon: *Josephine* (New York, 1977)
L. Haney: *Naked at the Feast: a Biography of Josephine Baker* (New York, 1981)

SAMUEL S. BRYLAWSKI

Baker, Julius (*b* Cleveland, OH, 23 Sept 1915). Flutist. After studying with William Kincaid at the Curtis Institute, he was principal flutist with the Pittsburgh SO (1941–3), the CBS SO (1943–50), the Chicago SO (1951–3), and the New York PO (1964–83). From 1946 until 1964 he performed regularly with the Bach Aria Group, and after that time continued to play with the ensemble, though less often. His edition of flute solos from Bach's cantatas, Passions, and oratorios (1972) is a standard source for flutists. He has given the American premières of concertos by Ibert (with the CBS SO, 1947) and Imbrie (with the New York PO, 1979). He became a member of the faculty at the Juilliard School in 1954 and at the Curtis Institute in 1980.

BIBLIOGRAPHY

P. Estevan: *Talking with Flutists* (n.p., 1976)

KAREN MONSON

Baker, Kenny [Kenneth] (*b* Jenkins, KY, 26 June 1926). Country-music fiddler. He began playing the fiddle as a youth by imitating his father, and by the age of 16 had learned to play the guitar. His earliest musical influences were the local fiddlers Marion Samner and Chubby Wise as well as the jazz musicians Django Reinhardt and Stephane Grappelli. In the mid-1950s he played with the singer Don Gibson for four years and in 1957 he became the fiddle player for Bill Monroe's Blue Grass Boys; he played with the group from 1957 to 1959, 1962 to 1963, and 1967 to 1984. Though he continues his interest in jazz, Baker is better known for his bluegrass style of playing, the cool professionalism of which has been emulated by other country musicians and is widely admired. He has made a number of recordings as a soloist, on the County label.

For illustration *see* BLUEGRASS MUSIC.

BIBLIOGRAPHY

A. Foster: "Kenny Baker," *Bluegrass Unlimited*, iii/6 (1968), 8

RONNIE PUGH

Baker, Robert S(tevens) (*b* Pontiac, IL, 7 July 1916). Organist and teacher. He graduated from Illinois Wesleyan University in 1938 and received the DSM degree from the Union Theological Seminary School of Sacred Music, New York, in 1944. His teachers included Clarence Dickinson, Tertius Noble, Frederick Stock, and David McK. Williams. He himself taught at the school from 1946. After a 1947 début at the national convention of the American Guild of Organists, in St. Louis, he quickly established himself as an outstanding recitalist. In 1957 he gave the opening recital in the First International Congress of Organists at Temple Church in London; and in 1966 he was one of two American organists to play during the 900th anniversary celebration season at Westminster Abbey. He has served as organist and choirmaster at various churches including Fifth Avenue Presbyterian, Temple Emanu-El, and St. James's Episcopal in New York and, since 1975, at the First Presbyterian Church there. He was dean of the School of Sacred Music (at Union Seminary) from 1961 to 1973, when the school was closed. It was immediately re-established as the Yale Institute of Sacred Music at Yale University, with Baker as director.

VERNON GOTWALS

Baker, Theodore (*b* New York, 3 June 1851; *d* Dresden, Germany, 13 Oct 1934). Music scholar and lexicographer. He received his early education in New York and the Boston area, and for a time was an organist in Concord, Massachusetts. Trained as a young man for a business career, he decided rather on music and in 1874 he went to Germany to study. He was awarded the doctorate at Leipzig in 1882; his dissertation, based on field studies among the Seneca Indians in New York state, was the first serious work on American Indian music. (It was shown to MacDowell by Henry Gilbert, and provided themes for MacDowell's Second ("Indian") Suite for orchestra.) Baker returned to the USA in 1891 and became literary editor and translator for the music publishing firm of G. Schirmer (1892), a post he held until his retirement in 1926, when he went back to Germany. Besides making many translations into English of theory and harmony texts, librettos, and articles (the last especially for the *Musical Quarterly*, published by Schirmer), Baker compiled *A*

Dictionary of Musical Terms (1895) and the *Biographical Dictionary of Musicians* (1900, rev. 7/1984 by N. Slonimsky), the work for which he is best known. (*See also* DICTIONARIES, §2.)

H. WILEY HITCHCOCK

Baklanov [Bakkis], **Georgy (Andreyevich)** (*b* Riga, Latvia, 17 Jan 1881; *d* Basle, Switzerland, 8 Dec 1938). Latvian baritone. He received his early training in Russia, and made his début at Kiev in 1903. He then sang in Russia from 1905 to 1909, and after that appeared in various theaters in Europe and the USA. He joined the Boston Opera in 1909, and made his American début, as Barnaba in *La Gioconda*, on 8 November 1909, in the inaugural performance at the Boston Opera House. He sang in Boston in 1909–11 and 1915–17 and was consistently a favorite with the audiences there. While under contract in Boston Baklanov also sang in New York at the Metropolitan Opera in an exchange between the two companies. He moved to the Chicago Opera in 1917 and remained there until 1926. In 1930 he sang the title role in a production of the "original" version of *Boris Godunov* with the Philadelphia Orchestra under Stokowski. For several years afterwards he was a mainstay of the Russian Opera Company of New York. Baklanov was greatly admired for his dramatic talents, and his voice was rich and vibrant.

BIBLIOGRAPHY

H. Lahee: *The Grand Opera Singers of Today* (Boston, 1912)
Q. Eaton: *The Boston Opera Company* (New York, 1965)

HAROLD BARNES/KATHERINE K. PRESTON

Baksa, Robert Frank (*b* New York, 7 Feb 1938). Composer. He grew up in Tucson, Arizona, and studied composition at the University of Arizona (BA 1969). His teachers were Henry Johnson and Robert McBridge in Arizona and Lukas Foss at the Berkshire Music Center. From 1962 he lived in New York and worked as a music copyist. In his music Baksa prefers to achieve expressiveness through craft rather than experimentation. He has written more than 400 works, including a large quantity of chamber music and pieces for keyboard. Best known are his choral works and songs, among them settings of Shakespeare, Housman, Bierce, and Dickinson. His major works include the Serenade for string orchestra (1964) and two operas, *Aria da capo* (after E. St. Vincent Millay, 1966, rev. 1978) and *Red Carnations* (after L. Hughes, 1969), which was commissioned by Lincoln Center for the Metropolitan Opera Studio.

Balada, Leonardo (*b* Barcelona, Spain, 22 Sept 1933). Composer. The son of a tailor, he was trained as both a tailor and a pianist and attended the Barcelona Conservatory. In 1956 he won a scholarship to study at the New York College of Music; he graduated from the Juilliard School in 1960. His teachers included Copland, Tansman, and Persichetti for composition, and Igor Markevich for conducting. He taught at the United Nations International School from 1963 to 1970, then joined the music faculty at Carnegie-Mellon University, Pittsburgh, where he was named professor in 1975. Most of his works incorporate Spanish melodic inflections and are based on triadic harmonies, though colored freely with tone clusters, dense overlapping textures, and other constructionist features. From about 1966 Balada's experimentation with these techniques dominated almost to the exclusion of melody, as in *Cuatris* for chamber ensemble (1969) and *Cumbres* for band (1971); the two orchestral *Homages*, to Casals and Sarasate (1975), however, mark a return to a national melodic style. Balada favors bright colors and aggressive rhythms. Hard-edged tone, whether on piano, tuned percussion, pizzicato strings, or staccato brass, is typical. Similarly, human speech is treated as a percussion instrument in the stage works *Maria Sabina* (1969) and *No-Res* (1974), for which Balada coined the term "tragifonias" to signify that they combine the declamatory style of Greek tragedy with symphonic forces. Several of his works have been recorded; he was the subject of a radio program "Leonardo Balada: his Music and Thought," first broadcast by New York's public radio station WNYC in 1982.

WORKS

Stage: Maria Sabina (C. J. Cola), nars, chorus, orch, 1969; No-Res (J. Paris), nars, chorus, orch, 1974; Hangman, Hangman! (chamber opera, 1, L. Balada), 1982; Zapata! (opera, 2, T. Capobianco, G. Roepke), 1982–4

Vocal: 4 Canciones de la Provincia de Madrid, song cycle, 1v, pf, 1962; 3 Cervantinas, song cycle, 1v, pf, 1967; Las Moradas (S. Teresa de Jesus), chorus, 7 insts, 1970; 3 Epitafios de Quevedo, song cycle, 1v, pf, 1971; Voices no. 1, 1972; Torquemada (L. Balada), B/Bar, 14 insts, chorus, 1980

Orch: Musica Tranquila, str, 1960; Pf Conc., 1964; Gui Conc., 1965; Guernica, 1966; Sinfonia en Negro: Homage to Martin Luther King, 1968; Bandoneon Conc., 1970; Cumbres, band, 1971; Sinfonia concertante, gui, orch, 1972; Steel Sym., 1972; Auroris, 1973; Ponce de Leon, nar, orch, 1973; Conc., pf, winds, perc, 1974; Homage to Casals, 1975; Homage to Sarasate, 1975; Conc., 4 gui, orch, 1976; 3 Anecdotes, castanets/wood perc, orch, 1977; Sardana: Dance of Catalonia, 1979; Quasi Adelita, sym. wind, 1981; Quasi un pasodoble, 1981; Vn Conc., 1982

Chamber and inst: Musica en 4 Tiempos, pf, 1959; Vn Sonata, 1960; Conc., vc, 9 insts, 1962; The Seven Last Words, org, 1963; Geometrias: no. 1, fl, ob, cl, bn, tpt, perc, 1966, no. 2, str qt, 1967, no. 3, bandoneon, 1968; Cuatris, 4 insts, 1969; Minis, bandoneon, 1969; End and Beginning, rock ens, 1970; Mosaico, brass qnt, 1970; Elementalis, org, 1972; Tresis, fl/vn, gui, vc, 1973; 3 Transparencies of a Bach Prelude, vc, pf, 1976; Transparency of Chopin's First Ballade, pf, 1977; Persistencies, pf, 1978; Preludis obstinants, pf, 1979; Sonata, 10 wind, 1980

Gui: Lento with Variation, 1960; Suite no. 1, 1961; 3 Divagaciones, 1962; Analogias, 1967; Apuntes, 4 gui, 1974; Minis, 1975; 4 Catalan Melodies, 1978; Persistencies, 1979

Principal publishers: Belwin-Mills, General, G. Schirmer

BIBLIOGRAPHY

P. E. Stone: "He Writes for the Audience, but on his own Terms," *New York Times* (21 Nov 1982), §II, 17, 22
Leonardo Balada (Pittsburgh, 1982) [brochure of Carnegie-Mellon University]
P. E. Stone: "Leonardo Balada's First Half Century," *Symphony*, xxxiv/3 (1983), 85

DAVID WRIGHT

Balanchine [Balanchin], **George** [Balanchivadze, Gyorgy Melitonovich] (*b* St. Petersburg [now Leningrad], Russia, 22 Jan 1904; *d* New York, 30 April 1983). Choreographer. He was trained at the Imperial Ballet in St. Petersburg, where he created his first dance before graduating in 1921. He danced in the ballet company of the State Theater of Opera and Ballet and choreographed for the Young Ballet, which he himself organized. In 1924 he left Russia for western Europe, where he joined Diaghilev's Ballets Russes. When that company disbanded after Diaghilev's death in 1929 he worked for various European companies and musical revues until 1933, when he came to the USA at the invitation of Lincoln Kirstein. Balanchine founded the School of American Ballet in New York in 1934, and with dancers trained there he formed several ballet companies: the American Ballet (1935–8), the American Ballet Caravan (1941), the Ballet Society (1946–8), and the New York City Ballet (founded 1948).

During the early 1920s Balanchine had studied piano and composition for three years at the Petrograd State Conservatory. He gave many of his ballets the titles of the musical compositions from which they were created, for example *Kammermusik no. 2*

(Hindemith) and *Divertimento no.15* (Mozart). Balanchine's musical collaboration with Stravinsky, which began in 1925 with his revision of the choreography of *Le chant du rossignol*, was one of the most fruitful partnerships in the history of art; Balanchine produced 39 works from Stravinsky's music, and among them are some of the most innovative ballets of the 20th century, including *Apollo* (1928), *Orpheus* (1948), and *Agon* (1957). Balanchine's first work on an American theme was *Alma mater* (1935), composed by Kay Swift and orchestrated by Morton Gould, whose music Balanchine later chose for *Clarinade* (1964). He also choreographed four musicals by Richard Rodgers, notably *On your Toes* (1936), and ballets to the music of Ives (*Ivesiana*, 1954), Hershy Kay (*Western Symphony*, 1954, and *Union Jack*, 1976), Sousa (*Stars and Stripes*, 1958), Gershwin (*Who Cares?*, 1970), and others. He was the author of *Balanchine's Complete Stories of the Great Ballets* (1954; rev. as *Balanchine's New Complete Stories of the Great Ballets*, 1968; rev. and enlarged 1977).

See also DANCE, §III, 1 and fig.3.

BIBLIOGRAPHY

"George Balanchine," *Dance Index*, iv/2–3 (1945) [whole issue]
"Balanchine, George," *CBY 1954*
B. Taper: *Balanchine* (New York, 1963; rev. and enlarged as *Balanchine: a Biography*, 1974; rev. and enlarged, 1984)
Y. Slonimsky, trans. J. Andrews: "Balanchine: the Early Years," *Ballet Review*, v/3 (1976) [whole issue]
N. Reynolds: *Repertory in Review: Forty Years of the New York City Ballet* (New York, 1977)
B. H. Haggin: *Discovering Balanchine* (New York, 1981)
Choreography by George Balanchine: a Catalogue of Works (New York, 1982, rev. 1984)
N. Goodwin: "Balanchine and Music," *Dance and Dancers*, no.404 (1983), 21
B. Hastings: *Choreographer and Composer: Theatrical Dance and Music in Western Culture* (Boston, 1983), 122–60 [collaborations with Stravinsky]
M.-C. Kahn, compiler, and S. Au, ed.: "Balanchine: a Selected Bibliography," *Ballet Review*, xi/2 (1983), 9; xi/3 (1983), 97
K. LaFave: "Point Counterpoint: a Musician's Look at Balanchine," *Ballet News*, iv/12 (1983), 22
A. Kisselgoff: Obituary, *New York Times* (1 May 1983)
R. Maiorano and V. Brooks: *Balanchine's 'Mozartiana': the Making of a Masterpiece* (New York, 1985)
S. Volkov, trans. A. W. Bouis: *Balanchine's Tchaikovsky: Interviews with George Balanchine* (New York, 1985)

SUSAN AU

Balatka, Hans [John] (*b* Hoffnungsthal, nr Olmütz [now Olomouc, Czechoslovakia], ? 26 Feb 1825; *d* Chicago, IL, 17 April 1899). Conductor and composer. He studied music at Hoffnungsthal and later at the gymnasium and university in Olmütz, where he was a choirboy at the cathedral. From 1845 he studied music (under Simon Sechter and Heinrich Proch) and law at the University of Vienna, where he worked as a music copyist and a tutor. During the 1848 revolution he sided with the Academic Legion, and following its defeat he fled Europe. He arrived in Chicago in 1849 and went to Milwaukee, where he organized a male chorus (1849) and a string quartet (1850). From 1850 to 1860 he was music director of the Milwaukee Musical Society and conducted its first concert (May 1850) and its first oratorio, Haydn's *The Creation* (July 1851, in German; for illustration *see* MILWAUKEE), and directed and sang the role of the Burgomaster in its first opera, Albert Lortzing's *Zar und Zimmermann* (April 1853). He also founded a singing-school and served as music director of the German theater (1855–60). Because of his reputation with the Milwaukee Musical Society he was asked to conduct music festivals in Cleveland, Cincinnati, Detroit, and Chicago. His performance of Mozart's Requiem (Chicago, 1860) led to his appointment as director of the Chicago Philharmonic Society (1860–69); while in Chicago he also conducted the Musical Union, the Oratorio Society, and other singing groups. In 1871–2 he again conducted the Milwaukee Musical Society, but he returned to Chicago where he remained except for a short stay in St. Louis (1877). In 1879 he founded the Balatka Academy of Musical Art, which was important to music education in Chicago in the late 19th and early 20th centuries. He was also active as a journalist and regularly contributed columns on music to the Chicago newspaper *Daheim*.

Balatka wrote several orchestral fantasies, a piano quartet, and other piano music; his vocal works include about 30 songs, pieces for chorus such as *The Power of Song* (1856) for double male chorus, and a *Festival Cantata* (1869) for soprano and orchestra. Apparently he had a remarkable memory for music; in Milwaukee he reconstructed the score of Lortzing's *Zar und Zimmermann* from memory after it had been stolen. Balatka's significance lay in his conducting and educational activities: he was one of the first important figures for the development of music in the Midwest.

BIBLIOGRAPHY

"Hans Balatka: a Musician's Recollections of Fifty Years," *Sunday Chicago Tribune* (25 Feb 1895)
The National Cyclopedia of American Biography, x (New York, 1900), 197
J. J. Schlicher: "Hans Balatka and the Milwaukee Musical Society," *Wisconsin Magazine of History*, xxvii (1943–4), 40
——: "The Milwaukee Musical Society in Times of Stress," *Wisconsin Magazine of History*, xxvii (1943–4), 178
Dictionary of Wisconsin Biography (Madison, WI, 1960), 23
T. H. Schleis: *Opera in Milwaukee: 1850–1900* (diss., U. of Wisconsin, 1974)

THOMAS H. SCHLEIS

Baldwin. Firm of instrument makers, notably of pianos and organs. It was founded in Cincinnati in 1862 by Dwight Hamilton Baldwin (*b* North East, PA, 15 Sept 1821; *d* Cincinnati, OH, 23 Aug 1899). Before moving to Cincinnati in 1857 to teach music in schools, he had attended the preparatory department at Oberlin College (1840–42), which he left to become a minister and school singing teacher in Lewis County, Kentucky, and Ripley, Ohio.

The firm D. H. Baldwin & Co. was formed in June 1873 when Lucien Wulsin (*b* Louisiana, 1845; *d* 4 Aug 1912), a clerk in Baldwin's firm since 1866, became a partner. A branch at Louisville was opened in 1877 by Robert A. Johnson (*b* Mt. Leigh, Adams County, OH, 1838; *d* Louisville, 28 March 1884), who became a partner in 1880. Three more partners joined in 1884 after the death of Johnson; these were Albert A. van Buren, George W. Armstrong, Jr. (*b* Cincinnati, 18 Aug 1857; *d* Cincinnati, 27 June 1932), and Clarence Wulsin (*b* Cincinnati, 1855; *d* Indianapolis, 26 Feb 1897), who ran the Indianapolis branch. From the 1860s to the late 1880s the firm was one of the largest dealers in keyboard instruments in the Midwest, and agent for such makers as Bourne, Decker, Estey, Fisher, and Steinway.

In 1889 a subsidiary of the firm, the Hamilton Organ Co., Chicago, began to manufacture reed organs, and by 1891 the Baldwin Piano Co., Cincinnati, also a subsidiary, was making low-priced upright pianos. By 1898 the parent company also owned the Ellington Piano Co. (1893) and the Valley Gem Piano Co. (originally the Ohio Valley Piano Co., founded in 1871 in Ripley, Ohio). John Warren Macy provided technical advice in the early years of manufacturing, developing a piano of high quality that won the Grand Prix at the Paris Exhibition in 1900.

In July 1903 Lucien Wulsin and George Armstrong bought control of the company, which was led in turn by Wulsin until 1912, Armstrong from 1912 to 1926, and Lucien Wulsin, Jr. (*b* Cincinnati, 17 March 1889; *d* Cincinnati, 13 Jan 1964) from 1926 to 1964.

In the late 1920s, in conjunction with the physics department of the University of Cincinnati, the firm began a research program in electronics that resulted in the introduction of the Baldwin electronic organ in 1947. The original models were designed by Dr. Winston E. Kock, the company's director of electronic research from 1936; some were intended for use in churches, but the majority of Baldwin organs are smaller instruments (many of them "spinet" organs with two staggered manuals) for the home.

In 1965 the firm introduced a newly designed concert grand piano, the model SD-10. By the 1970s the parent company, D. H. Baldwin & Co. (now under the chairmanship of the founder's grandson, Lucien Wulsin (*b* Cincinnati, 21 Sept 1916)), had expanded into a large corporation; the music subsidiary, Baldwin Piano & Organ Co., continued to manufacture grand and upright pianos and electronic organs at factories in Greenwood (Mississippi) and Conway, Truman, and Fayetteville (Arkansas). In the 1960s the firm experimented with a concert grand piano whose sound was electronically enhanced. The instrument proved impractical to produce on a large scale, but it served as a prototype for the firm's later, more successful electronic and computerized keyboard instruments. After 1960 the company extended its range of electronic instruments, first with electric harpsichords, then, later in the decade, with electric guitars and pianos. It acquired several manufacturing operations, including those of Gretsch (makers of guitars, drums, and amplifiers), Kustom (piano makers) and Ode (banjo makers); these were sold in 1980 to Charles Roy, who formed the Kustom–Gretsch Company in Nashville. Baldwin imports Couesnon wind instruments from France, Ramponi flutes from Italy, Dorado guitars (made by Kawai) from Japan, and, from Korea, a Howard piano, which is manufactured jointly by Baldwin and the Korean-American Musical Instrument Corporation. In 1963 the Baldwin corporation took over Bechstein, which retains its own identity and continues to make pianos in its own style. In 1983 the firm's parent company (now the Baldwin-United Corporation) filed for bankruptcy after sustaining heavy losses in the insurance business. The Baldwin Piano & Organ Co. was sold the following year to a group of the company's executives; these included Harold Smith, who became president of the company, and R. S. Harrison, who became its chairman.

BIBLIOGRAPHY

A. Dolge: *Pianos and their Makers*, i (Covina, CA, 1911/*R*1972), 345
Baldwin Papers, *OCHP*

CYNTHIA ADAMS HOOVER

Baldwin, Dalton (*b* Summit, NJ, 19 Dec 1931). Pianist. He began his formal musical training at the Juilliard School, but gained the BM from the Oberlin College Conservatory. He continued his studies in Paris with Boulanger and Madeleine Lipatti and in 1954 began there his long and successful partnership with the baritone Gérard Souzay. Concentrating primarily on the song repertory, Baldwin was coached by such composers as Poulenc, Sibelius, Martin, and Barber. He has participated in a number of first performances (notably of Rorem's *War Scenes* in 1969, with Souzay as soloist) and has accompanied such other eminent singers as Elly Ameling, Jessye Norman, Marilyn Horne, Frederica Von Stade, Glenda Maurice, and William Parker. Perhaps his finest achievements have been his recordings of the complete songs of Debussy, Fauré, Poulenc, and Ravel. Baldwin's playing is characterized by a softness of touch and a superb legato, which allow him to phrase with the singer; he is supportive without being too subdued.

BIBLIOGRAPHY

E. Keats: "The Art of Singing Lieder," *HiFi/MusAm*, xxxi/12 (1981), 28

RICHARD LeSUEUR

Baldwin, Samuel A(tkinson) (*b* Lake City, MN, 25 Jan 1862; *d* New York, 15 Sept 1949). Organist. He studied organ in St. Paul with Frank Wood and while still a teenager served as organist of the House of Hope Presbyterian Church. Early in the 1880s he went to Germany and studied with Gustav Merkel at the Royal Conservatory of Dresden, graduating in 1884. He then returned to the USA and held positions as a church organist in Chicago, St. Paul, and Minneapolis, where he also founded and directed choral societies. In 1895 he became organist of the Church of the Intercession in New York, and seven years later succeeded Buck at Holy Trinity Church in Brooklyn, a position he held until 1911.

In 1907 Baldwin was appointed to the new chair of music at the City College of New York (later becoming head of the department), and on 11 February 1908 presented the inaugural recital of the 84-stop Skinner organ in the Great Hall, an instrument he had designed. This was the first of 1362 bi-weekly programs which he gave over a span of 24 years; it has been estimated that as many as 70,000 heard him play each season. His repertory, comprising about 2000 works, included Bach, Mendelssohn, Rheinberger, and Widor, many transcriptions (particularly of works by Wagner), and new pieces by his American contemporaries Bartlett, Foote, Lemare, Rogers, and Thayer. Baldwin gave recitals throughout the Northeast and performed at expositions in Chicago (1893), St. Louis (1904), and San Francisco (1915). A founder and Fellow of the American Guild of Organists, he also wrote a history of the organization (1946). Baldwin's compositions include organ pieces, a symphony, some chamber pieces, and songs and anthems.

WILLIAM OSBORNE

Bales, Richard (Henry Horner) (*b* Alexandria, VA, 3 Feb 1915). Composer and conductor. He graduated in 1936 from the Eastman School, where Howard Hanson was a decisive influence in shaping his interest in American music, and continued studies at the Juilliard School (1939–41) and with Serge Koussevitzky at the Berkshire Music Center (summer 1940). His musical activities have centered on the National Gallery of Art (Washington, DC) where he became the first music director in 1942 and founder and conductor of the National Gallery Orchestra the following year; in this position, which he has likened to that of an 18th-century Kapellmeister, he organized the National Gallery's Sunday evening concerts and contributed to them both as conductor and composer. His promotion of American music, particularly through the annual American Music Festival which he initiated at the Gallery in the spring of 1944, has provided opportunities for performers and composers from all over the country. Most of his compositions, characterized by pleasant melodies and a clear tonal idiom, were written for presentation at the Gallery. He retired from the National Gallery position on 3 August 1985.

WORKS

Orch: National Gallery Suites I, 1943, II, 1944, III "American Design," 1957, IV "American Chronicle," 1965; The Spirit of Engineering, suite, 1983–4; a few other works

Vocal: 3 cantatas [based on 18th- and 19th-century American music incl. patriotic and Civil War songs]: The Confederacy, 1953, The Republic, 1955, The Union, 1956; A Set of Jade (ancient Chin.), song cycle, 1v, pf, 1964, orchd, 1968; several songs and choral pieces

Chamber: Str Qt, 1944; pf suite, 1963; To Elmira with Love, pf suite, 1972, orchd, 1983; Diary Pages, 2 pf, 1978

Transcrs., arrs., most for orch

8 documentary film scores

Principal publisher: Peer-Southern

BIBLIOGRAPHY

"Bales, Richard," *Compositores de América/Composers of the Americas*, ed. Pan American Union, xv (Washington, DC, 1969)

M. Hunter: "A Music Maker for Sunday Nights," *New York Times* (6 Oct 1984)

JOANNE SHEEHY HOOVER

Balfa, Dewey (*b* Bayou Grand Louis, nr Mamou, LA, 20 March 1927). Fiddler and singer. He began playing fiddle at the age of 13 and later formed the Balfa Brothers Cajun band with his brothers Will, Burkeman, Harry, and Rodney. Their instrumentation consisted of two fiddles, a guitar, a triangle, and often an accordion, all typical of traditional Cajun music (*see* EUROPEAN-AMERICAN MUSIC, §II, 2(i)). The group was in great demand during the popularity of dance halls in the 1940s and was enthusiastically received at the Newport Folk Festival of 1964. Balfa then returned to Louisiana, where his activities as a teacher, performer, and advocate of Cajun music were influential in its national revival. Among his performances in the USA have been several at the Smithsonian Institution's Festival of American Folklife; he has also performed abroad, and his band has remained active despite the deaths of Will and Rodney Balfa in 1978. In 1982 he was awarded a National Heritage Fellowship by the NEA.

BIBLIOGRAPHY

B. Ancelet: "Dewey Balfa: Cajun Music Ambassador," *Louisiana Life*, i/4 (1981), 78

J. Broven: *South to Louisiana: the Music of the Cajun Bayous* (Gretna, LA, 1983)

B. J. Ancelet and E. M. Morgan: *The Makers of Cajun Music* (Austin, TX, 1984)

DANIEL SHEEHY

Ball, Ernest R. (*b* Cleveland, OH, 21 July 1878; *d* Santa Ana, CA, 3 May 1927). Composer and singer. After studying music at the Cleveland Conservatory he went to New York, where he became a pianist in vaudeville theaters, and later staff pianist and composer for Witmark. His first success was the ballad *Will you love me in December as you do in May?*, written in 1905 to lyrics by Jimmy Walker. Many of his most popular songs thereafter were composed for the Irish tenors John McCormack and Chauncey Olcott, with whom he also collaborated. Ball composed some 400 songs, including such standards as *Mother Machree* (1910), *When Irish eyes are smiling* (1913), and *A little bit of heaven* (1914). Much of the last decade of his life was spent performing in vaudeville.

BIBLIOGRAPHY

J. Burton: "Honor Roll of Popular Songwriters: Ernest R. Ball," *The Billboard*, lxi (14 May 1949), 38

DALE COCKRELL

Ballad opera. A form of opera that originated in England in the 18th century, in which spoken dialogue, usually of a humorous, satirical, or pastoral nature, alternates with strophic songs set to simple traditional or popular tunes. The first ballad opera known to have been performed in America was *Flora, or Hob in the Well*, which was given at the Courtroom in Charleston on 18 February 1735. By 1752 several other English ballad operas had become popular in America, including *The Beggar's Opera*, *Damon and Phillida*, *The Devil to Pay*, *The Honest Yorkshireman*, *The Mock Doctor*, and *The Virgin Unmasked*. Such works continued to dominate the American musical stage until the Revolution, though a number of newer forms, such as the ballad-burletta (in which spoken dialogue was replaced by rhymed recitation and concerted pieces in imitation of light Italian comic opera were added – for example, *Midas*), the pasticcio (which used music from the works of named composers – usually English – alongside traditional songs, as in *Love in a Village*, *Maid of the Mill*, *Lionel and Clarissa*), and operas written by a single composer (Charles Dibdin's *The Padlock*), had been performed in America by 1772.

The first native American to produce a ballad opera was James Ralph, who wrote *The Fashionable Lady* in 1730 after moving to London. In 1767 the *Philadelphia Gazette* announced that Andrew Barton's full-length comic opera, *The Disappointment, or The Force of Credulity* (ed. in RRAM, iii-iv, 1976), would be performed on 20 April. On 16 April, however, the *Gazette* reported that the opera "as it contains personal Reflections, is unfit for the stage." No 18th-century performance has been documented, but the libretto was published in 1767 and a second edition followed in 1796. The work, based on fact, is a social satire, in which several prominent Philadelphians are made to look foolish in a treasure-hunting scheme. Tunes are indicated for 18 airs and a dance; of these at least 13 are ballad tunes (most had previously been used in other operas), and at least four are contemporary popular songs. The tunes range in complexity from the simple *Yankee Doodle* to Thomas Arne's air *My fond shepherds*, reflecting the tendency, then current in England, to draw music from a variety of sources.

Although theatrical entertainment was forbidden in America during the Revolution, British soldiers in New York between 1778 and 1783 regularly presented shows, including ballad operas, for loyalist inhabitants and occupying troops. *The Blockheads, or Fortunate Contractor*, published in London in 1782 but described as "performed in New York," was probably part of their repertory. The author of the work is unknown, but the subject matter and the political sentiments expressed point to a loyalist or even a British soldier. 16 songs are indicated, but no titles or first lines are provided; it is probable, to judge from the statement "composed by several of the most eminent masters in Europe" on the title page, that the work was a pasticcio.

Theater was gradually reestablished after the Revolution, but by then pure ballad opera had been succeeded by the pasticcio. For the most part the music was still simple and unpretentious, but occasionally pieces in the more cultivated and ornate *galant* style were used. Royall Tyler's comic opera *May Day in Town, or New-York in an Uproar* was performed on 19 May 1787; neither libretto nor songs are extant, but the music was "compiled from the most eminent masters."

Another pasticcio, *The Better Sort, or The Girl of Spirit*, probably by William Hill Brown, was published in Boston in 1789, but only the prologue was performed. The plot is thin, but provides opportunities for the principal characters to discuss various social and political questions. Only seven of the 18 songs carry an indication of the tunes to be used for them: since theatrical presentations were prohibited in Boston until 1792, there was little chance that the work would be performed, and the author probably felt it unnecessary to supply tunes for all the songs. Of the eight tunes given (one song is furnished with an alternative tune), two are from popular songs and three have ballad origins; five had already appeared in other contemporary stage works.

William Dunlap's one-act afterpiece *Darby's Return*, first performed in New York on 24 November 1789, was written as a sequel to *The Poor Soldier*, probably the most popular opera in the USA at that time. *The Poor Soldier* is a conservative work, about two-thirds of its music having been taken from ballad sources, mostly Irish. Dunlap's text is entirely in verse, and his musical choices are also conservative; the songs that open and close the work are both from folk sources – in fact the opening tune is also that of the finale of *The Poor Soldier*. *Darby's Return* was moderately successful, largely owing to the performance of Thomas Wignell in the role of Darby.

Peter Markoe's *The Reconciliation, or The Triumph of Nature* (Philadelphia, 1790) was accepted by the Old American Company but never staged. Three airs, one with music (the tune is from Arne's *Artaxerxes*), were printed in the *Universal Asylum and Columbian Magazine* in June 1790, the first printing of music from any American opera (see illustration). The same magazine gave a critical report of the opera, concluding that "the want of humour, of variety in the dialogue, and the length of some of the soliloquies, render it less fit for the stage than for the closet."

Opening of the song "Truth from thy radiant throne look down" (set to music from Thomas Arne's opera "Artaxerxes") from Peter Markoe's comic opera "The Reconciliation, or the Triumph of Nature" (Universal Asylum and Columbian Magazine, 4 June 1790)

All 11 songs in the work use tunes that were widely available in published sources; five are ballads, and nine had appeared in other 18th-century operas. The influence of the *galant* style is very clear in the choice of music.

During the last decade of the 18th century both ballad operas and pasticcios were superseded by operas in which the majority of the music was newly written by a single composer. Benjamin Carr, Pelissier, Reinagle, and James Hewitt, for example, wrote new music for works performed in their respective theaters. An occasional reference to the use of pasticcio techniques is found in newspaper descriptions: *Little Yankee Sailor* was presented in Philadelphia in 1795 with music "selected from William Shield, James Hook, Rayner Taylor, Charles Dibdin, etc.," and arranged by George Gillingham. The most popular English ballad operas continued to be performed into the early 19th century, but no American ballad opera or pasticcio achieved lasting success. Whereas ballad opera in England originated as a vehicle for satire on popular Italian opera, and thus made a statement in musical terms about musical matters, in the USA it served only as a framework for the personal, social, or political statements of playwrights. Its importance as a genre, however, lies in its contribution to the establishment of a musical tradition in the American theater.

See also MUSICAL THEATER, §I; OPERA, §1; and POPULAR MUSIC, §I, 1.

BIBLIOGRAPHY

O. G. T. Sonneck: "Early American Operas," *SIMG*, vi (1904–5), 428–95
——: *Early Opera in America* (New York, 1915/*R*1963)
M. C. Diebels: *Peter Markoe (1752?–1792): a Philadelphia Writer* (Washington, DC, 1944)
T. Ridgway: "Ballad Opera in Philadelphia in the Eighteenth Century," *Church Music and Musical Life in Pennsylvania*, ed. Committee on Historical Research of the Pennsylvania Society of the Colonial Dames of America, iii, pt.2 (Philadelphia, 1947)
E. I. Zimmerman: *American Opera Librettos, 1767–1825: the Manifestation and Result of the Imitative Principle in American Literary Form* (diss., U. of Tennessee, 1972)
W. Rubsamen, ed.: *The Ballad Opera: a Collection of 171 Original Texts of Musical Plays Printed in Photo-facsimile* (New York, 1974)
J. Layng: "America's First Opera," *Opera Journal*, ix/3 (1976), 3
D. McKay: "*The Fashionable Lady*: the First Opera by an American," *MQ*, lxv (1979), 360
P. H. Virga: *The American Opera to 1790* (Ann Arbor, MI, 1982)
C. Rabson: " 'Disappointment' Revisited: Unweaving the Tangled Web," *American Music*, i/1 (1983), 12; ii/1 (1984), 1

SUSAN L. PORTER

Ballantine, Edward (*b* Oberlin, OH, 6 Aug 1886; *d* Oak Bluffs, MA, 2 July 1971). Composer. He studied at Harvard University (BA 1907) with Spalding and Converse, then went to Berlin, where he was a student of Artur Schnabel, Rudolf Ganz, and Philippe Rüfer (1907–9). In 1912 he was appointed to the music faculty of Harvard, and remained there until his retirement in 1947. His music, cast in a post-Romantic, tonal, and accessible style, is often marked by humor, occasionally by a satirical eclecticism. These traits are most apparent in his best-known pieces, two sets of piano variations on *Mary had a little lamb* (1924, 1943), in which each variation is in the style of a different composer, and in the *Four Lyrical Satires* for voice and piano. Besides piano pieces, songs, and a violin sonata, Ballantine's works include a musical play, *The Lotos Eaters* (1907), the orchestral *Prelude to "The Delectable Forest"* (1914), *The Eve of St. Agnes* (1917), *By a Lake in Russia* (1922), and *From the Garden of Hellas* (1923), and the choral *Song for a Future* and *Lake Werna's Water*.

His principal publishers were O. Ditson, G. Schirmer, and A. P. Schmidt.

H. WILEY HITCHCOCK

Ballard, James (*fl* 1830–50). Music teacher and writer, active in New York. He taught music in New York during the 1840s; advertisements in E. A. Poe's *Broadway Journal* (1845–6) describe him as "professor of the guitar, singing and the flute," with a studio at 135 (later 15) Spring Street. The third (and earliest known) edition of his work *The Elements of Guitar-playing* appeared in 1838; it is modeled on Fernando Sor's *Method for the Spanish Guitar* (in an English translation of 1832), and its unusually detailed text contains much valuable information about guitar technique of the period. A unique feature is Ballard's theory of teaching chords through "chord positions," an attempt to relate diatonic harmony directly to the fingerboard of the instrument. Ballard was also the author of a second method, *Ballard's Guitar Preceptor*, published about the same time, and he composed numerous arrangements for the instrument.

BIBLIOGRAPHY

P. Danner: "A Noteworthy Early American Guitar Treatise," *Soundboard*, ix (1981), 270

PETER DANNER

Ballard, Louis W(ayne) [Honganózhe] (*b* Miami, OK, 8 July 1931). Composer and educator. In his childhood Ballard, who is of Quapaw-Cherokee descent (Honganózhe is a Quapaw name), absorbed a large repertory of American Indian music, and subsequently he systematically studied the musics of many tribes. He studied composition at Tulsa University (BA 1954, MA 1962) and privately with Milhaud, Castelnuovo-Tedesco, and Surinach. While in Tulsa he taught in local schools and directed church choirs. He has won three NEA composer grants (1967, 1971, 1973) and a Ford Foundation study grant (1970), and has received commissions from the Harkness Ballet, the Tulsa PO, the St. Paul Chamber Orchestra, and the American Composers Orchestra, among others. From 1962 to 1966 he was music chairman at the Institute of American Indian Arts in Santa Fe (performing-arts chairman, 1966–9), and he was a percussionist in the Santa Fe SO (1962–4). From 1969 to 1979 he supervised the music curriculum in the US Bureau of Indian Affairs school system, and from 1976 to 1982 was the chairman of minority concerns in music education for New Mexico, by appointment of the Music Educators National Conference. He has written two textbooks on American Indian music, *My Music Reaches to the Sky* (1973) and *Music of North American Indians* (1975), as well as several articles, and he has developed extensive teaching material based on American Indian music including two kits, *Oklahoma Indian Chants for the Classroom* (1970) and *American Indian Music for the Classroom* (1972). His compositions combine American Indian melodic and rhythmic material (and occasionally Indian instruments) with mainstream 20th-century compositional techniques. He sometimes uses the pseudonym Joe Miami.

WORKS

3 ballets, incl. The Four Moons, orch, 1967

Large ens: Fantasy Aborigine I–IV, orch, 1964, str, 1976, orch, 1977, orch, 1984; Scenes from Indian Life, orch, 1964, arr. band, 1970; Why the Duck has a Short Tail (L. W. Ballard, R. Ballard, after American Indian myth), nar, orch, 1969 [staged as ballet, 1970]; Devil's Promenade, orch, 1972–3; Ocotillo Festival Ov., band, 1973; Siouxiana, ww, 1973; Incident at Wounded Knee, small orch, 1974; Ishi, America's Last Civilized Man, orch, 1975; Wamus-77, band, 1977; Nighthawk Keetowah, band, 1978; Xactce'oyan [Companion of Talking God], orch, 1982

Inst: Str Trio, 1959; American Indian Pf Preludes, 1963; Rhapsody for 4 Bn, 1963; Ritmo Indio, ww qnt, 1969; Cacega ayuwipi [The Decorative Drums], 4/5 perc, 1970; Katcina Dances, vc, pf, 1970; Midwinter Fires, cl, fl/Sioux fl, pf, 1970; Desert Trilogy, 8 insts, 1971; Kateri Tekawitha (L. W. Ballard), Mez, str qnt, wind qnt, 1973; Rio Grande Sonata, vn, pf, 1976; City of Silver, pf fantasy, 1981; City of Fire, pf fantasy, 1984

Cantatas: Espíritu de Santiago (L. W. Ballard), SATB, fl, gui, pf, 1963; The Gods Will Hear (L. New), SATB, orch/pf, 1964; Portrait of Will Rogers (L. W. Ballard, after Rogers), nar, SATB, orch/pf, opt. dancers, 1972; Thus Spake Abraham (Bible, L. W. Ballard, A. Lincoln), SATB, pf, 1976

Other: Sacred Ground, film score, 1977; teaching pieces

Principal publishers: Belwin-Mills, Bourne, New Southwest

BIBLIOGRAPHY

W. Terry: "World of Dance, The Four Moons," *Saturday Review* (18 Nov 1967), 60 [review]

M. Branham and M. Powers: "Louis Ballard, New World Composer of the Southwest," *New Mexico Magazine*, l/5 (1972), 33

J. Katz: "Louis Ballard, Quapaw/Cherokee Composer," *This Song Remembers* (Boston, 1980), 132

GENEVIEVE VAUGHN

Ballet. A type of theatrical dance; *see* DANCE, §§II, 2; III, 1, 2.

Balliett, Whitney (*b* New York, 17 April 1926). Jazz critic. After graduating from Cornell University (BA 1951), he joined the staff of the *New Yorker*. For the *Saturday Review* (1953–7) and then for the *New Yorker* he contributed reviews of jazz concerts, recordings, and books, and interviews with jazz musicians; these articles have been published separately in a continuing series of books (from 1959). He also published poetry in the same magazines and in *Atlantic Monthly* during the 1950s.

Balliett's writings are eloquent and highly stylized. The interviews portray his subjects with dignity, and his reviews often create effects that parallel those of the music being discussed. At his best, in an assessment of style or a description of an improvisation, Balliett has provided insights more penetrating than many formal musical analyses.

WRITINGS

The Sound of Surprise (New York, 1959/*R*1978)

Dinosaurs in the Morning (Philadelphia, 1962/*R*1978)

Such Sweet Thunder (Indianapolis, 1966)

Ecstasy at the Onion (New York, 1971)

Improvising (New York, 1977)

American Singers (New York, 1979)

BARRY KERNFELD

Ballin' the jack. A black social and theatrical dance performed in a serpentine pattern, thought to have originated in Sea Island, Georgia. The name comes from railroad language: "jack" was a colloquial southern term for locomotive and "high balling" a hand signal used to start rolling. The dance was introduced to theater audiences as a dance-song routine of the same name in the black musical *Darktown Follies* (1913, music Chris Smith, lyrics Jim Burris) and the *Ziegfeld Follies*. Burris's lyrics describe the movements:

> First you put your two knees close up tight
> Then you sway 'em to the left, then you sway 'em to the right
> Step around the floor kind of nice and light
> Then you twis' around and twis' around with all your might
> Stretch your lovin' arms straight out in space
> Then you do the Eagle Rock with style and grace
> Swing your foot way 'round then bring it back
> Now that's what I call "Ballin' the Jack."

The pelvic twisting motion mentioned in the fourth line caused enough scandal to inspire this line in a lyric for the James P. Johnson tune *Stop it, Joe* (1917): "I don't mind being in your company, but don't you Eagle Rock or Ball the Jack with me . . . this ain't no hall room, it's a ball room." (*See also* EAGLE ROCK.)

BIBLIOGRAPHY

M. Stearns and J. Stearns: *Jazz Dance: the Story of American Vernacular Dance* (New York, 1968)

L. F. Emery: *Black Dance in the United States from 1619 to 1970* (Palo Alto, CA, 1972)

LINDA MOOT, PAULINE NORTON

Ballou, Esther (Williamson) (*b* Elmira, NY, 17 July 1915; *d* Chichester, England, 12 March 1973). Composer, pianist, and educator. She studied piano and organ as a child and took degrees at Bennington (Vermont) College (1937), Mills College (1938), and the Juilliard School (1943); at Bennington she took composition lessons from Luening, and at Juilliard from Wagenaar and privately from Riegger. While in California she composed ballets for Louise Kloepper and José Limón and toured nationally as a pianist with various dance companies. From 1959 she taught at the American University, Washington, DC; during her career as an educator she put forward experimental methods for theory teaching at the college level. Her music, according to her own description, "tends towards classicism in that it stresses clarity of design and directness of expression." In 1963 she became the first American woman composer to have a work (the Capriccio for violin and piano) given its first performance at the White House. Her manuscripts, which include a pedagogical text, *Creative Explorations of Musical Elements* (1971), are in the American University Library, Washington, DC.

WORKS

Orch: Suite, chamber orch, 1939; Intermezzo, 1943; Blues, 1944; Pf Conc. no.1, 1945; Prelude and Allegro, pf, str, 1951; Concertino, ob, str, 1953; Adagio, bn, str, 1960; In memoriam, ob, str, 1960; Gui Conc., 1964; Pf Conc., no.2, 1964; Serenade, gui, str, 1964, withdrawn; Konzertstück, va, orch, 1969

Choral: Bag of Tricks (I. Orgel), SSAA, 1956; The Beatitudes, SATB, org, 1957; A Babe is Born (15th century), SATB, 1959; May the words of my mouth (Bible), SATB, 1965; I will lift up mine eyes, S, SATB, org, 1965; O the sun comes up-up-up in the opening sky (E. E. Cummings), SSA, 1966; Hear us!, SATB, brass, perc, 1967

Other vocal: 4 Songs (A. E. Housman), S, vc, pf, 1937; What if a much of a which of a wind (Cummings), S, Bar, B, wind qnt, 1959; Street Scenes (H. Champers), S, pf, 1960; Bride (Sorenson), S, org, 1962; Early American Portrait (E. Peck), 5 songs, S, chamber orch, 1962; 5-4-3 (Cummings), Mez, va, harp, 1966; other songs

Chamber: Impertinence, cl, pf, 1936; In Blues Tempo, cl, pf, 1937; Nocturne, str qt, 1937; War Lyrics, pf, tpt, perc, 1940; Christmas Variations, ob, hpd, 1954; Pf Trio, 1955, rev. 1957; Divertimento, str qt, 1958; Vn Sonata, 1959; A Passing Word, fl, vc, pf, ob, 1960; Capriccio, vn, pf, 1963; Dialogues, ob, gui, 1966, rev. 1969; Elegy, vc, 1968; Prism, str trio, 1969; Romanzo, vn, pf, 1969; several other works for 1–8 insts

Kbd: Dance Suite, pf, 1937; 2 pf sonatinas, 1941, 1964; 2 sonatas, 2 pf, 1943, 1958; Beguine, 8 hands, 1950, arr. 2 pf, 1957, arr. orch, 1960; Music for the Theatre, 2 pf, 1952; Pf Sonata, 1955; Variations, Scherzo, and Fugue, 1959; Rondino, hpd, 1961; Passacaglia and Toccata, org, 1962; Variations for Gail, pf, 1964; For Art Nagle on his Birthday, pf, 1968; Impromptu, org, 1968; other works incl. several teaching pieces

BIBLIOGRAPHY

R. D. Ringenwald: *The Music of Esther Williamson Ballou: an Analytical Study* (thesis, American U., 1960)

JAMES R. HEINTZE/R

Ball State University. State university in Muncie, Indiana, founded in 1918. Its music courses flourished during the 1930s. In 1983 the school of music enrolled approximately 600 students, of whom about 450 were undergraduates, and had a faculty of 65. BA, BM, BS, MA, MM, and DA degrees are offered in performance, theory-composition, music education, and music history (*see also* LIBRARIES AND COLLECTIONS, §3).

WILLIAM McCLELLAN

Balmer, Charles (*b* Mühlhausen, Germany, 21 Sept 1817; *d* St. Louis, MO, 15 Dec 1892). Organist, conductor, composer, and publisher. A child prodigy, he studied at the Göttingen Conservatory of Music and was assistant conductor there in 1833. He immigrated to the USA in 1836, settling in St. Louis in 1839. The following year he conducted the orchestra of the Jesuit College and was instrumental conductor of the St. Louis Sacred Music Society; he founded the St. Louis Oratorio Society in 1846 and served as its director until it ceased activities. He was organist at Christ Episcopal Church for 46 years. In 1848 he founded the BALMER & WEBER MUSIC HOUSE with Carl Heinrich Weber. He composed a large number of piano pieces, songs, organ works, and choral works, using a number of pseudonyms, including Charles Remlab, T. van Berg, Alphonse Leduc, Charles Lange, Henry Werner, August Schumann, T. Meyer, and F. B. Rider. Balmer conducted the music at Lincoln's funeral in Springfield, Illinois, in 1865.

BIBLIOGRAPHY

E. C. Krohn: *Missouri Music* (New York, 1971)

——: *Music Publishing in the Middle Western States before the Civil War* (Detroit, 1972)

JAMES M. BURK

Balmer & Weber Music House. Firm of music publishers. CHARLES BALMER (1817–92) and Carl Heinrich Weber (*b* Koblenz Germany, 3 March 1819; *d* Denver, CO, 6 Sept 1892) came to the USA in the 1830s; Balmer became an organist and conductor, Weber a cellist, and their early compositions were published in the East. In 1848 the two men entered into partnership and opened a shop in St. Louis. Gradually the firm absorbed most of its competitors including Nathaniel Phillips, James & J. R. Phillips, H. A. Sherburne, H. Pilcher & Sons, W. M. Harlow, Cardella & Co., and Compton & Doan. By the end of the century it had an exceptionally large and flourishing business in the publication of parlor music.

After the death of the partners, the business was managed by a company in which the Balmer family predominated. Lack of efficient direction and the rise of Kunkel Brothers, Shattinger, and Thiebes-Stierlin caused the business to deteriorate, and in 1907 the catalogue was sold to Leo Feist of New York. He attempted to ship the sheet music to New York down the Mississippi, but the vessel foundered off the coast of New Jersey and its cargo sank.

BIBLIOGRAPHY

E. C. Krohn: *Missouri Music* (New York, 1971)

——: *Music Publishing in the Middle Western States before the Civil War* (Detroit, 1972), 27

ERNST C. KROHN/R

Balsam, Artur (*b* Warsaw, Poland, 8 Feb 1906). Pianist. He studied in Łódź, where he made his début at the age of 12, and at the Berlin State Academy of Music. He received first prize in the International Piano Competition in Berlin in 1930, and then won the Mendelssohn Prize in 1931. He first toured North America in 1932 with Yehudi Menuhin, and immigrated after

Hitler came to power in Germany in 1933. He has given numerous recitals since 1918 and made many appearances with orchestras (including a series of six Mozart concertos for the BBC during the 1956 Mozart bicentenary); but he is most celebrated as an ensemble pianist, who most remarkably combines sensibility and a capacity for listening with strength of personality. Balsam has recorded about 250 works in the solo and chamber literature, including all Haydn's and Mozart's music for solo piano, all Mozart's sonatas with violin, and all Beethoven's sonatas with violin and cello. His partners in concert, and often on records, have included Francescatti, Goldberg, Fuchs, Rostropovich, Szigeti, Totenberg, Milstein, David Oistrakh, and Leonid Kogan. In 1960 he joined the Albeneri Trio (which then became the Balsam–Kroll–Heifetz Trio) in place of Erich Itor Kahn. A distinguished teacher, he has taught at the Eastman School of Music, Boston University, and the Manhattan School of Music; he has also led summer sessions for more than 30 years at Kneisel Hall in Blue Hill, Maine. Among his pupils is Murray Perahia, with whom he has performed. He edited and composed cadenzas for Mozart's piano concertos K37, 39–41, 175, and 238.

MICHAEL STEINBERG/DENNIS K. McINTIRE

Balthrop, Carmen Arlen (*b* Washington, DC, 14 May 1948). Soprano. She studied at the University of Maryland, College Park (BM 1970), and at the Catholic University of America (MM 1971). In 1975 she won first place in the Metropolitan Opera Auditions; the same year she sang (and in 1976 recorded) the title role of Scott Joplin's *Treemonisha* with the Houston Opera Company. After performing in Francesco Cavalli's *L'egisto* at Wolf Trap (1977), she made her début at the Metropolitan Opera as Pamina and then appeared as Roggiero in Rossini's *Tancredi* with the New York City opera in 1978. She is also active as a recitalist.

BIBLIOGRAPHY

SouthernB

P. Turner: *Afro-American Singers* (Minneapolis, 1977)

DOMINIQUE-RENÉ DE LERMA

Baltic-American music. *See* EUROPEAN-AMERICAN MUSIC, §III, 3.

Baltimore. The largest city in Maryland (pop.786,775, ranked ninth largest in the USA; metropolitan area 2,174,023). First settled in 1662, Baltimore became a town in 1730; by 1800, its population of more than 26,000 was larger than that of the state's capital, Annapolis. Baltimore has a music history which can be traced back to the American Revolutionary period. As early as 1784 concerts in the city were advertised in the press. These early programs were of great diversity, including works by Bach, Dittersdorf, Haydn, František Kočzwara, I. G. Pleyel, G. B. Viotti, and J. B. Vanhal, as well as by such musicians as Alexander Reinagle and Rayner Taylor, who had recently come to the USA and lived in Baltimore.

In 1794, a year after Benjamin Carr had established a music shop in Philadelphia, his father Joseph and brother Thomas inaugurated a similar enterprise in Baltimore. The first publication of *The Star-Spangled Banner* in sheet music form was by Joseph Carr in November 1814 (for illustration *see* PATRIOTIC MUSIC, fig.1).

1. Education. 2. Orchestras. 3. Concert organizations, halls. 4. Opera.

1. EDUCATION. The Peabody Conservatory (known first as the Academy of Music) was founded on 12 February 1857 by the philanthropist George Peabody, making it technically the oldest educational institution of its kind in the USA. Provision was made for it as part of the Peabody Institute, together with an extensive library, a fine-arts gallery, and a forum for scholars' and scientists' lectures. Construction of the original building (see fig.1), begun in 1861, was completed in 1866, but instruction was not offered until 1868. The conservatory's first director was Lucien Southard (1868–71). He was succeeded in 1871 by the Danish-born composer and conductor Asger Hamerik, a former pupil of Berlioz, whose distinguished tenure lasted until 1898. Other directors have been Harold Randolf (1898–1927), Otto Ortmann (1928–41), Reginald Stewart (1941–58), Peter Mennin (1958–62), Charles Kent (1963–8), Richard Franko Goldman (1968–77), Elliott W. Galkin (1977–82), and Robert O. Pierce, who succeeded Galkin as dean and acting director and was named director in 1983. From its earliest period, when Hamerik engaged the American poet and flutist Sidney Lanier to play in the Peabody Orchestra and give a series of lectures on Shakespeare, the activities of the conservatory have been imaginative and extensive. The faculty has included Nicolas Nabokov, Nadia Boulanger, Henry Brant, Earle Brown, Elliott Carter, Henry Cowell, Leon Fleisher, Ralph Gomberg, Ernst Krenek, Louis Persinger, Vittorio Rieti, and Benjamin Lees. The Institute, which attracts students from all over the world, became affiliated with the Johns Hopkins University in 1977, and offers instruction at undergraduate and graduate levels (including a

1. The Academy of Music (Peabody Conservatory) on North Howard Street, Baltimore: engraving, late 19th century

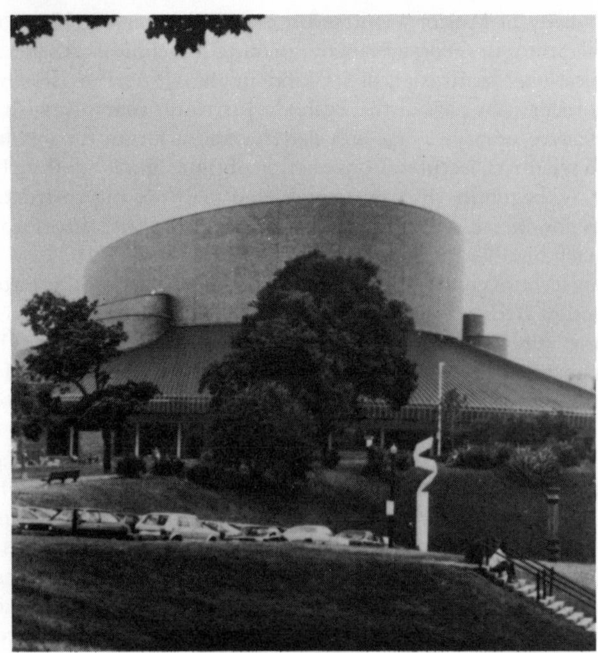

2. *The Joseph Meyerhoff Symphony Hall, Baltimore, opened in 1982*

DMA). It has an enrollment of approximately 430, as well as a preparatory division of 2000 students.

There are about two dozen institutions of higher education in Baltimore and its environs besides the Peabody Institute. The Johns Hopkins University and Goucher College both organize concert series with internationally recognized performers. The Baltimore Chamber Music Society (founded in 1950), in cooperation with the Baltimore Museum of Art, sponsors a controversial series of concerts consisting almost entirely of 20th-century works. In addition the Peabody Conservatory has since 1977 offered an annual series of concerts of contemporary music under the direction of Frederik Prausnitz. Res Musica was established in 1980 to sponsor performances of works by young and local composers.

2. ORCHESTRAS. In 1914 Baltimore became the first city in the USA to found an orchestra on a municipal appropriation (of $8000). The first conductor (until 1930) was Gustav Strube of the faculty of the Peabody Conservatory. Following Strube, the music directors were George Siemonn (1930–35), Ernest Schelling (1935–7), Werner Janssen (1937–9), Howard Barlow (1939–42), Reginald Stewart (1942–52), Massimo Freccia (1952–9), Peter Herman Adler (1959–68), Brian Priestman (as resident conductor 1968–9), and Sergiu Comissiona (1970–84). David Zinman was named principal guest conductor in 1983.

Reginald Stewart, also director of Peabody, devised a plan for the coordination of the pedagogical program of the conservatory and the orchestra's performances, based on Mendelssohn's direction of the Leipzig Conservatory and the Gewandhaus Orchestra. As a result, many of the principal players of the Baltimore SO were appointed to positions on the Peabody faculty; this practice continues and the orchestra is still financed by both the state of Maryland and the city of Baltimore. It is one of the most active orchestras in the USA for young peoples' concerts: since 1971 it has given an average of 104 concerts for student audiences each season. Under Comissiona's direction, the orchestra has commissioned and presented a new work by an American composer annually: symphonies by Robert Hall Lewis, Ross Lee Finney, and Elie Siegmeister, and works by Sessions, Rochberg, Schuller, Lazarof, Druckman, Donald Erb, and Morton Gould.

3. CONCERT ORGANIZATIONS, HALLS. With a large population of English and German extraction, the city has a rich tradition of choral societies and festivals, the most notable being the Bach Society of Baltimore, the Handel Society, and the Choral Arts Society. In 1859 a chorus of 4000 children was organized in the city.

Baltimore has six outstanding concert halls in current use, all aesthetically pleasing and acoustically effective. The oldest is the Lyric Theatre, constructed in 1894 and designed after the Neues Gewandhaus in Leipzig. After extensive renovation in 1980–81, the theater (capacity 2683) was reopened in 1982. In the same year the Joseph Meyerhoff Symphony Hall (fig.2; capacity 2467) was opened; designed by Pietro Belluschi, this dramatic structure, the home of the Baltimore SO, is named in honor of one of the city's most generous philanthropists. A second hall opened in 1982 is also named after him – the Joseph and Rebecca Meyerhoff Auditorium, a recital hall (capacity 363) in the Baltimore Museum of Art. The Kraushaar Auditorium at Goucher College, again designed by Belluschi, was opened in 1962; it has a small opera pit and a capacity of 995. The Shriver Hall (capacity 1100) of the Johns Hopkins University is the site of a distinguished chamber music series. Peabody Conservatory's concert hall (approximate capacity 800) reopened after two years of extensive repairs in the fall of 1983 as the Miriam A. Friedberg Concert Hall.

4. OPERA. Although opera was first heard in Maryland in the 18th century, it has not flourished in Baltimore, except by virtue of visiting companies. The Baltimore Civic Opera Company was founded in 1940. Renamed the Baltimore Opera Company, it presents three or four productions annually, usually of well-known 19th-century Italian and French works, using the Baltimore SO and its conductor.

See also LIBRARIES AND COLLECTIONS, §3.

BIBLIOGRAPHY

O. G. T. Sonneck: *Early Concert-life in America (1731–1800)* (Leipzig, 1907/ *R*1978)

S. J. Lafferty: *Names of Music Teachers, Musicians, Music Dealers, Engravers, Printers, and Publishers of Music, Conservatories of Music, Music Academies, Manufacturers of Pianos, Organs, and other Musical Instruments Appearing in the Baltimore City Directories from 1796–1900* (MS, Peabody Institute, Baltimore, 1937)

L. Kiefer: *Baltimore's Music: the Haven of the American Composer* (Baltimore, 1962)

R. E. Robinson: *A History of the Peabody Conservatory of Music* (diss., Indiana U., 1969)

ELLIOTT W. GALKIN

Bampton, Rose (Elizabeth) (*b* Lakewood, nr Cleveland, OH, 28 Nov 1909). Mezzo-soprano, later soprano. She studied with Horatio Connell and Queena Mario at the Curtis Institute for five years. Her operatic début was as Siebel in *Faust* with the Chautauqua Opera in 1929, and she went on to sing secondary roles with the Philadelphia Grand Opera (1929–32) and as a soloist (in *Gurrelieder*) with the Philadelphia Orchestra under Stokowski; on 28 November 1932 she made her Metropolitan Opera début as Laura in *La Gioconda*. Her début as a soprano, in a 1937 Town Hall recital, was soon followed by her first soprano role at the Metropolitan as Leonora (*Il trovatore*) on 29 May 1937; during her many years with the Metropolitan company (to 1945, and 1947–50), she won praise especially for Sieglinde, Kundry, and Donna Anna. She sang at Covent Garden (Amneris, 1937), Dresden, the Teatro Colón, Buenos Aires (from 1942 – in 1948 as Daphne in the first South American performance of Strauss's opera), the San Francisco Opera and in Chicago. In 1937 she married Pelletier, and after her retirement taught in New York and Montreal. Bampton's was not one of the great voices, but a fine one, supported by the sovereign musicianship that endeared her to Toscanini and Stokowski.

MAX DE SCHAUENSEE/DENNIS K. McINTIRE

Band, The. Rock group. It was led by (James) Robbie Robertson (*b* Toronto, Ont., 5 July 1944), guitarist and songwriter; its other members were Levon Helm (*b* Marvell, AR, 26 May 1942), drummer, Richard Manuel (*b* Stratford, Ont., 3 April 1945; *d* Winter Park, FL, 4 March 1986), pianist and songwriter, Rick Danko (*b* Simcoe, Ont., 9 Dec 1943), bass guitarist, fiddle and mandolin player, and songwriter, and Garth Hudson (*b* London, Ont., 2 Aug 1942), organist, saxophonist, and euphonium player. Except for Hudson, all members of the group also sang. Robertson had learned to play guitar at the age of five, and had worked with rock bands since his teens. In the late 1950s he and Helm joined Ronnie Hawkins's backing ensemble, with which they performed a repertory of country music, rockabilly, and blues throughout the USA and Canada. Manuel (who had led his own band, the Revols), Danko, and Hudson then joined Hawkins's group.

In 1964 the five left Hawkins and began performing on their own under various names (the Canadian Squires, the Crackers, Levon and the Hawks). John Hammond, Jr., a white blues singer, engaged them as a backing group after hearing them in a Canadian nightclub, and they performed and recorded with him until 1965, when they were similarly engaged by Bob Dylan. Helm and Robertson played in Dylan's first folk-rock concert (at Forest Hills, New York, in 1965); all five musicians accompanied him on his world tour in 1965–6 (though Mickey Jones replaced Helm as the group's drummer for its European and Australian performances), then joined him in Woodstock, New York, where he was recuperating from a motorcycle accident. There they developed a style of songwriting that combined Dylan's allusive lyrics with their own eclectic, stately, and enigmatic brand of rock. They recorded a number of songs that showed an extraordinary attention to detail despite the rough quality of the recording; these were widely issued illegally before their commercial release in 1975 on the album *The Basement Tapes*.

When Dylan started to record with country musicians from Nashville, The Band began to consider itself a distinct entity; initially its three principal songwriters were Robertson, Manuel, and Danko. In 1968 the group recorded *Music from Big Pink* (a reference to the house in Woodstock where they worked), which included original material (Robertson's song *The Weight* from the album later became a hit for Aretha Franklin), songs by Dylan and others written in collaboration with him, and *Long Black Veil*, a country song. The album is notable for the freedom with which the vocal lines intertwine and overlap with one another; in The Band's later recordings a more straightforward distinction is drawn between lead singer and backing textures. Before returning to live performances The Band recorded its second album, *The Band*, most of the material for which was by Robertson; some of the songs, such as *The Night they Drove Old Dixie Down* (with which Joan Baez had a hit), *Up on Cripple Creek*, and *King Harvest*, evoke an idealized American South. At this time The Band was briefly regarded as a country-rock group, but its arrangements, which were characterized by calm tempos, economical playing by Robertson and Helm, and the use of two keyboard instruments, also suggested hymns, parlor songs, Cajun

The Band, mid-1970s: (left to right) Levon Helm, Garth Hudson, Robbie Robertson, Rick Danko, and Richard Manuel

music, brass bands, blues, and a wide range of other American styles.

After *Cahoots* (1971) The Band recorded much less new material: *Rock of Ages* (1972), recorded in concert, included arrangements by Allen Toussaint, and *Moondog Matinee* (1973) revived old rock-and-roll songs. But the group retained its popularity, and in 1973 performed before an audience of half a million in Watkins Glen, New York, where they shared an all-day concert with the Grateful Dead and the Allman Brothers. They next rejoined Dylan to record his album *Planet Waves* (1974) and to make a tour of 21 American cities, which resulted in a live album, *Before the Flood* (1974). *Northern Lights – Southern Cross* (1975) and *Islands* (1977) contain the last songs written by members of the group; on these recordings Hudson added synthesizers to his keyboard instruments.

On Thanksgiving Day 1976, The Band gave its final concert at the Winterland auditorium in San Francisco. This performance, which included guest appearances by Dylan, Hawkins, Muddy Waters, Neil Young, Joni Mitchell, the Staple Singers, Neil Diamond (for whom Robertson had produced an album, *Beautiful Noise*), and others, was documented in Martin Scorsese's film *The Last Waltz* (1978). After The Band's last concert Robertson appeared in and wrote the score for the film *Carny* (1980), and assembled the soundtrack for Scorsese's *King of Comedy*. Helm recorded with a group called the RCO All-Stars and toured with the Cate Brothers; he also acted in the film *Coal Miner's Daughter* (1980). Danko and Manuel toured and performed separately and together, and sometimes with Helm. Hudson worked in a studio in California with various groups, including the new-wave band the Call, for which he produced two albums. In 1983 Danko, Manuel, Helm, and Hudson reunited and toured with the Cate Brothers, calling themselves The Band.

The Band's music drew on the basic vocabulary of rock, blues, and country music. It emerged as the psychedelic rock era was drawing to a close, and its restrained style can be seen as a reaction to the musical excesses of the period. The Band's first two albums contain some of the most deeply felt, carefully crafted rock ever recorded; as Robertson's productivity as a songwriter declined, however, the group's music became less consistently satisfying. Although some of its later songs (such as *The Shape I'm in* and the title song of *Stage Fright*) are of a high quality, most of The Band's later work became increasingly formulaic.

RECORDINGS

(selective list; recorded for Capitol unless otherwise stated)

Music from Big Pink (SKA02955, 1968); *The Band* (STA0132, 1969); *Stage Fright* (SW425, 1970); *Cahoots* (SN16003, 1971); *Rock of Ages* (SAAB11045, 1972); *Moondog Matinee* (SW11214, 1973); *Northern Lights – Southern Cross* (ST11440, 1975); *Islands* (SN11602, 1977); *The Last Waltz* (Warner Bros. 3146, 1978)

BIBLIOGRAPHY

G. Marcus: *Mystery Train: Images of America in Rock 'n' Roll Music* (New York, 1975, rev. and enlarged 2/1982)

JON PARELES

Band organ. A mechanical organ (known as "fairground organ" in Europe) used to provide music for carousels, and in amusement parks, circuses, and skating rinks. It produced loud music that could be heard above the noise of a crowd, and consisted of several ranks of organ pipes, with accompaniment generally provided by a built-in bass drum, snare drum, and cymbal. The band organ was usually built in an elaborately carved and colorfully painted case that sometimes incorporated moving figures in its façade. All but the very largest instruments were designed to be portable.

The earliest band organs, developed during the 18th century, were essentially barrel organs: they had a wooden cylinder or barrel covered with metal pins that formed a musical program. By 1880 these organs were being produced in large sizes; they had over 100 keys, several hundred pipes, and a variety of percussion effects. These large instruments were powered by steam or water engines and later by electric motors. In the USA Eugene DeKleist of North Tonawanda, New York, was an important builder of barrel-operated band organs. In 1892 the French firm of Gavioli in Paris developed a new system for playing organs whereby perforated cardboard sheets were hinged together to form a continuous strip which when folded up resembled a book. As the cardboard strip passed through the key frame, the music was "read" by a row of small metal keys extending through the perforations. Other keys operated percussion effects and turned ranks of pipes on and off. Unlike barrel-operated band organs, book-operated instruments could play musical selections of any length; the new system was also cheaper and more responsive. As a result barrel-organ manufacture declined after 1900, and the "book-music" system came to be used extensively by European builders. Organs built by Gavioli were distributed in the USA by the Berni Organ Co. of New York.

Shortly after 1900 the Rudolph Wurlitzer Company of North Tonawanda began to manufacture band organs using the paper-roll system, in which a perforated roll of paper passed across a tracker bar (a brass bar with a row of holes along it). When a hole in the tracker bar was uncovered by a perforation passing over it, air was sucked into the hole, triggering a pneumatic mechanism that actuated the proper note or function. Most band organs made in the USA used the paper-roll system, and read them with vacuum, or negative, pressure; an exception was the organ built in North Tonawanda by Artizan Factories, which, like European instruments, used positive pressure. Paper rolls could accommodate a large number of tunes; selections ranged from classical pieces to popular songs of the day.

The pipework used in band organs consisted of both flue and reed pipes voiced on 20 to 30 cm of pressure (as measured by water-filled tubes). Flue pipes were the organ's equivalent of flutes, piccolos, violins, and cellos; reed pipes imitated trumpets, clarinets, baritones, and trombones. Pipes were usually made of wood, but in earlier organs the reed pipes had polished brass resonators arranged symmetrically, for the sake of appearance, in the façade. The pipework was divided into bass, accompaniment, melody, and countermelody sections. On a small organ a typical distribution of notes in each section might be 5, 9, 14, and 13; on a large instrument it could be 21, 16, 21, and 38. Only in very large organs were these sections chromatic. Some notes of the scale were omitted in smaller organs to keep the size of the instrument to a minimum; this precluded correct performances of many pieces, and often made arrangements necessary.

For many years the American manufacture of band organs was centered in North Tonawanda. In 1893 DeKleist formed the North Tonawanda Barrel Organ Works to produce barrel-operated organs and pianos; the firm became a supplier to the Rudolph Wurlitzer Company in 1897, at which time it became the DeKleist Musical Instrument Manufacturing Co. Wurlitzer purchased the company in 1908, and continued to manufacture band organs in large quantities through the 1920s; production then declined and ended in 1939. Two other firms of band-organ makers that were formed in North Tonawanda by former employees of DeKleist were the North Tonawanda Musical Instrument Works, active from about 1906 to 1918, and Artizan Factories, which operated from 1922 through the late 1920s. In Brooklyn, New York, the B. A. B. Organ Company was in business from the 1920s to 1957; this firm manufactured folding cardboard music books and paper music rolls, and converted many band organs of other types to systems that used these devices.

Economic conditions and the advent of electronic sound reproduction forced most band-organ companies out of business, but a small number of band organs are still made. Reproductions and restored original instruments are found in museums, private collections, and a few amusement parks.

BIBLIOGRAPHY

R. DeWaard: *From Music Boxes to Street Organs* (Vestal, NY, 1967)

E. V. Cockayne: *The Fairground Organ: its Music, Mechanism and History* (Newton Abbot, England, 1970)

Q. D. Bowers: *Encyclopedia of Automatic Musical Instruments* (Vestal, NY, 1972)

A. A. Reblitz and Q. D. Bowers: *Treasures of Mechanical Music* (Vestal, NY, 1981)

DURWARD R. CENTER

Bands. The word "band" is used to denote many types of instrumental ensemble; it is thought to originate in the medieval Latin *bandum* ("banner," also "company" or "crowd"). In contemporary American usage "band" without qualification (see below) is commonly understood to mean a mixed wind and percussion group; this article deals mainly with the history of such ensembles in the USA, which include the concert band, the marching band, the military band, the circus band, and the symphonic band (also known as the symphonic wind ensemble, symphony of winds, or wind orchestra). (*See also* CIRCUS MUSIC, MILITARY MUSIC, MARCH, and INSTRUMENTS.)

In common parlance "band" is often used of any group of musicians or instruments, defined according to function (theater band, dance band), instrumentation (banjo band, percussion band, steel band, string band, wind band), or style of repertory (rock band, jazz band). For information on such groups *see* COUNTRY MUSIC, JAZZ, JUG BAND, POPULAR MUSIC, §IV, ROCK, and WASHBOARD BAND.

The terms "band" and "orchestra" were often in the past used interchangeably but have become increasingly distinct. What is now commonly referred to as a band is descended from the "high" (i.e. loud) instruments of the medieval period and from the civic waits and *Stadtpfeifer*, who generally performed outdoors and therefore used predominantly loud brass and percussion instruments; traditionally bands were mobile, had a vernacular appeal (they usually performed lighter forms of music and often gave free outdoor concerts), and were usually associated with military organizations and were thus uniformed. The orchestra, on the other hand, is descended from the medieval "low" (i.e., soft) instruments, which normally played indoors, using predominantly strings and softer wind instruments; traditionally orchestras were associated with the church or the nobility and later with formal concerts of more "serious" and sophisticated music for which audiences paid. As late as the early 20th century professional musicians were expected to be "double-handed," that is, competent on both wind and string instruments; the function (and therefore the name) of an ensemble determined its instrumentation, the same performers making up a wind band for outdoor occasions or an orchestra for indoor concerts and entertainments.

1. EARLY HISTORY. As with other areas of musical culture, European customs and traditions of band music were brought to America in the 17th century by the colonists. The snare drum was an important and necessary part of colonial life. It served not only to set the cadence for marching men but also to beat orders, warnings, and signals for both military and civilian activities. Whenever possible a fife, bagpipe, or other instrument was used to add melodic interest. These instruments, referred to as the "field music," were used primarily for functional purposes, and normally provided the camp duty calls that regulated the field or garrison (*see* MILITARY MUSIC).

Another European tradition, the "band of music" or military band, had developed in the army of Louis XIV of France; it usually consisted of three oboes and either a bass oboe or bassoon. British regiments had such bands by the end of the 17th century, and these must have been known to the American colonists. The band of music was also known in the larger American cities by the mid-18th century: a parade in Philadelphia in 1755 was "attended by a Band of Music." The following year Benjamin Franklin, as commander of a militia regiment, was preceded on parade by the "Hautboys and Fifes in Ranks." (It may be assumed that the term "hautboys," following European practice, referred to military musicians in general.) Other important American cities had similar bands, particularly in the militia units then being formed, as did the British regiments serving in America during the French and Indian War.

2. THE REVOLUTIONARY PERIOD AND EARLY 19TH CENTURY: "HARMONIEMUSIK" AND JANISSARY MUSIC. From about the mid-18th century court and household music in Europe was largely provided by wind bands (*Harmonien*): in an effort to reinforce inner voices and create a new timbre, two horns were added to the European band, and clarinets were introduced soon after. Trumpets were sometimes included, especially in the German states. This instrumentation became standard in what was eventually referred to as the *Harmoniemusik*. Until the end of the 18th century bands usually consisted of pairs of oboes, clarinets, bassoons, and horns, their music ranging from five to eight parts (Table 1, p. 128: 1781). Such bands had no drums; as signaling instruments, these remained with the field music. The many serenades, nocturnes, cassations, *Parthien*, and divertimentos composed for this combination constituted the repertory of the bands of the 18th century. All these attributes of European band music were brought to America by the immigrants.

British regimental bands gave concerts in New York, Boston, and Philadelphia before the Revolution, and Americans were quick to form bands of their own. Both British and American regiments supported bands during the war, and performances were frequent. The 3d and 4th artillery regiments of the Continental Army, commanded by colonels John Crane and Thomas Proctor, had bands as early as 1777, which served until the end of the Revolution; these achieved exceptional reputations, and may alone have provided sufficient basis for the establishment of an American band tradition. Colonel Crane's Band, also known as the Massachusetts Band, continued to give concerts following demobilization, and R. F. Goldman believes it to have been the basis for Gilmore's Boston Brigade Band. Other bands were also

TABLE 1: Comparative band instrumentation

Instruments	*1781* *Harmoniemusik*, Revolutionary period	*1818*	*1846*	*1854*	*1861*	*1878* Gilmore's 22d Regiment Band	*1918* US Army regimental band authorization	*1924* Sousa Band	*1944* US Army divisional band authorization	*1946* Goldman Band	*1948* University of Illinois Symphonic Band	*1962* College Band Directors National Association recommendation	*1983* US Army separate band authorization
Flute/piccolo		3				4	2	6	3	4	12	6	2
Oboe/english horn	2					2	2	3	1	2	8	2	1
Heckelphone											1		
Bassoon	2	2				2	2	2	1	2	6	2	1
Contrabassoon						1					1		
Contrabass sarrusophone							1						
A♭ clarinet						1							
E♭ clarinet						3	1		1	1		1	
B♭ clarinet	2	2				16	10	26	12	19	29	18	7
Alto clarinet						1	2	1	1		4	6	
Bass clarinet						1	2	2	1	1	5	3	
Contrabass clarinet											3	5	
Soprano saxophone						1							
Alto saxophone						1	1	4	4	1	3	1	2
Tenor saxophone						1	1	2	2	1	3	1	1
Baritone saxophone						1	1	1	1	1	1	1	1
Bass saxophone								1			1		
E♭ cornet			1	2	3	1						1	
B♭ cornet				2	2	4		6		4	7	3	
E♭ trumpet			2	1									
B♭ trumpet		2	1			2	4	2	10	3	4	3	7
B♭ flugelhorn		1	2			2	2				2		
French horn	2	2	2			4	4	4	4	4	9	4	4
Alto horn				2	2	2							
Alto ophicleide			2										
Tenor horn					2	2							
Trombone		1	3			3	4	4	6	6	9	4	4
Euphonium				1	1	2	2	2	2	2	6	3	2
Bass ophicleide			2										
Serpent		1											
Bass			2	2	4	5	4	6	5	4	8	3	3
Double (string) bass										1	3		
Percussion				2	3	4	3	3	2	3	9	5	3
Harp										1	2		
Piano													1
Guitar													1
Total	8	14	17	12	17	66	48	75	56	60	136	72	40

Instrumentation for 1818, 1846, 1854, and 1861 drawn from band books.

active in post-Revolutionary America: bands welcomed George Washington in almost every village and city that he visited on his grand tour in 1789; taverns, coffeehouses, theaters, and pleasure gardens all attracted customers by employing bands to perform medleys, excerpts from popular stage works, battle pieces, transcriptions of orchestral works, original compositions, marches, and patriotic songs. The *Massachusetts March*, a common-step march (half-note = 75) printed in Samuel Holyoke's *Instrumental Assistant*, ii (1807), is typical of the band music of the period (ex. 1).

The Militia Act of 1792, according to which all able-bodied, adult, white males were required to perform military service for at least two "muster days" each year, aided greatly the development of bands. A further impetus was supplied by the regular meetings, for drill and ceremonies, of élite organizations. No military, civic, festive, or holiday occasion was complete without music, and bands were organized to provide it; these were usually attached to militia units, and, while retaining their civilian status, the bandsmen normally wore uniforms, a mode of dress that became traditional. Tutors, such as Olmstead's *Martial Music* (1807), began to appear in print. Among the Revolutionary War bandmasters active into the Federal period were John Hiwell, the former Inspector of Music in the Continental Army, and Philip Roth. New leaders, such as Peter von Hagen, James Hewitt, and Gottlieb Graupner, immigrated with European military experience behind them.

Widespread interest in Turkish (janissary) music at the end of the 18th century led to the introduction into bands of the bass drum, cymbals, triangle, tambourine, crescent, and single kettledrum. The more exotic instruments soon fell into disuse, but the bass drum, often with a mounted cymbal, became standard in American bands and field musics alike. The separation between these two types of ensemble was retained, but combined performances became more frequent, and the snare drum soon became an integral part of each. Further development of the band's instrumentation ensued in the Federal period: woodwind instruments with additional keys, piccolos, bass clarinets, trombones, bass horns, and serpents were added to the *Harmoniemusik*; William Webb's *Grand Military Divertimentos* were published for an ensemble including these instruments (Table 1, 1818). Another new instrument, the keyed (or Kent) bugle, patented by Joseph Halliday of Dublin in 1810, was a regulation bugle with keys that permitted it to be fully chromatic (*see* KEYED BUGLE). It was made popular in New York through the performances of Richard Willis, who within a year of his arrival from Dublin in 1816 became the first Teacher of Music and leader of the band at West Point. Other virtuosos on the keyed bugle included Frank Johnson in Philadelphia and Edward Kendall in Boston. Keyed bass horns and ophicleides were also developed, and bands continued to increase in size. By 1832 US Army infantry regiments had bands consisting of 15 to 24 members, a range adopted for the bands of the militia. In that year, however, General Order 31 limited infantry bands to ten privates and a chief musician, a drastic reduction that led to the elimination of woodwind instruments in favor of the new, versatile, chromatic brass instruments.

Ex.1 The "Massachusetts March," from Samuel Holyoke: *Instrumental Assistant*, ii (1807)

3. THE MID-19TH CENTURY: DEVELOPMENT OF BRASS BANDS. The first all-brass band may have been the Boston Brass Band, led by Kendall, which gave its inaugural concert in 1835 (though it is possible that Dodworth's City Brass Band of New York (later the National Brass Band) or the Providence Brass Band (later the American Brass Band of Providence) was organized earlier). The precise instrumentation of this ensemble, which had up to 20 players, is not known, but it must have included keyed and valved horns, posthorns, bugles, trombones, and ophicleides; Kendall was the band's bugle soloist.

Over the next two decades the development of brass instruments led other bands to be reorganized along these lines. In Paris Adolphe Sax invented a family of saxhorns ranging from soprano to contrabass. In the USA such manufacturers as Thomas D. Paine of Woonsocket, Rhode Island, John F. Stratton of New York, Isaac Fiske of Worcester, Massachusetts, Samuel Graves of Winchester, New Hampshire (later of Boston), and J. Lathrop Allen and E. G. Wright of Boston developed valved, chromatic, brass or silver bugles with conical bores and deep-cupped mouthpieces that permitted ease of execution, accurate intonation, and an even, mellow timbre throughout their range. This homogeneous brass family soon supplanted the mixed woodwind and heterogeneous brass groups formerly in use. The change to all-brass instrumentation was so swift and complete that by 1856 the editor of *Dwight's Journal of Music* complained that "all is brass now-a-days – nothing but brass." The terms used to denote instruments were applied loosely, and bands consisting of the family of valved, conical-bore brass instruments were often known as cornet bands or saxhorn bands, as well as brass bands. In addition to bell-front and bell-upright brass instruments, valved, over-the-shoulder instruments were developed. Allen T. Dodworth claimed, perhaps incorrectly, that these instruments were first introduced by his family in 1838; he specified that they were intended for military bands, "as they throw all the tone to those who are marching to it," but that for general purposes those with their bells upward were "most convenient." He also advised that "care should be taken to have all the bells one way."

Dodworth, with his father and three brothers, established the Dodworth Band in the mid-1830s; for many years this was considered the finest band in the USA. Some of its members who later led their own ensembles included Alessandro Liberati, Carlo Cappa, D. L. Downing, and Theodore Thomas. The Dodworths were an enterprising family: all were proficient performers on more than one instrument, and all were composers. Harvey B. Dodworth was a brilliant soloist and proprietor of the family music store and publishing company. Allen Dodworth became a successful teacher of ballroom dancing, and first treasurer of the New York Philharmonic Orchestra Society, which the family was influential in establishing in 1842; he was also a member of the orchestra's violin section (three other members of the family played with the orchestra as well; *see* DODWORTH).

While some civilian bands were larger, official US Army bands in the early 19th century were still limited to ten musicians and a leader. In 1845 this number was increased to 16, and the men were mustered as a group, rather than as privates in the various companies. Since most civilian bands were associated with militia organizations patterned on army models, this change was significant.

1. The Boston Brass Band, with (right to left) four soprano saxhorns, four alto (or tenor) saxhorns, cymbals, drums, three over-the-shoulder trombones, and three bass saxhorns: from "Gleason's Pictorial Drawing Room Companion" (9 August 1851)

Brass bands flourished in the 1850s. Their instruments were fully developed, and both amateur and professional bands were much in evidence; some 3000 ensembles, with more than 60,000 members, were in existence in the years preceding the Civil War. While the level of musicianship in the amateur groups varied widely, there were a number of fine professional bands of the highest standard. The Salem (Massachusetts) Brass Band, led in the 1850s by Kendall and later by Gilmore, and the American Brass Band in Providence under Joseph C. Greene, were both highly reputed. Russel Munger's Great Western Band of St. Paul and Christopher Bach's Band of Milwaukee were well known among the many bands organized in the newly settled Midwestern states. A grand festival concert, a benefit for the American Musical Fund Society, was held at Castle Garden, New York, on 4 September 1852, and 11 outstanding bands performed, including the Dodworth Cornet Band, the Boston Brigade Brass Band, and Joseph Noll's 7th Regiment Band. The program, including overtures and potpourris from popular operas, solos and duets, and dances and marches, is representative of concerts of the time.

Little printed band music from this period is extant; most bands played from manuscript. Published piano music frequently included the statement "as performed by" followed by the name of a well-known band, mainly to increase sales, and often carried a note stating that parts for military band – presumably in manuscript form – were available from the publisher. In 1844 Elias Howe added "several New and Popular Pieces in 6 and 8 parts, for a Brass Band" to his collection of dances and other light numbers, the *First Part of the Musician's Companion*. In 1846 E. K. Eaton published *Twelve Pieces of Harmony for Military Brass Bands*, an excellent compilation for 17-piece ensemble (Table 1, 1846), which demanded advanced technical facility not only from the player of the high, E♭ bugle but from the entire group. To meet the "increasing demand for such a work, caused by the rapid advancement of the brass bands of our country," Allen Dodworth published his *Brass Band School* in 1853. In addition to the rudiments of music, he provided fingering charts, advice on rehearsing and choosing an instrument, and military regulations, tactics, and camp duties; he also included 11 popular airs and marches arranged for a band of 12 players, with drums and cymbals. His remarks indicate that the music may be played by as few as six or as many as 21 pieces (with doubling), but that for the first 14 only "instruments of like character be used, that is, valve instruments of large calibre." G. W. E. Friederich published his *Brass Band Journal* (1854), a collection of 24 pieces with similar instrumentation (Table 1, 1854), and in 1859 W. C. Peters & Sons published *Peters' Sax-horn Journal*. These printed collections consisted principally of patriotic songs, popular airs, arrangements of songs by Foster, operatic excerpts, waltzes, polkas, schottisches, and marches. The music was intended for a large audience and made few technical demands on its players. The better professional bands of the period seldom had recourse to these compilations but relied instead on extensive manuscript collections.

General Order 15 (4 May 1861) called for the raising of 40 volunteer regiments for the Union (39 of infantry, one of cavalry). Each infantry regiment was authorized "2 principal musicians [and] 24 musicians for band," and the cavalry regiment was authorized 16 band musicians; in addition two field musicians were allotted for each company. General Order 16 extended the same organization to the regular army, and later calls did so to additional volunteer regiments. Bufkin estimates conservatively that the Union Army, which had a total strength of more than two and a half million men, had 500 bands and 9000 players, in addition to the two field musicians assigned to each company. Confederate regulations, which were usually similar, allowed 16 privates to act as musicians, in addition to the chief musician. Many civilian and militia bands enlisted as a body in the new volunteer regiments. While most conformed to regulations, some (supported, as in the past, by the officers) exceeded their authorized strength and dressed in elaborate uniforms. The 24th Massachusetts Volunteer Infantry had 20 drummers, 12 buglers, and a 36-piece, mixed wind band led by Gilmore. The American Brass Band of Providence, led by Greene, enlisted as a unit in the 1st Rhode Island Regiment. Other prominent civilian bandmasters who, together with their bands, served in the war included Claudio S. Grafulla, Harvey Dodworth, E. B. Flagg, Thomas Coates, and Walter Dignam. Gustavus W. Ingalls enlisted a band of 22 men in the 3d New Hampshire Regiment, and their Port Royal Band Books constitute a primary source for instrumentation and repertory of the period; another important set of manuscript books is that of the 25th Massachusetts Regiment (Table 1, 1861); these are held at the American Antiquarian Society in Worcester. Eight members of the Salem (North Carolina) Brass Band enlisted in the 26th North Carolina Regiment, and their story (Hall, 1963) is typical of the experiences of many bands serving on both sides of the conflict.

Civil War bands served not only to provide music for military and civilian ceremonies, but to promote the esprit de corps of the soldiers through informal entertainments as well; bandsmen also served as medical assistants during battle. Nevertheless, there were those in Congress who felt that too much money was being expended on bands; in 1861 a moratorium was placed on the formation of new bands and the filling of vacancies in existing ones, and General Order 91 (1862) directed that all volunteer regimental bands be mustered out of service. Brigade bands of 16 musicians were authorized, but, with three to four regiments in each brigade, this authorization reduced considerably the number of bands and bandsmen. It was difficult, however, in so large an army to enforce regulations uniformly, and so some regimental, militia, and post bands continued to serve until the end of the war; thus the band of the 107th US Colored Infantry (see fig.2), which was typical in size and instrumentation of the many brigade bands in service, was actually a regimental unit.

Even during this heyday of all-brass bands, some retained woodwind instruments. Dodworth's concerts included works for mixed wind bands as early as 1852, and in that year the 7th Regiment (New York) Band was re-formed as a 42-piece woodwind and brass group, which under Joseph Noll, then Claudio Grafulla, achieved a reputation for excellence surpassed only by that of the Dodworth Band. Immigrant bandmasters, especially Italians, favored reed instruments, which were an important part of their musical heritage. Francis Scala, a virtuoso clarinetist, maintained the Italian woodwind tradition as leader of the US Marine Band from 1855 to 1871; Gilmore's Band had five reed instruments in 1862, and may have had them as early as 1859. These bands were large and of an exceptional quality; they were not typical of bands of the Civil War period, but rather prefigured the next period in American band history.

4. The late 19th and early 20th centuries.

(i) Gilmore, Sousa, and the flourishing of band music. PATRICK S. GILMORE may rightly be considered the father of the modern American symphonic band. A flamboyant, jovial Irishman, with seemingly boundless energy and enthusiasm, he arrived in the USA in 1849 and soon became leader of the Salem Brass Band. In 1859, his reputation secure, he established Gilmore's Band, and assumed personally all the organization's financial and busi-

2. *The band of the 107th US Colored Infantry at Fort Corcoran, Arlington, Virginia, November 1865*

ness responsibilities. After a brief period of service in the Civil War with the 24th Massachusetts Infantry, he was charged with organizing and training all the state's bands; in this capacity he assembled a band of 500 and a chorus of 6000 for the ceremonies held to inaugurate the governor of Louisiana in 1864. The huge National Peace Jubilee of 1869, and the even larger World Peace Jubilee of 1872, both of which he organized in Boston, brought him international attention. In 1873 he assumed leadership of New York's 22d Regiment Band, and soon established it as the finest professional band in the country. A skilled promoter, he attracted large audiences by choosing programs adeptly, and by engaging as soloists such outstanding musicians as the cornetists Matthew Arbuckle, Liberati, Herman Bellstedt, and Jules Levy, the saxophonist E. A. Lefebre, the euphonium player Joseph Raffayolo, and the sopranos Emma Thursby and Eugenie Pappenheim. Gilmore treated his musicians honestly and fairly, and paid them well. His 22d Regiment Band normally had a complement of 66 musicians (Table 1, 1878), far exceeding the limits imposed by military regulations of the time. The ensemble made an American tour in 1876 and a successful European tour two years later. During the 1880s they worked year-round: in summer at Manhattan Beach, in winter in New York at Gilmore's Garden (this was P. T. Barnum's Hippodrome) and the 22d Regiment Armory, and in autumn and spring on tour. At this time there were only four important professional symphony orchestras in the USA, and none of these had a full season; as a result the finest musicians sought employment with Gilmore. His band inspired other ensembles throughout the country to raise their level of performance and repertory, and to reintroduce the woodwind instruments that had fallen into disuse during the brass-band movement. He aspired to establish a permanent band of 100 musicians, but his death in 1892 aborted this venture.

There were other bandmasters active at the time, though none toured as extensively as Gilmore, or achieved his fame and reputation. Grafulla continued to conduct the 7th Regiment (New York) Band after the Civil War until his death in 1880; he was succeeded by Carlo Cappa, a trombonist who had left Kendall's band to serve under Grafulla. Cappa also appeared as a soloist with the Dodworth Band, and for a number of years was first trombonist with Theodore Thomas's orchestra. David Wallis Reeves, who had also been a soloist under Dodworth, in 1866 became leader of the American Band of Providence; he added woodwinds to it and created a professional ensemble. Arbuckle and Liberati, who had been soloists under Gilmore, formed bands of their own. Robert Browne Hall, one of the finest cornet soloists in the Northeast, directed bands in Maine from 1882 to 1902. Fred Weldon, Jean Missud, and Mace Gay are among the other bandmasters who acquired fine local reputations with their bands.

In 1889 *Harper's Weekly* estimated that there were more than 10,000 "military" bands active in the USA. In many western communities the local military post band provided the only music available. Many bands were associated with local militia units but, though uniformed, retained their civilian status. Professional and amateur bands appeared at military and civilian ceremonies and parades, concerts, amusement parks, seaside resorts, county and state fairs, and national and international expositions. Their repertory ranged from the ever popular marches, songs, waltzes, and novelty pieces to the classical standards of the day. Most Americans received their first, and in many instances their only, exposure to the music of Mozart, Beethoven, Rossini, Verdi, Liszt, and Wagner through band performances; sometimes entire grand operas were staged with band accompaniment. Marches were extremely popular, as were opera selections and variations performed by leading soloists. The texture of European marches was generally homophonic, usually consisting of a melody with rhythmic accompaniment. Reeves is generally credited with being the first to add countermelodies, and to develop a style that served as a foundation for later composers; his *2d Reg[imen]t Conn[ecticut] N[ational] G[uard] March* became a favorite of Ives, who quoted it in his *Decoration Day* (1912).

While large bands were led by conductors, smaller ones were frequently led by their solo cornetist, as in the days of brass bands. For this reason the solo cornet part in a printed band arrangement usually served also as the conductor's cue sheet. Carl Fischer of New York was one of the first firms to publish band music with separate, printed parts for each instrument, and to include a two- or three-line conductor's score. The firm engaged a number of outstanding editors, among them Louis Philippe Laurendeau, Frank H. Losey, Vincent F. Safranek, Theodore Moses Tobani, and Mayhew Lester Lake, many of whose arrangements are still performed. Thomas H. Rollinson prepared many arrangements during his 40 years with Ditson. Later important publishers of band music included Charles L. Barnhouse, John Church, Harry Coleman, Henry Fillmore, George F. Briegel, and several bandmasters who issued their own music, such as Missud, Fred Jewell, and Karl L. King.

The most important figure in the history of American band music was John Philip Sousa. He assumed leadership of the US Marine Band in 1880; by 1891 he had brought the ensemble to a high level of professionalism, and with it undertook an American tour. The tour's manager, David Blakely, who had been Gilmore's manager for many years, persuaded Sousa in 1892 to leave the Marine Corps and form his own band (for illustration and further discussion *see* SOUSA, JOHN PHILIP). This ensemble soon became dominant; on Gilmore's death in 1892 several of his important soloists joined Sousa, who was also able to obtain many of Gilmore's unfulfilled engagements. Sousa was an astute showman, but his meteoric rise was due in greater measure to his compositions and consummate musicianship. He engaged the finest available players for each position, and attracted such outstanding soloists as the cornetists Bohumir Kryl, Liberati, John Dolan, Herbert Clarke, Walter Rogers, Frank Simon, and Bellstedt, the trombonist Arthur Pryor, the euphonium players Simone Mantia and Joseph DeLuca, the violinists Maud Powell, Florence Hardeman, and Nicoline Zedeler, and the sopranos Estelle Liebling and Marjorie Moody. He experimented with his band's instrumentation, which at first resembled that of the Marine Band, and gradually increased its membership from 46 players to an average of 70 (Table 1, 1924). He made regular tours from 1892 until his death in 1932, including trips to Europe in 1900, 1901, 1903, and 1905, and a world tour in 1910–11. A typical Sousa program listed about nine titles, ranging from his own suites, medleys, and marches to novelty pieces, solos, orchestral transcriptions, and opera excerpts (such as selections from Wagner's *Parsifal*, which he performed a decade before its première at the Metropolitan Opera). His printed programs are deceptive, however, for after each scheduled work he normally added one or two encores; a program with nine offerings listed might in fact contain as many as 30. The encores were chosen spontaneously and were usually marches by Sousa himself.

Other major figures of the period included such veterans as Cappa, Missud, Francesco Fanciulli, Thomas P. Brooke, Monroe

A. Althouse, and Victor Herbert, several soloists from Sousa's Band who went on to form bands of their own (Liberati, Clarke, Kryl, Simon, Pryor, Mantia, Bellstedt, and Eugene LaBarre), and bandmasters, such as Giuseppe Creatore, Patrick Conway, Frederick Innes, and Edwin Franko Goldman, who organized new, professional ensembles; Goldman was remarkable for his practice of seeking out composers who were known chiefly for their work in other areas, and his band gave the first performances of pieces written for it by Percy Grainger, Ottorino Respighi, Jaromír Weinberger, and Albert Roussel, as well as the Americans Henry Hadley, C. C. White, D. G. Mason, Bainbridge Crist, and Leo Sowerby. Since women were not admitted to the professional bands except as violin, soprano, or harp soloists, they formed bands of their own, such as Helen May Butler's Ladies Brass Band (see fig.3).

In addition to the professional bands there were thousands of amateur ensembles, many of them connected with civic organizations. A town band was a mark of social status: "A town without its brass band is as much in need of sympathy as a church without a choir. The spirit of a place is recognized in its band" (Dana, 1878). A number of states passed "band laws," which provided for the levying of special taxes to support free band concerts. Many civic bands dated back to antebellum times, including the Allentown (Pennsylvania) Band (founded 1828), the Repasz Band (Williamsport, Pennsylvania, 1831), the Barrington (New Hampshire) Band (1832), the Ringgold Band (Reading, Pennsylvania, 1852), and the Naperville (Illinois) Band (1859). Most of these bands were unknown outside their own areas, but some had famous directors, such as the Fort Dodge (Iowa) Military Band, led for 38 years by King, and the Long Beach (California) Municipal Band, led by Clarke, then by Joseph J. Richards. Some bands were sponsored by fraternal and sororal organizations, such as the Shriners, whose bands were led by Jewell, Henry Fillmore, Ned Mahoney, and others, and after World War I the bands of the American Legion and the Veterans of Foreign Wars. The brass band tradition was maintained by the many bands of the Salvation Army. Industrial bands were a source of goodwill for their sponsors and of recreation for their members; among these were the Philco Band led by Herbert N. Johnston, the Armco Band led by Simon, former soloist with Sousa, the Arma Band led by Erik Leidzén, and the Metropolitan Life Insurance Company Band led by Briegel. Many of the bands' directors had several positions: Briegel, for example, in addition to leading the Metropolitan band, also directed the 22d Regiment (New York) Band, the New York City Fire Department Band, and the Kismet Temple Band; many of his musicians played in more than one of the groups. To train musicians for these ensembles, a number of schools were established, such as Hale A. VanderCook's College of Music (formed in Chicago in 1909), Losey's Military Band School (Erie, Pennsylvania, 1914), Ernest S. Williams's School of Music (Brooklyn, New York, 1922), Patrick Conway's Military Band School (Ithaca, New York, 1922), and Frederick N. Innes's Conn National School of Music (Chicago, 1923).

Some bands had specialized styles and repertories. Among these were the circus bands, which had traditions dating back to the 18th century. The best-known circus bandmasters and musicians included Joseph J. Richards, Charles E. Duble, Henry Fillmore, Jewell, King, Carl Clair, Perry G. Lowery, and Russell Alexander; they provided the music for such companies as Barnum & Bailey, Ringling Brothers, Forepaugh-Sells Brothers, Sells-Floto, Wallace and Hagenbeck, and others. They invariably played at a faster tempo ("circus" tempo) than did military or civic bands.

Another ensemble was the New Orleans brass band (*see* NEW ORLEANS, §3). This evolved from the brass bands of the Civil War, but had an Afro-American and Creole heritage. Often associated with benevolent societies, the bands provided music for

3. *Helen May Butler and her Ladies Brass Band at Minnesota State Fair,* 1909

club functions, including funerals. From the 18th century bands customarily played a solemn march on their way to the cemetery but a brisk quickstep, usually *Merry Men Home from the Grave*, on their return. A distinctive practice of the New Orleans bands was improvising on tunes (such as the spiritual *When the saints go marching in*), which resulted in an early form of jazz. There were many permanent black ensembles at the end of the 19th century, including the Onward, Excelsior, Eureka, and St. Bernard brass bands, and many leading jazz instrumentalists gained their first experience in these groups. Bands continued to develop jazz, even in the military; the bandmasters James Reese Europe and James "Tim" Brymn are credited with taking jazz to the Old World with their army bands during World War I.

The popularity of bands declined after World War I, in the face of competition from radio, phonograph recordings, and motion pictures. The development of the automobile contributed to the demise of amusement parks, at which bands had been an important attraction. Staples of the band repertory, such as the polka, waltz, and schottische, fell out of fashion, and jazz gained favor as an accompaniment to dancing. Sousa continued to draw enthusiastic crowds, but other bandmasters, such as Creatore and Kryl, had to be satisfied with appearances at fairs and expositions and on the Chautauqua circuit. The Depression dealt a final blow to the band tradition, and on Sousa's death in 1932 no bandmaster stood ready to take his place as leader of the movement, the focus of which soon shifted from the professional bandmaster to the educator.

(ii) The academic band movement. The roots of the academic band movement lie in the mid-19th century. Boston's Farm and Trades School had a band as early as 1848; Paul Schneider was hired in 1884 to form a band at the Christian Brothers High School in Memphis, Tennessee. At least four elementary-school bands participated in the Columbus Day celebrations in Columbus, Ohio, in 1892; Greenville, South Carolina, had at least one public-school band in 1893. The Jenkins Orphanage Band of Charleston, South Carolina, capitalized on the popularity of black boys' bands in plantation road shows, and was sufficiently accomplished to tour the northeastern USA and England for many years beginning in 1895. Junius K. Adams was teaching three different boys' bands in Live Oak, Florida, in 1896, and there were mixed as well as girls' bands all over the country.

University bands developed in close association with the military; the band of the Royal Irish Regiment (18th Foot) performed at the College of Philadelphia's commencement exercises of 1767 and 1773, and military bands continued to influence their counterparts in colleges and universities. Harvard and Yale universities both had bands around 1827, the College of Charleston had one as early as 1828, and the University of Indiana organized a brass band in 1832. The universities of Michigan (formed 1817) and Notre Dame (1842) had bands within a few years of their establishment. The Morrill Act of 1862, which provided public land grants for the establishment of educational institutions, required these colleges to offer courses in military training. Military ceremonies required music and there are records of bands at virtually all educational institutions following the Civil War. These were associated with and trained by the military, and uniformed and organized according to army regulations, which authorized 16-piece brass bands, each with a leader and an assistant. The leaders were usually students who had gained experience with municipal ensembles, and the instrumentation in many cases was fully balanced according to brass band principles. Members received military but not academic credit for their work. Military ceremonies, political rallies, parades, dedications, outdoor festivities, and sporting events were all enlivened by the music of these bands, which played popular overtures and medleys, spirited marches, and school songs.

Band participation at sporting events became increasingly important, and by the end of the 19th century performances before football games and at half-time were common. With the addition of woodwind instruments, the college and university bands increased in size and were organized more frequently like professional than military ensembles. Professional bandmasters, such as Conway at Cornell University (1895–1908) and Gustav Bruder at Ohio State University (1896–1929), were engaged part-time, and regular faculty replaced student directors. Paul Spotts Emrick began almost 50 years of service at Purdue University in 1905; in the same year Oregon State University engaged Harry L. Beard, and ALBERT AUSTIN HARDING became director of the University of Illinois Band. Harding, a friend of Sousa's and greatly influenced by him, believed that bands should, in the quality of their repertory and performance, aspire to the standards expected of the professional symphony orchestra. He sought to give the Illinois band a symphonic sound by making greater use of oboes, bassoons, alto and bass flutes and clarinets, the full saxophone family, flugelhorns, horns instead of altos, and a contrabassoon. Since arrangements for such a band did not exist, he made almost 150 transcriptions of orchestral works by such composers as Dohnányi, Ibert, Kodály, Prokofiev, Shostakovich, and Richard Strauss. The artistic standard of the University of Illinois Band soon equaled that of the best professional bands, and Harding's work was widely emulated.

World War I brought a renewed interest in military bands, and mobilization fostered an expanded musical instrument industry. A school for army bandleaders, directed by Arthur A. Clappé, had been organized through the efforts of Frank Damrosch in 1911; Walter Damrosch formed a similar school at Chaumont, France, in 1918. American regimental bands compared unfavorably with their European counterparts in size and instrumentation until their membership was increased from 20 to 48 (Table 1, 1918) and greater emphasis was placed on thorough musical training. Members of army bands returned to civilian life with enthusiasm, skill, and experience, and many became instrumental directors in public schools. Class instruction in band and orchestral instruments began to receive support from school officials by the close of World War I. The strongest emphasis was on orchestral groups, however, according to a study conducted in 1919 of instrumental music in the schools: of the 359 cities (in 36 states) that participated in the survey, only 88 had bands, while 278 had orchestras. (The figures are probably, however, somewhat misleading, since no note was taken of extracurricular bands or of community bands in which schoolchildren may have played. A similar survey in 1973 cited 2000 institutions of higher education with bands, orchestras, and choirs, and some 50,000 secondary-school bands, compared with about 5000 orchestras.)

Musical instrument manufacturers welcomed the new interest in instrumental music education, for the decrease in professional and amateur bands following the war threatened to diminish their market. To stimulate demand, they organized the first national school band contest, in Chicago in June 1923. Although many of the 25 bands that competed were local, the reaction to the event – of enthusiasm and demand for more such contests –

was extraordinary. The manufacturers asked the National Bureau for the Advancement of Music to sponsor later competitions. The Committee on Instrumental Affairs of the Music Supervisors National Conference, using funds provided by the manufacturers, developed state contests to stimulate greater participation at the national level. Success was so great that by 1937 the National School Band Association, which had been organized in 1926 to administer the contests, had formed ten regional organizations. By 1941 there were 562 bands (33,398 students) participating, in addition to many ensembles eliminated from the national competition at the district level.

While the growth of the symphonic band was due in large part to band contests, marching bands benefited principally from the popularity of intercollegiate football. Larger bands were needed to fill the huge stadiums that were built between the two world wars. Once freed from their association with the Reserve Officers' Training Corps, bands no longer marched on and off the field in military formation at half-time, but rather developed distinctive, original routines. The University of Illinois Band under Harding is generally credited with being the first to play opening fanfares from the goal line, and to march in a block-letter formation down the field. Many other bands followed its example; in 1936 the Ohio State University Marching Band, a 120-piece ensemble led by Eugene J. Weigel (1894–1973), formed the word "Ohio" in script, and thus began a tradition that has continued to the present (for illustration *see* EDUCATION IN MUSIC, fig.2).

At the same time measures were taken to raise the level of musicianship in both symphonic and marching bands. In 1928 Joseph E. Maddy founded the National Music Camp at Interlochen, Michigan, which became the most famous of many American summer music schools. As early as 1919 Harding had invited secondary-school band directors to observe his rehearsals at the University of Illinois, and to discuss specific problems and repertory; in 1930 he began a series of band "clinics" that exerted so great an influence that he came to be known as the "dean of university band directors." When the AMERICAN BANDMASTERS ASSOCIATION was organized in 1929, Harding was the only educator to be included in a group that otherwise consisted only of service and professional band directors. In 1941 William D. Revelli of the University of Michigan formed the COLLEGE BAND DIRECTORS NATIONAL ASSOCIATION (CBDNA) with the aims of conducting acoustical and tonal research, improving the musicianship of college band directors, and developing a standard instrumentation for bands (Table 1, 1962), a concept later rejected as being too restrictive. The association also commissioned original band music, making a practice of approaching composers who were already established in other areas of music.

5. THE POSTWAR ERA. World War II somewhat curtailed the school band movement, but the enthusiasm of the returning veterans inspired its revival. Through the League of Composers, then the American Bandmasters Association, Goldman commissioned works by Thomson, Piston, Mennin, Persichetti, Hanson, Creston, Morton Gould, and Robert Russell Bennett. In 1946 Kappa Kappa Psi (founded 1919), the national honorary band fraternity, entered into a cooperative arrangement with Tau Beta Sigma, its sororal counterpart (founded 1939; *see* GREEK-LETTER SOCIETIES, §2). New professional organizations were formed, such as the National Association of College Wind and Percussion Instructors (1951), the American School Band Directors Association (1953), the National Catholic Bandmasters' Association (1953), the National Band Association (1960), the Women Band Directors National Association (1969), and the Association of Concert Bands (1977). Football half-time shows developed into elaborate pageants and directors vied to create the most unusual, exotic, and spectacular show. Bands marched with higher and faster steps (the Florida A & M band in particular became known for its cadence of 320 steps per minute), and reached immense proportions, with much larger complements of brass and percussion instruments than formerly. The adherence to traditions inherited from field-music organizations, such as the use of a color guard, precision marching, learning by rote, and strong emphasis on percussion, became known as "corps style" and gained great popularity in marching bands. Symphonic bands also increased in size (Table 1, 1948). In reaction to such developments Frederick Fennell formed the Eastman Symphonic Wind Ensemble in 1952. This had a flexible instrumentation, stressed individual performers in the same fashion as chamber ensembles, and used no doubling unless instructed to do so by the composer. Repertory included the wind serenades of Mozart and Richard Strauss, the wind symphonies of Stravinsky and Hindemith, and other works ranging in time from Giovanni Gabrieli and Johann Christoph Pezel to Piston, Riegger, Schoenberg, and Varèse. Similar wind ensembles were organized in virtually every important university; in 1957 Robert A. Boudreau founded the American Wind Symphony as a professional ensemble (for illustration *see* PITTSBURGH). Fennell's work at Eastman was carried on from 1965 by Donald Hunsberger. Symphonic bands and wind ensembles have continued to flourish in junior and senior high schools, colleges, and universities, where students are involved in marching and concert performances, festivals, national and international tours, and composer-in-residence programs.

Many universities have a number of bands with different purposes and of different levels of competence. The band department at the University of Michigan, for example, has four concert bands (a symphonic band of 90 members (fig.4, p. 136), a concert band with 85, a university band with 80, and a campus band with 160), four athletic bands (a 250-piece marching band, and three separate "pep" bands, each with 40 members, for men's basketball, women's basketball, and hockey games), three wind ensembles (the Wind Ensemble, the Chamber Winds, and the Conductor's Wind Ensemble), and two jazz bands. Few students belong to more than one of the bands; academic credit is offered for participation in any of the groups except the Conductor's Wind Ensemble. Three full-time members of faculty are retained to train and direct the bands. The university also sponsors a wind ensemble for high-school students. The repertory of these groups is well represented in a set of 24 recordings, entitled *The Revelli Years*, issued on the Golden Crest label.

The professional band did not altogether disappear in the postwar era: Richard Franko Goldman, who assumed leadership of the Goldman Band (Table 1, 1946) on the death of his father, Edwin Franko Goldman, in 1956, continued the tradition of free outdoor concerts begun in 1911. He also continued his father's practice of commissioning new works: among those who wrote for him were Bergsma, Giannini, and Douglas Moore. In 1946 Leonard B. Smith organized the Detroit Concert Band, a professional ensemble that remains active and has made a series of successful recordings of older band music, including orchestral transcriptions, virtuoso solos, novelty pieces, and marches. In

4. *The University of Michigan Symphony Band with its conductor H. Robert Reynolds, 1978*

1956 an award was established by the Ostwald Uniform Company to honor the best band composition submitted each year to a jury of the American Bandmasters Association; winners have included Clifton Williams, Robert E. Jager, John Barnes Chance, Fisher Tull, Karl Kroeger, Roger Nixon, James Barnes, James E. Curnow, and Martin Mailman. The CBDNA has continued to commission works, from Krenek, Davidovsky, and others. Merle Evans, the bandmaster of the Ringling Brothers and Barnum & Bailey Circus, entertained audiences until his retirement in 1969; during his 50 years in the circus he is said to have performed for more than 165 million people.

In the military, reductions in the number and size of bands continued. The divisional band of 56 players current during World War II (Table 1, 1944) replaced as many as ten regimental bands; the present divisional or post band is a 40-piece musical unit that can serve many purposes (Table 1, 1983). The special bands of the armed services and the service academies (such as the US Army Band and the US Military Academy Band), however, include more than 140 players, choristers, and supporting personnel, and remain the country's leading professional wind ensembles. Community bands are enjoying a revival and some of the 2000 and more adult bands in the USA have achieved a professional standard of playing. Many bands have been in existence for more than a century, and some of the famous names of the past have been revived: the 26th North Carolina and 1st Wisconsin Brigade bands were resurrected for the Civil War Centennial, and the 3d and 4th Continental Artillery bands for the Bicentennial. The American Band of Providence and the Great Western Band of St. Paul are only two of the many bands that have taken on new life, and are again entertaining the citizens of their communities in the traditional manner.

BIBLIOGRAPHY

A. Dodworth: *Dodworth's Brass Band School* (New York, 1853/*R*1978)

G. F. Patton: *A Practical Guide to the Arrangement of Band Music* (Leipzig, Germany, 1875/*R*1981)

W. H. Dana: *J. W. Pepper's Practical Guide and Study to the Secret of Arranging Band Music, or The Amateur's Guide* (Philadelphia, 1878)

A. A. Clappé: *The Wind-band and its Instruments* (New York, 1911/*R*1976)

E. F. Goldman: *Band Betterment* (New York, 1934)

R. Dvorak: *The Band on Parade* (New York, 1937)

R. F. Goldman: *The Band's Music* (New York, 1938)

G. R. Prescott and L. W. Chidester: *Getting Results with School Bands* (New York, 1938)

C. B. Righter: *Success in Teaching School Orchestras and Bands* (Minneapolis, 1945)

L. W. Chidester: *International Wind-band Instrumentation* (San Antonio, 1946)

R. F. Goldman: *The Concert Band* (New York, 1946)

F. Fennell: *Time and the Winds* (Kenosha, WI, 1954)

F. N. Mayer: *A History of Scoring for Band* (diss., U. of Minnesota, 1957)

H. W. Schwartz: *Bands of America* (Garden City, NY, 1957/*R*1975) [see also R. F. Camus: "The Golden Age of Bands: a Second Look," *Journal of Band Research*, xv/2 (1980), 1]

Band Music Guide (Evanston, IL: Instrumentalist Company, 1959, 8/1982)

K. Berger: *Band Encyclopedia* (Evansville, IN, 1960)

J. Wagner: *Band Scoring* (New York, 1960)

R. F. Goldman: *The Wind Band* (Boston, 1961/*R*1974)

H. H. Hall: *A Johnny Reb Band from Salem* (Raleigh, 1963/*R*1980)

G. D. Bridges: *Pioneers in Brass* (Detroit, 1965)

H. H. Hall: *The Moravian Wind Ensemble: Distinctive Chapter in America's Music* (diss., George Peabody College for Teachers, 1967)

J. R. Smart: *The Sousa Band: a Discography* (Washington, DC, 1970)

A. G. Wright and S. Newcomb: *Bands of the World* (Evanston, IL, 1970)

J. T. Haynie: *The Changing Role of the Band in American Colleges and Universities, 1900 to 1968* (diss., George Peabody College for Teachers, 1971)

L. K. McCarrell: *A Historical Review of the College Band Movement from 1875 to 1969* (diss., Florida State U., 1971)

C. H. Tiede: *The Development of Minnesota Community Bands during the Nineteenth Century* (diss., U. of Minnesota, 1971)

R. E. Eliason: *Keyed Bugles in the United States* (Washington, DC, 1972)

D. Whitwell: *A New History of Wind Music* (Evanston, IL, 1972)

W. A. Bufkin: *Union Bands of the Civil War (1862–65): Instrumentation and Score Analysis* (diss., Louisiana State U., 1973)
C. Bryant: *And the Band Played On* (Washington, DC, 1975)
L. Smith: *A Study of the Historical Development of Selected Black College and University Bands as a Curricular and Aesthetic Entity 1867–1975* (diss., Kansas State U., 1976)
W. Suppan: *Lexikon des Blasmusikwesens* (Freiburg, Germany, 1976)
W. J. Schafer: *Brass Bands and New Orleans Jazz* (Baton Rouge, LA, 1977)
D. Whitwell and A. Ostling, Jr., eds.: *The College and University Band* (Reston, VA, 1977)
F. J. Cipolla: "Annotated Guide for the Study and Performance of Nineteenth Century Band Music in the United States," *Journal of Band Research*, xiv/1 (1978), 22
F. J. Cipolla: "A Bibliography of Dissertations Relative to the Study of Bands and Band Music," *Journal of Band Research*, xv/1 (1979), 1–31; xvi/1 (1980), 29
J. Newsom: "The American Brass Band Movement," *Quarterly Journal of the Library of Congress*, xxxvi (1979), 114
R. Garofalo and M. Elrod: "Heritage Americana," *Journal of Band Research*, xvii/1 (1981), 1
R. O. Olson: "A Core Repertoire for the Wind Ensemble," *Journal of Band Research*, xviii/1 (1982), 11
D. Whitwell: *The History and Literature of the Wind Band and Wind Ensemble* (Northridge, CA, 1982)
M. Good: "A Selected Bibliography for Original Concert Band Music," *Journal of Band Research*, xviii/2 (1983), 12; xix/1 (1983), 26

RAOUL CAMUS

Bandy, Moe [Marion F., Jr.] (*b* Meridian, MS, 12 Feb 1944). Country-music singer and guitarist. Born in the hometown of Jimmie Rodgers, he grew up listening to records of yodeling. His father, who led a country-music band, taught him to play guitar and influenced him to consider a country-music career. Upon graduation from high school in San Antonio, Texas, in 1962, he formed his first band, Moe and the Mavericks. Over the next 12 years he played in Texas dance halls and on a San Antonio television show, "Country Corner," and recorded for several small companies, but with little success. His first single was his own song, *Lonely Lady* (1964), issued by Satin. In 1972 Bandy persuaded the producer Ray Baker to produce a session for him; though Bandy had to finance it, the result was his first charted record, *I just started hatin' cheatin' songs today*. Originally released on Footprint, the record had national success and was reissued by General Recording Company, an Atlanta label, in 1973. Subsequent GRC releases included *Honky Tonk Amnesia* (1973), *It was always easy to find an unhappy woman* (1974), and *Don't anyone make love at home anymore* (1974). In the mid-1970s Bandy formed a new band, the Rodeo Clowns, and appeared on the "Grand Ole Opry" and in Europe. In 1975 he became contracted to Columbia Records, for which he made many successful recordings, beginning with *Hank Williams, you wrote my life* (1976). Among later releases were *Here I am drunk again* (1976), *Cowboys ain't supposed to cry* (1977), and a duet with Joe Stampley, *Just Good Ole Boys*, which reached no. 1 on the country chart in 1979. Bandy is known particularly for his performances of honky-tonk songs dealing with drinking and cheating. He makes no concessions to the country-pop style; his repertory is faithful to the hardcore country music that has traditionally attracted blue-collar audiences.

DON CUSIC

Bangs, Lester (*b* El Cajon, CA, 14 Dec 1948; *d* New York, 30 April 1982). Rock critic. His career as a critic started in 1969, when *Rolling Stone* began to print articles he wrote while attending San Diego State College. Once he was established as a writer his work as a rock critic was widely published; at the same time he wrote many essays, most of which remain unpublished, on such topics as sex, politics, and culture. From 1971 to 1976 he was an editor and writer for the Detroit magazine *Creem*, and his articles helped to set its irreverent tone. He moved to New York, where he inspired and influenced the nascent punk-rock movement and published books on Blondie (1980) and (with Paul Nelson) Rod Stewart (1981). Eventually he began to perform, in an energetic, if defiantly crude, punk style, and made the recordings *Let it blurt/Live* (Spy 003, 1979) and *Jook Savages on the Brazos* (Live Wire 3, 1981). Bangs was the best of those rock critics whose writings are informed with a rebellious energy that mirrors the music they love. Central to his work is a buoyant vitality, set against a more somber determination to overcome his nihilistic impulses. An anthology of his work, edited by Greil Marcus, is in preparation.

JOHN ROCKWELL

Banjo. A plucked lute with a long, guitar-like neck and a circular soundtable of tautly stretched parchment or skin (now usually plastic), against which the bridge is pressed by the strings. The banjo and its variants have had long and widespread popularity as folk, parlor, and professional entertainers' instruments.

1. Structure. 2. History.

1. STRUCTURE. The modern banjo is normally fitted with raised frets and strung with five steel wire strings, the lowest in pitch being overspun with fine copper wire. It is tuned *g'–c–g–b–d'* (C tuning) or *g'–d–g–b–d'* (G tuning). There are usually 24 or more screw-tightening brackets (for adjusting the skin tension) attached to the outer side of a tambourine-like rim of laminated wood about 28 cm (or slightly larger for concert instruments) in diameter. In banjos of high quality the upper edge over which the head is stretched is often of complicated design, as in the (1920s) "Mastertone" system by the firm of GIBSON, which used a metal "tone tube" resting on spring-supported ball-bearings (fig. 1*b*, p. 138); or the "Electric" design of A. C. FAIRBANKS. A pan-shaped, wooden "resonator" is often attached to the lower side of the otherwise open-backed body and serves to reflect outwards the sound emitted by the underside of the soundtable. The "thumb string," the short fifth string, is placed adjacent to the lowest-pitched string and secured by a peg inserted into the side of the neck at the fifth fret position.

Until the early 20th century banjos were normally strung with gut strings, and these or nylon strings are still used by "classical" banjoists. Raised frets were advocated by James Buckley in *Buckley's New Banjo Method* (New York, 1860) but did not become common until the 1880s. George C. Dobson's *"Victor" Banjo Manual* (Boston, 1887) describes frets inlaid flush with the fingerboard as position markers but states that "the latest and most modern manner . . . is with raised frets." Mid-19th-century commercial banjos were larger than modern ones and were tuned to the lower-pitched A tuning of *e'–a–e–g♯–b*. Smaller banjos and higher pitches later became increasingly popular, until by the 1880s most banjos were of modern proportions and commonly tuned to the modern C tuning. By 1890 in the USA the banjo was treated as a transposing instrument pitched in C with music still written in A, a situation that continued until 1909 when the American Guild of Banjoists, Mandolinists, and Guitarists voted to abandon the old A notation and write the music in C, or "English notation." In England both the written and tuning pitch were fixed at the modern level by the 1880s.

A number of hybrid and specialized banjos were developed during the late 19th and early 20th centuries, including cello and piccolo banjos (tuned an octave below and above the standard banjo); banjeaurines; guitar, mandolin, and ukulele banjos (strung and tuned like their parent instruments); and plectrum banjos (identical to standard banjos but lacking the fifth string). The tenor banjo (tuned *c–g–d′–a′*) is similar to the standard banjo but has a shorter neck and no fifth string. Like the plectrum banjo it was developed for use in jazz and dance orchestras and is played with a plectrum.

2. HISTORY. The development of the modern banjo began in the second quarter of the 19th century as a largely commercial adaptation of an instrument used by West African slaves in the New World as early as the 17th century. The earliest known illustration of the instrument is in Sir Hans Sloane's *A Voyage to the Islands of Madeira, Barbados, Nieves, S. Christopher and Jamaica* (London, 1707), written in 1688, which depicts two Jamaican black "strum-strums" with long, flat necks and skin-covered gourd bodies. In the French colonies, where the instrument was usually known as the *banza*, it was often associated with the calinda, a dance unsuccessfully suppressed by acts of the Martinique government as early as 1654 and as late as 1772.

In the British colonies the instrument was usually known as *banjer* or *banjar*, pronunciations still commonly used in the southern USA. The Rev. Jonathan Boucher, describing life in Maryland and Virginia before he returned to England in 1775, wrote in *Boucher's Glossary of Archaic and Provincial Words* (London, 1832): "The favorite and almost only instrument in use among the slaves there was a *bandore*; or, as they pronounced the word, *banjer*. Its body was a large hollow gourd, with a long handle attached to it, strung with catgut, and played on with the fingers." Thomas Jefferson, in his *Notes on Virginia* (Paris, 1784, and Richmond, Virginia, 1853), stated of the Blacks: "The instrument proper to them is the Banjar, . . . its chords [strings] being precisely the four lower chords of the guitar." The common English guitar of the period was tuned *C–e–g–c′–e′–g′*; hence the *banjar* would have been tuned either *C–e–g–c′*, if by "lower" Jefferson meant "lower in pitch," or else *g–c′–e′–g′*, if he meant "lower in position when held by the player." The former interpretation gives a scordatura tuning pattern still sometimes used for the banjo's four full-length strings; the latter gives the pattern of the modern G tuning.

The origin of the *banza* remains speculative, similar long-necked instruments with a skin soundtable being common in West Africa, the Middle East, and Asia. A virtually identical instrument, the *ramkie*, has existed in South Africa since the early 18th century. But a West African origin is more likely, and Samuel Charters, in *The Roots of the Blues: an African Search* (New York, 1982), points out that the *xalam*, an instrument of great age still played by the Wolof people in Senegal, bears a remarkable resemblance to the banjo in both its structure and the techniques for playing it.

A late 18th-century watercolor entitled *The Old Plantation* (painted in South Carolina and now in the Abby Aldrich Rockefeller Folk Art Center, Williamsburg, Virginia) shows a group of slaves dancing to the music of a banjo (*see* AFRO-AMERICAN MUSIC, fig. 1). The instrument, while otherwise similar to Sloane's "strum-strum," is interesting in that it provides one of the earliest known illustrations of the characteristic short thumb string. The picture clearly shows three full-length strings plus a fourth end-

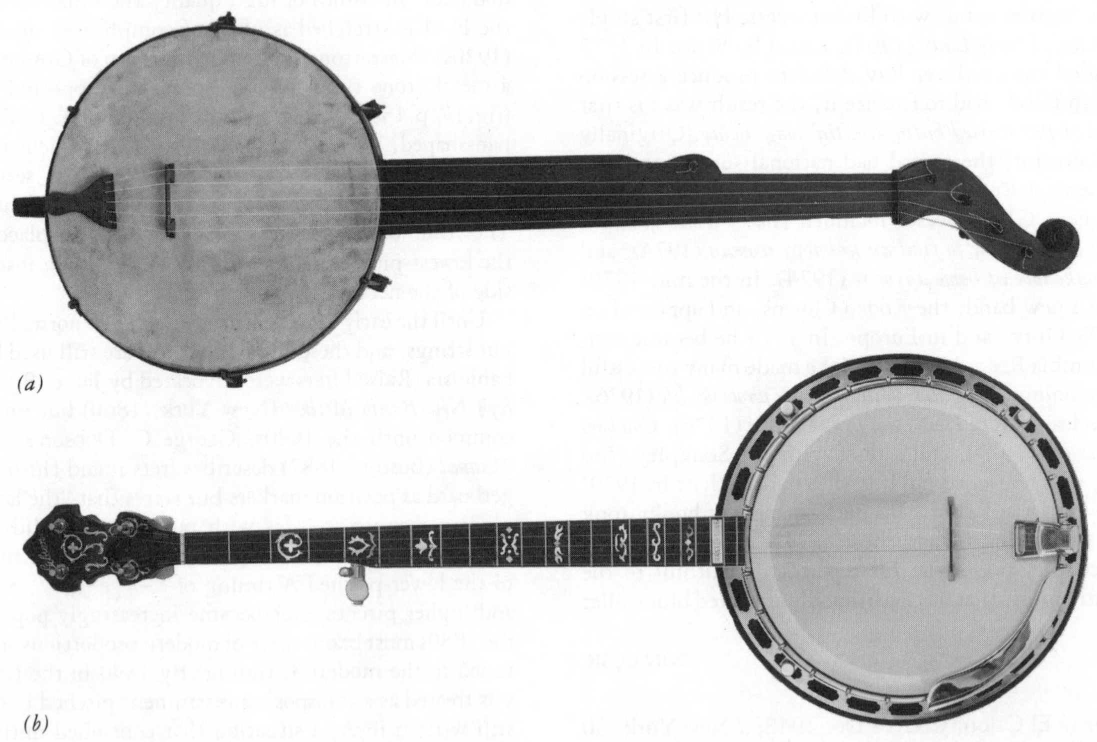

1. Five-string banjos: (a) by William Boucher, 1846; (b) Mastertone model by the Gibson company, c1924 (both Smithsonian Institution)

ing at a peg set into the neck on the bass side, about halfway from the bridge to the nut. Some confusion on this point has resulted from an inaccurate drawing of this instrument, showing four full-length strings, included in an article by Woodward (1949). The invention of the short string is often erroneously attributed to JOEL WALKER SWEENEY; nevertheless, as the first well-known and widely traveled white banjoist, Sweeney played a role in bringing the banjo to the attention of urban audiences in the USA and England and presumably in popularizing the type of banjo that he played. One made by him is in the Los Angeles County Museum (catalogue no. A.2543). Although fretless and of light construction, it had a short fifth string and screw-tightening brackets (now missing) for adjusting the skin tension, and it is similar to a modern banjo.

Through the influence of Sweeney, DAN EMMETT, and many other popular minstrel-show banjoists, the banjo was rapidly introduced to white urban culture and by the 1840s and 1850s was being commercially produced by such early makers as WILLIAM BOUCHER of Baltimore (see fig. 1*a*), whose banjos were almost identical with Sweeney's, and James Ashborn of Wolcottville, Connecticut, who applied an improved tuning-peg to a banjo in 1852 (US Patent 9268).

By the end of the Civil War the banjo had also taken root among traditional white musicians of the rural South, who had learned about it from direct contact with black musicians and, especially, touring minstrel shows, medicine shows, and circuses. The banjo joined the fiddle to initiate a tradition of what is now called "old-time string band music," and was also played as a solo instrument and to accompany songs. The black tradition remained fairly strong in the rural South through the 1930s, but by the 1980s there were few black players. Until the latter decades of the 20th century interplay between the black and white traditions was common.

Two general classes of playing styles, each with many variations, have developed. The first class involves down-stroking styles, those using the thumb and the back (nail) of the index or middle finger, always moving downwards as they hit the strings. Apart from numerous mentions of the banjo's use to accompany singing and dancing, no detailed descriptions or notations of pre-19th-century performances are known. However, the earliest minstrel style is known from mid-19th-century instruction books; called "stroke" playing, this downstroking style creates a sound in many early minstrel banjo solos that corresponds closely with the limited available descriptions of pre-minstrel black playing. This correspondence and other evidence suggest that pre-minstrel black playing was also a down-stroking style. The earliest style of rural southern white banjo players is basically the same down-stroking style, a style which is still used, with many variations, and now known generically as "frailing" or "clawhammer" style.

The second class of banjo styles, finger-picking, first appeared (it had been obliquely referred to earlier) in an 1865 instruction book by FRANK B. CONVERSE, though he credited the BUCKLEY family with being the first to play it. Called "guitar style" at first, and later "classical" or "classic" banjo, it is essentially an application of finger-style guitar playing techniques to the banjo. During the 1870s this style began displacing the older "stroke" styles on the minstrel, vaudeville, and concert stages and in the home as the banjo was increasingly used as a genteel parlor instrument for the performance of popular and light classical music.

2. Four-string banjo player, c1902

Finger-style playing began to enter the rural folk tradition among both black and white players around 1900, apparently in imitation of the classic style. At first, folk finger-styles were primarily "two-finger picking" (that is, thumb and index finger); in the 1940s a new folk "three-finger" style (thumb, index finger, and middle finger) developed; called "bluegrass picking," it is the most widely heard style in the 1980s.

As early as the 1860s the banjo was taken up by high society. An article in the *Boston Daily Evening Voice* (20 Oct 1866) noted that "the banjo has found its way into the highest public circles, and many of the ladies of the bon ton, infatuated with its music, have become expert in its management. Indeed it is not uncommon to find the banjo occupying a conspicuous corner in a Fifth Avenue parlor." By the 1880s, the new playing style was firmly established and the banjo's conquest of high society was complete. Concurrently, there was a vast expansion in the production of banjos and great elaboration in their design and decoration, by makers such as the Dobsons (New York and Boston), S. S. STEWART (Philadelphia), and A. C. FAIRBANKS (Boston). Besides making regular banjos, these makers (primarily Stewart) created a set of banjo orchestra instruments, all with five strings but of different sizes and pitches. From about 1890 to 1920 there was a craze for banjo, mandolin, and guitar clubs and orchestras; by the turn of the century most good-sized cities and colleges had such organizations. In this period specialized journals and great quantities of marches, rags, and transcriptions of popular and light classical music were published for banjo by Stewart, Walter Jacobs of Boston, Clifford Essex of London, and others.

The banjo's important relationship to popular music at that time is well illustrated in the case of RAGTIME. Nathan finds in some minstrel-show banjo tunes the earliest examples of the kinds of syncopation that later appear in the genre. Banjo pieces such as George Lansing's *The Darkie's Dream* (1887) are among the precursors of ragtime; ragtime itself immediately entered the banjo repertory, and banjo compositions from the middle 1890s on were heavily influenced by ragtime. The recorded output of the greatest turn-of-the-century banjo recording artists, VESS L. OSSMAN and FRED VAN EPS, includes many rags, and banjo recordings of ragtime (available long before ragtime piano recordings were issued) were influential in increasing its popularity. Thus, the banjo contributed significantly to the enormous impact that ragtime had on all of popular music. Other important concert banjo virtuosos of the time included Parke Hunter, ALFRED A. FARLAND, and FRED BACON.

By the 1920s the popularity of the five-string banjo was rapidly declining among urban players. It was displaced by the four-string tenor and plectrum banjos, which were favored as rhythm instruments in the jazz and dance orchestras of the day, largely because a pick-played banjo was better suited to the music for the fast, rhythmic new dance steps. The first true tenor banjo was probably the "banjorine" marketed by J. B. Schall of Chicago in 1907, which was advertised as "tuned like a mandolin and played with a pick." Such an instrument found ready acceptance among mandolinists and violinists, whose original instruments did not adapt well to the new music. Regular banjoists converted more easily to the plectrum banjo. Once introduced, these instruments did not long remain as mere accompanying rhythm instruments; solo styles developed, as did virtuoso soloists such as Eddie Peabody and Harry Reser. The "Jazz Age" created a new society craze for the banjo, this time in its four-string versions. By the 1940s, however, the four-string banjo was being replaced by the guitar, especially the electric guitar, as the rhythm instrument of choice.

The five-string banjo regained something of its former popularity after World War II, largely because of the influence of the American banjoists Pete Seeger (*see* SEEGER, (2)), who popularized traditional rural southern styles among urban players as one aspect of the folksong revival, and Earl Scruggs (*see* FLATT AND SCRUGGS), who became famous as the developer of the "bluegrass" style of banjo playing (*see* BLUEGRASS MUSIC).

In the southeast USA, many white traditional country musicians still play banjos, often homemade and fretless; their scordatura tunings, playing techniques and repertory include survivals of 19th-century minstrel and black performing practice. The Archive of Folk Culture, Library of Congress, Washington, DC, has a good collection of field recordings of such music. In the USA the American Banjo Fraternity promotes classic banjo playing and holds semiannual conventions.

Public instrument collections possessing banjos include the Smithsonian Institution, Washington, DC; the Metropolitan Museum of Art, New York; and the Stearns Collection of Musical Instruments, University of Michigan, Ann Arbor.

BIBLIOGRAPHY

The Cadenza, i/1–xxxi/22 (1894–1924)

The Crescendo, i/1–xxv/12 (1908–33)

P. Seeger: *How to Play the Five-string Banjo* (New York, 1948, 3/1961)

A. Woodward: "Joel Sweeney and the First Banjo," *Los Angeles County Museum Quarterly*, vii/3 (1949), 7

H. Nathan: *Dan Emmett and the Rise of Early Negro Minstrelsy* (Norman, OK, 1962)

D. J. Epstein: "Slave Music in the United States before 1860: a Survey of Sources," *Notes*, xx (1962–3), 195, 377

B. C. Malone: *Country Music U.S.A.: a Fifty-year History* (Austin, 1968, 2/1985)

A. Rosenbaum: *Old Time Mountain Banjo: an Instruction Method* (New York, 1968)

C. P. Heaton: "The Five-string Banjo in North Carolina," *Southern Folklore Quarterly*, xxxv (1971), 62

T. Adler: "The Physical Development of the Banjo," *New York Folklore Quarterly*, xxviii (1972), 187

D. J. Epstein: "African Music in British and French America," *MQ*, lix (1973), 61–91

——: "The Folk Banjo: a Documentary History," *EM*, xix (1975), 347

R. L. Webb: "Banjos on their Saddle Horns," *American History Illustrated*, xi/2 (1976), 11

R. B. Winans: "The Folk, the Stage, and the Five-string Banjo in the Nineteenth Century," *Journal of American Folklore*, lxxxix (1976), 407–37

D. J. Epstein: *Sinful Tunes and Spirituals: Black Folk Music to the Civil War* (Urbana, IL, 1977)

R. B. Winans: "Black Banjo Tradition in Virginia and West Virginia," *Journal of the Virginia Folklore Society*, i (1979), 7

——: "Black Instrumental Music Traditions in the Ex-slave Narratives," *Black Music Research Newsletter*, v/2 (1982), 2

S. Cohen: "Banjo Makers and Manufacturers," *Mugwumps*, vii (1983), 10

R. L. Webb: *Ring the Banjar! the Banjo in America from Folklore to Factory* (Cambridge, MA, 1984)

R. B. Winans: "Early Minstrel Show Music, 1843–1852," *Musical Theatre in America*, ed. G. Loney (Westport, CT, 1984), 71

JAY SCOTT ODELL, ROBERT B. WINANS

Banjo Joe. Pseudonym of GUS CANNON.

Bannock. American Indian group of the Great Basin area. *See* PAIUTE.

Baptist Church, music of the. The first Baptist church in America was founded by English immigrants at Providence in 1639. Some 17th-century English Baptists objected to the use of congregational singing in worship. However, there is evidence that several early Baptist churches in America practiced psalm-singing, probably using the Sternhold and Hopkins or Ainsworth psalters. In some cases singing was apparently abandoned when large numbers of non-singing English Baptists joined these churches. When objections to singing in Baptist worship began to die out in the early 18th century, many non-singing churches adopted or reintroduced psalmody, while newly formed churches sang from their inception.

The hymnals used by Baptists in America during the 18th and early 19th centuries were usually of English origin. The collection found most often among early 18th-century Baptists was Tate and Brady's *New Version of the Psalms*. This was succeeded during the second half of the century by various editions of Isaac Watts's psalms and hymns, frequently supplemented by J. Rippon's *Selection of Hymns* (London, 1787, repr. New York and Elizabethtown, 1792). Earlier editions of Watts were replaced by the *Psalms and Hymns of Dr. Watts Arranged by Dr. Rippon* (London, 1801, repr. Philadelphia, 1820), commonly known as "Rippon's Watts." The first Baptist hymnal compiled in America, *Hymns and Spiritual Songs*, was published anonymously at Newport, Rhode Island, in 1766. However, it was not until the publication of J. Winchell's *An Arrangement of . . . Watts* (Boston, 1819) that an American compilation seriously rivaled English hymnals among Baptists, especially in New England. "Rippon's Watts" continued in use in the Middle Atlantic States until both it and "Winchell's Watts" were superseded by B. Stow and S. F. Smith's *The Psalmist* (1843). In addition to its enormous popularity, *The Psalmist* was significant because it marked a turning away from "Watts entire" and from collections that were merely supplementary to Watts. A collection somewhat outside the mainstream of Baptist hymnody in the North was J. Smith's *Divine Hymns* (Portsmouth, 1791). This early collection of folk hymn texts had little impact on standard northern Baptist hymnals, but owing to its popularity in rural areas it did reach 12 editions. The collections noted here were words-only hymnals, but the Baptists also counted among their number several significant composers, including Oliver Holden and Oliver Shaw. The first tunebook published specifically for Baptists in America, Samuel Holyoke's *The Christian Harmonist* (1804), was apparently a failure.

During the 18th century Baptist hymnody followed much the same course in the North and South. After 1800, however, Baptists of the South began to rely increasingly upon the folk hymn. The most popular southern collections included J. Mercer's *The Cluster* (1810), S. Dupuy's *Hymns and Spiritual Songs* (1811), W. Dossey's *The Choice* (1820), and S. S. Burdett's *Baptist Harmony* (1834). Three widely used southern folk hymn tune collections, W. Walker's *The Southern Harmony* (1835), B. F. White and E. J. King's *The Sacred Harp* (1844), and J. G. McCurry's *The Social Harp* (1855), were compiled by Baptists. The 20th-century revival of interest in folk hymnody has encouraged the continued use of these tunebooks in certain southern congregations and annual shape-note singing meetings. Controversies among Baptists caused a division of the denomination into Northern and Southern Baptist Conventions in 1845. The *Baptist Psalmody* (1850) of B. Manly and B. Manly, Jr., gained immediate acceptance among Southern Baptists, holding much the same place that *The Psalmist* did among their northern brethren.

The most important influence on late 19th-century Baptist hymnody was the emergence of the gospel song. Many prominent gospel songwriters were Northern Baptists (for example, W. B. Bradbury, R. Lowry, and W. H. Doane). A few individuals advocated the widespread adoption of English liturgical hymnody among Baptists in the North. The most remarkable attempt in this direction was E. H. Johnson's *Sursum corda* (1898), although it never became popular. *The Baptist Hymnal* (1883) and similar collections that attempted to balance liturgical hymnody with the gospel song were more widely accepted. *The New Baptist Hymnal*, produced jointly by Northern and Southern Baptists in 1926, became quite popular in the North but did not find favor in the South. The most recent hymnals of Northern Baptists (since 1950 called the American Baptist Convention), *Christian Worship* (1941) and *Hymnbook for Christian Worship* (1970), were jointly compiled with the Disciples of Christ.

Late 19th-century Southern Baptists wholeheartedly embraced the gospel song, which almost entirely replaced the folk hymn as the basis of their congregational singing. This emphasis on the gospel song continued well into the 20th century in such books as R. H. Coleman's *The Modern Hymnal* (1926) and *The American Hymnal* (1933) and B. B. McKinney's *The Broadman Hymnal* (1940). The two most recent Southern Baptist hymnals, both titled *Baptist Hymnal* (1956 and 1975), have drawn from a wider range of hymnic styles and traditions.

Choirs were generally rejected in Baptist churches until after 1770. The earliest record of choral singing dates from the year 1771, when a choir was formed at the First Baptist Church of Boston. Other urban churches in the North soon imitated this practice, and by 1820 most of the larger churches had instituted choirs. A few urban churches in the South formed choirs in the early 19th century, but even as late as 1868 some Southern Baptist churches were struggling with the propriety of admitting choirs. Early Baptist choirs were generally composed of volunteers who sat in the balcony facing the pulpit. In the late 19th and early 20th centuries the influence of English liturgical movements prompted many Baptist churches to vest their choirs and place them in full view of the congregation.

Even more controversial than the use of choirs was the introduction of musical instruments. Despite considerable opposition, the bass viol began appearing in Northern Baptist churches shortly after 1800. About 1819 an organ was installed in the Baptist church at Pawtucket, Rhode Island, and the older, better-established New England Baptist churches soon began acquiring organs. Lingering objections to instruments prevented most Southern Baptist churches from acquiring organs until after 1850. Nearly all Baptist churches in the USA today use some sort of instrument – usually organ or piano – in their worship.

In recent years many of the larger Baptist churches have hired full-time ministers of music who are responsible for a church's entire music program. These programs frequently include separate choirs for different age groups, various types of instrumental ensemble, and direction of the congregational singing. In smaller churches the minister of music is frequently a part-time or volunteer worker with more limited responsibilities.

Two important factors in the development of Southern Baptist church music during the 20th century have been the establishment of the Church Music Department in 1941 and the influence of music schools in the seminaries operated by the Southern Baptist Convention. The Church Music Department provides literature, music, and training opportunities for church musicians. Graduate-level instruction in sacred music is offered at Southwestern Baptist Theological Seminary, Fort Worth; Southern Baptist Theological Seminary, Louisville; New Orleans Baptist Theological Seminary, New Orleans; and Golden Gate Baptist Theological Seminary, Mill Valley, California.

BIBLIOGRAPHY

H. S. Burrage: *Baptist Hymn Writers and their Hymns* (Portland, ME, 1888)
L. F. Benson: *The English Hymn* (New York, 1915/*R*1962)
A. L. Stevenson: *The Story of Southern Hymnology* (Salem, VA, 1931/*R*1970)
G. P. Jackson: *White Spirituals in the Southern Uplands* (Chapel Hill, 1933/*R*1965)
H. W. Foote: *Three Centuries of American Hymnody* (Cambridge, MA, 1940/*R*1968)
G. P. Jackson: *White and Negro Spirituals* (New York, 1943/*R*1964, 1975)
W. Dinneen: *Music at the Meeting House, 1775–1958* (Providence, 1958)
W. L. Hooper: *Church Music in Transition* (Nashville, 1963)
"Our Baptist Heritage in Church Music," *Church Musician*, xv (1963), 14
W. J. Reynolds: *A Survey of Christian Hymnody* (New York, 1963; 2/1978 ed. M. Price as *A Joyful Sound: Christian Hymnody*)
H. Eskew: "Hymnody of our Forefathers," *Church Musician*, xv (1964), 5
W. J. Reynolds: *Hymns of our Faith: a Handbook for the Baptist Hymnal* (Nashville, 1964, rev. 2/1967)
E. Lockwood and L. Ellinwood: "Christ, the Appletree," *The Hymn*, xxvi (1975), 25
W. J. Reynolds: *Companion to Baptist Hymnal* (Nashville, 1976)
——: "Our Heritage of Baptist Hymnody in America," *Baptist History and Heritage*, xi (1976), 204
D. Music: "The Introduction of Musical Instruments into Baptist Churches in America," *Quarterly Review: a Survey of Southern Baptist Progress*, xl/1 (1979), 55
H. Eskew and H. McElrath: *Sing with Understanding; an Introduction to Christian Hymnology* (Nashville, 1980)
D. Music: "Oliver Holden (1765–1844): the First Baptist Composer in America," *Quarterly Review: a Survey of Southern Baptist Progress*, xli/1 (1980), 46
——: "The First American Baptist Tunebook," *Foundations*, xxiii (1980), 267
——: "Music in the First Baptist Church of Boston, Massachusetts, 1665–1820," *Quarterly Review: a Survey of Southern Baptist Progress*, xlii/3 (1982), 37
C. R. Brewster: *The Cluster of Jesse Mercer* (Macon, GA, 1983)
T. H. Cook: *A History of Music at Central College during the Nineteenth Century* (diss., U. of Northern Colorado, 1983)
"Church Music in Baptist History," *Baptist History and Heritage*, xix (1984) [complete issue]
I. H. Murrell, Jr.: *An Examination of Southern Ante-bellum Baptist Hymnals and Tunebooks as Indicators of the Congregational Hymn and Tune Repertories of the Period*

with an Analysis of Representative Tunes (diss., New Orleans Baptist Theological Seminary, 1984)
D. Music: "Starke Dupuy, Early Baptist Hymnal Compiler," *Quarterly Review: a Survey of Southern Baptist Progress*, xlv/1 (1984), 43
J. T. Titon: "Stance, Role, and Identity in Fieldwork among Folk Baptists," *American Music*, iii/1 (1985), 16

DAVID W. MUSIC

Barab, Seymour (*b* Chicago, IL, 9 Jan 1921). Composer and cellist. At the age of 13 he performed as a church organist in Chicago. Later he studied cello with Piatigorsky and Edmund Kurtz and between 1940 and 1960 played in several major orchestras, including those of Indianapolis, Cleveland, Portland (Oregon), and San Francisco. Among the chamber ensembles he helped to organize are the Composers Quartet, and the New York Pro Musica, in which he played viola da gamba. During the 1960s Barab taught at Rutgers, the State University of New Jersey, and at the New England Conservatory.

A sojourn in Paris in 1952 fostered Barab's interest in composition; while there he wrote more than 200 art songs, and he continues to write mainly vocal works. He is best known for his more than 30 operas, most of which are in one act. Of these the most frequently performed are *Chanticleer* (libretto by M. C. Richards, after Chaucer; first performed in Aspen, 4 August 1956), *A Game of Chance* (E. Manacher; Rock Island, Illinois, 11 January 1957), *Little Red Riding Hood* (Barab, after J. and W. Grimm; New York, 13 October 1962), and *The Toy Shop* (Barab; New York, 3 June 1978). His more recent operas include *A Piece of String* (after G. de Maupassant; Greeley, Colorado, May 1985), and *The Maker of Illusions* (Barab; New York, 21 April 1985). Barab has also composed orchestral works, chamber pieces, and choruses; among his song settings are *The Child's Garden of Verses* and *Songs of Perfect Propriety*, both of which have been recorded.

Barati, George (*b* Győr, Hungary, 3 April 1913). Composer, conductor, and cellist. He took classes from Zoltán Kodály and studied composition with Leo Weiner at the Ferenc Liszt Academy of Music in Budapest (1932–8), and became well known as a cellist in Hungary. He came to the USA shortly before World War II and from 1939 to 1943 studied composition at Princeton University with Sessions. He played cello with the San Francisco SO from 1946 to 1950, and conducted the Honolulu SO from 1950 to 1967. Since then Barati has concentrated on composing and conducting, the latter with over 85 orchestras around the world. He has composed more than 50 works, which show the influence of Bartók and Kodály and, by his own assessment, that of the years he has spent living in Hawaii and touring the Far East. He received a Naumburg Award in 1959 and a Guggenheim Fellowship in composition in 1965.

WORKS
(selective list)

Str Qt no.1, 1944; Chamber Conc., 1952; Vc Conc., 1957; The Dragon and the Phoenix, orch, 1960; Str Qt no.2, 1962; Polarization, orch, 1965; Baroque Qt Conc., 1969; Pf Conc., 1973; Conc., gui, small orch, 1976, rev. 1982; Branches of Time, 2 pf, orch, 1981; Confluence, orch, 1982; The Ugly Duckling, film score, 1982, arr. orch suite, 1982; Indiana Triptych, 1983; Chant to Pele, fl, 1983; B. U. D. Pf Sonata, 1984

Principal publishers: ACA, Peters

KATHLEEN HAEFLIGER

Barbecue Bob [Hicks, Robert] (*b* Walnut Grove, GA, 11 Sept 1902; *d* Lithonia, GA, 21 Oct 1931). Blues singer and guitarist. As a youth he worked on a farm before moving to Atlanta, where he was employed first at a hotel and later as a cook in Tidwell's Barbecue Place in the wealthy suburb of Buckhead – a job that earned him his nickname. His characteristic vocal range and the ringing notes of his 12-string guitar played with a slide were demonstrated on his first recording, *Barbecue Blues* (1927, Col. 14205), which was a best seller. Although he did not see the Mississippi floods, his *Mississippi Heavy Water Blues* (1927, Col. 14222) was timely. He experimented with various blues forms, was continually inventive in his themes, as on *We Sure Got Hard Times Now* (1930, Col. 14558), and played occasional dance or comic songs such as *The Monkey and the Baboon* (1930, Col. 14523). Barbecue Bob became the central figure of a school of blues singers working in and around Atlanta, a group that included his elder brother Laughing Charlie Hicks, Curley Weaver, and several lesser-known musicians. He made a couple of records with his brother (who also recorded solo under the name of Charlie Lincoln); *Darktown Gamblin'* (1930, Col. 14531), with simulated crap and skin games, was typical of their vocal exchanges. Within three years Barbecue Bob appeared on over 70 recordings. His last were with the Georgia Cotton Pickers, which included Weaver on guitar and Buddy Moss on harmonica, an outstanding example being *She's coming back some cold rainy day* (1930, Col. 14577). Shortly afterwards he contracted influenza, leading to the pneumonia that caused his death at the age of 28. His brother was deeply depressed by the loss, became alcoholic and criminal, and died in jail in 1963.

BIBLIOGRAPHY

P. Oliver: "Barbecue Bob," *Music Mirror*, v/8 (1958), 6
P. Lowry: "Some Cold Rainy Day," *Blues Unlimited*, no.104 (1973), 15

PAUL OLIVER

Barber, Samuel (*b* West Chester, PA, 9 March 1910; *d* New York, 23 Jan 1981). Composer. Never stylistically in the vanguard, his music was consistently appreciated throughout his long career by performers and audiences and only slightly less so by critics. Few American composers of concert music and opera have seen such a high proportion of their works enter and remain in the repertory.

1. Career. 2. Style.

1. CAREER. He had his first piano lessons at the age of six and began composing when he was seven; he also had cello lessons briefly. Among his juvenile pieces was a short opera, *The Rose Tree*, which was performed by him and his sister Sara. This early attempt could be seen as the beginning of an inclination towards vocal music, an important area of his work as a mature composer. He was supported and encouraged in his respect by his mother's sister, the contralto Louise Homer, and her husband Sidney Homer, a composer who concentrated almost exclusively on song. (Barber edited an anthology of Homer's songs as a tribute to his uncle in 1943.) As a teenager Barber was organist at Westminster Presbyterian Church and attended the West Chester High School, graduating in 1926. His academic musical training began at the age of 14 when he entered the Curtis Institute as a member of its first class in 1924. (Its founder, Mary Louise Curtis Bok, was to become one of Barber's devoted benefactors.) There he was exposed to a group of talented musicians; he studied piano with Boyle and later with Vengerova, composition with Scalero, and conducting with Reiner. He was also interested in developing his baritone voice and studied singing with Emilio Edoardo de Gogorza. His vocal progress was encouraging enough for him to

1. Samuel Barber, c1972

entertain the notion for a time of pursuing a singing career. He gave vocal recitals at the Curtis Institute and, after graduation, studied with John Braun in Vienna and sang publicly there. In 1935 he was heard in recitals on NBC radio and recorded his *Dover Beach*.

During his eight years at the Curtis Institute, Barber's skill as a composer was firmly established. A number of the works composed during these years – such as the first two songs of op.2, the Serenade for string quartet, *Dover Beach*, and the Cello Sonata – are not those of a merely talented student: they are the products of an assured composer. These works, along with many later ones, became standards in the American repertory. Furthermore, elements of Barber's style that emerged during the student years – the long lyric lines, the felicitous text-setting, and the knowing exploitation of instrumental color and technique – were not radically changed in later years.

The first of Barber's numerous awards was the Bearns Prize of Columbia University in 1928 for his Violin Sonata. This enabled him to travel abroad (to Italy) for the first time. He won the Bearns Prize a second time in 1933, for the overture to *The School for Scandal*, his first work to be performed by a major orchestra. In 1935 and again in 1936 he traveled in Europe and composed at the American Academy in Rome as the result of Pulitzer Traveling Scholarships and the Rome Prize. The compositions produced during these years – the *Music for a Scene from Shelley*, the First Symphony, and the String Quartet – were performed immediately in New York and Rome. The symphony was played in the USA for the first time by Rodzinski and the Cleveland Orchestra in January 1937. Rodzinski conducted it again in July at the Salzburg Festival – the first time an American work was performed there. In 1935 Barber met Toscanini in Italy and showed him some of his work. Three years later Toscanini conducted the NBC SO in premières of two works by Barber on the same program, the *First Essay* for orchestra and the Adagio for Strings; the latter is an orchestral transcription of the second movement of the String Quartet. Toscanini also recorded the Adagio, and it became Barber's most popular and most frequently performed piece.

Barber returned to the Curtis Institute in 1939 as a teacher of composition and remained there until 1942, though he had no great liking for this kind of work and never again accepted a teaching position. He was elected to the National Institute of Arts and Letters in 1941 and in 1958 to the American Academy of Arts and Letters. In 1943 he purchased a house in Mount Kisco, New York, with Menotti, who had been a fellow student at the Curtis Institute and his traveling companion in Europe. Barber was to do most of his composing there until 1974, when he and Menotti sold the house. In April 1943 he was conscripted into the US Army and assigned to the Army Air Force. During the first year of his military service, spent largely in Fort Worth, he composed two works, the *Commando March* for band and the Second Symphony (dedicated to the Army Air Force), on commission from the Air Force. The latter work was performed by Koussevitzky and the Boston SO in Boston and New York, but it did not find wide acceptance. Barber revised the symphony in 1947 but apparently was never very satisfied with it; 24 years after its composition he withdrew it and destroyed the manuscript score and performance materials. The second movement, however, exists in a revised version as *Night Flight*.

Barber was released from military service at the end of World War II, and he returned to Europe almost immediately on a Guggenheim Fellowship. He was made a consultant to the American Academy in Rome in 1948. During the later 1940s and throughout the 1950s he composed a number of large works as the result of important commissions. The Cello Concerto (which won the 1947 New York Music Critics' Circle Award) was commissioned by John Nicholas Brown for Garbousova, and the ballet *Medea* (*The Cave of the Heart*) by the Ditson Fund for Martha Graham. Another dance score, *Souvenirs*, was commissioned by Lincoln Kirstein for the Ballet Society of New York. Three vocal works – *Knoxville: Summer of 1915*, *Hermit Songs*, and *Prayers of Kierkegaard* – were commissioned respectively by Eleanor Steber, the Coolidge Foundation of the Library of Congress, and the Koussevitzky Foundation. The Piano Sonata was written on a League of Composers commission.

The most ambitious work produced by Barber in the 1950s was the four-act opera *Vanessa*, completed in 1957, with a libretto by Menotti. After its première season the Metropolitan Opera staged the work during two other seasons, 1958–9 and 1964–5. It was also performed at the Salzburg Festival in 1958. Sargeant described the score as "both complex and highly charged with emotional meaning"; he also considered that Barber demonstrated "that an American composer with sufficient knowledge of and feeling for the great international operatic tradition can turn out a near masterpiece in the genre." *Vanessa* won the 1958 Pulitzer Prize for music.

A second Pulitzer Prize was awarded to Barber for his 1962 Piano Concerto, commissioned by his publisher, G. Schirmer, on its centenary. At its première Schonberg drew parallels between the concerto and Prokofiev's piano writing and found in the piece "a sense of confidence in the entire conception – the confidence that comes only from an experienced composer engaged in a work that interests him." Barber's biggest work of the decade, how-

2. *Excerpt from the vocal score of Barber's opera "Vanessa," completed in 1957: autograph MS (DLC)*

ever, was again a full-scale opera, *Antony and Cleopatra*, with a libretto by Zeffirelli after Shakespeare. It was commissioned by the Metropolitan Opera for the opening of its new house at Lincoln Center in September 1966. *Antony and Cleopatra* was largely a failure with the critics and with the public; the score was considered generally weak, but it was by no means condemned out of hand. While Peter Heyworth considered its "late romantic style" devoid of originality, "it clearly came from the workshop of a composer who knew what he was about, had pondered the problems of opera, of combining action and movement with the need for lyrical expansion, and who had a welcome feeling for the human voice." There was widespread agreement that the most prominent factor in the opera's failure was the production, designed and directed by Zeffirelli. Desmond Shawe-Taylor wrote that "throughout the evening there was a recurrent impression that Barber's music, rich in substance and sometimes very engaging, was being submerged beneath the glitter and complexity of the spectacle." With highly elaborate sets and costumes, a large chorus, dancers, hundreds of supernumeraries, and live animals, the production was decidedly old fashioned, clumsy, and often confused. Barber recalled the failure later with equanimity, but he left New York immediately after the première and remained in virtual seclusion for about five years in the Italian Alps. It was announced in April 1974 that *Antony and Cleopatra* would be revised and the libretto reshaped by Menotti. The première of this revised version was presented by the Opera Theater of the Juilliard School in New York on 6 February 1975; it was far more successful with critics and audiences than the original version.

Barber produced one distinct oddity in the late 1960s: a third version of his most famous piece, the Adagio for Strings, set as a choral work to the text of the *Agnus Dei*. He returned to the concert scene in 1971 with two commissioned works, *The Lovers* and *Fadograph of a Yestern Scene*. Barber composed little in his last years; he died of cancer at the age of 70.

2. STYLE. In his notice of the revised version of the First Symphony, Thomson commented that Barber's chief problem seemed to be "laying the ghost of romanticism without resorting to violence." This idea proved to be off the mark, however, for not only did Barber not lay the Romantic ghost (with or without violence), he apparently never wanted to: his music is always primarily an expression of personal emotion. He could be (and frequently has been) classified as a neoromantic, if indeed this too general term has much meaning. Barber's art is essentially lyric and dramatic, and his harmonic language is basically that

of the late 19th century. Much of his music is based on key relationships. In the 1940s he began to incorporate elements having more in common with the contemporary idiom. Some critics have pointed to the Violin Concerto, which has angular lines and diatonic dissonance in the last movement, as signaling a new stylistic "period" in Barber's music, but this is perhaps too strong an interpretation. The concerto demonstrated that Barber had simply (and importantly) added to his resources and broadened the scope of his artistic choices. His later orchestral scores have fairly dense harmonic textures but are always rooted in a key or tonal center. At least one movement of the flamboyant Piano Sonata, however, is based on the 12-tone technique (this appears to be a unique instance in his music). On the other hand he could produce a work of great simplicity, skirting triviality, such as *Souvenirs*, which recalls the elegant café style of Walton's *Façade*.

In his discipline and use of traditional forms, Barber could also be considered something of a classicist. The concertos, symphonies, and other instrumental works adhere loosely to sonata form; he has also used fugue (most notably in the Piano Sonata) and passacaglia (First Symphony). Further, his sense of proportion and total form is very keen. Barber's fondness for Romantic fullness and lyricism, combined with Classical procedures, places him in a position within his era somewhat similar to that of Brahms in his. Also, neither Barber nor Brahms was known as an innovator and both produced works of substance and beauty with a distinct personal stamp. If the entrepreneur and knowledgeable contemporary-music enthusiast Ashley Pettis could write in a letter to the *New York Times* in 1938 that he found Barber's music "utterly anachronistic as the utterance of a young man of 28, A.D. 1938," Hans Heinsheimer could write of it in 1980 that "it speaks its own language, [and] shows a very personal, recognizable handwriting which is the trademark of any important composer." Barber himself made a statement in 1971 that could serve as his credo as a composer:

> [When] I'm writing music for words, then I immerse myself in those words, and I let the music flow out of them. When I write an abstract piano sonata or a concerto, I write what I feel. I'm not a self-conscious composer . . . it is said that I have no style at all but that doesn't matter. I just go on doing, as they say, my thing. I believe this takes a certain courage.

See also ORCHESTRAL MUSIC, §3; for further illustrations *see* MENOTTI, GIAN CARLO and STRAVINSKY, IGOR.

WORKS

(all published unless otherwise stated)

op.

STAGE

– The Rose Tree (opera, A. S. Brosius), 1920, inc., unpubd; West Chester, PA

– One Day of Spring (incidental music, M. Kennedy), 1v, str, 1935, lost, unpubd; Winter Park, FL, 24 Jan 1935

23 Medea (Serpent Heart) (ballet, M. Graham), 1946, New York, 10 May 1946; rev. as The Cave of the Heart, New York, 27 Feb 1947; arr. as orch suite, 1947, Philadelphia, 5 Dec 1947, Philadelphia Orchestra, cond. Ormandy; Medea's Meditation and Dance of Vengeance, op.23a, 1953, New York, 2 Feb 1956, New York PO, cond. Mitropoulos

28 Souvenirs (ballet, T. Bolender), 1952, New York, 15 Nov 1955; arr. as suite, pf 4 hands, 1952, NBC television, July 1952; suite, orch, 1952, Chicago, 12 Nov 1953, Chicago SO, cond. Reiner

32 Vanessa (opera, 4, Menotti), 1956–7, New York, 15 Jan 1958, Metropolitan Opera, cond. Mitropoulos; rev. 1964

35 A Hand of Bridge (opera, 1, Menotti), 4 solo vv, chamber orch, 1953; Spoleto, Italy, 17 June 1959

40 Antony and Cleopatra (opera, 3, Zeffirelli, after Shakespeare), 1966, New York, 16 Sept 1966, Metropolitan Opera, cond. Schippers; rev. 1974, New York, 6 Feb 1975, cond. Conlon

ORCHESTRAL

5 The School for Scandal, ov., 1931–3; Philadelphia, 30 Aug 1933, Philadelphia Orchestra, cond. Smallens

7 Music for a Scene from Shelley, 1933; New York, 24 March 1935, Philharmonic Symphony Society, cond. W. Janssen

9 Symphony no.1, 1936, Rome, 13 Dec 1936, Augusteo Orchestra, cond. B. Molinari; rev. 1942

11 Adagio for Strings, 1936 [arr. of 2nd movt of Str Qt]; New York, 5 Nov 1938, NBC SO, cond. Toscanini

12 [First] Essay for Orchestra, 1937; New York, 5 Nov 1938, NBC SO, cond. Toscanini

14 Violin Concerto, 1939; Philadelphia, 7 Feb 1941, A. Spalding, Philadelphia Orchestra, cond. Ormandy

17 Second Essay, 1942; New York, 16 April 1942, Philharmonic Symphony Society, cond. Walter

– Funeral March [based on Army Air Corps Song], 1943, unpubd

– Commando March, band, 1943; Atlantic City, NJ, sum. 1943, Army Air Force Band, cond. Barber

19 Symphony no.2, 1944, Boston, 3 March 1944, Boston SO, cond. Koussevitzky; rev. 1947, Philadelphia, 21 Jan 1948; 2nd movt rev. as Night Flight, orch, op.19a, 1964, Cleveland, 8 Oct 1964, Cleveland SO, cond. Szell

21 Capricorn Concerto, fl, ob, tpt, str, 1944; New York, 8 Oct 1944, Saidenberg Little SO, cond. D. Saidenberg

22 Cello Concerto, 1945; Boston, 5 April 1946, R. Garbousova, Boston SO, cond. Koussevitzky

– Horizon, *c*1945, unpubd; Merrick, NY, 19 Jan 1985, Merrick SO, cond. C. Gouse

– Adventure, fl, cl, hn, harp, "exotic" insts, 1954, unpubd

36 Toccata festiva, org, orch, 1960; Philadelphia, 30 Sept 1960, P. Callaway, Philadelphia Orchestra, cond. Ormandy

37 Die natali, chorale preludes for Christmas, 1960; Boston, 22 Dec 1960, Boston SO, cond. Munch

38 Piano Concerto, 1962, New York, 24 Sept 1962, J. Browning, Boston SO, cond. Leinsdorf; 2nd movt transcr. fl, pf, 1961

– Mutations from Bach, brass choir, timp, 1967; New York, 7 Oct 1968

44 Fadograph of a Yestern Scene (after Joyce: Finnegans Wake), 2 solo vv, orch, 1971; Pittsburgh, 11 Sept 1971, B. Valente, J. Simon, Pittsburgh SO, cond. Steinberg

47 Third Essay, 1978; New York, 14 Sept 1978, New York PO, cond. Mehta

48 posth. Canzonetta, ob, str, orchd C. Turner, 1977–8; New York, 17 Dec 1981, H. Gomberg, New York PO, cond. Mehta

CHORAL

XIII Christmas Eve: a Trio with Solos, 2 solo vv, SAA, org, *c*1924, unpubd

8/1–2 The Virgin Martyrs (Siegebert of Gembloux, trans. H. Waddell), SSAA, 1935, Philadelphia, CBS radio, 1 May 1939; Let Down the Bars, O Death (E. Dickinson), SATB, 1936

– God's Grandeur, chorus, 1938, lost, unpubd; Bluefield, WV, 13 Feb 1938, Westminster Choir, cond. J. F. Williams

– Motetto (Job), 4vv, 8vv, *c*1938, unpubd

– Peggy Mitchell, 4vv, *c*1939, unpubd

15 A Stopwatch and an Ordnance Map (S. Spender), male vv, 3 kettledrums, 1940; Philadelphia, 23 April 1940

– Ave Maria (after Josquin Desprez), 4vv, *c*1940, unpubd

16 Reincarnation (J. Stephens): Mary Hynes, Anthony O'Daly, The Coolin', 4vv, 1937–40

– Ad "bibinem" cum me regaret ad cenam (V. Fortunatus), 4vv unacc., 1943

– Long Live Louise and Sidney Homer, canon, 1944, unpubd; Winter Park, FL, 9 Jan 1945

30 Prayers of Kierkegaard (Kierkegaard), S, A ad lib, T ad lib, chorus, orch, 1954; Boston, 3 Dec 1954, L. Price, St. Cecilia Chorus, Boston SO, cond. Munch

– Chorale for Ascension Day (Easter Chorale) (P. Browning), chorus, brass, timp, org ad lib, 1964; Washington, DC, 7 May 1964

11 Agnus Dei, chorus, org/pf, 1967 [arr. of 2nd movt of Str Qt]

42 Twelfth Night (L. Lee), To be Sung on the Water (L. Bogan), 4vv unacc., 1968

43 The Lovers (P. Neruda), Bar, chorus, orch, 1971; Philadelphia, 22 Sept 1971, T. Kraus, Temple University Choirs, Philadelphia Orchestra, cond. Ormandy

CHAMBER

– Fantasie, 2 pf, 1924, unpubd
XVI Sonata in Modern Form, 2 pf, *c*1925, unpubd
1 Serenade, str qt/str orch, 1928; Philadelphia, 5 May 1930, Swastika Quartet
4 Violin Sonata, f, 1928, lost, unpubd; Philadelphia, 10 Dec 1928, G. Gilbert, Barber
6 Cello Sonata, 1932; New York, 5 March 1933, O. Cole
11 String Quartet, 1936; Rome, 14 Dec 1936, Pro Arte Quartet [arrs. for str and chorus, org, see op.11, ORCHESTRAL and CHORAL]
– Commemorative March, vn, vc, pf, unpubd
31 Summer Music, wind qnt, 1955; Detroit, 20 March 1956
38a Canzone (Elegy) fl, pf, 1961 [transcr. of 2nd movt of Pf Conc.]

SOLO INSTRUMENTAL

I/3 Melody in F, pf, 1917, unpubd
– Sadness, pf, 1917, unpubd
I/4 Largo, pf, 1918, unpubd
I/5 War Song, pf, 1918, unpubd
III/1 At Twilight, pf, 1919, unpubd
III/2 Lullaby, pf, 1919, unpubd
X/2 Themes, pf, *c*1923, movts 2–3 unpubd [movt 1 = Three Sketches no.3]
– Three Sketches, pf: Love Song (to Mother), To my Steinway (to Number 220601), Minuet (to Sara) [= Themes: movt 1], 1923–4
– [Untitled work] ("Laughingly and briskly"), pf, *c*1924, unpubd
– Petite berceuse (to Jean), pf, *c*1924, unpubd
– Prelude to a Tragic Drama, pf, 1925, unpubd
– To Longwood Gardens, org, 1925, unpubd
– Fresh from West Chester (Some Jazzings): Poison Ivy, a Country Dance, 1925; Let's Sit it out, I'd Rather Watch (I Sam Barber did it with my little hatchet, a walls [sic]), 1926; unpubd
– Three Essays, pf, 1926, unpubd
– Four Chorale Preludes, kbd, 1927, unpubd
– Four Partitas, kbd, 1927, unpubd
– Prelude and Fugue, b, org, 1927, unpubd; Philadelphia, 10 Dec 1928, C. Weinrich
– Pieces for Carillon: Round, Allegro, Legend, 1930–31, unpubd; Mountain Lake, FL
– Suite for Carillon, 4 pieces, 1932
– Two Interludes (Intermezzi), pf, 1931–2, unpubd; New York, 1 March 1939, J. Behrend
20 Excursions, pf, 1942–4; New York, 1945, Horowitz
26 Sonata, pf, 1949; Havana, 9 Dec 1949, Horowitz
– Wondrous Love, variations on a shape-note hymn, org, 1958
33 Nocturne (Homage to John Field), pf, 1959; New York, 1959, Browning
– Variations on Happy Birthday [to Eugene Ormandy], 1970, unpubd
46 Ballade, pf, 1977; Fort Worth, Sept 1977, S. De Groote

SONGS

(1v, pf, unless otherwise stated)

– Sometime (to Mother), Mez, 1917, unpubd; West Chester, PA, 25 April 1926
– Why Not (K. Parsons), 1917, unpubd
II/3 In the Firelight, 1918, unpubd
II/4 Isabel (J. G. Whittier), 1919, unpubd
– An Old Song (C. Kingsley), 1921, unpubd
– Hunting Song (J. Bennett), Bar, pf, cornet, *c*1921, unpubd
V/2 Thy Will be Done (3 verses from The Wanderer), *c*1922, unpubd
VII Seven Nursery Songs (to Sara), S, 1920–23, unpubd; West Chester, PA, 25 April 1926
– October Weather (Barber), S, *c*1923, unpubd; West Chester, PA, 25 April 1926
– Dere Two Fella Joe, high v, 1924, unpubd; West Chester, PA, 25 April 1926
– Minuet, S, A, pf, *c*1924, unpubd
XIV My Fairyland (R. T. Kerlin), 1924, unpubd; West Chester, PA, 25 April 1926
– Summer is Coming (after A. Tennyson), 2 solo vv, pf, *c*1924, unpubd; West Chester, PA, 4 June 1927
– Two Poems of the Wind (F. MacCleod): Little Children of the World, Longing, 1924, unpubd; West Chester, PA, 25 April 1926
– A Slumber Song of the Madonna (A. Noyes), 1v, org, 1925, unpubd; West Chester, PA, 25 April 1926
– Fantasy in Purple (L. Hughes), 1925, unpubd; West Chester, PA, 25 April 1926
– Lady when I Behold the Roses (anon.), 1925, unpubd; West Chester, PA, 25 April 1926
– La nuit (A. Meurath), 1925, unpubd; West Chester, PA, 25 April 1926
– Two Songs of Youth: I Never Thought that Youth would Go (J. B. Rittenhouse), Invocation to Youth (L. Binyon), 1925, unpubd; West Chester, PA, 25 April 1926
– Addio di Orfeo (C. Monteverdi), 1926, arr. 1v, str, hpd, unpubd
– An Earnest Suit to his Unkind Mistress not to Forsake him (Sir T. Wyatt), 1926, unpubd
– Ask me to Rest (E. H. S. Terry), 1926, unpubd
– Au clair de la lune, 1926, unpubd; West Chester, PA, 25 April 1926
– Hey Nonny No (Christ Church MS), 1926, unpubd
– Man (H. Wolfe), 1926, unpubd; West Chester, PA, 25 April 1926
– Music when Soft Voices Die (P. B. Shelley), *c*1926, unpubd; West Chester, PA, 25 April 1926
– Thy Love (E. Browning), 1926, unpubd; West Chester, PA, 25 April 1926
– Watchers (D. Cornwell), 1926, unpubd; West Chester, PA, 25 April 1926
– Dance (J. Stephens), 1927, lost, unpubd; London, 25 June 1935
– Mother I cannot Mind my Wheel (W. S. Landor), 1927, unpubd
– Only of Thee and Me (L. Untermeyer), *c*1927, lost, unpubd; West Chester, PA, 4 June 1927
– Rounds: A Lament (Shelley); To Electra (R. Herrick); Dirge: Weep for the World's Wrong; Farewell; Not I (R. L. Stevenson); Of a Rose is al myn Song (anon., 1350); Sunset (Stevenson); The Moon (Shelley); Sun of the Sleepless (G. G. Byron); The Throstle (Tennyson); When Day is Gone (R. Burns); Late, Late, so Late (Tennyson: Guinevere); 3 vv, pf, 1927, unpubd
– There's Nae Lark (A. Swinburne), 1927, unpubd
2 Three Songs: The Daisies (Stephens), 1927, With Rue my Heart is Laden (A. E. Houseman), 1928, Bessie Bobtail (Stephens), 1934; London, 25 June 1935
– The Shepherd to his Love and the Nymph's Reply, 1928, unpubd
3 Dover Beach (M. Arnold), Mez/Bar, str qt, 1931; New York, 5 March 1933
– Love at the Door (from Meleager, trans. J. A. Symonds), 1934, unpubd
– Serenades (G. Dillon), 1934, unpubd
– Love's Caution (W. H. Davies), 1935, unpubd
– Night Wanderers (Davies), 1935, unpubd
– Of that so Sweet Imprisonment (J. Joyce), 1935, unpubd
– Peace (from Bhartirihari, trans. P. E. More), 1935, unpubd
– Stopping by Woods on a Sunny Evening (R. Frost), 1935, unpubd
– Strings in the Earth and Air (Joyce), 1935, unpubd
10 Three Songs (Joyce: Chamber Music): Rain has Fallen, Sleep Now, 1935, Rome, 22 April 1936; I Hear an Army, 1936, Philadelphia, 7 March 1937, arr. 1v, orch
– The Beggar's Song (Davies), 1936, unpubd; Rome, 22 April 1936
– In the Dark Pinewood (Joyce), 1937, unpubd
13 Four Songs: A Nun Takes the Veil (G. M. Hopkins), 1937; The Secrets of the Old (W. B. Yeats), 1938, New York, 12 Feb 1939; Sure on this Shining Night (J. Agee), 1938, arr. 1v, orch, and chorus, pf; Nocturne (F. Prokosch), 1940, arr. 1v, orch; perf. complete, Philadelphia, 4 April 1941
– Song for a New House, 1v, fl, pf, 1940, unpubd
– Between Dark and Dark (K. Chapin), 1942, lost, unpubd
18 Two Songs: The Queen's Face on a Summery Coin (R. Horan), 1942; Monks and Raisins (J. G. Villa), 1943; New York, 22 Feb 1944
24 Knoxville: Summer of 1915 (Agee), high v, orch, 1947, unpubd, Boston, 9 April 1948, E. Steber, Boston SO, cond. Koussevitzky; rev. 1v, chamber orch, 1950, Washington, DC, Dumbarton Oaks, 1 April 1950
25 Nuvoletta (from Joyce: Finnegans Wake), 1947
27 Melodies passagères (R. M. Rilke): Puisque tout passe, Un cygne,

Tombeau dans un parc, Le clocher chante, Départ, 1950–51; nos. 1, 4, and 5 perf. Washington, DC, 1 April 1950; perf. complete, Washington, DC, 21 Jan 1952

29 Hermit Songs (Irish texts of 8th–13th centuries): At Saint Patrick's Purgatory (trans. S. O'Faolain), Church Bells at Night (trans. H. Mumford Jones), Saint Ita's Vision (trans. C. Kallman), The Heavenly Banquet (trans. O'Faolain), The Crucifixion (anon., from The Speckled Book, trans. Mumford Jones), Sea-snatch (trans. W. H. Auden), Promiscuity (trans. Auden), The Monk and the Cat (trans. Auden), The Praises of God (trans. Auden), The Desire for Hermitage (trans. O'Faolain), 1952–3; Washington, DC, 30 Oct 1953, L. Price, Barber

39 Andromache's Farewell (from Euripides: The Trojan Women, trans. J. P. Creagh), S, orch, 1962; New York, 4 April 1963, M. Arroyo, New York PO, cond. Schippers

41 Despite and Still: A Last Song (R. Graves), My Lizard (T. Rilke), In the Wilderness (Graves), Solitary Hotel (from Joyce: Ulysses), Despite and Still (Graves), 1968–9; New York, 27 April 1969

45 Three Songs: Now I have Fed and Eaten Up the Rose (G. Keller, trans. Joyce), A Green Lowland of Pianos (J. Harasymowicz, trans. C. Milosz), O Boundless, Boundless Evening (G. Heym, trans. C. Middleton), 1972; New York, 30 April 1974

MSS in *DLC*

Principal publisher: G. Schirmer

BIBLIOGRAPHY

A. Copland: "From the '20's to the '40's and Beyond," *MM*, xx (1942–3), 80
R. Horan: "Samuel Barber," *MM*, xx (1943), 161
"Barber, Samuel," *CBY 1944*
N. Broder: "The Music of Samuel Barber," *MQ*, xxxiv (1948), 325
H. Dexter: "Samuel Barber and his Music," *MO*, lxxii (1949), 284
N. Broder: "Current Chronicle: New York," *MQ*, xxxvi (1950), 276
H. Tischler: "Barber's Piano Sonata Opus 26," *ML*, xxxiii (1952), 352
N. Broder: *Samuel Barber* (New York, 1954)
R. Friedewald: *A Formal and Stylistic Analysis of the Published Music of Samuel Barber* (diss., U. of Iowa, 1957)
C. Turner: "The Music of Samuel Barber," *Opera News*, xxii/13 (1958), 7
"Classified Chronological Catalog of Works by the United States Composer Samuel Barber," *Inter-American Music Bulletin*, no. 13 (1959), 22
"Samuel Barber," *Compositores de América/Composers of the Americas*, ed. Pan American Union, v (Washington, DC, 1959), 14
L. S. Wathen: *Dissonance Treatment in the Instrumental Music of Samuel Barber* (diss., Northwestern U., 1960)
J. Briggs: "Samuel Barber," *International Musician*, lx/6 (1961), 20
B. Rands: "Samuel Barber: a Belief in Tradition," *MO*, lxxxiv (1961), 353
"Barber, Samuel," *CBY 1963*
W. A. Dailey: *Techniques of Composition Used in Contemporary Works for Chorus and Orchestra on Religious Texts as Important Representative Works of the Period from 1952 through 1962* (diss., Catholic U., 1965)
E. Salzman and J. Goodfriend: "Samuel Barber: a Selective Discography," *HiFi/Stereo Review*, xvii/4 (1966), 88
E. Salzman: "Samuel Barber," *HiFi/Stereo Review*, xvii/4 (1966), 77
J. E. Albertson: *A Study of Stylistic Elements of Samuel Barber's 'Hermit Songs' and Franz Schubert's 'Die Winterreise'* (diss., U. of Missouri, Kansas City, 1969)
R. L. Larsen: *A Study and Comparison of Samuel Barber's 'Vanessa,' Robert Ward's 'The Crucible,' and Gunther Schuller's 'The Visitation'* (diss., Indiana U., 1971)
L. L. Rhoades: *Theme and Variation in Twentieth-century Organ Literature: Analyses of Variations by Alain, Barber, Distler, Dupré, Duruflé, and Sowerby* (diss., Ohio State U., 1973)
S. L. Carter: *The Piano Music of Samuel Barber* (diss., Texas Tech U., 1980)
H. Heinsheimer: "Samuel Barber: Maverick Composer," *Keynote*, iv/1 (1980), 7
H. Gleason and W. Becker: "Samuel Barber," *20th-century American Composers*, Music Literature Outlines, ser. iv (Bloomington, IN, rev. 2/1981), 1 [incl. further bibliography]
D. A. Hennessee: *Samuel Barber: a Bio-bibliography* (Westport, CT, 1985)
B. Heyman: *Samuel Barber: a Documentary Study of his Works* (diss., CUNY, in progress)
J. Sifferman: *The Solo Piano Works of Samuel Barber* (diss., U. of Texas, in progress)

RICHARD JACKSON (text), BARBARA B. HEYMAN (work-list)

Barbershop quartet singing. A style of singing that originated in the USA in the late 19th century. It is characterized by four-voice parallel harmonies in 3rds, 4ths, and 5ths; chromatic voice-leading creates diminished and dominant 7th chords, augmented 6th chords, and triads with added 6ths, usually in close positions (major 7ths, flatted 9ths, and chords of the 13th are considered stylistically inappropriate). The melody is carried by the "lead" (second) tenor, another tenor harmonizes above, the bass provides the foundation, and the baritone completes the harmony, frequently crossing above the melodic line. Chord progressions known as "swipes" often compensate for the lack of an instrumental accompaniment, and are particularly effective when employed as a coda to a piece (ex. 1).

Ex.1 Barbershop "swipe"

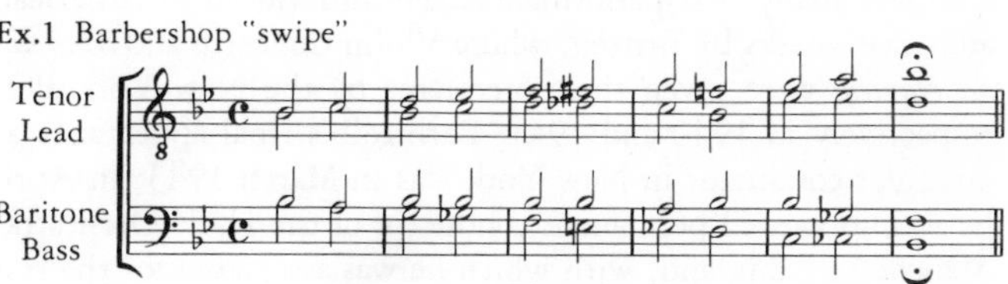

The barbershop quartet movement, which flourished between about 1895 and 1930, was given impetus by the fledgling recording industry. Performances by such professional groups as the Manhansett, Haydn, American, and Peerless Quartets became widely available and gave rise to the formation of thousands of amateur groups throughout the country during the movement's peak years (1910–25). A fundamental change in the American popular song also contributed to the development of barbershop harmony. Many tunes in the earlier decades of the 19th century were constructed around the tonic octave of the scale, but by about 1895 melodies with a dominant-to-dominant range had evolved. This meant that the bass part was less likely to double low melody notes and it also allowed the upper tenor part to flow in a smooth line above the lead, mostly in 3rds and 6ths. By the late 1920s the increasing popularity of jazz, sound films, and the radio had led to a decline in the number of active quartets. In 1938 the SOCIETY FOR THE PRESERVATION AND ENCOURAGEMENT OF BARBER SHOP QUARTET SINGING IN AMERICA was founded, with affiliated clubs in Britain, Scandinavia, and Germany. Two organizations for women barbershop singers, Harmony Incorporated and Sweet Adelines, have also been formed.

BIBLIOGRAPHY

J. W. Johnson: "The Origin of the 'Barber Chord,'" *The Mentor*, xvii/1 (1929), 53
S. Spaeth: *Barbershop Ballads* (Englewood Cliffs, NJ, 1940)
D. K. Antrim: "The Barbershop Brotherhood," *The Etude*, lxxii/11 (1954), 11
D. Martin: "Three Eras of Barbershop Harmony," *The Harmonizer*, xv/2 (1955), 20
J. L. McClelland: *Of, By, and For the People: a History of Barbershop Harmony* (thesis, College of Wooster, PA, 1959)
D. Martin: "The Evolution of Barbershop Harmony," *Music Journal Annual* (1965), 40

VAL HICKS

Barbirolli, Sir **John** [Giovanni Battista] (*b* London, England, 2 Dec 1899; *d* London, 29 July 1970). English conductor and cellist of French-Italian descent. He won scholarships to Trinity College (1911–12) and the Royal Academy of Music (1912–17), London, and made his début as a cellist at the age of 11. He played in orchestras and ensembles in London and began his conducting career in the late 1920s, working with numerous orchestras including those at Covent Garden and Sadler's Wells. His growing international reputation prompted an invitation from the New York PO to serve as guest conductor for ten weeks during the 1936–7 season; his American début was on 5 November 1936. He made such a favorable impression that he was offered a three-year contract as principal conductor, to succeed Toscanini. The contract was renewed for two years through 1941–2, the orchestra's centenary season, when the conducting was shared with Toscanini and other eminent colleagues. During holiday periods Barbirolli conducted in other cities including Chicago, Los Angeles, Seattle, Cincinnati, and Vancouver, British Columbia.

During his period in New York, Barbirolli programmed much contemporary music, including works by American composers, and gave many first performances. He introduced to American audiences works by Britten, whose Violin Concerto and *Sinfonia da requiem* were given their premières by the New York PO, respectively in 1940 and 1941. Barbirolli's final appearance as a regular conductor in New York was in March 1943; in April he was appointed permanent conductor of the Hallé Orchestra, Manchester, England, with which he was associated for the rest of his life. He also worked with the Berlin PO.

Barbirolli's New York years were not without problems. His manner was much more restrained than Toscanini's, and New York audiences, accustomed to a more virtuoso style, were lukewarm in their reaction to him. However, to succeed Toscanini was a formidable task, and Barbirolli not only stayed with the orchestra for five years but was invited back several times as guest. In 1960 he was appointed music director of the Houston SO, succeeding Stokowski; when he resigned in 1967, he was named conductor emeritus. Barbirolli was much honored in England, and also received awards from the governments of Italy and Finland.

BIBLIOGRAPHY

M. Kennedy: *Barbirolli* (London, 1971/*R*1982) [with discography by M. Walker]
C. Reid: *John Barbirolli* (New York, 1971)
H. Shanet: *Philharmonic: a History of New York's Orchestra* (Garden City, NY, 1975)
D. Ewen: *Musicians since 1900* (New York, 1978), 39

KATHERINE K. PRESTON

Barbour, J(ames) Murray (*b* Chambersburg, PA, 31 March 1897; *d* Homestead, PA, 4 Jan 1970). Acoustician, musicologist, and composer. He studied at Dickinson College, Pennsylvania (MA 1920), and Temple University (BMus 1924). From 1926 to 1929 he taught at Wells College, New York, leaving with a fellowship to the universities of Cologne and Berlin. After studies at Cornell University (PhD 1932, with a dissertation on the history of equal temperament), he taught at Ithaca College, New York (1932–9), and then until 1964 at Michigan State College (later University). He was awarded the DMus at the University of Toronto (1936). In 1957–8 he was president of the American Musicological Society.

Barbour's *Tuning and Temperament: a Historical Survey* (1951, 2/1953) is widely accepted as the most authoritative account of the history and theory of temperaments, a study to which he applied his talents as mathematician, historian, and musician. He also published books on William Billings (1960) and brass instruments (1964). His scholarly articles appeared in mathematical as well as musical journals and were marked by precision, clarity, and concision. With Fritz A. Kuttner he issued three recordings illustrating the history of tuning systems. His compositions include a Requiem, the symphonic poem *Childe Rowland*, solo and choral songs, works for organ and piano, and some chamber music.

JON NEWSOM/R

Bare, Bobby [Robert Joseph] (*b* Ironton, OH, 7 April 1935). Country-music singer and songwriter. In his teens he performed as a singer and guitarist in a country band in Ohio; by the late 1950s his style had gravitated towards rock. He recorded his first hit song, *All American Boy* (1958), for the Ohio label Fraternity on the day before he entered the army; it was released under the name Bill Parsons, and though it reached no.2 on the pop chart Bare received neither royalties nor credit. After his discharge from the army, he toured with the Dave Clark Five, Jay and the Americans, and Bobby Darin. Beginning in the mid-1960s he recorded many hit singles, including *Shame on me* (1962), *500 miles away from home* (1963), *Detroit City* (1963), *Miller's Cave* (1964), and *How I got to Memphis* (1970). In 1964 he appeared in the film *A Distant Trumpet* but chose a singing career over a theatrical one; he moved from California to Nashville in the late 1960s. He resumed a country-music orientation and performed many songs by Shel Silverstein. His deep, rich baritone voice lent itself particularly well to folk material and narrative songs, and his innovative concept albums, *Lullabyes, Legends, and Lies* (1973), *Singin' in the Kitchen* (1974), and *Hard Time Hungrys* (1975), anticipated folk-rock and progressive country styles. About 1970 Bare founded a publishing company, Return Music, whose writers included Billy Joe Shaver (*Ride me down easy*, *I'm just an old chunk of coal*) and Roger Murrah (*We're in this love together*, *Southern Rains*). Bare is also known for promoting the careers of Waylon Jennings, Kris Kristofferson, and Mickey Newbury.

RECORDINGS

(selective list)

All American Boy (Fraternity 835, 1958) [as Bill Parsons]; Shame on me (RCA 8032, 1962); Detroit City (RCA 8183, 1963); 500 miles away from home (RCA 8238, 1963); Miller's Cave (RCA 8294, 1964); How I got to Memphis (Mer. 73097, 1970); *Lullabyes, Legends, and Lies* (RCA CPL2-0290, 1973); Marie Laveaux (RCA APBO0261, 1974); *Singin' in the Kitchen* (RCA 10096, 1974); *Hard Time Hungrys* (RCA APL1-0906, 1975); *Sleeper Wherever I Fall* (Col. KC35645, 1978)

BIBLIOGRAPHY

P. Carr: "An Interview with Bobby Bare," *Country Music*, ix/9 (1981), 36

DON CUSIC

Bargy, Roy F(rederick) (*b* Newaygo, MI, 31 July 1894; *d* Vista, CA, 16 Jan 1974). Popular composer and pianist. He began to study piano at the age of five in Toledo, Ohio. By the time he was 17 he had discarded his ambitions to become a concert pianist, having become fascinated with ragtime pianists in Toledo's red-light district, including the famous exponent of eastern ragtime Luckey Roberts. After playing professionally in movie theaters and organizing a dance band, he was engaged in 1919 by the ragtime composer Charley Straight to edit, play, arrange, and compose for Imperial Player Rolls. Bargy's association with Straight led to his acquaintance with the agent Edgar Benson, who assembled a band directed by Bargy to record for Victor. Bargy later joined Isham Jones's orchestra for two years and, in 1928, began a 12-year association with Paul Whiteman's band, for which he is best remembered today. Later he served as conductor and arranger for Larry Ross's radio show, and from 1943 he was music director for Jimmy Durante, a position he held until his retirement 20 years later.

Bargy is noted for his contribution to the ragtime-based style of novelty piano. Like the work of his contemporary Zez Confrey, his compositions may be viewed as advanced rags: he routinely employed 10ths in the bass (a feature more readily associated with early jazz than ragtime), but favored right-hand patterns found in ragtime of the 1910s, recalling at times the work of Straight and the classic ragtime composer James Scott. Although Bargy's works are not as ambitious or imaginative as Confrey's, they represent a charming recasting of the language of midwestern ragtime in the more vivacious mode of the late 1910s and the 1920s.

WORKS

Selective list; unless otherwise indicated, all are printed works for pf published in Cleveland.

Rufenreddy (collab. C. Straight) (1921); Slipova (1921); Knice and Knifty (collab. Straight) (1922); Sunshine Caper (1922); Behave Yourself (1922); Jim Jams (1922); Justin-tyme (1922); Pianoflage (1922); Sweet and Tender (Chicago, 1923); A Blue Streak; Omeomy

BIBLIOGRAPHY

D. A. Jasen: *Recorded Ragtime, 1897–1958* (Hamden, CT, 1973)

D. A. Jasen and T. J. Tichenor: *Rags and Ragtime: a Musical History* (New York, 1978)

DAVID THOMAS ROBERTS

Bari, Joe. The stage name used early in his career by TONY BENNETT.

Bar-Illan, David (Jacob) (*b* Haifa [now in Israel], 7 Feb 1930). Pianist. A graduate of the Haifa Music Institute, he then studied at the Juilliard School and at Mannes College. He made his début in 1946 with the Palestine Broadcasting Service Orchestra, first played in England (Wigmore Hall) in 1953, and gave his first American concerts the following year. He presented the première of Starer's Piano Concerto no.2 with Mitropoulos and the Israel PO in 1959, and Starer has since written another concerto for him. A pianist with an expansive style well suited to 19th-century music, Bar-Illan has performed widely in Europe, the USA, Latin America, and Israel, as a recitalist and soloist. The music of Liszt is of particular interest to him and he has published articles on that subject and on Israeli music. Besides works by Liszt, he has recorded music by Beethoven, Schubert, Weber, Mendelssohn, and Schumann. He became a member of the piano faculty of the Mannes College in 1980.

BIBLIOGRAPHY

K. Courhie: "David Bar-Illan," *Virtuoso*, i/3 (1980), 3

MICHAEL STEINBERG/R

Barker, Sister (Ruth) Mildred (*b* Providence, RI, 3 Feb 1897). Shaker singer and songleader. After her father died, when she was seven, she lived with the Shaker Society in Alfred, Maine; she later became a member of the society and lived there until it disbanded in 1931. With other members she moved to the Shaker Society at Sabbathday Lake, New Gloucester, Maine, where for many years she tended to young people and from 1947 was a trustee; she became the spiritual leader of the community in 1972. She learned by ear several hundred spirituals and gospel hymns in the traditional Shaker repertory, and also studied piano; her excellent singing voice and reliable memory enabled her to become the songleader in Shaker services. She wrote several commentaries on early songs, as well as biographical, historical, and devotional articles and poems for the *Shaker Quarterly*; she also cooperated in the filming of song performances and in the production of recordings by scholars. She received a National Heritage Fellowship from the NEA in 1983.

BIBLIOGRAPHY

D. W. Patterson: *The Shaker Spiritual* (Princeton, NJ, 1979)

DANIEL W. PATTERSON

Barkin, Elaine (Radoff) (*b* Bronx, NY, 15 Dec 1932). Composer and writer. She studied with Karol Rathaus, Saul Novack, and Leo Kraft at Queens College, CUNY (BA 1954), with Irving Fine, Harold Shapero, and Arthur Berger at Brandeis University (MFA 1954, PhD 1971), and with Boris Blacher at the Berlin Hochschule für Musik (1956–7). After teaching at Queens College (1964–70) and the University of Michigan (1970–74) and serving as visiting lecturer at Princeton University (1974), she joined the faculty of UCLA. Barkin has been guest composer at the universities of Washington, British Columbia, Illinois (1980), and Virginia (1981), as well as at Yale University, and Oberlin (1982), Bard (1983), and Wheaton (1984) colleges. She has held fellowships from the Fulbright Commission (1956–7), Princeton University (1974), the Rockefeller Foundation (1980), and the MacDowell Colony (1980). Her honors include commissions from the ISCM (1974), the NEA (1974, 1976, 1978), and UCLA (1981), and an ACA recording award (1974).

In her compositions, Barkin has used serial procedures to determine larger musical structure, and she frequently links short, open sections to form larger formal units, as in her String Quartet. In the String Trio, slow harmonic motion supports long, lyrical contours in a polyphonic web of lines and shifting timbres. More recently, she has investigated various manners of text setting, beginning with the *Two Dickinson Choruses* and extending this interest to include collaborative and interactive performance in "realtime" compositions such as *Media Speak*. As analyst and critic, Barkin has written extensively on 20th-century music and questions of perception, attempting to discover "ways and words that can produce and evoke qualitative responses to music and images similar to those experienced." Her articles have been published in various journals including *Perspectives of New Music*, of which she became co-editor in 1964.

WORKS

Theater: De amore (A. Capellanus, various poets), 4 male/female pfmrs, gui, va, harp, db, perc, 1980; Media Speak, 9 speakers, sax, slides, 1981; Women's Voices (various texts), 4 female reciters, tape, slides, 1983

Orch: Essay, 1957; Plus ça change, str, perc, 1971–2

Chamber: Brandeis 1955, pf, 1956; Refrains, fl, cl, vn, va, vc, pf, 1967; 6 Pieces, pf, 1968–9; Str Qt, 1969; Prim Cycles, fl, cl, vn, vc, 1973; Sound Play, vn, 1974; Mixed Modes, cl, b cl, vn, va, vc, pf, 1974–5; For Suite's Sake, hpd, 1975; Inward & Outward Bound, 13 insts, 1975; Str Trio, 1976; Ebb Tide, 2 vib, 1977; Plein chant, a fl, 1977; Impromptu, pf, vn, vc, 1981; In its Surrendering, tuba, 1981; At the Piano, pf, 1982; N.B. Suite, 2 or more fl, db, 1982; Still Life, bar sax, vib, 1983

Vocal: 2 Dickinson Choruses, SATB, 1978; The Supple Suitor (Dickinson), S, fl, ob, vc, vib, hpd/pf, 1978–9

Principal publishers: ACA, Association for the Promotion of New Music, Mobart

BIBLIOGRAPHY

E. Cory: "Barkin's String Quartet," *MQ*, lxii (1976), 616

T. Cleman: "Mixed Modes and String Trio," *Notes*, xxxvi (1979–80), 472

RICHARD SWIFT

Barlow, Harold (*b* Boston, MA, 15 May 1915). Writer on music and composer. He graduated from the Boston University College of Music (BM 1937), where he studied the violin. With Sam

Morgenstern he compiled two indexes, *A Dictionary of Musical Themes* (1948) and *A Dictionary of Vocal Themes* (1950): both employ an alphabetic system, devised by Barlow, for identifying a theme when only the melody is known. As a composer, Barlow is perhaps best known for his 1949 song *I've got tears in my ears from lyin' on my back in my bed while I cry over you*, for which he wrote both the words and the music.

PAULA MORGAN

Barlow, Howard (*b* Plain City, OH, 1 May 1892; *d* Bethel, CT, 31 Jan 1972). Conductor. He studied law and made his conducting début at a MacDowell Colony festival in 1919. He formed and conducted the American National Orchestra (1923–5), to which he admitted only musicians born in the USA. He was associated with CBS as a conductor (1927–32) and as general music director (1932–43). He was also conductor of the Baltimore SO (1940–43) and director of the NBC radio series "The Voice of Firestone" from 1943 to 1961 (televised from 1949). A committed exponent of American music, he commissioned works from Copland, Harris, and Randall Thompson among others. In 1940 he was awarded a certificate of merit from the National Association of American Composers and Conductors as "the outstanding native interpreter of American music."

BIBLIOGRAPHY

D. Ewen: *Dictators of the Baton* (Chicago and New York, 1943, rev. 2/1948)
"Barlow, Howard," *CBY 1954*
Obituary, *New York Times* (2 Feb 1972)
J. Holmes: *Conductors on Record* (Westport, CT, 1982)

SORAB MODI

Barlow, Samuel L(atham) M(itchell) (*b* New York, 1 June 1892; *d* Wyndmoor, PA, 19 Sept 1982). Composer, writer, and liberal activist. He studied at Harvard University (BA 1914), then in New York with Percy Goetschius and Franklin Robinson, in Paris with Isidore Philipp, and in Rome with Ottorino Respighi (orchestration, 1923). Before World War I, and for two decades thereafter, he was very active in New York civic and professional groups formed to promote music, and in liberal political action groups. He was the first chairman of the New York Community Chorus, chairman of the Independent Citizens Committee for the Arts, Sciences, and Professions, governor of the ACA, chairman of the American Committee for the Arts, director of the China Aid Council, and vice-president of the American Committee for Spanish Freedom. In addition, he taught in various settlement schools and was a frequent contributor to *Modern Music*.

Barlow's opera *Mon ami Pierrot*, to a libretto by Sacha Guitry on the life of Lully and purporting to show the origin of the French children's song *Au clair de la lune*, was the first by an American to be produced at the Opéra-Comique in Paris (11 January 1935); his "symphonic concerto for magic lantern," *Babar* (after Brunoff's picture books), uses slide projections. Despite such novelties, Barlow's style was relatively conservative: he admitted that "tunes which wouldn't shock Papa Brahms keep sticking their necks out."

WORKS

(selective list)

Stage: Ballo sardo, ballet, 1928; Mon ami Pierrot (opera, Guitry), 1934; Amanda, opera, 1936; Amphitryon 38 (incidental music, Giraudoux), 12 orch pieces, 1937

Orch: Vocalise, 1926; Alba, sym. poem, orch/chamber orch, 1927; Pf Conc., 1931; Babar, sym. conc., slides, 1936; Leda, 1939; Sousa ad Parnassum, 1939

Inst.: Ballad, Scherzo, str qt, 1933; Spanish Quarter, pf suite, 1933; Conversation with Tchekhov, pf trio, 1940; Jardin de Le Nôtre, pf suite

Vocal: choruses and songs, incl. 3 Songs from the Chinese, T, 7 insts, 1924

Principal publishers: Choudens, Joubert, G. Schirmer

BIBLIOGRAPHY

S. L. M. Barlow: *The Astonished Muse* (New York, 1961) [autobiography]
Obituary, *New York Times* (21 Sept 1982)

H. WILEY HITCHCOCK

Barlow, Wayne (Brewster) (*b* Elyria, OH, 6 Sept 1912). Composer and teacher. He studied composition with Edward Royce, Bernard Rogers, and Howard Hanson at the Eastman School (1930–37), where he received the MMus and the PhD degrees, and with Schoenberg at the University of Southern California (1935). In 1937 he joined the faculty of the Eastman School, eventually becoming chairman of the composition department, director of the electronic music studio (1968), and dean of graduate studies (1973); in 1978 he was named professor emeritus. He has received two Fulbright scholarships (1955–6, 1964–5) and numerous commissions, and has traveled widely as lecturer, guest composer, and conductor of his own works. He also served as organist and choirmaster at two churches in Rochester, St. Thomas Episcopal (1946–76) and Christ Episcopal (1976–8). He is a prolific composer in an eclectic, tonal, free 12-tone style, and has published the book *Foundations of Music* (1953/*R*1983).

WORKS

Orch: The Winter's Passed, ob, str, 1938; Night Song, 1957; Rota, chamber orch, 1959; Images, harp, orch, 1961; Sinfonia da camera, 1962; Conc., sax, band, 1970; Hampton Beach, ov., 1971; Soundscapes, orch, tape, 1972; 2 ballet scores, 9 others

Vocal: Psalm xxiii, chorus, org/orch, 1944; Mass, G, chorus, orch, 1951; Missa Sancti Thomae, chorus, org, 1959; Wait for the Promise of the Father, cantata, T, Bar, chorus, orch, 1968; Voices of Darkness, reader, pf, perc, tape, 1974; Voices of Faith, reader, S, chorus, orch, 1975; 7 others

Chamber: Triptych, str qt, 1953; Trio, ob, va, pf, 1964; Dynamisms, 2 pf, 1967; Elegy, va, pf/orch, 1967; Intermezzo, va, harp, 1980; 7 others

Org pieces incl. Hymn Voluntaries for the Church Year, 4 vols., 1963–81; 4 Chorale Voluntaries, 1979–80

3 tape pieces incl. Soundprints in Concrete, 1975

Principal publishers: Concordia, C. Fischer, J. Fischer, Gray, Presser

BIBLIOGRAPHY

EwenD

W. THOMAS MARROCCO

Bärmann, Karl. *See* BAERMANN, CARL.

Barnabee, Henry Clay (*b* Portsmouth, NH, 14 Nov 1833; *d* Jamaica Plains, MA, 16 Dec 1917). Actor and singer. He began performing in amateur theatricals and concerts while working as a clerk in a dry-goods store. He became professional in 1865 but did not gain widespread recognition until he was recruited by the Boston Ideal Opera Company in 1879 (he was one of its original members). When the group was later reorganized as the Bostonians Barnabee was elected one of its officers; he remained with the company for the rest of its existence and the rest of his career. His most celebrated role was the Sheriff of Nottingham, which he created in the operetta *Robin Hood* by De Koven and H. B. Smith (1891), and which he sang more than 2000 times. His other notable roles included Sir Joseph Porter in Gilbert and Sullivan's *H.M.S. Pinafore*, Izzet Pasha in Franz von Suppé's *Fatinitza*, and Lord Allcash in Daniel Auber's *Fra Diavolo*. He was admired for his excellent bass-baritone voice and restrained but deft comedy. He wrote a volume of reminiscences, *My Wanderings* (1913).

GERALD BORDMAN

Barn dance. Originally a rural meeting for dancing, held in a barn or similar large building. Beginning in the 1920s the term was used to designate variety radio programs of folklike entertainment; the first program so described was broadcast on radio station WBAP in Fort Worth, Texas, in 1923, though many southern radio stations had presented programs of country music in the previous year. The most important of the broadcast barn dances were the NATIONAL BARN DANCE (WLS, Chicago, 1924–70), and the "WSM Barn Dance" (WSM, Nashville, started 1925), which as the GRAND OLE OPRY was still running in the mid-1980s; both were started by GEORGE D. HAY. Other programs included the "Renfro Valley Barn Dance" (WLW, Cincinnati, started 1937), the "Tennessee Barn Dance" (WNOX, Knoxville, Tennessee, started 1942), the "Old Dominion Barn Dance" (WRVA, Richmond, Virginia, started 1946), and the "WHN (New York) Barn Dance." Similar programs that used different titles were the "Louisiana Hayride" (KWKH, Shreveport, Louisiana, started 1948), the "Midwestern Hayride" (WLW, Cincinnati, started 1937), the "Big D Jamboree" (KRLD, Dallas, Texas, started 1924), and the "World's Original WWVA Jamboree" (Wheeling, West Virginia, started 1926). By 1949 some 650 radio stations were broadcasting live country-music performances, but by the mid-1950s such shows had nearly disappeared, with the notable exception of the "Grand Ole Opry," which benefited from the growth of the country-music industry in Nashville. (*See* COUNTRY MUSIC.)

BIBLIOGRAPHY

L. Gentry: *A History and Encyclopedia of Country, Western and Gospel Music* (Nashville, 1961/*R*1972), esp. 168–75
B. C. Malone: *Country Music U.S.A.: a Fifty-year History* (Austin, 1968, 2/1985)
T. A. Patterson: "Hillbilly Music among the Flatlanders: Early Midwestern Radio Barn Dances," *Journal of Country Music*, vi/1 (1975), 12

Barnet, Charlie [Charles Daly] (*b* New York, 26 Oct 1913). Jazz saxophonist and bandleader. He was born into a wealthy family, but rebelled in his teens to become a musician. Though never a major jazz improviser, he led a very popular dance band during the swing period, which was also admired for its jazz playing. Barnet was one of the first white bandleaders to employ Blacks, usually as solo stars, among them Roy Eldridge, Charlie Shavers, Benny Carter, and Frankie Newton (who joined the band as early as 1937). Barnet was especially influenced by the Duke Ellington Orchestra, and played many arrangements which frankly imitated Ellington's. In 1939 his hit recording of Billy May's arrangement of *Cherokee* made him one of the most popular swing bandleaders. However, with the decline of the big bands in the late 1940s, he was forced to disband his orchestra, which thereafter regrouped only for special occasions.

For illustration *see* KAYE, DANNY.

RECORDINGS
(selective list)

The Gal from Joe's (1939, Bluebird 10153); Cherokee (1939, Bluebird 10373); The Duke's Idea/The Count's Idea (1939, Bluebird 10453); The Sergeant was Shy (1940, Bluebird 10862); Skyliner (1945, Decca 18659); Portrait of Edward Kennedy Ellington, pts I–II (1949, Cap. 60010)

BIBLIOGRAPHY

E. Edwards and others: *Charlie Barnet and his Orchestra* (Whittier, CA, 1965, rev. 2/1970)
J. Burns: "Charlie Barnet," *Jazz Monthly*, no.183 (1970), 9
C. Garrod: *Charlie Barnet and his Orchestra* (Spotswood, NJ, 1973)
C. Barnet and S. Dance: *Those Swinging Years* (Baton Rouge, LA, 1984)

JAMES LINCOLN COLLIER

Barnett, Alice (Ray) (*b* Lewiston, IL, 26 May 1886; *d* San Diego, CA, 28 Aug 1975). Composer, teacher, and patron. She studied with Ganz and Borowski at the Chicago Musical College (BM 1906) and with Heniot Levy and Adolf Weidig at the American Conservatory, Chicago; she also studied composition in Chicago with Wilhelm Middleschulte and in Berlin with Hugo Kaun (1909–10). From 1917 to 1926 she taught music at the San Diego High School. A respected and influential leader of musical life in San Diego, her many activities included writing program notes for concerts given by the Los Angeles SO, helping to found the Musical Merit Foundation, the San Diego Opera Guild, and the San Diego Civic SO (of which she was chairwoman for 14 years), and serving on the board of directors of the Amphion Club (1920–48). Barnett wrote some 60 art songs, 49 of which were published by G. Schirmer and Summy between 1906 and 1932. They display a lyrical gift, sure tonal sense, and, despite her German training, strong French harmonic influence. They are often exotic and colorful, especially *Chanson of the Bells of Oseney* (1924) and the Browning cycle *In a Gondola* (1920), which is also dramatic; others of her songs are *Panels from a Chinese Screen* (1924), *Harbor Lights* (1927), and *Nirvana* (1932). She also wrote instrumental music, including a piano trio (1920) and *Effective Violin Solos* (1924). Although Barnett stopped composing in the late 1930s, she maintained her musical activities in San Diego. Her manuscripts and papers are at the San Diego Historical Society.

BIBLIOGRAPHY

W. T. Upton: "Some Recent Representative American Song-composers," *MQ*, xi (1925), 398
—: *Art-song in America* (Boston, 1930/*R*1969), 214 [incl. music examples]
A. F. Block and C. Neuls-Bates, eds.: *Women in American Music: a Bibliography of Music and Literature* (Westport, CT, 1979)

ADRIENNE FRIED BLOCK

Barnett, John (Manley) (*b* New York, 3 Sept 1917). Conductor. He studied piano, violin, and trumpet, and took courses in conducting at the Manhattan School of Music, and then studied with Bruno Walter, Weingartner, Enesco, and Malko in Europe. After an apprenticeship under Leon Barzin with the National Orchestral Association, he became a staff conductor with the WPA Federal Music Project of New York (1939–42); in this capacity he conducted a variety of orchestras, including the Federal Knickerbocker Orchestra, as an assistant to Klemperer, and the New York City SO. During this period, he also conducted the Stamford (Connecticut) SO. Following wartime service in the army, he was associate conductor of the Los Angeles PO (1946–58) and in 1956 went with the orchestra on its tour of the Far East; he remained in Tokyo for a time to organize and train the Japan-America PO, made up of Japanese musicians and members of the US Armed Forces Band. He returned to New York in 1958 to become music director of the National Orchestral Association, which he led until 1970. In 1976 Barnett served as musical artistic consultant to the NEA.

GENE BIRINGER

Barnhouse, Charles Lloyd (*b* Grafton, WV, 20 March 1865; *d* Oskaloosa, IA, 29 Nov 1929). Music publisher, bandmaster, and composer. As a child, he was given cornet lessons by his uncles. He became a proficient soloist, and by the age of 18 was director of the Grafton Band. He then toured for several years with musical comedy companies. In 1886 he moved to Mount Pleasant, Iowa, where he directed the local band and set up a music publishing business. He moved his family and business first to Burlington, Iowa, in 1891, and then to Oskaloosa in 1895. For many years he directed the Iowa Brigade Band, for which he built a permanent rehearsal hall. He published more than 100 of his own band compositions, including cornet solos, marches, galops, waltzes, and dirges; some works appeared under the pseudonyms Jim Fisk and A. M. Laurens. A number of his marches are recorded in the series Heritage of the March (compiled by ROBERT HOE, JR). His publishing business flourished, becoming the second largest family-owned music house in the country. In addition to his own compositions, he published the works of such important band composers as Jewell, VanderCook, Karl King, Russell Alexander, and Walter English. The company bearing his name continues to publish band music of high quality under the direction of his grandsons Robert and Charles.

RAOUL CAMUS

Barnum, P(hineas) T(aylor) (*b* Bethel, CT, 5 July 1810; *d* Bridgeport, CT, 7 April 1891). Impresario. After an early success exhibiting Joyce Heth (advertised as George Washington's 160-year-old nurse), Barnum purchased a moribund collection of curiosities, and by relentless promotion made Barnum's Museum one of New York's central attractions. By 1850 his management of such novelties as the celebrated midget Tom Thumb had established him as America's leading showman, and the lecture hall at the Museum became an early venue for "family" minstrelsy and variety. In 1844 Barnum capitalized on the enthusiasm for Tyrolean acts by introducing the often parodied "Swiss Bell Ringers" (who actually came from Lancashire, England). He sponsored the Irish soprano Catherine Hayes on a tour of California (1852), and as president of the New York Crystal Palace he played an important role in Jullien's "Grand Musical Congress" (1854).

Barnum's greatest triumph, however, was a tour by Jenny Lind (1850–51); under his management she gave 95 concerts in 19 cities, attracting unprecedented receipts of $712,161.34 (*see also* TAYLOR, BAYARD). Barnum traveled with the troupe and, with inspired publicity and an eye for sensation, promoted Lind much like an exhibit; though Lind eventually broke with him, they remained on good terms. This was the first major tour in the USA to be managed by a nonperformer, and it marked the rise of a separate class of agents and promoters. Barnum's methods influenced popular entertainers as well as impresarios such as Max Maretzek and the Strakosch brothers; his impact on America's music industry was lasting and profound.

BIBLIOGRAPHY

P. T. Barnum: *The Life of P. T. Barnum, written by himself* (New York, 1855; rev. as *Struggles and Triumphs*, 1869); ed. G. S. Bryan as *Struggles and Triumphs, or The Life of P. T. Barnum, written by himself* (New York, 1927)

N. Harris: *Humbug: the Art of P. T. Barnum* (Boston, 1973)

W. P. Ware and T. C. Lockard, Jr.: *P. T. Barnum Presents Jenny Lind: the American Tour of the Swedish Nightingale* (Baton Rouge, LA, 1980)

A. H. Saxon, ed.: *Selected Letters of P. T. Barnum* (New York, 1983)

WILLIAM BROOKS

Baron, Samuel (*b* Brooklyn, NY, 27 April 1925). Flutist and conductor. He studied at Brooklyn College (1940–45), and at the Juilliard School (1942–8) with Georges Barrère, Arthur Lora (flute), and Edgar Schenkman (conducting). He gained orchestral experience with the New York SO, the New York City Opera, and the Minneapolis SO (principal flute), and in 1949 was a founder-member of the New York Woodwind Quintet, with which he played regularly (1949–69, and again from 1980), making many notable recordings and giving many first performances. In the mid-1950s he turned increasingly to chamber

P. T. Barnum escorting Jenny Lind ashore at the Canal-Street Wharf on her arrival in New York, 1 September 1850: engraving from Barnum's "Struggles and Triumphs" (1869)

music and until 1965 was associated successively with the American Chamber Orchestra, the New York Chamber Soloists, and the Contemporary Chamber Ensemble. In that year, he joined the BACH ARIA GROUP, of which he became music director in 1980. As a soloist his repertory is large, and he has given many first performances.

A distinguished teacher, Baron has been on the staff of the Yale School of Music (1965–7), Mannes College (1969–72), SUNY, Stony Brook (from 1966), and the Juilliard School (from 1977). He was founder and conductor, in 1948, of the New York Brass Ensemble, which he has directed in many recordings. He has edited Bach's Flute Sonata in A BWV1032 (1974) with a reconstruction of the first movement, and his arrangement of the *Art of Fugue*, for string quartet and five wind instruments, though unpublished, has been recorded. Baron has written *Chamber Music for Winds* (1969).

BIBLIOGRAPHY

P. Estevan: *Talking with Flutists* (n.p., 1976), 21

PHILIP BATE/R

Barons of Rhythm. Jazz band formed in 1935 by COUNT BASIE.

Barrelhouse. A style of piano playing that originated among black American blues musicians in the early 20th century. It was first practiced in the makeshift saloons of lumber camps in the South and is related to BOOGIE-WOOGIE (i), which may have preceded it as a blues piano style (*see* BLUES, §4). Whereas boogie developed as fast music largely of eight beats to the bar, barrelhouse was played in regular 4/4 meter. Ragtime bass figures or the heavy left-hand vamp known as "stomping" were often employed with occasional "walking" bass variations. Characteristic early recordings are *Barrel House Man* (1927, Para. 12549) by the Texas pianist Will Ezell, *The Dirty Dozen* by Speckled Red (Rufus Perryman) (1929, Bruns. 7116), and *Soon This Morning* by Charlie Spand (1929, Para. 12790); Perryman and Spand worked in Detroit after leaving the South. *Diggin' My Potatoes* (1939, Bluebird 8211), by Washboard Sam with Joshua Altheimer on piano, and *Shack Bully Stomp* (1938, Decca 7479), by Peetie Wheatstraw, are examples of the persistence of the style. Many barrelhouse themes became standards, and were played by blues pianists after other styles had superseded the form. The term "barrelhouse" was also used to mean "rough" or "crude," as in *"Mooch" Richardson's Low Down Barrel House Blues* (1928, OK 8554), and several blues singers, among them Nolan Welch, Buck McFarland, and Bukka White, were known by this nickname.

BIBLIOGRAPHY

S. Calt, J. Epstein, and N. Perls: Liner notes, *Barrelhouse Blues 1927–1936* (Yazoo 1028, 1971)
E. Kriss: *Barrelhouse and Boogie Piano* (New York, 1974)

PAUL OLIVER

Barrère, Georges (*b* Bordeaux, France, 31 Oct 1876; *d* Kingston, NY, 14 June 1944). Flutist. He studied at the Paris Conservatoire with Joseph-Henri Altès and Paul Taffanel, then held a number of important posts leading to appointments in the orchestras of the Opéra and the Théâtre Colonne. In 1895 he founded the Société Moderne des Instruments à Vent, which replaced Taffanel's group of the same name, disbanded in 1893; with this ensemble Barrère introduced over 80 new works. He came to New York in 1905 to play first flute with Damrosch's New York SO, a post he held until 1928. He taught concurrently at the Institute of Musical Art (until 1930) and the Juilliard School (from 1931). In the USA, as in France, he founded chamber groups: the Barrère Ensemble of Wind Instruments (1910; expanded in 1914 to 13 players to become the Barrère Little Symphony), which for 30 years performed new and rarely heard works; the Barrère–Britt Concertino; the Trio de Lutèce (1914); and the Barrère–Britt–Salzedo Trio (1932). As a soloist, and with various of his chamber groups, Barrère gave a number of first performances of American works, including Griffes's *Poem* (1919); David Stanley Smith's *Fête galante* (1920); Suzanne Bloch's Suite for flute and piano (1933); Varèse's *Density 21.5* (1936; composed at Barrère's request); and Wagenaar's Triple Concerto (1938). He also participated in Cowell's New Music Quarterly Recordings series, performing in Cowell's Suite for wind quintet, Berezowsky's Suite for wind quintet, Piston's Three Pieces (all released 1935), and the finale of Riegger's Divertissement (released 1934). As one of the greatest flutists, Barrère's influence was profound; he was much sought-after as a teacher in New York. He wrote many articles, contributed to flute tutors, made several nationwide concert tours, and also composed. He became an American citizen in 1937.

BIBLIOGRAPHY

G. Barrère: *Georges Barrère* (New York, 1929)
George Barrère Flutist (New York, n.d.)
The Platinum Flute and Georges Barrère (New York, 1935)
L. de Lorenzo: *My Complete Story of the Flute* (New York, 1951), 182
D. Ewen: *Musicians since 1900* (New York, 1978), 47

RUTH B. HILTON

Barrett (Campbell), Delois (*b* Chicago, IL, 3 Dec 1926). Gospel singer. At the age of 17 she joined the Roberta Martin Singers, where her unusually clear and strong soprano voice made her a valuable soloist. She achieved her first national success in 1949 with the group's recording of *What a blessing in Jesus I've found.* As a member of the Martin Singers she traveled throughout the USA and appeared at the Festival of Two Worlds in Spoleto, Italy, with the composer Menotti. In the early 1950s she married Frank Campbell, pastor of the Beersheba Baptist Church in Chicago, and after her marriage and the birth of her four children she curtailed her travels with the Martin Singers in order to assist her husband at the church. At the suggestion of Martin, Barrett formed the Barrett Sisters with her two sisters, Billie Barrett Greenbey and Rhodessa Barrett Porter; Martin served the trio as accompanist for a time. Although the Barrett Sisters are traditional gospel singers, they are also known for their rendition of such songs as John Stainer's *God so loved the world* and Rodgers and Hammerstein's *You'll never walk alone.* The Barrett Sisters have appeared at the Apollo Theater in Harlem, in Carnegie Hall, and on national television. Barrett was one of the participants in the reunion concert of the Roberta Martin Singers that was held at the Smithsonian Institution in February 1981.

BIBLIOGRAPHY

SouthernB
H. C. Boyer: "Contemporary Gospel Music: Characteristics and Style," *BPiM*, vii (1979), 22
T. Heilbut: *The Gospel Sound: Good News and Bad Times* (New York, 1971/*R*1975)
W. T. Walker: *Somebody's Calling My Name* (Valley Forge, PA, 1979)

HORACE CLARENCE BOYER

Barretto, Ray(mond) (*b* Brooklyn, NY, 29 April 1929). Bandleader and conga player. Although he is of Puerto Rican extraction, he came to salsa music via jazz. He first played in jam sessions while serving with the US Army in Germany, and continued to play with several important jazz musicians on his return to Harlem. Before forming his own group in 1961 he was a member of Tito Puente's band and also played with Herbie Mann. He recorded with such musicians as Cannonball Adderley, Red Garland, and Dizzy Gillespie. Barretto's first band was a *charanga* (flute supported by violins). His recording *El watusi* (1962) was a substantial rhythm-and-blues hit, and he spent some years trying to repeat that success before moving to Fania Records in 1967. In that year he issued his important Latin-jazz fusion album *Acid*, and from then was recognized as one of the leading salsa bandleaders. In the late 1970s he signed a contract with Atlantic Records, for which he recorded the jazz-influenced albums *Eye of the Beholder* (1977) and *Can You Feel It?* (1978); the hoped-for success in the Anglo-American market, however, did not take place. During the early 1980s Barretto continued to play salsa concerts in the USA and abroad, and to appear in New York jazz clubs.

BIBLIOGRAPHY

J. S. Roberts: *The Latin Tinge* (New York, 1979)

JOHN STORM ROBERTS

Barron, Louis (*b* Minneapolis, MN, 23 April 1920). Composer. He and his wife Bebe (née Charlotte Wind, *b* Minneapolis, 16 June 1927) have written pioneering works in the field of electroacoustic music. Louis Barron studied piano and wrote jazz criticism while a student at the University of Minnesota. After college he worked for the Gallup organization as a social psychologist. Bebe Barron received an MA in political science from the University of Minnesota, where she studied composition with Cordero. In 1947 she studied with Riegger and Cowell in New York while working as a researcher for *Time*. That same year the Barrons were married and began to experiment with manipulations of electronic sounds using an ordinary tape recorder; in 1948 in New York they established one of the earliest electroacoustic music studios. It contained both disc and tape equipment, with sine- and square-wave oscillators, mixers, and filters. Louis Barron's knowledge of electronics allowed him to design and build so-called behavioral circuits, based on Norbert Wiener's science of cybernetics. Their experiments led the Barrons to use and develop the characteristics of individual circuits to create different types of sound events which they considered "gestalts." Eventually they constructed a large collection of cybernetic circuits for use in processing sounds and in composing. Their first fully realized work was the electronic composition *Heavenly Menagerie* (1951). During 1952 and 1953 the Barrons' studio was used by Cage for the preparation of his first tape works. In 1956 the Barrons composed the score for *Forbidden Planet*; it was the first electronic score for a commercial film and because of its wide dissemination it has had a considerable impact on the development of electronic music. In 1962 the Barrons moved to Los Angeles, where, although divorced in 1970, they continued to collaborate on compositional projects.

WORKS

(all elec, composed with Bebe Barron)

Dramatic: Legend (American Mime Theatre), 1955; Ballet (P. Feigay), 1958; incidental music for 4 plays, 1957–62

Tape: Heavenly Menagerie, 1951; For an Elec Nervous System, 1954; Music of Tomorrow, 1960; Spaceboy, 1971, arr. film score, 1973; The Circe Circuit, 1982; Elegy for a Dying Planet, 1982

Film scores: Bells of Atlantis (I. Hugo), 1952; Miramagic (W. Lewisohn), 1954; Forbidden Planet (F. M. Wilcox), 1956; Jazz of Lights (I. Hugo), 1956; Bridges (S. Clarke), 1959; Crystal Growing (Western Electric), 1959; The Computer Age (IBM), 1968; Spaceboy (R. Druks), 1973; More than Human (A. Singer), 1974; Cannabis (Computer Graphics), 1975

BIBLIOGRAPHY

P. Glanville-Hicks: "Tapesichord," *Vogue*, cxxii/1 (1953), 42
L. Barron and B. Barron: "Forbidden Planet," *Film Music*, xv/5 (1956), 18
C. Harmon: "Music of the Future," *Time*, lxviii/1 (1956), 36
P. Manuell and J. Huntley: *Technique of Film Music* (New York, 1957)
A. Nin: *The Diary of Anaïs Nin*, v–vii (New York, 1974–80)
S. Rubin: "Retrospect: Forbidden Planet," *Cinefantastique*, iv/1 (1975), 4
F. Clarke and S. Rubin: "Making Forbidden Planet," *Cinefantastique*, vii/2–3 (1979), 42
D. Schary: *Heyday* (Boston, 1979), 290

BARRY SCHRADER

Barrows, John (*b* Glendale, CA, 12 Feb 1913; *d* Madison, WI, 11 Jan 1974). Horn player. He studied at the Eastman School of Music (1930–32), San Diego State Teachers College (1933–4), and at Yale University (1934–8). He played horn with the Minneapolis SO (1938–42) and with the orchestras of the New York City Opera (1946–9) and the New York City Ballet (1952–5). Barrows was best known for the reliable virtuosity he exhibited with the New York Woodwind Quintet, an ensemble that he co-founded in 1952 and performed with until 1961. He taught at Yale (1957–61) and at New York University (1958–61); in 1961 he was appointed professor at the University of Wisconsin, Madison, where he remained until his death. He composed two string quartets, a wind quintet, and a string trio, and made many arrangements of orchestral works which are among the staples of the concert band repertory.

JAMES WIERZBICKI

Barth, Hans (*b* Leipzig, Germany, 25 June 1897; *d* Jacksonville, FL, 8 Dec 1956). Composer and pianist. As a child he attended the Leipzig Conservatory, studying under Carl Reinecke. He moved to the USA with his family in 1907 and made his New York recital début the next year. He became a citizen of the USA in 1912. Busoni inspired him to experiment with new scales, and Barth helped to invent a portable quarter-tone piano in 1928, for which he composed numerous works; he was acquainted with Ives and may have rekindled that composer's interest in quarter-tone music. Barth performed in the USA and Europe on the harpsichord, piano, and quarter-tone piano, and was a soloist with orchestras in Cincinnati, Havana, and Philadelphia; with the Philadelphia Orchestra he served for five years under Stokowski, and performed his Concerto for quarter-tone piano on 28 March 1930. He was a MacDowell Fellow, directed the Institute of Musical Art (Yonkers, New York) and the National School for Musical Culture (New York), and taught piano at the Mannes School and the Jacksonville College of Music (1948–56).

WORKS

Stage: *Miriagia* (operetta), op.2, 1938; Save me the Waltz (incidental music, B. Bernier)

Orch: Pf Conc., 1928; Conc., $\frac{1}{4}$-tone str, $\frac{1}{4}$-tone pf, op.11, 1930; Conc., $\frac{1}{4}$-tone pf, str, op.15, 1930; Drama Sym., 1940; Sym. "Prince of Peace," op.25, 1940; 10 Etudes, $\frac{1}{4}$-tone pf, orch, 1942–4

Chamber: 2 pf sonatas, opp.7, 14, 1929, 1932; Qnt, $\frac{1}{4}$-tone pf, str, 1930; Suite, $\frac{1}{4}$-tone str, brass, timp, 1930; 2 Suites, pf, opp.20, 23, 1938, 1941

Many songs

Principal publishers: Associated, Axelrod, Mills

BIBLIOGRAPHY

EwenD
"Barth at Miami Conservatory," *Musical Courier*, cxxxix (1 Jan 1949), 33

KATHERINE K. PRESTON

Bartholomew, Marshall (*b* Belleville, IL, 3 March 1885; *d* Guilford, CT, 16 April 1978). Choral conductor. He studied at the University of Pennsylvania (BM 1908) and at the Hochschule für Musik in Berlin (1912–14) with Horatio Parker, Engelbert Humperdinck, and Albert Coates. During World War I he was director of the Music Bureau of the National War Council. In 1921, the year he joined the faculty of Yale University, he established the Yale Glee Club, which he conducted until 1953. He founded the International Student Music Council in 1930 and for several years was president of the International Music Council of the United States. During World War II he was a member of the music committee of the Cultural Division of the US State Department. In 1952, he was awarded an honorary MA from Yale; three years later he received the Yale Medal. To celebrate his 90th birthday, he conducted 2000 former members of the Yale Glee Club. Bartholomew composed a number of vocal works including *Song in the Night*, *April Song*, and *Call of Spring*; he was also an arranger and editor.

BIBLIOGRAPHY

M. Kaplan: Obituary, *New York Times* (18 April 1978), 42

SORAB MODI

Bartlett, Daniel B. Instrument dealer and maker, active in Concord, New Hampshire, during the 1840s in partnership with DAVID M. DEARBORN.

Bartlett, Ethel (1896–1978). Pianist, who performed the two-piano repertory with her husband, RAE ROBERTSON.

Bartlett, Homer N(ewton) (*b* Olive, NY, 28 Dec 1846; *d* Hoboken, NJ, 3 April 1920). Composer and organist. He studied piano, organ, and composition in New York, where he began a career as a church organist at the age of 14. He spent 12 years at the Marble Collegiate Church, New York, and over 30 years at the Madison Avenue Baptist Church, retiring in 1912. A founding member of the American Guild of Organists, he was also active in the rival National Association of Organists (president 1910–11) and the New York Manuscript Society.

Bartlett was a prolific composer: his published opus numbers reached 271. Some of his early salon pieces, for example the *Grande polka de concert* (1867), achieved great popularity and were published in several editions. Other works include *La vallière* (opera, 1887), *Magic Hours* (operetta, 1910), an oratorio, *Samuel*, church music, violin and cello concertos, and the symphonic poem *Apollo* (1911). He also composed chamber music, organ works, character pieces for piano, over 80 solo songs, and part-songs. Late in his career he became fascinated with Japanese themes. The piano pieces *Kuma saka* (1907) and *Dondon-bushi* (1918) display this exotic preoccupation, though they are not based on any real understanding of Japanese music.

BIBLIOGRAPHY

R. Hughes: *Contemporary American Composers* (Boston, 1900), 317
S. Salter: "Bartlett, Homer Newton," *DAB*

WILLIAM OSBORNE

Bartók, Béla (*b* Nagyszentmiklós [now Sînnicolau Mare, Romania], 25 March 1881; *d* New York, 26 Sept 1945). Hungarian composer, ethnomusicologist, and pianist. He lived in the USA during his last five years.

1. Life and works. 2. Posthumous success in the USA.

1. LIFE AND WORKS. Bartók studied piano and composition at the Budapest Academy of Music (1899–1903), and was influenced at a young age by the works of Wagner, Liszt, and Richard Strauss. In 1903–4 he appeared in concerts outside of Hungary for the first time and was introduced as a composer. His music began to be published in 1904, the year in which he made his first transcription of a Hungarian peasant song – a response to increasing national sentiment in Hungary. In 1905 he met Zoltán Kodály, and the two began a lifelong collaboration in folksong research. Bartók taught piano at the Budapest Academy from 1907 to 1934, which gave him enough financial security to extend his folksong research to other nationalities. In his own compositions he began to synthesize art music and peasant song in the 14 Bagatelles op. 6 (1908), the String Quartet no. 1 (1908), and the Two Pictures (1910) for orchestra. By 1918 he had collected over 9000 folksongs, all the while composing intensively, notably the one-act opera *Bluebeard's Castle* (1911). His first popular success was *The Wooden Prince* (1917); he was striving for concise effects in the Piano Suite op. 14 (1916) and the Second String Quartet op. 15 (1915–17). Within several years Bartók was making regular recital tours through Europe, which resulted in the composition of a number of piano works, neoclassical in style, to fulfill his needs as a performer: two piano concertos (1926, 1930–31), the Sonata (1926), and the suite *Out of Doors* (1926).

Between December 1927 and February 1928 Bartók made a tour of the USA. After his American début (in New York on 22 December 1927, playing the Rhapsody op. 1 with the New York PO under Willem Mengelberg), he made 25 appearances, many of them lecture-recitals on new Hungarian national music (including Kodály's), sponsored by the Pro-Musica Society. Among the cities he visited were San Francisco, Los Angeles, Portland, Seattle, Denver, Kansas City, Chicago, and St. Paul; he was also soloist in orchestral concerts in Cincinnati, Philadelphia, and New York again before his return to Budapest. The next few years were among his most prolific; he completed the two rhapsodies for violin and piano (and arrangements of both for violin and orchestra and of the first for cello and piano) and the Fourth String Quartet (all 1928), the *Cantata profana* (1930) and other choral works, the Second Piano Concerto (1931), and the 44 Violin Duos (1931).

In 1934 Bartók was relieved of his formal teaching duties and accepted a commission from the Hungarian Academy of Sciences to prepare the publication of his Hungarian folksong collection; but his teaching efforts continued in lectures on folk music and in the composition of *Mikrokosmos* (1926–39), a set of six volumes (153 pieces) of progressive piano studies. His important compositions of the 1930s were written to commission: the Fifth String Quartet (1934) was composed for Elizabeth Sprague Coolidge, the Music for Strings, Percussion, and Celesta (1937) and the Divertimento (1939) for Paul Sacher (conductor of the Basle Chamber Orchestra), the Sonata for two pianos and percussion (1937) for the Basle ISCM chapter, the Violin Concerto (1937–8) for the violinist Zoltán Székely, and *Contrasts* (1938), com-

Béla Bartók during his final voyage to the USA, 1940

missioned by Benny Goodman, for Goodman and Joseph Szigeti. These works display many of the metrical and rhythmic characteristics – and especially the palindromic form – that are perhaps the most original features of Bartók's style.

Bartók's anti-fascist views and actions resulted in attacks against him in the Hungarian and Romanian newspapers. He became concerned for the safety of his manuscripts and sent them abroad for safekeeping, and he began to consider emigrating, especially after the annexation of Austria by Nazi Germany in 1938. He made a second American tour (11 April–18 May 1940), during which he gave a concert with Szigeti in the Library of Congress, recorded *Contrasts* in New York with Szigeti and Goodman, and lectured on folk music. He learned then too of the existence at Harvard University of the Milman Parry collection of some 2600 discs of Yugoslav folk music. With help from members of the music faculty at Columbia University a research grant to enable him to work in the collection was made available from the Alice M. Ditson Fund; under the grant he received a music assistantship at Columbia for the period from March 1941 through December 1942 with an honorarium of $3000 a year. He returned home to settle his affairs and in autumn 1940, with his second wife, the pianist Ditta Pásztory, left Hungary forever; they disembarked in New York on 30 October. Bartók's last significant European composition had been the Sixth String Quartet (1939), a lament punctuated by "scenes from life"; its *mesto* conclusion is the only one of Bartók's late works not to end joyously.

Soon after arriving in the USA Bartók was awarded an honorary doctorate by Columbia University and, after a week in Cleveland, settled in an apartment in Forest Hills, New York. During 1940–42 he completed no new work, though he arranged the Sonata for pianos and percussion (1937) as a double piano concerto (December 1940) and transcribed the Second Suite (1905–7) for two pianos (1941), both for concerts with his wife. From April 1942 his health began to decline. On 21 January 1943 he performed for the last time in public, playing with his wife in the American première of the Concerto for Two Pianos at a New York PO concert under Reiner. Medical tests resulted in a diagnosis of leukemia, treatment for which was paid for by ASCAP. He spent the summers of 1943–5 at a sanatorium on Saranac Lake, New York; during the first one he completed the Concerto for Orchestra which had been commissioned that spring by Koussevitzky for the Boston SO. In November 1943 he met Yehudi Menuhin, who asked him to write a violin sonata; it was completed in March 1944, after a salubrious winter (financed by ASCAP) in Asheville, North Carolina.

Bartók worked on three new compositions in 1945. The Third Piano Concerto was completed but for the orchestration of the last few bars; the Viola Concerto, commissioned by William Primrose, was left in sketch form (both works were completed by Tibor Serly). He also arranged the Ukrainian folksong *A férj keserve* ("The husband's grief") and began work on a cycle of Ukrainian folksongs. Bartók also planned a seventh quartet, but in September 1945 his health suddenly took a turn for the worse. From Saranac Lake he returned to New York, where he died in West Side Hospital.

The music of this final period of Bartók's life was less rigorous, less strictly organized, more fluid, more confessional, and more marked by extremes. The brilliant orchestral coloring of these works, new to his music, undoubtedly played a part in their subsequent success. Each is, moreover, somewhat exceptional. *Contrasts* (1938) has a certain jazz coloring (in Bartókian style), perhaps reflecting the recordings by the Goodman band sent by Szigeti to Bartók. The Concerto for Orchestra ([?1942–]1943), which contains material originally intended for a ballet, stands by itself if only because of its genre; it also was clearly designed to display Koussevitzky's orchestra. The Sonata for solo violin (1944) contains the quintessence of Bartókian melody and strives for the utmost concentration of expression. The clear Mozartian mold of the Third Piano Concerto and its easier, less personal style than that of the other two concertos, is unique in Bartók's output.

2. POSTHUMOUS SUCCESS IN THE USA. Bartók may have foreseen the immense success his music was to enjoy in the USA after his death, for he was present at the triumphant premières in late 1944 of the Sonata for solo violin (by Menuhin on 26 November in Town Hall, New York) and the Concerto for Orchestra (by the Boston SO under Koussevitzky on 1 December), and commissions were flowing in, not only that from Primrose for the Viola Concerto, which he was able to sketch fully, but others that he was not able to fulfill at all: from his publisher Ralph Hawkes for a seventh string quartet and from the two-piano team of Bartlett and Robertson for a double concerto. The posthumous success was, ironically, swift in coming: already in 1948–9 American orchestras played works by Bartók more often than those by any other 20th-century composer except Strauss and Prokofiev. For a time, also, younger American composers were strongly attracted to Bartók's music and influenced by it, especially its formal, rhythmic, and contrapuntal techniques. Even adherents of 12-tone composition found the intellectual rigor and protoserialism of some of the works worthy of their attention

(see Babbitt, 1949; Forte, 1960; Perle, 1977). Ultimately, however, Bartók's language and his aesthetics proved to be too personal (perhaps too national) and resistant to adaptation; no "Bartók school" crystallized in the USA. Many of Bartók's writings have been published as *Béla Bartók Essays* (ed. B. Suchoff, 1976).

BIBLIOGRAPHY

M. Babbitt: "The String Quartets of Bartók," *MQ*, xxxv (1949), 377

H. Stevens: *The Life and Music of Béla Bartók* (New York, 1953, rev. 2/1964)

A. Fassett: *Béla Bartók's American Years: the Naked Face of Genius* (Boston, 1958)

A. Forte: "Bartók's Serial Composition," *MQ*, xlvi (1960), 233

V. Bator: *The Béla Bartók Archives: History and Catalogue* (New York, 1963)

F. Bonis: *Béla Bartóks Leben in Bildern* (Budapest, 1964, enlarged 2/1972 in Hung. and Ger.; Eng. trans., 1972)

J. Vinton: "Bartók on his own Music," *JAMS*, xix (1966), 232

E. Lendvai: *Béla Bartók: an Analysis of his Music* (London, 1971)

M. Carner: "Béla Bartók," NOHM, x (1974), 274

J. McCabe: *Bartók Orchestral Music* (London, 1974)

D. Dalton: "The Genesis of Bartók's Viola Concerto," *ML*, lvii (1976), 117

Y. Lenoir: *Vie et oeuvre de Béla Bartók aux États-Unis d'Amérique 1940–1945* (diss., U. of Louvain, Belgium, 1976)

B. Suchoff: "Bartók in America," *MT*, cxvii (1976), 123

G. Perle: "The String Quartets of Béla Bartók," *A Musical Offering: Essays in Honor of Martin Bernstein* (New York, 1977)

L. Somfai: "Bartók's Writings," *MT*, cxviii (1977), 395 [review of *Béla Bartók Essays*, ed. B. Suchoff (1976)]

H. G. Miskin: "Bartók at Amherst," *Amherst* (1978), win., 14

S. Kovacs: "Reexamining the Bartók/Serly Viola Concerto," *SM*, xxiii (1981), 295

M. Gillies: "Bartók's Last Works: a Theory of Tonality and Modality," *Musicology*, vii (1982), 120

E. Antokoletz: *The Works of Béla Bartók: a Study of Tonality and Progression in Twentieth-century Music* (Berkeley, CA, 1984)

L. Somfai and V. Lampert: "Bela Bartók," *Modern Masters*, The New Grove Composer Biography Series (New York, 1984), 1–101 [incl. full list of works]

VERA LAMPERT, LÁSZLÓ SOMFAI/H. WILEY HITCHCOCK

Barzin, Leon (Eugene) (*b* Brussels, Belgium, 27 Nov 1900). Conductor and educator. Taken to the USA at the age of two, he studied the violin with his father, who was first viola in the Metropolitan Opera orchestra, and later with Edouard Deru, Pierre Henrotte, and Ysaÿe. He joined the New York PO in 1919 and was appointed first viola in 1925, a position he retained until 1929. The next year he was named principal conductor and music director of the National Orchestral Association, a proving ground for young professionals. In occasional public concerts and in weekly rehearsals, which reached a wide audience through the New York municipal radio station, he groomed his players in performances of the standard repertory. His method was deliberate and considerate, and the results were impressive. He led the ensemble until 1958, and returned as principal conductor from 1970 to 1976. He also appeared as guest conductor with the New York PO, was conductor of the Hartford (Connecticut) SO, 1938–40, and took charge of education at the New England Conservatory. He received the Columbia University Ditson Award and the Gold Medal of Lebanon, and was made a member of the Légion d'honneur in 1960.

GEORGE GELLES/R

Barzun, Jacques (*b* Créteil, Val-de-Marne, France, 30 Nov 1907). Historian and critic. He came to the USA in 1919 and was a pupil of Carlton J. H. Hayes at Columbia University (BA 1927), where he was awarded the doctorate in 1932. During his long association with Columbia he served as lecturer (1927), professor (1945), and provost (1958–67); he was Seth Low professor of history there from 1960 until his retirement. His writings have dealt mainly with 19th-century European and 20th-century American culture; his work in music has centered on Berlioz, the subject of his large and exhaustively documented *Berlioz and the Romantic Century* (1950, rev. 2/1956 as *Berlioz and his Century*, rev. 3/1969), a pioneering reappraisal of Berlioz's standing and achievement approached from a cultural rather than musicological standpoint. Its influence on Berlioz appreciation was profound. He has also edited a volume of Berlioz's letters and translated *Les soirées de l'orchestre*. Barzun's critical views (summarized in *Critical Questions on Music and Letters, Culture and Biography, 1940–1980*, 1982) are wide-ranging and demonstrate a special understanding of the Romantic movement and its belief that music begins to speak at the point where words stop. He has consistently propounded the chief Romantic virtues of energy, sincerity, diversity, and imagination as antidotes to the sicknesses of 20th-century society.

HUGH MACDONALD/PAULA MORGAN

Basie, Count [William] (*b* Red Bank, NJ, 21 Aug 1904; *d* Hollywood, CA, 26 April 1984). Jazz bandleader and pianist. He was a leading figure of the swing era in jazz and, alongside Duke Ellington, an outstanding representative of big-band style.

1. Life. 2. Ensemble style. 3. Solo style.

1. Life. After studying piano with his mother, as a young man he went to New York, where he met James P. Johnson, Fats Waller (with whom he studied informally), and other pianists of the Harlem stride school. Before he was 20 he toured extensively on the Keith and TOBA vaudeville circuits as a solo pianist, accompanist, and music director for blues singers, dancers, and comedians, an early training that was to prove significant in his later career. Stranded in Kansas City in 1927 while accompanying a touring group, he remained there, playing in silent-film theaters. In July 1928 he joined Walter Page's Blue Devils which, in addition to Page (double bass), featured the singer Jimmy

Count Basie

Rushing; both later figured prominently in Basie's own band. Basie left the Blue Devils early in 1929 to play with two lesser-known bands in the area; later that year he joined Bennie Moten's Kansas City Orchestra, as did the other key members of the Blue Devils shortly after. When Moten died suddenly in 1935 the band continued under Buster Moten, but Basie left soon thereafter. The same year, with Buster Smith and several other former members of the Moten orchestra, Basie organized a new, smaller group of nine instruments which included Jo Jones (drums) and later Lester Young (tenor saxophone); as the Barons of Rhythm it began a long engagement at the Reno Club in Kansas City. The group's radio broadcasts led in 1936 to contracts with a national booking agency and the Decca Record Company; it expanded and within a year the Count Basie Orchestra, as it had become known, was one of the leading big bands of the swing era. By the end of the 1930s the band had acquired international fame with such pieces as *One O'Clock Jump* (1937), *Jumpin' at the Woodside* (1938) and *Taxi War Dance* (1939), but gradual recourse to written arrangements began to lead it towards stylization and conformity, and to subdue its personality to the personalities of its arrangers. Except for the years 1950–51, when financial considerations forced him to use a six- to nine-instrument combo, Basie continued to direct a big band throughout the next four decades with considerable popular and artistic success, though it never matched the excellence or importance of its early years. In 1954 the band made the first of its many European tours, and in later years it won numerous awards and led popularity polls both in the USA and abroad.

2. Ensemble style. Like all bands in the Kansas City tradition, the Count Basie Orchestra was organized about its rhythm section, which supported the interplay of brass and reeds and served as a backdrop for the unfolding of solos. Using an elliptical style of melodic leads and cues, Basie was able to control his band firmly from the keyboard while blending perfectly with his rhythm section. This celebrated group, consisting of Basie (piano), Page (bass), Jones (drums), and, from 1937, Freddie Green (rhythm guitar), altered the ideal of jazz accompaniment, making it more supple and responsive to the wind instruments and helping to establish "four-beat" jazz (with four almost identically stressed beats to a bar) as the norm for jazz performance. Of particularly far-reaching significance was Jones's technique of placing the constant pulse in the hi-hat cymbal instead of the bass drum, thereby immeasurably lightening the timbre of jazz drumming. Another important factor was the accuracy and solidity of Page's "walking" bass technique, which obviated the need for left-hand patterns in the piano and imparted a buoyant swing to the ensemble. To attain its unique timbre and swing, Basie's rhythm section practiced for hours independently of the rest of the band. It was supreme in its day, and its innovations served as models for the even more spare and flexible rhythm sections of the bop school.

During the band's heyday in the late 1930s Basie preferred light, readily expandable arrangements particularly noted for the use of riffs, a legacy of the Moten band and of Southwest ensemble jazz generally. Ex.1 shows a typical Basie riff pattern (another can be found in Riff, ex. 1), which might easily have been developed in rehearsal and played by rote as a "head" (rather than notated) arrangement. This sort of ensemble accompaniment, which contrasts with the more elaborate group writing of Ellington, Don Redman, and Sy Oliver, gave full freedom to Basie's outstanding soloists. These included Harry Edison and Buck

Ex.1 Riff from *Shout and Feel it* (air-shot recording, 1937), transcr. J. B. Robinson

Clayton (trumpets), Dicky Wells and Benny Morton (trombones), Helen Humes and Jimmy Rushing (singers), and two excellent tenor saxophonists, Herschel Evans and Lester Young, whose widely differing styles and artistic personalities gave added breadth and tension to the group's performances. All of these soloists are prominently featured on the band's Decca and Vocalion recordings between 1937 and 1941, which represent some of the finest recorded jazz of the period (Evans, who died in 1939, plays only on the Decca sides). Basie also issued small-group recordings with his band's rhythm section and soloists (notably Young), which are masterpieces of their kind.

In his bands of the 1950s and 1960s Basie retained his swing-style rhythm section but chose soloists with more modern leanings, particularly Thad Jones (cornet, trumpet, flugelhorn), Eddie "Lockjaw" Davis and Frank Foster (tenor saxophones), Marshall Royal (alto saxophone and section leader), and Frank Wess (flute). Though the band's sound tended to change with its current arrangers (most notably Neal Hefti, Benny Carter, Quincy Jones, and Thad Jones), it was unequaled for its relaxed precision and control of dynamics. Basie's later bands, though musically less satisfying, never lost their large popular following. In the end, the Count Basie Orchestra proved the most long-lived and durable in jazz.

3. Solo style. Basie's eminence as a bandleader tended to overshadow his considerable achievements as a jazz pianist. Early recordings with Moten such as the introduction to *Moten Swing* (1932) reveal his mastery of the ragtime and stride idioms. By the mid-1930s, however, Basie had adopted a highly personal, laconic, blues-oriented style, compounded of short melodic phrases, often nothing more than jazz clichés, expertly placed and accented with wit and ingenuity. These seemingly fragmentary and disjoint solos, of which ex.2 is typical, were nevertheless capable

Ex.2 Solo from *One O'Clock Jump* (air-shot recording, 1937), transcr. J. B. Robinson

of generating great forward momentum and cumulative energy, and of leading in the next soloist, a gift for which Basie was justly famed. Though sometimes wrongly attributed to laziness,

Basie's "minimal" style, with its avoidance of the ornate mannerisms to which other pianists of the time were prone, was in fact deliberately abstracted from the more elaborate jazz piano styles of his day to meet the demands of large-ensemble improvisation. It was of seminal importance to John Lewis and the cool pianists of the West Coast school in the early 1950s. Jazz pianists as diverse as Oscar Peterson and Mary Lou Williams have freely acknowledged their debt to Basie.

See also JAZZ, §IV, 3.

RECORDINGS
(selective list)

SWING PERIOD
(big band; recorded for Decca unless otherwise stated)

Swinging at the Daisy Chain (1937, 1121); One O'Clock Jump (1937, 1363); Good Morning Blues (1937, 1446); Sent for you yesterday and here you come today (1938, 1880); Every Tub (1938, 1728); Doggin' Around (1938, 1965); Jumpin' at the Woodside (1938, 2212); Shorty George (1938, 2325); Jive at Five (1939, 2922); Oh! Lady be Good (1939, 2631); Rock-a-bye Basie (1939, Voc. 4747)

Taxi War Dance (1939, Voc. 4748); Miss Thing, pts i-ii (1939, Voc. 4860); Clap Hands, here Comes Charlie (1939, Voc. 5085); Ham 'n' Eggs (1939, Col. 35357); Tickle-Toe (1940, Col. 35521); Gone with "What" Wind (1940, OK 5629); The World is Mad, pts i-ii (1940, OK 5816); Stampede in G Minor (1940, OK 5987); Diggin' for Dex (1941, OK 6365); The King/Blue Skies (1945, Col. 37070)

(small group)

Shoe Shine Boy (1936, Voc. 3441); Oh! Lady Be Good (1936, Voc. 3459); Oh! Red/Fare thee, Honey, Fare thee Well (1939, Decca 2780); Dickie's Dream/Lester Leaps in (1939, Vic. 5118)

LATER BANDS

The Count (1947–9, Camden 395); *Dance Session* (1953, Clef 626); *Sixteen Men Swinging* (1953–4, Verve 22517); *Count Basie Swings and Joe Williams Sings* (1955, Clef 678); *Basie Plays Hefti* (1958, Roul. 52011); *Chairman of the Board* (1959, Roul. 52032); *The Count Basie Story* (1960, Roul. RB1); *The Legend* (1961, Roul. 52086); *Basie at Birdland* (1961, Roul. 52065); *L'il Ol' Groovemaker* (1963, Verve 68549); *Basie Jam* (1973, Pablo 2310718); *On the Road* (1979, Pablo 2312112)

BIBLIOGRAPHY

SouthernB

W. Basie: *Blues by Basie* (New York, 1943)

B. Harding, ed.: *Count Basie's Boogie Woogie Styles* (New York, 1944)

J. Hammond: "Count Basie Marks 20th Anniversary," *Down Beat*, xxii/22 (1955), 11; repr. in *Eddie Condon's Treasury of Jazz*, ed. E. Condon and R. Gehman (New York, 1956/*R*1975), 250ff

N. Shapiro and N. Hentoff, eds.: *Hear me Talkin' to ya* (New York, 1955), 257ff

R. Horricks: *Count Basie and his Orchestra: its Music and Musicians* (London, 1957)

N. Shapiro: "William 'Count' Basie," *The Jazz Makers*, ed. N. Shapiro and N. Hentoff (New York, 1957/*R*1975), 232

E. Towler: "Vintage Basie," *Jazz Monthly*, iii/6 (1957), 2

A. Hodeir: "Du côté de chez Basie," *Jazz Review*, i/2 (1958), 6

B. Schiozzi: *Count Basie* (Milan, 1961)

A. Hodeir: *Toward Jazz* (New York, 1962), 97ff

J. Burns: "Lesser Known Bands of the '40s: Count Basie," *Jazz Monthly*, no.171 (1969), 8

J. G. Jepsen, B. Scherman, and C. Hallstrom: *A Discography of Count Basie* (Copenhagen, n.d. [*c*1969])

M. Williams: *The Jazz Tradition* (New York, 1970), 107ff

R. Russell: *Jazz Style in Kansas City and the Southwest* (Berkeley, CA, 1971, 2/1973)

A. McCarthy: *Big Band Jazz* (London, 1974), 47ff

J. Aikin: "Count Basie," *Contemporary Keyboard*, iii/7 (1977), 10

Jazz magazine, no. 251 (1977) [Basie issue; see esp. A. Brunet: "Vers un classicisme: sur quelques arrangements exemplaires," pp. 22ff]

L. Feather: "Count Basie," *Contemporary Keyboard*, iv/3 (1978), 55

S. Dance: *The World of Count Basie* (New York, 1980)

J. S. Wilson: Obituary, *New York Times* (27 April 1984)

J. BRADFORD ROBINSON

Basquin, Peter (John) (*b* New York, 19 June 1943). Pianist. He studied at Carleton College (Minnesota) under William Nelson (BA 1963), and at the Manhattan School under Dora Zaslavsky (MM 1967). In 1971 he won second prize (the highest awarded) in the Montreal International Music Competition and on 8 March made his concert début at Alice Tully Hall, New York. Since then he has been soloist with the Boston SO, the Minnesota Orchestra, and the Montreal SO. An accomplished chamber musician, he was a founder-member of the American Chamber Trio in 1972 and began an association with the Aeolian Chamber Players in 1981. He is known particularly for his performances of neglected 19th-century works (he has played a number of programs of such pieces at the Newport Music Festival) and of the music of contemporary American composers; his recordings include sonatas by Karel Husa and Marga Richter, and chamber works by Roy Harris and David Diamond. Basquin began teaching at Hunter College, CUNY, in 1970 and became an associate professor there in 1977. He is a co-author, with Gerald Pincess, Marlies Danziger, and Wayne Dynes, of *Explorations in the Arts* (1984).

KAREN MONSON

Bassett, Leslie (Raymond) (*b* Hanford, CA, 22 Jan 1923). Composer and teacher. He studied at the University of Michigan with Finney, by whose teaching he was particularly influenced, and he also had lessons with Boulanger (1950–51), Gerhard (1960), and Davidovsky (electronic music, 1964). In 1952 he joined the faculty of the University of Michigan, becoming head of the composition department in 1970 and Albert A. Stanley Professor in 1977; he was also a founder-member of the university's electronic studio, and he directs the Contemporary Directions Performance Project. Among the awards he has received are the Rome Prize (which took him to the American Academy in Rome, 1961–3), a Pulitzer Prize (1966 for the Variations for orchestra), Guggenheim Fellowships (1973–4, 1980–81), and a Naumburg Foundation recording award for the Sextet for piano and strings (1974); his *Echoes from an Invisible World* was commissioned by the Philadelphia Orchestra for the Bicentennial. In 1976 he was elected a member of the Institute of the American Academy and Institute of Arts and Letters. Bassett's music is carefully structured, its formal processes clear; conventional pitch materials are frequently deployed in an original manner. Even his writing for voices is instrumental in character, a quality he uses to advantage in the choral works, where voices and instruments are cohesively combined. A strong religious feeling is evident in the serious and often serene tone of his work.

WORKS

ORCHESTRAL

5 Movts, 1961; Variations, 1963; Designs, Images and Textures, band, 1964; Colloquy, 1969; Forces, vn, vc, pf, orch, 1972; Echoes from an Invisible World, 1975; Conc., 2 pf, orch, 1976; Sounds, Shapes and Symbols, band, 1977; Conc. grosso, brass qnt, wind, perc, 1982; Conc. lyrico, trbn, orch, 1983; Colors and Contours, band, 1984

CHAMBER

Trbn Qt, 1949; Hn Sonata, 1952; Brass Trio, 1953; Trio, va, cl, pf, 1953; Qnt, str qt, db, 1954; Trbn Sonata, 1954; Cl Duets, 1955; Va Sonata, 1956; 5 Pieces, str qt, 1957; Suite, trbn, 1957; Ww Qnt, 1958; Vn Sonata, 1959; Vc Duets, 1959; Pf Qnt, 1962; Str Qt no. 3, 1962; Music for Vc and Pf, 1966; Nonet, wind qnt, tpt, trbn, tuba, pf, 1967; Music for Sax and Pf, 1968; Sextet, pf, va, str qt, 1971

Sounds Remembered, vn, pf, 1972; Music for 4 Hns, 1974; 12 Duos, 2/4 trbn, 1974; Wind Music, fl, cl, ob, a sax, hn, bn, 1975; Soliloquies, cl, 1976; Str Qt no. 4, 1978; Sextet, fl, a fl, cl, b cl, vc, db, 1979; Temperaments, 5 gui, 1979–83; A Masque of Bells, carillon, 1980; Trio, vn, cl, pf, 1980; Conc. da camera, fl, cl, tpt, vn, vc, pf, perc, 1981

CHORAL

The Lamb (Blake), SATB, pf, 1952; Out of the Depths, SATB, org, 1957; For City, Nation, World, cantata, T, SATB, children's chorus ad lib, congregation, 4 trbn, org, 1959; Moonrise (Lawrence), SSA, 9 insts, 1960; Remembrance (Rupert), SATB, org, 1960; Eclogue, Encomium and Evocation, SSA, 4 insts, 1962; Follow now that Bright Star (carol), SATB, 1962; Prayers for Divine Service (Lat.), TTBB, org, 1965; Hear my Prayer, O Lord (Ps. lxiv), SA, org, 1965; Notes in the Silence (Hammarskjöld), SATB, pf, 1966

Collect, SATB, tape, 1969; Moon Canticle, amp nar, SATB, vc, 1969; Celebration: in Praise of Earth, amp nar, SATB, orch, 1970; Of Wind and Earth (Shelley, Bryant, St. Francis), SATB, pf, 1973; A Ring of Emeralds (Irish poets), SATB, pf, 1979; Sing to the Lord (Ps. xcv), SATB, org, 1981; Lord, who hast formed me (G. Herbert), SATB, org, 1981

OTHER WORKS

Kbd: 6 Pf Pieces, 1951; Toccata, org, 1955; Voluntaries, org, 1958; Mobile, pf, 1961; 4 Statements, org, 1964; Elaborations, pf, 1966; Liturgies, org, 1980

Solo vocal: 4 Songs (Blake, Herbert, E. A. Robinson), 1953; Easter Triptych (Bible), T, 15 brass, 5 perc, 1958; To Music (Jonson, Herrick, Billings), 3 songs, 1962; The Jade Garden (oriental), 1973; Time and Beyond (Emerson, Tagore, Van Doren), B, cl, vc, pf, 1973; Love Songs (Gk. anon., Landor, Brodstreet, Emerson, Harrington), 1975

Elec: 3 Studies in Elec Sound, 1965; Triform, 1966

*c*20 works now withdrawn, incl. 2 syms., 1949, 1956, 2 str qts, 1949, 1951

Principal publishers: ACA, King, Merion, Peters

BIBLIOGRAPHY

EwenD

A. Brown: "Leslie Bassett," *Asterisk*, ii/2 (1976), 8 [incl. list of works]

EDITH BORROFF

Bass viol. Bowed string instrument. Although in modern usage the term refers to a six- or seven-string instrument of the viol family often called viola da gamba, in the 18th and 19th centuries in the USA and occasionally in Britain "bass viol" meant a four-string instrument tuned in 5ths like a cello. It was probably a shortened version of the term "bass violin." Such instruments were of two kinds: the first like a cello except for certain local constructional details, the second of larger body size but with the same string length and fingerboard as a cello, with a short neck (accommodating playing only up to the second position without recourse to thumb positions). Instruments of both kinds were occasionally made with five strings, but no contemporary instruction book refers to the practice or indicates the tuning. The large-sized instruments are called "church basses." Certain archaisms in construction reflect earlier European building techniques, the commonest being an f-hole in which small connecting bridges of wood are left at the turns, a groove or channel routed in the wood of the back and belly into which the ribs were fitted and glued, and the use of a footlike extension of the neckblock (almost always integral with the neck itself) projecting into the body and fixed to the wood of the back by a butted glue joint and a screw. A peculiarly American feature is the use of plank-sawn wood in the belly and back, giving the instruments a curious florid appearance; but the best makers used quarter-sawn wood according to traditional European practice.

From the late 18th century up to the mid-19th there was an active American industry in the manufacture of these instruments, probably created partly by the demand for bass instruments to accompany the church choirs which had been relieved of their Puritan obligation to perform unaccompanied. By the 1830s there were makers specializing in the production of bass viols; over 35 are known to have been working in New England in this period. The earliest known maker was Crehore of Boston, who is reported to have made his first bass for a local music master in 1785; he made basses of both sizes. The most prominent and prolific was ABRAHAM PRESCOTT, who made his first instrument in 1809. The popularity of the instrument declined around the time of the Civil War, partly because the pipe or reed organ had superseded it in church music.

FREDERICK R. SELCH

Batson, Flora (*b* Washington, DC, 16 April 1864; *d* Philadelphia, PA, 1 Dec 1906). Soprano. She grew up in Providence, singing in public there and in Boston while still quite young. She first appeared in New York (at Steinway Hall) and Philadelphia in 1885, at which time she became a member of James Bergen's Star Concert Company, replacing Nellie Brown. She married Bergen in 1887. During the years 1887–96 she toured internationally, singing before Pope Leo XIII and the royal families of Hawaii and England, and in New Zealand and Africa; her later tours with the bass Gerard Millar included a visit to Australia in 1899. She also sang in opera excerpts with the South Before the War Company, as well as at Boston's Music Hall. Her repertory was much like that of other traveling singers of her time, and included both ballads and arias, mostly from operas by Bellini, Donizetti, and Rossini.

BIBLIOGRAPHY

SouthernB

M. C. Hare: *Negro Musicians and their Music* (Washington, DC, 1936/*R*1974), 219

DOMINIQUE-RENÉ DE LERMA

Battle, Kathleen (*b* Portsmouth, OH, 13 Aug 1948). Soprano. After studying singing with Franklin Bens at the Cincinnati College-Conservatory (BM 1970, MM 1971), she came to the attention of Thomas Schippers, then the music director of the Cincinnati SO, who arranged for her formal début at Spoleto in Brahms's *German Requiem* under his direction (1972). At about the same time, she was engaged by James Levine for both the Ravinia Festival and the Metropolitan Opera, where she has become one of the most successful of the younger artists. At the Metropolitan she has appeared in such roles as Mozart's Blonde, Despina, and Pamina, Rosina, Strauss's Zdenka and Sophie, and Oscar (*Un ballo in maschera*). She has sung with the major American and European orchestras, with the principal American opera companies, and at the Salzburg Festival; she is also an engaging recitalist. Battle is gifted with a high, sweet soprano of considerable intrinsic charm, which she governs with technical finesse; she also has an exceptionally attractive and vivacious stage presence, and her work is invariably skillful and stylish, if not always highly individual.

BIBLIOGRAPHY

"Battle, Kathleen," *CBY 1984*

RICHARD DYER

Battle Hymn of the Republic. Title of a poem written to the melody "Glory hallelujah" during the Civil War, and by extension the title of the resulting national song; *see* PATRIOTIC MUSIC, §1, and BOSTON (i), fig.6.

Battle music. Program music depicting battles. The genre goes back at least to the Renaissance. By the 18th and 19th centuries battle pieces usually displayed the same general form. An introduction depicting a peaceful scene is followed by trumpet signals and the call to arms. The composer's imagination is shown in the battle section, and a third section suggests the cries of the wounded or lamentation for the slain, represented by a slow tempo and chromaticism. Shouts of victory or trumpet fanfares introduce the final section, which then depicts a celebration, usually with a fast dance or a march. American battle music was modeled on European works, in particular František Kočžwara's *The Battle of Prague* (*c*1788), which was published in the USA from *c*1793 through the 19th century. It was followed by editions of at least 15 European battle pieces, mainly for piano but sometimes arranged for other instruments, before 1825. They are characterized by special keyboard and compositional techniques: extended tremolos, persistent diminished 7th chords, expansive scales and arpeggios, and unusual harmonic progressions and modulations. A special feature, to imitate cannon shots or gunfire, was a cluster of keys in the bass, played by one or both hands and designated by a special sign such as ⊗ (used by Bernard Viguerie) or a fermata (used by Heinrich Simrock). A work by an otherwise unknown composer, Ogilvy, from Tannadice, Scotland, was second in popularity only to Kočžwara's; Ogilvy's *The Battle of Waterloo* (1818), which ends with a triumphal chorus instead of the usual dance or march, was published in the USA throughout the century, usually under the name of the original arranger for piano, "G. Anderson." Most of the other European battle pieces published in the USA use national songs such as *God Save the King*, *La marseillaise*, Haydn's *Kaiserhymne*, and *Yankee Doodle*. Nearly all printed editions include program captions and some have illustrated covers; two works by Peter Weldon, *The Battle of Baylen* (1809) and *The Siege of Gerona* (1810–12), have particularly elaborate engravings depicting the battle and the leaders.

The first American battle piece seems to have been James Hewitt's *Overture in Nine Movements Expressive of a Battle*, performed in 1792 but no longer extant. The early examples display the same characteristics as the European type, and some are nationalistic not only in their melodies. Hewitt's *The Battle of Trenton* (1797), Benjamin Carr's *The Siege of Tripoli* (1804), and Francesco Masi's *The Battles of Lake Champlain and Plattsburg* (1815; see illustration) feature the fife and drum. Masi's also represents the American army in the right hand with sixteenth-notes, and the slower British in the left with eighth- and quarter-notes. Peter Ricksecker's *The Battle of New Orleans* (1816) uses Viguerie's symbol for bass clusters and (uniquely for such pieces on either side of the Atlantic) modulates through a complete circle of 5ths to all 12 keys. Percussion stops were available on some pianos, and Denis-Germain Etienne specified two of them in his *Battle of New Orleans* (1816). A descriptive work related to the battle piece is Hewitt's *The Fourth of July* (1801), which describes the marching, riding, shouting, and gunfire associated with the American holiday.

The most prolific 19th-century composer of battle pieces in the USA was Charles Grobe, who from the late 1840s on wrote no fewer than 12 "descriptive fantasies," as well as other pieces, on battles of the Mexican and Civil wars. *The Battle of Manassas* (about the Battle of Bull Run in Virginia; ed. Hinson, 1975) by Thomas Bethune was played many times by the composer and became a best-selling publication. The pianist is to imitate a train by saying "chu-chu" and whistling; otherwise the piece consists mainly of relevant popular tunes and marches, though it also, inexplicably, includes *La marseillaise*.

Gottschalk's *Bataille, étude de concert* op.63 (?1867–8) has some of the martial rhythms and certainly the virtuosity of a battle piece, but without programmatic captions. Related to it are the

Title page of Francesco Masi's sonata "The Battles of Lake Champlain and Plattsburg" (1815)

Chant du soldat op.23 (?1855) and the *Chant de guerre* op.78 (1857–9), again for solo piano. Gottschalk also wrote *El sitio de Zaragoza* for ten pianos, performed in Madrid on 13 June 1852, but this is not extant in the original version. The practice of including national tunes, however, is represented in his *Union, paraphrase de concert* op.48 (1852–62).

Other 19th-century American composers of battle pieces include Francis Buck, William Stirby, Theodore Moelling, Joseph Turner, and James C. Beckel. Among 20th-century examples of the tradition are the battle pieces of E. T. Paull, published between 1905 and 1922 with elaborate lithographed covers in five colors. Charles Ives commemorated another type of battle in his *Yale–Princeton Football Game* (?1898).

BIBLIOGRAPHY

J. E. Henning: *Battle Pieces for the Pianoforte Composed and Published in the United States between 1795 and 1820* (diss., Boston U., 1968)

M. Hinson, ed.: *Piano Music in Nineteenth Century America* (Chapel Hill, 1975)

J. BUNKER CLARK

Bauer, Harold (*b* London, England, 28 April 1873; *d* Miami, FL, 12 March 1951). Pianist. He made his first public appearance at the age of nine as a violinist and it was not until 1892 that, partly on the advice of Paderewski with whom he had worked informally, he decided to pursue his career as a pianist. The next year he played in Paris and then toured Russia. Subsequently he appeared with great success throughout Europe and established a position not only as a fine soloist but as a chamber musician of the first rank. He frequently played in trios with Thibaud and Casals. Bauer first appeared in the USA as a soloist with the Boston SO in 1900, and about the time of World War I, having made seven tours to more than 60 American cities, he immigrated and began to exert an important influence on musical life. He founded the Beethoven Association of New York (1918–41), a leading chamber music society to which artists gave their services, and he constantly pursued a purely artistic ideal and showed himself ready to subordinate personal prestige to higher ends. He was especially associated with the music of Brahms, Schumann, and Franck but his repertory also included the works of most other major composers including some, such as Debussy and Ravel, who were his contemporaries. He wrote *Harold Bauer, his Book* (1948). Many of his papers are at the Library of Congress.

BIBLIOGRAPHY

H. C. Schonberg: *The Great Pianists* (New York, 1963), 377

R. R. Gerig: *Famous Pianists and their Technique* (Washington and New York, 1974), 367

H. C. COLLES/RONALD KINLOCH ANDERSON/R

Bauer, Marion (Eugenie) (*b* Walla Walla, WA, 15 Aug 1887; *d* South Hadley, MA, 9 Aug 1955). Composer, teacher, and writer on music. She studied in Portland, Oregon, and in Paris and Berlin, her teachers including Boulanger, Huss, Campbell-Tipton, and Rothwell, and John Paul Ertel, André Gédalge, and Raoul Pugno. From 1926 to 1951 she taught at New York University, where she was made associate professor in 1930; she was on the faculty of the Juilliard School from 1940 to 1944. She also taught at other institutions, and from 1928 she lectured almost annually at Chautauqua. An enthusiastic supporter of American music, she was a co-founder of the American Music Guild (1921) and a board member of the League of Composers. She contributed numerous articles to music journals and was New York editor of the *Musical Leader*. Her music remained basically impressionist, showing clarity of texture and a strong sense of form.

WORKS

Orch: Indian Pipes, 1927, orchd M. Bernstein, arr. pf, 1928; Lament on African Themes, chamber orch, 1928; Sym. Suite, str, op.34, 1940; Pf Conc. "American Youth," op.36, 1943; Sym., 1947–50

Vocal: Orientale, S, orch, 1914, orchd 1934; 4 Poems (J. G. Fletcher), 1v, pf, op.16, 1916; 3 Noëls, female vv, 1929; Ragpicker's Love, song cycle, 1v, str qt, 1935; 4 Songs, S, str qt, 1936; A garden is a lovesome thing, chorus, pf, op.28, 1938; The Thinker, chorus, op.35, 1938; China (B. Todrin), chorus, orch, op.38, 1944; At the New Year (K. Patchen), chorus, op.42, 1949; Death spreads his gentle wings (E. P. Crain), chorus, 1949; A foreigner comes to earth on Boston Common (H. Gregory), chorus, 1951; other songs and choruses

Chamber: Allegro giocoso, 11 insts, 1920; Vn Sonata no. 1, op. 14, 1922; Fantasia quasi una sonata, vn, pf, op.18, 1928; Str Qt, 1928; Suite (Duo), ob, cl, 1932; Sonata, va/cl, pf, op.22, 1935; 5 Greek Lyrics, fl, 1938; Concertino, ob, cl, str qt, op.32b, 1939–43; Sonatina, ob, pf, op.32a, 1940; 2 trio sonatas, fl, pf, vc, no. 1, op.40, 1944, no.2, 1951; 5 Pieces, str qt, 1946–9; Aquarelle, ww ens/chamber orch, 1948; Patterns, ww ens, 1948; Prelude and Fugue, fl, str, 1948

Pf: In the Country, suite, 1913; Up the Ocklawaha, 1913, arr. vn, pf, arr. orch; From the New Hampshire Woods, 1921; Sun Splendor, 1926, arr. 2 pf, arr. orch; 4 Pf Pieces, 1930; Dance Sonata, 1932; Two Aquarelles, 1945

Other works: Prometheus Bound (incidental music, Aeschylus), 2 fl, 2 pf, 1930; Pan and Syrinx (choreographic sketch for film), chamber ens, 1937; 3 Moods for Dance, 1950; Meditation and Toccata, org, 1951

Principal publisher: G. Schirmer

WRITINGS

with E. Peyser: *How Music Grew: from Prehistoric Times to the Present Day* (New York, 1925, rev. 2/1939)

——: *Music through the Ages: a Narrative for Student and Layman* (New York, 1932, rev. 2/1946, rev. and enlarged 3/1967 by E. Rogers as *Music through the Ages: an Introduction to Music History*)

Twentieth Century Music (New York, 1933/*R*1978, rev. 2/1947)

Musical Questions and Quizzes: a Digest of Information about Music (New York, 1941)

with E. Peyser: *How Opera Grew: from Ancient Greece to the Present Day* (New York, 1956)

BIBLIOGRAPHY

EwenD

C. Ammer: "Bauer, Marion Eugénie," *NAW*

BARBARA H. RENTON

Baur, Clara (*b* nr Stuttgart, Germany, 1835; *d* Cincinnati, OH, 18 Dec 1912). Music educator who founded the Cincinnati Conservatory of Music in 1867 (*see* CINCINNATI, §4).

Baxter, J(esse) R(andall, Jr.) (*b* Lebanon, AL, 8 Dec 1887; *d* Dallas, TX, 21 Jan 1960). Publisher and composer of gospel songs. He attended singing-schools in Alabama where he studied under some of the foremost gospel hymn writers, including James Rowe and Charles Gabriel. He became proficient in writing both words and music, and probably wrote more convention songs than any other gospel-music composer of his time (a compilation of his songs, *Precious Abiding Peace*, was published in 1960). He was also an outstanding singing-school teacher and conducted his own schools until 1922, when the publisher A. J. Showalter asked him to manage one of his offices, in Texarkana, Texas. In 1926 Baxter joined V. O. Stamps in the foundation of the Stamps–Baxter Music Company at Jacksonville, Texas. When the company moved to Dallas in 1929, Baxter opened a branch office in Chattanooga, Tennessee. The business was extremely successful, becoming one of the foremost publishers of gospel music in seven-shape notation. After Stamps's death in 1940, Baxter moved to Dallas and became president of the firm. In 1949 an article in *Time* likened the company to a gospel Tin Pan Alley: at that time the firm employed 50 people; its journal, *Gospel Music News*, had a circulation of 20,000.

See also GOSPEL MUSIC, §I, 2, and SHAPE-NOTE HYMNODY, §5.

BIBLIOGRAPHY

C. Baxter and V. Polk: *Biographies of Gospel Song Writers* (Dallas, 1971)

S. Beary: *The Stamps–Baxter Music and Printing Company: a Continuing Tradition, 1926–1976* (diss., Southwestern Baptist Theological Seminary, 1977)

SHIRLEY BEARY

Bayes, Nora [Goldberg, Dora] (*b* ?Milwaukee, WI, 1880; *d* Brooklyn, NY, 19 March 1928). Actress and singer. Her baptismal name is variously given as Dora, Leonora, and Eleanor. She began her career in vaudeville in Chicago in 1899 and made her Broadway début in *The Rogers Brothers in Washington* (1901). She achieved fame after she married JACK NORWORTH, with whom she appeared in Ziegfeld's *Follies of 1908*, introducing that show's most popular song, Norworth's *Shine on, harvest moon*. The two appeared together frequently in vaudeville and on Broadway, where they were billed as "Nora Bayes, Assisted and Admired by Jack Norworth." After their divorce Bayes continued to appear both in vaudeville and on Broadway in such shows as *Maid in America* (1915), *Ladies First* (1918), *Her Family Tree* (1920), *Snapshots of 1921* (1921), and *Queen o' Hearts* (1922). Among the many songs associated with her were *Take me out to the ball game*, *Over there*, and *Japanese Sandman*.

GERALD BORDMAN

Bayley, Daniel (*b* Rowley, MA, 27 June 1729; *d* Newburyport, MA, 29 Feb 1792). Tunebook compiler and publisher. He moved to Newburyport with his family as a boy, and by 1761 was proprietor of a pottery shop. He identified himself in some publications as "Chorister of St. Paul's Church, Newburyport," and though no surviving records confirm that he held that title, he did receive the church's thanks in 1775 "for his Services as Clerk for sundry years past." His son, Daniel Bayley, Jr. (1755–99), with whom he has sometimes been confused, played the organ at St. Paul's from 1776.

Bayley's publications borrow heavily from the works of others. He began his prolific career as a compiler by bringing out *A New and Complete Introduction* (Newburyport, 1764), drawn from successful works by Thomas Walter of Massachusetts and the Englishman William Tans'ur. In 1768 he issued Tans'ur's *The Royal Melody Complete* (first published in London in 1754, in Boston in 1767); he then combined it with Aaron Williams's *Universal Psalmodist* (1763) under the title *The American Harmony*, several editions of which were published between 1769 and 1774. Bayley's earlier works had been printed in Boston, but by 1769 he had acquired a press, and from that time his collections were issued from Newburyport. Publications of the early 1770s included *The Essex Harmony* (1770–72), a tune supplement for metrical psalters, *The New Universal Harmony* and *A New Royal Harmony* (1773), both devoted mostly to anthems and set-pieces, and John Stickney's *The Gentleman and Lady's Musical Companion* (1774), a large compendium printed mostly from plates engraved for *The American Harmony*. After the War of Independence, Bayley pirated the title and part of the contents of Andrew Law's successful *Select Harmony* (1779), despite Law's vigorous protests. His last tunebooks, *The Essex Harmony* (1785) and *The New Harmony of Zion* (1788), are eclectic mixtures of British and American pieces, following the model introduced by Law.

In the decade preceding the war, Bayley was by far the most active American compiler and publisher, accounting for some two-thirds of the 21 sacred music collections that survive from the years 1764–74. His tunebooks introduced to New England a large repertory of mid-century British sacred music, including several works that came to be standard favorites.

BIBLIOGRAPHY

F. J. Metcalf: *American Writers and Compilers of Sacred Music* (New York, 1925/*R*1967)

I. Lowens and A. P. Britton: "Daniel Bayley's 'The American Harmony': a Bibliographical Study," *Papers of the Bibliographical Society of America*, xlix (1955), 340

I. Lowens: *Music and Musicians in Early America* (New York, 1964), 67

R. Crawford: *Andrew Law, American Psalmodist* (Evanston, IL, 1968/*R*1981), 20

I. F. Auger: *Music in Newburyport: Daniel Bayley* (thesis, Brown U., 1970)

R. Crawford and D. W. Krummel: "Early American Music Printing," *Printing and Society in Early America*, ed. W. Joyce (Worcester, MA, 1983), 197

RICHARD CRAWFORD

Baylor University. University chartered by the Republic of Texas in 1845 and sponsored by the Texas Union Baptist Association (from 1848 the Baptist State Convention). In 1886 it merged with Waco University and moved to its present site at Waco. A college of fine arts was organized in 1919, offering courses in music and expression, but was replaced in 1921 by the school of music. By 1980 the school of music enrolled nearly 400 students and had a full-time faculty of 43 under Elwyn Wienandt as dean. It offers BM and MM degrees, with emphasis on performance, church music, music history and literature, and theory and composition, and BMEd and MMEd degrees; the BFA degree in musical theater is offered jointly with the department of fine arts. The school of music sponsors an opera workshop and opera theater, as well as a number of performing ensembles. The Crouch Music Library, containing around 23,000 volumes, is especially strong in sacred music, particularly American hymnals and psalters, and contains the Mrs. J. W. Jennings collection of medieval manuscripts (*see also* LIBRARIES AND COLLECTIONS, §3). Indigenous Western and some non-Western musical instruments are housed in the Baylor University Strecker Museum and the Baylor University Texas Collection.

GRAYDON BEEKS

Bay Psalm Book. The name by which the first American metrical psalter, *The Whole Booke of Psalmes Faithfully Translated into English Metre* (Cambridge, MA, 1640), is commonly known. *See* PSALMS, METRICAL, §§1(iv), 2 (ii); *see also* NOTATION, fig. 1, PSALMODY, §1, and PUBLISHING AND PRINTING OF MUSIC, fig. 1.

Bazelon, Irwin (Allen) (*b* Evanston, IL, 4 June 1922). Composer. After graduating from DePaul University (BA 1944, MA 1945), he studied with Milhaud at Mills College (1946–8) and then settled in New York in 1948. He has held fellowships at the MacDowell Colony (1948, 1950, 1951) and the Yaddo Festival (1969) and was composer-in-residence at the Wolf Trap Farm Park (1974); other honors include an NEA grant (1976) and several commissions. Bazelon's music is dramatic and forceful, arising from his energetic personality and from his experience of city life. To convey "the rebellious mutterings, cross-rhythms and nervous tension and energy of the city" Bazelon has created a rhythmic language remarkable for its breadth and sophistication. Exciting, unpredictable rhythmic patterns drive the music forward. Unexpected accents produce false downbeats. Sudden contrasts occur as long-breathed melodic phrases articulated by imaginative syncopations sound alone or are supported by a carefully positioned harmonic background.

Bazelon favors the sounds of brass, wind, and percussion; many of his chamber works combine brass and percussion, and his concerto *Propulsions* is an important contribution to the percussion ensemble repertory. He regards the brass quintet as the equivalent of the string quartet in the 20th century, a concept developed in his Brass Quintet, in *Cross Currents* for brass quintet and percussion, and in *De-tonations*, a concerto for brass quintet and orchestra. Works such as *Churchill Downs* show the influence of jazz rhythms.

Bazelon's memorable though often embryonically simple thematic material is given an extensive and complex treatment, with literal repetition kept to a minimum; otherwise, ideas unfold by a process of continual variation and transformation. To give structure to such continuous development, Bazelon used patterns of pitch relationships and loosely applied serial procedures in the earlier works; in the 1970s he turned instead to more aurally perceptible outlines in which a succession of textural patterns and tempo sequences shape the form. A gradual stylistic purification culminated in an unusually restrained work for chamber orchestra, *A Quiet Piece for a Violent Time* (1975); the essence of Bazelon's music is contained within the contradictions implicit in its title. Bazelon is the author of *Knowing the Score: Notes on Film Music* (1975).

WORKS

Orch: Concert Ov., 1951–2; Ov. to Shakespeare's "The Taming of the Shrew," 1959; Ballet-centauri 17, concert ballet, 1960; 7 syms., no. 1, 1962, no. 2 "Testament to a Big City," 1962, no. 3, brass, perc, pf, str sextet, 1962, no. 4, 1964–5, no. 5, 1967, no. 6, 1969, no. 7, ballet for orch, 1980; Sym.

concertante, 1963; Dramatic Movt, 1964–5; Excursion, 1965; Churchill Downs, chamber conc., brass, perc, str septet, 1970–71; A Quiet Piece for a Violent Time, chamber orch, 1975; De-tonations, conc., brass qnt, orch, 1975–6; Spirits of the Night, 1976; Junctures, S, orch, 1979; Memories of a Winter Childhood, 1981; Spires, tpt, small orch, 1981; Tides, cl, orch, 1982; Fusions, chamber orch, 1983; Pf Conc., 1983

Chamber: Suite for Young People, pf, 1950; Pf Sonatina, 1950; 5 Pieces, pf, 1950; 5 Pieces, vc, pf, 1950; Brass Qnt, 1963; Early American Suite, ww qnt, hpd, 1965; Duo, va, pf, 1963, rev. 1969–70; Phenomena, S, chamber ens, 1972; Propulsions, perc ens, 1974; Ww Qnt, 1975; Concatenations, perc qt, va, 1976; Double Crossings, tpt, perc, 1976; Sound Dreams, sextet, fl, cl, va, vc, pf, perc, 1977; Triple Play, 2 trbn, perc, 1977; Imprints, pf, 1978; 3 Men on a Dis-course, cl, vc, perc, 1979; Cross Currents, brass qnt, perc, 1980; Partnership, timp, mar, 1980; For Tuba with Str Attached, tuba, str qt, 1982; Re-percussions, 2 pf, 1982

Principal publishers: Boosey & Hawkes, Novello

BIBLIOGRAPHY

EwenD

D. H. Cox: "A World of Violent Silence: a Note on Irwin Bazelon," *MT*, cxxiii (1982), 683

DAVID HAROLD COX

Beach, Amy Marcy (Cheney) [Mrs. H. H. A. Beach] (*b* Henniker, NH, 5 Sept 1867; *d* New York, 27 Dec 1944). Composer and pianist. She was the first American woman to succeed as a composer of large-scale art music and was celebrated during her lifetime as the foremost woman composer of the USA.

1. Childhood. 2. Early professional life. 3. Years on tour. 4. Personal characteristics. 5. Works.

1. CHILDHOOD. Amy Marcy Cheney, a descendant of a distinguished New England family, was the only child of Charles Abbott Cheney, a paper manufacturer and importer, and Clara Imogene (Marcy) Cheney, a singer and pianist. Amy was a precocious child: at the age of one she could sing 40 tunes accurately and always in the same key; before the age of two she improvised alto lines against her mother's soprano melodies; at three she taught herself to read; and at four she mentally composed her first piano pieces and later played them, and could also play hymns by ear in correct four-part harmony. The Cheneys moved to Chelsea, Massachusetts, about 1871. Amy's mother agreed to teach her piano when she was six, and at seven she gave her first public recitals, playing works by Handel, Beethoven, and Chopin as well as her own pieces. In 1875 the family moved to Boston, where Amy's parents were advised by some of Boston's leading musicians that she could enter a European conservatory; but they nevertheless decided on a local private school and engaged Perabo and later Baermann as piano teachers for her. In composition, Gericke prescribed a course of independent study using the masters as models. She had one year of harmony and counterpoint with Junius W. Hill, then taught herself orchestration and fugue, translating treatises by Berlioz and François-Auguste Gevaert. Her youthful development as a pianist was monitored by a circle including Goetschius, Longfellow, Oliver Wendell Holmes, William Mason, and Henry Harris Aubrey Beach (1843–1910), a socially prominent physician who lectured on anatomy at Harvard and was a well-schooled amateur singer and pianist; she was to marry him in 1885.

2. EARLY PROFESSIONAL LIFE. At her highly successful début in Boston (24 October 1883) Amy played Chopin's Rondo in E♭ and Moscheles's G minor Concerto with an orchestra led by Adolf Neuendorff; at her début with the Boston SO (28 March 1885), the first of several appearances with that orchestra, she performed Chopin's F minor Concerto with Gericke conducting. After her marriage to Dr. Beach, and in respect of his wishes, she curtailed her performances, donating the fees to charity, and concentrated on composition.

Beach's first published work was *The Rainy Day* (1880), a setting of Longfellow's well-known poem, issued in 1883 by Oliver Ditson (it was Arthur P. Schmidt, however, who published two-thirds of her compositions, beginning in 1885). Her major works during the period 1885–1910 include the Mass in E♭ op.5; *Eilende Wolken* op.18; the Symphony op.32; and the Piano Concerto op.45 – all introduced by such ensembles as the Boston Handel and Haydn Society, the Boston SO, and the Symphony Society of New York. Among her commissioned works were the *Festival Jubilate* op.17, written for the dedication (1 May 1893) of the Women's Building of the World's Columbian Exposition, Chicago, and the *Song of Welcome* op.42, for the Trans-Mississippi Exposition, Omaha (1898); others were the *Panama Hymn* op.74, for the International Exposition, San Francisco (1915), and the Theme and Variations for Flute and String Quartet op.80, written for the San Francisco Chamber Music Society. Beach performed in annual solo recitals and introduced her works, playing with orchestral, choral, and chamber groups.

3. YEARS ON TOUR. Dr. Beach died on 28 June 1910. On 5 September 1911 Beach sailed for Europe determined to establish a reputation there as both performer and composer and to promote the sale of her own works. Beginning in the autumn of 1912 she gave recitals in a number of German cities, playing her concerto, sonata, and quintet, and accompanying her songs; several German orchestras played her symphony. The reviews were favorable: one journal stated that Beach was the leading American composer, and the critic Ferdinand Pfohl called Beach a "virtuoso pianist" who had "a musical nature tinged with genius."

At the outbreak of World War I Beach returned to the USA in triumph, with 30 concerts already scheduled in the East and Midwest, and in 1915 moved to New York. Thereafter she spent winters on tour and summers practicing and composing in Hillsboro, Vermont; in Centerville on Cape Cod, Massachusetts, where she had a cottage purchased with the proceeds of her song *Ecstasy* op.19 no.2; and, from 1921, as a fellow at the MacDowell Colony. She made several trips abroad, including one in 1929 to play a benefit concert at the American Embassy in Rome, where she also finished her String Quartet op.89. In 1942, to celebrate Beach's 75th birthday, Elena de Sayn, a violinist and critic from Washington, DC, organized two retrospective concerts of her music. Beach died of a heart ailment in 1944.

4. PERSONAL CHARACTERISTICS. Beach was a highly disciplined composer, capable of producing large-scale works in a few days. She was energetic in the promotion of her compositions, arranging for performances as soon as works were completed. Equally gifted as a pianist, she had a virtuoso technique and an extraordinary memory. She was interested in philosophy and science, and was fluent in German and French; an Episcopalian, she was deeply religious and was generous, using her status in music and in Bostonian society to further the careers of many young musicians. She served as leader of several organizations including the Music Teachers National Association and the Music Educators National Conference, and was co-founder in 1926 and the first president of the Association of American Women Composers. Her will assigned her royalties to the MacDowell Colony.

5. WORKS. Beach wrote in a late Romantic style typical of the Bostonian composers of her youth (among whom were Chadwick

1. *Opening of Beach's song "Elle et moi" (autograph MS, DLC) published as one of "Three Songs" in 1893*

2. *Amy Marcy Beach (seated) with members of the Brooklyn Chamber Music Society of New York, including (far right) Carl Tollefsen, March 1940*

and Foote); it is marked by lyricism, intensity, rich textures, chromaticism, and a restlessness stemming from frequent modulation. The Piano Quintet shows her indebtedness to Brahms, while other works, especially the piano pieces, show a French influence. Some of the later works – for example the String Quartet and *Five Improvisations* for piano – are leaner and more dissonant. Her vocal works are effective, with long soaring lines, and in her songs she uses a wide variety of piano accompaniments that are often virtuoso yet establish a mood and support the voice (as in *Elle et moi* and *Dark is the Night*). Her writing for chorus and orchestra is idiomatic, even in her earliest major work, the Mass. Beach's piano music is at times brilliant, as in the *Ballad* and *Fireflies*, and at times delicate, as in the *Valse-caprice*. A number of works incorporate Eskimo, American Indian, Scottish, and Gaelic folk elements, as well as bird songs that she collected in transcription.

Beach's songs were favorites in the repertories of such leading singers as Emma Eames and Marcella Craft, and concerts devoted entirely to her works were given, especially by women's and music clubs. Her most popular works were the three Browning songs op.44, especially *The Year's at the Spring*, and the songs *Ecstasy*, *Juni*, and *Shena Van*; the Piano Quintet; the Symphony; the Violin Sonata; *Fireflies* and the two *Hermit Thrush* pieces for piano; and, among the secular choral works, *The Chambered Nautilus*. Her sacred works, in particular *The Canticle of the Sun*, have remained in the church repertory. Although in her later years her compositions were considered old-fashioned, they have returned to the concert stage as a result of the renewed interest in Romantic music and in works by women. Many have been recorded.

WORKS

(printed works published in Boston unless otherwise stated)

fs – full score   os – organ score

ps – piano score

Sources: An extensive collection of MSS, correspondence, printed music, scrapbooks, and photographs is in *NhU*; further MSS, printed editions, and correspondence are in *DLC*; orchestral scores are in *MBCM* and *PP*; a smaller collection of printed music and MSS, including juvenilia, is in *MoKU*.

Edition: *Amy Beach: Piano Music*, Women Composers, ser. x (New York, 1982) [WC]

op.

OPERA

149 Cabildo (1, N. B. Stephens), solo vv, vn, va, vc, db, pf, 1932, *MoKU*; Athens, GA, 27 Feb 1947

ORCHESTRAL

18 Eilende Wolken, Segler die Lüfte (Schiller), A, orch, 1892, vs (1892); New York, 2 Dec 1892

22 Bal masque, New York, 12 Dec 1893 [see also KEYBOARD]

32 Symphony "Gaelic," e, 1894, fs (1897); Boston, 30 Oct 1896

45 Piano Concerto, c♯, 1899; Boston, 6 April 1900; arr. 2 pf (1900)

53 Jephthah's Daughter (Mollevaut, after Judges xi.38; It. trans. I. Martino; Eng. trans. A. M. Beach), S, orch, vs (1903)

CHAMBER

23 Romance, vn, pf (1893)

34 Violin Sonata, a, 1896 (1899/*R*1985); Boston, 14 March 1899

40/1–3 Three Compositions: La captive, Berceuse, Mazurka, vn, pf (1898); arr. vc (1903)

55 Invocation, vn, pf/org, vc obbl (1904)

67 Piano Quintet, f♯, 1907 (1909/*R*1979); Boston, 27 Feb 1908

80 Theme and Variations, fl, str qt, 1916 (New York, 1920)

– Caprice, fl, vc, pf, 1921, *MoKU*

89 String Quartet, 1 movt, 1929 [orig. op.79], *DLC*

90 Pastorale, fl, vc, pf, 1921, *MoKU*

125 Lento espressivo, vn, pf, *NhU*

150 Piano Trio, 1938 (New York, 1939)

151 Pastorale, ww qnt (New York, 1942)

KEYBOARD

(pf unless otherwise stated)

3 Cadenza to Beethoven: Pf Conc. no.3, op.37, 1st movt (1888)

4 Valse-caprice (1889), WC

6 Ballad (1894), WC

15/1–4 Four Sketches: In Autumn, Phantoms, Dreaming, Fireflies (1892), WC

22 Bal masque (1894)

25 Children's Carnival (1894)

28/1–3 Trois morceaux caractéristiques: Barcarolle, Minuet italien, Danse des fleurs (1894), WC

36/1–5 Children's Album: Minuet, Gavotte, Waltz, March, Polka (1897)

47 Summer Dreams, pf 4 hands (1901)

54/1–2 Scottish Legend, Gavotte fantastique (1903)

60 Variations on Balkan Themes, 1904 (1906), rev. 1936, arr. 2 pf (1942)

64/1–4 Eskimos: Four Characteristic Pieces: Arctic Night, The Returning Hunter, Exiles, With Dog Teams (1907), rev. (1943)

65 Suite: Les rêves de Columbine (1907)

81 Prelude and Fugue (New York, 1918), WC

83 From Blackbird Hills (1922)

87 Fantasia fugata (Philadelphia, 1923), WC

91 The Fair Hills of Eire, pf/org (1922), rev. org as Prelude on an Old Folk Tune (New York, 1943)

92/1–2 The Hermit Thrush at Eve, The Hermit Thrush at Morn (1922)

97/1–5 From Grandmother's Garden: Morning Glories, Heartsease, Mignonette, Rosemary and Rue, Honeysuckle (1922)

102/1–2 Piano Compositions: Farewell Summer, Dancing Leaves (1924)

104 Suite for Two Pianos Founded upon Old Irish Melodies (Cincinnati, 1924)

106 Old Chapel by Moonlight (Cincinnati, 1924)

107 Nocturne (Cincinnati, 1924), WC

108 A Cradle Song of the Lonely Mother (1924), WC

111 From Olden Times

114 By the Still Waters

116 Tyrolean Valse-fantaisie (1926), WC

119 From Six to Twelve (1927)

– A Bit of Cairo (Philadelphia, 1928)

128/1–3 Three Pianoforte Pieces: Scherzino, Young Birches, A Humming Bird (Philadelphia, 1932), WC

130 Out of the Depths (1932)

148 Five Improvisations (New York, 1938)

CHORAL

(sacred; 4vv, org, unless otherwise stated)

5 Mass, E♭, 4vv, orch, 1890, os (1890); Boston, 7 Feb 1892

7 O Praise the Lord, all ye Nations (Ps. cxvii) (1891)

8/1–3 Choral Responses: Nunc dimittis (Luke ii.29), With Prayer and Supplication (Philippians iv.6–7), Peace I Leave with You (John iv.27) (1891)

17 Festival Jubilate (Ps. c), D, 7vv, orch, 1891, ps (1892); Chicago, 1 May 1893

24 Bethlehem (G. C. Hugg) (1893)

27 Alleluia, Christ is Risen (after M. Weisse, C. F. Gellert, T. Scott, T. Gibbons) (1895), arr. with vn obbl (1904)

33 Teach me thy Way (Ps. lxxxvi.11–12), 1895, *MoKU*

38 Peace on Earth (E. H. Sears) (1897)

50 Help us, O God (Pss. lxxix.9, 5; xlv.6; xliv.26), 5vv (1903)

52 A Hymn of Freedom: America (S. F. Smith), 4vv, org/pf (1903); rev. with text O Lord our God Arise (1944)

63 Service in A, S, A, T, B, 4vv, org: Te Deum, Benedictus (1905); Jubilate Deo, Magnificat, Nunc dimittis (1906)

74/1–2 All Hail the Power of Jesus' Name (E. Perronet), 4vv, org/pf, A Panama Hymn (W. P. Stafford), 4vv, orch, arr. 4vv, org/pf (New York, 1915)

76 Thou Knowest, Lord (J. Borthwick), T, B, 4vv, org (New York, 1915)

78/1–4 Canticles: Bonum est, confiteri (Ps. xcii.1–4), S, 4vv, org, Deus misereatur (Ps. lxvii), Cantate Domino (Ps. xcviii), Benedic, anima mea (Ps. ciii) (New York, 1916)

84 Te Deum, f, T, 3-part male chorus, org (Philadelphia, 1922)

95 Constant Christmas (P. Brooks), S, A, 4vv, org (Philadelphia, 1922)

96 The Lord is my Shepherd (Ps. xxiii), 3-part female chorus, org (Philadelphia, 1923)

98 I will Lift up mine Eyes (Ps. cxxi), 4vv (Philadelphia, 1923)

103/1–2 Benedictus es, Domine, Benedictus (Luke i.67–81), B, 4vv, org (1924)

105 Let this Mind be in You (Philippians ii.5–11), S, B, 4vv, org (Cincinnati, 1924)

109 Lord of the Worlds Above (I. Watts), S, T, B, 4vv, org (1925)

115 Around the Manger (R. Davis), 4vv, org/pf (1925); rev. 3-part female chorus, org/pf (1925); rev. 4-part female chorus, org/pf (1929) [see also SONGS]

121 Benedicite omnia opera Domini (Daniel iii.56–8) (1928)

122 Communion Responses: Kyrie, Gloria tibi, Sursum corda, Sanctus, Agnus Dei, Gloria, S, A, T, B, 4vv, org (1928)

123 The Canticle of the Sun (St. Francis), S, Mez, T, B, 4vv, orch, os (1928)

125/2 Evening Hymn: the Shadows of the Evening Hours (A. Procter), S, A, 4vv (1936) [arr. of song]

132 Christ in the Universe (A. Meynell), A, T, 4vv, orch, os (New York, 1931)

133 Four Choral Responses (New York, 1932)

134 God is our Stronghold

139 Hearken unto Me (Isaiah li.1, 3; xliii.1–3; xl.28, 31), S, A, T, B, 4vv, orch, os (1934)

141 O Lord, God of Israel (1 Kings viii.23, 27–30, 34), S, A, B, 4vv, 1941

– Hymn: O God of Love, O King of Peace (H. W. Baker), 4vv, 1941 (New York, 1942)

146 Lord of All Being (O. W. Holmes) (New York, 1938)

147 I will Give Thanks (Ps. cxi), S, 4vv, org (1939)

– Pax nobiscum (E. Marlatt), 3-part female chorus/3-part male chorus/4vv, org (New York, 1944)

(secular)

9 The Little Brown Bee (M. Eytinge), 4-part female chorus (1891)

16 The Minstrel and the King: Rudolph von Hapsburg (Schiller), T, B, 4-part male chorus, orch, ps (1890)

26/4 Wouldn't that be Queer (E. J. Cooley), 3-part female chorus, pf (1919) [arr. of song]

30 The Rose of Avon-town (C. Mischka), F, S, A, 4-part female chorus, orch, ps (1896)

31/1–3 Three Flower Songs (M. Deland): The Clover, The Yellow Daisy, The Bluebell, 4-part female chorus, pf (1896)

37/3 Fairy Lullaby (Shakespeare), 4-part female chorus (1907) [arr. of song]

39/1–3 Three Shakespeare Choruses: Over Hill, over Dale; Come unto these Yellow Sands; Through the House Give Glimmering Light, 4-part female chorus, pf (1897)

42 Song of Welcome (H. M. Blossom), 4vv, orch, os (1898)

43/4 Far Awa' (Burns), 3-part female chorus, pf (1918) [arr. of song]

44/1–2 The Year's at the Spring (R. Browning), 4-part female chorus, pf (1909); Ah, Love, but a Day (Browning), 4-part female chorus, pf (1927) [arr. of songs]

46 Sylvania: a Wedding Cantata (F. W. Bancroft, after W. Bloem), S, S, A, T, B, 8vv, orch, ps (1901)

49 A Song of Liberty (F. L. Stanton), 4vv, orch, 1902, ps (1902), arr. 4-part male chorus, pf (1917)

51/3 Juni (E. Jensen), 4vv, pf (1931), 3-part female chorus (1931) [arr. of song]

56/4 Shena Van (W. Black), 3-part female chorus/4-part male chorus (1917) [arr. of song]

57/1–3 Only a Song (A. L. Hughes), One Summer Day (Hughes), 4-part female chorus (1904); Indian Lullaby, 4-part female chorus (n.p., 1895)

59 The Sea-fairies (Tennyson), S, A, 2-part female chorus, orch, 1904, ps (1904)

66 The Chambered Nautilus (Holmes), S, A, 4-part female chorus, orch, org ad lib, ps (1907)

75/1, 3 The Candy Lion (A. F. Brown), Dolladine (W. B. Rands), 4-part female chorus (New York, 1915)

82 Dusk in June (S. Teasdale), 4-part female chorus (New York, 1917)

86 May Eve, 4vv, pf, 1921 (New York, 1933)
94 Three School Songs, 4vv (n.p., 1933)
101 Peter Pan (J. Andrews), 3-part female chorus, pf (Philadelphia, 1923)
110 The Greenwood (W. L. Bowles), 4vv (1925)
118/1–2 The Moonboat, 4vv (New York, 1929); Who has Seen the Wind (C. G. Rossetti), 4vv (New York, 1930)
126/1–2 Sea Fever (J. Masefield), The Last Prayer, 4-part male chorus, pf (1931)
127 When the Last Sea is Sailed (Masefield), 4-part male chorus (1931)
129 Drowsy Dream Town (R. Norwood), S, 3-part female chorus, pf (1932)
140 We who Sing have Walked in Glory (A. S. Bridgman) (1934)
144 This Morning Very Early (P. L. Hills), 3-part female chorus, pf (1937)

SONGS

(1v, pf, unless otherwise stated)

1/1–4 Four Songs: With Violets (K. Vannah) (1885), Die vier Brüder (Schiller) (1887), Jeune fille et jeune fleur (Chateaubriand) (1887), Ariette (Shelley) (1886)
2/1–3 Three Songs: Twilight (A. M. Beach) (1887), When far from Her (H. H. A. Beach) (1889), Empress of Night (H. H. A. Beach) (1891)
10/1–3 Songs of the Sea: A Canadian Boat Song (T. Moore), S, B, pf, The Night Sea (H. P. Spofford), 2 S, pf, Sea Song (W. E. Channing), 2 S, pf (1890)
11/1–3 Three Songs (W. E. Henley): Dark is the Night (1890), The Western Wind, (1889), The Blackbird (1889)
12/1–3 Three Songs (R. Burns): Wilt thou be my Dearie?, Ye Banks and Braes o' Bonnie Doon, My Luve is Like a Red, Red Rose (1887)
13 Hymn of Trust (O. W. Holmes) (1891), rev. with vn obbl (1901)
14/1–4 Four Songs: The Summer Wind (W. Learned), Le secret (J. de Resseguier), Sweetheart, Sigh no More (T. B. Aldrich), The Thrush (E. R. Sill), 1890 (1891); nos.2–3 rev. (1901)
19/1–3 Three Songs: For me the Jasmine Buds Unfold (F. E. Coates), Ecstasy (A. M. Beach), 1v, pf, vn obbl, Golden Gates (1893)
20 Across the World: Villanelle (E. M. Thomas) (1894)
21/1–3 Three Songs: Chanson d'amour (V. Hugo), Extase (Hugo), Elle et moi (F. Bovet) (1893)
26/1–4 Four Songs: My Star (C. Fabbri), Just for This (Fabbri), Spring (Fabbri), Wouldn't that be Queer (E. J. Cooley) (1894); no.4 arr. chorus
29/1–4 Four Songs: Within thy Heart (A. M. Beach), The Wandering Knight (anon., Eng. trans. J. G. Lockhart), Sleep, Little Darling (Spofford), Haste, O Beloved (W. A. Sparrow), 1894 (1895)
35/1–4 Four Songs: Nachts (C. F. Scherenberg), Allein! (Heine), Nähe des Geliebten (Goethe), Forget-me-not (H. H. A. Beach), 1896 (1897)
37/1–3 Three Shakespeare Songs: O Mistress Mine, Take, O Take those Lips Away, Fairy Lullaby (1897); no.3 arr. chorus
41/1–3 Three Songs: Anita (Fabbri), Thy Beauty (Spofford), Forgotten (Fabbri) (1898)
43/1–5 Five Burns Songs: Dearie, Scottish Cradle Song, Oh were my Love yon Lilac Fair!, Far Awa', My Lassie (1899); no.3 arr. 2 S, pf (1918), no.4 arr. chorus
44/1–3 Three [R.] Browning Songs: The Year's at the Spring, Ah, Love, but a Day, I Send my Heart up to Thee (1900); no.2 arr. S, T, pf (1917), arr. with vn obbl (1920); nos.1–2 arr. chorus
48/1–4 Four Songs: Come, ah Come (H. H. A. Beach), Good Morning (A. H. Lockhart), Good Night (Lockhart), Canzonetta (A. Sylvestre) (1902)
51/1–4 Four Songs: Ich sagete nicht (E. Wissman), Wir drei (H. Eschelbach), Juni (E. Jansen), Je demande à l'oiseau (Sylvestre) (1903); no.3 arr. chorus
56/1–4 Four Songs: Autumn Song (H. H. A. Beach), Go not too Far (F. E. Coates), I Know not how to Find the Spring (Coates), Shena Van (W. Black), 1904 (1904); no.4 arr. with vn obbl (1919), arr. chorus
61 Give me not Love (Coates), S, T, pf (1905)
62 When Soul is Joined to Soul (E. B. Browning) (1905)
68 After (Coates) (1909)
69/1–2 Two Mother Songs: Baby (G. MacDonald) (Springfield, OH, 1908), Hush, Baby Dear (A. L. Hughes) (1908)
71/1–3 Three Songs: A Prelude (A. M. Beach), O Sweet Content (T. Dekker), An Old Love-story (B. L. Stathem) (1910)
72/1–2 Two Songs: Ein altes Gebet, Deine Blumen (L. Zacharias) (New York, 1914)
73/1–2 Two Songs (Zacharias): Grossmütterchen, Der Totenkranz (New York, 1914)
75/1–2 A Thanksgiving Fable, Prayer of a Tired Child (New York, 1914)
76/1–2 Two Songs: Separation (J. L. Stoddard), The Lotos Isles (Tennyson) (New York, 1914)
77/1–2 Two Songs: I (C. Fanning), Wind o' the Westland (D. Burnett) (New York, 1916)
78/1–3 Three Songs: Meadowlarks (I. Coolbrith), Night Song at Amalfi (Teasdale), In Blossom Time (Coolbrith) (New York, 1917)
– A Song for Little May (E. H. Miller), 1922, *MoKU*
– The Arrow and the Song (Longfellow), 1922, *MoKU*
– Clouds (F. D. Sherman), 1922, *MoKU*
85 In the Twilight (Longfellow) (1922)
88 Spirit Divine (A. Read), S, T, org (Philadelphia, 1922)
93 Message (Teasdale) (Philadelphia, 1922)
99/1–4 Four Songs: When Mama Sings (A. M. Beach), Little Brown-eyed Laddie (A. D. O. Greenwood), The Moonpath (K. Adams), The Artless Maid (L. Barili) (Philadelphia, 1923)
100/1–2 Two Songs: A Mirage (B. Ochsner), Stella viatoris (J. H. Nettleton), S, vn, vc, pf (1924)
112 Jesus my Saviour (A. Elliott) (Philadelphia, 1925)
113 Mine be the Lips (L. Speyer) (1921)
115 Around the Manger (Davis), 1v, pf/org (1925) [see also CHORAL]
117/1–3 Three Songs (M. Lee): The Singer, The Host, Song in the Hills (Cincinnati, 1925)
120 Rendezvous (Speyer), with vn obbl (1928)
– Mignonnette (n.p., 1929)
124 Springtime (S. M. Heywood) (New York, 1929)
125/1–2 Two Sacred Songs: Spirit of Mercy (anon.) (1930), Evening Hymn: the Shadows of the Evening Hours (A. Procter) (1934); no.2 arr. chorus
131 Dark Garden (Speyer) (1932)
135 To one I Love (1932)
136 Fire and Flame (A. A. Moody), 1932 (1933)
137 May Flowers (Moody), 1932 (1933)
142 I Sought the Lord (anon.), 1v, org (1937)
143 I shall be Brave (Adams) (1932)
145 Dreams
152 Though I Take the Wings of Morning (R. N. Spencer), 1v, org/pf (New York, 1941)
– The Heart that Melts, *MoKU*
– The Icicle Lesson, *MoKU*
– If Women will not be Inclined, *MoKU*
– Time has Wings and Swiftly Flies, *MoKU*
– Whither (W. Müller) [after Chopin: Trois nouvelles études, no.3], *MoKU*

OTHER WORKS

– Arr.: Beethoven: Pf Conc. no.1, 2nd movt, pf 4 hands, 1887
– St. John the Baptist (St. Matthew, St. Luke), lib., 1889, *MoKU*
– Arr.: Berlioz: Les Troyens, Act 1 scene iii, 1v, pf, 1896
49 Transcr. of R. Strauss: Ständchen, pf (1902)
– Arr.: On a Hill: Negro Melody (trad.), 1v, pf (1929)

JUVENILIA

Air and Variations, pf, 1877, *MoKU*; Mamma's Waltz, pf, 1877, *MoKU*; Menuetto, pf, 1877, *MoKU*; Romanza, pf, 1877, *MoKU*; Petite valse, pf, 1878, *MoKU*; The Rainy Day (Longfellow), 1v, pf, 1880 (1883), *MoKU*; Allegro appassionata, *MoKU*; Moderato, pf

4 Chorales: Come ye Faithful (J. Hupton); Come to Me (C. Elliott); O Lord, how happy should we be (J. Anstice); To Heav'n I Lift my Waiting Eyes, 4vv, 1882, *MoKU*

INDEX TO VOCAL WORKS

A Canadian Boat Song, op.10 no.1; Across the World: Villanelle, op.20; After, op.68; Ah, Love, but a Day, op.44 no.2; A Hymn of Freedom: America, op.52; Allein!, op.35 no.2; Alleluia, Christ is Risen, op.27; All Hail the Power of Jesus' Name, op.74 no.1; A Mirage, op.100 no.1; Anita, op.41 no.1; An Old Love-story, op.71 no.3; A Panama Hymn, op.74 no.2; A Prelude, op.71 no.1; Ariette, op.1 no.4; Around the Manger, op.115; The Arrow and the Song, 1922; The Artless Maid, op.99 no.4; A Song for Little May, 1922; A Song of Liberty, op.49

A Thanksgiving Fable, op.75 no.1; Autumn Song, op.56 no.1; Baby, op.69 no.1; Benedic, anima mea, op.78 no.4; Benedicite omnia opera Domini, op. 121; Benedictus, op. 103 no. 2; Benedictus es, Domine, op. 103 no. 1; Bethlehem, op. 24; The Blackbird, op. 11 no. 3; The Bluebell, op. 31 no. 3; Bonum est, confiteri, op. 78 no. 1; [3] Browning Songs, op. 44; [5] Burns Songs, op. 43; The Candy Lion, op. 75 no. 1; Cantate Domino, op. 78 no. 3; The Canticle of the Sun, op. 123; Canticles, op. 78; Canzonetta, op. 48 no. 4

The Chambered Nautilus, op. 66; Chanson d'amour, op. 21 no. 1; [4] Chorales, 1882; Choral Responses, op. 8; [4] Choral Responses, op. 133; Christ in the Universe, op. 132; Clouds, 1922; The Clover, op. 31 no. 1; Come, ah Come, op. 48 no. 1; Come to Me, 1882; Come unto these Yellow Sands, op. 39 no. 2; Come ye Faithful, 1882; Communion Responses, op. 122; Constant Christmas, op. 95; Dark Garden, op. 131; Dark is the Night, op. 11 no. 1; Dearie, op. 43 no. 1; Deine Blumen, op. 72 no. 2; Deus misereatur, op. 78 no. 2; Dolladine, op. 75 no. 3; Dreams, op. 145; Drowsy Dream Town, op. 129; Dusk in June, op. 82

Ecstasy, op. 19 no. 2; Ein altes Gebet, op. 72 no. 1; Elle et moi, op. 21 no. 3; Empress of Night, op. 2 no. 3; Evening Hymn: the Shadows of the Evening Hours, op. 125 no. 2; Extase, op. 21 no. 2; Fairy Lullaby, op. 37 no. 3; Far Awa', op. 43 no. 4; Festival jubilate, op. 17; Fire and Flame, op. 136; [3] Flower Songs, op. 31; Forget-me-not, op. 35 no. 4; Forgotten, op. 41 no. 3; For me the Jasmine Buds Unfold, op. 19 no. 1; Give me not Love, op. 61; God is our Stronghold, op. 134; Golden Gates, op. 19 no. 3; Go not too Far, op. 56 no. 2

Good Morning, op. 48 no. 2; Good Night, op. 48 no. 3; The Greenwood, op. 110; Grossmütterchen, op. 73 no. 1; Haste, O Beloved, op. 29 no. 4; Hearken unto Me, op. 139; The Heart that Melts [1941]; Help us, O God, op. 50; The Host, op. 117 no. 2; Hush, Baby Dear, op. 69 no. 2; Hymn of Trust, op. 13; I, op. 77 no. 1; Ich sagete nicht, op. 51 no. 1; The Icicle Lesson [1941]; If Women will not be Inclined [1941]; I Know not how to Find the Spring, op. 56 no. 3; In Blossom Time, op. 78 no. 3; Indian Lullaby, op. 57 no. 3; In the Twilight, op. 85

I Send my Heart up to Thee, op. 44 no. 3; I shall be Brave, op. 143; I Sought the Lord, op. 142; I will Give Thanks, op. 147; I will Lift up mine Eyes, op. 98; Je demande à l'oiseau, op. 51 no. 4; Jesus my Saviour, op. 112; Jeune fille et jeune fleur, op. 1 no. 3; Juni, op. 51 no. 3; Just for This, op. 26 no. 2; The Last Prayer, op. 126 no. 2; Let this Mind be in You, op. 105; The Little Brown Bee, op. 9; Little Brown-eyed Laddie, op. 99 no. 2; The Lord is my Shepherd, op. 96; Lord of all Being, op. 146

Lord of the Worlds Above, op. 109; The Lotos Isles, op. 76 no. 2; Mass, op. 5; May Eve, op. 86; May Flowers, op. 137; Meadowlarks, op. 78 no. 1; Message, op. 93; Mignonnette (1929); Mine be the Lips, op. 113; The Minstrel and the King, op. 16; The Moonboat, op. 118 no. 1; The Moonpath, op. 99 no. 3; [2] Mother Songs, op. 69; My Lassie, op. 43 no. 5; My Luve is Like a Red, Red Rose, op. 12 no. 3; My Star, op. 26 no. 1; Nachts, op. 35 no. 1; Nähe des Geliebten, op. 35 no. 3; The Night Sea, op. 10 no. 2; Night Song at Amalfi, op. 78 no. 2; Nunc dimittis, op. 8 no. 1

O God of Love, O King of Peace, 1941; Oh were my Love yon Lilac Fair!, op. 43 no. 3; O Lord, God of Israel, op. 141; O Lord, how happy should we be, 1882; O Lord our God Arise, op. 52; O Mistress Mine, op. 37 no. 1; On a Hill: Negro Lullaby (1929); One Summer Day, op. 57 no. 2; Only a Song, op. 57 no. 1; O Praise the Lord, all ye Nations, op. 7; O Sweet Content, op. 71 no. 2; Over Hill, over Dale, op. 39 no. 1; Pax nobiscum (1944); Peace I Leave with You, op. 8 no. 3; Peace on Earth, op. 38; Peter Pan, op. 101

Prayer of a Tired Child, op. 75 no. 2; The Rainy Day, 1880; Rendezvous, op. 120; The Rose of Avon-town, op. 30; [2] Sacred Songs, op. 125; [3] School Songs, op. 94; Scottish Cradle Song, op. 43 no. 2; The Sea-fairies, op. 59; Sea Fever, op. 126 no. 1; Sea Song, op. 10 no. 3; Le secret, op. 14 no. 2; Separation, op. 76 no. 1; Service, op. 63; [3] Shakespeare Choruses, op. 39; [3] Shakespeare Songs, op. 37; Shena Van, op. 56 no. 4; The Singer, op. 117 no. 1; Sleep, Little Darling, op. 29 no. 3

Song in the Hills, op. 117 no. 3; Song of Welcome, op. 42; Songs of the Sea, op. 10; Spirit Divine, op. 88; Spirit of Mercy, op. 125 no. 1; Spring, op. 26 no. 3; Springtime, op. 124; Stella viatoris, op. 100 no. 2; The Summer Wind, op. 14 no. 1; Sweetheart, Sigh no More, op. 14 no. 3; Sylvania: a Wedding Cantata, op. 46; Take, O Take those Lips Away, op. 37 no. 2; Teach me thy Way, op. 33; Te Deum, op. 84; This Morning Very Early, op. 144; Thou Knowest, Lord, op. 76; Though I Take the Wings of Morning, op. 152

Through the House Give Glimmering Light, op. 39 no. 3; The Thrush, op. 14 no. 4; Thy Beauty, op. 41 no. 2; Time has Wings and Swiftly Flies [1941]; To Heav'n I Lift my Waiting Eyes, 1882; To One I Love, op. 135; Der Totenkranz, op. 73 no. 2; Twilight, op. 2 no. 1; Die vier Brüder, op. 1 no. 2; The Wandering Knight, op. 29 no. 2; The Western Wind, op. 11 no. 2; We who Sing have Walked in the Glory, op. 140; When far from Her, op. 2 no. 2; When Mama Sings, op. 99 no. 1; When Soul is Joined to Soul, op. 62; When the Last Sea is Sailed, op. 127; Whither [1941]

Who has Seen the Wind, op. 118 no. 2; Wilt thou be my Dearie?, op. 12 no. 1; Wind o' the Westland, op. 77 no. 2; Within thy Heart, op. 29 no. 1; With Prayer and Supplication, op. 8 no. 2; With Violets, op. 1 no. 1; Wir drei, op. 51 no. 2; Wouldn't that be Queer, op. 26 no. 4; The Year's at the Spring, op. 44 no. 1; Ye Banks and Braes o' Bonnie Doon, op. 12 no. 2; The Yellow Daisy, op. 31 no. 2

Principal publishers: Ditson, Presser, G. Schirmer, Schmidt

BIBLIOGRAPHY

EwenD; *NAW*

L. C. Elson: *The History of American Music* (New York, 1904; enlarged 2/1915; enlarged by A. Elson, 3/1925/*R*1971), 293

P. Goetschius: *Mrs. H. H. A. Beach* (Boston, 1906) [incl. analytical sketch of Sym. op. 32 and list of works]

"Mrs. H. H. A. Beach," *Musikliterarische Blätter*, i (Vienna, 1904), 1

G. Cowen: "Mrs. H. H. A. Beach, the Celebrated Composer," *Musical Courier*, no. 60 (6 June 1910), 14

"Mrs. Beach's Compositions," *Musical Courier*, no. 70 (24 March 1915), 37

H. Brower: *Piano Mastery* (New York, 1917), 179

B. C. Tuthill: "Mrs. H. H. A. Beach," *MQ*, xxvi (1940), 297

E. L. Merrill: *Mrs. H. H. A. Beach: her Life and Music* (diss., U. of Rochester, 1963)

M. G. Eden: *Anna Hyatt Huntington, Sculptor, and Mrs. H. H. A. Beach, Composer* (diss., Syracuse U., 1977) [incl. list of works]

A. F. Block: Introduction to *Amy Beach: Quintet in F-Sharp Minor, op. 67* (Boston, 1979), v

C. Ammer: *Unsung: a History of Women in American Music* (Westport, CT, 1980)

ADRIENNE FRIED BLOCK

Beach, Frank A(mbrose) (*b* Weedsport, NY, 20 Sept 1871; *d* Emporia, KS, 21 Jan 1935). Music educator. He studied at the School of Fine Arts, Syracuse University (1890–93), and the University of Michigan (BA 1895). After studying singing at the Juliani School of Opera in Paris (from 1905), he returned to the USA, becoming chairman of the music education department at the Kansas State Normal School in Emporia in 1908 and then chairman of its music department (1913–35). Beach was a pioneer in the use of recorded listening lessons in the public schools and at Emporia in 1915 organized the first state-wide school music contests. In 1920 he developed a standardized test of musical achievement, the first of its type, and in 1929 devised the contest rating system which is still in use in American school music competitions. He continued his research on music tests and measurements from 1920 until his death. Beach was president of the Music Supervisors National Conference in 1922 and was an active participant in many other professional organizations.

BIBLIOGRAPHY

S. M. Baldwin and R. M. Baldwin, eds.: *Illustriana Kansas* (Hebron, NE, 1933), 83–4

"Frank A. Beach, Musical Contest Founder, Dies," *Topeka Daily Capitol* (22 Jan 1935)

C. E. Strouse and R. M. Taylor: *A History of the Department of Music* (Emporia, KS, 1963)

"KMEA Hall of Fame," *Kansas Music Review*, xxxvii/2 (1975), 24

M. K. Kastendieck: *Frank Ambrose Beach: his Life and Career in the Music Educators National Conference* (thesis, U. of Kansas, 1984)

GEORGE N. HELLER

Beach, John Parsons (*b* Gloversville, NY, 11 Oct 1877; *d* Pasadena, CA, 6 Nov 1953). Composer. He studied piano at the New England Conservatory, Boston. In 1900 he obtained a position as a piano teacher at the Northwestern Conservatory, Minneapolis, and from 1904 to 1910 taught first in New Orleans and afterwards in Boston. He then went to Europe, where he studied with André Gédalge (composition) and Harold Bauer (piano) in Paris, and with Malipiero in Venice. On returning to Boston he took further composition lessons with Loeffler. He finally settled in Pasadena. Beach's opera *Pippa's Holiday* (after

Browning) was staged in Paris in 1915, and a ballet, *Phantom Satyr*, was performed in Asolo, Italy, in 1925; another ballet, *Mardi Gras*, was performed in New Orleans in 1926. His orchestral works include *Asolani* (performed in Minneapolis, 1926), *New Orleans Street Cries* (Philadelphia, 1927; Stokowski conducting), and *Angelo's Letter*, for tenor and chamber orchestra (New York, 1929). Beach also composed a number of chamber works and many songs and piano pieces. His music favors the rich sonorities of late Romanticism and almost invariably has programmatic associations.

ELIZABETH A. WRIGHT

Beach Boys. Rock group. Formed in 1961 in California, the group consisted of three brothers, Brian Wilson (*b* Hawthorne, CA, 20 June 1942), singer, pianist, and bass guitarist, Dennis Wilson (*b* Hawthorne, 4 Dec 1944; *d* Marina del Rey, CA, 28 Dec 1983), singer and drummer, and Carl Wilson (*b* Hawthorne, 21 Dec 1946), singer and guitarist; their cousin Mike Love (*b* Los Angeles, CA, 15 March 1941), singer and drummer; and Alan Jardine (*b* Lima, OH, 3 Sept 1942), singer and guitarist. At various times other musicians played with the band, including Bruce Johnston (*b* Chicago, IL, 24 June 1944), Glen Campbell (*b* Delight, AK, 22 April 1936), Daryl Dragon (*b* Los Angeles, 27 Aug 1942), Blondie Chaplin, Rick Fataar, and David Marks.

The Beach Boys, early 1960s: (left to right) Alan Jardine, Dennis Wilson, Brian Wilson, Carl Wilson, and Mike Love

The Beach Boys' first hit, *Surfin'* (1961), was devoted to the West Coast sport that was to give its name to the style of pop music that the group perfected. It was followed by other songs on the same subject, which extolled the youth culture of California in Wilson's whimsical, hedonistic lyrics. The vocal sound on these early recordings recalls that of such groups as the Four Freshmen and the Everly Brothers, but the harmonies have an uneasiness that subtly suggests emotional uncertainty. *Surfer Girl*, issued in 1963, was the first album produced by Brian Wilson and it established him as the group's principal songwriter and unofficial leader; its sound, characterized by close lush harmonies and thick layers of instrumentation, is highly distinctive. The production techniques employed by Wilson for this recording remained essentially unchanged in all the Beach Boys' later work. The next few years were the group's most fertile period: they recorded a series of enormously successful songs, including *I get around* (no. 1, 1964), *Help me, Rhonda* (no. 1, 1965), and *California Girls* (no. 3, 1965). Wilson's methods were most lavishly applied on *Good Vibrations* (no. 1, 1966), at once the most baroque and the most adventurous pop song of the time; it took six months to record and used Jew's harp, harpsichord, and theremin, in addition to the usual complement of rock instruments. With its multitracked vocal sound and allusive lyrics, *Good Vibrations* well represents the mannered naivety that Wilson contrived to create in the best of the group's music. Also in 1966 the Beach Boys recorded an album, *Pet Sounds*, that was unsuccessful commercially but was notable for some innovative studio techniques; it included the haunting song *God only knows*, remarkable for an unusual instrumental interlude, and *Wouldn't it be nice*.

At this time Brian Wilson envisioned and began producing an elaborate "concept" album to be entitled *Smile*. This project, intended as an American reply to the Beatles' *Sgt. Pepper's Lonely Hearts Club Band*, was never completed, but 15 songs were written; nine of them – interesting, quirky, and somewhat overwrought – were included in later albums released by the Beach Boys. This was the last musical project produced solely by Wilson, who withdrew from performing and was increasingly less involved with the group; in later efforts other members participated in the writing and production of songs. In 1968 the band performed in Czechoslovakia; on their return they recorded the album *Sunflower* (1970), then went to Amsterdam and recorded *Holland* (1973). They continued to perform new material, but increasingly their repertory remained focused on their hits of the early to mid-1960s. In the late 1970s, when nostalgia for rock-and-roll was at its peak, their work was the subject of renewed interest, and their early recordings were often repackaged and reissued. They continued to record and perform into the 1980s.

The Beach Boys were the foremost exponents of the brand of rock-and-roll called surf music, which they brought to a high level of sophistication. They became one of the most enduring groups in American popular music; over a period of activity spanning more than 20 years, their basic style has changed little. The group's later work includes little that can be compared to the songs of the 1960s, and it sometimes slips into self-parody; a striking exception is the album *The Beach Boys Love you* (1977), a collection of alluring fripperies worked up from snatches of melody, and mostly written by Brian Wilson.

RECORDINGS

(selective list; recorded for Capitol unless otherwise stated)

Surfin' (Candix 301, 1962); *Surfin' Safari* (1808, 1962); *Surfin' U.S.A.* (1890, 1963); *Surfer Girl* (1981, 1963); *All Summer Long* (2110, 1964); Fun, fun, fun (5118, 1964); I get around/Don't worry baby (5174, 1964); California girls (5464, 1965); Help me, Rhonda (5935, 1965); *Summer Days (and Summer Nights)* (2354, 1965); Good Vibrations (5676, 1966); *Pet Sounds* (2458, 1966); *Smiley Smile* (9001, 1967); *Wild Honey* (2859, 1967); *Sunflower* (Rep. 6382, 1970); *Surf's Up* (Rep. 6453, 1971); *Holland* (Rep. 2118, 1973); *The Beach Boys Love you* (Rep. 2258, 1977); *The Beach Boys* (Caribou FZ 39946, 1985)

BIBLIOGRAPHY

D. Leaf: *The Beach Boys and the California Myth* (New York, 1978)

B. Elliott: *Surf's Up!: the Beach Boys on Record, 1961–1981* (Ann Arbor, MI, 1982)

KEN TUCKER

Bean. *See* HAWKINS, COLEMAN.

Beans, Gus. Pseudonym of HENRY FILLMORE.

Beardslee, Bethany (*b* Lansing, MI, 25 Dec 1927). Soprano. After studying at Michigan State University and the Juilliard School, she made her New York début in December 1949. At Juilliard she met Jacques-Louis Monod, whom she married, and with whom for five years she gave recitals, presenting premières of a number of American works; she became known as a specialist in 20th-century music, and in the same period gave the first American performances of works by Schoenberg, Berg, Stravinsky, and Krenek. She was remarried in 1956, to the composer Godfrey Winham. In 1962 the American Composers Alliance awarded her its Laurel Leaf "for distinguished achievement in fostering and encouraging American music." In 1964, with a Ford Foundation grant, she commissioned and performed Babbitt's *Philomel* for soprano and recorded tape. Her wide range, impressive accuracy, and silvery lyric soprano have also proved effective in medieval and Renaissance music with the now defunct New York Pro Musica (1957–60), in Bach, and in recordings of Haydn and Pergolesi. In 1972 she performed *Pierrot lunaire* (earlier recorded under Robert Craft) with Boulez and members of the Cleveland Orchestra. Her recordings of American music include works by Babbitt, Perle, Randall, and Mel Powell. In 1981 she began a partnership with Richard Goode in recitals of lieder. Although she announced her retirement from singing, in the mid-1980s she continued to perform. Beardslee taught at Westminster Choir College (from 1976) and was professor of singing at the University of Texas, Austin (1981–2); on leaving Austin she spent a year as performer-in-residence at the University of California, Davis, and in 1983 began to teach at Brooklyn College, CUNY. She was awarded an honorary doctorate at Princeton University in 1977.

MARTIN BERNHEIMER/R

Bethany Beardslee

Beatles. English pop group. The Beatles grew out of a group formed in 1955 in Liverpool, England, by John Lennon (*b* Liverpool, 9 Oct 1940; *d* New York, 8 Dec 1980), rhythm guitarist and singer, which was later joined by Paul McCartney (*b* Liverpool, 18 June 1942), bass guitarist, keyboard player, and singer, and George Harrison (*b* Liverpool, 25 Feb 1943), lead guitarist and supporting singer, with Pete Best playing drums and Stu Sutcliffe guitar. In 1962 the three principal musicians were joined by Ringo Starr (Richard Starkey; *b* Liverpool, 7 July 1940), drummer and supporting singer. All the members wrote songs, but Lennon and McCartney were the most important songwriters.

Tours throughout Great Britain, coupled with the release of the group's first fresh-sounding recordings, led to an explosion of popularity ("Beatlemania") in 1963. The Beatles came to the USA in 1964, and their appearance on "The Ed Sullivan Show" on 9 February, before 73 million viewers, established their popularity (for illustration *see* BROADCASTING, fig.2); their success was confirmed by their first North American tour in August. The Beatles' music at the time was strongly influenced by such American idioms as blues, rhythm-and-blues, and rock-and-roll, and performers such as Chuck Berry, Elvis Presley, and Bill Haley.

During the middle years of their career the Beatles toured the USA twice more: in August 1965, when they performed for an audience of 56,000 in New York's Shea Stadium, and in August 1966; the final concert of the 1966 tour, on 29 August in San Francisco, was the group's last public concert. This period also saw the Beatles adopt social, cultural, and political positions that were imitated by American youth. At the same time they pursued new musical ideas that led away from their early stage-band sound and format towards investigation of the different textures and structures available in the recording studio, richer poetic tapestries, and an eclectic musical view, extending to Indian music and the avant garde. Each new album released during these years broke new musical ground, notably *Rubber Soul* (1965), *Revolver* (1966), and *Sgt. Pepper's Lonely Hearts Club Band* (1967).

Whereas the Beatles' second period was marked by experimentation, their third was one of unmalicious parody and a return to their origins. *The Beatles* (or the "white album," 1968) includes parodies of country music, the British music-hall tradition, the Beach Boys, Karlheinz Stockhausen, sentimental ballads, blues, and, most often, themselves. *Abbey Road* (1969) was the last album they recorded, and stylistically it summarized their career. The first side contains songs by all four members, pointing up individual qualities; the second side is integrated, the parts depending for their effect on contextual relationships, and the tripartite structures suggesting organic growth, development, and conclusion.

The Beatles were the most popular performers of the 1960s, making an unprecedented series of top-selling recordings and attracting worldwide audiences. They were among the first British popular musicians for many years to achieve great success in the USA, and at each stage of their career their ideas and innovations affected the course of American popular music. In many ways – musical, social, even economic – the Beatles were arguably the most influential musicians of the era.

After the Beatles disbanded in 1970, its members fashioned important individual careers. In 1970 JOHN LENNON moved to the USA, where he became involved in radical causes and, through his wife, Yoko Ono, in experimental movements in the arts. These experiences are manifest in the music he produced in the last decade of his life. McCartney's muse has never been as hesitant or as troubled as Lennon's was, and he has continued to record and perform regularly; he has built a large following among an audience that favors soft rock music with a pop flavor. Both Harrison and Starr have lived in the USA intermittently since 1980; Starr in particular has been drawn to American music, often making use of country-music idioms and performers for his recordings.

See also POPULAR MUSIC, §IV, 2, and ROCK, §2.

BIBLIOGRAPHY

H. Davies: *The Beatles: the Authorised Biography* (London, 1968, rev. 2/1978)
J. Eisen, ed.: *The Age of Rock* (New York, 1969)
J. Wenner: *Lennon Remembers* (New York, 1971)
P. McCabe and R. Schonfeld: *Apple to the Core: the Unmaking of the Beatles* (London, 1972)
W. Mellers: *Twilight of the Gods: the Beatles in Retrospect* (London, 1973)
R. Carr and T. Tyler: *The Beatles: an Illustrated Record* (London, 1975) [complete annotated discography]
H. Castleman and W. Podrazik: *All Together Now: the First Complete Beatles Discography: 1961–1975* (New York, 1975)
——: *The Beatles Again* (Ann Arbor, MI, 1977)
N. Schaffner: *The Beatles Forever* (Harrisburg, PA, 1977)
C. Campbell and A. Murphy: *Things we Said Today: the Complete Lyrics and a Concordance to the Beatles' Songs, 1962–1970* (Ann Arbor, MI, 1980)
N. Schaffner: *The Boys from Liverpool: John, Paul, George, Ringo* (New York, 1980)
T. Schultheiss: *The Beatles: a Day in the Life; the Day-by-day Diary, 1960–1970* (Ann Arbor, MI, 1980)
G. Stokes: *The Beatles* (New York, 1980)
J. Blake: *All you Needed was Love: the Beatles after the Beatles* (New York, 1981)
P. Norman: *Shout! The Beatles in their Generation* (New York, 1981)
D. Sheff and B. Golson: *The Playboy Interviews with John Lennon & Yoko Ono: the Final Testament* (New York, 1981)
B. Woffinden: *The Beatles Apart* (New York, 1981)
G. Martin: *All you Need is Ears* (New York, 1982)
H. Castleman and W. Podrazik: *The End of the Beatles* (Ann Arbor, MI, 1983)
R. Cepican and W. Ali: *The Long and Winding Road* (New York, 1983)
T. O'Grady: *The Beatles: a Musical Revolution* (Boston, 1983)
C. Terry: *Here, There and Everywhere: the First International Beatles Bibliography, 1962–1982* (Ann Arbor, MI, 1983)
J. Vollmer: *Rock 'n' Roll Times: the Style and Spirit of the Early Beatles and their First Fans* (New York, 1983)

DALE COCKRELL

Beatty, Josephine. Pseudonym of ALBERTA HUNTER.

Beaux Arts String Quartet. String quartet founded in 1955. *See* TARACK, GERALD.

Beaux Arts Trio. Piano trio. It was formed in 1955 and gave its first concert at the Berkshire Music Festival, Tanglewood. Two of the founder-members, the pianist Menahem Pressler and the cellist BERNARD GREENHOUSE, have remained; the violinist Daniel Guilet was succeeded on his retirement in 1968 by Isidore Cohen. Pressler (*b* Magdeburg, Germany, 16 Dec 1923) studied in Palestine with Rudiakov and Leo Kestenberg and in California with Egon Petri. At the age of 17 he won the Debussy Competition in San Francisco. In 1955 he took up a post at Indiana University, where he became a professor of music in 1958; he also teaches at the Jerusalem Music Center. Greenhouse (*b* Newark, NJ, 3 Jan 1916) studied with Casals for two years after graduating from the Juilliard School. He is on the faculties of the Manhattan School and SUNY, Stony Brook. His instrument is the "Stanlein" Stradivari of 1707. Cohen (*b* New York, 16 Dec 1922) also studied at the Juilliard School, with Galamian; he was with the Juilliard Quartet from 1958 to 1966, and has led the Casals and Mostly Mozart festival orchestras and the Little Orchestra Society, New York. The trio has recorded much of the standard repertory for the medium, including all the trios of Haydn, Beethoven, Schubert, Brahms, Mozart, and Dvořák, as well as Brahms's piano quartets (with the violist Trampler). It has toured widely, to North and South America, eastern and western Europe, Africa, the Middle East, Japan, Australia, and New Zealand. The smoothness and precision of its ensemble, its fire, and its grasp of style have won high praise.

The Beaux Arts Trio: (left to right) Isidore Cohen, Menahem Pressler, and Bernard Greenhouse

BIBLIOGRAPHY

H. Waleson: "Beaux Arts Trio an Enduring Sound," *New York Times Magazine* (18 Nov 1984), 76
E. Seckerson: "Three's Company," *The Strad*, xcv (1984–5), 672
N. Delbanco: *The Beaux Arts Trio* (New York and London, 1985)

Bebop. *See* BOP.

Bechet, Sidney (Joseph) (*b* New Orleans, LA, 14 May ?1897; *d* Paris, France, 14 May 1959). Jazz clarinetist and soprano saxophonist.

1. LIFE. He was a black Creole, a group which played a major role in the formation of jazz. He claimed to have taken up the clarinet as a young boy, but this assertion may have been made to tally with a falsified birthdate. He studied sporadically with the older clarinetists Lorenzo Tio, Jr., "Big Eye" Louis Nelson, and George Baquet, but was primarily self-taught. By about 1910 he was working with some of the incipient jazz bands in the city, but around 1914 he left New Orleans to wander (a habit which stayed with him into middle age), playing in touring shows and carnivals throughout the South and Midwest. He arrived in Chicago in 1917, and played with bands led by the New Orleans pioneers Freddie Keppard, King Oliver, and Lawrence Duhé.

In 1919 he was discovered by Will Marion Cook, who was about to take his large concert band, the Southern Syncopated

Orchestra, to Europe. The orchestra played mainly concert music in fixed arrangements with little improvising, but featured Bechet (who could not read music) in jazz specialties. In London the Swiss conductor Ernest Ansermet heard the band, and in an article that has been widely reprinted referred to Bechet as "an extraordinary clarinet virtuoso" and an "artist of genius."

While in London Bechet purchased a soprano saxophone and taught himself to play it. It became his primary instrument for the rest of his life, though he continued to play clarinet frequently. The soprano, although difficult to play in tune, has a powerful, commanding voice, and with it Bechet was able to dominate jazz ensembles.

In 1919 Bechet broke away from the Southern Syncopated Orchestra to work in England and France with a small ragtime band led by drummer Benny Peyton; throughout the 1920s he traveled constantly between Europe and the USA, even touring Russia with a jazz band. Crucially, probably in 1925, he worked for two or three months in New York with the Duke Ellington Orchestra. In 1924 the band had acquired trumpeter Bubber Miley, a growl specialist under the influence of King Oliver. Miley had awakened Ellington's musicians to the new jazz music, but the band was in a transitional period, still playing much ordinary jazz-flavored popular music. Bechet had by this time acquired a capacity to swing that was matched only by Louis Armstrong's, and his example led the band further towards jazz. Not long afterwards Bechet opened his own club, the Club Basha, in Harlem, and engaged the young alto saxophonist Johnny Hodges from Boston to play in his band. Hodges was profoundly influenced by Bechet, and from his commanding position in the Ellington orchestra from 1928 he extended this influence widely and deeply.

In 1924 and 1925 Bechet made a group of recordings with Armstrong which were variously issued under the names Clarence Williams's Blue Five and the Red Onion Jazz Babies. These constitute one of the most important bodies of New Orleans jazz, and were influential with musicians of the time. Through the next few years Bechet continued to wander, traveling in Europe and the USA. In the 1930s, as hot dance music lost its popularity to more sentimental styles, Bechet dropped into obscurity, playing when he could find work and, for a brief period around 1933, comanaging a tailor's shop. However, with the New Orleans revival from about 1939 Bechet was extolled by critics as one of the greatest jazz pioneers and his fortunes improved. He made several recordings, including some with Mezz Mezzrow (see illustration). In 1949 he returned to Europe for the first time in almost 20 years. He was received there with adulation and reverence, and in 1951 he settled permanently in France, where he lived out his final years as a show-business star.

2. Music. Bechet was one of the second generation of New Orleans jazz pioneers who spread out from the city in the years around World War I, giving the music its first national popularity. As one of the three or four best jazz musicians of the postwar period, he exerted a strong influence on northern musicians, and is regarded today as one of the consummate artists produced by this music. Because he traveled so much, especially abroad, he never developed the large popular following that he might have had if he had chosen to emulate Armstrong or Ellington in leading a large dance band. He was frequently bristly and difficult, with the *amour propre* of a star even in obscurity. His passions were free: he was expelled from both England and France for fighting, and spent almost a year in jail in Paris. He was certainly not temperamentally suited to the kinds of compromise that Armstrong and Ellington made to achieve popular success. But this same, barely controlled passion is one of the hallmarks of his playing, which is everywhere filled with feeling, from the

Sidney Bechet (soprano saxophone, right) with Mezz Mezzrow (clarinet), late 1940s

wild exuberance of *Sweetie Dear* (1932) to the brooding melancholy of *Blue Horizon* (1944). Bechet mastered the soprano saxophone to such a degree that few other jazz musicians were willing to challenge him, and until John Coltrane renewed the popularity of the instrument in the 1960s he had the field virtually to himself.

Like most of the New Orleans pioneers, Bechet tended to work out his figures in advance, and once he had arrived at a way of playing a tune he seldom changed it. But his playing was nonetheless passionate: his music was filled with movement, at fast tempos dashing headlong through the melody, at slow tempos swirling up and down the full range of the instrument in free-floating arpeggios. Because Bechet was such a solitary figure, his influence on jazz tended to be indirect, exercised through Ellington, Hodges, Buster Bailey (who managed a fair approximation of Bechet's style on soprano saxophone, which he adopted briefly), and a generation of younger players, including Bob Wilber, caught up in the New Orleans revival of the 1940s; but however indirect, it should not be undervalued.

RECORDINGS

(selective list)

As leader: Summertime (1939, BN 6); China Boy (1940, HRS 2001); Make me a Pallet on the Floor (1940, Bluebird 8509); Blue Horizon (1944, BN 43); *Sidney Bechet avec Claude Luter et son orchestre* (1949, Vogue 5.13)

As sideman: C. Williams: Texas Moaner Blues (1924, OK 8171), Mandy Make up your Mind (1924, OK 40260); Red Onion Jazz Babies: Cake Walking Babies (1924, Gennett 5627); New Orleans Feetwarmers: Sweetie Dear/Maple Leaf Rag (1932, Vic. 23360)

BIBLIOGRAPHY

SouthernB

E. Ansermet: "Bechet and Jazz Visit Europe, 1919," *Frontiers of Jazz*, ed. R. de Toledano (New York, 1947, 2/1962)

H. Lyttelton: *I Play as I Please* (London, 1954)

R. Mouly: *Sidney Bechet, notre ami* (Paris, 1959)

S. Bechet: *Treat it Gentle* (New York, 1960/*R*1975)

M. Williams: *Jazz Masters of New Orleans* (New York, 1967)

G. Schuller: *Early Jazz: its Roots and Musical Development* (New York, 1968)

H. J. Mauerer: *A Discography of Sidney Bechet* (Copenhagen, 1969)

R. Blesh: *Combo: USA* (Philadelphia, 1971/*R*1979), 33

H. Lyttelton: *The Best of Jazz: Basin Street to Harlem* (London, 1977)

J.-R. Hippenmeyer: *Sidney Bechet* (Geneva, Switzerland, 1980)

W. Balliett: *Jelly Roll, Jabbo and Fats* (New York, 1983), 31

B. Priestley: "Blues to Bechet," *The Wire*, no.3 (1983), 14

M. Hazeldine: "Dear Wynne: a Review of the Events of 1945–6, concerning Bunk Johnson, Sidney Bechet, Boston and Beyond," *Footnote*, xv/5 (1984), 4

JAMES LINCOLN COLLIER

Beck, Jean [Johann Baptist] (*b* Gebweiler, Alsace, Germany, 14 Aug 1881; *d* Philadelphia, PA, 23 June 1943). Philologist and musicologist. He studied in Paris and later in Strasbourg, where he received the doctorate in 1907. In his *Die Melodien der Troubadours und Trouvères* (1908, which incorporated his dissertation), he proposed the application of modal rhythm to medieval secular song. The French scholar Pierre Aubry became independently convinced of the same theory, and a bitter dispute ensued between the two men as to who had conceived the idea; in 1909 a judicial tribunal of scholars upheld Beck's claim. The lamentable outcome of this affair was Aubry's death in 1910 while fencing, apparently in preparation for a duel with Beck. In the face of unpopularity, Beck immigrated to the USA, where he held positions at the University of Illinois (1911–14), Bryn Mawr College (1914–20), and the Curtis Institute (from 1920). He was made a member of the executive board of the American Musicological Society at its inauguration (1934). Beck planned a collected edition in 52 volumes, with facsimiles, transcriptions, and commentary, of all troubadour and trouvère songs surviving with melodies, but the series ran to only two publications, the second edited jointly with his wife Louise Beck.

IAN D. BENT/R

Beck, Johann H(einrich) (*b* Cleveland, OH, 12 Sept 1856; *d* Cleveland, 26 May 1924). Conductor, composer, violinist, and teacher. He studied at the Leipzig Conservatory from 1879 to 1882, and made his European début as a violinist at the Leipzig Gewandhaus in his own String Quartet in C minor. On his return to Cleveland he continued activity with the Schubert String Quartet, which he had organized in 1877, and the Beck String Quartet, giving frequent concerts during the 1880s and 1890s. After 1878 he was active as a conductor. He directed the Detroit SO (1895–6) and local Cleveland orchestras during the early years of the 20th century, and appeared frequently with major orchestras in other cities. He conducted his own works with much success. Numerous contemporary articles and reviews give him high praise; Henry Krehbiel wrote of the String Sextet: "We doubt whether there is a composer in this country who could match his slow movement" (*New York Tribune*, 23 November 1887). Only his *Elegiac Song* op.4 no.1 seems to have been published, however. Beck was active in the Music Teachers National Association and the Ohio Music Teachers' Association. An extensive collection of his manuscripts and memorabilia is in the Cleveland Public Library.

WORKS

Stage: Salammbo (J. H. Beck), begun 1887, unfinished

Orch: Sym., "Sindbad," op.1, *c*1875–7, unfinished; 4 ovs., 1875–85; Skirnismael, cycle of 5 sym. poems, *c*1887–93, 3 unfinished; 2 scherzos, 1885–95, 1889; Aus meinem Leben, tone poem, 1917

Vocal: 6 tone poems, 1v, orch, 1877–89, incl. Elegiac Song, 1v, vn, pf, op.4 no.1 (Cleveland, 1877), 2 unfinished; Deukalion (B. Taylor), 4 solo vv, chorus, orch, ?1877, unfinished; Wie schoen bist du, T, orch; Meeresabend (M. Strachwitz, trans. Beck), Mez/T, orch, ?1908; Salvum fac regem, 4vv, pf; partsongs; songs

Inst: 4 str qts, 1877–80; Str Sextet, 1885–6; Vn Sonata, unfinished; pf pieces, incl. Sonata, unfinished, Canone all'ottave, 1875, 1 set of variations; others, incl. piece for fl, pf

BIBLIOGRAPHY

"Biographies of Noted American Musicians, no.119: Johann H. Beck," *Brainard's Musical World*, xxiv (1887), 364

"American Composers: Johann H. Beck," *The Musician*, ii (1897), 1

R. Hughes: *Contemporary American Composers* (Boston, 1900), 406

W. T. Upton: "Beck, Johann Heinrich," *DAB*

M. H. Osburn: *Ohio Composers and Musical Authors* (Columbus, OH, 1942), 28

J. H. Alexander: *It Must be Heard: a Survey of the Musical Life of Cleveland, 1836–1918* (Cleveland, 1981), 22

J. HEYWOOD ALEXANDER

Beck, Sydney (*b* New York, 2 Sept 1906). Music scholar and librarian. He was educated at the College of the City of New York, New York University, the Institute of Musical Art, and the Mannes College, his studies including violin and chamber music with Louis Sveçenski, composition with Bernard Wagenaar and Hans Weisse, and musicology with Sachs and Reese. He worked at the Music Division of the New York Public Library as head of the Rare Book and Manuscript Collections, editor of music publications, and curator of the Toscanini Memorial Archives (1931–68), and taught at Mannes (1950–68). From 1968 to 1976 he was director of libraries and a member of the faculty at the New England Conservatory. Beck's principal fields of study have been early string techniques and performance practice, textual analyses and criticism, and instrumental teaching and study, with an emphasis on English Renaissance music; as director and performer he has himself appeared with various concert groups. Between 1942 and 1959 he edited for the New York Public Library chamber works by Francesco Geminiani, William Holborne, Matthew Locke, and Jean-Marie Leclair, among other composers.

PAULA MORGAN

Becker. Family of violin makers. Carl G. Becker (*b* Chicago, IL, 20 Sept 1887; *d* Chicago, 6 Aug 1975) was the son of a prominent violinist and teacher; his maternal grandfather, Herman Macklett, had been a violin maker. He began as a craftsman in 1901 and a year later joined the firm of Lyon & Healy, where he worked under John Hornsteiner until 1908. When Hornsteiner left to start his own business Becker went with him, staying as an assistant until 1923. By 1924 he had become an outstanding violin maker, repairer, and connoisseur, and he took a position with William Lewis & Son, another Chicago firm; before 1924 he had already made about 100 violins in his spare time. After he joined Lewis he spent at least three summer months doing new work at Pickerel, Wisconsin; from 1925 to 1947 he made 389 new violins, violas, and cellos, each with its serial number (100–488). For the rest of each year he supervised the repair workshop of Lewis & Son, or accompanied the president of the firm on his journeys in search of old instruments.

His son, Carl F. Becker (*b* Chicago, 16 Dec 1919), inherited his father's ability, and worked with him from 1936. Between them they developed the art of violin restoration to a high level, introducing a number of important innovations and technical improvements. Carl F. Becker's particular specialty is varnish restoration. From 1948 to 1967 new instruments (nos. 489–726) were produced by father and son in Wisconsin in association with Lewis & Son.

By 1968 the Beckers' understanding of their craft and their perfectionism had become incompatible with the increasing pace of big business, and they left Lewis & Son to work on their own. Both new work (now over 750 instruments) and restoration continue to the same high standard. In the years before the elder Becker's death they each made a few instruments individually. Geraldine Becker (*b* Chicago, 14 Aug 1955), daughter of Carl F. Becker, has begun working with her father.

CHARLES BEARE

Becker, John J(oseph) (*b* Henderson, KY, 22 Jan 1886; *d* Wilmette, IL, 21 Jan 1961). Composer. He belongs, together with Ives, Ruggles, Cowell, and Riegger, to the group named the "American Five" of avant-garde music. Over several decades he served as the group's militant crusader for new music in the Midwest, seeking to establish a national music with experimental tendencies drawn from the American experience rather than from Europe.

Becker graduated from the Cincinnati Conservatory in 1905 and received the doctorate in composition from the Wisconsin Conservatory in 1923. His principal teachers were Alexander von Fielitz, Carl Busch, and the noted contrapuntist Wilhelm Middelschulte. He taught piano and theory at the North Texas College Kidd-Key Conservatory in Sherman, Texas, from 1906 until about 1914, an otherwise obscure period in his life. In 1917 he began a long career of teaching and administration in Midwestern Catholic institutions, among them the University of Notre Dame (1917–27), the College of St. Thomas in St. Paul, Minnesota (1929–33), and Barat College in Lake Forest, Illinois (1943–57). After meeting Cowell in 1928, he became an energetic member of the newly organized Pan American Association of Composers. In addition to lecturing and writing (his writings include articles on various 20th-century composers, the aesthetics of music, and education in music), he conducted Midwestern premières of works by Ives, Ruggles, and Riegger in the early 1930s. His warm friendship with Ives, fully documented in a remarkable correspondence between the two men (1931–54), resulted in his orchestration of Ives's *General William Booth Enters into Heaven* for baritone, male chorus and small orchestra in 1934–5. From 1935 to 1941 he was the controversial director of the Federal Music Project in Minnesota and was associate editor of the *New Music Quarterly*. A devout Catholic, he was chosen as the American musical representative to the First International Congress of Catholic Artists in Rome in 1950. His musical activity slackened somewhat in his later years because of declining health and years of continual neglect of his music.

Becker's early symphonies and songs reveal the influence of German Romanticism and, to a lesser extent, French impressionism. In the late 1920s his musical style underwent a radical change, leading to the highly dissonant yet lyrical *Symphonia brevis* of 1929. His creativity culminated in the 1930s in such works as *Abongo*, the Horn Concerto, *Concertino pastorale*, and a unique series of "Soundpieces," abstract chamber works of diversified instrumentation. His most significant contributions were large-scale stage works fusing dance, color, mime, stage design, and music into shapes prophetic of the "mixed-media" theater. He considered his masterpiece to be his Stagework no. 3: *A Marriage with Space* (1935), written in collaboration with the Chicago poet Mark Turbyfill. Becker favored such contrapuntal forms and procedures as chorale, fugue, and canon and preferred a

John J. Becker, c1950

dissonant, atonal counterpoint reminiscent of 16th-century polyphony in its even flow. His music employs abstract polytonal rhythmic patterns and large chordal outbursts with overtones calculated to blend with and transform the basic sonority. An unusually clear orchestration is characterized by strongly contrasting colors and much use of percussion. The swift change of moods from violent to darkly tragic is most clearly revealed in the brilliant Violin Concerto (1948), Becker's last completed work for orchestra. His work, although occasionally gentle and serene, is frequently satirical and forcefully expresses a feeling of social protest. At a time when neoclassicism and a return to folk sources dominated American music, Becker continually insisted on the responsibility of the composer to "add new resources, evolve new techniques, develop new sound patterns."

WORKS

(unpubd unless otherwise stated)

STAGE

The Season of Pan (ballet suite), small ens, *c*1910

The City of Shagpat (opera, 3, Becker, after G. Meredith), *c*1926–7, inc.

Salome (cinema opera, 1, Becker), *c*1931, inc.

Dance Figure: Stagework no.1 (ballet, Pound), S, orch, 1932 [incl. music from Salome]

The Life of Man: Stagework no.4 (ballet, after L. Andreiev), speaking chorus, orch, 1932–43, inc.

Abongo, a Primitive Dance: Stagework no.2 (ballet), wordless vv, 29 perc, 1933, pubd; New York, 16 May 1963

A Marriage with Space: Stagework no.3 (ballet, after M. Turbyfill), speaking chorus, orch, 1935, pubd [incl. music from Sym. no.3], arr. as Sym. no.4 "Dramatic Episodes," 1940

Nostalgic Songs of Earth (ballet), pf, 1938; Northfield, MN, 12 Dec 1938

Vigilante 1938 (ballet), pf, perc, 1938; Northfield, MN, 12 Dec 1938

Privilege and Privation: Stagework no.5c (opera, 1, A. Kreymborg), 1939, pubd; Amsterdam, 22 June 1982

Rain down Death: Stagework no.5a (incidental music, Kreymborg), chamber orch, 1939, earlier orch version, A Prelude to Shakespeare, 1937, rev. as Orch Suite no.1, 1939

Dance for Shakespeare's Tempest (incidental music), pf, chamber orch, 1940, inc., arr. M. Benaroyo as The Tempest, 2 pf, 1954

When the Willow Nods: Stagework no.5b (incidental music, Kreymborg), speaker, chamber orch, 1940 [incl. music from 4 Dances, pf, and Nostalgic Songs of Earth], rev. as Orch Suite no.2, 1940, pubd

Antigone (incidental music, Sophocles), orch, 1940–44

Trap Doors (incidental music, Kreymborg), speaking chorus, pf, n.d., inc.

Deirdre: Stagework no.6 (opera, 1, Becker, after J. M. Synge), 1945, inc. [unorchd]

Julius Caesar (film score, Shakespeare), brass, perc, 1949

Faust: a Television Opera (monodrama, Goethe, trans. B. Taylor), T, pf, 1951, pubd; Los Angeles, 8 April 1985

The Queen of Cornwall (opera, Hardy), 1956, inc.

Madeleine et Judas (incidental music, R. L. Bruckberger), orch, 1958; Paris radio broadcast, 25 March 1959

The Song of the Scaffold (film score, Bruckberger), 1959, inc.

ORCHESTRAL

Sym. no.1 "Etude primitive," 1912, last movt arr. as Sym. Movt "Americana," pf, *c*1912, arr. as Sonate American, vn, pf, *c*1925; 2 Orch Sketches (Cossack Sketches), 1912 [2nd movt = arr. of The Mountains]; A Tartar Song, *c*1912; Sym. no.2 "Fantasia tragica," 1920, lost, rev. *c*1937 [incl. music from Pf Sonata]; Sym. no.3 "Symphonia brevis," 1929, arr. pf, 1929, both pubd

Conc. arabesque, pf, 12 insts/small orch, 1930, pubd; Horn Conc., 1933, pubd; Concertino pastorale: a Forest Rhapsodie, 2 fl, orch, 1933; Mockery: a Scherzo, pf, dance orch, 1933; A Prelude to Shakespeare, 1937 [arr. of part of Rain down Death]; Va Conc., 1937; Pf Conc. no.2 "Satirico," 1938 [incl. music from Mockery]; Orch Suite no.1, 1939 [from incidental music from Rain down Death]; Orch Suite no.2, 1940, pubd [from incidental music from When the Willow Nods]; Sym. no.5 "Homage to Mozart," 1942; Victory March, 1942 [from Sym. no.6]; The Snow Goose: a Legend of the Second World War (after P. Gallico), 1944; Vn Conc., 1948, pubd

Orchestration of Ives: General William Booth Enters into Heaven, B, male vv, chamber orch, 1934–5, pubd

For sym. no.4 see under STAGE, and for syms. nos.6–7 see under CHORAL

CHORAL

Rouge bouquet (J. Kilmer), T, male vv, tpt, pf, 1917; Jesu dulcis memoria (offertory), male vv, org ad lib, 1919; Martin of Tours (C. L. O'Donnell), T/B, male vv, org, pf, 1919; Choral Mass, c, chorus, org, *c*1921, inc.; The Pool (H. Doolittle), 1923, arr. female vv, pf, *c*1947; Out of the Cradle Endlessly Rocking (Whitman), cantata, speaker, S, T, chorus, orch, 1929

Missa symphonica, male vv, 1933; Pater noster, unacc., 1935; Sym. no.6 "Out of Bondage" (Kreymborg, A. Lincoln), speaker, chorus, orch, 1942; Mass in Honor of the Sacred Heart, 3 equal vv, 1943; Mater admirabilis (offertory), female vv, 1944; A Little Easter Cycle (J. B. Tabb), S, female vv, 1944; Song of the Cedar Tree (anon.), (female vv)/(unison chorus, pf), 1944

Moments from the Passion (Goday, trans. McLaren), cantata, solo vv, chorus, org, 1945, pubd; Nunc sancte nobis spiritus (St. Ambrose), *c*1945; Morning Song (H. P. Horne), double chorus, 1946; Tantum ergo, female vv, 1946; Unison Mass in Honor of St. Madeleine Sophie Barat, female vv, pf, 1946; Ecce sacerdos, female vv, 1947

O domina mea, female vv, 1947; The Seven Last Words, female vv/male vv, 1947; Moments from the Liturgical Year (G. von Le Fort, trans. M. Chanler), speaker, speaking chorus, 1v, chorus of 3 equal vv, 1948; Mass in Honor of St. Viator, (unison chorus, org)/2vv, 1949; Sym. no.7 (Becker, the Beatitudes, Dante), speaking chorus, female vv, orch, 1954, inc.

CHAMBER

Pf Sonata "The Modern Man I Sing," *c*1910; The Mountains, pf, *c*1912; My Little Son, 18 Months Old: Studies in Child Psychology, pf, 1924; 2 Architectural Impressions, pf, 1924; 2 Chinese Miniatures, pf, 1925, pubd, arr. R. F. Kraner, orch, 1928; 2 Mockeries, pf, *c*1927, lost

Soundpiece [no.1], pf, str qt, 1932, arr. as no.1a, pf, str qnt, 1935, arr. as no.1b, pf, str, 1935; Soundpiece no.2a "Homage to Haydn": Str Qt no.1, 1936, arr. as no.2b, str, 1936, both pubd; Soundpiece no.3: Vn Sonata, 1936, pubd; Soundpiece no.4: Str Qt no.2, 1937, pubd; Soundpiece no.5: Pf Sonata, 1937, pubd; 4 Dances, pf, 1938; Soundpiece no.6: Sonata, fl, cl, 1942, pubd; Soundpiece no.7, 2 pf, 1949; Soundpiece no.8: Str Qt no.3, 1959, inc.; Improvisation, org, 1960; kbd arrs. of orch works, incl. Fantasia tragica, org, 1920, pubd

SONGS

(for 1v, pf, unless otherwise stated)

John Becker's Songbook, 1907–9: The evening breeze, Repentance, My wild rose (A. Austin); A love note (F. Stanton); The lake (A. Upson); Love without wings (M. F. Robinson), song cycle: We sat where shadows darken, How is it possible you should forget me, I know you love me not, And so I shall meet you again, my dear, O death of things that are; The moon hath fully risen (Heine)

2 Simple Songs: At Auction (H. A. Waithman), A Broken Song (M. O'Neil), *c*1917; 4 Songs: The grapes (C. Doris), O love me truly (Keats), I fear thy kisses (Shelley), Memory (H. Cook), 1918–20, nos.2–3 arr. S, str qt, 1919; Little Sleeper (Hafiz, trans. P. le Gallienne), S, str qt, 1919; 2 Songs (G. O'Neil): You are not here this April, Death of the Roses, 1921; 2 Songs from H. D.: The Pool, Whirl up Sea, 1923; 2 Songs: A Song (Gentle Lady) (Joyce), You and I (E. W. McCourt), 1923

2 Songs: Favours of the Moon (Baudelaire, trans. Symons), Naomi the Beautiful (G. B. Hallowell), 1923; A Heine Song Cycle (trans. J. Thompson): For many thousand ages, The earth is so fair and the violets so blue, The lotus flower doth languish, The pine tree, The violets blue of the eyes divine, Say, where is the maiden sweet?, My darling we sat together, I gazed upon her picture, In the Rhine, 1924–5

From the Story of Bhavanar (G. Meredith): Even's star yonder, Take me to thee, *c*1926, inc.; 2 Poems of Departure (Rihaku, trans. Pound): Separation on the River Kiang, Taking Leave of a Friend, 1927; 4 Songs from the Japanese (Basho, trans. C. H. Page): Quick falling dew, Friend sparrow, O cricket, The Frog, 1933; The Lark (Schubert) (A. Kreymborg), 1934

3 Songs to Poems by Mary Cecilia Becker: Open your arms to me, High to the altar of sacrifice, I should like to dance, 1935; Psalms of Love (P. Baum, trans. J. Bitchell): The nights moan, Thine eyes with gloom are gleaming, When the roses wonder, When the night goes hence, 1935; The Stars about the Lovely Moon (Sappho, trans. E. Arnold), 1943; At Dieppe (A. Symons): After Sunset, On the Beach, The Squall, Requies, 1959

MSS in *NN*

Principal publishers: Peters, Presser

BIBLIOGRAPHY

J. K. Sherman: "Becker the Crusader," *Northwest Musical Herald*, vii (1932), 5

C. R. Reis: *American Composers* (New York, 2/1932, rev. and enlarged, 4/1947/*R*1977 as *Composers in America: Biographical Sketches*)

H. Cowell: "John Becker," *American Composers on American Music* (Stanford, CA, 1933/*R*1962), 82
——: "John Becker: a Crusader from Kentucky," *Southern Literary Messenger*, i (1939), 657
D. Ewen: *American Composers Today* (New York, 1949)
H. Cowell: "Current Chronicle: New York," *MQ*, xxxix (1953), 426
G. Chase: *America's Music* (New York, 1955, 2/1966)
E. M. Becker: *John J. Becker: American Composer* (MS, *DLC*, 1958)
W. Riegger: "John J. Becker," *ACAB*, ix/1 (1959), 2
J. W. Downey: "Homage to John J. Becker," *Focus Midwest*, i (1962), July, 18
V. Perlis: *Charles Ives Remembered* (New Haven, 1974)
D. C. Gillespie: Preface to *Symphonia brevis* (New York, 1975)
——: "John Becker, Musical Crusader of St. Paul," *MQ*, lxii (1976), 195
——: *John Becker: Midwestern Musical Crusader* (diss., U. of North Carolina, 1977)
——: "John Becker's Correspondence with Ezra Pound: the Origins of a Musical Crusader," *Bulletin of Research in the Humanities*, lxxxiii (1980), 163
K. Gann: "The Percussion Music of John J. Becker," *Percussive Notes*, xxii/3 (1984), 26

DON C. GILLESPIE

Beddoe, Dan (*b* Aberaman, Wales, 16 March 1863; *d* New York, 26 Dec 1937). Welsh tenor. Though he won an Eisteddfod gold medal when only 19, his career as a singer made little headway till 1903. He had immigrated to the USA, living in Pittsburgh and Cleveland, where he worked in a steel factory and sang with choirs and in oratorio. He had a remarkable voice, however, and attracted the attention of Walter Damrosch in New York. He was engaged first to sing the solo part in Berlioz's Requiem as part of the centenary celebrations of 1903, and was then heard in a concert performance of *Parsifal*. Many important occasions followed, such as the New York première of Strauss's *Taillefer*, some of the first performances in the USA of Mahler's *Das Lied von der Erde*, and a performance of Beethoven's Ninth Symphony with Mahler himself conducting. The Cincinnati Festival heard him first in 1910 and for the last time in 1927. He continued to sing with a wonderfully well-preserved voice as late as 1934 when he was tenor soloist in *Messiah* at New York. He never sang on the operatic stage, but concert versions of *Die Meistersinger*, *Aida*, and *Samson et Dalila* were in his repertory. He returned occasionally to England and Wales, his last concerts there being given in 1924. He died after an automobile accident in 1937. His highly prized recordings include some made in 1928 when, at the age of 65, the beauty, evenness, and power of his voice seem scarcely to have diminished. Peculiarities of pronunciation and sometimes a shortness of breath prevent his earlier recordings from being completely acceptable as models of their kind, but they make quite credible the story that Caruso himself once attended one of Beddoe's concerts to learn from his art.

J. B. STEANE

Bedient, Gene R. (*b* Alliance, NE, 23 Aug 1944). Organ builder. After graduating from the University of Nebraska, he was apprenticed to Charles McManis of Kansas City and in 1969 established his own firm in Lincoln, Nebraska. In 1971 he received the master's degree from the same university. Notable organs include those built for the Wesley Foundation, Lincoln (1975), and Ripon College, Ripon, Wisconsin (1984). Bedient's organs are strongly influenced by historic north German models and are usually tuned in unequal temperaments.

BIBLIOGRAPHY

U. Pape: *The Tracker Organ Revival in America* (Berlin, n.d. [?1977])

BARBARA OWEN

Beecher. Family of clergymen, authors, and reformers active in the 19th century. Lyman Beecher (1775–1863), a Presbyterian minister and renowned evangelical leader, was a strong advocate of reform in church music and congregational singing. He was pastor of the Hanover Street Church, Boston, where he helped Lowell Mason in his career as a musical reformer; Mason served as Beecher's music director from 1827 to 1832. Beecher then moved to Cincinnati, where his music director was Mason's brother Timothy. Three of Beecher's 13 children were of importance in the development of American hymnody. Henry Ward Beecher (1813–87), who was pastor of Plymouth Church, Brooklyn, from 1847, edited the *Plymouth Collection* (New York, 1851, 2/1855), an influential hymnal which included two hymns by his brother Charles Beecher (1815–1900), also a minister and one of the music editors for the hymnal (*see* HYMNODY, §3(i)). Their sister Harriet Beecher Stowe (1811–96), who wrote the novel *Uncle Tom's Cabin* (1855), contributed three hymns to the collection, and published other hymns in her *Religious Poems* (1867). Her most popular hymn text, "Knocking, knocking, who is there," was adapted and set to music by G. F. Root; it became widely sung as a gospel song after its inclusion by Sankey and Bliss in their first collection, *Gospel Hymns and Sacred Songs* (1875).

BIBLIOGRAPHY

F. M. Bird: "Stowe, Harriet," *A Dictionary of Hymnology*, ed. J. Julian (New York, 1892, 2/1907/*R*1957), ii, 1096
J. Mearns: "Beecher, Charles," *A Dictionary of Hymnology*, ed. J. Julian (New York, 1892, 2/1907/*R*1957), i, 125
L. F. Benson: *The English Hymn* (New York, 1915/*R*1962), 473

PAUL C. ECHOLS

Beefheart, Captain. *See* CAPTAIN BEEFHEART.

Beeson, Jack (Hamilton) (*b* Muncie, IN, 15 July 1921). Composer and teacher. He attended the Eastman School (BM 1942, MM 1943) as a pupil of Burrill Phillips, Bernard Rogers, and Howard Hanson, and had private lessons with Bartók in New York (1944–5). From 1945 to 1948 he did graduate work in conducting and musicology at Columbia University, where he was an accompanist and conductor for the opera workshop; this apprenticeship strengthened the leaning towards opera which he had had from childhood. In 1945 he began to teach at Columbia, becoming MacDowell Professor of Music in 1967 and serving as chairman of the music department (1968–72); meanwhile he also lectured at the Juilliard School (1961–3) and at various other universities in the USA. Among the awards he has received are a Rome Prize (1948–50), a Fulbright Fellowship (1949–50), a Guggenheim Fellowship (1958–9), the Marc Blitzstein Award for the Musical Theater (1968), and the Gold Medal of the National Arts Club (1976). He has held office in many music organizations, including the American Music Center (1967–76), Composers Forum (from 1950), Alice M. Ditson Fund of Columbia University (from 1961), CRI (from 1967), American Academy in Rome (from 1975), and the American Academy and Institute of Arts and Letters (from 1980); he was elected to its Institute in 1976.

Beeson's operas may be considered to continue some of the qualities of those of Douglas Moore, one of his predecessors at Columbia. Though his style is of a later generation, it shares with Moore's a feeling for lyrical line, occasionally suggesting an American folk idiom; and Beeson, like Moore, has shaped successful opera subjects from American life and literature.

WORKS
(all pubd unless otherwise stated)

OPERAS

Jonah (2/3, Beeson, after P. Goodman), 1950, unpubd

Hello out There (chamber opera, 1, Beeson, after W. Saroyan), 1954; New York, 27 May 1954

The Sweet Bye and Bye (2, K. Elmslie), 1956; New York, 21 Nov 1957

Lizzie Borden (3, Elmslie), 1965; New York, 25 March 1965; Margret's Garden Aria, Abbie's Bird Song arr. S, pf, rev. 1967, pubd separately

My Heart's in the Highlands (chamber opera, 2/3, Beeson, after Saroyan), 1969; National Educational Television, 17 March 1970

Captain Jinks of the Horse Marines (romantic comedy, 3, S. Harnick, after C. Fitch), 1975; Kansas City, 20 Sept 1975

Dr. Heidegger's Fountain of Youth (1, Harnick, after Hawthorne), 1978; New York, 17 Nov 1978

CHORAL

A Round for Christmas (St. Luke), 1942, rev. 1951; 3 Psalms (Pss. cxxxi, xlvii, xxiii), 1951; 3 Psalms (Pss. cvii, cxxi, cxl), 1951; The Tides of Miranda (S. Moore), madrigal, 1954; The Bear Hunt (Lincoln), 1957; Evening Prayer (Matthew, Mark, Luke, and John) (trad. nursery rhyme), 1959; Nursery Rhyme Rounds: Hickup Snicup, Swan Song, Give the Poor Singer a Penny (trad. nursery rhymes), 1959; Greener Pastures (anon.), 1965; Boys and Girls Together (anon.), 1965

Homer's Woe (anon.), 1966; To a Lady who Asked for a Cypher (anon.: Mrs. Partington's Carpetbag of Fun), 1969; In Praise of the Bloomers (anon.: Mrs. Partington's Carpetbag of Fun), 1969; Everyman's Handyman (Beeson, after E. W. Smith), 1970; The Model Housekeeper (Beeson, after Smith), 1970; Knots: Jack and Jill for Grown-ups (R. D. Laing), 1979; Hinx, Minx (trad. nursery rhyme), 1980

SOLO VOCAL

3 Love Songs (Yeats), A, pf, 1944, rev. 1959; Lullaby (Yeats), A, pf, 1944, rev. 1959; 3 Songs (Blake), S, pf, 1945, rev. 1951; 5 Songs (F. Quarles), S, pf, 1946, rev. 1950; Eldorado (Poe), high v, pf, 1951; Piazza Piece (J. C. Ransom), S, T, pf, 1951; Big Crash out West (P. Viereck), Bar, pf, 1951; 2 Songs (J. Betjeman), Bar, pf, 1952; Six Lyrics (Eng. and American poets), high v, pf, 1952

2 Concert Arias, S, orch: The Elephant (Lawrence), 1953, The Hippopotamus (Eliot), orig. for 1v, pf, 1951, rev. and orchd, 1952; Indiana Homecoming (Lincoln), Bar, pf, 1956; Leda (Huxley), reciter, pf, 1957; Against Idleness and Mischief and in Praise of Labor (I. Watts), high v, pf, 1959; Fire, Fire, Quench Desire (G. Peele), high v, pf, 1959; To a Sinister Potato (Viereck), Bar, pf, 1970

A Creole Mystery (Beeson, after L. Hearn), Mez/Bar, str qt, 1970; The You should have Done it Blues (Viereck), S, pf, 1971; Death by Owl Eyes (R. Hughes), high v, pf, 1971; The Day's no Rounder than its Angles Are (Viereck), Mez/Bar, str qt, 1971; From a Watchtower (Wordsworth, Auden, Hopkins, De la Mare), 5 songs, high v, pf, 1976; Cat (Keats), S, pf, 1979; Cowboy Song (C. Causley), Bar, pf, 1979

INSTRUMENTAL

Orch: Hymns and Dances (from The Sweet Bye and Bye), 1958, arr. band, 1966; Sym. no.1, A, 1959; Transformations, 1959; Commemoration, band, chorus ad lib, 1960; Fanfare, brass, wind, perc, 1963, unpubd

Chamber: Song, fl, pf, 1945; Interlude, vn, pf, 1945, rev. 1951, unpubd; Pf Sonata no.4, 1945, rev. 1951; Pf Sonata no.5, 1946, rev. 1951; Va Sonata, 1953; 2 Diversions, pf, 1953, rev. of Pf Sonata no.3, 1944, withdrawn; Sketches in Black and White, pf, 1958, unpubd; Round and Round, pf 4 hands, 1959; Sonata canonica, 2 a rec, 1966; The Hoosier Balks, The Hawkesley Blues, 10 insts, 1967, unpubd [after Pf Conc., 1944, withdrawn]; Old Hundredth: Prelude and Doxology, org, 1972

53 works written before 1950 incl. 2 pf concs., piece for chorus and orch, 6 sonatas, various chamber works, songs, choruses, all unpubd, withdrawn

Principal publishers: Boosey & Hawkes, MCA, Mills, Presser

BIBLIOGRAPHY

EwenD

Q. Eaton: *Opera Production: a Handbook* (St. Paul, 1961–74) [entries on *Hello out There*, *The Sweet Bye and Bye*, *Lizzie Borden*, and *My Heart's in the Highlands*]

D. Johns: "Connections: an Interview with Jack Beeson," *MEJ*, lxvi/2 (1979), 44

HOWARD SHANET

Beglarian, Grant (*b* Tbilisi, Georgia, 1 Dec 1927). Music administrator and composer. On his arrival in the USA in 1947, he enrolled at the University of Michigan, where he was a pupil of Ross Lee Finney (BM 1950, MM 1952, DMA 1958); he also studied at the Berkshire Music Center with Copland in 1959–60. During a wide-ranging career he has been an editor with Prentice-Hall (1960–61), director of the Contemporary Music Project for the Ford Foundation (1961–9), and dean of the school of performing arts at the University of Southern California (1969–82). He became president of the National Foundation for Advancement in the Arts in Miami in 1982. An effective administrator, he has, as he explains, "designed activities to demonstrate that the artist shapes cultural and social institutions." His compositions (published by Piedmont) include sonatas for cello and violin with piano, *A Hymn for our Times* for bands, *And all the Hills Echoed* for solo baritone, chorus, timpani, and organ, *Elegy* for solo cello, and *Fables, Foibles, and Fancies* for narrator and cello. His style reflects the influence of his principal teachers, Finney and Copland.

KAREN MONSON

Béhague, Gerard (Henri) (*b* Montpellier, France, 2 Nov 1937). Musicologist. He studied piano and composition at the National School of Music of the University of Brazil and at the Brazilian Conservatory, Rio de Janeiro, then worked under Jacques Chailley at the Institut de Musicologie of the University of Paris before settling in the USA, where he studied with Gilbert Chase at Tulane University (PhD 1966). He then joined the music faculty at the University of Illinois, and later became professor of music at the University of Texas (1974). He was associate editor of the *Yearbook for Inter-American Musical Research* (1969–75), editor of the music section of the *Handbook of Latin American Studies* (1970–74), and editor of *Ethnomusicology* (1974–8) and *Latin American Music Review* (from 1980). Although he has been specially concerned with American music, theory, and methods of musical research, Béhague's main interest has been Latin American music (on which he was editorial adviser and a principal contributor to *The New Grove*); he has concentrated particularly on the music of Brazil, which he has studied as both historian and ethnomusicologist. He is the author of *The Beginnings of Musical Nationalism in Brazil* (1971) and *Music in Latin America: an Introduction* (1977).

PAULA MORGAN

Behrend, Jeanne (*b* Philadelphia, PA, 11 May 1911). Pianist and composer. She graduated from the Curtis Institute (1934), where she studied piano with Josef Hofmann and composition with Rosario Scalero. Recommended by Villa-Lobos, who called her a "heroine of the Americas," she was sponsored by the US State Department in a good-will tour of South America in 1945–6. She founded and directed the Philadelphia Festival of Western Hemisphere Music (1959–60), which opened with her *Festival Fanfare: Prelude to the National Anthem*, performed by members of the Philadelphia Orchestra. Her other compositions include a string quartet, *Lamentation* for viola and piano, *Quiet Piece* and *Dance into Space* for piano, songs, and a cantata. In 1965 Behrend was awarded the Order of the Southern Cross from the Brazilian government for her services to Brazilian music. She taught piano at the Juilliard School, the Curtis Institute, and Western College (Oxford, Ohio), and gave courses in American music at Juilliard, the Philadelphia Conservatory, and Temple University. In 1969 she joined the piano faculty of the Philadelphia College of Performing Arts, and in 1974 instituted a course for adult beginners, "It Is Never Too Late!." She edited a selection of piano music by Gottschalk (1956) and songs by Foster (1964), Gottschalk's *Notes of a Pianist* (1964), and a volume of early American fuging-tunes (1976).

JOHN G. DOYLE

Behrman, David (*b* Salzburg, Austria, 16 Aug 1937). Composer. The son of the playwright S. N. Behrman and a nephew of Heifetz, he was brought up in New York, where he studied composition privately with Riegger. At Harvard (BA 1959) he was a pupil of Piston. He then went to Europe on a Paine Traveling Fellowship and studied with Pousseur and Stockhausen. After returning to the USA he received an MA degree in music theory from Columbia University. He was from 1966 a member of the Sonic Arts Union, a cooperative of composers of electronic music, with which he toured extensively in the USA and Europe. In the years 1965–70 he produced a notable series of recordings of experimental music for Columbia Masterworks (including Terry Riley's *In C*), and from 1970 to 1976 he worked with Cage, Tudor, and Mumma for the Merce Cunningham Dance Company. He has been artist-in-residence at several universities, including Mills College, Oakland, California, where he served as co-director of the Center for Contemporary Music.

Behrman designed his first electronic circuitry in 1966; this resulted in *Runthrough* (1967). Since then homemade or home-adapted electronics systems which involve sound synthesizers, microcomputers, and video have been integral to his music: "The form of the music," he has said, is "a slow unfolding of the possibilities of the system." Many of Behrman's systems are pitch-responsive, in that a microcomputer responds to a pitch or pitch sequence improvised by the performers, answering them in pre-programmed ways. More recently he has created sound installations (often in collaboration with Paul De Marinis), some of them interactive, with listeners able to play simple instruments and contribute to the audio-visual effect. No matter what electronics he uses, Behrman writes music that is prevailingly lyrical, even pastoral, and thus eloquently refutes the notion that electronic music must be futuristic and dehumanizing.

WORKS

(selective list)

cms – computer music system

Players with Circuits, 2 pf/zithers/gui, elec (2 pfmr), 1966; Wave Train, 2 amp pf (2–4 pfmr), 1966 (Source 4, 1966); Runthrough, elec (4 pfmr), 1967 (Mainstream 5010, 1968), rev. as Sinescreen, 1970; For Nearly an Hour (choreographer M. Cunningham: Walkaround Time), elec (3 pfmr), 1968; Reunion, performance piece, elec, collab. J. Cage, L. Cross, M. Duchamp, T. Duchamp, G. Mumma, D. Tudor, 1968; Runway, v, tape, elec, collab. Mumma, 1969; A New Team Takes Over, 2 speakers, elec, 1969; Pools of Phase-locked loops, synth, 1972, new version as Home-made Synth Music with Sliding Pitches, 1973; Cloud Music, sound installation, elec, collab. B. Diamond, R. Watts, 1974–9; Voice with Tpt and Melody-driven Elec, 1v, tpt, cms, 1974

Cello with Melody-driven Elec, vc, cms, 1975; Voice with Melody-driven Elec (choreographer Cunningham: Rebus), 1v, cms, 1975; Figure in a Clearing, vc, cms, 1977 (Lovely Music 1041, 1978); On the Other Ocean, insts, cms, 1977 (Lovely Music 1041, 1978); Indoor Geyser, sound installation, cms, 1979–81; Touch Tones, sound installation, cms, 1979; Singing Stick, cms, 1980–81, rev. as Flute, Rebab, Singing Stick, 1981; She's Wild, performance piece, collab. P. De Marinis, T. Hanlon, F. Friedman, 1981 (Record Records, 1981); Sound Fountain, sound installation, cms, video graphics, collab. De Marinis, 1982

6-Circle, 2 tpt, cms, cptr graphics, 1983–4; Orch Construction Set, orch, 1984; Interspecies Smalltalk (choreographer Cunningham: Pictures), vn, elec kbd, cms, cptr graphics, 1984; Installation for La Villette, sound installation, cms, cptr graphics, collab. G. Lewis, 1985–

BIBLIOGRAPHY

J. Rockwell: "Electronic & Computer Music & the Humanist Reaction: David Behrman," *All American Music: Composition in the Late Twentieth Century* (New York, 1983), 133

JOHN ROCKWELL

Beiderbecke, (Leon) Bix (*b* Davenport, IA, 10 March 1903; *d* New York, 6 Aug 1931). Jazz cornetist. As a boy he had a few piano lessons, but was self-taught on the cornet and learned an unorthodox technique by playing with records. His family disapproved of his interest in jazz, and sent him in 1921 to Lake Forest Academy, but the opportunity to play and hear jazz in nearby Chicago caused frequent truancy and eventually his expulsion. After several months working for his father in Davenport he turned to a career in music. Based in Chicago, he became known through his work and recordings with the Wolverines in 1924 (for illustration *see* JAZZ, fig.2). In the same year he began a long association with the saxophonist Frank Trumbauer, recording with him in New York. After working with Jean Goldkette's dance band (1924), he joined Trumbauer's group in St. Louis (1925–6). His association with Trumbauer broadened his musical experience and developed his music reading, in which, however, he was never to become adept. In late 1926 he and Trumbauer joined Goldkette, and were prominently featured with his group in New York until it disbanded in September 1927. They then joined Paul Whiteman's band, with which, and with various groups under their own names, they made a series of influential recordings. Beiderbecke's alcoholism caused his health to deteriorate and he was frequently unable to perform. He left Whiteman in September 1929; hopes of rejoining the group after recuperation were not realized. Until his death he worked in

Bix Beiderbecke

New York, in a radio series and in a few jobs with the Dorsey brothers, with the Casa Loma Orchestra, and with Benny Goodman.

From relatively undistinguished influences Beiderbecke developed a beautiful and original style. His distinctive, bell-like tone (his friend Hoagy Carmichael described it as resembling a chime struck by a mallet) achieved additional intensity through his unorthodox fingering, which often led him to play certain notes as higher partials in lower overtone series, imparting a slightly different timbre and intonation to successive pitches. With his basically unchanging tone as a foil, Beiderbecke relied for expressiveness on pitch choice, pacing, and rhythmic placement (as opposed to Louis Armstrong, who systematically used variety of timbre). Beiderbecke also improvised at the piano and wrote a few piano pieces, such as *In a Mist* and *Flashes*, which reflect certain aspects of impressionism; however, his cornet playing, nearly always in settings over which he had no control, had to conform to the harmonic usages of contemporary jazz and popular music. His playing was largely diatonic with sparing use of nondiatonic 9ths and 13ths as well as the lowered 3rds and 7ths common to jazz. By avoiding harmonically functional chromatic pitches his improvisations often seemed to transcend the ordinary harmonic progressions of their accompaniment without contradicting them, as exemplified in his solo on *Royal Garden Blues* of 1927 (ex. 1). This characteristic, together with his unique timbre, gave his work a restrained, introspective manner and often set his playing apart from its surroundings.

Ex.1 Solo from *Royal Garden Blues* (1927, OK 8544), transcr. J. Dapogny

Beiderbecke's originality caused him to be one of the first white jazz musicians admired by black performers; Louis Armstrong recognized in him a kindred spirit, and Rex Stewart reproduced some of his solos exactly on recordings. Beiderbecke's influence was decisive on such white players as Red Nichols and Bunny Berigan. Although he was largely unknown to the general public at the time of his death, he acquired an almost legendary aura among jazz musicians and enthusiasts; on account of such popularized accounts of his life as Dorothy Baker's highly romanticized biography *Young Man with a Horn* (1938), he soon came to symbolize the "Roaring Twenties" in the popular imagination. Only in recent years has legend been sufficiently sifted from fact to put Beiderbecke's career and achievement into a balanced perspective.

RECORDINGS

(selective list)

As leader: In a Mist (Bixology) (1927, OK 40916); At the Jazz Band Ball/Jazz Me Blues (1927, OK 40923); Royal Garden Blues (1927, OK 8544); Since My Best Girl Turned Me Down (1927, OK 41001); Louisiana (1928, OK 41173)

As sideman with F. Trumbauer: Singin' the Blues (1927, OK 40772); Riverboat Shuffle (1927, OK 40822); I'm Coming Virginia (1927, OK 40843); Blue River (1927, OK 40879); Humpty Dumpty (1927, OK 40926)

As sideman with others: Wolverine Orchestra: Jazz Me Blues (1924, Gennett 5408); P. Whiteman: Dardanella (1928, Vic. 25238)

BIBLIOGRAPHY

D. Baker: *Young Man with a Horn* (Boston, 1938)

E. Nichols: "Bix Beiderbecke," *Jazzmen*, ed. F. Ramsey, Jr. and C. E. Smith (New York, 1939/*R*1977), 143

G. Johnson: "The Wolverines and Bix," *Frontiers of Jazz*, ed. R. de Toledano (New York, 1947, 2/1962)

N. Shapiro and N. Hentoff, eds.: *Hear me Talkin' to ya* (New York, 1955/*R*1966), 132ff

B. James: *Bix Beiderbecke* (London, 1959); repr. in *Kings of Jazz*, ed. S. Green (New York, 1978)

——: *Essays on Jazz* (London, 1961), 96ff

B. Green: *The Reluctant Art* (London, 1962), 18ff

R. Hadlock: *Jazz Masters of the Twenties* (New York, 1965)

G. Schuller: *Early Jazz: its Roots and Musical Development* (New York, 1968), 187ff

M. Williams: *The Jazz Tradition* (New York, 1970, rev. 2/1983)

V. Castelli and others: *The Bix Bands: a Bix Beiderbecke Disco-biography* (Milan, 1972)

R. Berton: *Remembering Bix* (New York, 1974)

A. McCarthy: *Big Band Jazz* (London, 1974), 72ff

R. M. Sudhalter and P. R. Evans: *Bix: Man and Legend* (New Rochelle, NY, 1974)

J. P. Perhonis: *The Bix Beiderbecke Story: the Jazz Musician in Legend, Fiction, and Fact* (diss., U. of Minnesota, 1978)

JAMES DAPOGNY/J. BRADFORD ROBINSON

Beissel [Beisel], **(Johann) Conrad** [Konrad] (*b* Eberbach, Germany, 1 March 1691; *d* Ephrata, PA, 6 July 1768). Composer and hymnodist. He was apprenticed as a boy to a baker who was a musician, from whom he learned violin. After his conversion to Pietism in 1715 his religious views incurred the displeasure of church authorities; he immigrated to America in 1720 and settled among some German Baptists in Germantown, Pennsylvania. In 1732 he moved to Ephrata, where he took the name Father Friedsam and founded a semimonastic community which became the EPHRATA CLOISTER.

Beissel was a prolific writer with a literary style that was mystical, metaphorical, erotically symbolic, and filled with scriptural allusions. Three of his hymn collections were published by Benjamin Franklin (1730, 1732, 1736), and Christopher Sauer issued his *Zionitischer Weyrauchs Hügel* (1739), a large collection of hymns and other poetry (including some European authors). After a quarrel with Sauer, Beissel obtained his own printing press, which became, next to Sauer's, the most important colonial German press. *Das Gesäng der einsamen und verlassenen Turtel-Taube* (1747) was the first major hymnal from the Ephrata press: like the earlier hymnals, it contains only texts, but whereas the earlier books listed standard European hymn tunes, this and subsequent Ephrata hymnals adopted Beissel's own melodies.

Beissel developed his own method for singing and composition, outlined in the "Verrede über die Sing-Arbeit" ("Foreword on the art of singing") in the *Turtel-Taube*, from one of his followers, Edward Blum. He took the tonic triad as the center of any given tonality, designating the tones of that triad as "masters" and the remaining tones of the scale as "servants";

accented or concluding syllables of verses usually fell on a "master" tone, unaccented ones on a "servant." Beissel's rules for harmonization take as their foundation the soprano line rather than the bass, which often results in extensive parallel movement; while dominant–tonic progressions are common at cadences, other chord progressions are random. Rhythms closely follow the accentuation of the words, but without establishing a set metrical relation between long and short notes, thus creating unusual metric flexibility.

The *Paradisisches Wunder-Spiel* (1754) is the only Ephrata publication to include music; since the community press lacked musical type, the notation was entered by hand. The *Wunder-Spiel* contains 49 pieces, most of which are for four voices, though some are in as many as seven parts. (A second *Wunder-Spiel*, published in 1766, included only texts, taken primarily from earlier Ephrata hymnals.) Musical production at Ephrata ceased about 1762, and the community declined after Beissel's death in 1768. The unique nature of the music limited its performance almost exclusively to the community itself, and even the hymn texts by Beissel and his followers found only limited acceptance among Pennsylvania Germans. A few are in German tunebooks published by Joseph Doll (1810), Johannes Rothbaust (1821), and Michael Bentz (1827), and 43 are in the Harmony Society's *Gesangbuch* (1827), but not with the Ephrata tunes.

WORKS

Collection: [*10*] *Ephrata Cloister Chorales*, ed. R. P. Getz (New York, 1971)

Das Gesäng der einsamen und verlassenen Turtel-Taube (Ephrata, PA, 1747)
Paradisisches Wunder-Spiel (Ephrata, 1754)
Hymns in: Göttliche Liebes und Lobes gethöne (Philadelphia, 1730); Vorspiel der Neuen-Welt (Philadelphia, 1732); Jacobs Kampff- und Ritter-Platz (Philadelphia, 1736); Zionitischer Weyrauchs Hügel (Germantown, PA, 1739); Nachklang zum Gesäng der einsamen Turtel-Taube (Ephrata, 1755); Neuvermehrtes Gesäng der einsamen Turtel-Taube (Ephrata, 1762)

BIBLIOGRAPHY

Lamech and Agrippa: *Chronicon ephratense* (Ephrata, PA, 1786; Eng. trans. J. M. Hark, 1889/*R*1972)
J. F. Sachse: *The Music of the Ephrata Cloister* (Lancaster, PA, 1903/*R*1971)
P. S. Leinbach: "Beissel, Johann Conrad," *DAB*
W. C. Klein: *Johann Conrad Beissel, Mystic and Martinet* (Philadelphia, 1942)
H. T. David: "Hymns and Music of the Pennsylvania Seventh-day Baptists," *American-German Review*, ix/5 (1943), 4
E. E. Doll and A. M. Funke: *The Ephrata Cloisters: an Annotated Bibliography* (Philadelphia, 1944)
L. G. Blakely: "Johann Conrad Beisel and Music of the Ephrata Cloister," *JRME*, xv (1967), 120
O. Kilian: "Konrad Beissel (1691–1768): Founder of the Ephrata Cloister in Pennsylvania," *Bach: the Quarterly Journal of the Riemenschneider Bach Institute*, vii (1976), no.3, p.25; no.4, p.31; viii/1 (1977), 23
L. A. Viehmeyer: *First-line Index to Ephrata Hymody* (unpubd computerized index, *OYU*)

EDWARD C. WOLF

Belafonte, Harry [Harold George] (*b* New York, 1 March 1927). Popular singer and actor. He lived in Kingston, Jamaica, for five years (1935–40), returning to New York in 1940. In 1945 he began a career as an actor, having studied in Erwin Piscator's drama workshop at the New School of Social Research. He experienced greater commercial success, however, as a popular singer, making his début at the Royal Roost, New York, in 1949. The following year he rejected his popular song repertory and began to sing traditional melodies from Africa, Asia, America, and the Caribbean, which he collected in folk-music archives. Having secured an RCA recording contract in 1952, Belafonte went on to become the most popular "folk" singer in the USA. His interpretations of Trinidadian calypso music between 1957 and 1959 won him his greatest success and marked the pinnacle of his career. His mass appeal through the 1950s, moreover, enabled him to resume his work as an actor, and he appeared in several motion pictures. During the 1960s and 1970s his popularity waned, but he continued to record, and to perform in nightclubs and theaters for a predominantly white, middle-class audience. In 1976 and again in 1979 he made world tours, performing his folk-inspired songs for large crowds of dedicated followers.

BIBLIOGRAPHY

"Belafonte, Harry," *CBY 1956*
D. Cerulli: "Belafonte: the Responsibility of an Artist," *Down Beat*, xxiv (1957), no.5, p.17; no.6, p.14; no.7, p.17
A. Shaw: *Belafonte; an Unauthorized Biography* (New York, 1960)
"Harry Belafonte," *Variety* (25 April 1976), 54

RONALD M. RADANO

Belasco, David (*b* San Francisco, CA, 25 July 1853; *d* New York, 14 May 1931). Playwright. After making his début as an actor for a repertory theater in California (1871) he became a prolific and highly successful playwright and director. He wrote over 50 plays and produced over 350 for theaters on Broadway and stock companies. In March 1900 *Madame Butterfly*, his adaptation of a magazine story by John Luther Long, scored a tremendous hit at the Herald Square Theater, New York. A few weeks later Belasco took his production of *Madame Butterfly* to London, where it was seen that summer by Puccini, in London for the English première of *Tosca*. The composer decided immediately to make *Butterfly* the subject of his next opera. While visiting New York early in 1907 for the first performance of *Madama Butterfly* at the Metropolitan Opera, Puccini saw three of Belasco's plays in a search for a suitable operatic subject. These included *The Girl of the Golden West*, which had first been produced at Pittsburgh in 1905. Although not as struck by this as he had been by *Butterfly*, Puccini decided to adapt it as *La fanciulla del West*, which received its world première at the Metropolitan in December 1910. Belasco published a two-volume autobiography, *My Life's Story*, in 1915.

ELIZABETH FORBES

Belasco, F. *See* ROSENFELD, MONROE H.

Belcher, Supply (*b* Stoughton, MA, 29 March 1752; *d* Farmington, ME, 9 June 1836). Composer and tunebook compiler. He began a career as a merchant in Boston, but by 1776 was back in his home town, where he purchased a farm and operated a tavern; he was also a member of the Stoughton Musical Society. In 1785 he and his family moved to Maine and spent six years in Hallowell (now Augusta). A local newspaper reported in 1796, of a public ceremony marking the Hallowell Academy's first year of operation: "The exercises were enlivened by vocal and instrumental music under the direction of Mr. Belcher, the 'Handel of Maine'." Belcher then settled in Farmington, where he spent the rest of his life. He played a leading role in the community, as town clerk, magistrate, representative to the state government, selectman, and schoolmaster, and was also known as a violinist and singer; he is said to have organized the town's first choir.

Almost all Belcher's 60-odd published compositions appear in his tunebook *The Harmony of Maine* (Boston, 1794/*R*1972), devoted entirely to his own music. In 1797 he brought out a smaller work including the *Ordination Anthem* and "a number of other fuging pieces, never before published," but no copies have been located. His music is rooted in New England psalmody, yet shows other modern stylistic influences. Several of his pieces are in three rather than four voices, and move the melody from the tenor to the treble voice. Several more set secular texts, often with copious melodic ornamentation and even appoggiaturas (for example, "Invitation"). Unusually frequent and precise performance directions ("Crescendo," "Divoto," "Vigoroso," "Pianissimo") suggest that Belcher was a demanding leader. He was a talented, communicative composer, though his music was not popular and was never widely reprinted.

BIBLIOGRAPHY

F. Butler: *History of Farmington, Franklin County, Maine* (Farmington, 1885), 378

F. J. Metcalf: *American Writers and Compilers of Sacred Music* (New York, 1925/ *R*1967), 83

E. Owen: *The Life and Music of Supply Belcher* (diss., Southern Baptist Theological Seminary, 1969)

RICHARD CRAWFORD

Belknap, Daniel (*b* Framingham, MA, 9 Feb 1771; *d* Pawtucket, RI, 31 Oct 1815). Composer, tunebook compiler, and singing master. He received a common-school education, then worked in his native town as a farmer and a mechanic, also teaching singing-schools from the time he was 18. He married around 1800, then in 1812 moved to Pawtucket.

Almost all his 86 known compositions were first printed in his own tunebooks, an exception being his most widely published piece, "Lena," which was introduced in *The Worcester Collection* (Boston, 5/1794). Belknap's *The Harmonist's Companion* (Boston, 1797), a brief 32-page collection, contains only his own compositions, which are written in an American idiom untouched by European-inspired reform. His later compilations, *The Evangelical Harmony* (Boston, 1800), *The Middlesex Collection* (Boston, 1802), and *The Village Compilation* (Boston, 1806), are devoted almost entirely to American music; they include pieces by Massachusetts composers such as Bartholomew Brown, Joseph Stone, and Abraham Wood, as well as many of his own pieces. Unlike many of his fellow psalmodists, Belknap also wrote secular music. His compilation *The Middlesex Songster* (Dedham, 1809) contains *Belknap's March*, his only known instrumental composition.

BIBLIOGRAPHY

Vital Records of Framingham, Massachusetts, to 1850 (Boston, 1911)

Vital Records of Carlisle, Massachusetts, to the End of the Year 1849 (Salem, MA, 1918), 70

F. J. Metcalf: *American Writers and Compilers of Sacred Music* (New York, 1925/ *R*1967), 146

R. J. Wolfe: *Secular Music in America 1801–1825: a Bibliography* (New York, 1964)

RICHARD CRAWFORD

Belknap, Frank. Pseudonym under which HENRY F. GILBERT published songs.

Bell, Thom (*b* Philadelphia, 27 Jan 1943). Record producer, arranger, and songwriter. In the 1960s he worked as a pianist for Cameo Records in Philadelphia, and was a member of the group Kenny Gamble and the Romeos; Gamble later became Leon Huff's production partner, and Bell collaborated with them on a number of projects. Bell had his first success as an independent record producer in 1968 with the Delfonics' *La la means I love you* (no.4), and two years later was responsible for another of their hits, *Didn't I blow your mind this time* (no.10, 1970). He went on to create the refined, silky pop-soul sound of the Stylistics, who, like the Delfonics, made prominent use of falsetto in crooning ballads such as *You are everything* (no.9, 1971) and *Betcha by golly, wow* (no.3, 1972). Bell's melodic style was heavily indebted to Burt Bacharach, and his sparkling orchestrations, using strings, woodwind, horns, and delicately scored percussion, were among the most ingenious quasi-symphonic, pop-soul arrangements of the 1970s. His equally fine work with the Spinners (including *I'll be around*, no.3, 1972; and *They just can't stop it*, no.5, 1975) featured intricate vocal harmonies and a more sinewy sound. In the late 1970s Bell produced a three-song EP with Elton John and in the early 1980s he collaborated with Deniece Williams in the writing and producing of two of her albums, *My Melody* (1981) and *Niecy* (1982).

BIBLIOGRAPHY

SouthernB

STEPHEN HOLDEN

Bellamann, Henry [Heinrich] **(Hauer)** (*b* Fulton, MO, 28 April 1882; *d* New York, 16 June 1945). Author, pianist, and teacher. He attended Westminster College in Fulton (1899–1900) and the University of Denver (1900–03), and then continued his studies in London and New York, and in Paris, where he worked with Isidore Philipp (piano) and Charles Widor (organ and composition). He was dean of the School of Fine Arts at Chicora College for Women in Columbia, South Carolina (1907–24), where he developed a reputation as a pianist and expert on modern French music. He was chairman of the examining board of the Juilliard School (1924–6) and dean of the Curtis Institute (1931–2). Bellamann composed a piano concerto, chamber music, and choral works. His literary output includes several novels (*King's Row*, the most successful of them, was later adapted as a film), some volumes of poetry, and articles on music (in *Musical Quarterly* and other journals). He was one of the first to write and lecture on the music of Ives (Ives set two of Bellamann's poems, *Yellow Leaves* and *Peaks*).

BIBLIOGRAPHY

P. Pathun: "*Concord*, Charles Ives, and Henry Bellamann," *Student Musicologists at Minnesota*, vi (1975–6), 66

PAULA MORGAN

Bellison, Simeon (*b* Moscow, Russia, 4 Dec 1883; *d* New York, 4 May 1953). Clarinetist. He learned first from his father, and at nine was playing in bands conducted by him. From 1894 to 1901 Bellison studied under Joseph Friedrich at the Moscow Imperial Academy. He was first clarinet for the opera orchestras in Moscow (1904–14) and St. Petersburg (1915). During the Russo-Japanese War and World War I he was in the army. In 1920 he settled in the USA and was first clarinet in the New York PO from 1920 to 1948. He organized and played in several ensembles, including Zimro (which toured the Far East, the USA, and Canada, 1917–20) and the Clarinet Ensemble (75 players, formed in 1927 to tour the USA). Bellison had a high reputation as a teacher in Russia and the USA. He published many arrangements for clarinet, and wrote articles for *The Clarinet* (nos.9–12, 1952–3); he also wrote a novel, *Jivoglot*.

BIBLIOGRAPHY

W. King: *The Philharmonic-Symphony Orchestra of New York* (New York, 1939)

PAMELA WESTON/R

Bellringing. The art of bellringing was brought to the USA from England and the Low Countries, and is found in all three of its main aspects: change ringing on swinging bells, the playing of carillons (stationary bells), and handbell ringing. European techniques were adopted for change ringing and for playing carillons and have remained effectively unchanged, but a distinctive American style of handbell ringing has evolved and there is a large body of American music for handbells. The first active ring (or set of bells used in change ringing) was installed in Christ Church (or Old North Church), Boston, in 1744. The first tower peal (a sequence of "changes" or patterns in which the order of sounding of the bells is altered systematically from one pattern to the next, and no pattern recurs) was rung in Philadelphia by the handbell ringers brought to the USA by P. T. Barnum in 1844; the peal consisted of 5040 changes. Interest in this kind of ringing (which was borrowed from the English practice of change ringing) waned after the Civil War, but was revived at the end of the 19th century by Arthur Nichols at Old North Church and elsewhere. Another revival took place in the 1960s, initiating an increase in the number of towers with swinging bells. In 1985 there were 18 operable rings in the USA, most of which were installed after 1960; the National Cathedral in Washington, DC (1964, ten bells), is among the most active centers for change ringing. The North American Guild of Change Ringers was formed in 1971 and the following year began publication of a quarterly newsletter, *The Clapper*.

The first carillon in the USA came from France and was installed at Notre Dame University in 1856; the second was erected in 1895 at Iowa State College. It was not until the 1920s that carillons became more prevalent. By 1985, however, there were nearly 200, of which 30 have 50 or more bells: the carillon at the University of Kansas (see illustration) has, for example, 53, that at Kirk in the Hills, Bloomfield Hills, Michigan, has 77, that at Riverside Church, New York, 74, and the instrument at the University of Chicago, 72. Eight carillons include bells by Meneely of Troy, New York, which were cast between 1919 and 1941, though all other bells have come from English, French, and Dutch foundries. The early carillonneurs also came from Europe. Several American players studied with the Belgian master Kamiel LeFevere, who played the carillon in Cohasset, Maine, and later that in Riverside Church, and to whom belongs much of the credit for the popularity of the carillon in the USA. Other prominent carillonneurs include James Lawson (Riverside Church) and Percival Price (University of Michigan). American interest was also stimulated by the writings of William Gorham Rice. The Guild of Carillonneurs in North America was founded at Ottawa in 1936, and the University of Michigan introduced the carillon as a degree subject in music performance, under Price, in 1939; an annual carillon festival was begun in the early 1960s. Electronic carillons, which have a similar sound to that of the true instrument, are manufactured in the USA by Schulmerich of Sellersville, Pennsylvania, and are very widely used.

From about 1840 teams of handbell ringers began to tour the eastern USA, and for a while many of these flourished in the Chautauqua programs and on vaudeville circuits. An amateur team was founded in Boston in 1895 by Nichols, and his daughter Margaret Shurcliff organized the Beacon Hill Ringers there in 1923. She established the New England Guild in 1937 and was influential in the formation of the American Guild of English Handbell Ringers in 1954 (*c*6500 members in 1985). In the 1940s Scott Parry and Doris Watson of Brick Presbyterian Church, New York, began to incorporate handbell ringing into services; American churches have since played a large part in spreading the popularity of handbell ringing. Other factors contributing to the increase of interest in the art have been the annual festival held since 1954 and the tours and broadcast performances of professional teams such as the Spartan Ringers of Michigan State University. Ringing is practiced in many schools and has been successfully used in music therapy. A large amount of material is now published for handbells, including original compositions, arrangements, and instruction manuals, and the journal *Overtones*. Handbells (usually in two- to five-octave sets – tuned respectively g to g'' and C to c'''') are manufactured in the USA by Schulmerich, and Malmark of New Britain, Pennsylvania.

World War II memorial bell tower (1951) at the University of Kansas

With the greater popularity of handbell ringing, new playing techniques and adaptations of older ones have been introduced to bring variety to the sweet, pure sound of the bells: swinging, shaking, plucking (in which the clapper is struck against the bell with the fingers), martellato (in which the mouth of the bell is struck on a padded table to create a strong, percussive effect), and precision damping (though some bellmasters prefer minimal damping so that the characteristic reverberation is heard). Variety may also be obtained by solo ringing.

BIBLIOGRAPHY

Meneely Bells (Troy, NY, 1920)

W. G. Rice: *Carillon Music and Singing Towers of the Old World and the New* (New York, 1925)

S. N. Coleman: *Bells: their History, Legends, Making, and Uses* (Chicago and New York, 1928/*R*1971)

S. B. Parry: *The Story of Handbells* (Boston, 1957)

M. H. Shurcliff: "English Bells," *Old-time New England*, xlix (1959), 57

E. Hatch: *The Little Book of Bells* (New York, 1964)

W. G. Wilson: *Change Ringing: the Art and Science of Change Ringing on Church and Hand Bells* (New York, 1965)

L. E. Springer: "The Search for Americana," *The Collector's Book of Bells* (New York, 1972), 115–46

——: *That Vanishing Sound* (New York, 1976)
B. Ashurst: "Bells as Folk Music," *College Music Symposium*, xix (1979), 30
E. Bradford: *The First Quarter-century, '54–'79* (Wilmington, DE, 1979)
R. C. Gruen: "Change Ringing on Tower and Handbells," *Overtones*, xxv (1979), 15
R. E. Coughlin: "The Practice of Change Ringing in the United States: the Historical Record," *The Clapper*, viii (1980), 9
R. H. von Grabow, ed.: *Directory: Carillons in North America* (Ottawa, rev. 1981)
D. Allured: *Musical Excellence in Handbells* (Nashville, 1982)

ELLEN JANE LORENZ

Bellson [Balassoni], **Louis (Paul)** (*b* Rock Falls, IL, 26 July 1924). Jazz drummer, bandleader, and composer. He won a nationwide drumming contest sponsored by Gene Krupa in 1940, and played professionally with Benny Goodman when he was only 17. From 1946, after military service, he quickly became a leading big-band drummer, playing with Goodman, Tommy Dorsey, Harry James, Count Basie, and especially Duke Ellington (1951–3), who performed some of Bellson's early arrangements. After leaving Ellington he led his own big bands and performed frequently with his wife, the singer Pearl Bailey.

Bellson's excellent, precise technique and flamboyant solo style have placed him, with Buddy Rich, among the foremost big-band drummers of the post-swing period. He is particularly known for his tight ensemble playing and his virtuoso control of two pedal-operated bass drums, a technique he ascribes to his childhood training as a tap dancer. Besides contributing many of the scores for his bands, he has also composed a jazz ballet, *The Marriage Vows* (1962), and other pieces for jazz groups and symphony orchestra.

RECORDINGS
(selective list)

As leader: *Louis Bellson Quintet* (1954, Norgran EPN 70-3); *The Dynamic Drums of Louis Bellson* (1968, Col. TW0322); *Dynamite!* (1979, Conc. 105)
As sideman with Duke Ellington: *Duke Ellington's Coronets* (1951, Mercer 1005); *Ellington Uptown* (1952, Col. ML4639)

BIBLIOGRAPHY

P. Willard: "Louis Bellson," *Down Beat*, xliii/11 (1976), 12
Z. Knauss: *Conversations with Jazz Musicians* (Detroit, 1977), 2

J. BRADFORD ROBINSON

Bellstedt, Herman (*b* Bremen, Germany, 21 Feb 1858; *d* San Francisco, CA, 8 June 1926). Bandmaster, cornetist, composer, and arranger. He immigrated to the USA with his family in 1867, and settled in Cincinnati in 1872. He studied music with his father and with Mylius Weigand, and was acclaimed as a prodigy when he first performed a cornet solo in public at the age of 15. A year later he joined the Cincinnati Reed Band, with which he continued to play until 1879. He then became cornet soloist with the Red Hussar Band at Manhattan Beach, New York, and for this ensemble wrote many cornet solos. He rejoined the Cincinnati Reed Band in 1883. From 1889 to 1891 he was soloist with the Gilmore Band; by this time his reputation equaled that of his contemporaries William Paris Chambers and Jules Levy. He returned once again to Cincinnati, and in 1892 he founded the Bellstedt-Ballenger Band, with which he appeared as conductor and cornet soloist. In 1904 he joined the Sousa Band, alternating as soloist with Herbert L. Clarke and Walter Rogers, but he left Sousa in 1906 to join Innes's Band as soloist and assistant conductor. He directed the Denver Municipal Band from 1909 to 1912. In 1913 he became professor of wind instruments at the Cincinnati Conservatory, where he won respect as a teacher and numbered among his students Frank Simon, who also played with Sousa. Bellstedt composed works for piano, violin, orchestra, and band, and is best known for his cornet solos *La mandolinata* and *Napoli*. The Heritage of the March series of recordings (compiled by ROBERT HOE, JR.), subseries 31, includes a sample of his work.

BIBLIOGRAPHY

F. R. Seltzer: "Famous Bandmasters in Brief," *Jacobs' Band Monthly*, iv/3 (1919), 14
G. D. Bridges: *Pioneers in Brass* (Detroit, 1965), 6

RAOUL CAMUS

Belmont Music Publishers. Firm of music distributors and publishers. It was founded in Los Angeles in the early 1960s by Gertrud and Lawrence Schoenberg, wife and son of the composer, to make Schoenberg's music more readily available in the USA. In addition to publishing his music, Belmont distributes European editions of Schoenberg's works (among them those of Universal Edition, Schott, and Faber & Faber) and hires out parts. The firm also deals in editions of his theoretical writings and offers slides of his works of art.

FRANCES BARULICH

Belmonts. Rock-and-roll vocal group led by DION.

Belt, Philip R(alph) (*b* Hagerstown, IN, 2 Jan 1927). Fortepiano maker. He began his career as a piano technician and repairer in a music store at New Castle, Indiana, where he experimented with thin wire. He was first inspired to make reproductions of early pianos by seeing an illustration of an instrument by the German maker Johann Andreas Stein (1728–92) and examining an antique German square piano. While apprenticed to Frank Hubbard (1965–7) he made his first replica of the fortepiano by the Flemish maker Johan Lodewijk Dulcken (i) (formerly attributed to Stein) at the Smithsonian Institution, on which he based nine instruments. In 1966 he established his own workshop in Center Conway, New Hampshire, which later moved to Battle Ground, Indiana (1971), Pawcatuck, Connecticut (1978), and New Haven (1982). He was also associated with Zuckermann Harpsichords (1975–9). After restoring the Stein instrument at the Toledo (Ohio) Museum of Art, Belt produced two Stein replicas, and in 1972 a Stein fortepiano kit. Following research in Europe (1973) he made five reproductions of fortepianos by the Austrian maker Anton Walter (1752–1826). Belt's thorough understanding of the principles of German and Viennese action is reflected in his instruments, which have a clear sound and a fluid touch. In the 1970s his pioneering replicas of the fortepiano helped to promote Classical keyboard performance practice in the USA.

BIBLIOGRAPHY

W. J. Zuckermann: *The Modern Harpsichord* (New York, 1969), 85f

MARIBEL MEISEL

Belwin-Mills. Firm of music publishers. Belwin, Inc., was founded in 1918 by Max Winkler, and Mills Music Publishers started a year later under the aegis of Jack and Irving Mills; the two organizations merged as the Belwin-Mills Publishing Corporation in 1969, with Martin Winkler as director. The company, located in Melville, New York, has become one of the most important publishers of educational music, producing many widely used piano series as well as a number of class band methods and material for teaching string instruments. The firm represents such composers as Arlen, Chávez, Creston, Crumb, Davidovsky, Dello Joio, Duke Ellington, Morton Gould, Krzysztof Penderecki, Sessions, Toch, and John Vincent, and also issues popular music. Divisions of the company include J. Fischer, H. W. Gray, McAfee Music, Musicord Publications, and Pro Art Publications. In 1973 it became sole distributor for Edward B. Marks Music and formed a joint venture between MCA Music and the Mills Music division of the company.

W. THOMAS MARROCCO, MARK JACOBS/R. ALLEN LOTT

Benary, Barbara (*b* Bay Shore, NY, 7 April 1946). Composer and gamelan performer. She studied at Sarah Lawrence College (BA 1968) and at Wesleyan University (MA, PhD in ethnomusicology, 1973). She has received a Woodrow Wilson dissertation fellowship (1972), a commission from the NEA (1981–2), and several Meet the Composer awards. Initially a violinist, she also plays string instruments of India, China, and Bulgaria. Her output includes several music-theater works, dance scores, and a sourcebook for improvisation, *System Pieces for a Droning Group* (1971). In 1974, using designs by Dennis Murphy, she built the Gamelan Son of Lion, an ensemble of Javanese instruments that includes traditional metallophones and gongs with hubcaps and food cans as resonators. She composed 25 works for this ensemble between 1975 and 1983, including *Gamelan NEA* (1982), composed in collaboration with Philip Corner, Daniel Goode, and Peter Griggs; some are in the style of traditional Javanese court music, and in others she has adapted the methods and aesthetics of the avant garde to ethnic instruments and has integrated contemporary forms and structures with traditional Javanese vocal and instrumental styles. *Braid*, written for the Gamelan Son of Lion, uses a 14-note sequence within interlocking rhythmic structures; in *Sleeping Braid* this becomes the subject of a canon. Several of her gamelan pieces have been recorded.

WORKS

Gamelan: Convergence, 1975; Braid, 1975; No Friends in an Auction, 1976; In Time Enough, 1978; Sleeping Braid (B. Benary), female v, gamelan insts, 1979; The Zen Story (K. Maue), female v, gamelan, 1979; In Scrolls of Leaves (anon.), 2 female vv, gamelan insts, 1980; Moon Cat Chant, 1980; Singing Braid, 1980; Solkattu, 1980; Sun Square, 1980; Exchanges, 1981; Gamelan NEA, collab. Corner, Goode, Griggs, 1982; Hot-rolled Steel, 1984; others

Music-theater: 3 Sisters who are not Sisters (Stein), 1967, Paramus, NJ, 1967; The Only Jealousy of Emer (1, Yeats), 1970, New York, 1970; The Interior Castle (3, J. Braswell), 1973, Bronxville, NY, 1973; The Gauntlet (2, Braswell), 1976, New York, 1976; Sanguine (Braswell), 1976, New York, 1976; The Tempest (Shakespeare), 1981, New York, 1981; a few others

Dance scores: Night Thunks, 1980; A New Pantheon, 1981; Engineering, 1981; Mas Damn, 1981; others

Other: System Pieces for a Droning Group, sourcebook of 15 pieces for vocal and percussion improvisation, 1971; Exlasega, sym. band, 1981; music for puppet shows, 1977–81

BIBLIOGRAPHY

T. Johnson: "Barbara Benary brings Java to Jersey," *Village Voice* (17 July 1976)
Zummo: "Benary Builds Gamelan," *Soho Weekly News* (19 May 1977)
J. Rockwell: "Recordings: the Gentle Magic of Javanese Gamelan," *New York Times* (12 Aug 1979)
T. Johnson: "Composers in Collaboration," *Village Voice* (1 June 1982)

STEPHEN RUPPENTHAL

Benét, Stephen Vincent (*b* Bethlehem, PA, 22 July 1898; *d* New York, 13 March 1943). Writer. He wrote poetry and prose with great facility, producing a wide variety of works – light verse, short stories, novels, essays, reviews, and long poems. Though their quality is uneven, they include several important works, notably the epic poem *John Brown's Body* (1928). Most of Benét's subjects come from American history or folklore. Among the many American composers who have been drawn to his poetry are Randall Thompson, Leslie Bassett, Gail Kubik, and Douglas Moore (who also set poems by Benét's brother William Rose Benét, 1886–1950). Moore was a lifelong friend of Benét's, and the two worked closely together on the one-act opera *The Devil and Daniel Webster*. This tale first appeared in 1936 as a short story in the *Saturday Evening Post*. Its spectacle of bringing the dead to life and the drama of its final courtroom scene make it excellent material for the stage. The opera version, first produced in 1939 by the American Lyric Theater in New York, met with considerable popular and critical success.

Simplicity, directness, and strong poetic rhythm are the qualities that make much of Benét's verse well suited for musical setting, particularly in traditional musical styles. These qualities are most evident in *A Book of Americans* (1933), a collection of 55 short poems for children by Benét and his wife, Rosemary Carr Benét. Several composers, including Josef Alexander, Earl George, Kubik, and Arnold Shaw, have written sets of pieces using selections from this book.

BIBLIOGRAPHY

C. A. Fenton: *Stephen Vincent Benét* (New Haven, 1958)
P. Stroud: *Stephen Vincent Benét* (New York, 1962)
M. Hovland: *Musical Settings of American Poetry: a Bibliography* (Westport, CT, in preparation) [incl. list of settings]

HOWARD NIBLOCK

Benge, Elden (*b* Winterset, IA, 12 July 1904; *d* Burbank, CA, 12 Dec 1960). Trumpeter and trumpet manufacturer. He studied cornet with William Eby, Vladimir Drucker, and Harold Mitchell. After playing in movie theater orchestras and recording studios in California he trained as first trumpet in the Chicago Civic Orchestra. He was first trumpeter with the Detroit SO (1929–30), and with the Chicago SO (1930–40). From then until 1952, he played with the Chicago PO and the radio station WGN staff orchestra. Benge made his first trumpet in 1937; in 1952 he moved to Burbank to devote himself exclusively to manufacturing. On his death the business passed to his son Donald (*b* Chicago, 4 Nov 1933). About 1971 it was bought by KING MUSICAL INSTRUMENTS; the plant was moved to Anaheim, California, and on its closure in 1983 to Eastlake, Ohio.

The firm produces over 20 models of trumpet (in B♭, C, D/E♭ and piccolo B♭/A), cornet and flugel horn. Like VINCENT BACH, Benge took the French Besson B♭ trumpet as his point of departure, but sought a more brilliant tone and more flexible intonation. Benge trumpets are very widely used, particularly on the West Coast, by trumpeters in symphony orchestras as well as in commercial entertainment.

EDWARD H. TARR

Bennett, Harold. Pseudonym of HENRY FILLMORE.

Bennett, Robert Russell (*b* Kansas City, MO, 15 June 1894; *d* New York, 18 Aug 1981). Orchestrator, conductor, and composer. He studied with Carl Busch in Kansas City (1912–15), with Nadia Boulanger in Paris (1926–31), and in Berlin and London. After working as a dance-band musician and as a copyist for New York publishers, in 1919 he was commissioned by the publishers T. B. Harms to orchestrate theatrical songs, the earliest including Cole Porter's *An Old Fashioned Garden* (1919). From the 1920s to the 1960s he was the leading orchestrator for

Broadway musicals; he scored some 300, among them the best-known works of Kern, Friml, Gershwin, Porter, Rodgers, Berlin, and Loewe. Bennett established standards that influenced other Broadway orchestrators during the period and raised the status of the orchestrator to equal that of the authors and composers of musical shows. From 1930 he worked in Hollywood film studios and from 1937 to 1940 was president of the American Society of Musical Arrangers. He was the recipient of numerous awards and honors, and wrote a book on orchestration, *Instrumentally Speaking* (1975).

There are many stylistic similarities between Bennett's original compositions and his Broadway arrangements. His concert works, which include several symphonies, concertos, and overtures, two operas, a ballet-operetta, and pieces for chamber groups and for wind band, often incorporate elements from various popular idioms, and his arrangements demonstrate a thorough grounding in symphonic techniques. The pieces for band, a medium for which he had a special affinity, are the most frequently performed of his original works. All his music shows a mastery of instrumentation, accompaniment, and countermelody, but his scoring is sometimes superior to his musical material. Although he thought he had a tendency to over-orchestrate, Bennett demonstrated a distinctive awareness of how to achieve the maximum effect with the minimum of resources, and to do so with an originality that widely influenced other professional arrangers.

WORKS
(selective list)

STAGE

Endymion (ballet-operetta), 1927; Maria Malibran (opera), 1935; The Enchanted Kiss (opera, 1), 1944

Orchestrations of musicals: Wildflower (V. Youmans), 1923; Rose Marie (R. Friml), 1924; Show Boat (J. Kern), 1927; Of thee I Sing (G. Gershwin), 1931; Anything Goes (C. Porter), 1934; Oklahoma! (R. Rodgers), 1943; Carmen Jones (after Bizet's Carmen), 1943; Annie Get your Gun (I. Berlin), 1946; Kiss me, Kate (Porter), 1948; South Pacific (Rodgers), 1949; The King and I (Rodgers), 1951; Pipe Dream (Rodgers), 1955; My Fair Lady (F. Loewe), collab. P. Lang, 1956; Flower Drum Song (Rodgers), 1958; The Sound of Music (Rodgers), 1959; Camelot (Loewe), collab. P. Lang, 1960

INSTRUMENTAL

Orch: Charlestown Rhapsody, 1926; Paysage, 1928; Sights and Sounds, 1929; March, orch, 2 pf, 1930; Abraham Lincoln Sym., 1931; Early American Ballade on Melodies of Stephen Foster, 1932; Variations on a Theme by Jerome Kern, 1933; Adagio eroico, 1935; Hollywood Scherzo, 1936; 8 études, 1938; Sym., D, 1941; Vn Conc., 1941; Four Freedoms Sym., 1943; Classic Serenade, str, 1945; Ov. to an Imaginary Drama, 1946; Sym., 1946; A Dry Legend, 1947; Pf Conc., 1948; Variations, vn, orch, 1949; Commemoration Sym., 1959; Conc., harp, vc, orch, 1960; Conc., vn, pf, orch, 1962; Sym., 1962; Gui Conc., 1970

Chamber: Vn Sonata, 1927; Org Sonata, 1929; Hexapoda, vc, vn, pf, 1940; A Song Sonata, 1947; Rose Variations, tpt, pf, 1955; Qnt, org, str qt, 1962; Org Sonata; Water Music, str qt

Wind band: Suite of Old American Dances, 1949; Conc. grosso, 1957; Ohio River Suite, 1959; West Virginia Epic, 1960; Kentucky, 1961; 3 Humoresques, perf. 1961; Zimmer's American Greeting, perf. 1974; Twain and the River (1977); Ov. to Ty, Tris and Willie

BIBLIOGRAPHY

EwenD
J. T. Howard: *Our American Music* (New York, 1931, rev. 4/1965)
R. R. Bennett: "Eight Bars and a Pencil," *New York Times* (7 June 1947)
——: "All I Know About Arranging Music," *International Musician*, xlvii/8 (1949), 9
H. W. Wind: "Another Opening, Another Show," *New Yorker*, xxvii (17 Nov 1951), 46
M. Goss: *Modern Music Makers* (New York, 1952), 181
"Man Behind the Tune," *Newsweek*, xlii (20 July 1953), 86
"Bennett, Robert Russell," *CBY 1962*
R. R. Bennett: "A Look at Music Arranging," *MJ*, xxii/3 (1964), 37
F. Fennell: "Basic Band Repertory: Suite of Old American Dances," *The Instrumentalist*, xxxiv/2 (1979), 28
Obituary, *New York Times* (19 Aug 1981)

RONALD BYRNSIDE/ROBERT SKINNER

Bennett, Tony [Benedetto, Anthony Dominick; Bari, Joe] (*b* New York, 3 Aug 1926). Popular singer. He sang with military bands during World War II and then studied singing with Miriam Spier at the American Theatre Wing school. He appeared on Arthur Godfrey's television shows "Talent Scouts" and "Songs for Sale" and was discovered by Bob Hope in 1950 while performing in a New York nightclub with Pearl Bailey; it was Hope who suggested he change his stage name from Joe Bari to Tony Bennett. Bennett signed a recording contract with Columbia Records in 1950 through the director of popular music, Mitch Miller, and had a series of hit singles that included *Boulevard of Broken Dreams* (1950), *Because of you* (1951), *Cold, Cold Heart* (1951), *Blue Velvet* (1951), and *Rags to Riches* (1953). In 1962, after a slump in his career attributable to the rise of rock-and-roll, Bennett returned to the charts with what became his signature song, *I left my heart in San Francisco*; this helped to establish him as a sophisticated, versatile popular stylist, and he went on to perform with swing bands as well as popular orchestras and to record with the jazz pianist Bill Evans.

In the early 1950s Bennett became one of the most popular male ballad singers in the romantic Italian-American bel canto tradition of Frank Sinatra. But unlike the young Sinatra and Vic Damone, who exemplified the same tradition, Bennett had a lyric baritone with a distinctively husky edge, which served him well as he matured into an increasingly jazz-oriented saloon singer. An admirer of classic jazz, he claims to have modeled his breathing and phrasing on the playing of the jazz pianist Art Tatum and his relaxed delivery on that of the singer Mildred Bailey.

BIBLIOGRAPHY

"Bennett, Tony," *CBY 1965*
W. Conover and others: "20 Years with Tony," *Billboard*, lxxx (30 Nov 1968), 1–40 [incl. discography]
W. Balliett: "A Quality that Lets you in," *New Yorker*, xlix (7 Jan 1974), 33

STEPHEN HOLDEN

Bennington College. Liberal arts college located in Bennington, Vermont. From its opening as a women's college in 1932, it has offered an experimental approach to education in which the visual and performing arts are of central importance. Kurt Schindler was Bennington's first director of music (1933–4). He was succeeded by Otto Luening, who remained at Bennington until 1944. Under Luening's directorship the college excelled in musical performance and was unique during the 1930s for the innovative concert programs it sponsored. Later it continued to attract distinguished performers and composers to its faculty. The institution began admitting men in 1969 and in 1982 had an enrollment of approximately 600. It offers the BA and MFA in music, and a strong program in black music.

BIBLIOGRAPHY

T. P. Brockway: *Bennington College: in the Beginning* (Bennington, VT, 1981)

NINA DAVIS-MILLIS

Benson, George (*b* Pittsburgh, PA, 22 March 1943). Jazz and pop guitarist and singer. From 1962 to 1965 he spent apprentice years with organist Jack McDuff, but otherwise has mainly led his own groups. In the 1960s he attracted attention in jazz circles for his speed and agility on the electric guitar, which he played in an original style based on that of Wes Montgomery and somewhat touched by rock-and-roll. Having established his jazz credentials (he even recorded with Miles Davis in 1968), Benson began in the early 1970s to make a series of commercially oriented jazz recordings for CTI which gained him a large popular audience. After leaving CTI for a contract with Warner Bros. his first recording, *Breezin'* (1976), elevated him to the status of a major pop star. Since then, he has issued a long succession of popular hits, but he has also returned occasionally to a jazz setting for club or recording engagements.

RECORDINGS
(selective list)

As leader: *Benson Burner* (1966–7, Col. 33569); *Giblet Gravy* (1967, Verve 68749); *Shape of Things* (1968, A&M 3014); *Beyond the Blue Horizon* (1971, CTI 6009); *White Rabbit* (1971, CTI 6015); *Breezin'* (1976, WB 3111); *Weekend in L.A.* (1977, WB 3139); *Give me the Night* (1980, WB HS3453)
As sideman: M. Davis: *Miles in the Sky* (1968, Col. CS9628)

BIBLIOGRAPHY

C. Mitchell: "Breezin' along with a Bullet," *Down Beat*, xliii/15 (1976), 16
L. Feather: "Superstar Update," *Down Beat*, xlv/7 (1978), 13
J. Sievert: "George Benson: Platinum Jazz," *Guitar Player*, xiii/7 (1979), 86
G. T. Simon: *The Best of the Music Makers* (New York, 1979)
L. Lyons: *The 101 Best Jazz Albums* (New York, 1980)
G. Giddins: *Riding on a Blue Note* (New York, 1981), 266ff

LEE JESKE

Benson, Joan (*b* St. Paul, MN, 9 Oct 1929). Keyboard player. After attending the University of Illinois (BM, MM 1951) and Indiana University (1953), she studied in Europe with Edwin Fischer, Messiaen, Viola Thern, and Guido Agosti. Her growing interest in early music and the clavichord led to further work with Fritz Neumeyer, Ruggero Gerlin, and Macario Santiago Kastner before she returned to the USA in 1960 following a tour of the Middle East. After a highly successful recording in 1962, Benson began concert appearances on the clavichord and, in time, the fortepiano. Her début on the clavichord was at the 1963 Carmel Bach Festival, where she played the American première of C. P. E. Bach's Freie Fantasie in F♯ minor, w67. Since 1965, she has made many concert and lecture tours of North America, Europe, and Asia and has performed on instruments of most of the major music collections. After teaching at Stanford University (1968–76), she accepted an appointment in 1976 at the University of Oregon and also joined the faculty of the Aston Magna Festival in 1980. Benson has been praised for unusually sensitive and stylish interpretations in concert and on recordings of a repertory that spans keyboard music from the Renaissance to the Viennese Classics and includes also contemporary works, some of which have been written for her. Her work has been crucial in the revival of interest in the fortepiano and the music of C. P. E. Bach.

BIBLIOGRAPHY

M. Bargreen: "Profile: Joan Benson, Clavichordist," *Clavier*, xix/10 (1980), 42

HOWARD SCHOTT

Benson, Warren (Frank) (*b* Detroit, MI, 26 Jan 1924). Composer and teacher. He studied music theory at the University of Michigan (BM 1949, MM 1951) but is essentially self-taught as a composer. He was timpanist with the Detroit SO in 1946. He has conducted and taught composition at Anatolia College in Salonica, Greece (1950–52, as a Fulbright scholar), Mars Hill (North Carolina) College (1952–3), Ithaca (New York) College (1953–67), where he organized the Ithaca College Percussion Ensemble, and the Eastman School (from 1967); he was also active in the Contemporary Music Project from its inception, developing its first pilot project. As a composer he has written especially successfully for percussion and wind ensembles and has received numerous commissions and awards, including a Guggenheim Fellowship (1981–2). His music is varied and selective in technique; lyricism is prominent in it, as is colorful instrumentation. He is the author of *Creative Projects in Musicianship* (1967) and *Compositional Processes and Writing Skills* (1974).

WORKS

Orch: A Delphic Serenade, 1953; 5 Brief Encounters, str, 1961; Theme and Excursions, str, 1963; Chants and Graces, str, pic, harp, perc, 1964; Bailando, 1965; Hn Conc., 1971; The Man with the Blue Guitar, 1980; Beyond Winter: Sweet Aftershowers, str, 1981; Concertino, fl, str, perc, 1983
Band: 8 works, incl. The Leaves are Falling, 1963; The Passing Bell, 1974; Sym. no.2 "Lost Songs," 1982
Wind ens: Concertino, a sax, wind, 1954; Sym., drums, wind orch, 1962; Recuerdo, ob/eng hn, wind, 1965; Star-edge, a sax, wind, 1965; Helix, tuba, wind, 1966; The Solitary Dancer, 1966; The Mask of Night, 1968; Shadow Wood (T. Williams), S, wind, 1971; The Beaded Leaf (A. Hecht), B, wind, 1974; Other Rivers, 1984; Wings, 1984
Perc: Variations on a Handmade Theme, 8 handclappers, 1957; Perc Trio, 1957; 3 Pieces, perc qt, 1960; Streams, 7 perc, 1961; 3 Dances, 1962; Rondino, 8 handclappers, 1967; Winter Bittersweet, 6 perc, 1981
Chamber: 15 pieces for solo inst, pf, 1951–66; Marche, ww qt, 1955; Qnt, ob/s sax, str, 1957; Wind Rose, sax qt, 1967; Str Qt, 1969; Capriccio, pf qt, 1972; The Dream Net, a sax, str qt, 1976; Largo Tah, b trbn, mar, 1977; Qnt, perc, str, 1984; other inst pieces
Choral: Psalm xxiv, SSAA, str, 1957; 27 pieces for SATB, incl. Songs of O, SATB, brass qnt, mar, 1974; Earth, Sky, Sea (K. Rexroth), SATB, fl, b trbn, mar, 1975; Meditation, Prayer and Sweet Hallelujah (E. Bullins), chorus, pf, 1979; A Song of Praise, SATB, 1983
Solo vocal: Nara (E. Birney), S, fl, pf, 2 perc, 1970; 5 Lyrics of Louise Bogan, Mez, fl, 1977; Songs for the End of the World (J. Gardner), Mez, eng hn, hn, vc, mar, 1980; Moon Rain and Memory Jane, song cycle, S, 2 vc, 1982; The Putcha Putcha Variations (Gardner), 1v, 1983; 8 others

MSS in *NRU-Mus*
Principal publishers: C. Fischer, MCA, E. C. Schirmer, Presser

BIBLIOGRAPHY

EwenD
R. Ricker: "Composer's Profile: Warren Benson," *Saxophone Symposium*, iv/1 (1979), 4
D. Hunsberger: "A Discussion with Warren Benson [about] *The Leaves are Falling*," *College Band Directors National Association Journal*, i/1 (1984), 7 [incl. list of wind compositions]

JERALD C. GRAUE/R

Bent [née Bassington], **Margaret (Hilda)** (*b* St. Albans, England, 23 Dec 1940). English musicologist. She studied at Girton College, Cambridge (BA 1962, MusB 1963, PhD 1969), working under Thurston Dart in her research on the Old Hall MS. She taught at Cambridge and London (from 1963), King's College, London (1965–75), and Goldsmiths' College (from 1972); in the USA she has been on the faculties of Brandeis University (1975–81) and Princeton University (from 1981). Much of her work on English music of the 14th and 15th centuries has grown out of her detailed study of the Old Hall MS, which she published with Andrew Hughes (1969–73); central to her research was a paleographic and diplomatic investigation of the manuscript and its concordances, which revealed its original plan. She has also worked extensively with French and Italian music of the same period. Her interests include manuscript studies, notation, performance-related matters such as *musica ficta* and word-setting, and problems of musical transmission. She is the author of *Dun-*

staple (1981). In 1983 she was elected president of the American Musicological Society.

DAVID SCOTT/PAULA MORGAN

Benton, Rita (*b* New York, 28 June 1918; *d* Paris, France, 23 March 1980). Musicologist and music librarian. She studied at the Juilliard School, taking a diploma in piano in 1938; she received the BA at Hunter College the following year. After graduate work in musicology at the University of Iowa (MA 1951, PhD 1961), where she became music librarian in 1953, she was appointed to the faculty of the department of music in 1967. She was president of the Music Library Association (1962–3) and editor of *Fontes artis musicae* (from 1976). Among Benton's interests was French music of the late 18th century. She endeavored to solve the difficult bibliographical problems associated with Ignace Pleyel, and published a thematic catalogue of his works (1977). Her translation (1970) of Frits Noske's *La mélodie française de Berlioz à Duparc* has been praised for the fluidity of its English and fidelity to the author's literary style. As a music librarian, she was active in the International Association of Music Libraries. Her four-volume *Directory of Music Research Libraries* provides a wealth of information about major library collections of music.

PAULA MORGAN

Benzell, Mimi (*b* Bridgeport, CT, 6 April 1922; *d* Manhasset, NY, 23 Dec 1970). Soprano. She studied at Hunter College, CUNY, and then under Olga Eisner at the Mannes College. She made her operatic début in 1944 in Mexico City, where she appeared as Zerlina and the Queen of Night, both under Sir Thomas Beecham. The latter role was also that in which she made her Metropolitan Opera début in 1945, under Bruno Walter; her other major roles at the Metropolitan included Gilda, Mozart's Blonde, Musetta, and Philine in *Mignon*. In 1949 she gave up her operatic career to concentrate on popular music, first in concerts and nightclubs and on radio and later in the musical theater. She is remembered primarily for her work in Jerry Herman's successful Broadway musical *Milk and Honey*, which ran from 1961 to 1963. Her few recordings, which include the role of Musetta, reveal a modest voice but a very distinctive timbre.

RICHARD LESUEUR

Beranek, Leo L(eroy) (*b* Solon, IA, 15 Sept 1914). Acoustician. He was educated at Cornell College (BA 1936) and Harvard University (MS 1937, DSc 1940). He taught physics and communication engineering at Harvard (1940–43); in 1947 he joined the faculty of the Massachusetts Institute of Technology. The following year he was a founder of the acoustical consulting firm Bolt, Beranek and Newman, of which he was president from 1953 to 1969, retiring in the early 1970s. Before writing his classic *Music, Acoustics and Architecture* (1962) Beranek traveled through 20 countries, listening and making measurements in many halls and interviewing acousticians and others. He was acoustic consultant for Fredric R. Mann Hall, Tel-Aviv, Israel (1957), the remodeling of the Tanglewood Music Shed (1960), Philharmonic Hall, New York (1962), the National Arts Centre, Ottawa (1969), the Musical Arts Center, Indiana University, Bloomington (1972), the Centro de Bellas Artes, San Juan, Puerto Rico (1981), and the reconstruction of the Filene Center at Wolftrap Farm Park, Vienna, Virginia (1984). Beranek's work is notable for its application of scientific method to room acoustics while keeping in view the aesthetic demands of music.

R. W. B. STEPHENS/PAULA MORGAN

Berberian, Cathy [Catherine] (*b* Attleboro, MA, 4 July 1925; *d* Rome, Italy, 6 March 1983). Singer. Varied training and early experience helped to equip this versatile artist: courses in mime, writing, and opera at Columbia University and New York University (1942–3); Hindu and Spanish dancing; work as soloist with an Armenian dance group and in summer repertory; and vocal study in Milan with Giorgina del Vigo. She made her début in Naples in 1957, at an Incontri Musicali concert. The following year, at a John Cage concert in Rome, she sang his *Aria with Fontana Mix*. Her American début was at the Berkshire Music Festival, in 1960, with Berio's *Circles* (she also taught singing at the Berkshire Music Center). In a series of works (notably *Circles*, *Sequenza III*, *Visage*, and *Recital I*) inspired by her vocal virtuosity, darting, witty intelligence, and vivid presence, LUCIANO BERIO (to whom she was married from 1950 to 1966) in effect limned the voices, styles, and temperament of this remarkable performer. The long list of composers who wrote for her includes Stravinsky (*Elegy for JFK*), Henze, and Haubenstock-Ramati. Her repertory embraced 17th-century opera, folksong of all countries, and the salon *morceaux* – ranging from exquisite miniatures to such *trouvailles* as Griepenkerl's vocal version of the "Moonlight" Sonata – gathered in her recital "Une Soirée chez Mme Verdurin." Her compositions include *Stripsody* for solo voice (1966) and *Morsicat(h)y* for piano (1971).

BIBLIOGRAPHY

D. J. Soria: "Artist Life," *HiFi/MusAm*, xx/7 (1970), 4
N. Soames: "Profile on Cathy Berberian," MO, xcix (1975–6), 210
——: "Cathy Berberian," *Music and Musicians*, xxvi/6 (1978), 8
Obituary, *New York Times* (8 March 1983)

ANDREW PORTER

Berezowsky [Berezovsky], **Nicolai** [Nikolay] **(Tikhonovich)** (*b* St. Petersburg [now Leningrad], Russia, 17 May 1900; *d* New York, 27 Aug 1953). Composer, conductor, and violinist. He studied at the court chapel in St. Petersburg (1908–16) and played the violin at the Saratov opera (1917–19) and the Bolshoi (1919–20). In 1920 he left the USSR; he studied violin with Robert Pollack in Vienna and in 1922 reached New York where he was a member of the New York PO (1923–9). In 1927 he held a fellowship to study composition with Goldmark and violin with Kochanski at the Juilliard School; he also conducted the Atwater Kent Radio Concerts (1926–7). In 1928 he became an American citizen. The following year he left the USA to live in Europe, but returned after two years and from 1935 to 1940 was a member of the Coolidge String Quartet; he was also assistant conductor at CBS radio (1932–6 and 1941–6). He received a grant from the National Institute of Arts and Letters (1944) and a Guggenheim Fellowship (1948). His style blended Russian folk melos, Rimsky-Korsakovian orchestral expertise, and mild dissonance. The palatable symphonies, championed by Koussevitzky, won immediate critical acclaim, as did the concertos introduced by Primrose and Piatigorsky. His children's opera *Babar the Elephant* was widely performed.

WORKS

Selective list; dates in parentheses are those of publication, others are those of first performance.

Orch: 4 syms., op.12, 1931, op.18, 1934, op.21, 1937, op.27, 1943; concs., for vn, op.14, 1930, vc (Conc. lirico), op.19, 1935, va, op.28, 1941, cl, op.29 (1941), harp, op.31, 1945, theremin (Passacaglia), 1948; Sinfonietta, op.17, 1932; Introduction and Allegro, small orch, op.8 (1945)

Vocal: Gilgamesh, cantata, nar, solo vv, chorus, orch, op.32, 1947; Babar the Elephant (children's opera, 1, D. Heyward), op.40, 1953

Chamber: Thème et variations, cl, str, pf, op.7, 1926; Str Qt, op.16 (1933); Duo, va, cl, op.15 (1941); Suite, wind qnt, op.22 (1941); Brass Suite, 7 brass, op.24 (1942); Fantasy, 2 pf, op.9 (1944); Sextet Conc., str, op.26 (1951)

Principal publishers: Boosey & Hawkes, Edition Russe

BIBLIOGRAPHY

Baker7; *EwenD*

J. T. Howard: *Our Contemporary Composers* (New York, 1941), 184

A. Berezowsky: *Duet with Nicky* (Philadelphia, 1943)

ROBERT STEVENSON

Berg, T. van. Pseudonym of CHARLES BALMER.

Berger, Arthur (Victor) (*b* New York, 15 May 1912). Composer. Between the ages of 11 and 16 he studied the piano, and his first compositions were written while he was in high school. From 1928 to 1930 he attended the City College of New York; he received his first formal instruction in composition at New York University (BS 1934). In these years he became acquainted with the avant garde (Ives, Varèse, Cowell) and joined the Young Composers Group, formed by Copland. As a fellowship student he enrolled in the Longy School of Music (1935–7) and concurrently attended Harvard (MA 1936), where he was taught by Piston, Davison, and Leichtentritt. During the years 1937–9 he studied in Paris with Boulanger. He then taught at Mills College (1939–42) and also studied composition with Milhaud, who helped him secure a commission to write a woodwind quintet for members of the San Francisco SO. Berger subsequently taught at Brooklyn College (1942–3), the Juilliard School, and Brandeis University (from 1953); in 1979 he became a member of the faculty of the New England Conservatory. Long active as a writer and editor, he has been music critic for the *Boston Transcript* (1943–7), *New York Sun* (1943–6), and *New York Herald Tribune* (1946–53); served as editor of the *Musical Mercury* (1934–7) and *Perspectives of New Music* (1962–3), of which he was a co-founder; and contributed articles to many journals, notably *Modern Music*, *Saturday Review*, *Atlantic Monthly*, *High Fidelity*, and *Score*. He also wrote a monograph on Copland (1953). Among his awards have been an American Council of Learned Societies grant (1936), a Fulbright scholarship (1960), an NEA grant (1967), and a Guggenheim Fellowship (1975–6). He is a member of the American Academy of Arts and Sciences and of the Institute of the American Academy and Institute of Arts and Letters.

While in Paris (1937–9) Berger's interest in Stravinsky's music was heightened, and this in turn had considerable influence on the development of his style, and led to the publication of several articles on Stravinsky's music. Berger is almost invariably categorized as a Stravinskian neoclassicist with regard to his music of the period 1940–57, and as a serial or post-Webern composer for his later works. Although he has admitted the early influence of Stravinsky and Schoenberg, particularly of the latter's *Die glückliche Hand* and Piano Suite op.25, it would be simplistic to classify him in this way, for he has developed his own procedures that lend special and highly effective qualities to his music. Paramount is a concern with musical space, both vertical and horizontal. To maintain the clarity of vertical pitch relationships he uses a lean, spare texture, whereas horizontal connections are delineated by wide-spaced leaps. In his vocabulary of linear procedures, 7ths and 9ths are commonplace and function normatively, as do conjunct intervals in traditional tonal music; they are not used "as a means of speaking in a raised voice" (Berger). Frequently interrupted, rhythmically fragmented lines also contribute to the openness of the textures. His concern with the structuring of musical space does not spring from an abstract interest, nor is it the result of formulaic manipulations; Berger believes simply that such treatment enhances the beauty of pitch relationships and sonorities.

During the early 1950s Berger's harmonic idiom was essentially diatonic, but because he often displaced the elements of chords, exploding them by means of fragmentation, vertical octave spacings, or delayed progression, his music hardly seemed diatonic. Comparisons with Webern undoubtedly stemmed from his use of such techniques, yet the diatonic skeleton provided a connection with Stravinskian neoclassicism; indeed, Babbitt used the term "diatonic Webern" in a review of the Duo for cello and piano (1951), and Berger himself hinted at a merging of the two styles in his work when he described the Chamber Music for 13 players (1956) as "neoclassic twelve-tone." His Five Pieces for piano (1969) display a sophisticated arsenal of procedures, including the use of combinatorial sets as well as refined techniques of pitch selection and of registration. In a number of works he has used a group of five source-trichords whose pitch classes provide vertical sonorities and, in a linear fashion, are arpeggiated as melodic fragments.

Since 1961, when he wrote the Three Pieces for two prepared pianos, Berger's music has tended to be less rigorously systematic in its serialism. In his words, "cells, often of a tone-cluster variety," are used to create vertical organization in which individual pitch classes are dispersed by means of widely shifting octave dispositions. Since 1958 his output has not been large; at the same time he has shown increasing stylistic independence. Having ended his reliance on dodecaphony and neoclassicism, he finds it necessary to derive new constraints and assumptions for each work in order to replace those previously provided by external procedures.

WORKS

Orch: 3 Pieces for Str Orch, 1945; Ideas of Order, 1952; Polyphony, 1956; Chamber Conc., 1960, 3rd movt rev. as Movt for Orch, 1964, 1st, 2nd, 3rd movts rev. as Perspectives I, II, III, 1978

Inst: Qt in C, fl, ob, cl, bn, 1941; Serenade concertante, vn, 11 insts, 1944, rev. 1951; 3 Pieces, str qt, 1945; 4 duos, vn, pf, 1948, vn, pf, 1950, vc, pf, 1951, ob, cl, 1952, arr. cl, pf, 1957; Chamber Music, 13 insts, 1956; Str Qt, 1958; Septet, fl, cl, bn, vn, va, vc, pf, 1965–6; Trio, gui, vn, pf, 1972; Pf Trio, 1980; Wind Qnt, 1984

Pf: 2 Episodes, 1933; Entertainment Pieces, ballet music, 1940; Fantasy, 1942; Rondo, 1945; Capriccio, 1945; 3 Bagatelles, 1946; Partita, 1947; Intermezzo, 1948; 4 Two-part Inventions, 1948–9; 3 One-part Inventions, 1954; 3 Pieces, 2 prepared pf, 1961; 5 Pieces, 1969; Composition, pf 4 hands, 1976; An Improvisation for A[aron] C[opland], 1981; Perspectives III, pf 4 hands, 1982 [arr. of orch work]

Vocal: Words for Music, Perhaps (3 Songs) (Yeats), S/Mez, (fl, cl, vc)/pf, 1939–40; Garlands (Askepiades), Mez, pf, 1945; Psalm xcii, SATB, 1946; Boo Hoo at the Zoo: Tails of Woe (J. Mullan), 2vv, 1978; 5 Songs (Horace, Rilke, Valéry, Belli, Rossetti), T, pf, 1978–9; Love, Sweet Animal (D. Schwartz), SATB, pf 4 hands, 1982

Principal publishers: Associated, Boelke-Bomart, C. F. Peters, E. B. Marks, G. Schirmer, Lawson-Gould, Mercury, New Music

BIBLIOGRAPHY

EwenD

P. Glanville-Hicks: "Arthur Berger," *ACAB*, iii/1 (1953), 2

J. M. Perkins: "Arthur Berger: the Composer as Mannerist," *PNM*, v/i (1966),

75, repr. in *Perspectives on American Composers*, ed. B. Boretz and E. T. Cone (New York, 1971)

Festschrift for Berger, *PNM*, xvii/1 (1978), 1–91 [incl. interview by J. Coppeck; articles by E. Baskin, S. Silver, and others; bibliography of writings by P. Jones; and list of works]

E. Barkin: "Arthur Berger's Trio for Violin, Guitar and Piano," *Breaking the Sound Barrier*, ed. G. Battcock (New York, 1981)

B. Northcott: "Arthur Berger – an Introduction at 70," *MT*, cxxiii (1982), 323

P. Driver: "Arthur Berger and his Unmistakable Music," *Boston Globe* (28 Dec 1983)

CHARLES H. KAUFMAN

Berger, Henry [Heinrich Wilhelm] (*b* Potsdam, Germany, 4 Aug 1844; *d* Honolulu, HI, 14 Oct 1929). Bandmaster and composer. He studied music in Treuenbrietzen, Germany, and at the age of 17 entered the Conservatory of Military Music in Berlin, where he remained for three years. He played with orchestras led by Johann Strauss the younger in Berlin, Paris, and Vienna. He moved to Honolulu in 1872, on leave from the German army, to conduct His Hawaiian Majesty's Band (later the Royal Hawaiian Military Band); apart from one visit to Germany in 1876–7 he retained leadership of the ensemble until his retirement in 1915. He organized many orchestras and bands, as well as the first string quartets to be formed in Hawaii, and was the original conductor of a group that later became the Honolulu SO. He conducted more than 32,000 band concerts, and arranged more than 1000 Western musical works and 200 Hawaiian songs. Of the 75 Hawaiian songs and over 500 marches that he composed, the best-known are *Ka Hea A Hiku*, *Kohala March*, *Liholiho*, *Beautiful Ilima*, *Ahi Wela*, and *Hula March*. Berger's impact on Hawaiian music was twofold: he fostered its evolution from *hīmeni* (missionary hymns) to secular, modern forms, while at the same time helping to preserve the vernacular musical tradition.

BIBLIOGRAPHY

G. S. Kanahele: *Hawaiian Music and Musicians: an Illustrated History* (Honolulu, HI, 1979), 34

Berger, Jean (*b* Hamm, Germany, 27 Sept 1909). Composer and conductor. The son of Orthodox Jews, he grew up in Alsace-Lorraine and attended the universities of Heidelberg and Vienna. He studied musicology first with Egon Wellesz and then Heinrich Bessler, and in 1931 received the PhD in musicology from Heidelberg. After serving briefly as assistant conductor at the Darmstadt Opera (1932–3), he moved to France and studied composition in Paris with Louis Aubert and Pierre Capdevielle and conducted Les Compagnons de la Marjolaine, a mixed choir. In 1937 his choral work *Le sang des autres* won first prize at an international competition in Zurich. For two years after the outbreak of World War II he taught at the Conservatorio Brasileiro de Musica in Rio de Janeiro and worked as an opera coach; in 1941 he moved to New York, where he worked as a vocal coach and arranger for CBS and NBC. He became an American citizen in 1943. He taught at Middlebury College beginning in 1948 and later at the University of Illinois, Urbana (1959–61), and the University of Colorado (1961–8). In 1964 he founded the John Sheppard Music Press in Boulder, Colorado. As a musicologist, he has edited several 17th-century works and has written on the Italian composer Giacomo Perti.

Berger describes his idiom as "unflinchingly tonal." Yet even in his choral works, which constitute the bulk of his output, he avoids an academic style, preferring a pragmatic blend of Franco-German folk music, South American melody and rhythm, and polyphonic modality. *Brazilian Psalm* (1941) has entered the standard American choral repertory, and it remains Berger's most popular composition.

WORKS

Stage: Pied Piper (play with music, after R. Browning), dancers, solo vv, choruses, small orch, 1968; Birds of a Feather: an Entertainment (C. Gilman), 1971; Yiphth and his Daughter (opera, Berger), 1972; The Cherry Tree Carol (liturgical drama), 1975

Orch: Caribbean Conc., harmonica, orch, 1942; Creole Ov., orch, 1949; Petit Suite, str, 1952; Short Ov., str, 1958; Divertissement, str, 1970; Concert Piece, 2 fl, str, 1972; Short Sym., 1974; Diversion, str, 1977; other works

Inst: 5 Compositions, pf, 1944; Sonatina, pf, 1952; Suite, fl, pf, 1955; Divertimento, 3 tr insts, 1957; Caribbean Cruise, 2 pf, 1958; 6 Short Pieces, ww qnt, 1962; 3 Duets, tr insts, 1968; Partita, ww qnt, 1970; Diversions, kbd, 1980; other works

Choral: Le sang des autres, 1937; Brazilian Psalm (J. de Lima), SATB, 1941; Vision of Peace (Bible), 1949; Magnificat, S, vv, fl, perc, 1960; Fiery Furnace (Bible), dramatic cantata, 1962; Song of Seasons, soloists, several choruses, orch, 1967; The Exiles (S. Funaroff), 2vv, 2 pf, perc, 1976; numerous other anthems and partsongs

Songs: 4 Sonnets (L. de Camoens), 1942; 4 Songs (L. Hughes), 1951; The Instruments (Dryden), 1952; 3 Canciones (15th-century anon.), 1968; other works

Principal publishers: AMP, Augsburg, Broude Bros., J. Sheppard

BIBLIOGRAPHY

W. D. Pritchard: "The Choral Style of Jean Berger," *American Choral Review*, viii/4 (1965), 4

J. Berger: "B on B," *Diapason*, lviii/6 (1967), 42

K. E. Smith: *The Choral Music of Jean Berger* (diss., U. of Iowa, 1972)

NED QUIST

Berger, Karl(hanns) (*b* Heidelberg, Germany, 30 March 1935). Jazz vibraphonist and educator. In Heidelberg he studied piano from the age of 10 and learned to play jazz vibraphone at a local jazz club. He also studied musicology and philosophy at Heidelberg and Berlin (PhD 1963). In March 1965 he joined Don Cherry's free jazz quintet, then based in Paris. When the group recorded in New York in September 1966 Berger remained in the USA, playing in schools with Horacee Arnold's group for Young Audiences, Inc. (1967–71), and periodically touring with his own groups. In autumn 1972, with Ornette Coleman, he cofounded the Creative Music Studio in Woodstock, New York. As its director he has created a program that concentrates on bringing out students' own ideas rather than directing them towards established jazz styles. Sam Rivers, Jack DeJohnette, Anthony Braxton, and Lee Konitz are among the musicians who have assisted Berger in workshops and concerts in Woodstock and New York.

RECORDINGS

(selective list)

As leader: *Karl Berger Quartet* (1966, ESP 1041); *Tune In* (1970, Mlst. 9026); *We are You* (1971, Calig 30607); *With Silence* (1972, Enja 2022); *Live at the Donaueschingen Music Festival* (1979, MPS 68250)

As sideman: D. Cherry: *Symphony for Improvisors* (1966, BN 84247); L. Konitz: *The Lee Konitz Duets* (1967, Mlst. 9013); D. Cherry: *Eternal Rhythm* (1968, Saba MPS15204); M. E. V.: *United Patchwork* (1977, HORO 15-16)

BIBLIOGRAPHY

R. DiNardo: "Karl Berger," *Coda*, xi/12 (1974), 2

E. Jost: *Free Jazz* (Graz, Austria, 1974)

P. Occhiogrosso: "Karl Berger: Music Universe c/o Woodstock, N.Y.," *Down Beat*, xliii/11 (1976), 18

"Karl Berger: l'école de Woodstock," *Jazz magazine*, no.280 (1979), 28

M. Ullman: *Jazz Lives: Portraits in Words and Pictures* (Washington, DC, 1980/*R*1982)

BARRY KERNFELD

Bergmann, Carl (*b* Ebersbach, Germany, 12 April 1821; *d* New York, 16 Aug 1876). Conductor and cellist. He studied under Zimmermann at Zittau and Adolf Friedrich Hesse at Breslau. Involved in the German Revolution of 1848, he immigrated to New York in 1849, having had orchestral experience in Breslau, Vienna, Pest, Warsaw, and Venice. He joined the Germania Musical Society, serving for a time as cellist, then as conductor until 1854. In 1852–4 he also conducted the concerts of the Boston Handel and Haydn Society. When the Germania Society disbanded in 1854, he settled in New York, becoming conductor of the Männergesangverein Arion, cellist of the Thomas chamber ensemble, and, in 1855, conductor (alternating with Eisfeld) of the New York Philharmonic Society orchestra. His surprising success in performances of the radical new music of Wagner (the overture to *Tannhäuser* on 21 April 1855, and other works later in the spring) led to his being appointed sole conductor for the 1855–6 and 1858–9 seasons of the Philharmonic. He then shared the conductorship with Eisfeld until the latter's retirement in 1865, after which he retained the post alone until failing health compelled his resignation in March 1876. He was also conductor for several years of the Brooklyn Philharmonic Society orchestra. Among his most noteworthy performances as an opera conductor was that of *Tannhäuser* on 4 April 1859 at the New York Stadt-Theater: it was the first hearing in America of a complete Wagner opera.

Bergmann was an important force in shaping the New York Philharmonic into a great orchestra, and his taste not only for Mozart, Beethoven, and Schumann but for the more modern Liszt, Berlioz, Wagner, and Tchaikovsky (he scheduled the American première of Tchaikovsky's *Romeo and Juliet* for late spring 1876, but could not conduct) influenced attitudes about the "standard" orchestral repertory.

BIBLIOGRAPHY

H. E. Krehbiel: *The Philharmonic Society of New York: a Memorial* (New York, 1892); ed. H. Shanet in *Early Histories of the New York Philharmonic* (New York, 1979)

C. N. Boyd: "Bergmann, Carl," *DAB*

H. E. Johnson: "The Germania Musical Society," *MQ*, xxxix (1953), 75

H. Shanet: *Philharmonic: a History of New York's Orchestra* (Garden City, NY, 1975)

H. WILEY HITCHCOCK

Bergsma, William (Laurence) (*b* Oakland, CA, 1 April 1921). Composer and teacher. He studied at Stanford University (1938–40) and at the Eastman School (1940–44, BA, MA), where his principal composition teachers were Hanson and Rogers. In 1946 he was appointed to teach composition at the Juilliard School; there he was deeply involved in the curricular reforms of the 1940s, directing the new department of literature and materials of music, and he served as associate dean from 1961 until 1963, when he was made professor and director of the school of music at the University of Washington, Seattle. In 1972–3 he was visiting professor at Brooklyn College, CUNY. Among the grants he has received are two Guggenheim fellowships (1946, 1951), a Phelan Award (1955), another award from the American Academy of Arts and Letters (1965), and a fellowship from the NEA (1979). In 1967 he was elected to the National Institute of Arts and Letters. He has received commissions from the Seattle SO (1978), and the Chamber Music Society of Lincoln Center, the Los Angeles Chamber Orchestra, and the Y Chamber Symphony, New York (all 1981). Bergsma's music is resourceful and imaginative, essentially tonal, texturally conventional, and predominantly lyrical. In later works he has incorporated avant-garde ideas, and his technique, particularly in form and orchestration, is formidable. Recordings of his works include the Third String Quartet (by the Juilliard String Quartet), excerpts from *The Wife of Martin Guerre*, and a collection of chamber music.

WORKS

(selective list)

STAGE

Paul Bunyan (ballet), 1938, San Francisco, 22 June 1939, orch suite, 1938, rev. 1945; Gold and the Señor Commandante (ballet), 1941, Rochester, 1 May 1942; The Wife of Martin Guerre (opera, 3, J. Lewis), 1956, New York, 15 Feb 1956; The Murder of Comrade Sharik (opera, 2, Bergsma, after M. Bulgakov), 1973

ORCHESTRAL

Dances from a New England Album, 1939, rev. 1969; Music on a Quiet Theme, 1943; The Fortunate Islands, str, 1947, rev. 1956; Sym. no. 1, 1949; A Carol on 12th Night, 1954; March with Tpts, band, 1956; Chameleon Variations, 1960; In Celebration, 1963; Documentary 1 "Portrait of a City," 1963, rev. 1968; Serenade "To Await the Moon," chamber orch, 1965; Vn Conc., 1966; Documentary 2 "Billie's World," 1968; Changes, 1971; Sym. no. 2 "Voyages," solo vv, chorus, orch, 1976; Sweet was the Song the Virgin Sung: Tristan Revisited, va, orch, 1978

VOCAL

Choral: In a Glass of Water Before Retiring (S. V. Benét), 1945; Black Salt, Black Provender (L. Bogan), 1946; On the Beach at Night (Whitman), 1946; Let True Love Among us be, 1948; Riddle me This, 1957; Praise (Herbert), chorus, org, 1958; Confrontation (Job), chorus, kbd/orch, 1963, rev. 1966; The Sun, the Soaring Eagle, the Turquoise Prince, the God (Florentine MS), chorus, brass, perc, 1968; Wishes, Wonders, Portents, Charms, mixed vv, insts, 1974

Songs: 6 Songs (Cummings), 1944–5; Bethsabe, Bathing (G. Peele), 1961; 4 Songs (trad., Peele), medium v, cl, bn, pf, 1981

CHAMBER AND INSTRUMENTAL

Suite, brass qt, 1940; 5 str qts, 1942, 1944, 1953, 1970, 1982; Pastorale and Scherzo, rec/fl, 2 va, 1943; 3 Fantasies, pf, 1943, rev. 1983; Tangents, pf, 1951; Conc., wind qnt, 1958; Fantastic Variations on a Theme from Tristan and Isolde, va, pf, 1961; Illegible Canons, cl, perc, 1969; Clandestine Dialogues, vc, perc, 1976; Blatant Hypotheses, trbn, perc, 1977; Qnt, fl, str qt, 1980, rev. 1981; The Voice of Coelacanth, hn, vn, pf, 1981; Four All, cl, trbn, vc, perc, 1981; Symmetries, ob, bn, pf, 1982; Variations, pf, 1984

Principal publishers: C. Fischer, Galaxy, Hargail

BIBLIOGRAPHY

A. Skulsky: "The Music of William Bergsma," *Juilliard Review*, iii/2 (1956), 12

W. Bergsma: "The Laboratory of Performance," *College Music Symposium*, ix (1969), 23

KURT STONE

Berigan, Bunny [Roland Bernart] (*b* Hilbert, WI, 2 Nov 1908; *d* New York, 2 June 1942). Jazz trumpeter and bandleader. He began playing in local groups while a teenager, and in the early 1930s moved to New York as a freelance musician and sometime member of such important bands as Hal Kemp's, Paul Whiteman's, the Dorsey Brothers', Benny Goodman's, and Tommy Dorsey's. In 1933 he made a number of recordings under his own name, and from 1937 led his own successful big band. He rejoined Dorsey for a few months in 1940, then briefly led his own group until his death. Berigan and Bix Beiderbecke are often compared for the similarities of their lives and musical conceptions. As did many white trumpeters of his generation, Berigan showed the influence of Louis Armstrong in the variety of his timbre and attack, his wide range, and use of chromatic pitches. He showed too the influence of Beiderbecke in his use of "ghost" notes, lengthy concentrations of eighth-notes played with bell-like attack, and melodic lines that encompass more than one contrapuntal part. Berigan integrated these elements and a fine harmonic sense into a distinctive, uninhibited style, heard to good advantage on Tommy Dorsey's *Marie* (1937).

RECORDINGS

(selective list)

As leader: I can't get Started (1936, Voc. 3225); I nearly let Love go Slipping through my Fingers (1936, Voc. 3254); I can't get Started (1937, Vic. 36208)

As sideman: B. Goodman: King Porter Stomp (1935, Vic. 25090); B. Holiday: Billie's Blues (1936, Voc. 3288); T. Dorsey: Marie (1937, Vic. 25523)

BIBLIOGRAPHY

G. Frazier: "Bunny Berigan," *Jam Session*, ed. R. Gleason (New York, 1958), 42

W. Mellers: *Music in a New Found Land* (London, 1964), 380

I. Crosbie: "Bunny Berigan," *Jazz Journal*, xxvii/9 (1974), 8

A. McCarthy: *Big Band Jazz* (London, 1974), 187

V. Danca: *Bunny* (Rockford, IL, 1978)

JAMES DAPOGNY/R

Berio, Luciano (*b* Oneglia, Imperia, Italy, 24 Oct 1925). Italian composer, conductor, and teacher. He studied composition with Giorgio Federico Ghedini at the Milan conservatory, obtaining his diploma in 1950. In the same year he married the singer CATHY BERBERIAN, the chosen interpreter of many of his works (even after their marriage was dissolved in 1966). A first journey to the USA, which he visited on their honeymoon, was followed by another in 1951, when he attended Dallapiccola's classes at the Berkshire Music Center on a Koussevitzky Foundation scholarship. The encounter with Dallapiccola encouraged a spiritual and technical transformation; even more momentous was the contact with the American musical world as a whole, which Berio welcomed as a way of escaping from provincial backwaters. This is demonstrated by his early interest in electronic music, which was stimulated by his experience in 1952 of the first tape-music compositions of Luening and Ussachevsky, and began to take shape in 1953 with his composition of the musical soundtracks for a series of films for Italian television. With Bruno Maderna he persuaded the Milan station of the Italian state radio to set up the first studio for electronic music in Italy, the Studio di Fonologia Musicale, which he directed from 1955 to 1961.

In 1960 Berio returned to the Berkshire Music Center as a teacher and composer-in-residence, and directed on 1 August the première of his important work *Circles* (to texts by Cummings) for voice, harp, and two percussionists, which had been commissioned by the Fromm Foundation. Disliking being tied down to a permanent post, and frustrated by the bureaucratic difficulties that were hampering the development of the Milan studio, Berio resigned from the radio in 1961, and was free to accept an appointment to teach at Mills College, Oakland, California (1962–3). He remained in the USA for almost a decade, teaching also at Harvard University (1966–7) and the Juilliard School (1965–6, 1967–71), where he also conducted the Juilliard Ensemble which he had founded to perform contemporary music. But he tired of teaching ("I began to feel like a dentist") and returned in 1972 to Europe; he worked in Paris at IRCAM and in Rome as artistic director of the Accademia Filarmonica Romana (1976), and eventually composed and conducted from a base in a Tuscan town near Siena.

Among the most important works of Berio's American years were several in a series of "archetypal" compositions, titled simply for the genre they represent, such as the four- (later five-) movement symphony *Sinfonia* (commissioned for the 125th anniversary season of the New York PO and given its première performance by that orchestra and the Swingle Singers, under Berio's direction, on 10 October 1968), the opera *Opera* (first performed by the Santa Fe Opera Company, 12 August 1970), and the recital work *Recital I (for Cathy)* for solo singer and 17 instrumentalists (completed by Berio in 1972, after his return to Europe). The second movement of *Sinfonia* is an arrangement of the earlier *O King* (1967) for singer and five players; its text consists only of syllables in the name of Martin Luther King, Jr. Also from Berio's American period came most of the solo works titled *Sequenza* – *Sequenza II* (harp, 1963); *III* (female voice), *IV* (piano), and *V* (trombone), all 1966; *VI* (viola, 1967); and *VII* (oboe, 1969) – and the set of *Folk Songs* (1964) for soprano and seven instruments, settings of texts in various languages, among them *Black is the color of my true love's hair* and *I wonder as I wander*. The pianist Peter Serkin joined Berio at the keyboards in the première performance of *Memory for Electric Piano and Electric Harpsichord* (New York, 12 March 1971).

BIBLIOGRAPHY

M. Donat: "Berio and his 'Circles,'" *MT*, cv (1964), 105

M. Bortolotto: "Luciano Berio o dei piaceri," *Fase seconda: studi sulla nuova musica* (Turin, Italy, 1969), 128

M. Donat: "Berio's 'Sinfonia,'" *The Listener*, lxxxii (1969), 89

"Berio, Luciano," *CBY 1971*

D. Avron and J. F. Lyotard: "'A few words to sing': Sequenza III," *Musique en jeu* (1971), no.2, p.28

G. Krieger and W. M. Stroh: "Probleme der Collage in der Musik aufgezeigt am 3. Satz der 'Sinfonia' von Luciano Berio," *Musik und Bildung*, iii (1971), 229

L. A. Neill: *The Harp in Contemporary Chamber and Solo Music* (diss., UCLA, 1971) [incl. analyses of *Circles* and *Sequenza II*]

E. Schwartz: "Current Chronicle: The Netherlands," *MQ*, lviii (1972), 653 [on a Berio concert series]

M. Donat: "Forking Paths," *The Listener*, lxxxix (1973), 125

V. Ravizza: "Die Melos-Analyse: Sinfonia für acht Singstimmen und Orchester von Luciano Berio," *Melos*, xli (1974), 291

I. Stoianowa: "Verbe et son: 'centre et absence': sur *Cummings ist der Dichter* de Boulez, *O King* de Berio et *Für Stimmen . . . Missa est* de Schnebel," *Musique en jeu* (1974), no.16, p.79

G. W. Flynn: "Listening to Berio's Music," *MQ*, lxi (1975), 388

D. Osmond-Smith: "Berio and the Art of Commentary," *MT*, cxvi (1975), 871

P. Altmann: *Sinfonia von Luciano Berio. Eine analytische Studie* (Vienna, 1977)

P. Schnaus: "Anmerkungen zu Luciano Berios *Circles*," *Musik und Bildung*, x (1978), 489

R. W. Miller: *A Style Analysis of the Published Solo Piano Music of Luciano Berio* (diss., Peabody Conservatory, 1979)

S. F. Pellman: *An Examination of the Role of Timbre in . . . Sequenza V by Luciano Berio* (diss., Cornell U., 1979)

R. Dalmonte, ed.: *Luciano Berio: Intervista sulla musica* (Rome, 1981; Eng. trans., ed. D. Osmond-Smith, in *Luciano Berio: Two Interviews with Rosanna Dalmonte and Bálint András Varga*, New York, 1985)

B. Schrader: "Interview with Luciano Berio," *Introduction to Electro-acoustic Music* (Englewood Cliffs, NJ, 1982), 179

D. Osmond-Smith: *Playing on Words: a Guide to Luciano Berio's "Sinfonia"*, Royal Musical Association Monographs, i (London, 1985)

CLAUDIO ANNIBALDI/H. WILEY HITCHCOCK

Berkeley. City in California, part of the SAN FRANCISCO Bay area. The University of California established a campus at Berkeley in 1868; the music department was founded 33 years later (*see* CALIFORNIA, UNIVERSITY OF; *see also* LIBRARIES AND COLLECTIONS, §3).

Berkeley, Busby [Enos, William Berkeley] (*b* Los Angeles, CA, 29 Nov 1895; *d* Palm Springs, CA, 14 March 1976). Choreographer and film director. The son of theatrical parents, he made his stage début at the age of five. He acted, directed stock companies, choreographed, and produced a Broadway show before going to Hollywood to direct the musical numbers in the film version of *Whoopee* (1930). Berkeley is best known for the production numbers he created for films made by Warner Bros. in the 1930s. These were among the first in Hollywood to exploit cinematic techniques for theatrical effects that were impossible to achieve on the stage: unusual camera angles and movements highlighted elaborate sets, symmetrical architectural patterns, and extended, often surreal and absurd musical narratives. In many cases his camera moved more than his dancers. In *Footlight Parade* (1933) chorus girls slid down waterfalls; in *Gold Diggers of 1933* they played violins outlined in neon lights, combining to form a giant violin; *Fashions of 1934* included a chorus of girls pretending to play mock harps, the pillars of which were formed by other girls. Though none of his later films are as noteworthy as those for Warner Bros., he made an important contribution to the Alice Faye–Carmen Miranda color extravaganza *The Gang's all Here* (1943) and was credited with supervising the revival in 1971 of *No, No, Nanette*.

See also MUSICAL FILM, fig. 1.

BIBLIOGRAPHY

"Berkeley, Busby," *CBY 1971*

T. Thomas, J. Terry, and B. Berkeley: *The Busby Berkeley Book* (Greenwich, CT, 1973)

E. Mordden: *The Hollywood Musical* (New York, 1981)

SAMUEL S. BRYLAWSKI

Berklee College. School of music founded in Boston in 1945; *see* BOSTON (i), §9 (i).

Berkshire Music Center. Former name of the Tanglewood Music Center, an educational institution in Lenox, Massachusetts. An international festival of music (known as the Berkshire Music Festival until 1985) is held annually on the same site. *See* TANGLEWOOD.

Irving Berlin, 1947

Berlin, Irving [Baline, Israel] (*b* Tyumen', Russia, 11 May 1888). Songwriter. His father Moses Baline (*d* 1896) was a Jewish cantor who immigrated to the USA with his family and settled in New York in 1893. The young Baline first worked as a street singer, then as a singing waiter at Pelham's Café in Chinatown. From 1907 he wrote lyrics, and his first published song was *Marie from Sunny Italy* (1907), with music by the café's pianist, M. Nicholson; a printer's error on the cover gave him the name "Berlin." He subsequently became a song plugger and made his stage début, performing his own songs in a revue, *Up and Down Broadway* (1910). He achieved international success with the song *Alexander's Ragtime Band* (1911), for which he wrote the words and music; this became the theme song of a new style of social dance and was the most popular of the Tin Pan Alley ragtime songs (*see* POPULAR MUSIC, §III, 2 and fig. 3). Berlin's first ballad was *When I lost you* (1912), written after his wife's death; his first complete score and lyrics were written for *Watch your Step* (1914, with the song "Play a simple melody"), a musical comedy with the dancers Vernon and Irene Castle. By 1918 Berlin had contributed to several New York revues and operettas, including the *Ziegfeld Follies* (1911) and *The Century Girl* (1916), and had performed in London as the "King of Ragtime" (1917). His American patriotism was expressed in an all-soldier revue, *Yip, Yip, Yaphank* (1918, with the song "Oh! how I hate to get up in the morning"). In 1913 he had become a partner in a publishing firm with Ted Snyder; in 1919 he formed his own publishing company, Irving Berlin Music, Inc., and in 1921 (with Sam H. Harris) built the Music Box Theatre, where he staged four revues which included some of his most popular songs. His last successful revues were *As Thousands Cheer* (1933, with the song "Easter Parade") and *This is the Army* (1942).

From 1935 Berlin wrote songs for some of the most successful Hollywood film musicals. The careers of leading popular performers such as Bing Crosby, Ethel Merman, Fred Astaire, and Ginger Rogers are permanently linked to Berlin's songs in *Top Hat* (1935), *On the Avenue* (1937), *Holiday Inn* (1942), and other films up to the mid-1950s. He also wrote his most popular musicals for Merman: *Annie Get your Gun* (1946, with the songs "There's no business like show business" and "Anything you can do") and *Call me Madam* (1950, with "The hostess with the mostes' ").

Berlin has been perhaps the most versatile and successful American popular songwriter of the 20th century. He was self-taught as a pianist and plays in an unconventional manner, using predominantly the black keys on an instrument that has a lever under the keyboard for automatic transposition. It has traditionally been said that he cannot read music and has always been dependent on assistants to transcribe his ideas, yet he has published about 1500 songs, a remarkable number of which are familiar throughout the world. Many of his best songs are sentimental ballads lightened by elements of popular styles like ragtime or swing. His tunes generally imply strong harmonic progressions; unlike most popular songs, their first phrase is usually unrepeated, and they are often in rare forms (e.g., *ABCD*) or have uneven phrase lengths (frequently to conform with choreographic demands). *Alexander's Ragtime Band* quotes from Stephen Foster's *Old Folks at Home* and is one of the first Tin Pan Alley songs with verse and refrain in different keys; *White Christmas*, perhaps the best-selling song of all time, is a sentimental ballad with an unusually chromatic tune.

See also PATRIOTIC MUSIC, §2.

WORKS

STAGE

Works for which Berlin wrote all or much of the score; lyrics are by Berlin. Names of librettists are given in parentheses; dates are those of first New York performance.

Ziegfeld Follies of 1911 (revue, G. V. Hobart), 26 June 1911
Watch your Step (musical, H. B. Smith), 8 Dec 1914 [incl. Play a simple melody]
Stop! Look! Listen! (musical, Smith), 25 Dec 1915 [incl. The girl on the magazine cover, I love a piano]
The Century Girl (revue, collab. H. Blossom), collab. V. Herbert, 6 Nov 1916
The Cohan Revue of 1918, collab. G. M. Cohan, 31 Dec 1917
Yip, Yip, Yaphank (revue), 2 Sept 1918 [incl. Mandy; Oh! how I hate to get up in the morning]
Ziegfeld Follies of 1919 (revue), 16 June 1919 [incl. A pretty girl is like a melody, You'd be surprised]
Ziegfeld Follies of 1920 (revue), 22 June 1920 [incl. Tell me, little gypsy]
Music Box Revue 1921–22, orchd F. Tours, M. DePackh, S. Jones, H. Akst, 22 Sept 1921 [incl. Say it with music]
Music Box Revue 1922–23, orchd Tours, DePackh, Jones, Akst, 23 Oct 1922 [incl. Lady of the evening]
Music Box Revue 1923–24, orchd Tours, DePackh, Jones, Akst, 22 Sept 1923
Music Box Revue 1924–25, orchd Tours, DePackh, Jones, Akst, 1 Dec 1924
The Cocoanuts (musical, G. S. Kaufman), 8 Dec 1925; film, 1929
Ziegfeld Follies of 1927 (revue), 16 Aug 1927 [incl. Shaking the blues away]
Face the Music (musical, M. Hart), 17 Feb 1932 [incl. Let's have another cup o' coffee, Soft lights and sweet music]
As Thousands Cheer (revue, Hart), orchd Tours, A. Deutsch, H. Kresa, 30 Sept 1933 [incl. Easter Parade, Heat Wave]
Louisiana Purchase (musical, M. Ryskind), orchd D. Walker, 28 May 1940 [incl. It's a lovely day tomorrow]; film, 1942
This is the Army (revue), 4 July 1942 [incl. I left my heart at the stage door canteen; This is the army, Mr. Jones]; film, 1943
Annie Get your Gun (musical, H. Fields, D. Fields), orchd P. J. Lang, R. R. Bennett, T. Royal, 16 May 1946 [incl. Anything you can do, Doin' what comes natur'lly, The girl that I marry, I got the sun in the morning, There's no business like show business, They say it's wonderful]; film, 1950
Miss Liberty (musical, R. Sherwood), orchd Walker, 15 July 1949
Call me Madam (musical, H. Lindsay, R. Crouse), orchd Walker, 12 Oct 1950 [incl. The best thing for you, The hostess with the mostes' on the ball, It's a lovely day today, Marrying for love, They like Ike, You're just in love]; film, 1953
Mr. President (musical, Lindsay, Crouse), orchd Lang, 20 Oct 1962

FILMS

(not all scores wholly by Berlin)

The Awakening, 1928
Hallelujah, 1929
Puttin' on the Ritz, 1930
Mammy, 1930
Reaching for the Moon, 1931
Kid Millions, 1934
Top Hat, 1935 [incl. Cheek to Cheek; Isn't this a lovely day?; Piccolino; Top hat, white tie, and tails]
Follow the Fleet, 1936 [incl. I'm putting all my eggs in one basket, Let's face the music and dance]
On the Avenue, 1937 [incl. I've got my love to keep me warm, This year's kisses]
Alexander's Ragtime Band, 1938
Carefree, 1938 [incl. Change partners]
Second Fiddle, 1939
Holiday Inn, 1942 [incl. Be careful, it's my heart; White Christmas]
Blue Skies, 1946
Easter Parade, 1948 [incl. Better luck next time, It only happens when I dance with you]
White Christmas, 1954 [incl. Count your blessings]
There's No Business Like Show Business, 1954

OTHER SONGS

(selective list; lyrics by Berlin)

Marie from Sunny Italy (music M. Nicholson), 1907; Alexander's Ragtime Band, 1911; Everybody's doin' it, 1911; When I lost you, 1912; When the midnight choo choo leaves for Alabam', 1912; International Rag, 1913; Snooky Ookums, 1913; When I leave the world behind, 1914; Someone else may be there while I'm gone, 1917; I've got my captain working for me now, 1919; All by myself, 1921; Always, 1925; Remember, 1925; Blue Skies, 1927; Russian Lullaby, 1927; The song is ended, 1927; Say it isn't so, 1932, How deep is the ocean?, 1932; God bless America, 1938 [chorus written 1918]

Principal publisher: Berlin

BIBLIOGRAPHY

A. Woolcott: *The Story of Irving Berlin* (New York, 1925)
S. Green: *The World of Musical Comedy* (New York, 1960, rev. 2/1968)
"Berlin, Irving," *CBY 1963*
D. Ewen: *Composers for the American Musical Theater* (New York, 1968)
D. Jay: *The Irving Berlin Songography* (New Rochelle, NY, 1969)
A. Wilder: *American Popular Song* (New York, 1972)
M. Wilk: *They're Playing our Song* (New York, 1973)
M. Freedland: *Irving Berlin* (New York, 1974)
C. Hamm: *Yesterdays: Popular Song in America* (New York, 1979)
M. Knapp: "*Watch your Step*: Irving Berlin's 1914 Musical," *Musical Theatre in America: Greenvale, NY, 1981*, ed. G. Loney (Westport, CT, 1984), 245

DEANE L. ROOT
GERALD BORDMAN (work-list)

Berlinski, Herman (*b* Leipzig, Germany, 18 Aug 1910). Organist and composer. He studied piano and composition at the State Conservatory of Leipzig (where Karg-Elert taught him composition) and attended the Ecole Normale de Musique in Paris, where he was a pupil of Cortot and Boulanger. He immigrated to the USA in 1941. At the Seminary College of Jewish Music in New York he studied organ and musicology with Joseph Yasser and was awarded the PhD. Berlinski was organist at the Temple Emanu-El in New York (1954–63) and then minister of music at the Washington (DC) Hebrew Congregation (1963–77). He has spent his life as a liturgical musician and composer, and his music contains historical Jewish materials inseparably joined to personal invention. His widely performed organ toccata *The Burning Bush* (1957) fully succeeds in fusing Hebrew imagery with sacred musical media. He is a gifted recitalist and his recordings reflect an international Jewish background coupled with brilliant technical achievement.

BIBLIOGRAPHY

M. Kayden: "The Music of Herman Berlinski," *ACAB*, vii/3 (1959), 2
K. S. Mervine: "Herman Berlinski after 'The Burning Bush': an Interview," *American Organist*, xvi/5 (1982), 46

VERNON GOTWALS

Bernal Jiménez, Miguel (*b* Morelia, Mexico, 16 Feb 1910; *d* León, Guanajuato, Mexico, 26 July 1956). Mexican composer. He studied music in Morelia as a boy before enrolling at the Pontificio Istituto di Musica Sacra in Rome (1928–33). After graduation he returned home to teach, was appointed director of the Escuela Superior de Música Sagrada (1936), and in 1939 founded the monthly *Schola cantorum*, which he edited until 1953. He toured widely in Mexico and the USA as a concert organist, choral conductor, and lecturer. His last nine years were spent in New Orleans as a choral director, member of the board of directors of the New Orleans SO, and dean of the music faculty at Loyola University (1954–6). Credited with reviving the composition of sacred music in Mexico, he also wrote operas, ballets, orchestral and instrumental music, and film scores (mostly before coming to the USA). Whatever the genre, Bernal Jiménez's music was the most tasteful composed by a conservative Mexican of his generation.

BIBLIOGRAPHY

M. Querol Gavaldá: "Bernal Jiménez, Miguel: la técnica de los compositores," *AnM*, x (1955), 224

O. Mayer-Serra: *Música y músicos de Latinoamérica*, i (1957), 105
H. de Grail: "Miguel Bernal Jiménez," *Músicos mexicanos* (Mexico City, 1965), 214
A. S. Lemmon: "Miguel Bernal Jiménez," *Heterofonía*, vii/4 (1974), 6

ROBERT STEVENSON/R

Bernheimer, Martin (*b* Munich, Germany, 28 Sept 1936). Music critic. He studied at Brown University (BA 1958), the Hochschule für Musik in Munich (1958–9), and under Reese at New York University (MA 1961). He was on the music staff of the *New York Herald-Tribune* (1959–62), assistant to Irving Kolodin at the *Saturday Review* (1962–5), music critic for the *New York Post* (1961–5), and from 1965 music critic of the *Los Angeles Times*. He won the Deems Taylor Award for music criticism in 1974 and 1978 and the Pulitzer Prize for criticism in 1982. Bernheimer is a widely respected and influential critic, who is particularly knowledgeable about opera and the voice. In addition to his activities as a journalist, he has taught criticism in various schools and universities, and has written for music journals and *The New Grove*.

PATRICK J. SMITH

Bernstein, Elmer (*b* New York, 4 April 1922). Composer and conductor. He was trained as a pianist but also studied composition with Citkowitz, Sessions, Ivan Langstroth, and Wolpe. He attended New York University, then in 1942 enlisted in the Army Air Corps; he arranged and composed music for some 80 programs for the Armed Forces Radio Service. For three years after his discharge he was active as a concert pianist. Norman Corwin then engaged him to score a radio drama, and this led to an offer to compose for films. *Sudden Fear*, Bernstein's third film, attracted favorable attention, and in 1955 he came suddenly to prominence for his jazz score for *The Man with the Golden Arm*. He has composed the scores for more than 100 feature films, as well as music for many documentary films and television shows. He writes in a distinctive style, the chief characteristics of which are a pronounced jazz element (e.g., *Walk on the Wild Side*), a fresh, youthful-sounding lyricism, clean-cut economical instrumental textures, extreme versatility, and a fondness for thematic metamorphosis (notably in *The Great Escape*).

In 1974 he founded the Film Music Collection to further the cause of good film music through writings and recordings; during the four years of its existence the organization published 13 issues of *Film Music Notebook* and issued 14 record albums of music conducted by Bernstein. He also appeared in a film, *Music for the Movies*, discussing the history and technique of film music.

WORKS
(selective list)

FILM SCORES

Saturday's Hero, 1951; Sudden Fear, 1952; Never Wave at a WAC, 1953; Make Haste to Live, 1954; The Man with the Golden Arm, 1955; The View from Pompey's Head, 1955; The Ten Commandments, 1956; Men in War, 1957; Sweet Smell of Success, 1957; Desire under the Elms, 1958; God's Little Acre, 1958; Some Came Running, 1958; The Miracle, 1959; From the Terrace, 1960; The Magnificent Seven, 1960; By Love Possessed, 1961; Summer and Smoke, 1961; Birdman of Alcatraz, 1962; Walk on the Wild Side, 1962

The Great Escape, 1963; Love with the Proper Stranger, 1963; To Kill a Mockingbird, 1963; Baby the Rain Must Fall, 1964; The Hallelujah Trail, 1965; Hawaii, 1966; Return of the Seven, 1966; Thoroughly Modern Millie, 1967; The Bridge at Remagen, 1969; True Grit, 1969; A Walk in the Spring Rain, 1970; See No Evil, 1971; Cahill, United States Marshal, 1973; The Trial of Billy Jack, 1974; The Shootist, 1976; National Lampoon's Animal House, 1978; The Great Santini, 1979; Airplane!, 1980; The Chosen, 1981; Five Days One Summer, 1982; Trading Places, 1983; Ghostbusters, 1984; The Black Cauldron, 1985; Spies Like Us, 1985

Scores for documentary films, television music

OTHER WORKS

How Now, Dow Jones (musical, lib. by M. Shulman, lyrics by C. Leigh), New York, 7 Dec 1967; 3 suites, orch; 2 song cycles; works for pf, va and pf

BIBLIOGRAPHY

E. Bernstein: "What Ever Happened to Great Movie Music?," *HiFi/MusAm*, xxii/7 (1972), 55
T. Thomas: *Music for the Movies* (South Brunswick, NJ, and New York, 1973), 185
I. Bazelon: *Knowing the Score: Notes on Film Music* (New York, 1975), 170
E. Bernstein: "On Film Music," *Journal of the University Film Association*, xxviii/4 (1976), 7
T. Thomas, ed.: *Film Score: the View from the Podium* (South Brunswick, NJ, and New York, 1979), 154
S. Vertlieb: "Soundtrack," *Cinemacabre*, no.3 (1980), 56

CHRISTOPHER PALMER/CLIFFORD McCARTY

Bernstein, Lawrence F (*b* New York, 25 March 1939). Musicologist. He graduated from Hofstra University (BS 1960) and at New York University studied with LaRue and Reese (PhD 1969). He taught at the University of Chicago, 1965–70, and then joined the faculty of the University of Pennsylvania, where he was chairman of the department of music, 1974–7. He was editor-in-chief of the *Journal of the American Musicological Society*, 1975–7. Bernstein's interests include French secular music of the 16th century and the pre-Classical symphony. His research on the 16th-century chanson has centered on the uses of pre-existing material, including cantus firmus and parody techniques (on which he wrote his dissertation); in 1974 he received the Alfred Einstein Award of the American Musicological Society for an article on the chanson in Italy (*JAMS*, xxvi, 1973, pp.1–68). He has contributed editions of music by Jhan Gero and a collection of chansons to the series Masters and Monuments of the Renaissance.

PAULA MORGAN

Bernstein, Leonard (*b* Lawrence, MA, 25 Aug 1918). Composer, conductor, teacher, and pianist. As a composer, he has straddled the worlds of serious and popular music, playing a major role in lifting the Broadway musical theater towards the realm of opera. Through his appearances on television, Bernstein has probably done more than any educator for the general understanding of music. He was the first American to be appointed music director of the New York PO; also a gifted pianist, he has often performed simultaneously as soloist and conductor.

1. Childhood and student years: 1918–43. 2. Early career: 1944–50. 3. Years of path-breaking activity: 1951–63. 4. Later years: from 1963.

1. CHILDHOOD AND STUDENT YEARS: 1918–43. Bernstein is a first-generation American whose artistic temperament derives as much from his Russian-Jewish roots as from his American experience. His father, Samuel, the oldest child of a scholar-rabbi, was 16 when he left the Ukraine for New York, where he took a job in the Fulton fish market; his mother, Jennie Resnick, was seven when she arrived in Lawrence, where she worked in the mills from the age of 12. The eldest of three children, Leonard attended the highly competitive Boston Latin School. His introduction to music came late for one who was to become a professional musician; he was ten when the family acquired an upright piano. Immediately he was drawn to it, but his father bitterly opposed this interest, expecting him to join his beauty supply

business. Bernstein began lessons, however, with a neighbor, Frieda Karp, and went on to study with Susan Williams, a faculty member of the New England Conservatory; Helen Coates, an assistant to Heinrich Gebhard, Boston's foremost piano teacher; and finally with Gebhard himself.

In 1935 Bernstein entered Harvard University, where he studied with Edward Ballantine, Edward Burlingame Hill, A. Tillman Merritt, and Walter Piston. While an undergraduate he wrote incidental music for a production of *The Birds* (Aristophanes), directed and played the piano for Blitzstein's left-wing musical *The Cradle will Rock*, and met Dimitri Mitropoulos, who exerted a profound influence on his musical life. After graduating in 1939 (BA), Bernstein studied at the Curtis Institute: piano with Isabella Vengerova, score reading with Renée Longy, orchestration with Randall Thompson, and conducting with Fritz Reiner (winters of 1939–40 and 1940–41). He also studied conducting with Koussevitzky at the Berkshire Music Center (summers of 1940 and 1941), where in 1942 Koussevitzky appointed him his assistant. Meanwhile, he had become involved with the Revuers (a group of popular entertainers that included Adolph Green and Betty Comden), who composed and sang sophisticated songs at the Village Vanguard, New York, where Bernstein often spent the evening and occasionally played the piano (without pay). In the autumn of 1942 he began working at Harms-Remick, arranging popular songs for piano, transcribing band pieces, and notating improvisations by such jazz artists as Coleman Hawkins and Earl Hines; these were published under the pseudonym Lenny Amber (Amber being an English translation of the German Bernstein).

In August 1943 Artur Rodzinski, the newly appointed music director of the New York PO, named Bernstein his assistant conductor. On 14 November 1943 Bruno Walter, who was scheduled to conduct the orchestra, fell ill, and Bernstein substituted for him in a concert that was broadcast throughout the USA. His performance was reviewed on the front page of the *New York Times* and in other newspapers across the country; the widespread publicity not only launched his conducting career, it made him instantly recognizable to millions.

2. Early career: 1944–50. After serving in 1944–5 as guest conductor of seven major orchestras, including the Pittsburgh SO and the Boston SO, Bernstein was appointed music director of the New York City SO, replacing Stokowski. During his tenure with the orchestra (1945–8), he conducted mostly 20th-century compositions, concentrating on works by Stravinsky, Bartók, Chávez, Hindemith, Prokofiev, and Shostakovich; although he did present excerpts from Berg's *Wozzeck* (with Rose Bampton), he felt little affinity for the music of the Second Viennese School. In the summer of 1946 he conducted the American première of Britten's *Peter Grimes* at the Berkshire Music Center. That year he also led the Czech PO in two programs devoted to American music including pieces by Copland, Barber, Roy Harris, Schuman, Gershwin, and himself. He proved to be an effective ambassador for American music; not only did he look the role, with his wide smile and informal manner, but he captured American music, with its special inflections and particular rhythms, more successfully than anyone else. In Tel Aviv in 1947 he conducted the first of a series of concerts with the Palestine PO (later Israel PO), to which he was music adviser during 1948–9. Also in 1948 he conducted a concert given by concentration camp survivors in a refugee camp near Munich, appeared with orchestras in Milan, Vienna, Budapest, Paris, Munich, and Scheveningen (the Netherlands), and in the USA was appointed to the faculty at the Berkshire Music Center. He was not yet 30.

The Clarinet Sonata (1941–2) was Bernstein's first published composition. His works of this period possess both the vitality of popular genres and the restraint normally associated with art music. The first such work for orchestra was the Symphony no. 1 "Jeremiah," which he conducted with the Pittsburgh SO in January 1944; it won the New York Music Critics' Circle Award as the best American work of the year. In April, at the Metropolitan Opera, Hurok presented *Fancy Free*, a ballet choreographed by Jerome Robbins; it became the basis for the musical *On the Town* (with book and lyrics by Comden and Green), which opened on Broadway in December of that year and enjoyed great popularity as well as considerable critical acclaim. During these years Bernstein also continued his activities as a pianist and in 1949 appeared as soloist under Koussevitzky in his Symphony no. 2 "The Age of Anxiety."

3. Years of path-breaking activity: 1951–63. After Koussevitzky died in June 1951, Bernstein became head of the orchestra and conducting departments at the Berkshire Music Center. In the same year he married Felicia Montealegre Cohn, a Chilean actress, and was appointed professor of music at Brandeis University, where he served until 1955. He continued to compose works for the stage: *Trouble in Tahiti*, his first opera (one act), was produced at Brandeis in 1952; *Wonderful Town* opened on Broadway in 1953; and *Candide*, a comic operetta based on Voltaire's novel, was completed in 1956. The musical theater work *West Side Story*, conceived and choreographed by Robbins, was finished in 1957. The last, widely acclaimed as a musical of unprecedented dramatic, choreographic, and musical integrity, was to become extraordinarily successful in the USA and abroad in both stage and film versions. Other works of this period include the *Serenade*, commissioned by the Koussevitzky Foundation, and music for the film *On the Waterfront* (starring Marlon Brando), which was released in 1954.

In 1953 Bernstein became the first American to conduct at La Scala when he directed Callas in Cherubini's *Medea*. And, after serving in 1957 as co-director (with Mitropoulos) of the New York PO, he became in 1958 the first American-born music director of that orchestra, organizing its seasons around themes such as "Keys to the 20th Century," "The Middle European Tradition," "Spring Festival of Theater Music," and "The Gallic Approach." In 1960 he conducted the orchestra in a Mahler festival (Bernstein has since come to be identified with the anguished composer-conductor, and he claims that, while Copland was his musical father, Beethoven and Mahler were his forefathers), and in September 1962 he conducted it at the opening concert of Philharmonic Hall at Lincoln Center. At the inaugural gala for John F. Kennedy, he presented his *Fanfare I* written specially for the occasion.

During the 1950s and early 1960s Bernstein's international reputation flourished. He was the first to take the New York PO to South America, Israel, Japan, New Zealand, the USSR, Turkey, and several European countries; his first book, *The Joy of Music*, was published in 1959; *West Side Story* was performed widely in the USA and abroad; and he made his début at the Metropolitan Opera conducting Verdi's *Falstaff* (1963). Espe-

1. *Part of the vocal score of Bernstein's "Tonight" from "West Side Story," completed 1957: autograph MS (DLC)*

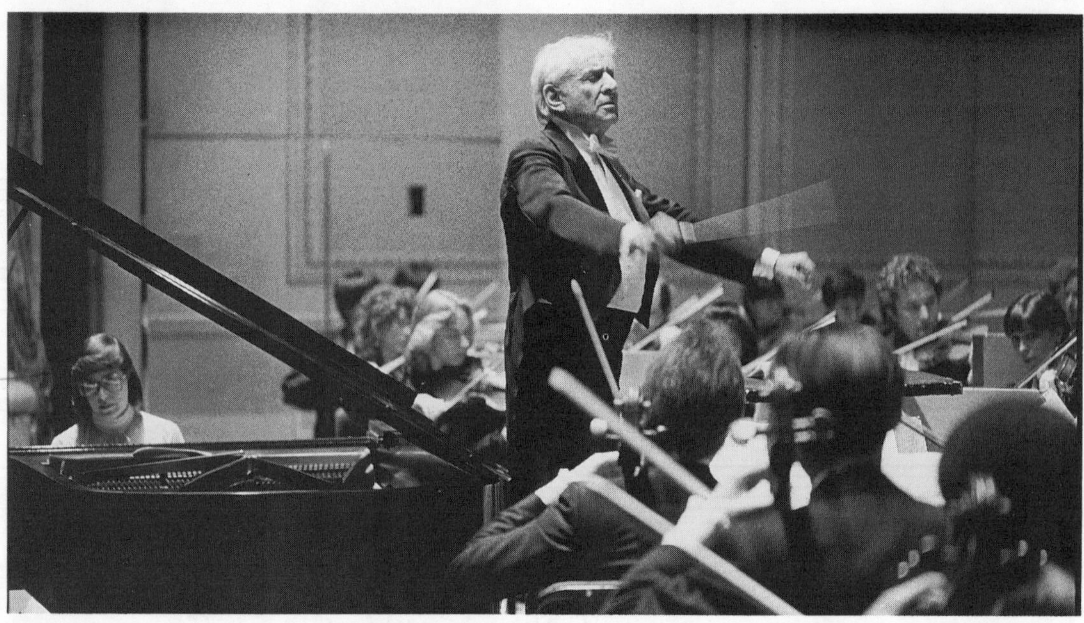

2. *Leonard Bernstein conducting the Symphony Orchestra of the Curtis Institute, with Susan Starr (piano) in a performance of his Symphony no.2 "The Age of Anxiety" at a concert celebrating the institute's 60th anniversary, 22 April 1984*

cially important to Bernstein's career at this time was his recognition of the potential of television for reaching a large audience. After his remarkable success as a lecturer on the television series "Omnibus" in 1954, he began other series in 1958 – the "Young People's Concerts," which ran for 15 years, and two programs for adults, "Lincoln Presents" and "Ford Presents," all with the New York PO. These televised lectures appealed to the musically literate but were also accessible to people with no knowledge of music, and in them Bernstein set the standard for those who would follow him. He has said that his efforts to teach music to his own children (born in 1952, 1955, and 1962) lay behind his success with his television programs.

From the beginning of his career, Bernstein had profited from exposure in the mass media. It was fortunate for him that the concert in which he substituted for Walter was broadcast nationally: others were not. Radio brought him initial recognition, and then print, recordings, and television increased his popularity. He played a central role in the burgeoning of performing arts and the building of cultural centers in the USA, and he transformed the image of the American musician from a somewhat forlorn figure to a remarkable and exciting one.

4. LATER YEARS: FROM 1963. Partly because he was welcome at the White House and partly because he thought the youthful President shared many of his liberal political views, Bernstein exulted in the brief period of Kennedy's tenure. On 22 November 1963 the President was assassinated. In many public statements made since, Bernstein has returned obsessively to that event, and it marked a turning point in his career. Although negative criticism of his conducting style had begun as early as 1947, it escalated in the early 1960s; in the *New York Times*, the music critic Harold Schonberg consistently ridiculed his gestures, once saying "Bernstein rose vertically, à la Nijinsky, and hovered there a good 15 seconds by the clock." This was also a difficult period for Bernstein as a composer. The widespread use of 12-tone techniques among his contemporaries, including his friend and mentor Aaron Copland, as well as criticisms leveled against him for adhering to tonality undoubtedly undermined his confidence.

In November 1963 Bernstein completed his Symphony no.3 "Kaddish"; in it he uses serial techniques in the first part and tonal writing in the second, a lullaby. Bernstein explains this alternation of language thus: "the agony expressed with 12-tone music has to give way . . . to tonality and diatonicism." In order to confront 12-tone music, Bernstein arranged for a sabbatical from the orchestra in 1964. He claims that during this period he threw away more 12-tone pieces and bits of pieces than he had written otherwise. At the end of the sabbatical he confirmed his commitment to tonality with the *Chichester Psalms*.

It was not as a composer, however, that Bernstein enjoyed international renown throughout the 1960s and 1970s but as a conductor, and he was invited to conduct on many notable occasions. The Viennese in particular held him in high regard. In 1966 he conducted *Falstaff* at the Staatsoper; in 1969, to celebrate the Staatsoper's centennial, he conducted Beethoven's *Missa solemnis*; and in 1970 (in honor of Beethoven's 200th anniversary) he conducted *Fidelio*. In Berlin Bernstein began filming a series of concerts of Mahler's music with the Vienna PO (1971), and he also led the Vienna Staatsoper and the Vienna PO in performances at La Scala to celebrate the latter's 200th anniversary (1978).

Bernstein remained as music director of the New York PO until 1969, when he retired as conductor laureate. His concerts had attracted capacity audiences, and during his tenure the orchestra made more recordings than ever before. Additional income from television programs brought about unprecedented financial stability. On 15 December 1971 Bernstein returned to conduct his 1000th concert with the New York PO, and he has continued to tour with the orchestra. Despite his reputation as a conservative, Bernstein has conducted numerous nontonal works including more than 40 world premières, among them Carter's Concerto for Orchestra, Babbitt's *Relata II*, Schuller's *Triplum*, and Cage's *Atlas eclipticalis*. In the late 1970s, however, he began to devote himself primarily to the standard repertory, and he has emerged as America's most overtly Romantic conductor; he has refined his approach to Brahms and Schumann, continued to explore Mahler, and in 1983 recorded Wagner's *Tristan und Isolde*.

Bernstein was also in demand as a public speaker, and as Charles Eliot Norton Professor of Poetry at Harvard University (1973), he gave a series of lectures in which he discussed music ranging from Hindu ragas through Mozart to Copland; these were later published as *The Unanswered Question* (1976). All music, Bernstein believes, is rooted in a universal language comparable to Noam Chomsky's universal grammar of speech, and this conviction underlies these lectures (as well as his earlier television series and even his undergraduate thesis); it also illuminates his belief that good music can be found in jazz and popular song as well as in the symphony. His own compositions are an eloquent testimony to this belief. Bernstein's works from the early 1970s include *Mass*, composed for the opening of the Kennedy Center (8 September 1971). He wrote relatively little during the remainder of the decade, perhaps due to his wife's long illness and her death (1978), but in 1980 he began the opera *A Quiet Place* (commissioned by the Houston Opera, La Scala, and the Kennedy Center), which he considers his most important work. Conceived as a sequel to *Trouble in Tahiti*, it was first performed on a program with that opera; later *Trouble in Tahiti* was incorporated into *A Quiet Place* as a flashback. Despite problems of structure and text, the work is bold and ambitious, and contains some of Bernstein's most complex and beautiful music. In 1984 *A Quiet Place* became the first American opera ever to be performed at La Scala. Bernstein was elected to the Academy of the American Academy and Institute of Arts and Letters in 1981 and in 1985 received the Academy's Gold Medal for Music, in recognition of him as a composer.

Bernstein has not, in his music, expanded the boundaries of musical thought; nor has he crystallized a style associated with a past era. What he has done above all is proclaim that an American can be a remarkable and exciting musician. No musician of the 20th century has ranged so wide. As a composer, he has written symphonies, chamber and vocal music, and opera, as well as music for dance, film, and Broadway. As a public personality, he has conducted, written books, appeared on television, lectured at universities, and remained a thoroughly professional pianist. As a conductor, he has not only shown himself a searching interpreter but has also introduced American works around the world. He has in sum achieved an unparalleled renown.

See also MUSICAL, §6 and fig.4; NEW YORK, §5; ORCHESTRAL MUSIC, §4.

WORKS

(all published unless otherwise stated)

DRAMATIC

The Birds (incidental music, Aristophanes), vv, chamber orch, 1938, unpubd; Cambridge, MA, 21 April 1939

The Peace (incidental music, Aristophanes), chorus, inst ens, 1940, unpubd; Cambridge, MA, 23 May 1941

Fancy Free (ballet, J. Robbins), 1944; New York, 18 April 1944

On the Town (musical, B. Comden, A. Green, Bernstein), orchd H. Kay, Bernstein, 1944; Boston, 13 Dec 1944

Facsimile (ballet, Robbins), 1946; New York, 24 Oct 1946, cond. Bernstein

Peter Pan (incidental music, Bernstein, after J. M. Barrie), orchd Kay, 1950; New York, 24 April 1950, cond. B. Steinberg

Trouble in Tahiti (opera, 1, Bernstein), 1951; Waltham, MA, 12 June 1952, cond. Bernstein

Wonderful Town (musical, Comden, Green, after J. A. Fields, J. Chodorov: My Sister Eileen), orchd D. Walker, 1953; New Haven, 19 Jan 1953

On the Waterfront (film score), 1954; film, dir. E. Kazan, released 28 July 1954

The Lark (incidental music, L. Hellman, after J. Anouilh), 7 solo vv, 1955; Boston, 28 Oct 1955

Salome (incidental music, Wilde), vv, orch, 1955, unpubd

Candide (comic operetta, Hellman, R. Wilbur, J. La Touche, D. Parker, Bernstein, after Voltaire), orchd Kay, Bernstein, 1956, Boston, 29 Oct 1956; rev. 1973 (Wilbur, La Touche, Sondheim, Bernstein, after H. Wheeler, after Voltaire), Brooklyn, NY, 20 Dec 1973, cond. J. Mauceri

West Side Story (musical, Sondheim, after A. Laurents), orchd S. Ramin, I. Kostal, Bernstein, choreographed Robbins, 1957; Washington, DC, 19 Aug 1957

The Firstborn (incidental music, C. Fry), 1958, unpubd; New York, 20 April 1958

Mass (theater piece, S. Schwartz, Bernstein), orchd J. Tunick, Kay, Bernstein, 1971, Washington, DC, 8 Sept 1971, cond. M. Peress; arr. S. Ramin for chamber orch, Los Angeles, 26 Dec 1972, cond. Peress

Dybbuk (ballet), 1974; New York, 16 May 1974, cond. Bernstein

By Bernstein (revue) [based on unpubd and withdrawn theater songs], 1975, withdrawn; New York, 23 Nov 1975

1600 Pennsylvania Avenue (musical, A. J. Lerner), orchd Ramin, Kay, 1976; Philadelphia, 24 Feb 1976

A Quiet Place (opera, 1, S. Wadsworth), 1983, Houston, 17 June 1983, cond. J. De Main; rev. 1984 in 3 acts, incl. Trouble in Tahiti

ORCHESTRAL

Fancy Free, suite [based on ballet], 1944; Pittsburgh, 14 Jan 1945, Pittsburgh SO, cond. Bernstein

On the Town, 3 dance episodes [based on musical], 1945, San Francisco, 13 Feb 1946, San Francisco SO, cond. Bernstein; transcr. concert band

Facsimile, choreographic essay [based on ballet], 1946; Poughkeepsie, NY, 5 March 1947, Rochester PO, cond. Bernstein

Symphony no.2 "The Age of Anxiety," after Auden, pf, orch, 1949, Boston, 8 April 1949, Boston SO, cond. Koussevitzky; rev. 1965

Prelude, Fugue and Riffs, cl, jazz ens, 1949, ABC television, 16 Oct 1955, cond. B. Goodman; choreographed J. Clifford, New York, 15 May 1969

Serenade [after Plato: Symposium], vn, str, harp, perc, 1954; Venice, Italy, 12 Sept 1954, I. Stern, Israel PO, cond. Bernstein

On the Waterfront, sym. suite [based on film score], 1955; Lenox, MA, 11 Aug 1955, Boston SO, cond. Bernstein

West Side Story, sym. dances [based on musical], 1960; New York, 13 Feb 1961, New York PO, cond. Foss

Fanfare I [for inauguration of J. F. Kennedy], 1961; Washington, DC, 19 Jan 1961, cond. Bernstein

Fanfare II [for 25th anniversary of the High School of Music and Art], 1961; New York, 24 March 1961, cond. Richter

Two Meditations from Mass, 1971; Austin, TX, 31 Oct 1971, cond. Peress

Meditation III from Mass, 1972, withdrawn; Jerusalem, 21 May 1972, Israel PO, cond. Bernstein

Dybbuk Suite nos.1–2 (Dybbuk Variations) [based on ballet], 1974; no.1, Auckland, New Zealand, 16 Aug 1974, cond. Bernstein; no.2, New York, 17 April 1977, cond. Bernstein

Three Meditations from Mass, vc, orch, 1977, arr. vc, pf, 1978; Washington, DC, 11 Oct 1977, Rostropovich, National SO, cond. Bernstein

Slava!, ov., 1977; Washington, DC, 11 Oct 1977, National SO, cond. Rostropovich

CBS Music, 1977; pts.1 and 5, CBS television, 1 April 1978

Divertimento, 1980; Boston, 25 Sept 1980, cond. S. Ozawa

A Musical Toast, 1980; New York, 11 Oct 1980, cond. Z. Mehta

Halil, nocturne, fl, str, perc, 1981; Jerusalem, 23 May 1981, cond. Bernstein

CHORAL AND VOCAL

Symphony no.1 "Jeremiah" (Bible), Mez, orch, 1942; Pittsburgh, 28 Jan 1944, Pittsburgh SO, cond. Bernstein

Hashkivenu (Heb. liturgy), T, chorus, org, 1945; New York, 11 May 1954, cond. M. Helfman

Yidgal (Heb. liturgy), chorus, pf, 1950

Harvard Choruses (Lerner): Dedication, Lonely Men of Harvard, 1957; New York, 7 March 1957, cond. G. W. Woodworth

Symphony no.3 "Kaddish" (Heb. liturgy, Bernstein), S, speaker, chorus, boys' chorus, orch, 1963, Tel Aviv, 10 Dec 1963, Israel PO, cond. Bernstein; rev. 1977, Mainz, Germany, 25 Aug 1977, cond. Bernstein

Chichester Psalms (Bible), Tr, chorus, orch, 1965; New York, 15 July 1965, J. Bogart, Camerata Singers, New York PO, cond. Bernstein

Warm-up, mixed chorus, 1970 [incorporated into Mass]

A Little Norton Lecture (Cummings), male vv, 1973, unpubd, arr. as no.8 in Songfest; Cambridge, MA, 1973

Songfest: To the Poem (F. O'Hara), The Pennycandy Store beyond the El (L. Ferlinghetti), A Julia de Burgos (J. de Burgos), To What you Said (Whitman), I, too, Sing America (L. Hughes), Okay "Negroes" (J. Jordan), To my Dear and Loving Husband (A. Bradstreet), Storyette H. M. (G. Stein), If you can't eat you got to (Cummings), Music I Heard with You (C. Aiken), Zizi's Lament (G. Corso), What Lips my Lips have Kissed (Millay), Israfel (Poe), 6 solo vv, orch, 1977; Washington, DC, 11 Oct 1977, National SO, cond. Bernstein

Olympic Hymn (G. Kunert), chorus, orch, 1981; Baden-Baden, Germany, 23 Sept 1981

Arrs.: Simchu Na (Heb. folksong), SATB, pf, 1947; Reena (Heb. folksong), chorus, orch, 1947, unpubd

CHAMBER

Piano Trio, 1937, unpubd

Music for Two Pianos, 1937, unpubd [incl. in On the Town]; Brookline, MA, 12 June 1938

Piano Sonata, 1938, unpubd

Music for the Dance, nos. 1 and 2, 1938, unpubd [incl. in On the Town]; Brookline, 12 June 1938

Scenes from the City of Sin, pf 4 hands, 1939, unpubd

Violin Sonata, 1940, unpubd

Four Studies, 2 cl, 2 bn, pf, *c*1940, unpubd; radio broadcast, Philadelphia, 1940

Clarinet Sonata, 1941–2; Boston, 21 April 1942

Seven Anniversaries, pf, 1943; Boston, 14 May 1944

Four Anniversaries, pf, 1948; Cleveland, 1 Oct 1948

Brass Music, tpt, hn, trbn, tuba, pf, 1948; New York, 8 April 1959

Five Anniversaries, pf, 1954

Shivaree, brass, perc, 1969 [incorporated into Mass]; New York, 28 Sept 1970

Touches, pf, 1981

Arr. Copland: El salón México, pf/2 pf; Boston, 18 Nov 1941

SOLO VOCAL
(all with pf acc.)

Psalm cxlviii, 1932

I Hate Music (Bernstein), song cycle: My Name is Barbara, Jupiter Has Seven Moons, I Hate Music, A Big Indian and a Little Indian, I'm a Person Too, 1943; Lenox, MA, 24 Aug 1943

Lamentation, 1943 [arr. of 3rd movt of Sym. no. 1 "Jeremiah"]

Afterthought (Bernstein), 1945, withdrawn; New York, 24 Oct 1948

La bonne cuisine (4 recipes, Bernstein), 1947; New York, 10 Oct 1948

Two Love Songs (Rilke): Extinguish my eyes, When my soul touches yours, 1949; New York, 13 March 1963

Silhouette (Galilee) (Bernstein), 1951; Washington, DC, 13 Feb 1955

On the Waterfront (La Touche), 1954, withdrawn

Get Hep! (Bernstein), 1955, withdrawn

So Pretty (Comden, Green), 1968; New York, 21 Jan 1968

Mad Woman of Central Park West, My New Friends, Up! Up! Up!, 1979; Buffalo, NY, 6 April 1979

Piccola serenata, 1979; Salzburg, Austria, 27 Aug 1979

Principal publishers: Amberson, Harms, Jalni

WRITINGS

The Joy of Music (New York, 1959)

Young People's Concerts for Reading and Listening (New York, 1962, rev. and enlarged 2/1970)

The Infinite Variety of Music (New York, 1966)

The Unanswered Question (Cambridge, MA, 1976)

Findings (New York, 1982)

BIBLIOGRAPHY

EwenD

P. Gradenwitz: "Leonard Bernstein," *MR*, x (1949), 191

W. Hamilton: "On the Waterfront," *Film Music*, xiv/1 (1954), 3

D. Drew: "Leonard Bernstein: *Wonderful Town*," *Score*, no. 12 (1955), 77

H. Keller: "On the Waterfront," *Score*, no. 12 (1955), 81

H. C. Schonberg: "New Job for the Protean Mr. Bernstein," *New York Times Magazine* (22 Dec 1957), 14, 31

H. Stoddard: *Symphony Conductors of the U.S.A.* (New York, 1957), 26

D. Gow: "Leonard Bernstein, Musician of Many Talents," *MT*, ci (1960), 427

J. Briggs: *Leonard Bernstein, the Man, his Work, and his World* (Cleveland, 1961)

A. Holde: *Leonard Bernstein* (Berlin, 1961)

J. Gottlieb: *The Music of Leonard Bernstein: a Study of Melodic Manipulations* (diss., U. of Illinois, 1964)

——: "The Choral Music of Leonard Bernstein, Reflections of Theater and Liturgy," *American Choral Review*, x (1968), 156

J. Gruen: *The Private World of Leonard Bernstein* (New York, 1968)

W. W. Tromble: *The American Intellectual and Music: an Analysis of the Writings of Suzanne K. Langer, Paul Henry Lang, Jacques Barzun, John Dewey, and Leonard Bernstein – with Implications for Music Education* (diss., U. of Michigan, 1968)

E. Ames: *A Wind from the West: Bernstein and the New York Philharmonic Abroad* (Boston, 1970)

M. Cone: *Leonard Bernstein* (New York, 1970)

G. Jackson: "*West Side Story*: Thema, Grundhaltung und Aussage," *Maske und Kothurn*, xvi (1970), 97

D. Wooldridge: *Conductor's World* (New York, 1970), 310

H. Berlinski: "Bernstein's Mass," *Sacred Music*, xcix/1 (1972), 3

J. Gruen: "In Love with the Stage," *Opera News*, xxxvii/3 (1972), 16

E. Salzman: "Quo vadis Leonard Bernstein?," *Stereo Review*, xxviii/5 (1972) 56

N. Goemanne: "Open Forum: the Controversial Bernstein Mass: Another Point of View," *Sacred Music*, c/1 (1973), 33

A. Pearlmutter: "Bernstein's Mass Revisited: a Guide to Using a Contemporary Work to Teach Music Concepts," *MEJ*, lxi/1 (1974), 34

J. W. Weber: *Leonard Bernstein* (Utica, NY, 1975) [discography]

R. Chesterman: "Leonard Bernstein in Conversation with Robert Chesterman," *Conversations with Conductors* (Totowa, NJ, 1976), 53, 69

G. Gottwald: "Leonard Bernsteins Messe oder der Konstruktion der Blasphemie," *Melos/NZM*, ii (1976) 281

J. Ardoin: "Leonard Bernstein at Sixty," *HiFi/MusAm*, xxviii/8 (1978), 53

P. Davis: "Bernstein as Symphonist," *New York Times* (26 Nov 1978), §II, 17

J. Gottlieb: *Leonard Bernstein: a Complete Catalogue of his Works* (New York, 1978)

A. Keiler: "Bernstein's *The Unanswered Question* and Problems of Musical Competence," *MQ*, lxiv (1978), 195

J. Gottlieb: "Symbols of Faith in the Music of Leonard Bernstein," *MQ*, lxvi (1980), 287

J. Hiemenz: "Bernstein on Television: Pros and Cons," *HiFi/MusAm*, xxx/4 (1980), 14

B. Bernstein: "Personal History: Family Matters," *New Yorker*, lviii (22 March 1982), 53, (29 March 1982), 58; repr. as *Family Matters* (New York, 1982)

H. Matheopoulos: *Maestro: Encounters with Conductors of Today* (London, 1982), 3

P. Robinson: *Bernstein* (New York, 1982)

U. Schneider: "Die Wiedergeburt der Musik aus dem Geist des Dreiklangs – Leonard Bernstein als verbaler Musikdeuter," *HiFi Stereophonie*, xxi/1 (1982), 56

S. Lipman: "Lenny on our Minds," *New Criterion*, iii/10 (1985), 1

J. Peyser: [biography] (New York, in preparation)

JOAN PEYSER

Bernstein, Martin (*b* New York, 14 Dec 1904). Writer on music and music educator. He studied at New York University (BS 1925, BMus 1927), where he began teaching in 1926; he became professor in 1947, and served as chairman of the department of music from 1955 until his retirement in 1972. In addition to teaching, Bernstein was a member of the double bass section of the New York PO (1926–8), a conductor for the American Bach Society (1951–3), and a lecturer on music in a weekly radio program for WCBS, New York (1955–7). His publications include *Score Reading* (1932, rev. 2/1947) and *An Introduction to Music* (1937, rev. 2/1951; rev. with M. Picker, 3/1966, 4/1972). A collection of essays in his honor (edited by E. H. Clinkscale and C. Brook) was published in 1977.

PAULA MORGAN

Berry, Chu [Leon Brown] (*b* Wheeling, WV, 13 Sept 1908; *d* Conneaut, OH, 30 Oct 1941). Jazz tenor saxophonist. He grew up in a musical family, and was inspired by Coleman Hawkins to take up saxophone. He played the alto instrument in high school and during his three years at West Virginia State College, then in 1929 received his first important professional engagement on tenor saxophone in Sammy Stewart's Chicago-based big band. The following year he settled in New York, where he worked in many leading bands, including those of Benny Carter (1932) and Charlie Johnson. He also took part in Spike Hughes's famous recording sessions in New York in 1933. After periods with Teddy Hill (1933–5) and Fletcher Henderson (1935–6), which established his reputation, he joined Cab Calloway's band in 1937, remaining as its star soloist until his death in an automobile accident. From 1935 he was also a prolific freelance recording artist.

Berry was strongly influenced by Coleman Hawkins, but soon developed his own distinctive style, and even became influential in his own right during Hawkins's long absence from the American jazz scene (1934–9). His sound was less voluptuous than Hawkins's and his melodic imagination not as fertile, but he was the older man's equal in harmonic sophistication and his superior when it came to swing and drive. Berry excelled at performing in fast tempos, where his remarkable breath control, unerring sense of time, and even, strong tone-production stood him in good stead. His early ballad playing was sometimes too florid, but in recordings such as *A Ghost of a Chance* and *Lonesome Nights* (both made with the Calloway band in 1940) a new maturity became evident. Had he lived, Berry might well have offset the overwhelming influence of Lester Young on later tenor saxophonists.

RECORDINGS

(selective list)

As leader: Indiana (1937, Variety 587); Sittin' In/Forty-Six West Fifty-Second (1938, Com. 516); Blowin' Up a Breeze (1941, Com. 541)

As sideman: R. Norvo: Blues in E Flat (1935, Col. 3079D); H. Allen: Rosetta (1935, Voc. 2965); L. Hampton: Sweethearts on Parade (1939, Vic. 26209), Shufflin' at the Hollywood (1939, Vic. 26254), Ain't Cha Comin' Home? (1939, Vic. 26362), Hot Mallets (1939, Vic. 26371); C. Basie: Oh! Lady Be Good (1939, Decca 2631); C. Calloway: A Ghost of a Chance (1940, OK 5687), Bye Bye Blues (1940, OK 6084), Lonesome Nights (1940, OK 5827)

BIBLIOGRAPHY

SouthernB

D. Morgenstern: "Three Forgotten Giants," *DBY 1965* (Chicago, 1964)

J. Evensmo: *The Tenor Saxophone of Chu Berry* (Hosle, Norway, 1976)

D. Chamberlain and R. Wilson, eds.: "The Otis Ferguson Reader," *December Magazine*, xxiv/1–2 (1982), 58

DAN MORGENSTERN

Berry, Chuck [Charles Edward Anderson] (*b* San Jose, CA, 15 Jan 1926). Rock-and-roll singer, songwriter, and guitarist. He was one of the originators of rock-and-roll, forging it into a massively commercial, socially revolutionary musical force. A brilliant lyricist, inventive composer, innovative guitarist, and captivating performer, he was one of the genre's first black performers to appeal to a white mainstream audience. His national reputation, which began in the mid-1950s, lasted far longer than those of most other popular musicians; he enjoyed considerable success in 1964, at the height of the "British invasion," and continued to perform and record into the mid-1980s.

1. Life. 2. Style and Influence.

1. Life. Berry deliberately obscured his early years; sources differ as to his date of birth, and the year was long given as 1931. Raised in St. Louis and Wentzville, Missouri, he spent his childhood in comfortable, working-class circumstances. He attended Antioch Baptist Church, where his father was a bass in the choir. At Sumner High School in St. Louis Berry studied guitar with his music teacher, Julia Davis; he also learned piano and saxophone. During World War II he was sent to a reform school for three years for attempted robbery; when he was released at the age of 21 he worked in a General Motors plant and studied cosmetology. With the pianist Johnny Johnson and the drummer Ebby Harding he formed a trio; this was known first as the Johnny Johnson Trio, but Berry, after changing from saxophone to voice and guitar, assumed leadership of the group by the mid-1950s. They played in nightclubs and at house parties in St. Louis before auditioning for Leonard Chess, the owner of Chess Records, to whom Berry had been introduced by Muddy Waters. Their audition included some blues numbers, notably a song of which they were especially proud, *Wee wee hours,* and a parodistic rockabilly song, *Ida Red*, which Chess, a musically ungifted but commercially shrewd impresario, suggested be retitled *Maybellene* and recorded with a "bigger beat." *Maybellene* was issued in 1955, backed with *Wee wee hours*, as Berry's first recording.

Maybellene became one of the first enormously popular rock-and-roll songs, and the first single recording to reach high positions on the pop, country, and rhythm-and-blues charts. During the next few years Berry wrote and recorded many memorable songs: *Thirty Days* in 1955; *Roll over Beethoven* (also part of the first Chess audition), *Havana Moon*, and *Brown-eyed Handsome Man* in 1956; *School Day* and *Rock and Roll Music* in 1957; *Around and Around*, *Johnny B. Goode*, *Sweet Little Rock and Roller*, *Sweet Little Sixteen*, and *Reelin' and Rockin'* in 1958; *Back in the U.S.A.*, *Memphis, Tennessee*, and *Little Queenie* in 1959; and *Let it Rock* in 1960. During this period he toured constantly and made an ebullient impression in concert; he became well-known for his stage deportment, in particular his "duck walk," which involved bending his knees and slithering across the stage. He also appeared in several early rock-and-roll films, of which the best-known are *Rock Rock Rock* (1958) and *Go Johnny Go* (1959); these were thinly disguised concert films, in which musical numbers were linked by tenuous plots.

In 1959 Berry was arrested for a violation of the Mann Act; he was convicted in 1961 and sent to the Federal penitentiary in Terre Haute, Indiana. By the time of his release in 1963 his nightclub had closed and his family had left him. His years in prison had also affected his personality: once cheerful and optimistic, he was now sullen, bitter, and suspicious, especially in his dealings with promoters and record company executives; his stage shows, however, retained their joyous spirit. He lived for a time in Wentzville, where he developed an amusement park that bore his name. But he soon resumed his musical career, encouraged by a number of English and American rock musicians who admired his work. In the face of the "British invasion" he made a triumphant return with songs like *Nadine* and *No Particular Place to Go* (both from 1964), which rank with his best work. After this new flurry of success, however, Berry faded until 1972, when he recorded *My Ding-a-ling*, a sexual novelty song that became his only recording to reach no. 1 on the pop chart. He began to perform frequently on the "nostalgia circuit," often as part of programs organized by the promoter Ralph Nader. Although he usually played with hastily assembled backup bands, his performances rarely fell below a level of workmanlike professionalism: after an engagement at a discothèque in New York, Robert Palmer wrote in the *New York Times* that Berry had given "a magnificent show"; he "seemed to be offering a kind of crash course in American vernacular music." In 1979 Berry was convicted of income-tax evasion for failing to report $110,000 in income from concerts he had given in 1973; he served four months in the Federal penitentiary in Lompoc, California. Two months before entering prison he performed at the White House.

2. Style and influence. Berry was the leading pop-music poet of teenage life. His music combines the virtuoso guitar playing

Chuck Berry, 1979

of country music and rockabilly with the rhythm-guitar riffs and 12-bar structure of blues and rhythm-and-blues. His lyrics, which celebrate cars, high school, girls, and the redemptive power of rock-and-roll, helped shape rock's themes for decades. His descriptions of teenage social rituals came just as the American youth movement began to change the repressive ambiance of the 1950s, and hence his was a key voice in the artistic articulation of that revolution.

St. Louis in the 1930s was a lively center for gospel, blues, and jazz. Among the musicians who seem particularly to have affected Berry were Charlie Christian, who developed a unique style with the electric guitar, making use of the ominous roughness obtainable through amplifier distortion; T-Bone Walker, who blended brilliant musicianship with amiable clowning; the rhythm-and-blues singer Louis Jordan; and Big Joe Turner (Berry once sang an impassioned version of his *Confessin' the Blues* at a high-school musicale). Other influences on Berry extended beyond blues and jazz to include black and white pop singers of the day, especially Nat "King" Cole and Frank Sinatra. From 1955 his songs constitute a tangled web of country and black influences; southern Whites and Blacks shared a common destiny of poverty and isolation from the mainstream of society and often influenced each other's music.

The structural basis of Berry's songs is the blues, in formal variants ranging from eight to 24 bars, with a strong emphasis on the backbeat. He had an easy, conversational baritone, the inflections shorn of classic blues ornamentation, and crisp enunciation; on the radio he was sometimes mistaken for a white performer. As a guitarist he employed speeded-up blues and rhythm-and-blues licks, infusing them with bluegrass influences, and adapting them to pop-song formats. He exploited the electric guitar's potential for rhythmic chording and ringing overtone effects in a way that has influenced rock guitarists ever since. A skillful leader, he could elicit a strong performance from a rhythm section, even with an informally organized ensemble.

Berry's lyrics treat cars as symbols of individual liberty, rock as an anthem on freedom and sexuality, and high school as a prison and microcosm. His songs portray the world of the typical teenager, and achieve much of their impact from their wit and telling detail. His musical influences and themes varied widely. *Roll over Beethoven* is a humorous but explicit cry of self-assertion by vernacular music; *Havana Moon* is one of the first American pop-calypso songs; *Brown-eyed Handsome Man* is an early attestation of black pride; *Sweet Little Sixteen* is an affectionate tribute to his fans.

While he never attained the legendary status in popular culture of Elvis Presley, Berry is perhaps the most critically acclaimed of the early rock-and-roll stars. In Marsh's words, "Chuck Berry is to rock what Louis Armstrong was to jazz." His enormous influence can be seen in the number of musicians who recorded his material. The Beach Boys' early hit, *Surfin' USA* (1963), was musically a copy of *Sweet Little Sixteen.* Buddy Holly recorded his songs, as did the Beatles (*Roll over Beethoven* and *Rock and Roll Music*); Mick Jagger and Keith Richards of the Rolling Stones met as teenagers when they discovered their common interest in Berry's music, and the Stones recorded many songs by and about him in their early years. Linda Ronstadt's album *Living in the USA* (1978) was inspired by Berry, and includes his song *Back in the USA*. In a more general, internalized way, innumerable rock musicians have borrowed his musical signatures and poetic themes, and emulated his mischievous, insouciant stage manner.

RECORDINGS

(selective list; recorded for Chess unless otherwise stated)

Maybellene/Wee wee hours (1604, 1955); Thirty Days (1610, 1955); Brown-eyed Handsome Man (1635, 1956); Havana Moon (1645, 1956); Roll over Beethoven (1626, 1956); Rock and Roll Music (1671, 1957); School Day (1653, 1957); *After School Sessions* (1426, 1958); Around and Around/Johnny B. Goode (1691, 1958); Sweet Little Rock and Roller (1709, 1958); Sweet Little Sixteen/Reelin' and Rockin' (1683, 1958); Back in the U.S.A./Memphis, Tennessee (1729, 1959); Little Queenie (1722, 1959); Let it Rock (1747, 1960); *Rockin' at the Hops* (1448, 1960); Nadine (1883, 1964); No Particular Place to Go (1898, 1964); *St. Louis to Liverpool* (1488, 1964); *Chuck Berry in Memphis* (Mercury 61123, 1967); *The London Chuck Berry Sessions* (60020, 1972); My Ding-a-ling (2131, 1972); *Rockit* (Atco 38-118, 1979)

BIBLIOGRAPHY

SouthernB

R. Christgau: "Chuck Berry," *The Rolling Stone Illustrated History of Rock & Roll*, ed. J. Miller (New York, 1976, rev. 2/1980), 58

M. Lydon: "Chuck Berry," *Rock Folk: Portraits from the Rock 'n' Roll Pantheon* (New York, 1971, 2/1973), 1

"Chuck Berry," *CBY 1977*

D. Marsh: "Berry, Chuck," *The New Rolling Stone Record Guide*, ed. D. Marsh and J. Swenson (New York, 1979, 2/1983), 38

H. De Witt: *Chuck Berry: Rock 'n' Roll Music* (New York, 1981, rev. 2/1985)

R. Denyer: *The Guitar Handbook* (London, 1982), 10

K. Reese: *Chuck Berry: Mr. Rock n' Roll* (New York, 1982)

JOHN ROCKWELL

Berry, Wallace (Taft) (*b* La Crosse, WI, 10 Jan 1928). Composer, theorist, and teacher. He studied at the University of Southern California (PhD 1956) and at the Paris Conservatoire with Boulanger on a Fulbright scholarship (1953–4). In 1952 the vocal and orchestral work *Spoon River* brought him to national attention. He has taught at the University of Southern California (1956–7) and the University of Michigan (1957–77), where he was made head of the music theory department in 1968, and from 1978 has served as head of the music department at the

University of British Columbia. From 1982 to 1985 he was president of the Society for Music Theory. He is the author of *Form in Music* (1966), *Eighteenth-century Imitative Counterpoint* (with E. L. Chudacoff, 1969), and *Structural Functions in Music* (1976).

WORKS

Stage: The Admirable Bashville (chamber opera, Shaw), 1954

Orch: 4 Movts, chamber orch, 1954; Fantasy, D, 1958; 5 Pieces, small orch, 1961; Pf Conc., 1964; Canto elegiaco, 1968; Intonation: Victimis hominum inhumanitatem in memoriam, 1972; Acadian Images, 1977–8

Choral: No Man is an Island (Donne), 1959; Heaven-haven (G. M. Hopkins), 1960; Spring Pastoral (E. Wylie), 1960

Solo vocal: Limericks, 1v, pf, 1951; Paean from the Grave, 1v, pf, 1951; Spoon River (E. L. Masters), S, Bar, orch, 1952; Anthea, T, pf, 1953; Canticle on a Judaic Text, S/T, orch, 1953; 4 Songs of the Sea, 1v, pf, 1957; 3 Songs of April, S/T, str qt, 1959; Des visages de France, S, Mez, ens, 1967; Credo in unam vitam, T, hn, vc, ens, 1969; Lover of the Moon Trembling Now at Twilight, S/T, ens, 1971; Of the Changeless Night and the Stark Ranges of Nothing, Mez, vc, pf, 1978–9

Inst: Cl Sonata, 1950; Suite, str trio, 1950; 3 Pieces on Arabic Songs, fl, ob, tom-tom, 1950; Pf Qnt, 1951; Divertimento, hpd, ob, eng hn, vc, 1952; Variations, pf, 1952; 8 20th-century Miniatures, pf, 1955; Canons, 2 cl, 1959; 4 str qts, 1960, 1964, 1966, 1982; Duo, vn, pf, 1961; Fantasy on "Von Himmel hoch," org, 1963; Threnody, vn, 1963; Divertimento, wind qnt, pf, perc, 1964; Canto lirico, va, pf, 1965; Composition for Pf and Elec Sounds, 1967; Fantasy in 5 Statements, cl, pf, 1967; Duo, fl, pf, 1968; Pf Trio, 1970; 3 Anachronisms, vn, pf, 1973; 3 Essays in Parody, tr inst, pf, 1973; 10 Pieces, tr inst, pf, 1973–4; Pf Sonata, 1975; Variations on a "Martyrs' Tune," org, 1976

Principal publishers: C. Fischer, Presser, Southern

EDITH BORROFF/R

Berteling, Theodore (*b* Germany, 1821; *d* New York, 1890). Maker of flutes, clarinets, and oboes. He began his career in Boston with E. G. Wright in 1849. During the next few years he worked successively with Graves & Co. and J. Lathrop Allen, setting up in business for himself in 1855. In 1857 he moved to New York, where his business continued until 1915.

In 1850 and again in 1856 Berteling won silver medals for his instruments in exhibitions of the Massachusetts Charitable Mechanic Association in Boston. US patents 76,389 of 1868 and 264,611 of 1882 were obtained by Berteling for improvements in his flutes. Berteling instruments are made of wood but make extensive use of metal linings, metal reinforcing at joints, and metal coverings. A piccolo at the Smithsonian Institution is entirely covered with nickel silver in addition to being lined with brass.

Most Berteling instruments have an elaborate key mechanism. His flutes often have foot extensions to *b* and *b♭*. Early Boehm system flutes with conical bore as well as cylindrical examples are among Berteling's instruments in the Dayton C. Miller collection at the Library of Congress. A Berteling oboe is in the collection of the Henry Ford Museum, Dearborn, Michigan.

BIBLIOGRAPHY

N. Groce: *Musical Instrument Making in New York City during the Eighteenth and Nineteenth Centuries* (diss., U. of Michigan, 1982)

ROBERT E. ELIASON

Besoyan, Rick [Richard] (*b* Reedley, CA, 2 July 1924; *d* Sayville, NY, 13 March 1970). Composer and lyricist. He wrote his first musical score in 1942 for a high-school production. After serving in the US Army during World War II he toured with the Savoy Light Opera Company. He left it to go to New York and study at the American Theatre Wing and with Stella Adler. In 1957 he wrote both music and lyrics for a revue, *In your Hat*; one of its songs was so successful that he expanded the idea into *Little Mary Sunshine*, which opened off Broadway in 1959. This was a spoof on old-fashioned operetta of the Romberg and Friml variety and was a huge success, running for 1143 performances. Besoyan followed it with *The Student Gypsy* (1963) and *Babes in the Wood* (1964), but *Little Mary Sunshine* had apparently exhausted the demand for this kind of work, and neither was successful. At the time of his death Besoyan was working on a dramatization of Paul Gallico's *Mrs. 'Arris Goes to Paris*.

RICHARD C. LYNCH

Bessaraboff, Nicholas [from 1945 Nicholas Bessaraboff Bodley] (*b* Voronezh, Russia, 13 Feb 1894; *d* New York, 10 Nov 1973). Writer. Actively interested in music from childhood, he was trained as a mechanical engineer in St. Petersburg (1912–15). In 1915 he was sent to the USA to join a Russian Artillery Commission seeking to procure munitions. After the 1917 Revolution Bessaraboff stayed in the USA, working as an engineer in Rochester, New York; it was there that he began the serious study of instruments. In 1927 he became a naturalized American citizen. Four years later he moved to Boston, where in 1935 he began a short catalogue that grew into a general compendium of western European instruments, arranged in the form of a systematic classification of instruments. *Ancient European Musical Instruments: an Organological Study of the Musical Instruments in the Leslie Lindsey Mason Collection at the Museum of Fine Arts, Boston* was published in 1941, after which time Bessaraboff devoted himself mainly to his engineering career and to the study of prime numbers.

BIBLIOGRAPHY

D. D. Boyden: "Nicholas Bessaraboff's *Ancient European Musical Instruments*," *Notes*, xxviii (1971–2), 21

DAVID D. BOYDEN

Bethlehem Bach Festival. Annual festival featuring the music of J. S. Bach, inaugurated at Bethlehem, Pennsylvania, in 1900. It is presented by the Bach Choir of Bethlehem, founded in 1898 by John Frederick Wolle, organist of the Central Moravian Church, and is held at Packer Memorial Church, Lehigh University, on the second and third weekends of May. The origins of the festival are rooted in the religious traditions of the Moravians, who settled in the area in the 18th century. The festival itself was initiated on 27 March 1900 with the first American performance of Bach's B minor Mass, conducted by Wolle. Festivals were held in 1901, 1903, and 1905; after reorganization of the choir in 1911 they were resumed annually under Wolle (1912–32), whose successors include Ifor Jones (1939–69), Alfred Mann (1970–80), William Reese (1981–3), and Greg Funfgeld (from 1983). From 1912 to 1947 the orchestral ensemble was drawn from members of the Philadelphia Orchestra. Soloists have included such renowned artists as Rose Bampton, Helen Boatwright, Phyllis Curtin, Charles Bressler, and Phyllis Bryn-Julson. In 1976 the choir appeared in Germany at the 51st International Festival of the New Bach Society in Berlin and at the Thomaskirche, Leipzig.

BIBLIOGRAPHY

R. Walters: *The Bethlehem Bach Choir* (Boston, 1918, 2/1923)
——: "Bach at Bethlehem, Pennsylvania," *MQ*, xxi (1935), 179
M. A. D. Howe: " 'Venite in Bethlehem' – the Major Chord," *MQ*, xxviii (1942), 174

SARA VELEZ, RITA H. MEAD

Bethune (Green), Thomas [Blind Tom] (*b* Columbus, GA, 25 May 1849; *d* Hoboken, NJ, 13 June 1908). Pianist and composer. He was blind from birth and was bought as a slave with his parents in 1850 by James N. Bethune, a journalist, lawyer, and politician in Columbus. He demonstrated musical aptitude and exceptional retentive skills by his fourth year and was given musical instruction by Bethune's daughter Mary. He was exhibited throughout the state by his master in 1857, and then hired out to Perry Oliver, a planter of Savannah, who took him on an extensive concert tour throughout the slave-holding states; this included a command performance at Willard Hall in Washington for visiting Japanese dignitaries. His programs included works by Bach, Beethoven, Chopin, Liszt, Thalberg, and other European masters, improvisations on operatic tunes and popular ballads, and several of his own published and unpublished compositions. He could perform difficult pieces after one hearing, sing and recite poetry or prose in several languages, duplicate lengthy orations, and imitate the sounds of nature, machinery,

Sheet-music cover of Thomas Bethune's "Oliver Gallop" and "Virginia Polka" (1860)

and various musical instruments. On the outbreak of the Civil War, he was returned to the Bethunes, who continued to exhibit him in the South to raise money for the Confederacy. After the Bethunes were successful in a guardianship trial in July 1865, Tom was taken abroad, with W. P. Howard of Atlanta as his musical tutor; he received testimonial letters from such musicians as Ignaz Moscheles and Charles Hallé. The Bethunes moved to Warrenton, Virginia, on their return, and Tom was shown throughout the USA and Canada; he studied with Joseph Poznanski in New York during the summers. In 1887 Bethune's son's widow gained legal control over Tom, and continued to exhibit him in major concert halls and as a vaudeville attraction. His final appearances were on the Keith Circuit, in 1904–5.

Tom wrote more than 100 piano works which are typical examples of 19th-century parlor pieces; they include *The Rainstorm* (1865), *The Battle of Manassas* (1866), *March Timpani* (1880), *Cyclone Galop* (1887), *Blind Tom's Mazurka* (1888), and *Grand March Resurrection* (1901). His vocal compositions reveal a familiarity with revival hymns.

BIBLIOGRAPHY

SouthernB

Blind Tom: the Great Negro Pianist (Baltimore, 1867)

J. Becket: "Blind Tom as he is To-day," *Ladies' Home Journal*, xv/10 (1898), 13

A. Tutein: "The Phenomenon of 'Blind Tom'," *The Etude*, xxxvii (1918), 91

E. Abbott: "The Miraculous Case of Blind Tom," *The Etude*, lviii (1940), 517

E. M. Thornton: "The Mystery of Blind Tom," *Georgia Review*, xv (1961), 395

N. T. Robinson: "Blind Tom: Musical Prodigy," *Georgia Historical Quarterly*, li (1967), 336

G. H. Southall: "Blind Tom: a Misrepresented and Neglected Composer-Pianist," *BPiM*, iii (1975), 141

——: *Blind Tom: the Post-Civil War Enslavement of a Black Musical Genius* (Minneapolis, 1979)

——: *The Continuing "Enslavement" of Blind Tom, 1865–1887* (Minneapolis, 1982)

GENEVA H. SOUTHALL

Beversdorf, (Samuel) Thomas (*b* Yoakum, TX, 8 Aug 1924; *d* Bloomington, IN, 15 Feb 1981). Composer. He studied with Kennan at the University of Texas (BM 1945), with Rogers and Hanson at the Eastman School (MM 1946, DMA 1957), and with Copland and Milhaud at the Berkshire Music Center (summer 1947). He taught at the University of Houston and was first trombonist with the Houston SO, 1946–8, and from 1949 until his death he was professor of music at Indiana University. He held the Hoblitzel Fellowship while a student at the University of Texas and in 1956 was awarded a Danforth Teaching Fellowship. He received a commission from the Cincinnati SO (for *Ode*, 1952) and one from the Houston SO (for *New Frontiers*, 1953). From 1944 to 1959 Beversdorf composed prolifically and rapidly, his music characterized by standard timbral combinations, but thereafter he worked more slowly, producing introspective compositions on a larger scale with more unusual instrumentation; all his works reflect a sensitivity to the practical needs of a variety of ensembles and circumstances. He also wrote two opera librettos: *Metamorphosis* (after Kafka), 1955–66, and *Amphitryon 99, or I Hope it isn't a Cold Marble Couch* (after Plautus and Giraudoux), 1977–8.

WORKS

Stage: The Hooligan (opera, 1, Beversdorf, after Chekhov: The Boor), 1964–9; Vision of Christ (mystery play, J. Wheatcroft, after Langland), 1971

Choral: 17 Antiphonal Responses, chorus, org, 1949; The Rock, oratorio (T. S. Eliot), 1958; Mini Motet from Micah, S, Bar, SATA, org, 1969; 2 Amen settings, chorus, org, 1969

Orch: 4 syms., 1946, 1950, 1954 rev. 1958, 1960, no.3, wind, perc; Mexican Portrait, small orch, 1948, rev. 1952; Conc. grosso, ob, chamber orch, 1948; Conc., 2 pf, orch, 1951; Ode, 1952; New Frontiers, 1953; Serenade, wind, perc, 1957; Vn Conc., 1959; Variations (Threnody), 1963; Murals, Tapestries, and Icons, wind, elec b gui, elec pf, 1975; other works

Brass: Hn Sonata, 1945; Cathedral Music, brass ens, 1950, brass qt, org, 1953; 3 Epitaphs, brass qt, 1955; Tuba Sonata, 1956; Tpt Sonata, 1962; Walruses, Cheesecake, and Morse Code, tuba, pf, 1973; Conc., tuba, wind, 1975

Inst: Suite on Baroque Themes, cl, vc, pf, 1947; 2 str qts, 1951, 1955; Vn Sonata, 1964–5; Fl Sonata, 1965–6; Divertimento da camera, fl + pic, ob

+ eng hn, db, hpd, 1968; Vc Sonata, 1968–9; Sonata, vn, harp, 1977; Corelliana Variations, fl + pic, fl + pic + a fl, vc, 1980; other works

Other: 6 pf works, incl. Pf Sonata, 1944, Toccata, 2 pf, 1953; 3 Songs (Cummings), S, pf, 1955; other songs

Principal publishers: Invention, Southern Music

BIBLIOGRAPHY

EwenD

DAVID COPE

Bezanson, Philip (Thomas) (*b* Athol, MA, 6 Jan 1916; *d* Hadley, MA, 11 March 1975). Composer and teacher. He studied at Yale University (BM 1940) and with Clapp at the State University of Iowa (MA 1948, PhD 1951), where he joined the faculty in 1947 and succeeded Clapp as principal professor of composition in 1954. In 1964 he was called to head the music department at the University of Massachusetts, Amherst; in 1973 he relinquished that post to teach full-time at the university. Bezanson's honors include a commission from Mitropoulos for the Piano Concerto (1952), an award from the Fromm Foundation (1953, for the Piano Sonata), and a Guggenheim Fellowship (1971). Many of his pupils later achieved prominence as composers, among them T. J. Anderson, Dodge, Felciano, Edwin London, Sollberger, and Olly Wilson. Bezanson's works fall within the mainstream of 20th-century music in the generation after Stravinsky, Bartók, and Hindemith. It is rooted in diatonicism but has frequently changing scales and tonal centers; shifting major and minor 3rds are common. Standard meters, often irregularly accented, predominate. In 1981 a Bezanson archive was established at the University of Massachusetts, Amherst.

WORKS

Operas: Western Child (3, P. Engle), 1959, U. of Iowa, 28 July 1959, rev. as Golden Child, NBC television, 16 Dec 1960; Stranger in Eden (3, Reardon), 1963

Vocal: Requiem for the University of Iowa Dead (Engle), chorus, orch, 1955; The Word of Love (Engle), song cycle, 1v, pf, 1956; Song of the Cedar (Engle), cantata, chorus, orch, 1958; Songs of Innocence (Blake), song cycle, 1v, chamber orch/pf, 1959; Contrasts (Herrick, K. Gunderson, Blake), 1v, pf, 1966; Morning, Noon, Evening (J. Langland), unacc. chorus, 1966; That Time may Cease and Midnight never Come (Marlowe), Bar, orch, 1968, arr. Bar, pf; Dies Domini magnus (Bible), chorus, pf, 1971; St. Judas (N. Kazantzakis), oratorio, chorus, orch, 1973; Memory (A. Lincoln), chorus, chamber ens, 1975

Orch: 2 syms., 1946, 1950; Cyrano de Bergerac, ov., 1949; Dance Scherzo, small orch, 1950; Fantasy, Fugue and Finale, str, 1951; Pf Conc., 1952, rev. 1960; Rondo-prelude, 1954; Anniversary Ov., band, 1956; Capriccio concertante, 1967; Concertino, ob, str, 1968; Sinfonia concertante, 1971

Chamber and inst: Divertimento, 8 wind, 1947; 2 str qts, 1948, 1961; 2 vn sonatas, 1949, 1953; Pf Sonata, 1951; Str Trio, 1954; Cl Sonata, 1955; Sextet, 5 ww, pf, 1955; Homage to Great Americans, ww qnt, 1958; Prelude and Dance, 6 brass, 1958; Pf Trio, 1963; Divertimento, org, brass, timp, 1964; Trio, cl, hn, pf, 1966; Diversion, tpt, hn, trbn, 1967; Petite Suite, 7 ww, 1973; Brass Sextet, 1974; several inst duos, pf pieces

MSS in *IaU*, *MU*

Principal publisher: ACA

FREDERICK CRANE

B-52s. Rock group. It was formed in 1976 in Athens, Georgia, and its members are Fred Schneider (Frederick W. Schneider, III; *b* Ocean Port, NJ, 1 July 1951), vocalist and songwriter; Kate Pierson (*b* Rutherford, NJ, 27 April 1953), vocalist, keyboardist, and songwriter; Ricky (Richard Hilton) Wilson (*b* Athens, GA, 19 March 1953), guitarist and songwriter; Keith Strickland (*b* Athens, 26 Oct 1953), drummer, keyboardist, guitarist, and songwriter; and Cindy (Cynthia Leigh) Wilson (*b* Athens, 28 Feb 1957), vocalist and songwriter. The B-52s took their name from a local expression for the exaggerated "beehive" hairstyle worn by Cindy Wilson and Kate Pierson. The simple, earthy dance beat of the group's music is founded on Ricky Wilson's five-string guitar riffs and Strickland's loud, precise drumming. Toy instruments, go-go dancing, and electronic sound effects supplement Schneider's campy declamation to create a style of party music that is both arty and unpretentious, nostalgic and futuristic at once. The album *The B-52s* (WB 3255), released in 1979, included *Rock Lobster*, a song about a surreal beach party, which became a hit. Their second album, *Wild Planet* (WB 3471, 1980), and a mini-LP (*Mesopotamia*, WB 3641, 1982) produced by David Byrne of the Talking Heads, were less successful, but marked Cindy Wilson's emergence as a powerfully emotional lead singer. *Whammy!* (WB 23819, 1983) included two more dance hits, *Whammy Kiss* and *Song for a Future Generation*. The group is as effective in live performances as it is on record, the flamboyant dress of the women contributing to the party atmosphere created by the music. *Party Mix*, a six-track album of remixed versions of songs mostly from *The B-52s*, was released in 1981; it is an early example of the application by white artists of a technique well-established among black groups, which makes music more suitable for dancing by boosting bass and percussion and heightening sound effects.

JOHN PICCARELLA

Bible, Frances (L.) (*b* Sackets Harbor, NY, 26 Jan 1927). Mezzo-soprano. After studying with Belle Julie Soudant and Queena Mario at the Juilliard School (1939–47), she made her début in 1948 at the New York City Opera, where she remained a leading artist until 1977. Although over the course of her long career she sang virtually the entire standard repertory for her voice, she was particularly noted for her Cenerentola and her interpretations of trouser roles such as Cherubino, Hansel, and Oktavian. She took part in the world premières of Douglas Moore's *The Ballad of Baby Doe* and Robert Ward's *The Crucible*, both of which she recorded, William Grant Still's *Troubled Island*, and David Tamkin's *The Dybbuk*, and in a number of important American premières. She also sang in Europe (participating in the Glyndebourne recording of *L'incoronazione di Poppea*) and with various American regional companies. She taught at Rice University, Houston (1979–82), and was artist-in-residence there in 1982–3. Bible's voice was warm, her technique assured; in the early years of her career she was a lively and charming presence on stage, and later she excelled in roles demanding authority. Her qualities made her a prominent and well-loved presence in the American theater.

RICHARD DYER

Bibliographies. Music bibliography has been defined as the study and description, especially in published form, of musical documents and of the literature about music. As a whole it entails two separate but interdependent areas of investigation. Analytical and descriptive bibliography are concerned with the study and identification of books as physical objects, and involve such matters as paper, design, typography or engraving, printing, and binding. Reference bibliography is concerned with access to information about musical materials and the literature of music – their existence, identity, contents, and availability – and is usually embodied in lists that are known as "bibliographies." This article is concerned exclusively with reference bibliographies that cover music published in or otherwise distinctive to the USA.

1. Introduction. 2. Access by period. 3. Access by place. 4. Access by content. 5. Access by bibliographical form.

1. Introduction. The bibliographical record of American music has been described numerous times, notably in Guy Marco's *Information on Music* (1977) and G. Thomas Tanselle's general *Guide to the Study of United States Imprints* (1971). Here it is discussed in terms of four dimensions: the historical period of the item in question; the geographical context; the content (artistic, intellectual, or as otherwise embodied in particular musical genres); and the physical form of the item in question (e.g., manuscript, broadside, etc.). All four dimensions are necessarily manifest in any single musical document and thus bibliographies inevitably overlap in coverage and emphasis. Even so, these dimensions are useful to readers, who are confronted by the vast and rapidly proliferating bibliographical record of American music. Furthermore, as extensive as that record is, viewed in the light of these dimensions it is seen to be nevertheless very uneven, for some topics are covered with admirable authority while others, such as 19th-century manuscripts, still await their first survey.

2. Access by period. An important aspect of chronologically delimited lists is the inclusion or exclusion of sheet music; if such lists do not exclude it, they are overwhelmed by it. Sheet music may be defined negatively as any publication that cannot be defined as a book, that is, as the output of a book-trade publisher, or an item long and physically substantial enough to be bound; treatises, hymnals, songbooks, other anthologies, and books about music are normally listed in bibliographies from which sheet music is excluded. The lists that do include sheet music are generally directed towards performers, who need to know what repertory exists and where it can be found.

Materials from the earliest decades in American history are covered in two landmark bibliographies: for books in general, Charles Evans's *American Bibliography* (1903–34, extended in several later studies), and for music in particular, Oscar Sonneck's *Bibliography of Early Secular American Music* (1905), which has been essentially superseded by William Treat Upton's extensive revision of 1945. Evans excluded many forms of ephemera, and the early sheet music he included, most of it undated, proved ill-suited to his annalistic arrangement; in the 1970 supplement to the work, Roger Bristol included some sheet music on the basis of Upton's assigned datings in the Sonneck revision, but he excluded the titles Upton had been unable to date. Most books cited in the Evans work are now accessible in microprint publications, justifying the guides to it published by Donald Hixon and Priscilla Heard respectively in 1970 and 1975. Evans offered, besides a partial coverage of sheet music, a listing of most tunebooks and songsters, though these are better covered in Allan Britton's survey of early American tunebooks (1949) and Irving Lowens's songster bibliography (1976). The Sonneck–Upton work includes not only sheet music but also librettos, writings about music, and song anthologies (with their contents).

Only recently has there been any serious systematic attempt to chart the vast bibliographical map of American music published after 1800. Understandably, the resulting works have been modeled on the lists that cover the 18th century. Richard Wolfe's *Secular Music in America, 1801–1825* (1964) essentially continues the Sonneck–Upton bibliography in scope and conception, though it wisely abandons Sonneck's arrangement by title in favor of one by composer. The scope of the Evans work is being extended in the continuing *American Bibliography*, the first volume of which, by Shaw and Shoemaker, was published in 1958 and the contents of which are now also available in microform; the continuation of Evans's annalistic arrangement, however, once again makes for curious placements of undated sheet music, especially in the volumes that were published before Wolfe's more authoritative work. Lowens's songster bibliography extends to 1820, and the tunebook bibliography begun by Britton and Lowens and being completed by Richard Crawford extends Britton's list of 1949 to 1810.

The burgeoning output of the American press in the middle of the 19th century has largely discouraged compilers interested in this important period. The list of copyright publications prepared in 1851 by Charles Coffin Jewett during his brief period at the Smithsonian Institution is of a respectable quality but covers only a short time span. Other bibliographies, such as the two general ones by Orville Roorbach (*Bibliotheca americana*, 1852–61) and James Kelly (*American Catalogue of Books*, 1866–71), as well as the massive *Complete Catalogue of Sheet Music and Musical Works* issued in 1870 by the Board of Music Trade, are vast in scope but limited in publication details. Valuable unpublished records for this period do exist, notably in the district court copyright records (the uses of which are described by Tanselle in *Studies in Bibliography*, xxii, 1969, pp.77–124). A few bibliographies of works written between 1826 and 1890 in certain geographical areas or in particular musical genres have been published (see §§3 and 4 below), but this period is essentially the darkest in American music bibliography. With the *American Catalogue of Books* issued by *Publishers Weekly* (1876–1910) and ostensibly limited to items in book format, the improvement in bibliographical controls began to be discernible.

The US Copyright Office began to publish its copyright registers in 1891 (though the volumes issued before 1897 are not widely available); music entries have been collected separately since 1895. Varying entry practices during the early years, however, and a lack of good indexes to the weekly or monthly listings make the set very difficult to use. It is therefore generally easier to locate a publication through a copyright search in the card catalogues at the Library of Congress. Nevertheless, for all its faults, the set of copyright registers remains the country's best attempt at a current national music bibliography. The improved format and highly selective approach to cataloguing begun in 1949 were unfortunately abandoned in 1956, partly in deference to the Library of Congress's improved music catalogue, *Music and Phonorecords* (1958), which has been part of the *National Union Catalog* (*NUC*) program since the 1950s. In 1957 the Copyright Office reverted to its former practice of listing the basic data for new registrations, and volumes are now published semiannually and by title, with a separate section for copyright renewals.

Music coverage in the *NUC* was until the 1970s restricted by the arbitrary and awkwardly implemented exclusion of musical materials, which justified the catalogue of printed music for 1953–72 published by members of the Music Library Association in 1974 under the leadership of Elizabeth Olmsted. For cataloguing information in general, librarians have learned to use the Olmsted set alongside the massive *National Union Catalog: Pre-1956 Imprints* (1968–81). While music was officially excluded from this listing, over a million music entries are to be found there in addition to hymnals, songbooks, and writings about music, and although coverage is international, the main-entry arrangement calls attention to many obscure editions by American composers and writers on music.

As the historical record of American music extends into the present to become the current record of new music publication, the specific needs of performers and readers are usefully differentiated into what is new, recommended, or available in print. New music titles are listed in the copyright registers in their comprehensive way, in the *NUC* (which addresses the needs of library cataloguers), and in music journals. The quarterly issues of the Music Library Association's journal *Notes*, which lists music submitted to it for review and books about music received at the Library of Congress, are important sources for this information. Other journals also list new works of special interest to their particular readers, such as the *Sonneck Society Newsletter*, which has listings of new books, articles, editions, and recordings of interest to the general community of American-music specialists.

For recommended titles and critical evaluations of new publications, *Notes* and a number of other journals listed below (see List) include general sections of book and music reviews. Limited in coverage, these reviews vary in authority from the casual and dubious to the highly reputable and discerning. Performers and readers generally find less than adequate guidance from such evaluations and rely on the advice of knowledgeable colleagues and retailers or on the informal "recommended lists" prepared and distributed by professional groups and respected musicians.

Currently available books about music have long been listed in the general lists of the book trade, such as the *Publisher's Trade List Annual* (1873–), but only recently has there been a successful attempt to produce lists devoted entirely to music in print. The breakthrough came with Margaret Farish's *String Music in Print* (1965), which led in time to the invaluable Music in Print series published by Musicdata since 1974. Publishers' catalogues often provide essential information, although availability can change quickly. Music retailers and librarians also have at their disposal unified reference materials classified in broad categories of repertory that enable them to learn what is currently available from music publishers.

In addition to the lists that attempt to cover all or most of the imprints produced in the USA, there are others designed to promote American music in particular historical periods. For example, bibliographies of early American music, especially the music of colonial America, were issued in connection with the US Bicentennial; among these are John Specht's list of early vocal music (1974), various classified lists in the *Music Educators Journal* during the years 1975–6, *American Music before 1865* (1976), and Richard Jackson's bibliography of early music in editions published 1970–76 (1977). Publications designed on the other hand to promote the modern repertory include two catalogues issued in 1975 and 1978 by the American Music Center, an organization that promotes serious works in this area. Current lists of the works of individual composers have been prepared by publishers and by organizations such as the American Composers Alliance and the performing rights societies, or as part of promotional projects for contemporary music in general. Groups of composers from particular historical periods have also been promoted collectively through bibliographical lists, such as Alexander Janta's surveys of early 19th-century Polish-American music (1961–5, 1982). Many of the content and form lists discussed below also highlight repertories of particular periods, whether through prose discussions, classified arrangement, annotations, or indexes.

3. ACCESS BY PLACE. Local and regional imprint lists, as surveyed in section A of Tanselle's *Guide* (1971), typically include writings about music and often songbooks, hymnals, and instruction books as well; rarely do they list any sheet music. Notable exceptions are the lists of Confederate music published by Richard Harwell in 1955 and 1957 and complemented by Frank Hoogerwerf's bibliography (1984), and Dena Epstein's survey of the Chicago music trade before the 1871 fire (1969). Some of the reasons for limited coverage of sheet music in regional bibliographies are suggested by Ralph Holibaugh and D. W. Krummel in an essay in *Fontes artis musicae* (1981).

Other regional lists describe the music of local and regional composers of the present rather than the past, ranging in coverage from modest pamphlets and biographical dictionaries (*see* DICTIONARIES) to works such as the report of the Boston Composers Project coordinated by Linda Solow (1983). Library classification schemes often provide regional and local coverage, and many sheet-music collectors have established particular geographical categories, but in general other attributes of documents almost always take precedence in classification over location, so that a great deal of the work of collecting titles pertaining to particular cities, states, and regions remains to be done.

4. ACCESS BY CONTENT. Different musical repertories often call for special documents, appropriately covered in special lists as well as in general catalogues and bibliographies. Bibliographies of specific kinds of music can be found in this dictionary in the books cited in the articles on various genres (such as BANDS, FOLK MUSIC, JAZZ, OPERA, and ORCHESTRAL MUSIC). It should be remembered that until recently large-scale American musical works have rarely been published, at least in the USA. A few were issued by European publishers (for example, the quartets of Carl Perkins, published in Leipzig), but most are extant, if at all, only in manuscript and are bibliographically cited only if their composers are the subject of scholarly study. Important repertory guides have been prepared by Judith Carman and her team on early art song (1976), by Patricia Lust on postwar vocal chamber music (1985), by Marilou Kratzenstein (1980) and Prudence Curtis (1981) on organ music, by John and Anna Gillespie on piano music (1984), by Dean Arlton on piano sonatas (1968), and by Jerome Landsman on violin music (1966). Other genre lists call attention to current works; among them are the Central Opera Service directory of contemporary operas (1967), Kenneth Berger's band music guides (beginning in 1953), Richard Weerts's list for wind and percussion music (1973), Angelo Eagon's general guides to concert music (1964), and the catalogues of ASCAP (1959) and BMI (1963). Numerous other lists of international scope also include American works in proportion to the importance and extent of the American repertory. Happily, the extended and serious musical works are the ones most likely to be catalogued in music libraries, where the prospect of better coverage through improved cooperative subject cataloguing is eagerly awaited.

If folk and popular music are somewhat less adequately described in their notated forms, part of the reason is that many of the repertories are more distinctively embodied in sound recordings (and therefore are covered in DISCOGRAPHIES). Many of the major bibliographies are thus devoted not to the music itself but to writings about the music, and the user of these bibliographies is advised to consider not only the scope of the work promised in the title, but the peripheral areas that may or may not be included depending on the predilections of the compiler (popular music, for example, may or may not include jazz, folksong may or may not include parlor music, rock may or may not include blues, country music may or may not include ragtime). Notable among the general works are Charles Haywood's *A Bibliography of North American Folklore and Folksong* (1951), Larry Sandberg's and Dick Weissman's *The Folk Music Sourcebook* (1976), Mark Booth's *American Popular Music* (1983), and Paul Taylor's critical guide (1985). Ray Lawless (1965) covers the folk-music movement at one of its high points, Frank Hoffman's list is devoted to rock (1981), and Gargan and Sharma (1984) provide useful bibliographical access to current tunes. The first important compiler of a list for jazz was Jane Ganfield (1933), who was followed by Robert Reisner (1954), Alan Merriam and Robert Benford (1954, whose work is the most comprehensive in scope), Donald Kennington (1970), and Steven Winnick (1974).

American sacred tunebooks are particularly well documented in bibliographies. The early 1800s are covered fairly comprehensively in works by James Warrington (1898), Frank Metcalf (1917), and Allen Britton (1949), all of which will be superseded for the period to 1810 by Crawford's tunebook bibliography. Sacred music in later periods is surveyed only broadly, as for example by Waldo Selden Pratt in the *Grove American Supplement* (1920). The Hymn Society of America's *Bibliography of American Hymnals* (1983) carries the list up to 1978, citing 7500 titles from both North and South America. Katherine Diehl's index (1966) remains the best general source for locating standard hymns. Among the notable denominational bibliographies are Edward Wolf's list of Lutheran titles and the *Mennonite Bibliography* by Springer and Klassen (both 1977). Specialized repertory lists include those by Richard Stanislaw (1978) on four-shape tunebooks, Nicholas Temperley and Carl Manns (1983) on fuging-tunes, and Samuel J. Rogal (1983) on sacred collections for the young.

Among the bibliographies concerned with miscellaneous other repertories are the lists of pedagogical books for string players by Jerome Landsman (1966) and Charles Sollinger (1974); Richmond Browne's listings of music theory (1977–8); the film music surveys of Clifford McCarty (1953), Win Sharples, Jr. (1978), Martin Marks (1979–80), and Claudia Gorbman (1980); and the bibliographies of works by black composers in particular genres by Dominique-René De Lerma (1975) and Evelyn Davidson White (1981).

The bibliographical search for particular songs is often difficult, not only because the field is so vast and the collections so poorly organized but because the information with which to begin a search is often incomplete. The source itself may either be a piece of sheet music or an anthology. For efficient bibliographical work with song titles, three kinds of reference books – chronologies, guides to stage productions, and analytical indexes – must be used in a complementary way, along with library catalogues, copyright registration records (for obscure titles when a date is known), and other sources. Chronologies are particularly valuable insofar as titles often prove to be distinctive to their periods (i.e., songs mentioning mother often date from the time of the Civil War, mock-Irish comic and coon songs from the early 20th century, big-band tunes and songs with nonsense titles from the 1930s and 1940s).

Analytical indexes serve both as reference books and as buying guides, particularly for small libraries. The first of these to index song anthologies was Minnie Sears's *Song Index* (1926); among its successors, *Songs in Collections* by De Charms and Breed (1966) is the most respected. Coverage in these works and in the indexes by Robert Leigh (1964) and Patricia Havlice (1975) extends to folksongs and foreign works as well; similarly, Florence Brunnings's *Folk Song Index* (1981) contains much more than folk music. The *UTK Song Index* (1981) offers a computer microfiche format (COM), which is easily updatable, as is *Folio-dex* (1974), which provides access to the contents of the major "song folio" anthologies through a loose-leaf service. The BBC *Song Catalogue* (1966) cites a good many earlier American works, and patriotic songs are listed by Harry Dichter and Elliott Shapiro (1941) and Dichter alone (1947–66). Several song indexes provide occasional subject groupings, mostly informal in their construction and reflecting known or anticipated needs; often the first words of a song identify the subject as well.

In addition to genre bibliographies, content bibliographies include listings of the outputs of individual composers and groups of composers classified into large historical or geographical categories. Surveys of the works of black composers include Ora Williams's bibliography of black women in the arts (1978) and the general list of Samuel Floyd and Marsha J. Reissner (1983). Women composers are also surveyed by various reference guides, such as those compiled by Donald Hixon and Don Hennessee (1975), Joann Skowronski (1978), and Adrienne Fried Block and Carol Neuls-Bates (1979). The annual listings in the winter issues of *Pan Pipes of Sigma Alpha Iota* serve to update the published work-lists of composers. For numerous examples of biographical dictionaries, which frequently contain work-lists as well as dates of first performances, *see* DICTIONARIES, List, §3.

Bibliographies of other kinds of books about American music include David Horn's *The Literature of American Music* (1972), which includes unusual writings especially on popular music, but with no indication of scope of coverage; Richard Jackson's survey *United States Music* (1973) and Marco's *Information on Music* (1977), both useful to reference librarians; Tanselle's *Guide* (1971); Delli (1979); and *Resources of American Music History* (1981). (For further bibliographies of music history books, *see* HISTORIES and the bibliographies in the history books themselves.) The few bibliographies of writings of and about American composers and musicians are cited in section C of Tanselle's *Guide* (1971). Other distinguished bibliographies have been compiled by American scholars. Among the more important of those that include some American coverage are the general surveys by Robert Darrell (1951), James Coover (1952), and Vincent Duckles (1964), the series indexes of Anna Harriet Heyer (1944, 1957), the ethnomusicology lists by Bruno Nettl (1961), the guide to criticism by Harold Diamond (1979), and the list of autobiographies by John Adams (1982). Many musical settings of texts by major American poets are cited in Tanselle's *Guide*, in Jacob Blanck's *Bibliography of American Literature* (1955–), and in Michael Hovland's *Musical Settings of American Poetry* (in preparation). Material of special interest to educators was summarized in 1968 by Thomas Clark Collins. An extensive survey of music therapy materials, *Music the Healer*, was published in 1970, and the field is now described in the *Music Therapy Index* (1976–) and the *Music Psychology Index* (1978–). Tests have been surveyed by C. W. Flemming (1936) and P. R. Lehman (1969), among others.

5. ACCESS BY BIBLIOGRAPHICAL FORM. Most of the distinctive forms of musical document are devoted to particular repertories and characteristics of particular historical periods and hence are usually accessible through the lists described above. As a last resort in searching, the reader or performer can consult special

lists devoted to particular kinds of physical objects that embody the record of American music.

With regard to manuscripts, two surveys of early American handwritten documents, by James Fuld and Mary Wallace Davidson (1980) and Kate Van Winkle Keller (1981), overlap in that the former covers some of the items in the latter, but in greater detail. No comprehensive catalogue of American musical manuscripts after 1801 has yet been published, though locations of these materials appear in various resource materials on library collections. In the area of printed ephemera, Gillian Anderson's *Freedom's Voice in Poetry and Song* (1977) covers song texts in newspapers from the Revolutionary War period; and mid-19th-century broadsides are listed in works by Earle Rudolph (1950) and Edwin Wolf (1963). Bibliographies of printed ephemera also include Lowens's list of songsters (1976), which normally contain no musical notation. Original American music source materials of all kinds are listed in *Resources of American Music History* (1981).

American dissertations concerned specifically with music were first listed in 1932 by Oliver Strunk in a bulletin published by the American Council of Learned Societies. His list was updated by Daugherty, Ellinwood, and Hill in 1940 and continues with *Doctoral Dissertations in Musicology*, begun by the Music Teachers National Association and the American Musicological Society in 1952 and from 1977 a part of the international index by Adkins and Dickinson. The current updatings for newly accepted and completed American doctoral dissertations, which for many years appeared in the *Journal of the American Musicological Society*, are now issued separately by the society. The general record of American doctoral dissertations in all fields began in 1938; it is now available on line, which allows useful "key word" access to musical and other topics. Among the special subject lists are Kenneth Hartley's for sacred music (1966), Rita Mead's for American music topics in all areas (1974), and Frank Cipolla's for band music (1979–80); the lists by Dominique-René De Lerma (1970) and James Heintze (1985) enter the vast domain of master's theses in a highly selective way.

Music periodicals, listed retrospectively by Charles Wunderlich (1962) and William Weichlein (1970), as well as elsewhere in this dictionary (*see* PERIODICALS), are also cited in several special bibliographies, including those prepared by Frank Campbell for choral conductors (1952). For several decades *Notes* has included occasional lists of new periodical titles (summarized for 1963–84 in vol.xli, 1984–5, p.14). Joan Meggett surveyed the music periodical literature in 1978. Indexes to the periodical literature have also been prepared by Sheila Keats on American composers (1954), by Hazel Gertrude Kinscella on American music of all kinds in the *Musical Quarterly* (1958), and by Dean and Nancy Tudor on popular music (1974). Two music periodical indexes cover current writings: *RILM Abstracts*, begun in 1967 and devoted to scholarly writings (ethnomusicological writings are placed in class 35; the entries on American art music are scattered, though accessible under "U.S.A." in the index or by means of subject headings), and *Music Index*, begun in 1949 and considerably less sophisticated than *RILM* in its indexing practices, though it includes a much wider range of timely and popular writings of particular relevance to the student of American music.

Of the so-called "basic lists" that have been developed to aid small libraries in the selection of music collections, the earliest was begun in 1935 by the National Association of Schools of Music. The original list and a series of supplements were gathered together and published in 1967 as *A Basic Music Library*; the updated edition of 1977, by Michael Winesanker, was organized in a single alphabetical sequence for the convenience of library searching, while the revision of 1979 is classified by subject. General lists were published by Pauline Bayne's Music Library Association committee in 1978 and 1983, and others have been prepared by J. Bunker Clark and Marilyn Clark (1969) and Krummel (1976–7) respectively for high school and college libraries.

Catalogues of American music prepared for collectors are often valuable to scholars as well. In addition to codifying the corpus of recognized "collectors' items," for instance, *Early American Sheet Music* by Dichter and Shapiro (1941) provides an invaluable directory for the confirmation of publishers' names and the dating of editions. Dichter's three handbooks of the same repertory (1947–66), which are essentially lists of items for sale, are still useful for their citations and pricing suggestions. James Fuld's 1955 study seeks to establish the first editions of the most popular music through a specification of the collector's "points" and illustrated covers; his book of 1966, though international in scope, includes many American works.

LIST

The following is a selective list of bibliographies of, and works about, American music. A number of important library catalogues have been included either for their extensive scope or for their comprehensive coverage in a particular area of music. (For other archival catalogues, see the bibliographies for the institutions concerned in LIBRARIES AND COLLECTIONS.) Period of coverage is given, where appropriate, in brackets.

"Appendix to the Librarian's Report: Copy-right Publications . . . Part II: List of Musical Compositions," *Fifth Annual Report of the Board of Regents*, ed. Smithsonian Institution (Washington, DC, 1851), 223–33, 186–322 [for 1846–50; 554 items, mostly from East Coast publishers; in the government publications serial set under "Senate, Special Session, March 1851: Miscellaneous"]

O. A. Roorbach: *Bibliotheca americana, 1820–61* (New York, 1852–61, repr. 1939), 4 vols. [occasional music references; indexed in master's papers prepared for Kent State U. by K. Dempsey, 1972, and M. J. Kuceyeski, 1975]

J. Kelly: *American Catalogue of Books Printed . . . from January 1861 to January 1871* (New York, 1866–71, repr. 1938), 2 vols. [occasional music references]

Complete Catalogue of Sheet Music and Musical Works, ed. Board of Music Trade (New York, 1870/*R*1973) [lists nearly 100,000 titles issued by affiliated music publishers; abbreviated entries, no indexes; see D. J. Epstein's masterly introduction to reprint, and *Notes*, xxxi (1974–5), 7]

Publisher's Trade List Annual (New York, 1873–; author and title indexes 1948– as *Books in Print*) [collected catalogues of major American publishers]

American Catalogue of Books, ed. *Publishers Weekly* (New York, 1876–1910, repr. 1941), 21 vols. in 15 bks [originally a list of books in print, but in time a record of new titles; author, title, subject listings]

Catalogue of Title Entries, later *Catalogue of Copyright Entries*, ed. US Copyright Office (Washington, DC, 1891–) [now issued biannually; from 1895 with separate music section]

J. Warrington: *Short Titles of Books Relating to or Illustrating the History and Practice of Psalmody in the United States, 1620–1820* (Philadelphia, 1898/*R*1971) [lists chiefly American items after 1720; largely superseded by Metcalf, 1917]

C. Evans: *American Bibliography: a Chronological Dictionary of All Books, Pamphlets, and Periodical Publications Printed in the United States of America from . . . 1639 . . . to . . . 1820* (Chicago, 1903–34; suppl., 1955; suppl. by R. P. Bristol, 1970), 12 vols. plus index and suppls. [other indexes: R. P. Bristol: *Index to Printers, Publishers, and Booksellers . . . in American Bibliography* (Charlottesville, VA, 1961); C. K. Shipton and J. E. Mooney: *National Index of American Imprints through 1800: the Short-title Evans* (Worcester and Barre, MA, 1969); see also Hixon, 1970, and Heard, 1975]

O. G. T. Sonneck: *A Bibliography of Early Secular American Music* (Washington, DC, 1905, rev. and enlarged W. T. Upton 2/1945/*R*1964) [first edn lists materials through 1801, rev. edn includes an additional 800 secular works, mainly sheet music]

F. J. Metcalf: *American Psalmody, or Titles of Books Containing Tunes Printed in America from 1721 to 1820* (New York, 1917/*R*1968) [lists holdings of 23 collections and references from important bibliographies extending into the

1830s; largely supersedes Warrington, 1898]

W. S. Pratt: "Tune Books," *Grove AS*, 385 [useful for mid-19th-century works]

M. E. Sears: *Song Index* (New York, 1926/*R*1966; suppl., 1934) [lists songs in important collections, based on card files in *NN-L*]

Union List of Serials in the Libraries of the United States and Canada, ed. W. Gregory (New York, 1927, 2/1943, rev. E. B. Titus 3/1965; suppls., Washington, DC, 1973– as *New Serial Titles*, from 1982 in 3-month cumulations)

Periodicals Directory (New York, 1932–, from 1965/6 as *Ulrich's International Periodicals Directory*) [issued biennially]

O. Strunk: *State and Resources of Musicology in the United States* (Washington, DC, 1932) [includes lists]

J. Ganfield: *Books and Periodical Articles on Jazz in America from 1926–1932* (New York, 1933)

"A List of Books on Music," *National Association of Schools of Music Bulletin*, no.3 (1935; suppls., 1936–57) [see also 1967]

C. W. Flemming: *A Descriptive Bibliography of Prognostic and Achievement Tests in Music* (New York, 1936)

Microfilm Abstracts (Ann Arbor, MI, 1938–, from 1952 as *Dissertation Abstracts*, from 1969 as *Dissertation Abstracts International*) [issued monthly; from 1966 music in ser.A: Humanities and Social Science]

D. H. Daugherty, L. Ellinwood, and R. S. Hill: *A Bibliography of Periodical Literature in Musicology and Allied Fields and a Record of Graduate Theses* (Washington, DC, 1940–43/*R*1973), 2 vols.

Bio-bibliographical Index of Musicians in the United States of America since Colonial Times, ed. Historical Record Survey (Washington, DC, 1941, rev. 2/1956/*R*1972)

H. Dichter and E. Shapiro: *Early American Sheet Music: its Lure and its Lore, 1768–1889* (New York, 1941/*R*1977 with revisions and addns as *Handbook of Early American Sheet Music*) [includes a directory of early sheet-music publishers]

A Catalog of Books . . . to July 31, 1942, ed. Library of Congress (Ann Arbor, MI, 1942–6/*R*1967; suppl., 1948/*R*1967 [1 Aug 1942 to 31 Dec 1947]), 167 vols. plus 42 suppls.

A. H. Heyer: *Check-list of Publications of Music* (Ann Arbor, MI, 1944)

Cumulative Catalog of Library of Congress Printed Cards [title varies], ed. Library of Congress (Washington, DC, 1947–55), 46 vols. [also published in cumulations; superseded by the *NUC*, 1958–69]

H. Dichter: *Handbook of American Sheet Music* (Philadelphia, 1947–66), 3 vols. [essentially antiquarian dealer's lists]

M. M. Mott: "A Bibliography of Song Sheets: Sports and Recreation in American Popular Songs," *Notes*, vi (1948–9), 379; vii (1949–50), 522–61; ix (1951–2), 33–62; continued by G. D. McDonald, xiv (1956–7), 325–52, 507–33

A. P. Britton: *Theoretical Introductions in American Tune-books to 1800* (diss., U. of Michigan, 1949)

The Music Index (1949–)

E. L. Rudolph: *Confederate Broadside Verse* (New Braunfels, TX, 1950)

R. D. Darrell: *Schirmer's Guide to Books on Music and Musicians: a Practical Bibliography* (New York, 1951)

C. Haywood: *A Bibliography of North American Folklore and Folksong* (New York, 1951, rev. 2/1961)

F. C. Campbell: *A Critical Annotated Bibliography of Periodicals* (New York, 1952) [lists 44 periodicals on choral music]

J. B. Coover: *A Bibliography of Music Dictionaries* (Denver, 1952, rev. 3/1971 as *Music Lexicography, Including a Bibliography of Music Dictionaries*)

Doctoral Dissertations in Musicology, ed. Music Teachers National Association and American Musicological Society (Denton, TX, 1952, rev. H. Hewitt 2/1958, rev. C. Adkins 5/1971, 7/1984; suppls. in *JAMS* and *American Music Teacher*; new ser., 1984–)

J. Mattfeld: *Variety Music Cavalcade* (New York, 1952, rev. 3/1971) [lists 40,000 works, by year]

K. Berger: *Band Music Guide* (Evansville, IN, 1953, rev. 8/1982)

A. P. Britton and I. Lowens: "Unlocated Titles in Early Sacred American Music," *Notes*, xi (1953–4), 33

Z. W. George: *A Guide to Negro Folk Music: an Annotated Bibliography of Negro Folk Music and Art Music by Negro Composers or Based on Negro Thematic Material* (diss., New York U., 1953) [prose discussion complemented by unpublished card index at Howard U.]

Library of Congress Author Catalog: a Cumulative List of Works Represented by Library of Congress Printed Cards, 1948–1952 (Ann Arbor, MI, 1953), 24 vols.

C. McCarty: *Film Composers in America: a Checklist of their Work* (Glendale, CA, 1953/*R*1972)

S. Keats: "Reference Articles on American Composers: an Index," *Juilliard Review*, i/3 (1954), 21

A. Merriam and R. Benford: *A Bibliography of Jazz* (Philadelphia, 1954/*R*1970)

R. Reisner: *The Literature of Jazz* (New York, 1954, rev. and enlarged 2/1959)

J. Blanck and others: *Bibliography of American Literature* (New Haven, CT, 1955–), 7 vols. to 1984 [summarized in *Notes*, xxi (1963–4), 337]

Compositores de América: datos biográficos y catálogos de sus obras/Composers of the Americas: Biographical Data and Catalogs of their Works, ed. Pan American Union (Washington, DC, 1955–) [includes extensive work-lists]

J. J. Fuld: *American Popular Music (Reference Book), 1875–1950* (Philadelphia, 1955; suppl., 1956) [lists first edns of the 265 most popular works in each year]

R. B. Harwell: "Sheet Music," in M. L. Crandall: *Confederate Imprints: a Check List Based Principally on the Collection of the Boston Athenaeum*, ii (Boston, 1955), 561–669, 719–21; suppl. in Crandall's *More Confederate Imprints* (Richmond, VA, 1957), 225, 250 [lists 731 items of sheet music and 24 hymnals]

Library of Congress Catalog Books: Subjects (Ann Arbor, MI, 1955– [1950–]) [in 5-year cumulations; from 1953 music scores no longer included]

J. Burton: *The Index of American Popular Music* (Watkins Glen, NY, 1957) [indexes songs in anthologies compiled by Burton]

A. H. Heyer: *Historical Sets, Collected Editions, and Monuments of Music: a Guide to their Contents* (Chicago, 1957, rev. 3/1980), 2 vols.

H. G. Kinscella: "Americana Index to the Musical Quarterly, 1915–1957," *JRME*, vi/2 (1958), 1–144 [lists 7000 texts by or about Americans]

R. R. Shaw and R. H. Shoemaker: *American Bibliography: a Preliminary Checklist* (New York, 1958–63 [1801–19]; continued by Shoemaker, G. Cooper, and others, New York and Metuchen, NJ, 1964– [1820–] as *A Checklist of American Imprints*; indexes and suppls., 1965–6, 1972–3 [1801–29]), 1 vol. for each year plus suppls. [continues Evans, 1903–34; summary by D. W. Krummel in *Yearbook for Inter-American Research*, xi (1975), 168]

The National Union Catalog: a Cumulative Author List Representing Library of Congress Printed Cards and Titles Reported by Other American Libraries, ed. Library of Congress (Ann Arbor, MI, 1958–69 [1953–67]; suppl., 1961 [1952–5]), 154 vols. plus suppl. [cumulated by the Gale Research Company, 1969–71, and superseded by the *NUC*, 1968–80]

The National Union Catalog: Music and Phonorecords, ed. Library of Congress (Ann Arbor, MI, 1958 [1953–7]; New York, 1963 [1958–62]; Ann Arbor, 1969 [1963–7]; 1973 [1968–72]; Totowa, NJ, 1978 [1973–7]; Washington, DC, 1979– [1978–] as *Music, Books on Music, and Sound Recordings*), 19 vols. to 1978

ASCAP Symphonic Catalog, ed. ASCAP (New York, 1959, rev. 3/1977)

J. Edmunds and G. Boelzner: *Some Twentieth-century American Composers: a Selective Bibliography* (New York, 1959–60), 2 vols. [lists writings by and about 32 major composers]

A. Janta: "Early XIX Century American-Polish Music," *Polish Review*, vi (1961), 73–105; x (1965), 59 [lists 70 edns pubd in the USA]

B. Nettl: *Reference Materials in Ethnomusicology* (Detroit, 1961, rev. 2/1967)

R. Houser: *Catalogue of Chamber Music for Woodwind Instruments* (Bloomington, IN, 1962/*R*1973)

C. Wunderlich: *A History and Bibliography of Early American Musical Periodicals, 1782–1852* (diss., U. of Michigan, 1962; Ann Arbor, MI, 1977)

A. P. Basart: *Serial Music: a Classified Bibliography of Writings on Twelve-tone and Electronic Music* (Berkeley and Los Angeles, 1963)

Symphonic Catalogue, ed. BMI (New York, 1963, rev. 2/1971)

E. Wolf, II: *American Song Sheets, Slip Ballads and Poetical Broadsides, 1850–1870* (Philadelphia, 1963) [photobibliography of musical ephemera at the Library Company of Philadelphia]

S. Bull: *Index to Biographies of Contemporary Composers* (New York, 1964–74)

V. Duckles: *Music Reference and Research Materials: an Annotated Bibliography* (New York, 1964, rev. and enlarged 3/1974)

A. Eagon: *Catalog of Published Concert Music by American Composers* (Washington, DC, 1964, rev. 2/1969; suppls., 1971–4)

Early American Periodicals Index to 1850 (New York, 1964) [microprint of O. Cargill's card index, completed in 1934 and maintained at New York U. by N. F. Adkins; 8000 titles are listed in Series E: "Songs"; cards F 226–35 of "General Articles" relate to music; titles of periodicals indexed are listed in *The Pamphleteer Monthly*, i/7–8 (1940)]

R. Leigh: *Index to Song Books* (Stockton, CA, 1964/*R*1972)

N. Shapiro: *Popular Music: an Annotated Index of American Popular Songs* (New York, 1964–73), 6 vols. [chronological groupings]

R. J. Wolfe: *Secular Music in America, 1801–1825: a Bibliography* (New York, 1964), 3 vols. [lists more than 10,000 titles]

M. K. Farish: *String Music in Print* (New York, 1965, rev. 2/1973/*R*1980; suppls., 1968–)

R. M. Lawless: *Folksingers and Folkways in America* (New York, 1965) [extensive lists of collections and writings, pp.271–430]

D. De Charms and P. F. Breed: *Songs in Collections: an Index* (Detroit, 1966) [index to 411 collections]

K. S. Diehl: *Hymns and Tunes: an Index* (New York, 1966) [index to 78 hymnals, mainly American]
J. J. Fuld: *The Book of World-Famous Music: Classical, Popular and Folk* (New York, 1966, rev. 2/1971) [lists and traces the first appearance in print of 1000 melodies, over half of them American; includes incipits]
K. R. Hartley: *Bibliography of Theses and Dissertations in Sacred Music* (Detroit, 1966)
J. L. Landsman: *An Annotated Catalogue of American Violin Sonatas, Suites . . . 1947–1961* (diss., U. of Southern California, 1966; Urbana, IL, 1968)
Song Catalogue, ed. BBC Music Library (London, 1966) [title index in vols.iii and iv valuable for Anglo-American repertory]
A Basic Music Library for Schools Offering Undergraduate Degrees in Music, ed. National Association of Schools of Music (Washington, DC, 1967) [supersedes the association's lists, 1935–57; lists books, periodicals, and scores]; rev. M. Winesanker as *A List of Books on Music* (Reston, VA, 2/1977, rev. Winesanker as *Books on Music: a Classified List* 3/1979) [list books and periodicals]
L. M. Cross: *A Bibliography of Electronic Music* (Toronto, 1967)
"Directory of American Contemporary Operas," *Central Opera Service Bulletin*, x/2 (1967) [complete issue]
RILM Abstracts (1967–)
The CMP Library, ed. Music Educators National Conference (Washington, DC, 1967–8, rev. V. B. Lawrence 2/1969), 3 vols. [prepared by Contemporary Music Project, as described in *Notes*, xxvi (1969–70), 482; lists by genre works for school performing groups]
D. L. Arlton: *American Piano Sonatas of the Twentieth Century: Selective Analysis and Annotated Index* (diss., Columbia U., 1968)
J. B. Clark and M. Clark: "A Music Collection for the High School Student," *Notes*, xxv (1968–9), 685 [includes bibliography]
T. C. Collins: *Music Education Materials: a Selected Annotated Bibliography* (Washington, DC, 1968)
The National Union Catalog, Pre-1956 Imprints: a Cumulative Author List, Representing Library of Congress Printed Cards and Titles Reported by Other American Libraries (London, 1968–80; suppls., 1980–81), 685 vols. and 69 suppls. [supersedes for pre-1956 imprints the four *NUC* series covering 1942–62]
D. J. Epstein: *Music Publishing in Chicago before 1871: the Firm of Root & Cady, 1858–1871* (Detroit, 1969), 85–146 [lists 1000 titles published by Root & Cady]
P. R. Lehman: "A Selected Bibliography of Works on Music Testing," *JRME*, xvii/4 (1969), 427
Library of Congress and National Union Catalog Author Lists, 1942–1962: a Master Cumulation, ed. Gale Research Company (Detroit, 1969–71), 152 vols. [consists of the four *NUC* series covering 1942–62; superseded by the *NUC*, 1968–80]
E. B. Carlson: *A Bio-bibliographical Dictionary of Twelve-tone and Serial Composers* (Metuchen, NJ, 1970)
D.-R. De Lerma: *A Selective List of Masters' Theses in Musicology* (Bloomington, IN, 1970)
R. S. Denisoff: *American Protest Songs of War and Peace* (Los Angeles, 1970, rev. 1973 as *Songs of Protest, War & Peace*)
D. L. Hixon: *Music in Early America: a Bibliography of Music in Evans* (Metuchen, NJ, 1970) [reorganizes music entries in Evans, 1903–34, alphabetically by entry and includes titles not available in microprint]
D. Kennington: *The Literature of Jazz* (London, 1970, rev. with D. L. Read, Chicago, 2/1980)
Music the Healer: a Bibliography, ed. Institutional Library Services, Washington State Library (Olympia, WA, 1970)
W. J. Weichlein: *A Checklist of American Music Periodicals, 1850–1900* (Detroit, 1970) [lists 309 titles]
W. R. Ferris, Jr.: *Mississippi Black Folklore: a Research Bibliography and Discography* (Hattiesburg, MS, 1971)
D. W. Krummel: "The Facsimiliad," *Yearbook for Inter-American Music Research*, vii (1971), 135 [on reprints of American music books]
H. B. Peters: *The Literature of the Woodwind Quintet* (Metuchen, NJ, 1971)
G. T. Tanselle: *Guide to the Study of United States Imprints* (Cambridge, MA, 1971), 2 vols. [analysis of music coverage, with addns, by D. W. Krummel in *Yearbook for Inter-American Music Research*, viii (1972), 140]
S. R. Charles: *A Handbook of Music and Music Literature in Sets and Series* (New York, 1972)
D. Daniels: *Orchestral Music: a Source Book* (Metuchen, NJ, 1972)
D. Horn: *The Literature of American Music* (Exeter, England, 1972, rev. Metuchen, NJ, 2/1977, as *The Literature of American Music in Books and Folk Music Collections*) [lists 1388 books and articles]
E. C. Krohn: *Music Publishing in the Middle Western States before the Civil War* (Detroit, 1972) [regional listings]
C. R. Arnold: *Organ Literature: a Comprehensive Survey* (Metuchen, NJ, 1973)
R. Jackson: *United States Music: Sources of Bibliography and Collective Biography*, ISAMm, i (Brooklyn, NY, 1973, rev. 2/1976) [lists 90 important American music reference books, notably those with biographical entries]
H. Voxman and L. Merriman: *Woodwind Ensemble Music Guide* (Evanston, IL, 1973)
R. K. Weerts: *Original Manuscript Music for Wind and Percussion Instruments* (Washington, DC, 1973)
Folio-dex: Vocal, Piano, and Organ Music Finding List (Loomis, CA, 1974–) [looseleaf index to folio anthologies]
S. Kostka: *A Bibliography of Computer Applications in Music* (Hackensack, NJ, 1974)
R. H. Mead: *Doctoral Dissertations in American Music: a Classified Bibliography*, ISAMm, iii (Brooklyn, NY, 1974) [lists 1226 works]
Music in Print (Philadelphia, 1974–) [series, see Nardone, Nardone, and Resnick, 1974; Nardone, 1975; Farish, 1978; Farish, 1979]
T. R. Nardone, J. H. Nardone, and M. Resnick: *Choral Music in Print* (Philadelphia, 1974; suppls., 1976, 1981–3), 2 vols. plus suppls. [part of Music in Print series]
E. Olmsted: *Music Library Association Catalog of Cards for Printed Music, 1953–1972* (Totowa, NJ, 1974) [lists titles from libraries other than the Library of Congress]
D. Phillips: *A Selected Bibliography of Music Librarianship* (Urbana, IL, 1974)
C. Sollinger: *String Class Publications in the United States, 1851–1951* (Detroit, 1974)
R. J. Specht: *Early American Vocal Music in Modern Editions* (Albany, NY, 1974)
D. Tudor and N. Tudor: *Popular Music Periodicals Index* (Metuchen, NJ, 1974)
S. Winnick: *Rhythm: an Annotated Bibliography* (Metuchen, NJ, 1974)
D.-R. De Lerma: *Black Concert and Recital Music: a Provisional Repertoire List* (Bloomington, IN, 1975)
J. G. Finell: *Catalog of Choral and Vocal Works* (New York, 1975) [lists works in the American Music Center; see also Famera, 1978]
P. Havlice: *Popular Song Index* (Metuchen, NJ, 1975; suppls., 1978, 1984)
P. S. Heard: *American Music, 1698–1800: an Annotated Bibliography* (Waco, TX, 1975) [reorganizes music entries in Evans, 1903–34, in 3 chronological sequences: books with musical notation, books about music, books not available in microprint]
D. Hixon and D. Hennessee: *Women in Music: a Biobibliography* (Metuchen, NJ, 1975) [lists dictionaries and encyclopedias containing biographies]
T. R. Nardone: *Organ Music in Print* (Philadelphia, 1975) [part of Music in Print series]
"Selective List of American Music for the Bicentennial Celebration," *MEJ*, lx/8 (1975), 54; lxi/9 (1975), 48; lxii/2 (1975), 66; lxii/6 (1976), 55
J. Voigt and R. Kane: *Jazz Music in Print* (Winthrop, MA, 1975, rev. Boston, 3/1982 as *Jazz Music in Print and Jazz Books in Print*)
American Music before 1865 in Print and on Records: a Biblio-discography, ISAMm, vi (Brooklyn, NY, 1976) [lists 199 performing editions for Bicentennial events, among other works]
J. E. Carman and others: *Art-song in the United States: an Annotated Bibliography* (New York, 1976; suppl., 1978)
D. W. Krummel: "Musical Editions: a Basic Collection," *Choice*, xiii (1976–7), 177
I. Lowens: *A Bibliography of Songsters Printed in America before 1821* (Worcester, MA, 1976) [lists 649 books with song texts]
Music Therapy Index (Lawrence, KS, 1976–)
L. Sandberg and D. Weissman: *The Folk Music Sourcebook* (New York, 1976)
C. Adkins and A. Dickinson: *International Index of Dissertations and Musicological Works in Progress* (Philadelphia, 1977, 2/1984; American-Canadian suppl., 1979)
G. Anderson: *Freedom's Voice in Poetry and Song* (Wilmington, DE, 1977) [lists 1455 titles of political and patriotic lyrics in colonial newspapers, 1773–83]
R. Browne: "Index of Music Theory in the United States, 1955–1970," *ITO*, iii/7–11 (1977–8) [complete issue]
R. Jackson: *U.S. Bicentennial Music* (Brooklyn, NY, 1977) [lists about 500 editions of early American music published 1970–76]
G. A. Marco: "The Americas," *Information on Music: a Handbook of Reference Sources in European Languages* (Littleton, CO, 1977) [extensive list of bibliographies and other reference books]
N. P. Springer and A. J. Klassen: *Mennonite Bibliography, 1631–1961*, ii (Scottdale, PA, 1977), 285 [lists 365 hymnals]
E. C. Wolf: "Lutheran Hymnody and Music Published in America, 1700–1850: a Descriptive Bibliography," *Concordia Historical Institute Quarterly*, l (1977), 164
P. S. Bayne: *A Basic Music Library* (Chicago, 1978, rev. 2/1983) [Music Library

Association committee recommendations]
K. M. Famera: *Catalog of the American Music Center Library*, ii: *Chamber Music* (New York, 1978) [see also Finell, 1975]
M. K. Farish: *Orchestral Music in Print* (Philadelphia, 1978–9; suppls., 1980–), 2 vols. plus suppls. [part of Music in Print series]
J. M. Meggett: *Music Periodical Literature: an Annotated Bibliography of Indexes and Bibliographies* (Metuchen, NJ, 1978)
Music Psychology Index (Lawrence, KS, 1978–)
W. Sharples, Jr.: "A Selected and Annotated Bibliography of Books and Articles on Music in the Cinema," *Cinema Journal*, xvii/2 (1978), 36–67
J. Skowronski: *Women in Music: a Bibliography* (Metuchen, NJ, 1978)
R. J. Stanislaw: *A Checklist of Four-shape Shape-note Tunebooks*, ISAMm, x (Brooklyn, NY, 1978)
O. Williams: *American Black Women in the Arts and Social Sciences: a Bibliographic Survey* (Metuchen, NJ, 1978)
A. F. Block and C. Neuls-Bates: *Women in American Music: a Bibliography of Music and Literature* (Westport, CT, 1979)
F. J. Cipolla: "A Bibliography of Dissertations Relative to the Study of Bands and Band Music," *Journal of Band Research*, xv/1 (1979), 1–31; xvi/1 (1980), 29
B. Delli: "Music," *Arts in America: a Bibliography*, ed. B. Kappel (Washington, DC, 1979), iii
H. J. Diamond: *Music Criticism: an Annotated Guide to the Literature* (Metuchen, NJ, 1979)
M. K. Farish: *Orchestral Music in Print* (Philadelphia, 1979; suppls., 1980–82) [part of Music in Print series]
I. V. Jackson: *Afro-American Religious Music: a Bibliography and a Catalogue of Gospel Music* (Westport, CT, 1979)
M. Marks: "Film Music: the Material, Literature, and Present State of Research," *Notes*, xxxvi (1979–80), 282–325 [includes bibliography]
J. J. Fuld and M. W. Davidson: *Eighteenth-century American Secular Music Manuscripts: an Inventory* (Philadelphia, 1980)
C. Gorbman: "Bibliography on Sound in Film," *Yale French Studies*, no.60 (1980), 269
M. Kratzenstein: "The United States," *Survey of Organ Literature and Editions* (Ames, IA, 1980), 178
H. Sampson: *Blacks in Blackface: a Source Book on Early Black Musical Shows* (Metuchen, NJ, 1980), 131–327
R. C. Von Ende: *Church Music: an International Bibliography* (Metuchen, NJ, 1980)
F. E. Brunnings: *Folk Song Index* (New York, 1981) [lists 50,000 titles in 896 collections in her personal archive]
P. B. Curtis: *American Organ Music North of Philadelphia before 1860: Selected Problems and an Annotated Bibliography* (diss., Manhattan School of Music, 1981)
D.-R. De Lerma: *Bibliography of Black Music* (Westport, CT, 1981–), 4 vols. to 1984 [i–iv list black music, vi planned as a bibliography of writings on black music]
F. Hoffmann: *The Literature of Rock, 1954–1978* (Metuchen, NJ, 1981)
K. Van W. Keller: *Popular Secular Music in America through 1800: a Preliminary Checklist of Manuscripts in North American Collections* (Philadelphia, 1981)
D. W. Krummel and others, eds.: *Resources of American Music History* (Urbana, IL, 1981)
E. Meadows: *Jazz Reference and Research Materials: a Bibliography* (New York, 1981)
J. M. Meggett: *Keyboard Music by Women Composers: a Catalog and Bibliography* (Westport, CT, 1981)
UTK Song Index (Knoxville, 1981) [microcard index to the collection]
E. D. White: *Choral Music by Afro-American Composers: a Selected, Annotated Bibliography* (Metuchen, NJ, 1981)
J. L. Zaimont and K. Famera: *Contemporary Concert Music by Women: a Directory of the Composers and their Works* (Westport, CT, 1981)
J. L. Adams: *Musicians' Autobiographies: an Annotated Bibliography of Writings Available in English 1800 to 1980* (Jefferson, NC, 1982)
A. Janta: *A History of Nineteenth Century American-Polish Music* (New York, 1982)
D. B. Wilmeth: *Variety Entertainment and Outdoor Amusements: a Reference Guide* (Westport, CT, 1982)
Bibliography of American Hymnals, ed. Hymn Society of America (New York, 1983) [microfiche]
M. Booth: *American Popular Music: a Reference Guide* (Westport, CT, 1983)
S. A. Floyd and M. J. Reisser: *Black Music in the United States: an Annotated Bibliography of Selected Reference and Research Materials* (Millwood, NY, 1983)
M. Maguire: *American Indian and Eskimo Music: a Selected Bibliography through 1981* (Washington, DC, 1983)
S. Rogal: *The Children's Jubilee: a Bibliographical Survey of Hymnals for Infants, Youth, and Sunday Schools Published in Britain and America, 1655–1900* (Westport, CT, 1983)
L. I. Solow and others: *The Boston Composers Project: a Bibliography of Contemporary Music* (Cambridge, MA, 1983)
N. Temperley and C. G. Manns: *Fuging Tunes in the Eighteenth Century* (Detroit, 1983)
W. Gargan and S. Sharma: *Find That Tune: an Index to Rock, Folk-rock, Disco, and Soul in Collections* (New York, 1984) [index to 203 anthologies]
J. Gillespie and A. Gillespie: *A Bibliography of Nineteenth-century American Piano Music* (Westport, CT, 1984)
J. R. Heintze: *American Music Studies: a Classified List of Master's Theses* (Detroit, 1984)
F. W. Hoogerwerf: *Confederate Sheet-music Imprints*, ISAMm, xxi (Brooklyn, NY, 1984) [lists 800 items published during the Confederacy]
P. Lust: *American Vocal Chamber Music, 1945–1980: an Annotated Bibliography* (Westport, CT, 1985)
P. Taylor: *Popular Music since 1955: a Critical Guide to the Literature* (London, 1985)
M. A. Hovland: *Musical Settings of American Poetry: a Bibliography* (in preparation)

PERIODICALS CONTAINING LISTS AND REVIEWS

Numbers at the ends of citations refer to PERIODICALS.

General

Pan Pipes of Sigma Alpha Iota (1909–), 398
Notes (1943/4–), 594
The American Music Teacher (1951–), 679
The Sonneck Society Newsletter (1975–), 986

Choral and sacred

The Hymn (1949–), 664
Journal of Church Music (1957–), 715
American Choral Review (1958–), 723
The Choral Journal (1959/60–), 746
Church Music (1966–), 812
Pastoral Music (1976/7–), 1005

Instrumental

The American Organist (1918–70), 464
The Instrumentalist (1946–), 613
The Piano Quarterly (1952/3–), 690
Woodwind/Brass and Percussion (1957–), 722
Clavier (1962–), 764
Percussive Notes (1962–), 770
T.U.B.A. Journal (1973–), 945
Soundboard (1974–), 960

Popular

Down Beat (1934–), 536

Educational

Music Educators Journal (1914/15–), 435
The NATS Bulletin (1944/5–), 601, 915

Scholarly

The Musical Quarterly (1915–), 451
Journal of the American Musicological Society (1948–), 633
Ethnomusicology (1953/7–), 692
American Music (1983–), 1090

Bibliographical

The Music Index (1949–), 668

BIBLIOGRAPHY

O. G. Sonneck: "The Bibliography of American Music," *Papers of the Bibliographical Society of America*, i (1904–6), 50
H. Dichter and E. Shapiro: *Early American Sheet Music: its Lure and its Lore, 1768–1889* (New York, 1941/R1977 with revisions and addns as *Handbook of Early American Sheet Music*)
W. T. Upton: "Early American Publications in the Field of Music," *Music and Libraries*, ed. R. S. Hill (Washington, DC, 1943), 50
D. W. Krummel: "Graphic Analysis: its Application to Early American Sheet Music," *Notes*, xvi (1958–9), 213
D. W. Krummel and J. B. Coover: "Current National Bibliographies: their Music Coverage," *Notes*, xvii (1959–60), 375
E. C. Krohn: "On Classifying Sheet Music," *Notes*, xxvi (1969–70), 473
G. T. Tanselle: "Copyright Records and the Bibliographer," *Studies in Bibliography*, xxii (1969), 77–124 [incl. inventory of district court copyright records, 1790–1870]
D. W. Krummel, ed.: *Guide for Dating Early Published Music* (Hackensack, NJ, 1974), esp. 229ff; suppl. in *FAM*, xxiv (1977), 175

R. J. Wolfe: *Early American Music Engraving and Printing* (Urbana, IL, 1980)
R. Holibaugh and D. W. Krummel: "Documentation of Music Publishing in the U.S.A. in the Nineteenth Century," *FAM*, xxviii (1981), 94
For further bibliography *see* PUBLISHING AND PRINTING OF MUSIC.

D. W. KRUMMEL

Bickford (Revere), Vahdah Olcott [née Olcott, Ethel Lucretia] (*b* Norwalk, OH, 17 Oct 1885; *d* Los Angeles, CA, 18 May 1980). Guitarist and teacher. She grew up in Los Angeles, where she received her first guitar instruction from George Lindsey, a music retailer. In 1903–4 she studied in Berkeley with Manuel Ferrer, who taught her the repertory and techniques of the European classical guitar. In 1914 she moved to New York, where she played concerts and gave guitar lessons; she also assisted Philip J. Bone in the publication of his book *The Guitar and Mandolin.* In 1915 she married Myron Bickford (1886–1971), a mandolin virtuoso and leader of a mandolin orchestra. (They soon took the astrological names Vahdah and Zarh.) Vahdah gave the American première of Mauro Giuliani's Concerto no.3 for guitar and string quartet at Town Hall. She returned to Los Angeles in 1923 and was the founder of the Los Angeles (later the American) Guitar Society. She performed in and led various ensembles of fretted instruments in Los Angeles, and taught guitar. Although she published more than 140 works, Bickford was best known for her *Guitar Method*, op.25, and her *Advanced Course*, op.116, published by Ditson; these influenced numerous guitarists. She consistently promoted the guitar as a chamber instrument, and remained active as a performer in ensembles at meetings of the American Guitar Society into the early 1970s.

BIBLIOGRAPHY

P. J. Bone: "Bickford, Vahdah Olcott," *The Guitar and Mandolin: Biographies of Celebrated Players and Composers* (London, 1914, 2/1954/*R*1972), 37
"The Bickfords," *Fretted Instrument News*, xix/2 (1950), 8
R. C. Purcell: "In memoriam Vahdah Olcott Bickford Revere," *Soundboard*, vii/3 (1980), 120
——: *Vahdah Olcott Bickford Revere, 1885–1980* (Los Angeles, 1980) [booklet for a memorial service held by the American Guitar Society]

THOMAS F. HECK

Biedermann, Edward J(ulius) (*b* Milwaukee, WI, 8 Nov 1849; *d* Freeport, NY, 26 Nov 1933). Organist and composer. Little is known of his career other than that he studied in Germany from 1858 until 1864 and then returned to the USA to become a church organist, first in Newburgh, New York, and then in New York City at Old St. Mary's on Grand Street and at St. Francis de Sales. Failing eyesight caused him to retire from active church work in 1918. For many years he was associated with the editorial department of the publishing firm J. Fischer. He wrote four masses and many songs and piano pieces, and also compiled collections of organ literature and an anthology of vocal duets. Beaver College awarded him an honorary DMus in 1906.

WILLIAM OSBORNE

Big apple. A lively and strenuous circle dance, popular between 1937 (the year it was observed in a nightclub of the same name in Columbia, South Carolina) and the early 1940s. Of black-American origin, the dance was rearranged by Arthur Murray into a ballroom favorite and frequently performed to swing music, such as the arrangements of Tommy Dorsey. The dance required a caller to signal step changes, and it incorporated the most active dance steps of the era: the Suzie-Q, truckin' (with its shuffle step and waving index finger), the shag, and the organ grinder. Interludes gave individual dancers (or "shiners") a chance to exhibit their dancing prowess in the center of the circle, where they performed such steps as the lindy hop, the flea hop, the bunny jump, and "peckin' and posin'." The whole sequence of dances ended with arms raised and a shouted "Praise Allah!". Tin Pan Alley hit upon the craze almost immediately, and in 1937 two songs were copyrighted, *The Big Apple* by Bob Emmerich and Buddy Bernier and *Big Apple* by Lee David and John Redmond. The noted dancer and teacher Ted Shawn expressed the belief that the big apple was "a genuine folk expression and . . . a desirable successor to the selfish modern Fox Trot and Waltz." The little apple, a popular variant of the dance, involved the same steps but was performed by individual couples rather than by a large group.

BIBLIOGRAPHY

J. Bonomo: *Improve Your Dancing* (Brooklyn, NY, 1938)
A. Murray: *How to Become a Good Dancer* (New York, 1938)
M. Stearns and J. Stearns: *Jazz Dance: the Story of American Vernacular Dance* (New York, 1968)

LINDA MOOT

Bigard, Barney [Albany Leon] (*b* New Orleans, LA, 3 March 1906; *d* Culver City, CA, 27 June 1980). Jazz clarinetist. Born into a musical Creole family (his cousin Natty Dominique was a noted cornetist), Bigard began on E♭ clarinet, studying with Lorenzo Tio, Jr., and using an Albert system instrument. Discouraged on the clarinet, he adopted the tenor saxophone and joined Albert Nicholas's band late in 1922. After working briefly with Oke Gaspard and Amos White, he returned to Nicholas, with whom he traveled to Chicago late in 1924. There they joined King Oliver for an important engagement at the Plantation Cafe from February 1925 to March 1927. On four titles recorded in 1926 with a contingent from Oliver's band (under the leadership of Luis Russell), Bigard displayed a cleanly executed saxophone style in the "slap tongue" manner characteristic of that era. In the same year he began a long series of recordings with Oliver for the Vocalion label.

As Oliver altered his band's personnel, Bigard was occasionally called upon to play clarinet, which soon became his principal instrument. He also recorded with Jelly Roll Morton and, in April 1927, with Johnny Dodds and Louis Armstrong. At the end of April, Bigard went with the Oliver band to New York, where they played for a fortnight at the Savoy Ballroom. The band broke up later while on tour, and Bigard joined Charlie Elgar's group in Milwaukee for the summer. He then returned to New York, playing with Russell for two months before joining Duke Ellington at the end of 1927 or beginning of 1928.

Except for a brief absence in summer 1935, Bigard remained with Ellington until June 1942. This was the high-water mark of his career. During this period, he perfected a highly individual clarinet style characterized by a warm tone in all registers, sweeping chromatic runs, and long, continuous glissandos. He quickly became a distinctive voice in the Ellington orchestra, and was prominently featured on hundreds of recordings, most notably on *Clarinet Lament* (*Barney's Concerto*), which he wrote with Ellington in 1936 (Bigard also collaborated on *Mood Indigo*, *Ducky Wucky*, and *Saturday Night Function*, among others). In addition he made many recordings with contingents of the Ellington band, and found time to record again with Oliver in 1928 and to produce four outstanding titles with Morton in 1929.

After leaving Ellington, Bigard continued to play and record with his own groups in Los Angeles and New York. His work during the autumn of 1946 with Louis Armstrong in the film *New Orleans* led to his next important association, as clarinetist with the Armstrong All-Stars. During his long tenure with this group (1947–52, 1953–5, 1960–61), he toured the world and took part in many outstanding recording sessions. Bigard went into semiretirement in 1962, but continued to play occasionally at concerts, recording dates, television appearances, and numerous American and international jazz festivals.

RECORDINGS
(selective list)

As leader: Barney Goin' Easy (1939, Voc. 5378); Step Steps Up/Step Steps Down (1944, Signature 28114); Rose Room/Coquette (1945, Keynote 617); *Clarinet Gumbo* (1973, RCA APLI-1744)

As sideman with Duke Ellington: Sweet Mama (1928, Harmony 577-H); Saturday Night Function (1929, Vic. 38036); Mood Indigo (1930, Bruns. 4952); Ducky Wucky (1932, Bruns. 6432); Clarinet Lament (Barney's Concerto) (1936, Bruns. 7650); Across the Track Blues (1940, Vic. 27235)

As sideman with others: L. Russell: 29th and Dearborn/Sweet Mumtaz (1926, Voc. 1010); King Oliver: Too Bad (1926, Voc. 1007); A. Wynn: That Creole Band (1926, OK 8350); J. Dodds: Weary Blues (1927, Voc. 15632); King Oliver: Showboat Shuffle (1927, Voc. 1114); J. Morton: That's like it ought to be (1929, Vic. 38601); L. Armstrong: Tea for Two, pts. i–ii (1947, Decca 9-28099–9-28100); C Jam Blues (1947, Decca 9-28102), Just you, Just me (1951, Decca 9-28175)

BIBLIOGRAPHY

L. Feather: "Barney Bigard Blindfold Test," *Down Beat*, xxxvi/12 (1969), 30
B. Bigard: "Me and Brother Satch," *Jazz hot*, no.263 (1970), 16
S. Dance: *The World of Duke Ellington* (New York, 1970), 81
R. Stewart: "Illustrious Barney Bigard," *Jazz Masters of the Thirties* (New York, 1972/*R*1980), 113
E. K. Ellington: *Music is my Mistress* (Garden City, NY, 1973/*R*1976), 114
D. Koechlin: *50 ans de Barney Bigard* (Darnetal, France, 1979)
B. Bigard: *With Louis and the Duke* (New York, 1986)

LEWIS PORTER

Big band. A type of dance band popular in the 1930s and 1940s, consisting of ten to 15 instruments, predominantly wind; a distinctive feature of the music played by such bands was the pitting against each other of the reed and brass sections.

See JAZZ, §IV.

Big Brother and the Holding Company. Blues and rock group, formed in 1965, of which JANIS JOPLIN was for a time a member.

Biggs, E(dward George) Power (*b* Westcliff on Sea, Essex, England, 29 March 1906; *d* Boston, MA, 10 March 1977). Organist. He studied at the Royal Academy of Music in London. He began to play in the USA in 1930 and became an American citizen in 1937, pursuing a career as a recitalist, broadcaster, and recording artist that did much to popularize the concert organ and organ music as well as the artist. From 1942 to 1958 he broadcast weekly solo programs over a nationwide radio network. Originating in the Germanic (now Busch–Reisinger) Museum at Harvard, these recitals on an Aeolian-Skinner "classic style" organ brought the sound of organ mixtures, mutations, and Baroque reeds, as well as the music itself, to many listeners for the first time. Biggs was meanwhile an indefatigable public performer. A product of both activities was an extensive series of phonograph recordings, made in the USA and in many European cities, including "Historic Organs of England" and "The Glory of Gabrieli," the Handel organ concertos, various Bach projects, and others with instrumental ensembles; after 1958, when the Aeolian-Skinner instrument was replaced, his recordings from the Busch–Reisinger Museum were made on an organ by the Dutch builder Dirk Flentrop (see illustration). Biggs published editions of early music and performed new works (by Hanson, Piston, Quincy Porter, Sowerby, and others). His career was marked by interest in organ music of all eras and in many kinds of organs most suitable to its interpretation, and by unfailing energy in performance. He played with most major American orchestras, and in 1962 joined Catharine Crozier and Virgil Fox in inaugurating the organ at Philharmonic Hall, New York. His ultimate achievement was to surpass everyone else in the USA where the extent and variety of his repertory, selfless devotion to the instrument, and a proper understanding of it are concerned.

E. Power Biggs playing the Flentrop organ in the Busch–Reisinger Museum, Harvard University

BIBLIOGRAPHY

"E. Power Biggs," *Music: the A.G.O. and R.C.C.O. Magazine*, xii/3 (1978), 23, 42 [4 of Biggs's articles with list of edns. and discography]

VERNON GOTWALS

Biglow & Main. Firm of music publishers. A partnership was formed in New York in 1867 between Lucius Horatio Biglow (1833–*c*1910) and Sylvester Main (1819–73) in order to continue the publishing activities of William Bradbury, who had become seriously ill during the previous year. Bradbury served the firm as music editor until his death in January 1868. Main had formerly been Bradbury's assistant, but it was his son Hubert Platt Main (1839–1925) who was responsible for shaping the editorial policy of the company and who built it into one of the foremost 19th-century firms of gospel-song publishers. Among the composers whose works he issued were Philip P. Bliss, William H. Doane, William J. Kirkpatrick, Robert Lowry, McGranahan, G. F. Root, Sankey, Sherwin, Stebbins, Sweney, and Whittle. Lowry succeeded Bradbury as music editor in 1868, and a number of other composers also had editorial relationships with the firm. The poet Fanny Crosby worked closely with many of Biglow & Main's composers, contributing a total of almost 6000 texts; she formed a particularly successful collaboration with Doane.

Ira Sankey became president of the firm on the retirement of Biglow in 1895. On his death in 1908 he was succeeded by his son I. Allan Sankey (1874–1915), and for the next few years the firm was run by the Sankey family. Biglow & Main was purchased in 1922 by the Hope Publishing Co., and merged in 1933 with the E. O. Excell Co., but the company's publications continue to be issued under its own name. Hubert Main's extensive collection of books concerning 19th-century American hymns and hymn writers is now in the Newberry Library, Chicago.

CAROLINE RICHMOND

Big Sid. *See* CATLETT, SID.

Big 3 Music Corporation. Firm of music publishers. It was formed in 1939 by Metro-Goldwyn-Mayer, which acquired three major publishers of popular music, Robbins Music Corporation, Leo Feist, Inc., and Miller Music, in order to gain control of copyrights for music used in films. The resulting company, the Big 3 Music Corporation, continues to expand its catalogue with popular music, film scores, and television theme music; among its successes have been *You don't have to say you love me*, *Batman's Theme*, *The shadow of your smile*, and *Somewhere my love*. It also publishes arrangements of such tunes for use by schools in editions for chorus and for marching band. In 1973 MGM sold Big 3 to United Artists.

FRANCES BARULICH

Bikel, Theodore (*b* Vienna, Austria, 2 March 1924). Actor and singer. He spent his youth in Europe and Israel, where he made his stage début during the 1943–4 season. In 1946 he moved to London and took up a career as a stage and film actor. He immigrated to the USA in 1954 and became a naturalized American in 1961. After making his concert début at Carnegie Recital Hall, New York, in 1956, he played several character parts in the theater before being cast in the role of Georg von Trapp in the Rodgers and Hammerstein musical *The Sound of Music* (1959). During his long theater career Bikel has appeared in numerous films, plays, and musicals, and has been active in theater guilds and politics. He also built up an international reputation as a singer of ethnic folk music, exploiting his strong baritone voice and considerable skill as a guitarist; his scholarly approach to his material and knowledge of many languages combine with a keen sense of humor to create authentic, zestful performances. His many recordings cover a wide range of folk material from four continents, though most of his repertory derives from Europe and Israel; he is perhaps best known for his interpretations of Russian folk and gypsy songs, with the moods of which he has a particular affinity. He has appeared in many folk festivals and presented his own folk-music radio program from 1957 to 1962; he published the book *Folksongs & Footnotes* in 1960. Beginning in the late 1960s, he concentrated more on theater work than concert performances, appearing in such musicals as *Fiddler on the Roof* and *The Rothschilds* by Bock and Harnick, and Kander's *Zorba*.

BIBLIOGRAPHY

"Bikel, Theodore," *CBY 1960*

A. Hano: "The Star Nobody Knows," *Coronet*, xlvii/3 (1960), 156

R. Gaines and M. Saunders: "A Dynamo Named Bikel," *Hi-fi/Stereo Review*, vii/4 (1961), 45

G. Milstein: "Theodore Bikel: Charisma and Chutzpah," *Esquire*, lv/4 (1961), 110

O. Brand: *The Ballad Mongers* (New York, 1962)

R. Lawless: "Theodore Bikel," *Folksingers and Folksongs in America* (New York, 1965), 43

CRAIG A. LOCKARD

Billings, Bud and Joe. Country-music duo, the members of which were FRANK LUTHER and CARSON J. ROBISON.

Billings, William (*b* Boston, MA, 7 Oct 1746; *d* Boston, 26 Sept 1800). Composer and singing teacher. He exerted a strong influence on the development of church music in New England during the 1770s and 1780s, and subsequently throughout the USA, where his tunes and anthems were widely sung in churches, singing-schools, and at social gatherings. The contemporary diarist William Bentley described him as "the father of our New England music."

1. Life. 2. Works.

1. LIFE. Little is known of Billings's early life, but it is probable that he had only a rudimentary formal education. In 1760 after the death of his father, a Boston shopkeeper, he was apprenticed to a tanner, a trade which he seems to have worked at for much of his life. His musical education is undocumented, but it is likely that he attended singing-schools in Boston, and may also have participated in informal choral societies that met for the recreational singing of psalmody. It has been claimed by Lindstrom, without evidence, that Billings studied with the Boston singing master John Barry. He may also have received some instruction from Josiah Flagg and William Selby, though this was probably only occasional advice and criticism of his early compositions. It is thought that Billings was largely self-taught in music, gaining his knowledge from the study of the compositions and theoretical writings of such English psalmodists as William Tans'ur, Aaron Williams, John Arnold, and Uriah Davenport.

Billings began to teach singing-schools as early as 1769. Most of his activities were centered in and around Boston, although he taught briefly in Providence in 1774 and the same year taught a school in Stoughton, Massachusetts, where one of his pupils was Lucy Swan, whom he married on 26 July 1774. The couple had nine children. Billings was described by Bentley as "a singular man, of moderate size, short of one leg, with one eye, without any address, and with an uncommon negligence of person. Still he spake and sung and thought as a man above the common abilities." Nathaniel D. Gould added that he had "a stentorian voice," one arm that was somewhat withered, and a propensity for taking large quantities of snuff (*Church Music in America*, 1853/*R*1972). In spite of his physical handicaps, Billings was a very successful singing master, teaching at the fashionable Boston churches, including Brattle Street Church, Old South Church, First Church, and Stone Chapel. By 1780 he was affluent enough to purchase a house at 89 Newbury Street, and was a pew holder at the Hollis Street Church.

In the late 1780s, however, Billings's fortunes declined, and he accepted a succession of minor municipal appointments – scavenger, hogreeve, and sealer of leather. In 1790 a public concert was held for his benefit, the advertisement assuring the public that his "distress is real." Soon afterwards Billings mortgaged his house and tried to sell the rights to his music to the publishing firm of Thomas & Andrews. The firm did issue Billings's final tunebook in 1794, not as the business venture Billings proposed, however, but as a charitable enterprise sponsored by several musical societies in Boston and paid for by subscription. Billings's wife died in March 1795, leaving him with six children under the age of 18. He continued his activities as a singing master and retained the post of sealer of leather until 1796. On his death he left an estate valued after the payment of debts at slightly more than $800, and he was buried in an unmarked grave, probably in the Boston Common.

2. WORKS. Billings wrote over 340 compositions. Most of these are psalm and hymn tunes, but there are also 51 fuging-tunes, 4 canons, and 52 anthems and set-pieces. All his music is for four-voice unaccompanied chorus, although he included parts for unspecified instruments in two of his anthems; such instruments as flute, clarinet, bassoon, violin, viola, and cello could also double the vocal parts. The principal melody in his psalm and hymn tunes was assigned to the tenor voice, but Billings expressed the wish that some treble voices should double the tenor an octave higher, and vice versa, producing a full choral sound in which the tenor and treble lines are closely intertwined and vie for the listener's attention. Billings employed an additive compositional technique, in which the tenor melody was composed first, then the bass according to rules of consonant counterpoint, then the treble to provide a countermelody to the tenor, and finally the counter (or alto). All parts often share common musical motifs, but each usually maintains a good deal of rhythmic and melodic independence. The harmony is contrapuntally derived and, while related to functional tonality (particularly at cadences), does not usually follow common 18th-century European harmonic formulas.

The New-England Psalm-singer (1770) was the first of Billings's six tunebooks, and the first collection to be devoted exclusively to American compositions and to the music of a single American composer. The variety of its contents, ranging from psalm tunes of stark simplicity to florid hymn tunes and fairly complex polyphonic anthems, suggests that Billings had been composing for a number of years; the announcement in its preface that a second volume of music "consisting chiefly of Anthems, Fuges, and Chorus's" would be published if the first met "with Encouragement" supports this hypothesis. (The publication of the second volume was delayed by the political events of the 1770s, appearing only in part and undoubtedly greatly revised, as *The Psalm-singer's Amusement* in 1781.) Paul Revere engraved the frontispiece for *The New-England Psalm-singer*, which shows a group of gentlemen sitting around a table singing from several open tunebooks (see illustration). There is no evidence to support the popular belief that Revere engraved the music in the book, however, which task may have been undertaken by Billings himself. The volume includes a lengthy essay "On the Nature and Properties of Sound" by Charles Stockbridge, and Billings's own somewhat discursive but informative theoretical introduction, in which he states: "I don't think myself confined to any Rules for Composition laid down by any that went before me," and "it is best for

The frontispiece to William Billings's "New-England Psalm-singer" (1770) showing a psalm tune in canonic form: engraving by Paul Revere

every *Composer* to be his own *Carver*." These remarks are considered by some writers to be Billings's declaration of musical independence, but they do not seem so radical when read in the context in which Billings made them. Although Billings surpassed most other Anglo-American psalmodists of his day, he did not attempt to forge a new style or create new modes of expression. He accepted the forms and techniques passed on to him by earlier church composers, adapting them to his needs through his own unique abilities.

The music of *The New-England Psalm-singer* is uneven in inspiration and insecure in technique. Some psalm tunes and all the anthems have prosodical problems, causing conflicts between the accents of the words and the music. The collection includes some of Billings's most popular tunes, however, such as "Amherst," "Brookfield," "Chester," and "Lebanon." Billings denounced the contents in 1778, saying that "many of the pieces in that Book were never worth my printing, or your inspection," but the volume remains one of the most important American musical documents, setting the tone for and giving direction to American psalmody for 30 or 40 years following its publication.

In 1772 Billings received legislative approval of copyright for *The New-England Psalm-singer*, but the governor of Massachusetts, for reasons undisclosed, refused to sign the act to bring it into law. Only one piece by Billings, the fuging-tune "Lanesborough," appeared before his next collection; printed anonymously in John Stickney's *The Gentleman and Lady's Musical Companion* (1774), "Lanesborough" shows significant musical growth.

Billings's second tunebook, *The Singing Master's Assistant* (1778), was written for his singing-schools, and clearly shows the extent of his development during the intervening years. Not only are problems of prosody completely eliminated, but the texts are set more imaginatively and with greater attention to musical effect; the melodies are more fluid and the counterpoint more deftly handled. Popularly known as "Billings's Best," *The Singing Master's Assistant* went through four editions between 1778 and 1789. Billings characterized it as "An Abridgement of the New-England Psalm-Singer," but over two-thirds of its contents were newly published pieces; he thoroughly revised tunes reprinted from *The New-England Psalm-singer*, and provided a better organized, more succinct theoretical introduction. To increase its utility as a textbook, it was organized (apart from the first two pieces) to move progressively from simple to more complex pieces. The music clearly shows the various sides of Billings's personality: the conscientious and capable singing master, the ardent patriot, and the humorous wag. Among the patriotic pieces is "Chester," reprinted with four new verses including the line "And gen'rals yield to beardless boys"; *Lamentation over Boston* ("By the rivers of Watertown"), a deeply felt paraphrase of Psalm cxxxvii; and the exuberant *Independence* ("The states, O Lord"), containing the words "Down with this earthly king, No king but God!" Billings's sense of humor is shown in his literary satire in the introduction ("An Historical Account of G. Gamut") and mock dedication ("To the Goddess of Discord"), and in his musical joke, "Jargon," in which he deliberately misapplied the rules of composition to produce a work of unresolved dissonance. *The Singing Master's Assistant* also includes a variety of music in other moods, such as the lyrical anthem "I am the rose of Sharon"; the majestic psalm tune "Majesty" ("The Lord descended from above"); the touching set-piece *David's Lamentation* ("David, the king, was grieved and moved"); the somber *Funeral Anthem* ("I heard a great voice from heav'n"); and the madrigalistic fuging-tune "Dunstable" ("With earnest longings of the mind"). The collection richly deserved its high reputation and served later tunebook compilers as a major source for Billings's music, which (because it was not protected by copyright) was reprinted without permission of or compensation to the composer.

Music in Miniature (1779) was designed to be bound with a metrical psalter, and was directed towards the congregational singer; it was quite different from Billings's other tunebooks in that it contained only psalm tunes. Nearly half its 72 pieces were reprinted from *The Singing Master's Assistant* or *The New-England Psalm-singer*, and Billings also included ten standard English psalm tunes in his own arrangements, the only instance of his publishing music other than his own. The music was printed without text, facilitating the singing of a tune to any psalm or hymn text which matched the meter of the music.

The Psalm-singer's Amusement (1781), according to Billings "not for Learners," was issued to meet the needs of more advanced singers. In the variety of its settings and the virtuosity of its contents it holds a unique position in 18th-century psalmody. It is the smallest of Billings's tunebooks, containing only 24 works, but nearly half of these are substantial anthems and set-pieces. In his brief prefatory remarks Billings stated that "This work is a Part of the Book of Anthems, which I have so LONG promised." Although it cannot be determined precisely when any of Billings's pieces were composed – it is known that he held some works back for years before publishing them while others were never printed – it seems certain that any music in *The Psalm-singer's Amusement* dating from early in his career was thoroughly revised. There is no evidence of technical weakness in any of the pieces: in choice of keys, text setting, fugal counterpoint, musical structure, and variety of effect, Billings may have reached his apex as a composer.

Among the noteworthy works in *The Psalm-singer's Amusement* are two concert pieces, *Modern Musick* and *Consonance*, which describe the experience of attending a choral concert such as often closed a singing-school session. Several anthems make use of unusual keys, for example "And I saw a mighty angel" (B major) and *Euroclydon* ("They that go down to the sea"; F♯ major) – both almost unknown in parish church psalmody. Others, such as "Who is this that cometh," present an advanced complex of musical and textual imagery. The fuging-tune "Rutland" is also unusual in that, from a beginning in A minor, it makes a modulation (uncommon in parish church psalmody) to D minor, then ends in C major.

In *The Suffolk Harmony* (1786) Billings seems to have been working towards a more refined style based on tuneful melody, greater variety of texture, closer integration of words and music, and a less flamboyant and more controlled musical language. Unlike his earlier tunebooks, *The Suffolk Harmony* does not seem to have been directed towards a particular group of users; it contains three anthems, four fuging-tunes, and 25 psalm and hymn tunes. There are 18 settings of texts by the English Universalist poets James and John Relly which, along with several by Watts and Billings's own Christmas hymn "Shiloh," have been described as "lovely part-songs on religious texts" rather than standard hymn tunes. *The Suffolk Harmony* was Billings's first collection to enjoy copyright protection (limited to the state of Massachusetts, however), and perhaps because of this and the intimate nature of the music, few pieces were reprinted by later tunebook compilers. Only "Jordan" enjoyed a popularity commensurate with Billings's earlier pieces.

The Continental Harmony (1794), published as a charitable act when the composer was in financial distress, appears to be a collection of pieces which Billings had composed at various times during his career. "Cobham" and "Victory," for example, are found in a manuscript dating from the early 1780s. The anthem "I charge you, o ye daughters" is so close in style to "I am the rose of Sharon" (in *The Singing Master's Assistant*) that it is difficult not to conclude that they were composed at the same time. The fuging-tune "Great Plain" has prosodical problems not found in any piece by Billings outside *The New-England Psalm-singer*, and the *Anthem for Ordination* ("O thou to whom all creatures bow") contains whole sections of music which had been published earlier in *Retrospect* ("Was not the day," in *The Singing Master's Assistant*) and *Peace* ("God is the king," *c*1783). Other tunes, such as "Adams," "Cross Street," "Hopkinton," and "Sudbury," and anthems, including *An Anthem for Thanksgiving* ("O clap your hands"), *Deliverance* ("I will love thee"), and *Variety without Method* ("O God, thou hast been displeased"), seem to follow the stylistic paths laid out in *The Suffolk Harmony*. Although the theoretical introduction to *The Singing Master's Assistant* was reprinted in *The Continental Harmony*, Billings supplemented it with an extended commentary on the rules of music in the form of a dialogue between a master and a scholar. This commentary provides many insights into Billings's thought and style and clearly indicates that he was familiar with a wide range of historical and theoretical literature on music (*see* THEORY, §2).

In addition to his six collections Billings published a small number of pieces independently during the 1780s and 1790s. These include *An Anthem for Easter* ("The Lord is ris'n indeed"; 1787, rev. 1795), which remains the most popular anthem by an 18th-century American composer. He may also have allowed a few of his unpublished tunes to be issued by others: "Union" appeared in *The Worcester Collection* (2/1788) and "Mansfield" in *The Boston Collection* (*c*1799). Billings's last known composition was *A Piece on the Death of Washington* (1799), mentioned in a list of his works drawn up after his death by Nahum Mitchell. Billings probably did not live to publish the work, which does not appear to have survived in manuscript. Some of his unpublished tunes – not in his hand, however – are found in manuscripts at the University of Michigan, Ann Arbor, the Massachusetts Historical Society, the Watkinson Library at Trinity College, Hartford, the Lincoln Center Library, and the private collection of Mrs. Dorothy Waterhouse of Boston. These manuscripts also contain tunes which are rhythmic, melodic, or structural variants of published pieces, suggesting the recycling of old works.

Billings also engaged in literary activity and was a poet of imagination if not distinction. Each of his tunebooks (apart from *Music in Minature*) includes some of his poetry and prose; "Shiloh" (in *The Suffolk Harmony*) is perhaps the most successful of his texts. The words for most of his anthems were arranged from biblical verses, but Billings frequently altered them, supplying new words and phrases to create a stronger image, a more definite mood, or to provide opportunities for musical development. In 1783 he edited one issue of the *Boston Magazine* which so upset Boston's gentlemen that he was relieved of the editorship. The following year he published a satire on Puritan hypocrisy entitled *The Porcupine, Alias the Hedge-hog, or Fox Turned Preacher*. It is possible that he issued other pamphlets which have not survived.

Billings's music reached the height of its popularity in the 1780s and 1790s when it was reprinted and performed throughout the USA. In 1786 the publisher Isaiah Thomas wrote: "For the progress of Psalmody in this country the Publick are in a great measure indebted to the music abilities of Mr. WILLIAM BILLINGS, of Boston." In 1788 a Philadelphia critic posed Billings as "the rival of Handel," predicting that "the English will pay proper tribute to his merits as soon as they are acquainted with his productions." That acquaintance came the following year when Thomas Williams included two of Billing's tunes, "Marshfield" and "New England" (i.e., "Hartford"), in his *Psalmodia Evangelica* and about five years later John Rippon included "Spillman" (i.e., "Consolation") in his *Selection of Psalm and Hymn Tunes* (*c*1795). These are among the very few American pieces to find a place in English tunebooks.

See also PSALMODY, esp. §2 and exx.4, 6, and 10.

WORKS

Edition: *The Complete Works of William Billings*, ed. K. Kroeger and H. Nathan (Charlottesville, VA, and Boston, 1977–)

Collections: *The New-England Psalm-singer* (Boston, 1770) [NEPS]
The Singing Master's Assistant, or Key to Practical Music (Boston, 1778/*R*, 4/1786–9/*R*) [SMA]
Music in Miniature (Boston, 1779) [MM]
The Psalm-singer's Amusement (Boston, 1781/*R*1974) [PSA]
The Suffolk Harmony (Boston, 1786) [SH]
The Continental Harmony (Boston, 1794/*R*1961) [CH]

Waterhouse MS, private collection of D. Waterhouse, Boston [W]

PSALM AND HYMN TUNES

* – *version with fugal chorus listed under "Fuging-tunes"*

Adams, CH; Africa, NEPS, rev. SMA, MM; Albany, NEPS; America, NEPS, rev. SMA, MM; Amherst, NEPS, rev. SMA, MM; Andover (i), NEPS; Ashford, NEPS; Ashham, SMA; Asia (i), NEPS; Asia (ii), MM; Attleborough, NEPS; *Aurora, MM; Baltimore, SMA; Baptism, SH; Barre, NEPS; Bedford, in *Sacred Harmony* (Boston, *c*1788) [variant of Waltham]; Bellingham, CH; Beneficence, SH; Bennington, W [variant of Friendship]; Berlin, PSA; *Bethlehem, MM; Bolton, SMA; Boston, NEPS, rev. SMA; Bradford, W [variant of Consolation]; Braintree, NEPS; Brattle Square, SH

Brattle Street, NEPS; Brest, MM; Bridgwater, NEPS; Brookfield, NEPS, rev. SMA, MM; Brookline, NEPS, rev. MM; Brunswick, SMA; Burlington, SH; Calvary, MM, rev. CH as St. Thomas; Cambridge, NEPS, rev. SMA, MM; Camden, SH; Charlston, NEPS; Chelsea (i), NEPS; Chelsea (ii), SH; Chester, NEPS, rev. SMA, MM; Chesterfield, NEPS; Chocksett, SMA, MM; Claremont, CH; Cobham (Raynham), CH; Columbia, SMA, MM; Concord, NEPS; Connection, SMA, MM, CH; Conquest, SH; Consolation, SMA; Corsica, NEPS; *Creation, MM; Cross Street, CH; *Crucifiction, MM; Cumberland, NEPS; Danbury, MM

Dedham (i), NEPS; Deerfield, see Thomas-town; Delaware, MM; Dickinson, NEPS; Dighton, NEPS; Dorchester, NEPS, rev. SMA; Dublin, MM; Dudley, MM; Dunstable (i), *MHi* [variant of Saybrook]; *Dunstable (ii), MM; Duxborough, NEPS, rev. SMA, MM; Eastham, NEPS; East Sudbury, CH; Easttown, NEPS; Eden, SH; The 18th Psalm, NEPS; Election, SH; Emanuel, PSA; Emmaus, SMA, MM; Essex, NEPS; *Europe, MM; Exeter, SMA; Fairfield, NEPS; Fitchburgh, MM; *Framingham, MM; Franklin, MM; Freedom, NEPS; Friendship, NEPS; Georgia (i), NEPS; Georgia (ii), MM; Germantown, *MHi*; Gloucester, SH

Golgotha, PSA; Gospel Pool, in J. Ingalls: *Christian Harmony* (Exeter, NH, 1805) [excerpt from Was not the day, see "Anthems and set-pieces"]; Greenland, NEPS; Hacker's Hall, W; Halifax, SMA, MM; Hampshire (i), NEPS; Hampshire (ii), MM; Hamton, NEPS; Hanover, NEPS; Hanover New, NEPS; Hartford, PSA, SH; Harvard, NEPS; Hatfield, first pubd in posth. edn of PSA (n.p., *c*1804); Haverill, NEPS; Hebron (i), NEPS, rev. SMA, MM; Hingham, NEPS; Holden, NEPS; Hollis, NEPS; Hollis Street, NEPS, rev. SMA; Hull, SH; Ipswich, NEPS; Jamaica (i), NEPS; Jamaica (ii), MM; Jargon, SMA; Jerusalem, SH; Jordan, SH; Judea, SMA

Lancaster (Shirley), NEPS; The Lark (Boston, 1790); Lebanon, NEPS, rev. SMA, MM; Lewis-town, CH; Lexington, NEPS; Liberty, NEPS; Lincoln, NEPS; Lynn, NEPS; Madrid, MM, SH; Majesty, SMA; Malden, NEPS; *Manchester, MM; Mansfield (i), MM; Mansfield (ii), in *The Boston Collection* (Boston, *c*1799); Marblehead, NEPS, rev. SMA; Marshfield, NEPS, rev. SMA, MM; *Maryland, MM; Massachusetts, NEPS; Medfield, NEPS, rev. SMA; Medford, NEPS; Mendom, PSA, SH; Middlesex, NEPS; Middletown, NEPS; Moravia, SH; Moriah, SH; *Morpheus, MM; Morriston, W [variant of Medfield]

Nantasket, NEPS; Nantucket, NEPS; Nazareth, MM; New Boston, NEPS;

Newburn, MM; New-castle, MM; New Haven, W [variant of Duxborough]; New Hingham, NEPS, rev. SMA, MM [variant of Hingham]; New North, NEPS, rev. SMA, MM; Newport, NEPS; New South, NEPS, rev. SMA, MM; New Town, NEPS; Norfolk, CH; North River, NEPS; No.45, NEPS; Nutfield, NEPS; Old Brick, NEPS; Old North, NEPS; Old South, NEPS; Orange Street, NEPS; Orleans, NEPS; Oxford, MM; Paris, MM; Pembroke, NEPS; Pembroke New, NEPS; Petersburgh, SH; *Philadelphia, MM; Philanthropy, SH

Pitt, NEPS; Plainfield, NEPS; Pleasant Street, NEPS; Plymouth New, in J. French; *Harmony of Harmony* (Northampton, MA, 1802); Plymton, NEPS; Pomfret, NEPS; Pownall, NEPS; Princetown, NEPS, rev. SMA, MM; Providence, NEPS; Pumpily, NEPS, rev. SMA, MM; Purchase Street (i), NEPS; Purchase Street (ii), MM; Queen Street, NEPS; Raynham, see Cobham; Resignation, PSA; Restoration, SH; Resurrection (Boston, 1787); *Revelation, MM; Richmond, SMA, SH; Rochester, CH; Roxbury (i), NEPS; Roxbury (ii), SMA, MM; St. Elisha's, NEPS; St. John's, CH

St. Peter's, in A. Pilsbury: *United States Sacred Harmony* (Boston, 1799) [variant of Savannah]; St. Thomas, CH [rev. of Calvary]; St. Vincent's, in *Sacred Harmony* (Boston, *c*1788) [variant of Concord]; Sappho, NEPS, rev. SMA; Savannah, SMA; Saybrook, MM; Scituate, NEPS; Sharon, SMA; Sherburne, SMA, MM; Shiloh, SH; Shirley, see Lancaster; Sinai, SH; Smithfield, NEPS; South-Boston, CH; Spain, SMA, MM; Spencer, W [variant of Bolton]; Stockbridge, SMA; Stoughton, NEPS; Sturbridge, MM; Sudbury (i), NEPS; Sudbury (ii), CH; Suffolk, NEPS, rev. SMA, MM; Sullivan, SMA

Summer Street, NEPS; Sunday, SMA; Swanzey, NEPS; Thomas-town (Deerfield), CH; Tower Hill, NEPS; Trinity-new, MM; Union (i), NEPS; Union (ii), in *The Worcester Collection* (Worcester, MA, 2/1788); Unity, NEPS; Uxbridge, NEPS; Vermont, SMA; Victory, CH; Waltham, NEPS, rev. SMA, MM; *Wareham, MM; Warren, SMA; Water Town, NEPS; Wellfleet, NEPS; West Boston, SH; Westfield, NEPS; West-Sudbury, CH; Wheeler's Point, NEPS; Wilks, NEPS; Williamsburgh, NEPS; Worcester, SMA; Wrentham, SMA, MM

FUGING-TUNES

** – version without fugal chorus listed under "Psalm and hymn tunes"*

Adoration, PSA; Andover (ii), PSA; Assurance, PSA; *Aurora, SMA; Benevolence, SMA; *Bethlehem, SMA; The Bird (Boston, 1790); Brattle Street, SH; Broad Cove, CH; Cohasset, CH; *Creation, CH; *Crucifiction (Boston, 1787); Dartmouth, W [variant of New North, see "Psalm and hymn tunes"]; Dedham (ii), CH; *Dunstable, SMA; Egypt, CH; *Europe, NEPS; *Framingham, PSA; Gilead, CH; Great Plain, CH; Hadley, *CtHT-W* [variant of opening section of Hark, hark, hear you not, see "Anthems and set-pieces"]; Heath, SMA; Hebron (ii), in A. Pilsbury: *United States Sacred Harmony* (Boston, 1799) [variant of Northborough]; Hopkinton, CH; Invocation, CH; Kittery, SH

Lanesborough, in J. Stickney: *The Gentleman and Lady's Musical Companion* (Newburyport, MA, 1774); *Manchester, PSA; *Maryland, SMA; Medway, SMA; Milton, NEPS; Morning-hymn, CH; *Morpheus, W; New Plymouth, CH; Northborough, SH [variant of Lanesborough]; North Providence, SMA; *Philadelphia, SMA; Phoebus, SMA; Redemption, PSA, *Revelation, CH; Rocky Nook, CH; Rutland, PSA; St. Andrew's, CH; St. Enoch, CH; Sheffield, in J. Huntington: *Apollo Harmony* (Northampton, MA, 1807); Taunton, NEPS; *Wareham, PSA; Washington, SMA; Washington Street, CH; Weymouth, CH; Wheeler's Point, SH

ANTHEMS AND SET-PIECES

And I saw a mighty angel, PSA; As the hart panteth, NEPS; The Beauty of Israel, PSA; Behold how good and joyful (Union), SH; Blessed is he that considereth (i), NEPS; Blessed is he that considereth (ii), PSA; By the rivers of Watertown (Lamentation over Boston), SMA; David, the king, was grieved and moved (David's Lamentation), SMA; Down steers the bass (Consonance), PSA; Except the Lord build the house (Boston, *c*1787–90); God is the king (Peace) (Boston, *c*1783)

Hark, hark, hear you not (Anthem for Christmas), CH; Have pity on me, *MHi* [variant of Samuel the priest]; Hear, hear, o heav'ns (Anthem for Fast Day), CH; Hear my prayer, o Lord (i) (Anthem for Fast Day), NEPS; Hear my prayer, o Lord (ii), SMA; The heavens declare (Sublimity), CH; I am come into my garden, CH; I am the rose of Sharon, SMA; I charge you, o ye daughters, CH; I heard a great voice from heav'n (Funeral Anthem), SMA; I love the Lord (Gratitude), SMA; I will love thee (Deliverance), CH; Is any afflicted, SMA; Let ev'ry mortal ear attend, PSA; Lift up your eyes, SH

The Lord descended from above, NEPS; The Lord is King, NEPS; The Lord is ris'n indeed (Anthem for Easter) (Boston, 1787), rev. pubd 1795, lost, repr. in *The Village Harmony* (Exeter, NH, 5/1800); Mourn, mourn, mourn (Anthem for Fast Day), CH; My friends I am going (The Dying Christian's Last Farewell), CH; O clap your hands (Anthem for Thanksgiving) (Boston, *c*1787–90); O God, my heart is fixed, CH; O God, thou hast been displeased (Variety without Method), CH; O praise God (Universal Praise), CH; O Praise the Lord of heaven (Anthem for Thanksgiving), CH

O thou to whom all creatures bow (Anthem for Ordination), CH; Praise the Lord, o my soul, *NN-L*; Samuel the priest (Funeral Anthem), SH; Sanctify a fast, CH; Sing praises to the Lord (Anthem for Thanksgiving Day Morning), CH; Sing ye merrily, SMA; The states, o Lord (Independence), SMA; They that go down to the sea (Euroclydon), PSA; Thou, o God, art praised, PSA; Vital spark of heav'nly flame (The Dying Christian to his Soul), PSA; Was not the day (Retrospect), SMA; We are met for a concert (Modern Musick), PSA; We have heard with our ears, CH; When the Lord turned again, CH; Who is this that cometh from Edom?, PSA

CANONS

(all in NEPS)

Thus saith the high, the lofty one; Wake ev'ry breath; When Jesus wept; Canon 4 in 1 [no text]

LOST WORKS

I was glad when they said unto me, anthem, perf. Boston, 13 March 1785; A Piece on the Death of Washington, 1799, listed by Mitchell

WRITINGS

ed.: *The Boston Magazine* (Oct 1783)

The Porcupine, Alias the Hedge-hog, or Fox Turned Preacher (Boston, 1784)

BIBLIOGRAPHY

"An Account of Two Americans of Extraordinary Genius in Poetry and Music," *Columbian Magazine*, ii (1788), 211

N. Mitchell: "William Billings," *Musical Reporter*, i (1841), 297

C. Lindstrom: "William Billings and his Times," *MQ*, xxv (1939), 479

A. Garrett: *The Works of William Billings* (diss., U. of North Carolina, 1952)

J. M. Barbour: *The Church Music of William Billings* (East Lansing, MI, 1960)

H. Nathan: Introduction to facs. of W. Billings: *The Continental Harmony* (1794) (Cambridge, MA, 1961)

J. M. Barbour: "Billings and the Barline," *American Choral Review*, v (1963), 1

H. W. Hitchcock: "William Billings and the Yankee Tunesmiths," *Hi Fi/Stereo Review*, xvi/2 (1966), 55

H. Nathan: "William Billings: a Bibliography," *Notes*, xxix (1972–3), 658

R. Crawford and D. McKay: "The Performance of William Billings' Music," *JRME*, xxi (1973), 318

——: "Music in Manuscript: a Manuscript Tunebook of 1782," *Proceedings of the American Antiquarian Society*, lxxxiv (1974), 43

G. Anderson: " 'Samuel the Priest Gave up the Ghost' and *The Temple of Minerva*: Two Broadsides," *Notes*, xxxi (1974–5), 493

D. P. McKay and R. Crawford: *William Billings of Boston: Eighteenth-century Composer* (Princeton, NJ, 1975)

H. Nathan: *William Billings: Data and Documents* (Detroit, 1976)

G. Anderson: "Eighteenth-century Evaluations of William Billings: a Reappraisal," *Quarterly Journal of the Library of Congress*, xxxv (1978), 48

K. Kroeger and H. Nathan: Letter, *JAMS*, xxxi (1978), 176

K. Kroeger: "William Billings's Music in Manuscript Copy and some Notes on Variant Versions of his Pieces," *Notes*, xxxix (1982–3), 316

KARL KROEGER

Bilson, Malcolm (*b* Los Angeles, CA, 24 Oct 1935). Pianist and fortepianist. After receiving his BA from Bard College in 1957, he studied with Grete Hinterhofer at the Akademie für Musik und Darstellende Kunst in Berlin, with Reine Gianoli at the Ecole Normale de Musique in Paris, and with Stanley Fletcher and Webster Aitken at the University of Illinois (DMA 1968). He was appointed to the faculty of Cornell University in 1968, and became a full professor in 1976. In 1969 he purchased one of the first five-octave fortepianos by Philip Belt, based on a Louis Dulcken original in the Smithsonian Institution, and in 1977 he acquired a copy by Belt of Mozart's Walter concert instrument. Bilson was one of the first artists in the USA to make a persuasive case for the use of period instruments in Viennese Classical music. He achieved this through stylish and imaginative performances that took the idiomatic capabilities of the fortepiano as their starting-point; he has played all over the USA and in Europe. With Sonya Monosoff and John Hsu, he formed the Amadé Trio in 1974 and has made several recordings with the ensemble; in 1983 he embarked on a complete recording of Mozart's piano concertos. His solo recordings of Mozart, Haydn, and Beethoven sonatas have received high praise for the new light they throw on a well-established repertory.

ROBERT WINTER

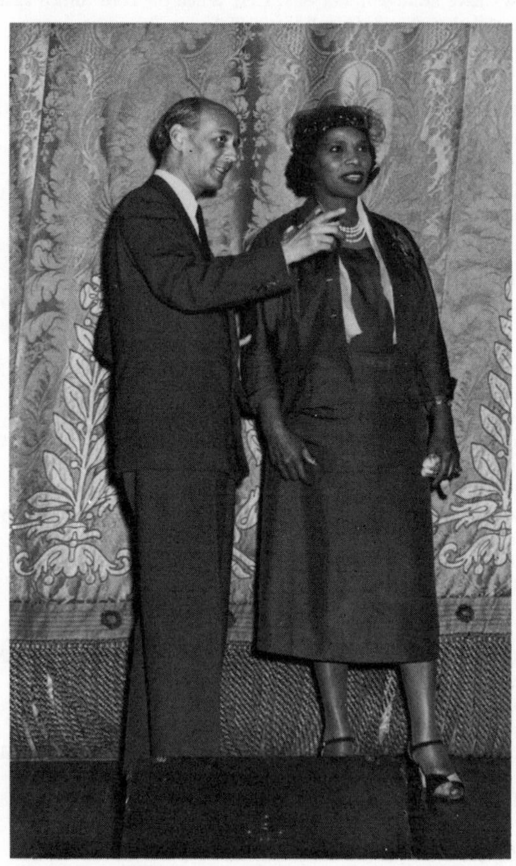

Rudolf Bing welcoming the contralto Marian Anderson to the Metropolitan Opera, 7 October 1954

Bing, Sir Rudolf (*b* Vienna, Austria, 9 Jan 1902). British opera impresario. The son of an iron and steel magnate, he began his career in a Viennese bookshop whose proprietor soon branched out as an impresario of artistic events. In the 1920s he worked in Berlin before becoming assistant to Carl Ebert at the Hessisches Staatstheater in Darmstadt (1928–30), assistant to the Intendant of the Charlottenburg Opera, Berlin (1930–33), and general manager of the Glyndebourne Opera (1936–49). In 1946 he took British nationality and helped to found the Edinburgh Festival, of which he was artistic director (1947–9). In 1950 he became general manager of the Metropolitan Opera, New York.

Bing's tenure at the Metropolitan (until 1972) was the second longest in its history: he had a great influence on both the company and American opera in the 1950s and 1960s, particularly because of his autocratic attitudes. In his early years there he improved standards of performance and direction. His emphasis on scenic design and imaginative direction reflected his European experience, and was new to the USA. Bing introduced a number of black singers and dancers to the company and extended the season to fill the whole year; he also supervised the move to the new house in the Lincoln Center. In the latter part of his tenure, however, like his predecessor Gatti-Casazza, he failed to develop new ideas for coping with the economic and artistic climates of the period, although the house continued to have notable individual successes. In 1973 he was appointed Consultant for Special Projects by Columbia Artists Management. His autobiography *5000 Nights at the Opera* (1972) relates some of the many vicissitudes of his career; he subsequently provided additional information in *A Knight at the Opera* (1981). He was knighted in 1971.

See also NEW YORK, §4.

BIBLIOGRAPHY

J. Higgins: "Sir Rudolf Bing: a Lion in Winter," *HiFi/MusAm*, xxxii/11 (1982), 18

PATRICK J. SMITH

Bingham, Seth (*b* Bloomfield, NJ, 16 April 1882; *d* New York, 21 June 1972). Organist and composer. He studied under Horatio Parker at Yale (BA 1904; B Mus 1908) and in Paris with Vincent d'Indy, Charles-Marie Widor, Alexandre Guilmant, and Harry Jepson (1906–7). After teaching at Yale from 1908 until 1919, he was a member of the music faculty of Columbia University until his retirement in 1954; he also held classes in advanced composition at the Union Theological Seminary and was for 35 years organist and music director at the Madison Avenue Presbyterian Church. A prolific composer, particularly of liturgical choral and organ works, Bingham also wrote numerous concertos, suites, and sonatas in a conservative, lyrical vein; perhaps his best-known secular work is the Concerto for brass, snare drum, and organ.

WORKS

Opera: La charelzenn, 1917

Choral: Let God Arise, male vv, 1916; The Strife is O'er, 1916; Come thou Mighty King, 1916; Wilderness Stone, nar, solo vv, chorus, orch, 1933; Canticle of the Sun, chorus, orch, 1942; Perfect through Suffering, chorus, org, 1971; many other sacred choral works

Orch: Wall Street Fantasy, 1916; Passacaglia, 1918; Memories of France, 1920; Pioneer America, 1925; The Breton Cadence, 1928; Org Conc., 1946; Conc., brass, snare drum, org, 1954

Chamber: Suite, 9 wind, 1915; Str Qt, 1916; Tame Animal Tunes, 18 insts, 1918; Connecticut Suite, org, str, 1953; sonatas, suites

Org: Roulade, 1920–23; Suite, 1923; Pioneer America, 1926; Harmonies of Florence, 1928; Carillon de Château-Thierry, 1936; Pastoral Psalms, 1937; 12 Hymn-preludes, 1942; Baroques, suite, 1943; Variation Studies, 1950; 36 Hymn and Carol Canons, 1952; many other org pieces

Pubd songs, incl. An Old Song (1908), Brahma, The 4-way Lodge, 2 Japanese Songs

Principal publishers: J. Fischer, Gray, Peters, G. Schirmer

BIBLIOGRAPHY

P. J. Basch: "Seth Daniels Bingham: a Tribute," *Music: the A.G.O. and R.C.C.O. Magazine*, vi/4 (1972), 32 [incl. list of works]

H. WILEY HITCHCOCK

Binkerd, Gordon (*b* Lynch, NE, 22 May 1916). Composer. He received the BMus in 1937 from South Dakota Wesleyan University, where Russell Danburg and Gail Kubik were influential in his decision to become a composer. His later studies were at the Eastman School (MMus 1941), where he studied with Bernard Rogers, and Harvard University (MA 1952), where he studied musicology and, with Piston and Irving Fine, composition. Binkerd's later music was deeply influenced by Piston's teaching, and by his association with Fine. Professor of Music at the University of Illinois from 1949 until 1971, Binkerd received a Guggenheim Fellowship in 1959 and an award from the National Institute of Arts and Letters in 1964. He has received commissions from the St. Louis SO, the Ford and Fromm foundations, the McKim Fund of the Library of Congress, and various choral organizations. Since his retirement he has devoted himself to composition and is best known for his many choral works, which have been praised for their expressive use of vocal tone-colors and careful attention to the texts. Binkerd's style is characterized by a richly chromatic but tonal harmonic language and contrapuntal textures. His ability to sustain long lines within a complex texture is most apparent in the Piano Sonata.

WORKS

Orch: 3 syms., 1955, 1957, 1959; 3 Canzonas, brass, 1960; A Part of Heaven (2 Romances), vn, orch, 1972; The Battle (after Frescobaldi), brass, perc, 1972; Movement, rev. 1972; several transcrs. of org works for orch, wind ens

Inst: Vc Sonata, 1952; Trio, cl, va, vc, 1955; 4 pf sonatas, 1955, 1981, 1982, 1983; Org Service, 1957; 2 str qts, 1958, 1961; Entertainments, pf, 1960; Concert Set, pf, 1969; Pf Miscellany, 1969; Vn Sonata, 1977; Str Trio, 1979; a few other chamber pieces and short pf pieces, org works

Choral: Autumn Flowers (J. Very), 1968; To Electra (Herrick), 9 choruses, 1968–73; In a Whispering Gallery (Hardy), 1969; Nocturne (W. C. Williams), chorus, vc, 1969; A Christmas Caroll (Herrick), 1970; A Scotch Mist (Burns), 3 choruses, male vv, 1976; Choral Strands (Freud, Tennyson), 4 choruses, 1976; Sung under the Silver Umbrella (Chesterton, Blake, J. Stephens, S. Mead, T. Moore), 6 choruses, tr vv, pf, 1977; Requiem for Soldiers lost in Ocean Transports (H. Melville), 1983–4; Houses at Dusk (Longfellow, H. Belloc, F.-G. Halleck, trad.), 4 choruses, male vv, pf, 1984; Dakota Day (Tennyson), mixed vv, fl, ob, cl, harp, 1985; *c*70 other choral works

Songs: Shut out that Moon (Hardy), S/T, pf, 1968; 3 Songs (Herrick, A. Crapsey), Mez, str qt, 1971; Portrait intérieur (Rilke), 1v, vn, vc, 1972; 4 Songs, 1976; Secret-love (Dryden), Mez, vc, harp, 1977; Heart Songs (Burns), 1980; many other songs, 1v, pf

Principal publisher: Boosey & Hawkes

BIBLIOGRAPHY

D. Hagan: "Gordon Binkerd," *ACAB*, x/3 (1962), 1
D. Cohen; "Music from the Radical Center," *PNM*, iii/1 (1964), 131
L. Hawthorne: *The Choral Music of Gordon Binkerd* (diss., U. of Texas, 1973)
E. M. Miller: *A Stylistic Study of the Songs of Gordon Binkerd* (diss., U. of Oklahoma, 1974)
R. Schackelford: "The Music of Gordon Binkerd," *Tempo*, no.114 (1975), 2
P. B. Griffith: *The Solo Piano Music of Gordon Binkerd* (diss., Peabody Conservatory, 1984)
D. A. Saladino: *The Influence of Poetry on Compositional Practices in Selected Choral Music of Gordon Binkerd* (diss., Florida State U., 1984)

RICHARD A. MONACO/R

Binkley, Thomas (Eden) (*b* Cleveland, OH, 26 Dec 1931). Musicologist, lutenist, and player of early wind instruments. He graduated from the University of Illinois (BM 1954) and then went to Germany to study musicology at the University of Munich. In 1959 in Munich he founded the Studio für alte Musik for the performance of early music; the other members were the mezzo-soprano Andrea von Ramm, the tenor Nigel Rogers, and the string player Sterling Jones. This group, later known as the Studio der frühen Musik, toured throughout the world until 1972, when it moved to Basle in Switzerland to take up residence at the Schola Cantorum Basiliensis. Binkley returned to the USA in 1978 as a visiting professor at Stanford University. In 1979 he became director of the Early Music Institute at the School of Music of Indiana University. Binkley's publications include articles on performance practice. He has made more than 40 recordings with the Studio der frühen Musik, for which he has been awarded many European prizes, including the Edison Award, Amsterdam (1964 and 1974), the Grand Prix du Disque, Paris (four times between 1968 and 1974), and the Preis der deutscher Schallplattenkritik, Berlin (seven times between 1965 and 1982).

LARRY PALMER

Birch, Raymond. Pseudonym of CHARLES L. JOHNSON.

Bird. *See* PARKER, CHARLIE.

Bird, Arthur H. (*b* Belmont, MA, 23 July 1856; *d* Berlin, Germany, 22 Dec 1923). Composer and pianist. He received his early training from his father and uncle, who were composers and compilers of hymn tunes. He showed a particular talent for improvisation, and in 1875 was admitted to the Berlin Hochschule, where he became a pupil of K. A. Haupt, A. Loeschhorn, and E. Rohde. In 1877 he returned to the USA and was appointed organist at St. Matthew's, Halifax, Nova Scotia; he also taught piano at the Young Ladies' Academy and the Mount St. Vincent Academy, and founded the Arion Club, a men's chorus. During his second stay in Germany (1881–6) he studied composition under H. Urban and became a close friend and disciple of Liszt. At the invitation of the North American Saengerbund he returned to the USA in 1886 to direct the Milwaukee Musical Festival, where his compositions were favorably received. He then returned permanently to Berlin. He became the Berlin correspondent for the Chicago journal *Musical Leader* and also wrote for other musical magazines such as *The Etude* and *The Musician*. Bird's music was well known in Germany, and most of it was published there, but after about 1895 he composed relatively little. Contemporary critics agreed that his works, late Romantic in style, were pleasing and melodious, and that he was an excellent contrapuntist. He was elected to the National Institute of Arts and Letters in 1898.

WORKS

STAGE

Daphne, or The Pipes of Arcadia (operetta, 3), New York, private perf., 13 Dec 1897; Volksfest (ballet), op.13, 1886, perf. 1887, lost [also version for pf 4 hands]; Rübezahl (ballet), Berlin, 1886, pf score pubd

ORCHESTRAL

Serenade, str, 1882; Suite, E, str, op.1, 1882 [incl. Gavotte, op.7]; Concert Ov., D, 1884; Eine Carneval Szene, op.5, 1884 (Breslau, 1887); First Little Suite, 1884, lost [also version for pf 4 hands]; Second Little Suite, op.6, 1884–5; Sym., A, op.8, 1885 (Breslau, 1886); Melody and Spanish Dance, vn, chamber orch, op.9, 1885; 3 Characteristic Marches, op.11, 1885; [Piece], g, vc, chamber orch, 1885; Introduction and Fugue, d, org, orch, op.16, 1886; Oriental Scene and Caprice, fl, chamber orch, op.17, 1887; 2 Episodes, 1887–8; 2 Poems, op.25, 1888; 2 Pieces, str, op.28, 1888

Third Little Suite (Souvenirs of Summer Saturdays), C, op.32, 1890 (Boston, 1892); Romance, vn, chamber orch, 1890; Variations on an American Folksong, fl, chamber orch, op.34, 1891; Galop, band, *c*1909; Symphonic Suite, E♭, *c*1910, rev. *c*1918

CHAMBER

Andante and Allegro, vn, pf, 1878; Adagio, fl, vn, vc, pf, 1879; Nonet (Marche miniature), ww, 1887; Suite, D, 10 wind insts, 1889; Mazurka, vn; Melody and Tarantella, vn, pf, op.38, 1896; Serenade, 10 wind insts, op.40, 1898; transcrs.

KEYBOARD

Pf: 3 Pieces, op.2, 1882; Sonata, 1883; Allegro con moto, 1883; Gavotte, Album Leaf, and Lullaby, op.3, 1883; Rondo Humoreske, 1883; 6 Sketches, 1883; 2 Pieces, 1883–4; Sonatina, 1885; 4 Pieces, op.10, 1886; 3 Waltzes, op.12, 1886; 8 Sketches, op.15, 1886; Gavotte, Waltz, and Minuet, op.18, 1887; 5 Puppet Dances, op.19, 1887; 7 Pieces, op.20, 1887; 3 Pieces, op.21, 1887; Piano Pieces for 4 Children, op.22, 1887; 4 Album Leaves, op.24, 1888; 4 Pieces, op.26, 1888; Theme and Variations, op.27, 1889; 4 Romances, op.29, 1889; 3 Pieces, op.31, 1890; 4 Pieces, op.33, 1890; Album Leaf and Scherzando, op.35, 1891; 3 Pieces, 1896; 2 Clog Dances and an Album Leaf, 1905; 4 Pieces, op.46, 1910; The Springlet, Elegiac Waltz, and a Fragment, op.49,

1911; 3 Miniature Poems (after Longfellow), op.50, 1912

Pf 4 hands: French Ov., 1878; 3 Marches, 1881; Waltz; Fantastic Caprice, 1883; First Little Suite, op.4, 1884 [also version for orch]; Volksfest, 1886 [also version for orch]; 3 Characteristic Waltzes, op.14, 1886; American Melodies, op.23, 1887

Org: Fugue on A.H., 1881; 4 Fugues and a Canon Trio, 1881; 4 Sonatas, 1882; 3 Oriental Sketches, op.42, 1898 (New York, 1903); Marcia, 1902; Concert Fantasia, 1904; Toccatina, 1905

Reed org: 10 Pieces, op.37, 1897; 3 Pieces, op.39, 1898; Tempo di minuetto and Spring, op.41, 1898; 4 Pieces, op.44, 1902; 3 Sketches, op.45, 1903; Prelude and Fuga, a, 1907; Prelude and Fuga, C, 1907; Postlude, 1909

VOCAL

The passions are at peace within, T, org, 1878; Lied, B, pf; The World's Wanderers (P. B. Shelley), B; 3 Quartettes (Shelley, Lessing), male vv; 4 Quartets, male vv, 1885; Frau Holde (Baumbach), song cycle, male vv, pf; Wanderlieder (Hammerling), male vv, pf, op.30, 1891; 5 Songs, female vv, pf, op.36, 1896; Hush, my child, and slumber (Wisby), S, pf, 1898; All the Summer Long (Liliencron), Bar, reed org, 1903

MSS in *DLC*

BIBLIOGRAPHY

EwenD
L. C. Elson: *The History of American Music* (New York, 1904, enlarged 2/1915)
W. T. Upton: "Bird, Arthur," *DAB*
W. C. Loring, Jr.: "Arthur Bird, American," *MQ*, xxix (1943), 78
——: *The Music of Arthur Bird* (Atlanta, rev. 2/1974)

W. THOMAS MARROCCO

Birge, Edward Bailey (*b* Northampton, MA, 12 June 1868; *d* Bloomington, IN, 16 July 1952). Music educator. He attended Brown University (BA 1891) and taught music in public schools and teacher-training schools in New England before becoming public school music director in Indianapolis (1901–21). There he made instruction in music available to all elementary school students, organized bands and orchestras, and introduced courses in music theory and literature. During these years he also taught at the Jordan College of Music and the American Institute of Normal Methods. From 1921 to 1938 he headed the public school music department and directed the university chorus at Indiana University. Birge wrote 45 articles for professional publications and edited or co-edited six major series on school music; his *History of Public School Music in the United States* (1928, rev. 1937/*R*1966) is still widely used. He was a founder of the Music Supervisors National Conference and edited its journal (1930–44). He was also an officer of the National Education Association and the Music Teachers National Association.

BIBLIOGRAPHY

J. W. Beattie: "Appreciation of a Colleague," *MEJ*, xxv/1 (1938), 16
W. Earhart: "A Tribute to a Colleague," *MEJ*, xxx/6 (1944), 13, 59
C. F. Schwartz, Jr.: *Edward Bailey Birge: his Life and Contributions to Music Education* (diss., Indiana U., 1966)

GEORGE N. HELLER

Birmingham. City in Alabama (pop. 284,413; metropolitan area 847,487). Founded in 1871, it grew rapidly as a steel-producing center and by World War II had become the industrial, economic, and cultural heart of the state. As early as 1874 the city fathers considered establishing a music department in the Free Public School, but the plan was abandoned because of lack of funds. A city brass band active in the 1870s and a Mendelssohn Glee Club (organized in 1887 and renamed the Mendelssohn Society in 1890) were among the earliest musical organizations.

The Birmingham SO was founded in 1933 but was not in continuous operation until 1946. Its first conductor and music director was Dorsey Whittington (1933–48), succeeded by Arthur Bennett Lipkin (1948–60), Arthur Winograd (1960–64), and Amerigo Marino (1964–85), during whose tenure the orchestra's name was changed to the Alabama SO (1976). Birmingham is also the headquarters of two professional opera companies (Southern Regional Opera and the Birmingham Civic Opera; formerly also the Alabama Opera), as well as the Birmingham Chamber Music Society, the Birmingham Civic Chorus, and the Birmingham Music Club. Other musical events are sponsored annually by a number of churches, secondary schools, and private organizations. The Alabama School of Fine Arts in Birmingham has been state-supported since 1971 and offers musical training for students in grades 7–12. The colleges offering four-year accredited courses in music include Birmingham-Southern College and Samford University (formerly Howard College). Music plays an important part in the nationally acclaimed Birmingham Festival of the Arts (founded in 1951), which salutes a different country each spring with a program of arts and educational events.

The Birmingham Public Library and the Samford University School of Music Library contain extensive holdings of local musical memorabilia (notably the Fred Grambs Scrapbooks, chronicling the early history of the city's musical life, at *AB*) as well as collections of printed music, hymnals, sound recordings, and personal correspondence of various local musical figures (including the Ruth Hannas Papers, with correspondence of Ernst Krenek, at *AB*).

BIBLIOGRAPHY

J. R. Hornady: *The Book of Birmingham* (New York, 1921)
C. E. Roebuck: *The History of Birmingham from 1871 to 1890* (thesis, U. of Alabama, 1931)
M. C. McMillan: *Yesterday's Birmingham*, Seeman's Historic Cities Series, xviii (Miami, 1975)

ROBERT J. NICOLOSI

Biscardi, Chester (*b* Kenosha, WI, 19 Oct 1948). Composer. He studied English literature (BA 1970), Italian literature (MA 1972), and music (MM 1974) at the University of Wisconsin in Madison; his composition teachers were Les Thimmig and (for electronic music) Burt Levy. He then studied composition with Robert Morris, Penderecki, Yehudi Wyner, and Toru Takemitsu at Yale University (MMA 1976). He has won many awards including a Charles Ives scholarship from the American Academy and Institute of Arts and Letters (1975–6), a Rome Prize (1976), a Guggenheim Fellowship (1979–80), a MacDowell Colony Fellowship (1981), and grants from the American Music Center (1980) and the Martha Baird Rockefeller Fund (1982). In 1977 Biscardi joined the faculty of Sarah Lawrence College in Bronxville, New York.

Like the music of his most influential teacher, Takemitsu, Biscardi's compositions are generally of a delicate nature, with transparent textures and understated events articulated by lengthy pauses; many of his instrumental pieces of the early 1980s include experimental playing techniques, but usually the nontraditional sounds are used only to create gentle resonances and purely sonic gestures.

WORKS

Opera: Tight-rope (9 scenes, H. Butler), 1984–5; Madison, WI, 5 Oct 1985

Orch and choral: Heabakes, 5 Sapphic Lyrics, S, S, A, SATB, perc, 1974; At the Still Point, orch, 1977; Eurydice (H. D.), SA, chamber orch, 1978; Goodbye my Fancy (Whitman, M. D'Alessio), SATB, nar, 1982; Pf Conc., 1983

Inst: Tartini, vn, pf, 1973; Orpha, str qt, mar, vib, 1974; Tenzone, 2 fl, pf, 1975; They had Ceased to Talk, vn, va, hn, pf, 1975; Pf Trio, 1976; Mestiere, pf, 1979; Trasumanar, 12 perc, pf, 1980; Di vivere, cl, fl, vn, vc, pf, 1981; Incitation to Desire, pf, 1984

Songs: Turning (C. Biscardi), S, vn, str trio, 1973; Indovinello (I. Veronese), 12 solo vv, 1974; Trusting Lightness (J. Anderson), S, pf, 1975; Chez vous (S. Harnick), S, pf, 1983

Incidental music: The Duchess of Malfi (J. Webster), 1976; Witch Dance (A. Ganson, after M. Wigman), 1983

Principal publishers: American Composers Edition, Peters, Presser

JAMES WIERZBICKI

Bishop [née Riviere], **Anna** (*b* London, England, 9 Jan 1810; *d* New York, 18 March 1884). English soprano. She studied singing with Henry Bishop and made her professional début in London on 20 April 1831. She married Bishop on 9 July 1831 but eloped with the harpist Nicholas Bochsa in 1839. In 1847 she and Bochsa came to New York, where she made her American début in Donizetti's *Linda di Chamounix* at the Park Theatre on 4 August 1847. She took part in the American premières of Michael Balfe's *The Maid of Artois* (Park Theatre, 5 Nov 1847) and Friedrich Flotow's *Martha* (Niblo's Garden, 1 Nov 1852). She made several world tours; on one, in 1856, Bochsa died in Australia and on another, in 1866, she was shipwrecked off Wake Island with her second husband, Martin Schultz (whom she had married in 1858). Her last public appearance was in Steinway Hall, New York, on 20 April 1883.

Anna Bishop possessed a high soprano voice and a brilliant technique, though her singing was said to lack the expressive power of Jenny Lind's. Scrapbooks containing details of her concerts are now in Boston Public Library (MS 446.10) and the archives of the Metropolitan Opera.

BIBLIOGRAPHY

Travels of Anna Bishop in Mexico, 1849 (Philadelphia, 1852)

G. G. Foster: *Biography of Anna Bishop* (New York, 1853)

Obituaries: *American Art Journal*, xl (1884), 356; MT, xxv (1884), 212

W. B. Squire: "Bishop, Anna," *DNB*

JEAN BOWEN

Bishop-Kovacevich, Stephen (*b* Los Angeles, CA, 17 Oct 1940). Pianist of Yugoslav parentage. Until 1975 he was known as Stephen Bishop. He studied with Lev Schorr from 1948 and made his first public appearance in San Francisco in 1951. In 1959 he moved to London to study with Myra Hess. Included in his highly successful London début recital (1961) were Beethoven's Diabelli Variations; this work best demonstrates that structural mastery, achieved in commanding yet lucidly sensitive playing, which marks him as one of his generation's most searching Beethoven interpreters. An authoritative technician but not an effortless virtuoso, Bishop-Kovacevich can on occasion produce an impression of brusque force; no performance in a large repertory is ever thoughtless or cold. He has won the Edison Award for a recording of Bartók and Stravinsky and has also distinguished himself in recordings of Mozart and Beethoven, among others. He has edited a Schubert anthology and contributed to *Myra Hess and her Friends* (1966).

MAX LOPPERT/R

Bispham, David (Scull) (*b* Philadelphia, PA, 5 Jan 1857; *d* New York, 2 Oct 1921). Baritone. After seven years working in his uncle's wool business, he decided at the age of 30 to pursue a singing career; he went first to Milan to study with Vannuccini and Francesco Lamperti and then to London to work with William Shakespeare and Albert Randegger. He made his operatic début as Longueville in Messager's *Basoche* at the English Opera House (3 November 1891), where his comic acting ability and singing brought him immediate success. He sang Kurwenal (*Tristan und Isolde*) the following year at Drury Lane, and later sang at Covent Garden as well. He made his début at the Metropolitan Opera as Beckmesser on 18 November 1896 and remained with the company until 1903. Much in demand in England and the USA in opera and oratorio and on the recital stage for several decades, he excelled in the Wagnerian roles (of which he considered Kurwenal and Beckmesser to be his best) and was versatile in light, comic, and grand opera, with 58 roles in his repertory.

Bispham was ardently in favor of using the English language in operas and songs, and to this end, helped to form the Society of American Singers in 1917, which presented comic operas in English using American casts; he toured with the troupe for several years both as singer and administrator. He also developed lecture-recital programs, in which he talked about the pieces he was performing, and he promoted the works of English and American composers by including them in his programs.

A highly skilled actor, Bispham appeared as Beethoven in Hugo Müller's play *Adelaide* (1898) in both England and America. In his later years, he developed a repertory of more than 25 monologues of poetry and prose which he performed to musical accompaniment, often provided by famous groups of the day; notable among his recitations were parts of *A Midsummer Night's Dream*, to Mendelssohn's music (first given with the New York PO under Frank Damrosch in 1902), and Sophocles' *Antigone* (performed at the Orpheus Club, Philadelphia, under Horatio Parker in 1908). From 1902 he was also an influential teacher in Philadelphia. The Opera Society of America established a Bispham Memorial Medal in 1921 for an opera in English by an American composer. Bispham's musical papers and other materials are preserved in the New York Public Library.

BIBLIOGRAPHY

D. Bispham: *A Quaker Singer's Recollections* (New York, 1921/*R*1977)

Obituary, *MusAm*, xxxiv/24 (1921), 1

F. H. Martens: "Bispham, David Scull," *DAB*

O. Thompson: "David Bispham," *The American Singer* (New York, 1937/*R*1969), 204

J. Dennis: "David Bispham," *Record Collector*, vi (1951), 5 [with discography]

J. B. Richards: "Bispham, David Scull," *Le grandi voci*, ed. R. Celletti (Rome, 1964)

RICHARD ALDRICH/DEE BAILY

Bitgood [Wiersma], **Roberta** (*b* New London, CT, 15 Jan 1908). Composer and organist. She studied music at Connecticut College (BA 1928) and then attended the Guilmant Organ School, from which she graduated in 1930. She also received degrees from Columbia University (MA 1932) and the School of Sacred Music, Union Theological Seminary (MSM 1935, DSM 1945). She held positions as an organist and choir director in New York, New Jersey, California, Michigan, and Connecticut. As an organ recitalist and adviser on church music she has made tours nationwide; she has also been active as a violist in local orchestras. From 1935 to 1947 she served as music director of Bloomfield (New Jersey) College. As president of the American Guild of Organists, 1975–81, she displayed a special concern for upgrading professional standards and improving the morale of church musicians. Bitgood's own compositions reflect a lifelong involvement with church music, especially young people's choirs. Her style ranges from the intimate, as in the anthem *Wise Men Seeking Jesus* (1960), with its flowing, archaic-sounding melodies, to large-scale works for religious festival occasions that use an impressive chordal and melodically more disjunct technique.

WORKS

Cantatas: Job (Bible, D. B. Judah), 1947; Joseph (Bible, N. Selnecker), 1960; Let There Be Light (M. L. Kerr), 1965

Choral: 20 choruses, incl. Give me a Faith (C. L. Reynolds), 1945, Except the Lord Build the House (Bible), 1956, Lord may we Follow (E. Osler), 1974; 17 works for junior choir, incl. Christ Went Up into the Hills (K. Adams), 1943, Holy Spirit Hear Us (W. H. Parker), 1958, How Excellent is Thy Name (Bible), 1965; 6 works for chorus and children's chorus, incl. Hosanna (Moravian liturgy), 1935, Glory to God, 1943; 4 collections of responses

Solo vocal: The Greatest of These is Love (Bible), 1934; Be Still and Know that I am God (Bible), 1940

Org: 5 choral preludes, incl. Choral Prelude on Jewels, 1942; 9 other works, incl. On an Ancient Alleluia, 1958, Rejoice, Give Thanks, org, brass, 1970

Principal publishers: Choristers Guild, H. W. Gray, Flammer, Sacred Music, Westminster

MARIBEL MEISEL

Bjoerling [Björling], **Jussi** [Johan] **(Jonaton)** (*b* Stora Tuna, Sweden, 5 Feb 1911; *d* Stockholm, Sweden, 9 Sept 1960). Swedish tenor. He was first taught by his father, David Björling, a professional tenor, and from 1916 made many concert tours with his father and two brothers as a treble in the Björling Male Quartet, which made a few commercial recordings in the USA in 1920. In 1928 he entered the Stockholm Conservatory. He made his recognized début at the Royal Swedish Opera in 1930 as Don Ottavio. Until 1938 he was a regular member of the Stockholm Opera, but he was soon in general demand in the leading European operatic centers, and his international status was confirmed by his successful débuts at Chicago in *Rigoletto* (8 December 1937), at the Metropolitan Opera in *La bohème* (24 November 1938), at Covent Garden in *Il trovatore* (12 May 1939), and at San Francisco in *La bohème* (18 October 1940). His New York recital début was at Town Hall on 4 January 1938; he had previously sung at Carnegie Hall, however, for a radio broadcast in November 1937. In the USA he became an indispensable favorite, returning regularly to the Metropolitan and other houses except during the war years of 1941–5.

Although Bjoerling's repertory had by this time become almost entirely Italian, his appearances were infrequent in Italy itself, where the purity and restraint of his style may perhaps have disconcerted a public used to a more overt and impassioned display. American audiences, on the other hand, who had long admired similar classic qualities in the work of Martinelli, were specially delighted by the refined art of the Swedish singer. His voice was a true tenor of velvety smoothness, though capable also of ringing high notes of considerable power; admirably schooled, it showed remarkable consistency from top to bottom of his register and throughout the 30 years of his career. To the end, its beautiful quality and his impeccable musicianship provided ample compensation for a stage presence that was rather a matter of deportment than of acting. His smooth legato was well suited to Gounod's Faust and Romeo; but the center of his repertory consisted of Verdi's Duke of Mantua, Manrico, Riccardo, and Don Carlos and Puccini's Rodolfo, Cavaradossi, and Des Grieux. Having a voice ideally adapted to the phonograph, he made a large number of delightful and valuable recordings, including many complete operas, among which his Rodolfo in the famous Beecham set of *La bohème* well illustrates the distinction of his tone and phrasing. In 1935 he married Anna-Lisa Berg, who occasionally appeared with him as Mimì (Stockholm, 1948) and Juliet (San Francisco, 1951).

BIBLIOGRAPHY

F. F. Clough and C. J. Cuming: "Jussi Bjoerling: a Discography," *American Record Guide*, xii (1945–6), 84

J. Björling: *Hed bagaget i stupen* (Stockholm, 1945) [autobiography]

C. L. Bruun and K. Stubington: "Jussi Björling," *Record News*, iv (Toronto, 1959–60), no.4, p.117; no.5, p.176 [with discography]

Obituary, *New York Times* (10 Sept 1960)

L. Trimble: "Farväl Guldstrupan! Death comes to Sweden's Golden Throat – Jussi Bjoerling," *MusAm*, lxxx/11 (1960), 34

H. Rosenthal: *Great Singers of Today* (London, 1966)

E. S. Lund and H. Rosenberg: *Jussi Björling: a Record List* (Copenhagen, 1969)

D. Ewen: *Musicians since 1900: Performers in Concert and Opera* (New York, 1978)

J. Porter and H. Henrysson: *A Jussi Björling Discography* (Indianapolis, 1982)

DESMOND SHAWE-TAYLOR/R

Black, Frank (J.) (*b* Philadelphia, PA, 29 Nov 1894; *d* Atlanta, GA, 29 Jan 1968). Conductor and composer. At Haverford College he studied piano and chemistry. He began the serious study of music with Joseffy, and wrote songs for vaudeville. He was conductor at the Fox Theater in Philadelphia from 1923, having started as assistant to Erno Rapee. In 1928 he was appointed music director of NBC, and served as general music director from 1932 to 1948. Active in recording studios, he accompanied such artists as Leonard Warren and Bidú Sayão; with Oscar Levant he recorded Gershwin's *Rhapsody in Blue*. His recordings with the NBC orchestra include works by C. P. E. Bach, Brahms, Roussel, Sibelius, and others. In the 1930s he coached the Revelers, a popular vocal quartet. Among Black's compositions are *Bells at Eventide* and *A Sea Tale*. He scored Edna St. Vincent Millay's *The Murder of Lidice* and Alice Duer Miller's *The White Cliffs of Dover*, and also made arrangements of works by Bach and Beethoven.

BIBLIOGRAPHY

W. G. King: "About Frank Black, Guest Conductor of the NBC Symphony – at the Stadium," *New York Sun* (22 July 1939), 12

D. Ewen: *Dictators of the Baton* (Chicago and New York, 1943, rev. and enlarged 2/1948), 273

J. Holmes: *Conductors on Record* (Westport, CT, 1982)

SORAB MODI

Black, Mrs. Morris. *See* CAHIER, MME. CHARLES.

Black, Robert (Carlisle) (*b* Dallas, TX, 28 April 1950). Pianist and conductor. He attended Oberlin College Conservatory (BM in piano 1972) and the Juilliard School (MM 1974, DMA 1977), studying with Beveridge Webster, Roger Sessions, and Gustave Reese. His recital début was in 1976 at Carnegie Recital Hall. As a pianist, he has been praised for his technical command and dramatic intensity, particularly in his interpretations of Liszt, Beethoven, and contemporary music; his first performances include Shapey's *Fromm Variations* (1979) and *Passacaglia* (1983), Rudhyar's *Epic Poem* (1982), and, with Kalish, Stravinsky's *Three Movements* (piano four hands, 1981). As conductor of the New York New Music Ensemble from 1975, Speculum Musicae from 1978, and the New York orchestra Prism (which he founded in 1983), he has presented a wide variety of music from the standard repertory as well as contemporary music. His premières as a conductor include Shapey's *Three for Six* (1981), Schwantner's *Music of Amber* (1981), and Wuorinen's *New York Notes* (1982). Among his American premières as a pianist and conductor are works by the French composer Jean Barraqué. Black has toured extensively and made numerous recordings. He has taught at Princeton University (1976–83), the University of California, Santa Barbara (1981–2), and from 1983 at Columbia University.

MICHAEL CANICK

Black-American music. The various musical styles of black Americans are discussed in general terms in AFRO-AMERICAN MUSIC; for more detailed discussions *see* BLUES, COON SONG, DISCO, DOO-WOP, FUNK, GOSPEL MUSIC, JAZZ, MINSTRELSY, MOTOWN, RAGTIME, RAP, RHYTHM-AND-BLUES, SOUL MUSIC, SPIRITUAL; *see also* POPULAR MUSIC, §§II, 3; III, 1, 2, 4; IV, 6.

Black bottom. A quick-tempo social dance performed in the 1920s to the music of the big bands. It is thought to have originated in the early 1900s in the "juke" (black) bawdy houses of the "Bottoms," the black quarter of Nashville. The movements of the dance are described in Perry Bradford's song *The Original Black Bottom Dance* (1919) thus:

> Hop down front and then you Doodle back
> Mooch to your left and then you Mooch to your right,
> Hands on your hips and do the Mess Around,
> Break a Leg until you're near the ground.
> Now that's the Old Black Bottom Dance.

The "doodle" was a slide, and the "break a leg" referred to a hobbling step. The dance also involved a twisting motion of the body (similar to the shimmy), hops forward and back, side turns, stamps, a skating glide performed with deep knee bends, and, according to the Stearns, "a genteel slapping of the backside"; as a theatrical dance, it included kicks and high leaps. The popularity of the black bottom and other related dances, such as the charleston (*see* CHARLESTON (ii)), developed from the success of the black revue *Shuffle Along* (1921). The first theatrical adaptation of the black bottom occurred in the show *Dinah* (1924), produced by Irving C. Miller in Harlem, but it was Ann Pennington's performance of the dance to the song "Black Bottom" (music by Ray Henderson, lyrics by Buddy DeSylva and Lew Brown) in *George White's Scandals of 1926* that led to its widespread popularity.

BIBLIOGRAPHY

M. Stearns and J. Stearns: *Jazz Dance: the Story of American Vernacular Dance* (New York, 1968)

L. F. Emery: *Black Dance in the United States from 1619 to 1970* (Palo Alto, CA, 1970)

P. Oliver: *The Meaning of the Blues* (New York, 1972)

For further bibliography *see* DANCE.

PAULINE NORTON

Blackfoot (i) [Siksika]. American Indians of a northern Plains culture, now primarily in Montana and southern Canada (*see* INDIANS, AMERICAN, fig. 1); they are distributed among three tribes, the Piegan, Blood (Kainah), and Northern Blackfoot. The amount of music and the association of musical performances with other activities in Blackfoot culture indicate that music fulfills a broad and generalized role (although less now than in the late 19th century). Songs, religious and secular, are symbols of real events and do not exist for their own sake; the main function of song is to serve as an authenticating device for ceremonial acts and as a statement of tribal identity even today.

The Blackfoot view the origin of songs as supernatural: songs are learned in dreams or visions, or are borrowed from other cultures. When a song is performed, credit must be given to the person who dreamed it or the tribe from which it is borrowed. The prescribed learning technique is not a phrase-by-phrase repetition but careful listening to the song in its entirety; the cassette recorder is a valuable device for the dissemination of songs, especially those sung on the powwow circuit. Songs are considered valuable to the Blackfoot, and there is a traditional scale of values for songs according to the degree to which they fulfill their function. The most highly valued are those relating to ceremonies, but within each ceremony some are more powerful than others. Since the mid-20th century some songs seem to be valued for purely aesthetic reasons. The age of a song is considered important in determining its value, old songs being held in high esteem. Traditionally the knowledge of powerful songs was considered more important than technical ability, but now, perhaps through exposure to European musical values, a "good voice" has become a more important element of good singing. Various performances rules have also changed over the last 100 years. The rule requiring performance of songs at the "right time only" has been relaxed except among a few traditionalists, and the restriction of repetitions to the sacred number of four has changed to repetition for as long as the singers (or dancers) may desire.

Song may be either ceremonial or social. Ceremonial songs include those related to the Sun Dance, medicine bundles (collections of ceremonial objects wrapped in clothes or skins, especially those objects associated with the beaver and horse cults), men's societies (seven age-grade societies), and healing. Entertainment, both individual and group, often includes riding songs, songs associated with sports (horse races and hand games), and various social dance-songs such as the Grass Dance, the Rabbit Dance, and the Forty-niner Dance, popular in the Plains area. In general the Blackfoot musical style conforms to that of other Plains cultures. An old and a new repertory, with some stylistic differences, can be distinguished. The old is derived from the music of older ceremonial practices, such as the Sun Dance and medicine-bundle ceremonies. Fairly complex and varied, this material is often sung solo in a chest voice with typical Plains-style pulsations. Song texts generally are lexical. The new repertory conforms to the intertribal powwow style established in the 1940s. It consists of songs with sharply descending melodic contours, using scales of four or five tones in which the intervals of minor 3rd and major 2nd occur frequently; tessitura is generally high and vocal delivery tense. The typical form consists of a short section sung by a soloist and repeated by a second singer, followed by several phrases sung by the group and then repeated by the group (*AABCA'BCA'*, in which *A'* represents octave displacement of *A*).

Instruments are less prominent among the Blackfoot than among other Indian cultures. In the 19th century the Blackfoot had two kinds of drum, a large double-headed drum and a smaller single-headed frame drum. The larger, used for the Sun Dance, was made from a hollowed-out tree trunk covered with two skin heads; as a result of contact with Whites a large washtub covered with a single head was often substituted, as later was the bass drum. The smaller drum, a hoop covered with one head, was used for various ceremonies. In the 1950s small double-headed drums also became common. The container rattle, usually made from rawhide, is the most varied and important instrument, though many of them are more important as ceremonial objects than as sound-producers. Musically their function is to provide a percussive accompaniment like that of the drum. However, unlike drums, rattles are used in more intimate contexts such as the various bundle ceremonies in which medicine bundles are unwrapped while prescribed songs are sung. Certain types of rattle, pertaining to men's societies and medicine cults, are rarely played. The eagle-bone whistle is also a ceremonial object among the Blackfoot; as with other Plains tribes, this instrument is used

Blackfoot powwow, Montana, c1893

almost exclusively for the Sun Dance and is played simultaneously with the drum. The flute is rare; its appearance and use may be a borrowing from other Plains tribes.

Contact with non-Blackfoot peoples has always had an influence on music in Blackfoot culture. The practice of "borrowing" individual songs from neighboring Indian cultures is documented in the 19th century, and today entire groups of songs may be "borrowed" by performers traveling thousands of miles a year on the powwow circuit. Another major outside influence has been the music of various Anglo groups: religious, educational, and popular. Performance of this so-called "white music" by Blackfoot musicians began in the early 20th century, reached a peak in the 1920s, then nearly disappeared before being revived in the 1950s. In the 1980s there are dozens of groups, formal and informal, performing religious songs, band music, and (among the young) country, rock, and gospel music. The practitioners of "white music" do not perform traditional Blackfoot songs, though the audience for both may often be the same.

Recordings of Blackfoot music made in the field are in the holdings of the Archives of Traditional Music at Indiana University, Bloomington, and the American Museum of Natural History, New York.

See also INDIANS, AMERICAN, esp. §I, 4(ii)(a).

DISCOGRAPHY

Indian Music of the Canadian Plains (FW P464, 1955) [with liner notes by K. Peacock]

Twelve Blackfoot Songs (Indian Records 220, 1965)

Blackfoot A-1 Club Singers (IH 4001-2, 1973)

From the Land of the Blackfoot (Can. C6095, 1973)

Blackfoot A-1 Singers (Can. C6132, 1975)

Songs from the Blood Reserve: Kai-Spai Singers (Can. C6133, 1975)

An Historical Album of Blackfoot Indian Music (FW FE34001, 1979) [with liner notes by B. Nettl]

BIBLIOGRAPHY

C. Wissler: *Social Organization and Ritualistic Ceremonies of the Blackfoot Indians* (New York, 1912)

A. Nevin: "Two Summers with the Blackfeet Indians of Montana," *MQ*, ii (1916), 158

J. Ewers: *The Blackfoot: Raiders on the Northwestern Plains* (Norman, OK, 1958)

B. Nettl: "Blackfoot Music in Browning, 1965, Functions and Attitudes," *Festschrift für Walter Wiora zum 30 December 1966* (Kassel, Germany, 1967), 593

——: "Studies in Blackfoot Indian Musical Culture," *EM*, xi (1967), 141, 293; xii (1968), 11–48, 192

——: "Biography of a Blackfoot Indian Singer," *MQ*, liv (1968), 199

R. E. Witmer: *The Musical Culture of the Blood Indians* (thesis, U. of Illinois, 1970)

——: "Recent Change in the Musical Culture of the Blood Indians of Alberta, Canada," *Yearbook for Inter-American Musical Research*, ix (1973), 64

J. RICHARD HAEFER

Blackfoot (ii) [Sihasapa]. American Indians belonging to the Teton subgroup of the SIOUX. They are unrelated to the Blackfoot (i) Indians.

Blackmar, A(rmand) E(dward) (*b* Bennington, VT, 1826; *d* New Orleans, LA, 28 Oct 1888). Music publisher and dealer. He moved to Cleveland in 1834, graduated from Western Reserve College in 1845, and worked as a music teacher in Huntsville, Alabama (1845–52), and at Centenary College, Jackson, Louisiana (1852–5). In 1858 he joined E. D. Patton's music store in Vicksburg, Mississippi, which he bought out the following year with his younger brother Henry Blackmar (1831–1909). The brothers moved to New Orleans in 1860, where they operated publishing firms and music stores jointly, separately, and often with others. From 1861 to 1866 Henry also ran a store in Augusta, Georgia. Armand was imprisoned briefly in 1862 by the Union Army for his rabid espousal of the Southern cause; he issued more CONFEDERATE MUSIC than any other publisher in New Orleans, including one of the earliest editions of *Dixie* (1861), and *The Bonnie Blue Flag* (1861) and *Maryland! My Maryland!* (1862). He frequently arranged or composed music himself under the pseudonym A. Noir. Blackmar was in San Francisco between 1877 and 1880, but was publishing again in New Orleans from 1881 to 1888.

BIBLIOGRAPHY

R. B. Harwell: *Confederate Music* (Chapel Hill, 1950)

P. C. Boudreaux: *Music Publishing in New Orleans in the 19th Century* (thesis, Louisiana State U., 1977)
R. Powell: *A Study of A. E. Blackmar and Bro., Music Publishers of New Orleans, Louisiana, and Augusta, Georgia, with a Checklist of Imprints in Louisiana Collections* (thesis, Louisiana State U., 1978)
F. W. Hoogerwerf: *Confederate Sheet-music Imprints*, ISAMm, xxi (Brooklyn, NY, 1984)

JOHN H. BARON

Black Patti. *See* JONES, SISSIERETTA.

Blackwell, Ed(ward Joseph) (*b* New Orleans, LA, 1927). Jazz drummer. He was early influenced by the dixieland drummer Paul Barbarin, and in the late 1940s he played with a rhythm-and-blues band led by Plas and Raymond Johnson. In 1953 he moved to Los Angeles, where for several years he played with Ornette Coleman. He returned to New Orleans in 1956, but rejoined Coleman in New York in 1960, replacing Billy Higgins in Coleman's quartet. Throughout the 1960s he worked with Coleman, adopting the marching rhythms of New Orleans music to the new free-jazz style; he also made a series of celebrated recordings with Coleman's former associate, Don Cherry. Blackwell toured Africa with Randy Weston in 1965–6, and recorded with Archie Shepp in 1967. Stricken with kidney disease in 1974, he performed much less frequently in the later 1970s. He was artist-in-residence at Wesleyan University for several years beginning in 1975. In 1976 he began to tour with Old and New Dreams, a group dedicated to playing Ornette Coleman's compositions. One of the most melodic of jazz drummers, Blackwell often concentrates on the sonorities of his tom-toms and bass drum, sometimes producing nearly sing-song rhythms.

RECORDINGS
(selective list)

As co-leader of Old and New Dreams: *Old and New Dreams* (1976, Black Saint 0013); *Old and New Dreams* (1979, ECM 1154)
As sideman: O. Coleman: *This is our Music* (1960, Atl. 1353); *Twins* (1960, Atl. 1588); *Free Jazz* (1960, Atl. 1364); *Ornette on Tenor* (1961, Atl. 1394); E. Dolphy: *Eric Dolphy at the Five Spot* (1961, New Jazz 8260); D. Cherry: *Complete Communion* (1965, BN 84226); *Symphony for Improvisers* (1966, BN 84247); *Where is Brooklyn* (1966, BN 84311); *Mu*, pt.i (1969, BYG 529301); *Mu*, pt.ii (1969, BYG 529331); O. Coleman: *Science Fiction* (1971, Col. KC31061); D. Cherry: *El Corazon* (1982, ECM 1230)

BIBLIOGRAPHY

B. Mintz: *Different Drummers* (New York, 1975)
R. Palmer: "Ed Blackwell: Crescent City Thumper," *Down Beat*, xliv/12 (1977), 17
S. Fish: "Ed Blackwell: Singin' on the Set," *Modern Drummer*, v/8 (1981), 14

MICHAEL ULLMAN

Blackwell, Scrapper (1903–63). Blues guitarist and singer, partner of LEROY CARR.

Blackwood, Easley (*b* Indianapolis, IN, 21 April 1933). Composer and pianist. He studied with Messiaen at the Berkshire Music Center (1949), with Hindemith at Yale (1950–54), and, on a Fulbright scholarship, with Boulanger in Paris (1954–7). In 1958 he was appointed to the University of Chicago, where he became professor in 1968. He has received a first prize from the Koussevitzky Foundation (1958), the Brandeis Creative Arts Award (1968), and commissions from the Chicago SO and the Library of Congress. As a pianist he has distinguished himself in North America and Europe in the contemporary repertory, notably the second sonatas of Ives and Boulez and the solo works of Schoenberg, Berg, and Webern. His compositions are highly controlled, with complex chromatic, polyrhythmic textures, and wide-ranging melodic contours. In the early 1980s his interest in nontempered tuning led to a set of 12 intriguing microtonal etudes for synthesizer (*see* TUNING SYSTEMS, §2(iii)).

WORKS

Orch: Sym. no.1, op.3, perf. 1958; Sym. no.2, op.9, perf. 1961; Cl Conc., op.13, 1964; Sym. no.3, op.14, perf. 1965; Sym. Fantasy, op.17, 1965; Ob Conc., op.19, 1965; Vn Conc., op.21, 1967; Fl Conc., op.23, 1968; Pf Conc., op.24, 1970; Sym. no.4, 1973; Sym. no.5, 1978
Vocal: Un voyage à Cythère (Baudelaire), S, wind, op.20, 1966; 4 Letter Scenes from Gulliver's Last Voyage, Mez, Bar, tape, op.25, 1972
Inst: Va Sonata, op.1, 1953; Chamber Sym., op.2, 1954; Str Qt no.1, op.4, 1958; Concertino, 5 insts, op.5, 1959; Str Qt no.2, op.6, 1960; Vn Sonata, op.7, 1960; Fantasy, vc, pf, op.8, 1960; Chaconne, carillon, op.10, 1961; Pastorale and Variations, wind qnt, op.11, 1961; Sonata, fl, hpd, op.12, 1962; Fantasy, fl, cl, pf, op.15, 1965; 3 Short Fantasies, pf, op.16, 1965; Sym. Episode, org, op.18, 1966; Pf Trio, op.22, 1967; Sonata, vn, pf, 1973; 12 Microtonal Etudes, synth, 1982

Principal publisher: G. Schirmer

JAMES R. McKAY

Blades, Rubén (*b* Panamá, Panama, 16 July 1948). Popular singer and songwriter. He graduated from the Universidad Nacional de Panama in 1974 with a degree in law but, despite an offer of employment at the Panamanian Embassy in Washington, DC, went to New York to pursue a musical career. While working in the mailroom at Fania Records he came to the attention of the bandleader Ray Barretto, with whom he made his début as lead singer in Madison Square Garden. He later became associated with the trombonist and bandleader Willie Colon on a number of recordings; songs such as *Pablo pueblo*, *Plastico*, and *Siembra* gave rise to Blades's popularity as a performer and writer of material dealing with social and political subjects. Blades created an acronym – Focila – to define sounds associated with Latin-American urban folk traditions; examples are *What happened* (a bilingual piece) and *El tren #6*, both recorded by Bobby Rodriguez and La Compania. His first album for an American recording company (Elektra/Asylum), *Buscando a America* (1984), continues to touch upon the struggles of Latin-American countries against social, economic, and political oppression. Blades made his film début in *Crossover Dreams* (1985), for which he also provided the music.

BIBLIOGRAPHY

P. Grein: "Blades Seeks Cut of Pop Market," *Billboard*, xcvi (5 May 1984), 53
J. Cocks: "The Keen Edge of Rubén Blades," *Time*, cxxiv (2 July 1984), 82
P. Bloom: "Discovering Rubén Blades," *High Fidelity*, xxxiv/8 (1984), 74
E. Levin: "A Novelist's Eye, A Humanist's Heart and a Hot Band Make Rubén Blades Salsa's 'Numero Uno,'" *People Weekly*, xxii (13 Aug 1984), 75
E. Fernández: "Chilling Out with Rubén Blades," *Village Voice*, xxx (5 March 1985), 79
"Ruben Blades: Searching for America," *The First Rock & Roll Confidential Report*, ed. D. Marsh (New York, 1985)

TONY SABOURNIN

Blaisdell, Frances (*b* Tellico Plains, TN, 5 Jan 1912). Flutist. A pupil of Ernest Wagner and Georges Barrère, she graduated from the Juilliard School, having won the concerto competition at the age of 18, and studied in France with Marcel Moyse. She played in New York on Broadway, with the Phil Spitalny All Girls' Band, and as accompanist to Lily Pons. In 1938 she formed the Blaisdell Wind Quintet with Bruno Labate (oboe), Alexander Williams (clarinet), Benjamin Cohen (bassoon), and Richard Moore (horn); active until 1941, the group played mainly on the radio and was often heard on the CBS and NBC networks. One of the first women to become a member of an orchestra, Blaisdell was first flutist with the National Orchestra Association and, for 15 years, with the New York City Ballet. She appeared as a soloist with the New York PO, the National Orchestra Association, and the New York SO; in Radio City Music Hall, Madison Square Garden, and major American cities; and on BBC radio. Blaisdell has been on the faculties of the Manhattan School of Music, New York University, and Mannes College, and in 1973 began teaching at Stanford University. She also gives flute seminars in the USA, South America, and New Zealand. Blaisdell's playing combines the full tone and musical phrasing of the French school with her own vigorous rhythmic interpretation and an individual use of tone color. She was among the first women to achieve fame as a professional flutist.

MARTHA WOODWARD

Blake, Blind [Arthur] (*b* ?Jacksonville, FL, *c*1895; *d* ?Florida, 1933–5). Songster, blues singer, and guitarist. He is known to have played extensively in Florida, and was well known as a songster and guitarist in Georgia and the eastern states. Although he was blind, he traveled as far as Tennessee and Detroit. Between 1926 and 1932 he recorded some 80 titles, including a number of instrumental pieces, of which *Blind Arthur's Breakdown* (1929, Para. 12892) demonstrated his unparalleled technique. His playing, which was light and flowing, showed a strong ragtime influence in common with eastern guitarists. Many of his songs were ideal for dancing, such as *Come on boys, let's do that messin' around* (1926, Para. 12413), while others clearly derived from the medicine show repertory, for example *He's in the jail house now* (1927, Para. 12565). In Detroit he formed a partnership with the boogie-woogie pianist Charlie Spand, with whom he recorded several titles including the exhilarating *Hastings Street* (1929, Para. 12863), remarkable for its integration of instrumental lines. Blake had a melancholy voice that was particularly effective on such blues recordings as *Search Warrant Blues* (1928, Para. 12737) and *Cold Hearted Mama Blues* (1928, Para. 12710). He also accompanied other singers, including Bertha Henderson and Leola B. Wilson, and influenced later singers, Blind Boy Fuller and the songster Bill Williams among them.

BIBLIOGRAPHY

SouthernB

S. Charters: "Blind Blake," *Sweet as the Showers of Rain* (New York, 1977)

P. Oliver: *Songsters and Saints: Vocal Traditions on Race Records* (New York, 1984)

PAUL OLIVER

Blake, Charles Dupee (*b* Walpole, MA, 13 Sept 1847; *d* Brookline, MA, 24 Nov 1903). Composer. He studied piano and composition from an early age with, among others, John Knowles Paine and J. C. D. Parker. He entered into an exclusive contract with White-Smith in Boston to publish his compositions; this arrangement lasted until 1888 when Blake began to publish his work himself. He may have written as many as 5000 works, many of which are for the piano but which also include songs and a light opera, *The Light-Keeper's Daughter* (1882). He published under ten or more different pseudonyms. *Rock-a-bye baby* is probably his best-known song today, although *Clayton's March* might have claimed that distinction in the 19th century. The style throughout is a simple one, fitted to the skills of most amateur pianists and vocalists; as his contemporaries realized, Blake aimed "at producing music for the masses, in which he [was] successful to an unusual degree" (Jones).

BIBLIOGRAPHY

EwenD

F. O. Jones, ed.: *A Handbook of American Music and Musicians* (Canaseraga, NY, 1886/*R*1971)

W. S. B. Mathews, ed.: *A Hundred Years of Music in America* (Chicago, 1889/*R*1970)

DALE COCKRELL

Blake, Eubie [James Hubert] (*b* Baltimore, MD, 7 Feb 1883; *d* New York, 12 Feb 1983). Ragtime pianist and composer. When he was six years old his parents, who had been slaves, purchased a home organ and arranged for him to have lessons. Later he studied music theory with a local musician, Llewelyn Wilson. Despite the disapproval of his mother, an extremely religious woman, Blake began to play professionally in a Baltimore nightclub at the age of 15, and in 1899 wrote his first piano rag, *Charleston Rag*. In 1915 he met the singer Noble Sissle. The two men formed a songwriting partnership and had an immediate success with *It's all your fault*, performed by Sophie Tucker. Blake and Sissle went to New York and joined Europe's Society Orchestra, and after World War I they formed the Dixie Duo, a vaudeville act. In 1921 they produced an extremely successful musical, *Shuffle Along*, which ran for more than 14 months on Broadway and subsequently went on tour. Blake continued to write songs with Sissle and other lyricists for several Broadway and London shows during the 1920s and 1930s, and toured as music director for United Service Organizations productions during World War II. He first recorded in 1917, and continued to record as soloist and with his orchestra into the 1930s. He retired in 1946 and returned to the study of composition at New York University, completing the Schillinger system of courses three years later. During the ensuing years he spent much time notating many of his compositions.

A ragtime revival in the 1950s focused attention on Blake as the nation's foremost rag pianist and launched him on a new career as a touring player and lecturer. He returned to recording in 1969 with the album *The Eighty-six Years of Eubie Blake* (Col. C2S-847), and in 1972 established his own publishing and record company, Eubie Blake Music. He also made piano rolls for the QRS Company (1973). Blake became a legendary figure, performing constantly on television and at jazz festivals in the USA and abroad. He received awards from the music and theater industries and from civic and professional organizations; he was awarded the Presidential Medal of Freedom (1981) and honorary degrees from Brooklyn College (1973), Dartmouth College (1974), Rutgers University (1974), the New England Conservatory (1974), and the University of Maryland (1979). His life was celebrated in documentary films and on Broadway in such shows as *Eubie* (1978).

Blake's music is distinguished by an enormous diversity, reflecting tastes in popular music in the early and middle decades of the 20th century. Many of his more than 300 songs are infused with the syncopated ragtime rhythms that swept Tin Pan Alley between 1900 and 1920. His tunes tend to have a large melodic range and exhibit disjunct motion, while his harmonic language includes many altered blues chords and chromatic progressions. The broad range of Blake's music can be seen in his ethnic songs ("If you've never been vamped by a brownskin"), which derive from the earlier coon song, in musical-theater ballads ("Love will find a way"), in spiritual songs ("Roll, Jordan"), or in *double-entendre* novelty songs ("My handyman ain't handy any more"). His piano music, which consists mostly of rags, displays many

Eubie Blake (left) with Noble Sissle: photograph autographed for Eileen Southern by Blake, 1969

of the melodic, harmonic, and rhythmic characteristics of the songs. With their use of broken-octave basses, highly embellished melodies, and arpeggiated figurations, they give a good indication of Blake's own virtuosity at the keyboard. His rags, along with others written in the 1920s by composers such as Fats Waller and James P. Johnson, had a direct influence on the development of the Harlem stride-piano school of the following decade.

WORKS
(selective list)

STAGE

Unless otherwise stated, all are musicals; some music written in collaboration with N. Sissle. Librettists and lyricists are given in that order in parentheses. Dates are those of first New York performance.

Shuffle Along (F. E. Miller, A. Lyles; N. Sissle), 23 May 1921 [incl. Everything reminds me of you, If you've never been vamped by a brownskin, I'm just wild about Harry, Love will find a way]

Elsie (C. W. Bell; Sissle), 2 April 1923

The Chocolate Dandies (orig. title In Bamville) (Sissle, L. Payton; Sissle), 1 Sept 1924 [incl. That charleston dance, Bandanaland, Jazztime baby, The sons of old black Joe]

Lew Leslie's Blackbirds (revue, Miller, A. Razaf; Razaf), 22 Oct 1930 [incl. Memories of you, My handyman ain't handy any more, Who said blackbirds are blue?, Roll, Jordan]

Shuffle Along of 1933 (Miller; Sissle), 26 Dec 1932 [incl. Harlem Moon]

Swing It (C. Mack), 22 July 1937 [incl. Ain't we got love]

Tan Manhattan (revue, Razaf), 1940 [incl. Tan Manhattan, We are Americans too, Weary]

Others, unperf.

SONGS

Some associated with Broadway shows; unless otherwise stated, all lyrics are by N. Sissle.

It's all your fault (1915); At the Pullman porter's full dress ball (1916); Floradora Girls (1920); Vision Girl, in Midnight Rounders, 1920; Serenade Blues (1922); You were meant for me, in London Calling, 1923; When the Lord created Adam (Razaf) (1931); Blues – why don't you let me alone (A. Porter) (1937)

PIANO

Charleston Rag (orig. title Sounds of Africa) (1899); Corner of Chestnut and Low (In Baltimo') (1903); Tricky Fingers (1904, rev. 1969); The Baltimore Todalo (1908); The Chevy Chase (1914); Just a Simple Little Old Blues (Blue Rag in 12 Keys) (1919); Tickle the Ivories (1928); Eubie's Boogie (1942); Dicty's on 7th Avenue (1955); Eubie's Classical Rag (1972); Eubie Dubie (1972); The High Muck de Mucks (1972)

BIBLIOGRAPHY

R. Blesh and H. Janis: *They All Played Ragtime* (New York, 1950, rev. 4/1971)
R. Blesh: *Combo: USA: Eight Lives in Jazz* (Philadelphia, 1971)
E. Southern: *The Music of Black Americans: a History* (New York, 1971, rev. 2/1983)
P. Bailey: "A Love Song to Eubie," *Ebony*, xxviii/9 (1973), 94
W. Bolcom and R. Kimball: *Reminiscing with Sissle and Blake* (New York, 1973) [incl. work-list, discography]
W. J. Schafer and J. Riedel: *The Art of Ragtime* (Baton Rouge, LA, 1973/*R*1977)
E. Southern and B. King: "Conversation with Eubie Blake," *BPiM*, i (1973), 50, 151
"Blake, Eubie," *CBY 1974*
D. A. Jasen and T. J. Tichenor: *Rags and Ragtime: a Musical History* (New York, 1978)
L. Carter: *Eubie Blake: Keys of Memory* (Detroit, 1979)
A. Rose: *Eubie Blake* (New York, 1979)
E. A. Berlin: *Ragtime: a Musical and Cultural History* (Berkeley, CA, 1980)
L. Norment: "Farewell to Ragtime's Apostle of Happiness," *Ebony*, xxxviii/7 (1983), 27
A. Woll: *Dictionary of the Black Theatre* (Westport, CT, 1983)
K. Bloom: *American Song: the Complete Musical Theatre Companion, 1900–1984* (New York, 1985)

EILEEN SOUTHERN, JOHN GRAZIANO

Blake, George E. (*b* England, ?1775; *d* Philadelphia, PA, 20 Feb 1871). Music engraver and publisher. He immigrated to the USA before 1793 and in 1794 began teaching flute and clarinet. In 1802 he acquired the piano manufactory of John I. Hawkins in Philadelphia, and soon after began to publish and to operate a circulating music library. His production included many American compositions (*c*1808) and political songs (*c*1813); an early piracy of Thomas Moore's *Irish Melodies* (1808–*c*1825); a serial, *Musical Miscellany* (from 1815); and the first American edition of *Messiah* (*c*1830), along with other major vocal works by Handel. Most numerous among his output, however, were songs of the Philadelphia theater, based on London publications. Blake also issued typeset opera librettos and engraved tunebooks. He continued to be active throughout the 1830s, in later years also issuing minstrel music and excerpts from Italian opera. At the height of his career (*c*1810–30) he was America's most prolific music publisher.

BIBLIOGRAPHY

Obituary, *Philadelphia Evening Transcript* (21 Feb 1871)

J. C. White: *Music Printing and Publishing in Philadelphia, 1729–1840* (thesis, Columbia U., 1949)

D. W. Krummel: *Philadelphia Music Engraving and Publishing* (diss., U. of Michigan, 1958), 98–108

R. J. Wolfe: *Secular Music in America, 1801–1825: a Bibliography* (New York, 1964)

——: *Early American Music Engraving and Printing* (Urbana, IL, 1980)

D. W. KRUMMEL

Blakey, Art [Buhaina, Abdullah Ibn] (*b* Pittsburgh, PA, 11 Oct 1919). Jazz drummer and bandleader. He received some piano lessons at school and by seventh grade was playing music full-time, leading a commercial band. Shortly afterwards he changed to drums, on which he taught himself to play in the aggressive swing style of Chick Webb, Sid Catlett, and Ray Bauduc. In autumn 1942 he joined Mary Lou Williams for an engagement at Kelly's Stables in New York. He then played with the Fletcher Henderson Orchestra (1943–4), including a long tour of the South. On leaving Henderson Blakey briefly led a big band in Boston before joining Billy Eckstine's new band in St. Louis. During his years with Eckstine (1944–7) Blakey became associated with the modern jazz movement along with his fellow band members Miles Davis, Dexter Gordon, Fats Navarro, and others.

When Eckstine disbanded his group in 1947 Blakey organized the Seventeen Messengers, a rehearsal band, and recorded with an octet called the Jazz Messengers, the first of his many groups bearing this name. He then traveled in Africa, probably for more than a year, to learn about Islamic culture. In the early 1950s he performed and broadcast with such musicians as Charlie Parker, Miles Davis, and Clifford Brown, and particularly with the pianist Horace Silver, his kindred musical spirit of this time. After recording together several times, in 1955 Blakey and Silver formed a cooperative group with Hank Mobley and Kenny Dorham, retaining the name Jazz Messengers. When Silver left the following year the leadership of this important group passed to Blakey, and he has been associated with it since then. It was the archetypal "hard bop" combo of the late 1950s, playing a driving, aggressive extension of bop with pronounced blues roots. Over the years the Jazz Messengers have served as a springboard for young jazz musicians such as Donald Byrd, Johnny Griffin, Wayne Shorter, Freddie Hubbard, Keith Jarrett, Chuck Mangione, Woody Shaw, JoAnne Brackeen and Wynton Marsalis. In addition to his numerous tours and recordings with the Messengers, Blakey also made a world tour in 1971–2 with the Giants of Jazz (with Dizzy Gillespie and Thelonious Monk) and frequently appeared as a soloist at the Newport Jazz Festival in New York, most memorably in a drum battle with Max Roach, Buddy Rich, and Elvin Jones (1974).

Blakey is a major figure in modern jazz and an important stylist on his instrument. From his earliest recording sessions with Eckstine, and particularly in his historic sessions with Thelonious Monk in 1947, he exudes power and originality, creating a dark cymbal sound punctuated by frequent loud snare- and bass-drum accents in triplets or cross-rhythms. Although Blakey discourages comparison of his own music with African drumming, he adopted several African devices after his visit in 1948–9, including rapping on the side of the drum and using his elbow on the tom-tom to alter the pitch. Later he organized recording sessions with multiple drummers, including some African musicians and pieces. His much-imitated trademark, the forceful closing of the hi-hat on every second and fourth beat, has been part of his style since 1950–51. A loud and domineering drummer, Blakey also listens and responds to his soloists. His contribution to jazz as a discoverer and molder of young talent over three decades is no less significant than his very considerable innovations on his instrument.

RECORDINGS

(selective list)

As leader: Message from Kenya/Nothing but Soul (1953, BN 1626); *A Night at Birdland*, i–iii (1954, BN 5037-9); *Drum Suite* (1956–7, Col. CL1002); *A Message from Blakey: Holiday for Skins* (1958, BN 4004); *Des femmes disparaissent* (1958, Fontana, 660224); *The Freedom Rider* (1961, BN 84156); *Buttercorn Lady* (1966, Lml. 86034); *Jazz Messengers '70* (1970, Catalyst 7902); *Anthenagin* (1973, Prst. 10076); *Recorded Live at Bubba's* (1980, Who's Who in Jazz 21019); *Album of the Year* (1981, Timeless 155)

As sideman: B. Eckstine: Blowin' the Blues Away (1944, De Luxe 2001), Mister Chips, on *Together!* (1945, Spotlite 100), I Love the Rhythm in a Riff (1945, National 9014); T. Monk: Who Knows (1947, BN 1565); M. Davis: Weirdo (1954, BN 45-1650); H. Silver: Doodlin', on *Horace Silver and the Jazz Messengers* (1954, BN 5058)

BIBLIOGRAPHY

H. Frost: "Art Blakey in St. Louis," *Metronome*, lxiii/2 (1947), 26

H. Lovett: "Art Blakey," *Metronome*, lxxii/6 (1956), 17

J. Tynan: "The Jazz Message," *Down Beat*, xxiv/21 (1957), 15

R. Horricks: *These Jazzmen of our Time* (London, 1959, 2/1962), 131

Z. Carno: "Art Blakey," *Jazz Review*, iii/1 (1960), 6

J. Goldberg: *Jazz Masters of the Fifties* (New York, 1965/*R*1980), 45

B. Mintz: *Different Drummers* (New York, 1975), 43

J. Litweiler: "Bu's Delights and Laments," *Down Beat*, xliii/6 (1976), 15

A. Taylor: *Notes and Tones: Musician to Musician Interviews* (Liège, Belgium, 1973/*R*1982), 251

I. Gitler: "Art Blakey Speaks his Mind," *Jazz Magazine*, iv/1 (1979), 40

H. Nolan: "New Message from Art Blakey," *Down Beat*, xlvi/17 (1979), 19

"Art Blakey and the Jazz Messengers," *Swing Journal*, xxxiii (Feb 1979), 224 [discography]

P. Danson: "Art Blakey," *Coda*, no.173 (1980), 14

M. Paudras: "Art Blakey: le message," *Jazz hot*, nos.374–5 (1980), 16

B. Rusch: "Art Blakey: Interview," *Cadence*, vii (1981), no.7, p. 8; no.9, p. 12

LEWIS PORTER

Bland, Bobby ("Blue") [Robert Calvin] (*b* Rosemark, TN, 27 Jan 1930). Blues singer. His first contact with music came through his involvement in a gospel ensemble, the Miniatures. When he was 17 his family moved to Memphis, and he became associated with a group called the Beale Streeters, which included B. B. King, Johnny Ace, Roscoe Gordon, and Junior Parker. His first solo recordings, made for the Modern label in 1951, were inauspicious, but he had greater success once he had begun to work with the arranger and producer Joe Scott at Duke Records. In the late 1950s Bland recorded rough, hard blues songs with strong guitar obbligatos: *Farther up the road* (1957) is an example of this intense early style. *I'll take care of you* (1959) marked an abrupt change of direction: Bland's later singles were painstakingly crafted, and he became adept at projecting warmth and intimacy, often punctuating the vocal line with growls and cries; Scott tempered his phrasing and added dazzling horn fanfares to the arrangements, which were based on Wayne Bennett's supple guitar playing, reminiscent of T-Bone Walker. In the 1970s and 1980s he continued to record, but without Scott's participation his songs often lacked the vitality of his earlier work.

RECORDINGS

(selective list; recorded for Duke unless otherwise stated)

Farther up the road (170, 1957); I'll take care of you (314, 1959); Turn on your love light (344, 1961); That's the way love is/Call on me (360, 1963); Ain't nothing you can do (375, 1964); Good Time Charlie (402, 1966); Chains of Love (449, 1969); *Dreamer* (ABC 50169, 1974); *B. B. King and Bobby Bland: Together for the First Time . . . Live* (ABC 50190, 1974); *Reflections in Blue* (ABC 1018, 1977); *I Feel Good, I Feel Fine* (MCA 3157, 1979)

BIBLIOGRAPHY

SouthernB

J. Dufour: "Good Time Bobby," *Soul Bag*, no.41 (1974), 2

K. Mohr and E. Choisnel: "Bobby Bland," *Soul Bag*, no.41 (1974), 6 [discography; addns in no.44 (1974)]

P. Guralnick: *Lost Highway* (Boston, 1979), 68

JOSEPH McEWEN

Bland, James A(llen) (*b* Flushing, NY, 22 Oct 1854; *d* Philadelphia, PA, 5 May 1911). Minstrel performer and songwriter. He was educated in Washington, DC, where he enrolled in the law department of Howard University, but left at the end of his second year through lack of interest. He spent a great deal of time listening to the songs and tales of the laborers on the university campus, most of whom had formerly been slaves, and was deeply moved by the spirituals and the rhythm and harmony of the work songs. He learned to play the banjo, taught himself the rudiments of harmony, and began composing songs. He organized musical groups, becoming active in the Manhattan Club (a group of musically gifted young Blacks employed in government), and performed at various social functions, where he soon became known as a versatile entertainer. He found the perfect outlet for his musical and theatrical talents in the minstrel show, and joined the Original Black Diamonds of Boston as a leading performer in 1875. A year later he became a member of the Bohee Minstrels, and then of Sprague's Georgia Minstrels. In order to overcome racial discrimination from white concert-hall owners, this group was sold to George B. Callender (becoming Callender's Original Georgia Minstrels), and went on to achieve nationwide success and fame. It was then taken over by Jack Haverly to become Haverly's Genuine Colored Minstrels, and then Haverly's Colossal Carnival and Genuine Colored Minstrels.

Haverly took his Genuine Colored Minstrels to London, opening at Her Majesty's Theatre on 30 July 1881. Bland was a star performer, and became famous for his rendition of *Oh, dem golden slippers* with a special comic routine at the end; another favorite with his audiences was *The Colored Hop*. He also displayed his varied talents in "An Ethiopian Specialty," which consisted of singing, dancing, and acrobatic stunts. The show met with huge success and received glowing press reports. When the company sailed for New York on 5 August 1882 Bland and a few others remained in London, and subsequently toured the country. Bland became a member of English companies for a short time, but achieved his greatest success as a solo performer: he was advertised as "the Idol of the Music Halls."

Bland returned to the USA in 1890 at the peak of his career and fame. He toured with W. S. Cleveland's Colossal Colored Carnival Minstrels billed as "the eccentric original James Bland"; Bland and Tom McIntosh were advertised as "the Two Greatest Comedians of their Race." He remained with this company for about a year, but his subsequent appearances became fewer and his itinerary is unclear. The claim that he returned to Europe in 1891 lacks documentation. W. C. Handy states in his autobiography, *Father of the Blues* (1941), that he met Bland in Louisville in 1897, but he was no longer such a dazzling entertainer. A year later he sang for a short time with Black Patti's Troubadours, but the black minstrel era was nearing its end, and another musical theater was developing. Bland tried to meet the new challenge by writing a musical comedy, *The Sporting Girl*, but it was a failure. Eventually he returned to Philadelphia, where, penniless and ill, he died of tuberculosis. He was buried in an unmarked grave in the Colored Cemetery in Merion, Philadelphia; a gravestone was not erected until 15 July 1946.

It is doubtful whether Bland composed the 600 songs that are repeatedly claimed for him by various writers and are referred to on his gravestone; only a tenth of that total survives which is verifiably by him. He was always most anxious and careful to secure copyrights for his songs and the Library of Congress has 40 such copies, but although Bland spent some ten years of his life in England, the British Library does not list a single British copyright except for a few of the songs originally copyrighted in the USA. He wrote his songs and dances for specific performances, shaping the melodies, texts, and rhythms to suit the situation and the character. They range from sentimental ballads to vigorous dances and sturdy marches. His musical inspiration was drawn from black spirituals, gospel hymns, and work songs, with their rhythmic pulse and leader-response elements. Bland's most famous song, *Carry me back to old Virginny*, was adopted by the State of Virginia in 1940 as its official state song.

WORKS

Edition: *J. A. Bland: Album of Outstanding Songs*, ed. C. Haywood (New York, 1946)

Unless otherwise indicated, all works are minstrel songs with texts by Bland and all were published in Boston.

The Farmer's Daughter (1874); Carry me back to old Virginny (1878); Close dem windows (1879); Fascinating Coon (New York, 1879); Father's growing old (1879); Flowers will come in May (1879); In the morning by the bright light (1879); Lucy, the pride of the South (1879); My old home in Mississippi (1879); Oh, dem golden slippers (1879); Old Homestead (1879); Old Plantation Lonely (1879); Pretty Little South Carolina Rose (1879); Rambling through the Clover (1879); Silver Slippers (1879); Take good care of mother (1879); Uncle Joe, or The Cabin by the Sea (1879); Whisper softly, baby's dying (1879)

De angels am a coming (New York, 1880); Dancing on the kitchen floor (1880); Darkey's Request (New York, 1880); Darkie's Jubilee (1880); Dashing Harry May (New York, 1880); De Golden Wedding (1880); In the evening by the moonlight (New York, 1880); Keep dem golden gates wide open (New York, 1880); Kiss me goodnight, mother (1880); Listen to the silver trumpets (1880); Oh, my brother! (1880); Sister Hannah (n.p., 1880); Sons of Ham (New York, 1880); Way up yonder (1880); Won't we have a jolly time? (New York, 1880); The Colored Hop (Philadelphia, 1881); Come along, Sister Mary (n.p., 1881); Dandy Black Brigade (New York, 1881); Darkie's Moonlight Picnic (New York, 1881); Gabriel's Band (New York, 1881); I'll name the boy Dinnes, or no name at all (n.p., 1881); Mid'st Pretty Violets (1881); My own Sweet Wife to be (n.p., 1881)

Oh, Lucinda! (Philadelphia, 1881); Oh, why was I so soon forgotten? (n.p., 1881); The Old Fashioned Cottage (n.p., 1881); Only to hear her voice (n.p., 1881); Rose Pachoula (n.p., 1881); Taddy, please, scare me again (n.p., 1881); Tell all de children good bye (Philadelphia, 1881); Tell 'em I'll be there (New York, 1881); Traveling back to Alabama (n.p., 1881); You could have been true (New York, 1881); Christmas Dinner (1889); Tapioca (n.p., 1891); Happy Darkies (New York, 1892)

Climbing up the Golden Stairs, lost; Kingdom Coming; The Missouri Hound Dog; The Old Log Cabin in the Dell

The Sporting Girl (musical comedy), *c*1900

Principal publishers: B. W. Hitchcock, J. F. Perry, Pauline Lieder

BIBLIOGRAPHY

SouthernB

T. H. R. Clarke: "James Bland," *Negro History Bulletin*, ii (1938–9), 48

K. Miller: "James A. Bland: the Negro Stephen Foster," *The Etude*, lvii (1939), 431, 472

C. Haywood: *James A. Bland: Prince of the Colored Songwriters* (Flushing, NY, 1944)
E. J. R. Isaacs: *The Negro in the American Theatre* (New York, 1947)
J. J. Daly: *A Song in his Heart* (Philadelphia, 1951)
C. Haywood: *A Bibliography of North American Folklore and Folksong* (New York, 1951, rev. 2/1961)
T. Fletcher: *100 Years of the Negro in Show Business* (New York, 1954)
L. Hughes: "James A. Bland, Minstrel Composer, 1854–1911," *Famous Negro Music Makers* (New York, 1955), 29
E. K. Emurian: "Carry me back to old Virginny," *Living Stories of Famous Songs* (Boston, 1958), 11
L. Hughes and M. Meltzer: *Black Magic: a Pictorial History of the Negro in American Entertainment* (Englewood Cliffs, NJ, 1967)
J. B. Bland: *James Allen Bland, Negro Composer: a Study of his Life* (MMEd thesis, Howard U., Washington, DC, 1968)
E. Southern: *The Music of Black Americans: a History* (New York, 1971, rev. 2/1983)
E. Southern, ed.: *Readings in Black American Music* (New York, 1971)
I. Simond: *Old Slacks Reminiscences and Pocket History of the Colored Profession from 1865 to 1891* (Bowling Green, OH, 1974)
R. C. Toll: *Blacking Up: the Minstrel Show in Nineteenth-century America* (New York, 1974)
——: *On with the Show* (New York, 1976)
C. Hamm: *Yesterdays: Popular Song in America* (New York, 1979)

CHARLES HAYWOOD

Blank, Allan (*b* New York, 27 Dec 1925). Composer. He studied at the Juilliard School, where he held a fellowship in conducting (1945–7), New York University (BA 1948), the University of Minnesota (MA in composition, 1950), and Columbia University Teachers College (1954–7). From 1950 to 1952 he was a violinist in the Pittsburgh SO, and he taught instrumental music in New York high schools between 1956 and 1965. He then taught theory and composition at Western Illinois University, Macomb (1966–8), Paterson (New Jersey) State College (1968–70), and Lehman College, CUNY (1970–77), before becoming associate professor at Virginia Commonwealth University, Richmond, in 1978, where he is director of the New Music Ensemble. In 1983 he received an NEA composers' grant and was awarded the George Eastman Prize for his Duo for bassoon and piano. Blank writes music with flowing, arabesque-like lines; out of these is realized a sonorous polyphony in which each instrument or voice remains distinct.

WORKS

Stage: Aria da capo (chamber opera, E. St. Vincent Millay), 1958–60; Excitement at the Circus (children's play, I. Leitne), vv, pf, 1968; The Magic Bonbons (8 scenes, A. Blank, after L. G. Baum), 1980–83; incidental music for 2 plays

Large ens: Concert Piece, band, 1960–63; Music for Orch, 1964–7; 6 Miniatures and a Fantasia, orch, 1972; 6 Significant Landscapes, chamber orch, 1972–4; Divertimento, tuba, band, 1979; Kreutzer March, band, 1981; Concertino, bn, str, 1984

Chamber: Wind Qnt, 1968–70; Bicinium II, cl, bn, 1974; Coalitions, 2 cl, trbn, pf, 2 perc, 1975; Trio, tpt, hn, trbn, 1975; An American Medley, brass qnt, fl, perc, 1976; Coalitions II, sax qt, 1976; Paganini Caprices, 4 hn, 3 tpt, 3 trbn, tuba, 1976; Ceremonies, tpt, perc, 1977; Duo, bn, pf, 1978; 4 Inventions, bn, pf, 1979; Introduction and Rondo Fantastico, bn, pf, 1979; Str Qt, 1981; Fantasy on Cantillation Motives, vn, va, vc, 1983; Trio, fl, vc, pf, 1983; other works incl. 3 wind qnts

Solo inst: Rotation, pf, 1959–60; A Song of Ascents, va, 1968; 3 Pieces, tpt, 1969; 3 Novelties, a sax, 1971; Music for Vn, 1972; 2 Studies, cl, 1972; Restatement of Romance, pf, 1973

Vocal: Buy me an ounce & I'll sell you a pound (Cummings), SATB, pf, 1956; Poem (Cummings), S, cl, vc, harp, 1963; 2 Ferlinghetti Songs, S, bn, 1964; 2 Parables by Franz Kafka, S, vn, va, 1964; 13 Ways of Looking at a Blackbird (W. Stevens), S, fl + pic, cl + b cl, pf, vn + va, vc, 1964–5; Esther's Monologue (M. Blank), cantata, S, ob, va, vc, 1970; Lines from Proverbs, SATB, 1973; American Folio (trad.), SATB, pf/insts, 1976; 2 Holy Sonnets (Donne), A, ob + eng hn, va, harp, 1977; Some Funnies and Poems (O. Nash, E. Lear, Cummings, M. Blank, A. Blank), nar, pf, 1982; 11 other works

Principal publishers: Associated, CFE, Dorn, Music for Percussion, Presser, Seesaw, Smith

ELAINE BARKIN/MARTIN BRODY

Blanton, Jimmy [James] (*b* Chattanooga, TN, Oct 1918; *d* Los Angeles, CA, 30 July 1942). Jazz double bass player. He played locally in combos led by his mother, a pianist, and attended Tennessee State College briefly before moving in the late 1930s to St. Louis, where he performed in the Jeter–Pillars band and in Fate Marable's riverboat groups. There he was discovered in late 1939 by Duke Ellington, who engaged him immediately for his orchestra. Blanton's playing subtly altered the Ellington sound, stabilizing the band's rhythm and greatly enhancing its swing; it also ushered in Ellington's most creative period as a composer, particularly in masterpieces such as *Ko-Ko* and *Concerto for Cootie*, where Blanton's bass part is especially prominent. Blanton also took part in informal jam sessions at Minton's Playhouse in New York, contributing to the early genesis of the bop style. From 1941 his playing became somewhat erratic, and late that year he was obliged by ill health (diagnosed as congenital tuberculosis) to take up residence in a California sanatorium, where he died shortly afterwards.

In his tragically brief career Blanton revolutionized jazz bass playing, and until the advent of the free-jazz styles of Scott LaFaro and Charlie Haden in the 1960s all modern bass players drew on his innovations. He possessed great dexterity and range, roundness of tone, accurate intonation, and above all an unprecedented swing. His strong sense of harmony led him to incorporate many nonharmonic passing tones in his accompaniment lines, giving them a contrapuntal flavor and stimulating soloists to their own harmonic explorations. Blanton also contributed the earliest fully satisfying jazz solos on this instrument, which depart in their inventive melody and flexible rhythms from the "walking" bass style that was then prevalent. Despite his short career Blanton left a large recorded legacy, not only in his 130-odd recordings with the Ellington orchestra, but also in many small-group performances with Ellington sidemen, and especially in a remarkable series of piano–bass duos with Ellington himself. As adapted by his followers Oscar Pettiford, Ray Brown, and Charles Mingus, Blanton's innovations also led indirectly to the creation of the bop rhythm section.

RECORDINGS
(selective list)

Duos with Duke Ellington: Plucked Again/Blues (1939, Col. 35322); Pitter Panther Patter/Sophisticated Lady (1940, Vic. 27221); Body and Soul/Mr. J. B. Blues (1940, Vic. 27406)

As sideman with Duke Ellington: Jack the Bear (1940, Vic. 26536); Conga Brava/Ko-Ko (1940, Vic. 26577); Concerto for Cootie (1940, Vic. 26598); Sepia Panorama/Harlem Air Shaft (1940, Vic. 26731); In a Mellotone (1940, Vic. 26788)

As sideman with others: B. Bigard: Lost in Two Flats (1939, OK 5422); C. Williams: Black Butterfly (1940, OK 5618); J. Hodges: Squatty Roo (1941, Bluebird 11447)

BIBLIOGRAPHY

SouthernB
R. G. Reisner: *The Jazz Titans* (Garden City, NY, 1960)
I. Kanth: *A Discography of Jimmy Blanton* (Stockholm, 1970)
E. K. Ellington: *Music is my Mistress* (Garden City, NY, 1973/*R*1976)

J. BRADFORD ROBINSON

Blauvelt, Lilian Evans (*b* Brooklyn, NY, 16 March 1874; *d* Chicago, IL, 29 Aug 1947). Soprano. As a child she studied violin, and at the age of eight she gave a recital in Steinway Hall, New York. At 15 she entered the National Conservatory in New York as a singing student and was taught by Jacques Bouhy and Emmy Fursch-Madi; when Bouhy returned to Paris Blauvelt followed him there. She made her début in Brussels on 6 September 1891 in Gounod's *Mireille*. She spent a winter in St. Petersburg where she immediately met with success. In 1899 she performed for Queen Victoria, and in 1902, by special command, she sang the coronation ode for Edward VII, who awarded her the Coronation Medal. She made her Covent Garden début in 1903 as Marguerite in *Faust*. Her popularity was greatest in England, but she was nevertheless in constant demand in the USA as a recitalist and festival soloist. Although it was rumored that she might join the Metropolitan Opera, she sang no opera in New York, but she did appear in Hosmer's operetta *Rose of Alhambra* in 1906–7. After study with Alexander Savine (whom she married in 1914) it was announced that she had become a dramatic soprano, and in 1919 she appeared in Savine's opera *Xenia* in Zurich. In later years she taught in New York and Chicago. Her voice was described as a high soprano of very pure timbre, but dramatic in quality, with a range from *g* to *d'''*. Her recordings, though rather primitive, show an exceptionally brilliant technique.

PHILIP LIESON MILLER

Bledsoe, Jules [Julius] (*b* Waco, TX, 29 Dec 1898; *d* Hollywood, CA, 14 July 1943). Baritone. He studied at Central Texas College, Bishop, and Virginia Union College and may have also studied at the Chicago Musical College and in Rome and Paris. Following army service, he matriculated at the Columbia University Medical School in 1919 (though he continued private study with Claude Warford, Lazar Samoiloff, and Parisolti), but he had abandoned plans for a medical career by the time he made his début at New York's Aeolian Hall in April 1924. After appearing in W. Frank Harling's hybrid opera *Deep River* and singing in performances of Gruenberg's *The Creation* and *In Abraham's Bosom* in 1926, he created the role of Joe in Jerome Kern's *Showboat* on Broadway (1927), which he also sang in the film version of 1929. He toured Europe as a recitalist in 1931. The following year he was in Cleveland, where he took the role of the Voodoo Man in Shirley Graham du Bois' *Tom-Tom* and, at short notice, sang Amonasro in *Aida*. His other roles included Boris Godunov (1933) and Gruenberg's Emperor Jones, both of which he performed in the USA and Europe, and he made a second film, *Drums of the Congo*, in 1942.

BIBLIOGRAPHY

SouthernB

M. C. Hare: *Negro Musicians and their Music* (Washington, DC, 1936/*R*1974), 173, 332, 358

DOMINIQUE-RENÉ DE LERMA

Blegen, Judith (*b* Missoula, MT, 27 April 1941). Soprano. She learned to play the violin as a child; at the Curtis Institute from 1959, her principal studies were violin (under Toshiya Eto) and singing (under Euphemia Gregory). In 1963, while still a student, she sang with the Philadelphia Orchestra; following an earlier apprenticeship at the Santa Fe Festival (to which she later returned as a principal), she was engaged for concerts at Spoleto in 1963. After further study as a Fulbright scholar in Italy, she went in 1964 to Nuremberg, and during her two years there took such varied roles as Lucia, Susanna, and Zerbinetta (*Ariadne auf Naxos*). Engagements followed in Vienna, Salzburg, Paris, and the major American houses; her début role of Papagena at the Metropolitan Opera (19 January 1970) led to performances as Marcellina (*Fidelio*), Mélisande, Ascanius (*Les troyens*), and Sophie in *Werther* and *Der Rosenkavalier*. She has also appeared with leading orchestras in the USA, and given lieder recitals. Her singing is notable for its charm, intelligence, and polish; she avoids soubrette clichés, and makes the most of a voice that is exceptionally pure and sweet, if not particularly large or colorful. She has both sung and creditably played the violin in Menotti's *Help, Help, the Globolinks!* and *Die Fledermaus* (as Adele). On record and in recitals she has sung duets with Frederica von Stade.

BIBLIOGRAPHY

"Blegen, Judith," *CBY 1977*

MARTIN BERNHEIMER/R

Blesh, Rudi [Rudolph] **(Pickett)** (*b* Guthrie, OK, 21 Jan 1899; *d* Gilmanton, NH, 25 Aug 1985). Writer on music. He attended Dartmouth College and earned a BS in architecture at the University of California in Berkeley. In the 1940s he served as jazz critic for the *San Francisco Chronicle* and the *New York Herald Tribune*. He wrote a pioneering serious history of jazz, *Shining Trumpets* (1946), and with Harriet Janis was co-author of the first history of ragtime, *They All Played Ragtime* (1950). The latter work established him as the leading authority in this field, and eventually prompted a revival of the music. Also with Janis, he founded Circle Records, a small but significant jazz label which became the first to issue the Library of Congress recordings of Jelly Roll Morton. In 1953 they sold Circle Records – apart from the Morton recordings – to Jazzology Records. From 1947 to 1950, and again in 1964, Blesh wrote and narrated radio programs on jazz and American folk music. Beginning in 1956 he taught jazz history at Queens College and New York University, and in the 1970s he contributed jacket notes for numerous ragtime recordings. Blesh also edited ragtime piano music and wrote books on modern art and the cinema.

WRITINGS

This is Jazz: a Series of Lectures Given at the San Francisco Museum of Art (San Francisco, 1943)

Shining Trumpets: a History of Jazz (New York, 1946, rev. and enlarged 2/1958/*R*1975)

with H. Janis: *They All Played Ragtime* (New York, 1950, rev. 4/1971)

Combo: USA: Eight Lives in Jazz (Philadelphia, 1971)

"Scott Joplin: Black-American Classicist," *The Collected Works of Scott Joplin*, ed. V. B. Lawrence (New York, 1971)

BIBLIOGRAPHY

J. E. Hasse: "Rudi Blesh and the Ragtime Revivalists," *Ragtime: its History, Composers, and Music* (New York, 1985)

S. Holden: Obituary, *New York Times* (28 Aug 1985)

JOHN EDWARD HASSE

Bley [née Borg], **Carla** (*b* Oakland, CA, 11 May 1938). Jazz composer and bandleader. She learned the fundamentals of music from her father, a church musician, but is otherwise self-taught. At the age of 17 she moved to New York where she worked intermittently as a pianist and cigarette girl, writing jazz tunes for musicians such as George Russell, Jimmy Giuffre, and her husband at the time, Paul Bley. In 1964, with the trumpeter Mike Mantler, she formed the Jazz Composers' Guild Orchestra, known from 1965 as the Jazz Composer's Orchestra. In 1966 she helped found the Jazz Composer's Orchestra Association, a novel nonprofit organization which commissions, produces, and distributes commercially unviable jazz. Though already highly regarded by this time among critics, she first came to public notice with *A Genuine Tong Funeral* (1967), a cycle of pieces recorded with the Gary Burton Quartet, and with her compositions and arrangements for Charlie Haden's *Liberation Music Orchestra* (1969). During these years she also completed her most substantial work, the eclectic "jazz opera" *Escalator over the Hill*. This work was extraordinarily well received by the international jazz press, and led to several composing grants. Since that time Bley has continued to compose, expanded the activities of the Jazz Composer's Orchestra Association, and led her own ten-piece touring band. An indifferent keyboardist, Bley is an outstanding jazz composer with a wide range of styles at her command. Much of her best work is infused with a spirit of parody and sardonic humor. Her *3/4* for piano and orchestra has been performed by musicians as varied as Keith Jarrett, Ursula Oppens, and Frederic Rzewski.

RECORDINGS

(selective list)

As leader or co-leader: with G. Burton: *A Genuine Tong Funeral* (1967, RCA LSP3988); *Escalator over the Hill* (1968–71, JCOA EOTH [1003–5]); *Tropic Appetites* (1973–4, Watt 1); 3/4, on *13 3/4* (1975, Watt 3); *Dinner Music* (1976, Watt 6); *European Tour* (1977, Watt 8); *Musique Mécanique* (1978, Watt 9); *Social Studies* (1980, Watt 11)

As sideman: C. Haden: *Liberation Music Orchestra* (1969, Imp. 9183)

BIBLIOGRAPHY

G. Buhles: "Die Jazzkomponistin Carla Bley: Kurzbiographie, Werkanalyse, Würdigung," *Jazzforschung*, viii (1976), 11

H. Mandel. "Carla Bley: Independent Ringleader," *Down Beat*, xlv/11 (1978), 18

B. Primack: "Carla Bley: First Lady of the Avant-Garde," *Contemporary Keyboard*, v/2 (1979), 9

R. Zabor: "Carla Bley: the Toast of the Continent," *Musician*, no.35 (1981), 64

L. Dahl: *Stormy Weather* (New York, 1984), 202

D. Palmer: "Carla Bley Returns to Form," *New York Times* (10 Feb 1985)

J. BRADFORD ROBINSON

Blind Tom. *See* BETHUNE, THOMAS.

Bliss, Anthony A(ddison) (*b* New York, 19 April 1913). Music administrator and lawyer. After attending Harvard University (BA 1936), he pursued graduate studies at Columbia University (1936–8) and law at the University of Virginia (LlB 1940); he practiced law in New York. In 1949 he became a member of the board of directors of the Metropolitan Opera Association, and served as its president (1956–7), executive director (1974–81), and general manager (1981–5). He has also held administrative or board positions with a number of arts organizations, including the Joffrey Ballet in New York, the American Arts Alliance, Lincoln Center, the NEA (music and dance panels), and the New York Foundation of the Arts. Among the changes Bliss initiated in the Metropolitan's operations, the expanding of its season and the introduction of sounder financing were especially important.

BIBLIOGRAPHY

"Bliss, Anthony A(ddison)," *CBY 1979*

WILLIAM McCLELLAN

Bliss, Philip P(aul) (*b* Clearfield Co., PA, 9 July 1838, *d* Ashtabula, OH, 29 Dec 1876). Gospel hymnwriter and compiler of gospel hymnbooks, singer, and composer. He began his career as a singing-school teacher, leader of musical conventions, and concert singer. In 1874 he was persuaded by Moody to enter evangelistic work in association with Whittle. Bliss wrote some 95 secular songs; 303 sacred pieces bear his name, as either author or composer or both. The majority of his published works appeared in one of the seven books which he edited alone or with Sankey. The terms "gospel song" and "gospel hymn" first appeared in the titles of his *Gospel Songs* (Cincinnati, 1874) and *Gospel Hymns and Sacred Songs* (Cincinnati, 1875). The latter was edited jointly with Sankey, as was a second volume, *Gospel Hymns no.2* (Cincinnati, 1876); after Bliss's death Sankey edited four more collections with other collaborators and the entire series, published together as *Gospel Hymns nos.1–6 Complete* (1894/*R*1973), became the main source of gospel hymns during the remainder of the 19th century. Bliss's most popular hymns include *Sing them over again to me*, *When peace like a river attendeth my way*, and *"Man of Sorrows!" What a name*. (*See also* GOSPEL MUSIC, §I, 1(iii).)

BIBLIOGRAPHY

D. W. Whittle, ed.: *Memoirs of Philip P. Bliss* (New York, 1877)

R. D. Kalis: "The Poet of Gospel Song," *Bread of Life* (March 1964) [monthly magazine of the Ridgewood Pentecostal Church, Brooklyn, NY]; repr. in *The Hymn*, xxv (1974), 101; xxvi (1975), 46

B. J. Neil: *Philip P. Bliss (1838-1876): Gospel Hymn Composer and Compiler* (diss., New Orleans Baptist Theological Seminary, 1977)

D. J. Smucker: *Philip Paul Bliss and the Musical, Cultural and Religious Sources of the Gospel Music Tradition in the United States, 1850–1876* (diss., Boston U., 1981)

BOB J. NEIL

Blitzstein, Marc (*b* Philadelphia, PA, 2 March 1905; *d* Fort de France, Martinique, 22 Jan 1964). Composer. He was the first composer to develop a convincing music-theater idiom representative of American vernacular speech style. Deeply committed to the doctrine of "art for society's sake," a doctrine adopted from Hanns Eisler, Bertolt Brecht, Kurt Weill, the Soviet composers, and the *Gebrauchsmusik* school, he devoted much of his talent for dramatic and musical characterization to topics of social commentary and political satire.

1. Up to 1930. 2. 1931–42. 3. 1942–64. 4. Style.

1. UP TO 1930. Blitzstein began to study music at the age of three. He performed publicly as a pianist two years later and began composing at seven. He entered the University of Pennsylvania at 16 and continued his musical and academic training with distinction. He turned his full attention to music only after a scholarship granted by the university was discontinued because of an unsatisfactory evaluation in a physical education class. He received an award as pianist from the Philharmonic Society of Philadelphia in 1922. After leaving the university he studied piano with Alexander Siloti in New York. When the Curtis Institute was founded in 1924 Blitzstein enrolled as a student of composition with Scalero. Shortly before leaving for study in Europe, he performed as solo pianist in July 1926 with the Philadelphia Orchestra under Hadley.

The greater part of the next two years was spent studying with Boulanger in Paris and with Schoenberg in Berlin. In 1928 he heard Weill's and Brecht's *Die Dreigroschenoper*, a work he found enjoyable but of no particular significance in relation to his own style of composition at the time. In that year he also made his first major appearance in New York as composer-pianist (Sonata for piano, 1927) and, in the periodical *Modern Music*, as a music critic. His contributions to the magazine were considered significant; he continued writing for *Modern Music* until 1943 and also contributed to several other periodicals, including the *Musical Quarterly* and *New Masses*. Although his compositions were not well received, critics could not overlook his obvious talent and potential, sensing that a prodigious, albeit angry, young man had burst upon the American musical scene. In May 1929 his first stage work, *Triple Sec*, was performed at a privately sponsored program in Philadelphia. The following year it was chosen to be part of the Theatre Guild's musical revue *Garrick Gaieties*. Although not a critical success, the revue ran for half a year, and the score was published by Schott in Germany. Until 1934 he traveled frequently between the USA and Europe, supporting himself by conducting lecture-recital series on 20th-century music while continuing to compose and to write about musical activities.

2. 1931–42. The years from 1931 to 1935 represent a transitional period in Blitzstein's creative attitude. His writings about music show a new-found respect for the music-theater of New York revues and a continuing respect for the work of Schoenberg. His compositions reveal both an extraordinary facility for musical satire (*The Harpies* is a parody of Stravinsky's neoclassicism) and his acceptance of social issues as suitable subject matter for dramatic music (*The Condemned* was inspired by the trial and execution of Sacco and Vanzetti). He also continued his previous abstract aestheticism.

In 1935 Blitzstein attended lectures by Eisler on "The Crisis in Music" at the New School for Social Research in New York, where both men later taught. Eisler's presentation convinced him that one could not talk about music without analyzing its relationship to the social conditions in which it was created. Blitzstein was at this time secretary of the Composers Collective of New York, in which Eisler also was involved. In the same year Blitzstein saw the Theatre Union production of Brecht's *Die Mutter* in an American adaptation by Paul Peters, with music by Eisler. Blitzstein's wife, the writer Eva Goldbeck, analyzed the role of music in that production and in other socially significant theater pieces in the first detailed and sympathetic studies of Brecht's "epic theater" published in the USA. Blitzstein met Brecht at that time and performed his sketch *Nickel under the Foot*, which was later incorporated into *The Cradle will Rock*, the play in music that Blitzstein dedicated to Brecht. His writings from this period to the end of the decade show Blitzstein to be an ardent promoter of Eisler's dictum: the creative artist must "transform himself from a parasite (on society) to a fighter (on behalf of society)."

From 1936 until 1942 Blitzstein was chiefly engaged in expressing his left-wing social awareness through dramatic works for the theater and other media: *The Cradle will Rock*, originally intended for production by the Federal Theatre Project, but independently produced by Orson Welles and John Houseman under the auspices of the Mercury Theatre after Federal authorities found its theme (the organization of a union in Steeltown, USA) too controversial; *I've Got the Tune*, an autobiographical radio song-play that serves as an artistic credo; and *No for an Answer*, an opera exposing the injustices suffered by the immigrant working class and pointing to the positive role the middle class can play in social struggles. Blitzstein also wrote film scores for *Valley Town* (Willard Van Dyke, director), a study of unemployment, and *Native Land* (Paul Strand, Leo Hurwitz, and others), a full-length portrayal of fascist tendencies in corporate America. In 1940–41 and 1941–2 he received Guggenheim Fellowships.

Marc Blitzstein, London, 1943

3. 1942–64. From August 1942 until summer 1945 Blitzstein was a member of the US 8th Army Air Force in England. Regarding the Allied cause as entirely just, he composed music for projects designed to entertain and encourage both military and civilian fighters; *Freedom Morning*, for orchestra, and the *Airborne Symphony* for orchestra and male chorus, commissioned by the Army, are the principal works from this period. He also served as music director of the American Broadcasting Station in Europe, based in London (see illustration), and traveled in newly liberated areas of France to gather songs of the resistance movement.

In 1946 the Koussevitzky Foundation commissioned an opera. Blitzstein chose to adapt Lillian Hellman's play *The Little Foxes*; intended for the Broadway stage, it included spoken dialogue in the style of an *opéra comique*. It was produced as *Regina* in 1949, revised in 1953 and 1958, and staged numerous times thereafter. Throughout the 1950s he continued to compose for the stage, both incidental music and full-scale musical plays. He persisted as a social critic in *Reuben Reuben* and *Juno*, the latter based on Sean O'Casey's *Juno and the Paycock*. His greatest public acclaim came from his translation and adaptation of *Die Dreigroschenoper* as *The Threepenny Opera*, first produced in 1952. In 1956 he began a similar adaptation of *Mutter Courage* and in 1958 of *Aufstieg und Fall der Stadt Mahagonny*, both by Brecht; neither project was completed. In 1959 he became a member of the National Institute of Arts and Letters.

The Metropolitan Opera Association recommended Blitzstein for a Ford Foundation grant in 1960, and he chose the subject of Sacco and Vanzetti for a three-act opera. He pursued this project until his death with only one interruption – acceptance of an appointment in 1962–3 as playwright-in-residence at Bennington College. There he became friends with Bernard Malamud and began to set two of Malamud's short stories. He was killed while on a working residency in Martinique, in a late-night altercation at a waterfront bar.

4. STYLE. The change in Blitzstein's conception of the function of the artist in society was accompanied by a change in musical style. Before the mid-1930s his works exemplify respect for the craft of composition and a penchant for uncompromising dissonance handled within the bounds of neoclassical principles of expression. Both characteristics reflect his international schooling. After his turn to Eisler's credo for the 20th-century composer, Blitzstein adopted stylistic traits that functioned successfully for purposes of agitation and propaganda. This "agit-prop" style consisted of a modified but consistent use of dissonance, more traditional melodic contours with rhythms closely patterned after the American vernacular, and song forms based on standard 12-bar blues, 32-bar popular songs, speech patter, aria, and arioso. In short, he used whatever style, medium, or method he felt necessary to accomplish his extra-musical goals for the texts he set. The results were a mixture of his contemporary idiom with techniques founded on the proletarian precepts of Eisler. In the 1940s, as Blitzstein became less militant, though by no means less socially aware, he continued to adopt and adapt various current or experimental styles. *Regina* was almost operatic, *Reuben Reuben* almost a Broadway musical, and his second *King Lear* (1955), using electronic music by Luening and Ussachevsky, almost avant-garde incidental music. His unwillingness to comply with the usual characteristics of accepted categories in music invariably presented difficulties for audiences and critics. The influence of his social attitudes and work is still found in the music of his close friend Leonard Bernstein (*Trouble in Tahiti*, 1951, dedicated to Blitzstein, and *Mass*, 1971).

See also OPERA, §5 and fig.3.

WORKS

DRAMATIC

Triple Sec (opera-farce, 1, R. Jeans), 1928; Philadelphia, 6 May 1929, cond. A. Smallens

Parabola and Circula (opera-ballet, 1, G. Whitsett), 1929

Cain (ballet), 1930

The Harpies (opera, 1, Blitzstein), 1931; New York, 25 May 1953, cond. H. Ross

The Condemned (choral opera, 1, Blitzstein), 1932

Send for the Militia (theater sketch, Blitzstein), 1v, pf, 1935

The Cradle will Rock (play in music, 10 scenes, Blitzstein), 1936–7; New York, 16 June 1937, cond. Blitzstein

I've Got the Tune (radio song-play, Blitzstein), 1937; New York, CBS, 24 Oct 1937, cond. B. Herrmann

F. T. P. Plowed Under (theater sketch, Blitzstein), 1937

No for an Answer (opera, 2, Blitzstein), 1938–40; New York, 5 Jan 1941, cond. Blitzstein

Labor for Victory (radio series, Blitzstein), 1942

Goloopchik (musical play, Blitzstein), 1945, inc.

Show (ballet), 1946

Regina (opera, 3, L. Hellman, Blitzstein), 1946–9; New York, 31 Oct 1949, cond. M. Abravanel; rev. 1953, 1958

The Guests (ballet), 1948; New York, 20 Jan 1949, cond. Barzin

Reuben Reuben (musical play, 2, Blitzstein), 1950–55; Boston, 10 Oct 1955, cond. S. Krachmalnick

Juno (musical play, 2, J. Stein, Blitzstein, after O'Casey), 1957–9; New York, 9 March 1959, cond. R. E. Dolan

Sacco and Vanzetti (opera, Blitzstein), 1959–64, inc.

The Magic Barrel (opera, 1, Malamud, Blitzstein), 1963, inc.

Idiots First (opera, 1, Malamud, Blitzstein), 1963, inc., completed by L. Lehrman; Ithaca, NY, Aug 1974, cond. Lehrman

Incidental music: Julius Caesar (Shakespeare), 1937; Danton's Death (Büchner), 1938; Androcles and the Lion (Shaw), 1946; Another Part of the Forest (Hellman), 1946; King Lear (Shakespeare), 2 versions: 1950, 1955; Volpone (Jonson), 1956; A Midsummer Night's Dream (Shakespeare), 1958; A Winter's Tale (Shakespeare), 1958; Toys in the Attic (Hellman), 1960

Film scores: Hände, 1928; Surf and Seaweed, 1931; War Department Manual, 1935; Chesapeake Bay Retriever, 1936; The Spanish Earth, 1936–7, collab. V. Thomson; Valley Town, 1940; Native Land, 1940–41; Night Shift, opera, 1942; The True Glory, 1945–6 [composed but not used for the film]

Trans. and adaptation of Weill: Die Dreigroschenoper as The Threepenny Opera, 1950–52; Waltham, MA, 14 June 1952, cond. Bernstein

VOCAL

As if a Phantom Caress'd me (Whitman), 1v, pf, 1925; After the Dazzle of Day (Whitman), 1v, pf, 1925; Into my Heart an Air (Housman), 1v, pf, 1925; Gods (Whitman), Mez, str, 1926; 4 Whitman Songs, Bar, pf, 1928; Is Five (Cummings), S, pf, 1929; Cantatina, female chorus, perc, 1930; Children's Cantata, chorus, 1935; Jimmie's Got a Goil (Cummings), 1v, pf, 1935

A Child Writes a Letter, Bar, pf, 1936; Invitation to Bitterness (Blitzstein), ATB, 1938; The Airborne Symphony (Blitzstein), T, B, narrator, male chorus, orch, 1943–6, New York, 1 April 1946, cond. Bernstein; Displaced (Blitzstein), 1v, pf, 1945; This is the Garden (Blitzstein), chorus, orch, 1957, New York, 5 May 1957, cond. H. Aks; 6 Elizabethan Songs (Shakespeare), 1v, pf, 1958; From Marion's Book (Cummings), 1v, pf, 1960

INSTRUMENTAL

Sarabande, orch, 1926; Romantic Piece, orch, 1930; Piano Concerto, 1931; Surf and Seaweed, suite, orch, 1933; Variations, orch, 1934; Freedom Morning, sym. poem, orch, 1943, London, 28 Sept 1943, cond. Weisgall; Native Land, suite, orch, 1946; Lear: a Study, orch, 1958, New York, 27 Feb 1958, cond. Mitropoulos

Sonata, pf, 1927; Piano Percussion Music, 1929; Scherzo, pf, 1930; Str Qt, 1930; Serenade, str qt, 1932; Discourse, cl, vc, pf, 1933; Suite, pf, 1933; Le monde libre, march, pf, 1944; Show, suite, pf, 1947; The Guests, suite, pf, 1949

MSS in *WHi*

Principal publisher: Chappell (New York)

BIBLIOGRAPHY

EwenD

H. Brant: "Marc Blitzstein," *MM*, xxiii/3 (1946), 170

J. O. Hunter: "Marc Blitzstein's 'The Cradle Will Rock' as a Document of America, 1937," *American Quarterly*, xvi (1964), 227

M. Lederman: "Memories of Marc Blitzstein, Music's Angry Man," *Show*, iv (1964), 18

W. H. Mellers: *Music in a New Found Land* (New York, 1964/*R*1975)

P. M. Talley: *Social Criticism in the Original Theatre Librettos of Marc Blitzstein* (diss., U. of Wisconsin, 1965)

J. Peyser: "The Troubled Time of Marc Blitzstein," *Columbia University Forum*, ix/1 (1966), 32

J. Gruen: *Close-up* (New York, 1968), 166

R. J. Dietz: "Marc Blitzstein and the 'Agit-Prop' Theatre of the 1930s," *Yearbook for Inter-American Musical Research*, vi (1970), 51

——: *The Operatic Style of Marc Blitzstein* (diss., U. of Iowa, 1970)

J. Houseman: *Run-through: a Memoir* (New York, 1972)

L. J. Lehrman: *A Musical Analysis of "Idiots First"* (thesis, Cornell U., 1975)

C. Davis: *The Sun in Mid-career* (New York, 1975)

E. Gordon: "The Roots of 'Regina'," *Performing Arts*, iii/8 (1980), 6

——: "Of the People: Marc Blitzstein Remembered," *Opera News*, xliv/19 (1980), 26

ROBERT J. DIETZ/ERIC GORDON

Bloch, Ernest (*b* Geneva, Switzerland, 24 July 1880; *d* Portland, OR, 15 July 1959). Composer and teacher. He became a naturalized American in 1924.

1. LIFE. He studied in his native city with Louis Rey (violin) and Emile Jaques-Dalcroze (composition) during the 1890s. On

the encouragement of Martin Marsick, he journeyed first to Brussels, where he continued his studies under Eugène Ysaÿe (violin) and François Rasse (composition) from 1897 to 1899, and then to Frankfurt am Main, where his principal teacher was Iwan Knorr (1900), who, Bloch acknowledged, taught him to think independently and to develop his own musical personality. He spent the period 1901–3 in Munich, where he was largely his own mentor, although he took a few lessons with Ludwig Thuille. After a year in Paris, he returned to Geneva, where he married Margarethe Schneider and entered his father's clock business. In the ensuing years he conducted orchestral concerts at Neuchâtel and Lausanne (1909–10) and lectured on aesthetics at the Geneva Conservatory (1911–15); his spare time was devoted to composition.

Bloch came to the USA for the first time in 1916 as conductor for Maud Allan and her dance company. He was engaged primarily in teaching during the years 1917–20, both privately and at the Mannes College; in addition, he conducted orchestral concerts of his own works and established a reputation as a "Jewish" composer. His Viola Suite (1919) was awarded the Coolidge Prize, and it quickly earned a place in the repertory of eminent violists. Bloch served as the first director of the Cleveland Institute (1920–25), where he proposed reforms, such as the abandoning of examinations and textbooks in favor of direct musical experience, which found no sympathy among the advocates of a "practical" curriculum and resulted in his resignation. He served as director of the San Francisco Conservatory from 1925 to 1930. In 1927 he was awarded the first prize in a contest sponsored by *Musical America* for his epic rhapsody in three parts, *America*.

For most of the 1930s Bloch lived principally in Switzerland, with occasional visits to various European capitals to conduct his works. Because of anti-Semitic feeling and also because he wished to retain his American citizenship, he returned to the USA and in 1940 took a position as professor of music at the University of California, Berkeley, where he taught summer courses until his retirement in 1952. In these later years, Bloch was accorded numerous honors, including the first Gold Medal in Music of the American Academy of Arts and Sciences (1947), two New York Music Critics' Circle awards (1952) for outstanding contributions to chamber music (String Quartet no.3) and orchestral music (Concerto grosso no.2), and membership in the National Institute of Arts and Letters (1937) and in the American Academy of Arts and Letters (1943). In 1958, suffering from cancer, Bloch underwent surgery which proved to be unsuccessful. In spring 1968 an Ernest Bloch Society was established in the USA, largely through the efforts of the three Bloch children, Suzanne, Lucienne, and Ivan. A Bloch Society in London, under the leadership of Alex Cohen, flourished during the late 1930s.

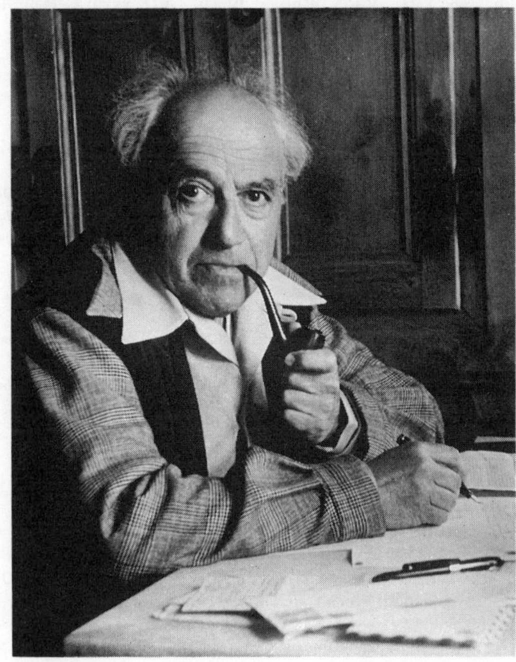

Ernest Bloch, 1949

2. WORKS. The works composed during Bloch's student days in Geneva (e.g., the *Symphonie orientale*) are highly Romantic in style and somewhat undisciplined, often too expansive for the material presented. From the period in Munich and Paris there are two major efforts, the Symphony in C♯ minor and the pair of symphonic poems, *Hiver–Printemps*. Both works are largely derivative, the former influenced by Strauss in melody, harmony, and orchestration, the latter by Debussy in the use of color, particularly in the woodwind and harp solos and in the closing reflective coda.

Macbeth, a lyric drama in seven scenes, produced at the Opéra-Comique in November 1910, established Bloch as a dramatic composer. The work synthesized elements drawn from Wagnerian music-drama, from Debussy's *Pelléas et Mélisande*, and from Mussorgsky's *Boris Godunov* with Bloch's own emerging originality. Certain characteristics are already evident: frequent changes of meter, tempo, and tonality, melodic use of the augmented and perfect 4th at crucial moments, open 4ths and 5ths, cross-relations, modal flavor, dark instrumentation, repeated-note patterns, many ostinatos and pedal points, and ever-present cyclic formal procedures (the last refined and developed through study with Rasse, a pupil of Franck).

With a series of highly-charged epics on a broad scale, biblical in subject and known as the "Jewish Cycle," Bloch's search for a musical identity found fulfillment. In these deeply emotional pieces he painted sweeping musical canvases with a rich and diverse orchestral palette; their oriental or quasi-Hebrew character is heightened by many passages containing the augmented 2nd, as well as by prominent parts for harp and celesta. The Scotch-snap rhythm, with its many variants, is pervasive. In general, little use is made of authentic Hebrew material (the symphony *Israel* is an exception in quoting from the *Song of Songs*), but certain of the characteristics listed above take on a new meaning in the context of the cycle; for example, the repeated-note patterns and the augmented and perfect 4th motifs in *Schelomo* evoke the call of the shofar as it is sounded in the synagogue on the high holy days, while the unfettered rhythmic flow is not unlike that found in much Jewish chant. Further, the frequent accents on the last or penultimate beat of a bar have analogies in the Hebrew language.

After the "Jewish" works, Bloch's adoption of a neoclassical aesthetic is apparent to varying degrees in such works as the two violin sonatas, the First Piano Quintet (which uses quarter-tones in the first and last movements) and in the first Concerto grosso. Even here, however, certain references are revealed (e.g., to the Gregorian mass *Kyrie fons bonitatis* in the Second Violin Sonata or the "Dirge" and "Pastorale" movements of the Concerto grosso). In the 1930s Bloch returned to epic compositions, producing the monumental *Avodath hakodesh* and the Violin Concerto with its American-Indian motto (which also contains the Scotch-snap rhythm). The use of a unifying motto, as in the earlier *America*, became an important structural feature of many of the late works. The compositions after 1941 are essentially a summation of Bloch's compositional career; in the main they are less subjective than those of earlier years. Some may be categorized as neoclassical (the Concerto grosso no.2), some as neoromantic (the *Concerto symphonique* for piano and orchestra), and others as expressionist (the *Sinfonia breve*). These later pieces are generally devoid of the kaleidoscopic and sometimes rhetorical features of the "Jewish Cycle."

Bloch had many distinguished pupils (among them Sessions, Porter, and Rogers), whom he taught to develop and to create according to their individual temperaments and talents. He did not found any school nor did he blaze new paths; he molded into a distinctive style the ingredients he found already in use, including new techniques such as atonality and 12-tone themes. Admitting unashamedly that most of his works were inspired by poetic or philosophical ideas, he proclaimed the primacy of melody in his creative thinking. For Bloch music was a spiritual expression. The quality of Bloch's output is, on the whole, high, particularly in the orchestral and chamber media, where he felt completely at home. The best compositions, with a few exceptions, are those in which he avoided preconceived forms or subject matter; he did not succeed well when his work was selfconscious, as in the two patriotic efforts, *America* and *Helvetia*. His firm beliefs in his own work and his faith in the spirituality of mankind make him a singular figure of 20th-century music.

WORKS

(all pubd unless stated otherwise)

ORCHESTRAL

Helvetia, 1900–29; Chicago, 18 Feb 1932
Symphony in c♯, 1901–2; Geneva, 1910
Hiver–Printemps, sym. poems, 1904–5; New York, 3 Dec 1917
Three Jewish Poems, 1913; Boston, 23 March 1917
Schelomo, vc, orch, 1915–16; New York, 3 May 1917
Suite, va, orch, 1919
In the Night, 1922
Concerto grosso no.1, str, pf obbl, 1924–5; Cleveland, 1 June 1925
Four Episodes, chamber orch, 1926
Voice in the Wilderness, orch, vc obbl, 1936; Los Angeles, 21 Jan 1937
Evocations, 1937; San Francisco, 11 Feb 1938
Violin Concerto, 1937–8; Cleveland, 15 Dec 1938
Suite symphonique, 1944; Philadelphia, 26 Oct 1945
Concerto symphonique, pf, orch, 1947–8; Edinburgh, Scotland, 3 Sept 1949
Scherzo fantasque, pf, orch, 1948; Chicago, 2 Dec 1950
Concertino, fl, va, str, 1950
Suite hébraïque, va/vn, orch, 1951; Chicago, 1 Jan 1953
Concerto grosso no.2, str, str qt, 1952; London, England, 11 April 1953
In memoriam, 1952
Sinfonia breve, 1952; London, England, 11 April 1953
Symphony, trbn, orch, 1954; Houston, 4 April 1956
Symphony in E♭, 1954–5; London, England, 15 Feb 1956
Proclamation, tpt, orch, 1955
Suite modale, fl, str, 1956; Kentfield, CA, 11 April 1965
Two Last Poems, fl, orch, 1958

VOCAL

Historiettes au crépuscule (C. Mauclair), 1v, pf, 1904
Macbeth (opera, 3, E. Fleg, after Shakespeare), 1904–9; Paris, France, 30 Nov 1910
Poèmes d'automne (B. Rodès), Mez, orch, 1906
Israel, 5 solo vv, orch, 1912–16; New York, 3 May 1917
Prelude and Two Psalms (Pss. cxiv, cxxxvii), S, orch, 1912–14
Psalm xxii, A/Bar, orch, 1914
America: an Epic Rhapsody (Bloch), chorus, orch, 1926; New York, 20 Dec 1928
Avodath hakodesh (sacred Heb.), Bar, chorus, orch, 1930–33; Turin, Italy, 12 Jan 1934

CHAMBER

Str Qt no.1, 1916; Pf Qnt no.1, 1921–3; 3 Nocturnes, pf trio, 1924; In the Mountains, str qt, 1925; Night, str qt, 1925; Paysages, str qt, 1925; Prelude, str qt, 1925; 2 Pieces, str qt, 1938–50; Str Qt no.2, 1945; Str Qt no.3, 1952; Str Qt no.4, 1953; Str Qt no.5, 1956; Pf Qnt no.2, 1957

OTHER INSTRUMENTAL

Str: Suite, va, pf, 1919; Vn Sonata no.1, 1920; Baal shem, vn, pf, 1923, orchd 1939; From Jewish Life, vc, pf, 1924; Méditation hébraïque, vc, pf, 1924; Nuit exotique, vn, pf, 1924; Vn Sonata no.2 (Poème mystique), 1924; Abodah, vn, pf, 1929; Melody, vn, pf, 1929; Two Pieces, va, pf, 1951; 3 suites, vc, 1956, 1956, 1957; 2 suites, vn, 1958; Suite, va, 1958
Pf: Ex-voto, 1914; Four Circus Pieces, 1922; In the Night, 1922; Poems of the Sea, 1922, orchd; Danse sacrée, 1923; Enfantines, 1923; Nirvana, 1923; Sonata, 1935; Visions and Prophesies, 1936
Org: 6 Preludes, 1949; Four Wedding Marches, 1950

JUVENILIA 1895–1900

(all unpubd)

Symphonie orientale; Vivre – aimer, sym. poem; Str Qt; Orientale, orch; Vn Conc.; Vc Sonata; Poème concertante, vn, orch; vn pieces incl. Fantaisie, Pastorale; songs incl. Là-bas, Larmes d'automne, Musette, Près de la mer

MSS in *CU-MUSI*, *DLC* [juvenilia]
Principal publishers: American Music, Boosey & Hawkes, Broude, Carisch, Eschig, C. Fischer, Leuckart, Mills, G. Schirmer, Summy-Birchard, Suvini Zerboni

BIBLIOGRAPHY

EwenD
O. Downes: "Ernest Bloch, the Swiss Composer, on the Influence of Race in Composition," *Musical Observer*, xv (1917), 11
G. Gatti: "Ernest Bloch," *MQ*, vii (1921), 20
R. Sessions: "Ernest Bloch," *MM*, v/1 (1927–8), 3
M. Tibaldi-Chiesa: *Ernest Bloch* (Turin, 1933)
——: "The History of Bloch's Macbeth," *Messagerie musicali* [Eng. version] (1939), 1
M. Minsky: *Ernest Bloch and his Music* (diss., George Peabody College, 1945)
D. Newlin: "The Later Works of Ernest Bloch," *MQ*, xxxiii (1947), 443
J. Hastings: "Ernest Bloch and Modern Music," *MR*, x (1949), 115
E. Chapman: "Ernest Bloch at 75," *Tempo*, no.32 (1955), 6
The Music of Ernest Bloch: a Program Manual, ed. National Jewish Music Council (New York, 1956), 44ff
W. M. Jones: *The Music of Ernest Bloch* (diss., Indiana U., 1963)
D. Z. Kushner: *Ernest Bloch and his Symphonic Works* (diss., U. of Michigan, 1967)
M. Griffel: "Bibliography of Writings on Ernest Bloch," *CMc*, no.6 (1968), 142
D. Z. Kushner: "Ernest Bloch: Teacher-Thinker," *American Music Teacher*, xviii/1 (1968), 29
——: "A Singular Ernest Bloch," *MJ*, xxviii/1 (1970), 40, 51, 53
——: "The Revivals of Bloch's Macbeth," *Opera Journal*, iv/2 (1971), 9
——: *Ernest Bloch and his Music* (Glasgow, Scotland, 1973)
E. Raditz: *An Analytical Study of the Violin and Piano Works of Ernest Bloch* (diss., New York U., 1975)
S. Bloch and I. Heskes: *Ernest Bloch, Creative Spirit: a Program Source Book* (New York, 1976)
R. Strassburg: *Ernest Bloch, Voice in the Wilderness: a Biographical Study* (Los Angeles, 1977)
D. Z. Kushner: "Ernest Bloch: a Retrospective on the Centenary of his Birth," *College Music Symposium*, xx/2 (1980), 77
——: "The 'Jewish' Works of Ernest Bloch," *Journal of Musicological Research*, iii/3–4 (1981), 259; repr. in *Journal of Synagogue Music*, xiv/1 (1984), 28
E. Brody: "Romain Rolland and Ernest Bloch," *MQ*, lxviii (1982), 60
D. Z. Kushner: "Ernest Bloch's *Enfantines*," *College Music Symposium*, xxiii/1 (1983), 103
——: "Ernest Bloch: Music Educator," *International Journal of Music Education* (Nov 1984), 37

DAVID Z. KUSHNER

Blomstedt, Herbert (*b* Springfield, MA, 11 July 1927). Swedish conductor. He grew up in Sweden (taking citizenship there), and from 1950 to 1955 studied conducting with Igor Markevich, Jean Morel (at the Juilliard School), and Bernstein (at the Berkshire Music Center, where he won the Koussevitzky conducting prize in 1953). He was music director of a number of Scandinavian orchestras (including the Oslo PO, 1962–8), with which he recorded many Scandinavian compositions, most notably the orchestral works of Nielsen. In 1975 he became music director of the Dresden Staatskapelle. He has toured with that orchestra throughout Europe, Asia, and the USA (1979, 1983). In the USA he has conducted the orchestras of Boston, Los Angeles, Pittsburgh, Minnesota, and San Francisco, as well as the National SO (Washington, DC). He has taught at the Aspen Music School and at the Los Angeles PO Conducting Institute. In 1985 he became music director of the San Francisco SO. Blomstedt's disciplined, fastidious technique results in performances of refreshing clarity, grace, and vision, especially in the standard repertory.

BIBLIOGRAPHY

M. Steinberg: "Making Music with Herbert Blomstedt," *Symphony Magazine*, xxxvi/3 (1985), 69

Blondie. Rock group. Its members were Debbie (Deborah) Harry (*b* Miami, FL, 30 June 1946), singer; Chris Stein (*b* Brooklyn, NY, 5 Jan 1950), guitarist; Jimmy Destri (*b* Brooklyn, 8 April 1954), keyboard player; Frank Infante (*b* Jersey City, NJ), guitarist; Nigel Harrison (*b* Stockport, England), bass guitarist; and Clem(ent) Burke (*b* Bayonne, NJ, 24 Nov 1955), drummer. Harry was the group's most prominent member and, with Stein, its principal songwriter; she began her career as a singer with Wind in the Willows, a folk-rock group. Blondie was formed in New York in 1975, made an LP recording issued by Private Stock the following year, and toured the USA in 1977. Blondie was among the most successful of the new-wave bands, exploiting a pop-art, camp image that helped to defuse the rawness and violence of punk and transform it into a sleek, safe, salable style. This double-edged interpretation of pop culture, at once both subversive and subtly comic, was fully explored on *Parallel Lines* (1978), a tour de force that combined deadpan humor with hidden meanings; the disco remix of *Heart of Glass* from this album reached no. 1 on the American chart and was also an international hit. The group's later work was less consistent, though such experiments as an album-length video (*Eat to the Beat*) and a rap hit (*Rapture*, no. 1, 1981) kept it in the public eye. As its commercial success continued, Blondie dropped some of its defensive comedy, and turned instead to more explicit treatments of global and personal depression, which lacked both the entertainment value and the artistic thrust of the earlier music. From 1980 Stein and Harry began to undertake solo projects: Stein composed the score for the film *Union City* (1980) and in 1981 Harry recorded a solo album, *KooKoo* (Chrysalis 1347), which was produced by Nile Rodgers and Bernard Edwards of Chic; Harry later pursued a career as an actress, and appeared in David Cronenberg's film *Videodrome* (1982). Blondie disbanded in 1982.

RECORDINGS

(selective list; recorded for Chrysalis unless otherwise stated)

Blondie (Private Stock 2023, 1976); *Parallel Lines* (1192, 1978), incl. Heart of Glass; *Plastic Letters* (1166, 1978); *Eat to the Beat* (1225, 1979); *Autoamerican* (1337, 1980), incl. Rapture; *The Hunter* (1384, 1982)

BIBLIOGRAPHY

L. Bangs: *Blondie* (New York, 1980)

JOHN PICCARELLA

Blood [Kainah]. American Indian tribe of Montana, and Alberta, Canada; *see* BLACKFOOT (i).

Blood, Sweat and Tears. Rock group. It was formed in New York in 1968 by Al Kooper (*b* Brooklyn, 5 Feb 1944), a singer, songwriter, keyboard player, and record producer, with seven other musicians; it became popular after Kooper left the band later that year and David Clayton-Thomas (*b* Surrey, England, 13 Sept 1941) became its lead singer. From its inception the group made considerable use of brass instruments and elements drawn from jazz. Its first album, *Child is Father to the Man* (1968), included folk, blues, and pop songs (among them Billie Holiday's *God Bless the Child*), arranged in a style influenced by Maynard Ferguson and Stan Kenton. *Blood, Sweat and Tears* (1968), by far the most successful of the group's albums, won a Grammy Award; three of its songs, *You've made me so very happy*, *And when I die*, and *Spinning Wheel*, reached no.2 on the pop chart in 1969. Clayton-Thomas left the group in 1972 and returned in 1974; it disbanded in 1977. Notwithstanding the influence of jazz on its instrumentation and its attempt to create a jazz-rock fusion, Blood, Sweat and Tears seldom engaged in improvisation; among the ensembles inspired by its music is the group Chicago.

RECORDINGS

(selective list; recorded for Columbia unless otherwise stated)

Child is Father to the Man (9619, 1968); *Blood, Sweat and Tears* (9720, 1968); *3* (30090, 1970); *4* (30590, 1971); *New Blood* (31780, 1972); *No Sweat* (32180, 1973); *Mirror Image* (32929, 1974); *New City* (33484, 1975); *More than Ever* (34233, 1976); *Brand New Day* (ABC 1015, 1977)

STEPHEN HOLDEN

Bloom, Rube (*b* New York, 24 April 1902; *d* New York, 30 March 1976). Popular composer and songwriter. Although self-taught, he became an excellent pianist at an early age and in 1919 began work as an accompanist for vaudeville shows. He worked in dance bands and jazz groups throughout the 1920s, recording with such major artists as Bix Beiderbecke, the Dorsey brothers, Red Nichols, Frankie Trumbauer, Miff Mole, Noble Sissle, and Ethel Waters. In 1928 he was awarded first prize in the Victor Company's contest for his *Song of the Bayou*. He arranged songs for numerous publishing companies during the 1920s and recorded his piano pieces for Victor, Okeh, Harmony, and Cameo. Bloom's best piano music comprises some of the most original work in the novelty-piano idiom. His brilliant *Spring Fever* is still performed by pianists interested in the novelty repertory.

WORKS

(selective list; all printed works published in New York)

Pf: The Futuristic Rag (1923); Soliloquy (1926); Spring Fever (1926); Silhouette (1927); Jumping Jack (collab. B. Seaman and M. Smoley) (1928); Aunt Jemima's Birthday (1931); One-finger Joe (1931); Southern Charms (1931)

Songs: Song of the Bayou (Bloom) (1929); Truckin' (T. Koehler) (1935); Day in, day out (J. Mercer) (1939); Don't worry 'bout me (Koehler) (1939); Fools rush in (Mercer) (1940); Give me the simple life (H. Ruby) (1945); Lost in a dream (E. Leslie) (1949); Here's to my lady (Mercer) (1952)

Principal publishers: Mills, Robbins, Triangle

BIBLIOGRAPHY

D. A. Jasen: *Recorded Ragtime, 1897–1958* (Hamden, CT, 1973)

D. A. Jasen and T. J. Tichenor: *Rags and Ragtime: a Musical History* (New York, 1978)

DAVID THOMAS ROBERTS

Bloomfield, Theodore (Robert) (*b* Cleveland, OH, 14 June 1923). Conductor. After studying conducting (with Maurice Kessler) and piano at the Oberlin College Conservatory (BM 1944) he attended the Juilliard Graduate School where he studied conducting with Edgar Schenkman; further study followed with Arrau and Monteux. He made his début on 9 September 1945 conducting the New York Little SO in Carnegie Recital Hall and was apprentice conductor to Szell for the Cleveland Orchestra's 1946–7 season. He made his European début in Como, Italy, in 1952 and was appointed music director of the Portland (Oregon) SO in 1955. From 1959 to 1963 he was music director of the Rochester PO; he then went to Germany and became principal conductor of the Hamburg Staatsoper. After three seasons as music director of the Frankfurt am Main Opera (1966–8) and several years guest conducting in Europe, he became chief conductor of the Berlin SO (1975–82), winning the Berlin Critics' Circle music prize in 1977. Bloomfield has conducted the premières of works by Bernard Rogers, Ron Nelson, Frank Martin, and Goffredo Petrassi, and the first European performances of works by Avshalomov, Mennin, and Kubik. His interpretations are noted for their balance and clarity, and he has evinced a commitment to introducing rarely performed works by American composers to European audiences.

Bluebeat. Term, used chiefly in Britain, for SKA.

Blue Devils. Jazz band formed by WALTER PAGE in 1925.

Blue Grass Boys. Bluegrass group formed by BILL MONROE in 1938.

Bluegrass music. A style of COUNTRY MUSIC that grew in the 1940s from the music of Bill Monroe and his group, the Blue Grass Boys. It combines elements of dance, home entertainment, and religious folk music of the rural Southeast. A bluegrass band typically consists of four to seven individuals who sing and accompany themselves on acoustic string instruments: two rhythm instruments (guitar and double bass) and several melody instruments (fiddle, five-string banjo, mandolin, steel guitar, and second guitar). Lead instrumentalists take solo breaks between verses of a song and provide a harmonic and rhythmic background often in a responsorial relationship to the vocal part. Instrumental works have alternating solos as in jazz. Notable performers who have initiated bluegrass instrumental techniques are Earl Scruggs (banjo) and Monroe (mandolin). The vocal range of bluegrass music is higher than most country music singing, often reaching c''. In vocal duets the second (tenor) part lies above the melody; trios include a baritone part below the melody. In religious songs a fourth (bass) part is added. Usually these parts are harmonic, but in duets particularly they provide vocal counterpoint. The music is mostly in duple meter with emphasis on the offbeats. Tempos are generally fast: an average slow song has 160 quarter-notes per minute, a fast one 330.

The bluegrass repertory includes traditional folksongs but is dominated by newly composed music – sentimentally reminiscent secular songs, religious spirituals, revival hymns, and instrumental numbers. Phonograph records have always been important for disseminating the repertory and style. In the 1940s most groups played on the radio and toured rural communities in the South. During the 1950s they appeared on television and in so-called "hillbilly bars" in the urban Northeast. In the 1960s the folksong revival opened college concert halls, coffee houses, and folk festivals to bluegrass performers, and in 1965 Carlton Haney established the First Annual Blue Grass Festival in Fincastle, Virginia, the prototype for many such yearly events nationwide. During the 1970s and 1980s bluegrass music included many styles, from "traditional" bands – such as the Johnson Mountain Boys and Larry Sparks and the Lonesome Ramblers – performing the 1945–55 repertory to "progressive" and "newgrass" groups – such as the Seldom Scene and New Grass Revival – that combine

Bill Monroe and the Blue Grass Boys, mid-1970s, including Kenny Baker (fiddle), Monroe (mandolin), Bill Box (guitar), and Randy Davis (double bass)

rock songs and techniques with bluegrass instrumentation and performing style.

See also WASHINGTON, §5.

BIBLIOGRAPHY

L. M. Smith: "An Introduction to Bluegrass," *Journal of American Folklore*, lxxviii (1965), 245

N. V. Rosenberg: "From Sound to Style: the Emergence of Bluegrass," *Journal of American Folklore*, lxxx (1967), 143

G. O. Carney: "Bluegrass Grows all Around: the Spatial Dimensions of a Country Music Style," *Journal of Geography*, lxxiii (1974), 34

H. W. Marshall: "'Keep on the Sunny Side of Life:' Pattern and Religious Expression in Bluegrass Gospel Music," *New York Folklore Quarterly*, xxx (1974), 3–43

B. Artis: *Bluegrass* (New York, 1975)

C. K. Wolfe: *Kentucky Country* (Lexington, KY, 1982)

R. Cantwell: *Bluegrass Breakdown* (Urbana, IL, 1984)

N. V. Rosenberg: *Bluegrass: a History* (Urbana, IL, 1985)

NEIL V. ROSENBERG/R

Blue Jay Singers. Gospel quartet. It was organized in 1926 by Clarence Parnell, a pioneer figure in the black gospel-quartet tradition, and by the mid-1930s had become the most popular group of its type in the deep South. Besides Parnell (bass), its original members were Silas Steele (lead), Jimmie Hollingsworth (tenor), and Charlie Beale (baritone). Steele in particular became a model for other gospel-quartet soloists. Although the group was known for its "sweet" style of singing, performing in close harmony in a style reminiscent of early barbershop quartets, towards the end of the 1930s it adopted a more aggressive manner; the singers are regarded as the progenitors of the "hard" gospel style in vogue among quartets by 1950 (*see* GOSPEL MUSIC, §II, 2 (iii)). After moving to Chicago in the early 1940s, they helped to develop the midwestern "clank-a-lanka" style of gospel music (named after a rhythmic quartet response to the leader's solo). The Blue Jay Singers flourished until the 1960s, including among its later members Nathaniel Edmonds, Charles Bridges, and Willie Rose.

BIBLIOGRAPHY

Black American Quartet Traditions (Washington, DC, 1981)

Liner notes, *Birmingham Quartet Anthology: Jefferson County, Alabama, 1926–1953* (Clanka Lanka, 1981)

HORACE CLARENCE BOYER

Blue note. A microtonal lowering or "bending" of the third, seventh, or (less commonly) fifth degree of the diatonic scale, common in blues, jazz, and related musics. The pitch or intonation of blue notes is not fixed precisely but varies according to the performer's instinct and expression. Together with other, non-inflected pitches they make up the blues scale.

The origin of blue notes has been the subject of much speculation, and will probably never be clarified. Traditionally they were attributed to the difficulty experienced by the American slaves in adapting West African pentatonicism to European diatonicism, which caused them to invent two new scale degrees of indistinct pitch. However, the proponents of this view overlook the fact that some West African scales are diatonic, and that pitch inflection occurs in West African music and may thus form part of the African heritage of the blues. Further, they misrepresent the early blues scale as diatonic, whereas in practice it is a pentatonic scale (ex. 1, blue notes marked by asterisks) in which

Ex.1

the diatonic second and sixth degrees occur occasionally as extra-scalar passing notes and all scale degrees may be inflected to some extent. Whatever their origins, blue notes are universally associated with black-American music in North America, and are unaccountably absent from other Afro-American musics of the western hemisphere. (For a different interpretation, *see* AFRO-AMERICAN MUSIC, §5.)

The blues scale in jazz differs from that shown in ex. 1, being in essence merely the diatonic scale to which inflected third, fifth, and seventh degrees may be added to impart a blues flavor (ex. 2). The inflected fifth degree is rare in blues performances

Ex.2

and seems to have been invented by early jazz musicians by aural analogy with the blues. Blue notes were common in jazz from the earliest times, and have long been used as a criterion for separating authentic early jazz from jazz-related commercial music of the day. At first they were apparently associated with particular pitches (notably C♯–D in the key of B♭) and were not transposable, which probably indicates their dependence on certain characteristic instrumental fingerings; later, as jazz musicians gained greater fluency in remote keys, blue notes could be heard on other pitches as well. Eventually blues-like inflections were applied to other degrees of the scale, as can be heard in the "Saeta" from Miles Davis's *Sketches of Spain* (1959–60) and above all in the work of Ornette Coleman, who from the early 1960s applied blue-note inflections to all degrees of the chromatic scale. The characteristic sound of blue notes has also left an imprint on jazz harmony, examples being the familiar augmented 9th and augmented 11th chords whose semitone clashes may represent an attempt to "verticalize" the ambiguous pitch level of the third- and fifth-degree blue notes (ex. 3). Blue notes have

Ex.3

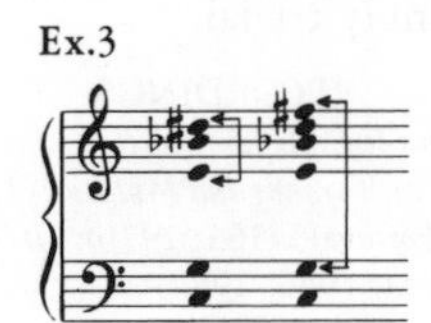

Ex.4

also influenced jazz pianism (where microtonal inflections are physically impossible), whether in the "crushed" notes familiar from the blues and boogie-woogie styles or in more complex figurations such as ex. 4, a pianistic equivalent of the "whinnying" vibrato of blues guitarists.

BIBLIOGRAPHY

W. Sargeant: "The Scalar Structure of Jazz," "The Derivations of the Blues," *Jazz: Hot and Hybrid* (New York, 1938/*R*1975)

E. Bornemann: "The Roots of Jazz," *Jazz*, ed. N. Hentoff and A. J. McCarthy (New York, 1959/*R*1974)

L. A. Pyke: *Jazz, 1920 to 1927: an Analytical Study* (diss., U. of Iowa, 1962), 78ff
G. Schuller: *Early Jazz: its Roots and Musical Development* (New York, 1968), 43ff
G. Bohländer and K. H. Holler: *Reclams Jazzführer* (Stuttgart, Germany, 1970), 740ff
J. Fahey: *Charley Patton* (London, 1970), 38ff
J. Shepherd and others: *Whose Music?* (London, 1977), 166ff

J. BRADFORD ROBINSON

Blue Notes. *See* MELVIN, HAROLD, AND THE BLUE NOTES.

Blue Oyster Cult. Rock group. Its members are Eric Bloom, singer, guitarist, and keyboard player; Donald "Buck Dharma" Roeser, guitarist and singer; Albert Bouchard, drummer and singer; Joseph Bouchard, bass guitarist; and Allen Lanier, guitarist, keyboard player, and singer. Roeser, Lanier, and Albert Bouchard belonged in the late 1960s to a group called Soft White Underbelly. Blue Oyster Cult was formed at SUNY, Stony Brook, in 1971. Under manager Sandy Pearlman and producer Murray Krugman, they have made recordings that both epitomize and parody the mystical elements of rock and its occult pretensions by the use of elaborate religious and military symbolism. All the members of the band, as well as Pearlman, are capable songwriters, but they have also used lyrics by the rock critic R. Meltzer and the rock singer Patti Smith. The albums *Blue Oyster Cult* (1972), *Tyranny and Mutation* (1973), and *Secret Treaties* (1974) are all characterized by Roeser's superior guitar playing, a heavy beat, vocal harmonies like those of pop songs, and eerie, fantastic lyrics. *Agents of Fortune* (1976) was a commercial success and gave the group the hit single *Don't fear the reaper*; the group's live performances from that time had to be given in large arenas and used elaborate electronic equipment and laser light. Originally a group that appealed chiefly to critics, by the early 1980s Blue Oyster Cult had a large audience of young people and had become the most sophisticated of the heavy-metal bands. Their studio recordings continued to display complexity and polish, but their songs became increasingly trivial.

RECORDINGS

(selective list; all recorded for Columbia)

Blue Oyster Cult (31063, 1972); *Tyranny and Mutation* (32017, 1973); *Secret Treaties* (32858, 1974); *Agents of Fortune* (34164, 1976); *Fire of Unknown Origin* (37389, 1981); *Extraterrestrial Live* (37946, 1982)

JOHN PICCARELLA

Blues. A secular black-American folk music of the 20th century, which has a history and evolution separate from, but sometimes related to, that of jazz. From obscure and largely undocumented rural American origins it became the most extensively recorded of all folk-music types. It has been subject to social changes that have affected its character. Since the early 1960s, blues has been the most important single influence on the development of Western popular music (*see* AFRO-AMERICAN MUSIC and POPULAR MUSIC).

1. Definition. 2. Origins. 3. The 1920s: first recordings. 4. Piano blues and the northern migration. 5. 1930s blues. 6. Urban blues. 7. Postwar blues. 8. Blues and the white audience. 9. Conclusion.

1. DEFINITION. The most important extra-musical meaning of "blues" refers to a state of mind. Since the 16th century "the blue devils" has meant a condition of melancholy or depression. But "the blues" did not enter popular American usage until after the Civil War; and as a description of music that expressed such a mental state among Blacks it may not have gained currency until after 1900. The two meanings are closely related in the history of the blues as music, and it is generally understood that a blues performer sings or plays to rid himself of "the blues." This is so important to blues musicians that many maintain one cannot play the music unless one has "a blue feeling" or "feels blue." Indeed, the blues is considered a perpetual presence in the lives of black Americans and is frequently personified in their music as "Mister Blues." It follows that "blues" can also mean a way of performing. Many jazz players of all schools have held that a musician's ability to play blues expressively is a measure of his quality. Within blues as folk music this ability is the essence of the art; a singer or performer who does not express "blues" feeling is not a "bluesman." Certain qualities of timbre employing rasp or growl techniques are associated with this manner of expression; the timbre as well as the flattened and "shaded" notes (produced by microtonal deviations from standard temperament; *see* BLUE NOTE) so distinctive to the blues can be simulated, but not, its exponents contend, blues feeling.

As the blues was created largely by illiterate musicians, scarcely any of whom could read music, improvisation, both verbal and musical, was an essential part of it, though not to the extent that it was in jazz. To facilitate improvisation a number of patterns evolved, of which the most familiar is the 12-bar blues (*see* BLUES PROGRESSION). Apparently this form crystallized in the first decade of the 20th century as a three-line stanza in which the second line repeated the first, thus enabling the blues singer to improvise a third, rhyming line while singing the second. This structure was supported by a fixed harmonic progression, which all blues performers knew and which they played almost automatically: it consists of four bars on the tonic, of which two might accompany singing and the fourth might introduce a flattened seventh; two bars on the subdominant, usually accompanying singing, followed by two further bars on the tonic; two bars on the dominant seventh, accompanying the rhyming line of the vocal part; and two concluding bars on the tonic. Such a progression could be played in any key, though blues guitarists favored E or A and jazz musicians B♭. Many variants exist, but this pattern is so widely known that "playing the blues" generally presupposes the use of it.

The term "blues" is also used to identify a composition that uses blues harmonic and phrase structure but which is intended to be performed as written, such as *Dallas Blues* (1912) by Hart Wand and Lloyd Garret, the first to use the form, or *St. Louis Blues* (1914) by W. C. Handy. There are numerous compositions that are in no way related to blues but that bear the name, like *Limehouse Blues* (1924) by Douglas Furber and Philip Braham. Published compositions in blues form, while at first bringing a new sound to a larger audience, contributed much to the confusion about the nature of blues as folk music, and helped to link the term in the popular mind with jazz. This association with jazz has retarded blues research and the independent consideration of its origins, traditions, forms, and exponents. Only since 1960 has it been extensively discussed in its own right.

2. ORIGINS. In its early years the blues was wholly black American. It has been suggested that it existed before the Civil War, but this view has no supporting evidence. Influential in its development were the collective unaccompanied WORK SONGS of the plantation culture, which followed a responsorial "leader-and-chorus" form that can be traced not only to pre-Civil War

origins but to African sources. Responsorial work songs died out when the plantations were broken up, but persisted in the southern penitentiary farms until the 1950s. After the Reconstruction era black workers either engaged in seasonal collective labor in the South or tended smallholdings leased to them by the system of debt-serfdom known as sharecropping. Work songs therefore increasingly took the form of solo calls or "hollers," comparatively free in form but close to blues in feeling. The vocal style of the blues probably derived from the holler (*see* FIELD HOLLER).

Blues instrumental style shows tenuous links with African music. Drumming was forbidden on slave plantations, but the playing of string instruments was often permitted and even encouraged, so the music of Africans from the savannah regions, with their strong traditions of string playing, predominated. The *jelli*, or *griots* – professional musicians who also acted as their tribe's historians and social commentators – performed roles not unlike those of the later blues singers. The banjo was a direct descendant of their *bania* or *khalam*.

In the 1890s the post-Reconstruction bitterness of southern Whites towards Blacks hardened into segregation laws; this in a sense forced the black communities to recognize their own identity, and a flowering of black sacred and secular music followed. Ballads in traditional British form extolling the exploits of black heroes (e.g., *John Henry*, *John Hardy*, *Po' Lazarus*, and *Duncan and Brady*) were part of this musical expansion, and blues emerged from the combination of freely expressive hollers with the music of these ballads. Few blues were noted by early 20th-century collectors, but those collected frequently had a four-line or rhyming-couplet form. Some of the ballads popular among black singers, for example *Railroad Bill*, *Frankie and Albert*, *Duncan and Brady*, and *Stack O'Lee*, had a single couplet with a rhyming third line as a refrain; in blues the "couplet" consisted of one repeated line:

> I'm troubled in mind, baby, feelin' blue and sad
> I'm troubled in mind, baby, feelin' blue and sad.
> The blues ain't nothin' but a good man feelin' bad.

See, See Rider, *Joe Turner Blues*, and *Hesitating Blues* were among the earliest songs of this type.

At first the blues was probably only a new song form in the repertory of the black songster (*see* SONGSTER (ii)), the titles providing a theme for a loose arrangement of verses (e.g., *Florida Blues*, *Atlanta Blues*, and *Railroad Blues*). Many songsters and early blues singers in the South worked in medicine shows, street entertainments promoted by vendors of patent medicines. Their travels helped to spread the blues, as did those of wandering singers who sang and played for a living. They followed the example of the street evangelists who at that time were popularizing gospel songs. By preferring the guitar to the banjo as an accompanying instrument the songsters represent a link between the older black song tradition and the blues. By the 1920s the blues singer, who sang and played only blues, began to replace the songster.

Blues songs had no fixed number of stanzas, and the inevitable return to the tonic after the stanza's third line gave shape to long improvisations. The ballad singers had concentrated on the exploits of legendary black heroes, but blues singers sang of themselves and those who shared their experiences. Many stanzas rapidly became traditional and certain images or lines entered the stock-in-trade of every blues singer. But the inventive singer expressed his anxieties, frustrations, hopes, or resignation through his songs. Some blues described disasters or personal accidents; themes of crime, prostitution, gambling, alcohol, and imprisonment are

1. Ma Rainey with her Georgia Jazz Band, c1924, with Thomas A. Dorsey (piano), Al Wynn (trombone), and Ed Pollock (trumpet)

2. *Blind Lemon Jefferson, c1929*

prominent in early examples and have persisted ever since. Some blues are tender but few reveal a response to nature; far more express a desire to move or escape by train or road to an imagined better land. Many are aggressively sexual, and there is much that is consciously and subconsciously symbolic of frustration and oppression.

3. THE 1920S: FIRST RECORDINGS. The earliest forms of blues were not the first to be recorded. Mamie Smith's recording of *Crazy Blues* (OK 4169) in August 1920 brought a popularized form to a large audience; Smith was a stage performer, and her blues, accompanied by a jazz band, were sung in vaudeville fashion. They set the pattern for numerous recordings by Edith Wilson, Sara Martin, Clara Smith, and many other black singers, most of whom were professional entertainers working with touring shows on the circuit of the Theater Owners Booking Agency, which managed black artists. Among them were singers whose songs were blues in name only; but others had a deep feeling for the new idiom, including Lottie Beamon from Kansas City, Missouri, and Ma Rainey from Athens, Georgia, both stocky women with powerful voices, as well as Ida Cox from Knoxville, Tennessee, who was much admired for her nasal intonation. But the "Empress of the Blues," as she came to be called, was Bessie Smith from Chattanooga, whose majestic recordings set a standard that few could emulate.

Many of these so-called "classic" blues singers came from the South or from border states and had heard rural singers whose blues they borrowed. Published blues, which had been available for some years, were performed with jazz band accompaniment to audiences in northern cities. With Papa Charlie Jackson's *Papa's Lawdy Lawdy Blues* (Para. 12219), recorded with banjo accompaniment in 1924, the recording industry began to make known the songs of the country tradition. Jackson's style was simple and his technique that of the songsters, but *Long Lonesome Blues* (1926, Para. 12354) by Blind Lemon Jefferson from Texas, had the authentic sound of rural blues.

Mississippi has been popularly regarded as the birthplace of blues and has been the source of many of the earthiest, least sophisticated recordings. Most Mississippi singers were guitarists who played a heavily accented accompaniment to their frequently guttural and always expressive singing. The most influential blues singer from the state was Charley Patton, who initiated a school of singer–guitarists on Dockery's plantation, near Clarksdale, before World War I. He influenced Tommy Johnson from the Jackson area, and they represented distinct, though linked, Mississippi styles: Patton, Son House, and Henry Sims, and their successors, Tommy McClennan and Bukka White, performed with deep, "heavy" voices and strong, persistent rhythms, while Johnson, Ishmon Bracey, and Bo Carter and the related Chatmon family used more complex, lighter rhythmic patterns and sang in higher voices, often using falsetto for final syllables. Bo Carter and the Chatmons had a string band called the Mississippi Sheiks which played blues and other forms of country music and was a link with the earlier songster tradition. In Memphis, north of the Mississippi delta region, similar bands were formed in which a jug was often played as a bass instrument (*see* JUG BAND and WASHBOARD BAND). Ensembles using improvised instruments to augment strings were started in many small towns, most notably in Memphis.

The Texas approach to blues was exemplified by Blind Lemon Jefferson. His words were original and often poetic:

> Sittin' here wondrin', will a match-box hold my clo's?
> Sittin' here wondrin', will a match-box hold my clo's?
> Ain't got so many matches, but I got so far to go.

This was one of the many images he created that passed into folk usage. Rambling Thomas followed his use of long lines, and his use of the guitar as an expressive "second voice" answering the words of the vocal line. Alger Texas Alexander was so close to the holler tradition that he did not play an instrument at all, but on his best recordings he was accompanied on the guitar by Lonnie Johnson from New Orleans, who worked in Texas, or Dennis "Little Hat" Jones from San Antonio.

Mobile units, notably those of Columbia, Victor, and Okeh, made field recordings of many singers who would otherwise have remained unknown. Some singers made few recordings, perhaps giving a false impression of their abilities. As only a few centers were used, vast areas of the South were unrepresented: hardly any recordings were made in the 1920s in Alabama, Arkansas, or Florida. In Atlanta, Georgia, a school of 12-string guitar players with rich voices was recorded: among them were Barbecue Bob Hicks, his brother Charlie Lincoln, Curley Weaver, Peg Leg Howell, and Blind Willie McTell. Several of them employed a knife, bottleneck or other slide to press the strings against the frets of their guitars. Some tuned their guitars to an open chord, producing a "cross-note" tuning, which enabled them to press the slide against all the strings while playing a blues sequence. By moving the slide along the frets, whining, mournful sounds in keeping with blues feeling could be produced. This adaptability of the guitar made it a favorite instrument of blues singers.

Of the early southern singers only a few women were recorded. Among them were Bessie Tucker, a powerful-voiced singer from Texas whose songs were largely about prison, and Lucille Bogan (Bessie Jackson) from Birmingham, Alabama, who sang robust blues about prostitution and lesbianism. The most notable was Memphis Minnie who, in Big Bill Broonzy's words, "played the guitar like a man." These women were admired for the masculinity of their musical attack: traditional femininity was replaced by a bragging sexuality.

4. Piano blues and the northern migration. The shadings and inflections of the blues can be obtained relatively simply on a guitar, but the blues pianist can produce the effect of blues grace notes and glissandos only by "crushing" the keys (striking them not quite simultaneously) and the effect of blues rhythm only by syncopation and strongly accented rhythmic phrases. Blues piano style may have derived partly from ragtime: the form known as Barrelhouse has affinities with improvised rags. Many blues pianists from Texas and Louisiana played in the makeshift lumber-camp saloons where barrelhouse style originated; among them was Little Brother Montgomery, who was an exponent of the *Vicksburg Blues* (1930, Para. 13006), a standard basis for extemporization with a climbing bass figure. His contemporary from Arkansas, Roosevelt Sykes, recorded it in 1929 under the alternative name of *44 Blues* (OK 8702).

Bass figures were important in the development of piano blues; the "walking" bass of broken or spread octaves repeated through the blues progression provided the ground to countless improvisations. Charles "Cow Cow" Davenport's recordings, including *Cow Cow Blues* (1928, Bruns. 80022), illustrate facets of the early piano blues that were unified in the playing of his protégé, Pine Top Smith, who popularized the name boogie-woogie (*see* Boogie-woogie (i)). Both went to Chicago from the South, as did hundreds of other blues singers, pianists, guitarists, and other instrumentalists in the decade after World War I. The many immigrants forced up rent prices in Chicago and Detroit, and pianists played for beer and tips at "rent parties" organized for mutual aid in the tenements. These became schools for other pianists, among them Meade "Lux" Lewis.

The many blues teams formed in Chicago included that of the pianist Georgia Tom Dorsey (see fig. 1) and the guitarist Tampa Red (Hudson Whittaker), who were both from Georgia but had worked with Ma Rainey. The combination of blues and vaudeville experience led them to a vein of "hokum," a combination of rural wit, sly urban sophistication, and bawdiness; it was a new type of blues, entertainment without serious intent, which mildly ridiculed country manners while helping southern immigrants to adjust to urban life. With Big Bill Broonzy, another member of the Hokum Boys, Georgia Tom and Tampa Red managed to go on making recordings when the financial crash of October 1929 stopped most blues recording.

5. 1930s blues. In the early 1930s the most popular blues singer was Leroy Carr, a pianist who was accompanied with uncanny rapport by the guitarist Scrapper Blackwell. Their approach had a strong southern character, but their lyrics had a considered, reflective quality, colored by disappointment rather than bitterness and reflecting the mood of many of their listeners. Carr was widely copied, and his classic performances, such as *How Long, How Long Blues* (1928, Voc. 1191) and *Midnight Hour Blues* (1932, Voc. 1703), were recorded by numerous singers, even in the 1970s, long after his death in 1935. The fatalism of his works is also found in those of his principal imitator, Bumble Bee Slim (Amos Easton), and of Walter Davis, a pianist based in St. Louis. Both had somewhat flat voices and a far less impassioned delivery than that of the previous generation of blues singers. Many of the 1930s blues are characterized by a cynicism prompted by the difficulties of the Depression. Several singers of this period were based in St. Louis, midway between North and South, and their blues reflected both southern and northern attitudes. Although he was still recording in 1934 (the year of his death), Charley Patton in Mississippi was already outdated, and 16 titles he made that year remained unissued. His generation of Mississippi bluesmen, including Tommy Johnson, Ishmon Bracey, and Son House, was still active but unrecorded; the cooler, less emotional singers of the younger generation had taken over. So it is perhaps surprising that a singer like Sleepy John Estes from Brownsville, Tennessee, with a country guitar and cracked voice, singing extremely parochial lyrics, should have been as extensively recorded as he was. He had a counterpart further east in Tennessee and the Carolinas in Blind Boy Fuller, a street singer with a gritty voice and ragtime guitar style. He was accompanied by a brilliant harmonica virtuoso, Sonny Terry; Estes was no less sympathetically supported by his own harmonica player, Hammie Nixon.

6. Urban blues. In Chicago the tough conditions of the 1930s stimulated a more aggressive, extrovert blues sound and collective performance. Tampa Red recorded some 200 titles in the decade, augmenting his plangent guitar with the heavier sound of his Chicago Five band. Its personnel varied but generally included Black Bob or Blind John Davis playing the piano, with other instruments such as tenor saxophone or trumpet taking the lead. A new departure in blues, it was followed by Big Bill Broonzy, the undisputed leader of Chicago folk music in the 1930s. Broonzy's groups were always subordinate to his singing and immaculate guitar playing, but he was the center of a school of urban singers of southern origin, including his reputed half-brother Robert Brown, known as Washboard Sam. Sam's washboard playing was matched by his loud, rough voice, and Broonzy often played in his groups. They were frequently joined by Sonny Boy Williamson (i), a highly influential harmonica player with a distinctive "tongue-tied" voice, who recorded extensively under his own name, and William "Jazz" Gillum, who also played the harmonica. Together they created an outgoing, topical form of

3. Leroy Carr (seated) and Scrapper Blackwell, c1934

4. *Washboard Sam, 1940s*

blues that did not lose its sense of contact with those newly arrived from the South, though the sound was essentially that of Southside Chicago.

In contrast to these developments in urban blues, a new generation of "down-home" singers from Mississippi, with a style firmly rooted in the Patton–House tradition, began to be recorded as the decade came to a close. Their blues were coarser and fiercer than their predecessors' and provided a powerful stimulus for the blues in the early 1940s, when the JIVE music of Louis Jordan and his contemporaries was reducing the stature of the blues with humorous novelty pieces intended only as entertainment. These later Mississippi singers included Tommy McClennan, Robert Petway, Bukka White, and above all Robert Johnson, who had the most lasting influence on the evolution of the blues. While still in his early 20s (1936–7) he recorded some 30 titles shortly before his death; these highly introverted, sometimes obsessive blues, with a whining guitar sound and throbbing beat, made a profound impression even on singers who recorded more than 20 years later. If one artist epitomized the range of performance and attitudes of the blues in the 1930s it was probably Broonzy, but the most memorable creations came from the singing and playing of Carr and Johnson.

7. POSTWAR BLUES. Until the end of World War II the recording of blues had been controlled by a few large companies, but in the late 1940s small companies, many owned by Blacks, started commercial production. Some were in southern cities like Memphis and Houston, some on the West Coast, where a smooth style of blues created by westward-moving migrants from Texas found a new market. New concerns also operated in Chicago and Detroit, so the combined output of blues records was considerable. Until then blues recordings had been classified and marketed as race records (*see* RACE RECORD). This segregation, which even entered sales catalogues, contributed to the development of postwar RHYTHM-AND-BLUES, a term free of racial connotations. Rhythm-and-blues encompassed many kinds of blues and related music, from the soft-toned West coast blues of Charles Brown to the technically brilliant guitar playing of T-Bone Walker. But, like the related rock-and-roll (*see* POPULAR MUSIC, §IV), it encompassed much else besides, including the harmonizing of the rhythm-and-blues quartets, the popular, nostalgic, blues-based vocals of the New Orleans pianist Fats Domino, the frenetic performances of Little Richard, and the witty lyrics of Chuck Berry and Bo Diddley. Their music was on the fringe of blues and thus outside the scope of a discussion of its main traditions.

Of postwar blues singers among the most notable is Muddy Waters (McKinley Morganfield). His early manner (as seen in his Chicago recordings of 1947) owed much to Robert Johnson, but he soon added a harmonica (Little Walter) and a piano, guitar, or drums to fill out the sound, as the Broonzy–Williamson groups had done. In the 1950s his music became increasingly threatening, with hoarse singing, slow blues–boogie piano playing by Otis Spann, and the complementary warbling harmonica of Little Walter, Walter Horton, or James Cotton. With all instruments amplified, the live sound was highly charged, and the recordings sold in large numbers. Muddy Waters's principal rival was Howlin' Wolf (Chester Burnett) – romantic sobriquets were still expected of blues singers. Howlin' Wolf developed a ferocious and energetic style, shown for instance in *Smokestack Lightnin'* (1956, Chess 1618). He derived much of his style from Charley Patton, whereas Robert Johnson inspired Elmore James, who was in many ways the archetypal postwar Chicago blues singer. James was technically quite limited, depending on a bottleneck slide and rhythms formulated by Johnson; he sang in a taut, constricted voice and, like many singers of his generation, paid greater attention to projection and volume than to content and subtle expression. This reflects a general change in the relationship of the blues singer to his audience: though "blues" still signified both music and mood, there was greater emphasis on performance to audiences, and lyrics became more stereotyped and less personal to the singer.

Many other southern blues singers were popular in the 1950s, among them John Lee Hooker, who left Mississippi to settle in Detroit and developed his own heavily accented guitar technique. Another was Jimmy Reed, whose loose vocals against insistent rhythms set him somewhat apart from his contemporaries but made him very popular with black audiences. In Texas, Lightnin' Hopkins extended the tradition of Blind Lemon Jefferson, dominating blues in that state. Even when the young, more urban singers from Memphis, Bobbie Bland and Little Junior Parker, settled in Texas to work and record, Hopkins did not lose his position.

8. BLUES AND THE WHITE AUDIENCE. Within jazz criticism blues had been treated with some respect, though it was seen as a precursor of jazz rather than as a distinct musical style with a parallel evolution. Leadbelly (Huddie Ledbetter), though primarily a songster, was widely acclaimed in New York in the 1940s among jazz enthusiasts and mourned at his death (1949) as "the last of the blues singers." This of course was not the case, not even in jazz itself, for the blues singers Joe Turner and Jimmy Rushing continued to sing in jazz groups, and blues recordings were prominent in rhythm-and-blues in the 1950s. When Big Bill Broonzy went to Europe in the early 1950s he too was seen as a rare survivor of the blues tradition; he helped to stimulate the growing interest in blues by the publication of his autobiography (1955). Soon after his death (1958) the team of Brownie

McGhee and Sonny Terry went to Europe, and during the 1960s a succession of blues singers visited Britain and the Continent; some remained, among them the pianists Memphis Slim, Eddie Boyd, Curtis Jones, and Champion Jack Dupree.

In 1959–60 the first serious studies of blues were published and field trips for research were undertaken, largely by Europeans. During the following years strenuous efforts were made to find early blues singers, with the result that Fred McDowell, Robert Pete Williams, Mance Lipscomb, and Robert Shaw were recorded for the first time, and Mississippi John Hurt, Bukka White, Sleepy John Estes, Son House, and others were rediscovered. Many veteran singers toured Europe, where they played to large and enthusiastic audiences. Skiffle, a quasi-country blues band music, had a fleeting popularity in Britain when Broonzy was alive, and the later visits of blues singers, the publication of many studies and magazines on the subject, the availability of recordings, and the consciousness of a "generation gap" (which seemed to parallel the segregation of Blacks in the USA) all contributed to the emergence of British pop groups whose early work was strongly influenced by blues. Of these the Beatles were the best known, but the Rolling Stones, the Animals, and the Who owed more to blues. Blues-based pop music was loud, heavily amplified, and augmented with sound-distorting devices; the performers were extravagantly dressed, and deliberately challenged established pop music. A similar movement followed in the USA, where the young musicians were, theoretically, closer to blues artists. Paul Butterfield, Mike Bloomfield, and the group Canned Heat depended closely on postwar blues based on the Chicago style.

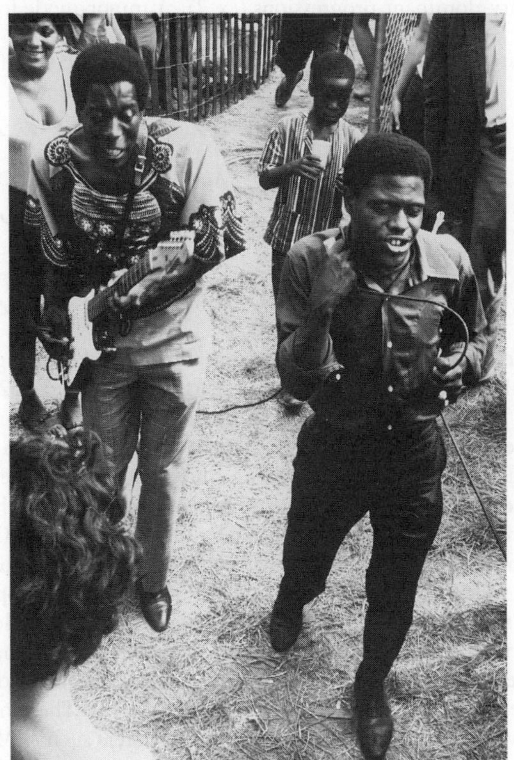

5. Buddy Guy (left) and Junior Wells at the Ann Arbor Blues Festival, 1970

9. Conclusion. The kindling of white interest in black music always presages or coincides with a departure from the idiom by the black population; when blues gained white enthusiasts it lost black audiences. Some singers, for example Otis Rush and J. B. Hutto, retained their integrity as artists, taking daytime jobs and performing in clubs when they could. Fortunate blues singers toured American universities; others returned to truck driving or crop raising. In black America Soul music predominated, with its gospel techniques and some element of blues expression. Few blues singers retained their following in the soul era; the most prominent was B. B. King, an articulate, expressive, technically accomplished guitarist with a large following. His namesakes Albert King and Freddie King worked in a similar vein, appearing at the large open-air concerts of the 1970s. Other singers of a younger generation, including Buddy Guy and Junior Wells, used the vocal techniques and stage mannerisms of soul singing, but they too were most successful performing at universities. In the mid-1970s there were only a few blues singers working steadily, and their audiences were mainly white, though the blues had gained an international audience, and blues singers were sponsored by the State Department for tours in Africa and Asia. A few black singers, notably Taj Mahal, departed from a sophisticated popular style to find some satisfaction in traditional blues, but they cannot be said to represent the culture in the sense that Jefferson, Carr, Johnson, or Muddy Waters once did. By 1980, however, there were signs of a renewed interest in blues in black communities as far apart as Chicago, Memphis, Houston, and Oakland, while younger Blacks who had formerly rejected the music were beginning to recognize it as part of their cultural inheritance. Soul-blues singer-guitarists such as Johnny Copeland, Z. Z. Hill, and Robert Cray have been welcomed in recent years. Though blues may not be a folk music for much longer it may survive as an ethnic art form.

Assessment of the importance of the blues in 20th-century American folk music has often been made in relation to jazz or to pop music. As a music of the people it had its mediocre exponents, but within the extensive corpus of recordings there are innumerable examples of folk compositions of genius and beauty, expressions of the human spirit that are both profoundly moving and complete in themselves as creative works. It is music that will increasingly be valued in its own right. Blues singers and musicians extended the expressive range of the guitar, piano, harmonica, and human voice and evolved many musical substructures within the framework of a recognizable and distinct idiom. Blues was also important as the primary artistic expression of a minority culture: it was created mainly by black working-class men and women, and, through its simplicity, sensuality, poetry, humor, irony, and resignation transmuted to aggressive declamation, it mirrored the qualities and the attitudes of black America for three-quarters of a century.

See also Jazz, §§II, 2, III, 6.

BIBLIOGRAPHY

H. W. Odum and G. B. Johnson: *The Negro and his Songs* (Chapel Hill, 1925)
R. Blesh: *Shining Trumpets* (New York, 1946/*R*1975), chaps.4–6
S. B. Charters: *The Country Blues* (New York, 1959/*R*1975)
P. Oliver: *Blues Fell this Morning* (London, 1960)
H. Courlander: *Negro Folk Music U.S.A.* (New York, 1963)
J. Godrich and R. M. W. Dixon: *Blues and Gospel Records, 1902–1942* (Hatch End, nr London, 1963, rev. and enlarged 3/1982 as *Blues and Gospel Records, 1902–1943*)
L. Jones: *Blues People* (New York, 1963)
P. Oliver: *Conversation with the Blues* (London, 1965)

C. Keil: *Urban Blues* (Chicago, 1966)
S. B. Charters: *The Bluesmen* (New York, 1967)
M. Leadbitter and N. Slaven: *Blues Records, 1945–1966* (London, 1968)
P. Oliver: blues entries, *Jazz on Record*, ed. A. McCarthy (London, 1968)
——: *Screening the Blues: Aspects of the Blues Tradition* (London, 1968)
——: *The Story of the Blues* (London, 1969)
H. Oster: *Living Country Blues* (Detroit, 1969)
R. M. W. Dixon and J. Godrich: *Recording the Blues* (London, 1970)
C. Gillett: *The Sound of the City* (New York, 1970)
P. Oliver: *Savannah Syncopators: African Retentions in the Blues* (London, 1970)
W. Ferris: *Blues from the Delta* (London, 1971)
R. Middleton: *Pop Music and the Blues* (London, 1972)
M. Rowe: *Chicago Breakdown* (London, 1973)
J. Broven: *Walking to New Orleans: the Story of New Orleans Rhythm and Blues* (Bexhill-on-Sea, England, 1974)
M. Haralambos: *Right On: from Blues to Soul in Black America* (London, 1974)
P. Garon: *Blues and the Poetic Spirit* (London, 1975/*R*1979)
G. Oakley: *The Devil's Music: a History of the Blues* (London, 1976)
P. Oliver: "Blue-Eyed Blues: the Impact of Blues on European Popular Culture," *Approaches to Popular Culture*, ed. C. W. E. Bigsby (London, 1976)
S. B. Charters: *Sweet as the Showers of Rain* (New York, 1977)
J. T. Titon: *Early Downhome Blues: a Musical and Cultural Analysis* (Urbana, IL, 1977)
S. Harris: *Blues Who's Who* (New Rochelle, NY, 1979)
R. Palmer: *Deep Blues* (New York, 1981/*R*1983)
D. Evans: *Big Road Blues: Tradition and Creativity in the Folk Blues* (Berkeley, CA, 1982)
P. Oliver: *Blues off the Record: Thirty Years of Blues Commentary* (Tunbridge Wells, England, 1984)
——: *Songsters and Saints: Vocal Traditions on Race Records* (London, 1984)

PAUL OLIVER

Blue Sky Boys. Country-music duo. Its members were the tenor and mandolin player William A. (Bill) Bolick (*b* Hickory, NC, 28 Oct 1917) and his brother the baritone and guitarist Earl Bolick (*b* Hickory, NC, 16 Dec 1919). Although they had sung with earlier country-music string bands, they began their career as a duo in 1935, when they sang on radio station WWNC in Asheville, North Carolina. The duo's name was inspired by the Blue Ridge Mountains and by the popular description of the area around Asheville as the "Land of the Sky." In 1936 they made their first recordings for RCA Victor, an association that lasted until after their official retirement. Their career was interrupted by military service during World War II, but afterwards they broadcast regularly on WNAO in Raleigh, North Carolina. The Bolicks became widely admired for their close vocal harmony and for their mandolin and guitar instrumentation. They specialized in sentimental parlor tunes, old-time ballads, and gospel songs; *The Sunny Side of Life* (1936), *Only One Step More* (1940), *Kentucky* (1947), and *Alabama* (1949) were among their most popular recordings. Unwilling to adapt to the upbeat, commercial idiom and the use of electric instruments popular in postwar country music, they officially retired in 1951. They did, however, make occasional appearances at folk festivals and college concerts, and recorded for Starday, Rounder, Camden, Capitol, and Bluebird. Their style of harmony and choice of songs have had a great impact on modern generations of country-music and folk singers.

BIBLIOGRAPHY

B. McCuen: "Blue Sky Boys Discography," *Country Directory*, no.1 (1960), 20
A. Green: liner notes, *Blue Sky Boys* (Camden CAL797, 1964)
E. Kahn: liner notes, *The Blue Sky Boys* (Cap. T2483, 1965)
B. C. Malone: *Country Music U.S.A.: a Fifty-Year History* (Austin, 1968, 2/1985)

BILL C. MALONE

Blues progression. The underlying harmonic structure of the blues. In the broad sense, the term can refer to the harmonic basis of any piece called a BLUES (an exhaustive survey of these progressions can be found in Dauer). In the narrow sense, it refers to a flexible, cyclic 12-bar structure, consisting of three four-bar phrases with the chord pattern shown in ex. 1. Many variants

Ex.1 Basic harmonic structure of the 12-bar blues progression

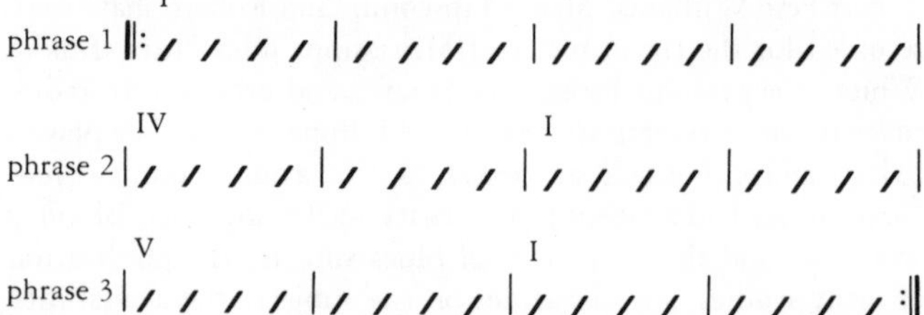

of this pattern are possible: frequently IV is used in place of I in bar 2, or in place of V in bar 10. The chord shape most commonly chosen for this pattern by blues musicians is a major triad with an added flatted seventh, though the functional implications that such chords carry in 18th-century classical music are not necessarily present in blues. Country or "downhome" blues guitarists characteristically vary the rhythms and harmonies of the basic progression, and sometimes discard harmonic function altogether by maintaining a tonic drone on the bass strings; in this case a blues harmonic progression may be intimated by the vocal and treble-string melodies. In jazz the simple 12-bar scheme of ex.1 is subject to a wide variety of substitute and passing harmonies, of which an extreme example is provided by Charlie Parker's *Blues for Alice* (1951), with its sequences of interpolated secondary-dominant progressions (ex.2). A minor-mode form of

Ex.2 Harmonic structure of C. Parker: *Blues for Alice* (1951, Clef 337)

phrase 1: F | Fmaj7 Em7–♭5 A7 | Dm7 G7 | Cm7 F7
phrase 2: B♭7 | B♭m7 E♭7 | Am7 D7 | A♭m7 D♭7
phrase 3: Gm7 | C7 | F7 (Dm7 | Gm7 C7)

the blues progression also exists, notably in Duke Ellington's *Ko-Ko* (1940; for illustration *see* ELLINGTON, DUKE, fig.2) and later in the soul jazz of the 1950s and in rock.

There is evidence to suggest that the blues progression originated as early as the 1890s among blues guitarists of the Mississippi delta and itinerant southern boogie-woogie pianists, though recordings of this music did not appear until the mid-1920s. By that time the blues progression had already been adapted to serve in other styles. Themes based on 12-bar blues progressions appeared in ragtime compositions from 1904; later, composer–collectors of the blues published multithematic "blues," combining 12-bar blues progressions with 16-bar ragtime themes and popular songs (e.g., W. C. Handy's *Memphis Blues*, 1912). These hybrid pieces were popularized by "classic" blues singers such as Mamie Smith and Bessie Smith from 1920. A few years later, in 1923, recordings by innovative black jazz ensembles from New Orleans revealed that there were several established variants from the standard blues pattern. Only later were field recordings made of rural blues musicians. Because of this confusion in the sources it is impossible to establish an original form of the blues progression.

BIBLIOGRAPHY

C. Keil: *Urban Blues* (Chicago, 1966)
G. Schuller: *Early Jazz: its Roots and Musical Development* (New York, 1968)
L. Koch: "Structural Aspects of King Oliver's 1923 Okeh Recordings," *Journal of Jazz Studies*, iii/2 (1976), 36
E. Newberger: "Archetypes and Antecedents of Piano Blues and Boogie Woogie Style," *Journal of Jazz Studies*, iv/1 (1976), 84
J. Titon: *Early Downhome Blues: a Musical and Cultural Analysis* (Urbana, IL, 1977)
J. L. Collier: *The Making of Jazz: a Comprehensive History* (Boston, 1978)
A. Dauer: "Towards a Typology of the Vocal Blues Idiom," *Jazzforschung*, xi (1979), 9–92
E. Berlin: *Ragtime: a Musical and Cultural History* (Berkeley, CA, 1980/*R*1984 with addns)

BARRY KERNFELD

Blues Project. Rock group. It was formed in 1965 in New York by Danny Kalb (*b* Brooklyn, NY, 1942), singer and guitarist, who had accompanied singers such as Judy Collins and had been one of Dave Van Ronk's Ragtime Jug Stompers; Steve Katz (*b* Brooklyn, 9 May 1945), singer, guitarist, and harmonica player, who had played with Van Ronk and with Jim Kweskin's Even Dozen Jug Band; Tommy Flanders, lead singer; Andy Kulberg (*b* Buffalo, NY, 1944), bass guitarist, who was a classically trained flutist and had studied modern jazz at New York University; Roy Blumenfeld, drummer; and Al Kooper (*b* Brooklyn, 5 Feb 1944), singer and keyboard player, who had played guitar with the Royal Teens and organ for Bob Dylan, and was one of the authors of *This Diamond Ring*, which was made a hit single by Gary Lewis and the Playboys. The diverse experience of the members of the group made for an unprecedentedly eclectic style; their music veered unpredictably from pop and feckless folk-rock to jazzy instrumentals and blues extravaganzas, distinguished by Kalb's frenzied guitar solos. With Paul Butterfield's Blues Band, the Blues Project was one of the first influential white blues groups in the USA, providing inspiration for early experimental and progressive rock musicians. But the group proved unstable: Flanders left in 1966, before the first album was completed; Kooper left the following year; and Kalb soon afterwards. The Blues Project disbanded (Kooper and Katz eventually formed Blood, Sweat and Tears, and Kulberg and Blumenfeld formed Seatrain), but in 1971 a number of its former members reunited to record an album (*Lazarus*, released in 1971) and went on to give a concert in Central Park, New York, in 1973; in 1983 the group re-formed again to make several live appearances.

RECORDINGS
(selective list)

Live at the Cafe au Go Go (Verve 3000, 1966); *Projections* (Verve 3008, 1967); *Planned Obsolescence* (Verve 3046, 1968); *Lazarus* (Cap. 782, 1971)

BIBLIOGRAPHY

A. Kooper and B. Edmonds: *Backstage Passes: Rock 'n' Roll Life in the Sixties* (New York, 1977), 83–134

KEN EMERSON

Blumenfeld, Harold (*b* Seattle, WA, 15 Oct 1923). Composer and conductor. He was educated at the Eastman School (1941–3), Yale University (BM 1948, MM 1949), and the University of Zurich (1948); his principal teachers in composition were Bernard Rogers and Hindemith. During several summers at the Berkshire Music Center, from 1949 to 1952, he trained as a conductor with Shaw and Bernstein and worked as stage director for Goldovsky, for whom he prepared an English-language production of Monteverdi's *L'incoronazione di Poppea*. Blumenfeld has held academic positions at Washington University, St. Louis (from 1950), and Queens College, CUNY (1971–2). He has received awards from the Martha Baird Rockefeller Fund (1975), the American Academy and Institute of Arts and Letters (1977), and the NEA (1980), as well as a Missouri Composer Commission. He has written on contemporary music and opera and in 1980 published a translation of part of Praetorius's *Syntagma musicum* (1614–20).

During the 1960s Blumenfeld devoted a major share of his energies to directing opera in St. Louis, where he campaigned for adequate production standards and cooperation within the local community. As director of the Opera Theatre of St. Louis (1962–6) and the Washington University Opera Studio (1960–71), he offered an innovative mixture of the standard repertory, Baroque opera, and 20th-century works.

Blumenfeld developed his early compositional style while under the influence of Hindemith, but later abandoned this course in favor of the approaches of such composers as Berio, Crumb, and Carter. About 1970 he began to relinquish his responsibilities as an opera director to concentrate on composing; all of his subsequent works focus on the declamation of texts, around which he weaves delicate, timbrally subtle accompaniments, often with chamber ensembles, percussion instruments, and extended techniques for piano. His music frequently employs contrapuntal textures and calls for the spatial separation of performance forces.

WORKS

Opera: Amphitryon 4 (3, after Molière), 1962, arr. orch, 1962; Fritzi (1, C. Kondek, after Molnar), 1979; Four-score: an Opera of Opposites (2, Kondek, after Nestroy: Haus der Temperamente), 1981–5

Orch: Miniature Ov., 1958; Contrasts, 1961–2

Inst: Transformations, pf, 1963; Expansions, ww qnt, 1964; Movts, brass septet, 1965; Night Music, gui, 1973, withdrawn

Choral: See Here the Fallen, SATB, orch, 1943; 3 Scottish Poems, male vv, 1948–50; War Lament (S. Sassoon), SATB, gui, 1970; Song of Innocence (Blake), T, Mez, large chorus, chamber chorus, orch, 1973; other works

Vocal: Rilke for One Voice and Gui, 3 songs, 1975; Circle of the Eye (T. McKeown), song cycle, medium v, pf, 1975; Starfires (P. Hanson), Mez, T, orch, 1975; La vie antérieure (Baudelaire), cantata, Bar, Mez, T, 13 insts, 1976; Voyages (H. Crane), cantata, Bar, va, gui, 3 perc, 1977; Uščnost' [Essence] (Mandelstam), 9 songs, medium v, pf, 1979, retitled Silentium; La voix reconnue (Verlaine), cantata, T, S, vc, pf, 1980; La face cendrée (Rimbaud), cantata, S, vc, pf, 1981; other works

Principal publishers: Belwin-Mills, Galaxy

BIBLIOGRAPHY

EwenD
S. Jenkins, Jr.: "Waiting at the Gateway," *Opera News*, xxxii/26 (1968), 19
J. Wierzbicki: "Blumenfeld's Music," *St. Louis Globe-Democrat* (3–4 Feb 1979)

RICHARD S. JAMES

Blyth, Samuel (baptized Salem, MA, 13 May 1744; buried Salem, 13 Jan 1795). Craftsman and organist. He worked all his life in Salem, where from 1766 to 1783 he occasionally played the organ at St. Peter's Church. He also ran a boarding-school for girls, and is recorded in Salem account books as a painter of ships, carriages, carpets, and canisters, a gilder, and a maker of Venetian blinds. Only one musical instrument by him is known: a spinet from about 1785, now in the Essex Institute, Salem. It is one of the few extant examples of 18th-century American plucked-string keyboard instruments, and is modeled on English types. The instrument has a range of *G/B* to f''' and has a mahogany case, with the painted inscription "Samuel Blyth SALEM Massachusetts Fecit" over the keyboard. A bill dated 7 February 1786 from Samuel Blyth to Mrs. Margaret Barton "To making a Spinnett for her daughter – L 18 . . 0–0" is also in the Essex Institute.

BIBLIOGRAPHY

R. Russell: *The Harpsichord and Clavichord* (London, 1959, 2/1973), pl.80

N. F. Little: "The Blyths of Salem: Benjamin, Limner in Crayon and Oil, and Samuel, Painter and Cabinetmaker," *Essex Institute Historical Collections*, cviii/1 (1972), 49

CYNTHIA ADAMS HOOVER

BMI. *See* BROADCAST MUSIC, INC.

Board of Music Trade. Trade organization founded in New York in 1855 by 27 leading music publishers in reaction to steps taken by the New York firm William Hall & Sons to halve the list prices of noncopyrighted music. The member publishers of the group, which included Oliver Ditson in Boston, S. Brainard & Sons in Cleveland, and Horace Waters in New York, were able to reach a compromise whereby the prices for this music would be reduced by only 20%. The board issued a *Complete Catalogue of Sheet Music and Musical Works* (1870/*R*1973), a comprehensive list of all the works published by its members and the closest the industry had come to producing a list of music in print. After a slow decline, the board held its last meeting in 1895; it was succeeded in the same year by the MUSIC PUBLISHERS' ASSOCIATION OF THE UNITED STATES. Any allusions to the Music Publishers' Association or the Music Publishers' Board of Trade in historical materials published before 1895 refer to the Board of Music Trade.

BIBLIOGRAPHY

D. J. Epstein: "Music Publishing in the Age of Piracy: the Board of Music Trade and its Catalogue," *Notes*, xxxi (1974–5), 7

DENA J. EPSTEIN

Boas, Franz (*b* Minden, Germany, 9 July 1858; *d* New York, 21 Dec 1942). Anthropologist and ethnomusicologist. He was trained as a physicist and geographer, and apparently went to North America in 1883 to perfect the mapping of the region inhabited by the Eskimo in Baffinland; while living among them, his career shifted from geography to ethnology. On his return to Berlin he became interested in the methods used by Carl Stumpf, Hornbostel, and Herzog in the study of music in other cultures. In 1886 Boas returned to North America to work among the Bella Coola Indians of the Pacific northwest. He took a post teaching anthropology at Clark University (Worcester, Massachusetts) in 1888 and settled in the USA, having decided to make American Indians the center of his anthropological work. He was professor of anthropology at Columbia University (1899–1937), and in his teaching he emphasized the importance of music in the study of primitive culture. With the advent of the phonograph he urged his students to collect music along with other ethnological data. He recorded much material among the Kwakiutl and neighboring tribes in British Columbia and among the Yoruba in Africa. His publications of the period 1887–1900 include many transcriptions of Indian melodies and served as models for later ethnological treatises that included music. After 1900 Boas developed a keen interest in linguistics and the closely linked oral arts and their accompanying forms – tale and myth, poetry, music, and dance – and his publications (over 600 items) often included song texts with translations.

BIBLIOGRAPHY

"Franz Boas, 1858–1942," *American Anthropologist*, xlv/3 (1943) [incl. complete list of writings]

M. J. Herskovits: *Franz Boas: the Science of Man in the Making* (New York, 1953)

B. Nettl: *North American Indian Musical Styles* (Philadelphia, 1954)

N. Judd: *The Bureau of American Ethnology: a Partial History* (Norman, Oklahoma, 1962)

SUE CAROLE DE VALE/R

Boatwright [née Strassburger], **Helen** (*b* Sheboygan, WI, 17 Nov 1916). Soprano. Of German parentage, she was the youngest of six children, all of whom sang. During her high-school years she studied with Anna Shram Irving, to whom she owes her grounding in the lieder repertory. At 19 she won a scholarship to Oberlin College, where her teacher was Marion Sims. After winning the state and district competitions of the National Federation of Music Clubs in 1941, she entered the national competition in Los Angeles, where she met Howard Boatwright, who was competing as a violinist. They married in 1943, a year after her operatic début (as Anna in a production in English of Otto Nicolai's *Die lustigen Weiber von Windsor* at the Berkshire Music Festival); from 1943 to 1945 she sang leading roles with opera companies in Austin and San Antonio, Texas. From 1945 to 1964 she and her husband lived and taught in New Haven, and in the latter year she was appointed Adjunct Professor of Voice at Syracuse University. Principally a concert artist and recitalist, Boatwright sang with most of the important orchestras and choral groups in the country, frequently in works outside the concert repertory. In March 1967 she made her New York recital début at Town Hall in a program that included Hindemith's *Das Marienleben* cycle (she had earlier performed as a soloist with Hindemith's collegium). She has made a number of recordings, notably one of 24 songs by Ives, in which she is accompanied by John Kirkpatrick.

PHILIP LIESON MILLER

Boatwright, Howard (Leake, Jr.) (*b* Newport News, VA, 16 March 1918). Composer, violinist and musicologist. He was trained as a violinist in Norfolk by Israel Feldman, made his début at Town Hall in New York in 1942, and was assistant professor of violin at the University of Texas, Austin, from 1943 to 1945. At Yale (BM 1947, MM 1948) he studied theory and composition with Hindemith, at whose urging he stayed on as assistant professor in music theory (promoted to associate professor, 1954). As music director at St. Thomas's Church, New Haven (1949–64), Boatwright established a reputation as a pioneer in the performance of early choral music. He has made several concert tours in the USA, Mexico, and Europe, sometimes with his wife, the soprano Helen Boatwright. While in New Haven he also served as conductor of the Yale University Orchestra from 1952 to 1960, and was concertmaster of the New Haven SO (1950–62). He became dean of the school of music at Syracuse University in 1964, and from 1971 was professor of music in composition and theory. Boatwright has pursued a varied career as a scholar. His writings include an *Introduction to the Theory of Music* (1956) and significant scholarly work on Hindemith, Quincy Porter, and Ives as well as on classical Indian music. He was a Fulbright lecturer in India during the year 1959–60 and received a Fulbright grant to study in Romania, 1971–2. He was elected to the board of directors of the Charles Ives Society in 1975.

Boatwright has composed prolifically throughout his career. At first he concentrated on sacred choral music but his compositions from the 1970s also included important instrumental works, notably the Symphony and the String Quartet no.2. His earliest choral works are modal; subsequently the chamber works in particular were influenced by Hindemith's middle-period style. About 1966 he began to develop a synthesis of 12-tone procedures and Schoenbergian sonorities, but with Hindemith's control of dissonance. His Quartet for clarinet and strings received the award of the Society for the Publication of American Music in 1962.

WORKS

Orch: A Song for St. Cecilia's Day, large str ens, 1948; Variations, small orch, 1949; Sym., 1976 [incl. Movt for Orch, Larghetto espressivo, Trio scherzando, and Passacaglia for Orch]

Inst: 2 str qts, 1947, 1974; Trio, 2 vn, va, 1948; Serenade, 2 str, 2 wind, 1952; Qt, cl, str, 1958; 12 Pieces for Vn Alone; Cl Sonata, 1980; other chamber and kbd works, incl. 4 org preludes

Choral: The Women of Trachis (Sophocles, trans. Pound), 6 choruses, female vv, chamber orch, 1955; Mass, C, 1958; The Passion According to St. Matthew, solo vv, SATB, org, 1962; Canticle of the Sun (St. Francis of Assisi), S, SATB, orch, 1963; Music for Temple Service, Bar, SATB, org, 1969; A Song for St. Cecilia's Day, S, SATB, orch, 1981; over 20 other works incl. 4 masses, many choral partsongs

Solo vocal: The Ship of Death (Lawrence), S, A, T, B, str qt, 1966; The Lament of Mary Stuart (Carissimi cantata text), S, hpd/pf, opt vc, 1968; 6 Prayers of Kierkegaard (trans. P. LeFevre), S, pf, 1978; *c*50 songs

Principal publishers: Galaxy, Oxford UP, Sacred Music, E. C. Schirmer, Valley

BIBLIOGRAPHY

EwenD

J. Knapp: "Howard Boatwright: an American Master of Choral Music," *American Choral Review*, vi/1 (1963), 1

TERENCE J. O'GRADY

Boatwright, McHenry (*b* Tennille, GA, 29 Feb 1928). Bass-baritone. He was educated at the New England Conservatory, where he obtained degrees in piano (BM 1950) and singing (BM 1954). During this time he won two Marian Anderson awards (1953 and 1954) and the Arthur Fiedler Voice Contest. His professional concert début was at Jordan Hall, Boston, in February 1956, though he had earlier performed in a recording of Berlioz's *La Damnation de Faust* with the Boston SO conducted by Munch. As a result of winning the National Federation of Music Clubs competition in 1957, he made his Town Hall début in January, 1958. That year he also made his operatic début, singing Arkel (*Pelléas et Mélisande*) with the New England Opera Theater. He has been heard in opera, in concert, and with orchestras around the world. He created the central role in Schuller's opera *The Visitation* in Hamburg, Germany (12 October 1966), and he repeated the role when the Hamburg company made its American début at the Metropolitan Opera House in 1967. Among his recorded roles is that of Crown in Gershwin's *Porgy and Bess*. He possessed strength and vibrancy in all registers, but it was as an interpreter that he was acclaimed, for fully projecting the inner drama, passion, and mood of the music he performed.

BIBLIOGRAPHY

SouthernB

D. J. Soria: "Artist Life," *HiFi/MusAm*, xvii/5 (1967), 5

THOR ECKERT, JR.

Bobri [Bobritsky], **Vladimir (Vassilievich)** (*b* Khar'kov, Ukraine, 13 May 1898). Guitarist and editor of Ukrainian origin. His study of art at the Imperial Khar'kov Art School was halted by the Russian Revolution. He immigrated to the USA in 1922, where he eventually became very successful in New York as a commercial artist. The classical guitar, to which Andrés Segovia first drew attention in New York on a tour in 1928, captured Bobri's interest. He became president of the Society of the Classic Guitar in 1936 and editor of its publication *The Guitar Review* (*Guitar Review* from 1961) in 1946. His own guitar pieces, editions of guitar music, pedagogical publications (e.g., *Complete Study of Tremolo for the Classic Guitar*, 1972), and contributions to *Guitar Review* for over 35 years attest to his devotion to the instrument. He wrote *The Segovia Technique* (1972) and compiled *A Musical Voyage with 2 Guitars* (1974), a collection of arrangements and original music by himself and Carl Miller.

THOMAS F. HECK

Bock, Jerry [Jerrold Lewis] (*b* New Haven, CT, 23 Nov 1928). Composer. He studied music at the University of Wisconsin (1945–9), where he composed music for collegiate productions. He then moved to New York, and wrote songs for revues, television ("Your Show of Shows"), and the weekly summer musicals at Camp Tamiment, Pennsylvania. He collaborated with the lyricist Larry Holofcener on several songs, including three in the Broadway revue *Catch a Star!* (1955); they achieved major success with their score for *Mr. Wonderful* (1956). From 1958 to 1970 Bock worked in collaboration with the lyricist Sheldon Harnick on seven shows, including *Fiorello!* (1959), which earned them a Pulitzer Prize for drama, *She Loves Me* (1963), and their most successful work, *Fiddler on the Roof* (1964), the first production of which ran for more than 3000 performances in New York. After his collaboration with Harnick came to an end in the early 1970s Bock produced no further works for the musical theater. His music was perhaps the most traditionally romantic of the modern Broadway composers; his scores are notable for their skill in conveying local color, their harmonic and structural invention, and fresh, memorable melodies.

WORKS

Selective list. Unless otherwise indicated, all are musicals, and dates are those of first New York performance. Librettists and lyricists are listed in that order in parentheses.

Mr. Wonderful (J. Stein, W. Glickman; L. Holofcener, G. Weiss), 22 March 1956 [incl. Mr. Wonderful; Too close for comfort]

Wonders of Manhattan (film score), 1956

The Body Beautiful (Stein, Glickman; S. Harnick), 23 Jan 1958

Fiorello! (G. Abbott, J. Weidman; Harnick), 23 Nov 1959 [incl. Little Tin Box; 'Til tomorrow; When did I fall in love?]

Tenderloin (Abbott, Weidman; Harnick), 17 Oct 1960

She Loves Me (J. Masteroff; Harnick), 23 April 1963 [incl. Dear friend; Ice Cream; She loves me]; television production, 1979

Fiddler on the Roof (J. Stein; Harnick), 22 Sept 1964 [incl. Matchmaker, matchmaker; Sunrise, sunset; To Life]; film, 1971

The Apple Tree (Bock, Harnick, J. Coopersmith), 18 Oct 1966

The Canterville Ghost (television music, Harnick), 1966

The Rothschilds (S. Yellen; Harnick), 19 Oct 1970

Songs in revues, incl. Catch a Star!, 1955; Ziegfeld Follies, 1957

BIBLIOGRAPHY

S. Green: *The World of Musical Comedy* (New York, 1960, rev. and enlarged 4/1980)

D. Ewen: *Popular American Composers* (New York, 1962; suppl 1972)

GERALD BORDMAN

Bodanzky, Artur (*b* Vienna, Austria, 16 Dec 1877; *d* New York, 23 Nov 1939). Conductor. He studied violin, and at 18 joined the orchestra of the Vienna Hofoper. In 1900 he made his début conducting Sidney Jones's *The Geisha* with the 18-man orchestra in České Budějovice. In 1903 he returned to the Vienna Opera as Mahler's assistant, soon making his way rapidly in theaters and concert halls in Vienna, Berlin, Prague, and Mannheim. In 1914 he introduced *Die Fledermaus* to Paris and *Parsifal* to London, the latter making such an impression that he was named successor to Alfred Hertz at the Metropolitan Opera. He made his American début conducting *Götterdämmerung* on 18 November 1915. Thereafter his career was centered on New York: at the Metropolitan (with a brief break in 1928) until his death; with the New SO, which he took over in 1919 from its first conductor, Varèse, until its merger with the Philharmonic in 1922; and with the Society of the Friends of Music from 1921, as successor to Stokowski, until 1931 when the society was dissolved.

Best known as a Wagnerian, Bodanzky was anything other than a narrow specialist. He was on the podium for Caruso's last Metropolitan performance, in Halévy's *La juive*, and his repertory there included Gluck, Richard Strauss, Tchaikovsky, Meyerbeer, Suppé, and the American premières of Jaromír Weinberger's *Shvanda the Bagpiper* and Krenek's *Jonny spielt auf*. At the Friends of Music his repertory ranged from *Dido and Aeneas* to Ildebrando Pizzetti and Zemlinsky, and his many American premières included those of Mahler's *Das Lied von der Erde*, Honegger's *Le roi David*, and Janáček's Glagolitic Mass. Physically, Bodanzky was like a much taller Mahler, from whom his "the facts, not the show" attitude derived. The typical Bodanzky performance was fast, intense, and heavily cut (however, he gave as well as taking away, composing recitatives and other additions for Weber's *Oberon* and *Der Freischütz*, *Die Zauberflöte*, and *Fidelio*).

MICHAEL STEINBERG/R

Bo Diddley [McDaniel, Elias] (*b* McComb, MS, 30 Dec 1928). Rock-and-roll singer. He was taken to Chicago at the age of five, and soon after began violin lessons, which he continued for 12 years. He was familiar with gospel music and the delta blues players of Chicago's southside, but he was most strongly influenced by Nat "King" Cole, Louis Jordan, and John Lee Hooker, whose *Boogie Chillen'* inspired him to play guitar. He formed a street-corner band, which attracted enough attention to be granted an audition with Chess Records in 1954. In early 1955 *Bo Diddley* was released as a single and reached no.2 on the rhythm-and-blues chart. It had bragging, nonsense lyrics, like many of his later songs, but its chief appeal lay in its shimmering rumba rhythm and violent, primitive guitar playing. Diddley stood outside the mainstream of rock-and-roll of the 1950s; he recorded unusual jazz instrumental pieces with weird sound-effects, doo-wop songs, blues, idiosyncratic rock-and-roll numbers, and rambling insult battles with Jerome Green, his maracas player. Many of his songs are based on a distinctive syncopated rhythm (ex. 1).

Ex.1

$\frac{4}{4}$

Diddley had few pop hits (only *Say Man* reached the Top 20 on the pop chart), but his influence on such performers as Jimi Hendrix, the Rolling Stones, and the Yardbirds was considerable; cover versions of his songs were recorded by many American and English groups. He owned a large collection of unusually shaped guitars, and was rarely photographed twice with the same instrument. His stage name is derived from the instrument known as a DIDDLEY BOW.

RECORDINGS

(selective list; all recorded for Checker)

Bo Diddley/I'm a Man (814, 1955); Crackin' Up (924, 1959); Say Man (931, 1959); Road Runner (942, 1960); You can't judge a book by its cover (1019, 1962); Boss Man (3007, 1966); Ooh Baby (1158, 1967)

BIBLIOGRAPHY

SouthernB
N. Nite: *Rock On* (New York, 1974), 184
J. Miller: "Bo Diddley," *The Rolling Stone Illustrated History of Rock & Roll* (New York, 1976), 328
R. Denyer: *The Guitar Handbook* (London, 1982), 13

JOSEPH McEWEN

Bodky, Erwin (*b* Ragnit [now Neman], Lithuania, 7 March 1896; *d* Lucerne, Switzerland, 6 Dec 1958). Pianist, harpsichordist, musicologist, and composer. He made his début as a pianist at the age of 12. After attending the Gymnasium in Tilsit he went to the Hochschule für Musik in Berlin, where he studied with Ernő Dohnányi, Paul Juon, Robert Kahn, and others, graduating in 1920. He then continued his studies under Busoni (piano) and Strauss (composition), and performed as a solo pianist. During the 1920s he wrote a piano concerto, a symphony for chamber orchestra, works for solo piano, and chamber music. Until 1938 he occupied various teaching posts at music schools in Berlin and Amsterdam. In that year he came to the USA, where he taught first at the Longy School of Music in Cambridge, Massachusetts, and founded the Cambridge Collegium Musicum (later the Cambridge Society for Early Music) in 1942; in 1949 he received the first music appointment at Brandeis University, where he taught music history. He was primarily interested in methods of performance of early keyboard music: he played both harpsichord and clavichord, and explored ways of rendering certain harpsichord effects on the modern piano. He published three scholarly works connected with these interests: *Der Vortrag alter Klaviermusik* (1932), *Das Charakterstück* (1933), and *The Interpretation of Bach's Keyboard Works* (1960). In 1955 he presented "Roads to Bach," one of the earliest programs on music seen on educational television. From 1967 the Cambridge Society for Early Music sponsored the Erwin Bodky International Competition for young performers of early music, the only such competition in the USA.

BIBLIOGRAPHY

H. S. Slosberg and others, eds.: *Erwin Bodky: a Memorial Tribute* (Waltham, MA, 1965)

WILLIAM D. GUDGER

Bodley, Nicholas Bessaraboff. *See* BESSARABOFF, NICHOLAS.

Boelke-Bomart. Firm of music publishers. It was founded by Margot and Walter R. Boelke in New York in 1948 and moved to Hillsdale, New York, in 1951. Affiliated to ASCAP, the firm specializes in the publication of contemporary music, and under the general editorship of Jacques-Louis Monod (1952–82), who succeeded Kurt List, built up a small but important catalogue. Among its composers are Berger, Casanova, Lansky, Lerdahl, Perle, Schoenberg, Spies, and Winkler. In 1975 a sister company, Mobart Music Publications (an affiliate of BMI) was founded; its composers include Babbitt, Gideon, Ives, Monod, Pollock,

Shifrin, Weber, and Webern. The distributor for both companies in the USA and Canada is Jerona Music Corporation.

BIBLIOGRAPHY

G. Sturm: "Encounters: Walter R. Boelke," *MadAminA!: a Chronicle of Musical Catalogues*, iv/1 (1983), 9

ALAN POPE/R. ALLEN LOTT

Boettcher Concert Hall. Principal concert hall in DENVER.

Bohannon [Bohannon, Hamilton Frederick] (*b* Newman, GA). Rhythm-and-blues drummer. He received a BA in music education from Clark College in Atlanta and taught music for a time. He then joined a local group and met Jimi Hendrix, who became a major influence on his style. Bohannon began his professional performing career in 1965 as a drummer for Stevie Wonder. In 1967 he became the leader of the Motown label's leading road band – known on radio as Bohannon and the Motown Sound – and spent the next five years on tour, backing such acts as Gladys Knight and the Pips, the Temptations, Diana Ross and the Supremes, the Spinners, Smokey Robinson and the Miracles, and the Four Tops. When Motown moved its headquarters from Detroit to Los Angeles, Bohannon left the company and signed a contract with Dakar, a small label based in Chicago. There he began writing and arranging his own disco music, and produced a series of disco albums, dominated by his percussion playing, which blended mellow funk with primitive, irrepressible rhythms. In 1975 his single *Footstompin' Music* reached the Top 40 on the rhythm-and-blues chart; Bohannon then moved to Mercury and recorded the scintillating *Let's start the dance* (1978), which reached the rhythm-and-blues Top 10. Later releases, however, such as *Let's start the dance again* (1981), had little success. Most of Bohannon's recordings are characterized by dominant percussion lines, simple guitar solos, and intermittent vocal passages. Although little known to the general public, he is respected within the music industry as a producer, arranger, and performer.

GARY THEROUX

Bojangles. *See* ROBINSON, BILL "BOJANGLES."

Bok (Zimbalist), Mary Louise Curtis (*b* Boston, MA, 6 Aug 1876; *d* Philadelphia, PA, 4 Jan 1970). Music patron. The daughter of the well-known Philadelphia newspaper publisher Cyrus H. K. Curtis, she married Edward Bok, editor of a Curtis publication, and devoted a long life to the support and encouragement of music. In 1917 she founded the Settlement School of Music and in 1924 the Curtis Institute of Music, both in Philadelphia, the latter with an endowment of $12\frac{1}{2}$ million dollars. She was president of the Curtis Institute until her death. From 1929 to 1934 she was also chairman of the board of the Philadelphia Grand Opera Company. After the death of Edward Bok, she married, in 1934, the violinist EFREM ZIMBALIST, at that time director of the Curtis Institute. She received the honorary degree of Doctor of Humane Letters from the University of Pennsylvania in 1932 and the MusD from Williams College in 1934. Her choice collection of musical autographs, which she gave to the Curtis Institute, included the Burrell Collection of Wagner's letters and music manuscripts, as well as compositions by J. S. Bach, Liszt, Mozart, Schubert, and Schumann; it was sold at auction at Christie's, New York, in 1980–82.

For illustration *see* PHILADELPHIA, fig.3.

BIBLIOGRAPHY

D. B. Thomas: "Zimbalist, Mary Louise Curtis Bok," *NAW*

E. A. Viles: *Mary Louise Curtis Bok Zimbalist: Founder of the Curtis Institute of Music and Patron of American Arts* (diss., Bryn Mawr College, 1983)

OTTO E. ALBRECHT

Bolcom, William (Elden) (*b* Seattle, WA, 26 May 1938). Composer, pianist, and author. He began composition studies with Verrall at an early age and continued with Milhaud at Mills College (1958–61) and with both Milhaud and Messiaen in Paris. A period of work with Leland Smith at Stanford University (1961–4) was followed by teaching at the University of Washington (1965–6) and Queens College, CUNY (1966–8). While in New York Bolcom developed the technique and style of playing ragtime that, through concerts and recordings, placed him in the forefront of the ragtime revival; he has also composed original rags, among them *The Graceful Ghost*. From 1968 to 1970 he was composer-in-residence at the Yale University Drama School and the New York University School of the Arts.

In 1971 Bolcom met the mezzo-soprano JOAN MORRIS, whom he married in 1975 and with whom he began to develop programs on the history of the American popular song. Their recitals and recordings of songs by Henry Russell, Henry Clay Work, and others have done much to arouse interest in parlor and music-hall songs of the 19th and early 20th centuries. Bolcom has also made solo albums of music by Gershwin, Milhaud, and himself. In 1973 he took a position at the University of Michigan, where he became associate professor of composition in 1977. With Robert Kimball he wrote the book *Reminiscing with Sissle and Blake* (1973); he also edited the collected writings of Rochberg, *The Aesthetics of Survival: a Composer's View of 20th-century Music* (1984).

Bolcom's intent to break down artificial distinctions between popular and serious music is realized in his own compositions, in which widely differing styles are often juxtaposed within the same work. An intensely dramatic atonality is contrasted with the song styles of World War I (as in the cabaret opera *Dynamite Tonite*), ragtime (*Black Host*), old popular tunes (*Whisper Moon*), or a waltz (Piano Quartet). Bolcom's ideology, rooted in the transcendentalism of Blake, inspires compositions concerned with momentous religious and philosophical themes, a concern expressed in intense, even flamboyant music of vivid illustrative power. These qualities are evident in *Frescoes*, and most notably in the monumental setting of the 46 poems in William Blake's *Songs of Innocence and Experience*. The latter work, a summation of Bolcom's achievements as a composer, was highly acclaimed at its world première in Stuttgart on 8 January 1984.

WORKS

STAGE

Dynamite Tonite (cabaret opera, 2, A. Weinstein), 2 actors, 1963

Greatshot (cabaret opera, 2, Weinstein), 2 actors, 1966

Theatre of the Absurd (paraphrase, Bolcom), actor, taped actors, wind qnt, pf, tapes, mechanized eyeballs, 1960

The Beggar's Opera (J. Gay), 1978 [completion of adaptation begun by Milhaud, 1937]

ORCHESTRAL

Sym., 1957; Concertante, vn, fl, ob, orch, 1961; Concerto Serenade, vn, str orch, 1964; Sym. (Oracles), 1965; Fives, vn, pf, 3 str groups, 1966; Commedia, chamber orch, 1971; Summer Divertimento, 1973; Pf Conc., 1976; Humoresk, org, orch (1979); Sym., chamber orch, 1979; Ragomania, 1982; Vn Conc., 1983

VOCAL

Songs of Innocence and Experience (Blake), 9 solo vv, 3 choruses, children's chorus, orch, 1956–81

Unacc. chorus: Satires (Bolcom), 1970; Vocalise from Songs of Experience, 1977

Songs: Morning and Evening Poems (Blake), A, T/Ct, ens, 1966; Open House (T. Roethke), T, small orch, 1975; 6 Cabaret Songs (Weinstein), 1v, pf, 1978; 3 Irish Songs (T. Moore), Mez/Bar, ens, 1978; 3 Donald Hall Songs, Mez/Bar, ens, 1979; 6 New Cabaret Songs (Weinstein), 1v, pf, 1983

CHAMBER AND INSTRUMENTAL

7 str qts, 1950–61, withdrawn; Concert Piece, cl, pf, 1958; Décalage, vc, pf, 1961; Pastorale, vn, pf, 1961; Octet, fl, cl, bn, vn, va, vc, db, pf, 1962; Session I, 7 insts, 1965; Str Qt no.8, 1965; Dream Music no.2, hpd, 3 perc, 1966; Phrygia, harp, 1966; Session II, vn, va, 1966; Session III, cl, vn, vc, pf, perc, 1967; Session IV, 9 insts, 1967; Dark Music, vc, timp, 1969; Duets for Qnt, fl, cl, vn, vc, pf, 1971

Fancy Tales, vn, pf, 1971; Whisper Moon, fl, cl, 2 vn, pf, 1971; Novella (Str Qt no.9), 1972; Duo Fantasy, vn, pf, 1973; Trauermarsch, fl, ob, elec hpd, elec vc, 1973; Seasons, gui, 1974; Pf Qt, 1976; Short Lecture, cl, 1976; Vn Sonata no.2, 1978; Afternoon, Rag Suite of Joplin, Lamb, Scott and Bolcom, cl, vn, pf, 1979; Brass Qnt, 1980; Aubade, ob, pf, 1982; Lilith, sax, pf, 1984

KEYBOARD

Romantic Pieces, pf, 1959; 12 Etudes, pf, 1959–60; Fantasy Sonata no.1, pf, 1961; Interlude, 2 pf, 1963; Dream Music no.1, pf, 1965; Black Host, org, perc, tape, 1967; Brass Knuckles, pf, 1968; Garden of Eden (Suite), pf, 1968; Praeludium, org, vib, 1969; Chorale and Prelude on Abide with me, org, 1970; Seabiscuits Rag, pf, 1970; The Graceful Ghost, pf, 1970

Frescoes, pf + hpd, pf + harmonium, 1971; Hydraulis, org, 1971; Raggin' Rudi, pf, 1972; Mysteries, org, 1976; Revelation Studies, carillon, 2 players, 1976; Fields of Flowers, 1978; 3 Gospel Preludes, org, 1979; Monsterpieces (and Others), pf, 1980; Gospel Preludes Bks II–III, org, 1982; The Dead Moth Tango, pf, 1983–4

Principal publishers: E. B. Marks, Presser

BIBLIOGRAPHY

EwenD

J. Hiemenz: "Musician of the Month: William Bolcom," *HiFi/MusAm*, xxvi/9 (1976), 4

G. Gelles: "New American Music," *New York Times* (11 April 1976)

A. Porter: *Music of Three Seasons: 1974–77* (New York, 1978), 290–92

M. Lorimer: "Bolcom's Seasons," *Guitar Player*, xv (1981), 120; xvi (1982), 98

P. J. Smith: "Keeping Outside Time," *The Times* (2 June 1984)

AUSTIN CLARKSON

Bolden, Buddy [Charles Joseph] (*b* New Orleans, LA, 6 Sept 1877; *d* Jackson, LA, 4 Nov 1931). Jazz cornetist and bandleader. The first of the New Orleans cornet "kings," he was highly regarded by contemporary black musicians in the city, who in their reminiscences embroidered his life with a great many legends and spurious anecdotes. A careful sifting of this data and contemporary records reveals that Bolden, unlike many of his peers, came late to music, adopting the cornet around 1894 after completing his schooling, and that he emerged not from the brass marching-band tradition but rather from the string bands which played for private dances and parties. By 1895 he was leading his own semiprofessional group with Frank Lewis (clarinet) and, later, Willie Cornish (valve trombone), though city records continue to refer to him as a plasterer. By 1901, when his name first appears in city directories as a professional musician, his group had stabilized into a six-piece unit with cornet, clarinet, valve trombone, guitar, double bass, and drums. Bolden's rise to fame coincided with the emergence of a black pleasure district – Black Storyville – at South Rampart and Perdido streets, where he soon became a local celebrity playing in the dives and tonks (but not the brothels). By 1905, when his fame was at its peak, his group performed regularly in the city's dance halls and parks, and undertook excursions to outlying towns. In the following year Bolden showed distinct signs of violent mental derangement, and his band rapidly disintegrated, eventually passing to the leadership of trombonist Frank Dusen. In 1907, in a state of hopeless indigence and alcoholism, Bolden was admitted to a mental institution in Jackson, where he spent his remaining years.

Contemporary musicians universally praised the power of Bolden's tone, his rhythmic drive, and the emotional content of his slow blues playing, often contrasting him with the more genteel Creole band tradition of John Robichaux and others. Bolden apparently did not improvise melodies freely in the manner of later jazz musicians, but found ingenious ways of ornamenting existing melodies, often incorporating a distinctive "lick" which functioned as a signature. Although he left no known recordings (a cylinder allegedly recorded in the late 1890s has never been located), Bolden undoubtedly had a formative influence on Freddie Keppard, Bunk Johnson, and other New Orleans cornetists and, by his example, helped to standardize the New Orleans jazz ensemble and repertory.

BIBLIOGRAPHY

SouthernB

M. Ondaatje: *Coming through Slaughter* (Toronto, 1976)

D. Marquis: "The Bolden–Peyton Legend: a Revaluation," *Jazz Journal*, xxx/2 (1977), 24

——: *Finding Buddy Bolden* (Goshen, IN, 1978)

——: *In Search of Buddy Bolden, First Man of Jazz* (Baton Rouge, LA, 1978)

J. BRADFORD ROBINSON

Bolet, Jorge (*b* Havana, Cuba, 15 Nov 1914). Pianist. First attracted to the piano at the age of nine, he made remarkable progress studying with local teachers. When he was 12 he entered the Curtis Institute as a scholarship student, studying with David Saperton (piano) and Reiner (conducting); his other piano instructors included Godowsky (1932–33) and Rosenthal (1935). Bolet made his European début in Amsterdam (1935); his American début, in Philadelphia (1937), was followed by further studies, with Serkin. After winning the Naumburg Prize (1937) and the Josef Hofmann Award (1938), he taught at Curtis as Serkin's assistant (1939–42). Military service took him to Japan, and in 1946 he conducted the Japanese première of *The Mikado*. He resumed his career after the war and spent some time working with Chasins. He has taught at Indiana University (1968–77), and in 1977 was appointed head of the piano department at Curtis. Since the early 1960s his artistry and virtuosity have been acclaimed as transcendent, and he is considered to be one of the last representatives of the grand tradition of Romantic piano playing. Bolet gave the first performances of Dello Joio's Third Piano Sonata and of concertos by John La Montaine and Joseph Marx; he has made many recordings, notably of the music of Liszt.

BIBLIOGRAPHY

B. Morrison: "Jorge Bolet," *Music and Musicians*, xxv/5 (1977), 16

A. Marcus: "Jorge Bolet," *Great Pianists Speak with Adele Marcus* (Neptune, NJ, 1979)

GREGOR BENKO/R

Bolt, Beranek and Newman. Firm of acoustic consultants founded in 1949 by LEO L. BERANEK.

Bomba (Sp.). A folkdance of Puerto Rico's coastal areas; *see* HISPANIC-AMERICAN MUSIC, §2 (ii).

Bond [Jacobs-Bond], **Carrie (Minetta)** (*b* Janesville, WI, 11 Aug 1861; *d* Hollywood, CA, 28 Dec 1946). Composer and publisher. She studied piano with the local teachers C. J. Titcomb and J. W. Bischoff, but an early marriage and the birth of a son prevented further study. The death of her second husband, Dr. Frank Bond, in 1895 forced her to attempt a career, and for six years she struggled to get several sentimental pieces and children's songs accepted for publication. After limited success dealing with unscrupulous publishers she formed her own publishing company, Carrie Jacobs-Bond and Son, in Chicago. She developed a network of enthusiastic supporters by performing her own music, accompanying her distinctive half-spoken, half-sung renditions in an improvisatory manner that was often more elaborate than the printed versions of the songs. She convinced amateur singers and then prominent professionals to include her songs in recitals: her first collection, *Seven Songs as Unpretentious as the Wild Rose* (1901), which included two of her most famous songs, *Just a-wearyin' for you* and *I love you truly*, was partially funded by Jessie Bartlett Davis. David Bispham sang an all-Bond recital, despite the protests of his manager, at Studebaker Hall in Chicago in 1901. Bond's most successful song, *A Perfect Day* (1910), sold over eight million sheet-music copies and five million records; it was issued in more than 60 versions, and the growing demand for it necessitated eight moves of the publishing company to progressively larger office quarters in Chicago. The *Half Minute Songs*, a witty collection of one-line pieces (1910–11), contains the six-second song *Answer the first rap*.

Forced by ill health to spend the winters away from Chicago, Bond sang in club cars for her railway fare to southern California and earned her room and board at a Hollywood hotel by arranging Sunday night musicales. In 1920 she moved her publishing company and its sales outlet, the Bond Shop, to Hollywood, where she became an intimate friend of many musicians and film stars, including Cadman, Schumann-Heink, and Gracie Fields. She published an autobiography, *The Roads of Melody* (1927), and also wrote for newspapers. After the suicide of her only son, Frederick Jacobs Smith, she ceased to compose for several years, but produced a small number of songs and piano pieces in the last two decades of her life. Her almost 200 compositions show a genuine lyrical gift, an ability to communicate a variety of emotions, and a level of craftsmanship that makes much of her work of lasting artistic value.

WORKS

(selective list; most works pubd in Chicago)

SONGS

(unless otherwise indicated, texts by Jacobs-Bond)

Po' Li'l Lamb! (P. L. Dunbar) (1901); Seven Songs as Unpretentious as the Wild Rose (1901): De Las' Long Res', Des hold my hands, I love you truly, Just a-wearyin' for you (F. Stanton), Parting, Shadows, Still unexprest; A Study in Symbols (C. Urmy) (1901); His buttons are marked "U.S." (M. N. Bradford) (1902, rev. 1918); A Vision (1905); He advertised (text from the *Cleveland Leader*) (1907); His Lullaby (B. Healy) (1907); Love and Sorrow (Dunbar) (1908); A Perfect Day (1910); Half Minute Songs (1910–11)

The Sandman (M. W. Slater) (1912); God remembers when the world forgets (C. Bingham) (1913); A little bit o' honey (W. G. Wilson) (1917); I've done my work (G. W. Caldwell) (1920); Little lost youth of me (E. M. Jewett) (1923); Roses are in bloom (1926); My Mother's Voice (1942); There's somebody waiting for me (1942); Because of the light (F. Carlton) (1944)

PIANO

The Chimney Swallows (1897); Tzigani Dances (1897); Memories of Versailles (1898); Uncle Sam's Victory for Liberty March (1898); Reverie (1902); Betty's Music Box (1917)

Principal publisher: Boston Music Co.

PHYLLIS BRUCE

Bond, Victoria (*b* Los Angeles, CA, 6 May 1945). Conductor and composer. She studied composition and singing at the University of Southern California before attending the Juilliard School, where she studied composition under Sessions and Persichetti and conducting under Morel, Ehrling, and Karajan (MMA 1975, DMA 1977); she was the first woman to be awarded a doctorate in conducting at Juilliard. She made her American début at Alice Tully Hall, New York, in 1973. After graduating from Juilliard, she was an Exxon/Arts Endowment conductor with the Pittsburgh SO and music director of both the Pittsburgh Youth Orchestra and the New Amsterdam SO (1978–80). She made her European début with the Radio Telefís Orchestra, Dublin, in 1982, and has appeared with a number of American orchestras, including the Houston SO and the Buffalo PO. In 1983 she was appointed music director of the Bel Canto Opera in New York and in 1984 became responsible for the programming and conducting of the Albany SO's youth concerts.

Although better known as a conductor, Bond devotes equal time to composition and has had many of her works – primarily chamber music and ballets – published (by Seesaw and Alexander Broude). Major works include two ballet scores choreographed by Lynn Taylor Corbett, *Equinox* (1977, commissioned by the Pennsylvania Ballet) and *Other Selves* (1979, commissioned by the Jacob's Pillow Dance Company), as well as two works for narrator and orchestra, *The Frog Prince* (1983–4) and *What's the Point of Counterpoint?* (1984–5).

BIBLIOGRAPHY

C. Apone: "Victoria Bond: Composer, Conductor," *HiFi/MusAm*, xxix/4 (1979), 28

J. W. Lepage: "Victoria Bond: Conductor, Composer," *Women Composers, Conductors, and Musicians of the Twentieth Century: selected Biographies* (Metuchen, NJ, 1980), 1

BARBARA JEPSON

Bonds [Richardson], **Margaret (Allison)** (*b* Chicago, IL, 3 March 1913; *d* Los Angeles, CA, 26 April 1972). Composer, pianist, and teacher. She began musical studies with her mother, whose home was a gathering place for young black writers, artists, and musicians including the composers Will Marion Cook and Florence Price. Bonds showed promise early, composing her first work, *Marquette Street Blues*, at the age of five. While in high school she studied piano and composition with Price and later with William Dawson; she received BM and MM degrees from Northwestern University (1933, 1934). She moved to New York in 1939 and in 1940 married Lawrence Richardson; at the Juilliard Graduate School she studied piano with Djane Herz and composition with Starer. Other teachers included Roy Harris, Emerson Harper, and Walter Gossett.

Bonds first came to public notice when she won the Wanamaker prize in 1932 for the song *Sea Ghost*; in 1933 she became the first black soloist to appear with the Chicago SO, in a performance of Price's Piano Concerto at the World's Fair. During the 1930s Bonds opened the Allied Arts Academy for ballet and music in Chicago, and was active as a solo and duo pianist in Canada and the USA. In New York she taught and served as music director for musical theater institutions, and organized a chamber society to foster the work of black musicians and composers. She also established a sight-singing program at Mount Calvary Baptist Church in Harlem. Later, she taught at the Inner City Institute and worked with the Inner City Repertory Theater in Los Angeles.

Bonds's output consists largely of vocal music. Her best-known works are spirituals for solo voice and/or chorus, but she also wrote large musical theater works, notably *Shakespeare in Harlem*, *Romey and Julie*, and *U.S.A.* As a popular-song writer she collaborated with Andy Razaf, Joe Davis, and Harold Dickinson; the best known of their works are *Peachtree Street* and *Spring will be so Sad*. Her works for orchestra and for piano are programmatic and reflect her strong sense of ethnic identity in their use of spiritual materials, jazz harmonies, and social themes (e.g., *Montgomery Variations* for orchestra, dedicated to Martin Luther King and written at the time of the march on Montgomery in 1965). Her last major work, *Credo*, was performed the month after her death by the Los Angeles PO under Mehta. Some of her arrangements of spirituals were commissioned and recorded by Leontyne Price during the 1960s.

WORKS

Stage: Shakespeare in Harlem (L. Hughes), perf. Westport, CT, 1959; Romey and Julie (R. Dunmore); U.S.A. (J. Dos Passos); The Migration, ballet, perf. 1964; Wings over Broadway, ballet; 4 other musical theater works

Chorus: The Ballad of the Brown King (Hughes), solo vv, chorus, orch, 1954; Mass, d, chorus, org, perf. 1959; Fields of Wonder (Hughes), song cycle, male chorus, pf, perf. 1964; Credo, Bar, chorus, orch, perf. 1972; many other sacred and secular works

4 orch works, incl. Montgomery Variations, 1965

42 songs, incl. Sea Ghost, 1932; The Negro Speaks of Rivers (Hughes), 1941; To a Brown Girl, Dead (Hughes), 1956; 3 Dream Portraits (Hughes), 1959; The Pasture (Frost), 1958; Stopping by the Woods on a Snowy Evening (Frost), 1963

14 popular songs, incl. Peachtree Street, collab. A. Razaf, J. Davis, 1939; Spring will be so Sad when she Comes this Year, collab. H. Dickinson, 1940; Georgia, collab. Razaf, Davis, *c*1939

Spirituals (all or most arrs.): 5 Spirituals, perf. 1942; Ezekiel saw the Wheel, 1v, pf (1959), arr. orch, 1968; I got a Home in that Rock, 1v, orch/pf (1959), rev. 1968; Sing Aho, 1v, pf (1960); Go Tell it on the Mountain, 1v/chorus, pf (1962); This little Light of mine, S, chorus, orch; Standin' in the Need of Prayer (1v, pf)/(S, chorus); He's got the Whole World in his Hands, 1v, pf (1963); Ev'ry Time I Feel the Spirit, 1v, pf (1970); I Wish I Knew how it would Feel to be Free, S, chorus, orch; Sinner, please don't let this Harvest Pass (1v, pf)/(S, mixed chorus); 6 others

4 pf works, incl. Spiritual Suite, Troubled Water, 1967

Principal publishers: Beekman Music, Dorsey, Mutual Music Society, Ricordi, Sam Fox, W. C. Handy

BIBLIOGRAPHY

SouthernB

H. J. Yuhasz: "Black Composers and their Piano Music Part I," *American Music Teacher*, xix/4 (1970), 24

Obituary, *Variety*, cclxvi (10 May 1972), 86

Obituary, *BPiM*, i (1973), 197

C. C. Harris, Jr.: "Three Schools of Black Choral Composers and Arrangers 1900–1970," *Choral Journal*, xiv/8 (1974), 11

M. D. Green: *A Study of the Lives and Works of Five Black Women Composers in America* (diss., U. of Oklahoma, 1975)

L. Berry: *Biographical Dictionary of Black Musicians and Music Educators* (Guthrie, OK, 1978)

C. Ammer: *Unsung: a History of Women in American Music* (Westport, CT, 1980)

A. Tischler: *Fifteen Black American Composers with a Bibliography of their Works* (Detroit, MI, 1981) [incl. list of works]

F. Berry: *Langston Hughes: Before and Beyond Harlem* (Westport, CT, 1983)

M. D. Green: *Black Women Composers: a Genesis* (Boston, 1983)

A. J. Thomas: *A Study of the Selected Masses of Twentieth-century Black Composers: Margaret Bonds, Robert Ray, George Walker and David Baker* (diss., U. of Illinois, 1983)

BARBARA GARVEY JACKSON

Bonelli [Bunn], **Richard** (*b* Port Byron, NY, 6 Feb 1887). Baritone. He studied at Syracuse University and later in Paris under Arthur Alexander and Jean de Reszke. He made his début as Valentin in *Faust* at the Brooklyn Academy in 1915 and joined the San Carlo Opera Company in 1922. His European début was at Modena in 1923 in Catalani's *Dejanice*. He first sang with the Chicago Grand Opera in 1925 and the San Francisco Opera in 1926, returning to both for several seasons. His début at the Metropolitan Opera on 1 December 1932 was as Germont with Rosa Ponselle. Although considered to be a Verdi specialist, the roles he sang most often were Valentin, Tonio (*Pagliacci*), and Sharpless (*Madama Butterfly*); his few performances as Wolfram were highly praised. His recordings show a lyric voice, with an excellent legato but without great power; one of the best is of the duet from *Martha*, with Mario Chamlee. Bonelli retired in 1945 and taught at the Curtis Institute and in New York.

BIBLIOGRAPHY

O. Thompson: *The American Singer* (New York, 1937/*R*1969), 378

RICHARD LeSUEUR

Bones [bone castanets]. Concussion idiophones, or clappers, of indefinite pitch. Originally made from animal rib bones, they now more commonly consist of flat hardwood sticks, about 15 cm long and slightly curved. They are played in pairs, with one pair usually held in each hand: one bone is held between the first and second fingers, pressed to the base of the thumb; the other, held between the second and third fingers, is struck against the first with a rapid flicking of the wrist. The bones produce a sound similar to that of castanets, and like them may be used to produce rhythms of great complexity.

The bones were played in China before 3000 BC, in Egypt around 3000 BC, in ancient Greece and Rome, and in Europe from medieval times. Although they are played in black Africa, their use is limited and, in some parts of the continent, of recent origin. In the USA the bones are associated principally with black music, and with the minstrel show in particular. It has been suggested that when slaves were forbidden the use of the drum in the 18th century they began to play the bones instead. In the early minstrel shows, in the 1840s, the bones were an essential rhythm instrument in an ensemble that otherwise consisted of fiddle, banjo, and tambourine; they were also used to play solos, often in imitation of drumbeats or the sounds of horses' hooves. The bones player was an "endman": he stood at one end of the minstrels' semicircle, and was the focus of much attention during the group's comic routines; in the early days of the minstrel show he was sometimes the master of ceremonies as well.

BIBLIOGRAPHY

O. Logan: "The Ancestry of Brudder Bones," *Harper's New Monthly Magazine*, lviii (1878–9), 687

H. Nathan: *Dan Emmett and the Rise of Early Negro Minstrelsy* (Norman, OK, 1962/*R*1977)

D. J. Epstein: *Sinful Tunes and Spirituals: Black Folk Music to the Civil War* (Urbana, IL, 1977)

R. B. Winans: "Black Instrumental Music Traditions in the Ex-slave Narratives," *Black Music Research Newsletter*, v/2 (1982), 2

——: "Early Minstrel Show Music, 1843–1852," *Musical Theatre in America*, ed. G. Loney (Westport, CT, 1984), 71

ROBERT B. WINANS

Bonner, Eugene MacDonald (*b* Washington, NC, 1889). Composer. He attended the Peabody Conservatory, Baltimore, and studied composition with Brockway and piano with Hutcheson. He went to England in 1911 and remained there until 1917, when he enlisted in the US Army. After the war Bonner worked in Paris, where he studied conducting under Albert Wolff, 1921–7. He then returned to New York and served as music critic for

The Outlook magazine (1927–9) and several newspapers, including the *Daily Eagle*, *Daily Mirror*, and *New York Herald Tribune*. In all Bonner composed five orchestral works, four chamber works, and five operas. The orchestral piece *Whispers of Heavenly Death* and a suite from his opera *La comédie de celui qui épousa une femme muette* were performed by the Baltimore SO.

WORKS

Operas: Barbara Frietchie, 1915–17, unperf.; La comédie de celui qui épousa une femme muette (after France), 1923, excerpts arr. as orch suite; The Venetian Glass Nephew (after E. Wylie), *c*1928; The Gods of the Mountain, 1936; Frankie and Johnnie

Orch: 3 Songs (Whitman), 1v, orch (1923); Whispers of Heavenly Death, 1925; White Nights, 1925; Taormina (1940); Concertino, pf, str

Chamber: Flûtes, Mez/Bar, fl, cl, bn, harp/pf, vc (1923); Pf Qnt, 1925; Suite sicilienne, vn, pf, 1926; Young Alexander, incidental music, wind, harp, perc, 1929

Principal publishers: Chester, J. Fischer

CHARLES H. KAUFMAN

Bonvin, Ludwig (*b* Sierre, Switzerland, 17 Feb 1850; *d* Buffalo, NY, 18 Feb 1939). Composer and musicologist. He studied medicine in Vienna and law in Switzerland, but was largely self-taught in music. He served as organist and choirmaster for a German Jesuit order in Exaeten, the Netherlands, and held various teaching posts before becoming ordained in England in 1885. He settled in the USA in 1887 and until he retired in 1929 was associated with Canisius College and other institutions in Buffalo.

Bonvin's compositions include a symphony and six tone poems for large orchestra; 17 works for chamber ensembles; 10 masses and other choral works with orchestra; 52 motets, litanies, offertories, and other sacred and secular choruses; 4 operas for children; 11 song cycles; and many character pieces for piano and organ. His work displays a firm technical mastery of post-Wagnerian harmony and counterpoint, with long, romantic lines, rich orchestral sonorities, and a fine sense of formal detail. He sometimes used the pseudonyms Georges De'Sierre, B. von Siders, and J. B. Rainer. Bonvin was a leading advocate for the application of mensural rhythm to Gregorian chant. He wrote a number of essays on the subject, including "On Syrian Liturgical Chant" (*MQ*, iv, 1918, p.593) and "The 'Measure' in Gregorian Music" (*MQ*, xv, 1929, p.16). He also recommended the admission of women to the congregational choir. The University of Würzburg awarded him an honorary doctorate of theology (1923) for his many contributions to sacred music. Collections of his manuscripts and memorabilia are in Buffalo at Canisius College, Daemen College, and the Buffalo and Erie County Public Library.

BIBLIOGRAPHY

Ludwig Bonvin: Verzeichnis sämtlicher Kompositionen und Schriften (Leipzig, 1907)

L. Bonvin: "Jubilee Address," *The Echo* (Buffalo) (23 Oct 1924)

O. E. Singenberger: "Ludwig Bonvin, SJ," *Caecilia*, lviii (1931), 170 [incl. list of pubd compositions]

ARTHUR J. NESS

Boogaloo. A social dance originating in New York and popular in the mid-1960s. Stepping diagonally, the dancer twisted each leg in alternation to the outside, bent the knee, and pointed the foot; with upturned hands, the arms were twirled from the elbows, which were pulled in and forward. Music for the boogaloo combined syncopated Latin bass and drum ostinatos with conventional soul songs. Hits during its brief vogue included Tom and Jerrico's *Boogaloo* (1965), Joe Cuba's *Bang, Bang* (1966), Hector Rivera's *At the Party* (1967), and Fantastic Johnny C.'s *Boogaloo Down Broadway* (1967).

BIBLIOGRAPHY

M. Stearns and J. Stearns: *Jazz Dance: the Story of American Vernacular Dance* (New York, 1968)

J. S. Roberts: *The Latin Tinge* (New York, 1979)

BARRY KERNFELD

Boogie-woogie (i). A percussive style of piano blues favored, for its volume and momentum, by bar-room, honky-tonk, and rent-party pianists. The term appears to have been applied originally to a dance performed to piano accompaniment, and its widespread use stems from the instructions for performing the dance on the recording *Pine Top's Boogie Woogie* (1928, Voc. 1245) by Pine Top Smith. The boogie style is characterized by the use of blues chord progressions combined with a forceful, repetitive left-hand bass figure; many bass patterns exist, but the most familiar are the "doubling" of the simple blues bass (ex.1) and the "walking" bass in broken octaves (ex.2).

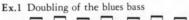

Ex.1 Doubling of the blues bass

Ex.2 "Walking" bass in broken octaves

Walking basses are reported to have been developed by ragtime pianists in the 19th century, and the first published example appears to be in Blind Boone's *Rag Medley no.2* (1909). Similar bass figures are used by Artie Matthews in his *Pastime Rag no.1* (published 1913), and are applied to a blues in his *Weary Blues* (1915). George Thomas used the same device in his *New Orleans Hop Scop Blues* (1911, published 1916) and on his recording *The Rocks* (1923, OK 4809), which he made under the pseudonym Clay Custer and which appears to be the first recorded example of a walking bass. Such figures consisted of even eighth-notes, dotted eighth- and 16th-notes, and triplets, and were loosely identified by musicians, sometimes by names such as the "Rocks," the "Chains," the "Fives." The right-hand configurations played against the bass patterns were both rhythmic and melodic, with sharp ostinato passages and sequences in 3rds and 6ths. Some performances, such as Meade "Lux" Lewis's *Bass on Top* (1940, BN 16), display subtly shifting patterns, while Wesley Wallace's train imitation *No.29* (1930, Para. 12958) employs 5/4 time in the bass and 4/4 in the treble. Such a feat is possible through the independence of the right-hand improvisations from the steady, rolling rhythm maintained by the left hand. Startling dissonances occur through the juxtaposition of the two strands, and cross-rhythms are also frequently created. Deliberate discords and rapid "crushed" or "press" notes, obtained by the striking of adjacent notes in rapid succession, are evident on Lewis's *Honky Tonk Train Blues* (1927, Para. 12896).

The first generation of boogie-woogie pianists – blues pianists who prominently featured walking bass and "eight-to-the-bar" rhythms – recorded some notable examples, among them Romeo Nelson's *Head Rag Hop* (1929, Voc. 1447), Arthur Montana Taylor's *Indiana Avenue Stomp* (1929, Voc. 1419), and Charles Avery's *Dearborn Street Breakdown* (1929, Para. 12896); these were rent-party pianists who were forgotten in the Depression years. In 1938 a revival was initiated by the record producer and critic John Hammond, who sought out Albert Ammons and Meade "Lux" Lewis, then working in Chicago as taxi-drivers. With Pete Johnson from Kansas City and his singer Joe Turner, the Boogie Woogie Trio became popular at Café Society, New York, and, linked with the swing craze, boogie-woogie enjoyed a brief vogue. These authentic boogie pianists made a number of outstanding recordings, including Pete Johnson's *Goin' Away Blues* (1938, Voc. 4607) with Big Joe Turner, and Albert Ammons's *Chicago in Mind* (1939, BN 4). The brief but widespread popularity of boogie-woogie also led to the discovery of Jimmy Yancey and "Cripple" Clarence Lofton, who brought singular rhythmic conceptions to their playing. The connection with swing is exemplified in such recordings as *Boogie Woogie* by Tommy Dorsey and his Orchestra (1938, Vic. 26054) and Count Basie's *Basie Boogie* (1941, OK 6330); some recordings, such as Will Bradley's *Boogie Woogie Conga* (1941, Col. 35994), Charlie Barnet's *Scrub me, Mama, with a boogie beat* (1940, Bluebird 10975), and the Andrews Sisters' *Boogie Woogie Bugle Boy* (1941, Decca 3598), despite their titles, bear little relation to the original idiom.

In the late 1940s boogie-woogie reverted to the blues, becoming a standard element in every blues pianist's playing. Chicago pianists gained inspiration from the recordings of Big Maceo (Major Merriweather), whose *Chicago Breakdown* (1945, Bluebird 34-0743) was a tour de force. From the 1950s innumerable boogie-woogie recordings were made by blues pianists, some of whom, such as Little Brother Montgomery and Otis Spann, showed comparatively sophisticated musicianship, while others, such as Memphis Slim (Peter Chatman) and Champion Jack Dupree, played in a more primitive style. Boogie-woogie has proved to be one of the most enduring elements in blues performance, and has provided the background for scores of recordings by the Chicago blues bands of Muddy Waters and Howlin' Wolf.

BIBLIOGRAPHY

W. Russell: "Boogie Woogie," *Jazzmen*, ed. F. Ramsey, Jr., and C. E. Smith (New York, 1939)

E. Borneman: "Boogie Woogie," *Just Jazz*, ed. S. Traill and G. Lascelles (London, 1957)

M. Harrison: "Boogie Woogie," *Jazz*, ed. N. Hentoff and A. J. McCarthy (New York, 1959/*R*1974)

P. Oliver: "Piano Blues and Boogie Woogie," *Jazz on Record*, ed. A. McCarthy (London, 1968)

P. Oliver: *The Story of the Blues* (London, 1969), 73ff, 114f

E. Kriss: *Barrelhouse and Boogie Piano* (New York, 1974)

PAUL OLIVER

Boogie-woogie (ii). A social dance and dance step of black-American origin characterized by high kicks, knee and lower-body twists, and swaying. It became popular in the early 20th century along with the ragtime or animal dances like the camel walk, but achieved even greater popularity in the 1930s when it was associated with the piano style of the same name and performed acrobatically by the tap dancer Nicholas Brothers in the film *Big Broadcast of 1936*. Music for the boogie-woogie included Tommy Dorsey's hit *T.D.'s Boogie Woogie* (1938), *Boogie Woogie Bugle Boy* (1941), made popular by the Andrews Sisters, and such songs as *Basin Street Blues*, *Bugle Call Rag*, *How Long Blues*, and *Darktown Strutters Ball*. In the late 1970s and early 1980s, the term "boogie-down" generally referred to rock dancing.

BIBLIOGRAPHY

M. Stearns and J. Stearns: *Jazz Dance: the Story of American Vernacular Dance* (New York, 1968)

P. Oliver: *The Meaning of the Blues* (New York, 1972)

For further bibliography, *see* DANCE.

PAULINE NORTON

Booker T. and the MGs. Instrumental group. It was formed in 1961 by members of the Mar-keys, a leading southern soul band which was important in the development of the Memphis sound. Booker T. Jones (*b* Memphis, TN, 11 Dec 1944), an organist, was studying music at Indiana University in 1961 when he met Steve Cropper (*b* Willow Springs, MO, 21 Oct 1941), who became the group's guitarist. The original bass guitarist, Lewis Steinberg, was soon replaced by Donald "Duck" Dunn (*b* Memphis, 24 Nov 1941); the drummer was Al Jackson (*b* Memphis, 27 Nov 1935; *d* Memphis, 1 Oct 1975). "MG" in the group's name stands for "Memphis Group." Booker T. and the MGs had the first of a series of successes with *Green Onions* (no.3, 1962). In the mid-1960s they became the house band of Stax Records in Memphis, playing on the recordings of such soul artists as Sam and Dave (*Hold on! I'm comin'*), Wilson Pickett (*In the midnight hour*), and Eddie Floyd (*Knock on wood*). Cropper collaborated in the writing of all these songs, and his terse, melodic guitar lines and Booker T.'s sweeping organ playing helped to define the Stax sound. They toured occasionally as part of the "Stax-Volt Revue." One of the group's final and best-known successes was *Time is tight* (no.6, 1969), part of the soundtrack which Jones composed for the film *Uptight*. The group disbanded in 1971, when the predominant style of soul music changed from the tight, skeletal sound that characterized Stax recordings to a lusher, more heavily orchestrated sound. With the exception of Jackson, the members all became session musicians; Cropper and Dunn were the most successful in this area, recording with the Blues Brothers (Dan Aykroyd and John Belushi) and appearing in their film of 1980. Jones has recorded solo albums as well as duets with Priscilla Coolidge (at one time his wife), and has produced recordings for Willie Nelson (*Stardust*, 1978, among others).

RECORDINGS

(selective list; all recorded for Stax)

Green Onions (127, 1962); Bootleg (169, 1965); Groovin' (224, 1967); Soul-limbo (0001, 1968); Hang 'em high (0013, 1969); Time is tight (0028, 1969)

BIBLIOGRAPHY

SouthernB ("Jones, Booker T.")

P. Garland: *The Sound of Soul* (Chicago, 1969)

JOHN MORTHLAND

Boone, Blind [John William] (*b* Miami, MO, 17 May 1864; *d* Warrensburg, MO, 4 Oct 1927). Pianist and composer. He was blind from infancy, but soon revealed musical abilities, and several prominent local families contributed funds to send him to the Missouri School for the Blind in St. Louis, where he could further develop his talents. Although he was later expelled from this school, he received some formal piano instruction and acquired a reputation as a prodigy. He earned his living as an itinerant musician until 1879, when he came to the attention of John Lange, Jr., a prominent black contractor in Columbia, Missouri, who took charge of the youth's musical career. Within five years Boone was giving regular concerts in a group with a banjoist, a violinist, and a child singer. They played an annual ten-month season from 1885 to 1915, performing six nights a week; by

1915 Boone had played 8400 concerts and traveled more than 200,000 miles.

During the years of his greatest success Boone published a number of compositions, including waltzes, coon songs, and classical character pieces. The best known of these are *Blind Boone's Southern Rag Medleys* nos. 1 and 2 (1908–9). His most spectacular composition, however, was apparently *Marshfield Tornado*, a musical depiction of a storm that struck this small Missouri town in the 1880s. Although Boone was reportedly offered thousands of dollars to reproduce this piece in sheet music or on a piano roll, he always refused, claiming that he wanted to reserve the work solely for his own use. In 1916 Lange died, and Boone's career began an inevitable decline that was hastened by his aversion to jazz. By the time of his final performance in the little town of Virden, Illinois, on 31 May 1927, much of his former enthusiasm and flamboyant manner had disappeared. His works were rediscovered during the ragtime revival of the 1970s, however. One of his instruments, an ornate Chickering grand piano, is displayed by the Boone County Historical Society in the Maplewood Mansion, Nifong Memorial Park, Columbia.

WORKS

Selective list; unless otherwise stated, all printed works published in Columbia, Missouri.

Pf: Caprice de concert (sur thèmes nègres) nos. 1–2 (St. Louis, 1893); Old Folks at Home (St. Louis, 1894); Sparks (St. Louis, 1894); Dance des nègres (Caprice de concert no. 3) (St. Louis, 1902); Blind Boone's Aurora Waltz (1907); Blind Boone's Southern Rag Medley no. 1 (1908; repr. in *Ragtime Rarities*, ed. T. J. Tichenor, New York, 1975); Blind Boone's Southern Rag Medley no. 2 (1909; repr. in *Ragtime Rarities*, ed. T. J. Tichenor, New York, 1975); Last Dream (1909); Love Feast (1913); Grand valse de concert op. 13 (Kansas City, MO, 1923)

Songs: Whar shill we go when de great day comes (New York, 1892); When I meet dat coon tonight (New York, 1892); Dinah's Barbeque (St. Louis, 1893); You can't go to gloria that a'way (St. Louis, 1893); That little German band (St. Louis, 1894); Melons Cool and Green (St. Louis, 1894); Dat morning in de sky (Kansas City, MO, 1899); Georgia Melon (1908)

Principal publishers: Allen, Kunkel

BIBLIOGRAPHY

SouthernB
M. Fuell: *Blind Boone: his Early Life and his Achievements* (Kansas City, MO, 1915)
N. T. Gentry: "Blind Boone and John Lange Jr.," *Missouri Historical Review*, xxxiv (1940), 232
G. T. Ashley: *Reminiscences of a Circuit Rider* (Hollywood, CA, 1941), 115
R. Blesh and H. Janis: *They All Played Ragtime* (New York, 1950, rev. 4/1971)
R. Darch: "Blind Boone: a Sensational Missouri Musician Forgotten," *Bulletin of the Missouri Historical Society*, xvii/3 (1961), 245
M. Harrah: "The Incomparable Blind Boone," *Ragtimer* (1969), July–Aug, 9
——: "Wayne B. Allen: 'Blind' Boone's Last Manager," *Ragtimer* (1969), Sept–Oct, 10
W. Parrish: "'Blind' Boone's Ragtime," *Missouri Life*, vii/5 (1979), 17

W. K. McNEIL, JAMES M. BURK (work-list)

Boone, Charles (*b* Cleveland, OH, 21 June 1939). Composer. He studied at the Academy of Music in Vienna (1960–61), the University of Southern California (BM, theory, 1963), and San Francisco State College (MA, composition, 1968); among his teachers were Karl Schiske, Adolf Weiss, and Krenek. From 1975 to 1977 he was composer-in-residence in Berlin under the auspices of the Deutscher Akademischer Austauschdienst; he has been awarded three NEA grants (1968, 1975, 1983) and was commissioned by the San Francisco SO to compose *First Landscape* (1971). Active as an organizer of performances of new music, he served in the 1960s as chairman of the San Francisco Composers' Forum and as coordinator of the Mills College Performing Group and Tape Music Center, and founded the San Francisco BYOP (Bring Your Own Pillow) concert series in the early 1970s. He writes and lectures on new music in Europe and the USA. From his early pointillism Boone evolved a more expansive style using static blocks of sound; the recent works are more monochromatic in instrumental color, and strive for a "complex simplicity" (his term), expressed through timbral relationships, overlapping sonorities, and changes of texture. A connoisseur and collector of art, he has been much influenced by the architecture of Alvar Aalto, whose clear and understated structures he seeks to emulate in elegantly balanced, rather classical compositions; although they fall well within the category of atonal modernism, Boone's works avoid allegiances to serial or narrative methods.

WORKS

(voices are untexted in works for which no author is given)

3 Motets (E. E. Cummings), SATB, 1962–5; Oblique Formation, fl, pf, 1965; Starfish, fl, cl, 2 perc, 2 vn, pf, 1966; A Cool Glow of Radiation, fl, tape, 1966; The Edge of the Land, orch, 1968; Not Now, cl, 1969; Qt, vn, vc, cl, pf, 1970; Vermilion, ob, 1970; Zephyrus, ob, pf, 1970; Chinese Texts (trans. K. Rexroth), S, orch, 1971; First Landscape, orch, 1971; Vocalise, S, 1972; Second Landscape, chamber orch, 1973, arr. orch, 1979; Raspberries, 3 perc, 1974; Linea meridiana, chamber ens, 1975; Fields/Singing, S, chamber ens, 1976; San Zeno/Verona, chamber ens, 1976; Shunt, 3 perc, 1978; Str Piece, str orch, 1978; Little Fl Pieces, 1979; Streaming, fl, 1979; Slant, perc, 1980; Springtime, ob, 1980; Winter's End, S, Ct, va da gamba, hpd, 1980; Trace, fl, 10 performers, 1981–3; The Watts Towers, 1 perc, 1981; Weft, 6 perc, 1982; Drum Bug, mechanical woodblocks, 1983; The Khaju Bridge, S, tpt, db, elec org, perc, tape, 1983–; Drift, octet, 1984–5

Principal publisher: G. Schirmer

CHARLES SHERE

Boone, Pat [Charles Eugene] (*b* Jacksonville, FL, 1 June 1934). Popular singer and actor. He began singing in public at the age of ten and, while a student at North Texas State University, appeared on his own radio show and on television in the "Ted Mack Amateur Hour" and "Arthur Godfrey's Talent Scouts." He began his recording career with Dot Records in 1955, and his success as a leading popular singer of the mid- and late 1950s was closely linked to the emergence of rock-and-roll as the music of American youth. Although he was generally identified by the public with the new music, only his earliest hits can be strongly related to it, and in them the elements of rhythm-and-blues and country music objectionable to the middle-class audience were minimized by the musical arrangements or neutralized by Boone's pleasant crooning and wholesome personality. Many of his early hits were cover versions of original recordings by black and country artists, such as *Ain't that a shame* (1955) and *Long Tall Sally* (1956). Later recordings, such as *Love Letters in the Sand* (1957), *April Love* (1957), and *The Exodus Song* (1961), were in the more traditional Tin Pan Alley style. Boone was widely imitated in the 1950s, but thereafter his singing career declined, although he continued to make occasional appearances and recordings and firmly established himself as a proponent of Christian causes. Between 1957 and 1970 he appeared in 15 films, and since 1970 has performed in theaters and clubs with his wife and four daughters.

BIBLIOGRAPHY

"Boone, Pat," *CBY 1959*
G. Wood: *An A–Z of Rock and Roll* (London, 1971)
M. R. Pitts and L. H. Harrison: *Hollywood on Record: the Film Stars' Discography* (Metuchen, NJ, 1978)
C. E. Boone: *Together: 25 Years with the Pat Boone Family* (Nashville, TN, 1979)
C. Hamm: *Yesterdays: Popular Song in America* (New York, 1979)

MICHAEL J. BUDDS

Boosey & Hawkes, Inc. Firm of music publishers and dealers in musical instruments. Based in New York, it is a subsidiary of Boosey & Hawkes Ltd. of London. The London firm was established in 1930 as the result of a merger between Boosey & Co. and Hawkes & Co. It has grown into a major international publishing house with branches throughout the world. Besides the standard repertory, it publishes much 20th-century music and represents, among others, Stravinsky, Bartók, Kodály, Strauss, Britten, Prokofiev, Peter Maxwell Davies, and Nicholas Maw. The New York firm was first established as a branch of Boosey & Co. in 1892 and became Boosey & Hawkes, Inc., in 1930. Under Ralph Hawkes and his successors as president, it has developed its own catalogue, which emphasizes the works of American composers, including Carter, Copland, Piston, Argento, Del Tredici, Kolb, Rorem, Floyd, and Lees. From 1965 to 1981 it issued a newsletter. In 1979 a musical instrument division was created for the sale of instruments manufactured by the London firm.

BIBLIOGRAPHY

Q. E[aton]: "Bread & Hyacinths," *Opera News*, xxx/16 (1966), 12

FRANCES BARULICH

Bootsy's Rubber Band. Rhythm-and-blues group led by BOOTSY COLLINS.

Bop [bebop, rebop]. A style of jazz developed in the early 1940s in New York, which came to full maturity by 1945 in the work of Dizzy Gillespie (trumpet), Charlie Parker (alto saxophone), Bud Powell and Thelonious Monk (piano), Kenny Clarke and Max Roach (drums), and others. The word "bop" is a shortened form of the vocables (nonsense syllables) "bebop" or "rebop," which were commonly used in scat singing to accompany the distinctive two-note rhythm shown in ex. 1. Although bop was solidly grounded in earlier jazz styles (dixieland and swing), it represented a considerable increase in complexity, and was considered revolutionary at the time of its development. Perhaps its most significant characteristic was the highly diversified texture created by the rhythm section, compared with the insistent four-beat approach of the swing era. In the newer style, the basic beat was stated by the double bass player and elaborated by the drummer on ride cymbal and hi-hat, while a variety of on- and off-beat punctuations were added on the piano, bass drum, and snare drum (ex. 2). These punctuations sometimes reinforced and sometimes complemented the melody, causing much rhythmic interplay during improvised solos; the best bop soloists were adept at improvising rapid melodies filled with asymmetrical phrases and accent patterns. Ex. 2 also illustrates the enriched harmonic vocabulary of the bop style, which made far more frequent use of altered 9th, 11th, and 13th chords than earlier jazz. Moreover, since many bop themes and improvisations were based largely on these chords, the melodies of bop were also more complex (i.e., more chromatic) than those of swing.

Ex. 1 L. Armstrong: *Hotter than That* (1927, OK 8535), transcr. T. Owens

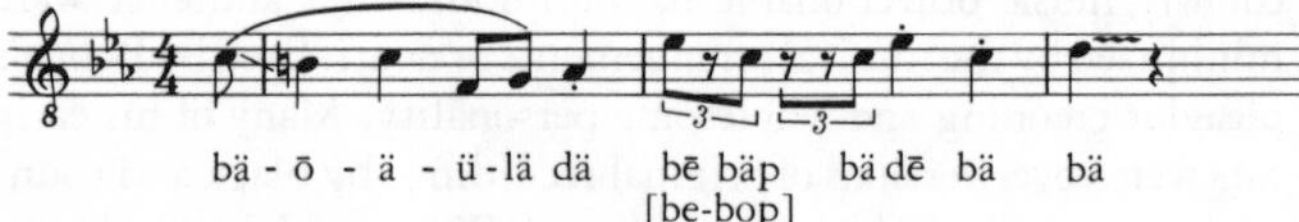

Ex. 2

Many early bop themes, such as *Ornithology* (Parker and Benny Harris), *Anthropology* (Parker and Gillespie), *Groovin' High* (Gillespie), *Donna Lee* (Parker), and *Hot House* (Gillespie), were intricate melodies based on the harmonic structures of earlier popular songs. However, by the late 1940s the most common themes had become simpler, and some were even based on the overworked swing-era device called the riff (e.g., Milt Jackson's *Bag's Groove* and Clifford Brown's *Blues Walk*). This shift from complex to simple themes had no effect on the procedures followed by the rhythm section or the style of the improvised solos. Other developments caused slight alterations in the character of the music. In the late 1940s and 1950s, for example, a number of bop musicians (the trumpeter Miles Davis, the alto saxophonist Paul Desmond, the tenor saxophonist Stan Getz, the baritone saxophonist Gerry Mulligan, the vibraphonist Milt Jackson, and the pianist John Lewis, among others) began playing in a soft, subtle manner later called COOL JAZZ. From the mid-1950s other bop players (including the alto saxophonist Cannonball Adderley, the pianist Horace Silver, the organist Jimmy Smith, and the drummer Art Blakey) began incorporating folk elements from the blues and black gospel traditions into their playing, attracting labels such as "soul-jazz," "funky jazz," and HARD BOP. In most cases the differences between bop and these subspecies were too minor to warrant reference to distinct styles.

Bop players generally rejected the elaborate written arrangements of swing music for a straightforward pattern: a unison statement of the theme, followed by a string of improvised solos and a concluding unison statement. They also preferred to play in small combos, consisting typically of the quintet instrumentation used by Charlie Parker (trumpet, saxophone, piano, double bass, and drums). Nonetheless, some short-lived big bands, formed in the 1940s, played in the bop style, notably those led by Billy Eckstine and Dizzy Gillespie. Permanent inroads into big-band style were made in the late 1940s and early 1950s, when swing bandleaders such as Woody Herman, Stan Kenton, and Count Basie began employing younger, bop musicians. Arrangers and players, finding that bop rhythm sections could support large brass and reed sections, and that the harmonies of swing-style riffs could be modernized, developed ways of fusing the two styles. Later bop bands, such as those led by Gil Evans, Thad Jones and Mel Lewis, Louis Bellson, Toshiko Akiyoshi and Lew Tabackin, and Rob McConnell, gained widespread acceptance in the jazz world.

In addition to the aforementioned musicians, other important bop players include the trumpeters Fats Navarro, Clifford Brown, and Freddie Hubbard; trombonists J. J. Johnson and Bob Brookmeyer; alto saxophonists Sonny Stitt, Jackie McLean, Art Pepper, and Phil Woods; tenor saxophonists Dexter Gordon, Sonny Rollins, John Coltrane, and Johnny Griffin; baritone saxophonists Serge Chaloff and Pepper Adams; pianists Billy Taylor, Bill Evans, and Oscar Peterson; guitarists Wes Montgomery and George Benson; double bass players Ray Brown, Oscar Pettiford, and Charles Mingus; and drummers Philly Joe Jones, Shelly Manne, and Elvin Jones.

See also JAZZ, §V.

BIBLIOGRAPHY

L. Feather: *Inside Be-bop* (New York, 1949/*R*1977 as *Inside Jazz*)
A. Hodeir: *Jazz: its Evolution and Essence* (New York, 1956/*R*1975), 99ff
A. Morgan and R. Horricks: *Modern Jazz: a Survey of Developments since 1939* (London, 1956/*R*1977)
M. Stearns: *The Story of Jazz* (New York, 1956/*R*1958), 155ff
L. Feather: *Jazz: an Exciting Story of Jazz Today* (Los Angeles, 1958)
R. Horricks and others: *These Jazzmen of our Time* (London, 1959, 2/1962)
R. Russell: "Bebop," *The Art of Jazz*, ed. M. Williams (New York, 1959), 187 [orig. pubd as 4 articles in *Record Changer*, vii–viii (1948–9)]
J. Goldberg: *Jazz Masters of the Fifties* (New York, 1965/*R*1980)
I. Gitler: *Jazz Masters of the Forties* (New York, 1966)
J. S. Wilson: *Jazz: the Transition Years 1940–1960* (New York, 1966)
L. Feather: *From Satchmo to Miles* (New York, 1972), 129ff
R. Russell: *Bird Lives: the High Life and Hard Times of Charlie (Yardbird) Parker* (New York, 1973)
T. Owens: *Charlie Parker: Techniques of Improvisation* (diss., UCLA, 1974)
M. Harrison and others: *Modern Jazz: the Essential Records, a Critical Selection* (London, 1975)
J. L. Collier: *The Making of Jazz: a Comprehensive History* (Boston, 1978), 341ff
D. Gillespie and A. Fraser: *To Be, or not . . . to Bop: Memoirs* (Garden City, NY, 1979)
S. Strunk: "The Harmony of Early Bop: a Layered Approach," *Journal of Jazz Studies*, vi/1 (1979), 4–53
R. Horricks: *Dizzy Gillespie and the Be-bop Revolution* (New York, 1984)

THOMAS OWENS

Borden, David (Russell) (*b* Boston, MA, 25 Dec 1938). Composer and keyboard player. He studied composition with Louis Mennini, Bernard Rogers, and Howard Hanson at the Eastman School (BM 1961, MM 1962) and with Billy Jim Layton, Leon Kirchner, and Randall Thompson at Harvard University (MA 1965). He also studied at the Berkshire Music Center with Wolfgang Fortner (summer 1961) and Gunther Schuller (summer 1966); on a Fulbright fellowship with Boris Blacher at the Berlin Hochschule für Musik (1965–6); privately with jazz artists Jimmy Giuffre and Jaki Byard; and with Robert Moog, inventor of the Moog synthesizer and other electronic instruments. After tenure in 1966–8 as Ford Foundation composer-in-residence for the Ithaca, New York, public school system, he became composer and pianist at the dance department of Cornell University in 1968. Borden is perhaps best-known for his work with Mother Mallard's Portable Masterpiece Co., a performing group comprising electronic keyboard instruments, synthesizers, and voices, which he formed in 1969. In addition to Borden, Mother Mallard's members have included Judy Borscher, Steve Drews, Linda Fisher, and Chip Smith; recordings by the group are available on the Earthquack label.

From 1967 Borden has used synthesizers in live performances, and through the use of solo improvisations, wave-form manipulation, and multi-track tape techniques he has developed a personal style of polyphonic music. His music from the early 1980s is minimal in style, characterized by a steady rhythmic pulse and running eighth-note lines with melodic counterpoint.

WORKS

Orch: Trbn Concertino, 1960; The Force, S, chamber orch, 1962; Cairn for JFK, orch, tape, 1965; All-American, Teenage, Lovesongs, wind ens, tape, 1967; Trudymusic, pf, orch, 1967; Variations, wind ens, tape, 1968

Chamber: 3 Pieces, ww qnt, 1958; 15 Dialogues, trbn, tpt, 1959–62; Short Trio, pf trio, 1964; Flatland Music, vc, elec gui, pf, perc, 1965; Pentacle & Epitaph, ob, va, harp, 1966; Omnidirectional Halo III, 2 S, 2 hpd, 2 vc, 1974; Counterpoint, fl, vc, harp, 1978

Synth ens: Cloudscape for Peggy, 1970; Easter, with tape, 1970; Endocrine Dot Pattern, with 2 brass, 1970; A. Art, with tape, 1971; Frank (i.e. Sin), with tape, 1971; Tetrahedron, 1971; All Set, 1972; Music, with tape, 1972; The Omnidirectional Halo, with wind ens, 1972; C-A-G-E, pts. I–III, 1973–5; The Continuing Story of Counterpoint, pts. 1–9, 1976–83; Anas platyrhynchos, 1977; Enfield in Winter, 1978

Other elec: Technique, Good Taste and Hard Work, 3 tapes, 1969; Esty Point, Summer 1978, elec pf, 4 synth, opt. s sax, 1981; Anatidae I, s sax, elec pf, 2 synth, tape, II, bar sax, elec gui, 2 synth, tape, 1984; Enfield in Summer, elec pf, 3 synth, 1984; The Heurtgen Forest, Germany, January 22 1945, elec pf, 3 synth, 1984

Principal publisher: Lameduck

JOAN LA BARBARA

Boretz, Benjamin (*b* New York, 3 Oct 1934). Composer and theorist. He began composing at an early age and studied philosophy as well as music in high school and at Brooklyn College (BA 1954). He received an MFA in composition at Brandeis University (1957), where he was a pupil of Arthur Berger and Irving Fine. He also studied with Foss at UCLA and Milhaud at Aspen. In 1970 he received the PhD from Princeton, where he had been a pupil of Sessions and Babbitt. From 1973 he taught at Bard College, Annandale-on-Hudson, New York. Among his awards have been the Fromm Composition Prize, 1956, a Fulbright scholarship, 1970–71, and a Princeton University Council of the Humanities fellowship, 1971–2.

His early work demonstrates concern for systematic design and the realization of complex and multiple networks of nested musical relationships. Later he explored contexts for improvisatory music making: scenarios and texts for group interaction, notational and gestural stimuli for performance, and so-called soundscores, i.e., taped sound intended as a "text" for performance. Beginning in 1980 he taped many hundreds of episodes of "solo and collaborative soundmaking expression."

Boretz's work as a writer and editor has had a particularly great impact. He was music critic for the *Nation*, 1962–9, and with Arthur Berger founded the journal *Perspectives of New Music* in 1962, of which he remained a co-editor (with Berger, Edward T. Cone, and Elaine Barkin, in succession) until 1982. The lengthiest of his writings, *Meta-Variations: Studies in the Foundation of Musical Thought*, which appeared in that journal in installments (1969–73), applies principles of empiricist philosophy in examining the possibility of discourse about music. In later writings, he investigated varieties of musical-verbal discourse in which the sonority of language, changes in narrative voice, and the graphic presentation of the text play a fundamental role. He has also written on other composers such as Sessions, Perle, and Babbitt.

WORKS

(selective list)

Conc. grosso, str, 1954; Partita, pf, 1955; Divertimento, ens, 1956; Vn Conc., 1956; Str Qt, 1957–8; 3 Donne Songs, S, pf, 1959–60; Brass Qnt, 1961–3; Group Variations I, chamber orch, 1964–7, II, tape, 1968–71; Liebeslied, pf, 1974; (". . . my chart shines high where the blue milks upset . . ."), pf, 1976; Language, as a Music: Six Marginal Pretexts for Composition, speaker, pf, tape, 1978; Soliloquy II, pf, 1979; -Forming, tape-recorded improvisations, 1980–; Soliloquy III, kbd, 1980; Musics for Two Composers, pfmrs, 1981; Soliloquy IV, pf, 1981; Soliloquy V, elec b gui, 1982; Midnight Music, pfmrs, 1982

Principal publisher: Lingua

MARTIN BRODY

Borge, Victor [Rosenbaum, Borge] (*b* Copenhagen, Denmark, 3 Jan 1909). Pianist, musical humorist, and conductor. After early training with his father, he gave a piano recital at the age of eight in Copenhagen, which won for him a scholarship to the conservatory; he later studied with Frederic Lamond and Egon Petri in Berlin. He performed in amateur musical reviews in Copenhagen, but his satires of Hitler placed him in danger and he fled, first to Sweden and then to the USA, where he later became a citizen. In New York in 1940 he began regularly to appear on Bing Crosby's "Kraft Music Hall" radio series, which led to a radio show of his own. Starting in the autumn of 1953 he gave nearly 850 daily recitals under the title "Comedy in Music" at the Golden Theater on Broadway. He has toured in many parts of the world and has appeared widely on radio and television and in films. His routines (which are partly improvised) are a mixture of verbal and musical humor, delivered at the piano; though his comic reputation is based on his continually forestalling and interrupting his own playing, he is an accomplished performer, as his elaborate musical jokes (such as the composite piano concerto consisting of well-known passages from the repertory skillfully run together) demonstrate.

When he was well into his 60s Borge began to appear as a guest conductor with such orchestras as the Amsterdam Concertgebouw and the New York PO. He sang and played with Beverly Sills in the Opera Company of Boston production of *Die Fledermaus* (25 January 1980), and made his opera conducting début in *Die Zauberflöte* with the New Cleveland Opera Company (30 November 1979). He has written two books, *My Favorite Intermissions* (1971) and *My Favorite Comedies in Music* (1980), and made several recordings. Among his many honors are knighthoods conferred by Denmark, Norway, Sweden, and Finland.

BIBLIOGRAPHY

R. King: "Victor Borge, Comedy's Music Man," *MJ*, xxxv/10 (1977), 4

B. Wechsler: "Victor Borge: Conductor and Concert Pianist," *MJ*, xxxviii/4 (1980), 35

J. Wagner: "Victor Borge: Clown Prince of Music," *Clavier*, xx/6 (1981), 15

KAREN MONSON

Bori, Lucrezia [Borja y Gonzales de Riancho, Lucrecia] (*b* Valencia, Spain, 24 Dec 1887; *d* New York, 14 May 1960). Spanish soprano. She studied first in Spain, then in Milan with M. Vidal, and made her début in 1908 at the Teatro Adriano, Rome, as Micaela in *Carmen*. In 1910, after auditioning for Toscanini, Gatti-Casazza, and Puccini, she was offered the title role in *Manon Lescaut*, given by the Metropolitan Opera during its first visit to Paris. She repeated the role in her official début with the company in New York two years later (opening night of the 1912–13 season), having in the meantime fulfilled engagements in Paris, at La Scala (where she sang Oktavian in the first Italian production of *Der Rosenkavalier*), and in Buenos Aires.

Bori performed at the Metropolitan for several seasons before undergoing a number of operations to remedy her increasing vocal problems. She was nevertheless able to return there for another 15 years before retiring at the end of the 1935–6 season. Among her important roles should be mentioned Norina (in Donizetti's *Don Pasquale*), Gounod's Juliet, and Fiora (in Montemezzi's *L'amore dei tre re*). Endowed with a voice of modest size, rather limited in the upper register, Bori used its clear and delicate timbre to draw characters of pathetic fragility (Mimì and Manon); she imbued them with intense and passionate feeling and, in the comic repertory, with gentle and stylized charm. She may be considered a modern version of the "sentimental" 18th-century prima donna.

BIBLIOGRAPHY

G. Gatti-Casazza: *Memories of Opera* (New York, 1941)

J. B. Richards: "Lucrezia Bori," *Record Collector*, ix (1954–5), 105 [with discography]

R. Celletti: "Lucrezia Bori," *Musiche e dischi*, no. 107 (1955), 10 [with discography by R. Vegeto]

G. Lauri-Volpi: *Voci parallele* (Milan, 1955), 37ff

M. de Schauensee: "Lucrezia Bori," *Opera News*, xxv/1 (1960), 26

R. Celletti: "Bori, Lucrezia," *Le grandi voci* (Rome, 1964) [with discography by R. Vegeto]

"Lucrezia Bori Discography," *Record Advertiser* (1971), no.2, p.3

L. Rasponi: "Lucrezia Bori," *The Last Prima Donnas* (New York, 1982), 433

RODOLFO CELLETTI/R

Bornschein, Franz (Carl) (*b* Baltimore, MD, 10 Feb 1879; *d* Baltimore, 8 June 1948). Composer. The son of a German-born violist and sometime orchestra leader, he studied violin in Baltimore with Lawrence Rosenberger and Julius Zech. He started to compose at the age of eight; in 1895 he entered Peabody Conservatory, where he studied violin with Joan C. Van Hulsteyn and harmony with Phillip L. Kahmer and Otis B. Boise (diploma 1902). He joined the faculty of the Peabody preparatory department in 1905 and also became Baltimore correspondent for *Musical America*. From 1910 to 1913 he served as music critic for the Baltimore *Sun* and from 1919 until his death taught violin, conducting, and composition at Peabody.

As a composer, Bornschein is known chiefly for his many choral works, of which *The Djinns*, *Onowa*, *Joy*, and *Conqueror Worm* were the most popular (for some of these he wrote his own texts under the pseudonym Frank Fairfield). He also wrote several well-received orchestral tone poems on American themes, including *Moon over Taos* and *The Earth Sings*, which were given their premières by Werner Janssen and Reginald Stewart, respectively. Bornschein was for many years active as a conductor of orchestras and choral groups in Baltimore.

WORKS

Stage: Mother Goose's Goslings (children's operetta, Bornschein), 1918; Willow Plate (operetta, D. Rose), 1932; Song of Songs (lyric opera, F. Coutts, Bornschein), 1934; 2 other operettas

Orch: Southern Nights, 1935; Leif Erikson, 1939; Moon over Taos, 1939; The Earth Sings, 1939; The Mission Road, 1939; Ode to the Brave, 1944; 9 other sym. poems; 2 vn concs., g, E; many suites for youth orch

Inst: Str Qt, 1900; Pf Qnt, 1904; Pan Dances (Prankish Pan), fl, str, 1933; Appalachian Legend, vc, pf, 1940; The Sprite, harp, 1945; 22 duos, vn, pf; 3 other duos, vc, pf; kbd works; arrs.; juvenilia for 1–2 insts

Vocal: over 80 choruses, incl. Wet-Sheet and Flowing Sea (A. Cunningham), 1906, The Djinns (V. Hugo), 1913, Onowa (F. H. Martens), 1915, Four Winds (C. Luders), 1921, The Sea (J. McLeod), 1923, The Knight of Bethlehem (S. Maugham), 1924; 7 cantatas, incl. Zorah (F. H. Martens), 1914, Conquerer Worm (Poe), 1939, Joy (The Mystic Trumpeter) (Whitman), 1942; Deodate (Bible), oratorio; 27 anthems; many choral arrs.; 30 songs; 10 recitations, lv, pf

MSS in *MdHi*, *MdBPC*

Principal publishers: Ditson, J. Fischer, G. Schirmer

BIBLIOGRAPHY

Choral Compositions by Franz Bornschein (Baltimore, 1940s) [copy in *MdBPC*]

E. M. Daniels: "A Checklist of the Bornschein Collection at the Maryland Historical Society" (MS, *MdHi*, *MdBPC*)

J. M. Gingerich: "Index of the Franz C. Bornschein Scrapbooks in the Peabody Conservatory Library" (MS, *MdBPC*)

NED QUIST

Borowski, Felix (*b* Burton in Kendal, nr Kendal, England, 10 March 1872; *d* Chicago, IL, 6 Sept 1956). Composer, teacher, and critic. He was educated in London and Cologne and began his career in Aberdeen, Scotland. In 1897 he joined the Chicago Musical College as teacher of violin, composition, and history. He became president of the college (1916–25) and then moved to Northwestern University, first as special lecturer in history and form, then as professor of musicology (1937–42). For several years he wrote program notes for the Chicago SO. His books *The Standard Operas* (Chicago, 1928) and *The Standard Concert Guide* (Chicago, 1932), republished together in 1936, were expansions of works by George P. Upton, whose role as Chicago's leading music critic (for the *Chicago Tribune*) Borowski inherited. He was also responsible for building the music collection of the Newberry Library, beginning soon after his arrival in Chicago and continuing as a part-time staff member (1920–56).

WORKS

(selective list)

Stage: Boudour (ballet), 1919; A Century of the Dance (ballet), 1934; Fernando del Nonsensico (opera), 1935

Orch: Pf Conc., 1914; Allegro de concert, org, orch, 1915; Elégie symphonique, 1917; 3 peintures, 1918; Le printemps passionné, 1920; Youth, 1922; Ecce homo, 1923; Semiramis, 1924; 3 syms., 1931, 1933, 1938; The Mirror, 1953

Other works: 3 str qts, 1897, 1928, 1944; 3 org sonatas; short vn pieces, incl. Adoration; short vocal and pf pieces

D. W. KRUMMEL

Borroff, Edith (*b* New York, 2 Aug 1925). Musicologist. She attended the Oberlin Conservatory and graduated from the American Conservatory, Chicago (BM 1946, MM 1948). After teaching at Milwaukee Downer College (1950–54), she enrolled at the University of Michigan for graduate work (PhD 1959). She was later on the faculties of Hillsdale College, Michigan (1958–62), and the University of Wisconsin (1962–6); in 1966 she was appointed professor of music at Eastern Michigan University and in 1974 joined the faculty of SUNY, Binghamton. Borroff's fields of research include French chamber music of the period 1690 to 1750, American music, and contemporary music. Combining scholarship with an interest in music education, she has written numerous articles in music education journals and has presented lectures on a general overview of history. She is the author of *Music of the Baroque* (1970), *Music in Europe and the United States: a History* (1971), and *Music in Perspective* (1976).

PAULA MORGAN

Bossa nova. A musical style of Brazilian origin blending elements of the samba and cool jazz; it was popular in the USA in the 1960s. Bossa nova music is subdued, and its challenging harmonies have elicited fine improvisations. In a typical song, a drummer and an acoustic guitarist superimpose soft, precise ternary figures on a duple meter (ex. 1). Characteristically, light

Ex.1 A typical bossa nova rhythm

syncopations delivered by a saxophonist or singer with a vibrato-free, breathy, quiet tone permeate the melody. 7th and 9th chords, rapid modulations, and major-minor alternations are common; lyrics, if present, are generally sung in Portuguese or English and convey bittersweet sentiments.

Bossa nova probably began in Brazil with João Gilberto's recording of Antonio Carlos Jobim's composition *Chega da saudade* (1959). The guitarist Charlie Byrd, having visited Brazil, initiated the bossa nova craze in the USA through his recording with Stan Getz, *Jazz Samba* (1962), which included Jobim's *Desafinado*. Jazz recording companies, in attempting to cash in on Getz's Grammy award-winning success, produced a disastrous concert at Carnegie Hall in November 1962 and numerous mediocre recordings, but neither failures in jazz nor distortions in pop (Eydie Gorme's 1963 hit *Blame it on the Bossa Nova*) destroyed the original style. João and Astrud Gilberto's rendition of Jobim's *The Girl from Ipanema* was the milestone among a number of other excellent recordings in the bossa nova style in the mid-1960s, including those of Herbie Mann, Paul Winter, and Sergio Mendes.

BIBLIOGRAPHY

M. Budds: *Jazz in the Sixties* (Iowa City, IA, 1978)

J. S. Roberts: *The Latin Tinge* (New York, 1979)

BARRY KERNFELD

Bostic, Earl (*b* Tulsa, OK, 25 April 1913; *d* Rochester, NY, 28 Oct 1965). Jazz alto saxophonist and arranger. During the early 1930s he worked in several bands in the Midwest before studying at Xavier University, New Orleans. He left Louisiana to tour with various groups, then moved to New York in 1938. He was featured in big bands led by Don Redman, Edgar Hayes, and Lionel Hampton, but was better known for work within his own small unit. In the 1930s and 1940s, Bostic was recognized as an accomplished saxophonist and as a skillful arranger, but was not considered to be a major soloist. However, after recording *Flamingo* (1951), he gained widespread fame, and subsequently his records sold in vast quantities. On them, he often overemphasized glissandos, and deliberately exaggerated his vibrato. Despite these inelegant effects, Bostic regularly showed that he retained considerable technical prowess, particularly in producing high harmonics – a skill he taught John Coltrane. Heart ailments curtailed his activities during the last decade of his life.

RECORDINGS

(selective list)

Flamingo (1951, King 4475); Cherokee (1952, King 4623); Indiana (1956, King 4954); Exercise (1957, King 5056); Answer Me (1957, King 5081); Twilight Time (1958, King 5136)

BIBLIOGRAPHY

SouthernB

R. Cage: "Rhythm & Blues Notes," *Down Beat*, xxi/26 (1954), 8

H. Friedrich: "Earl Bostic Discography," *Jazz Statistics*, no.4 (1956), 3; no.14 (1960), 2; no.17 (1960), 8

Obituary, *Down Beat*, xxxiv/10 (1967), 13

JOHN CHILTON

Boston (i). Capital of Massachusetts (pop. 562,994; metropolitan area 2,763,357). It was settled in 1630 and has become the principal city of the region of the six northeastern states called New England. Boston has long been known for the richness and variety of its cultural and educational activity and for the breadth and intensity of its musical life. Many distinguished American composers have been Bostonians by birth or by virtue of long residence in the city, and some have had an important impact on Boston's musical life. The city was already a center for composition in the 18th century, a tradition that has continued into the 20th. Boston was formerly an important seat of music publishing and instrument manufacture; the many new firms formed there since the mid-20th century have not, however, outweighed those lost by acquisition, merger, and consolidation elsewhere.

The departure of a large part of Boston's music industry is balanced, in maintaining the city's national importance, by the continued excellence and the expanded influence of its performing and educational institutions. Several politically independent municipalities, among them Cambridge and Wellesley, are here considered parts of "Greater Boston."

1. First settlers: Pilgrims and Puritans. 2. Early concert life: to 1881. 3. Concert life since 1881: the Boston SO and other orchestras. 4. Opera and musical theater. 5. Choruses. 6. Other ensembles and performers: (i) Smaller ensembles (ii) Vernacular traditions. 7. Theaters and concert halls. 8. Instruments. 9. Education and libraries: (i) Education (ii) Libraries. 10. Writers on music. 11. Printing and publishing.

1. First settlers: Pilgrims and Puritans. In 1620 separatists from the Church of England who had been in the Netherlands since 1609 set sail for Virginia, but landed at what is now the town of Plymouth in Massachusetts. They carried with them the psalter that Henry Ainsworth had published in Amsterdam in 1612 for the English-speaking Protestants there, which contained the psalms in English prose and in rhymed English verse, with the music of 39 tunes (borrowed from English, French, and Dutch psalters) to which all 150 psalms could be sung. Many members of the congregation in Leiden were said to be "very expert in music." Psalm singing was an important social and devotional activity, and the psalm tunes may well have occupied the place in the lives of the Pilgrims that folk melodies and theater songs had in less austere societies. (*See also* Psalmody, §1.)

In 1630 a Puritan group established the Massachusetts Bay Colony at Boston and quickly set about organizing a complex society that within ten years had established satellite communities, the "Latin School," Harvard College, and a book press. They, too, restricted their music to songs based on the psalms, and the version they brought to America was the one of Sternhold and Hopkins (London, 1562), though they also knew the music in Ravenscroft's psalter (1621).

The first Bostonians soon decided that these psalters did not suit their needs, and a group of 30 colonial divines devised new rhymed, metrical translations closer to the original Hebrew. This resulted in the Bay Psalm Book (1640), the first North American book in English. Its verses are simple and clear and can be sung to a small number of tunes. The first edition known to include music was the ninth (1698), but meanwhile this American book had also been printed in England and was in relatively wide use there. The 13 tunes in the 1698 edition are from Playford's *A Breefe Introduction to the Skill of Musicke*. These tunes were probably the everyday music of the ordinary people of Boston, along with a certain amount of folk balladry and other music remembered from England.

The few psalm tunes were generally learned by rote, but by 1647 enough had been forgotten about them to require the practice called "lining out," in which a precentor sang or declaimed a single line of text which the congregation then repeated in song. This solo-leader and choral-response practice led to slower tempos, in turn allowing greater variation in the congregation's singing, which then led to a kind of free and often dissonant heterophony. Lining out was not instituted in Plymouth until about 1681. In Boston, by the 1650s and 1660s, young people had gained familiarity with newer styles and with current English popular music and sought to bring musical instruments from England. After the turn of the century, moreover, the feeling arose that lining out had outlived its usefulness, that the time had come for the "old way of singing" to be replaced by "regular singing," that is, by musically literate singing according to the rules of art music. Singing-schools were organized to teach it, and the appetite for music they created gave rise in turn to the "first New England school" of American composers, the Yankee tunesmiths of the late 18th century (*see* New England composers, schools of).

2. Early concert life: to 1881. To the degree that local conditions allowed, early concert life in New England resembled that of England itself. Boston's earliest known public concert was given in 1731, a century after the arrival of the first settlers. The first concert with a large instrumental ensemble was organized in 1771 by Josiah Flagg, who persuaded the 64th Regiment Band to play at a concert of instrumental and vocal music by Handel, J. C. Bach, and others. In 1773 William Selby, organist of King's (later Stone) Chapel, used the band to accompany his chorus at a public concert in a program that included a Handel overture, the "Hallelujah" Chorus, and a coronation anthem.

The German musician Gottlieb Graupner had settled in Boston by 1797, and the von Hagen family (originally Dutch) arrived at about the same time. James Hewitt, who left England in 1792, lived in Boston from about 1811 to 1816. They were all active in varying degrees as composers, performers, teachers, and publishers, but Graupner's energy and talent as entrepreneur, organizer, and leader made an incomparable mark. In 1809 he and a group of other musicians met for the first time as the Boston Philo-Harmonic Society, for the purpose of studying and performing the symphonies of Haydn and other orchestral music (choral music was furthered by the foundation of the Handel and Haydn Society in 1815; see §5 below). Before long almost every professional instrumentalist in the city was a member, and accomplished amateurs joined in too. The society's concerts were an important part of the city's musical life until late in 1824.

The orchestra of the Boston Academy of Music (see §9 below), founded in 1833, was led by George James Webb. It introduced seven of Beethoven's symphonies to the city as well as symphonies of Mozart and Mendelssohn. Ole Bull, Henry Vieuxtemps, and Henri Herz were presented by the academy before its concerts were succeeded in 1847 by those of the Musical Fund Society, a musicians' cooperative organization with Webb as conductor, which played in Tremont Theatre (now Tremont Temple) and in the new Music Hall until 1855. Edward Kimball's Boston Brass Band, the first in the USA, gave its first public concert in March 1835.

The Germania musical society, a touring ensemble of young musicians from Berlin, made its first Boston appearance in 1849. For several years it made Boston its headquarters. In 1857 its flutist Carl Zerrahn, who remained in Boston after the orchestra disbanded in 1854, started a new series of Philharmonic concerts, but wartime conditions brought it to a halt in 1863. In that year 224 professionals established the Boston Musicians' Union.

In 1865 the Harvard Musical Association, which was founded in 1837 by 50 Harvard alumni who had been members of the undergraduate music club called the Pierian Sodality of 1808 (see §9 below), organized a new series of orchestral concerts that ran until 1882, when the one-year-old Boston SO took over. It was an orchestra of about 50 musicians under the direction of Zerrahn, and it played regular series of concerts in the Music Hall with programs that J. S. Dwight and his fellows on the organizing committee specified to be "pure. . .above all need of catering to low tastes. . .in which we might hear only com-

1. *Opening concert of the World Peace Jubilee in Boston (17 June 1872) with a chorus of 20,000, an orchestra of 1000, and a military band of 1000: engraving*

posers of unquestioned excellence, and into which should enter nothing vulgar, coarse, 'sensational,' but only such as outlives fashion," which is to say that there were to be no marches, dances, or opera potpourris (for details of the repertory see Dwight, 1881, pp.446–7, 449). In setting new high standards, Dwight aimed to improve on the light-music programs with which Jullien had toured in 1853–4, though even Dwight had to admit the excellence of Jullien's performances of symphonies by Mozart, Beethoven, and Mendelssohn.

In 1869 the largest orchestra ever organized in Boston, numbering about 1000 players, with Ole Bull as concertmaster, was assembled by Patrick S. Gilmore to participate in his five-day National Peace Jubilee and Musical Festival, along with a chorus of about 10,000 voices, in a huge, specially built coliseum that covered more than three acres and had 50,000 seats. President Grant, members of his cabinet, several governors, and many military leaders visited Boston for the series of events. Its great success was not duplicated by its sequel: the World Peace Jubilee and International Musical Festival of 1872 (see fig.1), which ostensibly marked the end of the Franco-Prussian War, had an orchestra and chorus doubled to 2000 and 20,000, a grand organ, 100 Boston firemen in uniform pounding real anvils in the Anvil Chorus from Verdi's *Il trovatore*, electrically fired cannon, and, as guest artists, two of the most popular composer-performers from Europe, Franz Abt and Johann Strauss.

The decline of the Harvard Musical Association concerts, beginning around 1872, had many contributory causes, chief of which was probably the competition of the much finer performances given by Theodore Thomas and his splendid touring orchestra during their sojourns in Boston. Around 1880 a third Philharmonic Society was organized by Bernhard Listemann, who had been Thomas's concertmaster and in 1881 became the first concertmaster of the new Boston SO.

3. Concert life since 1881: the Boston SO and other orchestras. The Boston SO, founded in 1881, has long been the city's central musical institution, supplying players and administrators to other performing organizations in the city, teachers to its schools, and performances to its composers. It is now a huge cultural conglomerate that serves the whole of Massachusetts throughout the year; its concerts, many of which are broadcast locally and nationally on radio and television, cover both light and serious music. For many years the orchestra was thought to be a peculiarly Brahmin institution and it probably was so, in large part, although it aspired from the very beginning to democratize the consumption of concert music. The practice of making a considerable number of unreserved seats available at low prices and without advance payment has been maintained even in periods when most of its concerts could be sold out by subscription, and its long history of broadcasting and recording are part of that tradition.

The Boston SO was founded by Henry Lee Higginson, a member of a Boston banking family who had studied music in Vienna from 1856 to 1860 and who saw the city's need for what he described as "a full and permanent orchestra, offering the best music at low prices, such as may be found in all the large European cities. . .The essential condition of such orchestras is their stability." That is to say that the members of his orchestra were not to be occasional workers but professional musicians employed exclusively by him and paid by him for the entire season's engagement. He estimated that his first season with an orchestra of 70 players could be budgeted at $140,000 and would have an operating deficit of $25,000.

The first concert was given in the Music Hall on 22 October 1881 under George Henschel. Higginson also instituted summer seasons of light music, which began on 1 July 1885 as the Promenade Concerts and eventually became known as the Boston Pops. He thought that the orchestra might start a music school of its own, but this did not happen until 1940, when the Berkshire Music Center held its first session, concurrently with the orchestra's Berkshire Festival, at Tanglewood, in Lenox, Massachusetts. It was not universally agreed that Higginson's monopolization of the Music Hall and of the services of so many local musicians was in the best interests of the whole community, but he controlled his orchestra almost as firmly as did the ruling prince of any German city-state, and he made it an example for the rest of the country. The first season's 20 concerts (and their 20 public dress rehearsals) had a total attendance of 83,359. The second season was extended to 26 concerts and rehearsals, and attendance increased to 111,777. In 1900 the orchestra and its administrative offices moved into the newly constructed Symphony Hall, whose acoustical excellence places it among the finest concert halls in the world (see §7 below). For many years the Boston SO was the only American orchestra that owned its auditorium and office space. In 1918 Higginson turned control of the orchestra over to a group of nine citizens, incorporated as the Trustees of the Boston Symphony Orchestra, who were pledged to hold the institution in trust for the people of Boston. In August 1982 the orchestra had 23 trustees, a 55-member Board of Overseers, a music director and two additional staff conductors, 99 playing musicians, an administrative staff of 23, and a large supporting staff. The length and variety of its seasons, and its property holdings in Boston and at Tanglewood, make its budget larger than that of any other American orchestra. For the year ending 31 August 1983 its total income was $25,066,891; its total expenses were $18,969,107; and its net worth was $32,555,392.

Until World War I the orchestra's resident, principal conductors were all central Europeans, but French influence predominated later: George Henschel (1881–4), Wilhelm Gericke (1884–9, 1898–1906), Arthur Nikisch (1889–93), Emil Paur (1893–8), Karl Muck (1906–8, 1912–18), Max Fiedler (1908–12), Henri Rabaud (1918–19), Pierre Monteux (1919–24), Serge Koussevitzky (1924–49), Charles Munch (1949–62), Erich Leinsdorf (1962–9), William Steinberg (1969–72), and Seiji Ozawa (from 1972).

In 1917 the Boston SO made its first recordings, for the company now known as RCA, with which it was exclusively allied for approximately 50 years. The hasty replacement of Muck in 1918 was the result of his arrest and internment as an enemy alien. In 1920 more than 30 players who wished to affiliate with the Boston Musicians' Protective Association, the local union of the American Federation of Musicians, went on strike and were replaced by musicians of Monteux's choice. The Boston SO was the last important American orchestra to join the union, in 1942.

Koussevitzky instituted a policy of frequent performance of new music by both American and European composers, which he pursued so vigorously that he created a school of American composers who, without the opportunities to be heard that he provided, might have turned their energy in other directions. Copland, Hanson, Harris, and Piston, of the first generation of this school, were followed by Barber, Schuman, Bernstein, and others. It was also under Koussevitzky that the orchestra took over the Berkshire Festival, acquired Tanglewood, and in 1940 founded the Berkshire Music Center (officially renamed the Tanglewood Music Center in 1985) as a school where young musicians might study with orchestra members, other performers, and composers (*see* TANGLEWOOD). In addition the orchestra offers a series of concerts at Tanglewood in the summer conducted by the music director and distinguished guests that make it the most celebrated and influential undertaking of its kind in the USA. Radio network broadcasting began in the Koussevitzky era, and during World War II he instituted his Bach–Mozart chamber orchestra summer concerts, the antecedent of many concert series, which were later continued at Tanglewood.

In the meantime, in 1929 Arthur Fiedler, who had been a member of the orchestra since 1915 (his father had joined in 1885), organized the Esplanade Concerts – free, outdoor programs of symphonic and light music, played in a band shell on the banks of the Charles River. In 1930 Fiedler succeeded Alfredo Casella as Pops conductor, a position he held until his death in 1979. He was succeeded in 1980 by John Williams. For the orchestra's 50th anniversary season (1930–31), Koussevitzky instituted the practice, then hardly known, of commissioning composers to write for the occasion. That season Stravinsky's *Symphony of Psalms*, Hindemith's *Konzertmusik*, and works by Copland, E. B. Hill, Honegger, Prokofiev, Respighi, and Roussel were commissioned.

During Munch's tenure, the orchestra's season expanded greatly and for the first time offered the musicians yearlong employment; regular television broadcasts and in-house production and syndication of radio concert-tapes were begun. Public dress rehearsals were reinstituted in Symphony Hall; the number of Boston SO concerts in the Berkshire Festival increased from 13 to 24, and there were also eight open rehearsals. Youth concerts in Symphony Hall were instituted in 1959 under the direction of Harry Ellis Dickson. Under Munch, and with Monteux as guest conductor, the orchestra made its first European tours in 1952 and

2. Boston SO conductors: (left to right) Pierre Monteux (1919–24), Serge Koussevitzky (1924–49), and Charles Munch (1949–62)

1956, when it was the first American orchestra to play in the USSR. Its first trans-Pacific tour (1960) took the orchestra to Taiwan, Japan, the Philippines, New Zealand, and Australia, with Copland as guest conductor. For its 75th anniversary season (1955–6) the Boston SO and the Koussevitzky Music Foundation jointly commissioned works by Barber, Bernstein, Copland, Dutilleux, Einem, Hanson, Ibert, Martinů, Milhaud, Petrassi, Piston, Schuman, Sessions, and Villa-Lobos.

The Boston Symphony Chamber Players were established in 1964, during the tenure of Leinsdorf, who was also responsible for instituting a short "pre-concert concert" as a preliminary to the main event, and important conferences on music education and other subjects at the Berkshire Music Center. Steinberg's ill-health during his three-year directorship prevented him from leaving a distinctive mark on the orchestra. Ozawa, who first came to the USA in 1960 to study at Tanglewood, is the first Berkshire Music Center alumnus to head the Boston SO. During his tenure, the orchestra commissioned for its 100th anniversary works by Sandor Balassa, Bernstein, John Corigliano, Peter Maxwell Davies, Harbison, Kirchner, Peter Lieberson, Donald Martino, Andrzej Panufnik, Sessions, Tippett, and Olly Wilson. Important Boston SO guest conductors and premières are too many to enumerate here.

Several communities in the area now maintain independent orchestras, many of which are conducted by Boston SO members. The Boston Orchestral Club, a social and musical organization, was an amateur orchestra established in 1884 with Charles Callahan Perkins as president, conducted until 1887 by Listemann and from then until 1892 by Chadwick. After a gap, a new organization was formed with the same name, conducted by Georges Longy from 1899 to 1913; its president was Elisa Hall, the saxophonist for whom Debussy wrote his *Rapsodie*. The MacDowell Club, a somewhat similar organization formed in 1896, included Longy and Arthur Fiedler among its conductors. The People's SO was formed around dismissed Boston SO strikers in 1920 with union support and under Emil Mollenhauer as conductor. It was disbanded in 1936 after two years under the direction of Fabien Sevitzky (Koussevitzky's nephew), who also conducted the orchestra of the Metropolitan Theatre and a youth orchestra. The Boston Civic SO was founded as a community orchestra and training orchestra in 1925 by Joseph F. Wagner, who led it until 1944. The Boston PO, conducted by Benjamin Zander, is a similar organization. A Greater Boston Youth SO is now affiliated with Boston University. The university's school of music and the two conservatories in Boston have several orchestras, and in addition there are orchestras at Harvard-Radcliffe, Massachusetts Institute of Technology (faculty members there also conduct the New Orchestra of Boston, an independent organization founded 1984), and Northeastern University.

For illustration *see* ORCHESTRAS, fig.2.

4. OPERA AND MUSICAL THEATER. Puritan traditions long inhibited the development of theater in Boston, both spoken and sung, and it was not until the 20th century that the city had a stable and more-or-less permanent opera company of the kind that New York and New Orleans, for example, had had long before. However, an anti-theater law of 1750 did not prevent presentation of "readings" of English ballad and comic operas, such as *Love in a Village* in 1769 and *The Beggar's Opera* in 1770. Before the end of the century, well over 150 ballad operas had been performed in Boston.

In the late 1820s the resident opera company of New Orleans brought its French repertory to Boston. Other smaller touring opera groups passed through, but none left much of a mark until spring 1847, when an Italian company based in Havana played the first of two seasons in the Howard Athenaeum, including works by Bellini, Donizetti, Mozart, Pacini, Rossini, and Verdi. Its appetite whetted, from about 1850 to 1860 Boston welcomed companies organized by William Henry Fry, Max Maretzek, and others. Traveling companies continued to visit during the next two decades. Opera in English opened at the grand new Boston Theatre in 1860, and in 1864 German opera took brief hold; Beethoven, Flotow, Mozart, Nicolai, Wagner, and Weber were heard along with German versions of Boieldieu, Gounod, and Halévy. A local composer, Julius Eichberg, had several comic operas performed during the 1860s. The Strakosch and Mapleson touring companies and others played in Boston, and a week-long Wagner Festival in 1877 presented three early works and *Die Walküre*. The American première of Gilbert and Sullivan's *H.M.S. Pinafore* was given in Boston on 25 November 1878, and in 1883 the new Metropolitan Opera Company of New York began its (occasionally interrupted) annual visits to Boston. In 1895–6 a season of opera – mostly light, French works sung in English by young Americans – was presented at the Castle Square Theatre by C. E. French. Charles A. Ellis, manager of the Boston SO, also presented an opera season early in 1899, with Gadski and Melba in the casts, the New York SO in the pit, and Walter Damrosch as both a business partner and conductor. *See also* BOSTON IDEAL OPERA COMPANY and FADETTE LADIES' ORCHESTRA OF BOSTON.

Eben D. Jordan, Jr., a merchant prince whose father had backed Gilmore's extravaganzas of 1869 and 1872 (see §2 above) and the establishment of the New England Conservatory, joined with the impresario Henry Russell (son of the songwriter) to found the Boston Opera Company, which was intended to function with the Metropolitan and the Chicago and Philadelphia companies in a kind of cartel with interlocking directorates. Jordan invested more than $1,000,000 in a splendid new Opera House, with about 2700 seats and with fine acoustic design by Wallace Clement Sabine of Harvard (whose masterpiece is Symphony Hall; see §7 below), and he guaranteed the company's deficit for three years.

The company opened on 8 November 1909 with Ponchielli's *La Gioconda* sung by a cast that included Louise Homer and Lillian Nordica. In its first season its repertory consisted of 21 operas, of which 88 performances were given in Boston and 47 on tour, in addition to some concerts and occasional entertainments. The company had its own orchestra and its conductors included André Caplet, Wallace Goodrich, Alexander Smallens, Walter Straram, and Felix Weingartner. Among other singers with the company who are still well remembered were Frances Alda, Lucrezia Bori, Lina Cavalieri, Emmy Destinn, Emma Eames, Olive Fremstad, Mary Garden, Frieda Hempel, Georgette Leblanc, Margarete Matzenauer, Nellie Melba, Leo Slezak, Luisa Tetrazzini, and Maggie Teyte.

A disastrously over-ambitious and costly spring season in Paris in 1914 kept the house dark in the following season and led to bankruptcy in 1915. During the next two years short seasons were presented by a successor company with an almost identical name, Boston Grand Opera Company, under the direction of Max Rabinoff, who also managed and presented Anna Pavlova and her dance company.

In 1917 the Chicago Opera began regular visits to the Opera House that continued for 15 years. In the meantime the house became part of the Shubert chain and was used for many theatrical purposes. Traveling ballet, operatic, and theatrical companies played there, as well as the Metropolitan and the WPA. In the 1950s a long campaign, mysteriously conducted by unnamed forces that had other purposes for the land on which the building stood, led to several changes in ownership and the sudden demolition of the house in 1958.

There was no important local opera production again until Boris Goldovsky established the New England Conservatory Opera Workshop in 1942 to present economical but technically advanced ensemble productions of high musical and theatrical quality, usually staged and conducted by Goldovsky, and often sung in his English translations. Goldovsky's former protégée Sarah Caldwell (with James Stagliano and Linda Cabot Black) formed a new company in 1958, known first as the Boston Opera Group, later renamed the Opera Company of Boston. Its first production was Offenbach's *Le voyage dans la lune* (in English) and it has since presented American premières of important operas by Berlioz, Nono, Prokofiev, Rameau, Schoenberg, Sessions, Tippett, and Zimmermann, and world premières of operas by Middleton and Schuller. Opera New England is a touring company that draws on the resources of the Opera Company of Boston. Another resident company is John Balme's Boston Lyric Opera. By about 1910 it was quite common for musicals to play in Boston before opening on Broadway so that any flaws discovered early might be remedied before the show moved to New York.

5. CHORUSES. The earliest choral singing in Boston was the first settlers' congregational psalm singing, which continued through later times of controversy over the relative virtues of the "crude" old style and the cultivated new style of music promoted in the singing-schools (see §1 above and §9 below). From the 1770s William Selby, organist of King's (Stone) Chapel, presented public concerts of choral music with orchestral accompaniment (see fig.3). The work of George K. Jackson, who in 1812 organized a concert of Handel's music and who was instrumental in broadening the musical repertory of Boston's churches, created conditions that eventually led to the foundation of the HANDEL AND HAYDN SOCIETY on 20 April 1815.

A choirboy in the Park Street Church (in 1810–14) many years later remembered that the 50-member choir was renowned for ignoring fuging-tunes and singing the hymn tunes and anthems of the best English composers. Out of this choir came many of the original members of the Handel and Haydn Society. The society was formed for the purpose of "cultivating and improving a correct taste in the performance of sacred music, and also to introduce into more general practice the works of Handel, Haydn and other eminent composers." The second oldest musical organization in the USA, it gave its first concert on 25 December 1815 and served as the prototype for similar organizations in other cities. At Christmas 1818, for its 17th concert, the society gave its first performance of a complete oratorio, *Messiah*; on 16 February 1819, *The Creation* followed. The first edition of *The Boston Handel and Haydn Society Collection of Church Music*, anonymously edited by Lowell Mason (president of the society 1827–

3. *Interior of King's (Stone) Chapel, Boston, during a music festival, 10 January 1786: engraving*

32), was published in 1822. In 1823 the Handel and Haydn Society attempted to commission an oratorio from Beethoven, who considered, Schindler told Thayer in 1854, sending the setting of J. K. Bernard's *Der Sieg des Kreuzes* that he was planning to write for the Gesellschaft der Musikfreunde in Vienna. Nothing ever came of the Vienna project, and Boston was not important enough in Beethoven's mind to justify so large a project – though he was evidently pleased with the knowledge of his recognition in so remote a place.

Other choruses generally had educational or religious purposes, or both, or were ad hoc assemblages without institutional permanence. The gigantic choruses brought together for the jubilees of 1869 and 1872 (see §2 above) included singers from distant states. Otto Dresel (see §6 below) led small singing societies that gave no public concerts but met in private homes to study works of J. S. Bach, Schubert, Schumann, and Robert Franz, then otherwise unknown in the USA. J. C. D. Parker, probably the first Harvard graduate to become a professional musician, organized the Parker Club in 1862 and performed programs of choral music that included many of his own compositions.

A mid-19th-century German *Liedertafel* was later transformed into the Orpheus Music Society, and several English style glee clubs were the ancestors of three long-lived choral societies: the Apollo Club of about 50 male voices, founded in 1871 and led by B. J. Lang; the Boylston Club, founded in 1873 as a male-voice group devoted to relatively light music and converted in 1877 into a chorus of mixed voices with a serious repertory; and the Cecilia Society, established in 1874 under Lang to perform with the orchestra of the Harvard Musical Association rather than with piano or organ. In 1877 it separated from the association, and in 1889 it gave the first of more than 100 performances with the Boston SO. Arthur Fiedler became its conductor in 1930.

The periods of greatest activity of these groups overlapped with those of the present-day choral societies, most of which are affiliated with educational institutions, and sometimes perform with the Boston SO. In 1912 A. T. Davison of the Harvard faculty took over the direction of the student glee club and quickly began to shift its repertory from drinking-songs and comic "novelty" numbers to serious music by important composers and folksongs in his own arrangements. In 1913 he also took over the Radcliffe (College) Choral Society, and the two groups often performed together as a mixed chorus with the Boston SO. In the late 1940s the Chorus pro Musica was organized by Alfred Nash Patterson, and the New England Conservatory Chorus came under the direction of Lorna Cooke de Varon. The Tanglewood Festival Chorus was organized in 1970 under John Oliver for the purpose of performing with the Boston SO both at Tanglewood and in Boston; it is sponsored by Boston University and the orchestra. (*See also* BOSTON FESTIVAL ORCHESTRA.)

6. OTHER ENSEMBLES AND PERFORMERS.

(i) Smaller ensembles. The public performance of chamber music acquired an important place in musical life with the organization of the Mendelssohn Quintette Club in 1849 under the leadership of Thomas Ryan, whose memoirs (1899) give the history of its expanding influence and of its climactic tour (1881–2) to the West Coast, New Zealand, and Australia. The German pianist and composer Otto Dresel (1826–90), a pupil of Hiller and Mendelssohn, settled in Boston in 1852 and was much admired for his tireless efforts on behalf of the music of J. S. Bach, Schumann, and Robert Franz. In 1858 B. J. Lang, who had been a member of the Liszt circle in Europe, returned to Boston to start an active career that included conducting the world première of Tchaikovsky's First Piano Concerto (1875) at the Music Hall, with Hans von Bülow as soloist. In 1874 the violinist and conductor Bernhard Listemann settled in Boston, where he, his brother, and his sons had long and varied careers. The Euterpe Society was organized in 1879 as a membership–subscription scheme for the presentation of serious chamber music concerts and sonata recitals.

The stability and skills of the members of the Boston SO provided a new kind of community artistic resource. Franz Kneisel, who became concertmaster in 1885, in 1886 organized the Kneisel Quartet, which made its reputation during its 20 years in Boston. The success of the Longy Club, organized in 1900, developed a new taste for French wind music, which was later featured by the Boston Flute Players Club, organized in 1920 under the direction of Georges Laurent. Both played much new music, including works of American composers. These independent outgrowths of the orchestra had many successors, among which were several different series of chamber orchestra concerts, presented at various times with various names. Directors included Arthur Fiedler, Bernard Zighera, and Fiedler's cousin, Josef Zimbler. The Boston Symphony Chamber Players were organized by the orchestra's management in 1964.

Concert series of broad general interest in the 1980s are presented under various auspices. The impresario Walter Pierce, successor to Aaron Richmond, works in collaboration with Boston University and other institutions. Other valued series are the Charles River Concerts and the International Artists Series. At Harvard, the Fanny Peabody Mason Foundation concerts are complemented by the Fromm Music Foundation concerts of contemporary music (*see* FROMM, PAUL). The Isabella Stewart Gardner Museum and the Museum of Fine Arts also present concert series.

The "early music movement" has a relatively long history in Boston, where interest in "original instruments" dates back to at least 1905, when Arnold Dolmetsch began to make them for the Chickering company and even members of the Boston SO learned to play them. In 1938 a group of string players from the orchestra formed the Boston Society of Ancient Instruments under Alfred Zighera. It was an adventurous group for its time, with a broad repertory, and it had the collaboration of Putnam Aldrich, Willi Apel, and Erwin Bodky, but later experts scoffed at its modernized bows and fretless fingerboards. Bodky's Cambridge Collegium Musicum, founded in 1942 and succeeded by the Cambridge Society for Early Music, established standards of performance nearer to those preferred today, and eventually the Boston Camerata, founded in 1954 by Narcissa Williamson and directed from 1968 by Joel Cohen, became one of the country's best-known groups of this kind. Another ensemble that is also capable of large-scale undertakings is Martin Pearlman's Banchetto Musicale. The Boston Museum Trio plays period instruments from the collections of the Museum of Fine Arts. The Boston Early Music Festival and Exhibition, first held in 1981, has continued its biennial sessions (see fig.4, p.270; *see also* EARLY-MUSIC REVIVAL).

Two influential contemporary music groups are Collage, derived from the Boston SO, and Boston Musica Viva.

(ii) Vernacular traditions. The vernacular tradition, which long resisted obliteration, more or less yielded to Lowell Mason and

4. *Scene from Handel's "Teseo" (Act 3 scene iv) performed at the Boston Early Music Festival, Boston College Theater Arts Center, 30 May 1985, with Christine Armistead (left, Clizia), Drew Minter (Arcane), Judith Nelson (Princess Agilea), and the festival orchestra (obbligato players standing facing the stage) conducted by Nicholas McGeegan from the harpsichord*

his school of the 1830s. It was not destroyed, but it went underground and has little documented history. Popular entertainment music was certainly heard in Boston, but for a long time relatively little of it originated there. The popular English songwriter and entertainer Henry Russell lived in Boston for a while in the 1830s, and Kendall organized his Boston Brass Band in 1835, but the blackface minstrels, the white singing families, the English balladeers, and the plays with music that eventually became the American "musical" generally came to Boston from elsewhere. Perhaps only Patrick S. Gilmore can be considered a Bostonian "crossover artist," bridging the "popular" and the "classical" (see §2 above).

There was more activity of this kind in the 20th century. In the 1920s the pianist Sid Reinherz contributed to the change in style from late rag to early stride, and Leo Reisman led a fine jazz-style big band in the Brunswick Hotel. Mal Hallett's popular band had a distinguished membership that in 1933 included Gene Krupa and Jack Teagarden. The bandleader Vaughn Monroe began his career as a singer with the Jack Marshard "society orchestra" in 1936. Other similar groups were led by Meyer Davis, Eddy Duchin, and Ruby Newman.

Distinguished individual jazz musicians from the area included Serge Chaloff, Bobby Hackett, and Max Kaminsky. George Wein, who began his career as a jazz pianist after leaving Boston University, became internationally known as a jazz impresario. Joan Baez began her career as a folksinger at Boston University. During the rock era the J. Geils Band (formed in 1967) and the band called Boston (1975) attained great popularity. Gunther Schuller's New England Ragtime Ensemble, with players from the New England Conservatory, was one of the principal participants in the rediscovery of ragtime music in the early 1970s and became a very popular touring attraction. Joshua Rifkin, while a faculty member at Brandeis University, also arranged and produced recordings by Judy Collins, and, as a pianist, made some of the first recordings in the Scott Joplin revival.

7. THEATERS AND CONCERT HALLS. Early public performances of music were organized in private homes, coffeehouses, and, when appropriate, religious meeting houses. A law of 1750, re-enacted in 1784, prohibited theatrical entertainments of all kinds, but it was commonly circumvented by billing such events as "lectures" or "readings." In 1792 an establishment called the New Exhibition Room was opened, but its "lectures, moral and entertaining" and its "gallery of portraits, songs, feats of tumbling and ballet pantomime" quickly got it into trouble with the law enforcement authorities, who closed it down in 1793.

Public demand brought swift change, however, and in 1793 the highly respectable Boston Theatre, designed by Charles Bulfinch to be the grandest in the USA, was opened. It was here that Graupner led the orchestra and the von Hagens were heard (see §2 above). It was often called the Federal Street Theatre, especially after the Haymarket Theatre opened in 1796, and spoken drama and ballad opera were popular on both stages. Graupner later had a concert room in the same building as his home and shop. His Philharmonic concerts took place in Pythian Hall, and later the Pantheon. The Handel and Haydn Society's early performances were given in churches such as Stone Chapel (the popular, anti-British name of King's Chapel; fig. 3) and then Boylston Hall. From 1835 to 1843 the Boston Theatre, remodeled and renamed the Odeon, was the home of Lowell Mason's and George J. Webb's Academy of Music. It provided commodious classroom space and an auditorium that seated 1500 and had standing room for 1000 more.

In 1827 the Tremont Theatre was built. After a fire, it was reopened as the Baptist Tremont Temple, which survives as rebuilt in the 1870s after another fire. It was the largest auditorium in the city until 1852, and even in the 20th century important performers have appeared there. The Lion Theatre of 1836, built for "dramatic and equestrian performances," taken over in 1839 by the Handel and Haydn Society and renamed the Melodeon, was the successor to the Odeon as Boston's leading concert hall. The academy's symphony concerts took place there in 1843–7, and the Germania concerts from 1849.

In 1845 the Millerite Tabernacle, which had failed to see the world come to an end, was refitted as a theater, the Howard Athenaeum, which in 1847 saw Boston's first important season of Italian opera. It was closed in 1953, after long years of service as the Old Howard, a famous burlesque house, and it was destroyed by fire in 1961. In the 1840s, the Chickering firm's showrooms were the site of such serious musical events as the Harvard Musical Association's chamber music concerts, and by the 1850s there was a Chickering Hall. Minstrel shows played at the Adelphi (opened 1847) and the Lyceum (1848).

In 1850 Jenny Lind gave two concerts in the largest indoor space in the city, the great hall of the Fitchburg Railroad Station, to audiences said (probably by the impresario P. T. Barnum) to have numbered 4000 each time; Ryan (1899) suggested a more realistic figure of 1800. The place was held to be so unworthy of her art that several members of the Harvard Musical Association in 60 days raised a construction fund of $100,000 for a new hall, and on 20 November 1852 they opened the Music Hall, whose auditorium seated about 2700. This hall provided a new and invigorating rallying point for the city's musical life. Its acoustical qualities are said to have been excellent, except during the years 1863–84, when the great organ (see §8 below) interfered with the projection of orchestral sound. Parts of the original Music Hall are thought to have been preserved in the Orpheum Theatre, a vaudeville and movie house that later occupied the site; from 1971 to 1978 it was the home of the Opera Company of Boston.

In 1854 the New Boston Theatre opened, and from 1860 various operas were produced there. The Continental Theatre opened in 1866 and prospered with a long run of the musical *The Black Crook*. Gigantic temporary pavilions held the performers and audiences at the Peace Jubilees of 1869 and 1872 (see §2 above). In 1876 Harvard's Memorial Hall had appended to it the 1400-seat Sanders Theatre, which became the university's principal auditorium and was the site of the Boston SO's Cambridge concert series for about 80 years. In 1896 the little Steinert Hall was opened by the Steinert Piano Co.

In the spring of 1893 Henry Lee Higginson said that he would discontinue maintenance of the Boston SO unless the Music Hall, which was then seen as a drafty firetrap on a site endangered by planned street and subway construction, could be replaced within little more than a year. The estimated cost of $400,000 was quickly subscribed. By the end of the year the land had been bought and the firm of McKim, Mead & White had begun to work on the design of the New Boston Music Hall, later named Symphony Hall (fig.5). The original plan, for an auditorium in the shape of a Greek theater, was changed to the long, narrow rectangle familiar from the old Music Hall and known to work well in Leipzig and Vienna. The collaboration of Wallace C. Sabine, then a young member of the Harvard physics department, made this the first scientifically designed auditorium; it is, by all accounts, one of the finest in the world. When the hall opened on 15 October 1900, its cost had risen to about $750,000. The auditorium has a capacity of about 2625, reduced to about 2365 in the Pops season, when tables are placed on the hall floor.

Jordan Hall (capacity 1019), built in 1908 at the New England Conservatory, is well suited to performances by smaller groups and solo recitals. In 1909 the 2700-seat Boston Opera House opened; its acoustic design too was by Sabine (see §4 above). The Metropolitan Theatre, opened in 1926 as a splendid vaudeville

5. *Symphony Hall, Boston, opened in 1900*

and movie palace and later used as an opera and ballet house (sometimes called the Music Hall or the Metropolitan Center), was closed in 1982 because of an unsafe roof. The next important piece of musical architecture in the area was the Hatch Memorial Shell, built in 1940 for the free, outdoor concerts given on the Charles River Esplanade by Arthur Fiedler and members of the Boston SO. Massachusetts Institute of Technology (MIT) opened its fine 1238-seat, general-purpose Kresge Auditorium in 1955. The practice of architectural acoustics, which originated with Sabine, was carried forward in mid-century by the firm of Bolt, Beranek & Newman; Leo L. Beranek's *Music, Acoustics and Architecture* (1962) is a basic work on the subject.

8. INSTRUMENTS. Before American independence almost all the musical instruments used in Boston had been imported from England. They later came from the Continent, but by the mid-19th century Boston was exporting instruments to Europe and South America. Collections of varied size and character are owned by the Boston Public Library, the Boston SO, Boston University, Harvard University, the Museum of Fine Arts, and the New England Conservatory.

The first organ in New England, probably the second in the Colonies, had been installed in the home of Thomas Brattle by 1711. In the mid-20th century it was in Portsmouth, New Hampshire, and in playable condition. The first locally built organ was left unfinished by Edward Bromfield, who also made the first American microscope; after his death in 1746 it was completed and installed in Old South Church. A contemporary report of the period 1810–15 said that only six Boston churches then had organs. Among early organ builders were William Goodrich, the firms of Hayts, Babcock & Appleton and Hook & Hastings, and John Rowe. In 1854 a very successful reed-organ business was begun by Henry L. Mason and Emmons Hamlin, with financial backing from Lowell Mason and Oliver Ditson. Its products became well known in Europe, and its profits helped to finance the manufacture of the very fine Mason & Hamlin pianos, begun in 1883, which eventually outweighed the reed-organ business in importance and resulted in its sale in 1911.

In 1855 a committee of citizens raised $10,000 "to obtain an organ of the first class, one that shall rival in power, in magnitude, and in excellence, the famous instruments of the Old World," for installation in the Music Hall, then three years old. An instrument was ordered from the German firm of Walcker in Ludwigsburg, which took five years to build it. Delivery was delayed by wartime conditions, but the organ was finally dedicated on 2 November 1863 by John Knowles Paine, B. J. Lang, and others. It was much the largest organ in North America and one of the three or four largest in the world, with four manuals plus pedals, and 17 pairs of bellows driven by a "hydraulic machine of about two horsepower, or four to eight men." Early accounts suggest that it did not take long to notice that its quality did not match its size. By the early 1880s the organ had fallen into disrepair. It was eventually moved, much altered, to Methuen, Massachusetts, where it was put into use again only in 1909; in 1931 it was purchased by Ernest M. Skinner, who had moved his organ-building firm, founded in 1901, to that town (*see* AEOLIAN-SKINNER ORGAN CO.).

A spinet built by John Harris in 1769 was probably the first keyboard string instrument made in the Colonies. Benjamin Crehore, originally a cabinetmaker, was building harpsichords and string instruments by 1792, and by 1797 he had begun to make pianos, probably using English Broadwoods as his models. He trained the Babcock brothers and the Bent brothers, had the von Hagens as partners for a while, and sold his instruments at Graupner's shop.

Jonas Chickering, who made his first piano in 1823, took out several important patents during the 1840s. The Chickering company prospered, and when its new factory opened in 1855 it was the second largest building in the country, exceeded in size only by the US Capitol. In 1927 the company moved to East Rochester, New York, as part of the American Piano Co. In 1883 Mason & Hamlin began producing pianos (as well as reed organs) which were used by such leading performers as Rachmaninoff and Harold Bauer; this firm also was absorbed and moved to East Rochester, in 1932. Several other makers active in Boston produced good pianos for home and school use, most of them products of firms that were ultimately absorbed by the AEOLIAN CORPORATION.

In the mid-1980s several makers of fine harpsichords and other early keyboard instruments were in business in and around Boston. William Dowd and Frank Hubbard, who established a joint workshop in 1949, worked independently from 1958. The Eric Herz workshop began operations in 1954. Jeremy Adams, who worked with Dowd, became an independent maker, restorer, and rebuilder in 1968.

A few early-17th-century settlers are believed to have brought viols to America. Within 50 years prosperous individuals were importing string instruments; Benjamin Crehore began to make them in Boston during the 18th century. George Gemunder, who trained in Paris under Vuillaume, and his brother August opened their shop in Boston in 1847, but moved to New York in 1851. The firm of J. B. Squier, organized in 1886, was later remembered principally as a manufacturer of strings.

William Callender began to make wind instruments in 1796, and others continued the trade through the 19th century, though with little distinction until William S. Haynes started his flute company in 1900. Haynes and his foreman Verne Q. Powell were influential in establishing the silver flute in the USA, although wooden piccolos began to make a comeback around mid-century. Powell started his own firm in 1926 and made Boston a leading center of flute making; in 1961 he sold it to a group of his employees. One of his former employees, Friedrich von Huene, began making early flute replicas and recorders in his own shop in 1960. Brannen Brothers, organized in 1977 by the former general manager of the Powell firm, was joined in 1978 by the English flute maker Albert K. Cooper. Nearly half its production since then has been in gold. In 1901 Cundy-Bettoney began to build woodwind instruments that were destined for the educational market, and in 1925 began to produce what were said to be the first metal clarinets.

Boston became a center of brass-instrument manufacture after the establishment of Edward Kendall's Boston Brass Band in 1835, but development of both the art and industry were impeded by non-standardization of instruments and instrumentation. Gilmore, the most influential bandmaster in the USA before Sousa, was a partner in the instrument-making firm of Gilmore, Graves & Co. in 1864–5, and he claimed that he personally tested every instrument made by the firm. The firms of E. G. Wright and Graves & Co. combined about 1869 to form the BOSTON MUSICAL INSTRUMENT MANUFACTORY, known for its fine band instruments during the late 1880s. In 1884 Thompson and Odell founded the Standard Brass Instrument Co., which also made guitars and banjos; it was later taken over by the Vega company.

George B. Stone started his business in percussion instruments in 1890. The Zildjian family's cymbal business, founded in Constantinople in 1623, moved to the Boston area in 1929.

9. EDUCATION AND LIBRARIES.

(i) Education. Early settlers in Boston gave musical education due concern, for the young there had to be taught to sing the praise of the Lord. This devotional art is said to have had a place in the original curriculum of Harvard College, which was founded in 1636. The first published musical teaching material is the "admonition to the reader," in the Bay Psalm Book of 1640 (see §1 above). The instructive introductions to 18th-century tune books extended and continued this practice. By 1720 (or perhaps as early as 1712) the traditional "old way of singing" came under attack from those who favored cultivated and musically literate "regular singing" and the establishment of singing-schools in which to achieve it.

Thomas Symmes began the "singing war" in 1720, and in 1721 it was picked up by the teachings of John Tufts and of Thomas Walter. Settlers had been in Massachusetts for a century by then, but another century was to pass before this movement was replaced by a new one, in the work of Lowell Mason. Music teaching, until then, was often the business of singing-schools organized by ill-paid itinerant instructors who set up class in one town after another and rarely earned their living expenses from music alone. A century of Yankee tunesmiths wrote and published the psalm settings and hymns that were their teaching pieces, but, from the early 1820s, Mason's collections quickly replaced their rugged vigor with a pseudo-Mendelssohnian gentility that Mason had learned from a descendant of one of Bach's colleagues.

Mason studied the methods of the Swiss educational theorist Pestalozzi and applied them to the children's music classes that he taught in churches and private schools. In the Boston Academy of Music, which he and G. J. Webb founded in 1833, he held teacher-training classes in addition to its concerts (see §2 above). In 1837 he introduced music to the curriculum of the Boston public schools at his own expense, and in the following year the Boston school board created the first program of free, public-school instruction in music, under his direction. He also served on a state board, organized regional teacher-training conventions, converted many of the peripatetic teachers from the singing-schools into public-school teachers with regular positions, and transformed the content of the old tunebooks into the kind of public school songbook that was still in use a century after his time.

Harvard University, in Cambridge, was the first college in the USA, founded to train young men for the ministry. Its evolution into a secular university was slow, and music at first had a place there only in connection with religion. As early as 1808 there was interest enough in music among Harvard undergraduates for them to organize a club, the Pierian Sodality, whose members formed the basis of the Harvard Musical Association, founded in 1837, though the name was not assumed until 1840 (for details of its orchestral activities see §2 above). It had no formal connection with the college but acted as an alumni advisory group, and in 1838 it first recommended that instruction in music be added to the curriculum. Its efforts had no effect, however, until 1862, when Harvard appointed John Knowles Paine to the post of college organist and instructor in music. In 1875 he became full professor of music, one of the first in the country. He taught four courses: harmony, counterpoint, history, and form and analysis, to an average enrollment of 30 students. The first advanced degrees in music in the USA were awarded at Harvard: the AM in 1875 (to Arthur Foote) and the PhD in 1905 (to Louis Adolphe Coerne). During his long tenure (until his death in 1906) Paine taught many important composers and music historians, some of whom became distinguished Harvard faculty members themselves, including A. T. Davison, E. B. Hill, Hugo Leichtentritt, and Walter R. Spalding (who taught from 1895 to 1935). Later musicologists who taught there include Elliot Forbes, Donald Grout, David G. Hughes, Lewis Lockwood, A. Tillman Merritt, Walter Piston, John M. Ward, Christoph Wolff, and G. Wallace Woodworth. Piston was responsible for expansion of the theory and composition programs in the 1930s. Merritt was chairman of the music department in the periods 1942–52 and 1968–72, and strengthened its programs in a number of ways, including the establishment of a graduate musicology program. An important component of Harvard's musical life has been its Glee Club, directed successively by Davison, Woodworth, Forbes (department chairman from 1972), and John T. Adams (see §5 above). Some of the composers who have taught at Harvard are Arthur Berger, Bernstein, F. S. Converse, Copland, Del Tredici, Irving Fine, E. B. Hill, Hindemith, Holst, Kim, Kirchner, Piston, Sessions, Stravinsky, I. Tcherepnin, and Randall Thompson. The music department had 20 faculty members, 50 graduate students, and 40 undergraduate music majors in 1984. It has always been largely concerned with training composers and scholars, not performers, and it grants advanced degrees in musicology and composition. The widespread activities of the Fromm Music Foundation on behalf of new music are based at Harvard (*see* FROMM, PAUL).

The Perkins Institution and Massachusetts School for the Blind (founded in 1832) added music to its program in 1833, with Mason as teacher. It soon specialized in training organists, pianists, and choral singers, and later supplied a large part of the faculty at a music school for the blind founded in England under the patronage of Queen Victoria. In the 1870s it added to its curriculum a long-influential course for piano technicians and tuners.

Two new music schools opened in February 1867. First was the Boston Conservatory, founded under the direction of the violinist and composer Julius Eichberg, who for a time was also superintendent of music in the public schools. He made violin teaching an early speciality of his conservatory, which in 1981 described itself as "a college of music-drama-dance." The New England Conservatory, now much the larger of the two, was established in 1867 by Eben Tourjée, with the assistance of Robert Goldbeck, on the model of a European conservatory. By 1881 it had almost 1500 students, but enrollment in the 1980s was reduced to about half that figure. Its directors (presidents since 1953) have included George Chadwick (1897–1930), Wallace Goodrich (1931–42), Harrison Keller (1946–58), and Gunther Schuller (1967–77). In addition to traditional areas of study, it has programs in early music and Afro-American performance and composition. The Department of Third Stream Studies was established in 1972; it explores the relationship between Western classical, jazz, and ethnic musical traditions, including improvisatory techniques. The College of Music at Boston University was organized in 1872 by Tourjée, who kept his conservatory post and engaged much the same faculty for both schools. The training of performers, composers, and teachers remains the principal focus of all three schools, and all draw heavily on the Boston SO for teachers of orchestral instruments.

Advanced musical education in Boston was long dominated by Germans and by Americans who had studied in Germany until in 1916 Georges Longy opened the school bearing his name, directed from 1978 by Roman Totenberg, to offer instruction in solfège and theoretical subjects as taught in France. The Malkin Conservatory, a small, private school that functioned from 1933 to 1954, is remembered principally for having enticed Schoenberg from Europe to teach for one year; Ernst Toch and Nicolas Slonimsky also taught there.

The Berklee College of Music was founded by Lawrence Berk in 1945 with 125 students, filling a need then largely ignored by traditional institutions: the training of professional musicians for work in jazz and the various popular traditions. It offers the BM degree and a professional diploma, with particular emphasis on performance and composition; there are courses in jazz, pop, rock, and Latin music, theater, film, television, and recorded music, as well as studio production and engineering techniques. Enrollment in 1982 was approximately 2600, 500 of whom were from 75 foreign countries. Among its graduates are Gary Burton, Keith Jarrett, Quincy Jones, Arif Mardin, Gabor Szabo, Stomu Yamash'ta, and Josef Zawinul.

There are many other institutions of higher education in which music has an important place. Brandeis University, in nearby Waltham, was founded in 1948, the first and only nonreligious Jewish-sponsored university in the USA. Erwin Bodky was appointed the first professor of music in 1949. In 1982 there were some 40 graduate students and 25 undergraduate majors in the music department, which offers a BA in music and MusM and PhD degrees in musicology and composition. The university's School of Creative Arts, which was given its direction by Irving Fine, has had Arthur Berger, Kenneth Levy, Joshua Rifkin, Harold Shapero, and Seymour Shifrin on its faculty. Other important institutions in the area are: Massachusetts Institute of Technology (with David Epstein, John Harbison, Marcus Thompson, and others on its humanities faculty); Northeastern University; Tufts University, whose music department was founded in 1895 under Leo Rich Lewis; and Wellesley College. Music is also taught at Curry, Emerson, Gordon, and Simmons colleges and at the various campuses of the University of Massachusetts. Joint programs of study have been offered by the two conservatories, Longy, Harvard, and Tufts, in various combinations.

There is a long-standing tradition of community music schools in the Boston area. The Elma Lewis School of Fine Arts, a highly valued institution in the center of the black community, has accomplished a great deal. Earlier music schools were maintained by the city's Italian, Jewish, and Lithuanian communities.

(ii) Libraries. The principal music libraries in Boston proper are the collection (begun in 1859) at the Boston Public Library, whose enormous archival value can hardly be assessed from the admirable published catalogues (of 1910 and 1972), and those at Boston University, the Harvard Musical Associaton, the Massachusetts Historical Society, and the New England Conservatory of Music. In Cambridge, Harvard's holdings are principally in three collections: the Houghton Library, the Isham Memorial Library, and the Eda Kuhn Loeb Library. Wellesley College also has a fine music library. At some distance from the city but of very great importance for their collections of Americana are the Essex Institute in Salem and the American Antiquarian Society in Worcester. A librarians' informal discussion group that first met in 1974 became a productive consortium of 16 institutions called Boston Area Music Libraries, which in 1983 issued the monumental publication *The Boston Composers Project*. (For further discussion of the holdings of these institutions, *see* LIBRARIES AND COLLECTIONS, §3, "Massachusetts.")

10. WRITERS ON MUSIC. The first book-length work of general musical literature published in the USA was probably John Rowe Parker's *A Musical Biography or Sketches of the Lives and Writings of Eminent Musical Characters, Interspersed with an Epitome of Interesting Musical Matter* (Boston, 1824). His *The Euterpiad, or Musical Intelligencer* (1820–23), the city's first musical periodical, was later described by Dwight as a fortnightly "of very high tone, in every way respectable, and ably seconding the efforts of those who were trying to elevate the standard of musical art, free from all the meretricious and commercial features of so many modern periodicals devoted nominally to music." Neither it nor several successors had long lives, but *Dwight's Journal of Music* (1852–81; *see* PERIODICALS, fig.1) covered local, national, and international musical topics and was enhanced by the writings of such contributors as Alexander Wheelock Thayer.

The Ditson firm, which published *Dwight's Journal* from 1868 and then several lesser journals, also published important books. Near the end of the 19th century, L. C. Page began to publish handsome editions of books by the Elsons, Lahee, and Rupert Hughes that have remained valuable.

William Foster Apthorp, who began publishing music criticism in the *Atlantic Monthly* in 1872, became in 1892 the program annotator for the Boston SO, a position at least as influential in forming public opinion in Boston as that of journalistic critics there. His successors have included Philip Hale, John N. Burk, Michael Steinberg, and Steven Ledbetter. Among the memorable Boston newspaper critics were Olin Downes, his son Edward O. D. Downes, Alfred H. Meyer, Moses Smith, and H. T. Parker. In the 1980s the most influential daily newspaper was the *Boston Globe*, of which Richard Dyer became music critic in 1976. Historical and theoretical studies in Boston were centered at Harvard University long before they were given the name "musicology." More recently scholars at Boston University, Wellesley College, and Brandeis University have made important contributions to musical scholarship as well (see §9 above). Willi Apel and Nicolas Slonimsky worked in Boston for many years as independent scholars. Richard C. Appel and Leonard Burkat, formerly of the Boston Public Library staff, published many historical, critical, and bibliographical studies. An important contribution to musical knowledge was made by William Schwann, who began publishing his authoritative catalogues of long-playing recordings and tapes in 1949.

11. PRINTING AND PUBLISHING. The first music known to have been printed and published in North America appeared in the ninth edition of the Bay Psalm Book (Boston, 1698), in which 13 tunes are printed from woodblocks. The next appeared in two psalm-singing instruction books, with the tunes set in three parts. One, by John Tufts, first published in 1721 or earlier, used a letter-and-staff notation. The other, by Thomas Walter, also issued in 1721, was printed by James Franklin, Benjamin's

older brother, and is probably the first North American music printed from engraved metal plates. Thereafter, psalm settings and hymns were published in Boston in constantly increasing numbers for about 100 years (*see* PUBLISHING AND PRINTING OF MUSIC, §1). Two collections by Josiah Flagg (1764 and 1766) and at least part of William Billings's *The New-England Psalm-singer* (1770) were engraved by Paul Revere, Boston's leading goldsmith (for illustration *see* BILLINGS, WILLIAM). Thomas Johnston, a craftsman of greatly varied talents, was more active than any other individual of his time in engraving, printing, and selling music. The first American set of type for printing music was cast in Boston by William (or possibly John) Norman, who was the first publisher of sheet music in the city. The earliest known example of the type's use is in the *Boston Magazine*, 1783, published by Isaiah Thomas, who was especially active in partnership with Ebenezer T. Andrews.

Between 1798 and 1804 P. A. von Hagen (father and son) issued about 100 publications. Gottlieb Graupner, who began publishing activities in 1802, was Boston's principal music publisher for about 25 years. His stimulation of Boston's concert life was not entirely disinterested but helped expand his market. The Handel and Haydn Society, which he helped organize, paid him five cents per page, then a considerable sum, for the music of Haydn's *Creation*. After his death in 1836, his plates went to a new firm that was to become the country's biggest and to be famous for a century as the Oliver Ditson company. James Hewitt published in Boston from about 1812 to 1817, and there were

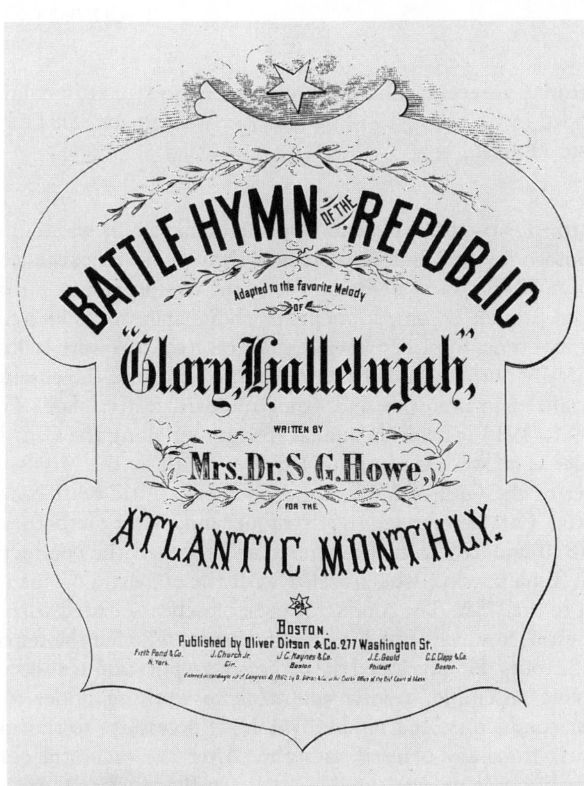

6. Cover to the sheet-music of the "Battle Hymn of the Republic," published in Boston by Oliver Ditson & Co., 1862; Julia Ward Howe's poem first appeared in the "Atlantic Monthly" in February 1862

other firms, but their catalogues were generally backed by very small editions and had short lives, while Ditson expanded and absorbed dozens of other publishers before it was itself absorbed by Theodore Presser in 1931. One of Ditson's acquisitions was the firm established in 1843 by Elias Howe.

In the meantime, the firm of George D. Russell served as a training ground for Arthur P. Schmidt, who in 1876 founded a new firm that energetically published the concert music of American composers, Bostonians especially, and went so far as to issue engraved full scores of orchestral works by Beach, Bird, Chadwick, Foote, Hadley, MacDowell, Paine, Stojowski, and others. The Schmidt catalogue is now owned by Summy-Birchard, as are those of McLaughlin & Reilly, established in 1904, which published music of Roman Catholic interest, and of C. C. Birchard, founded in 1901, which long specialized in school and community songbooks and also published major works by American composers. Cundy-Bettoney, dating back to 1868 and specializing in wind music, is now part of Carl Fischer; the Wa-Wan Press, founded in 1901 by Arthur Farwell, was acquired by G. Schirmer in 1912. Among engraving and printing firms that did not publish were M. D. Henning (established 1882) and John Worley (1904).

Specialty publishers include the firm of Robert King (established 1940), devoted to brass music until 1982, when it expanded to include other areas, and Berklee, which is affiliated with Berklee College (see §9 above). Two remaining older firms are the BOSTON MUSIC COMPANY (founded 1885), publisher of Ethelbert Nevin and of John M. Williams's piano-teaching material, which was long controlled by various branches of the Schirmer family, and E. C. Schirmer, founded in 1921, which is especially strong in choral music and published Piston's earliest theoretical work, early Copland, and such composers as Pinkham, Conrad Susa, and Randall Thompson. There are three publishing houses owned by composers (or their families): Dantalian, established by Donald Martino; Margun and the related house of Gunmar, established by Marjorie and Gunther Schuller in 1975 and 1979; and Glocken Verlag, managed by Franz Lehár's son as the American branch of the English firm based in London.

BIBLIOGRAPHY

G. Hood: *A History of Music in New England* (Boston, 1846/*R*1970)

The Great Organ in the Boston Music Hall, being a Brief History of the Enterprise (Boston, 1865)

J. S. Dwight: "Music in Boston," *The Memorial History of Boston*, ed. J. Winsor (Boston, 1881), iv, 415–64

Boston Symphony Orchestra Concert Bulletin (Boston, 1881–)

C. C. Perkins, J. S. Dwight, W. F. Bradbury, and C. Guild: *History of the Handel and Haydn Society of Boston, Massachusetts* (Boston and Cambridge, MA, 1883–1934/*R*1977–9)

W. F. Apthorp: *Musicians and Music Lovers, and other Essays* (New York, 1894/*R*1974)

C. E. French: *A Year of Opera at the Castle Square Theatre, from May 6, '95, to May 6, '96* (Boston, 1896)

T. Ryan: *Recollections of an Old Musician* (New York, 1899/*R*1979)

R. Hughes: *Contemporary American Composers* (Boston, 1900, repr. 1906 as *Famous American Composers*, rev. and enlarged 2/1914 as *American Composers*)

Catalog of the Allen A. Brown Collection of Music (Boston, 1910–16)

M. A. D. Howe: *The Boston Symphony Orchestra: an Historical Sketch* (Boston, 1914, rev. and enlarged 2/1931/*R*1978)

W. A. Fisher: *Notes on Music in Old Boston* (Boston, 1918/*R*1976)

B. Perry: *Life and Letters of Henry Lee Higginson* (Boston, 1921/*R*1973)

R. G. Appel: "Beethoven in Boston," *More Books*, ii (1927), 47

J. H. Railey: *The New England Conservatory of Music, 1867–1927* (Boston, 1927)

W. R. Spalding: *Music at Harvard: a Historical Review of Men and Events* (New York, 1935/*R*1977)

G. Brush: *Boston Symphony Orchestra: Charcoal Drawings of its Members, with Biographical Sketches* (Boston, 1936)
C. M. Ayars: *Contributions to the Art of Music in America by the Music Industries of Boston, 1640–1936* (New York, 1937/*R*1969)
A. Foote: "A Bostonian Remembers," *MQ*, xxiii (1937), 37
H. C. McCusker: *Fifty Years of Music in Boston, based on Hitherto Unpublished Letters in the Boston Public Library* (Boston, 1937)
H. W. Foote: "Musical Life in Boston in the Eighteenth Century," *Proceedings of the American Antiquarian Society*, new ser., xlix (1939), 293
Commemorative Record of the One Hundred Concerts given by the Boston Flute Players' Club (Boston, 1940)
H. E. Johnson: "Early New England Periodicals devoted to Music," *MQ*, xxvi (1940), 153
N. Bessaraboff: *Ancient European Musical Instruments: an Organological Study of the Musical Instruments in the Leslie Lindsey Mason Collection in the Museum of Fine Arts, Boston* (Cambridge, MA, 1941)
H. E. Johnson: *Musical Interludes in Boston, 1795–1830* (New York, 1943/*R*1967)
A. Copland: "Serge Koussevitzky and the American Composer," *MQ*, xxx (1944), 255
M. A. D. Howe: *The Tale of Tanglewood, Scene of the Berkshire Festivals* (New York, 1946)
H. Leichtentritt: *Serge Koussevitzky, the Boston Symphony Orchestra and the New American Music* (Cambridge, MA, 1946/*R*1978)
L. Burkat: "Music in the Berkshires," *Tempo*, no.5 (1947), 18
M. Smith: *Koussevitzky* (New York, 1947)
L. Burkat: "Current Chronicle: Boston," *MQ*, xxxiv (1948), 249
H. E. Johnson: *Symphony Hall, Boston* (Boston, 1950/*R*1979)
L. Burkat: "Boston Symphony Orchestra," *ReM*, no.212 (1952), 43
H. E. Johnson: "The Germania Musical Society," *MQ*, xxxix (1953), 75
C. Münch: *Je suis chef d'orchestre* (Paris, 1954; Eng. trans., 1955/*R*1978)
A. C. Buechner: *Yankee Singing Schools and the Golden Age of Choral Music in New England* (diss., Harvard U., 1960)
C. Manos: *Portrait of a Symphony* (New York, 1960)
L. L. Beranek: *Music, Acoustics and Architecture* (New York, 1962/*R*1979)
J. W. Thompson: *Music and Musical Activities in New England, 1800–1838* (diss., Peabody College for Teachers, 1962)
Q. Eaton: *The Boston Opera Company* (New York, 1965/*R*1980)
H. E. Johnson: *Hallelujah, Amen!: the Story of the Handel and Haydn Society of Boston* (Boston, 1965/*R*1981)
A Tanglewood Dream: the Berkshire Music Center 25th Anniversary Album, 1940–65 (New York, 1965)
B. Owen: *The Organs and Music of King's Chapel, 1713–1964* (Boston, 1966)
R. T. Daniel: *The Anthem in New England before Eighteen Hundred* (Evanston, IL, 1966/*R*1979)
P. E. Paige: *Musical Organizations in Boston, 1830–1850* (diss., Boston U., 1967)
C. R. Nutter: *History of the Harvard Musical Association, 1837–1962* (Boston, 1968)
H. E. Dickson: *"Gentlemen, More Dolce Please!": an Irreverent Memoir of Thirty Years in the Boston Symphony Orchestra* (Boston, 1969)
M. W. Lebow: *A Systematic Examination of the Journal of Music and Art edited by John Sullivan Dwight, 1852–1881, Boston, Massachusetts* (diss., UCLA, 1969)
D. K. Stigberg: *Congregational Psalmody in Eighteenth-century New England* (diss., U. of Illinois, Urbana, 1970)
Dictionary Catalog of the Music Collection, Boston Public Library (Boston, 1972–7)
L. J. Clarke: *Music in Trinity Church, Boston, 1890–1900: a Case Study in the Relationship between Worship and Culture* (diss., Union Theological Seminary, NY, 1973)
B. D. Wilson: *A Documentary History of Music in the Public Schools of the City of Boston, 1830–1850* (diss., U. of Michigan, 1973)
Leadership in the Arts: a Study on the Relocation of Authority (Cambridge, MA, 1975) [conversations with Erich Leinsdorf, Roger Voisin, Leonard Burkat, and others]
H. Kupferberg: *Tanglewood* (New York, 1976)
E. Leinsdorf: *Cadenza: a Musical Career* (Boston, 1976)
J. Baker-Carr: *Evening at Symphony: a Portrait of the Boston Symphony Orchestra* (Boston, 1977)
L. Snyder: *Community of Sound: Boston Symphony and its World of Players* (Boston, 1979)
B. Lambert, ed.: *Music in Colonial Massachusetts, 1630–1820*, i: *Music in Public Places* (Boston, 1980); ii: *Music in Homes and in Churches* (Boston, 1985)
B. Owen: *The Organ in New England* (Raleigh, NC, 1980)
D. A. Wood: *Music in Harvard Libraries: a Catalogue of Early Printed Music and Books on Music in the Houghton Library and the Eda Kuhn Loeb Music Library* (Cambridge, MA, 1980)
The Boston Composers Project: a Bibliography of Contemporary Music (Cambridge, MA, 1983)
H. T. Parker: *Motion Arrested: Dance Reviews*, ed. O. Holmes (Middletown, CT, 1983)
D. McKay: "Opera in Colonial Boston," *American Music*, iii/2 (1985), 133

LEONARD BURKAT
(9(i) with NINA DAVIS-MILLIS)

Boston [Boston dip] **(ii).** A slow ballroom dance related to the waltz. It originated in the USA during the 1870s and was the first modern ballroom dance requiring the feet to be kept pointing straight forwards rather than turned out, and to be performed mostly with the feet flat on the floor rather than on the toes. The Boston was danced with the hands on the partner's hips, the man's feet outside the woman's, and used few of the turning motions normally identified with the waltz. In the late 19th century it was performed to three counts, requiring a step on count one with the flat of one foot while bending or "dipping" the knee of the other leg, holding for count two, and rising onto the toes and pivoting for count three. The dance gained popularity in the early 20th century as the "hesitation waltz," in which the step pattern was performed to two bars of 3/4, one step for each of the first four counts and a pause or "hesitation" for counts five and six.

BIBLIOGRAPHY

A. Dodworth: *Dancing and its Relation to Education and Social Life* (New York, 1885; 3/1900 ed. T. G. Dodworth)
V. Castle and I. Castle: *Modern Dancing* (New York, 1914/*R*1980)

For further bibliography, *see* DANCE.

PAULINE NORTON

Boston Camerata. Ensemble of singers and instrumentalists founded in Boston in 1954 by Narcissa Williamson. *See* EARLY-MUSIC REVIVAL, §4.

Boston Festival Orchestra. Touring orchestra. It was founded in Boston in 1889 and was managed throughout its existence by George W. Stewart, a trombonist in the Boston SO; its purpose was to provide accompaniment for choirs at festivals and community events in places where orchestral resources were lacking. Generally numbering between 50 and 60 players, the ensemble specialized in oratorios and other standard festival fare. From 1889 to 1913 it made an annual spring tour along the Canadian border as far west as Minneapolis, then south by the Mississippi River to the Gulf of Mexico and up the Atlantic coast back to Boston. Carl Zerrahn led the first tour, and Victor Herbert those in 1890 and 1891; in the latter year he shared the conducting with Tchaikovsky, who traveled with the orchestra on his only visit to the USA. The conductor most closely associated with the orchestra, however, was Emil Mollenhauer, who led the remaining 22 tours. He developed the orchestra's reputation as an accompanying ensemble, readily adaptable to working under many guest conductors, and reputedly able, if necessary, to transpose an aria from any oratorio at sight. After the orchestra ceased touring it was reconstituted annually in Boston for many years under Mollenhauer's direction to accompany the concerts of the Handel and Haydn Society chorus.

BIBLIOGRAPHY

H. Woelber: "Famous Bandmasters: Emil Mollenhauer," *International Musician*, xxx/6 (1932), 12

——: "A Great Manager: George Washington Stewart," *International Musician*, xxxii/6 (1934), 19
E. N. Waters: *Victor Herbert: a Life in Music* (New York, 1955/R1978)

STEVEN LEDBETTER

Boston Ideal Opera Company [Bostonians]. Opera company. It was organized by Effie H. Ober, a singers' agent, in Boston in 1879. A local newspaper, critical of the performances of Gilbert and Sullivan's *H.M.S. Pinafore* that had been staged in the city in 1878, had called for an "ideal" production; the company responded with its highly successful version on 14 April 1879. Before long the troupe had a sizable repertory of contemporary comic operas and such works as Donizetti's *L'elisir d'amore* and Auber's *Fra Diavolo*, was making annual countrywide tours, and had earned a reputation as the finest American ensemble of its kind. In 1887 an internal dispute prompted several of the leading players, including Barnabee, Cowles, Jessie Bartlett Davis, Karl, and W. H. MacDonald, to assume the group's management, at which time its name was changed to the Bostonians. The company presented several first performances of Victor Herbert's works and became associated particularly with the operetta *Robin Hood* by De Koven and H. B. Smith, of which they gave the première in 1891. By 1898 the soprano Alice Nielsen had left the Bostonians to form her own company, taking with her several of its leading performers. This precipitated the group's demise, and it finally disbanded in 1905.

GERALD BORDMAN

Boston Musical Instrument Manufactory. Firm of band instrument makers. The company was established in about 1869 when a group of brass instrument makers working at 71 Sudbury Street in Boston combined their skills and resources. The original group included George C. Graves, William E. Graves, Elbridge G. Wright, Henry Esbach, Louis F. Hartman, and William G. Reed. All were partners and workmen in the firms of E. G. Wright and Graves & Co. A case of musical instruments exhibited at the Massachusetts Charitable Mechanic Association fair of 1869 won the new company a silver medal. It became a leading producer of band instruments during the late 1880s and made instruments for several of the leading band soloists as well as for hundreds of community bands across the country. The firm was known for its "three star" cornets and trumpets. In 1913 the factory was reincorporated as the Boston Musical Instrument Company; it was sold to Cundy-Bettoney in 1919. Instruments by this firm are found in most American collections, notably the Janssen Collection in Claremont, California; the Larson Collection in Vermillion, South Dakota; and the Essig Collection in Warrensburg, Missouri.

BIBLIOGRAPHY

C. M. Ayars: *Contributions to the Art of Music in America by the Music Industries of Boston, 1640–1936* (New York, 1937/R1969)

ROBERT E. ELIASON

Boston Music Company. Firm of music publishers. It was founded in 1885 by Gustave Schirmer, Jr. (*b* New York, 18 Feb 1864; *d* Boston, MA, 15 July 1907) and operated from premises at 2 Beacon Street, Boston; its first publication, Arthur Whiting's *Concert Etude* for piano, was issued the following year. The firm's large catalogue, which includes many works by Ethelbert Nevin and Carrie Jacobs-Bond, is predominantly educational. Among its popular instructional series are the piano methods by John M. Williams (the "Blue Books"), C. Paul Herfurth's series *A Tune a Day* (for various instruments), and *Junior Hymn Books* for piano by Rachael Beatty Kahl. Connections with the Schirmer family and firm remained close. Ernest Charles Schirmer, cousin of Gustave and founder of the E. C. Schirmer Music Company of Boston in 1921, was business manager and then partner, but left in 1917. On Gustave's death ownership passed to his son, also named Gustave (*b* Boston, 29 Dec 1890; *d* Palm Beach, FL, 28 May 1965), who engaged Carl Engel as editor and music adviser (1909–21), acquired catalogues of other publishers, and joined ASCAP (1924). In 1922 publication headquarters were moved to New York. The firm has long acted as agent for both domestic and foreign publishers. From 1965 to 1976 it was owned by the Frank Music Corp., then passed into the hands of CBS for a year, during which time it ceased to publish. Williamson Music took over from 1977 to 1979, when it was sold to William Hammerstein to become a division of the Hammerstein Music & Theater Company, Inc.

BIBLIOGRAPHY

W. A. Fischer: *One Hundred and Fifty Years of Music Publishing in the United States* (Boston, 1933/R1977)
C. M. Ayars: *Contributions to the Art of Music in America by the Music Industries of Boston, 1640–1936* (New York, 1937/R1969)

GERALDINE OSTROVE

Boston Society of Ancient Instruments. Chamber ensemble founded in Boston in 1938. *See* EARLY-MUSIC REVIVAL, §2, and BOSTON (i), §6(i).

Boswell, Connee [Connie] (*b* New Orleans, LA, 3 Dec 1907; *d* New York, 11 Oct 1976). Jazz singer. She was a member of the Boswell Sisters (Connee, Martha, and Helvetia), a vocal trio who specialized in intricately arranged close-harmony singing, and with whom she also performed occasionally on saxophone, trombone, and piano. The group achieved international fame during the early 1930s, their recordings with the Dorsey Brothers' Band being notably successful. Connee's voice, which was heavily featured, was rich in feeling, and her sense of timing and rhythmic phrasing made her a favorite with jazz enthusiasts. Despite having to spend most of her life in a wheelchair (as a result of poliomyelitis), she embarked on a successful career as a soloist in 1935. She was able to interpret a wide range of material with warmth and subtlety, and her work influenced many other singers, including Ella Fitzgerald. Boswell continued touring and appearing in films until the 1950s; thereafter she made occasional public appearances, and an admirable album (1956) with a re-formed version of the Original Memphis Five, including Miff Mole and Tony Spargo.

RECORDINGS
(selective list)

As soloist: I'm all dressed up with a broken heart (1931, Bruns. 6162); Me Minus You (1932, Bruns. 6405); *Connie Boswell and the Original Memphis Five* (1956, Vic. LPM1426), incl. Japanese Sandman
With the Boswell Sisters: You oughta be in pictures (1934, Bruns. 6798)
With Bob Crosby: Yes Indeed (1940, Decca 3689)

BIBLIOGRAPHY

Down Beat, v/8 (1938), 8
C. Ellis: "Connee Boswell," *Storyville*, no.71 (1977), 166

JOHN CHILTON

Botsford, George (*b* Sioux Falls, SD, 24 Feb 1874; *d* New York, 11 Feb 1949). Popular composer and arranger. He grew up in Iowa, where his first published work, *The Katy Flyer*, appeared in 1899. Shortly thereafter he moved to New York, and for the next few years he composed a number of moderately successful but undistinguished popular songs, though his *Sailing down the Chesapeake Bay* was a big hit in 1913. He also experimented unsuccessfully the following year with miniature opera to be sung by three or four musicians. From 1908 to 1916 he wrote more than 18 piano rags which received wide distribution and brought him considerable commercial success. During the 1920s Botsford was manager of the harmony and quartet department of the music publisher Jerome H. Remick, writing highly regarded vocal arrangements for quartets, glee clubs, and amateur minstrel shows. He also directed the New York City Police Department Glee Club, and worked as music director for various stage productions.

Botsford is most notable as a composer of piano rags. His excellent *Black and White Rag* (1908) is one of the most enduring pieces in the genre, and the *Grizzly Bear Rag* (1910) was very popular both as an instrumental piece and as a song (with lyrics by Irving Berlin). Although his rags were written to appeal to popular taste (many use a catchy three-over-four rhythm common at that time), they are well structured and unified, and often contain melodic trios reflecting midwestern folk roots.

WORKS

(selective list; unless otherwise stated, all printed works published in New York)

Pf: The Katy Flyer (Centerville, IA, 1899); Black and White Rag (1908); Klondike Rag (1908); Wiggle Rag (1908); Chatterbox Rag (1910); Grizzly Bear Rag (1910); Hyacinth (1911); Honeysuckle Rag (1911); Incandescent Rag (1913); Universal Rag, 1913

Songs: Travelling, or Iowa Corn Song (J. Devins) (1906); Pride of the Prairie (H. Breen) (1907); Grizzly Bear Rag (I. Berlin) (1910); Eskimo Rag (J. C. Havez) (1912); Sailing down the Chesapeake Bay, collab. Havez (1913); When big profundo sang low C (M. T. Bohannon) (1921)

Principal publisher: Remick

BIBLIOGRAPHY

"George Botsford: a Harmonious Blender of Quartet Music," *Metronome*, xxxix/9 (1923), 142

R. Blesh and H. Janis: *They All Played Ragtime* (New York, 1950, rev. 4/1971)

D. A. Jasen and T. J. Tichenor: *Rags and Ragtime: a Musical History* (New York, 1978)

RICHARD ZIMMERMANN

Bottje, Will Gay (*b* Grand Rapids, MI, 30 June 1925). Composer and flutist. He attended the Juilliard School, obtaining the BS in flute and the MS in composition (1947). Following several years as a freelance flutist, teacher, and conductor in western Michigan, he went to Europe on a Fulbright scholarship to study with Boulanger in Paris and Henk Badings in the Netherlands. In 1953 he enrolled at the Eastman School (DMA 1955), where he was a composition pupil of Rogers and Hanson and studied conducting with Paul White and flute with Joseph Mariano. He also studied at the electronic music studios of the University of Utrecht (1962–3) and the Stiftlesen in Stockholm (1973). Except for two years at the University of Mississippi (1955–7), his career as a teacher was spent at Southern Illinois University, Carbondale (1957–81), where in 1965 he founded and then directed the electronic music studio. On his retirement he returned to Grand Rapids to devote himself to composition.

Bottje's works are performed most frequently on college campuses and in concert series of new music. He has won a number of prizes and received commissions from Washington University, Illinois State University, and Southern Illinois University, as well as other institutions and ensembles. Bottje's particularly adept writing for flute, piccolo, and other woodwinds is evident in many of his chamber works and in the Concertino (1956). His musical language has been described as experimental and dissonant, but is nevertheless accessible to both performers and listeners. He is drawn especially to writing for like groups of instruments (as in the Quartet for Saxophones and the Chaconne for five guitars). His best-known work is probably the Sinfonia concertante for brass quintet and band (1961).

WORKS

Operas: Altgeld (Bottje), 1968; Root! (J. Maloon), 1971

Orch: Ballad Singer, 1951; Conc., fl, tpt, harp, str, 1955; Concertino, pic, orch, 1956; Sym. no.5, 1959; Pf Conc., 1960; Wayward Pilgrim (Dickinson), S, chorus, chamber orch, 1961; Rhapsodic Variations, va, pf, str, 1962; Tangents (Sym. no.7), 1970; Chiaroscuros, 1975; Tuba Conc., 1977; Mutations, small orch, 1977; Songs from the Land between the Rivers, chorus, orch, 1981; Conc., bn, ob, chamber orch/pf, 1981; Commentaries, gui/kbd, chamber ens/chamber orch, 1983; Sounds from the West Shore, 1983; Conc., vn, ob, small orch, 1984

Band/brass ens: Contrasts, band, 1952; Sym. no.4, band, 1956; Conc., tpt, trbn, band, 1959; What is Man? (Whitman), chorus, band, 2 pf, nar, 1959; Sinfonia concertante, brass qnt, band, 1961; Sym. no.6, large brass ens, org, perc, also arr. kbd, 1963; Sym. Allegro, brass ens, perc, 1971; Facets, pf, band, 1975; Vc Conc., band, 1975; Conc., band, 1982; other band works

Chamber: 4 str qts, 1950, 1959, 1962, 1982; Diversions, ww qnt, pf, nar, 1962; Qt, s, a, t, b sax, 1963; Interplays, hn, hpd, pf, tape, 1970; Chaconne, 5 gui, 1975; Dances: Real and Imagined, gui, str qt, 1976; Pf Trio, 1978; Gui Sonata, 1980; Sym., vc, pf 4 hands, 1980; Fl Sonata, 1981; Qnt, cl, bn, hn, vn, db, 1983; Conc., 2 fl/pf, 1984; Mallets, xyl, mar, vib, 1984; *c*70 other chamber works; kbd pieces, incl. Sparks from a New Flint, 3 vols., synth

Vocal: Quests of Odysseus (N. Kazantzakis, K. Friar), T, pf, 1960; In Caverns All Alone, 7 songs, T, fl, bn, pf, 1979; A Sentence once Begun (C. Fry), S, pf/str qt, 1982; Exhortation to the Dawn, SATB, org/pf/brass ens, 1984; other songs and vocal works

Other: From the Winds and the Farthest Spaces (L. Eiseley), tape, ww qnt, nar, dancers, slides, 1977; To Charm the Cloudy Crystal (Eiseley), chamber ens, 2 nar, dancer, 1983; other tape, mixed-media works; film music

Some early works withdrawn, incl. Syms. nos.1–3, 1946–53

Principal publishers: ACA, M. M. Cole, Robert King, Music for Percussion

BARBARA A. PETERSEN

Boucher, William (*b* Germany, 1822; *d* Baltimore, MD, 11 March 1899). Instrument maker. He was apparently first a drum maker. He came to the USA in 1845 and worked as an instrument maker in Baltimore until 1891. In the 1840s he began making five-string banjos in Baltimore and was probably the earliest commercial manufacturer of banjos. He won medals for his violins, drums, and banjos in the 1850s. The Smithsonian Institution has three of his banjos (from the years 1845–7; for illustration *see* BANJO, fig. 1*a*), donated by Boucher in 1890; the receipt for these identifies him as "the inventor of tightening banjo-heads by screw-fixtures. . . ." These banjos are characterized by heads of large diameter, thin but deep wooden rims, open backs, bracket systems for tightening the head, fretless fingerboards with one or more curves shaped into the side of the neck just below the fifth-string peg, and friction pegs. Boucher used several shapes for the peghead, but the most common was a scroll shape (like a violin peghead scroll turned sideways).

BIBLIOGRAPHY

L. Libin: *Our American Instruments* (New York, 1985)

ROBERT B. WINANS

Boudousquié, Charles (*b* New Orleans, LA, 29 Feb 1814; *d* New Orleans, 23 Aug 1866). Impresario. He was the third and last director of the Théâtre d'Orléans, succeeding Pierre Davis, son of the theater's founder, about 1853. He did much to create the reputation of the theater, which was especially important for its promotion of opera. In 1858 he married the noted French soprano Julie Calvé, who was prima donna at the theater from 1837 to 1846. The following year he left the Théâtre d'Orléans to build the new French Opera House, which was formally opened on 1 December 1859 with a performance, in French, of Rossini's *Guillaume Tell*. Under Boudousquié's brief but vigorous directorship, which saw the American première of Meyerbeer's *Dinorah* (1861, with Adelina Patti in the title role), the French Opera House quickly eclipsed the Théâtre d'Orléans as New Orleans's leading opera house.

See also NEW ORLEANS, §1.

JOHN JOYCE

Boulanger, Nadia (Juliette) (*b* Paris, France, 16 Sept 1887; *d* Paris, 22 Oct 1979). French teacher, conductor, organist, and composer. She was born into a musical family: her father, Ernest Boulanger, and her grandfather had taught singing at the Paris Conservatoire; her mother, the Princess Raissa Mychetsky, had been one of her father's students. Boulanger entered the Conservatoire at the age of ten and studied harmony with Paul Antonin Vidal, organ with Louis Vierne and Alexandre Guilmant, and composition with Charles-Marie Widor and Gabriel Fauré, the latter remaining a favorite composer throughout her life. In 1908 she was placed second in the Prix de Rome competition with her work *La sirène*. One of her first pupils, her younger sister Lili, became the first woman to win the Prix de Rome (1913). Lili's premature death in 1918 deeply affected Boulanger and influenced her to give up composing for a life of teaching. She taught at the Ecole Normale de Musique, Paris, from 1920 to 1939, and from 1921 at the American Conservatory at Fontainebleau, near Paris, of which she became director in 1950. She also taught at the Paris Conservatoire from 1946. She became the leading music teacher of the 20th century, and was particularly influential with American composers. After Copland, Melville Smith, and Virgil Thomson "discovered" her in 1921 hundreds of Americans went to France to study with her.

Boulanger first came to the USA in 1924 for her début as organist in a performance of Copland's Symphony for Organ and Orchestra, a work she had convinced Damrosch and Koussevitzky to commission from her student. In 1938 she became the first woman to conduct the Boston SO. During World War II she lived in the USA (1940–46) and taught in Massachusetts at Wellesley College, and Radcliffe College, Cambridge, and in New York at the Juilliard School.

During the 1920s and 1930s, as her reputation grew, her influence on the musical development of America became such that Thomson once described every town as having "a five-and-ten-cent store and a Boulanger student." Known as the "Boulangerie," they came year after year to her apartment on the rue Ballu in Paris or to the American Conservatory for summer courses. She taught harmony, counterpoint, analysis, composition, organ, and other musical subjects to composers, performers, conductors, and musicologists from all over the world. Among her most prominent American students were Copland, Thomson, Roy Harris, Elliott Carter, David Diamond, Douglas Moore, Piston, Talma, Siegmeister, and Blitzstein. Her European students included Jean Françaix, Igor Markevich, and Marcelle de Manziarly. At her famous Wednesday afternoon classes young musicians could meet and hear works by the foremost figures in the arts of the day, including Boulanger's close friend Stravinsky. The performances of Monteverdi and Gesualdo madrigals at these gatherings played an important role in their rediscovery. Boulanger was considered a strict and demanding disciplinarian by some, but for those who she thought had talent and sincerity her devotion and efforts were tireless. She was possessed of phenomenal ability and thorough knowledge of all periods and styles of music. Her many awards, honors, and decorations included a commandership of the Légion d'honneur, nomination as maître de chapelle to the Prince of Monaco, and membership in the American Academy of Arts and Sciences.

BIBLIOGRAPHY

"Boulanger, Nadia," *CBY 1962*
A. Kendall: *The Tender Tyrant: Nadia Boulanger* (London, 1976)
L. Rosensteil: *Nadia Boulanger: a Life in Music* (New York, 1982)
A. Shawm: "Nadia Boulanger's Lessons," *The Atlantic*, ccli/3 (1983), 78

VIVIAN PERLIS

Boulez, Pierre (*b* Montbrison, Loire, France, 26 March 1925). French composer, conductor, and theorist. He attended the Paris Conservatoire (1942–5), where he studied harmony with Olivier Messiaen, and received private instruction in serial techniques from René Leibowitz, a pupil of Schoenberg. By the age of 20 he had developed a musical language based on the works of Anton Webern, and thereafter his compositions hardly veered from that particular grammar. Boulez first won acclaim in the USA as the composer of *Le marteau sans maître* (1954), a recording of which was released in the mid-1950s. Boulez came to the USA for the first time in 1952 as the conductor of the Compagnie Renaud-Barrault. Then on friendly terms with John Cage, whom he had met in Paris in 1949, he stayed in Cage's loft in New York, where he attended a performance by David Tudor of his Second Piano Sonata. Also on the program was Cage's *Music of Changes*, a work so far removed from Boulez's in approach that it precipitated a quarrel that ended the friendship between the two composers.

Boulez returned with Barrault to New York in 1958; he also went to Los Angeles, where he conducted *Le marteau sans maître* at one of the Monday Evening Concerts, a series devoted to 20th-century music. In 1963, no longer working for Barrault, he appeared as Horatio Appleton Lamb Lecturer at Harvard University, where he discoursed on the aesthetics of composing, and he revisited Los Angeles to conduct *Improvisations I–II*.

George Szell heard about Boulez from members of the Concertgebouw Orchestra in 1965; by then conducting had displaced composition as Boulez's principal activity. Szell invited him to conduct the Cleveland Orchestra in 1965 and 1967, and he became principal guest conductor of that organization in 1969. That same year Boulez appeared as a guest conductor with four other major American orchestras. After he performed Stravinsky's *Le sacre du printemps* with the New York PO, the board of directors appointed him music director of the orchestra. He held the position from 1971 to 1977, concurrently serving as music director of the BBC SO in London in 1971–4.

Up to 1969 Boulez conducted the 20th-century repertory he admired, generating excitement in concerts that attracted audiences specially interested in that music. But in New York the same programs drove the traditional subscription audience from the concert hall. In order to guarantee the subscribers' continued attendance, Boulez compromised his ideal that progress in art takes precedence over commercial success and included more standard repertory in his programs.

On 5 January 1973 the Chamber Music Society of Lincoln Center gave the American première of *Explosante-fixe* (for unspecified forces), the only major work Boulez composed during his time in New York. Boulez returned to Paris in 1978 as director of IRCAM, an institute for training and research in composition, electronic and computer techniques, acoustics, and instrument building. After leaving the New York PO, he made his first conducting appearance in the USA with the Los Angeles PO on 13 May 1984, performing Carter's Symphony of Three Orchestras, a work he commissioned while music director of the New York PO.

See also NEW YORK, §5.

BIBLIOGRAPHY

Grove 6

"Boulez, Pierre," *CBY 1969*

P. Heyworth: "Profiles: Taking Leave of Predecessors: Pierre Boulez," *New Yorker*, xlix (24 March 1973), 45; xlix (31 March 1973), 45

J. Peyser: *Boulez: Composer, Conductor, Enigma* (New York, 1976) [reviewed by S. Lipman, *Times Literary Supplement* (London, 11 March 1977), 277]

P. Griffiths: *Boulez* (London, 1978)

M. Walsh: "Boulez ex machina," *Time*, cxviii (28 Dec 1981), 66

H. Matheopoulos: "Pierre Boulez," *Maestro: Encounters with Conductors of Today* (London, 1982), 25

JOAN PEYSER

Boulton [née Craytor], **Laura** (*b* Conneaut, OH, 1899; *d* Bethesda, MD, 16 Oct 1980). Ethnomusicologist. She studied at Western Reserve University, Denison University (BA), and the University of Chicago (PhD). From 1929 to 1979, she participated in 40 expeditions in which she recorded music of the peoples of Africa, the American Southwest, Central and South America, Alaska, Asia, Eastern Europe, and the South Pacific; her travels were sponsored by the US Department of the Interior, the American Museum of Natural History, and the University of Chicago, among other institutions. Boulton taught at the University of Chicago (1931–3) and the University of California (1946–9), and was director of the Laura Boulton Collection of Traditional and Liturgical Music at Columbia University (1967–72) and the Laura Boulton Collection of World Music and Musical Instruments at Arizona State University (1972–7). She produced and directed documentary films and radio and television programs, and she also was responsible for a number of recordings of traditional music. Her writings include *The Music Hunter: the Autobiography of a Career* (1969) and *Musical Instruments of World Cultures* (1972), based on her own collections.

PAULA MORGAN

Bowen, Eugene (Everett) (*b* Biloxi, MS, 30 July 1950). Composer and performer. After studies at the California Institute of the Arts with Harold Budd, Morton Subotnick, and Leonard Stein (1970–72), he was instructor in electronic music at Moorpark (California) College from 1975 to 1980. His compositional style combines the simplicity and lyricism of his mentor Budd with an understated use of electronics. He has collaborated with Budd and Daniel Lentz both in performance and on recordings such as Lentz's *After Images* (1981). Bowen's *Longbow Angels*, written for the double bass player Buell Neidlinger, was runner-up in a competition sponsored by the International Society of Bassists (1977). Bowen has been involved with folk and regional music; he has traveled extensively in Mexico and in 1971 was a lecturer on modern American music at the University of Guadalajara. His recording *Traditional Folk Music in Ventura County* (1977) employs both Mexican and Anglo performers. These folk influences have been significant in his work, which combines an American minimalism (rooted in folk music) with the most advanced electronic and acoustic processes.

WORKS

Casida del llanto (Lorca), 2 solo vv, elec, 1971; Longbow Angels, 5 db, 1974; Junkyard Pieces, perc ens, 1976; Jewelled Settings, S, pf, vib, vc, elec, 1980; Desert's Edge, tape, vib, Chinese bells, synth, 1981

Principal publisher: Soundings

PETER GARLAND

Bowers, Thomas J. (*b* Philadelphia, PA, *c*1823; *d* Philadelphia, 3 Oct 1885). Tenor. He studied organ with his older brother, John C. Bowers, whom he succeeded as organist at St. Thomas's African Episcopal Church, Philadelphia, about 1838. Yielding to his parents' desire that he devote his talents to sacred music, Thomas rejected a position in Frank Johnson's band. However, he studied singing with Elizabeth Taylor Greenfield, with whom he appeared in a duo recital at the Sansom Street Hall, Philadelphia, in February 1854; reviewers dubbed him the "American Mario" and the "colored Mario," judging him to be the equal of the tenor Giovanni Matteo Mario. Later tours with Greenfield took Bowers from Canada to Baltimore (where he appeared only before unsegregated audiences). His repertory, which included arias by Friedrich Flotow, Verdi, and Donizetti, was intended to set him off from the image of contemporary minstrelsy.

BIBLIOGRAPHY

SouthernB

J. M. Trotter: *Music and Some Highly Musical People* (Boston, 1881/*R*1968), 130

M. C. Hare: *Negro Musicians and their Music* (Washington, DC, 1936/*R*1974), 199

DOMINIQUE-RENÉ DE LERMA

Bowie, Lester (*b* Frederick, MD, 11 Oct 1941). Jazz trumpeter. He grew up in St. Louis and gained early musical experience with blues and rhythm-and-blues bands, including those of Albert King and Little Milton. In 1965 he moved to Chicago to become music director for his wife, the rhythm-and-blues singer Fontella Bass. There he became an organizer of the ASSOCIATION FOR THE ADVANCEMENT OF CREATIVE MUSICIANS, a group of young black jazz players who experimented with avant-garde forms. In 1969 Bowie was a founding member of the ART ENSEMBLE OF CHICAGO, an eclectic and highly theatrical avant-garde jazz group with which he has been associated ever since. When not touring with the Art Ensemble, Bowie can be found playing in many contexts – from solo concerts to appearances with his bands From the Root to the Source, which combines gospel music with jazz and rock, and Lester Bowie's Brass Fantasy. He is among the most original trumpeters in jazz, with a large stock of effects at his command.

RECORDINGS
(selective list)

Gittin' to Know Y'all (1969, MPS 2120728); *Fast Last* (1974, Muse 5055); *Rope-a-dope* (1975, Muse 5081); *The 5th Power* (1978, Black Saint 0020); *The Great Pretender* (1981, ECM 1209); *All the Magic!* (1982, ECM 23789)

BIBLIOGRAPHY

V. Wilmer: "Extending the Tradition," *Down Beat*, xxxviii/9 (1971), 13

R. Townley: "Lester . . . Who?" *Down Beat*, xli/2 (1974), 11

M. Luzzi: *Uomini e avanguardie jazz* (Milan, 1980)

B. McRae: "Avant Courier: Lester Bowie," *Jazz Journal International*, xxxiii/11 (1980), 12

J. Rockwell: "Jazz, Group Improvisation, Race & Racism: the Art Ensemble of

Chicago," *All American Music: Composition in the Late Twentieth Century* (New York, 1983), 164
H. Mandel: "Lester Bowie M.D.: Magical Dimensions," *Down Beat*, li/3 (1984), 14

LEE JESKE

Bowles, Paul (*b* Jamaica, NY, 30 Dec 1910). Composer and writer. In the late 1920s and early 1930s he studied with Copland, Thomson, and Boulanger, and lived in Europe and North Africa. Between 1936 and 1963 he occasionally wrote music for the New York theater, being associated with Orson Welles, William Saroyan, and Tennessee Williams. He received a Guggenheim Fellowship in 1941 to compose the opera *The Wind Remains*. In 1948 he returned to Tangier where he wrote a second opera after Lorca, *Yerma*, for the singer Libby Holman. In 1959 he was given a Rockefeller grant for ethnomusicological research, which occupied him in Tangier for the next decade. The major part of his compositional output dates from before 1949, the year in which his first novel, *The Sheltering Sky*, appeared. From that time he was more active as a writer and translator than as a composer. His literary output comprises novels, numerous short stories, poetry, essays, translations, and an autobiography, *Without Stopping* (1972). His music is nostalgic and witty, evocative in its use of American jazz, Mexican dance, and Moroccan rhythm, and exclusively in short forms – the operas are constructed as suites of songs. By contrast the fiction is dark, despairing, and formally extended.

WORKS
(selective list)

DRAMATIC

Yankee Clipper (ballet), 1936; The Ballroom Guide (ballet), 1937; Denmark Vesey (opera, C. H. Ford), 1938; Pastorela (ballet), 1941; The Wind Remains (opera, after F. G. Lorca), 1941–3; Colloque sentimental (ballet), 1944; Yerma (opera, after Lorca), 1948–55

Incidental music: My Heart's in the Highlands (W. Saroyan), 1939; Love's Old Sweet Song (Saroyan), 1940; Love like Wildfire (R. Hepburn), 1941; The Glass Menagerie (T. Williams), 1945; Summer and Smoke (Williams), 1948; Sweet Bird of Youth (Williams), 1959; The Milk Train doesn't Stop here Anymore (Williams), 1963; Edwin Booth (M. Geiger); In the Summer House (J. Bowles); Watch on the Rhine (L. Hellman); *c*12 others

16 film scores

INSTRUMENTAL

Orch: Iquitos, 1933; Pastorale, Havanaise et Divertissement, 1933; Suite, 1933; Romantic Suite, 6 ww, str, pf, 1939; Conc., 2 pf, wind, perc/orch, 1947; Danza mexicana, 1947

Chamber: Sonata, ob, cl, 1930; Fl Sonata no. 1, 1932; Scènes d'Anabase (St. J. Perse), T, ob, pf, 1932; Par le détroit, cantata, S, 4 male vv, harmonium, 1933; Vn Sonata no. 1, 1934; Pf Trio, 1936; Melodia, 11 insts, 1937; Music for a Farce, cl, tpt, perc, pf, 1938; 3 Pastoral Songs (anon., Canon Dixon, S. O'Sullivan), T, str, pf, 1944; Prelude and Dance, wind, brass, perc, pf, 1947; A Picnic Cantata (J. Schuyler), 4 solo vv, 2 pf, perc, 1952

Pf: 2 sonatinas, 1932, 1935; Nocturne, 2 pf, 1935; Suite, 2 pf, 1939; Iquitos, 1947; Orosí, 1948; Night Waltz, 2 pf, 1949; Sonata, 2 pf, 1949; at least 15 other pieces

SONGS
(all lv, pf, unless otherwise stated)

Edition: *Paul Bowles: Selected Songs*, ed. P. Garland (Santa Fe, NM, 1984) [G]

Danger de mort (G. Linze), 1934–5; David (F. Frost), 1935, G; Letter to Freddy (G. Stein), 1935, G; Memnon (Cocteau), 1935; Scènes d'Anabase III (Perse), 1935; Lullaby, chorus, 1939; Tornado Blues, chorus, pf, 1939; 2 Skies (J. Bowles), 1942; Night Without Sleep (Ford), 1943, G; Song of the Old Woman (Farther from the Heart) (J. Bowles), 1943, G; 4 Spanish Songs (Lorca), 1943, G; In the Woods (P. Bowles), 1945, G

Blue Mountain Ballads (Williams), 1946, G; Once a Lady was Here (P. Bowles), 1946, G; Three (Williams), 1946, G; Gothic Suite (Williams), song cycle, 1960, G; Her Head on the Pillow (Williams), 1961, G; Bluebell Mountain (J. Bowles); Green Songs (R. Thoma), G; Scenes from the Door (Stein); 6 Songs (P. Bowles); 3 Songs from the Sierras; many others

Arrs.: [4] *American Folk Songs*, 1940; *12 American Folk Songs*, ?1940

MSS in *TxU*

Principal publishers: G. Schirmer, Soundings

BIBLIOGRAPHY

EwenD
P. Glanville-Hicks: "Paul Bowles: American Composer," *ML*, xxvi (1945), 88
C. R. McLeod: *Paul Bowles: a Checklist 1929–1969* (Flint, MI, 1970) [list of writings incl. music criticism]
D. J. Soria: "Artist Life," *HiFi/MusAm*, xxi/8 (1971), 4
V. Thomson: *American Music since 1910* (New York, 1971), 126
N. Rorem: "Come Back Paul Bowles," *New Republic*, clxvi (22 April 1972), 24
P. Garland: "Paul Bowles and the Baptism of Solitude," *Americas: Essays on American Music and Culture, 1973–80* (Santa Fe, 1982), 186–218

NED ROREM

Bowman, Euday L(ouis) (*b* Fort Worth, TX, 9 Nov 1887; *d* New York, 26 May 1949). Ragtime composer. He reportedly worked as an itinerant pianist, beginning in "Hell's Half Acre," the former bordello district of Fort Worth. Bowman commemorated four streets in this district with piano rags. In 1914 he published the *12th Street Rag* at his own expense, then sold it to the music publisher J. W. Jenkins' Sons in Kansas City, Missouri. Its theme-and-variations structure (unusual for ragtime) and use of a repeating three-note motif (sometimes called "secondary rag") made the piece catchy and easy to play, and under the Jenkins imprint it became a major hit. Words were added, and it was issued in numerous arrangements, becoming an enduring standard among bandleaders, pianists, broadcasters, and the record-buying public. More than 120 versions were recorded on 78 r.p.m. records alone, and until the ragtime revival in the 1970s it ranked as the most popular rag of all time. Bowman recorded the piece in 1924 for Gennett and again in 1938 for ARC, but the recordings were never issued. Following Pee Wee Hunt's extraordinarily successful recording of the rag in 1948, Bowman tried to capitalize on its renewed popularity, issuing his own recording of it, but he died soon thereafter.

WORKS

Selective list; all are for pf and, unless otherwise indicated, printed works published in Kansas City, Missouri.

12th Street Rag (Fort Worth, TX, 1914); Sixth Street Rag, 1914; Tenth Street Rag, 1914; Petticoat Lane (1915); Shamrock Rag (Fort Worth, 1916); Eleventh Street Rag (1917); Chromatic Chords, 1926

BIBLIOGRAPHY

L. Laird: "The 12th Street Rag Story," *Kansas City Times* (23 Oct 1942); repr. in *Rag Times*, xiii (May 1979), 1
Obituary, *Kansas City Star* (5 June 1949)
D. A. Jasen and T. J. Tichenor: *Rags and Ragtime: a Musical History* (New York, 1978), 49

JOHN EDWARD HASSE

Boyden, David D(odge) (*b* Westport, CT, 10 Dec 1910). Musicologist. He studied at Harvard (BA 1932, MA 1938) and at Columbia University and the Hartt School of Music, West Hartford, Connecticut. From 1938 to 1975 he taught at the University of California, Berkeley, where he became a full professor in 1955; he served as chairman of the music department (1955–61). He has published three textbooks for students including the widely read *An Introduction to Music* (1956, 2/1970), but the bulk of his work has been on the history of string instruments and string playing. His *History of Violin Playing from its Origins* *to 1761* (1965) is a major work of scholarship informed by practical experience as well as scholarly judgment. In 1957 he was awarded an honorary doctorate by the Hartt School of Music. He has been twice vice-president of the American Musicological Society (1954–6, 1960–62), a Fulbright Fellow at Oxford University (1963), and three times the recipient of a Guggenheim Fellowship (1954, 1967, and 1970).

PHILIP BRETT/R

Boykan, Martin (*b* New York, 12 April 1931). Composer. He studied with Piston at Harvard University (BA 1951), and with Hindemith, first at the University of Zurich (1951–2) and then at Yale University (MM 1953). In 1953 he went to Vienna on a Fulbright scholarship, and in 1957 he joined the faculty of Brandeis University, where he was appointed professor in 1976. He received a commission from the Fromm Foundation in 1975; his awards include a grant from the Martha Baird Rockefeller Fund for Music (1977), an NEA grant (1983), and a Guggenheim Fellowship (1984).

Despite the tonal orientation of his principal teachers, Boykan's mature style is atonal and reflects the influences of Webern and the late music of Stravinsky, the respective subjects of his two most important articles ("'Neoclassicism' and the late Stravinsky," *PNM*, i/2, 1963, p.155, and "The Webern Concerto Revisited," *Proceedings of the American Society of University Composers*, iii, 1970, p.74). His String Quartet no.1 (1967) is partly serial; his later works use 12-tone techniques. A characteristically American feature of his music is the long line, which for him is rhythmically flexible and extends across a wide registral range. He favors long works for small ensembles; his pieces, though few in number, are carefully crafted. The first two string quartets have been recorded by CRI.

WORKS

3 early chamber works; Psalm cxxviii, chorus, 1965; Str Qt no.1, 1967; Conc., 13 insts, 1972; Str Qt no.2, 1975; Pf Trio, 1977; Elegy, S, fl, cl, vn, vc, db, pf, part i (Goethe, Leopardi, Ungaretti), 1979, part ii (Brentano, Dickinson, Li Ho), 1982; Str Qt no.3, 1984

BIBLIOGRAPHY

EwenD

J. Harbison and E. Cory: "Martin Boykan: String Quartet (1967), Two Views," *PNM*, xi/2 (1973), 204 [incl. score]

E. Cory: "Martin Boykan: String Quartet No.1 (1967)," *MQ*, lxii (1976), 616

STEVEN E. GILBERT

Boyle, George Frederick (*b* Sydney, Australia, 29 June 1886; *d* Philadelphia, PA, 20 June 1948). Pianist, composer, and teacher. He received his early musical training from his parents, and after concert tours in Australia went to Berlin in 1905 to study with Busoni. He spent five years performing in Germany, the Netherlands, and Great Britain before settling in the USA in 1910, where he taught at the Peabody Conservatory (1910–22), the Curtis Institute (1924–6), and the Institute of Musical Art (1927–39); he also gave recitals, in New York and elsewhere. As a composer, he is perhaps best known for his Piano Concerto, first performed by the Washington (DC) SO (Worcester Festival, 1911) and later by the New York PO (conducted by Boyle), both times with Ernest Hutcheson as soloist.

WORKS

(selective list)

The Black Rose (operetta)

Orch: Pf Conc., d (New York, 1912); Sym. Fantasy, 1915; Slumber Song and Aubade, 1915; Vc Conc., 1917; Pf Concertino, 1935

Inst: Pf Sonata, b, 1916; 3 pf trios; Va Sonata, 1918; Vc Sonata, 1928; Suite, 2 pf, 1932; Ballade élégiaque, pf trio, 1935; Vn Sonata, 1935; other chamber music, numerous pf pieces

Vocal: 2 cantatas, The Pied Piper of Hamelin (Browning), Don Ramiro (Heine), 1916; *c*50 songs, incl. 6 Songs (Heine: New Spring), S, pf (New York, 1909), La bonne chanson (Verlaine), 1v, pf (New York, 1911), 4 Poems (Heine: New Spring), 1v, pf (New York, 1912)

Principal publishers: Composers' Music Corp., Elkan-Vogel, G. Schirmer

RICHARD ALDRICH/DENNIS K. McINTIRE

Bozeman, George (*b* Pampa, TX, 1936). Organ builder. After graduating from North Texas State University, he served his apprenticeship with Otto Hofmann, Robert L. Sipe, and Fritz Noack. In 1967 he received a Fulbright scholarship to study organ building and playing in Austria. In 1971 he established his own firm in Lowell, Massachusetts, and the following year he entered into partnership with David V. Gibson (*b* 1944), moving to a new workshop in Deerfield, New Hampshire, soon after. The partnership was dissolved in 1982 and Bozeman continued to work independently. Bozeman's firm has built several new organs and restored a number of old ones; its most important instruments include those in Faith Lutheran Church, Syosset, New York (1978), and St. Paul's Episcopal Church, Brookline, Massachusetts (1982), as well as an organ based on the designs of Gottfried Silbermann for SUNY, Stony Brook (1985). The firm also builds a small, versatile "stock" design, the Cortez.

BIBLIOGRAPHY

U. Pape: *The Tracker Organ Revival in America* (Berlin, n.d. [?1977])

BARBARA OWEN

Bracey, Ishmon [Ishman] (1901–70). Blues singer and guitarist who frequently shared recording sessions with TOMMY JOHNSON.

Brackeen [née Grogan], **JoAnne** (*b* Ventura, CA, 26 July 1938). Jazz pianist. She learned jazz piano by imitating Frankie Carle solos from her parents' record collection. During the late 1950s she worked with the saxophonists Teddy Edwards, Harold Land, Dexter Gordon, and Charles Lloyd. She married the saxophonist Charles Brackeen during the early 1960s and moved to New York with him in 1965. There she began to attract attention as a pianist with Art Blakey's Jazz Messengers (1969–72) and with Joe Henderson's group (1972–5). At that point she began an eventful two years with Stan Getz's quartet, which brought a wider audience for her playing, much critical acclaim, and offers to record as a leader. Though clearly influenced by the pianists McCoy Tyner and Chick Corea, her musical approach is unique, particularly in regard to rhythmic development. From the mid-1970s she toured and recorded with her own groups, becoming a major figure among contemporary jazz pianists.

RECORDINGS

(selective list)

As leader: *Snooze* (1975, Choice 1009); *Tring-a-ling* (1977, Choice 1016); *Special Identity* (1981, Antilles 1001)

As sideman: A. Blakey: *Jazz Messengers '70* (1970, Catalyst 7902); S. Getz: *Live at Montmartre* (1977, Steeplechase 1073–4)

BIBLIOGRAPHY

C. J. Safane: "JoAnne Brackeen: Profile of an Emerging Jazz Piano Headliner," *Contemporary Keyboard*, v/11 (1979), 18

L. Feather: *The Passion for Jazz* (New York, 1980), 144

N. George: "JoAnne Brackeen: Pianist for a New Era," *Down Beat*, xlvii/7 (1980), 22

BILL DOBBINS

Bradbury, William Batchelder (*b* York Co., ME, 6 Oct 1816; *d* Montclair, NJ, 7 Jan 1868). Composer, teacher, organist, publisher, and piano manufacturer. In 1830 his family moved to Boston, where he studied music with Sumner Hill and attended Lowell Mason's Academy of Music; he also sang in Mason's Bowdoin Street church choir and later became organist there. From 1836 he taught music classes and gave private piano lessons in Machias, Maine, then in 1838 became a singing-school teacher in St. John's, New Brunswick. Bradbury moved to New York in 1840 as choir leader of the First Baptist Church, Brooklyn, and the following year accepted a position as organist at the Baptist Tabernacle in New York. He established singing classes for children similar to those of Mason in Boston; his annual music festivals with as many as 1000 children led to the introduction of music in New York's public schools. He also published his first collection, *The Young Choir* (1841), in association with Charles Walden Sanders. The music was later revised by Thomas Hastings, with whom Bradbury collaborated on four other collections, beginning in 1844 with *The Psalmodist*.

Bradbury spent the years 1847 to 1849 in Europe, visiting London and Berne, and studying in Leipzig with E. F. Wenzel (piano), Moritz Hauptmann (harmony), and Ignaz Moscheles (composition). During this time he saw Mendelssohn conduct at the Gewandhaus Concerts and met Liszt and Robert and Clara Schumann. He wrote letters to the *New York Observer* and the *New York Evangelist* describing his personal and musical experiences there.

Following his return to the USA Bradbury lived in New Jersey and New York and continued teaching music to children, composing, and compiling numerous collections of music; he also conducted at several music conventions. Between 1850 and 1854 he was choir director at Broadway Tabernacle, New York, and in 1854 became associated with Mason, Hastings, and G. F. Root in their normal musical institutes, where he taught harmony. During the same year he began the manufacture of pianos with his brother Edward G. Bradbury and F. C. Lighte. The Bradbury piano received the endorsement of Theodore Thomas, William Mason, Gottschalk and others, and in 1863 won first prizes at state fairs in New Jersey, New York, Illinois, Ohio, Pennsylvania, and Indiana. Following Bradbury's death the firm was controlled by F. G. Smith and was later absorbed into the Knabe Piano Company.

Bradbury composed, edited, and compiled numerous tunebooks, many of which were published by the firm he established in New York in 1861. Bradbury Publishers also issued a few compilations by other composers; after Bradbury's death it was taken over by Lucius Biglow and Sylvester Main to become Biglow & Main. Most of Bradbury's earlier works were designed for Sunday-school use and were exceedingly popular; an advertisement in the *New York Musical Gazette* in 1869 reported that over three million copies of *The Golden Chain* (1861), *The Golden Shower* (1861) and *The Golden Censer* (1864) had been sold, and another collection, *Fresh Laurels* (1867), sold 1,200,000 copies. He compiled eight books of secular music, including *The Alpine Glee Singer* (1850) and *The New York Glee and Chorus Book* (1855). Bradbury wrote 921 hymn tunes, many of which, including those of the hymns *Jesus loves me*, *Just as I am without one plea*, *Sweet hour of prayer*, *Saviour, like a shepherd lead us*, and *He leadeth me*, remain in present-day hymnals.

See also HYMNODY, esp. §3(ii) and ex.6.

WORKS

(selective list; all printed works published in New York)

Collections: The Young Choir (with C. W. Sanders, 1841); The Psalmodist (with T. Hastings, 1844); The Mendelssohn Collection (with Hastings, 1849); The Shawm (with G. F. Root, 1853); The Jubilee (1857); Cottage Melodies (1859); Oriola (1859); The Golden Chain (1861); The Golden Shower (1861); Pilgrim's Songs (1863); Bradbury's Devotional Hymn and Tune Book (1864); The Golden Censer (1864); Fresh Laurels (1867)

Cantatas: Daniel, or The Captivity and Restoration (Root, C. M. Cady), collab. Root, solo vv, chorus, pf (1853); Esther, the Beautiful Queen (Cady), solo vv, chorus, pf (1856)

921 hymn tunes, mostly pubd in collections, incl. Rest; The God of love will sure indulge; Just as I am without one plea; Caddo; Olive's Brow; Holy bible, book divine; Sweet hour of prayer; Saviour, like a shepherd lead us; The sweetest name; Jesus loves me; Solid Rock; He leadeth me; Will the angels come to me?

30 anthems, incl. O magnify the Lord (collab. Hastings), 4vv, pubd in The Psalmodist (1844); Heavenly Love, 4vv, pubd in The Jubilee (1857)

79 other sacred choral pieces

24 glees, incl. My home is on the mountain, pubd in The New York Glee and Chorus Book (1855)

77 other secular works, many pubd in The Alpine Glee Singer (1850)

Principal publishers: Bradbury, Ivison, Phinney & Co., Newman

BIBLIOGRAPHY

Obituary, *New York Musical Gazette*, ii (1867–8), 25

"William Bradbury," *New York Musical Gazette*, vii (1873), 65

F. J. Metcalf: *American Writers and Compilers of Sacred Music* (New York, 1925/*R*1967), 274ff

S. Salter: "Bradbury, William Batchelder," *DAB*

L. Ellinwood: "Bradbury, William Batchelder," *The Hymnal 1940 Companion* (New York, 1949), 385f

A. B. Wingard: *The Life and Works of William Batchelder Bradbury 1816–1868* (diss., Southern Baptist Theological Seminary, 1973)

ALAN B. WINGARD

Bradford, Alex (*b* Bessemer, AL, 23 Jan 1927; *d* Newark, NJ, 15 Feb 1978). Gospel singer and composer. At the age of 13 he joined the Protective Harmoneers, a children's gospel group in Bessemer, and had his own radio show on a local station. He attended Snow Hill Institute in Snow Hill, Alabama, and as a student teacher acquired the title "professor," which he maintained throughout his career. While traveling with Mahalia Jackson in 1941–2, he copied down the names of promoters from her address book and left her employ to organize his own group, the Bradford Singers. When they made no great impression on the gospel field, Bradford joined Willie Webb and his singers, with whom he recorded *Every day and every hour* (1950). On the strength of its success he organized the Bradford Specials, an all-male group who sang in robes with pastel stoles and choreographed most of their songs. In 1953 Bradford wrote and recorded *Too close to heaven*, which sold a million copies and received an award from the National Baptist Music Convention. A series of gospel recordings followed, and Bradford amassed a large following, not only for the beauty of his singing, marked by a throaty baritone and shrill falsetto, but his flamboyance as a stage personality and performer. In 1961 he turned to the theater and achieved a huge success in Langston Hughes's *Black Nativity* (1961), which then toured Europe and was broadcast nationwide on television in the USA. In 1972 he appeared on Broadway in *Don't Bother Me, I Can't Cope*, for which he won the Obie Award, and again in 1976 in *Your Arm's Too Short to Box with God*. He composed more than 300 gospel songs, including (besides *Too close to heaven*) *He'll wash you whiter than snow* (1955) and *After it's over* (1963).

BIBLIOGRAPHY

SouthernB
J. Haskins: "The Arts: Alex Bradford," *Now*, vi (1977), 48
Obituary, *BPiM*, vi (1978), 240

HORACE CLARENCE BOYER

Bradford, (John Henry) Perry [Mule] (*b* Montgomery, AL, 14 Feb 1893; *d* New York, 20 April 1970). Jazz pianist, composer, and organizer. He worked in minstrel shows and as a solo pianist before concentrating on song writing and musical direction. In 1921 he organized the first recording session to feature a black blues singer (Mamie Smith). That session produced *Crazy Blues*, which sold over a million copies and initiated a craze for blues singing. During the 1920s, recordings made under Bradford's name featured freelance work by Louis Armstrong, Buster Bailey, James P. Johnson, and other important early jazz musicians. In the same decade, Bradford achieved considerable success with various compositions, including *You can't keep a good man down*, *Evil Blues*, and *That thing called love*, but thereafter his songs were never again in vogue.

BIBLIOGRAPHY

P. Bradford: *Born with the Blues* (New York, 1965)
M. Stearns and J. Stearns: *Jazz Dance: the Story of American Vernacular Dance* (New York, 1968), chaps. 14, 15

JOHN CHILTON

Bradley, Owen (*b* Westmoreland, TN, 21 Oct 1915). Country-music record producer. In the 1930s he worked as a popular musician and arranger and in 1940 became a staff musician at radio station WSM, Nashville. During his service in the US Maritime Service in the early 1940s he played in the Ted Weems orchestra. After the war he returned to WSM to become its music director; he continued to lead the studio orchestra until 1958. In 1947 Bradley began working part-time as a producer for Decca Records, whose country-music operations were under the direction of Paul Cohen, and in 1958 he succeeded his mentor as director of country artists and repertory. In 1952, with his brother Harold, also a studio musician, Bradley established a recording studio in downtown Nashville (it later moved to 16th Avenue South); it became the cornerstone of Music Row, the geographical center of the Nashville music industry offices from the 1960s. This "Quonset hut" studio, with its echo chamber and three-track stereo console (a novelty at that time), was considered the finest in Nashville; it customarily logged more than 700 recording sessions annually and was used not only by country singers but also by popular artists from elsewhere, such as Connie Francis and Guy Mitchell. It was bought by Columbia Records in 1961. In 1965 Bradley built a new studio, Bradley's Barn, outside Nashville, where the informality of the atmosphere was conducive to excellent improvisations by the recording musicians.

Bradley made several technical innovations in country music recording: a lush sound that usually included background voices (generally the Jordanaires or the Anita Kerr Singers), generous echoes, and new methods of recording drums. He is also credited with playing a formative role in advancing the careers of such artists as Marty Robbins, Johnny Cash, Burl Ives, Patsy Cline, Loretta Lynn, Brenda Lee, and Conway Twitty.

NANCY TOFF

Braham, David (*b* nr London, England, 1834; *d* New York, 11 April 1905). Composer and conductor. He and his brother Joseph were violinists in London music halls before going to New York in 1856; there David was orchestra leader and composer for Pony Moore's Minstrels, at Tony Pastor's Opera House (from 1865), and at the Theatre Comique (from 1871). During these years he wrote variety-show songs to words by Gregory Hyde, G. L. Stout, Jennie Kemble, J. B. Murphy, and others. In 1872 he set some lyrics for *The Mulligan Guard* by the playwright EDWARD HARRIGAN; the resulting march-song (*see* MUSICAL, fig. 1), sold to publisher William A. Pond for only $50, became known worldwide and established the pair as a songwriting team. When Harrigan leased the Theatre Comique in 1876 Braham became his permanent orchestra leader.

Harrigan's sketches and plays found humor in the mundane life of the urban ethnic neighborhoods of New York, treating the subject with sympathetic insight rather than theatrical sensationalism or melodrama. Braham's music complemented Harrigan's scripts; he composed to finished lyrics, suiting range, rhythm, key, and tempo to the actor and role. He varied song forms and style, using a different meter for every song in a play, though he had a preference for strongly triadic and angular melodies. Braham's deceptively simple harmonies, rhythms, and melodies, his small details of variety in a seemingly commonplace technique, and his long-term association with a single lyricist and a single publisher made him the best-known American theater composer of the 1870s and 1880s. He produced about 200 published songs for voice and piano.

Braham's two sons were also musicians: David Braham, Jr., later became an actor, but George led David Belasco's orchestra and succeeded his father as Harrigan's music director and composer. Braham's daughter Annie married Harrigan. Of Joseph Braham's sons, John led the orchestra at the Boston Athenaeum, and directed the first American production of Gilbert and Sullivan's *H.M.S. Pinafore* in 1878; Harry conducted in New York theaters and was Lillian Russell's first husband; and Albert and William performed with the Boston Symphony Orchestra.

WORKS

SONGS

Selective list; all for 1v, pf, with lyrics by E. Harrigan, and published in New York.

The Mulligan Guard (1873); Patrick's Day Parade (1874); The Regular Army O! (1874); Skidmore Guard (1874); Slavery Days (1876); The Babies on our Block (1879); The Little Widow Dunn (*c*1879); Down in Gossip Row (1880); Hang the Mulligan Banner up (1880); Locked out after nine (1880); Mary Kelly's Beau (1880); The Mulligan Braves (1880); Never take the horse-shoe from the door (1880); Sandy-haired Mary in our area (1880); The Full Moon Union (*c*1880); Don't you miss the train (1881); Paddy Duffy's Cart (1881); Just across from Jersey (1883); Henrietta Pye (1885); Poverty's tears ebb and flow (1885)

Principal publisher: W. A. Pond

BIBLIOGRAPHY

E. J. Kahn: *The Merry Partners* (New York, 1955)
C. Hamm: *Yesterdays: Popular Song in America* (New York, 1979)
R. Moody: *Ned Harrigan* (Chicago, 1980)
D. L. Root: *American Popular Stage Music, 1860–1880* (Ann Arbor, MI, 1981)

DEANE L. ROOT

Braham, John (*b* London, England, 20 March 1774; *d* London, 17 Feb 1856). English tenor and composer. He made his début as a boy soprano at Covent Garden in 1787. He sang on the Continent after his voice broke, returning to England at the turn of the century, where he established a reputation as one of the country's leading tenors. He came to the USA in the autumn of 1840 and, at the age of 68, "surpassed all expectations" with the "pathos, sublimity, power, and wonderful execution" of his voice. He appeared first in concert, with a selection of tenor and baritone airs from opera and oratorio mixed with popular ballads. His American operatic début, at the Park Theatre in New York, was in Stephen Storace's *The Siege of Belgrade*, and he went on to re-create many of his famous roles, in Charles Horn's *The Devil's Bridge*, Thomas Dibdin's *The Cabinet*, and Weber's *Der Freischütz*. At one point he astonished audiences and critics by appearing in seven demanding roles in less than two weeks. He also sang in other American cities before returning to England in 1842.

Braham was famed for the expressiveness and the floridity of his delivery; the richness of his embellishment helped establish a new school of vocal ornamentation in Britain. He composed songs and operas, including *The English Fleet in 1342* (1803), and also wrote arias for interpolation in the operas of other composers, particularly for his own roles. "All's Well" from *The English Fleet* was the most popular duet in the USA during the first half of the 19th century; other favorite songs were *Tho' love is warm awhile*, *Is there a heart that never lov'd?*, and *No more sorrow*. These pieces are less formal and more directly expressive than the songs of many of Braham's British contemporaries.

BIBLIOGRAPHY

W. T. Parke: *Musical Memoirs* (London, 1830)

G. C. D. Odell: *Annals of the New York Stage*, iv (New York, 1928/R1970)

W. B. Squire: "Braham, John," *DNB*

J. M. Levien: *The Singing of John Braham* (London, 1945)

R. J. Wolfe: *Secular Music in America, 1801–1825: a Bibliography* (New York, 1964)

CHARLES HAMM

Brailowsky [Brailovsky], **Alexander** (*b* Kiev, Ukraine, 16 Feb 1896; *d* New York, 25 April 1976). Pianist. He studied with Pukhal'sky at the Kiev Conservatory and in 1911 went to Vienna, where he was a pupil of Theodor Leschetizky. During World War I he had lessons with Busoni in Switzerland, and he made his début in Paris in 1919. Thereafter he toured widely and in 1924 first appeared in New York, where his success was great. He made coast-to-coast tours in the USA, played in South America, and settled in New York. He continued to visit Europe and gave his first series of recitals of the complete piano works of Chopin in Paris in 1924; he later repeated these there as well as in New York in 1938. On the 150th anniversary of Chopin's birth in 1960 he again gave his complete piano works in New York and Brussels. Brailowsky's repertory consisted largely of the works of Romantic composers, particularly Chopin and Liszt, and he was usually regarded as an artist whose approach to pianism was that of a great virtuoso rather than an intellectual.

BIBLIOGRAPHY

K. Blaukopf: *Grosse Virtuosen* (Teufen, 1954); enlarged Fr. trans. as *Les grands virtuoses* (Paris, 1955), 217

"Brailowsky, Alexander," *CBY 1956*

A. Chasins: *Speaking of Pianists* (New York, 1957, rev. 3/1981), 150

RONALD KINLOCH ANDERSON/R

Brainard, Silas (*b* Lempster, NH, 14 Feb 1814; *d* Cleveland, OH, 8 April 1871). Music publisher. His family moved to Cleveland in 1834 and with Henry J. Mould opened a music store, Brainard and Mould, two years later. By 1845 the company was known as S. Brainard and in that year began to publish music; this business (known as S. Brainard & Sons from 1866) became one of the most important in the country. Brainard published popular music, mostly pieces for piano and songs for solo voice with piano accompaniment, but also a few sacred hymns and quartets. Also in 1845 Brainard bought Watson Hall (built 1840, known as Melodeon Hall, 1845–60, and then Brainard's Hall, until 1872), where many musical events took place. Brainard was a flutist who participated in and arranged music for musical organizations in Cleveland. He opened branches of the publishing company in New York, Louisville, and Chicago (where it was eventually based), and in 1864 established an influential journal, *Western Musical World*, which became *Brainard's Musical World* in 1869. Brainard married Emily Mould in 1840. Two of their seven children, Charles Silas Brainard and Henry Mould Brainard, assumed responsibility for the firm on their father's death, changing its name to S. Brainard's Sons. The firm ceased in 1931.

BIBLIOGRAPHY

K. Merz: "Silas Brainard," *Brainard's Musical World*, viii (May, 1871)

L. A. Brainard: *The Genealogy of the Brainerd-Brainard Family in America 1649–1908*, i (Hartford, 1908), 326

S. P. Orth: *A History of Cleveland, Ohio* (Chicago and Cleveland, 1910), 111, 200

H. Dichter and E. Shapiro: *Early American Sheet Music: its Lure and its Lore, 1768–1889* (New York, 1941/R1977)

E. C. Krohn: *Music Publishing in the Middle Western States before the Civil War* (Detroit, 1972)

J. H. Alexander: *It must be Heard: a Survey of the Musical Life of Cleveland, 1836–1918* (Cleveland, 1981)

J. HEYWOOD ALEXANDER

Branca, Glenn (*b* Harrisburg, PA, 6 Oct 1948). Art-rock composer and performer. He attended Emerson College, Boston, where he studied dramatic arts (1967–71). After moving to New York in 1976 he founded with Jeffrey Lohn an experimental rock group, Theoretical Girls. His first instrumental pieces for massed electric guitars date from 1979, and he began to attract widespread attention in 1981, following the première of his Symphony no. 1 (*Tonal Plexus*) at the Performing Garage. Subsequently he wrote four more "symphonies" and a dance for Twyla Tharp, *Bad Smells* (1982).

Branca, who received no formal musical training, has been influenced by Varèse and the *bruitisme* of the futurists, percussion composers of the 1930s, and the "no-wave" instrumental art-rock of New York in the late 1970s. His music, deafeningly amplified, employs rapidly strummed electric guitars, percussion, and brass; the more recent "symphonies" call for "mallet guitars," designed and constructed by Branca himself, which are essentially amplified dulcimers. Even though the harmonies are primordial and the rhythms plodding, the cumulative effect of his music, augmented by mystical subtitles and the bohemian raffishness of the performers, can be powerful. In 1982 at the New Music America festival in Chicago, John Cage provoked a controversy by calling Branca's music, in its forceful insistence, "fascist."

See also EXPERIMENTAL MUSIC, fig. 2.

WORKS

(selective list)

Anthropophagoi, music-theater work, Boston, 1975; Instrumental, 6 gui, 1979; Lesson no. 1, elec gui, 1979; The Ascension, rock band, 1980; Sym. no. 1 (Tonal Plexus), 1981; Bad Smells, ballet, 1982; Sym. no. 2 (The Peak of the Sacred), 1982; Sym. no. 3 (Gloria), 1983; Sym. no. 4 (Physics), 1983; Sym. no. 5 (Describing Planes of an Expanding Hypersphere), 1984; 14 songs, rock band, 1977–9

JOHN ROCKWELL

Brandeis University. University founded in Waltham, Massachusetts, in 1948; *see* BOSTON (i), §9 (i).

Branscombe, Gena (*b* Picton, Ont., 4 Nov 1881; *d* New York, 26 July 1977). Composer and conductor. Her teachers included Borowski and Ganz (composition and piano) at the Chicago Musical College, where she later taught piano, Engelbert Humperdinck (during a visit to Berlin, 1909–10), and Stoessel (conducting). After serving as head of the piano department at Whitman College, she moved to New York in 1910, where from the 1920s she was active in women's arts organizations and as a choral conductor, notably of the Branscombe Choral (1933–54), for which she wrote and arranged many works; she also tirelessly promoted contemporary and American music. In her own works textual expression is of prime importance and is achieved through a style emphasizing late-Romantic, richly textured harmony.

WORKS

(texts of vocal works by Branscombe unless otherwise stated)

Vocal, orch: The Bells of Circumstance (opera), 1920s, inc.; Pilgrims of Destiny, S, B, chorus, 1929; Quebec Suite, T, orch, 1930; Youth of the World, SSA, chamber orch, 1932; *c*35 works, mostly choral arrs.

Songs, 1v, pf, unless otherwise stated: Serenade (R. Browning), 1905; Autumn Wind, 1911; A Lute of Jade, song cycle, 1912; The Sun Dial (K. Banning), song cycle, 1913; I bring you heartsease, 1915; Three Unimproving Songs, 1922; Hail ye tyme of holie-dayes (Banning), 1924; Wreathe the holly, SSAA, pf, 1938; Coventry's Choir, SSAA, pf, 1944; Bridesmaids' Song, SSAA, pf, 1956; A Joyful Litany, SSAA, pf, 1967; *c*100 others; *c*70 choral arrs.

Chamber, inst: Concertstück, pf, 1906; Sonata, vn, pf, 1920; Procession, tpt, pf, 1930; Pacific Sketches, hn, pf, 1956; American Suite, hn, pf, 1959; *c*20 ens works; *c*30 pf pieces; *c*15 vn pieces

Principal publisher: Arthur P. Schmidt

BIBLIOGRAPHY

L. A. E. Marlow: *Gena Branscombe (1881–1977)* (diss., U. of Texas, 1980)

LAURINE ELKINS MARLOW

Brant, Henry (Dreyfuss) (*b* Montreal, Que., 15 Sept 1913). Composer. The son of a violinist, he developed his experimental attitude to music in boyhood: at the age of nine he was composing for his own homemade instruments and organizing performances with them. He studied at the McGill Conservatorium, Montreal (1926–9), the Institute of Musical Art in New York (1929–34), and the Juilliard Graduate School (1932–4), also taking private lessons from Riegger, Antheil, and Fritz Mahler (conducting) during the 1930s. Having settled in New York, he earned his living by composing, conducting, and arranging for radio, films, ballet, and jazz groups. In the 1950s and 1960s he extended his work in commercial music to Hollywood and Europe. He also taught composition and orchestration at Columbia University (1945–52), the Juilliard School (1947–54), and Bennington College (1957–80). His awards include two Guggenheim Fellowships (1947 and 1956), and he was the first American composer to win the Prix Italia (1955). In 1979 he was elected to the American Academy and Institute of Arts and Letters.

Brant's early published music shows marked contrasts in style from work to work and a pronounced interest in unusual timbral combinations. *Angels and Devils* (1931, revised in 1956 and 1979) is a concerto for flute with ten members of the flute family. Brant has continued to explore timbre in such works as *Origins* (1950), a percussion symphony with organ, and *Orbits* (1979), which requires 80 trombones with individual parts. A far-reaching innovation came in 1953 with *Antiphony I* for five widely separated orchestral groups positioned in the auditorium and on stage. This example of "spatial music" predated Stockhausen's *Gruppen*

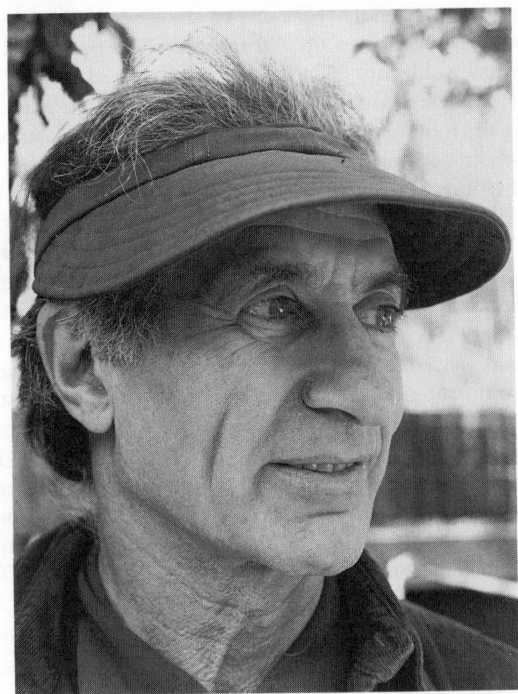

Henry Brant, 1982

by five years. Unlike Stockhausen, however, Brant followed and expanded Ives's concepts of stylistic contrast and spatial separation. In *Antiphony I* (1953) and almost all of Brant's subsequent "spatial" works each group is assigned music quite unrelated in timbre, texture, and style to the music of the other groups. Rhythmic coordination is maintained within each ensemble, often by conductors, but in order to allow for possible time lags in the hall Brant has devised procedures to permit overall noncoordination within controlled limits. These and similar techniques are employed in *The Grand Universal Circus* (1956), which presents simultaneous contrasted musical and dramatic events throughout the entire theater area, and *Voyage Four* (1963), a "total antiphony" in which musicians are located on the back and side walls and under the auditorium floor, as well as on stage. With *Meteor Farm* (1982) Brant presented a multicultural spatial work with Javanese, West African, and southern Indian ensembles, each retaining unaltered its own traditional music, performing alongside symphony and jazz orchestras and two choruses. He has also composed what he calls "instant music" – spatial works, written for particular occasions, that involve controlled improvisation, since detailed instructions are given for register and timbre, but not pitch.

Brant wrote that in 1950 he had "come to feel that single-style music . . . could no longer evoke the new stresses, layered insanities, and multi-directional assaults of contemporary life on the spirit." His use of space became central to his conception of a polystylistic music, and his experiments have convinced him that space exerts specific influences on harmony, polyphony, texture, and timbre. He regards space as music's "fourth dimension" (the other three being pitch, measurement of time, and timbre). In order to facilitate performance of his "elaborate but natural-sounding complexity," he has avoided writing music of unusual technical or rhythmic difficulty. Material for large groups is conventionally notated except where rhythmic noncoordination or indefinite vocal pitches require special indications; solo parts are treated similarly, though several have opportunities for virtuoso improvisation. Brant does not use electronic materials nor even permit amplification, for he considers his work to be fully intelligible only when heard live.

Brant is an adept and versatile performer on wind and percussion instruments (which he collects from non-Western cultures). In the 1970 recording of *Machinations* he himself played all ten parts, for E♭ flute, double flageolet, double ocarina, ceramic flute, steel harp, organ, glockenspiel, xylophone, chimes, and timpani. Perhaps because of the particular challenges of Brant's music, an unusually large number of his compositions, both spatial and nonspatial, have been recorded.

WORKS

WITH SPATIAL SEPARATION

Antiphony I, 5 orch groups, 1953, rev. 1968
Ceremony, triple conc., ob, vn, vc, S, A, T, B, wind, pf 4 hands, 4 perc, 1954
Millennium II, S, brass, perc, 1954
Conclave, Mez, Bar, tpt, trbn, pf, harp, timp, glock, 1955
December, S, T, speakers, choruses, orch groups, 1955
Encephalograms II, S, 7 insts, 1955
Labyrinth I, 20 solo str, str orch, 4 female vv ad lib, 1955
Labyrinth II, wind, 4 female vv ad lib, 1955
On the Nature of Things (after Lucretius), str, solo ww, glock, 1956
The Grand Universal Circus, theater piece, 8 solo vv, 32 vv, 16 insts, 1956
Hieroglyphics I, va, timp, chimes, cel, harp, org, distant vv, 1957
Millennium III, 6 brass, 6 perc, 1957
The Children's Hour, 6 solo vv, chorus, 2 tpt, 2 trbn, org, perc, 1958
In Praise of Learning, 16 S, 16 perc, 1958
Joquin, pic, 6 insts, 1958
Mythical Beasts, S/Mez, 16 insts, 1958
The Crossing, T, ob/s sax, glock, vn, vc, 1959
Atlantis, antiphonal sym., Mez, speaker, chorus, orch, band, perc, 1960
The Fire Garden, T/S, small chorus, pic, harp, pf, perc, 1960
Quombex, va d'amore, distant music boxes, org, 1960
Barricades, ob/s sax, T, cl, bn, trbn, pf, xyl, 4 str, 1961
Concerto with Lights, vn, 10 insts, lights, 1961
Feuerwerk (Brant), speaker, ww, hpd, chime, timp, 2 vn, 2 va, 1961
Fire in Cities (Brant), choruses, 2 pf, orch groups, 8 timp, 1961
Headhunt, trbn, b cl, bn, vc, perc, 1962
The Fourth Millennium, 2 tpt, hn, euphonium, tuba, 1963
Underworld, sax, pipe org, 1963
Voyage Four, orch, 1963
Dialogue in the Jungle, S, T, 5 ww, 5 brass, 1964
Sing o Heavens, S, A, T, Bar, chorus, tpt, trbn, pf, perc, 1964
Odyssey – Why not?, fl, fl obbl, 4 small orch groups, 1965
Hieroglyphics II, vn, cel, perc ad lib, pf ad lib, 1966
Verticals Ascending, 2 wind ens, 1967
Chanticleer, cl, pf, perc, str qt, 1968
Windjammer, hn, pic, ob, b cl, bn, 1969
Crossroads, vn, pic-vn, mez-vn, va, 1970
Kingdom Come, orch, circus band, org, 1970
The Immortal Combat, 2 bands, 1972
An American Requiem, 5 wind groups, bell groups, brass, perc, org, church bells, opt. S, 1973
Divinity: Dialogues in the Form of Secret Portraits, hpd, 2 tpt, 2 trbn, hn, 1973
Sixty, 3 wind ens, 1973, rev. 1982 as 60/70
Nomads, solo v, solo perc, solo brass, orch/wind ens, 1974
Prevailing Winds, wind qnt, 1974
Six Grand Pianos Bash plus Friends, pfs, perc, pics, 2 brass, 1974
Solomon's Gardens, 7 solo vv, chorus, 24 handbells, 3 insts, 1974
A Plan of the Air, S, A, T, B, Baroque org, 10 wind and perc groups, 1975
Curriculum, Bar, b fl, b cl, pf, timp, mar, va, vc, db, 1975
Homage to Ives, Bar, pf obbl, 3 orch groups, 1975
American Commencement, 2 brass and perc groups, 1976
American Debate, wind and perc in 2 groups, 1976
American Weather, 8 solo vv, chorus, tpt, trbn, chimes, glock, 1976
Spatial Concerto (Questions from Genesis), pf, 8 S, 8 A, orch groups, 1976
Antiphonal Responses, 3 solo bn, pf, orch, 8 isolated insts, 1978
Cerberus, pic, db, S, mouth org, 1978
Curriculum II, small orch groups, 1978
The $1,000,000 Confessions, 2 tpt, 3 trbn, 1978
Trinity of Spheres, 3 orch groups, 1978
Orbits, 80 trbn, S, org, 1979
The Glass Pyramid, solo ww, 2 pf, perc, str, ww trio, chimes, 1980
Inside Track, pf, sopranino obbl, 3 inst groups, projections, 1980
The Secret Calendar, orch groups, solo insts, org, 1v, 1980
Horizontals Extending, 2 small wind ens, jazz drums, karate artist, 1982
Meteor Farm, orch, 2 chorus, 2 perc groups, jazz orch, gamelan, West African drums and vv, Indian ens, 2 S, 1982
Desert Forest, large and small sym. groups, 1983
Litany of Tides, vn, 2 orch, 4 vv, 1983
Vuur onder Water [Fire under Water], ww, str, perc, vv, multi-track tape, 1983
Bran(d)t aan de Amstel [Burning/Brant on the Amstel], environmental piece, 100 fl, 3 orch, 4 hurdy-gurdy, 3 chorus, 4 opt. carillon, 1984
Western Springs, 2 orch, 2 chorus, 2 jazz combo, 1984

WITHOUT SPATIAL SEPARATION

(orch)

Cl Conc., 1938; Fisherman's Ov., 1938; Whoopee in D, 1938; City Portrait, ballet, perf. New York, 1940; Fantasy and Caprice, vn, orch, 1940; Rhapsody, va, orch, 1940; The Great American Goof, excerpts from ballet, 1940; Vn Conc., 1940; Downtown Suite, 1942; Sym., 1942, 1st and 2nd movts withdrawn, last movt entitled An Adventure

Dedication in Memory of Franklin D. Roosevelt, 1945; The 1930s, sym., 1945; Statements in Jazz, cl, dance orch, 1945; Jazz Cl Conc., cl, jazz band, 1946; The Promised Land, sym., 1947; Street Music, wind, perc, 1949; Origins, sym., 20 perc, org, 1950; Galaxy II, wind, timp, glock, 1954

(ens)

Angels and Devils, fl, 3 pic, 5 fl, 2 a fl, 1931, rev. 1956, rev. 1979; Variations for 4 Inst (Variations in Oblique Harmony), 1931; Music for a Five and Dime Store, vn, pf, kitchen hardware, 1932; Double-crank Hand Organ, 2 pf, perc, 1933; Prelude and Fugue, str octet, ww, 1934, rev. as Requiem in Summer, wind qnt, 1934, rev. 1955; The Marx Brothers, tone poem, tin whistle/fife/pic, fl, ob, harp, pf, va, vc, 1938; Variations on a Theme by Robert Schumann, 2 pf, tpt, timp, 1940; Conc., sax/tpt, fl, 6 cl, tuba, perc, 1941, rev. 1970

Downtown Suite, 9/11 insts, 1942; Imaginary Ballet, pic, vc, pf, 1946; Funeral Music for the Mass Dead, 2 bn, vc, db, 1947; All Souls' Carnival, fl, pf, accordion, vn, vc, 1949, rev. 1957; Millennium I, 8 tpt, chimes, glock, 1950; Signs and Alarms, pic, 2 cl, brass, perc, 1953; Stresses, tpt, pf, str, perc, 1953; Ice Age, ondes martenot/cl, pf, glock, xyl, 1954; Piri, fl, harp, pf, glock, 1954; Galaxy I, cl, hn, chimes, vib, 1954; Conversations in an Unknown Tongue, vn, va, t vn, vc, 1958

Sky Forest – Jazz Fugue, accordion qt, 1962; Consort for True Violins, 8 vn-type insts, 1965; Machinations, fl, double flageolet, double ocarina, ceramic fl, steel harp, org, perc, 1970 [not notated]; From Bach's Menagerie, 4 sax, 1975; Solar Moth, solo vn, fl, a fl, b fl, harp, pf, 4 vn, 4 va, mar/1v, timp, 1979 [not notated]

(inst)

Sonata, 2 pf, 1931; 4 Chorale Preludes, 2 pf, 1932; Mobiles, fl, 1932; Partita, fl, pf, 1932, rev. 1954; Duo, vc, pf, 1937, rev. 1962

(choral)

The 3-way Canon Blues, unacc. vv, 1947; Credo for Peace, vv, speaker, tpt, 1948; County Fair, vv, 10 insts, 1949; Madrigal en casserole, vv, pf, 1949

(film scores)

Capitol Story, 1944; The Pale Horsemen, 1944; Journey into Medicine, 1946; My Father's House, 1947; Outbreak, 1949; The Big Break, 1951; Ode to a Grecian Urn, 1953; The Secret Thief, 1956; Your Community, 1956; Doctor "B," 1957; Endowing our Future, 1957; United Nations Day, 1959; Early Birds, 1961

Several other works withdrawn

BIBLIOGRAPHY

EwenD; *VintonD*

S. Sankey: "Henry Brant's 'Grand Universal Circus'," *Juilliard Review*, iii/3 (1956), 21

Compositores de América/Composers of the Americas, ed. Pan American Union, vi (Washington, DC, 1960)

H. Brant: "Space as an Essential Aspect of Musical Composition," *Contemporary Composers on Contemporary Music*, ed. E. Schwartz and B. Childs (New York, 1967), 221

D. Drennan: *Henry Brant's Use of Ensemble Dispersion, as Found in the Analysis of Selected Compositions* (diss., U. of Miami, 1975)

K. Brion and J. E. Brown: "The Spatial Wind Music of Henry Brant," *The Instrumentalist*, xxx/6 (1976), 36

T. Everett: "Interview with Henry Brant," *The Composer*, vii (1976–7), 29

D. Drennan: "Henry Brant's Choral Music," *Choral Journal*, xvii/5 (1977), 27
H. Brant: "Spatial Music Progress Report," *Quadrille*, xii/3 (1979), 20
C. Gagne and T. Caras: "Henry Brant," *Soundpieces: Interviews with American Composers* (Metuchen, NJ, 1982), 53
G. Mott: "Weslyan University Orchestra and Weslyan Singers: Brant's *Meteor Farm*," *HiFi/MusAm*, xxxii/7 (1982), 36
E. Schwartz: "Henry Brant Embraces Amsterdam," *HiFi/MusAm*, xxxiv/12 (1984), 35

KURT STONE

Branzell, Karin (Maria) (*b* Stockholm, Sweden, 24 Sept 1891; *d* Pasadena, CA, 14 Dec 1974). Contralto. After three years of study she became a member of the Swedish Royal Opera (1912), with which she sang for six years, and from 1918 to 1923 she sang with the Berlin Staatsoper. She made her début at the Metropolitan Opera as Fricka in *Die Walküre* on 6 February 1924 and continued to sing major contralto roles with the company (including Brangäne with Melchior and Flagstad) until 1944, making guest appearances at Bayreuth (1930–31) and other leading houses throughout this period. After retiring from the stage, she taught, first in New York (at the Juilliard School from 1946), then (from 1969) in California; her pupils included Mignon Dunn, Jean Madeira, and Nell Rankin. She came out of retirement to sing Erda in *Siegfried* at the Metropolitan on 7 February 1951. Branzell's was one of the great voices of her day – rich, sumptuous, voluminous – and her tall figure and stage presence befitted the Wagnerian roles she was called upon to sing. Her large range enabled her to sing soprano roles as well, including Brünnhilde in *Die Walküre*.

BIBLIOGRAPHY

R. Celletti: "Branzell, Karin," *Le grandi voci* (Rome, 1964) [with discography by R. Vegeto]

MAX DE SCHAUENSEE/R

Brass band. A type of wind band consisting solely of brass instruments. It originated in the 1820s. *See* BANDS.

Brauchli, Bernard (*b* Lausanne, Switzerland, 5 May 1944). Swiss clavichord player. After piano studies in Lausanne (1963–7) and Vienna (1968–9), he became increasingly attracted to the clavichord and its repertory. He made his European début at Fribourg, Switzerland, in 1972 and his American début at Marlboro College, Vermont, in 1973. Having studied musicology at the New England Conservatory under Julia Sutton (MMus 1976), he began research in early Iberian keyboard music with Macario Santiago Kastner in Lisbon in 1977. He regularly tours North America and Europe, performing and recording a wide repertory of Renaissance and Baroque clavichord music, with an emphasis on Iberian composers; he has won high praise as a sensitive and tasteful interpreter. In contrast to most other modern clavichordists, he restricts himself to the fretted form of the instrument. He has given summer courses in Austria and Spain (1978–82) and lectures at the Boston Museum of Fine Arts (1978–83); he became professor of clavichord at the New England Conservatory in 1983. His publications include articles on the clavichord, its history, and iconography.

HOWARD SCHOTT

Braxton, Anthony (*b* Chicago, IL, 4 June 1945). Jazz alto saxophonist, contrabass clarinetist, and composer. In his teens he pursued jazz and European art music. After returning to Chicago from army service, he joined the Association for the Advancement of Creative Musicians in 1966, and in the following year formed the Creative Construction Company with Leroy Jenkins and Leo Smith. Later, in New York, he joined the Italian improvisation ensemble Musica Elettronica Viva (1970) and Chick Corea's free jazz quartet, Circle (1970–71). From 1972, following the delayed success of *For Alto*, the first album ever recorded for unaccompanied saxophone, he was invited to present numerous solo concerts. He also appeared frequently leading his own quartets, particularly with the double bass player Dave Holland. Although Braxton's recorded output stresses avant-garde jazz, his repertory expanded in the 1970s to include bop improvisation, humorous pieces for parade band, and compositions for piano.

RECORDINGS

(selective list)

As leader: *For Alto* (1968, Delmark 420–1); *Saxophone Improvisations Series F* (1972, America 30AM011–2); *In the Tradition*, i (1974, Steeplechase 1015); *Five Pieces 1975* (1975, Arista 4064); *Creative Orchestra Music 1976* (1976, Arista 4080); *Performance 9/1/79* (1979, Hat Hut 19); *For Two Pianos* (1980, Arista 9559)

As sideman: *Creative Construction Company*, i (1970, Muse 5071); Circle: *The Paris Concert* (1971, ECM 1018–19); D. Holland: *Conference of the Birds* (1972, ECM 1027)

BIBLIOGRAPHY

SouthernB
R. Townley: "Anthony Braxton," *Down Beat*, xli/3 (1974), 12
B. Smith and others: "Anthony Braxton," *Coda*, xi/8 (1974), 2
P. Occhiogrosso: "Anthony Braxton Explains himself," *Down Beat*, xliii/14 (1976), 15
G. Gazzoli: "Anthony Braxton: an Alternative Approach," *Jazz Forum*, no.62 (1979), 32
M. Ullman: *Jazz Lives: Portraits in Words and Pictures* (Washington, DC, 1980/*R*1982), 199
H. de Craen and E. Janssens: *Anthony Braxton Discography* (Brussels, 1982)
R. Radano: *Anthony Braxton and his Two Musical Traditions: the Meeting of Concert Music and Jazz* (diss., U. of Michigan, 1985)

BARRY KERNFELD

Bray, John (*b* England, 19 June 1782; *d* Leeds, England, 19 June 1822). Actor, composer, and arranger, active in Philadelphia, New York, and Boston from 1805 to 1822. He came to Philadelphia from England in 1805 as a member of Warren and Reinagle's theater company, and also acted in Charleston, New York, Richmond, and Baltimore. In 1815 he moved to Boston, where he remained active until the onset of his final illness, when he went back to Leeds.

Most of Bray's compositions are songs for the stage, patriotic songs, and sacred works. His most important work is the "Operatic Melo Drame" *The Indian Princess*, based on the story of Captain John Smith and Pocahontas; this was issued in 1808 in a vocal score which, besides songs and choruses, included the overture and instrumental background pieces for the scenes in melodrama – an unusually complete publication for the period (for illustration *see* OPERA, fig.1). Bray's musical style is less polished than that of his American contemporaries Reinagle, Graupner, and Taylor. Although his melodies are graceful and full of rhythmic variety, his piano textures, with their reliance on broken-chord and murky basses, their closely spaced triads, awkward voice-leading in inner parts, and infrequent modulations, often lack clarity. (*See also* MELODRAMA, §2, and ex.1.)

WORKS

Selective list; all published in Philadelphia, n.d., unless otherwise stated; estimated dates of publication are given in brackets.

Stage: The Indian Princess, or La belle sauvage (opera-melodrama, 3, J. N.

Barker), Philadelphia, 6 April 1808, vs (1808), lib pubd separately (1808/*R*1972); 5 melodramas, 7 operas and pantomimes, lost, listed in Parker

Songs, all for 1v, pf, unless otherwise stated: Soft as yon silver ray that sleeps ([?1807]); The Rose ([?1807]); Il ammonitore dell'amore, or Love's Remembrancer, 6 songs ([1807]); Henry and Anna ([?1807]); Aurelia Betray'd! ([?1809]); Looney M'Gra ([?1809]); The Heath this Night ([*c*1812]); Hull's Victory ([?1812]/*R*1956); Our Rights on the Ocean, or Hull, Jones, Decatur & Bainbridge ([?1813]); The Cypress Wreath ([?1813]); Columbia, Land of Liberty! ([?1815]); The Columbian Sailor ([?1816]); Where can peace of mind be found, 2v, pf (Boston, 1821)

Sacred: God is There!, 1v, pf (Boston, [?1818]); Peace and Holy Love, 1v, pf (Boston, 1820); Child of Mortality, 2 solo vv, 4vv (Portsmouth, [*c*1824])

Inst: General Harrison's Grand March, pf ([?1812]); Madison's March, pf, fl/vn, in *Musical Olio*, no.3 (1814), 25

BIBLIOGRAPHY

J. R. Parker: "Mr. Bray," *The Euterpeiad*, i (1820), 11 [incl. list of stage works]
W. Dunlap: *History of the American Theatre* (London, 2/1833), ii
C. Durang: "The Philadelphia Stage," *Philadelphia Sunday Dispatch* (1854, 1856, 1860) [series of articles; compiled by T. Westcott as *History of the Philadelphia Stage, between the Years 1749 and 1855*, 1868, *PU*; similar compilations as *The Philadelphia Stage* in *PPL*, *History of the Philadelphia Stage* in *PHi*]
H. E. Johnson: *Musical Interludes in Boston, 1795–1830* (New York, 1943)
G. C. D. Odell: *Annals of the New York Stage*, ii (New York, 1949/*R*1970), 289, 340, 373
H. W. Hitchcock: "An Early American Melodrama: The Indian Princess," *Notes*, xii (1954–5), 375
R. Wolfe: *Secular Music in America, 1801–1825: a Bibliography* (New York, 1964)
V. F. Yellin: Liner notes, *Two Early American Musical Plays* (New World 232, 1978)

ANNE DHU SHAPIRO

Brazos Valley Boys. Western swing group formed in the 1940s by HANK THOMPSON.

Bread. Pop group. Its members were David Gates, singer, guitarist, and keyboard player; James Griffin, guitarist; Mike Botts, drummer; and Robb Reyer and Larry Knechtel, keyboard players. Formed in Los Angeles in 1969, Bread was one of the most commercially successful of several West Coast pop groups that made glossy, romantic recordings using judiciously chosen rock instrumentation. Bread's leader and songwriter was Gates, whose pure, light tenor, without vibrato, was an ideal vehicle for his dreamy love-songs; these included *Make it with you*, *It don't matter to me*, and *Baby, I'm-a want you*. The group disbanded in 1973, reunited briefly in 1976, and made their last hit record, Gates's *Lost Without Your Love*, in the same year. With the Carpenters, Bread helped to define the pleasantly formulaic pop style known as "soft rock."

RECORDINGS

(selective list; all recorded for Elektra)

Make it with you (45686, 1970); It don't matter to me (45701, 1970); *Bread* (74044, 1969); *On the Water* (74076, 1970); *Manna* (74086, 1971); Baby I'm-a want you (45751, 1971); Guitar Man (45803, 1972); Lost Without Your Love (45365, 1976)

STEPHEN HOLDEN

Break. In jazz, a brief solo passage occurring during an interruption in the accompaniment, usually lasting one or two bars and maintaining the underlying rhythm and harmony of the piece. Breaks appear most frequently at the ends of phrases, particularly the last phrase in a structural unit (e.g., a 12-bar blues or a 32-bar song), or at the end of a 16-bar unit of a multithematic piece (e.g., a march or rag). The break probably formed an evolutionary link between brass band music and improvised jazz, at a stage when soloists were capable of creating short stretches of new material but not complete choruses; the first coherent, extended solos may have evolved from chains of breaks. The break may also have developed by analogy with the cadenza of art music.

Jelly Roll Morton stressed the importance of the break to early jazz in his Library of Congress recordings of 1938 (AAFS 1651). His performances of the 1920s, as well as the legendary duet breaks by King Oliver and Louis Armstrong in 1923 and Don Redman's arrangements for Fletcher Henderson's band, illustrate the compositional function of the break as a source of textural contrast. An improvisatory function is apparent in recordings of the same period by Armstrong and Sidney Bechet, who took advantage of the break for moments of unrestrained melodic spontaneity. Although the break fell out of fashion as a compositional device in the 1930s (except for the drum breaks at the end of many big-band recordings), it remains common as an improvisatory device, being often used to introduce a solo chorus. Transcriptions of 125 solo breaks by Armstrong were published in 1927 for study purposes, and a particularly spectacular break by Charlie Parker on an otherwise abortive take of *A Night in Tunisia* in 1946 (Dial matrix D1013-1) has been issued separately as *The Famous Alto Break*.

BIBLIOGRAPHY

G. Schuller: *Early Jazz: its Roots and Musical Development* (New York, 1968)

BARRY KERNFELD

Break dancing. A black-American spectacular dance performed by one to six dancers that originated as a competitive street dance in the ghettos of New York's South Bronx in the early 1970s. It is characterized by unique floor movements (such as spins performed on the head, hand, or back), acrobatic feats, mime, and martial arts motions, especially jabbing and thrusting gestures; some balletic and jazz movements have also been incorporated. Break dancing, or "breaking," technically refers only to the floor movements, but it has become more of a generic term and now encompasses a number of originally independent dances or dance steps: the "electric boogie" (which involves wave-like movements that start at one part of the body and move to another); "popping" (jerky movements, in which the bones seem to pop out of their joints); the "robot" (moving parts of the body in isolation from one another); "locking" (collapsing parts of the body, then snapping them back into position); and the "moonwalk" (a mime movement in which the dancer appears to walk while actually standing still; popularized by the singer Michael Jackson).

Break dancing is generally performed to a hard, electronic style of funk known as hip-hop, and often takes place in conjunction with other urban arts – scratching, rap, and graffiti painting. The popularity of break dancing increased enormously in 1983–4 through the films *Flashdance* (1983), *Breakdance*, and *Beat Street* (both 1984).

BIBLIOGRAPHY

M. Holman: *Breaking and the New York City Breakers* (New York, 1984)
B. Nadell and J. Small: *Break Dance* (Philadelphia, 1984)

PAULINE NORTON

Breakdown. (1) A black-American folk and spectacular dance characterized by rhythmic patterns created by the feet hitting the floor. It became a theatrical dance in the middle of the 19th century principally through the influence of William Henry Lane, who performed under the name "Juba." The dance often concluded the song-and-dance numbers in late 19th-century minstrel shows, and seems to be related to the "break" sections in these numbers, which consisted of short, two- or four-bar interludes of danced rhythmic patterns between the solo verse and the chorus (*see* DANCE, §II, 3). Both the dance itself and the idea of performing dance between the sections of a song influenced tap dance in the 20th century.

(2) A riotous dance or gathering (*see also* HOEDOWN). The fiddle or banjo music accompanying such dances, particularly in the white-American folk tradition from the late 19th century, often has rapid figurations, arpeggios, and triplets added to vary the melody. S. P. Bayard, in his *Hill Country Tunes* (1944), suggests that some animated pieces in the repertories of Appalachian fiddlers and fifers were played not as dance accompaniments but as "broken-down dance tunes."

(3) A synonym for REEL.

BIBLIOGRAPHY

P. Magriel, ed.: *Chronicles of American Dance* (New York, 1948)
L. F. Emery: *Black Dance in the United States from 1619 to 1970* (Palo Alto, CA, 1972)
For further bibliography *see* DANCE.

PAULINE NORTON

Brecht, George (*b* Philadelphia, PA, ?1926). Artist-composer. Trained as a pharmacist, he had no formal schooling in the arts. In the early 1950s he began to paint and, influenced by Dada and Eastern philosophy, developed (independently of Cage) a number of indeterminate methods in reaction to the abstract expressionists; these years are chronicled in his book *Chance-imagery* of 1965. In 1958 he studied with Cage at the New School for Social Research, New York. His fellow students included Dick Higgins, Allan Kaprow, and Mac Low who, with Robert Watts, joined FLUXUS, a group of avant-garde artists that gained prominence in the early 1960s. Brecht, whose interests centered on minimalist-like performance events, experimented with techniques involving theatrics, games, and "events." Most of his works of the 1960s and early 1970s draw attention to isolated occurrences in daily routine; their titles are frequently humorous, for example, *Solo for Violin Viola Cello or Contrabass* (1962), in which the performer polishes the instrument rather than plays it. Always preferring to think in musical terms, Brecht calls his instructions for performance events "scores." An event as understood by Brecht is a scene before an audience, containing one activity, whether brief or drawn out by means of repetition, resembling a children's game or an adult gag and ranging from an exercise in perception to the enactment of a basic metaphor. Brecht's other book, *Vicious Circles and Infinity: a Panoply of Paradoxes* (1965), was written with P. Hughes. Brecht moved to West Germany in 1970 and lives in Cologne.

BIBLIOGRAPHY

J. Van der Marck: "George Brecht: an Art of Multiple Implications," *Art in America*, lxii/4 (1974), 48
M. Nyman: "George Brecht: Interview," *Studio International*, cxcii (1976), 256

DAVID COPE

Brehm, Alvin (*b* New York, 8 Feb 1925). Composer, conductor, and double bass player. He studied double bass with Fred Zimmerman and orchestration with Vittorio Giannini at the Juilliard School (1942–3) and composition with Riegger at Columbia University (MA 1951). He made his début as a double bass player in 1942. He has been a member of the Contemporary Chamber Ensemble (1969–73), the Group for Contemporary Music (1971–3), the Philomusica Chamber Music Society (1973–83), and the Chamber Music Society of Lincoln Center (for illustration *see* CHAMBER MUSIC SOCIETY OF LINCOLN CENTER) as a regular guest since its opening season (1969) and as an artist member from 1984. He has also performed with the Guarneri, Budapest, Lenox, and Composers string quartets, with the New York PO and the Pittsburgh SO, of which he was a member in 1950–51, and as a recitalist. He made his début as a conductor in 1947, and since then he has given the premières of more than 50 works, both in guest appearances and as conductor of the Composer's Theatre Orchestra, which he founded in 1967.

Brehm is best known, however, as a composer, striving in his work for lyricism and structural clarity; various critics have described his compositions as accessible, intense, and "Stravinskian." Honors he has received include commissions from the Chamber Music Society of Lincoln Center and the St. Paul Chamber Orchestra and grants from the Naumburg Foundation, the NEA, and the Ford Foundation. Many of his works have been recorded. He has held teaching positions at various colleges including SUNY, Stony Brook (1968–75), the Manhattan School (1969–75), and SUNY, Purchase (from 1972), where he became Dean of the Music Division in 1982.

WORKS

Orch: Hephaestus Ov., 1966; Concertino, vn, str, 1975; Pf Conc., 1977; Db Conc., 1982; Tuba Conc., 1982

Chamber and inst: Theme, Syllogism, Epilogue, pf, 1951; Divertimento, tpt, hn, trbn, 1962; Dialogues, bn, perc, 1964; Divertimento, ww qnt, 1965; Variations, vc, 1965; Brass Qnt, 1967; Variations, pf, 1968; Colloquy and Chorale, bn qt, 1974; Vc Sonata, 1974; Quarks, fl, bn, str qt, pf, 1976; Sextet, pf, str, 1976; Metamorphy, pf, 1979; A Pointe at his Pleasure, Renaissance insts, 1979; AYU Variations, fl, gui, 1980; Tre canzone, va, pf, 1980; La bocca della verità, fl, cl, vn, vc, pf, 1984; Sextet, ww qnt, pf, 1984; Children's Games, fl, cl, vn, va, vc, pf, 1984–5; Sextet, wind qnt, pf, 1984–

Vocal: Cycle of 6 Songs (Lorca), 1965

Principal publishers: General Music, Piedmont

ELLEN HIGHSTEIN

Breil, Joseph Carl (*b* Pittsburgh, PA, 29 June 1870; *d* Los Angeles, CA, 23 Jan 1926). Singer, composer, and conductor. He began to study piano and violin at the age of 11, and singing at 16. He attended St. Fidelis College, Butler, Pennsylvania, and Curry University, Pittsburgh, before going to Leipzig to study law. While in Leipzig he decided to pursue a career in music and took courses at the Conservatory and studied singing with Ewald. He also had singing lessons in Milan and Philadelphia (with Giuseppe del Puente) and sang as principal tenor of the Emma Juch Opera Company (1891–2). Then he settled in Pittsburgh, where he taught singing and was choir director of St. Paul's Cathedral (1892–7); for six years thereafter he worked for a variety of theater companies, and from 1903 to 1910 as an editor.

Breil first gained recognition as a composer with his incidental music to *The Climax* in 1909; three years later he wrote and conducted one of the first scores composed expressly for a film (*Queen Elizabeth*). Breil's association with D. W. Griffith resulted in several film scores, including *The Birth of a Nation* (1915) and *Intolerance* (1916). The former included selections from the symphonic repertory and popular songs from the Civil War as well as much original music by Breil. His one-act opera *The Legend* was produced at the Metropolitan Opera in 1919.

WORKS
(selective list)

Stage: The Climax (incidental music, E. Locke), 1909; Love Laughs at Locksmiths (comic opera, Breil), 1910; The Seventh Chord (incidental music, A. Miller), 1913; The Sky Pilot (incidental music, F. Mandel and G. H. Brennan), 1917; The Legend (opera, J. Byrne), 1919; Der Asra (opera, Breil, after H. Heine), 1925

Film scores: Queen Elizabeth, 1912; The Prisoner of Zenda, 1913; Cabiria, 1914; The Birth of a Nation, 1915; The Martyrs of the Alamo, 1915; The Lily and the Rose, 1915; Double Trouble, 1915; The Penetentes, 1915; The Wood Nymph, 1916; Intolerance, 1916; The Lost Battalion, 1919; The White Rose, 1923; The Green Goddess, 1923; The White Sister, 1923; America, collab. A. Finck, 1924

Vocal: sacred works, incl. 2 masses, solo vv, SATB; 3 partsongs

MSS in *DLC*

Principal publishers: Berge, Chappell

BIBLIOGRAPHY

D. J. Teall: "Mr. Breil's 'Legend' Embodies his Theories of Practical Democracy," *MusAm*, xxviii/22 (1918), 5

B. D. Ussher: "Joseph Carl Breil," *MusAm*, xliii/15 (1926), 39 [obituary]

E. E. Hipsher: "Joseph Carl Breil," *American Opera and Its Composers* (Philadelphia, 1927), 87

M. Marks: *Report of Search on Joseph Carl Breil* (MS, *DLC*) [on film scores]

——: *Music for Silent Films, 1895–1930: Case Studies of the Relationship between Music and Image* (diss., Harvard U., in preparation)

KATHERINE K. PRESTON, MARTIN MARKS

Bremner, James (*b* England; *d* Philadelphia, PA, or nr Philadelphia, Sept 1780). Composer, teacher, organist, and harpsichordist. He may have been related to the Edinburgh and London publisher Robert Bremner. He came to America in 1763 and settled in Philadelphia, where he taught harpsichord, guitar, violin, and flute, and served as organist at St. Peter's Church. By 1767 he was organist at Christ Church, where he remained until 1774 or later, but he may have spent some of this period in England, for a "J. Bremner" published music in London during the years 1770–75. Bremner and one of his pupils, Hopkinson, often presented public concerts together. Hopkinson substituted as organist at Christ Church during Bremner's absence and wrote an ode on the occasion of Bremner's death. Four short harpsichord pieces and one arrangement by Bremner are in the Hopkinson manuscript collection at the University of Pennsylvania.

BIBLIOGRAPHY

O. G. T. Sonneck: *Francis Hopkinson . . . and James Lyon* (Washington, DC, 1905/*R*1967)

——: *A Bibliography of Early Secular American Music* (Washington, DC, 1905; rev. and enlarged by W. T. Upton 2/1945/*R*1964)

——: *Early Concert-life in America (1731–1800)* (Leipzig, 1907/*R*1978)

B. A. Wolverton: *Keyboard Music and Musicians in the Colonies and United States of America Before 1830* (diss., Indiana U., 1966)

J. BUNKER CLARK

Bresnick, Martin (*b* New York, 13 Nov 1946). Composer. He attended Hartt College (BA 1967) and Stanford University (MA 1969, DMA 1972), where he was a pupil of Chowning and Ligeti; during the year 1969–70 he was a Fulbright Fellow at the Vienna Academy of Music, where he studied under Gottfried von Einem and Friedrich Cerha. He has taught at the San Francisco Conservatory (1971–2), Stanford University (1972–5), and Yale University (from 1976). At both Stanford and Yale he has directed the university contemporary music ensembles. Bresnick's numerous commissions and awards include the American Academy's Rome Prize (1975), two NEA awards (1975, 1979), a MacDowell Colony Fellowship (1977), and the Premio Ancona (1980), for the chamber work *Conspiracies*.

Bresnick has written primarily for small ensembles, and shows a predilection for multiples of a single instrument; he is also involved with film music. A number of his works are explicitly programmatic, often dealing with themes of a political nature. He has explored computer-assisted methods of precompositional planning and combined synthesized and electroacoustic sounds with those of normal acoustic instruments in interesting ways, for example deploying different sound sources in all areas of the performance space and producing the Doppler effect by electronic means. Since 1970 he has concentrated on a contrapuntal heterophony that often involves canon and a very limited improvisation on thematic material.

WORKS

Dramatic: Ants (theater piece, M. Bresnick, R. Myslewski), 1976

Orch: Ocean of Storms, 1969–70; Wir weben, wir weben, 1976–8, arr. str sextet, 1980

Inst: Pf Sonata, 1963; Trio, 2 tpt, perc, 1965; Ww Qt, 1967; PCOMP, tape, 1968; Pour, tape, 1969; Introit, 8 ww, 8 brass insts, 1969; 3 Intermezzi, vc, 1971; Musica, 9 insts, 1972; B.'s Garlands, 8 vc, 1973; Conspiracies, 5 fl, 1979; Der Signál, 3 solo vv, tape, chamber ens, 1982; other works

Vocal: Aloysha, Bar, pf, 1964; Where is the Way, SATB, 1970; Stoneground, actor-singers, 1974

Film music: Arthur and Lillie (J. Else), 1976; The Day After Trinity (J. Else), 1980

Principal publisher: Bote & Bock

RICHARD S. JAMES

Bressler, Charles (*b* Kingston, PA, 1 April 1926). Tenor. He studied at the Juilliard School with Lucia Dunham and Sergius Kagen, and later with Marjorie Schloss. A founding member of the New York Pro Musica, Bressler toured with the group from 1953 to 1963. His performance of the title role in its production of the *Play of Daniel* won him the Best Male Singer award from the Théâtre des Nations festival in Paris, and his recording of the part is still unsurpassed. Bressler joined the New York Chamber Soloists in the year in which it was founded (1957) and has toured with the group in Europe, Asia, and Latin America. At Santa Fe he sang in the American premières of Henze's *Boulevard Solitude* (1967) and *The Bassarids* (1968), and at the Library of Congress in the first performance of Hugh Aitken's *Fables* (1975). His voice is a light, fluid tenor, heard to best advantage in medieval, Renaissance, and Baroque music, and in later works demanding intelligence and finesse more than sheer power; his recordings reflect the breadth and variety of this repertory. He has taught at a number of institutions, including the Mannes College, the Manhattan School, and Brooklyn College.

MICHAEL FLEMING

Brett, Philip (*b* Edwinstowe, England, 17 Oct 1937). Musicologist. He studied in England at King's College, Cambridge (BA 1958, MusB 1961). He then spent a year at the University of California, Berkeley, before returning to Cambridge (PhD 1965). In 1966 he joined the faculty of the department of music at Berkeley and was appointed professor in 1978. He became an American citizen in 1979. At Cambridge Brett collaborated with Thurston Dart on The English Madrigalists (1956), a revision of E. H. Fellowes's series The English Madrigal School (1913–24). He also worked on the music of the English composer William Byrd (1543–1623); his research has shown that many of the pieces accepted by Fellowes are of doubtful authenticity. In 1972 he became general editor of a new edition of Byrd's music. Brett has specialized in the performance of Handel's music, as conductor and harpsichordist. He is also interested in the works of Benjamin Britten and is the author of *Peter Grimes* in the series Cambridge Opera Handbooks (1983).

DAVID SCOTT/PAULA MORGAN

Brewer, John Hyatt (*b* Brooklyn, NY, 18 Jan 1856; *d* Brooklyn, 30 Nov 1931). Organist and composer. He was a boy soprano in various Brooklyn and New York churches (1864–71), and studied organ and composition with Buck. He served as organist in a number of Brooklyn churches: City Park Chapel (1871–3), Church of the Messiah (1873–7), Clinton Avenue Congregational Church (1877–81), and, for the last 50 years of his life, the Lafayette Avenue Presbyterian Church. From 1899 to 1906 he taught at Adelphi College. An energetic leader of amateur musical organizations, Brewer conducted the Boylston, Brooklyn Hill, Damrosch, Flatbush, and Orpheus glee clubs, the Cecelia Ladies' Vocal Society, and the Hoadley Amateur Orchestra. In 1903 he succeeded Buck as conductor of the all-male Apollo Club. He was also active as a recitalist and composed over 200 works. Brewer was a Fellow and Warden of the American Guild of Organists and in 1916 received an honorary DMus from New York University.

WORKS

(selective list)

Vocal: Hesperus (F. L. Mace), female vv, 1894; The Herald of Spring (J. Payne), female vv, 1895; The Birth of Love (Bulwer Lytton), male vv, 1895; The Holy Night, mixed vv, 1901; The Lord of Dunderberg (A. Guiterberg), male vv, 1905; The Conqueror, Spring (C. Feinthel), male vv, 1918; A Message of Music (F. W. Farber), male vv, 1928; songs

Inst: Str Qt, d; The Lady of the Lake, org, pf, vc, 1891; Suite, orch (1891); Reverie, org, harp, vn, bells, 1915; org works

Principal publishers: G. Schirmer, Schmidt

BIBLIOGRAPHY

R. Hughes: *Contemporary American Composers* (Boston, 1900), 331

L. Ellinwood: *The History of American Church Music* (New York, 1953/*R*1970), 203f

WILLIAM OSBORNE

Brewster, William Herbert, Sr. (*b* Somerville, TN, 2 July 1897 or 1899). Composer of gospel songs. He attended Roger Williams College in Nashville (BA 1922), then moved to Memphis to become dean of a proposed black seminary sponsored by the Southern Baptist denomination. The school did not materialize, however, and in 1928 he accepted the pastorate of the East Trigg Baptist Church in Memphis. He also served on the Education Board of the National Baptist Convention and as dean of Shelby County General Baptist Association, and founded and directed the Brewster Theological Clinic at Memphis, which has branches in 25 cities throughout the USA. Brewster is best known as a composer who makes use of sophisticated biblical texts. His first song, *I'm leaning and depending on the Lord*, was written in 1939; since that time he has contributed over 200 works to the repertory. Two of his pieces, *Move on up a little higher* (1946) and *Surely, God is able* (1949), were the first black gospel recordings to sell over a million copies. Mahalia Jackson, Clara Ward, Queen C. Anderson, and his own group, the Brewster Ensemble, popularized most of his songs. Brewster has also composed more than 15 biblical music dramas, one of which, *Sowing in Tears, Reaping in Joy*, was presented at the Smithsonian Institution in December 1982 during a weekend seminar devoted to his music.

BIBLIOGRAPHY

SouthernB

H. C. Boyer: *The Gospel Song: a Historical and Analytical Study* (thesis, Eastman School of Music, 1964)

——: "Contemporary Gospel Music: Characteristics and Style," *BPiM*, vii (1979), 22

T. Heilbut: *The Gospel Sound: Good News and Bad Times* (New York, 1971/*R*1975)

A Retrospective of Gospel Music Composer Reverend William Herbert Brewster (Washington, DC, 1982)

HORACE CLARENCE BOYER

Brian, Billy. Pseudonym of GENE PITNEY.

Brice, Carol (Lovette Hawkins) (*b* Sedalia, NC, 16 April 1918; *d* Norman, OK, 15 Feb 1985). Contralto. She studied at the Palmer Memorial Institute in Sedalia before attending Talladega (Alabama) College (BM 1939) and the Juilliard School (1939–43), where she trained under Francis Rogers. While still a student at Juilliard, she appeared with Bill Robinson in Mike Todd's production of *The Hot Mikado* at the New York World's Fair (1939) and was a soloist at St. George's Episcopal Church (New York, 1939–43), where she worked with the baritone Henry T. Burleigh. In 1941 she sang at a concert to mark the third inauguration of President Franklin Roosevelt and made her recital début in New York at the Chaplet. In 1943 she became the first black American to win the Naumburg Award. Following her Town Hall début (13 March 1945), she presented a recital on television (CBS, 1945) and appeared with the symphony orchestras of Pittsburgh (1945), Boston (1946), and San Francisco (1948). Her stage performances included the role of the Voodoo Princess in Clarence Cameron White's *Ouanga* (independently given at the Metropolitan Opera in 1956 and at Carnegie Hall), Addie in Blitzstein's *Regina*, Kakou in Arlen's *Saratoga*, Maude in *Finian's Rainbow* (1960), Queenie in Jerome Kern's *Showboat*, Maria in Gershwin's *Porgy and Bess* (1961, 1976), and Harriet Tubman in *Gentleman be Seated* (1963); from 1967 to 1971, she appeared at the Vienna Volksoper in *Porgy and Bess*, *Showboat*, and *Carousel*. In 1974 she joined her husband, the baritone Thomas Carey, on the faculty of the University of Oklahoma, establishing with him the Cimarron Circuit Opera Company. Her recordings include arias by Bach, Falla's *El amor brujo*, and Mahler's *Lieder eines fahrenden Gesellen*; she also participated in the recordings of *Regina* and *Saratoga*, both in 1959, and *Porgy and Bess*, for which she won a Grammy Award.

BIBLIOGRAPHY

SouthernB

P. Turner: *Afro-American Singers* (Minneapolis, 1977), 14

DOMINIQUE-RENÉ DE LERMA

Brice, Fanny [Fannie; Borach, Fannie] (*b* New York, 29 Oct 1891; *d* Hollywood, CA, 29 May 1951). Actress and singer. She began singing in her parents' saloon, then worked on the burlesque circuit playing comic roles, where she came to the attention of Ziegfeld. He gave her a part in his *Follies of 1910*, in which her performance of Berlin's "Good-bye Becky Cohen" and Joe Jordan's "Lovie Joe" stopped the show. She appeared in eight more editions of the *Follies* as well as numerous other Broadway musicals. She was known particularly for her performance of comic songs with a Yiddish accent, for example "I'm an Indian" from the *Follies of 1920*, and "Old Wicked Willage of Wenice" in *Fioretta* (1929; libretto by Earl Carroll, music by George Bagby and G. Romilli). She was also a superb torch-singer, and became associated with such ballads as James F. Hanley's *Rose of Washington Square* and Maurice Yvain's *My Man*. Brice was less successful in film roles, but won her widest recognition playing the brattish Baby Snooks on radio; she first presented the character on Broadway in the Ziegfeld *Follies of 1934*, performed it on the radio in the CBS program "Ziegfeld Follies of the Air" in 1936 and continued to play it on various programs until her death. She was married to the producer and songwriter Billy Rose.

BIBLIOGRAPHY

N. Katkov: *The Fabulous Fanny* (New York, 1951)
S. Green: *The Great Clowns of Broadway* (New York, 1984)

GERALD BORDMAN

Brico, Antonia (*b* Rotterdam, Netherlands, 26 June 1902). Conductor. She came to the USA at the age of six and graduated from the University of California, Berkeley, in 1923. Following further piano study with Stojowski in New York, in 1927–32 she pursued conducting in Germany, studying at the Hochschule für Musik in Berlin and privately with Muck. She made her début as a conductor in Berlin in 1930 and subsequently was a guest conductor for many European orchestras and at the Hollywood Bowl.

Brico returned to the USA in 1932, making appearances in New York with the Musicians SO, and orchestras sponsored by the Federal Music Project of the WPA; in 1934 she founded the Women's SO of New York, which she conducted until 1938. She also conducted orchestras in Detroit, Buffalo, Los Angeles, and San Francisco, and in 1938 at a Lewisohn Stadium concert she became the first woman to direct the New York PO. After that, however, the number of her engagements declined as the idea of a female conductor ceased to be a novelty.

During the 1941–2 season Brico settled in Denver, where in 1948 she founded and conducted the semiprofessional Antonia Brico SO. After World War II she traveled to Finland to conduct several concerts of Sibelius's music, and became associated with Albert Schweitzer. A documentary film, *Antonia*, made in 1974, about her career and the discouragements she experienced on account of her sex resulted in engagements to conduct leading orchestras once again. She has also taught classes in piano, conducting, and the history of opera, and worked as an opera coach.

CAROL NEULS-BATES

Brigham Young University. A private university in Provo, Utah. In 1875 members of the Church of Jesus Christ of Latter-day Saints founded the Brigham Young Academy; it became a university in 1903. In 1980 the department of music (in the College of Fine Arts) enrolled 500 majors and employed a full-time faculty of 39 under the chairmanship of James Mason. It offers an Associate of Science (AS) degree in piano technology; an Associate of Arts (AA) in piano pedagogy and church music; a BA in general music, or with emphasis on music history, church music, sound recording, or studio composition; BM and MM degrees in composition and theory, music education, performance, and pedagogy; a BFA in music theater; an MM in conducting; an MA in music education, musicology, or music theory; and the PhD. The Harold B. Lee Library contains the manuscript music collections of John Laurence Seymour, Percy Faith, and Republic Pictures; it also holds a number of sheet music collections, a large number of Mormon hymnals, and the William Primrose Viola Library. The music department's collection of musical instruments, built around the Van Buren Collection, comprises about 100 items. (*See also* LIBRARIES AND COLLECTIONS, §3.)

GRAYDON BEEKS

Brill Building. The building situated at 1619 Broadway, New York, in which, for several decades through the mid-1960s, many popular songwriters and music publishers had offices; the name is applied to the style of music that they wrote and published, especially from 1959 to 1965. This music, often referred to as "teenage pop," used elements of doo-wop and other types of rock-and-roll, and gospel music; it appealed chiefly to young, middle-class, white listeners.

The most important publisher of songs in the Brill Building style (notwithstanding its location at 1650 Broadway, across the street from most of its competitors), was Aldon Music; formed in 1958 by Don Kirshner and Al Nevins, its principal songwriting teams were Gerry Goffin and Carole King, Barry Mann and Cynthia Weil, and Howard Greenfield and Neil Sedaka. Among the most important firms to occupy the Brill Building was Trio Music, founded by the songwriting and production team of Leiber and Stoller, and with which Jeff Barry and Ellie Greenwich were later associated. Other songwriting partnerships in the Brill Building tradition include Doc Pomus and Mort Schuman, who wrote for the Drifters, and Burt Bacharach and Hal David, who wrote for Dionne Warwick.

Brill Building songs were of varying quality and adhered closely to formula. The best songs of Goffin and King (such as *Will you still love me tomorrow?*) and Mann and Weil (*You've lost that lovin' feeling*) are rock-and-roll ballads strongly influenced by gospel music; many of those written by Barry and Greenwich were arranged by Phil Spector and performed by girl groups. The Brill Building style declined with the advent of the Beatles and other English rock groups, who wrote most of their own material; by the late 1960s most Brill Building publishers had sold their companies, and most of the songwriters had moved to Los Angeles.

BIBLIOGRAPHY

G. Shaw: "Brill Building Pop," *The Rolling Stone Illustrated History of Rock & Roll*, ed J. Miller (New York, 1976, rev. 2/1980), 120
A. Betrock: *Girl Groups: the Story of a Sound* (New York, 1982)

STEPHEN HOLDEN

Briquet, Jean. Pseudonym of ADOLF PHILIPP.

Bristow, George Frederick (*b* Brooklyn, NY, 19 Dec 1825; *d* New York, 13 Dec 1898). Composer, performer, conductor, and teacher. He was the son of William Richard Bristow (1803–67), conductor, composer, and clarinetist in the New York area. He learned piano and violin with his father and the cellist W. Musgriff, then reportedly studied violin with Ole Bull and harmony, counterpoint, and orchestration with Henry Christian Timm and George Macfarren (although the latter is extremely doubtful).

Although important as a composer, Bristow was known in his lifetime equally as a performer, conductor, and teacher. He began his professional performing career as a violinist at the age of 13 with the Olympic Theatre Orchestra, a group of six that performed in popular musical comedies and occasional light operas. He was a member of the first violin section of the New York Philharmonic Society Orchestra from 1843 (not 1842 as reported in most other sources) until his retirement in 1879. He also performed in and often led the violin section of such notable orchestras as Jullien's (1853–4) and those that accompanied Jenny Lind (1850–51) and Marietta Alboni (1852). As a conductor Bristow led such major choral groups as the New York Harmonic Society (1851–63) and the Mendelssohn Society (1867–71) in performances of large choral and orchestral works. He also held posts as choir director and organist in several New York churches, among them St. George's Chapel (1854–60).

With Heinrich and Fry, Bristow contributed to the awareness and support of native composers. In New York he became a leader in establishing local music groups that had varying degrees of nationalistic purpose, such as the American Musical Fund Society (1852; an early type of musician's protective organization found in other American cities), American Music Association (1856), and Metropolitan Music Association (1859). He joined the heated controversy in the press in 1853–4 between the traditionalist Richard Storrs Willis and the Americanist Fry and, to protest what he thought was a lack of encouragement for American composers, resigned his post in the Philharmonic for the season.

Although the organizations for the support of native talent were generally short-lived, Bristow continued to express his sentiments through his compositions, where he frequently drew on American subject matter (e.g. *Rip Van Winkle*, *Jibbenainosay*, *The Great Republic*, *Columbus*, *The Pioneer*, *Niagara Symphony*). However, his music remained typically European in harmonic, melodic, rhythmic, and formal characteristics. From the early student works of the 1840s (the Sinfonia in E♭, string quartets, and string duos), which are Classical in proportion and style, Bristow's development reflects the significant changes in trends and tastes in New York in the mid-19th century for works in the style of Beethoven and Mendelssohn rather than those after Haydn. His later works (*Niagara Symphony* and *Daniel*) often employ large vocal and instrumental resources. The instrumental and vocal repertory with which he became acquainted as a performer greatly influenced his compositional style. His orchestration exhibits solid craftsmanship, but his chamber works, written during the 1840s when few American composers exploited the medium, are especially notable.

Bristow contributed significantly to music education in New York as a public school teacher from 1854; he also taught privately and wrote several pedagogical works. In his instruction books for singers he combined a solid basic method (including note-reading, use of vocal exercises, solfeggio syllables, and a controlled two-voice method of improvisation) with a broad selection of European and American musical literature. In order to encourage quality in his students' performances, he often enlisted the aid of prominent professional musicians.

See also ORCHESTRAL MUSIC, §2.

WORKS

Printed works published in New York unless otherwise indicated; MSS of unpublished works mainly in *NN-L*. For more detailed list see Rogers.

DRAMATIC

Rip Van Winkle (opera, 3, J. H. Wainwright, after W. Irving), op.22, 1852–5; New York, Niblo's Garden, 27 Sept 1855; rev. 1878–82 (J. W. Shannon), vs pubd (1882/*R*1982)

Daniel (oratorio, W. A. Hardenbrook), solo vv, SATB, orch, op.42, 1866, lib. pubd (1867)

King of the Mountains (opera, M. A. Cooney), op.80, 1894, unfinished

SACRED VOCAL

(for SATB, org, unless otherwise indicated)

To the Lord our God (sentence), S, A, T, B, op.15, 1850

I will arise (sentence), [op.23], ?1853

Morning Service (Te Deum, Jubilate, Kyrie), E♭, op.19 (1855), Te Deum separately pubd (1888)

Gloria Patri, Praise to God, solo vv, SATB, orch, op.31, vs pubd as op.33 (Boston, 1860)

Evening Service (Bonum est, Benedic anima mea), op.36 (1865)

Christ our Passover (Easter Anthem), op.39, ?1866

The Lord is in his holy temple (sentence), S, A, T, B, org, op.40, ?1866; rev. 1891 (inc.)

*c*130 hymns, chants, ?1867

Four Offertories, op.48, ?1870

Morning Service (Te Deum, Benedictus), op.51, ?1873; Te Deum pubd (1873)

Easy Morning Service, F, [op.58], ?1881

There is joy today, SATB, pf, in Tonic Sol-fa Advocate (Nov 1882)

Holy Night, SATB, pf, in Tonic Sol-fa Advocate (Nov 1884)

Evening Service, G, [op.56], ?1885

Mass, C, solo vv, SATB, orch, op.57, 1885

Christmas Anthem (Light flashing into the darkness) (J. Elmendorf), op.73, 1887

O bells of Easter morning, SATB, pf, in Tonic Sol-fa Advocate (March 1887)

Where the holly boughs are waving, SATB, pf, in Tonic Sol-fa Advocate (Nov 1887)

Easter Anthem, solo vv, SATB, org, [op.77], ?1894

Except the Lord build the house, S, A, chorus, org, [op.79], ?1894

Sweet is the prayer [after pf study by S. Heller], op.81, ?1894

Come ye that love the Saviour's name [after H. Praher]

I heard a voice from heaven, S, A, T, B, org

Oh that the salvation of Israel, SATB, pf/org

O Lord, thy mercy, my sure hope, SATB, [op.76] (sketch)

There's rest for all in heav'n, 1v, pf

SECULAR VOCAL

(choral)

Ode, S, female vv, orch, [op.29], ?1856

The Pioneer (H. C. Watson), cantata, solo vv, SATB, orch, op.49, ?1872 [orig. intended as prol. to Arcadian Symphonie, see "Orchestral"]

The Great Republic, Ode to the American Union (W. O. Bourne), solo vv, SATB, orch, op.47, vs pubd (1880)

Niagara Symphony, solo vv, SATB, orch, op.62, 1893

The Bold Bad Baron, male vv, ?1896

Call John, SATB

Ode Written for G. S., 1v, SATB, kbd (kbd part inc.)

(songs, for 1v, pf, unless otherwise indicated)

Thine eye hath seen the spot, ?1846, inc., part quoted in W. T. Upton: *Art-song in America* (Boston, 1930/*R*1969 with suppl. 1938); The Welcome Back (Boston, 1848); I would I were a favorite flower, in The Message Bird: a Literary and Musical Journal (1 Dec 1849); The opening day (W. H. Carew), glee, SATB, pf, in The Message Bird (15 Feb 1850); The dawn is breaking o'er us, ?1852; Spring time is coming (J. H. Wainwright) (Springfield, MA, 1852); The abode of music (M. Marseilles), canzonet, op.31, 1855

The Cantilena: a Collection of Songs, Duets, Trios and Quartetts (1861) [130 works]; Keep step with the music of the Union, unison vv, orch, 1862, vs in The Centennial School Singer, ed. G. H. Curtis and W. O. Bourne (1876); Lily Song (1869); A Song of the Hearth and Home (W. P. Durfee) (1869); Only a little shoe (A. D. T. Cone) (1884); Woman's Love, ?1887; The ghost came bobbing up (J. W. Shannon); When morning's bright sun, 1v, orch

ORCHESTRAL, CHAMBER

Orch: Ov., E♭, op.3, 1845; Sinfonia, E♭, op.10, 1848; Captain Raynor's Quickstep, 1849; Serenade Waltz, 1849; Waltz, ?1849; La cracovian, vn, orch, op.13, 1850 [rev. of Duetto concertante, vn, pf, op.1, 1844]; Jullien Sinfonia, d, op.24, ?1853; Winter's Tale, ov., op.30, 1856; Symphonie, f♯, op.26, 1858; Columbus, ov., op.32, 1861; Arcadian Symphonie, op.50, 1872; Fantasie cromatica con fuga [arr. of J. S. Bach], op.53, 1879; Jibbenainosay, ov., op.64, ?1889

Chamber: Duetto concertante, vn, pf, op.1, 1844 [rev. as La cracovian, vn, orch, op.13, 1850]; Fantasie Zampa, vn, pf, op.17, 1844; Duo no.2, g, vn, va, 1845; Duo no.3, G, vn, va, op.8, 1845; Quartetto, str, F, op.1, ?1849; Quartetto, str, g, op.2, 1849; Violin Sonata, G, op.12, ?1849; Friendship, vn, pf, op.25, ?1855; The Judge, march, pf, perc, op.60, ?1886

KEYBOARD

(pf)

Rory O'Moore, variations (1842); Grand waltz de bravura, op.6 (1845); Grand duo . . . sur . . . La fille du regiment, pf 4 hands, op.7, 1845; Septour, pf duet, op.16, 1846; Dream of the Ocean [arr. of J. Gungl] (1849); Duo La fille du regiment, 2 pf, op.5, 1849; Andante et polonaise, op.18, ?1850 (n.d.); A life on the ocean wave, op.21, ?1852; Souvenir de Mount Vernon, op.29 (1861); Eroica, op.38, ?1865; Raindrops, op.43, ?1867

La vivandiere, op.51, ?1884; Dreamland, op.59, ?1885; Saltarello, [op.61] ?1886; March, op.69, ?1887; Marche-caprice, op.51 (1890); School March, op.63 (Boston, 1893); Impromptu, [op.76], ?1894 (inc.); Plantation Pleasures, op.82, ?1894; Plantation Memories no.2, op.83, ?1895; Plantation Memories no.3, ?1895; March Columbus (inc.); A Walk Around (inc.); arrs., transcrs.

(org)

[53] Interludes, in Melodia sacra: a Complete Collection of Church Music, ed. B. F. Baker, A. N. Johnson, and J. Osgood (Boston, 1852); Pot pourri, op.28, 1856; Impromptu Voluntaries, op.45, pubd as Six Pieces (1883); Six Easy Voluntaries, op.72, in George F. Bristow's New and Improved Method for the Reed or Cabinet Organ (1887)

PEDAGOGICAL WORKS

with F. H. Nash: Cantara, or Teacher of Singing (1866, enlarged, 2/1868)

George F. Bristow's New and Improved Method for the Reed or Cabinet Organ (1887)

Bristow's Two-part Vocal Exercises, op.75 (1890–95)

LOST WORKS

La belle Amerique, nocturne, op.4; L'etoile du soir, nocturne, C♭, op.7; La pensee, nocturne, op.9; La belle de la joi, op.11; Innocence, nocturne, op.14; La belle nuit, nocturne, op.20; Blue Bell, nocturne, op.27; Valse, E♭, op.29; Burial Service, op.34, ?1861, *NN-L* (text only); Valse, E/D, op.35; Le canari, pf, op.37; Epigram, pf, op.41; Morceau, A♭, pf, op.46

Te Deum and Jubilate, C, op.51; No More from Great Republic, op.52; Te Deum and Benedictus, B♭, 1v, org, op.54; Te Deum and Jubilate, F, op.58; Morceaux, org, op.65; Introduction and Fugue, op.66; Belteshazzar from Oratorio, op.67; Darius from Oratoria, op.68; Trois morceaux, org, op.70; Chant Te Deum, op.71; Remember me, male vv, op.74; Vocal Exercises for Schools, bk 1, op.75; Le serenade, nocturne, 1851/2

Principal publishers: Pond, G. Schirmer, Ditson, Dodworth

BIBLIOGRAPHY

EwenD

J. W. Moore: *Appendix to Encyclopedia of Music* (Boston, MA, 1875)

W. M. Thoms: "George F. Bristow," *American Art Journal*, xxxvii (1882), 241

F. O. Jones, ed.: *A Handbook of American Music and Musicians* (Canaseraga, NY, 1886/*R*1971)

J. D. Champlin and W. F. Apthorp, eds.: *Cyclopedia of Music and Musicians*, i (New York, 1888)

G. H. Curtis: "G. F. Bristow," *Music*, iii (1893), 547

"Violinist and Composer; Sketch of his Life," *Music*, xv (1899), 471

W. Rieck: "When Bristow's Rip was Sung at Niblo's Garden," *MusAm*, xliii/7 (1925), 3

C. N. Boyd: "Bristow, George Frederick," *DAB*

"Bristow, George Frederick," *The National Cyclopedia of American Biography*, xxiii (New York, 1933/*R*1967)

D. D. Rogers: *Nineteenth-century Music in New York City as Reflected in the Career of George Frederick Bristow* (diss., U. of Michigan, 1967)

B. F. Kauffman: *The Choral Works of George F. Bristow (1825–1898) and William H. Fry (1815–1864)* (diss., U. of Illinois, 1975)

K. E. Gombert: *"Leonora" by William Henry Fry and "Rip Van Winkle" by George Frederick Bristow: Examples of Mid-nineteenth-century American Opera* (diss., Ball State U., 1977)

DELMER D. ROGERS

Britain, Radie (*b* Silverton, TX, 17 March 1908). Composer. After graduating with honors from the American Conservatory, Chicago (BM, piano, 1924), she went to Europe, where she studied composition and theory in Munich with Albert Noelte and organ in Paris with Marcel Dupré. She returned from Europe in 1926 and continued to work with Noelte, then at the Chicago Conservatory, and subsequently spent two seasons at the MacDowell Colony. She also studied piano with Godowsky and organ with Yon. From 1930 to 1934 she taught harmony and composition at the Girvin Institute of Music, Chicago, and from 1934 to 1939 was on the faculty of the Chicago Conservatory; she taught piano and composition privately in Hollywood from 1940 to 1960. She received an Award of Merit from the National League of American Pen Women. Over 50 of her compositions have received national or international awards, including *Epic Poem* (1927), *Light* (1935), and *Cosmic Mist Symphony* (1962); in 1945 she became the first woman to receive the Juilliard Publication Award, for *Heroic Poem*. She wrote *Composer's Corner* (1978) and three other books.

Although she experimented with atonal and serial techniques in some of her later works, Britain's primary concerns have been lyric expression and the creation of atmosphere in music. Many of her programmatic or pictorial works are inspired by American geography and scenery, especially that of her native Southwest. She has written: "I wish to feel in American music the conquest of the pioneer, the determined man of the soil, the gigantic beauty of a sunset, the nobility of the Rockies, the wonder of the Grand Canyon, the serenity of the hidden violet and the purity of the wild flower."

WORKS

Dramatic: Ubiquity (musical drama, L. Luther), 1937; Happyland (operetta, A. Greenfield), 1946; Carillon (opera, R. Hughs), 1952; The Spider and the Butterfly (children's operetta, 3, L. P. Hasselberg), 1953; Kuthara (chamber opera, 3, L. Luther), 1960; 5 ballets, 1929–64, incl. Wheel of Life, 1933, Lady in the Dark, 1960, Western Testament, 1964

Orch and choral: Sym. Intermezzo, 1928, arr. 5 insts, 1976; Heroic Poem, 1929; Rhapsody, pf, orch, 1933; Light, 1935; Drouth, 1939, arr. pf, 1939; Ontonagon Sketches, 1939; Suite, str, 1940; Phantasy, ob, orch, 1942, arr. fl, pf, 1962; We Believe, 1942; Serenata sorrentina, small orch, 1946, arr. pf, 1946; Cactus Rhapsody, orch, 1953, arr. 2 pf, 1965, rev. orch, 1974; Nisan (K. Hammond), SSAA, pf, str, 1961, arr. SATB, pf, 1961; Cosmic Mist Sym., 1962; Brothers of the Clouds, male vv, orch, 1964, arr. SATB, pf; Anwar Sadat (In Memory), orch, 1982; many other works

Inst: Epic Poem, str qt, 1927; Str Qt, 1934; Prison (Lament), str qt, 1935; Pastorale, 2 pf, 1935, arr. orch, 1939, arr. ob, harp, hpd, 1967, arr. fl, harp, 1977; The Chateau, pf, harp, 1938; Chipmunks, ww, 1940, arr. ww, harp, perc, 1940; Serenade, vn, pf, 1944; Barcarola, vn, pf, 1948, arr. S, 8 vc, 1958; Pf Sonata, 1958; In the Beginning, 4 hn, 1962; The Famous 12, pf, 1965, arr. 12 insts as Les fameux douze, 1966; Recessional, 4 trbn, 1969; Phantasie, ww trio, 1975; Adoration, brass qt, 1976; Translunar Cycle, vc, pf, 1980; Ode to NASA, brass qnt, 1981; Soul of the Sea, vc, pf, 1984; many other works

Vocal: Many choruses, incl. Drums of Africa (Jenkins), 1934, Noontide (Nietzsche), 1935, Harvest Heritage (Britain), 1963; over 50 songs; several song cycles

MSS in *DLC*, *CLU-MUS*, *TxAm*, *TxU*, *WyU*, Moldenhauer Archives, Spokane, WA

Principal publishers: Clayton Summy, C. Fischer, Green, Henroico, Kjos, Ricordi, Wilmark

BIBLIOGRAPHY

EwenD

C. Reis: *Composers in America: Biographical Sketches* (New York, 4/1947/*R*1977, rev. and enlarged edn of *American Composers*)

M. Goss: *Modern Music Makers* (New York, 1952)

J. L. Zaimont and K. Famera: *Contemporary Concert Music by Women* (Westport, CT, 1981)

KATHERINE K. PRESTON

British-American music. *See* EUROPEAN-AMERICAN MUSIC, §II, 1.

British invasion. A term used to describe the sudden popularity in the USA of a number of English rock groups in the mid-1960s, including the Beatles, the Rolling Stones, The Who, the Yardbirds, the Kinks, and the Animals; *see* ROCK, §2.

Britton, Allen P(erdue) (*b* Elgin, IL, 25 May 1914). Music educator. He graduated from the University of Illinois (BS 1937, MA 1939) and continued his studies at the University of Michigan (PhD 1950). After teaching in the public schools of Griffith, Indiana (1938–41), he joined the faculty of Eastern Illinois University (1941–3). He was appointed professor of music at the University of Michigan in 1949, and from 1969 until his retirement in 1979 he was dean of the school of music. Britton was president of the Music Educators National Conference, 1960–62, and founding editor of both the *Journal of Research in Music Education*, 1953–72, and *American Music* (from 1983). He is also editor of the textbook series *Foundations of Music Education* (1964–). His research has centered on early American tunebooks and he is co-author (with Irving Lowens) of "The Easy Instructor, 1798–1831: a History and Bibliography of the First Shape Note Tune Book" (1953; repr. in Lowens: *Music and Musicians in Early America*, 1964).

PAULA MORGAN

Broadcasting. The transmission of sound or images, or both together, by radio or television. The word "broadcast" is now commonly applied to radio transmissions and the word "telecast" has been coined to describe transmissions by television. This article deals with the history of music broadcasting in the USA.

1. Early broadcasting. 2. Commercial development to 1940. 3. Expansion and diversification to the 1950s. 4. Developments in television. 5. FM radio. 6. Trends in the 1980s.

1. EARLY BROADCASTING. The first music to be broadcast over radio waves was transmitted on Christmas eve 1906 from Brant Rock, Massachusetts, by Reginald Fessenden. His broadcast, which included a phonograph recording of the Largo from Handel's *Serse* and a performance on the violin, was heard over a wide area, mainly by shipboard wireless operators. In 1907 Lee de Forest, the inventor of the three-element vacuum tube (the "audion"), began experimental transmissions of recorded and live music; on 5 March 1907 he transmitted a performance of Rossini's *William Tell* overture from Telharmonic Hall in New York to the Brooklyn Navy Yard, and on 13 January 1910 he broadcast excerpts from *Cavalleria rusticana* and *Pagliacci*, sung by Caruso, from the stage of the Metropolitan Opera House in New York. As the number of amateur radio broadcasters grew, so did the problem of simultaneous transmissions on the same frequency from different locations, and in 1912 the US Congress passed the first radio licensing law, allocating different points on the radio-wave frequency spectrum to different transmitters.

As early as 1916 David Sarnoff proposed to his employer, the American firm of Marconi, the development of a "radio music box" as a household utility similar to the piano or the phonograph. In 1919, after the lifting of wartime restrictions on any but military broadcasting, General Electric established the Radio Corporation of America (RCA), with Sarnoff in a managerial role. The rival Westinghouse firm turned to an employee, Frank Conrad, and proposed an expansion of his experimental amateur station 8XK in Pittsburgh, over which he had been broadcasting recorded music daily. Beginning operations on 2 November 1920 as KDKA, it was one of the first commercial broadcasting stations in the USA. Other commercial stations were soon on the air: WWJ in Detroit, WJZ in Newark, New Jersey (which later moved to New York), WBAY (later renamed WEAF) in New York, WNAC in Boston, KYW in Chicago, and KWG in Stockton, California; the opening broadcast of KWG on 22 November 1921 was graced by one of the leading sopranos of the Metropolitan Opera, Ernestine Schumann-Heink.

2. COMMERCIAL DEVELOPMENT TO 1940. In the early period of commercial radio many different ideas for program content were tried. By far the most important element, however, was popular music, and the broadcasting of live performances was preferred over recorded music (then in its infancy and far from satisfactory acoustically). "Remote" broadcasts (that is, those made from locations other than radio studios), often by dance orchestras from hotel ballrooms, began as early as 1921 and were commonplace by 1924. Performers were quick to discover the promotional value of radio and often broadcast without compensation. Music publishers, through their song pluggers, also soon exploited the medium. Songs about radio even began to appear, possibly the earliest of which was *The Radio Kiss* (1922) by B. K. Hanchette and E. R. Steiner, a waltz-song that promised "amidst the static's growl and shriek, thro' sputtering tubes that hiss," the sound of a "luscious kiss." The inauguration by the owners of WEAF of "toll broadcasting" (i.e., advertising) in 1922 laid the foundation for the large-scale commercialization of radio. The advertisers ("program sponsors") or agencies working on their behalf usually produced their own programs, often naming the musical groups employed after the product being advertised (hence the Ipana Troubadours and the Cliquot Club Eskimos, named respectively for brands of toothpaste and soft drinks).

Also in 1922, station WSB in Atlanta began broadcasting hillbilly music. BARN DANCE programs were aired elsewhere, such as Fort Worth (WBAP's "Barn Dance," 1923), Chicago (WLS had the "Chicago Barn Dance" program, subsequently retitled the "National Barn Dance"), and Nashville (WSM's "Barn Dance," which began in 1925 and later became the "Grand Ole Opry"). Black music was largely ignored by early commercial radio, although in a 1922 broadcast Ethel Waters sang with a band led by Fletcher Henderson, and in 1924 Henderson began broadcasting live "remotes" from the Roseland Ballroom in New York over WHN.

The proliferation of broadcast music prompted ASCAP as early as 1922 to demand fees for the playing on radio of the music it licensed. In a protective reaction, the National Association of Broadcasters (NAB) was formed the following year.

Network broadcasting, that is, the simultaneous broadcasting of a single program by connected stations in different locations, had been developed by the mid-1920s. The National Broadcasting Company (NBC) inaugurated its network on 15 November 1926 with a gala four-hour broadcast from New York; it included performances by the New York SO under Walter Damrosch, the New York Oratorio Society, the tenor Titta Ruffo of the Metropolitan Opera, Edwin Franko Goldman's band, and "remotes" by the soprano Mary Garden in Chicago and dance bands led by Vincent Lopez, Ben Bernie, and others. A rival network owned by the Columbia Phonograph Broadcasting System (which later became CBS) opened on 18 September 1927. Its first day of programming included a performance of Deems Taylor's opera *The King's Henchmen*, with Metropolitan Opera singers conducted by Howard Barlow. By that time some seven million radio receivers were in operation in the USA, and many more came into use after the introduction in the same year of automobile radios.

1. Part of an advertisement (late 1920s) for the weekly broadcasts on KDKA radio by Dilworth's Little German Band, directed by Gus Smaltz, with Schnitzel the dog

A number of sponsored music programs were introduced in the late 1920s. These were, typically, weekly programs with a variety-show format and a wide range of repertory, from operatic selections to popular songs and jazz. Among the longest running were the "Palmolive Hour," "The Bell Telephone Hour," and "The Voice of Firestone." The last, which began in 1928, presented such singers as Lawrence Tibbett and Richard Tucker accompanied by an orchestra led by a series of conductors identified with radio, notably Alfred Wallenstein and Barlow. In 1949 "The Voice of Firestone" was one of the first music programs to be "simulcast" (broadcast simultaneously over radio and television).

Virtually every popular-music star of the Depression era was a radio performer. Some, like the singer Kate Smith, built their careers on radio appearances. The intimate vocal style of crooning, associated first with Rudy Vallee and Bing Crosby and later with Frank Sinatra, was made possible by the radio microphone. The swing era of jazz was ushered in by remote broadcasts, usually late at night, by big bands; two well-known series of this kind of music were "The Camel Caravan" and "Let's Dance," which led Benny Goodman's band to national renown. The symbiotic relationship between the various popular music media of the time – sheet music, recordings, and radio broadcasts – was underscored by the extraordinarily large radio audience that developed for the weekly program "Your Hit Parade" (1935–58), which transmitted the most popular songs of the preceding week.

Concert music and opera were also broadcast during these peak years of network radio, most often on the "sustaining" (as opposed to "sponsored") programs presented by the networks themselves to fulfill the commitment to public service they were required by law to demonstrate. While many music programs were single concerts or short series, some continued for years and became important in the American cultural scene. In 1928 RCA began its weekly "RCA Educational Hour," which became the "NBC Music Appreciation Hour" and continued until 1942. Through this weekly series, directed by Walter Damrosch, hundreds of thousands of schoolchildren were introduced to symphonic and other concert music. CBS began weekly broadcasts of concerts by the New York PO in 1930, and these continued in one form or another until 1967. Other pioneers in initiating symphony orchestra broadcast series were Stokowski and the Philadelphia Orchestra, Koussevitzky and the Boston SO, Gabrilowitsch and the Detroit SO, and Alfred Hertz and the San Francisco SO. In 1937 NBC established its own symphony orchestra for Arturo Toscanini, who conducted it in regular weekly broadcasts from 25 December 1937 to 4 April 1954; since its dissolution, no American network has maintained a full orchestra. One of the longest-standing series on national radio is the broadcast of the Saturday matinée performances of the Metropolitan Opera, which began on 25 December 1931 with Engelbert Humperdinck's *Hänsel und Gretel*. Even older, though less of a regular institution, is the series of broadcasts from Salt Lake City by the Mormon Tabernacle Choir, which began in 1929.

While dance music has always been the mainstay of broadcast programming in the USA, commercial radio has had a few brief flirtations with American composers of concert music. On 1 May 1932 Eugene Goossens conducted a radio concert of the works of five composers – Philip James, Max Wald, Carl Eppert, Florence Galajikian, and Nicolai Berezowsky – which had been selected from 573 manuscripts submitted in a contest sponsored by NBC; the first prize of $5000 was awarded to James for his suite *Station WGZBX*. During the 1936–7 season CBS commissioned orchestral works from Copland, Hanson, Roy Harris, Piston, and Still, stipulating length and instrumentation ("that of the average radio concert orchestra – 37 players," wrote CBS's consultant on music to Copland), and inviting the composers to come to the CBS studios for a demonstration of instrumental effects possible with a microphone. Copland's response was *Music for Radio*. Gruenberg produced a "non-visual radio opera" called *Green Mansions*, and Blitzstein, interested in the enormous audience of the decade's principal mass medium, composed the radio song-play *I've Got the Tune*, which received its première on CBS on 24 October 1937. An especially successful radio work (originally intended for the musical revue *Sing for your Supper*) was *Ballad for Americans*, a "statement of democracy" for voice and orchestra by Earl Robinson to a text by John Latouche; with the bass Paul Robeson as soloist, the work had its première in a CBS studio on 5 November 1939, and was later broadcast again, performed in concert, and recorded.

3. Expansion and diversification to the 1950s. Besides the two major national networks, NBC and CBS, and two others – the Mutual Broadcasting System (MBS) established in 1934, and the American Broadcasting Corporation (ABC) established in 1943 – and the local stations affiliated with the networks, there developed hundreds of smaller, unaffiliated stations. Their need to compete with the networks' resources in artistic talent and program production was met partly by independently syndicated programs distributed on phonograph discs called "electrical transcriptions" (ETs). These 16-inch discs, recorded at $33\frac{1}{3}$ r.p.m., contained fully produced programs, complete with advertising, which often included a new musical genre, the "singing commercial" (*see* Advertising, music in). Commercial music recordings, too, provided program material for both the networks and the unaffiliated stations. It was to present and coordinate programs consisting of such music that the radio disc jockey, who was to preside over an astonishing proportion of radio air time, was introduced. In one week in 1938, for example, the Federal Communications Commission discovered in a national survey that 51.6% of all programs, both sponsored and sustaining, were based on recordings of popular and light music, most of it chosen, sequenced, and presented by disc jockeys. One of the earliest disc jockeys to become well known was Martin Block, who in 1935 began "Make Believe Ballroom" (WNEW, New York), using recordings to simulate performances in a fictitious hotel ballroom; by 1941 the program was receiving 12,000 letters each month from listeners. WNEW became the first station to broadcast 24 hours a day when it introduced "Milkman's Matinee," an all-night disc-jockey show.

In 1939, faced with the threat of a demand by ASCAP for payments of $7\frac{1}{2}$% of the networks' gross receipts, the NAB retaliated by refusing to pay, and formed its own performing rights organization, Broadcast Music, Inc. (BMI) (*see* Performing rights societies, §2(ii)). From 1 January to 13 May 1941 no music licensed by ASCAP was played on the networks. Since most of the composers of the time belonged to ASCAP, this created a programming shortfall, which was met by the broadcasting of a variety of music not controlled by ASCAP – Latin, hillbilly, and folk music, and the black music that later came to be known as rhythm-and-blues, as well as music licensed by BMI, music in the public domain, and other unlicensed music. These broadcasts marked the beginning of a commercial foothold in the popular music world of a broader spectrum of music than the Tin Pan Alley songs that had formerly predominated overwhelmingly. Rural stations contributed to this diversification in their emphasis on hillbilly music, and in the late 1940s some stations began to broadcast specifically to black audiences. An important early example of such programming was "King Biscuit Time," a live blues program featuring Sonny Boy Williamson (i) and Robert Lockwood, which began in 1941 on KFFA in Helena, Arkansas. WDIA in Memphis seems to have been the first station (1949) to present only black music.

World War II brought to American broadcasting an international role and a new network, the Armed Forces Radio Service (AFRS), which by the end of 1943 had 306 outlets in 47 countries. Initially intended for American bases abroad, AFRS was soon recognized as a potentially powerful instrument of propaganda for local populations. Other radio enterprises sponsored or supported by the government were also created, such as Voice of America, Radio Free Europe, and Radio Liberation. All of these broadcast American music, especially popular music and jazz, which increasingly influenced the light music of other countries and prepared the ground for the international pop and rock musical culture of the 1960s. In the USA that ground was partially prepared by disc jockeys such as Alan Freed, who in 1951 on WJW in Cleveland capitalized on an unexpectedly favorable response to black rhythm-and-blues recordings among the largely white, youthful audience of his "Moon Dog Show" (later called "The Moon Dog House Rock 'n' Roll Party").

4. Developments in television. A television broadcast was first transmitted in 1928. The radio networks supported intensive research and development of the medium in the 1930s, and by May 1940 23 stations were telecasting in the USA. After World War II commercial television developed rapidly, becoming by the 1950s the dominant American mass medium, especially during the evening hours.

The major networks virtually abandoned radio for television. Music was to be heard constantly, but usually only as theme music, as an element in variety shows, as incidental background for drama, or in commercials. Nevertheless, the promotional power and influence of a music performance on television was enormous, as was demonstrated vividly by Elvis Presley's appearances in the mid-1950s on "The Jackie Gleason Show" and Ed Sullivan's "Talk of the Town." Similarly, the "New York Philharmonic Young People's Concert" series, telecast by CBS under Leonard Bernstein's direction in the 1950s and 1960s, reached an audience of millions and raised Bernstein to the status of a cultural idol. Other important events included the first national television broadcast by a symphony orchestra, the Philadelphia Orchestra under Ormandy (CBS, 20 March 1948); the first full-length opera transmission, Verdi's *Otello* from the stage of the Metropolitan (ABC, 29 November 1948); and the first opera commissioned for television, Menotti's *Amahl and the Night Visitors* (on NBC's "Television Theater," 24 December 1951). Annual Christmastide telecasts of Menotti's short opera helped to make it immensely popular and stimulated hundreds of local live productions annually; in 1984 almost 500 were staged. Other television operas commissioned and transmitted by NBC, none as successful as *Amahl*, were Martinů's *The Marriage* (première on 7 February 1953), Foss's *Griffelkin* (6 November 1955), Dello Joio's *The Trial at Rouen* (8 April 1956), Stanley Hollingsworth's *La grande Bretêche* (10 February 1957), and Menotti's *Labyrinth* (3 March 1963). Possibly the most spectacular failure among television opera performances was the première of Stravinsky's *The Flood*, commissioned by CBS and telecast on 14 June 1962.

The great change in popular music from Tin Pan Alley to

rock-and-roll was reflected in (and encouraged by) radio broadcasts and the recordings that fed them, then later by television in the same way. Ed Sullivan's Sunday evening programs introduced to television audiences groups such as the Dave Clark Five, the Beatles, and the Rolling Stones, whose music was already familiar from radio (fig.2). Television even adopted the disc-jockey format in such programs as "American Bandstand," in which the host Dick Clark presided every afternoon for 90 minutes over a studio full of teenagers dancing to recorded music. ABC-TV, already presenting the weekly folk-music program "Hootenanny," introduced in 1965 a weekly rock series, "Shindig"; NBC offered "Hullabaloo."

With the rise of rock-and-roll came the Top 40 radio programming format, in which music broadcasting was limited to a comparatively small number of hit records (as determined by popularity charts published in such weekly magazines as *Billboard*) to the virtual exclusion of any other music. This practice invited corruption (paying for airplay, or "payola") and led to government investigation in 1959 and eventually to legislation forbidding such payments.

5. FM RADIO. Early commercial radio was exclusively amplitude-modulation (AM) radio. Frequency modulation (FM) was invented about 1933 by Edwin H. Armstrong, whose first experimental FM station went on the air in 1939. By World War II several hundred FM broadcasting licenses had been granted; by the end of the 1960s there were some 2000 FM stations in operation (as opposed to 4200 AM stations), and the majority of these were either noncommercial stations or carried the same programs as their owners' AM stations. In 1968 the Federal Communications Commission ordered most of the owners of both AM and FM stations in the same area to carry different programs on each. Since FM radio had a wider range of frequencies and dynamics, was virtually immune from interference and static, and was capable of carrying a stereophonic signal (a facility that was developed only later for AM), it invited music programming, particularly after the development of stereophonic recording in 1960 and the resulting interest in "hi-fi" (high-fidelity) audio equipment. By the late 1970s FM had become the dominant medium for radio music, and many AM stations abandoned music entirely for "talk-show" formats. The balance between AM and FM stations changed dramatically: in 1984, while AM stations numbered 4741 (not many more than in the 1960s), FM stations had increased to 3680, with an additional 1169 devoted to educational programming.

One limitation of FM radio is that transmissions can be received only by line-of-sight contact (whereas AM signals, especially those transmitted by the powerful "clear channel" 50,000-watt stations, can be received thousands of miles from the point of transmission). This limitation tended to make FM commercially unattractive, since the size of the audience for any station was comparatively small and advertising correspondingly difficult to attract; when this was added to the cost of meeting the requirement imposed by the 1968 FCC order that AM and FM programming be different, many commercial stations could no longer afford to continue FM broadcasting. These factors, however, did not apply to small, noncommercial stations, and many FM stations were set up by colleges and universities; some of these emulated commercial stations in their programming, but more provided outlets for kinds of music neglected by commercial radio, especially classical concert music, jazz, experimental music, and avant-garde pop and rock. Besides college stations, stations supported by listeners in a few major cities – notably the Pacifica Foundation stations KPFA in Berkeley, California, and WBAI in New York – began to offer eclectic, progressive programs.

Most of the music broadcast from FM stations is prerecorded; program material is provided not only by commercial disc recordings but, increasingly as tape-recording technology has improved, by tapes of live concerts. By the early 1980s listeners to FM radio on both the National Public Radio (NPR) and the commercial stations were being offered series by practically every major American orchestra (for example, the Minnesota Orchestra, the St.

2. Ed Sullivan (center) with the Beatles in the CBS Studios, New York, 9 February 1964

Louis SO, and the St. Paul Chamber Orchestra on NPR, and the Boston SO, the Philadelphia and Cleveland orchestras, and the Detroit SO on commercial stations), as well as European musical events such as the Salzburg Music Festival and the Utrecht Early Music Festival.

NPR was established in 1970 as a nonprofit, private corporation with funding provided by the Corporation for Public Broadcasting, membership fees (from listeners to individual stations), and grants from corporations, foundations, and federal agencies. The primary role of NPR is to provide a variety of programming and other support services to affiliated stations, most of them at colleges or universities or municipally owned. The music programming of NPR, which tends not to emphasize rock and pop, relies heavily on recordings of live concerts and operas; its "World of Opera" series has included broadcasts of such American operas as the San Diego Opera production of Menotti's *La loca*, Sarah Caldwell's production of Sessions's *Montezuma*, and the production by the Atlanta SO of Joplin's *Treemonisha*. Works produced by the San Francisco Opera are broadcast each autumn. The tendency of NPR to homogenize the programming of otherwise independent stations was offset to some degree in the late 1970s when it began to offer satellite transmission time to any of its affiliates that wished to syndicate programs to other member stations. NPR's television counterpart is the Public Broadcasting Service (PBS), which offers operas from the Metropolitan, symphonic concerts by the New York PO, and other concerts (such as those given by the Chamber Music Society of Lincoln Center, which are broadcast in the series "Live from Lincoln Center"). PBS also broadcasts special concerts, such as those by the Vienna PO under Bernstein, and presents the long-running country-music program "Austin City Limits," which began in the mid-1970s.

6. Trends in the 1980s. Broadcasting in the USA refuses to be homogeneous. The decentralized ownership of broadcast licenses allows all kinds of music to be transmitted. There is even a small number of commercial radio stations broadcasting classical music, notable among which are WQXR and WNCN (New York), KFAC (Los Angeles), WTMI (Miami), WCRB (Boston), WQRS (Detroit), KFUO (St. Louis), KSCM (San Francisco), and WGMS (Washington, DC). These compete with stations that the radio industry classifies as "beautiful music" or "easy listening" stations, which broadcast nonintrusive, gentle instrumental music (or its vocal counterpart, called "adult contemporary"). Many cities and towns in the USA have, moreover, at least one full-time religious music station; for purposes of audience targeting, the music these stations offer is termed by the industry "contemporary Christian" (if white) or "inspirational" or "gospel" (if black). Since the late 1940s there has also been an increasing amount of music broadcast for ethnic communities whose language is other than English. With the divestiture of unprofitable AM outlets by large broadcasting corporations, music of minority interest has moved increasingly to the AM band. Additionally, large parts of the USA can receive music from Mexican AM stations, which often transmit at much higher levels of power than American broadcasters are allowed.

Cable television services, which developed rapidly in major metropolitan areas in the early 1980s, have included a wide repertory of music on special arts channels and brought one major musical innovation to television audiences: music video. MTV (Music Television), for example, a 24-hour-a-day rock-music cable service, presented to about 24 million homes in 1984 what might be called "picture radio." Eschewing television's traditional half-hour-long program modules, it offers brief video vignettes based on recorded versions of currently popular songs; these are rotated rapidly, in a pace like that of a rock-oriented radio show, and are introduced by a "video jockey."

In the mid-1980s there is speculation about direct satellite-to-home broadcast service, now in the initial phases of development. And some envision a telephone-line music-delivery service to home recording systems, to supplement or replace purchase of discs or tapes for play at home.

BIBLIOGRAPHY

P. W. Dykema: *Music as Presented by the Radio* (New York, 1935)
H. G. Kinscella: *Music on the Air* (New York, 1937)
W. R. Sur: *Experimental Study of the Teaching of Music Understanding by Radio* (diss., U. of Wisconsin, 1942)
T. W. Adorno: "A Social Critique of Radio Music," *Kenyon Review*, vii (1945), 208
M. J. Haggans: *The Broadcasting of Sacred Music* (Boston, 1945)
G. Chase, ed.: *Music in Radio Broadcasting* (New York, 1946)
E. LaPrade: *Broadcasting Music* (New York, 1947)
R. U. Nelson and W. Rubsamen: "Bibliography of Books and Articles on Music in Film and Radio," *HMYB 1949–50*, 318
L. C. Hood: *The Programming of Classical Music Broadcast over the Major Radio Networks* (New York, 1956)
H. B. Summers: *A Thirty-year History of Programs Carried on National Radio Networks in the United States, 1926–1956* (Columbus, OH, 1958/*R*1971)
R. C. Burke: *A History of Televised Opera in the United States* (Ann Arbor, MI, 1963)
S. Shemel and M. W. Krasilovsky: *This Business of Music* (New York, 1964, rev. and enlarged 5/1985)
E. Barnouw: *A History of Broadcasting in the United States* (New York, 1966–70)
W. B. Emery: *National and International Systems of Broadcasting: their History, Operation and Control* (Ann Arbor, MI, 1969)
R. Nye: *The Unembarrassed Muse* (New York, 1970), pt 6
A. Passman: *The Deejays* (New York, 1971)
J. Bornoff and L. Salter: *Music and the Twentieth Century Media* (Florence, Italy, 1972)
J. R. Williams: *This Was "Your Hit Parade"* (Rockland, ME, 1973)
E. Helm, ed.: *Music and Tomorrow's Public* (Paris, 1975)
L. W. Lichty and M. C. Topping: *American Broadcasting: a Source Book on the History of Radio and Television* (New York, 1975)
C. Hamm: *Yesterdays: Popular Song in America* (New York, 1979)
T. A. DeLong: *The Mighty Music Box: the Golden Age of Musical Radio* (Los Angeles, 1980)
T. K. Eberly: *Music in the Air: America's Changing Tastes in Popular Music, 1920–1980* (New York, 1982)
"Radio," *Ear*, viii/5 (1984) [whole issue]

For further bibliography *see* Performing rights societies.

RITA H. MEAD/NED SUBLETTE

Broadcast Music, Inc. (BMI). Performing rights licensing organization founded in 1940. In addition to its primary activity of licensing the works of its writer and publisher affiliates to the users of music in copyright (*see* Performing rights societies, §2), BMI sponsors the BMI-Lehman Engel Musical Theatre Workshop, the BMI Awards to Student Composers competition (founded 1951), the Los Angeles Songwriters Showcase, and numerous symposia for songwriters around the country; it also gives annual awards in the fields of pop and country music. The New York office maintains the BMI/Carl Haverlin Archives, which is available for scholarly research (*see* Libraries and collections, §3); selections from its holdings are seen in occasional traveling exhibitions. There are other main offices in Los Angeles and Nashville, as well as regional licensing offices in other large cities. BMI publishes a quarterly news magazine *The Many Worlds of Music* (1963–), a handbook for writer and publisher affiliates, documentary brochures on over 70 of its affiliated composers, and numerous other promotional and educational pamphlets.

For bibliography, *see* COPYRIGHT; PERFORMING RIGHTS SOCIETIES.

BARBARA A. PETERSEN

Broadfoot, Eleanor. *See* CISNEROS, ELEONORA DE.

Brockton, Lester. Pseudonym of MAYHEW LAKE.

Brockway, Howard (*b* Brooklyn, NY, 22 Nov 1870; *d* New York, 20 Feb 1951). Composer, pianist, and teacher. He studied piano with H. O. C. Kortheuer and in 1890 went to Berlin, where he remained for five years, studying composition with Otis Boise and piano with Heinrich Barth. A concert of his chamber and orchestral pieces was given by the Berlin PO on 23 February 1895, and the maturity of his work made a striking impression; he also acquired a publisher in Berlin. On his return to the USA, he began a career in New York. During the years 1903–9 he taught at the Peabody Institute; back in New York, he taught at the Institute of Musical Art and later at the Mannes College, and also gave concerts and lecture-recitals. In 1910 he was elected to the National Institute of Arts and Letters. He produced few original works after 1911, but his arrangements of Kentucky folksongs, collected with Loraine Wyman, enjoyed popularity in the USA and England. Retiring from the Juilliard School (the successor to the Institute) in 1940, he continued teaching privately. Brockway was a gifted composer, with a rare sensibility and unique warmth of melody and harmony. Notable among his large works are the Violin Sonata and the Cello Suite.

WORKS

(*selective list*)

Orch: Ballad, op.11, 1894; Sym., op.12, 1894; Cavatina, vn, orch, op.13 (1895); Sylvan Suite, op.19 (1900); Scherzo (Scherzino), n.d., lost; Pf Conc., n.d., inc., lost

Chamber: Vn Sonata, op.9 (1894); Moment musical, vn, pf, op.16 (1897); Romance, vn, pf, op.18 (1897); 3 Compositions: Aria, The Coquette, Romance, vn, pf, op.31 (1906); Suite, vc, pf, op.35 (1908); Pf Qnt, ?op.38, lost; Fugue, 2 vn, pf, n.d.

Choral: Cantate Domino, op.6, 1892; 2 Choruses: Wings of a Dove, Hey Nonino, op.24 (1899); Des Saengers Fluch, op.27 (1902); Herr Oluf, op.37 (1913); Matin Song (Heywood), op.40 (1911)

Pf pieces incl. Dreaming; Unrest; At Twilight; An Idyl of Murmuring Water; 2 Preludes, 1925, unpubd

Songs incl. Would thy faith were mine, Intimations, The Mocking Bird, An Answer; folksong arr. incl. Lonesome Tunes (New York, 1916); 20 Kentucky Mountain Songs (Boston, 1920)

MSS in *DLC*

Principal publishers: G. Schirmer, Schlesinger (Berlin), Church (Cincinnati)

BIBLIOGRAPHY

R. Hughes: *Contemporary American Composers* (Boston, 1900, 3/1914)

BARTON CANTRELL/R

Broder, Nathan (*b* New York, 1 Dec 1905; *d* New York, 16 Dec 1967). Editor and writer on music. He attended City College, New York, and studied music privately, but as a music scholar he was largely self-educated. He was associate editor of the *Musical Quarterly* (1945–67) and manager of the publications department at G. Schirmer (1945–54); he subsequently became executive director of the American Section of RISM (1961–5) and music editor at W. W. Norton & Co., New York (1963–7). He also taught at Columbia University (1946–52, 1959–62) and served as president of the American Musicological Society (1963–4).

Although Broder's career was devoted largely to guiding and publishing the work of others, he was himself a productive scholar. He published a book of essays, *The Great Operas of Mozart* (1962; it includes librettos translated by W. H. Auden and others), several articles on Mozart, and a standard edition of Mozart's piano sonatas and fantasias. He also assisted Reese in writing *Music in the Middle Ages* (1940) and wrote on contemporary Americans, including Barber (1954).

JON NEWSOM/R

Brombaugh, John (*b* Dayton, OH, 1 March 1937). Organ builder. A graduate of the University of Cincinnati, he was apprenticed to Charles Fisk, Fritz Noack, and Rudolph von Beckerath before establishing his own business in Middletown, Ohio, in 1968. Unlike many small builders, he felt it important to maintain a complete operation in which pipes, keyboards, and other components were made in his own workshop rather than by subcontractors. After several small but distinguished instruments, he built his first sizable organ in 1970, for the First Lutheran Church of Lorain, Ohio. Brombaugh's engineering skills are complemented by a scholarly interest in historic instruments, and he has been a pioneer in creating organs incorporating historic visual, tonal, and mechanical principles, principally derived from north European Renaissance and Baroque practices. One of the

Organ by John Brombaugh & Co. in the Ashland Avenue Baptist Church, Toledo, Ohio

first organs to be built exclusively according to these principles was completed by Brombaugh's company in 1972 and is in the Ashland Avenue Baptist Church, Toledo, Ohio (see illustration). In 1977 Brombaugh moved his firm to larger quarters in Eugene, Oregon, having completed an important instrument for the Lutheran Church there in 1976. His practice organs and positives have been popular with educational institutions. Some of his instruments incorporate features such as swell divisions that permit historically faithful performances of the Romantic repertory. One of Brombaugh's mechanical innovations is a drawknob with three positions that regulates the level and amplitude of wind pressure by controlling the concussion bellows and the Tremulant. Notable instruments can be found in the United Methodist Church, Oberlin, Ohio (1974), Grace Church, Ellensburg, Washington (1974), St. Mark's Church, Storrs, Connecticut (1978), Fairchild Chapel, Oberlin College (1981), and the Seventh Day Adventist Church, Collegedale, Tennessee (1985).

BIBLIOGRAPHY

D. Boe: "The Brombaugh Organ at Toledo, Ohio," *Organ Yearbook*, v (1974), 115

U. Pape: *The Tracker Organ Revival in America* (Berlin, n.d. [?1977])

J. Hamilton: "An Emerging US Organ-building Movement," *MT*, cxxv (1984), 347, 407

BARBARA OWEN

Bronson, Bertrand H(arris) (*b* Lawrenceville, NJ, 22 June 1902). Scholar of English literature and folksong. He studied English literature at the University of Michigan (BA 1921), Harvard University (MA 1922), and Yale University (PhD 1927); he also received an MA at Oxford University (1929). After teaching at the University of Michigan (1925–6), he joined the English department of the University of California, Berkeley, in 1927, later becoming professor (1945) and professor emeritus (1969). In addition to writing on Chaucer and 18th-century English literature, Bronson is the author of an important study, *The Ballad as Song* (1969), and has edited a four-volume collection, *The Traditional Tunes of the Child Ballads* (1959–72).

PAULA MORGAN

Brook, Barry S(helley) (*b* New York, 1 Nov 1918). Musicologist. He studied at the City College of New York (BS 1939), and at Columbia University (MA 1942), and received the doctorate from the Sorbonne in Paris in 1959. In 1945 he joined the faculty of Queens College and in 1967 was appointed executive officer of the PhD program in music at CUNY. Brook has studied musical iconography, the sociology of music, and music and aesthetics of the 18th and 19th centuries. His doctoral dissertation, *La symphonie française dans la seconde moitié du XVIIIe siècle* (published in 1962), is an exemplary study of the development of the French symphony in the second part of the 18th century. He is the general editor of the anthology series *The Symphony: 1720–1840* (1969–). As editor of a facsimile edition of the Breitkopf Thematic Catalogues (1966), he assembled into a single volume the many parts of the earliest and largest printed thematic catalogue; he has also published a bibliography of thematic catalogues (1972). He is general editor of *RILM Abstracts*. His investigations of computer applications for music documentation include the development of the "Plaine and Easie Code System" for notating music, which he presented in *Musicology and the Computer: Musicology 1966–2000* (1970). A central figure in the inception and administration of international musicological projects, he has done much to further collaboration on music-bibliographical projects, including, besides RILM, the Répertoire International d'Iconographie Musicale (RIdIM).

PAULA MORGAN

Brookmeyer, Bob [Robert] (*b* Kansas City, MO, 19 Dec 1929). Jazz valve trombonist and pianist. He studied at the Kansas City Conservatory and began his career as a pianist in various dance bands. In 1952 he took up the valve trombone, and immediately became an important figure in the West Coast style of jazz, particularly after replacing Chet Baker in Gerry Mulligan's "pianoless" quartet (1953–4); at the same time he continued to perform on piano, most notably in a revealing duet album with Bill Evans (1959). In the early 1960s he led a popular combo with the trumpeter and flugelhorn player Clark Terry. He was a founding member of the Thad Jones – Mel Lewis Orchestra (1965), for whom he wrote several outstanding arrangements. From 1968 he was a studio musician on the West Coast, and frequently played as a sideman with well-known mainstream jazz musicians. Brookmeyer was the first noteworthy jazz musician since Juan Tizol to specialize on valve trombone, but unlike Tizol he was an excellent soloist, playing in a good-humored linear style with, at times, pronounced overtones of blues and swing. As a pianist he developed a distinctive percussive and dissonant manner entirely outside the main traditions of jazz pianism.

RECORDINGS
(selective list)

As leader: *The Blues Hot and Cool* (1960, Verve 68385); *Gloomy Sunday* (1961, Verve 68455)

As leader with others: B. Evans: *The Ivory Hunters* (1959, UA4044); C. Terry: *Tonight* (1964, Mainstream 6043); *The Power of Positive Swinging* (1964, Mainstream 6054); *Gingerbread Men* (1966, Mainstream 6086)

As sideman: G. Mulligan: [*Paris Concert*] (1954, Vogue 7381/7383)

BIBLIOGRAPHY

L. Feather: "Brookmeyer's Tale of Three Cities," *Down Beat*, xxii/18 (1955), 9

B. Coss: "Bob Brookmeyer: Strength and Simplicity," *Down Beat*, xxviii/2 (1961), 19

D. Morgenstern: "Bob Brookmeyer: Master of the Brass Stepchild," *Down Beat*, xxxiv/2 (1967), 14

M. Williams: "Giuffre, Brookmeyer Reunion," *Down Beat*, xxxv/2 (1968), 15

"A Gallery of BMI Jazz Composers," *BMI: the Many Worlds of Music* (1981), no.3, p.25

J. BRADFORD ROBINSON

Brooks, Patricia (*b* New York, 7 Nov 1937). Soprano. At the age of ten she won an award from the radio station WQXR for her solo playing in a Mendelssohn piano concerto. She studied music at the Manhattan School, but at 15 took up dancing, studying with Martha Graham; having injured her knee, she turned to drama, appearing off-Broadway in Pirandello and O'Neill before deciding to become a singer. Having made her New York City Opera début on 12 October 1960, as Marianne in *Der Rosenkavalier*, she soon graduated to Sophie, to a leading role in Robert Ward's *The Crucible*, Violetta, Massenet's Manon, Leoncavallo's Nedda, Gilda, Lucia, and, perhaps most memorably, Mélisande. She made her Covent Garden début as the Queen of Shemakhan in *The Golden Cockerel* in December 1969, and appeared at Chicago, San Francisco, Toronto, and Santiago (Chile). In 1974 she played Berg's Lulu at Santa Fe and later at Houston. Brooks is a highly individual actress, and her performances were more often notable for theatrical impact than vocal perfection. She appeared in concerts throughout the USA. After her retirement from singing in 1978, Brooks taught at SUNY, Purchase, until 1981.

MARTIN BERNHEIMER/R

Brooks, Shelton (Leroy) (*b* Amesburg, Ont., 4 May 1886; *d* Los Angeles, CA, 6 Sept 1975). Songwriter, pianist, and vaudeville entertainer. He grew up in Detroit, where he taught himself music. For nearly half a century he toured the USA and Canada as an entertainer; he visited Europe with Lew Leslie's *Blackbirds of 1923* and appeared in a command performance for King George V and Queen Mary. Later he was a member of Ken Murray's successful revue *Blackouts* (1949). Although he never learned to read music, in the years around World War I he wrote a number of songs popularized by artists such as Sophie Tucker, Al Jolson, Mae West, Benny Goodman, and Ella Fitzgerald, including the highly successful *Some of these days* (1910) and *Darktown Strutters' Ball* (1917). The brash, often sexually suggestive style of these songs appealed to an age looking for relief from the stuffiness of Victorian morality. Brooks continued to compose songs until late in life, and long after the demand for his particular type of song had disappeared; by the time of his death he was almost completely forgotten as one of the most innovative and original songwriters of the early part of the century.

WORKS

Selective list of songs; unless otherwise stated, all are printed works published in Chicago, and all lyrics are by Brooks.

You ain't talkin' to me (M. Marshall) (1909); Honey Gal (1910); Some of these days (1910); Jean (New York, 1911); There'll come a time (1911); All Night Long (1912); You ain't no place but down South (C. Smith) (n.p., 1912); Rufe Johnson's Harmony Band, collab. M. Abrahams (New York, 1914); Walkin' the Dog (1916); Darktown Strutters' Ball (1917); I wonder where my easy rider's gone (n.p., 1929)

Principal publisher: Rossiter

BIBLIOGRAPHY

SouthernB

J. Burton: *The Blue Book of Tin Pan Alley*, ii (New York, 1965)

I. Whitcomb: "Shelton Brooks is Alive and Strutting," *Los Angeles Times Calendar* (18 May 1969), 12

SAM DENNISON

Brooks, William (Firdyce) (*b* New York, 17 Dec 1943). Musicologist and composer. He studied music and mathematics at Wesleyan University (BA 1965) and then attended the University of Illinois, receiving degrees in musicology (MM 1971) and composition and theory (DMA 1976). His instructors included Hamm in musicology and Johnston, Gaburo, Brun, and Cage in composition. He taught at the University of Illinois (1969–73) and at the University of California, Santa Cruz (1973–7); more recently he has been active as a freelance composer, scholar, and performer, and has taught at the University of Keele, England (1977–8), Middlebury College (1982), and the Institute for Studies in American Music, Brooklyn College (1983). He was awarded Woodrow Wilson and Danforth teaching fellowships and a Smithsonian Institution Fellowship (1979–80), and in 1982 received an NEA composers' grant. Brooks serves on the editorial board of *Popular Music* and was also adviser on 19th-century music for this dictionary. In his compositions Brooks has been strongly influenced by electronic sounds. He frequently uses American popular or folk idioms in his works, but challenges the listener (often humorously or cunningly) to hear old sounds in unexpected ways by recasting, juxtaposing, and transforming these familiar elements. He has sung as a tenor with several vocal ensembles, among them the Extended Vocal Techniques Ensemble (1976–7), Pomerium Musices (1977), and Electric Phoenix (1980–83).

WORKS

Stage: Untitled (Borges), 8 solo vv, 2 speakers, 1972; The Legacy (chamber opera, Brooks), 4 solo vv, live elec, 4 opt. actors, 1982–3; incidental music for 3 plays, 1985

Inst: Poempiece I: whitegold blue, fl, 1967; Poempiece II: how I fooled the Armies, b trbn, 1968; Bryant's Ridge Disco Phase no. 1 (R. Madison), singers, disco band, 1978; Wallpaper Pieces, pf, 1979–; Footnotes, gui, 1981–4; Doors, S, mixed chorus, pf, wind, perc, 1983

Vocal: Gertrude Stein Trilogy: I, Many Returns, 50 songs, Mez, pf, 1977, II, Medley, 7 songs, Mez, pf, 1978, III, Parlor Music, 1v, 1979–; Madrigals (O. Gibbons, S. Foster, Brooks), amp SATB qt, 1977–8; Duets, 8 untexted pieces, 1v, live elec, 1978–9

KATHERINE K. PRESTON

Broonzy, Big Bill [William Lee Conley] (*b* Scott, MS, 26 June 1893; *d* Chicago, IL, 14 Aug 1958). Blues singer and guitarist. He grew up in Arkansas, where he lived on a farm until he was in his late 20s. After working as a fiddle player in the rural South, he settled in Chicago in 1920. There he learned to play guitar, on which he was already an outstanding performer when he began to record ten years later. In the late 1930s and the 1940s he was sympathetically supported by Joshua Altheimer or Black Bob on piano in a manner reminiscent of Leroy Carr and Scrapper Blackwell. Broonzy sang in France in 1951 and subsequently made several visits to Europe, where he rediscovered the old country songs he had played in his early years. He also recorded more than 200 titles, including several versions of *John Henry* (1951, Vogue 118) and the protest song *Black, Brown and White* (1951, Vogue 125).

Big Bill Broonzy

One of the most prolifically recorded of blues singers, Broonzy formed a link between the country and urban blues traditions, playing with a light, lilting style. Some of his recorded blues are wistful, poetic statements, complemented by moaning notes on the guitar, such as *Big Bill Blues* (1932, Champion 16400) and *Friendless Blues* (1934, Bluebird 5535), while others are of a gently ribald or "hokum" character, including *Keep your hands off her* (1935, Bluebird 6188) and *Good Jelly* (1935, Bluebird 5998). He was later one of the first blues singers to use trumpet and saxophone in small-band accompaniments, but the several recordings he made in this form were less successful than his earlier work. Broonzy's generosity, his considerable talents, and his support of younger singers, combined with a homely wit, made him one of the most popular of all blues musicians.

BIBLIOGRAPHY

Y. Bruynoghe and W. Broonzy: *Big Bill Blues* (London, 1955/*R*1964)
S. B. Charters: *The Country Blues* (New York, 1959)
P. Oliver: *The Story of the Blues* (London, 1969)
S. Harris: *Blues Who's Who* (New Rochelle, NY, 1979)
Living Blues, no.55 (1982–3) [several articles]

PAUL OLIVER

Broude, Alexander. Firm of music publishers, distributors, importers, and exporters. Alexander Broude (*b* New York, 1 Jan 1909) was originally associated with his brother, Irving, in Broude Brothers, and began publishing music in the 1930s in New York. In 1954 Alexander severed the association and founded his own company, Alexander Broude, Inc. (ABI Music), which from 1962 published music for all media, including educational materials and music textbooks. 20th-century American composers in the Alexander Broude catalogue include Bales, Ruth Crawford, Dahl, Etler, Frost, Daniel Kessner, Alan Schulman, Elliott Schwartz, Riegger, and Westergaard. European composers of all periods, including Rachmaninoff, Casals, and Dallapiccola, are also published by the firm. Alexander Broude retired in 1970. In 1982 the company was bought by Michael Lefferts (president) and Dean Streit (vice-president).

W. THOMAS MARROCCO, MARK JACOBS/R

Broude Brothers. Firm of music publishers. Founded in the 1930s by Irving and Alexander Broude, it publishes scholarly editions and reference works as well as performing editions of works by modern and older composers. Its projects have included new editions of the collected works of Dietrich Buxtehude, Jean-Baptiste Lully, Marin Marais, Luca Marenzio, and Jean-Philippe Rameau. It publishes the series Monuments of Music and Music Literature in Facsimile, as well as historical sets such as Tudor Church Music, Masters and Monuments of the Renaissance, and Music at the Court of Ferrara. Among 20th-century composers published by the firm are Babbitt, Bacon, Berger, Bloch, Duke, Herrmann, Hovhaness, Krenek, La Montaine, Lockwood, Messiaen, Nin-Culmell, and Rozsa. Alexander Broude left the organization in 1954 and established his own firm. Irving Broude's widow, Anne, took over the firm after her husband's death in 1973; when Mrs. Broude retired in 1979, her son Ronald became president. The Broude Trust for the Publication of Musicological Editions was formed in 1981 to provide financial support for the preparation of the collected editions and historical sets.

W. THOMAS MARROCCO, MARK JACOBS/R

Brougham, John (*b* Dublin, Ireland, 9 May 1810; *d* New York, 7 June 1880). Playwright and actor. He was active in London from 1830 to 1842, then made his New York début on 4 October 1842. He toured widely in the USA, performing in Boston in 1846–8, then settled in New York, where he starred at Burton's Theatre. On 23 December 1850 he opened Brougham's Lyceum, but the venture failed and the house closed on 17 March 1852. From 1852 to 1860 Brougham acted at Wallack's and Burton's theaters and managed the Bowery. He spent five years in London, and on his return in 1865 he acted in and wrote for several different theaters in Boston, Philadelphia, and New York. He opened Brougham's Theatre in New York on 25 January 1869, but soon after was forced by the owner, Jim Fisk, to step down. From 1870 to 1877 he performed at Daly's and Wallack's theaters on Broadway and toured with stock companies. The following year his friends rescued him from destitution by organizing a benefit (17 January 1878), which provided him with an annuity for his last two years.

Brougham was a comic actor of great skill. He wrote more than 100 plays; most of the comedies used music extensively. *Little Nell and the Marchioness* (1867) became Lotta Crabtree's principal vehicle, but Brougham was best known for his burlesques: *Met-a-mora, or The Last of the Pollywogs* (1847), *Columbus el Filibustero!* (1857), *Much Ado about a Merchant of Venice* (1869), and especially *Po-ca-hon-tas, or The Gentle Savage* (1855; ed. R. Moody in *Dramas from the American Theater*, 1966, p.397). In these the musical references ranged from Meyerbeer to minstrelsy, with startling and hilarious juxapositions; by elevating music to a central place, Brougham enriched the burlesque form and prepared the way for later genres.

BIBLIOGRAPHY

Obituary, *New York Mirror* (12 June 1880)
W. Winter, ed.: *Life, Stories, and Poems of John Brougham* (Boston, 1881)
W. Winter: *Other Days* (New York, 1908/*R*1970)
"Notable Players of the Past and Present: John Brougham," *New York Clipper*, lviii (19 Feb 1910), 2
W. Winter: *The Wallet of Time* (New York, 1913/*R*1969)
D. Hawes: *John Brougham: American Playwright and Man of the Theatre* (diss., Stanford U., 1954)
P. M. Ryan, Jr.: "John Brougham: the Gentle Satirist," *Bulletin of the NYPL*, lxiii (1959), 619 [incl. list of works]
W. Brooks: "*Pocahontas*: her Life and Times," *American Music*, ii/4 (1984), 19

WILLIAM BROOKS

Brown, Clifford [Brownie] (*b* Wilmington, DE, 30 Oct 1930; *d* Pennsylvania, 26 June 1956). Jazz trumpeter. He studied mathematics at Delaware State College and music at Maryland State College. During these years he attracted attention through his exceptional performances with the college jazz band and his brief appearances in Philadelphia with leading jazz musicians such as Fats Navarro, Dizzy Gillespie, and Charlie Parker, all of whom praised and encouraged him. He spent a year in the hospital after an automobile accident in 1950, but then resumed his career in Philadelphia and in March 1952 made his first recordings with Chris Powell's Blue Flames. Brown joined the Tadd Dameron band for a recording session (later issued as *The Clifford Brown Memorial Album*) and for appearances in summer 1953 at Atlantic City, New Jersey. In September 1953 he toured Europe with Lionel Hampton's big band, making several recordings with American and European jazz musicians. On his return he performed with several East Coast groups, including a newly formed ensemble led by the drummer Art Blakey. In 1954 he and the drummer Max Roach formed the Brown-Roach Quintet, with which he was associated until he was killed in an automobile accident two years later. This quintet was one of the most significant jazz groups of the 1950s, and had a major influence on the establishment of the style later known as "hard bop."

Brown was one of the outstanding jazz trumpeters of the 1950s, and his reputation as an extraordinary improviser endures. His

Clifford Brown, early 1950s

playing reflected a synthesis of certain stylistic aspects of Gillespie, Miles Davis, and Navarro; it was characterized by a rich, broad tone and percussive attack, unusually long yet carefully shaped phrases, extraordinary virtuosity, and a seemingly unending flow of logically developed musical ideas. His most mature work was with the Brown-Roach Quintet, as reflected in their albums *Study in Brown* and *At Basin Street*. His style exerted a pervasive influence on jazz improvisation in the 1960s and 1970s, and represented an alternative approach to the subdued manner of Davis. His influence may be seen most directly in the work of Lee Morgan and Freddie Hubbard.

RECORDINGS
(selective list)

As co-leader: with A. Farmer: *Swedish All-stars* (1953, Prst. 167); with M. Roach: *Study in Brown* (1955, EmArcy 36037); *At Basin Street* (1956, EmArcy 36070)
As sideman: C. Powell: Ida Red (1952, OK 6875); T. Dameron: *A Study in Dameronia* (1953, Prst. 159); A. Blakey: *A Night at Birdland*, i-iii (1954, BN 5037-9); S. Rollins: *Sonny Rollins plus Four* (1956, Prst. 7038)

BIBLIOGRAPHY

A. Hodeir: *Jazz: its Evolution and Essence* (New York, 1956/*R*1975)
R. Atkins: "Clifford Brown," *Jazz Review*, ii/11 (1959), 24
——: "Clifford Brown," *Jazz Monthly*, vi/6 (1960), 4
A. Morgan: "Clifford Brown," *Jazz on Record*, ed. A. McCarthy (London, 1968), 29
R. Bolton: "Clifford Brown," *Jazz Journal*, xxii/5 (1969), 6
J. G. Jepsen: "Clifford Brown: a Complete Discography," *Down Beat Music: 15th Yearbook* (1970), 109
M. L. Stewart: *Structural Development in the Jazz Improvisational Technique of Clifford Brown* (diss., U. of Michigan, 1973); pubd in *Jazzforschung*, vi-vii (1974–5), 141–273
C. Sheridan: "A Study in Brown," *Jazz Journal*, xxix/6 (1976), 4
M. L. Stewart: "Some Characteristics of Clifford Brown's Improvisational Style," *Jazzforschung*, xi (1979), 135
B. Weir: *Clifford Brown Discography* (Cardiff, Wales, 1983)

OLLY WILSON

Brown, Earle (Appleton, Jr.) (*b* Lunenburg, MA, 26 Dec 1926). Composer. He was a leading representative of the "New York school" established in the early 1950s in association with Cage, Tudor, Feldman, and Wolff. After training in engineering and mathematics at Northeastern University, Boston, he studied composition with Roslyn Brogue Henning (1947–50) and theory with McKillop at the Schillinger School (1946–50). He taught the Schillinger system privately in Denver (1950–52) and then, motivated by his interest in the art of Alexander Calder and Jackson Pollock and by his contacts with Cage, he moved to New York to participate in the Project for Music for Magnetic Tape with Cage and Tudor. His development of graphic notation in 1952 and of open form in 1953 established him as a leader of the American avant garde. Also at this time he was actively involved in various European festivals, principally the Darmstadt summer courses. He worked as an editor and recording engineer for Capitol Records and in 1960 was made director of the "contemporary sound series" of Mainstream Records. From 1968 to 1973 he was professor of composition and composer-in-residence at the Peabody Conservatory, Baltimore, where he received an honorary DMus in 1970; he has been visiting professor at several institutions, including SUNY, Buffalo (1975), the University of California, Berkeley (1976), and Yale University (1980–81). He was composer-in-residence in the Künstler Programm in West Berlin (1970–71), with the Rotterdam PO (1974), at the California Institute of the Arts (1974–83), and at the Aspen Music Festival (1975, 1981); in 1981 he was guest conductor with the Saarbrücken Rundfunk orchestra. His honors include a Guggenheim Fellowship (1965–6), an award from the National Institute of Arts and Letters (1972), an NEA grant (1974), and the Brandeis University Creative Arts Award (1977), as well as commissions from Merce Cunningham, Pierre Boulez, Luigi Nono, Lukas Foss, the Denver SO, and many others.

Early in his career Brown realized that total reliance on an

1. Earle Brown, 1985

aural system (such as the serial method of Webern or Babbitt) was a limitation to his music. In a foreword to the series of pieces published as *Folio* (1952) and *Four Systems* (1954) he outlined his approach to composition: "to have elements exist in space . . . the score being a picture of this space at one instant . . . a performer must set all this in motion . . . either sit and let it move or move through it at all speeds." Brown's first significant works were written in "time notation," i.e., with rationally chosen pitch relationships but no metrical obstruction to the flow of the music. The Music for Violin, Cello and Piano (1952) is an example of 12-tone technique in a free and spacious organization. Webern's influence is obvious in these early pieces, particularly in their reliance on silence and on novel string techniques, and this type of melodic composition remained a part of Brown's style, even in much later works involving some use of graphics.

November 1952 and *December 1952* were the first pieces by Brown written in graphic notation. The former, subtitled *Synergy*, eliminated standard staves for a completely lined sheet with conventional note-heads and markings of duration and intensity; instrumentation, clefs, attacks, and distances between notes were to be decided by the performer. For *December 1952* Brown conceived the first wholly graphic notation, removing all traditional symbols (see fig. 2). The score presents black rectangles of various sizes irregularly disposed on a white background, to be interpreted along the lines of the quotation above. The introduction of open-form notation was a less radical step but an essential development in escaping from what had become, for Brown, an increasingly confining system. In open-form composition the ordering and combination of the written-out material is left to the choice of the performers or conductor. The first such piece was Brown's *Twenty-five Pages* (1953), a score consisting of 25 pages to be arranged in any order. Brown's open-form technique may be considered an aural application of an essentially visual procedure, developed principally in Calder's mobiles. His first orchestral work in open form was *Available Forms I* (1961), in which the material is given in several large sections, each divided into five subsections. The conductor decides the sequence of sections and subsections. This principle was expanded in *Available Forms II* (1962) for large orchestra with two conductors.

Brown's basic concern in his notational innovations has been for the involvement of the performer as a musician aware of his capabilities to work within a framework provided by the composer. The aim was to free the player from confusing and arduous tasks, at the same time increasing the identification of the musician with the material and heightening the spontaneity and uniqueness of the performance. In addition to composed musical structuring, almost all of Brown's music after 1960 has employed both graphics and open form, the major works of this later period being *Corroboree*, *Modules I* and *II*, *Cross Sections and Color Fields*, *Windsor Jambs*, and *Sounder Rounds*. Many of his works have been recorded.

See also NOTATION, §2.

WORKS

All published unless otherwise stated; most places and dates of first performance unavailable.

Fugue, pf, 1949, unpubd; Home Burial, pf, 1949, unpubd; Trio, cl, bn, pf, 1949, inc., unpubd; Passacaglia, pf, 1950, unpubd; Strata, 2 pf, 1950, unpubd; Str Qt, 1950, unpubd; 3 Pieces, pf, 1951; Perspectives, pf, 1952; Music for Violin, Cello and Piano, 1952

Folio, unspecified instrumentation, 1952–3: October 1952, November 1952 (Synergy), December 1952, MM 87 and MM 135, Music for Trio for Five Dancers, 1953 [title]; arr. chamber ens, 1981

Music for "Tender Buttons" (G. Stein), speaker, fl, hn, harp, 1953, unpubd

Octet I, 8 tapes, 1952–3, unpubd

Twenty-five Pages, 1–25 pf, 1953; New York, 14 April 1954

Four Systems, unspecified instrumentation, 1954, arr. chamber ens, 1981

Indices, concert and ballet versions, chamber orch, 1954, unpubd

Music for Cello and Piano, 1954–5

Four More, pf, 1956, unpubd

Octet II, 8 tapes, 1957, unpubd

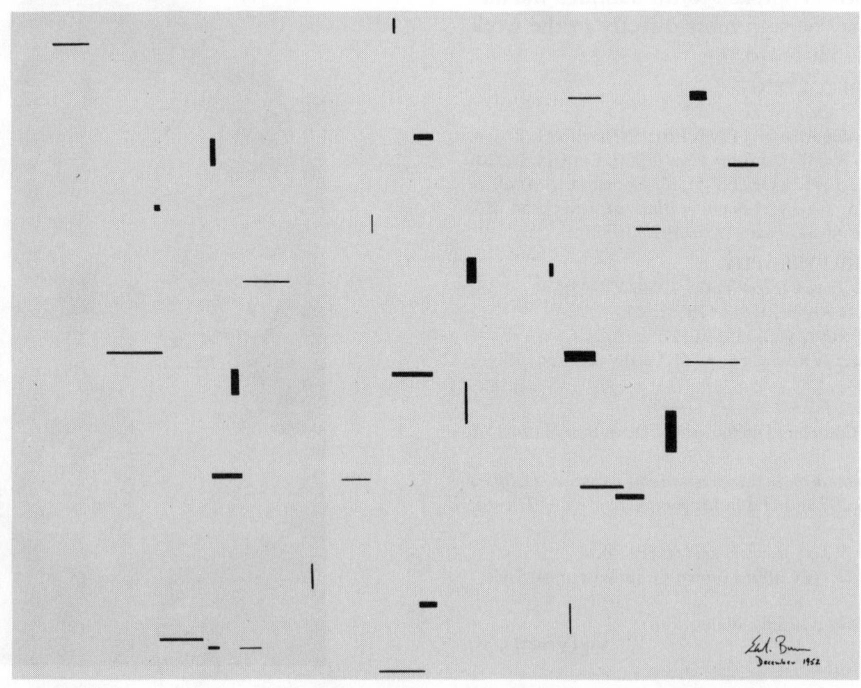

2. *The score of Brown's "December 1952"*

Pentathis, fl, b cl, tpt, trbn, harp, pf qt, 1957–8
Hodograph I, fl, pf + cel, bells + vib + mar, 1959
Available Forms I, 18 insts, 1961
Light Music, large orch, lights, elec, 1961, unpubd
Available Forms II, large orch, 2 conductors, 1962
Novara, fl, b cl, tpt, trbn, harp, pf qt, 1962
From Here, 4S, 4A, 4T, 4B, 20 insts, 1963
Times Five, fl, trbn, harp, vn, vc, 4-track tape, 1963
Corroboree, 3/2 pf, 1964
Nine Rarebits, 1/2 hpd, 1965
String Quartet 1965, 1965
Calder Piece, 4 perc, mobile, 1963–6, unpubd
Modules I–II, orch, 1966, III, 1969
Event: Synergy II, 11 ww, 8 str, 1967–8
Small Pieces for Large Chorus, 1969–70
Syntagm III, fl, b cl, vib, mar, harp, pf + cel, vn, vc, 1970
New Piece Loops, 17 insts, 1971–2, part of projected Folio II
Time Spans, large orch, 1972
Centering, vn, chamber orch, 1973
Sign Sounds, 18 insts, 1972
Cross Sections and Color Fields, orch, 1975
Windsor Jambs (Transients) (wordless text), Mez, fl, cl, pf, perc, vn, va, vc, 1980
Folio II, unspecified insts, 1981
Sounder Rounds, orch, 1982; Saarbrücken, Germany, 12 May 1983, cond. E. Brown
Tracer, fl, ob, bn, vn, vc, db, 4-track tape, 1984; West Berlin, Germany, 8 Feb 1985

Principal publishers: Associated, Schott, Universal

BIBLIOGRAPHY

EwenD
J. Cage: *Silence* (Middletown, CT, 1961, 2/1966)
G. Chase, ed.: *The American Composer Speaks* (Baton Rouge, LA, 1966
J. Cage: *A Year from Monday* (New York, 1967)
——: *Notations* (New York, 1969)
D. Henahan: "Earle Brown: they love him in Baden-Baden," *New York Times* (21 June 1970)
V. Thomson: *American Music since 1910* (New York, 1971)
H. Russcol: *The Liberation of Sound* (Englewood Cliffs, NJ, 1972)
M. Nyman: *Experimental Music: Cage and Beyond* (London, 1974), 45ff, 58
D. Rosenberg and B. Rosenberg: "Earle Brown," *The Music Makers* (New York, 1979), 79
J. LaBarbara: "Earle Brown's Homage to Alexander Calder," *HiFi/MusAm*, xxx/7 (1980), 12
H.-J. Herbort: "New Discoveries of 'Open Form,'" *Die Zeit* (5 June 1981)
P. L. Quist: *Indeterminate Form in the Works of Earle Brown* (diss., Peabody Conservatory of Music, 1984)

WILLIAM BLAND/JAMES WIERZBICKI

Brown, Francis H(enry) (*b* Newburyport, MA, 6 April 1818; *d* Stamford, CT, 23 June 1891). Pianist, composer, and teacher. He lived for a time in Boston, where he was a protégé of Jonas Chickering. After an injury to his hand prevented study abroad, he went to Providence in 1849 and became organist there at the First Baptist Church in America. In 1856 he moved to New York, where he joined the faculty of the Spingler Institute on Union Square. Following the Civil War he built a conservatory with a 400-seat concert hall in Stamford, and expanded his teaching to Bridgeport and other communities in southern Connecticut. Brown published more than 200 compositions as well as several pedagogical works, including the *Institute Chorus Book* (1857). Many of his songs and piano pieces were very successful: *Will you come to my mountain home?* (1845) sold 60,000 copies, and *Pride Polka* (1850) over 100,000.

BIBLIOGRAPHY

A. R. Coolidge: "Francis Henry Brown 1818–1891: American Teacher and Composer," *JRME*, ix (1961), 10–37 [incl. list of works]

ARLAN R. COOLIDGE

Brown, Frankie. Pseudonym of TED DAFFAN.

Brown, Howard Mayer (*b* Los Angeles, CA, 13 April 1930). Musicologist and editor. He graduated from Harvard College (BA 1951), studied privately in Vienna, and returned to Harvard in 1953 (MA 1954, PhD 1959). He first taught at Wellesley College (1958–60) and in 1960 was appointed assistant professor at the University of Chicago, becoming professor in 1967. In 1972 he succeeded Thurston Dart as the King Edward Professor of Music, King's College, University of London; he returned to Chicago in 1974. He served as president of the American Musicological Society in 1979–80. As his practical editions, performances, and recordings indicate, Brown represents a new breed of musicologist which emerged from the American universities beginning in the 1950s. These scholars seek to put their knowledge to use not only in research, teaching, and publishing, but also in performing and conducting early music. Brown's studies on Renaissance music have been especially valuable in two areas: the late 15th- and early 16th-century chanson and 16th-century instrumental music. His *Instrumental Music Printed before 1600: a Bibliography* is the standard and fundamental work from which all modern studies proceed. His *Musical Iconography* (with Joan Lascelle) offers the first comprehensive method for cataloguing and thus gaining access to the huge reservoir of information concerning music to be found in the visual arts of the West. He is also the editor of the facsimile series *Italian Opera, 1640–1770* (1977–). Brown was elected a Fellow of the American Academy of Arts and Sciences in 1980, and in 1984 he won the Otto Kinkeldey Award of the American Musicological Society for his edition *A Florentine Chansonnier from the Time of Lorenzo the Magnificent* (1983).

WRITINGS

Music in the French Secular Theater, 1400–1550 (diss., Harvard U., 1959; Cambridge, Mass., 1963)
Instrumental Music Printed before 1600: a Bibliography (Cambridge, Mass., 1965)
with J. Lascelle: *Musical Iconography: a Manual for Cataloguing Musical Subjects in Western Art before 1800* (Cambridge, Mass., 1972)
Sixteenth-century Instrumentation: the Music for the Florentine Intermedii, MSD, xxx (1973)
Embellishing Sixteenth-century Music (London, 1976)
Music in the Renaissance (Englewood Cliffs, NJ, 1976)

H. COLIN SLIM/R

Brown, James (*b* nr Augusta, GA, 3 May 1933). Popular singer, dancer, songwriter, and bandleader. After a tough early life that included at least one term in a state prison, he first worked as a professional musician in Macon, Georgia, in the mid-1950s, singing with a vocal quartet called the Famous Flames, who remained a part of his revue for the next ten years. He signed a recording contract with King Records of Cincinnati and in 1956 his recording of the pleading, almost devotional song *Please, please, please* became a hit on the rhythm-and-blues chart. Brown had an impeccable sense of timing and a harsh, rasping voice. He developed a varied repertory that reflected the styles of singers who had influenced him: gospel and blues songs like those of Ray Charles, frenetic dance tunes like Little Richard's, and sweet ballads like Billy Eckstine's. After the ballad *Try me* reached no. 1 on the rhythm-and-blues chart in 1958, Brown signed a contract with the national booking agency Universal Attractions, which established a band for him (the J.B.s), and arranged concerts at theaters in the larger northern cities. Slowly Brown began to perfect his live act, develop an original approach to songwriting, and attract a national black audience.

In 1963 Brown released *The James Brown Show*, a recording of a concert at the Apollo Theater in Harlem; it sold over a million copies, an unprecedented feat for a black musician. By then, Brown had become a consummate performer, not only as a singer (in which he was helped by the backing of a band that achieved an exhilarating precision) but also as a dancer: he combined leaps, splits, knee-drops, and a breathtaking step in which he appeared to skate on air while making backwards pedaling motions, in a mesmerizing choreography. As if to match the energy of his live performances, he began in his recordings (which after 1964 were all made under his supervision) to break away from the conventional structures of the popular song, and began to emphasize those elements of the music that most related to movement. While melody became less important, rhythms were articulated by repeated bass phrases reminiscent of Caribbean and African music, stuttering electric guitar, churning, polyrhythmic percussion lines, often played by two or three drummers, and jabbing wind parts, which sometimes delineated a simple riff based on one chord without change for five minutes or more (as in *There was a time*, 1968).

Brown's new, sparse style was first heard in 1964 on the song *Out of Sight* and became widely popular with the hit single of 1965 *Papa's got a brand new bag*. In these and later recordings Brown virtually invented the style now known as "funk." It was excellent for dancing to, and Brown's singles consistently reached the Top Ten on the rhythm-and-blues chart during the next ten years, making him the best-selling rhythm-and-blues artist of his era. He continued to record prolifically, and although many of his efforts, such as *Lowdown Popcorn* (1969), were ephemeral dance pieces, the fiery *Say it loud, I'm black and I'm proud* (no. 14, 1968) became an anthem for black teenagers, and the single *King Heroin* (no.40, 1972) featured an impassioned lecture on the evils of drugs. He also recorded a few experiments: *Super Bad* (1970), for example, contains a startlingly dissonant and highly effective saxophone solo that recalls the free jazz style of Albert Ayler.

Although his audience declined in the mid-1970s because of the predominance of the smoother disco style, Brown became prominent once more as younger musicians rediscovered funk at the end of the decade. This popularity was based largely on his almost legendary status as the "Godfather of Soul" (a title that Brown first used for himself in the early 1970s), the reputation of his early recordings, his appearance in 1980 in *The Blues Brothers*, a film with John Belushi and Dan Aykroyd, and his influence upon other artists. The last was evident mainly in the dazzling dance steps of Michael Jackson and the music of numerous funk groups, including Parliament/Funkadelic and Kool and the Gang, but it was not restricted to artists in the rhythm-and-blues tradition: David Bowie adopted Brown's hypnotic beat for songs such as *Fame* and *Golden Years*, and the Talking Heads used hard, plangent funk rhythms on their album *Remain in Light* (1980). The lean, streamlined sounds of rap and hip-hop, which emerged in New York in the early 1980s, also owe much to Brown's innovations: the pioneer of hip-hop, Afrika Bambaataa, who has acknowledged his debt to Brown, collaborated with him in 1984 on the single *Unity*. In 1983 Brown recorded an album, *Bring it On*, which received some critical acclaim, and he continues to perform sporadically.

At the height of his popularity in the late 1960s, Brown became an advocate of racial pride and of moderation in black politics; his concerts were regarded by white politicians as a safe outlet for black discontent, and in 1968 his endorsement was solicited by Hubert Humphrey, the Democratic presidential candidate.

James Brown, c1972

For further illustration *see* POPULAR MUSIC, fig. 10.

RECORDINGS

(selective list; recorded for King unless otherwise stated)

Singles: Please, please, please (Federal 12258, 1956); Try me (Federal 12370, 1956); Out of sight (Smash 1919, 1964); It's a man's world (6015, 1965); There was a time (6144, 1968); Say it loud, I'm black and I'm proud (6187, 1968); Lowdown Popcorn (6250, 1969); Super Bad (6329, 1970); King Heroin (Pol. 14116, 1972); Get on the good foot (Pol. 14139, 1972); Papa don't take no mess (Pol. 14255, 1974); Unity (Tommy Boy 847, 1984)

LPs: *The James Brown Show Live at the Apollo* (826, 1963); *Pure Dynamite* (883, 1964); *Raw Soul* (1016, 1967); *Sex Machine* (1115, 1970); *Hot Pants* (4054, 1971); *The Payback* (Pol. 3007, 1974); *Body Heat* (Pol. 6093, 1976); *Bring it On* (Churchill/Augusta 22001, 1983)

BIBLIOGRAPHY

SouthernB

C. White: Liner notes, *James Brown: Solid Gold* (Pol. 2679044, 1977)

A. Shaw: *Honkers and Shouters: the Golden Years of Rhythm and Blues* (New York, 1978)

R. Palmer: "James Brown," *The Rolling Stone Illustrated History of Rock & Roll*, ed. J. Miller (New York, rev. 2/1980), 136

G. Hirshey: *Nowhere to Run: the Story of Soul Music* (New York, 1984)

R. Palmer: "Return of James Brown," *New York Times* (11 July 1984), §C, p. 18

JIM MILLER

Brown, Les(ter Raymond) (*b* Reinerton, PA, 14 March 1912). Bandleader, arranger, and composer. He received his musical training at Ithaca (New York) College (1926–9), where his teachers included Patrick Conway and Wallingford Riegger, at the New York Military Academy (1929–32), and at Duke University (1932–6), where he also led his first dance band, the Duke Blue Devils (1935–6). After this band split up, he worked as an arranger in New York, then in 1938 formed a 12-piece dance orchestra. During the 1940s his band made many radio broadcasts, toured extensively, appeared in leading hotels, and had hit recordings with *Sentimental Journey* (1944, with Doris Day) and *I've got my love to keep me warm* (1948). 1947 marked the beginning of a long association with Bob Hope as music director for the entertainer's radio and television shows; with Hope he went on 16 Christmas tours around the world to entertain American troops. From the 1950s Brown's activities centered on television work in Hollywood where, with his "Band of Renown," he took part in such programs as "The Steve Allen Show" (1959–61) and "The Dean Martin Show" (1963–72). He also appeared as guest conductor with, among others, the orchestra of the Hollywood Bowl. Brown has written several songs, including *It's the time to be jolly*, *My number one dream came true*, *Are you still in love with me?*, and *Comes the sandman*.

BIBLIOGRAPHY

G. Simon: *The Big Bands* (New York, 1967, 4/1981), 99ff

C. Garrod: *Les Brown and his Orchestra 1936–1952* (Zephyrhills, FL, 1974) [discography]

MARK TUCKER

Brown, Lew [Brownstein, Louis] (*b* Odessa, Ukraine, 10 Dec 1893; *d* New York, 5 Feb 1958). Lyricist. He came to the USA with his family when he was five and began to write lyrics and parodies of songs while a teenager. In 1912 he began a collaboration with Albert Von Tilzer, achieving success with a number of songs, such as "I may be gone for a long, long time" (interpolated in *Hitchy-koo*, 1917) and "Oh, by jingo" (in *Linger Longer Letty*, 1919). Brown started to work with composer RAY HENDERSON in 1922; in 1925 they were joined by Buddy DeSylva and for a short time became the most successful songwriting team on Broadway. Brown continued to produce similar shows with Henderson after DeSylva's departure, but the vogue for politically slanted musicals in the early 1930s meant that their work no longer achieved the same popularity. Brown wrote one unsuccessful revue, *Calling All Stars* (1934), in collaboration with Harry Akst, before going to work as a producer in Hollywood. He wrote songs for several films, including "Baby, take a bow" (in *Stand Up and Cheer*, 1934), "Life begins when you're in love" (in *The Music Goes Round*, 1936), "The Lady Dances" (in *Strike Me Pink*, 1936), "That Old Feeling" (in *New Faces of 1937*, 1937), and "Don't sit under the apple tree" (in *Private Buckaroo*, 1942). He returned to Broadway only once, with *Yokel Boy* (1939, including "Comes Love"), which was also filmed.

Brown, Milton (*b* Stephenville, TX, 8 Sept 1903; *d* Crystal Springs, TX, 18 April 1936). Country-music singer and bandleader. In 1918 Brown moved to Fort Worth, where he sang in a barbershop quartet. In 1931, at a country dance, he met Bob Wills, then primarily a fiddler, and began to work with him on radio, first in a band called the Aladdin Laddies (on WBAP, Fort Worth) and later with the Light Crust Doughboys. Using the name Fort Worth Doughboys, Wills and Brown made their first recordings, *Nancy Jane* and *Sunbonnet Sue*, for Victor on 9 February 1932; these two sides are often considered to be the seminal recordings of the western swing movement. In 1932 Wills and Brown left the Doughboys to form separate bands; Brown's, the Musical Brownies, included violinist Cecil Brower and jazz pianist Fred Calhoun. The band's repertory, represented on its first recordings (made for Bluebird in 1934), included fiddle breakdowns, pop ballads, blues, cowboy songs, and jazz tunes, all played on string instruments. Later in 1934 Bob Dunn joined the band, playing the electric steel guitar, which was at that time a novelty. Regular radio appearances over the powerful station KTAT in Fort Worth soon made the Brownies as popular in Texas as Wills's band was in Oklahoma, and its recorded output grew: 18 sides for Victor (1934) and 84 sides for Decca (1935–6). At the peak of his popularity Brown was killed in an automobile accident. His brother Durwood continued the band for a time, but key personnel left, and in 1938 the Musical Brownies broke up.

BIBLIOGRAPHY

B. Pinson: "The Musical Brownies," *Old Time Music*, no.1 (1971), 14

——: "Musical Brownies Discography," *Old Time Music*, no.5 (1972), 21

C. Townsend: *San Antonio Rose: the Life and Music of Bob Wills* (Urbana, IL, 1976)

T. Russell: Liner notes, *Taking Off* (String 804, 1977)

CHARLES K. WOLFE

Brown, Miss. Name under which the composer Harriet Mary Browne (sister of FELICIA HEMANS) was sometimes known.

Brown, Nacio [Ignatio] **Herb** (*b* Deming, NM, 22 Feb 1896; *d* San Francisco, CA, 28 Sept 1964). Popular songwriter. His family moved in 1902 to Los Angeles, where he attended the Manual Arts High School and, at home, was taught piano by his mother; later he studied composition formally. From 1916 to 1920 he ran a successful menswear store in Beverly Hills, after which he amassed a small fortune in real estate. During these years he wrote songs as a hobby, including one called *When Buddha Smiles* (to words by Arthur Freed) which became a national hit in 1921. In 1926 his "novelette" *Doll Dance*, written for *The Hollywood Music Box Revue*, became an international hit. Still he felt no need, either artistic or financial, to become a full-time songwriter. But in 1929, at the urging of the MGM executive Irving Thalberg, he and Freed provided the songs for the first full-length film musical, *The Broadway Melody*. This immediately produced three international hits: *The Wedding of the Painted Doll* (using a catchy triplet motif from *Doll Dance*), where the tunes are linked by sparkling modulations, *You were meant for me*, and *The Broadway Melody*, all written in a spare, breezy style.

For the next few years the songwriting team of Brown and Freed dominated Hollywood film musicals. For *The Hollywood Revue of 1929* they contributed "Singin' in the Rain," the catchy octave leaps of which were later employed by Brown in such songs as "You are my lucky star" (from *Broadway Melody of 1936*); "The Pagan Love Song" was written for Ramon Novarro in *The Pagan* (1929); "Paradise," full of innuendo, was sung by Pola Negri in *A Woman Commands* (1931), and prompted a sequel, "Temptation," in *Going Hollywood* (1933). In 1934 their song "All I do is dream of you" was introduced by Joan Crawford and Gene Raymond in *Sadie McKee*; it soon became a standard, and its simple tonic and dominant harmonies were repeated in "Good morning" (from *Babes in Arms*, 1939). For *Ziegfeld Girl* (1941), an MGM extravaganza, Brown created an evergreen in "You stepped out of a dream," this time in collaboration with Gus Kahn; a highly original song with daring chromaticism, it is still sometimes used as a model in harmony courses.

During the 1940s Brown gradually abandoned songwriting for other pursuits while Freed, a film producer from 1939, supervised many of MGM's greatest musicals, culminating in *Singin' in the Rain* (1952), which took its songs from the Brown and Freed repertory. By this time Brown had announced his official retirement.

BIBLIOGRAPHY

I. Whitcomb: *After the Ball: Pop Music from Rag to Rock* (New York, 1973)

IAN WHITCOMB

Brown (Mitchell), Nellie E. (*b* Dover, NH, 1845; *d* Boston, MA, Jan 1924). Soprano. She was a pupil of Caroline Bracket in Dover and sang in local churches before going to Boston, where she studied with Mrs. J. Rametti (around 1874) and at the New England Conservatory (diploma 1879). In 1874, while still a student, she gave four recitals in Boston and made her New York début (at Steinway Hall); she also participated in the 1876 Centennial Musical Festival in Boston. Brown was "prima donna soprano" with James Bergen's Star Concerts from 1882 until 1885; meanwhile she continued her activities at various churches in Boston until 1886, when she established the Nellie Brown Mitchell Concert Company (Mitchell was her married name). She began teaching singing at the Hedding Chautauqua Summer School, East Epping, New Hampshire, during the summer of 1888. Brown retired from the concert stage in the 1890s, after which she devoted her time largely to private teaching.

BIBLIOGRAPHY

SouthernB
J. M. Trotter: *Music and Some Highly Musical People* (Boston, 1881/*R*1968), 192
M. C. Hare: *Negro Musicians and their Music* (Washington, DC, 1936/*R*1974), 218

DOMINIQUE-RENÉ DE LERMA

Brown, Pete [James Ostend] (*b* Baltimore, MD, 9 Nov 1906; *d* New York, 20 Sept 1963). Jazz alto saxophonist. He worked in a variety of musical settings in Baltimore before moving to New York in 1927. He played freelance in many New York bands before becoming, in 1937, an original member of John Kirby's group. A year later he left Kirby to lead his own bands. Brown was a highly original musician whose terse, intensely rhythmic phrasing made him a central figure in the "jump band" movement that flourished in Harlem during the 1930s. His wheezy tone, and the seemingly inexhaustible flow of his cryptic improvisations, made his alto saxophone style instantly recognizable; he also recorded on trumpet and tenor saxophone. Brown might have been more famous had he accepted offers to play in big swing bands instead of preferring to work and record in small groups. Echoes of his saxophone phrasing were later heard in the work of many rhythm-and-blues players; his harsh, reedy sound was also much copied.

RECORDINGS
(selective list)

As leader: It all depends on you (1944, Keynote 1312)
As sideman: F. Newton: Please don't talk about me when I'm gone (1937, Variety 518); W. "the Lion" Smith: The Old Stamping Ground (1937, Decca 1380); J. Noone: Four or Five Times (1937, Decca 1621); J. Marsala: Three O'Clock Jump (1940, General 3001)

BIBLIOGRAPHY

L. Feather: "Forgotten Man of Jazz," *Melody Maker* (28 Dec 1940), 3
G. Hoefer: "The Hot Box," *Down Beat*, x/20 (1943), 16

JOHN CHILTON

Brown, Ray(mond Matthews) (*b* Pittsburgh, PA, 13 Oct 1926). Jazz double bass player. He moved to New York around 1945 and immediately established himself in the emerging bop scene. He played on a number of important early bop recordings with Charlie Parker, Dizzy Gillespie, Bud Powell, and others, and was the bass player in Gillespie's first big band (1946–8). Thereafter he toured for several years as music director for his wife, Ella Fitzgerald. In 1951 he began a long affiliation with the Oscar Peterson Trio which brought him international recognition and a popular following; for over a decade he dominated jazz popularity polls on his instrument. Around 1960, following the example of Oscar Pettiford, he took up the cello, adapting his instrument by adding a fingerboard like that of the double bass and additional strings, and using a bass tuning. After leaving Peterson's trio in 1966 Brown settled on the West Coast, where he became an active freelance and studio musician. He recorded at least nine albums with the L. A. Four (Brown, Laurindo Almeida, Bud Shank, and Shelly Manne). Along with Pettiford and Charles Mingus, Brown was the leading bassist in the bop style, playing in a manner noted for its precision, beauty of tone, and tasteful solo style.

RECORDINGS
(selective list)

As leader or co-leader: *Jazz Cello* (1960, Verve 68390); with Duke Ellington: *This One's for Blanton* (1972, Pablo 2310721)
As sideman: D. Gillespie: One Bass Hit, pts.i–ii (1946, Musicraft 404), Two Bass Hit (1947, Vic. 20-2603); How High the Moon, on O. Peterson: *At the Stratford Shakespearean Festival* (1956, Verve 8024); I got Plenty of Nothin', on O. Peterson: *Porgy and Bess* (1959, Verve 8340); L. A. Four: *Montage* (1981, Conc. 156)

BIBLIOGRAPHY

M. Gaudry and M. Peynet: "This is Ray Brown," *Jazz Hot*, no.167 (1961), 28; no.168 (1961), 10
G. Lees: "In Walked Ray," *Down Beat*, xxviii/18 (1961), 18
L. Feather: "The New Life of Ray Brown," *Down Beat*, xxxiv/5 (1967), 24
J. Tracy: "Rhythm + Rosin = Royalty: Ray Brown," *Down Beat*, xliii/2 (1976), 12
L. Lyons: "The L. A. Four–Journeymen United," *Down Beat*, xliv/15 (1977), 18
M. Hennessey: "First Bass," *Jazz Journal International*, xxxv (1982), no.7, p.8; no.8, p.10

J. BRADFORD ROBINSON

Brown, Trisha (*b* Aberdeen, WA, 25 Nov 1936). Choreographer. She graduated from Mills College and also studied with Anna Halprin and Robert Dunn as well as at the American Dance Festival. She has taught at Mills College, Reed College, New York University, and other institutions. Brown was a founding member of the Judson Dance Theater and the Grand Union, and in 1970 she formed the Trisha Brown Company. Like many postmodern choreographers, Brown has often rejected music entirely or given it a subordinate role in her dances. During the early 1960s she performed improvised and "task" dances, which she later varied in a series of "equipment pieces" requiring what she called "external support systems," such as ropes, pulleys, and mountain-climbing gear. The "accumulation" and "structured" pieces of the early 1970s involved the systematic ordering of movement. In 1979 Brown began to create several large-scale dance works in collaboration with such artists as Robert Rauschenberg, Donald Judd, and Fukijo Nakaya, and with the composers Robert Ashley and Laurie Anderson; in these works she included music as a dominant element for the first time.

BIBLIOGRAPHY

S. Banes: "Trisha Brown: Gravity and Levity," *Terpsichore in Sneakers: Post-modern Dance* (Boston, 1980), 76

SALLY BANES

Brown, William (*fl* 1783–8). Flutist and composer. After making his début in New York on 8 August 1783, he appeared in Philadelphia, Baltimore, and Charleston. In New York in 1785 he was a founder of and performer in a series of subscription concerts and he was also one of the organizers and performers in the City Concerts of Philadelphia (with Henri Capron, Alexander

Reinagle, and Alexander Juhan, 1786–8). Brown is best known as the composer of the first keyboard music to be published in the USA: *Three Rondos for the Piano Forte or Harpsichord, Composed and Humbly Dedicated to the Honourable Francis Hopkinson Esqr.* (Philadelphia, 1787; the first is edited in A. McClenny and M. Hinson, eds.: *A Collection of Early American Keyboard Music*, 1971, and the third in RRAM, i, 1977). The name of one subscriber, "Miss Christiane Brown, in Cassel," suggested to Carl Engel that Brown may be the Wilhelm Braun who played flute at the Hofkapelle in Cassel in 1770–80, and who later was living in Hanau in 1805–6. The subscription list (reprinted in Engel's article) includes many other names from Europe, as well as prominent names of the USA.

BIBLIOGRAPHY

O. G. T. Sonneck: *A Bibliography of Early Secular American Music* (Washington, DC, 1905; rev. and enlarged by W. T. Upton, 2/1945/*R*1964)

——: *Early Concert-life in America (1731–1800)* (Leipzig, 1907/*R*1978)

C. Engel: "Introducing Mr. Braun," *MQ*, xxx (1944), 63

B. A. Wolverton: *Keyboard Music and Musicians in the Colonies and United States of America before 1830* (diss., Indiana U., 1966)

J. BUNKER CLARK

Browne (Garrett), Augusta (*b* Dublin, Ireland, 1820; *d* Washington, DC, 11 Jan 1882). Composer and writer on music. Her family came to the USA by 1830, and during the 1840s and 1850s she was organist at the First Presbyterian Church in Brooklyn, New York. She was described as a "professor of music" on her compositions published in New York and Boston between 1842 and 1855. One of the most prolific women composers in the USA before 1870, she wrote mainly parlor songs and salon piano pieces; Moore, in one of the few published acknowledgments of an American woman composer before 1900, attributes "over 200" compositions to her and describes her as "a composer of note." Her songs are often in modified *ABA* form; the best known include *The Chieftain's Halls* (1844) and *The Warlike Dead in Mexico* (1848). She made use of English and Irish musical sources (for example, John Braham's *The Death of Nelson* was a model for *The Warlike Dead*, and Thomas Moore's *A Selection of Irish Melodies* supplied the themes for *The Hibernian Bouquet* variations), and she resisted any vernacular American styles, describing them as "taste-corrupting." Browne was confused in her own lifetime with another composer: Cheney describes her (in *The American Singing Book*, 1879/*R*1980) as best known for *The Pilgrim Fathers*, a work actually written by Harriet Mary Browne, sister of Felicia Hemans. Browne became a prominent author in the late 1840s, writing two books and contributing articles on musical taste to various magazines, including the *Columbian Lady's and Gentleman's Magazine* and the *Musical World and New York Musical Times*. In her article "A Woman on Women" (*Knickerbocker Monthly*, lxi/1, 1863, p. 10) she asserted the right of women to a thorough musical education.

WORKS

(selective list; unless otherwise stated, printed works published in New York)

Vocal: The Family Meeting (C. Sprague) (1842); Grand Vesper Chorus (R. Heber) (n.d. [1842]); The Chieftain's Halls (Boston, 1844); A Song for New England (H. W. Elsworth) (n.d. [1844]); The Volunteer's War Song (Mrs. Balmanno) (1846); The Reply of the Messenger Bird (E. Young) (Philadelphia, 1848); The Warlike Dead in Mexico (Balmanno) (1848); Song of Mercy (J. Bunyan) (1851)

Pf: The Caledonian Bouquet, variations (1841); The French Bouquet, variations, op.31 (1841); The American Bouquet, variations (Philadelphia, 1844); The De Meyer Grand Waltz (1846); The Hibernian Bouquet, variations (n.d. [1840s]); The Mexican Volunteer's Quickstep (n.d. [*c*1850]); Angels Whisper, variations (Philadelphia, n.d. [1850s]); The Merry Mountain Horn, variations (Philadelphia, n.d. [1850s]); The Ethereal Grand Waltz (n.d.)

Principal publisher: Firth & Hall

BIBLIOGRAPHY

J. Moore: *Appendix to the Encyclopedia of Music* (Boston, 1875)

C. Ammer: *Unsung: a History of Women in American Music* (Westport, CT, 1980)

J. Tick: *American Women Composers before 1870* (Ann Arbor, MI, 1983)

JUDITH TICK

Browne, Harriet Mary (*d* 1858). Composer. She was the sister of and frequently collaborated with FELICIA HEMANS; she has been confused with AUGUSTA BROWNE.

Browne, Jackson (*b* Heidelberg, Germany, 9 Oct ?1949). Folk-rock singer, songwriter, guitarist, and pianist. He grew up in Orange County, California, but began his career performing in New York clubs in the late 1960s. It was not, however, until he returned to the West Coast in the early 1970s that he reached artistic maturity, as one of a group of singers and songwriters (including Glenn Frey and Don Henley of the Eagles, John David Souther, Jack Tempchin, and Danny O'Keefe) who were influenced by Bob Dylan. Together they defined a style of southern California folk-rock that evoked Los Angeles as a modern frontier city in which the pop star was a figurative cowboy; their music was characterized by a long-lined ballad style that blended pop, folk-rock, and echoes of traditional cowboy melodies. While the main preoccupation of this group was the social ethos of Los Angeles, Browne's songs were more personal and romantic, concerned with the psychological nuances of erotic relationships and the search for transcendent love; their frequent hymn-like cadences give many of them a devotional flavor. Another theme, that of an earthly paradise imperiled by pollution, is most intensely presented in the title song of the album *For Everyman* (1973) and "Before the Deluge" (from *Late for the Sky*, 1974), which with their apocalyptic images have the aura of solemn populist hymns.

On his fourth album, *The Pretender* (1976), Browne followed the example of Bruce Springsteen and moved away from intimate acoustic folk towards a more grandiose folk-rock style; its title song, one of his finest, directly addresses the choice between commitment and complacent consumerism that Browne saw as central for his generation. This change of approach gained him still more popularity – the live album *Running on Empty* (1977) sold more than four million copies – but it also strained his vocal and compositional capabilities. Never prolific, Browne's output dwindled after *The Pretender*, as he became increasingly involved in the antinuclear movement; he was one of the founders, in 1979, of MUSE (Musicians United for Safe Energy) and contributed substantial financial support to the *No Nukes* film and album. Browne intensified the exhortatory tone of *The Pretender* on *Hold Out* (1980), where it took on a preaching quality. His career took on a new impetus in 1983 with the success of the well made but conventional album *Lawyers in Love*.

RECORDINGS

(selective list; all recorded for Asylum)

Jackson Browne (5051, 1972), incl. Doctor my eyes; *For Everyman* (5067, 1973); *Late for the Sky* (7E1017, 1974); *The Pretender* (7E1079, 1976), incl. Here come those tears again; *Running on Empty* (6E113, 1977), incl. Stay; *Hold Out* (511, 1980), incl. Boulevard, That girl could sing; *Lawyers in Love* (602681, 1983)

STEPHEN HOLDEN

Browne, J(ohn) F(ace) (*b* London, England, *c*1815; *fl* New York, *c*1840–1873). Harp maker. He immigrated to New York in the late 1830s. In August 1840 the first advertisement appeared: "J. F. Browne, harpmakers of London and New York, respectfully informs his friends and the Musical World that he has established himself in New York for the manufacture and importation of these very beautiful instruments." His work was advertised regularly in the music periodicals and business directories of 1840–72. Browne's first showroom was at 295 Broadway; by 1867 he was at 581 Broadway. He continued in business until 1873, when the firm of J. F. Browne & Co. was taken over by Edgar J. Browne and George H. Buckwell; a harp firm of Browne & Buckwell continued until 1942.

The harp method by the renowned French harpist and composer N. C. Bochsa (Eng. trans. of pt. 1 as *A History of the Harp*, 1853) includes a page testifying to the splendid quality of Browne's six-and-a-half octave, double-action harp. In 1853 Browne received the Franklin Medal of the Society of Arts, Philadelphia, for "his splendid improvements in this delightful instrument." Tonally, his instruments were described as having "an extraordinary addition of sweetness, purity and power" (*Musical Times*, Baltimore, 21 March 1853).

LUCIEN THOMSON

Browning, Jean. *See* MADEIRA, JEAN.

Browning, John (*b* Denver, CO, 22 May 1933). Pianist. He made his first public appearance in Denver when he was ten. As a boy he studied in Los Angeles with Lee Pattison, a Schnabel pupil, and in 1953 went to Rosina Lhévinne at the Juilliard School (BM, MM 1956). He rapidly made his way to prominence by winning the Steinway Centennial Award in 1954 and the Leventritt in 1955. He made his début, with the New York PO under Mitropoulos, in 1956, the same year in which he won second prize in the Queen Elisabeth International Competition in Brussels; thereafter he became one of the American pianists most in demand. In addition to many appearances as a soloist and recitalist, he has given master classes at Northwestern University, Evanston, Illinois, and at the Manhattan School of Music, and has served as a juror at the Queen Elisabeth Competition. He has been awarded honorary doctorates in music from Ithaca College (1972) and Occidental College (1975).

Browning had particular success introducing Barber's Piano Concerto (24 September 1962, with Leinsdorf and the Boston SO at Lincoln Center). Except for Barber, Prokofiev (all of whose concertos he recorded with Leinsdorf in Boston), and Rachmaninoff, his repertory has tended to center on the 19th century and Mozart. He is a tasteful, somewhat humorless, not deeply searching player, blessed with one of the easiest, most brilliant techniques of any pianist before the public.

BIBLIOGRAPHY

"Browning, John," *CBY 1969*

A. Marcus: "John Browning," *Great Pianists Speak with Adele Marcus* (Neptune, NJ, 1979), 144

MICHAEL STEINBERG/R

Brownlee, Archie (*b c*1925; *d* New Orleans, LA, 8 Feb 1960). Gospel singer. In 1939 he formed a gospel group, the Cotton Blossom Singers, from among his fellow blind students at the Pineywood School in Piney Woods, Mississippi. When they began to earn their tuition fees by singing at local churches and auditoriums they changed their name to the Jackson Harmoneers, and then to the Original Five Blind Boys of Mississippi. Besides Brownlee, early members of the group were Percell Perkins, Lloyd Woodard, Lawrence Abrams, and Joseph Ford (who was replaced in 1948 by J. T. Clinkscales). Brownlee was influenced by Robert H. Harris, and was one of the first gospel singers to perform in the "hard" gospel style, emphasizing a very strident falsetto and employing wails and screams. Two of the group's most popular recordings are *Lord, I've tried* (1946) and *I'm gonna leave you in the hands of the Lord* (1958).

BIBLIOGRAPHY

P. Williams-Jones: "Afro-American Gospel Music: a Brief Historical and Analytical Survey, 1920–1970," *Development of Materials for a One Year Course in African Music for the General Undergraduate Student*, ed. V. E. Butcher (Washington, DC, 1970), 199–239

T. Heilbut: *The Gospel Sound: Good News and Bad Times* (New York, 1971/*R*1975)

HORACE CLARENCE BOYER

Brownlee, John (Donald Mackensie) (*b* Geelong, Australia, 7 Jan 1901; *d* New York, 10 Jan 1969). Baritone and educator. He studied in Melbourne and Paris, and made his London début in 1926, at Melba's farewell appearance at Covent Garden; until 1936 he was a prominent member of the Paris Opéra. He also sang at Glyndebourne and toured widely. Following his début with the Metropolitan Opera on 17 February 1937 (as Rigoletto), he joined the company, remaining until 1958. His singing, while neither so rich nor so resonant as to place him among the greatest baritones, was admirably schooled and always distinguished in style.

Brownlee played a prominent part in American musical life. In the summer of 1955 he established the Empire State Music Festival, near Ellenville, New York, having bought the land and built the facilities. At the Manhattan School of Music, where he became director in 1956 and served as president from 1966 until his death, he did much innovative work with student opera and drama productions, and increased the breadth of the curriculum. From 1953 to 1967 he was president of the American Guild of Musical Artists.

BIBLIOGRAPHY

B. MacKenzie and F. MacKenzie: *Singers of Australia* (Melbourne, 1967), 117

M. deSchauensee: Obituary, *Opera News*, xxxiii/18 (1969), 34

DESMOND SHAWE-TAYLOR/R

Brown's Ferry Four. Country-music gospel quartet formed by GRANDPA JONES, MERLE TRAVIS, and the DELMORE BROTHERS; it made its first recording in 1945.

Brownson, Oliver (*b* Bolton, CT, 13 May 1746; *d* Smithfield, NY, 1815). Composer, singing master, and printer. He was prominent among the Connecticut composers who contributed many psalm and fuging-tunes to the repertory of 18th-century choral music. Brownson taught in several parts of Connecticut, and from 1775 to 1797 was mostly in Litchfield, Simsbury, West Simsbury, and New Hartford. He was associated with Asahel Benham, Timothy Swan, and Alexander Ely in the sale of music books. He settled in Peterboro, New York, sometime between 1797 and 1800.

Brownson's compositions were first published in Law's *Select Harmony* (Cheshire, 1779). Brownson's own *Select Harmony*, issued in four editions (probably in Hartford) between 1783 and 1791,

The Dave Brubeck Quartet: Joe Morello (drums), Eugene Wright (double bass), Dave Brubeck (piano), and Paul Desmond (alto saxophone)

contained a large number of new pieces by Americans with "Author's Names set over the tunes," as well as 22 original works. The title page, engraved by Isaac Sanford, depicts a church choir arranged around three sides of the gallery, the leader at the center with a pitchpipe in hand (*see* CHORAL MUSIC, fig. 1). Brownson also published *A New Collection of Sacred Harmony* (Simsbury, 1797).

BIBLIOGRAPHY

R. Crawford: "Connecticut Sacred Music Imprints, 1778–1810," *Notes*, xxvii (1970–71), 445, 671

R. M. Wilson: *Connecticut's Music in the Revolutionary Era* (Hartford, 1979)

A. Britton, I. Lowens, and R. Crawford: *A Bibliography of American Sacred Music Imprints through 1810* (Worcester, MA, in preparation)

RUTH M. WILSON

Brown University. Institution of higher education in PROVIDENCE, Rhode Island, founded in 1764 as Rhode Island College (*see also* LIBRARIES AND COLLECTIONS, §3).

Brubeck, Dave [David Warren] (*b* Concord, CA, 6 Dec 1920). Jazz composer, pianist, and bandleader. He received early training in classical music from his mother, a pianist, and by the age of 13 he was performing professionally with local jazz groups. In 1941–2, while a music major at the College of the Pacific in Stockton, California, he led a 12-piece band; he also studied composition with Milhaud at Mills College in Oakland. During World War II he was sent to Europe to lead a service band (1944). On his discharge in 1946 he resumed his studies with Milhaud and, with fellow students, founded the experimental Jazz Workshop Ensemble, which recorded in 1949 as the Dave Brubeck Octet. Also in 1949, with the drummer-vibraphonist Cal Tjader and double bass player Norman Bates (later Ron Crotty), he organized the Dave Brubeck Trio. This group existed until 1951 when, with the addition of the alto saxophonist Paul Desmond, Brubeck formed his first quartet. The "classic" Brubeck quartet was created when Brubeck and Desmond were joined by the drummer Joe Morello (1956) and double bass player Eugene Wright (1958); this group remained together until 1967 (see illustration).

The Brubeck quartet was immensely popular on college campuses in the 1950s; the album *Jazz at Oberlin*, recorded in concert at that college in 1953, contains some of Brubeck's and especially Desmond's finest improvisations. In 1954, as a sign of his growing popularity, Brubeck's picture appeared on the cover of *Time* and he left Fantasy for Columbia Records. During the 1950s and 1960s he began experimenting with time signatures unusual to jazz, such as 5/4, 9/8, and 11/4. By 1959 he had recorded the first jazz instrumental piece to sell a million copies – Paul Desmond's *Take Five* (in 5/4 meter), which was released with his own *Blue Rondo à la Turk* (in 9/8, grouped 2+2+2+3). Only the drummer Max Roach had preceded Brubeck in the successful integration of irregular meters and jazz forms.

Brubeck, who considers himself in essence "a composer who plays the piano," has written and, in some instances, recorded several large-scale compositions since the 1960s, including two ballets, a musical, an oratorio, four cantatas, a mass, works for jazz combo and orchestra, as well as many pieces for solo piano. In the 1970s he organized several new quartets which at various times included one or more of his sons: Darius (keyboards), Chris (bass guitar and bass trombone), and Danny (drums). Brubeck has appeared at the Newport (1958, 1972, 1981), Monterey (1962, 1980), Concord (1982), and Kool jazz festivals as well as at the White House (1964, 1981). During the 1950s and 1960s he was a frequent winner of the *Down Beat*, *Metronome*, and *Playboy* popularity polls.

RECORDINGS

(selective list)

Dave Brubeck Octet (1949, Fan. 4019–20); Squeeze Me/How High the Moon (1950, Fan. 515); *Jazz at College of the Pacific* (1953, Fan. 4054–5); *Jazz at Oberlin* (1953, Fan. 3245); *Jazz Goes to College* (1954, Col. B1940/B1943); *Brubeck Plays Brubeck* (1956, Col. CL878); *Solo Piano* (1957, Fan. 3259); *Jazz Impressions of Eurasia* (1958, Col. CL1251); *Time Out* (1959, Col. CL1397), incl. Take Five, Blue Rondo à la Turk; *Dialogues for Jazz-Combo and Orchestra* (1959, Col. CL1466); *Time Further Out* (1961, Col. CS8490)

Jazz Impressions of Japan (1964, Col. CS9012); *Jazz Impressions of New York* (1964, Col. CS9075); *Elementals for Jazzcombo, Orchestra and Baritone-Solo* (1970, Decca

DL71081); *Adventures in Time* (1972, Col. CG30625); *Two Generations of Brubeck* (1973, Atl. 1645); *Brubeck and Desmond: Duets* (1975, Hor. 703); *The Dave Brubeck Quartet 25th Anniversary Reunion* (1976, Hor. 714); *Concord on a Summer Night* (1982, Conc. 198)

WORKS
(selective list)

Stage: A Maiden in the Tower (ballet), 1956; Points on Jazz (ballet), 1961; The Real Ambassador (musical), 1962

Chorus, orch: The Light in the Wilderness (I. Brubeck), oratorio, 1968; The Gates of Justice (I. Brubeck, after Bible), cantata, 1969; Truth is Fallen (I. Brubeck, after Isaiah, Jeremiah), cantata, 1971; La fiesta de la posada (I. Brubeck, after Bible), cantata, 1975; Beloved Son, oratorio, 1978; Festival Mass to Hope, 1980

Jazz combo, orch: Dialogues, 1959, collab. Mulligan; Elementals, Bar, jazz combo, orch, 1970; Fugal Fanfare, jazz soloists, orch, 1970; They all Sang Yankee Doodle, orch, opt. jazz improvisation, 1975, arr. pf/2 pf

Pf: Reminiscences of the Cattle Country, 1946

Principal publishers: Associated Music, Delaware Water Gap, Hansen, Shawnee

BIBLIOGRAPHY

EwenD

D. Brubeck: "Jazz Evolvement as Art Form," *Down Beat*, xvii (1950), no.1, p.12; no.2, p.13

"Brubeck, Dave (W.)," *CBY 1956*

I. Brubeck and D. Brubeck: "Jazz Perspective," *Jam Session*, ed. R. Gleason (New York, 1958)

Dave Brubeck (New York, 1961) [list of works]

D. Morgenstern: "Two Generations of Brubecks: a Talk with Dave, Darius, and Chris," *Down Beat*, xxxix/10 (1972), 12

Biography of Dave Brubeck (New York, 1972)

C. J. Stuessy: *The Confluence of Jazz and Classical Music from 1950 to 1970* (diss., U. of Rochester, 1978), 296–320, 396ff

"Dave Brubeck," *Swing Journal*, xxxiv/2 (1980), 164 [discography]

I. Storb: "Dave Brubeck, Komponist und Pianist," *Jazzforschung*, xiii (1981), 9–43 [incl. list of works]

RICHARD WANG

Brubeck, Howard R(engstorsff) (*b* Concord, CA, 11 July 1916). Composer, brother of Dave Brubeck. He began his musical studies with piano lessons from his mother and then attended San Francisco State College (BA 1938) and Mills College (MA 1941), where he was a pupil of Milhaud. In 1944, after a few years of high school teaching, he became an assistant to Milhaud at Mills College. In 1950 he joined the faculty of San Diego State College as a teacher of composition and in 1953 became chairman of the music department of nearby Palomar College. He retired in 1978, having served at Palomar as Dean of Humanities for 12 years.

Brubeck's works are further in style from jazz than those of his brother, yet he always avoided academicism and successfully combined strictly notated orchestral scores with improvisatory solo combos. The influence of Milhaud – and sometimes echoes of Copland – can be heard in his music; a flair for orchestral writing, secure craftsmanship, and sophisticated wit are also evident. In the late 1950s performances of both *California Suite* (in San Francisco and Brussels) and *Dialogues* (performed by the Dave Brubeck Quartet with the San Diego SO and the New York PO) brought him to international prominence.

WORKS

Orch: Gigue, str, 1939; Alleluia, S, chorus, orch, 1941; Elizabethan Suite, SA, chamber orch, 1944; California Suite, 1945; Ov., The Devil's Disciple, 1954; 4 Dialogues, jazz ens, orch, 1956; Sym. Movt on a Theme of Robert Kurka, 1958; The Gardens of Versailles, 1960; several arrs. for jazz ens, orch, of works by D. Brubeck, incl. Summer Song, Brandenburg Gate, Cathy's Waltz, In Your Own Sweet Way; band transcrs., other ovs., pieces for chorus, orch

Stage: Latin-American Dance Suite (dance music), 2 pf, 1942; Harmony at Evening (dance music), speaker, pf, 1947; Mother's Day (film score), bn, tpt, vn, prepared pf, 1948; Of Strife Resounding (dance music), 7 perc players, pf, 1950; Ritual of Wonder (dance music), pf, 1950; Daphni (film score), small orch, 1951; incidental music for plays by Molière, Regnard, Lorca, Euripides, Shaw, Ibsen, 1941–50

Other: inst works, incl. pf teaching pieces; choruses, songs

Principal publishers: Derry

BARBARA A. PETERSEN

Bruce, (Frank) Neely (*b* Memphis, TN, 21 Jan 1944). Composer, pianist, conductor, and musicologist. He studied piano with Roy McAllister at the University of Alabama (BM 1965) and with Soulima Stravinsky at the University of Illinois (MM 1966, DMA 1971), where he also studied composition with Ben Johnston. From 1974 he has taught at Wesleyan University and conducted the Wesleyan Singers, commissioning works from such composers as Wolff, Oliveros, and Brant. He is the founder (1977) and director of the American Music/Theater Group. Bruce's compositions fall into three distinct periods. From 1962 to 1972 he wrote a number of large works using serial techniques and information theory, including Fantasy for Ten Winds and Percussion and the Quintet, his most rigorously serial piece. During 1971–6 he began to exploit the possibility of juxtaposing widely contrasting or seemingly incompatible styles in such works as *The Trials of Psyche*, an opera first performed at the University of Illinois (1971), and the first in a series of *Grand Duos* for various solo instruments and piano. From 1976 he has made a conscious effort to incorporate his understanding of the American music tradition into his own work, making use of elements of ragtime, bluegrass, and sentimental ballad style, as well as tunes in four-bar phrases based on 18th- and 19th-century models; works in this style include a second series of *Grand Duos* and *Perfumes and Meanings*, commissioned by the London Sinfonietta and first performed at the Queen Elizabeth Hall, London (1980).

As a pianist Bruce specializes in American music and has given the premières of such works as *HPSCHD* (Cage and Hiller), *The Time Curve Preludes* (Duckworth), and the Piano Sonata op.113 of Farwell. He made his New York début playing works by Hiller at the Electric Circus (1968) and first appeared in Europe at the Warsaw Festival (1972) accompanying the American baritone David Barron in a concert of songs by Ives. He has both played and conducted in recordings of a wide variety of American music and directed a historic panorama of scenes from American operas at the Holland Festival (1982). Bruce was a member of the editorial committee of New World Records (1974–8), founder (1976) and chairman (1976, 1979, 1982) of the New England Sacred Harp Singing, and Senior Research Fellow at the Institute for Studies in American Music at Brooklyn College, CUNY (1980).

WORKS

Stage: Pyramus and Thisbe (chamber opera, 1, Shakespeare), 1965; Au clair de la lune, mime, 2-track tape, 1969; Membrane (incidental music, R. Fisher), 1971; The Trials of Psyche (opera, 1, J. Orr, after Apuleius), 1971; Music for Dancing, dancers, S, fl, elec pf, perc, 1979; Americana, or, A New Tale of the Genii (opera, 4, T. Connor), 1983

Inst: Fantasy, 10 wind, perc, cptr-generated 2-track tape, 1967; Perc Conc., 1967; 3 Canons, mar, 1967; Ww Qnt, 1967; 8 Grand Duos, 1 inst, pf, 1971–83; Conc., vn, chamber orch, 1974; Rondo, fl, tuba, pf, 1976; For Jim Fulkerson, trbn, 1977; a few other large ens works; *c*20 other chamber pieces for various insts; numerous pf pieces, incl. 6 sonatas, 1957–73

Choral: The Death of a Soldier (W. Stevens), 1969; Psalm i (Bay Psalm Book), 1971; 3 Choruses on Poems by Herman Melville, 1971; There was a child went forth (Whitman), 1972; Lines Written on the Roof of 110 Thompson Street (anon.), 1974; 7 Mass settings, 1959–76; Perfumes and Meanings, 16 solo vv, 1980; more than 60 other works, many to texts of the Roman Catholic liturgy

Solo vocal: A Feast of Fat Things, cantata, S, 7 insts, 1977; over 150 songs, incl. 5 Songs on Poems by John Finlay, 1v, pf, 1964, Psalm xxiii, 1v, 1968, 7 Songs on Poems by Emily Dickinson, 1v, pf, 1970, Juliana and the Lozenges (T. Canning), 1v, pf, 1974, The Blades o' Bluegrass Songbook (late 19th-century Kentuckian), 1v, pf, 1974–81, 5 Songs on Poems of John Ferdon, 1v, pf, 1978, The Pond in Winter (Thoreau), 1v, pf, 1980, Marriage (S. K. Bayles), cycle of 9 songs, S, fl, pf, 1980, Chinese Love Poems (various poets), cycle of 17 songs, 1v, pf, 1980, Whitman Fragments, 1981

Principal publisher: Media

WILLIAM DUCKWORTH

Brulé. American Plains Indian group belonging to the Teton division of the SIOUX.

Brün, Herbert (*b* Berlin, Germany, 9 July 1918). German composer. He left Germany to escape the Nazi regime and studied with Wolpe at the Jerusalem Conservatory (1936–8); later he attended Columbia University (1948–9). Until 1963 he worked primarily as a freelance composer, living in Israel and Germany and writing for the theater, radio, and television. He also lectured for Bavarian Radio (Munich), at the Darmstadt summer courses, and on several tours of the USA; his German lectures were published in three collections (1960, 1961, 1962).

From 1955 to 1962 Brün conducted research in Paris, Cologne, and Munich on the application of electroacoustic and electronic methods of sound production to composition. In 1963 he joined the faculty of the University of Illinois, where he expanded his research to include the significance of computer systems for composition. He was visiting professor at the University of Ohio, Columbus, in 1969–70. While continuing to compose for traditional instruments, Brün has used computers both for sound generation and as a compositional aid. He has written extensively on the use of computers in music and on the function of music in society and the political significance of musical ideas. Several of his compositions have been recorded, including *Anepigraphe*, *Futility 1964*, *Gestures for Eleven*, and *More Dust*.

WORKS

Orch: Concertino, 1947; Mobile, 1958

Chamber: 5 Pieces, pf, 1945; Sonatina, fl, 1948; Sonatina, va, 1950; Pf Sonata, 1951; 3 str qts, 1952, 1957, 1961; Gestures for Eleven, 11 insts, 1964; Soniferous Loops, fl + pic, tpt, db, xyl, mar, perc, tape, 1964; Trio, fl, db, perc, 1964; Gesto, pic, pf, 1965; Non sequitur VI, fl + pic, vc, harp, pf, 2 perc, tape, 1966; Trio, tpt, trbn, perc, 1968; Nonet, 1969; Six for Five by Three in Pieces, ob + eng hn, cl + b cl, 1971; Twice upon Three Times, b cl, tuba, 1980; other solo and ens works

Elec: Anepigraphe, 1958; Klänge unterwegs (Wayfaring Sounds), 1962; Futility 1964, 1964; Infraudibles, 1968; Piece of Prose, 1972; Dust, 1976; More Dust, 1977; Dustiny, 1978; A Mere Ripple, 1979; U-turn-to, 1980; I told you so, 1981; other works

Cptr: Mutatis mutandis, 1968; Polyplots, 1971; Links, 1973; other works

Ballets

Principal publishers: Lingua, Smith (Baltimore), Tonos (Darmstadt)

BIBLIOGRAPHY

B. J. Levy: "Herbert Brün: Three Works for Percussion," *PNM*, viii/1 (1969), 136

T. Blum: "Herbert Brün: Project Sawdust," *Computer Music Journal*, iii/1 (1979), 6

S. Smith: "A Portrait of Herbert Brün," *PNM*, xvii/2 (1979), 56

P. Hamlin and C. Roads: "Interview with Herbert Brün," *Composers and the Computer*, ed. C. Roads (Los Altos, CA, 1985), 1

NEIL B. ROLNICK

Brunis, Georg [Brunies, George Clarence]. Jazz trombonist, co-founder of the NEW ORLEANS RHYTHM KINGS.

Brunswick, Mark (*b* New York, 6 Jan 1902; *d* London, England, 26 May 1971). Composer and teacher. After studies with Rubin Goldmark (harmony, counterpoint, and fugue) and Bloch (composition) he lived in Europe (1925–38), where he studied with Boulanger. He also associated with a group of Viennese musicians that included Webern, who admired his Two Movements for string quartet. Back in the USA he was made chairman of the National Committee for Refugee Musicians (1938–43), and he taught at Black Mountain College (1944) and Kenyon College (1945) before his appointment as chairman of the music department of the City College of New York (1946–67). He was also president of the American section of the ISCM (1941–50) and of the College Music Association (1953). Brunswick's music, from the earliest works, is economical, nonrhetorical, and extremely intense. His dissonant linear writing shows the influence of 16th-century polyphony, to which he was very much drawn, and an imaginative and individual use of color is apparent in each of his works. Most of the vocal pieces are settings of his own verse or ancient Latin or Greek poetry. He contributed to the *Musical Quarterly* and the *Saturday Review of Literature*.

WORKS

Opera: The Master Builder (3, after Ibsen), 1959–67, inc.

Orch: Sym., B♭, 1945; Air with Toccata, str, 1967

Vocal: Lysistrata (Aristophanes), suite, S, female vv, orch, 1930; Eros and Death: Death (Lucretius), Fragment of Sappho (Sappho), Hymn to Venus (Lucretius), Potiundi tempori (Lucretius), Death and Eros (Lucretius), Epilogue (Hadrian), choral sym., Mez, chorus, orch, 1932–54; 4 Madrigals and a Motet (Brunswick), 1960; 4 Songs (Brunswick), T, pf, 1964; 5 Madrigals, chorus, 1965; Voce vita (A. de St. Victor), motet, n.d.

Chamber: 2 Movts, str qt, 1926; Fantasia, va, 1932; 7 Trios, str qt, 1956; Septet, wind qnt, va, vc, 1957; 6 Bagatelles, pf, 1958; Qt, vn, va, vc, db, 1958; Choral Prelude, Das alte Jahr vergangen ist, org, n.d.

MSS in *NNR*

Principal publishers: Bomart, G. Schirmer, Universal

BIBLIOGRAPHY

EwenD

M. Gideon: "The Music of Mark Brunswick," *ACAB*, xiii/1 (1965), 1

G. Warfield: "An Interview with Mark Brunswick," *Contemporary Music Newsletter*, iii/3–4 (1969), 1

MIRIAM GIDEON

Brusilow, Anshel (*b* Philadelphia, PA, 14 Aug 1928). Violinist and conductor. He studied the violin with Zimbalist at the Curtis Institute (1943), and at the Philadelphia Musical Academy, where he obtained a diploma after study with Jani Szanto (1947). In 1944 at the age of 16 he was the youngest pupil ever accepted by Monteux, with whom he studied conducting for the next ten years; also in 1944 he made his solo début with the Philadelphia Orchestra under Ormandy. In 1955 he was appointed concertmaster of the Cleveland Orchestra by Szell, and four years later he became concertmaster of the Philadelphia Orchestra. He retained that position until 1966 when he founded the Chamber Symphony of Philadelphia and became the ensemble's conductor. The Dallas SO appointed him resident conductor in 1970; he was then the orchestra's music director and conductor (1971–3). He was a member of the faculty at North Texas State University, Denton, from 1973 to 1982, when he joined the faculty at Southern Methodist University.

A proponent of contemporary music, Brusilow gave the first performances of Yardumian's Violin Concerto, in its original version in 1951 and its expanded version in 1961, both with Ormandy and the Philadelphia Orchestra, and he conducted the

Chamber Symphony of Philadelphia in the first performance of Yardumian's Mass in 1967.

BIBLIOGRAPHY

J. Creighton: *Discopaedia of the Violin, 1889–1971* (Toronto, 1974), 100

GEORGE GELLES/R

Bryant, Boudleaux (*b* Shellman, GA, 13 Feb 1920). Country-music songwriter. He works in collaboration with his wife, Felice Bryant (*b* Milwaukee, WI, 7 Aug 1927). He was trained as a violinist and spent a season with the Atlanta SO in 1938. He then performed with a succession of country groups as a singer, fiddler, and guitarist, and while on tour in 1945 he met Felice in Milwaukee. After their marriage they began to write songs, which they tried to place with publishers in the mid-1940s; they were unsuccessful until Fred Rose arranged for Little Jimmy Dickens to record their *Country Boy* in 1949. At Rose's suggestion they moved to Nashville in 1950, where they wrote for Acuff–Rose and Tannen Publishers. As Bud and Betty Bryant they recorded some of their own material for MGM (1951–3), for whom Boudleaux also recorded as a soloist (under the name Bood Bryant), and for Hickory (1954–9), but the recordings had little success. The Bryants have composed songs for Carl Smith (*It's a lovely, lovely world* and *Hey Joe*), Eddy Arnold (*I've been thinking* and *The Richest Man*), and the Everly Brothers, who launched their career with *Bye bye love* and later recorded *Wake up little Susie*, *All I have to do is dream*, and *Bird Dog*. *Rocky Top*, which the Bryants wrote in the mid-1960s, has become one of the state songs of Tennessee. Their later songs include *Devoted to you*, recorded by James Taylor and Carly Simon in 1978, and *Hey Joe, Hey Moe*, which Boudleaux wrote for Joe Stampley and Moe Bandy in 1981. The Bryants were among the first Nashville songwriters to establish a reputation solely on the basis of their compositional talents without becoming well-known as performers. They are notable in the history of country music for the longevity of their success and their productivity.

BIBLIOGRAPHY

K. Delaney: "200,000,000 Records Later . . . Boudleaux and Felice Bryant: All they had to do was Dream," *Songwriter*, iv/3 (1978), 24

RONNIE PUGH

Bryant [O'Brien], **Dan(iel Webster)** (*b* Troy, NY, 1833; *d* New York, 10 April 1875). Minstrel performer and manager. He began as a performer in the late 1840s, and made his first New York appearance with Charley White's Serenaders in 1851. From 1852 to 1854 he and his brother Jerry performed with Wood's Minstrels in New York, and late in the 1854 season he formed Bryant and Mallory's Minstrels with Ben Mallory. By this time he was being advertised as "the unapproachable Ethiopian comedian." In February 1857 he formed Bryant's Minstrels with his brothers Jerry and Neil. As a versatile and brilliant performer, Bryant quickly became a public idol; the troupe performed with great success in New York until Bryant's death in 1875, and also toured in California and elsewhere in 1867–8. Bryant's Minstrels excelled in the portrayal of black "plantation life," marking a return to the classic type of minstrelsy of the 1840s; they were also innovators, placing a greater emphasis on burlesque skits. Their continued popularity in the 1860s and 1870s was due not only to the talents of individual performers such as Bryant himself, but also to a constant stream of hilarious, topical burlesques of current plays or events. Bryant engaged Dan Emmett in 1858 as performer and composer, and it was for Bryant's troupe that Emmett wrote *I wish I was in Dixie's Land* (1859) and other walk-arounds; Emmett enjoyed a second heyday with the Bryants until 1866.

Bryant was the leading minstrel performer of his day, appearing as comedian, dancer, musician, and singer. He was one of minstrelsy's greatest dancers, and his widely imitated song-and-dance skits *The Essence of Old Virginny* and *Shoo Fly don't Bodder me* are regarded as true classics of minstrelsy. As a musician his primary instrument was the banjo, but he also played tambourine and bones. He was an extremely talented blackface comedian and a master of the comic-stage black dialect. He also had a secondary career as a whiteface Irish comedian during summer seasons from 1863 to at least 1870, winning great acclaim in *Handy Andy* and *The Irish Emigrant*. He wrote the lyrics "Turkey in the Straw" (1861) to G. W. Dixon's tune *Zip Coon*.

BIBLIOGRAPHY

E. L. Rice: *Monarchs of Minstrelsy* (New York, 1911)

C. Wittke: *Tambo and Bones: a History of the American Minstrel Stage* (Durham, 1930)

G. C. D. Odell: *Annals of the New York Stage*, v–ix (New York, 1931–7/*R*1970)

H. Nathan: *Dan Emmett and the Rise of Early Negro Minstrelsy* (Norman, OK, 1962/*R*1977)

R. C. Toll: *Blacking Up: the Minstrel Show in Nineteenth-century America* (New York, 1974)

ROBERT B. WINANS

Bryant, William Cullen (*b* Cummington, MA, 3 Nov 1794; *d* New York, 12 June 1878). Poet. He attended Williams College in Williamstown, Massachusetts (1810–11), but withdrew to study law. Admitted to the bar in 1815, he practiced law in Massachusetts, then in 1825 moved to New York to begin his career as a journalist. In 1829 he became editor of the *New York Evening Post*, a position he held for almost half a century. As a prominent leader of the Unitarian movement, an influential liberal democrat, and, later, an active organizer of the Republican Party, he became a dominant force in both public affairs and literature.

Bryant achieved recognition with the publication in 1817 of his poem *Thanatopsis*. Soon after, in 1820, Henry D. Sewall invited him to contribute to a new Unitarian hymnbook, for which he produced five hymns, the first of many he wrote throughout his life. Although he is not considered a great hymn writer, his hymns were popular in his day, particularly "O Thou whose own vast temple stands," "Mighty One, before whose face," and "As shadows cast by cloud and sun."

The earliest settings of Bryant's poetry, published in the mid-1830s, were four songs by Elam Ives, Jr., based on the poems *The Hunter's Serenade*, *The New Moon*, *A Song of Pitcairn's Island*, and *Song of the Greek Amazon*. Bryant was a serious and earnest poet whose principal poetic concerns were nature, religion, and the transience of earthly things. His most frequently set poems include *The Serenade* and *The Siesta* (both translated from the Spanish); these are among the few he wrote in the style of the conventional song lyrics of the period. Settings of one or both were made by Leslie Bassett, Bainbridge Crist, Henry Cutler, W. R. Dempster, Luther Emerson, Howard Hanson, Margaret Ruthven Lang, and Huntington Woodman. Although Bryant is the least set of the major 19th-century poets, his lyrics have held a steady, if limited, appeal for composers.

BIBLIOGRAPHY

"Bryant, William Cullen," *A Dictionary of Hymnology*, ed. J. Julian (New York, 1892, rev. 2/1907/*R*1957)

H. A. Clarke: "The Relations of Music to Poetry in American Poets," *Music*, vi (1894), 163
C. S. Lennart: *Musical Influence on American Poetry* (Athens, GA, 1956)
K. S. Diehl: *Hymns and Tunes: an Index* (New York, 1966)
C. H. Brown: *William Cullen Bryant* (New York, 1971)
H. E. Johnson: "Musical Interests of Certain American Literary and Political Figures," *JRME*, xix (1971), 272
M. A. Hovland: *Musical Settings of American Poetry: a Bibliography* (in preparation) [incl. list of settings]

MICHAEL HOVLAND

Bryn-Julson, Phyllis (Mae) (*b* Bowdon, ND, 5 Feb 1945). Soprano. Trained as a pianist at Concordia College in Moorhead, Minnesota, she was heard by Gunther Schuller, who was struck by her facility at sight-reading 12-tone music. At his instigation she studied singing at the Berkshire Music Center, where she received additional encouragement from Erich Leinsdorf. After further study at Syracuse University she made her official début with the Boston SO in Berg's *Lulu* Suite (28 October 1966), which led to numerous concert engagements in the USA and Europe. Although her repertory is broad and eclectic, she has achieved her greatest successes in an extraordinary variety of modern works, many written specially for her by such composers as Phillip Rhodes, Perera, Lybbert, and Del Tredici; her recordings include many of these and other contemporary pieces. The clarity and pure timbre of her voice, her perfect pitch, three-octave range, and ability to sing accurately (even in quarter-tones) have made her a valued exponent of the music of Boulez, Crumb, Ligeti, and Foss. Her first operatic role was Malinche in the American première of Sessions's *Montezuma* under Sarah Caldwell (Boston, 1976). She has served on the faculties of Kirkland-Hamilton College (Clinton, New York) and the University of Maryland, and has given master classes in the USA and Europe. Her husband is the organist Donald Sutherland, with whom she has performed in recital and on record.

MARTIN BERNHEIMER/R

Bucci, Mark (*b* New York, 26 Feb 1924). Composer. His grandfather was a professional bassoonist and his father played the contrabassoon with the Cleveland Orchestra (1939–60). Bucci studied in New York with Serly (1942–5), and at the Juilliard School (BS 1951) with Jacobi and Giannini; subsequently he was a pupil of Copland at the Berkshire Music Center. He has been the recipient of numerous awards and prizes, including an Irving Berlin Scholarship (1948–52), the Piatigorsky Award (1949), two MacDowell Colony Fellowships (in 1952 and 1954), two Guggenheim Fellowships (1953–4, 1957–8), and a National Institute of Arts and Letters grant (1959). His one-act opera *Tale for a Deaf Ear* was commissioned for performance at the Berkshire Music Festival in the summer of 1957; in 1966 he was named co-winner of the Prix Italia, an international television award, for *The Hero*, an opera that had been commissioned by the Lincoln Center Fund and broadcast from New York the previous year.

The great majority of Bucci's works are for the stage: in addition to operas, he has composed musicals, film scores, and incidental music. He has also written several plays, including works for children; the book and lyrics for a pop opera, *Myron its Deep down Here*; the format for the game show "Keyboard"; and a science-fiction musical, *Time and Again*. An admirer of Puccini, Bucci writes in a modern yet lyric style, utilizing marked rhythms and catchy harmonies and melodies.

WORKS

Operas: The Boor (E. Haun, after Chekhov), 1949; The Beggar's Opera (after Gay), 1950; Sweet Betsy from Pike (Bucci), 1953; The Dress (Bucci), 1953; Tale for a Deaf Ear (after E. Enright), 1957; The Hero (after Gilroy), 1965; The Square One (jazz opera, T. Brown); Myron its Deep down Here (pop opera, Bucci), 1972; Midas (H. Hackaday), 1981

Musicals: Caucasian Chalk Circle (Brecht), 1948; The Thirteen Clocks (Bucci, after J. Thurber), 1953; The Adamses (Bucci, after P. Jacobi), 1956; Time and Again (Bucci), 1958; The Girl from Outside (T. Brown, Bucci), 1959; Chain of Jade (D. Rogers), *c*1960; Pink Party Dress (Rogers), 1960; The Old Lady shows her Medals (Rogers) (1960); Cheaper by the Dozen (Rogers, after F. Gilbreth and E. Carey), 1961; Johnny Mishuga (Rogers), 1961; Our Miss Brooks (Rogers, after R. J. Mann), 1961; The Best of Broadway (revue, Rogers), 1961; Ask any Girl (Rogers), *c*1967; Second Coming (S. S. Ackerman, Bucci), 1976

Incidental music: Cadenza (Dills), 1947; Elmer and Lily (Saroyan), 1952; Summer Afternoon (Bucci), 1952; The Western (mime play), 1954; The Sorcerer's Apprentice (C. Fuller), arr. of Dukas, 1969

Other: 3 stage plays, 1960–67; inst works, incl. Conc. for a Singing Inst, any solo inst, str, 1959; Fl Conc., several choral works, songs

Principal publishers: S. French, Frank

KATHERINE K. PRESTON

Buchla, Donald (Frederick) (*b* Southgate, CA, 17 April 1937). Electronic instrument designer and builder, composer, and performer. He graduated from the University of California, Berkeley (BA in physics 1961), and shortly afterwards became affiliated with the San Francisco Tape Music Center (SFTMC), where he worked with Subotnick, Oliveros, and Sender, composing *musique concrète* (1962) and designing and building acoustic sound sculptures and electronic devices for generating and processing sound. In 1963, with the aid of a Rockefeller Foundation grant, he built the Modular Electronic Music System (part of the Buchla 100 series; see illustration); in 1966 the first complete Buchla synthesizer was installed at the SFTMC. He formed Buchla Associates (later Buchla & Associates) in Berkeley in 1966 to manufacture synthesizers; apart from a brief period (1969–71) during which it was owned by CBS Musical Instruments the company has remained independent. From 1970 most of Buchla's designs incorporated computerized elements. His products are the Electric Music Box (Series 200), the Music Easel (nicknamed "Wea-

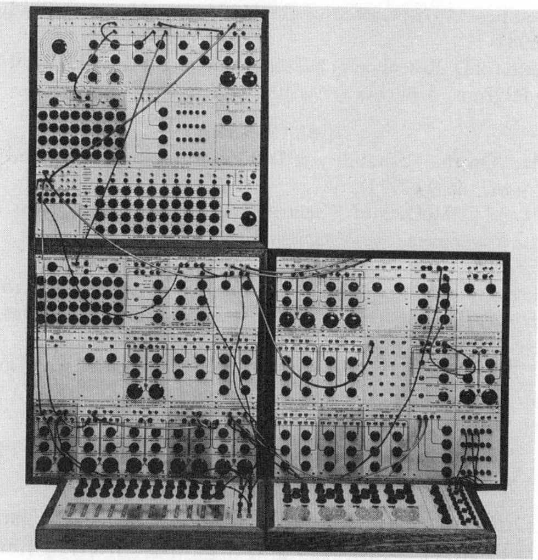

The Buchla Series 100 (1966), a modular analog synthesizer appropriate for studio use; the modules are interconnected by means of patchcords

sel"), the hybrid Series 500, the Series 300, the Touché, and the Buchla 400. Of these the last four named are digital systems, and all except the last two are modular or quasi-modular. A feature of both his analog and digital systems and their accompanying software (of his own design) is their flexibility in performance and adaptability to a wide range of compositional styles (*see* ELECTROACOUSTIC MUSIC, §4).

In addition to electronic instruments Buchla has designed electronic music studios including those of Fylkingen and the Royal Academy of Music in Stockholm and IRCAM, Paris, and some facilities of the Columbia-Princeton Electronic Music Center. He was technical director of the California Institute of the Arts (Los Angeles, 1970–71) and of the Electric Symphony (1971), and has also performed with and served as electronic music consultant for the Arch Ensemble. He has co-directed the Artists' Research Collective, Berkeley, from 1978, and in 1980 he became a consultant to IRCAM. In 1978 he received a Guggenheim Fellowship to study computer languages and in 1981 an NEA grant.

In 1975, with Strange, Buchla co-founded the Electric Weasel Ensemble, a performance group for live electronic music. In his excerpt from the collaborative work *Anagnorisis* (1970) the emotional content of the Joan of Arc legend is communicated through sounds dispersed in space. Such compositions as *Five Video Mirrors* (1966), *Harmonic Pendulum* (1972), and *Consensus Conduction* (1981) are written for specific electronic installations and integrate the roles of composer, performer, and audience. Buchla allows interaction between performer and instrument, a form of directed improvisation, in pieces such as *Keyboard Encounter* (1976) and *Silicon Cello* for amplified cello and electronics (1979). Rhythmic motifs, which are constantly regenerated electronically, and coloristic timbres are characteristic of his work, as is the control through voltage changes of such elements as timbre, pitch, tempo, and modulation.

WORKS

(all with elec insts)

Cicada music, *c*2500 cicadas, 1963; 5 Video Mirrors, audience of 1 or more, 1966; Anagnorisis, 1 player, 1v, 1970 [excerpt from collaborative work]; Harmonic Pendulum, Buchla Series 200 synth, 1972; Garden, 3 players, 1 dancer, 1975; Keyboard Encounter, 2 pf, 1976; Q, 14 insts, 1979; Silicon Cello, amp vc, 1979; Consensus Conduction, Buchla Series 300 synth, audience, 1981

Orchestration of D. Rosenboom: How much Better if Plymouth Rock had Landed on the Pilgrims, 2 Buchla Series 300 synth, 1969

BIBLIOGRAPHY

D. Buchla: "On the Desirability of Distinguishing between Sound and Structure," *Source*, no.9 (1971), 68

D. Buchla and C. McDermid: "Genesis of an Instrument," *Synthesis*, i/1 (1971)

A. Strange: *Programming and Metaprogramming in the Electro-organism: an Operating Directive for the Music Easel* (Berkeley, CA, 1974) [manual]

D. Buchla and others: *Programming and Metaprogramming in the Electro-organism: a Preliminary Operating Directive for the Series 500 Electric Music Box* (Berkeley, CA, 1975) [manual]

J. Aikin: "The Horizons of Instrument Design: a Conversation with Don Buchla," *Keyboard*, viii/12 (1982), 8

H. Davies: "Buchla," *Grove I*

STEPHEN RUPPENTHAL

Buck, Dudley (*b* Hartford, CT, 10 March 1839; *d* West Orange, NJ, 6 Oct 1909). Composer and organist. In 1855 he began to study piano; in the same year he entered Trinity College, Hartford. After two years at Trinity he left to study music in Leipzig, where his teachers were Moritz Hauptmann, Julius Rietz, Johann Schneider, and Ignaz Moscheles. In 1860 he went with Schneider, his organ teacher, to Dresden, where he remained for a year. In 1862, after a year in Paris, he returned to Hartford, where he taught music and played organ in the North Congregational Church.

In 1869 Buck moved to Chicago, where his reputation as an organist increased as a result of several concert tours. After the Chicago Fire in 1871 he became organist for the Music Hall Association in Boston and a member of the faculty of the New England Conservatory of Music. In Boston he wrote his first successful large-scale compositions, *The Legend of Don Munio* and *The Forty-sixth Psalm*; the latter was performed at the Third Triennial Festival of the Handel and Haydn Society in 1874. Buck went to New York in 1875 as the assistant conductor of the Theodore Thomas Orchestra and settled in Brooklyn. He became organist and choirmaster of the Holy Trinity Church and musical director of the Apollo Club of Brooklyn, positions that he held until his retirement in 1903.

Throughout his career Buck composed a large number of anthems, hymns, and other church music; however, his reputation as a composer rested mostly upon his large-scale secular cantatas. In 1876, at the request of the US Centennial Commission, Buck and Sidney Lanier wrote *The Centennial Meditation of Columbia* which was performed at the Centennial Celebration in Philadelphia. In 1880 Buck's cantata *The Golden Legend* was performed at the Cincinnati May Festival, and in 1889 *The Light of Asia* was given its première at Novello's Oratorio Concerts in London. He also composed a number of significant works for the organ, including the first organ sonata written by a native American. In 1898 Buck was elected to the National Institute of Arts and Letters.

His son Dudley Buck (1869–1941) was a tenor and teacher active in London, New York, and Chicago.

WORKS

(selective list; all printed works published in New York unless otherwise indicated)

STAGE

Deseret, or A Saint's Affliction (comic opera, W. A. Croffut), New York, 11 Oct 1880, lost; selections pubd (1880)

Serapis (opera, 3, D. Buck), 1889; vs (1891)

INSTRUMENTAL

Orch: Andante et allegro de concert, pf, orch, op.12, lost; Culprit Fay Ov., op.44, 1870, lost; Sym. "In Springtime," E♭, op.70, lost; Romanza, 4 hn, orch, op.71, *c*1875; Marmion (after W. Scott), ov., 1878; Festival Ov. on . . . The Star-Spangled Banner, *c*1879; Canzonetta et bolero, vn, orch, 1887, version for vn, pf (1887)

Org: Grand Sonata, E♭, op.22 (1866); Concert Variations on The Star-Spangled Banner, op.23 (1868); Impromptu-pastorale, op.27 (1868); At Evening (Idylle), op.52 (1871); Variations on a Scotch Air (Annie Laurie), op.51 (1871); Sonata no.2, g, op.77 (1877); Variations on The Last Rose of Summer, op.59 (1877); Variations on Old Folks at Home (1888); other short pieces, transcrs.

Chamber: Concert Variations on The Last Rose of Summer, str qnt, op.68, 1875; Romanza and Scherzo, fl, 2 vn, va, vc, db, 1883; 3 Fantasias, cl, pf, op.5

6 works, pf; 3 works, pf 4 hands

VOCAL

Sacred: The Forty-sixth Psalm, solo vv, chorus, orch (Boston, 1872); Midnight Service for New Year's Eve, chorus, org (1880); Communion Service, C, chorus, org (1892); The Story of the Cross (Buck), cantata, solo vv, chorus, org (1892); The Triumph of David (Buck), cantata, solo vv, chorus, org (1892); The Coming of the King (Buck), cantata, solo vv, chorus, org (1895); Christ, the Victor (Buck), cantata, chorus, org (1896); 55 anthems; *c*20 sacred songs

Secular cantatas: The Legend of Don Munio (Buck, after W. Irving), solo vv, chorus, orch, op.62 (Boston, 1874); The Centennial Meditation of Columbia (S. Lanier), chorus, orch (1876); The Nun of Nidaros (Longfellow), T, male chorus, fl, str qnt, pf, reed org, op.83, 1878 (1879); Scenes from The Golden Legend (H. W. Longfellow), solo vv, chorus, orch, 1879 (1880); King Olaf's

Christmas (Longfellow), solo vv, male chorus, str qnt, pf, reed org, op.86, vs (1881); Chorus of Spirits and Hours (P. B. Shelley), T, male chorus, fl, str qnt, pf, org, op.90 (1882); The Voyage of Columbus (Buck, after Irving), solo vv, male chorus, orch (1885); The Light of Asia (E. Arnold), solo vv, chorus, orch, vs (London, 1886); Bugle Song (A. Tennyson), male chorus, orch (1891); Paul Revere's Ride (Longfellow), male chorus, orch (1898)

*c*50 sacred and secular choruses, male, female, or mixed vv, incl. Festival Hymn (Buck), op.57 (Boston, 1872); *c*50 secular songs; 4 duets, vv, pf

Principal publishers: Ditson, Novello, Presser, G. Schirmer
MSS in *MB*, *DLC*

WRITINGS

Illustrations in Choir Accompaniment with Hints in Registration (New York, 1877/*R*1971)
The Influence of the Organ in History (London, 1882)

BIBLIOGRAPHY

Dudley Buck: a Complete Bibliography (New York, 1910) [list of works]
F. H. Johnson: *Musical Memories of Hartford* (Hartford, 1931/*R*1970)
R. G. Cole: "Buck, Dudley," *DAB*
W. K. Gallo: *The Life and Church Music of Dudley Buck* (diss., Catholic U. of America, 1968)

WILLIAM K. GALLO/R

Buck and wing. A black-American dance of the late 19th and early 20th centuries. As an immediate predecessor of the tap dance (the terms "tap dancing" and "buck and wing" were often used interchangeably in the early 1900s), the buck and wing grew out of earlier dances of black and white origin, including the buck, soft shoe, clog dance, jig, wing, and pigeon wing. Like the buck and clog dances, it was performed on the flat foot, though not as a shuffle; the wing step consisted of several taps, a scrape, and an upward spring. Any standard 32-bar tune served as a suitable accompaniment.

BIBLIOGRAPHY

M. Stearns and J. Stearns: *Jazz Dance: the Story of American Vernacular Dance* (New York, 1968)
L. F. Emery: *Black Dance in the United States from 1619 to 1970* (Palo Alto, CA, 1972)

For further bibliography, *see* DANCE.

PAULINE NORTON

Buckley. Family of minstrel performers of English origin. James Buckley (*b* Manchester, England, 1803; *d* Quincy, MA, 27 April 1872) came to the USA with his family in 1839 and formed the Congo Melodists in Boston in 1843. The troupe moved to New York after 1845, later becoming famous as the New Orleans Serenaders and then as Buckley's Serenaders. They made two trips to England (1846–8 and 1860–61). James Buckley's sons were members of the troupe. R. Bishop Buckley (*b* England, 1826; *d* Quincy, 1867) was famous for his playing of the Chinese fiddle, and Fred Buckley (*b* Bolton, England, 12 Oct 1833; *d* Boston, MA, 12 Sept 1864) was a superb violinist. George Swayne Buckley (*b* Bolton, Aug 1829; *d* Quincy, 25 June 1879) was the most versatile, appearing as a singer, dancer, and burlesque actor, as well as playing several instruments (he was particularly known as a banjoist and bones player). In the early 1840s he toured with banjoist Joel Sweeney as "Young Sweeney." According to Converse, Buckley was probably the first to play the banjo in the "guitar" style, where the fingers are used to pluck the strings, rather than in the original "stroke" style.

Buckley's Serenaders were influential in the late 1840s and early 1850s, particularly since they were the first company to produce burlesque blackface opera, a genre in which they excelled. After his father's retirement and the death of his brothers, George Swayne Buckley reorganized the troupe in 1867 and toured until about 1876.

BIBLIOGRAPHY

F. B. Converse: "Banjo Reminiscences," *The Cadenza*, vii–ix (1901–2) [series of articles]
E. L. Rice: *Monarchs of Minstrelsy* (New York, 1911)
C. Wittke: *Tambo and Bones: a History of the American Minstrel Stage* (Durham, 1930)
N. Howard: *The Banjo and its Players* (MS, 1957, *NN-L*)

ROBERT B. WINANS

Buckley, Emerson (*b* New York, 14 April 1916). Conductor. After studying at Columbia University (BA 1936), he held his first conducting post with the Columbia Grand Opera, 1936–8. Over the next decade, he held a variety of positions in opera, ballet, symphonic music, and broadcasting. He served as music director of the Miami Opera, 1950–73, and then became its artistic director and resident conductor; in 1963 he was appointed conductor of the Fort Lauderdale SO and in 1964 music director of the Seattle Opera. He has conducted numerous other companies, including the New York City Opera, and has appeared as guest conductor with major orchestras, among them the Toronto SO, Minneapolis SO, and Boston SO. He presented world premières of Moore's *The Ballad of Baby Doe* (1956) and Robert Ward's *The Crucible* (1961) and *Minutes till Midnight* (1982). Also active as an educator, Buckley has served on the faculties of the University of Denver (1956), Columbia University (1957–8), the Manhattan School (1958–70), Temple University (1970), and the North Carolina School of the Arts (1971). While at the Manhattan School he produced many operas from the French repertory, including such little-known works as Thomas' *Hamlet*, Berlioz's *Béatrice et Bénédict*, Massenet's *Werther* and *Thaïs*, and Gounod's *Mireille*. In 1963 he received the Alice M. Ditson Award for conducting, and in 1970 he was made a Chevalier of the Ordre des Arts et Lettres by the French government; his son Richard (*b* New York, 1 Sept 1953), also a conductor, was appointed music director of the Oakland SO in 1983.

MICHAEL FLEMING

Buckwheat notation. One of the names used for the notation of SHAPE-NOTE HYMNODY.

Budapest Quartet. String quartet of Hungarian origin. The original members, Emil Hauser, Imre Poganyi, Istvan Ipolyi, and Harry Son, all played in the Budapest Opera Orchestra; the quartet gave its first concert in 1917 and made several European tours in the 1920s. During its subsequent history, the membership changed completely: by 1936 it consisted of Joseph Roisman (first violin), ALEXANDER SCHNEIDER (second violin), Boris Kroyt (viola), and Mischa Schneider (cello). Though these players were Russians and Ukrainians, the quartet's name remained unchanged and it was in this form that it became famous on both sides of the Atlantic.

In 1938, after extensive tours of Europe, the players settled in the USA. From that year until 1962 they were quartet-in-residence at the Library of Congress, where they gave 20 concerts a year. In 1944 Alexander Schneider was replaced as second violinist by Edgar Ortensky; Ortensky was subsequently replaced by Jac Gorodetzky, but in 1955 Schneider resumed his former position. For the string quintet repertory they were often joined by Katims and, after 1955, Trampler. In 1962, the quartet assumed residency at SUNY, Buffalo, but it continued to undertake world tours, becoming especially renowned for its interpretation of Beethoven's quartets. The group made its last public appearance in 1967, after which the illness first of Mischa Schneider and, within a year, of Roisman and Kroyt forced it to disband. Roisman retired in 1969 at the age of 68, and in the same year Kroyt died at the age of 72; the other two members continued to teach at Buffalo. Under Roisman's leadership the Budapest Quartet became known for its forthright brilliance and unanimity of style. During its last 30 years, it achieved not only a high level of critical esteem, but a remarkable popular success.

BIBLIOGRAPHY

R. Gelatt: "Budapest String Quartet," *Music-Makers* (New York, 1953), 178
J. Wechsberg: "Profiles: the Budapest," *New Yorker*, xxxv (14 Nov 1959), 59
B. James: "The Budapest Quartet," *Audio and Record Review*, iii/3 (1963), 15 [with discography by F. F. Clough and G. J. Cuming]
S. Smolian: Discography, *American Record Guide*, xxxvii (1970–71), 220

ROBERT PHILIP/R

Budd, Harold (*b* Los Angeles, CA, 24 May 1936). Composer. He attended Los Angeles City College and San Fernando Valley State College (BA 1963), where he was a pupil in composition of Aurelio de la Vega, and studied with Dahl at the University of Southern California (MM 1966). From 1970 to 1976 he was a faculty member at the California Institute of the Arts, Valencia; as a teacher he influenced a number of younger composers, including Eugene Bowen, Peter Garland, and Michael Byron. Budd has been awarded two NEA grants (1974, 1979–80). His early work (until 1972) made use of open structures: *The Candy-apple Revision*, for example, consists simply of a D♭ major chord. At that time he worked frequently in performance with Oliveros and Lentz, and with the visual artist Wolfgang Stoerchle. His later music is characterized by an extreme lyricism and lushness, partly the result of a skillful use of chromatic harmony and of his choice of instruments – electric pianos, harps, vibraphones, and female voices. Works from this period are of a radical simplicity, yet subtle and refined. Black musicians, including Albert Ayler, Pharoah Sanders, and Marion Brown (the last of whom he has collaborated with), have exerted an influence on his sense of melodic statement, while from Eno he learned to regard the recording studio as a musical medium (since 1979 his compositions have not been notated and are subject to much studio modification). In the early 1980s Budd successfully merged contemporary and new-wave music elements.

WORKS

NOTATED

The Candy-apple Revision, any inst(s), 1970; Madrigals of the Rose Angel, female vv, harp, cel, elec pf, perc, 1972; Butterfly Sunday, Mez, harp, 1973; Let Us Go into the House of the Lord, Mez, harp, 1974; Song of Paradise: 17 Illuminations on the Holy Koran, B-Bar, harp, glock, vib, perc, 1974; Bismillahi 'Rrahmani 'Rrahim, a sax, elec pf, cel, vib, mar, perc, 1974–5; Juno, perc ens, 1975; Basheva Songs (D. G. Rossetti, P. Bethsebe), 1978

STUDIO

(titles are those of individual works; details in parentheses are of recordings)

Coeur d'Orr (Advance FGR–16, 1972); The Oak of the Golden Dream (Advance FGR–16, 1972); The Plateaux of Mirror, collab. B. Eno (Editions EG 202, 1980); The Serpent (in Quicksilver) (Cantil 181, 1981); Abandoned Cities (Cantil 384, 1984); Dark Star (Cantil 384, 1984); The Pearl, collab. Eno (Editions EG 37, 1984); Wonder's Edge, collab. E. Bowen (Cold Blue L 10, 1984)

Works up to 1970 and some others, withdrawn

BIBLIOGRAPHY

J. Silberman: Interview with Harold Budd, *LA Reader* (Los Angeles, 31 Oct 1981)
B. Jackson: "Harold Budd," *BAM Magazine* (San Francisco, 12 Feb 1982)
G. Sandow: "Music for a Rainy Day," *Village Voice* (23 Oct 1984) [review of *Abandoned Cities*]

PETER GARLAND

Buelow, George J(ohn) (*b* Chicago, IL, 31 March 1929). Musicologist. He studied at the Chicago Musical College (BM 1950, MM 1951) and in 1951 began graduate studies in musicology at New York University (PhD 1961). From 1961 to 1968 he taught at the University of California, Riverside. He was then professor of music successively at the University of Kentucky, from 1968 until 1969, and at Rutgers University to 1977, when he became professor of musicology at Indiana University. Buelow specializes in German music of the 17th and early 18th centuries, with emphasis on performance practice, theory, and opera. His study of Heinichen's treatise on thoroughbass accompaniment (1966) is one of the principal works in English on German Baroque theory. His work on the operas of Mattheson includes an edition of *Cleopatra* (EDM, 1975). He also wrote a study of Strauss's *Ariadne auf Naxos* (1975, with Donald G. Daviau). Buelow is the series editor for musicology of the UMI Research Press.

PAULA MORGAN

Buffalo. City in western New York state (pop. 357,870; metropolitan area 1,242,826). The frontier village of Buffalo, situated at the eastern tip of Lake Erie and abutting Canada, was settled in 1803 and incorporated in 1832. Its early musical life was dominated by German settlers; its rise to prominence as a musical center coincided with its industrial growth in the late 19th century.

1. Early history. 2. Performing ensembles. 3. Concert venues and organizations, ballet, and opera. 4. Education and libraries. 5. Instrument making. 6. Broadcasting.

1. EARLY HISTORY. In 1812 the First Presbyterian Church and its choir were founded; the first singing group, the Musica Sacra Society, was organized by about 60 residents in 1820. A village band was formed in 1824, and a military band was established in 1829. The first professional musician, James D. Sheppard, arrived in Buffalo in 1827; he started a music store (which from 1838 was headquarters of the Handel and Haydn Society), taught music, and gave the first performances on the first organ in the village, installed in St. Paul's Episcopal Church in 1829. The Philharmonic Society, a singing society, was formed in 1830; during the latter half of the 19th century many other singing societies flourished, of which the best-known were the Buffalo Liedertafel (established in 1848 and active well into the 20th century), the Liederkraenzchen (formed 1853), and the Buffalo Saengerbund (formed 1855; first performance 1862). These ethnic societies were followed by such groups as the Continental Singing Society (1862), the St. Cecelia Society (1863), the Ladies Morning Musicale (formed by Mrs. Lawrence Rumsey in 1870), the Choral Union (formed by Carl Adam in 1871), and the Guido Chorus (formed by Seth Clark in 1904). A number of ethnic singing societies are still functioning, of which the Polish Chopin Singing Society is the most active; it has made several European tours. The largest community chorus in the city is the Buffalo Schola Cantorum, which performs regularly with the Buffalo PO in addition to presenting concerts of its own.

2. PERFORMING ENSEMBLES. The first orchestra in Buffalo was the short-lived Beethoven Musical Society, formed in 1869. After

its demise, orchestral music was performed by visiting ensembles. In 1883 Leopold Damrosch brought the New York Symphony Society, an orchestra of over 100 players, to Buffalo for the 23rd Saengerfest of the German North American Saengerbund. Theodore Thomas visited annually with his orchestra from 1884, and Walter Damrosch conducted his orchestra in 1887. The same year the Buffalo Orchestral Association was formed, with John Lund as its conductor; this group lasted for nine years, and was supported principally by Frederick C. M. Lautz, a local businessman. In 1901 Victor Herbert and his orchestra performed at the Pan American Exposition in Buffalo; their concerts proved popular, and the orchestra was invited to give another series of performances the following year. In 1906 Louis Whiting Gai and Mai Davis Smith, who were local impresarios, inaugurated Buffalo's first regular series of concerts by visiting orchestras. The Philharmonic Society of Buffalo was formed in 1908; this group sponsored performances by Frederick Stock and the Chicago SO from 1909 to 1917.

In 1921 Arnold Cornelissen formed a 70-piece orchestra, the Buffalo SO, which performed six times a year with visiting soloists and conductors. During the Depression the city's musical life was supported by public funds; members of the Buffalo SO became part of the Mayor's Committee for Unemployment in 1933 under the direction of John Lund, and during the next several years the orchestra was financed by such federal agencies as the Temporary Emergency Relief Administration, the Federal Music Project, and the WPA. In 1935 the Buffalo PO was established under the conductorship of Franco Autori; the orchestra was conducted by William Steinberg from 1945 to 1952, and by Josef Krips from 1953 to 1963. Lukas Foss, who was music director from 1963 to 1970, emphasized the modern repertory, and under him the orchestra recorded works by such composers as Cage, Penderecki, and Xenakis. The Buffalo PO was led by Michael Tilson Thomas from 1971 to 1978, by Julius Rudel from 1979 to 1985, and by Semyon Bychkov from 1985. In the early 1980s the orchestra had 87 members and gave over 150 concerts annually, including 18 subscription concerts in Buffalo, a series of concerts in local churches that often included works for organ and orchestra, and a number of performances as a visiting orchestra throughout the region and nationally. The orchestra also gives "pops" and children's concerts; some of its members administer and coach the Greater Buffalo Youth Orchestra, and participate in educational programs sponsored by Young Audiences of Western New York. Other orchestras active in the Buffalo area include the community orchestra of Cheektowaga (formed 1960), the Clarence Summer Orchestra (formed in 1959 by Joseph Wincenc), and the community orchestras of Orchard Park (1949) and Amherst (1946), both also formed by Wincenc. There are several chamber orchestras that include members of the Buffalo PO; perhaps the best-known of these is the Ars Nova Orchestra (1974), conducted by Marylouise Nanna, which presents an annual Vivaldi festival.

According to several accounts a string quartet was first heard in Buffalo in the late 1870s. In 1884 the Buffalo Philharmonic Society was organized "to establish and maintain a quartet of stringed instruments"; as a result the Dannreuther String Quartette of New York was engaged for several series of concerts. The Buffalo Symphony Society was organized in 1921 and incorporated in 1924; it sponsored performances by some of the leading chamber ensembles of the day. The first concerts were given in the Hotel Statler ballroom. The society (renamed the Buffalo Chamber Music Society in 1940) later presented concerts by such performers as Andrés Segovia, Jean-Pierre Rampal, the Albeneri and Beaux Arts trios, the Budapest, Cleveland, Flonzaley, Hungarian, and Juilliard quartets, the Vienna Octet, and I Solisti Veneti; the society now sponsors a series of five concerts each year.

3. Concert venues and organizations, ballet, and opera. Until the mid-19th century most concerts and recitals were held in private homes. When Jenny Lind gave a recital in 1851, the need for a concert hall became evident. St. James Hall, built in 1835, was used for musical performances from 1859. The city's opera house was in use from 1862 to 1874, and the Metropolitan

Kleinhans Music Hall, Buffalo

Theatre, built in 1852, was renovated and renamed the Academy of Music in 1868. In 1883 the German Young Men's Christian Association built a music hall; this was destroyed by fire in 1885, and a second hall was built in 1887. The new building had an auditorium seating 2500 and a smaller concert hall seating 1100. In 1901 an ornate Temple of Music was constructed as part of the Pan American Exposition; this contained an impressive pipe organ and a Steinway grand piano.

The principal concert hall in Buffalo is Kleinhans Music Hall (see illustration). In 1934 Edward L. Kleinhans and Mary Seaton Kleinhans left their estates to the City of Buffalo for the purpose of constructing a concert hall; such a facility was greatly needed, as the old Elmwood Music Hall (the remodeled 74th Armory), which had been the site of most large musical events since 1912, was inadequate and structurally unsound. Kleinhans Music Hall, designed by Eliel Saarinen, was begun in 1939 and dedicated on 12 October 1940, at a concert by the Buffalo PO. The hall is known for its simple, elegant architecture and its excellent acoustics. Its main auditorium seats 2839, and its Mary Seaton Room, used principally for chamber music concerts and receptions, seats 850. Kleinhans Music Hall is used by the Buffalo PO, the Buffalo Chamber Music Society, and other local organizations.

A number of concerts are held at Holy Trinity Lutheran Church; its organ, built by Moeller and Van Zoren, is one of the largest electronically assisted instruments in the USA. A five-manual chancel console and a two-manual gallery console were completed in 1984 expressly for use in performances by the Buffalo PO. Shea's Buffalo Theater, built in 1926, regularly presents musicals, ballets, and operas on a modest scale. In Amherst, New York, the Frank B. and Cameron Baird Music Hall and the 700-seat Frederick C. and Alice Slee Chamber Hall were dedicated in 1981 at the University of Buffalo's new suburban campus.

During the summer months, an outstanding series of opera, ballet, and Broadway productions, and performances by the Rochester PO, are presented at Artpark in Lewiston, north of Buffalo. This facility, opened in the summer of 1974, is located on the Niagara River, and includes a 2324-seat theater, with additional seating outdoors. In the summer of 1984 the Buffalo PO Society dedicated a new Waterfront Performing Arts Facility, a tent-like structure suitable for popular concerts; in the past such concerts have been held at Rich Stadium, and in the 18,000-seat Memorial Auditorium. Popular music is also heard at the Tralfamadore Cafe in Buffalo's theater district; this and the Hotel Statler are popular venues for jazz.

One of the city's leading concert organizations is the Chromatic Club, formed in 1898; modeled after a Boston club of the same name, it sponsored concerts by its own members and other performers. Its support of Buffalo's orchestras began in 1921, when it paid for the first concert of the Buffalo Orchestra Association, and it has continued to sponsor concerts and recitals, and to encourage young musicians by awarding scholarships. In the 1940s the impresario Zorah B. Berry was responsible for bringing talented artists and orchestras from around the world to Buffalo. From 1973 QRS, a local manufacturer of piano rolls, promoted recitals and concerts by celebrated musicians, and in 1978 it established a nonprofit arts foundation to organize this program. Two of the more active local promoters of popular music are Festival East Concerts and Harvey and Corky Productions.

Buffalo has never been able to support ballet or opera on a large scale, but the Empire State Ballet and the Western New York Opera Theatre are strong local companies.

4. Education and libraries. Buffalo has a long tradition of fine music instruction, and its educational programs enjoy wide support. The First Settlement Music School was established in 1924. The University of Buffalo (from 1962 part of SUNY) has an important music department, which was founded by Cameron Baird in 1951; Baird brought Hindemith to Buffalo in 1939 when the composer fled Germany. The university has attracted to its faculty such prominent figures as composers Morton Feldman and Lejaren Hiller, librarian and bibliographer James Coover, musicologist Jeremy Noble, and such performing groups as the Budapest and Cleveland quartets. For many years, beginning in 1964, the university was the headquarters of the Center for the Creative and Performing Arts. Founded by Lukas Foss and Allen Sapp, chairman of the music department, the center brought young composers and instrumentalists to Buffalo for one-year residencies to compose and perform new music. The program did much to establish Buffalo as a center of contemporary music in the USA; it attracted such musicians as Sylvano Bussotti, George Crumb, Cornelius Cardew, Terry Riley, Niccolò Castiglioni, Vinko Globokar, Yuji Takahashi, and Paul Zukofsky. Through the professorship for composition, endowed by the Frederick and Alice Slee bequest, Nabokov, Haieff, Smit, Kirchner, Hiller, Copland, Rorem, Thomson, Rochberg, Carlos Chávez, Henri Pousseur, David Diamond, and Mauricio Kagel have been composers-in-residence at the university. The Slee bequest has also, since 1956, supported annual performances of the complete cycle of Beethoven's string quartets by such ensembles as the Budapest, La Salle, Guarneri, Juilliard, and Orford quartets. The university's music department confers the BFA and the BA, the MFA in performance, and masters' and doctoral degrees in theory, music education, music history, and composition. It has an enrollment of about 290 (180 undergraduate, 110 graduate) and 28 full-time faculty members.

The music department of the State University College of New York at Buffalo, for many years led by Joseph Wincenc, has traditionally trained music educators for the Buffalo area. In addition to the fine music library located at SUNY, Buffalo, the city has one of the country's leading public library music collections at the main branch of the Buffalo and Erie County Library; the former collections of the Buffalo Museum of Science, the Grosvenor Reference Library, and the Buffalo Public Library are housed there. The library's many scores, recordings, librettos, and books include strong collections of American folk music and of popular sheet music. The library also houses the NBC SO–Toscanini collection of scores, purchased by the Buffalo PO in 1958; the collection contains 2000 titles, including first editions, and scores bearing Toscanini's notations on technical and stylistic matters. (*See also* Libraries and collections, §3.)

5. Instrument making. The history of musical instruments in Buffalo from the 18th century to the 1930s is documented in a collection of 200 instruments in the Buffalo and Erie County Historical Society. Included in the collection are fifes, drums, and bugles from the War of 1812, the Civil War, and World War I, American Indian instruments, a Steinway piano from the 1901 Pan American Exposition, and such rarities as a giraffe piano, a Gibson harp-guitar, and a leather-covered Russian bassoon.

One of Buffalo's most important instrument manufacturers was the George A. Prince Company, which distributed more than 40,000 melodeons worldwide. The Rudolph Wurlitzer Co.

long had an office in the Buffalo suburb of North Tonawanda, and Farny Wurlitzer (1883–1972) was an important musical figure in Buffalo for decades. Two of Wurlitzer's theater organs are still extant in Buffalo: the instrument at the Riviera Theater in North Tonawanda is used regularly in concerts and recitals, and the organ at Shea's Buffalo Theater was restored in 1984. Wurlitzer's North Tonawanda factory also manufactured band organs, as did a number of other concerns in the town, including North Tonawanda Musical Instrument Works and Artizan Factories.

Tonawanda is the home of the Schlicker Organ Company, formed in 1932 by the organ builder Herman Leonhard Schlicker, which manufactures pipe organs. In Buffalo the QRS company continues to make piano rolls.

6. BROADCASTING. One of the more notable musical institutions to become established in Buffalo is its local concert music station. WNED-FM, a National Public Radio station, began broadcasting concert music in 1977. It broadcasts classical music exclusively, and produces locally a "Music in Buffalo" series. For several years WNED-TV's telecasts of the Buffalo PO's Martin Luther King, Jr., Concerts were nationally broadcast.

BIBLIOGRAPHY

A. A. Van De Mark: *The Year Book of the American Artist's Club, Season 1924–1925* (Buffalo, 1925)

M. Larned and E. Choate: *Music in Buffalo from 1882–1932* (Buffalo, 1932)

——: *The First Fifty Years of Music in Buffalo* (Buffalo, 1932)

S. Pascal: *A History of Musical Preparation and Performed Musical Activity in the Community of Buffalo during the First Half of the 19th Century* (Buffalo, 1950)

W. L. Barnette, Jr.: *An Informal History of the Buffalo Chamber Music Society* (Buffalo, 1973)

The Chromatic Club: Seventy-fifth Anniversary, 1898–1973 (Buffalo, 1973)

P. Hart: "Buffalo Philharmonic Orchestra," *Orpheus in the New World: the Symphony Orchestra as an American Cultural Institution* (New York, 1973), 212

Mrs. W. J. Mangan: *Inside the Buffalo Philharmonic Orchestra* (Buffalo, 1980)

JUDITH A. COON

Buffalo Springfield. Rock group. It was formed by Stephen Stills (*b* Dallas, TX, 3 Jan 1945; singer and guitarist), Richie (Paul Richard) Furay (*b* Yellow Springs, OH, 9 May 1944; singer and guitarist), and Neil Young (*b* Toronto, Ont., 12 Nov 1945; singer and guitarist). This central trio was augmented by Dewey Martin (singer and drummer) and Bruce Palmer (bass guitarist). The group's first album, *Buffalo Springfield* (1967), consisting entirely of songs by Stills and Young, offered plaintive vocal harmonizing and rock fervor over a folk-rock base, a sound that was made better known by the group Crosby, Stills and Nash (later joined by Young). Buffalo Springfield began to break up soon after its recording début; later members of the group included Jim Felder, bass guitarist; Doug Hastings, guitarist; and Jim Messina, guitarist. In addition to Crosby, Stills, Nash and Young and its various spinoffs, and Poco, which was formed by Furay and Messina, Buffalo Springfield was also the basis or inspiration for the duo Loggins and Messina, the Souther–Hillman–Furay Band, and the Eagles, and launched the solo careers of many of these musicians.

Buffalo Springfield lasted only from 1966 to 1969, but its work helped determine the pattern of the eclectic, commercially successful folk-rock and country-rock Los Angeles groups made up of members of widely diverging styles. It also helped establish southern California's music industry as a commercial challenge to the dominance of London's during the mid- to late 1960s, though the group itself had only one hit single, *For what it's worth* (no.7, 1967).

RECORDINGS

(selective list; all recorded for Atco/Atlantic)

Buffalo Springfield (33-200, 1967); For what it's worth (6459, 1967); *Buffalo Springfield Again* (33-226, 1968); *Last Time Around* (33-256, 1969)

BIBLIOGRAPHY

D. Koepp: "Buffalo Springfield: a Trouser Press Retrospective," *Trouser Press*, vi/1 (1979), 25

JOHN ROCKWELL

Buhaina, Abdullah Ibn. *See* BLAKEY, ART.

Buhlig, Richard (*b* Chicago, IL, 21 Dec 1880; *d* Los Angeles, CA, 30 Jan 1952). Pianist and teacher. He studied in Chicago and in Vienna with Theodor Leschetizky, and made his début in Berlin in 1901. He then toured Europe and the USA, where he made his début with the Philadelphia Orchestra in New York on 5 November 1907. In 1923 he returned to Europe with two of his pupils, Henry Cowell and Wesley Kuhnle; Cowell and Buhlig gave concerts in Berlin and Vienna. On his return to the USA, Buhlig became associated with Cowell's New Music Society and gave recitals in Los Angeles and San Francisco. He was a teacher of piano at the Institute of Musical Art in New York. He also taught John Cage.

Buketoff, Igor (*b* Hartford, CT, 29 May 1915). Conductor. He studied at the University of Kansas (1931–2), the Juilliard School (BS 1935, MS 1941), and the Los Angeles Conservatory (honorary doctorate 1949), and taught at Juilliard (1935–45), the Chautauqua School of Music (1941–7), and Columbia University (1943–7). In 1942 he won the first Alice M. Ditson Award for Young Conductors. He has held the directorships of the Chautauqua Opera (1941–7), the Fort Wayne PO (1948–66), the Iceland State SO (1964–5), the St. Paul Opera (1968–74), and the Texas Chamber Orchestra (1980–81). He also taught at Butler University (1953–63) and the University of Texas (1977–9). A champion of contemporary music, he founded the World Music Bank for International Exchange and Promotion of Contemporary Music in 1957 and headed the Contemporary Composers Project for the Institute of International Education from 1967 to 1970. In collaboration with RCA Victor, he has recorded compositions by Lees, Mennin, Sessions, and Yardumian, and other 20th-century works. In 1984 he conducted the world première of the fragment of Rachmaninoff's opera *Mona Vanna* with the Philadelphia Orchestra at the Saratoga (New York) Arts Center.

THOR ECKERT, JR.

Bukofzer, Manfred F(ritz) (*b* Oldenburg, Germany, 17 March 1910; *d* Oakland, CA, 7 Dec 1955). Musicologist. He entered Heidelberg University to study law but soon decided on musicology as a career. After musical studies in Berlin, he entered Basle University (PhD 1936). In 1937 he was lecturer at the Volksschule of Basle University; he immigrated to the USA in 1939. After a year at Western Reserve University in Cleveland (1940–41), he joined the faculty at the University of California, Berkeley, and remained there until his death.

Bukofzer's doctoral dissertation, on the history of English discant, firmly established his reputation as one of the most brilliant scholars of his generation. There followed many other pioneering studies on English music of the 14th and 15th centuries, including writings on Dunstable (whose works he edited for Musica Britannica, 1953) and the documents of pre-Tudor

English polyphony. Bukofzer's scholarly interests, however, extended well beyond English music of the Renaissance. He did research in ethnomusicology, he was a capable conductor, and although he disclaimed being a specialist in Baroque music, his *Music in the Baroque Era* (1947) remains a standard survey. He is also the author of *Studies in Medieval and Renaissance Music* (1950). Bukofzer was keenly interested in the nature and purpose of musicology and its relationship to other academic disciplines; some of this work appears in *The Place of Musicology in American Institutions of Higher Learning* (1957/*R*1977). He was the first American chairman of the committee of RISM and represented musicology in the American Council of Learned Societies.

SYDNEY ROBINSON CHARLES/R

Bulgarian-American music. *See* EUROPEAN-AMERICAN MUSIC, §III, 4.

Bull, Amos (*b* Enfield, CT, 9 Feb 1744; *d* Hartford, CT, 23 Aug 1825). Singing master, composer, and schoolteacher. He grew up in Enfield and Farmington and probably received his musical training in singing-school. When he was 22, he advertised proposals for an ambitious three-part compendium of church music: rules of music; psalm tunes; and services, chants, hymns, and anthems. There is no evidence that subscriptions were sufficient to enable publication. Bull's peripatetic life as singing master took him from New London and New Haven to Connecticut River valley towns and back. In 1774 the New London (Connecticut) *Gazette* advertised for sale Bull's *The Gamut or Rules of Music*. He may have invented this popular and inexpensive teaching aid, which first appeared in Connecticut about 1760 and was usually bound into commonplace books compiled for and by singing-school students.

Bull was teaching in New York during the Revolutionary War: he became parish clerk and master of the Charity School of Trinity Church from April 1778 to 1782, when he resigned and returned to Connecticut. In 1788, he established a store and school at his Hartford residence. The Second Ecclesiastical Society (South Church) employed him to instruct their choir for over 25 years. He was an Episcopalian, and although his collection of psalms and anthems *The Responsory* was reportedly designed for the South Church choir, it contained 12 anthems by Bull on prayerbook texts, set for the unusual combination of two trebles, tenor, and bass. The collection, published in 1795, was largely of American compositions and was the first by a Connecticut composer to be printed typographically. Bull's house still stands as a Hartford landmark.

See also PSALMODY, esp. ex.7.

BIBLIOGRAPHY

E. P. Parker: *History of the Second Church of Christ in Hartford* (Hartford, 1892)
R. Daniel: *The Anthem in New England before 1800* (Evanston, 1966)
R. Crawford: "Connecticut Sacred Music Imprints, 1778–1810," *Notes*, xxvii (1970–71), 445, 671
D. O. White: "Amos Bull and the House that would not Die," *Connecticut Antiquarian*, xxv/1 (1973), 4
R. M. Wilson: *Connecticut's Music in the Revolutionary Era* (Hartford, 1979)

RUTH M. WILSON

Bull, Ole (Bornemann) (*b* Bergen, Norway, 5 Feb 1810; *d* Lysøen, nr Bergen, 17 Aug 1880). Norwegian violinist and composer. He was trained in Norway, and remained devoted to Norwegian culture and the cause of Norwegian independence throughout his life. He made several tours in Europe during the 1830s and 1840s, which established him as one of the greatest violin virtuosos of his time; when he returned to Norway in 1838, he was welcomed as a national hero. He toured in America from November 1843 to December 1845, having spectacular success; the *New York Herald* estimated that he traveled 100,000 miles and gave over 200 concerts. Bull returned to Norway in October 1848, and devoted the next three years to promoting Norwegian folk culture; in July 1849 he founded a national theater in Bergen.

Ole Bull: drawing (1839) by Josef Kriehuber (private collection)

In January 1852 Bull returned to the USA to found a colony for Norwegian immigrants; he bought 11,144 acres in Potter County, Pennsylvania, and spent much time and money supporting settlers and building the colony's first capital, Oleana. Legal and logistical problems proved insurmountable, however, and in September 1853 Bull sold his holdings and the scheme collapsed. He began touring again, this time with Maurice Strakosch and Strakosch's ten-year-old sister-in-law Adelina Patti. From November 1852 to December 1853 they traveled as far west as Chicago and as far south as New Orleans, and in 1854 Bull and Strakosch went to California. Early in 1855 Bull joined with Strakosch and Max Maretzek in an unsuccessful attempt to sponsor a season of opera in New York. For the next two years Bull was harassed by lawyers and beset by illness; he performed often, but spent much time in New York and Boston, where he was an honored guest in literary circles. On 29 July 1857 he sailed again for Norway, and during the next decade lived primarily in Bergen.

From 1867 to 1873 Bull made winter tours of the USA and spent his summers in Norway. In 1870 he married Sara Thorp, the 20-year-old daughter of a Wisconsin senator, and in 1872 he sponsored a fund for the purchase of a collection of Scandinavian literature for the University of Wisconsin. During the same year he built a large estate on Lysøen, an island near Bergen, where, from 1873, estranged from his wife, he lived for much of the time, performing in Europe most winters. He returned to the USA in 1876, after he and his wife were reconciled; he also settled his differences with Maurice Strakosch, who managed his tours from 1877. Bull remained a great attraction in America and performed with undiminished success almost until his death.

Bull's devotion to independence and democracy, his engaging individualism, and his enterprising idealism were all in accord with mid-19th-century American ideology, with its blend of initiative, sentiment, and visionary thought. By 1845 Bull was describing himself as America's "adopted son," and during his second visit he was more citizen than musician, entangled in schemes, promotion, and litigation. His popularity was universal, from Boston salons to frontier steamboats, and depended as much on his colorful personality and his genuine affection for common people as on the remarkable virtuosity that made his name a byword for "fiddle" playing of legendary quality.

BIBLIOGRAPHY

S. C. Bull: *Ole Bull: a Memoir* (Boston, 1883/*R*1978)
M. B. Smith: *The Life of Ole Bull* (Princeton, 1943/*R*1973)
O. Linge: *Ole Bull* (Oslo, 1953)
I. Bull: *Ole Bull's Activities in the United States between 1843 and 1880* (Smithtown, NY, 1982)

WILLIAM BROOKS

Bumbry, Grace (Melzia Ann) (*b* St. Louis, MO, 4 Jan 1937). Mezzo-soprano and soprano. She studied at Boston University, Northwestern University, and the Music Academy of the West, Santa Barbara, where she was taught by Lotte Lehmann from 1955 to 1958, the year she was joint winner (with Martina Arroyo) of the Metropolitan Opera auditions. After gaining further prizes, she went to Europe and made her stage début at the Paris Opéra in 1960 as Amneris. That year she joined the Basle Opera where she built up her repertory. In 1961 she appeared at Bayreuth – the first black artist to sing in that house – as Venus (*Tannhäuser*). In 1963 she made her début at Covent Garden as a very impressive Eboli (*Don Carlos*), the role in which she made her first Metropolitan appearance in 1965. At Salzburg she sang Lady Macbeth in 1964–5 and Carmen in 1966–7. She has also appeared at La Scala, the Rome Opera, and the Vienna Staatsoper, where in 1970 she sang Mascagni's Santuzza, her first soprano role. That year she sang her first Salome (at Covent Garden) and in 1971 her first Tosca (at the Metropolitan), repeating it at Covent Garden in 1973. Her Jenůfa at La Scala in 1974 was praised as musically and dramatically convincing, and she was imposing as Dukas' Ariane at the Opéra in 1975. Since the mid-1970s she has left the mezzo repertory, with the rare exception of Eboli, in favor of soprano roles. She undertook Bess in *Porgy and Bess* at the Metropolitan in 1985. Also active throughout her career as a recitalist (she is an accomplished lieder singer), she joined Shirley Verrett in an 80th birthday tribute to Marian Anderson at Carnegie Hall in January 1982. On occasion she has also performed with Frank Sinatra. Bumbry's voice, warm and voluminous in the lower and middle registers, tends to lose quality in the upper, though she certainly has a soprano range. She achieves her considerable acting successes by her commanding personality on the stage and her effective but economical gestures; her Carmen and Amneris are interpretations to treasure. Her recordings include opera, lieder, and oratorio.

BIBLIOGRAPHY

SouthernB
"Bumbry, Grace," *CBY 1964*
A. Blyth: "Grace Bumbry," *Opera*, xxi (1970), 506
M. Hoelterhoff: "Interview with Grace Bumbry," *MJ*, xxxv/9 (1977), 4
M. Mayer: "Musician of the Month: Grace Bumbry," *HiFi/MusAm*, xxix/11 (1979), 4
S. Rubin: "Amazing Grace," *Opera News*, xliv/4 (1981), 11
H. C. Schonberg: "A Bravo for Opera's Black Voices," *New York Times Magazine* (17 Jan 1982), 24

ALAN BLYTH/R

Bunny hop. A popular social dance of the 1950s; *see* CONGA.

Burschstein, Raisa. *See* RAISA, ROSA.

Burge, David (Russell) (*b* Evanston, IL, 25 March 1930). Pianist and composer. He studied at Northwestern University (BM 1951, MM 1952) and the Eastman School (DMA 1956), and was a pupil of Pietro Scarpini (piano) while in Florence on a Fulbright scholarship (1956–7). In 1959 he began a series of annual American concert tours, winning recognition from critics and composers for technical prowess and his receptiveness to new ideas. He was appointed in 1962 to teach at the University of Colorado, where he founded and directed the Contemporary Music Festival and became professor of music. Burge conducted the Boulder PO (1965–72) and was chairman of the American Society of University Composers (1970–74), although at the same time he was giving his attention increasingly to the performance of 20th-century piano music rather than to composition. He joined the faculty of the Eastman School, where he is chairman of the piano department, in 1975 and was named Kilbourn Professor of Music in 1978. He is a frequent contributor of articles and reviews to *Keyboard*, *Notes*, and other journals. Burge has made dozens of recordings and has given first performances of many works of American composers, including Albright, Bedford, Crumb, Curtis-Smith, and Barton McLean. His own music reflects Burge's occasionally capricious and theatrical character as a performer.

WORKS
(selective list)

Eclipse II, pf, 1964; Sources II, vn, cel, pf, 1966; Sources III, cl, perc, 1967; Aeolian Music, fl, cl, pf, vn, vc, tape, 1968; A Song of Sixpence, S, pf, 1968; That no one knew, vn, orch, 1969; Twone in Sunshine, an Entertainment for Theater, 1969; 3 Variations on Simple Gifts, pf, 1980

Principal publishers: Bowdoin College Press, A. Broude, CPE

ELAINE BARKIN/R

Burgin, Richard (*b* Warsaw, Poland, 11 Oct 1892; *d* Gulfport, FL, 29 April 1981). Violinist and conductor. He made his first public appearance at the age of 11 with the Warsaw PO and toured the USA as a soloist in 1907. From 1908 to 1912 he was enrolled in Auer's class at the St. Petersburg Conservatory; subsequently he was concertmaster of the Helsinki SO (1912–15) and the Oslo SO (1916–19). In 1920 he joined the Boston SO as concertmaster and remained in the post for 42 years, adding the duties of associate conductor in 1943. During his long tenure, he conducted over 300 concerts (including many premières and works by Mahler, Bruckner, Schoenberg, and Shostakovich), appeared as soloist, and led his own string quartet. He was head of the string department of the New England Conservatory of Music and in 1959 joined the violin faculty of Boston University; he also taught conducting at the Berkshire Music Center. In

1962 Burgin moved to Florida, where he joined the faculty of Florida State University as violin professor (1963–72) and served as a member of the Conducting Symposium held at Jacksonville University in 1973 and 1974. He was active as a guest conductor (including a week with the Puerto Rico SO at the invitation of Casals) and was also a member of the Florestan Quartet; he gave his last concert in June 1980 at Florida State University. Burgin was a musician of amazing versatility and tireless enthusiasm, equally adept as a violinist, conductor, and educator. He influenced Boston's musical life significantly, particularly during the Koussevitzky era, and was instrumental in establishing the Auer tradition of violin playing in the USA. In 1940 he married the violinist RUTH POSSELT.

BIBLIOGRAPHY

A. Mell: "Where are they Now?: Richard Burgin," *Journal of the Violin Society of America*, ii/2 (1976), 41
Obituary, *New York Times* (1 May 1981)

BORIS SCHWARZ

Burk, John N(aglee) (*b* San Jose, CA, 28 Aug 1891; *d* Boston, MA, 6 Sept 1967). Writer on music. He studied at Harvard (BA 1916). He succeeded Philip Hale as program annotator for the Boston SO in 1934, and in 1935 he edited a collection of Hale's program notes from the years 1901 to 1933 (*R*1971). He also edited and annotated the letters of Richard Wagner from the Burrell Collection, at that time the property of the Curtis Institute (1950). Burk wrote three biographies: *Clara Schumann: a Romantic Biography* (1940), *The Life and Works of Beethoven* (1943), and *Mozart and his Music* (1959).

PAULA MORGAN

Burkat, Leonard (*b* Boston, MA, 21 July 1919). Librarian, administrator, and writer on music. He studied at Boston, Columbia, and Harvard universities. From 1937 to 1947 he worked at the Boston Public Library, becoming assistant head of the music department. In 1946 he was appointed librarian of the Berkshire Music Center, of which he was later administrator (1957–63); from 1947 he also served as assistant librarian of the Boston SO, a position created for him by Koussevitzky. He was later assistant to Charles Munch (1953–7) and then artistic administrator of the orchestra. From 1963 to 1973 Burkat was employed by CBS, first as director of Columbia Masterworks, then as vice-president of Columbia Records, and finally as vice-president of CBS/Columbia Records Group. In 1975 he began his own syndicated program-note firm. He wrote reviews and articles for the *Boston Globe* and *Evening Transcript* from 1938 to 1944; he has also contributed to *Notes*, *Tempo*, and the *Musical Quarterly*.

PAULA MORGAN

Burke, Joseph (*b* Galway, Ireland, 9 May 1817; *d* New York, 19 Jan 1902). Violinist and actor. He had a sensational career as a child actor, making his début in Dublin in 1824. He appeared with equal facility in comedy and tragedy, played the violin, and sang. As "Master Burke the Irish Roscius" he first appeared on the American stage on 22 November 1830 at the Park Theatre, New York. In 1840 he left the theater to study and practice law in Albany, New York, then in 1844 went to Europe to study violin with Charles-Auguste de Bériot. He returned to the USA the following year, undertook lengthy tours of the country with Leopold de Meyer (1846–7), Richard Hoffman (1847–8), and Jenny Lind (1850–52), and appeared with Gottschalk (1855–6) and Thalberg (1857). He performed several times with the New York Philharmonic Society, with which he gave the American première of Mendelssohn's Violin Concerto (24 November 1849); he also served as the society's president. He ceased to perform shortly after, but continued to teach (chiefly piano) in New York until about 1880, when he retired to his farm in Alexander, near Batavia, New York.

BIBLIOGRAPHY

Biography of Master Burke (Philadelphia, 1830)
Obituary, *Daily News* (Batavia, NY, 20 Jan 1902)
G. C. D. Odell: *Annals of the New York Stage*, iii–vii (New York, 1928–31/*R*1970)
C. L. Carmer: *Dark Trees to the Wind* (New York, 1949), 151
R. A. Lott: *The American Concert Tours of Leopold de Meyer, Henri Herz, and Sigismond Thalberg* (diss., City U. of New York, in preparation)

R. ALLEN LOTT

Burke, Solomon (*b* Philadelphia, PA, 1936). Rhythm-and-blues singer. He became a soloist in his church at the age of nine, and at 12 he was appearing on a local radio program as "the Wonder-Boy Preacher." His first recordings, made for Apollo in 1955, showed stylistic uncertainty. In 1960, he met Jerry Wexler, a vice-president of the Atlantic company, and in 1961 he had his first success, with *Just out of reach of my two empty arms*, a country-music ballad. The following year he recorded another hit, *Cry to me*, which showed gospel influences. Unlike other soul singers of the 1960s, who sang with unflagging intensity, often verging on hysteria, Burke was a master of control; his work was majestic and dignified, yet as powerful as the most volatile performances recorded by Wilson Pickett. He was a convincing storyteller and an eclectic songwriter and singer, capable of absorbing a range of idioms and influences. However, after several attempts to adapt to the shifting tastes of the 1970s, he returned to his earlier style on several gospel albums issued by Savoy Records.

RECORDINGS

(selective list; recorded for Atlantic unless otherwise stated)

Just out of reach of my two empty arms (2114, 1961); Cry to me (2131, 1962); Goodbye baby (2226, 1964); Got to get you off my mind (2276, 1965); *Rock 'n' Soul* (8096, 1966); *King Solomon* (8158, 1968); *Music to Make Love by* (Chess 60042, 1975); *Into my Life you Came* (Savoy 14679, 1982); *Take me, Shake me* (Savoy 14717, 1983)

BIBLIOGRAPHY

N. Nite: *Rock On* (New York, 1974), 75
J. Futrell and others: *The Illustrated Encyclopedia of Black Music* (New York, 1982), 41

JOSEPH McEWEN

Burleigh, Cecil (*b* Wyoming, NY, 17 April 1885; *d* Madison, WI, 28 July 1980). Composer, violinist, and teacher. He studied violin and theory as a child, and while in high school composed incidental music and began improvising at the piano. From 1903 to 1905 he attended the Klindworth-Scharwenka Conservatory, Berlin, where he studied violin with Anton Witek and composition with Leichtentritt. Upon his return to the USA he enrolled at the Chicago Musical College, studying violin with Emile Sauret and composition with Felix Borowski. He appeared as a soloist with major orchestras and in joint recitals in Canada and the USA between 1907 and 1909; he then taught violin at the Western Institute of Music and Drama in Denver until 1911, violin and theory at Morningside College, Sioux City, Iowa (1911–14), and at Montana State University, Missoula. He left teaching in 1919 to resume his studies in New York: violin with Auer, composition with Bloch, and orchestration with Rothwell. He also played violin professionally. From 1921 to his retirement in 1955 he taught violin, theory, and composition at the University of Wisconsin, Madison. Except for three violin concertos and three other orchestral works, Burleigh, heavily influenced by MacDowell's character pieces, composed mostly in smaller forms until 1940 (the year of his second marriage); thereafter he began to compose more ambitious works in larger forms.

WORKS

(selective list)

Orch: 3 vn concs., op.25, 1915, arr. vn, pf, 1915, op.43, 1919, op.60, 1928; The Village Dance [after pf piece], op.16 (1921); Evangeline, op.41, 1929; Mountain Pictures, op.42, 1917–19 (1930); Leaders of Men, 1943; 3 syms., Creation, Prophecy, Revelation, ?1944; From the Muses, small orch, 1945

Chamber and inst: 4 Rocky Mountain Sketches, vn, pf, op.11, 1914; Scherzando fantastique, vn, pf, op.12, 1914; Sonata "The Ascension," vn, pf, op.22, 1914; 6 Nature Studies, vn, pf, op.23, 1915; 4 Prairie Sketches, vn, pf, op.13, 1916; A Ballad of Early New England, pf, op.58, 1924; Sonata "From the Life of St. Paul," vn, pf, op.29, 1926; 2 Sketches from the Orient, pf, op.55, 1926, arr. band, 1928; 3 Mood Pictures, pf, op.56, 1926; Mountain Pictures [after orch work], 2 pf (1931); Hymn to the Ancients, pf qnt, 1940; 2 Essays in Str Qt: Illusion, Transition, 1945; Leaders of Men [after orch work], suite, 2 pf, 1945; 47 others, incl. 25 for vn, pf, 20 for pf, children's pieces

Songs, 1v, pf, unless otherwise stated: The Letter (Tennyson), op.8, 1917; The Lighthouse (Longfellow), op.32/5, *c*1917; Philomel (Shakespeare), op.32/1, *c*1917; The Sea hath its Pearls (Heine, trans. Longfellow), op.32/2, *c*1917; O Mountains of the North (J. G. Whittier), op.33/4, 1918; Song of the Brook (Tennyson), op.33/5, 1918; What does Little Birdie Say? (Tennyson), op.33/6, 1918; Break, Break, Break (Tennyson), op.47/2, 1920; Sunrise (Emerson), op.49/1, 1920; To the Past, To the Future (from 2 Songs after Lowell), op.45, 1920; Wings (V. W. Mackall), op.61, 1927; Westward (Longfellow), *c*1928; Fragments from Sappho (trans. W. S. Landor and W. E. Leonard), 1v, vc, pf, 1945; Translations from Literature (Hawthorne, Emerson, Antoninus), 1v, vc, pf, 1946; *c*50 others

MSS in *DLC*, *NN*

Principal publishers: Boston Music, Composers' Music, Ditson, C. Fischer, Presser, G. Schirmer, Summy

BIBLIOGRAPHY

EwenD

B. Berry: "Cecil Burleigh, Composer," *Music and Musicians*, i/10 (1915), 6

L. Mackall: "Cecil Burleigh has Found in Great West Rich Vein of Musical Inspiration," *MusAm*, xxiii/6 (1915), 37

G. Saenger: "Cecil Burleigh, American Solo Violinist and Composer," *Musical Observer*, xii/11 (1915), 659

J. Harold: "Cecil Burleigh, Violinist Composer," *Musical Observer*, xviii/10 (1919), 33

J. T. Howard: *Cecil Burleigh*, in Studies of Contemporary American Composers (New York, 1929)

"Among the Composers: Cecil Burleigh," *Etude*, lxi/4 (1943), 227

MARGERY MORGAN LOWENS

Burleigh, Harry [Henry] **T(hacker)** (*b* Erie, PA, 2 Dec 1866; *d* Stamford, CT, 12 Sept 1949). Composer and singer. From 1892 to 1895 he studied at the National Conservatory of Music in New York, where he was influenced by many notable musicians, especially the conservatory's director, Antonín Dvořák. In February 1894 he was selected to join the choir of St. George's Church, one of the most prominent and wealthy churches in the USA, as baritone soloist. He was also soloist at Temple Emanu-El from 1900 to 1925. He worked as a music editor for Ricordi from 1913 until his death.

Burleigh wrote 265 vocal compositions, including three song cycles – *Saracen Songs* (1914), *Passionale* (1915), and *Five Songs on Poems of Laurence Hope* (1915) – and 187 choral arrangements of black spiritual melodies (issued in *Old Songs Hymnal*, 1929). He also compiled a collection of black minstrel melodies (1910). He was a pioneer in the arrangement of spirituals for solo voice with piano accompaniment, and it was his setting of *Deep River* (1917) that established his fame, though another arrangement for unaccompanied mixed chorus (1913) is probably better known. Other popular compositions are *Love's Garden* (1902), *Jean* (1903), *Ethiopia Saluting the Colors* (1915), *The Young Warrior* (1915), and *Little Mother of Mine* (1917).

BIBLIOGRAPHY

SouthernB

M. Cuney-Hare: *Negro Musicians and their Music* (Washington, DC, 1936/*R*1974)

E. Janifer: "H. T. Burleigh Ten Years Later," *Phylon: the Atlanta University Review of Race and Culture*, xxi (1960), 144

R. L. Allison: *Classification of the Vocal Works of Harry T. Burleigh (1866–1949) and Some Suggestions for their Use in Teaching Diction in Singing* (diss., Indiana U., 1966)

E. Southern: *The Music of Black Americans: a History* (New York, 1971/*R*1983)

"In Retrospect . . . Harry T. Burleigh (1866–1949)," *BPiM*, ii (1974), 75

E. Southern: "America's Black Composers of Classical Music," *MEJ*, lxii/3 (1975), 46

ROLAND L. ALLISON

Burlesque [burletta]. A term used in the early 19th century to denote a dramatic production that ridicules stage conventions and literary forms, and from the late 19th century to mean principally a variety show in which striptease is the chief attraction.

From the late 1830s William Mitchell presented burlesques of operas and romantic plays at his Olympic Theatre, New York, and the English immigrant John Brougham wrote and acted in numerous burlesques from 1842 until he retired in 1879. Brougham's *Po-ca-hon-tas* (1855, after H. W. Longfellow's narrative poem) is peopled with "Salvages," its dialogue is a string of *doubles entendres*, and its songs were selected from such popular tunes as "Widow Machree" and "Rosin the Bow," and Tyrolean melodies. Several minstrel troupes presented such satires; in the 1860s the Kelly & Leon Negro Minstrels performed burlesques of Offenbach (*La Belle L. N.*, *Grand Dutch S.*) throughout the northeastern states, and Sanford's Minstrel Burlesque Opera Troupe advertised a "change of programme every night."

From about 1860 burlesque often provided the framework for elaborate spectacles, beginning with those produced in New York by Laura Keene, who employed ballet troupes of women whose costumes exposed their legs. One of the most successful shows of the decade was *The Black Crook* (1866), in which dancing girls in pink tights caused a sensation (*see* MUSICAL THEATER, fig. 1). By the 1870s a well-defined standard format for burlesque had evolved, consisting of variety acts, musical numbers, and short skits or "bits," all of which emphasized rowdy humor. Particular character types, such as the straight-man comedian, the ingénue, the soubrette, the prima donna, and the character comedian, performed in stock comedy situations. Nearly all New York theaters, however, presented shows that relied less for their effect on dramatic elements, wit, or satire than on female beauty, and the term "burlesque" gradually shifted in meaning from the ridicule of stage conventions to an emphasis on women in various degrees of undress. Although music was incidental to the proceedings, a small pit orchestra was usually present to perform standard light classics and popular tunes to introduce or accompany the acts.

With the rise of the Mutual Burlesque Association in the 1920s, lowbrow comedy sketches began to be replaced by increasingly more sensual displays of the female form, rapidly progressing from the nude tableau to the striptease. At the same time the Minsky brothers added a new dimension to their shows by constructing a runway from the stage down the middle of the theater, allowing a closer interaction between the performer and her audience. Performances of burlesque in New York were brought to an end in 1937, when the mayor, Fiorello La Guardia, acceded to the demands of its detractors and banned it and the Minsky name from all the city's theaters. Although it continued to be offered in other cities, burlesque increasingly failed to attract audiences. By the 1960s the sexual revolution, which led to the publication of explicit magazines and an increasing acceptance of nudity in films and on stage, meant that burlesque was no longer regarded as a risqué form of entertainment.

See also DANCE, §II, 3.

BIBLIOGRAPHY

B. Sobel: *Burleycue* (New York, 1931)
W. Green: *A Survey of the Development of Burlesque in America* (thesis, Columbia U., 1950)
W. H. Rubsamen: "The Ballad Burlesques and Extravaganzas," *MQ*, xxxvi (1950), 551
A. Green and J. Laurie: *Show Biz from Vaude to Video* (New York, 1951)
I. Zeidman: *The American Burlesque Show* (New York, 1967)
D. B. Wilmeth: *Variety Entertainment and Outdoor Amusements* (Westport, CT, 1982), 152

DEANE L. ROOT, JOHN GRAZIANO

Burns, Ralph (*b* Newton, MA, 29 June 1922). Jazz arranger, composer, and pianist. He studied at the New England Conservatory in 1938–9 and worked in the band of Charlie Barnet, who recorded his piece *The Moose* in 1943. Burns then joined Woody Herman, playing an important role in the band's rhythm section during 1944–5. He withdrew in order to work freelance, but continued writing for Herman and recorded under his own name until the late 1950s. A period of concentration on orchestrating for the Broadway stage led to considerable film work in the 1970s.

Burns's early arrangements for the Herman band, however, are his most important contribution. As well as intelligent versions of contemporary popular songs, his original pieces *Apple Honey* and *Bijou* effectively harnessed the ensemble's power and that of its soloists. More ambitious works such as *Lady McGowan's Dream* and *Summer Sequence* (the last part of which became a song with lyrics by Johnny Mercer under the title *Early Autumn*) betray the rewarding but not predominant inspiration of Ellington. Many of Burns's arrangements of the last 20 years or more have not required the creation of original material, but he has been associated with some significant film directors, arranging the film scores of Woody Allen's *Bananas* (1971), Bob Fosse's *Sweet Charity* (1969), *Cabaret* (1972), and *Lenny* (1974), and Martin Scorsese's *New York, New York* (1977). The two last-named projects, by calling on Burns's jazz experience, lent authenticity to an area too often bowdlerized in the film industry.

RECORDINGS
(selective list)

As leader: Places Please (1951, Clef 8971); Someday, Somewhere/Spring Is (1951, Clef 8974); *Very Warm for Jazz* (1958, Decca 9207)

As sideman with W. Herman: Apple Honey (1945, Col. 36803); Bijou (1945, Col. 36861); Lady McGowan's Dream, pts.i–ii (1946, Col. 38365-6); Summer Sequence, pts.i–iv (1946–7, Col. 38365-7)

BRIAN PRIESTLEY

Burnson, George. *See* LONDON, GEORGE.

Burton, Gary (*b* Anderson, IN, 23 Jan 1943). Jazz vibraphonist and bandleader. He taught himself to play the vibraphone and toured South America with his own group as early as 1962 before rising to prominence in George Shearing's quintet (1963) and Stan Getz's quartet (1964–6). In 1971 he joined the staff of the Berklee School of Music in Boston. He has frequently toured and recorded with his own small ensembles, his duo performances with the pianist Chick Corea being especially well received.

A virtuoso vibraphonist, Burton developed an original style of improvisation quite distinct from his influential predecessors on this instrument, Lionel Hampton and Milt Jackson. He has promoted a playing style that makes use of four mallets at once; he sometimes uses electronic distorting devices to produce fuzz tone and reverberation, and has performed on a vibraphone that has no pulsator. In many ways Burton created a compromise between modern jazz piano styles (he cites Bill Evans and Thelonious Monk as his inspiration) and jazz wind style. He is one of the few modern jazz improvisers not to draw substantially from the melodic conceptions of bop musicians Charlie Parker and Dizzy Gillespie, creating instead a fresh vocabulary that emphasizes 20th-century art music as well as country music. His accompaniments are frequently rich in vamps and pedal points, reminiscent both of country and Latin American styles.

RECORDINGS
(selective list)

As leader: *Duster* (1967, RCA LSP3835); *Country Roads and other Places* (1968, RCA LSP4098); Alone at Last (1971, Atl. 1598); Hotel Hello (1974, ECM 1055); *Easy as Pie* (1980, ECM 1184); *Picture This* (1982, ECM 1226)

Duos with C. Corea: *Crystal Silence* (1972, ECM 1024); *Duet* (1978, ECM 1140); *In Concert, Zürich* (1979, ECM 1182-3)

BIBLIOGRAPHY

P. Rivelli and R. Levin, eds.: *The Rock Giants* (New York, 1970)
M. Ruppli and E. Raben: "Discographie de Gary Burton," *Jazz hot*, no.342 (1977), 26
C. Stern: "Vibist Gary Burton," *Down Beat*, xlv/21 (1978), 16; xlvi/1 (1979), 17
N. Tesser: "Many Facets of Burton," *Jazz Magazine*, iii/3 (1979), 44

MARK C. GRIDLEY

Busch, Adolf (Georg Wilhelm) (*b* Siegen, Germany, 8 Aug 1891; *d* Guilford, VT, 9 June 1952). German violinist and composer, brother of Fritz Busch. He was taught violin by his father, and when only 11 he entered the Cologne Conservatory as a pupil of Willy Hess and Bram Eldering; he was later taught there by Fritz Steinbach. He went to Bonn in 1908 to study composition with Hugo Grüters. In 1912 he became concertmaster of the Konzertverein orchestra in Vienna, under Ferdinand Löwe. With Löwe's encouragement, he founded the Wiener Konzertvereins-Quartett the following year, but World War I put a stop to its activities, and it was not until 1919 that it was reformed as the Busch Quartet.

Busch settled in Basle in 1927, and adopted Swiss nationality in 1935. He toured in many countries as a soloist and with his quartet. He also formed a piano trio with his brother Hermann Busch, a cellist, and Rudolf Serkin. In 1939 all three musicians moved to the USA, and a year later Gösta Andreasson and Karl Doktor, the other two members of the quartet, followed. While in the USA, Busch continued to perform as a soloist, in chamber works with Serkin, as leader of the Busch Chamber Players, and also as a conductor of larger-scale orchestral works. In 1950 he and his brother Hermann, Serkin, and Marcel and Louis Moyse founded the Marlboro School of Music in Vermont.

Busch was greatly admired as a soloist, especially in the concertos of Beethoven and Brahms, but his outstanding importance was as a player and director of chamber music. His quartet was especially famous for its fervent and lucid performances of Beethoven, and for its ability to make the supposedly difficult late quartets perfectly comprehensible. His recordings include string quartets by Beethoven, Brahms, and Schubert, Bach's complete Brandenburg Concertos and orchestral suites, and, with Serkin, several works by Brahms. His compositions, rarely performed, show the influence of Reger, with whom he was associated from 1907, and include orchestral and choral works, concertos, songs, and a large number of chamber works. Busch was a distinguished teacher, and Yehudi Menuhin was among his pupils.

BIBLIOGRAPHY

J. Creighton: *Discopaedia of the Violin, 1889–1971* (Toronto, 1974)

ROBERT PHILIP/R

Busch, Carl (Reinholdt) (*b* Bjerre, Denmark, 29 March 1862; *d* Kansas City, MO, 19 Dec 1943). Teacher, conductor, and composer. He studied at the Copenhagen Royal Conservatory with J. P. E. Hartmann and Niels Gade (1882–5), at the Brussels Conservatory (1885), and in Paris with Benjamin Godard (1886). In 1887 he immigrated to the USA and settled in Kansas City. He founded and conducted several musical organizations, including the Kansas City SO (1911–18), and appeared as guest conductor with orchestras throughout the USA and Europe. He was a noted teacher of string instruments and theory and composition, numbering among his pupils Robert Russell Bennett and William Dawson. From 1924 to 1938 he taught at the Chicago Musical College, Brigham Young University, Notre Dame University, Kansas City-Horner Conservatory, and Kansas City University. As a composer, he was especially noted for works based on American subjects, particularly the American Indian; his several award-winning compositions include *A Chant from the Great Plains*, which won the first Goldman Band Composition Contest (1920). He was knighted by the kings of Denmark and Norway.

WORKS

Orch: 6 suites, 1890–1928, 3 pubd (1928); 2 rhapsodies, 1897, (1905); 14 works, str orch, 1897–1918, 6 pubd (1897–1918); Sym., 1898; March, 1898; 4 sym. poems, 1898–1924, 2 pubd (1914, 1924); Prologue (1899); Vc Conc., 1919

Inst: 4 str trios (1893–1926); 44 str solos (1893–1926); 8 ww solos, 1893–1940, 4 pubd (1893–1940); Vn Sonata, 1897; Str Qt, 1897; Str Qnt, 1897; 24 str études (1909); 26 works, ww ens (1930–43)

Vocal: 13 choruses, female vv, 1887–1930, 8 pubd (1900–30); 69 songs, 1891–1925, 61 pubd (1891–1925); 15 choruses, male vv, 1893–1928, 12 pubd (1893–1925); 22 cantatas, 15 with orch, 1894–1929, 19 pubd (1894–1929); 14 choruses, mixed vv, 1900–35, 11 pubd (1900–26)

Other: 8 works, band, 1906–34, 6 pubd (1921–32)

Principal publishers: Breitkopf & Härtel, Ditson, FitzSimons, C. Fischer

BIBLIOGRAPHY

D. R. Lowe: *Sir Carl Busch: his Life and Work as a Teacher, Conductor, and Composer* (diss., U. of Missouri, 1972)

DONALD R. LOWE

Busch, Fritz (*b* Siegen, Germany, 13 March 1890; *d* London, England, 14 Sept 1951). German conductor and pianist, brother of Adolf Busch. The son of an instrument maker and violinist, he began his music education at home. In 1906 he entered the Cologne Conservatory, where he studied with Fritz Steinbach, Wilfried Boettcher, and Otto Klauwell. His first professional post, in 1909, was as conductor and chorus director at the State Theater in Riga; he subsequently held posts in Gotha (1911–12) and Aachen (1912–18) before being appointed music director of the Stuttgart Opera in 1918. In 1922 he moved to the Dresden Staatsoper, where he gradually established a world reputation as an opera conductor and promoter of the modern repertory. He made guest appearances at Bayreuth (1924), London (1929), and New York, where he was guest conductor of the Symphony Society in the 1927–8 and 1928–9 seasons.

Because of his opposition to the Nazi regime, Busch left Germany for South America in 1933. During the following years he conducted in Buenos Aires, Copenhagen, Stockholm, and at the Glyndebourne Festival in England. In 1936 he was offered Toscanini's post with the New York PO but did not accept, preferring to retain his positions in England and Scandinavia. He returned to the USA in 1941 and served as music director and principal conductor of the short-lived New Opera Company of New York (founded that year). In January and February of 1942 he was guest conductor of the New York PO. His début at the Metropolitan Opera, with *Lohengrin*, was on 26 November 1945. He was principal conductor of the Metropolitan for the next four seasons but was never entirely at ease in New York; one concert promoter complained that he was "not a showman." Busch also conducted the Chicago SO in 1948–9 and 1950, then returned to Scandinavia and England. He was the soundest type of German musician; not markedly original or spectacular, but thorough, strong-minded, decisive in intention and execution, with idealism and practical sense nicely balanced. He wrote *Aus dem Leben eines Musikers* (1949; Eng. trans., 1953, as *Pages from a Musician's Life*).

BIBLIOGRAPHY

S. Hughes: *Glyndebourne: a History of the Festival Opera, 1934–1964* (London, 1965)
G. Busch: *Fritz Busch, Dirigent* (Frankfurt am Main, 1970) [with discography]
B. Dopheide: *Fritz Busch* (Tutzig, 1970)
R. Bing: *5000 Nights at the Opera* (London, 1972)

RONALD CRICHTON/R

Busch, Lou(is) [Bush, Louis Ferdinand; Carr, Joe "Fingers"] (*b* Louisville, KY, 18 July 1910; *d* Camarillo, CA, 19 Sept 1979). Ragtime pianist, composer, and recording executive. At the age of 16 he left home to tour as a pianist with the Clyde McCoy band, a popular dance orchestra of the 1930s. He later served as pianist and arranger with a series of big bands, notably those of George Olsen, Ray Noble, Vincent Lopez, and Henry Busse. In 1941 he settled in Los Angeles and, after a period as accompanist to Lena Horne, he was employed by the newly formed West Coast record label Capitol. When Euday Bowman's *Twelfth Street Rag*, recorded in 1948 by Pee Wee Hunt, sold more than three million copies worldwide, Busch was placed in charge of Capitol's artists and repertoire department and invited to capitalize on the success of the recording. He then adopted his pseudonym, Joe "Fingers" Carr, and agreed to be marketed on record covers as a barroom pianist with gartered sleeves, cigar, and derby hat; despite this promotional gimmickry, he played fine ragtime piano. He also wrote a long series of sturdy hit rags. His 36 singles and 14 albums during the 1950s created a congenial setting for the ragtime revival and inspired many young musicians who later developed the second revival in the late 1960s. Under the name Lou Busch he also enjoyed success in Britain with his recording *Zambesi* (1956). After moving to Warner Bros. Records he was associated, as music director, with the comedian Allan Sherman, and in the late 1970s he toured with a former pupil, Lincoln Mayorga, as a ragtime duo called the Brinkerhoff Piano Company.

BIBLIOGRAPHY

T. Waldo: *This is Ragtime* (New York, 1976)

D. A. Jasen and T. J. Tichenor: *Rags and Ragtime: a Musical History* (New York, 1978)

IAN WHITCOMB

Buswell, James Oliver, (IV) (*b* Fort Wayne, IN, 4 Dec 1946). Violinist and conductor. He graduated from Harvard and studied violin with Galamian at the Juilliard School. He made his professional début in St. Louis at the age of 16, and he gave a number of concerts while at Harvard. Following his highly acclaimed New York recital début (Philharmonic Hall, 1967), he appeared as a soloist with many of the leading American orchestras and made several visits to Europe, playing for the first time in Britain with the London SO in 1971. In addition to continuing a solo career, he has been active as a chamber musician, playing with the Chamber Music Society of Lincoln Center (for illustration *see* CHAMBER MUSIC SOCIETY OF LINCOLN CENTER) and participating regularly in the Santa Fe Chamber Music Festival. He taught at the University of Arizona (1972–3), and in 1974 joined the faculty of the Indiana University School of Music, where he has conducted a number of operas. The clarity, tonal strength, and spontaneity of his playing are heard on his recording (with Valenti) of Bach's violin sonatas. He owns a Stradivari violin of 1720, the "Levêque."

BIBLIOGRAPHY

B. Schwarz: *Great Masters of the Violin* (New York, 1983), 558

RICHARD BERNAS/DENNIS K. McINTIRE

Butler, Jerry (*b* Sunflower, MS, 8 Dec 1939). Rhythm-and-blues singer. He moved to Chicago in 1942 and at the age of 15 joined a gospel choir, where he met Curtis Mayfield, Sam Gooden, and Arthur and Richard Brooks. They formed a rhythm-and-blues close-harmony group, which in 1958 took the name the Impressions and signed a recording contract with Vee Jay Records. On its first release, *For your precious love* (1958), the group was billed as Jerry Butler and the Impressions, and when the record became a hit, Butler left to pursue a solo career. His rich baritone voice, smoother and more popular-sounding than that of most rhythm-and-blues singers but more mature than the tenor falsetto of Sam Cooke and those who imitated him, gave Butler several more hits, including *He will break your heart* (1960), *Moon River* (1961), and *Let it be me* (1964), a duet with Betty Everett. In 1967 he began to record with the producers Kenneth Gamble and Leon Huff for Mercury Records; their collaboration resulted in two outstanding albums, *Ice on Ice* and *The Ice Man Cometh* (both 1969), as well as the successful singles *Lost* (1967), *Hey Western Union man* (1968), *Never give you up* (1968), *Moody Woman* (1969), and *Only the strong survive* (1969). Butler subsequently recorded for a variety of labels but with only sporadic success, often in duets with such partners as Gene Chandler, Brenda Lee Eager, and Thelma Houston.

RECORDINGS

(selective list)

For your precious love (Abner 1013, 1958); He will break your heart (Vee Jay 354, 1960); Moon River (Vee Jay 405, 1961); Let it be me (Vee Jay 613, 1964) [with B. Everett]; Lost (Mer. 72764, 1967); Hey Western Union man (Mer. 72850, 1968); Never give you up (Mer. 72850, 1968); *The Ice Man Cometh* (Mer. 61198, 1969); *Ice on Ice* (Mer. 61234, 1969); Moody Woman (Mer. 72929, 1969); Only the strong survive (Mer. 72898, 1969); What's the use of breaking up (Mer. 72960, 1969)

DAVE MARSH

Butler University. Privately endowed university founded in Indianapolis in 1855; *see* INDIANAPOLIS, §4.

Butterfield Blues Band, Paul. Blues sextet. Formed by Paul Butterfield (*b* Chicago, IL, 17 Dec 1942), who sang and played harmonica, its members were Elvin Bishop (*b* Tulsa, OK, 21 Oct 1942), guitar; Mike Bloomfield (*b* Chicago, 28 July 1944; *d* 15 Feb 1981), guitar; Jerome Arnold, electric bass guitar; Sam Lay, drums (replaced after the group's first album by Billy Davenport); and Mark Naftalin, keyboards. Butterfield learned to play flute at the age of six; while in his teens, he became fascinated by urban blues, and learned rhythm-and-blues techniques from Little Walter, Muddy Waters, and other notable performers in nightclubs in the Chicago area. He formed his group in 1963 and within two years its reputation had earned it a recording contract with the Elektra label. In 1965 the group gained worldwide publicity through its appearance at the Newport Folk Festival, where it backed Bob Dylan in his controversial performance using electric instruments for the first time. The notoriety, however, did little to boost sales of the Butterfield band's first album; in 1966 its second album, *East-West*, sold nearly twice as many copies, yet climbed no higher than no.65 on the popular album chart. In desperation, the group changed its style to soul music; this was the first of several stylistic shifts that it made as it slowly lost direction. Bloomfield left in 1968; after recording several albums with Al Kooper and Stephen Stills, he performed for a while as a soloist, then wrote scores for pornographic films. Bishop also left in 1968; he formed his own blues-rock band, which had a hit in 1976 with *Fooled around and fell in love* (this included an uncredited lead vocal by Mickey Thomas, later a member of the Jefferson Starship). Butterfield dissolved his group in 1972 and subsequently formed a short-lived group called Butterfield's Better Days. In the late 1970s he toured with Levon Helm's R.C.O. All-Stars, and with the bass guitarist Rick Danko, a former member of The Band, formed the Danko-Butterfield Band, also short-lived. After a serious illness in 1980–81, Butterfield performed only occasionally, and his recordings for the Bearsville label had little success. Although never more than a cult favorite, the Paul Butterfield Blues Band is credited with helping to popularize black urban blues among white audiences in the mid-1960s.

RECORDINGS

(selective list; all recorded for Elektra)

The Paul Butterfield Blues Band (7294, 1965); *East-West* (7315, 1966); *The Resurrection of Pigboy Crabshaw* (74015, 1968); *Live* (7E2001, 1970); *Golden Butter* (7E2005, 1972)

GARY THEROUX

Byas, Don [Carlos Wesley] (*b* Muskogee, OK, 21 Oct 1912; *d* Amsterdam, Netherlands, 24 Aug 1972). Jazz tenor saxophonist. He played in a variety of jazz bands during the 1930s, including those led by Lionel Hampton, Buck Clayton, Don Redman, Lucky Millinder, and Andy Kirk. In 1941, he joined the Count Basie band, occupying the chair formerly held by Lester Young. From 1943 to 1946, he played in small groups with Coleman Hawkins, Dizzy Gillespie, and others. In autumn 1946, he traveled to Europe with the Don Redman band; soon he took up permanent residence there – first in France, then, in the mid-1950s, in Holland. He returned to the USA only once, in 1970. Byas began his career as one of the many imitators of Coleman Hawkins, but by the mid-1940s he had became an important transitional figure who combined the tone quality and vibrato of Hawkins with some of the rhythmic and melodic ideas of Charlie Parker and other bop players. He produced many fine recordings, two of the most remarkable being duets with the double bass player Slam Stewart recorded during a concert in 1945.

RECORDINGS
(selective list)

As soloist: Riffin' and Jivin' (1944, Savoy 582); Laura (1945, American 1001-4); How High the Moon (1945, Savoy 597)
Duos with S. Stewart: Indiana (1945, Jazz Star 47101); I got rhythm (1945, Jazz Star 47102)
As sideman: Men from Minton's: Stardust, pt.i, on *The Harlem Jazz Scene* (1941, Esoteric 4); Count Basie: Harvard Blues (1941, OK 6564)

BIBLIOGRAPHY

R. Horricks: *Count Basie and his Orchestra: its Music and Musicians* (London, 1957), 177ff
D. Byas: "In my opinion," *Jazz Journal*, xiv/3 (1961), 5
J. Burns: "Don Byas," *Jazz Journal*, xviii/9 (1965), 5
M. Hennessey: "Don Byas: Emphatic Expatriate," *Down Beat*, xxxiv/15 (1967), 23
W. F. van Eyle: *Don Byas Discography* (Zaandam, Netherlands, 1967)
D. Morgenstern: Liner notes, *Savoy Jazz Party* (Savoy 2213, 1976)
D. B. Wilke: "A Don Byas Discography 1938–1972 (Part 1: 1938–1943)," *Micrography*, no.46 (1978), 17

THOMAS OWENS

Byrd, Donald(son Toussaint L'Overture) (*b* Detroit, MI, 9 Dec 1932). Jazz trumpeter, flugelhorn player, and educator. He studied at Wayne State University in Detroit (BM 1954) and the Manhattan School (MA in music education). While at Manhattan he became the favorite studio trumpeter of the bop label Prestige (1956–8) because of his masterful technique and warm tone. He gave performances with George Wallington, Art Blakey, Max Roach, Sonny Rollins, John Coltrane, and others, before settling into a partnership with Pepper Adams (1958–61). After studying composition in Europe (1962–3) he began a career in black music education, teaching at Rutgers University, the Hampton Institute, Howard University, and (after receiving a law degree, 1976) North Carolina Central University; in 1983 he was awarded a doctorate at Columbia Teachers College. In the 1970s he took up a danceable jazz-rock style. His *Black Byrd*, the best-selling album on the Blue Note record label up to that time, led to the formation of his students into the Blackbyrds, a hit group of the mid-1970s.

RECORDINGS
(selective list)

As leader: *Byrd in Flight* (1960, BN 4048); *Royal Flush* (1961, BN 84101); *Free Form* (1961, BN 84118); *A New Perspective* (1963, BN 84124); *Electric Byrd* (1970, BN 84349); *Black Byrd* (*c*1972, BN LA047); *Street Lady* (1973, BN LA140)
As co-leader: A. Farmer: *Two Trumpets* (1956, Prst. 7062); P. Woods: *The Young Bloods* (1956, Prst. 7080)
As sideman: J. McLean: *Lights Out* (1956, Prst. 7035); A. Blakey: *The Jazz Messengers* (1956, Col. CL897); H. Silver: *Six Pieces of Silver* (1956, BN 1539); S. Rollins: *Sonny Rollins* (1956, BN 1542); R. Garland: *All Mornin' Long* (1957, Prst. 7130); J. Coltrane: *Lush Life* (1958, Prst. 7188); P. Adams: *10 to 4 at the 5 Spot* (1958, Riv. 265); D. Gordon: *One Flight Up* (1964, BN 84176)

BIBLIOGRAPHY

M. James: "Donald Byrd," *Jazz Monthly*, ix/1 (1963), 6
N. Hentoff: "Donald Byrd," *BMI: the Many Worlds of Music* (June 1967), 17
B. Quinn: "Donald Byrd: Campus Catalyst," *Down Beat*, xxxviii/17 (1971), 19
H. Nolan: "Donald Byrd: 'Infinite Variations'," *Down Beat*, xl/13 (1973), 18
B. Palmer: "Black Byrd's Jazz Flies High," *Rolling Stone*, no.184 (10 April 1975), 22

BARRY KERNFELD

Byrds. Rock group. Its leader, Roger (James) McGuinn (*b* Chicago, IL, 13 July 1942), a guitarist and songwriter, began his career in Chicago during the folk revival of the late 1950s as a backing musician for the Limelighters and Bobby Darin; he was also a member of the Chad Mitchell Trio for two years in the early 1960s. In 1964 he formed the Jet Set with four other folk musicians in Los Angeles: the guitarist David Crosby (Van Cortland; *b* Los Angeles, CA, 14 Aug 1941), formerly of Les Baxter's

The Byrds, early 1970s: (left to right) Clarence White, Roger McGuinn, Gene Parsons, and Skip Battin

Balladeers; the guitarist Gene Clark (*b* Tipton, MO, 17 Nov 1944), formerly of the New Christy Minstrels; the bass guitarist Chris Hillman (*b* Los Angeles, 4 Dec 1942), former leader of the Hillmen; and the studio drummer Mike Clarke (*b* New York, 3 June 1945). The group changed its name to the Beefeaters and then to the Byrds. It began recording in 1964 and had its first success the following year with Bob Dylan's *Mr. Tambourine Man* (no.1, 1965), on which McGuinn played a Rickenbacker electric 12-string guitar; he, Clark, and Crosby sang on the recording, but studio musicians supplied the backing. (For illustration of the group in 1965, *see* ROCK, fig.2.)

Initially the Byrds recorded similar versions of other writers' material (they had a hit with Pete Seeger's *Turn! Turn! Turn!* in 1966) and songs by Gene Clark; when Clark left (to return to folk and bluegrass groups, and eventually to record solo albums), McGuinn and Crosby began to write songs for the Byrds. Their *Eight Miles High* (1966) introduced psychedelic rock to a large audience; its lyrics (about flying at 40,000 feet), McGuinn's fast, modal obbligato on 12-string guitar, and an enveloping haze of electronic sound persuaded some critics that the song celebrated the drug culture and it was banned by several radio stations. Struggles for control of the group, which sometimes led to fist fights on stage, resulted in the departure of Crosby and Clarke after the recording of *Younger than Yesterday* (1967); Crosby formed a group with Stephen Stills and Graham Nash, and Clarke went to work with Gene Clark.

McGuinn leaned towards country music on his next two albums. *The Notorious Byrd Brothers* (1968) was recorded with studio musicians, and *Sweetheart of the Rodeo* (1968) included songs written by Gram Parsons (Cecil Connor) (*b* Winter Haven, FL, 5 Nov 1946; *d* Joshua Tree National Monument, CA, 19 Sept 1973), a singer and guitarist; these modernized the themes of sin and redemption that characterize much country music, and helped to prepare the way for country-rock. In 1968 Parsons and Hillman left the Byrds to form the Flying Burrito Brothers. Later that year McGuinn re-formed the Byrds with the bluegrass guitarist Clarence White, the drummer Gene Parsons, and the bass guitarist John York, who was replaced by the bass guitarist and songwriter Skip Battin (formerly of Skip and Flip). *Wasn't Born to Follow* by Gerry Goffin and Carole King, from the soundtrack to the film *Easy Rider* (1969), was a minor hit, and the album *Untitled* (1970) included a song (*Chestnut Mare*, written by McGuinn and Jacques Levy) that McGuinn has played regularly in his solo sets. The original members of the Byrds reunited briefly in 1973 but the group disbanded shortly afterwards. McGuinn began working as a soloist with his own bands; he took part in Dylan's "Rolling Thunder Revue" in 1975–6. In 1979 McGuinn, Clark, and Hillman formed a band, but it was short-lived; McGuinn and Hillman then stayed together for another year before returning to solo work.

The Byrds were one of the most influential rock groups of the 1960s, and their chiming guitar sound recurred in the music of such punk and post-punk groups as Television and R. E. M. From a background in folk and country music the original members of the group evolved the styles known as folk-rock and country-rock, which they then popularized. Their vocal sound, distinguished by close, bluegrass-style harmony, exercised a strong influence on West Coast pop, and one of the most pervasive sounds in rock music – folk guitar licks played on electric guitar – can be traced to McGuinn.

RECORDINGS

(selective list; recorded for Columbia unless otherwise stated)

Mr. Tambourine Man (8172, 1965); *Fifth Dimension* (9349, 1966), incl. Eight Miles High; Turn! Turn! Turn! (43424, 1966); *Younger than Yesterday* (9442, 1967); *Notorious Byrd Brothers* (9575, 1968); *Sweetheart of the Rodeo* (9670, 1968); *Untitled* (30127, 1970); *The Byrds* (Asy. 5058, 1973)

JON PARELES

Byron, Michael (*b* Chicago, IL, 7 Sept 1953). Composer and performer. After attending the California Institute of the Arts (1971–3), where he studied composition with Budd, Tenney, and Teitelbaum, trumpet with Mario Guarneri and Thomas Stevens, and South Indian singing with Jon Higgins, he studied at York University, Ontario (BA 1974). He has received grants from York University (1975), the Ontario Arts Council (1977), the NEA (1979), and the New York State Council on the Arts (1982). Byron's interest in special areas of neglected new music led him to compile and edit *Pieces* (1973–8), an anthology of unusually notated scores by other composers. He also edited *Music with Roots in the Aeather* (in preparation), a transcription of the video work by Robert Ashley containing discussions between Ashley and various contemporary composers. Byron's own compositions are written in a Romantic style tempered by a minimalist aesthetic. Recordings of his music include *Tidal* (Neutral Records), *Marimbas in the Dorian Mode* (Cold Blue Records), and *Starfields* (Telus Records).

WORKS

Song of the Lifting up of the Head, pf, 1972; Starfields, pf 4 hands, 1974; Entrances, 4 pf, 1975; Morning Glory, perc, 1975; Marimbas, 1976; A Living Room at the Bottom of a Lake, orch, 1977; Music for One Piano, 1978; Three Mirrors, perc ens, 1978–9; Music of Steady Light: 158 Pieces for Str Insts, 1979–82; Tidal, vn, va, vc, db, pf, elec kbds, 1980–81; Double Str Qt, 1984

Other works in collaboration with the performance art group Maple Sugar

Principal publishers: A. R. C. Publications, Fuge Magazine, Parachute Magazine, Pieces, Soundings

JOAN LA BARBARA

C

Cabrillo Music Festival. International festival of orchestral and chamber music, solo recitals, and staged works, established in 1963 in Aptos, California. It was founded by Lou Harrison, the bassoonist Robert Hughes, and Ted Teows, an instructor at Cabrillo College. Held for two weeks in late August in the Cabrillo College Theater (capacity 540) and at various other locations, such as the Mission San Juan Bautista, the festival is noted for its innovative programming and emphasis on the works of living composers; over 50 world premières had been given by the mid-1980s, and it won the ASCAP Award for Adventurous Programming in 1983 and 1984. The first music director, Gerhard Samuel, was succeeded by Richard Williams in 1969, Carlos Chávez in 1970, and Dennis Russell Davies in 1974. Davies has stressed making the artists more accessible to their audiences through workshops and "Meet the Composer" sessions, open rehearsals, and a composer-in-residence program, in which Bolcom, Cage, Copland, and Keith Jarrett have participated; guest artists have included Janos Starker, Jorge Mester, and Romuald Tecco. The festival orchestra consists of about 65 musicians from leading orchestras in the USA and Canada.

SARA VELEZ

Cadman, Charles Wakefield (*b* Johnstown, PA, 24 Dec 1881; *d* Los Angeles, CA, 30 Dec 1946). Composer. His maternal great-grandfather, Samuel Wakefield (1799–1895), was a composer of hymns and built the first pipe organ west of the Allegheny Mountains. Cadman received formal instruction in organ from William Steiner, piano from Edwin L. Walker, and theory from Lee Oehmler. He pursued advanced studies in theory and conducting with Luigi von Kunitz and Emil Pauer, leader and conductor of the Pittsburgh SO. In 1908 Cadman became accompanist of the Pittsburgh Male Chorus and from 1907 to 1910 served as organist at the East Liberty Presbyterian Church, Pittsburgh; he was music editor and critic of the *Pittsburgh Dispatch* from 1908 to 1910.

Cadman became interested in the music of the American Indians after reading articles by Alice C. Fletcher, a Washington ethnologist, and Francis La Flesche, son of a chief of the Omaha tribe. In January 1909 he arranged and published Four American Indian Songs op.45, of which *From the Land of the Sky-blue Water* became enormously popular. During the summer of that year Cadman and La Flesche visited the Omaha and Winnebago reservations and made recordings of tribal songs. In February Cadman organized a series of lecture-performances entitled "American Indian Music Talk," which after 24 April 1913 were given with the aid of Princess Tsianina Redfeather, a Cherokee-Creek Indian. After a successful tour of Europe with the series, Cadman moved to Denver, and in 1916 to Los Angeles, where he devoted himself to composing and teaching. In 1918 the Metropolitan Opera produced *Shanewis or The Robin Woman*, based on events in the life of Princess Redfeather (*see* OPERA, fig.2). The culmination of Cadman's works on American Indian themes, *Shanewis* was highly successful, and in the following year was given an unprecedented second staging at the Metropolitan. During 1919–33 Cadman composed more operas, and in 1926 received an honorary doctorate from the University of Southern California. He also composed several film scores and in 1929 worked under contract for Fox Studios. He was a founder of the Hollywood Bowl and a member of the National Institute of Arts and Letters.

Cadman's music is marked by well-made melodies, if conventional harmony. He belongs to that group of American composers – which also included Farwell, Gilbert, Nevin, and Skilton – who "idealized" (i.e., set into a conservative 19th-century harmonic idiom) the music of the American Indians. Although his early works were mostly sentimental household songs, the Trio in D major (1914) revealed in the composer a keen instrumental flair, also evident in later orchestral works. Cadman also wrote articles on American music (*MQ*, i (1915), 387; *The Etude*, lxi (1943), 705).

WORKS

(several pubd in other arrs.)

STAGE

The Land of the Misty Water (opera, R. La Flesche, N. R. Eberhart), 1909–12, unperf., rev. as Ramala

Shanewis or The Robin Woman (opera, 2, Eberhart), New York, 23 March 1918

The Rubaiyat of Omar Khayyám (film music, dir. F. P. Easle), 1919–21; film, retitled A Lover's Oath, first shown 1925

The Sunset Trail (operatic cantata, 2 scenes, G. Moyle), Denver, 5 Dec 1922

The Garden of Mystery (opera, 1, Eberhart), New York, 20 March 1925

Rappaccini's Daughter (incidental music, Hawthorne), 1925

The Ghost of Lollypop Bay (operetta, 2, C. and J. Roos), 1926

Lelawala (operetta, G. M. Brown), 1926

A Witch of Salem (opera, 3, Eberhart), Chicago, 8 Dec 1926

The Belle of Havana (operetta, Brown), 1928

South in Sonora (operetta, 3, C. and J. Roos), 1932
The Willow Tree (radio score), NBC, 3 Oct 1932
Music for *c*6 other films, some orig., some arrs. of vocal works

INSTRUMENTAL

Orch: Thunderbird Suite, 1914; Oriental Rhapsody (after Omar Khayyám), 1921; To a Vanishing Race, str, 1925; Hollywood Suite, 1932; Dark Dancers of the Mardi Gras, pf, orch, 1933; Trail Pictures, suite, 1934; American Suite, str, 1936; Suite on American Folktunes, 1937; Sym. "Pennsylvania," e, 1939–40; Aurora Borealis, pf, orch, 1944; A Mad Empress Remembers, vc, orch, 1944; Huckleberry Finn Goes Fishing, ov., 1945

Pf: Carnegie Library March, 1898, unpubd; Melody, G♭, 1905; Prairie Sketches, suite, 1906, arr. orch, 1923; Idealized Indian Themes, 1912; Pf Sonata, A, 1915; Oriental Suite, 1921; several other works

Chamber: Pf Trio, D, 1914; Vn Sonata, G, 1932; Pf Qnt, g, 1937

VOCAL

Choral: The Vision of Sir Launfal (J. R. Lowell), male chorus, 1909; The Sunset Trail (Moyle), 1925; The Father of Waters (Eberhart), 1928; The Far Horizon (J. Roos), 1934; other works, incl. *c*10 sacred anthems

Over 300 songs, incl. At Dawning (Eberhart), 1906; Four American Indian Songs (Eberhart), 1909; Sayonara (Eberhart), song cycle on Japanese themes, 1910; From Wigwam and Teepee (Eberhart), song cycle on Indian themes, 1914; The Willow Wind (Chin.), song cycle, 1922

Principal publishers: O. Ditson, J. Fischer, H. Flammer, Galaxy, Presser, White-Smith, Willis

BIBLIOGRAPHY

EwenD
A. W. Kramer: "An Important Addition to American Chamber Music," *MusAm*, xx/22 (1914), 19
"Charles Wakefield Cadman: an American Composer," *Musician*, xx (1915), 687
J. F. Porte: "Charles Wakefield Cadman: an American Nationalist," *The Chesterian*, no.39 (1924), 223
C. W. Wakefield: *Complete Musical Works of Charles Wakefield Cadman* (Los Angeles, 1937) [catalogue]
N. C. Fielder: *Complete Musical Works of C. W. Cadman* (Los Angeles, 1951) [catalogue]
H. D. Perison: *Charles Wakefield Cadman: his Life and Works* (diss., Eastman School, U. of Rochester, 1978)
——: "The 'Indian' Operas of Charles Wakefield Cadman," *College Music Symposium*, xxii/2 (1982), 20

DAVID E. CAMPBELL

Cady, Calvin Brainerd (*b* Barry, IL, 21 June 1851; *d* Portland, OR, 29 May 1928). Music educator. He studied music at the Oberlin Conservatory and under Ernst Friedrich Richter, Benjamin Papperitz, and Oscar Paul at the Leipzig Conservatory (1872–4). After a period of teaching the piano and harmony at Oberlin (1874–9), he went to Ann Arbor to become the first director of the University School of Music (later absorbed into the University of Michigan). In 1888–94 he taught at the Chicago Conservatory, then taught privately in Boston; from 1907 he taught music education in New York, at Columbia University Teachers College (1907–10) and the Institute of Musical Art (1908–13). In 1913 he founded the Music-Education School in Portland. His three-volume manual *Music-Education* (Chicago, 1902–7) emphasized the study of music as a gateway to all the liberal arts, as did his school in Portland.

BRUCE CARR

Caesar, Shirley (*b* Durham, NC, 13 Oct 1938). Gospel singer. She made her first appearance at the age of eight and by the age of 12 was known throughout the South as "Baby Shirley." She studied business education at North Carolina State College, but left after two years when the opportunity came in 1958 to join Albertina Walker and the Caravans. While with the group she specialized in songs performed in a fast tempo in which she sang at the very top of her range; she used a great deal of ornamentation, adding extra notes, scoops, and growls to the melody as well as words to the original text (e.g., *Sweeping through the city*, 1960; *I won't be back*, 1962). Her performances were also marked by high energy: she was known for her "runs" and "shouts for Jesus." She became an evangelist in 1961 and left the Caravans in 1966 to seek a solo career. She moved from the energetic song to the "song and sermonette" form developed by Edna Gallmon Cooke in the 1950s. Caesar won a Grammy Award in 1972 for her recording of *Put your hand in the hand of the man from Galilee*. The years 1966 to 1980 were marked by a series of songs dealing with mother (e.g., *Don't drive your mama away*, 1969; *No Charge*, 1978; *Faded Roses*, 1980). She moved from Roadshow to Myrrh/Word records in 1980 and refined her style, resulting in a larger, multiracial following and a Dove Award in 1982. She has been named Best Female Gospel Singer three times by *Ebony* magazine.

BIBLIOGRAPHY

SouthernB
"First Lady of Gospel," *Ebony*, xxxvii/11 (1977), 98
R. Anderson and G. North: *Gospel Music Encyclopedia* (New York, 1979)

HORACE CLARENCE BOYER

Cage, John (Milton, Jr.) (*b* Los Angeles, CA, 5 Sept 1912). Composer, philosopher, and writer on music. He has been at the center of the avant garde in the USA for several decades. The influence of his compositions and his aesthetic thought has been felt all over the world, particularly since World War II; he has had a greater impact on world music than any other American composer of the 20th century.

1. John Cage, 1971

1. Chromatics. 2. Dance, percussion, prepared piano. 3. Zen, I Ching, chance. 4. Tape, theater, indeterminacy. 5. Fame and notoriety. 6. "Everything we do is music." 7. Reunions and celebrations.

1. CHROMATICS. The son of an inventor, Cage excelled in Latin and oratory at Los Angeles High School, and on graduating in 1928 he was elected one of 13 "Ephebians" by faculty vote, on the basis of his "scholarship, leadership, and character." After attending Pomona College in Claremont for two years, he went in the spring of 1930 to Europe, traveling to Paris, Berlin, Madrid, and other cities and devoting himself to the study of music, art, and architecture. On his return to California he continued to write poetry and music and to paint, holding a series of jobs and studying with the pianist Richard Buhlig. In 1933 he went to New York for a year to study theory and composition with Weiss. He also attended Cowell's classes in non-Western, folk, and contemporary music at the New School for Social Research. Back in California in the autumn of 1934 he studied counterpoint with Schoenberg and also took courses in theory at UCLA. There he became involved for the first time with a dance group, as accompanist and composer. In 1938 he moved to Seattle as composer-accompanist for Bonnie Bird's dance classes at the Cornish School; there he met Merce Cunningham, with whom he was to collaborate thenceforth (*see* DANCE, §III, 2).

His earliest compositions are based on a schematic organization of the 12 pitches of the chromatic scale. Such works as the Six Short Inventions (1934) and the *Composition for Three Voices* (1934) deal with the problem of keeping repetitions of notes among the different voices as far apart as possible, even though each voice uses the same 25-pitch range and must itself state all 25 pitches before repeating any one of them. *Music for Wind Instruments* (1938) and *Metamorphosis* (1938) use fragments of 12-tone series transposed to various pitches determined by the intervallic structure of the series itself. These works are all for small combinations of instruments and show the influence of the theories and compositions of his teachers.

2. DANCE, PERCUSSION, PREPARED PIANO. Cage organized a percussion orchestra in Seattle in 1938. In 1940 he moved to San Francisco, where he and Lou Harrison gave concerts of percussion music, and in 1941 he went to Chicago to give a course in new music at the Chicago Institute of Design. He accompanied for the dance classes of Katherine Manning and organized several percussion concerts. In the spring of 1943 he went to New York, which has remained his base. A program of percussion music under his direction presented by the League of Composers at the Museum of Modern Art on 7 February 1943, including three of his own works, brought him major public attention for the first time, being reviewed and reported even in such popular channels as *Life* magazine. He wrote music for Cunningham and toured with Cunningham's company as accompanist, eventually becoming its music director.

Almost all of Cage's music during this period was written for percussion or for prepared piano (a piano transformed into a percussion instrument of diverse timbres by the insertion of various objects between the strings at certain points). Among his first compositions for prepared piano was *Bacchanale*, written for the dancer Syvilla Fort in Seattle in 1940, when he had wanted to accompany a dance with percussion music but without using a number of instruments. By the late 1940s Cage had established a reputation as a talented and innovative composer. A performance at Carnegie Hall of his major work for prepared piano, Sonatas and Interludes, by Maro Ajemian in January 1949 was an important event of the New York music season, and Cage received awards that year from the Guggenheim Foundation and the National Institute of Arts and Letters, which cited him for "having thus extended the boundaries of musical art."

2. *Detail of a piano "prepared" by Cage, 1940*

The prepared piano gave a wide range of percussive sounds; each note could have a distinctive timbre, determined by what objects were inserted in the strings and at what point (see fig. 2; for further illustration *see* PREPARED PIANO). And in his music for percussion ensembles Cage used a large variety of usual and unusual instruments. His *First Construction (in Metal)* of 1939 has the six percussionists play orchestral bells, thundersheets, piano, sleigh bells, oxen bells, brake drums, cowbells, Japanese temple gongs, Turkish cymbals, anvils, water gongs, and tam-tams. While in Chicago Cage had access to the sound-effects collection of a local radio station, and afterwards he began to use electrically produced sounds. For example, *Imaginary Landscape no.3* (1942) employs audio-frequency oscillators, variable-speed turntables for the playing of frequency recordings and generator whine, an electric buzzer, an amplified coil of wire, and an amplified marimba.

Many of the sounds produced by the prepared piano and some percussion instruments are of indeterminate or extremely complex pitch, and Cage quite logically turned from structures based on pitch organization to ones built on rhythmic patterns. The first 16 bars of *First Construction* are broken into the pattern 4 + 3 + 2 + 3 + 4, which is repeated 16 times. The String Quartet (1949–50) has a rhythmic structure of $2\frac{1}{2} + 1\frac{1}{2} + 2 + 3 + 6 + 5 + 1\frac{1}{2} + 1\frac{1}{2}$; the pattern of *Music for Marcel Duchamp* (1947) is 11 × 11 (2 + 1 + 1 + 3 + 1 + 2 + 1).

Patterns built on additive groups provide the basis for rhythmic structures in some Eastern music; as used by Cage, they give his music a static quality quite different from the linear, goal-oriented thrust of most western European and American art music, and he has explained that the expressive intent of certain of these pieces reflects Eastern attitudes. The ballet *The Seasons* (1947) attempts to express the traditional Indian view of the seasons as quiescence (winter), creation (spring), preservation (summer), and destruction (autumn); the Sonatas and Interludes (1946–8) express the "permanent emotions" of Indian tradition: the heroic, the erotic, the wondrous, the mirthful, sorrow, fear, anger, and the odious, and their common tendency towards tranquillity.

3. ZEN, I CHING, CHANCE. The external events of Cage's career in the late 1940s and early 1950s resembled those of the previous years, with continued activity in composition and work with the Cunningham Dance Company. He spent several summers teaching at Black Mountain College in North Carolina, he gave occasional classes at the New School for Social Research, and he went twice to Europe: in late 1949 with Cunningham and in 1954 with the pianist-composer David Tudor. The important events of these years were internal; it was at this time that the most dramatic changes in his thinking about music occurred.

In the late 1940s Cage had begun a study of Eastern philosophies with Gita Sarabhai and of Zen Buddhism with Daisetz T. Suzuki of Columbia University. By 1950 he was studying the I Ching, the Chinese book of changes; and in 1951 he began a series of pieces using various methods of composition in which elements of chance were introduced into the process of creation or performance, works in which Cage as the composer relinquished at least some control over what the final sounds of the piece would be. In *Music of Changes* (1951) – a lengthy piano work in four volumes – pitches, durations, and timbres were determined not by a conscious decision on the part of the composer but by the use of charts derived from the I Ching and the tossing of three coins. *Music for Piano I* (1952) is notated completely in whole notes, with the performer determining durations; pitches were chosen by ruling staves on pages of paper and then making notes where imperfections were observed on the page. *Imaginary Landscape no.4* (1951) is performed with 12 radios with two performers at each, one manipulating the knob that changes stations and the other the volume control; the notation is precise, but of course the sounds for any given performance vary according to what is on the air.

Cage's aim in these works was "to make a musical composition the continuity of which is free of individual taste and memory (psychology) and also of the literature and 'traditions' of the art." Later he explained his philosophical basis for creating chance or random music. He came to believe that it should not be man's role to shape the world around him to his own desires and habits, but rather to adapt himself to the objects and people surrounding him. In music, as in life, one should make the best of the world oneself, should find for oneself what is beautiful and meaningful. "Now structure is not put into a work, but comes up in the person who perceives it himself. There is therefore no problem of understanding but the possibility of awareness." His *4′33″* (1952), which may be performed by any instrument or combination of instruments, epitomizes this attitude. The performer(s) sit silently on stage for the duration of the piece; the music consists of whatever noises are made by the audience and whatever sounds come from outside the auditorium during this time.

Until he moved into chance operations Cage had been slowly yet steadily building a reputation as a talented and serious innovator. But performances of such pieces as *Music of Changes*, consisting of a string of unrelated notes often separated by long silences and timed by a stopwatch held by the performer, or of the piece for 12 radios, were met with amusement, amazement, or hostility. Few musicians or critics understood what he was trying to do. A handful of men – Morton Feldman, David Tudor, Christian Wolff, Earle Brown – worked with him and exchanged ideas during these years; together they founded the Project of Music for Magnetic Tape. Otherwise he found stimulation and encouragement from people in other arts: the visual artists Robert Motherwell, Robert Rauschenberg, and Jasper Johns, the poet Mary Caroline Richards, and the dancer Merce Cunningham.

4. TAPE, THEATER, INDETERMINACY. Cage had used electronic sounds in earlier pieces, but *Imaginary Landscape no.5* (1952) was his first piece prepared on magnetic tape. Made as an accompaniment for a dance by Jean Erdman, it was put together by transferring the sounds from 42 phonograph records to tape, chopping these into fragments of varying lengths and reassembling them according to chance operations (*see* NOTATION, §2). *Williams Mix* (1952) was a much more complex piece. About 600 tapes of various sounds, musical and nonmusical, were assembled, fragmented, and then combined on eight tracks according to precise measurements and combinations arrived at by chance operations derived from the I Ching. The collecting, measuring, and splicing of these occupied Cage and Brown for many months.

In the summer of 1952, at Black Mountain College, Cage conceived and brought about an event that was an important precursor of the "happenings" of the following decade. This piece of "concerted action" involved simultaneous, uncoordinated music for piano and phonograph, poetry reading, dancing, lecturing, films, and slides. Other pieces of this time were planned to have visual as well as aural interest: *Water Music* (1952) is written for a pianist who must pour water from pots, blow whistles under water, use a radio and a pack of cards, and perform other actions to engage the eye.

Cage's chance music of the early 1950s had been constructed by one of several methods that ensured a random collection of notes, but once such a process had taken place the piece was fixed, was notated precisely, and would be just the same in each performance. A next step was to make pieces that would not be fixed, that would change from performance to performance. *Music for Piano 4–19* (1953) consists of 16 pages, the notes derived by chance operations; these pages "may be played as separate pieces or continuously as one piece or:" (sic). *Music for Piano 21–36* and *37–52* (1955) are two groups of pieces to be played alone or together or with *Music for Piano 4–19*. *Music for Piano 53–68* (1956) and *Music for Piano 69–84* (1956) complete the set of pieces, all of which may be performed, in whole or in part, by any number of pianists. *26′ 1.1499″* for a string player (1955), with notes selected partly by chance and partly by observation of imperfections in the paper on which it was written, may be played as a solo, or several different sections may be played simultaneously by various instruments to make duets, trios, quartets, etc. The most ambitious piece of this sort is the Concert for Piano and Orchestra (1957–8). There is no master score; parts for each instrument of the orchestra were written using chance methods. The piece may be peformed by any number of players as a solo, ensemble piece, symphony, aria, or concert for piano and orchestra. Each player selects from his part any number of pages to play, in any sequence, and coordination is by elapsed time, with the conductor's arms functioning as the hands of a clock.

5. FAME AND NOTORIETY. Attitudes towards Cage and his work, always strong, became even more intense during this most radical period. Vigorously and violently attacked for what he was saying

and doing, he was at the same time increasingly in demand as a lecturer, teacher, and performer. He and Tudor made a concert tour of Europe in 1954, performing in Cologne, Paris, Brussels, Stockholm, Zurich, Milan, and London and at the Donaueschingen Festival in Germany. Reaction was largely hostile, but soon afterwards such European composers as Stockhausen began discussing and experimenting with chance music. Back in the USA, Cage spent much of his time touring with the Cunningham Dance Company, which was performing more and more frequently. When in New York, he sometimes taught classes at the New School, attracting as students Dick Higgins, Allan Kaprow, George Brecht, Al Hansen, and Jackson MacLow, each of whom was to make a mark on the avant-garde scene. A retrospective concert of Cage's music, with a selection of pieces covering a span of 25 years, was given at New York's Town Hall in May 1958. The reception was mixed; audience response to the newly composed Concert for Piano and Orchestra was as violent as that which had greeted the first performance of *The Rite of Spring*, but a three-disc album of the concert, put out by George Avakian, made it possible for critics to evaluate Cage's development in a more informed way than before.

Cage was in Europe again that summer (1958), giving concerts and lectures and teaching a class in experimental music at Darmstadt. Luciano Berio invited him to Milan, where he spent four months working in the tape studio operated by the Milan radio station, making the tape piece *Fontana Mix*. During this stay he appeared on the Italian television quiz show "Lascia o raddoppia," successfully answering questions on mushrooms over a five-week period, winning a large prize, and creating and performing several compositions (*Water Walk* and *Sounds of Venice*) as a prelude to the competition sessions. Back in New York in 1959 he taught courses in experimental music and mushroom identification at the New School, was commissioned to write a large orchestral work by the Montreal Festivals Society, was a co-founder of the New York Mycological Society, and accepted his first appointment at a degree-granting academic institution: he was a Fellow at the Center for Advanced Studies at Wesleyan University, Middletown, Connecticut, for the academic year 1960–61.

Bernstein undertook a performance of *Atlas eclipticalis* with the New York PO at Lincoln Center in February 1964. Contact microphones attached to each instrument fed sound into an elaborate electronic system, whence it was distributed to six loudspeakers in various parts of the auditorium. Most of the audience walked out during the first presentation, and in succeeding performances members of the orchestra hissed the composer and attempted to sabotage the piece. More positive events of these years were a six-week concert tour of Japan in 1962 with Tudor, appointments as composer-in-residence at the University of Cincinnati (1967), associate of the Center for Advanced Study at the University of Illinois (1967–9), and artist-in-residence at the University of California, Davis (1969), and election to the National Institute of Arts and Letters in 1968.

6. "EVERYTHING WE DO IS MUSIC." Beginning with such works as *Music of Changes* (1951) and *Imaginary Landscape no.4*, Cage had employed notation expressing a relation between time and space such as exists when sound is recorded on tape. In the former piece 2.5 cm equals a quarter-note or its equivalent. Performers were given increasing freedom to choose what they were to play in pieces written in the later 1950s, but Cage's scores had more

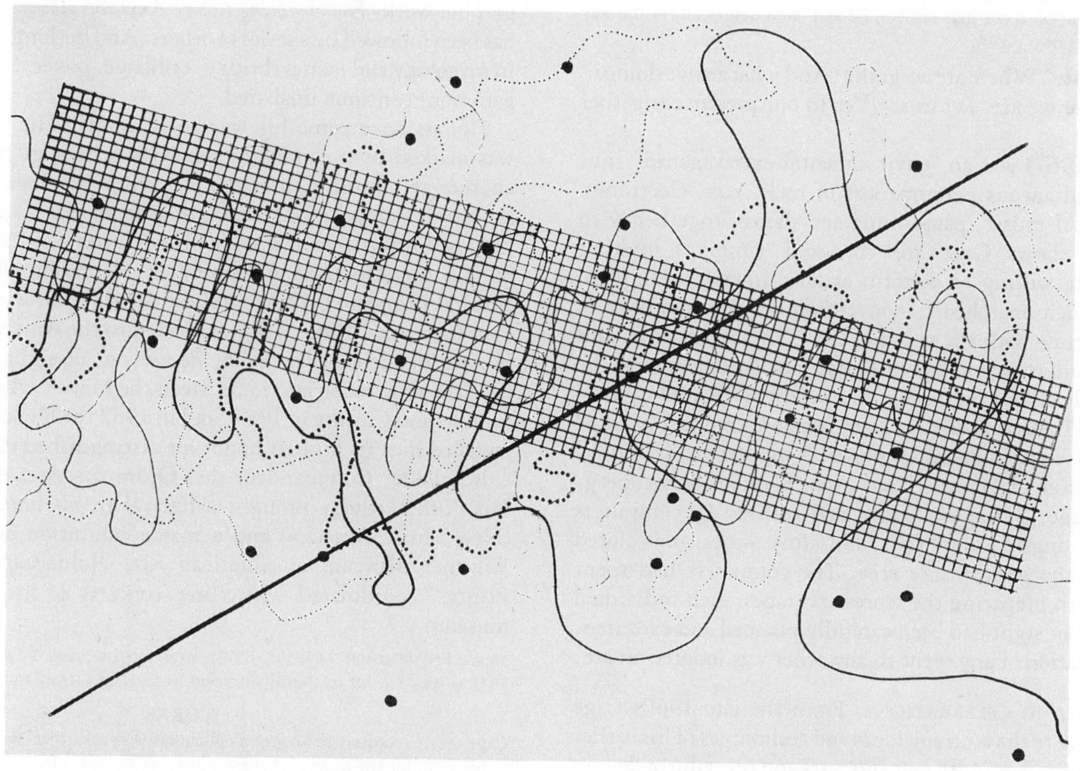

3. *Graphic notation from Cage's "Fontana Mix" (1958)*

or less precisely notated pitches, and a performance was to be coordinated within a precisely notated or decided period of time. In 1958, however, Cage began creating works that were "compositions indeterminate of their performances." The scores of *Fontana Mix, Music Walk*, and Variations I consist of transparent templates with lines or dots, to be superimposed over one another in any way, the performer making his own part (fig. 3). Variations I may be performed by any number of players using any number and kind of instruments; Variations II (1961) requires "any number of players, and sound-producing means"; Variations IV (1963) is for "any number of players, any sounds or combinations of sound produced by any means, with or without other activities." These "scores" suggest to the performer only in the most general way what he is to play or do: sounds and actions almost completely of the performers' choosing are the result. *0′0″* (1962), as performed by Cage himself in the mid-1960s, consisted in his preparing and slicing vegetables, putting them in an electric blender, and then drinking the juice, with the sounds of these various actions amplified throughout the hall.

Such things were taken by many to be the actions of a madman or a charlatan. Cage's explanation, given in his lectures and writings, was that distinctions between life and art should be broken down, that he as a composer should, through his compositions, make his audiences more aware of the world they are living in. Expecting "art" because they had come to a specific place at a planned time in response to an announced program, they would be offered a collection of sounds and sights such as they might encounter elsewhere at other times. If they could learn to respond to these, they could do the same when they were not in the concert hall. As Cage wrote in *Silence* (1961):

> Our intention is to affirm this life, not to bring order out of chaos or to suggest improvements in creation, but simply to wake up to the very life we're living, which is so excellent once one gets one's mind and one's desires out of the way and lets it act of its own accord.

And in his lecture "Where are we going? And what are we doing?" he wrote: "Here we are. Let us say Yes to our presence together in Chaos."

Musicircus (1967) was an "environmental extravaganza" consisting of simultaneous performances of rock, jazz, electronic, piano, and vocal music, pantomime and dance, together with films and slide shows. Cage's role consisted "simply in inviting those who were willing to perform at once (in the same place and time)." Such anarchistic, convention-defying affairs were very much in tune with the mood of the USA at that time, and Cage enjoyed unprecedented popularity, particularly among the young and radical and on college campuses. *HPSCHD* (1967–9), made with Lejaren Hiller, was an immense complex of sight and sound. Seven harpsichordists played computer-realized mixtures of the music of Mozart, Beethoven, Chopin, Schoenberg, Hiller, and Cage, 51 tapes planned and realized by computers were played through 51 amplifiers, and films, slides, and colored lights bathed the performance area. The composers had spent many months in preparing the scores and tapes; each individual event of sound or sight had been carefully planned and executed, though the relation of any event to any other was indeterminate.

7. Reunions and celebrations. From the late 1960s Cage has been willing to draw on any ideas and techniques of his earlier periods, or to mix these with new interests and procedures. Scores may be precisely and intricately notated, or they may give only the most general guide to the shape and content of the piece. He writes for conventional instruments, for electronic sounds, and for amplified and distorted sound materials drawn from the natural world, or he draws on previously recorded material. Pieces may be designed for performance in conventional concert halls, in dance theaters, at home, or outdoors. One thing may become another: a chess game played on an amplified board becomes a musical composition in *Reunion* (1968); tiny drawings retrieved from Thoreau's *Journals* are used as a musical score in *Score* (1974); poetry is transformed into part of a musical piece in *62 Mesostics re Merce Cunningham* (1971). Yet however disparate their methods or media, all these pieces are unmistakably Cageian, having in common his continuing desire to utilize various chance procedures and improvisations to create sound patterns divorced from self-expression.

Typical is *Etudes australes* (1974–5), a virtuoso piece for piano that has a precisely notated score derived from tracing astronomical charts onto music staves. *Cheap Imitation*, written for piano in 1969 and orchestrated in 1972, is based on a piece by Satie; the original rhythmic patterns are kept but pitches are replaced with notes selected through chance procedures. *Child of Tree* (1975) and *Branches* (1976) make use of amplified plant sounds; *Roaratorio, an Irish Circus on Finnegans Wake* (1979) is an electronic piece built of thousands of sounds mentioned in Joyce's novel, many of them recorded in places mentioned in the book. *A Dip in the Lake* (1978), written for performance in Chicago and its surrounding area, is scored for "two places, three places and four places"; participants are instructed to "go to the places and either listen to, perform at and/or make a recording of" a number of quicksteps, waltzes, and marches. Thoreau and Joyce have joined Satie and Duchamp as persons of unusual interest to Cage. He often uses a computer to perform chance operations more efficiently and dispassionately than any human. His first major graphic work, *Not Wanting to Say Anything about Marcel* (1969), has been followed by a series of others. And his long-time interests in mycology and games (bridge, cribbage, poker, Scrabble, backgammon) continue unabated.

Honors have come his way increasingly. His 60th birthday was marked by a concert at the New School in July 1972 and another at Lincoln Center the following January. Commissions for major compositions have come from the Canadian Broadcasting Corporation (*Lecture on the Weather*, 1975), the Boston SO for the American Bicentennial celebration (*Renga*, 1976), IRCAM (*Roaratorio*, 1979), and the Cabrillo Music Festival (*Dance Four Orchestras*, 1981). He was elected to the American Academy of Arts and Sciences in 1978, he was one of eight New Yorkers (and the only musician) to be given the Mayor's Award of Honor for Arts and Culture in 1981, and in 1982 the French government awarded him its highest honor for distinguished contribution to cultural life, Commandeur de l'Ordre des Arts et des Lettres. His 70th birthday brought a festival in his honor in Chicago (New Music America) and a major exhibition at New York's Whitney Museum of American Art, "John Cage: Scores and Prints," coordinated with three concerts of his music at the museum.

See also Environmental music; Experimental music, esp. §2 and fig. 1; Orchestral music, §4; for further illustration *see* Cunningham, Merce.

WORKS

Cage created various nonnotated collaborative works that he does not claim as his own; for the most part these works are excluded from this list. All works are published unless otherwise stated.

Three Songs (G. Stein), 1v, pf, 1932

Sonata, cl, 1933
Sonata for Two Voices, 2 or more insts, 1933
Solo with Obbligato Accompaniment of Two Voices in Canon, and Six Short Inventions on the Subject of the Solo, 3 or more insts, 1933–4
Composition for Three Voices, 3 or more insts, 1934
Music for Xenia (A Valentine out of Season), prepared pf, 1934
Six Short Inventions, a fl, cl, tpt, vn, 2 va, vc, 1934
Quartet, 4 perc, 1935
Quest, 2nd movt, pf, 1935
Three Pieces, 2 fl, 1935
Two Pieces, pf, c1935, rev. 1974
Trio, suite, 3 perc, 1936
Five Songs (Cummings), A, pf, 1938
Metamorphosis, pf, 1938
Music for Wind Instruments, wind qnt, 1938
First Construction (in Metal), 6 perc, 1939
Ho to AA (C. Tracy), 1v, pf, 1939, unpubd
Imaginary Landscape no.1, 2 variable-speed turntables, frequency recordings, muted pf, cymbal, 1939
Bacchanale, prepared pf, 1940
Living Room Music, perc and speech qt, 1940
Second Construction, 4 perc, 1940
Double Music, 4 perc, 1941, collab. L. Harrison
Third Construction, 4 perc, 1941
And the Earth shall Bear Again, prepared pf, 1942
The City Wears a Slouch Hat (K. Patchen), radio play, perc, 1942, unpubd
Credo in Us, 4 perc, 1942
Forever and Sunsmell (Cummings), 1v, 2 perc, 1942
Imaginary Landscape no.2 (March no.1), 5 perc, 1942
Imaginary Landscape no.3, audio-frequency oscillators, variable-speed turntables, elec buzzer, amp wire, amp mar, 1942
In the Name of the Holocaust, prepared pf, 1942
Primitive, prepared ("string") pf, 1942
Totem Ancestor, prepared pf, 1942
The Wonderful Widow of Eighteen Springs (Joyce), 1v, closed pf, 1942
Amores, 2 prepared pf solos, 2 perc trios, 1943
A Room, pf/prepared pf, 1943
Our Spring will Come, pf, 1943
She is Asleep, qt for 12 tomtoms, duet for 1v, prepared pf, 1943
Tossed as it is Untroubled (Meditation), prepared pf, 1943
A Book of Music, 2 prepared pf, 1944
Four Walls (M. Cunningham), pf, vocal interlude, 1944
The Perilous Night, prepared pf, 1944
Prelude for Meditation, prepared pf, 1944
Root of an Unfocus, prepared pf, 1944
Spontaneous Earth, prepared pf, 1944
The Unavailable Memory of, prepared pf, 1944
Three Dances, 2 amp prepared pf, 1944–5
Daughters of the Lonesome Isle, prepared pf, 1945
Mysterious Adventure, prepared pf, 1945
Party Pieces (Sonorous and Exquisite Corpses), c1945, 20 pieces by Cage, Cowell, Harrison, Thomson [arr. fl, cl, bn, hn, pf, by R. Hughes]
Experiences, duo for 2 pf, solo for 1v (Cummings), 1945–8
Ophelia, pf, 1946
Two Pieces, pf, 1946
Sonatas and Interludes, prepared pf, 1946–8
Dreams that Money can Buy, film score, 1947, unpubd
Music for Marcel Duchamp, prepared pf, 1947
Nocturne, vn, pf, 1947
The Seasons (ballet, 1), orch/pf, 1947
Dream, pf, 1948
In a Landscape, harp/pf, 1948
Suite, toy pf/pf, 1948
String Quartet, 1949–50
A Flower, 1v, closed pf, 1950
Six Melodies, vn, kbd, 1950
Concerto, prepared pf, chamber orch, 1950–51
Imaginary Landscape no.4 (March no.2), 12 radios, 1951
Music of Changes, pf, 1951
Sixteen Dances, fl, tpt, 4 perc, vn, vc, 1951
Two Pastorales, prepared pf, 1951
For M.C. and D.T., pf, 1952
4′33″, tacet for any inst/insts, 1952
Imaginary Landscape no.5, tape, 1952
Music for Carillon no.1, 1952
Music for Piano 1, 1952
Seven Haiku, pf, 1952
Waiting, pf, 1952
Water Music, pianist, 1952
Williams Mix, 8 1-track/4 2-track tapes, 1952
59½″, any 4-string inst, 1953
Music for Piano 2, 1953
Music for Piano 3, 1953
Music for Piano 4–19, 1953
Music for Piano 20, 1953
26′ 1.1499″, str player, 1953–5
Music for Carillon nos.2–3, 1954
34′ 46.776″, prepared pf, 1954
31′ 57.9864″, prepared pf, 1954
Music for Piano 21–36, 1955
Music for Piano 37–52, 1955
Speech, 5 radios, newsreader, 1955
26′ 1.1499″, str player, 1955
Music for Piano 53–68, 1956
Music for Piano 69–84, 1956
Radio Music, 1–8 radios, 1956
27′ 10.554″, perc, 1956
For Paul Taylor and Anita Dencks, pf, 1957
Winter Music, 1–20 pf, 1957
Concert for Piano and Orchestra, 1957–8
Aria, 1v, 1958
Fontana Mix, tape, 1958
Music Walk, pf (1 or more players), 1958
Solo for Voice 1, 1958
TV Koeln, pf, 1958
Variations I, any number of players, any insts, 1958
Sounds of Venice, TV piece, 1959
Water Walk, TV piece, 1959
Cartridge Music, amp sounds, 1960
Music for Amplified Toy Pianos, 1960
Music for The Marrying Maiden (J. MacLow), tape, 1960
Solo for Voice 2, 1960
Theatre Piece, 1–8 pfmrs, 1960
WBAI, auxiliary score for perf. with other works, 1960
Where are we going? And what are we doing?, lecture on 4 1-track tapes, 1960
Atlas eclipticalis, any ens from 86 insts, 1961
Music for Carillon no.4, 1961, rev. 1966
Variations II, any number of players, any means, 1961
4′ 33″ (no.2) (0′ 0″), solo for any player, 1962
Variations III, any number of people performing any actions, 1962–3
Variations IV, any number of players, any means, 1963
Electronic Music for Piano, pf + elec, 1964
Rozart Mix, tape, 1965
Variations V, audio-visual perf., 1965
Variations VI, plurality of sound systems, 1966
Variations VII, any number of players, any means, 1966, unpubd
Music for Carillon no.5, 1967
Musicircus, mixed-media event, 1967
Newport Mix, tape loops, 1967, unpubd
HPSCHD, 1–7 amp hpd, 1–51 tapes, 1967–9, collab. L. Hiller
Reunion, diverse pfmrs, 1968, unpubd, collab. D. Behrman, L. Cross, Mumma, Tudor
Cheap Imitation, pf, 1969, orchd 1972, vn version 1977
Sound Anonymously Received, any insts, 1969, unpubd
33⅓, any recordings, audience, 1969, unpubd
Song Books (Solos for Voice 3–92), 1970
Les chants de Maldoror pulvérisés par l'assistance même, French-speaking audience of not more than 200, 1971
62 Mesostics re Merce Cunningham, amp 1v, 1971
WGBH-TV, composers and technicians, 1971
Bird Cage, 12 tapes, 1972
Mureau, mix from Thoreau's writings, 1972
Etcetera, small orch, tape, 1973
Score (40 Drawings by Thoreau) and 23 Parts, any insts/vv, 1974
2 Pieces, pf, 1974
Etudes australes, 32 pieces, pf, 1974–5
Child of Tree, perc using amp plant materials, 1975
Lecture on the Weather, 12 insts/vv, tapes, film, 1975

Apartment House 1776, mixed media, 1976
Branches, perc solo/ens, amp plant materials, 1976
Quartets I–VIII, 24/41/93 insts, 1976
Renga, 78 insts/vv, 1976
Quartet, 12 amp vv, concert band, 1976–8
49 Waltzes for the Five Boroughs, any number of players, any means, 1977
Inlets, conch shells, tape, 1977
Primitive: Music for Dance, pf, 1977
Telephones and Birds, 3 pfmrs, 1977
The Unavailable Memory of:, prepared insts, 1977
Freeman Etudes, vn, 1977–80
A Dip in the Lake: Ten Quicksteps, 62 Waltzes, and 56 Marches for Chicago and Vicinity, listener, pfmr and/or recorder, 1978
Chorals, vn, 1978
Etudes borealis, pf and/or vc, 1978
Letters to Erik Satie, 1v, tape, 1978, unpubd
Someday, radio event, 1978, unpubd
Some of the Harmony of Maine, org, 3/6 assistants, 1978
Il treno, prepared trains, 1978, unpubd
Variations VIII, poster, 1978
Hymns and Variations, 12 amp vv, 1979
Roaratorio, an Irish Circus on Finnegans Wake, elec, 1979
Sonata for Two Voices, any 2 or more insts, 1979
Improvisations III, duets, 1980, unpubd
Litany for the Whale, 2 solo vv, 1980
Composition in Retrospect, computer, 1981
Dance Four Orchestras, 1981
30 Pieces for 5 Orchestras, 1981
A House Full of Music, 1982
Atlas borealis, orch, vv, 1982
Improvisations IV, 1982
Instances of Silence, installation, tapes, 1982, unpubd
Postcard from Heaven, 1–20 harps, 1982
Ear for Ear, vv, 1983
Souvenir, org, 1983
30 Pieces for String Quartet, 1983
A Collection of Rocks, orch without cond., 1984
Nowth upon Nacht, 1v, pf, 1984
Music for ——, fl, cl, vn, vc, 3 perc, pf, trbn, 1984–5
Ryoanji, vv, fl, ob, db, perc, small orch, 1984–5

Principal publisher: Peters

GRAPHIC WORKS

with C. Sumsion: Not Wanting to Say Anything about Marcel (1969)
with L. Long and A. Smith: Mushroom Book (1972)
Series re Morris Graves (1974)
Score without Parts (40 Drawings by Thoreau), (1978)
Seven-day Diary (Not Knowing) (1978)
17 Drawings by Thoreau (1978)
Signals (1978)
Changes and Disappearances (1979–82)
On the Surface (1980–82)

WRITINGS

with K. Hoover: *Virgil Thomson: his Life and Music* (New York, 1959)
Silence (Middletown, CT, 1961) [essays and lectures]
A Year from Monday (Middletown, 1967) [essays and lectures]
To Describe the Process of Composition Used in Not Wanting to Say Anything about Marcel (Cincinnati, OH, 1969)
with A. Knowles: *Notations* (New York, 1969)
M (Middletown, CT, 1973) [writings, 1967–72]
Writings through Finnegans Wake (Tulsa, OK, and New York, 1978)
Empty Words (Middletown, CT, 1979) [writings, 1973–8]
with S. Barron: *Another Song* (New York, 1981)
Mud Book (New York, 1982) [with illustrations by L. Long]
Themes and Variations (New York, 1982)

BIBLIOGRAPHY

CATALOGUE

R. Dunn, ed.: *John Cage* (New York, 1962) [annotated]

GENERAL STUDIES

(1945–65)

K. List: "Rhythm, Sound and Sane," *New Republic*, cxiii (1945), 870
S. Goldstein: "John Cage," *Music Business* (1946), April
P. Glanville-Hicks: "John Cage," *MusAm*, lxviii/10 (1948), 5, 20
R. Maren: "The Musical Numbers Game," *Reporter*, xviii (6 March 1958), 37
H. G. Helms: "John Cage's Lecture 'Indeterminacy'," *Die Reihe*, v (1959), 83–121
L. A. Hiller and L. M. Isaacson: *Experimental Music* (New York, 1959)
K. G. Roy: "The Strange and Wonderful Sonic World of John Cage," *HiFi/Stereo Review*, v/5 (1960), 62
V. Thomson: "John Cage Late and Early," *Saturday Review*, xliii (30 Jan 1960), 38
M. Wilson: "John Cage," *Canadian Music Journal*, iv/4 (1960), 54
"Cage, John (Milton, Jr.)," *CBY 1961*
T. Ichiyanagi: "John Cage," *Ongaku geijutsu*, xix/2 (1961)
N. Slonimsky: "If Anyone is Sleepy, Let him Go to Sleep," *Christian Science Monitor* (14 Dec 1961), 11
J. Johnston: "There is No Silence Now," *Village Voice* (8 Nov 1962)
K. McGary: "I have Nothing," *Antioch Review*, xxii (1962), 248
B. Markgraf: "John Cage: Ideas and Practices of a Contemporary Speaker," *Quarterly Journal of Speech*, xlviii (1962), 128
W. Mellers: "The Avant-garde in America," *PRMA*, xc (1963–4), 1
D. Heckman: "The Sounds and Silences of John Cage," *Down Beat*, xxxi/11 (1964), 20
G. Steinem: "Music, Music, Music, Music," *Show* (1964), Jan, 59
C. Tomkins: "Figure in an Imaginary Landscape," *New Yorker* (28 Nov 1964), 64, 68
D. Charles: "Entr'acte: 'Formal' or 'Informal' Music?," *MQ*, li (1965), 144
W. Mellers: *Music in a New Found Land* (New York, 1965), 177
C. Tomkins: *The Bride and the Bachelors: the Heretical Courtship in Modern Art* (New York, 1965)

(1966–75)

E. Morris: "Three Thousand Seven Hundred Forty-seven Words about John Cage," *Notes*, xxiii (1966–7), 468
L. B. Meyer: "The End of the Renaissance?," *Music, the Arts and Ideas* (Chicago, 1967), 68
U. Dibelius: "John Cage oder gibt es kritische Musik?," *Melos*, xxxv (1968), 377
S. Kubota: *Marcel Duchamp and John Cage* (New York, 1968)
C. Tomkins: *Ahead of the Game: Four Versions of the Avant-garde* (Harmondsworth, England, 1968)
W. Bartsch and others: *Die unvermeidliche Musik des John Cage* (Kolb, Switzerland, 1969)
R. Kostelanetz: "The American Avant-garde, Part II: John Cage," *Stereo Review*, xxii/5 (1969), 61; repr. in *Master Minds* (New York, 1969)
W. E. Lewinski: "Where do we Go from Here?: a European View," *MQ*, lv (1969), 193
E. Salzman: "Milton Babbitt and John Cage, Parallels and Paradoxes," *Stereo Review*, xxii/4 (1969), 60
S. Sontag: "The Esthetics of Silence," *Styles of Radical Will* (New York, 1969), 3
R. C. Clark: "Total Control and Chance in Musics: a Philosophical Analysis," *Journal of Aesthetics and Art Criticism*, xxviii (1970), 355; xxix (1970), 53
P. Gaboury: "Electronic Music: the Rift between Artist and Public," *Journal of Aesthetics and Art Criticism*, xxviii (1970), 345
R. Kostelanetz, ed.: *John Cage* (New York, 1970)
M. Siegel: "Come in, Earth, are you There?," *Arts in Society*, vii (1970), 70
E. J. Snyder: *John Cage and Music since World War II: a Study in Applied Aesthetics* (diss., U. of Wisconsin, 1970)
D. Charles: "Cage et l'expérience du non-vouloir," *ReM*, nos. 276–7 (1971), 19
Chou Wen-Chung: "Asian Concepts and Twentieth-century Western Composers," *MQ*, lvii (1971), 211
M. Nyman: "Cage and Satie," *MT*, cxiv (1973), 1227
C. Cardew: *Stockhausen Serves Imperialism and Other Articles* (London, 1974)
M. Nyman: *Experimental Music: Cage and Beyond* (New York, 1974)
V. Toncitch: "Kants Denkkategorien verpflichet: zur Ästhetik und Musik von John Cage," *Melos/NZM*, i (1975), 7

(from 1976)

B. E. Johnson: "John Cage," *Nutida Musik*, xxi (1977–8), 8
D. Charles: *Gloses sur John Cage* (Paris, 1978)
S. Emmerson: "John Cage," *Music and Musicians*, xxvii/3 (1978), 74
H. K. Metzger and R. Riehn: *John Cage* (Munich, 1978)
H. Åstrand: "Glosor om John Cage," *Nutida Musik*, xxii (1978–9), 54
J. Bell: "John Cage," *Art News*, lxxiii/3 (1979), 61
E. Lo Bue: "Nothing to say: John Cage come letterato," *Italia musicale*, xiv/1 (1979), 155

D. Bither: "John Cage: a Grand Old Radical," *Horizon*, xxiii/12 (1980), 48
S. Buettner: "Cage," *IRASM*, xii (1981), 141
P. Griffiths: *Cage* (New York, 1981)
T. J. O'Grady: "Aesthetic Value in Indeterminate Music," *MQ*, lxvii (1981), 306
P. Gena and J. Brent, eds.: *A John Cage Reader: in Celebration of his 70th Birthday* (New York, 1982)
S. Montague: "Significant Silences of a Musical Anarchist," *Classical Music* (London, 22 May 1982), 11
R. Stevenson: "John Cage on his 70th Birthday: West Coast Background," *Inter-American Music Review*, v/1 (1982), 3
C. Hamm: "The American Avant-garde," *Music in the New World* (New York, 1983), 580–617
J. Rockwell: "The American Experimental Tradition & its Godfather," *All American Music: Composition in the Late Twentieth Century* (New York, 1983), 47
D. Vaughan: "Duet: the Forty-year Collaboration of Avant-gardists Merce Cunningham and John Cage," *Ballet News*, iv/9 (1983), 21
T. DeLio: *Circumscribing the Open Universe: Essays on Cage, Feldman, Wolff, Ashley and Lucier* (Washington, DC, 1984)

WORKS

J. Pence: "People call it Noise – but he calls it Music," *Chicago Daily News* (19 March 1942), 4
"Percussion Concert," *Life*, xiv/11 (1943), 42, 44
L. Harrison: "The Rich and Varied New York Scene," *MM*, xxi (1945), 181
D. M. Hering: "John Cage and the 'Prepared Piano'," *Dance Magazine*, xx/3 (1946), 21, 52
S. Finkelstein: "John Cage's Music," *New Masses*, lxii (7 Jan 1947), 30
V. Thomson: "Expressive Percussion," *The Art of Judging Music* (New York, 1948), 164
P. Yates: "Music for Prepared Piano," *Arts and Architecture*, lxvi/4 (1949), 21
H. Cowell: "Current Chronicle," *MQ*, xxxviii (1952), 123
H. Curjel: "Cage oder das wohlpräparierte Klavier," *Melos*, xxii (1955), 97
G. Avakian: "About the Concert," *The 25-year Retrospective Concert of the Music of John Cage* (matrix no. KOBY 1499–1504, 1959) [liner notes]
A. Frankenstein: "In Retrospect – the Music of John Cage," *HiFi*, x/4 (1960), 63
J. Hollander: Review of *Silence*, *PNM*, i/2 (1963), 137
P. Dickinson: "Way Out with John Cage," *Music and Musicians*, xiv/3 (1965), 32
L. Austin: "HPSCHD," *Source*, ii/2 (1968), 10
R. Filliou: *Lehren und Lernen als Aufführungskünste* (New York, 1970)
S. Kisielewski: "Awangarda czy bezsilnosc," *Ruch muzyczny*, no.13 (1970), 10
W. E. Duckworth: *Expanding Notational Parameters in the Music of John Cage* (diss., U. of Illinois, 1972)
D. Charles: *Pour les oiseaux* (Paris, 1977; Eng. trans. as *For the Birds*, Salem, NH, 1981)
M. Fürst-Heidtmann: "Det preparerade Pianots Idé och Teknik," *Nutida Musik*, xxi (1977–8), 9
M. Fürst-Heidtmann: *Das präparierte Klavier des John Cage* (Regensburg, Germany, 1979)
V. Thomson: "Cage and the Collage of Noises," *A Virgil Thomson Reader* (Boston, 1981)
S. Husarik: "John Cage and Lejaren Hiller: HPSCHD, 1969," *American Music*, i/2 (1983), 1

INTERVIEWS

M. Kirby and R. Schechner: "An Interview," *Tulane Drama Review*, x/2 (1965), 50
L. G. Bodin and B. E. Johnson: "Semikolon: Musical Pleasure (interview with John Cage)," *Dansk musiktidskrift*, xli (1966), 36
D. Charles: "Soixante réponses à trente questions," *Revue d'esthétique*, xxi/2–4 (1968), 9
W. Zimmermann: "John Cage," *Desert Plants: Conversations with 23 American Musicians* (Vancouver, BC, 1976)
A. Gillmor: "Intervju med John Cage," *Nutida Musik*, xxi (1977–8), 13
R. Reynolds: "John Cage and Roger Reynolds: a Conversation," *MQ*, lxv (1979), 573
T. Everett: "10 Questions: 270 Answers," *Composer*, x–xi (1980), 57–103
C. Gagne and T. Caras: "John Cage," *Soundpieces: Interviews with American Composers* (Metuchen, NJ, 1982)
S. Montague: "John Cage at Seventy: an Interview," *American Music*, iii (1985), 205

CHARLES HAMM

Cahier, Mme. Charles [née Layton Walker, Sarah (Jane); Black, Mrs. Morris] (*b* 8 Jan 1870; *d* Manhattan Beach, CA, 15 April 1951). Contralto. She studied singing first in Indianapolis, then with Jean de Reszke in Paris, as well as Gustav Walter in Vienna and Amalie Joachim in Berlin. Two years after her operatic début at the Opéra in Nice (1904), she was engaged by Mahler to sing at the Vienna Hofoper, where she subsequently appeared for six seasons in roles that included Carmen and several in Wagner operas. She made her Metropolitan Opera début on 3 April 1911 as Azucena, and during the next two years sang Amneris and Fricka with the company; elsewhere her most famous role was Carmen. Her concert work was, however, the most significant part of her career. She was particularly well known for her performances of Mahler's music; in 1911 Bruno Walter chose her to sing in the posthumous world première of *Das Lied von der Erde* in Munich. After the close of her performing career, she taught in Sweden, Salzburg, and New York. The few recordings that she made document an imposing voice (if somewhat uncentered in tone) and a stately style. One of them, *Urlicht* from Mahler's Second Symphony, is of considerable historic importance because of her association with the composer.

RICHARD DYER

Cahill, Marie (*b* Brooklyn, NY, 7 Feb 1870; *d* New York, 23 Aug 1933). Actress and singer. She made her début in 1888 and appeared in small roles in several Broadway plays before spending some time performing in Paris and London. She returned to the USA in 1895 to accept a small part in the musical *Excelsior, Jr.*, then assumed the title role in the show's national tour. She subsequently appeared in such musicals as Victor Herbert's *The Gold Bug* (1896), in which she stopped the show with "When I first began to marry, years ago," and *The Wild Rose* (1902), in which she introduced "Nancy Brown"; she achieved stardom in *Sally in our Alley* (1902) with her most famous song, "Under the bamboo tree." Cahill continued to play leading roles – in *Nancy Brown* (1903), *It Happened in Nordland* (1904), *Moonshine* (1905), *Marrying Mary* (1906), *The Boys and Betty* (1908), *Judy Forgot* (1910), *The Opera Ball* (1912), and *Ninety in the Shade* (1915), many of which were produced by her husband, Daniel V. Arthur. When her popularity began to wane she appeared increasingly in vaudeville, and her last Broadway assignment was in *The New Yorkers* (1930). A short, thick-set, belligerent actress, she was notorious for her quarrels with producers over her insistence on choosing her own interpolations; on a number of occasions these battles cost her important parts. Many of her songs were written by Blacks in a ragtime idiom, and Cahill earned a reputation as a "coon shouter."

GERALD BORDMAN

Cahill, Thaddeus (*b* Mount Zion, IA, 1867; *d* New York, 12 April 1934). Inventor of the Telharmonium, an electromechanical keyboard instrument; *see* ELECTROACOUSTIC MUSIC, §7.

Cahn [Cohen, Kahn], **Sammy** [Samuel] (*b* New York, 18 June 1913). Lyricist. His first assignments as a lyricist were for specialty material for dance bands. In 1937 he and Saul Chaplin, with whom he had earlier led a dance band, adapted a Yiddish theater song into a very successful song for the Andrews Sisters, *Bei mir bist du schön*. With Chaplin, Jimmy Van Heusen, Nicholas Brodszky, and Jule Styne, he wrote many successful songs for Hollywood films, notably for Frank Sinatra, and won many Academy nominations and awards. His talent for adapting lyrics for special occasions and personalities has brought him many commissions for song parodies for industrial shows, benefits, and television. *High Button Shoes* (1947), written with Jule Styne, was a successful Broadway stage show, as was an autobiographical revue, *Words and Music* (1974).

WORKS

STAGE

(dates are those of first New York performance)

High Button Shoes (J. Styne), 9 Oct 1947 [incl. I still get jealous; Papa, won't you dance with me?]

Skyscraper (J. Van Heusen), 13 Nov 1965 [incl. Everybody has a right to be wrong]

Walking Happy (Van Heusen), 26 Nov 1966

Words and Music (revue), various composers, 16 April 1974

FILMS

Youth on Parade (Styne), 1942 [incl. I've heard that song before]; Carolina Blues (Styne), 1944 [incl. There goes that song again]; Anchors Aweigh (Styne), 1945 [incl. I fall in love too easily, The charm of you]; It Happened in Brooklyn (Styne), 1947 [incl. Time after time]; Romance on the High Seas (Styne), 1948 [incl. It's magic]; The Toast of New Orleans (N. Brodszky), 1950 [incl. Be my love]; Our Town (television) (Van Heusen), 1955 [incl. Love and marriage]; High Time (Van Heusen), 1960 [incl. The second time around]; Robin and the Seven Hoods (Van Heusen), 1964 [incl. My kind of town]

SONGS

(most associated with films)

Bei mir bist du schön (S. Chaplin), 1937; I'll walk alone (Styne), in Follow the Boys, 1944; I should care (P. Weston, A. Stordahl), in Thrill of a Romance, 1945; Because you're mine (Brodszky), in Because you're Mine, 1952; Three Coins in the Fountain (Styne), in Three Coins in the Fountain, 1954; I'll never stop loving you (Brodszky), in Love me or Leave me, 1955; The Tender Trap (Van Heusen), in The Tender Trap, 1955; All the way (Van Heusen), in The Joker is Wild, 1957; High Hopes (Van Heusen), in A Hole in the Head, 1959; Pocketful of Miracles (Van Heusen), in Pocketful of Miracles, 1961; Call me irresponsible (Van Heusen), in Papa's Delicate Condition, 1963

BIBLIOGRAPHY

"Cahn, Sammy," *CBY 1974*

S. Cahn: *I Should Care* (New York, 1974)

SAMUEL S. BRYLAWSKI

Cahuilla. American Indian tribe, who spoke a Uto-Aztecan language and lived in south-central California, south of the San Bernardino Mountains (*see* INDIANS, AMERICAN, fig.1). Cahuilla aboriginal music was typical of Indian musical style in southern California. Almost entirely vocal, and highly functional, it consisted of songs sung to accompany the various rituals in Cahuilla life. Song was the basis of the oral tradition, providing a vehicle for the transfer of knowledge and traditional practice from one generation to another. Thus there were songs for rites of passage, such as birth and puberty, and for entrance into certain societies. There were songs for work, play, and gambling, shamanistic songs for healing and to invoke power (for love, competition, etc.), and priestly songs for commemoration, prayer, and dedication, which were cosmological in nature.

Since song was so central to daily life, it was natural for all members of the society to sing and to know their family songs; however, the institution of ceremonial singing was entrusted to a select few, the *hauiniktam*, who occupied inherited positions requiring long and arduous training and preparation. Although these clan leaders were male, there was a female complement that assisted in the ceremonies, which were performed to long song cycles, sometimes of an epic nature, sung in unison. Singers and dancers, both men and women, were required to perform nightly (the whole night through) in the week-long annual ceremonies. Physical and mental endurance, and vocal longevity, were normal. The best singers and dancers were usually older people, but the participation of all ages, especially in social dancing (e.g., the Bird Dance *wikikmalem*), was expected.

The formal plan of Cahuilla music was basically a two-part song form: a first part, which generally had four repetitions, an upward motion to the second part (the so-called "rise"), and an ending formula which differed with each song type. A typical form was *AAAA BABA AAAA BABA C*. The songs usually occurred in groups. A pair of songs related textually (often related musically as well) were referred to as "brothers." The songs in a cycle relied upon one another for meaning; this led to lengthy song series. Meter was predominantly complex, compound, and compound-complex. Metric organizations of fives, sixes, sevens, and nines abounded. Syncopation was a prime ingredient of this

Ex.1 Bird Song of the Cahuilla
= 192
kwe le me le me yo ko - we kwe le me le me yo ko - we kwe
le me le me yo ko - we kwe
trans.: "the rabbit's floppy ears . . ."

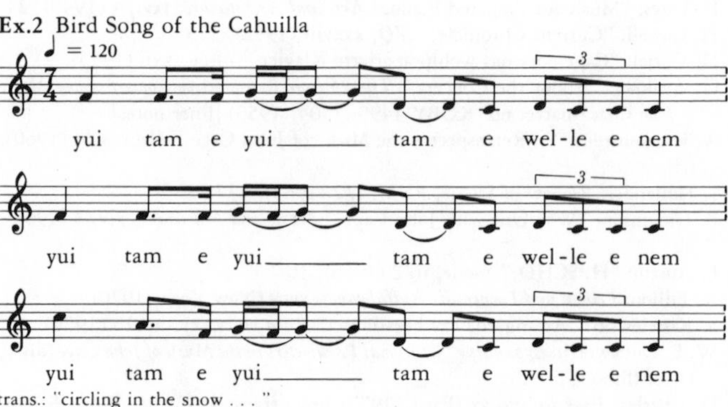
Ex.2 Bird Song of the Cahuilla
= 120
3
yui tam e yui tam e wel-le e nem
yui tam e yui tam e wel-le e nem
yui tam e yui tam e wel-le e nem
trans.: "circling in the snow . . ."

music (exx. 1–2). The extended pentatonic scale was widely used among the various song types, but more specific to Cahuilla musical style was the use of glissando (this means that any attempt to use standard notation can be only approximate). 3rds and 7ths, in particular, tended to be neutral (neither major nor minor) (ex.3).

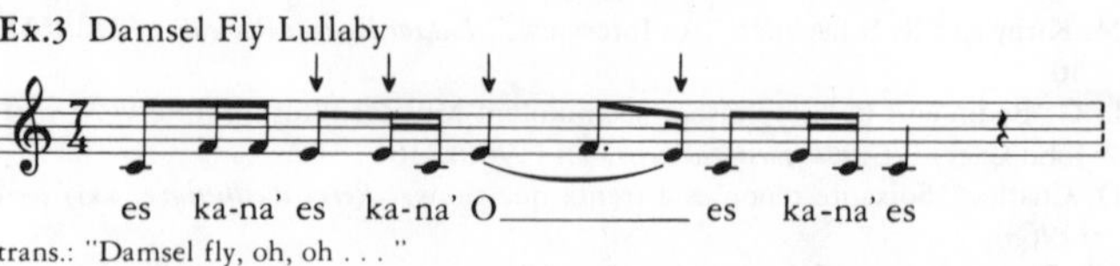
Ex.3 Damsel Fly Lullaby
es ka-na' es ka-na' O es ka-na' es
trans.: "Damsel fly, oh, oh . . ."

all examples rec. and transcr. E. H. Siva

Instrumental music was secondary, serving mainly to accompany singing. Various sorts of rattle were used in accompaniment, an appropriate one for each song type (e.g., deer-hoof rattle for commemoration of the deer). The split-stick, or clapper, was used for the twirling Eagle Dance. Bone whistles were used for certain ceremonials. The end-blown, four- or six-hole wooden flute was a personal instrument; it sometimes played a part in courting. The bullroarer served to summon the people to ceremonial gatherings.

Recordings of Cahuilla music are in the holdings of the Lowie Museum of Anthropology, University of California, Berkeley; the Library of Congress, Washington, DC; the Malki Museum, Banning, California; the Southwest Museum, Los Angeles, California; and the Ethnomusicological Archive, UCLA.

See also INDIANS, AMERICAN, esp. §I, 4 (ii)(c).

BIBLIOGRAPHY

T. T. Waterman: "Native Musical Instruments of California," *Outwest*, viii (1908), 277

L. Hooper: "The Cahuilla Indians," *American Archaeology and Ethnology*, xvi/6 (1920), 315–80

A. L. Kroeber: *Handbook of the Indians of California* (Washington, DC, 1925)

G. Herzog: "The Yuman Musical Style," *Journal of American Folklore*, xli (1928), 183

W. D. Strong: "Aboriginal Society in Southern California," *American Archaeology and Ethnology*, xxix/1 (1929), 1–358

L. J. Bean: *Mukat's People* (Berkeley, CA, 1972)

J. McGrath: *My Music Reaches to the Sky: Native American Musical Instruments* (Washington, DC, 1974)

W. J. Wallace: "Music and Musical Instruments," *Handbook of North American Indians*, viii: *California*, ed. R. F. Heizer (Washington, DC, 1978), 642

ERNEST H. SIVA

Cailliet, Lucien (*b* Châlons-sur-Marne, France, 22 May 1891; *d* California, 27 Dec 1984). Composer, arranger, and conductor. While stationed in Dijon for military service, he studied at the national conservatories there and in Paris, graduating in 1913. He was successively a drum major, solo clarinetist and assistant bandmaster, and bandmaster in the French Army. While touring the USA in 1915 with a French band, he decided to leave the army and immigrate; he became an American citizen in 1923. In 1919 he joined the Philadelphia Orchestra as a clarinetist and arranger under Stokowski; he made a number of orchestral arrangements, some of which, with his agreement, were performed and recorded under Stokowski's name. He remained with the Philadelphia Orchestra until 1938. During this period he taught clarinet at the Curtis Institute, and earned the doctor of music degree at the Philadelphia Musical Academy (1937). From 1938 to 1945 he taught orchestration (on which he wrote a textbook, unpublished), counterpoint, and conducting at the University of Southern California. Between 1945 and 1957 he appeared as a guest conductor with many orchestras, composed 25 film scores, and made numerous orchestrations, including that for the soundtrack of Cecil B. DeMille's *The Ten Commandments*. In 1957 he was appointed educational and musical director for the G. Leblanc Corporation, a position he filled until 1976. He wrote many arrangements for band, orchestra, and clarinet choir, and a number of original compositions, of which *Variations on "Pop Goes the Weasel"* is perhaps the best-known. His name was often (though incorrectly) spelled Caillet.

WORKS

(selective list)

Sym. band: *c*20 works, incl. American Holiday, Campus Chimes, Festivity Ov., Galaxy, Victory Fanfare; *c*100 arrs. of works by various composers, incl. Bach, Bizet, Massenet, Rossini, Tchaikovsky, Wagner

Orch: Fantasy, cl, orch; Memories of Steven Foster; Our United States; Spirit of Christmas; Rhapsody, vn, orch

Other inst: 5 works, cl ens; 9 arrs., cl ens; 4 works, sax qt, incl. Carnaval; 3 works, cl, pf; other arrs.

Principal publishers: Boosey & Hawkes, Fox, Southern

BIBLIOGRAPHY

L. Fisher: "Lucien Cailliet: his Contributions to the Symphonic Band, Orchestra, and Ensemble Literature," *Journal of Band Research*, xviii/2 (1983), 48 [incl. complete list of works]

RAOUL CAMUS

Cajun music. *See* EUROPEAN-AMERICAN MUSIC, §II, 2 (i).

Cakewalk. A 19th-century dance of black-American origin, popularized and diffused through imitations of it in blackface minstrel shows (especially their WALK-AROUND finales) and, later, vaudeville and burlesque. It seems to have originated in slaves parodying their white owners' high manners and fancy dances. The name supposedly derives from the prize (presumably a cake) given to the best dancers among a group of slaves, but it may go back little further than the 1890s, when "cakewalk contests" among dancing couples were organized as public entertainments in northern American cities. Although no specific step patterns were associated with the dance, it was performed as a grand march in a parade-like fashion by couples prancing and strutting arm in arm, bowing and kicking backwards and forwards (sometimes with arched backs and pointed toes), and saluting to the spectators. The cakewalk was popularized and refined through the all-black musicals of the late 1890s (notably Will Marion Cook's *Clorindy, or The Origin of the Cakewalk*, 1898) and the dancing of Charles Johnson and the vaudeville team of Bert Williams and George Walker, who gave it international fame in the early 1900s through their performances in *In Dahomey* (1902) and *In Abyssinia* (1905). The cakewalk was associated with a syncopated music akin to ragtime, of which the most phenomenally successful example was the march/two-step by Kerry Mills, *At a Georgia Camp Meeting*, recorded many times beginning in 1898 by Sousa's band. The popularity it achieved led to its acceptance in the white social milieu and eventually, to the incorporation of some of the cakewalk steps into white-American dance forms. (For illustration *see* DANCE, fig.2.)

BIBLIOGRAPHY

M. Stearns and J. Stearns: *Jazz Dance: the Story of American Vernacular Dance* (New York, 1968)

W. M. Cook: "Clorindy, the Origin of the Cakewalk," *Theatre Arts*, xxxi (1947), 61; repr. in *Readings in Black American Music*, ed. E. Southern (New York, 1972), 217

L. F. Emery: *Black Dance in the United States from 1619 to 1970* (Palo Alto, CA, 1972)

E. A. Berlin: *Ragtime* (Berkeley, CA, 1980/*R*1984 with addenda)

H. WILEY HITCHCOCK,
PAULINE NORTON

Caldwell, Sarah (*b* Maryville, MO, 6 March 1924). Opera impresario, conductor, and director. She was educated at the University of Arkansas, Hendrix College (Arkansas), and at the New England Conservatory, where she studied violin under Richard Burgin. In 1946 she won a scholarship as a violist at the Berkshire Music Center, where the next year she staged Vaughan Williams's *Riders to the Sea*. She then studied with Boris Goldovsky. From 1952 to 1960 she was head of the Boston University opera workshop; in 1958 she founded what was to become the Opera Company of Boston.

She established herself as a conductor and as an innovative director of a wide range of operas in Boston and, subsequently, throughout the USA, and has given the American premières of such works as Prokofiev's *War and Peace*, Luigi Nono's *Intolleranza*, Schoenberg's *Moses und Aron*, and Roger Sessions's *Mon-*

Sarah Caldwell, early 1970s

tezuma. In 1976 she became the first woman conductor of the Metropolitan Opera (*La traviata*). She is also an orchestral conductor, and has appeared with the New York PO, the Pittsburgh SO, and the Boston SO. She has always been known for her interest in staging difficult and demanding works under adverse conditions, and enjoys producing variant editions of standard works (e.g., the first version of *Boris Godunov* and *Don Carlos* in French). In 1982 her company arranged a collaboration to develop opera in the Philippines; and the next year she was appointed artistic director of the New Opera Company of Israel. As a director she is considered a follower of Walter Felsenstein, but in fact her approach to each opera is wholly her own; and she is to be regarded as one of the most influential opera directors in the USA.

BIBLIOGRAPHY

"Caldwell, Sarah," *CBY 1973*

PATRICK J. SMITH/R

Caldwell, William (*fl* Maryville, TN, 1834–7). Composer and tunebook compiler. He is known to have been associated with Ananias Davisson, at least through his use of *Kentucky Harmony* (1816) and *A Supplement to the Kentucky Harmony* (1820), from both of which he borrowed extensively for his own compilation, *Union Harmony: or Family Musician* (Maryville, TN, 1837). *Union Harmony* in turn influenced later Tennessee tunebooks, such as John B. Jackson's *Knoxville Harmony* (1838), Andrew W. Johnson's *American Harmony* (1839), and W. H. and M. L. Swan's *Harp of Columbia* (1848). Caldwell claimed 42 tunes in *Union Harmony*, which he indicated were "not entirely original" but carried his harmonizations. These tunes are predominantly in the American folk-hymn idiom.

See also SHAPE-NOTE HYMNODY, §2.

BIBLIOGRAPHY

G. P. Jackson: *White Spirituals in the Southern Uplands* (Chapel Hill, 1933/*R*1965)
G. E. Webb, Jr.: *William Caldwell's "Union Harmony" (1837)* (thesis, Southern Baptist Theological Seminary, 1975)

HARRY ESKEW

California, University of. State university with campuses at Berkeley, Davis, Los Angeles, Santa Barbara, Riverside, San Diego, Irvine, and Santa Cruz. The university was established by state legislature in 1868; by the early 1980s student enrollment had reached over 139,000, with a faculty of about 8000.

The music department of the Berkeley campus (in the College of Letters and Sciences) was founded in 1901, 33 years after the founding of the campus itself; its curriculum was largely shaped by Charles Seeger, chairman from 1912 to 1919, who introduced the first courses in musicology offered in the USA. The department continued to develop significantly from 1937 to 1951 under the chairmanship of Albert I. Elkus, who brought to the faculty such figures as Bloch, Sessions, Bliss, Imbrie, and Bukofzer. Elkus, himself a composer as well as a pianist and teacher, established the importance of composition in the department, and by 1983 seven of the 16 full-time faculty members were composers. The department enrolls some 150 undergraduate and graduate music students. Ethnomusicology was added to the curriculum in the 1970s, and in this area the department has become one of the most distinguished in the country. It offers a BA degree in general music and an MA and PhD in composition or scholarship and criticism, and it sponsors a small number of performing ensembles (including a gamelan), which often perform works directly related to the research interests of the faculty. The Music Library, established in 1947 and directed by Vincent Duckles (1947–81) and Michael Keller (from 1981), contains the Alfred Cortot, Sigmund Romberg, and Harris D. H. Connick collections of opera scores, a large number of early Italian opera librettos, manuscript instrumental music of the Tartini school, and the papers and music of several well-known California composers and scholars, including Oscar Weil, Hertz, Einstein, Bloch, Elkus, Bukofzer, Denny, Imbrie, Felciano, and Charles Seeger. In 1976 it began publishing its own newsletter, *Cum notis variorum*, in which the collections are regularly discussed. The department's collection of musical instruments, built around the Ansley K. Salz Collection of violins, violas, and bows, contains over 100 instruments (mostly Western), and the Robert H. Lowie Museum of Anthropology maintains a collection of over 1000 ethnic instruments from around the world and an archive of sound recordings.

The University of California at Davis (founded in 1906) offered its first BS degrees in 1922, but the music department (in the College of Letters and Sciences) was not founded until 1958. By 1980 it enrolled around 60 students and had a full-time faculty of ten. It offers a BA in general music, an MA in composition or musicology, and an MAT. The department sponsors a small number of ensembles that perform works related to the research interests of the faculty. The music library contains materials relating to the opera house in Woodland, California, and music by Larry Austin, Robert Bloch, Andrew Frank, George Perle, Jerome Rosen (i), Richard Swift, and William Valente.

Founded in 1919 as the southern branch of the University of California, the University of California at Los Angeles adopted its present name in 1927 and moved to its current site two years later; the music department (in the College of Fine Arts) was founded in 1919 and in the 1980s had an enrollment of about 450 undergraduate and graduate music students, with a full-time faculty of nearly 50. It offers a BA in general music, an MA and PhD in historical musicology, ethnomusicology, systematic musicology, composition, or music education, and an MFA in instrumental and vocal performance, opera, or conducting. The music department sponsors a number of performing ensembles, and the music library (established in 1942) includes strong holdings in ethnomusicology, ballad opera, and 17th- and 18th-century opera librettos. It contains the collections of Fannie Charles Dillon, Hal Levy, Earl Lowry, and Edward B. Powell, as well as the archive collections of Mary Carr Moore, Mader, Toch, Vincent, and Zeisl; it is also strong in the music of Chihara, Friml, Lazarof, Roy Harris, and Gardner Read. The William Andrews Clark Memorial Library specializes in English music and ballad opera, and the University Research Library holds the George Pullen Jackson collection of hymnody. There are also extensive music holdings in the John Edwards Memorial Foundation at the Center for the Comparative Study of Folklore and Mythology, the Archive of Popular American Music, the Center for Study of Comparative Folklore and Mythology research collection, the Ethnomusicology Archive, the Oral History Archives, and the Theater Arts Research Library. The music department maintains an instrument collection built around the Erich Lachmann Collection of string instruments. In addition, the Institute of Ethnomusicology houses a collection of some 1000 instruments with an emphasis on non-Western high-art cultures, and the Museum of Cultural History holds some 300 instruments, most from New Guinea and Africa. (*See also* LOS ANGELES, §4 (v).)

The Santa Barbara State College was incorporated into the University of California system in 1944 and moved to its present site in 1954, the year it inaugurated graduate-level programs. The music department (in the College of Letters and Sciences) had an enrollment of nearly 200 majors and graduate students in the 1980s, with a full-time faculty of 20. In addition to undergraduate degrees, it offers an MA in performance and the MA and PhD in composition, theory, or musicology; a single-subject teaching credential is also offered through the Graduate School of Education. The music department sponsors a small number of performing ensembles. The university library maintains the Lotte Lehmann, Bernard Herrmann, and Goethe collections, and the Arts Library holds the Anthony Boucher Archival Record Collection. The university publishes the Series of Early Music edited by Karl Geiringer.

The campus for the University of California at Riverside was approved by the state legislature in 1949 and declared a general campus of the state university system in 1959; a graduate division was established in 1960. The music department (in the College of Letters and Sciences) employed a full-time faculty of eight in 1980. In addition to a BA, it offers an MA in theory and composition, music history, or performance practice. The department sponsors a small number of performing groups, including a collegium musicum for which it maintains a collection of 30–35 modern reproductions of Renaissance and Baroque instruments. The affiliated San Bernardino County Museum houses nearly 30 instruments, some from local Indian cultures. The music library contains the Oswald Jonas, Niels Gade, and Marcella Craft collections, as well as materials from the WPA Southern California Music Project.

Not until 1964 was a campus of the university opened at San Diego. The music department (in the College of Letters and Sciences) was founded in 1966, and in 1980 enrolled some 150 students with a full-time faculty of 17. It offers a BA (both as a major and as a combined music and humanities major), an MA in composition, performance, computer music, or theoretical studies, and a PhD in composition and theoretical or experimental studies. The department sponsors a variety of performing groups, including Sonor, an ensemble drawn from faculty members specializing in modern music. According to its catalogue, there is a strong emphasis on "experimental research and its applications in electronics, computers, acoustics, extended instrumental techniques, and possible social contexts for music," and the department sponsors the Center for Music Experiment. The music library is strong in contemporary scores, notably those of Robert Erickson, Kenneth Gaburo, Joseph Julian, Wilbur Ogdon, Pauline Oliveros, and Roger Reynolds.

The seventh campus of the University of California, at Irvine, was founded in 1965 and the music department (in the School of Fine Arts) employs a full-time faculty of ten, offering BA and MFA degrees. Santa Cruz, also founded in 1965, has eight small residential colleges. The music department (in the Humanities and Arts Division) offers only a BA degree but sponsors several performing groups, notably a *mariachi* ensemble, a gamelan, and a Near Eastern music group.

See also ETHNOMUSICOLOGY, §3, and LIBRARIES AND COLLECTIONS, §3.

GRAYDON BEEKS (with ROBERT COMMANDAY)

California Indians. Group of American Indian tribes that share certain cultural traits. *See* CAHUILLA, CHUMASH, DIEGUEÑO, MAIDU, POMO, SHASTA, WINTUN, YOKUTS, and YUROK; *see also* INDIANS, AMERICAN, §I, 4 (ii)(c).

California Institute of the Arts. A private conservatory of the arts in Valencia, California. It was incorporated in 1961, following the merger of the Los Angeles Conservatory of Music (founded 1883) and the Chouinard Art Institute (1921), and moved to its present campus in 1971. It is made up of schools of art and design, dance, music, film and video, and theater, and a division of critical studies. The school of music (which in 1980 enrolled 150 students and employed a full-time faculty of 23 under the dean Nicholas England) offers a BFA in composition, performance, or general music, and an MFA and certificates of Fine Arts and Advanced Study in composition or performance. Strong emphasis is placed on the study and performance of chamber music, music of the 20th century, and ethnomusicology. The school sponsors student and faculty ensembles that specialize in contemporary music, and groups that perform African, Indian, and Indonesian music; it also supports annual festivals of contemporary and ethnic music. The institute's library contains some 50,000 books, 15,000 scores (including, notably, the works of its faculty members Earle Brown, Mel Powell, and Morton Subotnick), 11,000 sound recordings, and 5500 microfilms.

GRAYDON BEEKS

California mission music. The Spanish colonization of Alta California (the lower two-thirds of the present state of California) began in 1769 under the Franciscan Junípero Serra. By 1823 a chain of 21 missions had been established along the California coast as far north as the present town of Sonoma. The thriving musical life of the mission communities centered on the liturgical and festival services of the Roman Catholic Church. Much of the music used in the missions has survived, as well as considerable archival evidence relating to the cultivation of music in Spanish California. The Spanish and subsequent Mexican occupations of California lasted until the mid-19th century, though the cultivation of music at the missions was abruptly diminished after 1833, when the Mexican government ordered the missions to be secularized, their priests returned to Spain, and their lands sold; musical activity virtually ceased in 1846. This 80-year period is a paradigm for studying Spanish colonialism in North America and, in the case of the history of music in the USA, provides the only opportunity to examine the extent of the cultivation of music in a Spanish colony.

1. Franciscan musicians. 2. Musical repertory. 3. Performance practice. 4. Manuscript sources and notation.

1. FRANCISCAN MUSICIANS. Junípero Serra (1713–84) (see above) was a trained musician. He began his evangelization of native Californians by teaching them music, both plainsong and polyphony. The single liturgical manuscript identified as his, which is incomplete, consists predominantly of plainsong, but there is one polyphonic mass movement, the *Credo Parisiense*. Serra regularly presided over Solemn Masses at which the Proper and Ordinary were chanted, at first by other Franciscans and later by native Californians. He also encouraged the use of hymns in Spanish during processions on major feast days and rogation days, and at the beginning and end of each day, and he participated in the singing of them. From the beginning, music was considered an essential element in the liturgical life of each mission community. Even so, only six Franciscans in addition to Serra seem to have distinguished themselves as musicians: Juan Sancho (1772–1830), Narciso Durán (1776–1846), Felipe Arroyo de la Cuesta (1780–1840), Estevan Tapis (1756–1825), José Viader (*b* 1765), and Florencio Ibáñez (1740–1818).

Sancho was the most important of these musicians. He not only seems to have been the most highly trained of them, he also provided California with its first identifiable polyphonic repertory, which he began copying for his own use in Majorca in 1795. As it extended to many items by the time he arrived in California in 1804, it is not surprising that Mission San Antonio de Padua became well known for its music during his 26-year tenure there. Durán, an amateur, was as active a musician as Sancho. He seems to have been responsible for transmitting an unusual colored Spanish music notation throughout California (see §4). His main contributions to music in California were his establishment of a kind of scriptorium at Mission San José (1806–33), which produced a number of the extant music manuscripts, and his devising of pedagogical theories for simplifying the task of teaching music, both plainsong and polyphony, to native Californians. He proposed the abandonment of Gregorian modal theory in favor of the more modern major and minor system, and insisted that all musicians learn to sing and play an instrument, and that all music be accompanied.

Arroyo de la Cuesta too produced a number of music manuscripts. He seems to have been the only missionary who systematically attempted to catechize in native languages and this led him to produce a body of contrafacta to well-known hymns in the Mutsun dialect. His knowledge of music and music notation was comparable to that of Durán, from whom he received a number of polyphonic works. Ibáñez, like Serra, had been choirmaster of his convent in Spain. His missionary career was spent at Missions San Antonio de Padua (1801–3) and Nuestra Señora de Sóledad (1803–18). Contemporary accounts of the music he prepared for public occasions praise the skill of his Indian choir and orchestra. He composed a Nativity drama which was regularly produced on Christmas eve throughout California until about 1835. Viader, at Mission Santa Clara (1796–1833), and Tapis, at Mission San Juan Bautista (1815–25), supervised exceptionally large choirs and orchestras and the production of large music manuscripts. Unfortunately, the information about their musical activities is largely anecdotal, and devoid of concrete references to works performed and the manner of performance.

It must be assumed that other friars were actively involved with music in the 21 missions, for the unvarying routine of mendicant monasticism precisely prescribed the need for and place of music in the Mass, Office, and devotional services. This is most evident from the inventories which survive from nine missions. The collections of instruments assembled before 1833 range in size from seven instruments (Mission Nuestra Señora de Sóledad) to 43 (Mission Santa Barbara). Violins were the most common, but wind instruments of all types except trombones and bassoons were purchased, the most exotic being piccolos, oboes, and high trumpets. The large number of instruments in the various collections is difficult to explain, as sea trade with Mexico virtually ceased after 1810. Since few instruments noted in the inventories (1833–56) have survived, it is impossible to speculate about their origins.

2. MUSICAL REPERTORY. Plainsong was the staple music in the missions. All of the sizable manuscripts as well as a number of the fragments contain sections devoted to the principal feasts from the Sanctorale as well as portions of the Temporale from the Roman Missal. Far less music for the Office was documented; the most common was music for Lauds and First and Second Vespers on the patronal feast of a mission. With very few exceptions, the plainsong follows the Spanish use found in *Prontuario del canto-llano gregoriano*, ed. Vicente Pérez Martínez (Madrid, 1799–1800).

Polyphonic music was also important in the missions. It was copied into manuscripts prepared for the most prosperous and well-established as well as the newest missions. It has been estimated that at least as many music manuscripts have been lost as survive. 24 complete cycles of the Ordinary of the Mass remain, as well as seven individual Mass movements and five works for the Proper. Psalms, canticles, and hymns – but not antiphons – were set polyphonically for the Office. The largest group is that of Spanish-language hymns, composed for processions on major feasts, rogation days, benedictions, and the daily recitation of the doctrina. *Dios te salve* (ex. 1) is typical of these works, which are in two, three, or four parts. Conspicuous stylistic traits are the tonic–dominant harmonies, the doubling of the melodic line in 3rds, and the somewhat fluid metrical structure.

Ex.1

Dios te sal - ve...

Dios te sal-ve Ray-nay Ma - dre, de mi-se-ri-cor - di-a,
vi-day dul-zu-ra, es-per-an-za nu-es - tra: Di - os te sal - ve.

The greatest musical differences exist among the various settings of the Ordinary, which vary considerably in quality, length, and complexity. The most elaborate works are for chorus (in two, three, or four parts) and instrumental accompaniment (orchestra and/or organ). The most outstanding setting is one without title by Ignacio Jerusalem (*c*1710–1769) now in the Santa Barbara Mission Archive Library. The four movements which survive, in choral parts only (possibly from a work for eight-part chorus, soloists, and orchestra), are typical of Jerusalem's elaborate style, which makes use of choral fugues, extensive melismatic writing for soloists, and bold tutti passages.

By contrast, such works as the anonymous two-part *Misa Viscayína* require only the most modest musical forces, and also contain a great deal of unison writing. The diversity of styles found in the remaining polyphony is consistent not only with the differences in the origins of the music and with the size and capability of the various mission orchestras and choruses but also with the varying degrees of solemnity required for the various feasts, Sundays, and ferials. The ubiquitous polyphonic settings of the Ordinary in all of the large manuscripts make it clear that polyphony for the Ordinary of the Mass was a *sine qua non* at every mission.

3. PERFORMANCE PRACTICE. There is no question that native Californians throughout the region responded positively to the music offered by the Franciscans. The Indians learned music quickly and showed great aptitude for playing instruments and singing. The choirs and orchestras of the missions were restricted to men and boys. Those selected for them were taught to read music, Latin, and Spanish, and to play instruments. Though a number of manuals survive which discuss the composition of polyphony, there appears to be no comparable volumes for the training of instrumentalists, and there is therefore no direct evidence to show how the Indians were taught to play. Durán, the only Franciscan to leave any instructions, insisted that his instrumentalists play and sing at the same time, and he also had the instrumentalists double all vocal parts in the Mass, and presumably in the Office also, be it plainsong or polyphony. His chorus and orchestra at Mission San José are known to have totaled over 30 musicians.

With one exception, the eyewitness accounts of visitors to California express astonishment and praise for the music during liturgical celebrations at the missions. Unfortunately, no Franciscan or trained musician left a detailed description of the music of a major liturgical event. It must be assumed that performance practices varied from mission to mission but were generally consistent with European musical standards at the time. Missions with a capable leader, a music library, highly developed ensembles, and extensive instrument collections must have produced elaborate music – especially a mission such as Santa Barbara, which boasted a pipe organ too. Smaller and less prosperous missions probably produced much more modest music. There is no evidence that the Franciscans intentionally diluted or compromised the performance standards that they would have learned in Spain or Mexico. Nor did they seek to establish a cathedral musical tradition in California; the music they knew from their home convents and parishes was more appropriate for their needs.

4. MANUSCRIPT SOURCES AND NOTATION. The 45 extant manuscripts and fragments, housed in eight different archives and libraries in California, are extremely varied in their appearance and musical contents; nearly all were intended as choirbooks. No printed music other than that found in the tutors and chantbooks has survived. Virtually all of the remaining manuscripts must have been produced before the Mexican government edict of 1833 (see introduction above). Plainsong in the choirbooks and fragments is in chant notation. Virtually all of the polyphony in them is notated, however, in an unusual square notation. Two-, three-, and four-part works are notated on a six-line staff in score format. The parts are differentiated from each other by the use of colors, probably introduced by Durán (see §1 above). The notational symbols are squares and diamonds, the shapes associated with the long-abandoned mensural notation employed from the 13th century to the 16th; the perpetuation of this practice can certainly be traced to the Spanish tradition of using mensural notation in tutors on music well into the 19th century.

See also HISPANIC-AMERICAN MUSIC, §1.

BIBLIOGRAPHY

H. H. Bancroft: *History of California* (San Francisco, 1883–90)
Z. Engelhardt: *The Missions and Missionaries of California* (San Francisco, 1908–15)
H. E. Bolton, ed.: *Historical Memoirs of New California* (Berkeley, 1926)
O. da Silva: *Mission Music of California* (Los Angeles, 1941)
E. B. Webb: *Indian Life at the Old Missions* (Los Angeles, 1952)
M. Geiger: *The Life and Times of Fray Junípero Serra* (Washington, DC, 1959)
——: *Mission Santa Barbara 1782–1965* (Charlotte, NC, 1965)
L. Spies and T. Stanford: *An Introduction to Certain Mexican Archives* (Detroit, 1969)
N. Benson: "Mission Music in the California Missions: 1602–1848," *Student Musicologists at Minnesota*, iii (1968–9), 128; iv (1969–70), 104
T. Göllner: "Two Polyphonic Passions from California's Mission Period," *Yearbook for Inter-American Musical Research*, vi (1970), 67
R. Stevenson: *Renaissance and Baroque Musical Sources in the Americas* (Washington, DC, 1970)
——: *Christmas Music from Baroque Mexico* (Berkeley, 1974)
M. Geiger: "Harmonious Notes in Spanish California," *Southern California Quarterly*, lvii (1975), 243
T. Göllner: "Unknown Passion Tones in Sixteenth-century Hispanic Sources," *JAMS*, xxviii (1975), 46
M. Geiger: *As the Padres Saw Them* (Santa Barbara, 1976)
M. Crouch, with W. Summers and K. Lueck-Michaelson, eds.: "An Annotated Bibliography and Commentary Concerning Mission Music of Alta California from 1769–1834," *CMc*, no.22 (1976), 88
W. Summers: "The Organs of Hispanic California," *Music (AGO-RCCO) Magazine*, x (1976), 50
——: "Music of the California Missions: an Inventory and Discussion of Selected Printed Music Books used in Hispanic California, 1769–1836," *Soundings, University of California Libraries, Santa Barbara*, ix (1977), 13
R. Stevenson: "16th- through 18th-century Resources in Mexico, iii," *FAM*, xxv (1978), 156
W. Summers: "Correspondence," *CMc*, no.27 (1979), 24
——: "Orígenes hispanos de la música misional de California," *Revista musical chilena*, no.149–50 (1980), 34
——: "Santa Barbara Mission Archive Library," *Resources of American Music History*, ed. D. W. Krummel (Urbana, IL, 1981), 41
——: "Spanish Music in California, 1769–1840: a Reassessment," *IMSCR*, xii *Berkeley 1977*, ed. D. Heartz and B. Wade (Kassel, 1981), 360
R. Stevenson: "California Music, 1806–24: Russian Reportage," *Inter-American Music Review*, iv/2 (1982), 59
W. Summers: "Correspondence," *Latin American Music Review*, iii/1 (1982), 130
G. A. Harshbarger: *The Mass in G by Ignacio Jerusalem and its Place in the California Mission Music Repertory* (diss., U. of Washington, 1985)

WILLIAM SUMMERS

California State University. Name applied in 1982 to a state system of 19 campuses, formerly known as the California State University and Colleges. In 1960 13 independent state colleges and two state polytechnic colleges were organized into a statewide system with a board of trustees and a chancellor. Additional schools were subsequently founded, and by 1980 16 of the 19 campuses had achieved university status; in 1982 the system enrolled more than 300,000 students and had a faculty of some 18,000 members.

All of the former state normal schools offer strong programs in music education. Although Humboldt State University (founded in 1913; enrollment of 7500 in 1980), offers only a BA, the campuses at Chico (1887; 13,000) and at Fresno (1911; 16,000) offer an MA as well. San Jose and San Diego state universities (1857 and 1879), with enrollments of nearly 30,000 students each, award BA, BM, and MA degrees; San Diego also offers special studies in world music, piano pedagogy, and Suzuki string pedagogy. San Francisco State University (1899; 24,000) offers in addition to the BA an MM in performance and houses the Frank V. de Bellis Music Collection of Italian music, donated to the state college system in 1963.

California State Polytechnic University, San Luis Obispo, was founded in 1901 as an independent vocational high school, and became part of the state system in 1960 (enrollment of 15,600 in 1978); the music department offers only a minor in music. A southern branch of the college was founded in Pomona in 1938 and became a state university in 1978 (enrollment of 16,000 in 1980); its music department offers a BA degree with emphasis on performance, composition, jazz, or ethnomusicology.

The state system of higher education was expanded after World War II with the establishment of a number of new schools, all with substantial music programs. The campuses at Los Angeles and Sacramento (both 1947; 22,000), Long Beach (1949; 33,000), Fullerton (1957; 21,000), and Northridge (1956; 28,000) offer BA and BM degrees in music and MA degrees in composition, music history, performance, and music education; in addition, Fullerton offers an MM in composition, conducting, or performance. The John F. Kennedy Memorial Library at the Los Angeles campus houses a collection of 213 annotated scores from the library of Otto Klemperer and numerous works by Roy Harris, and the music library at Long Beach holds the Metro-Goldwyn-Mayer Library, film scores, and the Wesley Kuhnle Collection of materials relating to tuning and temperament.

California State University in Hayward (1957; 10,000) and at Dominguez Hills (1960; 8000), Sonoma State University (1960; 5000), and three members of the state university system that have not achieved university status (the Stanislaus (1957; 4200), and Bakersfield and San Bernardino (both 1965; 3100) campuses of California State College) all have more limited music programs.

See also LIBRARIES AND COLLECTIONS, §3.

GRAYDON BEEKS

Calinda. A black-American dance that spread through Spanish America and the southern USA. The earliest known description dates from 1698, when Père Lavat (*Nouveau voyage aux isles d'Amérique*, ii, 51), who called it the *calenda*, recorded having seen it danced, with a drum accompaniment, on Martinique. It was considered indecent by some Christian communities and subsequently forbidden, but was not wholly suppressed among the slaves.

BIBLIOGRAPHY

R. Nettel: "Historical Introduction to 'La Calinda'," *ML*, xxvii (1946), 59

EUGÈNE BORREL/R

Callas [Kalogeropoulou], **(Cecilia Sophia Anna) Maria** (*b* New York, 4 Dec 1923; *d* Paris, France, 16 Sept 1977). Greek soprano.

Maria Callas as Leonora in Verdi's "Il trovatore"

In 1937 she left the USA for Greece and became a pupil of the well-known soprano Elvira de Hidalgo at the Athens Conservatory. Four years later she sang Tosca, her first leading role, at the Athens Opera (4 July 1941), and went on to sing Santuzza (*Cavalleria rusticana*), Marta (in Eugen d'Albert's *Tiefland*), and Leonore (*Fidelio*) during the next three years. Returning to New York in 1945, she was heard by Giovanni Zenatello, who engaged her for Ponchielli's *La Gioconda* in Verona. This successful appearance (2 August 1947) under Serafin was the start of her real career, and she was soon in demand in Italian theaters for such heavy roles as Aida, Turandot, Isolde, Kundry (*Parsifal*), and Brünnhilde. A versatility perhaps unmatched since the days of Lilli Lehmann was shown in Venice in 1949, when only three days after singing a *Walküre* Brünnhilde she deputized for an indisposed colleague in the florid bel canto role of Elvira in Bellini's *I puritani*. Gradually, under the guidance of Serafin, she relinquished her heavier roles in order to concentrate on the earlier Italian operas. Besides adding to her repertory Leonora, Violetta, Gilda, Lucia di Lammermoor, Rosina, Amina (in Bellini's *La sonnambula*), and Norma, she was in constant demand whenever rare and vocally taxing operas of the older school were revived; she sang in memorable productions of Haydn's *Orfeo ed Euridice*, Gluck's *Alceste* and *Iphigénie en Tauride*, Cherubini's *Médée*, Spontini's *La vestale*, Rossini's *Armida* and *Il turco in Italia*, Donizetti's *Anna Bolena* and *Poliuto*, and Bellini's *Il pirata*. Her greatest triumphs were won as Norma, Cherubini's Medea, Anna Bolena, Lucia, Verdi's Lady Macbeth, Violetta, and Tosca, many of which she repeated in the major opera houses of the world, where her fame reached a level that recalled the careers of Caruso and Chaliapin.

Callas made her début at La Scala as Aida (12 April 1950); her first appearances at Covent Garden (8 November 1952), the Lyric Theatre of Chicago (1 November 1954), and at the Metropolitan Opera (29 October 1956) were as Norma. Her relations with the Bing regime at the Metropolitan were uneasy, and unfortunately, the same could be said, in latter days, of those with the managements of the Rome Opera and of La Scala. Over the years, this scrupulous artist became the subject of sensational and harmful publicity suggesting that she was a difficult and jealous colleague, an accusation refuted and resented by many of those who worked with her most closely. The truth was probably that an exacting, self-critical temperament coupled with recurrent vocal troubles often forced her into a difficult choice between withdrawal from contractual engagements and singing below her best form.

Of Callas's artistic pre-eminence there can be no doubt. Among her contemporaries she had the deepest comprehension of the classical Italian style, the most musical instincts, and the most intelligent approach, together with exceptional dramatic powers. There was authority in all that she did, and in every phrase that she uttered. Her voice, especially during the early 1950s, was in itself an impressive instrument, with its penetrating, individual quality, its rich variety of color, and its great agility in florid music. During the 1960s vocal troubles led to her gradual withdrawal from the stage, and she made her last operatic appearance at Covent Garden, as Tosca, on 5 July 1965; she became a Greek citizen the following year. In 1971–2 she gave a series of master classes (mainly in New York), and in 1973 made an extensive concert tour of Europe, the USA, and the Far East with her former colleague Giuseppe di Stefano, revealing unimpaired artistic powers but sadly diminished vocal resources.

It remains uncertain whether Callas's vocal defects (inequality of registers, harshness in the middle voice, and tremolo on sustained high notes) were mainly due to inadequate training or to some physical intractability; nor can it ever be determined whether (as has been claimed) these vocal faults were really no more serious than those noted by contemporaries in the work of Pasta, Malibran, and Schroeder-Devrient. At least it is significant that the name of Callas can evoke such comparisons. Fortunately, numerous recordings, including many complete operas, remain to show that her technical defects were far outweighed by her genius.

BIBLIOGRAPHY

"Callas, Maria," *CBY 1956*
W. Mann: "Maria Meneghini Callas," *Gramophone Record Review*, no.43 (1957), 533 [with discography by F. F. Clough and G. J. Cuming]
E. Callas: *My Daughter – Maria Callas*, transcr. L. G. Blochman (New York, 1960, enlarged 2/1967/*R*1977)
G. Jellinek: *Callas: Portrait of a Prima Donna* (New York, 1960)
L. Riemens: *Maria Callas* (Utrecht, Netherlands, 1960)
F. Herzfeld: *La Callas* (Berlin, rev. 2/1962)
S. Galatopoulos: *Callas: La divina* (London, 1963, rev. 2/1966, rev. and enlarged 3/1976 as *Callas: prima donna assoluta*) [with discography]
R. Celletti: "Callas, Maria," *Le grandi voci* (Rome, 1964) [with discography by R. Vegeto]
H. Rosenthal: "Maria Callas," *Great Singers of Today* (London, 1966), 32
C. Cederna: *Chi è Maria Callas?* (Milan, 1968)
M. Picchetti and M. Teglia: *El arte de Maria Callas como metalenguaje* (Buenos Aires, 1969)
J. Ardoin and G. Fitzgerald: *Callas* (New York, 1974)
D. Hamilton: "The Recordings of Maria Callas," *HiFi/MusAm*, xxiv/3 (1974), 40 [with discography]
H. Wisneski: *Maria Callas: the Art behind the Music* (New York, 1975) [with peformance annals 1947–74, and discography of private recordings by A. Germond]
J. Ardoin: *The Callas Legacy* (New York, 1977, rev. 2/1982)
"Callas Remembered," *Opera News*, xlii/5 (1977) [incl. articles on Callas by W. Legge, p.9; C. Cassidy, p.13; D. J. Soria, p.15]
P.-J. Rémy: *Callas: une vie* (Paris, 1978)
P.-J. Rémy: *Maria Callas: a Tribute* (New York, 1978)
S. Segalini: *Callas: les images d'une voix* (Paris, 1979; Eng. trans., London, 1981)
S. Linakis: *Diva: the Life and Death of Maria Callas* (Englewood Cliffs, NJ, 1980)
C. Verga: *Maria Callas: mito e malinconia* (Rome, 1980)
C. G. Chiarelli: *Maria Callas: vita, immagini, parole, musica* (Venice, 1981)
G. B. Meneghini: *Maria Callas mia moglie* (Milan, 1981; Eng. trans. as *My Wife Maria Callas*, New York, 1982)
A. Stassinopoulos: *Maria Callas: the Woman behind the Legend* (New York, 1981)
L. Rasponi: "Maria Callas," *The Last Prima Donnas* (New York, 1982), 577

DESMOND SHAWE-TAYLOR/R

Callaway, Paul (Smith) (*b* Atlanta, IL, 16 Aug 1909). Organist and choirmaster. After attending Westminster College in Fulton, Missouri, he studied further with Leo Sowerby (1936) and with Marcel Dupré (1938). Positions in New York and Grand Rapids led to his appointment in 1939 as organist and choirmaster of the Cathedral Church of St. Peter and St. Paul in Washington, DC, a post he held until 1977. As well as preparing the musical portions of the weekly service and directing the choir, from 1941 he conducted the Cathedral Choral Society's annual oratorio performances. He was music director of the Opera Society of Washington from its inception in 1956 until 1967, and of the Lake George Opera Festival in Glens Falls, New York, from 1967 until 1977. Particularly interested in contemporary music, he conducted the première of Menotti's *The Unicorn, the Gorgon and the Manticore* at the Coolidge Festival of the Library of Congress in 1957, and in the same year conducted the first performance of Dallapiccola's *Cinque canti*, also at the Library of Congress. He played the solo organ part in Barber's *Toccata festiva* with the Philadelphia Orchestra in 1960; he is also active as a recitalist.

BIBLIOGRAPHY

"Paul Callaway," *The Diapason*, lxviii/3 (1977), 9

GEORGE GELLES

Calliope. A musical instrument intended for outdoor use and operated by steam or compressed air. It was invented by Joshua C. Stoddard (*b* 26 Aug 1814; *d* 4 April 1902), who settled in Worcester, Massachusetts, in 1845; he supported himself by keeping bees while working on a variety of inventions and experiments. His invention of the calliope (named for the Greek muse of eloquence) is said to have been inspired by his noticing the great carrying power of locomotive steam whistles.

Stoddard's completed instrument was first introduced to the public in 1855. It consisted of a steam boiler, a set of valves,

Steam-operated calliope by Arthur S. Denny: engraving from the "Illustrated London News" (3 December 1859)

and 15 graded steam whistles, played from a pinned cylinder. It was claimed that it could be heard for five miles – the Worcester City Council banned Stoddard from playing it within the city limits. Having nevertheless secured financial backing from some Worcester industrialists, he developed a keyboard model and founded the American Steam Piano Co. After financial difficulties a few years later, Stoddard was supplanted as head of the company by Arthur S. Denny, who changed the firm's name to the American Steam Music Co., and later claimed Stoddard's invention as his own. In 1859 Denny took to England a 37-note calliope that played from both keys and barrels (see illustration). A low-pressure (5 lbs) model, it was exhibited in the Crystal Palace, London, but Denny assured potential purchasers that outdoor models were available that employed up to 150 lbs of steam pressure and could be heard for 12 miles. The instrument never caught on in the British Isles, although it achieved popularity in a variety of applications in the USA.

As early as 1858 calliopes were installed on river showboats, either on the top deck or on a steam towboat, and their music became familiar to several generations of dwellers along the banks of the Mississippi and other great rivers. One such steamboat, the *Delta Queen*, continues to maintain a regularly played calliope in the 1980s; at night its clouds of steam are illuminated by colored spotlights. One of the few calliopes to be exported in the 19th century was used by the Pasha of Egypt on his private steamer. Calliopes also replaced the large and cumbersome barrel organs of some circuses and fairgrounds, doubtless because they were considerably louder. After the turn of the century compressed-air calliopes were developed; these proved more popular (and more portable) for such purposes and were even used in parades and political rallies, while steam instruments were retained for riverboats with their ready supply of steam. The air calliopes could be played from either a keyboard or a paper roll, and were manufactured by the Artizan Co. (Air-Calio), the Tangley Co. (Calliaphone), the Harrington National Calliope Co., and the Han-Dee Co. Some had as many as 58 notes, but the ones heard at carnivals and in parades are usually much smaller, and almost always played from a keyboard.

The one feature common to all calliopes is their whistle construction, which is the same as that of factory and locomotive steam whistles: a mouth surrounds the circumference of the pipe, the top and bottom being attached by four brackets or ears. Those in steam calliopes are always made of heavy brass; other materials are sometimes used for air calliopes. The music played, often in just two parts on short-compass instruments, is always of a simple nature, consisting usually of familiar songs, dances, and marches; a calliope makes an appearance in the film *Showboat* (1951).

BIBLIOGRAPHY

P. Graham: "Showboats and Calliopes," *Midwest Folklore*, v (1955), 229

A. W. J. G. Ord-Hume: *Barrel Organ: the Story of the Mechanical Organ and its Repair* (London, 1978)

L. C. Swanson: *Steamboat Calliopes* (Moline, IL, 1981, rev. 2/1983)

BARBARA OWEN

Calloway, Cab(ell) (*b* Rochester, NY, 25 Dec 1907). Popular singer and bandleader. He spent his childhood in Baltimore and began his professional career in Chicago as a singer and dancer. In 1928–9 he led such groups as the Alabamians in Chicago and New York and the Missourians in New York, where in 1929 he appeared in the revue *Hot Chocolates*. In 1930 the Missourians played and recorded under Calloway's name; they appeared with great success at the Cotton Club, New York, in 1931–2, and soon replaced Duke Ellington's band as house orchestra. The group toured Europe in 1934, appeared in several films, and made a large number of recordings until 1948, when it was disbanded. Calloway then performed mainly in musical theater, taking the role of Sportin' Life in Gershwin's *Porgy and Bess* and performing in *Hello, Dolly*, but he occasionally assembled bands for specific performances or tours.

Calloway was one of the most successful bandleaders of the 1930s and 1940s, and was famous for his extroverted singing and flamboyant appearance (Gershwin modeled the role of Sportin' Life on him), as well as for his scat singing, from which his sobriquet "the Hi-de-ho Man" derived. He also composed a large number of his band's songs. The band's most important contribution, however, was to promote the careers of a great many jazz musicians, among them Chu Berry, Ben Webster, Milt Hinton, Cozy Cole, Jonah Jones, and Dizzy Gillespie, and with these soloists Calloway made a number of excellent recordings.

RECORDINGS

(selective list)

Minnie the Moocher (1931, Bruns. 6074); The Scat Song (1932, Bruns. 6272); Reefer Man (1932, Banner 32944); Ratamacue (1939, Voc. 4700); Special Delivery (1941, OK 6147); Hey Doc (1941, OK 6354)

BIBLIOGRAPHY

SouthernB

O. Fluckiger: *Discography and Soligraphy of Cab Calloway* (Reinach, Switzerland, 1960)

G. T. Simon: *The Big Bands* (New York, 1967)

S. Dance: *The World of Swing* (New York, 1974)

C. Calloway and B. Rollins: *Of Minnie the Moocher and me* (New York, 1976)

J. Popa: *Cab Calloway and his Orchestra* (Zephyr Hills, FL, 1976)

D. Gillespie and A. Frazer: *To Be or Not to Bop* (New York, 1979)

D. Travis: *An Autobiography of Black Jazz* (Chicago, 1983), 219

JOSÉ HOSIASSON/R

Calvé [Calvet] **(de Roquer), (Rosa-Noémie) Emma** (*b* Decazeville, France, 15 Aug 1858; *d* Millau, France, 6 Jan 1942). French soprano. She made her début as Marguerite in *Faust* in Brussels in 1881, and three years later appeared in Paris and from 1887 at La Scala, Milan. Calvé soon became one of the first favorites of the international public, especially in London and New York, where her Santuzza and above all her Carmen were considered incomparable. (Her début at the Metropolitan Opera, on 29 November 1893, was in the former role; she sang the latter a month later.) Although these parts were to dominate her repertory, Massenet wrote two roles for her, the heroines of *La navarraise* and of *Sapho*. At the Metropolitan, she gave the American premières of *La navarraise* (1895) and De Lara's *Messaline* (1902). In 1904, having taken part in the 1000th performance of *Carmen* at the Opéra-Comique, she announced her intention of leaving the stage and did not thereafter reappear at the Metropolitan, but she sang at Oscar Hammerstein's Manhattan Opera House in 1907 and 1908 and continued to give concerts in the USA – including appearances in vaudeville – until 1927. Her voice – a luscious, finely trained soprano with the addition of strong chest-tones and some very pure high notes (originally extending to high F), the secret of which she claimed to have learned from Domenico Mustafà, the Italian castrato who became director of the Sistine Chapel Choir – derived a peculiar charm from its combination of absolute steadiness with rich color. As an interpreter she was intensely dramatic and impulsive, to the point of capriciousness in later life. Her recordings, though disappointingly limited in repertory, are none the less extraordinary.

BIBLIOGRAPHY

A. Gallus [pseud. of A. Wisner]: *Emma Calvé: her Artistic Life* (New York, 1902)
E. Calvé: *My Life* (New York, 1922)
——: *Sous tous les ciels j'ai chanté* (Paris, 1940)
J. A. Haughton: "Calvé, Most Famous of Carmens, is Dead," *MusAm*, lxii/1 (1942), 5
D. Shawe-Taylor: "Emma Calvé," *Opera*, vi (1955), 220
H. Pleasants: *The Great Singers* (New York, 1966, rev. 2/1981), 303
H. Barnes and W. Moran: "Emma Calvé: a Discography," *Recorded Sound* (1975), no.59, p.450

DESMOND SHAWE-TAYLOR/R

Cambodian-American music. *See* ASIAN-AMERICAN MUSIC, §6(i)(b).

Cambridge. City in Massachusetts, situated on the Charles River north of Boston; it is the home of the main campus of Harvard University. *See* BOSTON (i), §9(i); *see also* LIBRARIES AND COLLECTIONS, §3.

Camden, Maine, Harp Colony [Salzedo School; Summer Harp Colony of America]. A summer school for professional and amateur harpists established by Carlos Salzedo in 1931. Up to 40 students, mostly women, were able to study with Salzedo twice each week from June through August. They followed a dress code he established and spent most of their days practicing in their rooms at village houses he had selected. When Salzedo died in 1961 his home was left to his chosen successor, Alice Chalifoux, a former student and principal harpist with the Cleveland Orchestra from 1931 to 1973. Under her direction, the colony became a nonprofit institution with a board of trustees, but has changed little apart from an increase in students (now up to 60 each season). A number of harpists who hold or have held the principal chair in major American orchestras studied at Camden, including Ann Hobson (Boston SO), Marilyn Costello (Philadelphia Orchestra), and Douglas Rioth (San Francisco SO).

JOANNE SHEEHY HOOVER

Camilieri, Lorenzo (*b* Corfu, Greece, 1878; *d* New York, 20 April 1956). Conductor, teacher, and composer. He entered the Royal Conservatory, Naples, at the age of 14 and took a diploma in 1895. Having conducted and taught in Athens for a time, he visited England and France as a conductor, and accompanied the singer Maria Barrientos on a tour. He settled in New York in November 1914 (he became an American citizen in 1921) and subsequently taught singing and formed the People's Liberty Chorus (1916, renamed the People's Chorus of New York in 1935), a mixed ensemble of from 300 to 566 amateurs whom Camilieri trained to read music and to sing. He directed the group in several concerts each year, presenting the music of Bach, Handel, Beethoven, and Schubert, selections from grand opera and operetta, and popular pieces such as the songs of Stephen Foster, at Carnegie Hall and Town Hall and in high school auditoriums, until 1955, when he disbanded it and retired. His compostions were mainly choral.

ERIC BLOM/R

Campanini, Cleofonte (*b* Parma, Italy, 1 Sept 1860; *d* Chicago, IL, 19 Dec 1919). Italian conductor and violinist. After study in Parma he was active as an opera conductor there and in Nice, Milan, where he led the premières of Francesco Cilea's *Adriana Lecouvreur* (1902) and Puccini's *Madama Butterfly* (1904), Spain, and South America. He was assistant conductor for the Metropolitan Opera in its inaugural season (1883–4). His brother Italo Campanini (1845–96) sang the title role in Gounod's *Faust* in the Metropolitan's opening production (22 October 1883); he had previously appeared in the USA with Mapleson's company (1878–82) and had sung Don José in the first American performance of *Carmen* (Academy of Music, 23 October 1878). In 1887 the brothers returned to the USA with a concert troupe and presented the first American performance of Verdi's *Otello* (Academy of Music, 16 April 1888), with Cleofonte conducting and his wife, Eva (sister of Luisa Tetrazzini), singing Desdemona. Cleofonte served as the principal conductor of Oscar Hammerstein's Manhattan Opera Company during its first three seasons (1906–9) and conducted the American premières of Massenet's *Thaïs* (1907), Charpentier's *Louise* (1908), and Debussy's *Pelléas et Mélisande* (1908). In 1910 he became music director of the Chicago Grand Opera Company and in 1913 its general manager, retaining the position when it was reorganized in 1915 as the Chicago Opera Association. He was responsible for many American premières with the Chicago company, conducting Herbert's *Natoma* (Philadelphia, 1911), producing Hadley's *Azora* (Chicago, 1917), and commissioning De Koven's *Rip Van Winkle* and Prokofiev's *The Love for Three Oranges*.

BIBLIOGRAPHY

LaMusicaD
G. Graziosi: "Campanini, Cleofonte," *ES*
E. C. Moore: *Forty Years of Opera in Chicago* (New York, 1930/*R*1977)
J. F. Cone: *Oscar Hammerstein's Manhattan Opera Company* (Norman, OK, 1966)
R. L. Davis: *Opera in Chicago* (New York, 1966)

R. ALLEN LOTT

Campbell, Aline. Pseudonym of MERLE MONTGOMERY.

Campbell, Frank C(arter) (*b* Winston-Salem, NC, 26 Sept 1916). Music librarian. He graduated from Salem College (BM 1938) and from the Eastman School of Music (MA 1942). After a further year of graduate studies he began work as a music cataloguer in the Sibley Music Library of the Eastman School. In 1943 he accepted a position in the music division of the Library of Congress. In 1959 he began his association with the New York Public Library, serving first as assistant chief and then, from 1966 to 1985 (when he retired), as chief of the music division.

Campbell's career combines training as a pianist and musicologist with experience in librarianship. From 1967 to 1969 he was president of the Music Library Association, and in 1970 he was appointed editor of the association's journal, *Notes*, having been music review editor from 1950 to 1966. While at the Library of Congress Campbell wrote on important musical holdings for the Library's *Quarterly Journal of Current Acquisitions*; he is also the author of articles on the music division of the New York Public Library.

PAULA MORGAN

Campbell, Glen (Travis) (*b* Delight, AR, 22 April 1936). Popular singer and guitarist. As a member of a large musical family he absorbed the music of rural Arkansas during his childhood and spent his early career performing with western bands in Albuquerque (1955–60). In Los Angeles from 1960 to 1967 he became a highly successful studio musician and sideman, respected for his versatility on guitar, banjo, mandolin, and fiddle.

He also worked in clubs, made several recordings, appeared on television in "Shindig" (1964–5), and performed with the Beach Boys (1965). By 1967 he had become a major artist; his singles *Gentle on my Mind* and *By the time I get to Phoenix* both won gold records. His varied experience in the folk, country, rock, and popular song traditions characterized the crossover in musical styles in popular music of the late 1960s and the 1970s. His singing of plaintive ballads in arrangements reflecting these diverse backgrounds was especially effective.

BIBLIOGRAPHY

"Campbell, Glen," *CBY 1969*

MICHAEL J. BUDDS

Campbell, Lucie Eddie (*b* Duckhill, MS, 30 April 1885; *d* Nashville, TN, 3 Jan 1963). Composer of gospel songs. When she was four years old her family moved to Memphis, where she studied piano and music theory. When she graduated from the Booker T. Washington High School in 1899 the school offered her a teaching position, which she held for the next 44 years. During the summers she studied at Rust College, Holly Springs, Mississippi (BA), and at the State University, Nashville (MA). Throughout her life she was active with the National Baptist Convention and in 1919 was one of the founders of the National Baptist Training Union, serving as its music director. It was for the convention that she wrote most of her 45 gospel songs beginning with the words for "Something within me" (1919). Her other compositions include *Footprints of Jesus* (1949), *He'll understand and say, well done* (1933), *In the upper room*, and *My Lord and I* (both 1947). Her songs have been recorded by major gospel singers, including Mahalia Jackson, Clara Ward, and Ruth Davis and the Davis Sisters. In 1946 she was a member of the National Policy Planning Commission of the National Education Association. She received numerous awards from the National Baptist Convention.

BIBLIOGRAPHY

SouthernB

H. C. Boyer: *The Gospel Song: a Historical and Analytical Study* (thesis, Eastman School of Music, 1964)

W. E. Washington, ed.: *Miss Lucy Speaks* (Nashville, 1971)

T. Heilbut: *The Gospel Sound: Good News and Bad Times* (New York, 1971/*R*1975)

I. V. Jackson: *Afro-American Religious Music: a Bibliography and Catalogue of Gospel Music* (Westport, CT, 1979)

W. T. Walker: *Somebody's Calling My Name* (Valley Forge, PA, 1979)

HORACE CLARENCE BOYER

Campbell-Tipton, Louis (*b* Chicago, IL, 21 Nov 1877; *d* Paris, France, 1 May 1921). Teacher and composer. He studied in Chicago and Boston, and from 1896 to 1899 at the Leipzig Conservatory, where his teachers included Gustav Schreck and Carl Reinecke. He taught theory and composition at the Chicago Musical College from 1901 to 1904, then moved to Paris and continued to compose and teach. His works are mostly on a small scale and include many songs. The *Four Sea Lyrics* (1907, facs. in V. B. Lawrence, ed.: *The Wa-Wan Press, 1901–1911*, 1970) are among his best works, as are *The Opium Smoker* and *A Memory* (both 1907); his last published work, *Day's End* (1921), is in his distinctive free recitative style. Among his finest works for piano are the *Sonata Heroic* (1904, facs. in Lawrence, 1970), the two *Legends* (1908), and the *Etude en octaves* (1912). He also wrote pieces for violin and piano, including a *Romanza appassionata*, *Suite pastorale*, and *Lament*. Larger works are in manuscript. Campbell-Tipton's early compositions show evidence of his German training, whereas his later works reflect his interest in French impressionism.

BIBLIOGRAPHY

W. T. Upton: "Our Musical Expatriates," *MQ*, xiv (1928), 143

JOHN GILLESPIE

Campion Society. Society for the presentation of songs in English, founded by JOHN EDMUNDS in San Francisco in 1946; it disbanded in 1953.

Campos-Parsi, Héctor (*b* Ponce, Puerto Rico, 1 Oct 1922). Composer. After early music studies in Ponce and a general arts education at the University of Puerto Rico in Río Piedras (1938–44), he went to the New England Conservatory (1947–50). Subsequently he studied with Copland and Messiaen at the Berkshire Music Center (1949 and 1950), and with Boulanger at Fontainebleau, near Paris (1951–3). He returned to Puerto Rico in 1955 and from then on has taken an active part in its educational and cultural life, notably as adviser to the government-sponsored free schools of music, as organizer of the cultural promotion program of the Institute of Puerto Rican Culture, as director of that agency's musical events, publications and research, and as professor of composition and theory at the Puerto Rico Conservatory. In 1980 he was named musical adviser to the newly created Administration for the Development of Arts and Culture of the Puerto Rican government. He was made a member of the Puerto Rican Academy of Arts and Sciences after receiving that organization's highest music award, the Gran Premio de Música, in 1970. Other prizes he has received include the Maurice Ravel Prize (Paris, 1953) and the publication prize of the Organization of American States (Washington, DC, 1954). His mature music has followed two parallel lines of development: one nationalist, incorporating elements of Puerto Rican folk music; the other international, progressing from the neoclassicism of his scores of the early 1950s to electronic and aleatory music. His writings on Puerto Rican music include a volume of *La gran enciclopedia de Puerto Rico* (1976).

WORKS

Ballets: Incidente, 1949; Melos, 1951; Juan Bobo y las fiestas, 1957; Urayoán, 1958; Areyto boriken, 1974; De Diego (J. Diego, H. Campos-Parsi), taped vv, elec, 1974

Orch: Divertimento de Sur, fl, cl, str, 1953; Oda a Cabo Rojo, 1959; Rapsodia elegíaca, str, 1960; Kollagia, orch, perc, tape, 1963; Dúo trágico, pf, orch, 1964; Tissú, accordion, small orch, 1984; Tureyareito, 1984; a few others

Chamber: Versículos, va, 1948; Serenata, str trio, 1949; Vn Sonata, 1949; Música, 3 vn, 1949; Str Qt, 1950; Dialogantes, vn, pf, 1952; 3 dúos, fl, cl, 1952; Sonatina, vn, pf, 1953; Conversaciones, vn, pf, 1954; Música per la stagione estiva, 2 fl, pf, 1956; El secreto, fl, ob, 2 cl, vc, pf, 1957; Petroglifos, pf trio, 1966; Arawak, vc, tape, 1970; Sleeping Beauty, incidental music, fl, harp, 2 pf, 1978; Fanfare for an American Festival, 3 tpt, 2 trbn, perc, 1982; Tiempo sereno, str, 1983; *c*25 other works

Solo vocal: 4 puntos cubanos (L. L. Torres), 1956; Majestad negra (L. P. Matos), 1959; Columnas y círculos (A. Trías), S, pf, 1966, rev., T, S, pf, vib, hpd, 1967; Ulises (J. A. Corretjer), 1973; 3 poemas revolucionarios (Torres), 1973; Poema total, elec, speakers, 1975; Glosa emilian ense, S, A, chamber ens, 1977; *c*10 other works

Choral: Aleluya, 1948; Ave María, 1949; La pastorcita (B. Silva), 1951; Ubao Moin (Corretjer), A, B, speaking chorus, chorus, orch, 1968; *c*12 other works

Pf: Plenas, 1947; Isleñas, 1948; Sonata, 1953; 3 fantasías, 1956; others

Principal publishers: Institute de Cultura Puertorrigueña, Peer

BIBLIOGRAPHY

D. Thompson: "Laud Ode by Campos Parsi," *San Juan Star* (21 Dec 1959), 8

——: "Music in Puerto Rico: Heritage of Four Centuries Flowers in Dynamic Commonwealth," *MusAm*, lxxx/8 (1960), 8

F. Caso: *Héctor Campos-Parsi in the History of Twentieth-century Music in Puerto Rico* (diss., Indiana U., 1972; Sp. trans., San Juan, 1980)
Compositores de América/Composers of the Americas, ed. Pan American Union, xix (Washington, DC, 1979), 13

DONALD THOMPSON

Cannon, Gus [Banjo Joe] (*b* Red Banks, MS, 12 Sept 1883; *d* Memphis, TN, 15 Oct 1979). Singer, banjoist, and jug player. The son of a former slave, he was brought up on a Mississippi plantation where, as a child, he made a banjo from a frying pan. In his early teens he worked on the railroad and as a farmer, and played at labor camps in the South. He formed a partnership with the harmonica player Noah Lewis about 1910 and in the ensuing years performed for country dances and for traveling medicine shows. His first recordings included items from the show repertory, such as a satirical song about Booker T. Washington, *Can you blame the colored man?* (1927, Para. 12571). The following year he was joined by Lewis and the guitarist Ashley Thompson for the first recordings by Cannon's Jug Stompers, on which Cannon played the bass line on the jug. *Minglewood Blues* (1928, Vic. 21267) was distinguished by Lewis's sensitive harmonica playing set against Thompson's high-pitched voice; Cannon himself sang with curious diphthong vowels, as on *Heart Breakin' Blues* (1928, Vic. 38523) and the fast *Feather Bed* (1928, Vic. 38515). Hosea Woods's kazoo playing with Cannon's jug gave a distinct country quality to the sound of the band, but their performances were carefully considered and well integrated, as comparision of two takes of *Viola Lee Blues* reveals (1928, Vic. 38523, RCA (E)RCX 202). Throughout the remaining 40 years of his life Cannon lived in poor circumstances in Memphis, occasionally entertaining but mainly working as a street cleaner.

Gus Cannon, Memphis, 1971

In 1963 the Rooftop Singers made a version of the Jug Stompers' *Walk Right In* (1929, Vic. 38611), bringing Cannon belated recognition and royalties, but at the age of 80 he was no longer able to perform with his former skill.

BIBLIOGRAPHY

SouthernB
B. Olsson: *Memphis Blues* (London, 1970)
——: Liner notes, *Cannon's Jug Stompers and Gus Cannon as Banjo Joe, 1927–30* (Herwin 208, 1973) [incl. discography]

PAUL OLIVER

Cantata Singers. New York choral group founded in 1934 by Paul Boepple. *See* EARLY-MUSIC REVIVAL, §1.

Cantor, Eddie [Itzkowitz, Isidore] (*b* New York, 31 Jan 1892; *d* Hollywood, CA, 10 Oct 1964). Actor and singer. It is thought that he made his début in vaudeville at the Clinton Music Hall, New York, at the age of 15. He worked as a singing waiter, and also performed in music halls in London. On his return to New York he took part in *Canary Cottage* (1917), where he came to the attention of Ziegfeld, and subsequently appeared in the *Ziegfeld Follies of 1917*. A short, thin, jumpy performer, he quickly became one of Ziegfeld's biggest stars, performing in the *Follies* of 1918, 1919, 1923, and 1927, as well as in *Kid Boots* (J. McCarthy, H. Tierney, 1923) and *Whoopee* (W. Donaldson, 1928). Songs that became associated with his name include *You'd be surprised* (Berlin), *Alabamy bound* (R. Henderson), *Dinah* (H. Akst), *If you knew Susie* (B. G. DeSylva, B. Green), *Margie* (C. Conrad, J. R. Robinson), *Ida, sweet as apple cider* (E. Leonard), and *Makin' whoopee* (Donaldson). From 1929 Cantor worked in Hollywood, where he appeared in numerous films and later had a popular radio show. He returned to Broadway only once, for the production of *Banjo Eyes* (V. Duke, 1941). He wrote three memoirs, *My Life in your Hands* (1928), *Take my Life* (1957), and *The Way I See it* (1959).

BIBLIOGRAPHY

"Cantor, Eddie," *CBY 1954*

GERALD BORDMAN

Cape, Safford (*b* Denver, CO, 28 June 1906; *d* Uccle, Brussels, Belgium, 26 March 1973). Conductor, musicologist, and composer. After early piano and composition studies in Denver, he went to Belgium in 1925 to study composition with Raymond Moulaert and musicology with Charles van den Borren, whose daughter he later married. During the period 1928–32 he concentrated on composition, producing a piano trio, a string trio, piano solos, and songs. In 1933, however, he gave up all other activity to devote his time to the authentic realization in performance of medieval and Renaissance music. He formed the Pro Musica Antiqua of Brussels, a vocal and instrumental ensemble specializing in 13th- to 16th-century music. As its conductor Cape toured throughout Europe and North and South America, and made many recordings, including several of documentary historical interest. Ill-health compelled him to retire in 1967.

HOWARD SCHOTT/R

Capobianco, Tito (*b* La Plata, Argentina, 28 Aug 1931). Opera director and administrator. He studied at the University of Buenos Aires and made his début as a director at the Teatro Argentino in his native town with *Aida* in 1953. He became technical director of the Teatro Colón in Buenos Aires (1958–62), and general director at the Teatro Argentino (1959-61). He first attracted serious notice in the USA in 1966 with his stagings for the New York City Opera during its first year at Lincoln Center; Alberto Ginastera's *Don Rodrigo* was presented in a hieratic manner, and the singers in Handel's *Giulio Cesare* were directed to move like "incorrigible courtiers." The world première of Ginastera's *Bomarzo*, given by the Opera Society of Washington, followed in 1967. Capobianco then became resident stage director for the New York City Opera, where he brought his broad, almost balletic sense of style to bear on works as dissimilar as Boito's *Mefistofele* and Donizetti's three "Tudor queen" operas for Beverly Sills. He has also designed as well as staged operas, and has worked in Europe, Australia, and the Canary Islands, where he has headed the Las Palmas Festival. He was artistic director of the Cincinnati Opera Festival (1961–5) and the Cincinnati Opera (1962–5) and in 1975 was appointed to the same position at the San Diego Opera. In July 1983 he became vice-president and general director of the Pittsburgh Opera. Capobianco's wife, the choreographer Elena Denda, has worked with him on some of his most celebrated productions. Capobianco was professor of acting and interpretation at the Academy of Vocal Arts, Philadelphia (1962–8), founded and directed the American Opera Center at the Juilliard School of Music (1967–9), and was appointed director of opera studies and festival stage director at Music Academy of the West, Santa Barbara, California, in 1983.

FRANK MERKLING

Cappa, Carlo Alberto (*b* Alessandria, Italy, 9 Dec 1834; *d* New York, 6 Jan 1893). Bandmaster, trombonist, and composer. He entered the Royal Academy at Asti, Italy, when he was ten, remained there for five years, then enlisted in the band of the Sixth Italian Lancers as a trombonist. He served in the Italian military for six years, and at the age of 21 enlisted in the US Navy and joined the band of the frigate *Congress*, which was moored at Genoa. He arrived in the USA in 1858 and joined Edward Kendall's band for a tour of several American cities; he then became a member of the Shelton Band of New York, which was led by Claudio S. Grafulla. Cappa joined the Seventh Regiment Band of New York when Grafulla became its leader. From 1869 to 1876 he was first trombonist in the Theodore Thomas Orchestra; he also played euphonium with the Mapleson Opera Company and appeared as a euphonium soloist with the Dodworth Band. In 1881 he became leader of the Seventh Regiment Band; under his direction it gave regular concerts at Central Park and Brighton Beach in New York, and made national tours. He was highly regarded for his superb musicianship and received knighthoods in Italy and Venezuela. Cappa composed several marches, including *The Sardinia March*, the *Seventh Regiment Knapsack Quickstep*, and *Col. Appleton's March*.

BIBLIOGRAPHY

"Carlo Cappa," *American Art Journal: Music, Art, Literature, and the Drama*, xliv (1886), 229
F. O. Jones, ed.: *A Handbook of American Music and Musicians* (Canaseraga, NY, 1886/*R*1971)
E. Clark: *History of the Seventh Regiment of New York, 1806–1889* (New York, 1890)
"Carlo Alberto Cappa," *Musical Courier*, no.22 (1891), 640
T. Rossi: "An Educator of the People," *Musical Courier*, no.25 (1892), 10
Obituaries: *Musical Courier*, no.26 (1893), 21; *New York Times* (7 Jan 1893)

FRANK J. CIPOLLA

Capron, Henri (*fl* 1785–95). Cellist, singer, impresario, and composer, of French origin. He is first mentioned in 1785 as a manager of subscription concerts in Philadelphia. He organized similar concerts in New York, generally in series of three: in 1788–9, with Reinagle as co-manager; in 1791–2; and in 1793–4 (the City Concerts, presented at the City Tavern). He performed in these as the soloist in cello concertos, as a member of chamber duos and quartets, and as a singer (often in duets with Mary Ann Pownall); he also played cello in the Old American Company's orchestra. From 1793 he was co-manager with John Christopher Moller of a music store in Philadelphia, and with Moller published four issues of *Moller and Capron's Monthly Numbers*, a periodical collection of music. In 1794 he became head of a French boarding school in Philadelphia. Among his few extant compositions (mostly appearing in the *Monthly Numbers*) are *A New Contredance* and the songs *Delia*, *Go Lovely rose*, *Julia see*, *New Kate of Aberdeen*, and *Softly as the breezes blowing*.

BIBLIOGRAPHY

O. G. T. Sonneck: *A Bibliography of Early Secular American Music* (Washington, DC, 1905; rev. and enlarged by W. T. Upton, 2/1945/*R*1964)
——: *Early Concert-life in America (1731–1800)* (Leipzig, 1907/*R*1978)
G. C. D. Odell: *Annals of the New York Stage*, i (New York, 1927)
J. T. Howard: *Our American Music* (New York, 1931, rev. 4/1965)

H. WILEY HITCHCOCK

Captain Beefheart [Van Vliet, Don] (*b* Glendale, CA, 15 Jan 1941). Avant-garde rock composer, singer, and instrumentalist. As a teenager he taught himself to play harmonica and saxophone, and worked with amateur rhythm-and-blues groups. He left Antelope Valley College, Lancaster, California, after one semester in 1959 to work with Frank Zappa, whom he had met in high school. They planned to form a group, the Soots, and to make a film, *Captain Beefheart Meets the Grunt People*; neither project was realized, but Van Vliet adopted the stage name Captain Beefheart, and formed his Magic Band in Lancaster in 1964. Beefheart and his group (the members of which have changed frequently) have recorded and performed periodically since then, though Beefheart's personal eccentricities, together with a lack of popular acceptance and incomprehension within the music business, have made for an erratic career. He has continued to collaborate with Zappa and made guest appearances as a singer on two of Zappa's albums, *Hot Rats* (1969) and *Bongo Fury* (1975). Zappa also produced *Trout Mask Replica*, which is widely regarded as Beefheart's first characteristic album.

The early Magic Band played a slightly warped form of blues and boogie, with Beefheart singing in a style reminiscent of Howlin' Wolf and John Lee Hooker (as on *The Legendary A&M Sessions*, recorded in 1965 but not released until 1984). His first released album (*Safe as Milk*, 1967) was made with a group that included the guitarist Ry Cooder. On *Trout Mask Replica* the Magic Band consisted of two slide guitars (often in two different open tunings), bass guitar, and drums, playing in strictly organized meters; over this foundation Beefheart played freer instrumental lines on the saxophone, bass clarinet, and harmonica, and sang in a variety of voices ranging from a bass growl to falsetto. The music is through-composed rather than in typical pop song form, and the lyrics are both earthy and surreal, filled with puns and free association. His more complex work is a form of chamber music for rock ensemble – often in shifting, irregular rhythms and uncertain tonalities – the parts of which are fully composed and not improvised; the musicians are taught the music by rote.

During the mid-1970s Beefheart returned to basic blues and rock on the albums *Unconditionally Guaranteed* and *Bluejeans and Moonbeams* (both 1974), but these were neither artistically nor commercially successful. As new-wave rock groups discovered his earlier work he returned to his original, harsher style; his compositions became still more complex and less melodic, and his singing style moved towards declamatory recitation. Some members of the Magic Band independently recorded their own material during the mid-1970s, using the name Mallard.

RECORDINGS
(selective list)

Safe as Milk (Buddah 5001, 1967); *Trout Mask Replica* (Straight 1053, 1969); *Lick my Decals off, Baby* (Straight 1063, 1970); *Clear Spot* (Rep. 2115, 1972); *The Spotlight Kid* (WB 2050, 1972); *Unconditionally Guaranteed* (Mer. 1709, 1974); *Bluejeans and Moonbeams* (Mer. 1018, 1974); *Shiny Beast (Bat Chain Puller)* (WB 3256, 1978); *Doc at the Radar Station* (Virgin 13148, 1980); *Ice Cream for Crow* (Epic 38274, 1982); *The Legendary A&M Sessions* (A&M 12510, 1984)

JON PARELES

Cara, Irene (*b* Bronx, NY, 18 March 1959). Popular singer, actress, and songwriter. Born into a musical family, Cara began appearing in variety programs on Spanish-language television when she was seven, and throughout her teens she won prominent roles in Broadway shows, television series, and films. Her acting and singing in the film *Fame* (1980) brought her national attention, as did her singing of the title song in the film *Flashdance* (1983), for which she wrote the lyrics; for *Flashdance . . . what a feeling* she received a Grammy Award for best female pop performance and an Academy Award for best song of the year. Cara has a strong, belting soprano voice and an appealing presence, but apart from her hit singles, she has not made a consistent impression.

RECORDINGS
(selective list)

Fame (RSO 1034, 1980); Out here on my own (RSO 1048, 1980); Anyone can see (Network 47950, 1981); Flashdance . . . what a feeling (Casablanca 812353-1, 1983)

JOHN ROCKWELL

Caramoor Festival. Annual summer concert series established in Katonah, New York, in 1946. Caramoor was once the elaborate Mediterranean-style country estate of Walter and Lucie Rosen, who began arranging musicales for invited audiences in the 1930s. The festival includes operas, orchestral concerts, chamber-music and solo recitals, dance, lectures, and special events for children, held in two open-air sites on the estate: the Venetian Theater (capacity 1500) and the Spanish Courtyard (capacity 500). Members of the St. Luke's Chamber Ensemble form the core of the festival orchestra, and such internationally renowned soloists and ensembles as Beverly Sills, Jessye Norman, Alicia de Larrocha, Garrick Ohlsson, the Beaux Arts Trio, the Tokyo String Quartet, and the Waverly Consort have appeared as guest artists. The first music director of the festival was Alfred Wallenstein, who was appointed in 1958; he was succeeded by Julius Rudel in 1963 and John Nelson in 1983.

SARA VELEZ

Carapetyan, Armen (*b* Eṣfahān, Iran, 11 Oct 1908). Musicologist and editor of Armenian origin. After taking a diploma at the American College in Tehran in 1927, he studied the violin and composition in Paris and New York, and became a composition pupil of Malipiero. He studied musicology at Harvard where he was awarded the MA in 1940 and the PhD in 1945, the year he founded the American Institute of Musicology, of which he has since been the director.

Carapetyan's principal interest is the music of the Middle Ages and the Renaissance. As general editor of Corpus Mensurabilis Musicae, Musicological Studies and Documents, and, for some years, Corpus Scriptorum de Musica, he is responsible for the publication of a growing number of important collected editions, scholarly monographs, and theoretical treatises. He has been editor of *Musica disciplina* since its first issue in 1946. He is publisher of all the American Institute of Musicology series, which include, in addition to those of which he is general editor, Corpus of Early Keyboard Music, Miscellanea, and Renaissance Manuscript Studies. His editorials in *Musica disciplina* have dealt with some of the basic issues of music scholarship, including the editing, publishing, and performing of early music.

PAULA MORGAN

Caravans. Gospel group formed in 1958 by ALBERTINA WALKER and others.

Carawan, Guy (*b* Los Angeles, CA, 28 July 1927). Folksinger. He attended Occidental College (BA 1952) and UCLA (MA 1953), learned to sing folksongs in the style of Woody Guthrie and Pete Seeger, and was associated briefly with the folksingers' organization People's Songs. In the mid-1950s he was one of only a few folksingers to perform at American schools and colleges; he also toured in Europe, China, and the USSR. Later he became active in the civil-rights movement in the South, and helped reintroduce the song *We shall Overcome* to southern Blacks, who had traditionally sung it as *I'll Overcome Some Day*. He became a resident musician and folklorist at the Highlander Folk School in Tennessee, and in the 1960s made field recordings and continued to perform. He organized a number of folk festivals and helped revive the singing traditions of the Georgia Sea Islands; in 1963 he formed the Sea Island Singers on Johns Island, North Carolina. Carawan performs on the six- and twelve-string guitars, banjo, autoharp, tin whistle, and hammered dulcimer. With his wife Candie Carawan he has written two books on traditional southern music (*Ain't you Got a Right to the Tree of Life*, 1967, and *Voices from the Mountains*, 1975), compiled collections of protest songs, and issued ten documentary recordings.

DAVID K. DUNAWAY

Card, June (*b* Dunkirk, NY, 10 April 1942). Soprano. She made her début in 1966 with the Central City Opera in Colorado as Elvira (*L'italiana in Algeri*) and the following year sang the title role in Janáček's *The Cunning Little Vixen* in Munich. In 1970 she began her association with the Frankfurt Opera and also fulfilled engagements in Vienna (Magda in Puccini's *La rondine*, 1971), Barcelona (1976), and other leading European houses. At the 1978 Edinburgh Festival she took part in the British première of Luigi Nono's *Al gran sole carico d'amore*. Her repertory includes such traditional roles as Donna Elvira, Senta, Nedda, Chrysothemis (*Elektra*), Zdenka (*Arabella*), and Janáček's Jenůfa, Kát'a Kabanová, and Emilia Marty, but she has also appeared in many later and less well-known operas such as Henze's *Der junge Lord* and *The Bassarids*, Franz Schreker's *Die Gezeichneten*,

Shostakovich's *Katerina Izmaylova*, Stravinsky's *The Rake's Progress*, and Bernd Alois Zimmermann's *Die Soldaten*, where the security of her singing and the intensity of her interpretation are of especial value.

ELIZABETH FORBES

Carden, Allen D(ickenson) (*b* Tennessee, 13 Oct 1792; *d* Franklin, TN, 29 March 1859). Singing-school teacher and tunebook compiler. Nothing is known of his early activities or training, but in 1817 he was active as a teacher in Tennessee, Kentucky, and Virginia, and in 1823 he taught singing-schools in Nashville. His first tunebook, *Missouri Harmony* (published in St. Louis, printed in Cincinnati, 1820, rev. 1850/*R*1975), was the most popular tunebook of the South and West until the Civil War, and went through 22 editions by 1857. Carden procured music type and published his other tunebooks himself; *The Western Harmony* (Nashville, 1824) and *United States Harmony* (Nashville, 1829) did not achieve the success of *Missouri Harmony*, however. Carden remained in and around Nashville from 1830 to 1850, when he moved to Williamson County (probably Franklin), Tennessee. *See also* SHAPE-NOTE HYMNODY, §2.

BIBLIOGRAPHY

E. C. Krohn: *Missouri Music* (New York, 1971)

D. L. Crouse: *The Work of Allen D. Carden and Associates in the Shape-note Tunebooks "The Missouri Harmony," "Western Harmony," and "United States Harmony"* (diss., Southern Baptist Theological Seminary, 1972)

DAVID L. CROUSE

Carhart & Needham. Firm of reed organ and melodeon makers. It was founded about 1846 by Jeremiah Carhart and Elias Parkman Needham in New York, and became one of the first American firms to produce melodeons and reed organs in large numbers. Carhart had previously worked for George A. Prince & Co., and was the holder of several patents for improvements to reed organs, including an early version of the suction bellows. Carhart & Needham manufactured both complete reed organs and reeds, and by 1866 had produced over 15,000 instruments, the largest having two manuals, pedals, and 14 sets of reeds. The firm remained in business until the 1870s.

BIBLIOGRAPHY

R. F. Gellerman: *The American Reed Organ* (New York, 1973)

N. Groce: *Musical Instrument Making in New York City during the Eighteenth and Nineteenth Centuries* (diss., U. of Michigan, 1982)

BARBARA OWEN

Caribbean-American music. *See* HISPANIC-AMERICAN MUSIC, §2 (ii).

Carillon. A set of stationary bells (normally set in a tower or on a high frame) for playing music; for a discussion of carillons in the USA, *see* BELLRINGING.

Carl, William Crane (*b* Bloomfield, NJ, 2 March 1865; *d* New York, 8 Dec 1936). Organist. A pupil of Samuel P. Warren, he became organist of First Presbyterian Church in Newark, New Jersey, in 1882. Later (*c*1890) he studied in Paris with Alexandre Guilmant, and in 1892 he became organist of Old First Presbyterian Church in New York. In 1899 he founded the Guilmant Organ School, apparently the first institution of its kind in the USA. As a teacher Carl advocated, in place of the older, rhythmically slack tradition, the "clean-cut playing of Guilmant." As a recitalist throughout the USA and abroad and as a teacher of organists, Carl introduced an expanded repertory, a more brilliant technique, and a broader view of church music. The Guilmant Organ School trained hundreds of professional church musicians, many of whom became well known. Although not himself a composer, Carl edited at least ten volumes of organ music between 1898 and 1919, including *Master-Studies for the Organ* (1907), a widely used organ method, and the *Historical Organ Collection* (1919); his anthologies contain mainly works by European composers (some now forgotten) and many transcriptions and are patterned after Guilmant's *Archives des maîtres de l'orgue*. Active for over 50 years, Carl instigated a number of changes in musical taste; he also influenced congregational and clerical attitudes on church music and helped improve the financial circumstances of church musicians.

VERNON GOTWALS

Carle, Frankie [Carlone, Francis Nunzio] (*b* Providence, RI, 25 March 1903). Pianist, composer, arranger, and bandleader. At the age of seven he appeared as a piano soloist and in 1918 he led his first band. His graceful and relaxed piano improvisations established him with the public and earned him the nickname "the Golden Touch." In 1933 he joined the band of Mal Hallett, which he left to join the Horace Heidt band in 1939. He formed his own big band in 1944 but abandoned it in the 1950s in favor of a smaller group. At the end of the decade Carle retired, but in 1972 he appeared briefly for a three-month tour with Freddy Martin in the show *Big Band Cavalcade*.

As a composer Carle has several hits to his credit, including *Sunrise Serenade*, which became Hit of the Year in 1938 and the following year sold over a million copies. Other successes are *Carle Boogie*, *Lover's Lullaby*, *Sunrise in Napoli*, and *Dreamy Lullaby* (with words by Benny Benjamin and George Weiss). Carle's arrangements were published in the collections *Modern Hot Piano Solos* (1937) and *Rhythm Classics* (1949). He also appeared in nine films.

SORAB MODI

Carlisle, Cliff(ord Raymond) (*b* nr Mount Eden, KY, 6 May 1904; *d* Lexington, KY, 5 April 1983). Blues singer, songwriter, and guitarist. Like many early country-music instrumentalists, he was caught up in the national fad for Hawaiian music after World War I; he emulated the guitar work of Sol Hoopi and Frank Ferera, and adapted a standard guitar to allow himself to play with a slide. After an apprenticeship with various vaudeville groups and tent shows, such as the Continental Red Path Chautauquas, he began to win fame by imitating the "blue yodel" style of Jimmie Rodgers. He made his first recordings in 1930 for Gennett, and early in his career also recorded one session with Rodgers for Victor. Carlisle soon established an independent reputation as the "Yodelin' Hobo," specializing in "new song stories." These abandoned the sentimental themes and images of country music of the 1920s in favor of lyrics that dealt with problems such as divorce, domestic fights, faithless lovers, and making ends meet: his *Seven years with the wrong woman* (1932), for instance, was one of the first country songs about divorce. Other songs chronicled hobo and prison life. Carlisle wrote about 500 compositions, mostly in an earthy, white blues style, and made more than 300 recordings, which demonstrate his unique playing technique on acoustic steel guitar.

In the late 1930s Carlisle began working with various members of his family, including his brother Bill (*b* Wakefield, KY, 19 Dec 1908), his son Tommy, and even his parents; his repertory broadened to include sentimental and gospel songs. The Carlisle brothers' last great success was *Rainbow at Midnight* (1946); Cliff retired in the early 1950s. Bill continued to perform with the family group as the Carlisles; they made regular appearances on the "Grand Ole Opry" and recorded some of Cliff's songs.

RECORDINGS
(selective list)

Shanghai Rooster Yodel (Romeo 5112, 1931); Seven years with the wrong woman (Per. 12861, 1932); Tom Cat Blues (Voc. 5492, 1932); The Girl in the Blue Velvet Band (ARC 5-12-61, 1934); Wildcat Woman and Tomcat Man (Bluebird 6350, 1936); It takes an old hen to deliver the goods (Bluebird 6493, 1937)

With Bill Carlisle: The Uncloudy Day (Decca 5716, 1939); Rainbow at Midnight (King 535, 1946)

BIBLIOGRAPHY

E. Earle: "Cliff and Bill Carlisle Discography," *Folk Style*, vii (1960), 7

C. K. Wolfe: *Kentucky Country* (Lexington, KY, 1982)

——: "Cliff Carlisle," *Bluegrass Unlimited* (Dec 1984), 56

CHARLES K. WOLFE

Carlone, Francis Nunzio. *See* CARLE, FRANKIE.

Carlos, Wendy [Walter] (*b* Pawtucket, RI, 14 Nov 1939). Composer. An early experimenter in electronic music, Carlos – a transsexual, formerly called Walter Carlos – worked with Ron Nelson at Brown University (AB 1962), then studied composition with Luening, Ussachevsky, and Beeson at Columbia University (MA 1965). From 1964 Carlos served as an adviser to Robert Moog in modifying and perfecting the Moog synthesizer. In collaboration with the producer Rachel Elkind, Carlos developed a method for creating electronic versions of orchestral sounds. The synthesizer gained recognition as a musical instrument and became the standard for electronic realizations owing to the enormous popularity of Carlos's recording *Switched-on Bach* (1968), which was made on a Moog synthesizer; more than a million copies of the album were sold. Carlos's virtuosity as a performer on the synthesizer and creativity as an arranger are convincingly displayed in her later albums, which include original compositions such as *Timesteps* (1970, used in the score for the film *A Clockwork Orange*, 1971), and *Pompous Circumstances* (1974–5). The popularity of these recordings led to experimentation in the merging of orchestral and synthesizer sounds, a technique which was successfully used in the film score *TRON* (1982). Aided by advanced technology, Carlos electronically produced hundreds of near-perfect replicas of instrumental voices. These were used in the first digitally synthesized orchestra for the album *Digital Moonscapes* (1985).

WORKS
(selective list)

Stage: Noah (opera), 1964–5

Elec, orch: Timesteps, synth, 1970; A Clockwork Orange, film score, synth, 1971; Sonic Seasonings, synth, tape, 1971; Pompous Circumstances, synth/orch, 1974–5; The Shining, film score, synth, tape, orch, 1978–80; Variations on Dies irae, orch, 1980; TRON, film score, synth, orch, 1981–2

Chamber: 3 Studies, fl, pf, tape, 1963–5; Vc Sonata, 1965–6; other works, ens, pf, synth, tape

Principal publishers: Hanson, Tempi

BIBLIOGRAPHY

D. Milano: "Wendy Carlos," *Contemporary Keyboard*, v/12 (1979), 32 [incl. discography]

——: "The Notation used by Wendy Carlos," *Contemporary Keyboard*, v/12 (1979), 38

R. Moog: "Wendy Carlos: New Directions for a Synthesizer Pioneer," *Keyboard*, viii/11 (1982), 51

——: "The Soundtrack of TRON," *Keyboard*, viii/11 (1982), 53

R. D. Larson: "The Sound of TRON," *CinemaScore*, nos. 11–12 (1983), 34

JUDITH ROSEN

Carmichael, Hoagy [Hoagland Howard] (*b* Bloomington, IN, 22 Nov 1899; *d* Rancho Mirage, CA, 27 Dec 1981). Songwriter, singer, pianist, and bandleader. He studied piano with his mother, Lida Carmichael, who played ragtime and popular songs in silent-movie theaters in Bloomington, and also learned the rudiments of jazz piano from Reginald DuValle of Indianapolis. While attending Indiana University in Bloomington he formed a college jazz band, and made his first recordings in 1925. He completed a law degree the following year and established a practice in Palm Beach, Florida, but when by chance he heard a recording of his *Washboard Blues* performed by Red Nichols he abandoned law altogether. He played piano with the Jean Goldkette band, then moved to New York about 1930 to pursue a career as a songwriter. He collaborated on popular songs with the lyricists Johnny Mercer, Frank Loesser, Paul Francis Webster, Stanley Adams, and others. Later he moved to Los Angeles and contributed songs to a number of motion pictures, including *Thanks for the Memory* (1938) and *To Have and Have Not* (1944).

From 1937 to 1954 Carmichael took musical or dramatic roles in 14 motion pictures, most notably *To Have and Have Not*, *The Best Years of our Lives* (1946), and *Young Man with a Horn* (1950). He usually portrayed an easy-going pianist with an unpretentious singing style. During the 1940s he served as host for several musical variety programs on network radio. Beginning in the 1950s he appeared on television, acting in 13 programs or series.

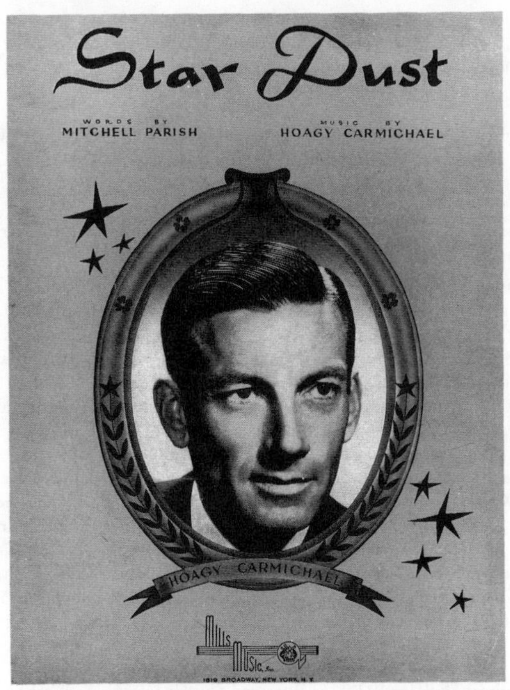

Hoagy Carmichael: Sheet-music cover of his song "Star Dust," with words by Mitchell Parish, published by Mills Music (1929)

In 1971 he was elected to the Songwriters Hall of Fame, and in the following year Indiana University awarded him an honorary doctorate.

Carmichael was one of the master songwriters of the 20th century: "the most talented, inventive, sophisticated, and jazz-oriented of all the great craftsmen" (Wilder). Beginning in the 1930s, along with Johnny Mercer, he legitimized regional songwriting and made it internationally popular; his chosen lyrics frequently celebrated small-town America. More than three dozen of his songs became hits. *Star Dust* (1929) became one of the most enduring of all pop standards, being recorded more than 1100 times and reportedly translated into 30 languages, and *In the cool, cool, cool of the evening* (1951) won an Academy Award for best song.

Carmichael was unusual among songwriters for having contributed many songs to both the popular and the jazz repertories. He began his career as a jazz musician, and composed his first piece, *Riverboat Shuffle* (1925), for his close friend, the jazz cornetist Bix Beiderbecke. Carmichael wrote a number of other instrumental jazz compositions, and recorded with Beiderbecke, Paul Whiteman, Louis Armstrong, Gene Krupa, Glenn Miller, and the Dorsey brothers. His songs have been adopted by musicians from most major genres of American popular music. His two autobiographies, *The Stardust Road* (1946) and *Sometimes I Wonder* (1965), illuminate his life and the worlds of popular song, film, and early jazz.

Collections of Carmichael's music manuscripts, sheet music, and recordings are held by Indiana University, in the Archives of Traditional Music, Lilly Library, and School of Music Library. Other materials are at the Monroe County Public Library, Bloomington; the Academy of Motion Pictures Library, Los Angeles; and the Los Angeles Public Library.

WORKS

(selective list)

Edition: *The Star Dust Melodies*, ed. R. S. Schiff (Melville, NY, 1983) [incl. list of works] [S]

STAGE

Walk with Music (G. Bolton, P. Levy, A. Lipscott; J. Mercer), New York, 4 June 1940 [incl. Way back in 1939 AD; S]

SONGS

Many associated with films. Music and, unless otherwise indicated, lyrics are by Carmichael; other lyricists are listed in parentheses.

Star Dust (M. Parish) (1929), S; Georgia on my mind (S. Gorell) (1930), S; Rockin' Chair (1930), S; Come easy, go easy, love (S. Clapp) (1931), S; Lazy River (S. Arodin) (1931), S; New Orleans (1932), S; Lazybones (Mercer) (1933), S; One Morning in May (Parish) (1933), S; How little we know (Mercer) (1934); Judy (S. Lerner) (1934), S; Little Old Lady (S. Adams) (1936), S; Heart and Soul (F. Loesser) (1938), S; Small Fry (Loesser), in Sing you Sinners, 1938, S; Two Sleepy People (Loesser), in Thanks for the Memory, 1938, S; I get along without you very well (J. B. Thompson) (1939)

Can't get Indiana off my mind (R. De Leon) (1940), S; The Nearness of you (N. Washington) (1940); The Lamplighter's Serenade (P. F. Webster) (1942), S; Skylark (Mercer) (1942), S; The Old Music Master (Mercer), in True to Life, 1943, S; How little we know (Mercer), in To Have and Have Not, 1944, S; Ole Buttermilk Sky (J. Brooks), in Canyon Passage, 1946, S; In the cool, cool, cool of the evening (Mercer), in Here Comes the Groom, 1951, S; My Resistance is Low (H. Adamson), in The Las Vegas Story, 1952, S

INSTRUMENTAL

Pf: Riverboat Shuffle (1925), S; Boneyard Shuffle (1926), S; Washboard Blues (1926), S; Manhattan Rag (1929), S; March of the Hoodlums (1929), S; Barbaric (1930); Cosmics (1933)

Orch: Brown County in Autumn; Johnny Appleseed Suite

Principal publishers: Famous, Frank, Mills, Peer-Southern, Warner Bros.

BIBLIOGRAPHY

A. Wilder: *American Popular Song: the Great Innovators, 1900–1950* (New York, 1972), 371ff

An Exhibition Honoring the 75th Birthday of Hoagland Howard Carmichael, Ll.B., 1926, D.M., 1972, Indiana University (Bloomington, IN, 1974) [catalogue]

D. Schiedt: *The Jazz State of Indiana* (Pittsboro, IN, 1977)

T. Buckley: "Profile of and Interview with Songwriter Hoagy Carmichael," *New York Times* (27 June 1979)

J. Lucas: "The Unknown Hoagy," *Second Line*, xxxii (aut. 1980), 20

Obituary, *New York Times* (28 Dec 1981)

J. E. Hasse: *The Works of Hoagy Carmichael* (Cincinnati, 1983)

——: "LP Recordings Devoted to Hoagy Carmichael," *Jazz Notes* (Oct 1983), 5

JOHN EDWARD HASSE

Carnegie, Andrew (*b* Dunfermline, Scotland, 25 Nov 1835; *d* Lenox, MA, 11 Aug 1919). Philanthropist and arts patron. Born in poverty, he immigrated to Allegheny, Pennsylvania, in 1848 and rose, in one of the most successful careers in American business history, to become the dominant figure in the international steel industry. He came to believe that the accumulator of a fortune had a duty to spend it for the good of mankind, and he devoted much energy during his last 40 years to benefactions. These centered on educational projects and the promotion of world peace, for which he endowed various foundations. He also supported some musical activities. He contributed about $6,000,000 to the building of organs for churches in the USA and the British Empire. Although he believed that concert organizations should be self-supporting, he lent his name and some of his time and money to several. These included the New York Oratorio Society and the New York SO, both of which were conducted by Walter Damrosch (son-in-law of Carnegie's good friend, the politician James G. Blaine) and for both of which Carnegie served as president briefly from 1888; he also supported the New York Philharmonic Society and was its president from 1901 until 1909. Apparently at Damrosch's urging, Carnegie contributed most of the construction costs of the New York Music Hall, which was opened in 1891 and was renamed Carnegie Hall in 1898, though not at his instigation. From about 1903 he gave an annual $5000 birthday gift to Damrosch.

After Carnegie's death, the Carnegie Corporation of New York (established by Carnegie in 1911) awarded various small grants for musical projects. It also gave over $750,000 between 1933 and 1943 to distribute, as a gift to universities, colleges, and secondary schools in the USA and the British Commonwealth, a phonograph and a set of classical recordings chosen, under the corporation's sponsorship, to represent the central tradition of Western art music.

See also PITTSBURGH, §§1, 2, and 4.

BIBLIOGRAPHY

B. J. Hendrick: "Carnegie, Andrew," *DAB*

W. Damrosch: *My Musical Life* (New York, 1930), 90ff

G. Martin: *The Damrosch Dynasty* (Boston, 1983), 94ff, 110ff, 187f

RICHARD CRAWFORD

Carnegie Hall. The name of several concert halls in American cities endowed by the philanthropist Andrew Carnegie, the most notable of which is the acoustically renowned hall in New York built in 1891; *see* NEW YORK, §3.

Carney, Harry (Howell) (*b* Boston, MA, 1 April 1910; *d* New York, 8 Oct 1974). Jazz baritone saxophonist. He first played piano and later turned to clarinet and alto saxophone. He was active professionally in Boston from the age of 13, and in 1927 moved to New York, where he began a lifelong association with Duke Ellington's orchestra (*see* JAZZ, fig.5), first playing several reed instruments, especially alto saxophone, and later almost exclusively baritone saxophone (occasionally bass clarinet). The baritone saxophone was Carney's preferred instrument, and he was the first (for many years the only) important jazz soloist on that instrument. In later years he made use of the technique of circular breathing, which allowed him to sustain the flow of sound indefinitely. His distinctive, rich tone was an essential element of the Ellington sound, and his deep and precise voice anchored the reed section and added an unmistakable touch to the orchestra's performances.

RECORDINGS

(selective list; all as sideman with Duke Ellington)

Doin' the Voom Voom (1929, Vic. 38035); Harlem Speaks (1933, Decca 800); Saddest Tale (1934, Bruns. 7310); Jumpin' Punkins (1941, Vic. 27356); Perdido (1942, Vic. 27880); Serious Serenade (1955, Cap. EAP3-679); Chromatic Love Affair, on *The Greatest Jazz Concert in the World* (1967, Pablo 2625704)

BIBLIOGRAPHY

SouthernB

G. Schuller: *Early Jazz: its Roots and Musical Development* (New York, 1968), 336f

S. Dance: *The World of Duke Ellington* (New York, 1970)

R. Stewart: *Jazz Masters of the Thirties* (New York, 1972/R1980), 129ff

JOSÉ HOSIASSON

Carpenter, John Alden (*b* Park Ridge, IL, 28 Feb 1876; *d* Chicago, IL, 26 April 1951). Composer. His father was a wealthy industrialist, his mother a church singer who had studied with Marchesi and William Shakespeare. After studying with Amy Fay and W. C. E. Seeboeck in Chicago, he studied composition with J. K. Paine at Harvard University, graduating in 1897. He then joined his father's firm of George B. Carpenter & Co., of which he was vice-president from 1909 to 1936. He was an admirer of Elgar's music, and after much persistence he succeeded in having some lessons with him during several months in Rome (1906). Returning to Chicago he studied with Bernhard Ziehn (1908–12). His first orchestral work, a humorous suite *Adventures in a Perambulator* (1914), proved to be an immediate and lasting success. He was elected to the National Institute of Arts and Letters in 1918 and the American Academy of Arts and Letters in 1942.

With the Piano Concertino, Carpenter began his mild but persistent flirtation with American popular music, including ragtime and jazz. He followed this formula with instant success in a "jazz pantomime" *Krazy Kat* (1921), based on the comic strip by George Herriman. It was produced at Town Hall, New York, on 20 January 1922 with choreography by Adolph Bolm and came to the attention of Diaghilev, who asked Carpenter to write an American ballet to be produced in Monte Carlo. The resulting work was *Skyscrapers*, "a ballet of modern American life." Plans for a production by Diaghilev fell through and instead it was given at the Metropolitan Opera on 19 February 1926. Two years later it was performed at the National Theater in Munich.

Carpenter's orchestral works – including two symphonies, a violin concerto, and two symphonic poems – were received with considerable acclaim, and earned for him such honors as the gold medal of the National Institute of Arts and Letters. His numerous songs for voice and piano greatly enhanced his reputation and brought him recognition as an outstanding song composer of his generation. Among his best songs are the cycles *Gitanjali* and *Water-colors*. The Four Negro Songs on texts by Langston Hughes reveal Carpenter's effective use of popular elements, particularly jazz-like rhythms. Turning to another aspect of Americana, Carpenter wrote *Young Man, Chieftain!*, an "Indian Prayer" with a text by Mary Austin.

Of his symphonic works the most successful is *Sea Drift*, a tone poem after Whitman. The orchestral *Danza* and a ballet *The Birthday of the Infanta* display the tinges of Spanish coloring to which Carpenter was partial, reflecting his affinity with Debussy and Ravel; his music as a whole is permeated by French impressionism. Apart from the merit of his songs, his place in American music is assured by the historical significance of his ballet *Skyscrapers* as an early attempt to depict "modern American life." Too simplistic in its repeated contrasts of work and play it nevertheless projects the impersonality, the variety, and the dynamism of the urban scene. The instrumentation includes three saxophones, a tenor banjo, and two red traffic lights played by means of a keyboard in the wings. There is also a chorus of six tenors and six sopranos on stage, reinforced by a chorus offstage. There are allusions to popular songs of the time, some mild syncopations, and a tinge of jazz. Carpenter's continued interest in jazz is indicated by his Jazz Orchestra Pieces, one of which, *A Little Bit of Jazz*, was dedicated to Paul Whiteman.

WORKS

STAGE

Strawberry Night Festival Music, 1896

Branglebrink (incidental music, R. M. Townsend, E. G. Knoblauch), collab. F. B. Whittemore, R. G. Morse, 1896

Selections from the Flying Dutchman (incidental music, H. T. Nichols), 1897

The Little Dutch Girl (pastoral play, 3, M. E. Stone, Jr., after Ouida: Two Little Wooden Shoes), 1900

The Birthday of the Infanta (ballet), 1917, rev. 1919, arr. suite, 1930, rev. 1940, arr. concert suite, 1949; Chicago, 23 Dec 1919

Krazy Kat (jazz pantomime), 1921, rev. 1940; Chicago, 23 Dec 1921

Skyscrapers (ballet), 1923–4; New York, 19 Feb 1926

ORCHESTRAL AND CHORAL

Suite for Orchestra, *c*1906–9

Berceuse, small orch, 1908

Adventures in a Perambulator, suite, 1914; Chicago, 19 March 1915

Piano Concertino, 1915, rev. 1948; Chicago, 10 March 1916

Symphony no. 1 "Sermons in Stones," 1917; Norfolk, CT, 5 June 1917

A Pilgrim Vision, sym. poem, 1920; Philadelphia, 23 Nov 1920

Jazz Orchestra Pieces (Oil and Vinegar), 1925–6

Song of Faith (Carpenter), SATB, orch, 1931, rev. 1936

Patterns, pf, orch, 1932; Boston, 21 Oct 1932

Sea Drift, sym. poem, after Whitman, 1933, rev. 1944; Chicago, 30 Nov 1933

Violin Concerto, 1936; Chicago, 18 Nov 1937

Danza, 1937, arr. pf, 1947

Symphony in C, 1940, based on Sym. no. 1; Chicago, 24 Oct 1940

Variation 9, in Variations on an American Folksong [12 variations each by a different composer], 1940

Song of Freedom (M. H. Martin), unison chorus, orch, 1941, arr. chorus, band, 1942

Symphony no. 2, 1942; New York, 22 Oct 1942

The Anxious Bugler, sym. poem, 1943; New York, 17 Nov 1943

Blue Gal, vc, orch, 1943

Dance Suite, 1943; 3 Nov 1943 [Danza and orchestrations of Polonaise américaine, Tango américain, see CHAMBER AND INSTRUMENTAL]

The Seven Ages, orch suite, after Shakespeare, 1945; New York, 29 Nov 1945

Carmel Concerto, pf, orch, 1948; 20 Nov 1949

Song of David, vc, women's vv, orch, 1951, inc.

CHAMBER AND INSTRUMENTAL

Minuet, pf, 1893; Twilight Reverie, pf, 1894; Pf Sonata no. 1, 1897; Miniature, vn, pf; Nocturne, pf, 1898; Valse triste, vn, pf; Vn Sonata, 1911, New York, 11 Dec 1912; Polonaise américaine, pf, 1912; Impromptu, pf, 1913; Little

Indian, pf, 1916; Little Dancer, pf, 1917; Tango américain, pf, 1920; Diversions, 5 pf pieces, 1922; Str Qt, 1927; Pf Qnt, 1934

SONGS
(all 1v, pf)

Love whom I have never seen (Carpenter), 1894; My Sweetheart (G. Alexander), 1894; Norse Lullaby (E. Field), 1896; Alas, how easily things go wrong (G. McDonald), 1897; In Spring (Shakespeare), 1897; Little John's Song (N. Hopper), 1897; Memory (from the *Athenaeum*), 1897; Mistress Mine (Shakespeare), 1897; Sicilian Lullaby (Field), 1897

Improving Songs for Anxious Children (R. Carpenter), 17 songs, 1901–2; When little boys sing (R. Carpenter), collection, 1904; Treat me Nice (P. L. Dunbar), 1905; Down in India (L. Hope); The cock shall crow (Stevenson), 1908; Go, lovely rose (E. Waller), 1908; May, the Maiden (S. Lanier), 1908; The Green River (L. A. Douglas), 1909; The Heart's Country (F. Wilkinson), 1909; Little Fly (Blake), 1909; Looking Glass River (Stevenson), 1909

Chanson d'automne (Verlaine), 1910; Le ciel (Verlaine), 1910; Dansons la gigue! (Verlaine), 1910; En sourdine (Verlaine), 1910; Il pleure dans mon coeur (Verlaine), 1910; Bid me to Love (Maeterlinck, trans. R. Herrick), 1911; A Cradle Song (Blake), 1911; Don't Ceäre (W. Barnes), 1911; Fog Wraiths (M. Howells), 1912; Her Voice (Wilde), 1912; To One Unknown (H. Dudley), 1912; Les silhouettes (Wilde), 1912

Gitanjali [Song offerings] (Tagore: Gitanjali, nos.57, 60–62, 80, 90), 1913, orchd 1934; The day is no more (Tagore: Gitanjali, no.74), 1914; The Little Prayer of I (A. Simpson), 1914; The Player Queen (Yeats), 1914; Wull ye come in early spring (W. Barnes), 1914; Water-colors (Li-Po, Yu-hsi, Li She, trad. Chin. coll. Confucius), 4 songs, 1916, orchd 1918; The Home Road (Carpenter), 1917, arr. SATB, arr. unison vv, pf

Khaki Sammy (Carpenter), 1917; The Lawd is smilin' through the do' (trad.) 1918; Berceuse de guerre (E. Cammaerts), 1918; Serenade (Sassoon), 1920; Slumber Song (Sassoon), 1920, orchd 1943; Les cheminées rouges (M. Havet), 1922; Le petit cimetière (Havet), 1923; O! Soeur divine (E. Calvé), 1923; Mountain, mountain (J. and R. Carpenter), 1926; Four Negro Songs (L. Hughes): Shake your Brown Feet, Honey, The Crying Blues, Jazz Boys, That Soothin' Song, 1926

America the Beautiful, 1928; Young Man, Chieftain! (M. Austin), 1929; The Hermit Crab (R. Hyde), 1929; Gentle Jesus, Meek and Mild (Carpenter), 1931; If (M. Stevenson), 1934; The Past Walkes Here (V. W. Cloud), 1934; The Pools of Peace (J. Campbell), 1934; Rest (incl. M. Simpson: The Dial), 1934; Worlds (A. Fischer), 1934; Morning Fair (incl. J. Agee: Sonnet xx from Permit me Voyage), 1935

MSS in *ICN*
Principal publisher: G. Schirmer

BIBLIOGRAPHY

EwenD
W. T. Upton: *Art-song in America* (Boston, 1930/*R*1969), 197
O. Downes: "J. A. Carpenter, American Craftsman," *MQ*, xvi (1930), 443
F. Borowski: "John Alden Carpenter," *MQ*, xvi (1930), 449 [incl. list of works]
T. C. Pierson: *The Life and Music of John Alden Carpenter* (diss., U. of Rochester, 1952)
G. Chase: "Carpenter, John Alden," *DAB*
H. Gleason and W. Becker: "John Alden Carpenter," *20th-century American Composers*, Music Literature Outlines, ser. iv (Bloomington, IN, rev. 2/1981) [incl. further bibliography]

GILBERT CHASE

Carr. Family of music publishers and musicians of English origin.

(1) Joseph Carr (*b* England, 1739; *d* Baltimore, MD, 27 Oct 1819). Music publisher. He was active in London until 1794, when on the urging of his son (2) Benjamin Carr he immigrated to the USA and established his publishing house in Baltimore. He issued contemporary European music as well as American dances, popular ballads, and patriotic songs, including the first edition of *The Star-Spangled Banner* (1814; for illustration *see* PATRIOTIC MUSIC, fig. 1). He also published the *Musical Journal for the Piano Forte*, edited by Benjamin, and *Carr's Musical Miscellany*, and sold keyboard instruments and guitars. On Carr's death the publishing firm was taken over by his son (3) Thomas Carr.

(2) Benjamin Carr (*b* London, England, 12 Sept 1768; *d* Philadelphia, PA, 24 May 1831). Music publisher, composer, and organist, son of (1) Joseph Carr. He learned the music trade in his father's shop in London, studied with the leading church musicians of the day (including Samuel Arnold and Charles and Samuel Wesley), and is said to have performed in programs given by the Concert of Ancient Music and at Sadler's Wells Theatre. He immigrated to the USA and settled in Philadelphia in 1793, and was followed the next year by the rest of his family, who went to Baltimore, where his father set up a music-publishing firm. Carr established thriving music businesses in New York (sold to James Hewitt in 1797) and in Philadelphia, then the nation's capital. There he was organist of St. Augustine's Catholic Church (1801–31) and of St. Peter's Episcopal Church. His amazing versatility as a publisher, editor, promoter, singer, pianist, organist, composer, teacher, and conductor, and his active leadership in civic musical affairs, including the founding of the Musical Fund Society of Philadelphia (1820), led him to be called the "Father of Philadelphia Music."

Carr's firm in Philadelphia was one of the first notable American music publishing establishments, and he and his family were leaders in supplying the young nation with patriotic music. He had an unusually fine business sense and is credited with a surprisingly large number of first American publications, including *Yankee Doodle*, *Pleyel's Hymn*, and *Adeste fideles*. His *Musical Journal for the Piano Forte* (issued weekly for 24 weeks during winter and spring in the years 1800–04) was the first American music publication in magazine form of consequence; alternate issues were devoted to vocal and instrumental music. A companion publication, *Musical Journal for the Flute or Violin*, was published concurrently on the same plan. Later *Carr's Musical Miscellany in Occasional Numbers* (1812–25) contributed significantly to the availability of good music.

Carr had an active interest in the theater, appearing as actor and singer with the Old American Company in New York in 1794–5. He wrote a number of operas (including *The Archers*, frequently cited as one of the earliest in the USA), and composed incidental music for several plays. Many of his songs were ballads which achieved significant popularity. In all he composed 275 secular works and 85 sacred works, including hymns, psalms, anthems, masses, and chants. He also wrote pedagogical works, such as *The Analytical Instructor* (1826), *Lessons and Exercises in Vocal Music* (1811), and *Short Methods of Modulating from One Key to Another* (n.d.).

Carr was an important figure particularly in the musical growth and development of Philadelphia. As a publisher he issued enormous amounts of music from England, Europe, and America. In his activities as a concert manager he promoted music of the best quality, and he was in great demand as singer, actor, conductor, and organist (he was reputed to be the finest organist in Philadelphia for many years). Important collections of Carr's music may be found at the New York Public Library, the Library of Congress, Columbia University, and the Edward I. Keffer Collection of the Musical Fund Society of Philadelphia.

WORKS

Selective list; printed works published in Philadelphia unless otherwise stated.
Edition: *B. Carr: Selected Secular and Sacred Songs*, ed. E. R. Meyer, RRAM (in preparation)

STAGE

Philander and Silvia, or Love Crown'd at Last (pastoral opera), London, Sadler's Wells, 16 Oct 1792

The Caledonian Frolic (pantomime), Boston, 1793, lost
Macbeth (incidental music), New York, 14 Jan 1795
Poor Jack (pantomime), New York, 1795, lost
The Archers, or Mountaineers of Switzerland (opera, W. Dunlap), New York, John Street, 18 April 1796; selections pubd, 1 song repr. in *Music in America*, ed. T. Marrocco and H. Gleason (New York, 1964)
Arrs. of English operas with additional music, incl. S. Arnold: The Children in the Wood, Philadelphia, 24 Nov 1794; C. Dibdin: The Deserter, New York, 19 May 1795; Linn: Bourneville Castle, New York, 16 Jan 1797; W. Holcroft: The Spanish Barber, 1800; other opera arrs., incidental music

OTHER WORKS

Vocal: 4 Ballads (1794); 3 Ballads, op.2 (1799); 6 Ballads from . . . The Lady of the Lake, op.7 (1810); 4 Ballads from . . . Rokeby, op.10 (Baltimore, ?1813); The History of England, 1v, pf, op.11 (Baltimore, ?1814/*R*1954); Musical Bagatelles, 1v, pf, op.13 (*c*1820); [6] Canzonets, op.14 (1824); numerous songs
Inst (for pf unless otherwise stated): Federal Overture, 1794, pf score (1794/*R*1957); 6 sonatas (1796), no.6 ed. in RRAM, i (1977); Dead March and Monody for General Washington, pf and vs (Baltimore, 1800); 3 divertimentos, in Musical Journal for the Piano Forte, i (1800); The Siege of Tripoli: Historical Naval Sonata, op.4 (1804), ed. in RRAM, i (1977); Applicazione adolcita, op.6 (1809); 6 Progressive Sonatinas, pf, vn/fl ad lib, op.9 (Baltimore, ?1812); other works, incl. marches, waltzes, variations
Pedagogical: Lessons and Exercises in Vocal Music, op.8 (Baltimore, 1811); Analytical Instructor, op.15 (1826); Short Methods of Modulating from One Key to Another (n.p., n.d.)

COLLECTIONS AND EDITIONS

With O. Shaw, The Gentleman's Amusement and Companion to the Flute (*c*1785–1800); Musical Journal for the Piano Forte (1800–04; repr. 1942) [pubd in 2 sections as Musical Journal Vocal Section and Musical Journal for the Flute or Violin]; Masses, Vespers, Litanies, Hymns, Psalms, Anthems & Motets (1805); Carr's Musical Miscellany in [85] Occasional Numbers (1812–25/*R*1982) [pf music and songs]; A Collection of Chants and Tunes for the Episcopal Churches of Philadelphia (1816); The Chorister (1820); Lyricks (1825); Le clavecin (1825); Sacred Airs, in 6 Numbers (1830)

(3) Thomas Carr (*b* England, 1780; *d* Philadelphia, 15 April 1849). Music publisher, composer, and organist, son of (1) Joseph Carr. In 1794 he went with his parents to Baltimore, where he was associated with his father's publishing firm and was organist of Christ Church (1798–1811). He was important as a composer and arranger of patriotic songs. In 1814, at the request of Francis Scott Key, he adapted the words of *The Star-Spangled Banner* to the tune *To Anacreon in Heaven*, and in 1840 he wrote songs in support of the Whig cause and General Harrison, including *Old Tippecanoe's Raisin'*. After his father's death in 1819 he continued the publishing firm for three years, but then sold the catalogue to George Willig and John Cole and moved to Philadelphia, where he continued intermittently to publish and compose, and was also active as a teacher.

BIBLIOGRAPHY

L. C. Madeira: *Annals of Music in Philadelphia and History of the Musical Fund Society from its Organization in 1820 to the Year 1858* (Philadelphia, 1896)
O. G. T. Sonneck: *A Bibliography of Early Secular American Music* (Washington, DC, 1905; rev. and enlarged by W. T. Upton, 2/1945/*R*1964)
——: *Early Concert-life in America (1731–1800)* (Leipzig, 1907/*R*1978)
——: *Report on "The Star-Spangled Banner," "Hail Columbia," "America," "Yankee Doodle"* (Washington, DC, 1909/*R*1972, rev. and enlarged 2/1914/*R*1969)
——: *Early Opera in America* (New York, 1915/*R*1963)
F. J. Metcalf: *American Writers and Compilers of Sacred Music* (New York, 1925/*R*1967), 139
A. Elson: "Carr, Benjamin," *DAB*
V. L. Redway: "The Carrs, American Music Publishers," *MQ*, xviii (1932), 150
W. A. Fisher: *One Hundred and Fifty Years of Music Publishing in the United States* (Boston, 1933)
R. A. Gerson: *Music in Philadelphia* (Philadelphia, 1940/*R*1970)
H. Dichter and E. Shapiro: *Early American Sheet Music* (New York, 1941/*R*1977)
G. Chase: *America's Music* (New York, 1955, rev. 2/1966/*R*1981)
H. Dichter: "Benjamin Carr's 'Music [*sic*] Journal'," *MJ*, xv/1 (1957), 17
D. W. Krummel: *Philadelphia Music Engraving and Publishing, 1800–1820: a Study in Bibliography and Cultural History* (diss., U. of Michigan, 1958)
J. Mates: *The American Musical Stage before 1800* (New Brunswick, NJ, 1962)
C. E. Wunderlich: *A History and Bibliography of Early American Periodicals, 1782–1852* (diss., U. of Michigan, 1962)
I. Lowens: *Music and Musicians in Early America* (New York, 1964)
R. J. Wolfe: *Secular Music in America, 1801–1825: a Bibliography* (New York, 1964)
H. E. Davis: "The Carrs: a Musical Family," *Pennsylvania Genealogical Magazine*, xxiv (1965), 56
R. L. Smith: *The Church Music of Benjamin Carr* (diss., Southwestern Baptist Theological Seminary, 1969) [with list of works]
C. A. Sprenkle: *The Life and Works of Benjamin Carr* (diss., Peabody Conservatory, 1970)
E. R. Meyer: "Benjamin Carr's *Musical Miscellany*," *Notes*, xxxiii (1976–7), 253
R. J. Wolfe: *Early American Engraving and Printing* (Urbana, IL, 1980)
J. B. Clark: "American Organ Music before 1830," *The Diapason*, lxxii/11 (1981), 1

W. THOMAS MARROCCO, MARK JACOBS/R (1), RONNIE L. SMITH (2), R. ALLEN LOTT (3)

Carr, Joe "Fingers." *See* BUSCH, LOU.

Carr, Leroy (*b* Nashville, TN, 1905; *d* Indianapolis, IN, 28 April 1935). Blues singer and pianist. In his early 20s he met and formed a partnership with the blues guitarist Scrapper Blackwell (Francis Hillman Black) (1903–63) and, although both men recorded as soloists, it was as a team that they were particularly esteemed. Carr generally took the vocal parts, accompanying himself in a smoothly rolling piano style influenced by boogie-woogie. His melancholy voice, against which Blackwell's clear-cut guitar playing acted as a strong foil, was comparatively sweet for blues singing, and his texts, jointly written with Blackwell, were deliberately poetic. The duo produced many masterpieces of the idiom, such as *How Long, How Long Blues* (1928, Voc. 1191), *Midnight Hour Blues* (1932, Voc. 1703), *Hurry down sunshine* (1934, Voc. 02741), and *Prison Bound* (1928, Voc. 1241), which soon entered the permanent repertory of blues singers and are unsurpassed in their integration of piano, guitar, and voice (for illustration *see* BLUES, fig.3). When Carr died from acute alcoholism he was mourned throughout the blues world and many blues were dedicated to his memory. Blackwell never recovered from the shock and ceased to perform.

BIBLIOGRAPHY

D. P. Schiedt: Liner notes, *Blues before Sunrise: Leroy Carr* (Col. 1799, *c*1960)
P. Oliver: *The Story of the Blues* (London, 1969)
B. Hall and R. Noblett: Liner notes, *Leroy Carr, 1930–1935* (Magpie 4407, 1978)

PAUL OLIVER

Carrell, James P. (*b* Lebanon, VA, 13 Feb 1787; *d* Lebanon, 28 Oct 1854). Composer and tunebook compiler. He was a Methodist minister. Records indicate that his compilation *Songs of Zion* was printed by Ananias Davisson in 1820 in Harrisonburg, Virginia, but no copies have been located. His more important tunebook, compiled with the Presbyterian elder David Little Clayton (*b* Marion Co., VA, 15 Jan 1801; *d* Frederick Co., VA, 17 Sept 1854), was *The Virginia Harmony* (Winchester, VA, 1831, 2/1836), in which he claimed 25 settings. Although *The Virginia Harmony* tends to reflect a more northern urban orientation than did Davisson's tunebooks, it has the distinction of including the earliest known printing of the anonymous pentatonic folk melody "Harmony Grove," now associated with *Amazing Grace*.

BIBLIOGRAPHY
G. P. Jackson: *White Spirituals in the Southern Uplands* (Chapel Hill, 1933/*R*1965)
H. Eskew: *Shape-note Hymnody in the Shenandoah Valley, 1816–1860* (diss., Tulane U., 1966)

HARRY ESKEW

Carreño, (Maria) Teresa (*b* Caracas, Venezuela, 22 Dec 1853; *d* New York, 12 June 1917). Venezuelan pianist and composer. When eight years old she was taken to New York, where she gave a recital on 25 November 1862, and took lessons from Louis Moreau Gottschalk. She lived mainly in Paris from 1866 to 1870, where she studied with Georges Mathias and, later, with Anton Rubinstein. She returned to the USA early in 1876 to study singing in Boston, but her career centered on Europe and she was particularly successful in Germany, where she lived and taught for over 30 years. She was married four times: to the violinist Emile Sauret in 1872, to baritone Giovanni Tagliapietra in 1875, to Eugen d'Albert in 1892, and to Tagliapetra's younger brother Arturo in 1902. While married to Giovanni Tagliapietra, she spent two years in Venezuela with him, organizing and conducting an opera company in which she also sang. She composed a String Quartet in B minor, though most of her other works were for piano. She introduced a number of compositions by her former pupil Edward MacDowell in the USA, performing the Andantino from his *Erste moderne Suite* in Saratoga in 1883 and his *Zweite moderne Suite* in Chicago in 1884; she performed the première of his Piano Concerto in D minor in 1888. Her last appearance with an orchestra in the USA was with the New York Philharmonic Society on 8 December 1916.

BIBLIOGRAPHY
J. B. Plaza: *Teresa Carreño* (Caracas, 1938)
M. Milinowski: *By the Grace of God* (New York, 1940/*R*1977)
I. Peña: *Teresa Carreño* (Caracas, 1953)

NORMAN FRASER/R

Carrillo(-Trujillo), Julián (Antonio) (*b* Ahualulco, San Luis Potosí, Mexico, 28 Jan 1875; *d* San Angél, Mexico, 9 Sept 1965). Mexican theorist, composer, and conductor of Indian extraction. He received his early musical training at the National Conservatory in Mexico City. While he was experimenting on his violin with the division of a string into multiple parts, he arrived at a "new sound" – a $\frac{1}{16}$-tone. Between 1899 and 1905 he studied in Europe at the conservatories of Ghent and Leipzig. On returning to Mexico in 1905 he assumed many administrative duties, among them a professorship in composition at the National Conservatory, where he later served as director (1913–14). Carrillo lived in New York from 1914 to 1918; during that time he organized the American SO, which had a regular concert season and competed favorably with the New York PO. Back in Mexico he again became director of the National Conservatory (1920), but in 1924 he retired from his official public duties and devoted himself to working out his theories of microtonality, which he called "sonido 13," and applying them in compositions for new or adapted instruments; he formulated a new system of notation suitable for their expression. In 1926 the League of Composers in New York commissioned a work from Carrillo for its concerts of new music, and he wrote his *Sonata casi-fantasia* for its Town Hall recital on 13 March. This concert marked the beginning of a long and fruitful friendship and artistic collaboration with Stokowski, who, on hearing of Carrillo's success with the *Sonata casi-fantasia*, commissioned a work for the Philadelphia Orchestra. The Concertino was performed with great acclaim at Carnegie Hall and later on tour with the Philadelphia Orchestra in Baltimore, Philadelphia, and Washington, DC. Stokowski persuaded Carrillo to retain the classical orchestra, playing in conventional tones and semitones, and to use a smaller group for the new microtones: the formal result was a resuscitation of the Baroque concerto grosso format, and one which allowed Carrillo to realize his concept of "metamorphosis," whereby there would be a continuum of traditional and new sounds in an ever-expanding development. Carrillo continued to experiment and compose with success throughout the remaining 40 years of his life. In 1930 he formed a complete orchestra capable of playing exclusively in microtones. This Orquesta Sonido 13 toured throughout Mexico in the 1930s, sometimes with Stokowski as its conductor. Carrillo also received another commission from Stokowski, that for the Concertino for $\frac{1}{3}$-tone piano with orchestra, introduced in Houston in 1962 with his daughter Dolores as soloist and Stokowski conducting.

BIBLIOGRAPHY
G. R. Benjamin: "Julián Carrillo and 'sonido trece'," *Yearbook, Inter-American Institute for Musical Research*, iii (1967), 33–68

GERALD R. BENJAMIN

Cars. Rock group. Formed in Massachusetts in 1976, its members are Ric Ocasek (Richard Otcasek; *b* Baltimore, MD), singer and guitarist; Ben Orr (Benjamin Orzechowski; *b* Lakeland, OH), singer and bass guitarist; Elliot Easton (Shapiro; *b* Brooklyn, NY), guitarist; Greg(ory) Hawkes (*b* Arlington, VA), keyboard player; and David Robinson (*b* Massachusetts), drummer. Ocasek, who has written or collaborated in writing all the group's songs, and Orr worked together in various groups from the late 1960s. Ocasek had been playing guitar since the age of 10; Orr had worked on a rock television program, "Upbeat," in Cleveland as a teenager and was later a producer and studio musician. The two recorded an album in 1972 as part of a folk trio called Milkwood, and settled in Cambridge, Massachusetts, where they played in several other groups. They were then joined by Hawkes, who had played keyboards in Milkwood's backup group, Robinson, who had been the drummer for the Modern Lovers, and Easton. The Cars' first album (*The Cars*, 1978) introduced their characteristic sound, marked by Ocasek's expressionless, melancholy vocals, Easton's succinct guitar licks, and Hawkes's one-handed keyboard playing. This and their second album, *Candy-o* (1979), each sold more than three million copies. Their later albums, which are notable for musical experiments and dense instrumental textures, were also commercially successful. *Panorama* (1980), the most innovative, includes songs in odd meters and several in which the lyrics make bitter reflections on celebrity. The group's members have been active as producers and operate a studio, Syncro Sound, in Boston; Ocasek has produced albums for the punk groups Suicide and Bad Brains. The Cars were the first new-wave group to bring songs focusing on the themes of nihilism and alienation to a wide pop audience. Their music combines influences from the Velvet Underground and Roxy Music with melodic elements from rock of the 1950s and 1960s.

RECORDINGS
(selective list; all recorded for Elektra)
The Cars (135, 1978), incl. Good times roll, Just what I needed, My best friend's

girl; *Candy-o* (507, 1979), incl. It's all I can do, Let's go; *Panorama* (514, 1980), incl. Touch and go; *Shake it Up* (567, 1981), incl. Shake it up, Victim of Love; *Heartbeat City* (60296, 1984)

JON PARELES

Carson, "Fiddlin'" John (*b* Fannin Co., GA, 23 March 1868; *d* Atlanta, GA, 11 Dec 1949). Country-music fiddler and singer. He was a well-known fiddler and balladeer in northern Georgia before World War I, and was particularly popular as a contestant at the annual Georgia Old-Time Fiddlers' Association convention in Atlanta; he was seven times voted state champion fiddler. He often performed for political campaigns in Georgia, and was an associate of the political leaders Tom Watson and Herman and Eugene Talmadge. He was one of the first white folk musicians to appear on radio, making his début on WSB in Atlanta on 9 September 1922. In June 1923 he recorded two of his best-known songs, *The little old log cabin in the lane* and *The old hen cackled and the rooster's going to crow*, for Okeh Records, a recording session that is considered to have marked the beginning of the hillbilly music industry. Carson was affiliated with Okeh until 1931; he recorded nearly 150 songs. In 1934 he signed with RCA Victor, for which he rerecorded some of his earlier repertory; often he was backed by a string band, the Virginia Reelers, whose personnel included his youngest child, Rosa Lee ("Moonshine Kate") Carson. He was noted for his elaborate vocal ornamentation as much as for his fiddling skills. His repertory included traditional American ballads, popular songs from the 1890–1910 era, and topical political songs, many dealing with the plight of the farmer.

BIBLIOGRAPHY

A. Green: "Hillbilly Music: Source and Symbol," *Journal of American Folklore*, lxxviii (1965), 204

R. Franklin: "'Fiddlin' John's been at it for 71 Years," *Atlanta Journal* (5 June 1949); excerpts repr. in *Old Time Music*, no.1 (1971), 20

B. Coltman: "Look Out! Here He Comes: Fiddlin' John Carson: One of a Kind and Twice as Feisty," *Old Time Music*, no.9 (1973), 16

N. Cohen: "Fiddlin' John Carson: an Appreciation and a Discography," *JEMF Quarterly*, x (1974), 138

M. Wilson: Liner notes, *The Old Hen Cackled and the Rooster's Going to Crow* (Rounder 1003, 1973)

N. Cohen: "Early Pioneers," *Stars of Country Music*, ed. B. C. Malone and J. McCulloh (Urbana, IL, 1975), 16

G. Wiggins: "John Carson: Early Road, Radio, and Records," *Journal of Country Music*, viii/1 (1979), 20

BILL C. MALONE

Carter, Benny [Bennett Lester] (*b* New York, 8 Aug 1907). Jazz instrumentalist, arranger, composer, and bandleader.

1. Life. 2. Music.

1. Life. Carter received early musical training from his mother and several neighborhood teachers, but was primarily self-taught. He first played trumpet, then tried the C-melody saxophone, and shortly thereafter changed to alto saxophone, which became his principal instrument. From 1923 to 1928 he played in the bands of June Clark, Earl Hines, and others, but first attracted widespread attention during a year in Fletcher Henderson's orchestra (1930–31), to which he contributed many important arrangements. After leaving Henderson he succeeded Don Redman briefly as music director of McKinney's Cotton Pickers in Detroit, then returned to New York to form his own highly respected orchestra in 1932. This group included at various times several major innovators in the early swing style: Bill Coleman (trumpet), Dicky Wells (trombone), Ben Webster and Chu Berry (tenor saxophone), Teddy Wilson (piano), and Sid Catlett (drums). Carter disbanded his group in late 1934 and moved the following year to Europe; he settled in London, where he served as staff arranger for the BBC dance orchestra (1936–8). During these years he met with resounding acclaim and did much to advance the cause of jazz, playing and recording with local musicians in England, France, and Scandinavia and leading his own interracial, multinational band in the Netherlands (1937); he regularly played alto and tenor saxophone, trumpet, and clarinet, and occasionally played piano and sang.

Carter returned to the USA in 1938 and formed a new orchestra which took up a residency at the Savoy Ballroom in Harlem through much of 1939 and 1940. After briefly leading a sextet, he traveled with a new big band to the West Coast, settling permanently in Los Angeles in 1942. There he continued to lead his orchestra (which in the mid-1940s included such modern jazz musicians as Miles Davis, J. J. Johnson, and Max Roach), but otherwise turned increasingly to studio work. Beginning with *Stormy Weather* (1943), he composed and arranged for several major films and, later, television productions. One of the first black musicians to find acceptance in the Hollywood studios, Carter was instrumental in facilitating the entry of other talented Blacks, and was a leading force in the amalgamation of the black and white Musicians' Union locals.

From 1946 Carter no longer led a regular orchestra, though he continued to be active in jazz through tours with Jazz at the Philharmonic, occasional big-band engagements, and many recordings. In the 1950s and 1960s he also wrote arrangements for most of the leading jazz singers, including Sarah Vaughan, Ella Fitzgerald, Ray Charles, Peggy Lee, and Louis Armstrong. Carter resumed a more active performing schedule in the 1970s: he appeared at major festivals and nightclubs, made annual tours of Europe and Japan, and, following a ten-year hiatus, resumed recording on a regular basis. He also began a new career as an educator, spending several periods in residence at universities. Princeton University, where he was a frequent lecturer, awarded him an honorary doctorate in 1974.

2. Music. Carter is an extraordinarily versatile musician, and has made major contributions to jazz in several areas. As an instrumentalist he is recognized, along with Johnny Hodges, as the leading creator of a jazz alto saxophone style before Charlie Parker. Even his early solos, such as *I'd Love It* (1929), show the pure tone, facility, varied dynamics, and sophisticated harmonies that set his work apart from that of his contemporaries; later recordings, such as *Crazy Rhythm* (1937), with their long lines, legato phrasing, and understated attack, presaged future developments on this instrument (see ex. 1). Carter's trumpet playing, if not as original as his alto saxophone style, is also distinctive, with a characteristic bright tone and delicate vibrato (*More than you Know*, 1939), while his relatively few recordings on clarinet

Ex.1 From *Crazy Rhythm* (1937, Swing 1), transcr. J. Mehegan

reveal him to be an accomplished player with a full, rich tone in the instrument's chalumeau register (*Shoe Shiner's Drag*, 1938). Carter has also recorded competent solos on piano, tenor and soprano saxophone, and trombone.

As an arranger, Carter was a principal architect of the big-band swing style; his arrangement for Fletcher Henderson of *Keep a Song in your Soul* (1930) in particular is often cited as a landmark in the evolution of jazz arranging. *Lonesome Nights* and *Symphony in Riffs* (both 1933) display the innovative block-chord writing for reed instruments that marked his early scores and later became part of the stock in trade of most swing arrangers. His later work of the 1940s is more balanced, while still containing flowing choruses for the reed instruments. Carter also composed a wide range of works, from popular novelty items to extended pieces and dramatic scores. His later recordings, such as *Further Definitions* (1961), continue to show his masterly writing for the reed section, as well as a new drive and momentum in his solo playing.

RECORDINGS
(selective list)

As leader: Lonesome Nights (1933, OK 41567); Symphony in Riffs (1933, Col. 2898D); More than you Know (1939, Voc. 5508) [tpt]; Sleep (1940, Voc. 5399); O.K. for Baby (1940, Decca 3294); I Surrender Dear (1944, Cap. 200) [tpt]; I Can't Escape from You (1944, Cap. 40048); Malibu (1945, Cap. 200); *Further Definitions* (1961, Imp. 12); *Benny Carter 4 – Montreux '77* (1977, Pablo Live 2308–204) [a sax, tpt]

As sideman: McKinney's Cotton Pickers: I'd Love It (1929, Vic. 38133) [a sax]; F. Henderson: Keep a Song in your Soul (1930, Col. 2352D); The Chocolate Dandies: Dee Blues (1930, Col. 2543D) [cl]; Once Upon a Time (1933, OK 41568) [tpt]; C. Hawkins: Honeysuckle Rose/Crazy Rhythm (1937, Swing 1); L. Hampton: I'm in the Mood for Swing [a sax]/Shoe Shiner's Drag [cl] (1938, Vic. 26011); The Chocolate Dandies: I can't believe that you're in love with me (1940, Com. 1506) [a sax]

BIBLIOGRAPHY

L. Feather: "Bennett L. Carter, Esquire," *Melody Maker* (31 Oct 1936), 2

C. Emge: "Jazz' Most Underrated Musician? Benny Carter," *Down Beat*, xviii/10 (1951), 2

L. Feather: "The Enduring Benny Carter," *Down Beat*, xxviii/11 (1961), 15

G. Schuller: *Early Jazz: its Roots and Musical Development* (New York, 1968), 272ff

R. Stewart: "The Benny Carter I Knew," *Jazz Masters of the Thirties* (New York, 1972/*R*1980), 168

S. Dance: *The World of Swing* (New York, 1974), 135

H. Lyttelton: *The Best of Jazz II* (New York, 1982), 132–56

J. Evensmo and others: *The Alto Saxophone, Trumpet and Clarinet of Benny Carter, 1927–1946* (Hosle, Norway, 1982)

M. Berger and others: *Benny Carter: a Life in American Music* (Metuchen, NJ, 1982)

E. Okin: "Benny Carter: the Cat with Nine Lives," *The Wire*, no.9 (1984), 16

EDWARD BERGER

Carter, Betty [Jones, Lillie Mae] (*b* Flint, MI, 16 May 1930). Jazz singer. She grew up in Detroit, where as a teenager she sang with Charlie Parker and other visiting bop musicians. In 1948 she began touring with Lionel Hampton's band, which brought her to New York in 1951. She worked intermittently for the next two decades, appearing frequently at the Apollo Theater, singing in Ray Charles's touring show (1960–63), and visiting Japan (1963), London (1964), and France (1968). In the late 1950s and early 1960s she was associated with several recording companies, but refused to make the concessions to popular taste that they demanded of her; instead she preferred complex renditions of popular songs which, though often carefully planned, captured the spirit of bop improvisation. In 1971 she founded her own recording company, Bet-Car Productions. Her appearance in 1975 in Howard Moore's musical *Don't Call Me Man* prompted a number of club engagements and enabled her to form her own trio (1975–80), led by the pianist John Hicks.

RECORDINGS
(selective list)

Betty Carter and Ray Bryant (1955, Epic 3202); *Out There* (1958, Progressive Jazz 90); *The Modern Sound of Betty Carter* (1960, ABC-Para. 363); *Ray Charles and Betty Carter* (1961, ABC-Para. 385); *'Round Midnight* (1962–3, Atco 33–152); *Finally Betty Carter* (1969, Roul. 5000); *Now it's My Turn* (1976, Roul. 5005); *Betty Carter and the Audience* (1979, Bet-Car 1003)

BIBLIOGRAPHY

B. McLarney: "Betty Carter: the 'In' Singer," *Down Beat*, xxxiii/15 (1966), 18

M. Jacobson: "Betty Carter is Alive in Bed-Stuy," *Village Voice*, xx (18 Aug 1975), 100

H. Nolan: "Betty Carter's Declaration of Independence," *Down Beat*, xliii/14 (1976), 23

D. Hollenberg: "Betty Carter," *Down Beat*, xliv/8 (1977), 44

L. Prince: "Betty Carter: Bebopper Breathes Fire," *Down Beat*, xlvi/9 (1979), 12

M. Ullman: *Jazz Lives: Portraits in Words and Pictures* (Washington, DC, 1980/*R*1982)

BARRY KERNFELD

Carter, Bo [Chatmon, Armenter] (*b* Bolton, MS, 21 March 1893; *d* Memphis, TN, 21 Sept 1964). Blues singer and guitarist. He came from a large musical family, and during World War I formed a family string band, the Mississippi Sheiks, which played for country dances and at functions for Whites. Its members included at various times his brothers Sam (guitar), Lonnie (violin), and Harry (piano), as well as another relative, Walter Vincson, on guitar and the mandolin and guitar player Charlie McCoy. The group's many recordings sometimes included Carter, examples being *Loose like that* (1930, OK 8820) and *Sales Tax* (1934, Bluebird 5453) which, despite their "hokum" elements, give a good impression of rural string-band music. Although Carter was a skilled carpenter, failing eyesight led him to take up music professionally, and he recorded extensively in the 1930s. His traditional Mississippi origins are evident in his guitar accompaniment to *Bo Carter's Advice* (1936, Bluebird 7073) and *New Stop and Listen* (1932, Para. 13134), both of which bear close stylistic similarities to Tommy Johnson's recordings. Carter's solo recordings were numerous and consistently good, ranging from the delicate song *I get the blues* (1936, Bluebird 6589), with its sensitively timed accompaniment, and *Shake 'em on down* (1938, Bluebird 7927), a resonant interpretation of a blues standard, to his many erotic songs and blues such as *Ram Rod Daddy* (1931, OK 8897) and *Pussy Cat Blues* (1936, Bluebird 6735), both distinguished by his engaging singing and excellent playing.

BIBLIOGRAPHY

P. Oliver: *Conversation with the Blues* (London, 1965)

S. Calt and J. Miller: Liner notes, *Bo Carter 1931–1940* (Yazoo 1034)

PAUL OLIVER

Carter, Elliott (Cook, Jr.) (*b* New York, 11 Dec 1908). Composer and writer on music. His reputation, which grew steadily from the 1950s, rests squarely on a cumulative sequence of large-scale works; at its best his music sustains an energy of invention that is unrivaled in contemporary composition.

1. Life. 2. Early works. 3. Transition. 4. Works of 1948–59. 5. The concertos. 6. Later works.

1. LIFE. Carter was educated at the Horace Mann School and at Harvard (1926–32, BA in English, MA in music). From 1932 to 1935 he studied at the Ecole Normale de Musique in Paris and privately with Boulanger. After returning to the USA he

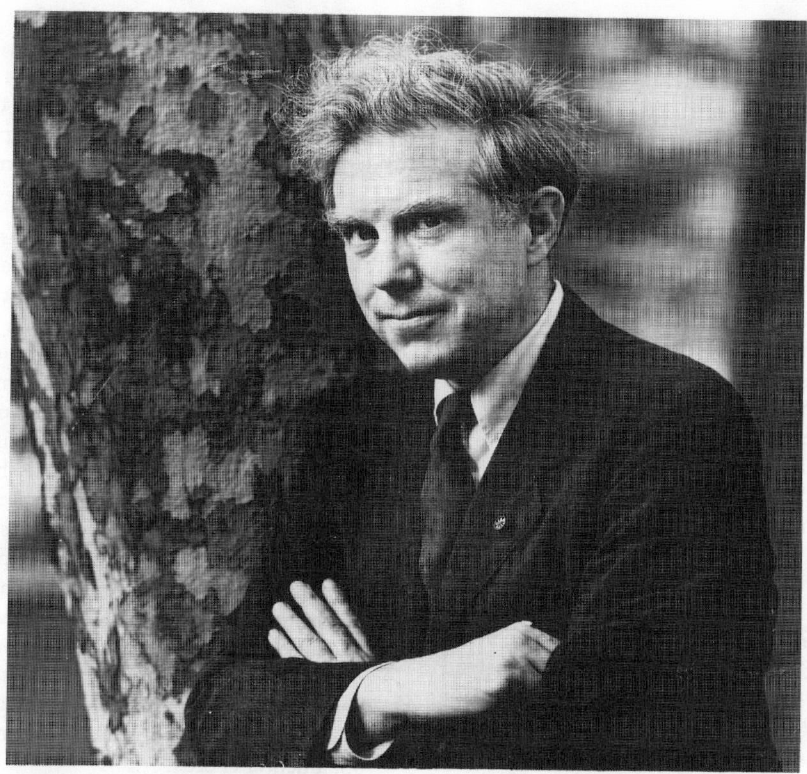

1. Elliott Carter

became music director of Ballet Caravan until 1940 and a regular contributor to *Modern Music* until 1946. In 1939 he married the sculptor Helen Frost-Jones, by whom he had one son. The suite from his ballet *Pocahontas* won the Juilliard Publication Award in 1940. From 1940 to 1942 he was on the faculty of St. John's College, Annapolis, teaching music and related subjects, and from 1943 to 1944 he worked as a consultant in the Office of War Information. In 1945 his *Canonic Suite* for four alto saxophones was awarded a BMI Publication Prize and his *Holiday Overture* won first prize in the Independent Music Publishers Contest; he also received a Guggenheim Fellowship. He was professor of composition at the Peabody Conservatory from 1946 to 1948, and at Columbia University from 1948 to 1950.

In 1950 a second Guggenheim Fellowship and a grant from the National Institute of Arts and Letters enabled him to work in seclusion in Arizona on his String Quartet no.1. This won first prize in the International Quartet Competition at Liège, Belgium, in 1953, and in the same year Carter received a fellowship to the American Academy in Rome, where he worked on his Variations for Orchestra, commissioned by the Ford Foundation for the Louisville Orchestra. In 1955–6 he was professor of composition at Queens College, New York; in 1956 he was elected a member of the National Institute of Arts and Letters, and his Sonata for flute, oboe, cello, and harpsichord received the Naumburg Prize. In 1958 he taught at the Salzburg Seminars. In 1960 his String Quartet no.2 won the Pulitzer Prize and the Critics' Circle Award, and in 1961 the same work gained the UNESCO Prize, also being nominated "best received contemporary classical composition" by the National Academy of Recording Arts and Sciences. Also in 1961 Carter received the Sibelius Medal and the Critics' Circle Award for his Double Concerto.

From 1960 to 1962 Carter was professor of composition at Yale. In 1963 he was elected a member of the American Academy of Arts and Sciences (Boston) and was appointed composer-in-residence at the American Academy in Rome. The following year he held a similar appointment in Berlin, where he worked on his Piano Concerto. In 1965 he received the Brandeis University Creative Arts Award, and in 1967 the Harvard Glee Club Medal. That year he returned for another year as composer-in-residence at the American Academy in Rome, also spending some of 1968 at the Villa Serbelloni at Bellagio, Italy, where he worked on his Concerto for Orchestra, commissioned by the New York PO for its 125th anniversary year. In 1969 he was elected a member of the American Academy of Arts and Letters.

In 1971 Carter was awarded the Gold Medal of the National Institute of Arts and Letters and he spent more time at the Villa Serbelloni, working on his String Quartet no.3. In 1967 he was appointed to teach composition at the Juilliard School and was also named Andrew D. White Professor-at-Large of Cornell University. He has also taught at the Dartington and Tanglewood summer schools and served in the League of Composers, the ISCM, and the ACA. He has received honorary doctorates from the New England Conservatory of Music (1961), Swarthmore College (1965), Princeton University (1967), Ripon College (1968), Oberlin College, and Boston, Yale, and Harvard universities (1970), as well as the Peabody Conservatory (1974) and the University of Cambridge (1983). He received the Handel Medallion in 1978, the Ernst von Siemens Prize in 1981, the Edward MacDowell Medal in 1983, the George Peabody Medal in 1984, and the National Medal of Arts in 1985.

Carter has avoided conducting or playing in public on the grounds of "poor performing nerves," but his writings on music cover an impressive range: he has published articles on many aspects of 20th-century music including the works of Ives, Piston, Riegger, Stravinsky, and Wolpe. A collection of these, *The Writings of Elliott Carter: an American Composer looks at Modern Music*, edited by E. Stone and K. Stone, was published in 1977.

2. EARLY WORKS. Carter had the good fortune to grow up during a progressive period of New York's cultural life. At the age of 16 he met Ives, who encouraged him to compose and took him to concerts. During his schooldays he heard not only *The Rite of Spring* and *Pierrot lunaire*, but also many first performances of Varèse, Ruggles, Ives himself, and later the young Sessions and Copland. Scriabin was another early enthusiasm. Scholar friends introduced him to Indian and Balinese music, and he took the opportunity of a visit to Vienna with his businessman father in 1925 to purchase all the available scores of the Second Viennese School, including Schoenberg's newly published Piano Suite op.25. Meanwhile his interest in the modern movement also extended to Proust, Joyce, Eisenstein, the German expressionist painters, and the visiting Moscow Arts Theater.

Wide reading in modern literature, together with subsidiary courses in mathematics, German, and Greek, also occupied much of his time at Harvard, which he chose largely in order to attend Koussevitzky's adventurous concerts with the Boston SO. But singing Bach in the Glee Club and sharing a room with the Elizabethan specialist Stephen Tuttle aroused his interest in the music of earlier centuries and he profited from the technical advice of Holst, who appeared as visiting professor for 1931–2. Vacations were spent exploring the German classics at the Salzburg and Munich festivals. Nonetheless, it was studying a range of material from Machaut to Stravinsky and furthering his command of strict counterpoint in up to 12 parts under Boulanger that proved crucial in focusing his musical understanding and technique. Contact with Stravinsky and the conducting of a French madrigal group were other musical gains of his years in Paris, during which observation of the events surrounding the Stavisky affair also matured his political outlook.

The darkening situation in Europe and the Depression to which he returned in 1935 were to affect his compositional direction. His first major orchestral score, the ballet suite *Pocahontas* (1938–9), displays variously the influence of Stravinsky and Hindemith, the English virginalists, and that mild vein of indigenous lyricism exemplified by Piston, but not a trace of German expressionism. Carter has explained that although the modern movement has remained for him a permanent core of ideas, the expressionist aesthetic had at that point come to seem like part of the madness that led to Hitler. His reaction was towards moderation and the practical. This took the form, on the one hand, of participation in a liberal arts college scheme to deploy music as a link study between mathematics, the sciences, and the ancient and modern languages and literature, and, on the other, of a deliberate simplification of compositional style towards a hoped-for accessibility.

This aim was undoubtedly achieved in the fresh, unpretentious diatonicism of such works as the *Three Poems of Robert Frost* (1943) and *The Harmony of Morning* (1944). Other works of this period nevertheless presage aspects of his mature style. Continual variation of material and its extension into sustained melodic paragraphs are already features respectively of the pellucidly bitonal *Pastoral* (1940) and the warmly intimate *Elegy* (1943) for cello and piano. The first movement of the Symphony no.1 (1942) belies the New England calm of its Coplandesque opening in subsequent flights of contrapuntal dialectic, while the ostensibly "popular" *Holiday Overture* (1944) not only employs a "Jacobean" technique of cross-rhythms in ways comparable with the quite independent usages of Michael Tippett but also superimposes slabs of contrasting texture and tempos for the first time in Carter's work.

3. TRANSITION. These developments, together with a rereading of Freud towards the end of World War II, led Carter increasingly to feel that the neoclassical aesthetic represented an evasion of vital areas of feeling and expression. In the fine Piano Sonata (1945–6) he accordingly attempted to free himself from traditional schemata by deriving his compositional substance from the interrelations of the tone-color and playing technique of the instrument itself. The hierarchical superimpositions of octaves, 5ths, 4ths, and 3rds that comprise the work's harmony embody the characteristic overtone resonances of the piano. Carter exploited his fundamental chord of 5ths, B–F♯–C♯–G♯–D♯–A♯, right from the beginning, setting up a tension between chordal paragraphs founded on B and A♯ that soon issues in arpeggios and then tirades of toccata-like figuration, constant in pulse but continually varied in rhythmic grouping. Only later, and in passing, do such textures separate out into something resembling theme and accompaniment. The magnificent second-movement fugue is similarly evolved out of, and dissolved back into, the fundamental chords.

Carter's next three works have a somewhat retrospective quality, as though he now felt the need to tidy away the loose ends of a "first period" before going on. Neoclassical gestures from then recent Stravinsky, notably the Symphony in Three Movements, are to be heard again in *The Minotaur* (1947), if for the last time in Carter's output. The declamatory male-voice choruses, *Emblems* (1947), have similarly remained the last of his choral works, and the Woodwind Quintet (1948), a kind of Les Six-type divertimento, is the last of his genre pieces, though the frenetic energy of its part-writing also looks forward to the next phase.

4. WORKS OF 1948–59. In the Sonata for cello and piano (1948) Carter resumed his exploitation of instrumental character itself by emphasizing the differences between his two protagonists. Although this contrast is still subsidiary to the character forms of the two inner movements – an "out-of-doors" scherzo and an impassioned elegy – the opposition of melodic content, tone, articulation, and pace between the two instruments during large stretches of the outer movements is so great as almost to create the impression that the players are simultaneously improvising independently. The "almost" is crucial, as the work adumbrated Carter's abiding aesthetic quest for a "focused freedom" and several of his most far-reaching coordinating techniques for the first time. Instead of relying on a received harmonic vocabulary, he permeated and "framed" his progressions by a recurrent chromatic aggregate of interlocking 3rds (the second movement is his last piece to bear a key signature), while by superimposing opposing rhythms – for instance, triplets on quintuplets – and shifting the basic pulse from one to another, he hit on the device later known as "metric modulation," a means of gearing continually fluctuating speeds in precise notation.

The drive and eloquence such techniques had helped to release in what is one of the finest 20th-century cello sonatas now encouraged Carter in a wider rethinking of the elements of musical discourse. He turned once more to the music of Ives, to the rhythmic formulations of Cowell's *New Musical Resources* and Nancarrow's earliest studies for player piano, and to medieval, oriental, and African music for devices to create modern equivalents of the dynamic continuities in the classics that interested him, notably the elliptical coherences of middle-period Haydn and the techniques of superimposition in the operatic ensembles of Mozart, Verdi, and Mussorgsky. Meanwhile he practiced elaborating structures from deliberately restricted materials in the Eight Etudes and a Fantasy for woodwind quartet (1949–50) and the Eight Pieces for four timpani (1950–66).

Scruples about outstripping the stamina of players and audiences notwithstanding, Carter at last felt compelled to allow the urgencies of his new explorations free play in a large-scale work. The monumental String Quartet no.1 (1950–51) superimposes independent melodies in polymetric relationships as complex as 3 against 7 against 15 against 21; and the pitch materials of its entire 40 minutes relate not to tonality but to a tetrachord, E–F–G♯–A♯, from which every interval may be obtained by permutation. Even more impressive, however, is the work's grandly unified sweep through four movements. These comprise a tumultuous opening stretch of seething four-part counterpoint opening out into a more aerated scherzo, not without resemblances to that of Berg's *Lyric Suite*, which in turn gives way to an Adagio where the contrast of tranced upper strings against passionate recitatives from viola and cello represents the widest point of textural definition before the volatile concluding variations work back again towards heterophony. Yet the whole vast sequence is also conceived as a kind of parenthesis in the opening cello cadenza, which the first violin resumes at the end.

Far from languishing in obscurity as Carter had feared, the String Quartet no.1 rapidly established his international reputation, encouraging him to rethink the possibilities of two further traditional ensembles with comparable boldness. Having worked hitherto with equal voices, he took Sylvia Marlowe's commission for the Sonata for flute, oboe, cello, and harpsichord (1952) as an opportunity to develop the structural possibilities of a group dominated by one. Here the somewhat acid timbre of the harpsichord is amplified by the other instruments, and its typical gestures are anticipated, echoed, and modified in terms of their individual characters. The long diminuendo that comprises the first movement, for instance, reflects the gradual subsidence of the fuzz of upper partials which the other instruments catch and reverberate from the harpsichord's percussive opening attack, while the capacity of the latter for precise, rapid figuration touches off some of Carter's most spontaneous flights of metrical modulation in the delectable finale.

With the Variations for Orchestra (1954–5; see fig.2, p.368) Carter faced the problem of deploying his greatly expanded sense of textural functions in an ensemble that retains the 19th-century concept of monolithic chordal tuttis in its very balance of forces. His solution was to build the work around not one but three elements, the theme itself and two ritornellos, the one a descending line that gets faster in its reappearances, the other a fast rising gesture transformed in reverse. As the three are frequently superimposed, Carter was able to create not only layered tuttis of considerable richness and power (ninth variation), but also a scherzando music by rapid switches of spotlight (first variation). Implicit here is yet another textural dimension to be developed in later pieces: the sense of perspective in bringing one idea into foreground definition while another simultaneously sinks back into an indistinct accompanying role. The overall trajectory is a reversal of the First Quartet's: starting from textural multiplicity, Carter worked inwards to a static neutrality in the fifth variation, which isolates the characteristic harmonies of the whole, and then out again towards variety. Whether or not the resemblance of the climax of the finale to Debussy's *Jeux* (a work with a comparable "time sweep") is deliberate, it remains the last moment in Carter's music to sound at all derivative.

With the String Quartet no.2 (1959) Carter achieved at last an "auditory scenario for the players to act out with their instruments" that is virtually independent of received formal procedures. Each instrument is assigned a different "vocabulary" of characteristic intervals, rhythms, and expressive gestures, the parts evolving not in terms of constant themes against varied backgrounds, but rather in terms of constant fields of possibilities realized in continually varied foreground shapes – as it were, the same tones of voice uttering ever new sentences. The conversational metaphor, which Carter doubtless derived from the precedent of Ives's Second Quartet, also accounts for the continuous nine-section form which is the direct result of the various controversies, dominations, and agreements among the four players. As these interactions proceed more or less at the speed of human speech, projecting the work presents difficulties that can be mitigated to some extent by spacing the players wider apart than usual, but that largely disappear in the fullness of quadraphonic recording. *See also* NOTATION, §2.

5. THE CONCERTOS. If the Second Quartet attempts to communicate meaning largely in terms of its own devising, the Double Concerto (1961) dramatizes the process of becoming meaningful. Its quasi-palindromic shape, a process of integration going backwards after the midpoint, arose from Carter's decisions first to assign contrasting intervallic and rhythmic sets to the solo piano and harpsichord and to back each with a differently constituted ensemble, and second to deploy the keyboards as intermediaries between the percussion and pitch-sustaining instruments in the groups. At the start antiphonal percussion establishes the basic rhythmic oscillations, suggesting the "giant polyrhythms" that underlie the whole structure – a procedure reversed at the end to produce a memorable image of dissolution. Moving inwards, these are gradually associated with the intervallic sets and the combined figures then developed in characteristic gestures by the keyboards in long concertante dialogues that lead towards and away from the work's center. This comprises the most sustained and expressive treatment of the pitch materials in a glowing chorale-like passage for wind and strings during which the soloists and percussion are reduced to simple retarding and accelerating patterns. Despite the innumerable local incidents, parentheses, and contradictions with which this scheme is animated and the almost bewildering ductility and friskiness of the keyboard writing, the Double Concerto probably remains Carter's most convincing cyclic structure.

The Piano Concerto (1964–5), by contrast, is sequential in form and develops the Beethovenian kind of confrontation between disparate forces to be sensed behind a number of earlier Carter passages. In the first half the piano presents a mosaic of contrasting, mostly lyrical character-paragraphs, often supported only by a "companionate" concertino of seven solo wind instruments and strings. The few orchestral irruptions, however, prove ominous precursors to the second half. In this the ripieno strings gradually pile up into densely inert chords while brass and wood-

2. *Opening of Variation 6 from Carter's Variations for Orchestra (1954–5): autograph MS (DLC)*

wind tick monotonously away in polyrhythms that slowly approach synchronization, the combined effect of which is progressively to subdue the piano despite repeated attempts to break out and a series of long concertino solos offering "irrelevant suggestions." At breaking-point, the piano is assailed by the orchestra at its most brutal and insensitive, but survives as its quiet self. Unlike the previous works, the Piano Concerto has a somewhat heavy *espressivo* quality that doubtless befits its pessimistic scenario but may also reflect its innovative pitch system, in which varying superimpositions of three-note chords are extracted from a background formulation of two 12-note chords, one for the piano and concertino, and one for the orchestra.

Yet the flexibility with which Carter could handle an even more elaborate version of the same technique (with chords of five and seven notes) is just one of the ways in which the Concerto for Orchestra (1968–9) comprises both his most synoptic and his most exhilarating achievement. An evocation of the "poetry of change" inspired by verses of St. John Perse's *Vents*, it combines both cyclic and sequential procedures. There are four "close-up" movements, each dominated by a different concertino pack, in the background of which, however, sounds of the other three are continually to be heard. Another continuity, developed from the Variations, is the progressive slowing of the second-movement music against the quickening of the fourth, while the whole structure is "framed" in an awesome impressionist approach and retreat of the entire material at the beginning and end. After the dark opacity of the Piano Concerto, Carter's new-found orchestral brilliance and command of musical space is most impressive. This arises partly from the reappearance in the total chromatic of a diatonic or at least polytonal element, for instance in the tangy block progressions of the fourth-movement concertino (muted trumpets, oboes, and violas), and partly from the accession of an atmospheric quality, particularly in the swirling and soaring second-movement scherzo music.

6. Later works.

(i) 1960–81. If the slowly appearing pieces of the 1950s and 1960s constitute almost paradigmatic studies in relating the boldest formal concepts to the most individualized exploitation of the various chosen ensembles, Carter's productivity since 1970 suggests an increasing spontaneity in his mastery of the musical language he has elaborated for himself, enabling him to recover textural simplicity as a compositional resource and to resume vocal composition for the first time since 1947. Among the nonvocal works, the String Quartet no.3 (1971) is conceived as a continuous interplay between two duos, of which the first (violin I and cello) plays *quasi rubato* throughout against the *giusto sempre* of the second (violin II and viola). The first duo is allotted four complete movements to play against the six of the second, but all ten are segmented and shuffled in such a way that each is sooner or later heard in combination with each of the others. On paper the permutatory form-plan appears about the most schematic that Carter has elaborated. In performance the kaleidoscopic rapidity of the textural switches and the transcendental virtuosity of the instrumental part-writing create perhaps the most volatile and immediate impact of all his chamber works.

Despite its comparable instrumental demands and freer formal unfolding, the Duo for violin and piano (1973–4) makes a relatively contained, at times even intimate effect. The work dramatizes the contrast of bowed and struck strings, the violin's sustaining power and enormous variety of color and attack against the piano's greater range of pitch and volume. This contrast is presented in a long opening paragraph of passionate recitative for violin against a more regular, impersonal chiming for piano, after which the work evolves in a series of dialectical waves, each generated by aspects of the one before. Despite confrontations of considerable violence, the work achieves its most personal moments where the passing back and forth of common pitches between the instruments seems to set up fugitive pedal points of a poetic euphony; the conclusion in which violin and piano to some extent exchange the expressive characteristic of the opening also creates a formal symmetry reminiscent of the Cello Sonata.

The Brass Quintet (1974) reverts to the quasi-anthropomorphic approach of such pieces at the String Quartet no.2, starting metaphorically from the intention of the trumpets and trombones to play slow, solemn music, which is instantly and continually interrupted by the aberrant, egotistical horn. Yet the series of duos, trios, and "quodlibets" into which the subsequent arguments are marshaled creates a more formalistic impression than either the segmentation of the String Quartet no.3 or the symmetry of the Duo. The overall structure, however, is possibly the most boldly asymmetrical in Carter's output, a lengthy sequence of pungent, contentious sound blocks finally giving way to a balancing shorter section of striking simplicity and calm.

If the 15-minute span of A Symphony of Three Orchestras (1976) achieves at times an incandescent multiplicity beyond even that of the Concerto for Orchestra, its structure seems to derive rather from the chamber works: its extended central section is constructed, after the precedent of the String Quartet no.3, from the permutational overlappings of 12 movements, four assigned to each of the three large chamber orchestras into which the standard symphonic line-up is divided, and the work is "framed" by a solo obbligato completed at the end, analogous with the String Quartet no. 1. But in this instance the obbligato adumbrates not a rise but a descent, the surpassingly lyrical opening trumpet solo wheeling and banking downwards through ethereal string chords (expressly inspired by Hart Crane's vision of seagulls at dawn over New York in his long poem *The Bridge*) and the final catastrophic piano obbligato plunging to the depths, after a series of brutal tutti chords have pulverized the central section into broken phrases and aimless ostinatos, perhaps symbolizing the suicide of the poet himself.

Night Fantasies (1980), Carter's first solo piano piece since 1946, relates more closely in structure and tone to the Duo, its contrasting materials (initially suggested by the characters of the four well-known New York pianists who commissioned the work and, by analogy, the character suites of Schumann) being cross-cut in a continuous 20-minute sequence, a kind of fantastical nocturne "suggesting the fleeting thoughts and feelings that pass through the mind during a period of wakefulness at night." The piece begins with, and intermittently returns to, a remote "night music" comprising a static background of fixed pitches, out of which the "thoughts and feelings" erupt unpredictably as a contrasting series of figurations each dominated by a different interval plus its inversion – with the noninvertible tritone reserved for a stubborn "recitativo collerico" marking the center-point. The work's range of expression is epitomized when, after a final climax of grinding grandeur, the music "drops off" with almost ironic casualness.

Meanwhile, in returning to vocal writing (and the song cycle genre at that) with *A Mirror on which to Dwell* (1975), for soprano and nine players, Carter posed himself a double problem: how to rethink the possibilities of the voice in terms of his later style and how to interrelate a sequence of separate movements after a two-decade preoccupation with more or less continuous structures. His approach was to derive the contours and inflections of his vocal lines from reading Elizabeth Bishop's poems aloud, and to balance and clarify differently the accompaniment functions of picturesque illustration, emotional expression, and "objective" symbolism in each of the settings, so that the work as a whole would cohere as a sequence of bold contrasts. Thus, for instance, the opening setting, "Anaphora," inclines to the symbolic in the way its cyclical subject matter is mirrored in the permutations of a fixed scheme of registers and pitches; "A View of the Capitol from the Library of Congress" is more illustrative, with its almost Ivesian evocation of a distant military band; while, in function, the twittering oboe obbligato in "Sandpiper" falls somewhere between the two. A comparable approach can be discerned in the six Robert Lowell settings *In Sleep, in Thunder* (1981), for tenor and 14 players, in which, for example, the distant soprano who is overheard singing vocalises in the second poem, "Across the Yard: La Ignota," is evoked by a florid trumpet obbligato. But whereas *A Mirror* was unified by alternations of chosen poems on the general themes of nature, love, and isolation, *In Sleep, in Thunder*, which opens with a short, dedication-like setting of "Dolphin" accompanied by string quintet alone, is conceived as a "portrait" of the poet himself; and the wider range of the music, from the gently mocked New England pastoral simplicities of "Careless Night" to the jagged turbulence of "Dies irae," mirrors the greater emotional range of Lowell's poems, from human intimacy to religious wrath.

Between these works, however, Carter also sought to combine his new-found vocal style with the continuous structuring of his later instrumental music in *Syringa* (1978), an extended vocal duet with accompaniment for 11 players – difficult to classify but owing something in provenance both to opera and to the spiritual dialogues of the baroque. Here, a relatively conjunct setting for mezzo-soprano of John Ashbery's specially written eponymous text – a modern meditation upon the Orpheus myth – is counterpointed by an elaborate commentary for bass on Ancient Greek texts selected by Carter himself and set in the original, while a third continuity is sustained by a guitar obbligato suggestive of Orpheus's lute. *Syringa* is broadly cast in three wave-like sweeps of continuously evolving material, running to almost 20 minutes; the elaboration of this scheme is mitigated, out of consideration for the audibility of the texts, by the often exceptional delicacy of its scoring, but the piece remains among Carter's most demanding to grasp entire.

(ii) From 1981. Having rethought in his own terms each of the four standard voice-types in his trilogy of vocal works, Carter has turned since 1981 to new challenges in the purely instrumental sphere. As its title suggests, the *Triple Duo* (1982–3) splits its instrumentation by family into three pairs. But the commission (from the Fires of London) also specified that the work be performable without conductor, thus compelling Carter for once to relate his cross-tempos to a common pulse. His solution was to couch the argument of his flute/clarinet duo in rhythmic threes as against the fours of the violin/cello duo and the fives of the piano and percussion. As if in defiance of this apparent compromise, the beginning and end of the piece sound deceptively the most random of any of his works, while much of the intervening dialectic is conducted with the high spirits of a divertimento.

Penthode (1984–5), commissioned for the Ensemble Intercontemporain, is by contrast not only Carter's longest large-ensemble score since the 1960s but also his most elaborate study in multiple structure: its 20 players are divided into five quartets of mixed family (one quartet consists of trumpet, trombone, harp, and violin, another of flute, horn, marimba, and double bass, and so on), and an ever evolving melodic line is passed continuously among the quartets. Yet the viola solo which gradually summons the five groups into being at the outset seems also to relate, in its improvisatory style, to four short pieces completed between the *Triple Duo* and *Penthode*. The shortness is material: Carter appears deliberately to have set himself the task of concentrating some of his procedures into tighter time-spans. Certainly the cross-cutting of material and mood in *Changes* (1983) for solo guitar creates the sense of a microcosm of his larger works, just as its harmonic structure of intervallic permutations around a sequence of nodes (suggested by change-ringing) is a distillation of his more elaborate pitch schemes – to all of which *Riconoscenza* for solo violin (1984) sounds like a still shorter, purer double. By contrast, the bubblings of the flute and clarinet duet, *Esprit rude/esprit doux* ("Rough breathing/smooth breathing," 1984), compound more the effect of a single layer of one of Carter's multiple structures, for once extracted and exhibited for itself, while the *Canon for 4* (1984) is a masterly re-animation in his current manner of a strict contrapuntal procedure – canon by simultaneous inversion, retrograde, and retrograde inversion – which he essayed long before in the second movement of the *Canonic Suite*. That these short pieces in no way imply a slackening of Carter's grasp is confirmed not only by the scale of *Penthode* but by his contemplation, in 1985, of three further large commissions (a fourth string quartet, a violin concerto, and a work for symphony orchestra).

Carter's mature output reveals an enterprise somewhat at variance with most of his contemporaries, for the major achievements of Copland, Shostakovich, Dallapiccola, Lutosławski, Britten, and Tippett have been principally expressions of personal sensibility rather than attempts to expand the language. His aim to complement the innovations of the earlier modern masters in the handling of pitch (Schoenberg), rhythm (Stravinsky), and texture (Varèse) with parallel developments in the domain of timing, through the large-scale integration of tempo relationships and harmonic backgrounds, can be compared, in his own generation, only with that of Messiaen. But where Messiaen has amplified the static Debussian hierarchies, excelling in color and decoration, Carter is all dialectic and movement, displaying a grasp of dynamic form comparable, among 20th-century composers, only with Berg. The result is music of genuine difficulty, not only because of the complexities created, for instance, by cross-tempos, but also, as Rosen has pointed out, because of the way these banish coordinating strong beats. There was a period, in the 1950s and 1960s, when Carter's one arguable weakness – the packing of his scenarios with incident to the detriment of dramatic economy – seemed a real stumbling block for orchestras. But younger generations of virtuoso soloists and ensemble players have proved ever more eager to tackle, and quick to master, the unique challenges of each new Carter piece as it appears.

See also ORCHESTRAL MUSIC, §4.

WORKS

STAGE

Philoctetes (incidental music, Sophocles), T, Bar, male chorus, ob, perc, 1931, unpubd; Cambridge, MA, 15 March 1933

Mostellaria (incidental music, Plautus), T, Bar, male chorus, chamber orch, 1936, unpubd; Cambridge, MA, 15 April 1936
Pocahontas (ballet legend, 1), pf, 1936, Keene, NH, 17 Aug 1936, withdrawn, orch version, 1938–9; New York, 24 May 1939, cond. F. Kitzinger
Much Ado about Nothing (incidental music, Shakespeare), 1937, withdrawn
The Minotaur (ballet), 1947; New York, 26 March 1947, cond. L. Barzin

ORCHESTRAL

Symphony, 1937, withdrawn
The Ball Room Guide (ballet suite), 1937, inc., withdrawn [Polka used in Prelude, Fanfare and Polka]
English Horn Concerto, 1937, inc., withdrawn
Prelude, Fanfare and Polka, small orch, 1938, unpubd
Suite, from Pocahontas, 1939, rev. 1960
Symphony no.1, 1942, rev. 1954; Rochester, NY, 27 April 1944, cond. H. Hanson
Holiday Overture, 1944, rev. 1961; Frankfurt am Main, Germany, 1946, cond. H. Blümer
Suite, from The Minotaur, 1947
Elegy, str, 1952 [arr. of Elegy, vc, pf]; New York, 1 March 1953, cond. D. Broekman
Variations for Orchestra, 1954–5; Louisville, 21 April 1956, cond. R. Whitney
Double Concerto, hpd, pf, 2 chamber orch, 1961; New York, 6 Sept 1961, cond. G. Meier
Piano Concerto, 1964–5; Boston, 6 Jan 1967, cond. Leinsdorf
Concerto for Orchestra, 1968–9; New York, 5 Feb 1970, cond. Bernstein
A Symphony of Three Orchestras, 1976; New York, 17 Feb 1977, cond. Boulez
Penthode, 5 inst qts, 1984–5; London, 26 July 1985, cond. Boulez

CHORAL

Tom and Lily (comic opera, 1), 4 solo vv, mixed chorus, chamber orch, 1934, withdrawn
Tarantella (Ovid), male chorus, pf 4 hands/orch, 1936; orch version, unpubd [from incidental music to Mostellaria]
The Bridge (oratorio, H. Crane), 1937, inc.
Harvest Home (Herrick), unacc., 1937, unpubd; New York, spr. 1938
Let's be Gay (J. Gay), female chorus, 2 pf, 1937, unpubd; Wells College, spr. 1938
To Music (Herrick), unacc., 1937; New York, spr. 1938
12 madrigals, 3–8vv, 1937, most withdrawn [incl. To Music]
Heart not so heavy as mine (Dickinson), unacc., 1938; New York, 31 March 1939
The Defense of Corinth (Rabelais), speaker, male vv, pf 4 hands, 1941; Cambridge, MA, 12 March 1942
The Harmony of Morning (M. Van Doren), female vv, small orch, 1944; New York, 25 Feb 1945
Musicians Wrestle Everywhere (Dickinson), mixed vv, str ad lib, 1945; New York, 12 Feb 1946
Emblems (A. Tate), male vv, pf, 1947, perf. 1952

SOLO VOCAL

My Love is in a Light Attire (Joyce), 1v, pf, 1928, unpubd; other Joyce settings, late 1920s, lost
Tell me where is fancy bred? (Shakespeare), A, gui, 1938
Three Poems of Robert Frost, Mez/Bar, pf, 1943: Dust of Snow, The Rose Family, The Line Gang; arr. S/T, chamber orch, 1975
Warble for Lilac-Time (Whitman), S/T, pf/small orch, 1943, rev. 1954; Saratoga Springs, NY, 14 Sept 1946
Voyage (H. Crane), Mez/Bar, pf, 1943; New York, 16 March 1947; arr. with small orch, 1975, rev. 1979
The Difference (Van Doren), S, Bar, pf, 1944, unpubd
A Mirror on which to Dwell (E. Bishop), S, fl + pic + a fl, ob + eng hn, cl + E♭ cl + b cl, perc, pf, vn, va, vc, db, 1975: Anaphora, Argument, Sandpiper, Insomnia, A View of the Capitol, O Breath; New York, 24 Feb 1976
Syringa (J. Ashbery, Ancient Gk.), Mez, B, 11 players, 1978; New York, 10 Dec 1978
In Sleep, in Thunder (R. Lowell), T, 14 players, 1981: Dolphin, Across the Yard: La Ignota, Harriet, Dies irae, Careless Night, In Genesis; London, 27 Oct 1982

CHAMBER AND INSTRUMENTAL

Piano Sonata, late 1920s, withdrawn
3 string quartets, ?*c*1928, 1935, 1937, withdrawn
Sonata, fl, pf, 1934, withdrawn
Musical Studies, *c*1938; nos.1–3 rev. as Canonic Suite; no.4, Andante espressivo, withdrawn
Canonic Suite, 4 a sax, 1939; rev. for 4 cl, 1955–6; rev. for 4 sax, 1981
Pastoral, eng hn/va/cl, pf, 1940
Elegy, vc, pf, 1943; arr. str qt, 1946, arr. str orch, 1952, arr. va, pf, 1961
Piano Sonata, 1945–6; New York, broadcast 16 Feb 1947
Woodwind Quintet, 1948; New York, 21 Feb 1949
Sonata, vc, pf, 1948; New York, 27 Feb 1950
Eight Etudes and a Fantasy, fl, ob, cl, bn, 1949–50; New York, 28 Oct 1952
Eight Pieces for Four Timpani, 1 player, 1950–66
String Quartet no.1, 1950–51; New York, 26 Feb 1953
Sonata, fl, ob, vc, hpd, 1952; New York, 19 Nov 1953
String Quartet no.2, 1959; New York, 25 March 1960
String Quartet no.3, 1971; New York, 23 Jan 1973
Canon for 3: in memoriam Igor Stravinsky, 3 equal insts, 1971; New York, 23 Jan 1972
Duo, vn, pf, 1973–4; New York, 21 March 1975
Brass Quintet, 2 tpt, hn, 2 trbn, 1974; London, broadcast 20 Oct 1974
A Fantasy about Purcell's "Fantasia Upon One Note," 2 tpt, hn, 2 trbn, 1974; New York, 13 Jan 1975
Birthday Fanfare for Sir William Glock's 70th, 3 tpt, vib, glock, 1978, unpubd; London, 3 May 1978
Night Fantasies, pf, 1980; Bath, England, 2 June 1980
Triple Duo, vn, vc, fl, cl, pf, perc, 1982–3; New York, 23 April 1983
Changes, gui, 1983; New York, 11 Dec 1983
Canon for 4, Homage to William [Glock], fl, b cl, vn, vc, 1984; Bath, England, 8 June 1984
Esprit rude/esprit doux, fl, cl, 1984, ded. Boulez; Baden-Baden, Germany, 31 March 1985
Riconoscenza per Goffredo Petrassi, vn, 1984; Pontino, nr Rome, 15 June 1984

Principal publishers: Associated, Boosey & Hawkes

BIBLIOGRAPHY

P. Rosenfeld: "The Newest American Composers," *MM*, xv (1937–8), 157
R. F. Goldman: "Current Chronicle," *MQ*, xxxvii (1951), 83
A. Skulsky: "Elliott Carter (Study of his works)," *ACAB*, iii/2 (1953), 2
W. Glock: "A Note on Elliott Carter," *Score* (1955), no.12, p.47
R. F. Goldman: "The Music of Elliott Carter," *MQ*, xliii (1957), 151
Compositores de América/Composers of the Americas, ed. Pan American Union, v (Washington, DC, 1959)
H. Koegler: "Begegnungen mit Elliott Carter," *Melos*, xxvi (1959), 256
A. Copland: "America's Young Men of Music," *Music and Musicians*, ix/4 (1960), 11
O. Daniel: "Carter and Shapero," *Saturday Review*, xliii (17 Dec 1960), 11
R. F. Goldman: "Current Chronicle: New York," *MQ*, xlvi (1960), 361
"Carter, Elliott (Cook)," *CBY 1960*
M. Steinberg: "Elliott Carters 2. Streichquartett," *Melos*, xxviii (1961), 35
K. Stone: "Problems and Methods of Notation," *PNM*, i/2 (1963), 9
I. Stravinsky and R. Craft: *Dialogues and a Diary* (New York, 1963), 47ff
C. Wuorinen: "The Outlook of Young Composers," *PNM*, i/2 (1963), 58
M. Boykan: "Elliott Carter and Postwar Composers," *PNM*, ii/2 (1964), 125
R. Henderson: "Elliot Carter," *Music and Musicians*, xiv/5 (1966), 20
D. Hamilton: "New Craft of the Contemporary Concerto: Carter and Sessions," *HiFi*, xviii/5 (1968), 67
R. Kostelanetz: "The Astounding Success of Elliott Carter," *HiFi*, xviii/5 (1968), 41
R. Kostelanetz: *Master Minds: Portraits of Contemporary American Artists and Intellectuals* (New York, 1969), 289ff
K. Stone: "Current Chronicle: New York," *MQ*, lv (1969), 559
B. Boretz: "Conversation with Elliott Carter," *PNM*, viii/2 (1970), 1
A. Edwards: *Flawed Words and Stubborn Sounds: a Conversation with Elliott Carter* (New York, 1971)
R. Hurwitz: "Elliott Carter: the Communication of Time," *Changes in the Arts*, no.78 (1972), 10
B. Northcott: "Elliott Carter: Continuity and Coherence," *Music and Musicians*, xx/12 (1972), 28
N. Rorem: "Elliott Carter," *New Republic*, clxvi (26 Feb 1972), 22
R. Jackson, ed.: *Elliott Carter: Sketches and Scores in Manuscript* (New York, 1973)
A. Porter: "Mutual Ordering," *New Yorker*, xlviii (3 Feb 1973), 82 [on String Quartet no.3]
C. Rosen: "One Easy Piece," *New York Review of Books*, xx/2 (1973), 25; repr. in Rosen, 1984 [on Double Conc.]
R. Morgan: "Elliott Carter's String Quartets," *Musical Newsletter*, iv/3 (1974), 3
A. Whittall: "Elliott Carter," *1st American Music Conference: Keele 1975*, ed. P. Dickinson (Keele, England, n.d. [?1977]), 82
J. F. Weber: *Carter and Schuman*, Discography Series, xix (Utica, NY, 1978)

A. Clements: "Elliott Carter Views American Music," *Music and Musicians*, xxvi/7 (1978), 32 [review of *The Writings of Elliott Carter*]
M. Mayer: "Elliott Carter: Out of the Desert and into the Concert Hall," *New York Times* (10 Dec 1978)
B. Northcott: "America's Magna Carter," *Sunday Telegraph* (London, 17 Dec 1978)
——: "Carter in Perspective," *MT*, cxix (1978), 1039
Elliott Carter: a 70th Birthday Tribute (London, 1978) [incl. contributions by P. Boulez, P. Fromm, W. Glock, B. Northcott, R. Ponsonby]
M. Steinberg: "Elliott Carter: an American Original at Seventy," *Keynote*, ii/10 (1978), 8
A. Whittall: "The Writings of Elliott Carter," *Tempo*, no.124 (1978), 40
B. Northcott: "Carter's 'Syringa'," *Tempo*, no.128 (1979), 31
A. Porter: "Famous Orpheus," *New Yorker*, liv (8 Jan 1979), 56 [on Syringa]
D. Schiff: "Carter in the Seventies," *Tempo*, no.130 (1979), 2
L. Kerner: "Creators on Creating: Elliott Carter," *Saturday Review*, vii/12 (1980), 38
H. Gleason and W. Becker: "Elliott Carter," *20th-century American Composers*, Music Literature Outlines, ser. iv (Bloomington, IN, rev. 2/1981), 20 [incl. further bibliography]
A. Porter: "Music in the Silence of the Night," *New Yorker*, lvii (30 Nov 1981), 184
C. Gagne and T. Caras: "Elliott Carter," *Soundpieces: Interviews with American Composers* (Metuchen, NJ, 1982), 87 [on Night Fantasies]
D. Schiff: "'In Sleep, in Thunder': Elliott Carter's Portrait of Robert Lowell," *Tempo*, no.142 (1982), 2
J. Bernard: "Spacial Sets in Recent Music of Elliott Carter," *Music Analysis*, ii/1 (1983), 5
W. Crutchfield: "Paul Jacobs Talks about Carter and Messiaen," *Keynote*, vii/10 (1983), 18
D. Schiff: *The Music of Elliott Carter* (New York, 1983)
J. Rockwell: "American Intellectual Composers & the 'Ideal Public'," *All American Music: Composition in the Late Twentieth Century* (New York, 1983), 37
M. M. Coonrod: *Aspects of Form in Selected String Quartets of the Twentieth-century* (diss., Peabody Conservatory, 1984) [on String Quartet no.3]
R. M. Meckna: *The Rise of the American Composer-Critic: Aaron Copland, Roger Sessions, Virgil Thomson, and Elliott Carter in the Periodical "Modern Music," 1924–1946* (diss., U. of California, Santa Barbara, 1984)
B. Northcott: "Fascinatin' Modulation," *New York Review of Books*, xxxi/9 (1984), 18
W. C. Pflugradt: *Elliott Carter and the Variation Process* (diss., Indiana U., 1984)
C. Rosen: *The Musical Languages of Elliott Carter* (Washington, DC, 1984) [incl. interview and M. Cundiff: "A Guide to Elliott Carter Research Materials at the Library of Congress Music Division"]

BAYAN NORTHCOTT

Carter, Ron(ald Levin) (*b* Ferndale, MI, 4 May 1937). Jazz double bass player. He began to play cello at the age of ten. Four years later his family moved to Detroit where, encountering barriers to his career as a cellist owing to his race, he changed to double bass in 1954. His interest in jazz developed only gradually. He played in the Philharmonia Orchestra of the Eastman School of Music, where he gained the BM in 1959. On arriving in New York after graduating, he joined the Chico Hamilton quintet (with Eric Dolphy) and enrolled at the Manhattan School (MM 1961). He played as a freelance musician with Cannonball Adderley, Randy Weston, Thelonious Monk, Bobby Timmons, and others, before joining Miles Davis's quintet in 1963. He remained with Davis until 1968, participating in all his recordings and forming, with pianist Herbie Hancock and drummer Tony Williams, an essential part of Davis's innovative rhythm section. Carter soon became, and has remained, one of the most prolifically recorded double bass players, making hundreds of albums with scores of jazz and soul artists. His most notable associations after Davis were with the New York Jazz Quartet (from 1972), V.S.O.P. (1976–7), the Milestone Jazz Stars (1978), and his own quartet (from 1975), in which he plays melodies on piccolo bass. Carter has also published a method for jazz bass playing, *Building a Jazz Bass Line* (1966, 2/1970).

RECORDINGS
(selective list)

As leader: *All Blues* (1973, CTI 6037); *Piccolo* (1977, Mlst. 55004); *Peg Leg* (1977, Mlst. 9082)
As sideman: M. Davis: *E.S.P.* (1965, Col. CS9150); H. Hancock: *Maiden Voyage* (1965, BN 84195); W. Montgomery: *A Day in the Life* (1967–8, A&M 3001); A. Franklin: *Soul '69* (1969, Atl. 8212); New York Jazz Quartet: *Concert in Japan* (1975, Salvation 703); H. Hancock: *V.S.O.P.* (1976, Col. PG34688); *Milestone Jazz Stars in Concert* (1978, Mlst. 55006)

BIBLIOGRAPHY

D. Heckman: "Ron Carter," *Down Beat*, xxxi/9 (1964), 18
"Ron Carter," *Swing Journal*, xxix/7 (1975), 42 [discography]
E. Williams: "Ron Carter," *Down Beat*, xlv (1978), no.2, p.12; no.3, p.20
M. Hinton: "New Giant of the Bass," *Jazz Magazine*, ii/2 (1978), 46
C. Albertson: "Ron Carter," *Stereo Review*, xl/6 (1978), 78
S. Stephens: *Ron Carter Bass Lines* (New Albany, IN, 1983) [9 transcrs.]

BARRY KERNFELD

Carter, Shirley. *See* VERRETT, SHIRLEY.

Carter Family. Country-music group. Its members were Alvin Pleasant Carter (*b* Maces Spring, VA, 15 Dec 1891; *d* Maces Spring, 7 Nov 1960), his wife Sara Dougherty Carter (*b* Flat Woods, VA, 21 July 1898; *d* Lodi, CA, 8 Jan 1979), and his sister-in-law Maybelle Addington Carter (*b* nr Nickelsville, Scott Co., VA, 10 May 1909; *d* Madison, TN, 23 Oct 1978). They lived in Maces Spring, in the Clinch Mountains of Virginia, and made their first recordings in August 1927 for the Victor label; they later signed a contract with the American Record Company, with Columbia, and with Decca. By 1943 they had recorded more than 300 sides, but after that year they did not perform together (though A. P. Carter and his children, Janette and Joe, made a few recordings before his death). Maybelle Carter (later known as "Mother" Maybelle) continued performing on the "Grand

The Carter Family: Maybelle (guitar), Alvin Pleasant, and Sara (autoharp)

Ole Opry" with her children Helen (*b* 1927), June (*b* 1929), and Anita (*b* 1933) Carter; June Carter married JOHNNY CASH, and the four women performed on his road and television shows. June's daughter from an earlier marriage, Carlene, began her career singing with her grandmother, but then moved to London and became a rock singer.

The Carter Family became the most influential and widely popular country-music singing group in the USA. Their instrumental style, usually consisting only of Maybelle's melodic line on the guitar underscored by autoharp chords played by Sara, was immediately recognizable and, like their three-part singing, was widely copied. They built up an exceedingly large repertory of Anglo-American folksongs, religious material, and sentimental parlor songs; numerous country-music songs still performed (e.g., *Wildwood Flower*, *I'm thinking tonight of my blue eyes*, and *Jimmie Brown the Newsboy*) are referred to as "Carter Family songs." Their influence extended to urban youth who learned their songs second- or third-hand, particularly during the folk revival of the late 1950s and early 1960s, when the Carter repertory was used by such singers as Joan Baez and Jack Elliott. The original members of the Carter Family group were elected to the Country Music Hall of Fame in 1970.

See also GOSPEL MUSIC, §I, 3.

BIBLIOGRAPHY

B. C. Malone: *Country Music U.S.A.: a Fifty-year History* (Austin, 1968, 2/1985)
E. Kahn: *The Carter Family: a Reflection of Changes in Society* (diss., U. of California, Los Angeles, 1970)
J. Atkins: *The Carter Family* (London, 1973)
——: "The Carter Family," *Stars of Country Music*, ed. B. C. Malone and J. McCulloh (Urbana, IL, 1975), 95
T. Russell: liner notes, *The Carter Family* (TL CW–06, 1982)

BILL C. MALONE/R

Caruso, Enrico (*b* Naples, Italy, 27 Feb 1873; *d* Naples, 2 Aug 1921). Italian tenor. He studied with Guglielmo Vergine and made his début in Mario Morelli's *L'amico francesco* in Naples in 1894. He took further lessons from the conductor Vincenzo Lombardi while continuing to sing locally, and achieved his first real success in Ponchielli's *La Gioconda* at Palermo in 1897. During the next few years he laid the foundations of his career with engagements in Milan (which included the world premières of Francesco Cilea's *L'arlesiana* in 1897 and *Adriana Lecouvreur* in 1902), Buenos Aires, and Rome. Following a relatively unsuccessful appearance as Alfredo in *La bohème* at La Scala during the 1900–01 season, he triumphed there shortly afterwards in Donizetti's *L'elisir d'amore*.

Caruso made his Covent Garden début in 1902 as the Duke in *Rigoletto* and sang the same role again in his first appearance at the Metropolitan Opera on 23 November the following year (see illustration). Over the next decade he performed periodically at the Metropolitan, and in 1910 he created the role of Dick Johnson in Puccini's *La fanciulla del West*. From 1912 he sang with the company continuously, appearing in many of the great tenor roles in the Italian repertory – Canio (*Pagliacci*), Puccini's Rodolfo (*La bohème*), Cavaradossi (*Tosca*), and Verdi's Radames, Alfredo, and Riccardo (*Un ballo in maschera*); he repeated Dick Johnson in 1911 at the only appearance he made with the Chicago Grand Opera Company. He sang in a number of other American cities on tours with the Metropolitan and in concert (he was in San Francisco at the time of the 1906 earthquake). Caruso continued to make guest appearances in Europe, but sang in Italy on only two further occasions, both benefit engagements. He

Enrico Caruso as the Duke of Mantua in Verdi's "Rigoletto"

gave his last public performance at the Metropolitan on 24 December 1920, as Eléazar in Halévy's *La juive*. He died of pleurisy the following summer.

In his early years, before he achieved security in his high notes, Caruso's dark tone gave rise to ambiguities, and he was often regarded almost as a baritone. The exceptional appeal of his voice was, in fact, based on the fusion of a baritone's full, burnished timbre with a tenor's smooth, silken finish, by turns brilliant and affecting. The clarion brightness of his high notes, the steadiness of the sound, his exceptional breath control, and his impeccable intonation combined to form a unique vocal instrument. These qualities enabled him to sing the French and Italian lyric repertory (particularly Gounod's *Faust*, Bizet's *Les pêcheurs de perles*, Massenet's *Manon*, and Puccini's *Manon Lescaut*, *La bohème*, and *Tosca*), as well as lighter operas from the 19th century, such as *L'elisir d'amore* and Friedrich Flotow's *Martha*. His noble and incisive declamation, his broad, high-mettled phrasing, and his vigor in dramatic outbursts made him a notable interpreter of Verdi and *grand opéra*. In this repertory, too, his performances were characterized by the irresistible erotic appeal of his timbre. But the legend of Caruso, considered the greatest tenor of the century, was also due to a temperament as warm and vehement as his voice. He made numerous recordings in the USA, beginning as early as 1902, which made him universally famous.

For a drawing by Caruso, *see* GRUENBERG, LOUIS.

BIBLIOGRAPHY

M. H. Flint: *Caruso and his Art* (New York, 1917)
S. Fucito and B. J. Beyer: *Caruso and the Art of Singing* (New York, 1922)
P. V. R. Key and B. Zirato: *Enrico Caruso: a Biography* (Boston, 1922/*R*1972)
P. M. Marafioti: *Caruso's Method of Voice Production* (New York, 1922/*R*1981)
D. Caruso: *Wings of Song: the Story of Caruso* (London, 1928)
——: *Enrico Caruso: his Life and Death* (New York, 1945)

H. Steen: *Caruso: eine Stimme erobert die Welt* (Essen, Germany, 1946)
E. Gara: *Caruso: storia di un emigrante* (Milan, 1947/*R*1973)
T. R. Ybarra: *Caruso: the Man of Naples and the Voice of Gold* (New York, 1953)
F. Robinson: *Caruso: his Life in Pictures* (New York, 1957)
J. Freestone and H. J. Drummond: *Enrico Caruso: his Recorded Legacy* (Minneapolis, 1961)
A. Favia-Artsay: *Caruso on Records* (Valhalla, NY, 1965)
J. P. Mouchon: *Enrico Caruso: sa vie et sa voix* (Langres, France, 1966; Eng. trans., Gap, France, 1974)
H. Pleasants: "Enrico Caruso," *The Great Singers* (New York, 1966), 292
S. Jackson: *Caruso* (New York, 1972)
"A Century of Caruso," *Opera News*, xxxvii/16 (1973) [Caruso issue]
J. R. Bolig: *The Recordings of Enrico Caruso* (Dover, DE, 1975)
Caruso's Caricatures (New York, 1977)
B. Kellner: "All in his Voice," *Opera News*, xlv/1 (1980), 17
G. R. Marek: "Beneficent Ghost," *Opera News*, xlvi/2 (1981), 22
H. Greenfeld: *Caruso* (New York, 1983)

RODOLFO CELLETTI/R

Carvalho, Eleazar (de) (*b* Iguatu, Brazil, 28 July 1912). Brazilian conductor and composer. He played tuba and double bass in the band of the Brazilian Navy and graduated from the National School of Music in 1934. From 1930 to 1940 he played tuba in the orchestra of the Teatro Municipal in Rio de Janeiro; in 1941 he was appointed assistant conductor and thereafter conductor of the Brazilian SO, of which he was named Conductor for Life in 1965. Carvalho came to the USA in 1946 to study with Koussevitzky, who invited him to conduct the Boston SO in 1947. After guest conducting in the USA and Europe he became music director of the St. Louis SO in 1963 and its conductor emeritus in 1968. He served as conductor of the Pro Arte SO at Hofstra University, Hempstead, New York, from 1968 to 1973; in that year he returned to Brazil where he was appointed music director of the Orquestra Sinfônica Estadual in São Paulo. In 1983 he taught at the Juilliard School. Carvalho has conducted opera and is a notable interpreter of contemporary music. He is a champion of the works of the Second Viennese School, and these have influenced his own compositions, which include operatic, symphonic, instrumental, and vocal works, and at times incline to the post-Romantic grandeur of Mahler. He married the Brazilian pianist and composer Jocy de Oliveira.

BIBLIOGRAPHY

"Kousssevitzky's Grandchildren," *HiFi/MusAm*, xxviii/10 (1978), 88

SORAB MODI

Cary, Annie Louise (*b* Wayne, ME, 22 Oct 1841; *d* Norwalk, CT, 3 April 1921). Contralto. She studied in Boston with J. Q. Wetherbee and Lyman Wheeler, and from 1866 in Milan with Giovanni Corsi. She made her operatic début in Copenhagen as Azucena (*Il trovatore*) in 1867 and studied with Pauline Viardot at Baden-Baden between operatic engagements in Scandinavia. After further engagements, in Hamburg, Stockholm, Brussels, and London, she was brought to the USA in August 1870 by the impresario Max Strakosch. She made her début in a joint recital at Steinway Hall, New York, on 19 September 1870. Highlights of the next five seasons in the USA were her appearances with Theodore Thomas's orchestra at his first Cincinnati May Festival (1873) and her Amneris in the American première of *Aida* in New York (Academy of Music, 28 November 1873). After further tours and engagements in Europe and Russia (1875–7), she returned to the USA and toured with Thomas's orchestra. Cary became the first American woman to sing a Wagnerian role in the USA (Ortrud in *Lohengrin*, 1877). She joined Clara Louise Kellogg's English Opera Company for a few seasons, toured with J. H. Mapleson's Company (1880–82), and was successful in concert and oratorio in all the leading cities of the USA. After her marriage to Charles Monson Raymond in 1882, she retired from singing and spent the remainder of her life chiefly in New York and Norwalk, Connecticut.

BIBLIOGRAPHY

Obituaries: *Boston Transcript* (4 April 1921); *New York Times* (4 April 1921); *New York Times* (10 April 1921)
G. T. Edwards: *Music and Musicians of Maine* (Portland, 1928/*R*1970), 204
P. Key: "Cary, Annie Louise," *DAB*
O. Thompson: "Annie Louise Cary," *The American Singer* (New York, 1937/*R*1969), 79
H. E. Johnson: "Cary, Annie Louise," *NAW*

DEE BAILY

Cary, Mary Flagler (*b* New York, 15 Sept 1901; *d* New York, 27 Dec 1967). Philanthropist. She was from childhood closely involved with the intellectual and cultural life of New York. Her father, Harry Harkness Flagler, was president of the New York Symphony Society and its successor, the Philharmonic-Symphony Society of New York, and many well-known composers, conductors, and concert artists were friends of the family. She acquired an important collection of music manuscripts, subsequently given by the Mary Flagler Cary Charitable Trust to the Pierpont Morgan Library in New York. A skilled musician herself, she helped in 1930 to found the National Orchestral Association, a training orchestra for young players, of which she was president and principal financial sponsor until her death. The Trust, set up in 1968 under the terms of her will, provides continuing support for the association and also assists other music training and performing institutions in New York.

ELLEN HIGHSTEIN

Caryll, Ivan [Tilkin, Félix] (*b* Liège, Belgium, 12 May 1861; *d* New York, 29 Nov 1921). Composer and conductor. He studied at the Liège Conservatory, then in Paris, and in 1882 settled in London, where he became a piano teacher. His first stage score was produced there in 1886. He was appointed conductor at the Lyric Theatre, where he enjoyed his first big success with *Little Christopher Columbus* (1893), and at the Gaiety Theatre, for which he wrote, with Lionel Monckton, a number of highly successful musical comedies between 1894 and 1909. In all he composed about 40 light operas and musical comedies for London, Europe, and the USA (*The Ladies' Paradise*, 1901, was the first musical comedy to be presented at the Metropolitan Opera). In 1899 he became conductor of a light orchestra bearing his name; Elgar composed his *Sérénade lyrique* (1899) for it. In 1910 Caryll moved to the USA, eventually becoming a naturalized American. Most of his later works were first produced here, though he continued to divide his time between the USA, England, and France, and based many of his works on French sources. He died after collapsing during rehearsals for *The Hotel Mouse* (also known as *Little Miss Raffles*).

Caryll was an extravagant character, elegantly dressed, and with a magnificent forked beard. He was a prolific composer of lilting and undemanding music who, as fashions changed, adapted his musical style at will to embrace European operetta, Victorian balladry, American plantation songs, Edwardian musical comedy, and ragtime-inspired foxtrots. However, his sympathies probably lay with the expansiveness of 19th-century European operetta rather than the more direct 20th-century American styles. Although he was successful in writing musical comedy songs, including "Goodbye girls, I'm through" (*Chin-Chin*, 1914) and "Wait till the cows come home" (*Jack o'Lantern*, 1917), his most popular piece is the waltz from *The Pink Lady* (1911).

WORKS
(selective list)

STAGE

Only those first produced in the USA; all dates are those of first New York performance and, unless otherwise stated, works were published there in vocal score at the time of the first production.

Marriage à la carte (3, C. M. S. McLellan), Casino, 2 Jan 1911
The Pink Lady (The Satyr) (3, McLellan), New Amsterdam, 13 March 1911
Oh! Oh! Delphine (3, McLellan), Knickerbocker, 30 Sept 1912
The Little Café (3, McLellan), New Amsterdam, 10 Nov 1913
Chin-Chin (A. Caldwell, R. H. Burnside, J. O'Dea), Globe, 20 Oct 1914
Papa's Darling (H. B. Smith), New Amsterdam, 2 Nov 1914
Jack o'Lantern (Caldwell, Burnside), Globe, 16 Oct 1917
The Girl Behind the Gun (G. Bolton, P. G. Wodehouse), New Amsterdam, 16 Sept 1918, 11 nos. pubd in vs (1917); rev. as Kissing Time, London, 1919
The Canary (Smith, Wodehouse, Caldwell), Globe, 4 Nov 1918, 6 nos. pubd in vs (1918)
Tip Top (Caldwell, Burnside), Globe, 5 Oct 1920, 5 nos. pubd in vs (1920)
Kissing Time (G. V. Hobart, P. Johnson), Lyric, 11 Oct 1920, 8 nos. pubd in vs (1920) [not identifiable with rev. version of The Girl Behind the Gun]
The Hotel Mouse (Little Miss Raffles) (Bolton, C. Grey), Shubert, 13 March 1922, ?unpubd

OTHER WORKS

Many songs, dances, salon pieces

Principal publisher: Chappell

BIBLIOGRAPHY

Obituary, *MusAm*, xxv/7 (1921), 55
H. B. Smith: *First Nights and First Editions* (Boston, 1931)
C. Smith: *Musical Comedy in America* (New York, 1950, rev. 2/1981)
D. Ewen: *The Complete Book of the American Musical Theater* (New York, 1958, rev. 3/1970)
G. Hughes: *Composers of Operetta* (London, 1962)
G. Bordman: *American Musical Theatre: a Chronicle* (New York, 1978)
——: *American Operetta from H.M.S. Pinafore to Sweeney Todd* (New York, 1981)

ANDREW LAMB

Casa Loma Orchestra. Popular dance band. It was one of the first white swing bands to adopt a black big-band sound and to introduce this sound to a wide audience. The sophistication of the arrangements written for the band by GENE GIFFORD and the technical mastery of its ensemble playing made the Casa Loma a model for many later swing orchestras. It made its initial appearances in Detroit in 1927 as the Orange Blossoms, an offshoot of Jean Goldkette's band. It acquired several new members during the next three years, and was organized into a corporate ensemble with Glen Gray (Knoblaugh) as its president. In 1929 it appeared at the Roseland Ballroom in New York as the Casa Loma Orchestra and made its first recording with Okeh. The band experienced its greatest success during the years 1930 to 1935, recording for Brunswick, Victor, and Decca, scoring high on popularity polls, and attracting a large following, particularly among college audiences; in 1933–4 it appeared on the first radio series to broadcast a swing band. During the late 1930s its popularity waned, however, as original members began to leave and as new swing bands began to find favor with the public.

For illustration *see* POPULAR MUSIC, fig.6.

BIBLIOGRAPHY

M. Stearns: *The Story of Jazz* (New York, 1956)
G. Simon: *The Big Bands* (New York, 1967, rev. 3/1974)
A. McCarthy: *Big Band Jazz* (London, 1974)

RONALD M. RADANO

Casals, Pablo [Pau] (*b* Vendrell, Spain, 29 Dec 1876; *d* San Juan, Puerto Rico, 22 Oct 1973). Catalan cellist, conductor, pianist, and composer. The son of musical parents, he was accomplished on the piano, organ, and violin before first hearing a cello when he was 11. In 1887 he studied cello with José García at the Barcelona Municipal Music School, and piano and composition under José Rodoreda. Technical experiments with bowing and fingering early produced an individual style and unprecedented mastery. After his début at Barcelona on 23 February 1891, performances in cafés helped his finances; discovery of the Bach unaccompanied suites encouraged his serious approach to music and launched him on a lifetime's study. In 1893 the queen regent awarded him a scholarship to study at the Madrid Conservatory and in 1895 another for study at the Brussels Conservatory; a misunderstanding with his prospective cello teacher there led him to abandon the scholarship, however. In 1896 he returned to teach in Barcelona, becoming principal cellist at the Gran Teatro de Liceo; he joined a piano trio with the Belgian violinist Mathieu Crickboom and Enrique Granados, and later a string quartet led by Crickboom.

Casals made his international début in Paris in 1899 playing Edouard Lalo's concerto under Charles Lamoureux, and the event marked the beginning of his career as a soloist. Never a flamboyant performer, he sought tirelessly in practice and rehearsal for the truth and beauty he felt to be an artist's responsibility, and used his formidable powers with a simplicity and concentration that allowed no compromise. His playing was memorable as much for beauty of tone as intellectual strength. His artistry led to a new appreciation of the cello and its repertory; from 1905 he also set new standards in the piano trio repertory with Jacques Thibaud and Alfred Cortot; their ensemble gave historic performances on some of the earliest electrical recordings. Casals's international reputation, which had already reached its peak by 1914, was sustained during the 1920s by wide-ranging tours (which brought financial as well as artistic success).

In 1919 Casals founded the Orquestra Pau Casals in Barcelona; it became a body of players with which foremost soloists were proud to work. He conducted it until 1936 when, under threat of execution by the Franco regime, he moved to Prades, a Catalan village on the French side of the Spanish border. During World War II he gave many concerts in France in aid of the Red Cross and of his Catalan fellow exiles, and physically helped to distribute aid to these refugees. In 1945, having realized that no political moves would be taken against the Spanish regime, he stopped playing in public, but he ended his silence for the Bach bicentenary of 1950, when eminent musicians gathered at Prades to make music with him. In 1956 he settled finally in Puerto Rico.

Casals was extremely important to the development of musical life in Puerto Rico. The Festival Casals was established in 1957 with him as director; he was also instrumental in founding the Puerto Rico SO in 1958 (he conducted its first concert) and the Puerto Rico Conservatory, of which he became president when it opened in 1960. His third and final marriage was to the Puerto Rican cellist Marta Montañez in 1957. He resumed his international career, giving master classes in Siena, Italy, in Zermatt, Switzerland, and in Marlboro, Vermont, where he also performed as cellist and conductor. He played at the United Nations (1958) and to President Kennedy at the White House (1961), and launched a peace campaign with worldwide performances of his oratorio *El pessebre*. Of his own compositions, those dating from his time in Puerto Rico are mostly sacred or secular vocal works, traditional in style and simple in content, with no concessions to 20th-century developments.

BIBLIOGRAPHY

L. Littlehales: *Pablo Casals* (New York, 1929, rev. 2/1949) [with discography]
J. Alvin: "The Logic of Casals's Technique," *MT*, lxxi (1930), 1078
D. Cherniavsky: "Casals's Teaching of the Cello," *MT*, xciii (1952), 398
R. Gelatt: "Pablo Casals," *Music-makers* (New York, 1953), 149
J. M. Corredor: *Conversations avec Casals: souvenirs et opinions d'un musicien* (Paris, 1955; Eng. trans., 1956)
E. Christen: *Pablo Casals: l'homme, l'artiste* (Geneva, Switzerland, 1956)
P. Moeschlin and A. Seiler: *Casals* (Olten, Switzerland, 1956) [with discography]
M. Eisenberg: "Pablo Casals at Eighty: a Tribute," *Violins and Violinists*, xviii (1957), 4
J. García Borrás: *Pablo Casals, peregrino en América: tres semenanas con el maestro* (Mexico, 1957)
R. Montanez: "El significado del Festival Casals," *Artes y letras*, ii/5 (1957), 3
"Puerto Rico Toasts Casals," *Latin American Report*, i/12 (1957), 14
P. Casals: *Personal Statement to the Press . . . in Connection with his Acceptance to Participate in the United Nations Day Concert* (24 Oct 1958; repr. in Kirk, 506) [broadcast]
B. Taper: *Cellist in Exile: a Portrait of Pablo Casals* (New York, 1962)
J. Alavedra: *Pau Casals* (Barcelona, Spain, 1962; Sp. trans., 1963)
"Casals, Pablo," *CBY 1964*
A. Forsee: *Pablo Casals: Cellist for Freedom* (New York, 1965)
E. Vives de Fabregas: *Pau Casals* (Barcelona, 1966)
J. M. Corredor: *Casals: biografia ilustrada* (Barcelona, 1967)
P. Casals and A. E. Kahn: *Joys and Sorrows* (London, 1970)
A. Whitman: "Casals, the Master Cellist, Won Wide Acclaim in Career that Spanned 75 Years," *New York Times* (23 Oct 1973)
H. L. Kirk: *Pablo Casals: a Biography* (London, 1974) [with discography by T. N. Towe, and substantial but inc. list of works]
Hommage à Pablo Casals, Connaissance du Roussillon, iv (Paris, 1976)
D. Blum: *Casals and the Art of Interpretation* (London, 1977)

ROBERT ANDERSON/R

Case Western Reserve University. University founded in 1967 in CLEVELAND through the merger of Western Reserve University and the Case Institute of Technology.

Cash, Johnny [John R.] (*b* Kingsland, AR, 26 Feb 1932). Country-music singer and songwriter. He began recording country music in 1955 for the Sun label, accompanied by the Tennessee Two (electric guitarist Luther Perkins and bass player Marshall Grant). At that stage of his career he was one of a small group of singers influenced by rock-and-roll (others were Elvis Presley, Carl Perkins, and Jerry Lee Lewis) who were known as "rockabillies." He joined the "Louisiana Hayride" on radio station KWKH in Shreveport in 1955, and was a member of the "Grand Ole Opry" from 1956 to 1958. In 1958 he signed a new recording contract, with Columbia. Drummer Bill Holland joined Cash's band, henceforth known as the Tennessee Three, in 1960, and the group was extremely active on the concert and nightclub circuit. In the 1960s Cash had a successful road show whose personnel included the Statler Brothers (from 1964), the Carter Family (after Cash's marriage to June Carter in 1968), and Perkins. From 1969 to 1971 he was host of "The Johnny Cash Show" on ABC-TV, one of the first country-music programs to appear regularly on national television. Cash has become one of the best-known and most influential of country-music performers in the USA and Europe; his voice is a deeply resonant, relaxed baritone, and he often adopts a speech-song style. His repertory, one of the most eclectic in country music, includes rural, gospel, and popular songs; in the 1960s his texts often commented on the problems of American Indians, convicts, and impoverished rural southerners, and several, such as *The Ballad of Ira Hayes* (1964), were taken up as protest songs during the folksong revival of that period. He was elected to the Country Music Hall of Fame in 1980.

Johnny Cash, c1970, in the show "Grand Ole Opry," broadcast by WSM radio

RECORDINGS
(selective list)

With the Tennessee Two, all recorded for Sun: Hey porter/Cry, cry, cry (221, 1955); Folsom Prison Blues (232, 1955); I walk the line (241, 1956); Ballad of a Teenage Queen (283, 1958); Guess things happen that way (295, 1958)
As soloist, all recorded for Columbia: Don't take your guns to town (41313, 1958); I got stripes (41427, 1959); *Ride this Train* (CS8255, 1960); Ring of Fire (42788, 1963); Understand your man (42964, 1963); The Ballad of Ira Hayes (43058, 1964); *Johnny Cash at Folsom Prison* (CS9639, 1968); A Boy Named Sue (44944, 1969); Man in Black (45339, 1971); *Any Old Wind that Blows* (KC32091, 1973); *Ragged Old Flag* (32917, 1974); One piece at a time (10321, 1976); *The Rambler* (34833, 1977); *Gone Girl* (83323, 1978); Bull Rider (11237, 1980); Without Love (11424, 1981)

BIBLIOGRAPHY

J. L. Smith: *Johnny Cash Discography and Recording History, 1955–68*, John Edwards Memorial Foundation Special Series, ii (Los Angeles, 1969)
C. Wren: *Winners Got Scars Too: the Life and Legends of Johnny Cash* (New York, 1971)
J. Cash: *Man in Black* (Grand Rapids, MI, 1975) [autobiography]
F. Danker: "Johnny Cash," *Stars of Country Music*, ed. B. C. Malone and J. McCulloh (Urbana, IL, 1975), 289
——: Liner notes, *Johnny Cash* (TL CW03, 1982)
J. L. Smith: *The Johnny Cash Discography* (Westport, CT, 1985)

BILL C. MALONE

Cassel, (John) Walter (*b* Council Bluffs, IA, 15 May 1910). Baritone. In 1929 he was awarded first prize in singing and second prize in trumpet in the Iowa State Music Contest. He went to New York, where he studied with Frank La Forge, sang on several radio programs (including "Hammerstein Music Hall of the Air" and "Maxwell House Show Boat"), and made his début in 1942 as de Brétigny in Jules Massenet's *Manon* at the

Metropolitan Opera; he left the company in 1945, dissatisfied with its casting policy. He ventured into musical comedy with a long run in Romberg's *The Desert Song* and other productions, and continued to appear in opera with various companies, including those at Philadelphia, Pittsburgh, Cincinnati, New Orleans, and San Antonio. After World War II he went to Europe, where he sang at the Vienna Staatsoper and in Düsseldorf, Germany. He made his recital début in New York in 1948, appeared with the New York City Opera between 1948 and 1960, and in 1955 rejoined the Metropolitan, with which he remained until 1966. In 1956 he sang the role of Horace Tabor in the première of Douglas Moore's *The Ballad of Baby Doe* in Central City, Colorado, and in 1958 appeared as Petruchio in the New York City Opera's first production of Vittorio Giannini's *The Taming of the Shrew*. From 1970 to 1972 he sang the role of Johann Strauss, Sr., in a production of Korngold's *The Great Waltz* in London, then performed in Italy and Spain. In 1974 he began teaching at Indiana University, where in 1983 he sang the role of Horace Tabor. His well-modulated voice is suited to the works of Wagner (Frederick of Telramund in *Lohengrin*, the Dutchman in *Der fliegende Holländer*, Kurwenal in *Tristan und Isolde*) and Richard Strauss (Jokanaan in *Salome*, Orestes in *Elektra*, the Music Master in *Ariadne auf Naxos*).

BIBLIOGRAPHY

"Cassel, John Walter," *CBY 1943*

J. Ardoin: "Walter Cassel," *MusAm*, lxxix/12 (1959), 17

CHARLES JAHANT

Cassidy, Claudia (*b* Shawneetown, IL, 15 Nov 1899). Critic. She studied drama and journalism at the University of Illinois (BA 1921), and music privately. She wrote music, drama, and dance criticism for the *Chicago Journal of Commerce* (1925–41), the *Chicago Sun* (1941–2), and the *Chicago Tribune* (1942–65); she also appeared on a weekly radio program, "Critic's Choice," on the Chicago radio station WFMT, and contributed to *Chicago* magazine. Her criticism is for the most part unspecialized and oriented towards the performer; she wrote favorably of the work of such composers as Prokofiev, Hindemith, and Bartók early in their American careers. Much of her criticism is concerned with the Lyric Opera of Chicago and the Chicago SO; three of the orchestra's conductors – Kubelík, Jean Martinon, and Désiré Defauw – attributed their departures from Chicago to her unfavorable reviews. A collection of her reviews of European performances of the early 1950s was published as *Europe – on the Aisle* (1954).

See also CRITICISM, §4.

THOMAS WILLIS

Cassilly, Richard (*b* Washington, DC, 14 Dec 1927). Tenor. He studied at the Peabody Conservatory, and made his début as a concert singer in 1954. At the end of that year he sang in Menotti's *The Saint of Bleecker Street* on Broadway, and that led to his engagement with the New York City Opera as Vakula in Tchaikovsky's *Vakula the Smith*. In 1959 he appeared for the first time at the Chicago Lyric Opera, as Laca in *Jenůfa*. His European début was in the title role of Heinrich Sutermeister's *Raskolnikoff* at Geneva in 1965, the year he joined the Hamburg Staatsoper, where he made his début as Canio. His first appearance at Covent Garden was as Laca in 1968, and he returned to the house to sing Siegmund, Florestan, Othello, and a Tannhäuser particularly praised for its clear enunciation and total involvement in the character. In 1968 he sang Peter Grimes in a new production of Britten's opera for Scottish Opera at the Edinburgh Festival. In 1970 he made his débuts at the Vienna Staatsoper (Tannhäuser), Munich (Othello), and La Scala (Samson); in 1972 at the Paris Opéra (Siegmund); and in 1973 at the Metropolitan (Radames). In 1974 he sang Schoenberg's Aaron at Hamburg, and he has recorded the part under Boulez. He has in his repertory more than 55 roles, including most of the heroic tenor roles, and sings them with intelligence and intensity even if occasionally without perfect control. He was made a Hamburg *Kammersänger* in 1973.

ALAN BLYTH/R

Castaldo, Joseph (*b* New York, 23 Dec 1927). Music educator and composer. He began as a clarinetist and while stationed in Italy on military service studied at the Accademia di S. Cecilia, Rome (1947). On his return to the USA he continued his training at the Manhattan School with Giannini and then studied composition at the Philadelphia Conservatory with Persichetti. He received BM and MM degrees from the conservatory and joined its faculty, becoming chairman of the composition and theory department in 1960; when it merged with the Philadelphia Musical Academy he became president of the institution (its name was changed to the Philadelphia College of Performing Arts in 1976). He retired in 1983. Among his compositions are a cello concerto (1984), two string quartets, a woodwind quintet (*Dichotomy*), other chamber works including sonatas for piano, violin, and cello, a cantata (*Flight*, 1960), and choruses. His style was at first eclectic, showing the influence of Persichetti, but it became much more experimental in the late 1960s. Many of his later compositions, such as *Theoria* (1971, rev. 1972) for wind ensemble, piano, and percussion, and *Lacrimosa I* (1976) and *Lacrimosa II* (1977) for strings, are one-movement structures based on cumulative formal procedures and incorporating striking instrumental effects. His principal publishers are Peer-Southern and G. Schirmer.

PAUL C. ECHOLS

Castelnuovo-Tedesco, Mario (*b* Florence, Italy, 3 April 1895; *d* Beverly Hills, CA, 17 March 1968). Composer and pianist. He studied piano with Edoardo del Valle, then entered the Cherubini Conservatory in Florence where he received degrees in piano (at the age of 15) and composition (at 18), which he studied with Ildebrando Pizzetti. His earliest published work dates from 1909. Performances of his orchestral works were given by Vittorio Gui with the Augusteo Orchestra of Rome, by the Maggio Musicale Fiorentino, and by Toscanini with the Vienna PO. *I profeti* (Violin Concerto no.2) was first performed by Jascha Heifetz with the New York PO under Toscanini in 1933; the Cello Concerto by Piatigorsky with the same orchestra and conductor in 1935; and the Second Piano Concerto by the composer with Sir John Barbirolli and the New York PO in 1939. The political climate in Italy forced Castelnuovo and his family to immigrate, and assisted by Heifetz and Toscanini they came to the USA in 1939. After a year in Larchmont, New York, Castelnuovo settled in Beverly Hills, taking American citizenship in 1946.

Castelnuovo was a very prolific composer; major works written after he immigrated include the Concerto for Two Guitars (1962) and the overtures *A Midsummer Night's Dream* (1940) and *King John* (1941, commissioned for the centenary of the New York PO), two of a series of overtures for Shakespeare plays begun in

1930. His opera *The Merchant of Venice* won first prize in an international competition sponsored by La Scala in 1958. In Hollywood Castelnuovo composed numerous film scores (including those for *Gaslight*, *Ten Little Indians*, and *The Day of the Fox*); he also appeared frequently as a piano soloist and taught composition, mainly to composers of film scores. His response to the Tuscan landscapes of his upbringing, his affinity for Spanish music and culture, and his Jewish heritage have all influenced his compositions. His vocal music, in particular the songs, reveals a sensitive and expressive treatment of the voice. The American-period works are among the most frequently performed and Castelnuovo is perhaps best known for his many guitar solos, written mostly at the request of Andrés Segovia. His autobiography, *Una vita di musica*, remains unpublished.

WORKS

(only those composed in the USA; R – no. in Rossi, 1977)

DRAMATIC

Operas: The Merchant of Venice (Shakespeare), op. 181, 1956, Florence, Italy, 1961; All's Well that Ends Well (Shakespeare), op. 182, 1955–8, unperf.; Saul (V. Alfieri), op. 191, 1958–60, unperf.; The Importance of Being Earnest (chamber opera, Wilde), 8 solo vv, 2 pf, perc, 1961–2, Radio Italiana, 1972

Oratorios: The Book of Ruth, op. 140, 1949; Il libro di Giona, op. 151, 1951; The Song of Songs, op. 172, 1954–5; The Book of Esther, op. 200, 1962; Tobias and the Angel, op. 204, 1964–5

Ballets: The Birthday of the Infanta, op. 115, 1942, New Orleans, 1947; The Octoroon Ball (K. Dunham), op. 136, 1947

Film scores: Tortilla Flat, 1942; Dorian Gray, 1944; Gaslight, 1944; 10 Little Indians (And Then there were None), 1945; The Loves of Carmen, 1948; The Brave Bulls, 1950; The Mark of the Avenger, 1951; The Day of the Fox, 1956; 100 others, 1941–56

Other: Aucassin et Nicolette (chant-fable, 12th-century Fr., trans. Castelnuovo, Rossi), S, Bar, 10 insts, marionettes, op. 98, 1964 [rev. version, orig. composed 1919–38]; incidental music, incl. Morning in Iowa (R. Nathan), op. 158, 1952–3, Hollywood, 1964

ORCHESTRAL

Shakespeare ovs.: A Midsummer Night's Dream (Ov. to a Fairy Tale), op. 108, 1940; King John, op. 111, 1941; Anthony and Cleopatra, op. 134, 1947; The Tragedy of Coriolanus, op. 135, 1947; Much Ado about Nothing, op. 164, 1953; As You Like It, op. 166, 1953; also 4 dances for Love's Labour's Lost, op. 167, 1953

With solo insts: 2 gui concs., op. 99, 1939, op. 160, 1953; Vn Conc. no. 3, op. 102, 1939; Poem "Larchmont Woods," vn, orch, op. 112, 1942; Capriccio diabolico, gui, orch, op. 85b, 1945 [after op. 85, gui]; Serenade, op. 118, gui, orch, 1943; Capitan Fracassa [arr. op. 16, vn, pf, 1920], vn, orch, 1945; Conc. da camera, ob, 3 hn, timp ad lib, str, 1950; I nottambuli [arr. op. 47, vc, pf, 1927], vc, orch, 1960; Conc., 2 gui, orch, op. 201, 1962

Other works: Indian Songs and Dances, op. 116, 1942; An American Rhapsody, R117a, 1943; 5 Humoresques, op. 121 [on themes of Foster], 1943

CHORAL

A Lullaby (S. Foster), male/mixed chorus, orch, R119a, 1943; Sacred Service, Bar, chorus, org, op. 122, 1943, enlarged 1950; Kol nidrei, cantor, chorus, org, vc, R111b, 1944; Naomi and Ruth, cantata, female vv, pf/org, op. 137, 1947; Songs and Processions for a Jewish Wedding, chorus, org, op. 150, 1950; Romancero gitano (Lorca), mixed chorus, gui, op. 152, 1951; Naaritz'cho, cantor, chorus, org, R155a, 1952; The Queen of Sheba, cantata, female vv, pf, op. 161, 1953; Song of the Oceanides (Aeschylus), 2 female choruses, 2 fl, harp, op. 171, 1954; The Fiery Furnace, small cantata, Bar, children's vv, pf/org, perc, op. 183, 1958; Memorial Service for the Departed, cantor, chorus, org, op. 192, 1960; other works, 1939–60, esp. for female vv, pf

16 unacc. works, 1946–67

SOLO VOCAL

With insts: 6 Scottish Songs (Scott), S, T, harp, str, op. 100, 1939; The Princess and the Pea, miniature ov., nar, orch, op. 120, 1943; The Flood, nar, orch, R122c, 1944, for Genesis Suite, collab. Schoenberg, Stravinsky, and others; Song of the Shulamite (Bible), 1v, fl, harp, str qt, op. 163, 1953; 2 Schiller Balladen, nar, 2 pf, perc, op. 193, 1961; other vocal works with orch

Songs, 1v, pf: 28 Shakespeare Sonnets, 3 for chorus, op. 125, 1944–7, 4 more added 1963; 5 poesie romanesche (M. dell' Arco), op. 131, 1946; Il bestiario (A. Loria), op. 188, 1960; Poesie suedesi (trad.), op. 189, 1960

Songs, 1v, gui: Ballata dell'esilio (G. Cavalcanti), R180a, 1956; Vogelweide (W. von der Vogelweide), Bar, gui/pf, op. 186, 1959; Platero y yo (Jiménez), nar, gui, op. 190, 1960; The Divan of Moses-ibn-Ezra, op. 207, 1966

Many other songs

CHAMBER AND INSTRUMENTAL

Sonatas: vn, va, op. 127, 1945; cl, pf, op. 128, 1945; va, vc, op. 144, 1950; vn, vc, op. 148, 1950; 2 tpt sonatas, op. 179, 1955; vc, harp, op. 208, 1967

Other works, 2 or more insts: Meditation, vc, pf, R111a, 1941; Divertimento, 2 fl, op. 119, 1943; Sonatina, bn/vc, pf, op. 130, 1946; Str Qt, op. 139, 1948; Qnt, gui, str qt, op. 143, 1950; Fantasia, gui, pf, op. 145, 1950; Str Trio, op. 147, 1950; Suite 508, va, pf, op. 170/21, 1960; Quartettsatz, op. 170/28, 1960; Mélodie hébraïque, db, pf, 1963; Str Qt "casa al dono," op. 203, 1963; Sonatina, fl, gui, op. 205, 1965; Eclogues, fl, eng hn, gui, op. 206, 1966; several other works

Org: 5 Preludes, R122a, 1943; Fanfare, R152a, 1951; Prelude on the 12-tone Row, R152b, 1951; Chorale-prelude, op. 170, 1959; Fugue, op. 170, 1959; Introduction, Aria and Fugue, op. 159, 1967; Prelude, op. 170/49, 1967; a few others

Pf: Candide, op. 123, 1944; Napolitana, R127a, 1945; Suite nello stile italiano, op. 138, 1947; Evangélion, op. 141, 28 little pieces, 1949; 6 canons, op. 142, 1950; 6 pieces in form of canons, op. 156, 1952; El encanto, op. 165, 1953; Duo-pianism, op. 170/19, 1959; Sonatina zoologica, op. 187, 1960; several other works

Gui: Rondo, op. 129, 1946; Suite, op. 133, 1947; 21 items in op. 170 series, 1954–67; 3 preludi mediterranei, op. 176, 1955; La guarda cuydadosa, Escarraman, after Cervantes, op. 177, 1955; Passacaglia, op. 180, 1956; 3 preludi al Circeo, op. 194, 1961; 24 caprichos de Goya, op. 195, 1961; Sonatina canonica, 2 gui, op. 196, 1961; Les guitares bien temperées, op. 199, 2 gui, 1962; Appunti, op. 210, 1967–8, vols. 2 and 3, inc.; Fuga elegiaca, 2 gui, R210a, 1967

MSS of pubd works in *DLC*; unpubd MSS in private collection

Principal publishers: Bruzzichelli, Curci, C. Fischer, General Music, Marks, Presser

BIBLIOGRAPHY

EwenD

G. M. Gatti: "A Young Florentine," *Modern Music*, iii/4 (1926), 28 [on *La Mandragola*]

R. von Weber and others: "Mario Castelnuovo-Tedesco," *The Book of Modern Composers*, ed. D. Ewen (New York, 1942), 391; (3/1961), 108

G. Saleski: "Mario Castelnuovo-Tedesco," *Famous Composers of Jewish Origin* (New York, 1949), 31ff

B. Kremenliev: "Mario Castelnuovo-Tedesco," *Music of the West*, vii/8 (1952), 5

G. Pugliese: "Florence (ii): Aucassin et Nicolette," *Opera*, iii (1952), 470

A. Damerini: "*Il mercante di Venezia* di Mario Castelnuovo-Tedesco," *Musica d'oggi*, new ser., iv (1961), 114

M. Rinaldi: "Castlenuovo-Tedesco and the Merchant of Venice," *Ricordiana*, vi/4 (1961), 1

M. Castelnuovo-Tedesco: "The Song of Songs," *MJ*, xxi/8 (1963), 21 [incl. list of works]

J. C. G. Waterhouse: *The Emergence of Modern Italian Music (up to 1940)* (diss., U. of Oxford, 1968), esp. 655ff

G. M. Gatti: "Ricordo di Mario Castelnuovo-Tedesco," *Accademia nazionale di Santa Cecilia: annuario 1969* (Rome, 1969), 117

J. L. Thiel: *The Stylistic Trends found in a Comparative Analysis of Three Published Organ Works by Mario Castelnuovo-Tedesco* (diss., U. of Missouri, Kansas City, 1970)

R. C. Purcell: "Mario Castelnuovo-Tedesco and the Guitar," *Guitar Review*, no. 37 (1972), 2

M. L. Holmberg: *Thematic Contours and Harmonic Idioms of Mario Castelnuovo-Tedesco, as Exemplified in the Solo Concertos* (diss., Northwestern U., 1974)

N. Rossi: "Platero y Yo by Mario Castelnuovo-Tedesco," *The Realm of Music* (Boston, 1974)

——: "Castelnuovo-Tedesco: Aristocracy of Thought," *HiFi/MusAm*, xxv/5 (1975), 18

——: *Catalogue of Works by Mario Castelnuovo-Tedesco* (New York, 1977)

P. A. Higham: *Castelnuovo-Tedesco's Works for Guitar* (thesis, U. of Alberta, 1977)

N. Rossi: "Castelnuovo-Tedesco's 'Sonata for Clarinet and Piano'," *The Clarinet*, vii/2 (1980), 48

B. H. Scalin: *Operas by Mario Castelnuovo-Tedesco* (diss., Northwestern U., 1980)

N. Rossi: "Mario Castelnuovo-Tedesco," *Hearing Music* (New York, 1981)

NICK ROSSI

Castle [Blyth], **Vernon** (*b* Norwich, England, 2 May 1887; *d* Fort Worth, TX, 15 Feb 1918). Ballroom and exhibition dancer. He and his wife, Irene Castle (née Foote; *b* New Rochelle, NY, 7 April 1893; *d* Eureka Springs, AR, 25 Jan 1969) began to appear as a dance team in New York clubs in 1912. They danced in the musical *The Sunshine Girl* (1913), where their performance won wide appeal partly because of the enthusiasm among the upper classes in New York for the new steps of vernacular dance. By 1914 they had become the city's most popular social dance team, appearing in Broadway shows and silent films, and they enjoyed great success with their book *Modern Dancing* (1914/ *R*1980). The Castles owned several entertainment centers where they performed and taught social dancing; the dances that they popularized, including the Castle walk (a variant of the ONE-STEP, danced on the toes with stiff knees; see illustration), hesitation waltz, and foxtrot, merged patrician sophistication with sexual suggestiveness and lack of restraint. Their special brand of social dancing, accompanied by the "syncopated" music of their music director James Reese Europe and his orchestra, helped to popularize black urban music and paved the way for the dance styles and social life of the 1920s. A film of their lives, *The Castles*, was made by Fred Astaire and Ginger Rogers in 1939.

Vernon and Irene Castle performing the Castle walk in Irving Berlin's musical "Watch your Step" (1914)

See also DANCE, §III, 4.

BIBLIOGRAPHY

I. M. Fanger: "Castle, Irene," *NAW*
I. Castle: *My Husband* (New York, 1919)
F. L. Allen: "When America Learned to Dance," *Scribner's Magazine*, cii/3 (1937), 11, 42
D. Duncan: "Irene Castle in 1956," *Dance Magazine*, xxx/10 (1956), 87
I. Castle, B. Duncan, and W. Duncan: *Castles in the Air* (Garden City, NY, 1958)
W. Bolcom and R. Kimball: *Reminiscing with Sissle and Blake* (New York, 1973)

RONALD M. RADANO

Castleman, Charles (Martin) (*b* Quincy, MA, 22 May 1941). Violinist. He began studies at the age of four, his first teacher being Emanuel Ondříček. When he was six he appeared with Fiedler and the Boston Pops Orchestra, and he gave his first solo recital (at Jordan Hall, Boston) three years later. From 1957 until 1963 he studied with Galamian at the Curtis Institute and was coached on various occasions by Josef Gingold, David Oistrakh, and Henryk Szeryng. He also studied at Harvard College. His adult début was at New York (Town Hall) in 1964. He has toured Europe and Russia, and has been soloist with major orchestras on both sides of the Atlantic. In 1970 he founded and became director of the Quartet Program (in Saratoga, later in Troy, New York), which helps to develop professional chamber ensembles. With the violist Paul Doktor and the cellist Jennifer Langham, he played in the New String Trio of New York (1972–5). Since 1975 he has been a member of the Raphael Trio with the pianist Daniel Epstein and the cellist Susan Salm; the group has made several European tours. Castleman taught at the Philadelphia Musical Academy and in 1975 he became a professor of violin at the Eastman School of Music. As a participant in the Ford Foundation Concert Artists program, he commissioned and gave the world première of Amram's Violin Concerto in St. Louis in 1981. That year he also gave the first complete performance in New York of Ysaÿe's six unaccompanied violin sonatas, which he later recorded. He has edited Rochberg's *La bocca della verità*, and has published on the madrigals of Luzzasco Luzzaschi. He plays a violin by J. B. Guadagnini and owns a large and fine collection of bows.

BIBLIOGRAPHY

P. Mose: "Charles Castleman's Quartet Program," *HiFi/MusAm*, xxxi/12 (1981), 35–6, 38

MICHAEL STEINBERG/R

Castle walk. A variant of the ONE-STEP introduced by Vernon and Irene Castle in the 1910s.

Caston, Saul [Cohen, Solomon] (*b* New York, 22 August 1901; *d* Winston-Salem, NC, 28 July 1970). Conductor and trumpeter. A descendant on his mother's side of the distinguished Guzikow family of Polish musicians, Caston began studying trumpet at the age of eight with Max Schlossberg, who was then trumpeter of the New York PO. In 1918 he became second trumpeter and five years later principal in the Philadelphia Orchestra. He received a conducting diploma in 1935 from the Curtis Institute, where he taught from 1924 to 1942. He was appointed assistant conductor of the Philadelphia Orchestra in 1936 and was conductor of the Reading SO from 1941 to 1944. In 1945 he resigned from the Philadelphia Orchestra to become music director of the Denver SO. Under his leadership (1945–64), it increased its subscription and youth concerts and won critical recognition in the national press. Caston also inaugurated a concert series featuring audience–composer dialogue, which won four ASCAP awards for its contribution to the promotion of contemporary music.

BIBLIOGRAPHY

H. Stoddard: "Saul Caston," *Symphony Conductors of the U.S.A.* (New York, 1957), 38

BARBARA JEPSON

Catholic Church, music of the. *See* ROMAN CATHOLIC CHURCH, MUSIC OF THE.

Catholic University. University founded in Washington, DC, in 1887, with a music department from 1950; *see* WASHINGTON, §6.

Catlett, Sid(ney) ["Big Sid"] (*b* Evansville, IN, 17 Jan 1910; *d* Chicago, IL, 25 March 1951). Jazz drummer. He played in several minor Chicago bands before moving in 1930 to New York, where he began a freelance career, making many recordings and appearing with such important bands as Benny Carter's (1932), McKinney's Cotton Pickers (1934–5), Fletcher Henderson's (1936), and Don Redman's (1936–8). From 1938 to 1942 he was prominently featured in the big band led by Louis Armstrong, whose preferred drummer he became. After leading his own combos in various cities, he again joined Armstrong in the latter's small group, the All Stars, playing New Orleans jazz (1947–9).

Catlett was among the outstanding drummers of the swing period, and many jazz drummers of the postwar styles were influenced by his work. He had a bright, firm touch and absolute metrical precision in his right-hand ride patterns, which allowed him to create unpredictable cross-accents with the left, including his famous, expertly timed rim-shots. By almost imperceptibly rushing the beat he could at times generate enormous intensity in a big-band performance. He was an expert accompanist in a small-group setting, carefully adjusting his timbres to suit the soloist and sometimes anticipating the course of the improvisation. He also provided some of the most satisfying extended solos in premodern jazz drumming, revealing a clear sense of logical development and drum "melody" which set him apart from contemporaries such as Gene Krupa. Perhaps most remarkable was his individual way of adapting to all the jazz styles then available, as reflected in his many recordings with leading musicians in the New Orleans, Chicago, swing, and even bop styles. His unrestrained manner is well captured in the film *Jammin' the Blues* (1944).

RECORDINGS

(selective list)

As leader: I Never Knew/Love for Sale (1945, Cap. 10032)

As sideman: F. Henderson: Jangled Nerves (1936, Vic. 25317); T. Wilson: Warmin' up (1936, Bruns. 7684); B. Goodman: Tuesday at Ten (1941, Col. 36254); D. Gillespie: Salt Peanuts (1945, Guild 1003); L. Armstrong: Boff-boff, pt ii (1947, Decca 9-28102)

BIBLIOGRAPHY

SouthernB

W. Balliett: *The Sound of Surprise* (New York, 1959), 143

G. Hoefer: "Big Sid," *Down Beat*, xxxiii/6 (1966), 26

B. Esposito: "Big Sid Catlett," *Jazz Journal*, xxii/5 (1969), 10

J. BRADFORD ROBINSON

Catlin, George (*b* Wethersfield, CT, 1777 or 1778; *d* Camden, NJ, 1 May 1852). Musical instrument maker. He worked in Hartford from *c*1799 to at least 1813, and made a very wide variety of instruments including woodwinds, string instruments, harpsichords, pianos, and organs. He also advertised measuring and surveying instruments. He formed at least two partnerships of short duration before leaving Hartford. Bassoons signed Catlin & Bliss and Catlin & Bacon are known, and an organ for Christ Church, Hartford, was made by Catlin & Bacon in 1812. About 1810 Catlin invented a bass clarinet called the "clarion," which was the most successful instrument of its type for the following 15 or 20 years (*see* INSTRUMENTS, fig. 1).

By 1815 at the latest Catlin had moved to Philadelphia, where he continued his business on a smaller scale. He entered a flute in the Franklin Institute's second annual Exhibition of American Manufactures in 1825. The judging committee stated that "the ingenuity and skill of this artist are well known and the flute presented by him was a very fair specimen of his talent." Catlin also entered some "violin trimings" in the 17th exhibition of the Franklin Institute in 1847. His production could not have been large, judging from the number of surviving instruments; however, the bassoons and bass clarinets from his Hartford period were unusual accomplishments for a maker in the USA at that time. Of the seven known American bassoons made before 1860 four were made by Catlin and two by his probable protégés the Meacham brothers. Examples of Catlin's work are found at the Smithsonian Institution and at the Henry Ford Museum, Dearborn, Michigan.

BIBLIOGRAPHY

R. E. Eliason: "George Catlin: Hartford Musical Instrument Maker," *JAMIS*, viii (1982), 16

——: "George Catlin, Hartford Instrument Maker (Part 2)," *JAMIS*, ix (1983), 21

ROBERT E. ELIASON

Cayuga. Indian tribe of the IROQUOIS confederacy.

Cazden, Norman (*b* New York, 23 Sept 1914; *d* Bangor, ME, 18 Aug 1980). Composer, musicologist, and pianist. He received a teacher's diploma from the Juilliard Graduate School (1932) and a BS in social science at the City College, New York (1943); he studied musicology at Harvard University (PhD 1948), where he also took composition lessons with Piston and Copland. As a pianist he made his début in 1926 and until 1943 worked as composer-pianist for several modern dance groups. Throughout his career he appeared as a soloist and accompanist and taught theory and piano privately; for a year he was music director of the New York radio station WLIB. He held appointments at Vassar College and the universities of Michigan and Illinois before he joined the faculty of the University of Maine, Orono (1969), where he remained until his death. A versatile composer, he wrote music broad in expressive range, with marked rhythmic impulse, frequent use of polyphony (from sparse to massive in density), and widely expanded tonality. His melodies sometimes reflect his deep interest in folk music, the lifelong study of which led to collaborations on a number of published collections, and to a suggested alternative to modal terminology and traditional analytical methods (see *YIFMC*, iii (1971), 45–78). In addition to his dissertation, Cazden published a number of articles on the nature and perception of consonance and dissonance, challenging earlier theories and concluding that societal cultures and musical context, not acoustical laws, determine musical response (see especially *International Review of the Aesthetics and Sociology of Music*, iii (1972), 217, and xi (1980), 123–68; *Journal of Aesthetics and Art Criticism*, xx (1962), 301, which includes a critique of Helmholtz's theories).

WORKS

Stage: The Lonely Ones (ballet), pf/orch, op.44, 1944, Boston, 1944; Dingle Hill (dramatic cantata), op.70, 1958, Chichester, NY, 1958; The Merry

Wives of Windsor (incidental music), op.78, 1962; The Tempest (incidental music), op.83, 1963

Orch: Preamble, op.18, 1938; 6 Definitions, op.25, 1930–39; 3 Dances, op.28, 1940; Stony Hollow, op.47, 1944; Sym., op.49, 1948; 3 Ballads, op.52, 1949; Songs from the Catskills, band, op.54, 1950; Woodland Valley Sketches, op.73, 1960; Adventure, op.85, 1963; Chamber Conc., cl, str, op.94, 1965; Va Conc., op.103, 1972

Chamber: Str Qt, op.9, 1936; Conc., 10 insts, op.10, 1937; 3 Chamber Sonatas, cl, va, op.17, 1938; Qt, cl, str trio, op.23, 1939; Str Qnt, op.32, 1941; Hn Sonata, op.33, 1941; 10 Conversations, 2 cl, op.34, 1941; Fl Sonata, op.36, 1941; 3 Constructions, wind qnt, op.38, 1941; 3 Directions, 2 tpt, bar hn/trbn, trbn, op.39, 1941; 6 Discussions, wind ens, op.40, 1941–2; Suite, vn, pf, op.43, 1943; 4 Presentations, vn, pf, op.45, 1944; Suite, 2 tpt, hn, bar hn, trbn, tuba, op.55, 1964; Qnt, ob, str qt, op.74, 1960; 2 Elizabethan Suites, 2 tpt, hn, trbn, tuba, op.91, 1964, str qt, op.92, 1965; Wind Qnt, op.96, 1966; Pf Trio, op.97, 1969; 6 Sennets, 4 trbn, op.100, 1971; Bn Sonata, op.102, arr. vc, pf as op.102a, 1971; Eng Hn Sonata, op.104, arr. va, pf as op.104a, arr. cl, pf as op.104b, 1974; Tuba Sonata, op.105, arr. db, pf as op.105a, 1974

Pf: Sonatina, op.7, 1935; Sonata, op.12, 1938; Variations, op.26, 1940; Passacaglia, op.46, 1944; 3 New Sonatas, op.53, 1950; 3 Sonatinas, op.69, 1959; Sonatina, op.88, 1964; "Sunshine" Sonata, op.101, 1971; 6 Preludes and Fugues, op.106, 1974

Vocal and choral works; other dance, orch, and chamber pieces; inst music for amateurs; over 12 collections of folk music arrs.

MSS in *OU*; pubd works and holographs in American Music Center, New York
Principal publisher: MCA

WRITINGS

Musical Consonance and Dissonance (diss., Harvard U., 1948)
A Book of Nonsense Songs (New York, 1961)
with H. Haufrecht and N. Studer: *Folk Songs of the Catskills* (Albany, 1982)

BIBLIOGRAPHY

EwenD
H. Haufrecht: "The Writings of Norman Cazden: Composer and Musicologist," *ACAB*, viii/2 (1959), 2

RUTH B. HILTON

CBS Musical Instruments. A division created in 1966 by the Columbia Broadcasting System, Inc. (CBS, Inc., from 1974), to manage and expand its instrument business. The corporation had entered the field in 1965 with the acquisition of Fender (electric guitars and electric bass guitars, Fender-Rhodes pianos, and V. C. Squier strings) and Electro-Music (Leslie speakers for electronic organs), to which Rogers (drums) was added in 1966. CBS Musical Instruments operated first as part of the Columbia Records Division, both of which became part of a corporate group in 1966. Later acquisitions were Buchla (synthesizers, 1969–71), Steinway (pianos, 1972), Gulbransen (electronic organs, 1973), Gemeinhardt (flutes, 1977), Lyon & Healy (harps, 1977), and Rodgers (electronic organs, 1977); from 1982 to 1985 the Chroma synthesizer and two electronic pianos, acquired from ARP, were marketed by the Fender unit. Leslie was sold in 1980 and Fender in 1985, when CBS, Inc., announced its plans to sell the remaining components of the instrument division.

LEONARD BURKAT

Cecil, Winifred (*b* Staten Island, NY, 31 Aug 1907; *d* New York, 13 Sept 1985). Soprano and pedagogue. She studied at the Curtis Institute, as well as privately with Sembrich in New York and Elena Gerhardt in Leipzig. She began her professional career on the radio program "Show Boat," which starred Lanny Ross. After a recital début at Town Hall, New York (14 December 1935), she made several concert tours and appeared with various American orchestras. Having declined a contract with the Metropolitan Opera, she went to Italy in 1937 and made her opera début at the Teatro San Carlo, Naples, in the title role of Respighi's *Maria Egiziaca*. Engagements followed in Prague and Vienna, and at La Scala, Milan; her roles included Aida, Tosca, Madeleine (*Andrea Chenier*), Fiora (*L'amore dei tre re*), Elsa (*Lohengrin*), Elisabeth (*Tannhäuser*), Donna Anna, and the Countess. She also made concert appearances, notably in England. During World War II she lived in retirement in Italy, where she was involved in unofficial diplomatic work with the American and Italian troops; for her services she was made an Honorary Dame of the Order of Malta. After the death of her husband, she returned to New York (1950), where she gave recitals and taught. In 1957 she instituted a course for singers called "Joy in Singing," in which she emphasized deportment, repertory, and communication with the audience. For a time she contributed reviews of recordings to the *Saturday Review*.

PHILIP LIESON MILLER

Ceely, Robert (Paige) (*b* Torrington, CT, 17 Jan 1930). Composer. He attended the New England Conservatory (BM 1954) and Mills College (MA 1961), where he was a pupil of Milhaud; at the Berkshire Music Center (summer 1955) and at Princeton (1957–9) he was a pupil of Sessions. He worked with Vercoe on computer music at the Massachusetts Institute of Technology (summer 1958) and took courses at Darmstadt during the summers of 1962 and 1964. He was music director at Robert College, Istanbul, 1961–3, and after a year as an audio engineer at Harvard (1965–6) he joined the faculty of the New England Conservatory. In 1965 he founded and became director of Boston Experimental Electronic Music Projects (now known as BEEP) and in 1967 director of the electronic music program at the Conservatory. His awards include a Fromm Foundation award (1969), two Cine Golden Eagle awards for film scores (*Incendio* and *Bleve*) and an NEA grant (1979). Ceely is especially recognized as a composer of electronic music, on which subject he has contributed articles for various journals including *Electronic Music Review*.

WORKS

Stage: Beyond the Ghost Spectrum (ballet), ens, tape, 1969; The Automobile Graveyard (opera, 2, Arrabal), 1981–

Inst: Str Trio, 1953; Orch Variations, 1954; Ww Qnt, 1954; Composition for 10 Insts, 1963; Modules, 7 insts, 1967–8; Logs, 2 db, 1969; Hymn, vc, db, 1969; Slide Music, 4 trbn, 1973; Rituals, 40 fl, 1974–6; Bottom Dogs, 4 db, 1980; Pf Piece, 1980; Roundels, wind, tape, 1981; Pf Variations, 1981–2; Totems, ob, tape, 1982; Dialogues, fl, 1983; Giostra, ob, pf, 1984; Pianetude, pf, 1984; Pitch Dark, jazz ens, 1984

Elec: Stratti, tape, 1963; Elegia, tape, 1963–4; Vonce, tape, 1966–7; MITSYN Music, 1968–71; La fleur, les fleurs, 1975; Frames, tape, 1978; Infractions, tape, 1983; several other tape pieces

Other: vocal works, incl. Lullaby (G. Gascoigne), S, trbn, 1978; Flee, Floret, Florens (after Chaucer, de Vitry), 15 solo vv, 1978; 7 film scores, incl. Incendio, 1975, Bleve, 1976

Principal publishers: ACA, Association for the Promotion of New Music

BARBARA A. PETERSEN

Celestin, Papa [Oscar Phillip] (*b* LaFourche, LA, 1 Jan 1884; *d* New Orleans, LA, 15 Dec 1954). Jazz trumpeter and bandleader. In 1906 he moved to New Orleans, where his Original Tuxedo Orchestra (later known as the Tuxedo Jazz Orchestra), with its emphasis on popular songs and novelty pieces, enjoyed considerable success from 1917 until Celestin's death. Although his band was always popular with dancers, and toured (mostly in the South) during the 1920s and 1930s, it only became nationally known during the early 1950s through appearing on television and in films. In 1953 Celestin played a command performance for President Eisenhower.

Celestin's long-lasting popularity was due to his personality and to the way he presented his band's music rather than to his skills as a jazz trumpeter. He rarely promoted his own trumpet playing and was not a natural improviser, though he occasionally created muted solos that were full of feeling, and his singing was usually robust and cheerful. Some idea of the enthusiasm that the group engendered is apparent on *Li'l Liza Jane* (1950, RWP 9–10).

BIBLIOGRAPHY

SouthernB

J. G. Curren: "Oscar 'Papa' Celestin," *Second Line*, vi/1–2 (1955), 1

G. Hoefer: Obituary, *Down Beat*, xxii/2 (1955), 2

G. Hulme: "Oscar 'Papa' Celestin," *Matrix*, no.47 (1963), 3; no.53 (1964), 18 [discography]

P. R. Haby: "Oscar 'Papa' Celestin, 1884–1954," *Footnote*, xii/5 (1981), 4

JOHN CHILTON

Celli, Joseph (*b* Bridgeport, CT, 19 March 1944). Composer and oboist. He studied at the University of Hartford's Hartt School of Music (BMEd 1967), at Northwestern University (MM 1971), and at Oberlin Conservatory; his principal teachers were Albert Goltzer and Ray Still. From 1975 Celli has been director of Real Art Ways, an organization which he founded with other Connecticut artists to provide space for and promote avant-garde events in Hartford. In 1984 Real Art Ways served as host for the New Music America Festival. As a performer Celli gave the American premières of Stockhausen's *Spiral* and *Solo*. In order to extend the oboe repertory, he has commissioned more than 35 compositions from a variety of American composers, including Oliveros, Niblock, Cope, Lucier, Fulkerson, and Goldstein; among the new works are pieces for acoustic or electric oboe combined with various instrumental ensembles, mixed-media works, and directed improvisations. As a composer Celli often includes improvisatory elements in his works and uses extended techniques for oboe and english horn. In 1981 he received a joint commission from the Wesleyan Singers and the Connecticut Council on the Arts for a work for chorus and tape entitled *To Be Announced*.

WORKS

. . . in the bag . . ., dancer, live elec, 1976; Sky: S for J, 5 eng hn without reeds, 1976; Ringing, antique cymbals, 1978; Improvisations, eng hn, 1979–82; Improvisations, ob, vn, 1979–82; Ring Ritual, 2 pfmrs, 1981; To Be Announced, 8 groups of vv, 8-track tape, 1981

JOAN LA BARBARA

Centennial Exhibition. A commemorative exhibition established by Act of Congress on 3 March 1871 and officially called the "International Exhibition of Arts, Manufactures, and Products of the Soil and Mine." It marked the centennial of the Declaration of Independence and took place in Philadelphia from 10 May to 10 November 1876. Invitations to participate were accepted by 17 states and 39 foreign countries, and nearly ten million visitors viewed displays in over 200 buildings. Two of these, Horticultural Hall and Memorial Hall, became permanent additions to Fairmount Park, the site of the exhibition.

At the opening ceremonies, attended by over 100,000 people, an orchestra of 150 and a chorus of 1000 were conducted by Theodore Thomas, assisted by Dudley Buck. The program began with national airs from the USA and participating countries, and included a Centennial March, commissioned from Richard Wagner at a fee of $5000. Two other works written for the occasion were the *Centennial Hymn* op.27 by John Knowles Paine and *The Centennial Meditation of Columbia*, a cantata by Dudley Buck. The "Hallelujah" chorus from Handel's *Messiah* was also performed, accompanied by artillery salutes and ringing chimes.

In the center of the largest exhibition building, the Main Hall, was a bandstand big enough for an orchestra of 65 players, and concerts were given daily by choirs, string quartets, singers, pianists, and bands, including the Gilmore Band from New York, the US Marine Band, and the First Brigade Band from Philadelphia. More than 40 new odes and hymns were performed at these concerts and at Centennial concerts given elsewhere in Philadelphia, among them the *Agricultural Grand March* by Edward Mack, *Centennial Ode* by Julia M. Swift, *The Great Centennial* by Howard Paul, and *Souvenir de Philadelphia: Grand Caprice Centennial* by Henry Herz Andrews.

The most popular concerts were sponsored by the builders of the two great organs in the Main Hall. The larger organ, with four manuals and 2704 pipes, was built by Hook & Hastings of Boston at a cost of $15,000 and incorporated the latest improvements in organ design. The other, built by Hilborne Lewis Roosevelt of New York for $20,000, included a main organ, an electric suspended organ, and an electric "echo" organ. Among other instruments of all kinds displayed at the exhibition were 200 pianos by 64 different manufacturers, and an "electro-magnetic orchestra," or orchestrion, invented by William F. and H. Schmoele of Philadelphia, which simulated a band of 12 instruments.

A National Commemoration, held on 4 July at Independence Square in Philadelphia, began with an overture, *The Great Republic*, based on the song *Hail! Columbia* as arranged by Bristow. The closing ceremony included Wagner's Centennial March and the "Dettingen" *Te Deum* by Handel.

BIBLIOGRAPHY

J. D. McCabe: *History of the Centennial Exhibition* (Philadelphia, 1876)

F. Leslie: *Historical Register of the United States Centennial Exposition* (New York, 1877)

United States International Exhibition, 1876: Report of the Director General (Washington, 1880), i, ii, vii

S. E. Trout: *The Story of the Centennial of 1876* (n.p., 1929)

R. A. Gerson: *Music in Philadelphia* (Philadelphia, 1940)

J. Maass: *The Glorious Enterprise* (New York, 1973)

MARTHA FURMAN SCHLEIFER

Central City Opera Festival. An annual summer opera festival established in Central City, Colorado, in 1932. It is thought to be the earliest such festival in the USA. Most of the festival events are held in the elegant and beautifully restored Victorian opera house (capacity 800) inaugurated in 1878, which had presented burlesque, opera, Gilbert and Sullivan operettas, and serious drama until the turn of the century. As the silver and gold deposits around Central City declined, so did the fortunes of the opera house: it became a cinema in 1908 and was closed down in 1927. After acquisition by the University of Denver in 1931 and some months of restoration, the house re-opened under the auspices of the Central City Opera House Association (formed 1932), which decided on a summer festival format. Programs are also given at Williams Stables and Teller House Bar. The festival was suspended in 1942–5 and for one season in 1982. In addition to productions of the standard repertory (performed in English) and world premières of new works, including Douglas Moore's *The Ballad of Baby Doe* in 1956, the festival offers Victorian salon recitals, apprentice productions of single scenes from opera, dance, and jazz concerts; performances from the festival occasionally tour to neighboring cities. Artists who have appeared at Central City include Charles Bressler, Jerome Hines, Spiro Malas, Judith Raskin, and Benita Valente.

SARA VELEZ, SANFORD A. LINSCOME

Central Opera Service. Organization founded in 1954 by Eleanor (Mrs. August) Belmont and sponsored by the Metropolitan Opera National Council. Its 2000 members include opera companies and workshops, professionals involved with opera, and interested individuals. The organization provides information about performance material and repertory, and its staff performs a wide range of services including organizational counseling and advice about public relations and fund-raising techniques. Since 1959 it has published a bulletin (now quarterly), several complete issues of which consist of important directories: *Opera Companies and Workshops in the United States and Canada* (annually since 1962), *Directory of American Contemporary Operas* (1967 and supplements), *Directory of English Opera Translations* (3/1974 and supplements), *Directory of Operas and Publishers* (1976), *Career Guide for the Young American Singer* (3/1978 and quarterly addenda), and *Directory of Sets and Costumes for Rent: Operas – Operettas – Musicals* (3/1979 and annual addenda). In 1984 the administrative director of the organization was Maria F. Rich; its headquarters are in New York.

JOHN SHEPARD

Centre for American Music. A program for study, research, and performance of American music, based at Keele University, Staffordshire, England. It was founded in 1974 by Peter Dickinson, the first professor of music at the university's newly established department of music. The center, which has probably the finest collection of American music materials in Europe, has sponsored the Ives centenary concerts (1974) and three conferences (1975, 1978, and 1983, the last in collaboration with the Sonneck Society); in 1975 it introduced an MA in American music. Composers and performers who have given lectures and recitals there include Copland, Carter, Crumb, Glass, Ben Johnston, Alan Mandel, Reich, Charles Rosen, Elliott Schwartz, and Christian Wolff. Holders of Fulbright-Hays Visiting Professorships, each for an academic year, have been William Brooks (1977), Dwight Peltzer (1978), and Cecil Lytle (1979); Karl Kroeger was Leverhulme Research Fellow in 1980.

BIBLIOGRAPHY

P. Dickinson: "Recent Research on Musical Traditions of the United States: a View from Britain," *IMSCR*, xii *Berkeley 1977*, ed. D. Heartz and B. Wade (Kassel, 1981)

——: "British-American Interactions: Composers and Students," *MT*, cxxiv (1983), 411

PETER DICKINSON

Cepeda-Atiles, Rafael (*b* San Juan, Puerto Rico, 10 July 1910). Singer, drummer, and dancer. Seven generations of his family have performed the *bomba*, a Puerto Rican dance characterized by the use of drums, responsorial singing, and spontaneous dancing by individuals and couples within a circle of participants. He had learned the basic *bomba* steps by the time he was ten; he also learned the *plena*, a type of short, narrative song with a marked African influence. In 1942 he organized a dance group that included Ramón Cepeda, Adolfo Rosa, Julio Domena, Francisco García, Tito el Indio, Higinio Benítez, and Alejo Cruz; later he organized another group, La Familia Cepeda, with his wife, 11 children, and other members of his family. He has written more than 600 compositions. In 1983 he received a National Heritage Fellowship from the NEA.

HECTOR VEGA-DRUET

Cha cha cha. A social couple dance that peaked in popularity in 1959. Derived from the MAMBO, the cha cha cha involves a shuffle step (with a rocking of the hips) performed to a rhythm that seems to have given the dance its name (ex. 1). Songs like

Ex.1 A typical cha cha cha rhythm

Everybody Loves to Cha Cha Cha (1959), written by Barbara Campbell and recorded by Sam Cooke, popularized the cha cha cha, but music for the dance has been frequently arranged from existing tunes, as in the case of Enoch Light's *I Want to Be Happy Cha Cha* and *Tea for Two Cha Cha*, arranged and recorded by Warren Covington and the Tommy Dorsey Orchestra.

BIBLIOGRAPHY

P. Buckman: *Let's Dance: Social, Ballroom, & Folk Dancing* (New York, 1978)

J. S. Roberts: *The Latin Tinge: the Impact of Latin American Music on the United States* (New York, 1979)

PAULINE NORTON

Chadabe, Joel (A.) (*b* New York, 12 Dec 1938). Composer. He studied with Will Mason at the University of North Carolina, Chapel Hill (BA 1959), and with Elliott Carter at Yale (MM 1962). From 1965 he taught at SUNY, Albany, where in 1966 he established an electronic music studio. In 1978 he became president of Composers' Forum, New York. Chadabe has been awarded a Ford Foundation Fellowship (1964) and grants from the NEA (1976) and the Rockefeller Foundation (1977); he has received commissions from the Center for the Creative and Performing Arts, Buffalo, and from Robert Stierer and Yvar Mikhashoff. He contributed a discussion of the technology of synthesizers to *The Development and Practice of Electronic Music* (1975; ed. J. Appleton and R. Perera) and articles by him on aspects of electronic and computer music have appeared in *Perspectives of New Music*, *Electronic Music Review*, *Computer Music Journal*, and elsewhere.

From 1965 to 1977 Chadabe was engaged in creating tape compositions that use electronic sound sources, and mixed-media works that combine live and electronic forces. From 1977 he has worked primarily with computers, producing a body of music notable for an imaginative use of technology and for accessibility and variety; in *Rhythms* (1980), for example, the percussionist improvises a duet with a computer/synthesizer that composes as it plays, its tuneful variations, somewhat Caribbean in flavor, changing with Chadabe's signals. Other computer works range from the icy, atonal *Scenes from Stevens* to the sociable *Playthings*, a public-interactive installation that invites people to "play" the computer by manipulating proximity-sensitive antennas. Chadabe has given concerts and demonstrations with his portable minicomputer/synthesizer system throughout North America, Europe, and Australia.

WORKS

Inst: Prelude to Naples, 4 insts, 1965; Monomusic, 8 insts, 1969 [withdrawn]; From the 14th On, vc, 1973; Variation 1983, pf, 1983; The Long Ago and Far Away Tango, pf, 1984

Tape: Street Scene, eng hn, tape, slides, 1967; Drift, 1970; with L. Foss: Map, insts, tape, 1970, rev. 1972 by Foss; Ideas of Movement at Bolton Landing,

1971; Echoes, 1 inst, elec, 1972; Shadows and Lines, 1972; with L. Foss: Chamber Music, perc, tape, 1974; Flowers, 1 str inst, tape, 1974; Dancers, 1975; Settings for Spirituals, 1977 [cptr-generated sounds]

Cptr: Playthings, installation, 1978; Solo, cptr/synth, 1978; Scenes from Stevens, cptr/synth, 1979; Rhythms, cptr/synth, perc, 1980; Follow Me Softly, cptr/synth, perc, 1984

Principal publisher: C. Fischer

BIBLIOGRAPHY

J. Fulkerson: "What Defines a Piece of Music?" *The Composer*, v/1 (1973), 15

T. Johnson: "New Music," *HiFi/MusAm*, xxv/9 (1975), 2

LINDA SANDERS

Chadwick, George Whitefield (*b* Lowell, MA, 13 Nov 1854; *d* Boston, MA, 4 April 1931). Composer, teacher, conductor, pianist, and organist. He was a leading figure of the Second School of New England composers. Highly regarded in his lifetime as a composer, he was also largely responsible for the effective reorganization of the New England Conservatory and was one of the most influential teachers in American music.

1. Early years up to 1880. 2. 1880–97. 3. 1897–1931. 4. Style.

1. EARLY YEARS UP TO 1880. Chadwick's father and mother were musical amateurs who probably met at a New Hampshire singing-school conducted by Nathaniel Gould. Because of his mother's early death and his father's remarriage, Chadwick was left to his own resources at an early age. He thus developed the self-reliance and independence that were to characterize his music as well as his academic life. He learned music from his older brother and by the age of 15 was active as an organist. From this time on he had to pay for his own musical instruction, as his father, a businessman, was opposed to his pursuing a career in music. He did not complete high school, but went to work as a clerk in his father's insurance office. By 1872 he had become the regular organist of a Congregational church, while continuing his studies as a special student at the New England Conservatory, where his organ teachers were Dudley Buck and Eugene Thayer.

In 1876 Chadwick accepted a temporary post as professor of music at Olivet College in Michigan. While at Olivet he became a founding member of the Music Teachers National Association and read a paper on popular music at its first convention. Determined to receive a more systematic musical education, Chadwick traveled in the autumn of 1877 to Leipzig where, after three months of private study with Salomon Jadassohn, he enrolled at the conservatory on 3 January 1878. His success as a composer was as surprising as it was rapid. The first two movements of his String Quartet no. 1 were played in a concert of student works in May and favorably received. In the spring of 1879 his String Quartet no.2 and the concert overture *Rip Van Winkle* were judged the best compositions at the annual conservatory concerts. *Rip Van Winkle* quickly received further performances in Dresden and Boston. Greatly encouraged, Chadwick decided to gain additional training in Munich with Josef Rheinberger; but before studying with him he joined a group of young, vagabond American painters under the informal tutelage of Frank Duveneck (1848–1919). He journeyed with the "Duveneck boys" to Giverny, France, and in the autumn he entered the Munich Hochschule für Musik. The impromptu excursion contributed to the francophile attitudes which are noticeable in his later compositions.

2. 1880–97. Chadwick returned to Boston in May 1880; he began a career as an organist, teacher, and conductor, and quickly made his mark as a composer in virtually every genre. He was not a virtuoso keyboard performer, and though he held organ posts for many years, they were secondary to his other interests. He rarely appeared as a pianist except in performances of his own works.

In Boston there were many active choral organizations; Chadwick composed a number of choral works, including *The Viking's Last Voyage* for the Apollo Club, and directed the Arlington Club men's chorus. He also directed an amateur orchestral ensemble, the Boston Orchestral Club, for several years. The presence of such major orchestras as the Boston SO and the Philharmonic Society during the 1880s spurred Chadwick's contributions to the orchestral medium, in which he felt especially at home. The success of *Rip Van Winkle* made it relatively easy for him to obtain performances of new works. The Philharmonic Society played his waltz *Beautiful Munich* (1881), the Harvard Musical Association orchestra performed the Symphony no. 1 (1882), and the Boston SO played the "overture to an imaginary comedy" *Thalia* (1883). This "took all hearts by storm" (*Boston Evening Transcript*) and opened the way for the first performance of the Scherzo from the as yet incomplete Symphony no.2 in March 1884. The Scherzo was so much liked that the audience demanded an immediate repetition, the first ever granted in the history of the Boston SO. By the time the symphony received its first complete performance in 1886, Chadwick was regarded especially as a masterly composer of lighter movements. But the piece most often performed, the "overture to an imaginary tragedy" *Melpomene* (1887), was considered finer simply because the composer was at last writing music deemed entirely "serious."

1. *George Whitefield Chadwick*

The founding of the Kneisel Quartet was important to Chadwick's career. The group gave the first performance of his Quartet no.3, and the composer wrote Quartet no.4 and the Piano Quintet especially for them. The Quartet no.5 was written for the Adamowski Quartet.

Chadwick's earliest works for the theater were composed for private clubs to which he belonged. They were strongly influenced by the Gilbert and Sullivan operettas then making their first appearance in the USA. *Tabasco* (1893–4), commissioned by an amateur troupe for a fund-raising benefit, was sufficiently popular to justify a professional revival by the Seabrooke Opera Co., and it toured extensively.

Immediately after his return from Munich in 1881 Chadwick had set himself up as a private teacher. By the spring of the following year he had joined the faculty of the New England Conservatory, with which he remained affiliated until his death, becoming director in 1897. His leadership brought the growth and modernization of the conservatory from its original form (essentially a school of piano playing for training teachers) to a full-fledged conservatory on the European model. Chadwick's innovations included an opera workshop, a student repertory orchestra, and courses in orchestration and harmony based on the study of actual music rather than abstract principles. His textbook *Harmony: a Course of Study* (1897/*R*1975) was printed in many editions and became a standard text.

Chadwick had become a prominent figure in American music by the early 1890s; in 1892 he was commissioned to compose an ode for the opening festivities of the World's Columbian Exposition in Chicago. His grandiose score in three movements, for large chorus and orchestra with three additional brass bands, was performed (without the quiet middle movement) by a chorus of 5000 and an orchestra of 500. In Boston a few weeks later it was presented by a vocal octet with Chadwick accompanying on the organ.

Chadwick's third (and last) symphony was awarded a prize by the National Conservatory of Music in 1894, during the directorship of Antonín Dvořák, a composer with whom Chadwick shared a remarkable similarity of musical outlook. It is not surprising that Dvořák's "American" String Quartet op.96, which received its first performance by the Kneisel Quartet in Boston early in 1894, should seem to have directly inspired Chadwick's Fourth Quartet, first performed by the same ensemble late in 1896.

For some years Chadwick was the director and conductor of the Springfield Festival (1890–99) and the Worcester Festival (1897–1901), at which he championed such works as Berlioz's *La damnation de Faust*, Franck's *Les béatitudes*, Brahms's *German Requiem*, Glazunov's Symphony no.6, and a concert version of Saint-Saëns's *Samson et Dalila*. These festivals also inspired some of his major compositions; for Springfield he wrote the cantata *Phoenix expirans* and a colorful setting of Scott's *Lochinvar* for baritone and orchestra, and for Worcester he composed his largest score, the lyric drama *Judith*, based on his own scenario adapted from the Apocrypha. The dramatic action and some of the orchestral sonorities are clearly inspired by *Samson et Dalila* (which Chadwick had conducted a year before beginning his own score), though the influence of Mendelssohn's choral writing is also evident. Though it has never been staged, *Judith* is a colorful, large-scale opera much of which could be acted to telling effect. This is especially true of the central scene of seduction and murder, one of the most expertly constructed and tautly lyrical passages in American dramatic music. Sections emphasizing the chorus, on the other hand, are more like oratorio scenes. Chadwick almost certainly realized that the work would probably not achieve a theatrical performance, and he may have consciously chosen a middle path between opera and oratorio.

3. 1897–1931. After Chadwick assumed the directorship of the New England Conservatory in 1897 he found that the demands of the institution forced him to limit his composing largely to the summer months, which he usually spent on Martha's Vineyard, off Cape Cod. He took his responsibilities as administrator and teacher seriously; conservatory students remembered his steady and close attention to their progress and his somewhat daunting presence at every recital. He also developed the conservatory's orchestra, which he himself usually directed. Much of his teaching was given over to advanced composition students, among them Horatio Parker, who became a lifelong friend, Frederick Shepherd Converse, Edward Burlingame Hill, Daniel Gregory Mason, Farwell, Shepherd, and Still.

After the turn of the century Chadwick's multi-movement orchestral works were generally lighter in character; he continued also to produce programmatic concert overtures and symphonic poems. The Sinfonietta in D, *Symphonic Sketches*, and *Suite symphonique*, cast in four movements, mark an apparent decision to avoid the traditional abstract qualities of the symphony. The Sinfonietta is entirely abstract, but it is much lighter in character than the three earlier symphonies. The *Symphonic Sketches* and the *Suite symphonique* have programmatic features, and in fact Chadwick indicated that each of the *Sketches* could be performed independently. They quickly became established as among the brightest and most "American" orchestral compositions of the time. The *Suite Symphonique* was an attempt to repeat the success of the *Sketches*, but though it won a National Federation of Women's Clubs prize, it did not make so consistently strong an impression as the earlier score, despite a clever "Intermezzo and humoresque" movement containing a cakewalk in 5/4 and a parody of Debussy. One other abstract score of this period, the Theme, Variations, and Fugue for organ and orchestra, was on a smaller scale. Its successful blending of the solo instrument with the orchestra recommended it to many organists.

Chadwick continued to write orchestral works with titles that in some way reflect classical antiquity: *Euterpe* (1903), *Cleopatra* (1904), and *Aphrodite* (1910–11) continue in the path of *Thalia* and *Melpomene*, though only *Euterpe*, an abstract concert overture, can be linked to the earlier scores (and its ebullient syncopations sound anything but classically European). *Aphrodite* was inspired by a classical head of the goddess in the Museum of Fine Arts, Boston. Chadwick's last large orchestral score, *Angel of Death*, was similarly inspired by sculpture – in this case a work of Daniel Chester French. Chadwick also wrote two orchestral tributes to deceased friends: *Adonais* (1899), a richly sombre, somewhat Wagnerian score for the pianist Frank Fay Marshall, and an *Elegy* for Horatio Parker.

There is little doubt that the work on which Chadwick pinned his greatest hopes was his *verismo* opera *The Padrone*. Set in an unnamed city on the American east coast (presumably Boston), the opera tells a realistic story of poor Italian immigrants whose lives are ruined by a small-time mafioso figure who controls them. The composer originally intended that the immigrants should sing in Italian and the "Americans" in English, though this plan was not carried out; the entire opera is in English. It

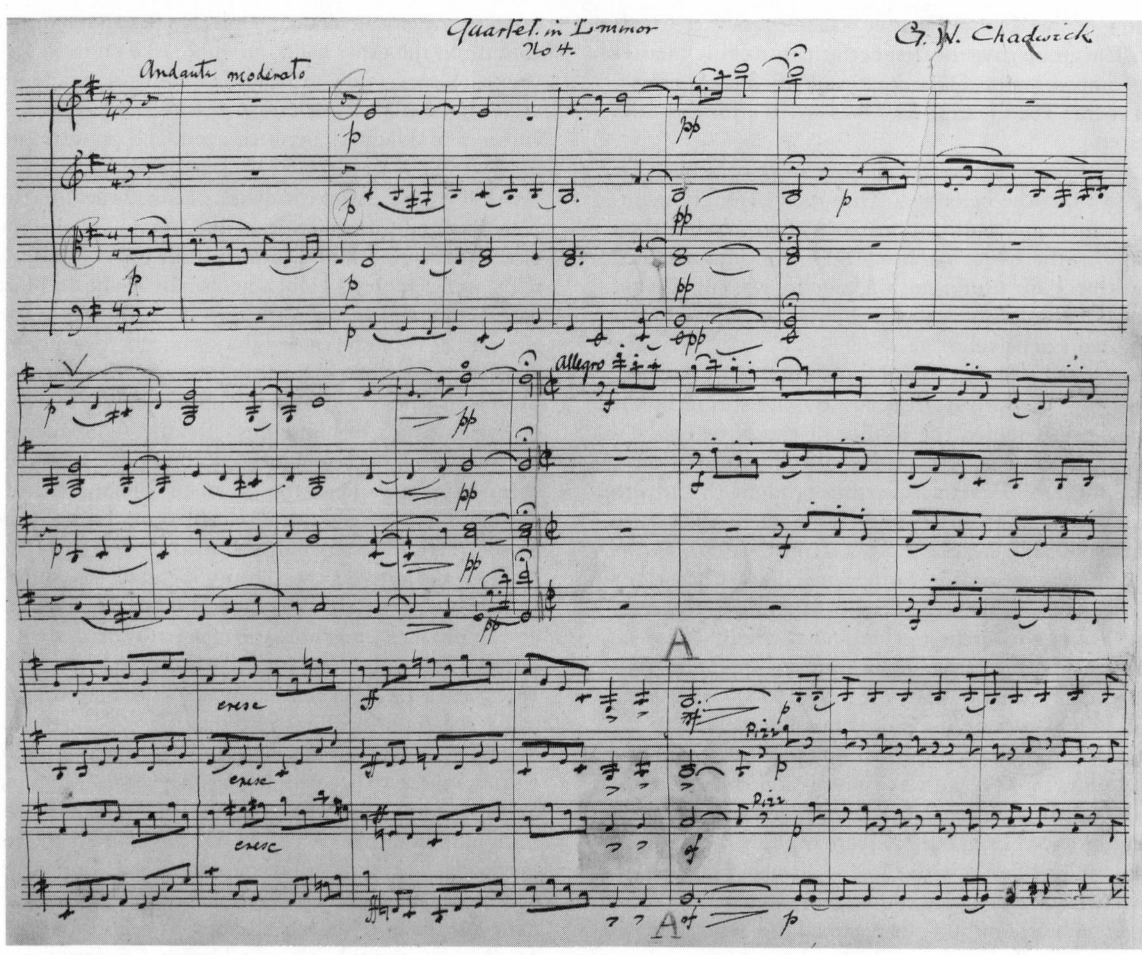

2. *Opening of Chadwick's String Quartet no.4 (1896): autograph MS (DLC)*

is colorfully scored and fast-paced, reflecting careful study of the late works of Verdi and the major scores of Puccini. It is rare among American operas in that it avoids both the mythological or distant historical settings and the exotic themes of American Indians found in other American operas of the time. *The Padrone* is an opera of modern life, reflecting the current social situation. Had it been produced, it might well have pointed the way to a new manner of operatic composition in the USA, one making the most of Americans' traditional directness and realistic outlook. Instead the score was turned down by the Metropolitan Opera. Chadwick learned from H. E. Krehbiel that the Metropolitan's manager Gatti-Casazza "disliked the book because it was a drama of life among the humble Italians, – and probably too true to life" (Chadwick's diary). A possible production in Chicago fell through when the impresario there suddenly died, and *The Padrone* remains unperformed.

Aside from *The Padrone*, most of Chadwick's major works in the decade 1909–18 were composed for the Norfolk Festival; these include his Christmas oratorio *Noel* (1909), the symphonic fantasy *Aphrodite* (1912), *Tam O'Shanter* (1915), and *Anniversary Overture* (1922). Chadwick was so delighted with the rehearsal conditions and the quality of the performances of *Noel* and *Aphrodite* that he offered *Tam O'Shanter* as a gift to the festival in appreciation of its work. *Noel* was popular with choral societies for some years, and *Aphrodite* obtained several performances with American orchestras (including the Chicago SO under Frederick Stock). But it is *Tam O'Shanter* that has so far showed the greatest staying power; a kind of American *Till Eulenspiegel*, it is Chadwick's homage to his own Celtic heritage, lovingly evoking the Robert Burns poem with warmth and humor.

Chadwick's creativity declined in his last years. He suffered regularly from gout, and a shipboard injury received in 1898 never healed properly, forcing him to use a cane in his later years. In the 1920s he wrote little, though he did rework *Rip Van Winkle* for publication, and his monograph on Horatio Parker appeared (1921/*R*1971). Chadwick received many honors; in addition to prizes for his compositions, he was a member of the National Institute and the American Academy of Arts and Letters (elected in 1898 and 1909, respectively); the latter awarded him a gold medal in 1928. In his later years there were occasional all-Chadwick concerts and Chadwick's contribution to the creation of an American musical language was recognized.

4. STYLE. Although Chadwick has sometimes been called a "Boston classicist," with all of its connotations of stuffiness, both his life and his music indicate the contrary. His music and his personality had indeed an academic flavor; but as an American of rural stock, a high-school dropout, and vagabond scholar he was hardly a stereotype. Numerous anecdotes testify to his sense of humor and his outspokenness, which often gave the impression

of gruffness. His best works show him to have been a pioneer in freeing American musical expression from German conservatory style. Very early in his career commentators noted "American" traits in his music, as in the String Quartet no.2 and the scherzos of his first two symphonies. Some works, such as the lyric drama *Judith*, show an interest in French sonorities, while *The Padrone*, for all its evocation of American urban life, draws on the techniques of *verismo* opera. In the Symphony no.2 he uses in the Scherzo a pentatonic melody resembling Negro song nine years before Dvořák included the better-known example in his Symphony "From the New World." Most movements of Chadwick's symphony use a variant of the introductory horn call, another pentatonic idea. Some melodies are related to hymnody and folksong. Chadwick's most representative works – the Symphony no.2, String Quartet no.4 (see fig.2), *The Padrone*, *Symphonic Sketches*, *Tam O'Shanter*, and many of the songs – illustrate a recognizable American style characterized by the unique rhythms of Anglo-American psalmody, Afro-Caribbean dance syncopations, parallel voice-leading (4ths and 5ths), and virtuoso orchestration. And his vocal works frequently display a sensitivity, unusual for the time, to characteristic syncopated or sprung rhythms of the English language, though there are also passages that could just as easily be settings of German or Latin.

The vagaries of Chadwick's reputation have paralleled that of the Second New England School in general. From a zenith of popularity achieved only after years of struggle for acceptance before World War I, it fell to a nadir of neglect during the postwar years. Then, after scholarly research into the roots of the present American musical establishment was begun after World War II, interest in Chadwick was again aroused, the conflict of the generations having been forgotten.

WORKS

Fragments, exercises, and most lost or incomplete works omitted. Numbers from Ledbetter (1984).

Publishers are indicated by means of abbreviations as follows: C. C. Birchard, Boston [Bi], Boston Music Co., Boston [Bo], J. Church, Cincinnati [C], O. Ditson, Boston [D], H. W. Gray, New York [G], T. B. Harms, New York [H], J. B. Millet, New York [M]; Novello, London [N], L. Prang, Boston [P], G. Schirmer, New York [S], A. P. Schmidt, Boston [Sm], C. Scribner, New York [Sc], Silver Burdett, Boston [SB], B. F. Wood, Boston [W]

I: STAGE

No.	*Title*	*Genre, no. of acts*	*Libretto*	*Composition*	*First performance*	*Sources and remarks*
1	The Peer and the Pauper	comic operetta, 2	R. Grant	1884		incorporates II:2, *MBCM* (inc.), lib. lost
2	A Quiet Lodging	operetta, 2	A. Bates	1892	Boston, 1 April 1892	MS lost except for no.5, "The first man I married," in private collection of V. F. Yellin, New York; lib., *MBCM*
3	Tabasco	burlesque opera, 2	R. A. Barnet	1893–4	Boston, 29 Jan 1894; professional production, 9 April 1894	uses material from I:1, see Yellin, 1957, pp.173–5; *MBCM*, vs (W 1894)
4	Judith	lyric drama, 3	W. C. Langdon, after scenario by Chadwick based on *Book of Judith* [Apocrypha]	1899–1900	Worcester Festival, 23 Sept 1901	*DLC*, vs (S 1901/*R* in Earlier American Music, iii, New York, 1972)
5	Everywoman: her Pilgrimage in Quest of Love	incidental music, 5	W. Browne	1910	Hartford, CT, 9 Feb 1911; New York, 27 Feb 1911	uses material from I:1, see Yellin, 1957, p.224, also II:19; vs (H 1911)
6	The Padrone	opera, 2	D. Stevens, after scenario by Chadwick	1912–13		*MBCM*
7	Love's Sacrifice	pastoral opera, 1	Stevens	1916–17	Chicago, 1 Feb 1923	school opera, partly orchd by Chadwick's students; *MBCM*, vs (Bi 1917)

II: ORCHESTRAL

(for full orch, with multiple wind, unless otherwise stated)

No.	*Title, genre, scoring*	*Composition*	*First performance*	*Sources and remarks*
1	Rip Van Winkle, ov.	1879	Leipzig, 18 March 1879	ded. J. Jefferson; *DLC*, *MBCM* (copy); rev. 1920s (Bi 1930)
2	Schön München (Beautiful Munich), waltz	1880	Boston, 7 Jan 1881	reused in I:1; *MBCM*
3	Symphony no.1, C, op.5	1881, begun ?1878	Boston, 23 Feb 1882	*MBCM*

No.	Title, genre, scoring	Composition	First performance	Sources and remarks
4	Andante, G, str orch	1882	Boston, 13 April 1882	arr. from Andante of V: 2
5	Thalia, ov.	1882	Boston SO, 12 Jan 1883	subtitled "overture to an imaginary comedy"; *MBCM*
6	Symphony no.2, B♭	1883–5	Scherzo, 1884; complete, Boston SO, 10 Dec 1886	(Sm 1888/*R* in Earlier American Music, iv, New York, 1972)
7	The Miller's Daughter (Tennyson), song and ov., Bar, orch	1886	San Francisco, 18 May 1887	1st part arr. from VII:4; *MBCM*
8	Melpomene, dramatic ov.	1887	Boston SO, 23 Dec 1887	subtitled "overture to an imaginary tragedy"; *DLC*; arr. pf 4 hands, VIII:12
9	A Pastoral Prelude	1890	Boston SO, 30 Jan 1892	*DLC*
10	Serenade, F, str orch	1890		*MBCM*
11	Symphony no.3, F	1893–4	Boston SO, 19 Oct 1894	ded. T. Thomas (Sm 1896)
12	Tabasco March, band/orch	1894	perf. with I:3, Boston, 29 Jan 1894	arr. pf (W 1894)
13	Adonais, ov.	1899	Boston SO, 2 Feb 1900	subtitled "in memoriam Frank Fay Marshall (amici probe et fidelis)," *DLC*
14	Euterpe, ov.	1903	Boston SO, 22 April 1904	*DLC* (S 1906)
15	Symphonic Sketches	1895–1904	Boston SO, 7 Feb 1908	*DLC* (S 1907)
	Jubilee	1895		
	Noel	1895		
	Hobgoblin	1904		
	A Vagrom Ballad	1896		
16	Cleopatra, sym. poem	1904	Worcester Festival, 29 Sept 1905	*DLC*
17	Sinfonietta, D	1904	Boston, 21 Nov 1904	(S 1906)
18	Theme, Variations, and Fugue, org, orch	1908	Boston, 13 Nov 1908	arr. org, IX:28
19	Everywoman Waltz	1909		pf score, *MBCM*, entitled "S. S. [?Suite symphonique] Waltz," but used in I:5
20	Suite symphonique, E♭	1905–9	Philadelphia, 29 March 1911	ded. F. A. Stock (Sm 1911)
21	Aphrodite, sym. fantasy	1910–11	Norfolk Festival, 4 June 1912	ded. Mr. and Mrs. C. Stoeckel, *DLC*
22	Tam O'Shanter, sym. ballad	1914–15	Norfolk Festival, 3 June 1915	after poem by R. Burns; ded. H. Parker, *DLC* (Bo 1917)
23	Angel of Death, sym. poem	1917–18	New York Symphony Society, 9 Feb 1919	ded. W. Damrosch, *DLC*
24	Jericho March	?1919		orch version of VII:119, *MBCM*
25	Elegy	1920		subtitled "in memoriam Horatio Parker," arr. of IX:29; *DLC*
26	Anniversary Overture	?1922	Norfolk Festival, 7 June 1922	? composed as early as 1917, as Illyria; *MBCM*
27	Tre pezzi: 1 Overture Mignon, 2 Canzone vecchio, 3 Fuga giocosa	1923		*DLC*

III: CHORAL WITH ORCHESTRA

No.	Title, genre	Text	Scoring	Composition	First performance	Sources and remarks
1	The Viking's Last Voyage	S. Baxter	B, TTBB, orch	1881	Boston, 22 April 1881	*MBCM*, vs (Sm 1881)
2	The Song of the Viking	Mrs. Craigin	TTBB, orch	1882, orchd 1914		for 50th anniversary of Concordia Gesang-Verein, Leipzig, with Ger. text as Das Lied des Viking; orchestration of VI:3; *MBCM*
3	Dedication Ode	H. B. Carpenter	S, A, T, B, SATB, orch	1883	Boston, 1883	for ded. of New Hollis Street

No.	Title, genre	Text	Scoring	Composition	First performance	Sources and remarks
						Church; *MBCM*, vs, as op.15 (Sm 1886)
4	Lovely Rosabelle, ballad	Scott	S, T, SATB, orch	1889	Boston, 10 Dec 1889	*DLC*, vs (Sm 1889)
5	Lullaby		SSAA, str orch	?1889		arr. of VI:10
6	The Pilgrims	F. D. Hemans	SATB, orch	1890	Boston, 2 April 1891	*MBCM* (copy), vs (Sm 1890)
7	Phoenix expirans, cantata	anon. Lat. hymn	S, A, T, B, SATB, orch	1891	Springfield Festival, 5 May 1892	*DLC*, *MBCM*, vs (Sm 1892)
8	Ode	H. Monroe	S, T, SATB, wind ens, orch	1892	Chicago, 21 Oct 1892	for the opening of the World's Columbian Exposition; *DLC* (entitled "Columbia"), vs (C 1892)
9	The Lily Nymph, dramatic cantata	Bates	S, T, B, B, SATB, orch	1894–5	New York, 7 Dec 1895	*DLC*, vs (Sm 1895)
10	Ecce jam noctis	St. Gregory	TTBB, orch	1897	New Haven, 30 June 1897	for Yale commencement at which Chadwick received hon. MA; *DLC*, vs (Sm 1897)
11	Noel	compilation	S, A, T, B, SATB, orch	1907–8	Norfolk Festival, 2 June 1909	*DLC*, vs (G 1909)
12	Elfin Song	J. R. Drake	SSAA, orch	1913		orch arr. of VI:26; *MBCM*
13	Silently swaying on the water's quiet breast	V. von Scheffel	SSAA, orch	?1916		orch arr. of VI:38; *MBCM* (2 different versions)
14	Jehovah reigns in majesty	Ps. xcix	TTBB, brass, org	?1916		arr. of VI:105
15	Land of our hearts	J. H. Ingham	SATB, orch	1917	Norfolk Festival, 4 June 1918	*DLC*, vs (C 1918)
16	These to the front	M. A. D. Howe	TTBB, orch	1918		orch arr. of VI:44
17	The Fighting Men	Howe	unison vv, orch	?1918		orch arr. of VI:41; *MBCM*
18	Joshua	R. D. Ware	TTBB, orch	?1919		orch arr. of VI:45; *MBCM* (entitled "Jericho March")
19	Mexican Serenade	A. Guiterman	SATB, orch	?1921		orch arr. of VI:52; *MBCM*
20	Fathers of the Free	E. E. Brown	SATB, orch	?1927		*MBCM* (partly autograph), vs (G 1927)
21	Commemoration Ode	J. R. Lowell	SATB, orch	?1928		presumably for World War I commemoration; *MBCM*, vs (D 1928)

IV: SOLO VOCAL WITH ORCHESTRA

No.	Title	Text	Voice	Composition	First performance	Sources and remarks
1	Lochinvar	Scott	Bar	1896	Springfield Festival, 7 May 1896	ded. M. Heinrich, *DLC*, vs (Sm 1896)
2	A Ballad of Trees and the Master	S. Lanier	low/medium	?1899		orch arr. of VII:87; *MBCM*
3	Aghadoe	J. Todhunter	A	1910		*DLC*, vs (Sm 1911)
4	The Curfew	Longfellow	low/medium	?1914	Boston, 17 Feb 1924	orch arr. of VII:112; *MBCM*
5	The Voice of Philomel	Stevens	low/medium	?1914	Boston, 17 Feb 1924	orch arr. of VII:107; *MBCM*
6	Joshua	Ware	medium	?1919		orch arr. of VI:45; *MBCM*
7	Drake's Drum	H. Newbold	low/medium	?1920	Boston, 17 Feb 1924	orch arr. of VII:121; *MBCM*
8	Pirate Song	A. Conan Doyle	Bar	?1920		orch arr. of VII:122; *MBCM*

V: CHAMBER

No.	*Title, scoring*	*Composition*	*First performance*	*Sources and remarks*
1	Trio, c, ?str	?1877	Leipzig, 1878	lost
2	String Quartet no. 1, g, op. 1	1878	Leipzig, 29 May 1878 (2 movts)	*MBCM*; Andante arr. str orch, II:4
3	String Quartet no. 2, C, op. 2	1878	Leipzig, 30 May 1879	*MBCM*
4	String Quartet no. 3, D	?1885	Boston, 9 March 1887	MS in private collection of D. Kelleher, New York; parts only, *MBCM*
5	Quintet, E♭, pf, 2 vn, va, vc	1887	Boston, 23 Jan 1888	*DLC* (Sm 1890)
6	String Quartet no. 4, e	1896	Boston, 21 Dec 1896	*DLC*; parts only (S 1902)
7	String Quartet no. 5, d	1898	Boston, 12 Feb 1901	*MBCM*; parts pubd privately (1910)
8	Romanze, vc, pf	1911		(Sm 1911)
9	Easter Morn, vn/vc, pf	?1914		(Sm 1914); arr. 4 vn, harp, org, *MBCM*
10	Fanfare, 3 tpt, 3 trbn, timp	1925	Boston, 3 Nov 1925	for unveiling of J. S. Sargent mural at Museum of Fine Arts; *MBCM*

VI: OTHER CHORAL
(keyboard reductions of choral works with orchestra not listed)

No.	*Title*	*Text*	*Scoring*	*Remarks and publication*
		secular		
1	Margarita	Scheffel	TTBB	(Sm 1881)
2	Reiterlied (Trooper's Song)		TTBB	(Sm 1881)
3	The Song of the Viking	Craigin	TTBB, pf	(Sm 1882); orchd 1914, III:2
4	Spring Song, op. 9		SSAA, pf	(Sm 1882)
	Four Partsongs		TTBB	(Sm 1886)
5	The Boy and the Owl	J. L. Breck		
6	Serenade	Breck		
7	Drinking Song	Bates		
8	When love was young	Bates		
9	Jabberwocky	L. Carroll	TTBB	(Sm 1886)
10	Lullaby		SSAA, pf	(Sm 1889); orchd ?1889, III:5
	Four Songs of Brittany	Bates	SSA, pf	(Sm 1890); arr. from VII:46, 48, 49, 51
11	The autumn winds are chill			
12	Love is fleeting			
13	My sweetheart gave a crimson blossom			
14	The lark that sang when morning broke			
15	Stormy Evening	R. L. Stevenson	children's vv	(Bi 1901)
	Two Four-part Choruses		SSAA	(S 1902)
16	Stabat mater speciosa	G. da Todi		
17	Thistle Down	A. Macy		
	Two Four-part Choruses		SSAA	(S 1903)
18	Rondel (canon)	J. C. Grant		
19	Behind the lattice	S. M. Peck		
	Three Choruses	Meleager	SSA, pf	(S 1904)
20	To Heliodora			
21	At the bride's gates			
22	Dorcas			
	Three Part-songs		TTBB	(Sm 1910)
23	Darest thou now, O soul	Whitman		
24	Credo	W. M. Thackeray		
25	Pack, clouds, away	T. Heywood	with pf ad lib	
26	Elfin Song	Drake	SSAA, pf	(Sm 1910); orchd 1913, III:12
27	In a China Shop	G. C. Hellman	SSAA, pf	(Sm 1910)
28	Inconstancy (Sigh no more, ladies)	Shakespeare	SATB/SSAA/TTBB, pf ad lib	(Sm 1910)
29	It was a lover and his lass	Shakespeare	SSA, pf/TTBB, pf ad lib	(Sm 1910)
30	Mary's Lullaby	C. A. Matson Dolson	SSAA, pf ad lib	(Sm 1910)
31	Miss Nancy's Gown	Z. Cooke	SSA, pf	(Sm 1910)
32	The Spring Beauties	H. G. Cone	SSA, pf	(Sm 1911)
33	Busy Lark	Chaucer	children's vv	(Bi 1912)
34	Noble's Traditions	R. W. Rivers	children's vv, pf	(Boston, 1913)
35	Hail us doctors of song	J. Koren	TTBB, pf	pubd in The Sängerfest (Boston, 1914)
36	The Lamb	Blake	children's vv	(Bi 1914)

No.	Title	Text	Scoring	Remarks and publication
37	Sons of Herman	J. L. Sanford	children's vv	(D 1914)
38	Silently swaying on the water's quiet breast	Scheffel	SSAA, pf	(D 1916); with orch acc., III:13
39	The Bluebells of New England	T. B. Aldrich	SSA, pf	(D 1917)
40	Dolly	A. Dobson	SSA, pf	(D 1917)
41	The Fighting Men	Howe	unison vv, pf	=VII:118 (Bi 1918); with orch acc., III:17
42	Here comes the flag	Macy	children's vv	(Bi 1918)
43	June	J. H. Smith	SSA, pf	(D 1918)
44	These to the front	Howe	TTBB, pf	(D 1918); with orch acc., III:16
45	Joshua	Ware	TTBB, pf	(D 1919); for arrs. see II:24, III:18, IV:6, VII:119
46	Buie Annajohn	B. Carman	SATB, pf	(SB 1923)
47	Caravan Song	A. H. Hyatt	SATB, pf	(SB 1923)
48	Chorus of Pilgrim Women	J. P. Peabody	SSAA, pf	from the Pilgrim Tercentenary Pageant, 1921; (SB 1923)
49	Deep in the soul of a rose	Hyatt	SSA, pf	(SB 1923)
50	The Immortal (Spring Song)	C. Y. Rice	SATB, pf	(Bi 1923)
51	Little Lac Grenier	W. H. Drummond	SSATTB, pf	(SB 1923)
52	Mexican Serenade	Guiterman	SATB, pf	(SB 1923); with orch acc., III:19
53	Mister Moon	Carman	SSAA, pf	(SB 1923)
54	A Christmas Greeting		SATB, pf ad lib	pubd privately (1925)
55	A Madrigal for Christmas	?Chadwick	SATB	pubd privately (*c*1926)
56	A Ballad of Trees and the Master	Lanier	SATB, pf/org	(D 1929); arr. of VII:87, 1927
	Holiday Songs			(D 1928)
57	Angel of peace	O. W. Holmes	SATB, pf ad lib	for Armistice Day; *DLC*
58	Concord Hymn	R. W. Emerson	SATB, pf	for Patriot's Day
59	Evening	S. Baring-Gould	SATTBB, pf ad lib	
60	In the hammock we swing	C. S. Pratt	SSA, pf	for Mother's Day, arr. of VII:32
61	A May Carol	F. D. Sherman	SATB, pf	
62	The Mistletoe Bough		SATB, pf ad lib	
63	New Year's Song	G. E. Troutlock	SATB, pf ad lib	
64	The Runaway	Rice	SATB, pf	
65	A Valentine	M. B. Edwards	SATB, pf	
66	What say?	G. F. Norton	SATB, pf	
67	Saint Botolph	Macy	TTBB, pf	(D 1929); arr. of VII:97

sacred

No.	Title	Text	Scoring	Remarks and publication
	Three Sacred Anthems, op.6		SATB, org	(Sm 1882)
68	Praise the Lord			
69	Blessed be the Lord (Benedictus)			
70	O Thou that hearest			
	Three Sacred Quartets, op.13		SATB, org	(Sm 1885)
71	As the hart pants	Ps. xlii		
72	God who madest earth and heaven			
73	God to whom we look up blindly	B. Taylor		
74	Abide with me		SAT, org	(Sm 1888)
75	Brightest and best	R. Heber	SATB	(Sm 1888); version for 1v, pf, VII:131
76	O cease, my wandering soul		SAB, org	(Sm 1888)
77	O day of rest		ATB, org	(Sm 1888)
78	There were shepherds		SATB	(Sm 1888)
79	Thou sendest sun and rain		SATB	(Sm 1889)
80	Art thou weary?		SATB	(Sm 1890)
81	God be merciful		SATB, org	(Sm 1890)
82	Behold the works of the Lord		SATB	(Sm 1891)
83	Come hither, ye faithful		SATB	(Sm 1891)
84	Saviour, like a shepherd		SATB	(Sm 1891)
85	While thee I seek		SATB	(Sm 1891)
86	Awake up my glory		SATB	(Sm 1895)
87	The Beatitudes		SATB, org	(Sm 1895)
88	Jubilate, B♭	Ps. c	SATB, org	(Sm 1895)
89	Lord of all power and might		SATB, org	(Sm 1895)
90	Peace and light		SATB, org	(Sm 1895)
91	Sentences and Responses		SATB, org	(Sm 1895)
92	Thou who art divine	adapted O. B. Brown	SATB	(Sm 1895)
93	Welcome happy morn		SATB	(Sm 1895)
94	When the Lord of love was here		SATB	(Sm 1895); hymn tune: Armstrong
95	O holy child of Bethlehem	Phillips Brooks	A, SATB, org	(Sm 1896)

No.	Title	Text	Scoring	Remarks and publication
96	Shout, ye high heavens	Plaudite coeli, trans. J. L. Hayes	SATB, org	(Sm 1897)
97	While shepherds watched		SATB	(Sm 1899)
98	Hark! hark, my soul	W. F. Faber	A, SATB, org	(S 1903); version for 1v, pf, VII:137
99	Morn's roseate hues	from The Hymnal, nos. 120, 121	SATB, pf/org	(N 1903)
100	Teach me, O Lord			(D 1903)
	Two Anthems		SATB, org	(S 1904)
101	Come unto me			
102	Thou shalt love the Lord thy God			
103	Saviour, again to thy dear name	J. Ellerton	SATB, pf/org	(N 1904)
104	Sun of my soul	J. Keble	T, SATB, org	(N 1904)
105	Jehovah reigns in majesty	Ps. xcix	TTBB, org	(D 1916); arr. with brass, III:14

VII: SOLO SONGS

All with piano or organ accompaniment. The incipit is given only when it differs from the title. Separately published extracts from larger works are not included.

No.	Title	Incipit	Text	Remarks and publication
		secular		
	Three Songs by J. W. Chadwick			(D 1881)
1	So far away			
2	Good Night	The moon is sinking fast, my love		
3	Across the hills		P. W. Lyall	
4	The Miller's Daughter	It is the miller's daughter	Tennyson	(Sm 1881); arr. Bar, orch, II:7
	Three Love Songs, Bar, op.8		Bates	(Sm 1882)
5	Rose Guerdon	I kiss the rosebud which you wore		
6	Serenade	While stars above thee glow		
7	Before the Dawn	In the hush of the morn		
	Three Little Songs, op.11			(Sm 1883)
8	Request	Is my lover on the sea?	B. Cornwall	
9	Gay little Dandelion			
10	Thou art so like a flower		after Heine	
	Six Songs			(Sm 1885)
11	The Danza	If you never have danced the danza	Bates	
12	He loves me	Over and over with ceaseless motion	N. MacIntosh	
13	In bygone days		Breck	
14	I know two eyes			
15	Sweet wind that blows		O. Leighton	
16	Lullaby	Lullaby, baby		
17	King Death	King Death was a rare old fellow		(Sm 1885)
18	The Sea King	Come sing of the great Sea King	Cornwall	(Sm 1885)
	Two Songs		T. B. Aldrich	(Sm 1886)
19	Nocturne	Up to her chamber window		
20	Song from the Persian	O sad are they who know not love		
21	The Mill	Winding and grinding	Miss Mulock	(Sm 1886)
22	Allah	Allah gives light in darkness	Longfellow	(Sm 1887)
23	The Lament (Egyptian Song from "Ben Hur")	I sigh as I sing of the story land	L. Wallace	(Sm 1887)
24	The Lily	Far up the steep a lily grows	A. Salvini, trans. T. R. Sullivan	(Sm 1887)
	Baby's Lullaby Book		C. S. Pratt	(P 1888)
25	January: The snowflakes float down from the skies			
26	February: The snowbirds that chirped in the sun			
27	March: Hark and hear the March wind blowing			
28	April: On the roof the rain is dripping			
29	May: This sweet May day, my dear			
30	June: O the red rose tree has a bud my dear			
31	July: If I were a lily			
32	August: In the hammock we swing			arr. SSA, pf, VI:60
33	September: O Moon, round Moon			
34	October: Through the day the Heavenly Father			
35	November: Summer birds have taken wing			
36	December: Long years ago in eastern Heaven			
37	Green grows the Willow	O I love my love the best	H. Aïde	(Sm 1888)
38	Sorais' Song	As a desolate bird that through darkness	H. Rider Haggard	(Sm 1888)
	Three Ballads			(Sm 1889)
39	A Bonny Curl	I have a curl, a bricht brown curl	A. Rives	
40	The Maiden and the Butterfly	There wandered once a maiden		
41	A Warning	A gentle innocent she was	E. Breck	
42	Bedouin Love Song	From the desert I come to thee	Taylor	(Sm 1890)

No.	Title	Incipit	Text	Remarks and publication
	Songs of Brittany		Bates	(Sm 1890)
43	Loud trumpets blow			
44	Proudly, Childe Haslin			
45	How flowers fade			
46	The autumn winds are chill			
47	As summer wind			arr. SSA, pf, VI:11
48	Love is fleeting			
49	My sweetheart gave a crimson blossom			arr. SSA, pf, VI:12
50	How youth with passion plays			arr. SSA, pf, VI:13
51	The lark that sang when morning broke			
52	Proudly at morn the hunter rode			arr. SSA, pf, VI:14
53	The trumpet sounds and calls away			
54	The distaff whirled			
	A Flower Cycle		Bates	(Sm 1892/*R*1980)
55	The Crocus	Brave crocus, out of time and rash		
56	The Trilliums	Wake Robin, the trilliums call		
57	The Water Lily	Where the dark waters lave		
58	The Cyclamen	Over the plains where Persian hosts		
59	The Wild Briar	The wild briar dabbles his fingertips		
60	The Columbine	Gay in her red gown trim and fine		
61	The Foxglove	In grandma's garden in shining rows		
62	The Cardinal Flower	When days are long and steeped in sun		
63	The Lupine	Ah Lupine, with silvery leaves		
64	The Meadow Rue	The tall white rue stands like a ghost		
65	The Jasmine	The soft, warm night wind flutters		
66	The Jacqueminot Rose	'Twas a Jacqueminot rose that she gave me at parting		
	Two Folk Songs			(Sm 1892)
67	O love and joy			
68	The Northern Days		C. Rossetti	
69	Armenian Lullaby	If thou wilt close thy drowsy eyes	E. Field	(Sc 1896)
70	Kissing Time	'Tis when the lark goes soaring	Field	(Sc 1896)
	Lyrics from "Told in the Gate"		Bates	(Sm 1897/*R*1980)
71	Sweetheart, thy lips are touched with flame			
72	Sings the nightingale to the rose			
73	The rose leans over the pool			
74	Love's like a summer rose			
75	As in waves without number			
76	Dear love, when in thine arms I lie			
77	Was I not thine			
78	In mead where roses bloom			
79	Sister fairest, why art thou sighing?			
80	Oh, let night speak of me			
81	I said to the wind of the south			
82	Were I a prince Egyptian			
83	Farewell to the Farm	The coach is at the door at last	Stevenson	(Sc 1898)
84	I have not forgotten		W. M. Chauvenet	(C 1898)
85	The Land of Counterpane	When I was sick and lay abed	Stevenson	(Sc 1898)
86	Since my love's eyes		Chauvenet	(C 1898)
87	A Ballad of Trees and the Master	Into the woods my master went	Lanier	(D 1899); with orch acc., IV:2; arr. SATB, VI:56
	Six Songs			(S 1902)
88	Euthanasia	O drop your eyelids down, my lady	Macy	
89	The Aureole	Oh, love is like an aureole	Macy	
90	Adversity	A soft eye's drooping lid	Macy	
91	The Wishing Stream	Fair stream, whose arms from snows above	Chauvenet	
92	The Honeysuckle	'Twas a tender little honeysuckle vine	Macy	
93	The Stranger-man	Now what is this, my daughter dear?	Macy	
	Three Songs, Mez/Bar			(S 1902)
94	In my Beloved's Eyes	I looked into the midnight deep	Chauvenet	orig. pubd (Sc 1897)
95	The Brink of Night	Upon the brink of night I stand	Chauvenet	
96	Thou art to me		Macy	
97	Saint Botolph	Saint Botolph flourished in the olden time	Macy	(W 1902); arr. TTBB, VI:67
	Four Irish Songs			(Sm 1910)
98	Larry O'Toole	You've all heard of Larry O'Toole	Thackeray	
99	The Lady of Leith	There was a lady lived in Leith	W. Maginn	
100	Nora McNally	I met her in Thundercut Alley	A. Moor	
101	The Recruit	Sez Corporal Madden to Private McFadden	R. W. Chambers	
	Five Songs			(Sm 1910)
102	When stars are in the quiet skies		B. Lytton	
103	Love's Image	My love o'er the water	J. Thomson	
104	Gifts	Give a man a horse he can ride	Thomson	

No.	*Title*	*Incipit*	*Text*	*Remarks and publication*
105	When I am dead		Rossetti	
106	O Love stay by and sing		Sullivan	
	Five Songs		Stevens	(S 1914)
107	The Voice of Philomel	With melody the air is thrilling		later orchd, IV:5
108	The Bobolink	The violet and the iris were in flower		
109	Roses	Sylvia stood by the trellis below		
110	When she gave me her hand			
111	When Phillis looks			
112	The Curfew	Solemnly, mournfully, dealing its dole	Longfellow	(Sm 1914); later orchd, IV:4
113	The Daughter of Mendoza	O lend to me sweet nightingale	M. B. Lamar	(Sm 1914)
114	Fulfillment	'Twas beneath an autumn sky	Stevens	(Sm 1914)
115	Periwinkle Bay	Her starry eyes, like summer skies	Stevens	(Sm 1914)
116	That golden hour		Stevens	(Sm 1914)
117	Yesterday	Comes the morning	Stevens	(Sm 1914)
118	The Fighting Men	Away to the front, in France or Flanders	Howe	=VI:41 (Bi 1918); with orch acc., III:17
119	Joshua	Joshua was the son of Nun	Ware	arr. of VI:45 (D 1920)
	Three Nautical Songs			
120	The Admirals	Sat there the Queen	Ware	
121	Drake's Drum	Drake, he's in his hammock	Newbold	later orchd, IV:7
122	Pirate Song	A trader sailed from Stepney town	Conan Doyle	later orchd, IV:8
123	A Christmas Limerick	A boy had a chum	?Chadwick	pubd privately (1927)
124	If I were you			recorded, but no MS or pubd copy extant; see C. Oja, ed.: *American Music Recordings* (Brooklyn, NY, 1982), no. 1690
125	Ladybird			ibid., no. 1691
126	The Morning Glory			ibid., no. 1693
127	Time Enough			ibid., no. 1711
		sacred		
	Three Sacred Songs			(Sm 1887)
128	When our heads are bowed with woe		H. H. Milman	
129	O Mother dear, Jerusalem		F. Baker	
130	Let not your heart be troubled			
131	Brightest and best		Heber	version for SATB, VI:75
132	Hail, all hail the glorious morn		I. S. Taylor	(Sm 1892)
133	He maketh wars to cease			(Sm 1892)
134	There is a river			(Sm 1892)
135	Faith	My faith is mighty as the tide	Macy	(C 1899)
136	The Good Samaritan, with vn obbl	A poor wayfaring man of grief	J. Montgomery	(C 1900)
137	Hark! hark, my soul		Faber	version for SATB, VI:98

VIII: PIANO

(for pf solo unless otherwise stated)

1–6 Six Characteristic Pieces, op.7: Congratulations, ded. F. F. Marshall; Please do, ded. Marie Chadwick, Leipzig; Scherzino, ded. A. Preston, Boston; Reminiscence; Irish melody, ded. W. McEwen, Munich; Etude, ded. G. Heubach, Brooklyn (Sm 1882)

7–8 Two Caprices, C, g (Sm 1888)

9–11 Drei Walzer, f, E♭, A♭ (Sm 1890)

12 Melpomene, ov., pf 4 hands (Sm 1891); arr. of II:8

13 Chanson orientale (M 1895)

14 Nocturne (M 1895)

15–24 Ten Little Tunes for Ten Little Fingers, pedagogical pieces (W 1903)

25–9 Five Pieces: Prélude joyeux, ded. A. Foote; Dans le canot: Barcarolle, ded. A. Whiting; Le ruisseau, ded. H. Hopekirk; Le crépuscule, ded. T. Adamowski; Les grenouilles: Humoresque, ded. H. Hopekirk (S 1905)

30 Aphrodite, 2 pf, ?1911, *MBCM*; arr. of I:21

31 The Aspen, pedagogical piece (St. Louis, 1924)

32–3 Diddle Diddle Dumpling, Ye Robin, pedagogical pieces from A Second Book of Piano Pieces (Boston, 1928)

34 The Footlight Fairy, inc., *MBCM*

35 Novelette, *MBCM*

36 Prelude and Fugue à la hornpipe, G, *MBCM* (copy)

37 Prelude and Fugue, a, *MBCM* (copy)

38 Prelude and Fugue, c, *MBCM*

IX: ORGAN

1–10 Ten Canonic Studies, op.12, ded. H. M. Dunham (Sm 1885)

11–20 [10] Progressive Pedal Studies (Sm 1890)

21–3 Three Compositions: Prelude, Response, March (Sm 1890)

24 Pastorale (M 1895)

25 Requiem, *MB* (dated "Oct 8/95") (M 1896)

26 Canzonetta, G, *MB* (M 1896)

27 Introduction and Theme, E♭, *MB* (M 1896)

28 Theme, Variations, and Fugue, 1908 (Bo 1923); arr. of II:18

29 Elegy, in memoriam Horatio Parker (Bo 1920); arr. orch, II:25

30 Suite in Variation Form: Prelude, Recitative, Cipher (Pastorale), Romance, Tema, Finale (Fuga) (G 1923)

31 In Tadaussac Church (1735) (G 1926)

INDEX TO THE VOCAL WORKS

weary?, VI:80; As a desolate bird that through darkness, VII:38; As in waves without number, VII:75; A soft eye's drooping lid, VII:90; As summer wind, VII:47; As the hart pants, VI:71; A trader sailed from Stepney town, IV:8, VII:122; At the bride's gates, VI:21; The Aureole, VII:89; The autumn winds are chill, VI:11, VII:46; A Valentine, VI:65; Awake up my glory, VI:86; A Warning, VII:41; Away to the front, in France or Flanders, III:17, VI:41, VII:118

Baby's Lullaby Book, VII:25–36; The Beatitudes, VI:87; Bedouin Love Song, VII:42; Before the Dawn, VII:7; Behind the lattice, VI:19; Behold the works of the Lord, VI:82; Benedictus, VI:69; Blessed be the Lord, VI:69; The Bluebells of New England, VI:39; The Bobolink, VII:108; The Boy and the Owl, VI:5; Brave crocus, out of time and rash, VII:55; Brightest and best, VI:75, VII:131; The Brink of Night, VII:95; Buie Annajohn, VI:46; Busy Lark, VI:33

Caravan Song, VI:47; The Cardinal Flower, VII:62; Chorus of Pilgrim Women, VI:48; The coach is at the door at last, VII:83; The Columbine, VII:60; Come hither, ye faithful, VI:83; Come sing of the great Sea King, VII:18; Comes the morning, VII:117; Come unto me, VI:101; Commemoration Ode, III:21; Concord Hymn, VI:58; Credo, VI:24; The Crocus, VII:55; The Curfew, IV:4, VII:112; The Cyclamen, VII:58; The Danza, VII:11; Darest thou now, O soul, VI:23; The Daughter of Mendoza, VII:113

Dear love, when in thine arms I lie, VII:76; Dedication Ode, III:3; Deep in the soul of a rose, VI:49; The distaff whirled, VII:54; Dolly, VI:40; Dorcas, VI:22; Drake's Drum, IV:7, VII:121; Drinking Song, VI:7; Ecce jam noctis, III:10; Egyptian Song from "Ben Hur," VII:23; Elfin Song, III:12, VI:26; Euthanasia, VII:88; Evening, VI:59; Fair stream, whose arms from snows above, VII:91; Faith, VII:135; Farewell to the Farm, VII:83; Fathers of the Free, III:20; Far up the steep a lily grows, VII:24

The Fighting Men, III:17, VI:41, VII:118; 4 Irish Songs, VII:98–101; 4 Songs of Brittany, VI:11–14; The Foxglove, VII:61; From the desert I come to thee, VII:42; Fulfillment, VII:114; Gay in her red gown trim and fine, VII:60; Gay little Dandelion, VII:9; Gifts, VII:104; Give a man a horse he can ride, VII:104; God be merciful, VI:81; God to whom we look up blindly, VI:73; God who madest earth and heaven, VI:72; Good Night, VII:2; The Good Samaritan, VII:136; Green grows the Willow, VII:37

Hail, all hail the glorious morn, VII:132; Hail us doctors of song, VI:35; Hark and hear the March wind blowing, VII:27; Hark! hark, my soul, VI:98, VII:137; He loves me, VII:12; He maketh wars to cease, VII:133; Here comes the flag, VI:42; Her starry eyes, like summer skies, VII:115; Holiday Songs, VI:57–66; The Honeysuckle, VII:92; How flowers fade, VII:45; How youth with passion plays, VII:50; If I were a lily, VII:31; If I were you, VII:124; If thou wilt close thy drowsy eyes, VII:69; If you never have danced the danza, VII:11

I have a curl, a bricht brown curl, VII:39; I have not forgotten, VII:84; I kiss the rosebud which you wore, VII:5; I know two eyes, VII:14; I looked into the midnight deep, VII:94; I met her in Thundercut Alley, VII:100; The Immortal, VI:50; In a China Shop, VI:27; In bygone days, VII:13; Inconstancy, VI:28; In grandma's garden in shining rows, VII:61; In mead where roses bloom, VII:78; In my Beloved's Eyes, VII:94; In the hammock we swing, VI:60, VII:32; In the hush of the morn, VII:7

Into the woods my master went, IV:2, VI:56, VII:87; I said to the wind of the south, VII:81; I sigh as I sing of the story land, VII:23; Is my lover on the sea?, VII:8; It is the miller's daughter, VII:4; It was a lover and his lass, VI:29; Jabberwocky, VI:9; The Jacqueminot Rose, VII:66; The Jasmine, VII:65; Jehovah reigns in majesty, III:14, VI:105; Joshua, III:18, IV:6, VI:45, VII:119; Jubilate, VI:88; June, VI:43; King Death, VII:17; Kissing Time, VII:70; Ladybird, VII:125; The Lady of Leith, VII:99; The Lamb, VI:36

The Lament, VII:23; The Land of Counterpane, VII:85; Land of our hearts, III:15; The lark that sang when morning broke, VI:14, VII:51; Larry O'Toole, VII:98; Let not your heart be troubled, VII:130; The Lily, VII:24; The Lily Nymph, III:9; Little Lac Grenier, VI:51; Lochinvar, IV:1; Long years ago in eastern Heaven, VII:36; Lord of all power and might, VI:89; Loud trumpets blow, VII:43; Love is fleeting, VI:12, VII:48; Lovely Rosabelle, III:4; Love's Image, VII:103

Love's like a summer rose, VII:74; Lullaby, III:5, VI:10, VII:16; The Lupine, VII:63; Lyrics from "Told in the Gate," VII:71–82; The Maiden and the Butterfly, VII:40; Margarita, VI:1; Mary's Lullaby, VI:30; The Meadow Rue, VII:64; Mexican Serenade, III:19, VI:52; The Mill, VII:21; The Miller's Daughter, VII:4; Miss Nancy's Gown, VI:31; Mister Moon, VI:53; The Mistletoe Bough, VI:62; The moon is sinking fast, my love, VII:2; The Morning Glory, VII:126; Morn's roseate hues, VI:99; My faith is mighty as the tide, VII:135

My love o'er the water, VII:103; My sweetheart gave a crimson blossom, VI:13, VII:49; New Year's Song, VI:63; Noble's Traditions, VI:34; Nocturne, VII:19; Noel, III:11; Nora McNally, VII:100; The Northern Days, VII:68; Now what is this, my daughter dear?, VII:93; O cease, my wandering soul, VI:76; O day of rest, VI:77; Ode, III:8; O drop your eyelids down, my lady, VII:88; Oh, let night speak of me, VII:80; Oh, love is like an aureole, VII:89; O holy child of Bethlehem, VI:95

O I love my love the best, VII:37; O lend to me sweet nightingale, VII:113; O love and joy, VII:67; O Love stay by and sing, VII:106; O Moon, round Moon, VII:33; O Mother dear, Jerusalem, VII:129; On the roof the rain is dripping, VII:28; O sad are they who know not love, VII:20; O the red rose tree has a bud my dear, VII:30; O Thou that hearest, VI:70; Over and over with ceaseless motion, VII:12; Over the plains where Persian hosts, VII:58; Pack, clouds, away, VI:25; Peace and light, VI:90

Periwinkle Bay, VII:115; Phoenix expirans, III:7; The Pilgrims, III:6; Pirate Song, IV:8, VII:122; Praise the Lord, VI:68; Proudly at morn the hunter rode, VII:52; Proudly, Childe Haslin, VII:44; The Recruit, VII:101; Reiterlied, VI:2; Request, VII:8; Rondel, VI:18; Rose Guerdon, VII:5; The rose leans over the pool, VII:73; Roses, VII:109; The Runaway, VI:64; Saint Botolph, VI:67, VII:97; Sat there the Queen, VII:120; Saviour, again to thy dear name, VI:103; Saviour, like a shepherd, VI:84

The Sea King, VII:18; Sentences and Responses, VI:91; Serenade, VI:6, VII:6; Sez Corporal Madden to Private McFadden, VII:101; Shout, ye high heavens, VI:96; Sigh no more, ladies, VI:28; Silently swaying on the water's quiet breast, III:13, VI:38; Since my love's eyes, VII:86; Sings the nightingale to the rose, VII:72; Sister fairest, why art thou sighing?, VII:79; The snowbirds that chirped in the sun, VII:26; The snowflakes float down from the skies, VII:25; So far away, VII:1

The soft, warm night wind flutters, VII:65; Solemnly, mournfully, dealing its dole, IV:4, VII:112; Song from the Persian, VII:20; The Song of the Viking, III:2, VI:3; Songs of Brittany, VII:43–54; Sons of Herman, VI:37; Sorais' Song, VII:38; The Spring Beauties, VI:32; Spring Song, VI:4, VI:50; Stabat mater speciosa, VI:16; Stormy Evening, VI:15; The Stranger-man, VII:93; Summer birds have taken wing, VII:35; Sun of my soul, VI:104; Sweetheart, thy lips are touched with flame, VII:71; Sweet wind that blows, VII:15

Sylvia stood by the trellis below, VII:109; The tall white rue stands like a ghost, VII:64; Teach me, O Lord, VI:100; That golden hour, VII:116; There is a river, VII:134; There wandered once a maiden, VII:40; There was a lady lived in Leith, VII:99; There were shepherds, VI:78; These to the front, III:16, VI:44; This sweet May day, my dear, VII:29; Thistle Down, VI:17; Thou art so like a flower, VII:10; Thou art to me, VII:96; Thou sendest sun and rain, VI:79; Thou shalt love the Lord thy God, VI:102

Thou who art divine, VI:92; 3 Little Songs, VII:8–10; 3 Love Songs, VII:5–7; 3 Nautical Songs, VII:120–22; 3 Sacred Anthems, VI:68–70; 3 Sacred Quartets, VI:71–3; Through the day the Heavenly Father, VII:34; Time Enough, VII:127; 'Tis when the lark goes soaring, VII:70; To Heliodora, VI:20; The Trilliums, VII:56; Trooper's Song, VI:2; The trumpet sounds and calls away, VII:53; 'Twas a Jacqueminot rose that she gave me at parting, VII:66

'Twas a tender little honeysuckle vine, VII:92; 'Twas beneath an autumn sky, VII:114; Upon the brink of night I stand, VII:95; Up to her chamber window, VII:19; The Viking's Last Voyage, III:1; The violet and the iris were in flower, VII:108; The Voice of Philomel, IV:5, VII:107; Wake Robin, the trilliums call, VII:56; Was I not thine, VII:77; The Water Lily, VII:57; Welcome happy morn, VI:93; Were I a prince Egyptian, VII:82; What say?, VI:66; When days are long and steeped in sun, VII:62; When I am dead, VII:105; When I was sick and lay abed, VII:85

When love was young, VI:8; When our heads are bowed with woe, VII:128; When Phillis looks, VII:111; When she gave me her hand, VII:110; When stars are in the quiet skies, VII:102; When the Lord of love was here, VI:94; Where the dark waters lave, VII:57; While shepherds watched, VI:97; While stars above thee glow, VII:6; While thee I seek, VI:85; The Wild Briar, VII:59; Winding and grinding, VII:21; The Wishing Stream, VII:91; With melody the air is thrilling, IV:5, VII:107; Yesterday, VII:117; You've all heard of Larry O'Toole, VII:98

BIBLIOGRAPHY

EwenD; *GroveAS*

F. O. Jones: "Chadwick, George W.," *A Handbook of American Music and Musicians* (Canaseraga, NY, 1886/*R*1971), 31

J. Tiersot: *Musiques pittoresques: promenades musicales à l'Exposition de 1889* (Paris, 1889), 55

R. Hughes: *Contemporary American Composers* (Boston, 1900), 210ff

L. C. Elson: *The History of American Music* (New York, 1904; enlarged 2/1915; enlarged by A. Elson, 3/1925/*R*1971), 170ff

C. Engel: "George W. Chadwick," *MQ*, x (1924), 438
J. T. Howard: *Our American Music* (New York, 1931, rev. 4/1965), 325ff
A. L. Langley: "Chadwick and the New England Conservatory of Music," *MQ*, xxi (1935), 39
G. Chase: *America's Music* (New York, 1955, 2/1966/*R*1981), 368ff
V. F. Yellin: *The Life and Operatic Works of George Whitefield Chadwick* (diss., Harvard U., 1957)
H. W. Hitchcock: *Music in the United States: a Historical Introduction* (New York, 1969, 2/1974), 132ff
V. F. Yellin: "Chadwick, American Realist," *MQ*, lxi (1975), 77
S. Ledbetter: Introduction to *George W. Chadwick: Songs to Poems by Arlo Bates* (New York, 1980)
S. Ledbetter: "George W. Chadwick: a Sourcebook" (1984, MS, *MBCM*)
A. McKinley: "Music for the Dedication Ceremonies of the World's Columbian Exposition in Chicago, 1892," *American Music*, iii/1 (1985), 42

STEVEN LEDBETTER (text and work-list), VICTOR FELL YELLIN (text)

Chakmakjian, Alan Hovhaness. *See* HOVHANESS, ALAN.

Chaliapin, Feodor (Ivanovich) (*b* nr Kazan, Russia, 13 Feb 1873; *d* Paris, France, 12 April 1938). Russian bass. Widely considered the greatest singing actor of his day, he was largely self-taught. From the age of 17 he sang – first in the chorus and later in progressively more important roles – in small provincial opera and operetta troupes. After study (1892–3) in Tbilisi with D. A. Usatov, he successfully sang a wide variety of roles in Tbilisi and St. Petersburg. From 1894 to 1896 he belonged to the Imperial Opera in St. Petersburg, but left to join Savva Mamontov's private opera in Moscow. It was there that he further developed his musical and artistic powers and became renowned for his carefully thought-out performances. He was a member of the Bolshoi Opera in Moscow from 1899 to 1914, and made frequent guest appearances in St. Petersburg and in provincial opera houses.

Chaliapin's international career began in 1901 at La Scala. He made his American début at the Metropolitan Opera on 20 November 1907, in Boito's *Mefistofele*, and during the 1907–8 season sang Don Basilio (*Il barbiere di Siviglia*), Leporello, and Faust, but his reception was cool and for the next 14 years he did not appear in the USA. In the interim he sang in Paris, London, and Russia, leaving his homeland in 1921. When he returned to the Metropolitan on 9 December 1921 to sing Boris (in Russian), the vocal and dramatic impression was overpowering. He remained with the Metropolitan through the 1928–9 season, adding Philip II (*Don Carlo*) and Massenet's Don Quixote to the roles he had sung earlier. He also sang with the Chicago Opera (1922–4) and toured the USA as the head of his own opera troupe. His first American recital was at the Manhattan Opera House (13 November 1921); he gave numerous others during this period. After his return to Europe in 1929 he sang no more opera in the USA but made a final recital tour in 1935. He appeared in two films: *Tsar Ivan the Terrible* (1915) and *Don Quixote* (1933), made some 200 recordings, and wrote two autobiographical books (translated as *Pages from my Life*, 1927, and *Man and Mask*, 1932; excerpts from these were included in *Chaliapin: an Autobiography as Told to Maxim Gorky*, 1968).

Chaliapin's voice was sufficiently flexible to allow him to sing baritone roles like Rubinstein's Demon, Tchaikovsky's Eugene Onegin, and Valentine (*Faust*), as well as such bass roles in the Italian and French repertory as Boito's and Gounod's Mephistopheles, Oroveso (*Norma*), Philip II, and Don Basilio. In *Prince Igor* he sang Galitsky, Konchak, and Igor. He was a perfectionist where his own makeup, costuming, musical, and dramatic preparation were concerned, and untiring in his attention to the staging of the operas in which he took part. He inspired, particularly as Boris, a series of imitators who have attempted to reproduce his every inflection. The accounts of people who worked with him in the theater or knew him offstage all reveal a man with an almost superhuman vital force, warm and responsive to a large circle of friends, and fiercely intolerant of musical or artistic mediocrity.

BIBLIOGRAPHY

H. T. Finck: "Chaliapine, the Russian Mephistopheles," *The Century*, new ser., lxxxi (1910–11), 230
R. Newmarch: *The Russian Opera* (London, 1914)
B. Semeonoff: "Feodor Chaliapine," *Record Collector*, v/6 (1950), 124 [with discography]
E. Grosheva, ed.: *Fyodor Ivanovich Shalyapin: literaturnoye nasledstvo* [Literary legacy] (Moscow, 1960) [incl. lists of roles, concert repertory, discography]
H. Pleasants: *The Great Singers* (New York, 1966, rev. 2/1981), 319
B. Semeonoff: "Chaliapin's Repertoire and Recordings," *Record Collector*, xx/8–10 (1972), 173 [with discography by A. Kelly]
D. Ewen: *Musicians Since 1900: Performers in Concert and Opera* (New York, 1978)

HAROLD BARNES/R

Challis, Bill [William H.] (*b* Wilkes Barre, PA, 8 July 1904). Jazz arranger. He started on piano, then took up the saxophone, and later led the student band at Bucknell University. In 1926 he joined Jean Goldkette's band as staff arranger, beginning a close association with the cornetist Bix Beiderbecke which continued when both men joined Paul Whiteman's band the following year. Challis wrote some of Whiteman's most jazz-oriented arrangements, including *Lonely Melody*, *Changes*, and *Dardanella*, giving Beiderbecke ample solo space and sometimes scoring his cornet improvisations for the trumpet section. He also wrote excellent scores for smaller groups formed for recording sessions from Whiteman's band and led by the saxophonist Frank Trumbauer. Challis's best work of this period reveals a tasteful synthesis of jazz and dance-band elements, a sure grasp of the new jazz style, and an awareness of the strengths of Whiteman's and Goldkette's musicians. After leaving Whiteman in 1930 Challis became a freelance arranger for, among others, Trumbauer, Fletcher Henderson, the Dorsey brothers, the Casa Loma Orchestra, Lennie Hayton, and a number of radio orchestras. In later years he turned to popular music, remaining active into the 1960s. In 1974 he arranged Beiderbecke's piano compositions (which he had notated and edited for publication in 1930) for guitar quintet.

RECORDINGS

(selective list)

For J. Goldkette: Cover Me up with Sunshine/My Pretty Girl (1926–7, Vic. 20588); Hoosier Sweetheart (1927, Vic. 20471)
For P. Whiteman: Changes (1927, Vic. 21103); Lonely Melody (1928, Vic. 21214); Dardanella (1928, Vic. 25238)
For others: F. Trumbauer: Ostrich Walk/Riverboat Shuffle (1927, OK 40822); F. Henderson: Singing the Blues (1931, Vic. 22721)

BIBLIOGRAPHY

R. M. Sudhalter and P. R. Evans: *Bix: Man and Legend* (New Rochelle, NY, 1974)

DAN MORGENSTERN

Challis, John (*b* South Lyon, MI, 9 Jan 1907; *d* New York, 6 Sept 1974). Harpsichord maker. He began piano lessons at the age of seven and later, while at college in Michigan, studied organ with Frederick Alexander. From his father, a skilled jeweler and watchmaker, he learned to use precision tools and to do metalwork of great delicacy and refinement. An attempt in 1925 to build a clavichord based on his organ teacher's Dolmetsch-Chickering instrument led to his going to England in 1926 to study early keyboard instruments and their construction with Arnold Dolmetsch. He was awarded the first Dolmetsch Foundation Scholarship for craftsmen in 1928. In 1930 he returned to the USA and established his workshop at Ypsilanti, Michigan, later moving to Detroit, and finally to New York.

Challis was a highly creative and innovative builder who rejected as sterile the copying of historical instruments. The extremes of climate in large areas of North America led him to experiment continually with new materials and techniques of construction in an effort to produce instruments with a stability comparable to that of the modern piano. In this he was eminently successful. While remaining faithful to a decorative scheme in the tradition of Dolmetsch's later instruments, he based the interior structure of his instruments increasingly on components of metal and plastic. In his last years he even used metal soundboards, thereby gaining stability in tuning without sacrificing the characteristic Challis tone quality (distinctive timbres that he favored and approved while conceding that they were not those of historical instruments). The extraordinary craftsmanship displayed in all his instruments compelled admiration even from his critics.

In addition to harpsichords of various sizes, Challis also produced clavichords and a small number of pedal harpsichords for organists. One of these pedal harpsichords, built in 1968, may well be the most complex instrument of its type ever produced. His experimental activities extended as well to the piano, resulting first in a piano (*c*1944) freely derived from the Viennese instruments of Mozart and Haydn, and then (after 1960) a hybrid instrument: iron-framed but not overstrung, double-strung throughout, with the full compass of the modern piano, and a Herz-Erard double escapement action. Several of Challis's apprentices have attained distinction as harpsichord makers, notably William Dowd and Frank Rutkowski.

BIBLIOGRAPHY

[H. L. Haney:] "Portrait of a Builder: John Challis," *The Harpsichord*, ii/3 (1969), 14

HOWARD SCHOTT

Chaloff, Serge (*b* Boston, MA, 24 Nov 1923; *d* Boston, 16 July 1957). Jazz saxophonist. He studied piano and clarinet formally but was self-taught on the baritone saxophone, being influenced by Harry Carney of Duke Ellington's band and Jack Washington of Count Basie's. He worked in various minor bands from 1939 to 1944; in 1945 he moved to Boyd Raeburn's group, then a progressive force in the definition of postwar jazz styles. In that year he also joined George Auld's band and was decisively influenced by Charlie Parker, quickly absorbing the devices of melodic construction, harmonic vocabulary, and rhythmic variety needed to give his swing-based style a wider range of expression. His most important lengthy engagement was with Woody Herman in 1947–9. Persistent ill-health made Chaloff less active in the 1950s, though he continued to record almost up to his death.

Chaloff was an important figure of the bop movement and one of the most significant improvisers on the baritone saxophone. Early performances such as *The Most* (1949) show him to have been a virtuoso, while others, for example *Gabardine and Serge* (1947), demonstrate the logic of his improvising and its often sombre emotional content. Despite illness he continued to advance during the 1950s, adding to his style an integral use of dynamic and tonal shading and carefully varied degrees of intensity.

RECORDINGS

(selective list)

Pumpernickel (1947, Savoy 956); Gabardine and Serge (1947, Savoy 978); Chickasaw/Bop Scotch (1949, Futurama 3003); The Most (1949, Futurama 3004); Fabel of Mable (1954, Storyville 426); *Blue Serge* (1956, Cap. T742), incl. The Goof and I, Stairway to the Stars

BIBLIOGRAPHY

A. Morgan: "Serge Chaloff," *Jazz Monthly*, iii/8 (1957), 24

I. Gitler: *Jazz Masters of the Forties* (New York, 1966), 39

A. McCarthy: *Big Band Jazz* (London, 1974), 236

M. Harrison: *A Jazz Retrospect* (Newton Abbot, England, 1976), 161

P. Moon: "Serge Chaloff Discography," *Discographical Forum*, nos.38–41 (1977–8)

MAX HARRISON/R

Chamber music. A term commonly applied to instrumental music for small ensembles of solo players, written for performance in intimate surroundings; this article deals with the composition and practice of such music in the USA. A broader interpretation of "chamber music" might comprehend vocal and theatrical forms for small numbers of performers, and much jazz, pop, and rock music; for discussions of these *see* ART SONG, CHORAL MUSIC, OPERA, ORCHESTRAL MUSIC, JAZZ, POPULAR MUSIC, and ROCK. A number of chamber ensembles are dealt with in individual entries and in articles about the cities in which they are based; *see also* EARLY-MUSIC REVIVAL and ELECTROACOUSTIC MUSIC.

1. To 1840. 2. 1840 to 1920. 3. After 1920.

1. TO 1840. The chamber music brought from Europe by early immigrants to America was domestic music, both instrumental and vocal; its performance in the colonies must at first have been rarer and simpler than in the established communities from which the settlers came. Instrumental chamber music, as it is now generally understood, arrived relatively late in North America, for it required certain social structures (which could result only from the "civilizing" and urbanizing process of colonial development) to flourish; this kind of chamber music is undocumented in early Spanish and French North America. The music of the late 18th-century Yankee tunesmiths, though ostensibly written and taught for use in sacred services, functioned also – in the popular singing-schools led by such men as William Billings, Daniel Read, Timothy Swan, and Andrew Law – as a kind of vocal chamber music. Early instrumental instruction books, which were in many ways modeled on the vocal tunebooks, contained the first examples of American instrumental chamber music, though it was not usually in the sonata-based forms that were the essence of contemporary European chamber music. The first such book was Samuel Holyoke's *The Instrumental Assistant* (Exeter, NH, 1800), which included popular and patriotic songs as well as extracts from longer European compositions in arrangements for three instrumental parts. Its success led to a second volume (1807), with pieces for as many as seven instruments, addressed to the increasing number of local clubs for instrumentalists that came to be known as "social orchestras." A similar collection by Oliver Shaw, *For the Gentlemen*, was also published in 1807.

English and European chamber music, composed primarily for the pleasure of its players rather than for an audience, is known to have been played in America by the 1770s. Members of the Philadelphia circle that included Francis Hopkinson and Governor John Penn (a violinist) played chamber works by Arcangelo Corelli, George Frideric Handel, and Johann Stamitz. According to a report of 1774, the library of the Virginia planter

Robert Carter included Handel's flute sonatas. Thomas Jefferson's collection of string instruments was probably used in the performance of chamber music other than the duets he played with Patrick Henry. Benjamin Franklin may not have composed the odd quartet for three violins and cello attributed to him, but the very attribution makes it worthy of notice.

Professional musicians recently arrived from Europe became increasingly important in post-Revolutionary American musical life. Many had been active composers and performers of chamber music before coming to the New World, and they brought their music with them. Joseph Gehot, for example, who had published string duos, trios, and quartets in London in the 1770s and 1780s, undoubtedly brought some to the USA when he immigrated in 1792, and before the turn of the century, chamber music by such resident composers as von Hagen, Moller, Reinagle, Selby, and Rayner Taylor had been performed at public concerts.

The German-speaking communities of Moravians and other central Europeans, concentrated in Pennsylvania and the Carolinas, had an especially active musical culture, of which chamber music was an important part. John Antes's three string trios of 1779–81, written after he had gone to Egypt as a missionary and published in London (*c*1790), are the first chamber works composed by a native American. (He is thought to have composed a set of string quartets before he left America, but if he did so they are now lost.) Johann Friedrich Peter's six string quintets, dated 1789 in Salem, North Carolina, are the earliest extant chamber works composed in the USA. The *Parthien* for wind sextet by David Moritz Michael, who was in Pennsylvania from 1795 to 1815, constitute a significant beginning to chamber music for winds in the New World. Haydn's string quartets are thought to have been first heard in America in Bethlehem, Pennsylvania, where trios by Mozart entered the American repertory in 1785.

2. 1840 TO 1920. In the USA, as in Europe, chamber music was at first performed in public concerts with other kinds of music. In 1842, for example, the first concert of the Philharmonic Society of New York included a quintet by Johann Nepomuk Hummel as well as orchestral music. But in 1844 the Harvard Musical Association, under J. S. Dwight's leadership, initiated an annual series of six concerts of chamber music that continued for some five years. In 1849 in Boston five string players, two of whom doubled on flute and clarinet, formed the Mendelssohn Quintette Club (see Ryan), the first long-lived, professional American chamber music ensemble. Beginning in 1859 the group toured North America, and in 1881–2 they played along the entire West Coast, as well as in Hawaii, Australia, and New Zealand, presenting chamber music of the Classical and Romantic European repertory to many in its audiences for the first time. The occasional inclusion of lighter music on their programs earned Dwight's disapproval in the first issue of his *Journal* (1852), but later (1881) he published an admiring summary of their repertory.

In 1850–60 chamber music concert series like those of the Mendelssohn Quintette Club in Boston were established in other cities. Theodor Eisfeld organized a series of concerts in 1851 in New York. William Mason and Theodore Thomas began another series there on 27 November 1855 with a program that included the first public performance of the Piano Trio no.1 op.8 by Brahms (whom Mason had met in Weimar in 1853); the Mason–Thomas concerts continued for 13 years, during which time more

1. Members of the Mason–Thomas chamber ensemble (left to right): George Matzka (viola), Joseph Mosenthal (second violin), Frederick Bergner (cello), Theodore Thomas (first violin), and William Mason (piano); from Thomas's "A Musical Autobiography" (1905)

than 70 performances were given (see fig. 1). In Chicago a series of chamber music concerts was initiated at the Briggs House in 1860, and it is likely that similar series were presented in other Midwestern cities, many of which had large populations of central European immigrants.

By the middle of the 19th century the repertory of chamber music by Americans was still small. It included idiosyncratic works by Heinrich, among them "some pieces of a national character . . . calculated for the lovers of the violin" (as he described them) such as *The Yankee Doodleiad* (1820), a quintet for piano, three violins, and cello or double bass. It also included two string quartets by Fry and two by Bristow (1849), and a piano trio and two string quartets by C. C. Perkins, which were issued in 1854 and 1855 by Breitkopf & Härtel in Leipzig and seem to have been the first American music published by that important firm. Many members of the next two generations of American composers studied in Germany and wrote well-crafted pieces in the styles of Mendelssohn, Schumann, and Brahms. Among them were John Knowles Paine (String Quartet, *c*1859; two piano trios, *c*1875) and William Wallace Gilchrist (undated Piano Quintet and Nonet) and the somewhat younger George Chadwick (string quartets nos. 1, 3, and 5, 1878–98; Piano Quintet, 1887), Arthur Bird, Henry Holden Huss, Edgar Stillman Kelley, and Arthur Whiting; Chadwick's broader stylistic interests are reflected in his second and fourth string quartets (1878, 1896). Arthur Foote wrote especially well for piano with strings, in a series of violin sonatas, and piano trios, quartets, and quintets; his *A Night Piece* (1922) is still a popular work for flute and string quartet or quintet. Daniel Gregory Mason also worked skillfully in an eclectic but basically German style (Piano Quartet, 1909–11; *String Quartet on Negro Themes*, 1918–19); his Divertimento for wind quintet (1926) reflects the growing American interest in chamber music for winds.

As the 19th century ended and the 20th began, several important and long-lived chamber ensembles were organized. The Kneisel Quartet (1885–1917), the first great American string quartet, was formed by Franz Kneisel, the concertmaster of the Boston SO, and three other members of the orchestra; it was the model for many later stable and long-lasting American quartets, and toured widely. The Kneisel Quartet favored the central European repertory, and it gave, in New York, the world premières of many European works, including Dvořák's "American" Quartet op. 96, Quintet op. 97, and Quartet op. 105. The Flonzaley Quartet, led by Adolfo Betti, was formed in 1902 in New York; before disbanding in 1928 the group played some 2500 concerts in the USA, particularly favoring recent Russian and French works. These were also prominent in the repertories of the wind and mixed ensembles led by Georges Longy in Boston from 1900 to 1925. All of these groups played a substantial amount of music by Americans.

The predominantly Austro-German cast of American chamber music of the later 19th century gave way in the early 20th to a wider variety of styles. Chamber works by Amy Beach (notably her Violin Sonata, 1896; Piano Quintet, 1907; Theme and Variations for flute and string quartet, 1916; Piano Trio, 1938), Charles Martin Loeffler (*Poème païen* for 13 instruments, 1902; Music for Four Stringed Instruments, 1917–19), Charles T. Griffes (*Three Tone-pictures*, 1910–12; *Two Sketches*, 1918–19), Arthur Shepherd (*Triptych*, 1925; Piano Quintet, 1940), John Alden Carpenter (String Quartet, 1927; Piano Quintet, 1934), and Edward Burlingame Hill (Sextet for piano and winds, 1934; String Quartet, 1935) show the increasing influence of new French music, while those by Frederick Converse (three string quartets, 1896–1935; Septet, 1897; *Two Lyric Pieces* for brass quintet, 1939), Arthur Farwell (String Quartet "The Hako," 1922; Piano Quintet, 1937), and Henry Gilbert (String Quartet, 1920) represent an attempt to cultivate an independent American style by incorporating elements of folk and national music. In the same period Ives composed many idiosyncratic chamber works (*From the Steeples and the Mountains*, 1901–?1902; *Halloween*, 1906; *All the Way Around and Back*, 1906), as well as pieces with more conventional scoring and structure (two string quartets, 1896–1913; a piano trio, 1902–?1903; four violin sonatas, 1902–?1916).

3. After 1920. By the time the generation of American composers born around 1900 – Piston, Cowell, Porter, Sessions, Thomson, Copland, Roy Harris, and Ruth Crawford, among others – came to maturity in the 1920s, the practice and composition of chamber music were firmly established in the USA, and thereafter most composers wrote some chamber music. Especially valuable are the neoclassical contributions of Piston (five string quartets, 1933–51, and other works); the outputs of Porter (ten quartets, 1922–58) and Harris (Piano Quintet, 1936; Concerto for piano, clarinet, and string quartet, 1926; Concerto for string sextet, 1932); the stylistically varied works of Cowell (five string quartets, 1916–56, and a piano trio, 1918–19; *Ostinato pianissimo*, 1934, *A Set of Five*, 1952, and *Persian Set*, 1957, all emphasizing percussion; and *Toccanta* for soprano and chamber ensemble, 1940), Copland (single examples of works in several chamber media), and Thomson (a neobaroque *Sonata da chiesa*, 1926; *Stabat mater* for soprano and string quartet, 1931; and other unconventional works, in addition to two string quartets, 1931–2); and Crawford's unique String Quartet (1931).

The 1920s also saw many European chamber ensembles begin to make regular tours of the USA, and a number of them, including the Busch, Kolisch, Lener, Pro Arte, and Roth quartets, subsequently took up residence here. Preeminent until the 1960s was the Budapest Quartet, founded in 1917, which settled in the USA in 1938 and was quartet-in-residence at the Library of Congress under the Gertrude Clarke Whittall Foundation (1938–62). The Library of Congress was also long the center of the chamber music activities supported by ELIZABETH SPRAGUE COOLIDGE, who had first organized a regular chamber music festival in Pittsfield, Massachusetts, in 1918. Under the Coolidge Foundation, established at the library in 1925, a suitable auditorium was built and an active program of commissions and prizes begun. The catalogue (1950, 1964) of autograph scores she collected shows the great breadth of Coolidge's taste.

Several of the American composers who came to maturity in the 1930s made important contributions to the chamber music repertory. Barber tended, like Copland, to write single, masterly works in each medium he used (*Dover Beach* for baritone and string quartet, 1931; Cello Sonata, 1932; String Quartet, 1936, the slow movement of which was arranged as the Adagio for Strings; *Summer Music* for wind quintet, 1955). Schuman produced a series of energetic string quartets, as did Kirchner and Diamond (who wrote ten). The three by Carter (1950–71) eclipsed all others by revealing new sonorous, textural, and structural possibilities in the traditional medium. Babbitt's chamber music ranges from pieces in conventional media (five string quartets, 1948–82; Woodwind Quartet, 1953) through others of more

2. Elizabeth Sprague Coolidge with the Manhattan String Quartet, NBC studios, New York, 1935: (clockwise from left) Oliver Edel (cello), Julius Shaier (viola), Walter Koons of NBC, Coolidge, Rachmael Weinstock (first violin), and Harris Danziger (second violin)

unusual instrumentation (Composition for Four Instruments, 1948; Composition for 12 Instruments, 1948; *All Set* for jazz ensemble, 1957) to vocal works with tape (*Vision and Prayer*, 1961; *Philomel*, 1964; *Phonemena*, 1975). Less easy to summarize is the chamber music of Cage. Although he too wrote for traditional ensembles (String Quartet, 1950; music for violin and piano), he also composed works for unconventional combinations, including percussion (several works titled *Construction in Metal*, 1939–41) and radios (*Imaginary Landscape no.4* for 12 radios, 1951).

As the 20th century progressed, chamber music in the broadest sense became an increasingly popular genre among American composers, and employed ever more varied instrumentation. Many composers wrote for traditional ensembles, though occasionally in new forms or tunings, but even more found their individual voices through unusual combinations of instruments, sometimes with singers, live and electronic music in combination, and the use of mixed media, which blurs the distinctions between abstract instrumental music, vocal chamber music, and theater. Johnston pursued an interest in untempered tunings in his string quartets nos.2 and 3 (1964–73). Hiller and Isaacson wrote the *Illiac Suite* (1955–6) for string quartet, the first complete large-scale composition to have been created with the aid of a computer. Reich's early pulse and phase music is mostly for chamber ensembles (as are the similar but unrelated early works of Glass), and one might say that Reich treats the individual tape tracks of such works as *Come Out* (1966; entirely electronic except for the single spoken phrase that is its sound source) almost like members of a chamber group. Rochberg shifted style dramatically from one chamber composition to the next, as is evident in the neoclassical String Quartet no.1 (1952), the Webernian String Quartet no.2 (1959–61), and the String Quartet no.3 (1972) with its neotonal evocation of the styles of Beethoven and Mahler. Crumb explored unusual sonorities in the acclaimed *Ancient Voices of Children* (1970), for singer, boy's voice, and chamber ensemble, in *Black Angels* (1970), for electric string quartet, and in *Vox balaenae* (1971), for flute, cello, and piano (all amplified); the last work approaches the theatrical in that the players are to be masked and to perform under special lighting. Theatrical elements also appear in chamber works by Reynolds (*The Emperor of Ice Cream*, 1962, in which the singers change their positions on stage several times during the course of the performance), Druckman (*Animus I–IV*, 1966–77), and Davidovsky (*Synchronisms nos.1–8*, 1963–74, with their interactions between live performers and tape music).

After World War II there was a great increase in the number of professional chamber ensembles. Among string quartets, the Budapest Quartet remained preeminent until the Juilliard String Quartet (formed in 1946) rivaled it with new standards of performance of the most difficult 20th-century works; the group's performances and recordings of the quartets of Bartók, Schoenberg, Ives, and Carter are especially highly regarded. It has been associated with the Juilliard School since 1946, as well as with the Library of Congress since 1962 and Michigan State University since 1977, and was one of the first chamber ensembles to be "in residence" at educational institutions. This arrangement allows the members of a group to join the faculty of the institution concerned while continuing to give concert performances and make tours. The University of Wisconsin began this practice with its appointment in 1940 of the Pro Arte Quartet of Brussels; in 1947 the Walden Quartet, after a year in residence at Cornell University, joined the University of Illinois. Many other such affiliations followed, involving string quartets, piano trios, woodwind and brass ensembles, and early-music groups.

There were other indications that chamber music was flourishing: festivals devoted to it (the Santa Fe Chamber Music Festival; the Sitka Summer Music Festival in Sitka, Alaska; and the Festival of American Chamber Music in Washington, DC) and opportunities for specialized study at other festivals (including those held at Aspen, Colorado; Marlboro, Vermont; Portland, Oregon; and Lenox, Massachusetts) (*see* FESTIVALS), sponsorship by symphony orchestras of small ensembles formed from their members (such as the Boston SO Chamber Players, formed in 1964, and the New York PO Ensembles, 1983), and stable, professional organizations offering complete seasons of concerts (most prominently the CHAMBER MUSIC SOCIETY OF LINCOLN CENTER in New York). A growing interest in chamber music among amateur performers was reflected in the establishment of AMATEUR CHAMBER MUSIC PLAYERS, formed in 1947 to facilitate contact between such players; by the mid-1980s there were 3000 members in North America, 1000 elsewhere, and yet another 1000 in the affiliated French Association des Musiciens Amateurs. The interests of professional chamber music players and groups have been served since 1977 by CHAMBER MUSIC AMERICA; in 1984 its membership included 76 string quartets, 38 new-music groups, 38 early-music groups, 35 piano trios, 33 wind ensembles, 25 brass ensembles, 8 vocal groups, and more than 180 other ensembles, in addition to other individual and organizational members.

BIBLIOGRAPHY

T. Ryan: *Recollections of an Old Musician* (New York, 1899/R1979)
O. Downes and E. T. Rice: "American Chamber Music," *Cobbett's Cyclopedic Survey of Chamber Music*, ed. W. W. Cobbett (London, 1929/R1963), i, 11
A. L. Goldberg: "American Performing Organizations," *Cobbett's Cyclopedic Survey of Chamber Music*, ed. W. W. Cobbett (London, 1929/R1963), 18
C. Hughes: *Chamber Music in American Schools* (New York, 1933)
R. P. Phelps: "American Chamber Music before 1875," *Woodwind Magazine*, ii/3 (1949)
Autograph Musical Scores in the Coolidge Foundation Collection (Washington, DC, 1950; suppl. 1964)
R. P. Phelps: *The History and Practice of Chamber Music in the United States from Earliest Times up to 1875* (diss., U. of Iowa, 1951)
E. Sagul: *Development of Chamber Music Performance in the United States* (diss., Columbia U., 1952)
V. B. Danek: *A Historical Study of the Kneisel Quartet* (DME diss., Indiana U., 1962)
N. Slonimsky: "Chamber Music in America," *Cobbett's Cyclopedic Survey of Chamber Music*, iii, ed. C. Mason (London, 1963), 152–91
J. L. Landsman: *An Annotated Catalogue of American Violin Sonatas, Suites . . . 1947–1961* (diss., U. of Southern California, 1966; Urbana, IL, 1968)
C. R. Doherty: *Twentieth-century Woodwind Quintet Music of the United States* (diss., U. of Missouri, Kansas City, 1971)
D. M. Geeting: *A Comparative Study of Sonatas for Clarinet and Piano Published in the United States from 1950–1970* (diss., U. of Oregon, 1974)
N. E. Tawa: "Secular Music in the Late Eighteenth-century American Home," *MQ*, lxi (1975), 511
A. Horne: *Twentieth-century Solo and Ensemble Music for Woodwinds by Black Composers* (diss., U. of Iowa, 1976)
American Ensemble (1978–83)
K. M. Famera: *Catalog of the American Music Center Library, ii: Chamber Music* (New York, 1978)
B. R. Compton: *Amateur Instrumental Music in America, 1765 to 1810* (diss., Louisiana State U., 1979)
Chamber Music America: Membership Directory (New York, 1981–)
Chamber Music: Performance and Study at Music Training Institutions, ed. National Association of Schools of Music (Reston, VA, 1982)
Amateur Chamber Music Players North American Directory (Washington, DC, 1983)
Chamber Music Magazine (1984–)
Symphony Orchestras and Chamber Music (Chicago, 1984) [survey]
M. Berger: *Guide to Chamber Music* (New York, 1985)
P. Lust: *American Vocal Chamber Music, 1945–1980: an Annotated Bibliography* (Westport, CT, 1985)

LEONARD BURKAT (with GILBERT ROSS)

Chamber Music America. Organization of professional chamber music groups in the USA and Canada, incorporated in 1977. Its purposes are to "promote the welfare of chamber music by acting as an advocate and coordinator in developing major government, foundation, corporate, and private funding support for the field" and to serve "in an advisory, informational, consulting, and referral capacity not only to professionals in the field but also to all persons interested in chamber music." Chamber Music America achieves these goals by publishing a journal (*Chamber Music Magazine*, which succeeded *American Ensemble* in 1984) and special directories (including *A Directory of Summer Chamber Music Workshops, Schools & Festivals*, 1984), administering grant and residency programs, publicizing its activities, and holding semi-annual conferences. After its first year, Chamber Music America was chosen to administer the Chamber Music Residency project of the C. Michael Paul Foundation, which places new chamber ensembles with host institutions (museums, broadcast facilities, churches, businesses, and other performing arts organizations) for a limited period to give them the opportunity to develop the management skills necessary for a regular performance schedule. In 1983 Chamber Music America established a commissioning program through which grant money was channeled to New York City ensembles seeking to commission new works; the program was extended to national ensembles in 1985, and grants to eight groups were made in the first year. Headquarters are in New York.

BIBLIOGRAPHY

H. C. Schonberg: "The Chamber-music Boom," *New York Times* (28 Jan 1979), §2, p.19

JOHN SHEPARD

Chamber Music Society of Lincoln Center. Chamber ensemble. Resident in New York at Alice Tully Hall of the Lincoln Center for the Performing Arts, it gave its first performance on 11 September 1969. The society was conceived by William Schuman, the president of Lincoln Center, who appointed the pianist CHARLES WADSWORTH as the society's artistic director. Among the musicians Wadsworth assembled to perform for the opening season (1969–70) were Charles Treger (violin), Walter Trampler (viola), Leslie Parnas (cello), Paula Robison (flute), Leonard Arner (oboe), Gervase de Peyer (clarinet), Loren Glickman (bassoon), and Richard Goode (piano). By 1984 the society had grown to 18 members, and the season's schedule to over 90 concerts (including 40 at Alice Tully Hall; others in New York, Washington, and Chicago, and a national tour). Members have included the pianists André-Michel Schub and Lee Luvisi, the English french-horn player Barry Tuckwell, mezzo-soprano Frederica von Stade, the Emerson String Quartet, cellist Fred Sherry, double bass player Alvin Brehm, and violinists Jaime Laredo, James Oliver Buswell, and Ani Kavafian (see illustration, p.402).

The society won immediate critical acclaim, its success owing much to Wadsworth's imaginative programming, his personable manner of introducing the music, and his augmentation of the ensemble with internationally known artists (including occasionally some from jazz); other guests have included Dietrich Fischer-Dieskau, Leonard Bernstein, Sills, Boulez, Perlman, and Chick Corea. The society's commissions, about 50 in number, include works by Schuman, Boulez, Barber, Stanley Silverman, and the Austrian Friedrich Cerha. Its concerts have been broadcast on National Public Radio and the Public Broadcasting System's series "Live from Lincoln Center."

BIBLIOGRAPHY

H. Klein: " 'Charlie,' A Good Man for Chamber Music," *New York Times* (12 Oct 1969)
H. C. Schonberg: "New York's Finest," *New York Times* (29 Oct 1972), §2, p.19
A. Rich: "Charles Wadsworth," *New York Magazine*, xi (18 Sept 1978)
B. Holland: "The Man Behind the Boom in Chamber Music," *Saturday Review*, viii/9 (1981), 10
P. G. Davis: "A Musical Birthday Card to Haydn and Stravinsky," *New York Times* (11 Sept 1981)

JAMES CHUTE

Chambers, Paul (Laurence Dunbar, Jr.) (*b* Pittsburgh, PA, 22 April 1935; *d* New York, 4 Jan 1969). Jazz double bass player. From the age of 13 he lived in Detroit, where he took up the double bass in 1949 and was soon working with Kenny Burrell and other Detroit jazzmen. A tour with Paul Quinichette

The Chamber Music Society of Lincoln Center, 1984: (left to right) the Emerson String Quartet (Eugene Drucker and Philip Setzer, violin; David Finckel, cello; and Lawrence Dutton, viola); Paula Robison, flute; Leonard Arner, oboe; Loren Glickman, bassoon; Alvin Brehm, double bass; Frederica von Stade, mezzo-soprano; Fred Sherry and Leslie Parnas, cello; Charles Wadsworth, artistic director and pianist; James Oliver Buswell, violin; Walter Trampler, viola; Richard Goode and Lee Luvisi, piano; Gervase de Peyer, clarinet; and Ani Kavafian, violin

took him in 1955 to New York, where he was immediately accepted by the bop elite. He joined Miles Davis's quintet in October of that year, forming with Red Garland and Philly Joe Jones a rhythm section that, for its propulsive swing, had no rivals. He also played on many recordings by John Coltrane, then his fellow sideman with Davis. A conservative musician in the tonal "walking" bass style, Chambers faded unjustifiably into obscurity as jazz styles changed in the early 1960s. In 1963 he left Davis together with Wynton Kelly and Jimmy Cobb to form a short-lived trio, but his subsequent activities were hampered by ill health.

RECORDINGS
(selective list)

As leader: *Bass on Top* (1957, BN 1569)

As sideman with M. Davis: *'Round about Midnight* (1955–6, Col. CL949); *Steamin'* (1956, Prst. 7200); *Cookin'* (1956, Prst. 7076); *Kind of Blue* (1959, Col. CL1355); *Someday My Prince Will Come* (1961, Col. CS8456)

As sideman with J. Coltrane: *Black Pearls* (1958, Prst. 7316); *Stardust* (1958, Prst. 7268); *The Believer* (1958, Prst. 7292); *Bahia* (1958, Prst. 7353)

As sideman with others: C. Adderley: *Presenting Cannonball Adderley* (1955, Savoy MG12018); S. Rollins: *Tenor Madness* (1956, Prst. 7047); W. Kelly: *Smokin' at the Half Note* (1965, Verve 68633)

BIBLIOGRAPHY

V. Wilmer: "Paul Chambers Talks to Valerie Wilmer," *Jazz Journal*, xiv / 3 (1961), 15

J. Renaud: "Paul Chambers 1935–69," *Jazz hot*, no.248 (1969), 32

"Dictionnaire de la contrebasse," *Jazz Magazine*, no.166 (1969), 33

J. Stinnett: *The Music of Paul Chambers* (n.p., 2 / 1984) [20 transcrs.]

BARRY KERNFELD

Chambers, Stephen Alexander. *See* HAKIM, TALIB RASUL.

Chambers, William Paris (*b* Newport, PA, 1 Nov 1854; *d* Newville, PA, 1 Nov 1913). Cornetist, bandmaster, and composer. When he was quite young his parents moved to Newville, where he studied cornet. By the time he was 18 he was soloist and conductor of the Keystone Cornet Band, and at 25 he became director of the Capitol City Band of Harrisburg. In 1888 he was appointed director of the Great Southern Band of Baltimore; when he led the band on a trip to Denver in 1892, his feat of performing a cornet solo at the summit of Pike's Peak was widely reported. Chambers next became manager of the C. G. Conn retail store in New York, and continued to perform and teach; he toured Europe and Africa in 1903 and 1905. In 1908 he was described in *Holton's Harmony Hints* as "the greatest cornet soloist in the world," and as having "absolute command of every tone of the chromatic scale of five complete octaves." Chambers wrote a number of cornet solos, waltzes, and overtures, but is remembered principally as a composer of marches, of which *Chicago Tribune*, *Boys of the Old Brigade*, and *Hostrauser's March* are the most popular. A number of his compositions are recorded in the Heritage of the March series (compiled by ROBERT HOE, JR.), subseries 4, D, W, and AA.

BIBLIOGRAPHY

H. L. Clarke: "Famous Cornetists of the Past: W. Paris Chambers," *Jacobs Bard Monthly*, xvi / 10 (1931), 4

G. D. Bridges: *Pioneers in Brass* (Detroit, 1965), 19

C. M. Barr, Jr.: *William Paris Chambers (1854–1913): his Life and Contribution to Music* (thesis, Indiana U. of Pennsylvania, 1973) [incl. discography and list of works]

R. Hoe, Jr., ed.: "Brief Biographies of Famous March Composers," *Journal of Band Research*, xiv / 1 (1978), 55

RAOUL CAMUS

Chamlee, Mario [Cholmondeley, Archer] (*b* Los Angeles, CA, 29 May 1892; *d* Los Angeles, 13 Nov 1966). Tenor. He studied with Achille Alberti in Los Angeles and then (having made his début as Edgardo in 1916) in New York. Scotti secured his début at the Metropolitan (*Tosca*, 1920), where he remained until 1928.

After a period in Europe he sang Lohengrin and Walther in San Francisco and appeared again at the Metropolitan (in the première of Hageman's *Caponsacchi*, title role, 1937, and in Menotti's *Amelia al ballo*). He retired in 1939. Chamlee was admired for his legato singing and the rich, dark timbre of his voice; his recordings, which betray a less than distinguished sense of style, are probably unrepresentative.

J. B. STEANE

Chance, John Barnes (*b* Beaumont, TX, 20 Nov 1932; *d* Lexington, KY, 16 Aug 1972). Composer. He began studying composition at the age of 15, and received the BM and MM degrees from the University of Texas, where he was a pupil of Clifton Williams, Kent Kennan, and Paul Pisk; he won the Carl Owens Award for student composition in 1956 and 1957. He performed as timpanist with the Austin SO, and was an arranger for the Fourth and Eighth US Army Bands. From 1960 to 1962 he was composer-in-residence in Greensboro, North Carolina, for the Ford Foundation Young Composers Project. He was a member of the faculty at the school of music of the University of Kentucky from 1966 until his death. He composed works for band, chorus, orchestra, solo instruments, and chamber groups; his most popular compositions include the *Variations on a Korean Folk Song* (which received the American Bandmasters Association Ostwald Award in 1966), *Incantation and Dance*, Elegy, *Blue Lake Overture*, Introduction and Capriccio for piano and winds, and the brilliant Symphony no.2 for winds and percussion, completed just before his death.

WORKS

Orch: Sym. no. 1 (1956); Ov. to a Fairy Tale (1957); Fiesta! (1960); Satiric Suite, str (1961)

Vocal: Blessed are they that Mourn, chorus, str, hns, bass drum (1961); The Noiseless, Patient Spider, female vv, multiple fl (1961); Alleluia, chorus, band (1962); Ballad and March, chorus, band (1962); 3 Songs (E. E. Cummings), S, fl, pf (1962); Kyrie and Alleluia, chorus, orch (1967)

Band: Incantation and Dance (1963); Introduction and Capriccio, 24 ww, pf (1966); Variations on a Korean Folk Song (1967); Blue Lake Ov. (1971); Elegy (1972); Sym. no.2, wind, perc (1975)

Inst: Credo, tpt, pf (1959)

Principal publisher: Boosey & Hawkes

BIBLIOGRAPHY

D. A. Anthony: *The Published Band Compositions of John Barnes Chance* (EdD diss., U. of Southern Mississippi, 1981)

RAOUL CAMUS

Change ringing. An art of BELLRINGING in which a given number of bells (from four to ten or 12) is rung according to a sequence of permutations (changes) in which no bell moves more than one step from one pattern to the next and no pattern recurs.

Changes. Jazz musicians' term for sequences of harmonies – e.g., "blues changes," referring to BLUES PROGRESSION.

Chanler, Theodore (Ward) (*b* Newport, RI, 29 April 1902; *d* Boston, MA, 27 July 1961). Critic and composer. He studied the piano and composition with Hans Ebell and theory with Arthur Shepherd, and in 1919 he entered the New York Institute of Musical Art, where he was a pupil of Buhlig (piano) and Goetschius (counterpoint). Later he worked under Bloch at the Cleveland Institute, attended Oxford University (1923–5), and then studied composition for three years with Boulanger in Paris. Returning to the USA in 1933, he became music critic of the *Boston Herald* in 1934 for a short time. In 1940 he won the League of Composers Town Hall Award with *Four Rhymes from Peacock Pie*, and in 1944 he was awarded a Guggenheim Fellowship. He taught at the Peabody Conservatory (1945–7) and later at the Longy School, Cambridge, Massachusetts. One of the most perceptive and articulate American composer–writers of his day, he was a regular contributor to *Modern Music*. His compositions are marked by lyrical melody and polytonality; he was at his best in smaller forms, and it was through the songs, particularly the two sets of *Epitaphs* (1937, 1940), based on poems of De la Mare, that he made his name. He was also interested in piano teaching, and worked at developing a simplified technique for that instrument.

WORKS

Stage: Pas de trois (ballet), pf, orch, 1942; The Pot of Fat (chamber opera), Cambridge, MA, 8 May 1955

Choral: Mass, 2 female vv, org, 1930; 4 Chorals for Summer (L. Feeney), 1947; several other works

*c*50 songs, all 1v, pf, incl. These, my Ophelia (MacLeish), 1925; Agnus Dei, 1930; The Doves (Feeney), 1931; Memory (Blake), 1934; 8 Epitaphs (De la Mare), 1937; 3 Epitaphs (De la Mare), 1940; 4 Rhymes from Peacock Pie (De la Mare), 1940; The Lamb (Blake), 1940; I rise when you enter (Feeney), 1942; The Flight (Feeney), 1944; The Children (Feeney), 1945; The Policeman in the Park (Feeney), 1946; The Patient Sleeps (Henley), 1946; 21 others, all inc.

Inst: Sonata, vn, pf, 1927; other vn works, org pieces

Pf: *c*25 works, incl. 5 Short Colloquies, 1936; 3 Short Pieces, 1939; Toccata, 1939; Aftermath, 1941; The Second Joyful Mystery, 2 pf, 1942; A Child in the House, 1949

Principal publishers: Associated, G. Schirmer

BIBLIOGRAPHY

EwenD

E. A. Nordgren: *An Analytical Study of the Songs of Theodore Chanler (1902–1961)* (diss., New York U., 1980)

DAVID E. CAMPBELL

Chantels. Rock-and-roll vocal group. Formed in New York in 1956, they were the first successful female rock ensemble. They were led by Arlene Smith (*b* 5 Oct 1941), who was inspired by Frankie Lymon and the Teenagers, and who is regarded by some as having the most powerful and expressive voice of any rock-and-roll singer; the other members of the group were Lois Harris, Sonia Goring, Jackie Landry, and Rene Minus. The group was produced first by Richard Barrett for the End label, then by George Goldner, the company's director, who had produced recordings for Lymon, the Crows, and the Harptones; he later produced the Isley Brothers and the Shangri-Las. Goldner used a small instrumental ensemble with heavy reverberation that was the principal inspiration for Phil Spector's "wall of sound" in the early 1960s. The Chantels' performances were distinguished by their emotional intensity; most notable were the hits *Maybe* and *I love you so*, and the superb *If you try* (all from 1958). In 1959 Smith left the Chantels, who went on to make undistinguished but commercially successful recordings with Barrett on the Carlton label; in 1961 she made two little-known recordings with Spector, including *Love, love, love* (Big Top 3073). She later attended the Juilliard School and worked as a teacher in New York; in the 1970s and early 1980s she appeared periodically in rock-and-roll revival shows.

RECORDINGS
(selective list)

He's Gone (End 1001, 1957); *The Chantels* (End 301, 1958); Every night (End 1015, 1958); If you try (End 1030, 1958); I love you so (End 1020, 1958); Maybe (End 1005, 1958); Look in my eyes (Carlton 555, 1961); Well, I told you (Carlton 564, 1961)

BIBLIOGRAPHY

L. Winner: "The Chantels," *The Rolling Stone Record Review* (New York, 1971), 85

G. Marcus: "Girl Groups," *The Rolling Stone Illustrated History of Rock & Roll*, ed. J. Miller (New York, 1976, rev.2/1980), 160

GREIL MARCUS

Chapel Hill, Raleigh, Durham. A group of cities in North Carolina, of which Raleigh (pop. 150,255) is the capital; Durham (pop. 100,831) and Chapel Hill (pop. 32,421) are situated northwest of Raleigh. The metropolitan area (pop. 531,167) is often referred to as the "Research Triangle," owing to the presence in the area of a number of colleges and universities, notably the University of North Carolina at Chapel Hill and Duke University at Durham.

In the earliest days of settlement (the 1790s) the Raleigh and Chapel Hill area was overshadowed by the coastal city of Wilmington; Durham, the newest of the three cities, was not established until after 1851. Throughout the 19th century community music in the state was dominated by brass bands, which in the 1880s included such groups as the Raleigh Brass Band, the Durham Cornet Band, and the Colored Band of Durham. There were a number of prominent music teachers in the area during the 19th century. Among them were Gustave Blessner (1840s), whose compositions are in the Early American Music Collection at the University of North Carolina at Chapel Hill (as are those of James Aykroyd and Mrs. L. H. Whitaker), L. von Meyerhoff (1875), who came from Vienna and had been a pupil of Rubinstein, and Carl S. Gaertner.

The University of North Carolina at Chapel Hill was chartered in 1789, and was the first state university to accept and graduate students. The notable music department was formed in 1919 with Paul John Weaver as its first professor of music. The department experienced its greatest growth during the chairmanship of Glen Haydon (1934–66). Under the chairmanship of James Pruett (from 1976) the department had in 1983 150 undergraduates and 75 graduate majors with 40 full-time faculty members. BM, BMEd, BA, MA, and PhD degrees are offered in performance, music education, composition, and musicology. An institute of folk music was founded at the university in 1932 by Lamar Stringfield. The music library (described in *CMc*, no.17, 1974, p.54) has over 100,000 items including books, recordings, scores, and periodicals, and supports the strong graduate program in musicology as well as other interests. Special collections include 5000 pieces of early American sheet music (among them music by the local composers Aykroyd and Whitaker), a shape-note hymnal collection, and the Folk Music Recordings Archive (*see also* LIBRARIES AND COLLECTIONS, §3).

A music program was established in 1961 at Duke University in Durham. The BA degree is offered in music history, theory, composition, and performance; MA and PhD degrees are offered in musicology and composition. The composition department sponsors a series of contemporary concerts under the title "Encounters," and a visiting composer program, which has brought Iain Hamilton and Vincent Persichetti, among others, to the university. The music library has over 60,000 volumes. At least seven other colleges and universities in the area also offer music programs.

The North Carolina SO was founded in 1932 by the composer, flutist, and conductor Lamar Stringfield. Benjamin Swalin, conductor of the orchestra from 1944 to 1972, and his wife Maxine were also influential in the establishment of the orchestra, which is state-supported and has its home at Memorial Auditorium in Raleigh. John Gosling was the orchestra's conductor from 1972 to 1980; it then lacked a permanent conductor until 1982 when Gerhard Zimmerman was appointed. The orchestra's Symphony Society sponsors the Kathleen and Joseph M. Bryan Young Artists Competition.

The National Opera Association, founded as Grass Roots Opera in 1948, is based in Raleigh and regularly tours the country. The A. J. Fletcher Educational and Opera Foundation, also in Raleigh, extends its support to the National Opera as well as to many of the music programs of nearby private colleges. North Carolina is one of the few states to have a cabinet-level arts administration.

There are many community chamber, orchestral, choral, gospel, brass, folk, rock, popular, bluegrass, country, and other groups in the area. Touring international performers attract large audiences at the Civic Center and at Reynolds Coliseum in Raleigh, as well as at smaller halls. Durham has been of some importance for popular music, jazz, and blues. The jazz musicians Donald Byrd and Mary Lou Williams were active at both Duke University and North Carolina Central University in Durham. Sonny Terry, who lived in North Carolina from 1934, was one of the most important popularizers of the blues from the 1940s to the 1960s.

Musical instrument makers were active as early as 1828, when Sesley Whitaker was in business in Raleigh. Of those makers based in the cities in the 1980s the harpsichord builder John Watson is the most noted. A major collection of historical musical machines and instruments is located west of Durham at Daniel Boone Village.

BIBLIOGRAPHY

A. Washburn: *A Descriptive Catalogue of Confederate Music in the Duke University Collection* (thesis, Duke U., 1936)

North Carolina Musicians: a Selective Handbook, ed. North Carolina Federation of Music Clubs (Chapel Hill, 1956)

A. P. Hudson: *Songs of the Carolina Charter Colonists, 1663–1763* (Raleigh, 1962)

J. H. Craig: *The Arts and Crafts in North Carolina, 1689–1846* (Winston-Salem, NC, 1965) [exhibition catalogue]

H. T. Pearsall: *The North Carolina Symphony Orchestra from 1932 to 1962: its Founding, Musical Growth, and Musical Activities* (MEd thesis, Indiana U., 1969)

NANCY R. PING-ROBBINS
(with MARIE KROEGER)

Chapin. Family of musicians active principally in Ohio, Kentucky, and Pennsylvania in the 19th century. The brothers Lucius Chapin (*b* Springfield, MA, 25 April 1760; *d* Cincinnati, OH, 24 Dec 1842) and Amzi Chapin (*b* Springfield, 2 March 1768; *d* Northfield, OH, 19 Feb 1835) were well-known and highly respected singing-school teachers. Although they were proponents of the music and musical values of Andrew Law, both wrote folk hymns. Five of their tunes, "Ninety-third," "Rockbridge," "Rockingham," "Twenty-fourth," and "Vernon," are included in Wyeth's *Repository of Sacred Music, Part Second* (1813). As many as 16 hymns were attributed to the Chapins in such 19th-century collections as Carden's *Missouri Harmony* (1820) and Funk's *A Compilation of Genuine Church Music* (1832), although only seven of these can be credited to them with any assurance; uncertainty still remains as to which brother composed which tune. Four tunes ("Ninety-third," "Olney," "Twenty-fourth," and "Vernon") remain in modern editions of the southern tunebooks *Christian Harmony* and *Sacred Harp*, and the two most popular, "Ninety-third" and "Twenty-fourth," are included in such major

Protestant hymnbooks as the *Methodist Hymnal* and the *Lutheran Book of Worship*.

Lucius Chapin had five sons, three of whom were also singing-school teachers: Lucius Rousseau Chapin (1794–1861) taught in Ohio and possibly Kentucky and Indiana; Amzi Philander Chapin (1795–*c*1835) was active in Kentucky, south-central Virginia, and North Carolina; and Cephus Lysander Chapin (1804–28) traveled to Kentucky, Alabama, and Mississippi.

BIBLIOGRAPHY

G. P. Jackson: *White Spirituals in the Southern Uplands* (Chapel Hill, 1933/*R*1965)

——: *Down-east Spirituals and Others* (New York, 1943)

C. Hamm: "The Chapins and Sacred Music in the South and West," *JRME*, viii (1960), 91

I. Lowens: "John Wyeth's *Repository of Sacred Music, Part Second* (1813): a Northern Precursor of Southern Folk-hymnody," *Music and Musicians in Early America* (New York, 1964)

J. W. Scholten: *The Chapins: a Study of Men and Sacred Music West of the Alleghenies, 1795–1842* (diss., U. of Michigan, 1972)

——: "Amzi Chapin: Frontier Singing Master and Folk Hymn Composer," *JRME*, xxiii (1975), 109

——: "Lucius Chapin: a New England Singing Master on the Frontier," *Contributions to Music Education*, iv (1976), 64

JAMES SCHOLTEN

Chapin, Schuyler G(arrison) (*b* New York, 13 Feb 1923). Impresario and music administrator. He attended the Longy School in Cambridge, Massachusetts (1940–41), where he was a pupil of Boulanger, and then worked for NBC (1941–51). He was general manager of Tex and Jinx McCary Enterprises (1951–3) and then a booking director with Columbia Artists Management, before becoming head of the Masterworks division of Columbia Records in 1959. In 1963 he joined the staff of Lincoln Center, where as vice-president in charge of programming he organized international festivals in the summers of 1967 and 1968 and began the Great Performers series and the Mostly Mozart festival. From 1969 to 1971 he served as executive producer for Amberson Enterprises. As general manager of the Metropolitan Opera (1972–5) he appointed James Levine music director and John Dexter director of production, and brought new works into the company's repertory (including Britten's *Death in Venice* and Berlioz's *Les troyens*). Chapin became dean of the School of the Arts at Columbia University in 1976, and chairman of the board of the American Symphony Orchestra League in 1982. In 1983 he was appointed to the President's Committee on the Arts and the Humanities. *Musical Chairs: a Life in the Arts* (1977) is his autobiography.

BIBLIOGRAPHY

S. E. Rubin: "A Met Understudy Makes it to the Top," *New York Times Magazine* (23 Sept 1973), 36

"Chapin, Schuyler G(arrison)," *CBY 1974*

ELLEN HIGHSTEIN

Chappell. Firm of music publishers. The original London firm began publishing in 1811. The American company was established in New York in 1935 by Max Dreyfus (*b* Kuppenheim, Germany, 1 April 1874; *d* Brewster, NY, 12 May 1964) who had earlier been associated with Harms; his brother, Louis Dreyfus (*b* Kuppenheim, 11 Nov 1877; *d* London, England, 2 May 1967), had bought the English firm in 1929. Louis became president of the London branch of Chappell, and Max created an affiliate company in New York. Chappell became the leading publisher of show music in America, producing scores by such composers as Romberg, Kern, Gershwin, Porter, Rodgers, Loewe, as well as works by Noël Coward, Ivor Novello, Gilbert and Sullivan, Styne, Weill, Harburg, and Rome. Philips (North America) bought the company in 1968, and a year later an office was opened in Nashville. The extensive show and standard catalogue (including sacred music) has been maintained under the name of Chappell, but the emphasis has been shifted to rock and popular music, including works by Pink Floyd, Randy Goodrum, Devo, the Police, Marvin Hamlisch, and Carole Bayer Sager. Chappell became a division of Polygram in 1972. Presser includes Chappell publications in its rental department.

BIBLIOGRAPHY

C. Mair: *The Chappell Story, 1811–1961* (London, 1961)

FRANCES BARULICH

Character notation. One of the names used for the notation of SHAPE-NOTE HYMNODY.

Charles, Ray [Robinson, Ray Charles] (*b* Albany, GA, 23 Sept 1930). Rhythm-and-blues and soul singer, pianist, arranger, and songwriter. Raised in Greenville, Florida, in a very poor family, at the age of five he contracted glaucoma; it went untreated and within a year he was blind. At five he also began playing piano. Two years later he went to the St. Augustine School for the Deaf and the Blind, where he studied composition and learned to write music scores in braille. In school he also learned to play trumpet, alto saxophone, clarinet, and organ. In 1945 Charles was orphaned and left school to form a combo, which toured northern and central Florida. He was determined to get as far from home as possible, and after he had saved $600 he left for Seattle. There he played in a number of jazz trios, developing a piano and vocal style heavily influenced by Charles Brown, then with Johnny Moore's Three Blazers, and Nat "King" Cole. It was also at about this time that he changed his name to Ray Charles, in order to avoid confusion with the prizefighter Sugar Ray Robinson. Charles acquired a substantial following in Seattle, in 1949 becoming a member of the first black group to have a sponsored television show. Soon after, he began to record for a variety of labels, including Jack Lauderdale's Swing Time, with which he had his first rhythm-and-blues hits, *Baby let me hold your hand* (1951) and *Kiss me baby* (1952). Swing Time had limited distribution and resources, however, and in late 1952 Lauderdale sold Charles's contract to Atlantic Records for $2500. (Charles had recorded in 1947 for Atlantic as a sideman with the trumpeter Joe Morris.)

Up to this point, Charles was distinguished more as an arranger than as a performer. He had toured with the blues guitarist and singer Lowell Fulson during his Swing Time days, and he had later traveled to New Orleans, where he arranged *The things that I used to do* for the gravel-voiced, gospel-influenced bluesman Guitar Slim, whose recording of it was a hit on the rhythm-and-blues chart and sold a million copies. In general, however, he remained more conversant with the urban jump-blues styles of Nat "King" Cole, Pete Brown, and Louis Jordan than with the southern blues of Fulson and Guitar Slim. But his work with those two musicians seems to have affected Charles's own style deeply, because soon after joining Atlantic he made his first musical breakthrough – a merger of his sophisticated technique with the new type of rhythm-and-blues that was developing into rock-and-roll at that period. His first Atlantic releases, in 1954, were novelty jump blues, but with *I've got a woman* (1955) Charles immediately established himself as a major figure in the new style. *I've got a woman* violated one of the most deeply felt taboos of black culture by mingling the coarse sexuality of the blues with the emotional intensity of gospel music as practiced in Baptist and Pentecostal services. The song consisted of solo vocal phrases accompanied only by the rhythm section of the backup group, interspersed with instrumental passages based on the 16-bar chord sequences of gospel song, in which Charles's piano figures were doubled by the group. During this period Charles took many of his song ideas from the gospel repertory. For instance, *I've got a woman* is directly derived from a hymn by Alex Bradford, his great *Lonely Avenue* came from the Pilgrim Travelers' *I've got a new home*, and *Nobody but you* was a simple contraction of *Nobody but you Lord.*

Ray Charles, c1959

Charles was not the only American singer of the early 1950s to explore the borrowing for secular popular music of the material and performance characteristics of gospel: Sonny Til and the Orioles (*Crying in the chapel*, 1952) had pioneered the fusion, which Elvis Presley, Clyde McPhatter of the Drifters, and Little Richard were also exploiting by 1955. But Charles's approach was perceived as more pernicious (he was attacked for his improprieties by both the blues singer Bill Broonzy and certain jazz critics) because he adopted a manner of delivery associated with the intense testifying of the Holiness and Apostolic churches and applied those vocal techniques (moans, grunts, and ecstatic incoherences) to the most explicitly sexual material that had ever found success on the popular charts. Charles still sang straight, sophisticated blues – *Drown in my own tears* of 1956 is one of the greatest performances of urban blues recorded since World War II – but his most successful songs were those performed in his sensual gospel style, such as *Hallelujah, I love her so* (1956), *The Right Time* (1959), and *What'd I say* (1959); the last effectively recreates the ambience of a Pentecostal service in its manic, swinging fervor.

Ironically, Charles may have achieved so many hits with such material precisely because of the unfamiliarity of white Americans with the conventions of blues and gospel. Such listeners were captured by the combination of emotionalism and virtuosity on Charles's recordings, for however simple the subject matter and emotions of his songs, his performances always created the impression of a highly developed and controlled technique. This allowed him to broaden his palette to a degree previously unprecedented in rhythm-and-blues, which made him acceptable to audiences devoted to many different styles of music, from rock-and-roll and white pop to jazz; Frank Sinatra called him "the only genius in the business" (an accolade that Atlantic fully exploited). On the album that Charles recorded at the Newport Jazz Festival in 1958 he established himself as a testifying rock-and-roll preacher, a smooth, sophisticated popular singer, a big-band leader, and a swinging post-bop pianist. By that time he was recording as many albums as singles, working with such versatile arrangers as Ralph Burns and Quincy Jones (the latter had taken music lessons from Charles during his youth in Seattle), and touring with a big band and a female backup chorus modeled on gospel groups – supporting forces of a size that for economic reasons had seldom been used since the war.

By the end of the 1950s Charles had outgrown the commercial confines of Atlantic, which was a rhythm-and-blues and jazz company; having explored the possibilities open to a black singer recording with black musicians for a black audience, he had become an ambassador for black culture to white audiences. In consequence in late 1959 he signed with ABC/Paramount Records, a popular label owned by the ABC television network. At first, this change of labels made no essential difference to Charles's approach. (Indeed, one of his purposes in making the move was to gain more creative control over his recordings, though this seems to have amounted to no more than his being granted royalties as a producer as well as a performer.) Even his most adventurous project, the recording of two albums entitled *Modern Sounds in Country & Western Music*, was foreshadowed – on his final Atlantic album, *The Genius of Ray Charles* – by a version of Hank Snow's country song, *I'm movin' on*. The best of the early ABC hits – *Georgia on my mind, One mint julep, Hit the road Jack, I can't stop loving you, You don't know me, Busted* – have the same searing intensity, musical inventiveness, and sly wit as the earlier successes. It was as a result of these recordings, as much as his first hits, that Charles became a dominant influence on such important performers of the 1960s as Aretha Franklin, Stevie Wonder, Steve Winwood, the Righteous Brothers, James Brown, and Eric Burdon of the Animals. However, eclecticism proved to have as many pitfalls for a black performer in the blues tradition such as Charles as it did for a white one such as Presley. And like Presley's his music deteriorated towards the end of the sixties, not because it paled in comparison with new developments in hard rock, but because the material became increasingly sentimental and banal. Charles was, in addition, damaged by an arrest in 1965 for possessing heroin (it transpired that he had been an addict for his entire adult life, but he was apparently quickly and completely cured). After an absence from performing of a year following the arrest, Charles recorded some successful singles, including (ironically) *Let's go get stoned* (1966) and at least one great album (*A Message from the People*, 1972). But his power was diminished by his own acceptance of the conventions of supper-club show business. Although almost all of his later recordings include a remarkable moment or two, and his concerts have continued to be stimulating, Charles has never again recaptured the consistent unity of vision that marked his first decade as a performer.

Yet Charles must be regarded as a musician of fundamental importance and far-reaching influence. It can be argued that he was the principal architect of the transformation of black popular music from the rhythm-and-blues style to soul. There has been almost no performer in the latter genre who has not been deeply affected by Charles's vocal and arranging styles. And within the mainstream of popular jazz Charles's instrumental recordings, particularly those made for Atlantic with the vibraphone player Milt Jackson of the Modern Jazz Quartet, have been equally influential. Furthermore, it is difficult to name another performer whose recorded work so completely expresses the scope of American popular-music ambition and achievement from the 1950s to the 1980s. All of these qualities decisively mark Charles not only as one of the most original popular artists of the 1950s, but as one of the most important American musicians of any style to have emerged in the postwar period.

RECORDINGS
(selective list)

Baby let me hold your hand (Swing Time 250, 1951); Kiss me baby (Swing Time 274, 1952); I've got a woman (Atl. 1050, 1955); Drown in my own tears (Atl. 1085, 1956); Hallelujah, I love her so (Atl. 1096, 1956); Lonely Avenue (Atl. 1108, 1956); The Right Time (Atl. 2010, 1959); What'd I say (Atl. 2031, 1959); *The Genius of Ray Charles* (Atl. 1312, 1960); Georgia on my mind (ABC 10135, 1960); *Genius + Soul = Jazz* (Imp. 2, 1961); Hit the road Jack (ABC 10244, 1961); One mint julep (Imp. 200, 1961); I can't stop loving you (ABC 10330, 1962); *Modern Sounds in Country & Western Music*, i–ii (ABC/Para. 410, 435, 1962); You don't know me (ABC 10345, 1962); Busted (ABC 10481, 1963); *Ingredients in a Recipe for Soul* (ABC/Para. 465, 1963); Let's go get stoned (ABC 10808, 1966); *A Message from the People* (ABC 755, 1972); *True to Life* (Atl. 19142, 1977)

BIBLIOGRAPHY

J. Maher: "Ray Charles Carried the Ball – then Everybody Else Began Scoring Big," *Billboard*, lxxiv (10 Nov 1962), 34

"Charles, Ray," *CBY 1965*

P. Ackerman and others: "A Touch of Genius: the Ray Charles Story," *Billboard*, lxxvii (15 Oct 1966), §RC, p.1

B. Fong-Torres: "Ray Charles," *Rolling Stone*, no.126 (18 Jan 1973), 28

L. Goddet: "Ray Charles pas à pas . . . ," *Jazz hot*, no.329 (1976), 8

P. Welding: "Ray Charles: Senior Diplomat of Soul," *Down Beat*, xliv/9 (1977), 12

R. Charles and D. Ritz: *Brother Ray: Ray Charles' Own Story* (New York, 1978)

R. Palmer: "Soul Survivor Ray Charles," *Rolling Stone*, no.258 (9 Feb 1978), 11

W. Balliett: *American Singers* (New York, 1979), 50

L. Feather: "Piano Giants of Jazz: Ray Charles," *Contemporary Keyboard*, vi/7 (1980), 62

DAVE MARSH

Charles, Teddy [Cohen, Theodore Charles] (*b* Chicopee Falls, MA, 13 April 1928). Jazz vibraphonist, composer, and arranger. He studied percussion at the Juilliard School in 1946, but taught himself to play vibraphone; later he studied composition with Hall Overton. After playing for a number of bandleaders from 1946 to 1952, he began leading various experimental jazz groups of his own, with which his career subsequently became associated. He has been particularly concerned with the interaction of improvisation and composition in jazz, and has both commissioned and recorded some unusually intelligent examples of jazz composition and arrangement, such as George Russell's *Lydian M-1*, Jimmy Giuffre's *Quiet Time*, and Gil Evans's *You go to my head*. In his own compositions, too, Charles broke away from the conventional formal pattern of popular songs to write such works as his *Variations on a Motive by Bud* (1953), which has a 48-bar chorus made up of eight-bar sections in the form *ABCDED*. The written and improvised contrapuntal textures of his works of this period looked forward to the collective extemporization in the jazz of the 1960s; the modality of *Etudiez le cahier* and polytonal elements of *Further Out* show a strong harmonic sense. Charles has throughout his career been an outstanding vibraphonist, but is perhaps most important for his efforts to bring more diverse musical materials to jazz.

RECORDINGS
(selective list)

Teddy Cohen Trio (1951, Prst. 132); *New Directions* (1953, Prst. 164); *Teddy Charles Tentet* (1956, Atl. 1229); *A Word from Bird* (1956, Atl. 1274)

BIBLIOGRAPHY

T. Charles and I. Gitler: "Dialogue on Modern Jazz," *Jazz*, i (1959), 161

R. Atkins: "Teddy Charles," *Modern Jazz: the Essential Records*, ed. M. Harrison (London, 1975), 30

M. Harrison: *A Jazz Retrospect* (Newton Abbot, England, 1976), 43

MAX HARRISON/R

Charleston (i). City in South Carolina (pop. 69,510; metropolitan area 430,462). It was founded in 1670 by Lord Anthony Ashley Cooper (later 1st Earl of Shaftesbury) as Charles Town, after Charles II, and rapidly became the commercial and cultural center of the colonial South. In the 18th century Charleston grew from a small seaport into the fourth largest city in the USA. The pre-war years (*c*1830–60) saw the culmination of the city's golden age of commerce and culture and Charleston dominated the intellectual, cultural, commercial, and political life of the South until the Civil War. It is now a modern shipping and industrial center.

The first documented account of musical activity in Charleston dates from 1732, when the *South Carolina Gazette* reported a "Consort of Musick" presented "for the benefit of Mr Salter" on 12 April, the second known public concert in America. Charleston was also the site of the first opera performance in America, when *Flora, or Hob in the Well* was given at "the Courtroom" on 18 February 1735.

Colonial Charleston had several musicians of high caliber. Among these were John Salter, first organist at St. Philip's Church (and the same "Mr Salter" mentioned above), and his successor, Charles Theodore Pachelbel, son of the German composer and organist Johann Pachelbel. Charles Theodore Pachelbel was an organist and church musician in Charleston from 1737 until his death in 1750. Also prominent at this time were two English organists, Peter Valton and Benjamin Yarnold. Peter Albrecht von Hagen and Gottlieb Graupner were briefly active in Charleston before going north to Boston.

The mainstay of Charleston's 18th-century musical life was the St. Cecilia Society, thought to be the first musical society in America. Founded in 1762, the society comprised a fellowship of "gentlemen amateurs" supplemented by professional musicians engaged by the season. Its original purpose was to foster the growth and cultivation of music in Charleston and to provide a means of entertainment for its members. Its heyday was in the 1770s, when its concerts were affairs of great elegance and noteworthy musical interest. Typical programs included overtures, oratorio selections, songs, and piano pieces by contemporary European composers. These concerts continued until 1822 when increasing difficulty in obtaining musicians led to the society's lapse into an exclusive social cotillion. (St. Cecilia's modish dancing assemblies continue today.)

Charleston's musical traditions reached their apex in the fashionable social milieu of the pre-Civil War period. The social season from October to May offered a round of pleasures including concerts, balls, and theatrical productions. Audiences heard a host of performers among both local and visiting artists, many of whom were internationally renowned, such as Mme Anna Bishop, Ole Bull, Jenny Lind, Adelina Patti, and Sigismund Thalberg. Concerts included a variety of genres: the genteel air, opera and oratorio selections, and instrumental solos and ensembles. Apart from contemporary Italian opera, which was highly favored, the concert repertory bore a distinct British imprint, for the most popular composers were either active in London, or born in England or Ireland (Haydn, Handel, Thomas Moore, Henry Bishop, Thomas Arne, John Braham, Muzio Clementi, John Stevenson, Matthew King, and others).

Among noteworthy local musicians was Jacob Eckhard, Sr., composer and organist at St. Michael's from 1809 to 1833, who maintained high standards in church music. Others included Charles H. Gilfert, a composer, pianist, and theatrical entrepreneur who lived and worked in Charleston from 1807 to 1825; Henry Wellington Greatorex, the "American psalmodist"; and Samuel Dyer, an English church musician who lived and worked in Charleston from 1819 to 1822. Filippo Trajetta, son of Tommaso Traetta, briefly made Charleston his home during the first decade of the 19th century. Six local music societies presented regular concerts, most of which were organized for charity and the cultivation of music among the citizens. None enjoyed more than an ephemeral existence.

Musical programs were given in the churches and in several concert halls, among which were South Carolina Institute Hall (capacity 3500), Hibernian Hall (2500), and Military Hall and Charleston Theatre (both 1200). Moreover, there were numerous "long rooms," saloons, and hotels featuring music. Summer pleasure gardens were also popular, the favorite being Vauxhall Gardens, modeled after its British counterpart.

Cultural events naturally diminished sharply during the Civil War, in which the city was directly involved. After it, Charleston again enjoyed a flourishing musical life. Music societies and amateur performing groups abounded. The Charleston Conservatory was opened in 1884 under the leadership of Otto Müller. In 1869 the Academy of Music opened; for more than 30 years numerous musical and dramatic artists of international stature appeared on its stage. The leading musical personality of the late 19th century was "Mme Barbot" (formerly Hermina Petit), a teacher, conductor, and upholder of local musical standards and traditions. She was born in Brussels in 1842, the daughter of the Belgian musician Victor Petit, and in 1852 was successfully presented as a child prodigy in a piano recital at Niblo's Gardens in New York. Her family moved to Charleston in 1853. She organized the Charleston Musical Association in 1875 and conducted more than 40 oratorios from the standard repertory, part of a career that spanned more than 60 years. Other notable residents in the early 20th century included the composer Karl Theodore Saul; the German tenor Anton Schott, who lived and taught in Charleston from 1905 to 1910; the pianist Alexander Zenier; and Karl Metz, a composer and leader of "Metz's Band." A series of concerts (1919–24) sponsored by Maud Gibbon, a local patron of music, brought to the city such artists as Casals, Thibaud, Lhévinne, Kreisler, and Rachmaninoff. Another local fixture was the Jenkins Orphanage Band, a group of black children that achieved international recognition in the early 20th century with tours of the USA and Europe. The Siegling Music House (1819–1970), among the longest lasting music shops in the USA, was also active in music publishing during the 19th century.

The Charleston PO was organized by G. Theo Wichmann in 1925. This orchestra of about 75 musicians gave numerous concerts of standard orchestral works until World War II. It grew out of the Charleston String Symphony, founded in 1936 by Maud Gibbon (who had in 1919 organized a concert with an orchestra of 65 musicians conducted by Martha Laurens Patterson). The string orchestra gave three concerts a year, conducted by Tony Hadgi (1936–40) and David Sackson (1940–41). In 1942 this group was expanded into a full orchestra with Albert Fracht as conductor until 1959; his successors have been Donn Mills (1959–63), Lucien DeGroote (1963–83), and Mark Cedel (from 1983).

The Charleston Choral Society, an amateur association founded in 1944 by its conductor Vernon Weston, gave two or three oratorio performances a year until 1966, when it became the Charleston Opera Company with Weston continuing as director; its first production was of Puccini's *Tosca*.

In 1977 Charleston became the site for the annual Spoleto Festival (USA), the American branch of Menotti's Festival of Two Worlds. It encompasses opera, chamber music, symphony concerts, choral concerts, jazz, country music, theater, and dance, as well as exhibitions of the visual arts; between 125 and 140 events may be offered. Further musical life is provided in the city by two ballet companies, an active community concert association, and many performances of church music.

See also LIBRARIES AND COLLECTIONS, §3.

BIBLIOGRAPHY

C. Fraser: *Reminiscences of Charleston* (Charleston, 1854/*R*1969)
B. St. Julien Ravenel: *Charleston: the Place and the People* (New York, 1907)
O. G. T. Sonneck: *Early Concert-life in America (1731–1800)* (Leipzig, 1907/*R*1978)
E. P. Simons: *Music in Charleston from 1732–1919* (Charleston, 1927)
E. Willis: *The Charleston Stage in the XVIII Century* (New York, 1933)

Hermina Barbot

F. P. Bowes: *The Culture of Early Charleston* (Chapel Hill, 1942)
W. S. Hoole: *The Ante-Bellum Charleston Theatre* (Tuscaloosa, AL, 1946)
G. W. Williams: *St. Michael's Charleston, 1751–1951* (Columbia, 1951)
V. L. Redway: "Charles Theodore Pachelbell, Musical Emigrant," *JAMS*, v (1952), 32
G. W. Williams: "Eighteenth Century Organists of St. Michael's, Charleston," *South Carolina Historical and Genealogical Magazine*, liii (1952), 146
——: "Early Organists at St. Philip's, Charleston," *South Carolina Historical and Genealogical Magazine*, liv (1953), 83
——: "Charleston Church Music, 1562–1833," *JAMS*, vii (1954), 35
——: "Jacob Eckhard and His Choirmaster's Book," *JAMS*, vii (1954), 41
M. J. Curtis: *The Early Charleston Stage, 1703–1798* (diss., Indiana U., 1968)
G. C. Rogers, Jr.: *Charleston in the Age of the Pinckneys* (Norman, OK, 1969)
J. J. Hindman: *Concert Life in Ante Bellum Charleston* (diss., U. of North Carolina, Chapel Hill, 1971)
G. W. Williams: *Jacob Eckhard's Choir-master's Book of 1809* (Columbia, SC, 1971)

JOHN JOSEPH HINDMAN

Charleston (ii). Lively, social dance of the 1920s, said to have originated in Charleston, South Carolina, as a black-American dance form. It appeared for the first time in theatrical dance in the black musical comedy *Liza* (1922; produced by Irving C. Miller, music by Maceo Pinkard) and achieved enormous popularity in 1923 as a dance song, "The Charleston," by James P. Johnson and Cecil Mack (ex. 1), in the black musical *Runnin' Wild*. Other shows produced in that year and featuring the dance

Ex.1 C. Mack and J. Johnson: *Charleston* (1923)

included *How Come?* and the *Ziegfeld Follies*. It became the symbol of the "Roaring Twenties," the jazz age, the Black Renaissance, flappers, the period of prohibition, organized crime, and "big spending," and the frenzied social gaiety that came abruptly to an end with the Wall Street crash of 1929.

The movements of the charleston were based on those of other black-American exhibition dances, especially the ones introduced in the black revue *Shuffle Along* in 1921. They included shimmying (rapid shaking of the upper torso, hips, thighs, and buttocks), exuberant and on occasion violent kicking of the legs and swinging of the arms, and slapping of parts of the body with the hands, all of which were performed in the seemingly awkward posture of a half-squat, with hunched shoulders, knees together, and toes pointing inward; the effect, however, was one of grace and lighthearted abandon. As a stage dance its movements included vigorous side kicks, flailing of the arms, and swinging of the torso. During its few years of popularity in about 1925–8 it was modified by the English gliding style of dance, and the abrupt motions were replaced by subtler ones with hands on the knees or swaying of the torso while rotating the hands with the palms out. In the late 1920s the charleston died out but it was revived as a stage dance in the 1950s and 1960s, notably for nostalgic musicals. The music was fast, about 50–60 bars per minute. The characteristic syncopated rhythm is usually notated as in ex. 1; the same rhythm is used in other dances of black-American origin, notably the BLACK BOTTOM.

BIBLIOGRAPHY

M. Stearns and J. Stearns: *Jazz Dance: the Story of American Vernacular Dance* (New York, 1968)
L. F. Emery: *Black Dance in the United States from 1619 to 1970* (Palo Alto, CA, 1972)

For further bibliography *see* DANCE.

PAULINE NORTON

The charleston: "Music Hath Charms," cartoon by Ralph B. Fuller in "Judge," xc (17 April 1926)

Charters, Samuel (Barclay) (*b* Pittsburgh, PA, 1 Aug 1929). Jazz, blues, and folk-music scholar. He was born to a family of jazz musicians, and attended Sacramento City College, from which he received an associate's degree in 1949, and Tulane University (1954); he studied music with Imbrie and Denny at the University of California, Berkeley (BA 1956). His field recordings of blues performances in the New Orleans area, which he submitted to the Vanguard record company in 1954 at the suggestion of Frederic Ramsey, Jr., were the first of his many recordings of ethnic music. From 1970 to 1984 he lived in Sweden, studying indigenous folk music; his research resulted in a book, *Spelmännen* (1979), about Swedish folk fiddling. Other fieldwork has taken him to the British Isles, Mexico, and the Bahamas. He has been active as a producer of folk music recordings; a series of albums of African music entitled *African Journey* was issued by Vanguard in the mid-1970s, and he has supervised other projects for Folkways. In 1979 he received an ASCAP-Deems Taylor award for *Roots of the Blues* (1979, 2/1982), and a Grammy Award for Clifton Chenier's recording *I'm Here*, which he produced. Charters has also written novels and poetry, and combined his musical and literary interests in his book *Jelly Roll Morton's Last Night at the Jungle Inn: an Imaginary Memoir* (1984).

WRITINGS

Jazz: New Orleans, 1885–1957 (Belleville, NJ, 1958, rev. 2/1963)
The Country Blues (New York, 1959)
Jazz: a History of the New York Scene (Garden City, NY, 1962)
Bluesmen: the Story and the Music of the Men who Made the Blues (New York, 1967)
Spelmännen (Stockholm, 1979)
Roots of the Blues (New York, 1979, 2/1982)
Jelly Roll Morton's Last Night at the Jungle Inn: an Imaginary Memoir (New York, 1984)

KATHLEEN HAEFLIGER

Chase, Gilbert (*b* Havana, Cuba, 4 Sept 1906). Music historian and critic. He studied at Columbia University and the University of North Carolina (BA), and privately in New York and Paris.

From 1929 to 1935 he was music critic in Paris for *Musical America* and other journals. From 1940 to 1943 he served as Latin American specialist in the music division of the Library of Congress. In 1955 he was appointed director of the School of Music of the University of Oklahoma. He was on the faculty of Tulane University, 1961–6, where he founded and directed the Inter-American Institute for Musical Research. Afterwards he worked independently as a scholar, author, editor, and lecturer. From 1975 to 1979 he was a visiting professor at the University of Texas, Austin.

Chase is a prolific writer on Spanish and American subjects. *The Music of Spain* (1941, rev. 2/1959) was the first comprehensive account of the subject in any language. *America's Music* (1955, rev. 2/1966) was the first historical study of music in the USA to treat folk and popular music as seriously as art and religious music. In other writings Chase has increasingly addressed himself to the history of Latin American and American music in its cultural context. He founded and edited the yearbook of Tulane's Inter-American Institute (1965–75).

See also HISTORIES, §1.

H. WILEY HITCHCOCK/PAULA MORGAN

Chasins, Abram (*b* New York, 17 Aug 1903). Writer and broadcaster on music, pianist, and composer. He studied at the Juilliard School, Columbia University, and the Curtis Institute. From 1926 to 1935 he was a teacher at Curtis, and after touring regularly as a pianist between 1925 and 1946, he became music director of the New York radio station WQXR in 1947. His radio work, both in this post and previously (he initiated the "Abram Chasins Music Series" (1932–8) and the "Master Class of the Air"), earned him a high reputation. After his retirement from WQXR in 1965 he became musician-in-residence at the University of Southern California and director of KUSC, the university radio station, which he developed into a major station of the National Public Radio network. Among his compositions are piano concertos in F minor (1928) and F♯ minor (1931), *Three Chinese Pieces* for piano (1928, orchestrated 1929), *Parade* for orchestra (1930), and many other piano pieces.

WRITINGS

Speaking of Pianists (New York, 1957)
The Van Cliburn Legend (New York, 1959)
The Appreciation of Music (New York, 1966)
Music at the Crossroads (New York, 1972)
Leopold Stokowski: a Portrait (New York, 1979)

BIBLIOGRAPHY

"Chasins, Abram," *CBY 1960*

KARL KROEGER/PAULA MORGAN

Chatham, Rhys (*b* New York, 19 Sept 1952). Composer. He studied composition with La Monte Young, Morton Subotnick, and Maryanne Amacher. In 1971, when he was 18, he co-founded and became director of the music program at the Kitchen, which later became New York's foremost experimental-music performing space; two years later he left the Kitchen and worked intermittently as a bartender and freelance composer, but from 1977 to 1980 again acted as music director there. Since 1980 he has devoted himself fully to composing. Chatham has collaborated with, among others, the visual artists Robert Longo (who played in his band) and Charles Atlas, and the choreographer Karole Armitage, with whom he toured in Europe, performing his score for the striking work, *Drastic Classicism* (1981).

Chatham was one of the first to combine the structural techniques of the experimental avant-garde with the often acerbic sound of punk and art rock (in 1978). His rock-influenced works – which he has played both in concert spaces and in rock clubs – create sandstorms of noise, subtly textured by means of the high overtones generated by the varied, often eccentric, but always precisely defined tunings of the electric guitars in his band (his interest in overtones may be due to his having tuned harpsichords during his teenage years). In 1982, as the result of a commission from the Groupe de Recherche Contemporaine of the Paris Opéra, Chatham re-created the sound of his music for electric guitars in a piece scored for brass octet and percussion (*For Brass*), demonstrating triumphant energy and, particularly in its instrumental writing, extraordinary finesse.

WORKS

Ear Ringing, sine-wave generator, 1977; Gui Trio, 3 elec gui, drums, 1977; The Out of Tune Guitar, 3 elec gui, drums, 1979; Acoustic Terror, elec gui, drums, 1981; Drastic Classicism, 4 elec gui, drums, 1981; The Decibel Diary, elec gui, film, 1982; For Brass, 4 tpt, 2 trbn, b trbn, tuba, perc, 1982; *c*20 other works

BIBLIOGRAPHY

G. Sandow: "The New New Music," *Village Voice* (13 May 1981)

GREGORY SANDOW

Chatianov, Samuel. *See* CHOTZINOFF, SAMUEL.

Chatman, Stephen (George) (*b* Faribault, MN, 28 Feb 1950). Composer. After studying piano with Maria Syllm, he entered the Oberlin Conservatory (BM 1972), where his principal teachers were Walter Aschaffenburg and Joseph Wood. At the University of Michigan, he studied with Bassett, Bolcom, Finney, and Eugene Kurtz (DMA 1977). A Fulbright Scholarship enabled him to study for a year in Cologne (1974). He also received three BMI student composer awards (1974–6), an Ives Award from the American Academy and Institute of Arts and Letters (1975), and commissions from the NEA, the Canadian Arts Council, and the Ontario Arts Council. In 1976 he joined the faculty of the University of British Columbia, where he was appointed associate professor in 1982. A strong programmatic element underlies Chatman's works, as in *Occasions* (1976–7), a depiction of a series of moods, and *Wild Cat* (1971–5). Such works are free in form and varied in style. His keen sense of humor is evident in *Whisper, Baby* (1975) and *Variations on "Home on the Range"* (1979). Consistent use of collage techniques, veiled references, and a counterpoint of styles suggest an affinity with Ives, but Chatman's textures are clearer, perhaps as a result of his concern with audience communication.

WORKS

Orch: Two Followers of Lien, 1973; Occasions, 1976–7; Grouse Mountain Lullaby, 1978; They all Replied, 1978; Crimson Dream, 1982–3

Inst: Wild Cat, fl, 1971–5; O lo velo, a sax, perc, 1973; On the Contrary, cl, chamber ens, 1973–4; Quiet Exchange, cl, perc, 1976; Hesitation, vn, cel, 1977; Amusements, pf, 1977–8; 5 Scenes, fl, gui, 1978; Variations on "Home on the Range," str qt/sax qt, 1979; Fleeting Thoughts, gui, 1980; Black and White Fantasy, pf, 1981; Gossamer Leaves, cl, pf, 1981; Fanfare, 3 tpt, 3 trbn, 1982; other chamber and solo inst works

Vocal: Whisper, Baby (S. Chatman), SATB, pf, perc, 1975; 11 songs, 3 choral partsongs, 2 anthems

Principal publishers: Berandol, E. B. Marks

BIBLIOGRAPHY

R. MacMillan: "Canadian Distinctiveness Influencing Chatman Works," *Music Scene*, no.313 (1980), 9

MICHAEL MECKNA

Chautauqua and lyceum. The names of two interrelated groups of institutions that, since the 1820s, have provided a platform for musical performance and a framework for musical education in the USA and Canada.

1. History. 2. Performers.

1. History. The American lyceum movement was begun in Massachusetts in 1826 through the efforts of Josiah Holbrook (1788–1854), who conceived a nationwide (even worldwide) network of local groups in which the members would improve each others' minds by lectures, discussions, and presentations. The idea spread very rapidly, and soon there were thousands of groups located all over the USA; their existence in such numbers gave rise to a throng of professional speakers who largely replaced the original local presenters. Music had only a small place in the early lyceums: it was occasionally the topic of a lecture, and Lowell Mason and John Sullivan Dwight were among those who addressed lyceum audiences. There was a little singing instruction, but musical performances were rare.

A new phase began after the Civil War with the formation of professional lyceum bureaus for the management of the traveling talent. The most important was the Redpath Lyceum Bureau, founded by James Redpath (1833–1891) in 1868, which eventually comprised a dozen semi-independent offices in all parts of the USA and one in Canada. Although the lyceum movement remained very high-minded, it now placed somewhat more emphasis on entertainment, and music began to occupy a large place in the programs. By the 1900s music had become the largest single element; lectures and performances were given throughout the fall, winter, and spring in theaters, opera houses, schools, and churches.

The Chautauqua movement took its name, and much of its nature, from the Chautauqua Institution, founded in 1874 on the shore of Chautauqua Lake, New York, by John Heyl Vincent (1832–1920) and Lewis Miller (1829–99). Originally a training camp for Sunday-school teachers, the Chautauqua Institution soon expanded its activities into a summer-long program of adult education in a wide variety of secular and religious subjects. Music was an important element from the beginning. Although the emphasis at first was on sacred music, secular music was soon added to the program. Instruction had an important place and before long Chautauqua was offering music teaching at conservatory level during its summer season, as well as lectures, instruction, and group activities for nonprofessionals. It also offered performances by both resident groups and visiting performers.

Only two years after the founding of the Chautauqua Institution, other assemblies scattered around the country began to imitate it, often calling themselves Chautauquas and offering similar programs of summertime education, entertainment, and recreation. By the turn of the century, the lyceum bureaus were major suppliers of talent to the Chautauquas; in 1904 they made the first attempts to rationalize the travels of lecturers and performers by grouping the institutions on planned circuits. But the Chautauquas were too individualistic to take to the arrangement, and the circuit plan worked only from 1907, when it was sold by the bureaus as a package to communities that had not previously established Chautauquas. Each of the circuits lasted from three to seven days; the program was given in the same order in each town, and the same groups of performers followed one another around from town to town all through the summer. The number of circuits rapidly increased, reaching a peak in the early 1920s, when there were about 100, using over 500 tents to serve nearly 10,000 assemblies and a total audience of about 40 million.

After 1924, the circuit Chautauquas as well as the independent groups rapidly declined in number. The last circuit organizations operated in the early 1930s, and only a few independent programs were still running by 1940. A handful of Chautauquas still exist: the Chautauqua Institution itself continues to thrive, as does its music, and Bay View, Michigan, which has always based its activities closely on those of the original foundation, though on a smaller scale, is one of the few others that survive. Like the Chautauquas, the lyceum movement also declined in the 1930s, in many cases giving way to civic music programs and lecture series that no longer used the name "lyceum."

2. Performers. Before the advent of broadcasting, the lyceum and Chautauqua movements provided the best opportunity for Americans outside the big cities to hear music performed. The two offered very similar programs: both were supplied by the eventually numerous lyceum bureaus, and to a very large extent the same performers appeared before Chautauqua and lyceum audiences, the former in the summer months and the latter during the rest of the year. Moreover, the types of performers and groups remained fairly stable over the 60 or 70 years of the bureaus' activities.

The independent Chautauquas often presented a mix of local performers and professionals engaged through the bureaus. If local musicians were used, efforts were made to obtain the services of the best that the town or nearby communities could offer – singers, instrumental soloists and ensembles, choruses, and, especially, bands. The bureaus managed both full-time professional musicians (many of whom traveled all the year round giving Chautauqua and lyceum programs for years or even decades) and, in the Chautauqua movement, semiprofessionals and students. The total number of musicians involved by the early 20th century was very large indeed: hundreds in any season, and many thousands in total.

The professional bands were among the biggest attractions at any Chautauqua. Numerous Italian bands toured in the first decades of the 20th century – Signor Pasquale Ferrante's Royal Italian Guards Band, Victor's Florentine Band, Creatore's, Liberati's, Ciricillo's, and Quintano's bands, and many others. Some strove to be different: the members of Thaviu's Oriental Band appeared in fantastic costumes, while Carmeliny's Old Colonial Band wore colonial dress and white wigs; several ensembles, including Ewing's Band, consisted entirely of women. Probably the longest-lived and greatest favorite of all Chautauqua and lyceum ensembles was Bohumir Kryl's Bohemian Band, which toured from 1906 until well after the demise of the movements.

Instrumental ensembles were of every sort and of every size from two to 20: the two McGrath Brothers, who played banjos, were active around 1909–18; the Harp Symphony (1926–7) consisted of five young women, who played flute, harp, violin, cello, and piano; the White Rose Orchestra of around 1911 had six string players and a pianist (see illustration, p.412); and the Bostonians, active around 1918, was an orchestra of 20 women. Versatility was a notable characteristic of most of the ensembles. For example, the three-member Boston Lyrics of 1911–12 presented songs and readings illustrated spontaneously with cartoons and pastels, monologues, skits, solos and duets on the marimbaphone, and cornet and trombone solos and duets with piano.

Postcard advertising the White Rose Orchestra, a touring group managed by the Redpath–Vawter Chautauqua bureaus, 1911

Bellringers were perennial favorites: Ralph Dunbar's Singing Bell Ringers toured from at least 1900 to 1927.

Other groups were mainly vocal. Some choruses toured, but quartets (male or female, or occasionally mixed) were favored. In the second decade of the century, particularly popular groups included the Whitney Brothers, the Weatherwax Brothers, the Chautauqua Preachers Quartette, and the (female) Marigold Quartette. Black singing groups were much in demand. Early on they included the Tennesseeans, the North Carolinians, and the Fisk Jubilee Singers. The last group became the model for many that came afterwards, also called "jubilee singers" and usually consisting of five to eight men and women, though some were male or mixed quartets.

Instrumental and vocal soloists were less common than ensembles, but some of them, such as the contraltos Elsie Baker, active from at least 1910 until 1927, and Sibyl Sammis, active 1898–1916, were among the best-loved of all the performers. Quite a few internationally known musicians appeared occasionally in Chautauqua and lyceum programs, including Maud Powell, Mischa Elman, David Bispham, Pol Plançon, Ernestine Schumann-Heink, Tamaki Miura, and Gladys Swarthout at the beginning of her career; in 1915 Alice Nielsen made a complete 118-day Chautauqua circuit, traveling in a private railroad car, and the next summer both she and Julia Claussen did the same.

Opera and light opera companies appeared over most of the life of the Chautauqua and lyceum movements. In many cases they toured with a single work at a time; in others they presented scenes and selections from several operas. The works were normally abridged and reduced in scope; a typical company was a mixed quartet with a pianist.

A great variety of European national ensembles was also engaged: Croatian tamburica orchestras, Russian balalaika orchestras, Romanian and Hungarian orchestras, Welsh singers, and Alpine yodelers. Exotic groups came from various parts of the world – South Africa, New Zealand, the Philippines, and Hawaii – to speak about their native lands and customs, and to present their songs and dances. There were also American Indian troupes, and Indian princesses were popular, notably the Penobscot Watahwaso and the Cherokee Te Ata.

In the late years of Chautauqua activity, musicians who had become known through radio, including country-music groups, made their way into the tent programs.

A good selection of Chautauqua and lyceum music was recorded between about 1908 and the mid-1920s, particularly on the Victor Black Label, and also on various minor labels. Such performers as the Whitney Brothers, Charles Ross Taggart, Elsie Baker, Princess Watahwaso, Kryl's Band, Homer Rodeheaver, and the Chautauqua Preachers Quartette all made best-selling recordings.

BIBLIOGRAPHY

C. F. Horner: *The Life of James Redpath and the Development of the Modern Lyceum* (New York, 1926)
G. MacLaren: *Morally we Roll Along* (Boston, 1938)
V. Case and R. O. Case: *We called it Culture: the Story of Chautauqua* (Garden City, NY, 1948)
H. P. Harrison: *Culture under Canvas: the Story of Tent Chautauqua* (New York, 1958)
L. J. Wells: *A History of the Music Festival at Chautauqua Institution, 1874–1957* (Washington, DC, 1958)
I. Briggs and R. F. DaBoll: *Recollections of the Lyceum & Chautauqua Circuits* (Freeport, ME, 1969)
R. H. Cowden: *The Chautauqua Opera Association, 1929–1958: an Interpretative History* (n.p., 1974)
T. Morrison: *Chautauqua: a Center for Education, Religion, and the Arts in America* (Chicago, 1974)

FREDERICK CRANE

Chauvin, Louis (*b* St. Louis, MO, 13 March 1881; *d* Chicago, IL, 26 March 1908). Ragtime pianist and composer. He began a career as a vaudeville entertainer in partnership with Sam Patterson, a trained musician who had grown up with Chauvin in St. Louis. According to Patterson, Chauvin became a superb all-round performer with a wide repertory of piano pieces, a fine tenor voice, and effective comedy and dance styles. The duo eventually drew high praise from leading vaudevillians such as Bert Williams and George Walker. Later they disbanded to concentrate on the more profitable trade of piano playing. They appeared together at the Louisiana Purchase Exposition in St. Louis in 1904, and in that same year Chauvin won the Rosebud Club piano contest, an annual competition under the aegis of the ragtime pianist Tom Turpin. By this time he had become known as the "King of Ragtime Players." However, his inability to read music and his dissipated life style prevented Patterson from taking him to New York when he left St. Louis in 1906. Around 1908 Chauvin moved to Chicago, where he died a few months later.

By the unanimous testimony of his peers, Chauvin was the finest performer among the early St. Louis ragtime figures. Patterson described his playing as being in a "speed" style with overhand octaves and octaves in contrary motion. He reported that Chauvin composed rags almost daily, and preferred to rearrange other composers' tunes in more difficult keys. Brun Campbell claimed to have incorporated Chauvin's barrelhouse style into some of his own recordings, and Charles Thompson, another St. Louis player, recounted that Chauvin played the blues, and was "stretching 10ths way ahead of his time." Chauvin's only surviving compositions are collaborative pieces: *The Moon is Shining in the Skies* (1903), written with Patterson, and the well-known *Heliotrope Bouquet* (1907), notated by Scott Joplin. The first half of the latter piece is probably by Chauvin; the implied tango of the *A* strain and the grace-note figures of the *B* strain (deceptively notated as triplets) are features of a style different from that of the more conventional Joplin of the *C* and *D* strains. A surviving song by Chauvin, *Babe, it's too long off* (1906), probably scored by Patterson, makes use of a melodic–harmonic figure that occurs prominently in the *A* strain of *Heliotrope Bouquet*. Chauvin's sparse legacy makes it all the more regrettable that the recording industry did not begin documenting black talent in St. Louis until the early 1920s.

BIBLIOGRAPHY

SouthernB

R. Blesh and H. Janis: *They All Played Ragtime* (New York, 1950, rev. 4/1971)

T. Tichenor: "Chestnut Valley Days: the 'Real Thing' as Recalled by Charley Thompson," *Ragtime Review*, ii (April 1963), 5; repr. in *Rag Times*, v (Nov 1971), 3

P. Oliver: *Conversation with the Blues* (London, 1965)

D. A. Jasen and T. J. Tichenor: *Rags and Ragtime: a Musical History* (New York, 1978)

TREBOR JAY TICHENOR

Chawi. American Indian tribe of the PAWNEE confederacy.

Cheatham, Doc [Adolphus Anthony] (*b* Nashville, TN, 13 June 1905). Jazz trumpeter. After working for years in the brass sections of various big bands, he began playing in smaller jazz groups and belatedly gained a reputation as an interesting and consistent improviser. His brief solos with Eddie Heywood's Sextet in the 1940s hinted at his jazz potential, but it was not until the 1970s that Cheatham's jazz playing received international recognition. Unusually for a jazz musician, and particularly so for a brass player, his talents seemed to flower when he was in his 70s, and most of his best recordings date from this late stage of his career.

Cheatham always possessed an admirable technique, and his articulation and clarity of tone were striking (he was particularly expressive when using a cup mute); in later years he often added a rough burr to his sound which gave an invigorating edge to his solos. He occasionally played in big bands during the 1970s, but always returned to small-band settings, where he was best able to display his graceful improvisations, his flexibility, and his glorious high register.

RECORDINGS

(selective list)

As leader or co-leader: *Adolphus "Doc" Cheatham* (1973, Jezebel 102), incl. Mandy, Make up your Mind; *Hey Doc!* (1975, Black and Blue 33090), incl. Rosetta; *John, Doc & Herb* (1979, Metronome 627), incl. Little Happy Caldwell; with S. Price: *Black Beauty* (1979, Sackville 3029), incl. Memphis Blues

As sideman: E. Heywood: I Can't Believe that You're in Love with Me (1944, Com. 577)

BIBLIOGRAPHY

SouthernB

J. H. Klee: "Send for Doc Cheatham," *Mississippi Rag*, iii/12 (1976), 6

J. P. Battestini: "Doc Cheatham," *Coda*, no. 161 (1978), 28

W. Vache: "Doc Cheatham," *Jazz Journal International*, xxxii/12 (1979), 6

M. Ullman: *Jazz Lives* (Washington, DC, 1980)

L. Jeske: "Rx for the Blues," *Down Beat*, xlviii/12 (1981), 25

W. Balliett: *Jelly Roll, Jabbo and Fats* (New York, 1983), 74

JOHN CHILTON

Checker, Chubby [Evans, Ernest] (*b* Philadelphia, PA, 3 Oct 1941). Rock-and-roll singer and dancer. Checker adopted his stage name as a variation on that of Fats Domino. In high school, he developed his talents as a drummer, pianist, and vocal impressionist, skills that he exploited in the novelty song *The Class* (1959), which reached the Top 40 on the pop chart. The next year Checker recorded Hank Ballard's *The Twist*, and undertook a rigorous round of personal appearances to demonstrate the new dance step. Unexpectedly, the twist became a worldwide dance phenomenon. More than two dozen variants appeared on the charts over the next four years, as performers as different as the Beatles and Frank Sinatra tried to take advantage of the twist's commercial success (Joey Dee and the Starliters' *The Peppermint Twist*, the Isley Brothers' and the Beatles' *Twist and shout*, Sam Cooke's *Twistin' the night away*, among others). Checker remained active in television, film, and concerts well into the 1960s; and more than 30 of his dance and folk singles reached the popular chart, and a dozen the rhythm-and-blues chart. His popularity faded after 1964, however, as the Beatles ushered in a new era of rock-and-roll, though he continued to tour and record intermittently. Checker had a wider appeal than many previous rock-and-roll stars; he created music that appealed equally to young and old, rich and poor.

RECORDINGS

(selective list)

As soloist: The Class (Parkway 804, 1959); The Hucklebuck (Parkway 813, 1960); The Twist (Parkway 811, 1960); Pony Time (Parkway 818, 1961); Limbo Rock/Popeye the Hitchhiker (Parkway 849, 1962); Slow Twistin' (Parkway 835, 1962); Loddy Lo (Parkway 890, 1963); Let's do the Freddie (Parkway 949, 1965); Back in the U.S.S.R. (Buddah 100, 1969); Running (MCA 51233, 1982)

With B. Rydell: Jingle Bell Rock (Cameo 205, 1961)

GARY THEROUX

Cheeks, Julius "June" (*b* Spartanburg, SC, 7 Aug 1929; *d* Miami, FL, 27 Jan 1981). Gospel singer. He left school after the second grade and worked in the cotton fields and at service stations. In 1946 when the gospel group of which he was a member, the Baronets, appeared on a local radio program with the Nightingales and Archie Brownlee and the Blind Boys of Mississippi, the Nightingales were impressed with his singing and invited him to join the group. Organized in 1945 in Philadelphia by Barney Parks, the Nightingales included Cheeks, Paul Owens, Jo Jo Wallace, Carl Coates, and Howard Carroll. Cheeks's extended vocal range and energetic preaching style, which later influenced James Brown and Wilson Pickett, quickly made him the star of the group. In the late 1940s he joined Robert H. Harris and the Soul Stirrers. Returning to the Nightingales in the early 1950s he recorded *See how they done my Lord* (1955), which became a hit. He began preaching in 1954, and left the Nightingales again in 1960 to form his own group, the Knights, which had a success with *The last mile of the way* (1960). In the late 1960s Cheeks disbanded his group and sang for a while with the Mighty Clouds of Joy. From 1970 he spent his time preaching in Baltimore, Newark, and Miami. Cheeks was one of the first exponents of "hard" gospel singing, cultivating falsetto, growls, and screams; he also helped to place gospel quartets in the mainstream of black American music.

BIBLIOGRAPHY

SouthernB

T. Heilbut: *The Gospel Sound: Good News and Bad Times* (New York, 1971/*R*1975)

Obituary, *BPiM*, ix (1981), 240

HORACE CLARENCE BOYER

Chemehuevi. American Indian group of the Great Basin area. *See* PAIUTE.

Cheney, Simeon Pease (*b* Meredith, NH, 18 April 1818; *d* Franklin, MA, 10 May 1890). Singer, singing-school teacher, and composer. He was the son of Moses Cheney (1776–1853), a well-known local musician. As a young man he was a member, with his three brothers, Nathaniel, Moses Ela, and Joseph Young, and his sister Elizabeth Ela, of the Cheney Singers, a family group that toured throughout New England performing glees, ballads, and hymns (1845–7). He taught singing-schools in Vermont for much of his life, and compiled *The American Singing Book* (1879/*R*1980), a volume containing biographies of earlier American composers and examples of their work, as well as 33 original hymn tunes and three anthems. At the time of his death he was preparing a catalogue of birdsong, *Wood Notes Wild: Notations of Bird Music* (published posthumously in 1892); he was also one of the first to transcribe field recordings made of American Indian music. His brother Moses Ela Cheney (*b* Sanbornton, NH, 10 Dec 1812; *d* Redfield, SD, Feb 1896) also became a singing-school teacher. The musical convention he organized in Montpelier, Vermont, in May 1839 was probably the first of its kind in the state, and perhaps in New England.

BIBLIOGRAPHY

M. Cheney: "Learning to Sing in the Long Ago," *Boston Musical Visitor*, ii (Jan 1842), 124

E. Swayne: "A Vermont Musical Family," *Music*, xi (1896–7), 117

C. W. Hughes: "The Cheneys: a Vermont Singing Family," *Vermont History*, xlv (1977), 155

DALE COCKRELL

Chenier, Clifton (*b* Opelousas, LA, 25 June 1925). Zydeco and blues singer and accordion and harmonica player. The son of an accordion player, he heard both white and black Cajun musicians as a child. He played music on weekends before moving in the mid-1950s to Houston, where he secured employment in dance halls attended by Blacks from Louisiana. He played the large piano accordion which was more versatile and suitable for blues in many keys. The success of his *Cliston Blues* (1954, Imper. 5532) made him the most esteemed of the zydeco musicians. He was later joined by his brother Cleveland Chenier, who played a corrugated metal "chest washboard" in the form of a breastplate; they had a hit recording, *Louisiana Blues* (1965, Bayou 509), a good example of Chenier's rich patois. His eminently danceable music, such as the songs *Monifique* (1967, Arhoolie 1038), a slow drag with a heavy beat, and *Tu le ton son ton* (*c*1970, Arhoolie 1052), had wide appeal, and in the 1970s he toured extensively. *Jambalaya* (1975, Arhoolie 1086), made in Montreux, Louisiana, demonstrated the buoyant, jazz-influenced playing of his later style, and elaborate guitar work by Paul Senegal. The essence of his work and his improvisational ability was captured in the film *Hot Pepper* (1973). In 1979 ill health curtailed his playing for a while, but he has since resumed an active concert and recording career. He received a National Heritage Fellowship from the NEA in 1984.

BIBLIOGRAPHY

S. Harris: *Blues Who's Who* (New Rochelle, NY, 1979)

J. Broven: *South to Louisiana: the Music of the Cajun Bayous* (Gretna, LA, 1983), chap.9

B. J. Ancelet: "Clifton Chenier and his red hot Louisiana Band," *The Makers of Cajun Music* (Austin, 1984), 89

PAUL OLIVER

Chennevière, Daniel. *See* RUDHYAR, DANE.

Cherkassky, Shura (*b* Odessa, Ukraine, 7 Oct 1911). Pianist. His first teacher was his mother; then, after he settled in the USA, he studied with Josef Hofmann at the Curtis Institute. He made his début in Baltimore at the age of 11, and five years later toured Australia and South Africa. Not until 1945 did he make his first extensive tour of Europe, winning outstanding acclaim in Germany. Performing in other parts of the world for many years at a time (notably during the 1950s and again in the late 1960s and early 1970s), his tours have included engagements at the leading festivals in Europe and concerts in the Far East, Australia, New Zealand, Africa, and in 1976 and a number of times thereafter, in his native Russia. Also in 1976 he returned once again after a long absence to the USA and has since continued to appear with leading orchestras here and in Canada, as well as in recital. Cherkassky is at his best in the Romantic repertory, especially music in which his remarkable technique, range of color, and immediacy of imaginative response are allowed full play. His wayward temperament, akin to the old virtuoso school, is less well suited to the Classical repertory, and a hint of the idiosyncratic in his interpretations may be thought to mar his recordings, but those he has made of Russian music, notably Tchaikovsky, Rachmaninoff, and Prokofiev, are famous.

BIBLIOGRAPHY

J. Horowitz: "Shura Cherkassky – a Pianist who Follows his Intuition," *New York Times* (2 April 1978)

JOAN CHISSELL/R

Cherokee. American Indian tribe, who speak an Iroquoian language. They lived in the southern Appalachian highlands from as early as AD 1000 and had an estimated population of more than 15,000 in 1775. Today a large group of Cherokee lives in the five northeastern counties of Oklahoma and a smaller, eastern band on the Qualla Reservation in western North Carolina (*see* INDIANS, AMERICAN, fig. 1).

Any attempt to reconstruct a history of Cherokee music would have to rely on the accounts of missionaries and travelers of the 18th century and on ethnographies, not concerned primarily with music, from the late 19th century to the present. Few musical transcriptions have been made. Although traditional music used to pervade every level of Cherokee life, including prayers to the Creator, public ceremonies and celebrations, games, social and animal dances, affective magic, and curing, in more recent years some Cherokee have replaced traditional music with Christian hymns and gospel songs while others have taken up fiddle or guitar and have embraced country-music genres.

Cherokee music shares features with that of the Iroquois of the Northeast as well as that of other southeastern tribes: the initial and final shouts, responsorial techniques, signaling instrumental tremolos, and song-cycle format. Exploring stylistic similarities in Cherokee and Iroquois music by comparing New York Seneca and Oklahoma Cherokee musical forms, Heth (1979, p. 134) found that (1) structural points in both result in a thin texture; (2) cuing by the soloist and leader is important and is accomplished by vocal and/or instrumental techniques; (3) the instruments are similar; (4) the vocal style and interaction of media are comparable; and (5) the creativity allowed the lead singer in improvisation and choice of songs is also similar.

Cherokee thought concerning ceremonies and ritual practice stresses the application of the ritual numbers four and seven to music and dance, the general notion that every act performed is for a purpose, the idea that nonsense syllables may be outward manifestations of secret formulae or song texts, and that the Cherokee are permitted to think, say, recite, or sing texts or formulae. Myth, magic, and symbolism are especially important.

From early contact with the tribe, as well as from drawings, paintings, and written descriptions the following list of instruments can be drawn up: frame drums, kettledrums (with and without water), gourd, coconut, and turtle-shell hand-held rattles, turtle-shell and deer-hoof strung rattles (on various parts of the body), a flute, and trumpets made of the thighbone of a crane and of a conch shell. Of these, the drums, the hand-held rattles, and the turtle-shell strung rattles worn on the dancers' legs have survived to the present. A recent addition is the set of tin-can leg rattles worn in place of the turtle shells.

Cherokee music is mostly vocal and monophonic, and is performed with or without rattle and drum accompaniment. Although affective songs for love, hunting, or other magic-making are sung solo, dance-songs are usually sung in unison or are responsorial (sometimes both) and are interspersed with shouts and animal cries, the whole underlaid with instrumental accompaniment. The Stomp and Friendship Dances of the Oklahoma Cherokee are in song-cycle form, while most animal dances and other ceremonial songs are strophic, having the same music for each stanza. Repetition, variation, and improvisation play an important part in spinning out each form.

The vocal quality is mostly nasal and moderately tense, with glottal stops and turns reminiscent of yodeling. The vocal line is broken up with shouts and animal cries; the melodic contour is undulating and slightly descending. As few as three pitches may be used in a scale, as in the Mosquito Dance (which may be of Cherokee or Natchez origin), or as many as seven or even more, as in the Cherokee Friendship Dance, where alternating auxiliary tones bring the number to eight (exx. 1 and 2). Generally, however, the songs are based on pentatonic scales, both hemitonic and anhemitonic (ex. 3).

Ex.1 Excerpt from the Mosquito Dance

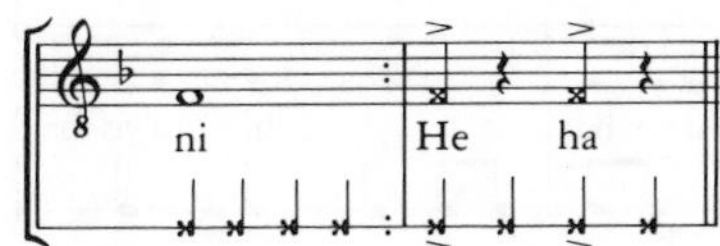

Ex.2 Excerpt from the Friendship Dance

Ex.3 Pentatonic scales
(a) hemitonic

(b) anhemitonic

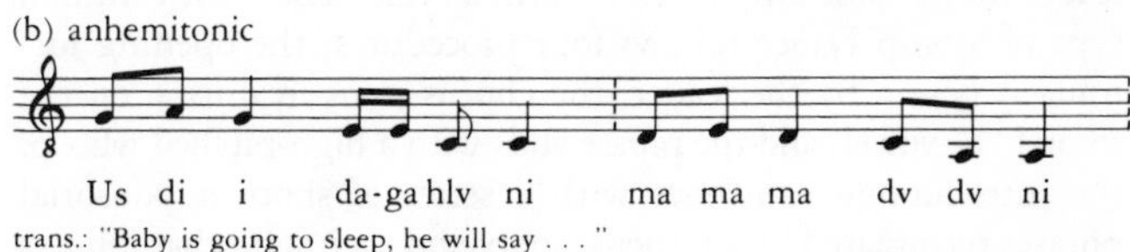

trans.: "Baby is going to sleep, he will say . . ."

The foundation of the various meters in the dance-songs is a steady alternation of accented and unaccented pulses outlined by the dancers' leg rattles. In the Stomp Dance cycles, the pulses in a leader's call may vary from two to seven, and in the chorus response from two to five, making some phrases as long as 11 beats (exx.4 and 5). Occasional overlapping phrases by leader and chorus may result in syncopation. The main rhythmic organizing principle, in addition to the accented–unaccented pulse, is isorhythm. It is not unusual for almost every phrase in a song to follow the same rhythmic pattern while melody and words change.

Ex.4 Excerpt from the Stomp Dance, 2 + 2 meter

Ex.5 Excerpt from the Stomp Dance, 5 + 6 meter

all examples transcr. C. Heth

In the Stomp Dance of the Oklahoma Cherokee, the most important traditional event using music, three basic forms are found: the opening Friendship Dance, the Stomp Dances, and the closing Old Folks' Dance. The Friendship Dance cycle consists of an introduction, seven songs, and a Stomp Dance. At the beginning, the leader uses four or seven sets of similar paired phrases, each followed by chorus shouts or whoops. Next, a leader–chorus unison pattern is set up that characterizes the rest of the piece. The leader sings a phrase, the chorus joins him in repeating it, and all sing in unison to the end of the section. A closing responsorial formula has the function of ending the song, introducing each of the following songs, and ending the cycle. Although more than a dozen Friendship Dance songs exist, the leader may choose only seven to form a cycle. The most common type of Stomp Dance follows four procedures: the opening formula is begun by the leader; the chorus joins in unison on the second "o" vowel, and the phrase ends with a high-pitched whoop; the introduction continues with a series of short responsorial phrases terminated by another whoop; and each song that follows (from four to 20 or more) is responsorial, leader and chorus alternating, and each ends with a shout. The Old Folks' Dance is strophic. Each verse begins with four similar phrases sung by the leader, each phrase followed by a chorus whoop. The verse that follows consists of a three-syllable phrase sung by the leader and a two-syllable response by the chorus. The leader–chorus pattern is repeated a number of times (usually 21) with no variation in words and little in pitch until the end of the strophe. Then a closing responsorial pattern is sung four times, and the entire cycle repeats four more times (Heth, 1979, pp.131f).

See also INDIANS, AMERICAN, esp. §I, 4(ii)(b).

DISCOGRAPHY

Delaware, Cherokee, Choctaw, Creek, recorded 1942–51 (Library of Congress AAFS L37, 1954)
Indian Songs of Today, recorded 1936–51 (Library of Congress AAFS L36, 1954)
Songs of Earth, Water, Fire, and Sky: Music of the American Indian, recorded 1975 (NW 246, 1976)
Songs and Dances of the Eastern Indians from Medicine Spring and Allegany, recorded 1975 (NW 337, 1985)

BIBLIOGRAPHY

T. Baker: *Über die Musik der nordamerikanischer Wilden* (Leipzig, Germany, 1882/*R*1976 with Eng. trans.)
J. Mooney: "The Cherokee Ball Play," *American Anthropologist*, iii (1890), 105
——: *Sacred Formulas of the Cherokees* (Washington, DC, 1891)
——: *Myths of the Cherokee* (Washington, DC, 1900)
J. Mooney and F. Olbrechts: *The Swimmer Manuscript* (Washington, DC, 1932)
G. Herzog: "African Influences in North American Indian Music," *PAMS 1939*, 130
F. G. Speck and L. Broom: *Cherokee Dance and Drama* (Berkeley, CA, and Los Angeles, 1951)
W. N. Fenton and G. P. Kurath: *The Iroquois Eagle Dance* (Washington, DC, 1953)
G. P. Kurath: "Antiphonal Songs of the Eastern Woodland Indians," *MQ*, xlii (1956), 520
——: "Effects of Environment on Cherokee-Iroquois Ceremonialism, Music, and Dance," *Symposium on Cherokee and Iroquois Culture: Washington, D.C. 1958*, ed. W. N. Fenton and J. Gulick (Washington, DC, 1961), 173
J. F. Kilpatrick and A. G. Kilpatrick: *Friends of Thunder* (Dallas, 1964)
——: *Walk in your Soul: Love Incantations of the Oklahoma Cherokee* (Dallas, 1965)
——: *Muskogean Charm Songs among the Oklahoma Cherokees* (Washington, DC, 1967)
——: *Run Toward the Nightland: Magic of the Oklahoma Cherokee* (Dallas, 1967)
R. Fogelson: "The Cherokee Ballgame Cycle: an Ethnographer's View," *EM*, xv (1971), 327
M. Herndon: "The Cherokee Ballgame Cycle: an Ethnomusicologist's View," *EM*, xv (1971), 339
C. Heth: *The Stomp Dance Music of the Oklahoma Cherokee* (diss., UCLA, 1975)
——: "The Mosquito Dance," *Chronicles of Oklahoma*, liv (1976–7), 519
——: "Stylistic Similarities in Cherokee and Iroquois Music," *Journal of Cherokee Studies*, iv/3 (1979), 128–62
M. Herndon: "Fox, Owl, and Raven," *Selected Reports in Ethnomusicology*, iii/2 (1980), 175

CHARLOTTE HETH

Cherokee Cowboys. Country-music band led by RAY PRICE.

Cherry, Don(ald Eugene) (*b* Oklahoma City, OK, 18 Nov 1936). Jazz trumpeter and bandleader. He first came to public notice as a regular member of Ornette Coleman's groups from 1957. He moved with Coleman to New York in 1959, and played on Coleman's first seven albums, including *Something Else!*, *Change of the Century*, and *Free Jazz*. After leaving Coleman in the early 1960s Cherry worked briefly with the saxophonists Steve Lacy and Sonny Rollins, then with Archie Shepp and Albert Ayler in Europe, and in 1963–4 with Shepp and John Tchicai in the New York Contemporary Five. From 1964 to 1966 he led a group based in Europe with the saxophonist Gato Barbieri and recorded his most widely praised albums *Complete Communion* and *Symphony for Improvisers*. He taught at Dartmouth College in 1970 and then based himself in Sweden for four years, visiting much of Europe and the Middle East, playing informally, and studying other styles of music. In the late 1970s and early 1980s he divided his time between playing with the rock star Lou Reed, a "world music" trio called Codona (with Collin Walcott and Nana Vasconcelos), and the band Old and New Dreams, whose members had formerly been sidemen with Coleman.

Cherry is a leading figure in free jazz. Although his improvisatory style derives largely from that of Coleman, he also cited the influence of the jazz trumpeters Fats Navarro, Clifford Brown, Miles Davis, and Harry Edison, as well as Mexican trumpet-playing style and the sounds achieved by players of the french horn and the conch trumpet. He plays with a rough-hewn quality and often unintentionally fluffs or splatters tones. On his recordings with Coleman his tone tends to be soft-textured and dry in quality; however, in a few of his later recordings he achieved a fuller, brassier sound. Lacking the speed, agility, and range of the average modern jazz trumpeter, he instead explores the varied tone qualities of his instrument, often changing tone dramatically within a single solo passage, using an uncommonly wide range of expressive devices. Cherry's improvisations are strikingly original: they are filled with ideas that do not generally depend on the bop melodic vocabulary. As an improviser Cherry is unusually flexible in that he is able to construct intelligent solo lines as well as contribute appropriately to simultaneous collective improvisations; in this respect he resembles the earliest jazz improvisers, who prized both solo capability and skill in collective interplay. His flexibility extends to an ability to switch back and forth between lines that swing and stay close to the beat and lines that go against the meter in a manner that suggests he is ignoring the beat and resisting swing feeling. Cherry's recorded improvisations usually dispense with preset song forms and accompanying chords, a characteristic they have in common with those of Coleman and also with the non-Western music Cherry has explored. This so-called "Third World music," or simply "world music," has led Cherry to write and play extensively in groups using tambūrā, sitar, gamelan instruments, finger cymbals, conch horns, and other exotica. He also learned to play flute, bamboo flute, percussion instruments, and the Brazilian berimbau. Cherry's world music makes use of drones and extended vamps, as well as mantras chanted and played over and over again. While his earlier jazz tunes derived from Coleman's distinctive melodic style, his more recent compositions draw on a wide array of sources, including Indian and Arabic–Turkish music, South African urban folk music, hymns, rhythm-and-blues, riff themes, and what Jost has called "endless melodies" – tunes with a cyclic layout and little harmonic or rhythmic differentiation.

Don Cherry, 1972

RECORDINGS

(selective list)

As leader: *Complete Communion* (1965, BN 84226); *Symphony for Improvisers* (1966, BN 84247); *Where is Brooklyn* (1966, BN 84311); *Eternal Rhythm* (1968, Saba MPS 15204); *Mu*, pt.i (1969, BYG 529301); *Mu*, pt.ii (1969, BYG 529331); *Human Music* (1969–70, Flying Dutchman 121); *The Creator has a Master Plan* (1971, Caprice 44); *Eternal Now* (1973, Antilles 7034); *Brown Rice* (1975, A&M Hor. 717); *Hear and Now* (1976, Atl. 18217); *The Journey* (1977, Chiaroscuro 187)

As sideman: O. Coleman: *Something Else!* (1958, Cont. 3551), *Change of the Century* (1959, Atl. 1327), *Free Jazz* (1960, Atl. 1364); J. Coltrane: *The Avant Garde* (1960, Atl. 1451); S. Lacy: *Evidence* (1961, New Jazz 8271); S. Rollins: *Our Man in Jazz* (1963, RCA LPM 2612); New York Contemporary Five: *Future I* (1963, Fontana 681013); A. Ayler: *New York Eye and Ear Control* (1964, ESP 1016); C. Haden: *Liberation Music Orchestra* (1969, Imp. 9183); JCOA: *Relativity Suite* (1973, JCOA 1008); C. Walcott: *Codona* (1978, ECM 1132), *Codona 2* (1980, ECM 1177)

BIBLIOGRAPHY

E. Jost: *Free Jazz* (Graz, Austria, 1974/*R*1981), 133

"Don Cherry Discography," *Swing Journal*, xxviii/4 (1974), 252

P. Occhiogrosso: "Emissary of the Global Muse: Don Cherry," *Down Beat*, xlii/21 (1975), 14

H. Mandel: "The World in his Pocket: Don Cherry," *Down Beat*, xlv/13 (1978), 20, 54

M. Hames: *The Music of Don Cherry on Disc and Tape* (Ferndown, Dorset, England, 1980–82)

F. Davis: "Don Cherry: a Jazz Gypsy Comes Home," *Musician*, no.53 (1983), 53

MARK C. GRIDLEY

Cheslock, Louis (*b* London, England, 25 Sept 1898; *d* Baltimore, MD, 19 July 1981). Composer, violinist, author, and teacher. He came to the USA as a child and acquired citizenship through his father's naturalization. He graduated from the Peabody Conservatory in violin (1917), harmony (1919), and composition (1921) and was appointed to the theory and composition faculty in 1922, having been a violin instructor in the school's preparatory department for six years; he remained there until his retirement in 1976. In 1964 he was awarded the DMus by the Peabody Institute. For 21 years (1916–37) he was a violinist in the Baltimore SO, serving for five years as assistant concertmaster and conducting his own works on a number of occasions. He participated in H. L. Mencken's Saturday Night Club from 1928 to 1950.

Cheslock's compositions have been widely performed. Neoromantic in style, they contain a rich and varied harmonic language, expansive melodic lines, and distinctive rhythms and meters. Although he preferred traditional forms and procedures, from the 1940s Cheslock's works incorporated jazz elements, whole-tone and polytonal sonorities, and aleatory and dodecaphonic techniques. He wrote an *Introductory Study on Violin Vibrato*

(1931), numerous magazine and newspaper articles, and edited *H. L. Mencken on Music* (1961).

WORKS

Stage: The Jewel Merchants (opera, J. B. Cabell), 1930; Cinderella (ballet), 1946

Orch: Vn Conc., 1921; 3 Tone Poems, 1922; Sym. Prelude, 1927; Serenade, str, 1930; Sym., D, 1932; Theme and Variations, hn, orch, 1934; Hn Conc., 1936; Legend of Sleepy Hollow, 1936; Rhapsody in Red and White, 1948; Set of Six, 1950; Suite, ob, str, 1953; Homage à Mendelssohn, str, 1960

Vocal: Psalm cl, SATB, 1931; David, oratorio, SATB, 1937; 3 Period Pieces (H. L. Mencken), SATB, 1940; The Congo (V. Lindsay), oratorio, SATB, 1942; 14 songs, 7 song cycles, 4 anthems, 2 partsongs

Chamber: Vn Sonata, 1917; Sonatina, pf, 1932; Shite Ami I (str qt, harp), II (vn, vc, harp), 1932; Str Qt, 1941; Sonatina, vc, pf, 1943; 7 Miniatures in a Curio Cabinet, pf, 1948; Concertinetto, brass, pf, perc, 1954; Descant, cl, 1970; 18 other str pieces; 12 other pf pieces

BIBLIOGRAPHY

EwenD

L. Keefer: *Baltimore's Music* (Baltimore, 1962)

E. R. Sprenkle: *The Life and Works of Louis Cheslock* (diss., Peabody Conservatory, 1979)

SAM DI BONAVENTURA

Chic. Disco group. Formed in New York in 1976, its members were Nile Rodgers (*b* 19 Sept 1952), guitarist; Bernard Edwards (*b* 31 Oct 1952), bass guitarist; Alfa Anderson (*b* 7 Sept 1946), singer; Norma Jean Wright, singer; and Tony Thompson, drummer. The group's first single recording, *Dance, dance, dance* (no.6, 1977), sold more than one million copies within a month of its release; the single *Le Freak* in 1978 reached no.1 on the chart, and remained in that position for five weeks. In 1979 the group made two more successful recordings, *I Want your Love* (no.7), and *Good Times* (no.1).

In 1983 Rodgers recorded a solo album, *Adventures in the Land of the Good Groove* (Mirage 90073). Chic's music is deceptively simple and shows a subtle, sardonic wit. Like those of other disco groups, their songs are repetitious, and the lyrics are often simple chants (*Good Times* has a chorus of singers repeating the words "Good times, these are the good times" for more than eight minutes). Within the rigid framework of disco, however, they forged a distinctive sound characterized by frequent syncopations, suggestions of polyrhythm, and wide-ranging melodic bass lines; the music is strikingly spare, the rhythm section supplying a light, quick beat to support Rodgers's airy guitar solos. As producers Rodgers and Edwards have worked together and individually with such performers as Sister Sledge, Carly Simon, Debbie Harry, Diana Ross, Aretha Franklin, and David Bowie.

RECORDINGS

(selective list; all recorded for Atlantic)

Chic (19153, 1977), incl. Dance, dance, dance; *C'est Chic* (19209, 1978), incl. Le Freak; *Risqué* (16003, 1979), incl. I Want your Love, Good Times; *Real People* (16016, 1980); *Take it Off* (19323, 1981)

KEN TUCKER

Chicago (i). City in Illinois (pop. 3,005,072, ranked second largest in the USA; metropolitan area 7,103,624).

1. Early history. 2. Opera and musical comedy. 3. Orchestras, choirs, and festivals. 4. Music schools and libraries. 5. Music publishers and instrument makers. 6. Composers and writers on music. 7. Jazz and blues. 8. Ethnic music.

1. Early history. Chicago was established in the late 17th century as a trading post near the southern end of Lake Michigan, and in 1803 Fort Dearborn was built there. The village was incorporated in 1833 and received its city charter in 1837. Much of the city was destroyed by fire in 1871, but it was rebuilt and soon became a center for trade and transport.

Chicago's concert activity until about 1880 was provided chiefly by touring artists and amateur music societies. The impresario P. T. Barnum brought musical attractions to Chicago as early as 1840. Later important touring artists included Adelina Patti, who made her first Chicago appearance in April 1853 with the violinist Ole Bull, and the pianist Louis Moreau Gottschalk, who performed there several times in the 1860s. Early concert halls included Rice's Theatre and McVicker's Theatre; the first auditorium designed for concerts was Tremont Music Hall, which opened in 1850 in the Tremont Hotel. As bigger theaters were built, opera companies, orchestras, and concert artists made regular visits to the city.

There were music schools and private music teachers in Chicago as early as 1835, and amateur performing groups soon followed. The Old Settlers' Harmonic Society (1835–6, sometimes called the Chicago Harmonic Society) was the first formal musical organization in the city. Other societies were the Chicago Choral Union (1846), the Mozart Society (1849), the Musical Union (1858–66), the Oratorio Society (1868–71), and the visiting GERMANIA MUSICAL SOCIETY. The Apollo Club, which has remained active, was organized as a male chorus by Silas G. Pratt and George P. Upton in 1872; women formed an occasional auxiliary chorus from 1874 and were admitted permanently in 1885.

2. Opera and musical comedy. Chicago's first opera performance was of Bellini's *La sonnambula* in 1850, but the second performance was interrupted by fire and the proposed week of performances was not completed. A second season in 1853 was successful, and from the third season in 1858 until 1871 touring opera companies made regular visits of one or two weeks to the city. Crosby's Opera House opened in 1865 with a stage suitable for full-scale grand opera; it was burned in the 1871 fire but had been rebuilt to accommodate touring companies by 1873. For the next decade light opera, operetta, and musical comedy dominated the city's stages, and grand opera was not revived until the early 1880s. During the 1883–4 season the rival New York companies of Henry Abbey and James Mapleson visited Chicago, and in 1889 the Metropolitan Opera of New York performed Wagner's complete *Ring* cycle there for the first time. A major operatic stage became available when the 4200-seat Auditorium Theatre opened on 10 December 1889 with a ceremony featuring Adelina Patti singing *Home, Sweet Home*. A four-week season by the Italian Grand Opera Company of New York followed. Until 1909 Chicago's opera seasons were provided by touring companies bringing to the Auditorium and other theaters famous singers and an extensive if not adventurous repertory.

In 1910 Chicago's first resident opera company, the Chicago Grand Opera Company, was formed with Harold McCormick, a financier, as president and Cleofonte Campanini as musical director. Its first production was *Aida*, and during the rest of the season the soprano Mary Garden, who as a child had lived in Chicago, performed in Debussy's *Pelléas et Mélisande*, Massenet's *Thaïs*, and Richard Strauss's *Salome*, among other operas. Amelita Galli-Curci made her American début with this company in 1916 as Gilda in Verdi's *Rigoletto*. Many of the company's singers were from New York; those more closely associated with Chicago included Edith Mason, Rosa Raisa, Claire Dux, Emma Abbott, and Jessie B. Davis.

Campanini became general director of the Grand Opera Company in 1913 and retained that position when the company was reorganized as the Chicago Opera Association (1915); after financial difficulties the company was headed by Mary Garden for the 1921–2 season. On 30 December 1921 Prokofiev conducted the company in the première of his opera *The Love for Three Oranges*, which had been commissioned by Campanini. Garden resigned as director and McCormick left at the end of the season, and the company was reorganized as the Chicago Civic Opera with Samuel Insull as president and Giorgio Polacco as musical director. In 1929 it moved from the Auditorium to the 3500-seat Civic Opera House. But support for opera waned after the stock market crash in 1929 and the company was dissolved in 1932. A second Chicago Grand Opera Company, relying heavily on singers from the Metropolitan Opera, presented brief seasons from 1933 to 1946 but was not successful.

The Lyric Theatre of Chicago, with Carol Fox as general manager, presented its first three-week season in November 1954, during which Maria Callas made her American début in Bellini's *Norma*. In 1956 the company was renamed Lyric Opera of Chicago. Although acclaimed by critics and the public as a local company, in its early seasons the Lyric Opera's repertory was chiefly Italian, and its leading singers and conductors were usually brought from Europe. Later, the scope of its repertory widened, and American performers made more frequent appearances. The Lyric Opera Center for American Artists, founded in 1973 as an apprentice program for the company and known for a time as the Opera School of Chicago, provides a training ground for American singers and a source of young artists who perform with the company. In 1973 the Lyric Opera commissioned the Polish composer Krzysztof Penderecki to write an opera in honor of the US Bicentennial. The work, *Paradise Lost*, although not completed in time for the 1976 celebration, was first performed on 29 November 1978, conducted by Bruno Bartoletti. In 1974 the Lyric Opera was host to the fourth international Verdi conference. Fox retired shortly before her death in 1981 and was succeeded by Ardis Krainik, who had been the company's artistic administrator. The company has a relatively short season (13 weeks, with seven or eight productions), and its performances are given at the Civic Opera House.

In addition to the Lyric Opera season, opera is performed in Chicago by numerous smaller groups, both amateur and partly or fully professional. The most important of these is the Chicago Opera Theater, a professional company founded in 1973 by Alan Stone. It presents three operas a year, each season including one from the standard repertory, one modern work, and one revival of an infrequently performed earlier opera; all performances are in English. A popular summer opera series was introduced at Ravinia Park, in the northern suburb of Highland Park, in 1915; it was suspended during the Depression of the 1930s, and although the Park was reopened in 1936 staged opera was no longer performed there (concert performances of opera have been continued at the summer orchestral festivals at Ravinia; see §3 below).

From the turn of the century to the outbreak of World War I Chicago was also a center for musical comedy. Many productions composed and produced there had long local runs and national tours, but did not necessarily enjoy success when transported to New York. Among the composers who wrote for this regional market were Reginald De Koven, whose operetta *Robin Hood* (1890) and opera *Rip Van Winkle* (1920) were first heard there; Gustav Luders (*King Dodo*, 1901; *The Sho-Gun*, 1904); Raymond Hubbell (*Chow-Chow*, 1902, later produced on Broadway as *The Runaways*); Ben Jerome (*Louisiana Lou*, 1911, a vehicle for Sophie Tucker; *The Girl at the Gate*, 1912); and the prolific Joseph E. Howard who between 1904 and 1915 wrote some 17 shows for the LaSalle Theatre. Later, musical comedy in Chicago was provided chiefly by touring companies of New York productions or revivals produced locally. An exception was the long-running Broadway musical *Grease* (New York opening, 1972), originally a successful Chicago production, greatly altered for New York.

Touring musical comedies are booked into many Chicago theaters, but those expected to draw large audiences play in the 4300-seat Arie Crown Theatre on the lake front. The Arie Crown is part of McCormick Place Convention Center (1971), the third example in Chicago of a complex including large, well-equipped performance spaces in structures which serve numerous other functions. The other two are the Auditorium (1889), which originally comprised a hotel and an office tower (later housing Roosevelt University) as well as the Auditorium Theatre, which is used chiefly to accommodate touring orchestras and ballet; and the Civic Opera House (1929), which is part of a skyscraper office building incorporating the Opera House and the 850-seat Civic Theatre.

3. ORCHESTRAS, CHOIRS, AND FESTIVALS. Chicago's first orchestra, the Philharmonic Society, performed from 1850 to 1868, conducted first by Julius Dyhrenfurth and later by Hans Balatka. Another orchestra performed under Henry Ahner from 1856 to 1858. The Chicago Orchestra was formed in 1891, with Ferdinand W. Peck as its first president. Theodore Thomas, who with his orchestra had visited Chicago for several seasons and was to be musical director of the World's Columbian Exposition (1893, with preliminary events from 1892), was appointed its first conductor. The orchestra performed in the Auditorium Theatre, and moved in 1904 to the new 2566-seat Orchestra Hall (see fig.1, p.420); the hall was extensively renovated in 1966 and 1981, when a Moeller pipe organ was installed.

Thomas's indefatigable efforts established the Chicago Orchestra as one of the most prestigious in the USA; from 1906 it was called the Theodore Thomas Orchestra, and in 1912 it was renamed the Chicago SO. The long tenure of Frederick Stock (1905–42), who was appointed assistant conductor in 1899 and succeeded Thomas on his death, was marked by performances of many new works, notably the premières of Prokofiev's Third Piano Concerto (1921, with the composer as soloist), Stravinsky's Symphony in C (1940, the composer conducting), and Kodály's Concerto for Orchestra (1941). Stock also instituted children's concerts and in 1919 established the Civic Orchestra of Chicago to train orchestral players. He was succeeded by Désiré Defauw (1943–7), followed by a brilliant if stormy season under Artur Rodzinski (1947–8). Rafael Kubelik (1950–53), although criticized for a narrow repertory, introduced over 70 new works, including Roy Harris's Seventh Symphony (1952). Under Fritz Reiner (1952–63), according to Stravinsky, the orchestra became "the most precise and flexible orchestra in the world." From 1963 to 1968 it was under the direction of the French conductor and composer Jean Martinon, from whom *Altitudes* (his Fourth Symphony, 1966) was commissioned for the orchestra's 75th anniversary. Georg Solti was appointed music director in 1969 but has continued an active international career, so that a number of guest conductors have worked with the Chicago SO, notably Carlo Maria Giulini (from 1968; principal guest conductor 1969–72) and Claudio Abbado (from 1971; principal guest conductor from 1982). Henry Mazer was appointed associate conductor in 1970,

1. *Orchestra Hall, Chicago*

with main responsibility for educational programs. Premières given by Solti in Chicago include Henze's *Heliogabalus Imperator* (1972) and Tippett's Fourth Symphony (1977). The orchestra's international renown is largely based on the excellence of its numerous recordings, particularly under Reiner and Solti, as well as its tours of Europe (1971, 1974, 1978, and 1981) and Japan (1977). *See also* ORCHESTRAS, §2 (vi).

The Chicago Symphony Chorus, founded in 1957 by Margaret Hillis (who has continued to direct it), was for many years the only professional organization of its kind in the USA. It has made tours and recordings, both independently and with the orchestra. Music of the Baroque, founded in 1971 by its conductor Thomas Wikman, is a professional chorus and orchestra. It presents five oratorio programs a year, each repeated at several locations in or near the city.

The Civic Music Association of Chicago was founded in 1913 to encourage the study of music. In addition to promoting park concerts and children's and community choruses, it helped Stock establish the Civic Orchestra. The Chicago Children's Choir, founded in 1956 by Christopher Moore, has about 450 members; it appears frequently in Chicago, and smaller groups drawn from the choir tour regularly.

Two important summer festivals are held annually in Chicago. Ravinia Park, built in 1904 as an amusement park, was the site of musical, dance, and theater events in the first decades of the century. Under the supervision of the businessman Louis Eckstein, orchestral concerts were given by the Damrosch, Chicago, and Minneapolis symphony orchestras. Single acts of operas were occasionally staged as part of the concerts. Whole evenings of opera were introduced in 1915, and from 1919 to 1931 great singers from the New York and Chicago companies (Lucrezia Bori, Elisabeth Rethberg, Giovanni Martinelli, Tito Schipa, and many others) were presented in elaborate Ravinia productions. The series was suspended during the Depression but was resumed in 1936 as the Ravinia Festival. Its music directors have included Seiji Ozawa (1964–8) and James Levine (from 1973). The festival now features concerts by the Chicago SO and visiting orchestras, chamber music ensembles, concert versions of operas, pop, jazz, theater, folk music, dance, young people's programs, and master classes. Besides Ozawa and Levine, conductors who have appeared at Ravinia include Ernest Ansermet, Josef Krips, André Kostelanetz, and Arthur Fiedler. Internationally known soloists have included the singers Eileen Farrell, Régine Crespin, and Leontyne Price, and the pianists Alicia de Larrocha and André Watts; among the dance companies have been the Ballet Russe de Monte Carlo, the New York City Ballet, the Martha Graham Company, and the San Francisco Ballet. Performances are held in the covered Ravinia Pavilion (capacity 3500 indoors, 15,000 on the lawn) and the more intimate Murray Theatre (capacity 923).

A municipally sponsored summer orchestra series was initiated in 1934 at Grant Park, on the lake shore near the center of the city. The Grant Park concerts were organized by the musicians' union official James C. Petrillo while he was a commissioner of Chicago parks; in 1978 the 40-year-old "temporary" bandshell erected by the WPA to house these concerts was replaced by a new structure, dedicated to Petrillo.

4. Music schools and libraries. Chicago's first important music conservatory was the Chicago Academy of Music, founded in 1867 by Florenz Ziegfeld; it later became the Chicago Musical College (1872) and then part of Roosevelt University (1954). Ziegfeld was its president until 1916; among his successors were Felix Borowski (1916–25) and Rudolph Ganz (1933–54). It offers BA, BM, and MM degrees in composition, performance, music education, and musicology. Hans Balatka opened an academy of music in 1879, but it did not survive long. Courses at the American Conservatory of Music, founded by John R. Hattstaedt in 1886, include the above degrees and a DMA in performance. The Sherwood Music School was founded in 1897 by the pianist William H. Sherwood, who had moved to Chicago in 1889. The University of Chicago has notable courses in Renaissance music studies and in composition, as well as a professional performing group, the Contemporary Chamber Players, and a collegium musicum, which performs early music. It offers BA, MA, and PhD degrees in composition, music theory, and musicology.

Northwestern University, in the northern suburb of Evanston, was founded in 1851 and began to offer music instruction in 1873. A school of music was established in 1895 under the direction of Peter Christian Lutkin, who served as dean until 1928. Lutkin also conducted the Chicago North Shore Festival (1909–30), which was organized by the school. The school has about 500 students and almost 100 instructors, and offers BM, BME, MM, DM, and PhD degrees in performance, music education, church music, musicology, and theory and composition. The library contains about 140,000 items; its collection of music published internationally since 1945 is particularly extensive, and has special collections of materials relating to Henry Cowell and John Cage, and part of the Moldenhauer Archive of 20th-century manuscripts. The Newberry Library has a rich collection of Renaissance and American music sources, and the music library of the University of Chicago has an important music history collection. The Chicago Historical Society contains documents of the city's musical history as does the Chicago Public Library, which also maintains a substantial collection of scores for performance. The Field Museum of Natural History has an important collection of musical instruments, including a gamelan which was brought to the USA for the World's Columbian Exposition in 1893 and thereafter remained in storage until it was restored to performance condition in 1977. Two newer repositories of source material for Chicago's musical history are the Chicago Jazz Archive, established at the University of Chicago in 1976, and the Chicago Blues Archive, founded in 1981 at the Chicago Public Library. In 1985 Samuel Floyd founded the Center for Black Music Research at Columbia College to continue the work of the Institute for Research in Black American Music set up earlier by Floyd at Fisk University. The sheet music collection of Walter N. H. Harding, a valuable source of research material, particularly for British and American popular song, went to the Bodleian Library, Oxford, in 1973 after its owner's death. (*See also* LIBRARIES AND COLLECTIONS, §3.)

5. Music publishers and instrument makers. Chicago has had many publishers of school music books, gospel music, and popular sheet music. The most important early firm was Root & Cady (1858–72); others included S. C. Griggs & Co. (1848–71), the first music publisher in Chicago; Joseph Cockcroft, the first in Chicago to print music from movable type (1853–4); Higgins Brothers, later H. M. Higgins Co. (1855–67; see fig. 2, p.422), publishers of the popular songs of H. P. Danks and J. P. Webster; and Clayton F. Summy, a leading publisher of educational music from 1888 to 1932. After 1920 New York's domination of popular music publishing forced many Chicago firms to move east or to go out of business. A notable exception is the firm of Will Rossiter, founded in 1891; it has remained active, and was the city's leading sheet music publisher until 1920. In 1964 the University of Chicago Press entered scholarly music publishing with the first volume of Monuments of Renaissance Music, a series of critical editions of important sources of 15th- and 16th-century music. Edward E. Lowinsky, its first general editor, was succeeded in 1977 by Howard Mayer Brown. In 1980 this press, in association with Ricordi in Milan, undertook the publication of the complete critical edition of the works of Verdi, with Philip Gossett as general editor.

Musical instrument manufacture, particularly of pianos and organs, was an important industry in Chicago from the mid-19th century. The W. W. Kimball Company, founded as a distributor in 1857, began manufacturing organs in 1880 and pianos in 1887. Lyon & Healy was established as a music shop in 1864 and began making instruments in 1885, becoming best known as harp makers. Organ builders have included Story & Clark, Wilcox & White, and Estey. The firm J. C. Deagan & Co., makers of bells, chimes, and other percussion instruments, was established in Chicago in 1896. The Ludwig firm of percussion makers was active in Chicago from 1909 to 1930.

6. Composers and writers on music. In the 19th century most composers who worked in Chicago wrote church and gospel music, light opera and musical comedy (see §2 above), popular songs, and music for school use. Popular songwriters who were active in Chicago in the mid-19th century include Henry Clay Work, who began as a music printer and later composed Civil War marching songs and parlor ballads; George F. Root, a partner in the firm of Root & Cady, also remembered for his patriotic songs of the Civil War; and Carrie Jacobs-Bond, also a publisher but better known for her sentimental ballads. The organist and composer Dudley Buck lived and worked in Chicago from 1869 to 1871, and P. P. Bliss, a composer of evangelist and gospel music, worked there from about 1864 until his death in 1876. Joseph E. Howard, besides his musical comedy scores, wrote popular songs in the ragtime style, including *Goodbye, my Lady Love* and *Hello, my Baby*. Howard's most famous song, *I wonder who's kissing her now*, was later attributed to Harold Orlob.

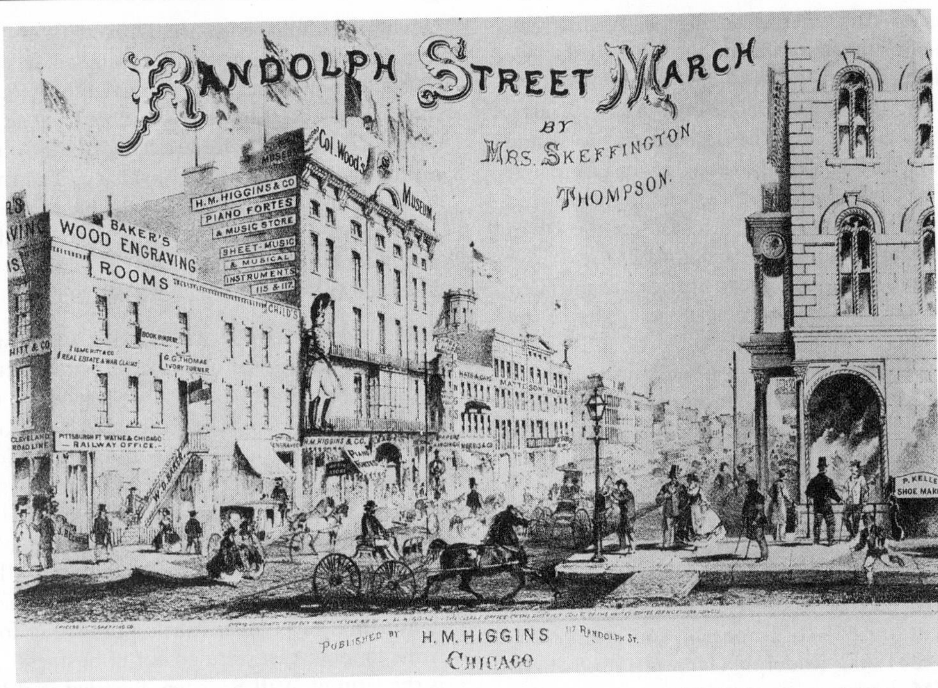

2. *Sheet-music cover of "Randolph Street March" (1866) showing the music store of the publisher H. M. Higgins on Randolph Street, Chicago*

20th-century composers who have been associated with Chicago include Felix Borowski, who taught and composed there from 1897 until his death in 1956; John Alden Carpenter, who enjoyed critical acclaim during the 1920s while also pursuing a successful business career; and Leo Sowerby, who taught at the American Conservatory from 1925 to 1962 and for most of that time was choirmaster at the Episcopal Cathedral of St. James. Ralph Shapey, Easley Blackwood, and Shulamit Ran have all been members of the faculty of the University of Chicago, and Alan B. Stout joined that of Northwestern University in 1963. Composers and performers of new music in Chicago and elsewhere are indebted to the philanthropist PAUL FROMM, who in 1952 endowed the Fromm Music Foundation which supports composers and performances of their works.

Important among the city's early writers on music are George P. Upton, who in 1863 became the first music critic on the *Chicago Tribune* and was a writer on opera and on individual composers; and W. S. B. Mathews (1837–1912), author of books on music education and founding editor of the journal *Music* (1892–1902). Chicago's academic institutions, particularly the University of Chicago, have attracted to their faculties a number of musicological scholars of international renown, including Lowinsky, Brown, and Gossett.

7. JAZZ AND BLUES. Chicago's role in the history of black-American musical forms has always been significant, and at times, especially in the case of the blues, decisive. The city's location (it is a major transportation center) and its night life have ensured favorable conditions for the growth of these musics from the earliest times. Visiting piano "professors" played ragtime at the time of the World's Columbian Exposition in 1893, before the first rags had appeared in print; by the early 1900s Chicago had become the center of ragtime piano playing. The New Orleans jazz pianists Tony Jackson and Jelly Roll Morton performed in Chicago as early as 1906, and in the next few years a number of black New Orleans musicians, attracted by the superior financial opportunities, began playing there on a regular basis. These included the "cornet kings" Freddie Keppard (1911), Manuel Perez (1913), and especially King Oliver (1918). White musicians from New Orleans followed suit, particularly a group called Stein's Dixie Jass Band, formed in Chicago in 1916; as the Original Dixieland Jazz Band, it soon occasioned the breakthrough of jazz into the popular-music market.

One important precondition for the growth of black music in Chicago was the so-called Great Black Migration from 1916 to 1920, when around 50,000 Southern blacks took up residence in Chicago, creating the Black Belt and its associated pleasure district. This, combined with the permissiveness of "Big Bill" Thompson's mayoralty and Chicago's lively cabarets and dance halls, created an appropriate setting in which jazz might flourish. Two important early events were the appearance of the New Orleans Rhythm Kings at Friar's Inn (1921) and King Oliver's Creole Jazz Band at the Lincoln Gardens dance hall (1922). Both groups recorded in Chicago for the first time during these years, creating what is widely regarded as the definitive documentation of the classic New Orleans style. Other important black New Orleans musicians working in Chicago at this time were Johnny Dodds, Baby Dodds, Zutty Singleton, Jimmy Noone, Jelly Roll Morton, and above all Louis Armstrong, who played with Oliver from 1922 and made his celebrated Hot Five recordings for Okeh from 1925 to 1928.

Alongside these immigrant New Orleans musicians there emerged an indigenous jazz culture of white Chicago musicians, beginning with the so-called Austin High School Gang of Jimmy McPartland (cornet), Frank Teschemacher (clarinet), Bud Freeman (tenor saxophone), Joe Sullivan (piano), Floyd O'Brien (trombone), Dick McPartland (banjo), and Dave Tough (drums). Other white musicians associated with the Chicago school included the Wolverine Orchestra, Benny Goodman, Gene Krupa, Ben Pollack, Jess Stacy, Muggsy Spanier, Pee Wee Russell, Eddie Condon, and, at times, Bix Beiderbecke, all of whom were active in Chicago in the mid-1920s and helped to create the New Orleans substyle known as CHICAGO JAZZ. By the end of the decade, however, most of these musicians had moved to New York, where the focus of jazz had shifted. Of the few to remain in Chicago in the 1930s, Jimmy Noone played regularly at the Apex Club, the Dodds brothers at various locations, and Earl Hines in his own big band at the Grand Terrace.

The Great Migration also brought many Southern blues musicians to Chicago, many of whom performed informally at private social functions in the Black Belt. Among these were Blind Lemon Jefferson from Texas, Big Bill Broonzy from Mississippi, Sonny Boy Williamson (i) from Tennessee, Blind Blake from Florida, and Georgia Tom Dorsey and Tampa Red from Georgia. These musicians all found superior recording conditions in Chicago, and much of their extant work was recorded there. Of special importance was the Chicago school of blues pianists, particularly "Cripple" Clarence Lofton, Jimmy Yancey, Meade "Lux" Lewis, Albert Ammons, Pine Top Smith, and others who performed at Chicago's rent parties. Yancey, Lewis, and Ammons in particular became important figures in the boogie-woogie craze of the late 1930s.

After World War II a specifically Chicago blues style, variously known as urban blues, city blues, or northern blues, emerged in the work of performers such as Elmore James, Little Walter, Muddy Waters, Howlin' Wolf, Otis Spann, Otis Rush, Jimmie Reed, Sonny Boy Williamson (ii), and Bo Diddley. This music, characterized by aggressive tempos, relatively sophisticated lyrics, and electronic amplification of all instruments, had an enormous impact on the development of popular music in the USA and abroad, particularly after being incorporated into the rock music of the late 1960s. Although interest in blues waned thereafter, Chicago continues to produce outstanding blues musicians, among the best being Buddy Guy.

Parallel to postwar blues developments there emerged an indigenous Chicago school of black avant-garde jazz. Here the groundwork was laid by the pianist-bandleader Sun Ra, who in the 1950s led an avant-garde collective whose performances were issued in small press runs on his private label, Saturn. Other jazz collectives arose after Sun Ra's departure for New York in 1960, the most significant being the Experimental Band, founded in 1961 by Muhal Richard Abrams. In 1965 this group and several other Chicago jazz collectives combined, under Abrams's leadership, to form the ASSOCIATION FOR THE ADVANCEMENT OF CREATIVE MUSICIANS, one of the earliest self-administered nonprofit organizations in jazz, which served as a model for similar ventures in other American cities. Among the important avant-garde jazz musicians associated with this organization were Anthony Braxton, Leroy Jenkins, Leo Smith, Steve McCall, and above all the members of the ART ENSEMBLE OF CHICAGO (Lester Bowie, Malachi Favors, Joseph Jarman, Roscoe Mitchell, and Don Moye), who best exemplify the blend of theatricality, humor, eclecticism, and wide-ranging timbral experimentation that characterizes Chicago's avant-garde jazz.

8. ETHNIC MUSIC. The population of Chicago, like that of most large American cities, is ethnically and racially diverse, and most groups strive to retain their own musical traditions. A directory

3. The Wolverine Orchestra (1924), who were associated with the Austin High School Gang: (left to right) Vic Moore, Bob Gillette, Jimmy McPartland, Dick Voynow, and George Johnson

4. *Street evangelist conducting a service on Sangamon Street, Chicago, in 1960; the guitarist is Blind James Brewer*

of ethnic performers in the Chicago area, published in 1982 and by no means exhaustive, lists more than 25 nationalities in its section on choruses alone. Black musicians contributed significantly to the development of jazz and blues in Chicago (see §7). The gospel music tradition in the city's black churches, arising in the 1930s and entirely different from the white evangelical gospel music of the 19th century, has also produced music and musicians of more than local importance, among whom the best known was Mahalia Jackson. The tradition of street evangelists, in which blind musicians were important, was curtailed by vagrancy laws after World War II but continued to the 1960s (see fig.4). Chicago's Polish population is one of the largest in the USA, and the city has served since the beginning of the 20th century as the center for recording, publishing, and distributing Polish music, as well as the home of numerous well-known performers and performing groups. The popularity of polka music and of Polish performers on radio and in recordings throughout the USA appears to have originated in Chicago, and the Sajewski Music Store, the largest Polish music specialty shop in the country, was founded there in 1897 and remained in business until 1981. Irish music has a long tradition in Chicago, and the city serves as a gathering place for both traditional and innovative performers. Francis O'Neill (*b* 1849), compiler of *Music of Ireland* (1903) and other collections of traditional Irish tunes, settled in Chicago in 1871. He was an amateur musician, and collected nearly 2000 tunes, many of them from Irish performers living in Chicago, forming a comprehensive repository of this music. Germans were influential in the early development of mainstream musical institutions in Chicago, and have also been enthusiastic supporters of amateur choral singing. Ethnic and folk music have a wide audience in Chicago, and there are numerous festivals, performance rooms, and organizations supporting both local and imported performers.

BIBLIOGRAPHY

A. T. Andreas: *History of Chicago* (Chicago, 1884–6)
F. Ffrench, ed.: *Music and Musicians in Chicago* (Chicago, 1899/*R*1979)
F. C. Bennett, ed.: *History of Music and Art in Illinois* (Philadelphia, 1904)
G. P. Upton: *Musical Memories: my Recollections of Celebrities of the Half Century, 1850–1900* (Chicago, 1908)
J. S. Currey: *Chicago: its History and its Builders* (Chicago, 1912)
P. A. Otis: *The Chicago Symphony Orchestra* (Chicago, 1924)
C. E. Russell: *The American Orchestra and Theodore Thomas* (Garden City, NY, 1927)
P. Gilbert: *Chicago and its Makers* (Chicago, 1929)
E. C. Moore: *Forty Years of Opera in Chicago* (New York, 1930/*R*1977)
K. J. Rehage: *Music in Chicago, 1871–1893* (diss., U. of Chicago, 1935)
B. L. Pierce: *A History of Chicago* (New York, 1935–57)
F. Ramsey: *Chicago Documentary: Portraits of a Jazz Era* (London, 1944)
L. L. Edlund: *The Apollo Musical Club of Chicago* (Chicago, 1946)
E. A. Johnson: *The Chicago Orchestra: 1891–1942* (diss., U. of Chicago, 1951)
N. Shapiro and N. Hentoff, eds.: *Hear me talkin' to ya* (New York, 1955/*R*1966), 80–164
J. Steiner: "Chicago," *Jazz*, ed. N. Hentoff and A. J. McCarthy (New York, 1959/*R*1974)
T. W. Thorson: *A History of Music Publishing in Chicago, 1850–1900* (diss., Northwestern U., 1961)
R. Hadlock: *Jazz Masters of the Twenties* (New York, 1965)
R. Davis: *Opera in Chicago* (New York, 1966)
C. Keil: *Urban Blues* (Chicago, 1966)
D. J. Epstein: *Music Publishing in Chicago before 1871: the Firm of Root & Cady, 1858–1871* (Detroit, 1969)
T. Hennessey: *From Jazz to Swing: Black Jazz Musicians and their Music, 1917–1935* (diss., Northwestern U., 1973), chap.7
M. Rowe: *Chicago Breakdown* (London, 1973)
L. E. McCullough: *Irish Music in Chicago: an Ethnomusicological Study* (diss., U. of Pittsburgh, 1978)
L. Ostransky: *Jazz City: the Impact of our Cities on the Development of Jazz* (Englewood Cliffs, NJ, 1979), chaps.4–6
R. Palmer: *Deep Blues* (New York, 1981)
R. K. Spottswood: "The Sajewski Story: Eighty Years of Polish Music in Chicago," *Ethnic Recordings in America* (Washington, DC, 1982), 133
A. McKinley: "Music for the Dedication Ceremonies of the World's Columbian Exposition in Chicago, 1892," *American Music*, iii/1 (1985), 42

ANNETTE FERN
(1–6, 8; 3 with SARA VELEZ, 4 with BRUCE CARR),
J. BRADFORD ROBINSON (7)

Chicago (ii). Rock group. The original members were Lee Loughnane (trumpet), James Pankow (trombone), Walter Parazaider (saxophone), Robert Lamm (piano), Terry Kath (guitar), Pete

Cetera (bass guitar), and Daniel Seraphine (drums); most of them also sang. The group was originally called Chicago Transit Authority, and this was also the title of their first album (Col. GP8, 1968), which included such hits as Lamm's *Does anybody really know what time it is?* and *Beginnings*. Many of the group's early songs were in the rhythmic style employed by Motown and James Brown, and their use of brass instruments and occasional improvised solos meant that they became known as a jazz-rock group. In the early 1970s, however, they changed their approach somewhat, shortened their name to Chicago, and released a number of pop ballads, the most successful of which was *If you leave me now* (Col. 10390, 1976). They continued to record in this style into the 1980s: *Hard to say I'm sorry* (Full Moon 29979, 1982) stayed at the top of the pop chart for two weeks.

BIBLIOGRAPHY

H. Siders: "Chicago: Jazz-rock Pioneers," *Down Beat*, xxxvii/21 (1970), 12

M. Hohman: "The Chicago Papers," *Down Beat*, xlii/2 (1975), 13, 42

MARK GRIDLEY

Chicago jazz. A subspecies of NEW ORLEANS JAZZ developed by young white musicians in the Chicago area during the early 1920s. A number of these musicians were associated with the so-called Austin High School Gang (Jimmy McPartland, Dave Tough, Frank Teschemacher, Joe Sullivan, and Bud Freeman); others such as Benny Goodman, Gene Krupa, and Muggsy Spanier were native to Chicago, while still others such as Eddie Condon, Pee Wee Russell, and Red McKenzie moved to Chicago early in their careers. Though only intermittently active in Chicago, Bix Beiderbecke and Frank Trumbauer are also sometimes associated with this school. At first the "Chicagoans" merely copied the New Orleans style of King Oliver and the New Orleans Rhythm Kings, but brought to it in some cases a superior instrumental technique (Goodman) and a more hectic and extrovert rhythmic basis (Krupa), together with a greater emphasis on solo playing. In general, however, they varied the basic features of New Orleans jazz rather than developing an independent style. With the suppression of Chicago's speakeasy culture in the late 1920s most of these musicians moved to New York, where several of them became important figures in the swing style of the 1930s.

See also JAZZ, §III, 4, 5, and CHICAGO, §7.

BIBLIOGRAPHY

J. Steiner: "Chicago," *Jazz*, ed. N. Hentoff and A. J. McCarthy (New York, 1959/*R*1974)

J. BRADFORD ROBINSON

Chicano. An American of Mexican descent; for Chicano musical traditions *see* HISPANIC-AMERICAN MUSIC, §2 (i).

Chickasaw Syncopators. Jazz band formed in 1927 by JIMMIE LUNCEFORD.

Chicken scratch [waila]. A form of acculturated popular music of the PIMA and PAPAGO Indians of southern Arizona, which blends Anglo, Hispanic, and Indian traditions. It is called "chicken scratch" by Anglo-Americans and the Pima, and "waila" (from Sp. *baile*: "social dance or gathering") by the Papago. Papago Indians were first exposed to European music by Jesuit and Franciscan missionaries in the 18th and early 19th centuries; later, on annual pilgrimages to Magdalena, Sonora, the Papago encountered Mexican popular music. It is probable that much of the chicken-scratch repertory was borrowed from Mexican traditions. Although the early history of chicken scratch is not well documented, a newspaper account and a description by an Anglo-American traveler confirm that it was in existence as early as the 1860s near Tucson; a Papago calendar stick from Indian Oasis (now Sells) dates the first such dance in that area in 1880.

The chicken-scratch repertory consists principally of the polka and *chota* (the word is taken from "schottische" but the dance is in fact a two-step), though local taste and changing fashions dictate the performance also of the waltz, *cumbia*, bolero, ma-

Chicken scratch ensemble: the Joaquin Brothers Papago Waila Band

zurka, *redowa*, and *ranchera*, and occasionally *pascola* tunes. The music is learned through oral tradition; an existing melody (sometimes doubled) is provided with a bass line, rhythmic underpinning, and harmony played by the inner voices on unaccented beats.

The earliest ensembles were acoustic string groups. In the 1920s new instruments, beginning with the clarinet, were introduced, probably through the influence of day schools and boarding-schools run by white Americans, which often had bands and orchestras. By World War II the fiddle was no longer used in most *waila* bands, but one or two all-string groups have made a comeback in the 1970s and 1980s. The typical chicken-scratch group consists of one or two melody instruments, usually accordion or saxophone, or both (playing the melody in 3rds and 6ths if there are two), a harmony guitar or *bajo sexto* (12-string bass guitar), bass guitar (usually electric), and drums. The major postwar change in *waila* instrumentation was the electrification of the instruments as electricity arrived in the Papago villages; except in the few all-string bands, all instruments but drums are now amplified.

Style varies from group to group; for example, Pima groups, such as the Gila River Six (Minus One), have a smoother, less driving style than Papago groups, such as the Molinas, and often prefer Latin rhythms. The repertory is essentially instrumental, though songs are occasionally performed with Spanish or Papago texts (the earliest chicken-scratch song with Papago text is *Oīk, oīk, oīk*, 1974). Papago bands often add a Mexican lead singer when performing for Mexican-American audiences at dance halls. Fashion often dictates the programming of chicken-scratch bands: in the early 1980s the *cumbia* was popular, and in 1983 the Verton Jackson Combo released a recording of *In the Mood* and *Angel Baby*, both without lyrics. Mexican influence has increased in the early 1980s. Loyal fans are devoted to particular bands, even though the membership may vary from month to month; their loyalty is shown by the purchase of recordings and by support at local "Battle of the Bands" events at off-reservation festivals.

DISCOGRAPHY

M. Enis and Company and El Conjunto Murrietta: *Chicken Scratch: Popular Dance Music of the Indians of Southern Arizona* (Can. 6085, 1972)
The American Indians Play Chicken Scratch (Can. 6120, 1974)
The Molinas: *Super Scratch Kings Number One* (Can. 6128, 1974)
Joaquin Brothers: *Polkas and Chotis* (Can. 6139, 1975)
Waila Social Dance Music (Can. 6155, 1976)
Gila River Six (Minus One): *Pima Chicken Scratch* (Can. 8050, 1978)
Chicken Scratch Fiesta (Can. 8055, 1981)
The Molinas: *"Los Papagos" Molinas: Papago Chicken Scratch* (Can. 8063C, 1982)
Verton Jackson Combo: *Pima Chicken Scratch* (Can. 8066C, 1983)

BIBLIOGRAPHY

J. Griffith: "*Waila*: the Social Dance Music of the Indians of Southern Arizona: an Introduction and Discography," *JEMF Quarterly*, xv (1979), 193
——: "*Waila* Music since 1979," *Southwest Folklore*, v (1981), 57

J. RICHARD HAEFER

Chickering. Firm of piano makers. It was founded as Stewart & Chickering in Boston in April 1823, when Jonas Chickering (*b* Mason, NH, 5 April 1797; *d* Boston, MA, 8 Dec 1853) went into partnership with the British maker James Stewart. Chickering had served an apprenticeship with John Gould, a cabinetmaker in New Ipswich, New Hampshire, and, after moving to Boston in 1818, had worked first with James Barker, also a cabinetmaker, and with John Osborne, a piano maker, from 1819 to 1823; Stewart had been trained in London, had built pianos in Baltimore (1812–19) and Philadelphia (1819–22), and had also worked with Osborne. Their firm was at 20 Tremont (or Common) Street, and their partnership was ended in 1826 when Stewart returned to London. Chickering worked alone for a few years, then formed a business relationship with John MACKAY that lasted from 1830 to 1841. During this period the firm operated at 416 Washington Street, Boston, and from 1838 to 1852 in a new factory at 334 Washington Street, where the pianos were finished; the initial manufacturing stages were completed in Lawrence, Massachusetts, and the veneering of the cases was carried out at Franklin Square, Boston. In 1837 the firm's name was Jonas Chickering & Co., from 1839 to 1841 Chickering & Mackays (Mackay's son William H. Mackay having become involved), and from 1842, after the death of John Mackay, Chickering & Mackay; after 1842 Chickering bought the Mackay interest.

Mackay was a shrewd, wealthy businessman who sought new commercial outlets and exploited the USA's rapidly growing railway and canal network, enabling the firm to export instruments and allowing Chickering to devote more time to making technical improvements. By 1837 he had developed a one-piece, cast-iron frame for the square piano (patent no. 1802, 8 Oct 1840) that improved on a design of Alpheus Babcock, who was then working for Chickering. By 1845 he had devised a circular scale that allowed for freer movement of the hammers, especially in the bass. Chickering was also the only important American maker by 1840 to manufacture grand pianos, for which, in 1843, he patented a one-piece cast-iron frame (patent no.3238, 1 Sept 1843), his most significant innovation. This was the first time such a device had been practically applied to the grand piano; it gave the instrument solidity, made it more resistant to severe American climates, and permitted higher string tension, which in turn meant that thicker strings, providing a richer tone, could be used. This successful one-piece metal frame laid the groundwork for the American system of piano manufacture that, by the 1870s, dominated the world market. The Chickering firm was awarded a medal for its square pianos and a commendation for its grand pianos at the Great Exhibition of 1851 at the Crystal Palace, London. The firm's grand pianos were praised for their fine, delicate tone by Gottschalk, who toured with Chickering pianos in the 1850s and 1860s.

In 1852 fire destroyed the factory; Chickering started to rebuild it at 791 Tremont Street in Boston, and after his death in 1853 its completion was overseen by his three sons, who carried on the firm as Chickering & Sons. The factory was equipped with a steam engine of 120 horse power, a sawmill, and rooms devoted to all the stages of piano making (except the foundry), and was said to be "probably the largest building in the United States, excepting only the National Capitol" (*see* PIANO, fig.2). Chickering's eldest son, Thomas E. Chickering (*b* Boston, 1824; *d* Boston, 14 Feb 1871), became president of the firm and remained in that position until his death. Frank (Charles Francis) Chickering (*b* Boston, 20 Jan 1827; *d* New York, 23 March 1891) moved to New York in 1859 to direct the company's operations there. He had considerable technical expertise, and was issued seven patents between 1861 and 1886; he was also active in New York social and musical societies. George Harvey Chickering (*b* Boston, 18 April 1830; *d* Milton, MA, 17 Nov 1899) managed the firm's factory in Boston.

Chickering & Sons won a gold medal at the Universal Exhibition of 1867 in Paris (resulting in a widely publicized conflict with Steinway over which firm won the highest award); Frank Chickering also received the Imperial Cross of the Légion d'honneur from Napoleon III. A Chickering grand piano built in the 1860s typically included a rosewood case, a one-piece, cast-iron frame with parallel supports, damper and una corda pedals, and a range of seven octaves and a minor 3rd (*A''* to *c''''*).

In 1886 P. J. Gildemeester, a relative of Gottschalk who had joined Chickering in 1878 and been business manager of the firm, became a partner. By the 1890s the firm's financial difficulties had led the Chickering brothers to share control of the company with C. H. W. Foster and George L. Nichols. From 1905 to 1911 ARNOLD DOLMETSCH worked with Chickering, establishing at the factory his own department that built harpsichords, clavichords, lutes, and viols. In 1908 Chickering became a division of the American Piano Company under the direction of C. H. W. Foster and George G. Foster. In 1926 a freely vibrating soundboard, independent of the piano's rim, was introduced. The plant was moved to East Rochester, New York, in 1927 and became part of the Aeolian American Corporation there in 1932.

Chickering established a number of concert halls in the late 19th and early 20th centuries. In Boston these included Tremont Temple (opened October 1853) and halls at the firm's factory at 334 Washington Street (July–1 December 1852), at the Chickering store at 246 Washington Street (November 1860 until it was demolished in May 1870), at the firm's national headquarters at 152 Tremont Street (seating 400; November 1883–January 1901), and at the Chickering building at 239–43 Huntington Avenue (seating 800; February 1901 until 1912, when it became the St. James Theatre). In New York Chickering Hall (seating 1400) was inaugurated in 1875 with a concert by Hans von Bülow, but financial uncertainty forced its sale in 1901; it was demolished the following year. A recital hall was included in the new Chickering Hall that opened on West 57th Street, New York, in 1924 as part of the firm's centennial celebrations.

BIBLIOGRAPHY

R. G. Parker: *A Tribute to the Life and Character of Jonas Chickering by one who Knew him Well* (Boston, 1854)
"The Late Col. Thomas E. Chickering," *Watson's Art Journal*, xiv/18 (1871), 212
"Supplement on Chickering Hall," *Musical and Dramatic Times and Music Trades Review*, i/5 (1876)
D. Spillane: *History of the American Pianoforte* (New York, 1890/*R*1969)
"Charles F. Chickering," *American Art Journal*, lvi/24 (1891), 369
"The Late George Harvey Chickering," *Music Trade Review*, xxix/22 (1899), 6
A. Dolge: *Pianos and their Makers*, i (Covina, CA, 1911/*R*1972), 270ff
R. E. M. Harding: *The Piano-forte: its History Traced to the Great Exhibition of 1851* (Cambridge, England, 1933, 2/1978)
C. M. Ayars: *Contributions to the Art of Music in America by the Music Industries of Boston, 1640 to 1936* (New York, 1937/*R*1969), 111
A. Loesser: *Men, Women and Pianos: a Social History* (New York, 1954)
M. Campbell: *Dolmetsch: the Man and his Work* (Seattle, WA, 1975), 168
C. Ehrlich: *The Piano: a History* (London, 1976)
N. A. Smith: "Boston Nineteenth Century Pianoforte Manufacture: the Contributions of Jonas Chickering," *Nineteenth Century*, viii (1982), 105
D. Campbell: *The Purveyor as Patron: the Contribution of American Piano Manufacturers and Merchants to Musical Culture in the United States 1851–1914* (diss., City U. of New York, 1984)

CYNTHIA ADAMS HOOVER

Chihara, Paul (Seiko) (*b* Seattle, WA, 9 July 1938). Composer. He studied composition with Robert Palmer at Cornell University (MA in English literature 1961, DMA 1965), and continued his studies with Boulanger in Paris (1962–3), Ernst Pepping in Berlin (1965–6), and Schuller at the Berkshire Music Center (1966). He joined the faculty of UCLA in 1966 and was associate professor of music until 1974; during those years he founded and directed the Twice Ensemble and conducted the collegium musicum. He was Andrew Mellon Professor at the California Institute of Technology in 1975 and taught at the California Institute of the Arts (1976). In 1980 he became composer-in-residence for the San Francisco Ballet. He has written over 15 film scores and has worked as a consultant and arranger for stage musicals, including Duke Ellington's *Sophisticated Ladies* (1981). He has received commissions from the Boston SO (Saxophone Concerto, 1981), Los Angeles PO (Symphony no.2, 1981), Fromm Music Foundation (Ceremony V, 1975), and the Sequoia String Quartet (Concerto for String Quartet and Orchestra, 1980), among others.

Chihara's works reflect his interest in oriental music through their emphasis on shifts in timbral coloring and limited pitch movement. *Logs* for double bass (1966) explores a group of brief phrases that may be repeated and combined in different orderings, or altered by the use of vibrato, accent, microtones, or unusual performance techniques. The resultant sonorities may be modified electronically. His later music develops these techniques, emphasizing the patternings of pitch and timbral units. Chihara also employs borrowed materials, as in the *Missa Carminum* which makes use of liturgical chant and traditional folksongs.

WORKS

Stage: ballets, incl. Shinju (Lovers' Suicide) (1, after Chikamatsu), 1975, Mistletoe Bride, 1978, The Infernal Machine, rev. as Oedipus Rag (musical, 1, J. Larson, after Cocteau), 1978–80, The Tempest (after Shakespeare), 1980
Orch: Forest Music, 1970; Windsong, vc, orch, 1971; Grass, db, orch, 1972; Ceremony III, fl, orch, 1973; Ceremony IV, 1973; Gui Conc., 1975; Sym. no.1 "Symphony in Celebration" (Ceremony V), 1975; Conc., str qt, orch, 1980; Sax Conc., 1981; Sym. no.2 "Birds of Sorrow," 1981; other early works, unpubd pieces
Chamber: Logs, db, 1966; Driftwood, str qt, 1967; Branches, 2 bn, perc, 1968; Willow Willow, fl, tuba, perc, 1968; Redwood, va, perc, 1971; Ceremony I, ob, 2 vc, db, perc, 1972; Ceremony II, amp fl, 2 amp vc, perc, 1974; Pf Trio, 1974; Elegy, pf trio, 1974; The Beauty of the Rose is in its Passing, bn, 2 hn, harp, perc, 1976; Str Qt (Primavera), 1977; Sinfonia concertante, 9 insts, 1980; Sequoia, str qt, tape, 1984
Choral: Magnificat, 6 female vv, 1965; Psalm xc, 1965; Ave Maria – Scarborough Fair (Lat., trad.), 6 male vv, 1971; Missa Carminum (Lat., trad.), 8 vv, 1975; short choral works
Over 15 film and television scores
Arrs. for musicals, incl. Ellington: Sophisticated Ladies, 1981

Principal publishers: Peters, G. Schirmer

BIBLIOGRAPHY

EwenD

RICHARD SWIFT

Child ballad. A term applied to any of the ballads contained in F. J. Child's *The English and Scottish Popular Ballads* (Boston, 1882–98/*R*1957, 1965); *see* EUROPEAN-AMERICAN MUSIC, §II, 1 (i).

Childs, Barney (Sanford) (*b* Spokane, WA, 13 Feb 1926). Composer and teacher. He was educated at Deep Springs College (1943–5), the University of Nevada (BA 1949), Oxford University (BA 1951, MA 1955), and Stanford University (PhD in literature, 1961); his composition studies were with Leonard Ratner (1952–3), Carlos Chávez (1953), Copland (1954), and Carter (1954–5). Childs taught English literature at the University of Arizona (1956–65) and at Deep Springs College (dean, 1965–9), then was composer-in-residence at Wisconsin College-Conservatory (1970) and fellow of Johnston College, University of Redlands (1971–3), where he became professor of composition and music literature in 1973. He was music and poetry editor for *Genesis West* and co-founder of Advance Recordings. He has edited a number of works by Frederic Ayres. Childs has served on the National Council and on the executive committee of the American Society of University Composers, the national advisory committee of the ACA, and the advisory board of the Charles Ives Center for American Music. He has also been a fellow of the MacDowell Colony (1963, 1970, 1974, 1978).

Childs's music is eclectic. He has explored indeterminacy, improvisation, and what he calls "self-generating structures" – music derived from the associations inherent in the assumed materials. In the early 1960s he wrote a number of works that are indeterminate in conception and performance, notably *Interbalances I–VI*. Works such as *Keet Seel* and *When Lilacs Last in the Dooryard Bloom'd* use nonfunctional triadic sonorities. During the mid-1970s Childs composed a number of intense and reflective works dedicated to several of his friends, for example the Trio of 1972 dedicated to the poet Paul Blackburn. More recent works are marked by free and linear, somewhat repetitive, shapes and multi-sectional, nonhierarchic overall structures. In addition to composing, Childs has published many articles in *Perspectives of New Music* and various other journals.

WORKS

Dramatic: The Roachville Project (theater piece), 4–10 people, 1967; ! Banana Flannelboard! (Childs, J. Newlove), 3 readers, tape, 1980

Orch: Sym. no.1, 1954; Conc., eng hn, hn, str, harp, perc, 1955; Sym. no.2, 1956; Music for almost Everybody, 1964; Music, pf, str orch, 1965; Variations on a Theme of Harold Budd, str orch, 1969; Cl Conc., 1970

Band: 6 Events, 58 players, 1965; Supposes: imago mundi, 1971; Concert Piece, tuba, band, 1973; The Golden Shore, 1974; Couriers of the Crimson Dawn, 1977; September with Band, 1978; A Continuance, 1979; Orrery, 1980

Chamber: Bn Sonata, 1953; Welcome to Whipperginny, 9 perc, 1961; Interbalances IV, tpt, reader, 1962; Music, 2 fl, 1963; Qt, fl, ob, db, perc, 1964; Any 5, 5 insts, 1965; Nonet, 1967; The Bayonne Barrel and Drum Company, solo wind ad lib, 13 wind, pf, 2 perc, 1968; Trio, cl, vc, pf, 1972; 4 Pieces, wind qnt, s/a sax, 1977; 13 Classic Studies, db, 1981; 4 brass qnts; 8 str qts; 5 wind qnts; *c*90 compositions for solo insts and chamber ens

Vocal: Keet Seel (Childs, Donne, Herbert, Shakespeare), chorus, 1970; Virtue (Herbert), S, pf, 1970; When Lilacs Last in the Dooryard Bloom'd (Whitman), solo vv, chorus, band, 1971; Lanterns and Candlelight (O. Gibbons), S, mar, 1975; Sunshine Lunchh, & Like Matters (Kipling, other texts chosen by singer), Bar, b cl, perc, elec, 1984; over 10 other vocal works

Principal publishers: ACA, Smith, Tritone

BIBLIOGRAPHY

EwenD; *VintonD*

RICHARD SWIFT

Childs, Lucinda (*b* New York, 26 June 1940). Choreographer. She attended Sarah Lawrence College and also studied with Hanya Holm, Helen Tamiris, Merce Cunningham, James Waring, and Robert Dunn. For the most part her works are danced in silence. Pieces from the 1960s such as *Street Dance* (1964) incorporated ordinary activities as dance movements; those of the 1970s and 1980s consist chiefly of stepping patterns (*Calico Mingling*, 1973; *Melody Excerpt*, 1977). Childs is perhaps best known for her role as dancer, actress, and speaker in the avant-garde opera *Einstein on the Beach* (1976), by Philip Glass and Robert Wilson; originally she choreographed only her own solo dance, but in the production staged at the Brooklyn Academy of Music in 1984 she served as choreographer of the entire work. Her participation in *Einstein on the Beach* led to a further collaboration with Glass, *Dance*, in which she used music for the first time; the work has been praised as her finest. Childs again used music in *Relative Calm* (1981), a work created in collaboration with Wilson and the American composer Jon Gibson, and in *Available Light* (1983), a collaboration with the composer John Adams and the architect Frank Geary.

BIBLIOGRAPHY

S. Banes: "Lucinda Childs: the Act of Seeing," *Terpsichore in Sneakers: Post-modern Dance* (Boston, 1980), 133

"Childs, Lucinda," *CBY 1984*

SALLY BANES

Chi-Lites. Soul vocal group. It was formed in Chicago, and the original members were Creadel Jones, Robert Lester, and Marshall Thompson, who had performed together in various local groups. Joined by Eugene Record (who became the group's lead singer, principal songwriter, and producer) they began recording in the mid-1960s, and had their first hit on the soul chart in 1969 with *Give it away*. A number of singles followed which were substantial successes on the pop chart, including *Have you seen her* (no.3, 1971) and *Oh girl* (no.1, 1972). The first of these was characterized by a sweet, mellow production sound and concise, smooth vocal harmonies, but the group's repertory was not restricted to love ballads: for example, *Give more power to the people* (no.26, 1971) displays an emotional anxiety that proves they were capable of addressing social problems with a skill uncommon among black vocal groups. Record and Jones left the group in 1975, and Record pursued a solo career which proved to be only intermittently successful. He rejoined the group in 1980, and in 1982 they had a hit on the black music chart with *Hot on a thing*.

RECORDINGS

(selective list; recorded for Brunswick unless otherwise stated)

Give it away (55398, 1969); Give more power to the people (55450, 1971); Have you seen her (55462, 1971); Oh girl (55471, 1972); A letter to myself (55491, 1973); Stoned out of my mind (55500, 1973); *Me and you* (20th Century-Fox 635, 1982), incl. Hot on a thing

ANTHONY MARKS

Chilton, Alex (*b* Memphis, TN, 28 Dec 1950). Rock singer and songwriter. He began his career as the lead singer of the Box Tops, who became known for their songs *The Letter* (no.1, 1967) and *Cry like a Baby* (no.2, 1968). After the group disbanded in 1970 he moved to New York, where an important experience for him was hearing performances by the Velvet Underground, then returned to Memphis, where he formed Big Star in 1971. This group never achieved commercial success, but its willfully anachronistic style (which, especially on the album *Radio City*, 1974, recalled the work of the Beatles) helped to define the "power pop" of the late 1970s. Big Star disbanded in 1975, and Chilton embarked on an eccentric career as a soloist, a producer for the Cramps, and a member of Tav Falco's Panther Burns; he influenced such diverse performers as Tom Petty and the Buzzcocks.

RECORDINGS

(selective list)

With the Box Tops: *Cry Like a Baby* (Bell 6017, 1968); *Non-Stop* (Bell 6023, 1968); *The Letter/Neon Rainbow* (Bell 6011, 1968)

With Big Star: *#1 Record* (Ardent 1501, 1972); *Radio City* (Ardent 2803, 1974); *Third* (PVC 7903, 1978)

JOHN PICCARELLA

Chilula. California Indian group. *See* YUROK.

Chinese-American music. *See* ASIAN-AMERICAN MUSIC, §2.

Chippewa. *See* OJIBWE.

Chiricahua. APACHE Indian group of the Southwest.

Choctaw. American Indian tribe of the Muskogean confederacy in the Southeast of the USA. Related to other Muskogean linguistic groups, the (sedentary) Choctaw formerly occupied a large territory in the present states of Mississippi and Alabama. As a result of treaties with the US Government, most of the population moved to Oklahoma in the 1830s; a small number remained in Mississippi (*see* INDIANS, AMERICAN, fig. 1). The descendants of the latter have retained significantly more of their culture, including music, than the western groups. The surviving Choctaw repertory includes pieces associated with the Stickball Game, a few miscellaneous songs, and many dance-songs (*hitla tuluwa*, also written *taloa*). Ethnographers have often defined the dance-songs as social dances, but evidence, especially the importance of animal symbols, suggests that they constituted a ritual repertory. The influence of Western society can be observed in the unique hymns (*abba isht tuluwa*) sung in the Christian churches, and in the fiddle and guitar repertory (*oboha hitla*) borrowed chiefly from Appalachia.

Traditionally held at night, the events at which the *hitla tuluwa* were presented were highly structured. The singing of the "first song" (*amona tuluwa*) was followed by cycles of seven songs; a Jump Dance (*tolobli hitla*), with a distinctive responsorial form, introduced each new cycle. When completing the series, the song leader (*entuluwa*) was allowed to select pieces from a large repertory. A Walk Dance (*itanoowa*) was sung at sunrise to conclude the occasion. The dance formations included circles, semicircles, and lines.

Choctaw music is unusual among North American Indian tribes in that the drum (*hathepa chitto*) is sounded only between songs, playing an ostinato rhythm (eighth-note followed by two 16ths). Concussion sticks (*etiboli*), played to sustain the underlying pulse of a piece, are used by the leader to accompany about half of the repertory. Sleigh bells, probably developed from an earlier idiophone, are worn by dancers. Early sources mention cane flutes and rasps, although neither has survived. Apart from the men's Jump Dances and a few examples in which the leader alone sings, the *hitla tuluwa* are sung by all participants in the dance. In all but the animal dances, most titles are generic terms for a number of variants. A common practice is to link two or more of these versions, which can be distinguished by a change in vocables. Except for the Quail Dance, all the dance-songs are monophonic, with women doubling the men's part at the octave. Musical compositions end with specific vocable patterns, primarily "ya ho! yo!," "we! ha!," or "ya! yu!" In some categories (e.g., the War Dances), a similar sequence may function as an introduction. The texts are made up primarily of nonlexical phrases, with the insertion of an occasional Choctaw word. The Choctaw singing style is distinguished by a nasal tone, and the voice production requires a relaxed throat.

In the oldest songs she recorded, Densmore noted the "period formation," defined as the repetition of large sections within a piece (1943). Except for the Jump Dances, the dance-songs are strophic. An obvious change in pitch or the insertion of different vocables introduces new sections within a piece; whoops and yells may also occur. The numbers four and seven often serve to organize internal patterns on various levels (common phrase patterns within sections include *ABAB*, *ABCB*, *ABBB*, etc.). Phrases may contain four vocables or seven pitches. Aspiration consistently indicates boundaries of musical phrases, and may occur simultaneously with other markers, such as upward glides, dynamic stresses, and glottal stops. Scales are primarily anhemitonic tetratonic or pentatonic, and tones outside these scales are invariably ornamental. The dance-songs are essentially isometric; there is a variety of melodic contours. Densmore's collection of cylinder recordings of Choctaw music is held in the Archive of Folk Culture at the Library of Congress.

See also INDIANS, AMERICAN, esp. §I, 4(ii)(b).

DISCOGRAPHY

American Indian Music of the Mississippi Choctaws, i–ii (Choctaw Central High School, Philadelphia, MS, 1971–2)

Choctaw–Chickasaw Dance Songs, i–ii (Sweetland, 1976–7)

BIBLIOGRAPHY

D. Bushnell: *The Choctaw of Bayou Lacomb, St. Tammany Parish, Louisiana* (Washington, DC, 1909)

J. Swanton: *Source Material for the Social and Ceremonial Life of the Choctaw Indians* (Washington, DC, 1931)

F. Densmore: *Choctaw Music* (Washington, DC, 1943)

G. Stevenson: *The Hymnody of the Choctaw Indians of Oklahoma* (diss., Southern Baptist Theological Seminary, 1977)

D. Draper: "Occasions for the Performance of Native Choctaw Music," *Selected Reports in Ethnomusicology*, iii/2 (1980), 147

——: "*Abba isht tuluwa*: the Christian Hymns of the Mississippi Choctaw," *American Indian Culture and Research Journal*, vi/1 (1982), 43

——: "Breath in Music: Concept and Practice among the Choctaw Indians," *Selected Reports in Ethnomusicology*, iv (1983), 285

DAVID E. DRAPER

Chookasian, Lili (*b* Chicago, IL, 1 Aug 1921). Contralto. She studied with Phillip Manuel and made her concert début in 1957 with the Chicago SO under Bruno Walter in Mahler's Symphony no.3. Her first stage appearance followed two years later when she sang Adalgisa (*Norma*) with the Arkansas Opera Theater in Little Rock.

After further study, with Rosa Ponselle, she made her New York début in Prokofiev's *Alexander Nevsky* with the New York PO under Schippers (1961), her Metropolitan Opera début as La Cieca (*La Gioconda*, 9 March 1962), and her European début at Bayreuth (1963). She has also sung with the New York City Opera (Menotti's *The Medium*, 1963) and with many other leading companies, including those of Mexico City and Hamburg (both in *Aida*) and Buenos Aires (Ulrica in *Un Ballo in maschera*), as well as at the Salzburg Festival. She created the role of the Queen in Pasatieri's *Inez de Castro* (April 1976), and her other roles include Azucena in *Il trovatore*, Madelon in Umberto Giordano's *Andrea Chenier*, and the three mezzo parts (Frugola, the Princess, and La Vecchia) in Puccini's *Il trittico*. Chookasian has appeared with most of the important American orchestras, and has recorded works ranging from Beethoven's Symphony no.9 and Mass in C to Yardumian's Symphony no.2, which was commissioned for her by the Philadelphia Orchestra. Her dark, rich voice is especially suited to the music of Mahler, which she performs frequently and has recorded on several occasions; important among these recordings are two of *Das Lied von der Erde*, made with the Philadelphia and the Cincinnati orchestras.

RICHARD LESUEUR

Choralcelo. A two-manual hybrid keyboard instrument, developed by Melvin L. Severy and George B. Sinclair, and first demonstrated in Boston in 1909; *see* ELECTROACOUSTIC MUSIC, §7.

Choral music. Music written for a group of singers, which is generally known as a chorus or choir. They may perform either in unison or, more commonly, in parts with one or more singers to a part. This article deals with the history and repertory of American choral music of the Western tradition. For further discussion of the different genres of choral music *see* PSALMODY, SINGING-SCHOOL, ANTHEM, FUGING-TUNE, SHAPE-NOTE HYMNODY, HYMNODY, SPIRITUAL, GOSPEL MUSIC, and GLEE. Other genres that use choral forces but are not customarily referred to as "choral" include OPERA, certain types of POPULAR MUSIC, and WORK SONGS. Information on the musical practices of religious denominations, some of which call for choral music, are to be found in the articles dealing with them (*see also* JEWISH-AMERICAN MUSIC and ISLAMIC MUSIC, AMERICAN). The vocal music of American Indians is discussed in articles on the individual tribes (*see also* INDIANS, AMERICAN), and that of the various immigrant ethnic groups in ASIAN-AMERICAN MUSIC and EUROPEAN-AMERICAN MUSIC; the choral music of black Americans is discussed in AFRO-AMERICAN MUSIC. A number of individual choirs are dealt with in their own entries, in articles on their conductors, or in articles concerning the cities in which they are based. Several choral groups devoted specifically to the performance of music of the Renaissance, Baroque, and Classical periods have flourished as a result of the EARLY-MUSIC REVIVAL. Choral music in schools and universities is discussed in the article on EDUCATION IN MUSIC. For information on choral music festivals *see* FESTIVALS.

I. History of choral singing. II. Repertory.

I. History of choral singing

1. 17th and 18th centuries. 2. 19th century. 3. 20th century.

1. 17TH AND 18TH CENTURIES. American choral music began with the congregational psalmody practiced by the early settlers in New England. Using psalters brought from Europe and, later, American revisions and editions, they sang metrical, rhymed translations of the psalms, without accompaniment and generally in unison. In the absence of trained musical leaders, congregations customarily had a very small repertory of tunes, which they learned by rote. A leader read or sang each line of the psalm or hymn before the congregation sang it (*see* LINING OUT). The singing style was characterized by extremely slow tempos, a consequently weakened sense of rhythm, and improvised, heterophonic melodic ornamentation.

Early in the 18th century, some New England clergymen decided that this style of congregational singing was unacceptable; they emerged as proponents of a reform movement intended to improve the quality of congregational singing. Around 1720, a controversy arose between those who preferred the "OLD WAY OF SINGING" and reformers who favored what they called "Regular Singing," "Singing by Rule," or "Singing by Note." The disputants argued primarily on theological grounds, but the outcome was of decided musical importance. The advocates of "Regular Singing" prevailed, and as a means of bringing about the desired reforms the formation of singing-schools was encouraged.

New England singing-schools were conducted by itinerant singing masters, of whom William Billings was the foremost representative. A typical school consisted of about 50 students and lasted between one and three months; schools were held in churches, meeting houses, or occasionally in taverns. Students were taught to read music (using solmization as a tool) and to sing in parts; attention was also given to vocal production, style of performance, and deportment. At the conclusion of a singing-school it was common to present a public demonstration. The singing, like the music, has been described as robust.

The enthusiasm of the early singing masters led to the formation of church and community choirs throughout New England from the 1750s. The Stoughton (Massachusetts) Musical Society, the oldest enduring community choral organization in the USA, was founded in 1786 under the influence of the singing-school movement. For the most part, the schools flourished in rural areas and in small villages and towns, but some singing masters resided permanently in metropolitan centers. In 1784 Andrew Adgate proposed a plan to found what he called an Institution for the Encouragement of Church Music in Philadelphia. The Uranian Academy, which resulted in 1787 from his efforts, provided free music instruction to large numbers of students and presented public concerts of sacred music. In 1786 Adgate led a chorus of 230 and an orchestra of 50 in a varied selection of sacred works including the "Hallelujah Chorus" from Handel's *Messiah* and Billings's *I am the rose of Sharon*. The Uranian Academy's concerts, and similar choral concerts presented by William Tuckey in New York and by William Selby in Boston, were exceptional events at a time when public concerts consisted predominantly of instrumental music.

There were also active choral traditions in certain minority religious sects, although most were isolated and had little lasting impact. Ann Lee, the founder of the American Shakers, communicated to her followers several songs in unorthodox notation which had been revealed to her in visions (*see* SHAKER MUSIC). Conrad Beissel, the leader of a Pennsylvania sect known as the EPHRATA CLOISTER or the Community of the Solitary, organized choirs and singing-schools for his followers, and produced an unconventional *Dissertation on Harmony* and two voluminous collections of hymns. In contrast to the idiosyncratic activities of the Shaker and Ephrata Cloister communities, the Moravian Church, officially known as the Unitas Fratrum, encouraged the production of a large body of remarkably sophisticated choral (and instrumental) music which compares favorably with Classical European compositions (*see* MORAVIAN CHURCH, MUSIC OF THE). The Moravians excelled in performance as well as in composition; in Bethlehem, a collegium musicum was formed in 1744, and in Salem, the Collegium Musicum der Gemeine was established in 1786. In addition, choral singing was practiced in the Spanish missions in the American Southwest (*see* CALIFORNIA MISSION MUSIC). Although the music in those early settlements was less refined than that of Mexico City and Lima – centers of the Spanish conquest – it is likely that American Indians of the Southwest were taught European musical skills and, quite possibly, organized into choirs before the time at which a musical culture was established in New England.

2. 19TH CENTURY. During the first half of the 19th century, the singing-school movement was supplanted in New England by the "better music movement." Its proponents, led by Lowell Mason, Thomas Hastings, and William B. Bradbury in the urban centers of the Northeast, criticized the unsophisticated compositions and performance standards of the earlier singing masters and substituted more dignified and decorous music. Emphasizing a need to refine taste and achieve progress through the application of "scientific" musical principles, these reformers advocated the adoption of European styles to improve American music. The favored performing style became more subtle, staid, and sober

1. Church choir accommodated in the gallery from where it leads the congregational singing; the figure in the center holds a pitchpipe with which he sets the starting note: engraving by Isaac Sanford for the title page of Oliver Brownson's "Select Harmony" (?Hartford, 1783)

than that of the 18th century. Mason and his colleagues turned away from American music of previous generations, and exercised a profound influence on the future of American choral music through their publications and their activities as teachers, organizers, and conductors. They promoted musical literacy by establishing vocal music as a subject in the curriculum of the public schools, raised the performance standards of church choirs, founded choral societies, and established "conventions" and "normal institutes" (the former short-term events, the latter longer summer study programs) in which American choral conductors, church musicians, and music educators received instruction. Mason's own church choir, at the Bowdoin Street Church in Boston, was a model for his contemporaries throughout the country; from 1831 to 1845 he taught the choir using the methods and techniques of the normal institutes.

The singing-school movement continued to flourish in the rural South and on the western frontier, where it adopted the shape-note notational system that had been introduced in the Northeast in the beginning of the 19th century. Shape-note singing was enormously popular, especially in the deep South. The repertory, mostly sacred, ranged from the music of Billings and his contemporaries to camp-meeting spirituals and adaptations of folksongs. Not only was the music performed by rural congregations and choirs, but people organized regional shape-note conventions or singings – festive events lasting up to several days in which music, religion, and conviviality were of equal importance. During the years before the Civil War, the original four-shape notational system was challenged by seven-shape systems (designed to promote solmization according to contemporary European standards; *see* NOTATION). This change, no doubt a sign of the inroads being made by the "better music movement," coincided with a general weakening of the shape-note tradition, though it continued through the rest of the 19th century and persists in the deep South, where shape-note singings, directly linked to the repertory and performance styles of an earlier time, are still held.

From 1800, revivalist activities in the pioneer settlements of the western frontier resulted in open-air services and social events, known as camp meetings, in which the singing of spirituals was an integral activity. Spirituals, although not exclusively choral music, contained a combination of secular folktunes and religious texts, which were used to "testify" to the joy of religion and to teach the young. Repetition of text and music was common, since participants had limited musical experience. Blacks and Whites mingled at the meetings (although they had separate religious meetings) and there was a free interchange of musical ideas. Black spirituals were otherwise associated principally with the unison singing in southern church congregations and in the fields, until the 1870s, when the Jubilee Singers of Fisk University began to include choral arrangements of spirituals on their programs.

By the late 19th century gospel music had begun to replace spirituals, especially in urban centers. Bradbury, a composer of hymns and compiler of collections, was at the forefront of the Sunday-school movement (1840–75). Gospel hymns were an important element of American religious music during the revivals led by Dwight L. Moody and Ira D. Sankey from 1875 to 1910, and later, during the Sunday-Rodeheaver era (1910–30). By the 1890s, there were published collections of black gospel hymns, which followed the white hymn tradition. Gospel choirs did not attain importance until the 1930s, especially among Blacks (see below).

Choral societies proliferated in the USA during the 19th century, often in conjunction with church choirs. Among the earliest were the Handel and Haydn Society of Boston, which in 1815 began an existence that continues to the present, and the Sacred Music Society of New York (founded 1823). Towards mid-century, German immigrants affirmed their cultural heritage by forming singing societies. In New York, the Deutsche Liederkranz was organized in 1847, and a rival organization, the Männergesangverein Arion, was set up in 1854. Across the country, wherever there were large German-American communities, similar convivial musical societies on European models were established; Milwaukee, Chicago, and Cincinnati were notable centers. Glee clubs, organized on English models, flourished from the beginning of the century; among the most notable were the Mendelssohn Glee Club (New York, 1866), the Apollo Club (Boston, 1871), the Apollo Musical Club (Chicago, 1872) and the Mendelssohn Club (Philadelphia, 1874). Germanic singing societies and glee clubs began almost invariably as all-male social organizations, but often evolved into large choral societies of mixed voices singing art music. The Apollo Musical Club of Chicago, for example, began with a small group of men in 1872, converted to mixed voices in 1875, and eventually became a major symphonic choral society of 250 voices. During the second half of the century, many societies were formed specifically to perform large-scale choral works with orchestra. The New York Oratorio Society, founded in 1873 by Leopold Damrosch, was the best-known civic chorus, but oratorio societies were established in most large cities. Other large choruses followed the example of the Handel and Haydn Society in naming themselves after major European composers: a Mendelssohn Society and a Beethoven Society were founded in Chicago, respectively in 1858 and 1873; a Mozart Society was founded in 1880 at Fisk University, and the Bethlehem Bach Choir, tracing its ancestry back to the Moravian collegium musicum of 1744, was founded in 1898 by J. Fred Wolle (1863–1933); he inaugurated the Bethlehem Bach Festival in 1900. The Mozart Society at Fisk University was among the first choral societies sponsored by an academic institution; others included the Oberlin Musical Union of Oberlin (Ohio) College (1860), the University Choral Union of the University of Michigan, Ann Arbor (1879), and the Madison Choral Union of the University of Wisconsin (1893).

Like the choral societies, American choral festivals usually followed English and German precedents. The Cincinnati May Festival, for example, goes back to a Sängerfest of 1849 in which several male Germanic singing societies formed a festival chorus of 118 singers. In subsequent years, Cincinnati's Männergesangverein festivals attracted more participants, and by 1870 nearly 2000 men were in the festival chorus. The next year Theodore Thomas was hired as music director, plans were made for the participation of choruses of mixed voices, and in 1873 the first May Festival took place with a chorus of 800 and an orchestra of over 100. In 1880, a permanent May Festival Chorus of 600 singers was established. The Handel and Haydn Society sponsored the first American festival for a chorus of mixed voices in 1856; 600 singers and an orchestra of 78 participated, and similar events held in 1865 and thereafter involved even more people. In Worcester, Massachusetts, festivals were presented from 1871 under the auspices of the Worcester County Musical Association, which had grown out of a normal institute begun in 1858. The largest festivals held in the USA during the 19th century, organized in Boston in 1869 and 1872 by Patrick S. Gilmore, surpassed in magnitude even the notoriously extravagant Handel commemorations presented earlier in the century at the Crystal Palace, London. Gilmore's Peace Jubilees were gargantuan affairs; in 1869 there were more than 10,000 choristers and 1000 instrumentalists, and the 1872 festival had a chorus of 20,000 and an orchestra of 2000 (*see* BOSTON, fig. 1).

American choral societies and festival choruses, having been organized on European models, used European repertory almost exclusively, especially the works of Handel, Haydn, Mozart, Beethoven, and Mendelssohn. Over the course of the century, however, some choral organizations presented works of American composers such as John Knowles Paine, Dudley Buck, William W. Gilchrist, and Horatio Parker, all of whom were well-versed in the favored European styles. By the end of the century, many amateur choral singers could read music and were participating in choirs and choruses which achieved a standard of performance comparable to that of their European counterparts.

3. 20TH CENTURY. The formation of music programs in American colleges and universities provided the basis for the greatest change in American choral music during the 20th century. Choral ensembles were organized to provide essential ensemble experiences for students majoring in music and cultural enrichment for other students. As a result of their institutional affiliations, these ensembles have had sufficient financial security to free them to explore diverse methods and repertory. Their example and their many alumni have resulted in the development of choirs and choruses away from the academy. Moreover, by allowing nonstudents to participate in their choruses, many colleges and universities have acted as patrons for community choruses. Two early collegiate choirs, created and nurtured by strong and idealistic conductors, achieved a standard of excellence which had a major impact on later developments: the St. Olaf Choir of St. Olaf College (Northfield, Minnesota), which was founded in 1912 and conducted until 1944 by F. Melius Christiansen, and the Westminster Choir (founded in 1921 as the choir of Westminster Presbyterian Church in Dayton, Ohio, but since 1926 affiliated with Westminster Choir College, and located since 1932 in Princeton, New Jersey), which was conducted until 1958 by its founder, John Finley Williamson. Another important collegiate conductor was Archibald Davison; as director of the all-male Harvard Glee Club from 1912 to 1933, he transformed a social society that sang a limited selection of college songs into a polished ensemble for the performance of art music. His example was followed by many college conductors, who led excellent men's and women's glee clubs. Of the many excellent recent collegiate choral ensembles, those of Robert Fountain (*b*1917), at Oberlin College and at the University of Wisconsin, Madison, have been particularly outstanding.

Universities have also been responsible for the training of choral conductors. Before the 1960s, this was generally a supplementary activity for students in other musical disciplines. Graduate programs, pioneered by such men as Charles Hirt (*b* 1911) at the University of Southern California and Harold Decker (*b* 1914) at the University of Illinois, now offer intensive training in choral literature and conducting.

In the early years of the 20th century, the singing of church choirs in the USA had deteriorated. Many congregations had ceased to maintain a choir and relied instead on a quartet of professional soloists. During this century American church music has improved remarkably. While professional singers continue to find employment as church musicians, their activities are usually integrated into well-conceived choral programs, and in many churches the parishioners themselves have formed excellent choirs without the aid of professionals. Williamson was among those responsible for the improved quality of church music in the USA; he realized his vision of a "ministry of music," which called for church musicians to function as full-time members of pastoral staffs, supervising graded choirs in a program of choral development.

During the 1920s and 1930s Williamson was at the forefront of what has come to be known as the *a cappella* choir movement. He and conductors such as Christiansen, Peter Christian Lutkin of Northwestern University, and Father William J. Finn, conductor of the Paulist Choristers of New York, led groups which sang a repertory of unaccompanied music (often with emphasis on the recently rediscovered polyphony of the Renaissance and Baroque periods). More important than the popularity of these *a cappella* choirs, however, the movement represented an attitude to performance based on the self-reliance of singing without accompaniment and the selflessness of achieving a uniformly blended ensemble. Attention was given to achieving unanimity in the smallest details of interpretation; the ultimate goal was the creation of the perfect choral instrument. Conductors disseminated their methods to large followings of disciples, and the term "*a cappella*" came to represent a call to achieve absolute homogeneity of sound, often with an almost religious zeal. Although the movement faded by mid-century, many of its goals remain; since then a more balanced programming of accompanied and unaccompanied repertory has prevailed among American choruses. The *a cappella* choir movement exercised a strong influence on the standard of choral performance and contributed to the creation of a wider and more discriminating public.

Choral music in the public schools benefited greatly from the *a cappella* choir movement. Young singers possessed clear and light voices, enthusiasm for an idealistic cause, and a willingness to participate in group activity. American educational administrators recognized that conspicuously excellent choral ensembles were of value not only culturally, but also in terms of community relations, and sought out trained music educators to create first-rate ensembles. Strong state organizations promoted excellence in choral singing by sponsoring contests, festivals, and honor choruses at regional and state levels. These state organizations were linked at the national level through their affiliations with the Music Educators National Conference and the American Choral Directors Association. The latter (founded in 1959) holds conventions and publishes a monthly journal; in the mid-1980s it had more than 11,000 members.

In the 1930s black musicians organized church choirs to draw on the repertory and performance style of gospel music. Thomas A. Dorsey formed the National Convention of Gospel Choirs and Choruses in 1932; the Cleveland-based choir Wings Over Jordan became nationally known through radio broadcasts from 1938. Gospel choirs in churches such as the Ebenezer Baptist Church (Chicago), Church of God in Christ (Memphis), Greater Harvest Baptist Church (Chicago), Washington Temple Church of God in Christ (Brooklyn), and Prayer Tabernacle Baptist Church (Detroit) emphasized a full four-part mixed chorus style until the 1960s, when James Cleveland and his Angelic Choir (First Baptist Church of Nutley, New Jersey) developed a style of solo singer with choral accompaniment that was widely admired. The Voices of Hope, formed in Los Angeles in 1957, continued to emphasize a choral sound. In the late 1960s gospel choirs were established in colleges and universities, first at those with large black enrollments (Howard University, Florida Agricultural and Mechanical University) and then at schools with predominately white enrollments (Macalester College, Mount Holyoke College, Harvard University). (*See* GOSPEL MUSIC, §II, 2 (iii).)

Large symphonic and oratorio choruses have continued to prosper in the 20th century; most major metropolitan centers have at least one chorus with more than 200 singers. However, the trend has been in the direction of smaller choruses, often called chorales, comprised of expert singers who are rigorously auditioned and selected. This was foreshadowed in 1893, when Frank Damrosch organized the Musical Art Society of New York, an ensemble advertised as a chorus of 70 professional singers. The *a cappella* choir movement and the quality of certain collegiate choruses were influential in this development, but there have been other contributing factors. Musicological studies of previously neglected areas of choral literature and performance practice have prompted a concern for authenticity, which has mandated smaller performance forces for certain kinds of repertory. Concert tours are also easier with smaller groups. The existence of a large pool of well-trained American choral singers provides personnel of a high caliber. Alongside the proliferation of small choruses has been the creation of specialized ensembles: singers devoted to the presentation of a relatively narrow repertory in stylistically appropriate performances. Many of these, including those designated "madrigal groups," perform older music; other ensembles, such as The Western Wind and the New Hutchinson Family Singers, are dedicated to avant-garde or American music.

The establishment of professional choral ensembles has had a profound impact on American choral music. Among the first professional groups in the USA were two choirs of black singers: the Eva Jessye Choir (active 1927–77) and the Hall Johnson Choir, which was established in 1930 and later became known as the Festival Negro Chorus of Los Angeles (see fig.2, p.434). Fred Waring's Pennsylvanians was a vocal-instrumental group formed in 1916 that had a continuous existence until his death in 1984. Waring capitalized on the national popularity of his professional touring ensemble to create a highly successful business organization, Shawnee Press, which sold large quantities of popular choral arrangements, held summer conducting workshops, and developed a copyrighted phonetic system of textual transliteration known as "tone syllables," which was intended to improve choral diction. Among Waring's protégés was Robert Shaw, who is widely regarded as the foremost choral conductor in the USA. In 1941 he founded the Collegiate Chorale, an amateur chorus of 120–200 voices which he led until 1954, and he was the founder and conductor of the Robert Shaw Chorale (1948–66), a 40-voice professional ensemble with which he toured internationally and made many recordings. As conductor of the Cleveland Orchestra Chorus (1956–67) and the Atlanta SO and Chorus (from 1967) Shaw has continued his work while becoming an influential orchestral director. Others who have formed their own professional groups are Roger Wagner and Gregg Smith.

Although economic factors require professional choral ensembles to exist with very modest numbers of singers (usually no more than 40 and often considerably fewer), there are a number of large choruses affiliated with symphony orchestras that operate primarily on a professional basis. The largest and best known is the Chicago Symphony Chorus, under the direction of Margaret Hillis, which has more than 200 members. The orchestras of Boston, Cleveland, St. Louis, and San Francisco also sponsor professional choruses. But in contrast to the many American orchestras that provide full-time employment for instrumental musicians, there is only one chorus in the USA in a comparable position, the Metropolitan Opera Chorus, which performs an operatic rather than a specifically choral repertory. Still, choral

2. *Hall Johnson in the 1940s with the Festival Negro Chorus of Los Angeles*

singing has become increasingly professional in recent years; by the 1980s the Association of Professional Vocal Ensembles (founded 1977) had a membership of more than 30 ensembles.

Professional choruses have set a standard, through performances, tours, and recordings, to which nonprofessional singers may aspire. More than ever before, choruses of all types perform a balanced repertory which includes not only European works of the past and present but also many works by American composers. This increased interest in American music is due in part to a growing sense of self-sufficiency which has freed choral musicians from their former reliance on a European *imprimatur*; it has also resulted from the emergence of composers who have created a repertory of considerable breadth and substance.

II. Repertory. The Puritan settlers who colonized New England in the 17th century brought with them a musical tradition rooted in Calvinist practice (*see* PSALMS, METRICAL). For almost a century and a half, English psalters such as those of Henry Ainsworth (Amsterdam, 1612), Thomas Ravenscroft (London, 1621), and Sternhold and Hopkins (London, 1562) served as the principal source of music in New England churches. The first book published in British North America was a psalter, the Bay Psalm Book of 1640; it was created to improve the translations of the psalms, not to change the tunes to which they were sung. The emergence in the early 1700s of the New England singing-schools was directed at the proper singing of the existing tune repertory, as were the first musical textbooks by John Tufts and Thomas Walter (both published in 1721). By the end of the 18th century, however, the singing-school movement had produced such activity that it stimulated a large and unique body of choral music by native Americans, beginning with *The New-England Psalm-singer* (1770) by William Billings; tunebooks by Andrew Law, Supply Belcher, Jacob French, Daniel Read, Timothy Swan, Jacob Kimball, Samuel Holyoke, and Oliver Holden soon followed (*see* NEW ENGLAND COMPOSERS, SCHOOLS OF). In published tunebooks, these composers created numerous choral compositions in five principal genres: plain tunes (homorhythmic settings of metrical psalms and hymns), fuging-tunes (similar to plain tunes but with at least one passage in which the voices enter successively in free imitation), anthems (through-composed settings of prose texts, usually scriptural), set-pieces (with secular texts), and canons. Of these, the anthems were the most ambitious musically. Four-part unaccompanied writing (treble, counter, tenor, and bass) was the norm, with the tenor carrying the main melody ("air"). Other stylistic characteristics included omission of the third degree of triads (particularly at cadences), consonances on strong beats, infrequent modulations, and modally inflected melody and harmony. Texts were predominantly sacred, although there were also secular texts reflecting patriotic themes (Billings's plain tune "Chester" and his anthem *Lamentation over Boston*) or the didactic and social aspects of the singing-schools (Billings's *Modern Musick* and *Down steers the bass*, the latter also set by Read). Temperley (1979) has shown certain similarities between American tunebooks and contemporaneous publications of English musicians who provided music for use in parish churches and in the meeting houses of dissenting sects.

Outside New England, an impressive choral repertory emanated from the several American Moravian communities established in Bethlehem, Pennsylvania, and Salem (now Winston-Salem), North Carolina, in the mid-18th century. Sophisticated choral works – chiefly anthems for mixed chorus, string orchestra, and organ – were written by both European- and American-born composers and performed by well-trained choristers and instrumentalists. German in background, composers such as Johannes Herbst, John Antes, Johann Friedrich Peter, and David Moritz Michael followed closely the procedures of European Classical style. Peter's festive Christmas anthem *Singet ihr Himmel* is typical in its opening orchestral ritornello, contrasting thematic material, homophonic texture, and tonic–dominant tonal polarity. The Moravian tradition extended well into the 19th century, though it exercised little direct influence on American musical life outside Moravian communities. Later composers include Peter Wolle, Francis Hagen, and Edward Leinbach, whose anthem *Hosanna* has been widely performed.

In the first decades of the 19th century, the New England singing-school movement, which had been born out of reform 100 years earlier, was itself subjected to reform. While the tradition was to survive in the shape-note hymnody of the South, the rough-hewn music of Billings and his contemporaries was supplanted in the East by European styles. Signs of reform were already apparent in the later compositions of Law and others, but it was men like Thomas Hastings, William B. Bradbury, and, especially, Lowell Mason who effectively brought the singing-school movement to a close in the Northeast. The prodigious publications of Mason and his disciples consisted mostly of adaptations of European compositions, although works by Mason, Hastings, George Webb, Bradbury, and others also appeared.

The growth of singing societies and choirs during the first half of the century stimulated serious composers to focus attention on choral music. John Knowles Paine, though primarily an instrumental composer, produced several notable large-scale choral works including a Mass in D (1865) and the oratorio *St. Peter* (1870–72). The Mass, which divides the Latin text into 18 large movements, owes much to Viennese Classicism and especially to Beethoven's *Missa solemnis*. Dudley Buck and Horatio Parker, whose music shows a certain affinity with the "new German school" of Liszt and Wagner, are conspicuous among their contemporaries for specializing in choral music, and each wrote cantatas and oratorios as well as anthems and other short works. Parker's oratorio *Hora novissima* (1893), an 11-movement setting of medieval Latin religious poetry, reveals a sure – and thoroughly European – mastery of musical structure and the manipulation of choral and orchestral forces. (It was presented as the year's novelty at the 1899 Three Choirs Festival in England.) Many composers wrote dramatic secular cantatas that were popular in the USA during the last decades of the 19th century: Buck's *Scenes from The Golden Legend* (1879), Chadwick's *The Viking's Last Voyage* (1881), Paine's *The Nativity* (1883), Foote's *The Wreck of the Hesperus* (1887–8), Gilchrist's *The Legend of Bended Bow* (1888), Parker's *Dream-king and his Love* (1891), and Gleason's *The Culprit Fay* op. 14 were among the best known.

Important developments also occurred in the vernacular choral music of the 19th century. The shape-note tradition that had originated in singing-schools in the Northeast around 1800 had its primary flowering in the South. Shape-note tunebooks preserved much of the 18th-century singing-school repertory while adding to it adaptations and arrangements of religious folk music, camp-meeting spirituals and revival songs, and new compositions. Tunebooks such as Ananias Davisson's *Kentucky Harmony* (1816), *The Southern Harmony and Musical Companion* (1835) of William Walker, and *The Sacred Harp* (1844) compiled by Benjamin Franklin White and E. J. King were thus the first notated examples of folk music that had previously existed only in the oral tradition. Of particular importance to the history of the white spiritual in the early 19th century were collections by Joshua Smith (*Divine Hymns*, 1794), Jeremiah Ingalls (*The Christian Harmony*, 1805), and John Wyeth (*Repository of Sacred Music, Part Second*, 1813). A compromise between the music of the camp-meeting spiritual and the more formal hymn style of Mason and Hastings was achieved in Joshua Leavitt's *The Christian Lyre* of 1830, a precursor to the later collections of gospel hymns by William B. Bradbury, P. P. Bliss, W. Henry Sherwood, Charles Albert Tindley, and others.

In the second half of the century, black folk music (especially the spiritual) was also notated. The establishment of choral organizations at Fisk University, Hampton Institute, and other black colleges initiated concert performances of black religious folksong, and this soon led to published collections of arranged spirituals such as Theodore Seward's *Jubilee Songs: As Sung by the Jubilee Singers of Fisk University* (1872 and 1884) and Thomas Fenner's *Cabin and Plantation Songs as Sung by the Hampton Students* (1874). Even though a precise rhythmic, melodic, and harmonic notation obscured elements of the folk style, these and similar collections brought to light an important body of American music, and the spiritual has assumed a solid position in the 20th-century choral concert repertory. Black composers, among them Harry T. Burleigh, Nathaniel Dett, and William Grant Still, have not only arranged spirituals but have appropriated their style for use in original compositions (such as Dett's oratorio *The Ordering of Moses*, 1937).

For popular songs of the 19th century, a refrain "chorus" concluded many sentimental, patriotic, and minstrel songs. In performances, it was not uncommon for vocal ensembles to sing the "chorus." Occasionally, Stephen Foster, George F. Root, Henry Clay Work, and others wrote out their song refrains in parts: Foster's *Come where my love lies dreaming* (1855) and Work's *Crossing the Grand Sierras* (1869) are set in parts throughout.

The music of Charles Ives synthesizes various musical traditions of the 19th century and at the same time foreshadows 20th-century developments. Ives's *The Celestial Country* (1898–9) has much in common with the Romantic cantatas of Parker and his contemporaries, while several early psalm settings prefigure more modern compositional techniques, such as the use of bitonality in Psalm lxvii (?1894). The quotation of familiar melodies, a typically Ivesian device, occurs in *Lincoln the Great Commoner* (1912), where scraps of patriotic tunes emerge spasmodically from dense textural surroundings, and in the first movement of the monumental Symphony no. 4 for chorus and orchestra (1909–16), in which Lowell Mason's hymn *Watchman, tell us of the night* is superimposed on a contrasting orchestral background. Perhaps most significant among Ives's more than 40 extant choral works are the three *Harvest Home Chorales* (?1898–?1901) and the massive setting of Psalm xc (1894–1924).

The eminence of American composers in the 20th century, along with the high standards of performance attained by many high school, collegiate, community, church, and professional ensembles, has resulted in an extensive modern repertory. Large compositions with orchestra remain common, but smaller works, often grouped into cycles or suites and demanding more than modest performing ability, have attracted increasing attention.

Among those composers who have perpetuated the 19th-century Romantic styles, Howard Hanson, Leo Sowerby, and Randall Thompson have written effectively for chorus. Thompson's works in particular, ranging from the short *a cappella Alleluia* (1940) to longer cycles such as *The Peaceable Kingdom* (1936) and *Frostiana* (1959), have taken firm root in the repertory. Also conservative in approach are the works of Paul Creston, Samuel Barber, Gian Carlo Menotti, and Ned Rorem. Menotti's *The Unicorn, the Gorgon and the Manticore* (1956) points to the renewed interest in the Renaissance madrigal that is shared by a number of American composers.

Conspicuous use of materials borrowed from vernacular styles of this and past centuries is to be found in the choral works of William Grant Still, Virgil Thomson, Henry Cowell, Roy Harris, Aaron Copland, Ross Lee Finney, William Schuman, and Leonard Bernstein, though not as an exclusive stylistic characteristic. Schuman, especially, has written much choral music in a wide diversity of styles, from the international style of the unaccompanied *Carols of Death* (1958) to the Americanisms of the cantata *Casey at the Bat* (1976). Copland's most important choral work, the narrative *In the Beginning* (1947) for mezzo-soprano and unaccompanied chorus, is decidedly international in idiom.

Stravinsky, Schoenberg, Bloch, and Hindemith (all of whom settled in the USA) have influenced successive generations of American composers, including Roger Sessions and Elliott Carter as well as more prolific choral composers such as Louise Talma, Irving Fine, and Daniel Pinkham. Talma's *Let's Touch the Sky* (1952), a three-piece cycle with flute, oboe, and bassoon, is neoclassical in style, while her unaccompanied *La corona* (1955) applies serial principles. Fine's suites *The Choral New Yorker* (1944) and *The Hour Glass* (1949) and Pinkham's cantatas and other church compositions are accessible and ingratiating. The choral compositions of Norman Dello Joio, Vincent Persichetti, and Alan Hovhaness have been influenced tangentially by international styles.

Before the mid-1950s experimentation in nontraditional sound resources and application of new principles of musical construction lay chiefly in the domain of instrumental (and electroacoustic) music. Since then, however, a number of choral composers, often aided by the use of graphic notation, have explored various avant-garde techniques. Particularly important has been the exploitation of both voiced and unvoiced sound effects such as pitch approximation, choral glissandos, speaking, shouting, hissing, breath sounds, tongue clicks, and other coloristic devices suggested by the sound potential of language itself. Salvatore Martirano's *O, O, O, O, that Shakespeherian Rag* (1958) is an almost lexicographical exposition of new devices. Prominent among American composers who have employed avant-garde techniques in various combinations are Earle Brown, Kenneth Gaburo, Richard Felciano, Roger Reynolds, and Olly Wilson. As a result of their work, techniques including spatially separated and changing sound sources, indeterminacy, and the integration of live and electronically produced sound components have found expression in American choral music.

BIBLIOGRAPHY

T. Symmes: *The Reasonableness of Regular Singing* (Boston, 1720/*R*1975)
S. Gilman: *Memoirs of a New-England Village Choir* (Boston, 1829)
T. Hastings: *Dissertation on Musical Taste* (New York, 1853)
P. S. Gilmore: *History of the National Peace Jubilee* (Boston, 1871)
C. C. Perkins and J. S. Dwight: *History of the Handel and Haydn Society of Boston, Massachusetts* (Boston and Cambridge, MA, 1883–1934/*R*1977–9)
H. E. Krehbiel: *Notes on the Cultivation of Choral Music and the Oratorio Society in New York* (New York, 1884)
R. Walters: *The Bethlehem Bach Choir* (Boston, 1918, 2/1923)
G. P. Jackson: *White Spirituals in the Southern Uplands* (Chapel Hill, 1933/*R*1965)
J. F. Williamson: "Training of the Individual Voice through Choral Singing," *MTNAP*, xxxiii (1938), 52
W. J. Finn: *The Art of the Choral Conductor* (Boston, 1939, rev. and enlarged 2/1960)
A. T. Davison: *Choral Conducting* (Cambridge, MA, 1940)
L. Bergmann: *Music Master of the Middle West: the Story of F. Melius Christiansen and the St. Olaf Choir* (Minneapolis, 1944/*R*1968)
A. T. Davison: *The Technique of Choral Composition* (Cambridge, MA, 1945)
F. Waring: *Tone Syllables* (Delaware Water Gap, PA, 1945)
A. Rich: *Lowell Mason: "the Father of Singing among the Children"* (Chapel Hill, 1946)
W. J. Finn: *Sharps and Flats in Five Decades* (New York, 1947)
A. P. Britton: *Theoretical Introductions in American Tune Books to 1800* (diss., U. of Michigan, 1950)
American Choral Review (1958–)
The Choral Journal (1959–)
R. S. Hines: *The Composer's Point of View: Essays on Twentieth Century Choral Music by those Who Wrote it* (Norman, OK, 1963)
E. A. Wienandt: *Choral Music of the Church* (New York, 1965/*R*1980)
H. Ades: *Choral Arranging* (Delaware Water Gap, PA, 1966)
R. T. Daniel: *The Anthem in New England Before 1800* (Evanston, IL, 1966/*R*1979)
H. Swan: "The Development of a Choral Instrument," *Choral Conducting: a Symposium*, ed. H. Decker and J. Herford (Englewood Cliffs, NJ, 1973), 4–55
J. Mussulman: *Dear People . . . Robert Shaw: a Biography* (Bloomington, IN, 1979)
N. Temperley: *The Music of the English Parish Church* (Cambridge, England, 1979)
R. Robinson: "John Finley Williamson: his Contribution to Choral Music," *Choral Journal*, xxii/1 (1981), 5
E. D. White: *Choral Music by Afro-American Composers* (Metuchen, NJ, 1981) [bibliography]
R. A. Reid: *Russian Sacred Music and its Assimilation into and Impact on the American A Capella Choir Movement* (diss., U. of Texas, 1983)

JAMES G. SMITH (I, bibliography), THOMAS BRAWLEY (II)

Chotzinoff [Chatianov], **Samuel** (*b* Vitebsk, Belorussia, 4 July 1889; *d* New York, 9 Feb 1964). Pianist, critic, and administrator. Brought to the USA in 1896, he attended public schools in New York and Westbury, Connecticut. He studied piano with Jeanne Franko and Oscar Shack, and in 1905 played Mozart's Piano Concerto in D minor K466 with the Educational Alliance Orchestra. Without ever having attended high school, he was accepted by Columbia University, where he studied with D. G. Mason. In 1911 he left without graduating to tour as accompanist for Alma Gluck and Efrem Zimbalist; from 1919 he also accompanied Jascha Heifetz, whose sister Pauline he married on 10 December 1925. In the same year, Chotzinoff succeeded Deems Taylor as music critic on *The World*, a position he held until the paper merged with the *New York Telegram* in 1931. From 1934 to 1941 he was music critic on the *New York Post*; among his projects for the promotion of music appreciation was a series of recordings made anonymously by well-known artists and organizations, distributed at cost by the newspaper. In 1936 he was appointed music consultant for NBC radio, and his first assignment was to induce Toscanini to organize and conduct the station's new symphony orchestra, which gave its first concert on Christmas Day 1937. Chotzinoff commissioned the first opera composed expressly for radio, Menotti's *The Old Maid and the Thief*, first performed on 22 April 1939. From 1938 he was the official commentator for the broadcasts of the New York PO. He also lectured on music for the Carnegie Corporation and taught at the Curtis Institute in Philadelphia. In January 1949 he was appointed general music director of NBC radio and television and he became a pioneer in televised opera, sponsoring the first opera composed for television, Menotti's *Amahl and the Night Visitors* (1951).

WRITINGS

Eroica: a Novel on the Life of Beethoven (New York, 1930)
A Lost Paradise: Early Reminiscences (New York, 1955)
Toscanini: an Intimate Portrait (New York, 1956)
Day's at the Morn (New York, 1964)
A Little Nightmusic (London, 1964) [conversations with Heifetz, Horowitz, Menotti, Price, Rodgers, Rubinstein, and Segovia]

PHILIP LIESON MILLER

Chou Wen-chung (*b* Chefoo, China, 28 July 1923). Composer and teacher. He took a bachelor's degree in civil engineering while in China; in 1946 he moved to the USA to study architecture but soon devoted himself to music, studying with Slonimsky at the New England Conservatory (1946–9) and with Luening at Columbia University (MA 1954). Perhaps most significantly, between 1949 and 1954 he studied privately with Varèse, whose musical executor he is and whose *Nocturnal* he completed according to the composer's sketches. He has held several academic positions and was appointed professor of music at Columbia in 1972. After about 1970 Chou composed but little, having turned his attention to editing the music of Varèse and to activities on behalf of improving Chinese-American cultural relationships. In 1982 he was elected to the Institute of the American Academy and Institute of Arts and Letters. He has contributed articles on Varèse and on the application of Asian concepts to 20th-century Western music to the *Musical Quarterly* and other journals. In 1984 he was appointed Fritz Reiner Professor and director of the Fritz Reiner Center for contemporary music of Columbia University.

Chou's music is a remarkably successful fusion of Chinese tradition and sophisticated Western vocabulary and style. Almost all his major works take as points of departure Chinese poetry, painting, calligraphy, or philosophical and aesthetic ideas, and he is conscious of his place in the long tradition of Chinese art. With particular reference to *Landscapes* (1949) he wrote: "I was influenced by the same philosophy that guides every Chinese artist, be he poet, painter or musician: affinity to nature in conception, allusiveness in expression, and terseness in realization."

Landscapes is based on traditional Chinese melodic patterns, combined with somewhat impressionist orchestration and harmony. *All in the Spring Wind* (1952–3) develops this style in other directions. Pentatonic or quasi-pentatonic patterns are still present (this trait persisted into the 1960s) but the predominantly soft dynamic range of *Landscapes* has been widened, and a characteristically repetitive yet continually changing texture, frequently oscillating between registral extremes, is established, along with flexibly mobile tempos. *And the Fallen Petals* (1954) extends this language: Varèse-like intervallic structures and dynamic gestures and sonorities appear.

Two of Chou's principal compositions, *The Willows are New* and *Yü ko*, are based on traditional works for the *qin*, a Chinese zither. His interest in this instrument is related to his concern for the variety and richness of which individual notes are capable: the *qin* tablature includes more than 100 symbols, in order to achieve, as Chou has written, "subtle inflections in the production and control of its tones as a means of expression." Care in the treatment of single notes is particularly evident in *Cursive*, the title of which bears witness to Chou's continuing concern with the simultaneous spontaneity and discipline of Chinese calligraphy. Microtonal variations and similar subtle adjustments are found in the flute part; in general, the performers are given an unusual degree of rhythmic freedom within a controlled scheme.

From the early 1960s Chou explored principles of the *I Ching* compositionally, in *Metaphors* for wind orchestra (1960–61) and, especially, *Pien* (1966). The word "pien" means transformation and change, and also refers to a mode, constantly mutating within itself. In the work Chou employs six modes, each linked to an *I Ching* trigram or "image." "The progression of these modes," he has noted, "takes the form of six interacting textures, each of which has not only six variable modes in pitch organization but also six each in the organizations of duration, intensity and articulation." Chou's procedures produce a work in which both continual complex change and invariability are simultaneously perceived. Several of his works have been recorded.

WORKS

(all pubd unless otherwise stated)

Orch: Landscapes, 1949; All in the Spring Wind, 1952–3; And the Fallen Petals, 1954; In the Mode of Shang, 1956; Metaphors, wind, 1960–61; Riding the Wind, wind, 1964; Pien, chamber conc., pf, perc, wind, 1966

Ens: Suite, harp, wind qnt, 1950; 2 Miniatures from the T'ang Dynasty, 10 insts, 1957; Soliloquy of a Bhiksuni, tpt, brass, perc, 1958; To a Wayfarer, cl, harp, perc, str, 1958; The Dark and the Light, pf, perc, vn, va, vc, db, 1964; Yü ko, 9 insts, 1965; Ceremonial, 3 tpt, 3 trbn, 1968, unpubd; Yün, 2 pf, 2 perc, wind sextet, 1969

Inst: 2 Chinese Folksongs, harp, 1950; 3 Folk Songs, fl, harp, 1950; Valediction, kbd, 1957, unpubd; The Willows are New, pf, 1957; Cursive, fl, pf, 1963

Vocal: 7 Poems of the T'ang Dynasty, S/T, ens, 1951; Poems of White Stone, chorus, ens, 1958–9, unpubd

5 documentary film scores, 1960–66

Edns: E. Varèse: *Nocturnal* (1973), *Amériques* (1974), *Intégrales* (1980), *Octandre* (1980)

Principal publisher: Peters

BIBLIOGRAPHY

EwenD

N. Slonimsky: "Chou Wen-chung," *ACAB*, ix/4 (1961), 2

K. Kroeger: "Chou Wen-Chung: *Landscapes. And the Fallen Petals. All in the Spring Wind*," *Notes*, xx (1962–3), 406

Chou Wen-chung: "Towards a *Re*-merger in Music," *Contemporary Composers on Contemporary Music*, ed. E. Schwartz and B. Childs (New York, 1967), 308

Compositores de América/Composers of the Americas, ed. Pan American Union, xv (Washington, DC, 1969), 224

A. Cohn: "Very Special: the Music of Chou Wen-chung," *American Record Guide*, xxxvi (1969–70), 886

A. Frankenstein: "The Sound World of Chou Wen-Chung," *HiFi*, xx/7 (1970), 84

B. Archibald: "Chou Wen-Chung: *Pien* and *Yu Ko. Cursive. The Willows are New*," *MQ*, lviii (1972), 333

E. Pulido: "Chou Wen-Chung," *Heterofonia*, xi/6 (1978), 10

EDWARD MURRAY

Chowning, John M. (*b* Salem, NJ, 22 Aug 1934). Composer. He studied at Wittenberg University, Springfield, Ohio (BM 1959), with Boulanger in Paris (1959–62), and at Stanford University (PhD 1966), where he began teaching in 1966 and where he has directed the Computer Music and Acoustics Group (1966–74) and the Center for Computer Research in Music and Acoustics (from 1975). His honors include NEA grants and commissions from IRCAM.

Chowning is a pioneer in the development of computer music. As a graduate student at Stanford he established computer sound-synthesis facilities in collaboration with Max Mathews, the creator of the first computer music languages. Using frequency modulation, he developed "Chowning FM," which has been widely and successfully used to imitate instrumental and vocal sounds, and to create original electronic sounds. Under Chowning's direction Stanford has become one of the world's leading centers for research in computer music and computer sound synthesis, attracting a wide variety of musicians and researchers in related scientific fields; Pierre Boulez's interest in the computer music technology developed at Stanford led to a close association between that facility and IRCAM, the center for research in electroacoustic music that Boulez organized in Paris.

Chowning's musical output is small, and his mature works

are exclusively for computer-generated quadraphonic sound. His pieces are characterized by their focus on aspects of computer sound generation which have simultaneously occupied him as research topics. *Turenas* for example is closely associated with the development of "Chowning FM" techniques and of special programs to simulate moving sound sources, and *Phōnē* reflects Chowning's exploration of the use of FM techniques to synthesize singing voices.

See also COMPUTERS AND MUSIC, §4, for a detailed discussion of *Stria*.

WORKS

Cptr: Sabelithe, 1972; Turenas, 1972; Stria, 1977; Phōnē, 1981

BIBLIOGRAPHY

C. Roads: "John Chowning on Composition," *Composers and the Computer* (Los Altos, CA, 1985), 17

NEIL B. ROLNICK

Christensen, Axel W(aldemar) (*b* Chicago, IL, 23 March 1881; *d* Los Angeles, CA, 17 Aug 1955). Popular pianist, teacher, and editor. He studied piano as a youth and in 1903 opened a teaching studio in Chicago with the advertisement "Ragtime Taught in Ten Lessons." He simplified Afro-American ragtime piano playing to three essential melodic-rhythmic patterns or "movements," and these became the basis for his teaching method and for a series of instruction books he brought out from 1904. *Christensen's Rag-time Instruction Book for Piano* went through numerous revisions and title changes to incorporate early jazz and, eventually, swing styles. One method book remained in print until at least 1955.

Early in his career Christensen began establishing branch schools to teach ragtime piano. By 1914 he had founded 50 branches, and by 1918 he had schools in most major cities in the USA and also some abroad. By 1935 these schools had taught ragtime, popular piano, and jazz piano to approximately 500,000 (mostly white) pupils.

From 1914 to 1918 Christensen edited and published the monthly *Christensen's Ragtime Review*, the only magazine of the period devoted to ragtime. The *Review* heavily promoted Christensen's schools and publications, covered vaudeville and early jazz, and occasionally published information on the "classic ragtime" of Scott Joplin and his peers. In April 1918 the *Ragtime Review* was absorbed by *Melody* magazine, for which Christensen continued to contribute a regular column.

By the 1910s Christensen had become known as the "Czar of Ragtime," and was later given the title the "King of Jazz Pianists." He composed a number of piano rags, several of which he recorded in the 1920s. He was also active as a pianist–entertainer and musical monologuist. The Indiana University Archives of Traditional Music has an oral history collected from Christensen's son Carle Christensen.

WORKS

(selective list; all printed works published in Chicago unless otherwise stated)

Pf: Irmena Rag (1908); The Cauldron Rag (1909); Star and Garter: Ragtime Waltz (1910); The Minnesota Rag (1913); Webster Grove Rag (1915); Teasing the Classics (1923); Axel Grease (1924); Nighty Night! (New York, 1924); Boogie Woogie Blues (1927)

Pedagogical: Christensen's Rag-time Instruction Book for Piano (1904, 8/1920 as Axel Christensen's New Instruction Book for Rag and Jazz Piano Playing); Christensen's Rag Time Instructor no.2, for Advanced Pianists (1909, 3/1925); Instruction Book for Vaudeville Playing, Books 1–5 (1912); Saxophone Rag Jazz Instructor (1922); Axel Christensen's Instruction Book for Jazz and Novelty Piano Playing (1927, 3/1933); Axel Christensen's Instruction Book for Modern Swing Music (1936, 3/1954)

Principal publisher: Christensen

BIBLIOGRAPHY

R. Blesh and H. Janis: *They All Played Ragtime* (New York, 1950, rev. 4/1971), 130

E. A. Berlin: *Ragtime: a Musical and Cultural History* (Berkeley, CA, 1980/*R*1984 with addenda), 68, 217

JOHN EDWARD HASSE

Christgau, Robert (*b* New York, 18 April 1942). Rock critic. He attended Dartmouth College (BA in English, 1962) and became one of the first widely read rock critics with a column called "Secular Music" in *Esquire*, 1967–9. He was a columnist for New York's *Village Voice* from 1969 to 1972 and was popular-music critic for *Newsday*, a Long Island newspaper, from 1972 to 1974. Then he was named music editor (subsequently senior editor) and chief rock critic for the *Village Voice*, for which he edited the "Riffs" section of rock and jazz reviews (until 1985) and oversees an annual "Pazz and Jop" critics' poll of the year's best records. He is the author of two books, *Any Old Way you Choose it* (1973), a collection of his early writings, and *Christgau's Record Guide* (1981), a collection, thoroughly revised, of his short record reviews from the 1970s. Self-styled as "dean of American rock critics," Christgau has earned the appellation with the fierce intelligence of his prose; in his capacity as editor at the *Village Voice* he has schooled a generation of younger critics.

JOHN ROCKWELL

Christian, Charlie [Charles] (*b* Texas, 29 July 1916; *d* New York, 2 March 1942). Jazz guitarist. He grew up in a slum in Oklahoma City. His father was a blind guitarist and singer, his brothers Edward and Clarence were musicians, and Charlie himself built and played cigar-box "guitars" during his elementary school days. When he grew up, he became a much-admired local musician in Oklahoma, playing an amplified acoustic guitar as early as 1937. Word of his skill reached the writer and record producer John Hammond, who arranged for Christian to travel to Los Angeles in August 1939 for an audition with Benny Goodman. Goodman, deeply impressed by Christian's playing, engaged him and soon featured him on weekly radio broadcasts and in recordings; before the year was over he was a nationally prominent jazz soloist. Unfortunately his success was as brief as it was immediate: he contracted tuberculosis in mid-1941 and died a few months later.

Christian was among the first jazz guitarists to amplify his instrument in order to match the volume of wind instruments, and he was clearly the most brilliant soloist of his time on electric guitar. He was emulated by many swing-style players, and his posthumous impact on younger bop guitarists was enormous.

Ex.1 Extracts from Christian's solos on B. Goodman: *Breakfast Feud* (1941, Col. 36039), transcr. T. Owens

Had he lived longer he doubtless would have become the first great bop guitarist, for he was a regular participant in the Harlem jam sessions at which Dizzy Gillespie, Kenny Clarke, Charlie Parker, and a few others played as they gradually developed the new idiom. Some of Christian's favorite melodic figures (especially the chromaticisms indicated in ex. 1) became common property among bop musicians. Though his rhythmic and harmonic conceptions lagged somewhat behind those of the new leaders, Christian nevertheless remains among the most creative soloists of the swing period and a seminal figure in the evolution of the jazz guitar. (For illustration *see* GUITAR, fig.2.)

RECORDINGS

(selective list)

As leader: Swing to Bop, Up on Teddy's Hill, on *The Harlem Jazz Scene* (1941, Esoteric 4)

As sideman with B. Goodman: Flying Home (1939, Col. 35254); Stardust (1939, Col. 26134); Seven Come Eleven (1939, Col. 35349); Gone with "What" Wind (1940, Col. 35404); Breakfast Feud (1941, Col. 36039); Good Enough to Keep (Air Mail Special) (1941, Col. 36099)

As sideman: E. Hall: Profoundly Blue (1941, BN 17)

BIBLIOGRAPHY

L. Feather: *The Book of Jazz* (New York, 1957), 112ff

R. Ellison: "The Charlie Christian Story," *Saturday Review*, xli (17 May 1958), 42

H. Edmonds and B. Prince: *Charlie Christian: Harlem Jazz* (New York, 1958) [transcrs.]

S. Dance, ed.: *Jazz Era: the 'Forties* (London, 1961), 74ff

B. Green: *The Reluctant Art* (London, 1962)

J. Hammond: "The Advent of Charlie Christian," *Down Beat*, xxxiii/17 (1966), 22

R. Blesh: *Combo: USA* (Philadelphia, 1971/*R*1979), 161ff

M. Takayanagi: *Charlie Christian Jazz Improvisation* (Tokyo, 1975) [transcrs.]

J. Evensmo: *The Guitars of Charlie Christian, Robert Normann, Oscar Aleman* (Hosle, Norway, 1976)

J. Hammond and I. Townsend: *John Hammond on Record: an Autobiography* (New York, 1977)

J. Callis: *Charlie Christian, 1939–1941: a Discography* (London, 1978)

J. L. Collier: *The Making of Jazz: a Comprehensive History* (New York, 1978), 342ff

R. Denyer: *The Guitar Handbook* (London, 1982), 9

THOMAS OWENS

Christian, Palmer (*b* Kankakee, IL, 3 May 1885; *d* Ann Arbor, MI, 19 Feb 1947). Organist. In Chicago he studied with Clarence Dickinson and was organist and music director of Hyde Park Presbyterian Church (1906–9). He studied abroad with Karl Straube in Leipzig (1909–10) and with Alexandre Guilmant in Paris (1910–11) and then returned to Chicago to become organist of Kenwood Church (1911–18). After a lengthy illness, probably tuberculosis, he served for two years (1920–21) as municipal organist in Denver. From 1924 until his death he was university organist and professor at the University of Michigan.

Christian toured extensively as a solo recitalist and a performer with leading American orchestras. At Michigan he taught many pupils who were later prominent. He gave frequent recitals on the large Skinner organ in Hill Auditorium in Ann Arbor and also arranged performances by visiting recitalists who enriched the musical scene and widened his students' horizons. A reviewer in 1935 reported that while Christian followed the old practice of "orchestrating" Bach at the console, he also commanded "clean-cut playing, convincing climaxes, delicate nuances, splendid phrasing, [and] fine color-sense."

VERNON GOTWALS

Christian Reformed Church, music of the. *See* DUTCH REFORMED CHURCH, MUSIC OF THE.

Christian Scientists, music of the. *See* CHURCH OF CHRIST, SCIENTIST, MUSIC OF THE.

Christiansen, F(rederik) Melius (*b* Eidsvold, Norway, 1 April 1871; *d* Northfield, MN, 1 June 1955). Conductor, educator, and composer. Born into a family of amateur musicians, he came to the USA in 1888 and first went to San Francisco. In 1890 he accepted a post as conductor of the Scandinavian Band in Marinette, Wisconsin. Two years later he entered Augsburg College in Minneapolis and then the Northwestern Conservatory of Music in the same city (graduating in 1894); from 1897 to 1899 he studied at the Leipzig Conservatory. In 1903 he became the head of the music department at St. Olaf College, a Norwegian-Lutheran school in Northfield, Minnesota. He founded the St. Olaf Choir in 1911 and remained its director until 1942, when he retired and was succeeded by his son Olaf (1901–84).

Christiansen created a distinctive ensemble sound that influenced choral singing in churches and schools throughout the Midwest. His goal was the blending of individual voices into a unified sound; he favored *a cappella* performances and demanded a straight tone, uniform color, fluid technical flexibility, and absolute precision of pitch.

Christiansen arranged hundreds of Lutheran chorales and Norwegian folk melodies into accessible and effective four-part settings. His St. Olaf Choir series, published by the Augsburg Publishing House in Minneapolis between 1919 and 1944, included 216 works in 12 volumes, many of which have become the mainstay of small-town choral literature. He also wrote three cantatas, an oratorio, two pieces for violin, one for piano, two for band, and two collections of organ works.

BIBLIOGRAPHY

L. N. Bergmann: *Music Master of the Middle West: the Story of F. Melius Christiansen and the St. Olaf Choir* (Minneapolis, 1944/*R*1968)

R. D. Hanson: *An Analysis of Selected Choral Works of F. Melius Christiansen* (EdD diss., U. of Illinois, 1970)

CAROL J. OJA

Christie, William (Lincoln) (*b* Buffalo, NY, 19 Dec 1944). Harpsichordist and conductor. After learning piano and organ, he had harpsichord lessons from Igor Kipnis at the Berkshire Music Center while studying history and the history of art at Harvard University (BA 1966). He then went to Yale University, studying harpsichord with Ralph Kirkpatrick, organ with Charles Krigbaum, and musicology with Claude Palisca and Nicholas Temperley (MMus 1970). He taught at Dartmouth College, Hanover, New Hampshire (1970–71), and moved to France in 1971. While a member of the Five Centuries Ensemble (1971–5), a quartet specializing in early and 20th-century works, he continued to appear as a solo harpsichordist and from 1972 as a member of the Concerto Vocale, a Renaissance and Baroque ensemble. In 1978 he formed *Les Arts Florissants* (borrowing for its name the title of a work by Marc-Antoine Charpentier), a vocal and instrumental group that performs the French and Italian Baroque repertory; it has become known particularly for its contribution to the revival of 17th- and 18th-century singing techniques, on which Christie is an acknowledged expert. He taught at the Sommer Akademie für alte Musik in Innsbruck, Austria (1977–83), and in 1982 became the first American to be appointed professor at the Paris Conservatoire. Both as harpsichordist and conductor Christie is a musician of sensitivity and high style. His recordings of Monteverdi and his contemporaries and the great French Baroque masters from Charpentier to Rameau have earned numerous awards, including several Grand Prix du Disque in France and the Prix Mondiale du Disque (1982) in Switzerland for Charpentier's *Le mariage forcé*.

HOWARD SCHOTT

Christy, Edwin Pearce (*b* Philadelphia, PA, 28 Nov 1815; *d* New York, 21 May 1862). Minstrel manager and performer. In 1842 while helping the widow Harriet Harrington to run a tavern at Buffalo, he joined her son George (who adopted the name Christy) and Thomas Vaughn to sing blackface songs. The troupe was augmented with Lansing Durand and others, and toured upstate New York in 1843–5. Acting as manager, interlocutor (center man on the minstrel semicircle), ballad singer, and banjo player, Christy took the six-man troupe to Palmo's Opera House in New York on 27 April 1846. From 15 February 1847 to 15 July 1854 they played at Mechanics Hall, perfecting a minstrel show in three sections that appealed to all levels of audience. On 25 August 1847, at the close of their second Cincinnati visit, Christy's Minstrels gave Stephen Foster a benefit performance that included *Oh! Susanna*. From that time the troupe specialized in Foster premières, and in 1851 at Foster's request Christy published *Old Folks at Home* as his original song.

Christy's Minstrels sailed on 20 September 1854 for San Francisco, where they played at Music Hall until early in 1855, when Christy retired from performing and the group returned to New York. He was then manager, and bought circus properties and theaters (called Christy's Opera Houses) from Brooklyn to Chicago. He never visited England, although the troupe licensed to use his name opened on 3 August 1857 at St. James's Theatre in London with such success that "Christy Minstrels" became the generic name for blackface minstrels in Great Britain.

The texts of the troupe's most popular songs were published in the five volumes of *Christy's Plantation Melodies* (Philadelphia, 1851–6). The fifth volume includes an article by Christy, "The Original Christy Minstrels," which cites a New York State Supreme Court decision supporting his claim to having originated blackface minstrelsy. Fearing that his business would be ruined by Civil War reverses, Christy committed suicide by jumping from a window of his New York house.

BIBLIOGRAPHY

[Surrogate's Court, County of New York]: *In the Matter of . . . the Last Will and Testament of Edwin P. Christy, Deceased* (New York, 1864)

W. E. Ballantine: "Christy Minstrelsy: its Origin and Development in America and England," *English Illustrated Magazine*, xlii (1909), May, 42

E. L. Rice: *Monarchs of Minstrelsy* (New York, 1911), 19, 45

The National Cyclopedia of American Biography, xxiii (New York, 1933/*R*1967)

E. F. Morneweck: *Chronicles of Stephen Foster's Family*, ii (Pittsburgh, 1944), 377, 396ff

F. C. Davidson: *The Rise, Development, Decline and Influence of the American Minstrel Show* (diss., New York U., 1952), 79ff

ROBERT STEVENSON

Christy [Harrington], **George** (*b* Palmyra, NY, 6 Nov 1827; *d* New York, 12 May 1868). Minstrel performer. He changed his family name of Harrington after joining (as a jig dancer) the troupe of his stepfather, Edwin Pearce Christy, at Buffalo in 1839. He appeared with Christy's Minstrels in New York from 1847 to 1853, creating such roles as Lucy Long and Cachuca, and distinguishing himself in every part from endman and bone player to wench. In 1853 he joined Henry Wood at 444 Broadway to form Wood and Christy's Minstrels. After a fire destroyed their premises in December 1854, the company went on tour;

Edwin Pearce Christy (inset top), George Christy, Thomas Vaughn, and the Christy Minstrels: sheet-music cover of "Christy's Melodies," published sequentially from 1847 by Jaques and Brother, New York

they later returned to New York and reestablished themselves on Broadway. Christy formed his own company, George Christy's Minstrels, in 1858, and played at Tom Maguire's Opera House in San Francisco. In May 1859 he attempted to resume occupancy of the rebuilt 444 Broadway in New York, but was enjoined from doing so by his erstwhile partner Wood. Christy later performed at Niblo's Saloon (1859), with J. W. Raynor's Company (1864), with R. M. Hooley in Brooklyn (1865), at Kelly and Leon's at 720 Broadway (1866), and with G. W. H. Griffin (1867). His last appearance was in Brooklyn with Hooley's Minstrels ten days before his death. Christy published collections of his songs, dialogues, and jokes, including *Essense of Kentucky* (1862), and collaborated with Charley White in *Christy and White's Ethiopian Melodies* (1854), an especially large collection, with 291 songs.

BIBLIOGRAPHY

A. Pastor: *George Christy: or the Fortunes of a Minstrel* (New York, 1885)

E. L. Rice: *Monarchs of Minstrelsy* (New York, 1911), 20

C. Lengyel, ed.: *Music of the Gold Rush Era* (New York, 1972), 194

ROBERT STEVENSON

Chuck Wagon Gang. Country- and gospel-music group. Formed in 1935 by David Parker ("Dad") Carter (*b* Columbia, KY, *c*1890), the group was at different times a quartet and a quintet, made up chiefly of changing combinations of Carter and eight of his children; one of the longest-lived ensembles in country music, it existed until the 1980s. Both Carter and his wife, Carrie Brooks, learned gospel music during their childhoods in Texas, and were brought up in the singing-school tradition that flourished there. Migratory farm workers, they moved to Lubbock, Texas, in the early 1930s, and Carter and his children Jim, Anna, and Rose began performing on the radio station KFYO as the Carter Quartet. By 1936 they had taken the name Chuck Wagon Gang. At first their repertory included a variety of old-time, sentimental, novelty, and gospel songs, but by 1937 they had acceded to audience requests and had begun to specialize in gospel music. They also appeared on WBAP/KGKO (Fort Worth) and made their first recording for the American Record Company in San Antonio in 1936. These activities won them a wide new audience who liked their simple arrangements, their lilting part-singing, and Rose's distinctive soprano.

World War II interrupted the group's career, but by 1948 it was broadcasting and recording again; much of its repertory came from the popular shape-note songbooks issued by the Dallas gospel publisher Stamps-Baxter. Among the songs that it made famous were *A Beautiful Life* (1936), *Jesus hold my hand* (1941), *I'll fly away* (1948), and *Travelling on* (1950). In 1948 the group began to perform at live concerts (which it had done only rarely before), including the first all-gospel concert at Carnegie Hall, on 7 June 1963. "Dad" Carter retired in 1955 and was replaced by a nephew, Pat McKeehan; the members of the group at that time also included Carter's children Anna, Rose, and Roy, and Anna's husband, Howard Gordon.

CHARLES K. WOLFE

Chumash. American Indians inhabiting the coast of California from north of Los Angeles to San Luis Obispo and inland (*see* INDIANS, AMERICAN, fig. 1). The Chumash are part of the California-Yuman musical region identified by Nettl. Because of epidemics in the 1800s, which severely reduced the population, and acculturation, traditional Chumash musical practices have almost disappeared.

There were several traditional genres of songs. Work songs coordinated the work of groups: of this sort was the Canoe Song, sung as the men rowed their boats in the Santa Barbara Channel. Ceremonial songs included those for the recently deceased, for ancestors, and for mythological characters such as Coyote and Swordfish, as well as songs performed by members of the Antap secret society, the members of which sought to exercise control over the natural and supernatural worlds.

One major function of music in Chumash society was to entertain. Rules as to the time of year when most dances might be performed do not seem to have been prescribed; dances might be requested by the wealthier Chumash (who could afford to pay the dancers and singers) or by the host of a festival. The dances most often requested became popular because of their complexity or beauty; until the late 1800s one such, a Swordfish Dance, was given at functions as diverse as weddings and mourning gatherings. Dances for entertainment and recreation had as many as five parts and were accompanied by two or three singers, who might also blow whistles or keep time with clappers. Dances performed at ceremonies such as puberty rites had more participants, and the initiates themselves also took part.

The musical instruments of the Chumash are those played by most Californian Indian groups – bone or reed whistles, flutes with four or six finger-holes, concussion sticks and split reeds to mark the rhythm, turtle-shell, tin-can, or deer-hoof rattles, and bullroarers. The musical bow is recorded as having been used by the Chumash, but it may have been introduced by the Yaqui Indians. The Chumash traditionally did not use drums, but in recent years they have introduced the large drums and drumming styles of the Plains Indians.

Though it varies widely, the predominant scale in Chumash songs is hemitonic hexatonic; the repetition of the tonic, major 2nd, minor 3rd, perfect 4th, major 3rd, minor 2nd, and perfect 5th are (in that order) the most commonly occurring intervals. Some songs have leaps of as much as a 13th. The vocal style is full-throated with occasional falsetto by both men and women. Many songs end with a series of rhythmic grunts, the meter of which is often unrelated to the song itself; these ending formulae ensure that singers and instrumentalists stop together. Songs are most often strophic with syllabic texts. The common meters are 4/4 and 6/8 (and subdivisions of those meters), and phrases of odd lengths occur frequently, sometimes to accommodate the text; conversely, words are altered to fit a regular meter, particularly in dance-songs, resulting in some words that are found only in song.

Although the traditional musical culture of the Chumash is all but extinct, through the efforts of the ethnologist John Harrington and several elderly Chumash a substantial collection of fieldnotes on Chumash culture has been amassed. In addition several dozen wax-cylinder recordings of Chumash songs were made by Harrison, which are now held in the Smithsonian Institution (taped copies are at the Library of Congress).

See also INDIANS, AMERICAN, esp. §I, 4(ii)(c).

BIBLIOGRAPHY

B. Nettl: *North American Musical Styles* (Philadelphia, 1954)

T. C. Blackburn: *December's Child: a Book of Chumash Oral Narratives* (Berkeley, CA, 1975)

D. T. Hudson and J. Timbrook: *Eye of the Flute* (Santa Barbara, CA, 1977)

G. Tegler: "An Index of Harrington's Chumash Recordings," *UCLA Institute of Archaeology Occasional Papers*, iii (1979), 22

D. T. Hudson: *Breath of the Sun* (Banning, CA, 1980)

GARY TEGLER

Chung. Family of instrumentalists of Korean origin.

(1) **Myung-Wha Chung** [Koo] (*b* Seoul, Korea, 19 March 1944). Cellist. At the age of 13, as the youngest performer to win the Korean National Competition, she made her début with the Seoul PO. From 1961 she studied with Rose at the Juilliard School (BA 1965) and in 1968 with Piatigorsky in Los Angeles. Her American début was in San Francisco in 1967 and her European in Italy at Spoleto in 1969; in 1971 she won first prize in the Geneva International Music Competition, Switzerland. She has performed with numerous orchestras abroad and in the USA (including the BBC, Hallé, and Royal PO in England, the Suisse Romande, and the San Francisco SO, Detroit SO, and Houston SO), and has recorded Tchaikovsky's Variations on a Rococo Theme with the Los Angeles PO. She also performs chamber music frequently with her sister (2) Kyung-Wha Chung and her brother (3) Myung-Whun Chung. She became an American citizen in 1971.

(2) **Kyung-Wha Chung** (*b* Seoul, Korea, 26 March 1948). Korean violinist, sister of (1) Myung-Wha Chung. She played Mendelssohn's Violin Concerto in Seoul at the age of nine, and three years later came to New York to study with Galamian at the Juilliard School. In 1967 she won the Leventritt Award jointly with Pinchas Zuckerman. Her New York PO début was a year later and in 1970 she made her first European appearance, with the London SO under Previn. She has toured widely, playing regularly with international orchestras. Her recordings include concertos by Tchaikovsky, Mendelssohn, Berg, Bartók, Beet-

hoven, Bruch, Elgar, Lalo, Prokofiev, Saint-Saëns, Stravinsky, and Walton. She performs chamber music regularly and makes frequent appearances with her sister and brother.

(3) **Myung-Whun Chung** (*b* Seoul, Korea, 22 Jan 1953). Pianist and conductor, brother of (1) Myung-Wha Chung. He made his début as a pianist at the age of seven with the Seoul PO. After coming to the USA he attended the Mannes College, studying piano with Reisenberg and conducting with Carl Bamberger. In 1974 he won second prize in the Tchaikovsky piano competition in Moscow. From 1975 to 1978 he studied conducting with Ehrling at the Juilliard School and then was associate conductor of the Los Angeles PO until May 1981. He has been appointed conductor with Saarland radio in Saarbrücken, Germany. He has appeared as guest conductor with many orchestras, including the London PO, Israel PO, Cleveland SO, National SO, and Detroit SO, and he has also conducted Puccini's *Madama Butterfly* in Philadelphia and San Francisco. As a pianist he has recorded with Charles Dutoit and the Los Angeles PO, and has toured internationally with the family chamber trio. He took American nationality in 1973.

ELIZABETH OSTROW

Church. Firm of music publishers. On 21 April 1859 Oliver Ditson of Boston bought the catalogue of Baldwin & Truax (established in 1851 by David Truax in Cincinnati, named Curtis & Truax in 1855 and Baldwin & Truax in 1857), and in association with John Church, Jr. (*d* Boston, MA, 19 April 1890), founded the firm of John Church, Jr., in Cincinnati. On 1 March 1869 Church bought the half-interest of Ditson and in partnership with his bookkeeper John B. Trevor established the firm of John Church & Co., which became incorporated in 1885 as John Church Co. Church bought the catalogue of George Root & Sons of Chicago in 1873, and at about this time William Sherwin joined the firm. In 1881 James R. Murray became chief director of publications and editor of the firm's periodical, *Music Visitor* (1871–97).

Church became notable for publishing the operas and, particularly, the celebrated marches of John Philip Sousa (*see* PATRIOTIC MUSIC, fig.2); the firm's other publications include operas and operettas by Julian Edwards and Reginald De Koven, as well as a set of piano pieces by Theodore Presser and works by contemporary American composers. At Church's death his son-in-law R. B. Burchard became president; W. L. Coghill became manager of publications in 1919, and in 1930 the entire catalogue was sold to Theodore Presser Co.

BIBLIOGRAPHY

W. S. B. Mathews, ed.: *A Hundred Years of Music in America* (Chicago, 1889/*R*1970), 394

H. Dichter and E. Shapiro: *Early American Sheet Music* (New York, 1941/*R*1977), 168, 181, 239

E. C. Krohn: *Music Publishing in the Middle Western States before the Civil War* (Detroit, 1972), 20

Thompson10, 420

ERNST C. KROHN

Church of Christ, Scientist, music of the. The church was founded in Boston in 1879 by Mary Baker Eddy, as a result of her discovery in 1866 of healing through prayer and her subsequent development of the doctrine of Christian Science; this teaches that all human ills are caused by the failure to understand and obey God, and that the cure for these ills can be achieved only through such understanding and obedience. When groups of Christian Scientists began to form, Eddy organized the Christian Science Mother Church, the First Church of Christ, Scientist, of which all other groups (though self-governing) are considered to be branches; the movement now has adherents worldwide.

There is no official service book for the Church of Christ, Scientist, and worship is extremely simple. There is no choir, nor are there special musical services. According to Eddy's *Manual of the Mother Church* (1895), the music shall be "of an appropriate religious character and of a recognized standard of musical excellence." It normally consists of organ (or piano) selections, three hymns, and, on Sunday, a solo. The choice of solos of "musical excellence" has on occasion proved difficult, and the Christian Science Publishing Society has therefore issued helpful volumes. Texts of hymns and solos are at all times carefully integrated with the subjects of the lesson-sermons, which are standard throughout the movement. A Christian Science hymnal was issued in 1892, and a second in 1912; the present hymnal (1932) includes 400 items, and a new hymnal is under consideration. Each hymnal has been a marked advance on its predecessor. In view of the church's international character, a number of hymns from other countries are included, particularly from England, Germany, and Scandinavia. Complete translations of the hymnal have been issued in French, German, Spanish, Danish, Dutch, Norwegian, and Swedish. Editions in Japanese, Portuguese, and Greek contain 110, 230, and 173 hymns respectively.

The Extension of the Mother Church in Boston, seating 5200, was built in 1903. Its four-manual organ, originally by Hook and Hastings, was extensively remodeled in 1951–2 by the Aeolian-Skinner Organ Co. The organists have included Walter Young (1912–24), Ruth Barrett Phelps (1932–61), and Thomas Richner (1972–). Among the church's solo singers Caroline Hudson Alexander, Mack Harrell, and Frederick Jagel were widely known. The church is occasionally host to the American Guild of Organists.

H. EARLE JOHNSON

Church of Jesus Christ of Latter-day Saints [Mormon Church], **music of the.** The Church of Jesus Christ of Latter-day Saints (frequently called the Mormon Church), which has a membership of more than five million worldwide (approximately three million in the USA and Canada), was formally organized by Joseph Smith in Fayette, New York, in 1830. The small original group saw itself as a "new Israel," invested with divine authority and commissioned by angelic messengers to re-establish the church of Jesus Christ after centuries of apostasy. The *Book of Mormon*, which the Church accepts as scripture along with the Bible, is an account of the ministry of Christ in ancient America to which Smith was led through a vision. The original community in New York state was followed by settlements at Kirtland, Ohio (1831–8), several in Missouri (1831–9), and around Nauvoo, Illinois (1839–46), all of which were abandoned for various social and political reasons. After Smith and his brother were killed at Carthage, Illinois, in 1844, Mormon leaders looked further west for a place of refuge and in February 1846 began an exodus towards the Rocky Mountains, reaching the valley of the Great Salt Lake in July 1847. This settlement was eventually established as SALT LAKE CITY, Utah, where the Church of Jesus Christ of Latter-day Saints has become a vital force in Christianity both nationally and internationally.

From its inception, the Church felt the need for a musical tradition that would reflect its unique origin and purpose. One of the first revelations that Smith received after the organization of the Church directed his wife, Emma, to "make a selection of sacred hymns": *A Collection of Sacred Hymns, for the Church of the Latter Day Saints*, containing 90 texts, was copyrighted in 1835. This vest-pocket edition, as the preface indicated, was to serve until "more are composed, or till we are blessed with a copious variety of the songs of Zion." *A Collection of Sacred Hymns*, edited by Parley P. Pratt, Brigham Young, and John Taylor, was published in England in 1840; it was later used in the USA, with 25 editions up to 1912 (as *Sacred Hymns and Spiritual Songs* from the ninth edition, 1851). The Church's General Music Committee published a volume of *Latter-day Saint Hymns* (Salt Lake City, 1927), which was followed by further revisions and enlargements in collections entitled simply *Hymns* in 1948 and 1950; a new hymnal, *Hymns* (1985), contains recently composed hymns as well as traditional favorites.

The dramatic history of the Church in its early decades and its wealth of new and sometimes startling theological principles provided a rich source of materials for poets and composers. Many new hymns focused on motifs associated with the "restoration of the Gospel." Others dealt with the Church's strong millennial expectations and the "gathering of Israel," the building of Zion, and themes of faith and courage through times of hardship and persecution.

Parley P. Pratt (1807–57) was perhaps the most skilled of the early writers. His restoration hymn "The morning breaks, the shadows flee," set by the Latter-day Saint composer George Careless (1839–1932), is typical. Eliza R. Snow (1804–87), a talented and prolific writer, contributed many texts. Perhaps the best known is "O my Father," which refers to the Latter-day Saint belief in a pre-mortal existence where mankind was prepared for the challenges of life on earth. The popular "Come, come, ye saints" by William Clayton (1814–79), set to an old English tune, is often regarded as a typical Mormon song. It is a hymn of affirmation, written in the midst of great trial and suffering as the pioneers crossed the plains and mountains in search of religious freedom. More than any other, it expresses the undaunted courage that sustained the Saints during their journey.

Forced to leave their settlements in the American Midwest, the Mormon pioneers, at the sacrifice of seemingly more important items, brought musical instruments and even the bell of their abandoned temple with them in their epic journey to the West. Singing and dancing at times alleviated the hardships of the exodus, and allowed them a way to express the joy they felt in their new-found freedom in the wilderness. Shortly after the pioneers had reached Salt Lake Valley, a temporary structure called the Bowery (1847–52) was erected for assembly and worship, including hymn singing. The appointment of the Welsh convert John Parry as choir leader in 1849 could be regarded as the foundation of the Salt Lake Mormon Tabernacle Choir, which, through its international tours, radio and television appearances, and numerous recordings, has become one of the best-known choirs in the world (see illustration). The 350-member choir sings for the Church's general conferences, held twice a year, and at other large assemblies in the Tabernacle, but reaches a wider audience through its Sunday morning broadcast "Music and the Spoken Word," a program of inspirational and devotional music begun in 1929, televised from 1962, and now carried by about 600 radio and 30 television stations in the USA and Canada. Conductors have included Anthony C. Lund (1916–35), J. Spencer Cornwall (1935–57), Richard P. Condie (1957–74), and Jerold D. Ottley (from 1975). The Tabernacle, with its domed roof and marvelous acoustics, was completed in 1867, and has served as a concert hall and public auditorium as well as a house of worship. The unusual shape of the building amplifies massed choral and organ sonorities and contributes greatly to the choir's quality of sound.

Latter-day Saint worship at its best is simple and dignified,

The Salt Lake Mormon Tabernacle Choir in the Mormon Tabernacle, Salt Lake City

with little emphasis on liturgy. A typical Sunday service includes an organ prelude and postlude and the singing of several hymns by the congregation. After the Sacrament (Communion) there is often a short musical performance by an individual or ensemble before one or more lay speakers address the worshipers. Each local congregation is expected to have a choir of its own to provide music for regular Sunday services and special occasions. Just as there are no paid clergy in the Church, so there are no paid musicians, and all music positions are filled by volunteers. Thus the cultivation of musical skills is encouraged in every family, and the Church maintains several programs to train lay musicians.

The Church fosters many types of musical activity: festivals, pageants, and musicals of all sorts, both sacred and secular. There are numerous regional choruses and instrumental groups, and the Church's colleges and universities, notably at the campuses of Brigham Young University at Provo, Utah, and in Hawaii, cultivate music extensively. Although there is little demand for extensive art music in the typical church service, Latter-day Saint composers have written a number of anthems and several fine oratorios, such as the *Oratorio from the Book of Mormon* by Leroy Robertson (1896–1971) and *The Redeemer* by the Tabernacle organist Robert Cundick (*b* 1926). Crawford Gates (*b* 1921) has written an impressive score for chorus and orchestra (1956) for the Hill Cumorah Pageant, staged each summer since 1937 near Palmyra, New York, and a popular musical, *Promised Valley*, commissioned for the centennial celebration of the founding of Salt Lake City (1947). Collections of Mormon folk music include A. M. Durham's arrangements of *Pioneer Songs* (1932), *Mormon Songs from the Rocky Mountains*, edited by T. E. Cheney (1968), and *Ballads of the Great West*, edited by Austin and Alta Fife (1970).

BIBLIOGRAPHY

E. W. Tullidge: *The History of Salt Lake City and its Founders* (n.p., 1885), esp. 774ff
L. M. Durham: *The Role and History of Music in the Mormon Church* (thesis, State U. of Iowa, 1942)
J. S. Cornwall: *A Century of Singing: the Salt Lake Mormon Tabernacle Choir* (Salt Lake City, 1958)
H. H. Macaré: *The Singing Saints: a Study of the Mormon Hymnal, 1835–1950* (diss., U. of California, Los Angeles, 1961) [incl. suppl.: "A Comprehensive List of all Hymns appearing in all Mormon Hymnals"]
N. B. Weight: *An Historical Study of the Origin and Character of Indigenous Hymn Tunes of the Latter-day Saints* (diss., U. of Southern California, 1961)
J. S. Cornwall: *Stories of our Mormon Hymns* (Salt Lake City, 1963)
J. L. Slaughter: *The Role of Music in the Mormon Church, School, Life* (diss., Indiana U., 1964)
L. M. Durham: "On Mormon Music and Musicians," *Dialogue: a Journal of Mormon Thought*, iii/2 (1968), 19
C. J. Kauman: *The Mormon Tabernacle Choir* (New York, 1979)
G. Petersen: *More than Music: the Mormon Tabernacle Choir* (Provo, Utah, 1979)
The Doctrine and Covenants (Salt Lake City, 1981), esp. §25

ROGER MILLER

Chusid, Martin (*b* Brooklyn, NY, 19 Aug 1925). Musicologist. He studied at the University of California, Berkeley (BA 1950, MA 1955, PhD 1961), and taught at the University of Southern California from 1959 to 1963. Since then he has been on the faculty of New York University, where he became professor in 1967; he was chairman of the department of music from 1967 to 1970 and associate dean of the graduate school of arts and science from 1970 to 1972. In 1976 he was appointed director of the American Institute for Verdi Studies at the university.

Chusid's principal fields of research are the music of Schubert and opera, particularly the operas of Mozart and Verdi. In addition to his articles he has contributed *A Catalog of Verdi's Operas* (1974) and the Norton Critical Score of Schubert's B minor Symphony (1968, 2/1971). In editing the symphony Chusid amended the version in the Breitkopf & Härtel collected edition on the basis of the autograph facsimile; the revised (Norton) edition incorporates a newly discovered scherzo fragment. Chusid is actively involved in the new critical edition of Verdi's works, for which he edited *Rigoletto* (1983).

PAULA MORGAN

Cibecue. American Indian group, subdivision of the Western Apache; *see* APACHE.

Cincinnati. City in Ohio (pop. 385,409; metropolitan area 1,401,470) on the Ohio River.

1. Early history. 2. May Festival and Symphony Orchestra. 3. Other musical organizations. 4. Music education. 5. Other musical activities.

1. EARLY HISTORY. Settled in 1788, Cincinnati became the first capital of the Northwest Territory in 1790 and was incorporated as a town in 1802. It was named after the Society of Cincinnati, an association of former officers of the Revolutionary Army. By 1840 it was the sixth largest city on the North American continent.

In the early years of the city, while it was part of the American frontier, Cincinnati gave little support to serious musical activity outside the church. When a traveling musician, Signor Muscarelli, gave a concert there in 1823 the climax of the evening was an imitation of dogs and cats on the violin; the violinist Joseph Tosso, a former pupil at the Paris Conservatoire who lived in Cincinnati from 1827 to 1887 and played an Amati, made his reputation with *The Arkansaw Traveler*, a well-known "specialty number" with recitation. But various choral organizations existed briefly during this period, instrumentalists played for dances and

1. Brass band in a Fourth of July procession at Cincinnati: engraving from "Frank Leslie's Illustrated Newspaper" (29 July 1865)

minstrel shows, and orchestras occasionally performed overtures by Handel or Mozart. The first showboats appeared on the Cincinnati riverfront in 1831.

During the 1840s immigration from Europe and particularly from Germany increased sharply, significantly affecting the cultural life of the city. By 1850 half the citizens were European-born, and almost 30% of the population was German. As Cincinnati acquired increasing numbers of trained musicians from Europe, amateur singing societies and instrumental ensembles became more professional. In 1849 the German and Swiss singing societies joined with similar ones from Louisville, Kentucky, and Madison, Indiana, to hold a Sängerfest in Cincinnati with a small orchestra and a combined chorus of 118, performing music by C. F. Zoellner, Mozart, Conradin Kreutzer, J. F. Reichardt, and F. W. Abt, among others. On this occasion the German Sängerbund of North America was formed. Annual Sängerfests were held thereafter in various cities, with Cincinnati as host again in 1851, 1867, and 1870. By 1870 the chorus had expanded to 2000 members, and the merchants of Cincinnati built for the Sängerfest a wooden exposition hall seating 5000. Brass bands performed for municipal occasions (see fig. 1).

The period after the Civil War marked the beginning of Cincinnati's formal cultural life. Of crucial importance was the role played by Theodore Thomas. Cincinnati was a stop on his first orchestral tour (1869) and for several years thereafter. In his autobiography he wrote:

> Cincinnati, one of the oldest settlements in the West, not only possesses wealth and culture, but it also has sincere and capable musicians, who by their influence as teachers developed a genuine love and understanding of music in that community. . . . For many years music has been a large part of the daily life of the Cincinnati people, and the city at that time [the 1870s] ranked second only to New York, Boston or Philadelphia, in musical achievement. When I made my first visit to Cincinnati with my orchestra, in 1869, even at that early time I found excellent choral societies there, and an orchestra superior to that of any city west of New York.

2. May Festival and Symphony Orchestra. During Thomas's 1871 visit he was invited to establish a music festival using choruses from throughout the West. Thomas agreed, and in May 1873 the festival was held in Exposition Hall for one week, using an expanded orchestra of 108 members and a chorus of 800; at each performance the hall was nearly filled. The festival was made a biennial affair, and Thomas continued as its music director. After the second festival in 1875 a group of citizens raised the money to replace the wooden Exposition Hall with a permanent brick structure. The new Music Hall (capacity 3600) opened with the third May Festival, which was postponed until the completion of the building in 1878. After the fourth festival a permanent May Festival chorus of Cincinnatians was established. Audiences traveled hundreds of miles for the event, which became annual in 1967. Next to the Worcester Music Festival (begun in 1858), it is the oldest music festival in the USA. Music directors succeeding Thomas (1873–1904) were Frank Van der Stucken (1906–12, 1923–7), Ernst Kunwald (1914–16), Eugène Ysaÿe (1918–20), Frederick Stock (1929), Eugene Goossens (1931–46), Fritz Busch (1948–50), Josef Krips (1954–60), Max Rudolf (1963–70), Julius Rudel (1971–2), James Levine, who was born in Cincinnati (1974–8), and James Conlon (from 1979).

The forerunner of the Cincinnati SO was the Cincinnati Orchestra, which began in 1872 under George Brand and augmented Thomas's orchestra for the May Festivals. In 1894 the Cincinnati Orchestra Association was founded, with stockholders and guarantors, to establish a symphony orchestra; Mrs. William

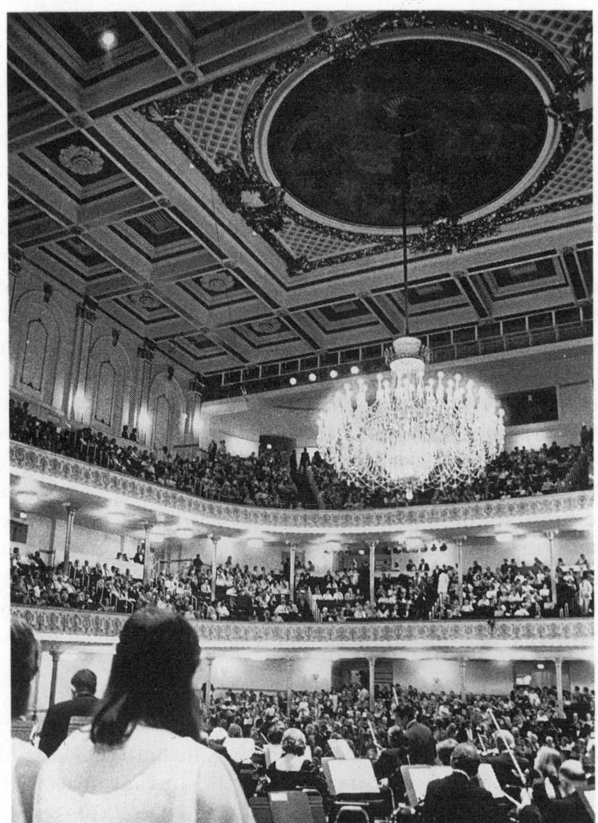

2. Interior of the Music Hall, Cincinnati, 1975

Howard Taft was its first president. In its first season it presented three series of concerts in Music Hall, conducted by Van der Stucken, Anton Seidl, and Henry Schradieck; for the following season Van der Stucken was engaged as permanent conductor. At the close of its 13th season (1906–7) the Orchestra Association, balking at demands made by the musicians' union, disbanded the orchestra. After a compromise it was reorganized in 1909 with Leopold Stokowski as conductor (1909–12). Succeeding conductors were Kunwald (1912–17), Ysaÿe (1918–22), Fritz Reiner (1922–31), Goossens (1931–47), Thor Johnson (1947–58), Max Rudolf (1958–70), Thomas Schippers (1970–77), Walter Susskind (music adviser, 1977–80), and Michael Gielen (1980–86). Jésus López-Cobos has been appointed to succeed Gielen in 1986. The orchestra has toured widely throughout the USA and Europe and was the first American orchestra to undertake a world tour (1967). A summer home for the orchestra, at a site on the Ohio River east of the city, opened in 1984. (*See also* Orchestras, §2(vi).)

3. Other musical organizations. In the late 19th and early 20th centuries touring companies brought opera to the city two or three times a year. In 1920 the Cincinnati Summer Opera Association was formed to present opera in an open-air band shell at the zoo. The enterprise was successful; later the audience area was covered against the weather, guarantee funds were raised, and internationally known artists were engaged. Fausto Cleva was music director from 1934 to 1963, and after a period with no regular music director, James de Blasis was appointed general director in 1974. Performances were transferred from the zoo to the Music Hall in 1972 and in 1975 the association's name was

changed to Cincinnati Opera, presenting an annual season of five or six operas from 1980.

In 1928 the Cincinnati Institute of Fine Arts was established with an endowment of $3,500,000 to support the Cincinnati SO and the Art Museum. After World War II the institute launched an annual fund drive, modeled on the community's united drive for social services, to support the Art Museum, the Taft Museum, the Cincinnati SO, and the Summer Opera. In 1978 the Fine Arts Fund expanded to include the Contemporary Arts Center, the Cincinnati Ballet, the Playhouse in the Park, and the May Festival. Cincinnati was the first city in the USA to inaugurate a fund drive involving the entire business and private community in support of the arts.

The Cincinnati Ballet was started as a resident company in Music Hall in 1970. Using mostly local performers, it presents an annual season of dance and undertakes tours of the region. The Cincinnati Composers' Guild was formed in 1978 to support and promote the work of local composers; it organizes concerts and lectures and publishes a quarterly newsletter. Other musical organizations include the Matinee Musicale (established 1911), the Cincinnati Chamber Music Society (1929), the Cincinnati Chamber Orchestra (1974), and the Cincinnati Pops Orchestra (1977).

In 1970–71 Music Hall was completely remodeled (fig.2); having excellent acoustics, it has served as the center of Cincinnati's musical activities, and houses the Cincinnati SO, the May Festival, the Summer Opera (since 1972), the Cincinnati Ballet, and a series of popular music concerts. Riverfront Coliseum (capacity 17,000), opened in 1975, is the home of many sports and entertainment attractions, especially rock groups.

4. MUSIC EDUCATION. Cincinnati was one of the first American cities to give regular music instruction in the public schools (from around 1845). Timothy B. Mason, son of Lowell Mason (i), was the first supervisor. In the 1840s and 1850s there were a few music schools and many private music teachers. In 1867 Clara Baur (1835–1912), a pianist and singer who had immigrated from Germany in 1849, founded the Cincinnati Conservatory of Music on the model of the Stuttgart Hochschule für Musik, where she had studied. The conservatory flourished under her direction, and after her death her niece Bertha Baur (1858–1940) continued the direction until her own retirement in 1930, when the Institute of Fine Arts took charge of the conservatory.

The College of Music of Cincinnati was founded in 1878 in Music Hall. Theodore Thomas moved to Cincinnati to be its first director but resigned in 1880 after a dispute with the board of directors. Like the conservatory, the College of Music appointed European musicians to its staff and offered training in performance for both professionals and amateurs, attracting students from all areas of the USA.

The College and the Conservatory merged in 1955, and in 1962, as the College-Conservatory of Music, it became part of the University of Cincinnati, occupying its own new building in 1967. In 1982 the school had over 125 instructors, including the LaSalle Quartet (in residence at the college from 1953). The academic staff includes many members of the Cincinnati SO, and the cross-fertilization between professional work and teaching draws excellent musicians to Cincinnati. The school has about 750 undergraduate and 300 graduate students. It offers BM, BFA, BA, MM, MA, DME, and PhD degrees, in performance (including dance), broadcasting, theater, arts administration, music education, theory, composition, and musicology. The library contains about 45,000 books and scores and 16,000 recordings, and includes the Harline collection of cinema and television music manuscripts, and the Chujoy collection of dance memorabilia, books, and periodicals. (*See also* LIBRARIES AND COLLECTIONS, §3.)

5. OTHER MUSICAL ACTIVITIES. Cincinnati was an important center of organ building in the 19th century. Two prominent makers of musical instruments, the Baldwin Piano & Organ Co. (founded 1865) and the Rudolph Wurlitzer Co. (1890, maker of the "Mighty Wurlitzer" theater organ and later of the jukebox), were in Cincinnati for many years, though both firms now manufacture their products elsewhere. Music publishing flourished in the 19th century, and in the early 1900s the important firm of music engravers and printers Otto Zimmerman & Son was active there; the Willis Music Co. and World Library Publications still carry on the city's publishing tradition. *Church's Musical Visitor* was an influential national periodical in the late 19th century; the music review *Billboard* was printed in Cincinnati from 1894 to 1982.

The Cincinnati Musicians' Protective Union (established 1881) was one of the first trade unions for musicians in the USA and played a leading role in founding the National League of Musicians (1886) and the American Federation of Musicians (1896). It was honored by becoming Local #1 of the American Federation of Musicians.

Cincinnati was an important center of ragtime composing and publishing, ranking perhaps fourth in the nation after New York, Chicago, and St. Louis. More than 110 ragtime works were issued there by publishers who included John Arnold, Great Eastern Publishing Co., the Groene Music Publishing Co., Joseph Krolage Music Publishing Co., and Mentel Bros. Publishing Co. Leading local composers of ragtime included Homer Denney, Henry J. Fillmore, Albert Gumble, Clarence M. Jones, Louis H. Mentel, and Floyd H. Willis. During the 1920s the Vocalstyle company issued player piano rolls. It was one of the first to print the words to popular songs on its rolls, and it also issued rolls by such musicians as Jelly Roll Morton. It was acquired in 1927 by the QRS Company of Chicago.

The city played its part in the development of rock-and-roll with the establishment there of King Records in 1945, one of the first companies to record rhythm-and-blues. King was responsible for discovering and promoting the music of James Brown, Clyde McPhatter, Hank Ballard, Bullmoose Jackson, Otis Redding, Bill Doggett, and Nina Simone, among others, and continued to be an important factor in popular music through the mid-1960s.

Among the varied personalities associated with the musical life of Cincinnati are Stephen Foster, who wrote many of his early songs while a clerk there in 1846–50; James Monroe Trotter, author of the first account of black musicians in America (*Music and some Highly Musical People*, 1878), who received his early musical training there; Henry E. Krehbiel, music critic of the *Cincinnati Gazette* from 1874 to 1880 before going on to the *New York Tribune*; the composers and bandmasters Henry J. Fillmore (who became known as the "March King" when Sousa's career was in decline), Frank Simon, and Herman Bellstedt, Jr.; and, more recently, Rembert Wurlitzer, the violin authority; Frank Foster, arranger for Count Basie and others; James Levine, the conductor; and Patricia and J. Ralph Corbett, whose philanthropy since the mid-1960s has been a vitalizing element in the musical life of the city.

BIBLIOGRAPHY

Church's Musical Visitor (1871–97)

F. E. Tunison: *Presto! From the Singing School to the May Musical Festival* (Cincinnati, 1888)

T. Thomas: *A Musical Autobiography* (Chicago, 1905/*R*1964, abridged)

C. F. Goss: *Cincinnati, the Queen City 1788–1912* (Chicago and Cincinnati, 1912)

F. R. Ellis: "Music in Cincinnati," *MTNAP*, viii (1913), 7

M. L. Storer: *History of the Cincinnati Musical Festivals and of the Rookwood Pottery by their Founder* (Paris, 1923)

Golden Jubilee: Cincinnati Music Hall 1878–1928 (Cincinnati, 1928)

L. C. Frank: *Musical Life in Early Cincinnati and the Origin of the May Festival* (Cincinnati, 1932)

"Clara Baur," *The National Cyclopedia of American Biography*, xxvi (New York, 1937/*R*1967), 438

C. de Chambrun: *Cincinnati: Story of the Queen City* (New York and London, 1939)

M. H. Osburn: *Ohio Composers and Musical Authors* (Columbus, OH, 1942)

J. Lewis: *An Historical Study of the Origin and Development of the Cincinnati Conservatory of Music* (diss., U. of Cincinnati, 1943)

H. R. Stevens: "The Haydn Society of Cincinnati, 1819–1824," *Ohio State Archaeological and Historical Quarterly*, lii (1943), 95

V. A. Orlando: *An Historical Study of the Origin and Development of the College of Music of Cincinnati* (diss., U. of Cincinnati, 1946)

O. D. Smith: "Joseph Tosso, the Arkansaw Traveler," *Ohio State Archaeological and Historical Quarterly*, lvi (1947), 16

H. R. Stevens: "Adventure in Refinement: Early Concert Life in Cincinnati 1810–1826," *Bulletin of the Historical and Philosophical Society of Ohio*, v (1947), no.3, p.8, no.4, p.22

——: "Folk Music on the Midwestern Frontier 1788–1825," *Ohio State Archaeological and Historical Quarterly*, lvii (1948), 126

F. Hodges: "Stephen Foster, Cincinnatian and American," *Bulletin of the Historical and Philosophical Society of Ohio*, viii (1950), 83

H. R. Stevens: "New Foundations: Cincinnati Concert Life 1826–1830," *Bulletin of the Historical and Philosophical Society of Ohio*, x (1952), 26

——: "The First Cincinnati Music Festival," *Bulletin of the Historical and Philosophical Society of Ohio*, xx (1962), 186

C. L. Gary: *A History of Music Education in the Cincinnati Public Schools* (diss., Western Reserve U., Cleveland, 1963)

J. E. Holliday: "Cincinnati Opera Festivals during the Gilded Age," *Cincinnati Historical Society Bulletin*, xxiv (1966), 131

Cincinnati Symphony Orchestra: a Tribute to Max Rudolf and Highlights of its History (Cincinnati, 1967)

J. E. Holliday: "The Cincinnati Philharmonic and Hopkins Hall Orchestras, 1856–1868," *Cincinnati Historical Society Bulletin*, xxvi (1968), 158

K. W. Hart: *19th Century Organ Builders of Cincinnati* (diss., U. of Cincinnati, 1972)

J. E. Holliday: "Grand Opera Comes to the Zoo," *Cincinnati Historical Society Bulletin*, xxx (1972), 7

I. Kolodin: "A Foresight Saga in Cincinnati," *Saturday Review* (20 May 1972), 38

P. Hart: "Cincinnati Symphony Orchestra," *Orpheus in the New World: the Symphony Orchestra as an American Cultural Institution* (New York, 1973), 264

J. S. Stern, Jr.: "The Queen of the Queen City: Music Hall," *Cincinnati Historical Society Bulletin*, xxxi (1973), 7

"100th Anniversary May Festival," *Cincinnati Enquirer* (18 May 1973), suppl.

R. T. Gifford: "Cincinnati's Music Hall: a Century of Continuity and Change," *Cincinnati Historical Society Bulletin*, xxxvi (1978), 79

Z. L. Miller and G. F. Roth: *Cincinnati's Music Hall* (Virginia Beach, VA, 1978)

R. C. Vitz: "Starting a Tradition: the First Cincinnati May Musical Festival," *Cincinnati Historical Society Bulletin*, xxxviii (1980), 33

R. McNutt and S. Rosen: "When King was King," *Cincinnati Enquirer Magazine* (5 July 1981), 14

J. Chute: "Progressive Programming in the Queen City," *Symphony Magazine*, xxxiii/3 (1982), 21

L. R. Wolz: *Opera in Cincinnati: the Years before the Zoo, 1801–1920* (diss., U. of Cincinnati, 1983)

J. E. Hasse: *Cincinnati Ragtime* (Cincinnati, 1983)

SAMUEL F. POGUE (with JOHN EDWARD HASSE)

Cinema organ. *See* THEATER ORGAN.

Circus music. A particular type of band music associated with traveling circuses. Since brass bands did not come into their own until about 1830, after the perfection of the keyed bugle, circus music from the 1790s consisted of fiddle and drum accompaniment. Large circuses in the 1880s, however, supported bands of 24 to 36 players, mostly of brass and timpani; they almost never included strings. Since the music for the show was almost continuous, there were often two or more lead trumpeters to share the solo work.

From about 1890 circus bandmasters realized the need for special music: a single act usually required several changes of mood, and the whole show might call for more than 200 cues and changes, all of which had to be smoothly executed. They wrote marches and "triumphal entries" to introduce the show's spectacles, fanfares and drum rolls to build excitement for major feats, and galops, schottisches, and other pieces in tempos chosen to match the requirements of the different acts. The players had to be flexible and keep time with the circus performers, sliding from one piece to the next in response to whistled cues from the circus equestrian director.

One of the earliest circus bandmasters was Edward Kendall; others of note were Albert Sweet, Ned Brill, Carl Clair (see illustration p.448), Henry Kyes, Eddie Woeckener, and Victor Robbins. Among those also prominent in the composition of circus music were Fred Jewell (*Quality Plus*, *Crimson Petal*, and *March to Mecca*), H. A. Vandercook (*Olevine*), Walter P. English, Charles E. Duble (*Bravura*, *Wizard of the West*, and *Under White Tents*), Russell Alexander (*Crimson Flush* and *Thunder and Blazes*), Henry Fillmore (*The Circus Bee* and *Rolling Thunder*), Merle Evans (*Fire Jump*, *Red Wagons*), and Karl L. King (*Robinson's Grand Entry*, *King Henry*, *Circus Days*, and perhaps the most popular circus march of all, *Barnum & Bailey's Favorite*). Many circus pieces are named for shows, and they are often dedicated to circus personalities.

After the 1895 season, when the Ringling Brothers Circus opened their shows with a performance of music by Liberati's concert band, circus bands often played a formal concert of classical music before the show. The main circus was often followed by a series of variety acts, which required orchestral (rather than band) accompaniment; some members of the band usually played in the orchestra. The circus would usually parade through each town on its tour to advertise its performances, led by the main band aboard an ornate wagon. Novelty instruments were also used, such as band organ, bagpipes, flageolet, shaker chimes, Una-Fon, and steam calliope; the last, in particular, became associated with the circus. The music chosen to arouse public interest in the show was rousing and the pieces were played without repeats. In addition, the parade might include a sideshow band, a clown band, and perhaps a band made up of ushers, cowboys, women, and children, or others associated with the circus. The sideshow band, consisting of about eight performers, played outside the circus sideshow to attract business, and inside to accompany the novelty acts and presentation of freaks. Continuing the traditional association of minstrel shows with circus performances, the sideshow bands played dixieland music, and after the turn of the century were nearly all made up of Blacks; they included many strong musicians and two outstanding leaders, Arthur Wright and P. G. Lowery.

The makeup of circus bands changed in the 1960s. A large circus would often employ just a bandleader, or a leader and a few players, and recruit local musicians, while smaller shows

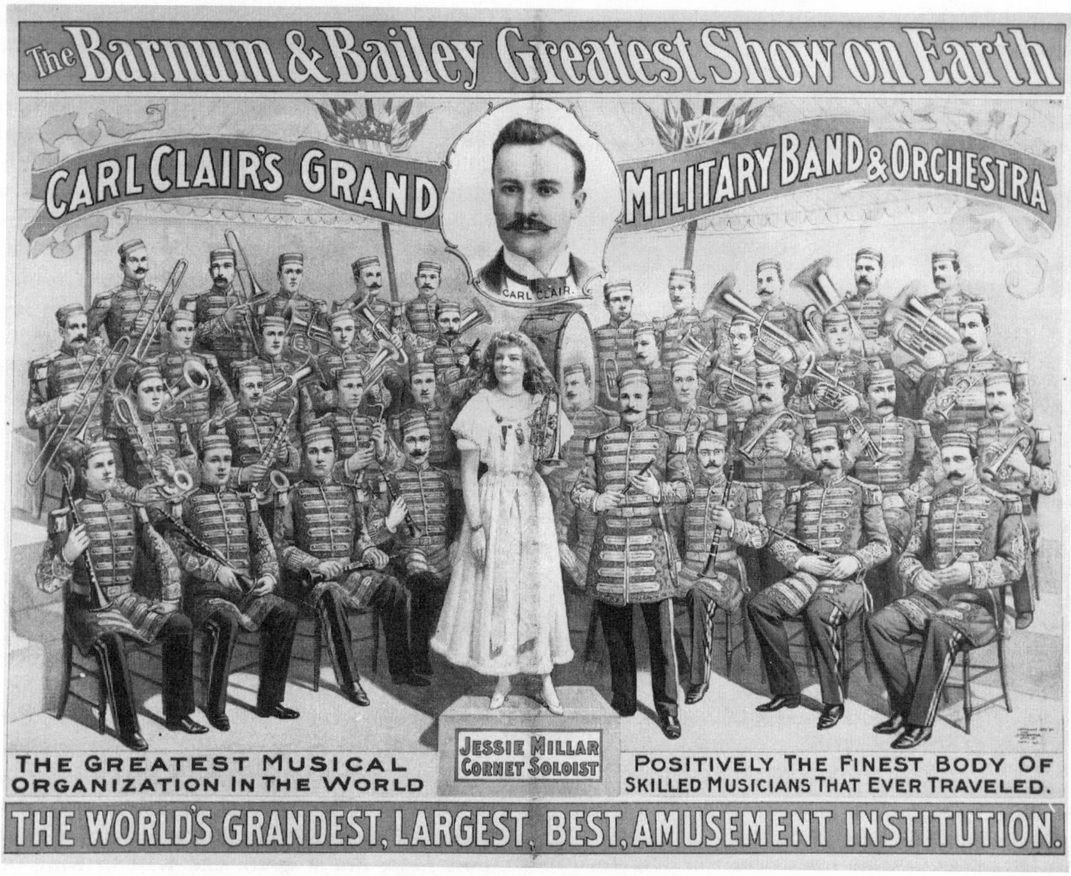

Advertisement for Barnum & Bailey's circus (1906), featuring Carl Clair's Grand Military Band and Orchestra

might carry a band of only six to 12 players, or even simply an electric organ accompanied by trumpet and drums. Sideshow bands disappeared, but were sometimes replaced by an air calliope. The traditional music, however, is still played by the professional circuses in operation today.

See also BANDS.

BIBLIOGRAPHY

T. Parkinson: "Big Tops Bloom but Chanteys Disappear," *The Billboard*, lxix/22 (1957), 1

H. R. North and A. Hatch: *The Circus Kings* (Garden City, NY, 1960)

C. P. Fox and T. Parkinson: *The Circus in America* (Waukesha, WI, 1969)

S. O. Braathen: "Circus Windjammers," *The Bandwagon*, xv/3 (1971), 12

——: "Chords and Cues," *The Bandwagon*, xv/5 (1971), 4

Circus Fanfare (1971–)

S. O. Braathen and F. O. Braathen: "The Parallel Development of Circuses and Bands in America," *The Bandwagon*, xvi/6 (1972), 4

TOM PARKINSON

Cisneros, Eleonora de [Broadfoot, Eleanor] (*b* Brooklyn, NY, 1 Nov 1878; *d* New York, 3 Feb 1934). Mezzo-soprano. She studied with Francesco Fanciulli and Adeline Murio-Celli in New York and sang for Jean de Reszke, who arranged for her to sing at the Metropolitan Opera. During the 1899–1900 season she performed Rossweise (*Die Walküre*) and Amneris (*Aida*) on tours and in New York, and claimed to be the first American-trained singer to perform at the Metropolitan. She went to Paris for further studies with Angelo Tabadello and at Turin in 1902 sang Wagner's Brünnhilde, Ortrud, and Venus, as well as Dalila and Amneris. From 1904 to 1908 she sang regularly at Covent Garden. At La Scala she was selected by Gabriele D'Annunzio to create the role of Candia in Alberto Franchetti's *La figlia di Iorio* in 1906; she also sang in the first performances there of Tchaikovsky's *The Queen of Spades* (1906) and Strauss's *Salome* (1906) and *Elektra* (1909). She claimed to be the first American singer to perform at Bayreuth, during the 1908 season. From 1906 to 1908 she was a leading singer at Hammerstein's Manhattan Opera House and then appeared with the Chicago-Philadelphia Opera Company (singing Amneris at the opening performance of the company in Chicago on 3 November 1910) until 1916. In 1911 she performed in London and Australia with the Melba Opera Company. She continued to sing, mostly in Europe, into the 1920s, but after making tours on behalf of the war effort during World War I her career suffered. With a large, statuesque bearing and a voice of remarkable volume and range, she was able to sing such dramatic soprano roles as Santuzza (*Cavalleria rusticana*), Gioconda, and Kundry (*Parsifal*), as well as mezzo-soprano and alto roles including Carmen, Laura (*La Gioconda*), Urbain (*Les Huguenots*), and Azucena (*Il trovatore*).

BIBLIOGRAPHY

"De Cisneros, Eleonora," *NAW*

SUSAN FEDER

Citkowitz, Israel (*b* Skierniewice [now in Poland], 6 Feb 1909; *d* London, England, 4 May 1974). Composer, teacher, and critic. He was brought to the USA at the age of three and became an American citizen. He studied with Copland and Sessions in New York, and from 1927 to 1931 with Boulanger in Paris. In 1932 his String Quartet was performed at the first Festival of Contemporary American Music at Yaddo. During the 1930s he published considerable criticism of new music, especially in *Modern Music* and *Musical Mercury*; his essay "The Role of Heinrich Schenker" (*MM*, xi, 1933, p. 18) was probably the first in English to treat that theorist. In 1939 he was appointed teacher of counterpoint and composition at the Dalcroze School of Music in New York. In 1969 he moved to London. Although not a prolific composer, he gained some recognition for his choral and chamber music.

WORKS
(*selective list*)

Unacc. choral: The Lamb, 1936; Songs of Protest, 1936

Songs: 5 Songs from "Chamber Music" (Joyce), 1930; Strings in the Air and Earth, 1930; song cycle (Blake), 1v, str qt, 1934; song cycle (Frost), 1936; Gentle Lady

Inst: Passacaglia, pf, 1927; Sonatine, pf, 1929; Str Qt, 1932; Andante tranquillo, str qt, 1932; Movements, str qt

BIBLIOGRAPHY

C. R. Reis: *Composers in America: Biographical Sketches* (New York, 3/1938 of *American Composers*, rev. and enlarged 4/1947/*R*1977)

M. Lederman: *The Life and Death of a Small Magazine*, ISAMm, xviii (Brooklyn, NY, 1983)

H. WILEY HITCHCOCK

Claflin, (Alan) Avery (*b* Keene, NH, 21 June 1898; *d* Greenwich, CT, 9 Jan 1979). Composer. In addition to studying law and banking, he studied music with Davison at Harvard University; in Paris, following the end of World War I, he encountered Satie, Auric, Poulenc, and Milhaud. In 1919 he entered the French-American Banking Corporation in New York, where he remained for 35 years, becoming president in 1947. Despite his career in business, Claflin found time for composing and for participation as a board member or officer in the ACA, CRI, Contemporary Music Society, and American SO. His dual interests invite comparison with Ives, whom he knew in New York business circles. *Lament for April 15*, his best-known composition, combines both his careers in that it is a five-voice setting of verbatim excerpts from the Internal Revenue Service 1040 Form ("Who must file . . ."). Its première at the Berkshire Music Festival (11 August 1955) was reported in *Time*, *Fortune*, *Cosmopolitan*, and the *New Yorker* as well as in *Le Figaro*, and in Australia. Many of his works date from after his retirement in 1954 and display a well-crafted, conservative style reminiscent of Poulenc's music. Claflin received the French Croix de Guerre in 1918 and the Légion d'honneur in 1948, and in 1965 the ACA awarded him its Laurel Leaf "for distinguished achievement in fostering and encouraging American music."

WORKS

Opera: The Fall of Usher (Claflin, after Poe), 1920–21; Hester Prynne (D. Claflin, after Hawthorne), 1929–33; La grande bretèche (G. R. Mills, after Balzac), 1946–8; Uncle Tom's Cabin (D. Claflin, after Stowe), 1964

Orch: Ballet Music from Hewlett, 1928–48; Moby Dick Suite, 1929, arr. 2 pf; Chapter III: a Sym., 1934–6; Concert Allegro, 1938; Sym. no. 2, 1941–3; Fishhouse Punch, 1945, arr. 2 pf, 1953; Teen Scenes, str orch, 1954–5; 4 Pieces for Orch (Sym. no. 3), 1956; Pf Conc. (Conc. giocoso), 1957, arr. 2 pf 6 hands; several other works

Other: 15 inst works, incl. Pf Trio, 1922, Str Qt, 1937, arrs. of orch works; 6 vocal works, incl. Mary of Nazareth, SSATTBB, org, 1948–54, Lament for April 15, SSATB, 1955, songs (Thurber, E. Lear, Cummings)

Principal publishers: ACA, Associated

BARBARA A. PETERSEN

Clapp, Philip Greeley (*b* Boston, MA, 4 Aug 1888; *d* Iowa City, IA, 9 April 1954). Composer and teacher. He studied composition, chiefly with Walter R. Spalding, at Harvard (BA 1908, MA 1909, PhD 1911). He worked on his dissertation at the British Museum, and studied composition and conducting with Max von Schillings in Stuttgart; while in Europe, he acted as special music correspondent for the *Boston Evening Transcript*, a position he held until 1919. An important influence on Clapp was his association with Muck, who made it possible for him to conduct the Boston SO in his First and Third Symphonies; he also appeared as a guest conductor with the Cincinnati SO (1913) and the American Orchestral Society (1929). Clapp was a teaching fellow at Harvard University (1911–12), director of music at the Middlesex School for Boys in Concord (1912–14), acting head of the Gloucester School of Music (1914–15), and director of music at Dartmouth College (1915–18); from June to December 1918 he was leader of the 73rd Coast Artillery Band. In 1919 he was appointed professor and head of the music department at the University of Iowa, where he remained until his death. The Bruckner Society of America awarded him the Bruckner Medal of Honor in 1940 and the Mahler Medal of Honor in 1942. Clapp's harmony derives directly from that of Wagner, Mahler, Strauss, and Debussy; his orchestration is remarkably clear, and his textures are generally homophonic, particularly in the symphonies. He favored established forms, often treating themes cyclically.

WORKS

Operas: The Taming of the Shrew (Clapp, after Shakespeare), 1945–8; The Flaming Brand (Clapp), 1949–53

Orch: 3 sym. poems, Norge, 1908, Song of Youth, 1910, Summer, 1912; 12 syms., E, 1908, e, 1911, E♭, 1916–17, A, 1919, D, 1926, B, 1926, A, 1928, C, 1930, E♭, 1931, F, 1935, C, 1942, B♭, 1944; Dramatic Poem with Solo Trbn, 1912, 3rd movt added 1940; A Highly Academic Diversion on 7 Notes, 1931; Ov. to a Comedy, 1933; Fantasy on an Old Plain Chant, 1938; Prologue to a Tragedy, 1939; Conc., b, 2 pf, orch, 1941; A Hill Rhapsody, 1945; The Open Road, ov., 1948

Other inst: Str Qt, 1909; Vn Sonata, 1909; Sonatina, pf, 1923; Suite, brass sextet, 1938; Prelude and Finale, wind qnt, 1938; Ballad, 2 pf, 1938; Concert Suite, 4 trbn, 1939; Fanfare Prelude, 1940

Vocal: O Gladsome Light (Longfellow), 1908; A Chant of Darkness (H. Keller), chorus, orch, 1919–24, rev. 1929, 1932–3; 3 partsongs, ?1940

MSS in *DLC*, *IaU*, *MB*, *NN*, *PP* (orch works)

Principal publishers: Boosey & Hawkes, Boston Music, J. Fischer

BIBLIOGRAPHY

EwenD

F. Swihart: "Philip Greeley Clapp," *Des Moines Register* (9 May 1948)

D. R. Holcomb: "Philip Greeley Clapp," *Books at Iowa*, no. 17 (1972), 3

——: *Philip Greeley Clapp: his Contribution to the Music of America* (diss., U. of Iowa, 1972)

DOROTHY REGINA HOLCOMB/R

Clappé, Arthur A. (*b* Cork, Ireland, 22 July 1850; *d* Washington, DC, 22 Nov 1920). Bandmaster, educator, administrator, and composer. He graduated from the Royal Military School of Music (Kneller Hall) in 1873, and became bandmaster of a British regiment stationed in India. In 1877 he was appointed director of the Governor-General's Foot Guards in Ottawa, Canada. On moving to New York in 1884 he became editor of *Metronome*, a magazine published by Carl Fischer, remaining in that position until 1891. On Gilmore's recommendation he was appointed teacher of music and director of the US Military Academy Band at West Point, New York; he served there until 1895. In 1893, at the request of the music publisher Harry Coleman, he founded *The Dominant*, becoming its owner and publisher in 1895, and continuing in that capacity until 1910. At his suggestion the US Army Music School was established under his leadership in 1911 at Fort Jay, New York, as a branch of the Institute of Musical Art. In 1918 he was commissioned a captain in the US Army and charged with the administration of a training school for bandmasters. After the armistice he was called to Washington to assist in drafting plans for the reorganization of the army, and to offer recommendations concerning its bands and bandmasters. Clappé's achievements as an educator and administrator made him one of the most important figures in the development of American military music. His compositions, many of which were written during his service in Canada, are for the most part unpublished. His published writings include *The Band Teacher's Assistant* (1888), *The Wind-band and its Instruments* (1911/*R*1976), and *The Principles of Wind-band Transcription* (1921).

BIBLIOGRAPHY

F. R. Seltzer: "Famous Bandmasters in Brief: Capt. Arthur A. Clappé," *Jacobs' Band Monthly*, iv/7 (1919), 10

RAOUL CAMUS

Clark [née Elliott], **Frances (Mary)** (*b* Angola, IN, 27 May 1860; *d* Salt Lake City, UT, 14 June 1958). Music educator. From 1884 to 1891 she taught in Indiana public schools and then held positions in Illinois (1891–6) and Iowa (1896–1903) before being appointed supervisor of music in Milwaukee (1903–11). In 1907, she presided over the founding meeting of the Music Supervisors (now Educators) National Conference and came to be regarded by music educators as the "Mother of the Conference." In 1911, Clark became head of the educational department of the Victor Talking Machine Co. at Camden, New Jersey, where she developed a comprehensive music appreciation program and promoted the use of recordings in the public schools, emphasizing especially folk music and dance. An early and enthusiastic supporter of music education by radio, she became a paid consultant to RCA Victor in 1936. She retired in 1947 and moved to Salt Lake City. Clark was co-organizer (with Percy Scholes) of the Anglo-American Music Conference in 1928, an officer of the Music Section of the National Education Association (1905–9), and a founder and life member of the National Federation of Music Clubs.

BIBLIOGRAPHY

E. B. Birge: "Supervisor Sketches: Frances Elliott Clark," *The Musician*, xxxvii/6 (1932), 9
"Clark Centennial Memorial Tributes," *MEJ*, xlvi/5 (1960), 78
J. F. Cooke, L. V. Hollweck, M. M. Keith, and H. G. Kinscella: "Frances Elliott Clark," *MEJ*, xlvi/5 (1960), 20
E. M. Stoddard: *Frances Elliott Clark: her Life and Contributions to Music Education* (diss., Brigham Young U., 1968)

GEORGE N. HELLER

Clark, Mattie Moss (*b* Selma, AL, 1928). Gospel singer and composer. After graduating from high school she moved to Detroit, where in 1958 she organized the Southwest Michigan State Choir of the Churches of God in Christ. This 300-voice choir gained national acclaim through its appearances at the national conventions of the Churches of God in Christ in Memphis and frequent performances in Chicago. Its first recording, *Save Hallelujah* (Savoy 14077, 1963), was enthusiastically received. Clark was a founding member of the Gospel Music Workshop of America (1968). In 1973 she became director of music for the International Churches of God in Christ, a position in which she directs the massed choirs of the churches at national conventions, and organizes and trains choirs for the crusades held by the church throughout the USA. She has inspired such gospel singers as Donald Vails, Beverly Glenn, and Rance Allen, all of whom were members of her choir. She has written more than 100 gospel songs, of which the best known is *Salvation is Free* (1963). Clark's brother is Bill Moss, leader of the gospel group known as the Celestials, and her daughters, led by Elbernita "Twinkie" Clark, have formed a group known as the Clark Sisters.

BIBLIOGRAPHY

T. Heilbut: *The Gospel Sound: Good News and Bad Times* (New York, 1971/*R*1975)

HORACE CLARENCE BOYER

Clark, Roy (Linwood) (*b* Meherrin, VA, 15 April 1933). Country-music singer, songwriter, guitarist, banjoist and fiddler. Born into a musical family, he learned to play banjo, fiddle, and guitar as a teenager. He won the national Country Music Banjo Championship in 1949 and 1950. He had by then moved to Washington, DC, where he played for square dances. During the 1950s he played guitar and banjo for Jimmy Dean, Marvin Rainwater, and George Hamilton IV, and recorded as a solo artist for several labels. In the early 1960s he toured with Wanda Jackson, and secured a solo contract with the label for which she recorded, Capitol Records, in 1961. He has had a succession of charted songs: *Tips of my fingers* (no.10, 1963), *Through the eyes of a fool* (no.31, 1964), *I never picked cotton* (no.5, 1970), and *Thank God and Greyhound* (no.6, 1970). A talented comedian as well as musician, Clark is especially popular on tours and in Las Vegas nightclubs, and has appeared on many television variety shows; beginning in 1969 he hosted the television show "Hee Haw" with Buck Owens. A versatile musician and entertainer whose personal popularity has been instrumental in increasing national acceptance of country music, Clark has also served as an international ambassador for the genre.

RECORDINGS
(selective list)

Tips of my fingers (Cap. 4956, 1963); Through the eyes of a fool (Cap. 5099, 1964); Yesterday, when I was young (Dot 17246, 1969); I never picked cotton (Dot 17349, 1970); Thank God and Greyhound (Dot 17355, 1970); Honeymoon Feeling (Dot 17498, 1974); If I had to do it all over again (Dot 17605, 1976)

BIBLIOGRAPHY

"Clark, Roy," *CBY 1978*

RONNIE PUGH

Clarke, Henry Leland (*b* Dover, NH, 9 March 1907). Composer and scholar. His father was a Unitarian minister in Saco, Maine (1914–44), where Clarke studied piano, organ, and violin, and began composing. His studies at Harvard University (1924–9, 1931–2, 1944–7) included a course in composition with Gustav Holst and culminated in a dissertation on John Blow. Clarke also studied in Paris with Boulanger (1929–31) and in New York and Bennington with Hans Weisse and Otto Luening (1932–8). He taught at Bennington College, Westminster Choir College, Vassar College, UCLA, and the University of Washington, Seattle (1958–77), from which he retired as professor emeritus.

A distinctive, ingenious treatment of scales appears in several of Clarke's works from the 1950s. *Monograph* for orchestra (1952) is restricted to the pitches C, D♯, E, F, G, A♭; *Six Characters* for piano, the Third Quartet, and *A Game that Two can Play* show various other restrictions. Clarke's essay "Musical Scales *ad hoc* and *ad hominem*" (*Journal of Aesthetics and Art Criticism*, xviii

(1959–60), 472) discusses the principle involved in these pieces and in a wide range of styles from folksong to Tcherepnin and John Verrall. More original and characteristic is the invention that Clarke calls "wordtones, that is, assigning a specific pitch in the melody to each word of the text and returning to that particular pitch every time the text returns to that particular word." This device first occurs unsystematically in the Cummings song *When any mortal* (1960), and is fully developed in the opera *Lysistrata* and many shorter works such as the cycle *William Penn Fruits of Solitude*. In *Lysistrata* the wordtones help to underline the perennial elements of satire, farce, suspense, radical hope, and complex heroism.

The function of both kinds of calculated limitation is to serve as a foil to the free harmonies and declamatory rhythms that openly present Clarke's political and religious concerns and comment wryly on human character. He was a member of the COMPOSERS COLLECTIVE OF NEW YORK, and used the pseudonym "J. Fairbanks" for songs written for the group. The wit and wisdom of Clarke's compositions, and of his essays (which appear in various journals and Festschriften), are as indigenous and independent as those of Charles Ives, though more urbane and concise.

WORKS

OPERAS

The Loafer and the Loaf (1, E. Sharp), 1951, perf. 1956

Lysistrata (2, J. Stevenson, after Aristophanes), 1968–72; Marlboro, VT, 9 Nov 1984

INSTRUMENTAL

Orch: Lyric Sonata, str, 1932, rev. 1960; Monograph, 1952; Saraband for the Golden Goose, 1957; Points West, wind, perc, 1960, arr. orch, 1970; Encounter, va, orch, 1961; Variegation, 1961

Chamber: 3 str qts, 1928, 1956, 1958; Danza de la muerte, ob, pf, 1937; Characters, pf, 1954; Nocturne, va, pf, 1955; A Game that Two can Play, fl, cl, 1959; Concatenata (Quodlibet), wind qnt, 1969; Danza de la vida, ob, pf, 1975; 3 from Foster, Fuguing Trio, fl, vn, vc, 1980–81; Drastic Measures, trbn, 1982; Salute to Justin Morgan, fl, vn, hpd, 1982; 7 shorter works for various insts; many pf and org pieces

CHORAL

Before Dawn (G. Thurber), SATB/SSAA, 1934, rev. 1949; Gloria in the Five Official Languages of the United Nations, solo vv, SATB, orch/org, 1950; Dona nobis pacem, TTBB, 1951; No Man is an Island (Donne), male vv/mixed chorus, band, 1951; Happy is the Man (Proverbs), 4vv, pf/org, 1953; Love-in-the-World (G. Taggard), S/T, SSA, pf, 1953; O God, by many Roads Unknown (Masefield), S, SSA, pf, 1953; Primavera (Taggard), SSA, str qt, 1953; 3 Madrigals (Clarke), 1957; Blessed is the Man (Ps. i), 1959

Lo, Here is Fellowschippe (F. Converse), 1960; L'allegro and Il penseroso (Milton), 1964; The Rewaking (W. C. Williams), 1966; Deering's Woods (Longfellow), 1969; The Young Dead Soldiers (MacLeish), 1970; Kyrie from the Mass for All Men, SB, pf, org, opt. perc, 1971; Mass for All Souls, 1975; Patriot Primer, 1975; These are the Times that Try Men's Souls (Paine), SSA, pf, 1976; The Bounty of Athena, SSA, pf, 1978; Ah! Freedom is a Noble Thing (J. Barbour), SATB, pf, 1981, arr. low v, pf, as Freedom; Give All to Love (R. W. Emerson), SATB, pf, 1981; No Great, no Small (Emerson), SATB, pf, 1982; Choose Life (Deuteronomy xxx.19), SATB, pf, 1983

5 other unacc. and over 15 acc. choral works; 8 hymn tunes; 4 hymn anthems

SONGS

(all 1v, pf, unless otherwise stated)

Le soleil ni la mort (La Rochefoucauld), medium v, pf, 1930; Carmina pacifica (Clarke), 1934, 1965; Lark (Taggard), S, 1936; A Woman of Virtue (after Proverbs), A, ob, gong, 1937; Freedom (Barbour), low v, pf, 1941; 3 Clerihews (Bentley), 1946; Spirit of Delight (Shelley), 1954; When any mortal (Cummings), 1960; 4 Elements (Emerson, Taggard, Sandburg, Whitman), S, vc, 1962; I Died for Beauty (Dickinson), 1963; Life in Ghana (M. Markwell), 1966; The Lord is My Shepherd (Ps. xxiii), medium v, fl, db, timp, 1971

The Soliloquy (Shakespeare), medium v, pf, 1972, also version for str qt; William Penn Fruits of Solitude, 1972; Let me go (Emerson), 1v, 1976; The Spring (R. T. Weston), 1978; Opposites (R. Wilbur), 1v, va/vc, 1979; Beauty is Truth (Keats), medium v, pf, 1983; Loudmouse (Wilbur), medium v, pf, 1983; Every night and every morn (Blake), medium v, pf, 1984; over 15 others

MSS in ACA

Principal publishers: MCA, Presser

BIBLIOGRAPHY

EwenD

J. Verrall: "Henry Leland Clarke," *ACAB*, ix/3 (1960), 2 [with list of works specifying instrumentations and durations]

I. Jones: "Composer on Sabbatical: Music from Deerfield," *Greenfield* [MA] *Recorder* (27 April 1970)

WILLIAM W. AUSTIN

Clarke, Herbert L(incoln) (*b* Woburn, MA, 12 Sept 1867; *d* Long Beach, CA, 30 Jan 1945). Cornetist and bandmaster. He was the best-known cornetist of his time, associated as a soloist with Sousa's Band (1893–1917) and Gilmore's Band (1892, and from 1893–8 in its reorganized form under Victor Herbert). He played second trumpet (on cornet) with the New York PO in December 1898, and first trumpet (on trumpet) with the Metropolitan Opera during the following season. He was cornet tester for C. G. Conn Co. (1913–15), and in 1916 he developed a medium-length "Holton-Clarke" model cornet with the Holton Co., with which he was formally associated in 1917–18. Later he was a bandmaster, in Huntsville, Ontario (1918–23), and with the Long Beach Municipal Band (1923–43).

Although Clarke was self-taught, he gained a considerable reputation as a teacher, beginning with the development of his own method of diaphragmatic breathing in 1906–7. Besides revising the Arban method, he issued *Technical Studies for the Cornet* (1912), a set of exercises based on breath control and finger-tongue coordination which is still popular. He also published a book, *The Cornet and the Cornetist* (1970). There are numerous recordings of Clarke playing with Sousa's Band, the earliest dating from 1899.

BIBLIOGRAPHY

H. L. Clarke: *How I became a Cornetist* (St. Louis, 1934)

G. Bridges: *Pioneers in Brass* (Detroit, 1965), 22ff [with discography]

EDWARD H. TARR

Clarke, Hugh Archibald (*b* Toronto, Ont., 15 Aug 1839; *d* Philadelphia, PA, 16 Dec 1927). Organist, music educator, conductor, and composer. He was trained by his father, the Scottish organist James Paton Clarke. In 1859 he went to Philadelphia, where he remained for the rest of his life, serving as organist of several churches in succession. He also conducted the Abt Male Chorus. In 1875 the University of Pennsylvania appointed him professor of music (one of the first in the USA), and he held that post until his death. He was awarded an honorary doctorate in 1886. His textbooks, especially *A System of Harmony*, were widely used for many years, although they had become outdated by the end of his life. He made several unsuccessful attempts to develop a music typewriter. His daughter Helen Archibald Clarke (1860–1926), author, editor, and founder of the periodical *Poet Lore*, was also an amateur composer.

WORKS

(all printed works published in Philadelphia)

Incidental music: Acharnians (Aristophanes), Philadelphia, 14 May 1886, vs (1886); Iphigenia in Tauris (Euripides)

Other: 3 Sonatinas, pf (1874); The Music of the Spheres, cantata, male vv (1880); Jerusalem, oratorio, vs (1890); 2 songs (R. Browning: Pippa Passes), 1899, *MB*

Ed.: Songs of the University of Pennsylvania (1897); Songs of Bryn Mawr College (1903)

WRITINGS

(published in Philadelphia unless otherwise indicated)

Harmony (1880)
Theory Explained (1892)
Pronouncing Dictionary of Musical Terms (1896)
A System of Harmony (1898)
Music and the Comrade Arts (Boston, 1899)
The Elements of Vocal Harmony (New York, 1900)
Counterpoint (1901)
Highways and Byways of Music (New York, 1901)

BRUCE CARR

Clarke, Kenny [Kenneth Spearman; Klook; Salaam, Liaquat Ali] (*b* Pittsburgh, PA, 9 Jan 1914; *d* nr Paris, France, 26 Jan 1985). Jazz drummer and bandleader. A member of a musical family, he studied several instruments in high school and began performing as a professional drummer with the Leroy Bradley band in Pittsburgh when he was still a teenager. He later joined Roy Eldridge's band and then played drums in several major jazz groups in the Midwest and East, including the Jeter–Pillars band in St. Louis and the bands of Lonnie Simmons, Edgar Hayes, Claude Hopkins, and Teddy Hill in New York. While playing with Hill in 1939–49 he and his fellow band member Dizzy Gillespie began to experiment with new rhythmic conceptions that were ultimately to influence the development of modern jazz. In the early 1940s, he played regularly at Minton's Playhouse in New York, where his association with Gillespie, Thelonious Monk, Bud Powell, and others led to the development of improvisational techniques that later became characteristic of the bop style. After military service in Europe from 1943 to 1946, he returned to the USA and recorded with Gillespie, Tadd Dameron, and Fats Navarro. He was a founding member of the MODERN JAZZ QUARTET, with which he played from 1952 to 1955. In 1956 he settled in France, where he played in a trio with Bud Powell (1959–62) and in 1960 organized the Clarke–Boland Big Band with the Belgian pianist and arranger Francy Boland. He also appeared in two films, *Lift to the Scaffold* (1957) and *Les liaisons dangereuses* (1959), and wrote music for the films *On n'enterre pas dimanche* (1959) and *La rivière du hibou* (1961).

Clarke was generally considered the principal innovator in modern jazz drumming. During his years with Gillespie he revolutionized jazz drumming by shifting the steady 4/4 pulse from the bass drum to the ride cymbal, thereby allowing the use of the bass and snare drums for independent counter-rhythms in support of the improvising soloists. This resulted in a polyrhythmic background that complemented the asymmetrical phrasing of the soloists, an ideal that became standard for modern jazz drumming. Among Clarke's compositions are the well-known *Salt Peanuts* (composed with Gillespie) and *Epistrophy* (with Monk).

RECORDINGS

(selective list)

As leader or co-leader: Epistrophy/Oop-bop-sh'bam (1946, Swing 224); with E. Wilkins: *Kenny Clarke/Ernie Wilkins Septet* (1955, Savoy 12007), incl. Plenty for Kenny; *Bohemia after Dark* (1955, Savoy 12017); *The Trio* (1955, Savoy 12023); *Klook's Clique* (1956, Savoy 12065), incl. Volcano; with F. Boland: *Francy Boland Big Band* (1963, Atl. 1404), *Blue Flame* (1976, MPS 229106)

As sideman: Men from Mintons: Swing to Bop, on *The Harlem Jazz Scene* (1941, Esoteric 4); D. Gillespie: Cubana Be/Cubana Bop (1947, Vic. 203145); Modern Jazz Quartet: La Ronde (1952, Prst. 828)

BIBLIOGRAPHY

SouthernB
L. Feather: *Inside Jazz* (New York, 1949)
N. Shapiro and N. Hentoff: *Hear me Talkin' to ya* (New York, 1955), 299ff
R. Russell: "Bop Rhythm," *The Art of Jazz*, ed. M. Williams (New York, 1959), 187
M. Harrison: "Kenny Clarke," *Jazz Era: the 'Forties*, ed. S. Dance (London, 1961), 76
G. Hoefer: "Kenny Clarke's Early Recordings," *Down Beat*, xxx/8 (1963), 23
B. Korall: "View from the Seine," *Down Beat*, xxx/31 (1963), 17
W. Mellers: *Music in a New Found Land* (New York, 1964/*R*1975), 334f
I. Gitler: *Jazz Masters of the Forties* (New York, 1966), 174ff
T. D. Brown: *A History and Analysis of Jazz Drumming to 1942* (diss., U. of Michigan, 1976), 476ff, 521f
B. Quinn: "Kenny Clarke: Rhythm Revolutionary," *Jazz Times* (Nov 1980), 12

OLLY WILSON

Clarke [Friskin], **Rebecca (Thacher)** (*b* Harrow, England, 27 Aug 1886; *d* New York, 13 Oct 1979). English composer and violist of German-American parentage. She studied composition with Charles Stanford at the Royal College of Music, London, and viola privately with Lionel Tertis, and performed throughout the world as soloist and in chamber groups from the 1910s to the 1930s. In 1912 she was among the first women asked to join a professional London orchestra – the (New) Queen's Hall Orchestra, which was one of only two Western European orchestras to hire women. Her Viola Sonata tied for first place with Bloch's Viola Suite in the 1919 Coolidge Competition (though the prize ultimately went to Bloch), establishing her reputation as a composer. Clarke's instrumental works are rhapsodic, post-impressionist in harmonic idiom, and characterized by sophisticated yet lively rhythms and idiomatic string writing. In 1944, at the age of 58, she married the pianist and composer JAMES FRISKIN and settled in New York. From that time she increasingly devoted her energies to teaching, lecturing, and promoting chamber music, at the expense of composing and performing. She wrote the articles on Bloch and the viola in *Cobbett's Cyclopedic Survey of Chamber Music* (1929, 2/1963) and articles for other publications; her correspondence with Elizabeth Sprague Coolidge is in the Library of Congress. In 1980 her Piano Trio was recorded.

WORKS

Va Sonata, 1919; Pf Trio, 1921; Vc Rhapsody, 1923; Prelude, Allegro, and Pastorale, cl, va, 1941; 20 other chamber and inst works; over 50 vocal works, incl. 41 songs, 6 partsongs

MSS in *DLC, NN*

Principal publishers: Chester, Oxford UP, Rogers

BIBLIOGRAPHY

Grove5
Cobbett's Cyclopedic Survey of Chamber Music, ed. W. W. Cobbett (London, 1929/*R*1963)
C. Johnson: *Rebecca Clarke: a Thematic Catalogue of her Works* (MS, 1977, *NNCU-G*)
E. Lerner: *A Modern European Quintet, c1900–c1960* (MS, 1981, rev. 1985, *NN-L*)

ELLEN D. LERNER

Clarke, William Horatio (*b* Newton, MA, 8 March 1840; *d* Reading, MA, 11 Dec 1913). Organ builder and author. He served as a church organist in several Massachusetts localities, 1856–66. There is some evidence that he then traveled in Europe before moving to Dayton, Ohio, as a school music supervisor in 1871. By 1874 he had established an organ-building firm in Indianapolis in partnership with Stephen P. Kinsley, a voicer formerly with the firm of Hook & Hastings. In the next four years he installed substantial instruments in Indianapolis, Louisville, Dayton, and Kokomo. While in Indianapolis he continued to work as a church organist, and from 1878 accepted other positions in churches in Boston, Toronto, and Rochester. After ill health compelled him to retire in 1884, he occupied himself by writing and consulting (by correspondence) on organ design. In 1890 he built an estate with a concert hall in Reading but his hopes of establishing a school in organ instruction were frustrated by ill health. Clarke wrote several treatises on organ building and organ playing, composed voluntaries, anthems, and other organ music, and produced a fictitious autobiography, *The Organist's Retrospect*, describing the artistic development of one Ernest Onslow (1896). Among his five sons, who were all musicians, was Herbert L. Clarke, noted bandmaster and cornetist.

BIBLIOGRAPHY

Obituary, *Diapason*, v/2 (1914), 1
B. Owen: *The Organ in New England* (Raleigh, 1979)

WILLIAM OSBORNE, BARBARA OWEN

Clayton, Buck [Wilbur Dorsey] (*b* Parsons, KS, 12 Nov 1911). Jazz trumpeter and arranger. His early career was spent in California, where he organized a big band which toured China in 1934. After returning to the USA he became a leading soloist in the band that Count Basie first took to New York in 1936. Here he was known for an attractive, burnished tone, a good technique, and a feeling for melodic improvisation; the sensitivity of his style made him an ideal accompanist for singers, notably Billie Holiday. Clayton also arranged and composed items that were performed by the bands of Count Basie, Duke Ellington, and Harry James. During the 1950s, after leaving Basie, Clayton became one of the central figures of mainstream jazz. Illness interfered with his playing schedules from 1967 onwards, but he continued to arrange for various American and European bands throughout the 1970s and early 1980s.

RECORDINGS
(selective list)

As leader: Robbin's Nest (1953, Col. B1836); Lazy River (1953, Vogue 5182)
As sideman: B. Holiday: He's funny that way (1937, Voc. 3748); C. Basie: Fiesta in Blue (1941, OK 6440); S. Bechet: *Brussels Fair '58* (1958, Col. CL1410), incl. All of me

BIBLIOGRAPHY

SouthernB
G. Hoefer: "Buck Clayton – a Brief Biography," *Down Beat*, xxviii/2 (1961), 16
H. McNamara: "Travelin' Man," *Down Beat*, xxxi/13 (1964), 13
V. Wilmer: "One for Buck," *Jazz People* (London, 1970), 125
S. Dance: *The World of Count Basie* (New York, 1980), 37

JOHN CHILTON

Clayton, David Little (1801–54). Tunebook compiler who, with JAMES P. CARRELL, compiled *The Virginia Harmony* (Winchester, VA, 1831, 2/1836).

Clayton, Norman John (*b* Brooklyn, NY, 22 Jan 1903). Radio evangelist and composer of gospel hymns. From the age of 12 he played a pump organ in the South Brooklyn Gospel Church, and later took up the trumpet. While continuing to serve as an organist he held various jobs, until in 1942 he joined the staff of the radio evangelist Jack Wyrtzen for his "Word of Life" rallies in New York. Clayton served this organization for 15 years as organist, vibraphonist, and director of the inquiry room. During this period he also worked with Erling C. Olsen on the "Sunday Morning Radio Bible Class," and with the Bellerose Baptist Church on their radio programs. During the period 1945 to 1959 Clayton published some 30 gospel songbooks; he then became associated with the Rodeheaver Company as a writer and editor. His best-known gospel hymn is *Now I belong to Jesus*, first published in his *Word of Life Melodies no.1* (1943). In their texts and harmonies, Clayton's songs represent a trend toward a romantic style of gospel hymnody.

BIBLIOGRAPHY

W. J. Reynolds: *Companion to Baptist Hymnal* (Nashville, 1976)
D. P. Hustad: *Dictionary-handbook to Hymns for the Living Church* (Carol Stream, IL, 1978)

HARRY ESKEW

Clemens (Gabrilowitsch), Clara (*b* Elmira, NY, 8 June 1874; *d* San Diego, CA, 19 Nov 1962). Contralto, author, and actress, daughter of MARK TWAIN. She intended to become a pianist, and studied with Moritz Moszkowski in Berlin, Helen Hopekirk in London, and Theodor Leschetizky in Vienna. Once she made the decision to become a singer, she trained in Hamburg with Marianne Brandt and in London with Blanche Marchesi. Her professional début occurred in Norfolk, Connecticut, in 1904; in 1908 she made her London début (16 June) and her New York début (November). She married the pianist OSSIP GABRILOWITSCH on 6 October 1909; they gave joint recitals in the USA and Europe, in which his songs were performed. Her repertory was wide and it was claimed that she was the first singer in New York to present a recital that surveyed the development of song from its folk origins to her day. She never sang opera, and her acting career was limited and brief. She was praised for her rich contralto voice, which had occasional blemishes in the upper range, and was reticent in projecting character for some of the more extrovert songs of her extensive repertory. Among her books are *The Development of Song* (1924), *My Father Mark Twain* (1931), and *My Husband Gabrilowitsch* (1938).

THOR ECKERT, JR.

Clements, Vassar (*b* nr Kinards, SC, April 1928). Country, bluegrass, and jazz fiddler. A self-taught musician, he began playing guitar professionally with the Blue Grass Boys as a teenager, and remained with the group until 1956. From 1958 to 1961 he was a member of Jim and Jesse's backup ensemble, the Virginia Boys. He performed with many other musicians, including Faron Young, Jimmy Martin, John Hartford, Earl Scruggs, Paul McCartney, the Allman Brothers Band, Linda Ronstadt, the Grateful Dead, and the Nitty Gritty Dirt Band. In 1975 he formed the Vassar Clements Band, whose style of music has been described as an "intensely exciting, disciplined and reckless . . . [mixture of] every kind of American music – swing, dixieland, blues, rock, country, and bluegrass, performed with the most impressive precision and virtuosity." Since the late 1970s he has been the foremost proponent of western swing, a hybrid of jazz and fiddle music characterized by jazz improvisations on folk, country, or bluegrass tunes. A widely respected and much sought after backup musician in Nashville, Clements owes much of his improvisatory, eclectic mixture of styles to swing-band and bluegrass music he heard while growing up; he was also influenced by Stephane Grappelli (although his fiddle style has a heavier tone and slower vibrato than Grappelli's) and Django Reinhardt. The use of sonorous double stops is integral to his playing technique. While principally a fiddler, he is also a proficient player of the viola, cello, double bass, guitar, and mandolin.

RECORDINGS
(selective list)

Southern Country Waltzes (Rural Rhythm VC 236, 1971); *Superbow* (Mer. MCR 41-1058, 1975); *Vassar Clements* (Mer. SRM 1-1022, 1975); *Bluegrass Session*

(Flying Fish 038, 1977); *Crossing the Catskills* (Rounder 0016, 1977); *Hillbilly Jazz* (Flying Fish 101, 1977); *Vassar Clements Band* (MCA 2270, 1977); *Nashville Jam* (Flying Fish 073, 1979) [with D. Jernigan, J. McReynolds, and B. Spicher]

BIBLIOGRAPHY

B. Silver: "Vassar Clements out West," *Bluegrass Unlimited*, xii/11 (1978), 18

KATHERINE K. PRESTON

Clemm [Clem], **Johann Gotlob.** *See* KLEMM, JOHANN GOTLOB.

Cleva, Fausto (Angelo) (*b* Trieste [now in Italy], 17 May 1902; *d* Athens, Greece, 6 Aug 1971). Conductor. He studied at the Trieste Conservatory and at the Verdi Conservatory in Milan, where he made his début conducting *La traviata* at the Teatro Carcano. Immigrating to the USA in 1920 (he became an American citizen in 1931), he met with immediate success, beginning a long association with the Metropolitan Opera the same year, first as chorus master and later as conductor: between 1950 and 1971 he conducted over 650 performances at the Metropolitan Opera alone. His work in New York was interspersed with periods of activity in Cincinnati, where he was music director of the Summer Opera from 1934 to 1963, at the San Francisco Opera, where he conducted in the 1942–3 season and again between 1949 and 1955, and in Chicago, where, as artistic director of the Chicago Opera Company from 1944 to 1946, he played an important part in the postwar raising of the city's operatic standards. A widely admired operatic maestro in the familiar Italian mold, he made guest appearances with the San Antonio SO and with opera companies abroad.

BERNARD JACOBSON

Cleve, George (Wolfgang) (*b* Vienna, Austria, 8 July 1936). Conductor. He came to the USA with his family in 1940 and later studied at the Mannes College; he then worked with Pierre Monteux, George Szell, and Franco Ferrara. He was associate conductor of the St. Louis SO during the 1967–8 season, leaving that post to become music director of the Winnipeg SO in Canada; the relationship, however, was an unhappy one, and Cleve departed after two seasons. He spent the 1971–2 season as principal guest conductor of the Iceland SO, then returned to the USA as music director of the San Jose (California) SO. In 1974 he founded the Midsummer Mozart Festival in northern California. As a guest conductor he has appeared with the San Francisco SO, the American SO, the Royal PO (London), the San Jose Opera, and the Opera Company of Philadelphia.

A talented and versatile conductor, Cleve has not achieved the kind of renown due his ability, in part because of a fiery temper. His personality calmed considerably, however, after he was nearly killed in a fire in March 1978; in spite of major injuries he returned to the podium seven months later. Cleve specializes in the large-scale works of the repertory, particularly the symphonies of Nielsen, Sibelius, and Mahler. He is also devoted to British music, and frequently performs works by Vaughan Williams, Elgar, and Tippett.

MICHAEL WALSH

Cleveland. City in Ohio (pop. 573,822; metropolitan area 1,898,720). Early settlers brought with them a rich and diverse heritage to this outpost community in Connecticut's Western Reserve. Music-making developed naturally from the community, especially the church. By the mid-1830s singing-schools were beginning to flourish and brass bands were popular. Choral and instrumental groups active after the city charter was granted in 1836 included the Cleveland Mozart Society (founded 1837), the Cleveland Harmonic Society (1837), the Cleveland Sacred Music Society (1842), the Cleveland Mendelssohn Society (1850), and the St. Cecilia Society (1852). The Cleveland Gesangverein (1854) gave performances of opera with orchestra, for example Flotow's *Alessandro Stradella* (1858) and Gustav Schmidt's *Prince Eugen* (1860). The city initially belonged to the musical tradition emanating from Boston (Lowell Mason conducted a series of workshops in Cleveland during the 1840s) and was for many years under the musical shadow of Cincinnati; local achievements nonetheless took on increasing importance.

The years following the Civil War were ones of tremendous growth for Cleveland. Waves of immigrants from Europe made the city the seventh largest in the USA by 1900. German influence was strong: members of the GERMANIA MUSICAL SOCIETY settled in Cleveland when that ensemble disbanded in 1854, and five Sängerfests were organized (1855, 1859, 1874, 1893, and 1927). Many of the musicians active in the city, including Reinhold Henninges (1836–1913) and Emil Ring (1863–1922), were German or Austrian by birth, while others, such as Johann H. Beck (1856–1924), James Rogers (1857–1940), and Wilson Smith (1855–1929), were born in the USA and studied in Germany. Also influenced by European ideals were Alfred Arthur (1844–1918), the city's foremost choral conductor during the period and founder of the Cleveland Vocal Society (1873–1902), N. Coe Stewart (1837–1921), a disciple of Lowell Mason who became the city's first full-time supervisor of music in the public schools (1869–1907), and the violinist Charles V. Rychlik (1875–1962), a student of Beck and Rogers who studied in Prague.

Orchestral music began to take hold in the 1870s and 1880s. Alfred Arthur directed orchestral programs at Brainard's Piano Ware Rooms in 1872 and conducted the Cleveland Vocal Society at the city's May festivals (1880–86 and 1895–7), which he organized; he also established an orchestra to play with that group for a time. The Cleveland Philharmonic Society was formed in 1881 under Ferdinand Puehringer with 36 players; he was succeeded by Mueller Neuhoff, Franz Arens, and Ring (from 1888). Ring and Beck conducted orchestras of the early 1900s, notably the Cleveland SO (1900–1901), the Cleveland Grand Orchestra (1902–9), and another Cleveland SO (1910–12). Local artists were sometimes featured with these ensembles, as were such groups as the Singers Club (founded 1891) under Albert Rees Davis, the Cleveland Opera and Oratorio Society under Adolph Liesegang, and the Harmonic Club under J. Powell Jones. The Dutch violinist Christiaan Timmner conducted an orchestral series (1913–16) with an orchestra which came to be supported by the city as the Cleveland Municipal SO. The culmination was reached in the founding of the Cleveland Orchestra in 1918 (see below).

Also important during the early years were chamber music, band music, parlor music, and publishing activity. The Cecilian String Quartet (1875–7) and the Schubert String Quartet (1877–*c*1890) were among significant ensembles. Band music, heard in numerous summer concerts and at festivals, was highly popular. These events were well reported in the local press and in the *Musical World* (1864–95; in *OClWHi*), the house journal of S. Brainard's Sons. This influential firm published a wide variety of parlor music after 1845.

Early in the 20th century Cleveland came to international musical prominence, a position it has held ever since. By that time public interest and accumulated wealth resulting from substantial business enterprises could sustain significant cultural events. An unprecedented series of concerts in the city was organized between about 1900 and 1920 by Adella Prentiss Hughes (1869–1950), who, through the Fortnightly Musical Club and the National Federation of Music Clubs, brought leading international performers to the city. A Chamber Music Society was formed in 1918, and the Cleveland Museum of Art, founded in 1916, soon began to include music in its program. Its McMyler organ (1922), the first in the USA to be installed in an art museum, was moved to a new auditorium in the museum and rebuilt in 1971.

The Cleveland Orchestra (called in its first season Cleveland's SO) was founded largely through the efforts of Adella Prentiss Hughes and with the support of the Musical Arts Association (founded 1915). It gave its inaugural concert under Nicolai Sokoloff at Grays' Armory (1893, capacity 5000) on 11 December 1918. The critic Wilson Smith wrote the next day in the *Cleveland Press*: "Sokoloff . . . is destined to lead our ever existing nucleus out of the house of bondage into the land of honey and pleasant pastures." Concerts were later given in the Masonic Auditorium (1920, capacity 2238) until the orchestra moved in 1931 to its permanent home, Severance Hall (see illustration; capacity 2000). Children's concerts were inaugurated in 1929. Sokoloff remained as music director until 1933, when he was succeeded by Artur Rodzinski (until 1943) and Erich Leinsdorf (1943–6). George Szell took over in 1946 and remained until his death in 1970 with James Levine as assistant conductor (1964–70). During his tenure the orchestra grew to 107 members, its season was expanded to the full year, and it achieved international acclaim, with tours to Europe in 1957 and 1967 and to the Far East in 1970. Pierre Boulez (guest conductor, 1967–74) and Louis Lane (associate conductor, 1956–73) conducted frequently in the interim until 1972, when Lorin Maazel was appointed music director, a post he held until 1982. After two seasons of guest conductors (including Leinsdorf), Maazel was succeeded in 1984 by Christoph von Dohnányi. The first permanent Cleveland Orchestra Chorus (from 1955) quickly rose to the highest level under Robert Shaw's direction (1956–67) and has maintained a high standard under its subsequent directors. A children's chorus, affiliated with the orchestra, was formed in 1967. The Cleveland Orchestra gives about 30 concerts annually at its summer home, the Blossom Music Center (inaugurated 1968) in Cuyahoga Falls; 40 additional dance and "popular" events make up a summer season lasting from June to September.

The Metropolitan Opera first visited Cleveland in 1899 and has appeared there frequently ever since. In addition there are two local professional companies: the Cleveland Opera (founded in 1976 under the direction of David Bamberger), which mounts an annual season of opera in English using both local and imported singers at the State Theatre (from 1984); and the Lyric Opera Cleveland, which began as the Cleveland Opera Theatre at the Cleveland Institute of Music in 1973, became autonomous in 1976, and offers performances of a broad-based repertory at the institute's Kulas Auditorium under the artistic direction of Michael McConnell (from 1982). Dance flourishes in the city, particularly through the fine work of the Cleveland Modern Dance Association (1956) and the Cleveland Ballet (1974).

Music education in the public schools advanced rapidly, especially in courses on music appreciation. By the early 20th century several music schools had been established: the Cleveland School of Music (incorporated 1885), the West Side Musical College (*c*1900), the Hruby Conservatory of Music (1918), and the music department at Western Reserve College (1826). The Cleveland

Severance Hall, Cleveland

Music School Settlement was founded by Almeda Adams in 1912. From an initial enrollment of 50 the school had grown to over 5000 by the 1980s; the largest community school in the USA, it has several branches and affiliates and a nationally acclaimed program in music therapy. Howard Whittaker was head of the school from 1947 to 1984, when he was succeeded by Malcolm Tait.

The Cleveland Institute of Music was founded in 1920, with Ernest Bloch as its first director and teachers including Roger Sessions and Quincy Porter. Bloch's successors have been Mrs. Franklyn B. Sanders (1925–32), Beryl Rubinstein (1932–52), Ward Davenny (1954–61), and Victor Babin (1961–72), during whose tenure the institute moved to new premises (1961) and the curriculum was expanded. Grant Johannesen served as consultant after Babin's death and was appointed director in 1974 (president from 1977); he was succeeded by David Ceroue in 1985. A joint music program is offered with Case Western Reserve University's music department.

Having settled in Cleveland in 1920 as assistant conductor of the Cleveland Orchestra, the composer Arthur Shepherd taught at Western Reserve College (later renamed Western Reserve University) from 1926 to 1950, also serving as the music department's chairman from 1933 to 1948. Western Reserve merged with the Case Institute of Technology to become Case Western Reserve University in 1967, of which John Suess became music department chairman in 1968, succeeded by Peter Webster in 1984. The composer Edwin London became chairman of the music department at Cleveland State University (founded 1964) in 1978. Significant contributions are also made by such neighboring educational institutions as Baldwin Wallace College (Berea), which includes a conservatory and Bach library and sponsors a Bach Festival, the OBERLIN COLLEGE CONSERVATORY OF MUSIC, and Kent State University.

Composers who have been active in Cleveland since about 1935 include Victor Babin, Rudolph Bubalo, Marcel Dick, Dennis Eberhard, Herbert Elwell, Donald Erb, Edwin London, J. D. Bain Murray, Eugene O'Brien, Klaus George Roy, Beryl Rubinstein, and Arthur Shepherd. Such composers as Ernest Bloch, Douglas Moore, Quincy Porter, Roger Sessions, and Raymond Wilding-White made substantial contributions to the city's musical life, though for comparatively brief periods. There is an active Cleveland Composers' Guild, formed during the 1920s.

The Department of Musical Arts was presented to the Cleveland Museum of Art in 1920 as an endowed gift in memory of P. J. McMyler. T. W. Surrette, the first musical curator there, established classes in music appreciation. He was succeeded by Walter Blodgett (1940–74) and Karel Paukert (from 1974). Organ recitals and concerts (principally of chamber music) include works that are infrequently performed. The museum's Musart Society (1946) and the McMyler Fund help support the concerts. Financial support for the city's musical life is also provided by the Kulas Foundation, established in the 1940s, and the Bascom Little Fund, among others.

Local libraries with significant music collections include the Cleveland Public Library, and the libraries of the Western Reserve Historical Society, which has a large collection of Shaker music, Case Western Reserve and Cleveland State universities, and the Cleveland Institute of Music (*see* LIBRARIES AND COLLECTIONS, §3).

Cleveland's musical life is enriched through many concerts given by local and visiting artists. In addition to the Cleveland Orchestra the city enjoys programs by other orchestral ensembles including the Cleveland Women's Orchestra, founded in 1935 by its conductor Hyman Shandler, the Suburban Symphony (1954), conducted by Martin Kessler, the Ohio Chamber Orchestra (1971), conducted by Dwight Oltman, and the Cleveland Chamber Symphony (1980), directed by Edwin London. Cleveland Public Library's fine arts department offered a series of concerts featuring local musicians from 1940 until 1967; the Cleveland Chamber Music Society was organized in 1949 and brings concerts of chamber music of the highest quality to the city. Choral groups that have remained active include the Singers Club (founded 1891), Cleveland Messiah Civic Chorus (1921), Singing Angels (1964), the William Appling Singers and Orchestra (1979), and the West Shore Chorale (1968). The American Guild of Organists maintains a strong chapter which sponsors an annual recital series.

Significant among the city's instrument builders are the Holtkamp Organ Co., founded by Gottlieb Votteler in 1855, and King Musical Instruments, one of the earliest manufacturers of distinguished brass instruments in the USA, founded in 1893 as the H. N. White Company. Other recent builders include the string makers Edward Crevoi, the Schmidt Brothers, Eastman Violin Shop, Jerry Forestiere, Otto Luderer, and Ponziani Violin; the harpsichord builders Cucciara Harpsichord Co., Walter O'Brien (both Garretsville) and Jan Leik (Oberlin); and the organ builders Tim Hemry, Jan Leik, Charles Ruggles, and the Ruhland Organ Co.

Cleveland has also played an active role in the history of popular song, jazz, Americanized polka, musical theater, and rock-and-roll. The songwriter Ernest R. Ball was born in the city, and Art Tatum frequently played in Cleveland jazz clubs during the early 1930s. Among the most important later jazz musicians from Cleveland have been the composer Tadd Dameron, the reed player Benny Bailey, the saxophonist Albert Ayler, the pianist and composer Bobby Few, and the trombonist Haydn "Jiggs" Wigham; others include the bass player Abraham Laboriel, the guitarist and composer Jim Hall, the trombonist and arranger Robert Curnow (long associated with Stan Kenton), and the reed player Ernie Krivda. Cleveland's numerous ethnic neighborhoods add rich variety to the city's popular-music scene; Ritchie Vadnal's Polka Kings and Frankie Yankovic's Polka Band are in great demand. The American musical theater has been enriched through the work of Clevelanders Noble Sissle, Jr., and John-Michael Tebelak. But it is with the influence of rock-and-roll that Cleveland has made the greatest change on the face of American popular music. The local disc jockey Alan Freed, working with Leo Mintz, brought the genre to prominence in the early 1950s, before it achieved its phenomenal international popularity.

See also ORCHESTRAS, §2(ii).

BIBLIOGRAPHY

R. Henninges: *Musical Evenings with Professor Waldmann and his Friends* (Cleveland, 1893)

J. Orth: "Music," *A History of Cleveland, Ohio*, ed. S. Orth (Chicago and Cleveland, 1910), i, 449

M. H. Osburn: *Ohio Composers and Musical Authors* (Columbus, 1942)

W. H. Porter: *Musical Development of the Western Reserve* (thesis, Western Reserve U., 1946)

A. P. Hughes: *Music is my Life* (Cleveland and New York, 1947)

W. G. Rose: *Cleveland: the Making of a City* (Cleveland and New York, 1950)

D. R. Breitmayer: *Seventy-five Years of Sacred Music in Cleveland, Ohio, 1800–1975* (thesis, Union Theological Seminary, 1951)

F. H. Grant: *Foundations of Music Education in the Cleveland Public Schools* (diss., Western Reserve U., 1963)

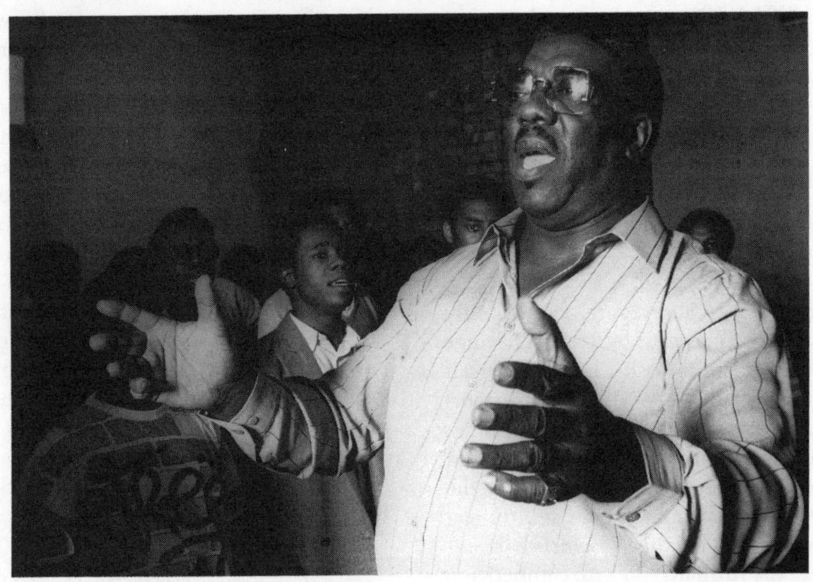

James L. Cleveland, 1985

R. C. Marsh: *The Cleveland Orchestra* (Cleveland and New York, 1967)
F. K. Grossman: *From Log Cabin to Severance Hall: the History of Music in Cleveland from 1800* (MS, *OCl*)
——: *A History of Music in Cleveland* (Cleveland, 1972)
B. Penyak: "Cleveland," *Grove 6*
J. H. Alexander: *It Must be Heard: a Survey of the Musical Life of Cleveland, 1836–1918* (Cleveland, 1981)

J. HEYWOOD ALEXANDER

Cleveland, James L. (*b* Chicago, IL, 5 Dec 1932). Gospel singer, composer, and pianist. He started singing in Thomas A. Dorsey's choir at the Pilgrim Baptist Church in Chicago, and made his first solo appearance with it at the age of eight. He joined the Thorn Gospel Singers as a teenager, and remained with them for eight years. After his voice began to break he strained to reach high notes, however; this resulted in a throaty and gravelly quality, which has increased with the years. He began composing in his early teens and had his first great success, *Grace is Sufficient*, at the age of 16. Between 1956 and 1960 he was a member of the Caravans, the Gospelaires, the Gospel Chimes, and the Gospel All-Stars. During this period he was most prolific as a composer, writing as many as three songs a week; his best-known songs include *He's using me* (1955), *Walk on by faith* (1962), and *Lord, help me to hold out* (1973). In the mid-1960s he joined the Rev. Lawrence Roberts's Angelic Choir in Nutley, New Jersey, and made a number of successful recordings (*see* GOSPEL MUSIC, §II, 2 (iii)). In *Peace, be still* (1963) Cleveland half croons, half preaches the verse, shifting to a musical sermon at the refrain; towards the end of the song the choir repeats a motif over which Cleveland extemporizes a number of variations. This style of performance is evident on all Cleveland's subsequent recordings. He has issued more than 50 albums, and has been awarded six gold records and two Grammy awards. In August 1968 he organized the Gospel Music Workshop of America, which had 500,000 members in 47 states by the mid-1980s. Since 1971 he has served as pastor of the Cornerstone Institutional Baptist Church, Los Angeles.

BIBLIOGRAPHY

SouthernB
T. Heilbut: "The Crown Prince of Gospel," *The Gospel Sound: Good News and Bad Times* (New York, 1971/*R*1975), 233
W. P. Burrell: "Reverend James L. Cleveland: King of Gospel," *Black Stars*, iii (1974), 24
R. Anderson and G. North: *Gospel Music Encyclopedia* (New York, 1979)
M. E. Casey: *The Contributions of James Cleveland* (thesis, Howard U., 1980)
"Cleveland, James," *CBY 1985*

HORACE CLARENCE BOYER

Cleveland Quartet. String quartet. It was formed in 1968 at the Marlboro Festival, Vermont, where it made its début the following year; the members are Donald Weilerstein, Peter Salaff, Atar Arad (who replaced Martha Strongin Katz in 1980), and Paul Katz. In 1969 the ensemble became quartet-in-residence at the Cleveland Institute, where Weilerstein taught, and two years later succeeded the Budapest Quartet at SUNY, Buffalo, where it gave annual performances of all Beethoven's quartets under the auspices of the Slee Beethoven Quartet Cycle bequest; it joined the faculty of the Eastman School in 1976. The quartet has toured throughout the USA and in Europe, Australia, and New Zealand, and has participated in the Festival Casals and the South Bank Summer Festival (London), among others. It has frequently collaborated with other performers, such as the pianist Alfred Brendel, with whom it recorded Schubert's "Trout" Quintet, and Pinchas Zukerman and Bernard Greenhouse, with whom it recorded Brahms's sextets. Other recordings include Brahms's string quartets, for which the quartet received several awards and was acclaimed for its precision and technical command as well as richness of tone, and the complete quartets of Beethoven. In addition to the standard repertory, the ensemble plays works by Ives, Bartók, and Sergei Slonimsky. The playing of the quartet combines muscularity and vigor with a refined suavity that is alive to the music's nuances. Its performances give the impression of four virtuoso musicians who, while complementing each other and achieving perfect ensemble, have not allowed their individual personalities to be submerged.

BIBLIOGRAPHY

R. Maycock: "The Cleveland Quartet," *Music and Musicians*, xxii/12 (1974), 10 [interview]

G. Freedman: "Mostly Beethoven: an Interview with the Cleveland Quartet," *MJ*, xxxiii/9 (1975), 10

A. Kozinn: "Four 'Clevelanders' who Adopted Beethoven," *New York Times* (6 Aug 1978), §D, p.13

L. Blandford: "The Strains of a String Quartet," *New York Times Magazine* (23 March 1980), 44

S. Modi: "The Cleveland Quartet: Adjusting to Change," *Ovation*, iv/1 (1983), 13

Cliburn, Van [Harvey Lavan, Jr.] (*b* Shreveport, LA, 12 July 1934). Pianist. Until he was 17, when he went to Rosina Lhévinne at the Juilliard School, his only teacher was his mother, herself a pupil of Arthur Friedheim. He made his recital début at four; at 13 he won a competition in Texas, by then the family's home, which secured him an engagement with the Houston SO, and the following year he played in Carnegie Hall as winner of the National Music Festival Award. His talent was consistently recognized: he won the Dealey Award and the Kosciuszko Foundation's Chopin prize in 1952, the Juilliard concerto competition in 1953 and Roeder Award in 1954, and, most important, the Leventritt Competition later that year. But in spite of the prizes and occasional appearances with major orchestras, he was little known when he won the International Tchaikovsky Competition in Moscow in April 1958. It was six months after the launching of *Sputnik*, and the USA was ready for a victory in the USSR, even that of a classical pianist; when Cliburn came home, he was welcomed by a New York ticker-tape parade. He made four tours of the USSR between 1960 and 1972. The Van Cliburn International Piano Competition was founded in 1962; it is held quadrennially in Fort Worth.

In his early career Cliburn was admired for the completeness of his technical command and for his massive, unpercussive tone. Even more remarkable was his musical taste, which, although it could produce rather distant performances of Mozart and Beethoven, gave his playing of the Romantic repertory an extraordinary character of grandeur combined with both chastity and warmth, as his 1958 recordings of the Tchaikovsky B♭ minor and Rachmaninoff D minor concertos reveal. From the mid-1960s it seemed that he could not cope with the loss of freshness: his repertory was restricted; his playing, always guided primarily by intuition, took on affectations; and the sound itself became harsher. In 1964 he began to conduct (after studying with Walter), but this was not followed up; and he has composed an (unperformed) piano sonata. He stopped performing in public in 1978.

BIBLIOGRAPHY

A. Chasins: *The Van Cliburn Legend* (Garden City, NY, 1959)

M. Fleming: "Van Cliburn Reflects on the Past and a Possible Future," *New York Times* (9 June 1985), §II, p.24

MICHAEL STEINBERG/R

Clifton, Arthur [Corri, P(hilip) Antony] (*b* Edinburgh, Scotland, ?1784; *d* Baltimore, MD, 19 Feb 1832). Composer, singer, pianist, and teacher, son of the Italian composer Domenico Corri. As P. Antony Corri he was well established as a composer in London (where his father had settled in about 1790) by *c*1808–13, when a great many of his piano pieces and songs were published, mainly by Chappell. His *L'anima di musica* (1810) is the most extensive piano tutor of its period. He was one of the organizers of the London Philharmonic Society in 1813, and sang in its first concerts. Sometime afterwards he immigrated to the USA (apparently because of marital problems), where he appeared in New York and Philadelphia, and then settled in Baltimore, possibly as early as 1814 and certainly by November 1817. There he was christened Arthur Clifton on 31 December 1817 at St. Paul's Episcopal Church, and married Alphonsa Elizabeth Ringgold on 1 January 1818. He served as organist at the First Presbyterian Church in 1818 and became organist and choirmaster at the First Independent Church (Unitarian), a position he kept until his death. He taught singing and probably also piano, appeared in concerts as a singer and pianist, and was music director for a theater for at least two seasons. Clifton's *Concerto da camera* was performed in New York on 3 February 1818; he continued to compose many songs and piano pieces, which were published in Baltimore beginning in 1820. His opera *The Enterprise; or, Love and Pleasure* was more ambitious than the usual English ballad opera yet probably lacked the recitatives of Italian opera.

WORKS

(only those published in the USA; for a fuller list see Wolfe, 1964)

Opera: The Enterprise; or, Love and Pleasure (1822); Baltimore, 27 May 1822 [18 nos. pubd separately (1823)]

Songs: Bliss! (1820); The Myrtle Cottage Maid (1820); True Beauty (1820); Hark, hark! Over valley and hill, Light skims thro' the air, Morning dews the sun dispelling [incidental music for Cherry and Fair Star, (1826–9)]; I still may boast my will is free, duet (1827); Lady, why art thou so fair? (1827); Annual Coronation Ode (1831); at least 35 others

Pf: Military Serenade, with fl, vc (1820); An Original Air, variations (1820); 2 Waltzes (1820); Independence and Union Waltzes (1823); The Bonnie Boat, variations (?1828); The Carrollton March (1828), perf. at the opening ceremony of the Baltimore & Ohio Railroad, 4 July 1828; Medley Ov., orch, arr. pf (?1832–3); 4 dances, 2 marches, 2 variations, 1 medley, and 1 ov.

Principal publishers: Clifton, Willig

EDITIONS

An Original Collection of Psalm Tunes (Baltimore, 1819)

New Vocal Instructer [sic] (Baltimore, 1820, 3/1846)

New Piano Forte Preceptor (Baltimore, 1820)

Clifton's New and Improved Piano Forte Preceptor (Baltimore, 1827, 3/1839, ?1843 as Clifton's Instructions for the Piano Forte)

BIBLIOGRAPHY

EitnerQ

J. H. Hewitt: *Shadows on the Wall* (Baltimore, 1877/*R*1971)

F. J. Metcalf: "Philip Anthony Corri and Arthur Clifton," *Choir and Musical Journal*, clx (1923), 75

——: *American Writers and Compilers of Sacred Music* (New York, 1925/*R*1967)

W. D. Gettell: "Arthur Clifton's *Enterprise*," *JAMS*, ii (1949), 23

L. Keefer: *Baltimore's Music* (Baltimore, 1962)

R. J. Wolfe: *Secular Music in America, 1801–1825: a Bibliography* (New York, 1964)

J. B. Clark, ed.: *Anthology of Early American Keyboard Music, 1787–1830* (Madison, 1977)

L. Frickey: "The Life and Vocal Works of Arthur Clifton, Baltimore's Unknown Composer" [NEH paper, U. of Kansas, 1978]

B. E. Wilson, compiler: *The Newberry Library Catalog of Early American Printed Sheet Music* (Boston, 1983)

J. BUNKER CLARK

Clifton, Bill (*b* Riderwood, MD, 5 April 1931). Country-music singer, guitarist, and autoharp player. Influenced by the recordings of the Carter family, he gave his earliest performances on local radio stations in Virginia, where he sang and accompanied himself on the guitar. In 1953 he formed the Dixie Mountain Boys, a bluegrass group. When it disbanded in 1957 he joined the "World's Original Jamboree" on radio station WWVA in Wheeling, West Virginia. Best known for his bluegrass singing (on recordings such as *All the good times are past and gone*, 1955;

Little Whitewashed Chimney, 1957; and *Springhill Disaster*, 1958), he is also one of the few country-music autoharp players to have made commercial recordings (including the album *Autoharp Centennial Celebration*, ELF101). During the 1960s Clifton arranged tours of England by such bluegrass performers as Bill Monroe, the Stanley Brothers, and the New Lost City Ramblers. He has toured the Philippines, New Zealand, Japan, the Netherlands, and Germany, where his foreign record releases have achieved high acclaim.

BIBLIOGRAPHY

R. K. Spottswood: "An Interview with Bill Clifton," *Bluegrass Unlimited*, ii (1968), no.9, p.3; no.10, p.9; no.11, p.7

R. J. Ronald and R. Petronko: "Bill Clifton Discography," *Bluegrass Unlimited*, vi/4 (1971), 13

D. Spottswood: "A Bluegrass Experiment: the First Generation," *Bluegrass Unlimited*, xiii/2 (1978), 22

RONNIE PUGH

Clinch Mountain Boys. Bluegrass group formed by the STANLEY BROTHERS in 1946.

Cline, Patsy [Hensley, Virginia Patterson] (*b* Winchester, VA, 8 Sept 1932; *d* Camden, TN, 5 March 1963). Country-music singer. As a teenager she sang with country bands in clubs in her home town, sometimes accompanying herself on guitar. She made her first recordings for the Four Star label in 1955, but achieved her greatest success on the Decca label after 1961. She gained valuable professional experience and reached a wider audience through her appearances on "Town and Country Time," a radio and television variety show in Washington, DC, but her career reached a turning point when, on 28 January 1957, she won first place on "Arthur Godfrey's Talent Scouts" on CBS television, singing *Walkin' after Midnight*. In 1960 she became a member of the "Grand Ole Opry." She preferred to sing traditional country music, and used such vocal tricks as yodeling and growling, but her voice was more suited to the country-pop music that became dominant in the late 1950s; her recordings of songs in that style, such as *I fall to pieces* and *Crazy* (both 1961), appealed to many people outside the usual country-music audience. Cline was at the height of her career when she was killed in an airplane crash. She was elected to the Country Music Hall of Fame in 1973.

BIBLIOGRAPHY

E. Nassour: *Patsy Cline* (New York, 1981)

J. Jensen: "Patsy Cline's Recording Career: the Search for a Sound," *Journal of Country Music*, ix/2 (1982), 34

D. Roy: "The Patsy Cline Discography," *Journal of Country Music*, ix/2 (1982), 47–115

BILL C. MALONE

Clinton, George (*b* Kannapolis, NC, 22 July 1940). Popular songwriter, record producer, entrepreneur, and singer. He grew up in New Jersey and formed a vocal group, the Parliaments, while he was still in his teens; its original members were Calvin Simon, Raymond Davis, Grady Thomas, and Fuzzy Haskins. In the 1960s Clinton worked on the fringes of the music business in the New York area. The Parliaments moved to Detroit and made their first successful recording, *I wanna testify*, in 1967. Beginning with *All your goodies are gone* (no.80, 1967), they began to show the influence of psychedelic rock, especially the work of Hendrix and Sly and the Family Stone, which helped Clinton to find his own style. In the late 1960s, as a result of a legal dispute, the Parliaments became known as Parliament, and Clinton put together another group, Funkadelic, which began recording for the Westbound label; these two groups consisted of a loose collection of musicians who at different times included, besides the original members of Parliament, Bernie Worrell (*b* New Jersey, 19 April 1944), keyboard player, BOOTSY COLLINS, bass guitarist, Eddie Hazel (*b* 10 April 1950), singer and guitarist, Raymond "Tiki" Fulwood (*b* 23 May 1944), drummer, Michael Hampton, guitarist, Gary Shider, singer and guitarist, and Walter "Junie" Morrison, keyboard player. Clinton sang, produced recordings, and wrote songs (usually with Worrell, Shider, or Collins), but his main function was to create a mythology into which the various groups, songs, and singers could be fitted.

Clinton's most influential recordings were made in the 1970s. *Osmium* (1970) is an extraordinarily adventurous album ranging in style and content from unwholesome sexual parody to metaphysical gospel, from country music to acid rock; one exquisite song, "The Silent Boatman," uses bagpipe. In the mid-1970s Clinton's musical and organizational ingenuity began to bring financial rewards. Neil Bogart signed up Parliament for Casablanca Records, and after making two excellent albums, though with only modest commercial success, the group released *Mothership Connection*, which sold several million copies, in 1976; the blend of rap (to science fiction lyrics) and heavy funk rhythms so caught the public's imagination that the group's abbreviated name, "P. Funk," and the title of the hit single from the album *Tear the roof off the sucker* became common phrases among black Americans. Parliament continued to make albums that sold well, culminating in the remarkable *Funkentelechy vs. the Placebo Syndrome* (1978), which used synthesizer, rather than bass guitar, as the source of its syncopated ostinato bass line. At around this time Clinton established Bootsy Collins with his own Rubber Band, recording on the Warner Bros. label, for which the Parliament and Funkadelic groups also turned out yet more highly successful albums. The best of the recordings made by Clinton's groups was *One Nation under a Groove* (1978), by a new combination of musicians known as Funkadelic. The title track, a dance number which reached no.28 on the pop chart, preserved Funkadelic's characteristic hard-rock guitar sound and its dubious scatological versifying.

Besides Parliament and Funkadelic, Clinton's activities gave rise to half a dozen groups that recorded successfully on most of the major labels. Clinton himself created the Rabelaisian stage persona of Dr. Funkenstein, who descended into performances from a flying saucer, reveling in his own good humor and extolling hedonism and personal freedom; a feature of his three- to six-hour-long concerts was the mass chanting of the phrase "Think! It ain't illegal yet!" In the late 1970s the success of Clinton's enterprises began to fade; Parliament, Funkadelic, and Collins's Rubber Band released albums of reasonable quality but uncertain focus. In 1982 Clinton embarked on a solo career that perpetuates the humor, myth-making, and musical style of the groups; *Atomic Dog* is as effective as the best of *One Nation under a Groove*.

With Sly and the Family Stone, Clinton's musicians were the most influential performers of black psychedelic rock and funk, distinguished by rhythmic complexity and generous use of electronic effects; their influence is heard not only in the music of many black groups but also in the work of such new-wave performers as Talking Heads, with whom Worrell played in the early 1980s.

RECORDINGS

(selective list)

Parliaments: I wanna testify (Revilot 207, 1967); All your goodies are gone (Revilot 211, 1967)

Parliament: *Osmium* (Invictus 7302, 1970); *Up for the Down Stroke* (Cas. 7002, 1974); *Mothership Connection* (Cas. 7022, 1976); *Funkentelechy vs. the Placebo Syndrome* (Cas. 7084, 1977), incl. Flash Light, Bop Gun

Funkadelic (recorded for Westbound unless otherwise stated): *Funkadelic* (216, 1970); *Free your Mind and your Ass will Follow* (2001, 1970); *Maggot Brain* (2007, 1971); *America Eats its Young* (2020, 1972); *Cosmic Slop* (2022, 1973); *Let's Take it to the Stage* (215, 1975); *Tales of Kidd Funkadelic* (227, 1976); *One Nation under a Groove* (WB 3209, 1978); *Uncle Jam Wants you* (WB 3371, 1979); *The Electric Spanking of War Babies* (WB 3482, 1981)

As soloist: *Computer Games* (Cap. 12246, 1982); Atomic Dog (Cap. 5201, 1983)

DAVITT SIGERSON

Clog dance. A step dance of English and Irish origin, performed with metal bars attached to the soles of the shoes to accentuate the rhythms sounded by the feet hitting the floor. In the USA it became a folk dance of the Appalachian Mountains region, and is danced on hardsoled shoes, either with or without metal taps. The step involves the placement of the entire foot, with particular emphasis on the sound and accent made by the heel. The dance is performed to music with the fast, driving beat and lively rhythms (either duple or 6/8 meter) characteristic of Appalachian fiddle tunes. Commonly performed tunes include *Devil's Dream*, *Old Joe Clark*, *Cripple Creek*, and *Ragtime Annie*. Music is performed by any combination of the instruments normally associated with the string band: the banjo, guitar, fiddle, mandolin, double bass, and/or guitar. Clog dancing has become a regular feature at folk and craft fairs, and competitions are frequently held, the major ones including the United States National Clogging Competition, Indiana, the National Clogging Hall of Fame, North Carolina, and the state clogging competitions of Georgia and Tennessee.

BIBLIOGRAPHY

P. Buckman: *Let's Dance: Social, Ballroom and Folk Dancing* (New York, 1978)

For further bibliography, *see* DANCE.

PAULINE NORTON

Clooney, Rosemary (*b* Maysville, KY, 23 May 1928). Popular singer. She first formed a duo with her sister Betty and worked for radio station WLW in Cincinnati, then sang for two years with Tony Pastor's band. In 1951 she made a recording of *Come on-a my house*, a song by the novelist and playwright William Saroyan and his cousin Ross Bagdasarian, which made her nationally famous; the following year three of her recordings, *Tenderly*, *Botch-a-me*, and *Half as Much*, sold a million copies. She sang in a hard voice with a driving beat, in a style derived from rhythm-and-blues that became known as "belting" and was cultivated among white singers in the early 1950s. She had further successes in 1954 with *Hey there* (from the musical *The Pajama Game* by Richard Adler and Jerry Ross), *This ole house*, and *Mambo italiano*. She also appeared in a number of films in the early 1950s, including *Here Come the Girls* (with Bob Hope) and *White Christmas* (with Bing Crosby). Although she remained inactive during the 1960s, Clooney began to record and give concerts again in the 1970s, by which time her singing style had become more akin to jazz.

BIBLIOGRAPHY

"Clooney, Rosemary," *CBY 1957*

A. Shaw: *The Rockin' 50s* (New York, 1974)

ARNOLD SHAW

Clough-Leiter, Henry (*b* Washington, DC, 13 May 1874; *d* Wollaston, MA, 15 Sept 1956). Music editor and composer. He studied organ with George William Walter and held various positions in Washington as a church organist. After moving to Providence in 1899 and then to Boston in 1901, he was a music editor for the firm of Ditson (1901–8), the Boston Music Co. (1908–21), and E. C. Schirmer (editor-in-chief, 1921–56). He composed many short choral works and songs, the cantatas *The Righteous Branch* and *Christ Triumphant*, and the symphonic ode (with soloists and double chorus) *The Christ of the Andes*.

BIBLIOGRAPHY

GroveAS

H. WILEY HITCHCOCK

Clovers. Rhythm-and-blues and rock-and-roll vocal group. Formed in Washington, DC, in the late 1940s, its members were Charlie White (*b* Washington, DC, *c*1930), John "Buddy" Bailey (*b* Washington, *c*1930), Matthew McQuater, Harold "Hal" Lucas, Jr., and Harold Winley, singers; and Bill Harris, guitarist. They began recording for Atlantic Records in 1951; their first two releases, *Don't you know I love you* and *Fool, Fool, Fool* (both 1951), reached no. 1 on the rhythm-and-blues chart. The witty songs with which Atlantic's staff writers provided them usually concerned hapless encounters with women, or alcohol, and prepared the way for the far more famous Coasters. The Clovers continued to make successful recordings through the 1950s, but achieved mass popularity only with *Love Potion no.9* (1959), which was, ironically, an imitation of the Coasters' style. Their work epitomized the anonymous creativity of black musicians which formed the basis for the rise to popularity of rock-and-roll in the 1950s. Although the Clovers produced mostly dance music, their harmonies were based not on jump blues but on gospel music and helped to lay the foundation for the emergence of soul music in the 1960s.

RECORDINGS

(selective list; recorded for Atlantic unless otherwise stated)

Yes sir, that's my baby (Rainbow 122, 1950); Don't you know I love you (934, 1951); Fool, Fool, Fool (944, 1951); One Mint Julep (963, 1952); Good Lovin' (1000, 1953); Nip Sip (1052, 1954); Your cash ain't nothin' but trash (1035, 1954); Lovey Dovey (1022, 1954); *The Clovers* (1248, 1956), incl. Down in the Alley [recorded 1953]; Devil or Angel (1083, 1956); Love, Love, Love (1094, 1956); Love Potion no.9 (UA 180, 1959)

BIBLIOGRAPHY

A. Shaw: *Honkers and Shouters: the Golden Years of Rhythm and Blues* (New York, 1978)

N. Tosches: "The Clovers: Absalom, Absalom! Doo-Wah, Doo-Wah!," *Unsung Heroes of Rock 'n' Roll* (New York, 1984), 96, 175 [incl. discography]

GREIL MARCUS

CMS. *See* COLLEGE MUSIC SOCIETY.

Coasters. Popular vocal group. A black quartet, it began as the Robins, a rhythm-and-blues vocal group, in 1949, and had its first successes with material written and produced by Leiber and Stoller – *Riot in Cell Block no.9* (1954), which highlighted the voice of Richard Berry (who later wrote *Louie Louie*), and *Smokey Joe's Café* (1955). The Robins then disbanded, but several of its members formed the Coasters (named after their Los Angeles base), which became the principal vehicle for Leiber and Stoller. These included Carl Gardner (lead singer), Billy Guy (who was responsible for most of the comic voices that characterized its hits), Cornell Gunter, and Will "Dub" Jones (bass). Their biggest successes were *Searchin'* (no.5, 1957), *Yakety yak* (no.1, 1958), *Charlie Brown* (1958; no.2, 1959), *Along came Jones* (no.9, 1959), and *Poison Ivy* (no.7, 1959).

The Coasters were known for the catchy arrangements and wry lyrics of the songs they performed; their facetious renderings made Stoller's ambitious, referential music palatable to a mass audience and enabled Leiber to discuss subjects that would otherwise have been considered unfit for airplay. Only Chuck Berry's lyrics surpass Leiber's work for the Coasters in literary subtlety and allegorical conscience. The deliciously lewd *Little Egypt* (1961) and *Poison Ivy*, a song that might be about a girl with a social disease, managed to penetrate popular radio during its most conservative years; *Framed* (1955), *Shoppin' for Clothes* (1960), and the classic *Riot in Cell Block no.9* discussed the oppression of black Americans in a way that made the problem real and approachable to the least enlightened listeners. The violins and *mariachi* touches of Leiber's and Stoller's innovative productions aptly suggested that the Coasters were the most frivolous of Top 40 acts, but they were also pioneers of social realism in pop music.

BIBLIOGRAPHY

S. Propes: *Those Oldies but Goodies: a Guide to 50's Record Collecting* (New York, 1973), 30 [discography]
R. Palmer: Liner notes, *Young Blood* (Atl./Deluxe AD2-4003, 1982)

DAVITT SIGERSON

Coast Salish. American Indian group of the northwest coast; *see* SALISH.

Coates, Dorothy Love (*b* Birmingham, AL, 30 Jan 1928). Gospel singer and composer. She was born into a musical family and by the age of ten was playing the piano for her church. As a teenager she sang with the Royal Travelers and a family group, the McGriff Singers. In 1945 she joined the Original Gospel Harmonettes, an all-female group in Birmingham, whose members were Vera Kilb, Mildred Miller Howard, Odessa Edwards, Willie Mae Newberry, and the pianist Evelyn Starks. Their first recordings, *I'm sealed*, followed by *Get away Jordan* (1951), placed them in the front ranks of gospel singers. The group made several successful recordings and appearances during the next seven years, performing predominantly works by Coates. Her compositional style is simple in its melody, harmony, and rhythm; her lyrics make use of favorite church sayings and "wandering couplets" taken from older hymns and spirituals (for example, *He may not come when you want him, but he's right on time*, 1953; *I've got Jesus and that's enough*, 1956). In her own performances she captures the emotion of the text by forcing her voice at the extremes of its range. Her songs have been recorded by such singers as Mahalia Jackson, Clara Ward, and Johnny Cash. Coates has appeared at all the major gospel festivals and frequently at the Newport Jazz Festival.

BIBLIOGRAPHY

SouthernB
T. Heilbut: *The Gospel Sound: Good News and Bad Times* (New York, 1971/*R*1975)
I. V. Jackson: *Afro-American Religious Music: a Bibliography and Catalogue of Gospel Music* (Westport, CT, 1979)

HORACE CLARENCE BOYER

Cobham, Billy [William C.] (*b* Panama, 16 May 1944). Jazz-rock drummer. When he was three he moved with his family to New York, where he later attended the High School of Music and Art. In the late 1960s he played in jazz groups with Billy Taylor and Horace Silver before helping to form a short-lived early fusion band, Dreams, in 1969–70. During these years he also played on Miles Davis's jazz-rock fusion recordings and, in 1971, became a member of John McLaughlin's Mahavishnu Orchestra. The power and precision of his playing with McLaughlin had an enormous impact on later jazz-rock drumming and placed him with Tony Williams and Alphonse Mouzon among the leading drummers in this new style. From the mid-1970s he led his own fusion groups and played in a large number of studio bands with Stanley Turrentine, Ron Carter, and other jazz musicians. He is also active as a teacher in university and conservatory workshops.

RECORDINGS

(selective list)

As leader: *Dreams* (1970, Col. C30225); *Spectrum* (1973, Atl. 7268); *Total Eclipse* (1974, Atl. 18121); *George Duke/Billy Cobham Band Live on Tour in Europe* (1976, Atl. 18194); *Observations &* (1982, Elek. 60123)
As sideman: H. Silver: *Serenade to a Soul Sister* (1968, BN 84277); M. Davis: *A Tribute to Jack Johnson* (1970, Col. KC30455); J. McLaughlin: *Inner Mounting Flame* (1971, Col. PC31067)

BIBLIOGRAPHY

L. Underwood: "Cymbals – a Sonic Galaxy: Billy Cobham and Louis Bellson," *Down Beat*, xliv/18 (1977), 13
J.-P. Patillot: "Billy's Bounce," *Jazz hot*, no.361 (1979), 8
C. Iero: "Billy Cobham," *Modern Drummer*, iii/4 (1979), 10
"Billy Cobham: Team Player," *Jazz Forum*, no.77 (1982), 34 [international edn]
B. Cleall: "Blues March," *Modern Drummer*, vi/3 (1982), 54 [transcr.]

J. BRADFORD ROBINSON

Cochiti. Pueblo Indian group. *See* PUEBLO, EASTERN.

Cochran, Eddie (*b* Oklahoma City, OK, 3 Oct 1938; *d* London, England, 17 April 1960). Rock-and-roll singer, songwriter, and guitarist. He began his career as a country-music singer in the mid-1950s, at which time he was living in Los Angeles and working with Hank Cochran (unrelated), who later became a leading writer of country songs in Nashville. *Sittin' in the balcony*, his first single, was released in 1956, but it was not until 1958 that he had his first success, with *Summertime Blues*; this song became an anthem for disaffected teenagers, and the hit songs that followed it, such as *C'mon everybody* (no.35, 1958) and *Somethin' else* (no.58, 1959), helped further to define the experience of young people in the 1950s. Cochran's virile tenor was the key element in the success of these songs, but he is best known for the primitive intensity of his guitar playing; he employed techniques and produced a sound that are normally associated only with much later rock musicians, and that influenced players such as Pete Townshend and new-wave performers. Cochran appeared in the film *The Girl can't Help it* (1956), in which he sang the song *20 Flight Rock*. He achieved his greatest popularity in England, where he died in an automobile accident while on tour.

RECORDINGS

(selective list; recorded for Liberty unless otherwise stated)

Sittin' in the balcony (55056, 1956); *Singin' to my Baby* (3061, 1957); Summertime Blues (55144, 1958); C'mon everybody (55166, 1958); Somethin' else (55203, 1959); *Eddie Cochran*, Legendary Masters, iv (UA 9959, 1972) [collected album, with extensive liner notes by L. Kaye]

JOHN MORTHLAND

Cochran, William (*b* Arlington, VA). Tenor. Educated at Wesleyan University, he studied singing at the Curtis Institute with Martial Singher. After winning the Lauritz Melchior Heldentenor Foundation Award in 1969, he became a member of the Frankfurt

Opera (1970) and the Vienna Opera, and has sung in many other European houses as well as in concert with the New York PO (1971), the Boston SO, and a number of other American orchestras. He made his London début at Covent Garden in 1974 as Laca (*Jenůfa*) and returned to San Francisco in 1977 (having sung Froh in *Das Rheingold* there in 1968) to sing Tichon (*Kát'a Kabanová*). In addition to all the German heroic tenor roles, his repertory includes Idomeneus, Jason (Cherubini's *Médée*), Otello, Canio (*Pagliacci*), Herod (Strauss's *Salome*), and the Pretender Dmitri (*Boris Godunov*). His well-placed voice and fine musicianship were also effectively displayed in Janáček's *The Makropulos Affair*, Busoni's *Doktor Faust*, Shostakovich's *Lady Macbeth of the Mtsensk District*, Bernd Alois Zimmermann's *Die Soldaten*, and Stravinsky's *The Rake's Progress*, in which he took the title role at Frankfurt in 1983.

ELIZABETH FORBES

Coci, Claire (*b* New Orleans, LA, 15 March 1912; *d* New Jersey, 30 Sept 1978). Organist. She began to study piano at the age of five and organ at ten, and at 14 she became an organist at the Church of the Immaculate Conception in her native city. Her first public organ recital was at Christ Church there in 1933. Her early training was with William C. Webb. She studied in the summers of 1935 and 1936 and during the academic year 1937–8 with Palmer Christian at the University of Michigan, and then in New York with Charles Courboin and in Paris with Marcel Dupré. She made her New York début, in Calvary Church, in 1938. In 1939 she became the first woman to give an organ recital in Cadet Chapel at West Point, where she later made a recording. In addition to making extensive concert tours, she taught at Oberlin Conservatory (from 1942), at Westminster Choir College in Princeton, New Jersey, and in New York at Mannes College, the Dalcroze School, and the School of Sacred Music at Union Theological Seminary; she also taught at Hartwick College in Oneonta, New York. From 1952 to 1955 she was official organist of the New York PO, the first and only woman to hold the post. In 1958 she founded the American Academy of Music and Art in Tenafly, New Jersey. She was killed in an automobile accident as she was returning to her home in Tenafly. Coci's career was a brilliant one owing to her solid technique, strong personality, and outstanding stage presence, and she was known for her interest in the music of contemporary composers.

Claire Coci, c1955

VERNON GOTWALS

Coe, David Allan (*b* Akron, OH, 6 Sept 1939). Country-music singer, guitarist, and songwriter. The product of a broken home, he spent nearly 20 of his first 30 years in reform schools and prisons. He learned to play guitar while in prison, and began to write songs, which he performed in penitentiary shows. After his release from the Ohio State Penitentiary in 1967, he went to Nashville, where he attempted to establish himself as a singer and songwriter. His unconventional performances and lifestyle appealed to the new audiences who came to country music from the rock culture. Shelby Singleton issued his first album, *Penitentiary Blues*, on his SSS label in 1968. Among his compositions are *Would you lay with me in a field of stone* (a no. 1 hit for Tanya Tucker in 1973) and *Take this job and shove it* (recorded by Johnny Paycheck in 1978). In 1978 Coe was one of the founders of Captive Music, a publisher of songs by prison inmates.

RECORDINGS

(selective list; recorded for Columbia unless otherwise indicated)

Penitentiary Blues (SSS 9, 1968); *The Mysterious Rhinestone Cowboy* (KC32942, 1974); *Once Upon a Rhyme* (PC33085, 1976); *Long-haired Redneck* (PC33916, 1976); *David Allan Coe Rides Again* (KC34310, 1977); *Tattoo* (PC34780, 1977); *Human Emotions* (KC35535, 1978)

BIBLIOGRAPHY

D. A. Coe: *Just for the Record* (Big Pine Key, FL, 1978) [autobiography]

DON CUSIC

Coerne, Louis (Adolphe) (*b* Newark, NJ, 27 Feb 1870; *d* Boston, MA, 11 Sept 1922). Conductor, teacher, and composer. He studied violin with Kneisel and composition at Harvard University with J. K. Paine (1888–90); from 1890 to 1893 he studied organ and composition in Munich with Joseph Rheinberger. After holding various church and conducting appointments in Buffalo, New York, and Columbus, Ohio, he returned to Germany, where he lived from 1899 to 1902 and completed Rheinberger's unfinished Mass in A minor. From 1903 to 1904 he taught at Smith College and at Harvard, where he wrote his thesis, *The Evolution of Modern Orchestration* (1908/*R*1979), and in 1905 received the first PhD in music given by an American university.

Coerne visited Germany again from 1905 to 1907. His opera *Zenobia* (op.66) was produced in Bremen in 1905; it was the first American opera to be heard in Germany, and also the only one of Coerne's stage works to be produced anywhere. His last posts included those of music director at Troy, New York (1907–9), director of the conservatory at Olivet (Michigan) College (1909–10), director of the school of music at the University of Wisconsin (1910–15), and professor at Connecticut College for Women, New London (1915–22).

Coerne wrote more than 500 works, some 300 of which were published. His dramatic works include *A Woman of Marblehead* (op.40), *Sakuntala*, a melodrama after Kalidasa (op.67), and *The Maiden Queen* (op.69). He also wrote incidental music for *The*

Trojan Women of Euripides, overtures and symphonic poems (including *Hiawatha*) for orchestra, *Romantic Concerto* for violin and orchestra, a string quartet, *Swedish Sonata* for violin and piano, and some piano pieces, songs, and partsongs. His manuscripts are in the Boston Public Library.

BIBLIOGRAPHY

GroveAS [incl. list of works]
A. Elson: "Coerne, Louis Adolphe," *DAB*

RICHARD ALDRICH/R

Cohan, George M(ichael) (*b* Providence, RI, 3/4 July 1878; *d* New York, 5 Nov 1942). Songwriter, actor, playwright, and producer. From boyhood he toured in New England and the Midwest with his parents and sister in an act called the Four Cohans, which by 1900 had become one of the leading performances on the vaudeville circuit. He played violin in the pit orchestra when he was nine and began writing sketches for the family act when he was 11 and songs when he was 13. During the 1890s he assumed a swaggering walk, brash speech, and rapid delivery, forming an image of a song-and-dance man that later became archetypal. In 1901 he extended his vaudeville sketch *The Governor's Son* into a full-length musical show, and in 1903 did the same with *Running for Office*: both were moderately successful items in the family's repertory.

Cohan's first original musical comedy was *Little Johnny Jones* (1904), for which he wrote the book, lyrics, and music, and in which he took the leading part. It was tried out in Hartford (10 October) before opening in New York, and became a considerable success on its subsequent tour. The fast-moving plot was a vehicle for elaborately choreographed dances, flag-waving parades, and songs that included "Yankee Doodle Boy" and "Give my regards to Broadway." In contrast with contemporary Broadway operetta the subject matter and characters were American, the speech vernacular, and the songwriting direct and easily memorable. In 1906 Cohan consolidated his reputation with *George Washington, Jr.* (again taking the leading role) and *Forty-five Minutes from Broadway*, written for Fay Templeton. He continued to write and, sometimes, to appear in musical comedies until the 1920s. Although the limited range of expression of these works restricted the inroads they made into the current vogue for operetta and, later, spectacular revue, they helped greatly to establish the taste for an essentially American style of musical comedy that was taken up most notably by Jerome Kern.

From 1904 Cohan was in partnership with Sam H. Harris, producing musical comedies, revues, and straight plays by Cohan as well as occasionally by other writers. Around 1907 they formed their own publishing company. They also acquired interests in several theaters in New York and owned their own playhouses, the George M. Cohan Theatre and the Cohan and Harris Theatre. The partnership ended in 1920 when Cohan lost his opposition to the unionization of actors, but Cohan continued to produce alone. As an actor he also gave distinguished performances in Eugene O'Neill's *Ah, Wilderness* (1934) and the political satire *I'd Rather be Right* (1937) by Rodgers and Hart.

Cohan wrote more than 500 songs, of which *Over there* (1917) was the most popular morale song for two world wars. It is for this and a few other spirited, slangy, and patriotic songs that he is chiefly remembered, helped by the film *Yankee Doodle Dandy* (1942) and the Broadway musical *George M!* (1968), which were based on his life and used many of his songs. Cohan was an untrained musician, who professed only to write songs in the standard format of introduction, two verses, and chorus, with simple harmonies and undemanding vocal range. However, his significance in bringing vaudeville elements into the mainstream musical theater to establish the essentially American brand of fast-moving musical comedy was profound.

George M. Cohan: commemorative postal stamp, designed by Jim Sharpe and issued by the US Postal Service, 3 July 1978

See also MUSICAL, fig.2; MUSICAL THEATER, §III, 1; PATRIOTIC MUSIC, §2.

WORKS

Musicals and revues; words by Cohan; all dates are those of first New York performance.

The Governor's Son, Savoy, 25 Feb 1901
Running for Office, 14th Street, 27 April 1903; rev. as The Honeymooners, Aerial Gardens, 3 June 1907
Little Johnny Jones, Liberty, 7 Nov 1904 [incl. Yankee Doodle Boy, Give my regards to Broadway]
Forty-five Minutes from Broadway, New Amsterdam, 1 Jan 1906 [incl. Forty-five minutes from Broadway, Mary's a grand old name, So long, Mary]
George Washington, Jr., Herald Square, 12 Feb 1906 [incl. You're a grand old flag, All aboard for Broadway]
The Talk of New York, Knickerbocker, 3 Dec 1907
Fifty Miles from Boston, Garrick, 3 Feb 1908 [incl. Harrigan]
The Yankee Prince, Knickerbocker, 20 April 1908
The American Idea, New York, 5 Oct 1908
The Man who Owns Broadway, New York, 11 Oct 1909
The Little Millionaire, George M. Cohan, 25 Sept 1911
Hello, Broadway!, Astor, 25 Dec 1914
The Cohan Revue, Astor, 9 Feb 1916
The Cohan Revue of 1918, collab. I. Berlin, New Amsterdam, 31 Dec 1917
The Voice of McConnell, Manhattan Opera, 25 Dec 1918
The Royal Vagabond, collab. A. Goetzl, Cohan and Harris, 17 Feb 1919
Little Nellie Kelly, Liberty, 13 Nov 1922
The Rise of Rosie O'Grady, Liberty, 25 Dec 1923

The Merry Malones, Erlanger's, 26 Sept 1927
Billie, Erlanger's, 1 Oct 1928

c500 songs, incl. Why did Nellie leave her home?, 1893; Venus, my shining love, 1894; Hot Tamale Alley, 1895; I guess I'll have to telegraph my baby, 1898; Over there, 1917

Principal publisher: Marks

BIBLIOGRAPHY

G. M. Cohan: *Twenty Years on Broadway and the Years it Took to Get There* (New York, 1924)
W. Morehouse: *George M. Cohan: Prince of the American Theater* (Philadelphia, 1943)
C. Smith: *Musical Comedy in America* (New York, 1950, rev. 2/1981)
S. Green: *The World of Musical Comedy* (New York, 1960, rev. 4/1980)
J. McCabe: *George M. Cohan: the Man who Owned Broadway* (New York, 1973)
D. Ewen: *All the Years of American Popular Music* (Englewood Cliffs, NJ, 1977)
S. M. Vallillo: "George M. Cohan's *Little Johnny Jones*," *Musical Theatre in America: Greenvale, NY 1981*, ed. G. Loney (Westport, CT, 1984), 233

RONALD BYRNSIDE/ANDREW LAMB

Cohen, Isidore (*b* 1922). Violinist who joined the BEAUX ARTS TRIO in 1968.

Cohen, Joel (Israel) (*b* Providence, RI, 23 May 1942). Conductor and lutenist. After studying composition and musicology at Brown University (BA 1963) and Harvard University (MA 1965), he worked in theory and composition in Paris with Boulanger (1965–7). He returned to the USA to become the director of the Boston Camerata, an instrumental ensemble founded in Boston in 1954, of which he had been a member during his student years. Under Cohen's direction the group was augmented by a chamber chorus, and its concert and recorded repertory encompassed medieval and Renaissance music as well as Baroque works. From 1975 the Camerata has regularly offered workshops and performed in the USA and in France. Individually Cohen is also active in France as a producer of early-music programs on television and radio as well as conductor and continuo lutenist at major music festivals. He also sings baritone. An imaginative and resourceful musician in his special domain, Cohen has lectured extensively at universities and conservatories in the USA and Europe on the performance of early music.

HOWARD SCHOTT

Cohen, Paul (*b* Chicago, IL, 10 Nov 1908; *d* Bryan, TX, 1 April 1971). Country-music record producer. In 1927 he began working for the Columbia Phonograph Company and in 1934 became a salesman for Decca Records. In the 1940s he took over direction of Decca's country division from Dave Kapp and began to concentrate his operations in Nashville in order to draw on the resources of the "Grand Ole Opry." In 1947 he hired OWEN BRADLEY, then music director of radio station WSM, as his deputy. In the spring of 1945 Cohen recorded Red Foley in WSM's Studio D, which was probably the first commercial recording session in Nashville. He built Decca's artist roster into the finest in country music; it included such seminal figures as Bill Monroe, Ernest Tubb, Foley, Bob Wills, Jimmy Wakeley, Webb Pierce, Kitty Wells, and Spade Cooley. Cohen left Decca in 1958 for Coral Records, and in 1960 established his own label, Todd Records. He subsequently held positions with Kapp Records and ABC Records, and was influential in the foundation of the Country Music Association.

Cohen, Theodore Charles. *See* CHARLES, TEDDY.

Cohn, Arthur (*b* Philadelphia, PA, 6 Nov 1910). Composer, conductor, and author. Trained at the Combs Conservatory of Music, the University of Pennsylvania, and the Juilliard Graduate School, Cohn studied violin with Sascha Jacobinoff and composition with Rubin Goldmark. He organized the Dorian Quartet and the Stringart Quartet, ensembles specializing in contemporary music, in the 1930s. From 1934 to 1952 Cohn was director of the Fleisher Music Collection of Philadelphia, and was head of the music department at the Free Library of Philadelphia from 1946 to 1952. He has been executive director of the Settlement School, Philadelphia, head of the Symphonic and Foreign Departments, Mills Music, New York, director of "serious music" for MCA Music, New York, and, in 1973, became director of "serious music" for Carl Fischer. Cohn has conducted the Philadelphia Orchestra and the National Orchestra of Mexico. Since 1958 he has been conductor of the Haddonfield (New Jersey) SO.

In addition to an active career on radio and television, Cohn has lectured widely in the USA, especially at the Berkshire Music Center. He has been critic for the *American Record Guide*, *Musical Courier*, and the *Rochester Times-Union*. His awards include first prize (1940) from the American Society of Ancient Instruments and 20 ASCAP awards (1962 to 1982). His works show a natural grasp of instrumentation, expressive lyricism, and a colorful sense of harmony.

WORKS

52 works, incl. 5 str qts, 1928–45, no.1 transcr. str orch as 4 Preludes, no.4 transcr. str orch as Histrionics; 5 Nature Studies, orch, 1932; Suite, e, vn, pf, 1932; Music for Brass Insts, 4 tpt, 3 trbn, 1935; Retrospections, str orch, 1935; Machine Music, 2 pf, 1937; The Pot-bellied Gods (R. Abramson), Bar, str qt, 1937; Suite, va, orch, 1937; Music for Ancient Insts, 1938; 4 Sym. Documents, 1939; Preludes, pf, 1939; Conc., 5 ancient insts, orch, 1940; The 12 (Russian), nar, str qt, 1940; Fl Conc., 1941; Declamation and Toccata, Hebraic Study, bn/(bn, pf), 1944; Variations, cl, sax, str orch, 1945; Music for Bn, 1947; Quotations in Perc, 103 perc, 6 pfmrs, 1958; Kaddish, orch, 1964; Perc Conc., 1970

MSS in *DLC*, *NN*

Principal publishers: Belwin-Mills, Elkan-Vogel, MCA

WRITINGS

The Collector's Twentieth-century Music in the Western Hemisphere (Philadelphia and New York, 1961/*R*1972)
Twentieth-century Music in Western Europe (Philadelphia and New York, 1965/*R*1972)
Recorded Classical Music (New York, 1981)
An Encyclopedia of Chamber Music (in preparation)

JAMES G. ROY, JR./R

Colburn, William F. (*fl* 1834–95). Music teacher, dealer, and publisher, active in Cincinnati. He formed the Eclectic Academy of Music with T. B. Mason in 1834 and became the first music teacher in the Cincinnati public schools in 1844. In 1849 he was a partner in the music publishing firm of Mason, Colburn & Co., but by 1851 was in partnership with Joel Field; an advertisement in the *Cincinnati Enquirer* reads "Colburn and Field, successors to Mason and Colburn . . . sole agents for Jonas Chickering's pianos." He was later in business by himself as a dealer in musical instruments. By 1859 he appears to have ceased publishing on his own account, but a W. F. Colburn joined the John Church Co. in 1890. City directories indicate that Colburn continued to deal in Chickering pianos as late as 1868, but his name ceases to appear after 1895.

BIBLIOGRAPHY

C. T. Greve: *Centennial History of Cincinnati and its Representative Citizens* (Chicago, 1904)

D. J. Epstein: Introduction, *Complete Catalogue of Sheet Music and Musical Works Published by the Board of Music Trade* (New York, 1870/*R*1973), p.xxiii

RICHARD D. WETZEL

Colby, Edward E(ugene) (*b* Oakland, CA, 5 July 1912). Music librarian. He received the BA in music at the University of California, Berkeley (1935), and the MA at Stanford University (1956); he received a certificate of librarianship at Berkeley in 1941 and a certificate in Far Eastern studies from Pomona College in 1944. From 1946 to 1949 Colby was acting chief of the music division of the Oakland Public Library, and then served as music librarian at Stanford University until his retirement in 1978; he was also archivist of the Archive of Recorded Sound at Stanford (1958–78), and lecturer in music (1951–79). Colby held the office of president of the Music Library Association from 1950 to 1952. He is the author of several journal articles dealing with sound recording archives.

PAULA MORGAN

Cole, Bob [Robert Allen] (*b* Athens, GA, 1 July 1863; *d* Catskill, NY, 2 Aug 1911). Lyricist, composer, and vaudeville entertainer. After graduating from Atlanta University he went to New York, where he became playwright for, and manager of, the All-Star Company at Worth's Museum. In 1896 he wrote a show for Black Patti's Troubadours, but left the company shortly afterwards because of a dispute with its managers. He then teamed up with Billy Johnson to write *A Trip to Coontown* (1898), the first musical comedy created, produced, managed, and performed entirely by Blacks; it was extremely successful, and toured for four years. Cole also wrote a number of coon songs with Johnson, most notably *La Hoola Boola* (1897), considered to be the original version of Yale University's *Boola Boola*. Cole then formed a songwriting partnership with the brothers J. Rosamond Johnson and James Weldon Johnson (no relation to Billy Johnson). Working as a trio, or more often in pairs, they produced an impressive number of hit songs, including *Under the Bamboo Tree* (1902), an enduring standard loosely based on the melody of the spiritual *Nobody knows the trouble I've seen* and introduced by Marie Cahill in Englander's *Sally in our Alley*. They contributed songs to other white Broadway musicals, including *The Belle of Bridgeport* (1900), *In Newport* (1904), and *Humpty Dumpty* (1904), and also produced two successful musicals of their own, *The Shoo-fly Regiment* (1907) and *The Red Moon* (1909). Cole's songs are typical of the many coon songs written around the turn of the century, but it would be a gross error to assume, as does Spaeth, that the racism inherent in the genre left him unaffected; he suffered a mental breakdown on the final night of an engagement at Keith's Fifth Avenue Theatre where he was performing with J. Rosamond Johnson, and committed suicide shortly afterwards.

WORKS
(selective list)

STAGE

Unless otherwise stated, librettos and/or lyrics are by Cole, and music is by J. R. Johnson, some probably in collaboration with Cole; dates are those of first New York performance.

A Trip to Coontown, collab. B. Johnson, 4 April 1898

The Shoo-fly Regiment, 6 Aug 1907 [incl. Won't you be my little brown bear?]

The Red Moon, 3 May 1909 [incl. On the road to Monterey]

SONGS

In collaboration with B. Johnson: La Hoola Boola (1897); I wonder what is that coon's game (1898); The Luckiest Coon in Town (1899); The Wedding of the Chinee and the Coon (1899); No Coons Allowed (1899)

Lyrics by Cole, J. W. Johnson, J. R. Johnson, music by Cole and/or J. R. Johnson: I ain't gwine ter work no mo', in The Belle of Bridgeport, 1900; The Maiden with the Dreamy Eyes (1901); Nobody's lookin' but de owl an' de moon (1901); Tell me, dusky maiden (1901); Oh, didn't he ramble (1902); Under the Bamboo Tree, in Sally in our Alley (1902); Moonlight on the Mississippi (1903); Scandal, in In Newport, 1904; Sambo and Dinah, in Humpty Dumpty, 1904; My Lulu San (1905); The Sweetest Gal in Town (1908)

BIBLIOGRAPHY

SouthernB

S. Spaeth: *A History of Popular Music in America* (New York, 1948/*R*1962)

J. W. Johnson: *Along This Way* (New York, 1933, repr. 1954)

T. Riis: *Black Musical Theater in New York, 1890–1915* (diss., U. of Michigan, 1981)

S. Dennison: *Scandalize my Name: Black Imagery in American Popular Music* (New York, 1982)

SAM DENNISON

Cole, Cozy [William Randolph] (*b* East Orange, NJ, 17 Oct 1906 or 1909; *d* Columbus, OH, 29 Jan 1981). Jazz drummer. Early in his career he worked with Jelly Roll Morton, Benny Carter, Willie Bryant, Stuff Smith, and many other bandleaders, gaining a wide range of experience which served as the basis of his later versatility. He achieved fame during his four years (1938–42) with Cab Calloway's Orchestra, with whom he made several outstanding recordings. He later studied at the Juilliard School and subsequently worked as a percussionist in studio and theater ensembles; he resumed touring as a member of Louis Armstrong's All Stars from 1949 until 1953. He left Armstrong to manage a drum school in New York, in partnership with Gene Krupa. In 1959 a recording of *Topsy* featuring Cole's drum solo achieved large international sales; as a result Cole organized his own regular band, which enjoyed success in the 1960s. He later joined a quintet led by his former colleague in the Cab Calloway band, trumpeter Jonah Jones.

RECORDINGS
(selective list)

As leader: Thru' for the Night (1944, Keynote 1301); Concerto for Cozy (1944, Savoy 575); Drum Fantasy (1954, MGM EP 622); Topsy, pts. i–ii (1957–8, Love 5004)

As sideman: C. Calloway: Crescendo in Drums (1939, Voc./OK 5062), Paradiddle (1940, Voc./OK 5467); R. Eldridge: St. Louis Blues (1944, Keynote 607); L. Armstrong: Way Down Yonder in New Orleans (1951, Decca 9.28169)

BIBLIOGRAPHY

SouthernB

S. Dance: *The World of Swing* (New York, 1974), 183

P. Vacher: "Cozy Conversing," *Mississippi Rag*, v/6 (1978), 10

JOHN CHILTON

Cole, John (*b* Tewkesbury, England, 1774; *d* Baltimore, MD, 17 Aug 1855). Composer, tunebook compiler, and publisher. He came to the USA with his family in 1785 and settled in Baltimore. Cole's reputed attendance there at singing-schools conducted by Andrew Law, Thomas Atwill, and Ishmael Spicer during the years 1789–92 has not been verified. In the preface to *The Devotional Harmony* (1814), he wrote of his training: "The authour has never had what is called a musical education . . . he is a self taught genius, scarcely able to finger his own compositions on a keyed instrument." He nevertheless seems at one time to have held the post of organist and choirmaster of St. Paul's Episcopal Church in Baltimore.

Cole's career as a compiler of sacred tunebooks spanned almost half a century; he produced nearly 30 different issues, from *Sacred Harmony* (1799), adapted to the Methodist hymnbook, to *Laudate*

Dominum (1846), for the Protestant Episcopal Church. He became involved in the printing trade as early as 1802 and published and printed several of these works himself, as well as composing some of the pieces that appeared in them. During the War of 1812 he served in the Maryland military, apparently acting as leader of a militia band in which he played clarinet. He taught at least one singing-school in Baltimore in 1819. In 1822 he opened a music store, and from then until 1839 worked as a publisher, specializing in secular sheet music, of which, by the late 1820s, he was Baltimore's leading purveyor. The Maryland Historical Society owns a nearly complete run of Cole's musical publications, a total of some 900 items.

BIBLIOGRAPHY

J. H. Hewitt: *Shadows on the Wall, or Glimpses of the Past* (Baltimore, 1877)
S. P. Cheney: *The American Singing Book* (Boston, 1879/*R*1980), 186
F. J. Metcalf: *American Writers and Compilers of Sacred Music* (New York, 1925/*R*1967)
L. H. Dielman: "Old Baltimore Music and its Makers," *Peabody Bulletin* (May 1934), 26
R. J. Wolfe: *Secular Music in America 1801–1825: a Bibliography* (New York, 1964)
——: *Early American Music Engraving and Printing* (Urbana, IL, 1980)

RICHARD CRAWFORD

Cole, Nat "King" [Coles, Nathaniel Adams] (*b* Montgomery, AL, 17 March 1917; *d* Santa Monica, CA, 15 Feb 1965). Jazz pianist and popular singer. His family moved to Chicago when he was four, and by the age of 12 he was playing organ and singing in the church where his father was pastor. At high school he came under the influence of the music educators N. Clark Smith and Walter Dyett. His three brothers (Eddie, Fred, and Isaac) were also jazz musicians, and he made his recording début for Decca in 1936 with Eddie Cole's band the Solid Swingers. The rhythmically vital playing of Earl Hines was a strong influence on Cole's piano style, and his own early groups, the Rogues of Rhythm and the Twelve Royal Dukes, often played Hines's arrangements. Cole left Chicago in 1936 to lead a band in a revival of Eubie Blake's revue *Shuffle Along*, and he set up permanent residence in Los Angeles after the show disbanded there the following year. He later formed a trio with Oscar Moore (guitar) and Wesley Prince (double bass), which performed at the Swanee Inn in Hollywood as King Cole and his Swingsters before becoming known as the King Cole Trio. The group's instrumentation proved musically stimulating and historically influential: Art Tatum adopted a similar trio format in 1943, as did Oscar Peterson and Ahmad Jamal during the early 1950s. Cole retained his trio (with some changes of personnel) until 1951, recording regularly for Decca and, from 1943, for Capitol.

Some of Cole's most influential jazz recordings date from the early 1940s. Among these were four masterpieces from a session in Los Angeles in 1942 with the tenor saxophonist Lester Young and the double bass player Red Callender – an event of seminal importance for both Cole and Young; *Indiana*, *Body and Soul*, *I Can't Get Started*, and *Tea for Two* document Cole's impeccable jazz credentials as well as the continuing growth and mastery of Young. The King Cole Trio sometimes sang in unison on their early recordings, but in 1943 Cole had a national hit with his solo song *Straighten Up and Fly Right*. His immaculate diction and liquid vocal style made this recording accessible to white audiences and launched his career as a popular singer. From this point he gradually appeared less often with his trio, though from 1944 to 1946 he gave concerts and recorded with Jazz at the Philharmonic. His hit recording *The Christmas Song* (1946) was the first of his solo vocal recordings to be accompanied by a studio orchestra.

Cole was the first black jazz artist to have his own weekly radio show (1948–9), and by the early 1950s was internationally known – perhaps the first black male singer since Louis Armstrong to attract worldwide recognition. Until 1965 he toured widely, performing in supper clubs, theaters, and concert halls, and appeared in several films, including *St. Louis Blues* (1958, in which he portrayed W. C. Handy). In the 1956–7 season he had a weekly show as a soloist on television.

It is Cole's work as a jazz pianist, however, that is of greatest musical significance. He developed the intricate right-hand style initiated by Hines and the sparse, rhythmic left-hand style of Count Basie, and his influence on other jazz pianists was enormous, as attested by artists as varied as Erroll Garner, Peterson, Red Garland, and Bill Evans. Although in later years the piano was ancillary to his career as a popular singer, his place in the history of jazz piano is secure.

RECORDINGS

(selective list)

As leader or co-leader: Sweet Lorraine (1940, Decca 8520); with L. Young: Indiana/Body and Soul (1942, Philo 1000), I Can't Get Started/Tea for Two (1943, Philo 1001); Straighten Up and Fly Right (1943, Cap. 20009); It's Only a Paper Moon/Easy Listening Blues (1943–4, Cap. 20012); The Christmas Song (1946, Cap.311); When I Take my Sugar to Tea (1947, Cap. 813); Nature Boy (1948, Cap. 15054); Mona Lisa (1950, Cap. 1010); *After Midnight* (1956, Cap. T782); *The Swinging Side of Nat King Cole* (1958, Cap. T1724)

As sideman: E. Cole: Thunder/Honey Hush (1936, Decca 7210); L. Hampton: Jack the Bellboy (1940, Vic. 26652); H. Haymer: Kicks, pts. i–ii (1945, Swing 370)

BIBLIOGRAPHY

"Cole, Nat King," *CBY 1956*
R. Gleason: "Just Can't See for Lookin'," *Jam Session* (New York, 1958)
G. Hall: *Nat "King" Cole: a Jazz Discography* (Laurel, MD, 1965)
"Nat 'King' Cole, 1917–1965," *Down Beat*, xxxii/7 (1965), 14
M. Cole and L. Robinson: *Nat King Cole: an Intimate Biography* (New York, 1971)
H. Pleasants: *The Great American Popular Singers* (New York, 1974), 213ff
L. Feather: "Piano Giants of Jazz: Nat King Cole," *Contemporary Keyboard*, iv/4 (1978), 57
D. Travis: *An Autobiography of Black Jazz* (Chicago, 1983), 179
J. Haskins and K. Benson: *Nat King Cole* (New York, 1984)

BILL DOBBINS, RICHARD WANG

Cole, Rossetter Gleason (*b* nr Clyde, MI, 5 Feb 1866; *d* Lake Bluff, IL, 18 May 1952). Teacher and composer. While attending high school in Ann Arbor, Michigan, he studied harmony with Francis L. York. He studied engineering and then liberal arts at the University of Michigan, taking some music courses under Calvin B. Cady. He was chapel organist and glee club leader and played organ in local churches while at the university, and in his final year he composed his first large work, *The Passing of Summer*, a cantata for soloists, chorus, and orchestra, which was performed by the University Musical Society the night before his graduation in 1888. For the next two years, he taught English, Latin, and German at high schools in Aurora, Illinois, and Ann Arbor. In 1890 he went to Berlin, where he won a three-year scholarship to the Königliche Meisterschule and studied with Max Bruch (violin), Wilhelm Middelschulte (organ), Heinrich van Eyken (composition and counterpoint), and Gustav Kogel (conducting). He returned, however, in 1892 to the USA and became professor and director of the music department at Ripon College, Wisconsin (1892–4), then professor at Grinnell College, Iowa (1894–1901), and professor at the University of Wisconsin (1907–9).

From 1901 to 1907 and from 1909 he taught privately in Chicago, composed, and was organist at the First Church of Christ, Scientist, Evanston; he was also co-editor of *Good Music* (1903–7). From 1915 he headed the theory department at the Cosmopolitan School in Chicago, where he became dean in 1935; he also directed the summer sessions of Columbia University's music department (1908–39). He served as president of the Music Teachers' National Association in 1903, 1909, and 1910, as dean of the Illinois Chapter of the American Guild of Organists (1912–14, 1929–31), and as president of the Society of American Musicians (1939–41). He contributed the volume *Choral and Church Music* (1916) to the Art of Music series published by the National Society of Music. Cole composed some 100 works in a variety of genres. He described his style (in D. Ewen, 1949) as " 'liberal' with decided modernistic tendencies, yet clinging more or less to a certain nineteenth century warmth of harmony and clear melodic outline."

WORKS

(selective list)

Dramatic: Hiawatha's Wooing (melodrama, Longfellow), nar, pf, op.20, 1904; King Robert of Sicily (melodrama, Longfellow), nar, pf/(pf, org)/orch, op.22, 1906; Pierrot Wounded (W. A. Roberts after P. Alberty), nar, pf, op.33 (1917); The Maypole Lovers [orig. Merrymount] (C. Ranck), 1919–31

Choral: The Passing of Summer (E. J. Cooley), cantata, solo vv, chorus, orch, op.14, 1887–8, rev. 1902; The Broken Troth (F. Martens), cantata, solo female vv, female chorus, pf, orch, op.32, 1917; The Rock of Liberty (A. F. Brown), cantata, solo vv, chorus, orch, op.36, 1919–20; partsongs

Orch: Symphonic Prelude, op.28, 1914 [orig. Fantaisie symphonique, org, 1912]; Pioneer Ov., op.35, 1918; Heroic Piece, org, orch, op.39, 1925, arr. orch, 1938; 2 Suites from The Maypole Lovers, 1934, 1942; Rhapsody, op.30, 1914–42 [orig. org]

Chamber and inst: March Celeste, org, op.6, 1888; Vn Sonata, D, op.8, 1891; Ballade, vc, pf, op.25, 1905–6 [orig. pf]; From a Lover's Notebook, pf, op.13, 1913; Meditation, org, op.29, 1914; Rhapsody, org, op.30, 1914; Legend, pf, op.31, 1916; 3 Songs, vc, pf, 1922; many other works for various inst ens; *c*20 other pf and org pieces

Songs, 1v, pf: *c*40 songs, incl. Auf Wiedersehen (J. Stewart), A Kiss and a Tear (C. F. Bragdon), When Love is in her Eyes, op.12/2–4, 1898; Absence (Anon.), op.17/3, 1903; When thou Art Nigh (T. Moore), op.23/2, 1907; Your Lad and my Lad (R. Parrish), 1918; In my Father's House are many Mansions (John xiv.1–3), 1919; Halcyon Days (W. A. Heidel), Lilacs (W. B. Crane), Love's Invocation (P. Carey), op.37, 1922

Principal publishers: Ditson, Gray, G. Schirmer, Schmidt

BIBLIOGRAPHY

EwenD

R. Hughes and A. Elson: *American Composers* (Boston, 1914), 514

"Find three 'Merry Mount' Operas in Existence," *MusAm*, li/8 (1931), 10

H. G. Kinscella: *Music on the Air* (New York, 1934), 292

"Mr. Rossetter G. Cole," *American Organist*, xvii (1934), 474

"Distinguished Composer Honored; Rossetter Cole Awarded Medal by American Opera Society," *Musical Leader*, lxvii/2 (1935), 9

D. Ewen, ed.: "Rossetter Gleason Cole," *American Composers Today* (New York, 1949), 62

MARGERY MORGAN LOWENS

Coleman, Cy [Kaufman, Seymour] (*b* Bronx, NY, 14 June 1929). Composer and pianist. He gave his first piano recital at the age of six, and later studied in New York at the High School of Music and Art and the College of Music. In 1947 he formed a trio with which he performed in local nightclubs. Shortly afterwards he began writing songs, first with the lyricist J. A. McCarthy, and from 1957 with Carolyn Leigh. His earliest successes included *Witchcraft* (1957), *Firefly* (1958), and *The best is yet to come* (1959); his first full Broadway score was *Wildcat* (1960). He subsequently achieved major successes with *Sweet Charity* (1966) and *Seesaw* (1973), both written in collaboration with Dorothy Fields. Coleman's early songs are lighthearted, jazz-influenced pieces with immediate appeal. In later shows, however, he has shown himself more venturesome, writing melodies that are less immediately engaging though no less artful; none has achieved the popularity of his earlier works.

WORKS

Selective list, Broadway musicals only; librettists and lyricists are listed in that order in parentheses, and dates are those of first New York performance.

Wildcat (N. R. Nash; C. Leigh), 16 Dec 1960 [incl. Hey, look me over]

Little Me (N. Simon; Leigh), 17 Nov 1962 [incl. I've got your number]

Sweet Charity (Simon; D. Fields), 29 Jan 1966 [incl. Baby, dream your dream, Big Spender, If my friends could see me now]; film, 1969

Seesaw (M. Bennett; Fields), 18 March 1973

I Love my Wife (M. Stewart), 17 April 1977

On the Twentieth Century (lib. and lyrics by B. Comden, A. Green), 19 Feb 1978

Barnum (M. Bramble; Stewart), 30 April 1980

GERALD BORDMAN

Coleman, Ornette (*b* Fort Worth, TX, 9 March 1930). Jazz saxophonist and composer.

1. Life. 2. Musical style.

1. LIFE. He began playing alto saxophone at the age of 14, and developed a style predominantly influenced by Charlie Parker. His early professional work with a variety of southwestern rhythm-and-blues and carnival bands, however, seems to have been in a more traditional idiom. In 1948 he moved to New Orleans and worked mostly at nonmusical jobs. By 1950 he had returned to Fort Worth, then went to Los Angeles with Pee Wee Crayton's rhythm-and-blues band. Wherever he tried to introduce some of his more personal and innovative ideas he met with hostility, both from audiences and musicians. While working as an elevator operator in Los Angeles he studied (on his own) harmony and theory textbooks, and gradually evolved a radically new concept and style, seemingly from a combination of musical intuition born of southwestern country blues and folk forms, and his misreadings – or highly personal interpretations – of the theoretical texts.

While working sporadically in some of the more obscure clubs in Los Angeles, Coleman eventually came to the attention of the double bass player Red Mitchell and later Percy Heath of the Modern Jazz Quartet. Coleman's first studio recording (for Contemporary in 1958) reveals that his style and sound were, in essence, fully formed at that time. At the instigation of the pianist John Lewis, Coleman (and his trumpet-playing partner Don Cherry) attended the Lenox School of Jazz in Massachusetts in 1959. There followed engagements at the Five Spot nightclub in New York, and a series of recordings for Atlantic entitled *The Shape of Jazz to Come* (which included his compositions *Lonely Woman* and *Congeniality*) and *Change of the Century* (with *Ramblin'* and *Free*). These recordings, which occasioned worldwide controversy, revealed Coleman performing in a style freed from most of the conventions of modern jazz. His recording *Free Jazz* (1960) for double jazz quartet, a 37-minute sustained collective improvisation, was undoubtedly the single most important influence on avant-garde jazz in the ensuing decade. On another recording from that year, *Jazz Abstractions*, Coleman is heard in a variety of more structured pieces, including Gunther Schuller's serial work *Abstraction* for alto saxophone, string quartet, two double basses, guitar, and percussion.

In 1962 Coleman retired temporarily from performing in pub-

Ornette Coleman, late 1970s

lic, primarily to teach himself trumpet and violin. His unorthodox treatment of these instruments on his return to public life in 1965 provoked even more controversy and led to numerous denunciations of his work by a number of influential American jazz musicians, including Miles Davis and Charles Mingus. However, Coleman was well received in Europe during his first tour there in 1965, giving a major impetus to the burgeoning European avant-garde jazz movement. In the mid-and late 1960s he also became interested in extended, through-composed works for larger ensembles, and produced among other pieces *Forms and Sounds* for woodwind quintet (1965) and *Skies of America*, a 21-movement suite for symphony orchestra (1972).

By the early 1970s Coleman's influence had waned considerably, while John Coltrane's dominance of saxophone styles had spread correspondingly. As Coleman turned increasingly to more abstract and mechanical compositional techniques (as in *Skies of America*), his playing lost some of its earlier emotional intensity and rhythmic vitality. But a visit to Morocco in 1973 and the gradual influence (especially rhythmic) of certain popular rock, funk, and fusion styles seemed to have revitalized his ensemble performances, a direction clearly discernible in Coleman's powerful electric band Prime Time (founded in 1981).

2. MUSICAL STYLE. Coleman's music cannot be understood solely in terms of the concept that has generally prevailed since the late 1920s – that jazz is primarily a form of expression for a virtuoso soloist. It is conceived essentially as an ensemble music; founded on traditional roots, it makes consistent use of spontaneous collective interplay at the most intimate and intricate levels. This accounts for its extraordinary unpredictability, freedom, and flexibility. Coleman's improvisations are highly mobile in tonality, rhythmic continuity, and form; they liberated the jazz solo both from an adherence to predetermined harmonic "changes" and a subservience to melodic variation. They also abandon traditional chorus and phrase structure, reinterpreting jazz rhythm, beat, and swing along freer, nonsymmetrical lines. Although it appeared to many to be incoherent and atonal, Coleman's playing was (and remains) essentially modal in concept, rooted in older, simpler black folk idioms – in particular a raw blues feeling. His wailing saxophone sound (produced in his early years on a plastic instrument) is never far removed from the plaintive human voice of Afro-American musical folklore. This essentially lyric approach, best heard on *Lonely Woman* (1959) and *Sex Spy* (1977), is linked to his "horizontal" concept of improvisation, a tendency explored earlier by such players as Lester Young and Miles Davis (in his post-bop modal style). Released from a strict adherence to harmonic functions and conventional form and phrase patterns, Coleman's solos are intrinsically linear, evolving in a sometimes fragmented musical discourse (ex. 1). His improvisations at fast

Ex.1 Coleman's second "chorus" from *Congeniality* (1959, Atl. 1317), transcr. G. Schuller

tempos are marked by flurries of notes, or gliding, swooping, and at times bursting phrases, played with great intensity and conviction. Occasionally his work seems burdened by the overuse of sequential patterning. But it is the strength of conviction of his playing (especially when aided by like-minded colleagues such as Cherry, the double bass player Charlie Haden, and the drummer Billy Higgins) that produces a sense of the inevitable in Coleman's art.

Technically Coleman plays as much "from his fingers" as by ear, an approach frequently resulting in nontempered intonation and unique tone colors. These effects are even more noticeable in his less convincing performances on trumpet and violin, although even on these instruments Coleman can sometimes produce compelling improvisations by sheer instinct and musical energy.

Coleman's style has changed little since the early 1960s. Whether he is working in Moroccan musical traditions, in atonal classically oriented works or, indeed, in rock- or funk-influenced idioms, his playing seems, in both sound and substance, to be capable at once of dominating and being assimilated by its surroundings.

In recent years Coleman has espoused a theory which he calls "harmolodic." It is apparently based on the untransposed reiteration in varied clefs and "keys" of the same musical materials (lines, themes, melodies), thus producing a simplistic organum-like "polyphony," primarily in unrelieved parallel motion. It is not clear, however, how this theory functions in Coleman's own improvisatory style. He is also noted for his use of obscure, often contradictory epigrams. Some observers see in these the "philosophical" analogs to his musical theories and concepts. Similarly, his notation of his own compositions – of which he has written several hundred – is imprecise, gestural, and in a sense graphic, leaving the performer free to give individual and differing interpretations.

While it may be impossible as yet to define specifically Coleman's influence in jazz (as one can do with Coleman Hawkins, Lester Young, Charlie Parker, or Coltrane), it is nonetheless clear that he opened up unprecedented musical vistas for jazz, the wider implications of which have not yet been fully explored – least of all by his many lesser imitators.

RECORDINGS
(selective list)

Something Else (1958, Cont. 3551); *Tomorrow is the Question* (1959, Cont. 3569); *The Shape of Jazz to Come* (1959, Atl. 1317), incl. Lonely Woman, Congeniality; *Change of the Century* (1959, Atl. 1327), incl. Ramblin', Free; *This is our Music* (1960, Atl. 1353); *Free Jazz* (1960, Atl. 1364); *Jazz Abstractions* (1960, Atl. 1365); *Ornette* (1961, Atl. 1378); *Ornette on Tenor* (1961, Atl. 1394); *Ornette Coleman at the Golden Circle I–II* (1965, BN 84224–5); *Crisis* (1969, Imp. 9187); *Science Fiction* (1971, Col. KC31061); *Body Meta* (1975, Artists House 1); *Soapsuds* (1977, Artists House 6), incl. Sex Spy

BIBLIOGRAPHY

B. Abel: "The Man with the White Plastic Sax," *Hi-fi Stereo Review*, v/2 (1960), 40
G. Russell: "Ornette Coleman and Tonality," *Jazz Review*, iii/5 (1960), 7
A Collection of [26] Compositions by Ornette Coleman (New York, 1961) [with preface by G. Schuller]
N. Hentoff: "Biggest Noise in Jazz," *Esquire*, lv/3 (1961), 82
——: *The Jazz Life* (New York, 1961), 222
H. Pekar: "Tomorrow is the Question," *Jazz Journal*, xv/11 (1962), 8
T. Martin: "The Plastic Muse," *Jazz Monthly*, x (1964), no.3, p.13; no.4, p.14; no.6, p.20; xi/3 (1965), 21
J. Goldberg: *Jazz Masters of the 50s* (New York, 1965), 228
D. Heckman: "Inside Ornette Coleman," *Down Beat*, xxxii (1965), no.19, p.13; no.26, p.20
J. Cooke: "Coleman Revisited," *Jazz Monthly*, xii/5 (1966), 9
M. Harrison: "Coleman and the Consequences," *Jazz Monthly*, xii/4 (1966), 10
A. Spellman: *Four Lives in the Bebop Business* (New York, 1966), 77
J. Cooke: "Ornette and Son," *Jazz Monthly*, xiii/5 (1967), 13
W. Mellers: *Caliban Reborn* (London, 1967), 135
E. Jost: "Zur Musik Ornette Colemans," *Jazzforschung*, ii (1970), 105
M. Williams: *Jazz Masters in Transition* (New York, 1970), 54, 203, 277, 282
——: *The Jazz Tradition* (New York, 1970), 207
M. Bourne: "Ornette's Innerview," *Down Beat*, xl/19 (1973), 16
J. Pailhé: "Ornette Coleman 1965," *Jazz hot* no.302, (1974), 21
E. Jost: "Ornette Coleman," *Free Jazz* (Graz, Austria, 1974/*R*1981)
M. Harrison: *A Jazz Retrospect* (Newton Abbot, England, 1976)
A. Taylor: "Ornette Coleman," *Notes and Tones* (Liège, 1979/*R*1982), 31
D. Wild and M. Cuscuna: *Ornette Coleman 1958–1979: a Discography* (Ann Arbor, MI, 1980)
C. Sheridan: "Ornette Coleman," *Jazz Journal International*, xxxiii/11 (1980), 22; xxxiv/1 (1981), 16
W. Balliett: "Ornette," *Jelly Roll, Jabbo, and Fats* (New York, 1983), 187
J. Rockwell: "Free Jazz, Body Music and Symphonic Dreams," *All American Music: Composition in the Late Twentieth Century* (New York, 1983), 185

GUNTHER SCHULLER

Coles, George. Pseudonym of GEORGE C. STEBBINS.

Colgrass, Michael (Charles) (*b* Chicago, IL, 22 April 1932). Composer and percussionist. After graduating from the University of Illinois (BMus 1956), he went to New York, where he supported himself in further studies and compositional activity by working as a percussionist. His principal composition teachers were Milhaud, Riegger, Weigel, Foss, and Ben Weber; Paul Price was his chief percussion instructor, although his skills in this direction were developed largely through his professional work. Colgrass has played with a wide variety of ensembles, from the Columbia SO (conducted by Stravinsky in his commercial recordings) to that for Bernstein's *West Side Story*, and also Dizzy Gillespie's band. Since 1967 he has made his living exclusively as a composer. He has received two Guggenheim fellowships (1964 and 1968), a Rockefeller grant (1968) to study theater arts (principally the Commedia dell'Arte in Milan and Grotowski's ensemble in Poland), and a Ford Foundation grant (1972). In 1978 he won the Pulitzer Prize for *Déjà vu*. He has had works commissioned by many organizations including the Fromm Foundation (1966), the Boston SO (1968), the Corporation for Public Broadcasting (1969), the Detroit SO (1975), the Minnesota Orchestra (1976), the New York PO (1977), the Chamber Music Society of Lincoln Center, and the Toronto SO (1982).

Colgrass's music reflects his widespread interests. His early pieces (1950–56) were mainly for percussion, but during the next decade he wrote a number of atonal chamber works marked by light lyricism, humor, and often by an undercurrent of jazz. After this period he began to write songs, theatrical concert works, and operas to his own texts, using a diversity of styles and emphasizing social comment and satire. *New People* (1969) was the first of Colgrass's works to contain a combination of several different styles. He continued to use this technique in works such as *Letter from Mozart* and *Déjà vu*, and later extended it by adding extramusical elements such as poetry recitation, dance, and pantomime. In 1971 Colgrass began giving creativity workshops (the first was at Indiana State University) to teach these performance techniques and to explore the possibilities of improvisation in performance. He has frequently conducted programs of his works, narrated his own texts at performances, and produced his dramatic pieces in universities and colleges throughout the USA. He has written several articles for the *New York Times*. Many of his vocal and orchestral works and some instrumental pieces have been recorded. During the 1970s he settled in Toronto.

WORKS

Stage, all texts by Colgrass: Virgil's Dream (music-theater, 1), 1967, Brighton, England, 1967; Nightingale Inc. (comic opera, 1), 1971, Champaign, IL, 1975; Something's Gonna Happen (children's musical, 1), 1978, Toronto, 1978

Inst: Light Spirit, fl, va, gui, perc, 1963; As Quiet As, orch, 1966; Auras, harp, orch, 1973; Concertmasters, 3 vn, orch, 1975; Letter from Mozart, orch, 1976; Wolf, vc, 1976; Flashbacks, 5 brass, 1979; Tales of Power, pf, 1980; Metamusic, pf, 1981; Memento, 2 pf, orch, 1982; Chaconne, va, orch; Delta, cl, vn, perc orch, 1979; Demon, amp pf, perc, tape, radio, orch, 1984; Winds of Nagual, ww ens, 1985

Perc: 3 Brothers, 9 perc, 1951; Perc Music, 4 perc, 1953; Variations, 4 drums, va, 1957; Fantasy Variations, solo perc, 6 perc, 1960; Divertimento, 8 drums, pf, str, 1961; Rhapsodic Fantasy, 15 drums, orch, 1965; Déjà vu, 4 perc, orch, 1977

Vocal, all texts by Colgrass unless otherwise stated: The Earth's a Baked Apple, chorus, orch, 1969; New People, Mez, va, pf, 1969; Image of Man, 4 solo vv, chorus, orch, 1974; Theatre of the Universe, solo vv, chorus, orch, 1975; Best Wishes USA, 4 solo vv, double chorus, 2 jazz bands, folk insts, orch, 1976; Night of the Raccoon (S. Takashima), harp, fl, kbd, perc, 1978; other works

Principal publishers: C. Fischer, MCA, Music for Percussion

BIBLIOGRAPHY

EwenD
G. Freedman: "Michael Colgrass," *MJ*, xxxv/7 (1977), 5

M. L. Humphrey: "Michael Colgrass: Music's Pulitzer Prize-winning Pitcher," *MJ*, xxxvi/10 (1978), 24

J. Horowitz: "Musician of the Month: Michael Colgrass," *HiFi/MusAm*, xxviii/11 (1978), 8

O. Hardy: "Freeing that Force Within is Composer's Way of Making Music," *Courier-Journal* (Louisville, 24 Feb 1982)

D. H. Smith: "What's this: a Composer who Wants All to Understand his Music?," *Christian Science Monitor* (27 May 1982)

D. Webster: "To this Composer, Time Lag is a Way of Life," *Philadelphia Inquirer* (13 Feb 1982)

KURT STONE

College Band Directors National Association. Professional organization founded in Chicago in 1941 by William D. Revelli, to serve the interests of bandmasters teaching in institutions above high-school level. As stated in the by-laws, the purpose of the association is to assist its members in seeking individual and collective growth as musicians, teachers, conductors, and administrators. Revelli was president during the association's formative years; a *Declaration of Principles* was formulated, principally by Mark Hindsley, by which the members dedicate themselves to the members of their bands, to their institutions, and to music as an art and a profession. An associated organization of the Music Educators National Conference, the association began publishing the *Journal of Band Research* (now biannual) in 1964. The association's headquarters are in Austin, Texas.

BIBLIOGRAPHY

R. Lasko: *A History of the College Band Directors National Association* (diss., U. of Cincinnati, 1971)

RAOUL CAMUS

College Music Society (CMS). Organization established in 1957 as a result of the merger of the Society for Music in Liberal Arts Colleges and the College Music Association. Its first meeting (1958) was at Harvard University. It provides a forum for the exchange of ideas within the academic music profession. Membership is open to teachers of music in colleges, universities, and conservatories in the USA and Canada. The organization sponsors annual meetings with symposiums and concerts and publishes a newsletter and a biannual journal, the *College Music Symposium* (founded in 1961; annual until 1977). Its other publications include a biennial *Directory of Music Faculties in Colleges and Universities, U.S. and Canada* (1967–), Bibliographies in American Music (1974–), including volumes on Gershwin, Billings, Griffes, Arthur Foote, and Gottschalk, and the series of monographs *CMS Reports*, which has included studies on such issues as the status of women in college music and racial and ethnic directions in American music. Acting as a national clearinghouse for information on the availability of music faculty positions in higher education, the society compiles and distributes to its members Music Faculty Vacancy lists. Its headquarters are at the University of Colorado in Boulder.

RITA H. MEAD

College songs. Official or traditional songs sung at ceremonial, festive, or athletic events to generate enthusiasm and school spirit, or to support the school's sports teams. They include "alma maters" (or school anthems; the Latin term *alma mater*, meaning "benign mother," is frequently applied by alumni to their school or college), "fight" songs, and nostalgic songs.

Popular songs such as glees, drinking songs, hymns, and ballads have traditionally been appropriated by students and adapted for school use at functions and festive occasions, but it was not until the 19th century that songs were commissioned expressly for such purposes by American schools and colleges. The earliest of these, *Fair Harvard*, written in commemoration of the 200th anniversary of Harvard University (1836), was set to the tune of the traditional song *My lodging is on the cold ground*, better known in the later version, *Believe me, if all those endearing young charms*

Ex.1 Derivation of Harvard University's alma mater

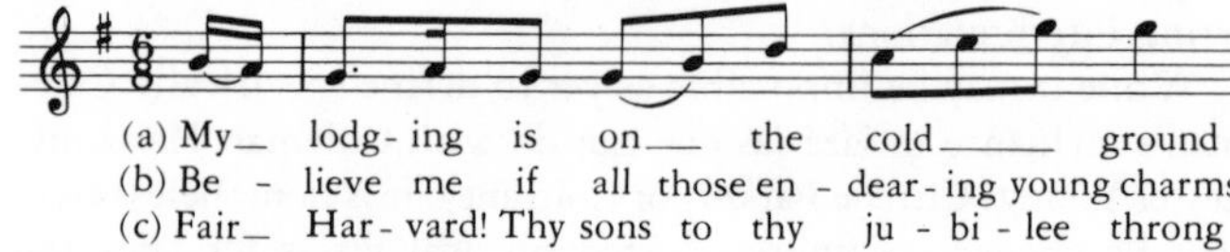
(a) My— lodg- ing is on— the cold— ground
(b) Be - lieve me if all those en - dear - ing young charms
(c) Fair— Har - vard! Thy sons to thy ju - bi - lee throng

(a) Traditional melody, first printed in *Vocal Music* (London, 1775)
(b) Words by T. Moore, *c*1807
(c) Words by S. Gilman, 1836

(ex.1); later, the same tune was adapted by other institutions, among them the University of Iowa. Other early examples of specially commissioned songs include the alma mater of Williams College in Williamstown, Massachusetts, an original song written by a member of the class of 1859, and the alma mater of Brown University in Rhode Island, set to the tune of *Araby's Daughter* by J. A. DeWolf in 1861.

Ex.2 Derivation of Cornell University's alma mater

(a) Down where the wav-ing wil-lows, 'neath the sun-beams smile
(b) Far above Ca - yu - ga's wa - ters, with its waves of blue

(a) H. Thompson, *Annie Lisle* (1858)
(b) Words by A. C. Weeks and W. M. Smith, 1872

Among the other traditional melodies that have become school songs through adaptation, the ballad *Annie Lisle* (ex.2) has been one of the most popular, and it is probably better remembered today as the tune of *Far above Cayuga's waters* (Cornell University) than in its original version; the alma maters of Swarthmore College in Pennsylvania and the University of Kansas are also set to this tune. Adaptations have also been made of Haydn's *Kaiserhymne* (ex.3), among them those used for the alma maters of

Ex.3 Derivation of the University of Pittsburgh's alma mater

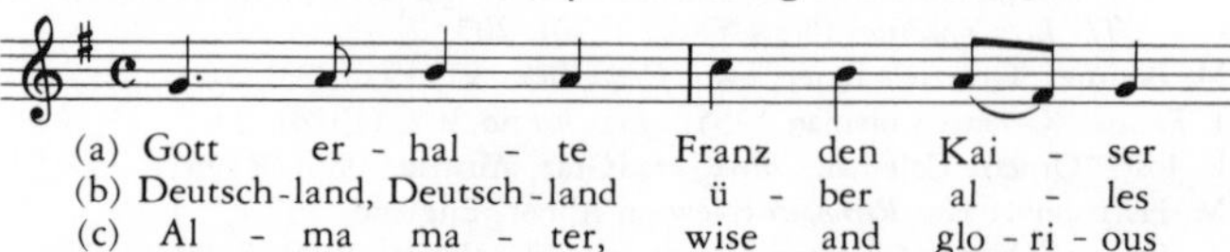
(a) Gott er - hal - te Franz den Kai - ser
(b) Deutsch-land, Deutsch-land ü - ber al - les
(c) Al - ma ma - ter, wise and glo - ri - ous

(a) Austrian national anthem (1797–1922), words by L. L. Haschka, music by J. Haydn, 1797
(b) German national anthem, from 1922, words by A. H. Hoffmann von Fallersleben, 1841
(c) Words by G. M. P. Baird, 1929

Columbia University and the University of Pittsburgh. Other sources of music include the traditional songs *O Tannenbaum* (Cornell University and the University of Maryland), *The Old Oaken Bucket* (Brown University), *Auld Lang Syne* (the University of Virginia), and the *Battle Hymn of the Republic* (the University of Colorado and the University of Georgia); a Sousa march (the University of Minnesota); and music from Brahms's Academic Festival Overture (Brandeis University), Gounod's *Messe brève et salut* (University of Wisconsin), and Elmer Bernstein's musical *How now, Dow Jones* (the University of South Carolina). *Tiger Rag*, which was attributed to D. J. La Rocca and the Original

Dixieland Jazz Band when it was first published in 1917, has been used as a fight song by a number of schools (e.g., Louisiana State and Memphis State universities).

The first American college songbook was issued by Yale University in 1853: *Songs of Yale*, compiled by Nathaniel W. T. Root and J. K. Lombard, contained only words, which were to be sung to popular tunes. The first anthology to include music as well was *Carmina yalensia*, compiled and arranged by F. V. D. Garretson (1867).

A large proportion of college songs were written during the first four decades of the 20th century, most in response to song contests sponsored by the colleges. Quite successful during this period was Thornton Allen, who wrote and published songs for a number of institutions, including the University of Arizona, Louisiana State University (publisher), and the University of Tennessee (co-composer). Few college songs have been written since World War II, and some of the newer institutions have no official songs at all. Although many are still played and sung in various arrangements for college bands, choruses, or orchestras, their importance seems to be diminishing.

The following list of songs is arranged alphabetically by state and institution. Each entry contains the title or, where titles are merely generic, the first line; the type of song, indicated by the letter a (alma mater) or f (fight song) (no letter is given for songs of a nostalgic or general nature); composer or derivation; author of the text, in parentheses (if no author is given, the composer is also the author of the text unless otherwise stated); and the date of composition and/or date of publication (publication information is given in parentheses). State songs associated with particular institutions are not normally included.

LIST

ALABAMA

AUBURN U. "On the rolling plains of Dixie" (a), B. Wood [music only]; *War Eagle* (f)

ALASKA

U. OF ALASKA, Fairbanks. "Though far we wander" (a), C. M. Franklin (M. J. Walker and C. M. Franklin); "Fight for Alaska" (f), C. M. Franklin; "Fight, fight, for our Alaska" (f) (C. W. Davis)

ARIZONA

ARIZONA STATE U., Tempe. "Where the bold sahuaros" (a), M. Dresskell and E. J. Hopkins; *Maroon and Gold* (f), F. K. McKernan, 1964

U. OF ARIZONA, Tucson. *All hail, Arizona* (a), D. H. Monroe (E. C. Monroe) (New York, 1926); *Bear down, Arizona* (f), J. Lee; *Fight, Wildcats, fight!* (f), T. Allen and D. Holsclaw (D. Holsclaw) (New York, 1930)

ARKANSAS

U. OF ARKANSAS, Fayetteville. *University of Arkansas Hymn* (a), H. D. Tovey (B. Payne) (Fayetteville, n.d.); *Arkansas Fight Song* (f), arr. J. Leach (San Antonio, TX, n.d.)

CALIFORNIA

MILLS COLLEGE, Oakland. *Fires of Wisdom* (a), E. F. Schneider (F. R. Carpenter), pubd in *Mills College Songs* (Oakland, 1913)

SAN JOSE STATE U. *New Spartan Fight Song* (f), G. Lease and F. Erickson; *Spartan Fight Song* (f), J. Wiles, 1939; *Hail, Spartans, hail!*, G. Erwin, 1933

STANFORD U. *Hail, Stanford, hail!* (a), M. R. Coolidge (A. W. Smith), 1941 (New York, n.d.); *Sons of Stanford Red* (f), W. C. Achi (G. F. Morgan), 1940 (New York, n.d.); *Come join the band*, to R. B. Hall's *New Colonial March* (A. Ellerbeck) (Cincinnati, 1901)

U. OF CALIFORNIA. *Hail to California* (a), C. R. Morse; *Big C* (f), H. P. Williams and N. S. McLaren

——, Berkeley. *All hail, Blue and Gold* (a), H. Bingham; *Fight for California* (f), E. E. McKoy (R. N. Fitch) (New York, 1909)

——, Davis. *Aggie Fight* (f), arr. L. Austin; *Sons of California* (f), C. R. Morse

——, Los Angeles. *Hail to the hills of Westwood* (a), J. M. Emerson; *Sons of Westwood* (f), F. K. James, J. Livingston, and B. Hansen (Beverly Hills, 1963)

——, Santa Barbara. *The Lonely Bull* (f), S. Lake (1962); *Go, Gauchos* (f), E. Bernstein and N. Gimbel

U. OF SOUTHERN CALIFORNIA, Los Angeles. " 'Mid storied lands" (a), J. O. Wilson; *Fight on for U.S.C.* (f), M. Sweet (G. Grant and M. Sweet)

COLORADO

U. OF COLORADO, Boulder. "Hail, all hail, our alma mater" (a), H. McMillan (J. Ogilvey), *c*1958; *Glory, glory, Colorado* (f), to *Battle Hymn of the Republic*; *Go, Colorado* (f), W. Simon (New York, 1958)

CONNECTICUT

U. OF CONNECTICUT, Storrs. *Old Connecticut* (a), A. S. Davis; *UConn Husky* (f), H. A. France, 1946, pubd in *University of Connecticut Songs* (Storrs, rev. 2/1954)

WESLEYAN U., Middletown. "Come, raise the song" (a), W. B. Davis (F. L. Knowles); *Battle Cry* (f), C. L. Waite; *Secrets*, C. R. Smith (F. L. Knowles): all pubd in *The Wesleyan Song Book*, ed. L. J. Patricelli (Middletown, 1901, 8/1953)

YALE U., New Haven. *Bright College Years* (a), C. Wilhelm (H. S. Durand), 1934; *Bulldog* (f), C. Porter, *c*1910; *Boola*, A. M. Hirsch, 1901: all pubd in *Songs of Yale*, ed. M. Bartholomew (New York, 16/1953)

DELAWARE

U. OF DELAWARE, Newark. "Hail to thee, proud Delaware" (a), A. J. Loudis (R. C. Currie), 1946; *Delaware Fight Song* (f), G. Kelly (H. Lawson), 1933

DISTRICT OF COLUMBIA

AMERICAN U., Washington, DC. "Firm on a sweep of campus" (a), R. D. Sure (P. A. Frederick), 1929

FLORIDA

FLORIDA STATE U., Tallahassee. *Alma mater* (a), J. Lawrence, 1947; *F.S.U. Fight Song* (f), T. Wright and D. Alley, 1950; *Hymn to the Garnet and Gold*, J. D. Smith

GEORGIA

U. OF GEORGIA, Athens. "From the hills of Georgia's north land" (a), to *Amici*, arr. H. Hodgson (J. B. Wright, Jr.); *Glory* (f), to *Battle Hymn of the Republic*, arr. H. Hodgson; *I want to go back*, C. T. Conyers; *Hail to Georgia*, G. W. Walter: all pubd in *Georgia Songs and Yells* (Athens, 1943)

HAWAII

U. OF HAWAII, Manoa. *In green Manoa Valley* (a), M. Gay (D. Rowell), 1921; *Fight for old Hawaii* (f), D. George, *c*1930

IDAHO

U. OF IDAHO, Moscow. *Here we have Idaho* (a), S. Hume-Douglas's *Garden of Paradise* (B. Packenham and M. Helm) (Caldwell, 1931); *Go, Vandals! Go!* (f), J. M. O'Donnell (Caldwell, 1933)

ILLINOIS

NORTHWESTERN U., Evanston. *Quaecumque sunt vera* (a), to St. Antony chorale, attrib. (probably wrongly) J. Haydn, HII:46, composed *c*1784, arr. P. C. Lutkin (J. S. Clark); *Go, U Northwestern* (f), T. C. Van Etten, 1912; *Northwestern Push On Song*, D. G. Robertson: all pubd in *Northwestern University Songbook* (1917, 3/1930)

U. OF CHICAGO. "Today we gladly sing the praise" (a), M. Evans (E. Lewis); *Wave the flag of old Chicago* (f), G. Erickson

WHEATON COLLEGE. "A Song of Alma Mater" (a), pubd in *Wheaton College Song Book* (1929); *Orange and Blue Fight Song* (f), R. C. Loveless [music only]

INDIANA

BALL STATE U., Muncie. "Dear alma mater, hear our vow of faith and trust in thee" (a), G. S. Chrisman; "Fight, team, fight" (f), C. L. Hoffer, *c*1930

BUTLER U., Indianapolis. *Gallery of Memories* (a), F. W. Wolff; *The Butler War Song* (f), J. Heiney: both pubd in *Songs of Butler University*, ed. F. E. Shera, F. Renn, and V. Taylor (1930)

INDIANA U., Bloomington. *Hail to old I.U.* (a), J. T. Giles (Bloomington, 1908); *Chimes of Indiana* (a), H. Carmichael (New York, 1937); *Indiana, our Indiana* (f), K. L. King and R. P. Harker (R. P. Harker) (Bloomington, 1913)

VALPARAISO U. *Hail to the Brown and Gold* (a), to F. W. Kücken's *Ach, wie wärs möglich dann*, Eng. version *How can I leave thee*; *On to Victory* (f), A. Bucci (G. G. Dye, M. J. Marquardt, and E. A. Anderson) (1930)

IOWA

DRAKE U., Des Moines. "With broad and firm foundation" (a), C. Bloom (E. J. Scott), 1925; *Here's to the Man Who Wears the D* (f)

U. OF IOWA, Iowa City. *Old Gold* (a), to *My lodging is on the cold ground*, pubd 1775 (J. C. Parish), pubd in *University of Iowa Song Book* (Iowa City, n.d.); *Iowa Fight Song* (f), M. Willson (New York, 1951); *On, Iowa*, W. R. Law, 1904, pubd in *University of Iowa Song Book* (Iowa City, n.d.)

KANSAS

U. OF KANSAS, Lawrence. *Crimson and the Blue* (a), to H. S. Thompson's *Annie Lisle*, pubd 1858 (G. B. Penny); *I'm a Jayhawk* (f), G. H. Bowles (1920); *The*

Banner of Old K. U., F. Waring, T. Waring, and P. Ballard (Delaware Water Gap, PA, 1930): all pubd in *The Songs of Old KU* (Lawrence, 1966)

WICHITA STATE U. "Our alma mater Wichita" (a), arr. T. Lieurance; *Hail! Hail, Wichita!* (f), T. Lieurance

KENTUCKY

U. OF KENTUCKY, Lexington. "Hail, Kentucky, alma mater" (a), C. A. Lampert (J. Funkhouser); *On, on, U. of K.* (f), C. A. Lampert (T. Perkins), 1947

U. OF LOUISVILLE, Belknap. "We, thy loyal sons" (a), J. N. Young and J. Powell, 1949; *Fight, U. of L.* (f), R. B. Griffith, *c*1962

LOUISIANA

LOUISIANA STATE U., Baton Rouge. "Where stately oaks" (a), L. Funchess, arr. J. F. Edmunds (H. Downey) (New York, 1935); *Fight for L. S. U.* (f), C. Carazo, arr. J. F. Edmunds (W. G. Higginbotham) (New York, 1937); *Tiger Rag* (f), to music by D. J. La Rocca and the Original Dixieland Jazz Band, pubd 1917 (New York, 1945)

TULANE U., New Orleans. "We praise thee" (a), W. H. Ruebush (E. J. Williams) (New Orleans, 1927); *The Olive and Blue* (f), W. Goldstein (M. ten Hoor)

——, Newcomb College. "Where stars arise" (a), W. Goldstein (F. H. Lea)

MAINE

BOWDOIN COLLEGE, Brunswick. *Rise, sons of Bowdoin* (a and f), C. T. Burnett (K. C. M. Sills); *Forward the White* (f), G. Sumner (K. A. Robinson); *Bowdoin Beata*, to *Wake, Freshmen, Wake* (H. H. Pierce): all pubd in *Songs of Bowdoin* (Brunswick, 1958)

U. OF MAINE, Orono. *The University Hymn* (a), H. M. Estabrooke; *For Maine* (f), C. D. Bartlett, 1924; *The Maine Stein Song*, to E. A. Fenstad's *"Opie" Two-Step*, pubd 1901 (L. Colcord; words pubd separately in 1905) (New York, 1910)

MARYLAND

JOHN HOPKINS U., Baltimore. *The John Hopkins Ode: Veritas vox liberabit* (a), E. E. Starr, arr. D. Coultes (W. L. Devries), 1892; *To Win* (f); *Johnny Hopkins on to victory* (f), E. C. Stollenwerck; *Dear Old Johnny Hopkins*, arr. O. P. Steinwald

U. OF MARYLAND, College Park. *Maryland, my Maryland* (a), to *Es lebe doch*, pubd 1799, later *O Tannenbaum*, arr. T. Allen (J. R. Randall) (1861)

MASSACHUSETTS

AMHERST COLLEGE. *To the Fairest College* (a), D. C. Bartlett; *Old Amherst's out for business* (f), arr. J. S. Hamilton; *Lord Jeffrey Amherst*, J. S. Hamilton

BOSTON U. "O glorious thy name" (a), J. P. Marshall (D. L. Marsh), 1928; *Go, B. U.* (f), R. Weeks and B. Fazioli; "For Boston University" (f), K. Hutchinson; *Clarissima*, B. C. Patterson (R. W. Taylor) (Boston, 1910)

BRANDEIS U., Waltham. "To thee, alma mater, we'll always be true" (a), to Brahms's Academic Festival Overture, composed 1880; *The Blue and the White* (f), I. Fine, 1959

HARVARD U., Cambridge. *Fair Harvard* (a), to *My lodging is on the cold ground*, pubd 1775, arr. L. Anderson (S. Gilman), 1836; *Ten thousand men of Harvard* (f), M. Taylor (A. Putnam)

MASSACHUSETTS INSTITUTE OF TECHNOLOGY, Cambridge. *Stein Song* (a), F. F. Bullard (R. Hovey) (1898); *Take me back to Tech*, to F. Seaver's *Solomon Levi* (I. W. Litchfield), pubd in *Technology Songs* (Boston, rev. 3/1929); *Sons of MIT*, J. B. Wilbur, pubd in *Technology Review* (March 1944)

SMITH COLLEGE, Northampton. *Oh! fairest alma mater* (a), H. D. Sleeper (H. Sperry) (Boston, 1908)

TUFTS U., Medford. "We come beside thy knee" (a), L. R. Lewis (D. L. Maulsby); *Tuftonia's Day* (f), E. W. Hayes; both pubd in *Tufts Songs Nineteen-Fifteen* (Medford, 1915)

U. OF MASSACHUSETTS, Amherst. "When twilight shadows deepen" (a), F. D. Griggs, 1917; *Fight, Massachusetts* (f), E. F. Sumner, 1931; *Roll down the field* (f), J. Bilik, 1964; *Sons of old Massachusetts*, B. Chadwick (H. L. Knight), 1903

WHEATON COLLEGE, Norton. "Long ago the pilgrims landed" (a), R. S. Capers (Norton, n.d.); *A Wheaton Hymn*, H. J. Jenny (J. E. Park), 1935

WILLIAMS COLLEGE, Williamstown. *The Mountains* (a), W. Gladden (Williamstown, n.d.); *Yard by Yard* (f), C. F. Brown and H. B. Wood (C. F. Brown and L. S. Potter) (Williamstown, 1909)

MICHIGAN

MICHIGAN STATE U., East Lansing. *M. S. C. Shadows* (a), B. Traynor, arr. H. O. Reed, adopted in 1949 (New York, n.d.); *Michigan State Fight Song* (f), F. I. Lankey, 1919 (New York, n.d.)

U. OF MICHIGAN, Ann Arbor. *Laudes atque carmina* (a), A. A. Stanley (C. M. Gayley); *Varsity* (f), E. V. Moore (J. F. Lawton); *Victors* (f), L. Elbel; *The Yellow and Blue*, M. Balfe (C. M. Gayley): all pubd in *The University of Michigan Songbook*, ed. P. A. Duey (Ann Arbor, 1967)

MINNESOTA

U. OF MINNESOTA, Minneapolis. *Hail, Minnesota* (a), T. E. Rickard (R. Upson and A. Upson) (Minneapolis, 1936); *U. of M. Rouser* (f), F. M. Hutsell (Minneapolis, 1936); *Trio of the Minnesota March* (f), J. P. Sousa (M. J. Jalma) (New York, 1927)

MISSISSIPPI

U. OF MISSISSIPPI, University. "Way down south in Mississippi" (a), W. F. Kahle (Mrs. A. W. Kahle), rev. by R. McNeil 1937; *Rebel March* (f), E. F. Yerby and R. R. Coats (F. Whitfield), 1942

MISSOURI

U. OF MISSOURI, Columbia. *Alma mater* (a); *Mizzou Chant* (f); *Old Missouri*: all pubd in *University of Missouri Songs*, ed. J. T. Quarles (Columbia, 2/1929)

WASHINGTON U., St. Louis. "Dear alma mater, thy name is sweet" (a), to F. W. Kücken's *Ach, wie wärs möglich dann*, Eng. version *How can I leave thee* (M. B. Roshenheim and G. B. Logan), pubd in *Washington University Song Book* (St. Louis, 1922)

MONTANA

MONTANA STATE U., Bozeman. *Fair M. S. U.* (a), anon. (M. K. Hall); *Stand up and Cheer* (f), P. P. McNeely (E. A. Duddy); *Montana State College [University]*, to S. Adams's *A Warrior Bold* (M. Eckels): all pubd in *Bobcat Song Book* (Bozeman, 1931)

NEBRASKA

U. OF NEBRASKA, Lincoln. *Dear old Nebraska U.* (a), H. Pecha, 1923; *Hail, Varsity* (f), W. Chenowith (W. Joyce Ayres), 1936; *The Cornhusker*, R. W. Stevens, 1909

NEVADA

U. OF NEVADA, Reno. "Where the Truckee's snow-fed waters" (a), anon. (J. H. Morse); *Nevada, my Nevada*, C. Haseman: both pubd in *University of Nevada Song Book* (Reno, 1924)

NEW HAMPSHIRE

DARTMOUTH COLLEGE, Hanover. *Men of Dartmouth* (a), H. R. Wellman (R. Hovey); *Dartmouth's in town again* (f), R. C. Hopkins (H. L. Armes); *Dartmouth Undying*, H. P. Whitford (F. McDuffee): all pubd in *Dartmouth Songbook* (Hanover, 6/1950)

U. OF NEW HAMPSHIRE, Durham. "New Hampshire, alma mater, all hail!" (a), to H. Smart's *Lancashire* (H. F. Moore); *The Line-up* (f), F. V. Cole [music only]; *New Hampshire Hymn*, A. E. Richards

NEW JERSEY

FAIRLEIGH DICKINSON U., Rutherford. "Praise to thee, o alma mater" (a), L. W. Goodhart (J. Davis); *Marching Song* (f), L. W. Goodhart (J. Davis); *O Fairleigh Dickinson*, R. Wingert (J. F. Doering)

PRINCETON U. *Old Nassau* (a), C. Langlotz (H. P. Peck) (1869); *The Princeton Cannon Song* (f), J. F. Hewitt and A. H. Osborn (Cincinnati, 1906); *Going back to Nassau Hall*, K. S. Clark (New York, 1910)

NEW MEXICO

U. OF NEW MEXICO, Albuquerque. "New Mexico! New Mexico! We sing to honor thee" (a), H. N. Summers and C. Summers, 1948; "Hail to thee, New Mexico" (f), L. Clauve (Dr. Sinclair), 1930

NEW YORK

CITY U. OF NEW YORK, Baruch College. "Standing high above the city's mighty roar" (a), M. Blech, 1976; *Baruch, yes* (f), B. R. Oppenheim (E. W. Mammen)

——, Brooklyn College. "On campus green" (a), S. Fine Kaye, arr. W. Boswell (R. Friend)

——, City College. *Lavender, my Lavender* (a), W. R. Johnson (E. Lieberman), 1919, pubd in *Songs of C.C.N.Y.* (New York, 1926)

——, Lehman College. "The challenge of the coming years" (a), E. Lisinsky (K. Blackman), 1968

——, Queens College. *Queens College Alma Mater Hymn* (a), E. J. Stringham (D. Durling); *The Day of the Knight* (f), M. J. Mandelbaum

COLUMBIA U., New York. *Stand, Columbia!* (a), to J. Haydn's *Kaiserhymne*, pubd 1797 (G. O. Ward); *Sans souci* (a), arr. L. M. Bingham (P. Fridenberg); both pubd in *Columbia University Songs*, compiled W. B. Donnell and others (Boston, 1904); *Roar, Lion, Roar* (f), R. Webb and M. W. Watkins (C. Ford)

CORNELL U., Ithaca. "Far above Cayuga's waters" (a), to H. S. Thompson's *Annie Lisle*, pubd 1858 (A. C. Weeks and W. M. Smith), pubd in *Songs of Cornell*, (Ithaca, 1960); *The Big Red Team* (f), C. E. Tourison (R. Berry), pubd in *Songs of Cornell* (Ithaca, 1960); *Evening Song*, to *Es lebe doch*, pubd 1799, later *O Tannenbaum* (H. Tyrrell) (1877)

NEW YORK U. *The Palisades* (a); *Old New York University*: both pubd in *New York University Song Book* (New York, 1921)

U. OF ROCHESTER. "Full many fair and famous streams" (a), arr. H. D. Wilkins (T. T. Swinburne); *Football Song* (*March, men of Rochester*) (f), C. R. Wright; *The Dandelion Yellow*, C. F. Cole (R. L. Greene)

STATE U. OF NEW YORK, Albany. "College of the Empire State" (a), A. W. Lansing (Mrs. F. Hubbard)

——, Buffalo. "Where once the Indian trod" (a), W. S. Goodale (S. B. Botsford), *c*1906, pubd in *Song Book 1916* (Buffalo, 1916)

SYRACUSE U. "Where the vale of Onondaga" (a), D. R. Walsh (J. W. Stevens); *Down, down the field* (f), C. H. Lewis (R. Murphy); *The Saltine Warrior*, D. R. Walsh (S. E. Darby, Jr.): all pubd in *Syracuse University Nostalgic Songs* (Syracuse, 1911)

VASSAR COLLEGE, Poughkeepsie. "Hark, alma mater, through the world is ringing" (a), G. C. Gow (A. W. Stone), 1898, rev. and adopted 1921

NORTH CAROLINA

DUKE U., Durham. *Dear old Duke* (a), R. H. James, 1930; *Blue and White* (f), G. E. Leftwich, Jr., 1930: both pubd in *Duke Songs* (Durham, 1951)

U. OF NORTH CAROLINA, Chapel Hill. *Hark the sound* (a), to *Amici*, arr. E. Slocum (W. S. Myers); *Tar heels on hand* (f), arr. E. Slocum (K. Kyser): both pubd in *Songs of the University of North Carolina at Chapel Hill* (Chapel Hill, 1977)

NORTH DAKOTA

U. OF NORTH DAKOTA, Grand Forks. "Hail to thee, o alma mater" (a), to J. Haydn's *Kaiserhymne*, pubd 1797, arr. J. Macnie (J. Macnie), 1899; *Stand up and cheer* (f), adapted by R. LaMeter and N. Nelson, *c*1928

OHIO

KENT STATE U. *Hail to thee, our alma mater* (a), D. Steere (E. T. Stump), pubd in *Official Songs of Kent State College* (Kent, 1931); *Fight on for K. S. U.* (f), E. Siennicki, pubd in *Songs: Kent State University* (Kent, 1951); *K. S. U. Victory March* (f), D. Chapman (R. E. Hartzell), pubd in *Songs: Kent State University* (Kent, 1951)

MIAMI U., Oxford. *Old Miami* (a), R. H. Burke (A. H. Upham), 1921; *Miami Fight Song* (f), P. C. Christman, 1949: both pubd in *Miami University Songs* (n.p., n.d.)

OBERLIN COLLEGE. "Sing of our glorious alma mater" (a), L. U. Rowland (A. S. Shuart) (1914); *A Song of Victory* (f), J. P. Scott (1914); *Ten thousand strong*, J. N. Pierce, 1913 (1914)

OHIO STATE U., Columbus. *Carmen Ohio* (a), to 17th-century tune arr. B. Carr in 1824 as *Spanish Chant* (F. A. Cornell), 1916; *Across the field* (f), W. A. Dougherty, Jr., 1915; *Buckeye Battle* (f), F. Crumit, 1919; *I wanna go back*

OKLAHOMA

OKLAHOMA STATE U., Stillwater. "Proud and immortal" (a), R. McCulloh, 1958; *Ride 'em, cowboys* (f), J. K. Long (E. Ward), 1934; *Oklahoma State*, F. Waring, T. Waring, and P. Ballard: all pubd in *Songs of Oklahoma State*, ed. M. A. Mitchell (Stillwater, n.d.)

U. OF OKLAHOMA, Norman. *The O.U. Chant* (a), J. L. C. Gilkey, 1936; *Boomer Sooner* (f), to Yale's *Boola*, arr. L. Haug (anon.), 1938; *O.k., Oklahoma*, F. Waring (New York, 1939); *Oklahoma!*, R. Rodgers (O. Hammerstein II), 1943

OREGON

U. OF OREGON, Eugene. *Oregon Pledge Song* (a), J. S. Evans, 1917; *Mighty Oregon* (f), A. Perfect (D. W. Gilbert), 1913

PENNSYLVANIA

BUCKNELL U., Lewisburg. *Dear Bucknell* (a), S. S. Merriman, pubd in *Bucknell Song Book* (1897); *Ray Bucknell* (f), arr. M. Le Mon, 1938; *Go, Bisons* (f), C. Rutledge, arr. M. Le Mon, 1938

INDIANA U. OF PENNSYLVANIA. "To our noble alma mater's name" (a), Mrs. H. E. Cogswell, 1905 (Cincinnati, n.d.); *The Spirit of Indiana* (f), H. E. Cogswell (Cincinnati, 1912)

PENNSYLVANIA STATE U., University Park. "For the glory of old State" (a), to C. C. Converse's *Lead me on* (F. L. Pattee), 1901, pubd in *Songs of the Pennsylvania State College*, ed. H. H. Atherton and J. B. Wyckoff (New York, 1906); *Fight on, State* (f), J. Saunders (New York, *c*1936); *The Nittany Lion*, J. A. Leyden, 1919

SWARTHMORE COLLEGE. "Staunch and gray" (a), to H. S. Thompson's *Annie Lisle*, pubd 1858 (E. J. Taylor)

U. OF PENNSYLVANIA, Philadelphia. *Hail, Pennsylvania* (a), to A. L'vov's *God save the tsar*, first national anthem of Russia, arr. E. M. Dilley *Fight on, Pennsylvania* (f), D. Zoob (B. S. McGiveran), 1923; *The Red and the Blue*, W. J. Goeckel (H. E. Westervelt): all pubd in *Songs of the University of Pennsylvania* (Philadelphia, 4/1923)

U. OF PITTSBURGH. "Alma mater, wise and glorious" (a), to J. Haydn's *Kaiserhymne*, pubd 1797 (G. M. P. Baird), 1929; *The Chant* (a), C. S. Harris (H. C. Scott), 1929; *Hail to Pitt* (f), L. M. Taylor (G. M. Kirk), 1910; *The Panther* (f), H. C. Scott (C. S. Harris) (New York, 1927)

RHODE ISLAND

BROWN U., Providence. "Alma mater, we hail thee" (a), to G. Kiallmark's *Araby's Daughter*, pubd 1822, later *The Old Oaken Bucket* (J. A. DeWolf); *The Brown Cheering Song* (f), H. S. Young (R. B. Jones); *Ki-yi-yi* (f), E. W. Corliss; *Ever True to Brown*, D. Jackson: all pubd in *Songs of Brown University*, ed. W. T. Hastings, T. B. Appleget, and J. B. Archer (Providence, 1928)

SOUTH CAROLINA

U. OF SOUTH CAROLINA, Columbia. "We hail thee, Carolina" (a), G. A. Wauchope, arr. D. Pritchard (Columbia, n.d.); *Carolina Fight Song* (f), C. Salley, arr. D. Pritchard (Columbia, n.d.); *The fighting game cocks lead the way* (f), to E. Bernstein's *Step to the rear* from the musical *How now, Dow Jones*, arr. J. Pritchard (C. Leigh)

SOUTH DAKOTA

U. OF SOUTH DAKOTA, Vermillion. *Pioneer Song* (a), W. R. Colton (M. K. Richardson), 1922.

TENNESSEE

MEMPHIS STATE U. "Stand firm, alma mater" (a), to song of H.T. Smart (?*Lancashire*), arr. T. C. Ferguson (J. W. Brister), *c*1930 (1983); *Go, Tigers, go!* (f), T. C. Ferguson, and T. Allen (E. Hubbard), 1961; *Tiger Rag*, to music by D. J. La Rocca and the Original Dixieland Jazz Band, pubd 1917, arr.

U. OF TENNESSEE, Knoxville. "On a hallowed hill" (a), Mrs. J. L. Meek (Knoxville, 1928); *Fight, Vols, fight!* (f), T. W. Allen and G. Sweet (G. Sweet) (New York, 1939); *Rocky Top* (f), B. Bryant and F. Bryant (1967)

TEXAS

BAYLOR U., Waco. *That good old Baylor line* (a), to G. Evans's *In the Good Old Summertime*, pubd 1902, arr. J. Goode and D. I. Moore (E. E. Markham) (1973); *Baylor Fight Song* (f), F. Boggs and D. Baker, 1945

NORTH TEXAS STATE U., Denton. *Glory to the Green and White* (a), J. Smith (G. Langford), 1966 (New York, 1969); *Fight, North Texas* (f), F. Stroup, 1939, arr. M. D. Summerlin

U. OF TEXAS, Austin. *The Eyes of Texas* (a), to *I've been working on the railroad*, pubd 1894 (J. L. Sinclair), pubd in *Songs from the 40 Acres* (Austin, n.d. [1918]); *Texas Taps* (f), W. S. Hunnicutt (B. Pharr), pubd in *Songs from the 40 Acres* (Austin, n.d. [1918]); *Deep in the heart of Texas*, D. Swander (J. Hershey) (New York, n.d. [1941]); *Texas, our Texas*, W. J. Marsh (G. Y. Wright and W. J. Marsh) (Fort Worth, 1925); *Yellow Rose of Texas*, J. K. (New York, 1858)

UTAH

BRIGHAM YOUNG U., Provo. *College Song* (a), to traditional tune, arr. W. F. Hanson (A. P. Greenwood), 1927; *The Cougar Song* (f), C. D. Sandgren, 1947; *The Old "Y" Bell*, C. D. Sandgren, arr. H. Walser 1958; *The Trail of the "Y"*, W. F. Hanson (T. E. Pardoe), 1934

VERMONT

MIDDLEBURY COLLEGE. "Walls of ivy, paths of beauty" (a), to J. Hughes's hymn tune "Cwm Rhondda" (anon.); *Victory* (f), F. P. Lang (R. E. Bundy); *The College on the Hill* (f), R. Rowe, pubd in *Middlebury Song Book* (Middlebury, 1942)

U. OF VERMONT, Burlington. "Old Vermont upon the hillside" (a) (C. H. Waddell), pubd in *The University of Vermont Song Book*, ed. H. R. Dane and K. H. Owens (New York, 1913)

VIRGINIA

U. OF VIRGINIA, Charlottesville. *The Good Old Song* (a), to G. Thomson's *Auld Lang Syne*, pubd 1799 (E. A. Craighill) (New York, 1906); *Virginia, Hail, all Hail!* (a), J. A. Morrow (n.p., 1935); *Just another touchdown for U. Va.* (f), to *When Johnny comes marching home*, pubd 1863 (S. M. O'Brien) (n.p., 1935); *From Rugby Road to Vinegar Hill*, to traditional tune, by 1972

WASHINGTON

U. OF WASHINGTON, Seattle. *Alma mater* (a), R. H. Allen and G. Hager, 1909; *Bow down to Washington* (f), L. J. Wilson, 1913; *Victory for Washington*, T. Herbert and G. Larson, 1937; all pubd in *Husky Song Book* (Seattle, n.d.)

WASHINGTON STATE U., Pullman. *Washington, my Washington* (a), J. D. Cline, 1914 (Pullman, 1932); *The Fight Song* (f), P. Sayles (Z. Melcher) (Pullman, 1932)

WEST VIRGINIA

WEST VIRGINIA U., Morgantown. *Alma, our alma mater* (a), L. Corson; *Hail, West Virginia* (f), E. Miller and E. McWhorter (F. B. Deem), 1915, pubd in

West Virginia Song Book (Charleston, WV, 1918); *Take me home, country roads*, B. Danoff, T. Nivert, and J. Denver, 1981; *The West Virginia Hills*, H. E. Engle (Lancaster, PA, n.d.)

WISCONSIN

U. OF WISCONSIN, Madison. *Varsity* (a), to "Salvum factus est" from Gounod's *Messe brève et salut*, arr. H. D. Sleeper (H. D. Sleeper), pubd as *Toast to Wisconsin* in *U.W. Songs* (Madison, 1898); *On, Wisconsin* (f), W. T. Purdy (C. Beck) (Chicago, 1909); *Songs to thee, Wisconsin*, ? to music by L. Spohr, pubd in *U. W. Songs* (Madison, rev. 2/1909)

WYOMING

U. OF WYOMING, Laramie. "Where the western lights" (a), J. E. Downey, 1949; *Cowboy Joe* (*Ragtime Cowboy Joe*) (f), L. Muir, G. Clarke, M. Abrahams, 1912

BIBLIOGRAPHY

J. Fuld: *The Book of World-Famous Music* (New York, 1966, rev. and enlarged 2/1971)

DEE BAILY

Colley, Sarah Ophelia. *See* PEARL, MINNIE.

Collins, Bootsy [William] (*b* Cincinnati, OH, 26 Oct 1951). Funk singer, songwriter, and bass guitarist. A member of James Brown's backup band, the J.B.s, while in his teens, he joined Parliament/Funkadelic in 1971. He worked closely with GEORGE CLINTON, contributed both lyrics and music to the band's songs, and helped shape its brand of social commentary, street humor, and science-fiction iconography. When Clinton signed a contract with Warner Bros. in 1976, he negotiated a separate, solo contract for Collins, who continued nevertheless to play with Parliament/Funkadelic as well. Collins's recordings from the late 1970s, with a backup group known as the Rubber Band, were designed ostensibly to appeal to young teenagers and were more successful commercially than Clinton's. They combined busy electronic effects, bizarre characters and musical dramas, and an ever-present, driving funk beat. Collins also worked as a songwriter and producer for other musicians, including Brown, Sly Stewart, Johnnie Taylor, the Sweat Band, and Zapp.

RECORDINGS

(*all recorded for Warner Bros.*)

Stretchin' out in Bootsy's Rubber Band (2920, 1976); *Ahh . . . the Name is Bootsy, Baby!* (2972, 1977); *Bootsy? Player of the Year* (3093, 1978); *This Boot is Made for Fonk-N* (3295, 1979); *Ultra Wave* (3433, 1980); *The One Giveth and the Count Taketh Away* (3667, 1982)

JOHN ROCKWELL

Collins, Judy (Marjorie) (*b* Seattle, WA, 1 May 1939). Popular singer, guitarist, and songwriter. As a child she was encouraged to take up a career as concert pianist by the conductor Antonia Brico, with whom she studied in Denver (1949–56). At the age of 16, however, she began to play guitar and to direct her interest towards folk music. She studied at MacMurray College, Jacksonville, Illinois, and the University of Colorado, where her involvement with folk music deepened. She began singing in clubs in Colorado in 1959; by 1961, after appearances in Chicago and New York, she had signed her first recording contract. During the 1960s she became a major figure in the folksong revival. Not only did she present distinguished performances of conventional folk material (Anglo-American ballads, songs of social protest, and so-called "urban folk music"), she also enlarged her repertory to include cabaret songs by Jacques Brel, theater songs by Weill and Sondheim, and contemporary introspective ballads by Leonard Cohen and Joni Mitchell, as well as her own compositions. Collins's voice may be characterized as cool, clear, sweet, and well-focused; her respect for lyrics is evident in flawless diction. Her somewhat narrow range of interpretation, marked by a well-controlled sense of emotional detachment, is amply compensated for by her musicianship. Collins has been strongly associated with social causes throughout her career.

Judy Collins, 1977

RECORDINGS

(*selective list; all recorded for Elektra*)

A Maid of Constant Sorrow (7209, 1961); *Judy Collins #3* (7243, 1964); *In my Life* (74027, 1966); *Wildflowers* (74012, 1967); *Who Knows where the Time Goes* (74033, 1968); *Whales and Nightingales* (75010, 1970); *Living* (75014, 1971); *Judith* (7E1032, 1975); *Hard Times for Lovers* (6E171, 1979); *Running for my Life* (6E253, 1980); *Times of our Lives* (60001, 1982)

BIBLIOGRAPHY

"Collins, Judy," *CBY 1969*
K. Baggelaar and D. Milton: *Folk Music* (New York, 1976)
V. Claire: *Judy Collins* (New York, 1977)

MICHAEL J. BUDDS

Colombo, Franco. Music publisher. He joined the New York branch of RICORDI in 1937 and later made it into his own company.

Colon, Willie [William Anthony] (*b* New York, 28 April 1950). Trombonist and bandleader. Of Puerto Rican extraction, he formed his first band at the age of 14. He had great success only three years later with his first album, *El malo*, recorded in the *bugalú* style of the 1960s. The band included two trombones and the singer Hector LaVoe (an important agent in Colon's early success), whose lyrics caught the strong and distinctive flavor of New York. By the early 1970s Colon was experimenting with different South American rhythms; "Che che colé," the most popular track on the album *Cosa nuestra* (1972), was based on a West African children's song and mixed several Latin rhythms. Colon also introduced Puerto Rican *jibaro* country music into salsa. In mid-1974, tired with the format of his band, he transferred the leadership to LaVoe. His next album, *The Good, the Bad, the Ugly* (1975), with the singer Rubén Blades, was a highly flexible blend of salsa, rock, *jibaro*, and big-band mambo elements. In the late 1970s he began singing himself as well as producing and recording with other artists such as Celia Cruz. He also made several albums of a socially conscious nature with Blades, including *Siembra* (1978) and *Tiempo pa matar* (1984);

the latter incorporates a number of Colon's typically original arrangements.

BIBLIOGRAPHY

J. S. Roberts: *The Latin Tinge* (New York, 1979)

JOHN STORM ROBERTS

Coltrane [née McLeod], **Alice** (*b* Detroit, MI, 27 Aug 1937). Jazz pianist, organist, and harpist. She played locally in Detroit and toured with vibraphonist Terry Gibbs for a year before meeting John Coltrane in 1963. Early the following year they married, and in 1966 she replaced McCoy Tyner in her husband's band. Coltrane introduced her to the harp, which she mastered on her own; he also exposed her to Eastern religions and a universal concept of music. After Coltrane's death in 1967 she formed several groups which included former players from her husband's band. She also pursued a vigorous study of Buddhism, which caused her increasingly to restrict her musical activities. Though influenced in her early years by the bop pianist Bud Powell, she developed a more sweeping and penetrating style, especially in her organ playing, after she joined her husband. This was the result partly of Coltrane's teaching and partly of the influence she derived from the harp. Her playing is vibrant, fresh, innovative, and uncompromising, with a very light and dexterous right hand accompanied by drone-like chords in the left.

RECORDINGS

(selective list)

With J. Coltrane: *Concert in Japan* (1966, Imp. 9246); *Live at the Village Vanguard Again* (1966, Imp. 9124); *Expression* (1967, Imp. 9120); *Cosmic Music* (1968, Imp. 9148)

Other: McCoy Tyner: *Extensions* (1970, BN 84424); A. Coltrane: *Ptah the El Daoud* (1970, Imp. 9196)

BIBLIOGRAPHY

SouthernB

P. Rivelli: "Alice Coltrane," *Black Giants*, ed. P. Rivelli and R. Levin (New York, 1970)

BILL COLE

Coltrane, John (William) (*b* Hamlet, NC, 23 Sept 1926; *d* New York, 17 July 1967). Jazz tenor and soprano saxophonist, bandleader, and composer. He was, after Charlie Parker, the most revolutionary and widely imitated saxophonist in jazz.

1. Life. 2. Music. 3. Influence.

1. Life. Coltrane grew up in Highpoint, North Carolina, where he learned to play E♭ alto horn, clarinet, and (at about the age of 15) alto saxophone. After moving to Philadelphia he enrolled at the Ornstein School of Music and the Granoff Studios; service in a navy band in Hawaii (1945–6) interrupted these studies. He played alto saxophone in the Joe Webb and King Kolax bands, then switched to tenor to join the alto saxophonist Eddie "Cleanhead" Vinson (1947–8). He performed on either instrument as circumstances demanded while working for Jimmy Heath, Howard McGhee, Dizzy Gillespie (with whom he made his first recording in 1949), Earl Bostic, and lesser-known rhythm-and-blues musicians. But by the time of his membership in Johnny Hodges's septet (1953–4) he was firmly committed to the tenor instrument. He performed infrequently over the next year, then leaped to fame in Miles Davis's quintet with the pianist Red Garland, the double bass player Paul Chambers, and the drummer Philly Joe Jones (1955–7). Throughout the 1950s addiction to drugs and then alcoholism disrupted his career. Shortly after leaving Davis, however, he overcame these problems; his album *A Love Supreme* celebrated this victory and the profound religious experience associated with it.

Coltrane next played in Thelonious Monk's quartet (July–December 1957), but owing to contractual conflicts took part in only one early recording session of this legendary combo. He rejoined Davis in various quintets and sextets with Cannonball Adderley, Bill Evans, Paul Chambers, Philly Joe Jones, and others (1958–60). While with Davis he discovered the soprano saxophone, purchasing his own instrument in February 1960.

Having led numerous studio sessions, established a reputation as a composer, and emerged as the leading tenor saxophonist in jazz, Coltrane was now prepared to form his own group. It gave its début at New York's Jazz Gallery in early May 1960. After briefly trying the pianist Steve Kuhn and drummers Pete LaRoca and Billy Higgins, he hired two musicians who became long-standing members of his quartet, the pianist McCoy Tyner (1960–65) and the drummer Elvin Jones (1960–66); the third, the double bass player Jimmy Garrison, joined in 1961. With these sidemen Coltrane's quartet soon acquired an international following. At times Art Davis added a second double bass to the group; Eric Dolphy also served as an intermittent fifth member on bass clarinet, alto saxophone, and flute from 1961 to 1963, and Roy Haynes was the most regular replacement for Elvin Jones during his incarceration for drug addiction in 1963.

Coltrane turned to increasingly radical musical styles in the mid-1960s. These controversial experiments attracted large audiences, and by 1965 he was surprisingly affluent. From autumn 1965 his search for new sounds resulted in frequent changes of personnel in his group. New members included the tenor saxophonist Pharoah Sanders, the pianist Alice Coltrane (his wife), Rashied Ali (a second drummer until Jones's departure), several drummers as seconds to Ali, and a number of African-influenced percussionists. In his final years and after his death, Coltrane acquired an almost saintly reputation among listeners and fellow musicians for his energetic and selfless support of young avant-garde performers, his passionate religious convictions, his peaceful demeanor, and his obsessive striving for a musical ideal. He died at the age of 40 of a liver ailment.

2. Music. The success of Coltrane's performances in the 1950s depended largely upon their tempo: though mature in his ballad playing and often imaginative at medium tempos, he was frequently shallow in his fast bop solos. At times he rendered ballad themes with little or even no adornment, as in his 1959 performances of *Naima* (named after his first wife). In other ballads, such as his version of Monk's *'Round Midnight* (September–October 1956), he alternated paraphrases of the theme with complex elaborations in which brief thematic references served as signposts. In either case, his priority was beautiful sounds. However esoteric his music became in later years, Coltrane remained a great romantic interpreter of ballads.

One of Coltrane's main objectives was to elaborate the full implications of bop chord progressions. At moderate speeds he could do this without ignoring rhythmic and expressive nuance, for example in his widely varying improvisations on *All of You* (1956), *Blues by Five* (1956), and *Blue Trane* (1957). But the faster the piece, the more concentrated was his exploration of harmony at the expense of other considerations. Like Charlie Parker, Coltrane improvised rapid bop melodies from formulae: but unlike Parker he drew on a small collection of formulae, failed to juxtapose these in new combinations, and tended to

John Coltrane

place them in predictable relationships to the beat. Early solos on *Salt Peanuts* and *Tune-up* (both 1956) exemplify this practice, which culminated in a blistering performance in his composition *Giant Steps* (1959). This solo was impressive because of Coltrane's huge driving tone, his astonishing technical facility, and his complex harmonic ideas; but rigid, repetitious eighth-note formulae lay just beneath the surface.

By seeking to escape harmonic clichés, Coltrane had inadvertently created a confining, one-dimensional improvisatory style. In the late fifties he pursued two alternative directions. First, his expanding technique enabled him to play what critic Ira Gitler called "sheets of sound," as exemplified in his very fast 16th-note runs during a live performance of *Ah-leu-cha* recorded at Newport in 1958 (ex.1). Such flurries gradually replaced the clarity of his approach in *Giant Steps* and disguised his excessive reiteration of formulae. Second, when Miles Davis discarded bop chord progressions in favor of relaxed ostinatos, Coltrane abandoned formulae in favor of true motivic development. Davis's *So What* on the album *Kind of Blue* (1959) was the first recording on which Coltrane systematically varied motifs throughout a solo (ex.2). This process became increasingly prominent in his most famous recordings, including *My Favorite Things* and *Equinox* (1960), *Teo* and *Impressions* (1961), *Crescent* (1964), and the album *A Love Supreme* (1964). Initially he developed motifs only in performances at slow or medium tempos and harmonic rhythms. Eventually he was also able to avoid repetitive responses at high speeds; for example, large portions of *Impressions*, played at a metronome marking of 310, gained coherence by his continuous, inventive manipulation of distinctive eighth-note formulae. (These famous recordings of the early 1960s are often referred to as being "modal," or as exemplifying "modal improvisation" or "modal playing." The concept has less to do with Coltrane himself – whose complex, chromatic lines usually defy modal analysis – than with Tyner's accompaniments, some of which suggest modal scales; for example, in *My Favorite Things* the ostinato based on minor 9th chords on E and F♯ gives rise to a Dorian scale starting from E: E–F♯–G–A–B–C♯–D; *see also* MODAL JAZZ.)

While consolidating his new manner of organizing melody, Coltrane embarked on a quest for new sonorities. Following Lester Young, Illinois Jacquet, and others, he used "false" fingerings to extend the tone-color and upper range of his instrument. The same quest led him to rescue from oblivion the soprano saxophone, which soon rivaled the tenor as his principal instrument. On both he learned to leap between extreme registers at seemingly impossible speed, and thus to convey the impression of an overlapping dialogue between two voices, as in the latter part of the 1963 version of *My Favorite Things*. Radical timbres akin to human cries dominate his late improvisations as his concern with tonality and pitch waned.

At this time Coltrane also developed a type of meditative, slow, rubato melody based upon black gospel preaching. In *Alabama* (1963), he interpreted a speech by Martin Luther King, Jr.; later, in *Psalm* from *A Love Supreme* (1964), he instrumentally "narrated" his own prayer (ex.3, with underlaid text from the album jacket). This technique also appears without obvious reference to a written source in several late recordings, including *Reverend King* (1966) and the album *Expression* (1967).

Ex.2 Motivic relationships in Coltrane's improvisation (tenor saxophone) on M. Davis, *So What*, from *Kind of Blue* (1959, Col. CL1355), transcr. A. White and B. Kernfeld

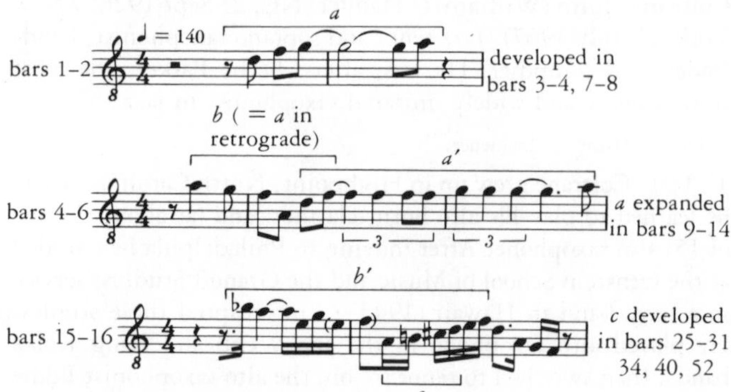

Ex.1 Coltrane's improvisation (tenor saxophone) on M. Davis, *Ah-leu-cha*, from *Miles and Monk at Newport* (1958, Col. CL2178), transcr. A. White and B. Kernfeld

Ex.3 Opening of *Psalm*, from *A Love Supreme* (1964, Imp. 77), transcr. L. Porter

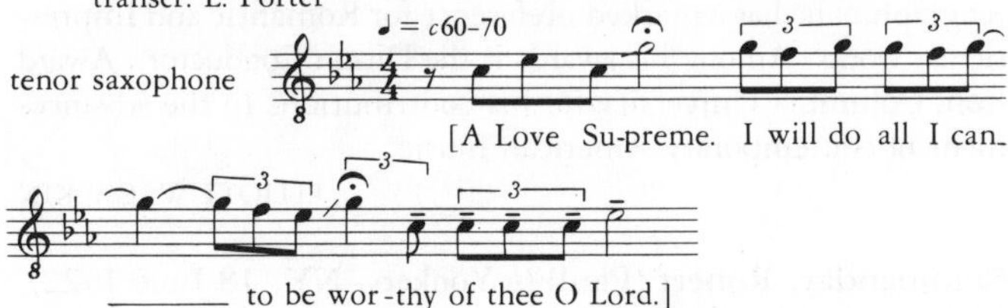

Coltrane's expansion of individual sonority went hand-in-hand with an expansion of group texture. In the quartet, Tyner often kept time and established tonal centers with chordal oscillations, thus freeing Jones to create swirling masses of drum and cymbal accents. Jones (later, Rashied Ali) and Coltrane frequently engaged in extended coloristic duets. The addition of Art Davis's bass, Eric Dolphy's bird- and speech-like sounds on wind instruments, and Pharoah Sanders's screaming tenor saxophone intensified the group's textures. Coltrane moved to the forefront of experimental jazz with *Ascension* (1965), which featured a sustained density of dissonant sound previously unknown to jazz. Two altos, three tenors, two trumpets, a pianist, two double bass players, and a drummer played through a scarcely tonal, loosely structured scheme; their collective improvisation and many of their "solos" stressed timbral and registral extremes rather than conventional melody. Thereafter, Coltrane's ensembles concentrated on maintaining extraordinary levels of intensity by filling a vast spectrum of frequencies, tone-colors, and (when he utilized extra percussionists) accents. The albums *Om* and *Meditations* of 1965, the late versions of *My Favorite Things* and *Naima* (1966), and many other recordings exemplify this final stage of his musical evolution.

3. INFLUENCE. Coltrane's impact on his contemporaries was enormous. Countless players imitated his sound on the tenor saxophone, though few could approach his technical mastery. He alone was responsible for recognizing and demonstrating the potential of the soprano saxophone as a modern jazz instrument; by the 1970s most alto and tenor saxophonists doubled on this once archaic instrument. Finally, by selling hundreds of thousands of albums in his final years, he achieved the rare feat of establishing avant-garde jazz, temporarily, as a popular music.

See also JAZZ, §VI, 2, 4.

RECORDINGS

(selective list)

AS LEADER

The First Trane (1957, Prst. 7105); *Lush Life* (1957–8, Prst. 7188); *Traneing In* (1957, Prst. 7123); *Blue Trane* (1957, BN 1577); *The Last Trane* (1957–8, Prst. 7378); *Soultrane* (1958, Prst. 7142); *Trane's Reign* (1958, Prst. 7213); *Black Pearls* (1958, Prst. 7316); *The Believer* (1958, Prst. 7292); *Standard Coltrane* (1958, Prst. 7243); *Stardust* (1958, Prst. 7268); *Bahia* (1958, Prst. 7353); *Giant Steps* (1959, Atl. 1311), incl. Naima; *Coltrane Jazz* (1959, Atl. 1354); *My Favorite Things* (1960, Atl. 1361)

Coltrane Plays the Blues (1960, Atl. 1382); *Coltrane's Sound* (1960, Atl. 1419), incl. Equinox; *Africa/Brass* (1961, Imp. 6); *Olé Coltrane* (1961, Atl. 1373); *Live at the Village Vanguard* (1961, Imp. 10); *Impressions* (1961–3, Imp. 42); *Coltrane* (1962, Imp. 21); *Selflessness* (1963–5, Imp. 9161), incl. My Favorite Things; *Live at Birdland* (1963, Imp. 50), incl. Alabama; *Crescent* (1964, Imp. 66); *A Love Supreme* (1964, Imp. 77), incl. Psalm; *Transition* (1965, Imp. 9195); *Ascension* (1965, Imp. 95); *Sun Ship* (1965, Imp. 9211); *Live in Seattle* (1965, Imp. 9202-2)

Om (1965, Imp. 9140); *Kulu Se Mama* (1965, Imp. 9106); *Meditations* (1965, Imp. 9110); *Cosmic Music* (1966, Coast Recorders 4950), incl. Reverend King; *Live at the Village Vanguard Again* (1966, Imp. 9124), incl. My Favorite Things, Naima; *Interstellar Space* (1967, Imp. 9277); *Expression* (1967, Imp. 9120)

AS SIDEMAN

M. Davis: *Miles* (1955, Prst. 7014); *'Round about Midnight* (1955–6, Col. CL949), incl. All of You, 'Round Midnight; *Relaxin'* (1956, Prst. 7129); *Steamin'* (1956, Prst. 7200), incl. Salt Peanuts; *Workin'* (1956, Prst. 7166); S. Rollins: *Tenor Madness* (1956, Prst. 7047); M. Davis: *Cookin'* (1956, Prst. 7094), incl. Tune up, Blues by Five; 'Round Midnight (1956, Prst. 45–413); T. Monk: *Thelonious Monk with John Coltrane* (1957, Jazzland 46); R. Garland: *All Mornin' Long* (1957, Prst. 7130); *Soul Junction* (1957, Prst. 7181); M. Davis: *Milestones* (1958, Col. CL1193); *Jazz Track* (1958, Col. CL1268); *Miles and Monk at Newport* (1958, Col. CL2178), incl. Ah-leu-cha; *Jazz at the Plaza*, i (1958, Col. C32470); C. Adderley: *Cannonball Adderley Quintet in Chicago* (1959, Mer. 20449); M. Davis: *Kind of Blue* (1959, Col. CL1355), incl. So What; *Someday my Prince will Come* (1961, Col. CS8456), incl. Teo; D. Ellington: *Duke Ellington and John Coltrane* (1962, Imp. 30)

BIBLIOGRAPHY

I. Gitler: "Trane on the Track," *Down Beat*, xxv/21 (1958), 16

A. Blume: "An Interview with John Coltrane," *Jazz Review*, ii/1 (1959), 25

Z. Carno: "The Style of John Coltrane," *Jazz Review*, ii (1959), no.9, p.17; no.10, p.13

J. Coltrane: "Coltrane on Coltrane," *Down Beat*, xxvii/20 (1960), 26

J. Goldberg: *Jazz Masters of the Fifties* (New York, 1965)

A. Spellman: "Trane: A Wild Night at the Gate," *Down Beat*, xxxii/26 (1965), 15

J. Cooke: "Late Trane," *Jazz Monthly*, no.179 (1970), 2

F. Kofsky: "Revolution, Coltrane, and the Avant-Garde," *Black Giants*, ed. P. Rivelli and R. Levin (New York, 1970)

B. McRae: "John Coltrane: the Impulse Years," *Jazz Journal*, xxiv/7 (1971), 2

A. White: *The Works of John Coltrane* (Washington, DC, 1973) [transcr. solos]

E. Jost: *Free Jazz* (Graz, Austria, 1974)

J. C. Thomas: *Chasin' the Trane: The Music and Mystique of John Coltrane* (Garden City, NY, 1975)

C. O. Simpkins: *Coltrane* (New York, 1975)

D. Wild: *The Recordings of John Coltrane: a Discography* (Ann Arbor, MI, 1977, 2/1979)

D. Baker: *The Jazz Style of John Coltrane* (Lebanon, IN, 1980)

B. Kernfeld: *Adderley, Coltrane, and Davis at the Twilight of Bebop: the Search for Melodic Coherence (1958–59)* (diss., Cornell U., 1981)

——: "Two Coltranes," *Annual Review of Jazz Studies*, ii (1983), 7–66

L. Porter: *John Coltrane's Music of 1960 through 1967: Jazz Improvisation as Composition* (diss., Brandeis U., 1983)

BARRY KERNFELD

Columbia String Quartet. String quartet founded in 1977 as the Schoenberg String Quartet; it changed its name to Columbia String Quartet the following year. The original members were Benjamin Hudson (*b* Decatur, IL, 14 June 1950), first violin; Carol Zeavin (*b* San Bernardino, CA, 2 May 1948), second violin; Janet Lyman Hill, viola; and André Emelianoff (*b* New York, 18 March 1942), cello. The quartet stopped performing in 1981 but re-formed in 1983 with Sarah Clarke (*b* Washington, DC, 18 March 1953) replacing Hill and Eric Bartlett (*b* Brattleboro, VT, 30 April 1957) replacing Emelianoff. It has performed much contemporary music and given several premières, including those of Wuorinen's *Archangel* (1978, with trombonist David Taylor) and Second String Quartet (1980), Roussakis's *Ephemeris* (1979), and quartets by Feldman (1980), Wayne Peterson (1984), and Larry Bell (1985). With Beardslee the Columbia String Quartet gave the première in 1979 of Berg's *Lyric Suite* in its newly discovered version with soprano. Among the works the quartet has recorded are Foss's Quartet no.3 and Rorem's *Mourning Song* (the latter with William Parker, baritone). The quartet has received two NEA grants (1979–80, 1980–81). Its performances are marked by instrumental virtuosity and stylistic refinement in both the contemporary and standard repertory.

BIBLIOGRAPHY

L. Kerner: "Pluralizing the Chamber Music Audience," *Village Voice* (6 March 1978)

SORAB MODI

Columbia University. Privately endowed university in New York with an important department of music and library; *see* NEW YORK, §12, and LIBRARIES AND COLLECTIONS, §3.

Comanche. American Indian tribe; offshoot of the Wyoming Shoshone. *See* SHOSHONE, and INDIANS, AMERICAN, fig.5.

Comden, Betty (*b* New York, 3 May 1915). Librettist and lyricist. She began her professional career as a member of the Revuers, performing satirical shows in nightclubs in New York. Most of the group's sketches were written by Comden in collaboration with fellow member Adolph Green (*b* New York, 2 Dec 1915). Their writing partnership, the longest in American theatrical history, became firmly established with their first work for Broadway, *On the Town* (1944, based on Leonard Bernstein's ballet *Fancy Free*), in which they also performed. They worked again with Bernstein on *Wonderful Town* (1953), and produced several works in collaboration with Jule Styne: *Two on the Aisle* (1951), *Peter Pan* (1954), *Bells are Ringing* (1956), *Say Darling* (1958), *Do Re Me* (1960), *Subways are for Sleeping* (1961), *Fade Out – Fade In* (1964), and *Hallelujah, Baby!* (1967). Other Broadway successes include *Applause* (1970, music by Charles Strouse) and *On the Twentieth Century* (1978, Cy Coleman). With few exceptions, the subject matter of their shows is their native New York, which they examine sardonically but lovingly. Comden and Green also wrote screenplays and lyrics for films. Although none of their film songs attained any real popularity, their screenplays for *Singin' in the Rain* (1952) and *The Band Wagon* (1953) were major achievements.

BIBLIOGRAPHY

"Comden, Betty; Green, Adolph," *CBY 1945*

GERALD BORDMAN

Comissiona, Sergiu (*b* Bucharest, Romania, 16 June 1928). Conductor. After studying conducting at the Bucharest Conservatory and then with Silvestri and Lindenberg, he began his professional career as a violinist in the Bucharest Radio Quartet. He made his début as a conductor with the Romanian State Opera orchestra in 1946, was appointed assistant conductor of the Romanian State Ensemble of musicians, chorus, and dancers in 1948, and served as its music director from 1950 to 1955. He then became principal conductor of the Romanian State Opera (1955–9). He emigrated to Israel and became music director of the Haifa SO from 1959 and of the Israel Chamber Orchestra, which he founded, from 1960. That year he made his British début, and he appeared frequently with the Royal Ballet at Covent Garden, 1962–6. His American début, with the Philadelphia Orchestra, was in 1965. He became music director of the Göteborg SO in 1966 and principal conductor of the Ulster Orchestra (Belfast) in 1967. In 1969 he became music director of the Baltimore SO, a post he retained through the 1983–4 season. In 1976 he was appointed artistic director of the Temple University Music Festival at Ambler, Pennsylvania, the summer home of the Pittsburgh SO, and from 1978 to 1982 was music adviser and principal conductor of the American SO, New York. In 1983 he was appointed chief conductor of the Netherlands Radio PO, and beginning with the 1983–4 season he became music director of the Houston SO. As an opera conductor he returned to Covent Garden with *Il barbiere di Siviglia* in 1975 and made his New York début with *La fanciulla del West* in 1977. Comissiona, who became an American citizen in 1976, is a colorful performer, with gestures instinctively dramatic and choreographic; he has a marked preference for Romantic and Impressionist works. Among his awards is the Ditson Conductor's Award from Columbia University for his contributions to the advancement of contemporary American music.

ELLIOTT W. GALKIN

Commanday, Robert (Paul) (*b* Yonkers, NY, 18 June 1922). Music critic. He studied theory and history at Harvard University (BA 1943), piano at the Juilliard School (1946), and musicology at the University of California, Berkeley (MA 1952). He taught music at Ithaca College (1947–8), the University of Illinois (1948–50), and the University of California, Berkeley (1951–61), where he directed the university's choral association (1950–63). He also directed the chorus of the Oakland SO from 1961 to 1965. In 1964 he succeeded Alfred Frankenstein as music and dance critic of the *San Francisco Chronicle*, a post he continues to fill. An erudite and informed writer, he is a champion of local composers and musical organizations and one of the leading critics on the West Coast. He received the John Swett Award of the California Teachers Association in 1975 and the Deems Taylor Award from ASCAP for 1975–6. From 1981 to 1985 he was president of the Music Critics Association. He is the author of the article on San Francisco in this dictionary.

PATRICK J. SMITH

Commander Cody and his Lost Planet Airmen. Country-rock group. It was formed in Ann Arbor, Michigan, in 1968 and its principal members were Commander Cody (George Frayne), pianist and singer; John Tichy, guitarist and singer; Andy (Andrew) Stein, fiddle player and saxophonist; Billy (William) C. Farlow, guitarist and singer; and Bill (William) Kirchen, guitarist and singer. Several other musicians belonged to the group at various times. Commander Cody and his Lost Planet Airmen first came to prominence after moving to San Francisco in 1969; it was among the first rock bands to explore the country-music style, recording country standards and writing its own songs in the same vein, which often had an element of parody about them. The group also performed boogie-woogie, Western swing, rockabilly, and early rock-and-roll, all in a raucous barroom style that concentrated on atmosphere rather than polished technique. *Hot Rod Lincoln* (no.9, 1972) was its only hit song, but the group influenced a number of country-rock bands of the 1970s. The Lost Planet Airmen disbanded in 1976, its members joining other groups; Cody has enjoyed sporadic success with the Commander Cody Band (*Rock and Roll Again*, Arista 4125, 1977) and as a solo performer, but has been more active as a painter.

RECORDINGS

(selective list; recorded for Paramount unless otherwise stated)

Lost in the Ozone (6017, 1971); Hot Rod Lincoln (0146, 1972); *Hot Licks, Cold Steel and Truckers' Favorites* (6031, 1972); *Live from Deep in the Heart of Texas* (1017, 1974); *We've Got a Live One Here* (WB 2939, 1976)

BIBLIOGRAPHY

J. Grissim: "Cajuns, Truckers and Commander Cody," *Country Music: the White Man's Blues* (New York, 1970), 248

G. Stokes: *Starmaking Machinery: inside the Business of Rock and Roll* (New York, 1977)

JOHN MORTHLAND

Commodores. Soul and funk group. Its members were LIONEL RICHIE (*b* 20 June 1950), lead singer and saxophonist; Thomas McClary (*b* 6 Oct 1950), guitarist; William King (*b* 30 Jan 1949), trumpet player; Milan Williams (*b* 28 March 1949), keyboard player; Ronald LaPread (*b* 4 Sept 1950), electric bass guitarist; and Walter Orange (*b* 15 April 1947), drummer. Formed at Tuskegee (Alabama) Institute in the late 1960s, the group initially played energetic funk in the style of James Brown. After extensive tours of the East and South, in 1971 they signed a contract with Motown to perform as an opening act for the Jackson Five. Three years elapsed, however, before the Commodores were allowed to record. Their first hits, such as *Machine Gun* (1974) and *Slippery when wet* (1975), were in a ragged, rhythm-and-blues style, which appealed primarily to fans of funk; the group's first song to reach the Top Ten on the pop chart was the uncharacteristically tender *Sweet Love* (1976). In an effort to continue such lucrative recording sales, the Commodores subsequently confined their singles almost exclusively to gentle love ballads, written for the crossover market by Richie and sung by him; these included *Just to be close to you* (1976), *Easy* (1977), *Three times a lady* (1978), *Still* (1979), *Sail on* (1979), and *Oh no* (1981). In concert, though, the group continued to play hard-driving rhythm-and-blues, which was jarring to audiences who knew the Commodores only as romantic balladeers through the playing of their recordings on the radio. The difficulty they experienced in projecting a coherent public image was exacerbated by Richie's swift development as a solo artist; when he left the group in 1982 most of the public's allegiance went with him and the Commodores' record sales plummeted. In 1984, however, they enjoyed renewed success on the pop chart with the nostalgic single *Nightshift*, which appeared the following year on an album of the same name.

RECORDINGS

(selective list; all recorded for Motown)

Machine Gun (1307, 1974); Slippery when wet (1338, 1975); Just to be close to you (1402, 1976); Sweet Love (1381, 1976); Brick House (1425, 1977); Easy (1418, 1977); Three times a lady (1443, 1978); Too hot ta trot (1432, 1978); Sail on (1466, 1979); Still (1474, 1979); Oh no (1527, 1981); *Nightshift* (6124, 1985)

GARY THEROUX

Common Way of Singing. *See* OLD WAY OF SINGING.

Commuck, Thomas (*b* Charlestown, RI, 18 Jan 1805; *d* Calumet Co., WI, 25 Nov 1855). Composer of Narragansett (Indian) ancestry. He lived at Brothertown, New York, from about 1825 to 1831, when he and his bride moved west, eventually settling at Brotherton, Wisconsin, where they had ten children; he died by drowning. In 1845 Commuck published *Indian Melodies . . . Harmonized by Thomas Hastings*, a collection of 120 tunes named mostly after chiefs or tribes. Two of his tunes were used by MacDowell: *Old Indian Hymn* in the fifth of the *Woodland Sketches* op.51 and *Shoshonee* in the third movement of the Second ("Indian") Suite op.48.

BIBLIOGRAPHY

R. Stevenson: "English Sources for Indian Music until 1882," *EM*, xvii (1973), 412

ROBERT STEVENSON

Como, Perry (*b* Canonsburg, PA, 18 May 1912). Popular singer. He began his career as a vocalist with dance bands and sang with the Ted Weems band for six years. In 1945 four of his recordings, *Till the end of time*, *If I loved you* (from the musical *Carousel* by Rodgers and Hammerstein), *A hubba-hubba-hubba*, and *Temptation*, sold a million copies. He continued to make hit records throughout the 1950s, notably of ballads such as *If* and *Catch a falling star*, as well as novelty numbers such as *Papa loves Mambo*. His popularity on the radio program "Chesterfield Supper Club" and on his own television show and "The Kraft Music Hall" was such that he became known simply as "Mr. C." In 1970, after an absence of ten years, he achieved another hit with the song *It's impossible*. Como's smooth baritone voice and magnetic delivery have made him an outstanding exponent of the crooning style of ballad singing; he is one of the most commercially successful of all pop recording artists.

BIBLIOGRAPHY

"Como, Perry," *CBY 1947*
A. Shaw: *The Rockin' 50s* (New York, 1974)

ARNOLD SHAW

Composers Collective of New York. A group of composers of music for the working class. The Collective, which grew out of a seminar in the writing of mass songs organized in 1933 by Jacob Schaefer, Leon Charles, and Cowell, sought to make an American contribution to the international working-class music movement then flourishing in Europe under writers such as Bertolt Brecht and composers such as Hanns Eisler. At first a part of the Pierre Degeyter Club (named after the composer of the work *Internationale*, 1871), the group soon became independent; for some time its members held weekly round-table discussions in which general musical and political ideas were aired and newly composed works held up to scrutiny. The organ of the American Music League, *Unison*, in 1936 listed Blitzstein as secretary of the Collective and the following as members or former members: Lan Adomian, Norman Cazden, Robert Gross, Herbert Howe, Alex North, Earl Robinson, Leon Charles, Jacob Schaefer, and Elie Siegmeister. Not mentioned were some composers such as Charles Seeger and H. L. Clarke who for professional reasons did not want their work with the group widely known (some, including Seeger, Siegmeister, and Clarke, used pseudonyms for the songs they wrote for the Collective).

Although they were for the most part highly trained, members accepted the guidance of several experts. Schaefer, long the director of the Yiddish-language Freiheit Gezang Farein, provided examples of skillful choral writing. Eisler, a leading composer of the mass song in German, visited New York in 1934 and took an active part in the discussions of the Collective; his speech "The Crisis in Music," delivered in Town Hall and printed by the Downtown Music School, exerted a major influence. Victor J. Jerome, an editor of the *Daily Worker*, served the Collective as editor, translator, and adviser. The two-volume *Workers Songbook* (1934–5), published by the Workers Music League, is devoted principally to works by Collective members and shows the wide range of their songs. Many were shaped by the free give-and-take process of the Collective, but divergent styles are evident: close to the American vernacular are the rounds of "Carl Sands" (Charles Seeger) and "L. E. Swift" (Elie Siegmeister), the United Front song of "J. Fairbanks" (H. L. Clarke), and notably the songs of Earl Robinson, whose *Joe Hill* later became an integral part of the folksong repertory. But experimental harmonies predominate in George Maynard's setting of Mike Gold's *John Reed, our Captain* and Copland's setting of Alfred Hayes's *Into the Streets May First*. (The latter had been judged the best setting of the text assigned for May Day 1934; Ashley Pettis reported (*New Masses*, 1 May 1934) that it was preferred to "catchy" settings submitted by regular Collective members.)

By the end of 1938 the Collective had disbanded. Though shortlived, it set the stage for Blitzstein's opera *The Cradle will Rock* and Robinson's *Ballad for Americans*, and all that followed from them. It also provided an example for Alan Lomax, Woody Guthrie, Pete Seeger, and other pioneers of the activist folksong movement.

BIBLIOGRAPHY

Foreword, *Workers Songbook*, no.1 (New York, 1934)

Foreword, *Workers Songbook*, no.2 (New York, 1935)

M. Blitzstein: "The Composers Collective of New York," *Unison*, i (June 1936) [whole issue]

E. Siegmeister: *Music and Society* (New York, 1938)

R. S. Dorisoff: *Great Day Coming: Folk Music and the American Left* (Urbana, IL, 1971)

R. Reuss: *American Folklore and Leftwing Politics, 1927–1957* (diss., Indiana U., 1971)

——: "Roots of American Left-wing Interest in Folksong," *Labor History*, xii (1971), 259

D. K. Dunaway: "Unsung Songs of Protest: the Composers Collective of New York," *New York Folklore*, v/i (1977), 1 [incl. further bibliography]

B. Achter: *Americanism and American Art Music, 1929–1945* (diss., U. of Michigan, 1978)

D. K. Dunaway: "Charles Seeger and Carl Sands: The Composers' Collective Years," *EM*, xxiv/2 (1980), 159

For further bibliography, *see* POLITICAL MUSIC.

HENRY LELAND CLARKE

Composers' Forum. Organization formed in 1935 by Ashley Pettis, with funding by the WPA's Federal Artist Project, to present the work of emerging American composers; it has also been known as Composers' Forum-Laboratory. It sponsored concerts that included forums, or moderated question and answer sessions involving the audience; this format became popular with other WPA composer organizations and universities. The first forum concert was held on 30 October 1935 in New York with support from Antheil, Copland, Varèse, Roy Harris, Marion Bauer, Daniel Gregory Mason, and Isadore Freed. Pettis wrote: "Here at Composers' Forum-Laboratory will be offered an opportunity to observe the composer at work for us – the audience. We will observe every type of music written by competent musicians – music expressive of every shade of thought and feeling peculiar to this moment in history. A panoramic view will be had of what is happening in a musical way about us." By 1940 more than 1600 works by hundreds of composers had been presented. When the WPA was ended, the forum moved to San Francisco under private patronage; it continued for two seasons until the outbreak of World War II. Composers' Forum was revived in 1947 under the joint sponsorship of the New York Public Library and Columbia University. An archive was established to house letters, transcripts, programs, and, from 1951, sound recordings of concerts and discussions. Composers' Forum was incorporated in 1972 and continues to present contemporary music.

B. C. VERMEERSCH

Composers String Quartet. String quartet formed in 1963. Its original members were Matthew Raimondi, Anahid Ajemian, Bernard Zaslav, and Seymour Barab; Zaslav was succeeded in turn by Jean Dupouy and Jean Dane, and Barab by Michael Rudiakov and Mark Schuman. Although it was founded largely to perform contemporary music, the quartet has increasingly played the standard repertory as well. For several seasons it was quartet-in-residence at the New England Conservatory, where in 1970 it established the biennial Composers Quartet Composition Prize, which guaranteed the winner the publication of his or her work and its public performance and recording by the quartet. Its foreign tours have included visits to the USSR and Bulgaria (1972), where it was the first American ensemble to perform after World War II, Europe, Africa, India, and the Middle East. It has recorded works by Carter, Perle, Crawford, and Babbitt, as well as by Mendelssohn, Dohnányi, and Hindemith. In 1974 it was appointed quartet-in-residence at Columbia University.

DENNIS K. McINTIRE

Computers and music. A computer is an electronic machine capable of storing, retrieving, and manipulating information at high speeds in response to a set of instructions known as a "program." Computers are customarily distinguished according to their method of operation: analog computers work by means of continuously varying voltages; digital computers use discrete units of information in the form of numbers. This article deals chiefly with the use in the USA of digital computers in musical composition, especially sound synthesis, but it also covers other areas in which computers have been employed, including theory, musicology, and the notation of music.

1. Automated composition. 2. The principles of digital sound synthesis. 3. History and development of digital sound synthesis. 4. The musical potential of digital sound synthesis. 5. Other applications of computers in music.

1. AUTOMATED COMPOSITION. The computer was first used by composers as an aid in working out the details of a musical composition. Using this process, the composer determines a number of rules to be followed in a given order (known in computer science as an "algorithm"). The computer works through these rules and produces a "score" in some form, which the composer may then transcribe into traditional notation.

Lejaren Hiller and Leonard M. Isaacson at the University of Illinois, Urbana-Champaign, were the first seriously to investigate the application of digital computers to composition in the USA. Their *Illiac Suite* for string quartet (1955–6) was followed by the *Computer Cantata* (1963; including computer-generated tape), created by Hiller and Robert A. Baker (both recorded on Heliodor 25053, 1967). Much of the early work done in this area was based on operations with random numbers. The computer was programmed to generate a series of random numbers, which could be used to determine pitches, durations, dynamics, choice of instrumentation, and other musical elements. The random numbers were screened according to criteria (such as the rules of species counterpoint) programmed by the composer; to determine the next in a sequence of pitches, for example, the computer generated new random numbers until one that complied with the rules appeared. In this manner an entire composition could be generated. Other composers have used the computer to manipulate tone rows, and Iannis Xenakis has evolved what he terms "stochastic" music, in which the computer is programmed to calculate the properties of individual musical events according to the statistics of the work as a whole.

2. THE PRINCIPLES OF DIGITAL SOUND SYNTHESIS. The computer can also be used to produce sound (comparably with a musical instrument) and to record and reproduce sound (comparably with the conventional phonograph disc or tape recorder). In the latter process sound is received by a microphone, the output from which is passed through a device known as an analog-to-digital converter (ADC); this converts the electrical impulses

from the microphone into a series of numbers which are then stored in the computer memory. (The same process is employed in digital recording without a computer, but in this case the storage medium is magnetic tape or the "compact disc.") To reproduce sound stored digitally, the numbers are passed through another device called a digital-to-analog converter (DAC), which is connected to an amplifier and loudspeaker. The essential difference between digital recording and the traditional phonograph disc or tape recording is that information is stored in the form of numbers. This has certain advantages. When a new copy of the recording is made no "tape hiss" is added, as happens with tape recordings, and the numbers themselves are not sensitive to variations in humidity and temperature, or susceptible to damage of other kinds, as are phonograph discs. (*See also* SOUND RECORDING, §3.)

In order to synthesize new (previously unrecorded) sounds, the composer must develop some method for creating the appropriate series of numbers. These numbers, generated "from scratch," can be played back by means of the DAC, amplifier, and loudspeaker in the same way as the numbers derived from a digital recording. The principal technique in the composition of computer music is the designing of appropriate methods (called "synthesis techniques") for generating the series of numbers that will produce the desired musical result; then, having chosen a synthesis technique for creating sound, the composer must be able to control the technique during the synthesis of the composition.

3. HISTORY AND DEVELOPMENT OF DIGITAL SOUND SYNTHESIS. Digital hardware was first used to record and perform musical compositions in the late 1950s. Much of the development of computer music has taken place in the context of the tradition of electric and electronic music, which began in the 19th century (*see* ELECTROACOUSTIC MUSIC). The first usable programs for the synthesis of musical sound were developed in 1957 at the Bell Telephone Laboratories in Murray Hill, New Jersey, by Max V. Mathews, a pioneer in computer music; he created a series of programs called "music compilers" (see Roads, 1980). Such a program allows the composer to deal with notes (or, more properly, musical events) by specifying their starting time, duration, loudness, pitch, and other characteristics. It also makes possible the strict specification of elements that are difficult to control in conventional musical performance: the "brightness" or "dullness" of each sound, for example. Using the early music compilers, the composer could instruct the computer to calculate all of the individual numbers required to produce every aspect of the music; the composition could be heard as sound when the digital information was passed through a DAC, amplifier, and loudspeakers. Works by Mathews and his collaborators can be heard on *Voice of the Computer* (Decca 710180, 1970). The music compilers quickly began to be used in a small group of electronic music studios: John Chowning at Stanford University was among the first (1964) to use these programs outside the Bell Laboratories; they were also used at Princeton University (by J. K. Randall, Godfrey Winham, and Hubert S. Howe) and Queens College, CUNY. Examples of computer music from this era are recorded on *Computer Music* (Nonesuch 71245, 1970).

In the early days of computer synthesis, computers did not work fast enough to calculate numbers at the rate at which they might be needed for making musical sound. For example, a particularly dense, two-minute portion of Randall's *Lyric Variations* for violin and computer, realized at Princeton in 1965–8 (and recorded on Cardinal 10057, 1969), took nine hours to compute. Computer synthesis was thus a two-step operation: first the numbers for the entire composition were calculated by the computer and stored in the correct order in its memory; then they were transferred to the DAC at the rate required to create the music as sound in time. Although this method of synthesis opens almost unlimited possibilities to the composer, it is cumbersome and precludes quick assessment of musical results. One solution to this problem is to join the advantages of computer control with a nondigital sound synthesizer to form a "hybrid" system. In 1968 Mathews and his colleagues at the Bell Laboratories developed one of the first hybrid systems, known as GROOVE (Generated Real-time Operations on Voltage-controlled Equipment). A computer-controlled synthesizer "played back" the composer's prepared score; at the same time, the characteristics of certain elements of the sound could be modified by a performer manipulating the synthesizer, and these modifications could be recorded by the computer for later editing and playback. Emmanuel Ghent's *Brazen* (1975) was recorded using this system (*New Directions in Music*, Tulsa Studios, 1978). Another pioneering system was the SalMar Construction assembled in the early 1970s by Salvatore Martirano and others at the University of Illinois. Most of the instruments built by Donald Buchla are also of this type (music that uses Buchla synthesizers in live performance is recorded on *Rosenboom and Buchla: Collaboration in Performance*, 1750 Arch Records 1774, 1978).

In the 1970s, with advances in digital technology, it became possible to replace the hybrid systems with digital synthesizers, instruments designed specifically to combine the sound-generating and -processing capabilities of the analog synthesizer with the programmability of the digital computer. Digital synthesizers create sound by means of streams of numbers in the same way as a computer, and using the same kinds of electronic circuit; but owing to their special design, they can generate the numbers as fast as they are needed to produce sound. This is known as "real-time" operation. One such device is the large Samson Box, designed by P. R. Samson, constructed by Systems Concepts, and delivered to Stanford University in 1977. Another is Dean Wallraff's DMX-1000, which is in use, for example, at Dexter Morrill's studio at Colgate University. This development spurred the design of commercial digital keyboard synthesizers. Jon Appleton at Dartmouth College was among the first to use these devices for composition (some of his works, using an early forerunner of the commercial instruments, are recorded on *The Dartmouth Digital Synthesizer*, Folkways 33442, 1976).

4. THE MUSICAL POTENTIAL OF DIGITAL SOUND SYNTHESIS. Digital synthesis offers the composer the possibility of producing sounds that cannot be created by other means. An early breakthrough was Tracy Lind Petersen's "cross-synthesis," in which a recording of a voice is combined with a musical recording so that the music is clearly audible but yet the speech is intelligible (Petersen, 1975). Paul Lansky, working at Princeton, manipulated one reading of Thomas Campion's poem *Rose-cheekt Lawra, come* in a variety of ways in his *Six Fantasies on a Poem by Thomas Campion* (1978–9; recorded on CRI 456, 1982). It is possible to retune a musical passage, or even one syllable from a recording of a singer, using digital techniques (see L. Rush, "The Tuning of Performed Music," in Blum and Strawn, 1983); for example, Charles Dodge transformed the voice of Caruso (on an early recording) into a *basso profondo* in his *Any Resemblance is Purely*

Coincidental (1980; Folkways 37475, 1982), realized at Brooklyn College, CUNY.

Composers are not, however, merely interested in effects: digital techniques make it possible for them to explore areas that were formerly inaccessible, since they have access to and can manipulate the sound in units of a fraction of a second; they can therefore exploit with absolute rigor and control the structure of the sound itself and its relationship to the compositional structure in which it occurs. Herbert Brün's *Infraudibles* (1967), realized at the University of Illinois, investigates this and other possibilities. In John Chowning's *Stria* (1977) the harmonic ratio of the octave (1 : 2) is replaced by the ratio of the "Golden mean" (1 : 1.618); under normal circumstances this would result in intervals that would sound terribly out of tune, but by manipulating the inner structure of the individual sounds according to the same ratio Chowning eliminates the impression of dissonance. The computer thus offers to the composer the opportunity of entering the relatively unexplored area of alternative tuning systems without being hampered by possibly unwanted dissonance, and at the same time allows the creation of a new form of unity between the sounds themselves and the pitches at which they are heard.

In working along such lines, musicians have become interested in learning more about musical sound. Almost from the beginning, computer-music facilities were involved in or associated with work on acoustics, perception, and the like. If composers can discover how the ear and brain perceive musical sound they increase their chance of creating sounds that will produce the effect they intend. This type of research (see Grey) has already revealed methods of avoiding timbres that are too artificially "electronic," and of imitating the sounds of orchestral instruments to a high degree of accuracy; for example, Dexter Morrill, working at Colgate University, has successfully synthesized trumpet tones (his Studies for trumpet and tape, 1974–5, are recorded on Golden Crest 7068, 1976). Explorations of the nature of sound and perception have also led to an understanding of ways in which the ear can be tricked by the composer. Many computer-music compositions are recorded and played back through stereophonic or quadraphonic equipment. As with earlier forms of synthesis, it is possible to "expand" the apparent size of the listening space by adding reverberation to the recording. It is even possible for the composer to control exactly the apparent location and distance from the listener of the sound source, and the apparent speed at which different sounds are played back; these possibilities are exploited in Chowning's *Turenas* (1972) and Gary Kendall's *Five-Leaf Rose* (1980), the latter realized at the studio at Northwestern University.

Although many computer-music compositions are tape works played back through amplifier and loudspeakers, a large number combine a computer-generated tape with live performance. Randall's *Lyric Variations* (mentioned above) is for violin and computer, and Vercoe's *Synapse* (1976; CRI 393, 1978) for viola and computer, while Morrill's *Six Dark Questions* (1978–9; Redwood 10, 1979) uses soprano and tape. Once real-time synthesis became available, composers started to favor live performance whenever possible, if only to avoid the reduction in sound quality that occurs when a composition is recorded on and played back from tape.

5. Other applications of computers in music. The use of computers in music is by no means limited to composition and synthesis. They can be used to aid or even automate the process of transcribing a sound recording into written notation. This has a variety of applications, from ethnomusicological fieldwork to the transcription of improvised performances. Music printing can be facilitated with computers. In the case, for example, of a complicated score, involving difficult rhythmic subdivisions over a large number of parts, the computer can easily calculate the placement of the notes on the page; it can also save the copyist time by performing tasks such as beaming automatically. Moreover the computer offers the composer the possibility of inventing new notational symbols and placing them wherever they are required on the page.

Computerized systems have also been devised to aid the composer–arranger; Mockingbird, developed by Severo Ornstein at the Xerox Palo Alto Research Center in Palo Alto, California, is a system of this sort. Music played on a conventional (piano-

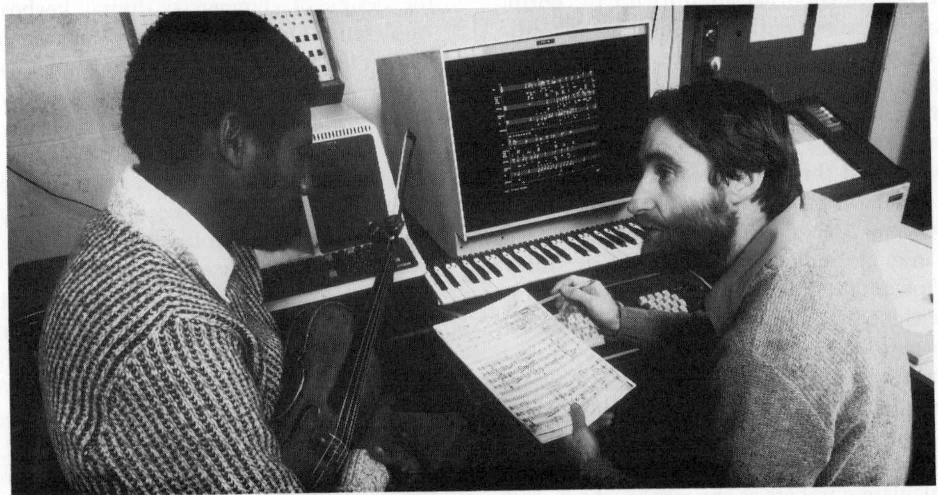

Barry Vercoe (right) with violist Marcus Thompson discussing Vercoe's "Synapse" (1976) for viola and computer-generated tape, MIT experimental music studio, Cambridge, Massachusetts, 1981

like) keyboard is instantaneously "transcribed" by the computer into musical notation, which is displayed on the monitor. The computer can then be used to help the composer to make changes in the notation: if, for example, the composer specifies a different key signature from the original, the computer can convert all of the accidentals into sharps, flats, or naturals as necessary; the composer, naturally, retains the ability to override such blanket instructions in individual cases.

Computers have many other applications in music. The quality of old recordings can be significantly improved by computer processing, as is demonstrated by Thomas Stockham's work on the album *Caruso: a Legendary Performer* (RCA CRM1–1749, 1976). Computer-assisted instruction (CAI) can take much of the drudgery out of teaching and learning basic music skills, such as harmony and aural skills. Computers are used in music theory and music history for a wide variety of tasks: they can facilitate the preparation of catalogues of incipits, simplify the task of producing critical editions, and assist in musical analysis. (For further details of such applications see Kassler and Howe.) Research in all aspects of the use of computers in music is shared at the annual International Computer Music Conference, held under the auspices of the Computer Music Association, which has its headquarters in San Francisco.

BIBLIOGRAPHY

L. A. Hiller, Jr., and L. M. Isaacson: *Experimental Music: Composition with an Electronic Computer* (New York, 1959)
L. A. Hiller, Jr., and R. A. Baker: *Computer Cantata: a Study in Composition using the University of Illinois IBM 7090 and CSX-1 Electronic Digital Computers*, University of Illinois School of Music Electronic Music Studios Technical Report, viii (Urbana, IL, 1963)
J. C. Tenney: "Sound Generation by Means of a Digital Computer," *JMT*, vii (1963), 24
L. A. Hiller, Jr., and R. A. Baker: "*Computer Cantata*: a Study in Compositional Method," *PNM*, iii/1 (1964), 62
Computers and the Humanities (1967–)
M. F. Somville: *Vowels and Consonants as Factors in Early Singing Style and Technique* (diss., Stanford U., 1967)
L. A. Hiller, Jr.: *Music Composed with a Computer: an Historical Survey* (Urbana, IL, 1969)
M. V. Mathews and others: *The Technology of Computer Music* (Cambridge, MA, 1969)
H. von Foerster and J. W. Beauchamp, eds.: *Music by Computers* (New York, 1969)
H. B. Lincoln, ed.: *The Computer and Music* (Ithaca, NY, 1970)
M. V. Mathews and F. R. Moore: "GROOVE: a Program to Compose, Store, and Edit Functions of Time," *Communications of the Association for Computing Machinery*, xiii (1970), 715
T. L. Rhea: *The Evolution of Electronic Musical Instruments in the United States* (diss., George Peabody College for Teachers, 1972)
S. M. Kostka: *A Bibliography of Computer Applications in Music* (Hackensack, NJ, 1974)
J. W. Beauchamp and J. Melby, eds.: *Proceedings of the Second Annual Music Computation Conference: Urbana, IL, 1975* (Urbana, 1975)
J. M. Grey: *An Exploration of Musical Timbre* (diss., Stanford U., 1975)
H. S. Howe, Jr.: *Electronic Music Synthesis: Concepts, Facilities, Techniques* (New York, 1975)
T. L. Petersen: "Vocal Tract Modulation of Instrumental Sounds by Digital Filtering," *Proceedings of the Second Annual Music Computation Conference: Urbana, IL, 1975*, ed. J. W. Beauchamp and J. Melby (Urbana, 1975), pt I, p.33
Computer Music Journal (1977–)
M. Battier and B. Truax, eds.: *Computer Music: Composition musicale par ordinateur: Århus 1978* (Ottawa, 1979)
C. P. Morgan, ed.: *The BYTE Book of Computer Music* (Peterborough, NH, 1979)
E. Stein: *The Use of Computers in Folklore and Folk Music: a Preliminary Bibliography* (Washington, DC, 1979)
D. Wallraff: "The DMX-1000 Signal Processing Computer," *Computer Music Journal*, iii/4 (1979), 44
W. Bateman: *Introduction to Computer Music* (New York, 1980) [see also J. M. Strawn, *Computer Music Journal*, v/1 (1981), 65]
H. Chamberlin: *Musical Applications of Microprocessors* (Rochelle Park, NJ, 1980)
M. Kassler and H. S. Howe, Jr.: "Computers and Music," *Grove 6*
C. Roads: "Interview with Max Mathews," *Computer Music Journal*, iv/4 (1980), 15
C. Roads, ed.: *Proceedings of the International Computer Music Conference: Evanston, IL, 1978* (Evanston, 1980)
P. R. Samson: "A General-purpose Digital Synthesizer," *Journal of the Audio Engineering Society*, xxviii (1980), 106
"Computer-assisted Instruction," *College Music Symposium*, xxi/2 (1981) [articles by J. Eddins, G. D. Peters, D. Gross and R. E. Foltz, D. L. Schrader, R. N. Killiam and others, F. T. Hofstetter]
D. S. Davis: "Computer Applications in Music: a Bibliography," *Proceedings of the International Computer Music Conference: New York, 1980* (San Francisco, 1981), 653–824
H. S. Howe, Jr., ed.: *Proceedings of the International Computer Music Conference: New York, 1980* (San Francisco, 1981)
C. Roads, ed.: *Proceedings of the International Computer Music Conference: San Diego, 1977* (San Francisco, 1981)
S. L. Tjepkema: *A Bibliography of Computer Music: a Reference for Composers* (Iowa City, IA, 1981)
L. Austin and T. Clark, eds.: *Proceedings of the International Computer Music Conference: Denton, TX, 1981* (Denton, 1982)
B. Blesser, B. Locanthi, and T. G. Stockham, Jr., eds.: *Digital Audio: Rye, NY, 1982* (New York, 1983)
T. Blum and J. Strawn, eds.: *Proceedings of the International Computer Music Conference: Venice, 1982* (San Francisco, 1983)
R. Pellegrino: *The Electronic Arts of Sound and Light* (New York, 1983)
P. Manning: "Computer," *GroveI*
C. Dodge and T. A. Jerse: *Computer Music: Synthesis, Composition, and Performance* (New York, 1985)
C. Roads, ed.: *Composers and the Computer* (Los Altos, CA, 1985)
C. Roads and J. Strawn, eds.: *Computer Music Tutorial* (Cambridge, MA, 1985)
——: *Foundations of Computer Music* (Cambridge, MA, 1985)
P. R. Samson: "Architectural Issues in the Design of the Systems Concepts Digital Synthesizer," *Digital Audio Engineering: an Anthology*, ed. J. Strawn (Los Altos, CA, 1985)
J. M. Strawn, ed.: *Digital Audio Engineering: an Anthology* (Los Altos, CA, 1985)
——: *Digital Audio Signal Processing: an Anthology* (Los Altos, CA, 1985)
C. Roads: *Computer Music History* (Los Altos, CA, in preparation)

JOHN STRAWN

Con Brio. A digital synthesizer, developed in 1979; *see* ELECTROACOUSTIC MUSIC, §4.

Concordia. Firm of music and book publishers. Concordia Publishing House was founded in St. Louis in 1869 by immigrant German Lutherans for the purpose of printing their hymnals and other church literature, and takes its name from the Lutheran Book of Concord (1580). Its catalogue, which has included music since 1880, consists of sacred pieces for solo voice and chorus, music for organ, organ and other instruments, handbells, and books on the liturgy, church music, and organs. From 1966 to 1980 the firm issued the periodical *Church Music*. Concordia is a nonprofit organization and the official publishing firm of the Lutheran Church–Missouri Synod.

FRANCES BARULICH

Concord String Quartet. String quartet. Founded in 1971, it won the Naumburg Award for chamber music the same year, which provided for its début at Alice Tully Hall in 1972 and the commissioning of Rochberg's Third String Quartet. Resident at Dartmouth College, New Hampshire, from 1974, the quartet has developed a reputation as a strong advocate of American music, and has maintained its original members. Mark Sokol (*b* Oberlin, OH, 16 July 1946), first violinist, studied with Robert Mann and Dorothy DeLay at the Juilliard School. Andrew Jennings (*b* Buffalo, NY, 3 Nov 1948), second violinist, studied with Galamian at the Juilliard School. John Kochanowski (*b*

South Bend, IN, 7 Jan 1949), violist, studied at the Interlochen Arts Academy, Michigan, and with Mann and Trampler at the Juilliard School. Norman Fischer (*b* Plymouth, MI, 25 May 1949), cellist, studied at the Interlochen Arts Academy and with Richard Kapuscinski at the Oberlin College Conservatory.

Rochberg continued to collaborate with the Concord, writing for the ensemble his Piano Quintet (1975), his Fourth (1977), Fifth (1978), and Sixth (1978) String Quartets (the "Concord Quartets," recorded by the ensemble), his Seventh String Quartet (1979), and his String Quintet (1982). Other composers who have written for the quartet include Foss (Third String Quartet), Ben Johnston (*Crossings*), and Druckman (Third String Quartet). The ensemble has been strongly influenced by the Juilliard Quartet in its energetic and aggressive style of playing.

BIBLIOGRAPHY

P. K. Mose: "The Concord String Quartet: a Ten-year Success Story," *HiFi/MusAm*, xxxii/2 (1982), 34

H. Kupferberg: "The Concord Quartet Embarks upon its Second Decade," *Ovation*, iii/11 (1982), 12

JAMES CHUTE

Condon, Eddie [Albert Edwin] (*b* Goodland, IN, 16 Nov 1905; *d* New York, 4 Aug 1973). Jazz banjoist and guitarist. He first played the ukulele, then the tenor banjo, plectrum banjo, tenor lute, and four-string guitar. He played with the Austin High School Gang in Chicago, and promoted and organized many important sessions, beginning with the McKenzie–Condon Chicagoans in 1927 and culminating in a series of albums for Columbia (1953–7). After making a reputation as a hard-hitting rhythm banjoist and guitarist Condon went on to specialize in organizing jam sessions which matched the early jazz repertory with the most accomplished instrumentalists on the New York scene. He organized a series of jazz concerts at Town Hall and Carnegie Hall (1942–6) and presented one of the earliest jazz programs on television (1942). He frequently led his own band at Nick Rongetti's club, and was co-owner (with Pete Pesci) of Condon's club, which opened in 1945. Condon was known for his dry wit, and was the co-author of three valuable sourcebooks on jazz.

RECORDINGS

(selective list)

Home Cooking (1933, Col. 35680); Love is just around the Corner (1938, Com. 500); A Good Man is Hard to Find, pts i–iv (1940, Com. 1504–5); Beale Street Blues, on *Jam Session Coast to Coast* (1953, Col. CL547); There'll be some Changes Made (1954, Col. B1967)

Eddie Condon, early 1940s

WRITINGS

with T. Sugrue: *We Called it Music: a Generation of Jazz* (New York, 1947/*R*1970)

ed. with R. Gehman: *Eddie Condon's Treasury of Jazz* (New York, 1956/*R*1975)

with H. O'Neal: *The Eddie Condon Scrapbook of Jazz* (New York, 1973)

BIBLIOGRAPHY

B. Esposito: "Remembering Eddie Condon," *Jazz Journal*, xxvi/10 (1973), 2

M. Jones: "The Father of Chicago Jazz," *Melody Maker* (11 Aug 1973), 20

W. H. Kenney, III: "He Played Rhythm: Eddie Condon, the Musician," *Journal of Jazz Studies*, iv/2 (1977), 72

B. White: *The Eddie Condon 'Town Hall Broadcasts' 1944–5: a Discography* (Oakland, CA, 1980)

W. H. Kenney, III: "Jazz and the Concert Halls: the Eddie Condon Concerts, 1942–48," *American Music*, i/2 (1983), 60

WILLIAM H. KENNEY, III

Conductors' Guild. Organization established by the AMERICAN SYMPHONY ORCHESTRA LEAGUE in 1975 to promote the interests of American conductors.

Cone, Edward T(oner) (*b* Greensboro, NC, 4 May 1917). Critic, composer, and pianist. He studied composition with Sessions at Princeton University (BA 1939, MFA 1942), where he held a Woodrow Wilson Fellowship (1945–6); he joined the faculty there in 1947. He was Ernest Bloch Professor at the University of California, Berkeley (1972), and was appointed Andrew D. White professor-at-large at Cornell University in 1979. Among the awards he has received are a Guggenheim Fellowship (1947–8), an Old Dominion Fellowship (Princeton University, 1964–5), and an ASCAP-Deems Taylor Award (1975). He has been on the editorial boards of *Perspectives of New Music*, *19th Century Music*, and *Studies in the Criticism and Theory of Music*.

An influential analyst and critic, Cone writes authoritatively about complex musical questions in lucid and supple prose. He brings to criticism generous humanistic and musical backgrounds that provide a firm base for his work in analysis and stylistic criticism. While much of his criticism has been devoted to modern music, especially that of Schoenberg and Stravinsky, he is equally illuminating on 18th- and 19th-century music.

Cone's criticism has focused upon three general areas: musical language, relationships between texts and music, and analytical and critical method. In *Musical Form and Musical Performance*, elements of harmony, rhythm, and phrasing suggest aspects of global structure that may be projected by performers and perceived by listeners. Tracing the contextual working-out of stylistic processes, as in "Stravinsky: the Progress of a Method" (*PNM*, i/1, 1962, p.18), has led Cone to penetrating conclusions about musical structure and style. In *The Composer's Voice* Cone attempts to resolve perplexing problems of communication, expression, and meaning in music. Other, later essays, such as "Three Ways of Reading a Detective Story – Or a Brahms Intermezzo" (*Georgia Review*, xxxi, 1977, p.554), expound upon links between literary narrative modes and musical settings. Cone's essays on analytical and critical method, from "Analysis Today" (*MQ*, xlvi, 1960, p.172) to "The Authority of Music Criticism" (*JAMS*, xxxiv, 1981, p.1), raise questions about analytical skills and their pertinence to specific musical contexts and styles, and suggest instead flexible ways of approaching the functions of background compositional procedures, how such functions may be explained, and how perceived. He has published many other articles in the *Musical Quarterly*, *Perspectives of New Music*, *19th*

Century Music, and the *Journal of the American Musicological Society*.

Cone's own music employs functions of extended tonality as a basis for thematic and harmonic elements. Hexachordal properties often provide the materials for the shaping of harmonic and large-scale tonal relationships, as in the String Sextet and *Page from a Diary*.

WORKS

Orch: Sym. (1953); Nocturne and Rondo, pf, orch, 1957; Conc., vn, chamber orch, 1959; Music, str, 1964; Cadenzas, vn, ob, str orch, 1979; several other orch pieces

Chamber: Prelude, Passacaglia and Fugue, pf, 1957; Str Sextet, 1966; Serenade, fl, vn, va, vc, 1975; Page from a Diary, pf, 1977; other chamber works; many pf pieces

Vocal: 9 Lyrics from In Memoriam (Tennyson), Bar, pf, 1978; other songs, choral works

Principal publishers: Marks, Rongwen

WRITINGS

Musical Form and Musical Performance (New York, 1968)

ed., with B. Boretz: *Perspectives on Schoenberg and Stravinsky* (New York, 1968, rev. 2/1972)

ed.: Berlioz: *Fantastic Symphony*, Norton Critical Scores (New York, 1971)

ed., with B. Boretz: *Perspectives on American Composers* (New York, 1971)

ed., with B. Boretz: *Perspectives on Contemporary Music Theory* (New York, 1972)

The Composer's Voice (Berkeley, CA, 1974)

ed., with B. Boretz: *Perspectives on Notation and Performance* (New York, 1976)

ed.: *Roger Sessions on Music* (Princeton, NJ, 1979)

BIBLIOGRAPHY

EwenD

R. Morgan: "E. T. Cone, String Sextet," *PNM*, viii/1 (1969), 112

RICHARD SWIFT

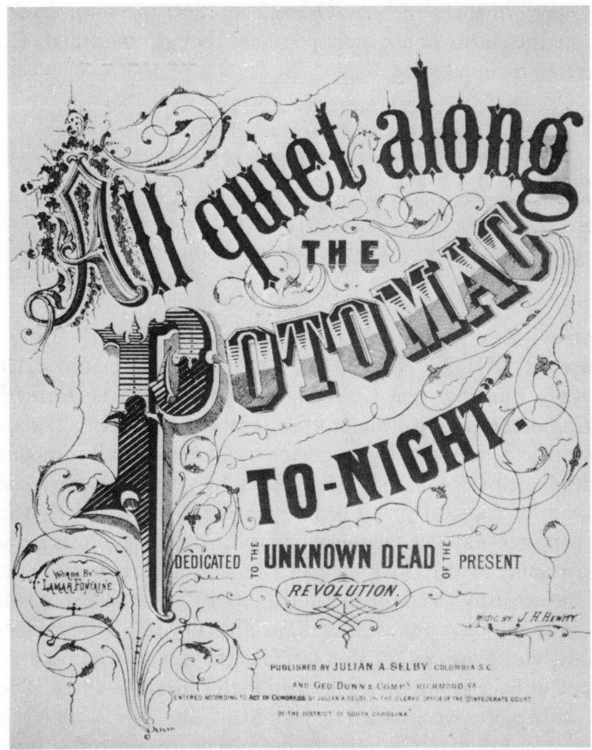

Confederate music: sheet-music cover (1860s) of "All quiet along the Potomac tonight" (music by John Hill Hewitt, words by Lamar Fontaine)

Confederate music. A term used to refer to music written in support of Southern political and ideological views around the time of the American Civil War (roughly 1860–65). This includes songs and piano pieces published as sheet music, texts printed in songsters and other sources, and manuscript music of various types, such as operettas and music for wind band. Since sympathy for Southern viewpoints was not confined to the seceding Southern states, this category includes a large quantity of music published in support of the Confederate cause in such Northern cities as Baltimore, and as far away as Canada and England.

In a stricter sense the term refers to music actually published in the South during the existence of the Confederate States of America. Such publications, referred to as "Confederate imprints," comprise a unique bibliographic category whose special character and history reveal much about Southern ideals, sentiments, and fortunes. For the South the publication of a regional repertory was a matter of considerable urgency and pride. As A. J. Bloch of Mobile, Alabama, counseled in his sheet-music series, Southern Flowers, "The South must not only fight her own battles but sing her own songs and dance to music composed by her own children." After the South's secession from the Union and the outbreak of hostilities, printing establishments in the South increased enormously their efforts to replace dwindling prewar stocks of music and to supply the new type of patriotic and topical repertory in public favor. There were some 35 music publishers active in the South during the war, the most important being A. E. Blackmar (New Orleans, and Augusta, Georgia), G. Dunn (Richmond, and Columbia, South Carolina; see illustration), J. A. McClure (Nashville and Memphis), J. C. Schreiner (Macon and Savannah, Georgia), and P. P. Werlein (New Orleans).

Songs relating to Southern patriotism naturally make up the largest single category of Confederate music. A significant portion of the parlor piano literature, too – marches, quicksteps, schottisches, polkas, and the like – could readily assume a respectable (and profitable) Southern viewpoint by patriotic title alone. There are music sheets devoted to virtually every significant leader or military hero, items referring to specific events or battles, songs relating to soldiering, various invocations of the Confederate flag, and songs of a generalized patriotic appeal as well as exhortations to the Deity. Among Confederate imprints there are also numerous songs depicting home life and idealized loved ones, or the more disquieting events of war – sentimental ballads in the genteel tradition, many of which were popular in both North and South.

The composer most closely associated with the Confederate repertory is undoubtedly John Hill Hewitt (1801–90). Active in Richmond at the beginning of the war, Hewitt subsequently moved to Augusta, where many of his songs, plays, and Confederate operettas were presented. Although most of Hewitt's efforts were decidedly partisan (such as the ballad opera *King Linkum the First*), he also wrote songs reflecting the misery of war for the common man, such as *All quiet along the Potomac tonight* (see illustration). Harry B. Macarthy (1834–88), successful as both songwriter and performer, popularized songs such as *The Bonnie Blue Flag* in "personation concerts," a fascinating road show that mixed buffoonery, sentiment, and overt appeals to patriotism. Theodore von La Hache (1822/3–69), active in New Orleans, was another significant Confederate composer. The song most frequently associated with the South, *Dixie*, was first published in the North, Dan Emmett having employed it as a "walk-around" for Bryant's Minstrels in New York in 1859.

After performances in New Orleans in 1860 the song came to assume the status of a widely popular, though unofficial, Confederate "national song."

BIBLIOGRAPHY

R. B. Harwell: *Confederate Music* (Chapel Hill, 1950)

——: "Confederate Carrousel: Southern Songs of the Sixties," *Emory University Quarterly*, vi (1950), 84

F. Hoogerwerf: "Confederate Sheet Music at the Robert W. Woodruff Library, Emory University," *Notes*, xxxiv (1977–8), 7

——: *Confederate Sheet Music Imprints*, ISAMm, xxi (Brooklyn, NY, 1984)

FRANK HOOGERWERF

Confrey, Zez [Edward Elzear] (*b* Peru, IL, 3 April 1895; *d* Lakewood, NJ, 22 Nov 1971). Composer and pianist. After studying music at the Chicago Musical College he formed a touring orchestra with his brother James about 1915. Through his work as a pianist and arranger for various piano-roll companies he developed a popular style known as NOVELTY PIANO, a combination of classical piano technique with syncopated rhythms and peppy tunes. The technical possibilities of piano rolls helped inspire some of the flashy keyboard effects and rhythmic tricks that influenced later composers in the novelty-piano idiom. Among his most popular pieces were *Stumbling* (1922), *Dizzy Fingers* (1923), and *Kitten on the Keys* (1921), the last of which he performed at Paul Whiteman's Aeolian Hall concert in 1924. These and other pieces were issued by Jack Mills, Inc. as *Modern Novelty Piano Solos* (1923). The novelty craze soon ceased to be novel, but Confrey continued to compose concert, popular, and student pieces into the 1940s.

BIBLIOGRAPHY

D. A. Jasen: "Zez Confrey: Creator of the Novelty Rag," *Rag Times*, v/3 (1971), 5

D. A. Jasen and T. J. Tichenor: *Rags and Ragtime: a Musical History* (New York, 1978), 214ff

E. A. Berlin: *Ragtime: a Musical and Cultural History* (Berkeley, CA, 1980), 162ff

MARK TUCKER

Conga. A Latin-American carnival road march that came to the USA around 1937. The bandleader Desi Arnaz was chiefly responsible for transforming it into a social dance craze, especially through his appearances in Rodgers and Hart's Broadway musical *Too Many Girls* (1939; film version, 1940). The conga experienced a revival in the 1950s. The music for the dance is built on a repeated rhythm (ex.1), which corresponds to three shuffle

Ex.1 A typical conga rhythm

steps and a kick, with the torso twisting from side to side. Couples can perform the conga by moving apart and back together again, but more characteristically it is performed in a long line, with the outstretched arms of each dancer placed on the shoulders or waist of the preceding dancer. A variation of the conga that also became popular in the 1950s is the bunny hop, which is per-

Ex.2 Bunny hop rhythm

formed in a moderate 4/4 (ex.2) as a line dance. The pattern of steps consists of two kicks to the right, two kicks to the left, a hop forward, a hop back, and three hops forward.

BIBLIOGRAPHY

A. P. Wright and D. Wright: *How to Dance* (Garden City, NY, 1942, 2/1958)

J. S. Roberts: *The Latin Tinge* (New York, 1979)

BARRY KERNFELD, PAULINE NORTON

Congregational Church. The Congregational Church in America, which grew out of the Congregational Way of 16th-century England, was defined as a distinctive movement in 1640 and organized as a national denomination in 1852. It was united with the Christian Church in 1931 and with the German and Evangelical churches in 1957 to form the United Church of Christ. For a discussion of the music of the Congregational Church, *see* UNITED CHURCH OF CHRIST, MUSIC OF THE.

Conjunto (Sp.). An instrumental ensemble developed in northern Mexico in the 19th century and used in the *norteño* folk music style; *see* HISPANIC-AMERICAN MUSIC, §2(i).

Conlon, James (*b* New York, 18 March 1950). Conductor. After graduating from the New York High School of Music and Art, he entered the Juilliard School in 1968, where he studied with Morel (BM 1972). He made his professional début as an opera conductor in Spoleto, Italy, with *Boris Godunov* in 1971. His conducting of *La bohème* at Juilliard a year later marked the beginning of an international career. Soon afterwards he received the conducting award of the National Orchestral Association, with which he subsequently made his first appearance at Carnegie Hall. In 1974 he became the youngest person to conduct a subscription concert of the New York PO. He first conducted at the Metropolitan Opera in 1976, directing a performance of *Die Zauberflöte*. He succeeded Levine as music director of the Cincinnati May Festival in 1979; in the 1980 season he led orchestral performances in Cleveland, Philadelphia, Boston, Chicago, and New York, made his first appearance with the Berlin PO, and conducted at the Metropolitan and Covent Garden. He was named music director of the Rotterdam PO in 1983. Conlon has carefully considered each step in his musical and professional development. His highly serious approach to music is offset by an almost childlike delight in performing it.

BIBLIOGRAPHY

A. Kozinn: "At 31, a Busy Guest Conductor Contemplates Settling Down," *New York Times* (2 Aug 1981)

M. Hoelterhoff: "James Conlon's Quick Rise to Conducting's Front Ranks," *Wall Street Journal* (12 Feb 1982)

JAMES CHUTE

Conn. Firm of instrument manufacturers and distributors, primarily of band instruments. The company was founded by Charles Gerard Conn (*b* Ontario Co., NY, 29 Jan 1844; *d* California, 1931), developer of a special type of mouthpiece for brass instruments. Conn originally produced it for his own use after a lip injury made it impossible for him to play a conventional cornet, but finding it was of interest to other cornetists he set up a small workshop. In 1875 he joined with Eugene Dupont, a skilled horn maker from France, to establish the Conn-Dupont Co. in Elkhart, Indiana. It produced first cornets and then other brass instruments. In 1887, as the C. G. Conn Co., the firm opened a subsidiary plant in Worcester, Massachusetts, buying out Fiske, one of the longest established instrument makers in the USA. A year later it produced the first saxophone built in the USA. By the 1980s the company offered an extensive range of brass instruments, flutes, clarinets, and saxophones of its own make, as well as imported wind instruments. Conn-made instruments were endorsed by several leading band directors, including Sousa. The company also manufactured a range of "Wonder" string instruments.

Despite increasing sales the company had financial difficulties, and in 1915 Conn sold it to Carl D. Greenleaf, who changed the name to C. G. Conn Ltd and converted the firm from a mail-order business to one operated through retail dealers. Greenleaf speeded production and reduced costs by introducing assembly-line production, and (in 1928) established a research department for the improvement of instrument design. During this time sales to professional touring bands and amateur town bands were diminishing, but Conn continued to grow, helped by the emerging interest in music in the schools, which the company (as well as other manufacturers) encouraged.

From the 1920s Conn's primary market was school bands and orchestras. It purchased the Leedy Manufacturing Co. in 1927 and the firm of Ludwig & Ludwig in 1930, and combined their production of drums and other percussion instruments in the Elkhart factory; the Leedy and Ludwig businesses were sold in 1955. In the 1960s Conn purchased or became affiliated with various instrument manufacturers: the New Berlin Instrument Co. (New Berlin, New York), producing clarinets, piccolos, oboes, and bassoons; the Artley Flute Co. (Elkhart, Indiana), manufacturing a range of student flutes; and the Best Manufacturing Co. (Nogales, Arizona), producing student alto saxophones. Slingerland and Deagan were also part of the group (1970–84).

The main Conn factory in Elkhart produced all the brass instruments, saxophones and flutes, and many instrument accessories. A second Elkhart plant was devoted to making electronic organs and devices such as the Stroboconn and Strobotuner tuning aids. After these factories at Elkhart were closed in the 1970s the electronic organ division moved first to Oak Brook, near Chicago, as Conn Organ and later to nearby Carol Stream as Conn Keyboards. In 1980 the keyboard divisions were sold to the Kimball firm and the other operations (with headquarters still at Elkhart) to Daniel J. Henkin of the Mardan company. Brass instruments are now made at Abilene, Texas. The company also offers violins and other string instruments imported from Germany and assembled in Cleveland, Ohio, and a range of guitars manufactured in Japan.

CAROLYN BRYANT

Connecticut Opera Association. Opera association formed in 1942 in HARTFORD.

Consoli, Marc-Antonio (*b* Catania, Italy, 19 May 1941). Composer. He came to the USA in 1956, and studied with Rieti at the New York College of Music, with Krenek at the Peabody Conservatory, with Schuller and Crumb at the Berkshire Music Center, and with Alexander Goehr at Yale University, where he received the DMA in composition in 1976. He also studied with Franco Donatoni at the Accademia Chigiana (Siena) and at the Warsaw Conservatory on a Fulbright Scholarship (1972–4). Honors he has received include two Guggenheim Fellowships (1971, 1978), two NEA grants (1979, 1980), an award from the American Academy of Arts and Letters (1975), and residencies at the MacDowell Colony and Yaddo. In 1976 Consoli founded the contemporary-music ensemble Musica Oggi, directing it until 1981; in 1984 he took over Rinaldo Music Press, a company devoted to the publication of new music. He has had works commissioned by the Steirischer Herbst Festival (Graz, Austria), the International Festival of Contemporary Art (Royan, France), and the Koussevitzky and Fromm foundations. His music has been performed at ISCM festivals in Finland (1978) and Belgium (1981) and by leading ensembles throughout Europe and the USA, among them the New York PO and the American Composers Orchestra.

Consoli's music is dramatic and brilliantly colored. A typical example, the virtuoso concerto for orchestra *Odefonia*, uses contrasting sonorities, rather than themes, to delineate an almost Classical structure. Since 1975 Consoli's works have become more lyrical, while remaining forceful and dynamic. Some of his music shows the influence of his Sicilian backgroud: *Vuci siculani* (1979) incorporates folk melodies, religious imagery, and the exotic sounds of the flute-like *fiscalettu*.

WORKS

Orch: Profiles, 1972–3; Music for Chambers, 1975; Odefonia, 1976; Naked Masks (3 Frescos from a Dream), ballet, 1980; The Last Unicorn, ballet, 1981; Afterimages, 1982

Vocal: Equinox I (W. Suiha, trans. G. Bownas, A. Thwaite), S, chamber ens, 1967; Equinox II (M. Shuoshi, trans. Bownas, Thwaite), S, chamber ens, 1968; Isonic (Consoli), S, fl, 2 pf, perc, 1970; Lux aeterna, 8-part chorus, 1972; Canti trinacriani (Consoli), Bar, tape, ens, 1975; 3 canzoni (Consoli), S/Mez, fl, vc, 1976; Vuci siculani (Consoli, Lat.), Mez, chamber ens, 1979; Fantasia celeste (Dante), S, chamber ens, 1983

Chamber and inst: Brazilian Fantasy, B♭ cl, pf, 1965; Sonatina, t sax, pf, 1965; Interactions: I, fl, ob, cl, bn, hn, tpt, trbn, timp, 1970, II, pf trio, 1971, rev. 1975, III, fl, harp, 1971, rev. 1975, IV (The Aftermath), hn, tpt, trbn, perc, db, 1971, rev. 1975, V (The Consequence), fl, str qt, 1972, rev. 1976; Pezzo, pf, 1970; Sciuri novi, fl, 1974; Ellipsonics, 1–4 insts, 1975; Memorie pie, pf, 1976; Sciuri novi II, db, tape/2 db, 1976; Orpheus Meditation, gui, 1981; Str Qt, 1983; Cantillation, vc, pf, 1984; a few others

Early works; some withdrawn works

Principal publishers: ACA, Margun, Presser, Rinaldo

MYRNA S. NACHMAN

Continental Vocalists. Male quartet. It was formed in 1853 in Pawtucket, Rhode Island, by four singers from Connecticut: William Dwight Franklin, John Wesleyan Smith, William Frisbie, and Charles Huntington. Three of them had met at the Boston Teachers Institute, where they studied with Lowell Mason, George J. Webb, and George F. Root. The group developed an American repertory, much of it patriotic, and many of their songs were written by Franklin, including *The Power of the Mighty Dollar*, *The Old Man's Soliloquy*, and *The Mountain Bugle's Echo*; *The Continental Vocalists Glee Book* (1855) also included works by many other contemporary composers. The group concentrated on excellent singing and exploited their gift for entertaining, avoiding controversial programming. They performed in costumes of the Federal Era, displayed flags, and accompanied themselves on flute, violin, cello, and melodeon. They made extensive annual tours from fall to spring during the 1850s and early 1860s, averaging four concerts weekly and playing to packed halls; in the 12 years of their existence they amassed over $70,000. Newspaper reviews were numerous and favorable; an undated review in the Buffalo *Express* is typical: "The Continentals are not to be likened to either the numerous bands of negro singers on the one hand, or to the namby-pamby don't be naughty school led by the Hutchinsons. These gentlemen are artists, in the best sense of the term." While there were many changes of personnel in the quartet, Franklin remained a member throughout. He and

Smith were still performing as a duo in the 1890s; by that time they had abandoned their earlier political themes and were singing for the temperance cause.

PHYLLIS BRUCE

Contradanse. *See* COUNTRY DANCE.

Converse, Frank B. (*b* Westfield, MA, 17 June 1837; *d* New York, 5 Sept 1903). Banjo player and teacher. He was attracted to the banjo after hearing George Swayne Buckley play in 1851, and neglected the piano to take up the instrument. He played at first in the "stroke" style (essentially the folk style now called "frailing"). He began his professional career as a minstrel performer in the mid-1850s and played with many different minstrel companies. Converse gained a reputation as an innovative and influential banjo player and teacher. He had studios at various times in Memphis, St. Louis, San Francisco, and, after he retired from the stage in 1883, New York. He wrote five widely used instruction books; one of these (1865) introduced the "guitar" or "classical" style of banjo playing, in which two or three fingers and the thumb are used to pluck the strings, as with the classical guitar. Converse was said to be the first to play in this style, though in his reminiscences he suggested that members of the Buckley troupe preceded him; but whether or not he invented it, Converse was very important in spreading this technique, which by the 1880s had become the dominant professional and parlor banjo style.

BIBLIOGRAPHY

F. B. Converse: "Banjo Reminiscences," *The Cadenza*, vii–ix (1901–2) [series of articles]

N. Howard: *The Banjo and its Players* (MS, 1957, *NN-L*)

E. L. Rice: *Monarchs of Minstrelsy* (New York, 1911)

ROBERT B. WINANS

Converse, Frederick Shepherd (*b* Newton, MA, 5 Jan 1871; *d* Westwood, MA, 8 June 1940). Composer, teacher, and administrator. He was the youngest of seven children born into a New England family. At the age of ten he began to study piano, and he showed an interest in composition almost from the start. After a good education in the public and private schools of Newton, Converse entered Harvard College in 1889, where he studied under John Knowles Paine. He received the BA with highest honors in music in 1893, and then tried to carry out his father's wish that he pursue a business career. But his nature was unsuited to commercial life, and after a few unhappy months in an office he decided to devote all of his energies to a career in music. He resumed his study of piano with Baermann and of composition with Chadwick. Recognizing the need for further study, Converse went to Munich in 1896 to the Royal Academy of Music; there he came under the influence of Joseph Rheinberger, with whom he studied counterpoint, composition, and organ. He graduated in 1898.

On returning to the USA, Converse soon became active in the musical life of Boston. Around 1900 he moved to a large country estate in Westwood where he farmed, participated in vigorous outdoor sports, and brought up a large family. At the same time he continued to compose, study, and teach. From 1900 to 1902 he was an instructor in harmony at the New England Conservatory; from 1903 to 1907 he taught at Harvard College, first as an instructor, later as an assistant professor. While at Harvard, he composed several major works which gained him a reputation as one of the outstanding composers of the USA. In 1905 he was asked by Percy McKaye to write the music for his play *Jeanne d'Arc;* this marked the beginning of a long and intimate friendship, and the two collaborated on several major works. Converse resigned from Harvard in 1907 to devote more time to composition.

From 1907 to 1914 Converse was at the height of his career as a composer; he was elected to the National Institute of Arts and Letters in 1908 and also served as vice-president of the Boston Opera Company (1908–14). He oversaw several performances of his operas, including the Metropolitan Opera Company's production of *The Pipe of Desire*. Completed in 1905 and first produced in Boston, this romantic opera was presented at the Metropolitan Opera on 18 March 1910, and was the first American opera to be performed there. However, the majority of the critics attacked the undramatic nature of the libretto and criticized the score for its lack of originality; praise was reserved mostly for Converse's skillful and effective orchestration. His second opera, *The Sacrifice* (1910), was more favorably received.

During World War I, Converse served in the Massachusetts State Guard and was a member of the National Committee on Army and Navy Camp Music. He returned to the New England Conservatory in 1920 to become head of the theory department. In 1931 he was appointed dean of the faculty, a position he held until 1938 when he was forced to retire because of illness.

Converse was a versatile composer who knew his métier. He was one of the earliest American composers to write successful symphonic poems; *The Mystic Trumpeter* is probably his best work. His music was widely performed during his lifetime. He received the David Bispham Medal from the American Opera Society of Chicago in 1926 and in 1937 was elected to the American Academy of Arts and Letters.

WORKS

OPERAS

The Pipe of Desire (G. E. Barton), 1905; Boston, 31 Jan 1906

The Sacrifice (F. S. Converse, J. A. Macy), 1910; Boston, 6 Jan 1911

Beauty and the Beast (Sinbad the Sailor) (P. MacKaye), 1913, unperf.

The Immigrants (MacKaye), 1914, unperf.

ORCHESTRAL

Youth, ov., 1895, rev. 1897; Sym. no. 1, d, 1898; Festival March, 1899; Festival of Pan, romance after Keats' Endymion, 1899; Endymion's Narrative, after Keats, 1901; Night and Day, 2 poems after Whitman, pf, orch, 1901; Vn Conc., 1902; Euphrosyne, ov., 1903; The Mystic Trumpeter, fantasy after Whitman, 1904; Jeanne d'Arc (incidental music, MacKaye), 1906; Ormazd, tone poem after the ancient Persian Bundehesch, 1911; Ave atque vale, tone poem, 1916; Sym. no.2, c, 1919; Sym. no.3, e, 1921; Song of the Sea, tone poem after Whitman: On the Beach at Night, 1923

Puritan Passions (film score, MacKaye: The Scarecrow), 1923; Elegiac Poem, 1925; Flivver Ten Million, epic tone poem, 1926; California, descriptive tone poem, 1927; American Sketches (Seeing America First), sym. suite, 1928; Pf Concertino, 1932; Sym. no.4, F, 1934; Salutation, concert march, 1935; Song at Evening, A, small orch, 1937 [arr. of movt from pf sonata]; 3 Old-fashioned Dances, chamber orch, 1938; Rhapsody, cl, orch, 1938; Haul Away, Jo!, variations on an American sea shanty, 1939; Sym. no.5, f, 1939; Indian Serenade, small orch, n.d. [arr. of vocal work]

VOCAL

La belle dame sans merci (Keats), Bar, orch, 1902; Laudate Dominum, male chorus, brass, org, 1906; Job, oratorio, solo vv, chorus, orch, 1906; Serenade, S, T, male chorus, fl, harp, small orch, 1907; Hagar in der Wüste (dramatic narrative, F. von Saar), A, orch, 1908

Masque of St. Louis, 1914; The Peace Pipe (Longfellow), cantata, 1915; The Answer of the Stars (M. A. D. Howe), cantata, 1919; The Flight of the Eagle (C. B. Fenno), cantata, 1930; Prophecy, tone poem, S, orch, 1932

Also *c*24 choral works for mixed/female/male chorus; *c*24 songs, 1v, pf

CHAMBER AND INSTRUMENTAL

Str Qt no.1, E♭, 1896, rev. 1901; Septet, cl, bn, hn, pf, str trio, 1897; Str Qt no.2, a, 1904; Pf Trio, e, 1932; Str Qt no.3, e, 1935; Prelude and Intermezzo, brass sextet, 1938; 2 Lyric Pieces, brass qnt, 1939

Also *c*12 chamber works; sonatas for vn, vc, pf; *c*24 pf pieces

MSS and papers in *DLC*

Principal publishers: H. W. Gray, G. Schirmer, C. C. Birchard, New England Conservatory Music Store, Boston Music

BIBLIOGRAPHY

EwenD

R. Severence: *The Life and Works of Frederick Shepherd Converse* (diss., Boston U., 1932)

R. J. Garofalo: *The Life and Works of Frederick Shepherd Converse (1871–1940)* (diss., Catholic University of America, Washington, DC, 1969)

ROBERT GAROFALO

Conway, Patrick (*b* nr Troy, NY, 4 July 1867; *d* Ithaca, NY, 10 June 1929). Conductor, bandmaster, and educator. As a young man he studied cornet with Charles Bates. He joined the Homer Band, which was led by Bates, and became its director while still in his teens. He attended the Ithaca Conservatory of Music and Cornell University; to support himself, he played in a country-dance group. He moved to Cortland, New York, in 1893, but returned to Ithaca two years later, where he directed the Cornell University Cadet Band until 1908. He also organized a municipal band in Ithaca, which gave summer concerts; during the winter he conducted the Lyceum Theater orchestra. His leadership of the two ensembles enabled him to offer year-round employment to his players, and as a result his groups attracted musicians of a high caliber. He formed a professional band (known, from 1908, as Patrick Conway and his Band) with some members of Ithaca's municipal ensemble; in 1903 he led the band in a series of concerts at Willow Grove Park, Pennsylvania, where it appeared regularly for the next 17 years. During this period he became a friend of Sousa, whose band also performed at Willow Grove; the two bands were engaged at the Panama-Pacific Exposition of 1915 in San Francisco, and on some occasions they performed together.

In 1908 Conway moved to Syracuse, where he formed the Syracuse SO and directed the orchestra of the principal theater. He made a number of recordings for Victor. In 1916 he was commissioned a captain in the US Army Air Service and charged with establishing a music program and an official band. He retained his commission and continued his work after the war, and is generally regarded as having laid the foundations of the band tradition of the US Air Force (successor to the Army Air Service). In 1922 he founded the Conway Military Band School in affiliation with the Ithaca Conservatory of Music. He led his band on the "General Motors Family Hour" in 1928 and 1929.

As a conductor, Conway was noted for his exacting standards, and for the consistent excellence of his band's performances; unlike many of his contemporaries, he had an economical conducting style. His band had a vast repertory: during a four-week engagement, it could give as many as 100 concerts without repeating a program. Music, recordings, and memorabilia related to Conway are held at the DeWitt Historical Society of Tompkins County, at Ithaca College, and in Colonel George S. Howard's personal papers at the American Bandmasters Association Research Center at the University of Maryland.

BIBLIOGRAPHY

F. R. Seltzer: "Patrick Conway," *Musical Messenger*, xiii/9 (1917), 3

G. S. Howard: "Patrick Conway," *Journal of Band Research*, xvii/1 (1981), 47

RAOUL CAMUS

Cooder, Ry(land) (*b* Los Angeles, CA, 15 March 1947). Guitarist, bass guitarist, mandolin player, and singer. He began playing guitar at the age of three, and by the early 1960s was performing with folk groups in southern California. In 1965–6 he formed the Rising Sons with Taj Mahal; he recorded with Captain Beefheart and the Magic Band (*Safe as Milk*, 1967), the Rolling Stones (*Let it Bleed*, 1969), and Little Feat (*Little Feat*, 1971). He began recording under his own name in 1970, producing albums of carefully selected, inventively syncopated blues and country songs, notably *Into the Purple Valley* (1972). His later recordings, which usually consist of songs from the 1960s or earlier, include material from such diverse genres as rock, rhythm-and-blues, jazz (the pianist Earl Hines performed on his album *Paradise and Lunch*, 1974), and vaudeville (*Jazz*, 1978). Through the 1970s he continued to work as a backing musician, and in that capacity made recordings with Randy Newman, Linda Ronstadt, and Arlo Guthrie; he wrote the scores for a number of films, including Walter Hill's *The Long Riders* (1980), Tony Richardson's *The Border* (1982), Wim Wenders's *Paris, Texas* (1984), and Louis Malle's *Alamo Bay* (1985). He also produced a recording by the Hawaiian guitarist Gabby Pahinui. A virtuoso performer on fretted instruments, Cooder combines elements of rock with various regional styles, including Mexican *música norteña* (the accordionist Flaco Jimenez is heard on his albums *Chicken Skin Music*, 1976, and *Showtime*, 1977) and a syncopated style of Bahamian guitar playing of which an important exponent is Joseph Spence. Because he is not a songwriter or a distinctive singer, Cooder has found it difficult to expand his cult following; he is widely respected among musicians.

RECORDINGS
(selective list)

Ry Cooder (Rep. 6402, 1970); *Boomer's Story* (Rep. 2117, 1972); *Into the Purple Valley* (Rep. 2052, 1972); *Paradise and Lunch* (Rep. 2179, 1974); *Chicken Skin Music* (Rep. 2254, 1976); *Showtime* (WB 3059, 1977); *Jazz* (WB 3197, 1978); *The Long Riders* (WB 3448, 1980); *The Border* (Backstreet 6105, 1982); *Alamo Bay* (Slash 25311-1, 1985)

JON PARELES

Cook, Barbara (Nell) (*b* Atlanta, GA, 25 Aug 1927). Singer and actress. She studied singing and acting and appeared in revues in the Catskill Mountains before making her Broadway début in the unsuccessful musical *Flahooley* (1951). During the 1950s she also appeared in revivals of *Oklahoma!* and *Carousel* at the New York City Center, and created the role of Cunegonde in Leonard Bernstein's *Candide* (1956); her recording of Cunegonde's mock-coloratura aria "Glitter and be gay" continues to be the performance by which others are judged. Cook also created the roles of Marion in Meredith Willson's *The Music Man* (1957) and Amalia in Bock's *She Loves me* (1963). That all three of these roles continue to be associated with her can be attributed to her acting talent and a natural, resonant voice, which effectively combines classical and popular vocal tehniques. Since 1973 she has devoted herself to nightclub and stage appearances, usually with her accompanist and music director Wally Harper.

BIBLIOGRAPHY

"Cook, Barbara," *CBY 1963*

SAMUEL S. BRYLAWSKI

Cook, Will Marion (*b* Washington, DC, 27 Jan 1869; *d* New York, 19 July 1944). Composer and conductor. He revealed musical talent early and at 13 was sent to study violin at Oberlin Conservatory. Later he studied in Germany with Joseph Joachim.

He returned to New York during the 1890s and matriculated at the National Conservatory. After a brief period as a concert violinist he began to work in the field of musical comedy as a director and composer; all his musical comedies were first performed in New York. In 1898 he produced on Broadway the first Negro musical-comedy sketch composed and directed by black men: *Clorindy, or The Origin of the Cakewalk*. During the years 1900–08 Cook was director and composer-in-chief for the Bert Williams/George Walker productions, which opened a golden era for the black musical theater with *The Sons of Ham* (1900), *In Dahomey* (1902), *In Abyssinia* (1906), and *In Bandanna Land* (1908). He also worked with other musical groups and continued to write his own musicals. In 1918 Cook organized a "syncopated" symphony orchestra that toured the USA and Europe, giving a command performance for King George V in 1919. After returning to the USA in 1922, he settled in New York and was active as a conductor, concert promoter, teacher, and musical adviser. Cook's music consistently exploits themes and idioms derived from Negro folklore and folk music. His basically neoromantic style is notable for its sophisticated melodies, bold and expressive harmonies, and vigorous rhythms. The rare recordings of his songs (made for Victor) include *Bon bon Buddy* (1908), *Who dat say chicken* (1902), and *Darktown is out tonight* (1902).

WORKS

(selective list)

Stage: several musicals, incl. Clorindy, or The Origin of the Cakewalk (P. Dunbar), 1898; Jes' Lak White Fo'ks (Dunbar), 1899; The Cannibal King (Dunbar, J. R. Johnson), 1901; The Southerners (W. Mercer, R. Grant), 1904; The Traitor (A. Creamer), 1913; Darkeydom (H. Troy, L. Walton), 1915; Swing Along, collab. W. Vodery, 1929; inst and choral music for the Williams/Walker musicals (J. Shipp)

Choral: partsongs, incl. Swing Along; many songs, incl. Exhortation, Rain Song

Principal publishers: Keith, Prowse, & Co.; Witmark

BIBLIOGRAPHY

SouthernB

M. Cuney-Hare: *Negro Musicians and their Music* (Washington, DC, 1936/*R*1974)

W. M. Cook: "Clorindy, the Origin of the Cakewalk," *Theatre Arts*, xxxi (1947), 61; repr. in *Readings in Black American Music*, ed. E. Southern (New York, 1971, rev. 2/1983), 227

E. Southern: *The Music of Black Americans: a History* (New York, 1971, rev. 2/1983)

A. Levy: "Cook, Will Marion," *DAB*

H. Sampson: *Blacks in Blackface* (Metuchen, NJ, 1980)

T. Riis: *Black Musical Theatre in New York, 1890–1915* (diss., U. of Michigan, 1981)

J. Green: "In Dahomey in London in 1903," *BPiM*, xi (1983), 22

A. Woll: *Dictionary of the Black Theatre* (Westport, CT, 1983)

K. Bloom: *American Song: the Complete Musical Theatre Companion, 1900–1984* (New York, 1985)

M. Carter: *Will Marion Cook: Afro-American Violinist, Composer and Conductor* (diss., U. of Illinois, in preparation)

EILEEN SOUTHERN

Cooke, Edna Gallmon (*b* Columbia, SC, 1918; *d* Philadelphia, PA, 4 Sept 1967). Gospel singer. She studied music at Temple University and subsequently became a school teacher. In 1938 she heard Willie Mae Ford Smith sing gospel music in Washington, DC, and decided to adopt the style. She began singing in towns in the Washington area, where she soon became known as the "Sweetheart of the Potomac," a title that remained with her throughout her career. She began recording in the early 1950s and by 1953 was one of the major gospel stars, specializing in the "song and sermonette" (where the first half of the song is delivered as a sermon and the second half is sung). Her most popular recordings, all made during the 1950s, include *Amen*, *Evening Sun*, and *Stop Gambler*. She performed most often with the support of a male quartet, beginning a song softly and subtly, then building in volume and drama as the song progressed.

BIBLIOGRAPHY

T. Heilbut: *The Gospel Sound: Good News and Bad Times* (New York, 1971/*R*1975)

H. C. Boyer: "An Overview: Gospel Music Comes Of Age," *Black World*, xxiii/1 (1973), 42, 79

HORACE CLARENCE BOYER

Cooke [Cook], **Sam(uel)** (*b* Chicago, IL, 22 Jan 1931; *d* Los Angeles, CA, 10 Dec 1964). Gospel and rhythm-and-blues singer and songwriter. The son of a Baptist minister, he first sang publicly in a group with his brothers, the Singing Children, at the age of nine. In his teens Cooke joined the Highway Q.C.'s, a gospel quartet, several of whose members subsequently sang with the Soul Stirrers, then the leading male group in the field. In 1950 Cooke was selected to replace R. H. Harris as lead tenor in the Soul Stirrers. Harris was one of the most influential singers in gospel music, and Cooke built on his style, adding a smoother falsetto, lyrical purity, delicate melisma, and something approaching a yodel on such recordings as *Touch the hem of his garment* and *The last mile of the way*. He immediately became one of the most important figures in gospel music, sending teenage girls into a frenzy and exercising a strong influence on other male singers.

In 1956 Cooke and his producer, Bumps Blackwell, decided to attempt secular songs, then forbidden in gospel circles. Cooke's first secular recording, *Lovable*, was released under the name Dale Cooke, but his style was so distinctive that the ruse was immediately obvious. He soon abandoned sacred gospel songs altogether and made a series of hit recordings for Keen Records, all of them imbued with his gospel style: *You send me* (1957), his first successful Keen release, reached no. 1 on both the popular and rhythm-and-blues charts; it was followed by *I love you for sentimental reasons*, *Everybody likes to cha cha cha*, *Only sixteen*, *Win your love for me*, and several others. These pieces were slight compared to the gloomy splendor of Cooke's best religious material, and he was unable to do much to redeem most of them; but *You send me* and *Only sixteen*, at least, were given fine performances, less closely related to hard rhythm-and-blues or rock-and-roll than to the older tradition of black popular singers such as Nat "King" Cole. In 1960 Cooke moved to RCA Records, where he worked with the producers Hugo and Luigi. Although his arrangements continued to be more elaborate than soulful, the material was often superior to his earlier popular songs. *Sad Mood*, *Having a party*, *Bring it on home to me*, *Another Saturday night*, and *Good Times* were especially successful in capturing both the innocence suggested by the purity of Cooke's tone and the yearning wistfulness implicit in his gospel-derived phrasing. He even managed to give a memorable and highly personal performance of a twist dance-song, *Twistin' the night away*.

Although Cooke's smooth, pop arrangements and the supper-club style of his material, which included such trifles as *The Banana Boat Song*, offended rhythm-and-blues purists as much as his conversion to a popular style had offended the gospel community, he had more influence than any other singer on such artists of the 1960s as Eddie Floyd, Marvin Gaye, Otis Redding, and Curtis Mayfield. All of these performers and a number of others, including white singers such as Rod Stewart, adopted elements of Cooke's vocal style, and for a decade after his death many of them also recorded songs from his repertory. Cooke wrote some of the best songs that he sang (notably *Bring it on home to me*, *Having a party*, *A change is gonna come*, and *Twistin' the night away*); he produced recordings by other performers for his Sar label; he ran Kags Music, a publishing company; and in general assumed a greater variety of roles in the popular music industry with more competence than had any earlier black performer.

Sam Cooke, c1955

Cooke died under mysterious circumstances in a gun fight in a Hollywood motel. His funeral was one of the largest in Chicago's history, as thousands of fans (of both gospel and pop music) turned out to pay tribute to him. His final recording, *A change is gonna come*, was a beautiful fusion of pop and gospel idioms, which also heralded a turn towards black consciousness in soul and rhythm-and-blues performances.

RECORDINGS
(selective list)

With the Soul Stirrers: Jesus gave me water (Specialty 802, *c*1951); Jesus wash away my troubles/Touch the hem of his garment (Specialty 896, *c*1956); The last mile of the way (Specialty 921, *c*1956)

As soloist: Lovable (Specialty 596, 1956) [issued under pseud. Dale Cooke]; I love you for sentimental reasons (Keen 4002, 1957); You send me (Keen 34013, 1957); Win your love for me (Keen 2006, 1958); Everybody likes to cha cha cha (Keen 2018, 1959); Only sixteen (Keen 2022, 1959); Sad Mood (RCA 7783, 1960); Having a party/Bring it on home to me (RCA 8036, 1962); Twistin' the night away (RCA 7983, 1962); Another Saturday night (RCA 8164, 1963); Good Times (RCA 8368, 1964); A change is gonna come (RCA 8486, 1964)

BIBLIOGRAPHY

SouthernB

T. Heilbut: *The Gospel Sound: Good News and Bad Times* (New York, 1971/*R*1975)

J. McEwen: *Sam Cooke: a Biography in Words and Pictures*, ed. G. Shaw (New York, 1977) [incl. discography]

——: "Sam Cooke," *The Rolling Stone Illustrated History of Rock & Roll*, ed. J. Miller (New York, rev. 2/1980), 113

G. Hirshey: *Nowhere to Run: the Story of Soul Music* (New York, 1984)

DAVE MARSH

Cooley, Spade [Donnell Clyde] (*b* Pack Saddle Creek, OK, 17 Dec 1910; *d* Oakland, CA, 5 Nov 1969). Country-music fiddler, singer, and bandleader. The grandson and son of talented fiddlers, his earliest musical training was in classical violin and cello. By the age of eight he was playing the fiddle with his father. His family moved to California in 1931, and in the early 1940s he appeared as a stand-in for Roy Rogers in several musical western films; he subsequently toured as a fiddler for Rogers. In 1942 he became the leader of an 11-piece band (originally formed by Jimmy Wakely) that performed at the Venice Ballroom in Venice, California; Cooley added three fiddlers and three singers (Tex Williams, Deuce Spriggins, and Smokey Rogers) to the group, which continued to grow, until it was the largest country-music ensemble in existence. He then operated his own ballroom in Santa Monica, California; its success led to a recording contract with Okeh, and his *Shame on you* reached no. 1 on the chart in 1945. About this time Cooley began calling himself the "King of Western Swing." He had his own television show, the "Hoffman Hayride," on KTLA, Los Angeles, from 1947 to 1956, when changing musical tastes and competition from Lawrence Welk's orchestra undermined his popularity; he then left television and eventually the music business. In 1961 he was imprisoned for the murder of his wife. He died of a heart attack while performing at a benefit concert in Oakland, California.

BIBLIOGRAPHY

J. Wakely: Liner notes, *Spade Cooley* (Col. FC37467, 1982)

RONNIE PUGH

Coolidge, Elizabeth (Penn) Sprague (*b* Chicago, IL, 30 Oct 1864; *d* Cambridge, MA, 4 Nov 1953). Patron of music. Her maiden name was Sprague and on 12 November 1891 she married Frederic Shurtleff Coolidge at Chicago. The Berkshire festivals of chamber music, held under her patronage at Pittsfield, Massachusetts, were begun in autumn 1918 as the South Mountain Chamber Music Festival. As an outgrowth of the festivals she created the Elizabeth Sprague Coolidge Foundation in 1925 at the Library of Congress by placing in trust a large sum of money, the income of which is paid to the library. The trust was intended, among other things, to enable the Music Division of the library to conduct music festivals, to give concerts, to offer and award a prize or prizes for any original composition or compositions performed in public for the first time at any festival or concert given under the auspices of the library, and to further the purposes of musicology through the Music Division of the library. Among the works that have resulted from commissions by the foundation are Copland's *Appalachian Spring*, Stravinsky's *Apollon-Musagète*, and Crumb's *Ancient Voices of Children*.

In 1925 Elizabeth Coolidge presented the library with an auditorium (capacity 511) costing over $90,000 exclusive of the organ, which was also her gift (it was removed in 1954). Her numerous benefactions also included contributions towards the gift of a music building to Yale University (primarily the gift of her mother, Nancy Ann Sprague), an endowment for the first pension fund for the Chicago SO (1916, in memory of her par-

Elizabeth Sprague Coolidge: detail from a bronze medal by Henry Kitson, presented by Coolidge to commemorate the 20th anniversary of the Berkshire Festival, 1938

ents), and the establishment of a tuberculosis hospital and a school for crippled children at Pittsfield. In 1932 she instituted the Elizabeth Sprague Coolidge Medal "for eminent services to chamber music," which was awarded annually to one or more recipients. She was an accomplished pianist and an experienced ensemble player. She began to write music in the 1890s, and composition later became for her primarily a spiritual refuge from the deafness which began to afflict her in her thirties.

For her contributions to education Coolidge received an honorary MA from Yale University, Smith College, and Mills College, as well as a DLitt from Mt. Holyoke College, a DMus from Pomona College, and an LLD from the University of California. She brought many European composers and performers to the USA and contributed towards cultural activity in Europe. In recognition of her European activities she received decorations from several foreign governments as well as the Medal of Citizenship from the city of Frankfurt am Main, and the Cobbett Medal from the Worshipful Company of Musicians in London.

The Elizabeth Sprague Coolidge Papers at the Library of Congress contain business and personal correspondence as well as books from her library, photographs, and scrapbooks. The Library of Congress also holds the papers of the Elizabeth Sprague Coolidge Foundation, which contain correspondence and autograph scores by many major 20th-century composers, programs, photographs, and other materials relating to contemporary music and musicians.

The following is a list of composers who have received commissions either from the Elizabeth Sprague Coolidge Foundation (marked by an asterisk) or at the instigation of Elizabeth Coolidge herself. Full documentation regarding these commissions is being prepared by the Library of Congress.

*Hugh Aitken, Franco Alfano, *Milton Babbitt, *Sándor Balassa, George Barati, *Samuel Barber, *Béla Bartók, Ernesto Bartolucci, Arnold Bax, *Gustavo Becerra, Conrad Beck, Herbert Bedford, *Nicolai Berezowsky, *William Bergsma, Balthasar Bettingen, *Thomas Beveridge, *Arthur Bliss, Ernest Bloch, Renzo Bossi, Domenico Brescia, Frank Bridge, Benjamin Britten, Hans Burian, Adolph Busch, *Roberto Caamaño, Francisco Casabona, Alfredo Casella, Mario Castelnuovo Tedesco, *Carlos Chávez, Raymond Chevreuille, *Rebecca Clark

Anthony Collins, *Aaron Copland, *Roque Cordero, Mario Corti, *Henry Cowell, *Paul Creston, *George Crumb, *Luigi Dallapiccola, Eric De Lamarter, *Norman Dello Joio, Marcel Dick, Mme Albert Domange, Henry Eichheim, *Jean-Claude Eloy, George Enescu, Arthur Farwell, Jacobo Ficher, *Irving Fine, *Ross Lee Finney, Jerzy Fitelberg, Johan Franco, Friedrich Frischenschlager, *Blas Galindo Dimas, *Miriam Gideon, *Henry Gilbert, *Alberto Ginastera, *Eugene Goossens, *Marcel Grandjany, *Camargo Guarnieri, *Cristobal Halffter, *Iain Hamilton

*Howard Hanson, *Donald Harris, *Roy Harris, *Paul Hindemith, Mary Howe, Henry Holden Huss, Josef Hüttel, Albert Huybrechts, Tadeusz Iarecki, Frederick Jacobi, Erich Itor Kahn, Jenö Kerntler, *Leon Kirchner, Rudolph Kolisch, Emil Kornsand, Boris Koutzen, William Kroll, Mario Labroca, László Lajtha, Wesley La Violette, Miguel Llobet, Normand Lockwood, *Charles Martin Loeffler, Nikolai Lopatnikoff, *Gian Francesco Malipiero, *Riccardo Malipiero, Bohuslav Martinů, Renzo Massarani, *Yoritsune Matsudaira, *Peter Mennin, *Gian Carlo Menotti

Georges Migot, *Darius Milhaud, *Lyndol Mitchell, Roderick Mojsisovics, Nicolas Nabokov, *Luigi Nono, Leo Ornstein, *Juan Orrego-Salas, George Nelson Page, *Robert Palmer, Raymond Petit, *Goffredo Petrassi, *Burrill Phillips, Gabriel Pierné, *Walter Piston, *Ildebrando Pizzetti, Quincy Porter, *Francis Poulenc, *Mel Powell, *Sergey Prokofiev, Maurice Ravel, Alois Reiser, Ottorino Respighi, Wallingford Riegger, George Rogati, Jean Rogister, Julius Röntgen, Cyril Rootham, *Ned Rorem, Alfred Rosé, Feri Roth, Albert Roussel, Beryl Rubinstein, *Ahmet Adnan Saygun, Arnold Schoenberg

*Gunther Schuller, *William Schuman, Roger Sessions, *Ralph Shapey, *Elie Siegmeister, James Simon, David Stanley Smith, Leo Sowerby, *Frederick Stock, *Igor Stravinsky, Gustav Strube, Théodore Szántó, *Josef Tal, Alexandre Tansman, Lionel Tertis, Randall Thompson, *Virgil Thomson, Ernst Toch, Burnet C. Tuthill, Ludwig Uray, *Aurelio de la Vega, *Heitor Villa-Lobos, H. Waldo Warner, Anton Webern, Leo Weiner, Egon Wellesz, Eric Walter White, Willy White, F. Wigglesworth, Clara Wildschut, *Russell Woollen

See also WASHINGTON, §3, and CHAMBER MUSIC, fig.2.

BIBLIOGRAPHY

L. S. Mitchell: *Two Lives* (New York, 1953)

W. C. Bedford: *Elizabeth Sprague Coolidge; the Education of a Patron of Chamber Music: the Early Years* (diss., U. of Missouri, 1964)

J. Rosenfeld: *Elizabeth Sprague Coolidge: a Tribute on the One Hundredth Anniversary of her Birth* (n.p., 1964)

M. T. Wilson: "Coolidge, Elizabeth Penn Sprague," *DAB*

G. B. Anderson: "Coolidge, Elizabeth Sprague," *NAW*

H. Temianka and D. Leavitt: "The Boundless Legacy of Elizabeth Sprague Coolidge," *Chamber Music Magazine*, ii/1 (1985), 14

GUSTAVE REESE/R

Coolidge Quartet. String quartet. It was the resident quartet of the Coolidge Auditorium, the chamber music hall established by the Elizabeth Sprague Coolidge Foundation at the Library of Congress; the first documentation of the Coolidge Quartet is in the Founder's Day program of 30 October 1936. The original members were William Kroll and Nicolai Berezowsky, violins; Nic(h)olas Molderan, viola; and Victor Gottlieb, cello. Kroll remained the first violinist of the quartet; the other members changed frequently. In 1940 Jack Pepper joined as second violinist; in 1941 David Dawson became violist and Naoum Benditzky cellist. In 1942 Leon Rudin replaced Jack Pepper as second violinist, succeeded in 1943 first by David Gillet and then by Louis Graeler with David Saidenberg as cellist. October 1943 seems to be the date of the Coolidge Quartet's last concert; by the Founder's Day concert of October 1947, the performing group listed in the program is the Kroll Quartet. The Coolidge Quartet's programs included both the standard 18th- and 19th-century repertory and numerous 20th-century works, including commissions by the Coolidge Foundation or by Elizabeth Sprague Coolidge herself, to whom many of the works were dedicated.

ELIZABETH OSTROW

Cool jazz. A label applied to diverse styles of modern jazz variously perceived as subdued, understated, or emotionally cool.

There was some implication that performers in this style were emotionally detached from their creation; however, the players themselves often voiced distaste for the label because this style was as taxing to play as other styles and was by no means devoid of emotion.

Most saxophonists of the cool school were disciples of Lester Young, a prominent tenor saxophonist in Count Basie's band of the 1930s. Young's emulators tried to match his relaxed rhythmic sense, his tuneful approach to improvisation, his soft, dry, lightweight tone, and his slow vibrato. Many cool saxophonists played in the Woody Herman and Stan Kenton big bands at some time during the late 1940s or early 1950s; among the most prominent were Lee Konitz, Stan Getz, Art Pepper, and Zoot Sims. Many cool trumpeters drew from the style of Miles Davis, who used almost no vibrato, placed great emphasis on simplicity and lyricism, and avoided the upper register; Chet Baker and Shorty Rogers are among the best-known trumpeters in this style. Cool drummers played more quietly and conservatively than other modern jazz drummers. Although there is no well-defined cool jazz piano style, George Shearing and John Lewis are sometimes classified as cool because of their light, clean touch and their stress on economy and lyricism in improvisation. Sometimes the term is also applied to Lennie Tristano, a pianist active in New York whose style is a modern alternative to bop, though this seems to contradict the high degree of intensity in Tristano's work.

The most influential arrangers in cool jazz were Claude Thornhill and Gil Evans, whose concepts supplied the foundations for Miles Davis's nonet recordings of 1949-50, later reissued collectively as *Birth of the Cool*. Five of the 11 arrangements in this series were contributed by Gerry Mulligan, a baritone saxophonist who led several bands during the 1950s that used instrumentation similar to that of Davis's group. (Gil Evans revived this instrumentation for several albums with Davis between 1957 and 1962.) The Davis nonet was originally seen as the smallest unit capable of reproducing the flavor of Thornhill's big band of the mid-1940s. It was unusual in that the tenor saxophone was frequently excluded and tuba (sometimes playing the melody line) and french horn added. The musicians played without vibrato, using a dry tone. While many of the large ensemble pieces had the floating, almost motionless quality associated with Thornhill's *Snowfall* (1941), others gave way to the jumpier character of bop, though with soft tone-colors sometimes described as "pastel."

Prototypical cool groups of the 1950s and 1960s include the Modern Jazz Quartet, George Shearing Quintet, Dave Brubeck Quartet, Gerry Mulligan Quartet, and many combos led by the saxophonist, clarinetist, and composer Jimmy Giuffre. Some critics consider that the modern jazz produced on the West Coast during the 1950s (*see* WEST COAST JAZZ) constitutes a category of cool jazz. It is more accurate to designate as cool only a few communities of white jazz musicians playing at that time in Los Angeles, San Francisco, New York, and Boston, as well as the output of the Modern Jazz Quartet and some of the music made by the Miles Davis combos; these last two groups comprised black musicians who, though rooted in the bop style of the 1940s, often played in a smoother, less fiery manner than did most bop bands. Indeed, although much cool jazz of the 1950s owes a large stylistic debt to the Count Basie and Lester Young combos of the late 1930s, cool musicians did not ignore the bop approaches that had emerged in the mid-1940s. Some cool saxophonists may have drawn almost exclusively on Lester Young, but most also incorporated the bop ideas of Charlie Parker. Furthermore, most used bop tunes rather than those associated with Basie.

In cool jazz, improvised counterpoint of the type practiced in the earliest days of combo jazz underwent a revival. The pianist John Lewis improvised lines simultaneously with the vibraphonist Milt Jackson in some performances by their Modern Jazz Quartet, as did the pianist Dave Brubeck with the saxophonist Paul Desmond, and the trombonist Bob Brookmeyer with Gerry Mulligan and Jimmy Giuffre.

See also JAZZ, §V, 6.

BIBLIOGRAPHY

M. Williams: "Bebop and After," *Jazz*, ed. N. Hentoff and A. J. McCarthy (New York, 1959/*R*1974), 287

A. Hodeir: *Toward Jazz* (New York, 1962)

J. Berendt: *The Jazz Book* (Westport, CT, 1975)

J. L. Collier: *The Making of Jazz: a Comprehensive History* (Boston, 1978)

M. Gridley: *Jazz Styles: History and Analysis* (Englewood Cliffs, NJ, 1978, rev. 2/1985)

MARK C. GRIDLEY

Coon song. A genre of comic song, popular from around 1880 to the end of World War I, with words in a dialect purporting to be typical of black Americans' speech. The term "coon" in early blackface minstrel songs had usually referred to the raccoon, whose meat was supposedly preferred by plantation slaves, as in Charles Mathews's *Possum up a Gum Tree* (*c*1830). Soon the term became synonymous with the slave himself, as in *Zip Coon* (1834) and *Whar did you cum from?* or *Oh Mr. Coon* (1850). By 1880 the term "coon" was used disparagingly of Blacks in general, as in the mockery of Blacks' social aspirations in *The Full Moon Union* (1880) by Edward Harrigan and David Braham:

> Dere isn't a coon
> But what am a luminary in
> A half a quarter moon.

Ef de party wins, a political song of the same year, points out the Blacks' loss of political and social influence following the end of the Reconstruction period:

> de ones for good luck, 'cordin' to my notion,
> Am de sort ob coons dat happen to be white.

J. P. Skelly's *The Dandy Coon's Parade* (1880) and *The Coons are on Parade* (1882) may be considered precursors of the coon song as a genre; with the addition of ragtime elements in the 1890s the coon song sprang into prominence as a national favorite. Words typical of the coon song were sometimes added to the final chorus of earlier rags, and ragtime elements of syncopation and harmony were borrowed for the coon song, but it is incorrect to consider the rag and the coon song as synonymous. Fundamental differences exist in form, style, and mood between the two genres.

The coon song was often performed on the vaudeville stage by white female "coon shouters," foremost among whom was May Irwin (see illustration). Her performance of Charles E. Trevathan's *The Bully Song* (1895) was influential in establishing the stereotype of the razor-carrying, jealously belligerent black male. Other coon songs explored every conceivable black characteristic, real or imagined, for its comic possibilities: black aspirations to a useful place in society (*When a coon opens a department store*, *The Coontown Billionaire*, and *When a coon sits in the presidential chair* by G. R. Wilson); the supposed aspirations of

Blacks to become Whites (*She's getting mo' like the white folks every day*); the supposed preferences of Blacks for certain foods (*Parson Johnson's Chicken Brigade*); the imagined propensity of Blacks for theft (*Appearances dey seem to be against me*); and gambling and luck (*I'm the luckiest coon in town* by Bob Cole and Billy Johnson).

Black songwriters produced songs fully as demeaning of their race as those by white composers, examples being Gussie Lord Davis's *When I do the hoochy-coochy in de sky* and Ernest Hogan's regrettable *All coons look alike to me*. Bob Cole surpassed all other black composers in this respect: in collaboration with the Johnson brothers, James Weldon and J. Rosamond, he wrote dozens of coon songs, the most famous of which was *Under the Bamboo Tree*. With Billy Johnson, Cole also wrote *No coons allowed*, *I wonder what is that coon's game?*, and many more such songs.

Coon song: sheet-music cover (1869) of "Crappy Dan de spo'tin' man" (words and music by Charles E. Trevathan) featuring May Irwin

Skits, entertainments, and whole shows were developed from the coon song, and coon songs found their way into legitimate theatrical productions as unrelated interpolations. John Philip Sousa's famous band popularized the genre both in America and abroad with songs such as Lee Johnson's *My Darktown Gal* and many others, including some composed by his assistant director, Arthur Pryor. At the peak of its popularity, the coon song was ubiquitous at every level of entertainment, and songwriters labored to supply the insatiable demand.

As a social phenomenon, the coon song epitomized white attitudes of the period towards Blacks. Musically, it was often exciting and innovative; only the words were responsible for the low opinion in which the coon song is held.

BIBLIOGRAPHY

SouthernB
I. Goldberg: *Tin Pan Alley: a Chronicle of the American Popular Music Racket* (New York, 1930/*R*1961)
D. Ewen: *The Life and Death of Tin Pan Alley* (New York, 1964)
S. Dennison: *Scandalize my Name: Black Imagery in American Popular Music* (New York, 1982)

SAM DENNISON

Cooper, Alice [Furnier, Vincent] (*b* Detroit, MI, 25 Dec 1945). Rock singer and songwriter. He formed a rock band in Phoenix that was known first as the Earwigs, then as the Spiders, and then as the Nazz; it moved to Los Angeles in 1968 (where the group became known as Alice Cooper, after its leader), then to Detroit. Its first successful album was *Love it to Death* (1971), which included the hit song *Eighteen* (no.21). By this time Cooper was known for his bizarre stage shows, in which he dressed in drag, introduced live chickens and snakes, and used such props as guillotines, gallows, and giant toothbrushes; he also appeared regularly on the television program "Hollywood Squares." Aided by his producer, Bob Ezrin, he became one of the few hard-rock artists to base his work on songs, and he made a number of very successful recordings in the early 1970s. In 1975 he embarked on a solo career with the tender ballad *Only women bleed* (no.12), but his later songs were less distinguished. His album *From the Inside* (1978), which chronicles his experience of alcoholism, marked the start of a less commercially successful but artistically more mature period, during which Cooper has continued to record and has also branched out into acting.

RECORDINGS

(selective list; recorded for Warner Bros. unless otherwise stated)

Love it to Death (1883, 1971), incl. Eighteen; *Killer* (B2567, 1971); School's Out (7596, 1972); Elected (7631, 1972); No more Mr. Nice Guy (7691, 1973); Only women bleed (Atl. 3254, 1975); I never cry (8228, 1976); You and me (8349, 1977); *From the Inside* (3263, 1978), incl. How you gonna see me now; *Flush the Fashion* (3436, 1980); *Special Forces* (3581, 1981); *Zipper Catches Skin* (23719, 1982)

BIBLIOGRAPHY

B. Greene: *Billion Dollar Baby* (New York, 1974)

JOHN PICCARELLA

Cooper, George (*b* New York, 1840; *d* New York, 26 Sept 1927). Lyricist. He studied law, but abandoned his career on account of the Civil War, in which he served briefly. His love of popular music led him to work with Stephen Foster; the two eventually collaborated on more than 20 songs, mainly of a comic or war-related nature. Cooper came to be one of the composer's closest friends. The text he wrote for Henry Tucker's music *Sweet Genevieve* (1869) has proved his most popular; other well-known songs for which he composed the lyrics are *Mother, kiss me in my dreams*, and *God bless the little church around the corner*. Cooper also worked with Tony Pastor (i) and Lillian Russell. He published more than 200 song texts, and was one of the first Americans to make his living from this occupation alone.

DALE COCKRELL

Cooper, Kenneth (*b* New York, 31 May, 1941). Harpsichordist, pianist, and musicologist. He studied harpsichord at the Mannes College with Sylvia Marlowe (1960–63) and musicology at Columbia University with Paul Henry Lang, Joel Newman, Douglas Moore, and Otto Luening (BA 1962, MA 1964, PhD 1971). He made his international début in London in 1965 and his American début in New York's Alice Tully Hall on 2 February

1973, with a program that included the world première of *Drive*, written for him by George Flynn. He has appeared frequently in festivals in the USA and Europe, and has performed as soloist with the American Opera Society, the Little Orchestra Society, and the Clarion Concerts Orchestra; as a representative of the US State Department he has toured the USSR, Romania, Greece, and England. He has also performed chamber music, with the Chamber Music Society of Lincoln Center, the Fine Arts Quartet, and such artists as Henry Schuman, Paula Robison, and Gerard Schwarz, and has made over a dozen recordings of 18th-century music. Highly regarded for the textual accuracy and musical vitality of his performances of the Baroque and Classical keyboard repertory, he also plays ragtime and contemporary music.

Cooper has taught at Barnard College (1967–71), Brooklyn College, CUNY (1971–3), Montclair State College (from 1977), and Mannes, where he became professor of harpsichord in 1975. Among his publications are a complete edition of Monteverdi's *Tirsi e Clori* (1967) and several articles for the *Musical Quarterly* and *High Fidelity*.

JAMES WIERZBICKI

Cooper, Paul (*b* Victoria, IL, 19 May 1926). Composer and teacher. He studied at the University of Southern California with Ingolf Dahl, Raymond Kendall, and Halsey Stevens (BMus and BA 1950, DMA 1955) and at the Paris Conservatoire with Boulanger on a Fulbright scholarship (1953). After teaching at the University of Michigan (1955–68), he served at the Cincinnati College-Conservatory as composer-in-residence and professor of composition and theory (1968–74), positions he subsequently took up at the Shepherd School of Music, Rice University (1974). His formally economical and varied music ranges in style from the highly dissonant to the quiet and contemplative. The Violin Concerto, a work of rich, nontonal harmony, spins a high, finely drawn solo line, which interacts with thick sonorities, overlapping lines, and widely spaced chords in the orchestra. By contrast, the *Cantigas* are harmonically spare and modal; their concern is with the mystical quality of the texts, and some of the material is taken from the original 13th-century melodies. Other works use aleatory or controlled overlapping techniques. Committed neither to the old nor to the new, Cooper uses in an original manner whatever techniques can best communicate his musical ideas. His honors include many commissions, and grants or awards from the Guggenheim, Ford, and Rockefeller Foundations, the NEA, and the American Academy and Institute of Arts and Letters. He is the author of *Perspectives in Music Theory* (1973, 2/1981).

WORKS

INSTRUMENTAL

Orch: 5 syms., no.1 "Concertant," solo ww, brass, str qt, perc, str, 1966, no.2 "Antiphons," ob, wind, 1971, no.3 "Lamentation," str, 1971, no.4 "Landscape," fl, tpt, va, orch, 1973–5, no.5, 1983; Vn Conc. no.1, 1967; Liturgies, wind, brass, perc, 1968; A Shenandoah/For Ives' Birthday, fl, tpt, va, orch, 1974; Descants, va, chamber orch, 1975; Homage, fl, tpt, va, orch, 1976; Vc Conc., 1976–8; Variants, 1978; Fl Conc., 1980–81; Vn Conc. no.2, 1980–82; Org Conc., 1982; Sax Conc., 1982; Sym. in 2 Movts, 1982–3

Chamber: 6 str qts, 1952, rev. 1978, 1954, rev. 1979, 1959, 1963–4, "Umbrae," 1973, 1977; Va Sonata, 1961; Divertimento, 2 fl, 1962; Vn Sonata, 1962; Sonata, pic, fl, a fl, pf, 1962–3; Vc Sonata no.1, 1962–3; Db Sonata, 1964; Vc Sonata no.2, 1965; Concert for 4, fl, ob, hpd, db, 1965; Concert for 5, wind qnt, 1965; Variations, vn, pf, 1967; Epitaphs, a fl, harp, db, 1969; Soliloquies, vn, pf, 1970; Variants II, va, pf, 1972; Chimera, vn, va, vc, pf, 1973; Concert for 3, cl, vc, pf, 1977; Canons d'amour, vn, va, 1981; Canti, va, pf, 1981; Chamber Music I, fl, 2 cl, vn, vc, pf, 1982, rev. as Chamber Music II, 1983

Kbd: Pf Sonata, 1962–3; Partimento, pf, 1967; Cycles, pf, 1969; Variants, org, 1972; Changes, pf, 1973; Requiem, org, perc, 1978; 4 Intermezzi, pf, 1980

Many other works, withdrawn

VOCAL

(all texts by C. E. Cooper unless otherwise stated)

Choral: Credo, double chorus, orch, 1970; Psalm of Penitence, double chorus, 1971; Cantigas, S, double chorus, orch, 1972; Equinox, chamber chorus, fl, vc, pf, 1976; Refrains, S, Bar, double chorus, orch, 1976; Celebration, speaker, chamber chorus, org, 1983; Voyagers, chorus, orch, brass, 1983

Song cycles: Silences, S, fl, ob, db, hpd, 1973; Tomorrow's Songs, S, a fl, pf, 1974; Coram morte, S/Mez, synth, 12 inst, 1978; Songs of Antigone, S, 7 inst, 1979; From the Sacred Harp (sacred folksongs), Mez, pf, 1982

Many other works, withdrawn

Principal publisher: Hansen-Chester

BIBLIOGRAPHY

E. Borroff: "Current Chronicle," *MQ*, lv (1969), 396

——: "A New Notation: *Soliloquies* for Violin and Piano (1971) by Paul Cooper," *Notations and Editions: a Book in Honor of Louise Cuyler* (Dubuque, IA, 1974/*R*1977), 191

EDITH BORROFF/R

Cooper, William M. (*fl* Dothan, AL, 1902–9). Composer and tunebook compiler. In 1902 he published in Dothan a revision of B. F. White's and E. J. King's *The Sacred Harp* (1844), one of the most popular of all southern tunebooks, as *The Sacred Harp: Revised and Improved*, changing the keys and the titles of many of the pieces and including a number of new gospel hymns. He systematically added alto parts to the three-part harmonizations of the original tunes, thereby in many cases altering the harmonic structure. Further editions of the "Cooper revision" were brought out in 1907, 1909, and 1927, and a retitled version, *The B. F. White Sacred Harp*, in 1949 and 1960. Although Sacred Harp singers in Georgia and northern Alabama and Mississippi use S. M. Denson's revision of *The Sacred Harp*, Cooper's revision is still used for singings in western Florida, southern Alabama and Mississippi, and eastern Texas.

BIBLIOGRAPHY

B. E. Cobb: *The Sacred Harp: a Tradition and its Music* (Athens, GA, 1978)

BUELL E. COBB, JR.

Cooper [née Leary], **Wilma Lee** (*b* Valley Head, WV, 7 Feb 1921). Country-music singer. As a child she sang with the Leary Family, a gospel vocal group consisting chiefly of her relatives. She married Dale T. "Stoney" Cooper (*b* Harmon, WV, 16 Oct 1918; *d* Nashville, 22 March 1977) after he joined the Leary Family as a fiddler in 1938; by 1942 they had begun to perform as a duo. After appearing on several radio stations, in 1947 they joined the "World's Original Jamboree" on radio station WWVA in Wheeling, West Virginia, where they remained for a decade; at the same time they made their first recordings for Rich-R-Tone (including *This world can't stand long*, 1947) and Columbia (*Willy Roy* and *No one now*, 1949; *The Legend of the Dogwood Tree*, 1950; and *Walking my Lord up Calvary Hill*, 1951), accompanied by their band, the Clinch Mountain Clan. From 1957 they made regular appearances on the "Grand Ole Opry," and continued to record, now on the Hickory label, which released their *Big Mountain Special* (1958) and *There's a big wheel* (1959). After Stoney Cooper's death, Wilma Lee continued to perform as a soloist, both on the "Opry" and on tours with the Clinch Mountain Clan. She has an intensely emotional vocal style in the tradition of the great female hillbilly singers, and plays rhythm guitar as well as banjo. She has received honors from Harvard University (1950) and an award from the Smithsonian Institution ("First Lady of

Bluegrass," 1974), and has been named Honorary State Colonel of Louisiana and Alabama.

BIBLIOGRAPHY

D. B. Green: "Wilma Lee and Stoney Cooper," *Bluegrass Unlimited*, viii/9 (1974), 25

R. Cogswell: " 'We Made our Name in the Days of Radio': a Look at the Career of Wilma Lee and Stoney Cooper," *JEMF Quarterly*, xi (1975), 67

RONNIE PUGH

Coover, James B(urrell) (*b* Jacksonville, IL, 3 June 1925). Music librarian and bibliographer. He attended Northern Colorado University, where he studied theory and composition (BA 1949, MA 1950). In 1953 he graduated (MALS) from the library school of the University of Denver, having served during his time there as bibliographer and assistant director of the Bibliographical Center for Research in Denver (1950–53). He was head of the music library of Vassar College from 1953 until 1967, when he became professor of music and director of the music library at SUNY, Buffalo. Coover has compiled several valuable bibliographies, notably *A Bibliography of Music Dictionaries* (1952, rev. 3/1971 as *Music Lexicography*), an extensive catalogue of music dictionaries with a historical introduction, and *Musical Instrument Collections* (1981), a listing of catalogues and cognate literature referring to collections, exhibitions, and expositions. An active member of the Music Library Association, he was its president in 1959–60.

PAULA MORGAN

Cope, David (Howell) (*b* San Francisco, CA, 17 May 1941). Composer, writer, and instrument maker. He studied composition with Grant Fletcher at Arizona State University (BM 1963), and with Halsey Stevens, Ingolf Dahl, and George Perle at the University of Southern California (MM 1965). He then taught at Kansas State College (1966–8), California Lutheran College (1968–9), the Cleveland Institute (1970–73), Miami University of Ohio (1973–7), and the University of California, Santa Cruz (from 1977). He has received two NEA grants (1976, 1980) and various other awards. Cope's music employs a wide range of performance forces and musical structures, from the traditional to the avant-garde. Contemporary techniques involving unconventional manners of playing, prepared instruments or those he has invented himself, microtonal scales (such as his 33-note system of just intonation), atonality, or polyrhythms are often found in his pieces. An interest in the Navajo people has led Cope to borrow ideas and forms from their music for his own; *Vortex*, *Rituals*, *Parallax*, and *Teec nos pos* are based on Navajo ceremonies. As editor of *The Composer* (1969–81), Cope published many informative, often controversial, interviews with composers such as I. A. Mackenzie, Pierre Boulez, Halsey Stevens, and John Cage. His books, especially *New Directions in Music*, are central to the literature on contemporary music.

WORKS

Orch: Tragic Ov., str, timp, 1960; Variations, pf, wind orch, 1965; Contrasts, 1966; Music for Brass and Str, 1967; Streams, 1973; Requiem for Bosque Redondo, brass choir, perc, 1974; Re-birth, concert band/wind ens, 1975; T Sax Conc., 1976; Threshold and Visions, 1977; Pf Conc., 1980; Afterlife, original insts, orch, 1983

Inst: 4 pf sonatas, 1960–67; 2 str qts, 1961, 1963; Iceberg Meadow, prepared pf, 1968; Cycles, fl, db, 1969; Margins, tpt, vc, perc, 2 pf, 1972; Koosharem: a Ceremony of Innocence, cl, db, perc, pf, 1973; Triplum, fl, pf, 1973; Parallax, pf, 1974; Rituals, vc, 1976; Vectors, 4 perc, 1976; Vortex, fl, trbn, pf, 3 perc, 1976; The Way, various insts incl. aluminum bells, musical glasses, 1981; Corridors of Light, original insts, 1983; other works for ens, many other pieces for 1–2 insts

Tape: Spirals, tuba, tape, 1972; Arena, vc, tape, 1974; Paradigm, vn, pf, tape, 1974; Teec nos pos, 1975; Glassworks, 2 pf, tape, 1979

Choruses, many songs

Principal publishers: C. Fischer, Seesaw

WRITINGS

Notes in Discontinuum (Los Angeles, 1970)

New Directions in Music (Dubuque, IA, 1971, rev. and enlarged 2/1976, rev. and enlarged 3/1981)

New Music Composition (New York, 1976)

New Music Notation (Dubuque, IA, 1976)

DALE COCKRELL

Copland, Aaron (*b* Brooklyn, NY, 14 Nov 1900). Composer. While his operas and symphonies are heard only occasionally, his major piano works hold a firm place in the American repertory, some of his orchestral suites and his *Lincoln Portrait* are widely admired, and his *Fanfare for the Common Man* is better known than his name. Copland is also a lecturer, a writer "from the composer's standpoint," a lifelong pianist, eventually a conductor, a teacher or preferably consultant to younger composers, a tireless instigator and tactful coordinator of musical activity, and a prominent representative for several decades of new music in the USA and American concert music abroad: in his own words he is "a good citizen of the Republic of Music."

1. Life. 2. Works. 3. Style.

1. LIFE. His parents immigrated, at different times and by different routes, from villages in the Polish and Lithuanian parts of Russia. His father came to New York as an adolescent, late in the 1870s, after some time in England, where the spelling of his name was established: Harris Morris Copland. His mother, Sarah Mittenthal, had grown up and attended school in a series of Midwestern and Texan cities before arriving in New York in 1881. In the 1890s the family store prospered; Harris Copland became president of the oldest synagogue in Brooklyn. Aaron, the fifth child, was seven years younger than his nearest sister. He learned what she could teach him at the piano and then, on his own initiative, went to Leopold Wolfsohn. After about three years with him, Copland advanced to study piano with Victor Wittgenstein and Clarence Adler. He had already begun to attend New York SO concerts under Damrosch at the Brooklyn Academy of Music. He was stirred by performances by Paderewski, Cyril Scott, Isadora Duncan, and the Diaghilev ballet, particularly in *Scheherazade* and *L'après-midi d'un faune*.

Beginning in 1917, and then more intensively after his graduation from the Boys' High School (1918), Copland studied harmony, counterpoint, and sonata form under Goldmark, whose fidelity to Beethoven, Wagner, and Fuchs increased his pupil's independent enthusiasm for Mussorgsky, Debussy, Ravel, Scriabin, and Scott. Ives's "Concord" Sonata, glimpsed on the piano in Goldmark's studio, attracted Copland, but his teacher prevented him from becoming "contaminated" with it. Copland forgot Ives for a decade. A literary friend, Aaron Schaffer, encouraged his idealism, guided his reading of *Jean-Christophe* and *The Dial*, and urged him to go to Paris. When he was 20, having saved just enough from his allowance and earnings in summer jobs, he set off to attend the new American Conservatory at Fontainebleau near Paris.

There Copland found a "powerful," "exhilarating" teacher in Boulanger; he stayed with her until 1924 and recruited other Americans to join and follow him. Something of the attitude he learned was promptly expressed in his essay on Fauré, whom he called "the French Brahms." His growing skills he employed in the Stravinsky-like rhythms and transparent instrumental sounds of his first big work, music for an unperformed ballet *Grohg* (1922–4), parts of which became the prize-winning *Dance Symphony* (1930). Copland's years in Paris brought fruitful contacts with Roussel, Prokofiev, Milhaud, and Koussevitzky. He attended the Diaghilev ballets, heard Koussevitzky conduct the première of Ravel's orchestration of Mussorgsky's *Pictures*, and studied French piano music under Viñes. Copland was less impressed by Satie than was Thomson, and less impressed by Honegger and Dukas than was Piston. He visited England, Belgium, and Italy; the summers were spent, on Boulanger's advice, in Berlin, Vienna, and Salzburg, where he responded to what he heard of Webern, Bartók, Hába, Hindemith, Weill, and many others. Mahler he took as a useful model of counterpoint as well as orchestration. He began to cultivate an interest in jazz. Wishing to be as recognizably American as Mussorgsky and Stravinsky were Russian, Copland applied some syncopated and polymetric rhythms and some "blue" intervals in his next works, most memorably in the suite *Music for the Theatre* (1925). At the same time he cultivated his own "idea of the grandiose, of the dramatic and the tragic, which was expressed to a certain extent in the Organ Symphony [1924, proposed by Boulanger for her first American tour] and very much in the *Symphonic Ode* [1927–9, for the 50th anniversary of the Boston SO]." The deliberate Americanism and the grandiosity were characteristics that recurred in various guises and various combinations throughout his later works. He continued to cherish the ideals of economy and refinement represented by Fauré, and to be fascinated by Stravinsky in all his phases. But amid all these diverse lures and standards, Copland developed his own musical personality, growing from his earlier spontaneous affinities with Mussorgsky and Scriabin.

1. Aaron Copland

He shared an apartment in Paris with Harold Clurman, then studying dramatic literature at the Sorbonne; Clurman provided the scenario for *Grohg*. Back in New York the two young men responded to the same currents of thought and fashion; their careers ran parallel through the optimistic 1920s, through what Clurman later called "the fervent years" of the 1930s, and thereafter. Clurman's ideas on art and society helped Copland to form his own without the influence of systematic reading or argument. Both were determined to "make clear to our countrymen the value attached in all lands to the idea of the creative personality" and to assert the "possibility of the coexistence of industrialism and creative activity." Their determination, like their friendship, was immune to all successes and failures. Clurman's article (1946) on the critic Paul Rosenfeld gives a valuable account of the young men's early admiration and gratitude, their slightly diverging responses to changing times, and their renewed appreciation of Rosenfeld's individualism.

Copland tried at first in 1924 to establish himself as a private teacher. Soon his compositions won the support of Rosenfeld (though Varèse still claimed Rosenfeld's most rapturous approval), then of the patron Alma Morgenthau Wertheim, of the Boston SO's new conductor Koussevitzky, of the MacDowell Colony, and of the Guggenheim Foundation – he had returned at a lucky moment when advanced New Yorkers were hoping to outdo Diaghilev's Paris. He later joined the League of Composers and, with his reporting, enriched its journal *Modern Music*; he paid due respect to Varèse, Bloch, Cowell, and Carpenter. In the summers of 1926, 1927, and 1929 he was able to go back to Europe to learn more of the latest musical news, to report, and to organize American collaborations. He enlisted Sessions, who continued to live in Europe, to join him in sponsoring an important series of concerts of new music in New York (the Copland–Sessions Concerts, 1928–31). In the next years Copland was among the founders of the Yaddo Festivals, the Arrow Music Press, and the ACA (president, 1937–45). At the New School for Social Research he succeeded Rosenfeld as lecturer to laymen (1927–37). His lectures and articles took enduring shape in the books *What to Listen for in Music* and *Our New Music*, both of which were widely read and admired, and translated into many languages. On the invitation of Chávez, whose music he had extolled with rare enthusiasm, he visited Mexico (1932); he toured Latin America on behalf of the Coordinator of Inter-American Affairs (1941) and the State Department (1947), and in many ways he exemplified the "good neighbor policy" of Franklin Roosevelt – Copland's Americanism was always more neighborliness than chauvinism.

During the terms when Piston took leave (1935, 1944) Copland taught at Harvard. In 1951 he revisited Europe for six months, went to Israel for the first time, and then returned to Harvard for a year as Norton Professor of Poetics – the first American composer in this chair. His lectures, published as *Music and Imagination*, were worthy successors to Stravinsky's *Poetics* and Hindemith's *Composer's World*, without the dogmatism of the former or the bitterness of the latter. In 1940, when Koussevitzky established a summer school at the Berkshire Music Center to supplement the festivals of the Boston SO there, he turned to Copland as teacher and adviser. Soon Copland became chairman of the faculty, a position he held each summer until he retired in 1965. As a teacher or colleague he generously helped composers from Chávez and Citkowitz to Takemitsu and Del Tredici. His help was always more encouragement than guidance in a particular direction, even though he shyly hoped that younger composers would surpass him and his contemporaries in progressing towards a "solid American tradition." He shared this concern with Piston, Sessions, Thomson, Harris, and Blitzstein, who constituted what he called in 1941 "a nascent American school." Their differences increased with time. Copland's valuing solidarity did not interfere with his support for such composers as Ives, Cowell, and Cage, whose successes he warmly welcomed although their styles did not conform to any tradition he envisioned.

Copland has received many honors: the Pulitzer Prize (1945), the New York Music Critics' Circle award (1945), the Academy of Motion Picture Arts and Sciences "Oscar" (1950), the Gold Medal of the National Institute of Arts and Letters (1956), the Presidential Medal of Freedom (1964), the Commander's Cross of the Order of Merit of the Federal Republic of Germany (1970), the Howland Prize of Yale University (1970), honorary degrees from Princeton (1956), Oberlin, Harvard, Brandeis, and a number of other universities, memberships or fellowships in the American Academy of Arts and Letters (of which Copland was eventually president), the American Academy of Arts and Sciences (Boston), the Accademia di S. Cecilia (Rome), the Royal Academy of Music and the Royal Society of Arts (London), the Academia Nacional de Belles Artes (Buenos Aires), and the University of Chile. He served as director or board member of the American Music Center, the American branch of the ISCM, the Koussevitzky Foundation, the Edward MacDowell Association, the Charles Ives Society, and the Naumburg Foundation, and as advisory editor of *Perspectives of New Music*. The Aaron Copland School of Music was founded in 1982 at Queens College, CUNY.

Between 1959 and 1972 Copland appeared as speaker, pianist, or conductor on 59 television programs, including a series of 12 for the National Educational Television network, several valuable interviews for the BBC, and programs with complete performances of the First Symphony, the Violin Sonata, the *Tender Land* suite, and the 12 Poems of Emily Dickinson. He continued touring as conductor and speaker through another decade before ending his conducting career in 1983 with a performance of *Appalachian Spring* in New York. Copland's recording of a rehearsal of that work is among his most vivid legacies.

2. WORKS. Copland's first considerable piece of chamber music was the trio *Vitebsk* (1929) and his first big piano work the Variations (1930). For orchestra, the early *Grohg* and *Music for the Theatre* were soon followed by a piano concerto, the Short Symphony, a hasty compilation for ballet, *Hear ye! Hear ye!* (1934, for Ruth Page), and a more distinctive major work, *Statements* (1932–5). As the world economic and political crisis deepened and war approached, Copland intensified his concerns for explicit social significance, for the theater (including dance and cinema), and for school music. His short opera for children, with a chorus of parents, *The Second Hurricane* (1936), is the clearest expression of these concerns. A more relaxed, and better-known, expression of related concerns is *El salón México* (1933–6), which led to Copland's permanent contract with Boosey & Hawkes as his publisher.

Beginning in 1938 he produced a series of ballets that reached wide audiences and for a decade exerted wide influence: *Billy the Kid* (1938, commissioned by Lincoln Kirstein for Eugene Loring), *Rodeo* (1942, for Agnes de Mille), and *Appalachian Spring* (1943–4, for Graham, who chose the title from a poem (*The Dance*) by Hart Crane; see fig.2). Then the Clarinet Concerto that he wrote for Benny Goodman (1947–8) was used by Robbins for the ballet *Pied Piper*, and the series was continued with *Dance Panels* (1959, revised 1962, for Heinz Rosen, Munich).

Copland's eight scores for films – documentaries and versions of plays by Wilder, Steinbeck, and others – set new standards for Hollywood. The previously established style, which Copland

2. Scene from the première of Copland's ballet "Appalachian Spring," performed by the Martha Graham Dance Company at the Coolidge Auditorium, Library of Congress, 30 Oct 1944

3. *Opening of the autograph short score of Copland's "Inscape," composed in 1967*

described as "Dvořák-Tchaikovsky generalized music" was replaced by a freedom to choose among all kinds of styles whatever could best "evoke a specific landscape." Copland's own range of rhythms and instrumental effects, as Hamilton has observed, "soon became the common coin of Hollywood hacks," and the freedom for greater variety came into force only over the next decades.

A still different kind of success was the result of a commission from Kostelanetz for one of a series of musical portraits of American heroes by various composers. At first Copland proposed to portray Whitman, but Kern had already started to work on Twain and Kostelanetz wished to avoid another literary figure. Copland next considered Jefferson and finally Lincoln; his friend Thomson, long practiced at musical portraiture, tried to dissuade him from anything so exalted. (Thomson's choice was Fiorello LaGuardia.) But Copland was well enough aware of the dangers, remembering Goldmark's orchestral threnody of 1919, *Requiem suggested by Lincoln's Gettysburg Address*, in which trumpets try to proclaim the American creed. Copland proceeded to make a new kind of portrait; his music, borrowing some American tunes of Lincoln's time and earlier, became the humble prelude and accompaniment for spoken excerpts from Lincoln's addresses and letters. Though he never convinced Thomson that his choice or his procedure was right, and though friends like Berger felt obliged to defend him long afterwards from "the belittling effect the Copland of *Lincoln Portrait* has, for some listeners, on the Copland of the Sextet," still the *Portrait* found many uses, and more performances even than *Appalachian Spring*. Among all the celebrated readers of the Lincoln text, the best was the Lincolnian Illinois statesman and Copland's exact contemporary, Adlai Stevenson. Copland's own reading of the text was more moving; a performance broadcast on television in 1980, with some moments from the rehearsal shown beforehand, demonstrated how he worked with the conductor Bernstein to preserve true meaning through his own nuances in timing. (*See also* MELODRAMA, §4.)

Berger and Mellers have found worthier successors to the Piano Variations in the Piano Sonata (1939–41), the Violin Sonata (1942–3), the Third Symphony (1944–6), and the Piano Quartet (1950), in which Copland for the first time made extensive use of 12-tone techniques within his free and distinctive harmonic style. The cycle of 12 Poems of Emily Dickinson (1944–50) was singled out by Stravinsky with songs by Ruggles and Babbitt. On the other hand, Copland's full-length opera, *The Tender Land* (1952–4), satisfied neither his large public nor his élite critics, although the orchestral suite became a favorite of some listeners. The orchestration of the Variations (1957) was a further disappointment. Then came the Piano Fantasy (1952–7), a long and complex work. The Nonet for Strings (1960) was regarded by admirers like Salzman as a temporary retreat from dodecaphony; it pleased such older friends as Kirkpatrick.

For the opening of Philharmonic Hall at Lincoln Center, New York, Copland composed *Connotations* (1962) and for the New York PO's 125th anniversary *Inscape* (1967; see fig.3). To listeners and critics at their first performances these pieces seemed to reveal Copland as a follower of new trends. Looking back in 1970, Bernstein, who had regarded him in the 1930s and 1940s as "a substitute father," recalled how in the 1950s young composers "gradually stopped flocking to Aaron; the effect on him – and therefore on American music – was heartbreaking." Perhaps just because Bernstein could not make *Connotations* compelling in performance, as he had so many of the earlier works, it seemed to him that Copland "tried to catch up – with twelve-tone music, just as it too was becoming old-fashioned to the young." But Copland himself never expressed "heartbreak." He was as little dismayed by misunderstanding and neglect as he was spoiled by official honors. As always, Copland's main concern continued to be the mysterious process of "exteriorising inner feelings." Always he was exploring his own "inscape" and finding the sounds with the right "connotations" to let any imaginative listener "relive in his own mind the completed revelation of the composer's thought."

Moreover, in the *Dance Panels* (1959), the *Music for a Great City* (1964), and the Duo for Flute and Piano (1971) he continued his explorations by means of triads and major scales, as he had done since *Music for the Theatre*. He found fresh ideas in these, in new relations between them and in the chromatic and dissonant materials that were also long familiar to him. *Night Thoughts* (1972) continued a progression from the Variations through the Sonata and the Fantasy, while the two *Threnodies* (1971, 1973) added weight to the list of chamber music; all three of these later works cast new light and shadow on all that had come before them, and they suggest a closer relationship to Ives and Stravinsky. His work as a whole has escaped chronological pigeonholes, and critics have recognized the integrity of Copland's style and the range of his concerns at every stage of his development.

3. STYLE. Copland's orchestration is well described by Thomson: "plain, clean-colored, deeply imaginative . . . theatrically functional . . . it has style." *Appalachian Spring* offers particularly interesting examples of Copland's orchestration, because the well-known suite for full orchestra may be compared with the original scoring for 13 instruments (flute, clarinet, bassoon, piano, and strings). Both confirm all of Thomson's points.

In the first climax (ex.1, fig.9) the discreet and ingenious doublings of the fuller version make a continually changing blend: the trumpets lead the slow lyric melody while the strings, piano, and xylophone pursue the leaping counterpoint; the tutti lasts for only two chords before the oboes and clarinets drop out; then the flutes rest for a deep chord with divided trumpets in unison with the horns; then the xylophone falls silent; then, after an extension of the phrase, the oboes and clarinets replace the piano. The same passage in the original version keeps the lyrical melody in the strings, the leaping counterpoint in the flute, clarinet, and piano; the bassoon is important just before and after the passage, linking larger continuities with a subordinate motif. In Copland's words as reported by Cole (*Tempo*, no.76, 1966), "orchestral know-how consists in keeping instruments out of each other's way" and, as Cole pointed out, in both early and late works this "know-how" serves for extreme clarity in counterpoint. The sound is never quite conventional, nor complacent in its novelty. Moreover, the sounds are always at the service of what Copland has called "the expressive idea," recognizing in each timbre and combination of timbres a specific "emotional connotation." Above all, the ever-changing details of sound are planned to express the emotional development of the whole work. The beginning and end of *Appalachian Spring*, with the "white tone" of the clarinet set off against hushed strings, makes the perfect frame for the clarinet's one long solo – its statement of the Shaker dance-prayer *The Gift to be Simple*, which is the theme for a set of variations. Often Copland's orchestration seems magically simple. When he added brass, drums, cymbals, glockenspiel, and xylophone to the originally very limited range of colors, he risked losing the simplicity. But his way of using the new timbres saved it.

With respect to rhythm, Copland's orchestral music is different from his piano and chamber music. The difference in notation is greater than that in sound, because Copland's experience in rehearsing convinced him of the lasting advantages of a traditional placement of bar-lines. But the orchestral music relies more often and for longer stretches on traditional patterns of dance and march, with steady tempos enlivened by odd accents and phrasings. (The complex rhythms of the Second Symphony are unmatched by anything in the later orchestral music.) The lively theme in ex.1 (fig.9) establishes a four-bar norm as well as the emphatic four-beat norm; the lyrical theme has four phrases in asymmetrical balance – 16 beats, 13, 12, and 15 – so that there are occasional bars that take three or five beats instead of four. Regularity is reinforced by the transitional fugato; then the overlapping entry of the theme makes a surprise; the fading-out of the passage, after the example, permits the *marcato* motif to break up into fragments and when, after a silent bar, motion resumes, there is even a bar of 7/8 before regularity returns. (In most of his music there are effective passages in 5/8 and 7/8, but no whole movement maintains such a meter.) In slower passages Copland calls for fluctuations of tempo as well as changes of meter and accent. Such fluctuations are used with particular virtuosity in the *Dance Panels*, where a waltz is more a lingering memory or shy hope than a whirling dance. His rhythms in solo instrumental music are often so subtle that the most elaborate notation cannot specify them precisely, but a performer who is at home with the style and who studies each piece thoroughly can make them convincing.

The combination of nervously animated and trance-like swaying rhythms is present in most of Copland's works, each time with a different relation between the contrasting types. In *Appalachian Spring* Carter has noted the procedures by which the animation is restrained and subdued. (Carter's Piano Sonata, written just after *Appalachian Spring*, may owe more to Copland in this respect than in harmony or timbre.) In Copland's Piano Sonata the slow finale, with bell effects, goes to an extreme of the trance type. In the Piano Fantasy, *Connotations*, and *Inscape*, there are marvelous transitions that bind the fast central movements into the slow beginnings and endings.

Copland's way of using familiar intervals is no more conventional than his orchestration, and no more indebted to Stravinsky or any other model. He finds new contexts for conventional intervals, without relying on them to shape his phrases, much less his long forms. When his contexts are very dissonant and chromatic, he still returns occasionally to triads, or to bare 5ths, 6ths, and particularly 10ths, for the sake of their sound and for the emotional connotations that he values so much. The critic Theodore Chanler remarked on Copland's characteristic 10ths in the works of the 1920s; they are still prominent in *Appalachian Spring* and *Inscape*. Very often he prefers a wide-spaced texture of few notes, alternating dissonance with pure consonance and playing with enharmonic ambiguities – for instance, the germinal diminished 4th or major 3rd of the Piano Variations. When he makes a major scale dominate, as in the phrases of *Appalachian Spring* shown in ex.1, Copland provides pungent clashes between melody and accompaniment, and he makes his abrupt cadences on a tonic with only its major 3rd. He leads up to this passage through a modulating fugato (ex.1, fig.8) with free collisions of the parts.

In many characteristic passages there are few clear harmonic progressions; even if a clear tonic and dominant are implied, the voice-leading may prolong indefinitely a single chord of approximately subdominant character. Forte has analyzed the third Piano Blues to show this procedure convincingly. In *Appalachian Spring*, however, perfect cadences are frequent; what keeps the music moving is melodic expectation.

A melody like that of the trumpet in ex.1 (fig.9) is rare, yet it could be recognized as Copland's even without its instrumentation and counterpoint. It avoids the leading tone of the scale

Ex.1 *Appalachian Spring*, 1943–4

it emphasizes the tonic as a high note, but otherwise touches the tonic only lightly; and it conforms to no accompanying triad, but rather suggests a broken 4th chord, with the repeated rising 4ths and the falling 7th.

This melody returns at three important points in the ballet, transformed each time. At the end of the Allegro, soft strings play the melody while a solo flute gasps the last fragments of the dance; here the melody's phrases are regularized to 14 beats each. Then at the end of the central Presto, before the variations on the Shaker tune (rehearsal number 51), a solo violin and oboe in octaves play a variant of the melody, with the concluding downward leap expanded to a 10th, but with the rhythm compressed to phrases of only eight and six beats. Finally, at the end of the work, flute and strings play the melody stretched out to phrases of 20 beats or more, and with its final leap quieted, first to a 5th and at last to a step onto the tonic. These variants of the melody, together with some motivic connections with other melodies, give coherence and a satisfying shape to the whole ballet; they make it a more symphonic composition than the suites derived from *Billy*, *Rodeo*, and *Our Town*. The final form of Copland's melody is like the gift of simplicity referred to in the Shaker text; it is no mere coda after the glorified variations but a fulfillment to which all the variations and the intervening hesitant prayer had led.

The Shaker tune in *Appalachian Spring* is an exception among all Copland's borrowed melodies: it is the only one that he does not modify with syncopation or changing meter, the only one that he dwells on through a set of variations. His earliest ventures in borrowing were travesties of *The Star-Spangled Banner* and Mendelssohn's Wedding March in *Hear ye! Hear ye!* In *El salón México*, *Billy the Kid*, *Rodeo*, and the *Lincoln Portrait*, the tunes may be presented straight once or twice, but generally durations are stretched unexpectedly or notes omitted, motifs are detached, new phrases are formed, so that the flow of the music is by no means determined by the tunes; and the forms never resemble Thomson's rondos. In the *Lincoln Portrait* there is something like an Ivesian blending of tunes: a hint of *Yankee Doodle* links the lyric *Springfield Mountain* and the boisterous *Camptown Races*. Even in the simplest arrangements of *Old American Songs*, Copland tampers with rhythms, at least between phrases, and in the accompaniments. *Simple Gifts* is one of the songs in his first set, and here its accompaniment is altogether different from that in any of the ballet's variations – most of the chords are syncopated. In *Appalachian Spring* the exceptional procedure may be essential to make clear the communal expression, for the sober tune and the Shaker community in which it was used are not so familiar as *So long, old Paint*, nor so colorful as *El mosco* and its Mexican dance hall atmosphere. (*Simple Gifts*, after Copland made it famous, was adopted into the repertories of schools, churches, and the popular "folksingers" of the 1960s.) If all these borrowings are simpler than the melodies of the Piano Variations, the simplicity of *Simple Gifts* is extraordinary, and Copland's use of the tune is in fine accord with its simplicity. Moreover, *Appalachian Spring* is a marvelous movement towards *Simple Gifts*; the music acknowledges the claims of solitariness and the possibilities of violence, but always turns toward true simplicity.

After *Appalachian Spring* and *The Tender Land*, Copland's interest in borrowed melodies was apparently exhausted; even the influence of such melodies on his own melodic invention declined. He never depended on them to the extent that Vaughan Williams, Janáček, and Bartók depended on what they had absorbed from folk music. Yet in all the works that led up to *Appalachian Spring*, as Carter observed, "there is a keen awareness in the choice of folk-material and in their handling that transforms everything into the Coplandesque." After that work Copland proceeded to develop his own kinds of declamatory and lyrical melody. Listeners all over the world continued to respond to the individual quality he had given so many borrowed melodies, and to recognize that quality in more and more of his music.

For further illustrations *see* FROMM, PAUL and STRAVINSKY, IGOR.

WORKS

(all published unless otherwise stated)

OPERAS

The Second Hurricane (school play-opera, E. Denby), 1936, New York, 21 April 1937, Henry Street Settlement Music School, cond. L. Engel

The Tender Land (opera, 2, H. Everett, after E. Johns), 1952–4, New York, 1 April 1954, New York City Opera, cond. Schippers; rev. 3 acts, 1955, Oberlin, OH, 20 May 1955; orch suite, 1956, Chicago, 10 April 1958, Chicago SO, cond. Reiner

BALLETS

Grohg, 1922–5, unpubd; excerpt Cortège macabre, orch, 1922–3, Rochester, 1 May 1925, cond. Hanson, unpubd; excerpts arr. as Dance Symphony, 1930, Philadelphia, 15 April 1931, cond. Stokowski; excerpt Dance of the Adolescent, arr. 2 pf, before 1932

Hear ye! Hear ye!, 1934, Chicago, 30 Nov 1934, cond. Ganz, unpubd

Billy the Kid, 1938, Chicago, 6 Oct 1938; orch suite, 1939, New York, 9 Nov 1940, NBC SO, cond. W. Steinberg; excerpts Prairie Night, Celebration, Waltz, n.d.; excerpts arr. 2 pf, n.d., New York, 17 Oct 1946, U. Appleton, M. Field

Rodeo, 1942, New York, 16 Oct 1942, cond. F. Allers; arr. pf, 1962; Rodeo: 4 dance episodes, orch, 1942, Boston, 28 May 1943, Boston Pops Orch, cond. Fiedler; excerpt Hoedown, str (1945)

Appalachian Spring, fl, cl, bn, pf, 4 vn, 2 va, 2 vc, db, 1943–4, Washington, DC, 30 Oct 1944, cond. Horst; suite, orch, 1945, New York, 4 Oct 1945, New York PO, cond. Rodzinski; suite, orch, 1970, Los Angeles, 14 Aug 1970, Los Angeles PO, cond. Copland; complete ballet, orch, n.d.; excerpt Variations on a Shaker Song, school orch (1967)

Dance Panels, 1959, rev. 1962, Munich, 3 Dec 1963, cond. Copland; arr. pf, 1965

FILM SCORES

The City, dir. O. Serlin, 1939, unpubd; excerpt Sunday Traffic incl. in Music for Movies, see ORCHESTRAL

Of Mice and Men (after Steinbeck), dir. L. Milestone, 1939, unpubd; excerpts incl. in Music for Movies

Our Town (after Wilder), dir. S. Wood, 1940; orch suite, 1940, Boston, 7 May 1944, Boston Pops Orch, cond. Bernstein; 3 excerpts arr. pf, 1944; excerpts incl. in Music for Movies

North Star (after L. Hellman), dir. Milestone, 1943, unpubd; excerpts Song of the Guerrillas and The Younger Generation pubd separately, see CHORAL

The Cummington Story, 1945, unpubd; excerpt In Evening Air, arr. pf, 1966

The Red Pony (after Steinbeck), dir. Milestone, 1948; orch suite, 6 scenes, 1948, Houston, 30 Oct 1948, Houston SO, cond. Kurtz; band suite, 4 scenes, 1966

The Heiress (after James: Washington Square), dir. W. Wyler, 1948, unpubd

Something Wild (after A. Karmel, J. Garfine), dir. Garfine, 1961, unpubd

ORCHESTRAL

Symphony, org, orch, 1924, New York, 11 Jan 1925, Boulanger, New York SO, cond. W. Damrosch; arr. without org as Symphony no. 1, 1928, Berlin, 9 Dec 1931, Berlin SO, cond. Ansermet; Prelude, chamber orch, 1934

Music for the Theatre, suite, 1925, Boston, 20 Nov 1925, Boston SO players, cond. Koussevitzky

Piano Concerto, 1926, Boston, 28 Jan 1927, Copland, Boston SO, cond. Koussevitzky

Symphonic Ode, 1927–9, Boston, 19 Feb 1932, Boston SO, cond. Koussevitzky; rev. 1955

Short Symphony (Symphony no. 2), 1932–3, Mexico City, 23 Nov 1934, Orquesta Sinfónica de México, cond. Chávez

Statements: Militant, Cryptic, Dogmatic, Subjective, Jingo, Prophetic, 1932–5, New York, 7 Jan 1942, New York PO, cond. Mitropoulos

El salón México, 1933–6, Mexico City, 27 Aug 1937, Orquesta Sinfónica de México, cond. Chávez

Music for Radio (Prairie Journal), 1937, New York, 25 July 1937, CBS RO, cond. H. Barlow

An Outdoor Overture, 1938, New York, 16 Dec 1938, High School of Music and Art Orch, cond. A. Richter; arr. band, 1941, New York, June 1942, Goldman Band, cond. Copland

Quiet City [arr. chamber piece], eng hn, tpt, str, 1939, New York, 28 Jan 1941, Saidenberg Little SO, cond. D. Saidenberg

From Sorcery to Science, puppet show score, 1939, New York World's Fair, 1[illegible] May 1939, unpubd

John Henry, chamber orch, 1940, New York, 5 March 1940, CBS SO, cond. Barlow; rev. 1952

Fanfare for the Common Man, brass, perc, 1942, Cincinnati, 12 March 1943, Cincinnati SO, cond. Goossens

Lincoln Portrait, speaker, orch, 1942, Cincinnati, 14 May 1942, W. Adams, Cincinnati SO, cond. Kostelanetz

Music for Movies [from film scores The City, Of Mice and Men, Our Town], small orch, 1942, New York, 17 Feb 1943, Saidenberg Little SO, cond. Saidenberg

Letter from Home, 1944, New York, 17 Oct 1944, cond. P. Whiteman; rev. 1962

Jubilee Variation on theme of Goossens, 1944, Cincinnati, 23 March 1945, Cincinnati SO, cond. Goossens, unpubd

Danzón cubano [arr. 2 pf piece], 1944, Baltimore, 17 Feb 1946, Baltimore SO, cond. R. Stewart

Symphony no. 3, 1944–6, Boston, 18 Oct 1946, Boston SO, cond. Koussevitzky

Clarinet Concerto, cl, str, harp, pf, 1947–8, New York, 6 Nov 1950, Goodman, NBC SO, cond. Reiner

Preamble for a Solemn Occasion, speaker, orch, 1949, New York, 10 Dec 1949, Olivier, Boston SO, cond. Bernstein; arr. org, 1953; arr. band, 1973

Orchestral Variations [arr. pf piece], 1957, Louisville, 5 March 1958, Louisville Orch, cond. Whitney

The World of Nick Adams (television score), 1957, Columbia Television Network, 10 Nov 1957, cond. A. Antonini

Connotations, 1962, New York, 23 Sept 1962, New York PO, cond. Bernstein

Music for a Great City [based on film score Something Wild], 1964, London, 26 May 1964, London SO, cond. Copland

Down a Country Lane [arr. pf piece], school orch, 1964, London, 20 Nov 1964, London Junior Orch, cond. E. Read

Emblems, band, 1964, Tempe, AZ, 18 Dec 1964, Trojan Band of the U. of Southern California, cond. W. Schaefer

CBS (Signature), 1967, CBS television, 29 Jan 1967

Inscape, 1967, Ann Arbor, 13 Oct 1967, New York PO, cond. Bernstein

Inaugural Fanfare (Ceremonial Fanfare), wind, 1969, Grand Rapids, MI, June 1969, Grand Rapids SO, cond. G. Millar; rev. 1975

3 Latin American Sketches: Estribillo, Paisaje mexicana, Danza de Jalisco, 1972, New York, 7 June 1972, New York PO, cond. Kostelanetz

CHAMBER

Capriccio, vn, pf; Poème, vc, pf; Lament, vc, pf; 2 Preludes, vn, pf; Piano Trio inc.; all *c*1916–21, unpubd

2 Pieces, str qt: Rondino, 1923, Fontainebleau, France, 1924; Lento molto, 1928, New York, 6 May 1928; arr. str orch, 1928

Lento espressivo, str qt, *c*1923, New York, 18 Oct 1984, Alexander Qt

2 Pieces, vn, pf: Nocturne, Ukelele Serenade, 1926, Paris, 1926, Dushkin, Copland

Vitebsk, Study on a Jewish Theme, pf trio, 1929, New York, 16 Feb 1929, W. Gieseking, A. Omnou, R. Maas

Miracle at Verdun (incidental music, H. Chlumberg), 1931, 16 March 1931, unpubd

Elegies, vn, va, 1932, New York, 2 April 1933, C. Karman, I. Karman, withdrawn

Sextet [arr. Short Symphony], cl, pf, str qt, 1937, New York, 26 Feb 1939

The Five Kings (incidental music, Shakespeare scenes), 5 insts, 1939, unpubd

Quiet City (incidental music, I. Shaw), cl, sax, tpt, pf, 1939, unpubd

Violin Sonata, 1942–3, New York, 17 Jan 1944, Posselt, Copland; arr. cl, pf, 1983, Rochester, 1983, M. Webster, B. Lister-Sink

Piano Quartet, 1950, Washington, DC, 29 Oct 1950, A. Schneider, Katims, F. Miller, Horszowski

Nonet, 3 vn, 3 va, 3 vc, 1960, Washington, DC, 2 March 1961, cond. Copland

Duo, fl, pf, 1971, Philadelphia, 3 Oct 1971, E. Shaffer, H. Menuhin
Threnody I: Igor Stravinsky, in memoriam, fl, str trio, 1971, London, ?April 1972, London Sinfonietta
Vocalise [arr. vocal piece], fl, pf, 1972, D. Dwyer
Threnody II: Beatrice Cunningham, in memoriam, G-fl, str trio, 1973, Ojai, CA, 1 June 1973

KEYBOARD

Moment musical, pf, 1917; Danse caractéristique, pf duet/orch, 1918; Waltz Caprice, pf, 1918; Sonnets I, III, 1918–20; Piano Sonata, G, 1920–21; all unpubd
Sonnet II, pf, *c*1919, New York, 26 Oct 1985, B. Lerner
Scherzo humoristique: Le chat et la souris, pf, 1920, Fontainebleau, 21 Sept 1921, Copland
Three Moods: Embittered, Wistful, Jazzy, pf, 1920–21, 1981, L. Smit
Petit Portrait, pf, 1921
Passacaglia, pf, 1921–2, Paris, Jan 1923, D. Ericourt
Sentimental Melody, pf, 1926, 1927, Copland
Piano Variations, 1930, New York, 4 Jan 1931, Copland; orchd 1957
Dance of the Adolescent [arr. excerpt from ballet Grohg], 2 pf, before 1932
Sunday Afternoon Music, pf, The Young Pioneers, pf, 1935, New York, 24 Feb 1936, Copland
Piano Sonata, 1939–41, Buenos Aires, 21 Oct 1941, Copland
Episode, org, 1940, March 1940, W. Strickland
Danzón cubano, 2 pf, 1942, New York, 9 Dec 1942, Copland, Bernstein; orchd 1944
Our Town [arr. film score], 3 excerpts, pf, 1944
2 Piano Pieces: Midday Thoughts, Proclamation for Piano, 1944–82, New York, 28 Feb 1983, B. Lerner
4 Piano Blues, 1947, 1934, 1948, 1926, no.4, Montevideo, 1942, H. Balzo
Piano Fantasy, 1952–7, New York, 25 Oct 1957, Masselos
Preamble for a Solemn Occasion [arr. orch piece], org, 1953
Down a Country Lane, pf, 1962
Rodeo [arr. ballet], 1962
Danza de Jalisco, 2 pf, 1963; orchd 1972
Dance Panels [arr. ballet], 1965
In Evening Air [arr. excerpt from film score The Cummington Story], pf, 1966
Night Thoughts (Homage to Ives), pf, 1972, Fort Worth, 30 Sept 1973, V. Viardo
Midsummer Nocturne, pf, 1977

CHORAL

4 Motets, 1921, Fontainebleau, 1924, Paris-American-Gargenville Chorus, cond. M. Smith
The House on the Hill (E. A. Robinson), SSAA, 1925, New York, spr. 1925, Women's U. Glee Club, cond. G. Reynolds
An Immorality (Pound), S, SSA, pf, 1925, New York, spr. 1925, Women's U. Glee Club, cond. G. Reynolds
Into the Streets May First (A. Hayes), unison vv, pf, 1934, New York, 29 April 1934, Workers Music League
What do we plant? (H. Abbey), SSA, pf, 1935, New York, Henry Street Settlement Girls Glee Club
Lark (G. Taggard), B, SATB, 1938, New York, 13 April 1943, Collegiate Chorale, cond. R. Shaw
Las agachadas (Sp. trad.), SSAATTBB, 1942, New York, 25 May 1942, Schola Cantorum, cond. H. Ross
Song of the Guerrillas (I. Gershwin), Bar, TTBB, pf, 1943 [from film score North Star]
The Younger Generation (I. Gershwin), SATB, pf, 1943 [from film score North Star]
In the Beginning (Genesis), Mez, SATB, 1947, Cambridge, MA, 2 May 1947, N. Tangeman, Robert Shaw Chorale, cond. Shaw
Stomp your Foot, The Promise of Living [from opera The Tender Land], SATB, pf, *c*1954, arr. orch
Canticle of Freedom (J. Barbour), 1955, Cambridge, MA, 8 May 1955, Chorus and Orch of the Massachusetts Institute of Technology, cond. K. Liepmann; rev. 1965, Atlanta, 19 Oct 1967, Atlanta SO, cond. Shaw

SONGS

(for 1v, pf, unless otherwise stated)

Melancholy (J. Farnol), 1917; Spurned Love (T. B. Aldrich), 1917; After Antwerp (E. Cammaerts), 1917; Night (A. Schaffer), 1918; A Summer Vacation, 1918; My heart is in the east, 1918; Simone (R. de Gourment), 1919; Music I heard (C. Aiken), 1920; all unpubd
Old Poem (Waley), 1920, Paris, 10 Jan 1922, C. Hubbard and Copland
Pastorale (E. P. Mathers), 1921, Paris, 10 Jan 1922, Hubbard and Copland
Alone (Mathers), 1922, New York, 4 Dec 1985, J. DeGaetani, unpubd
As it fell upon a day (R. Barnefield), S, fl, cl, 1923, Paris, 6 Feb 1924, A. MacLeish
Poet's Song (Cummings), 1927, New York, 11 Oct 1935, E. Luening
Vocalise, S/T, pf, 1928, New York, 11 Oct 1935, Luening
12 Poems of Emily Dickinson, 1944–50, New York, 18 May 1950, A. Howland, Copland; 8 Poems orchd, 1958–70, New York, 14 Nov 1970, G. Killebrew
Old American Songs [arrs.]: The Boatmen's Dance [D. Emmett, 1843], The Dodger [collected Lomax], Long Time Ago [1830s], Simple Gifts [Shaker, 1840s, ed. E. D. Andrews, 1940], I bought me a cat, 1950, Aldeburgh, 17 July 1950, P. Pears, Britten; arr. medium v, orch, Los Angeles, 7 Jan 1955, W. Warfield, Los Angeles PO, cond. A. Wallenstein
Old American Songs, set 2 [arrs.]: The Little Horses [collected Lomax], Zion's Walls [attrib. J. G. McCarry, ed. G. P. Jackson, 1942], The Golden Willow Tree [version of The Golden Vanity], At the River [R. Lowry, 1865], Ching-a-ring Chaw [1830s], 1952, Ipswich, MA, 1953, W. Warfield, Copland; arr. medium v, orch, Ojai, CA, 25 May 1958, G. Bumbry, Ojai Festival Orch, cond. Copland
Dirge in Woods (Meredith), 1954, Fontainebleau, 1954
Laurie's Song [from opera The Tender Land], S, pf, *c*1954

MSS in *DLC*
Principal publisher: Boosey & Hawkes

WRITINGS

What to Listen for in Music (New York, 1939, 2/1957)
Our New Music (New York, 1941, rev. and enlarged 2/1968 as *The New Music 1900–1960*)
Music and Imagination (Cambridge, MA, 1952, repr. 1959)
Copland on Music (New York, 1960) [selected essays]

For a list of articles see Smith, 1955, and Gleason and Becker, 1981

BIBLIOGRAPHY

BIBLIOGRAPHIES, DISCOGRAPHIES

D. Hamilton: "Aaron Copland: a Discography of the Composer's Performances," *PNM*, ix/1 (1970), 149
——: "The Recordings of Copland's Music," *HiFi*, xx/11 (1970), 52
H. Gleason and W. Becker: "Aaron Copland," *20th-century American Composers*, Music Literature Outlines, ser. iv (Bloomington, IN, rev. 2/1981), 33
C. Oja: "Aaron Copland," *American Music Recordings* (New York, 1982), 62
J. Skowronski: *Aaron Copland: a Bio-bibliography* (Westport, CT, 1985)

LIFE AND WORKS

V. Thomson: "Aaron Copland," *MM*, ix (1932), 67
A. Berger: *Aaron Copland* (New York, 1953) [review by H. Clurman, *Saturday Review*, xxxvi (28 Nov 1953), 36]
J. F. Smith: *Aaron Copland: his Work and Contribution to American Music* (New York, 1955) [incl. letters and summaries of writings]
R. F. Goldman: "Aaron Copland," *MQ*, xlvii (1961), 1
W. H. Mellers: *Music in a New Found Land* (London, 1964), 81
H. Cole: "Aaron Copland," *Tempo*, no.76 (1966), 2; no.77 (1966), 9
B. Northcott: "Copland in England," *Music and Musicians*, xviii/3 (1969), 34
L. Bernstein: "Aaron Copland: an Intimate Sketch," *HiFi*, xx/11 (1970), 53
E. Valencia: "Aaron Copland, el hombre, el músico, la leyenda," *Heterofonía*, iv/24 (1972), 9, 47
P. Dickinson: "Copland at 75," *MT*, cxvi (1975), 967
D. Rosenberg and B. Rosenberg: "Aaron Copland," *The Music Makers* (New York, 1979), 31
L. Kerner: "Aaron Copland's Time and Place," *Village Voice* (10 Dec 1980), 95
J. Rockwell: "Copland Conducts Copland at Tanglewood," *New York Times* (7 July 1980)
E. Rothstein: "Fanfares for Aaron Copland at 80," *New York Times* (9 Nov 1980), §D, p.21
W. Schuman: Tribute to Aaron Copland, Kennedy Center Honoree, 1979, *American Record Guide*, xliv/1 (1980), 6
R. Silverman: "Aaron Copland: Happy Birthday," *Piano Quarterly*, xxvii (1980), 5 [with articles also by L. Smit and D. Newlin]
H. W. Hitchcock: "Aaron Copland and American Music," *PNM*, xix (1980–81), 31 [with musical tributes by many composers, incl. Berger, Del Tredici, Diamond, Kirchner, Orrego-Salas, Persichetti, Ramey, Rorem, Shapero, Talma, and Thomson]
V. Perlis: "Copland and the BSO: a Lasting Friendship," [The Boston SO:] *The First Hundred Years*, ed. C. E. Hessberg and S. Ledbetter (Boston, 1981), 28
E. Salzman: "Aaron Copland: *the* American Composer is Eighty," *Stereo Review*, xlvi/2 (1981), 66
A. Copland and V. Perlis: *Copland 1900 through 1942* (New York, 1984) [auto-

biography] [review by A. Berger, *New York Review of Books*, xxxii/3 (1985), 21]

INTERVIEWS

E. T. Cone: "Conversations with Aaron Copland," *PNM*, vi/2 (1968), 57
"Interview with Aaron Copland," *1st American Music Conference: Keele 1975*, 4
N. Kenyon: "The Scene Surveyed: Nicholas Kenyon Talks to Aaron Copland," *Music and Musicians*, xxiv/3 (1975), 22
P. Rosenwald: "Aaron Copland Talks about a Life in Music," *Wall Street Journal* (14 Nov 1980), 31
L. Smit: "A Conversation with Aaron Copland," *Keyboard*, vi/11 (1980), 6 [with musical tributes by 12 composers, incl. K. Emerson's *Variations on Simple Gifts*]
C. Gagne and T. Caras: "Aaron Copland," *Soundpieces: Interviews with American Composers* (Metuchen, NJ, 1982), 101

WORKS, GENERAL STUDIES

P. Rosenfeld: "Copland without the Jazz," *By Way of Art* (New York, 1928), 266
——: "Aaron Copland's Growth," *New Republic*, lxvii (27 May 1931), 46
F. Sternfeld: "Copland as Film Composer," *MQ*, xxxvii (1951), 161
H. Overton: "Copland's Jazz Roots," *Jazz Today*, i (1956), 40
R. Evett: "The Brooklyn Eagle," *Atlantic Monthly*, ccxxxiv (1969), 135
H. Cole: "Popular Elements in Copland's Music," *Tempo*, no.95 (1971), 4
N. Kay: "Aspects of Copland's Development," *Tempo*, no.95 (1971), 23
D. Matthews: "Copland and Stravinsky," *Tempo*, no.95 (1971), 10
D. Young: "The Piano Music," *Tempo*, no.95 (1971), 15
S. Lipman: "Copland as American Composer," *Commentary*, lxi (1976), 70
C. Palmer: "Aaron Copland as Film Composer," *Crescendo International* (1976), May
T. Magrini: "Per una critica del 'populare' in Aaron Copland," *Ricerchi musicali*, ii/2 (1978), 5
B. Northcott: "Notes on Copland," *MT*, cxxii (1980), 686
P. Ramey: "Copland and the Dance," *Ballet News*, ii/5 (1980), 8
L. Starr: "Copland's Style," *PNM*, xix (1980–81), 68
N. M. Case: *Stylistic Coherency in the Piano Works of Aaron Copland* (diss., Boston U., 1984)

STUDIES OF PARTICULAR WORKS

P. Rosenfeld: "Musical Chronicle," *The Dial*, lxxviii (1925), 258 [Symphony]
A. Berger: "The Piano Variations of Aaron Copland," *Musical Mercury*, i (1934), 85
A. Goldberg: "Salome and New Ballets Occupy Chicago Stage," *MusAm*, liv/19 (1934), 11 [*Hear ye! Hear ye!*]
C. Sand [pseud. of C. Seeger]: "Copeland's [sic] Recital at Pierre Degeyter Club," *Daily Worker* (22 March 1934), 5 [several pieces]
C. M. Smith: "Copland's Hear ye! Hear ye!," *MM*, xii (1935), 86
P. Rosenfeld: "Current Chronicle," *MQ*, xxv (1939), 372 [*An Outdoor Ov.*, *The City*, *Billy the Kid*, and others]
J. Kirkpatrick: "Aaron Copland's Piano Sonata," *MM*, xix (1942), 246
A. Berger: "Copland's Piano Sonata," *Partisan Review*, x (1943), 187
E. Carter: "Theatre and Films," *MM*, xxi (1943), 50 [*North Star*]
——: "What's New in Music," *Saturday Review*, xxviii (20 Jan 1945), 13 [Vn Sonata, pf arrs. of *Our Town* and *Billy the Kid*]
——: "New Publications," *Saturday Review*, xxix (26 Jan 1946), 34 [*Appalachian Spring*]
A. Forte: *Contemporary Tone Structures* (New York, 1955), 63 [Piano Blues no.3]
A. Berger: "Aaron Copland's Piano Fantasy," *Juilliard Review*, v/1 (1957), 13
W. H. Mellers: "The Tender Land," *MT*, ciii (1962), 245
A. Salzman and P. Des Marais: "Aaron Copland's Nonet: Two Views," *PNM*, i/1 (1962), 172
P. Evans: "Copland on the Serial Road: an Analysis of Connotations," *PNM*, ii/2 (1964), 141
W. H. Mellers: "The Teenager's World," *MT*, cv (1964), 500 [on *Second Hurricane*]
R. P. Locke: *Aaron Copland's Twelve Poems of Emily Dickinson* (diss., Harvard U., 1970)
D. Whitwell: "The Enigma of Copland's Emblems," *Journal of Band Research*, vii/2 (1972), 5
D. Young: "Copland's Dickinson Songs," *Tempo*, no.103 (1972), 33
E. Salzman: "Copland's Appalachian Spring," *Stereo Review*, xxxix/4 (1974), 108
R. Swift: "Aaron Copland: Night Thoughts," *Notes*, xxxi (1974–5), 158
R. M. Daugherty: *An Analysis of Aaron Copland's "Twelve Poems of Emily Dickinson"* (diss., Ohio State U., 1980)
J. Anderson: "Dance: Copland Conducts for Graham," *New York Times* (18 June 1982), §C, p.8 [*Appalachian Spring*]
P. Fuller: *Copland and Stravinsky* (diss., UCLA, 1982) [*Appalachian Spring*]
D. Conte: *A Study of Aaron Copland's Sketches for Inscape* (diss., Cornell U., 1983)

OTHER LITERATURE

V. Thomson: "The Cult of Jazz," *Vanity Fair*, xxiv/4 (1925), 54
M. Graham: "The Dance in America," *Trend*, i/1 (1932), 5
A. Mendel: "What is American Music?"; "The American Composer," *Nation* cxxxiv (1932), 524, 578
P. Rosenfeld: "A Musical Tournament," *New Republic*, lxxi (15 June 1932), 119
V. Thomson: *The Musical Scene* (New York, 1945), 125
H. Clurman: "Paul Rosenfeld," *MM*, xxiii (1946), 184
V. Thomson: *The Art of Judging Music* (New York, 1948), 51, 74, 161, 201
——: *Music Right and Left* (New York, 1951), 120
R. Sessions: *Reflections on the Music Life in the United States* (New York, 1956) 156
I. Stravinsky and R. Craft: *Dialogues and a Diary* (New York, 1963), 47
V. Thomson: *Virgil Thomson* (New York, 1966), 71, 138, 146, 243, 277, 411
H. Clurman: *All People are Famous (Instead of an Autobiography)* (New York, 1974)
A. Croce: "The Blue Glass Goblet," *New Yorker*, l (6 May 1974), 130
W. Schuman: "Americanism in Music: a Composer's View," *Music in American Society 1776–1976*, ed. G. McCue (New Brunswick, NJ, 1977), 15
M. Siegel: "The Cake with the Stripper Inside," *Hudson Review*, xxxi (1978), 137
C. J. Oja: "The Copland-Sessions Concerts and their Reception in the Contemporary Press," *MQ*, lxv (1979), 212
C. Alexander: *Here the Country Lies: Nationalism and the Arts in 20th-century America* (Bloomington, IN, 1980)
B. Zuck: *A History of Musical Americanism* (Ann Arbor, MI, 1980)
R. Friedberg: *American Art Song and American Poetry* (Metuchen, NJ, 1981), 117
L. Bernstein: *Findings* (New York, 1982), 57, 284, 314, 336
M. Lederman: *The Life and Death of a Small Magazine (Modern Music, 1924–1946)*, ISAMm, xviii (Brooklyn, NY, 1983)
A. H. Levy: *Musical Nationalism: American Composers' Search for Identity* (Westport, CT, 1983)
A. Porter: "American Symphonists," *New Yorker*, lviii (31 Jan 1983), 94
R. M. Meckna: *The Rise of the American Composer-critic: Aaron Copland, Roger Sessions, Virgil Thomson, and Elliott Carter in the Periodical "Modern Music"* (diss., U. of California, Santa Barbara, 1984)
M. Meckna: "Copland, Sessions, and *Modern Music*: the Rise of the Composer-critic in America," *American Music*, iii/2 (1985), 198

WILLIAM W. AUSTIN
(work-list with VIVIAN PERLIS)

Coppock, William R. (*b* 1805; *d* Buffalo, NY, 17 Sept 1863). Music teacher and composer. He lived in Brooklyn from about 1821 to 1829, then in Buffalo from 1832 until his death. Most of his compositions are works for the piano, many on a modest scale and evidently designed for his students. His sonata *Le retour de Braddock's*, for example, consists only of two simple pieces, a waltz and a rondo. Some rondos and variations, however, are more suitable for the advanced student and accomplished amateur, occasionally displaying harmonic imagination and challenging keyboard techniques, as in the *Home Sweet Home* variations. A number of waltzes and marches are functional pieces for the ballroom and public ceremonies. The rondo *La belle Mary* (1841) was dedicated to "Master Rossini Coppock," presumably Coppock's son. Coppock also wrote a number of songs.

WORKS

Unless otherwise stated, all printed works were published in New York; estimated dates of publication are given in brackets.

PIANO

Variations: Home Sweet Home ([1827–31]); Oh No, we Never Mention her (1829); Jessie, the Flower o'Dumblane ([1842]); Carolina Dance, or Dandy Jim from Carolina (1844); Come Sing me that Sweet Air Again (1846); Rosa Lee, or Don't be Foolish Joe (1848); 4 other sets

Waltzes: The Brooklyn Waltz (Philadelphia, [1825]); Grand Military Waltz ([1829–35]); Le retour de Niagara (1835); [4 waltzes]: Le printemps, L'été, L'automne, L'hiver (1841); Arabella Waltz (1845); The Vine Cot Waltzes, à la cinq temps (1849); *c*6 others

Others: Le retour de Braddock's, sonata ([1827–31]); Le retour d'Alleghany, cotillion ([1827–31]); The Brooklyn Grand March, fl/vn ad lib ([1831–43]); Rise Gentle Moon, rondo (1839); La belle Mary, rondo (1841); The Minstrel's Return from the War, rondo (1845); Evergreen Divertimento (1851); 4 marches, 3 rondos, 2 divertimentos

SONGS

The Arcade ([1821–5]); When Zephyr comes freshning (Philadelphia, [1825–6]); The harp that I strung (1834); They said I must not sing of love (1834); I would be near thee (1848)

Principal publishers: Hall, Pond

BIBLIOGRAPHY

R. J. Wolfe: *Secular Music in America, 1801–1825: a Bibliography* (New York, 1964)

B. A. Wolverton: *Keyboard Music and Musicians in the Colonies and United States of America before 1830* (diss., Indiana U., 1966)

J. BUNKER CLARK

Copyright. The legal right in literary, musical, and artistic property.

1. Copyright legislation before 1976. 2. The 1976 act. 3. Exclusive rights in copyrighted matter. 4. Acquiring ownership. 5. Duration of copyright protection. 6. Compulsory licensing. 7. The manufacturing clause. 8. International aspects of US copyright. 9. Personal convenience versus the public good.

1. COPYRIGHT LEGISLATION BEFORE 1976. Copyright was not an unfamiliar concept to the signatories of the Declaration of Independence or the leaders of the Continental Congress, for as British subjects they had been living since 1710 under the world's first true copyright act, the Statute of Anne. Some of them would also have known about the first two leading cases in British copyright law – in 1769 and 1774 – the verdicts in which were flatly contradictory. American copyright law until the beginning of the 20th century was based largely on the Statute of Anne and English common law, and it thus inherited some of the English uncertainty about the exact relationship between the two. Common law, though not formally expressed in statutes, consisted then (as it does now) of a huge body of case law and legal tradition going back many centuries. It applied to such crimes as murder and theft, including the theft of products of the mind as long as they remained unpublished. Once published, those products could be protected for a limited time by the copyright statute, but after the statutory protection expired, according to the 1769 judgment, they returned to protection under common law; then in 1774 it was decided they would instead pass into the public domain.

Leaders in the 13 states were not slow to provide an American replacement for the Statute of Anne. By 2 May 1783, when the Continental Congress passed a resolution urging copyright action upon the states, three of them had already passed copyright acts and nine others did so within the next three years; only Delaware remained silent. Meeting in 1787, the Constitutional Convention lost no time in authorizing the Congress, which was about to assemble, "to promote the Progress of Science and useful Arts, by securing for limited Times to Authors and Inventors the exclusive right to their respective Writings and Discoveries." The first Congress enacted the young nation's first copyright act on 31 May 1790, establishing protection for maps, charts, and books for a term of 14 years, which was renewable upon further registration for another 14 years.

A number of additions were made in 1802 and 1819, but it was not until 1831 that Congress enacted the first general revision of the 1790 act; in the new legislation, "musical compositions" were mentioned for the first time, although some music had already been accepted under the category of "books." After further additions, made over the course of the next few decades, the second general revision of the act (1870) established the Library of Congress as the sole agency for the administration of copyright matters in the USA. A further advance came in 1891 when protection was extended for the first time to the works of foreign nationals.

The third general revision (1909) of the act improved the copyright situation in some areas, but not significantly in music. No attempt was made to define publication, an all-important issue in determining where the shadowy common law ended and where the statute began, and the definition of "writings" as used in the Constitution was not updated to include sound recordings and piano rolls. Performing rights were extended to music as well as to drama, but only when works were performed "for profit" – another ambiguous concept that was introduced but not adequately defined in the revised law. In 1912, motion pictures were added to the group of protected materials. Many amendments were proposed during the next six decades and some became law, but the problems specific to the performance, publication, and recording of music were not yet fully resolved. The complicated situation surrounding the uses of cable television delayed agreement on a comprehensive law even further, so that it was not until 1976 that a completely new statute was finally enacted.

2. THE 1976 ACT. Public Law 94-553 (94th Congress, Oct. 19, 1976, Title 17, US Code, Copyrights) took effect on 1 January 1978 and changed the aspect of copyright in the USA. For the first time in the country's history a single system of statutory protection was established for all copyrightable works. The amorphous concept of common-law protection over unpublished materials was preempted, as were a number of state statutes that had sought to codify and clarify that concept. Gone, too, were the formulae of copyright duration based on multiples of seven years (which is said to have been derived by those who drafted the Statute of Anne from the seven-year term of apprenticeship in printing and other trades), as well as the all-important but often moot question of what constituted publication, and the concept of "performance for profit," which could be defined in more than one way. On the other hand, the first statutory recognition of the principle of "fair use" of copyrighted materials was introduced, accompanied by an attempt to delineate as many instances of such fair use as could be managed. The compulsory licensing requirements for certain uses of copyrighted material (e.g., in jukeboxes and for television secondary transmissions) were greatly extended in order that a degree of fiscal responsibility on the part of its users could be imposed.

For the first time in American law the definition of what constitutes copyrightable matter was made both broad and succinct. Under section 102 of the title copyright protection is given to:

> original works of authorship fixed in any tangible medium of expression, now known or later developed, from which they can be perceived, reproduced, or otherwise communicated, either directly or with the aid of a machine or device. Works of authorship include the following categories:
> (1) literary works;
> (2) musical works, including any accompanying words;
> (3) dramatic works, including any accompanying music;
> (4) pantomimes and choreographic works;
> (5) pictorial, graphic, and sculptural works;
> (6) motion pictures and other audiovisual works; and
> (7) sound recordings.

Copyright still does not extend to ideas, procedures, systems, methods of operation, principles, discoveries, or concepts of any kind, nor to titles, names, or slogans, but rather to the perceptible and tangible expressions of these intellectual phenomena. Such phenomena are protected not by copyright law, but by patent statutes or such common-law concepts as unfair competition. (Copyright also differs from patent law in at least two other important respects: the degree of originality required and the force of law represented by their respective grants. A discernible degree of originality is significant in the area of copyright, and the copyright certificate is evidence only of a claim, not of its proven merit.)

Under the 1976 statute, "publication" – so treacherous in definition – no longer governs whether a work can be given full protection under the statute, for the only requirement of Title 17 is "fixation in any tangible medium of expression," present or future. By definition (section 101 of the statute), a work is "fixed" when

> its embodiment in a copy or phonorecord, by or under the authority of the author, is sufficiently permanent or stable to permit it to be perceived, reproduced, or otherwise communicated for a period of more than transitory duration. A work consisting of sounds, images, or both, that are being transmitted, is "fixed" for purposes of this title if a fixation of the work is being made simultaneously with its transmission.

The composer, for instance, acquires the copyright in his work as he goes along, movement by movement or even note by note. Whether he chooses pencil and manuscript paper or microphone and audio tape, or, as in the case of *musique concrète*, fashions the work on the tape itself, the medium of expression is tangible. In the case of random or aleatory compositions, where the medium is not fixed, and in unnotated and unphotographed choreography, extemporaneous speeches, truly improvised cadenzas, musical passages played in different ways by a teacher demonstrating a point to a pupil – in fact, in any case where material is "unfixed" but can be copied by a listener or spectator with a hidden microphone or a good memory, common law still plays a part.

Collective works, such as Festschriften or separate issues of a periodical, can be copyrighted as a whole by the editor or publisher of the whole, but the individual contributions are the property of their respective authors and remain so, unless the copyrights are expressly transferred. Section 201 of Title 17 specifies that "the owner of copyright in the collective work is presumed to have acquired only the privilege of reproducing and distributing the contribution as part of that particular collective work," or a revision of it. On the other hand, materials produced by individuals working on salaries as part of their prescribed duties fall into the category of works "made for hire," and the copyrights in these contributions belong to the employer. Similarly, "supplementary works" (e.g., editorial notes, musical arrangements, and illustrations), specially commissioned for use in collective works, can also be considered works for hire if the parties so agree in a written and signed statement. Any copyright claimed by a compiler (of, for example, a collection of preexisting songs by different composers) or by the creator of a derivative work (such as a story adapted for use in an animated film) has no effect upon the status of the original works.

3. Exclusive rights in copyrighted matter. Section 106 of Title 17 codifies for copyright owners their exclusive right

> (1) to reproduce the copyrighted work in copies or phonorecords;
> (2) to prepare derivative works based upon the copyrighted work;
> (3) to distribute copies or phonorecords of the copyrighted work to the public by sale or other transfer of ownership, or by rental, lease, or lending;
> (4) in the case of literary, musical, dramatic, and choreographic works, pantomimes, and motion pictures and other audiovisual works, to perform the copyrighted work publicly; and
> (5) in the case of literary, musical, dramatic, and choreographic works, pantomimes, and pictorial, graphic, or sculptural works, including the individual images of a motion picture or other audiovisual work, to display the copyrighted work publicly.

One of the important changes from earlier legislation is that in the 1976 statute the entire right of performance in public – not only performances "for profit" – is reserved (with certain limitations described below) to the copyright owner. Equally important is the admission for the first time (save for the limited antipiracy provisions that became effective in 1972) of sound recordings into the copyright provisions. With the proliferation in the 20th century of media and devices capable of reproducing musical sounds (radio, television, audio and video tape, disc recordings of several kinds, and musical software for use with computers), the protection offered by the Constitution of 1787 to "writings" has been rendered inadequate. Written music, whether printed or in manuscript, is commercially much less important than the musical sounds purveyed by any of these means. Even with the extended provisions of the 1976 statute, however, it is only the works themselves that are protected; the performance as a performance is still not copyrightable. The performers and record manufacturers can receive no royalties at all for the music they provide through the media of radio and jukeboxes.

The five exclusive rights of the copyright owner cited above are printed on less than half a page of the octavo booklet containing the law, whereas the delineation and elucidation of the exceptions to those rights occupy almost 22 full pages more. First comes a general statement of principle concerning "fair use" (section 107), which constitutes use of copyrighted matter "for purposes such as criticism, comment, news reporting, teaching (including multiple copies for classroom use), scholarship, or research." Four factors to be considered in assessing fair use are then set out:

> (1) the purpose and character of the use, including whether such use is of a commercial nature or is for nonprofit educational purposes;
> (2) the nature of the copyrighted work;
> (3) the amount and substantiality of the portion used in relation to the copyrighted work as a whole; and
> (4) the effect of the use upon the potential market for or value of the copyrighted work.

Of these factors, the first is the best understood and the least debated; the second is probably the least understood, especially among musicians who tend to equate a score with a book and to overlook the thorny performing rights problems, which a book does not have; and the third involves a principle more easily acknowledged than carried out in practice. The fourth factor is the most crucial and at the same time the most disregarded. The putative copier likes to think of his immediate need as "unique" and harmful to no one. He forgets that a few dozen similarly "unique" uses can make all the difference between profit and loss for the producers of the work. Without a viable market, the publisher or manufacturer cannot afford to produce a new work, the creator has no way of getting his work to the public and no recompense for his creation, and the public has one work fewer to enjoy.

Following these general statements concerning fair use, sections 108–12 of Title 17 list in great detail the dozens of possible exceptions (and exceptions to exceptions) to the exclusive rights of the copyright owner. Several of these are of general interest:

(i) Libraries and archives, provided they are open to the public or at least to researchers outside their own employ, and provided no direct or indirect commercial advantage is involved, may for reasons of preservation or security, copy unpublished works in their collections for themselves or for other libraries or archives meeting the same requirements. Published works may similarly be copied to replace lost, damaged, or deteriorating copies, provided a reasonable effort to purchase a new copy at a fair price has been unsuccessful. In the case of unperformable or nondisplay materials, a complete or a substantial part of a work may be copied for a private user, provided a reasonable investigation by the library or archives has shown a new copy to be unavailable to the user at a fair price, and provided the copy made is not part of a systematic or multiple-copy photoduplication project either by the user or the library. A somewhat routine proviso requiring the placement of signs warning of copyright infringement on or near its unsupervised copying machines relieves the library and its employees of liability for infringement by the general public.

(ii) Educational institutions, churches, and other noncommercial organizations may make copies under certain circumstances for such classroom and other purposes as scholastic uses, religious services, and aid to the blind or otherwise physically handicapped. By reason of an amendment to section 110, paragraph 4, of Title 17, which became law on 25 October 1982 (Public Law 97-366), copyright is not infringed if a nondramatic literary or musical work is performed

> in the course of a social function which is organized and promoted by a nonprofit veterans' organization or a nonprofit fraternal organization to which the general public is not invited, but not including the invitees of the organizations, if the proceeds from the performance, after deducting the reasonable costs of producing the performance, are used exclusively for charitable purposes and not for financial gain. For purposes of this section the social functions of any college or university fraternity or sorority shall not be included unless the social function is held solely to raise funds for a specific charitable purpose.

A group or individual (such as the owner of a bar or cocktail lounge) may, by using a single receiving apparatus and speakers of the domestic kind and making no direct charge, communicate copyrighted music and other transmitted matter without infringement. Record shops or other vending establishments open to the public without admission charge may allow prospective buyers or others to play sound recordings (the word "phonorecords" is used in the statute) of nondramatic musical works, provided the performance is not transmitted beyond the establishment, takes place in the sales area, and is for the sole purpose of promoting sales of the sound recordings. Hotels, motels, and apartment houses may relay broadcasts to the rooms of their guests or residents provided no cable system is used and no direct charge is made for the service.

(iii) With regard to computer programs (whether the matter stored is music or a communication in any language), by an amendment to Title 17 that took effect on 12 December 1980

> it is not an infringement for the owner of a copy of a computer program to make or authorize the making of another copy or adaptation of that computer program provided:
>
> (1) that such a new copy or adaptation is created as an essential step in the utilization of the computer program in conjunction with a machine and that it is used in no other manner, or
>
> (2) that such new copy or adaptation is created for archival purposes only and that all archival copies are destroyed in the event that continued possession of the computer program should cease to be rightful.
>
> (3) Any exact copies prepared in accordance with the provisions of this section may be leased, sold, or otherwise transferred, along with the copy from which such copies were prepared, only as part of the lease, sale, or other transfer of all rights in the program. Adaptations so prepared may be transferred only with the authorization of the copyright owner.

4. Acquiring ownership. Under section 201 of Title 17, every new work or part of an unfinished work becomes the property of its creator the moment he fixes it in some tangible medium of expression; the creators of a "joint work" are two or more authors whose intention it is to merge their contributions into "inseparable or interdependent parts of a unitary whole." The concept of copyright as "an indivisible bundle of rights" that cannot be broken up, which under the earlier law made for much cumbersome licensing and uncertain ownership, is gone. An owner may at any time sell, give away, or otherwise transfer ownership of either the whole or any one of the five rights; he may also license the use of all or any one of those rights while still retaining ownership.

Transfers of ownership, other than by operation of law, must be in writing and be signed by the conveyor; recordation of the conveyance with the Copyright Office is not obligatory to make the transfer legal, but it is required before any infringement action under Title 17 can be brought by the transferee. Because the renewal requirement or option under the former legislation is gradually being phased out, a new mechanism – termination of transfers – has been introduced under Title 17. The "widows' and orphans' clause" of the 1909 act returned ownership of a copyright to the author or his heirs when renewal time came, giving them the chance to make a new and better sale or other disposition. Section 203 of Title 17 achieves the same result through providing for a termination of transfer; this may be made by the original owner or his heirs during the five-year period beginning at the end of the 35 years from the date that the transfer (by sale, gift, or any other means except, of course, bequest) was executed. The termination of transfer is not possible in the case of works made for hire.

The formalities of recordation that have characterized American copyright since 1790 have been altered by the various congressional statutes but are still present.

(i) As stipulated in sections 401 and 402, all published works must bear a copyright "notice," including the word "Copyright," the abbreviation "Copr.," or the symbol for copyright (© for all items except sound recordings, for which the symbol is ℗), the year, and the name or other recognized identification of the owner. The notice must be placed on the copies "in such manner and location as to give reasonable notice of the claim of copyright." The law now allows some latitude in the case of notices inadvertently omitted, together with some lenience for innocent infringers deceived by the lack of notice.

(ii) What was, 100 years ago, the tail of the copyright donkey is now the head: deposit is at last of primary concern. Section 407 states that for all works published with a copyright notice within the USA, the owner of the publication right must, within three months after publication, deposit two copies of the best edition (or two discs, in the case of sound recordings) with the Copyright Office for the use or disposition of the Library of Congress. Failure to make the proper deposit does not affect the validity of the copyright claim, but if that failure continues after the Copyright Office has demanded compliance, it lays open the owner to fines ranging from $250, in addition to the total retail price of the two copies, up to $2500. With unpublished works, contributions to collective works, and works first published outside the USA, only one deposit copy is required. In the case of very expensive or very limited editions and in a few other circumstances, the Register of Copyrights is empowered to alter the deposit requirement, as long as a satisfactory archival record is secured for the Library of Congress.

(iii) Section 408 of Title 17 refers to registration as "permissive," since the procedure of registering is not necessary to ensure the validity of the copyright, although it is required before any action can be brought for an infringement. In the case of published works, no statutory damages or attorney's fees can be recovered if the alleged infringement took place more than three months after publication and the work was still unregistered (lacking therefore a public notice of its existence). One new feature in the present law is that a work registered as unpublished need not be reregistered when it is published. Another new feature, less attractive, is that once a registration form has been accepted, any error on that form cannot be corrected; a supplemental application must be filed to correct the information, but the original application is not removed.

5. DURATION OF COPYRIGHT PROTECTION. The new law (section 302) changed the term of copyright protection for works created on or after 1 January 1978 from 56 years (28 upon registration and 28 more after renewal) to "the life of the author and fifty years after the author's death," or what is known in copyright jargon as "life plus 50." In the case of joint authorship, the expiry date is calculated from the death of the last surviving author. When the owner is a company registering a work for hire, and in the case of anonymous or pseudonymous authors (i.e., when the identity of the author has not been revealed to the Copyright Office), the term is either 75 years from the year of publication or 100 years from creation in fixed form, whichever expires first. The need for renewal has been abolished for all works created on or after 1 January 1978, but not for works that were already in their first term at that date. For the early years of the Title 17 era, then, copyrighted works are subject to a range of possibilities as to duration:

(i) Works first copyrighted before 19 September 1906 are now in the public domain (as of 19 September 1934 or earlier if not renewed, as of 31 December 1981 or earlier if renewed).

(ii) Works first copyrighted between 19 September 1906 and 31 December 1949 and subsequently renewed had their renewal terms kept alive by a series of congressional enactments that began on 19 September 1962. Under section 304 of Title 17, all copyrights that were in their renewal terms at any time between 31 December 1976 and 31 December 1977 inclusive, or for which renewal registration was made between those two dates, had their renewal terms extended to the end of the 75th calendar year from the year in which they were originally copyrighted.

(iii) Works first copyrighted between 1 January 1950 and 31 December 1977 inclusive still had or have to have those copyrights renewed if they are not to enter the public domain at the end of the 28th year. The renewal term is 47 rather than 28 years.

(iv) A work created – not simply worked out in the mind, but fixed in a tangible medium of expression – before 1 January 1978 but neither published nor copyrighted under previous laws before that date is (in section 303) automatically given a term of "life plus 50":

> In no case, however, shall the term of copyright in such a work expire before December 31, 2002; and, if the work is published on or before December 31, 2002, the term of copyright shall not expire before December 31, 2027.

The intent of the act clearly is that expiration shall not take place before 1 January in each instance: all terms mentioned in the title that end after 31 December 1977 extend to the end of the calendar year involved, not, as was the case in earlier legislation, to the last day of an exact term (so that a copyright granted, for example, on 28 September 1923 expired on 28 September 1951 unless renewed).

With regard to duration of copyright in sound recordings, the first federal antipiracy legislation went into effect on 15 February 1972. That law and its successor, the Piracy and Counterfeiting Amendments Act of 1982 (Public Law 97-180), which increased the maximum fine from $25,000 to $250,000 and the maximum term of imprisonment from two to five years, affect only those sound recordings fixed since 15 February 1972. For recordings fixed before that date, copyright under Title 17 will not preempt common law and state statutes until 15 February 2047.

6. COMPULSORY LICENSING. The Act of 1909 stipulated that once a copyright owner had authorized for public distribution a recording of a nondramatic musical work (including background music to spoken works such as poetry), any other person was free to make and sell his own recording of the same work as long as he paid the copyright owner the statutory sum of 2¢ per side. (The rate was changed in the new law to accommodate LPs, tapes, and other recording media. It specifies either $2\frac{3}{4}$¢ per side or $\frac{1}{2}$¢ per minute of playing time, whichever is larger; it is likely that with the introduction of further recording innovations, playing time will become the standard component in future rates.) The policy of compulsory licensing, which usurps the copyright owner's right to select and deal exclusively with the performers and recording firm of his choice, came about in the aftermath of Theodore Roosevelt's trustbusting presidency. Title 17 retains compulsory licensing for sound recordings, and, as a means of collecting monies for copyright owners where practical considerations render a more just and accurate mechanism impossible, it defines three further categories of use that must be licensed:

(i) secondary ("boosting") transmissions by cable antenna television systems (section 111), the charge for which includes royalty amounts for the home delivery of music and other copyrighted matter;

(ii) jukeboxes (officially known as "coin-operated phonorecord players," section 116), which are for the most part owned and regulated by the Amusement and Music Operators' Association of America; and

(iii) Public Broadcasting and other noncommercial broadcasting groups (section 118), which of course use much copyrighted music and other matter.

Sections 801–10 of the new law created a Copyright Royalty Tribunal to collect and distribute the monies generated by these compulsory licensing provisions and by those added later by amendments to the title. A governmental equivalent of the performing rights societies (ASCAP, BMI, and SESAC Inc.; *see* PERFORMING RIGHTS SOCIETIES, §2), the tribunal is not part of the Copyright Office, but an independent agency in the legislative branch of the federal government, responsible directly to the Congress. It also determines whether the royalty rates prescribed for various uses are reasonable and, if they are not, makes adjustments to them.

7. THE MANUFACTURING CLAUSE. In 1891 American copyright protection was extended to books and other matter "consisting preponderantly of nondramatic literary material that is in the English language" by citizens of other countries, provided that such matter was manufactured in the USA. The 1976 act (section 601) contained the remnants of the original prescription but for the first time allowed material in English manufactured in Canada equal protection with that manufactured in the USA. It specified, however, that the manufacturing clause would cease to be effective on 1 July 1982. As that date approached, the printing and binding and other manufacturing trades continued to fear that without such a proviso American publishers would send their manuscripts abroad to be manufactured, where costs were lower. They were able, through lobbying, to secure an extension of the life of the clause for four years (to 1 July 1986) in spite of a veto cast by President Ronald Reagan to demonstrate his administration's intention to strengthen free trade.

8. INTERNATIONAL ASPECTS OF US COPYRIGHT. Works of foreign nationals are protected in the USA in several different ways.

(i) Unpublished works are protected under section 104 of Title 17, regardless of the nationality or domicile of the author.

(ii) A work first published in the USA, or by the United Nations or any of its subsidiary agencies, or by the Organization of American States, is protected under Title 17, regardless of the nationality of its author.

(iii) A work by a foreign national published outside the USA is protected if, on the date of first publication, the author (or any one of the authors of a joint work) is a national of a country that is a party to the Universal Copyright Convention or to another copyright convention or copyright treaty to which the USA is also a party; or if he is a national of a country recognized by a presidential proclamation as offering reciprocal protection to works by US nationals; or if he is a stateless person.

Works of US nationals are protected abroad under:

(i) the Universal Copyright Convention (of which the USA is a member) in all other member countries, provided the copyright notice described in §4, if required by that country, is properly affixed to the work;

(ii) any other copyright convention or treaty to which the USA and the country in which protection is sought are both parties, as long as the work is published in compliance with the conditions of that treaty or convention; and

(iii) the domestic copyright laws of certain countries, provided the specific requirements of those laws are met.

9. PERSONAL CONVENIENCE VERSUS THE PUBLIC GOOD. The 1976 statute redressed some of the worst inequities of the earlier legislation. Yet, even as members of the Congress and numerous special-interest groups were striving towards that achievement, innovations in the field of communications were beginning to have serious ramifications for various copyright issues. Slow and costly photographic processes were replaced by fast and inexpensive copying devices, and the clumsy acetate phonodisc was superseded by tapes of various kinds. Television in the home was barely 20 years old before video tape recorders were on the market, enabling anyone to capture the images and sounds received by his set. All these devices have led to widespread abuses of copyright law (particularly in the form of tape-to-tape, disc-to-tape, and "off-the-air" copying), which have an indirect but deadly effect on the market. Yet there has been a curious diffidence in copyright circles about testing legislation that might be invoked to dictate what a citizen may and may not do in the privacy of his own home. No such diffidence would be felt were he to make multiple copies to be sold in competition with those of the original producer and copyright holder, but the implications for the market of private copying for personal use are not much less serious.

There is no mechanism at present for providing creators (authors, composers, graphic artists, performers, publishers, and record companies) with due compensation for all the uses of their works. Without such a mechanism, as the uses continue to multiply the markets will dwindle until only works that are certain to be successful will reach the public. In time, fewer new and imaginative creators will be able to acquire an audience for their works. The biggest loser will be the public, and it is specifically for the benefit of the public that the US Constitution assigns to Congress the power – and duty – to enact copyright laws that will promote creative activity by ensuring creators some reward for their work. How can the public protect itself against the continuing erosion of its benefits from copyright? The compulsory licensing mechanism is a poor tool at best, and of no avail against individual infringements at home or in libraries. It would be possible to apply a tax to copying devices, levied at the time of purchase, which could fund payments to copyright holders, but such a system would be complicated and difficult to administer fairly. The invention of new copying devices, use of which can be denied to all except those who rightfully acquire a key, may offer protection in certain areas. But public recognition that copyrighted material must be paid for offers the best hope – and perhaps even the last hope – of maintaining the copyright-based culture that the Anglo-American world has shared for more than 200 years.

BIBLIOGRAPHY

L. R. Patterson: *Copyright in Historical Perspective* (Nashville, 1868)

T. Solberg: *Copyright Enactments 1783–1900* (Washington, DC, 1900; rev. 5/1973 as *Copyright Enactments: Laws Passed in the United States since 1783 Relating to Copyright*)

H. A. Howell: *The Copyright Law: an Analysis of the Law of the United States Governing Registration and Protection of Copyright Works* (Washington, DC, 1942; rev. 5/1979, by A. Latman, as *The Copyright Law: Howell's Copyright Law Revised and the 1976 Act*)

B. Kaplan and R. S. Brown, Jr.: *Cases on Copyright, Unfair Competition, and Other Topics Bearing on the Protection of Literary, Musical, and Artistic Works* (Brooklyn, NY, 1960, rev. 2/1974, rev. 3/1978)

S. Shemel and M. W. Krasilovsky: *This Business of Music* (New York, 1964, rev. and enlarged 5/1985)

M. B. Nimmer: *Cases and Materials on Copyright and Other Aspects of Law Pertaining to Literary, Musical, and Artistic Works* (St. Paul, 1971, rev. and enlarged 2/1979)

B. Ringer: *The Demonology of Copyright* (New York, 1974)

——: *Two Hundred Years of Copyright in America* (Washington, DC, 1976)

W. Lichtenwanger: "94-553 and All That: Ruminations on Copyright Today, Yesterday, and Tomorrow," *Notes*, xxxv (1978–9), 803; xxxvi (1979–80), 837

J. G. Erickson, E. R. Hearn, and M. E. Halloran: *Musician's Guide to Copyright* (New York, 1983)

For further bibliography *see* PERFORMING RIGHTS SOCIETIES.

WILLIAM LICHTENWANGER

Copyright collecting societies. *See* PERFORMING RIGHTS SOCIETIES.

Cordero, Ernesto (*b* New York, 9 Aug 1946). Guitarist and composer. He was brought up from infancy in Puerto Rico; he studied guitar and theory at the Madrid Conservatory (1967–70), the Accademia di S. Cecilia in Rome, and the Accademia Musicale Chigiana, Siena (1973–4). As a guitarist he has made many recital appearances in Puerto Rico, Europe, and the USA, performing Spanish and Latin American music as well as his own works, receiving high recognition and several awards. Since 1971 he has been a member of the faculty of the University of Puerto Rico, teaching both guitar and composition. Cordero composes primarily for guitar. His style is characterized by neoclassical adherence to traditional harmony and forms, with occasional dissonance related to certain aspects of guitar tuning and technique.

WORKS

Gui: Fantasía, gui, orch, 1975; Mapeyé, 1975; 5 Preludes, 1977; Concierto evocativo, gui, orch, 1978; Sonata, 1980; Due canzoni populari andaluze, 1981; Concierto antillano, gui, orch, 1983; many other works for solo gui, gui, orch

Other works: 3 canciones (M. Alonso, A. C. Ríos, M. Machado), 1v, orch, 1968–73; Canciones (various Puerto Rican poets), 11 songs, 1v, orch, 1983; other works for 1v, gui/1v, pf

Principal publishers: Institute of Puerto Rican Culture, Spanish Music Center, Zanibon

DONALD THOMPSON

Cordero, Roque (*b* Panamá, Panama, 16 Aug 1917). Panamanian composer, conductor, and teacher. He began composing as a youth, and after pursuing musical studies in his native city he obtained in 1943 a scholarship to attend the University of Minnesota. There he studied conducting with Mitropoulos, who took a great interest in his career and advised him to study counterpoint and composition with Krenek, then teaching at nearby Hamline University. On 5 April 1946 Mitropoulos conducted the first performance of Cordero's *Obertura panameña no.2* with the Minneapolis SO. Cordero continued to study conducting, with Stanley Chapple at the Berkshire Music Center and with Barzin in New York. He returned to Panama in 1950 as professor of composition at the National Institute of Music, a post he held until 1966; he was concurrently director of the Institute (1953–64) and conductor of the National Orchestra of Panama (1964–6). In 1966 he was appointed professor of composition at Indiana University, where he was also assistant director of the Latin-American Music Center. He went to New York in 1969 as music consultant for the publishing firm of Peer-Southern. In 1972 he joined the faculty of Illinois State University as professor of composition. Among his numerous awards and commissions are a Guggenheim Fellowship (1949) and commissions from the Koussevitzky Foundation (for the Violin Concerto) and the Kennedy Center (for the Double Concerto without Orchestra).

While disclaiming any intent to write "nationalistic" music, Cordero has stated that to be true to himself he must express something that belongs to his people, and this he tries to do through melodic figures and dance rhythms related to Panamanian folk music, such as the *mejorana* and *tamborito*. Thus several early works are in an overtly folkloric vein, although in later ones such allusions tend to be recondite. The *Sonatina rítmica* for piano (1943) is in this respect a transitional work, as it combines Panamanian dance rhythms with strictly classical forms.

Up to 1945 Cordero's music was generally tonal. In 1944 he experimented with 12-tone composition in the *Eight Miniatures* for small orchestra, revised in 1948. He first employed an adapted 12-tone technique in Sonatine for violin and piano (1946), in which the basic series is used freely, with melodic and harmonic repetitions, octave doublings, and frequent occurrences of the interval of the 7th. His mature 12-tone writing is most impressively displayed in the Second and Third Symphonies, the Violin Concerto, and the three string quartets. In spite of his long residence in the USA and his wide-ranging international career as a conductor, Cordero has always considered himself a specifically Panamanian composer.

WORKS

Orch: 8 Miniatures, 1944, rev. 1948; Obertura panameña no.2, 1944; Pf Conc., 1944; 3 syms., 1945, 1946, 1965; Movimiento sinfónico, str, 1946; Vn Conc., 1962; Circumvolutions and Mobiles, 57 insts, 1967; Concertino, va, str, 1968; Elegy, str, 1973; Momentum jubilo, 1973; 6 Mobiles, 1975; Ov. of Salutation, 1980; a few other short works

Chamber: Sonatine, vn, pf, 1946; Qnt, fl, cl, vn, va, pf, 1949; 3 str qts, 1960, 1968, 1973; 3 Short Messages, va, pf, 1966; Permutations 7, cl, tpt, timp, pf, vn, va, db, 1967; Paz, Paix, Peace, 4 trios, harp, 1969; Música veinte, vv, insts, 1970; Variations and Theme for Five, ww qnt, 1975; Soliloquios no.1, fl, 1975, no.2, sax, 1976, no.3, cl, 1976, no.4, perc, 1981, no.5, db, 1981; Double Conc. without Orch, vn, pf, 1978; Music for 5 Brass, brass qnt, 1980; other works

Vocal: Cantata (Lincoln, Ghandi, Kennedy, King), 1974; unacc. choral works

Pf: Sonatina rítmica, 1943; Rhapsody, 2 pf, 1945; Sonata breve, 1946; Sonata breve, 1966; 3 Piececillas para Alina, 1978; other works

2 ballets

Principal publisher: Peer-Southern

BIBLIOGRAPHY

G. Chase: "Composed by Cordero," *Americas*, x/6 (1958), 7; repr. in *Inter-American Music Bulletin*, no.7 (1958), 1

——: "Creative Trends in Latin American Music – II," *Tempo*, no.50 (1959), 25

R. R. Sider: *The Art Music of Central America: its Development and Present State* (diss., U of Rochester, 1967)

——: "Roque Cordero: the Composer and his Style," *Inter-American Music Bulletin*, no.61 (1967), 1

E. Ennett: *An Analysis and Comparison of Selected Piano Sonatas by three Contemporary Black Composers: George Walker, Howard Swanson, and Roque Cordero* (diss., New York U., 1973)

G. Béhague: *Music in Latin America: an Introduction* (Englewood Cliffs, NJ, 1979), 261, 304

A. de la Vega: "Latin American Composers in the United States," *Latin American Music Review*, i (1980), 162

GILBERT CHASE/R

Corea, Chick [Armando Anthony] (*b* Chelsea, MA, 12 June 1941). Jazz pianist and composer. He began playing the piano at the age of four, learning the fundamentals of music from his father (a professional musician). By listening regularly to the recordings of Dizzy Gillespie, Charlie Parker, and Billy Eckstine, he developed an interest in jazz at an early age, and began to transcribe and memorize the tunes and improvised solos of the pianist Horace Silver; he also came under the influence of Bud Powell. His first important professional engagements were in the Latin bands of Mongo Santamaria and Willie Bobo (1962–3), and a love of Latin music has been evident throughout his career. He then worked extensively with the jazz trumpeter Blue Mitchell (1964–6), recording his own compositions for the first time on Mitchell's sessions for Blue Note records. His interest, during this period, in the music of Joe Henderson, McCoy Tyner, Bill Evans, and Herbie Hancock can be clearly heard in his first recordings as a leader, *Tones for Joan's Bones* (1966) and *Now He Sings, Now He Sobs* (1968).

In 1968 Corea joined Miles Davis's group, which was then involved in an abstract form of electronic jazz–rock that initiated

Chick Corea, late 1970s

the so-called "fusion" movement of the 1970s. Corea's involvement with Davis marked the beginning of his extensive exploration of free improvisation, but his desire to develop a more individual, nonelectronic approach to free jazz prompted him, along with the double bass player Dave Holland, to leave the group in 1970. Inspired by the earlier work of Paul Bley and Gary Peacock, they formed a trio with the drummer Barry Altschul, later adding Anthony Braxton on reed instruments. This group, Circle, was very influential on the avant-garde jazz scene, but Corea soon felt a need to establish a more lyrical context for his music. The solo albums *Piano Improvisations*, i–ii, recorded in 1971 shortly before Circle disbanded, clearly reflect this urge. Corea also began the study of Scientology during this period, the dynamics of which greatly affected his subsequent work.

From 1972 to 1973 Corea attracted a wider audience with the first of his groups called Return to Forever, which made use of expansive melodies, romantic vocal lines, and infectious Latin rhythms. The second Return to Forever group was a powerful rock band in which Corea played the Fender-Rhodes electric piano, Hohner Clavinet, Yamaha organ, Minimoog and ARP Odyssey synthesizers, and various electronic gadgets and pedals; by the late 1970s he had become very popular with rock audiences. He continued to develop as a composer throughout this period, often augmenting his basic group with small string and brass ensembles, and utilizing elements from the Latin, Spanish, and classical traditions. Several of his tunes, including *Windows*, *Spain*, and *Crystal Silence* have become jazz standards. Unlike many "crossover" artists who left jazz for commercial rock, Corea has continued to perform and record regularly in a wide variety of acoustic jazz settings. These include solo performances, duos with the vibraphonist Gary Burton or the pianist Hancock, a quartet with Michael Brecker (saxophone), Eddie Gomez (double bass), and Steve Gadd (drums), and the group Trio Music with the double bass player Miroslav Vitous and the drummer Roy Haynes (1981–).

RECORDINGS
(selective list)

As leader: *Tones for Joan's Bones* (1966, Vortex 2004); *Now He Sings, Now He Sobs* (1968, Solid State 18039); *Is* (1969, Solid State 18055); *The Song of Singing* (1970, BN 84353); *Piano Improvisations*, i–ii (1971, ECM 1014 and 1020); *Return to Forever* (1973, ECM 1022); *Light as a Feather* (1973, Pol. 5525); *Hymn of the Seventh Galaxy* (1973, Pol. 5536); *My Spanish Heart* (1976, Pol. 2-9003); *The Mad Hatter* (1979, Pol. 1-6130); *Three Quartets* (1980, WB 3552)

As co-leader: G. Burton: *Crystal Silence* (1972, ECM 1024); H. Hancock: *An Evening with Herbie Hancock and Chick Corea* (1978, Col. PC35664-5); G. Burton: *In Concert, Zürich* (1979, ECM 1182/3)

As sideman: M. Davis: *Miles Davis at Fillmore West* (1970, CBS-Sony 39/40)

BIBLIOGRAPHY

L. Kart: "The Chick Corea File," *Down Beat*, xxxvi/7 (1969), 21

J. Toner: "Chick Corea," *Down Beat*, xli/6 (1974), 14

T. Darter: "Chick Corea: Multi-keyboard Giant," *Contemporary Keyboard*, i/1 (1975), 20

L. Underwood: "Chick Corea: Soldering the Elements, Determining the Future," *Down Beat*, xliii/17 (1976), 13

"Chick Corea," *Swing Journal*, xxxii/7 (1978), 290 [discography]

L. Underwood: "Armando in Wonderland," *Down Beat*, xlvi/5 (1979), 14

L. Feather: "Piano Giants of Jazz: Chick Corea," *Contemporary Keyboard*, vi/6 (1980), 60

BILL DOBBINS

Corigliano, John (i) (*b* New York, 28 Aug 1901; *d* Norfolk, CT, 1 Sept 1975). Violinist, father of the composer John Corigliano (ii). He studied violin with Giacomo Quintano, Alois Trnka, and Auer, made his début at Aeolian Hall, New York, in 1919, and first appeared as soloist with the New York PO in 1921. After touring as a soloist for some years, he became concertmaster of the CBS SO in 1934. He joined the New York PO in 1935 as assistant concertmaster and in 1943 became its first American-born and -trained concertmaster. In his frequent solo appearances he performed concertos by Elgar, Karol Szymanowski (no. 1), Vaughan Williams (*Concerto accademico*), and Walton, as well as the standard repertory; in 1938 he gave the American première of Delius's Violin Concerto with Barbirolli conducting. In 1956 he began giving recitals regularly with the pianist Helda Hermanns. He also was a soloist with the Cleveland Orchestra and the St. Louis SO. After his retirement in 1966 from the New York PO, he became concertmaster of the San Antonio SO, a position he held until his death. A lyrical and tasteful musician, Corigliano was at times a reticent soloist. Vittorio Giannini's Violin Concerto was dedicated to him.

MICHAEL FLEMING

Corigliano, John (Paul) (ii) (*b* New York, 16 Feb 1938). Composer, son of the violinist John Corigliano (i). He received his first formal training in music and composition at Columbia University (BA 1959), where he was a pupil of Luening; he later studied with Giannini at the Manhattan School and privately with Creston. From 1959 to 1964 he worked in New York as a music programmer, first for WQXR-FM and later for WBAI-FM; he has also been an associate producer of musical programs for CBS television (1961–72) and music director for the Morris Theatre in New Jersey (1962–4). Since 1968 he has taught composition, first at the College of Church Musicians, Washington, DC, later at the Manhattan School (from 1971) and Lehman College, CUNY (from 1974). He received a Guggenheim Fellowship in 1968 and an NEA grant in 1976.

The Violin Sonata, which won a prize at the Spoleto Festival in 1964, revealed a generally conservative tendency that Corigliano has since followed, and which is particularly evident in the four concertos (1968–81) and the *Dylan Thomas Trilogy* (1961–

76). The Clarinet Concerto (1977) has come to be viewed as a watershed in his career; commissioned by the New York PO and first performed by its principal clarinetist, Stanley Drucker, it was enthusiastically received, and has since been performed widely in the USA and elsewhere. During the late 1960s and early 1970s Corigliano briefly experimented with nontraditional performing forces, arranging rock music for Kama Sutra and Mercury records, using a synthesizer to make commercials, and composing *The Naked Carmen* (1970), an "electric rock opera" after Bizet. He has since written other dramatic music, including the film score to Ken Russell's *Altered States* for which he won an Academy Award nomination in 1980, and the opera *A Figaro for Antonio* (1984–5), commissioned by the Metropolitan Opera.

Corigliano deliberately writes in an accessible style that is often lyrical, with tonal harmonies, brilliant orchestration, virtuoso instrumental writing, and some bombastic touches; serial techniques, atonality, and disjunct melodic movement are also sometimes employed for purposes of piquant contrast. A few works, including the Flute Concerto (*Pied Piper Fantasy*), are programmatic. Corigliano has suggested that, with its eclecticism, film music has changed contemporary listening habits, and his own music, which is both eclectic and popular, has a similar appeal.

WORKS

Titles of individual movts performed separately not noted unless material has been revised.

Stage: The Naked Carmen (mixed-media opera, after Bizet), 1970; A Figaro for Antonio (opera, 2, W. Hoffman), 1984–5

Orch: Elegy, 1965; Tournaments Ov., 1967; Pf Conc., 1968, arr. 2 pf; Creations: 2 Scenes from Genesis, nar, chamber orch, 1972; Gazebo Dances, band, 1973, arrs. pf 4 hands, orch; Aria, ob, str, 1975; Ob Conc., 1975, arr. ob, pf; Voyage, str, 1976, arr. fl, orch, 1983; Cl Conc., 1977; Fl Conc. (Pied Piper Fantasy), 1981; Promenade Ov., 1981; 3 Hallucinations, 1981; Echoes of Forgotten Rites, 1982

Vocal: Fern Hill (D. Thomas), SATB, orch, 1961, arr. Mez, SATB, pf; What I Expected Was (Spender), SATB, brass, perc, 1962, arr. SATB, pf; The Cloisters (W. Hoffman), 4 songs, Mez, orch, 1965, arr. Mez, pf; Poem in October (D. Thomas), T, orch, 1970, arrs. T, 8 insts, and T, pf; L'invitation au voyage (Baudelaire, trans. Wilbur), SATB, 1971; A Black November Turkey (R. Wilbur), SATB, 1972; Poem on his Birthday (D. Thomas), Bar, SATB, orch, 1976, arr. Bar, SATB, pf; Psalm viii, SATB, 1976; several other works

Other: Kaleidoscope, 2 pf, 1959; Vn Sonata, 1963; Scherzo, ob, perc, 1975; Etude Fantasy, pf, 1976; 3 film scores, incl. Altered States, 1980, arr. as orch suite, Revolution, 1985

Principal publisher: G. Schirmer

BIBLIOGRAPHY

EwenD

W. M. Hoffman: "John Corigliano on Cracking the Establishment," *Village Voice* (21 Feb 1977)

E. W. Jeter: *The Study, Analysis and Performance of Selected Original Two-piano Music of Contemporary American Composers* (diss., Columbia U., 1978) [incl. analysis of *Kaleidoscope*, pp.50–66]

D. Cariaga: "John Corigliano: Composer who Writes to Order," *Los Angeles Times* (4 Feb 1979)

A. Kozinn: "The 'Unfashionably Romantic' Music of John Corigliano," *New York Times* (7 April 1980)

B. Holland: "Highbrow Music to Hum," *New York Times Magazine* (31 Jan 1982), 24

DALE COCKRELL

Cormier, Joe [L(aurent) Joseph] (*b* Cheticamp, NS, 19 March 1927). Fiddler. He grew up in an isolated French Acadian village in a home that was the center of local musical activity. He displayed exceptional musical skill in his childhood, and performed at dances and house parties by the time he was 12. His early musical influences included the French Quebec style and repertory of such outstanding fiddlers as Placide Odo, Joseph Allard, and Joe Bouchard. Cormier also gained familiarity with Cape Breton's Scottish music, in particular the work of Winston Fitzgerald of White Point, with whom he played for five years in Sydney, Angus Allan Gillis of Margaree, and Angus Chisholm of Margaree Harbor. He learned jig tunes of Scottish, French, and Irish origin. He also received classical training from his uncle Marcellin, a violinist and teacher educated in New England, and from Marcellin's son Pat. In 1962 Cormier moved with his family to Waltham, Massachusetts. He performs frequently in local Franco-American clubs, and has appeared at the Smithsonian Institution's Festival of American Folklife (1981) and the National Folk Festival, Wolf Trap, Virginia (1980 and 1982); he made a goodwill tour of Southeast Asia for the US State Department in 1982. He received a National Heritage Fellowship from the NEA in 1984. He has recorded for Rounder and Ambience, and appeared in a documentary film, *New England Fiddles* (1984).

LINDA MORLEY

Cornell University. Private university in Ithaca, New York. It was founded in 1865 and its music department was established in 1903. The department's original chairman, Hollis Dann, was succeeded by Otto Kinkeldey (1923–7), who also served as university librarian (1930–46) and professor of musicology (1930–58); his was the first musicology chair in the USA. Under Kinkeldey the department emphasized both scholarship and performance; he was instrumental in launching Cornell's graduate programs in music, including MA and PhD programs in musicology. Cornell was the first American university to grant the PhD in musicology (in 1932 to J. Murray Barbour). Later department chairmen included Donald J. Grout (1962–70). In addition to degrees in musicology the department offers the MA in theory and the MFA and DMA in composition; in 1985 its enrollment was approximately 30 graduate students. Notable library holdings include collections of 18th- and 19th-century opera scores, autograph scores and composers' letters, and American vocal sheet music (*see also* LIBRARIES AND COLLECTIONS, §3).

BIBLIOGRAPHY

H. E. Samuel: "The First Hundred Years of Music at Cornell," *Cornell University Music Review*, viii (1965), 3

D. Seaton, ed.: "Important Library Holdings at Forty-One North American Universities," *CMc*, no.17 (1974), 16

NINA DAVIS-MILLIS

Corner, Philip (*b* New York, 10 April 1933). Composer. He studied with Mark Brunswick at the City College of New York (BA 1955) and then attended the Paris Conservatoire (1956–7), where he came under the influence of Messiaen; at Columbia University (MA 1959) he was a pupil of Luening and Cowell. He became deeply interested in Eastern music while in Korea with the US Army in 1959–60, and after returning to New York was an early member of several important experimental groups, including Fluxus, the Judson Dance Theater, and Tone Roads. In 1974 he founded Sounds Out of Silent Spaces, which was heard regularly at the Experimental Intermedia Foundation, New York. Corner has been closely associated with Son of Lion, an American gamelan ensemble; *Gamelan* (1975) was commissioned by this group. Corner has collaborated frequently with choreographers, among them Lucinda Childs and Elaine Summers, and with several theater groups in the USA and in Europe. From 1972 he has been a faculty member at Rutgers University, where he introduced a new approach to music theory instruction that embraces concepts common to diverse cultures. He has also taught in New York at the New Lincoln School and the New School for Social Research. He has received grants from the NEA and the New York State Council on the Arts, and in 1983 was awarded a residency grant for West Berlin by the Deutscher Akademischer Austauschdienst.

Corner regards influences from Asian and other non-Western cultures as an essential aspect of modernism; as a young composer he had found that the concerns of certain contemporary American composers (Cage in particular) with timbre, microtones, and individual sound characteristics were also present in Asian music. One aspect of his affinity with Eastern thought, an interest in meditation, led him to explore the extent to which musical materials can be simplified, the extreme result of which was *Elementals* (1976), while other works written during the 1970s (the *OM* series, *Metal Meditations*, *Pulse*) also reflect this inclination. An important aspect of Corner's compositional technique is the integration of methodical and improvisational procedures, as applied to traditional instruments and natural objects. His innovative graphic notation has a particularly calligraphic quality, and his scores are to be appreciated visually as much as aurally (Corner uses the Korean pseudonym Gwan Pok – "Contemplating Waterfall" – in the oriental manner as a seal that is affixed to his scores). The numerical implications of Indonesian gamelan music have inspired him to create a "gamelan" series, beginning with *Gamelan*, of works in open form designed to be realized on many different kinds of instruments, some containing theatrical and vocal elements. Although for Corner, "gamelan" signifies an open-ended approach to music making available to Western as well as Eastern ensembles and solo performers, the works in the "gamelan" series include the possibility of being performed by a true gamelan.

One of the first to assimilate the influence of Cage, and a pioneering minimalist as well, Corner has integrated chance and systematic procedures, noise with silence and expression, and repetition and improvisation into a coherent body of compositions that clearly reflects his ongoing creative encounter with Eastern musical traditions. Several of his works have been recorded.

WORKS

Orch: This Is It . . . This Time, 1959

Inst: 13 ens works, incl. Passionate Expanse of the Law, 1958, Sang-teh [Situations], 1959, Air Effect, 1961, Certain Distilling Processes, 1962, Composition With or Without Beverly, 1962, Pond, 1968, OM Emerging, 1970, Elementals, 1976; 3 duos; 8 solos, incl. Stücke, fl, 1956, Pulse, vn/any other inst, OM series, vv or insts, 1970–74; 2 works with spoken text; 2 works with elec

Pf: 7 Joyous Flashes, 1958; Ink Marks for Performance, 1961–2; Pictures of Pictures from Pictures of Pictures, 1980; The Flight of the System, 1981; several other works, incl. 4-hand compositions

"Gamelan" (instrumentation given denotes that used in a particular performance, but in general the works are open scores): Gamelan, 1975; Gamelan II, 1975; Gamelan IX, 1975; The Barcelona Cathedral, 1978; Gamelan P. C., 1979; Gamelan LY (Lyra), gamelan ens, erhu, cl, 1979; Gamelan IRIS, gamelan ens, fl, 1980; Gamelan CONCERT! O, gamelan ens, hpd, elec gui, 1980; Gamelan CORN, vn, 1982; Gamelan ANTIPODE, vn, 1984; many other works

Theater music: 2nd Finale, 1961; Carrot Chew Performance, 1963; Solo With, 1965; Rationalize Outside Sounds, 1966; Pf Work, 1970; Metal Meditations, 1973; Democracy in Action, 1979; several other works

Other: Flares, mixed media, 1963; 4 elec works, 1962–79

Principal publishers: CFE, Peters

BIBLIOGRAPHY

H. Sohm, ed.: *Happenings and Fluxus* (Cologne, 1970)
T. Johnson: "New Music," *HiFi/MusAm*, xxv/1 (1975), 8
P. Corner: "Sang-teh (Situations)," *Painted Bride Quarterly*, iii/2 (1976), 18
W. Zimmermann: *Desert Plants: Conversations with 23 American Musicians* (Vancouver, 1976), 69
T. Johnson: "The Changing of the Avant Garde," *Boston Phoenix* (31 May 1977)
P. Job: "Les musiciens de métal," *Libération* (16 June 1978)
H. Ruhé: *Fluxus, the Most Radical and Experimental Art Movement of the Sixties* (Amsterdam, 1979)

MARGARET LENG TAN

Corri, P(hilip) Antony. *See* CLIFTON, ARTHUR.

Corrido (Sp.: "romance"). The principal ballad form of Mexican music; *see* HISPANIC-AMERICAN MUSIC, §2 (i).

Corsaro, Frank (Andrew) (*b* New York, 22 Dec 1924). Opera director. He was trained at the City College of New York, the Yale University School of Drama, and the Actors Studio, and worked for several years as a theater director in New York. He made his operatic début in 1958 at the New York City Opera with Carlisle Floyd's *Susannah*. This is a naturalistic work and it set the tone for many of Corsaro's subsequent productions with the same company, which included Verdi's *Rigoletto* and *La traviata*, Borodin's *Prince Igor*, Puccini's *Madama Butterfly*, and Gounod's *Faust*. His bold and innovative stagings of these works provoked considerable controversy for their departure from the traditional norms, and he has made novel use of projections and film clips in his productions of such 20th-century operas as Janáček's *The Makropulos Affair* and Delius's *A Village Romeo and Juliet*. Corsaro's world premières include Floyd's *Of Mice and Men* (1970) at the Seattle Opera, Hoiby's *Summer and Smoke* (1971) at the St. Paul Opera, and Pasatieri's *The Seagull* (1974) at the Houston Grand Opera, where he became associate artistic director in 1977. Another Houston première was the first professional production of Scott Joplin's *Treemonisha* (1975). Corsaro has close ties with the Glyndebourne Festival in England, where he joined with designer Maurice Sendak in a production of Prokofiev's *The Love for Three Oranges*; Sendak also worked with him on Janáček's *The Cunning Little Vixen*, at the New York City Opera in 1981. In January 1984 Corsaro made his début at the Metropolitan Opera with *Rinaldo*, the first of Handel's operas to be performed there. He has taught an acting class for singers in New York since 1969.

BIBLIOGRAPHY

D. Henahan: "When the Stage Director takes on the Opera," *New York Times Magazine* (12 Nov 1972), 44
D. Seabury: "In a Class with Corsaro," *Opera News*, xxxix/17 (1975), 26
"Corsaro, Frank (Andrew)," *CBY 1975*
F. Corsaro: *Maverick: a Director's Personal Experience in Opera and Theater* (New York, 1978)

FRANK MERKLING

Cortés, Ramiro, Jr. (*b* Dallas, TX, 25 Nov 1938; *d* Salt Lake City, UT, 2 July 1984). Composer of Mexican parentage. He studied with Halsey Stevens and Ingolf Dahl at the University of Southern California (BM 1955) and with Vittorio Giannini at the Juilliard School (MM 1962); he was also a pupil of Cowell (Charles Ives Scholarship, summer 1952), Donovan (at Yale University, 1953–4), Goffredo Petrassi (in Rome, 1956–8), and Sessions (at Princeton University, 1958). As a student he received several prizes for composition and a Fulbright-Hays Rome fellowship. After working in 1963–6 as a computer programmer, he taught at UCLA (1966–7) and at the University of Southern California (1967–72); in Los Angeles he was active as a pianist and as a conductor of new music. In 1972–3 he served as composer-in-residence at the University of Utah, and the following year he joined the faculty there, becoming chairman of the theory and composition department. Cortés's works, many of which were written on commission, have been performed by the New York PO, the Pittsburgh SO, the Los Angeles PO, and the Utah SO, among others. Until the late 1960s his music was serially organized, under the influence of late Stravinsky and Dallapiccola; thereafter it became more freely structured while remaining fully chromatic.

WORKS

Dramatic: The Christmas Garden (children's opera, S. Brakhage), 1955; Prometheus (opera, after Aeschylus), 1960; The Patriots (musical, after S. Kingsley), 1975–6, rev. 1978; The Eternal Return (opera, Cortés), 1981; dance scores, incidental music, film score, inc. works

Orch: Night Music, chamber orch, 1954; Sinfonia sacra, 1954, rev. 1959; Chamber Conc., vc, 12 wind, 1957–8, rev. 1978; Meditation, str orch, 1961; The Eternal Return, 1963, rev. 1966; Conc., vn, str, 1964–5, rev. 1983; Conc., hpd, str orch, 1970–71; Movts in Variation, 1972; Pf Conc., 1975; Sym. Celebration, 1979; Contrasts, sym. band, 1979–80; Music for Str, 1983; *c*5 other orch works

Chamber: Elegy, fl, pf, 1952; Divertimento, fl, cl, bn, 1953; Pf Qnt, 1953; Pf Sonata no.1, 1954; Pf Trio, 1959, rev. 1965; Str Qt no.1, 1962; The Brass Ring, 2 tpt, 3 trbn, 1967; Duo, fl, ob, 1967; Wind Qnt, 1967–8; Homage to Jackson Pollock, va, 1968; 3 Movts for 5 Winds, 1968; Partita, vn, 1970–71; Capriccio, ww qt, 1971; Vn Sonata, 1971–2; Vc Sonata, 1976–7; Charenton Variations, 11 insts, 1978; Little Suite, 8 insts, 1978; Tpt Sonata, 1978; Pf Sonata no.3, 1979; Suite, vn, pf, 1980; Trio, cl, vc, pf, 1981; Bridges, wind ens, 1982; Str Qt no.2, 1983; several other pf pieces, a few more chamber works

Vocal: Missa brevis, female vv, pf, 1954; America (Melville), cycle of 4 songs, S, str orch, 1958; Ode to a Nightingale (Keats), 1v, pf, 1970–71; Rêve parisien (Baudelaire), S, str qt, 1971–2; De profundis (Eng. poets), song cycle, 1v, pf, 1977; To the Sacred Moon (Theocritus), concert aria, S, pf, 1980; many other songs and choruses

Principal publishers: Boosey & Hawkes, Chappell, Elkan-Vogel, Peer, Peters, Presser, Wimbledon

Coryell, Larry (*b* Galveston, TX, 2 April 1943). Jazz-rock guitarist and bandleader. He worked with the drummer Chico Hamilton's group in 1965, then with an early jazz-rock band called Free Spirits. He received his widest exposure while playing with Gary Burton's quartet (1967–8), which was one of the first bands to combine jazz with country music. From 1969 to 1973 Coryell performed in a group called Foreplay with the saxophonist Steve Marcus and the pianist Mike Mandel, and in 1973 formed the Eleventh House with Marcus, Mandel, the drummer Alphonse Mouzon, the bass guitarist Danny Trifan, and the trumpeter Randy Brecker. He has worked sporadically with the double bass player Miroslav Vitous and the guitarist John McLaughlin, most notably recording a series of outstanding unamplified guitar duets with the latter, including *Rene's Theme* on Coryell's album *Spaces*. Coryell has excellent technique and is versatile and imaginative; though he cannot be identified consistently with a particular style, he is one of the most original improvisers on his instrument to have emerged during the 1960s and 1970s. A collection of his own transcriptions of his playing were published as *Improvisations from Rock to Jazz* (n.d.).

RECORDINGS
(selective list)

As leader: *Lady Coryell* (1968, Van. 6509); *Spaces* (1970, Van. 6558); *Fairyland* (1971, Flying Dutchman 515000); *Barefoot Boy* (1971, Flying Dutchman 10139); *The Eleventh House with Larry Coryell* (1974, Van. 79342); *Tributaries* (1979, Arista Novus 3017)

As sideman: *Free Spirits* (1966, ABC 593); C. Hamilton: *The Dealer* (1966, Im[illegible] 9130); G. Burton: *Duster* (1967, RCA LSP3835)

BIBLIOGRAPHY

N. Tesser: "Larry Coryell – Leveling Off," *Down Beat*, xliii/4 (1976), 12
M. Brooks: "The Eleventh House," *The Guitar Player Book* (New York, 1978 72
M. Gridley: *Jazz Styles: History and Analysis* (Englewood Cliffs, NJ, 1978, re[illegible] 2/1985)
"Larry Coryell," *Swing Journal*, xxxiv/3 (1980), 172 [discography]
D. Pritchard: *Larry Coryell: Jazz Guitar Solos* (Hialeah, FL, 1980) [20 transcrs

MARK C. GRIDLE[illegible]

Cos Cob Press. Music publishing firm. It was founded in 192[illegible] by Alma M. Wertheim as a nonprofit-making organization fo[illegible] aiding and disseminating the music of American composers. It[illegible] catalogue included works by Citkowitz, Copland, Gruenber[illegible] (including his opera *The Emperor Jones*), Harris, Piston, Sessions[illegible] Thomson, Wagenaar, and Whithorne. In 1938 the catalogu[illegible] was leased to the newly founded Arrow Music Press, which i[illegible] turn was acquired by Boosey & Hawkes in 1956.

BIBLIOGRAPHY

"Cos Cob Press is Launched," *MusAm*, xlix/7 (1929), 53

W. THOMAS MARROCCO, MARK JACOBS/[illegible]

Costello, Marilyn (*b* Cleveland, OH, 1924). Harpist. She attende[illegible] the Curtis Institute (diploma 1949), where she studied wit[illegible] Salzedo. While still a student at Curtis she joined the Philadel[illegible]phia Orchestra (1945) and became principal harpist in 1946. A[illegible] a soloist she has appeared with the Philadelphia Orchestra an[illegible] other major orchestras. She is also active as a recitalist, chamber music performer, and recording artist in the USA and Europe[illegible] In Switzerland, she has been a soloist at the Menuhin and Mon[illegible]treux festivals and given recitals for Radio Zurich and Radi[illegible] Suisse Romande; in the USA, she has performed at the Vermon[illegible] Mozart and the Minnesota Orchestra Mozart festivals. Costell[illegible] is noted for a brilliant technique, clear sound projection, an[illegible] vigorous and colorful interpretations; she received the Phono[illegible]graphic Critics' Award of Italy in 1965 and the Philadelphi[illegible] Orchestra's C. Hartmann Kuhn Award in 1973. She is head [illegible] the harp department at the Curtis Institute.

MARTHA WOODWAR[illegible]

Cotillion. Social dance of 18th-century French origin (*cotillon*[illegible] which became popular in the USA in the 1790s at the time [illegible] the large French immigration to this country following the Frenc[illegible] and Haitian revolutions. The anglicized name of the dance[illegible] "cotillion," appeared in American references to the danc[illegible] throughout the 19th century. (*See also* DANCE, §§I; II, 1.) Ini[illegible]tially, the American cotillion was danced in squares of four cou[illegible]ples and, like the quadrille and country dances, it involved geometri[illegible] patterns and figures. The dance consisted of two parts, whic[illegible] alternated in the manner of verse and chorus: the "change" (whic[illegible] was the same for all cotillions) and the "figure" (which was uniqu[illegible] to the particular cotillion). Each cotillion consisted of ten change[illegible] and one figure, and the entire dance could be repeated from seve[illegible] to 14 times.

Music for the cotillion was generally arranged from existin[illegible] tunes in 2/4 or 6/8, consisting of two to four strains, each eigh[illegible] bars in length and repeated. The basic walking step of the danc[illegible] was often elaborated in the late 18th and early 19th centuries t[illegible] display a dancer's skill and agility. The tempo for the cotillio[illegible] was about 120, like that of the quadrille, and in fact the tern[illegible] "cotillion" was often used to refer to the quadrille in the middle of the century. Jigs and reels (e.g., *York Fusilears* and the *Marlbrouk* song) were used in the 18th and early 19th centuries; beginning in the 1820s, opera tunes like those from Daniel Auber's *Fra Diavolo* and Vincenzo Bellini's *La sonnambula* were popular choices. Marching tunes like the *Steamboat Quickstep* were often used in the middle of the century. The "game" or "favor" cotillion, often called the "German," was introduced around this time as well. Lasting an hour or an hour and a half, it consisted of dances, games, and tricks, with the nature and order of figures determined by the caller.

BIBLIOGRAPHY

A Collection of the Newest Cotillions and Country Dances (Worcester, MA, 1800)
A Selection of Cotillons & Country-Dances (Boston, 1808)
V. Masi: *The Cotillion Party's Assistant and Ladies Musical Companion* (Boston, 1818)
The Ball-room Manual of Contra Dances and Social Cotillions, with Remarks on Quadrilles and Spanish Dance (Belfast, ME, and Boston, 1863)
H. Thurston: "The French Country-dance, the Quadrille, and the Cotillion," *English Dance and Song*, xxxiv (1972), 89
J. E. Morrison: *Twenty-Four Early American Country Dances, Cotillions & Reels for the Year 1976* (New York, 1976)
For further bibliography, *see* DANCE.

PAULINE NORTON

Cotten, Elizabeth (*b* nr Chapel Hill, NC, 1893). Guitarist and folksinger. As a child she taught herself banjo and guitar, which, since she was left-handed, she played upside down. When she was 12 she wrote her best-known song, *Freight Train*, which has often been mistakenly attributed to others. By the time she was 14 she had a large repertory of rags and dance tunes, some of which she had written herself. After undergoing a religious conversion during her teens she suspended her musical activities for nearly 50 years; she resumed them while working as a housekeeper for the Seeger family. At age 90 she made a national tour; she received a National Heritage Fellowship from the NEA in 1984. Cotten plays in a lyrical, syncopated style that evokes both blues and salon music.

Cotton, Ben (*b* Pawtucket, RI, 27 July 1829; *d* New York, 14 Feb 1908). Minstrel performer. He ran away from home to join a circus in 1845, and first gained prominence with Matt Peel's Minstrels in the mid-1850s, when he was a great success in the blackface role of "Old Bob Ridley," performing the song of the same name. He also played on the steamer *Banjo* on the Mississippi, which allowed him to observe southern Blacks at first hand, and he became particularly noted for his impersonations of black characters, especially old men. He achieved great fame as a minstrel performer in the 1860s and 1870s, sometimes in companies bearing his own name, and worked primarily in New York, San Francisco, and Chicago. Toward the end of his career, he played character parts in popular plays, including *Faithful Bob* (later known as *True Devotion*), which he produced with his wife and daughter.

BIBLIOGRAPHY

"Interview with Ben Cotton," *New York Mirror* (3 July 1897)
E. L. Rice: *Monarchs of Minstrelsy* (New York, 1911)

ROBERT B. WINANS

Country dance. A lively (but not rustic or rural) dance of 17th-century English origin known in France as the "contredanse," by which name it soon came to be called in England as well. In the USA, "contre" became "contra," and the name "contradanse" has been used interchangeably with "country dance" to the present day. It can be performed in a circle or square, but the form used almost exclusively in this country has been longways, with two lines of dancers facing each other. Like the cotillion and quadrille, the country dance is executed geometrically, and the progressive movements down the columns of dancers import a smoothness and precision that is satisfying both to the dancer and to the observer (*see also* DANCE, §I).

The music for country dances has generally been arranged from existing tunes, such as jigs (in 6/8) and reels (in 2/4), and performed on the fiddle and/or transverse flute. Some tunes have become associated with particular figurations, so that today country dances like *Money Musk* and *Pop Goes the Weasel* refer to both the tune and the dance pattern itself. The tunes generally consist of two strains, each eight bars in length and repeated (*AABB*). The tempo is about 120, and the beat and step have a springing, or in the case of jig tunes, a skipping quality.

In recent years, the revival of country dances in New England and the efforts of organizations like the Country Dance and Song Society have stimulated interest in this form of dance throughout the country. In its revived form, however, it is a rustic dance, with musical accompaniment provided by such instruments as the piano, fiddle, banjo, guitar, mandolin, bone castanets, hammered dulcimer, tin whistle, melodeon, flute, string bass, clarinet, *bohdrán* (Irish frame drum), and euphonium. Commonly performed country dances and dance tunes included *Hull's Victory*, *Soldier's Joy*, *College Hornpipe*, *White Cockade*, *Fisher's Hornpipe*, and *Rory O'More*.

BIBLIOGRAPHY

Cantelo: *Twenty-four American Country Dances as Danced by the British during their Winter Quarters at Philadelphia, New York & Charles Town* (London, England, 1785)
A Collection of Contra Dances: Containing the Newest, Most Approved and Fashionable Figures (Stockbridge, MA, 1792)
R. Holden: *The Contra Dance Book* (Newark, 1956)
K. Van W. Keller and R. Sweet: *A Choice Selection of American Country Dances of the Revolutionary Era 1775–1795* (New York, 1976)
J. E. Morrison: *Twenty-Four Early American Country Dances, Cotillions & Reels for the Year 1976* (New York, 1976)
V. J. Tufo: *Contra-dancing in Maine: the Revival of an American Tradition* (thesis, U. of Michigan, 1979)
For further bibliography, *see* COTILLION; DANCE.

PAULINE NORTON

Country Gentlemen. Bluegrass group. It was organized in July 1957 in the Washington, DC, area by the banjoist Bill Emerson, who initially recruited the guitarist and lead singer Charlie Waller and the mandolin player John Duffey. Jim Cox joined as banjoist and double bass player in 1958, and banjoist Eddie Adcock, who had played with Mac Wiseman, in 1960. There have been numerous changes in the group's personnel, which has included such bluegrass luminaries as the mandolin player Doyle Lawson, the fiddler and guitarist Ricky Skaggs, and the dobro player Mike Auldridge. Several of the members later formed SELDOM SCENE. The original Country Gentlemen were distinguished by vocal combinations and timbres that are unusual in bluegrass music: Duffey's loud, rich, full tenor, Adcock's breathy baritone, and Waller's deep tenor. Duffey and Adcock also contributed extremely showy mandolin technique. The most distinctive feature of the Country Gentlemen is their eclectic choice of repertory, which has drawn not only from traditional bluegrass sources (Flatt and Scruggs, the Stanley Brothers), but also from popular, folk, and rock performers (Harry Belafonte, the Kingston Trio, Simon and Garfunkel, Bob Dylan, Lefty Frizzell, Glen Campbell, Kris Kristofferson, James Taylor, Gordon Lightfoot). Although in the early 1970s the group added the dobro to its traditional string instruments, it performs even its nonbluegrass repertory in a definitively bluegrass style. It has made frequent appearances at bluegrass festivals, successfully toured Japan in 1972, and has recorded more than 300 titles for such labels as Folkways, Rebel, and Vanguard. With the return of Emerson in 1970, the group moved into the vanguard of progressive bluegrass. The Country Gentlemen were the most influential bluegrass group of the 1960s and 1970s, both in attracting new listeners to the genre and inspiring other performers.

BIBLIOGRAPHY

D. Tuchman: "The Country Gentlemen," *Pickin'*, i/2 (1974), 4

B. Artis: *Bluegrass* (New York, 1975)

B. Evans: "Good Music, Good Friends: the Country Gentlemen," *Bluegrass Unlimited*, xii/12 (1978), 18

D. Freeman: Liner notes, *Country Gentlemen: Twenty-fifth Anniversary* (Rebel 2201, 1982)

RONNIE PUGH

Country Joe and the Fish. Rock group. Its members were Joe (Joseph) McDonald (*b* El Monte, CA, 1 Jan 1942), lead singer and guitarist; "Chicken" Hirsch (*b* CA, 1940), drummer; Bruce Barthol (*b* Berkeley, CA, 1947), bass guitarist; Barry Melton (*b* Brooklyn, NY, 1947), guitarist; and David Cohen (*b* Brooklyn, 1942), guitarist and keyboard player. McDonald and Melton, who had been folk musicians in the early 1960s, formed the group in Berkeley in 1965. They began as a jug band performing protest songs and evolved into a group with conventional rock instrumentation in 1966. Although they made a number of artistically and commercially successful albums over the next few years, their most distinctive songs, including "Bass Strings" and "Section 43," are contained on the EP *Country Joe and the Fish* (1966); their most powerful piece, the instrumental "Untitled Protest," was never properly recorded. Always left-wing, as time went on Country Joe and the Fish became important representatives of the counterculture. The group disbanded in 1970 and McDonald embarked on a solo career, recording a number of albums in a folk style; they reunited briefly in 1977.

RECORDINGS

(selective list)

Country Joe and the Fish (EP, Rag Baby 1001, 1966); *Electric Music for the Mind and Body* (Van. 79244, 1967); *I-Feel-Like-I'm-Fixin'-to-Die* (Van. 79266, 1967); *Together* (Van. 79277, 1968); *Reunion* (Fan. 9530, 1977)

BIBLIOGRAPHY

S. Darlington: "Daredevil Meets Easter Bunny"; "The Story of a Band: Country Joe and the Fish," *Rock and Roll will Stand*, ed. G. Marcus (Boston, 1969), 87, 150

Country music. A popular music style. It is a commercial extension of the folk music of the rural South and was at first known as HILLBILLY MUSIC. It originated from the folk music brought by British settlers into the southern back-country, and evolved through contact with Afro-American, Cajun, Latin American, and other ethnic music, as well as with urban commercial music. At first it included the fiddle (the most popular instrument on the frontier), the five-string banjo (most common in the mountains of the Southeast), and the guitar. After 1900 other instruments such as the mandolin, string bass, and Hawaiian steel guitar appeared in country string bands. In the 1930s, led principally by WESTERN SWING bands, country groups began to add drums, pianos, and electric instruments. By the 1970s the electric guitar was widely used, and the traditional acoustic instruments were generally heard only in bluegrass bands (*see* BLUEGRASS MUSIC).

Until the 1920s, country music was performed largely at home, in church, or at such local functions as pie suppers, house parties, and county fairs. Rural entertainers, however, were never immune from the lure of commercialism; particularly talented fiddlers, balladeers, and string bands were often remunerated, and they sometimes attained a semblance of professionalism with performances in medicine shows, fiddle contests, itinerant tent shows, and vaudeville.

Country music began evolving towards an industry in 1920–25, when it was discovered and commercially exploited through show business. Country musicians found important new media through which to demonstrate and advertise their talents when radio stations, for example in Atlanta (WSB, 1922), Fort Worth (WBAP, 1922) and Nashville (WSM, 1925), began operating. By 1925 barn dance programs had become an institution on American radio (*see* BARN DANCE); the most famous of these, the "WSM Barn Dance," became the "Grand Ole Opry." After 1922 the recording industry began to cultivate the southern rural market. Although he was not the first country performer to record, "Fiddlin'" John Carson made a recording (1923) that sold so well that other companies were encouraged to seek similar talent. Thus began the development of the hillbilly recording industry, which had its first substantial success with Vernon Dalhart's recording of *The Prisoner's Song* (1924). In 1927 a former railway worker from Mississippi, Jimmie Rodgers, and a Virginia family trio, the Carter Family, made their first recordings, inaugurating two of the most important careers and styles in country-music history. In the mid-1930s the singing cowboys of the films became folk heroes and gave country music a glamorous, national forum (*see* COWBOY SONG).

Thereafter, country music gradually moved away from its southern rural identification to become both an industry and an eclectic genre with international appeal. Despite the Depression the music not only survived but, through radio, sustained and comforted rural people during hard times. World War II was the catalyst that converted country music from a regional phenomenon to a national one; the war economy prompted population shifts that brought people of diverse backgrounds into closer contact. Musical forms became more closely amalgamated. Meanwhile, southern servicemen carried their taste for country music all over the world. Such singers as Roy Acuff and Ernest Tubb were as popular among military personnel as Frank Sinatra and Bing Crosby. By 1950, when Hank Williams reached the peak of his career, country music had become established in American entertainment; the "Grand Ole Opry" was the most significant country radio show and Nashville the acknowledged center of the country-music industry. The quest for respectability and national acceptance within the industry was reflected in the replacement of the word "hillbilly" by "country" or "country-western" (a term representing the fusion of southeastern and southwestern styles).

Country music was even more popular during the 1960s and 1970s. Newer centers such as Bakersfield, California, and Aus-

"The Sources of Country Music," including players of the Appalachian dulcimer, fiddle, banjo, and guitar: mural (completed 1975) by Thomas Hart Benton (Country Music Hall of Fame and Museum, Nashville)

tin, Texas, challenged Nashville's preeminence, though the term NASHVILLE SOUND became virtually synonymous with country music. The "Grand Ole Opry," while remaining popular, declined in importance; such performers as Merle Haggard, Buck Owens, Charley Pride, Johnny Cash, and Willie Nelson no longer relied on an affiliation with it.

From the 1970s, country music reflected the growing homogenization of American life, as well as the ambivalence in an increasingly urban population often only one generation removed from a rural past. The music still shows its folk origins while persistently absorbing elements from a broader popular culture. Leaders of the country-music industry have striven to make the music acceptable to a national urban audience while preserving some image of small-town informality. Country music undoubtedly has a much wider range than during its early hillbilly years. It once conveyed an image of white, Anglo-Saxon, male Protestantism, but from the late 1960s it has had eminent black (Charley Pride), Chicano (Johnny Rodriguez), and female (Loretta Lynn, Dolly Parton) performers. Through its flirtation with rock, country music has become more attractive to young audiences (e.g., in the music of Kris Kristofferson, Willie Nelson, and Waylon Jennings). Efforts to fuse rock and country music (at Austin) led to a style known as PROGRESSIVE COUNTRY MUSIC; the Public Broadcasting Service television show "Austin City Limits," which began in the mid-1970s, has been influential in the dissemination of this style.

Despite the blending of styles and the international popularity of country music, the force of tradition persists. Most country singers still treat such themes as mother and home, the rambling man, prison, hard work, disappointed love, and traditional religion. Many singers (Johnny Cash, Merle Haggard, and Loretta Lynn) demonstrate respect for their own and the music's rural origins; older ones (Grandpa Jones, Roy Acuff) perform in styles that predate the Nashville sound; and bluegrass performers, though they have broadened their repertory to absorb rock and popular songs, remain loyal to the traditional acoustic instruments.

See also POPULAR MUSIC, §§III, 3, and IV, 6.

BIBLIOGRAPHY

L. Gentry, ed.: *A History and Encyclopedia of Country, Western, and Gospel Music* (Nashville, 1961, rev. 2/1969)

A. Green: "Hillbilly Music: Source and Symbol," *Journal of American Folklore*, lxxviii (1965), 204

R. Shelton and B. Goldblatt: *The Country Music Story: a Picture History of Country and Western Music* (Indianapolis, 1966, 2/1971)

B. C. Malone: *Country Music U.S.A.: a Fifty-year History* (Austin, 1968, 2/1985)

P. Hemphill: *The Nashville Sound: Bright Lights and Country Music* (New York, 1970)

C. Hagan: *Country Music Legends in the Hall of Fame* (Nashville, 1972)

D. Horstman: *Sing your Heart out, Country Boy* (New York, 1975)

B. C. Malone and J. McCulloh, eds.: *Stars of Country Music* (Urbana, IL, 1975)

D. B. Green: *Country Roots: the Origins of Country Music* (New York, 1976)

N. Tosches: *Country Music: the Biggest Music in America* (New York, 1977, rev. 2/1985)

C. K. Wolfe: *Tennessee Strings* (Knoxville, TN, 1977)

M. Bane: *The Outlaws: Revolution in Country Music* (New York, 1978)

C. F. Gritzner: "Country Music: a Reflection of Popular Culture," *Journal of Popular Culture*, xi (1978), 857

P. Carr, ed.: *The Illustrated History of Country Music* (Garden City, NY, 1979)

B. C. Malone: *Southern Music, American Music* (Lexington, KY, 1979)

P. Carr: "Vassar Clements: a Gentle Man with Music in his Soul," *Country Music*, ix/2 (1980), 10

C. K. Wolfe: *Kentucky Country* (Lexington, KY, 1982)

J. N. Rogers: *The Country Music Message* (Englewood Cliffs, NJ, 1983)

I. Tribe: *Mountaineer Jamboree: Country Music in West Virginia* (Lexington, KY, 1984)

BILL C. MALONE/R

Country Music Association (CMA). Organization founded in 1958 as an outgrowth of the Country Music Disc Jockeys' Association established four years earlier. The CMA was the first trade organization formed to promote a particular genre of music. As such, its initial goal was to increase radio and television airplay and advertising for country music, and it was greatly responsible for the commercial success of this kind of music in the 1960s and 1970s. In addition to congressional lobbying and the dissemination of information relating to the industry, the CMA has sponsored or supported Country Music Month, a nationally recognized annual celebration in November promoting country music; the prestigious Country Music Association Awards (founded 1967), to top country performers; the DJ Awards, to prominent disc jockeys in various markets; the Country Music Hall of Fame (established in 1961), which honors the greatest names in the industry; *CMA Close-up* (1959–), a monthly publication; the annual International Country Music Fan Fair (initiated in 1972), co-sponsored by the "Grand Ole Opry"; and country-music films (e.g., *Country Music on Broadway*, 1963, and *Your Cheatin' Heart*, 1964). The Country Music Hall of Fame Museum was opened in 1967 and is administered by the Country Music Foundation. It is generally acknowledged that the CMA tends to favor the music and musicians of Nashville, where it is located. A branch office has been opened in London, England.

BIBLIOGRAPHY

Behind the Record of the Country Music Association (Nashville, n.d.)

H. Stone: "The Country Music Association," *The Country Music Who's Who* (Denver, 1960), 79

"CMA – a Success Story," *The 1970 Country Music Who's Who* (New York, 1970), pt vi, p. 18

RITA H. MEAD

Country Music Foundation. Educational organization founded in Nashville in 1964 and administered by a staff of scholars, educators, curators, and librarians. The foundation oversees the Country Music Hall of Fame and Museum (founded in 1961; museum building opened in 1967) and the Country Music Foundation Library and Media Center (*see* LIBRARIES AND COLLECTIONS, §3). It is governed by a board of trustees made up of the most distinguished leaders of the country-music industry. Although the museum and library are the most visible of its activities, the foundation fosters an interest in the history of country music through a number of educational and scholarly projects. The Hall of Fame and Museum education department organizes lectures and demonstrations in Tennessee schools, and the Country Music Foundation Press publishes reprints and new works on country music to ensure the widest availability of historical works in the field. The foundation's *Journal of Country Music* (1970–), which contains scholarly articles written by specialists in many academic disciplines, is the primary vehicle through which the organization facilitates communication between the industry and those who study country music. In a broader sense, the organization speaks for the legitimacy and importance of all forms of American folk and popular music. As the largest research organization in the world devoted to a single genre of popular music, the foundation continues to argue in every forum for the equality of all artistic endeavors in commercial, popular, and folk music.

BIBLIOGRAPHY

D. Deen: "Country Music Hall of Fame Opens," *Music City News*, iv/10 (1967), 4

RITA H. MEAD

Country-rock. A style of popular music in which the sound and subject matter of country music are combined with a rock beat and instrumentation. It was foreshadowed in the 1950s and 1960s by singers such as the Everly Brothers, Roy Orbison (*Only the Lonely*, 1960), and Bobbie Gentry (*Ode to Billy Joe*, 1967). In the late 1960s a number of folk-rock performers, notably Bob Dylan (*John Wesley Harding*, 1968) and Joan Baez (*One Day at a Time*, 1970), began to turn away from the protest songs of the urban folk music revival and incorporate references to the traditional concerns of country music (the simple life, the warm South, nostalgia for the rural past, etc.) in their lyrics. Such themes and the country-style melodies to which they were set were developed in different ways by the Eagles, The Band, the Byrds, Crosby, Stills and Nash, Gram Parsons (at first with the Byrds, then with the Flying Burrito Brothers, then as a soloist), and Linda Ronstadt. Later performers whose work includes songs in the country-rock style are Dolly Parton, Kenny Rogers, Waylon Jennings, and Loretta Lynn.

Courboin, Charles M. (*b* Antwerp, Belgium, 2 April 1884; *d* New York, 13 April 1973). Organist. He was trained at the Brussels Conservatory and was an organ pupil of Alphonse Mailly. After coming to the USA in 1904, he held organ posts in Oswego and Syracuse, New York, and in Springfield, Massachusetts. He became increasingly associated with Alexander Russell in musical direction at the Wanamaker department stores in New York and Philadelphia (each of which housed a large pipe organ), and during the 1920s organized musical programs for Wanamaker that presented to the American public many European artists, including Stokowski and Marcel Dupré. In 1942, during the wartime absence of Virgil Fox, Courboin was appointed head of the organ department of Peabody Conservatory and the following year he became organist and music director at St. Patrick's Cathedral in New York, where he served until 1970. Through his activities as a church organist and concert organizer, as well as through his recitals and recordings (many of them for RCA Victor), teaching, and expertise in organ design, Courboin exercised a long and beneficial influence on American organs and organ playing.

VERNON GOTWALS

Courting flute. Duct flute of the American Indians. It was traditionally made of wood or cane, with an external duct. It was used by young men for serenading and had a fairly wide distribution, but it was most highly concentrated through the central USA in the Plains–Plateau–Southwest area. Tribes known to have used the courting flute include the Iroquois, Winnebago, Sioux, Omaha, Crow, Nez Percé, Northern Ute, Apache, and Seminole.

The method of construction was such that no two instruments were identical. Plains flutes were commonly made of red cedar, although other straight-grained woods were also used in the Plains–Plateau area; cane flutes were made in the Southwest. More recently, flutes have been made from metal gun barrels and nickel tubing. The instruments were generally about 4 cm in diameter and 50 to 54 cm long. A typical Plains flute was made from a straight section of wood split lengthwise and hollowed out to form a cylindrical bore. A block was left inside, creating a partition between the upper and lower chambers. The upper chamber was proportionally shorter (1 : 4) than the body of the instrument. On the front surface a small hole was cut in each chamber just above and below the partition. The surface around the hole was made flat and smooth and a thin wooden or metal plate was laid over it. A rectangular hole in the plate

1. *Courting flute of the Apache Indians with rawhide thongs (Museum of the American Indian, New York)*

fitted exactly over the two holes in the cylinder. A wooden block or saddle, flat on the underside and carved on top, was tied over the plate. Air blown into the end of the upper chamber flattens into a thin stream as it passes out of the upper hole and between the partition and the block. At the entrance to the lower chamber, the airstream impinges on the sharp edge or lip of the plate and makes the column of air within the flute vibrate. The flute could have two to eight finger-holes, but six holes in two groups of three was the most common arrangement. The instrument was often bound in several places with colored cord or leather thongs, which were not merely decorative but served to hold the two halves together.

Although occasional reference is made to the use of the flute in ceremonies and as a warning or war signal, its most common use was as a man's solo courting instrument. Because of its personal nature, the flute was usually made by the man who intended to play it and it was rarely lent or borrowed. Melodies for the flute were also individual creations and personally owned. The flute and its music often had supernatural associations.

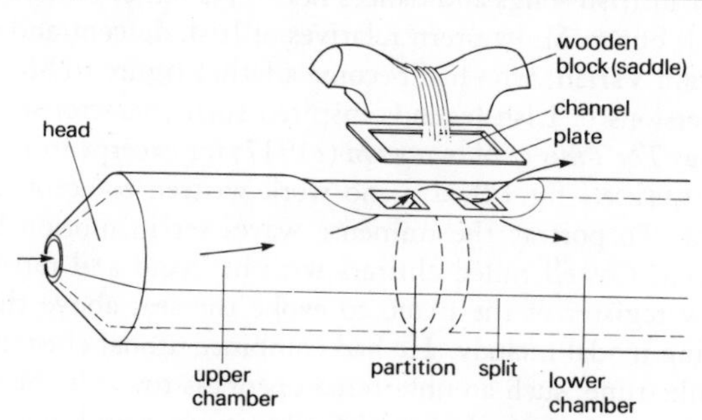

2. *Diagram of the windway of the courting flute*

Flute melodies, though individual, nevertheless have stylistic features in common. Most characteristic is their "spacious" and rhapsodic quality, which is often created by free and unmetered rhythm, and by leaps of octaves, 4ths, and 5ths within the melodic line; trills, grace notes, and downward glissandos; and rising releases at phrase endings. Long-held, pulsating notes – a vibrato-like effect that is created by acoustical beats on the fundamental note of the instrument – often act as an introduction and ending and may also clearly demarcate sections within the piece.

BIBLIOGRAPHY

F. Densmore: *Teton Sioux Music* (Washington, DC, 1918)
D. C. Miller: "Flutes of the American Indian," *The Flutist*, ii (1921), 509
L. E. Gilliam and W. Lichtenwanger: *The Dayton C. Miller Flute Collection* (Washington, DC, 1961)
A. P. Merriam: *Ethnomusicology of the Flathead Indians* (Chicago, 1967)
M. F. Riemer: *Instrumental and Vocal Love Songs of the North American Indians* (thesis, Wesleyan U., Middletown, CT, 1978)
A. L. Olsen: "The Nez Perce Flute," *Northwest Anthropological Research Notes*, xiii (1979), 36
D. T. Nevaquaya: Liner notes, *Comanche Flute Music* (Folkways FE4328, 1979)

MARY RIEMER-WELLER

Covelli, John (Thomas) (*b* Chicago, IL, 12 Oct 1936). Conductor and pianist. He studied music at Columbia University (BS 1960), making his début as a pianist at Town Hall, New York, while still a student (1957). He then served in the US Army (1960–62), first as official piano soloist with and then as conductor of the 7th Army SO in Europe. In 1962–3 he worked as assistant conductor of the London SO under Pierre Monteux, with whom he had studied conducting during the summers in the late 1950s. As a pianist, he won prizes in both the Busoni and Queen Elisabeth of Belgium competitions in 1964. Among the organizations with which he has held conducting positions are the Harkness Ballet (1967–8), the New York City Opera (1969–70), the St. Louis SO (1970–71), the Kansas City PO (1971–2), and the Milwaukee SO (1974–6); he has also been music director of the Flint (Michigan) SO (1976–82), and the Binghamton (New York) SO. In 1979 Covelli made his début as conductor-pianist with the Boston Pops Orchestra, and since then his guest conducting activities have been primarily in the "pops" field.

JAMES WIERZBICKI

Cover. A term used in the popular music industry usually for a recording of a particular song by performers other than those responsible for the original recorded version; it may also be applied to a rerecording of a song by the original performers (generally using pseudonyms) for a rival record company. In the 1950s and 1960s a cover typically entailed the rerecording of a song, aimed in its original recorded form at a particular sector of the record-buying public, for the purposes of disseminating it among a broader, or different, sector. At this time many international popular music hits were in fact cover versions by established white performers of songs originally recorded by Blacks on small regional labels.

By the late 1960s the term had largely lost these purely commercial connotations. It became fashionable for rock and soul singers to record their own versions of songs which had often already been hits in their own right. Thus many early rhythm-and-blues or soul songs received new treatments by rock singers: John Lennon, for example, had a hit with Ben E. King's *Stand by me* in 1975. A cover can simply be a straightforward copy of the original song, or a more radical reinterpretation of it: the Talking Heads' rendition of Al Green's *Take me to the river* actually appears to be an analysis of the song, and Tina Turner's version of the Beatles' *Help* changes the melody and harmony so fundamentally that it is scarcely the same song as that written by Lennon and McCartney.

While the term "cover" is not often applied to such reworkings, the principle of the cover version is present in "dub" remixes of reggae songs. Reggae artists use the term "version" for rerecordings of their own songs, in which they may completely alter the sound of the original by adding echo and other electronic effects. Cover versions of a rather different nature were made during the disco craze, when many record producers had a predilection for adding a dance rhythm to music of other genres; works by Beethoven and Mozart, for example, were subjected to this treatment.

ROBERT WITMER/ANTHONY MARKS

Cowboy song. A type of song describing cowboys and their life. Such songs began to appear in popular newspapers, as broadsides, in magazines (such as stockmen's journals), and in songbooks in the late 19th century; they became increasingly romanticized when they were taken over by Tin Pan Alley songwriters (such as Billy Hill) and by Hollywood composers. They are generally written in ballad style, but are melodically and structurally indebted to traditional popular, folk, and religious songs. The first significant collections were N. H. Thorp's *Songs of the Cowboy* (1908) and J. A. Lomax's *Cowboy Songs and other Frontier Ballads* (1910, rev. and enlarged 2/1938/*R*1965). The first commercial recordings of cowboy songs were probably those made by Charles Nabell for Okeh in 1924; Charles T. Sprague, known as the "Original Singing Cowboy," made a very successful recording of *When the work's all done this fall* for Victor in 1925. Other early cowboy singers were the Cartwright Brothers, Goebel Reeves (the "Texas Drifter"), Jules Verne Allen ("Longhorn Luke"), and Harry McClintock, but the true union of cowboy song and COUNTRY MUSIC did not come until after 1934, when GENE AUTRY began his career as a singing cowboy in Hollywood films. He popularized such songs as *Back in the saddle again* and *Riding down the canyon*; he and the singers he influenced (such as Roy Rogers, Tex Ritter, and the Sons of the Pioneers) did much to implant the romantic image of the cowboy in country music.

BIBLIOGRAPHY

F. G. Hoeptner: Liner notes, *Authentic Cowboys and their Western Folksongs* (RCA LPV522, 1965)

B. C. Malone: *Country Music, U.S.A.: a Fifty-year History* (Austin, 1968, 2/1985)

A. E. Fife and A. S. Fife, eds.: *Cowboy and Western Songs: a Comprehensive Anthology* (New York, 1969)

J. White: *Git Along, Little Dogies: Songs and Songmakers of the American West* (Urbana, IL, 1975)

D. B. Green: *Country Roots: the Origins of Country Music* (New York, 1976)

J. Tuska: *The Filming of the West* (Garden City, NY, 1976)

D. B. Green: "The Singing Cowboy: an American Dream," *Journal of Country Music*, vii/2 (1978), 4–61

C. Seemann: Liner notes, *Back in the Saddle Again* (NW314-15, 1984)

BILL C. MALONE

Cowell, Henry (Dixon) (*b* Menlo Park, CA, 11 March 1897; *d* Shady, NY, 10 Dec 1965). Composer, pianist, and writer on music. His enthusiasm, experimental open-mindedness, and energetic activity did much to promote novel techniques, and his prophetic compositional discoveries have continued to influence European and American musical practice.

1. Life. 2. Works.

1. LIFE. Cowell's father Harry immigrated from Ireland to British Columbia in order to manage a fruit orchard, which his father, the Dean of Kildare Cathedral, had given him. The venture failed and Harry moved to San Francisco, where he married Clarissa Dixon, who was from an Indiana-Iowa farming family. Their son Henry was born in a tiny cottage in the California foothills which was to be his home until 1936. At the age of five he began violin lessons, and for three years his father encouraged him as a child prodigy, but the strain was too much for his health and lessons were stopped; nevertheless he decided to become a composer. His parents were divorced in 1903 and Cowell and his mother spent the years 1906–10 visiting relatives in Iowa, Kansas, and Oklahoma, while his mother pursued a professional writing career between periods of illness. She was to die in 1916. In 1908 Cowell began his first long piece, a monodic setting of Longfellow's *Golden Legend*. It remained unfinished, and survives only as the second theme of the piano piece *Antinomy* (1917).

Back in California from 1910, Cowell bought his first piano in 1912. He studied with various local piano teachers and composed constantly, unencumbered by systematic training in composition or by any formal schooling: his parents were "philosophical anarchists," and their ideas of complete educational freedom led him to accept readily the many sounds around him as valid musical material. Important and lasting influences were the sounds of nature and the noises of man, his mother's Midwestern folktunes, and the rich variety of oriental musical cultures that existed in the San Francisco Bay area. He grew up hearing more Chinese, Japanese, and Indian classical music than he did Western music and never became familiar with the bulk of the European repertory, either as pianist or listener. Cowell owed his lifelong interest in Irish songs and dances not to his father (who was not musical) but to Midwestern relatives of Irish descent and to the poet John Varian, who had become a father figure to him. Varian's versions of Irish legends inspired such characteristic early pieces as *The Tides of Manaunaun* (?1917; for excerpt from score, *see* NOTATION, fig. 12), a piano work written to accompany a pageant. To portray the immense waves set in motion by the Irish god, Cowell rolled clusters with his hand and forearm in the low register of the piano to evoke the sea; above this is a sweeping modal melody. He had combined atonal clusters with a folklike tune; such an unfettered openness towards the gamut of musical resources and unusual combinations would characterize the breadth of Cowell's output. He played groups of his piano pieces at small concerts in San Francisco as early as 1912 but first received attention in print at his début concert as a composer-pianist (San Francisco, 5 March 1914) when his *Adventures in Harmony* (1913) and its tone clusters drew comment. By then he had written over a hundred pieces in various styles. His basic musical personality, that of the enthusiastic, spontaneous, and fluent trail-blazer, was firmly established.

Cowell's formal training began in 1914 with Charles Seeger, then at the University of California, Berkeley. Seeger arranged for him to acquire a solid technical foundation by studying harmony and counterpoint with E. G. Stricklen, Wallace Sabin, and the organist Uda Waldrop. At the same time he was to pursue free composition. In 1916 he registered at the Institute of Musical Art in New York, but, impatient with its stultifying academicism, he returned to California after one term. He resumed his exchange of ideas with Seeger and studied English compo-

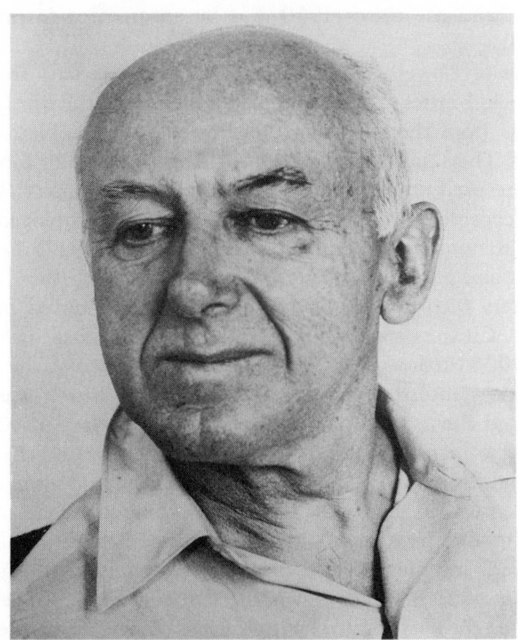

1. *Henry Cowell, 1959*

sition with Samuel Seward of Stanford University. At Seeger's insistence he worked out a systematic technique for the new materials he had already explored; with Seward he learned how to express his ideas in words. The result was the book *New Musical Resources* (1930/*R*1969), written between 1916 and 1919 and revised before its publication. This remarkable treatise describes, systematizes, and suggests new notations for Cowell's procedures, including clusters, free dissonant counterpoint, polytriadic harmony, counterrhythms, shifting accents, and a method for relating rhythm and pitch according to overtone ratios. (*See also* THEORY, §4(i).)

In February 1918 Cowell enlisted in the army, serving until May 1919. For most of this time he played the flute in military bands at army posts in Allentown, Pennsylvania, and Oswego, New York. About the same time he began to attract considerable attention as a performer of his own works and as a persistent advocate of the avant garde. By the mid-1920s he had extended his innovative piano techniques to include various types of cluster; stopping, strumming, scraping, plucking, and playing harmonics on the strings; and introducing various objects into the harp of the piano to produce percussive sounds. On 29 November 1919 he presented an all-Cowell recital in New York, then acquired professional management and inaugurated a series of five tours of Europe as composer-pianist (1923–33) that made him an international figure. His recitals of 1923 in Germany and in Paris, Budapest, and London were met with both outrage and intense interest, and he came to know well most of the major composers of Europe. Bartók wrote to him for permission to use his "invention" the cluster (the letter is lost), Schoenberg asked him to play for his class, and in 1932 Webern conducted the Scherzo movement of his Sinfonietta for chamber orchestra in Vienna. After his 1923 tour of Europe, Cowell returned to New York, where he made his formal American débuts (Carnegie Hall, 4 February 1924; Town Hall, 17 February 1924). These concerts received sensational reviews in the press and national wire services; he became a national celebrity, and annual concert-lecture tours of the USA followed, as well as, later, more appearances in Europe and, after 1956, Asia. In 1929 Cowell became the first American composer invited to the USSR. His sensational performances alarmed the authorities but excited his audiences, and the state publishing house printed two piano pieces, *Lilt of the Reel* (1928) and *Tiger* (1930).

From the early 1920s Cowell wrote and acted extensively on behalf of modern music, and he contributed several essays to the volume *American Composers on American Music* (1933/*R*1962), which he edited. In 1925 he founded the New Music Society in Los Angeles, moving it to San Francisco the following year. The Society gave concerts of European and American "ultramodernist" works until 1936. In 1927 he single-handedly launched NEW MUSIC, "a quarterly of modern compositions" in which contemporary works appeared. The inaugural issue contained Ruggles's *Men and Mountains*. North and South American compositions predominated, but *New Music* also published music by Europeans, including Schoenberg (op.33b), Webern (op.17 no.2), and Varèse (*Density 21.5*). Music by Ives, whom Cowell had met in 1927, appeared regularly; indeed, such important works as *The Fourth of July*, *Washington's Birthday*, the second movement of the Fourth Symphony, and many songs were first published in *New Music*. Cowell became Ives's most important link with the larger musical world. In addition to aiding *New Music* (from 1947 *New Music Edition*) and New Music Quarterly Recordings, which Cowell founded in 1934, Ives supported the concerts of American orchestral music that Cowell organized in major European cities in his role as director of the North American section of the Pan American Association of Composers (founded by Varèse, Salzedo, Chávez, and Cowell in 1928). Cowell took every opportunity to discuss Ives's work in lecture-concerts and in print throughout his life, and *Charles Ives and his Music* (1955), which he wrote with his wife, remains an important study.

Cowell turned in the mid-1920s to the serious study of non-European musics. In 1931–2 he worked with the comparative musicologist Erich von Hornbostel, with Professor Sambamoorthy of Madras, and with Raden Mas Jodjhana of Java, all in Berlin, under a Guggenheim Foundation grant. His preoccupation with new sounds continued with an unending quest for new ethnic contagions. Cowell began a deliberate attempt to synthesize "ultramodern" materials with the many possibilities offered him by other musical cultures. During these years, however, he embraced conservative idioms for certain commissions, teaching pieces, and music for amateurs. His writings of this period indicate a desire to compose "useful music" in a "neo-primitive" vein. Music could assist in the education of children as well, and could serve other arts such as film and dance, without dominating them. This led Cowell to what may be his most explosive notion, "elastic form." In a series of articles on dance (1934–41) he suggested that performers themselves choose the order of various segments of music provided by the composer: the music was to adapt to the dancers' forms. This implied at least a partial relinquishing by the composer of the total control over the finished product which had been basic to Western musical thought. Two books of this period, *Rhythm* (?1935) and *The Nature of Melody* (?1938), remain unpublished.

In both musical and personal matters Cowell was kind, trusting, and almost childlike. This perhaps explains why he initially deemed the presence of a defense attorney unnecessary when he was brought to court on a morals charge in 1936. Sentenced to imprisonment, he was sent to San Quentin penitentiary until pressure from many different sources, including fellow composers, led to his parole in 1940. He moved to New York, spent a year as secretary to Percy Grainger, and in 1941 married Sidney Hawkins Robertson, a writer, folksong collector, and photographer. In 1942 the governor of California pardoned Cowell at the request of the judge and the prosecuting attorney, who had come to the conclusion that the composer was innocent.

During the war Cowell served as senior music editor of the overseas division of the Office of War Information, having been engaged for his wide knowledge of the traditional musics of several continents. In 1941 he had resumed his teaching career at the New School for Social Research, New York, where in 1930 he had initiated "Composers Forum," a program, still in existence, that presents two composers and their music in discussion with the audience. Also at the New School he lectured about music of the world's peoples and was in charge of musical activities until he resigned in 1963. Cowell also held posts at the Peabody Conservatory (1951–6) and at Columbia University (1949–65), and he lectured at over 50 conservatories and universities throughout the USA, Europe, and Asia. Cage and Harrison were among his pupils, as were, more briefly, George Gershwin and Burt Bacharach. Cowell received many awards, grants, and honorary degrees; he was elected to the National Institute of Arts and Letters in 1951 and served as president of the ACA from 1951 to 1955. His last years were extraordinarily productive: from 1946 until his death he wrote over 100 compositions and published over 100 essays on music. Especially important among the latter is his series of 40 reviews of contemporary music for the *Musical Quarterly* (1947–58). A culmination of his constant search for fresh musical experiences was his world tour during 1956–7; the sponsorship of the Rockefeller Foundation and the US State Department enabled him to listen first-hand to the music of many cultures in their natural surroundings. A widely acknowledged international musical statesman, he represented the USA at the International Music Conference in Teheran and at the East-West Music Encounter in Tokyo (1961). He continued to compose throughout a series of debilitating illnesses from 1957 until his death in 1965.

2. WORKS. Cowell was an indefatigable musical explorer, discoverer, and inventor; his vast output might be characterized by an enthusiastic statement he made in 1955: "I want to live in the *whole world* of music!" His work reflects a bold but ingenuous openness towards many sound materials, novel compositional procedures, and a wide array of non-European and folk influences. He has been described (by Weisgall) as temperamentally incapable of excluding from his work any idea which interested him, and his ecumenical, if uncritical, approach helped provide the "open sesame" for new music in America, to quote Cage. Cowell seems not to have been interested in style *per se*, nor in the gradual evolution of a single, personal, idiomatic stamp. An idea that interested him for compositional development had, for Cowell, to determine the ultimate language and form of the resultant work. Composition was for him sometimes the result of long and deliberate consideration but more often was a spontaneous response to some recent musical experience. Three general periods of Cowell's work can be discerned, each reflecting an overall focus of attention, not a separate stylistic direction. The first (1912–35) is characterized chiefly by experiment and innovation, the second (1935–50) by various kinds of traditional or folklike models, and the third (1950–65) by an attempt to integrate them all.

Many of Cowell's early innovations were derived from the latent possibilities of the grand piano. He coined the word "tone clusters" from their look on the printed page (*see* NOTATION fig.12). They could be played with fingers, fists, or forearms and were used at first chiefly for programmatic effect (Cowell always considered these sounds as "chords" and employed them usually to reinforce melodic lines). *Advertisement* (1917) uses both diatonic and semitonal clusters; *Tiger* integrates a greater variety of clusters with free dissonance and more pronounced melodic writing. Clusters appear in Cowell's orchestral music as early as about 1924 (in *Some More Music*) and are exploited to the hilt in the Piano Concerto (1928). Another early invention was what he termed the "string piano." In *The Aeolian Harp* (*c*1923; see fig.2), the piano strings are to be strummed inside the piano while chords on the keys are depressed silently, and some strings are to be plucked; in *Sinister Resonance* (1930) strings are stopped and harmonics produced; and *The Banshee* (1925; *see also* NOTATION, §2, and fig.14) is to be played entirely on the strings while an assistant holds down the damper pedal. Cowell also originated the idea of introducing various objects inside the piano to produce new timbres, an innovation developed by Cage into the prepared piano. (*See also* PIANO MUSIC, §3(iii).)

Besides discovering unusual piano sounds, Cowell explored exotic instruments and percussion. Three southwest American Indian thundersticks (bullroarers) originally accompanied two movements of *Ensemble* for string quintet (1924). Cowell used graphic notation for dynamics at the beginning of the thunderstick parts, then gave instructions for the performers to improvise through to the end. In 1931 he collaborated with Lev Termen to develop the Rhythmicon, an electronic machine that could play complicated polyrhythms. For it he wrote the concerto *Rhythmicana* (1931) for a performance in Paris, which, however, did not take place. (In 1971 Leland Smith realized the solo part on a computer, and Sandor Salgo with the Stanford Orchestra gave the first performance under the title "Concerto for Rhythmicon and Orchestra.") As early as the 1920s Cowell composed, but did not always notate, percussion music for dance using found objects, and is generally considered the founder of the "West Coast School" of percussion (with Cage, Harrison, and Strang). His *Ostinato pianissimo* (1934) with its delicate gamelan-like sound remains a standard repertory piece for percussion ensemble. Certain symphonic works make elaborate use of percussion (Symphony no.11, 1953). The Percussion Concerto (1958) combines the metrically even rhythms of *Ostinato* with melodic writing in clusters, modality, and an orchestral counterpoint.

Among Cowell's most forward-looking ideas was his "rhythm–harmony" system, in which interval ratios from the overtone series are translated into corresponding rhythms. In the *Quartet Romantic* (1917) and the *Quartet Euphometric* (1919) the rhythms of four independent melodic strands are derived from a simple four-part substructure that Cowell called the "theme." Though harmonic resting points taken from the theme provide some sense of harmonic direction, the pitches in the quartets are chosen freely. The attractiveness of the sounds attests to the sensitivity of Cowell's ear. Long considered unplayable, the two quartets have recently been published, performed, and recorded. The indeterminacy implicit in the free thunderstick parts and original open-ended instrumentation of *Ensemble* became explicit in the

2. *Opening of Cowell's "The Aeolian Harp" (c1923): autograph MS (DLC)*

Mosaic Quartet (String Quartet no.3, 1935). Cowell's note in the score instructs that "The Mosaic Quartet is to be played, alternating the movements at the desire of the performers, treating each movement as a unit to build the mosaic pattern of the form." The teaching piece *Amerind Suite* for piano (1939), which permits students at various levels of proficiency to play simultaneously, leaves similar choices to the performers. *Ritournelle* for piano (from the incidental music *Les mariés de la Tour Eiffel*, 1939) perhaps most closely realizes Cowell's theory of "elastic form," and in one of his last pieces, *26 Simultaneous Mosaics* for five players (1963), musical sections of totally different character may be played at random. The principle, its original relation to dance, and the composer's oriental concerns point directly to the work of Cage.

At the time when he formulated his concept of indeterminacy, Cowell's tonal materials were becoming simpler, more oriented around a tonal center. Of the two important quartets from these years, the *Mosaic Quartet* simplifies the internal structure within its short movements. Separate strands of material tend towards diatonicism, while the composite sound alternates between "wrong-note" harmony and free dissonance. The String Quartet no.4 (the "United," 1936) is one of Cowell's earliest attempts at a "more universal music style," as he put it in a kind of apologia prefacing the original edition of the work. The drones, modal scales, unchanging harmonic areas, and frequent stretches of pizzicato most strongly recall eastern European folk music.

From 1936 onwards Cowell more often wrote tonally, and his rhythms became increasingly regular, with an ever stronger basis in traditional folk idioms. During the 1940s Eastern exoticism waned. The Irish jig, which he had always favored, was to provide a "scherzo" in many works, and the rugged diatonicism of early American hymnody, which he knew from William Walker's tunebook *The Southern Harmony* (1835), led to the series of 18 hymns and fuguing tunes for various instrumental combinations (1944–64). Their bisectional form, which Cowell described as "something slow followed by something fast," offered him a concise, down-to-earth form which suited his prolific and expeditious compositional habits. The streamlined style of this "American music," of his functional music for brass ensembles and for band, and of his SATB arrangements for the United Nations illustrated his eagerness to write music for a great variety of performers. He was later to explain the pervasive tonality in his works by pointing out that tonality, not atonality, was common to most musical cultures.

The music from the last two decades of Cowell's life is marked by a partial return to dissonant counterpoint and the amalgamation of previous innovative materials, especially clusters, with his fresh experiences with traditional musics from India (the "Madras" Symphony no.13, 1956–8), Indonesia (Percussion Concerto and Symphony no.19, 1965), Iran (*Persian Set* for orchestra, 1957, and *Homage to Iran* for violin and piano, 1957), and Japan (*Ongaku* for orchestra, 1957, and the two koto concertos, 1961–2, 1965). In the Percussion Concerto and Symphony no.11 ("Seven Rituals of Music," 1953), clusters act as melodic conglomerates within a modal context; the symphony is something like a compendium of his mature practice, each movement being in a different style. Cowell would continue to refashion previous works into new ones: an example is Symphony no.15 ("Thesis," 1960), in which he used music from his second and third quartets. His long concern with the manipulation of small melodic cells is represented by two fine late works, the Variations for Orchestra (1956) and the Trio for violin, cello, and piano (1965).

For further illustration, *see* NOTATION, fig.13.

WORKS

Catalogue: W. Lichtenwanger: *The Music of Henry Cowell: a Descriptive Catalog*, ISAMm (Brooklyn, NY, 1986)

Fragments, sketches, composition exercises, and most lost and incomplete works are omitted. Numbers are from Lichtenwanger; letter suffixes denote arrangements, and numbers following a diagonal indicate a movement or part of a larger work. To facilitate cross-references between sections letter prefixes have been added. Titles follow the forms found on Cowell's MSS, except for those in brackets, which are from Lichtenwanger. Cowell's MSS and sketches are in *DLC*; his papers and some MSS are held on deposit at *NN*.

AP – anniversary piece (Cowell composed 85 short pieces for his wife Sidney Robertson Cowell for various anniversaries beginning in 1941)

pf-str – piano strings (an indication that the part should be played directly on the strings of the piano)

Index: A – orchestral and band; B – concertante; C – choral; D – solo vocal; E – chamber (5 or more insts); F – chamber (3–4 insts); G – chamber (2 insts); H – chamber (solo inst); I – keyboard; J – dramatic; K – arrangements

< – arranged as/developed into > – arranged from/developed from

* – published work

A: ORCHESTRAL AND BAND

(for orch unless otherwise stated)

147 The Birth of Motion, *c*1914, inc. [part <A:221a]

213/2a What's This?, 1920 [>I:213/2]

221a Some Music, 1922 [>lost pf piece and A:147]

245 Symphony [no.1], b, 1918, rev. 1940

246 Camp March, small orch, 1918–19, lost

253 March, 1918–19

254 [Waltz], band, 1918–19, lost

289 A Symphonic Communication, 1919

305a Vestiges, 1922 [>I:305]

387a Manaunaun's Birthing, 1944, lost [>D:387]

404 Some More Music, ?*c*1924, inc.

415a Slow Jig, 1933 [>I:415]

439 Three Pieces for Chamber Orchestra, 1928, lost [? = A:443]

443 *Sinfonietta, chamber orch, 1928; as Marked Passages, Boston, 28 April 1928, cond. N. Slonimsky [? = A:439; movts 1 and 2 >movts 1 and 2 of E:380; movt 3 >I:429]

463/1a Reel (Lilt of the Reel), small orch, 1932; New York, 17 May 1933, cond. B. Herrmann [>no.1 of I:463]

463/1b Reel for CBS Orchestra, 1942 [>no.1 of I:463]

464 *Synchrony of Dance, Music, Light, retitled Orchesterstück: Synchrony, 1930; Paris, 6 June 1931, cond. Slonimsky

475 [untitled], ?1920–30

484 Two Appositions: One Movement for Orchestra, 1932, lost; Paris, 21 Feb 1932, cond. Slonimsky [arr. str, 484a; <I:484b]

486 Four Continuations for String Orchestra, 1932; Brooklyn, NY, 10 Dec 1933, cond. J. Edward Powers

493 Horn Pipe, 1933; Havana, 22 Oct 1933, cond. A. Roldán

498 Symphonic Episode, ?orch, ?1923–33, inc.

499 Suite for Small Orchestra, 1934; New York, 21 May 1934, cond. C. Vrionides

506 Reel no.2, small orch, 1934; Minneapolis, 9 Jan 1941, cond. J. Becker

523 How they Take It: Prison Moods, band, 1936, lost [arr. theater orch, 523a, ?1937, lost]

527 Jig in Four, 1936

528 Oriental Dance, concert band, 1936, lost

531 In the Style of a Popular Song, theater orch, 1937, lost

535 Reel Irish, military band, 1937, lost

541 Symphony no.2 "Anthropos," 1938: 1 Repose, 2 Activity, 3 Repression, 4 Liberation; Brooklyn, NY, 9 March 1941, cond. Cowell

543 *Celtic Set, concert band, 1938: 1 Interlochen Camp Reel, 2 Caoine, 3 Hornpipe; Selinsgrove, PA, 6 May 1938, cond. Grainger [arr. orch, 543a, 1944; <I:543b, <G:543c]

545 Air, band, 1938

547a *Symphonic Set, op.17, 1938; Chicago, 1 April 1940, cond. I. Solomon [>F:547]

550a Herman's Wedding March, band, 1938, lost [>I:550]

567 *Old American Country Set, 1939: 1 Blarneying Lilt, 2 Meetinghouse Chorale, 3 Comallye, 4 Charivari, 5 Cornhusking Hornpipe; Indianapolis, 28 Feb 1940, cond. F. Sevitzky [no.1 arr. small orch, 567/1a, 1940, lost, arr. band, 567/1b, 1941]

571 *Shoonthree (The Music of Sleep), band, 1939; Mansfield, PA, 3 May 1940, cond. R. F. Goldman

573 Crystal Set, 1939, lost

574 Quaint Minuet, band, 1939, lost [arr., 574a, lost]

576 Vox humana, 1939 [arr. band, 576a, lost]

577 Andante, orch ens, 1939, lost

578 Chorale, orch ens, 1939, lost

579 The Exuberant Mexican: Danza latina, band, 1939

580 Hornpipe, orch ens, 1939, lost

581 Menuet, orch ens, 1939, lost

582 Orientale, orch ens, 1939, lost

584 Spanish Waltz, orch ens, 1939, lost

587 *Pastoral and Fiddler's Delight, 1940; New York, 26 July 1940, cond. Stokowski

594 American Melting Pot, chamber orch, 1940: 1 Chorale (Teutonic-American), 2 Air (Afro-American), 3 Satire (Franco-American), withdrawn, 4 Alapna (Oriental-American), 5 Slavic Dance (Slavic-American), 6 Rhumba with added 8th (Latin-American), 7 Square Dance (Celtic-American), withdrawn; New York, 3 May 1943, cond. F. Petrides

595 58 for Percy, band, 1940 [<F:595a]

597 *Ancient Desert Drone, 1940; South Bend, IN, 12 Jan 1941, cond. Grainger [<G:597a]

598 Purdue, 1940; West Lafayette, IN, 19 Dec 1940, cond. Sevitzky

599 A Bit o' Blarney (This One is a Wise-cracker), band, 1940, inc.

602 Reel, 1940, lost

610 Indiana University Overture, 1941

617 *Shipshape Overture, band, 1941; State College, PA, 31 July 1941, cond. R. F. Goldman

625 Festive Occasion, band, 1942; New York, 3 July 1942, cond. Cowell

634 *Fanfare to the Forces of our Latin-American Allies, brass, perc, 1942; Cincinnati, 30 Oct 1942, cond. E. Goossens

636 Gaelic Symphony (Symphony no.3), band, str, 1942; movt 1, West Saugerties, NY, 24 July 1942, cond. E. Williams

645 American Pipers, 1943; New Orleans, 12 Jan 1949, cond. P. Henrotte

647 *Philippine Return: Rondo on Philippine Folk Songs, orch, 1943: 1 Introduction, 2 Iluli si nonoy [Iloilo cradle song], 3 An mananguete [Leyte coconut gatherer's song], 4 Pispis ining pikoy [Visayan game song], 5 Kalusan [Bataues rowing song]

648 United Music, 1943; Detroit, 23 Jan 1944, cond. K. Krueger

651a Hymn and Fuguing Tune [no.1], sym. band, 1944; New York, 14 June 1944, cond. E. F. Goldman [>I:651]

652 Improvisation on a Persian Mode for Orchestra, 1943

656 Symphonic Sketch, *c*1943, inc.

657 Hymn and Fuguing Tune no.2, str orch, 1944; WEAF radio, New York, 23 March 1944, cond. H. Nosco

659 *Animal Magic of the Alaskan Esquimo, band, 1944

660 *Hymn and Fuguing Tune no.3, 1944; Los Angeles, 14 April 1951, cond. I. Dahl [<I:660a]

673a Hymn and Fuguing Tune no.5, str orch, ?1946; Saratoga Springs, NY, 15 Sept 1946, cond. F. C. Adler [>C:673, <movts 1 and 2 of A:788]

679 Big Sing, 1945: 1 Fanfare, 2 Hymn, 3 Testimonials, 4 Great Rejoicing; Fresno, CA, 27 May 1946, cond. ?Cowell

686 Air, band, ?1940–45, inc.

687 Band Piece, ?1940–45

688 Hymn for Strings, str orch, 1946; Denton, TX, 22 March 1946, cond. Cowell

689 *Grandma's Rhumba, band, 1946

692 Festival Overture for Two Orchestras, 1946; Interlochen, MI, 11 Aug 1946, cond. W. E. Knuth

693 Congratulations! To Mr. and Mrs. Howard Hanson, str orch, 1946

697 *Symphony no.4 (Short Symphony), 1946: 1 Hymn, 2 Ballad, 3 Dance, 4 Introduction and Fuguing Tune; Boston, 24 Oct 1947, cond. R. Burgin [movt 4 >fuguing tune of I:696]

705/3a *Ballad, str orch, 1954; Tucson, AZ, 27 Nov 1956, cond. F. Balazs [>movt 3 of G:705, <E:705/3b]

719 *Saturday Night at the Firehouse, 1948

722 *Symphony no.5, 1948; Washington, DC, 5 Jan 1949, cond. H. Kindler

732 *A Curse and a Blessing, sym. band, 1949; Brooklyn, NY, 21 July 1949, cond. R. F. Goldman

744 *Overture for Large Orchestra, 1949; Santa Rosa, CA, 1 Dec 1968, cond. C. Brown

746 Commencement Parade, band, ?*c*1949, inc.

757 Andante and Allegro, 1950, inc.

767 Air of the Glen/Song of the Glen, band, ?*c*1950–51: 1 Andante

– Trio, 2 Schottische; movt 1 arr. as Air for String Orchestra, 767/1b, 1953, inc. [movt 1 <B:767/1a]

769 Fantasie (Enigma Variations) on a Theme by Ferdinand Kücken, band, 1952; West Point, NY, 30 May 1952, cond. F. Resta

770 Symphony no.6, 1952; Houston, 14 Nov 1955, cond. Stokowski

774 Rondo for Orchestra, 1952; Indianapolis, 6 Dec 1953, cond. Sevitzky

776 Symphony no.7, small orch, 1952; Baltimore, 25 Nov 1952, cond. R. Stewart

778 Symphony no.8, opt. A, chorus, orch, 1952; Wilmington, OH, 1 March 1953, cond. T. Johnson

787 Symphony no.9, 1953; Green Bay, WI, 14 March 1954, cond. R. Holder [movt 1 >hymn of G:758]

788 Symphony no.10, 1953; New York, 24 Feb 1957, cond. F. Bibo [movts 1 and 2 >A:673a, movts 5 and 6 >F:713]

790 *Symphony no.11 "Seven Rituals of Music," 1953; Louisville, 29 May 1954, cond. R. Whitney

797 *Singing Band, concert band, 1953

801/1 In Memory of a Great Man, 1954, inc., = no.1 of [6] Memorial Pieces [for nos.2–4, 6, see I:801/2, C:801/3, I:801/4, G:801/6; 801/5, frag.]

807 Toward a Bright Day, 1954: 1 Reel, 2 Vivace

810 Air, 1955, inc.

816 Dalton Suite, school orch, 1955; New York, 16 April 1956

821 Suite, str, ?1951–5

830 *Symphony no.12, 1955–6; Houston, 28 March 1960, cond. Stokowski

833 Variations for Orchestra, 1956, rev. 1959; Cincinnati, 23 Nov 1956, cond. Johnson

838 *Persian Set, chamber orch, 1957; Teheran, Iran, 17 Sept 1957, cond. A. Dorati

839 Teheran Movement, chamber orch, 1957

842 Music for Orchestra, 1957; Athens, Greece, 3 Sept 1957, cond. Dorati

846 Ongaku, 1957; Louisville, 26 March 1958, cond. Whitney

848 *Symphony no.13 "Madras," 1956–8; Madras, India, 3 March 1959, cond. T. Scherman

865 Antiphony for Divided Orchestra, 1959; Kansas City, MO, 14 Nov 1959, cond. H. Schwieger

867 Mela/Fair, 1959, inc.: 1 Thanksgiving, 2 Sowing after Rain, 3 Harvest; broadcast New Delhi, India, 13 Dec 1959

869 Characters, 1959: 1 Cowboy, 2 The Mysterious Oriental, 3 The Profound One, 4 Deep Thinker, 5 The Frightened Scurrier, 6 The Celestial Soul, 7 The Jaunty Irishman

874 Symphony no.14, 1959–60; Washington, DC, 27 April 1961, cond. H. Hanson

887 *Symphony no.15 "Thesis," 1960; Murray, KY, 7 Oct 1961, cond. Whitney [movts 1–4 >F:518, movt 6 >F:450]

892 Chiaroscuro, 1961; Guatemala City, 13 Oct 1961, cond. J. M. F. Gil

904 Andante, 1962

909/2a *Carol, 1965; Tulsa, OK, 16 Nov 1968, cond. F. Autori [>movt 2 of B:909]

912 Symphony no.16 "Icelandic," 1962; Reykjavík, Iceland, 21 March 1963, cond. W. Strickland

916 Symphony no.17, 1963

921a Hymn and Fuguing Tune no.16, 1964; New York, 6 Oct 1966, cond. Bernstein [>G:921]

930 *Symphony no.18, 1964

932 The Tender and the Wild: Song and Dance, 1964

942 Twilight in Texas, 1965; New York, 20 June 1968, cond. A. Kostelanetz

943 Symphony no.19, 1965; Nashville, TN, 18 Oct 1965, cond. W. Page

945 Symphony no.20, 1965, inc., movt 3 completed and orchd L. Harrison

946 Symphony no.21, 1965, sketches

B: CONCERTANTE

96 [concerto], ?A♭, pf, orch, 1914, lost

440 *Concerto for Piano and Orchestra, 1928; movts 1 and 2, New York, 26 April 1930, Cowell (pf); complete, Havana, 28 Dec 1930, Cowell, cond. P. Sanjuan [movt 1 >movt 1 of E:406]

452 Irish Suite, conc., pf-str, chamber orch, 1928–9: 1 The Banshee, 2 The Leprechaun, 3 The Fairy Bells; Boston, 11 March 1929, Cowell, cond. Slonimsky [movt 1 >I:405, movt 2 >I:448, movt 3 >I:447]

481 Concerto for Rhythmicon and Orchestra, 1931, orig. entitled Rhythmicana; realized cptr, orch, Palo Alto, CA, 3 Dec 1971, L. Smith, cond. S. Salgo

605 Four Irish Tales, pf, orch, 1940: 1 The Tides of Manaunaun, 2 Exultation, 3 The Harp of Life, 4 The Lilt of the Reel; New York, 24 Nov 1940, Cowell, cond. F. Mahler [no.1 >I:219/1, no.2 >I:328, no.3 >I:384, no.4 >no.1 of I:463]

620 Suite for Piano and String Orchestra, 1941, pf pt inc., reconstructed D. Tudor; Boston, 11 Jan 1942, Cowell, cond. J. Wolffers; movts 3–5 arr. as Little Concerto, pf, band, 620a, 1941, West Point, NY, 25 Jan 1942, Cowell, cond. F. Resta; movts 3–5 also arr. as Little Concerto, pf, orch, 620b, 1945

767/1a Air, vn, str orch, 1952 [>movt 1 of A:767]

771 *Flirtatious Jig (Fiddler's Jig), vn, str orch, 1952

813 Hymn and Fuguing Tune no.10, ob, str orch, 1955 [not = H:798]

861 *Concerto for Percussion and Orchestra, 1958; Kansas City, MO, 7 Jan 1961, cond. Schwieger

878 *Concerto brevis for Accordion and Orchestra, 1960

882 Variations on 3rds for Two Violas and String Orchestra, 1960; New York, 10 Feb 1961, cond. D. Antoun

894 Duo concertante, fl, harp, orch, 1961; Springfield, OH, 21 Oct 1961, J. Baker, G. Agostini, cond. J. Wiley

897 *Air and Scherzo for Alto Saxophone and Small Orchestra, 1963 [>G:897]

908 Concerto for Harmonica, 1962

909 Concerto for Koto and Orchestra [no.1], 1961–2; Philadelphia, 18 Dec 1964, K. Eto, cond. Stokowski [movt 2 <A:909/2a]

917 Concerto grosso, fl, ob, cl, vc, harp, str orch, 1963; Miami Beach, FL, 12 Jan 1964, cond. Sevitzky

940 Concerto no.2 for Koto and Orchestra in the Form of a Symphony, 1965; Hanover, NH, 8 May 1965, S. Yuize, cond. M. di Bonaventura

947 Concerto for Harp and Orchestra, 1965

C: CHORAL

53 O salutaris (liturgical), SATB, pf, 1913

95 Maker of Day, Mez, A, Bar, chorus, timp, pf, 1914

148 [untitled choral sketch], 4vv, *c*1914

154 The Wave of D. . ., 3vv, pf, ?*c*1914

218 The Light of Peace, chorus, pf, 1917

236 The Sun Shines: Chorale, 9vv, *c*1917

276a *Psalm cxxi, chorus, 1953 [>D:276]

533a *The Road Leads into Tomorrow (D. Hagemeyer), 8vv, pf ad lib, 1947 [arr. from lost song]

536 *The Morning Cometh (T. Chalmers Furness), chorus, 1937

546 *The Coming of Light (Hagemeyer), 4-pt female vv/4 solo vv, 1938

562 *Spring at Summer's End (Hagemeyer), SSA, ?*c*1938

586 Easter Music, chorus, band, 1940, lost: 1 The Passion, 2 The Vigil at the Cross, 3 The Resurrection

640 *Fire and Ice (R. Frost), male vv, band, 1943

641 *American Muse (S. V. Benét), 2-pt female vv, pf, 1943: 1 American Muse, 2 Swift Runner, 3 Immensity of Wheel

655 Hail, Mills! (L. Seltzer), SSA, pf, *c*1943

673 Hymn and Fuguing Tune no.5, 5vv, 1945 [arr. as A:673a]

675 *The Irishman Lilts (Henry Cowell), female vv, pf, 1945

690 *Air Held her Breath (A. Lincoln), canon, SATB, 1946

691 *To America (Hagemeyer), SSAATTBB, 1946

707 Union of Voices, 6-pt female vv, ?1945–6

712 *Day, Evening, Night, Morning (P. L. Dunbar), 6-pt male vv, 1947

715 *The Lily's Lament (E. H. Lomax), SSA, pf, 1947

716 *Sweet was the Song the Virgin Sung (Sweet Christmas Song) (early 17th-century), SATB, pf/org/str, 1948

723 *Luther's Carol for his Son (Luther), TTBB, 1948

727 *Do you Doodle as you Dawdle? (Henry Cowell), chorus, pf, drums ad lib, 1948

728 *Evensong at Brookside: a Father's Lullaby (Harry Cowell), male vv, 1948

731 Do, Do, Do, is C, C, C (Henry Cowell), children's chorus, pf, ?*c*1948

733 *Ballad of the Two Mothers (Lomax), SSATBarB, 1949

750 *To a White Birch (Hagemeyer), chorus, 1950
759 *Song for a Tree (Hagemeyer), SSA, opt. pf, 1950
775 With Choirs Divine (J. T. Shotwell), SSA, 1952
781 Mountain Tree (Hagemeyer), chorus, 1952
782 The Golden Harp, spiritual, 4-pt boys' chorus, 1952
796 Psalm xxxiv, SATB, unacc./org, 1953
801/3 A Thanksgiving for Ruth Strongin (S. R. Cowell), SSATB/S, pf/org/any 5 insts, 1954, no.3 of [6] Memorial Pieces [see also A:801/1]
818 . . .if He please (E. Taylor), chorus, boys' chorus, orch/pf, 1955
819 *The Tree of Life (Taylor), chorus, 1955
829 Lines from the Dead Sea Scrolls, TTTBBB, orch, 1956
873 [untitled, proposed Malayan national anthem], vv, band, 1959
881 Edson Hymns and Fuguing Tunes (L. Edson, Jr.), suite, chorus, orch, 1960; *arr. chorus, org, 881a, ?1960; arr. chorus, band, 881b
902 *Supplication: Processional (Henry Cowell), org, 2 tpt, 2 trbn, unison vv, timp ad lib, 1962
919 The Creator (G. R. Derzhavin), oratorio, S, A, T, B, chorus, orch, 1963
929 *Ultima actio (J. de Diego, trans. J. Machlis), SSATB, 1964
938 Zapados sonidos, SSAATTBB, tap dancer, 1964

9 other choral works, acc. and unacc., lost

D: SOLO VOCAL

(all for 1v, pf, unless otherwise stated)

93 Maternal Love (L. Smith Wood), ?*c*1913; 100 Follow to the Wild Wood Weeds, 1914; 104/8 That Sir which serves and seeks for gain (Shakespeare), 1914 [see I:104]; 104/9 And will he not come again? (Shakespeare), 1914 [see I:104]; 104/10 If she be made of red and white (Shakespeare), 1914, lost [see I:104]; 104/11 You that choose not by the view (Shakespeare), 1914, lost [see I:104]; 106 Sonnet on the Sea's Voice (G. Sterling), 1914; 123 Among the Rushes (C. Dixon), 1914; 125 The Fish's Toes (Dixon), 1914

129 Bed in Summer (R. L. Stevenson), 1914; 131 Rain (Stevenson), 1914; 134 Time to Rise (Stevenson), 1914; 135 Looking Forward (Stevenson), 1914; 136 At the Seaside (Stevenson), 1914; 145 Where Go the Boats (Stevenson), 1914; 146 A Baby's Smile (Smith Wood), *c*1914; 151 The Prelude (J. O. Varian), *c*1914; 152 *St. Agnes Morning (M. Anderson), *c*1914; 157 My Auntie (Dixon), 1915; 159 A Song of Courage (Dixon), 1915; 161 Jealousy (Dixon), 1915; 164 God of the Future (Varian), 1915; 174 White Death (C. A. Smith), 1915; 175 The Dream Bridge (Smith), 1915

177 I dreamed I lay where flowers were springing (Burns), 1915; 182 Light and Joy (Dixon), 1915; 192 The First Jasmines (R. Tagore), 1v, vn, pf, 1916; 198 The Wisest Wish (Dixon), 1916; 204 Christmas Song (E. R. Veblen), 1916; 207 Invocation (Varian), 1916; 215 March Men of the Earth (Varian), 1v/vv, pf, *c*1916 [acc. inc.]; 216 Psalm vii [recte Ps. viii], *c*1916; 222 Oh, could I mount on fairy wings (F. G. Currier), 1917; 226 Look Deep, 1917; 228 Angus Og (Varian), 1917; 230 Consecration (Currier), 1917

238 The Chauldron (Varian), S, A, T, B, pf, ?*c*1916–17; 244 The Morning Pool (Smith), 1918; 248 Democracy (Varian), 1918–19; 250 April (E. Pound), 1918–19; 251 Mother (T. Helburn), 1918–19; 256 Homing (L. Brower), 1918; 258 Systym (Stevenson), 1918–19; 261 My Summer (W. Brooks), 1918–19; 268 A Vision (L. Brown), 1918–19; 270 We'll Build our Bungalows (?Henry Cowell), 1v/vv, pf, ?1918, refrain lost; 274 Prayer for Mary, 1919

276 Psalm cxxi, 1919 [<C:276a]; 278 There is a Light (Varian), 1919; 282 Oh, let me breathe into the happy air (Keats), 1919; 291 The Daga's Song of the Hero Sun (Varian), *c*1919; 296 The Sun's Travels (Stevenson), ?1917–19; 297 To a Skylark (Shelley), 1920; 299 To my Valentine, 1920; 317 Forget me not, *c*1920; 319 Grief Song (Veblen), *c*1920; 322 Before and After (text and tune, T. Glynn), ?1915–20; 329 My Love (Harry Cowell), 1921

331 Auntie's Skirts (Stevenson), 1921; 337 Olivia (Harry Cowell), *c*1921; 344 Allegro and Burden, ?1916–21; 358 Music, when Soft Voices Die (Shelley), 1922; 363 The Song of the Silence (Harry Cowell), 1922; 364 The Dream of My Life, 1v, unacc., ?*c*1922; 365 Sentence (W. Bynner), ?*c*1922; 366 Vox celeste (Harry Cowell), ?*c*1922; 387 *Manaunaun's Birthing (Varian), 1924 [<A:387a]; 400 *Where she Lies (E. St. Vincent Millay), 1924

414 The Fairy Fountain (Harry Cowell), ?*c*1925; 417 Our Sun (Varian), ?*c*1925; 419 Reconciliation (G. W. Russell), T, org, ?*c*1920–25; 420 Shelter my soul, O my love (S. Naidu), ?*c*1920–25; 421 The Willow Waltz, ?*c*1920–25; 425 Carl's Birthday [Ruggles] (?Henry Cowell), ?1926; 436 Dust and Flame (J. Rantz), *c*1927; 455 Renewal, 1929; 474 Milady of Dreams, ?1920–30; 477 *How Old is Song? (Harry Cowell), 1931 [<G:477a]; 492 *Sunset, Rest (C. Riegger), 2 songs, 1933

497 Proletarian Songs and a March, 1v/vv, pf/unacc., ?1930–33: 1 Canned, 2 Free Nations United!, 4 Proletarian Song, 5 We can win together, 6 Working men unite, we must put up a fight! [for no.3 see I:497/3]; 504 Introspection (E. White), 1934; 507 Relativity (S. Giffin), 1934; 509 Plan ahead (C. W. Eliot), ?*c*1934; 538 6 Songs on Mother Goose Rhymes, 1v/vv, pf, 1937: 1 Curly Locks, 2 Polly put the Kettle on, 3 Three Wise Men, 4 Dr. Foster went to Gloucester, 5 Goosey, 6 Tommy Trot

542 3 Anti-modernist Songs, 1938: 1 A sharp where you'd expect a natural, 2 Hark! From the pit a fearsome sound, 3 Who wrote this fiendish "Rite of Spring"?; 566 Return, 1v, 3 perc, 1939; 575 Up from the Wheelbarrow (O. Nash), 1939; 604 Mice Lament (E. Grainger), 1v, pf-str, 1940; 665 *The Pasture (Frost), 1944 [AP]; 671 *United Nations: Songs of the People (trad.), 1945; 694 *Daybreak (Blake), 1946; 695 *The Donkey (G. K. Chesterton), 1946

698 *March on Three Beats (J. W. Beattie), 1v/vv, pf, 1946; 702 Family Ruellan-Taylor, 3 solo vv, 1946; 760 Signature of Light (Hagemeyer), 1951; 762 Her smile is as sweet as a rose (? Henry Cowell), 1v, ?unacc., 1951; 783 *The Little Black Boy (Blake), 1952, rev. 1954; 803 The Commission (C. McPhee), sym. cantata, 4 solo vv, orch, 1954, not orchd; 808 *Spring Comes Singing (Hagemeyer), 1954; 814 St. Francis' Prayer for Our Day, 4 solo vv, 1955 [AP]

820 Because the Cat (B. A. Davis), ?1951–5; 824 Septet for [5] Madrigal Singers, Cl, and Kbd, 1956; 825 Crane (P. Colum), 1956; 826 I heard in the night (Colum), (1v, pf/cl/va)/(S, fl), 1956; 827 Night Fliers (Colum), 1956; 864 Spring Pools (Frost), ?*c*1958; 879 High Let the Song Ascend (hymn), 1v, fl, pf, 1960; 891 Music I Heard (C. Aiken), 1961; 910 *Firelight and Lamp (G. Baro), 1962; 935 3 Songs (L. Hughes), 1v, fl/vn, cl, vc, 1964: 1 Demand, 2 Moonlight, 3 Fulfillment; 939 The Eighth-note Jig (R. Brown), ?1960–64; *c*80 others, most lost

CHAMBER

E: *5 or more insts*

328a *Exultation, 4 vn, 2 va, 2 vc, db, 1930 [>I:328]; 340 Carl's Birthday [Ruggles], 3 cl, hn, str qt, pf, *c*1920–21; 380 *Ensemble: Str Qnt with Thunder Sticks, 1924, *rev. 1956, 380b [movts 1 and 2 <movts 1 and 2 of A:443]; 406 A Composition, pf-str, ens, 1925 [movt 1 <movt 1 of A:440; movt 2 <I:406/2a]; 458 *Polyphonica, 12 insts/chamber orch, 1930; 491b *Suite for Ww Qnt, 1934 [>movts 2, 4, 5, 6, of G:491]; 505 *Ostinato pianissimo, 8 perc, 1934; 521 Dance Forms, 3 insts, 2 perc, 1936

548 4 Assorted Movts, fl, ob, cl, b cl, bn, hn, pf ad lib, 1938: 1 Hoedown, 2 Taxim, 3 Tala, 4 Chorale; 565 *Pulse, perc, 1939; 639 *Action in Brass, brass qnt, 1943: 1 Dancing Brass, 2 Singing Brass, 3 Fighting Brass; 643 This is America 1943, fanfare, 4 tpt, 3 trbn, tuba, 1943; 684 *Party Pieces (Sonorous and Exquisite Corpses), ?*c*1945, 20 pieces by Thomson, Cowell, Cage, and Harrison, Cowell contributed to nos.3, 9, 10, 12–20 [arr. fl, cl, bn, hn, pf, by R. Hughes]

705/3b *Ballad, ww qnt, 1956 [>A:705/3a]; 709 *Tall Tale, brass sextet, 1947; 717 Tune Takes a Trip, cl choir/qnt, 1948; 729 Grinnell Fanfare, brass, org, 1948; 772 4 Trumpets for Alan [Hovhaness], 4 tpt, muted pf, 1952; 837 Taxim, Round and F[uguing] T[une], inst ens, 1957, fuguing tune inc.; 851 *Rondo for Brass, 3 tpt, 2 hn, 2 trbn, 1958; 888 Suite, 2 vn, va, vc, db, ?1950–60; 923 *26 Simultaneous Mosaics, cl, vn, vc, pf, perc, 1963

F: *3–4 insts*

24 Pf Quartette, 3 vn, pf, ?1912; 160 Scenario, 2 vn, vc, pf, 1915; 162 Quartett, str qt, 1915; 166 Minuetto, str qt, 1915; 197 *Str Qt [no.1] (Quartett Pedantic), 1916; 223 *Quartet Romantic, 2 fl, vn, va, 1917; 283 *Quartet Euphometric, str qt, 1919; 332 Movt, str qt, 1921; 383 *4 Combinations for 3 Insts, vn, vc, pf, 1924; 408 *7 Paragraphs, vn, va/vn, vc, 1925; 438 4 Little Solos for Str Qt, 1928; 450 *Movt for Str Qt (Str Qt no.2), 1928 [>movt 6 of A:887]

518 *Mosaic Qt (Str Qt no.3), 1935 [<movts 1–4 of A:887]; 522 *Str Qt no.4 "United," 1936; 524 *Vocalise, 1v, fl, pf, 1936; 547 *Toccanta, S, fl, vc, pf, 1940, arr. as Music Lovers' Set of Five, fl, vn, vc, pf, 547b, 1940, lost [<A:547a]; 595a 58 for Percy, 3 harmonium, 1940 [>A:595]; 628 60 for 3 Sax, 1942; 650 R[uellan]-T[aylor] "Family Suite," s rec, s/a rec, t rec, 1943; 662 Sonatina, Bar, vn, pf, 1944 [AP]; 664 Hymn and Fuguing Tune no.4, (s rec, a rec, b rec)/ww/str, 1944 [AP]

668 Sonatina, Bar, vn, pf, 1944; 713 Hymn, Chorale, and Fuguing Tune no.8, str qt, 1947 [<movts 5 and 6 of A:788]; 737 *Sailor's Hornpipe: the Sax-happy Qt, 4 sax, 1949; 741 Christmas for Sidney 1949, s rec, a rec, t rec, kbd, 1944 [AP]; 779 *Set of Five, vn, pf, perc, 1952; 786 *For 50, s rec, a rec, t rec, 1953, pubd as no.2 of 3 Pieces for 3 Rec; 789 Song for Claire, 3 rec, kbd, 1953; 800 Sonata, duet, sopranino/s rec, s rec, a rec, 1954; 802 *Qt for fl, ob, vc, hpd, 1954, arr. fl, ob, vc, harp, 802a, 1962

806 *Pelog, 2 s rec, a rec, 1954 [AP], pubd as no. 1 of 3 Pieces for 3 Rec; 809 *Jig, s rec, s/a rec, a rec, 1955 [AP], pubd as no. 3 of 3 Pieces for 3 Rec; 832 *Str Qt no. 5, 1956; 843 Wedding Anniversary Music, a rec/vn, vn/cl/hn, vc/bn/hn, 1957 [AP]; 850 *Hymn and Fuguing Tune no. 12, 3 hn, 1958; 890 Sax Qt, 1961; 898 Family Rondo, 3 kotos, 1961; 901 Love on June 2, 1962, vn, fl, pf, 1962 [AP]; 903 *Trio for fl, vn, harp, 1962; 941 *Trio in 9 Short Movts, vn, vc, pf, 1965

G: *2 insts*

71 [A Prince who was Apart]: 1 March, 2 Wedding Music, vn, pf, lost [no. 2 ? = no. 12 of J:70]; 74 Rondo, vn, pf, 1913; 104/1 Vn Stucke, vn, pf, 1914 [= no. 1 of I:104]; 150 Minuetto, vn, pf, *c*1914; 153 Vn Piece no. 1, vn, pf, ?*c*1914; 158 Vc Sonata, 1915; 180 Vn Piece no. 2: Phantasmagoria, vn, pf, 1915; 199 Air, vn, pf, 1916; 263 Vn Song (Love Song), vn, pf, 1918–19; 264 Va Song, va, pf, 1918–19; 304 Mazurka, e, vn, pf, 1920; 320 Reminiscence, vn, pf, *c*1920; 352 Gavotte, vn, pf, 1922

357 Minuetto, vn, pf, 1922; 368 Chiaroscuro, vn, pf, 1923; 392 Paragraph for Leo, vn, pf, 1924; 393 Passage, vn, pf, 1924; 397 *Suite, vn, pf, 1924; 398 Trugbild (Phantasmagoria), vn, pf, 1924; 407 Fiddel Piece, vn, pf, 1925; 432 A Remembrance for Leo Linder, vn, pf, ?1926; 477a *How Old is Song?, vn, pf, 1942 [>D:477]; 491 *6 Casual Developments, cl, pf, 1933 [<J:491a, movts 2, 4, 5, and 6 <E:491b]; 517 7 Associated Movts, vn, pf, 1935

529 A Bit of a Suite, vn, va, 1937; 532 *3 Ostinati with Chorales, ob, pf, 1937; 552 [4 Pieces for Pereira], vn, pf, 1938, no. 4 inc.; 568 *Triad, tpt, pf, 1939; 597a Ancient Desert Drone, 2 harmonium, 1940 [>A:597]; 611 *Two-Bits, fl, pf, 1941; 649 Carol 1943, 2 rec, 1943; 653 Stonecrop, 2 rec, 1943; 674 Hymn, vn, pf, 1945 [AP; = movt 1 of G:705]; 676 For Sidney, 2 rec, 1945 [AP]

700 *Tom Binkley's Tune, euphonium, pf, 1946; 701 Family Cowell Duet, a rec, b rec, 1946 [AP]; 705 *Vn Sonata, 1946 [movt 1 = G:674, movt 3 <A:705/3a]; 710 *Hymn and Fuguing Tune no. 7, va, pf, 1947; 714 122,547th Two Part Invention, s rec, a rec, 1947 [AP]; 730 Set of Two, vn, pf-str, 1948; 736 *4 Declamations with Return, vc, pf, 1949; 756 Duet for Recorders, 1950 [AP]; 758 *Hymn and Fuguing Tune no. 9, vc, pf, 1950 [hymn <movt 1 of A:787]

763 Scherzo, s rec, a rec, 1951 [AP]; 766 Duet for Sidney with Love from Henry, vn, vc, 1951 [AP]; 773 Two Part Invention, s rec, a rec, 1952 [AP]; 777 11th Anniversary, s rec, s/a rec, 1952 [AP]; 784 A Set of Four, s rec, a rec, 1952; 791 Duet, s rec, a rec, 1953 [AP]; 793 Merry Christmas to Sidney, 2 rec, 1953 [AP]; 801/6 In Memory of Nehru, (sitar/vīṇā/vn/1v), (tambura/"sanoi"/pipes/harmonium), 1964, no. 6 of [6] Memorial Pieces [see also A:801/1]; 804 Invention, a rec, kbd, 1954 [AP]

811 Beethoven Birds, 2 rec/pf, 1955 [AP]; 812 Set of Two, vn, hpd, 1955; 815 Invention, 2 fl/2 rec, 1955 [AP]; 831 Two Part Invention, s rec, a rec, 1956 [AP]; 834 15th Anniversary, 2 tr insts, 1956 [AP]; 835 Sidney Xmas '56, vn, pf, 1956 [AP; = G:862]; 840 Love to Sidney, s rec, a rec, 1957 [AP]; 844 Christmas 1957, s rec, a rec, 1957 [AP]; 845 *Homage to Iran, vn, pf, 1957; 854 Birthday Piece, 2 tr insts, 1958 [AP]

855 [Duet], 2 tr insts, 1958 [AP]; 857 Introduction and Allegro, va, hpd/pf, 1958; 859 Duet, 2 s insts, 1958 [AP]; 862 Love to Sidney, Christmas 1958, s inst, pf, 1958 [AP; = G:835]; 866 Duet, 2 vn, 1959 [AP]; 870 Duet, 2 tr insts, 1959 [AP]; 872 Sidney's Christmas Stretto, 2 tr insts, 1959 [AP]; 875 *Hymn and Fuguing Tune no. 13, trbn, pf, 1960; 876 Stretto, 2 tr insts, 1960 [AP]; 880 Love to Sidney, 2 tr insts, 1960 [AP]

883 Love for Sidney, s rec, a rec, 1960 [AP]; 893 Duet: Hymn and Fuguing Tune no. 15a, 2 insts, 1961 [AP]; 896 Duet, 2 tr insts, 1961 [AP]; 897 *Air and Scherzo, a sax, pf, 1961 [<B:897a]; 899 Triple Rondo, fl, harp, 1961; 906 Love Christmas 1962, 2 tr insts, 1962 [AP]; 907 Duet, 2 insts, 1962 [AP]; 914 Sixty with Love, vn, vc, 1963 [AP]; 915 Hymn and Fuguing Tune no. 15b, vn, vc, 1963; 918 August Duet, 2 vn, 1963 [AP]

921 *Hymn and Fuguing Tune no. 16, vn, pf, 1963 [<A:921a]; 924 Christmas 1963, 2 vn, 1963 [AP]; 928 Hymn and Fuguing Tune no. 18, s sax, cb sax, 1964; 933 Duet, 2 a rec/2 vn/2 fl/2 ob, 1964 [AP]; 936 For Sidney with Love, s rec, a rec, 1964 [AP]; 937 Stretto for Claflins, 2 insts, 1964; 944 Duet for Sidney, s rec, a rec, 1965 [AP]; 948 Sidney's Tune, s rec, a rec, 1965 [AP]; 951 A Melodie for Charlie [Seeger], vn, vc, 1965; 952 Duet for Our Anniversary, vn, va/vc, 1965 [AP]

H: *solo inst*

280 For Unacc. Vc, 1919; 418 [Presto], vn, *c*1925; 699 *The Universal Fl, shakuhachi, 1946; 798 Hymn and Fuguing Tune no. 10, carillon, ?1952–3, fuguing tune not composed [not = B:813]; 849 Henry's Hornpipe, tr inst, 1958; 852 André's Birthday Song [Andree Ruellan], tr inst, 1958; 853 Lullaby for Philio, tr inst, 1958; 856 Wedding Rondo [for] Sidney Reisberg, cl, 1958

868 *Iridescent Rondo in Old Modes, accordion, 1959; 877 *Perpetual Rhythm, accordion, 1960, orig. version, 1949, lost; 884 Merry Christmas for Blanche [Walton], tr inst, 1960; 895 Birthday Melody for Blanche [Walton], tr inst, 1960; 913 To my Valentine, 1963 [AP]; 922 *Gravely and Vigorously, in memory of President John F. Kennedy, vc, 1963; 927 Solo for Alto Rec, 1964 [AP]; 931 The Birthday Child, a Day Late, a rec, 1964; 934 Solo for Alto Rec, a rec, t rec ad lib, 1964 [AP]

I: KEYBOARD

(pf solo unless otherwise stated)

5 Waltz, *c*1910; 9 The Wierd Night, *c*1910–11; 10 The Night Sound: a Sonata, 1910–11; 15 Rippling Waters, Waltz, *c*1911; 22 Ghoul's Gallop, ?1912; 27 Op. 1 for Pf, 1912: 1 School March, 2 Tarantelle, 3 Lullaby, 4 Flashes of Hell Fire: a Dance of Devils, 5 The Cloudlet, 6 The Frisk, 7 Imaginings, 8 The Last Match, 9 The Lotus, 10 Scherzo, 11 Etude, 12 Sonatine, all lost except nos. 2 and 4; 29 Nocturne, 1913; 30 Freak de concert, 1913 [= no. 13 of J:70]; 31 Polish Dance, 1913

32 Prelude no. 2, 1913 [= no. 1 of J:70]; 33 Prelude [no. 1] after the Style of Bach, 1913 [= no. 2 of J:70]; 34 Valse lente, 1913 [= no. 3 of J:70]; 35 Bersuse, 1913 [= no. 6 of J:70]; 36 Fairys Dance no. 3 in a Popular Style, 1913 [= no. 7 of J:70]; 37 Invention quasi Bach, a tre voce, 1913 [= no. 8 of J:70]; 38 Brownie's Dance, 1913 [= no. 10 of J:70]; 40 Savage Suite, 1913: 1 Savage Dance, 2 Savage Music, 3 War Dance, 4 Sad Fragment, 5 Melodie, 6 Fire Dance, 7 Funeral March of Natives, 8 Joy Dance, inc., 9 A Savage Rhythm, 10 A War [no. 8 = no. 16 of J:70]

41 A Fragment, 1913; 42 Etude-cadenza, 1913; 43 Lullaby, 1913; 44 Hunting Song, 1913; 45 The Awakening, 1913; 46 Message from Mars, 1913; 47 Quasi Mozart, 1913; 48 Largo, 1913; 51 Etude, d, 1913; 54 Wrinkle Rag, 1913 [= no. 4 of J:70]; 55 Love Dance (Valse), 1913 [= no. 14 of J:70]; 56 3 Sonatas, 1913: 1 Sonata, A, inc., 2 Sonate, E♭, 3 Sonate, B; 57 Romance, 1913 [= no. 11 of J:70]; 58 Dirge, 1913

59 Adventures in Harmony (A Novelette), 1913; 60 Sounds from the Conservatory, 2 pf, 1913; 63 Album Leaflet, 1913; 64 Hash, 1913; 65 Mist Music no. 1, 1913 [= no. 17 of J:70]; 66 Mist Music no. 2, 1913; 73 The Anaemic Rag (A Burlesque), 1913 [= no. 9 of J:70]; 75 Etude [no. 2], C, 1913; 76 Valse, 1913; 78a The Cauldron, ?1913–18 [arr. from lost pf piece]; 81 Sprites' Dance, 1913 [= Wind Spirits' Dance, no. 15 of J:70]

82 [Christmas-thoughts Pieces], 1913: 1 Etude-chimes, 2 Xmas Thoughts for Baby, 3 Reindeer Dance, 4 Xmas Bells, 5 Xmas Stocking Dance, 6 Watching for Santa, 7 The Tin Soldier, 8 The Xmas Tree, 9 Valse, 10 Tarantelle, 11 March, 12 For Phyllis, 1913, nos. 9–12 lost; 83 Sonate progressive, 1913: 1 Classic, 2 Romantic, 3 Modern, 4 Humoreske; 84 Orchestra Stucke, 1913 [?>lost orch work]; 86 Descriptive Piece, 1913; 87 The Battle Sonata, 1913; 91 [Andante], A♭, ?*c*1913

92 Jesus was born at Christmas, ?*c*1913; 94 Theme, with 3 variations, 1914; 97 In the Tropics, 1914; 98 Sea Picture, 1914 [= no. 5 of J:70]; 99 Etude no. 3, 1914; 102 Piece, 1914; 104 [Musical Letters to Mrs. Veblen], 1914: 2 Dance, 3 Maid and Hero, 4 Theme, 5 Tango Theme, 6 *Anger Dance "Mad Dance," 7 Modern Stucke, lost, 12 (Etude) Classic, 13 Etude no. 4 "The Winds," 14 Themelet, 15 Valse, 16 Snake Piece [for no. 1, see G:104/1, for nos. 8–11, see D:104/8–11]

105 Vio doloroso, 1914; 108 Imitations in Style of Various Composers: Chopin, Brahms, Schumann, Grieg, 4 pieces, 1914; 109 Popular Melodie, 1914; 114 Sonate Movt, F, 1914; 115 Sonate Movt, f, 1914; 119 Sonate Movt, c♯, 1914; 120 Resumé in 10 Movts, 1914: 1 Savage Music, 2 Choral Music, 3 Contrapuntal Music, 4 Classic Sonate, 5 Folk Music, lost, 6 Romantic, 7 Operatic, 8 Oriental, 9 Modern, 10 Futurist; 139 Skylight, 1914

213 [Dynamic Motion and encores]: 1 *Dynamic Motion, 1916, 2 *What's This?, 1st encore, 1917 [<A:213/2a], 3 *Amiable Conversation, 2nd encore, 1917, 4 *Advertisement, 3rd encore, 1917, 5 *Antinomy, 4th encore, 1917, 6 *Time Table, 5th encore, 1917; 214 The Rogues' Gallery: Portraits, 1916, 8 pieces, all lost except no. 6 Mrs. Bartlett; 217 Letter [to J. O. Varian], ?1915–16; 219/1 *The Tides of Manaunaun, ?1917 [= no. 1 of J:219, no. 1 of I:354; <no. 1 of B:605]

224 Sixth Etude (A Tragedy), 1917; 225 Sonate, 1917, movt 4 inc.; 227 Prelude and Canon, 1917; 229 Olive, 1917; 234 Antique Dance, 1917; 239 [untitled], A♭, ?*c*1916–17; 240 Prelude, ?*c*1916–17; 243 Telegram, ?1916–17; 262 Child's Song, 1918–19; 269 [Waltz], ?1918–19; 273 Sonate, c, 1919; 279 Prelude interrhythmique, 1919; 281 Sonate Movt, B, 1919; 292 [Expressivo], *c*1919; 294 Mrs. Barrett, ?1917–19; 295 One Moment, Please, ?1917–19; 298 Prelude specifique, 1920

302 Fugue, c, 1920; 303 Double Fugue, c, 1920; 305 Vestiges, 1920 [<A:305a]; 307 *Fabric, 1920; 308 The New Born, 1920; 310 Prelude diplomatique, 1920; 312 For Xmas '20: an Idiosyncrasy, 1920; 315 Episode, b♭, 1920; 323 Episode [no. 2], d, 1921; 324 *Episode [no. 3], g♯, 1921; 326 Singing

Waters, 1921; 327 Romance, E♭, 1921; 328 *Exultation, 1921 [<E:328a, <no.2 of B:605]; 335 Xmas 1921, 1921

336 Tom's Waltz, for Tom Moss to Play, 1921; 339 Cantabile, *c*1920–21; 342 March, *c*1920–21; 350 Dance Obsequious, 1922; 353 [Ings]: 1 *Floating, ?1922, 2 *Frisking, ?1922, 3 *Fleeting, 1917, 4 *Scooting, 1917, 5 *Wafting, 1917, 6 *Seething, 1917, 7 *Whisking, 1917, 8 *Sneaking, 1917, 9 *Swaying, 1924, 10 Sifting, 1917, lost, 11 Wafting no.2, 1917, 12 Landscape no.3: Trickling, 1917, 13 Whirling, ?1930, lost, 14 Rocking, 1955 [nos. 1–6 orig. pubd as series, Six Ings]

354 3 Irish Legends: 1 *The Tides of Manaunaun, ?1917, 2 The Hero Sun, 1922, 3 The Voice of Lir, 1920 [no.1 = I:219/1, <no. 1 of B:605]; 355 *It isn't It, 1922, pubd as Scherzo; 361 Scherzo, 1922; 362 Seven and One Fourth Pounds, 1922; 367 The Sword of Oblivion, pf-str, *c*1920–22; 369 The Vision of Oma, 1923; 370 *The Aeolian Harp, pf-str, *c*1923; 371 Love Song, ?*c*1923; 372 Love Song, ?*c*1923; 377 A Rudhyar, 1924; 378 Xmas Greetings for Olive, 1924

381 Exuberance, 1924; 382 The Fire of the Cauldron, 1924; 384 The Harp of Life, 1924 [<no.3 of B:605]; 388 March of the Feet of the Eldana, 1924; 389 2 Movts for Pf, 1924: 1 *Piece for Pf with Strings, 2 Allegro maestoso–Largo–Con moto, inc.; 390 Paragraph, 1924; 395 *The Snows of Fuji-yama, 1924; 399 The Trumpet of Angus Og (The Spirit of Youth), 1918–24; 401 Chromatic Inst Fugue, ?1924; 403 March of the Fomer, ?*c*1924

405 *The Banshee, pf-str, 1925 [<movt 1 of B:452]; 406/2a Duett to St. Cecilia, pf-str, 1925 [>movt 2 of E:406]; 409 *Prelude for Org, 1925; 412 The Battle of Midyar, ?*c*1925; 415 Irish Jig, ?*c*1925 [<A:415a]; 422 [?F. L.] D. on Birthday, ?*c*1920–25; 426 Domnu, the Mother of Waters, 1926; 429 *Maestoso (Marked Passages), 1926 [<movt 3 of A:443]; 433 The Sleep Music of the Dagna, pf-str, 1926; 435 How Come?, 1927

442 When the Wind Chases You, 1928; 446 [10 children's pieces for piano], 1928: 1 *The Nimble Squirrel, 2 *An Irish Jig, 3 *The Spanish Fiesta, 4 *In Colonial Days, 5 *The Hand Organ Man, titles of nos.6–10 unknown, nos. 1–5 pubd as by Henry Dixon; 447 *The Fairy Bells, pf-str, by 1928 [<movt 3 of B:452]; 448 The Leprechaun, pf-str, 1928 [<movt 2 of B:452]; 449 I Wish I had an Ice Cream Cone, 1928; 451 *2 Woofs, 1928; 453 *The Fairy Answer, pf-str, 1929; 454 Euphoria, 1929; 456 Next to Last, ?pf, ?1919–29

462 *Sinister Resonance, 1930; 463 *Dve piesy [2 pieces]: 1 V ritme "rilya," irlandskiĭ tanets, 1928 [Lilt of the reel], 2 Tigr [Tiger], 1930 [no.1 <A:463/1a and b, no.4 of B:605; no.2 >inc. pf piece]; 469 March of Invincibility, 1930; 470 Whirling Dervish, 1930; 473 For a Child, ?1920–30; 479 [Gig], 1931; 484b 2 Appositions, 1932 [>A:484]; 487 Rhythm Study, 1932; 489 Expressivo, ?1928–32; 496 On the 8th Birthday of the Princess (Magic Music): a Measure for Each Year, ?1930–33

497/3 Move Forward!, no.3 of Proletarian Songs and a March, D:497, ?1930–33, inc.; 514 *The Harper Minstrel Sings, 1935; 515 *The Irishman Dances, 1935; 530 Back Country Set: Reel, Jig, Hornpipe, 1937; 543b *Celtic Set (1941) [>A:543]; 543c *Celtic Set, 2 pf (1941) [>A:543]; 549 Set of 2 Movts, 1938: 1 Deep Color, 2 High Color, 1938; 550 Wedding March, 1938 [<A:550a]; 557 *Rhythmicana, 1938; 560 [Jig], ?pf, ?*c*1938; 564 *Amerind Suite, 1939: 1 The Power of the Snake, 2 The Lover Plays his Flute, 3 Deer Dance

607 Christmas Duet (Noel), pf 4 hands, 1940; 613 Granny O'Toole's Hornpipe, 1941; 614 *Homesick Lilt, 1941; 631 *Square Dance Tune, 1942; 635 *Processional, org, 1942; 646 2nd Anniversary, 1943 [AP]; 651 Hymn and Fuguing Piece, 1943 [<A:651a]; 654 Fabric Ending (Finale), ?1943; 658 *Mountain Music, 1944; 660a Hymn and Fuguing Tune no.3, *c*1948 [AP; >A:660]; 667 *Kansas Fiddler, 1944: 1 Fiddle Air, 2 Fiddle Jig, 3 Fiddle Hornpipe, 4 Fiddle Reel; 670 Elegie for Hanya Holm, ?1941–4

678 For Sidney Christmas 1945, 1945 [AP]; 683 Lookit! I'm a Cowboy, ?*c*1945; 685 Playing Tag is Keen, ?*c*1945; 696 Hymn and Fuguing Tune no.6, kbd, 1946 [AP; fuguing tune <movt 4 of A:697, part <I:711]; 703 Irish Epic Set, pf-str, kbd, 1946; 711 6th Two Part Invention for Sidney, 1947 [AP; part >I:696]; 718 Invention for Sidney, ?kbd, 1948 [AP]; 720 *All Dressed Up, 1948; 721 Deirdre of the Sorrows, 1948; 724 7th Two-part Invention, 1948 [AP]; 725 *The Good Old Days, 1948

726 Two Part Invention, 1948 [AP]; 734 Madman's Wisp, 1949: 1 Throwing the Curse, 2 Dancing the Spell; 735 Two Part Invention, kbd/2 rec, 1949 [AP]; 738 *Pa Jigs them all Down (Perpetual Jig), 1949; 739 *Pegleg Dance, 1949; 740 Two Part Invention, 1949 [AP]; 749 Two Part Invention, kbd, 1950 [AP]; 751 Two Part Invention, kbd, 1950 [AP]; 752 Two Part Invention with [pedal point on] G, 1950 [AP]; 754 *Two Part Invention in 3 Parts, 1950 [AP]; 755 Improvisation, 1950; 764 10th Anniversary, 1951 [AP]; 780 Invention, 1952 [AP]; 799 *Toccatina, 1954

801/2 Chorale to the Memory of Marie K. Thatcher, org, 1954, no.2 of [6] Memorial Pieces [see also A:801/1]; 801/4 Used in Org Piece for Allen McHose's Mother-in-law, org, 1961, no.4 of [6] Memorial Pieces [see also A:801/1]; 817 Ground and Fuguing Tune, org, 1955; 822 *Bounce Dance, 1956; 828 *Sway Dance, 1956; 841 Wedding Music, ded. H. and E. Rugg, 1957; 847 Wedding Piece for Krissi and Davy, 1957; 860 Jim's B'day, 1958; 886 *Set of Four, pf/hpd, 1960; 889 Perpetual Motion, 1961 [AP]; 900 *Hymn and Fuguing Tune no.14, org, 1962; 905 September 27, 1962, 1962 [AP]; 920 The Twenty-second, pf/(vn, vc), 1963 [AP]; 949 Tune for Avery [Claflin], pf/(vn, vc), 1965

J: DRAMATIC

70 Music for Creation Dawn (incidental music, T. Kanno), 27 pieces, pf, 1913: nos.1–17 composed separately [see I:32, 33, 34, 54, 98, 35, 36, 37, 73, 38, 57, G:71/2, I:30, 55, 81, 40/8, 65], 18 Sunset Music, 19 Fairy's Dance no.2, 20 Thy lily bells, 21 Extacy, 22 Sad Music, 23 Music for Saavashi, 24 Dance Music for Sagano, 25 Sleepy Music, 26 Extra Music: Melodie, 27 Moonlight Music (the finale); Carmel, CA, 16 Aug 1913, Cowell

184 Red Silence (incidental music, Jap. drama, F. L. Giffin), 10 pieces, speaker, fl, vn, vc, pf, 1915, no.7 inc., no.8 lost; San Francisco, 20 Jan 1916

219 The Building of Bamba (Irish mythological opera, 14 scenes, Varian), solo vv, mixed chorus, pf, 1917, inc., Halcyon, CA, 18 Aug 1917; rev. 1930, 219a, Halcyon, 7 Aug 1930, cond. Cowell [scene 1 = I:219/1, no.1 of I:354 <no.1 of B:605]

423 Atlantis (ballet, 9 movts), S, A, Bar, pf, orch, 1926

457 Men and Machines (dance music, E. Findlay), pf, 1930; Brooklyn, NY, 27 Feb 1930

476 Steel and Stone (dance music, C. Weidman), ?pf, 1931, lost, New York, 4 Feb 1931; arr. as Dance of Work, 10 insts, 476a, New York, 5 Jan 1932, cond. A. Weiss

482 Dance of Sport (dance music, Weidman), orig. entitled Competitive Sport, pf, also arr. fl, ob, cl, bn, str, 482a, 1931; New York, 5 Jan 1932

483 Heroic Dance (dance music, ded. M. Graham), 10 insts, ?1931; *arr. pf, 483a, ?1931

491a Six Casual Developments (dance music, Graham), chamber orch, 1934, lost; New York, 25 Feb 1934, cond. L. Horst [>G:491]

495 Three Dances of Activity (dance music, S. Delza), fl, pf, perc, 1933, lost: 1 Labor, 2 Play, 3 Organization; New York, 10 Dec 1933

500 Trojan Women (dance music, R. Radir), chamber orch, 1934

513 Fanati (incidental music, prol., 5 scenes, R. E. Welles), vv, pf, perc, 1935, lost; Palo Alto, CA, 7 June 1935

516 Salutation (dance music, H. Holm), fl, pf, perc, 1935, lost; Millbrook, NY, 28 Feb 1936

534 Sarabande (dance music, Graham), ob, cl, perc, 1937, lost; Bennington, VT, 30 July 1937, cond. Horst

537 Deep Song (dance music, Graham), ww, perc, 1937, lost; New York, 19 Dec 1937, cond. Horst

539 Ritual of Wonder (dance music, M. Van Tuyl), pf, perc, ?*c*1937

563 Les mariés de la Tour Eiffel (incidental music, J. Cocteau), pf, perc, 1939: 1 *Hilarious Curtain-opener, 2 *Ritournelle, 3 Two Ritournelles, 4 The Train Finale; Seattle, 24 March 1939, pf, dir. J. Cage

596 Fanfare: Variations (dance music, Van Tuyl), chaconne with 7 variations, 1940, lost; Oakland, CA, 27 July 1940

606 King Lear (incidental music, Shakespeare), male chorus, pf, orch, 1940; New York, 14 Dec 1940, dir. E. Piscator

609 *Trickster (Coyote) (dance music, E. Hawkins), ww, perc, 1941; New York, 20 April 1941

622 Hanya Holm Music (dance music, Holm), pf, 1941, inc.: 1 Dance of Introduction, 2 Evocation, 3 For a Dancer; no.1, New York, 17 March 1941

624 Woman in War (dance music, S. Chen), pf, 1942, lost; New York, 23 April 1942

627 Mr. Flagmaker (film music, M. E. Bute), SAATB, wind, ?pf, str, 1942

630 Banners: a Choreographic Chorale (dance music, 2 scenes, Whitman), S, chorus, chamber ens, 1942

637 Killer of Enemies (dance music, Hawkins), 1942, lost

644 Chinese Partisan Fighter (dance music, Chen), pf, 1943, lost; Redlands, CA, 27 Aug 1943

666 Derwent and the Shining Sword (incidental music, radio play, Bute), 1944

680 Hamlet (incidental music, Shakespeare), male vv, inst ens, 1945

743 O'Higgins of Chile (opera, 3, Lomax), 1949, not orchd

753 A Full Moon in March (dance music, G. Lippincott, W. B. Yeats),

male v/hn/vc/trbn, pf, 1950; Fargo, ND, 1 Dec 1950
761 Clown (dance music, Hawkins), pf, 1951
768 The Morning of the Feast (incidental music, M. Connelly), solo vv, inst ens, 1952
805 Changing Woman (dance music, J. Erdman), pf, drums, harmonium, 1954; San Francisco, 18 Dec 1954
836 Music for Ploesti (film music), ?1955–6, inc.
885 Here by the Water's Edge (film music, C. Pratt, L. Hurwitz), cl, bn, tuba, str, 1960, inc.

K: ARRANGEMENTS

525 C. Ives: Calcium Light Night, 6 wind, 2 drums, 2 pf, arr. and ed., 1936
572 J. S. Bach: Christ lag in Todesbanden BWV278, arr. band, 1939
588 F. Chopin: Polonaise, arr. band, 1936–40, lost
589 C. W. von Gluck: Andante, arr. orch ens, 1936–40, lost

folksong arrangements

612 *The Lost Jimmie Whalen (American trad.), 4vv, 1941
623 La Valenciana (Iberian trad.), S, A, mixed chorus, fl, bn, 2 gui, castanets, tap dancer, 1942
633 Ballynure Ballad (Irish trad.), chorus, bagpipe, 1942
672 *The Irish Girl (Irish trad.), SATB, pf, 1945
742 *Lilting Fancy (Nickelty, Nockelty) (Irish trad.), SATB, 1949
794 *Garden Hymn for Easter, SATB, 1953
795 *Granny does your dog bite?, SATB, 1953

Principal publishers: Associated, Boosey & Hawkes, C. Fischer, Peer-Southern, Peters, Presser, G. Schirmer

BIBLIOGRAPHY

M. Bauer: "New Musical Resources," *MM*, vii/3 (1929–30), 43
N. Slonimsky: "Henry Cowell," *American Composers on American Music*, ed. H. Cowell (Stanford, CA, 1933/*R*1962)
A. Farwell: "Pioneering for American Music," *MM*, xii (1934–5), 116
C. Seeger: "Henry Cowell," *Magazine of Art*, xxxiii (1940), 288
E. Gerschefski: "Henry Cowell," *ACAB*, iii/4 (1953–4), 3, 18
J. S. Harrison: "Cowell: Peck's Bad Boy of Music," *ACAB*, iii/4 (1953–4), 5
H. Brant: "Henry Cowell – Musician and Citizen," *The Etude*, lxxv (1957), no.2, p.15; no.3, p.20; no.4, p.22
J. Edmunds and G. Boelzner: *Some Twentieth-century American Composers*, i (New York, 1959), 37ff [incl. further bibliography]
H. Weisgall: "The Music of Henry Cowell," *MQ*, xlv (1959), 484
J. Cage: "The History of Experimental Music in the United States," *Silence* (Middletown, CT, 1961/*R*1973), 67
E. Helm: "Henry Cowell – American Pioneer," *MusAm*, lxxxii/4 (1962), 32
O. E. Albrecht: "Henry Cowell (1897–1965)," *JAMS*, xix (1966), 432
G. Chase: "Henry Cowell," *Inter-American Institute for Musical Research Yearbook*, ii (1966), 98
R. F. Goldman: "Henry Cowell (1897–1965): a Memoir and an Appreciation," *PNM*, iv/2 (1966), 23
various authors: "Henry Cowell: a Dancer's Musician," *Dance Scope* (1966), spr., 6
H. Oesch: "Henry Cowell, Pionier und Aussenseiter der Neuen Musik," *Melos*, xl (1973), 287
S. E. Gilbert: " 'The Ultramodern Idiom': a Survey of New Music," *PNM*, xii/1–2 (1973–4), 282
O. Daniel: "American Composer Henry Cowell," *Stereo Review*, xxxiii/6 (1974), 72
B. Saylor: *The Writings of Henry Cowell*, ISAMm, vii (Brooklyn, NY, 1977)
"Three Libraries to House Cowell Music and Recordings," *Clavier*, xvii/5 (1978), 56
B. Silver: "Henry Cowell and Alan Hovhaness: Responses to the Music of India," *Contributions to Asian Studies*, xii (1978), 54
D. S. Augustine: *Four Theories of Music in the United States, 1900–1950: Cowell, Yasser, Partch, Schillinger* (diss., U. of Texas, 1979)
R. H. Mead: "Cowell, Ives and *New Music*," *MQ*, lxvi (1980), 538
——: *Henry Cowell's New Music, 1925–1936: the Society, the Music Editions, and the Recordings* (Ann Arbor, 1981)
H. Gleason and W. Becker: "Henry Cowell," *20th-century American Composers*, Music Literature Outlines, ser. iv (Bloomington, IN, rev. 2/1981), 58 [incl. further bibliography]
M. L. Manion: *Writings about Henry Cowell: an Annotated Bibliography*, ISAMm, xvi (Brooklyn, NY, 1982)
F. Koch: *Reflections on Composing: Four American Composers: Elwell, Shepherd, Rogers, Cowell* (Pittsburgh, 1983)
R. H. Mead: "The Amazing Mr. Cowell," *American Music*, i/4 (1983), 63
H. W. Hitchcock: "Henry Cowell's *Ostinato Pianissimo*," *MQ*, lxx (1984), 23
D. Hall: "New Music Quarterly Recordings – a Discography," *Journal* [Association of Recorded Sound Collections], xvi/1–2 (1984), 10
B. Saylor: "The Tempering of Henry Cowell's 'Dissonant Counterpoint'," *Essays on Modern Music*, ed. M. Brody, ii (Boston, 1985), 3
W. Lichtenwanger: *The Music of Henry Cowell: a Descriptive Catalog*, ISAMm (Brooklyn, NY, 1986)

BRUCE SAYLOR (text),
WILLIAM LICHTENWANGER (work-list,
with ELIZABETH A. WRIGHT)

Cowles, Eugene Chase (*b* Stanstead, Que., ?1860; *d* Boston, MA, 22 Sept 1948). Actor and singer. He was brought up in Vermont, and later moved to St. Paul, where he studied singing. He achieved fame when he joined the Bostonians, particularly for his performance as Will Scarlet in the operetta *Robin Hood* by De Koven and H. B. Smith (1891), in which he introduced the song "Brown October Ale." His other notable roles included Romero in Victor Herbert's *The Serenade* (1897) and Sandor in Herbert's *The Fortune Teller* (1898), in which he introduced "Gypsy Love Song." Cowles continued to perform, particularly in works by Gilbert and Sullivan, until World War I, when he retired from the stage and taught singing.

GERALD BORDMAN

Cox [née Prather], **Ida** (*b* Toccoa, GA, 25 Feb 1896; *d* Knoxville, TN, 10 Nov 1967). Blues singer. She joined a minstrel show as a child and was singing in theaters at the age of 14. Although her career paralleled that of other classic blues singers, she depended less on vaudeville songs, and most of her repertory consisted of blues in traditional form. The first of her many recordings, *Any Woman's Blues* (1923, Para. 12053), was a composition by her pianist Lovie Austin, and demonstrated the characteristic resonant, rather nasal quality of her singing. With appropriate material, particularly her own blues compositions, she was among the finest women singers. *Ida Cox's Lawdy Lawdy Blues* (1923, Para. 12064) and *I've got the blues for Rampart Street* (1923, Para. 12063), both with excellent accompaniment by Tommy Ladnier on cornet and a trio including Austin, are strong yet relaxed. For several years Cox was accompanied professionally by the pianist Jesse Crump, who is heard playing a somber organ setting in *Coffin Blues* (1925, Para. 12318). After 1929, when she recorded *Jail House Blues* (Para. 12965) with the trombonist Roy Palmer, Cox did not record for ten years. *Four Day Creep* (1939, Voc. 05298), although recorded with a larger band than usual (including Hot Lips Page on trumpet), showed that she was still in excellent form. Between then and 1950 she worked intermittently as a singer, but made no recordings. In 1961 at the age of 65 she recorded a final session, including a remake of *Wild women don't have the blues* (on the album *Blues for Rampart Street*, Riv. 374). Her voice had lost its quality, however, and she retired from active performing thereafter.

BIBLIOGRAPHY

SouthernB
P. Oliver: *Conversation with the Blues* (London, 1965)
D. Stewart-Baxter: *Ma Rainey and the Classic Blues Singers* (New York, 1970)
——: Liner notes, *Ida Cox 1923 Recordings* (Fountain Vintage Blues 301, 1973)

PAUL OLIVER

Cox, Jean (*b* Gadsden, AL, 14 Jan 1922). Tenor. He studied at the University of Alabama, the New England Conservatory, and in Rome on a Fulbright scholarship with Luigi Ricci and Bertelli.

He made his début as Lensky in Tchaikovsky's *Eugene Onegin* in Boston with the New England Opera Theater, and, as Rodolfo, sang for the first time in Europe at the Teatro Sperimentale, Spoleto, in 1954. After seasons at Kiel and Brunswick (1953–9), he was engaged by the Mannheim Opera, which became his base. From 1956 he sang the Steersman, Lohengrin, Parsifal, Walther, and Siegfried at Bayreuth. As Siegfried (which he also sang at La Scala and Covent Garden) he looks and moves well, but he lacks the full stamina and vocal resources for the part. Cox has made occasional appearances in the USA, notably as Bacchus (*Ariadne auf Naxos*) at the Chicago Lyric Opera and as Walther in his début at the Metropolitan Opera (2 April 1976). His repertory also includes Don Carlos, Othello, Saint-Saëns' Samson, Števa (Janáček, *Jenůfa*), Apollo (Strauss, *Daphne*), Sergey (Shostakovich, *Katerina Izmaylova*), and the Cardinal (Hindemith, *Mathis der Maler*). With James King and Jess Thomas, Cox is among the most convincing heroic tenors of the post-war period.

HAROLD ROSENTHAL/R

Crabtree, Lotta [Charlotte Mignon] (*b* New York, 7 Nov 1847; *d* Boston, MA, 25 Sept 1924). Entertainer. She was guided by her mother throughout her career, which began in California, where from 1853 she learned singing and dancing from local entertainers. She toured mining towns in Mart Taylor's company from 1855, and appeared in variety halls in San Francisco in fall 1856. In 1861 she toured with Jake Wallace and his troupe, from whom she learned minstrelsy and to play the banjo. From 1859 to 1864 she made regular appearances in San Francisco theaters, where she was a great favorite. Her New York début at Niblo's Saloon on 1 June 1864 was coolly received, but she gained increasing fame from tours of the Midwest (1864–6). In Chicago in 1867 she played both title roles in John Brougham's *Little Nell and the Marchioness*, which was written especially for her; other notable successes included *Firefly* (1868), *Heart's Ease* (1870), *Zip* (1874), and *Musette* (1876). Regular tours with her own company made her a national figure, and she became the country's most highly paid actress. Her career began to wane in the mid-1880s, and she retired in 1892 after an injury. Her will left about $4 million to charities.

Crabtree's appeal rested primarily on her captivating presence; she improvised hilariously and interacted unpredictably with her audiences, managing to be both provocative and innocent. Her routines linked minstrelsy with musicals, frontier brashness with urban wit; her verve and humor greatly influenced later female vaudeville performers.

BIBLIOGRAPHY

C. Rourke: *Troupers of the Gold Coast, or The Rise of Lotta Crabtree* (New York, 1928)

H. M. Bates: *Lotta's Last Season* (Brattleboro, VT, 1940)

D. K. Dempsey and R. P. Baldwin: *The Triumphs and Times of Lotta Crabtree* (New York, 1968)

L. Rather: *Lotta's Fountain* (Oakland, CA, 1979)

I. F. Comer: "Lotta Crabtree and John Brougham: Collaborating Partners in the Development of American Musical Comedy," *Musical Theatre in America: Greenvale, NY, 1981*, ed. G. Loney (Westport, CT, 1984), 99

WILLIAM BROOKS

Craft, Robert (*b* Kingston, NY, 20 Oct 1923). Conductor and writer on music. He graduated from the Juilliard School (BA 1946). From 1950 to 1968 he was a conductor of the Evenings-on-the-Roof and the Monday Evening Concerts in Los Angeles. His main repertory interests were older music (Monteverdi, Schütz, Bach, and Haydn) and contemporary music (the Second Viennese School, Stockhausen, Varèse, and Boulez). He conducted the first performance of Varèse's *Nocturnal* and, with the Santa Fe Opera, the American premières of Berg's *Lulu* and Hindemith's *Cardillac*. He also directed the first recordings of the complete works of Webern and most of Schoenberg's music.

From 1948 Craft was closely allied with Igor Stravinsky, first as his assistant, later in a closer, almost filial relationship. Over 23 years he shared more than 150 concerts with Stravinsky, collaborated on seven books, and conducted the world premières of a number of Stravinsky's later works, notably *In Memoriam Dylan Thomas* and *Requiem Canticles*. Besides his Stravinsky collaborations, Craft has written extensively on music and literature, mainly for the *New York Review of Books*. After Stravinsky's death he worked on a three-volume biography of the composer. His works include *Chronicle of a Friendship* (1972), which contains sections from the collaborations, *Stravinsky in Photographs and Documents* (1976, with Vera Stravinsky), and the collections of criticism *Prejudices in Disguise* (1974), *Current Convictions* (1976), and *Present Perspectives* (1984). He is the translator and editor of Stravinsky's *Selected Correspondence* (1982–5).

BIBLIOGRAPHY

J. Peyser: "Stravinsky–Craft, Inc.," *American Scholar*, lii (1983), 513

"Craft, Robert," *CBY 1984*

PATRICK J. SMITH/PAULA MORGAN

Craighead, David (*b* Strasburg, PA, 24 Jan 1924). Organist. He studied privately in Los Angeles, then graduated in 1946 from the Curtis Institute where he was a pupil of McCurdy. A brilliant and technically secure recitalist, he began touring in 1944 and has played at national conventions of the American Guild of Organists. He has held important church and teaching posts, being organist of the Bryn Mawr Presbyterian Church (1942–6), the Pasadena Presbyterian Church (1946–55), and St. Paul's Episcopal Church in Rochester (from 1955); he has been a faculty member at Westminster Choir College, Princeton (1945–6), and at Occidental College, Los Angeles (1948–55), and chairman of the organ department at the Eastman School from 1955. He gave the first performances of Samuel Adler's Organ Concerto (1971) and Persichetti's *Parable* (1972). In 1983 Craighead received the International Performer of the Year Award, given by the New York City chapter of the American Guild of Organists. He married Marian Reiff, a professional organist, in 1948.

BIBLIOGRAPHY

J. Ferguson: "An Interview with David Craighead," *American Organist*, xvii/5 (1983), 84

VERNON GOTWALS

Crane, Julia E(ttie) (*b* Hewitville, NY, 19 May 1855; *d* Potsdam, NY, 11 June 1923). Educator and administrator. She attended the Normal School in Potsdam, graduating in 1874. In 1886 she founded the Crane Normal Institute of Music, for the training of music supervisors, at Potsdam College; the institute was the first of its kind in the USA to be connected with a teacher-training college. In 1887 she published her *Music Teacher's Manual*, which gained a reputation as the most complete guide to have been prepared for teachers of public school music. Throughout her career she worked to improve the quality of school music in the USA through lecturing, teaching, and involvement in professional organizations.

BIBLIOGRAPHY

E. B. Birge: *History of Public School Music in the United States* (Washington, DC, 1937)

W. D. Claudson: *The History of the Crane Department of Music, the State University of New York from 1884–1964* (diss., Northwestern U., 1965)

——: "The Philosophy of Julia E. Crane and the Origin of Music Teacher Training," *JRME*, vii (1969), 399

MARGARET WILLIAM McCARTHY

Crawford, Jesse (*b* Woodland, CA, 2 Dec 1895; *d* Sherman Oaks, CA, 27 May 1962). Theater organist. He grew up in Washington and Oregon orphanages and was entirely self-taught. He made his career first by playing for silent films and later as a performer on network radio and in the recording studio. His first success followed his appointment in 1917 to Sid Grauman's theater in Los Angeles. In 1921 Balaban & Katz brought him to the Chicago Theatre, where he met Helen Anderson (1899–1943), a cinema organist, whom he married; a second four-manual console was installed in the theater so that they could perform as a duo. From 1926 to 1932 they appeared together at the Paramount Theatre in New York and in 1933 Jesse Crawford appeared at the Chicago World's Fair. After his wife's death he continued as a solo performer of popular tunes. He later taught in New York and, after 1952, in Los Angeles. A writer for the *American Organist* (1962) considered his playing to represent "a perfection seldom found, in the realm of the theatre, the church or the concert hall."

BIBLIOGRAPHY

J. W. Landon: *Jesse Crawford: Poet of the Organ, Wizard of the Mighty Wurlitzer* (Vestal, NY, 1974)

VERNON GOTWALS

Crawford, Randy (*b* Macon, GA, 18 Feb 1952). Jazz and soul singer. She was brought up in Cincinnati and began singing as a child; by the time she was 15 she was working regularly in local nightclubs. Her first major performance was with George Benson in New York in 1972, and this led to her being booked for several major concerts throughout the USA. Her first album, *Everything Must Change* (1976), displayed her ability to interpret songs in a variety of styles with a voice that was rich in inflection and capable of a wide range of expression. Her first hit was as the guest singer on the title song of the Crusaders' album *Street Life* (1979), which was released as a single (MCA 41054) and reached no.36 on the pop chart. The Crusaders appeared on her album *Now We May Begin* (1980); they also wrote much of the material for this, including the hit single *One day I'll fly away*. Since then Crawford has worked with a number of producers and arrangers on several successful albums; she also gives frequent concert performances.

Crawford, Richard (Arthur) (*b* Detroit, MI, 12 May 1935). Musicologist. He attended the University of Michigan (BM 1958, MM 1959, PhD 1965) and began teaching there in 1962; he was appointed professor in 1975. He was president of the American Musicological Society, 1982–4, and Bloch Professor at the University of California, Berkeley, in 1985. Crawford's main interest is American music. He was a senior research fellow at the Institute for Studies in American Music at Brooklyn College, CUNY, in 1973–4; his fellowship lectures there, on American studies and musicology, were published in 1975, and his *Studying American Music* (which includes a list of his writings) was issued as one of the institute's special publications in 1985. He is the author of books on Andrew Law (1968) and (with D. P. McKay) William Billings (1975), and also compiled *The Civil War Songbook* (1977). He was the adviser on 18th-century music for this dictionary.

BIBLIOGRAPHY

"Richard Crawford, American Musicologist," *Music at Michigan*, xviii/1 (1984), 6

PAULA MORGAN

Crawford (Seeger), Ruth (Porter) (*b* East Liverpool, OH, 3 July 1901; *d* Chevy Chase, MD, 18 Nov 1953). Composer and educator. She received her early musical training largely at the School of Musical Art, Jacksonville, Florida, where she later taught piano. In 1921 she entered the American Conservatory in Chicago, studying piano with Heniot Levy and Louise Robyn and theory and composition with John Palmer and Adolf Weidig. Further piano studies with Djane Lavoie-Herz served to introduce her to a new musical circle which led her in 1929 to New York;

Ruth Crawford: portrait from life by Carl Bohnen, mid-1920s (private collection)

there she studied composition with Charles Seeger, whom she married in 1931 (*see* SEEGER family, (1) Charles). In 1930 she received a Guggenheim Fellowship which took her to Berlin and Paris for further study. In 1933 her Three Songs were chosen to represent the USA at the ISCM Festival.

Crawford pursued two musical interests in addition to her own composition throughout her life: American folk music, and teaching young children. She transcribed, arranged, and edited hundreds of folksongs from recordings in the Archive of American Folk Song at the Library of Congress, and composed piano accompaniments for some. Many were published in *Our Singing Country* by John and Alan Lomax and in her own collections, *American Folk Songs for Children* (1948), *Animal Folk Songs for Children* (1950), and *American Folk Songs for Christmas* (1953), which she used for teaching purposes.

Most of Crawford's innovative and experimental compositions are atonal with a natural predilection for tight organization. Her early compositions (1924–9) show influences of Scriabin's harmonic approach, traces of impressionism, and a fondness for the tritone and other dissonant intervals. Works from the early 1930s reveal intensified dissonance, highly patterned organization of several parameters, individual use of tone clusters, use of vocal and instrumental glissandos (unconventional at that time), innovative treatment of dynamics, and foreshadowing of metric modulation. Her high regard for both Berg and Bartók is also apparent in her works from these years. Crawford's last scores incorporate a simpler harmonic vocabulary and employ folk tunes in a distillation of her earlier art music techniques. Among her recorded works are Three Songs, the Suite for Small Orchestra, the String Quartet, the Violin Sonata, and several piano pieces.

WORKS

CHAMBER

Violin Sonata, 1926; Chicago, 22 May 1926
Suite, 5 wind, pf, 1927, rev. 1929
Suite no.2, str, pf, 1929
Three Songs (C. Sandburg), A, ob, perc, pf, opt. orch, 1930–32: Rat Riddles, 1930, New York, 21 April 1930; In Tall Grass, Berlin, 10 March 1932; Prayers of Steel, Amsterdam, 14 June 1933
Four Diaphonic Suites, 1930: no.1, 2 vc/(bn, vc); no.2, 2 cl; no.3, fl; no.4, ob/va, vc
String Quartet, 1931; New York, 13 Nov 1933
Suite for Wind Quintet, 1952; Washington, DC, 2 Dec 1952

OTHER

Vocal: Adventures of Tom Thumb (R. Crawford, after Grimm brothers), nar, pf, 1925; 5 Songs (Sandburg), Home Thoughts, White Moon, Joy, Loam, Sunsets, 1v, pf, 1929; 3 Chants, no.1, To an Unkind God, female chorus, no.2, To an Angel, S, SATB, no.3, S, A, female chorus, 1930; 2 Ricercari (H. T. Tsiang), no.1, Sacco, Vanzetti, no.2, Chinaman, Laundryman, 1v, pf, 1932
Orch: Suite for Small Orch, fl, cl, bn, 4 vn, 2 vc, pf, 1926; Rissolty Rossolty, 1939
Pf: 5 Preludes, 1924–5; 4 Preludes, 1927–8; Pf Study in Mixed Accents, 1930

MSS in *DLC*
Principal publishers: Continuo Music Press, New Music

FOLKSONG ARRANGEMENTS AND TRANSCRIPTIONS

C. Sandburg: *American Songbag* (New York, 1927) [4 arrs.]
19 American folk tunes, pf, unpubd, 1936–8
J. A. Lomax and A. Lomax: *Our Singing Country* (New York, 1941)
G. Korson: *Coal Dust on the Fiddle* (Philadelphia, 1943)
with C. Seeger: *J. A. Lomax and A. Lomax: Folk Song U.S.A.* (New York, 1947)
American Folksongs for Children (Garden City, NY, 1948)
G. Korson: *Anthology of Pennsylvania Folklore* (New York, 1949)
Animal Folksongs for Children (Garden City, 1950)
B. A. Botkin: *Treasury of Western Folklore* (New York, 1951)
American Folk Songs for Christmas (Garden City, 1953)
Let's Build a Railroad (New York, 1954)
E. Garrido de Boggs: *Folklore Infantil do Santo Domingo* (Madrid, 1955) [transcr.]
with D. Emrich and C. Seeger: 1001 Folksongs, inc., unpubd [13 vols.]

BIBLIOGRAPHY

EwenD
P. Rosenfeld: *An Hour with American Music* (Philadelphia, 1929)
M. Bauer: *Twentieth Century Music* (New York, 1933)
C. Seeger: "Ruth Crawford," *American Composers on American Music*, ed. H. Cowell (Stanford, CA, 1933), 110
S. R. Cowell: "Ruth Crawford Seeger," *JIFMC*, vii (1955), 55
Compositores de América/Composers of the Americas, ed. Pan American Union, ii (Washington, DC, 1956), 36
G. Perle: "Atonality and the 12-tone System in the United States," *Score*, no.27 (1960), 51
A. Porter: "Musical Events," *New Yorker*, xlviii (10 Feb 1972), 96 [on String Quartet]
M. Gaume: *Ruth Crawford Seeger: her Life and Works* (diss., Indiana U., 1973)
J. Rockwell: "Musical Spotlight puts Ruth Seeger in Focus Sharply," *New York Times* (21 Feb 1975)
A. Frankenstein: "Ruth Crawford Seeger: Three Songs," *Works by Henry Cowell, Ruth Crawford Seeger, Wallingford Riegger, John J. Becker* (New World 285, 1978) [liner notes]
M. Gaume: "Crawford-Seeger, Ruth Porter," *NAW*
M. M. Coonrod: *Aspects of Form in Selected String Quartets of the Twentieth Century* (diss., Peabody Conservatory, 1984)

MATILDA GAUME

Creatore, Giuseppe (*b* Naples, Italy, 21 June 1871; *d* New York, 15 Aug 1952). Conductor, impresario, and composer. He studied music at the conservatory in Naples, and by the age of 17 was conductor of the city's municipal band. He left this position after eight years to play trombone in another band during its American tour. Encouraged by the wealth of performing opportunities in the USA, he decided to form his own ensemble. He recruited 40 musicians for this purpose during a trip to Italy in 1902, then traveled with them to New York, where the band's opening concert was well received. In the next few years he toured the USA and Canada. He appeared on the Chautauqua circuit from 1910 to 1916. In 1918 he organized an opera company, which continued for five years; at the same time he pursued his band activities. The Depression brought about a decline in professional bands, and in 1936 he became conductor of the New York City Symphonic Orchestra, formed under the auspices of the WPA. A year later he became bandmaster of the New York State Symphonic Band, also a WPA group. In 1939 he attempted to bring grand opera to the Bronx, New York, but soon had to cancel this overambitious project, despite two successful performances. He continued to make appearances as a guest conductor; these commitments forced him to resign from the WPA program in 1940. He gave his last concert in New York at the age of 75.

Creatore was a flamboyant, imposing figure, with a powerful physique, long hair, and a formidable moustache; an exhibitionist on the podium, he gained some notoriety for his exploits in exhorting his players and mesmerizing his audiences. Publicists described him as the "Svengali of the baton." The full extent of Creatore's compositional output is unknown; six sets of manuscript scores and parts from the early 1900s are at Yale University, and a number of his compositions are recorded in the Heritage of the March series (compiled by ROBERT HOE, JR.), subseries 17.

RAOUL CAMUS

Creedence Clearwater Revival. Rock group. Its original members were John Fogerty (*b* Berkeley, CA, 28 May 1945), singer, lead guitarist, and keyboard player; his brother Tom Fogerty (*b* Berkeley, 9 Nov 1941), rhythm guitarist; Stu Cook (*b* Oakland, CA, 25 April 1945), bass guitarist; and Doug Clifford (*b* Palo Alto, CA, 24 April 1945), drummer. The group was formed by Tom Fogerty in El Cerrito, California, in 1959 as the Blue Velvets and played at local functions. In 1964 it became the Golliwogs and made a series of undistinguished single records for the Fantasy label in Berkeley, which achieved only local exposure; the name Creedence Clearwater Revival was adopted in 1967. The group's first hit recording, a version of Dale Hawkins's rockabilly-blues hit *Suzie Q* (no.11, 1968), was influenced by the psychedelic

Creedence Clearwater Revival, c1970: (from left to right) John Fogerty, Stu Cook, Tom Fogerty, and Doug Clifford

rock of the period and marred by superficial electronic effects. John Fogerty, the group's principal songwriter and by this time effectively its leader in his brother's place, then turned against what he saw as the specious cult of instrumental virtuosity and mystical vagueness associated with psychedelic rock; he began to produce short, tightly arranged songs about specific situations and the emotional responses to them, which drew on the early rock-and-roll, blues, and country music styles of Fats Domino, Carl Perkins, Elvis Presley, Howlin' Wolf, and Little Richard. The group had a series of commercial and artistic successes with lyrical singles and passionate, intelligent tracks recorded on albums (including *Proud Mary*, no.2, 1969; *Bad Moon Rising*, no.2, 1969; *Green River*, no.2, 1969; *Up around the bend*, no.4, 1970; *Lodi*; *Don't look now*; *Effigy*; and *Hideaway*). Fogerty's lyrics took the American South as a metaphor for freedom, and delineated an ethic of responsibility and compassion to counteract psychedelic hedonism. His singing, rough in style but fervently committed, and resonant guitar playing, with hard, distinct rhythms in fast tempos, characterized the music. The two albums *Creedence Clearwater Revival* (1968) and *Green River* (1969) presented as far-seeing an account of the limitations and opportunities of the American way of life as the rock idiom has produced. Between 1969 and 1972 Creedence Clearwater Revival enjoyed considerable commercial success: it performed at Woodstock, toured Europe and made nine singles and five albums that reached the Top Ten. Though it also impressed the critics, the group was derided by other musicians as simplistic and retrogressive, and internal difficulties (the departure of Tom Fogerty and the demands of Cook and Clifford for equal prominence with John Fogerty as singers and songwriters) led to its decline; it disbanded in 1972.

John Fogerty then pursued a solo career, making recordings on which he accompanied his singing by overdubbing the guitar, bass guitar, drum, saxophone, and keyboard parts. He applied this technique to country music standards, calling himself the Blue Ridge Rangers, and also to recordings of early rock songs and original material which he issued under his own name. In both cases, however, the music was uninspired, and after 1976 Fogerty released no recordings until the album *Centerfield* (1985), which he again played and produced on his own. It reached no. 1, and although the performances were often stiff and the lyrical scope of the songs very restricted, its success did indicate a revival in Fogerty's popularity.

RECORDINGS

(selective list; recorded for Fantasy unless otherwise stated)

Creedence Clearwater Revival (8382, 1968), incl. I put a spell on you, Suzie Q; *Bayou Country* (8387, 1969), incl. Born on the Bayou, Proud Mary; *Green River* (8393, 1969), incl. Bad Moon Rising, Commotion, Lodi, Wrote a song for everyone; *Willy and the Poorboys* (8397, 1969), incl. Don't look now, Down on the Corner, Effigy, Fortunate Son; *Cosmo's Factory* (8402, 1970), incl. Lookin' out my back door, Travelin' Band, Up around the bend, Who'll stop the rain?; *Pendulum* (8410, 1970), incl. Have you ever seen the rain?, Hey tonight, Hideaway; *Mardi Gras* (9404, 1972), incl. Someday never comes, Sweet hitchhiker

John Fogerty solo: *The Blue Ridge Rangers* (9415, 1973); *John Fogerty* (Asy. 1046, 1975); *Centerfield* (WB 25203, 1985)

BIBLIOGRAPHY

R. Gleason: "John Fogerty," *The Rolling Stone Interviews* (New York, 1971), 331–61

R. Christgau: "Creedence: Where do you Go from the Top?"; "Whatever Happened to Creedence Clearwater Revival?," *Any Old Way you Choose it: Rock and Other Pop Music, 1967–1973* (Baltimore, 1973), 178; 277

GREIL MARCUS

Creek. American Indian group belonging to the Muskogean confederacy. They lived in towns along major river courses in Alabama and Georgia (hence the name "Creek") from as early as 1000 to the 1830s. In the 1980s most of the approximately

17,000 Creeks live in Oklahoma, but small groups remain in Florida, Georgia, and Alabama (*see* INDIANS, AMERICAN, fig. 1). A history of Creek music would have to be reconstructed from accounts given by soldiers, travelers, and traders in the 18th century and by missionaries and ethnographers from the mid-19th century to the present.

Music still pervades much of the life of the Creek people; it includes songs for public ceremonies and celebrations (both seasonal and cyclical), social dances, and animal dances, and music associated with games, prayers to the Creator, affective magic, and curing. Because missionaries made little impact on the Creeks until comparatively late (the 1840s) the singing of Christian hymns is less pervasive in Creek culture than among some other southeastern tribes.

The ceremonial season begins in the spring with night-time stomp and social dances. These are held at the square grounds, variously called "stomp grounds," "ceremonial grounds," or "tribal towns." These "towns" are reconstructed versions of those that existed in the Southeast before the forced removal of the Indians to Indian territory in the 1830s. Ceremonial activities include, besides dancing, the practicing of dances, taking medicine, the renewal of the clan arbors around the square, playing ball, and feasting. As time for the midsummer Green Corn Ceremony or Busk draws closer, activities increase, culminating when the astronomers determine the two most important days for the start of the ceremony. The Green Corn Ceremony is the highlight of the year, showing respect and thanksgiving to the deities for the ripe corn and the earth's goodness. Its major dances, the Feather, Ribbon, and Buffalo, occur, along with renewal and purification ceremonies, during daylight hours. Although in the past the ceremony took two weeks, it is now held as close to a weekend as possible so that everyone may attend. The dances take place, for the most part, in the center of the square ground around a sacred fire that has logs oriented to the four cardinal directions; the sacred number four and multiples of it control most of the ceremonial activities, including the music and dance. The ceremony is directed from the chief's arbor (or bed) on the west, but the songleaders usually sit in the south arbor; the north and east arbors, when all four are present, also contain seating, usually for males and arranged by clan. Almost every movement of the dancers, singers, medicine men, fire-keepers, and others is counterclockwise around the fire, the ball-game pole, or the square ground.

The Creeks use only three types of instrument in their dance-songs: a hand-held rattle, constructed by stringing a gourd, coconut, or terrapin shell (containing pebbles) on a stick; a drum, generally a keg or crock, partly filled with water and covered at one end with a soft, wet hide, stretched and tied on (a "hard," double-headed drum is now sometimes substituted); and terrapin-shell or tin-can rattles attached to pieces of hide or old boot tops, worn on both legs by female dancers. A flageolet was formerly used for love-songs and amusement, and is now enjoying a revival.

Like Cherokee and Seminole music, Creek music is primarily vocal and monophonic, with rattle and sometimes drum accompaniment, though a few solo songs, such as lullabies and medicine, magic, love, and hunting songs, are unaccompanied; all the dance-songs require either the leg or hand rattles. The song cycle is the major form of Creek music. Repetition, variation, and improvisation, based on a fixed body of music, take the place of new composition. Creek songs have an undulating melodic contour, the predominant movement of which is descending. The scales, which are mainly anhemitonic pentatonic, have between two and seven or more pitches. Isorhythm is an important metric organizing principle, based on a steady, accented–unaccented pulse. Prescribed shouts, cries, and opening and closing formulae function as cues for the activities accompanied by the songs. The vocal quality is not only less nasal and tense than that of the Cherokee, but also contains more pulsations, voiced aspirations, and glottal shakes. Overlapping phrases between leader and chorus create momentary polyphony or harmony, while some songs, such as that for the Buffalo Dance, have complicated vertical textures in several parts.

Animal dances can be performed either to song cycles or to strophic songs, depending on the number of animal songs known for a particular genre: if only one song and refrain is known, the form is strophic with variations, as in the Gar Dance; if more songs are known, the leader may choose from among them in creating the dance. With many animal dances, the length of the dance is determined by the number of participants; in the Gar Dance, for example, the song continues until the first female dancer reaches the position behind the leader. Solo songs, along with animal dances, tend to have simpler melodies and forms than the Stomp and Friendship dances. The Creek Lullaby (ex. 1)

Ex.1 Creek lullaby (solo song), transcr. C. Heth

trans.: "Baby, sleep. Mother has gone to hunt turtles. She said she'd come back soon. Baby, sleep."

shows the common *ABA* form of a solo song. The forms of the Stomp, Friendship, and Old Folks' dances are analogous to those of the CHEROKEE, although performance details, style, and language differ. In all but the solo songs, responsorial singing of one type or another is the hallmark of Creek musical style.

See also INDIANS, AMERICAN, esp. §I, 4(ii)(b).

DISCOGRAPHY

Delaware, Cherokee, Choctaw, Creek, recorded 1942–51 (Library of Congress AAFS L37, 1954)

Songs of the Muskogee Creek (IH 3001–2, 1970)

Songs of Earth, Water, Fire, and Sky: Music of the American Indian, recorded 1975 (NW 246, 1976)

Stomp Dance (IH 3003–4, 1978)

Songs and Dances of the Eastern Indians from Medicine Spring and Allegany, recorded 1975 (NW 337, 1985)

BIBLIOGRAPHY

T. Baker: *Über die Musik der Nordamerikanischer Wilden* (Leipzig, Germany, 1882/*R*1976 with Eng. trans.)

F. G. Speck: *The Creek Indians of Taskigi Town*, Memoirs of the American Anthropological Association, ii/2 (Lancaster, PA, 1907)

——: "Ceremonial Songs of the Creek and Yuchi Indians," *University of Pennsylvania Museum Anthropological Publications*, i/2 (1911), 157–245
J. R. Swanton: *Early History of the Creek Indians and Their Neighbors* (Washington, DC, 1922)
——: "Aboriginal Culture of the Southeast," "Religious Beliefs and Medical Practices of the Creek Indians," "Social Organization and Social Usages of the Indians of the Creek Confederacy," *Annual Report of the U.S. B[ureau of] A[merican] E[thnology]*, xlii (1928), 673–726; 473–672; 23–472
——: *The Indians of the Southeastern United States* (Washington, DC, 1946)
J. F. Kilpatrick and A. G. Kilpatrick: *Muskogean Charm Songs among the Oklahoma Cherokees* (Washington, DC, 1967)
J. Howard: *The Southeastern Ceremonial Complex and its Interpretation*, Memoir: Missouri Archeological Society, no.6 (Columbia, MO, 1968)

CHARLOTTE HETH

Crehore, Benjamin (*b* Milton, MA, ?18 Feb 1765; *d* Milton, 14 Oct 1831). Maker of string and keyboard instruments. Although Spillane stated that Crehore was known as a maker of violins, cellos, guitars, drums, flutes, and harpsichords by 1792, only cellos remain to document this claim. He was especially renowned for his pianos (which he was making by 1797, according to a letter of November 1797 addressed to him), and may be said to be the founder of the New England piano industry.

Crehore lived and worked in Milton. His earliest surviving instrument, however, is a large cello (or "bass viol"), which, according to its label, was made by him in nearby Dorchester in 1788. In 1791 he entered into a partnership with Lewis Vose to build a shop that he rented from Vose from March 1792 until May 1796. In this shop, and in a later one constructed on property owned by his wife's family, he produced his instruments and trained such builders as Lewis and Alpheus Babcock and William and Adam Bent. He was associated with several professional musicians who were attracted to Boston by the opening of the Federal Street Theatre in the 1790s. Among these was Peter von Hagen, who, with his son, was Crehore's partner in music publishing, and in the sale and tuning of pianos, from May 1798 to June 1799. In 1801 two other musicians, Francis Mallet and Gottlieb Graupner, advertised "a large assortment of American Piano Fortes, manufactured by Benjamin Crehore," and in 1807 Graupner advertised a piano with a transposing keyboard "made, under his direction, after a plan of the Germans, by Messrs. Crehore and Babcock of Milton."

Never successful in forming a lasting business partnership, Crehore entered into an agreement with William Goodrich in 1804 to make hybrid piano-organs; the text of the agreement is at the Boston Public Library. He worked with the Babcocks on the Graupner transposing piano in 1807, and seems to have been associated with them until the death of Lewis Babcock in 1817. By 1816 Crehore may have been semiretired, for he stopped paying personal taxes. He is described in his will as a cabinet maker.

At least four cellos and five pianos by Crehore survive. The cellos (one in a private collection, one at the Boston Museum of Fine Arts, one at the Smithsonian Institution, and one at the New England Conservatory) have deeply cut scrolls and a typical body length of 73.6 cm. The five square pianos, similar in construction to English pianos of the period, usually have mahogany cases resting on stands with tapered legs, hand-stops to raise the dampers, a range of five or five and a half octaves, Zumpe action, and a long soundboard extending across the key frame. Two are still owned by the Crehore family; the others are at the Essex Institute in Salem, Massachusetts, the Boston Public Library, and the Metropolitan Museum of Art in New York.

BIBLIOGRAPHY

A. K. Teele: *The History of Milton, Mass. 1640 to 1887* (Boston, 1887), 149f, 377ff
D. Spillane: *History of the American Pianoforte* (New York, 1890/*R*1969), 50ff
O. G. T. Sonneck: *A Bibliography of Early Secular American Music* (Washington, DC, 1905; rev. and enlarged by W. T. Upton, 2/1945/*R*1964), 585f
C. L. Crehore: *The Benjamin Crehore Piano* (Boston, 1926)
C. M. Ayars: *Contributions to the Art of Music in America by the Music Industries of Boston, 1640 to 1936* (New York, 1937), 104f, 194f
H. E. Johnson: *Musical Interludes in Boston, 1795–1830* (New York, 1943), 269ff
A. C. Falcon: *Crehore and Kin* (Wellesley, MA, 1962), 20ff
Vose Papers (MS, *MMHi*) [account books]

CYNTHIA ADAMS HOOVER

Creshevsky, Noah (*b* Rochester, NY, 31 Jan 1945). Composer. He received his early musical training in the preparatory division of the Eastman School (1950–61) and then attended SUNY, Buffalo (MS 1966), and the Juilliard School (MFA 1968), where he was a pupil of Berio. During the year 1963–4 he studied at the Ecole Normale de Musique, Paris, with Boulanger. From Thomson he had informal lessons in form and analysis. He has held teaching positions at Juilliard and Hunter College, and in 1969 joined the faculty of Brooklyn College. He has received commissions from the choreographers Anna Sokolow and Rudy Perez and in 1981 was awarded an NEA grant.

Creshevsky's music was nurtured by the New York avant garde of the 1960s and early 1970s. *In Other Words: Portrait of John Cage* (1976), a "sound-text" work, uses a recording of Cage speaking as its only sound source; the words and phrases are reordered according to Creshevsky's notion of musical inflection and meaning inherent in speech, and a musical form emerges with the repetition and juxtaposition of speech fragments. The material used in *Highway* (1979), which further develops these techniques, is drawn from radio broadcasts and is combined into a rich polyphonic texture. In all Creshevsky's works humor and satire prompt the listener to re-evaluate the musical content of language and the contextual meaning of words. A number of his compositions have been recorded by Opus One Records.

WORKS

Tape: Circuit, 1971; Broadcast, 1973; In Other Words: Portrait of John Cage, 1976; Portrait of Rudy Perez, 1978; Highway, 1979; Sonata, 1980; Nightscape, 1982; Celebration, 1983

Mixed-media: Vier Lieder, theater piece, nar, pf, 1966; 3 Pieces in the Shape of a Square, 4 pfmrs (incl. 2 pianists), tape, 1967; Monogenesis, solo vv, double chorus, chamber orch, tape, 1968; Variations, (4 pianists, tape)/(perc, tape), 1969; Mirrors, dancers, tape, 1970

Inst: Chaconne, pf/harp, 1974; Guitar, gui, tape, 1975; Great Performances, any 2 insts, tape, 1977

Principal publisher: A. Broude

NOEL B. ZAHLER

Creston, Paul [Guttivergi, Giuseppe] (*b* New York, 10 Oct 1906; *d* San Diego, CA, 24 Aug 1985). Composer and teacher. Born into a poor immigrant family, he had no training in theory or composition although he did take piano and organ lessons with Dethier and Yon respectively. He did not decide on a career in composition until 1932. In 1938 he received a Guggenheim Fellowship and in 1941 the New York Music Critics' Circle Award for his Symphony no. 1; from that time he was among the most widely performed American composers. Creston made rhythm the keystone of his style, his technique depending primarily on constantly shifting subdivisions of a regular meter. The other main features of his music are long, florid, but motivically generated melodies; lush, impressionistic harmony; and very full orchestration. The texture is generally homophonic, the tonality free, and the form classical in its clarity and concision despite the flamboyantly romantic gestures. In sum Creston's work is brash and vital, spontaneous and intense, yet it is highly organized and displays remarkable ingenuity in thematic development. Creston received many awards and commissions; he was president of the National Association for American Composers and Conductors (1956–60) and was a director of ASCAP (1960–68). From 1968 to 1975 he was professor of music and composer-in-residence at Central Washington State College, Ellensburg.

He is the author of *Principles of Rhythm* (1964), *Rational Metric Notation* (1979), and numerous articles. In his writings he analyzes four centuries of rhythmic practice, and proposes revisions in notation aimed at eliminating irrationalities and inconsistencies.

WORKS

ORCHESTRAL

Partita, fl, vn, str, op.12, 1937; Threnody, op.16, 1938; 2 Choric Dances, op.17, 1938; Sym. no.1, op.20, 1940; Marimba Concertino, op.21, 1940; Sax Conc., op.26, 1941; Legend, band, op.31, 1942; Fantasy, pf, orch, op.32, 1942; Frontiers, op.34, 1943; Sym. no.2, op.35, 1944; Poem, harp, orch, op.39, 1945; Zanoni, band, op.40, 1946; Fantasy, trbn, orch, op.42, 1947; Pf Conc., op. 43, 1949

Sym. no.3, op.48, 1950; 2-Pf Conc., op.50, 1951; Sym. no.4, op.52, 1951; Walt Whitman, op.53, 1952; Invocation and Dance, op.58, 1953; Celebration Ov., band, op.61, 1954; Dance Ov., op.62, 1954; Sym. no.5, op.64, 1955; Vn Conc. no.1, op.65, 1956; Lydian Ode, op.67, 1956; Toccata, op.68, 1957; Accordion Conc., op. 75, 1958; Prelude and Dance, band, op.76, 1959; Janus, op.77, 1959

Vn Conc. no.2, op.78, 1960; Corinthians: XIII, op.82, 1963; Choreografic Suite, op.86, 1965; Pavane Variations, op.89, 1966; Chthonic Ode, op.90, 1966; Thanatopsis, op.101, 1971; Jubilee, band, op.102, 1971; Liberty Song, band, op.107, 1975; Suite, str, op.109, 1978; Festive Ov., band, op.116, 1980; Sādhanā, vc, orch, op.117, 1981; Sym. no.6, org, orch, op.118, 1981; *c*15 other works

VOCAL

4 Songs (Tagore), 1v, pf, op.7, 1935; 3 Sonnets (Ficke), 1v, pf, op.10, 1936; 3 Chorales (Tagore), SATB, op.11, 1936; Requiem, TB, org, op.15, 1938; Psalm xxiii, S, SATB, pf, op.37, 1945; Missa solemnis, SATB/TTBB, org/orch, op.44, 1949; Mass "Adoro te," SA/SATB, pf, op.54, 1952; The Celestial Vision (Dante, Whitman, Arjuna), TTBB, op.60, 1954; Isaiah's Prophecy (Christmas Oratorio), op.80, 1962

Nocturne (Auden), S, wind qnt, str qnt, pf, op.83, 1964; The Psalmist, A, orch, op.91, 1967; Mass "Cum jubilo," SATB, op.97, 1968; Hyas Illahee, SATB, orch, op.98, 1969; Leaves of Grass (Whitman), SATB, pf, op.100, 1970; Calamus (Whitman), TTBB, brass, perc, op.104, 1972; *c*15 other solo and choral works

CHAMBER AND INSTRUMENTAL

5 Dances, pf, op.1, 1932; 7 Theses, pf, op.3, 1933; 3 poems from Walt Whitman, vc, pf, op.4, 1934; Suite, sax, pf, op.6, 1935; Str Qt, op.8, 1936; Pf Sonata, op.9, 1936; Suite, va, pf, op.13, 1937; 5 2-part Inventions, pf, op.14, 1937; Suite, vn, pf, op.18, 1939; Sonata, sax, pf, op.19, 1939; 6 Preludes, pf, op.38, 1945; Suite, fl, va, pf, op.56, 1952; Suite, vc, pf, op.66, 1956

3 Narratives, pf, op.79, 1962; Metamorphoses, pf, op.84, 1964; Concertino, pf, wind qnt, op.99, 1969; Ceremonial, perc ens, op.103, 1972; Rapsodie, sax, pf/org, op.108, 1976; Rhythmicon 1–10, 123 studies, pf, 1977; Suite, sax qt, op.111, 1979; Pf Trio, op.112, 1979; other works incl. solo pf, band, inst pieces

Principal publishers: Belwin-Mills, Music Graphics, G. Schirmer

BIBLIOGRAPHY

EwenD

H. Cowell: "Paul Creston," *MQ*, xxxiv (1948), 533

——: "Creston's Symphony no.3," *MQ*, xxxvii (1951), 78

A. Cohn: *The Collector's Twentieth-century Music in the Western Hemisphere* (New York, 1961), 82ff

C. Walgren: "Paul Creston: Solo Piano Music," *American Music Teacher*, xxiv/4 (1975), 6

W. Simmons: "Paul Creston: Maintaining a Middle Course," *Music Journal*, xxxiv/10 (1976), 12

——: "Paul Creston: a Genial Maverick," *Ovation*, ii/9 (1981), 29

P. Snook: "Creston's Band Works," *Fanfare*, v/3 (1982), 94 [review]

Obituary, *New York Times* (26 Aug 1985)

WALTER G. SIMMONS

Crickets. Rock-and-roll group formed by BUDDY HOLLY.

Crist, Bainbridge (*b* Lawrenceburg, IN, 13 Feb 1883; *d* Barnstable, MA, 7 Feb 1969). Composer. He received the LLB degree from George Washington University and practiced law in Boston for six years, composing in his spare time. In 1912 he went to Europe to study theory and orchestration in Berlin with Paul Juon and in London with Claude Landi, and singing with William Shakespeare, Charles W. Clark, and Franz Emerich. He taught singing in Boston (1915–21) and Washington, DC (1922–3), then returned to Europe and taught until 1927 in Florence, Paris, Lucerne, and Berlin. After returning to Washington and teaching there, he settled finally in South Yarmouth, Massachusetts, in 1939. Nearly 200 of Crist's works were published, including 29 for orchestra (mostly with voice), three stage works, 13 for chorus, and many songs. The last were for a time frequently performed and broadcast and are noteworthy for the skillful handling of the voice, the sensitivity of the melodic line, and the aptness and variety of harmony; a number of them (like some of the smaller instrumental works) reflect an interest in the Orient (*Chinese Mother Goose Rhymes*, *Drolleries from an Oriental Doll's House*, *Colored Stars*). Crist published *The Art of Setting Words to Music* (1944).

WORKS

(selective list)

Stage: Le pied de la momie, choreographic drama, 1913; Pregiwa's Marriage, Javanese ballet, 1922; The Sorceress, choreographic drama, 1926

Orch: Abhisarika, vn, orch, 1921; Intermezzo, 1921; 3 dances, 1922; Yearning, 1924; 3 sym. poems, La nuit revécue, 1933, Hymn to Nefertiti, 1936, American Epic 1620, 1943; Vienna 1913, 1933; Frivolité, 1934; Fête espagnole, 1937

1v, orch: A Bag of Whistles, 1915; The Parting, 1916; Chinese Mother Goose Rhymes, 1917; O Come Hither!, 1918; Drolleries from an Oriental Doll's House, 1920; Coloured Stars, 4 songs, 1921; Remember, 1930; Evening, 1931; Noontime, 1931; The Way that Lovers Use, 1931; By a Silent Shore, 1932

Pf: Egyptian Impressions, 1913; Chinese Sketches, 1925

Choral works, many songs, inst pieces

Principal publishers: C. Fischer, G. Schirmer, Witmark

BIBLIOGRAPHY

J. T. Howard: *Bainbridge Crist* (New York, 1929)

W. T. Upton: *Art-song in America* (Boston, 1930/*R*1969 with suppl. 1938)

H. WILEY HITCHCOCK

Criticism.

1. The character of American criticism. 2. 1800–50. 3. 1850 to World War I. 4. Between the wars. 5. World War II to the present. 6. Jazz and rock.

1. THE CHARACTER OF AMERICAN CRITICISM. The character of American music criticism, which differs sharply from that of European, is derived primarily from a historical development in which the news element of criticism has played an important part. "As known and practiced in this country musical criticism is a department in the complicated service of the daily newspaper." This pragmatic generalization seems as true in the 1980s as it was in 1915 when it was formulated by William J. Henderson, one of the most respected critics this country has produced (in his influential essay "The Function of Musical Criticism," in

the first issue of the *Musical Quarterly*). But to allow that statement to stand as an implied summary of two centuries of criticism, or even of Henderson's own thoughtful essay, would be a distortion.

Henderson disliked the title "music critic," preferring to be known as a reporter specializing in music. Like most of his distinguished colleagues, he was a crusader: the great cause of his early years was Richard Wagner. He shared with the best American critics enthusiasms that a daily newspaper could not wholly accommodate and that therefore overflowed into magazine articles and books. Indeed, some of the best American criticism, written by musicians who never held a newspaper appointment, has appeared in literary magazines from the early 19th-century *Albion* to 20th-century "little magazines." It is nevertheless true that the mainstream of American criticism has flowed through the daily press; and it is to the development of this press that one must look for the influences that have made music criticism in this country different from the older, European tradition.

To the American reader the most surprising trait of the continental European press in the last 150 years has been its open partisanship. Many illustrious newpapers have seemed primarily journals of opinion and only secondarily newspapers. Music criticism in such papers, although rarely responsive to direct political pressures, has tended to voice the views of rival schools. The polemical reviews of such composer-critics as Berlioz, Schumann, Hugo Wolf, and Debussy are among the outstanding examples of continental criticism. Since World War II, however, rising costs of publication and shrinking circulation have curtailed the traditional duels of opinion and political propaganda. By contrast, American newspapers of the last 150 years have put increasing emphasis on sheer news: not (initially) out of any great idealism but because of crass financial interest. It started with imitations of the English penny press. As early as the 1830s editors discovered an untapped market of readers more interested in ephemeral news (murders, scandals, criminal trials, and the like) than in political opinion. This new mass of readers created rapidly increasing circulation figures. Competition in speedy news-gathering grew, especially during the Civil War, when the exploits and heroism of star correspondents enhanced the prestige of reportage. By the end of the war it was apparent that news rather than opinion was going to be the central strength of American newspapers, and this applied not only to politics but also to the arts. Editors emphasized the reportorial function even of their critics, and critics themselves took increasing pride in reportorial feats.

This emphasis led to another striking difference between continental European and American practices. In Europe reviews normally appear several days after the event, when it is no longer "news" in the American sense. American tradition, like the British, has demanded the publication of reviews the morning after the event or as soon as possible thereafter. There are critics who feel that such deadlines impose undue strains and who argue that an intelligent opinion needs a day or two to mature and to achieve cogent expression. But some of the finest critics have felt that their impression is most complete and vivid at the moment they leave the concert hall and suffers if the immediate impact is given time to wear off.

2. 1800–50. In the late 1700s musical performances were still too sporadic, even in the older cities of the eastern seaboard, to call for sustained attention in much of the daily press. The earliest printed review of an opera, the New-World première of the ballad opera *Love in a Village* by Thomas Arne and others, dates from 1767 in Philadelphia. It was presented as the report not of a professional but of "a gentleman contributor." This practice (familiar from the English press) of offering critiques in the form of letters to the paper persisted throughout the 18th century. As late as May 1786 a lengthy, detailed concert review (in the *Philadelphia Packet*) was still such a rarity that Oscar Sonneck called it a "noteworthy historic document."

In the early years of the 19th century the quantity and quality of American music criticism varied as widely as did the scattered concert life of the young republic. Operatic offerings developed under the shadow of a slowly fading tradition that the theater was the realm of the Evil One. Oratorio, being associated with religion, was more fortunate in community support and in the public prints. In Boston, the Handel and Haydn Society (founded in 1815) soon attracted sympathetic support. At the society's rehearsals for the American premières of *Messiah* and *The Creation* in the spring of 1817, for example, the critic of the *Boston Centinel* reported hearing moments that were "highly sublime." Yet he found the actual concerts deserving of praise "not so much from their positive merit as from the promise . . . of a more mature and chaste style of execution at some future period." The critic followed his tactful rebuke with such a list of technical and interpretive details as could have been offered only by a trained musician.

The increasing commercial importance of New York and its growing artistic leadership were soon underscored by the city's first season of Italian grand opera, introduced by Manuel García in 1825. His venture attracted wide public and journalistic attention on three counts: first, the sheer magnitude of the operation (a ten-month season of repertory ranging from Mozart's *Don Giovanni* to Rossini's *Otello*); second, the glamor that New York society found in an entertainment long regarded, according to the *New York Post*, as "the most elegant and refined among the amusements of the upper classes of the old world"; and third, the artistic caliber of the troupe. García had been Rossini's first Almaviva in *Il barbiere di Siviglia*. His son, also called Manuel, was to become the most sought-after singing teacher of the 19th century. And his daughter was the future Maria Malibran. The critic of the *New York Post* singled her out as "a fine contra-alto," whose voice, he said, encompassed three octaves with apparently effortless grace. The paper also praised her restraint in embellishment, in contrast to "the florid style of her father."

Through most of the 19th century, criticism in the American press was rarely signed or even initialed. (Probably the first and for many years the unique example of a signed music review appeared in 1839 in the *Boston Daily Evening Transcript* over the name Burchall.) A few individual critics can, however, be identified, chiefly by virtue of their eminence in other fields, by admiring mention by their colleagues, or by their vigorous self-advertisement. One of the most distinguished American critics of the mid-century, William Henry Fry, is identified by all three of these means. Although Fry is usually mentioned today as a composer, it has been said that his greatest importance lies in his criticism. He was only 23 (yet with at least one performance of an orchestral work behind him) when he joined the staff of his father's paper, the *National Gazette* of Philadelphia; for five years (1836–41) he worked as both composer and critic. Despite his youth he assessed with equal penetration the first American productions of such disparate recent masterpieces as Beethoven's *Fidelio* and Bellini's *Norma*.

Meanwhile, New York music criticism received a lift from the arrival in 1840 of a precocious young Englishman, Henry C. Watson. Armed with considerable experience of opera in London and with introductions to several eminent Americans, including Horace Greeley, Watson plunged into New York musical life. The year after his arrival he became one of the founders of the New York PO and soon he was contributing criticism to a series of daily and periodical publications in New York, including *The Albion*, the chief literary arbiter of the country. Indeed he may have been the author of the long and generally positive, though not uncritical, review in *The Albion* of the inaugural concert of the New York PO on 7 December 1842. By 1846, when he contributed elaborate program notes for the American première of Beethoven's Ninth Symphony by the New York PO, Watson was known as one of the leading critics in New York.

Up to the middle of the century the importance of music periodicals seems to have been slight. There were many of them, starting with the *Euterpeiad, or Musical Intelligencer* (Boston, 1820–23), but all were short-lived (*see* PERIODICALS). Few lasted more than two years, none for six. However, periodicals of more general scope carried occasional articles on music. Among these may be noted, in the years 1835–50, a small but influential group of transcendentalist magazines whose exalted ethical, intellectual, and critical concepts derived as much from New England puritanism as from Plato, Kant, and Ralph Waldo Emerson. The chief musical spokesman of Transcendentalism, "virtually the transcendental pope of music," according to Irving Lowens, proved to be John Sullivan Dwight. Shortly after his graduation from Harvard Divinity School, Dwight gave up the ministry and joined the utopian community of Brook Farm, to teach Latin and music. Soon he was drawn to the community's influential weekly, *The Harbinger*, for which he wrote over 100 articles during the years 1845–9. These were important experiences for his foundation shortly afterwards of *Dwight's Journal of Music*.

3. 1850 TO WORLD WAR I. At the middle of the century, American music criticism took on fresh vigor with the appearance of Richard Grant White (1851), William Henry Fry (1852), the foundation of *Dwight's Journal of Music* (1852), and the launching of two national magazines, *Harper's New Monthly Magazine* (1850) and the *Atlantic Monthly* (1857), which gave an important place to music. White, a lawyer, an important Shakespeare scholar, and father of the architect Stanford White, was co-editor of James Webb's *Morning Courier and New York Inquirer*, for which he also wrote anonymous but widely admired music criticism (1851–7). "My articles," White declared much later, in a *Century Magazine* article on opera, "did much to spoil and break up the business of musical criticism, so-called, in New York which was then in the hands of a few old hack newspaper writers, men equally incompetent and venal."

In 1852, Fry returned to New York after six years in Paris and London as political–cultural correspondent for several American newspapers, including Horace Greeley's recently founded *New York Tribune*. When Fry returned to become its political and general editor, as well as music critic, the *Tribune* was the most powerful newspaper in the country, partly by virtue of its popular weekly edition, which was read as far west as Chicago. Already an aggressive campaigner for higher standards of repertory and performance, and for American music (including his

William Henry Fry

own), Fry now became a crusader for criticism itself. The exaggerated fervor of his writing, with its generous mixture of self-praise, earned him occasional but richly deserved ridicule. Yet his concept of an American ideal of music criticism, first published in the *Musical World and Times* of 21 January 1854 and reprinted in *Dwight's Journal of Music*, has retained its validity:

> In the capacity of musical critic, I deem it inseparable from the honest performance of my duty to write, however late at night I may sit down to the task, a full notice of any musical performance of particular novelty, so that it may be spread before the readers of that journal the very morning after the performance . . . For example, when *Le Prophète* . . . was produced lately at Niblo's [25 November 1853] I deemed it my duty to get the full score from the manager and study every page, and on the night of the first performance when it closed near midnight, to sit down in my editorial room and write some three columns of analytical criticism . . . all of which appeared the next morning in print, though of course I did not get to bed until dawn.

Fry's prominence as a composer gave his critical opinions, however controversial, a technical foundation matched by few if any of his colleagues. He was a sensitive observer and his taste was unusually catholic, except for a growing conservatism. He believed that opera had been clearly in decline since Bellini's *Norma*. Reviewing the American première of Gounod's *Faust*, he found it wanting in "the indispensable vitality of divine melody." Wagner's *Tannhäuser*, he declared, ignored "most of the established laws of musical beauty and truth." This notion of immutable laws of beauty and truth may be traced through much of American music criticism far into the 20th century. In his later years, while Fry may have followed musical opinion as often as he led it, his influence remained powerful until ill-health forced his resignation a few months before the end of the Civil War. Looking back over this period half a century later, W. S. B. Mathews, the Chicago editor, critic, and historian of American music, declared that Fry had been the first American music critic to wield nationwide influence. He was succeeded on the *Tribune* by Henry Watson, who had already made a name for himself in the 1840s and now during his *Tribune* tenure (1863–7) was widely acknowledged the ablest music critic in the country.

Despite the achievements of the three contemporaries Watson, White, and Fry, it was long before many American dailies took music as seriously as the *Tribune* did. More typical of serious American newspapers in the 1850s and 1860s was the *New York Times*, which published a regular Monday morning column summarizing the "Amusements" of the past week, including concerts and recitals – although operas often rated a separate account the day after.

In 1852, the year of Fry's return to the USA, Dwight founded his famous weekly, *Dwight's Journal of Music*, which he edited for 30 years. Without advanced musical training (he had difficulty following an orchestral score) but with intense love for the art, a keen mind, literary flair, ability to attract distinguished colleagues and correspondents, and language skills that enabled him to translate from European periodicals, he established his journal as the most comprehensive as well as the most high-minded music periodical in the country. In addition to contributions from such illustrious correspondents as Alexander Wheelock Thayer, W. S. B. Mathews, and William Foster Apthorp, Dwight published serial installments from such current European works as Liszt's biography of Chopin and source works like Forkel's biography of Bach.

Like many American critics, Dwight aimed to educate. His critical judgments were conservative or even reactionary and were often proclaimed *ex cathedra*. His true loves were the Viennese Classics and Mendelssohn. He found Verdi vulgar, Brahms depressing and unedifying, and Wagner "the denial of music." Yet his idealism was genuine, and his influence enormous. When he ceased to publish his journal in 1881, his educational aims had been achieved and, as he observed somewhat sadly, public taste had passed him by. Dwight is an outstanding exemplar of a strong and originally puritan tendency in American criticism which contributed as late as 1907 to thunderous condemnations of Strauss's *Salome* and which lasted well into the second half of the century.

The foundation of the more generally cultural magazine, like *Harper's* and the *Atlantic Monthly*, in the 1850s was followed in 1870 by the *Century Illustrated Monthly Magazine* and by *Scribner's Magazine* in 1887. This quartet of dignified, literate periodicals catered to what is sometimes called the genteel tradition of educated middle-class professional or moneyed Americans, who sought more serious instructive reading than could be found in most newspapers. These magazines also provided an outlet for long, serious critical essays by the more thoughtful newspaper critics, which could hardly be accommodated in a daily paper, even on a Sunday, when the chief critic customarily contributed a general article commenting on trends and events in the musical world. It is interesting that the most frequent contributors on music to these intellectual magazines were the music critics of the leading daily papers.

For over a decade before the Civil War the westward shift of population was accelerated by refugees from the European revolutions of 1848 and 1849. By 1850 the population of Cincinnati, an important "western" center of music, was 30% German-born. Many German immigrants were music lovers or professional musicians, who helped to staff the budding symphony orchestras and chamber music groups or to swell their audiences. Some became music critics on the growing number of German-language newspapers and periodicals, such as the *Deutsche Musik Zeitung* (Philadelphia), several called *New-Yorker Musik Zeitung*, and the *New York Staatszeitung*, which, founded in 1832, was still appearing in 1985 as the oldest continuously published newspaper in any language in the USA.

It was in 1856 and 1859 that the German-born Theodore Thomas made his first visits to Chicago, described by his American wife as "a brisk little western city, already beginning to take an interest in things musical." On these occasions Thomas met and laid the foundations of a lifelong friendship with George P. Upton, then on the threshold of an illustrious career as Chicago's first and greatest music critic and a potent force in the city's fast-developing musical life. Upton, a Bostonian, graduated from Brown University in 1854, then, attracted by the westward development of America, moved to Chicago. He was engaged by the *Chicago Evening Journal* as a commercial reporter, but soon advanced to city editor and started a music column, the first in any newspaper in Chicago. By 1863 he was music critic of the *Chicago Tribune*, the most influential newspaper in the city. After a brief and sensationally successful stint as a Civil War correspondent, he returned to the *Tribune*, where he became city editor and editor for drama, art, and literature in addition to music.

Upton campaigned for instrumental music (which he considered the highest form of the art) and for the formation of a Chicago symphony orchestra. He supported American composers and performers, particularly those of western origins, almost to the point of chauvinism. Like many American critics, he also pursued educational aims. His Sunday newspaper articles prepared his readers for coming performances, even coaching them on audience behavior. During some 20 years on the *Tribune*, Upton continued to be a dynamic, constructive force in Chicago's musical evolution. Since his articles were not signed, it is not known exactly when he wrote his last musical pieces; he appears to have withdrawn gradually from writing about music while remaining on the *Tribune* editorial board.

Meanwhile the *New York Tribune* confirmed its national leadership in music criticism by appointing a distinguished successor to Fry and Watson: John Rose Green Hassard (1836–88), a man of alert musical intelligence and poetic gifts. Hassard is remembered particularly for his lengthy, enthusiastic articles, five in all, on the Bayreuth première of Wagner's *Ring* in 1876. Republished in pamphlet form, these articles stand out as the finest of the many American reports on the first Bayreuth Festival. The expanding horizons of American criticism in the 1870s are emphasized by the number of American colleagues who joined Hassard in Bayreuth. Prominent among them was Henry T. Finck, who reported for the *New York World* and *Atlantic Monthly* and even reviewed the second and third Bayreuth cycles of 1876 for the *New York Tribune* as a postscript to Hassard's reports.

The *New York Times* used the Bayreuth Festival to stage a technical coup. It was the first newspaper in the western hemisphere to publish cabled reports from a music critic; on the morning after each of the four *Ring* operas it published a review by its correspondent Frederick W. Schwab. The *Times* suggested editorially that the time might not be far distant "when we shall record and judge the production of another opera on another planet." The reports themselves were less impressive. Schwab praised Siegmund's "Winterstürme" as "a dainty love song" but found *Götterdämmerung* on the whole disappointing. Bayreuth had a profound effect not only on musicians and intellectuals but ultimately on public attitudes to music and the arts, and this may have convinced some American newspaper publishers that interest in serious music was greater than they had realized. For whatever reason, the years after the first Bayreuth Festival saw a remarkable consolidation of music criticism, particularly in the daily press of Boston and New York. In rapid succession, the leading newspapers of those cities engaged a group of strong-minded, relatively young critics. For over 40 years, first as crusaders and finally as a conservative old guard, but always as idealists and educators at heart, this small group exerted enormous influence not only in their own communities but in large areas of the country.

The first of these men was William Foster Apthorp, a man of broad training and background. Educated in France, Germany, and Italy, and under John Knowles Paine at Harvard, he became music critic of the *Atlantic Monthly* in 1876. He also began to contribute to two Boston dailies, the *Courier* and *Evening Traveler*. In 1881 the *Boston Evening Transcript* established its first regular music department with Apthorp as its chief. He was influenced by what he saw as a French style of personal criticism. "To my mind," he wrote, "criticism should be nothing but an expression of enlightened opinion – as enlightened as possible but never dogmatic." The critic's true position, he claimed, was that of "an interpreter between . . . composer or performer and the public."

Apthorp's younger contemporary, Philip Hale, was also trained abroad (Berlin, Munich, Paris) and studied law. He was admitted to the bar in 1880, but found his true vocation in music. In Paris he had fallen in love with French civilization. As a music critic he was an early defender of Debussy and an enthusiastic admirer of Richard Strauss. Starting in 1889, Hale wrote for three different Boston dailies before taking over the music and drama columns of the *Boston Herald* (1904–33). Like many of his colleagues in Boston and Philadelphia, he made frequent trips to New York to hear important new works. In 1907 he attended the single performance of Strauss's *Salome* at the Metropolitan Opera House. While Henry Krehbiel, then critic of the *New York Tribune*, found *Salome* the "apotheosis of that which is indescribably, yes, inconceivably gross and abominable," Hale ridiculed the moral approach. "*Salome* has been produced in New York," he wrote, "and there was no perturbation of nature, no shower of fiery, consuming rain; no fall of scarlet stars; no earthquake shock." At the end of a long and vivid report Hale concluded: "It is now possible to record only first impressions and the chief of these is that *Salome*, however distasteful the subject may be to some, is a stupendous work by a man of indisputable, if irregular and abnormal genius."

The only outright conservative, indeed reactionary, among the leading Boston critics of the day was Louis Charles Elson, a trained musician of German descent who presided from 1888 to 1920 as critic of the *Boston Advertiser*. The youngest of the Boston group, and in some ways the most brilliant, was Henry Taylor Parker (1867–1934), always known as "H.T.P." He too was educated at Harvard and traveled abroad, where he developed strong interests in many artistic fields. He wrote a curiously convoluted prose, often flavored with archaic turns of phrase. But he was not a trained musician, and it was said that he could not read music. This did not prevent him, however, from developing sharp, sympathetic insights into new musical tendencies, which won him the admiration of musicians and laymen alike. For the last 20 years of his life Parker was, in succession to William Foster Apthorp, music and drama critic of the *Boston Evening Transcript*.

During this same period the powerful group of new New York critics were conservative, more German-oriented, and sometimes pontifical. The central experience of their early years was Wagner, at a time when Wagner needed defenders. As noted above, Henry T. Finck, the oldest of the group, reported the Bayreuth Festival of 1876 for three American publications. He spent four more years in Germany before returning to New York to serve for 44 years as music critic of both *The Nation* and the *Evening Post*. The fact that, in his last years, he became an almost implacable conservative, arousing the ire and even disgust of younger musicians and critics, should not obliterate his early enthusiastic crusades.

If Upton typified those easterners who moved west to become community leaders, the career of Henry E. Krehbiel may illustrate the reverse trend of middle Americans who moved east to positions of responsibility. Born in Ann Arbor, Michigan, in 1854, Krehbiel served on the *Cincinnati Gazette* (1874–80) before he was invited to the *New York Tribune*, eventually to succeed to the influential post previously held by Fry, Watson, and Hassard. He started as assistant to Hassard, who continued to write occasional articles until the mid-1880s. Krehbiel's colleagues – except Finck, with whom he had a 40-year feud – admired him for his scholarship, for his "native intellectual power and vigor that would have put him among the leaders of any profession he might have adopted," and for his powerful advocacy of Wagner. On the occasion of the New York première of *Tristan und Isolde* in December 1886, Krehbiel wrote three long articles, published on successive days: the first and second on the opera's historical background, the third on the music. His scholarship was less impressive. He made the first English edition of Thayer's great Beethoven biography, revising and completing it using Thayer's original text and the published German editions (his added material has, however, proved unreliable). His great enthusiasms were Beethoven, Bach, Wagner, and string quartets. Conservative by nature, he tended to thunder his disapprovals. His younger admirer Richard Aldrich, later music critic of the *New York Times*, admitted:

> Krehbiel had something like a certainty that there were unchangeable laws, not man-made but inherent in the nature of things, in the art of music; that he knew what they were, and that it was his function to lay them down and expound them, as a final jurisdiction, from which he recognized no appeal.

The most brilliant New York critic of this period was William James Henderson. Some have regarded him as the greatest American critic. A graduate of Princeton, Henderson had studied piano, singing, and music theory and history. Beginning at the *New York Times* in 1883 as a reporter, he was soon covering important musical events as assistant to Frederick Schwab. When Schwab left in 1887, Henderson became the paper's first distinguished music critic. He soon put the *New York Times* in the front rank of musical authority with his acute reasoning, broad background, lucid literary style, and impressive and growing knowledge of the history and practice of the art. Henderson served the *Times* for 15 years until 1902, when he moved to the *New York Sun*. There he remained for the next 35 years (except for a four-year period on the *New York Herald*, 1920–24, because of a brief juggling of newspaper ownership).

Henderson shared his New York colleagues' passion for Wagner, still a controversial figure. In 1888, reviewing the American première of *Götterdämmerung*, he called the final scene "a fitting culmination to the most remarkable series of musical-dramatic works ever conceived by the mind of man." He was also an enthusiastic advocate of Brahms, whom he visited in Germany.

Henderson had a passionate hatred of sham and mediocrity and was one of the few critics to make clear the standards by which he judged. Briefly put, these were beauty, sincerity, emotional expressiveness, melody, clarity of structure, and moral and spiritual character. The problem of defining such attributes as beauty or spiritual character does not seem to have bothered him any more than it did his colleagues. Thus, though he loved Wagner, whom he considered the only 19th-century composer comparable to Beethoven, he called the conduct of Siegmund and Sieglinde in *Die Walküre* "outrageous." The morals of Puccini's Bohemians he considered "infinitely worse than those of the Wagner dramas." Henderson disliked most post-Verdi Italian opera, though he called Puccini "a wizard of stagecraft." In 1907 he agreed with his colleagues on *Salome*: "The whole story wallows in lust, lewdness, bestial appetites, and abnormal carnality." Although Henderson had little love for any music that ventured beyond 18th- and 19th-century norms, he made industrious, often successful efforts to understand. When, as late as 1924, Stravinsky's *The Rite of Spring* was introduced to New York, he admired it greatly. But later musical styles, starting with neoclassicism, he tended to regard as the little fads of emotionally sterile men, or as arrant bluff.

In 1902, when Henderson left the *Times* for the *New York Sun*, he recommended that Richard Aldrich succeed him. Aldrich was an altogether gentler character, less given to pontificating than Krehbiel or to the deflating epigrams for which Henderson was noted. Aldrich had won his journalist's spurs with the *Providence Journal* and the *Evening Star* of Washington, DC. These prepared him for a more serious, ten-year apprenticeship in New York as assistant to Krehbiel on the *Tribune* (1891–1901). Although his tastes tended to be conservative, his was the conservatism of a thoughtful man. He was all too aware of the ridicule heaped upon earlier critics whose judgments had been reversed by history. When he felt his own traditional standards did not apply to new music, he demanded what the new standards might be:

> Old fogies groping in the fog of the past would like to know if there are any other tangible or comprehensible principles for estimating the music of the new fashion. . . . Of course the young are very sure that they are right: they ought to be. . . . But it would be greatly to be desired to have and present to the groping elders some method of judging and comparing among the heirs of the ages.

One indication of Aldrich's standing in the musical world was that, after he left the *New York Times* in the spring of 1923, he spent autumn that year as guest critic of the London *Times*.

James Gibbons Huneker, the youngest of the New York group and the most forward-looking, was not a university man, but he studied music in Philadelphia and Paris, and at the National Conservatory in New York, where he later taught piano. Between 1891 and 1921 he wrote for New York dailies, various American periodicals, and journals in London, Paris, Berlin, and Vienna. For breadth and intensity of critical activity among all the arts, Huneker had no equal in the USA in his time. Closer to the Francophile Boston critics than to his New York colleagues, Huneker distanced himself from Wagner. "Richard of the Footlights," he called him; "the last of the great Romantics, he closed a period, did not begin one." In the cross-currents of contemporary art, Huneker felt at home. At a time when Strauss still seemed to many people a questionable figure on the horizon, Huneker wrote: "He is the living issue in music today; no other master has his stature." He called *Also sprach Zarathustra* "a cathedral in tone, sublime and fantastic, with its grotesque gargoyles, hideous flying abutments, exquisite traceries, . . . huge and resounding spaces, gorgeous façades, and heaven-splitting spires – a mighty musical structure." On the eve of World War I, when *Pierrot lunaire* puzzled most and irritated others, Huneker (who heard the first performance, in Berlin) reacted with a characteristic blend of artistic insight, technical grasp, and verbal virtuosity:

> What did I hear? At first, the sound of delicate china shivering into a thousand luminous fragments in the welter of tonality that bruised each other as they passed and repast. . . . What kind of music is this, without melody in the ordinary sense: without themes, yet every acorn of a phrase contrapuntally developed by an adept; . . . music that can paint . . . the abysm of a morbid soul, the man in the moon, the faint sweet odours of an impossible fairy-land, and the strut of the dandy from Bergamo?

4. Between the wars. The two decades between the wars were a time of drastic change in American music criticism. At issue was the 20th-century revolution in musical style, which only now hit the USA with full force. The critical struggle was sharper and the outcome more dramatic in New York than in other American cities, partly because the pre-war and wartime programs there had been far more conservative than those of Philadelphia, Boston, and other cities. Also, the still admired old guard (Krehbiel, Finck, Henderson, and Aldrich) was more firmly entrenched than were the conservatives of other cities, and the champions of modern music were more numerous, more vocal, and ultimately more organized than elsewhere. Further, the steadily declining number of daily papers concentrated power in the hands of the survivors. The critics fell into three distinct groups: the conservative old guard, their middle-of-the-road replacements – Deems Taylor, Lawrence Gilman, Olin Downes – and the crusaders, led first by Huneker, until his death in 1921, then by Paul Rosenfeld in the magazine *The Dial*, and finally by the League of Composers' quarterly, *Modern Music*.

Having dominated the New York critical scene for a few more years after the war, the old guard suddenly disintegrated. In March 1923 Krehbiel died. A few weeks later, Aldrich left the *Times*, and in 1924 Finck withdrew from the *Post* to write his memoirs, leaving only Henderson on the *Sun* as the last old-guard representative. On the *World* Huneker had already been replaced by the composer Deems Taylor. Now Krehbiel was succeeded by Lawrence Gilman, Aldrich by Olin Downes, and Finck by a series of brief appointments to the *Post*: Ernest Newman (for one year a guest critic from London), Olga Samaroff, Oscar Thompson, and Samuel Chotzinoff.

As a group these new arrivals were a quarter of a century younger than the pundits they replaced. They welcomed divergences of style and opinion. Gilman had long maintained that there could be "no such things as ascertainable standards of judgment; no such things as recognized conceptions of ideal excellence; no such things as touchstones: and, indeed, in relation to the art of music, there obviously are not."

Gilman went to the *Tribune* in 1923, after 23 years as music critic of *Harper's Weekly* and the *North American Review*. Early in life he had wanted to be a painter; he composed (in a post-Debussyan style) and was interested in modern poetry. All of this showed in his cultivated and colorful literary style. Like Huneker, whom he admired, Gilman was one of the most perceptive commentator–analysts of Strauss and Debussy. In *Pelléas* he praised the "music of twilight beauty and glamour that persuades and insinuates, that persistently enslaves the mind. . . . There is passion in [Debussy's] music, but it is the passion of the desire, less of life than of the shadow of life." His enthusiasms embraced Bartók and Stravinsky, and his intense curiosity brought him, score in hand, to many a rehearsal of contemporary music. He did not always like what he studied. Indeed, he misread and disliked whole areas of modern music, including the so-called neoclassical trend of the 1920s. And he never felt the need, as so many progressive musicians did, to repudiate his early admiration for Wagner. In 1925, when the Metropolitan Opera revived *Götterdämmerung* for the first time after World War I, Gilman was shaken:

> We are very fine fellows indeed, with our undeluded, challenging brains and our swift, spare, vital, sensitive art: but one page from a score like *Götterdämmerung* – one gleam from that luminous, kindling godlike eye, one sweeping gesture of that titanic arm, is enough to remind us who and what we are and who is still lord of the eternal heavens, unvanquishable and secure.

Olin Downes was appointed to the *New York Times* in 1924, having been for almost two decades music critic of the *Boston Post* (1906–24), at that time the largest daily newspaper in the country. A professional pianist, he was 19 when he became the first music critic of the *Post*. For the rest of his life he felt keenly his lack of traditional academic training, but his appetite for literature and the unorthodox guidance of his own enthusiasm helped him form a writing style of his own which was at best powerfully moving. He was an early supporter of Debussy, Strauss, Prokofiev, Stravinsky, and Shostakovich. Eventually, of course, they became the new orthodoxy. But Downes rather preferred the role of maverick. Early in his career he also fell in love with the music of Sibelius, then little known in the USA and dismissed by Downes's seniors, the French-oriented arbiters of taste in Boston. He played a major role in establishing Sibelius in the affections of the American public. Years later, when Sibelius's popularity was for a time on a par with that of Tchaikovsky, he grew tired of being labeled the champion of Sibelius. Another of his maverick tastes was a passion for the vitality and wit he found in ragtime and jazz, before the term "jazz" was known in print. He was quick to admire the Gershwin brothers' musical comedies. In the last year of his life (1955) he wrote: "If one asks what kind of contemporaneous music has the most vitality, the most spontaneity, invention, and freshness of approach, the answer is obvious. Of course it is jazz, which has come up from the ground and the genius of simple people."

Although Deems Taylor inherited Huneker's position on the *New York World* (1921–5), he did not share his curiosity and enthusiasm for innovative music. Indeed, the more Taylor heard of what he called "ultra modern" music, the more it bored him. That he was himself a successful composer was no help. Contrary to a widespread theory that composers make the best critics, Taylor's blandly accessible music was, if anything, an obstacle to his understanding of more radical contemporary works.

It was not a composer but a *littérateur*, a critical jack-of-all-trades, who crusaded most passionately and most memorably for new music in the 1920s. Paul Rosenfeld was not a musician by training. But his intuitive penetration of contemporary music may have been deepened by his grasp of avant-garde literature and visual arts and their key roles in the works of Schoenberg, Stravinsky, and others. From 1916 Rosenfeld contributed essays and reviews to *Seven Arts* (of which he was a co-founder), *Vanity Fair*, the *New Republic*, *Modern Music*, and *The Dial*, to which he contributed a regular "Musical Chronicle" from 1920 to 1927. He carried on the tradition of Huneker with colorful, subjective vocabulary and extravagant metaphors. He was greatly admired by many critical colleagues from other fields, including Lewis Mumford and Edmund Wilson, who judged that he fulfilled the functions of "appreciator, romantic critic" more satisfactorily than anyone else.

In 1924 the newly founded League of Composers launched its famous quarterly, *Modern Music* (originally the *League of Composers' Review*), as a forum for discussion, news, and reviews of new music, particularly in the USA. It was an audacious undertaking. Under the editorship of Minna Lederman an impressive number of leaders of contemporary music in the USA and abroad made thoughtful and provocative contributions for almost a quarter of a century. Among the most prominent American contributors were Marc Blitzstein, Aaron Copland, Henry Cowell, Randall Thompson, and Virgil Thomson.

Outside the older centers of the eastern seaboard, symphony orchestras seem to have played a more prominent role in the life of their communities and to have had closer relations with local music critics, the importance of each contributing to that of the other. In Chicago, where George Upton had made the establishment of the Chicago SO one of his goals, the outstanding critic of the inter-war years was Claudia Cassidy. An aggressive critic, Cassidy seemed to feel fiercely protective of the orchestra, and her vehement, sometimes strident rhetoric was feared. She was a powerful factor in Chicago's musical life. Her vivid descriptive powers were widely relished and made her one of the few critics between the two coasts who were read outside their own communities.

In the twin cities of Minneapolis and St. Paul, the establishment in 1903 of the Minneapolis SO was followed in 1904 by the appointment of a first music critic, Caryl B. Storrs, to the *Minneapolis Tribune*. Storrs was succeeded for most of the years between the wars by James Davies, a bluff, hearty critic with sharp opinions, hotly defended. During the same period the similarly brash Paul Bliss wrote under the pen-name of Southworth Alden for the *Minneapolis Star*; he was replaced in 1926 by his assistant, John K. Sherman, a far more thoughtful critic and a widely respected musician and scholar, who held his post until 1971. In St. Paul the most important critic of the time was Frances Boardman, who wrote chiefly for the *St. Paul Pioneer-Press*.

In San Francisco and Los Angeles, whose orchestras likewise had been founded early in the century, music criticism was also firmly established in a number of newspapers. Alfred Frankenstein, music critic for the *San Francisco Chronicle* from 1934, was probably the most distinguished music critic of his day on the West Coast. He was also art critic of the *Chronicle* and in 1965 gave up music to concentrate on art.

In the Southwest, from 1925 onwards, John Rosenfield of the *Dallas Morning News* played a major role in establishing the Dallas SO on a more regular footing. He was, according to Lehman Engel, the chief cultural arbiter in the Southwest for several decades, speaking out on music, theater, and film as well as the visual arts, dance, and books. He was sensitive to promising talent and was influential throughout Texas, Oklahoma, and Louisiana.

5. World War II to the present. In New York, the death of Lawrence Gilman in 1939 and the appointment of Virgil Thomson to replace him on the *New York Herald-Tribune* marked the beginning of a new era in music criticism. Thomson's virtuosity as critic of the *Herald-Tribune* should have surprised no

one acquainted with his long literary activity, starting with undergraduate contributions to the Harvard *Crimson*. From Paris, which he visited early and long, he wrote critical reports to the *Boston Evening Transcript* and *Modern Music*. His admiration for French prose as well as French music may have helped shape his deceptively simple, clear, elegant, and frequently witty style. He never attempted to translate the emotional storms of music into purple prose. Thomson's professional mastery of the craft of music, his wide acquaintance with modern idioms, and his particular sympathy for the composer's point of view made inviting reading. Despite a certain objectivity, his writing often seemed partisan. Yet he believed that the sole justifiable purpose of reviewing was "to inform the public; any other is an abuse of confidence. . . . No responsible newspaper owner would consider the use of his valuable columns for a private pulpit." Thomson's long familiarity with European reviews must have made him doubly aware of such a danger, and he never attempted to make a private pulpit of the columns of the *Herald-Tribune*. After 14 years of brilliantly successful reviewing there, he resigned to give himself more time to compose and conduct.

Despite the steadily shrinking number of daily newspapers across the country, there appeared to be a growing interest in music criticism, particularly when controversy was involved. This seemed apparent even in the older centers like Boston, where for some 12 years (1964–76) Michael Steinberg's brilliant, iconoclastic reviews outraged many performers, managers, and even the players of the Boston SO, who at one point petitioned their management to have him banned from their concerts. Nevertheless, Steinberg's work was also greatly admired, even outside Boston. Ironically, when he resigned from the newspaper it was to become the orchestra's program annotator.

In Chicago, Claudia Cassidy continued her stormy reign as music, dance, and drama critic–editor, now of the *Tribune*, until 1966, when she became critic-at-large. She was then succeeded as music critic by Thomas Willis, who was followed in 1977 by John von Rhein. In 1947, after a period as Cassidy's associate on the *Tribune*, Albert Goldberg moved to Los Angeles as critic of the *Los Angeles Times*. There he was succeeded in 1965 by Martin Bernheimer. A man of cosmopolitan background, with a musician's training and a broad knowledge of the art, Bernheimer often ruffled feathers with his exacting standards and sometimes caustic wit.

In Dallas, the widely respected John Rosenfield continued his warmly supported pioneering until 1966, when he was succeeded by one of the more enterprising and imaginative younger critics, John Ardoin. In Minneapolis, the veteran John Sherman of the *Star* was succeeded in 1971 by his assistant, Peter Altman, a man of impressively broad background in theater and literature as well as music. In the same year Michael Anthony, who has a solid musical training and literary flair, became music critic of the *Minneapolis Tribune*. Anthony is widely admired for his high standards and fine judgment and for the tact with which he formulates his opinions.

The intensive postwar development of musical life in Washington, DC, commanded the services of two highly trained and literate critics: Paul Hume of the *Washington Post* and, on the *Washington Star*, Irving Lowens, who was also a founding member of the Music Critics Association. In Baltimore, which is close enough to share the musical life of Washington, Elliott W. Galkin, a conductor and faculty member and dean of the Peabody Conservatory, was also music critic of the respected *Baltimore Sun* (1962–77). One of the most cultivated critics of an older generation was Max de Schauensee, who wrote for the *Philadelphia Bulletin* from the outbreak of World War II to his death in 1982. A strong European-American background and a wide knowledge of related arts gave his writing particular scope and authority.

Among the younger critics whose work has attracted attention outside their immediate communities are James Roos of the *Miami Herald*, a former student of Virgil Thomson and Irving Kolodin at the University of Southern California; James Wierzbicki, formerly of the *Cincinnati Post* and the *St. Louis Globe-Democrat*, later music critic of the *St. Louis Post Dispatch*; and Will Crutchfield, from 1984 on the music staff of the *New York Times*.

In 1954 Virgil Thomson's resignation from the *New York Herald-Tribune* led to another surprise. His successor, Paul Henry Lang, brought to his office an eminence in the field of scholarship that was new to American music criticism, though long familiar in Europe. Lang's multifarious activities as professor of musicology at Columbia University, editor of the *Musical Quarterly*, vice-president of the American Musicological Society, and president of the International Musicological Society combined with his early experience as a professional pianist and chorus répétiteur of the Royal Budapest Opera to give him an enviable perspective for his journalistic venture.

The year after Thomson's resignation, Olin Downes died, having served 33 years as music critic of the *New York Times*. He was succeeded by Howard Taubman, long an associate in the *Times* music department. A lively-minded and responsible critic, Taubman was a first-class newspaperman and investigator who never shrank from an awkward assignment that demanded a courageous stand. Taubman was succeeded in 1960 by Harold C. Schonberg, a man of incisive literary style, who had trained as a professional pianist and brought a rare breadth of interests to his work. He had studied painting with Kuniyoshi and was a passionate chess player and connoisseur of the history of the game and its relation to music. Schonberg was followed in 1980 by Donal Henahan. John Rockwell, a younger member of the department, has been distinguished by his active exploration of contemporary American music both serious and popular.

The steadily shrinking number of daily newspapers and music critics has been accompanied by an increase of music coverage in the periodical press, chiefly in the form of record reviews. This has been due in large part to the phenomenal development of the long-playing record, which revolutionized the recording industry and hence also listening habits world-wide. A dramatic illustration of these complementary trends involved the *New York Sun* and the *Saturday Review of Literature* at mid-century. During the last, declining seasons of the *Sun*, Irving Kolodin, then first music critic of the paper, inaugurated a weekly record column which proved popular. At the same time the *Saturday Review*, through a poll of its readers, discovered a growing interest in musical subjects, especially recordings. Kolodin was invited to start a record column in the *Saturday Review*. By 1950, when the *Sun* ceased publication, the *Saturday Review* column was a fast-growing music department. In effect, the increasing popularity of long-playing records caused the transfer of Kolodin and his department from the *Sun* to the *Saturday Review*, where a staff of assistants was soon required; these included John Ardoin, Martin Bernheimer, Oliver Daniel, Robert Jacobson, and H. C. Robbins Landon, all of whom soon went on to more important positions.

Record reviewing has, of course, an extended history, predating the advent of long-playing records by at least a quarter of a century. The *New York Times* pioneered a weekly record column in the 1920s. But other newspapers were slow to follow its example. The oldest and one of the best periodicals devoted to records is the *American Record Guide*, founded in 1926 as the *Phonograph Monthly Review* and edited from 1957 until his death in 1973 by James Lyons. The long roster of its contributors includes some of the most devoted scholars in the recording field. Until the early 1980s *High Fidelity* (founded 1951) and *Stereo Review* (1958) were two leading American periodicals in the field. For almost a quarter of a century both magazines featured detailed record reviews by large staffs of true specialists. But between 1980 and 1984 both magazines reduced most of their reviews to token length. Launched only in 1977, but quickly risen to top rank among record magazines, is *Fanfare*, with the subtitle "Magazine for Serious Record Collectors." This bulky bi-monthly averages between 300 and 400 pages and lists some 30 regular contributors. Its scope is as wide as the record industry. By contrast, a magazine of narrowly specialized scope, the *Journal for the Association of Recorded Sound Collections*, reviews reissues of historical, predominantly vocal, recordings.

Other specialized types of criticism are the reviews of opera productions in the Metropolitan Opera Guild's magazine *Opera News* and the substantial book review section in *Opera Quarterly*. *Notes*, the quarterly journal of the Music Library Association, includes brief but very professional reviews of recently published contemporary works and scholarly editions.

In 1939 Paul Rosenfeld started a "Current Chronicle" column in the *Musical Quarterly*. His column did not last, but in 1948 its title was revived under the editorship of Paul Henry Lang for a regular section of analytical reviews of new compositions performed in European as well as American centers. Among American contributors to this valuable feature were Elliott Carter, Aaron Copland, Henry Cowell, Richard F. Goldman, Irving Lowens, and Virgil Thomson. The "Current Chronicle" was discontinued in 1976.

Among general periodicals *The Nation* stands out for its distinguished series of long-tenured music critics, including Henry T. Finck, Bernard H. Haggin, and David Hamilton. In the 1980s Samuel Lipman has been admired for the scope and cogency of his critical essays in *Commentary* magazine.

For nearly 40 years, the musicologist and professor Joseph Kerman, of the University of California at Berkeley, has contributed provocative music criticism to various journals, including the *Hudson Review*, the *New York Review of Books*, and *Opera News*. Other musicians not primarily critics who have often contributed important essays to lay periodicals include such prominent figures as Elliott Carter, Aaron Copland, Robert Craft, Ned Rorem, and Charles Rosen.

The new arrival on the American scene most admired by musicians and laymen alike is Andrew Porter, music critic of the *Financial Times* of London (1955–72) and from 1972 of the *New Yorker*. Porter inaugurated here a type of criticism based on a practice familiar in the daily press of Europe, though to a lesser extent in England. The *feuilleton* or broad essay-review, in which historical background may bulk larger than the "news event" under review, finds its closest American analogue in the "Sunday article" (or "Saturday article" in an evening newspaper) on a general topic of current interest. Porter's column in the *New Yorker* is related to both traditions but enlarged both in length and content. In his own words, it is "part descriptive chronicle" (i.e. always tied to a specific event or several related events), but he usually presents the event as the latest addition to a long history, invoking personal experiences as well as his scholarly awareness of the remoter past. His critical evaluations are usually implicit in the background he cites. They are also explicitly formulated, but often quite briefly, depending on the quality and importance of the event itself. Porter's opinions and background excursions gain a particular interest, first, from his 20 years of reviewing performances throughout Europe as a London-based music critic; second, from the enthusiasm and thoroughness with which he fulfills his self-set critical tasks; and third, from his selection of events to review, which leans towards the unhackneyed (new works by contemporary composers, less familiar works by early composers, or innovative performances of familiar works).

In recent years the education of music critics has become an increasing concern. In the USA the first formal academic course in music criticism appears to have been inaugurated by Oscar Thompson at the Curtis Institute in 1928. Since then many music schools and universities have offered similar one-year courses. In 1952 Olin Downes and Virgil Thomson, feeling the need for an organization to improve standards of music criticism, began consultations with colleagues which resulted in the formation of the MUSIC CRITICS ASSOCIATION, incorporated in 1958. Its first major educational project was a series of two-year programs administered at the University of Southern California by Raymond Kendall, dean of its school of music. With the help of a generous Rockefeller Foundation grant, each first year of the program consisted of seminars held on the Los Angeles campus. Each second year consisted of fieldwork in which student critics were assigned as assistants to established critics in several American cities. This experimental program continued for some 12 years during which a number of students were placed in professional positions. In another series of projects administered by the association, summer workshops lasting five days to two weeks at various locations have enabled young critics to work under the supervision of senior critics, professional performers, historians, and other musicians. More recently Irving Lowens held discussions with Elliott W. Galkin, his successor as president of the association, with a view to establishing a graduate program at the Peabody Conservatory of Music which would lead to a master's degree in music criticism. After Lowens's death in 1983 the project was carried to fruition by Galkin, and this program, the first such in the USA, was inaugurated in 1984; Galkin was appointed to an endowed chair in music criticism at the conservatory in January 1985.

6. JAZZ AND ROCK. The earliest generally acknowledged piece of jazz criticism dates from 1919 and from Europe: the Swiss conductor Ernest Ansermet's article on the touring Southern Syncopated Orchestra that featured Sidney Bechet. For several decades, Europeans anticipated Americans in the serious appreciation of this American vernacular art form. Still, in the 1920s, Americans gradually began according jazz critical attention. Many of the first American writers on jazz were better known for their interest in literature (Carl Van Vechten) or classical music (Virgil Thomson, R. D. Darrell, Bernard H. Haggin, Irving Kolodin, Winthrop Sargeant; Henry Pleasants and Gunther Schuller are later examples of this same dual interest).

Jazz writing took on a new urgency in the 1930s, as the music spread in popularity and left-wing populism permeated the intelligentsia. At this time, the term "jazz" was understood to include styles (e.g. swing and "sweet" ballad backings) that are now considered as much a part of popular music as jazz *per se*. American jazz writing expressed itself first in a variety of popular-music weeklies and monthlies published in New York and London. *Jazzmen* (1939), edited by Frederic Ramsey and Charles Edward Smith, was one of the earliest books to assess jazz of this period and remains among the most authoritative. Important jazz critics in the 1930s included John Hammond, who contributed articles from New York for the *Melody Maker* of London, Marshall Stearns, active at *Down Beat*, and George T. Simon at *Metronome*. Leonard Feather moved to the USA in 1935 from England and became an active champion of bop. There were few black writers on jazz before the 1950s. Langston Hughes was sympathetic, but wrote sparingly; it was not until Ralph Ellison, and later LeRoi Jones (now Amiri Baraka), that black writers began to contribute actively to jazz criticism.

After World War II, a new generation of jazz writers emerged, among them Nat Hentoff, Whitney Balliett, Martin Williams and Dan Morgenstern; while all have been active as critics, Hentoff and Williams are also noted for their pioneering oral histories. Major newspapers had begun to feature regular jazz writing: John S. Wilson joined the *New York Times* in 1952, and during the next decade Feather found a base at the *Los Angeles Times*. Americans had begun to produce important books on jazz, as well, such as Stearns's *The Story of Jazz* (1956) and Schuller's *Early Jazz* (1968).

In the 1960s, with the decline of jazz as a commercial force after the "British invasion" in rock and the concentration on popular music by the record companies, some older jazz writers moved into academic or archival work. Younger critics often found it necessary to pursue varied careers (Bob Blumenthal, Stanley Crouch, James Lincoln Collier) or to write about both jazz and rock (Robert Palmer at the *New York Times*); even Gary Giddins, best known as a jazz critic, also writes about books for the *Village Voice* in New York.

Jazz and rock and their respective critical champions long remained bitterly divided. Jazz has generally attracted a more sophisticated level of formal musical analysis than has rock (although in the 1930s and 1940s numerous jazz critics concentrated on personality profiles and loose musical metaphors). Rock criticism has its musicologically oriented formalists. But the humanistic directness of the music has been mirrored in the freedom with which most rock writers discuss their subject in literary, sociological, political, and moral terms, and make musical description more a matter of comparison and evocation than strict analysis. The news and discussion of Elvis Presley and other early rockers was carried on by reporters and feature writers, not specialist critics. But by the early 1960s, some newspapers had critics covering rock and folk music (e.g. Robert Shelton at the *New York Times* and Ralph J. Gleason at the *San Francisco Chronicle*, one of the few jazz critics to accept rock openly). Rock criticism as a distinctive form dates only from the mid- to late 1960s, with the birth of such rock-music publications as *Crawdaddy!* in New York and *Rolling Stone* in San Francisco. Such early rock writers as Paul Williams, Richard Goldstein, Jon Landau, Robert Christgau, and Ellen Willis determinedly placed music within the larger social context of the youth culture of the 1960s; indeed, for the lesser writers the context seemed more important than the music.

In the 1970s, rock criticism coalesced and cooled into a subgenre of its own. Nearly every major newspaper had a rock critic: Robert Hilburn joined the staff of the *Los Angeles Times* in 1970 and oversaw the growth of that paper's extensive coverage of the music, while John Rockwell became the *New York Times*'s first staff rock critic in 1974. But a more characteristic kind of rock criticism continued to flourish in journals. *Rolling Stone* featured such writers as Landau, Greil Marcus, and Paul Nelson. Dave Marsh, Lester Bangs, and others made *Creem* in Detroit a focus of Midwestern rock writing. Christgau at the *Village Voice* attracted numerous younger writers, as well as such distinctive stylists as Marcus, R. Meltzer, and Bangs. Ken Emerson and, later, Kit Rachlis supervised a similar center of rock writing at the *Boston Phoenix*.

The advent of punk and new-wave rock in the late 1970s generated an eruption of new magazines (e.g. *Trouser Press* and *New York Rocker* in New York, *Slash* in Los Angeles) and younger writers associated with that music. In the meantime, several of the older rock writers had begun to turn their primary attention to books (notably Marcus and Marsh). There were signs that the study of rock, as of jazz before it, was winning respectability as an academic discipline, notably with the founding in 1983 of the American chapter of the International Association for the Study of Popular Music, headed by Charles Hamm of Dartmouth College.

See also JAZZ, §§III, 7; IV, 6; V, 9; VI, 5.

BIBLIOGRAPHY

Dwight's Journal of Music (1852–81)
W. S. B. Mathews: *A Hundred Years of Music in America* (Chicago, 1889)
——: "Music Journalism and Journalists," *Music: a Monthly Magazine*, ii (1892), 231, 331, 515
——: "Musical Critics and Criticism," *Famous Composers and their Works*, i, ed. P. Hale (Boston, 1900), 1
O. G. T. Sonneck: "To be or not to be – a Critic," *The Musician*, viii (1903), 321
L. Karr: "Musical Critics of the New York Daily Press," *Musical Leader and Concert-goer*, ix/10 (1905), 16
W. J. Henderson: "The Function of Musical Criticism," *MQ*, i (1915), 69
S. P. Gibling: "Problems of Musical Criticism," *MQ*, ii (1916), 244
L. Gilman: "Taste in Music," *MQ*, iii (1917), 1
MM [*League of Composers' Review* to April 1925] (1924–46) [see also M. Lederman (1983) and R. M. Meckna (1984)]
O. Downes: "Placing the Critics," *MM*, ii/2 (1925), 33
H. Hanson: "Of Critics, Publishers, and Patrons," *MM*, iv/2 (1927), 28
H. Straus: "Honest Antagonism," *MM*, iv/2 (1927), 3
R. Myers: "Possibilities of Musical Criticism," *MQ*, xiv (1928), 387
J. E. Chamberlin: *The Boston Transcript: a History of its First Hundred Years* (Boston, 1930)
A. Copland: "The Composer and his Critic," *MM*, ix (1931–2), 143
A. Berger: "Rosenfeld's 'Experience and Criticism,'" *MM*, xiii/3 (1936), 53
O. Thompson: "An American School of Criticism: the Legacy Left by W. J. Henderson, Richard Aldrich, and their Colleagues of the Old Guard," *MQ*, xxiii (1937), 428
E. Carter: "Musical Reactions: Bold and Otherwise," *MM*, xv (1937–8), 199
R. Sabin: "Early American Composers and Critics," *MQ*, xxiv (1938), 210
W. Sargeant: *Jazz Hot and Hybrid* (New York, 1938/*R*1975)
C. Engel: "Views and Reviews," *MQ*, xxvi (1940), 113 [tribute to L. Gilman]
——: "Views and Reviews," *MQ*, xxvi (1940), 260 [review of T. M. Greene: *The Arts and the Art of Criticism* (Princeton, NJ, 1940)]
M. Graf: *Composer and Critic: Two Hundred Years of Musical Criticism* (New York, 1946)
V. Thomson: *The Art of Judging Music* (New York, 1948)
J. Kerman: "Music Criticism in America," *Hudson Review*, i (1949), 557
J. K. Sherman: *Music and Maestros* (Minneapolis, 1952)
R. Reisner: *The Literature of Jazz* (New York, 1954, rev. 2/1959)
W. T. Upton: *William Henry Fry: American Journalist and Composer-Critic* (New York, 1954) [see also review by C. Hatch, *MQ*, xl (1954), 606]
R. F. Goldman: "Music Criticism in the United States," *The Score*, no.12 (1955), 85

H. Pleasants: *The Agony of Modern Music* (New York, 1955)
C. R. Reis: *Composers, Conductors and Critics* (New York, 1955)
M. Stearns: *The Story of Jazz* (New York, 1956)
I. Lowens: "Writings about Music in the Periodicals of American Transcendentalism (1835–50)," *JAMS*, x (1957), 71
B. L. Karson: *Music Criticism in Los Angeles, 1881–1895* (thesis, U. of Southern California, 1959)
G. Schuller: *Early Jazz* (New York, 1968)
J. Mussulman: *Music in the Cultured Generation: a Social History of Music in America 1870–1900* (Evanston, IL, 1971)
C. Russell: "The Analysis and Evaluation of Music: a Philosophical Inquiry," *MQ*, lviii (1972), 161
M. Sherwin: *The Classical Age of New York Musical Criticism, 1880–1920: a Study of Henry T. Finck, James G. Huneker, W. J. Henderson, Henry E. Krehbiel, and Richard Aldrich* (thesis, City College, CUNY, 1972)
G. Marcus: *Mystery Train: Images of America in Rock and Roll Music* (New York, 1975)
B. Mueser: *The Criticism of New Music in New York 1919–1929* (diss., CUNY, 1975)
L. Engel: *The Critics* (New York, 1976)
L. Grossman: *A Social History of Rock Music* (New York, 1976)
H. C. Schonberg: "What Happens When Music Critics Get Together," *New York Times* (28 Aug 1977), §II, p.15
P. J. Smith: "American Criticism: the Porter Experience," *19th Century Music*, ii (1978–9), 254 [review of A. Porter: *Music of Three Seasons* (New York, 1978)]
H. J. Diamond: *Music Criticism: an Annotated Guide to the Literature* (Metuchen, NJ, 1979)
M. McKnight: *Music Criticism in the New York Times and the New York Tribune 1851–1876* (diss., Louisiana State U., 1979)
L. Feather: *The Passion for Jazz* (New York, 1980)
M. Lederman: *The Life and Death of a Small Magazine ("Modern Music," 1924–1946)*, ISAMm, xviii (Brooklyn, NY, 1983)
M. C. Gray, ed.: *Twenty Articles on the Art of Criticism* (Seattle, 1984) [repr. from *Northwest Arts*]
B. Jepson: "Women Music Critics in the United States," *The Musical Woman: an International Perspective 1983*, ed. J. L. Zaimont and others (Westport, CT, 1984), 244
R. M. Meckna: *The Rise of the American Composer-Critic: Aaron Copland, Roger Sessions, Virgil Thomson and Elliott Carter in the Periodical Modern Music 1924–1946* (diss., U. of California, Santa Barbara, 1984)

EDWARD O. D. DOWNES (1–5), JOHN ROCKWELL (6)

Croatian-American music. Croatian music in the USA is discussed as part of the Yugoslav tradition; *see* EUROPEAN-AMERICAN MUSIC, §III, 12(iv).

Croce, Jim [James] (*b* Philadelphia, PA, 10 Jan 1943; *d* Natchitoches, LA, 20 Sept 1973). Popular and folk singer and songwriter. At the age of five he learned to play the accordion; later, he was influenced by such varied artists as the Coasters, Fats Domino, Merle Haggard, and Gordon Lightfoot. While at Villanova (Pennsylvania) University, he formed several groups, whose eclectic repertories included blues, rock, and railroad songs. Success as a New York coffeehouse entertainer, beginning in 1967, earned Croce a contract with Capitol Records, but when his first album, *Jim and Ingrid Croce* (recorded with his wife in 1969), was unsuccessful, Croce gave up music to drive a truck. The producer Tommy West encouraged him to continue writing, however, and in 1972 he recorded several demonstration sides. ABC Records, which had previously rejected Croce, then signed a contract with him and released the album *You don't Mess around with Jim*, which included two hit singles, the title song and *Operator (That's not the way it feels)*. In 1973 Croce's *Bad, Bad Leroy Brown* reached no. 1 on the chart. While on a concert tour later that year, Croce was killed in a plane crash. Public sentiment helped ensure the success of such posthumous releases as *I got a name* (1973), *Time in a Bottle* (1973), and *I'll have to say I love you in a song* (1974). Lifesong Records rereleased all Croce's albums in 1977. A natural storyteller, Croce specialized in character songs and love-songs; he was one of the most popular singers and songwriters of the early 1970s.

RECORDINGS

(selective list; recorded for ABC unless otherwise stated)

Jim and Ingrid Croce (Cap. ST315, 1969); *You don't Mess around with Jim* (756, 1972), incl. Operator (That's not the way it feels); Bad, Bad Leroy Brown (11359, 1973); I got a name (11389, 1973); Time in a Bottle (11405, 1973); I'll have to say I love you in a song (11424, 1974); Workin' at the Car Wash Blues (11447, 1974)

GARY THEROUX

Crocker, Richard L(incoln) (*b* Roxbury, MA, 17 Feb 1927). Musicologist. He graduated from Yale College (BA 1950) and completed the doctorate under Schrade in 1957 with a dissertation on the Limoges *prosae*. After teaching at Yale (1955–63), he was assistant professor (1963–7), associate professor (1967–71), and full professor (from 1971) at the University of California, Berkeley. He became known for his independent ideas in *A History of Musical Style* (1966) and in his article "The Troping Hypothesis" (*MQ*, 1966), for which he was awarded the Einstein Prize by the American Musicological Society. In 1969 he received a Guggenheim Fellowship. His work at Berkeley in developing methods for teaching non-musicians is embodied in *Listening to Music* (with Ann Basart, 1971). Crocker's major scholarly contribution, however, is to the history and analysis of the medieval sequence, culminating in *The Early Medieval Sequence* (1977). His work on music theory and early polyphony has been important in providing the basis for a new understanding of principles of composition in the Middle Ages, particularly those connected with tonal order.

PHILIP BRETT/R

Crooks, Richard (Alexander) (*b* Trenton, NJ, 26 June 1900; *d* Portola Valley, CA, 29 Sept 1972). Tenor. He sang as a boy soprano, then studied with Sidney H. Bourne and Frank La Forge. Making his New York début in 1922 under Walter Damrosch, he was initially very successful as a recitalist and in appearances with orchestras. He first sang in opera at Hamburg as Cavaradossi in 1927, then made appearances with the Berlin Staatsoper and in other European centers. His American opera début was in Philadelphia, also as Cavaradossi, on 27 November 1930. Engaged by the Metropolitan Opera, he made his début there as Massenet's Des Grieux on 25 February 1933. He sang leading lyric roles, mostly French and Italian, with the company and elsewhere in the USA as a guest for the next ten seasons, then continued a concert career until 1946. Crooks had a beautiful voice which, though limited in the upper register, was admired for its consistently high standard of tone and production. A sound musician but an indifferent actor, he was one of America's most popular tenors, especially in recital, and on radio and recordings, where his repertory included much light music.

BIBLIOGRAPHY

S. Sheldon: "Richard Crooks," *Record News*, ii (1957–8), 307 [with discography]
K. S. Mackiggan: "Richard Crooks," *Record Collector*, xii (1958–60), 125 [with discography]
C. I. Morgan: "Richard Crooks Discography," *Record Advertiser*, iii/1 (1972), 2

MAX DE SCHAUENSEE/R

Crooning. A style of quiet, sentimental popular singing, current from the 1920s to the 1950s; the term is mostly used to describe male voices. Until about the 1920s there was no essential difference between "classical" and "popular" singing, though a fuller voice and greater technical accomplishment were demanded of opera singers than of those who sang operetta and popular songs. During and after the 1920s the two styles became separate as popular singers began to use the radio microphone, for which a technique aimed at projecting the voice was no longer required. It was harder for sound engineers to accommodate a loud, resonant voice than to amplify a soft one, and crooning originated as performers discovered that they could sing quietly and still be heard. The pioneers included "Whispering" Jack Smith, "Little" Jack Little, and Rudy Vallee, who was perhaps the first to transfer the style from radio to the electronic public-address systems of ballrooms and auditoriums. Later singers such as Russ Columbo, Bing Crosby, Perry Como, and Frank Sinatra learned to exploit the sensitive response of improved microphones and amplification systems, and sang with a fuller voice and a wider dynamic range.

BIBLIOGRAPHY

H. Pleasants: *The Great American Popular Singers* (New York, 1974)
W. Balliett: *American Singers* (New York, 1979)
C. Hamm: *Yesterdays: Popular Song in America* (New York, 1979)

HENRY PLEASANTS

Cropper, Steve (*b* 1941). Guitarist, songwriter, and record producer. In the 1960s he was a member of BOOKER T. & THE MGS.

Crosby, Bing (Harry Lillis) (*b* Tacoma, WA, 2 May 1904; *d* Madrid, Spain, 14 Oct 1977). Popular singer and actor. As a boy in Spokane he played drums and sang with small jazz groups. With Al Rinker (Mildred Bailey's brother) and Harry Barris he formed the Rhythm Boys, who appeared from 1926 to 1930 with the Paul Whiteman Orchestra. He began working independently about 1930; in 1931 he began a spectacularly successful career in radio (with the theme-song *When the blue of the night*) and film, notably in musical films such as *Holiday Inn* (1942, with a score by Irving Berlin that included the song *White Christmas*) and others with the comedian Bob Hope.

Crosby was one of the first singers to master the use of the microphone and, even more than Al Jolson (whose singing his early recordings reflect), he was important in introducing into the mainstream of American popular singing an Afro-American concept of song as a lyrical extension of speech. He was one of the first crooners, using the microphone not so much for singing as for apparently talking (or even whispering) to a melody. He did this by easing the weight of breath on the vocal cords, by passing into a head voice lower in the register than art-song performers, by using forward production to aid distinct enunciation, by singing on consonants (a practice of black singers shunned by classical ones), and by making discreet use of appoggiaturas, mordents, and slurs to emphasize the text. These techniques were emulated by nearly all later popular singers.

Crosby was the most popular singer of his generation; sales of his records have been estimated at 300,000,000. His voice remained remarkably unblemished by age; even on his last recordings, made when he was in his seventies and singing in a bass range, it retained the characteristics of timbre, utterance, and ostensible artlessness that communicated directly to a broad public and contributed greatly to the image he projected of an ordinary, sympathetic personality.

For illustration *see* POPULAR MUSIC, fig.4.

BIBLIOGRAPHY

B. Crosby and P. Martin: *Call me Lucky* (New York, 1953)
H. Pleasants: *The Great American Popular Singers* (New York, 1974)
——: "Bing Crosby: a Bel Canto Baritone whose Art Disguises Art," *New York Times* (5 Dec 1976)
W. Balliett: *American Singers* (New York, 1979)

HENRY PLEASANTS/R

Crosby, Bob [George Robert] (*b* Spokane, WA, 25 Aug 1913). Jazz singer and bandleader, brother of Bing Crosby. After singing with Anson Weeks and the Dorsey Brothers' Orchestra (1934–5), Crosby was appointed leader of a cooperative band made up of former members of the Ben Pollack band and newcomers recruited in New York. The group's unique brand of big-band dixieland jazz achieved international popularity during the late 1930s; its star soloists Eddie Miller, Yank Lawson, Billy Butterfield, Irving Fazola, Matty Matlock, Nappy Lamare, Ray Bauduc, and Bob Haggart also played in the widely acclaimed small group, the Bob Cats. An unpredictable vibrato marred many of Crosby's vocals, but his rhythmic phrasing did much to compensate. During World War II, he served with distinction in the US Marines, leading a service band in the Pacific area. He later became a compère and singer on radio and television shows, occasionally organizing reunion bands for specific engagements.

RECORDINGS

(selective list)

South Rampart Street Parade/Dogtown Blues (1937, Decca 15038); March of the Bob Cats (1938, Decca 1865); The Big Noise from Winnetka (1938, Decca 2208); Rose of Washington Square (1939, Decca 2474); Spain (1940, Decca 3248)

BIBLIOGRAPHY

C. Jones: *The Bob Crosby Band* (London, 1946)
G. Lombardi: "La storia dei 'Crosbiani'," *Musica jazz*, xxxiii (1977), 16
J. Chilton: *Stomp Off, Let's Go!* (London, 1983)

JOHN CHILTON

Crosby, Fanny [Frances] (**Jane**) [Van Alstyne, Fanny] (*b* South East, Putnam Co., NY, 24 March 1820; *d* Bridgeport, CT, 12 Feb 1915). Poet and author of gospel hymn texts. She was blind from the age of six weeks, and was educated and later taught at the New York Institution for the Blind; she married Alexander Van Alstyne, also a teacher at the school, in 1858. Crosby developed remarkable powers of memory and versification. During the 1850s she supplied texts for some of G. F. Root's most successful songs, notably *Hazel Dell* (1852), *There's music in the air* (1854), and *Rosalie, the Prairie Flower* (1858).

In 1864 Crosby turned her poetic talents to hymnwriting, and by 1900, using over 200 pen names, had written approximately 9000 texts, including "Jesus, keep me near the cross" (1869), "Praise Him, praise Him" (1869), "Pass me not, o gentle Savior" (1870), "Rescue the perishing" (1870), "Blessed assurance" (1873), "All the way my Savior leads me" (1875), and "Saved by grace" (1894). She was the most important writer of gospel hymn texts in the 19th century, and her name became a guarantee of success as composers sought her works for their tunes. Her words carried great power to arouse emotions through their simplicity of language and personal treatment of themes, and although her texts epitomize the era of 19th-century revivalism, they remain popular in the 20th century. Approximately 1000 of Crosby's unpublished hymns are held by the Hope Publishing Company in Carol Stream, Illinois (successor to Biglow & Main, Crosby's principal publisher). Among her published collections of poetry were *The Blind Girl and other Poems* (1844), *Monterey and other Poems* (1851), *A Wreath of Columbia's Flowers* (1858), and *Bells at Evening* (1903).

BIBLIOGRAPHY

J. Julian: "Van Alstyne, Frances Jane, née Crosby," *A Dictionary of Hymnology* (New York, 1892, 2/1907/*R*1957), ii, 1203
W. Carlton, ed.: *Fanny Crosby's Life Story by Herself* (New York, 1903)
F. Crosby and A. White, eds.: *Memories of Eighty Years* (Boston, 1906)
B. Ruffin: *Fanny Crosby* (Philadelphia, 1976)
D. Hustad, ed.: *Fanny Crosby Speaks Again* (Carol Stream, IL, 1977)

MEL R. WILHOIT

Crosby, John O('Hea) (*b* New York, 12 July 1926). Opera company general director and conductor. He was educated at Yale University (BA 1950), and was an accompanist, opera coach, and conductor in New York from 1951 to 1956. In 1957 he founded the Santa Fe Opera Company in New Mexico and became its general director and a staff conductor. Almost wholly owing to Crosby's vision, it established itself as an innovative and dynamic company, presenting many American and world premières. Crosby himself conducted the American stage première of Richard Strauss's *Daphne* (1964) and the world première of Floyd's *Wuthering Heights* (1958). He served as president of Opera America (1976–) and head of the Manhattan School of Music (1976–85), while continuing with his Santa Fe duties.

BIBLIOGRAPHY

"Crosby, John (O'Hea)," *CBY 1981*

PATRICK J. SMITH

Crosby, Stills and Nash. Folk-rock group. Formed in 1968, it consisted of three singers who wrote the group's songs and provided its guitar accompaniments; from 1969 to 1971 NEIL YOUNG was also a member of the ensemble, then known as Crosby, Stills, Nash and Young. When the group was formed all its members were already internationally known: David Crosby (Van Cortland) (*b* Los Angeles, CA, 14 Aug 1941) had been a founding member of the Byrds, Stephen Stills (*b* Dallas, TX, 3 Jan 1945) had, like Young, belonged to Buffalo Springfield, and Graham Nash (*b* Lancashire, England, 1942) had been a member of the Hollies. Their first album, *Crosby, Stills and Nash* (1969), was widely successful; they began touring the same year, performed at the Woodstock festival, and recorded a second album, *Déjà vu* (1970), which gave them three hit singles. The group became known for its distinctive, triadic vocal arrangements and refined, ethereal singing style, which obscured individual voices. All the members wrote songs: Crosby was best-known for his moody folk ballads, Stills for songs with a pronounced blues influence, and Nash for simple, innocent folk-pop tunes. Young, during his brief association with the group, earned a reputation as its most gifted songwriter; his plaintive, autobiographical folk ballad *Helpless*, from the *Déjà vu* album, is the finest song recorded by the ensemble. After leaving the group he enjoyed a successful career as a soloist; the remaining members disbanded and re-formed the ensemble repeatedly during the 1970s and early 1980s and undertook a number of solo projects. The most successful of these was Stills's album *Stephen Stills* (Atl. 7202, 1970), which included the hit song *Love the one you're with* (no. 14), recorded with Jimi Hendrix and Eric Clapton.

RECORDINGS

(selective list; all recorded for Atlantic)

Crosby, Stills and Nash (8229, 1969), incl. Marrakesh Express, Suite: Judy Blue Eyes; *Déjà vu* (7200, 1970), incl. Helpless, Our House, Teach your Children, Woodstock; Ohio (2740, 1970); *Four Way Street* (2/902, 1971); *CSN* (19104, 1977), incl. Just a song before I go; *Daylight Again* (19360, 1982), incl. Southern Cross, Wasted on the Way; *Allies* (80075, 1983)

STEPHEN HOLDEN

Cross, Lowell (Merlin) (*b* Kingsville, TX, 24 June 1938). Composer. He studied English, mathematics, and music at Texas Technological University (1956–63), where he established an electronic music studio in 1961, and at the University of Toronto (MA 1968), where he took courses in electronic music with Myron Schaeffer and Gustav Ciamaga and media technology with Marshall McLuhan. During his last year at Toronto he taught electronic music and was a research associate at the electronic music studio. He was director (with Gnazzo) of the Mills Tape Music Center (1968–9), where he also taught. As consulting artist and engineer at Experiments in Art and Technology, Inc. (1968–70), he designed the laser deflection system for Expo '70 in Osaka, Japan, and was guest consultant at the National Institute of Design in Ahmedabad, India. In 1971 Cross joined the faculty of the University of Iowa, where he became professor in 1981; in addition to teaching he serves as director and audio engineer of the recording studios at the School of Music. He published *A Bibliography of Electronic Music* (1967, rev. 1968, rev. 1970) and

Crosby, Stills, Nash and Young with Joni Mitchell, August 1970: (left to right) Stephen Stills, David Crosby, Graham Nash, Mitchell, and Neil Young

has contributed articles on electronic music to various scholarly journals.

WORKS
(selective list)

0.8 Century, tape, 1961–2; 3 Etudes, tape, 1965; Video II (B), Video II (C), tape, audio system, television, 1965–8; Musica instrumentalis, pfmrs, audio system, television, 1966–8; Reunion, diverse pfmrs, 1968, collab. Cage, M. Duchamp, D. Tudor, and others; Video III, pfmrs, audio system, elec, television, 1968, collab. Tudor; Video II (L), tape, audio system, krypton laser, X–Y laser deflection system, 1965–9; Video/Laser I–IV, audio visual works using laser deflection systems, 1969–80, I–II collab. Tudor, C. Jeffries, III collab. Tudor; several other works collab. Tudor

CHARLES SHERE

Crouch, Andrae (Edward) (*b* Los Angeles, CA, 1 July 1942). Gospel singer, pianist, and composer. As a child he served as a church pianist. After two years of study at Valley Junior College he withdrew to organize a gospel group, the Cogics (an acronym for the Church of God in Christ). This group, which included his twin sister Sandra, disbanded when their pianist Billy Preston took up a career in secular music, and in the late 1960s Crouch organized another group, the Disciples. Crouch's performance style is varied: some songs are typical of the traditional gospel style (*Soon and very soon*, 1976); fast songs are often executed with the driving beat of secular soul music, often to the accompaniment of a synthesizer, with the Disciples providing a slick backing in the manner of a pop group (*I will keep you in perfect peace*, 1976); gospel ballads are delivered in a crooning style associated with secular music (*Tell them*, 1975). His recordings thus appeal to a multiracial secular as well as a religious audience (he has won a large number of Grammy awards), and he has had more financial success than any other black American gospel singer. He has appeared throughout the USA as well as in Europe and the Far East, and is regarded as one of the leaders of contemporary gospel music. Crouch has written more than 300 gospel songs, many of which, such as *Through it all* (1971) and *Take me back* (1977), have become standards.

BIBLIOGRAPHY

SouthernB
A. Crouch: *Through It All: a Biography* (Waco, TX, 1974)
P. Salvo: "Andrae Crouch, New King Of Pop Gospel," *Sepia Magazine*, xxv/12 (1976), 50

HORACE CLARENCE BOYER

Crouch, Frederick Nicholls (*b* London, England, 31 July 1808; *d* Portland, ME, 18 Aug 1896). Cellist, singer, and composer. He studied music with his father and grandfather and had cello lessons from Nicholas Bochsa; around 1822 he entered the Royal Academy of Music in London. He was a chorister at Westminster Abbey and St. Paul's Cathedral, and a cellist in various London theater orchestras for some 30 years from 1817. In about 1832 he moved temporarily to Plymouth, where he worked as a professional singer and a traveling salesman; during this time he composed his famous song *Kathleen Mavourneen* (*c*1838). He gave lectures on the songs and legends of Ireland, became supervisor at D'Almaine & Co. music publishers, and is said to have invented zincography, an engraving process.

In 1849 Crouch began a peripatetic career in the USA, coming first to New York, where he worked as a cellist in the Astor Place Opera House. He then moved to Boston, and in 1850 to Portland, Maine, where he conducted Rossini's *Stabat mater*. He went to Philadelphia in 1856, conducted Mrs. Rush's Saturday Concerts, and produced Etienne-Nicolas Méhul's *Joseph*. He then became conductor of the choir at St. Matthew's Church in Washington, DC, and attempted with a colleague to establish an academy of music there; after its failure he moved to Richmond, Virginia, and sang in the choir of St. Paul's Church. He served as a trumpeter in the Confederate Army during the Civil War, and then settled as a singing teacher in Baltimore. In 1881 he was working as a varnisher in a factory there; a testimonial concert was given in Baltimore in 1883.

Besides the song that made his name famous, and hundreds of others, Crouch wrote two operas, *Sir Roger de Coverley* and *The Fifth of November, 1670*, an *Othello Travestie* (Philadelphia, 1856) and a monody (now in *MH-Mu*). Some of his manuscripts are in the New York Public Library. One of his 16 children, Emma Elizabeth (1842–86), was the famous Parisian courtesan "Cora Pearl."

BIBLIOGRAPHY

"The Composer of Kathleen Mavourneen," *Musical Courier*, iii (1881), 23
F. O. Jones, ed.: *A Handbook of American Music and Musicians* (Canaseraga, NY, 1886/*R*1971)
[Autobiographical sketch], *The Folio* (Boston, Jan 1887)
"Crouch, Frederick Nicholls," *Cyclopedia of Music and Musicians*, ed. J. D. Champlin and W. F. Apthorp (New York, 1888–90) [lists 14 song collections]
"The Composer of Kathleen Mavourneen," *MMR*, xxii (1892), 202
Obituary, *MT*, xxxviii (1896), 611

BRUCE CARR

Crow [Absaroke] (Absaroke: "children of the large-beaked bird"). American Indian tribe of the northern Plains whose language is part of the Siouan family. Formerly sedentary farmers of the Northeast, the Crow migrated westward during the 18th century and became nomadic buffalo-hunters. Their culture, based on the horse and buffalo, was typical of Plains dwellers; it came to an end in 1878 when the Crow were moved to the reservation they now occupy in Montana (*see* INDIANS, AMERICAN, fig. 1).

Central to the traditional Crow world view was the belief that every natural phenomenon had its spirit, and that some of these spirits could exert supernatural power. Contact with a spirit was sought through visions, during which an individual received its "medicine"; this usually took the form of a song, which was peculiar to the individual and would aid him in a specific aspect of life. Thus men with appropriate power sang game-charming songs before a buffalo hunt, and a warrior always sang his personal medicine song before encountering the enemy. The Crow viewed all songs as having supernatural origins. Received either in dreams or visions, they became an individual's personal property. Songs were also borrowed, proper recognition being always given to the tribe of origin.

As with many other Plains tribes, a man's social rank and status depended on success in warfare and raiding. Traditionally most males belonged to a military society, each having its distinctive regalia, songs, and dance. Their activities were both social and military. During dances, held most often in the spring and summer, members sang their medicine songs, recited deeds of bravery, and directed songs of mockery at rival societies. Crow warriors made frequent forays into enemy camps to "count coup" (i.e., to touch an enemy, however lightly, with the hand or a stick), and to capture horses and other property. Upon their successful return, a victory celebration was held; its principal feature was a slow-moving, clockwise circle dance, in which the circle was made up alternately of men and women, taking short steps and swaying from side to side. Praise and honoring songs were sung for the warriors, and gifts were presented to the singers.

Crow Indians playing frame drums at a tobacco-planting ceremony in Montana, c1920

With the advent of reservation life, military societies began to function as mutual benefit associations. Their major ceremony became the Hot Dance (adopted from the Hidatsa in the 1870s), which corresponds to the Omaha, Grass, or War Dance of other Plains tribes. The dance, still held as late as 1931 (Lowie, 1935), included honoring songs and the giving of gifts, a special dance by eight chief dancers, a Kettle Dance, and a dog-meat feast.

The dominance of warlike pursuits found expression even in the principal religious ceremony of the Crow, the Sun Dance. Unlike other Plains tribes, the Crow did not perform this dance annually but only when an individual used it to pledge vengeance for a relative killed in warfare. Despite a difference in purpose, the Crow Sun Dance had the same general ceremonial features as the sun dances of other Plains tribes: the preparation (taking several days) of the lodge and the participants, strenuous dancing without food and water, and self-torture. Because of government suppression, the Crow Sun Dance ceased to be performed in the 1880s, but in 1941 the Crow adopted the Sun Dance of the Wind River Shoshone.

The cultivation of sacred tobacco, a medicine for promoting general welfare, was another important Crow religious activity. The Tobacco Society oversaw the adoption of new members and the elaborate ritual of planting and harvesting. A gift of songs was made to an initiate by existing members, and he danced with them on the fourth night of his adoption ceremony. The elaborate planting ceremony (see illustration) occurred in May. Women led the procession to the garden, followed by men carrying frame drums. At each of four stops (four being a sacred number), the men sang and drummed while the women danced. After the planting, four dances were held to promote the growth of the plant. The ceremonial cycle ended with a Harvest Dance.

The Crow also performed a Sacred Pipe Dance to promote individual good fortune and ceremonial friendship in a "father–child" relationship. Its outstanding feature was an adoption ceremony in which two dancers, each holding a rattle and a pipe stem, danced with crouching, swooping movements. The Crow Pipe Dance, like the Omaha *Wa'wan*, belongs to the widespread ceremonial complex referred to as the Calumet Dance, which has its origin in the Pawnee *Hako*.

The Crow's principal musical instrument was the hand-held, single-headed frame drum, used to accompany both solo and group singing. A large double-headed bass drum was played during the Hot Dance. Rawhide container rattles, in both spherical and doughnut shapes, were part of the regalia of the military societies. In addition, members of the Big Dogs warrior society carried cluster rattles consisting of deer hooves tied to a long stick; during impromptu "sings," society members stood in a circle and used these rattles as beaters on pieces of rawhide. The Crow also possessed two wind instruments: the eagle-bone whistle, blown by participants in the Sun Dance, and the wooden duct flute with finger-holes, played by young men during courtship.

Crow musical style, as it exists today, has features common to many Plains groups. Songs tend to start high and descend in "terrace" fashion over a range of an octave or more. Melodies are mostly based on four- or five-note scales, using major 2nds and minor 3rds. Song form is most often of the incomplete repetition type (*AABCBC*), in which the opening section (*A*) is sung by the leader and repeated by one or more singers, and the remaining sections (*BC*) are then sung through twice by the ensemble. Crow singing is characterized by a lower tessitura than is generally found among northern Plains groups; the men sing with a fairly relaxed, open throat and the voice has a distinctive warbling quality. Songs of the older repertory (e.g., medicine songs and songs of the military societies) often have verbal texts with meaning, while the texts of modern compositions consist mostly of vocables. Drum accompaniment is usual, the beats characteristically falling either just ahead of or behind the pulse of the song. At the Crow Fair and Indian Powwow, both held annually in August, the Crow perform the popular powwow dances of the northern Plains such as the War, Round, Rabbit, Owl, and Stomp dances.

Recordings of Crow music are in the holdings of the Bureau of American Ethnology at the Smithsonian Institution, Washington, DC, and the University of California Museum of Ethnology at Berkeley, California.

See also INDIANS, AMERICAN, esp. §I, 4(ii)(a).

DISCOGRAPHY

Crow Tribal Sun Dance Songs/Northern Cheyenne Sun Dance Songs (American Indian Soundchiefs 705/700, n.d.)

BIBLIOGRAPHY

E. S. Curtis: *The North American Indian*, iv (Cambridge, MA, 1909)

R. Lowie: "Social Life of the Crow Indians," *American Museum of Natural History, Anthropological Papers*, no.9 (1912), 179–248

——: *The Crow Indians* (New York, 1935, rev. 2/1956)

MARY RIEMER-WELLER

Crozier, Catharine (*b* Hobart, OK, 18 Jan 1914). Organist. A 1936 graduate of the Eastman School, from which she holds the artist's diploma in organ and a master's degree in music literature, she made her début in Washington, DC, in 1941 at a national convention of the American Guild of Organists. She had joined the organ faculty at the Eastman School in 1938 and became head of the department in 1953. From 1955 to 1969 she was organ professor at Rollins College, Winter Park, Florida. Her own teachers included Joseph Bonnet, Yella Pessl (harpsichord), and HAROLD GLEASON, whom she later married. With him she has given innumerable master classes at many institutions. Her concert career has taken her to most European countries. In 1962 she joined Biggs and Virgil Fox in inaugurating the organ at Philharmonic Hall, New York; in 1975, with Biggs, André Marchal, Karl Richter, and Raver, she played at the inauguration of the organ at Alice Tully Hall. She won the 1979 International Performer of the Year award from the New York City chapter of the American Guild of Organists. Her memorized repertory is immense and historically inclusive although she has specialized in contemporary music. Her great control, precision, sense of style, and range of expression make her performances remarkable.

VERNON GOTWALS

Crumb, George (Henry) (*b* Charleston, WV, 24 Oct 1929). Composer. He received his first musical training from his parents, who were both musicians. He studied composition at the Mason College of Music and Fine Arts, Charleston (BM 1950), where his father was on the faculty. In 1949 he married Elizabeth May Brown, a pianist and fellow student. Crumb continued his studies at the University of Illinois (MMus 1953) and the University of Michigan (DMA 1959), where his principal teacher was Ross Lee Finney, who, after Crumb's father, had the greatest influence on the young composer. He received several awards during his student years, including a fellowship for study at the Berkshire Music Center (summer 1955), a Fulbright scholarship (1955–6), and a BMI student award (1956). After teaching at the University of Colorado (1959–64) and at SUNY, Buffalo (1964–5), Crumb became professor and composer-in-residence at the University of Pennsylvania in 1965. His numerous honors include a Pulitzer Prize (1968, for the orchestral work *Echoes of Time and the River*), a UNESCO International Rostrum of Composers Award (1971), a Koussevitzky recording award (1971), and grants from the Rockefeller (1964), Guggenheim (1967, 1973), Fromm (1973), and Ford (1976) foundations, as well as from the National Institute of Arts and Letters (1967), to which he was elected a member in 1975. (For illustration of Crumb in 1974, *see* DEGAETANI, JAN.)

Crumb's early style was based on short musical subjects in which timbre, rhythm, pitch, and idiomatic technique were given equal structural significance; this concept expanded as his style developed, producing a highly effective and widely influential musical language. His mature style, exemplified in *Black Angels: 13 Images from the Dark Land* and *Ancient Voices of Children* (both 1970), shows a special concern for sonorous elements, of which tone qualities and their combination are of primary importance. He often calls for the use of new techniques for playing traditional instruments (such as bottleneck banjo techniques), of instruments associated with other musical cultures or traditions (such as the musical saw, musical glasses), and of experimental sound sources. His music for piano, both as a solo instrument and a member of chamber ensembles, has been especially imaginative in its expansion of the available color palette; Crumb's gadgetless effects are "completely viable, often beautiful and never gimmicky" (S. Bradshaw: "Keyboard music," §III, 7, *Grove* 6). He has been perhaps even more inventive in his treatment of the voice. All of the remarkable sonorous effects of Crumb's music are produced from scores that are carefully notated and reflect a highly disciplined craft (*see* NOTATION, §2).

Dynamic levels also shape Crumb's music; like timbre, they are determined by dramatic rather than by mathematical or serial considerations. Although on occasion volume is electronically controlled, it is more directly related to tone color, both through instrumentation and through a telling use of register. The rhythmic life of Crumb's work is rich: dramatic timing, measured succession, and metrical sections interact to achieve both contrast and coherence. *Makrokosmos I*, no.11 (see illustration, p.552), for example, uses all three: relationships between the subjects are dramatic, being dependent on the acoustic and psychological elements of the particular performance; the treble layer is measured but not metered; and the quotations from Chopin's *Fantaisie-impromptu* are metered.

Crumb's larger sense of fabric is akin not to the post-Romantic, expressionist, and serial designs of his immediate predecessors but to late 17th- and early 18th-century Baroque principles: the instruments themselves – vying, uniting, countering, and becoming reconciled – project spatial, organic forms that are clearly related to *concertato* ideals. The presence of the performer as a musical personality is essential, providing, with its drama and risk, so rich a creative energy that Crumb has not been drawn to the computer or the synthesizer.

Whereas in matters of fabric and texture Crumb seeks the nonarithmetic (but uses layered textures in "modern" Gothic technique) in matters of form, he reaches back to a medieval admixture of the musical, the symbolic, and particularly the cosmic. He delights in incorporating numerology and mirror images (sections or movements are often in arch form). He approaches the heart of the medieval *quadrivium* in such works as *Makrokosmos I*, *Black Angels*, and *Star-child*, all of which display the astronomical, arithmetic, geometric, and musical elements vital to that concept. Symbols made visible in the notation (but hidden from the listener) are another link to a medieval aesthetic, and direct quotation of medieval fragments occasionally brings this relationship to the surface. In the style of performance symbolism is again apparent, with the wearing of masks, the recitations of numbers by string players, the procession of orchestral

The score of George Crumb's "Dream Images (Love-Death Music)," no.11 of "Makrokosmos I" (New York, 1974)

players, and so forth. From 1980, however, a simplification has occurred, a concentration upon potent musical expression without extra-musical reinforcement.

Crumb's works typically unfold in a succession of opulent images, each one complete, that are strung into a coherent whole through contrast, cross-reference, and a judicious balance. Crumb acknowledges his debt to Debussy and Bartók, concentrating on the relationship of the very particular sounds he imagines to the musical ideas they support and embody. In preferring the appropriate to the surprising, musical effectiveness to unconnected flamboyance, Crumb has joined those composers who have declined merely to astonish their listeners, seeking instead to enrich them. This is suggested by his statement "Music might be defined as a system of proportions in the service of a spiritual impulse" (publisher's catalogue, 1982).

WORKS

(all published unless otherwise stated)

VOCAL

(all texts by Lorca unless otherwise stated)

Night Music I, S, pf + cel, 2 perc, 1963; Paris, 30 Jan 1964, B. Blanchard

Madrigals, Book I, S, vib, db, 1965; Philadelphia, 18 Feb 1966, E. Suderberg, Penn Contemporary Players

Madrigals, Book II, S, fl + a fl + pic, perc, 1965; Washington, DC, 11 March 1966, J. DeGaetani, Contemporary Chamber Ens, cond. Weisberg
Songs, Drones, and Refrains of Death, Bar, elec gui, elec db, elec pf + elec hpd, 2 perc, 1968; Iowa City, IA, H. Heap, cond. Hibbard
Madrigals, Book III, S, harp, perc, 1969; Seattle, 6 March 1970, Suderberg, U. of Washington Contemporary Group
Madrigals, Book IV, S, fl + pic + a fl, harp, db, perc, 1969; Seattle, 6 March 1970, Suderberg, U. of Washington Contemporary Group
Night of the Four Moons, A, a fl + pic, banjo, perc, elec vc, 1969; Washington, PA, 6 Nov 1969, J. Barton, Philadelphia Composers' Forum, cond. J. Thome
Ancient Voices of Children, S, Tr, ob, mand, harp, elec pf + toy pf, 3 perc, 1970; Washington, DC, 31 Oct 1970, DeGaetani, M. Dash, Contemporary Chamber Ens, cond. Weisberg
Lux aeterna (Requiem mass), 5 masked musicians: S, b fl + tr rec, sitar, 2 perc, 1971; Richmond, VA, 16 Jan 1972, Philadelphia Composers' Forum
Star-child (after Dies irae, Massacre of the Innocents (13th century), John xii. 36), parable, S, children's chorus, orch, 1977; New York, 5 May 1977, Gubrud, New York PO, cond. Boulez
Apparition (from Whitman: When Lilacs Last in the Dooryard Bloom'd), S, pf, 1979; New York, 13 Jan 1981, DeGaetani, Kalish

INSTRUMENTAL

String Quartet, 1954, unpubd; 1955
Sonata, vc, 1955; Ann Arbor, aut. 1956, C. Doppmann
Variazioni, orch, 1959; Cincinnati, 8 May 1965, Cincinnati SO, cond. Rudolf
Five Pieces for Piano, 1962; Boulder, CO, 12 Feb 1963, Burge
Four Nocturnes (Night Music II), vn, pf, 1964; Buffalo, 3 Feb 1965, Zukofsky, Crumb
11 Echoes of Autumn, 1965 (Echoes I), a fl, cl, pf, vn, 1966; Brunswick, ME, 10 Aug 1966, Aeolian Chamber Players
Echoes of Time and the River (Echoes II), 4 processionals, orch, 1967; Chicago, 26 May 1967, Chicago SO, cond. I. Hoffman
Black Angels: 13 Images from the Dark Land (Images I), elec str qt, 1970; Ann Arbor, 23 Oct 1970, Stanley Quartet
Vox balaenae (Voice of the Whale), 3 masked musicians: elec fl, elec pf, elec vc, 1971; Washington, DC, 17 March 1972, New York Camerata
Makrokosmos I, 12 fantasy-pieces after the Zodiac, amp pf, 1972; Colorado Springs, CO, 8 Feb 1973, Burge
Makrokosmos II, 12 fantasy-pieces after the Zodiac, amp pf, 1973; New York, 12 Nov 1974, R. Miller
Music for a Summer Evening (Makrokosmos III), 2 amp pf, 2 perc, 1974; Swarthmore, PA, 30 March 1974, Kalish, J. Freeman, R. DesRoches, R. Fitz
Dream Sequence (Images II), vn, vc, pf, perc, 1976; Brunswick, ME, 17 Oct 1976, Aeolian Chamber Players
Celestial Mechanics (Makrokosmos IV), pf 4 hands, 1979; New York, 18 Nov 1979, Kalish, Jacobs
A Little Suite for Christmas, A.D. 1979, pf, 1980; Washington, DC, 14 Dec 1980, L. Orkis
Gnomic Variations, pf, 1981; Washington, DC, 12 Dec 1982, J. Jacob
Pastoral Drone, org, 1982; San Francisco, 27 June 1984, Craighead
Processional, pf, 1983; Lenox, MA, 26 July 1984, Kalish
A Haunted Landscape, orch, 1984; New York, 7 June 1984, New York PO, cond. Weisberg

MSS in *DLC*
Principal publisher: Peters

BIBLIOGRAPHY

EwenD; *VintonD*
R. H. Lewis: "George Crumb: *Night Music I*," *PNM*, iii/2 (1965), 13
D. Henahan: "Current Chronicle: Chicago – George Crumb Echoes of Time and the River," *MQ*, liv (1968), 83
——: [Record review of *Eleven Echoes of Autumn*], *MQ*, lv (1969), 280
D. Hamilton: "Three Composers of Today," *Musical Newsletter*, i/1 (1971), 16
B. Fennelly: "George Crumb: 'Ancient Voices of Children,' " *Notes*, xxix (1972–3), 560
C. Gamer: "Current Chronicle: Colorado Springs, Colorado," *MQ*, lix (1973), 462
"Crumb, George (Henry)," *CBY 1974*
L. Luck: "George Crumb: 'Makrokosmos Vol. I,' " *Notes*, xxxi (1974–5), 157
R. Moevs: "George Crumb: 'Music for a Summer Evening (Makrokosmos III),' " *MQ*, lxii (1976), 293
A. Frank: "George Crumb: 'Songs, Drones, and Refrains of Death,' " *Notes*, xxxiii (1976–7), 694
R. Steinitz: "George Crumb," *MT*, cxix (1978), 844
C. Gagne and T. Caras: "George Crumb," *Soundpieces: Interviews with American Composers* (Metuchen, NJ, 1982), 117
D. Ott: *The Role of Texture and Timbre in the Music of George Crumb* (diss., U. of Kentucky, 1983)
D. Gillespie, ed.: *George Crumb: Profile of a Composer* (New York, 1985)

EDITH BORROFF

Crusaders. Jazz group. Its original members were Wilton Felder (tenor saxophone and bass guitar), Joe Sample (keyboards), Stix [Nesbert] Hooper (drums), and Wayne Henderson (trombone), who began playing together while in college in Texas. They moved to Los Angeles in the late 1950s and began working as backup musicians for various singers. In the early 1960s they took the name the Jazz Crusaders, and attracted a following among jazz audiences. Changing their name to the Crusaders in the early 1970s, they began to play dance music notable for its concision, clarity, and wealth of melody. Several of their recordings were commercially successful (mostly on the rhythm-and-blues chart), and in 1979 they had a major pop hit with *Street Life* (no.36), with Randy Crawford as guest singer. Their music combines elements of jazz, funk, and pop, and is always impeccably played; their recordings are produced by the members themselves, and display a scrupulous attention to detail. Henderson left the group in 1977, and in 1983 Leon Ndugu Chancler replaced Hooper, who now works as a soloist and session musician.

Cruz, Celia (*b* Havana, Cuba, 21 Oct ?1924). Popular singer. She first began singing on Cuban radio in the late 1940s, and studied at the Conservatory of Music in Havana from 1947 to 1950. In 1950 she joined the Sonora Matancera Orchestra as lead singer. The following year the orchestra began an extensive tour of the Caribbean, South America, and the USA, and Cruz became associated with such songs as *Cao cao mani picao*, *El yerberito*, and *Burundanga* (for which she was awarded a gold record in 1957). Between 1951 and 1961 she also appeared in five films and recorded several albums with the orchestra. After Fidel Castro's revolution in 1959 Cruz worked with the orchestra in Mexico for a year before settling in the USA. She made annual tours of South America throughout the 1960s, and in 1966 began an association with the Tito Puente Orchestra, with which she recorded eight albums. By the early 1970s salsa music had become very popular in New York, and in 1973 Cruz sang the role of Gracia Divina in Larry Harlow's Latin opera *Hommy*. The following year she won a gold record with the album *Celia and Johnny*, recorded with the Johnny Pacheco Orchestra. She was honored in a special event at Madison Square Garden, New York, on 23 October 1982. Her voice is a deep, metallic contralto, and her special skills in the art of improvisational singing have earned her the title "Queen of Salsa."

BIBLIOGRAPHY

"Cruz, Celia," *CBY 1983*

TONY SABOURNIN

Cuban-American music. The music of Cuban immigrants to the USA is discussed as part of the Caribbean tradition; *see* HISPANIC-AMERICAN MUSIC, §2 (ii).

Cugat, Xavier (*b* Barcelona, Spain, 1 Jan 1900). Violinist and bandleader. He grew up in Cuba and became famous in the USA during the 1920s as a popularizer of Latin dance rhythms. He began with a tango orchestra in the late 1920s, but adopted a more general format in the 1930s with the rise in popularity of the Cuban rumba. His early band, which included a trumpet, a marimba, and an accordion, was designed to play the Cuban, Guatemalan, and Argentinian music popular at the time. Although except for publicity reasons Cugat never claimed to play authentic Latin music, some of his early recordings still retain a certain freshness and charm, and his career as a whole helped pave the way in the USA for more authentic Latin styles. Cugat's nationwide success was greatly abetted during the 1940s by his appearance in a large number of musical films, the best-known being perhaps *You Were Never Lovelier* (1942).

BIBLIOGRAPHY
"Cugat, Xavier," *CBY 1942*
M. Gomez-Santinos: *Xavier Cugat* (Barcelona, 1958)
J. S. Roberts: *The Latin Tinge* (New York, 1979)

JOHN STORM ROBERTS

Cullen, Countee P(orter) (*b* New York, 30 May 1903; *d* New York, 9 Jan 1946). Writer. The adopted son of the Rev. Frederick A. Cullen and his wife Carolyn M. Cullen, he was the only well-known member of the so-called "Harlem Renaissance" to come from that area. Cullen's upbringing in a Methodist parsonage and his education at New York University (BA 1925) and Harvard University (MA 1926) significantly influenced his poetic work. His spiritual questioning and meditations on God, his reliance on mythic Greek allusions, and his use of poetic diction and forms evocative of the English Romantics (especially Keats) distinguish him from his peers who were more obviously exploiting themes rooted in Afro-American folk culture. His most enduring work is published in the collection *On these I Stand* (1947).

Although Cullen resisted the label "Negro poet," most of his successful work deals directly with the problems of carrying the gifts and burdens of two, often opposing, cultures. The resulting tension, frustration, doubt, and resistance are the strongest features of his poetry, notably in the well-known *Yet Do I Marvel* and *Heritage*. Because his verse is traditional and classical in its construction – Cullen titled many of his poems "lyric," "ballad," or "song" and wrote in these forms – it lends itself well to musical setting. The romantic yearnings and introspection of his poetry seem also to have attracted composers.

Emerson Whithorne used Cullen's poems for his song cycles *The Grim Troubadour* and *Saturday's Child*, and Virgil Thomson set seven choruses from Cullen's translation of Euripides' *Medea*. Cullen and Arna Bontemps wrote the book for the musical play *St. Louis Woman* (music by Harold Arlen and Johnny Mercer) based on Bontemps' novel *God Sends Sunday*. Dorothy Rudd Moore also set several of Cullen's poems.

BIBLIOGRAPHY
B. E. Ferguson: *Countee Cullen and the Negro Renaissance* (New York, 1966)
D. T. Turner: *In a Minor Chord: Three Afro-American Writers and their Search for Identity* (Carbondale, IL, 1971)
J. Wagner: *Black Poets of the United States* (Urbana, IL, 1973)
M. S. Cole: "*Afrika singt*: Austro-German Echoes of the Harlem Renaissance," *JAMS*, xxx (1977), 72
R. C. Friedberg: *American Art Song and American Poetry* (Metuchen, NJ, 1981)
M. A. Hovland: *Musical Settings of American Poetry: a Bibliography* (in preparation) [incl. list of settings]

JOSEPH A. BROWN

Cumming, William. Pseudonym of William Cumming Peters (*see* PETERS).

Cummings, Conrad (*b* San Francisco, CA, 10 Feb 1948). Composer. He studied with Bülent Arel and Joan Panetti at Yale University (BA 1970) and with Arel, David Lewin, and Layton at SUNY, Stony Brook (MA 1973). In 1977 he obtained a DMA in composition at Columbia University after further studies with Davidovsky, Chou Wen-chung, and Ussachevsky. He also took summer courses in computer music at the Berkshire Music Center and at Stanford University. From 1974 to 1976 he was on the faculty of the Columbia-Princeton Electronic Music Center and from 1976 to 1979 he was electronic music coordinator at Brooklyn College. He then spent a year at IRCAM in Paris, developing and composing with a new system of computer synthesis of the singing voice. He was appointed assistant professor at Oberlin College in 1980.

Cummings has received many awards including an NEA grant, MacDowell Colony fellowships, and grants from the Martha Baird Rockefeller Fund. He has had commissions from choreographers, new-music ensembles, the Smithsonian Institution (*Dinosaur Music*, for the opening of Dinosaur Hall at the National Museum of Natural History in December 1981), and Oberlin College (for *Eros and Psyche*, to celebrate the college's 150th anniversary in November 1983). His music is imaginatively inventive in its whimsical architecture and kaleidoscopic sonorities. Reflecting his personality, it is amiable, witty, and joyous. He has contributed to *Computer Music Journal*, *Musical America*, and other periodicals.

WORKS

Opera: Eros and Psyche (3, C. Cummings), 1982–3; Cassandra (3, C. Cummings), 1984–5

Large ens: Morning Music, 7 wind, perc, xyl, pf, 5 solo str, 1973; Movement, orch, 1974–5; Composition, orch, 1977; After Eros and Psyche, chamber orch, tape, 1985–

Chamber: Père Ubu, pf, ww qt, 1969; Triptych, vc, 1971; Divertimento, ob, vc, gui, 1971; Remembered Voices, pf, 1972; Bone Songs, cl, tpt, db, 1974; Basstet for Times Square, 4 db, 1978; Skin Songs (J. Awad, T. Meyer, S. E. Case, D. Trainer), S, a fl, cl, b cl, bn, vn, vc, 1978; Tap Dancer, 6 perc, 1978; Beast Songs (M. McClure), S, fl, cl/b cl, vn, vc, pf, cptr-synth vv, 1979; Ricochet (T. Meyer), T, pf, synth vv, 1980; Second Basstet for Times Square, 4 db, 1980; Summer Air, nonet, 1980; 7 Songs (T. Meyer), T/Bar, pf, cptr-synth vv, 1981; Piece for Mean-tone Org, 1982; Zephyr's Lesson, fl, vc, perc, tape, 1984

Elec: Subway Songs, 4-track tape, 1974; Endangered Species, dance music, 1977; Dinosaur Music, 10-track tape, 14 loudspeakers, 1981; Music for "Starlore," stereo tape, 1982

Principal publisher: Belwin-Mills

BARBARA A. PETERSEN

Cummings, E(dward) E(stlin) [e. e. cummings] (*b* Cambridge, MA, 14 Oct 1894; *d* Silver Lake, NH, 3 Sept 1962). Poet. Before World War II his poems attracted the attention of several composers, including Copland, Diamond, and most notably Cage. Cage's settings show a response to Cummings's naivety of tone rather than to the novelty of his style, which included an inventive use of punctuation, layout, and neologism. These were, however, the features that commended his work to Boulez (*e. e. cummings ist der Dichter*) and Berio (*Circles*), both of whom first encountered it during visits to the USA in the early 1950s. Cummings's innovations seemed to them to parallel some of their own, and his sensitivity to phonetic values made his writing a valuable starting-point for new approaches to text-setting.

Among the more than 200 settings of Cummings's verse, the poems most frequently set have been "In Just," "Hist whist," "I thank you God for most this amazing," "Sweet spring is your," and "Tumbling-hair." Composers particularly attracted by his style include William Bergsma (Six Songs), Vincent Persichetti (*Glad and Very*, *Spring Cantata*), Dominick Argento (*Songs about Spring*), Marc Blitzstein (*From Marion's Book*), Brian Fennelly (*Songs with Improvisations*), and Paul Nordoff (many songs). David Diamond also wrote a ballet score (*Tom*) to a scenario by Cummings, as well as an orchestral work based on his novel *The Enormous Room*. Cummings himself made an English translation of the narration for the published score of Stravinsky's *Oedipus rex*.

BIBLIOGRAPHY

M. A. Hovland: *Musical Settings of American Poetry: a Bibliography* (in preparation) [incl. list of settings]

PAUL GRIFFITHS/R

Cunha, José da (*b* Rio de Janeiro, Brazil, 27 Feb 1955). Bow maker. He was apprenticed to Salchow in New York and subsequently joined his workshop. In 1978 and 1980 he was awarded gold medals for his work at the international competitions of the Violin Society of America. His bows, of excellent wood, are tastefully modeled after the Tourte-Peccatte school and are extremely well made.

JAAK LIIVOJA-LORIUS

Cunningham, Arthur (*b* Piermont, NY, 11 Nov 1928). Composer. He began to study piano at the age of six and wrote music for his own jazz band when he was 12. He received the BA in music from Fisk University (1951) and an MA from Columbia University Teachers College (1957), then studied further at the Juilliard School and privately. While serving in the US Army (1955–7) he wrote music for army bands, musical shows, and television. The compositions of his mature period reflect his eclecticism; he draws freely on traditional techniques, serialism, jazz, and rock – the last particularly in his later stage works. His career has included teaching and touring as a lecturer and conductor; from the 1970s he became particularly active as a conductor of his own works. Recordings of his works include *Lullabye for a Jazz Baby* and *Engrams*.

WORKS

(for fuller list see Tischler, 1981)

Stage: The Beauty Part (musical, S. J. Perelman), 1963; Violetta (musical, after Odiberti: Le mal coeur), 1963; Ballet, str qt, jazz qt, 1968; His Natural Grace (Louey, Louey) (rock opera, Cunningham), 1969; Shango (incidental music, Cunningham), African insts, 1969; Harlem Suite (ballet, Cunningham), 1971; Night Song (theater piece, Swahili, Gulla from Sea Islands), 1973; 2 children's musicals

Orch: Adagio, ob, str, 1954; Night Lights, 1955; Lights across the Hudson, tone poem, 1956; Dialogues, pf, chamber orch, 1966; Theatre Piece, 1966; Concentrics, 1968; Dim du mim (Twilight), eng hn/ob, chamber orch, 1968–9; Lullabye for a Jazz Baby, tpt, orch, 1969 [from Harlem Suite]; Db Conc., 1971; The Walton Statement, db, orch, 1971; The Prince, Bar, orch, 1973; Rooster Rhapsody, nar, orch, 1975; Crispus attucks, band, 1976; Night Bird, 1v, jazz qnt, orch, 1978

Vocal: Many choral partsongs and choral suites; solo songs, incl. Prometheus (Aeschylus, trans. Havelock), B, 1964; arrs. of spirituals; Studies for Singing the Blues, manual, 1974

*c*20 works for various inst ens; several duos, incl. Minakesh, ob, pf, 1969, Covenant, vc, db, 1972; solo inst works, incl. Eclatette, vc, 1971

*c*60 pf pieces incl. Engrams, 1970

Principal publishers: Presser, Remick

BIBLIOGRAPHY

SouthernB

E. Southern: *The Music of Black Americans: a History* (New York, 1971, rev. 2/1983)

A. Tischler: *Fifteen Black American Composers* (Detroit, 1981) [with complete list of works]

EILEEN SOUTHERN

Cunningham, Merce [Mercier] (*b* Centralia, WA, 16 April 1919). Choreographer. He attended the Cornish Institute in Seattle, where he met John Cage, with whom he formed a lasting and productive partnership. He also studied modern dance at Mills College and the Bennington School of the Dance. After performing for a time with Martha Graham's company, he began to present his own choreography in 1942; among his first works was *Totem Ancestor*, to music by Cage. He formed his own dance company in 1953 and established a school in 1959. He has worked with many experimental composers (among them Earle Brown, Morton Feldman, David Tudor, and Christian Wolff) and introduced new concepts in music and dance, particularly the use of aleatory procedures and open form. He views music and dance as independent entities that share only the same duration. He was among the first choreographers to use electronic music, both live and taped, and *musique concrète*. He is arguably the most innovative choreographer of the 20th century.

See also DANCE, §III, 2.

Merce Cunningham (left) and John Cage; Cage holds a stopwatch, a device used in their work to synchronize dance and music

BIBLIOGRAPHY

C. Tomkins: *The Bride and the Bachelors* (New York, 1965, 2/1968)

"Cunningham, Merce," *CBY 1966*

"Time to Walk in Space," *Dance Perspectives*, no.34 (1968) [whole issue]

M. Cunningham: *Merce Cunningham* (New York, 1975) [autobiography]

J. Lesschaeve: *Merce Cunningham: Le danseur et la danse: Entretiens avec Jacqueline Lesschaeve* (Paris, 1980)

D. Vaughan: "Duet: the 40-year Collaboration of Avant-gardists Merce Cunningham and John Cage," *Ballet News*, iv/9 (1983), 21

J. Anderson: "Cunningham's 'Events' are Audacious and Controversial," *New York Times* (14 Oct 1984), §II, p. 16

SUSAN AU

Cunningham, Virginia (*b* Bridgeport, IL, 23 Aug 1910). Music librarian. She studied English at Stephens College, Columbia, Missouri, and the University of Wisconsin (BA 1932), where she also received a certificate in library science. From 1936 to 1940 she undertook graduate work in musicology at Columbia

University. She held positions at the Wichita (Kansas) Public Library (1932–3), the New York Public Library (1933–4), and the Columbia University Music Library (1934–40). She joined the cataloguing department of the Library of Congress in 1942; in 1956 she was appointed head of the music section of the Library's descriptive cataloguing division, a position she held until her retirement in 1972. Cunningham was president of the Music Library Association from 1956 to 1958. She edited *Rules for Full Cataloguing*, the third volume of the *Code international de la catalogage de la musique* (Frankfurt am Main, Germany, 1971).

PAULA MORGAN

Curran, Alvin (*b* Providence, RI, 13 Dec 1938). Composer. He studied piano and trombone from an early age. At Brown University he studied composition with Ron Nelson (BA 1960) and at Yale he was a pupil of Elliott Carter and Mel Powell (MMus 1963); on graduating he received the Bearns Prize. In 1965 he moved to Rome, where with Teitelbaum and Rzewski he founded the group Musica Elettronica Viva (1966) for the production and performance of live electronic music. The group rapidly expanded its functions to include free improvisation, street music and theater, collaborations with untrained musicians (usually vocalists), and audience participation, frequently involving hundreds of people; it gave more than 200 concerts in the USA and Europe in 1966–70. Much of Curran's music written after 1970 reflects the collective process involved in experimental work with Musica Elettronica Viva as well as continuing to combine electronics, traditional instrumental techniques, and "natural" sounds. Performances of Curran's works may overflow the boundaries of a conventional concert hall: *Monumenti* (1982), commissioned by the Alte Oper in Frankfurt am Main, Germany, required all the available space in that opera house and much of the surrounding square as well; a series of environmental works entitled *Maritime Rites* (1978–84) employed ships in the harbor of La Spezia, Italy, foghorns along the coast of the Netherlands mixed live in an all-night broadcast on Dutch radio, and boats full of singers cruising on various European and North American lakes. *Songs and Views from the Magnetic Garden* (1973), *Light Flowers, Dark Flowers* (1974), and *The Works* (1978–83) are intimate pieces in which selective recording techniques are used to give natural sounds, such as the whining of a dog or footsteps crunching in gravel, symphonic or operatic proportions. The tape pieces as well as numerous smaller works for live performance, including *Music for Every Occasion* (1967–80), *For Cornelius* (1982), and *Era ora* (1985), continue the tradition of intimate chamber music in that they are intended to be heard by a small audience in the privacy of the home. In addition to his activities as a composer, Curran taught vocal improvisation and environmental music at the Accademia Nazionale d'Arte Drammatica, Rome, from 1975 to 1980.

FREDERIC RZEWSKI

Curtin [née Smith], **Phyllis** (*b* Clarksburg, WV, 3 Dec 1922). Soprano. She graduated from Wellesley College in 1943, and studied singing first with Olga Averino at the Longy School and later with the bass Joseph Regneas. Her first important opera appearances were with the New England Opera Theatre in Boston as Lisa in Tchaikovsky's *The Queen of Spades* and Lady Billows in Britten's *Albert Herring*, followed in 1953 by a début with the New York City Opera in Gottfried von Einem's *Der Prozess*. Her varied roles at the City Opera over the next ten years included all the major Mozart heroines, Violetta, Strauss's Salome, William Walton's Cressida, and Susannah in Floyd's opera, a role she created. Engagements in Vienna, Buenos Aires, and Frankfurt, and with the Metropolitan Opera (début, 4 November 1961), La Scala, and Scottish Opera in the 1960s brought her international repute. She made numerous recital and concert appearances throughout the USA and Europe and was particularly known for her singing of contemporary works, many of which were composed for her. She retired from singing in public in 1984. Although she lacked the star qualities of more celebrated operatic sopranos, Curtin's singing was always much respected for its cultivated musicality, interpretive grace, and vocal purity. She has taught at the Aspen School of Music and the Berkshire Music Center, and was a member of faculty at Yale University from 1974 until 1983, when she became dean of Boston University's School of the Arts.

For illustration *see* FROMM, PAUL.

BIBLIOGRAPHY

"Curtin, Phyllis," *CBY 1964*

R. Dyer: "Curtin Call," *Boston Globe Magazine* (8 March 1984), 9

PETER G. DAVIS

Curtis, Alan (Stanley) (*b* Mason, MI, 17 Nov 1934). Harpsichordist, conductor, and musicologist. He studied at Michigan State University (BM 1955), at the University of Illinois (MM 1956, PhD 1963), and in Amsterdam under Gustav Leonhardt (1957–9). In 1960 he joined the faculty of the University of California, Berkeley, where he became professor in 1970. His scholarly work has concentrated largely on early keyboard music and includes several editions and a book, *Sweelinck's Keyboard Music: a Study of English Elements in Seventeenth-century Dutch Composition* (1969, 2/1972); he has also edited (with Marita McClymonds) Nicolò Jommelli's opera *La schiava liberata*, which he conducted in the modern première with the Netherlands Opera (September 1982). In addition to his work as a scholar, he has a wide reputation as a harpsichordist, fortepianist, and conductor in the USA and Europe. He conducted Stefano Landi's *Il Sant'Alessio* for the Rome Opera (June 1981) in a production based on engravings of the original sets and costumes, and his own version of Rameau's *Dardanus* with choreography from 18th-century sources by Shirley Wynne (Basle, May 1981). Among his more important recordings are performances of Monteverdi's *L'incoronazione di Poppea*, Cavalli's *Erismena*, Handel's *Admeto*, and Stradella's oratorio *La Susanna* for which he was awarded the Deutsche Schallplattenpreis. His important recordings of early keyboard music include Bach's *Goldberg Variations* and C. P. E. Bach's *Rondos nebst eine Fantasie fürs Fortepiano* played on his own J. H. Silbermann piano of about 1770. His collection of keyboard instruments also includes harpsichords, spinets, virginals, and a clavichord, all by Martin Skowroneck.

PHILIP BRETT/R

Curtis, King [Ousley, Curtis] (*b* Fort Worth, TX, 7 Feb 1934; *d* New York, 13 Aug 1971). Rhythm-and-blues and jazz tenor saxophonist and bandleader. Inspired by Lester Young, he began playing saxophone at the age of 12. While he was in high school he performed in various bands in the Fort Worth area, which played a mixture of jazz, rhythm-and-blues, and popular music. He turned down several offers of college scholarships to accept a position in Lionel Hampton's band, where he polished his writing and arranging skills and learned to play guitar. With this valuable experience, he moved to New York in 1952 and quickly found work as a session musician, eventually backing hundreds of performers on recordings and in concerts, including the Shirelles, Buddy Holly, Sam and Dave, Wilson Pickett, Delaney and Bonnie, the Allman Brothers, and Eric Clapton. With his own group, the King Pins (originally called the Noble Knights), Curtis recorded extensively for the Prestige, Enjoy, Capitol, and Atco labels in the same hybrid style as that of his earlier groups. In 1962 he wrote his most successful song, *Soul Twist*, which sold more than 750,000 copies. Two later singles, *Memphis Soul Stew* and *Ode to Billie Joe* (both 1967), also reached the Top 40. Owing to his syncopated, almost percussive style, Curtis became one of the best-known and most sought-after studio saxophone players of the 1950s and 1960s. In 1971, shortly after he was appointed Aretha Franklin's music director, Curtis was stabbed to death in New York.

RECORDINGS

(selective list)

Beach Party (Cap. 4788, 1962); Soul Twist (Enjoy 1000, 1962); Memphis Soul Stew (Atco 6511, 1967); Ode to Billie Joe (Atco 6516, 1967); Whole lotta love (Atco 6779, 1971)

GARY THEROUX

Curtis (Burlin), Natalie (*b* New York, 26 April 1875; *d* Paris, France, 23 Oct 1921). Folksong collector and folklorist. She studied music at the National Conservatory and piano with Arthur Friedheim and Ferruccio Busoni in New York; she also studied at the Paris Conservatoire with Alfred-Auguste Giraudet. After visiting the St. Louis Exposition in 1904, where she first encountered American Indian music, she abandoned plans for a career as a concert pianist and began to work among the North American Indians; her research resulted in the publication of *The Indians' Book* (1907, rev. 2/1923/*R*1968), which contains remarkably faithful transcriptions of 200 songs collected from 18 tribes. Later work, among the black students at the Hampton Institute in Virginia, provided material for *The Hampton Series of Negro Folk Songs* (1918–19), a four-volume collection of spirituals and secular pieces accompanied by a discussion of the harmonic improvisation used in their performance; a study of the music and folklore of two African students at the institute resulted in *Songs and Tales from the Dark Continent* (1920).

The sensitivity Curtis showed toward the music she so meticulously transcribed reflected her concern for the lives of the people to whom it belonged. She was active in the struggle to preserve the society and culture of the Indians and became involved in the development of the music school settlements for deprived children in New York. Her numerous articles, which served to introduce the study of American ethnic music to a wide public, were published principally in *Southern Workman*, *Craftsman*, and *Musical Quarterly*. The extensive collection of her field work, descriptive commentaries, and musical transcriptions is deposited in the Music Division of the Library of Congress.

BIBLIOGRAPHY

Obituaries: *MusAm*, xxxv/2 (1921), 47; *New York Times* (6 Nov 1921); *Outlook*, cxxix (1921), 458

W. T. Upton: "Curtis Burlin, Natalie," *DAB*

C. Haywood: *Bibliography of North American Folklore and Folksong* (New York, 1951/*R*1961)

G. Chase: *America's Music: from the Pilgrims to the Present* (New York, 1955, rev. 2/1966), 253, 394

R. Smith: "Natalie Curtis Burlin at the Hampton Institute," *Resound*, i/2 (1982), 1

CHARLES HAYWOOD

Curtis Institute of Music. One of the foremost conservatories of music in the USA, founded in 1924; *see* PHILADELPHIA, §6, and LIBRARIES AND COLLECTIONS, §3.

Curtiss, Mina (*b* Boston, MA, 1896; *d* Bridgeport, CT, 1 Nov 1985). Biographer. She studied at Smith and Radcliffe colleges and at Harvard University, and was an associate professor of English at Smith in 1920–37 and 1940–48. While editing Proust's correspondence for *The Letters of Marcel Proust* (1949) she undertook research in Paris, where she discovered many of Bizet's papers and letters; these form the basis of her book *Bizet and his World* (1958), from which her importance as a musical biographer stems. She also oversaw the first publication of many letters and documents of French musicians and writers of the early 19th century. Her published writings include *A Forgotten Empress: Anna Ivanovna, 1730–1740* (1974), and a memoir, *Other People's Letters* (1978), which describes her documentary research.

KATHLEEN HAEFLIGER

Curtis-Smith, Curtis O(tto) B(ismark) (*b* Walla Walla, WA, 9 Sept 1941). Composer. From 1960 to 1962 at Whitman (Washington) College he studied piano with Burge, and later at Northwestern University (BM 1964, MM 1965) he was a pupil of Gui Mombaerts in piano. His teachers in composition have been Gaburo (1966) and Maderna (at the Berkshire Music Center, 1972). In 1968 he joined the faculty of Western Michigan University, Kalamazoo, where he became a full professor in 1982. He has received a number of awards, including the Koussevitzky Prize (1972), three NEA grants (1974, 1977, 1980), two grants from the Martha Baird Rockefeller Fund for Music (1975, 1976), the gold medal of the Concorso Internazionale di Musica e Danza G. B. Viotti (1975), and a Guggenheim Fellowship (1978–9). Among his commissions are *Winter Pieces*, 1974, written for the St. Paul Chamber Orchestra and the Louis Falco Dance Company, *Masquerades*, 1978, for William Albright, and the String Quartet no.3, 1980, for the Kronos String Quartet; more recently he composed two works for the guitarist Michael Lorimer.

Curtis-Smith employs a chromatic vocabulary in a highly intuitive way, and displays a flair for original timbres in works such as *Rhapsodies* (1973). Written for Burge, this piano piece calls for color-coded groups of 4-pound-test fishing line to be drawn across the strings, creating continuous single and clustered pitches (he was the first to use a flexible bow on piano strings); mallets, tuning mutes, thumb picks, and a wine bottle are also required. The music flows with a characteristic nervous lyricism, its mellifluous dialogues punctuated with bursts of intensity. Curtis-Smith provides exact notation for his works and makes great demands on performers, for whom he sometimes prepares video tapes as an aid for rehearsal.

WORKS

Orch: Yu sareba [Rice Leaves], 1967–8; Xanthie: Winter Pieces, chamber orch, 1974; Bells (Belle du jour), pf, orch, 1974–5; GAS! (The Great American Sym.), 1982; Songs and Cantillations, gui, orch, 1983; Chaconne à son goût (Chaconnes, Puns, and Fantasies on Three Notes), 1984–5

Inst: Fl Sonata, 1963; 3 str qts, 1964, 1965, 1980; Sections, fl, vc, db, 1967; Fanfare for the Dark, 9 insts, 1972; Mateus, fl, pf, 1972; A Song of the Degrees, 2 pf, perc, 1972–3; 5 Sonorous Inventions, vn, pf, 1973; Unisonics, a sax, pf, 1976; Music for Handbells, 10 pfmrs, 1976–7; Partita, fl, cl, pf, perc, vn, va, vc, 1976–7; Ensembles/Solos, 12 insts, 1977; Tonalities, cl, perc, 1978; Plays and Rimes, brass qnt, 1979; Preludes and Blues, gui, 1979; Sundry Dances, 7 wind, 3 brass, db, 1979–80; Black and Blues, pf, brass qnt, 1980; Music for an Orangewench, gui qt, 1980–81; GAGS (The Great American Guitar Solo), 1982; Pf Trio (Sweetgrass), 1982–3; Ragmala (A Garland of Ragas), gui, str qt, 1983; other works

Kbd: Pianacaglia, pf, 1967; Trajectories, pf, 1968; Piece du jour, pf, 1971; Rhapsodies, pf, 1973; Suite in 4 Movts, hpd, 1975; Tristana Variations, pf, 1975–6; Gargoyles, org, 1978; Masquerades, org, 1978; For Gatsby (Steinway #D81281), pf, 1980; Variations on Amazing Grace, org, 1983, arr. large orch, 1983–4; More Southpaw Pitching, pf, 1984

Tape: Fanaffair for Fanny, 9 tpt, 4-track tape, 1971; Elec Study/Gong Sounds, 4-track tape, 1972; Summerian Sunshine, musique concrète, 1973

Vocal: All Day I Hear (J. Joyce: Chamber Music), SATB, 1965; "Till Thousands Thee. LPS." A Secular Alleluia Without, 6 S, 2 tpt, perc, 1969; "Passant. Un. Nous passons. Deux. De notre somme passons. Trois." (Rilke, Joyce, Homer, and others), 19 vv, 9 insts, 1970; Canticum novum/Desideria, 10 vv, 11 insts, 1971; Comédie (S. Beckett and others), dramatic song cycle, 1972; Invocation (Raga Kedar), solo vv, SATB, 1982; Beastly Rhymes (D. Pacock, traditional), SATB, 1983–4

Principal publishers: Presser, Mel Ray, G. Schirmer

BIBLIOGRAPHY

D. Burge: "C. Curtis-Smith's *Rhapsodies*," *Contemporary Keyboard*, iii/5 (1977), 44

C. Curtis-Smith: "Bowing the Piano Strings," *Woodwind World, Brass and Percussion*, xv/i (1976)

DAVID COPE

Cushing, Charles (*b* Oakland, CA, 8 Dec 1905). Composer. He studied at the University of California, Berkeley (BA, MA), and won the Paris Prize Fellowship (1929), which took him to the Ecole Normale de Musique for composition lessons with Boulanger; he also studied violin, viola, clarinet, and piano. He taught at Berkeley (1931–68, professor 1948), where he conducted the University of California Concert Band (1934–52). His music is lyrical and makes use of impressionist harmonies; notable among his works is *Carmen saeculare*, which was performed under his direction at the Greek Theatre in Berkeley. He translated the texts of Milhaud's *Les malheurs d'Orphée* and Satie's *Socrate*, and he contributed articles to *Modern Music*. In 1952 he was admitted to the Légion d'honneur.

WORKS

(selective list)

Incidental scores: The Tempest (Shakespeare), 1964; 3 others (Giraudoux, Aristophanes)

Choral: Carmen saeculare (Horace), chorus, orch, 1935; Psalm xcvii, chorus, band, 1939; Wine from China (Chin., trans.), male vv, pf duet, 1945; Ursula and the Radishes (W. Stevens), A, male vv, fl, 2 cl, hn, 1946; What are Years? (M. Moore), 1954

Orch: Divertimento, str, 1947; Angel Camp, band, 1952; Cereus, poem, 1960; numerous arrs. for band incl. B. Bartók: Petite suite (New York, 1963)

Solo vocal: Lyric Set (textless), S, fl, va, 1946; Poem (Marvell: To his Coy Mistress), Bar, orch, 1958; over 40 songs

Inst: 3 Eclogues, 2 cl, bn, 1938; Fantasy, fl, cl, bn, 1949; Sonata, cl, pf, 1957; Laudate pueri, 2 cl, 1960; 2 str qts; 2 sonatas, vn, pf, many pf pieces

MSS in *CU-MUSI*

BIBLIOGRAPHY

D. Milhaud: "Through my California Window," *MM*, xxi (1943–4), 94

VALERIE BROOKS SAMSON

Cutler, Henry S(tephen) (*b* Boston, MA, 13 Oct 1825; *d* Boston, 5 Dec 1902). Organist. He was a pupil of George F. Root in Boston and completed his training in Frankfurt, Germany. While abroad he visited England, where he took a great interest in the male cathedral choir tradition; returning to the USA in 1846, he determined to implant the style in this country. His first appointments were in Boston at Grace Church and at the Church of the Advent, where in 1855 he established what was probably the earliest vested choir in the USA. The introduction of surpliced men and boys provoked much controversy, however, many regarding it as a "popish innovation." In 1858 he became organist of Trinity Church, New York, where he carried out similar reforms in the spirit of the Oxford Movement. In the 20 years following his dismissal from Trinity in 1865 for neglect of duty, he held at least eight other positions in New York and Brooklyn, Princeton, Philadelphia, Providence, and Troy, New York. Cutler is remembered chiefly for two hymns composed to texts by Reginald Heber: *The Son of God goes forth to War* and *Brightest and Best of the Sons of the Morning*. He also wrote at least 20 organ pieces and between 1864 and 1871 published five volumes of church music.

BIBLIOGRAPHY

W. S. B. Mathews, ed.: *A Hundred Years of Music in America* (Chicago, 1889/*R*1970), 270

A. H. Messiter: *A History of the Choir and Music of Trinity Church, New York* (New York, 1906/*R*1970)

L. Ellinwood: *The History of American Church Music* (New York, 1953/*R*1970)

WILLIAM OSBORNE

Cuyler, Louise E(lvira) (*b* Omaha, NE, 14 March 1908). Musicologist. She received the BM in violin from the Eastman School of Music in 1929 and was awarded the MM in theory and composition at the University of Michigan (1933). After serving in the American Red Cross during World War II, she returned to the University of Michigan and at the same time resumed studies at the Eastman School (PhD 1948). At Michigan she became professor of music (1953) and director of the department of musicology (1957). She also served for over two decades as music critic for the *Ann Arbor Daily News*, retiring in 1971. In 1975 she was made Neilson Distinguished Professor of Smith College. Although her interests are wide, Cuyler is best known for her studies of the Franco-Flemish Renaissance and music in Germany during the Josquin period; in particular she has discussed the political use of the motet and the interaction of church and state in musical commissions. Her publications include *The Emperor Maximilian I and Music* (1973) and an edition of the third book of Isaac's *Choralis Constantinus* (1950).

EDITH BORROFF/PAULA MORGAN

Cyrille, Andrew (Charles) (*b* New York, 10 Nov 1939). Jazz drummer. By the age of 15 he was playing with a local trio. He matriculated at the Juilliard School in 1958, and in the late 1950s and early 1960s played professionally with Roland Hanna, Rahsaan Roland Kirk, Illinois Jacquet, Coleman Hawkins, and others. In 1964 he began a ten-year association with the pianist Cecil Taylor which established him as a leading drummer in the free-jazz style. During these years he also performed with many other musicians, including Grachan Moncur, Marion Brown, and Jimmy Giuffre, and recorded a solo album in Paris (1969). Later, with drummers Rashied Ali and Milford Graves he formed the cooperative group Dialogue of the Drums (1971) and his own group, Andrew Cyrille and Maono (1975), which continued to record in the 1980s. In 1985 he was playing in a new version of the celebrated group Air with Henry Threadgill and Fred Hopkins. One of the most subtle avant-garde drummers of the 1960s, Cyrille is valued for his tasteful, often restrained melodic playing as well as for his ability to provide multirhythmic support for avant-garde soloists.

RECORDINGS

(selective list)

As leader or co-leader: *What About?* (1969, BYG 529.316); M. Graves: *Dialogue of the Drums* (1974, IPS 001); *The Loop* (1978, Ictus 0009); *Special People* (1980, Soul Note 1012)

As sideman: C. Taylor: *Unit Structures* (1966, BN 84237); C. Haden: *Liberation Music Orchestra* (1969, Imp. 9183); C. Taylor: *Spring of Two Blue-J's* (1973, Unit Core 30551); L. Jenkins: *The Legend of Ai Glatson* (1978, Black Saint 0022)

BIBLIOGRAPHY

E. Raben: "Diskofilspalten," *Orkester Journalen*, xxxvii (Oct 1969), 19

J. Welch: "Different Drummers: a Composite Profile," *Down Beat*, xxxvii/6 (1970), 18

"Andrew Cyrille in conversation with Val Wilmer," *The Wire*, no.9 (1984), 12

MICHAEL ULLMAN

Czechoslovak-American music. *See* EUROPEAN-AMERICAN MUSIC, §III, 5.

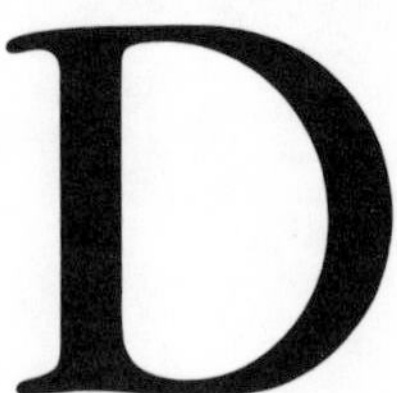

Da Capo Chamber Players. Ensemble specializing in the performance of contemporary music, founded in 1969 by JOAN TOWER.

D'Accone, Frank A(nthony) (*b* Somerville, MA, 13 June 1931). Musicologist. He studied with Geiringer and Gardner Read at Boston University (BMus, MMus) and with Pirrotta, Merritt, and Piston at Harvard University (MA 1955, PhD 1960). He was on the faculty of SUNY, Buffalo, from 1960 to 1968, when he was appointed professor of music at UCLA; he was also visiting professor at Yale University in 1972–3.

D'Accone is primarily interested in Florentine music of the 14th, 15th, and 16th centuries. His edition *Music of the Florentine Renaissance* (CMM, xxxii, 1966–73) constitutes a major source for students of the period, while his articles, which cover a wide variety of topics, give a broad view of the musical scene in the city during the Renaissance. More recently, D'Accone has turned his attention to the 17th century, publishing *Alessandro Scarlatti's Gli equivoci nel sembiante: the History of a Baroque Opera* (1985).

PAULA MORGAN

Da Costa, Noel (George) (*b* Lagos, Nigeria, 24 Dec 1929). Composer, violinist, and conductor. His parents were missionaries from Jamaica. He studied composition, theory, and conducting at Queens College, CUNY (BA 1952), and Columbia University (MA 1956), and on a Fulbright fellowship to Italy (1958–60) he studied composition with Luigi Dallapiccola. He has taught at Hampton (Virginia) Institute (1961–3), Queens and Hunter colleges, CUNY (1963–6), and at Rutgers, the State University of New Jersey (from 1970). He has conducted the orchestras of the Accademia Chigiana in Siena and of Queens and Hunter colleges, and is conductor and music director of the Triad Chorale, based in New York; he has also played violin with the Symphony of the New World and orchestras for opera, ballet, and Broadway musicals.

Da Costa's compositions cover a wide range of media and frequently combine dodecaphonic elements with black traditional practices.

WORKS

(for a fuller list, see Baker, Belt, and Hudson, 1978)

Dramatic: The Cocktail Sip (opera, T. Brewster), 1958; several children's theater works; incidental music

Vocal: The Confession Stone (O. Dodson), S, female vocal trio, inst ens, 1969; Counterpoint (Dodson), solo vocal qnt, double chorus, org/2 pf, 1970; I Have a Dream (M. L. King, Jr.), SATB, orch, 1971; November Song (G. Brooks), concert scene, S, vn, sax, pf, 1974; A Ceremony of Spirituals (trad.), S, s sax/t sax, chorus, orch, 1976; Sermon on the Warpland, nar, T, Bar, chorus, pf, org, 1980; many other solo vocal works and choruses; pieces for children's chorus

Inst: Occurrence for Six, fl, cl, b cl, t sax, tpt, db, 1965; 5 Verses with Vamps, vc, pf, 1968; In the Circle, 4 elec gui, elec b gui, perc, 1970; Jes' Grew, vn, elec pf, 1973; Magnolia Blue, vn, pf, 1975; Ukom Memory Songs, org, perc, 1981; many other pieces for 2–9 insts; works for various solo insts

Principal publisher: Atsoc

BIBLIOGRAPHY

SouthernB

E. Southern: *The Music of Black Americans: a History* (New York, 1971)

——: "America's Black Composers of Classical Music," *MEJ*, lxii/3 (1975), 46

D. Baker, L. Belt, and H. C. Hudson, eds.: *The Black Composer Speaks* (Metuchen, NJ, 1978)

CARMAN MOORE

Dadmun, J(ohn) W(illiam) (*b* Hubbardston, MA, 20 Dec 1819; *d* Boston, MA, 6 May 1890). Hymn tune composer and tunebook compiler. A Methodist minister, he became a prominent revival leader in New England in the late 1850s; from 1868 until his death he was chaplain at Boston's Deer Island prison. Nothing is known of his musical training, but between 1858 and 1866 he edited 13 tunebooks of various types, some with the help of professional musicians, and all containing simple but harmonically correct three- and four-voice arrangements. The first and most popular, *Revival Melodies* (Boston, 1858), sold almost 100,000 copies, before Dadmun replaced it with *The Melodeon* (Boston, 1860, later edns to 1866). Dadmun's collections epitomize the state of mid-19th-century northern, urban revival song in their eclectic mixture of traditional and contemporary hymn tunes,, Sunday-school songs, and reworked popular and folk melodies. His best-known tune, written with William McDonald, is "Rest for the Weary" (1858).

BIBLIOGRAPHY

F. J. Metcalf: *American Writers and Compilers of Sacred Music* (New York, 1925/*R*1967), 315

C. E. Claghorn: *Biographical Dictionary of American Music* (West Nyack, NY, 1973)

PAUL C. ECHOLS

Daffan, Ted [Theron Eugene] (*b* Beauregard Parish, LA, 21 Sept 1912). Country-music guitarist and songwriter. He grew up in Houston and played steel guitar with Leon Selph's Blue Ridge Playboys (1934–5) and the Bar X Cowboys (1936–40). His song *Truck Driver's Blues* (1939), reputedly the first trucking song in country music, became a hit for Cliff Bruner's Boys. In 1940 Daffan formed his own band, the Texans, and during the early 1940s recorded a series of successful songs, such as *Worried Mind*, *Blue Steel Blues*, *No Letter Today*, and the honky-tonk classic *Born to Lose*, many of which he published under the pseudonym Frankie Brown. The Texans disbanded during World War II, but after the war Daffan formed other groups in California and Texas. Throughout the late 1940s and 1950s his songs were recorded by such artists as Ernest Tubb, Les Paul and Mary Ford, Faron Young, and Hank Snow, and for a time in the mid-1950s Daffan had his own label, Daffan Records. From 1958 to 1961 Daffan and Snow were partners in a music publishing firm in Nashville, Silver Star, and though this firm ceased to operate when Daffan returned to Houston, he continued to be active in publishing.

RECORDINGS

(selective list; all recorded with the Texans, and for Okeh unless otherwise stated)

Truck Driver's Blues (Decca 5725, 1939); Worried Mind/Blue Steel Blues (05668, 1940); Put your little arms around me/I'm a fool to care (Voc. 05573, 1940); Weary, worried and blue (06253, 1941); Born to Lose/No Letter Today (06706, 1942); Headin' down the wrong highway (6744, 1945)

BIBLIOGRAPHY

B. Healy: "The Ted Daffan Story," *Country Directory*, no.4 (1962), 27

N. Tosches: "Nick Tosches Interviews Ted Daffan," *Old Time Music*, no.30 (1978), 6

RONNIE PUGH

Dahl, Ingolf (*b* Hamburg, Germany, 9 June 1912; *d* Frutigen, nr Berne, Switzerland, 6 Aug 1970). Composer, conductor, pianist, and music educator of Swedish-German parentage. He began his formal musical education at the Cologne Hochschule für Musik, then fled the Nazi regime to continue his studies in Switzerland at the Zurich Conservatory and the University of Zurich. Later he studied composition with Boulanger in California.

Dahl's professional career began with coaching and conducting at the Zurich Stadtoper. In 1938 he left Europe for the USA and settled in Los Angeles. From then on the range of his musical activities and involvements was immense, including work for radio and film studios, composing, conducting, giving piano recitals, and lecturing. He joined the faculty of the University of Southern California in 1945 and taught there until his death. Among his better-known former students is the conductor Michael Tilson Thomas.

In addition to teaching composition, conducting, and music history, Dahl directed the university's symphony orchestra (1945–58, 1968–9), performing much contemporary music. He introduced to the West Coast important new works by Americans (including Copland, Diamond, Foss, Ives, Piston, and Ruggles) and by Europeans (Berg's Chamber Concerto, Schoenberg's *Pierrot lunaire*, Hindemith's *Marienleben*, and Stravinsky's *The Wedding* and *Perséphone*), and promoted performances of early music. He also planned and conducted the famous Concerts on the Roof and the Monday Evening Concerts in Los Angeles. His close collaboration with Stravinsky resulted in numerous lectures and performances, and some arrangements of his music.

Dahl organized the Tanglewood Study Group at the Berkshire Music Center in 1952 and directed it for five years. He gave concerts in Europe (1961–2) sponsored by the US State Department, and directed and conducted at the Ojai Festival (1964–6). Among his awards are two Guggenheim Fellowships (1954 and 1958), two Huntington Hartford Fellowships (1954 and 1958), a grant from the National Institute of Arts and Letters (1954), and the 1964 Alice M. Ditson Award. From 1965 to 1968 he was a member of the National Policy Committee of the Ford Foundation's Contemporary Music Project, and in the summer of 1969 he was the featured composer at the East–West Music Festival in Honolulu. A series of annual Ingolf Dahl lectures on the history and theory of music was initiated at the University of Southern California in 1981.

Although Dahl wrote music from an early age, his output was fairly small; his varied career provided little time for composing, and he wrote slowly and meticulously. Though his work reflected the changes in his musical environment, the individuality of his style remained strong. His early works exhibit the dissonant and densely polyphonic texture typical of German expressionism in the 1920s. The impact of the USA and, later, his collaboration with Stravinsky resulted in increasing clarification of texture, a trend towards diatonicism, and a pronounced interest in timbre and instrumental virtuosity. Dahl used serial techniques in his music beginning with the Piano Quartet (1957), and evolved large, imaginatively conceived structures held together by motivic and tonal interrelationships and complex but compelling harmonic forces. This development led to his remarkable Sinfonietta for concert band (1961) with its unabashed leanings towards Stravinsky, then reached another peak in his formidable, almost neoromantic *Aria sinfonica* of 1965. Thereafter Dahl's works exhibit increasing concentration: leaner instrumentation, compact forms, and a stern focus on essentials.

WORKS

(selective list)

Orch: Conc., a sax, wind, 1949, rev. 1953; Sym. concertante, 2 cl, orch, 1952; The Tower of St. Barbara, sym. legend, 1954; Sinfonietta, concert band, 1961; Aria sinfonica, 1965; Quodlibet on American Folktunes (The Fancy Blue Devil's Breakdown) [arr. of pf work], 1965; Variations on a Theme by C. P. E. Bach, str, 1967; 4 Intervals, str orch, 1967, arr. pf 4 hands, 1967; Elegy Conc., vn, chamber orch, 1970, completed D. Michalsky, 1971

Chamber and instrumental: Allegro and Arioso, ww qt, 1942; Music for Brass Insts (Brass Qnt), 1944; Variations on a Swedish Folktune, fl, 1945, rev. 1962, arr. fl, a fl, 1970; Conc. a tre, vn, vc, cl, 1946; Duo, vc, pf, 1946, rev. 1948; Notturno, vc, pf, 1946; Divertimento, va, pf, 1948; Couperin Variations, rec/fl, hpd/pf, 1957; Pf Qt, 1957; Serenade, 4 fl, 1960; Pf Trio, 1962; Duettino concertante, fl, perc, 1966; IMC Fanfare, 3 tpt, 3 trbn, 1968; Fanfare on A and C, 3 tpt, hn, baritone, trbn, 1969, for Aaron Copland; Sonata da camera, cl, pf, 1970; 5 Duets, 2 cl, 1970; Little Canonic Suite, vn, va, 1970; Variations on a French Folksong, fl, pf, 1973

Vocal: 3 Songs (A. Ehrismann), S, pf, 1933; A Cycle of Sonnets (Petrarch), Bar, pf, 1968; A Noiseless, Patient Spider (Whitman), female chorus, pf, 1970

Pf: Rondo, 4 hands, 1938; Prelude and Fugue, 1939; Pastorale montano, 1943; Hymn and Toccata, 1947; Quodlibet on American Folktunes (The Fancy Blue Devil's Breakdown), 2 pf 8 hands, 1953; Sonata seria, 1953; Sonatina alla marcia, 1956; Fanfares, 1958; Sonata pastorale, 1959; Reflections, 1967

Arrs.: I. Stravinsky: Danses concertantes, 2 pf, 1944; Scènes de ballet, pf, 1944; Petite suite, 2 pf 4 hands, 1944

Principal publishers: Associated, Boosey & Hawkes, A. Broude, European American, Presser

EDITIONS

with J. Szigeti: *C. E. Ives: Violin Sonata no.3* (Bryn Mawr, 1951)

J. S. Bach: Violin Concerto in d, BWV1052a (New York, 1959)

BIBLIOGRAPHY

EwenD

H. Cowell: "Current Chronicle," *MQ*, xxxvi (1950), 589

K. Kohn: "Current Chronicle," *MQ*, l (1964), 227

H. Stevens: "In memoriam: Ingolf Dahl (1912–1970)," *PNM*, ix/1 (1970), 147

J. N. Berdahl: *Ingolf Dahl: his Life and Works* (diss., U. of Miami, 1975)

KURT STONE

Dakota [Santee]. American Plains Indian group belonging to the SIOUX.

Dalhart, Vernon [Slaughter, Marion Try] (*b* Jefferson, TX, 6 April 1883; *d* Bridgeport, CT, 14 Sept 1948). Tenor. He grew up in Texas ranch country, becoming familiar with cowboy songs of the area, and received some formal vocal training in Dallas. For several years, beginning in 1912, he sang light opera in New York; among his roles were Ralph Rackstraw in Gilbert and Sullivan's *H.M.S. Pinafore* (Century Opera Company) and Pinkerton in Puccini's *Madama Butterfly*. About 1915 he successfully auditioned for Thomas Edison and for 14 years recorded popular songs for Edison Diamond Discs. He also recorded for Columbia (1916–24), Victor (1918–38), and almost all the main labels, using more than 100 pseudonyms. His repertory included coon songs, arias from light operas, and patriotic, popular, and comedy songs. In 1924 he experimented with the hillbilly idiom and recorded *Wreck of the Old '97*, on which he was backed by CARSON J. ROBISON, and *The Prisoner's Song* for Victor; the latter appeared on more than 50 labels. After 1924 Dalhart recorded only country music, often with Robison as his duet partner (until 1928). His record sales decreased considerably in the 1930s as a result of the declining quality of his arrangements, which became less authentic in idiom and relied heavily on studio recording techniques.

Although he recorded every type of country song, Dalhart excelled in moralistic ballads that describe dramatic and generally tragic incidents (e.g., *The Death of Floyd Collins* and *The Fate of Edward Hickman*). More than 75 million copies of his records, over two thirds of which were of country music, were sold during his lifetime. His recordings made him the first country-music artist to attain international renown.

BIBLIOGRAPHY

B. C. Malone: *Country Music U.S.A.: a Fifty-year History* (Austin, 1968, 2/1985)

"A Preliminary Vernon Dalhart Discography, Parts 1–16," *JEMF Quarterly*, vi (1970), 160; vii (1971), 27, 59, 130, 153; viii (1972), 8, 90, 128, 212; ix (1973), 15, 83, 115; x (1974), 14, 95, 164

W. D. Haden: "Vernon Dalhart," *Stars of Country Music*, ed. B. C. Malone and J. McCulloh (Urbana, IL, 1975), 64

BILL C. MALONE

Dallas. City in Texas (pop. 904,078, ranked seventh largest in the USA; Dallas–Fort Worth metropolitan area 2,974,805). Founded in 1841 as a trading post by John Neely Bryan, it is a center of finance, fashion, film, and high technology and is one of the most important cultural centers in the southwestern USA. Although short-lived, the Fourier socialist colony established in 1854–8 at La Réunion near Dallas brought an artistic and cultural awareness unusual for a frontier town.

1. Opera. 2. Orchestras, concert life. 3. Educational institutions and libraries. 4. Composers and writers. 5. Blues, jazz, and country music.

1. OPERA. In 1875 Flotow's *Martha* was produced at Field's Opera House (opened 1873), a performance thought to be the first opera with orchestra given in Dallas. The Dallas Opera House opened on 15 October 1883 with a performance of Gilbert and Sullivan's *Iolanthe*; it served touring musicians, actors, and opera companies until it burned down in 1901. A new opera house was built in 1904 and in 1905 the Metropolitan Opera of New York performed *Parsifal*. In 1913 a grand opera committee brought the Chicago Grand Opera Company to Dallas; it continued to visit the city for about 20 years, with such singers as Garden, Tetrazzini, and Chaliapin among its artists. After the opera house burned in 1921, opera was given in the Fair Park Coliseum. During the 1930s and 1940s the impresario Fortune Gallo brought his San Carlo Touring Opera Company to Dallas. Its conductor in 1944 was Nicola Rescigno, co-founder in 1957 of the Dallas Civic Opera. In 1939 Arthur L. Kramer was instrumental in forming the Dallas Grand Opera Association, under whose auspices the Metropolitan Opera included Dallas on its annual tour. The Metropolitan company has continued to give about six performances each spring (except 1941–3 and 1961).

The Dallas Civic Opera was founded in 1957 with Lawrence Kelly, former manager of the Chicago Lyric Theatre, as general manager, and Rescigno as music director. The company mounted its first production in the State Fair Park Music Hall (capacity 4100) on 12 November 1957 with Rossini's *L'italiana in Algeri*, designed by Franco Zeffirelli and with Giulietta Simionato in the title role. It presents a wide repertory using internationally known and local singers. Callas sang Medea in 1958, inaugurating an annual autumn season of three or four productions. In

Scene from the first American performance of Vivaldi's opera "Orlando," presented by the Dallas Civic Opera at the State Fair Park Music Hall (28 November 1980), with Gwendolyn Killebrew and Marilyn Horne (foreground)

the following 25 seasons the company produced 61 works, including four American premières: Handel's *Alcina*, Cimarosa's intermezzo for baritone and orchestra *Il maestro di cappella*, Handel's oratorio *Samson*, and Vivaldi's opera *Orlando* (see illustration). Among the internationally known singers to have made their American début with the company are Joan Sutherland (in *Alcina*), Luigi Alva, Montserrat Caballé, Teresa Berganza, Jon Vickers, and Placido Domingo. Its orchestra draws from members of the Dallas SO. After Kelly's death in 1974, Rescigno also assumed the duties of general manager for two years, until Plato Karayanis was appointed general director in 1977. In 1981 the company's name was changed to the Dallas Opera.

The Music Theatre Company (formerly Lyric Theatre) of Southern Methodist University was established in the 1930s and gives five opera productions (both staged and concert performances) each year.

2. ORCHESTRAS, CONCERT LIFE. The amateur Dallas Philharmonic Society was formed in 1887, directed by Hans Kreissig, a German-born pianist and conductor. Many internationally known performers, including Ernestine Schumann-Heink, Nellie Melba, and Ignacy Paderewski, appeared in Dallas under the auspices of the St. Cecilia Club (1895–1906). In 1900 the Dallas Symphony Club was formed with Kreissig directing a 45-member orchestra with only five professionals; it was disbanded after two years. Walter J. Fried organized and conducted the Beethoven Symphony Orchestra from 1907 until 1911, when Carl Venth became conductor of the newly named Dallas SO. Venth left in 1913 and there was no orchestra until 1918, when Fried returned to conduct an ensemble drawn from professionals and students which he led until 1924. In 1925 Arthur L. Kramer organized a more professional orchestra under the direction of Paul Van Katwijk, then dean of music at Southern Methodist University, who was succeeded by Jacques Singer (1938–42). In 1945 it was reorganized as a fully professional orchestra under Antal Dorati, who left in 1949. Walter Hendl conducted the orchestra from 1949 to 1958, followed by Paul Kletzki from 1958 to 1961, the year in which Georg Solti was appointed senior conductor. He completed one season, leaving after disagreements with the symphony board, and was replaced in 1962 by the former assistant conductor Donald Johanos, who remained until 1970. His successor Anshel Brusilow tried unsuccessfully to combine the orchestra's popular and serious appeal; he was replaced in 1973–4 by Max Rudolf, with Louis Lane as principal guest conductor. A million dollars in debt, the orchestra suspended its activities in March 1974 but resumed concerts in February 1975 under Lane. Kurt Masur became principal guest conductor in 1976 and in 1977 Eduardo Mata was appointed principal conductor. Concerts were given in the 2500-seat McFarlin Memorial Auditorium at Southern Methodist University until 1973, when the orchestra moved to the State Fair Park Music Hall; a 2200-seat concert hall designed by I. M. Pei is under construction (scheduled opening 1988). In addition to its 22-week concert season, the orchestra plays for the Dallas Opera and takes part in the annual outdoor "Starfest" summer season. Until the formation of the Dallas SO Chorus in 1977, the 180-voice Grand Chorus of North Texas State University frequently appeared with the orchestra.

Other musical activities in Dallas include concerts sponsored by the Dallas Chamber Music Society (founded in 1942), a recital series sponsored by the Dallas Civic Music Association (1930), and a 12-week season of summer musicals (1941) in the State Fair Music Hall. The Dallas Civic Chorus (1960) gives several concerts yearly.

The *Dallas Morning News* G. B. Dealey Awards, first given in 1931, are a memorial to the newspaper publisher who established them (*see* AWARDS, §2(ii)). The contest is nationwide and is divided into an instrumental and a vocal section; the 13-year-old Van Cliburn won in 1952.

3. EDUCATIONAL INSTITUTIONS AND LIBRARIES. Dallas is the site of Southern Methodist University (SMU; founded 1915), whose music department was an independent school from 1917 until 1965; it then became part of the Meadows School of the Arts. The first BM degree was conferred in 1918, the first MM in 1946. The department, with a student enrollment of about 300 and a faculty of over 60 (including many principal players from the Dallas SO), offers courses leading to degrees in performance, pedagogy, music education, theory, history, composition, sacred music, and music therapy. The resident ensemble specializing in new music, Voices of Change, performs internationally. The Caruth Auditorium of the Owen Fine Arts Center and the McFarlin Auditorium are used regularly for both university and community musical events. The music library houses the Van Katwijk collection of papers, scores, and memorabilia.

The school of music at NORTH TEXAS STATE UNIVERSITY in nearby Denton is the second largest music school in the USA. Dallas Public Library Fine Arts Division houses several collections of musical interest, among them the John Rosenfield Collection of personal papers and an index of his *Dallas Morning News* articles (1925–66); the papers and memorabilia of Marion Flagg (1900–68), an influential music educator and musical consultant to the Dallas Independent School District; and the Rual Askew Memorial Collection of 7000 records bequeathed by the *Dallas Times Herald* music critic. (*See also* LIBRARIES AND COLLECTIONS, §3.)

4. COMPOSERS AND WRITERS. The composer David W. Guion, who died in Dallas, spent much of his life in northern Texas devoting many years to collecting and arranging American folksongs; among his works is the orchestral suite *Dallas* (1952). Donald Erb moved to Dallas in 1981, when he was named the first Meadows Distinguished Professor of Composition at SMU; in 1968–9 he had been associated with the Dallas SO. Other composers active in Dallas include Jerry Hunt, artist-in-residence at the Dallas Video Research Center (1974–7), and Robert X. Rodriguez, who joined the faculty of the University of Texas at Dallas in 1975 and was composer-in-residence with the Dallas SO under the auspices of the national "Meet the Composer/Orchestra Residencies Program" (1982–4). Others who have been influential in the musical life of the city include the choral director Lloyd Pfautsch (*b* 1921), who also teaches at SMU; Hermes Nye (1909–81), a folksinger and author of several books on folksinging; John Rosenfield (1900–66), amusements editor of the *Dallas Morning News*; and John Ardoin, who became music critic of the *Dallas Morning News* in 1966.

5. BLUES, JAZZ, AND COUNTRY MUSIC. The Dallas area made an important contribution to the early blues tradition. After the Civil War a freedman's town, known as Deep Ellum, was established on the eastern edge of Dallas and became a mecca to black musicians of northern Texas. Blind Lemon Jefferson began singing in the streets of various Texan towns in his youth, and his music later came to exemplify the "Texas blues style." Leadbelly wrote several ballads influenced by his years in Dallas, among

them *Fort Worth and Dallas Blues*. The first copyrighted piece of music with blues in the title was *Dallas Blues* (1912) by the Oklahomans Hart Wand and Lloyd Garret. Alex Moore (*b* 1899), a blues pianist who began playing in Deep Ellum, made his first recordings in 1929 and has remained active in Dallas.

The "Texas sound" has been legendary among jazz saxophone players from the 1920s, when "Buster" Henry Smith and Budd Johnson appeared frequently in Dallas, to such later players as David Newman and Jimmy Giuffre. The pianists Cedar Walton and Red Garland and the flutist Bobbi Humphrey have also contributed significantly to jazz in the city.

In 1950 the Dallas millionaire O. L. Nelms built the 2000-seat Bob Wills Ranch House for the country-music singer Bob Wills, who subsequently abandoned it for tax reasons. As the Longhorn Ballroom, it presents many touring country-music entertainers.

From Dallas have come such widely diverse personalities as Trini Lopez, Boz Scaggs, Ray Wylie Hubbard, and B. J. Thomas. The city is a frequent stopping place for touring performers, who can choose from a broad variety of local venues, including (besides those mentioned above) the Reunion Arena (capacity 18,500) and Dallas Convention Center (theater, 1770; arena 9816).

BIBLIOGRAPHY

J. W. Rogers: *The Lusty Texans of Dallas* (New York, 1951)

A. C. Greene: *Dallas: the Deciding Years: a Historical Portrait* (Austin, 1973)

S. Acheson: *Dallas Yesterday* (Dallas, 1977)

O. Chism: "Alex Moore: Singing the Blues at 79," *Dallas Times Herald* (19 Aug 1979)

DONNA MENDRO
(with SUSAN THIEMANN SOMMER, 1–2, ROBERT SKINNER, 3)

Dalmorès, Charles [Brin, Henri Alphonse] (*b* Nancy, France, ? 21 Dec 1871; *d* Los Angeles, CA, 6 Dec 1939). French tenor. He began his musical career as a horn player, performing in the Colonne and Lamoureux orchestras in Paris and teaching at the Lyons Conservatory. He studied singing at the Paris Conservatoire, and made his operatic début as Siegfried at Rouen in 1899, then sang with the Brussels Opera, at Covent Garden, and as Lohengrin at Bayreuth. He was one of the most valuable singers in Oscar Hammerstein's company at the Manhattan Opera House, New York (1906–10), where he made his début on 7 December 1906 as Gounod's Faust; he also appeared as Don José, Manrico in Verdi's *Il trovatore*, Turiddu in Mascagni's *Cavalleria rusticana*, Hoffmann, Pelléas, and Herod in Strauss's *Salome*. He also sang regularly with the Boston Grand Opera Company and the Philadelphia–Chicago Opera Company, and was a member of the Chicago Grand Opera Company (1910–18), where his roles included Tristan and Parsifal. He later taught singing in France and the USA. A sensitive musician and a colorful personality, he was also admired for his acting. His recordings show that he used his powerful voice with much technical accomplishment and a sense of style.

BIBLIOGRAPHY

E. C. Moore: *Forty Years of Opera in Chicago* (New York, 1930/*R*1977)

Q. Eaton: *The Boston Company* (New York, 1965/*R*1980)

J. F. Cone: *Oscar Hammerstein's Manhattan Opera Company* (Norman, OK, 1966)

R. L. Davis: *Opera in Chicago* (New York, 1966)

J. B. STEANE/R

Dameron, Tadd [Tadley Ewing] (*b* Cleveland, OH, 21 Feb 1917; *d* New York, 8 March 1965). Jazz composer, arranger, bandleader and pianist. After working with lesser-known groups he joined Harlan Leonard, scoring many of that band's records including *Dameron Stomp* and *A la Bridges*; he also wrote for Jimmy Lunceford, Coleman Hawkins (*Half Step Down, Please*), and Sarah Vaughan (*If you could see me now*). In the late 1940s Dameron arranged for the big band of Dizzy Gillespie, who gave the première of his large-scale orchestral piece *Soulphony* at Carnegie Hall in 1948. Also in 1948 Dameron led his own New York group including Fats Navarro, and was at the 1949 Paris Jazz Festival with Miles Davis. After forming another group of his own with Clifford Brown in 1953, he became inactive due to a problem with drugs, which led to his imprisonment in 1958. From 1961 he wrote scores for recordings by Milt Jackson, Sonny Stitt, and Blue Mitchell.

Dameron did not achieve full expression of his gifts as a composer because of his inability to maintain his own jazz group for long. Navarro was the finest interpreter of his pieces, as their many joint recordings show. The best of these exhibit a pithy thematic invention uncommon in jazz: *Sid's Delight* and *Casbah* (both 1949) reveal Dameron's powers at their height. Like Thelonious Monk, Dameron was repeatedly linked with bop, though he rarely employed its stylistic devices. With other arrangers for Gillespie he attempted to adapt bop to big bands, failing however to transfer the crucial rhythmic procedures of this essentially small-group style. In spite of this his best pieces for Gillespie (e.g., *Good Bait* and *Our Delight*) show particular melodic and harmonic substance. Other notable compositions by Dameron include *Fontainebleau* (1956), an extended piece without improvisation, *Hot House* (1945), recorded by a Gillespie–Charlie Parker group, and *Lyonia* (1949), recorded by Ted Heath in England.

RECORDINGS
(selective list)

As leader: The Squirrel/Our Delight (1947, BN 540); The Chase/Dameronia (1947, BN 541); Symphonette (1948, BN 1564); Sid's Delight/Casbah (1949, Cap. 60006); *Fontainebleau* (1956, Prst. 7037); *The Magic Touch* (1962, Riv. 419)

As composer: H. Leonard: A la Bridges (1940, Bluebird 10899), Dameron Stomp (1940, Vic. LPV531); C. Hawkins: Half Step Down, Please (1947, Vic. 20-3143); D. Gillespie: Hot House (1945, Guild 1002); S. Vaughan: If you could see me now (1946, Musicraft 398); D. Gillespie: Our Delight (1946, Musicraft 399), Good Bait (1947, Vic. 20-2878); T. Heath: Lyonia (1949, Decca 9255)

BIBLIOGRAPHY

J. Cooke: "Tadd Dameron," *Jazz Monthly*, vi/1 (1960), 23

B. Coss: "Tadd Dameron," *Down Beat*, xxix/4 (1962), 18

A. Morgan: "Tadd Dameron," *Jazz Monthly*, viii/2 (1962), 3

I. Gitler: *Jazz Masters of the Forties* (New York, 1966), 262

H. Woodfin: "The Complete Originality of Tadd Dameron," *Jazz & Blues*, iii/1 (1973), 4

M. Harrison: *A Jazz Retrospect* (Newton Abbot, England, 1976), 119

MAX HARRISON/R

Damrosch. Family of musicians.

(1) Leopold Damrosch (*b* Posen, Germany [now Poznań, Poland], 22 Oct 1832; *d* New York, 15 Feb 1885). Violinist, conductor, and composer. After receiving a degree in medicine from Berlin University in 1854, he decided, against his parents' wishes, to devote himself to the study of music. He became a pupil of Hubert Ries, S. W. Dehn, and Böhmer, and in 1857 Liszt appointed him leading violinist in the court orchestra at Weimar. In 1858–60 he was conductor of the Breslau Philharmonic Society, and in 1862 he organized the Orchesterverein of Breslau, of which he remained director until 1871.

In that year Damrosch was called to New York to become

conductor of the Männergesangverein Arion, a post he held until 1883. His energy, strong musical temperament, and organizing ability soon brought him influence in the musical life of New York, where in 1873 he founded the Oratorio Society, a choir devoted to the performance of oratorios and other works. After a financially unsuccessful season as conductor of the Philharmonic Society (1876–7) he formed his own orchestra, which gave the American première of Brahms's First Symphony, and which in 1878 was organized as the New York Symphony Society. He served as conductor of the Oratorio and Symphony societies until his death.

In 1880 Columbia College conferred the MusD on Damrosch. The following year he conducted the first great musical festival held in New York; with an orchestra of 250 and a chorus of 1200 he presented the American première of Berlioz's Requiem. In 1882 and 1883 he made successful tours through the western states with the Symphony Society. His compositions, some of which were published in the USA, included an oratorio, *Ruth and Naomi*, and a cantata, *Sulamith*, as well as other choral works and partsongs.

Damrosch was also instrumental in the establishment of German opera at the Metropolitan Opera, which had opened with an Italian season that was a disastrous financial failure. He presented a plan for German opera, gathered a company of German singers, and conducted nearly all the performances of the 1884–5 season.

See also NEW YORK, §§5, 7.

BIBLIOGRAPHY

H. E. Krehbiel: *Notes on the Cultivation of Choral Music and the Oratorio Society of New York* (New York, 1884/*R*1970)
F. H. Martens: "Damrosch, Leopold," *DAB*
E. T. Rice: "Personal Recollections of Leopold Damrosch," *MQ*, xxviii (1942), 269
G. Martin: *The Damrosch Dynasty: America's First Family of Music* (Boston, 1983)

(2) Frank (Heino) Damrosch (*b* Breslau, Germany [now Wrocław, Poland], 22 June 1859; *d* New York, 22 Oct 1937). Conductor and teacher, son of (1) Leopold Damrosch. He came to New York with his family in 1871, having studied composition and piano as a child. He first went into business in Denver, but soon devoted himself to music, founding the Denver Chorus Club in 1882 and being appointed supervisor of music in the Denver public schools in 1884. After his father's death he became chorus master at the Metropolitan Opera, where he remained until 1892. In that year he organized the People's Singing Classes in New York for instruction in sight-reading and choral singing; from this he developed in 1894 the People's Choral Union, with a mainly working-class membership of 500. He directed both groups until 1909. He also founded in 1893 the Musical Art Society of New York, a small chorus of professional singers devoted to the performance of *a cappella* choral works and modern choral music, and conducted it until it disbanded in 1920. From 1897 to 1905 he was supervisor of music in the New York public schools. He served as conductor of the Oratorio Society (1898–1912), succeeding his brother Walter, and presented a series of symphony concerts for young people. At various times he conducted choral societies in towns near New York, but resigned most of these posts to found in 1905 the Institute of Musical Art. He was its director until 1926, when it merged with the Juilliard Graduate School to form the Juilliard School of Music; he then served as dean until 1933 (*see* NEW YORK, §12). He was awarded an honorary MusD by Yale University in 1904.

WRITINGS

Popular Method of Sight-singing (New York, 1894)
Some Essentials in the Teaching of Music (New York, 1916)
Institute of Musical Art, 1905–1926 (New York, 1936)

BIBLIOGRAPHY

E. T. Rice: "A Tribute to Frank Damrosch," *MQ*, xxv (1939), 129
L. P. Stebbins and R. P. Stebbins: *Frank Damrosch: Let the People Sing* (Durham, 1945)
R. F. Goldman: "Damrosch, Frank Heino," *DAB*
G. Martin: *The Damrosch Dynasty: America's First Family of Music* (Boston, 1983)

(3) Walter (Johannes) Damrosch (*b* Breslau, Germany [now Wrocław, Poland], 30 Jan 1862; *d* New York, 22 Dec 1950). Conductor, music educator, and composer, son of (1) Leopold Damrosch. He was devoted to music from his childhood and studied composition and piano in Germany and in New York, where he came with his family in 1871. When his father began his season of German opera at the Metropolitan Opera in 1884 Walter became assistant conductor, and after his father's death he continued in that post under Anton Seidl until 1891. He succeeded his father as conductor of the Oratorio Society and New York Symphony Society, holding the former post until his resignation in 1898, and the latter, with a brief discontinuance, until the orchestra's merger in 1928 with the New York Philharmonic Society. He persuaded Andrew Carnegie to build Carnegie Hall as a home for the two societies, and brought Tchaikovsky to the USA for its opening in 1891. He presented the American premières of Tchaikovsky's Fourth and Sixth symphonies, and those of works by Wagner, Mahler, and Elgar. He also championed conservative American composers such as Carpenter, Loeffler, Daniel Gregory Mason, and Deems Taylor; he commissioned George Gershwin's piano concerto and conducted the première of his *An American in Paris*. In 1894 he organized the Damrosch Opera Company with German singers, giving performances in New York and throughout the country for five years. He was conductor of the German operas at the Metropolitan from 1900 to 1902 and of the New York Philharmonic Society in the 1902–3 season.

Damrosch was honored with the MusD by Columbia University in 1914. During World War I he organized a bandmasters' training school for the American Expeditionary Force in France and helped raise money for French musicians. These activities led in part to a tour of Europe by the Symphony Society in 1920 – the first European tour by an American orchestra – and to the founding of the American Conservatory at Fontainebleau, near Paris. In his later years Damrosch came to the fore as a director of broadcast orchestral music, and was the first to conduct an orchestral concert relayed across the USA. In 1927 he was appointed musical adviser to the NBC network; among other activities, he presented from 1928 to 1942 a "Music Appreciation Hour" for schoolchildren throughout the USA and Canada, an application to broadcasting of his lifelong work in giving children's concerts and lecture-recitals in New York. He was elected to the American Academy of Arts and Letters in 1932. Despite his untiring efforts for musical education and his busy conducting career, Damrosch never completely abandoned composition.

See also NEW YORK, §5, 7.

WORKS

(selective list)

OPERAS

The Scarlet Letter (3, G. P. Lathrop, after N. Hawthorne), Boston, 10 Feb 1896
The Dove of Peace (comic opera, 3, W. Irwin), Philadelphia, 15 Oct 1912
Cyrano de Bergerac (4, W. J. Henderson, after E. Rostand), New York, Metropolitan, 27 Feb 1913

The Man without a Country (2, A. Guiterman, after E. E. Hale), New York, Metropolitan, 12 May 1937

OTHER WORKS

Iphigenia in Aulis (incidental music, Euripides), Berkeley, CA, 1915
Medea (incidental music, Euripides), Berkeley, 1915
Electra (incidental music, Sophocles), New York, 1917
An Abraham Lincoln Song, Bar, chorus, orch, 1935
Dunkirk (R. Nathan), Bar, male chorus, chamber orch, 1943, NBC, 2 May 1943
Chamber music, songs

Principal publishers: G. Schirmer, Breitkopf & Härtel

BIBLIOGRAPHY

EwenD
W. Damrosch: *My Musical Life* (New York, 1923/*R*1972, enlarged 1930)
W. J. Henderson: "Walter Damrosch," *MQ*, xviii (1932), 1
G. Damrosch Finletter: *From the Top of the Stairs* (Boston, 1946)
F. T. Himmelein: *Walter Damrosch, a Cultural Biography* (diss., U. of Virginia, 1972)
W. R. Perryman: *Walter Damrosch: an Educational Force in American Music* (diss., Indiana U., 1972)
M. E. Goodell: *Walter Damrosch and his Contributions to Music Education* (diss., Catholic U. of America, 1973)
G. Martin: *The Damrosch Dynasty: America's First Family of Music* (Boston, 1983)

(4) Clara (Damrosch) Mannes (1869–1948). Pianist and music educator, daughter of (1) Leopold Damrosch and wife of DAVID MANNES.

H. E. KREHBIEL, RICHARD ALDRICH,
H. C. COLLES/R. ALLEN LOTT

Dana [Shindler; née Palmer], **Mary S(tanley) B(unce)** (*b* Beaufort, SC, 15 Feb 1810; *d* Shelbyville, KY, 8 Feb 1883). Poet and author of hymn texts. She married Charles E. Dana in 1835 and moved with him to Iowa; after his death four years later she returned to South Carolina and began her literary career. In 1851 she married Robert D. Shindler, a professor at Shelby College, Kentucky. She wrote three novels and a volume of sentimental poetry during the 1840s, but became best known as a writer of hymns and temperance verse. She published three collections of hymns, *The Southern Harp* (Boston, 1841), *The Northern Harp* (New York, 1842, 5/1843), and *The Western Harp* (Boston, 1860), all set to piano arrangements of popular songs, traditional Scottish and Irish tunes, and operatic airs; *The Temperance Lyre* (New York, 1842) is a small collection of temperance poems set to popular songs arranged for one, two, or three voices. Two of her hymns attained great popularity in the 1840s and 1850s: "O sing to me of heaven" (*c*1840), which entered the southern shape-note repertory set to various tunes, and "I'm a pilgrim, I'm a stranger" (published in *The Northern Harp*), set to a tune identified only as "Buona notte – Italian melody."

BIBLIOGRAPHY

T. B. Read: *The Female Poets of America* (Philadelphia, rev. 7/1857/*R*1978)
G. A. Wauchope: *The Writers of South Carolina* (Columbia, SC, 1910)
W. J. Burke and W. D. Howe: *American Authors and Books, 1640 to the Present Day* (New York, rev. 3/1972)
G. W. Ewing: *The Well-tempered Lyre* (Dallas, 1977), 83, 199

PAUL C. ECHOLS

Dana, William Henry (*b* Warren, OH, 10 June 1846; *d* Warren, 18 Feb 1916). Music educator. He graduated from the Williston Seminary in Easthampton, Massachusetts, then continued his education at Kullak's Academy of Music, Berlin, and the Royal Academy of Music, London. He was one of the founder-members of the Music Teachers National Association (1876) and later served that organization as treasurer; he also established Dana's Music Institute in Warren, Ohio, and was a member of the board of examiners of the American College of Musicians. An individualistic and pragmatic attitude underlies his instructional works, which include practical guides on thoroughbass and arranging for band and for orchestra, as well as a harmony textbook. Among his compositions are a *De profundis* for soloists, chorus, and orchestra, and motets, songs, and piano pieces.

PAULA MORGAN

Dance. Like all the arts, dance finds expression in a great range of styles, forms, and techniques, and is found in a number of contexts; its principal functions are as a social or communal activity and as a form of entertainment. This article deals with the history of the Western tradition of dance in the USA, the origins of which are European but which has been influenced by the music and dance practices of Africa mediated through black Americans (*see* AFRO-AMERICAN MUSIC), and to a lesser extent by those of Latin America. Social dances of the European tradition are discussed in some detail in EUROPEAN-AMERICAN MUSIC, §II, 1(ii). For information on country dancing *see* COUNTRY DANCE, BARN DANCE, HOEDOWN, and SQUARE DANCE. The dance of American Indians is dealt with in the article of that title (*see* INDIANS, AMERICAN, §2) and in articles on individual tribes. For the dances of European and Asian ethnic communities in the USA *see* EUROPEAN-AMERICAN MUSIC and ASIAN-AMERICAN MUSIC.

I. To 1800. II. The 19th century. III. The 20th century.

I. To 1800. During the 17th and 18th centuries social and theatrical dance existed as abstract physical movement, not yet colored by the emotive, expressive, and associative qualities that emerged during the course of the 19th century. All forms of dance at this period were governed by the regular pulse of metrical music and distinguished by tempo, meter, and rhythm. The relationship between the music of each dance and the steps themselves was extremely precise, and a knowledge of mathematics and geometry was considered requisite for the choreographer and dancing-master. The geometrical formations of each dance corresponded to particular strains in the music. Rhythms were characteristically "square" (based on multiples of four-bar units), and the steps and music shared an identity and a unity of expression. The simple, clear unfolding of a dance formation represented the aesthetic of mechanical movement held to be the ideal in all forms of dance throughout this period.

American social dances conformed to the European tradition of pairing or alternating a slow ceremonial dance, usually a march, with a lively, faster-paced dance, such as a JIG, REEL, or country dance. The private assembly or ball, which was a common social event of the upper classes, became more popular in the second half of the 18th century as the number of British military officers residing in the colonies increased. The British also helped to establish the "band of music," whose principal function was to play military music, but which doubled as a dance band, the musicians exchanging wind for string instruments; this practice continued throughout the 19th century. To arrange a ball immediately after a theatrical performance became an increasingly popular custom. The accompaniment for the dancing was provided by the musicians who had played at the theater for the evening's entertainment, and the formations were led by the actors and actresses. Dances were performed at other kinds of social gathering as well, such as weddings, Thanksgiving celebrations, and quiltings. The music for these informal activities was performed chiefly on the fiddle, and also, towards the end of the 18th century, the transverse flute.

French influence on American dance was strong throughout the period. Most of the dancing-masters were French by birth. They established schools in the North and were appointed on a private basis by the wealthier families in the South. But it was the large number of French dancers and musicians who immigrated to the USA after the French and Haitian revolutions that had the most profound effect on the forms and character of American dance. The French *cotillon* (referred to in the USA as the COTILLION) became an accepted form of social dance during the 1790s, and the association of "lighter" music and dance with French culture became firmly established at this time. French dancers were also active as choreographers and impresarios with theater companies and dance troupes.

Theatrical entertainments, ranging from drama to the circus, offered a variety of opportunities for seeing dance performed. Some theatrical dances were elaborate or stylized versions of the social forms that had already come into vogue; others involved new choreography and were eventually adapted as social dances. The processional MARCH was frequently used in theatrical entertainments, sometimes as the basis of a complete production; so integral was the march to 18th-century dance and its mechanical aesthetic that most theater choreography consisted of marchlike movements. Frequently a jig or HORNPIPE was performed to exhibit the skill of a particular dancer; they involved considerable physical and athletic prowess and acrobatics, and the rhythms were articulated by the sound of the feet hitting the floor in rapid patterns. America's first native stage dancer, John Durang, was particularly noted for his performances of these solo spectacular dances. He first performed the hornpipe before American audiences in 1785 to the tune *Billy the Fiddler*, composed for him by William Hoffmeister, a former drummer in the Continental Army. As performed by Durang, the hornpipe included both ballet and vernacular steps, such as the sisson, pigeon wing, whirligig, and glissade. PANTOMIME was virtually the only form of theatrical entertainment during much of this period to consist entirely of dance, gesture, and movement. The first *ballet d'action* (or drama composed entirely of danced movements) seen in the USA was the *Bird Catcher*, presented in 1792 by the company of the French dancer Alexander Placide.

II. The 19th century

1. Social dance. 2. Ballet. 3. Minstrelsy and musical theater.

1. SOCIAL DANCE. The enthusiasm of 19th-century Americans for dance was demonstrated principally in their love of social dancing. No longer the exclusive private assemblies of the 18th century, balls ranged greatly in style from the genteel events of the South and East to the more informal social gatherings of the California gold miners. As in the previous century, 19th-century balls were still choreographed: the individual dances were chosen in advance and the order of their performance was designed to provide the traditional contrast between slow and fast dances. Historically, various pairs of dances have at different times provided that contrast: the pavane and galliard, for example, were popular in the 16th century, and the courant and minuet in the 17th. In the 19th century, the contrast was provided by the march and waltz, of which, in essence, all 19th-century dances can be considered variations.

1. Sheet-music cover of "Queen Victoria's Dances," published by E. Ferrett & Co. in Philadelphia, c1845, depicting the Queen and Albert, Prince consort

Although it was introduced in the late 18th century, the WALTZ was not fully accepted as a ballroom dance in the USA until the 1820s and 1830s. With its innovative circular pattern, curved line, and emphasis on motion and speed, it represented the ideals expressed in Romantic ballet. It was the first of the "round" or "turning" dances in which couples, facing and holding each other, traced circular patterns across the dance floor. While the mechanical movement of the march was rejected as an aesthetic ideal in theatrical dance, it continued to function in social dance in the form of the opening grand march, the polonaise, and the march step and figures of the QUADRILLE and cotillion. The square shape of the cotillion provided another element of contrast with the circular pattern formed by the round dances.

The plain quadrille became enormously popular in the USA soon after it had been introduced in England (1815) and eventually became the standard form of the quadrille in this country. The GALOP (which became popular around 1829 and was commonly used to conclude the quadrille) and the POLKA (which was introduced to the USA in 1844) exploited perhaps better than any of the other round dances the speed and unhindered movement that were the ideals of social dance at this period. Several other round dances of the middle of the century, such as the MAZURKA, the *redowá*, and the *varsovienne*, were considered elaborations of the plain waltz and were occasionally referred to in the late 19th century as FANCY DANCES. In the second half of the century, the lancers became the most common form of the quadrille, and the SCHOTTISCHE (which the dancing-master Allen Dodworth claimed to have introduced in 1849) and TWO-STEP (a moderate version of the galop) became the most popular of the new round dances. The two-step was introduced in the late 1880s, when the march and dances in duple meter were especially favored, by an American dancing-masters' association, which chose for an accompaniment Sousa's march *The Washington Post* (1889).

Dancers in the early part of the century memorized the patterns of the cotillions and quadrilles, but in the 1840s the practice of "calling" or "prompting" became more widespread. Apparently a uniquely American phenomenon, calling was used either to announce or prompt the steps of known patterns or to allow the caller to improvise new patterns, which required great skill, since the coordination of the steps with the music was extremely precise. With the growing popularity of calling, the importance of the dancing-master declined. Instructions for social dances were published in ballroom guides, the most widely distributed of which were written by Elias Howe, Thomas Hillgrove, and Allen Dodworth.

As in the 18th century, the phrasing of dance music in the 19th century was square, while rhythms were characterized by strong accents and a steadiness of pulse and tempo that allowed for little or no rubato. The pieces were constructed as a series of repeated sections, to be played as many times as the situation demanded; embellishing the repeats, according to contemporary instructions on the performance of dance music, was one way in which musicians could sustain their interest in the music and consequently the liveliness of the rhythms that made for good dancing.

Music for American ballroom dancing was generally arranged from existing tunes, and especially popular were melodies from the operas of such well-known European composers as Rossini, Vincenzo Bellini, Gaetano Donizetti, Verdi, D.-F.-E. Auber, Giacomo Meyerbeer, and Michael Balfe. American popular songs and minstrel tunes, particularly those of Stephen Foster and Dan Emmett, were also frequently used. One of the more celebrated dance-band and parade leaders of the early 19th century, the black musician Frank Johnson (1792–1844), was said to have had a "remarkable taste in distorting a sentimental, simple and beautiful song into a reel, jig or country-dance."

American dance-band leaders also took pride in composing their own music. Johnson's *New Cotillions and March*, written in 1824 for General Lafayette, and the *Voice Quadrilles* published 15 years later were well received by ballroom dancers. Other 19th-century bandleaders who were known for their dance music include Benjamin Burditt (*Cadet Waltz*, 1866), Joseph Postlewaite (*Schottisch Quadrilles*, 1853), Simon Hassler (*La coterie blanche galop*, 1868), and Charles Kinkel (*Rosy Cheeks La Russe*, 1883). Dodworth, whose dance music was published as sheet music (his *Cally Polka*, 1846, appeared in at least four editions) led his own brass band, performed at dances, ran a dance academy (it was common for composers of dance music to serve as instructors in this period), and wrote one of the standard ballroom guides of the late 19th century. Other composers who taught dance included D. A. Carpenter of Philadelphia (who wrote the *Ladies Polka Quadrille*, 1849); A. M. Loomis of New Haven, whose dance series (including such works as the *Loomis Glide Mazurka*, 1888) became very popular in the late 1880s and 1890s; and L. DeGarmo Brookes of New York, especially known for his quadrilles (e.g., *Waltz Quadrilles*, 1875; *Quadrille russe*, 1860). Original music for dancing by European composers was commonly performed in American ballrooms throughout the 19th century. Josef Labitzky's *Aurora-Walzer* op.34, for example, appeared in numerous editions in the USA as the *Aurora Waltzes*, and the works of the French dancing-master C. L. N. d'Albert (1809–86), the English bandleader Daniel Godfrey (1831–1903), and all the members of the Strauss family enjoyed great popularity.

Dance musicians were often professionals belonging to bands that played outdoors in summer and functioned as dance bands or orchestras in the winter. Although most of them could play both wind or string instruments, dance music was generally performed on whatever instruments were available, a situation that contributed to the practice of making arrangements the parts of which could be played by any of several instruments. Dance bands varied in size from two to ten musicians playing various combinations of instruments, which included, most commonly, violin, piano, flute, clarinet, cornet, harp, cello, trombone, and ophicleide. Drums were not a common feature of dance bands until the end of the century, when they were used mainly in the grand march or to provide a very light rhythmic support for the quadrille.

2. Ballet. In reaction to the mechanical formality of the 18th century, 19th-century ballet emerged as a spontaneous expression of the emotions, fantasy, and the imagination in free and unhindered movement. Motion was achieved through quicker tempos, smoother and more lyrical rhythmic patterns, longer melodic phrases (now eight bars in length), and the elimination of elaborate embellishments and figurations in the patterns of steps in favor of choreography designed to cover distance and determine direction. The emotions were thought to be released in the dancer's submission to the rhythms, while the dramatized opposition of the female and male partners contributed to the emotional tension and dynamic energy.

The aesthetics of mid-19th-century "Romantic" ballet were introduced in Europe by the dancer Marie Taglioni in her father's production of *La sylphide* (1832; music by Jean Schneitzhöffer). Throughout the remainder of the 19th century it was the image and movements of the female dancer rather than her male partner that embodied the ideals of balletic movement. Dancing *en pointe*, which was introduced some time after 1795 and exemplified most notably in the work of Taglioni, became a fundamental aspect of the technique of women dancers and the primary means of achieving the flowing line and illusory images that characterized Romantic ballet. The series of dance numbers (*divertissements*) typical of 18th-century ballets was replaced in the first half of the 19th century by long sequences (*enchaînements*) of movements strung together not merely to show off a dancer's skill but to express an idea, concept, or emotion.

As 19th-century dancers sought greater expressiveness through their movements, they also sought greater expressiveness from the music itself, which was characteristically conceived in longer segments than the music composed for dance in the century before. Composers and dancers began to think of dance rhythm as something broader than the articulation of step patterns through the accents of the melody, and to develop ways in which it could reflect longer phrases and periods, as well as the patterns of harmonic change, emotional expressiveness, tone-color, and texture. It was not, however, until 1870 that, with Léo Delibes' *Coppélia* (American première New York, 1887), a musical score was composed for a ballet as a single dramatic work rather than as a series of individual dances. Tchaikovsky achieved even greater success with *Swan Lake* and *Sleeping Beauty*, first performed in the USA respectively in 1911 and 1916.

The history of 19th-century ballet concerns the gradual acceptance of the *ballet d'action* and theatrical dance as a form of artistic expression. Much choreographed dance continued to be used in the context of musical theater, where it was used in interludes between musical and dramatic scenes. Early Romantic ballets were often based on operas, especially French works such as Auber's *La muette de Portici* and Meyerbeer's *Robert le diable*, both of which were performed as ballets in the middle of the century. American composers seem rarely to have written music expressly for the ballet, although the identification of such works has been complicated by the 19th-century practice of not specifying the name of the choreographer or composer. *The Sisters*, produced for the renowned American ballerina Mary Ann Lee (1823–99) at New York's Bowery Theatre in 1839, is believed to be one of the very few American ballets. The ballet orchestra was the same as any other theater orchestra of the period; it consisted of between ten and 15 instruments, including first and second violins, viola, cello, and bass, and any combination of flute, clarinet, cornet, trombone, and drums.

The first widespread awareness and artistic acceptance of theatrical dance in the USA occurred in response to the Austrian ballerina Fanny Elssler, who toured the country between 1840 and 1842. In contrast with the ethereal image presented by Marie Taglioni, Elssler's dance was exotic and sensual; whereas Taglioni had executed her movements in silence, Elssler emphasized the rhythms in her dances with the sounds of her toes hitting the floor. Although her fame had developed from her performances of romantic ballets, Elssler's American repertory consisted primarily of *divertissements* and only eight ballets, including *La sylphide*, *Le dieu et la bayadère* (music by Auber), *La tarentule* (music by Casimir Gide), and *La somnambule* (music by Ferdinand Hérold). Especially popular with American audiences were her solo ethnic dances, the Spanish *La cachucha*, which she had choreographed in 1836 for Jean Coralli's ballet *Le diable boiteux* (music again by Gide), and the Polish *krakowiak*, which she danced to a particular melody known in the USA as the *Cracovienne*. The music for the two dances was published in the USA in sheet form, and the quickstep arrangement of the *Cracovienne* became a staple of the American brass-band repertory.

While no permanent ballet school or company was established in the USA during the 19th century, partly because there were no state or municipal opera houses such as those in Europe to support such enterprises, dancers could nevertheless receive formal training in American cities. Paul H. Hazard, who was born and trained as a dancer in Europe, instructed several of the best-known American dancers of the time, including the two most famous ballerinas, Mary Ann Lee and Augusta Maywood (1825–76). By providing instruction and performance opportunities, Elssler and her partner and ballet-master James Sylvain helped to develop a number of American dancers, including Lee, George Washington Smith (1820–99), the first native American *danseur noble*, and Julia Turnbull (1822–87), by exposing them to the finest European ballet technique. Lee and Maywood made their débuts together in 1837 at the Chesnut Street Theatre, Philadelphia, in *The Maid of Cashmere*, an English version of *Le dieu et la bayadère* (in 1842 Lee appeared in an American burlesque of the same ballet entitled *Buy it, Dear, t'is Made of Cashmere*). Maywood left the country in 1838 and became one of Europe's leading dancers, forming the first successful European private dance company. Lee remained in the USA (except for a year's study in Paris, in 1844–5) and staged the first American production of Adolphe Adam's *Giselle* in 1846. The following year, she and Smith, her partner, formed a company that toured the USA. Lee retired later in 1847 and was succeeded by Turnbull as the country's leading ballerina. These and other dancers who had been influenced or taught by Elssler left a legacy of knowledge and appreciation for the ballet that was realized in the formation of American companies in the 20th century.

In the second half of the century, interest in ballet waned both in Europe and the USA; only in the Russian Imperial Ballet did creative developments take place, though the results of that activity were not presented to American audiences until the early 20th century. Interest in theatrical dance in the USA focused rather on the forms it took in musical theater, vaudeville, and the music hall.

3. MINSTRELSY AND MUSICAL THEATER. The solo spectacular dance developed as a feature of blackface MINSTRELSY in the USA. It had its roots in several traditions, including the spectacular style established by John Durang, the 18th-century blackface tradition of English theater and especially the heightened sense of rhythm characteristic of black-American music and its African forebears. The musical accompaniment for these dances shows the influence of Irish jigs and reels, American quicksteps, and other forms that emphasized melody, duple meters (2/4 and 6/8), quick tempos, and a chordal, drum, or oscillating bass. Some of the most successful minstrel tunes, including *De Boatman's Dance* (1843) and *Dandy Jim from Caroline* (1844), were written by the well-known blackface performer Dan Emmett; other popular tunes of the 1840s and early 1850s were *Lucy Long*, *Stop Dat Knocking*, *Zip Coon*, *Old Dan Tucker*, and George Knauff's *Wait for the Wagon*.

The initial contribution made by black performers to early minstrel dance was a keen feeling for and ability to emphasize (sometimes by syncopation) the rhythms inherent in the music. The result was an increased looseness, ease, freedom, and spontaneity of body movement and a heightened joyousness of expression, qualities which permitted greater embellishment of the basic rhythm and metric pulse. The instruments used to accompany minstrel dances reinforced the musical rhythms: the banjo's percussive quality accentuated the rhythm in the melody line, while the tambourine and, especially, bones provided rhythmic embellishment.

The dance combined European and white-American steps and dances, such as the jig, CLOG DANCE, and pigeon wing, with such black steps and dances as the buck, BUCK AND WING, and BREAKDOWN. Thomas Dartmouth ("Daddy") Rice's *Jim Crow* (for illustration *see* RICE, THOMAS DARTMOUTH), which he first performed probably in 1828, is considered the first spectacular dance to show black influence. It consisted principally of a shuffle, whirl, and small jumps, to punctuate or accent the beat. A more direct influence was exercised by the black dancer William Henry Lane, who performed under the stage name "Juba" in the 1840s; he was regarded by his colleagues as unsurpassed in skill, grace, and endurance. Describing his dance as "a blur of legs," writers commented on the extraordinary command of his feet in beating out the rhythms, the "mobility of his muscles," his "elasticity of tendon," and his "natural grace," as well as his rejoicing laugh, sense of "fervent fun," and "mighty mirth." His movements created both abstract, embellished rhythms and "programmatic" rhythms, such as those made by a locomotive or a military drum.

The WALK-AROUND, performed at the end of an act, was essentially a grand march with solo and ensemble performances, involving a strutting walk and comical, cavorting movements. Its form and musical structure consisted of alternating song and instrumental sections and a concluding instrumental section four to eight bars in length. A similar form, with a four- or eight-bar instrumental conclusion, had appeared in Stephen Foster's early minstrel songs, such as *Oh! Susanna* (1848), *Camptown Races* (1850), *Nelly Bly* (1850), *Ring de banjo* (1851), and *Old Folks at Home* (1851). Dan Emmett, however, is considered most influential in establishing the form of the walk-around; two of his most famous examples are *I wish I was in Dixie's land* (1859) and *Old K.Y. Ky* (1860). Emmett's works anticipated the song-and-dance number, which emerged as a distinct musical genre in the 1860s. The song-and-dance concluded either with an instrumental section (expanded, however, to eight or 16 bars and designated as a dance section, often a breakdown, jig, reel, or march) or with a return to the vocal section to form an *ABA* structure. In the song section, solo voices alternating with a chorus were interspersed with "breaks," or interludes of dance two or four bars long; a break often concluded the dance section, functioning as a coda or "tag" ending. Two of the better-known performers billed in the 1860s as song-and-dance men were Frank Wood, remembered for his performance of *Gay & Festive Boy from the South* (1866), and Billy Emerson, who danced to *I'm happy, Little Ned* (1868; music by Frank Martin).

The "essence" dances, characterized by their shuffling steps and danced by black performers, became increasingly popular during the same period. The *Essence of Old Virginia* was perhaps the best-known of these dances, particularly in its performance by Billy Kersands, who danced it to Charles Pratt's *Wait 'till the clouds roll by* (1881). The essence was a predecessor of the SOFT SHOE, which appeared in the 1870s and was most memorably performed by George Primrose (1852–1919); his performance to Stephen Foster's *Old Folks at Home* established the song as a classic soft-shoe number. Both the essence and the soft shoe were performed to tunes in duple meter –the gentle Southern plantation songs were especially popular – the soft shoe most commonly to music in 4/4.

The first appearance of an element considered uniquely African – the involvement of the entire body in the articulation of multiple rhythms – first appeared in the late 1870s in dances commonly referred to as "characteristic," "eccentric," or "grotesque." The dances incorporated exaggerated and burlesqued movements, and were used both as spectacular dances and in social dancing; in the social forms the rhythms of existing tunes, usually those in duple meter (marches, polkas, two-steps, etc.), were syncopated, thus anticipating the rhythm of ragtime.

The first of the characteristic dances to acquire an identity of its own was the CAKEWALK, which was described as a "characteristic grand march." An example is Kerry Mills's well-known song *At a Georgia Camp Meeting* (1897), promoted as a "Characteristic March which can be used effectively as a Two-Step, Polka or Cakewalk." After the movements of the cakewalk became more refined in the black musicals of the late 1890s (e.g., Will Marion Cook's sketch *Clorindy, or The Origin of the Cakewalk*, 1898) and especially in the dance of Bert Williams and George Walker, the dance became acceptable in white musical theater and social dance.

In the second half of the 19th century the popularity of and emphasis on march movements greatly increased, not only in social dance and minstrelsy, but also in musical theater. In *The Black Crook* (1866), which contained songs and tunes by different composers, the march was performed as a precision drill by women dressed in tights and tunics that were designed to show off their legs (for illustration *see* MUSICAL THEATER, fig. 1). Commonly

2. *The cakewalk: wash drawing by George Scott from "The Graphic," 1906*

referred to as the "Amazon March," the title of the piece composed by Giuseppe Operti to accompany the drill in *The Black Crook*, the leg show became a standard feature in musical theater for the rest of the century. Lydia Thomson and her English troupe of blond young women further popularized the precision drill as performed by women; the tradition continues today in the choreography of the ROCKETTES at Radio City Music Hall, New York.

In the "Mulligan Guard" series of dramatic sketches, begun in 1878 as a burlesque of the then fashionable volunteer militia units, Edward Harrigan, Tony Hart, and David Braham introduced the era of the march-song musical or operetta; in this type the music consisted almost exclusively of numbers in which the performers simultaneously sang and marched about on stage. The march-songs in the operettas of Gilbert and Sullivan, which were introduced to American audiences in performances of *H.M.S. Pinafore* in 1878, were innovative for their full, rich sound of sung harmony. Sousa was influenced by this element and exploited it in his *El capitan* (1896), the most successful late 19th-century march-song operetta.

III. The 20th century

1. Classical theatrical dance. 2. Modern and post-modern dance. 3. Musical theater and the dance musical. 4. Social dance.

1. CLASSICAL THEATRICAL DANCE. In 1916 the Russian impresario Sergei Diaghilev toured the USA with his company, the Ballets Russes, performing in the major American urban centers as well as in a number of smaller cities such as Fargo, North Dakota; Duluth, Minnesota; Wichita, Kansas; and Dayton, Ohio. In addition to traditional ballets, the company's repertory included Stravinsky's *Petrushka* and *The Firebird*, and Debussy's *L'après-midi d'un faune*. American audiences and critics were receptive to Stravinsky's ballets, finding their "terrible dissonances" to be "amazingly appropriate" to the stage action. They were also receptive to the more romantic ballets in Diaghilev's repertory, such as Rimsky-Korsakov's *Sheherazade* and *Spectre de la rose* (based on Carl Maria von Weber's *Aufforderung zum Tanze* for solo piano).

Various other companies under the name Ballets Russes toured the country in the following years, but the first permanent school of classical ballet was not established until 1934, when the School of American Ballet, led by the Russian dancer GEORGE BALANCHINE and supported financially by Lincoln Kirstein and Edward M. M. Warburg, was opened in New York. Balanchine and Kirstein founded the school's resident company, the American Ballet, a year later; it became the Ballet Caravan and the Ballet Society before establishing quarters at the New York City Center in 1948 and adopting its present name, the New York City Ballet. The company has resided at Lincoln Center since 1964.

The first ballet music commissioned from an American composer was Copland's *Billy the Kid* (1938), written for a work that was choreographed by Eugene Loring and danced by the Ballet Caravan. Balanchine, who had been trained at the Imperial Ballet in St. Petersburg, considered most American ballet music to be "non-balletic." Nevertheless, he used American music for a number of his works, including *Ivesiana* (1954; music by Ives), *Stars and Stripes* (1958; Sousa), *Modern Jazz: Variants* (1960; Schuller), and *Who Cares?* (1970; Gershwin). For the most part, however, the music Balanchine selected for his ballets was written by European composers, most frequently Mozart, Tchaikovsky, and, especially, Stravinsky, from whose music he created 39 works; the status he accorded to the music is reflected by some of the

3. *George Balanchine rehearsing Stravinsky's "Variations" with Suzanne Farrell, May 1966*

titles, such as *Mozartiana* (two versions, 1934 and 1981; Mozart and Tchaikovsky) and *Concerto barocco* (1941; Bach). The intimate connection Balanchine recognized between ballet and music is exemplified in his observation that dance is music made visible and music is dance made audible.

Although he claimed that Russia was the home of Romantic ballet and the USA the home of classical, Romantic elements are nevertheless present in his choreography, notably in the stringing together of movements into ever longer *enchaînements*. The emotion in Balanchine's dances is the emotion aroused in the contemplation of pure, abstract beauty, a beauty so precisely conceived and possessing a tension so finely tuned that the slightest increase in that tension would cause the image to snap and shatter. Balanchine choreographed specifically for individual dancers and much of his creativity was inspired by his ballerinas, the most influential of whom were Tamara Toumanova, his two wives, Tanaquil Le Clerc and Maria Tallchief, and Suzanne Farrell (see fig.3). While Balanchine considered the role of the male dancer to be secondary – "prince consort" to his ballerinas – the strong classical male roles he created have received just as much recognition as the female parts. The best-known of his male dancers include Jacques d'Amboise, Edward Villella, Arthur Mitchell, Helgi Tomasson, and Peter Martins, who, with JEROME ROBBINS, succeeded Balanchine as "ballet-master in chief" of the New York City Ballet.

The American Ballet Theatre (ABT), founded in 1940, has been somewhat more diverse in its repertory and style. The strong influence of the Russian and English schools is evident in the choreographers and dancers of its early roster: Mikhail Fokine, Leonide Massine, ANTONY TUDOR, and Mikhail Baryshnikov. American themes and rhythms, which had generally been considered unsuitable for classical ballet, were present in ABT productions almost from the start, in such works as Jerome Robbins's *Fancy Free* (commissioned from Leonard Bernstein and first performed in 1944) and Agnes de Mille's *Fall River Legend* (commissioned from Morton Gould and first performed in 1948), the music for both of which has become part of the standard orchestral concert repertory. Generally, however, the company's ballets are choreographed to already existing music, in a wide variety of styles. Later eclectic productions include Eliot Feld's *Harbinger* (1967; music by Prokofiev), Alvin Ailey's *The River* (1970; Duke Ellington), Twyla Tharp's *Push Comes to Shove* (1976; Joseph Lamb and Haydn), and a revival of Balanchine's *Symphony Concertante* (1982; Mozart).

Diversity of style, in fact, characterizes most of the major American dance companies, among them the Joffrey Ballet (founded by ROBERT JOFFREY, 1954) and the Eliot Feld Ballet (1974; *see* FELD, ELIOT). The company founded in 1958 by ALVIN AILEY fosters black-American dance, music, and experience, and the Dance Theatre of Harlem, founded in 1971 by Arthur Mitchell, has sought to create opportunities for black dancers in classical choreography. The San Francisco Ballet Company, founded in 1933 and directed by Michael Smuin and Helgi Tomasson, and the Houston Ballet, founded in 1955 and directed by Ben Stevenson, are considered to be among the leading companies outside New York. Notable among the more successful newer companies are the Chicago City Ballet (1979), directed by Maria Tallchief and Paul Mejia, and the Pittsburgh Ballet Theatre (1969), directed by Patricia Wilde.

In addition to the contributions made by the important male dancers of the New York City Ballet and other American dance companies, the defection from the USSR to the West of Rudolf Nureyev, Baryshnikov, and others has helped to confirm the significance of the male dancer in American ballet. As permanent guest artist with London's Royal Ballet, Nureyev, with his brilliant, athletic technique, charismatic personality, and powerful physical presence, established a new image for the male ballet dancer, one that Baryshnikov has underscored not only through his skill but also through his ventures into other media, such as the successful Hollywood film *Turning Point* (1977), based on the personal lives of professional ballet dancers in New York. The Russian emphasis on athleticism struck a responsive chord in American attitudes towards dance and provoked, as did a similar movement in modern and post-modern dance (see below), an increased interest in theatrical dance.

The flowing, lyrical lines idealized in classical ballet began, in the late 1970s, to find a new medium of expression in the form of ice dancing.

2. MODERN AND POST-MODERN DANCE. Preoccupation with the question of what constitutes dance gave rise to both a new classicism and a new intellectualism in American dance in the 20th century. Choreographers and dancers rejected classical dance technique as an artificial medium – the legacy of a class-structured society – and sought to discover new forms of expression through physical movement. For many, new attitudes to dance led to a questioning of the role of music, and a rejection of the principle of rhythmic movement regulated by musical rhythms and hence of music itself. The fusion of music and dance cultivated by 19th-century choreographers gave way to a careful separation of the two elements and at the same time a recognition of the common aspects of dance and the visual arts.

The issues that have shaped what is known as the "modern" movement in dance were first addressed by three American women: Loïe Fuller, Ruth St. Denis, and ISADORA DUNCAN. The kind of physical movement that influenced these dancers came not from Romantic or classical ballet, in which they had little if any experience or training, but from social dance, physical education, acrobatics, and the dance of vaudeville, the music hall, and musical theater. While Fuller began her dancing career in New York in 1890, it was not until her appearance at the Folies-Bergère in Paris two years later that her influence on theatrical dance began. Through her skirt dances (particularly the serpentine) and spectacular lighting effects, Fuller was first to conceive of dance as a composite of art, theater, and abstract movement – a concept that became popular with many choreographers during the course of the century. St. Denis anticipated and influenced the psychological focus of the modern movement through the spiritual, exotic, and introspective nature of her dance; these characteristics were first manifested in *Rahda, the Mystic Dance of the Five Veils* (1905–6; music from Léo Delibes' *Lakmé*).

It was Duncan, however, who, in her writings and lectures as well as in her dance, confronted the issues of what constitutes danced movement and the relationship between dance and music. She came to regard the technique of classical ballet as an obstruction to the free and spontaneous expression of the emotions; instead, she looked to the simplicity and purity of classical architecture and its use of natural forms as a source of inspiration, to guide her creation of movements. Liberating herself from the blocked ballet shoe and restrictive costuming of the 19th century, Duncan danced with bare feet and in flowing Greek garments. With bemused unconcern for the reaction of her audiences, she began to dance to "art" music by composers such as Beethoven, Schumann, Wagner, and Chopin; because this music possessed artistic stature and existed independently of dance, her use of it made audiences conceive for the first time of music for dancing as something more than accompaniment or a backdrop written or adapted for the purpose. After performances by her in Budapest, Berlin, and Russia (1903–5), Duncan's revolutionary style and ideas concerning music for the dance achieved widespread recognition.

Athleticism played an important role in the dance of Fuller, St. Denis, and Duncan, as it had in other forms of American dance. The particular way in which these artists approached this element was influenced by the writings of the French philosopher François Delsarte (1811–71), who made spiritual and geometrical codifications of body movement, and by the Swiss musician Emile Jaques-Dalcroze (1865–1950), who developed a system of teaching music by translating gymnastics into rhythmic movements (called "eurhythmics").

The teachings of Delsarte first became popular in the USA in the late 19th century and those of Jaques-Dalcroze in the early 20th, at a time when health and physical education had become a major social concern; they motivated American colleges to include modern dance in their physical education curricula as a means of promoting a better understanding of movement. Delsarte's theories were of particular interest to Ted Shawn, who incorporated them into the curriculum of the Denishawn school of dance, which he founded with St. Denis in Los Angeles in 1915. Shawn also encouraged athleticism in dance through his efforts to reestablish the masculine aesthetic in theatrical dance: in the 1930s he formed the first all-male troupe of dancers. The national tours of the Denishawn troupe and the establishment of Denishawn schools around the country contributed much to the national acceptance and growth of the kind of dance envisioned by these early innovators. In 1932 Shawn established the Jacob's Pillow Dance Festival, in Massachusetts; it has become the nation's leading summer dance festival.

What is known as modern dance finally crystallized in the late 1920s and reached its peak in the 1930s and early 1940s. A highly individualistic art to which the concept of a standard technique is antithetical, modern dance is defined by the belief that truth in dance movement can be achieved only through the expression of the individual dancer's or choreographer's emotional experience. Perhaps it is for this reason that the dance of the great modern choreographers – Doris Humphrey, Mary Wigman, and MARTHA GRAHAM – has never been successfully restaged. Rather than a specific technique, these artists established certain principles of movement.

Doris Humphrey established one of the basic principles of modern dance, namely, "fall and recovery." Mary Wigman, who had studied with Jaques-Dalcroze and the Hungarian choreographer Rudolf von Laban, founded the German expressionist movement of modern dance, which was characterized by the balance between "emotional outbursts" and the "merciless discipline" of outer control. The greatest of all the modern choreographers was Martha Graham, who turned the concept of emotional expression into introspection and a relentless probing of the inner self.

Graham rejected the classical theories of movement that relied on a rigidly held pelvis and hips to free the arms and legs; instead she required dancers to allow every part of the body to move equally freely, and established the dynamic, opposing principles of "contraction and relaxation," "tension and release," as the most important in modern dance. Like the sharp contrast and reversals represented by these principles, Graham's movements opposed the smooth, flowing, lyrical rhythms of the 19th century, and reflected instead the sharp, angular, percussive rhythms she perceived in the restlessness and dissonance of 20th-century life. Her refusal to view dance as ornament and entertainment provoked the critic Eric Bentley to call her choreography the "dance of anxiety." While she rarely presented social or political issues in her dance, she captured the undercurrent of foreboding and the potential danger and power of the emotions that were present in those issues.

Graham's choreography was created before and therefore independently of the music, which was then composed expressly for it. The music may at times have enveloped the dance, intensified it, reflected various qualities in it, or guided the movements, but it did not provide the source of inspiration for it, as was the case for choreographers in the 19th century. In this way Graham broke with tradition, and her dance became a self-contained vehicle of expression. Louis Horst was the most significant of the composers who wrote for her. He had been with the Denishawn company for ten years before accepting the position of music director of her company in 1926, which he held until 1948. Horst wrote two of Graham's best-known works, *Primitive Mysteries* (1931; see fig.4) and *Frontier* (1935); others included Copland's *Appalachian Spring* (1944; for illustration *see* COPLAND, AARON, fig.2), Hunter Johnson's *Letter to the World* (1940), Menotti's *Errand into the Maze* (1947), and Dello Joio's *Diversion of Angels* (1948).

The freedom of the modern movement also permitted and encouraged exploration of non-Western dance forms. The choreography of Pearl Primus was based on African dance forms and movements and performed to the traditional chants and rhythms of African music. Katherine Dunham developed a dance style

4. Martha Graham and her company in "Primitive Mysteries" (New York, 1931)

5. *Alwin Nikolais Dance Theatre in "Sanctum" (New York, 1964)*

based on the rhythms of black-American and Caribbean dance and music; in establishing the Dunham School of Dance in New York (1945), Dunham also founded the first American school of black theatrical dance. The second generation of modern choreographers – including Erick Hawkins, Paul Taylor (who founded his own company in 1954), and Merce Cunningham (all of whom studied and performed with Graham), and José Limón and Ann Halprin – has been dominated primarily by men, who have continued to expand the role of the male theatrical dancer.

A highly intellectual attempt to isolate and abstract the minimalist essence of dance characterizes the post-modern period of the 1950s and 1960s, which is sometimes referred to as the "avant-garde" or "contemporary" movement in dance. The post-moderns discarded all the symbolic and associative mannerisms of dance, including its literary and dramatic references. Dance became arhythmic – free of the rhythmic regularity that had been used by 19th-century choreographers to create a sense of motion and forward propulsion – and its spatial quality was heightened. Of particular importance to post-modern choreographers were the theories of the French artist Marcel Duchamp, who argued that it was not the object itself but its setting and the attitude of the viewer that turned an object or event into art; following the same logic, any movement could become dance, given an appropriate context, environment, or attitude on the part of the audience.

ALWIN T. NIKOLAIS, who greatly expanded the visual palette of the choreographer with innovations in lighting and costuming, is considered one of the leading post-modern choreographers of dance as art, theater, and abstract movement. By ignoring the sexual identity of his dancers he removed the sexual polarity and tension that had created much of the emotional energy in earlier forms of theatrical dance. The "happenings" at the Judson Dance Theater in New York in the early 1960s represent at its most extreme the post-modern rejection of traditional dance and music and, instead, experimentation with dance as an experience of theater, art, and music expressed through spontaneous, unschooled movement. The theater was founded by Robert Dunn, a musician, and the dancer Judith Dunn, and drew on the creative talents of the choreographers and dancers Yvonne Rainer, Deborah Hay, and Steve Paxton, the composers Philip Corner and John Herbert McDowell, and the artists Robert Rauschenberg and Alex Hay. In its rejection of the proscenium stage in favor of a "space" that is created by the dance itself, the Judson Theater movement signaled an end to the cool withdrawal expressed in the dance of the 1950s by attempting to reestablish theatrical dance as a communal experience.

The most significant development in the music and dance of the post-modern period has come through the partnership, first formed in the 1940s, between the choreographer MERCE CUNNINGHAM and the composer John Cage. Cunningham's dance resembles classical dance in that it is built on a technique that requires intensive training and involves abstract movements more than emotional, symbolic, or literary representations. Most importantly, Cunningham has reaffirmed the importance of music to dance, but has turned the classical relationship of a composer and choreographer inside out: he emphasizes neither the regulatory role of music over dance nor the unity of the two, but rather a heightened sense of the differences between them, establishing the separateness of each through rhythmic disjunction or an avoidance of rhythmic coordination. It is the distance between the two elements that creates the emotional undertow of Cunningham's dance.

In the modern and post-modern movement, some choreographers rejected music entirely, and performances were danced in silence. It quickly became apparent, however, that the audience continued to be aware of sound, though now it was the sound created by the movements of the dancers and by extraneous activity. Influenced by this experience, some choreographers attempted to create music out of the sounds made by the dancers themselves. While Cage continued to compose music for the dance as an independent entity, he maintained the natural and spontaneous creation of sound present in the "silent" works through the element of chance, though according to his conception (based on the I Ching, the Chinese "book of changes") chance is an illusion and all events are determined and controlled by the laws of nature. In this way, the works of Cage and Cunningham represent not anarchy but the operation of natural laws, the meaning of which can be realized only in front of an audience, in whom the two points represented by the music and dance converge to complete the triangle of meaning. There is nothing free in their compositions. Without rhythmic cadence to guide the dancers, however, the beats have to be counted, and Cunningham uses a stopwatch to ensure that the music and dance end together.

Collaborations between Cage and Cunningham include *Suite for Five in Space and Time* (1956), *Antic Meet* (1958), *Landrover* (1972), and *Un jour ou deux* (1973). In *How to Pass, Kick, Fall, and Run* (1965) the sound accompaniment is supplied by readings from Cage's book *Silence*, and in *Variations V* (1965) the breaking of electromagnetic fields by the dancers' bodies causes changes in the accompanying electronic music and slide projections. Other composers who have worked with Cunningham include David Behrman (*Walkaround Time*, 1968), La Monte Young (*Winterbranch*, 1964), Pauline Oliveros (*Canfield*, 1969), Conlon Nancarrow (*Crises*, 1960), and Gordon Mumma (*Place*, 1965). Visual artists such as Robert Rauschenberg and Andy Warhol have also participated in their productions.

The spontaneity of the mixed-media approach to dance shifted in the 1980s to a more deliberate, academic, and intellectual approach, termed by those involved in the movement "interdisciplinary" and "collaborative." *Einstein on the Beach* (1976), with music by Philip Glass, production design by Robert Wilson, and choreography by LUCINDA CHILDS and Andrew de Groat, is considered to be the first of the interdisciplinary events. Childs creates her dances from the patterns of mathematical ratios. Similarly, Laura Dean, who creates a dance experience through the constant repetition of geometrical patterns performed to her own music and that of Steve Reich and other minimalist composers, believes the energy of dance to be worked out in mathematical structures. Her notated choreographies are in themselves works of art. The spontaneity and emphasis on natural movement associated with modern dance continues to be present in the work of such choreographers as TWYLA THARP, who combines the movements of social dance, the music hall, nightclub, classical ballet, and athletics with humor and unconventional settings. Her works include *Deuce Coup* (1973; music by the Beach Boys), *Give and Take* (1976; Gregor J. Werner, Sousa, Richard Goldman, and Art Tatum), and *The Catherine Wheel* (1981; created with the rock musician David Byrne).

The search for natural movement has also led dancers and choreographers to establish companies away from the urban setting of New York, such as the Deborah Hay Dance Company in Austin, and Pilobolus, founded by Moses Pendleton and Jonathan Wolken in New Hampshire in 1971. Born of the pastoral, "back-to-the-earth" movement of the late 1960s and early 1970s, Pilobolus takes the abstract forms of contemporary dance and, as its name implies, returns them to the earth; its emphasis on the natural world has led to a restoration of the sexual roles of the dancers and an affirmation of joyousness and life in a choreography that is created collectively by the company. The group uses existing music, as in *Day Two* (1981; music by Brian Eno, David Byrne, and Talking Heads) as well as original compositions that have been written to fit the choreography, as in *Ciona* (1974; Jon Appleton) and *Untitled* (1975; Robert Dennis).

The energy and spontaneity of black-American dance is expressed in the work of such companies as the Hubbard Street Dance Company in Chicago, which was founded by Lou Conte in 1978 from Urban Gateways (an educational arts program for inner-city schools) and specializes in jazz, tap, soft shoe, American ballroom dancing, and the drill and chorus-line routines of precision dancing.

3. MUSICAL THEATER AND THE DANCE MUSICAL. 19th-century rhythms and dance forms provided the structural basis for theater and film musicals of the 20th century, with the waltz replacing the march as the most popular of such forms. Although the waltz had been used successfully in such musicals as Victor Herbert's *Naughty Marietta* (1910), the real model for the waltz operetta was Franz Lehár's *Die lustige Witwe*, which was first performed in the USA (as *The Merry Widow*) in 1911. The continued popularity of this kind of musical is demonstrated by the success of such works as Rudolf Friml's *Rose Marie* (1924) and *The Vagabond King* (1925); Sigmund Romberg's *The Student Prince* (1924) and *The Desert Song* (1926); Richard Rodgers's *Oklahoma!* (1943) and *Carousel* (1945); and Stephen Sondheim's *A Little Night Music* (1973).

The black-American dance rhythms and forms that emerged out of late 19th-century minstrelsy and all-black shows continued to influence dance in the American musical theater of the 20th century. They became even more popular through the incorporation of routines based on the charleston (as in *Runnin' Wild*, 1923; *see* CHARLESTON (ii)) and the BLACK BOTTOM (in *Dinah*, 1924). Black-American dance had a particularly strong influence on spectacular dance, which took the form of tap. Much of the development of tap as a distinct style occurred in the dance musicals of the film industry, where black dancers taught their technique to white performers. BILL "BOJANGLES" ROBINSON, a "hoofer" (i.e., a dancer whose footwork is the essential feature of his skill), and a number of other well-known performers paved the way for black dancers to appear in films. Two of Robinson's most important dance sequences included the "stair" tap dance to Stephen Foster's *Oh! Susanna*, which he performed with Shirley Temple in *The Little Colonel* (1935), and his rendition of Harold Arlen's song *Stormy Weather* in the film of the same name (1943). "Eccentric" dances, involving movements made not only by the feet but by the entire body, were performed by John W. Bubbles in such films as *Cabin in the Sky* (1943; music by Vernon Duke) and *A Song is Born* (1948; music by Benny Goodman and other jazz instrumentalists) and by the Nicholas Brothers (Harold and Fayard), whose acrobatic style became known as "flash dance." The Nicholas Brothers began their career at the Cotton Club in 1932 and credited Balanchine for one of their more spectacular flash steps, the split-slide (a split performed by one dancer while sliding under the other), which was used for the first time in the musical *Babes in Arms* (1937) by Rodgers and Hart.

Influenced by the Broadway revue dance style of the early 20th century, Busby Berkeley, in the 1930s, also focused attention on dance in film through his elaborate choreography of geometric and drill patterns executed by chorus lines of women. Artistic acceptance and the increased importance of dance in film occurred primarily, however, through the dance and choreographical control of the "jazz tap" dancers FRED ASTAIRE and GENE KELLY. Astaire combined tap, elements of ballet, and social·dancing in a relaxed and easy yet elegant style. The music he used most frequently was the 32-bar song in 4/4 meter (*AABA*), and he choreographed not only to the melody but also the harmonic structure. Composers worked directly with him and often altered their music to accommodate the dance; Irving Berlin, for example, expanded his usual four-phrase structure to five in the song "Cheek to Cheek" for the film *Top Hat* (1935). Gene Kelly developed a wholesome, "all-American" athletic style out of tap, gymnastics, and ballet, and is considered the most successful of the film choreographers in integrating dance with the action. Kelly sought to make both the music and the dance intensify the characterization and flow out of a situation, a technique that was particularly significant in the films *On the Town* (1949; music by Leonard Bernstein), *An American in Paris* (1951; George Gershwin), and *Singin' in the Rain* (1952; Nacio Herb Brown).

One of the first appearances of ballet in musical films was Balanchine's choreography for "Slaughter on Tenth Avenue" in *On your Toes* (film 1939) by Rodgers and Hart, but it was the choreography by AGNES DE MILLE of the dream sequence in the film version of *Oklahoma!* (1955) that not only established ballet as an important vehicle of expression in the musical but showed that dance of any kind could be used to move the action along. Jerome Robbins's choreography for *West Side Story* (original stage version 1955, film 1961) was technically balletic, but he used jazz elements as well, inspired by the rhythms of Bernstein's score. Modern dance, which has been used in dance musicals particularly for introspective and highly emotional sequences, can be seen primarily in the work of De Mille, Charles Weidman (*Sing out, Sweet Land!*, 1944), Helen Tamaris (the revival of Kern's *Show Boat*, 1946; and Berlin's *Annie Get your Gun*, 1946, 1950), Hanya Holm (Loewe's *My Fair Lady*, 1956, 1964; and *Camelot*, 1960, 1967), Katherine Dunham (*Stormy Weather*, film, 1943), and Jack Cole (Styne's *Gentlemen Prefer Blondes*, 1949, film, with additional music by Carmichael, 1953; and the revival of *Kismet*, music by Borodin, 1953, film, 1955). Jack Cole is credited with the innovative "jazz style" in Broadway musicals, which involves "isolations," or movements of parts of the body (such as the hips, shoulders, head, and ribcage) in isolation from one another. Other choreographers who have varied that style through combinations of ballet, modern dance, jazz dance, and gymnastics include Eugene Loring, Michael Kidd, and Bob Fosse. The popularity of the dance musical declined in the late 1950s but revived in the mid-1970s with shows built on jazz dance, such as *A Chorus Line* (1975; music by Marvin Hamlisch), and the all-black revues *Bubbling Brown Sugar* (1976), *Ain't Misbehavin'* (1978), and *Eubie* (1978). In the USA a renewed general interest in dance is reflected in the success of Bob Fosse's *Dancin'* (1978), a Broadway show that contains neither plot nor songs but features dance of all kinds, performed to music in a wide range of styles by composers who include Bach, Sousa, and Cat Stevens. The important influence of theatrical dances on social dance forms in the 1970s and 1980s can be seen by the enormous success of films such as *Saturday Night Fever* (1977), *Grease* (1978), *Flash dance* (1983), and *Staying Alive* (1983), which featured (among others) the dancers John Travolta and Cynthia Rhodes and which contributed to the popularity of disco and break dancing, and the incorporation of jazz and ballet movements into social dancing.

4. SOCIAL DANCE. An important development in social dance in the 20th century was the demise of the ball, with its entirely predetermined program of dance selections. It was replaced from around 1911 by the cabaret and nightclub, both legitimate and respectable places of recreation, where people could eat, dance, drink, and be entertained by performances that had previously been regarded as socially unacceptable, particularly for women. The popular dances of the period were called "animal" or "ragtime" dances and had their origin in black dance; they included the TURKEY TROT, bunny hop (CONGA), GRIZZLY BEAR, TEXAS TOMMY, and camel walk, as well as the more erotic EAGLE ROCK,

6. *Jazz dancers at the Club Bali, Washington, DC, 1944*

SLOW DRAG, and buzzard lope. It was probably the popularity of the black styles, in which rhythms were articulated by the dancer's entire body, that led to the decline of the restrictive couple-embrace posture.

Irene and VERNON CASTLE, who made their first appearance in the USA in 1912 and helped to legitimize some of the new black dances, introduced the FOXTROT, which they performed to the accompaniment of W. C. Handy's *Memphis Blues*; Irene Castle, as well as Handy, claimed that the dance had been created by the Castles' music director and accompanist James Reese Europe specifically to fit Handy's music. The Castles also popularized the ONE-STEP and Latin rhythms in American social dancing (through their variations on the maxixe and TANGO).

In the 1920s the jazz dance bands of Nick LaRocca, Fletcher Henderson, Paul Whiteman, Red Nichols, and Jean Goldkette provided the music for many of the black dances, including the charleston and black bottom (which were both introduced to European audiences by the black-American dancer JOSEPHINE BAKER in 1926), the SHIMMY, BIG APPLE, and boogie-woogie (*see* BOOGIE-WOOGIE (ii)). In the 1930s the big bands of Benny Goodman, Duke Ellington, Glenn Miller, Tommy Dorsey, Count Basie, Artie Shaw, and Harry James made popular the expansive rhythms of "swing," which promoted the broad, athletic, off-the-floor movements of the LINDY and jitterbug.

In the 1940s and 1950s, as the bop and cool styles transformed jazz from dance music into concert music, Cuban dance bands led by such bandleaders as Perez Prado popularized Caribbean and Latin American social dances such as the BOSSA NOVA, CHA CHA CHA, CONGA, MAMBO, MERENGUE, RUMBA, and SAMBA. Young adults in the later 1950s preferred instead the black dances associated with rhythm-and-blues and rock-and-roll; in the 1960s dances like the BOOGALOO were popular. ROCK DANCES such as the chicken, frug, monkey, twist (popularized by Chubby Checker in 1960), and limbo were in many ways variants of the early ragtime dances, but their execution depended not on the interaction of two partners but on the individual dancer as part of the entire dancing group.

The steady, driving, propulsive beats of rock, funk, and soul music, sustained on guitars, brass, and drums and threatening to overpower the melody, inspired the concept of a never-ending dance that could be brought to a halt only by stopping the music abruptly or by slightly slowing the tempo. The idea was fully realized in the discothèques of the 1970s and 1980s, where taped music provides a constant stream of sound to which dancers can create any dance movements in endless sequences of their own choosing (*see* DISCO). BREAK DANCING, or breaking, a generic term for all forms of contemporary street dance performed to music derived from funk, achieved national popularity in 1983. It is a particularly acrobatic form of dance, which calls for a good deal of spinning on the back, head, and hands, and isolations of various parts of the body in broken or robot-like movements.

The popularity of exercising to music, or dance as exercise (dance aerobics), represents an old idea in a new form – the link between athleticism and music in cadenced rhythms, which has been a feature of American dance throughout its history.

See also JAZZ, §III, 1.

BIBLIOGRAPHY

GENERAL

C. Sachs: *Eine Weltgeschichte des Tanzes* (Berlin, 1933; Eng. trans., 1937/*R*1963)
J. Martin: *America Dancing* (New York, 1936/*R*1968)
P. Magriel, ed.: *Chronicles of American Dance* (New York, 1948)
A. Chujoy, ed.: *The Dance Encyclopedia* (New York, 1949, rev. and enlarged with P. W. Manchester 2/1967)
E. Denby: *Looking at the Dance* (New York, 1949/*R*1968)
W. Raffé: *Dictionary of the Dance* (New York, 1964)
A. Croce: *After Images* (New York, 1977)
H. Koegler: *The Concise Oxford Dictionary of Ballet* (New York, 1977)
E. Rogosin: *The Dance Makers: Conversations with American Choreographers* (New York, 1980)
C. Steinberg, ed.: *The Dance Anthology* (New York, 1980)
R. Copeland and M. Cohen: *What is Dance? Readings in Theory and Criticism* (New York, 1983)
P. Norton: *March Music in Nineteenth-century America* (diss., U. of Michigan, 1983)

SOCIAL AND VERNACULAR DANCE

Saltator: *A Treatise on Dancing* (Boston, 1802)
F. D. Nichols: *Instructor of Dancing in Boston: a Guide to Politeness* (Boston, 1810)
The Dancer's own Book, and Ball-room Companion (Philadelphia and New York, 1848)
J. Durang: *Durang's Terpsichore, or Ball Room Guide* (Philadelphia, 1848)
E. Howe: *Howe's Complete Ball-room Hand Book* (Philadelphia, 1858)
E. Ferrero: *The Art of Dancing* (New York, 1859)
E. Howe: *American Dancing Master and Ball-room Prompter* (Boston, 1862)
T. Hillgrove: *A Complete Practical Guide to the Art of Dancing* (New York, 1863)
E. B. Reilley: *The Amateur's Vademecum: a Practical Treatise on the Art of Dancing* (Philadelphia, 1870)
W. B. DeGarmo: *The Dance of Society* (New York, 1875, rev. and enlarged 5/1892)
L. Carpenter: *J. W. Pepper's Universal Dancing Master: Prompter's Call-book* (Philadelphia and Chicago, 1882, rev. and enlarged 2/1889)
A. Dodworth: *Dancing and its Relation to Education and Social Life* (New York, 1885, 3/1900 ed. T. G. Dodworth)
M. Wilson: *Dancing* (Philadelphia, 1899, repr. 1924)
V. Castle and I. Castle: *Modern Dancing* (New York, 1914/*R*1980)
B. Tolman and R. Page: *The Country Dance Book* (Guilford, VT, 1937)
A. C. Cole: "The Puritan and Fair Terpsichore," *Mississippi Valley Historical Review*, xxix/1 (1942), 3–34
A. P. Wright and D. Wright: *How to Dance* (New York, 1942, rev. 2/1958)
E. Reeser: *De geschiedenis van de wals* (Amsterdam, 1947; Eng. trans., ?1949)
M. Carner: *The Waltz* (New York, 1948)
B. C. Landauer: *Some Terpsichorean Ephemera* (New York, 1953)
S. F. Damon: *The History of Square Dancing* (Barre, MA, 1957)
N. A. Benson: *The Itinerant Dancing and Music Masters of Eighteenth Century America* (diss., U. of Minnesota, 1963)
G. A. Schneider: "Pigeon Wings and Polkas: the Dance of the California Miners," *Dance Perspectives*, no.39 (1969) [complete issue]
L. F. Emery: *Black Dance in the United States from 1619 to 1970* (Palo Alto, CA, 1972)
G. Giordano: *Anthology of American Jazz Dance* (Evanston, IL, 1975)
J. Van Cleef: "Rural Felicity: Social Dance in 18th-century Connecticut," *Dance Perspectives*, no.65 (1976) [complete issue]
K. Van W. Keller and R. Sweet: *A Choice Selection of American Country Dances of the Revolutionary Era 1775–1795* (New York, 1976)
R. Page: *Heritage Dances of Early America* (Colorado Springs, CO, 1976)
P. Buckman: *Let's Dance: Social, Ballroom & Folk Dancing* (New York, 1978)
J. S. Roberts: *The Latin Tinge: the Impact of Latin American Music on the United States* (New York, 1979)
V. J. Tufo: *Contra-dancing in Maine: the Revival of an American Tradition* (thesis, U. of Michigan, 1979)
S. A. Floyd, Jr., and M. J. Reisser: "Social Dance Music of Black Composers in the Nineteenth Century and the Emergence of Classic Ragtime," *BPiM*, viii (1980), 161–93
G. Schneider: "Using Nineteenth-century Social Dance Manuals," *Dance Research Journal*, xiv (1981), 39
H. Andreau: *Jazz Dance* (Englewood Cliffs, NJ, 1983)
C. A. Hoover: "Epilogue to Secular Music in Early Massachusetts," *Music in Colonial Massachusetts, 1630–1820*, ed. B. Lambert, ii (Boston, 1985), 729

THEATRICAL DANCE

I. Duncan: *My Life* (1927, 2/1933/*R*1955)
T. Shawn: *Dance we Must* (Lee, MA, 1940)
G. Amberg: *Ballet in America* (New York, 1949)
M. Lloyd: *The Borzoi Book of Modern Dance* (Brooklyn, NY, 1949)
A. de Mille: *Dance to the Piper* (Boston, 1952)
A. Franks: *Twentieth Century Ballet* (London, England, 1955)

G. Lippincott, ed.: *Dance Production* (Washington, 1956)
K. Dunham: *A Touch of Innocence* (New York, 1959)
J. Cage: *Silence* (Middletown, CT, 1961/*R*1967)
L. Horst and C. Russell: *Modern Dance Forms* (San Francisco, 1961)
M. Graham: *Martha Graham* (Brooklyn, NY, 1966)
L. Leatherman and M. Swope: *Martha Graham: a Portrait of an Artist* (New York, 1966)
L. Kirstein: *Three Pamphlets Collected* (Brooklyn, NY, 1967)
M. Stearns and J. Stearns: *Jazz Dance: the Story of American Vernacular Dance* (New York, 1968)
M. Cunningham: *Changes: Notes on Choreography*, ed. F. Starr (New York and London, 1969)
I. Guest: *Fanny Elssler* (London, 1970)
D. McDonagh: *The Rise and Fall and Rise of Modern Dance* (New York, 1970)
W. Terry: *Great Male Dancers of the Ballet* (Garden City, NY, 1970)
S. J. Cohen: *Doris Humphrey: an Artist First* (Middletown, CT, 1972)
M. Clarke and C. Crisp: *Ballet: an Illustrated History* (New York, 1973)
M. Cunningham: *Merce Cunningham* (New York, 1975)
M. Wigman: *The Mary Wigman Book*, ed. W. Sorell (Middletown, CT, 1975)
M. Hodgson: *Quintet: Five American Dance Companies* (New York, 1976) [on the Taylor, Ailey, Cunningham, Harlem, Feld companies]
D. McDonagh: *The Complete Guide to Modern Dance* (Garden City, NY, 1976)
N. Reynolds: *Repertory in Review: 40 Years of the New York City Ballet* (New York, 1977)
A. Livet, ed.: *Contemporary Dance* (New York, 1978)
C. Payne: *American Ballet Theatre* (New York, 1978)
E. Kendall: *Where she Danced* (New York, 1979)
G. R. Lishka: *A Handbook for the Ballet Accompanist* (Bloomington, IN, 1979)
J. Sherman: *The Drama of Denishawn Dance* (Middletown, CT, 1979)
M. B. Siegel: *The Shapes of Change: Images of American Dance* (Boston, 1979)
J. Delamater: *Dance in the Hollywood Musical* (Ann Arbor, MI, 1981)
S. Shelton: *Divine Dancer: a Biography of Ruth St. Denis* (Garden City, NY, 1981)
L. Theodore: "Preserving American Theatre Dance: the Work of the American Dance Machine," *Musical Theatre in America: Greenvale, NY, 1981*, ed. G. Loney (Westport, CT, 1984), 275

PAULINE NORTON

Daniel, Oliver (*b* De Pere, WI, 24 Nov 1911). Administrator and musicologist. He was educated at St. Norbert College, West De Pere (1925–9), and afterwards studied piano in Europe and at the New England Conservatory, Boston. He toured as a concert pianist and taught piano until 1942, when he became music director of the educational division of CBS radio; from 1947 to 1954 he produced and directed various broadcast series, including "Invitation to Music," "20th-century Concert Hall," and programs of the New York PO and the Boston SO. Daniel was cofounder in 1952 with Stokowski of the Contemporary Music Society. In 1954 he helped set up CRI, where he also served as a director, and from 1954 to 1977 he headed the concert-music division of BMI. He has been on the board of directors of many organizations, including the American SO (1962–72), the American Music Center (1966–78), the Society for Asian Music (1967–9), the Charles Ives Society (1973–83), and the American Composers Orchestra (honorary chairman, 1977–), and beginning in 1958 was long active in the affairs of the International Music Council of UNESCO. In 1956 he received the Laurel Leaf award of the ACA.

An ardent and effective advoçate of American composers, Daniel spurred the efforts to edit and perform Ives's Symphony no.4 that led to its première in 1965. Also active as a journalist, he contributed a regular column to *Saturday Review* (1957–68); other writings appeared in *The New Grove*, *The Etude*, *Musical America*, and *Stereo Review*. He edited several collections of early American music by such composers as Billings and Belcher, and wrote the biography *Leopold Stokowski: a Counterpoint of View* (1982).

CARL SKOGGARD

Daniels, Barbara (*b* Newark, OH, 7 May 1946). Soprano. Educated at Ohio State University and later at the Cincinnati College-Conservatory (MM), she made her début in 1973 with the West Palm Beach Opera as Mozart's Susanna. She was engaged at Innsbruck in 1974, where her roles included Fiordiligi and Violetta, then moved to Kassel two years later, adding Liù, Zdenka (*Arabella*), and Massenet's Manon to her repertory; there she also took part in the world première of Walter Steffans's *Unter den Milchwald* (1977), a musical adaptation of the play by Dylan Thomas. She made her début at Covent Garden in 1978 as Rosalinde (*Die Fledermaus*) and sang Norina (*Don Pasquale*) at the Kennedy Center (1979) and Zdenka at San Francisco (1980), before making her début at the Metropolitan Opera on 30 September 1983 as Musetta. Since 1978 she has sung at Cologne, where her roles have included Elisetta (*Il matrimonio segreto*), Lady Harriet (*Martha*), Micaela, and Alice Ford. A lyric soprano, she also has a facility for coloratura, which she demonstrated with great success as the Countess Adèle in *Le comte Ory* at Zurich (1981).

ELIZABETH FORBES

Daniels, Charles Neil (*b* Leavenworth, KS, 12 April 1878; *d* Los Angeles, CA, 23 Jan 1943). Songwriter and music publisher. He had popular success early in his career with the two-step *Margery* (1898), the song *You tell me your dream* (1899), and *Hiawatha* (1901), an "Indian intermezzo" (in fact an early ragtime song). He also purchased and published Scott Joplin's first piano rag, *Original Rags*, in 1898. He began working for Carl Hoffman, a local publisher in Kansas City, then formed his own firm, Daniels, Russel & Boone, which he sold to Whitney-Warner of Detroit in 1902 for a reputed $10,000, all based on the rights to the hugely popular *Hiawatha*. Later he established another publishing firm, Villa Moret, in Los Angeles. This took its name from one of Daniels's pseudonyms, Neil Moret, and was highly successful in the 1920s. Daniels contributed many enduring standards to the American popular song repertory, including *Moonlight and Roses* (1925), *Song of the Wanderer* (1926), *Chloe* (1927), *She's Funny that Way* (1928), and *Sweet and Lovely* (1931). His career epitomizes the work of the most ambitious and successful Tin Pan Alley musicians who were active during the ragtime era. His aid in promoting Joplin's music and the solid public and financial success of *Hiawatha* helped establish the music as an integral part of American popular culture.

BIBLIOGRAPHY

R. Blesh and H. Janis: *They All Played Ragtime* (New York, 1950, rev. 4/1971)
W. Schafer and J. Riedel: *The Art of Ragtime* (Baton Rouge, LA, 1973)
D. A. Jasen and T. J. Tichenor: *Rags and Ragtime: a Musical History* (New York, 1978)

WILLIAM J. SCHAFER

Daniels, Mabel Wheeler (*b* Swampscott, MA, 27 Nov 1878; *d* Boston, MA, 10 March 1971). Composer. Her father, George F. Daniels, was for ten years president of the Handel and Haydn Society in Boston. She studied at Radcliffe College (BA 1900) and with Chadwick in Boston. In 1904–5 she was a pupil of Ludwig Thuille in Munich and on returning published a valuable autobiography, *An American Girl in Munich: Impressions of a Music Student* (1905). She directed the Radcliffe Glee Club (1911–13) and was head of music at Simmons College, Boston (1913–18). Her largest work, the *Song of Jael* to a text by Edwin A. Robinson for the Worcester (Massachusetts) Festival (5 October 1940), was also her sole lengthy vocal work with text by a modern male author; she published a documented study, "Robinson's Interest in Music," in the *Mark Twain Quarterly* (ii/3, 1938). Although never daring or very individual, she was a competent composer who scored well for both voices and orchestra. She was known principally for her choral works. She received a MacDowell Fellowship (1931), awards from the National Federation of Music Clubs (1911) and the National Association of American Composers and Conductors (1958), and honorary doctorates from Boston University (1939), Wheaton College (1957), and New England Conservatory (1958).

WORKS

Operettas: A Copper Complication (R. L. Hooper) (1900); The Court of Hearts (Hooper), 1900; The Show Girl (R. A. Barnett) (1902), collab. D. K. Stevens

Opera sketch: Alice in Wonderland Continued, Brookline, MA, 1904

Choral with orch: The Desolate City (W. S. Blunt), Bar, chorus, orch, 1913; Peace with a Sword (A. F. Brown), op.25 (1917); Songs of Elfland (M. W. Daniels) (1924); The Holy Star (N. B. Turner), op.31/1 (1928), A Holiday Fantasy (Turner), op.31/2 (1928); Exultate Deo (Psalms), op.33 (1929); The Song of Jael (E. A. Robinson), S, chorus, orch, op.37 (1937); A Psalm of Praise (1954); others

Other choral works: In Springtime, choral cycle, female vv, 1910; Eastern Songs, female vv, pf, 2 vn, op.16/1, 1911; The Voice of my Beloved, female vv, pf, 2 vn, op.16/2, 1911; Flowerwagon (F. T. Patterson), SSA, pf (1914); The Girl Scouts Marching Song (Brown) (1918); Oh God of all our Glorious Past (A. E. Howe) (1930); Through the Dark the Dreamers Came (E. Marlatt), SSA/SATB, op.32/1, *c*1930, rev. (1961); The Christ Child (G. K. Chesterton), SATB, pf, op.32/2 (1931); A Night in Bethlehem (Daniels), SATB (1954); others

Orch: Suite, str, 1910; Deep Forest, small orch, op.34/1, 1931, arr. large orch, 1934; Pirates' Island, op.34/2, 1934; In memoriam, 1945; Digressions, ballet, str, op.41/2, 1947; Ov., 1951

Chamber: Pastoral Ode, fl, str, op.49, 1940; 3 Observations, 3 ww, 1943; 4 Observations, 4 str, 1945; Vn Sonata

Many songs

Principal publishers: J. Fischer, Gray, E. C. Schirmer, Schmidt

BIBLIOGRAPHY

EwenD

E. Kaledin: "Daniels, Mabel Wheeler," *NAW*

ROBERT STEVENSON

Danish-American music. The music of the Danish community in the USA is discussed as part of the Scandinavian tradition; *see* EUROPEAN-AMERICAN MUSIC, §II, 6.

Danks, H(art) P(ease) (*b* New Haven, CT, 6 April 1834; *d* Philadelphia, PA, 20 Nov 1903). Composer, singer, and conductor. He first studied music in Chicago, and built a local reputation as a church musician. In 1864 he moved to New York, where he became a singer and conductor in local churches as well as on the concert stage. During this time he published many sacred solo and choral pieces, and at his death at least 15 books of anthems alone bore his name. He also collaborated in the composition of three operettas, although these achieved little commercial success. Danks's widest reputation was made as a composer of popular songs: *Don't be Angry with me, Darling* (1870) sold tens of thousands of copies, and the ballad *Silver Threads among the Gold* (1872) more than three million – perhaps more than any other song of its day. Despite the revenues generated by this song, Danks died destitute and alone.

BIBLIOGRAPHY

G. Birdseye: "America's Song Composers: H. P. Danks," *Potter's American Monthly*, xii (1879), 333

W. S. B. Mathews, ed.: *A Hundred Years of Music in America* (Chicago, 1889/*R*1970), 98

C. Hamm: *Yesterdays: Popular Song in America* (New York, 1979), 264

DALE COCKRELL

Danly, Robert Clough (*b* Grundy County, IL, 1871; *d* Hinsdale, IL, 15 Dec 1938). Engineer and inventor. He was designer in charge of the tool room at the International Harvester Company, then president of his own firm, Accurate Engineering Company. He redesigned a trap drum pedal invented by his brother-in-law, William F. Ludwig, Sr., and mass-produced it in a rented Chicago barn; this led to the establishment in 1909 of Ludwig & Ludwig, as a small percussion manufacturing business that later expanded into larger quarters also housing the Danly Die Shop. Recognizing the need for a cheaper, more efficient, portable machine drum, the company produced the first American pedal timpani, a hydraulic model (patented in 1913). A foot pump acted on a rubber expansion tube that pressed a hoop against the head from inside the kettle. The tendency of the material to disintegrate and burst under pressure led to an improved model (patented in 1920), in which piano-wire cables were connected to the drum's tension screws and controlled by a pedal with a locking device. Danly sold his tool and die shop in 1914, and five years later became vice-president of Ludwig & Ludwig. He designed and engineered many new products, including an improved snare drum mechanism, a foot-activated cymbal striker, an all-metal drum shell, and the "Natural Way Balanced Action" timpani, which had a compression spring for tension balance of the pedal (patented 1923). In 1923 Danly formed a new business of his own, Danly Machine Specialties, Inc.

EDMUND A. BOWLES

Dann, Hollis Ellsworth (*b* Canton, PA, 1 May 1861; *d* Douglaston, NY, 3 Jan 1939). Music educator. After graduating from high school, he studied organ, piano, and singing privately (1881–4) and attended Elmira Business College (1886–7). His career as a music educator began with his appointment as supervisor of music for the Ithaca, New York, public schools (1887–1905); he was then head of the music department, Cornell University (1906–21), director of music for the state of Pennsylvania (1921–5), and head of the department of music education, New York University (1925–36). He was also on the faculty of the New School of Methods in Public School Music (1896–1906) and served as president of the Music Supervisors National Conference in 1920. He wrote many articles and books on music in schools and compiled collections of songs and teaching materials. Dann was one of the pioneers in fostering standards for public school music programs.

WILLIAM McCLELLAN

Da Ponte, Lorenzo [Conegliano, Emanuele] (*b* Ceneda [now Vittorio Veneto], Italy, 10 March 1749; *d* New York, 17 Aug 1838). Italian librettist and impresario. He was educated in the seminary at Ceneda and took holy orders. After a period spent teaching in Treviso, near Venice (1773–6), he made a living by writing occasional works. In 1781 he was appointed librettist to the newly founded Italian theater in Vienna, where he remained until 1792, collaborating most notably with Antonio Salieri, Vicente Martín y Soler, and Mozart. He then traveled to London, the Low Countries, and Italy, but by 1805 his financial difficulties became so pressing that he immigrated to the USA, arriving in Philadelphia on 4 June. He taught Italian in New York from 1807 to 1811 and after 1819 (from 1825 at Columbia College); from 1811 to 1818 he was in Sunbury, Pennsylvania.

Da Ponte assisted in a production of *Don Giovanni* during Manuel García's New York opera season of 1825. Heartened by the success, he corresponded with Giovanni Montresor, an impresario in Bologna, and sponsored concerts by his own niece Giulia in 1830. In 1832 Montresor brought a sizable company to New York and Philadelphia; its 59 performances were highly acclaimed, but, despite Da Ponte's efforts, the enterprise was a financial failure. Undismayed, the octogenarian launched plans for a $150,000 opera house in New York, and in 1833–4 he and a collaborator named Rivafinoli presented the first season of operas there. The house was much admired but the stockholders lost nearly $30,000; Rivafinoli disappeared and Da Ponte was forced to step down. After an equally costly second season, the Italian Opera House was used for theater performances; it burned down in 1839. Da Ponte's contribution to American music was small but significant; his early championship of Italian opera helped to introduce a style that remained influential throughout the 19th century.

BIBLIOGRAPHY

L. da Ponte: *Memorie di Lorenzo Da Ponte da Ceneda scritte da esso* (New York, 1823–7, rev. and enlarged, 2/1829–30); trans. E. Abbott as *Memoirs of Lorenzo Da Ponte*, ed. A. Livingston (Philadelphia, 1929/*R*1967)

——: *Storia della compagnia dell'opera italiana condotta da Giacomo Montresor in America* (New York, 1833)

——: *Frottola per far ridere* (New York, 1835)

J. L. Russo: *Lorenzo Da Ponte, Poet and Adventurer* (New York, 1922)

A Fitzlyon: *The Libertine Librettist: a Biography of Mozart's Librettist Lorenzo da Ponte* (London, 1955)

WILLIAM BROOKS

Darin, Bobby [Cassatto, Walden Robert] (*b* New York, 14 May 1936; *d* Los Angeles, 20 December 1973). Pop singer and songwriter. In 1958 he wrote and recorded *Splish Splash*, which became his first success on the chart; it was followed by *Dream Lover* and *Queen of the Hop*, both released in 1959. His next hit, a version of *Mack the Knife* from Weill's *Die Dreigroschenoper*, was a skillful rendition in a swing-influenced pop style. His performances reconciled the brashness of teenage pop with the more sophisticated club style of Sinatra. In the 1960s he became a leading nightclub performer; his diverse repertory embraced rhythm-and-blues, country-pop, and folk-rock material. A superb vocal mimic, Darin foreshadowed such mainstream performers as Billy Joel in his ability to adapt his singing to very different styles of music.

BIBLIOGRAPHY

"Darin, Bobby," *CBY 1963*

STEPHEN HOLDEN

Darracott, William, Jr. (*b* Milford, NH, 1799; *d* Milford, 1868). Maker of bowed string instruments. He was the son of a cooper, William Darracott, Sr. (1769–1825), and was described as a "mechanic" by trade, meaning that he used machinery and hand-tools to construct such custom-made items as spinning wheels and clocks. As an instrument maker he concentrated on the violin and "larger instruments of the same kind" (Ramsdell, 1901); he probably began this work around 1820. Few of his instruments survive: Howe (1916) mentions a three-string double bass dated 1827; another violin, dated 1837, is in the Selch collection, New York.

His son George L. Darracott (*b* Milford, 1831; *d* ? after 1898) followed his father as a mechanic and instrument maker, and a large bass viol by him, dated 1861, is in the Metropolitan Museum, New York. The instruments by both Darracotts are finely made, excellently finished works, not inferior to European manufacture; they are good examples of New England work before the Civil War, carried out in towns like Milford which had fine timber and water power for sawmills. Joseph Darracott is mentioned by Howe as working in Milford in 1809, but there is no other evidence of his existence. The well-known Hutchinson family of singers was also from Milford, and it is possible that the first violins used by Judson and John were supplied by one of the Darracotts.

BIBLIOGRAPHY

G. Ramsdell: *The History of Milford* (Concord, NH, 1901)

W. H. Howe: "Early American Violin Makers," *The Violinist*, xx/7 (1916), 15

FREDERICK R. SELCH

Darrell, R(obert) D(onaldson) (*b* Newton, MA, 13 Dec 1903). Writer on music. He studied at Harvard (1922) and the New England Conservatory (1923–6). He has written reviews and articles for *Phonograph Monthly Review* (1926–30), of which he was editor and publisher in 1930–31, *Music Lovers' Guide* (1932–4), *Down Beat* (1952), the *Saturday Review* (1953–5), and *High Fidelity*, of which he has been a contributing editor since 1956. He is best known as the compiler of the first general American discography, in which he included his own often very personal assessments, *The Gramophone Shop Encyclopedia of Recorded Music* (1936), the supplements to which he also edited from 1937 to 1939. He also edited the *Review of Recorded Music* (1947–50), and was the compiler of *Schirmer's Guide to Books on Music and Musicians* (1951).

BIBLIOGRAPHY

"Darrell, R(obert) D(onaldson)," *CBY 1955*

PAULA MORGAN

Dartmouth Digital Synthesizer. A digital synthesizer, developed by Sydney Alonso, Cameron Jones, and Jon Appleton in 1972–4; it was superseded by their Synclavier. *See* ELECTRO-ACOUSTIC MUSIC, §4.

Dashow, James (Hilyer) (*b* Chicago, IL, 7 Nov 1944). Composer. At Princeton University (BA 1966) he studied with Babbitt, Randall, Cone, and Kim; he was a pupil of Berger, Shifrin, and Boykan at Brandeis University (MFA 1969), and in Rome he studied with Goffredo Petrassi at the Accademia di Santa Cecilia (diploma 1971). He has taught at the Canneti Music Institute in Vicenza, Italy, and at Massachusetts Institute of Technology, and holds important posts in the Padua Computer Music Group, the Computer Music Association, and the Centro Sonologia Computazionale at the University of Padua; for some years Dashow has lived in Rome. His awards include two Wilson Fellowships, a Fulbright scholarship, two NEA grants, and a Rockefeller Foundation grant (for his opera *The Little Prince*, commissioned by the Venice Biennale); in 1984 he received an award from the American Academy and Institute of Arts and Letters. Dashow's vocal music makes original use of speechlike declamation. His main contribution to electronic music has been his manipulation by computer of electronic "generating pitches" to produce a complex of harmonically related "chords" and timbres, which he then uses to compose. Dashow has contributed several articles on computer music to *Interface*, *Computer Music Journal*, and other periodicals.

WORKS

Stage: The Little Prince (opera, after E. de Saint-Exupéry), vv, cptr, lasers, graphics, 1982–

Inst: Timespace Extensions, fl, pf, 2 perc, 1969; Duo, vn, pf, 1970; Ashbery Settings (J. Ashbery: Clepsydra), S, fl, pf, 1971–2; Astrazioni pomeridiane, orch, 1971–2; Maximus (C. Olson), S, 3 ww, pf, perc, 1972–3; Maximus, to Himself (Olson), S, fl, pf, 1973; Punti di vista, I, Forte Belvedere, pf, 1975–6, II, Montiano, pf, 1977

Solo v/inst with tape: Burst! (J. Kerouac: Desolation Angels), S, tape, 1971; Mappings, vc, tape, 1974; At Delphi (Sioux Indian, trans. F. Densmore), S, tape, 1975; Effetti collaterali, cl, tape, 1976; A Way of Staying (Ashbery: The Thief of Poetry), S, tape, 1977; Second Voyage (Ashbery: Voyage in the Blue), T, tape, 1977–9; Mnemonics, vn, tape, 1982–5

Tape: Whispers out of Time, 1975–6; Partial Distances, 1978; Conditional Assemblies, 1980; In Winter Shine, 1983; Sequence Symbols, 1984

BIBLIOGRAPHY

"Interview with James Dashow," *Composers and the Computer*, ed. C. Roads (Los Altos, CA, 1985), 27

BRUCE SAYLOR

D'Attili, Dario (*b* Rome, Italy, 26 March 1922). Violin maker and restorer. His family left Rome and immigrated to the USA in 1935; in 1938 he went to work at the bench of Fernando Sacconi in the shop of Emil Herrmann in New York. Apart from a period in the armed forces in World War II, he worked with Sacconi continuously until 1973. In 1951, when Herrmann moved from New York, they both joined the firm of REMBERT WURLITZER, establishing a workshop there that became second to none. Following Wurlitzer's death, D'Attili was appointed general manager in 1964. In spite of the demands of restoration work and (following the firm's acquisition of the Hottinger Collection of rare violins in 1965) of appraisals and other business, he continued to make new violins at his home until about 1974. His fine-sounding and much appreciated instruments show a keen understanding of violins by the Italian masters, and a special admiration for those of Pietro Guarneri of Mantua. D'Attili devoted much time to the study of violin varnish, with excellent results. When Wurlitzer closed in 1974, D'Attili became associated with William Moennig & Son of Philadelphia through that firm's purchase of the Hottinger Collection. He has continued to work as an independent appraiser, and is one of the most highly respected authorities on early violins and bows.

CHARLES BEARE

Davenport, (Jack) LaNoue (*b* Dallas, TX, 26 Jan 1922). Recorder player, editor, teacher, and conductor. His early musical experience included playing the trumpet in small jazz bands and in Broadway pit bands, and arranging music for shows in New York. While studying with Erich Katz at the New York College of Music he developed an interest in early music. Since 1949 he has played the recorder, crumhorn, sackbut, and viola da gamba and has arranged and directed much medieval and Renaissance music. He has edited music for the American Recorder Society, which has published several of his compositions, and later was general editor of the series *Music for Recorders* (Associated Music Publishers). He took part in the début of the New York Pro Musica under Greenberg in 1953 and rejoined them from 1960 until 1970; during this time he became director of the instrumental consort and assistant director of the Renaissance band. He toured internationally with them and took part in many recordings. In 1970 he joined the quartet Music for a While. Davenport has taught early music at several American universities and held an appointment as artist-in-residence at Sarah Lawrence College, where he has directed the graduate program in early music performance since 1975.

BIBLIOGRAPHY

J. M. Thomson: *Recorder Profiles* (London, 1972), 27ff

J. M. THOMSON/R

David, Hal (*b* Brooklyn, NY, 25 May 1921). Lyricist, brother of Mack David. He studied journalism before serving in the US Army during World War II, when he wrote sketches and lyrics for troop shows. His first successful song, *The Four Winds and the Seven Seas* (1949), was written while he was working for the bandleader Sammy Kaye. In the late 1950s he began a lengthy and fruitful collaboration with the composer BURT BACHARACH; many of their songs, such as *Walk on by* (1964), *What the world needs now is love* (1965), and *Alfie* (1966), were recorded by their protégée Dionne Warwick. They wrote many songs for films, and won an Academy Award for *Raindrops keep fallin' on my head* (1969, from *Butch Cassidy and the Sundance Kid*). In 1968 they collaborated on a successful Broadway musical, *Promises, Promises*, though a film musical, *Lost Horizon* (1973), was an expensive failure. Thereafter they ceased to work as a team, and David collaborated with Michel Legrand on another musical, *Brainchild*. In 1980 he was elected president of ASCAP.

BIBLIOGRAPHY

"David, Hal," *CBY 1980*

RICHARD C. LYNCH

David, Hans T(heodor) (*b* Speyer, Germany, 8 July 1902; *d* Ann Arbor, MI, 30 Oct 1967). Musicologist. He studied at the universities of Tübingen, Göttingen, and Berlin; he was awarded the doctorate at Berlin in 1928. He left Germany in 1933 for the Netherlands and in 1936 settled in the USA. In the following year he became music editor at the New York Public Library and later was appointed lecturer at New York University (1939), professor at Southern Methodist University (1945), and professor at the University of Michigan (1950). By the age of 26 he had established himself as a leading Bach scholar and later summed up his view of Bach in "Bach: a Portrait in Outline," in *The Bach Reader* (with Arthur Mendel, 1945, rev. 2/1966). His important editions of and commentaries on Bach's *Art of Fugue* and *Musical Offering* show his special interests in contrapuntal and canonic artifice and in cyclical works and unified collections. For the New York Public Library he produced a series of editions of music by the early Moravian settlers in Pennsylvania; for other publishers he edited numerous choral pieces of the 16th century to the 18th. A leading figure in the second generation of American musicologists, he brought the experience of German scholarship to the development of the discipline in the USA.

ARTHUR MENDEL/R

David, Mack (*b* New York, 5 July 1912). Lyricist and composer, brother of Hal David. He started writing lyrics for popular songs in the early 1930s, and has since written over 1000 songs, including many for film and television. He has received eight Academy Award nominations. "Bibbidi, bobbidi, boo" from Walt Disney's *Cinderella* (1949) was particularly popular and is typical of his work. In the early 1950s he wrote songs in collaboration with Jerry Livingston for three film musicals for Dean Martin and Jerry Lewis. He has contributed the title songs of many films, including *Walk on the Wild Side* (1962), *Hud* (1963), *It's a Mad, Mad, Mad, Mad World* (1963), and *The Dirty Dozen* (1967), and wrote the score for *Cat Ballou* (1965). In 1975 he was granted a patent for an "electronic composer," a system for composing a variety of different songs from fragmentary recordings.

RICHARD C. LYNCH

Davidovich, Bella (*b* Baku, Azerbaijan, 16 July 1928). Pianist. She began formal study of the piano at the age of six and made her début three years later in Baku, performing a Beethoven concerto. From 1947 to 1954 she attended the Moscow Conservatory, where she studied with Konstantin Igmunov and later with Yakov Fliyer. While still a student she won first prize in the Chopin Competition in Warsaw (1949), laying the foundation for a flourishing career that included annual concerts with the Leningrad PO from 1950. In 1962 she was appointed to a professorship at the Moscow Conservatory. Davidovich first appeared in the West in Holland in 1967, and in 1971 she made her first tour of Italy. Her foreign engagements were canceled after her son, violinist Dmitri Sitkovetsky (*b* 1954), defected to the USA in 1977, and she left the Soviet Union the following year (she became an American citizen in 1984). She made her American début at Carnegie Hall in 1979 and quickly reestablished her career, giving recitals and playing with leading orchestras throughout Europe and the USA. Her playing of the 19th-century repertory, with which she is most closely associated and of which she has made notable recordings, is colorful and intelligent, though markedly unsentimental.

MICHAEL FLEMING

Davidovsky, Mario (*b* Buenos Aires, Argentina, 4 March 1934). Composer. He studied violin as a child and began to compose at the age of 13. Subsequently he studied composition, theory, and history in Buenos Aires, where his principal teacher was Guillermo Graetzer; he also had lessons with Teodoro Fuchs, Erwin Leuchter, and Ernesto Epstein. In 1958 he studied at the Berkshire Music Center with Babbitt, who encouraged him to settle in the USA; in 1960 he began work at the Columbia-Princeton Electronic Music Center. He has taught at the University of Michigan (1964), the Di Tella Institute of Buenos Aires (1965), the Manhattan School (1968–9), Yale University (1969–70), City College, CUNY (1968–80), and Columbia University (from 1981), where he directs the Columbia-Princeton Electronic Music Center. From 1971 he also served as director of the Composers Conference at Wellesley College (formerly at Bennington College and Johnson State College). He was composer-in-residence at the Berkshire Music Festival in 1981. Davidovsky's many honors include a Koussevitzky fellowship (1958), two Rockefeller fellowships (1963, 1964), two Guggenheim fellowships (1960, 1971), the Brandeis University Creative Arts Award (1964), an award from the American Academy and Institute of Arts and Letters (1965), a Pulitzer Prize (1971), a Naumburg award (1972), and a Guggenheim award (1982). He has received commissions from such major institutions as the Pan American Union (1962), the Fromm Foundation (1963), and the Koussevitzky Foundation (1970; 1981 for Divertimento for Cello and Orchestra). In 1982 he was elected to the Institute of the American Academy and Institute of Arts and Letters.

Davidovsky is best known for his compositions combining live instrumental performance with recorded electronic sounds, and in particular for the *Synchronisms* nos. 1–8, in which he has concentrated on the unique quality of sound inherent to each instrument or group. The instruments use the 12-tone chromatic scale while the nontempered pitch continuum is employed in the tape part. Davidovsky uses extreme and rapid contrasts of speed, pitch, and timbre to create what he calls a "statistical curve of density," a technique found in many of his works. For tape music he draws on the full range of "classical" studio procedures, and he requires performers to match the inventiveness of his electronic composition by using an expanded spectrum of playing techniques. *Inflexions*, *Pennplay*, and the String Quartet no.4 are impressive examples of works for traditional instruments in which Davidovsky employs different kinds of multiple attack and decay, startling dynamic fluctuations, and highly unusual timbral combinations, creating sounds not previously considered possible. He has never been interested in "sound effects"; rather, his concerns are those of continuity and expression. He has sought to obviate the problem of the fixedness of tape music by approaching the limits of perception with regard to register, speed, and textural complexity, so that in repeated hearings the listener will always find something new.

WORKS

Synchronisms: no.1, fl, elec, 1963
no.2, fl, cl, vn, vc, elec, 1964
no.3, vc, elec, 1965
no.4 (Ps. xiii), male vv/mixed chorus, elec, 1967
no.5, perc ens, elec, 1969
no.6, pf, elec, 1970
no.7, orch, elec, 1973
no.8, ww qnt, elec, 1974

Orch: Concertino, perc, str, 1954; Suite sinfonica para "El payaso," 1955; Serie sinfonica, 1959; Contrastes no.1, str orch, elec, 1960; Planos, 1961; Transientes, 1972; Consorts, sym. band, 1980; Divertimento, vc, orch, 1984

Chamber: Str Qt no.1, 1954; Qnt, cl, str, 1955; 3 Pieces, ww qt, 1956; Noneto, 9 insts, 1956; Str Qt no.2, 1958; Trio, cl, tpt, va, 1962; Inflexions, chamber ens, 1965; Junctures, fl, cl, vn, 1966; Music for Solo Vn, 1968; Chacona, vn, vc, pf, 1971; Str Qt no.3, 1976; Pennplay, 16 players, 1978; Str Qt no.4, 1980; Str Trio, 1982; Capriccio, 2 pf, 1985

Vocal: Scenes from Shir-ha-shirim (Song of Solomon), S, 2 T, B, chamber orch, 1975; Romancero (14th–16th century Sp.), S, fl, cl, vn, vc, 1983

Tape: Elec Study no.1, 1961, no.2, 1962, no.3, 1965

Principal publishers: Marks, McGinnis & Marx, Peters

BIBLIOGRAPHY

EwenD

C. Wuorinen: "Mario Davidovsky: Contrastes no.1," *PNM*, iv/2 (1966), 144

S. M. Gryc: "Stratification and Synthesis in Mario Davidovsky's Synchronisms no.6," *ITO*, iv/4 (1978), 8

C. Gagne and T. Caras: "Mario Davidovsky," *Soundpieces: Interviews with American Composers* (Metuchen, NJ, 1982), 131

LESTER TRIMBLE/NOEL B. ZAHLER

Davidson, Mary Wallace (*b* Louisville, KY, 9 June 1935). Music librarian. She studied music at Wellesley College (BA 1957) and library science at Simmons College (MS 1962). After holding library positions in Brookline, Massachusetts (1962–4), and at Radcliffe College (1964–7), she was music librarian at Wellesley from 1967 to 1984, when she was appointed librarian of the Sibley Library at the Eastman School. She was co-author (with James J. Fuld) of *Eighteenth-century American Secular Music Manuscripts: an Inventory* (1980) as well as a member of the editorial staff of *The Boston Composers Project* (1983) and contributor of the article on North American libraries to *The New Grove Dictionary*. From 1983 to 1985 she served as president of the Music Library Association.

PAULA MORGAN

Davies, Dennis Russell (*b* Toledo, OH, 16 April 1944). Conductor. He made his début as a pianist with the Toledo SO in 1961, going on to study with Lonny Epstein and Sascha Gorodnitzki at the Juilliard School, where he also studied conducting under Morel and Mester (BMus 1966, MS 1968, DMA 1972). He made his conducting début in New York in 1968 with the Juilliard Ensemble (later re-formed as the Ensemble), which he cofounded with Berio and directed from 1968 to 1974; from 1969 they gave the "New and Newer Music" series at Lincoln Center. In 1970 Davies conducted the première of Berio's *Opera* at Sante Fe; the same year he appeared at the Royan Festival. His successful début with the Los Angeles PO in 1972 coincided with his appointment as music director of the St. Paul Chamber Orchestra. In 1973 he conducted *Pelléas et Mélisande* for the Netherlands Opera, and appeared at the Aspen and Alaska festivals. He made his Bayreuth début with *Der fliegende Holländer* in 1978, and in 1980 he became music director of the Württemberg State Opera, Stuttgart. He became principal conductor and program director of the Saratoga Performing Arts Center in 1985. Davies made the St. Paul Orchestra one of the most interesting chamber orchestras in the USA, with a repertory including both pre-Classical and contemporary works. He has given the first performances of works by Cage, Carter, Feldman, Berio, Patterson, Scherchen, and Rzewski with the Ensemble, and has conducted the American Composers Orchestra (of which he has been music adviser since 1976) in many concerts of American music. The precision and detail of his presentation of new works contrasts with his less incisive accounts of earlier music, but later concerts have shown a broadening and integration of these two stylistic approaches.

BIBLIOGRAPHY

A. Robertson: "Off and Running," *Opera News*, l/1 (1985), 16

H. Robinson: "Musician of the Month: Dennis Russell Davies," *HiFi/MusAm*, xxxv/7 (1985), 6

RICHARD BERNAS/DENNIS K. McINTIRE

Davis, Anthony (*b* Paterson, NJ, 20 Feb 1951). Jazz pianist and composer. He grew up in New York and studied music at Yale University (BA 1975), where he became the leading young pianist within a circle of musicians whose philosophy derived from the principles of the Association for the Advancement of Creative Musicians. In New Haven in 1973 he was co-founder of Advent, a free-jazz group which included the trombonist George Lewis, then joined the trumpeter Leo Smith's New Delta Ahkri band (1974–7). After moving to New York he played with the trio of the violinist Leroy Jenkins (1977–9), and since 1978 has co-led a duo and quartet with the flutist James Newton. He has also worked with Lewis and the cellist Abdul Wadud in several ensembles, such as the octet Episteme (formed in 1981), that bridge jazz and European classical traditions. As a composer Davis endeavors to control improvisation by providing strict notation. His works are often constructed around complex, ever-changing atonal lines, but they also explore simplicity, as in meditative passages of repeated material inspired by gamelan music. His

Dennis Russell Davies rehearsing with members of the St. Paul Chamber Orchestra

opera X, based on the life of Malcolm X, was developed in a series of workshops at the American Music Theater Festival and performed in Philadelphia in 1985.

RECORDINGS
(selective list)

As leader: *Of Blues and Dreams* (1978, Sackville 3020); *Lady of the Mirrors* (*c*1980, India Navigation 1047); *Episteme* (*c*1981, Gramavision 8101); *Variations in Dream-time* (*c*1983, India Navigation 1056)

As co-leader: with J. Newton: *Hidden Voices* (1979, India Navigation 1041); with J. Hoggard: *Under the Double Moon* (*c*1982, Pausa 7120)

As sideman: L. Smith: *Reflectativity* (1974, Kabell 2); O. Lake: *Life Dance of Is* (1978, Arista Novus 3003); L. Jenkins: *The Legend of Ai Glatson* (1978, Black Saint 0022)

BIBLIOGRAPHY

R. Zabor: "Funny, You *Look* like a Jazz Musician," *Village Voice*, xxiv (2 July 1979), 72

C. J. Safane: "Profile: Anthony Davis," *Down Beat*, xlvi/18 (1979), 64

R. Palmer: "Anthony Davis' New Musical Language," *Rolling Stone*, no.316 (1 May 1980), 26

F. Davis: "Anthony Davis," *Down Beat*, xlix/1 (1982), 21

BARRY KERNFELD

Davis, Ellabelle (*b* New Rochelle, NY, 17 March 1907; *d* New Rochelle, 15 Nov 1960). Soprano. She studied with Reina LeZar, then appeared in recitals with her sister Marie, a pianist, and toured with the Utica Jubilee Singers, before making her New York début at Town Hall on 25 October 1942. She made her operatic début as Aida (a role she also sang at La Scala, in 1949) at the Opera Nacional, Mexico City, on 23 June 1946, and in the same year appeared at the Teatro Gran Rex in Buenos Aires. She toured extensively as a recitalist with the pianist Kelley Wyatt in the USA, South America, Europe, and Israel, performing programs of spirituals, arias, and lieder. In addition to her activities in opera and recitals, she appeared in concerts, giving the première of Lukas Foss's *The Song of Songs* with the Boston SO under Koussevitzky in 1947; her first recital in Carnegie Hall took place the following year, and she also undertook another European tour, during which she sang at the Sibelius Festival in Helsinki. She was a soloist at the Berkshire Music Festival in 1950 and in 1959 performed Richard Strauss's *Vier letzte Lieder* with the National SO.

BIBLIOGRAPHY

SouthernB

R. Abdul: *Blacks in Classical Music* (New York, 1977), 95, 127

P. Turner: *Afro-American Singers* (Minneapolis, 1977), 22

DOMINIQUE-RENÉ DE LERMA

Davis, (Blind) Gary (*b* Lawrence County, SC, 30 April 1896; *d* Neutonville, NJ, 5 May 1972). Gospel and blues singer and guitarist. He was blinded as a child, but learned the harmonica, banjo, and guitar by the age of seven. His left wrist was broken and incorrectly set, and the distortion enabled him to play unorthodox chords. As a member of a country string band, Davis had a broad repertory of rags, reels, carnival tunes, and blues. His free-flowing blues technique, as in *I'm throwin' up my hand* (1935, ARC 35-10-16), had a great influence on other blues guitarists in the eastern USA. In 1933 Davis was ordained a minister in Washington, North Carolina, and afterwards played religious music almost exclusively. *Lord stand by me* (1935, ARC 6-05-65) is a rare recording of his preaching style. *Twelve Gates to the City* (1935, ARC 7-04-55), with its rolling rhythms, reveals his great speed and fluency on the guitar, alternating thumb and finger picking. In 1940 Davis moved to New York as a street singer in Harlem. *Blow Gabriel* and *If I had my way* (1956, Riv. 12-611) show his outstanding guitar technique with its slides and syncopations, and the husky, somewhat high-pitched and strained voice, interspersed with cries and comments, with which he sang his "holy blues." His importance as a leading religious singer was widely recognized only in the late 1960s.

BIBLIOGRAPHY

SouthernB

S. Grossman: Liner notes, *Reverend Gary Davis 1935–1939* (Yazoo 1023, 1970)

——: *Rev. Gary Davis: Blues Guitar* (New York, 1974)

PAUL OLIVER

Davis, Gussie Lord (*b* Dayton, OH, 3 Dec 1863; *d* New York, 18 Oct 1899). Songwriter. He had little formal training in music but studied privately with teachers at the Nelson Musical College, Cincinnati, where he was employed as a janitor. The moderate success of his first published song, *We sat beneath the maple on the hill* (1880), encouraged him to continue writing. Later he became a protégé of the songwriter James E. Stewart, who undoubtedly helped him to gain entry into the music publishing world. In 1890 he moved to New York and within three years had become one of the top songwriters of Tin Pan Alley; in 1895 he won second place in a contest sponsored by the *New York World* for the ten best songwriters in the USA. More than a million copies of his most popular song, *In the Baggage Coach Ahead* (1896), were sold (for title page, *see* AFRO-AMERICAN MUSIC, fig.3). Davis was the first black songwriter to win international acclaim for his ballads, which combined sweet lyrical melodies in waltz rhythms with heart-wrenching texts. He wrote more than 600 songs (sacred, comic, minstrel, and ethnic as well as lyrical), of which approximately 300 were published.

WORKS
(selective list)

Dramatic: A Hot Old Time in Dixie (musical), 1899; King Herod (cantata), 1892

*c*600 songs, lyrics by Davis unless otherwise stated, incl. We sat beneath the maple on the hill, 1880; Irene, Good Night, 1886; The Lighthouse by the Sea, 1886; 'Neath the Maples Long Ago, 1886; The Court House in de Sky (J. Macon), 1887; My Sailor Lad's Return (J. Ring), 1887; Wait till the tide comes in (G. Propheter), 1887; The Fatal Wedding (W. Windom), 1894; Picture 84, 1894; Down in Poverty Row, 1896; In the Baggage Coach Ahead, 1896; Send back the picture and the ring, 1896; Just set a light (H. Neal), 1897; My Creole Sue, 1898

MSS in *DLC*

Principal publishers: Haviland, Howley, G. Propheter, Spaulding & Gray

BIBLIOGRAPHY

SouthernB

D. Gilbert: *Lost Chords: the Diverting Story of American Popular Songs* (Garden City, NY, 1942/*R* 1971)

M. Marcuse: *Tin Pan Alley in Gaslight: Saga of the Songs that Made the Gray Nineties 'Gay'* (Watkins Glen, NY, 1959)

E. Southern: *The Music of Black Americans: a History* (New York, 1971, rev. 2/1983)

E. Southern and J. Wright: "In Retrospect: Gussie Lord Davis," *BPiM*, vi (1978), 188–250 [incl. list of more than 200 songs in the Whittlesey Files, Library of Congress, and reprints of 7 songs]

EILEEN SOUTHERN

Davis, Ivan (*b* Electra, TX, 4 Feb 1932). Pianist. A graduate of North Texas State University (BMus), he studied the piano with Silvio Scionti. He received a Fulbright award and worked with Carlo Zecchi at the Accademia di S. Cecilia, Rome (1955); on returning to the USA he was privately coached by Horowitz. He won the National Federation of Music Clubs Young Artists

(1955), Casella (1958), Busoni (1958), and Liszt (1960) competitions, and made his New York début with a much-praised solo recital at Town Hall in 1959. He received the New York City Handel Medallion in 1961, and made his first appearance with the New York PO at Carnegie Hall the following year. From 1965 to 1971 he was a piano professor at the University of Miami, Coral Gables, and taught at Indiana University, Bloomington, 1971–2. Davis's recordings of concertos by Liszt, Rachmaninoff, and Tchaikovsky display an unashamedly Romantic approach. His strong, metallic sound and brilliant technique are best heard in the most ebullient works of the late 19th-century repertory.

RICHARD BERNAS

Davis, Jessie Bartlett (*b* Morris, IL, Aug 1860; *d* Chicago, IL, 14 May 1905). Actress and singer. She studied in Chicago with F. W. Root and Sara Robinson Duff, and at the age of 15 became a member of Caroline Richings's Old Folks Opera Company. She joined the choir of the Church of the Messiah in Chicago and went on tour with the choir's "H.M.S. Pinafore" company in 1879, singing the role of Buttercup. After a further period of study in New York she made a successful début in Italian opera, performing with Patti in Gounod's *Faust* and Meyerbeer's *Dinorah* (1883). She sang with the Carleton Opera Company in its first season before joining the American Opera Company for two seasons. In 1888 she was engaged as principal contralto for the Bostonians, with whom she spent virtually the rest of her career; her best-known role was as Alan-a-Dale in *Robin Hood* by De Koven and H. B. Smith (1891), in which she introduced the song "Oh, promise me." Davis also wrote poetry, some of which she set to music.

BIBLIOGRAPHY

"Jessie Bartlett Davis," *Illustrated American*, xi (1892), 564

GERALD BORDMAN

Davis, Jimmie [James] **H(ouston)** (*b* Beech Springs, LA, 11 Sept 1902). Country-music and gospel singer. He studied at Louisiana College, Pineville (BA), and Louisiana State University (MS). In the late 1920s, while professor of history at Dodd College in Shreveport, Louisiana, he began singing throughout the Southwest. He was a self-confessed imitator of Jimmie Rodgers's yodeling style and was an accomplished blues performer. He sang hillbilly songs on radio station KWKH in Shreveport and made his first recording for that station's label, singing *Way out on the mountain* to piano accompaniment. He recorded for RCA Victor from 1929 to 1934, when he signed a contract with Decca. He was one of the first (and one of the few) country singers to record with a black accompanist; his principal collaborator was the blues musician Oscar Woods. His first hit for Decca was *Nobody's darlin' but mine* (1935); another was *You are my sunshine* (1940), which has been recorded more than 350 times. Since the early 1960s Davis has been identified almost exclusively with gospel music, recording for the Word label, and was still giving concerts in the early 1980s. He was elected to the Country Music Hall of Fame in 1972. Beginning in the 1930s Davis had an active civil service career in addition to his musical activities. He served two terms as Governor of Louisiana (1944–8 and 1960–64).

BIBLIOGRAPHY

G. McWhiney and G. B. Mills: "Jimmie Davis and his Music: an Interpretation," *Journal of American Culture*, vi/2 (1983), 54

BILL C. MALONE

Davis, John (*b* Paris, France, 1773; *d* Mandeville, LA, 13 June 1839). Entrepreneur and impresario. He arrived in New Orleans in 1809 and established himself in several commercial ventures. In 1819 he completed the rebuilding of the Théâtre d'Orléans (destroyed by fire in 1816), which under his management became a center of New Orleans musical life. Its ballroom was the most renowned in the city before 1840, and its opera company, owing to Davis's regular introduction of excellent French singers and instrumentalists, brought New Orleans to national prominence as a center of French opera. The company presented numerous American premières, including works by Auber, Meyerbeer, Rossini, Donizetti, and Weber, and between 1827 and 1833 undertook six acclaimed tours of the northeastern USA. In 1837 a management crisis and advancing illness forced Davis to retire; his son, Pierre Davis, succeeded him as director of the Théâtre d'Orléans. (*See also* NEW ORLEANS, §1.)

JOHN JOYCE

Davis, Miles (Dewey, III) (*b* Alton, IL, 25 May 1926). Jazz trumpeter, bandleader, and composer. An original, lyrical soloist and a demanding group leader, Davis was the most consistently innovative musician in jazz from the late 1940s through the 1960s.

1. Life. 2. Music.

1. LIFE. Davis grew up in East St. Louis, and took up trumpet at the age of 13; two years later he was already playing professionally. He moved to New York in September 1944, ostensibly to study at the Juilliard School but actually to locate his idol, the jazz saxophonist Charlie Parker. He joined Parker in live appearances and recordings (1945–8), at the same time playing in other combos and touring in Benny Carter's and Billy Eckstine's big bands. In 1948 he began to lead his own bop groups, and he participated in an experimental workshop centered on the arranger Gil Evans. Their collaborations with Gerry Mulligan, John Lewis, and John Carisi culminated in a series of nonet recordings issued under Davis's name and subsequently collected and reissued as *Birth of the Cool*. In 1949 he performed with Sonny Rollins and Art Blakey, and with Tadd Dameron, until heroin addiction interrupted his public career intermittently from mid-1949 to 1953. Although he continued to record with famous bop musicians, including Parker, Rollins, Blakey, J. J. Johnson, Horace Silver, and members of the Modern Jazz Quartet, he worked in clubs infrequently and with inferior accompanists until 1954.

In 1955 Davis appeared informally at the Newport Jazz Festival. His sensational improvisations there brought him widespread publicity and sufficient engagements to establish a quintet (1955–7) with pianist Red Garland, double bass player Paul Chambers, drummer Philly Joe Jones, and tenor saxophonist John Coltrane, who in 1956 was joined and later replaced by Rollins. In May 1957 Davis made the first of several remarkable solo recordings on trumpet and flugelhorn against unusual jazz orchestrations by Gil Evans. In the autumn he organized a short-lived quintet, later joined by alto saxophonist Cannonball Adderley; in the same year he wrote and recorded music in Paris for Louis Malle's film *Ascenseur pour l'échafaud*. Upon his return to the USA he re-formed his original quintet of 1955 with Adderley as a sixth member. For the next five years Davis drew the rhythm sections of his various sextets and quintets from a small pool of players: the pianists Garland, Bill Evans (1958–9), and Wynton

Miles Davis, 1969

Kelly; the drummers Jones and Jimmy Cobb; and the bass player Chambers. Personnel changes increased in early 1963, and finally Davis engaged a new rhythm section as the nucleus of another quintet: bass player Ron Carter (1963–8), pianist Herbie Hancock (1963–8), and drummer Tony Williams (1963–9). To replace Coltrane, who had left in 1960, Davis tried a succession of saxophonists, including Sonny Stitt, Jimmy Heath, Hank Mobley (1961), George Coleman (1963–4), and Sam Rivers; ultimately he settled on Wayne Shorter (1964–70).

These sidemen were by no means entirely faithful to Davis, because of his irascible temperament and his need for frequent periods of inactivity. Nevertheless, the combos of 1955–68 were more stable than his later ones of 1969–75. Often the instrumentation and style of his ever-changing recording groups (up to 14 players) diverged considerably from that of his working groups (generally sextets or septets). Influential new members joined him in the late 1960s and early 1970s: the keyboard players Chick Corea, Joe Zawinul, and Keith Jarrett; the electric guitarist John McLaughlin; the bass players Dave Holland and Michael Henderson; the drummers Jack DeJohnette, Billy Cobham, and Al Foster; and the percussionist Airto Moreira. As with Davis's previous colleagues, the excellence of these sidemen bore eloquent witness to his stature among jazz musicians.

For years Davis, who trained as a boxer, had always been physically equal to the exertions of playing jazz trumpet; however, in the mid-1970s, serious ailments and the effects of an automobile accident obliged him to retire. He suffered for five years from pneumonia and other afflictions. But in 1980 he made new recordings, and in the summer of 1981 began to tour extensively with new quintets and sextets. Although he was incapacitated by a stroke in February 1982, he resumed an active career in the spring of that year. Only the drummer Al Foster has remained in his groups through the mid-1970s and into the 1980s. New young members include another Bill Evans, on tenor and soprano saxophones (1980–84), the guitarist John Scofield (from 1983), and the saxophonist Branford Marsalis (from 1984).

2. Music. Davis rejected the standards set for jazz trumpeters in the 1940s by Dizzy Gillespie's bop improvisations, partly because of his limited technique (some of his early recordings were marred by errors), but principally because his interests lay elsewhere. He created relaxed, tuneful melodies centered in the middle register. Not reluctant to repeat ideas, he drew from such a small collection of melodic formulae that many solos seemed as much composed as improvised. Harmonically he was also conservative, and tended to play in close accord with his accompanists. Beneath this apparent pervasive simplicity lay a subtle sense of rhythmic placement and expressive nuance.

These characteristics have remained central to Davis's playing throughout his career. Their mature expression first came on the nonet sessions (1949–50), which inspired the cool jazz movement. Davis's liking for moderation meshed perfectly with his arrangers' concern for smooth instrumental textures, restrained dynamics and rhythms, and a balance between ensemble and solo passages. In the 1950s, as cool jazz became popular, Davis ignored this style, instead surrounding himself with fiery bop players.

Davis's fallow period in the early 1950s came to an end with his celebrated blues improvisation *Walkin'* (1954). In a session with Sonny Rollins in the same year he introduced the stemless harmon mute to jazz; its intense sound led to delicate recordings by his first quintet (*Bye Bye Blackbird*, 1956; *'Round Midnight*, September–October 1956), which are even more memorable than the fierce swing of the Garland–Chambers–Jones rhythm section on fast bop tunes. Many jazz trumpeters turned to flugelhorn after Davis had demonstrated its potential in his collaborations with Gil Evans; these recordings offer rare examples in jazz of lush orchestral settings with sustained emotional substance, and present an ideal foil for the relaxed tunefulness, melodic and harmonic simplicity, and subtle swing of Davis's improvisations (ex. 1).

Ex.1 Davis's improvisation on the first chorus of Gershwin's *Summertime*, from *Porgy and Bess* (1958, Col. CL1274), transcr. B. Kernfeld

By the late 1950s Davis had tired of bop structures, and turned to a new approach formulated at this time by Gil Evans and Bill Evans and later called "modal playing." However, the use of modes in Davis's 1958–9 recordings (*Milestones*, *So What*, *Flamenco Sketches*) had less significance for the future than the slowing of harmonic rhythm. In place of fast-moving, functional chord progressions, Davis used diatonic ostinatos ("vamps" in jazz parlance), drones, half-tone oscillations familiar from flamenco music, and tonic–dominant alternations in the bass line. (The inadvertent alteration of the titles *Flamenco Sketches* and *All Blues* on Bill Evans's liner notes to the famous album *Kind of Blue* has caused great confusion. *Flamenco Sketches* is a composition in five segments: the first and third are in major keys, the second and fifth suggest modal scales, and the fourth is based on a flamenco-like oscillation of D and E♭ major chords, giving the piece its name; *All Blues* is indeed, as Davis's later recordings of it prove, a 12-bar blues.)

Through 1964, on recordings and later in public, Davis's combos performed a small repertory of bop blues, popular songs, and ostinato tunes. During these years the technical and emotional compass of his playing expanded greatly. The addition to the group of Wayne Shorter led to a change in repertory that began with *E.S.P.* in 1965. Discarding standard tunes, Davis's groups recorded improvisations in a chordless, tonally ambiguous bop style, as well as new ostinato pieces on which the Hancock–Carter–Williams rhythm section found extraordinarily flexible ways of expressing 4/4 rhythms.

In 1968–9 Davis popularized a form of jazz subsequently called "fusion." *In a Silent Way* and *Bitches Brew* of 1969 blended acoustic sounds with electronic instruments, and melodic jazz improvisations with open-ended rock accompaniment. In the 1970s his assorted groups added electronically altered trumpet, Indian sitar and *tablā*, African or Brazilian percussion, and funky black-American dance rhythms to this music. Since resuming his career in the 1980s, Davis has returned principally to the conventions of jazz-rock which he had helped to establish, though he now also plays blues and, on occasion, popular songs from past decades. He concentrates on the trumpet, but also plays synthesizer. Already the innovator of more distinct styles than any other jazz musician, he remains a stimulating leader and masterful soloist.

See also JAZZ, §VI, 2, 4, and MODAL JAZZ.

RECORDINGS
(selective list)

TO 1951

As sideman with C. Parker: Billie's Bounce/Now's the Time (1945, Savoy 573); A Night in Tunisia/Ornithology (1946, Dial 1002); Yardbird Suite (1946, Dial 1003); Half Nelson (1947, Savoy 951); Ah-leu Cha (1948, Savoy 939); Au privave/Star Eyes (1951, Merc./Clef 11087)

As leader, all recorded for Capitol: Move/Budo (1949, 15404); Jeru/Godchild (1949, 60005); Boplicity/Israel (1949, 60011)

FROM 1951
(recorded for Prestige)

Morpheus/Blue Room (1951, 734); Dig (1951, 777); *Collector's Items* (1953, 1956, 7044); Four (1954, 898); Walkin' (1954, 45-157); *Miles Davis Quintet* (1954, 185); *Miles Davis Quintet* (1954, 187); *Miles Davis All Stars* (1954, 196); *Miles Davis All Stars* (1954, 200); *The Musings of Miles* (1955, 7007); *Milt and Miles* (1955, 7034); *Miles* (1955, 7014); *Relaxin'* (1956, 7129); *Steamin'* (1956, 7200); *Workin'* (1956, 7166); *Cookin'* (1956, 7094); 'Round Midnight (1956, 45-413)

(recorded for Columbia)

'Round about Midnight (1955–6, CL949), incl. Bye Bye Blackbird, 'Round Midnight; *Miles Ahead* (1957, CL1041); *Jazz Track* (1957–8, CL1268); *Milestones* (1958, CL1193); *Miles and Monk at Newport* (1958, CL2178); *Porgy and Bess* (1958, CL1274), incl. Summertime; *Jazz at the Plaza*, i (1958, C32470); *Kind of Blue* (1959, CL1355), incl. So What, Flamenco Sketches; *Sketches of Spain* (1959–60, CL1480)

Someday my Prince will Come (1961, CS8456); *In Person – Friday and Saturday Nights at the Blackhawk* (1961, C2S820); *Miles Davis at Carnegie Hall* (1961, CS8612); *Seven Steps to Heaven* (1963, CS8851); *Miles Davis in Europe* (1963, CS8983); *My Funny Valentine* (1964, CS9106); *Four and More* (1964, CS9253); *E.S.P.* (1965, CS9150); *Miles Smiles* (1966, CS9401)

Sorcerer (1967, CS9532); *Nefertiti* (1967, CS9594); *Miles in the Sky* (1968, CS9628); *Filles de Kilimanjaro* (1968, CS9750); *In a Silent Way* (1969, CS9875); *Bitches Brew* (1969, GP26); *Big Fun* (1969–72, PG32866); *A Tribute to Jack Johnson* (1970, KC30455); *Miles Davis at Fillmore* (1970, KG30038); *Live-Evil* (1970, KC30954)

Get Up with It (1970–74, KG33236); *On the Corner* (1972, KC31906); *Agharta* (1975, PG33967); *Star People* (1983, FG38657); *Decoy* (1983–4, FC38991)

BIBLIOGRAPHY

P. Harris: "Nothing but Bop? 'Stupid,' Says Miles," *Down Beat*, xvii/2 (1950), 18

A. Hodeir: *Jazz: its Evolution and Essence* (New York, 1956/*R* 1975)

N. Hentoff: "An Afternoon with Miles Davis," *Jazz Review*, i/2 (1958), 9

M. Davis: "Self-Portrait," *The Jazz Word*, ed. D. Cerulli (New York, 1960)

M. James: *Miles Davis* (New York, 1961); repr. in *Kings of Jazz*, ed. S. Green (New York, 1978)

N. Hentoff: *The Jazz Life* (New York, 1961/*R* 1975)

D. Heckman: "Miles Davis Times Three," *Down Beat*, xxix/23 (1962), 16

"Davis, Miles (Dewey, Jr.)," *CBY 1962*

J. Goldberg: *Jazz Masters of the Fifties* (New York, 1965/*R* 1980)

G. Hoefer: "The Birth of the Cool," *Down Beat*, xxxii/21 (1965), 24

——: "Early Miles," *Down Beat*, xxxiv/7 (1967), 16

D. DeMichael: "Miles Davis," *Rolling Stone*, no.48 (13 Dec 1969), 22

D. Locke: "Many Miles," *Jazz Monthly*, no.178 (1969), 18

L. Feather: *From Satchmo to Miles* (New York, 1972)

T. Hino, ed.: *Miles Davis: Jazz Improvisation* (Tokyo, 1975) [transcriptions]

T. Mortensen: *Miles Davis: den ny jazz* (Copenhagen, 1977)

S. Isacoff: *Miles Davis* (New York, 1978) [transcriptions]

M. Gridley: *Jazz Styles* (Englewood Cliffs, NJ, 1978)

F. Kerschbaumer: *Miles Davis: stilkritische Untersuchungen zur musikalischen Entwicklung seines Personalstils* (Graz, Austria, 1978)

B. Goldberg: *WKCR-FM Miles Davis Festival Handbook* (New York, 1979) [discography]

D. Baker: *The Jazz Style of Miles Davis* (Lebanon, IN, 1980)

B. Kernfeld: *Adderley, Coltrane, and Davis at the Twilight of Bebop: the Search for Melodic Coherence (1958–59)* (diss., Cornell U., 1981)

I. Carr: *Miles Davis* (New York, 1982)

D. Breskin: "Searching for Miles: Theme and Variations on the Life of a Trumpeter," *Rolling Stone*, no.405 (29 Sept 1983), 46

H. Brofsky: "Miles Davis and *My Funny Valentine*: the Evolution of a Solo," *Black Music Research Journal* (1983), 23
J. Chambers: *Milestones*, i: *The Music and Times of Miles Davis to 1960* (Toronto, 1983); ii: *The Music . . . since 1960* (New York, 1985)
H. Mandel: "Miles Davis," *Down Beat*, li/12 (1984), 16

BARRY KERNFELD

Davis, Peter G(raffam) (*b* Concord, MA, 3 May 1936). Music critic. He was educated at Harvard (BA 1958) and Columbia (MA 1962). From 1969 to 1981 he was on the music staff of the *New York Times*, and from 1981 has been music critic for *New York* magazine. Forthright in the expression of his opinions, Davis writes clearly and often with considerable passion, particularly about opera and singing, his special interests; he has a fondness for opera composers of the second rank, such as Massenet, Mascagni, and Schreker. Also noteworthy are his observations about recording and its place in the context of performance.

PATRICK J. SMITH

Davis, Richard (*b* Chicago, IL, 15 April 1930). Jazz double bass player. He studied privately from 1945 to 1954 while playing with a number of local orchestras in Chicago. His experience in dance bands led to engagements with Ahmad Jamal (1953–4) and Don Shirley (1954–5). In the late 1950s he worked largely with Sarah Vaughan, where his precision of time and tone became evident. The early 1960s were very productive for Davis, as documented on many recordings; during this period he also worked on a freelance basis in symphony orchestras, performing under Stravinsky and Leonard Bernstein. A highly sought-after player, he has recorded with musicians as varied as Jimmy Smith and Roland Kirk, and can be heard in the context of a large ensemble on recordings by the Thad Jones–Mel Lewis Orchestra. He has also published a tutor entitled *Introductory Lecture on Jazz Bass* (1972).

RECORDINGS
(selective list)

As sideman: E. Dolphy: *Out to Lunch* (1964, BN 84163); A. Hill: *Point of Departure* (1964, BN 84167); B. Ervin: *The Blues Book* (1964, Prst. 7340); B. Webster: *See You at the Fair* (1964, Imp. 65); T. Jones–M. Lewis: *Live at the Village Vanguard* (1967, Solid State 18016); *The Jazz Composer's Orchestra* (1968, JCOA 1001–2)

BIBLIOGRAPHY

SouthernB
D. Morgenstern: "Richard Davis: the Complete Musician," *Down Beat*, xxxiii/11 (1966), 23
D. C. Hunt: "The Contemporary Approach to Jazz Bass," *Jazz & Pop*, viii/8 (1969), 18
T. Tolnay: "Double Take: Ron Carter/Richard Davis," *Down Beat*, xxxix/9 (1972), 14
A. Berle: "Bassist Richard Davis: from Bo Diddley to Stravinsky," *Guitar Player*, xii/6 (1978), 30

BILL BENNETT

Davis, Ruth (*b* Philadelphia, PA, 1928; *d* Philadelphia, 2 Jan 1970). Gospel singer. In 1945 she formed a family group, the Davis Sisters, with her three sisters Thelma (1930–63), Audrey (1932–82), and Alfreda (*b* 1935); all had been members of the junior choir at the Mount Zion Fire Baptized Holiness Church in Philadelphia. Following their first appearance at Port Deposit, Maryland, early in 1946, they toured the Northeast performing in churches and schools. They began recording in 1947 and had their first hit, *Too close to heaven*, in 1953, followed by others including *He'll understand and say, well done* (1958) and *Twelve gates to the city* (1960). Ruth Davis, who subscribed to the "hard" gospel technique of straining the voice for spiritual and dramatic effect, provided the lead on these recordings. The group had a bluesy sound and their accompaniment, supplied by the pianist Curtis Dublin (*d c*1965), was full of jazz riffs. Imogene Greene and Jacqui Verdell also sang intermittently with them.

BIBLIOGRAPHY

T. Heilbut: *The Gospel Sound: Good News and Bad Times* (New York, 1971/*R*1975)
H. C. Boyer: "An Overview: Gospel Music Comes Of Age," *Black World*, xxiii/1 (1973), 42, 79

HORACE CLARENCE BOYER

Davison, A(rchibald) T(hompson) (*b* Boston, MA, 11 Oct 1883; *d* Brant Rock, MA, 6 Feb 1961). Music educator and choral conductor. He studied at Harvard University (BA 1906, MA 1907, PhD 1908). Except for his organ studies with Widor in Paris (1908–9), he was associated with Harvard throughout his career, as Austin Teaching Fellow (1909–10), organist and choirmaster (1910), lecturer (1912–17), assistant professor (1917–20), associate professor (1920–29), professor of choral music (1929–40), and James Edward Ditson Professor of Music (1940–54); he was also curator of the Isham Memorial Library (1941–55). As director of the Harvard Glee Club (1912–33) and the Radcliffe Choral Society (1913–28), he introduced the repertory of serious music, especially Renaissance *a cappella* music, to American collegiate choral societies. Davison published important educational works on choral conducting and composition, and several historical studies of church music and music education. The *Historical Anthology of Music*, compiled in collaboration with Apel (1946), is well known to students and teachers of music history, and his Concord Series of Educational Music was the most widely used in the USA before World War II. His compositions, written early in his career, include two comic operas, a musical, the symphonic poem *Hero and Leander*, and the *Tragic Overture*.

WRITINGS

The Harmonic Contributions of Claude Debussy (diss., Harvard U., 1908)
Protestant Church Music in America (Boston, 1920, enlarged 2/1933)
Music Education in America (New York, 1926)
Choral Conducting (Cambridge, MA, 1940)
The Technique of Choral Composition (Cambridge, MA, 1946)
ed., with W. Apel: *Historical Anthology of Music*, i (Cambridge, MA, 1946, rev. 2/1950); ii (Cambridge, 1950)
Bach and Handel: the Consummation of the Baroque in Music (Cambridge, MA, 1951)
Church Music: Illusion and Reality (Cambridge, MA, 1952)

BIBLIOGRAPHY

Essays on Music in Honor of Archibald Thompson Davison by his Associates (Cambridge, MA, 1957) [incl. complete list of writings, compositions, editions, and arrangements]
D. G. Tovey: *Archibald Thompson Davison: Harvard Musician and Scholar* (diss., U. of Michigan, 1979)

JON NEWSOM/R

Davison, Wild Bill [William Edward] (*b* Defiance, OH, 5 Jan 1906). Jazz cornetist. After touring with various bands he worked mostly in Chicago from 1927 to 1932; this was followed by a stay of several years in the Milwaukee area. After some of his recordings had been issued in 1940 Davison's playing began to attract widespread attention, and he moved to New York, where he became a stalwart of Eddie Condon's sessions and also frequently led his own groups. Through most of his career he preferred to play cornet rather than trumpet, and for one fascinating period he also doubled on E♭ valve trombone. During the 1970s and 1980s he undertook many overseas tours.

Davison's early recordings (from the 1920s) reveal a clear dependence on Bix Beiderbecke, but he soon developed a highly individual, robust style, exciting in fast numbers and warmly sentimental in ballads, that he maintained throughout his long career. His driving lead, couched in a flamboyant, husky tone, usually imparted tremendous zest to dixieland-type ensembles. His solos were never intricate, and his improvisations generally embellished the melody rather than delving deeply into the underlying harmonies.

RECORDINGS
(selective list)

As leader: Ghost of a Chance (1956, Col. CL871)

As sideman: A. Hodes: Shine (1945, BN 532); G. Wettling: Collier's Clambake (1951, Col. CL6189); E. Condon: I Can't Give you Anything but Love (1953, Col. CL547), At the Jazzband Ball (1955, Col. B2083)

BIBLIOGRAPHY

G. Hoefer: "The Hot Box," *Down Beat*, xv/7 (1948), 12

M. Jones: "Davison goes Commercial," *Melody Maker* (15 Nov 1975), 52

——: "Wild Man of the Cornet," *Melody Maker* (13 Jan 1979), 19

E. Cook: "On the Right Track," *Jazz Journal International*, xxxiv/4 (1981), 6

——: "Condon and Beyond," *Jazz Journal International*, xxxiv/5 (1981), 24

JOHN CHILTON

Davisson, Ananias (*b* Virginia, 2 Feb 1780; *d* Weyer's Cove, Rockingham Co., VA, 21 Oct 1857). Composer, printer, and tunebook compiler. His *Kentucky Harmony* (Harrisonburg, VA, 1816/*R*1976, 5/1826) was the first shape-note tunebook to be published in the South and the first of 13 shape-note tunebooks to be published before 1860 in the Shenandoah Valley. Davisson printed each of his tunebooks himself, following *Kentucky Harmony* with *Supplement to the Kentucky Harmony* (Harrisonburg, 1820, 3/1825), *An Introduction to Sacred Music* (Harrisonburg, 1821), and *A Small Collection of Sacred Music* (Mount Vernon, VA, ?1826). In spite of the term "Supplement" in its title, the *Supplement to the Kentucky Harmony* was the most innovative of Davisson's tunebooks, containing a much larger proportion of folk hymns and thus a greater orientation toward the South than his *Kentucky Harmony*. Davisson claimed 47 tune settings which are predominantly in the southern folk-hymn style; some of these, including the most popular, "Idumea" and "Tribulation," were among the tunes most frequently reprinted in later Shenandoah Valley tunebooks, as well as those of the deep South, such as William Walker's *Southern Harmony* (1835) and B. F. White and E. J. King's *The Sacred Harp* (1844).

See also HYMNODY, §2(i) and ex.2, and SHAPE-NOTE HYMNODY, §2.

BIBLIOGRAPHY

H. Eskew: *Shape-note Hymnody in the Shenandoah Valley, 1816–1860* (diss., Tulane U., 1966)

R. A. B. Harley: *Ananias Davisson: Southern Tune-book Compiler* (diss., U. of Michigan, 1972)

D. W. Music: "Ananias Davisson, Robert Boyd, Reubin Monday, John Martin, and Archibald Rhea in East Tennessee, 1816–26," *American Music*, i/3 (1983), 72

HARRY ESKEW

Davy, Gloria (*b* New York, 29 March 1931). Soprano. She studied with Belle Julie Soudent at the Juilliard School (1948–53). In 1953 she scored a notable success in a world tour of *Porgy and Bess* and then sang the Countess in the American première of *Capriccio* on 2 April 1954, the same year in which she made her Town Hall (New York) début with the Little Orchestra Society. After twice winning the Marian Anderson Prize, she made her European operatic début in 1957 at Nice as Aida, the role in which she also made her débuts at the Metropolitan Opera (12 February 1958), the Vienna Staatsoper (1959), and Covent Garden (1960). In 1958 her success as Gluck's Armida in a Milan concert, and in recitals at the Brussels World Fair, established her European career. She is also a performer of contemporary works, notably in the première of Henze's *Nachtstücke und Arien* at Donaueschingen (1957) and the 1972 version of Stockhausen's *Momente* (in concert and on record). The latter work especially demonstrates her dramatic authority, linguistic skills, and infectious sense of humor.

RICHARD BERNAS/R

Dawson, Alan (*b* Marietta, PA, 14 July 1929). Jazz drummer. He studied with Charles Alden in Boston in the early 1950s while working with many local jazz groups, and toured with Lionel Hampton in 1953. In 1957 he joined the percussion faculty of the Berklee School of Music, beginning an association that lasted until 1974. In addition to his academic commitments and continuing work in the Boston area Dawson has remained active as a touring and recording drummer; his most frequent and productive collaboration during the early 1960s was with the pianist Jaki Byard and the saxophonist Booker Ervin, with whom he made an excellent series of LPs for Prestige in 1963–5. From 1968 to 1974 he was a member of the Dave Brubeck Quartet, and recorded an outstanding solo on a new version of *Take Five* (1973, Atl. 1641). A gifted and resourceful drummer, Dawson is also an accomplished vibraphonist, and has published several tutors including *Blues and Odd Time Signatures* (1972) and, with Don DeMichael, *A Manual for the Modern Drummer* (1964).

BIBLIOGRAPHY

D. Morgenstern: "The Poll Winner as Teacher: Alan Dawson," *Down Beat*, xxxiii/19 (1966), 27

A. Dawson: "The Book," *Jazz Journal*, xxiii/11 (1970), 25

M. Gardner: "Alan Dawson," *Jazz Journal*, xxiv/4 (1971), 2

BILL BENNETT

Dawson, Mary Cardwell (*b* Meridian, NC, 14 Feb 1894; *d* Washington, DC, 19 March 1962). Opera director and teacher. She studied at the New England Conservatory and Chicago Musical College. In 1927 she founded the Cardwell School of Music in Pittsburgh, and later established the Cardwell Dawson Choir, which won prizes at the Century of Progress Exposition in Chicago (1933–4) and the New York World's Fair (1939–40). Her production of *Aida* for the 1941 meeting in Pittsburgh of the National Association of Negro Musicians (of which she was then president) led to the establishment that year of her National Negro Opera Company. The group's official début (in another performance of *Aida*) took place at the Syrian Mosque in Pittsburgh on 30 October 1941. During the next 21 years the company's repertory included Verdi's *La traviata*, R. Nathaniel Dett's *The Ordering of Moses*, and Clarence Cameron White's *Ouanga*, which was the first production at the Metropolitan Opera House to be staged by an outside company. Musicians who studied or worked with Dawson included Robert McFerrin, Camilla Williams, Lawrence Winters, McHenry Boatwright, Carol Brice, Edward Boatner, Ahmad Jamal, and Erroll Garner.

BIBLIOGRAPHY

SouthernB

Obituary, *New York Herald Tribune* (21 March 1962)

R. Adbul: *Blacks in Classical Music* (New York, 1977), 148

DOMINIQUE-RENÉ DE LERMA

Dawson, William Levi (*b* Anniston, AL, 23 Sept 1899). Composer and conductor. He graduated from Tuskegee Institute, then obtained degrees from the Horner Institute of Fine Arts, Kansas City (BMus), and the American Conservatory (MMus). He played trombone in the Chicago Civic Orchestra and taught in several colleges before returning to Tuskegee as director of music. Dawson's Tuskegee Choir gave many concerts in the USA and in Europe, establishing his reputation as a conductor. After he retired from Tuskegee in 1955 he was sent to Spain by the US State Department to tour as a conductor. His music, written in a neoromantic style, consistently employs black folksong idioms. Recordings of his works include *Negro Folk Symphony*, *Out in the Fields*, and *Spirituals*.

WORKS

(selective list)

Orch: Out in the Fields, S, orch, 1928; Scherzo, 1930; Negro Folk Sym., 1934, rev. 1952; A Negro Work Song, 1940

Chamber: Pf Trio, 1925; Vn Sonata, 1927

Vocal: Numerous choral partsongs, incl. An Easter Canticle; many choral and solo arrs. of spirituals and other Negro folksong

Principal publishers: Kjos, Shawnee, Warner

BIBLIOGRAPHY

EwenD; *SouthernB*

E. Southern: *The Music of Black Americans: a History* (New York, 1971, rev. 2/1983)

H. Roach: *Black American Music: Past and Present*, i (Malabar, FL, 1973, rev. 1985)

J. Spady: *William L. Dawson: A Umum Tribute* (Philadelphia, 1981)

M. H. Malone: *William Levi Dawson: American Music Educator* (diss., Florida State U., 1981)

H. Roach: *Black American Music: Past and Present*, ii (Malabar, FL, 1985)

EILEEN SOUTHERN

Day [Kappelhoff], **Doris** (*b* Cincinnati, OH, 3 April 1924). Singer and actress. She sang with the Bob Crosby band and Fred Waring before her recordings with Les Brown's Band of Renown, particularly *Sentimental Journey* (1944), brought her nationwide recognition. She made her first film, *Romance on the High Seas*, in which she introduced the song "It's Magic," in 1948, and won Academy awards for her performances of "Secret Love" in *Calamity Jane* (1954) and "Que sera, sera" in *The Man Who Knew Too Much* (1955). Her greatest success, however, was her role in *Love Me or Leave Me* (1955). She appeared in a total of 39 films including, in the 1960s, a series of sex comedies, in which she portrayed a naive, virginal heroine with freckles and a shy smile. Her singing, based on the style of Ella Fitzgerald, was mellifluous, ingratiating and even intimate.

BIBLIOGRAPHY

"Day, Doris," *CBY 1954*

A. E. Hotchner: *Doris Day: Her Own Story* (New York, 1976)

D. Ewen: *All the Years of American Popular Music* (Englewood Cliffs, NJ, 1977)

C. Young: *The Films of Doris Day* (New York, 1977)

ARNOLD SHAW

Dayton. City in Ohio (pop. 203,371; metropolitan area 830,070). It was settled in 1796. The first musical association was the Pleyel Society, organized in 1823 under the leadership of John W. Van Cleve, who played and taught a variety of instruments and was organist at Christ Church. The Dayton Philharmonic Society, formed in 1836 for the study of sacred music, and a series of concerts organized in 1840 by Lewis Huesman, a piano and organ teacher, followed. Pianos were manufactured by William Bourne from 1837 to 1840, during which time Dayton had only 1000 inhabitants. By 1849 the city had adopted music as a branch of study in its schools. After the Civil War several performing organizations were formed, including the Harmonia Society (a combination of the Sociale Sängerbund and Frohsinn Society, 1861), a later Dayton Philharmonic Society (1874), and the Young Men's Christian Association Orchestra (1886). The Mozart Musical and Literary Society (1888) and Chaminade Club (1902) merged in 1914 to form the Women's Music Club, which in 1928 was renamed the Dayton Music Club to allow the admission of men.

Sacred music has a strong tradition in Dayton. The Lorenz Publishing Co., founded in 1890 by E. S. Lorenz, specialized in Sunday-school music and periodical collections of anthems for the church service, eventually becoming one of the largest publishers of educational and religious music in the USA. The WESTMINSTER CHOIR COLLEGE grew out of the choir at the Dayton Westminster Church, where John Finley Williamson was engaged as director of music in 1920. Williamson founded the school in 1926 to train young people as church music directors. The college moved to Ithaca, New York, in 1929 and to Princeton, New Jersey, in 1932.

The Dayton PO was founded in 1933 by Paul Katz, who conducted the orchestra until 1975 when he was succeeded by Charles Wendelken-Wilson. From an ensemble of 26 players giving four concerts a season in the auditorium of the Dayton Art Institute (capacity 600), the orchestra had grown to over 100 by the 1980s and gives at least 25 concerts a season. The Victory Theatre (1250) was the orchestra's home from 1935 until 1943, when it moved to Memorial Hall (2500). In 1934 the orchestra instituted an annual series of four children's concerts. A Saturday Pops Series was added in 1978, presenting a cabaret-style program at the Dayton Convention and Exhibition Center (3000–5000). Guest performers of international reputation appear each season with the Dayton PO. Two string quartets, a woodwind quintet, a brass quintet, and a percussion trio are also sponsored by the orchestra. The Dayton Philharmonic Youth Orchestra was founded in 1937 by Katz. Other ensembles active for several years were the Dayton Piano Symphony (founded 1926) comprising 10 pianos, the Civic Concert Band (1933), the Dayton Civic Harmonica Band (1937), and many vocal groups. Two concert series, Vanguard Concerts and Soirées Musicales, bring well-known visiting artists to Dayton.

The Dayton Ballet Company was founded by Josephine and Hermene Schwarz as the Experimental Group for Young Dancers in 1937. It is considered one of the best regional dance companies in the USA, offering programs in Victory Theatre. The Dayton Contemporary Dance Company, founded by its artistic director Jeraldyne Blunden in 1968, has received wide recognition.

Choral groups active in the city are the Dayton Music Appreciation Choral Club (1934), the Dayton Rotary Boys' Choir (1943), and the Dayton Bach Society (1974).

The Dayton Opera Association (founded 1960) opened in 1961 with a performance of *Tosca*. It receives financial support from the Opera Guild (1963), which also organizes opera workshops, open dress rehearsals, and lecture-demonstrations at elementary, secondary, and adult-education levels.

Such institutions as the music departments of the University of Dayton (which offers bachelor's degrees in music, music therapy, and music education and also runs a Historic Keyboard Society), Wright State University (BM, BMEd, and MMEd), and Sinclair Community College contribute to the city's concert life, as do local churches, notably the Westminster Presbyterian Church and Grace United Methodist Church.

BIBLIOGRAPHY

History of Dayton, Ohio: with Portraits and Biographical Sketches of some of its Pioneer and Prominent Citizens (Dayton, 1889)

A. W. Drury: *History of the City of Dayton and Montgomery County, Ohio* (Chicago, 1909)

C. R. Conover, ed.: *Dayton and Montgomery County Resources and People* (New York, 1932)

C. H. Schisler: *A History of Westminster Choir College, 1926–1973* (diss., Indiana U., 1976)

D. Winkler, ed.: *Dayton Cultural Guide* (Miamisburg, OH, 1982)

BEVERLEY A. ERVINE

Deagan. Firm of instrument makers. John C. Deagan (*b* England, 1852; *d* Hermosa Beach, CA, 1932) established in 1880 the J. C. Deagan Musical Bells Co. of St. Louis, which moved to San Francisco in 1891 (becoming J. C. Deagan & Co. in 1895) and then to Chicago in 1897. He had some knowledge of acoustics, and his firm's instruments were manufactured to a high degree of precision; he was responsible for the recognition of $a' = 440$ as standard pitch. The first instrument manufactured by his firm was an orchestral glockenspiel that had steel bars tuned according to Hermann von Helmholtz's principles. This was followed by cathedral chimes (1886), the first xylophone of orchestral quality (1886), and tuned sleigh bells (1893). The firm's range of products was gradually expanded, mostly by the addition of novelty instruments, many of which were invented by Deagan himself; these included shaker chimes, tuned cowbells, tubaphones, tapaphones, and rattles. Later the company made orchestral bells, precision tuning forks and bars, and organ, orchestral, clock, and dinner chimes. By 1910 the Deagan catalogue consisted of 600 items, including 63 models of glockenspiels, 80 xylophones, and 60 sets of chimes; in 1916 the first large, electrically driven, tubular brass church bells were introduced. Two important innovations made by the firm were a vibraphone with aluminum alloy tone bars (1927) and the Celesta-Chime, an electric tower carillon (1937). In 1961 the firm introduced three new marimbas, a concert xylophone, "symphonic" orchestral chimes, a deluxe bell-lyra, and a new glockenspiel. In 1978 Deagan became associated with the Slingerland Drum Co. (*see* SLINGERLAND) as a division of C. G. Conn.

EDMUND A. BOWLES

Dearborn, David M. (*b* 1810; *d* 1865). Bass viol maker. He was apprenticed to Abraham Prescott and moved with him to Concord, New Hampshire, in 1833. Dearborn's first datable instrument is a five-string viol of 1836. He was in partnership with his brother Andrew in the late 1830s. From 1843 to 1847 he was in partnership with the instrument dealer and maker Daniel B. Bartlett as Dearborn & Bartlett and they maintained a music store in Concord on the main street. According to a broadside of the 1840s they sold "premium bass and double bass viols" of their own manufacture, and various brass and string instruments and accessories made in New York and Boston; they also had acquired "the stock and interest in the manufacture of melodions" from Charles Austin, a maker of seraphines, melodions, and other reed organs. Newspaper advertisements containing similar information appeared in 1843 and 1844. Although the firm of Dearborn & Bartlett is not listed in any of the Concord directories of the 1840s, the firm of Austin & Dearborn appears in the New England trade directory for 1849, and Liscom, Dearborn & Co. in a Concord directory of 1856. He also worked with his nephew, Lyman Dearborn, in the 1840s and 1850s. Dearborn's bowed string instruments are similar in design to Prescott's. The bass viols and double basses show a careful selection of woods and varnish and excellent workmanship.

FREDERICK R. SELCH

Dearie, Blossom (*b* East Durham, NY, 28 April 1926). Popular singer and pianist. She began her career as a member of the Blue Flames, a vocal group within Woody Herman's orchestra, and the Blue Reys, a similar group in Alvino Rey's band. In 1952 she went to Paris, where she performed with Annie Ross and also formed her own vocal group, the Blue Stars, whose jazz rendition of *Lullaby of Birdland* (sung in French) was a big hit in the USA. Two other vocal groups, the Double Six of Paris and the Swingle Singers, developed from the Blue Stars. Dearie returned to the USA in the late 1950s and subsequently appeared in nightclubs in New York and Los Angeles, accompanying herself at the head of her own trios. Her repertory includes much original material. She has a small, light voice, sometimes employing a thin, tight vibrato, and sings with intelligence, clarity, and originality. Her performance is enhanced by the way she strokes and caresses certain words and pounces upon and attacks others; she also makes use of blues effects. She is an elegant, refined, and witty singer. In 1985 she became the first recipient of the Mabel Mercer Foundation Award.

RECORDINGS

(selective list)

With the Blue Stars: Lullaby of Birdland, on *The Blues Stars of France* (1952, EmArcy 36067); *Blossom Dearie* (1956, Verve 2037); *Blossom Dearie Sings* (1974, Daffodil Records 101)

BIBLIOGRAPHY

J. S. Wilson: *The Collectors Jazz Modern* (Philadelphia, PA, 1959)

W. Balliett: "Absolutely Pure," *American Singers* (New York, 1979), 118

J. S. Wilson: "Cabaret: Blossom Dearie," *New York Times* (28 April 1983)

ED BEMIS

De Cisneros, Eleonora. *See* CISNEROS, ELEONORA DE.

Deems, Will. Pseudonym of HARVEY B. GAUL.

Defauw, Désiré (*b* Ghent, Belgium, 5 Sept 1885; *d* Gary, IN, 25 July 1960). Conductor and violinist. He studied violin with Johan Smit and was a founder and first violinist (1914–18) of the Allied Quartet (London). Returning to Belgium, he was director and professor of conducting at the Brussels Conservatory from 1926 to 1940. He appeared in New York as guest conductor with the NBC SO in 1938, and was conductor of the Montreal Société des Concerts Symphoniques from 1940 to 1943 and again from 1947 to at least 1951; during 1943–7 he was conductor of the Chicago SO but won little success. In the 1950s he conducted the Bloomington (Illinois) SO, Grand Rapids SO, Northwestern University Summer Orchestra, and the Gary SO (1950–58), after which he retired because of ill health. Defauw conducted several premières of American works and made a number of recordings with the Brussels Conservatory Orchestra and the Chicago SO, including what is probably the first recording of Prokofiev's *Scythian Suite* (with the Chicago SO).

BIBLIOGRAPHY

M. Herzberg: *Désiré Defauw* (Brussels, 1937)

ARTHUR JACOBS/RUTH B. HILTON

DeFranco, Buddy [Boniface Ferdinand Leonardo] (*b* Camden, NJ, 17 Feb 1923). Jazz clarinetist. After playing with the big bands of Gene Krupa and Charlie Barnet he became a prominent soloist in Tommy Dorsey's band (1944–8). He twice attempted (unsuccessfully) to lead his own big band, and otherwise performed in smaller groups, including Count Basie's octet (1950) and a quartet with Art Blakey and Kenny Drew (1952–3). He also toured Europe with Billie Holiday early in 1954. He gave the première of Nelson Riddle's *Cross-country Suite* in 1950. From 1958 he conducted jazz clinics at schools in California, during which time he formed a unique quartet with the bop accordionist Tommy Gumina (1960–63). In 1964 he made an acclaimed recording, *Blues Bag*, playing bass clarinet. Later he led the reconstituted Glenn Miller Orchestra (1966–74), but returned to teaching and playing intermittently in nightclubs. A talented improviser with a liquid tone and prodigious technique, DeFranco was frequently obliged to perform under circumstances that failed to challenge his abilities, because of the apparent incompatibility of his chosen instrument and bop, his preferred musical style.

RECORDINGS
(selective list)

As leader: A Bird in Igor's Yard, on L. Tristano: *Crosscurrents* (1949, Cap. 11060); Gone with the Wind/Lover Come Back to Me (1952, MGM 30679); Autumn in New York/Show Eyes (1953, Clef 89067); *Buddy DeFranco plays Benny Goodman* (1957, Verve 2089); *Cross-country Suite* (1958, Dot 9006); *Buddy DeFranco and Tommy Gumina* (1961, Mer. 20685); *Blues Bag* (1964, VeeJay 2506); *Free Sail* (1974, Choice 1008)

As co-leader: with A. Tatum: *Art Tatum–Buddy DeFranco Quartet* (1956, Verve 8229); with T. Gibbs: *Jazz Party: First Time Together* (1981, Palo Alto 8011)

BIBLIOGRAPHY

L. Feather: "Dance Biz Needs Younger Leaders: DeFranco," *Down Beat*, xviii/5 (1951), 1

"Buddy DeFranco's New Career," *Down Beat*, xxvi/2 (1959), 22

J. Burns: "The Forgotten Boppers," *Jazz and Blues*, ii/3 (1972), 5

S. Voce: "Buddy DeFranco," *Jazz Journal International*, xxxv (1982), no.1, p.8; no.2, p.24

BARRY KERNFELD

DeGaetani, Jan (*b* Massilon, OH, 10 July 1933). Mezzo-soprano. She studied at the Juilliard School and made her formal New York début in 1958. In November 1970 she gave the first performance of George Crumb's *Ancient Voices of Children* at the Library of Congress, and since then she has become a specialist in contemporary music. Her list of premières includes Peter Maxwell Davies's *A Stone Litany* (1973) and *Black Pentecost* (1982), Richard Wernick's *Visions of Wonder and Terror* (1976), Schuman's *In Sweet Music*, which she performed with the Chamber Music Society of Lincoln Center, and Carter's *Syringa*, with Speculum Musicae in New York (both in 1978). She performs regularly with the Contemporary Chamber Ensemble, with which she made a celebrated recording of *Pierrot lunaire* (which stresses its lyricism). In addition to the contemporary repertory, she has performed and recorded medieval music (*The Play of Herod* with the New York Pro Musica), Baroque cantatas, German lieder, and songs by John Dowland, Stephen Foster, Fauré, Ives, and many others.

A singer of remarkable intelligence and expressive power, with a voice clear and true throughout its wide range, DeGaetani has sung with many of the leading American and English orchestras. She made her first appearance with the New York PO in 1973, the same year she became a professor at the Eastman School and artist-in-residence at the Aspen Music Festival in Colorado. She frequently gives master classes and concerts at American universities, and, with Norman and Ruth Lloyd, she published *The Complete Sightsinger* (1980).

BIBLIOGRAPHY

R. Clark: "Jan DeGaetani," *Stereo Review*, xxxi/3 (1973), 77

B. Northcott: "A Complete Singer," *Music and Musicians*, xxi/5 (1973), 6

J. Hiemenz: "Musician of the Month: Jan DeGaetani," *HiFi/MusAm*, xxiv/4 (1974), 6

"DeGaetani, Jan," *CBY 1977*

H. Saal: "Queen of New Music," *Newsweek*, lxxxix (14 Feb 1977), 92

A. Kozinn: "From Cavalli to Cabaret with Jan DeGaetani," *New York Times* (1 Feb 1981)

MARTIN BERNHEIMER/R

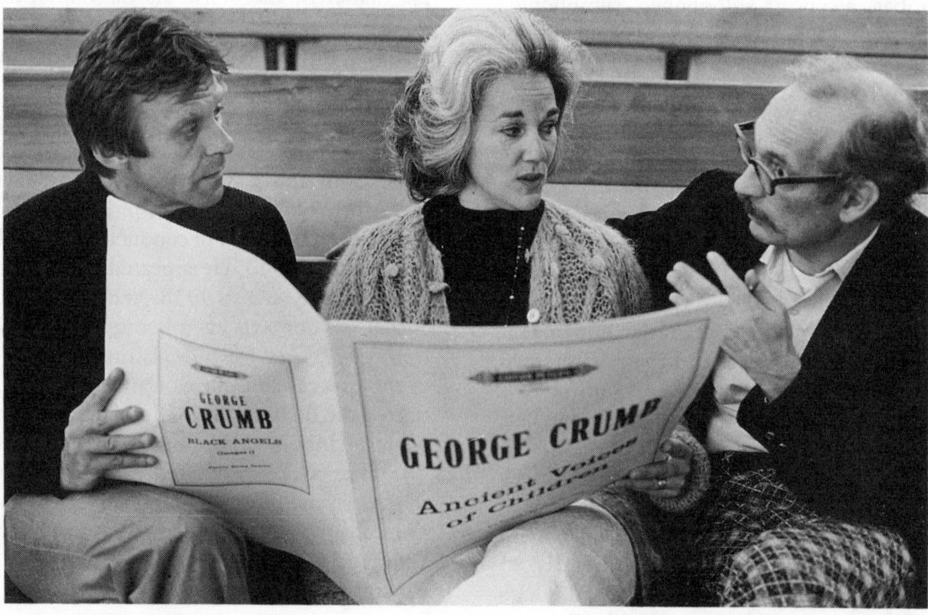

Jan DeGaetani with Richard Dufallo (left) and George Crumb, Aspen Music Festival, 1974

Degrees in music. *See* EDUCATION IN MUSIC, §II, 6.

Deis, Carl (*b* New York, 7 March 1883; *d* New York, 24 July 1960). Composer and organist. As a child he took piano lessons from his father, Otto Deis, a trombonist. Later he studied piano with Alexander Lambert and Richard Burmeister and harmony with A. W. Lilienthal, and attended the National Conservatory of Music and the New York College of Music. From 1906 he was active as a choral conductor and vocal coach, teaching at the Peddie Institute for Boys, the Collegiate School for Girls, and the Veltin School. From 1917 until 1953 as an editor for G. Schirmer, he prepared numerous editions of choral, vocal, and chamber music. He also served as organist at the Society for Ethical Culture (1919–33) and at Temple Emanu-el. He was member and governor of the Bohemians, an honorary member of the Laurier Club, and secretary of the Beethoven Association. As a composer, Deis is best known for his songs, among them *The Drums* (M. Irving), *New Years Day* (A. Tennyson), and *Were I a Star*. Among his other works are three pieces for string orchestra, a considerable quantity of original choral music as well as arrangements, and piano works.

BIBLIOGRAPHY

Obituary, *MusAm*, lxxx/11 (1960), 68

NED QUIST

DeJohnette, Jack (*b* Chicago, IL, 9 Aug 1942). Jazz drummer and pianist. He began playing the piano at the age of four, studying with a classical teacher for about ten years. By the time he reached high school he was playing blues and rock-and-roll on piano, but his interest soon turned to jazz and he started playing in small groups, emulating Ahmad Jamal. At about the age of 18 he began to study drums, which quickly became his primary interest. While in junior college he became involved with the Association for the Advancement of Creative Musicians; he was also profoundly impressed by an opportunity to perform with John Coltrane in the early 1960s. In April 1966 DeJohnette moved to New York, where he again performed several times with Coltrane and often appeared with Jackie McLean (1966–9). He first came to nationwide attention as a member of the popular Charles Lloyd Quartet, with which he recorded and toured worldwide for more than two years (1966–8). He then joined Miles Davis's group, where he replaced Tony Williams in 1969 and took part in the pathbreaking *Bitches Brew* recording sessions of that year. After leaving Davis in mid-1972 DeJohnette continued to be active in fusion groups, including several under his own leadership.

DeJohnette is a powerful and widely admired drummer. Although his original inspiration was Vernel Fournier, his major influences were Max Roach, Philly Joe Jones, and, later, Elvin Jones. In New York he also came under the influence of Tony Williams, especially in regard to cymbal technique. His groups Directions and Special Edition have received high critical acclaim, and he has recently resumed playing piano, revealing a skill and creativity to rival his drumming. Since 1975 he has been co-director with his wife of the Creative Music Agency in Woodstock, New York, a nonprofit enterprise for the management, performing, and teaching of jazz.

RECORDINGS

(selective list)

As leader: *Complex* (1968, Mlst. 9022); *Untitled* (1976, ECM 1074); *New Directions* (1978, ECM 1128); *Special Edition* (1979, ECM 1152); *New Directions in Europe* (1979, ECM 1157)

As sideman: C. Lloyd: *Dream Weaver* (1966, Atl. 1459), *Forest Flower* (1966, Atl. 1473); M. Davis: *Bitches Brew* (1969, Col. GP26), *Miles Davis at Fillmore* (1970, Col. KG30038)

BIBLIOGRAPHY

J. DeJohnette: "Jack DeJohnette Introduced his New Group, Compost," *Down Beat*, xxxviii/16 (1971), 19

——: "DeJohnette on DeJohnette," *Down Beat*, xlii/4 (1975), 16

B. Bennett: "Jack DeJohnette's 'Directions': Experimental Inheritors," *Down Beat*, xliv/6 (1977), 12

C. Stern: "Jack DeJohnette: South Side to Woodstock," *Down Beat*, xlv/18 (1978), 23

L. Jeske: "Jack DeJohnette: Naturally Multi-Directional," *Down Beat*, xlviii/3 (1981), 17

J. DeJohnette and C. Perry: *The Art of Modern Jazz Drumming* (New York, 1981)

P. Danson: "Jack DeJohnette," *Coda*, no.182 (1982), 12

H. Mandel: "Drummer, Drummer: Jack DeJohnette," *Down Beat*, lii/2 (1985), 16 [incl. discography]

LEWIS PORTER

De Koven, (Henry Louis) Reginald (*b* Middletown, CT, 3 April 1859; *d* Chicago, IL, 16 Jan 1920). Composer, conductor, and music critic. In 1872 he went to Europe. He studied the piano with Wilhelm Speidel at Stuttgart, took a degree at Oxford University (1879), studied theory with Dionys Pruckner in Stuttgart, singing with Luigi Vannuccini in Florence, and light opera with Richard Genée and Franz von Suppé in Vienna, and with Léo Delibes in Paris. In 1882 he returned to the USA, served as a music critic for *Harper's Weekly*, the New York *World*, *Herald*, and *Journal*, and the Chicago *Evening Post* (*c*1889–1912), and founded and conducted (1902–4) the Washington SO. De Koven's output includes an orchestral suite, a piano sonata and numerous other piano works, ballets, about 400 songs, and two grand operas written at the end of his career, but he is best known for his operettas, set in Europe or the Far East. *Robin Hood* (1890), which began the era when American operetta dominated the musical stage in the USA, was perennially in the repertory of the Bostonians, the first important operetta troupe after the introduction of Gilbert and Sullivan to America; and a song from it, "Oh promise me," has remained a popular wedding ballad. De Koven's music draws on both 19th-century Italian opera (in *Robin Hood* the grandiose finale of Act 2 is in the spirit of Rossini, and the Forest Song and Armorer's Song are reminiscent of Verdi) and folklike melody (*Rip Van Winkle*, and "When a maiden marries" from *Robin Hood*). He was elected to the National Institute of Arts and Letters in 1898.

WORKS

Unless otherwise stated, all are operettas, librettos are by H. B. Smith, and dates are those of first New York performance.

The Begum, 21 Nov 1887; Don Quixote, Boston, 1889; Robin Hood, Chicago, 9 June 1890; The Fencing Master, Boston, 1892; The Algerian, Philadelphia, 1893; The Knickerbockers, Boston, 1893; Rob Roy, Oct 1894; The Tzigane, 16 May 1895; The Mandarin, Cleveland, 1896; The Paris Doll, Hartford, 1897; The Highwayman, 13 Dec 1897; The Three Dragoons, 30 Jan 1899; The Man in the Moon (L. Harrison, S. Stange), collab. L. Englander, G. Keller, 24 April 1899; Papa's Wife, 13 Nov 1899; Broadway to Tokyo (Harrison, G. V. Hobart), collab. A. B. Sloane, 23 Jan 1900

Foxy Quiller, 5 Nov 1900; The Little Duchess, 14 Oct 1901; Maid Marian (after Robin Hood), Philadelphia, 4 Nov 1901; The Jersey Lilly (Hobart), collab. W. Jerome, J. Schwartz, 14 Sept 1903; Red Feather (book C. Klein; lyrics C. E. Cook), 11 Nov 1903; Happyland (F. Rancken), 2 Oct 1905; The Student King (Rancken, Stange), 25 Dec 1906; The Girls of Holland (Stange), 18 Nov 1907; The Golden Butterfly, 12 Oct 1908; The Beauty Spot (J. W. Herbert), 10 April 1909; The Wedding Trip, 25 Dec 1911; Her Little Highness, 13 Oct 1913; The Canterbury Pilgrims (opera, P. Mackaye), 8 March 1917; Rip Van Winkle (opera, Mackaye), Chicago, 2 Jan 1920

BIBLIOGRAPHY

A. F. De Koven: *A Musician and his Wife* (New York, 1926)

F. H. Martens: "De Koven, Henry Louis Reginald," *DAB*
J. W. Stedman, " 'Then Hey! For the Merry Greenwood': Smith and De Koven and Robin Hood," *Journal of Popular Culture*, xii (1978–9), 432

RONALD BYRNSIDE

De la Hache, Theodore. *See* LA HACHE, THEODORE VON.

De Lamarter, Eric (*b* Lansing, MI, 18 Feb 1880; *d* Orlando, FL, 17 May 1953). Organist, conductor, and composer. The son of a minister, he studied piano and organ as a child and was first employed as a church organist at the age of 15. He continued organ studies with George Herbert Fairclough in St. Paul and later with Wilhelm Middelschulte in Chicago, where he also studied piano with Mary Wood Chase and conducting with Theodore Spiering. After graduating from Albion College in 1900 he became organist and choir director at the New England Congregational Church in Chicago and remained in that post until 1912 (though he studied organ in Paris with Alexandre Guilmant and Charles-Marie Widor in the winter of 1901–2). He was also active as a music critic during this period, writing for three Chicago newspapers and the *Boston Transcript*. After serving briefly as organist at the Church of Christ Scientist in Chicago (1912–14) he became organist and choir director at the Fourth Presbyterian Church (1914–36).

De Lamarter succeeded Frederick Stock as conductor of the Musical Art Society in 1911, for two seasons, and in 1918 substituted for him for one season as conductor of the Chicago SO, thereafter serving as its assistant conductor until 1936. In that capacity he conducted the Chicago Civic Orchestra, the concerts of the Chicago SO at Ravinia for seven summers, and two concerts a day for ten weeks at the Century of Progress International Exposition in 1933. Beginning in 1924 he was for many years director of the concert series Chicago Allied Arts. He taught briefly at Olivet (Michigan) College (1904–5) and at the Chicago Musical College (1909–10), and for a longer period at the Gunn School of Music. On retirement from his positions in Chicago in 1936, he joined the staff of radio station WOR in New York for a year to direct orchestral concerts. In the 1940s, he taught at the University of Missouri, Columbia; Ohio State University, Columbus; and the University of Texas, Austin. De Lamarter received the Eastman School Publication Award (for *Psalm cxliv*) and the Society for the Publication of American Music award, and was elected to the National Institute of Arts and Letters in 1938.

De Lamarter is remembered chiefly for his organ and choral music, though in his own day he was noted for his performances with orchestra and recitals (many of which included new compositions), and for his own orchestral works of which many were first performed by such orchestras as the Chicago SO, the Philadelphia Orchestra, and the Cincinnati SO. His works were based on classical structures and, though they may incorporate both elements of dissonance and American popular idioms, are predominantly traditional in style.

WORKS
(selective list)

STAGE

The Betrothal (incidental music, M. Maeterlinck), New York, 1918
Dance of Life (ballet), 1931

ORCHESTRAL

The Faun, ov., 1914; 4 syms., no.1, D, 1914, no.2, g[after Whitman], 1926, no.3, e, 1931, no.4, 1932; 2 serenades, str, 1915; Masquerade, ov., 1916; Ballad on Song Themes by Leo Sowerby, 1917; Fable of the Hapless Folk Tune, 1917; The Betrothal, suite, 1918; Org Conc. no.1, E, 1920; The Giddy Puritan, ov., 1921; Org Conc. no.2, A, 1922; Weaver of Tales, org, chamber orch, 1926; Serenade near Taos, 1930–38; The Black Orchid, suite [from Dance of Life, ballet], 1931; Suite, str (1946); Huckleberry Finn, ov. (1948); Ol' Kaintuck, ov. (1948); At Christmastide (1948); Cluny, a Dialogue, va, orch (1949)

INSTRUMENTAL

Org: A Gothic Prelude (1937); Festival Prelude (1945); Suite (1945); Chorale Prelude, Ach bleib bei uns, Herr Jesu Christ (1948); From the Long Room of the Sea (1946); Minuet (1946); Scherzetto (1946); 4 Eclogues (1947); Ov. (1947); 4 Pieces (1947); At St. Etienne du Mont (1948); Chorale Prelude, Kommt her zu mir, spricht Gottes Sohn, rev. (1948); Thumb Box Sketches (1948); Chapel in the Smokies (1949); 6 Pieces (1949); Short Suite on Gregorian Themes (1950); Soliloquy (1950)

Chamber: Terzetto, vn, va, vc, 1911; Suite (in miniature), 1913; Vn Sonata, E♭, 1915; I've Got the Sowerby Blues, vc, pf, 1937; Str Qt no.1, G (1943), arr. str orch (1943); Apple Tree, str trio (1948); Ballad, hn, pf (1948); Foursome in C, 3 vn, va (1948); Poème, hn, pf (1948); 3 Pieces, vc, pf (1948); Str Qt no.2, F (1948); Serenade, d, str trio (1948); Triolet, D, vn, va/vc (1948); Arietta, bn, pf (1950); Folk Song, bn, pf (1950); Scherzetto, bn, pf (1950); Sketch Book in Eire, fl, ob, cl, bn (1950); Leprechaun Serenade, vn, pf (1951)

VOCAL
(to Biblical texts with keyboard accompaniment unless otherwise stated)

Noel: a Cycle of Ancient Carols (1920); Sing we to our God, cantata, 1v, org (1920); Psalm cxliv, Bar, orch, 1915, arr. Bar, org (1928); How Lovely are thy Dwellings, A, male chorus (1941); Responses, SATB (1941); O thou Eternal One, SATB (1946); The Bread of Life, A, SATB (1947); Forever, O Jehovah, thy Word, unacc. SATB (1947); God Be Merciful to Us, SSA (1947); Benedictus es Domine, B, SATB (1948); May Rain, SSA (O. Goulet) (1948); O Lord, how Excellent, SATB (1948); A Springtime Day, SSA (Goulet) (1948); They that Trust in the Lord, S, A, SATB (1948); How Lovely are thy Dwellings, A, SATB (1949); Blessed are the Pure in Heart, SATB (1951); other sacred works; songs

Principal publishers: Gray, Mills, Ricordi, Witmark

BIBLIOGRAPHY

EwenD
P. Christian: "Eric De Lamarter," *American Organist*, vii/4 (1924), 198
P. A. Otis: *The Chicago Symphony Orchestra: its Organization, Growth and Development 1891–1924* (Chicago, 1925/*R*1972)
T. C. Willis: *Music in Orchestra Hall* (diss., Northwestern U., 1966)

MARGERY MORGAN LOWENS

De La Martinez, Odaline. *See* MARTINEZ, ODALINE DE LA.

Delaney, Robert (Mills) (*b* Baltimore, MD, 24 July 1903; *d* Santa Barbara, CA, 21 Sept 1956). Composer. He studied at the University of Southern California (1921–2) and with Boulanger at the Ecole Normale de Musique in Paris (1922–7), where he was also a pupil of Lucien Capet and Honegger. In 1929 he was awarded a Guggenheim Fellowship and in 1933 a Pulitzer Prize for *John Brown's Song*, a choral symphony based on *John Brown's Body*. He taught at the Santa Barbara School, the Concord School of Music, and Northwestern University.

WORKS
(selective list)

Orch: The Constant Couple, suite, 1926; Don Quixote Sym., 1927; Pastoral Movt, 1930; Adagio, vn, str, 1935; Sym. Pieces nos.1–2, 1935, 1937; Work 22, ov., 1939; Going to Town, suite, 1941; Sym. no.1, 1942

Choral: John Brown's Song (S. V. Benét), choral sym., 1931; Blake Cycle, vv, orch; Night (Blake), vv, str orch, pf, 1934; Choralia nos.1–2, 1936, 1937; My soul, there is a country (Vaughan), vv, orch, 1937; Western Star, 5vv, orch, 1944

Chamber: Str Qts nos.2–3, 1930

Principal publisher: E. C. Schirmer

PEGGY GLANVILLE-HICKS/R

Delaney and Bonnie. Rock duo. It consisted of Delaney Bramlett (*b* Pontotoc County, MS, 1 July 1939) and his wife Bonnie

(Lynn) Bramlett (*b* Acton [now Langley], nr Sheffield, IL, 8 Nov 1944). They met in 1967 and began performing together soon after; in 1969 they met Eric Clapton, with whom they toured Europe. Their backup group, from 1969, included Carl Radle (drummer), Leon Russell (pianist), Jim Price (horn player), and Bobby Keys (saxophonist), and together they were known as Delaney and Bonnie and Friends. Their album *On Tour* (1970) was a fresh, easygoing amalgam of rhythm-and-blues, gospel, blues, and rock that was extremely influential. They continued to record together, and in 1971 made two hit recordings, *Never Ending Song of Love* (no. 13) and *Only you know and I know* (no. 20). After they made the album *Together* (1972), their marriage ended and they pursued separate careers with little success. As vocalists Delaney and Bonnie were unevenly matched; Delaney's voice was pleasant but somewhat hoarse and limited, while Bonnie's rich, coarse tenor was especially effective in conveying the weariness and despair that characterized many of the songs they wrote together.

RECORDINGS

(selective list)

Accept No Substitute (Elek. 74039, 1969); *Home* (Stax 2026, 1969); *On Tour* (Atco 33326, 1970); *To Bonnie from Delaney* (Atco 33341, 1970); *Genesis* (Crescendo 2054, 1971); *Motel Shot* (Atco 33358, 1971); *Together* (Col. KC31377, 1972)

KEN TUCKER

Delano, Jack [Ovcharov, Jascha] (*b* nr Kiev, Ukraine, 1 Aug 1914). Composer. He was brought to the USA as a child by his parents and studied at the Settlement Music School, Philadelphia (viola and composition, 1924–32) and at the Pennsylvania Academy of Fine Arts (1928–32). In 1946 he settled in Puerto Rico to assume various posts in governmental programs in radio, television, and rural community education, having already established a reputation as a documentary photographer. His general responsibility for films produced by the Division of Community Education led him to experiment with the mechanical and electronic alteration of recorded sound as early as 1948 in the score for the film *Desde las nubes*. He later composed works for such organizations as the Puerto Rico SO, the Ballet Infantil de Gilda Navarra, and the Ballets de San Juan. Except for early experiments directed towards solving specific problems connected with film music, Delano's style has been conservative but pleasantly spiced with dissonance; his principal contribution to music in Puerto Rico has been his incorporation of native rhythmic and melodic patterns into the forms, styles, and instrumentation of standard concert music.

WORKS

Ballets: Cucarachita Martina y Ratoncito Pérez (G. Navarra), 1951; La bruja de Loíza (A. García), 1956; Sanjuaneras (García), 1959; El sabio Doctor Mambrú (J. Anduze), 1962

Orch: Ofrenda musical, va, hn, str orch, 1959; Concertino clásico, tpt, small orch, 1965; La reina tembandumba, 1966

Chamber: Va Sonata, 1954; Fl Sonatina, 1958; Vn Sonata, 1961; 7 dúos a canon, 2 vn, 1967; Conc. piccolo, 8 vn, 1977; Preludio, gui, 1977; Str Qt, 1984

Vocal: La oración de Ximena (medieval Sp.), A, hpd/pf, 1955; Nocturno (L. Palés Matos), S, pf, 1959; Esta luna es mía (J. P. H. Hernández), S, female vv, 1962; 3 cancioncitas del mar (N. Vicéns), 1963; Me voy a Ponce (J. Balseiro), chorus, 1965; Canciones para Laura (E. Delgado), Mez, pf, 1977

Incidental music; film scores, incl. Desde las nubes, 1948

Other orch, chamber, and vocal works

BIBLIOGRAPHY

E. Hawes: "Jack Delano," *San Juan Star Magazine* (11 Dec 1977), 2

Compositores de América / Composers of the Americas, ed. Pan American Union, xix (Washington, DC, 1979), 22

DONALD THOMPSON

DeLay, Dorothy (*b* Medicine Lodge, KS, 31 March 1917). Violinist and teacher. She grew up in a musical environment: her father played cello and her mother was a pianist. She entered Oberlin College in 1933 and transferred the following year to Michigan State University, where she studied violin with Michael Press (BA 1937); she continued her studies in New York at the Juilliard School with Louis Persinger, Raphael Bronstein, and others (artist diploma 1941). During these years she was active as a soloist and in chamber ensembles, and she founded the Stuyvesant Trio with her sister Nellie as cellist and Helen Brainard as pianist. Her career was interrupted during World War II, but she resumed performing in 1946 and became interested in the method of Galamian, who had just been appointed to the Juilliard faculty. For the next 20 years DeLay was Galamian's chief and indispensable assistant. Their collaborative work came to an end when DeLay realized that she could contribute something decisively personal to a student's artistic development. Since forming her own class, she has won recognition as one of the outstanding violin teachers in the world; among her best-known students are Itzhak Perlman, Shlomo Mintz, Cho-Liang Lin, Mark Peskanov, and Christian Altenburger. DeLay is a singularly dedicated teacher, sensitive to the musical as well as the psychological needs of the student. She is on the faculties of the Juilliard School, Sarah Lawrence College, New England Conservatory, and Cincinnati College-Conservatory, and she teaches at the Aspen Music School; in addition she has given master classes in South Africa, China, Japan, and Israel, among other countries. She received the Artist Teacher Award of the American String Teachers Association in 1975 and an honorary DMus from Oberlin College in 1981.

BIBLIOGRAPHY

L. Jeffries: "Juilliard's First-string Family," *Keynote*, iii/10 (1979), 12

B. Schwarz: *Great Masters of the Violin* (New York, 1983)

BORIS SCHWARZ

Delius, Frederick [Fritz] **(Theodore Albert)** (*b* Bradford, England, 29 Jan 1862; *d* Grez-sur-Loing, France, 10 June 1934). English composer of German descent. He played the piano from an early age and was allowed to take violin lessons. On leaving school he bowed to the wishes of his father, who did not consider music a fit profession for his children, and entered the family wool company. In 1884 he persuaded his father to lend him enough money to join a friend in purchasing an orange plantation in Florida. This gave him longed-for freedom and enabled him to start serious composition. He lived on the plantation – Solano Grove, some 65 km from Jacksonville on the St. Johns River – neglected oranges, and acquired a friend and music tutor in Thomas F. Ward, an organist from New York then in Jacksonville. For six months Ward gave him a course in musical technique; Delius later stated that these were his only worthwhile lessons. At this time his sense of solitude in luxuriant natural surroundings and his immersion in the music of plantation Blacks were decisive to his artistic achievement.

Delius spent the winter and spring of 1886 in Danville, Virginia, having learned of an opportunity there for a private music teacher; he supported himself by teaching, singing, and playing the organ. After learning that his father had agreed to maintain him for an 18-month course in Germany at the Leipzig Conservatory he left the USA in June; he returned only once, briefly, in 1897, in the hope of leasing Solano Grove to a tobacco planter and so improving his financial position. Then he went back to

Europe and in the summer of 1897 settled in Grez-sur-Loing, which remained his home (except for a stay in England during World War I) until his death.

The first music by Delius to be published was issued at Jacksonville in 1892; it was a lively polka for piano, *Zum Carnival* (the title perhaps reflecting the Germanic bias of American music at the time). His style, slow to develop, was largely based on Wagner, whose endless flow and harmonic aura Delius attempted to emulate, and on Grieg, whose airy texture and nondeveloping use of chromaticism showed him how to lighten the Wagnerian load. Delius's works of the 1890s show a steady increase in the number of passages where the fusion of these elements sounds characteristic, reaching a peak in the opera *Koanga* (1895–7); its text is by Charles Keary and is drawn from an episode in *The Grandissimes*, a novel by George Washington Cable. Its tragic story of the deep South, in which an African prince is sold into slavery, enabled Delius to draw comprehensively on his Florida experiences. They were directly reflected in two other significant early works, the suite *Florida* (1887, rev. 1889) and the orchestral variations *Appalachia* (1896), on a tune Delius had apparently heard sung by plantation Blacks, which he later revised into a larger choral work (1898–1903). *Florida* is in four movements; the first (Sunrise) is based on "La Calinda," a tune that Delius used later in *Koanga*, and the Sunset movement on one that prefigures "I got plenty o' nuttin' " in Gershwin's *Porgy and Bess*. *Appalachia* covers a wider range of styles than Delius was later willing to admit; its première (in the revised version) in Germany in 1904, along with that of *Koanga* (in the same year), first brought him to international attention.

It would be difficult to claim other direct influences of his American sojourn on Delius's music and musical thought. Worth noting, however, is his fondness for the poetry of Walt Whitman, which is reflected in *Sea Drift* (1903–4) for baritone, chorus, and orchestra, widely considered his greatest achievement; *Songs of Farewell* (1930), powerfully concentrated and exultant settings for eight-part chorus and orchestra; and the *Idyll* ("Once I passed through a populous city") (1930–32) for soprano, baritone, and orchestra, his last work.

BIBLIOGRAPHY

P. Heseltine: *Frederick Delius* (London, 1923, rev. 2/1952/*R*1974)
G. Abraham: "Delius and his Literary Sources," *ML*, x (1929), 182 [repr. in *Slavonic and Romantic Music* (London, 1968), 332ff]
C. Delius: *Frederick Delius: Memories of my Brother* (London, 1935)
G. Tetley: "Delius Recalled as Virginia Town Music Teacher: Forgotten Interlude in Early Career disclosed by Old Resident of Danville," *MusAm*, lv/15 (1935), 14
E. Fenby: *Delius as I Knew him* (London, 1936, 2/1947/*R*1976, 3/1966, rev. 4/1981)
T. Beecham: *Frederick Delius* (London, 1959, rev. 2/1975)
A. Payne: "Delius's Stylistic Development," *Tempo*, no.60 (1961–2), 6
Delius Society Journal (London, 1963–) [quarterly]
C. Jahoda: *The Other Florida* (New York, 1967)
E. Fenby: *Delius* (London, 1971)
W. Randel: "Frederick Delius in America," *Virginia Magazine of History and Biography*, lxxix (1971), 349
——: " 'Koanga' and its Libretto," *ML*, lii (1971), 141
J. G. Brennan: "Delius and Whitman," *Walt Whitman Review*, xviii/3 (1972), 90
L. Carley and R. Threlfall: *Delius and America* (London, 1972)
M. Walker and S. Upton: *Delius Discography* (London, 1973)
R. Lowe: *Frederick Delius 1862–1934: a Catalogue of the Music Archives of the Delius Trust, London* (London, 1974)
C. Redwood, ed.: *A Delius Companion* (London, 1976)
R. Threlfall: *A Catalogue of the Compositions of Frederick Delius* (London, 1977)
L. Carley: *Delius: a Life in Letters 1862–1908* (London, 1983)
——: *Frederick Delius: a Short Biography* (London, 1984)

ANTHONY PAYNE/H. WILEY HITCHCOCK

Dello Joio, Norman (*b* New York, 24 Jan 1913). Composer and educator. It was as an organist at the Star of the Sea Church, New York, that he entered professional music at the age of 14. His father, Casimir, who immigrated from Italy early in the century, was also an organist. Dello Joio's godfather, the composer and organist Pietro Yon, was his principal teacher. He attended All Hallows Institute (1926–30) and the College of the City of New York (1932–4) before pursuing full-time musical training at the Institute of Musical Art (1936) and the Juilliard Graduate School (1939–41), where he studied composition with Wagenaar. In 1941 he studied with Hindemith at the Berkshire Music Center and at the Yale School of Music.

From the beginning of his career he received a number of grants and awards, and his works had regular performances. He won an Elizabeth Sprague Coolidge Award for his Piano Trio (1937), a Town Hall Composition Award for the orchestral work *Magnificat* (1942), and Guggenheim Fellowships in 1943 and 1944. In the following year he received a grant from the American Academy of Arts and Letters. His Variations, Chaconne and Finale, first performed by the New York PO under Walter, won the New York Music Critics' Circle Award for the best new orchestral piece of 1948; he won a second Critics' Circle Award in 1962 for the opera *The Triumph of St. Joan*. The Pulitzer Prize for music was awarded to him in 1957 for *Meditations on Ecclesiastes* for string orchestra. In 1961 he was elected to the National Institute of Arts and Letters. Among several scores composed for television, his music for the NBC program *The Louvre* won the 1965 Emmy award.

After working as music director in 1941–3 of Eugene Loring's Dance Players, Dello Joio began his teaching career at Sarah Lawrence College (1945–50). Later he was professor of composition at Mannes College (1956–72), and in 1959 he began a 14-year association with the Contemporary Music Project for Creativity in Music Education (supported by the Ford Foundation), through which young composers were placed in high schools throughout the USA to write new music for the school ensembles. Dello Joio conceived the project and was made chairman of the policy committee. In 1972 he became professor of music at Boston University and from 1972 to 1978 served as dean of the university's School of Fine and Applied Arts.

The relatively brief training with Hindemith was influential in shaping Dello Joio's musical thinking, though it was Hindemith's advice, rather than any technical instruction, that had most effect. He urged Dello Joio to speak naturally as a composer, without concern for models that had little relevance to his experience and temperament. The musical influences of Dello Joio's earlier life were 19th-century Italian opera, Catholic church music, and the popular music and jazz of New York in the 1920s and 1930s. Dello Joio fused elements of these to form the vocabulary for his subsequent creative work; the most prominent elements are Gregorian chant and a preoccupation with religious subjects. Such works as *Magnificat*, *Meditations on Ecclesiastes*, and *New York Profiles* use either literal quotations of chants or chant-like melodies. Dello Joio's treatment of the Joan of Arc story went through several revisions and transformations in operatic and symphonic form. The first was the opera *The Triumph of Joan*, which he withdrew after its première. A second opera was written for television as *The Trial at Rouen*, with a completely new text and score; this work was revised as *The Triumph of St. Joan* for the New York City Opera. A further version was *The Triumph of St. Joan Symphony*, a three-movement work based on material from the first opera; it was first performed with choreography by Graham. All of the St. Joan works contain much effective music in a pseudo-liturgical style.

His affinity with and enjoyment of popular music are apparent in numerous works. The flamboyant Fantasy and Variations for piano and orchestra, in its bursts of hammered-out repeated notes and jazz syncopation, suggests the same big-city stimulants that affected Gershwin. A flair for the theatrical is also evident: there is a fondness for big contrasts in dynamics, romantic tunes, grand gestures. This flair serves particularly well in his stage and television scores (*Air Power* is a prominent example). In general Dello Joio's music is extroverted, colorful, and well crafted.

WORKS

DRAMATIC

Prairie, see Sinfonietta under ORCHESTRAL

The Duke of Sacramento (ballet, Loring), 2 pf, 1942, withdrawn; New Hope, PA, 1942

On Stage (ballet, Kidd), orch, 1945, Boston, 1945; arr. orch suite, arr. pf suite

Diversion of Angels (Wilderness Stair) (ballet, Graham), orch, 1948; New London, CT, 1948

The Triumph of Joan (opera, J. Machlis), 1949, withdrawn; Bronxville, NY, 1950

The Triumph of St. Joan Symphony, based on the opera The Triumph of Joan, introduced as a ballet (Graham), 1951, Louisville, KY, 1951; rechoreographed as Seraphic Dialogue (Graham), New York, 1955

The Ruby (opera, W. Mass, after E. Dunsany: A Night at an Inn), 1953; Bloomington, IN, 13 May 1955

The Tall Kentuckian (incidental music, B. Anderson), 1953, Louisville, KY, 15 June 1953; Somebody's Coming and Sweet Sonny arr. SATB, pf, 1953

The Trial at Rouen (opera, Dello Joio), 1955, NBC television, 8 April 1956; rev. stage as The Triumph of St. Joan, 1959, New York, 1959

There is a Time, see Meditations on Ecclesiastes under ORCHESTRAL

Air Power (television score), music for 22 television programs, 1956–7, CBS, began 11 Nov 1956; arr. sym. suite, 1957

Profile of a Composer (television score), incl. A Ballad of the Seven Lively Arts, 1958; CBS, 1958

Here is New York (television score), incl. parts of New York Profiles, 1959, CBS, 1959; arr. orch suite

The Saintmaker's Christmas Eve (television score), 1959; ABC, 1963

Vanity Fair (television score, Thackeray), 1959; CBS, 1961

Anthony and Cleopatra (incidental music, Shakespeare), 1960; Stratford, CT, 1960

Blood Moon (opera, G. Hoffman), 1961; San Francisco, 1961

Time of Decision (television score), 1962

The Louvre (television score), 1965, NBC, 1965; arr. band, 1965

A Time of Snow (ballet, Graham), 1968, New York, 1968; arr. band as Heloise and Abelard

All is Still (theater piece), T, fl, ob, cl, harp, vas, vcs, db; America and Americans (television score); From Every Horizon: a Tone Poem to New York (film score); Spoon River (incidental music, E. L. Masters), pf, withdrawn

ORCHESTRAL

Pf Concertino, 1938, withdrawn; Fl Concertino, 1939, withdrawn; Ballad, str, 1940, withdrawn; Conc., 2 pf, orch, 1941, withdrawn; Sinfonietta, 1941, choreographed Loring as Prairie, 1942; Harmonica Concertino, 1942, withdrawn; Magnificat, 1942; To a Lone Sentry, 1943; Concert Music, 1944; Harp Conc., 1945, choreographed Tamaris as Women's Song, 1960

3 Ricercari, pf, orch, 1946; Serenade, 1947–8, choreographed Graham as Diversion of Angels, 1948; Variations, Chaconne, and Finale (3 Sym. Dances), 1947, choreographed Walker, 1963; Concertante, cl, orch, 1949, arr. cl, pf; New York Profiles, 1949; Epigraph, 1951; The Triumph of St. Joan Sym., 1951 [see also under DRAMATIC]

Meditations on Ecclesiastes, str, 1956, choreographed Limón as There is a Time, New York, 1956, choreographed Wilde as The Glass Heart, 1968; A Ballad of the 7 Lively Arts, pf, orch, 1957; Fantasy and Variations, pf, orch, 1961, arr. 2 pf; Variants on a Mediaeval Tune (In dulce jubilo), band, 1963; Antiphonal Fantasy on a Theme of Vincenzo Albrici, org, brass, str, 1965

Air, str, 1967; Fantasies on a Theme by Haydn, band/orch, 1968; Homage to Haydn, 1968–9; Songs of Abelard, band, opt. 1v, 1969; Choreography, 3 dances, str, 1972; Concertante, band, 1973; Lyric Fantasies, va, str, 1973, arr. va, pf; Satiric Dances, band, 1975 [from incidental music]; Colonial Ballads, band, 1976; Colonial variants: 13 Profiles of the Original Colonies, 1976; Arietta, str, 1978; Caccia, band, 1978; Ballabili, 1981; Aria and Roulade, band, 1983; East Hampton Sketches, str, 1983

Man from Independence; Southern Echoes

CHORAL

Chicago (Sandburg), SATB, 1939, withdrawn; Vigil Strange (Whitman), SATB, pf 4 hands, 1941; The Mystic Trumpeter (Whitman), SATB, hn, 1943; A Jubilant Song (Whitman), SATB/women's vv, pf, 1945; Sym. for Voices and Orch (after Benét: Western Star), 1945, withdrawn, later version entitled Song of Affirmation; A Fable (V. Lindsay), T, SATB, pf, 1946; Madrigal (Rossetti), SATB, pf, 1947

The Bluebird (Machlis), SATB, pf, 1950; A Psalm of David, SATB, str, brass, perc, 1950; Song of the Open Road (Whitman), SATB, tpt, pf, 1952; Song of Affirmation (Benét), cantata, S, SATB, nar, orch, 1953; Adieu, Mignonne, when you are Gone (O. Meredith), women's vv, pf, 1954; O Sing unto the Lord (Ps. xcviii), men's vv, org, 1958; To St. Cecilia (Dryden), SATB, pf/brass, 1958

Christmas Carol (Chesterton), SATB, pf 4 hands, 1960, arr. SSA, pf, arr. medium v, pf; Prayers of Cardinal Newman (Newman), SATB, org, 1960; The Holy Infant's Lullaby (A. E. Bennett), (unison vv, org)/(SATB, opt. org), 1961, arr. 1v, pf; Song's End (J. Payne), SSA, pf, 1963; 3 Songs of Chopin: The Lovers (from Dwojaki Koniec), The Ring (from Pierschien), The Wish (from Zyczenic), (SATB, orch)/(SA, orch/pf), 1964, arr. orch, arr. 1v, pf

Songs of Walt Whitman (Dello Joio, after Whitman): 1 I sit and look out upon the world, 2 The Dalliance of Eagles, 3 Tears, 4 Take our Hand, Walt Whitman, SATB, orch, 1966; Proud Music of the Storm (Whitman), SATB, brass, org, 1967; Christmas Music (trad.): Bright Star, God rest ye merry, gentlemen, Hark, the herald angels sing, Holy Infant's Lullaby, O come, all ye faithful, Silent Night, SATB, orch, 1968, arr. pf 4 hands [each no. also pubd separately in various arrs.]

Years of the Modern (Whitman), SATB, brass, perc, 1968; Mass (liturgy), SATB, brass, org/pf, 1969; Evocations: Visitations at Night (R. Hillyer), Promise of Spring (R. Hovey), SATB, opt. young vv, orch/pf, 1970; Come to me, my Love (Rossetti), SATB, pf, 1972; Psalm of Peace (Psalms), SATB, tpt, hn, org/pf, 1972; The Poet's Song (Tennyson), SATB, pf, 1973

Mass in Honor of the Eucharist (liturgy), SATB, cantor, congregation, brass, org, 1975; Notes from Tom Paine, SATB, pf, 1975; As of a Dream (Whitman), modern masque, solo vv, SATB, nar, dancers, orch, 1978; The Psalmist's Meditation (Bible), SATB, org/pf, 1979; Hymns without Words, SATB, pf/orch, 1980; Love Songs at Parting (Dello Joio), SATB, pf, 1981; I dreamed of an invincible city (Dello Joio), SATB, pf/org, 1984

Days of the Modern, withdrawn; Leisure, SATB, pf; Mass in Honor of the Blessed Virgin Mary, cantor, congregation, SATB, org, opt. brass; Of Crows and Clusters (V. Lindsay), SATB, opt. pf

CHAMBER AND INSTRUMENTAL

Pf Trio, 1937, withdrawn; Qt, 4 bn, 1937, withdrawn; Vc Sonata, 1937, withdrawn; Vn Sonata, A, 1937, withdrawn; Colloquy, vn, pf, 1938, withdrawn; Vn Sonata, 1938, withdrawn; Ww Qt, 1939, withdrawn; Suite, pf, 1940; Ww Trio, 1940, withdrawn; Fantasia on a Gregorian Theme, vn, pf, 1942; 3 pf sonatas, 1943, 1944, 1948; Prelude to a Young Dancer, pf, 1943; Prelude to a Young Musician, pf, 1943; Sextet, 3 rec, str trio, 1943

Trio, fl, vc, pf, 1944; Duo concertato, (vc, pf)/(2 pf), 1945; 2 Nocturnes, E, F♯, pf, 1946; Variations and Capriccio, vn, pf, 1948; Aria and Toccata, 2 pf, 1952; Family Album, pf 4 hands, 1962; Colloquies, vn, pf, 1963; Night Song, pf, 1963; Suite for the Young, pf, 1964; Laudation, org, 1965; 5 Images: Cortege, Promenade, Day Dreams, The Ballerina, The Dancing Sargeant, pf 4 hands, 1967, all arr. orch

Capriccio on the Interval of a Second, pf, 1968; Bagatelles, harp, 1969; Lyric Pieces for the Young, pf, 1971; The Developing Flutist, fl, pf, 1972; 3 Essays, cl, pf, 1974; Stage Parodies, pf suite, young players, pf 4 hands, 1974; Str Qt, 1974; Diversions, pf, 1975; 5 Lyric Pieces for the Young Organist, 1975; Salute to Scarlatti, pf/hpd, 1979; Tpt Sonata, 1979; Concert Variations, pf, 1980; Reflections on a Xmas Tune, ww qnt, 1981; Song at Springtide, pf 4 hands, 1983

SOLO VOCAL

(1v, pf unless stated otherwise)

Ballad of Thomas Jefferson (Jefferson), 1937; Gone (C. Sandburg), 1939, withdrawn; Joy (Sandburg), 1939, withdrawn; Mill Doors (Sandburg), 1939; New Born (L. G. Marshall), 1946; There is a lady sweet and kind (anon. Elizabethan), 1946; The Assassination: 2 Fates Discuss a Human Problem (R. Hillyer), 1947; Lament (C. Tichborne), 1947; 6 Love Songs: Eyebright (J. A. Symonds), Why so pale and wan fond lover? (J. Suckling), Meeting at Night (R. Browning), The Dying Nightingale (S. Young), All things leave me (Symonds), How do I love thee? (E. B. Browning), 1948

The Lamentation of Saul (after D. H. Lawrence: David), Bar, orch/6 insts, 1954; The Listeners (W. de la Mare), 1955; Un sonetto di Petrarca (Petrarch) (Songs of Adieu), cycle, 1959; A Christmas Carol (Chesterton), 1960; Bright Star (Hoffman), 1962; 3 Songs of Adieu: After Love (Symonds), Fade, Vision Bright (anon.), Farewell (Symonds), 1962; Songs of Remembrance (J. H. Wheelock), Bar, orch, 1977; Note Left on a Doorstep (L. Peter), medium v, pf

Principal publishers: Associated, C. Fisher, Marks, G. Schirmer

BIBLIOGRAPHY

EwenD

R. Sabin: "Norman Dello Joio," *MusAm*, lxx/12 (1950), 9

M. Powell: "Current Chronicle," *MQ*, xlii (1956), 383 [review and analysis of *The Trial at Rouen*]

"Dello Joio, Norman," *CBY 1957*

E. Downes: "The Music of Norman Dello Joio," *MQ*, xlviii (1962), 149

Compositores de América/Composers of the Americas, ed. Pan American Union, ix (Washington, DC, 1963)

D. L. Arlton: *American Piano Sonatas of the Twentieth Century* (diss., Columbia U., 1968) [incl. analysis of Pf Sonata no.3]

C. F. Del Rosso: *A Study of Selected Solo Clarinet Literature of four American Composers as a Basis for Performance and Teaching* (diss., Columbia U., 1969) [incl. analysis of *Concertante*]

J. R. Whalen: *A Comparative Study of the Sonata Number Three for Piano and the Variations, Chaconne, and Finale for Orchestra by Norman Dello Joio* (diss., Indiana U., 1969)

M. Hinson: "The Solo Piano Music of Norman Dello Joio," *American Music Teacher*, xix (1970), 34

T. A. Bumgardner: *The Solo Vocal Works of Norman Dello Joio* (diss., U. of Texas, Austin, 1973)

J. S. Wannamaker: *The Musical Settings of Walt Whitman* (diss., U. of Minnesota, 1975)

K. Matheson: *Interview with Norman Dello Joio* (MS, *NN-L*, 1978)

N. J. Boston: *The Piano Sonatas and Suites of Norman Dello Joio* (diss., Peabody Conservatory, 1984)

T. A. Bumgardner: *Norman Dello Joio* (in preparation)

RICHARD JACKSON

Delmore Brothers. Country-music duo. It consisted of Alton Delmore (*b* Elkmont, AL, 25 Dec 1908; *d* Nashville, TN, 4 July 1964) and Rabon Delmore (*b* Elkmont, AL, 3 Dec 1910; *d* Athens, AL, 4 Dec 1952). The sons of tenant farmers, as children they taught themselves to play fiddle and guitar. They learned to sing from black fieldhands, which gave their music the most prominent black blues influence of any country group in the prerock era. In 1930 they won a fiddling contest at the Limestone County fair, after which Alton wrote *Brown's Ferry Blues*, a classic country novelty song and the first of the more than 1000 tunes he composed. Rabon wrote about 200 songs.

In 1931, the Delmores auditioned for Columbia Records in Atlanta but recorded only one side. The following year they joined the "Grand Ole Opry," where they remained until 1938. During this period they also recorded for Victor, producing such country standards as *Southern Moon* and *The Fugitive's Lament*. Improvements in microphone technology enabled them to sing more softly than had any earlier country performers. That fact, coupled with the distinctive twang of Rabon's tenor guitar, had a great influence on the rising bluegrass movement, notably the Monroe Brothers and Blue Sky Boys. After 1938, the Delmores played on radio stations throughout the South. During the 1940s, they adapted black boogie-woogie to country harmony, resulting in the very successful *Blues stay away from me*. They also performed in a country-music gospel quartet, the Brown's Ferry Four, with Merle Travis and Grandpa Jones.

RECORDINGS

(selective list)

Brown's Ferry Blues (Bluebird B5403, 1933); Gonna lay down my old guitar (Bluebird B5299, 1933); Alabama Lullaby (Bluebird B6034, 1935); The Fugitive's Lament (Bluebird B6019, 1935); Southern Moon (Bluebird B6841, 1937); Broken Hearted Lover (Decca 5907, 1940); When it's time for the whippoorwill to sing (Decca DE5925, 1940); Blues stay away from me (King 803, 1949)

BIBLIOGRAPHY

A. Delmore: *Truth is Stranger than Publicity*, ed. C. K. Wolfe (Nashville, 1977) [incl. discography]

DAVE MARSH

Delogu, Gaetano (*b* Messina, Sicily, 14 April 1934). Italian conductor. He began to learn violin as a child and continued his musical education at the University of Catania, while studying for a law degree (1958). He then studied conducting with Franco Ferrara in Rome and Venice, and won a prize at the Young Conductor's Competition in Florence in 1964. After conducting for Italian Radio in Rome, Milan, Turin, and Naples, he won the Dimitri Mitropoulos Competition in New York in 1968. During the following season he worked with both the New York PO (under Bernstein) and with the National SO. After a period as conductor at the Teatro Massimo in Palermo (1975–8), he served as music director of the Denver SO from 1979 to 1986. Delogu has appeared as guest conductor with many leading orchestras, including the Vienna SO, the London PO, and the Czech PO (he has recorded with the last two). He has also been active in opera, specializing particularly in the works of Puccini.

BIBLIOGRAPHY

E. Forbes: "Delogu in Britain," *Music and Musicians*, xxii/10 (1974), 12

GENE BIRINGER

Delta Omicron International Music Fraternity. Professional music society for women, founded in 1909; *see* GREEK-LETTER SOCIETIES, §2.

Del Tredici, David (Walter) (*b* Cloverdale, CA, 16 March 1937). Composer. He trained first as a pianist, studying with Bernhard Abramowitsch in Berkeley, California, and with Robert Helps in New York, and at the age of 16 made his début with the San Francisco SO. In 1958 while participating as a pianist in the Aspen Music Festival he met Milhaud, who encouraged him to study composition. At the University of California, Berkeley (BA 1959), he studied with Elston and Shifrin and at Princeton University (MFA 1963) with Sessions and Kim. He taught at Harvard University (1966–72), at SUNY, Buffalo (1973), where he was a member of the Creative Associates group, and at Boston University (1973–84); in 1984 he joined the faculty of City College and Graduate School, CUNY. His honors include a Guggenheim Fellowship (1966), an award from the American Academy and Institute of Arts and Letters (1968), a Naumburg Award (1972), three NEA grants (1973, 1974, and 1984), a Pulitzer Prize (for *In Memory of a Summer Day*, 1980), and the Friedheim Award (for *Happy Voices*, 1982); he has received commissions from the Koussevitzky and Fromm foundations and such

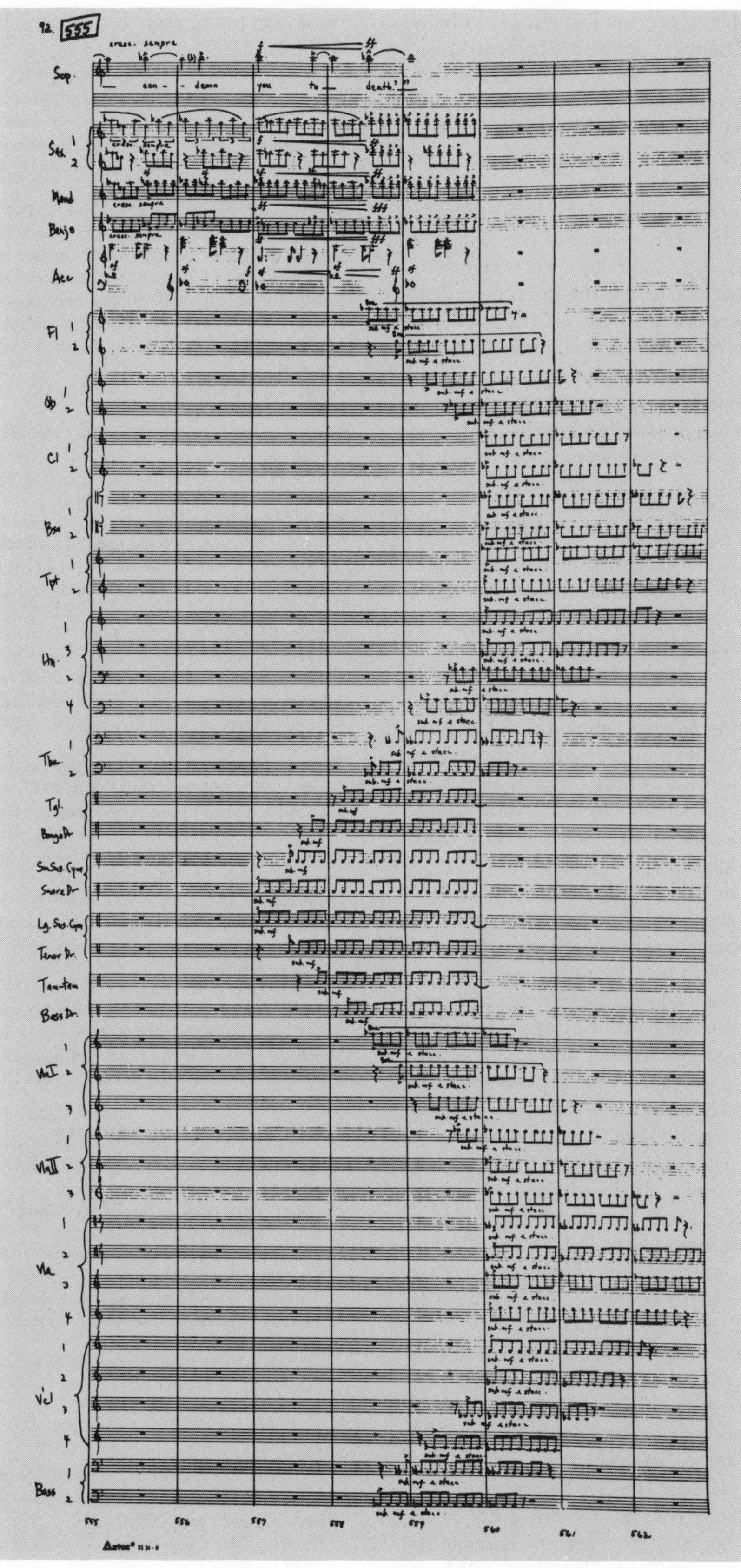

Score of "The Mouse's Tale" from David Del Tredici's "Adventures Underground" (1971)

orchestras as the Chicago, St. Louis, and San Francisco symphony orchestras, the Philadelphia Orchestra, and the Chamber Music Society of Lincoln Center (for *Haddocks' Eyes*, 1986). He has held residencies at the Marlboro Festival, the Berkshire Music Festival, and the Aspen Music Festival. In 1984 he was elected to the Institute of the American Academy and Institute of Arts and Letters.

Del Tredici's early works reflect the influence of his training at Princeton, which in the early 1960s was one of the centers of the serialist movement in the USA; although he temporarily abandoned his studies there because he felt the teaching of Sessions and Kim to be too doctrinaire, almost all the music he composed before 1968 employs the canon and palindrome, devices common to post-Webernian serialism. Except for a few instrumental works, the compositions from this period are settings of texts by James Joyce. Written in a rigorously schematic and often jarringly dissonant style, they are nonetheless rich in emotion, aesthetically more in the tradition of the pre-serial German expressionists than of the post-Webernians.

Del Tredici's style changed radically when he shifted his attention to Lewis Carroll's books *Alice's Adventures in Wonderland* and *Through the Looking Glass*: the whimsical, quizzical moods of Carroll's prose demanded a decidedly different musical language from the hard-edged melodic and harmonic style appropriate to Joyce's poetry. Del Tredici began to explore the possibilities of straightforward tonality, not in an effort to restore musical ideals of a past era but simply because the texts called for it. The puns and other word-play of Carroll's texts suggested a juxtaposition of musical idioms; all of the "Alice" works composed between 1968 and 1976 employ, in addition to amplified vocal soloist and full orchestra, a solo ensemble described either as a "rock group" (electric guitars, saxophones) or a "folk group" (banjo, mandolin, accordion, etc.). The "Alice" pieces written after 1976 are scored for orchestra and amplified soprano or for orchestra alone, but woven into their textures are many references to dance music, marches, and other vintage popular-music forms.

Final Alice was intended to be the last of Del Tredici's "Alice" works, but the success of its première by the Chicago SO resulted in a flurry of commissions, and Del Tredici decided to extend the cycle. *An Alice Symphony*, which may be divided into two independent works, *Illustrated Alice* and *In Wonderland*, was followed by the massive composition *Child Alice*, comprising *In Memory of a Summer Day* (part 1), and *Happy Voices*, *Quaint Events*, and *All in the Golden Afternoon* (part 2). In addition to sharing an orchestral style reminiscent of a tone poem by Richard Strauss laced with pungent dissonances, almost all of Del Tredici's "Alice" pieces include a "signature": near the end of the piece certain players count aloud from one to 13 in Italian, ending with an exaggerated pronunciation of the word "tredici."

Final Alice is in essence a theatrical work, its power resulting as much from its deft juxtaposition of contrasting idioms and sonorous "special effects" as from the individual and cumulative rhythmic energy of the various sections and the solidity of the composition's structure. The subsequent pieces are less dramatic and more lyrical, and they have been criticized as being unduly repetitious, unimaginative in content, and too obviously derivative of the Straussian style; but they have become enormously popular with the general public. Del Tredici has frequently been accused of pandering to the tastes of an increasingly conservative audience. He has seldom been regarded, however, as anything less than a first-rate musical craftsman, and his skills as an orchestrator win praise even from those adamantly opposed to his aesthetics.

WORKS

folk group – 2 s sax, mand, t banjo, accordion
rock group – s sax, s + t sax elec gui, elec b gui

Four Songs (J. Joyce): Dove Song, She Weeps over Rahoon, A Flower given to my Daughter, Monotone, 1v, pf, 1958–60; Berkeley, CA, 1 March 1961, M. Abramowitsch, Del Tredici

Soliloquy, pf, 1958; Aspen, CO, 1958, Del Tredici

String Trio, 1959; Berkeley, CA, 1 March 1961

Two Songs (Joyce): Bahnhofstrasse, Alone, 1959, rev. 1978; Washington, DC, 11 Feb 1983, P. Bryn-Julson, D. Sutherland

Fantasy Pieces, pf, 1959–60; San Francisco, CA, 1960, Del Tredici

Scherzo, pf 4 hands, 1960; Princeton, NJ, 1960, Del Tredici, R. Helps

I Hear an Army (Joyce), S, str qt, 1963–4; Lenox, MA, 12 Aug 1964, Bryn-Julson

Night Conjure-verse (Joyce), S, Mez/Ct, chamber ens, 1965; San Francisco, 3 March 1966, cond. Del Tredici

Syzygy (Joyce), S, hn, chamber ens, 1966; New York, 6 July 1968, Bryn-Julson, cond. R. Dufallo

The Last Gospel (John i.1–18), S, chorus, rock group, orch, 1967, rev. 1984; San Francisco, 15 June 1968, cond. Del Tredici

Pop-pourri (L. Carroll), amp S, Ct/Mez ad lib, mixed chorus, rock group, orch, 1968, rev. 1973; La Jolla, CA, 28 July 1968, Bryn-Julson, cond. M. Katims

An Alice Symphony (Carroll): 1 Speak Gently/Speak Roughly, 2 The Lobster Quadrille, 3 'Tis the Voice of the Sluggard, 4 Who Stole the Tarts?, 5 Dream-conclusion, amp S, folk group, orch, 1969; movt 2, London, 14 Nov 1969, cond. Copland; Illustrated Alice [= movts 1, 4, and 5], San Francisco, 8 Aug 1976, S. Harmon, cond. Del Tredici; In Wonderland [= movts 2, 3, and 5], Aspen, CO, 29 July 1975, S. D. Wyner, cond. Dufallo

Adventures Underground (Carroll): The Pool of Tears, The Mouse's Tale, amp S, folk group, orch, 1971, rev. 1977; Buffalo, NY, 13 April 1975, Wyner, cond. M. T. Thomas

Vintage Alice: Fantascene on A Mad Tea Party (Carroll), amp S, folk group, orch, 1972; Saratoga, CA, 5 Aug 1972, C. Commings, cond. Del Tredici

Final Alice (Carroll), amp S, folk group, orch, 1976; Chicago, 7 Oct 1976, B. Hendricks, cond. Solti; Acrostic Song pubd in various arrs.: 1v, pf; vv, pf/harp; unacc. chorus; gui; fl, pf/harp [Acrostic Paraphrase, harp, 1983, Virtuoso Caprice, pf, 1984, both based on Acrostic Song]

Child Alice (Carroll), pt 1: In Memory of a Summer Day, pt 2: Quaint Events, Happy Voices, All in the Golden Afternoon, amp S, orch, 1977–81; In Memory of a Summer Day, St. Louis, 23 Feb 1980, Bryn-Julson, cond. Slatkin; Quaint Events, Buffalo, NY, 19 Nov 1981, L. Shelton, cond. J. Rudel; Happy Voices, San Francisco, 16 Sept 1980, cond. E. de Waart; All in the Golden Afternoon, Philadelphia, 8 May 1981, B. Valente, cond. Ormandy; pt 2 perf. complete, Aspen, CO, 1 Aug 1984, D. Dorow

March to Tonality, orch, 1983–5; Chicago, 13 June 1985, cond. Thomas

Haddocks' Eyes (Carroll), S, chamber ens, 1985–6; New York, 2 May 1986, Bryn-Julson

Principal publisher: Boosey & Hawkes

BIBLIOGRAPHY

EwenD

H. Cole: "Del Tredici's The Lobster Quadrille," *Tempo*, no.91 (1969–70), 20

P. Earls: "David Del Tredici: Syzygy," *PNM*, viii/1 (1970), 304

D. Del Tredici and others: "Contemporary Music: Observations from those who Create It," *Music and Artists*, v/3 (1972), 12

O. Knussen: "David Del Tredici and 'Syzygy'," *Tempo*, no.118 (1976), 8

R. Holloway: "David Del Tredici and 'Adventures Underground'," *Tempo*, nos.133–4 (1980), 74

——: "David Del Tredici's 'All in the Golden Afternoon' at Philadelphia," *Tempo*, no.138 (1981), 51

"Del Tredici, David," *CBY 1983*

T. Page: "The New Romance with Tonality," *New York Times Magazine* (29 May 1983), 22

J. Rockwell: "David Del Tredici: the Return of Tonality, the Orchestral Audience and the Danger of Success," *All American Music: Composition in the Late Twentieth Century* (New York, 1983), 71

L. Brunner: "David Del Tredici: An Alice Symphony," *Notes*, xli (1984–5), 159

JAMES WIERZBICKI

De Luca, Giuseppe (*b* Rome, Italy, 25 Dec 1876; *d* New York, 26 Aug 1950). Italian baritone. In 1892 he entered the Santa

Cecilia conservatory in Rome to begin five years of vocal study with Vinceslao Persichini, and he made his operatic début at Piacenza on 6 November 1897 as Valentin in *Faust*. In 1903 he was chosen by La Scala for the premières of Giordano's *Siberia* (19 December 1903) and Puccini's *Madama Butterfly* (17 February 1904). He remained at La Scala for eight seasons. He first sang at the Metropolitan Opera in Rossini's *Il barbiere di Siviglia* on 25 November 1915, and for 20 consecutive seasons remained an invaluable and much appreciated member of the company, gradually assuming all the leading roles of the Italian repertory. His well-schooled baritone was less powerful than those of some contemporaries, but his mastery of the art of singing enabled him to retain his powers almost unimpaired to an advanced age. When he gave his last performances at the Metropolitan in *La traviata*, *La bohème*, and *Rigoletto*, taking leave of the scene of his old triumphs as Rigoletto on 12 March 1940, most of the professional singers and vocal enthusiasts in New York were present to pay their respects to him. On 7 November 1947, at the age of 70, just 50 years after his début, he gave his farewell New York recital. His many phonograph recordings, made over 45 years, are of fine quality; the early ones made for Fonotipia exhibit the brilliance of the young singer, while those for Victor made between 1917 and 1930 reveal the mature classical stylist and stand as models of the bel canto tradition.

BIBLIOGRAPHY

"De Luca, Giuseppe," *CBY 1947*

A. Favia-Artsay: "Giuseppe De Luca," *Record Collector*, v (1950), 56 [with discography]

Obituaries, *Musical Courier*, cxlii/5 (1950), 11; *New York Herald Tribune* (28 Aug 1950); *New York Times* (28 Aug 1950)

DESMOND SHAWE-TAYLOR/R

De Mille, Agnes (George) (*b* New York, 1909). Choreographer. After graduating from UCLA, she went to England where she danced with the companies of Marie Rambert and Antony Tudor. She toured the USA and Europe both as a solo performer and as the founder and director of several dance companies. In 1942 she created her most enduring and popular ballet, *Rodeo*, to music by Copland; many of her other works are similarly based on American themes and choreographed to music by American composers, including *Fall River Legend* (1948; music by Gould), *The Harvest According* (1952; Thomson), *The Four Marys* (1965; Trude Rittman), and *The Wind in the Mountains* (1965; Laurence Rosenthal, based on early American folksongs). De Mille also choreographed for many musicals and films, notably *Oklahoma!* (1943), by Rodgers and Hammerstein.

WRITINGS

Dance to the Piper (Boston, 1952/*R*1980)

And Promenade Home (Boston, 1958/*R*1980)

To a Young Dancer (Boston, 1962)

The Book of the Dance (New York, 1963)

Speak to me, Dance with Me (Boston, 1973)

Where the Wings Grow (Garden City, NY, 1978)

America Dances (New York, 1980)

Reprieve (Garden City, NY, 1981)

BIBLIOGRAPHY

"De Mille, Agnes," *CBY 1985*

SUSAN AU

Dempster, Stuart (Ross) (*b* Berkeley, CA, 7 July 1936). Trombonist and composer. After his initial training at San Francisco State College, he was appointed, between 1960 and 1966, assistant professor at California State College, Hayward, instructor at the San Francisco Conservatory, and member of the Performing Group at Mills College. He was first trombonist in the Oakland SO (1962–6), Creative Associate at SUNY, Buffalo, under Foss (1967–8), fellow at the Center for Advanced Study at the University of Illinois (1971–2), and senior Fulbright scholar to Australia (1973); he has also been awarded two NEA grants (1978, 1979) and a Guggenheim Fellowship (1981). In 1968 he became assistant professor and in 1978 associate professor at the University of Washington, Seattle.

Dempster is especially interested in new sounds and techniques, including those obtained through the study of non-Western instruments such as the Australian didjeridu. He has helped to enlarge the contemporary trombone repertory by commissioning and performing new works, notably Berio's *Sequenza V* (1966) and pieces by Imbrie, Krenek, Oliveros, Robert Erickson, and Robert Moran. He is the author of *The Modern Trombone: a Definition of its Idioms* (1979).

WORKS

Trbn: Sonata, b trbn, pf, 1961; Chamber Music 13, 1v, trbns, 1964; 10 Grand Hosery, ballet, trbn, dancers, sculptors, audience, 1971–2; Standing Waves, 1976; Life Begins at 40, 1976; Standing Waves, trbn, tape, 1978; Monty, 1979; Fog Calling, trbn, didjeridu, 1981; Gone with the Wind, 1981–; Sonic Breathing and Circular Meditations, trbn, didjeridu, 1981–; Harmonic Tremors, trbn, tape, 1982; Roulette, trbn, audience, 1983; Aix en Providence, 1983

Other works: 5 works, brass qt, 1957–9; Prelude and 2 Movts, vn, pf, 1959; Adagio and Canonic Variations, brass qnt, 1962; 2 Songs, 1v, harp, 1962; The Road not Taken, 1v, chorus, orch, 1967; Pipe Dream, pipes, dancers, slides, audience, sound sculpture ad lib, 1972; Didjeridervish, didjeridu, 1976; JDBBBDJ, didjeridu, audience, 1983; Don't Worry, it will Come, garden hoses, audience, 1983

Principal publisher: California UP

BIBLIOGRAPHY

F. L. McCarty: "An Interview with Stuart Dempster," *The Instrumentalist*, xxviii/10 (1974), 36

V. Samson: "An Interview with Stuart Dempster," *The Composer*, ix/18 (1978), 28

EDWARD H. TARR/R

Dempster, William Richardson (*b* Keith, Scotland, 1808; *d* London, England, 7 March 1871). Scottish singer and composer. He was apprenticed to a quill maker in Aberdeen, Scotland, but also pursued the study of music, which soon became his vocation. Hoping to further his career, he came to the USA, and sang at Niblo's Garden in New York on 4 September 1835. Though of inadequate strength to fill a large hall, his voice was admired for its sweetness and its affective projection of the sentiments in parlor ballads, especially those of his own composition. Dempster spent several years in America, then traveled back and forth to Great Britain, giving concerts on both sides of the Atlantic. He was always, however, more popular in America than in his own country; large numbers of Americans came to hear him and declared him to be the finest English ballad singer then appearing in the USA.

Dempster's compositions were in great demand, and Stephen Foster was among those who fell under their influence; Foster's *Oh! Susanna*, for example, bears some resemblance to the second part of Dempster's *The May Queen*. Dempster particularly liked to set the poems of Henry Wadsworth Longfellow and Alfred Tennyson. Among his most popular songs in America were *Lament of the Irish Emigrant* (1840), *The Blind Boy* (1842), *The May Queen* (1845), *The Rainy Day* (1947), *Footsteps of Angels* (1847), *Bird of the Wilderness* (1854), *The Deserted Road* (1864), and *Songs in the Idylls of the King* (1864).

BIBLIOGRAPHY

H. K. Johnson: *Our Familiar Songs* (New York, 1881), 620

F. Dean and H. K. Johnson, eds.: *Famous Songs and those who Made them* (New York, 1895), 521

G. C. D. Odell: *Annals of the New York Stage*, iv–vi (New York, 1928–31)

S. Spaeth: *A History of Popular Music in America* (New York, 1948), 87, 122

A. Stoutamire: *Music of the Old South* (Rutherford, NJ, 1972), 159, 164

N. E. Tawa: *Sweet Songs for Gentle Americans* (Bowling Green, OH, 1980)

NICHOLAS E. TAWA

Denny, William D(ouglas) (*b* Seattle, WA, 2 July 1910; *d* Berkeley, CA, 2 Sept 1980). Composer, teacher, and violist. After attending the University of California, Berkeley (BA 1931, MA 1933), he studied composition in Paris with Paul Dukas (1933–5) and at the American Academy in Rome (1939–41), where he was Horatio Parker Fellow. In June 1953 he won a Fromm Foundation award for his String Quartet no.2. He taught at Berkeley (1938–9), Harvard University (1941–2), and Vassar College (1942–4), before returning to Berkeley as professor in 1945. He remained on the faculty there until 1978, serving as vice-chairman of the department of music for more than 15 years and then as chairman from 1972 to 1975. As a conductor and violist Denny performed on many university occasions; he also conducted his own compositions with various orchestras.

Denny has been described as a "musicians' composer." His music is thoroughly personal and abstract, characterized by an intense lyricism with rhythmical elements predominating. The structure and symmetry of his works are flawlessly balanced, often within a complex contrapuntal texture, and his idiomatic writing for instruments has been particularly admired. Denny's harmonic language is dissonant yet oriented around tonal centers; his style has a definite similarity to the mature works of Piston. During the 1940s and 1950s he was one of the most respected composers active in the San Francisco Bay area, and his compositions were performed by the CBS and NBC symphony orchestras, the San Francisco SO, the Griller String Quartet, the Budapest String Quartet, the Juilliard String Quartet, and the University Chorus at Berkeley, among others.

WORKS

Orch: Bacchanale, 1935; Concertino, 1937; 3 syms., 1939, 1949, 1955–7; Sinfonietta, 1940; Suite, chamber orch, 1940; Ov., str, 1945; Praeludium, 1946; Introduction and Allegro, 1956

Chamber: 3 str qts, 1937–8, 1952, 1955; Va Sonata, 1943–4; Partita, org, 1958; Str Trio, 1965; Toccata, Aria, and Fugue, org, 1966

Choral: Most glorious Lord of Life, cantata, 1943; 3 Motets, 1946–7

MSS in *CU-MUSI*

JOHN A. EMERSON

Densmore, Frances (*b* Red Wing, MN, 21 May 1867; *d* Red Wing, 5 June 1957). Ethnomusicologist. She received her early musical education at Oberlin Conservatory; later she was a piano pupil of Carl Baermann in Boston and of Leopold Godowsky, and studied counterpoint at Harvard University. A pioneer in the study of American Indian music, she pursued this field with unflagging energy until her death. In 1901 she wrote down songs from a Sioux woman near Red Wing; then, in 1905, she visited the White Earth Reservation in Minnesota to observe the Chippewa, and made her first field trip at Grand Portage on the north shore of Lake Superior. In 1907 her work was recognized by the Bureau of American Ethnology of the Smithsonian Institution; she was given the title of Collaborator and, with the encouragement of the Smithsonian, began systematic field research that resulted in no fewer than 13 monographs on Indian music and five anthropological studies, all issued by the Smithsonian (1910–57). Already in her first book, *Chippewa Music* (1910–13), Densmore displayed her ability as an observant ethnographer and conscientious analyst of music. She contributed articles to many journals as a means of interpreting Indian culture to a larger public; her book *The American Indians and their Music* (1926, rev. 2/1937) was written as an introduction for the lay reader.

For illustration *see* ETHNOMUSICOLOGY, fig.2.

BIBLIOGRAPHY

T. Vennum, Jr.: "Densmore, Frances Theresa," *NAW*

WILLARD RHODES/R

Denson, Seaborn M(cDaniel) (*b* nr Arbacoochee, AL, 9 April 1854; *d* nr Helicon, AL, 18 April 1936). Singing-school teacher, composer, and tunebook compiler. He taught his first singing-school from B. F. White's and E. J. King's *The Sacred Harp* (1844) in 1874 and continued to conduct schools in the South for more than 50 years. He and his brother Thomas Jackson Denson (*b* nr Arbacoochee, AL, 20 Jan 1863; *d* nr Jasper, AL, 14 Sept 1935) taught countless thousands of rural singers from Georgia to Texas to read shape-note music. He served as music editor of J. S. James's revision of *The Sacred Harp, The Original Sacred Harp* (1911), adding alto parts to 327 three-part pieces. He and his brother contributed original compositions to this as well as to their own revision of the book, the *Original Sacred Harp, Denson Revision* (Haleyville, AL, 1936, rev. 2/1960, 4/1971), which they began but did not live to see published.

See also SHAPE-NOTE HYMNODY, §2.

BIBLIOGRAPHY

G. P. Jackson: "Sacred Harpers and their Conventions," *White Spirituals in the Southern Uplands* (Chapel Hill, 1933/*R*1965), 107

B. E. Cobb: *The Sacred Harp: a Tradition and its Music* (Athens, GA, 1978)

BUELL E. COBB, JR.

Denver. Capital city of Colorado (pop. 492,365; metropolitan area 1,620,902). It was founded in 1858, and the immense wealth that soon flowed from the gold and silver mines in the Rocky Mountains made possible the creation of a cultural and musical oasis in the isolated American West. The home, church, and theater were the centers of Denver's early musical life. The city's first piano was brought by a family of settlers in 1860. A local organ builder, Charles Anderson, placed a single-manual instrument in the H Street Presbyterian Church in 1872. The Rev. H. Martyn Hart, dean of the Episcopal Cathedral of St. John in the Wilderness, brought to Denver a series of English organists whose influence was lasting: the first was Arthur W. Marchant, who arrived in 1880 and had an organ by Hook & Hastings installed in the cathedral; he was succeeded by Walter E. Hall (1882), John H. Gower (1887), and Henry Houseley (1888). Houseley was also a teacher, composer, and conductor, and during the next 30 years contributed significantly to many areas of local musical life. In 1888 the musician and philanthropist Isaac E. Blake gave an 82-rank Roosevelt organ to Trinity Methodist Church, where Wilberforce Whiteman produced oratorio performances at the turn of the century. Whiteman's son, the bandleader Paul Whiteman, grew up in Denver, where his early musical training included playing viola in local symphony and theater orchestras.

An opera house was built in nearby Central City in 1877 and opened in 1878; it presented varied musical and dramatic fare until the turn of the century. In 1931 the building was acquired by Denver University and the house was reopened in 1932, when the Central City Opera House Association was formed; that year it became the site of the annual summer opera festival, the first in the USA (*see* CENTRAL CITY OPERA FESTIVAL).

Further interest in opera was stimulated in Denver when H. A. W. Tabor established the Tabor Opera House in 1881. The upholstery was of French brocade, the walls of mahogany. It opened with a performance of *Maritana*, an opera by the Irish composer Vincent Wallace, featuring Emma Abbott. The house declined after Tabor's financial ruin in 1893 and until the 1920s was used primarily for musicals; the building was demolished in 1963. Up to 1900 the Tabor Opera House and the Broadway Theatre were hosts to such opera singers as Adelina Patti, Etelka Gerster, Lillian Nordica, Francesco Tamagno, Nellie Melba, Emma Juch, and Johanna Gadski, but not all of Denver's opera was imported. The Reverend Joseph Bosetti organized the Denver Grand Opera Company and produced opera locally from 1915 until 1951. The Greater Denver Opera Company (1955–8) continued sporadic opera programs, as did the Denver Lyric Theatre from 1958 through the 1970s. Summer musicals were sponsored by the *Denver Post* from 1933 to 1972. The Denver Opera Repertory Company, active in the 1970s, was succeeded by Opera Colorado. Organized in 1981 with Nathaniel Merrill as director, this company gave its first season in 1983 at Boettcher Concert Hall, presenting Puccini's *La bohème* (in Italian and English) and Verdi's *Otello* (in Italian) with internationally known singers.

Denver's geographical isolation created a strong need for musical societies. Outstanding musicians were brought there in the early 1900s for the Tuesday Musical Club concerts. Robert Slack, the first impresario in the city, began in 1905 with contracts for Emma Eames, David Bispham, Ben Davis, Alfred Reisenauer, and Johanna Gadski; he remained active until his death in 1948 and his agency continued until the mid-1950s.

Interest in orchestral music was generated in the 1890s through summer garden concerts sponsored by Mary Elitch Long, and in 1900 Houseley founded an amateur symphony orchestra. Raffaelo Cavallo became its conductor in 1903 and was succeeded by Horace E. Tureman in 1911, when Cavallo set up his own rival orchestra, the Cavallo SO (see fig. 1). Tureman reorganized his orchestra, which had faltered during World War I, as the Denver Civic SO in 1921, and conducted its first performance in 1922. In 1934 union members left to become the Denver SO, nonunion members remaining as the Civic SO; Tureman conducted both groups. On Tureman's retirement in 1944 Saul Caston became director of the Denver SO, remaining until 1964; its concertmaster Henry Ginsburg also served as conductor of the Denver Civic SO. Subsequent conductors of the Denver SO have been Vladimir Golschmann (1964–70), Brian Priestman (1970–78), Gaetano Delogu (1979–86), and Philippe Entremont (from 1986). Boettcher Concert Hall became the orchestra's home on its opening in 1978. Several other orchestras have also been active in Denver. The semiprofessional Brico SO was founded by its conductor Antonia Brico as the Philharmonic Orchestra in 1948 (later known as the Businessman's SO). The Englewood Community Arts Orchestra, founded in 1954 by its director Gordon Parks, and the Denver Chamber Orchestra (known until 1981 as the Arapaho Chamber Orchestra) also draw their membership from both professionals and amateurs.

Wind bands have played an important role in Denver's musical life. The earliest known instrumental ensemble in Denver, the Sax Horn Band, was founded in 1860. It was followed by the Denver City Band (1861) and the Grand Army of the Republic Band (1869), directed by W. E. Reid. During the 1880s and 1890s the popularity of band music increased, and summer band concerts became a tradition. The First Brigade Band (1883), the Patrick S. Gilmore Band in 1888 and 1889, and the First Infantry Band under O. H. Richter helped sustain Denver's interest to the turn of the century. Also in the 1890s a band sponsored by

1. *Raffaelo Cavallo (center) with members of his symphony orchestra, Denver, c1912*

2. *Red Rocks outdoor theater, Denver*

the city itself grew in popularity and quality: the Denver Municipal Band, said to be the oldest surviving band of its type in the USA, began its 98th season in 1985. The band's early directors included Hermann Belstedt and Frederick Neal Innes; in 1919 a Denver businessman, Henry E. Sachs, became director, continuing until his death in 1970 at the age of 89. He was succeeded by Charles E. Lenicheck.

Denver's choral societies began with a Musical Union formed in 1867. A German Männerchor was established in 1870. Frank Damrosch, Denver's first public school music supervisor, organized a highly successful Choral Society in 1882 but returned to New York three years later. I. E. Blake started the Denver Choral Society in 1890; in 1894 its directorship went to Houseley, who gained for the ensemble a national reputation, with awards won at the Salt Lake City Welsh Eisteddfod in 1895 and the Louisiana Purchase Exposition, St. Louis (1904). David McK. Williams was the accompanist for the group. The Arion Singing Society was organized in 1904 and remained active through the 1930s. Other choral groups of the first half of the century were the Denver Philharmonic Chorus, the Treble and Bass Clef Clubs, and the Denver Municipal Chorus. The most popular and widely known group, however, was the choir of the Immaculate Conception Cathedral; under the direction of Monsignor Bosetti, it gave concerts in the Denver Auditorium from 1921 to 1932. Bosetti also had a strong influence on Denver's opera and choral performances from 1915 until the 1950s. Denver's strong choral heritage has continued with the Children's Chorale, founded in 1974 by Duain Wolf as a four-choir organization. The Classic Chorale, directed by Jerald Lipensky, began in 1972 as a community chorus, and in 1982 consisted of about 50 professional and amateur singers, augmented for large works with the Denver SO; it further offers a vocal and music education program to its members. Other choral groups are the Denver Concert Chorale (Nicholas Laurenti, musical director), the Denver Chamber Choir (William Jones), and the Colorado Choir and Chorus (Richard Eichenberger).

Fritz Thies, a local businessman, supported chamber music in Denver in the 1880s, leading to the formation of the Lehman Quartet (1892) and the Baker Quartet (1901). The Denver String Quartet, founded in 1921 by Henry Ginsburg, was the city's most popular chamber group and performed for over 20 years. The Friends of Chamber Music, established after World War II, owes its success to its founder, Jean Chappell Cranmer (1886–1974), who also founded the Applied Arts Society in 1920, was the first president of the Denver Symphony Society, and helped organize the nearby Aspen Music School. The Denver Early Music Consort was organized in 1976.

Of the concert facilities now available in Denver, the oldest summer theater in the USA is also the oldest structure in Denver still used for musical programs: built in 1891, the Elitch Garden Theater seats 1479 and offers musicals as part of its repertory. The excellent acoustical properties of Red Rocks, a natural outdoor theater, were known as early as 1911 when Mary Garden arrived there on a mule to do some impromptu "acoustical testing." Not until 1932, however, did George Cranmer, the local commissioner of parks, begin the transformation of Red Rocks into an actual theater (see fig.2). It was dedicated in 1941, when Helen Jepson sang to an audience of 10,000 Rotarians. While the Denver SO and many other musical organizations have occasionally appeared at Red Rocks, it is primarily used by hundreds of folk, popular, rock, and country music performers. Barry Fay of Fayline Inc. produces an all-pop festival at Red Rocks each summer. Other facilities used for these concerts are the Auditorium Arena (capacity 7300), McNichols Arena (20,000), and Rainbow Music Hall (1450). For many years Denver lacked a large, central concert hall to replace the 2400-seat Auditorium Theatre (1908) as a home for the Denver SO and an attraction for visiting orchestras and opera companies; the 2650-seat Boettcher Concert Hall, conceived as part of a center for the performing arts, was opened in 1978. The center also includes the Auditorium Theatre and the Helen Bonfils Theatre Complex. In 1981 the Business and Arts Council of Denver inaugurated a project entitled "Cultural Explorations in Metropolitan Denver" to stimulate financial and artistic cooperation.

Important private music schools in Denver have included the Denver University School of Music (founded 1879), the Denver Conservatory (1887), Colorado Women's College (1907), which merged with Denver University in 1982, the Liszt School (founded by James M. Tracey, 1906), Blanche Dingley Matthews School (1911), the Wolcott Conservatory (1920) and its offshoot under Edwin J. Stringham, the Denver College of Music (1925), and the Lamont School, now part of Denver University, founded in 1922 by Florence Lamont Hinman. Non-academic libraries include the Western History Room of the Denver Public Library and the State Historical Society Library.

BIBLIOGRAPHY

M. G. Wyer, ed.: *Music in Denver and Colorado* (Denver, 1927)
S. A. Linscome: *A History of Musical Development in Denver, Colorado, 1858–1908* (diss., U. of Texas, Austin, 1970)

SANFORD A. LINSCOME

Denver, John [Deutschendorf, Henry John, Jr.] (*b* Roswell, NM, 31 Dec 1942). Popular singer and songwriter. While studying architecture at Texas Tech University, Lubbock, he also performed as a folksinger. He moved to Los Angeles in 1964 and joined the Mitchell Trio, with whom he toured as the replacement for Chad Mitchell from 1965 until the group disbanded in 1968. By 1969 he had emerged as a major solo recording and concert artist, playing guitar and banjo, performing songs extolling simple pleasures and the outdoor life. He has been most successful with his own songs, pleasing amalgamations of folk, rock, and country elements, the most notable of which include *Leaving on a jet plane* (which was a success for Peter, Paul, and Mary in 1967), *Take me home, country roads* (1971), *Rocky Mountain High* (1972), and *Annie's Song* (1974). He reached the peak of his popularity in 1975, when he was named poet laureate of Colorado and received several country-music awards. He has recorded best-selling albums and made many concert tours and television appearances.

RECORDINGS
(selective list)

Rhymes & Reasons (Vic. 4207, 1969) [incl. Leaving on a jet plane]; *Poems, Prayers & Promises* (Vic. 4499, 1971) [incl. Take me home, country roads]; *Rocky Mountain High* (Vic. 47321, 1972); *Back Home Again* (Vic. 0548, 1974) [incl. Annie's Song]; *Windsong* (Vic. 1183, 1975); *Spirit* (Vic. 1649, 1976); *I Want to Live* (Vic. 2521, 1977)

BIBLIOGRAPHY

"Denver, John," *CBY 1975*
D. Dachs: *John Denver* (New York, 1976)
L. Fleischer: *John Denver* (New York, 1976)

MICHAEL J. BUDDS

De Paur, Leonard (*b* Summit, NJ, 18 Nov 1915). Conductor. He studied at the Institute of Musical Art, Columbia University Teachers College, and privately with Henry Cowell, Hall Johnson, Sergei Radamsky, and Pierre Monteux. After serving as assistant conductor of the Hall Johnson Choir (1932–6), he was music director of the Federal Theater Project in New York (1936–9), conducting, arranging, and composing music for various productions of Orson Welles, including *Macbeth*. In 1943, following a period of association with various Broadway shows, he began three years as choral director of the Air Force show "Winged Victory"; from this emerged the De Paur Infantry Chorus of the 372nd Regiment, with which De Paur toured extensively until 1957, meanwhile serving as choral director for the revivals of Thomson's *Four Saints in Three Acts* (1952) and Hammerstein's *Carmen Jones* (1956). He organized the De Paur Chorus in 1963, and, after two years of research into repertory, toured with it until 1969 in the USA and abroad, notably Africa, where the choir gave concerts in 15 countries. At the 1964 meeting of the National Association of Negro Musicians De Paur conducted the Orchestra of America at Philharmonic Hall, New York, in works by William Dawson, Coleridge-Taylor Perkinson, Ulysses Kay, and Duke Ellington. In 1971 he was appointed director of community relations of Lincoln Center, and until 1973 served as conductor of the Symphony of the New World. He conducted performances in 1971 and 1976 of William Grant Still's *A Bayou Legend* for Opera South in Jackson, Mississippi, and has recorded a wide range of works by black composers.

BIBLIOGRAPHY

SouthernB
R. Abdul: *Blacks in Classical Music* (New York, 1977), 57, 153, 210
P. Turner: *Afro-American Singers* (Minneapolis, 1977)

DOMINIQUE-RENÉ DE LERMA

DePreist, James (Anderson) (*b* Philadelphia, PA, 21 Nov 1936). Conductor. He studied at the University of Pennsylvania, and at the Philadelphia Conservatory of Music (1959–61) with Vincent Persichetti. In 1962 while on tour in the Far East he had poliomyelitis and became paralyzed in both legs. While convalescing he studied scores assiduously, and by late 1963 he was conducting in Bangkok. He won a first prize in the 1964 Dimitri Mitropoulos International Competition in New York, and Bernstein selected him as assistant conductor of the New York PO for the ensuing year. In 1967 he settled in Europe, and the next season made his continental début conducting the Rotterdam PO. He has conducted the Cleveland Orchestra, the Los Angeles PO, the Boston SO, the Philadelphia Orchestra, the Chicago SO, and the New York PO. He was associate conductor of the National SO of Washington from 1971 to 1974 and became its principal guest conductor in 1975. The following year he was named music director of the Quebec Symphony. In 1980 he became music director of the Oregon Symphony; his capable performances have won him much praise and have given the orchestra a respected regional profile. Among other awards, he has received honorary degrees from the University of Pennsylvania and from Laval University, Quebec.

BIBLIOGRAPHY

SouthernB
J. Hiemenz: "Musician of the Month: James DePreist," *HiFi/MusAm*, xxvii/3 (1977), 8

GEORGE GELLES/R

De Reszke, Edouard (*b* Warsaw, Poland, 22 Dec 1853; *d* Garnek, Poland, 25 May 1917). Polish bass. He studied with Filippo Coletti and Giovanni Sbriglia, then made his début in 1876 at the Paris Opéra as the King of Egypt in *Aida*. He appeared throughout Europe in roles such as Indra (in Massenet's *Le roi de Lahore*), the Count of St. Bris (*Les Huguenots*), Rossini's Don Basilio, Verdi's Fiesco (in the first performance of the revised version of *Simon Boccanegra*) and Silva (*Ernani*), and Leporello (in a special centennial performance of *Don Giovanni* at the Paris Opéra in 1887). He then came to the USA, where he frequently performed with his brother Jean de Reszke. He made both his American début (with the Abbey company in Chicago), as King

Henry in *Lohengrin*, and his début at the Metropolitan Opera, as Friar Lawrence in Gounod's *Roméo et Juliette*, in 1891. De Reszke specialized in the French repertory (his Mephistopheles and Friar Lawrence were particularly admired), and his huge voice and giant stature made him also a magnificent exponent of the Wagnerian roles, including Hans Sachs (*Die Meistersinger*), Daland (*Der fliegende Holländer*), King Marke (*Tristan und Isolde*), the Wanderer (*Siegfried*), and Hagen (*Götterdämmerung*). He retired in 1903, soon after his brother's retirement.

BIBLIOGRAPHY

C. Leiser: *Jean de Reszke and the Great Days of Opera* (London, 1933/R1970)
J. Dennis: "Edouard de Reszke," *Record Collector*, vi (1951), 101
P. G. Hurst: *The Operatic Age of Jean de Reszke* (New York, 1959)
R. Celletti: "Retszké, De," *Le grandi voci* (Rome, 1964)

ELIZABETH FORBES

De Reszke, Jean (*b* Warsaw, Poland, 14 Jan 1850; *d* Nice, France, 3 April 1925). Polish tenor. He studied with his mother, a talented amateur singer, and later with Ciaffei and Cotogni. After making his début at La Fenice, Venice (January 1874), he sang for several years in Europe as a baritone. Persuaded that his voice was naturally a tenor, he retired from the stage to study with Giovanni Sbriglia in Paris and made a triumphant return in the role of John the Baptist in the first Paris performance of Massenet's *Hérodiade* (1 February 1884). De Reszke sang with great success in Europe, often with his brother Edouard de Reszke, before making his American début with the Abbey company in Chicago as Lohengrin (1891) and his début at the Metropolitan Opera as Gounod's Romeo a few weeks later. For the next decade he appeared regularly in New York, where his popularity was enormous and his influence considerable. His beautiful voice, fine musicianship, and handsome stage presence were particularly admired in the French repertory, but he was also unsurpassed in Wagnerian roles. During his final season at the Metropolitan (1900–01), he sang Faust, Radames, Massenet's Le Cid, Meyerbeer's Raoul (*Les Huguenots*) and Vasco da Gama (*L'africaine*), Tristan, both Siegfrieds, Walther (*Die Meistersinger*), and Lohengrin. In 1903 he retired to Nice, where he taught singing until his death; among his pupils were Louise Edvina and Maggie Teyte.

BIBLIOGRAPHY

C. Leiser: *Jean de Reszke and the Great Days of Opera* (London, 1933/R1970)
J. Dennis: "Jean de Reszke," *Record Collector*, v (1950), 6
P. G. Hurst: *The Operatic Age of Jean de Reszke* (New York, 1959)
R. Celletti: "Retszké, De," *Le grandi voci* (Rome, 1964)
H. Pleasants: "Jean de Reszke," *The Great Singers* (New York, 1966), 254

ELIZABETH FORBES

De'Sierre, Georges. Pseudonym of LUDWIG BONVIN.

Des Marais, Paul (Emile) (*b* Menominee, MI, 23 June 1920). Composer and teacher. He studied composition with Sowerby in Chicago before attending Harvard University (BA 1949, MA 1953), where he studied with Piston, Merritt, and Gombosi. He spent two years in Europe on a John Knowles Paine Traveling Fellowship (1949–51), and studied with Boulanger. In 1960 he joined the faculty at UCLA, becoming professor of music in 1971. He has received a Thorne Award (1970–73) and a grant from the University of California Institute for Creative Arts.

The neoclassical language of his early music later moved towards a quasi-diatonic serialism in which ostinatos play a major role in the delineation of pitch centers. In his opera *Epiphanies*, open textures and simple pitch contexts are cultivated to permit full play in text setting; similar means are used in his large-scale choral works and in the later music for solo voice. Since the late 1970s Des Marais has become increasingly interested in music for the stage; *Triplum* was written for the choreographer Linda Sohl-Donnell. His writings include a book, *Harmony* (1962), and articles in *Perspectives of New Music*.

WORKS

Chamber opera: Epiphanies (H. Smith), 1964–8

Incidental music: A Secular Masque (Dryden), 1976; A Midsummer Night's Dream (Shakespeare), 1976; Oedipus (Sophocles), 1978; St. Joan (Shaw), 1980; Marriage à la Mode (Dryden), 1981; As You Like It (Shakespeare), 1983; The Man of Mode (G. Etherege), 1984

Dance pieces: Triplum, org, perc, 1981; Touch, 2 pf, 1984

Vocal: Le cimetière marin (P. Valèry), 1v, kbds, perc, 1971, withdrawn; Reflections on Fauré (Cummings), song cycle, 1v, pf, 1972; Brief Mass (Mass for the Seminarians), chorus, org, perc, 1973; Late Songs (P. Eluard, J. du Bellay, P. de Ronsard, A. de Lamartine), 4 songs, 1v, pf, 1978–9; Seasons of the Mind (G. Fletcher, R. Crashaw, E. Sitwell, T. Roethke), chamber chorus, pf 4 hands, cel, 1980–81

Kbd: 2 Movts, 2 pf, perc, 1972, rev. and enlarged as 3 Movts, 1975

RICHARD SWIFT

Des Moines. City in Iowa (pop. 191,003; metropolitan area 338,048). It became capital of the state in 1857. Its early musical life was shaped by Virgil Corydon Taylor (1817–1891), originally from Connecticut, and Maro Loomis Bartlett (1847–1919) of Ohio, who had been active in New York and Chicago. Taylor arrived in Des Moines in 1865; he organized music classes, conducted performances of his cantatas and other works, and served as organist of St. Paul's Episcopal Church. In 1868 F. Mills & Co., one of the earliest music publishers in the city, brought out his choral collection *The Praise Offering*. Bartlett was invited to become conductor of the 100-voice Des Moines Philharmonic Society in 1886. In his recollections of the city's musical life (*c*1915) he stated that the society had been first conducted by Willard Kimball of Grinnell and then by David Blakely of Minneapolis (later Sousa's business manager), who had brought Theodore Thomas and his orchestra and other groups to perform in Des Moines. Another important musical institution of this time was Gerberich's Grand Orchestra, a 38-member ensemble organized and conducted by the violinist and teacher Lyman S. Gerberich, which gave subscription concerts.

Bartlett quickly became an integral part of the musical life of Des Moines. In December 1886 he conducted his Philharmonic Society and Gerberich's orchestra in a performance of Handel's *Messiah*, which was given annually for the next decade. He also organized concerts by visiting artists, including Paderewski, Melba, and Kreisler, as well as the symphony orchestras of New York, Chicago, and Minneapolis. Amateur concerts were given by the Euterpe Club (*fl* 1880), the Apollo Club (1906–at least 1908), and other music societies. The Moore Opera House (1874–1929) and Foster's Opera House (1883–1911) offered varied fare, usually plays with or without music rather than opera. Further musical activity was provided by the Danish choir of Grand View College (founded 1896) and by Welsh music festivals held for a number of years from 1914 by the Des Moines Eisteddfod Association.

Bartlett founded the Des Moines Musical College in 1888 and served as dean of Drake University's College of Fine Arts, where he built a strong music department. Drake University (founded 1881) had one of the first music departments in the Midwest and offered the BM as early as 1886. Important musicians there have included Frederick Howard (*d* 1908), dean of the College of Fine Arts; the pianist Paul Stoye (1878–1971); the pianist, impresario, and composer George Frederick Ogden (1879–1930); Wallingford Riegger, head of the theory and cello departments from 1917 to 1922; and Francis Johnson Pyle (1901–1983), head of the theory and composition departments from 1937 to 1974.

The Civic Music Association was formed in 1925 to continue the tradition of inviting important performers and orchestras to Des Moines; its concerts were originally given in the KRNT Theatre (4000 seats) and from 1979 in the Civic Center of Greater Des Moines (2745). The Federal Concert Orchestra gave 690 concerts from March 1936 to July 1938, many of them summer concerts in Des Moines parks. The 86-member Drake–Des Moines SO was founded in 1937, with Frank Noyes of Drake as its conductor. In 1955 it was separated into two independent bodies, the Des Moines SO and the Drake SO. The former is a professional orchestra and gives 21 concerts a season in the Civic Center. Noyes continued as conductor until 1967, when he was succeeded by Robert Gutter (1967–9), Willis Page (1969–71), and Thomas Griswold (1971–3); after a season of guest conductors (1973–4), Yuri Krasnapolsky was appointed in 1974. Other concert organizations include the Des Moines Community Orchestra (founded 1976), the Greater Des Moines Youth Symphony (1963), the Des Moines Metro Opera (1973) of nearby Indianola, the Des Moines Choral Society (1980), the Concert Singers (1973), and the Des Moines Ballet (1970). In addition to the Civic Center, current concert halls include the Hoyt Sherman Place Auditorium (opened 1923; 1500 seats), Drake University Auditorium (1905; 1000), and the Hall of the Performing Arts in the Harmon Fine Arts Center (1973; 550).

The publishing firm of J. E. Agnew & Co., organized in 1911, specialized in band music until its demise in 1939. The local radio station WHO, established in 1924, broadcast only live music in its early years, including the popular Iowa Barn Dance Frolic, heard every Saturday night from about 1930 to 1957. It had its own orchestra, country band, and pop band until the early 1950s.

See also LIBRARIES AND COLLECTIONS, §3.

BIBLIOGRAPHY

M. L. Bartlett: *Des Moines as a Musical Center* (MS, *c*1915, *IaDm*)

Musical Iowana, 1838–1938: a Century of Music in Iowa, ed. Iowa Federation of Music Clubs (Des Moines, 1938)

N. E. Jones: *Music at Drake University, 1881–1931* (diss., U. of Michigan, 1964)

D. L. Parr: *Music Publishing in Iowa* (MA thesis, U. of Iowa, 1977)

D. P. Walker: "From 'Hawk-eye March and Quick Step' to 'Caprice Hongrois': Music Publishing in Iowa," *American Music*, i/4 (1983), 42

ZAIDE PIXLEY

Desmond [Breitenfeld], **Paul** (*b* San Francisco, CA, 25 Nov 1924; *d* New York, 30 May 1977). Jazz alto saxophonist. He studied clarinet at San Francisco State University and played in various groups before joining the Dave Brubeck Quartet in 1951 (for illustration *see* BRUBECK, DAVE). Because his career was almost solely with this group until its dissolution in 1967 he shared its success without receiving the recognition that was his due. Desmond was one of the most capable representatives of the "cool" tendency in alto saxophone jazz, of which Lee Konitz was the chief exponent, and which Lester Young, Benny Carter, and others had foreshadowed in the late 1930s. His tone had a luminous quality, consistent over the instrument's whole range, that was particularly reminiscent of Carter, but his most notable gift as an improviser was his power of sustained melodic invention, which depended in part on an unusually imaginative use of sequence. Desmond's independent recordings, with Gerry Mulligan and Jim Hall for example, do him more justice than his numerous ones with Brubeck, for whom he composed the popular *Take Five* in 5/4 time.

RECORDINGS

(selective list)

Desmond (1954, Fan. 321); *Paul Desmond and Friends* (1959, WB 1356); *Two of a Mind* (1962, RCA LSP2624); *Glad to be Unhappy* (1963–4, RCA LSP3407); *Skylark* (1973, CTI 6039); *The Paul Desmond Quartet Live* (1975, Hor. 850)

See also BRUBECK, DAVE.

BIBLIOGRAPHY

J. Goldberg: *Jazz Masters of the Fifties* (New York, 1965/*R*1980), 154ff

M. Williams: *Jazz Masters in Transition* (New York, 1970/*R*1980), 99ff

N. Hentoff: "The Solitary Floating Jazzman," *Village Voice*, xxi (22 Aug 1977), 35

MAX HARRISON/R

Dessoff Choirs. New York choral group founded by Margarete Dessoff. *See* EARLY-MUSIC REVIVAL, §1.

Destinn [Kittl], **Emmy** [Destinnová, Ema] (*b* Prague, Czechoslovakia, 26 Feb 1878; *d* České Budějovice, Czechoslovakia, 28 Jan 1930). Czech dramatic soprano. She studied singing under Marie Loewe-Destinn, adopting the latter's name in gratitude. On 19 July 1898 she made a highly successful début as Santuzza (*Cavalleria rusticana*) at the Berlin Kroll Opera, appearing two months later in the same role at the Royal Opera. She became a great favorite in Berlin, and remained there until 1908. Her international career began after a much acclaimed Senta (*Der fliegende Holländer*) at Bayreuth in 1901. From 1908 to 1915 she sang regularly at the Metropolitan Opera. Her début was as Aida, Toscanini conducting, on 16 November 1908. At the Metropolitan she created the part of Minnie in the première of *La fanciulla del West* (10 December 1910), and extended her Verdi roles to include *Il trovatore, Un ballo in maschera*, and Alice in *Falstaff*. Among her many other roles were Gioconda, Pamina (*Die Zauberflöte*), Nedda (*Pagliacci*), Marie (*The Bartered Bride*), and Santuzza. She made an extensive American tour in 1915–16, during which she opened the Chicago Opera season as Gioconda.

Her return to her native Bohemia during World War I led to her being interned by the Austrian government, as a declared sympathizer with the Czech national movement. After the war, her powers having by then begun to show signs of decline, she found it difficult to resume her former international position. She sang at Covent Garden, however, in 1919, and again at the Metropolitan during the seasons of 1919–21, and appeared in Dallas, Cleveland, Chicago, and Kansas City in 1919. Destinn was one of the greatest artists of her generation, equally gifted as singer and actress, with a voice of markedly individual timbre and emotional warmth, and of great flexibility; her trill, for example, was unusually distinct and even for so full a voice. She made over 200 recordings for several companies. She wrote a drama, *Rahel*, as well as poems and novels, and she also attempted composition.

BIBLIOGRAPHY

M. Stanley: "Emmy Destinn, Patriot, Tells of Life as Political Prisoner," *MusAm*, xxx/23 (1919), 4

A. Rektorys: *Ema Destinnová* (Prague, 1936) [contains bibliography and discography]

H. H. Harvey: "Emmy Destinn," *The Gramophone*, xvi (1938–9), 447 [incl. discography]

M. Martinková: *Život Ema Destinnové* [Destinn's life] (Plzeň, 1946)
M. J. Matz: "First Ladies of Puccini Premieres: Emmy Destinn," *Opera News*, xxvi/8 (1962), 14
A. Rektorys and J. Dennis: "Emmy Destinn," *Record Collector*, xx (1971), 5 [with discography]
V. Holzknecht and B. Trita: *E. Destinnová ve slovech a obrazech* [Destinn in words and pictures] (Prague, 1972)
M. Pospíšil: *Veliké srdce: život a umění Emy Destinnové* [Big-heart: the life and art of Destinn] (Prague, 1974) [with discography and list of roles]

DESMOND SHAWE-TAYLOR/R

DeSylva, Buddy [B. G.; George Gard] (*b* New York, 27 Jan 1895; *d* Hollywood, CA, 11 July 1950). Lyricist. He made his stage début in a benefit show at the Grand Opera House, Los Angeles, at the age of four. He left the University of Southern California after a year in order to work as a member of a "Hawaiian" orchestra in a local country club, where he played the ukulele and sang many of his own ballads. One of the club's patrons, Al Jolson, was impressed by the song " 'N Everything" and introduced it in *Sinbad* (1918); DeSylva eventually received royalties of $16,000. He then went to New York and produced more hits for Jolson, including "Avalon" (1920), "April Showers" (1921), and "California, here I come" (1921), and collaborated with George Gershwin on a Broadway score, *La La Lucille* (1919). He then worked with Kern on songs for *Sally* (1920, including "Look for the silver lining"), with Victor Herbert on the score for *Orange Blossoms* (1922, including "A Kiss in the Dark"), and with Gershwin again on *George White's Scandals of 1922* (including "I'll build a stairway to paradise"). From 1925 to 1931 DeSylva was a member of an exceedingly successful songwriting partnership with RAY HENDERSON and Lew Brown. After leaving the team he wrote songs for films and became a producer, supervising among others five musicals starring Shirley Temple. In 1939 he returned to Broadway, where he soon had three successful shows running simultaneously: *Du Barry was a Lady* (1939, music by Cole Porter), *Louisiana Purchase* (1940, Berlin), and *Panama Hattie* (1940, Porter). He was then recalled to Hollywood as head of Paramount Studios, but his work was curtailed by ill health.

CAROLINE RICHMOND

De Tar, Vernon (*b* Detroit, MI, 6 May 1905). Organist. He graduated from Syracuse University in 1927 and then studied piano with Franklin Cannon in New York, music theory with Clement Gale, and organ with David McK. Williams and Fernando Germani. He was organist and choirmaster at Calvary Episcopal Church (1932–39), and at the Church of the Ascension in New York from 1939 until his retirement in 1981. De Tar was also instructor in organ and church music at the School of Sacred Music of Union Theological Seminary (1945–72), at its successor, the Institute of Sacred Music at Yale University (1975–8), and at the Juilliard School (1947–82). As an outstanding practitioner for over 40 years in his post at the Church of the Ascension, and as a distinguished teacher of several generations of church organists, De Tar was instrumental in establishing high standards in performance and taste in the world of professional church music.

VERNON GOTWALS

Dethier, Gaston M(arie) (*b* Liège, Belgium, 19 April 1875; *d* New York, 26 May 1958). Organist. As a child he studied at the Liège Conservatory, where his father was a teacher of composition, and when he was 11 he became organist in the Church of St. Jacques. On Alexandre Guilmant's recommendation he went at the age of 19 to the USA to be organist of St. Francis Xavier in New York, a post he held until 1907. In 1904 he joined the faculty of the newly founded Institute of Musical Art and taught piano as well as organ. Among his pupils were Paul Creston, Norman Dello Joio, and Robert Noehren. After his retirement in 1945 he continued to teach privately. His many compositions for organ have largely passed out of the repertory; the effect of the "free pianistic and orchestral style of organ playing" that he helped to introduce to the country, however, endures. Dethier was a founder of the American Guild of Organists.

VERNON GOTWALS

Detroit. City in Michigan (pop. 1,203,339, ranked sixth largest in the USA; metropolitan area 4,353,413). Founded in 1701, the city had little significant musical life before 1850. The opening of the Erie Canal in 1824 brought settlers from the east, but almost 25 years passed before a sustained civic interest in music became evident. This interest grew during the 1850s, subsided during the Civil War, then reemerged with new vigor. Although older than many midwestern cities, Detroit lagged behind in musical activities. Perhaps the years of greatest development were the 1850s and the late 1860s, and, in the 20th century, the tenures with the Detroit SO of Ossip Gabrilowitsch and Antal Dorati.

1. Opera and choral societies. 2. Orchestras and concert halls. 3. Educational institutions and libraries. 4. Other activities.

1. OPERA AND CHORAL SOCIETIES. The first local attempts at opera were unstaged Italian works presented by the Detroit Philharmonic Society in 1855. Albert Lortzing's *Zar und Zimmermann*, given by the Harmonie Society in 1866, was the first opera staged by local performers. In 1869 the Detroit Opera House was built; with a seating capacity of over 2000, it was the largest hall the city had known. It was demolished on 4 May 1966, after which various theaters were used for operatic performances. The Masonic Auditorium (built in 1928) is used for many musical events, among which was an annual visit by the Metropolitan Opera (discontinued after the 1985 season). Thaddeus Wronski organized the Detroit Civic Opera Company in 1928; it was later associated with the Detroit SO in productions that were also presented in New York and Chicago, and continued until 1937. The Piccolo Opera Company was organized in 1961 for the purpose of performing operas in English for schools and other organizations. In 1971 David Di Chiera founded the Michigan Opera Theatre and became its artistic director. The company is resident in Detroit and tours throughout the state. It has its own orchestra and presents five works each season; it also sponsors an enterprising opera-in-residence program, whereby members of the company visit high schools for a week and work with students in producing an opera.

The first significant choral society was the Detroit Philharmonic Society (1855–9), directed by an Italian immigrant, Pietro Centemeri. Among the city's many choral societies the most notable have been the Harmonie (founded 1849), the Detroit Symphony Choir founded by Gabrilowitsch (1921–40), the Rackham Symphony Choir, formed in 1949 (as the University of Michigan Extension Choir) by Maynard Klein, and the Kenneth Jewell Chorale (1962), which, as the Detroit Symphony Chorale, became the nucleus of the 120-voice Detroit Symphony Chorus, formed in 1985.

2. ORCHESTRAS AND CONCERT HALLS. Among the early instrumental ensembles was the Stein and Buchheister Orchestra (1855–65), organized by two members of the Germania Musical Society, who settled in Detroit in 1854 when the society disbanded. As early as 1875, musical groups calling themselves the Detroit Symphony Orchestra appeared. The present Detroit SO was founded in February 1914 when Weston Gales organized 65 local musicians for an experimental symphony concert. Gabrilowitsch, who had been a guest soloist with the orchestra, was made permanent conductor in 1919. During his tenure he conducted the first complete symphony concert to be broadcast on radio (station WWJ) on 10 February 1922. He inaugurated the radio concert series known as the "Ford Sunday Evening Hour" in 1934; the program was broadcast nationally on CBS from 1936 to 1942. After Gabrilowitsch's death in 1936, Franco Ghione served as conductor from 1937 to 1940. The following season was shortened, and the orchestra ceased operation during the 1942–3 season. In 1943 it was reorganized as the Detroit Orchestra with Karl Krueger as conductor, but within six years it lapsed again. The Detroit SO was re-formed in 1951, when Paul Paray became permanent conductor. He retired in 1963 and was succeeded by Sixten Ehrling (1963–73), Aldo Ceccato (1973–7), and Antal Dorati (1977–81). The orchestra achieved new standards of excellence and worldwide recognition under Dorati: he organized festivals commemorating Beethoven (1977), Schubert (1978), Brahms (1980), and Bartók (1981); initiated televised concerts; arranged for the orchestra to resume recording, which it had ceased to do after Paray's tenure; and took the orchestra on its first European tour. Dorati resigned in a dispute with management over orchestra financing. The Israeli conductor, Gary Bertini, was appointed interim music adviser for two seasons, but in the following season the orchestra was without a permanent conductor and had to rely on guests, among them Dorati. Gunther Herbig became music director in September 1984.

Since its foundation the Detroit SO has been a pioneer in presenting young people's concerts. It offers one of the largest public service programs of any American orchestra through its school concerts and annual tours of the state. The orchestra gained recognition for summer concerts inaugurated at Belle Isle (an island in the Detroit River) in 1922 and at the Michigan State Fair Grounds in 1945. It served as the official orchestra for the annual autumn Worcester Music Festival in Massachusetts from 1958 to 1974, and in 1964 became the resident orchestra at the summer Meadow Brook Festival at Oakland University in Rochester, Michigan. In 1970 the orchestra instituted the Detroit Symphony Youth Orchestra to provide a training ensemble for talented young musicians.

Detroit's first concert hall was Firemen's Hall, an upstairs room of the fire station built in 1851 and seating 1000. The city's most famous concert hall, the 2100-seat Orchestra Hall, known for its fine acoustics, was built in 1919 at the insistence of Gabrilowitsch as a home for the Detroit SO. Lack of funds forced its abandonment in 1939; it fell into disuse, was later sold to a restaurant chain, and was eventually scheduled to be

Berry Gordy, Jr. (center), president of Motown, with his staff outside their headquarters at Hitsville in Detroit, early 1960s

torn down in 1970. A group of musicians from the Detroit SO launched a drive to purchase and restore the hall, and the first concert in the renovated building took place in the spring of 1976. In 1979 the Detroit SO returned to Orchestra Hall to play a concert marking the hall's 60th anniversary and the 40th anniversary of the orchestra's last appearance there. The orchestra usually performs at the Henry and Edsel Ford Auditorium (opened 1956; capacity 2900).

The Detroit Women's Symphony, founded in 1947, has remained active.

3. EDUCATIONAL INSTITUTIONS AND LIBRARIES. Attempts were made in 1818 to establish music schools, but lack of support doomed these to a short existence. However, in 1874 Jacob H. Hahn founded the Detroit Conservatory of Music, which lasted almost a century (until 1967). Among its directors was Francis L. York, who later became dean of the Detroit Institute of Musical Arts, founded in 1914. Since 1972 the facilities of the Institute have been shared by the Detroit Community Music School, which began in 1926 as the Music Settlement School. Detroit Teachers' College began offering music instruction in 1918; it merged with several other colleges to form a single institution that in 1934 became known as Wayne University and in 1959 as Wayne State University. It offers the BA, BM, MA, and MM degrees.

In 1943 the Detroit Public Library acquired the E. Azalia Hackley Collection, the largest collection in the USA devoted to black musicians and performing artists; that year the library also initiated an annual series of concerts featuring music by black composers (*see* LIBRARIES AND COLLECTIONS, §3).

4. OTHER ACTIVITIES. In 1851 Adam Couse, a friend of Stephen Foster's, issued the first music published in Detroit. Other important publishers of the period were Stein & Buchheister, J. Henry Whittemore, and Clark J. Whitney. Detroit was known in the 1890s for a vast output of ragtime hits from the publishers Whitney–Warner, Belcher & Davis, and others. In the early years of the 20th century Jerome H. Remick was one of the world's leading publishers of popular music. The Clough & Warren Organ Co., which was established as a melodeon factory in 1850, achieved world fame in the early 1880s when it built an organ for Liszt, to his specifications. In the 20th century the name of Grinnell Brothers, a leading music shop, was also associated with the manufacture of pianos; the firm went out of business in 1977.

For more than 30 years, Detroit was the home of one of the last Sousa-style community bands. The Detroit Concert Band was organized in 1946 by its conductor Leonard Smith to play summer concerts on Belle Isle. It offered annual concerts until 1980 when the season was canceled due to lack of funds. The recording company MOTOWN, in Detroit from its foundation in 1960 until it moved to Hollywood in 1971, has been particularly successful in promoting black American popular music. In 1980 the Montreux–Detroit International Jazz Festival, an annual summer event (renamed the Montreux–Detroit Kool Jazz Festival in 1982), was inaugurated in Detroit. Concerts are given throughout the city, some aboard the Bob-Lo excursion boats on the Detroit River.

In addition to the broadcast concerts of the Detroit SO, Karl Haas's radio program "Adventures in Good Music," begun in 1959, has achieved national recognition.

BIBLIOGRAPHY

M. Teal: *Musical Activities in Detroit from 1701 through 1870* (diss., U. of Michigan, 1964)

L. Mattson: *A History of the Detroit Symphony Orchestra* (diss., U. of Michigan, 1968)

J. Barron: "New Life for the Detroit Symphony," *New York Times* (14 April 1985), §II, p.21

MARY D. TEAL

Detroit Spinners. A name under which the SPINNERS recorded for Motown and by which they are often known in Europe.

Dett, R(obert) Nathaniel (*b* Drummondsville [now Niagara Falls], Ont., 11 Oct 1882; *d* Battle Creek, MI, 2 Oct 1943). Composer, pianist, and conductor. He was born into a musical family and given piano lessons as a child. He began the serious study of music at the Oliver Willis Halstead conservatory in Lockport, New York. In 1908 he graduated from Oberlin Conservatory, the first Black to receive the BMus degree there; he continued his music studies intermittently over the years at Columbia University, the University of Pennsylvania, the American Conservatory, Harvard University, with Boulanger in France (1929), and at the Eastman School (MMus 1932). His honors included the Bowdoin Literary Prize and the Francis Boott Music Award, both from Harvard, the Palm and Ribbon Award from the Royal Belgian Band, and the Harmon Foundation Award. He taught at two small colleges before accepting a long-term position as director of music at Hampton Institute (1913–31). In addition to teaching, he was active as a concert pianist and composer, publishing his first work in 1900. He developed the Hampton Institute Choir into a superior organization that won critical acclaim on tours in the USA and Europe and in 1919 helped to found the National Association of Negro Musicians. His last position was as a music director for the United Service Organizations in Battle Creek.

R. Nathaniel Dett

Dett wrote in a neoromantic, nationalistic style. He spoke on many occasions of the importance of black folk music and urged that "musical architects take the loose timber of Negro themes and fashion from it music . . . in choral form, in lyric and operatic works, in concertos and suites and salon music." Recordings of his music include *The Ordering of Moses*, by the Talladega College Choir and the Mobile SO, and *In the Bottoms*, by Natalie Hinderas.

For further illustration *see* AFRO-AMERICAN MUSIC, fig.4.

WORKS

Chorus, orch: 3 oratorios (Dett, after Bible): Music in the Mine (1916), The Chariot Jubilee (1921), The Ordering of Moses (1937) [all based on black folksongs]; American Sampler, 1937

Pf: 8 suites, incl. Magnolia (1911), In the Bottoms (1913), Enchantment (1922), The Cinnamon Grove (1928), Tropic Winter (1938), 8 Bible Vignettes (1941–3)

Several motets and partsongs, incl. Listen to the Lambs, I'll never turn back no more, Don't be weary, traveler

Numerous arrs. of spirituals, incl. 2 collections: Religious Folksongs of the Negro (1927), The Dett Collection of Negro Spirituals, i–iv (1936)

Other works for 1v, pf, vn, orch

Complete edn of pf music pubd by Summy (1973)

Principal publishers: J. Church, J. Fischer, Mills, Summy

BIBLIOGRAPHY

EwenD; *SouthernB*

M. Cuney-Hare: *Negro Musicians and their Music* (Washington, DC, 1936/*R* 1974)

E. Southern: *The Music of Black Americans: a History* (New York, 1971, rev. 2/1983)

W. Fisher: "Dett, Robert Nathaniel," *DAB*

D. de Lerma and V. McBrier: Introductions to *The Collected Piano Works of R. Nathaniel Dett* (Evanston, IL, 1973)

V. McBrier: *R. Nathaniel Dett: his Life and Works: 1882–1943* (Washington, DC, 1977)

J. Spencer: "R. Nathaniel Dett's Views on the Preservation of Black Music," *BPiM*, x (1982), 132 [incl. list of writings]

EILEEN SOUTHERN

Devil's Son-in-Law. *See* WHEATSTRAW, PEETIE.

Devo. Rock group formed in Akron, Ohio, in 1976. Its members are Mark Mothersbaugh, vocalist, keyboard player, and songwriter; Gerald V. Casale, bass guitar player and songwriter; Robert Mothersbaugh, guitarist; Robert Casale, guitarist; and Alan Meyers, drummer. The group's name comes from its concept of "de-evolution": the degeneration of modern people into technology-dependent, semiliterate inhabitants of a polluted environment. The group's *Q: Are we not Men? A: We are Devo* (produced by Brian Eno in 1978), which included songs such as *Space Junk*, *Jocko Homo*, and a version of the Rolling Stones' *Satisfaction*, used machine-like rhythms and electronic sounds. In the band's stage shows protective industrial uniforms and robot-like movements enhance the aural images of a mechanical music. Films made by Chuck Statler, which illustrate Devo's songs with precisely edited sequences of images that parody American life, remain among the best rock video projects; they include *The Truth about De-evolution* (1975). After a dull second album, Devo played up the comic content of their image and wrote more pop-oriented songs: *Freedom of Choice* yielded a hit single, *Whip it*, in 1980, and their version of Allen Toussaint's *Working in the coalmine* appeared on the soundtrack of the animated film *Heavy Metal* (1981). Devo's music and visual images have influenced the work of established artists such as Neil Young, as well as many new-wave bands.

RECORDINGS

(selective list; all recorded for WB)

Q: Are we not Men? A: We are Devo (3239, 1978); *Duty now for the Future* (3337, 1979); *Freedom of Choice* (3435, 1980); *New Traditionalists* (3595, 1981); *Oh no, it's Devo* (23741, 1982)

JOHN PICCARELLA

DeVoto, Mark (Bernard) (*b* Cambridge, MA, 11 Jan 1940). Composer, scholar, and teacher. The son of a distinguished author, DeVoto was exposed to a variety of intellectual stimuli at an early age. At Harvard University he studied composition with Piston and Randall Thompson (BA 1961); at Princeton (MFA 1963, PhD 1967) his principal teachers were Sessions, Babbitt, and Cone. He has taught at Reed College (1964–8), the University of New Hampshire (1968–81), and Tufts University (from 1981). The focus of his writings is the music of Berg, whose *Altenberg Lieder* are the subject of his doctoral dissertation. He was founding editor of the newsletter of the International Alban Berg Society (first published in 1970); he also revised and expanded Piston's *Harmony* for its fourth edition. As a composer, DeVoto has produced a series of interesting and varied works, including several for voice with specialized instrumental ensembles and four piano concertos. Of the latter, the second is dedicated to the memory of Varèse, and the third, subtitled "The Distinguished Thing," was written for a Fromm Foundation commission. In his early works Stravinsky and the Parisians of the 1920s were the major musical influences, in the later ones Varèse and Schoenberg.

WORKS

Orch and inst: Pf Conc. no.1, 1956; Night Songs and Distant Dances, 1962; 3 Little Pieces, 1964; Pf Conc. no.2, 1965–6; Pf Conc. no.3, The Distinguished Thing, 1968; 2 Etudes, pf left hand, 1971; The Caucasian Chalk Circle (incidental music, Brecht), vv, 9 insts, 1979–80; Pf Conc. no.4 (Rimbaud), pf, sym. wind ens, female vv, va obbl, 1983

Vocal: Planh (Pss., Ecclesiastes), S, 6vv, ob, cl, harp, 1960; American Songs (J. Lieberman, Rexroth, G. M. Hedin, J. W. Seymore), S, fl, va, trbn, harp, 1961; 3 Poe Songs, S, concertina, gui, hpd, 8 fl, 1967, rev. 1970; Fever-Dream Vocalise, S, fl, vc, pf, perc, 1968; Ornières (Rimbaud), S, pf, org, perc, 1974; H (Rimbaud), reciter, fl choir, bell, 1981

Arrs. for orch and band

STEVEN E. GILBERT

De Waart, Edo (*b* Amsterdam, Netherlands, 1 June 1941). Conductor. The son of a choral singer, he studied oboe with Haakon Stotijn at the Amsterdam Conservatory, and became co-principal oboe with the Amsterdam PO in 1961 and with the Concertgebouw Orchestra in 1963. During this time he was studying conducting, and a course at Hilversum in 1964 under Franco Ferrara brought about his début with the Netherlands Radio PO; later that year he won first prize in the Dimitri Mitropoulos conductors' competition in New York: the year's engagement as assistant conductor with the New York PO, 1965–6, however, proved to have less practical value than he had hoped. In 1965 he was engaged at the Spoleto Festival to conduct a double bill of *L'histoire du soldat* and Vieri Tosatti's *Partita a pugni*. In 1966 he became assistant conductor of the Concertgebouw Orchestra, and in the next year he formed and directed the Netherlands Wind Ensemble and was appointed co-conductor of the Rotterdam PO with Jean Fournet, whom he later succeeded as music director (1973–9). He also acquired experience as an opera conductor, leading performances of Menotti's *The Saint of Bleecker Street* (Netherlands Opera, 1970), *Der fliegende Holländer* (Santa Fe, 1971; his American opera début), and *Der Rosenkavalier*

(Houston, 1975). His Covent Garden début was in 1976 with *Ariadne auf Naxos*, and in 1979 he opened the Bayreuth Festival with *Lohengrin*. Having become principal guest conductor of the San Francisco SO in 1975, he was appointed music director there in 1977, a position he held until 1985, when he became music director of the Netherlands Opera. That year he was also named music director of the Minnesota Orchestra, to commence with the 1986 season. He conducted a *Ring* cycle at the San Francisco Opera (1985). His performances are clear and committed, if not notably individual, and his orchestral programs are wide-ranging in style. He has introduced a number of contemporary Dutch works to the USA and while he was at San Francisco the orchestra won several ASCAP Awards for Adventuresome Programming of Contemporary Music.

BIBLIOGRAPHY

C. Grier: "Edo de Waart," *Music and Musicians*, xviii/10 (1970), 28
A. Blyth: "Edo de Waart Talks," *Gramophone*, l (1972–3), 1303
P. Hart: "Edo de Waart," *Conductors: a New Generation* (New York, 1979, rev. 2/1983), 197
D. Schneider: *The San Francisco Symphony: Music, Maestros, and Musicians* (Novato, CA, 1983)

NOËL GOODWIN/R

Dexter, Al [Poindexter, Clarence Albert] (*b* Jacksonville, TX, 4 May 1905; *d* Lewisville, TX, 28 Jan 1984). Country-music songwriter, singer, and guitarist. For his earliest performances in his native eastern Texas, he was accompanied by a band of black musicians. His *Honky Tonk Blues* (1936), written with James Byron Paris, is the first known use of the term "honky tonk" in a country song. He later recorded with a studio group, which he called the Troopers (from Troup, Texas, where he spent many early years). His first big success was *Pistol Packin' Mama* (1942), which sold a million copies in six months and spent 14 successive weeks on the CBS "Lucky Strike Hit Parade." (*Life* magazine dubbed it "a national earache.") Throughout the 1940s, Dexter's songs remained consistently popular. In the 1950s and 1960s he performed at his own nightclub, the Bridgeport Club, in Dallas. He is remembered as the first prominent musician in the honky-tonk genre.

RECORDINGS
(selective list)

Honky Tonk Blues (Voc. 03435, 1936); Wine Women and Song (OK 05572, 1940); Pistol Packin' Mama/Rosalita (OK 6708, 1942); Too late to worry, too blue to cry (OK 6718, *c*1944); Guitar Polka/Honey do you think it's wrong? (Col. 36898, 1945); Texas Waltz (Col. 37881, 1947)

BIBLIOGRAPHY

N. Tosches: "Al Dexter," *Old Time Music*, no.22 (1976), 4
B. C. Malone: Liner notes, *Honky Tonkin'* (TL CW12, 1983)

RONNIE PUGH

Diamond, David (Leo) (*b* Rochester, NY, 9 July 1915). Composer. He studied at the Cleveland Institute, at the Eastman School with Bernard Rogers (1933–4), and at the Dalcroze Institute in New York with Paul Boepple and Roger Sessions (1934–6). After further study under Sessions, he went to France for lessons with Boulanger. He has received three Guggenheim Fellowships (1938, 1942, 1958) and many other awards and commissions from major institutions, among them the Fromm, Koussevitzky, and Rockefeller foundations. In 1936 he began work on the full-length ballet *Tom* to a scenario by Cummings and was sent to Paris by a private patron to complete the score in association with Léonide Massine. Diamond's first successful orchestral piece, *Psalm*, was written there that summer; it won the Juilliard Publication Award in the following year. The contacts he made in Paris with André Gide, Maurice Ravel, Albert Roussel, and Stravinsky broadened his artistic and philosophical ideas. From this period on his music was performed by leading conductors, including Hermann Scherchen, Koussevitzky, and Mitropoulos, the last of whom directed the New York PO in the first performances of the Symphony no. 1 and of *Rounds* (New York Music Critics' Circle Award, 1944). Diamond was appointed Fulbright professor at the University of Rome in 1951; in 1953 he settled in Florence, where he remained until his return to the USA for his 50th birthday celebrations, during which he conducted the New York PO, the Rochester PO, and other ensembles. He has taught at Salzburg, at the Harvard Seminar in American Studies, at SUNY, Buffalo (as Slee Professor, 1961, 1963), at the Manhattan School (1967–8, as chairman of the composition department), and, from 1973, at the Juilliard School. Diamond was elected to the National Institute of Arts and Letters in 1966 and was appointed its vice-president in 1974. In 1985 he was granted the William Schuman Award for his life's work as a composer.

David Diamond, 1985

Diamond's symphonies, quartets, and songs are the core of a very large and varied output. Clear structures, often evolved from contrapuntal or sonata-allegro procedures, are frequently fashioned into unusual one- or two-movement forms; among the later works are many masterly fugues and sets of variations. Diamond's writing for the orchestra is brilliant, and his work shows an intensely individual lyricism, occasionally austere but more often romantically tinged. His harmony has developed gradually from a diatonic-modal to a more chromatic style without losing a strong personal character. Diamond's meticulous craftsmanship and his sensibility have assured his position as a 20th-century classicist. (*See also* ORCHESTRAL MUSIC, §3.)

WORKS
(pubd unless otherwise stated)

STAGE
(all ballets unless otherwise stated)

A Myriologue, pf, 1935, unpubd
David (opera, D. H. Lawrence), 1935, inc., withdrawn

Formal Dance (M. Graham), pf, tpt, perc, 1935, unpubd; New York, 10 Nov 1935
Dance of Liberation, pf, 1936, unpubd; New York, 23 Jan 1938
Tom (Cummings), 1936, unpubd
Duet, cl, 1937, unpubd
Icaro (dance drama, after L. de Bossis), nar, pf, cl, perc, 1937, unpubd
Prelude, pf, 1937, unpubd
Twisting of the Rope (opera, Yeats), 1940, inc., withdrawn
The Dream of Audubon (G. Westcott), 1941, unpubd
The Tempest (incidental music, Shakespeare), 1944, rev. for large orch, 1946, 1968; New York, 25 Jan 1945
Labyrinth (M. Marchovsky), 1946, unpubd; New York, 5 April 1946
Romeo and Juliet (incidental music, Shakespeare), 1947, rev. 1950, unpubd; New York, 10 March 1951
The Rose Tattoo (incidental music, T. Williams), 1950–51; New York, 3 Feb 1951
Mirandolina (musical comedy, 4, P. Brown, after Goldoni), 1958
The Golden Slippers (musical folk play, 2, S. Citron, after Pérez Galdós), 1965; New York, 5 Dec 1965
The Noblest Game (opera, prologue, 2, K. Louchheim), 1971–5

RADIO AND FILM SCORES

Film: A Place to Live, 1941; Dreams that Money can Buy, 1943; Strange Victory, 1948; Anna Lucasta, 1949; Lippold's The Sun (dir. L. Hurwitz), 1965, unpubd; Life in the Balance, 1966
Radio: Hear it now, 1942; The Man behind the Gun, 1942

ORCHESTRAL

Symphony no.1, 1940–41; New York PO, cond. Mitropoulos, 21 Dec 1941
Symphony no.2, 1942; Boston SO, cond. Koussevitzky, 13 Oct 1944
Symphony no.3, 1945; Boston SO, cond. Munch, 3 Nov 1951
Symphony no.4, 1945; Boston SO, cond. Bernstein, 23 Jan 1948
Symphony no.5, 1951, rev. 1964; New York PO, cond. Bernstein, 26 April 1966
Symphony no.6, 1951–4; Boston SO, cond. Munch, 8 March 1957
Symphony no.7, 1959; Philadelphia Orchestra, cond. Ormandy, 26 Jan 1962
Symphony no.8, 1960; New York PO, cond. Bernstein, 27 Oct 1961
Symphony no.9 (Michelangelo Buonarroti), Bar, orch, 1985; American Composers Orchestra, cond. Bernstein, 17 Nov 1985
Full orch: Threnody, 1935, unpubd; Variations on a Theme by Erik Satie, 1935–6, unpubd; Psalm, 1936; Suite no.1 from Tom, 1936, unpubd; Vn Conc. no.1, 1936; Aria and Hymn, 1937; Ov., 1937; Vc Conc., 1938; Concert Piece, 1939; Vn Conc. no.2, 1947, unpubd; The Enormous Room, after Cummings, 1948; Timon of Athens, sym. portrait, 1949; Pf Conc., 1949–50; Sinfonia concertante, 1954–6; The World of Paul Klee, 1957; Pf Concertino, 1964–5; Vn Conc. no.3, 1967–8; Ov. no.2 "A Buoyant Music," 1970
Chamber orch: 25 early works; Hommage à Satie, 1934, withdrawn; Ballade, 1935, unpubd; Divertimento, pf, small orch, 1935, unpubd; Variations on an Original Theme, 1937; Heroic Piece, 1938; Elegy in Memory of Maurice Ravel, brass, harp, perc, 1938, rev. str, perc, 1938–9; Music, double str, brass, timp, 1938–9, rev. 1968; Conc., 1940; Rounds, str, 1944; Ceremonial Fanfare, brass, perc, 1950; Diaphony, org, brass, 2 pf, timp, 1955, rev. org, orch, 1968, unpubd; Elegies, fl, eng hn, str, 1962–3 [for Faulkner and Cummings]; Music for Chamber Orch, 1970; 3 other works, withdrawn
Orchestrations and arrs., most unpubd, incl. E. Satie: Chorale hypocrite, Messe des pauvres, Passacaille, 3 Gymnopédies; R. Sessions: Scherzino

VOCAL

*c*25 early and withdrawn songs; early works with orch
Choral: A Song for Shabuoth, children's chorus, pf, 1935; Paris this April Sunset (Cummings), 2-part female chorus, vc, db, 1937, unpubd; The Martyr (Melville), male chorus, opt. orch, 1950, rev. 1964; Mizmor L'David, sacred service, T, chorus, org, 1951; 2 Anthems (Diamond), mixed chorus, 1955; Prayer for Peace, chorus, 1960; This Sacred Ground (Lincoln), Bar, chorus, children's chorus, orch, 1962; To Music (J. Masefield, Longfellow), choral sym., T, B-Bar, chorus, orch, 1967; A Secular Cantata (J. Agee), T, Bar, chorus, small orch, 1976; many other acc. and unacc. works
Solo vv, insts: 2 Elegies (C. Rossetti), 1v, str qt, 1935, unpubd; Vocalises, 1v, va, 1935; The Mad Maid's Song (Herrick), 1v, fl, hpd, 1937, rev. 1953; Somewhere I have never travelled (Cummings), 1v, orch, 1938, unpubd; Ahavah, sym. eulogy, male nar, orch, 1954, unpubd
Song cycles: 4 Ladies (E. Pound), 1935, rev. 1962; 3 Epitaphs (S. T. Warner), 1938; 5 Songs from The Tempest (Shakespeare), 1944; L'âme de Claude Debussy (letters), 1949, unpubd; The Midnight Meditation (E. Olson), 1951; We Two (Shakespeare: Sonnets), 1964; Hebrew Melodies (Byron), 1967–8; Love and Time (K. Louchheim), 1968
Over 60 other songs

CHAMBER AND INSTRUMENTAL

4 or more insts: 6 Pieces, str qt, 1935; Chamber Sym., cl, bn, tpt, va, pf, 1935–6, unpubd; Conc., str qt, 1936; Qnt, fl, pf qt, 1937; Pf Qt, 1938; 10 str qts, 1940, 1943–4, 1946, 1951, 1960, 1962, 1963–4, 1964, 1966, 1966–8; Qnt, cl, 2 va, 2 vc, 1950; Wind Qnt, 1958; Night Music, accordion, str qt, 1961; Nonet, 3 vn, 3 va, 3 vc, 1961–2; Pf Qnt, 1972
1–3 insts: Partita, ob, bn, pf, 1935; Chamber Music for Young People, vn, pf, 1936; Vc Sonata, 1936, rev. 1938; Str Trio, 1937, unpubd; Vn Sonatina, 1937, unpubd; Vn Sonata, 1943–6; Canticle, vn, pf, 1946; Perpetual Motion, vn, pf, 1946; Chaconne, vn, pf, 1948; Pf Trio, 1951; Sonata, vn, 1954–9; Sonata, vc, 1956–9; Sonata, accordion, 1963; Introduction and Dance, accordion, 1966; Vn Sonata no.2, 1981
Pf: 8 Pf Pieces for Children, 1935; Sonatina, 1935; 4 Gymnopédies, 1937; 52 Preludes and Fugues, 1939–40; Conc., 2 pf, 1942; The Tomb of Melville, 1944–9; Album for the Young, 1946; 2 sonatas, 1947, 1972; A Private World, 1954–9; Then and Now, 1962; Alone at the Piano, 1967; Prelude, Fantasy and Fugue, 1983; many other pieces
Over 50 juvenile works, 1928–32; 6 withdrawn works

MSS in *PP* (Fleisher Collection)

Principal publishers: Associated, Boosey & Hawkes, C. Fischer, G. Schirmer, Southern

BIBLIOGRAPHY

EwenD
B. Lemmon: "A New American Symphonist," *The Etude*, lx (1942), 724
M. Goss: "David Diamond," *Modern Music Makers* (New York, 1952)
R. D. Freed: "Music is Diamond's Best Friend," *New York Times* (22 Aug 1965)
"Diamond, David (Leo)," *CBY 1966*
Compositores de América/Composers of the Americas, xiii, ed. Pan American Union (Washington, DC, 1970)
F. Corciata: "Our 'Youngest' Symphonic Composer Turns 60," *New York Times* (6 July 1975)
R. Friday: *Analyses and Interpretations of Selected Songs of David Diamond* (diss., New York U., 1984)
J. Peyser: "A Composer who Defies Categorization," *New York Times* (6 July 1985)
D. Diamond: *The Midnight Sleep* [unpubd autobiography]

FRANCIS THORNE

Diamond, Neil (*b* Brooklyn, NY, 24 Jan 1941). Pop singer, songwriter, and composer. In the mid-1960s Diamond worked as a songwriter for various New York music publishers and in 1966 his composition *I'm a believer* became a no.1 hit for the Monkees. The producers Jeff Barry and Ellie Greenwich subsequently helped Diamond to gain a contract with Bang Records as a singer, and several of his songs recorded with them, which had a strong country inflection, reached the Top 20. He moved to California in 1966 and signed with Uni Records; on this label he achieved his first no.1 hit as a performer, *Cracklin' Rosie* (1970). In 1972 he became the first pop-rock musician to present a concert production on Broadway. After he moved to Columbia Records in 1973, Diamond aspired to more ambitious projects, such as the soundtrack for the film *Jonathan Livingston Seagull* (1973). He reached a commercial peak in 1980 with his score for the film *The Jazz Singer*; though reviewers were critical it produced hit singles, including *Love on the rocks* and *America*.

The hallmark of Diamond's songs is a simple, aggressive melodicism, often heavily tinged with a Middle Eastern modality and the rhythmic pulse of Jewish folk dancing. His compositional style draws on popular, country, and classical influences to create songs that are simple, yet grandiose. Diamond's oratorical bass-baritone voice accentuates an often pretentious element of mysticism that runs through many of his later lyrics.

RECORDINGS
(selective list)

Cherry, cherry (Bang 528, 1966); Girl, you'll be a woman soon (Bang 542, 1967); Sweet Caroline (Uni 55136, 1969); *Touching you Touching me* (Uni 73071, 1969), incl. Holly, Holly; Cracklin' Rosie (Uni 55250, 1970); Song Sung Blue (Uni 55326, 1972); *Jonathan Livingston Seagull* (Col. JS32550, 1973) [film soundtrack]; *Beautiful Noise* (Col. JC33965, 1976); *The Jazz Singer* (Cap. 12120, 1980) [film soundtrack], incl. Love on the rocks, Hello again, America; *Love Songs* (MCA 5239, 1981)

BIBLIOGRAPHY

B. Fong-Torres: "The Frog who Would be King: the Importance of Being Neil Diamond," *Rolling Stone*, no.222 (23 Sept 1976), 100

"Diamond, Neil," *CBY 1981*

STEPHEN HOLDEN

Díaz, Justino (*b* San Juan, Puerto Rico, 29 Jan 1940). Bass. His studies at the University of Puerto Rico and the New England Conservatory were followed by training with Frederick Jagel. He first appeared with the New England Opera Theater in 1961 and, having won the Metropolitan Opera Auditions of the Air, made his début with the company on 23 October 1963 as Monterone in *Rigoletto*. Appearances with the American Opera Society and at the Casals Festival (Puerto Rico) and the Spoleto Festival followed, and in 1966 he sang Escamillo at the Salzburg Festival under Karajan. His career was firmly established when he was chosen to sing Antony in Barber's *Antony and Cleopatra* at the opening night of the Metropolitan's new house at Lincoln Center (16 September 1966). He subsequently appeared in Hamburg, Vienna, and Munich, at La Scala, and with the New York City Opera. He sang in the performance of Alberto Ginastera's *Beatrix Cenci* that inaugurated the opera house at the Kennedy Center in Washington in 1971 and made his Covent Garden début, again as Escamillo, in 1976. As one of the Metropolitan's leading basses, Díaz's evenly produced, warm *basso cantante* has been heard in a wide range of Italian roles. His recordings include Alfredo Catalani's *La Wally*, *Lucia di Lammermoor*, and oratorios by Handel.

BIBLIOGRAPHY

J. W. Freeman: "No Short Cut," *Opera News*, xxxi/9 (1966), 16

R. Zachary: "Song and Dance," *Opera News*, xxxvi/11 (1972), 14

RICHARD BERNAS/DENNIS K. McINTIRE

Di Bonaventura, Anthony (*b* Follensbee, WV, 12 Nov 1930). Pianist, brother of Mario di Bonaventura. He made his début with the New York PO at the age of 13, playing Beethoven's Third Piano Concerto. When he was 18 he entered the Curtis Institute, where he remained for six years, studying under Vengerova. After military service he went to Europe in 1958, and was soon appearing not only in recital but with leading European and American orchestras; in 1959 Klemperer chose him for a Beethoven concerto cycle with the London Philharmonia Orchestra. Di Bonaventura has always been a champion of contemporary music. Among the composers who have written works for him are Persichetti (Piano Concerto op.90), Berio (*Points on a Curve to Find*), Ginastera (Third Piano Sonata), Milko Kelemen (*Mirabilia*), and Leonardo Balada (*Transparency on Chopin's First Ballade*). Since making the first recording of Prokofiev's Eighth Sonata while still a student at Curtis, he has recorded music by Chopin, Debussy, Prokofiev, and, with notable distinction, Domenico Scarlatti. His playing is marked by extraordinary clarity, finished technique, and fastidious musicianship. He joined the faculty of Boston University in 1973.

RICHARD DYER

Di Bonaventura, Mario (*b* Follensbee, WV, 20 Feb 1924). Conductor, brother of Anthony di Bonaventura. He studied conducting with Igor Markevitch in Salzburg and Paris, making his début in 1952 when, as a winner of the Besançon International Conducting Competition, he led the Paris Conservatoire orchestra in the Prix de Paris competition. He also studied composition with Nadia Boulanger (1947–53) and was the recipient, in 1953, of the Lili Boulanger–Dinu Lipatti Memorial Prize in Composition. In the USA he has led a varied career as conductor of the Fort Lauderdale SO (1959–61), professor of music at Dartmouth College (1962–73), vice-president of G. Schirmer (1974–80), and director of Boston University's School of Music (1980–82). He has been guest conductor of many orchestras throughout Europe and the USA, including the Warsaw PO, the Wichita SO, and the Juilliard Contemporary Music Ensemble. Much of his career has been dedicated to promoting contemporary music; in 1960 he conducted the Fort Lauderdale SO in the première of Milhaud's Symphony no.9, and as organizer (1963) and then director (1963–70) of Dartmouth's summer contemporary music festival (the Congregation of the Arts) he conducted the first performances of numerous works, including Piston's Clarinet Concerto and Malipiero's *Endecatode* for chamber orchestra. In 1968 he received the Arnold Bax Memorial Award for Conducting.

MARGARET DOUTT

Dichter, Harry (*b* nr Warsaw, Poland, 25 Dec 1899; *d* Atlantic City, NJ, 27 Jan 1977). Collector of and dealer in sheet music. He immigrated to the USA in 1906. For some 40 years until his retirement in 1965 he worked as a waiter in Philadelphia. While operating a small bookshop, from 1929 to 1931, he developed a passionate interest in early American popular sheet music; he eventually collected and distributed approximately 500,000 sheets of the late 18th to late 19th centuries. Much of the music was purchased by universities and municipal libraries, many of which relied on Dichter as a consultant – from 1942 to 1945 he served the Free Library of Philadelphia in this capacity. With Elliott Shapiro, a sheet-music publisher, he wrote *Early American Sheet Music: its Lure and its Lore, 1768–1889* (1941/*R*1977 as *Handbook of Early American Sheet Music, 1768–1889*), still regarded as the leading reference work of its kind. Under his own name or that of Musical Americana he issued several collections of sheet music and other important publications, including J. J. Fuld's *American Popular Music 1875–1950* and his own *Handbook of American Sheet Music* (in three installments, 1947–66), and with G. Eckhardt edited the *Musical Americana Newsletter* (1956–63). During the 1940s he initiated a series of informative and convivial meetings with other leading collectors; these were held annually until 1972.

BIBLIOGRAPHY

L. S. Levy: "Sheet Music Buffs and their Collections: a Personal Memoir," *American Music*, i/4 (1983), 90

LESTER LEVY

Dichter, Misha (*b* Shanghai, China, 27 Sept 1945). Pianist of Polish descent. When he was two his parents settled in Los Angeles, where he studied piano from the age of six. At UCLA he attended a master class given in 1964 by Rosina Lhévinne, which led to a scholarship at the Juilliard School where he continued as her pupil. His crowning success came in 1966 when he won second prize in the third International Tchaikovsky Piano

Competition in Moscow. His American début was with the Boston SO at the Berkshire Music Festival in August 1966. He has toured extensively, making several return visits to the USSR. An all-rounder rather than a specialist, he is particularly at home in the 19th- and early 20th-century repertory, and plays most of the Romantic concertos. As a youthful interpreter he was sometimes criticized for being over-objective, but unidiosyncratic musicianship coupled with controlled virtuosity have always given his playing poise and authority. He has appeared regularly in concerts with his wife, the pianist Cipa Dichter (*b* Rio de Janeiro, 20 May 1944).

JOAN CHISSELL/R

Dickens, Little Jimmy [James C.] (*b* Bolt, WV, 19 Dec 1920). Country-music singer, guitarist, and songwriter. He was brought up on a ranch and at the age of 17 began performing on radio station WILS in Beckley, West Virginia, where he was known as Jimmy the Kid. He attended the University of West Virginia briefly, but singing interested him more; with a repertory of old sentimental and gospel songs, he gained experience performing on radio stations WIBC (Indianapolis), WLW (Cincinnati), and WKNX (Saginaw, Michigan). In 1948 he joined the cast of the "Grand Ole Opry" at the invitation of Roy Acuff, who helped him to obtain a contract with Columbia in 1949 and lent his own band to play for Dickens's first recording session; this produced the single that became Dickens's trademark, E. M. Bartlett's *Take an old cold tater*. It was the first of many comic songs in which Dickens celebrated rural life. He is also known for the brilliance of his backing bands and his encouragement of new instrumental techniques: his sideman Joel Price was the first country musician to play a Fender electric bass guitar; his fiddler Red Taylor contributed a jazz influence; his steel-guitar player Buddy Emmons used an innovative bar and pedal technique; and many of his novelty numbers from the mid-1950s featured electric-guitar duos by GRADY MARTIN and Jabbo Arrington in a style that anticipated rockabilly and rock-and-roll. After 1965 Dickens recorded for Decca, United Artists, Starday, and Little Gem, but had no major hits. He retained his following on the "Grand Ole Opry," however, and maintained a busy schedule of tours and television shows. His later career helped to prove that country singers can flourish even without chart successes.

Dickens's style is brash and exuberant, as his song *I'm little but I'm loud* (1950) claims. Influenced by Roy Acuff, Ernest Tubb, and Bill Monroe, he sings in a full-throated mountain style, with slurs, growls, and ornamentation. His ballad style owes much to the West Virginia folk tradition. He was elected to the Country Music Hall of Fame in 1983.

RECORDINGS

(selective list; recorded for Columbia unless otherwise stated)

Take an old cold tater (20548, 1949); A-sleepin' at the foot of the bed (20644, 1949); Country Boy (20585, 1949); Bessie the Heifer (20786, 1950); Hillbilly Fever (20677, 1950); I'm little but I'm loud (20769, 1950); May the bird of paradise fly up your nose (43388, 1965); When you're seventeen (Decca 32426, 1969); Try it, you'll like it (UA 50889, 1972)

CHARLES K. WOLFE

Dickenson, Vic(tor) (*b* Xenia, OH, 6 Aug 1906; *d* New York, 16 Nov 1984). Jazz trombonist. He was first regarded as a section trombonist, and rarely took solos, even during his tenure with Claude Hopkins (1936–9) and Count Basie (1940). However, in the early 1940s he emerged as a highly individual stylist whose improvisations exhibited a rare blend of humor and relaxation. One of the most consistent mainstream jazz musicians, Dickenson's professional career spanned over 60 years. His husky tone was always personal, and he was inventive at any tempo. He seemed equally at home with such diverse stylists as Sidney Bechet and Lester Young, and he was also a masterful accompanist of singers, plying them with soft asides that were always apt. A number of recordings made with his own septet for Vanguard in 1953–4 (with Ruby Braff and Edmond Hall) rank among the finest examples of mainstream jazz.

RECORDINGS

(selective list)

As leader: *The Vic Dickenson Septet*, i (1953, Van. 8001), incl. Jeepers Creepers; *The Vic Dickenson Septet*, iii (1954, Van. 8012), incl. When you and I were young Maggie

As sideman: S. Bechet: After you've gone (1943, V-disc 270); L. Young: D. B. Blues (1945, Aladdin 123)

BIBLIOGRAPHY

SouthernB

J. G. Jepsen: "Vic Dickenson diskografi," *Orkester journalen*, xxvi/2 (1958), 50

S. Dance: *The World of Swing* (New York, 1974/*R*1979), 301

L. Jeske: "Vic Dickenson: Swing Master Escapes London Gang," *Down Beat*, xlvii/3 (1980), 24

W. Balliett: *Jelly Roll, Jabbo and Fats* (New York, 1983), 111

JOHN CHILTON

Dickerson, Roger Donald (*b* New Orleans, LA, 24 Aug 1934). Composer. He studied piano and brass instruments as a child and played jazz and blues professionally in high school and college. After graduating from Dillard University, New Orleans (BA 1955), he studied composition with Heiden at Indiana University, Bloomington (MMus 1957). Military service followed, during which he played double bass with the Fort Smith SO and the US Army Headquarters band in Heidelberg, Germany. He then received a Fulbright scholarship and studied with Karl Schiske and Alfred Uhl at the Akademie für Musik und Darstellende Kunst in Vienna (1959–62). Returning to New Orleans, he continued to compose, teach composition, and perform. His honors include a John Hay Whitney Fellowship (1964) and the Louis Armstrong Memorial Award; in 1978 PBS produced a documentary film, *New Orleans Concerto*, built around his life and compositions. He was co-founder of the Creative Arts Alliance (1975). His compositions combine contemporary idioms with elements of jazz, blues, and soul.

WORKS

Orch: Concert Ov., 1957; A Musical Service for Louis, 1972; Orpheus an' his Slide Trbn, trbn, nar, orch, 1974–5; New Orleans Conc., pf, orch, 1976

Chamber: Prekussion, perc ens, 1954; Variations, ww trio, 1955; Str Qt, 1956; Music for Str Trio, 1957; Movt, tpt, pf, 1960; Cl Sonata, 1960; Wind Qnt, 1961; 10 Concert Pieces for Beginning Str Players, 1973

Band: Essay, 1958; Fugue 'n' Blues, 1959

Kbd: Sonatina, pf, 1956; Chorale Prelude (Das neugeborne Kindlein), org, 1956

Vocal: Fair Dillard, SATB, 1955; Music I Heard, S, pf, 1956; The Negro Speaks of Rivers (L. Hughes), S, pf, 1961; Psalm xlix, SATB, 3 timp, 1979

BIBLIOGRAPHY

H. West: "New Orleans Concerto," *Change*, x (1978), 60

A. Tischler: *Fifteen Black American Composers: a Bibliography of their Works* (Detroit, 1981)

DORIS EVANS McGINTY

Dickinson, Clarence (*b* Lafayette, IN, 7 May 1873; *d* New York, 2 Aug 1969). Organist and composer. He studied at Miami University, Oxford, Ohio, and at Northwestern University in Chicago. After further study in Berlin and in Paris with Moritz

Moszkowski (piano), Alexandre Guilmant (organ), and Gabriel Pierné (composition), he went to St. James's Episcopal Church in Chicago and then to the Brick Church (Presbyterian) in New York in 1909. In 1912 he became professor of church music at Union Theological Seminary where in 1928 he established the School of Sacred Music. He was its director until he retired in 1945. With his wife Helen Adell (Snyder) Dickinson (1875–1957), a writer, he produced a steady stream of church anthems and other music that contributed significantly to the improvement of taste in local churches. In 1917 they published *Excursions in Musical History*, a curious book intended to be "readable and popular," which reflected their views on many aspects of music. Dickinson edited Historical Recitals for Organ in 50 numbers, a series that educated generations of organists, widening horizons and elevating taste. His most famous organ work was the *Storm King Symphony* for orchestra and organ (1921); *In Joseph's Lovely Garden*, an Easter carol, was his best-known anthem. His *Technique and Art of Organ Playing* (New York, 1922) went into many editions, and the hymnal that he edited in 1933 for the Presbyterian Church was widely used. In 1954 he and his wife edited an important series of 18th-century Moravian anthems. At the time of his death he was the last surviving founder of the American Guild of Organists. The Clarence Dickinson Memorial Library of Church Music has been established at William Carey College in Hattiesburg, Mississippi. Dickinson's long life cast a lingering and benevolent shadow.

BIBLIOGRAPHY

S. Bingham: "Clarence Dickinson, 1873–1969," *American Organist*, lii/9 (1969), 8

G. L. Knight: "Clarence Dickinson: a Retrospect," *The Diapason*, lx/11 (1969), 16

VERNON GOTWALS

Dickinson, Emily (*b* Amherst, MA, 10 Dec 1830; *d* Amherst, 15 May 1886). Poet. After attending Amherst Academy, she spent a year at Mount Holyoke Female Seminary before returning to her home in Amherst, where she lived the rest of her life in increasing seclusion. Fond of music, she had taken singing and piano lessons in her youth. In her later years the theme of music, particularly the music of nature, became an important motif in her poetry. She wrote nearly 1800 poems, although only a handful were published in her lifetime. Most of her poems use meters derived from English hymnody, particularly common or ballad meter. Of all American poets, Dickinson ranks behind only Longfellow and Whitman in the number of poems that have been set to music; she and Whitman are the only 19th-century ones who remain substantial sources of texts for composers.

The earliest known settings are *Have you got a brook in your little heart?* (1896) by Etta Parker and Six Songs (1897) by Clarence Dickinson; most settings date from 1945 onwards. Composers have shown a marked preference for her earlier poems; among those most often set are "I'm Nobody! Who are you?," "If I can stop one heart from breaking," and "These are the days when birds come back." The innovative use of nontraditional rhymes, subtle metrical variations, concentrated images, and predominantly first-person dramatic voice, as well as the simple yet often passionate style of her poems make them well suited for musical setting. Moreover, the frequently used subjects of death and immortality, love and friendship, and nature provide a wealth of related verses for composers to set in song cycles.

Perhaps the best-known cycle of Dickinson poems is Copland's *Twelve Poems by Emily Dickinson*. Other cycles include *Six Poems by Emily Dickinson* by John Duke, *The Mob within the Heart* by Sergius Kagen, *Thirteen Poems of Emily Dickinson* by George Perle, *An Emily Dickinson Mosaic* by Daniel Pinkham, Jr., *Seven Choral Settings of Poems by Emily Dickinson* by Donald Grantham, *Songs to Poems of Emily Dickinson* by Otto Luening, Seven Songs for soprano and string quartet by Adolph Weiss, *Nature*, *Quiet Airs*, and *From Emily's Diary* by Ernst Bacon, and the melodrama *Magic Prison* by Ezra Laderman. Dorothy Gardner adapted her play *Eastward in Eden: the Love Story of Emily Dickinson* for opera, with music by Jan Meyerowitz. Other composers who have set a number of Dickinson poems include Robert Baksa, Arthur Farwell, and Thomas Pasatieri.

BIBLIOGRAPHY

J. Kerman: "American Music: the Columbia Series (II)," *Hudson Review*, xiv (1961), 408

M. W. England: "Emily Dickinson and Isaac Watts: Puritan Hymnodists," *Bulletin of the New York Public Library*, lxix (1965), 83–116; repr. in M. W. England and J. Sparrow: *Hymns Unbidden: Donne, Herbert, Blake, Emily Dickinson and the Hymnographers* (New York, 1966), 113–147

K. S. Diehl: *Hymns and Tunes: an Index* (New York, 1966)

D. T. Porter: *The Art of Emily Dickinson's Early Poetry* (Cambridge, MA, 1966)

W. J. Buckingham: *Emily Dickinson: an Annotated Bibliography* (Bloomington, IN, 1970)

D. Young: "Copland's Dickinson Songs," *Tempo*, no.103 (1972), 33

R. B. Sewall: *The Life of Emily Dickinson* (New York, 1974)

R. C. Friedberg: *American Art Song and American Poetry* (Metuchen, NJ, 1981)

O. Luening: "A Winding Path to Emily Dickinson," *Parnassus: Poetry in Review*, x/2 (1982), 225

M. A. Hovland: *Musical Settings of American Poetry: a Bibliography* (in preparation) [incl. list of settings]

MICHAEL HOVLAND

Dickinson, George Sherman (*b* St. Paul, MN, 9 Feb 1888; *d* Chapel Hill, NC, 6 Nov 1964). Music educator. He studied at Oberlin College (BA 1909), Oberlin Conservatory (BMus 1910), and at Harvard University (MA 1912); he became an associate of the American Guild of Organists (1910) and studied theory and composition in Berlin (1913–14). He worked as an organist and choirmaster in various churches (1902–21) and taught organ and theory at Oberlin Conservatory (1914–16) before joining the faculty at Vassar College (full professor 1922–53, music librarian 1927–53, chairman of the music department 1932–4). He was one of the principal founders of the American Musicological Society and its journal (*JAMS*), serving as chairman of its organizing committee (1934) and as president and chairman of the publication committee (1947–8) when the journal was established. Dickinson was active in the Music Library Association (president 1939–41). At Vassar he developed one of the best college music libraries in the country; his *Classification of Musical Compositions* is one of the bases of American music librarianship. Many of his other writings are concerned with musical style.

WRITINGS

The Growth and Use of Harmony (New York, 1927)

Classification of Musical Compositions: a Decimal-Symbol System (Poughkeepsie, NY, 1938)

The Pattern of Music (Poughkeepsie, NY, 1939)

Music as a Literature: an Outline (Poughkeepsie, NY, 1953)

The Study of Music as a Liberal Art (Poughkeepsie, NY, 1953)

The Study of the History of Music in the Liberal Arts College (New York, 1953)

A Handbook of Style in Music (Poughkeepsie, NY, 1965)

BIBLIOGRAPHY

Obituary, *Notes*, xxi (1964–5), 522

G. Haydon: "George Sherman Dickinson 1888–1964," *JAMS*, xviii (1965), 219

C. J. Bradley: *The Dickinson Classification: a Cataloguing and Classification Manual for Music* (Carlisle, PA, 1968)

JON NEWSOM

Dickinson, Peter (*b* Lytham St. Annes, England, 15 Nov 1934). English composer, pianist, and teacher. He attended Queens' College, Cambridge, where he was an organ scholar, studying under Philip Radcliffe and getting advice and encouragement from Lennox Berkeley. In 1958 he came to the USA on a Rotary Foundation fellowship and studied at the Juilliard School with Wagenaar; he also met and was influenced by Cage, Cowell, and Varèse. He worked as a pianist with the New York City Ballet and as a critic and lecturer before returning to England. In 1962 he was appointed to lecture at the College of St. Mark and St. John, Chelsea, and in 1966 moved to Birmingham, where he held university lectureships and was active as a performer and promoter of concerts of new music. In 1970 he resigned, and in 1974 accepted an appointment as the first professor of music at Keele University, where he founded what soon became one of the most important centers for the study of American music outside the USA (*see* CENTRE FOR AMERICAN MUSIC). In 1984 Dickinson left Keele in order to give more of his time to composing, performing, and lecturing. In texture, melody, and use of dissonance his early work shows affinities with that of middle-period Stravinsky; his early experimental and improvisational activity bore fruit in his works of the 1970s and 1980s. In its use of simple basic material in original ways Dickinson's music recalls that of Ives and Satie – composers in whom Dickinson has a special interest (as he does in Thomson and Lord Berners); it also evinces the influence of ragtime and blues. He has performed much American music in recitals and on recordings with his sister, the mezzo-soprano Meriel Dickinson, and he has written with sympathy and insight on American music, most often in the *Musical Times*.

HUGO COLE/H. WILEY HITCHCOCK

Dickman, Stephen (Allen) (*b* Chicago, IL, 2 March 1943). Composer. He studied theory and composition (with Druckman), cello (with Louis Garcia-Renard), and trumpet (with Emil Hauser) at Bard College (BA 1965), and theory and composition with Arthur Berger and Harold Shapero at Brandeis University (MFA 1968), and with Krenek at the Berkshire Music Center (1968). While at Brandeis he received many awards including the Joseph H. Bearns Prize for his String Quartet (1967) and two BMI Student Composer Awards (1968, 1969). In 1971 he won a Fulbright scholarship for study in Rome, with Petrassi for composition and with Giuseppe Selmi for cello. His *a cappella* opera of that time, *Real Magic in New York*, is highly contrapuntal and recalls chant; it uses generative rhythmic and melodic techniques, with each vocalist having his or her exclusive characteristics of pitch, interval, and tonality.

During the early 1970s Dickman traveled widely in Europe and Asia, and studied Indian music and the *sārangī*, a bowed instrument with sympathetic strings, in London and Bombay (1973–4). *Musical Journeys I–IV* document Dickman's thoughts while traveling. *Song Cycle* (1975–80), begun when he was in a hospital in Istanbul, shows the influence of traditional Turkish, Persian, and Indian music in its reliance on developing multiple repetitive rhythmic structures and in its melodic counterpoint, reminiscent of that of Indian ragas. Later pieces use the same rhythmic techniques. From 1976 to 1981 Dickman taught at the Tape Music Center, Mills College.

WORKS

Stage: Real Magic in New York (opera, R. Foreman), 1971; Str Trio: Dance (V. Matthews), 1980

Vocal: The Snow Man (W. Stevens), S, ens, 1966; On Mere Being (Stevens), S, ens, 1968; Continual Conversations with a Silent Man (Stevens), S, 1969; Song Cycle, multiple S, multiple vn, 1975–80: The Song of the Reed (Jalalul-Din Rumi), Love the Hierophant (Rumi), My Love Makes me Lonely (Dickman), I am a Lover (Dickman), Song (Dickman), Davani Shems-I-Tabrizi (Rumi); 10 Not Long Songs (Dickman), 1v, 1977; Magic Circle (Dickman, E. Frank), chorus, ens, 1980; At Night (Dickman), S, 1981; Orch by the Sea (Dickman), 4 S, orch, 1983

Chamber and tape: 2 str trios, 1965, 1970–71; Frei, tape, 1966; Lacerations, tape, 1966; Str Qt no.1, 1967; Damsel, 16 insts, 1968; Violoncello, 1969; 2 Violins, 1969; Pf Piece, 1971; 4 Pf Pieces, 1971; Musical Journeys I–IV, unspecified insts, 1972–6; Str Qts nos.2, 3, 1978; Str Qt no.4, On Themes by E. F., 1978; Influence of India, fl, vn, va, vc, pf, 1980; Everything and Everything, 3 tpt, str, 1982; Trees and Other Inclinations, pf, 1983; early chamber works

STEPHEN RUPPENTHAL

Dictionaries. Alphabetically ordered reference books, listing words or terms, or containing articles on a certain subject. The earliest American musical dictionaries were terminological, but during the course of the 19th century works of a more comprehensive kind, which included discussions of broader subjects and also biographies, were published by American compilers. Purely biographical dictionaries appeared in great numbers after 1900; interest in regional works of this kind became evident in the 1920s. A class of dictionaries that include no definitions of terms but contain information about musical works has been popular with music students and concertgoers since the 1950s. This article is devoted to musical dictionaries published in the USA by American compilers on subjects relevant to the history of American music. For periodical publications of American biography, *see* PERIODICALS.

1. Terminological. 2. Comprehensive. 3. Biographical.

1. TERMINOLOGICAL. American music lexicography began with William Billings's modest 140-entry "Musical Dictionary," which he included in *The Singing Master's Assistant* (1778). Its characteristically quirky, independent views were not taken up by Billings's successors: the first complete dictionaries published or reprinted in the USA were highly derivative of European antecedents. The two earliest, H. W. Pilkington's *A Musical Dictionary* (1812) and William Porter's *The Musical Cyclopedia* (1834), both emanating from Boston, as well as the first European dictionary to be reprinted here, Thomas Busby's *A Complete Dictionary of Music* (London, 1786; repr. Philadelphia, 1827/*R*), borrowed heavily from the works of Charles Burney, John Hawkins, J. W. Callcott, Jean Jousse, J.-J. Rousseau, and others (for a discussion of these books see J. Coover: "Dictionaries and encyclopedias of music," *Grove* 6).

Until Willi Apel's *Harvard Dictionary of Music* was published in 1944, American terminological dictionaries served as primers or short-definition lexicons; many of them, such as *Buck's New and Complete Dictionary of Musical Terms* (1873) and Theodore Baker's *A Dictionary of Musical Terms* (1895), also provided translations of foreign musical words. For fuller and more detailed explanations of musical terminology, musicians had to rely upon standard European dictionaries (e.g., John Stainer and W. A. Barrett's *A Dictionary of Musical Terms* (1876), George Grove's

A Dictionary of Music and Musicians (1878–90), and Hugo Riemann's *Musik-Lexikon* (1882)). A large number of these 19th- and early 20th-century books were "pronouncing" dictionaries; a more recent example of this now rare type is the *Pronouncing Dictionary of Musical Terms and Composers' Names* (1976).

Since the publication of the first edition of Apel's *Harvard Dictionary of Music*, a terminological dictionary with good, brief historical articles covering all aspects of music, and short but useful bibliographies, general terminological dictionaries have given way to specialized terminological ones on such subjects as musical instruments, church music, 20th-century music, jazz, and popular music. Notable among the special lexicons that have documented the changes in the jargon of popular and contemporary music are Arnold Shaw's *Lingo of Tin-Pan Alley* (1950), which had appeared a year earlier as an article in *Notes*, Robert Gold's *The Jazz Lexicon* (1964), and Robert Fink and Robert Ricci's *The Language of Twentieth Century Music* (1975).

2. COMPREHENSIVE. The first important American music encyclopedia was published in Boston by John Weeks Moore in 1852, a few years after he issued two numbers of a monthly lexicographic publication. For the terminological aspect of his *Complete Encyclopaedia of Music* (1852), Moore availed himself of the works of E. L. Gerber, A.-E. Choron, F. J. M. Fayolle, Burney, Hawkins, George Hogarth, Callcott, William Gardiner, Busby, J. A. Hamilton, Gustav Schilling, and F.-J. Fétis. More difficult for him to document were the various aspects of American musical life and the lives of American musicians. He pursued his work by sending out inquiries to large numbers of musicians in the USA and abroad, but the response was extremely poor and the information requested not fully supplied. Even though much of his biographical information was limited and was criticized for inaccuracy, Moore added an appendix to his encyclopedia in 1875 and published a second edition in 1880.

The next notable effort was the three-volume *Cyclopedia of Music and Musicians* (1888–90). Edited by John Denison Champlin with William Foster Apthorp, it was modeled on the successful *Cyclopedia of Painters and Paintings* (1886–7); it was lavishly illustrated with portraits of musicians, living and dead, and contained facsimile reproductions of scores by eminent composers.

In the first decades of the 20th century, two multi-volume encyclopedias were published by American compilers in the USA: *The American History and Encyclopedia of Music* (1908–10), edited by William Hubbard, and *The Art of Music* (1915–17), under the general editorship of Daniel Gregory Mason. Neither was alphabetically arranged, they both covered all aspects of music, and for the first time American music and musicians received substantial coverage in a comprehensive reference work.

The next two decades saw the publication of a number of comprehensive dictionaries compiled by a single person. *The New Encyclopedia of Music and Musicians* (1924) was edited by Waldo Selden Pratt, who had edited the American supplement (1920) to *Grove's Dictionary* (2/1904–10, 3/1927). Pratt was asked by Carl Fischer to prepare a new dictionary, which would be a one-volume condensation of the current edition of *Grove's Dictionary*, incorporating material in the American supplement; in the event, he also drew on the latest edition (1924) of the Riemann *Musik-Lexikon*.

In 1938 the Macmillan firm published the *Macmillan Encyclopedia of Music and Musicians* compiled and edited by Albert Wier. Wier was able to take advantage of the work done by Nicolas Slonimsky in correcting the errors in earlier reference works; Slonimsky had published details of these in his *Music since 1900* (1937). For one year Wier's was the most up-to-date and accurate music encyclopedia. In 1939 Oscar Thompson published *The International Cyclopedia of Music and Musicians*. Known for its scholarship and well-written articles, it has gone through ten editions, the last published in 1975. The editors of the later editions (Slonimsky, Robert Sabin, and Bruce Bohle) adhered to Thompson's original goal, namely, to have in one volume a "comprehensive and detailed treatment of a multitude of subjects that formerly required several volumes." Thompson felt the need to apologize for the large proportion of American composers included, saying that because they had not been fairly represented "in books of similar character issued abroad, the editor has preferred to err on the side of liberality in the factual statement of what they have achieved."

As in the case of terminological dictionaries, comprehensive dictionaries of terms, biographies, subjects, and theory have become more specialized in their coverage. Encyclopedias devoted to opera, dance, 20th-century music, popular music, and the music industry have appeared. It is interesting to note that until the publication of *The New Grove Dictionary of American Music*, Edward Jablonski's *Encyclopedia of American Music* (1981) was the only comprehensive dictionary covering all aspects of American music.

3. BIOGRAPHICAL. Since its publication in 1900, Theodore Baker's *A Biographical Dictionary of Musicians* has continued, through seven editions, to be the foremost international biographical dictionary in the English language. With the lexicographical sleuth Nicolas Slonimsky as editor for the last three editions, it remains an invaluable reference tool for musicians, students and concertgoers. Even though Baker himself included living musicians, he never intended his dictionary to be a "who's who" of music, such as those prepared by Dixie Hines and Harry P. Hanaford (1914), César Saerchinger (1918), and Pierre Key and Irene Haynes (1931). The longest-lived American work of this type was *Who is Who in Music*, which went through five editions (1927–51) under various titles. A new *Who's Who in American Music: Classical* appeared in 1983.

While biographical dictionaries have appeared since the 1950s for jazz (Leonard Feather's *The Encyclopedia of Jazz*, 1955), popular music (David Ewen's *Popular American Composers from Revolutionary Times to the Present*, 1962; suppl., 1972), and folk music (Ray Lawless's *Folksingers and Folksongs in America*, 1960), it was not until Lillian Roxon's comprehensive *Rock Encyclopedia* (1969) that material on rock musicians was made available. A rash of dictionaries in this area was published in the 1970s and 1980s, including another comprehensive dictionary, the glossy *Illustrated Encyclopedia of Rock* (1977), and purely biographical dictionaries by Michael Bane (1981), Brock Helander (1982), and Jon Pareles and Patricia Romanowski (1983).

The women's movement, beginning in the late 1960s, generated a new interest in women's studies, which led to the publication of a number of biographical dictionaries specializing in female musicians and composers. Some of the more notable are Don Hixon and Don Hennessee's *Women in Music* (1975), Susan Stern's *Women Composers* (1978), Jane LePage's two-volume *Women Composers, Conductors, and Musicians of the Twentieth Century* (1980–83), and Aaron Cohen's *International Encyclopedia of Women Composers* (1981; suppl., 1982).

Among other specialized biographical dictionaries are several covering black musicians. The first important compilation was W. C. Handy's *Negro Authors and Composers of the United States* (?1938). More recent studies include Henry Sampson's *Blacks in Blackface* (1980), *The Illustrated Encyclopedia of Black Music* (1982, under the editorial supervision of Jon Futrell), and Eileen Southern's important *Biographical Dictionary of Afro-American and African Musicians* (1982).

In addition to biographical dictionaries of national or international scope and those that deal with particular fields, regional dictionaries document scores of lesser-known musicians, whose names would otherwise be lost to history. The work of the regional chapters of the National Federation of Music Clubs, which promotes local musicians and publishes handbooks that include biographical sketches, has helped in the preservation or rediscovery of local musical history. Since the 1960s fewer regional dictionaries have been compiled. However, the Boston Area Music Librarians' *Boston Composers Project* (1983) has set a new standard for documenting the lives of local composers and should encourage others to publish similar studies.

LIST

The following list is divided into five main sections containing citations of comprehensive, terminological, and biographical works, as well as guidebooks to repertories and a number of miscellaneous dictionary-like listings and indexes. The first category contains citations of works that include terminological, biographical, and topical entries; repertory guidebooks may contain biographical information but do not have definitions of terms. It should be noted that dictionaries concerning a particular area of music (popular music, early music, etc.) may occur in any of the five categories. An asterisk indicates that the work so marked is a "pronouncing" dictionary or includes such a guide to pronunciation.

COMPREHENSIVE

J. W. Moore: *The Musician's Lexicon, or Encyclopedistical Treasury of Musical Knowledge* (Boston, and Bellows Falls, VT, 1845–6), 2 nos. [initiated as a monthly pubn]

——: *Complete Encyclopaedia of Music* (Boston, 1852, 2/1880/*R*1973; appx, 1875)

*——: *Dictionary of Musical Information* (Boston, 1876/*R*1971)

*W. S. B. Mathews: *Pronouncing Dictionary and Condensed Encyclopedia of Musical Terms, Instruments, Composers, and Important Works* (Chicago, 1880, ?5/1895)

F. O. Jones, ed.: *A Handbook of American Music and Musicians* (Canaseraga, NY, 1886/*R*1971)

J. D. Champlin and W. F. Apthorp: *Cyclopedia of Music and Musicians* (New York, 1888–90), 3 vols.

*W. M. Derthick: *Manual of Music* (Chicago, 1888, rev. 1890)

*J. M. Dungan: *The Normal Text-book* (Lafayette, IN, 1890)

*R. Hughes: *The Musical Guide* (New York, 1903, 2/1912 as *Music Lovers' Encyclopedia*, rev. and enlarged by D. Taylor and R. Kerr 3/1939)

L. J. de Bekker: *Stokes' Encyclopedia of Music and Musicians* (New York, 1908/*R*1974, 2/1924 as *Black's Dictionary of Music*, 3/1925 as *De Bekker's Music & Musicians*, 4/1937 as *The Encyclopedia of Music and Musicians*)

W. L. Hubbard: *The American History and Encyclopedia of Music* (Toledo, OH, and New York, 1908–10), 12 vols.

J. H. Clifford: *The Standard Musical Encyclopedia* (New York, 1910)

——: *The Musiclover's Handbook* (New York, 1911)

D. G. Mason, ed.: *The Art of Music: a Comprehensive Library of Information for Music Lovers and Musicians* (New York, 1915–17), 14 vols.

W. S. Pratt, ed.: *Grove's Dictionary of Music and Musicians: American Supplement* (New York, 1920, repr. 1925, rev. 2/1928, many reprs.)

W. S. Pratt: *The New Encyclopedia of Music and Musicians* (New York, 1924, rev. 2/1929/*R*1973)

A. A. Bachmann: *An Encyclopedia of the Violin* (New York, 1925/*R*1975)

N. Slonimsky: *Music since 1900* (New York, 1937, 4/1971) [incl. terminological dictionary in all edns; biographical dictionary in first 2 edns]

A. E. Wier: *Macmillan Encyclopedia of Music and Musicians* (New York, 1938; suppl., 1940)

O. Thompson: *The International Cyclopedia of Music and Musicians* (New York, 1939, rev. N. Slonimsky 4/1946, rev. R. Sabin 9/1964, rev. B. Bohle 10/1975)

A. Chujoy: *The Dance Encyclopedia* (New York, 1949, rev. and enlarged with P. W. Manchester 2/1967)

D. Ewen: *Encyclopedia of the Opera* (New York, 1955, rev. and enlarged 3/1971 as *The New Encyclopedia of the Opera*)

K. W. Berger: *Band Encyclopedia* (Evansville, IN, 1960)

P. Gammond and P. Clayton: *Dictionary of Popular Music* (New York, 1961)

I. Stambler: *Encyclopedia of Popular Music* (New York, 1965)

N. Lloyd: *The Golden Encyclopedia of Music* (New York, 1968)

L. Roxon: *Rock Encyclopedia* (New York, 1969, rev. 2/1978 as *Lillian Roxon's Rock Encyclopedia*)

C. Ammer: *Harper's Dictionary of Music* (New York, 1972)

Q. D. Bowers: *Encyclopedia of Automatic Music Instruments* (Vestal, NY, 1972)

M. Shestack: *The Country Music Encyclopedia* (New York, 1974)

J. Vinton, ed.: *Dictionary of Contemporary Music* (New York, 1974)

M. Nulman: *Concise Encyclopedia of Jewish Music* (New York, 1975)

K. Baggelaar and D. Milton: *Folk Music: More than a Song* (New York, 1976)

L. Orrey and G. Chase, eds.: *The Encyclopedia of Opera* (New York, 1976)

M. Clarke and D. Vaughan: *The Encyclopedia of Dance & Ballet* (New York, 1977)

G. S. Kanahele, ed.: *Hawaiian Music and Musicians: an Illustrated History* (Honolulu, 1979)

E. Katz: *The Film Encyclopedia* (New York, 1979)

B. Hadley, ed.: *Britannica Book of Music* (Garden City, NY, 1980) [articles on music from the *Encyclopaedia britannica*]

E. Jablonski: *The Encyclopedia of American Music* (Garden City, NY, 1981)

H. Rachlin: *The Encyclopedia of the Music Business* (New York, 1981) [pop music]

A. Shaw: *Dictionary of American Pop/Rock* (New York, 1982)

TERMINOLOGICAL

(general)

W. Billings: *The Singing Master's Assistant, or Key to Practical Music* (Boston, 1778/*R*, 4/1781/*R*) [incl. list of 140 terms]; ed. in *The Complete Works of William Billings*, ii, ed. H. Nathan (Boston, 1977)

T. A. Busby: *A Complete Dictionary of Music* (London, 1786; Philadelphia, 1827/*R*)

H. W. Pilkington: *A Musical Dictionary* (Boston, 1812)

W. S. Porter: *The Musical Cyclopedia. . .Embracing a Complete Musical Dictionary* (Boston, 1834)

J. S. Adams: *5,000 Musical Terms* (Boston, 1851, rev. 2/1865 as *Adams' New Musical Dictionary of Fifteen Thousand Technical Words*, ?3/1893)

*D. Buck: *Buck's New and Complete Dictionary of Musical Terms* (Boston, 1873, rev. 1901)

*W. Ludden: *Pronouncing Musical Dictionary of Technical Words, Phrases and Abbreviations* (New York, 1875, 2/1904)

J. Stainer and W. A. Barrett: *A Dictionary of Musical Terms* (London and Boston, 1876, 4/1898/*R*1974)

*J. C. Macy: *Pronouncing Pocket Dictionary of over 500 Musical Terms* (Boston, 1886)

J. D. Holcomb: *Holcomb's Polyglot Pocket Dictionary of Musical Terms* (Cleveland, 1893)

*T. Baker: *A Dictionary of Musical Terms* (New York, 1895, 21/1923/*R*1970, 25/1939)

*H. A. Clarke: *Pronouncing Dictionary of Musical Terms* (Philadelphia, 1896/*R*1977)

*C. W. Grimm: *Grimm's Pronouncing Pocket Dictionary of Musical Terms* (Cincinnati, 1896, 2/1907)

*W. S. B. Mathews and E. Liebling: *A Pronouncing and Defining Dictionary of Music* (Cincinnati and New York, 1896/*R*1973, 2/1925)

*H. S. Sawyer: *Music Teacher's Assistant. . .with a New Pronouncing Dictionary* (Chicago, 1900)

*T. Baker: *A Pronouncing Pocket Manual of Musical Terms* (New York, 1905, rev. 4/1978 as *Schirmer Pronouncing Pocket Manual of Musical Terms*)

*L. C. Elson: *Elson's Music Dictionary* (Boston, 1905/*R*1972, ?2/1909) [mainly a terminological dictionary]

*H. M. Redman: *Redman's Musical Dictionary and Pronouncing Guide* (Philadelphia, 1910)

*K. Bergmann: *Student's Pronouncing Dictionary of Musical Terms* (New York, 1911)

E. Duncan: *Encyclopedia of Musical Terms* (New York and Boston, 1914)

*J. Snyder: *Music Student's Pocket Dictionary of Musical Terms and How to Pronounce Them* (New York, 1927)

*W. Apel: *Harvard Dictionary of Music* (Cambridge, MA, 1944, rev. and enlarged 2/1969) [see also Randel, 1978]

R. Colvig: *Vocabulary of Musical Terms* (Berkeley, CA, 1958)

P. Gammond: *Terms used in Music* (New York, 1959, 2/1971)

W. Apel and R. T. Daniel: *The Harvard Brief Dictionary of Music* (Cambridge, MA, 1960/*R*1971)
*S. Barach: *An Introduction to the Language of Music* (Washington, DC, 1962)
J. M. and C. Watson: *Concise Dictionary of Music* (New York, 1965)
*W. P. Grant: *Handbook of Music Terms* (Metuchen, NJ, 1967)
C. Ammer: *Musician's Handbook of Foreign Terms* (New York, 1971)
T. Karp: *Dictionary of Music* (New York, 1973)
V. J. Picerno: *Dictionary of Musical Terms* (Brooklyn, NY, 1976)
**Pronouncing Dictionary of Musical Terms and Composers' Names* (Midland Park, NJ, 1976)
C. D. Grigg: *Music Translation Dictionary* (Westport, CT, 1978) [terms in 13 languages]
D. M. Randel: *Harvard Concise Dictionary of Music* (Cambridge, MA, 1978) [incl. material from Apel, 2/1969]
S. Levarie and E. Levy: *Musical Morphology: a Discourse and a Dictionary* (Kent, OH, 1983) [also unauthorized edn, 1980]

(specialized)

P. S. Donnerwetter [pseud.]: *Handy Music-lexicon* (Boston, 1894) [comic and satirical dictionary of musical terms]
G. A. Audsley: *Organ-stops* (New York, 1921)
S. Irwin: *Dictionary of Hammond Organ Stops* (New York, 1939, 4/1970)
L. Kirstein: *Ballet Alphabet: a Primer for Laymen* (New York, 1939/*R*1967)
A. Hughes: *Liturgical Terms for Music Students* (Boston, 1940/*R*1972)
*M. R. Oloff: *Balletic-dance Terms with English Pronounciations and Identifications* (St. Louis, 1949, ?2/1950)
A. Shaw: "The Vocabulary of Tin-Pan Alley Explained," *Notes*, vii (1949–50), 38; repr. as *Lingo of Tin-Pan Alley* (New York, 1950)
G. Grant: *Technical Manual and Dictionary of Classical Ballet* (New York, 1950, rev. 2/1967)
G. W. Stubbings: *A Dictionary of Church Music* (New York, 1950)
W. Granville: *The Theater Dictionary: British and American Terms in the Drama, Opera, Ballet* (New York, 1952)
H. Smither: *Critical Survey of Basic Terminology. . .in. . .20th-century Music* (diss., Cornell U., 1952)
B. Spinney: *Encyclopedia of Percussion Instruments and Drumming* (Hollywood, CA, 1955–9), 2 vols. [A–B only]
A. Berkman: *Singers' Glossary of Show Business Jargon* (Hollywood, CA, 1961)
W. F. Lee: *Music Theory Dictionary* (Huntsville, TX, 1961, 2/1966)
F. L. Moore: *Crowell's Handbook of World Opera* (New York, 1961) [terminological dictionary, pp.560–92]
S. Irwin: *Dictionary of Pipe Organ Stops* (New York, 1962, 2/1965)
J. R. Carroll: *Compendium of Liturgical Music Terms* (Toledo, OH, 1964)
R. S. Gold: *The Jazz Lexicon* (New York, 1964, 2/1975 as *Jazz Talk*)
S. Marcuse: *Musical Instruments: a Comprehensive Dictionary* (Garden City, NY, 1964/*R*1975)
W. G. Raffé: *Dictionary of the Dance* (New York, 1964)
E. T. Cone: "A Budding Grove," *PNM*, iii/2 (1965), 38
S. Irwin: *Dictionary of Electronic Organ Stops* (New York, 1968)
J. R. Davidson: *A Dictionary of Protestant Church Music* (Metuchen, NJ, 1975)
R. Fink and R. Ricci: *The Language of Twentieth Century Music: a Dictionary of Terms* (New York, 1975)
H. Risatti: *New Music Vocabulary* (Urbana, IL, 1975)
Musical Instruments of the World: an Illustrated Encyclopedia, ed. Diagram Group (New York, 1976)
The CAMEO Dictionary of Creative Audio Terms, ed. Creative Audio and Music Electronics Organization (Framingham, MA, 1980)
D. Delson and W. E. Hurst: *Delson's Dictionary of Radio and Record Industry Terms* (Thousand Oaks, CA, 1981)

BIOGRAPHICAL

(general and specialized)

L. Urbino: *Biographical Sketches of Eminent Musical Composers* (Boston, 1876) [arranged in chronological order]
F. Willard and M. Livermore: *A Woman of the Century* (Buffalo, 1893)
J. Towers: *Women in Music* (Winchester, VA, *c*1897)
*W. M. Breckenridge: *Pronouncing Dictionary of the Names of Prominent Musicians* (Chicago, 1899)
T. Baker: *A Biographical Dictionary of Musicians* (New York, 1900, rev. A. Remy 3/1919/*R*1970, rev. C. Engel 4/1940 as *Baker's Biographical Dictionary of Musicians*, rev. N. Slonimsky 5/1958/*R*1965, 6/1978, 7/1984; suppls., 1949, 1965, 1971)
O. Ebel: *Women Composers* (Brooklyn, NY, 1902, 3/1913)
O. G. T. Sonneck: *A Bibliography of Early Secular American Music* (Washington, DC, 1905, rev. and enlarged W. T. Upton 2/1945/*R*1964) [incl. biographies]
F. E. J. Lloyd: *Lloyd's Church Musicians Directory* (Chicago, 1910/*R*1974)
*W. J. Baltzell: *Baltzell's Dictionary of Musicians. . .with a Pronunciation of Foreign Names* (Boston, 1911, rev. 3/1918)
D. Hines and H. P. Hanaford: *Who's Who in Music and Drama* (New York, 1914) [vol. i of a proposed annual pubn]
C. Saerchinger: *International Who's Who in Music and Musical Gazeteer* (New York, 1918)
E. N. C. Barnes: *Who's Who in Music Education* (Washington, DC, 1925) [biographical dictionary, pp.1–40]
F. J. Metcalf: *American Writers and Compilers of Sacred Music* (New York, 1925/*R*1967)
*W. J. Baltzell: *Noted Names in Music* (Boston, 1927)
A. V. Frankenstein, ed.: *Who is Who in Music* (Chicago and New York, 1927, rev. S. Spaeth 2/1929, 1941)
E. E. Hipsher: *American Opera and its Composers* (Philadelphia, 1927/*R*1978, 2/1934)
J. T. H. Mize, ed.: *The International Who is Who in Music* (Chicago, 1927, 5/1951)
G. Saleski: *Famous Musicians of a Wandering Race* (New York, 1927, 2/1949 as *Famous Musicians of Jewish Origin*)
Dictionary of American Biography [*DAB*] (New York, 1928–36; 7 suppls., 1944–81; condensed version 1964, 2/1977 as *Concise Dictionary of American Biography*)
C. Reis: *American Composers of Today* (New York, 1930, enlarged 2/1932 as *American Composers*, enlarged 3/1938 as *Composers in America. . .1912–1937*, rev. and enlarged 4/1947/*R*1977)
P. V. R. Key and I. E. Haynes: *Pierre Key's Musical Who's Who* (New York, 1931)
D. Ewen: *Composers of Today* (New York, 1934, 2/1936) [superseded by his *American Composers Today*, 1949]
E. Barnes: *American Women in Creative Music* (Washington, DC, 1936)
W. C. Handy: *Negro Authors and Composers of the United States* (New York, ?1938/*R*1976)
Who's Who Today in the Musical World, 1936–37 (New York, 1938)
P. E. Miller: *Down Beat's Yearbook of Swing* (Chicago, 1939, 2/1943 as *Miller's Yearbook of Popular Music*)
D. Ewen: *Living Musicians* (New York, 1940; suppl., 1957)
R. Hughes: *The Biographical Dictionary of Musicians*, rev. and ed. D. Taylor and R. Kerr (New York, 1940) [separate pubn of the biographical entries as *Musical Guide*, 1903, 2/1912 as *Music Lovers' Encyclopedia*]
Bio-bibliographical Index of Musicians in the United States of America from Colonial Times, ed. Historical Records Survey (Washington, DC, 1941, 2/1956/*R*1972)
J. H. Fairfield: *Known Violin Makers* (New York, 1942/*R*1973 with appx)
W. G. Polack: *The Handbook to the Lutheran Hymnal* (St. Louis, 1942, rev. 3/1958) [biographical dictionary, pp.469–603]
The ASCAP Biographical Dictionary of Composers, Authors and Publishers (New York, 1948, 4/1980) [various editors]
D. Ewen: *American Composers Today* (New York, 1949) [supersedes his *Composers of Today*, 1934]
The Hymnal 1940 Companion, ed. Protestant Episcopal Church in the USA (New York, 1949, rev. 3/1956) [biographical dictionary, pp.365–608]
A. Haeussler: *The Story of our Hymns: the Handbook to the Hymnal of the Evangelical and Reformed Church* (St. Louis, 1952, 3/1954) [biographical dictionary, pp.517–1004]
Compositores de América: datos biograficos y catalogos de sur obras/Composers of the Americas: Biographical Data and Catalogs of their Works, ed. Pan American Union (Washington, DC, 1955–79), 19 vols. [incl. extensive work-lists]
L. G. Feather: *The Encyclopedia of Jazz* (New York, 1955, rev. and enlarged 2/1960 as *The New Edition of the Encyclopedia of Jazz*; suppls., 1966 as *The Encyclopedia of Jazz in the Sixties*, 1976 as *The Encyclopedia. . .in the Seventies*) [mainly a biographical dictionary]
Who's Who in Music and Records (New York, 1955)
D. Ewen: *Complete Book of the American Musical Theater* (New York, 1958, rev. 1970 as *New Complete Book. . .Theater*) [biographical dictionary, pp.609–734]
J. Roda: *Bows for Musical Instruments of the Violin Family* (Chicago, 1959) [mainly a biographical dictionary of bow makers]
The Country Music Who's Who (Denver, 1960, 3/1970)
R. M. Lawless: *Folksingers and Folksongs in America* (New York, 1960, rev. 2/1965 with suppl.)
L. Gentry: *A History and Encyclopedia of Country, Western, and Gospel Music* (Nashville, 1961/*R*1972, rev. 2/1969) [biographical dictionary, pp.359–598]
D. Ewen: *Popular American Composers from Revolutionary Times to the Present: a Biographical and Critical Guide* (New York, 1962; suppl., 1972)
C. E. Wunderlich: *A History and Bibliography of Early American Musical Periodicals, 1782–1852* (diss., U. of Michigan, 1962) [biographical dictionary of pub-

lishers, printers, engravers, editors, composers, and authors, appx C]
R. J. Wolfe: *Secular Music in America, 1801–1825: a Bibliography* (New York, 1964) [incl. biographical dictionary]
M. Montgomery: *Who's Who in the National Federation of Music Clubs* (New York, 1965, 2/1967)
D. Ewen: *Great Composers, 1300–1900* (New York, 1966)
A. Rose and E. Souchon: *New Orleans Jazz: a Family Album* (Baton Rouge, LA, 1967, rev. 2/1978, rev. and enlarged 3/1984) [biographical dictionary, pp.3–128]
G. T. Simon: *The Big Bands* (New York, 1967, 4/1981) [biographical dictionary, pp.450–514]
D. Ewen: *The World of Twentieth-century Music* (Englewood Cliffs, NJ, 1968)
A. K. Burks: *Follow the Pipers: a Guide to Contemporary Flute Artists and Teachers* (Westfield, NY, 1969)
D. Ewen: *Composers since 1900* (New York, 1969; suppl., 1981)
I. Stambler and G. Landon: *Encyclopedia of Folk, Country and Western Music* (New York, 1969, 2/1983) [mainly a biographical dictionary]
L. Brown and G. Friedrich: *Encyclopedia of Rock & Roll* (New York, 1970)
E. B. Carlson: *A Bio-bibliographical Dictionary of Twelve-tone and Serial Composers* (Metuchen, NJ, 1970)
F. D. Gealy: *Companion to the Hymnal: a Handbook to the 1964 Methodist Hymnal* (Nashville and New York, 1970) [biographical dictionary, pp.469–720]
D. L. Hixon: *Music in Early America* (Metuchen, NJ, 1970) [incl. biographical dictionary]
V. Thomson: *American Music since 1910* (New York, 1970) [incl. biographical dictionary]
T. Vallance: *The American Musical* (New York, 1970)
L. Brown and G. Friedrich: *Encyclopedia of Country and Western Music* (New York, 1971)
E. James: *Notable American Women, 1607–1950: a Biographical Dictionary* (Cambridge, MA, 1971; suppl., 1980)
J. R. Taylor and A. Jackson: *The Hollywood Musical* (New York, 1971) [biographical dictionary, pp.157–234]
J. Chilton: *Who's Who of Jazz: Storyville to Swing Street* (Philadelphia, 1972, rev. 2/1978, rev. and enlarged 3/1985)
C. R. Arnold: *Organ Literature: a Comprehensive Survey* (Metuchen, NJ, 1973, 2/1984) [biographical dictionary, 1973 edn, pp.294–597; 1984 edn, pp.17–557]
C. E. Claghorn: *Biographical Dictionary of American Music* (West Nyack, NY, 1973)
R. B. Fisher: *Musical Prodigies* (New York, 1973)
K. Thompson: *A Dictionary of Twentiety-century Composers, 1911–1971* (London, 1973)
R. D. Kinkle: *The Complete Encyclopedia of Popular Music and Jazz 1900–1950* (New Rochelle, NY, 1974), 4 vols. [biographical dictionary, vols.ii–iii]
N. Nite and R. M. Newman: *Rock On: the Illustrated Encyclopedia of Rock 'n' Roll* (New York, 1974–8, rev. 2/1982–4), 2 vols.
C. Pavlakis: *The American Music Handbook* (New York, 1974) [biographical dictionary, pp.259–360]
D. L. Hixon and D. Hennessee: *Women in Music: a Biobibliography* (Metuchen, NJ, 1975)
H. W. Jacoby: *Contemporary American Composers based at American Colleges and Universities* (Paradise, CA, 1975)
I. Stambler: *Encyclopedia of Pop, Rock and Soul* (New York, 1975) [mainly a biographical dictionary]
E. R. Anderson: *Contemporary American Composers: a Biographical Dictionary* (Boston, 1976, rev. 2/1982)
**Pronouncing Dictionary of Musical Terms and Composers' Names* (Midland, NJ, 1976)
W. J. Reynolds: *Companion to Baptist Hymnal* (Nashville, 1976) [biographical dictionary, pp.250–473]
M. F. Rich, ed.: *Who's Who in Opera: an International Biographical Dictionary* (New York, 1976)
F. Dellar, R. Thompson, and D. B. Green: *The Illustrated Encyclopedia of Country Music* (New York, 1977)
N. Logan and B. Woffinden: *The Illustrated Encyclopedia of Rock* (New York, 1977, rev. 4/1982 as *The Harmony Illustrated Encyclopedia of Rock*)
L. Berry, Jr.: *Biographical Dictionary of Black Musicians and Music Educators* (Guthrie, OK, 1978)
B. Case and S. Britt: *The Illustrated Encyclopedia of Jazz* (New York, 1978)
W. Craig: *Sweet and Lowdown: America's Popular Song Writers* (Metuchen, NJ, 1978)
D. Ewen: *Musicians since 1900: Performers in Concert and Opera* (New York, 1978)
A. Laurence: *Women of Notes: 1,000 Women Composers born before 1900* (New York, 1978)
S. Stern: *Women Composers: a Handbook* (Metuchen, NJ, 1978)
L. Walker: *The Big Band Almanac* (Pasadena, CA, 1978)
R. Anderson and G. North: *Gospel Music Encyclopedia* (New York, 1979) [mainly a biographical dictionary]
S. Harris: *Blues Who's Who: a Biographical Dictionary of Blues Singers* (New Rochelle, NY, 1979/R1981)
G. T. Simon: *The Best of the Music Makers* (Garden City, NY, 1979) [popular music performers]
C. W. Hughes: *American Hymns Old and New* (New York, 1980) [biographical dictionary, vol.ii, pp.289–609]
J. W. LePage: *Women Composers, Conductors, and Musicians of the Twentieth Century* (Metuchen, NJ, 1980–83), 2 vols.
H. T. Sampson: *Blacks in Blackface: a Source Book on Early Black Musical Shows* (Metuchen, NJ, 1980) [biographical dictionary, pp.328–454]
M. Bane: *Who's Who in Rock* (New York, 1981)
A. I. Cohen: *International Encyclopedia of Women Composers* (New York, 1981; suppl., 1982)
K. Kingsbury: *Who's Who in Country & Western Music* (Culver City, CA, 1981)
J. M. Meggett: *Keyboard Music by Women Composers: a Catalog and Bibliography* (Westport, CT, 1981)
S. J. Rogal: *Sisters of Sacred Song: a Catalogue of British and American Hymnodists* (New York, 1981)
J. L. Zaimont and K. Famera: *Contemporary Concert Music by Women: a Directory of the Composers and their Works* (Westport, CT, 1981)
C. E. Claghorn: *Biographical Dictionary of Jazz* (Englewood Cliffs, NJ, 1982)
B. N. Cohen-Stratyner: *Biographical Dictionary of Dance* (New York, 1982)
D. Ewen: *American Composers: a Biographical Dictionary* (New York, 1982)
J. Futrell and others: *The Illustrated Encyclopedia of Black Music* (New York, 1982) [mainly a biographical dictionary]
B. Helander: *The Rock Who's Who* (New York, 1982)
J. L. Holmes: *Conductors on Record* (Westport, CT, 1982)
G. Kehler: *The Piano in Concert* (Metuchen, NJ, 1982), 2 vols.
E. Southern: *Biographical Dictionary of Afro-American and African Musicians* (Westport, CT, 1982)
J. Pareles and P. Romanowski, eds.: *The Rolling Stone Encyclopedia of Rock & Roll* (New York, 1983)
Who's Who in American Music: Classical (New York, 1983)
N. Butterworth: *A Dictionary of American Composers* (New York, 1984)
M. White: *"You Must Remember This. . .": Popular Songwriters 1900–1980* (New York, 1985)
M. H. Holmes: *Fretted Instruments and their Makers: a Dictionary of American Musical Instrument Manufacturers* (in preparation)

(regional)

F. Gates: *Who's Who in Music in California* (Los Angeles, 1920)
Pennsylvania Composers and their Compositions, ed. Pennsylvania Federation of Music Clubs (Philadelphia, 1923)
E. C. Krohn: *A Century of Missouri Music* (St. Louis, 1924/R1971 with addns as *Missouri Music*)
G. C. Smith: *Creative Arts in Texas: a Handbook of Biography* (Nashville, 1926)
G. T. Edwards: *Music and Musicians of Maine* (Portland, ME, 1928/R1970) [incl. biographical dictionary]
B. D. Ussher: *Who's Who in Music and Dance in Southern California* (Hollywood, 1933, rev. by W. J. Perlman 2/1940 as *Music and Dance in California*, rev. by R. D. Saunders 3/1948 as *Music and Dance in California and the West*) [biographical dictionary, 1933 edn, pp. 161–267]
J. M. Fredericks: *California Composers: Biographical Notes* (San Francisco, 1934)
L. C. Graniss: *Connecticut Composers* (New Haven, 1935)
E. M. McCartney: *Virginia Composers* (n.p., 1935)
Indiana Composers, Native and Adopted, ed. Indiana Federation of Music Clubs (Bloomington, IN, 1936)
Washington State Composers, ed. Washington Federation of Music Clubs (Seattle, 1936)
O. J. Knippers: *Who's Who among Southern Singers and Composers* (Lawrenceburg, TN, and Hot Springs National Park, AR, 1937)
D. James: *Michigan Composers: Biographical Notes* (Ypsilanti, MI, 1938)
Musical Iowana 1838–1938: a Century of Music in Iowa, ed. Iowa Federation of Music Clubs (Detroit, ?1939) [biographical dictionary, pp.85–154]
Celebrities in El Dorado, WPA History of Music Project, iv (San Francisco, 1940/R1972)
Fifty Local Prodigies, WPA History of Music Project, v (San Francisco, 1940/R1972)
G. M. Rohrer: *Music and Musicians of Pennsylvania* (Philadelphia, 1940/R1970)
M. H. Osburn: *Ohio Composers and Musical Authors* (Columbus, OH, 1942)
H. W. Eichhorn and T. W. Mathis: *North Carolina Composers, as Represented in the Holograph Collection of the Library of the Woman's College* (Greensboro, NC, 1945)

Wisconsin Composers, ed. Wisconsin Federation of Music Clubs (n.p., 1948)
N. D. McGee: *Kentucky Composers and Compilers of Folk Music, Native and Adopted* (Frankfort, KY, 1950)
E. C. Whitlock and R. D. Saunders: *Music and Dance in Texas, Oklahoma, and the Southwest* (Hollywood, CA, 1950)
S. Spaeth: *Music and Dance in New York State* (New York, 1951)
R. D. Saunders: *Music and Dance in the Central States* (Hollywood, CA, 1952)
S. Spaeth: *Music and Dance in the Southeastern States* (New York, 1952)
——: *Music and Dance in the New England States* (New York, 1953)
——: *Music and Dance in Pennsylvania, New Jersey, and Delaware* (New York, 1954)
North Carolina Musicians, ed. North Carolina Federation of Music Clubs (Chapel Hill, 1956)
F. T. Wiggin: *Maine Composers and their Music: a Biographical Dictionary* (Rockland, ME, 1959–76), 2 vols.
Catalogue of Representative Works by Resident Living Composers of Illinois, also Brief Biographical Sketches (n.p., 1960)
A Directory of Contemporary California Composers, ed. Governor's Committee to Encourage the Selection, Performance, and Publication of Music of Merit by Western Composers (Sacramento, CA, 1961) [vol. i of a proposed series]
Southeastern Composers' League Catalogue (Hattiesburg, MS, 1962)
C. Boone: *The Composers' Forum Index of Bay Area Composers* (Berkeley, CA, 1964)
J. E. Mangler: *Rhode Island Music and Musicians, 1733–1850* (Detroit, 1965) [biographical dictionary, pp.3–49]
R. R. Fink and J. A. Johnson: *Annotated Directory of Michigan Orchestral Composers* (Detroit, 1967)
L. Panzeri: *Louisiana Composers* (New Orleans, 1972)
T. Todaro: *The Golden Years of Hawaiian Entertainment, 1874–1974* (Honolulu, 1974)
B. Owen: "Biographical Sketches of New-England Organ Builders," *The Organ in New England* (Raleigh, 1979), 396
C. H. Kaufman: *Music in New Jersey, 1655–1860* (Rutherford, NJ, 1981) [incl. biographical dictionary]
Boston Composers Project, ed. Boston Area Music Librarians (Cambridge, MA, 1983)

GUIDEBOOKS TO REPERTORY

J. Towers: *Dictionary-catalogue of Operas and Operettas* (Morgantown, WV, 1910/*R*1967)
H. Barlow and S. Morgenstern: *A Dictionary of Musical Themes* (New York, 1948, rev. 2/1975)
——: *A Dictionary of Vocal Themes* (New York, 1950, rev. 2/1976 as *A Dictionary of Opera and Song Themes, including Cantatas, Oratorios, Lieder, and Art Songs*) [notational index]
J. Burton: *The Blue Book of Tin Pan Alley* (Watkins Glen, NY, 1951, rev. 2/1965) [index in *The Index of American Popular Music*, 1957]
——: *The Blue Book of Broadway Musicals* (Watkins Glen, NY, 1952/*R*1969 with suppl.) [index in *The Index of American Popular Music*, 1957]
——: *The Blue Book of Hollywood Musicals* (Watkins Glen, NY, 1953) [index in *The Index of American Popular Music*, 1957]
R. G. McCutchan: *Hymn Tune Names, their Sources and Significance* (Nashville, 1957)
Q. Eaton: *Opera Production: a Handbook* (Minneapolis, 1961)
R. Lewine and A. Simon: *Encyclopedia of Theatre Music* (New York, 1961, 2/1973 as *Songs of the American Theater*)
J. Mattfeld: *A Handbook of American Operatic Premieres, 1731–1962* (Detroit, 1963)
H. E. Johnson: *Operas on American Subjects* (New York, 1964)
D. Ewen: *American Popular Songs from the Revolutionary War to the Present* (New York, 1966)
J. R. Taylor and A. Jackson: *The Hollywood Musical* (New York, 1971) [incl. index of films and biographical dictionary]
T. and M. Tumbusch: *Guide to Broadway Musical Theatre* (New York, 1972)
S. Green: *Encyclopaedia of the Musical Theatre* (New York, 1976)
A. L. Woll: *Songs from Hollywood Musical Comedies, 1927 to the Present: a Dictionary* (New York, 1976)
R. Lax and F. Smith: *The Great Song Thesaurus* (New York, 1984)

MISCELLANEOUS

B. Vanasek: *Dictionary of Chords and Scales* (New York, 1936)
N. Slonimsky: *Thesaurus of Scales and Melodic Patterns* (New York, 1947/*R*1970)
G. Read: *Thesaurus of Orchestral Devices* (New York, 1953/*R*1969)
F. P. Berkowitz: *Popular Titles and Subtitles of Musical Compositions* (Metuchen, NJ, 1962, 2/1975)
C. Colin and D. Schaeffer: *Encyclopedia of Scales* (New York, 1973)
M. Deutsch: *Lexicon of Symmetric Scales and Tonal Patterns* (New York, 1976)
N. Shapiro: *An Encyclopedia of Quotations about Music* (Garden City, NY, 1978)
H. E. Johnson: *First Performances in America to 1900: Works with Orchestra* (Detroit, 1979)
B. Krolick: *Dictionary of Braille Music Signs* (Washington, DC, 1979)
T. Wheeler: *American Guitars: an Illustrated History* (New York, 1982)

BIBLIOGRAPHY

A. B. Kroeger: *Guide to the Study and Use of Reference Books* (Boston and New York, 1902, rev. by E. P. Sheehy 9/1976 as *Guide to Reference Books*)
J. B. Coover: *A Bibliography of Music Dictionaries* (Denver, 1952, rev. 2/1958 as *Music Lexicography*, rev. 3/1971)
A. Berger: "New Linguistic Modes and the New Theory," *PNM*, iii/1 (1964), 1
R. L. Collison: *Encyclopedias: their History throughout the Ages* (New York, 1964)
V. Duckles: *Music Reference and Research Materials* (New York, 1964, rev. and enlarged 3/1974)
R. B. Slocum: *Biographical Dictionaries and Related Works* (Detroit, 1967; suppls., 1972, 1978)
V. Duckles: "Some Observations on Music Lexicography," *College Music Symposium*, xi (1971), 115
N. Williams and P. Daub: "Coover's Music Lexicography – Two Supplements," *Notes*, xxx (1973–4), 492
N. Findler and H. Vill: "A Few Steps towards Computer Lexiconometry," *American Journal of Computational Linguistics*, i (1974), 1–69
R. Stevenson: "American Musical Scholarship," *19th Century Music*, i (1977–8), 191
J. Vinton: "The Dictionary of Contemporary Music: a Post Mortem," *Essays after a Dictionary* (Lewisburg, PA, 1977), 17
P. H. Lang: "*Die Musik in Geschichte und Gegenwart*: Epilogue," *Notes*, xxxvi (1979–80), 271
R. S. Stevenson: "The Americas in European Music Encyclopedias," *Inter-American Music Review*, iii (1980–81), 159; v (1982–3), 109
D.-R. De Lerma: "A Concordance of Black-music Entries in Five Encyclopedias: Baker's, Ewen, Grove's, MGG, and Rich," *BPiM*, xi (1983), 190

DIANE O. OTA

Diddley, Bo. *See* BO DIDDLEY.

Diddley bow. Single-string chordophone of the southern states, known also as a one-string jitterbug. It usually consists of a length of wire whose ends are attached to a wall of a frame house, the house acting as a resonator. A cotton reel is frequently used as a bridge. A more portable version has the wire attached to a length of fence picket. The instrument is played with a glass bottleneck or nail. Many blues guitarists, including Big Joe Williams and Muddy Waters, learned to play first on the diddley bow. Lonnie Pitchford, a player from Mississippi, uses an electrically amplified version. The rock-and-roll singer Elias McDaniel reversed the instrument name for his professional pseudonym, Bo Diddley.

BIBLIOGRAPHY

D. Evans: "Afro-American One-stringed Instruments," *Western Folklore*, xxix (1970), 229

PAUL OLIVER

Di Domenica, Robert Anthony (*b* New York, 4 March 1927). Composer and flutist. He received the BS degree in music education from New York University in 1951 and pursued private studies in composition with Wallingford Riegger and Josef Schmid; his principal flute teacher was Harold Bennett. He joined the faculty of the New England Conservatory in 1969, and served (1973–6) as associate dean and dean. As an orchestral flutist he has performed with the Metropolitan Opera, New York City Opera, New York PO, and other orchestras; his ensemble work has included appearances with the Modern Jazz Quartet, Composers' Forum, Bach Aria Group, and the series Music in Our Time. For many years he also taught the flute privately. In 1972 he was awarded a Guggenheim Fellowship in composition.

A serial composer ever since his studies with Schmid (a pupil of Schoenberg), Di Domenica combines serial techniques with elements from jazz and American popular music. His music possesses an innate lyricism, reflecting his love of Italian opera, and in his piano works especially there are elements of fantasy, rhapsody, improvisation, and sometimes programmatic description. The opera *The Balcony* (1972) is a highly organized, atonal composition: every scene has its own tone row (each related to the next) and instrumental and tonal color, with a progressively ascending tessitura and growing tension. In later works Di Domenica has attached special importance to texts, whether setting them for solo voice or using them as background inspiration for instrumental compositions. He is particularly drawn to writing for the piano, and in this has received valuable assistance from his wife, Leona, a professional pianist. His music has been performed by leading orchestras, ensembles, and instrumentalists.

WORKS

Opera: The Balcony (2, Di Domenica, after Genet), 1972

Orch: Sym., 1961; Vn Conc., vn, chamber orch, 1962; 2 pf concs., 1963, 1982; Conc., wind qnt, str, timp, 1964; Music for Fl and Str Orch, 1967; The Holy Colophon, S, T, chorus, orch, 1980

Inst: Sextet, ww qnt, pf, 1957; Fl Sonata, 1957; Pf Sonatina, 1958; 4 Movts, pf, 1959; Qt, fl, hn, vn, pf, 1959; Qt, fl, vn, va, vc, 1960; Str Qt, 1960; Variations on a Tonal Theme, fl, 1961; Wind Qnt, S, ww qnt, 1963; Qnt, cl, str qt, 1965; Trio, fl, bn, pf, 1966; Vn Sonata, 1966; Saeculum aureum, fl, pf, tape, 1967; Sonata, a sax, pf, 1968; 11 Short Pieces, pf, 1973; Improvisations, pf, 1974; Music for Stanzas, fl, cl, bn, hn, tape, 1981

Songs: The First Kiss of Love (Byron), S, pf, 1960; 4 Short Songs (J. Bobrowski), S, chamber ens, 1975; Black Poems, Bar, pf, tape, 1976; Songs from Twelfth Night (Shakespeare), T, chamber ens, 1976; Sonata after Essays (Hawthorne: The Scarlet Letter), S, Bar, pf, fl + a fl, tape, 1977, arr. S, B, pf, chamber orch, tape, as Concord Revisited, 1978; Arrangements (Goethe), S, chamber ens, tape, 1979

Principal publishers: Margun, E. B. Marks, MJQ, Edition Musicus

BARBARA A. PETERSEN

Diegueño [Ipai-Tipai, Kumeyaay]. American Indian group, whose territory included most of what are now San Diego and Imperial counties, and Western Baja California, extending somewhat south of Ensenada (*see* INDIANS, AMERICAN, fig. 1). Like most Californian Indians, the Diegueño were never a tribe in a political sense, but a set of autonomous clans, each identified with a defined territory, and all speaking mutually intelligible dialects of a single language; the separate clans were linked to each other primarily by marriage and by social ties expressed in ceremonies and their accompanying dances and songs.

Solo instrumental music was rare among the Diegueño, as it was among other North American Indians. Young men played courtship melodies on the flute, and the musical bow and whistle were played for entertainment. The bullroarer was used as a call to ceremonies. Other instruments included scraped baskets, and rattles made of clay, gourds, turtle shells, or deer hooves. The Diegueño did not use drums. Most Diegueño sang, though many song types were restricted to shamans, or to men who had taken jimsonweed at initiation in an effort to obtain spiritual contacts. Singing played a central role in most social gatherings. It was also a necessary part of attempts to cure illness and to manage weather, and of all ceremonial occasions, including adolescence rites, religious ceremonies, and mourning rites. Much recreation involved singing, including a traditional gambling game, known by its Spanish name *Peon*. The repertory also included "bad songs," songs of ridicule directed at other clans; this type is exhibited throughout much of California and the Great Basin, but is not reported elsewhere in North America.

The Diegueño language belongs to the Yuman language family, and Diegueño music is part of the California-Yuman musical area, which includes many tribes in Arizona and extends north as far as the Pomo of north-central California. Diegueño songs have much in common with those of other Yuman tribes, especially the Mojave and Quechan. Non-Yuman tribes such as the Luiseño, Cupeño, and Cahuilla also have very similar music. All these groups had much contact with one another.

The California-Yuman musical style is typified by a relaxed, flowing vocal quality. One distinctive characteristic is an aspect of musical form called the "rise." Yuman melodies consist of two elements: a principal motif of narrow range that is constantly repeated, and other phrases, interspersed with these repetitions, which may repeat part of the main motif and which turn upwards, creating the "rise" (see Herzog). Although there is much variation in form, a simple example of a song in the Yuman style would be *AAA . . . RA*, with *R* (rise) introduced several times in the song after a variable number of repetitions of *A*.

The other distinctive characteristic of Yuman music is the organization of songs into long cycles, often consisting of over 100 songs. It often takes several days to sing the entire cycle. Learning and performing these song cycles are great feats, and require enormous stamina. The cycles are typically based on a myth, but the songs themselves do not tell the whole story (indeed, each song has only two or three real words in it, repeated over and over); instead each song quotes a character or names a place in the story. 16 song cycles were identified by Spier (1923) among the southern Diegueño. Many are shared with other tribes, and some have words in other languages, such as Quechan or Luiseño. Song cycles are performed during ceremonies or social gatherings. The songs are sung by a group, with the songleader in the center of the line holding a rattle. The singers also dance: in some songs the dance formation is a rotating circle; in others two lines (one of men and one of women) face each other and move back and forth.

The Diegueño now sing many modern American genres, such as hymns and country and popular songs. But the traditional song cycles are still heard at fiestas, funerals, and memorial ceremonies; *Peon* is widely played, and the songs associated with it are still sung.

See also INDIANS, AMERICAN, esp. §I, 4(ii)(c).

BIBLIOGRAPHY

T. T. Waterman: "The Religious Practices of the Diegueño Indians," *University of California Publications in Archaeology and Ethnology*, viii (1910), 271–358

L. Spier: "Southern Diegueño Customs," *University of California Publications in Archaeology and Ethnography*, xx (1923), 297–358

A. Kroeber: *Handbook of the Indians of California* (Washington, DC, 1925/*R*1953)

G. Herzog: "The Yuman Musical Style," *Journal of American Folklore*, xli (1928), 183–231

B. Nettl: *North American Indian Musical Styles* (Philadelphia, 1954)

K. Luomala: "Tipai and Ipai," *Handbook of North American Indians*, viii: *California*, ed. R. F. Heizer (Washington, DC, 1978), 592

L. Hinton and L. Watahomigie, eds.: *Spirit Mountain: an Anthology of Yuman Story and Song* (Tucson, AZ, 1984)

L. Hinton: "Musical Diffusion and Linguistic Diffusion," *Anthropology and Music: Essays in Honor of David P. McAllester*, ed. C. Frisbie (Detroit, in preparation)

LEANNE HINTON

Diemer, Emma Lou (*b* Kansas City, MO, 24 Nov 1927). Composer, teacher, and organist. At the age of seven she began writing short pieces for the piano and by 13 she had composed several piano concertos. At Yale University she studied under Donovan and Hindemith (BM 1949, MM 1950). A Fulbright scholarship (1952–3) enabled her to study at the Royal Conservatory in Brussels; she also studied at the Berkshire Music Center with Toch and Sessions (1954, 1955). She received the PhD from the Eastman School, where her teachers included Rogers, Hanson, and Craighead, in 1960. From 1959 to 1961 she was composer-in-residence for the secondary schools in Arlington, Virginia, under a Ford Foundation grant. During this period 22 of her compositions were published, including the *Symphonie antique*. She has served as professor of theory and composition at the University of Maryland (1965–70) and the University of California, Santa Barbara (from 1971). She has received many commissions and in 1981 received an NEA award for electronic music projects. An accomplished keyboard player, she performs on the organ, piano, harpsichord, and synthesizer. Her compositions, of which more than 125 are published, encompass a variety of musical textures. Energetic and direct, they display a skilled craftsmanship and distinctive originality. In the early 1970s she began to compose for tape but the bulk of her output continues to be for conventional forces. Several of her works have been recorded.

WORKS

ORCHESTRAL

Sym. no.1, 1952; Suite, 1954; Conc., hpd, chamber orch, 1958; Sym. no.2 (American Indian Themes), 1959; Youth Ov., 1959; Brass Menagerie, sym. band, 1960; Festival Ov., 1960; Rondo concertante, 1960; Sym. no.3 (Symphonie antique), 1961; Fl Conc., 1963; Concert Piece, org, orch, 1977; La Rag, sym. band, 1981; Winter Day, 1982; 2 other ovs.

CHAMBER AND INSTRUMENTAL

Vn Sonata, 1948; Pf Qt, 1954; Toccata, mar, 1955; Fantasie, org, 1958; Sonata, fl, pf/hpd, 1958; 10 Hymn Preludes, org, 1960; Ww Qnt no.1, 1960; Sextet, ww qnt, pf, 1962; Toccata, org, 1964; 7 Etudes, pf, 1965; Fantasy on "O Sacred Head," org, 1967; Toccata for Flute Chorus, 1968; Toccata and Fugue, org, 1969; Celebration, org, 1970; Music for Ww Qt, 1972; 3 Pieces for Carillon, 1972

Declarations, org, 1973; Movement, fl, ob, org, 1974; Pianoharpsichordorgan, pf, hpd, org, 1974; Movement, fl, ob, cl, pf, 1976; With Praise and Love I, org, 1978, II, org, 1979; Toccata, pf, 1979; Solotrio, xyl, vib, mar, 1980; Homage to Cowell, Cage, Crumb, and Czerny, 2 pf, 1981; Encore, pf, 1981; Echospace, gui, 1982; Summer of 82, vc, pf, 1982; other org works

VOCAL

Psalm cxxi, S/T, org, 1957; Songs of Reminiscence (D. D. Hendry), S, pf, 1958; Fragments from the Mass, female chorus, 1960; 3 Madrigals (Shakespeare), mixed chorus, pf/org, 1960; 3 Mystic Songs (Hindu poetry), S, Bar, pf, 1963; Sing a Glory (Hendry), chorus, orch, band, 1964; 4 Chinese Love Poems, S, hpd/pf, 1965; Verses from the Rubaiyat, SATB, 1967; The Prophecy (Bible), female chorus, pf, 1968

The 4 Seasons (Spenser), S, T, pf, 1969; Anniversary Choruses (Bible), SATB, orch, 1970; Madrigals 3 (Campion, Donne, Shakespeare), SATB, pf, 1972; Laughing Song (Blake), SATB, pf 4 hands, 1974; 4 Poems by Alice Meynell, S, chamber orch, 1976; Wild Nights! Wild Nights! (E. Dickinson), SATB, pf, 1978

Many other sacred and secular acc. and unacc. choral works, songs

WITH TAPE

Trio, fl, ob, hpd, tape, 1973; Qt, fl, va, vc, hpd, tape, 1974; Patchworks, tape, 1978; Add One no.1, amp pf, tape, 1981, nos.2–3, synth, tape, 1981; Hpd Qt, tape, 1981; Scherzo, tape, 1981; God is Love (Bible), chorus, tape, 1982; over 10 others

Principal publishers: Boosey & Hawkes, C. Fischer, Oxford, Seesaw

BIBLIOGRAPHY

C. Ammer: *Unsung: a History of Women in American Music* (Westport, CT, 1980)

E. L. Dalheim: "Emma Lou Diemer: Four Poems by Alice Meynell for soprano or tenor and chamber ensemble," *Notes*, xxxv (1978–9), 994

J. W. LePage: *Women Composers, Conductors and Musicians of the Twentieth Century* (Metuchen, NJ, 1980–83)

SALLY MERRILL

Dietz, Howard (*b* New York, 8 Sept 1896; *d* New York, 30 July 1983). Lyricist and librettist. He studied at Columbia University (where he was a contemporary of Lorenz Hart and Oscar Hammerstein II) and served in the US Navy before becoming director of publicity and advertising in 1919 for the Goldwyn Pictures Corporation (from 1924 Metro-Goldwyn-Mayer). He wrote verse in his spare time, and was asked by Jerome Kern to supply the lyrics for *Dear Sir* (1924). He also worked with Vernon Duke, Jimmy McHugh, and Ralph Rainger, but is best remembered for the numerous songs he wrote in collaboration with ARTHUR SCHWARTZ, beginning in 1929 with the revue *The Little Show* (with "I guess I'll have to change my plan"), including *Three's a Crowd* (1930) and *The Band Wagon* (1931, with "Dancing in the Dark"), and extending over a period of more than 30 years to the musical *Jennie* (1963). Dietz also directed some of these shows. His lyrics, which included those for some of the most admired revues of the 1930s, were praised for their urbanity and wit. He wrote an autobiography, *Dancing in the Dark* (1974).

BIBLIOGRAPHY

"Dietz, Howard," *CBY 1965*

GERALD BORDMAN

Diggle, Roland (*b* London, England, 1 Jan 1885; *d* Los Angeles, CA, 13 Jan 1954). Organist and composer. He was educated at the Royal College of Music and came to the USA in 1904. He was organist and choirmaster of St. John's Church, Wichita, Kansas (1907–11), and then at St. John's Cathedral, Quincy, Illinois. In 1914 he received the DMus from the Grand Conservatory of Music, New York; the same year he became a US citizen and moved to Los Angeles, where he was appointed organist and choirmaster of St. John's Church, a position he held for 40 years. In addition to conducting a 60-voice choir and giving recitals, Diggle composed prolifically, wrote for *The Diapason*, *American Organist*, *Etude*, and *Musical Opinion*, and took a leading role in the American Guild of Organists. Diggle's compositions, which range from the easy and melodious to the serious and difficult, have virtually disappeared from the repertory, although some of his works, notably the choral *Benedicite omnia opera*, were once very popular; his composing style was improvisatory and facile. He was, however, a figure of long-lasting influence, noted for his witty manner.

VERNON GOTWALS

Diggs, Benny (*b* New York, *c*1946). Gospel singer and pianist. He studied classical piano and singing as a teenager, but was attracted to gospel music through the work of J. C. White and Isaac Douglas, whom he met in 1969. He then served as pianist for the short-lived group the Isaac Douglas Singers before founding the New York Community Choir (NYCC) with Douglas in October 1970. The choir performed music that drew as much from contemporary secular styles (jazz and soul) as from the gospel tradition of James Cleveland, Mattie Moss Clark, and Thomas A. Dorsey. Their semisecular or contemporary style of gospel served as a fitting background to the recited poetry of Nikki Giovanni, with whom Diggs recorded *Like a ripple on a pond* (1973). For a short time during the mid-1970s he served as director for the soul group Revelation, but returned to gospel music in the late 1970s. Diggs is considered one of the leading artists of the contemporary style in gospel music.

HORACE CLARENCE BOYER

Di Giovanni, Edoardo. *See* JOHNSON, EDWARD.

Diller, Angela (*b* Brooklyn, NY, 1 Aug 1877; *d* Stamford, CT, 30 April 1968). Pianist and music educator. She studied at Columbia University and in Dresden. From 1899 to 1916 she headed the theory department of the Music School Settlement in New York, then joined the staff of Mannes College (1916–21). In 1921 she founded the Diller-Quaile School of Music with Elizabeth Quaile. The school emphasized the relationship between practical and theoretical studies of music. She retired as director in 1941 but was named director emeritus. She also taught at the University of Southern California, Mills College, and the New England Conservatory, and was co-founder of the Adesdi Chorus and A Cappella Singers of New York. Diller's numerous pedagogical publications include *First Theory Book* (1921), *Keyboard Harmony Course* (1936–49), and *The Splendor of Music* (1957).

BIBLIOGRAPHY

E. Hiebert: "Diller, Angela," *NAW*

PAULA MORGAN

Dilling, Mildred (*b* Marion, IN, 23 Feb 1894; *d* New York, 30 Dec 1982). Harpist. She was a pupil of Henriette Renié in Paris, where she made her professional début in 1911, followed by a New York début in 1913. In her long career she performed in a range of places from formal concert halls to the wartime camps. Celebrated international singers with whom she played included the sopranos Alma Gluck and Frances Alda, Edouard (bass) and Jean (tenor) De Reszke, the folk-singer Yvette Gilbert, and the baritone Nelson Eddy; she played for five American presidents. At the height of her career, she traveled over 30,000 miles a year, and throughout most of her life she taught privately, the actor Harpo Marx being one of her pupils. One of the founders of the American Harp Society in 1962, she also amassed the largest private collection of harps of all kinds in the world, 65 of which she used to keep in her New York apartment; on her death a representative sample was bequeathed to Indiana University. Two of her harp-music collections, *Old Tunes for New Harpists* (1934) and *Thirty Little Classics for the Harp* (1938), have become standard works.

BIBLIOGRAPHY

E. J. Kahn, Jr.: "The Harp Lady," *New Yorker*, xvi (3 Feb 1940), 25
Obituary, *New York Times* (3 Jan 1983)

THOR ECKERT, JR.

Dillon, Fannie Charles (*b* Denver, CO, 16 March 1881; *d* Altadena, CA, 21 Feb 1947). Pianist and composer. After graduating from Pomona College, Claremont, California, she studied in Berlin from 1900 to 1906 with the pianist Leopold Godowsky, the composer Hugo Kaun, and the theorist Heinrich Urban; later she studied with Goldmark in New York. Dillon made her début as a pianist in Los Angeles in 1908 and then toured as a concert artist on the West and East Coasts. On 9 February 1918 she gave a concert of her own works for the Beethoven Society in New York. She was a member of the music faculty at Pomona College from 1910 to 1913, and from 1918 until her retirement in 1941 she taught in the Los Angeles public schools. In 1921, 1923, and 1933 she was in residence at the MacDowell Colony. Her orchestral works include *In a Mission Garden*, *Celebration of Victory* (1918), *The Cloud* (1918), *The Alps* (1920), *Chinese Symphonic Suite* (1936), and *A Letter of the Southland*. Among her smaller works, the piano piece *Birds at Dawn* (published 1917) was especially popular.

BIBLIOGRAPHY

"California's Brilliant Composer-pianist, Fannie Dillon," *Musical Courier*, lxxiii/20 (1916), 45 [incl. list of works]

CAROL NEULS-BATES

Dinerstein, Norman (Myron) (*b* Springfield, MA, 18 Sept 1937; *d* Cincinnati, OH, 23 Dec 1982). Composer, educator, and administrator. He attended Boston University (BM 1960), Hartt College of Music (MM 1963), and Princeton University (PhD 1974), and studied further at the Hochschule für Musik, Berlin (1962–3), the Berkshire Music Center (1962, 1963), and the Darmstadt Summer School (1964). His teachers included Lutosławski, Schuller, Copland, Foss, Sessions, Babbitt, and Arnold Franchetti, whom he acknowledged as his principal teacher. He held academic posts at Princeton University (1965–6), the New England Conservatory (1968–9, 1970–71), Hartt College (as chairman of composition and theory, 1971–6), and the Cincinnati College-Conservatory (as chairman of composition, musicology, and theory, 1976–81; and dean, 1981–2).

Dinerstein's earliest compositions are tonal and lyrical. In 1961, influenced by Franchetti, he adopted a freely atonal and dissonant style of which the orchestral piece *Refrains* (1971) is a powerful example. His late works are tonal, expressive, and deeply humanistic. This is especially true of the pieces on Jewish themes such as *Zalmen* for violin (1975), performed at the ISCM festival in Israel in 1980; *Songs of Remembrance* for soprano and strings (1976–9), commissioned for the US Bicentennial; and *Hashkivenu* for tenor, chorus, and double bass (1981).

At the time of his death Dinerstein was simplifying his style in such works as *Golden Bells*, the second movement of a planned four-movement setting for chorus and orchestra of Poe's *The Bells*, which was completed after his death by Michael Schelle and performed by Michael Gielen and the Cincinnati SO.

WORKS

Orch: Cassation, 1963; Intermezzo, 1964; 3 Miniatures, str, 1966; Contrasto, 1968; Refrains, 1971; The Answered Question, wind ens, 1972

Vocal: 4 Settings (Dickinson), S, str qt, 1961; Schir ha Schirim (Bible), chorus, orch, 1963; Cricket Songs (H. Behn), unison tr vv, pf, 1967; Herrickana (Herrick), SATB, 1972; Poema ultrasonico (E. G. de Espinola), SATB, 1974; When David Heard (Bible), SATB, 1975; Songs of Remembrance (Yiddish, trans. J. Leftwich), S, str, 1976–9; Frogs (Behn), SATB, 1977; Love Songs (E. B. Browning, R. Browning, C. Rossetti, Song of Songs), song cycle, 1980; Hashkivenu (Heb.), T, chorus, db, 1981; Golden Bells (Poe), chorus, orch, 1980–82, completed by M. Schelle; 4 other song cycles; 5 unacc. choral works

Chamber and inst: 4 Movts for 3 Ww, fl, cl, bn, 1961; Terzetto, brass trio, 1961; Tizmoret Katan, vn, vc, 1961; 3 Wiegenlieder, pf, 1961; Satz, fl, 1963; Serenade, ob, cl, harp, vn, vc, 1963; Pezzi piccoli, fl, va, 1966; Pezzicati, db, 1967, rev. 1978; Short Suite for Young Players, fl, cl, a sax, hn, tpt, vn, va, 1967; Sequoia, jazz ens, 1969; Faster than a Rag, pf, 1974; Aeolus, org, 1975; Zalmen, or The Madness of God, vn, 1975; Tubajubalee, tuba ens, 1978

Principal publishers: Boosey & Hawkes, Contemporary Music Project, C. Fischer, G. Schirmer

JONATHAN D. KRAMER

Dion [DiMucci, Dion] (*b* New York, 18 July 1939). Rock-and-roll singer. In 1958 he formed a vocal group, the Belmonts; its other members were Fred Milano (*b* New York, 22 Aug 1939), Carlo Mastangelo (*b* New York, 5 Oct 1938), and Angelo d'Aleo (*b* New York, 3 Feb 1940). As Dion and the Belmonts they recorded *I wonder why* (1958), essentially an a cappella arrangement, but with some light, remarkably apt instrumentation; their later recordings, such as *A Teenager in Love* (no.5, 1959) and *Where or When* (no.3, 1960), were often more successful commercially but far less original. In 1960 Dion left the group, but he rejoined it for performances and recordings in 1967 and 1973 when his career as a soloist lost impetus. The Belmonts continued to record through the early 1970s; their album *Cigars, Acappella, Candy* (Buddah 5123, 1973) is an appealing, street-singers' revision of pop material in the style of rhythm-and-blues groups of the early 1950s.

On his own, Dion proceeded to make stylish, powerful recordings that owed much to Presley's songs from the 1950s. His songs expressed passion and humor; among the more notable were *Runaround Sue* (no.1, 1961), *The Wanderer* (no.2, 1961), and the exuberant *Lovers who wander* (no.3, 1962). From 1963 he was to an increasing extent inspired by the country blues of Robert Johnson and the urban folk music of Dylan; *Abraham, Martin and John* (no.4, 1968) showed these influences, as did the extraordinary blues song recorded on its reverse side, *Daddy rollin' (in your arms)*, which received little notice. A superb recording from 1970, *Your own backyard*, also won scant recognition. He continued to record albums through the 1970s, including *Born to Be with you* (1976), a moody collaboration with the producer Phil Spector, and *Return of the Wanderer* (1978). A product of the doo-wop tradition that dominated pop music in New York during the 1950s, Dion was the first important Italian-American rock-and-roll singer. His best recordings with the Belmonts, such as *I wonder why*, remain unparalleled as illustrations of the possibilities of group dynamics.

RECORDINGS

(selective list; recorded for Laurie unless otherwise stated)

With the Belmonts: I wonder why (3013, 1958); A Teenager in Love (3027, 1959); Where or When (3044, 1960)

As soloist: Runaround Sue (3110, 1961); The Wanderer (3115, 1961); Lovers who wander (3123, 1962); Abraham, Martin and John/Daddy rollin' (in your arms) (3464, 1968); Your own backyard (WB 7401, 1970); *Born to Be with you* (Phil Spector 002, 1976); *Return of the Wanderer* (Lifesong 35356, 1978)

BIBLIOGRAPHY

R. Price: "Hey, Dion my Man," *Rolling Stone*, no.218 (29 July 1976), 34

GREIL MARCUS

Dippel, Andreas (*b* Kassel, Germany, 30 Nov 1866; *d* Hollywood, CA, 12 May 1932). Tenor and impresario. He studied singing first with Nina Zottmayr in Kassel, and later with Julius Hey in Berlin, Alberto Leoni in Milan, and Johannes Ress in Vienna. He made his début at Bremen in 1887, remained with the company for five years, and sang at Bayreuth (1889), Breslau (1892–3), and the Vienna Hofoper (1893), as well as at Covent Garden in a *Ring* cycle (1897). He made his début at the Metropolitan Opera on 26 November 1890 in the title role of Alberto Franchetti's *Asrael*, and was a prominent member of the company from 1898 to 1908. Though not gifted with a remarkable voice, Dippel was a versatile artist and had a repertory of more than 150 operatic roles (notably the Wagnerian ones) and 60 oratorios. As the Metropolitan's standby tenor, he was able to step into any of those roles at a moment's notice.

In 1908 Dippel was appointed administrative manager of the Metropolitan company under Gatti-Casazza. He tried to extend its activities into Brooklyn, Philadelphia, and other areas, but his attempts were financially unsuccessful, and after two years he left owing to administrative differences. He became the director of the Philadelphia-Chicago Opera Company, but resigned once again over administrative clashes in 1913, even though this venture was a financial success. He then formed a light opera company of his own, which toured North America, and another group in 1924, which presented German operas in various mid-western cities. Dippel worked for Metro-Goldwyn-Mayer in Hollywood in the synchronization department between 1928 and 1932, and also taught singing.

DEE BAILY

Dippermouth. *See* ARMSTRONG, LOUIS.

Dirt Band. *See* NITTY GRITTY DIRT BAND.

Disc jockey. The person responsible for the selection, sequencing, and presentation of programs of recorded popular music, either on radio or in a discothèque. A radio disc jockey chooses the music to be played according to his own taste and that of his audience; his choice is often also governed by the current popularity charts (*see* BROADCASTING, §§3–6). He intersperses recordings with chatter, advertising jingles, and sometimes live interviews or telephone conversations. In a discothèque the disc jockey functions as a master of ceremonies, and, judging the mood of the clientèle, plays appropriate recordings to create and maintain the atmosphere. SCRATCHING, a technique that originated in New York in the 1970s, has turned the disc jockey from a master of ceremonies into an artist in his own right.

Disco. A style of dance music, usually recorded, which was popular in the USA in the late 1970s and early 1980s. The term, which came into currency in 1974, derives from the word "discothèque," used from the 1960s to describe a NIGHTCLUB where people dance to recorded music. Disco evolved out of the underground, dance-music culture, peopled largely by homosexuals and Blacks, that developed in New York's private clubs and lofts. Nonstop music was played by disc jockeys, who remixed dance recordings by boosting the bass and sequenced them into programmed, all-night marathons. The typical disco record features a relentless 4/4 beat and material organized around extended instrumental breaks that encourage free-style dancing. The lyrics are often erotic, or based on a series of dance-oriented chants. The prototypes for disco included the Motown soul-music repertory, and the propulsive orchestrated pop-soul recordings produced by Philadelphia International Records in the early 1970s; the Los Angeles singer and songwriter Barry White and his Love Unlimited Orchestra were among the earliest performers associated with disco.

As the music became more popular, different subgenres began to emerge and compete with one another. The most innovative was the ornate synthesizer-based music known as "Eurodisco." Giorgio Moroder, an Italian-Swiss who worked first in Munich and then in Los Angeles, was one of the most successful exponents of the Eurodisco style; with others, he wrote and produced his own material, and was one of those responsible for the rise of disco as a producer's medium. A clever synthesizer colorist, Moroder was co-writer and -producer of Donna Summer's recordings, beginning with the mock-orgiastic *Love to love you baby* (1975), and culminating with the elaborate two-disc suite *Bad Girls* (1979), which was one of the disco culture's finest products. Another recording that stands out is the album *Risqué* by Chic, a group of singers and instrumentalists led by the songwriters and producers Bernard Edwards and Nile Rodgers; this tempers disco mechanization with a sophisticated, minimalist, light-funk bass and guitar style. A third is the album *Saturday Night Fever* (1977), which featured the Bee Gees' dance hits *Stayin' Alive* and *Night Fever*. Taken from the soundtrack of the highly successful film of the same name, *Saturday Night Fever* became the best-selling album in American history up to that time, with sales of around 25 million two-disc sets, and was responsible for the widespread acceptance of disco into the mainstream of popular music.

After reaching a peak in late 1979 and early 1980, disco rapidly declined, as disc jockeys and the public turned against a style that had become too mechanized and overmarketed. Tastes in dance music changed: Chic's *Good Times* (1979) was one of the first disco recordings to incorporate a slower, less insistent beat, and, after this, disco music was gradually superseded by the sparser, more relaxed style known as FUNK. Many of the features of disco were absorbed into other genres of popular music: one of its most important legacies was the introduction of the synthesizer as a basic rhythmic and textural ingredient in pop instrumentation. But perhaps the most direct descendent of disco is the style known as "hi-energy," which is essentially a faster, more intense version of the classic disco sound.

STEPHEN HOLDEN

Discographies. Listings in which aspects of the physical characteristics, provenance, and contents of sound recordings are described. Data for such listings (which may include pictorial documentation) are acquired from the recordings themselves (with their containers and any accompanying written and iconographic materials), as well as from logbooks, lists, and catalogues compiled by the record producer or manufacturer, journals and other printed materials, and oral sources. Included in this discussion are other forms of discographical publication relevant to the study of discography in the USA: listeners' guides, review compilations and review indexes, and price guides. The early history of discography is largely that of jazz discography, to which a separate section is devoted in this article.

1. General. 2. Jazz discographies.

1. GENERAL. The key elements given for each recording in nearly all discographical listings are the name of the record label, issue number, and program contents (arranged alphabetically by composer or performer); the physical characteristics of the recording itself, such as type, size, the number of channels, playback speed, and type of groove, are also considered important features of true discographies. The complex catalogues that have come to be known as "systematic discographies" include such further details as master numbers (or matrix numbers for the earlier galvano-processed discs); take indicators (or transfer numbers for discs processed from tape sources); the date and location of, and the key participants in the recording session; and the date and place of publication, and publisher of the various issues (with label names and numbers). Before the development of long-playing (LP) recordings, a unique matrix number was etched, embossed, or stamped onto each surface of the disc near or under the label. Since it was a common practice for several versions of a performance to be made in case of mishap (such as the destruction of a master recording or the negative stampers made from it and used to produce commercial pressings), each of the versions (or "takes") was customarily assigned an additional number or letter, which was placed immediately after the matrix number. The convention of matrix and take numbers to designate discrete performances was abandoned with tape mastering, in which a fully edited master tape could be developed from all the material recorded during the sessions; successive modifications of a given master tape are identified on the finished disc by the transfer numbers. (*See also* SOUND RECORDING.)

Although lists of recordings appeared as early as the 1920s in magazines devoted to classical music, the first significant contributions to the field of discography in this country included listeners' guides (which are compendiums of opinions on available recordings intended to meet specific consumer requirements, such as buying on a limited budget, building a basic library, and finding the "best" performances), and compilations of record reviews. The first American discography, R. D. Darrell's *The Gramophone Shop Encyclopedia of Recorded Music* (1936), was essentially an alphabetized composer–title listing of art music on 78-r.p.m. electrical disc recordings issued commercially throughout the world. In the two decades that followed, relatively few important publications containing discographical information were produced in the USA. Among them were (in addition to those discussed in §2) the updated versions of Darrell's discography (one in 1942 by George Leslie and another in 1948 by Robert Reid); Gustavo Durán's *Recordings of Latin American Songs and Dances*, issued by the Music Division of the Pan American Union (1942); Julian Morton Moses's *Collectors' Guide to American Recordings, 1895–1925* (1949), devoted for the most part to vocal music recorded on preelectric lateral discs; and *Record Ratings* (1956) by Kurtz Myers, which was the first cumulation in book format of the quarterly index of LP record reviews published in the Music Library Association's journal *Notes*. From 1949 WILLIAM SCHWANN issued a monthly catalogue of available LP recordings, which he later extended to include tapes and compact discs. The late 1930s and 1940s also saw the initiation of several important critical surveys of the art-music repertory, each of which appeared in two or more editions: Bernard Haggin's *Music on Records* (1938, rev. 2/1942), David Hall's *The Record Book* (1940–48), and Irving Kolodin's *A Guide to Recorded Music* (1941–50). With the advent of the LP disc and a near quadrupling of the output of recordings, comprehensive surveys by single compilers were no longer feasible. The guides to LP records published by Alfred A. Knopf in 1955 consisted of volumes devoted to orchestral, chamber and solo instrumental, and vocal music, each prepared by a different compiler. The only outstanding one-man survey published after that time is Arthur Cohn's *Recorded Classical Music* (1981).

Systematic discography was gradually established as the norm, and American contributions to the field have covered virtually all musical genres. Many valuable discographies have appeared in the appendices to histories and other books devoted to a particular period or kind of music, and in similarly specialized studies published in journals. The growth of discographic bibliography may be measured by the expansion of the annually cumulated *Bibliography of Discographies* (1977–), which demonstrates that the number of discographies published in books and periodicals rose from 300 in 1978 to more than 800 in 1980. The number of periodicals devoted to discographic subjects has grown from the few published in the 1950s to more than 100 in the 1980s; among the most important of these are *Record Research* (founded in 1972), the quarterly journal of the John Edwards Memorial Foundation (1965–), the *Journal of Country*

Music published by the Country Music Foundation (1970–), and *Fanfare* (1977–).

Publication of other forms of discographic information also expanded with the recording industry. Collections of published commentary about sound recordings, usually appearing annually, included the *High-fidelity Record Annual* (1956–81, retitled *Records in Review* in 1957), *Down Beat Jazz Record Reviews* (1957–64), and the *Rolling Stone Record Review* (1971–4). Price guides have become an important source of information about sound recordings, particularly for collectors, since they give approximate market values for out-of-print recordings in particular subject areas. Because of the need to keep evaluations up to date, price guides are often revised more frequently than the published discographies and guidebooks in the same subject area; as a result, they often contain listings of recordings not yet cited in library catalogues or difficult to find in the Schwann catalogues. Important among these publications are Moses's *Price Guide to Collectors' Records* (1952), various surveys of popular music by Steve Propes (1973–), Jerry Osborne's *Original Record Collectors Price Guide* series (beginning in 1976), Peter Soderbergh's surveys of 78-r.p.m. records (1977–83), Les Docks's *1915–1965 American Premium Record Guide* (1980), and Ferguson and Johnson's *Mainstream Jazz Reference and Price Guide, 1949–1965* (1984).

The vast expansion of discographic literature that began in the 1960s was the result of a growing awareness of the cultural impact of sound recordings and their increasing popularity as a medium of entertainment. These factors led to the systematic development of private collections and, eventually, to recognition within the academic and library communities that sound recordings are legitimate tools of scholarship and worthy of acquisition, preservation, and cataloguing for purposes of scholarly research. Until that point, the field of discography remained largely in the hands of dedicated amateurs. The establishment in the late 1950s of sound archives supported by universities and libraries, in some cases with associated publishing programs, provided an environment within which discographic research could flourish, and led to the recognition of discography as a discipline in its own right. (*See also* SOUND AND FILM ARCHIVES.)

The most important general sound archives in the USA are those of the Motion Picture, Broadcasting, and Sound Recordings Division of the Library of Congress, the Rodgers and Hammerstein Archives of Recorded Sound in the Library and Museum of the Performing Arts at Lincoln Center, the Belfer Audio Archives at Syracuse University, the Archives of Recorded Sound at Stanford University, and the Collection of Historical Sound Recordings at Yale University; all possess major holdings in the area of American music. Important specialized sound collections include the International Piano Archives at the University of Maryland (College Park), the Archive of Folk Culture at the Library of Congress, the Archives of Traditional Music at Indiana University (Bloomington), the Institute of Jazz Studies at Rutgers University (Newark), the G. Robert Vincent National Voice Library at Michigan State University (East Lansing), the Center for the Study of Popular Culture at Bowling Green (Ohio) State University, and, in the area of country music, the Southern Documentary Recording and Film Collection at the University of North Carolina (Chapel Hill) and the library of the Country Music Foundation in Nashville. All of these archives have developed programs or publications to assist scholarly projects undertaken by individuals, corporations, and academic institutions. (The contents of these and other repositories of sound recordings are discussed in LIBRARIES AND COLLECTIONS.)

The year 1966 saw the establishment of the ASSOCIATION FOR RECORDED SOUND COLLECTIONS (ARSC), an organization of individual and institutional sound-recordings collectors whose aim it has been to foster the exchange of information relating to the field, to establish standards for archival restoration and preservation, and to make available the catalogues of important public and private sound collections. The association's *Journal* and special publications have been the most important means of achieving these ends. Its *Rules for the Archival Cataloging of Sound Recordings* (1980) was developed by a committee of representatives from the five leading general sound archives mentioned above, working cooperatively as the Associated Audio Archives. In 1982 this group began to implement an indexing program that has added a new dimension to discographic research methods. All the commercial disc holdings of the member archives are to be photographed and made available on microfilm; this process captures not only the record label but the embossed or etched information on the disc runoff area and the dimensions of the playing area as well. Publication of *The Rigler and Deutsch Record Index* (1985), which includes this photographic data and computer-produced indexes derived from it (arranged by issue number, matrix number, title, composer or author, performer, and holding institution), makes it possible for researchers to acquire a vast amount of information without having to visit the archive in which the recording is housed.

Data-processing technology began only in the 1980s to play a major role in discographic work; this trend is exemplified by such works as Carol J. Oja's *American Music Recordings* (1982), published by the Institute for Studies in American Music at Brooklyn College, and by the catalogue of the Institute of Jazz Studies at Rutgers (1980–), which is distributed in microfiche form and through computer network to online subscribers. The automated documentation of sound-recording registrations at the US Copyright Office (initiated in 1972) and the large automated cataloguing projects such as that of the ARSC promise a major expansion in the amount of information available in forms essential for discographic research. The growth of the communications industry and the proliferation of small computers continue to facilitate the widespread distribution of this information as it becomes available.

2. JAZZ DISCOGRAPHIES. Accurate information about recorded performances is essential in jazz, where recordings rather than scores or sheet music are the principal sources for study. The standard information contained in jazz discographies consists of the name of the leader or group, the date and place of recording, the players and their instruments, the titles of tunes, the matrix and take numbers, the label name, and the issue number. Take numbers are particularly important to the study of jazz, since two versions of the same piece, recorded only minutes apart, may differ significantly. With the advent of the LP and tape mastering in the late 1940s, the discographically convenient use of matrix and take designations was lost; an LP may contain many unrelated performances of diverse origins, the identification of which poses particular problems for the discographer. These difficulties are often compounded by insufficient or misleading information supplied by record manufacturers.

The first extensive discographical works were devoted to jazz.

The term "discography" itself was introduced in the 1930s as growing numbers of jazz enthusiasts sought to establish accurate information about personnel and recording dates. Early researchers also had to contend with the pseudonymous issuing of numerous recordings by well-known jazz bands. The field of jazz discography has been dominated from the start by Europeans. Two pioneering discographical works were published in 1936, Charles Delaunay's *Hot Discography* (in France) and Hilton Schleman's *Rhythm on Record* (in England). Delaunay's work laid the foundation for discographic research, notably in its use of matrix numbers to identify recordings, which has become standard. In 1942 Charles Edward Smith, with Frederic Ramsey and others, issued an important critical survey of jazz recordings entitled *The Jazz Record Book*, but the first true discography of importance by an American was Orin Blackstone's *Index to Jazz* (1945–8).

The most prominent jazz discographer since the early 1960s has been Brian Rust, an English recording historian whose *Jazz Records A–Z* (1961, rev. and enlarged 5/1983), though restricted to 78-r.p.m. issues, is the basic research tool for jazz recordings in the first half of the 20th century and the only general work with both artist and title indexes; it is complemented by two other works by him, published in 1973 and 1975, covering the popular and dance recordings of the period. The Danish discographer Jørgen Grunnet Jepsen extended coverage into the 1950s and 1960s with his 11-volume *Jazz Records*, now undergoing extensive revision (see below). The most recent attempt at a comprehensive jazz discography was made by the Belgian researcher Walter Bruyninckx, whose *60 Years of Recorded Jazz* (1978–82) covers all jazz and blues recordings to 1977.

As serious interest in jazz grew, discographers began to produce works that dealt with specific aspects of the music. Such specialized discographies may focus on a musical style (e.g., Eric Raben's *A Discography of Free Jazz*, 1969), a geographical area (lists of this sort deal with recordings made or issued in a particular region or country, or by performers of a certain nationality), a record label (e.g., the discographies published by Michael Ruppli), a recording format (e.g., piano rolls, phonograph cylinders, or radio transcription discs), or (most commonly) the work of an individual performer. Artist discographies trace not only the performer's recordings as both leader and sideman, but often his noncommercial recordings as well, including private tapes and airchecks (i.e., performances recorded off the air); some list solos by the performer and may even use incipits to distinguish between takes. Bio-discographies, such as W. C. Allen's *Hendersonia* (1973), a detailed chronicle of the career of Fletcher Henderson, integrate biographical and discographical information. A variant of the performer discography, the "solography," developed most notably by the Norwegian discographer Jan Evensmo, identifies all the recorded solos by an artist within a given period, listing lengths and tempos and offering critical commentary; the majority of the performers dealt with in solographies have been swing musicians. The Dutch discographer Dick Bakker, founder and editor of the important jazz periodical *Micrography* and author of discographies of Charlie Parker, Duke Ellington, Billie Holiday, and Teddy Wilson, has designed a system of abbreviations to identify the plethora of reissue LPs and to facilitate comparisons between them.

Jazz discographies are for the most part still being produced by dedicated amateurs, who usually work without the benefit of institutional affiliation or financial support. They are part of an informal, worldwide cooperative network, within which circulate drafts of discographic projects for review. A major effort of this type, involving dozens of contributors, has been devoted to the revision of Jepsen's *Jazz Records* (1963). Several organizations supplement the research efforts of these informal associations. The International Association of Jazz Record Collectors holds an annual convention and publishes the quarterly *IAJRC Journal* (1968–). Notable among other current periodical publications that regularly contain jazz discographies are *Down Beat* (founded in 1934), *Swing Journal* (1947), *Record Research* (1955), *Storyville* (1965), *Jazzforschung* (1969), the *Annual Review of Jazz Studies* (founded in 1973 as the *Journal of Jazz Studies*), and *Cadence* (1976).

LIST

Writings published in or otherwise distinctive to the USA. Period of coverage is given in brackets.

DISCOGRAPHIES

General

The National Union Catalog: Music and Phonorecords, ed. Library of Congress (Ann Arbor, MI, 1958 [1953–7]; New York, 1963 [1958–62]; Ann Arbor, 1969 [1963–7]; 1973 [1963–72]; Totowa, NJ, 1978 [1973–7]; Washington, DC, 1979– [1978–] as *Music, Books on Music, and Sound Recordings*)

Catalog of Copyright Entries, ser.3, pt xiv: *Sound Recordings*, ed. US Copyright Office (Washington, DC, 1972–7; as ser.4, pt vii, 1980– [coinciding with the implementation of the copyright act of 1976])

Sibley Music Library Catalog of Sound Recordings, ed. Eastman School (Boston, 1977)

B. Rust: *Discography of Historical Records on Cylinders and 78s* (Westport, CT, 1979) [includes songs of historical significance]

The Rigler and Deutsch Record Index – a National Union Catalog of Sound Recordings (Syracuse, NY, 1985) [pt 1 : 78-r.p.m. recordings in the holdings of members of the Association for Recorded Sound Collections; in microform]

J. R. Heintze: *Scholars Guide to Washington, D.C. for Audio Resources: Sound Recordings in the Arts, Humanities, and Social, Physical, and Life Sciences* (Washington, DC, 1985)

Art music

(by composer)

R. D. Darrell: *The Gramophone Shop Encyclopedia of Recorded Music* (New York, 1936, rev. G. Leslie 2/1942, rev. R. Reid 3/1948/*R*1970)

F. F. Clough and G. J. Cuming: *The World's Encyclopaedia of Recorded Music* (London, 1952–6/*R*1970)

American Music on Records: a Catalogue of Recorded American Music Currently Available, ed. American Music Center (New York, 1956)

R. Gilbert: *The Clarinetists' Solo Repertoire – a Discography* (New York, 1972–5)

D. Stahl: *A Selected Discography of Solo Song: a Cumulation through 1971* (Detroit, 1972; suppl., 1976 [1971–4])

D.-R. De Lerma: *A Discography of Concert Music by Black Composers* (Minneapolis, 1973)

American Music before 1865 in Print and on Records: a Biblio-discography, ISAMm, vi (Brooklyn, NY, 1976)

L. Rowell: *American Organ Music on Records* (Braintree, MA, 1976)

M. Kondracki, M. Stankiewicz, and F. C. Wielard: *Internationale Diskographie elektronischer Musik/International Electronic Music Discography* (Mainz, Germany, and New York, 1979)

C. J. Oja, ed.: *American Music Recordings: a Discography of 20th-century U.S. Composers* (Brooklyn, NY, 1982)

J. Frasier: *Women Composers: a Discography* (Detroit, 1983)

A. I. Cohen: *International Discography of Women Composers* (Westport, CT, 1984)

R. W. Shoaf: *Horn Discography* (Wilhelmshaven, Germany, 1985)

(by performer)

R. Bauer: *Historical Records* (Milan, Italy, 1937, rev. 1947/*R*1970 as *The New Catalogue of Historical Records, 1898–1908/09)*

J. M. Moses: *Collectors' Guide to American Recordings, 1895–1925* (New York, 1949/*R*1977)

L. G. Langwill: *The Bassoon and Contrabassoon* (New York, 1965)

A. L. Lowrey: *Trumpet Discography* (Denver, n.d.)

J. L. Creighton: *Discopaedia of the Violin, 1889–1971* (Toronto, 1974)

P. Turner: *Afro-American Singers: an Index and Preliminary Discography of Long-playing Recordings of Opera, Choral Music, and Song* (Minneapolis, 1977; suppl., 1977)

F. P. Fellers and B. Meyers: *Discographies of Commercial Recordings of the Cleveland Orchestra (1924–1977) and the Cincinnati Symphony Orchestra (1917–1977)* (Westport, CT, 1978)
P. C. Mawhinney: *Music Master: the 45 rpm Record Directory 1947 to 1982* (Allison Park, PA, 1983)
M. Kratzenstein: *Four Centuries of Organ Music* (Detroit, 1984)

(other)

F. P. Fellers: *The Metropolitan Opera on Record: a Discography of the Commercial Recordings* (Westport, CT, 1984) [arranged chronologically by recording session]
See also "Record labels"

Jazz

C. Delaunay: *Hot Discography* (Paris, 1936, rev. 3/1940/*R*1943, rev. W. E. Schaap and G. Avakian 5/1982 as *New Hot Discography: the Standard Directory of Recorded Jazz*)
C. E. Smith and others: *The Jazz Record Book* (New York, 1942)
O. Blackstone: *Index to Jazz* (Fairfax, VA, 1945–8/*R*1978 [1917–44])
D. Carey and A. McCarthy: *The Directory of Recorded Jazz and Swing Music* [cover title *Jazz Directory*] (Fordingbridge, England, later London, 1949–57)
F. Ramsey, Jr.: *A Guide to Long Play Jazz Records* (New York, 1954)
G. Avakian: *Jazz from Columbia: a Complete Jazz Catalog* (New York, 1956)
J. S. Wilson: *Collector's Jazz: Traditional and Swing* (Philadelphia, 1958)
——: *Collector's Jazz: Modern* (Philadelphia, 1959)
Bielefelder Jazzkatalog (Karlsruhe, Germany, 1960–)
Jazz Catalogue (London, 1960–)
B. Rust: *Jazz Records A–Z*, [i:] *1897–1931* (Hatch End, nr London, 1961, 2/1962 with index by R. Grandorge); [ii:] . . .*1932–1942* (Hatch End, 1965); i–ii as *Jazz Records A–Z, 1897–1942* (rev. London, 1969, rev. and enlarged New Rochelle, NY, 4/1978, rev. and enlarged 5/1983)
J. G. Jepsen: *Jazz Records, 1942–*[1969] (Holte and Copenhagen, Denmark, 1963–70) [alphabetical vols., A-Bl, Bl-Co, etc.; dates of coverage vary]
A. McCarthy and others: *Jazz on Record: a Critical Guide to the First 50 Years* (London, 1968)
E. Raben: *A Discography of Free Jazz* (Copenhagen, 1969)
T. Stagg and C. Crump: *"New Orleans, the Revival": a Tape and Discography of Negro Traditional Jazz Recorded in New Orleans or by New Orleans Bands 1937–1972* (Dublin, 1973)
R. D. Kinkle: *The Complete Encyclopedia of Popular Music and Jazz, 1900–1950* (New Rochelle, NY, 1974)
M. Harrison and others: *Modern Jazz: the Essential Records* (London, 1975)
J. Evensmo: *Jazz Solography Series* (Hosle, Norway, 1976–)
H. H. Lange: *The Fabulous Fives* (Chigwell, England, 1978)
W. Bruyninckx: *60 Years of Recorded Jazz, 1917–1977* (Mechelen, Belgium, 1978–82)
A Computerized Catalog of the Recorded Sound Collection of the Rutgers Institute of Jazz Studies (Newark, 1980–) [quarterly microfiche register and indexes]
T. Ikegami: *New Orleans Renaissance on Record* (Tokyo, 1980)
L. Lyons: *The 101 Best Jazz Records: a History of Jazz on Record* (New York, 1980)
R. Laing and C. Sheridan: *Jazz Records: the Specialist Labels* (Copenhagen, 1981)
H. Zwartenkot and others: *The Dutch Jazz & Blues Discography, 1916–1980*, ed. W. Van Eyle (Amsterdam, 1981) [lists recordings made abroad by C. Hawkins, B. Carter, etc.]
J. Litchfield: *The Canadian Jazz Discography, 1916–1980* (Toronto, 1982) [lists recordings made abroad by L. Armstrong, C. Parker, S. Lacey, A. Shepp, etc.]
W. Bruyninckx: *Modern Jazz* (Mechelen, Belgium, 1984–)
——: *Progressive Jazz* (Mechelen, 1984–)
J. Leder: *Women in Jazz: a Discography of Instrumentalists, 1913–1968* (Westport, CT, 1985)
W. Bruyninckx: *Modern Big Band* (Mechelen, in preparation)
See also "Record labels"

Popular music

H. R. Schleman: *Rhythm on Record: a Complete Survey and Register of All the Principal Recorded Dance Music from 1906 to 1936* (London, 1936/*R*1978)
One Spot Record Finder, from 1959 *One Spot New Release Reporter* (Oak Park, IL, 1956–8; Forest Park, IL, 1958–85)
J. C. Whitburn: *Top Country & Western Records, 1949–1971* (Menomonee Falls, WI, 1972; suppls., 1974–)
——: *Top Pop Records, 1955–1970* (Menomonee Falls, WI, 1972, rev. 2/1973 [1955–72], rev. 3/1979 [1955–78] as *Top Pop Artists & Singles*, rev. 4/1983 [1955–82] as *Top Pop Records*; suppls., 1974–)
D. A. Jasen: *Recorded Ragtime, 1897–1958* (Hamden, CT, 1973) [excludes jazz; includes novelty piano]
B. Rust and A. G. Debus: *The Complete Entertainment Discography – from the Mid-1890's to 1942* (New Rochelle, NY, 1973) [excludes jazz and blues]
J. C. Whitburn: *Top LPs, 1945–1972* (Menomenee Falls, WI, 1973; suppls., 1974–)
——: *Top Pop Records, 1940–1955* (Menomonee Falls, WI, 1973)
——: *Top Rhythm & Blues Records, 1949–1971* (Menomonee Falls, WI, 1973; suppls., 1975–)
F. L. Gonzalez: *Disco-file: the Discographical Catalog of American Rock & Roll and Rhythm & Blues Vocal Groups* (Flushing, NY, 1974, 2/1977 [1902–76])
R. D. Kinkle: *The Complete Encyclopedia of Popular Music and Jazz, 1900–1950* (New Rochelle, NY, 1974)
A. Leichter: *A Discography of Rhythm & Blues and Rock & Roll, circa 1946–1964* (Staunton, VA, 1975; suppl., 1978)
B. Rust: *The American Dance Band Discography, 1917–1942* (New Rochelle, NY, 1975) [excludes jazz bands]
J. C. Whitburn: *Top Easy Listening Records, 1961–1974* (Menomonee Falls, WI, 1975; suppls., 1975–)
R. D. Ferlingere: *A Discography of Rhythm & Blues and Rock 'n' Roll Vocal Groups, 1945 to 1965* (Pittsburg, CA, 1976)
C. F. Faber: *The Country Music Almanac* (Lexington, KY, 1978)
J. C. Whitburn: *Pop Annual, 1955–1977* (Menomonee Falls, WI, 1978)
T. Hounsome and T. Chambre: *Rock Record* (Southampton, England, 1979, New York, 1981, rev. 2/1983 as *New Rock Record*)
P. C. Mawhinney: *MusicMaster: the 45 rpm Record Directory 1947–1982* (Allison Park, PA, 1983)
F. W. Hoffmann: *The Cash Box Singles Charts, 1950–1981* (Metuchen, NJ, 1983)
J. Whitburn: *The Billboard Book of Top 40 Hits, 1955 to Present* (New York, 1983)
G. Albert and F. W. Hoffmann: *The Cash Box Country Singles Charts, 1958–1982* (Metuchen, NJ, 1984)
See also "Record labels"

Theater, film, radio, and television music

30 Years of Motion Picture Music: the Big Hollywood Hit Tunes since 1928, ed. ASCAP (New York, n.d. [?1959])
J. Limbacher: *Theatrical Events* (Dearborn, MI, 5/1968)
S. Smolian: *A Handbook of Film, Theater, and Television Music on Record, 1948–1968* (New York, 1970)
J. Limbacher: *Film Music: from Violins to Video* (Metuchen, NJ, 1974)
D. Hummel: *The Collector's Guide to the American Musical Theatre* (Grawn, MI, 1976, rev. 3/1984; suppl., 1979)
M. R. Pitts and L. H. Harrison: *Hollywood on Record: the Film Stars' Discography* (Metuchen, NJ, 1978)
G. W. Hodgins: *The Broadway Musical: a Complete LP Discography* (Metuchen, NJ, 1980)
J. R. Smart: *Radio Broadcasts in the Library of Congress, 1924–1941: a Catalog of Recordings* (Washington, DC, 1982)

Folk and ethnic music

Check-list of Recorded Songs in the English Language in the Archive of American Folk Song, to July, 1940, ed. Library of Congress, Music Division (Washington, DC, 1942)
G. Durán: *Recordings of Latin American Songs and Dances: an Annotated Selective List of Popular and Folk-popular Music* (Washington, DC, 1942, rev. 2/1950)
R. M. Lawless: *Folksingers and Folksongs in America: a Handbook of Biography, Bibliography, and Discography* (New York, 1960, rev. 2/1965/*R*1981)
J. Godrich and R. M. W. Dixon: *Blues & Gospel Records, 1902–1942* (Hatch End, nr London, 1963, rev. and enlarged 3/1982 as *Blues and Gospel Records, 1902–1943*)
M. Leadbitter and N. Slaven: *Blues Records, January, 1943 to December, 1966* (London, 1968) [excludes rhythm-and-blues, jazz blues, and urban blues]
A. P. Merriam: *African Music on LP: an Annotated Discography* (Evanston, IL, 1970)
A. Green: *Only a Miner: Studies in Recorded Coal-Mining Songs* (Urbana, IL, 1972)
A Catalog of Phonorecordings of Music and Oral Data Held by the Archives of Traditional Music, ed. Archives of Traditional Music, Indiana U. (Boston, 1975)
My Sister's Song (Milwaukee, 1975)
R. M. Stone and F. J. Gillis: *African Music and Oral Data: a Catalog of Field Recordings, 1902–1975* (Bloomington, IN, 1976)
P. Gronow: *Studies in Scandinavian-American Discography* (Helsinki, 1977)
D. S. Lee: *Native North American Music and Oral Data: a Catalogue of Sound Recordings, 1893–1976* (Bloomington, IN, 1979) [catalogue of the Archives of Traditional Music, Indiana U.]
D. Tudor and N. Tudor: *Black Music* (Littleton, CO, 1979)

——: *Grass Roots Music* (Littleton, CO, 1979)

R. A. Reuss: *Songs of American Labor, Industrialization, and the Urban Work Experience* (Ann Arbor, MI, 1983)

See also "Record labels"

Record labels

A. Koenigsberg: *Edison Cylinder Records, 1889–1912* (New York, 1969)

B. Rust: *The Victor Master Book*, ii: *1925–1936* (Stanhope, NJ, 1970) [projected vols. i:1903–25 and iii:1936–42 not pubd]

F. J. Karlin: *Edison Diamond Discs, 50001–52651, 1912–1929* (Santa Monica, CA, 1972)

K. Krueger: *The Musical Heritage of the United States – the Unknown Portion* (New York, 1973) [label: Society for the Preservation of the American Musical Heritage]

B. Randle: *The Columbia 1-D Series, 1923–1929* (Bowling Green, OH, 1974)

B. Rust: *The American Record Label Book* (New Rochelle, NY, 1978/*R*1984)

R. R. Wile: *Edison Disc Recordings* (Philadelphia, 1978)

M. Ruppli: *Atlantic Records* (Westport, CT, 1979)

R. Dethlefson: *Edison Blue Amberol Recordings* (Brooklyn, NY, 1980–81 [1912–29])

M. Ruppli: *The Prestige Label* (Westport, CT, 1980)

——: *The Savoy Label* (Westport, CT, 1980)

R. S. Sears: *V-Discs: a History and Discography* (Westport, CT, 1980)

J. R. Bennett: *Melodiya: a Soviet Russian L.P. Discography* (Westport, CT, 1981) [incl. works by Barber, Copland, Gershwin, etc.]

T. Fagan and W. R. Moran: *The Encyclopedic Discography of Victor Recordings: Pre-matrix Series . . . 12 January 1900 to 23 April 1903* (Westport, CT, 1983)

M. Ruppli: *The Chess Labels* (Westport, CT, 1983)

W. R. Daniels: *The American 45 and 78 rpm Record Dating Guide, 1940–1959* (Westport, CT, 1985)

M. Ruppli: *The King Labels* (Westport, CT, 1985)

OTHER LISTINGS

L – *listeners' guide*
P – *price guide*
PC – *periodical catalogue*
R – *compilation or index of reviews*

B. H. Haggin: *Music on Records* (New York, 1938, rev. 2/1942) (L)

D. Hall: *The Record Book: a Music Lover's Guide to the World of the Phonograph* (New York, 1940, rev. 3/1943/*R*1946; international edn, 1948) (L)

I. Kolodin: *A Guide to Recorded Music* (Garden City, NY, 1941, rev. 2/1947 as *New Guide to Recorded Music*; international edn, 1950) (L)

C. E. Smith and others: *The Jazz Record Book* (New York, 1942/*R*1978) (L)

Phonolog Reporter (Los Angeles, 1948–81; San Diego, 1981–) (PC)

Long Playing Record Catalog, from Jan 1972 *Schwann-1 Record & Tape Guide*, from Dec 1983 *The New Schwann* (Cambridge, MA, 1949–53; Boston, 1953–); artist index, 1953– (PC)

D. Hall: *Records: 1950 Edition* (New York, 1950) (L)

J. M. Moses: *Price Guide to Collectors' Records* (New York, 1952, rev. 3/1976) (P)

R. D. Darrell: *Good Listening* (New York, 1953) (L)

W. De Motte: *The Long Playing Record Guide* (New York, 1955, rev. 2/1962) (L)

D. Hall and A. Levin: *The Disc Book* (New York, 1955) (L)

The Guide to Long-playing Records (New York, 1955/*R*1978) [i: I. Kolodin, orchestral music; ii: P. L. Miller, vocal music; iii: H. C. Schonberg, chamber and solo instrumental music] (L)

B. H. Haggin: *The Listener's Musical Companion* (New Brunswick, NJ, 1956, rev. 3/1971 as *The New Listener's Companion and Record Guide*, rev. 4/1974) (L)

High-fidelity Record Annual (Philadelphia, 1956–81, from 1957 Great Barrington, MA, as *Records in Review* [1955–80]) (R)

K. Myers: *Record Ratings: the Music Library Association's Index of Record Reviews* (New York, 1956) (R)

Down Beat Jazz Record Reviews (Chicago, 1957–64 [1956–63]) (R)

J. S. Wilson: *The Collector's Jazz: Traditional and Swing* (Philadelphia, 1958) (L)

——: *The Collector's Jazz: Modern* (Philadelphia, 1959) (L)

Polart Index to Record Reviews (Detroit, 1960–67) (R)

A. Cohn: *Twentieth-century Music in Western Europe: the Compositions and the Recordings* (Philadelphia, 1965) (L)

Phonolog List-o-Tapes (Los Angeles, 1967–81; San Diego, 1981–) (PC)

A. McCarthy and others: *Jazz on Record – a Critical Guide to the First 50 Years, 1917–1967* (London, 1968) (L)

Rolling Stone Record Review (New York, 1971–4) (R)

A. O. Maleady: *Record and Tape Reviews* (Metuchen, NJ, 1972–5, San Anselmo, CA, 1976– [1971–]) (R)

J. Marinelli: *Jomars LP Price Guide* (n.p., 1973) (P)

S. Propes: *Those Oldies but Goodies* (New York, 1973) (P)

J. B. Steane: *The Grand Tradition – Seventy Years of Singing on Record* (New York, 1974) (L)

M. Harrison and others: *Modern Jazz: the Essential Records – a Critical Selection* (London, 1975, rev. 2/1978) (L)

S. Propes: *Golden Goodies* (Radnor, PA, 1975) (P)

D. Tudor: *Annual Index to Popular Music Record Reviews* (Littleton, CO, 1975–9 [1972–7]) (R)

J. Osborne: *Original Record Collectors Price Guide* (Phoenix, 1976–) [various guides for country, popular, rock, film music, blues, etc.] (P)

P. A. Soderbergh: *78 rpm Records and Prices* (Des Moines, 1977) (P)

M. Bookspan: *Consumers Union Reviews Classical Recordings* (Mount Vernon, NY, 1978) (R)

K. Myers: *Index to Record Reviews, Based on Material Originally Published in Notes . . . between 1949 and 1977* (Boston, 1978–80; suppl., 1984 [1978–83]) (R)

R. C. Hill: *The Official Price Guide to Collectible Rock Records* (Orlando, FL, ?2/1979, rev. ?3/1982) (P)

D. Marsh: *The Rolling Stone Record Guide* (New York, 1979, rev. 1983 as *The New Rolling Stone Record Guide*) (L)

D. Tudor and N. Tudor: *Contemporary Popular Music* (Littleton, CO, 1979) (L)

——: *Jazz* (Littleton, CO, 1979) (L)

L. R. Docks: *1915–1965 American Premium Record Guide: Identification and Values, 78's 45's and LP's* (Florence, AL, 1980, rev. 2/1982) (P)

S. Gould and R. Fredericks: *The Official Price Guide to Music Collectibles* (Orlando, FL, 1980) (P)

T. J. Hudgeons, ed.: *The Official Price Guide to Records* (Orlando, 1980, 6/1985)

P. A. Soderbergh: *Olde Records Price Guide, 1900–1947* (Des Moines, 1980) (P)

A. Cohn: *Recorded Classical Music – a Critical Guide to Compositions and Performances* (New York, 1981) (L)

E. A. Davis: *Index to the New World Recorded Anthology of American Music* (New York, 1981) (L)

Videolog (San Diego, 1981–) [incl. section "Musical and Performing Arts"] (PC)

J. L. Holmes: *Conductors on Record* (Westport, CT, 1982) (L)

R. K. Oermann: *The Listener's Guide to Country Music* (New York, 1983) (L)

P. A. Soderbergh: *Dr. Records' Original 78 rpm Price Guide* (Des Moines, 1983) (P)

Trouser Press Guide to New Wave Records (New York, 1983) (L)

D. Tudor: *Popular Music: an Annotated Guide to Recordings* (Littleton, CO, 1983) (L)

Ferguson and Johnson: *Mainstream Jazz Reference and Price Guide, 1949–1965* (Phoenix, 1984) (P)

J. Morthland: *The Best of Country Music* (New York, 1984) (L)

J. Swenson: *The Rolling Stone Jazz Record Guide* (New York, 1984) (L)

American journals and magazines giving discographical listings, including record catalogues that appear regularly, are listed in PERIODICALS.

BIBLIOGRAPHY

V. Duckles: "Discographies," *Music Reference and Research Materials* (New York, 1964, 3/1974), 407

D. Morgenstern: "Discography – the Thankless Science," *DBY 1966*, 57

W. C. Allen, ed.: *Studies in Jazz Discography* (New Brunswick, NJ, 1971/*R*1978) [only one vol. pubd; incorporated into *Journal of Jazz Studies*]

A. Briegleb, ed.: *Directory of Ethnomusicological Sound Recording Collections in the U.S. and Canada* (Ann Arbor, MI, 1971)

L. Foreman: *Discographies: a Bibliography of Catalogues of Recordings, Mainly Relating to Specific Musical Subjects, Composers and Performers* (London, 1973)

J. S. Patrick: "Discography as a Tool for Musical Research and Vice Versa," *Journal of Jazz Studies*, i/1 (1973), 65

D. E. Cooper: *International Bibliography of Discographies: Classical Music and Jazz & Blues, 1962–1972* (Littleton, CO, 1975)

Bibliography of Discographies (New York, 1977–) [i: classical music, 1925–75, ed. M. H. Gray and G. D. Gibson (1977); ii: jazz, ed. D. Allen (1981); iii: popular music, ed. M. Gray (1983)]

G. Gisondi: "Sound Recording Periodicals: a Preliminary Union Catalog of pre-LP-related Holdings in Member Libraries of the Associated Audio Archives," *Journal* [Association for Recorded Sound Collections], x/1 (1978), 37

B. Rust: *The American Record Label Book* (New Rochelle, NY, 1978/*R*1984)

Rules for the Archival Cataloging of Sound Recordings, ed. Association for Recorded Sound Collections (Manassas, VA, 1980)

B. Rust: *Brian Rust's Guide to Discography* (Westport, CT, 1980)

For further bibliography, see entries on individual sound archives in LIBRARIES AND COLLECTIONS, §3.

DAVID HALL, GARY-GABRIEL GISONDI (1)
EDWARD BERGER (2)

Distin, Henry (John) (*b* London, England, 22 July 1819; *d* Philadelphia, PA, 11 Oct 1903). Cornetist and brass instrument manufacturer. He was the second son of John Henry Distin, an English musician who in 1833 formed with his four sons a brass ensemble known as the Distin Family Quintet; after the death of the eldest son, in 1849 it became a quartet, touring the USA and Canada. In 1845 the family firm of Distin & Sons was founded to sell music in London, and in 1846 it became the first British agent for the new "saxhorn" of Adolphe Sax. Henry Distin, who had received his early training in music in London at the Royal Academy of Music, took over the firm in 1849. In 1850 the company began its own manufacture of brass instruments and, despite a breach with Sax in 1853, the business expanded steadily. In 1868 Distin sold the firm to Boosey & Son (which continued it as Distin & Co. until 1874).

Distin subsequently lost most of his wealth in unfortunate business endeavors and in 1877 he immigrated to New York. He set up shop at 79 East 4th Street (then 285 and 355 Bowery), but of the 1500 horns of this period most were made at 115-21 East 13th Street or in Moses Slater's factory at 42 Cortlandt Street. They included "echo" and "Paris" cornets and the first "melody horns" – instruments with crooks and an echo or muting valve intended as substitutes for french horns. By 1880 Distin was importing instruments for J. W. Pepper of New York and Philadelphia, and in the summer of 1882 he moved to Philadelphia to help Pepper establish a factory. Pepper, however, wished to sell cheaply to a mass market, so Distin, whose interest was in high-quality instruments, formed a partnership with Senator Luther R. Keefer and other businessmen to establish on 12 March 1886 the Henry Distin Manufacturing Co. Its factory in Williamsport, Pennsylvania, produced 22,000 Distin horns before February 1909, when Brua C. Keefer, Sr., purchased the company. He replaced Distin's name with his own, but instruments modeled on Distin's were manufactured until about 1940.

From 1884 to 1888 Distin published music and sold instruments in Philadelphia, first at 917 Filbert Street and then at 913 Arch Street. From 1889 he and his son William Henry, also an instrument maker, lived in Williamsport, but in 1890 Distin vested all rights with the company and retired to Philadelphia with a pension. His son is last reported, as a musician in Philadelphia, in 1909.

As a cornetist Distin spurred the growing popularity of early valve brass instruments, and as a manufacturer he improved their design, mechanism, and the tools of their construction. He sought 19 patents in his lifetime, including patents for percussion instruments and their accessories; he took out six patents in the USA. His "light piston valve" (patented in 1864) became the prototype for the modern cornet valve; his "center bore cornet" (patented in 1884), whose design freed the flow of air from abrupt bends in the tubing, became the standard of excellence in the USA. Every contemporaneous Philadelphia drum or brass instrument maker was influenced by Distin.

BIBLIOGRAPHY

New York Times (7 Aug 1881), 10
Williamsport Gazette and Bulletin (13 Oct 1903), 7
A. Carse: "Adolphe Sax and the Distin Family," *MR*, vi (1945), 193
P. Bate: *The Trumpet and Trombone* (New York, 1966)

ROBERT E. ELIASON, LLOYD P. FARRAR

Ditson, Oliver. Firm of music publishers. The company has the oldest continuous history of any music house in the USA, tracing its beginning to the firm of Ebenezer Battelle, who opened the Boston Book Store in 1783 and shortly afterwards began selling music as well. Two years later Benjamin Guild purchased the store, and he managed the firm until his death in 1792, when it was taken over by William Pinson Blake. William Pelham succeeded Blake in 1796, and Pelham, in turn, was succeeded by William Blagrove in 1804. Seven years later, the business became the property of Samuel H. Parker, who was the first of these owners to publish music. Oliver Ditson (*b* Boston, 20 Oct 1811; *d* Boston, 21 Dec 1888) served as an apprentice to Parker from 1823 to 1826 and then worked for two other Boston publishers, Isaac R. Butts and Alfred Mudge.

In 1835 Ditson began his own music publishing firm in the same building as Parker, and in 1836 the two became partners in the firm of Parker & Ditson. When the partnership was dissolved in 1842, Ditson acquired the remaining interest in the publishing company. Three years later John C. Haynes joined Ditson, becoming a partner when Oliver Ditson & Co. was formed in 1857. A period of vast expansion followed, during which Ditson bought more than 50 catalogues of other publishers throughout the country. The company acquired the old houses of Miller & Beacham of Baltimore, Lee & Walker of Philadelphia, William Hall & Son of New York, and John Firth & Son, also of New York, and during the same period established (in collaboration with others) the new companies of J. E. Ditson in Philadelphia, C. H. Ditson in New York, Lyon & Healy in Chicago, and the John Church company in Cincinnati. By 1890 Oliver Ditson & Co. was the largest music publisher in the USA, with a catalogue listing over 100,000 titles including vocal music (45,000), octavo music (4000), instrumental music (48,000), and books (3000). For illustrations of title pages, *see* BOSTON (i), fig.6, and BETHUNE, TOM.

Ditson published all types of music and music literature. The firm assumed the publication of *Dwight's Journal of Music* from 1858 until 1878, when it began its own *Musical Record* (renamed *Musical Record and Review* in 1901 and in 1903 incorporated into *The Musician*, which continued until 1918). In 1897 the Ditson company initiated a series of educational books entitled The Music Students Library; the best-known of these was The Musicians Library, a subseries of nearly 100 volumes of masterpieces of song and solo piano works, each edited by an authority in the field. In 1912 Ditson began a violin teaching series titled *Mitchell's Class Methods*, and in 1918 the 20-volume *Music Students Piano Course*. The last of these series, *A Study Course in Music Understanding*, was designed for the non-specialist. In 1931 the entire Ditson catalogue was acquired by the Theodore Presser Co.

BIBLIOGRAPHY

W. A. Fisher: *One Hundred and Fifty Years of Music Publishing in the United States* (Boston, 1933)

W. THOMAS MARROCCO, MARK JACOBS/R

Dittmer, Luther A(lbert) (*b* Brooklyn, NY, 8 April 1927). Musicologist. He was awarded the BA (1947) and the MA (1949) at Columbia University; he also took courses at the Juilliard School of Music and at Harvard. In 1949 he began studies at the University of Basle; he received the doctorate there in 1952. He then taught at Wagner College (1953–4), Adelphi College (1954–8), and the Manhattan School of Music (1955–7). In 1958 he became associated with Brooklyn College and later with the PhD music program at CUNY. He was director of the Institute of Mediaeval Music, which he founded in 1957. In 1976 he became head of the music department at Ottawa (Kansas) University.

Dittmer's interests include French and English polyphonic music of the 13th and 14th centuries and 16th-century Huguenot music. As director of the Institute of Mediaeval Music, he has provided scholars with facsimiles of manuscripts, including the major Notre Dame sources, and translations of theoretical writings.

PAULA MORGAN

Dixey, Henry E. (*b* Boston, MA, 6 Jan 1859; *d* Atlantic City, NJ, 25 Feb 1943). Comedian and singer. Following his début in his home town at the age of ten in *Under the Gaslight*, he came under the tutelage of the pantomimist James S. Maffitt. His New York début was as half of the heifer in the Manhattan première of E. E. Rice's popular musical burlesque, *Evangeline* (1874). He played increasingly more important comic parts in contemporary lyric pieces before he achieved stardom as the statue brought to life in *Adonis* (1884). This musical was the first play in Broadway's history to run for more than 500 consecutive performances; women flocked to gape at Dixey's handsome face and fine figure, and all sorts of playgoers returned to laugh at his sly interpretation of the miraculous statue, his spoof of Henry Irving, his hilarious routine in drag, and other comic highpoints. The show marked the apogee of his career, for although several other musicals were written especially for him, including *The Seven Ages* (1889) and *Rip* (1890), none was successful. Within a few seasons Dixey was reduced to accepting important supporting roles, though he occasionally starred in short-lived works.

GERALD BORDMAN

Dixie. Minstrel song, written by DAN EMMETT in 1859, which became a national song during the Civil War; *see* PATRIOTIC MUSIC, §1.

Dixie Dewdrop. Pseudonym used by UNCLE DAVE MACON in the 1930s.

Dixie Hummingbirds. Male vocal ensemble. It was formed by baritone James B. Davis in Greenville, South Carolina, in 1928, to perform gospel music. Early members were bass William Bobo (formerly with the Heavenly Gospel Singers), who joined the group about 1939 and remained until his death in 1976, and lead singer Ira Tucker, who previously had his own group, the Gospel Carriers, and who joined in 1939. It was in this year that the ensemble began its lengthy recording career. It moved to Philadelphia in 1942, but toured widely and also performed on radio, sometimes appearing as the Jericho Boys or the Swanee Quintet. Tenor Beachey Thompson joined in 1943, and Paul Owens was also a member during the early 1940s. By the 1950s the influence of rhythm-and-blues began to make itself felt; in 1952 guitarist Howard Carroll was added, and in 1954 bass James Walker joined Tucker as a second lead singer. The group continued the performance tradition of male gospel quartets, employing falsetto, melisma, portamento, and close harmony in a repertory of spirituals and contemporary sacred songs, many of which were arranged or composed by Walker, Tucker, or Tucker's son. The ensemble won a Grammy Award in 1973 for its own version of Paul Simon's *Loves me like a rock*, previously recorded with the composer. It celebrated its 50th anniversary in 1978, when it made several television appearances and a nationwide tour.

BIBLIOGRAPHY

SouthernB

B. W. Baker: *Black Gospel Music Styles, 1942–1975* (diss., U. of Maryland, 1978)

DOMINIQUE-RENÉ DE LERMA

Dixieland jazz. A term applied to the jazz played by white musicians of the early New Orleans school, but sometimes also to NEW ORLEANS JAZZ as a whole and often to the post-1940 revival of this music (also known as TRADITIONAL JAZZ). Owing to the absence of recorded evidence, the stylistic differences between early black jazz in New Orleans and its white counterpart played by groups such as Papa Jack Laine's and others is impossible to document. However, early commentators and observers are fairly unanimous in pointing out that white musicians were slower to grasp the rhythmic swing and blues inflections essential to jazz, though at the same time they made important contributions to its repertory and harmonic and melodic vocabulary. The name "dixieland" derives from the Original Dixieland Jazz Band, a white New Orleans group which became internationally successful through its tours and recordings from 1917; it played a bowdlerized form of jazz decorated with coloristic and novelty effects borrowed from black jazz. As later white jazz groups, such as the New Orleans Rhythm Kings, showed a fuller under-

The Dixie Hummingbirds with Ira Tucker (second from left) and William Bobo (guitar), c1958

standing of black jazz, it became less necessary to distinguish between the New Orleans and dixieland styles. From the 1950s, during the revival of New Orleans jazz, a number of older dixieland musicians were recorded, notably under the auspices of the New Orleans Jazz Club.

BIBLIOGRAPHY

G. Schuller: *Early Jazz: its Roots and Musical Development* (New York, 1968), 175ff

C. G. Herzog zu Mecklenburg: "Dixieland-Stil," *Stilformen des Jazz*, i (Vienna, 1973)

J. BRADFORD ROBINSON

Dixieliners. Country-music string band formed in 1932 by ARTHUR SMITH with Sam and Kirk McGee.

Dixon, Bill [William Robert] (*b* Nantucket, MA, 5 Oct 1925). Jazz trumpeter, composer, and music educator. He grew up in New York where, after studying painting at Boston University, he worked as a trumpeter and arranger. He was co-leader of a free-jazz quartet with Archie Shepp in 1962–3, and the following year presented "The October Revolution in Jazz," a series of concerts featuring performers who were then unknown. In 1965 he organized the Jazz Composers' Guild, an influential but short-lived collective, which endeavored to support the playing of jazz independently of nightclubs and booking agents. In the same year he also began a ten-year collaboration with the dancer Judith Dunn, with whom he presented a concert of free jazz and dance at the 1966 Newport Jazz Festival. Since 1968 he has taught at Bennington (Vermont) College, first assisting Dunn as a consultant in dance, though later he founded a department of black music. As a trumpeter Dixon has an unusual conception of improvised melody; he makes much use of squeezed notes, unconventional intonation, excessive vibrato, distorted tones, and other expressive devices. He has presented new compositions at the international jazz festivals in Paris (1976), Verona (1980), and Zurich (1981).

RECORDINGS
(selective list)

Archie Shepp-Bill Dixon Quartet (1962, Savoy 12178); *Bill Dixon 7-tette* (1964, Savoy 12184); *Intents and Purposes* (1967, RCA LSP3844); *In Italy*, i–ii (1980, Soul Note 1008, 1011); *November 1981* (1981, Soul Note 1037–8)

BIBLIOGRAPHY

D. Morgenstern and M. Williams: "The October Revolution: Two Views of the Avant Garde in Action," *Down Beat*, xxxi/30 (1964), 15

R. Levin: "The Jazz Composers Guild: an Assertion of Dignity," *Down Beat*, xxxii/10 (1965), 17

J. Anderson: "Judith Dunn and the Endless Quest," *Dance Magazine*, xli/11 (1967), 48

E. Jost: *Free Jazz* (Graz, Austria, 1974)

R. Riggins: "Prof. Bill Dixon: Intents of an Innovator," *Down Beat*, xlvii/8 (1980), 30

B. Rusch: "Bill Dixon: Interview," *Cadence*, viii (1982), no.3, p.5; no.4, p.20; no.5, p.14

BARRY KERNFELD

Dixon, (Charles) Dean (*b* New York, 10 Jan 1915; *d* Zug, Switzerland, 4 Nov 1976). Conductor. He studied at the Juilliard School and Columbia University, made his conducting début at Town Hall on 7 May 1938, and founded the New York Chamber Orchestra the same year. In a sense Dixon's career as a conductor paralleled Marian Anderson's as a singer: he opened several important doors to black musicians, being the first to appear as guest conductor of Toscanini's NBC SO (1941), of the New York PO (1942), and of the Philadelphia Orchestra (1943). In 1944 he founded the American Youth Orchestra and appeared for the first time with the Boston SO, and in 1948 he received Columbia University's Alice M. Ditson Award for outstanding contributions to modern American music. In 1949 he moved to Europe, holding appointments as principal conductor of the Göteborg SO in Sweden (1953–60) and from 1961 to 1974 as principal conductor of the Hesse Radio SO in Frankfurt am Main, Germany, where he made his home; he was also principal conductor of the Sydney SO (1964–7). In 1970 he began to unite the two strands of his career, adding a series of engagements with the leading American orchestras to his European commitments. Dixon's repertory combined an enthusiasm for American music with a taste for the main European tradition of Beethoven, Brahms, and Bruckner. His interpretations tended towards an engaging if occasionally wayward warmth rather than brilliance.

Dean Dixon

BIBLIOGRAPHY

SouthernB

K. Kristoffersen: "Dean Dixon," *HiFi/MusAm*, xx/8 (1970), 18

N. A. Trudeau: "When the Doors Didn't Open," *HiFi*, xxxv/5 (1985), 57

BERNARD JACOBSON

Dixon, George Washington (*b* 1808; *d* New Orleans, LA, 1861). Minstrel performer. He was most famous for his entr'acte performances of *Coal Black Rose*, the first blackface comic love-song, and *Long Tailed Blue*, the first song of the black dandy; both of these song types later became standard in the minstrel show, and both songs are in a simple musical style that was thought (mistakenly) to represent Afro-American music. Dixon claimed authorship of these songs (and, less credibly, of *Zip Coon*), and is credited as the first to perform them; he presented *Coal Black Rose* as early as 1827 in Albany and in 1828 brought it to New York, where he became highly popular. Capitalizing on this success, in 1829 he expanded the song into two comic skits (an interlude and an afterpiece) – *The Lottery Ticket* and *Love in a Cloud*; the latter has been cited as the first "negro play." Dixon performed throughout the 1830s, but by the 1840s he had been eclipsed by other minstrel performers; he went on to gain notoriety as a filibuster in Yucatan and as the editor of a New York scandal sheet.

BIBLIOGRAPHY

G. C. D. Odell: *Annals of the New York Stage*, iii, iv (New York, 1928)

C. Wittke: *Tambo and Bones: a History of the American Minstrel Stage* (Durham, 1930)

S. F. Damon: *Series of Old American Songs* (Providence, 1936)

C. Hamm: *Yesterdays: Popular Song in America* (New York, 1979)

ROBERT B. WINANS

Dixon, Henry. Pseudonym of HENRY COWELL.

Dixon, James (*b* Estherville, IA, 26 April 1928). Conductor. He studied at the University of Iowa, where his teachers included Imre Waldbauer, and privately with Mitropoulos (1949–60). He began his professional career conducting the 7th Army SO in Germany, where he introduced a number of American works. In later seasons he made regular appearances with the Minneapolis SO, of which he was associate conductor in 1961–2, the National Orchestra of Greece, the orchestras of North and West German Radio, the American Composers Orchestra, and the Boston Philharmonia; since 1965 he has been music director of the Tri-Cities SO, based in Davenport, Iowa. A gifted teacher, he has worked with student orchestras at the New England Conservatory (1959–61) and the University of Iowa (1954–9 and from 1962); he conducted a student group at the International Society for Contemporary Music Festival in Boston in 1976. Dixon has led premières of music by Wuorinen (Piano Concerto, *Concertone*, *Contrafactum*, *Grand Bamboula*), Thorne (*Liebesrock*), T. J. Anderson, Gideon, and William Matthews, and has recorded several of these works for CRI.

RICHARD DYER

Dixon, Jessy (*b* San Antonio, TX, 12 March 1938). Gospel singer, pianist, and composer. He studied piano at St. Mary's College, San Antonio, with the aim of becoming a concert pianist. He first heard gospel music as a teenager through the recordings and concerts of Clara Ward and the Ward Singers and Dorothy Love Coates and the Original Gospel Harmonettes. Leaving college after two years, he served for a time as accompanist for Brother Joe May, then in 1960 joined James Cleveland's Gospel Chimes. After five years with Cleveland he became director of the Thompson Community Singers, recording with them under the name of the Chicago Community Choir. In the late 1960s he organized the Jessy Dixon Singers, modeling their sound and style on that of Cleveland and his group; Dixon provided a baritone lead employing high falsetto in a repertory of call-and-response songs. From his piano study, Dixon developed an interest in progressive harmony, and when in the early 1970s he left the Savoy record label and moved to Light Records, his style changed to that of contemporary gospel, where the emphasis is on pure vocal sounds with melodies and harmonies borrowed from the popular music tradition, and accompaniment is provided by electronic instruments. In June 1980 Dixon was selected to represent contemporary gospel at the Golden Jubilee Year Celebration of Gospel Music held in Chicago. His best-known compositions include *The failure's not in God* (1964), *Bring the sun out* (1979), and *Satisfied* (1982).

BIBLIOGRAPHY

T. Heilbut: *The Gospel Sound: Good News and Bad Times* (New York, 1971/*R*1975)

R. Anderson and G. North: *Gospel Music Encyclopedia* (New York, 1979)

I. V. Jackson: *Afro-American Religious Music: a Bibliography and Catalogue of Gospel Music* (Westport, CT, 1979)

HORACE CLARENCE BOYER

Dlugoszewski, Lucia (*b* Detroit, MI, 16 June 1934). Composer. After being trained in physics at Wayne State University (1949–52), she moved to New York, where she studied piano with Grete Sultan from 1952 to 1955 and music analysis with Salzer at Mannes College in 1952–3; she also took lessons in composition from Varèse. As early as 1951 she devised the so-called timbre piano, a conventional piano whose strings are struck with beaters and played with a variety of bows and plectra. She developed a close association with the Erick Hawkins Dance Company, for whom she wrote many scores, and also invented a series of new percussion and friction instruments, executed by the sculptor Ralph Dorazio, 1958–60 (see illustration). During her early years in New York, she was noticed chiefly by New York School painters and poets including Robert Motherwell, John Ashbery, and Ad Reinhardt; the sculptor David Smith and the painter Herman Cherry sponsored her first New York concert in 1957,

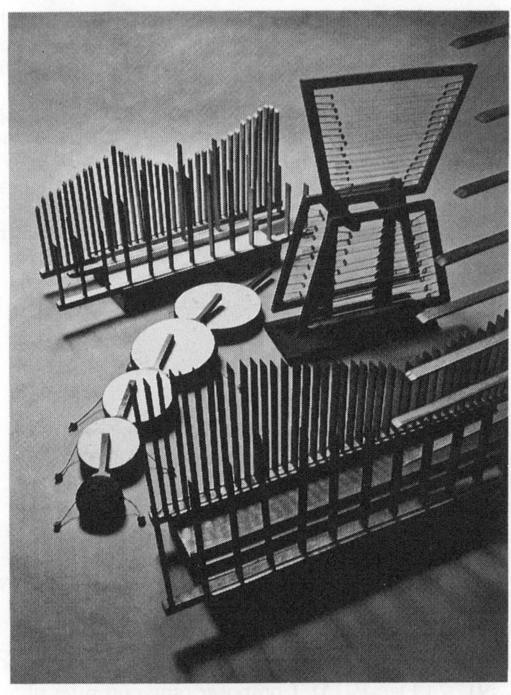

Some of Lucia Dlugoszewski's ladder harps and tangent rattles (constructed by Ralph Dorazio, 1958–60)

and Frank O'Hara was the first to review her music. Her orchestral works of the 1970s brought Dlugoszewski increasing recognition from musicians. She has received a Guggenheim Fellowship, grants from the Martha Baird Rockefeller Fund for Music and the Phoebe Ketchum Thorne Foundation, and an award from the National Institute of Arts and Letters; in 1977 she became the first woman to win the Koussevitzky International Recording Award, for *Fire Fragile Flight*. Her first major commission was from the New York PO and the NEA in 1975 for *Abyss and Caress*; other works have been composed for the Chamber Music Society of Lincoln Center, the Louisville Orchestra, and the American Composers Orchestra.

Dlugoszewski's timbral originality was apparent in her early works, both those for timbre piano, such as *Archaic Music* (1953–6), and those for large ensembles of her new percussion instruments (*Suchness Concert*, 1958–60). *Balance Naked Flung* (1966) revealed for the first time her "flung into" or "leaping" structures of recklessness and the architectonics of speed that she developed further in *Strange Tenderness of Naked Leaping* (1977) and other orchestral works of the next decade; the "leap" element of surprise is a specific technique for realizing a sensation of musical immediacy. From 1979 a new quality of elegance entered her work, the poetic essence of "elusivity" and "tilt" that informs *Wilderness Elegant Tilt* (1981–4). "Music," she has written, "must be intricate enough to slow up the murderous speed of our glibness [and] new enough to cheat the categories."

WORKS

Dramatic: 14 dance scores, incl. Here and Now with Watchers, 1954–7, 8 Clear Places, 1958–60, Cantilever, 1964, Lords of Persia, 1966–8, Black Lake, 1969, Angels of the Inmost Heaven, 1972, Avanti, 1983, and This Woman Duende Amor, 1984; incidental music for 2 plays, 1952–60; 3 film scores, 1952–73

Orch: Arithmetic Progressions, 1954; Orchestral Radiant Ground, 1955; Flower Music for Left Ear in a Small Room, 1956; Naked Flight Nageire, chamber orch, 1966; In Memory of my Feeling (F. O'Hara), T, chamber orch, 1972; Kireji: Spring and Tender Speed, 1972; Fire Fragile Flight, 1973–4; Abyss and Caress, tpt, orch, 1974–5; Strange Tenderness of Naked Leaping, 1977; Amor Now Tilting Night, chamber orch, 1978; Startle Transparent Terrible Freedom, 1981; Wilderness Elegant Tilt, conc., 11 insts, 1981–4; Quidditas Sorrow Terrible Freedom, 1983–4; Duende Amor, 1983–4; *c*10 other works

Inst: Archaic Music, timbre pf, 1953–6; Naked Wabin, fl, cl, perc, vn, db, timbre pf, 1956; Suchness Concert, large perc ens, 1958–60; Beauty Music, cl, perc, timbre pf, 1965; Balance Naked Flung, cl, tpt, b trbn, vn, perc, 1966; Naked Qnt, brass, 1967; Space Is a Diamond, tpt, 1970; Tender Theatre Flight Nageire, brass qnt, perc orch, 1972–9; Amor Elusive Empty August, ww qnt, 1979; Cicada Terrible Freedom, fl, str qnt, b trbn, 1980–81; Duende Newfallen, b trbn, timbre pf, 1982–3; Quidditas Str Qt, 1984; *c*15 other works

Principal publisher: Margun

BIBLIOGRAPHY

EwenD; *VintonD*
L. Dlugoszewski: "Is Music Sound?," *Jubilee*, ix/10 (1962), 28
P. Reps: *Accordingly, the Music of Lucia Dlugoszewski (Suchness Concert), in Unwrinkling Plays* (Rutland, VT, 1965)
T. Johnson: "Lucia Dlugoszewski," *HiFi/MusAm*, xxv/6 (1975), 4
J. Highwater: "Dlugoszewski Ascending," *New York Arts Journal*, viii/3 (1981), 6

J. HIGHWATER

Doane, William H(oward) (*b* Preston, CT, 3 Feb 1832; *d* South Orange, NJ, 24 Dec 1915). Composer, and compiler of Sunday-school and gospel hymnbooks. He was a highly successful manufacturer of woodworking machinery who became president of a number of businesses and received over 70 patents for his inventions. He had been well trained in music, and conducted the Norwich (Connecticut) Harmonic Society from 1852 to 1854. After he had suffered a nearly fatal heart attack at the age of about 30, Doane began to compose melodies for Sunday-school hymns, producing over 1000 tunes to texts by Fanny Crosby, and as many more to other authors' words; he also collaborated with Robert Lowry in the compilation of popular Sunday-school collections. His other works include *The Baptist Hymnal* (1883) and a number of Christmas (or "Santa Claus") cantatas, which became a popular genre. Doane's musical style reflects the influence of 19th-century popular songs. His best-known tunes include those of the hymns *Jesus, keep me near the cross* (1869), *More love to Thee, o Christ* (1870), *Pass me not, o gentle Savior* (1870), *Take the name of Jesus with you* (1871), *Draw me nearer* (1875), and *To God be the glory* (1875). About 25 of his hymn tunes are still in use. Doane was a generous contributor to the YMCA, Denison University, and the Cincinnati Art Museum, which houses his collection of musical instruments.

BIBLIOGRAPHY

J. H. Hall: *Biography of Gospel Song and Hymn Writers* (New York, 1914/*R*1971)
"Doane, William Howard," *The National Cyclopedia of American Biography*, xli (New York, 1956/*R*1971), 95
M. R. Wilhoit: *A Guide to the Principal Authors and Composers of Gospel Song in the Nineteenth Century* (diss., Southern Baptist Theological Seminary, 1982)

MEL R. WILHOIT

Dobbs, Mattiwilda (*b* Atlanta, GA, 11 July 1925). Soprano. She studied with Lotte Lehmann and Pierre Bernac. In 1948 she began her career as a concert singer and in 1951 won first prize in the Geneva Competition. During the next decade she went on to sing at the Metropolitan Opera, where she made her début as Gilda in *Rigoletto* (9 November 1956) and was particularly well known for her Olympia (*Les contes d'Hoffmann*). She also sang at La Scala, Covent Garden, the Paris Opéra, and the principal European festivals. After her marriage she lived in Sweden and sang much less frequently, though with continuing distinction; in 1967 she sang and recorded Constanze under Menuhin in the Phoenix Opera production of *Die Entführung aus dem Serail*, one of her last important appearances. Her small but buoyant voice, finished technique, and lively interpretations survive on a small number of recordings; perhaps the best of these is the first, a fresh and elegant performance of Leila (*Les pêcheurs de perles*) conducted by René Leibowitz.

BIBLIOGRAPHY

SouthernB
"Dobbs, Mattiwilda," *CBY 1955*

RICHARD DYER

Dobro. A guitar with one or more metal resonator discs mounted inside the body, under the bridge. It was developed in the USA by John Dopyera (*b* Czechoslovakia, June 1893), the son of a violin maker, and manufactured by the National String Instrument Corp. (formed by Dopyera and others) in Los Angeles from 1925. Dopyera left the company in about 1928 and set up the Dobro Corp. with two of his brothers, Emil ("Ed") and Rudolph ("Rudy"). The name "dobro," derived from the first syllables of "Dopyera brothers," was devised at this time (it is also the word for "good" in Slavonic languages). Besides dobros, the company marketed resonator ukuleles, banjos, mandolins, four-string tenor guitars, and double basses, and in 1932 produced what was probably the first Spanish electric guitar, which had magnetic pickups designed by Victor Smith.

Around 1933 changes in the management of the National String Instrument Corp. left another Dopyera brother, Louis, as the major stockholder, and a merger with the Dobro Corp. followed. The National Dobro Corp. moved to Chicago in 1936, and in the late 1930s added Hawaiian steel guitars and electric violins to its range of string instruments. It produced variants of the dobro for marketing under different names by distributors, and exchanged guitar bodies for metal and electrical parts with other companies. In 1942 it became the Valco Manufacturing Co. (named after Victor Smith, Al Frost and Louis Dopyera), which, after the war, concentrated on the making of electric guitars until its demise about 1964. Following a revival of interest in the dobro in the late 1950s, Emil Dopyera began to manufacture the instrument again around 1959 in El Monte, Los Angeles (later in nearby Gardena). His company was sold to

Mosrite around 1967, but the name "dobro" was regained by Emil Dopera, Jr., when his Original Musical Instrument Co. resumed the making of dobros in Long Beach, California, about 1971, moving to nearby Huntington Beach in 1972. In the early 1980s the company was sold to Gabriella Dopera Lazar, John Dopyera's sister.

The dobro was originally developed in response to the growing demand for a guitar that could produce a greater volume than the conventional instrument. It was superseded in many areas of popular music after World War II by the more efficient electric guitar. The dobro was used at first in country blues and hillbilly music; it was often played Hawaiian-style across the knees and with a bottleneck (indeed some models specifically adapted for Hawaiian playing were marketed); it is now heard mainly in bluegrass and related country music, though it is also played by some rock musicians.

BIBLIOGRAPHY

M. Brooks: "The Story of the Dobro [as told] by Ed Dopera," *Guitar Player*, v/8 (1971), 29; repr. in *The Guitar Player Book* (New York, and Saratoga, CA, 1978), 361

T. Wheeler: *The Guitar Book: a Handbook for Electric and Acoustic Guitarists* (New York, 2/1978), 38

——: *American Guitars: an Illustrated History* (New York, 1982), 286

HUGH DAVIES

Dockstader, Lew [Clapp, George Alfred] (*b* Hartford, CT, 7 Aug 1856; *d* New York, 26 Oct 1924). Minstrel performer and manager. He began his career as an amateur in Hartford in 1873, where he performed as a blackface song and dance man; he appeared with prominent minstrel organizations and with his own troupes. Between 1878 and 1883 he was Charles Dockstader's partner in a performing duo called the Dockstader Brothers, and in 1886 he formed his own Dockstader's Minstrels. He later formed a company with George Primrose (1898–1903), which was among the last minstrel troupes to tour the large cities. For the next 11 years he maintained his own company, and his last years were spent in vaudeville. Dockstader was an extremely successful organizer and director of minstrel productions and created many skits and afterpieces. His own talent lay particularly in burlesque and mimicry, and he was especially famous for his monologues and parodies of politicians, actors, and singers. He was one of the few to keep minstrelsy alive as a distinct form well into the 20th century, and his death symbolized the end of an American institution.

BIBLIOGRAPHY

E. L. Rice: *Monarchs of Minstrelsy* (New York, 1911)

C. Wittke: *Tambo and Bones: a History of the American Minstrel Stage* (Durham, 1930)

ROBERT B. WINANS

Dockstader, Tod (*b* St. Paul, MN, 20 March 1932). Composer. At the University of Minnesota he studied art and general subjects; he received no formal training in music. During the 1960s and early 1970s he composed tape music that reveals the influence of Varèse and his aesthetic. These pieces principally use the techniques of *musique concrète* and explore natural sound sources in straightforward statement–contrast–restatement structures. They contain ingenious timbral modulations of different sound events such as the swish of cymbals or the removal of adhesive tape. Beginning in the early 1970s Dockstader devoted himself to creating numerous brief film scores using electronic sound, all from one to three minutes in length. In discussing his works, Dockstader avoids references to "electronic music," preferring Varèse's term "organized sound." A number of his earlier compositions were recorded by Owl Records (Boulder, Colorado). In recent years he has worked in New York, where he is active as a film writer and editor, cartoonist, photographer, and industrial designer.

WORKS

Elec: 8 Elec Pieces, 1959–60; Traveling Music, 1960; Apocalypse, 1961; Luna Park, 1961; Drone, 1962; Water Music, 1963; Quatermass, 1964; 2 Moons of Quatermass, 1964; Telemetry Tapes, 1965; Omniphony 1, collab. J. Reichert, 1966–7; Counter, 1969; Whitewater, 1970, withdrawn, incl. in Animated Khartoum, 1971; *c*50 short film scores [recorded by Boosey & Hawkes]

DAVID COPE

Dr. Buzzard's Original Savannah Band. Pop group. Its members were Stony Browder, Jr. (*b* New York, 1949), guitarist and pianist; his half-brother August Darnell (Thomas August Darnell Browder) (*b* Montreal, Que., 1951), singer and bass guitarist; Cory Daye (*b* New York, 25 April 1952), singer; Andy Hernandez (*b* New York, 1950), vibraphonist; and Mickey Sevilla (*b* Puerto Rico, 1953), drummer. Formed in New York in 1974, it created a theatrical, fantastic music based on Hollywood films of the 1940s and incorporating elements of pop-soul, disco, calypso, and Latin music; Daye sang with curt insouciance in a hybrid of swing and disco styles. The group recorded three albums of highly original pop music, the impressionistic lyrics of which evoked an idealized vision of New York street life; the dense, almost symphonic arrangements (by Browder and Darnell, who also produced the recordings) owed something to the colorful big-band style of Cab Calloway and others, but the layered instrumentation often reinforced a novel kaleidoscopic bitonality that suggested the sound of two radios playing at the same time. Despite the inventiveness of the music, only the first of these albums was commercially successful.

When the group's schemes outgrew all the media they explored (including film and the theater) Darnell formed a new group, Kid Creole and the Coconuts (1980), which became the focus of the musicians' artistic energies. Darnell (songwriter, producer, bass player, and singer) and a constantly changing group of musicians (including Hernandez) specialized in what he called "mulatto music," another imaginative mixture of calypso, pop-soul, and Latin music. Although they presented a successful staged version of their second album, *Fresh Fruit in Foreign Places*, complete with rhymed narration, the same internal anarchy and unrealistic expectations that had plagued Dr. Buzzard's Original Savannah Band prevented Kid Creole and the Coconuts from realizing many of their more elaborate, mixed-media projects.

RECORDINGS

Dr. Buzzard's Original Savannah Band (RCA APLI 504, 1976), incl. Cherchez la femme; *Dr. Buzzard's Original Savannah Band Meets King Pennett* (RCA APLI 2402, 1978); *James Monroe H. S. Presents Dr. Buzzard's Original Savannah Band Goes to Washington* (Elek. 218, 1980)

STEPHEN HOLDEN

Dr. John [Rebennack, Malcolm John; Rebennack, Mac] (*b* New Orleans, LA, 1941). Rock singer, songwriter, and pianist. The son of a record-store owner, he grew up listening to Creole music and the legendary playing of the rhythm-and-blues pianist Professor Longhair, who performed in dance halls. By the late 1950s he was working as a session player with Longhair and the New Orleans rhythm-and-blues singers Frankie Ford and Joe Tex. He came to prominence as a rock-and-roll singer in the late 1960s, when he combined his early musical influences with an exotic live show, and recorded under the name Dr. John Creaux, the Night Tripper. His early albums (*Gris-Gris* and *Babylon*) were a fusion of jazz, psychedelic rock, and pop elements, and created a surprisingly original, eerie effect. But the work that best displays his dexterous keyboard abilities is *Gumbo*, an affectionate and lively tribute to the New Orleans rhythm-and-blues of Longhair, Huey Smith, and others. In 1973 Dr. John recorded *Right place wrong time*, which became a top ten hit, but the albums that followed were unfocused. His work of the early 1980s was more convincing but less commercially successful.

RECORDINGS
(selective list)

Gris-Gris (Atco 33-234, 1968); *Gumbo* (Atco 7006, 1972); *In the Right Place* (Atco 7018, 1973); Right place wrong time (Atco 6914, 1973); *Dr. John Plays Mac Rebennack* (Clean Cuts 706, 1981)

MIKAL GILMORE

Dodds, Baby [Warren] (*b* New Orleans, LA, 24 Dec 1898; *d* Chicago, IL, 14 Feb 1959). Jazz drummer, brother of Johnny Dodds. He played in New Orleans with Bunk Johnson, Papa Celestin, and others before joining Fate Marable's riverboat bands (1918–21), where he acquired a commanding reputation among New Orleans jazz musicians. In 1922 he was invited to San Francisco to join King Oliver, with whom he made his first recordings the following year in Chicago. Dodds remained in Chicago for the next two decades, recording freelance in historical sessions with Jelly Roll Morton and Louis Armstrong (1927) and playing in small groups led by his brother. With the revival of New Orleans jazz around 1940, Dodds was much sought after for small traditional groups led by Jimmie Noone, Bunk Johnson, Sidney Bechet, and others. He appeared regularly on radio in 1946–7 and toured Europe with Mezz Mezzrow in 1948. In the final decade of his life he was largely incapacitated by ill health, but he continued playing until 1957.

Dodds was the leading jazz drummer in the New Orleans style, and his equipment and technique became standard. Many younger drummers learned directly from him in Chicago, among them Dave Tough and Gene Krupa, to whom he imparted his secrets of drum accompaniment and tuning. Dodds's basic style derived from the short roll or ruff, played with a drive and precision that set him apart from his contemporaries. By varying his patterns throughout a performance he developed some of the earliest idiomatic accompaniments to improvised jazz ensembles and solos. Late in life he set down his knowledge of jazz drumming in a remarkable series of recorded solos with explanatory commentary, which serve as unique documents of New Orleans drumming style. (For illustration *see* OLIVER, KING.)

RECORDINGS
(selective list)

As leader: Careless Love (1945, BN 518); Drum Improvisation no.1 (1946, Circle 1001); Drum Improvisation no.2 (1946, Circle 1039); *Footnotes to Jazz*, i (1946–51, Folkways 30)

As sideman: King Oliver: I'm going to wear you off my mind (1923, Gennett 5134); J. R. Morton: Billy Goat Stomp (1927, Vic. 20772); L. Armstrong: Wild Man Blues (1927, OK 8474); J. Dodds: Weary City (1928, Vic. 38004); B. Johnson: In Gloryland (1945, American Music 101)

BIBLIOGRAPHY

G. Helliwell and P. Taylor: "Discography of Warren 'Baby' Dodds," *Jazz Journal*, iv (1951), no.3, p.3; no.4, p.19; no.5, p.17

N. Hentoff: "Warren 'Baby' Dodds," *The Jazz Makers*, ed. N. Shapiro and N. Hentoff (New York, 1957/*R*1975), 18

L. Gara: *The Baby Dodds Story* (Los Angeles, 1959)

B. King: "The Gigantic Baby Dodds," *Jazz Review*, iii/7 (1960), 12

G. Wettling: "A Tribute to Baby Dodds," *Down Beat*, xxix/7 (1962), 21

M. Williams: *Jazz Masters of New Orleans* (New York, 1967)

E. Lambert: "William Russell's New Orleans Recordings," *Jazz Monthly*, no.183 (1970), 3

T. D. Brown: *A History and Analysis of Jazz Drumming to 1942* (diss., U. of Michigan, 1976), 204–45

W. J. Schafer: *Brass Bands and New Orleans Jazz* (Baton Rouge, LA, 1977), 75ff

J. BRADFORD ROBINSON

Dodds, Johnny [John M.] (*b* New Orleans, LA, 12 April 1892; *d* Chicago, IL, 8 Aug 1940). Jazz clarinetist. He took up clarinet at the relatively late age of 17, and apart from some lessons from Lorenzo Tio, Jr., he was largely self-taught. Around 1912 he joined Kid Ory's band in New Orleans, where he played intermittently for the next six years. After touring in Fate Marable's riverboat bands (1917) and with a road show, he returned briefly to Ory's group in 1919, then left New Orleans permanently to join King Oliver in Chicago. During his years with Oliver he traveled to the West Coast, and took part in Oliver's historic Creole Jazz Band recordings in Richmond, Indiana, and Chicago (1923). A year later, also in Chicago, he assumed the leadership of Freddie Keppard's house band at Kelly's Stables. He directed this band for six years, during which time he also participated in studio recordings with Louis Armstrong (the Hot Fives and Hot Sevens), with Jelly Roll Morton, and with his brother, the drummer Baby Dodds, in small groups (including the Black Bottom Stompers, the Chicago Footwarmers, the Dixieland Thumpers, the State Street Ramblers, and the Washboard Band). With the decline of the New Orleans style in the 1930s, Dodds continued to lead a band part-time at various locations in Chicago, often in conjunction with his brother.

Dodds was a leading clarinetist in the New Orleans style, which to many he represented in its purest form. Unlike his contemporaries Jimmie Noone and Sidney Bechet, he had an uneven technical command, and his solos were sometimes marred by faulty execution; nevertheless his playing in ensembles was exemplary, as is attested by the several hundred small-band recordings he made with some of the leading jazz musicians of the day. Dodds's best work, played with a highly expressive vibrato centered slightly beneath true pitch, is permeated by a deep feeling for the blues, of which he was an outstanding early interpreter. (For illustration *see* OLIVER, KING.)

RECORDINGS
(selective list)

As leader: After you've Gone (1927, Bruns. 3568); Blue Clarinet Stomp (1928, Vic. 21554); Weary City (1928, Vic. 38004); Bull Fiddle Blues (1928, Vic. 21552)

As sideman: King Oliver: High Society Rag (1923, OK 4933); L. Armstrong: Alligator Crawl (1927, OK 8482), S.O.L. Blues (1927, Col. 35661); J. R. Morton: Wild Man Blues (1927, Bluebird 10256)

BIBLIOGRAPHY

SouthernB

A. Hodeir: *Jazz: its Evolution and Essence* (New York, 1956/*R*1975), 49ff

G. Lambert: *Johnny Dodds* (New York, 1962); repr. in S. Green, ed.: *Kings of Jazz* (New York, 1978)

M. Williams: *Jazz Masters of New Orleans* (New York, 1967), 87ff

G. Schuller: *Early Jazz: its Roots and Musical Development* (New York, 1968)

J. F. Riesco: *El jazz classico y Johnny Dodds su rey sin corona* (Santiago, Chile, 1972), 193–273

D. M. Bakker: "Johnny Dodds, 1923–1940," *Micrography*, no.44 (1977), 7 [discography]

H. Lyttelton: *The Best of Jazz: Basin Street to Harlem* (London, 1978)

J. BRADFORD ROBINSON

Dodds & Claus. Firm of piano makers, active in New York from 1791 to 1793. The brief partnership of Thomas Dodds (*b* England; *d* ?New York, *c*1799) and Christian Claus (*b* ?Stuttgart, Germany; *d* New York, after 1799) was among the first to establish the piano industry in New York.

Dodds arrived in New York from London in 1785. In an advertisement in the *Independent Journal* of 13 August 1785, he offered to sell, repair, and tune string, wind, and keyboard instruments at his house on Queen Street, and cited his experience as an organ, harpsichord, and piano maker for "upwards of twenty years." He was granted American citizenship in 1788. In 1789 he sold a piano to George Washington for his stepdaughter's lessons. He was also active as a mahogany merchant from 1789 to 1793. In 1783 Claus had received a patent in London for a key mechanism applied to the English guitar. In New York he continued to build English guitars and repair violins; he is listed in city directories from 1789 to 1799.

A square piano by Dodds & Claus at the Metropolitan Museum, New York, bears the signature of Archibald Whaites; presumably an apprentice to their firm, he later became an important piano builder in his own right. This instrument resembles John Broadwood's contemporary square pianos, but it is of inferior workmanship. An English guitar by Claus is also in the Metropolitan Museum.

BIBLIOGRAPHY

N. Groce: *Musical Instrument Making in New York City during the Eighteenth and Nineteenth Centuries* (diss., U. of Michigan, 1982)

L. Libin: *American Musical Instruments in the Metropolitan Museum of Art* (New York, 1985)

LAURENCE LIBIN

Dodge, Charles (Malcolm) (*b* Ames, IA, 5 June 1942). Composer. He studied composition at the University of Iowa (BA 1964) and Columbia University (MA 1966, DMA 1970), where his principal teachers were Hervig, Chou Wen-chung, and Luening; he also studied computer music at Princeton University with Godfrey Winham (1969–70). After teaching at Columbia (1970–77), he joined the faculty at Brooklyn College, CUNY (1977), where he directs the Center for Computer Music. He has done research in acoustics and computer music at the Bell Telephone Laboratories (1971–7), the University of California, San Diego (1974), and the Massachusetts Institute of Technology (1979). His numerous awards and honors include the Bearns Prize (1964, 1967), an American Academy of Arts and Letters Award (1975), Guggenheim Fellowships (1972, 1975), and NEA grants (1974, 1975, 1979). Among his commissions are those from the Fromm Foundation, the Koussevitzky Foundation, Nonesuch Records, the Arts Council of Great Britain, and Swedish National Radio. He has been president (1971–5) and chairman of the board of directors (1975–80) of the ACA and president (1979–82) of the American Music Center, has held offices in numerous other professional organizations, including the American Composers Orchestra, CRI, and the American section of the ISCM, and has served on the editorial board of *Perspectives of New Music* (1973–7).

Dodge has been active as a composer of computer music since the mid-1960s and has sought to extend the compositional technique and expressive range of this medium. *Earth's Magnetic Field* is a musical rendition of the effect of solar radiation on the magnetic field surrounding the earth. *Speech Songs* was his first work for synthesized voice; using sophisticated computer techniques he created a variety of vocal sounds which lend humor and irony to the text (by Mark Strand). In *Cascando*, a setting of the radio play by Samuel Beckett, the voice of a live performer, the Opener, "controls" two computer-synthesized audio channels, Voice and Music. Voice attempts to tell a story that will satisfy the Opener and allow Voice to remain silent, while Music represents a nonverbal response to the same situation. Dodge's works from the early 1980s focus on the confrontation between new, often dehumanizing technology and the musical expression of human thought and feeling: in *Any Resemblance is Purely Coincidental*, an operatic voice (originally that of Caruso) searches in vain among various computer sounds for a fitting accompaniment. In 1985 Dodge published *Computer Music: Synthesis, Composition, and Performance* (with T. A. Jerse).

WORKS

Composition in Five Parts, vc, pf, 1964; Washington, DC, 10 May 1964
Solos and Combinations, fl, ob, cl, 1964; Bennington, VT, 23 Aug 1964
Folia, fl, eng hn, b cl, tuba, vn, va, pf, 2 perc, 1965; Lenox, MA, 8 Aug 1965
Rota, orch, 1966; Iowa City, IA, 10 Nov 1966
Changes, cptr, 1969–70; Washington, DC, Oct 1970
Earth's Magnetic Field, cptr, 1970; first recorded, 1970
Speech Songs (M. Strand), cptr-synthesized vv, 1972; New York, 8 Dec 1972
Extensions, tpt, tape, 1973; New York, 5 May 1973
The Story of our Lives (Strand), cptr-synthesized vv, 1974
In Celebration (Strand), cptr-synthesized vv, 1975; New York, 15 Oct 1975
Palinode, orch, tape, 1976; New York, 7 Feb 1977
Cascando (radio drama, S. Beckett), actor, tape, 1978; Chicago, 2 Nov 1978
Any Resemblance is Purely Coincidental, pf, tape, 1980; Colorado Springs, CO, 3 April 1980
Han motte henne i parken (radio drama, R. Kostelanetz, trans. S. Hanson), cptr-synthesized vv, 1981; Venice, Italy, 1 Oct 1982
Distribution, Redistribution, cl, vn, pf, 1982; Brunswick, ME, 31 July 1982
He Met her in the Park (Kostelanetz), cptr-synthesized vv, 1983; Warsaw, Poland, 15 Sept 1983
The Waves (V. Woolf), female v, tape, 1984; Boston, 3 March 1984

Principal publishers: ACA, Cape North Alliance

BIBLIOGRAPHY

T. Johnson: "New Music," *HiFi/MusAm*, xxv/10 (1975), 10

P. Griffiths: *A Guide to Electronic Music* (London, 1979), 40, 49, 50, 52, 100

C. Gagne and T. Caras: "Charles Dodge," *Soundpieces: Interviews with American Composers* (Metuchen, NJ, 1982), 141

B. Schrader: *Introduction to Electro-Acoustic Music* (Englewood Cliffs, NJ, 1982), 156

JEROME ROSEN

Dodworth. Family of musicians and composers, prominent in the development of bands and band music in the 19th century. Thomas Dodworth (*b* Sheffield, England, 1790; *d* New York, 1876) arrived in New York in June 1828 with his eldest son, Allen T. Dodworth (*b* Sheffield, 9 Dec 1817; *d* Pasadena, CA, 12 Feb 1896); two other sons, Harvey B. Dodworth (*b* Sheffield, 16 Nov 1822; *d* West Hoboken, NJ, 24 Jan 1891) and Charles R. Dodworth (*b* Scotland, 1826; *d* Philadelphia, PA, 9 May 1894), arrived shortly afterwards. A fourth son, Thomas J. Dodworth (*b* New York, 13 Dec 1830; *d* New York, 7 May 1896), was the only one to be born in the USA.

Thomas Dodworth, Sr., played trombone and Allen was a gifted piccolo player; on their arrival, both men joined the Independent Band of New York, with which Allen appeared frequently as a soloist. The band changed its instrumentation in 1834 (becoming one of the first all-brass bands in the USA) and took the new name of City Band of New York. This organization broke up shortly after, and about half the members formed a new group, the National Brass Band, under Allen Dodworth.

In 1836 this became the Dodworth Band, and it quickly established a national reputation for excellent standards of performance. Harvey took over the leadership of the band in the late 1830s, relinquishing it in 1890 to his son Olean Dodworth (*b* 1843; *d* New York, 13 April 1916); he also developed the Dodworth Music Store and Publishing Co. Thomas J. Dodworth, who played the alto horn and cornet, joined the band in the early 1850s and remained with it until his death, though he also played in theater orchestras in New York. Charles, playing the flute and piccolo, was a member only until the late 1850s, when he moved to Philadelphia and took up a separate career as a performer and teacher. Allen continued to play with the band into the 1850s, but he became increasingly active as a dancing teacher and eventually devoted all his time to his studio, which became a center for the learning of the latest ballroom dances. He also wrote a series of articles called "The Formation of Bands" for the music journal *Message Bird* (1849), a brass band method – *Dodworth's Brass Band School* (1853/*R*1978) – eight booklets of instructions for various dances, and *Dancing and its Relation to Education and Social Life* (1885).

The Dodworth Band was usually under contract to a particular military regiment; at various times it performed for the 7th, 8th, 9th, 12th, 13th, 22nd, 55th, and 71st National Guard regiments of New York. Its longest attachment was to the 71st, and both Harvey and the younger Thomas served with this regiment during the Civil War. After the war, Harvey organized the first public concerts to be held in Central Park, for which he added to the band two helicons, a saxophone, and a bass clarinet. By the late 1870s the great era of the Dodworth Band was over, but its influence was still strongly felt. Patrick Gilmore wrote: "brass instruments were never played with greater delicacy or refinement than by the Dodworth organization . . . to be a member of this organization or to be graduated from it was to be looked upon as a star in the profession."

Many changes and innovations in the manufacture of brass instruments were brought about by the Dodworths or as a result of their influence. As early as 1838 they began to use valved instruments constructed so that the bell was directed over the player's shoulder (a shape designed for military use, to throw the sound back to the troops marching behind the band). These instruments also had a mellower tone, allowing a more sensitive style of concert performance, which was especially suited to accompanying vocal soloists. Most bands followed the lead of the Dodworth Band, and "over-the-shoulder" instruments remained popular until after the Civil War. Thomas, Sr., and Allen also developed the "ebor corno," a valved brass instrument with a range encompassing the alto and tenor registers to give a strong and homogeneous sound in the middle range.

Besides their activities as band musicians the Dodworths were influential figures in New York's musical life. They were among the founding members of the New York Philharmonic Symphony Society in April 1842; Allen was elected treasurer, and when the orchestra gave its first concert in December 1842 the personnel included Thomas (trombone), Allen and Harvey (violins), and Charles (piccolo). The family was also involved in the formation of the Musical Fund Society of New York. Several copies of sheet music by Allen, Harvey, and Charles are in special collections at the New York Public Library, the New-York Historical Society, and the Library of Congress.

DODWORTH'S
MUSICAL
FESTIVAL!!
AT
METROPOLITAN HALL,
LATE TRIPLER
On Friday Evening, February 20th, 1852,
On which occasion, in addition to their Superb Band of
50 PERFORMERS
They will be assisted by the following Eminent Artists,
Mrs. Laura A. Jones,
Mr. Henry Squires,
The American Tenor
Mr. George F. Bristow,
who will preside at the Piano Forte
Herr Kiefer,
Master Thomas,
Mr. Sedgwick,
Mr. Allen Dodworth.
Director, ... Harvey B. Dodworth.

PROGRAMME.

PART I.
1. Grand Military Overture by .... Felix Mendelsohn Bartholdy. First time in America. Dodworth's Full Band.
2. "Nay do not Weep" Poetry by J. H. Wainwright – Music from the Opera of "Rip Van Winkle." Mr. Squires .... G. F. Bristow
3. "Ernani Involami."—Cornetina Solo. Mr. Allen Dodworth .... Verdi
4. "We met by Chance" Mr. L. A Jones .... Kosken
5. Corno Bassetto Solo. Herr Kiefer .... Kiefer
6 Solo Concertina Mr. Sedgwick.
7. "The Bandit Quickstep." From Ernani .... Verdi. Arranged for the Cornet Band by D L Downing

PART II.
1. Grand Polka. "Bonnet du Concert." Full Band. Composed expressly for this occasion by .... Thomas Coates
2. "The Star of Love."—Cornet Band accompaniment. Mr. H Squires .... W. V. Wallace
3 Violin Solo—Theme & Variations from Otello. Mast. Thomas .. W. Ernst
4. "Giorno d'Orrore"—Duet from Semiramide .... Rossini. A. & H. B. Dodworth. Cornet Band accompaniment.
5 "The Dawn is breaking o'er us"—Cornet Obligato .... G. F. Bristow Mrs L. A. Jones.
6 "Trio from Norma" Messrs. Allen H B & C. R Dodworth —— Bellini
7. Urielle Quickstep H B Dodworth

Doors open at 7 o'clock, Concert to commence at 8 o'clock.
TICKETS....... 50 CENTS,
To be had at all the principal Music Stores, at No 483 Broadway, and at the door on the Evening of the Concert.

Playbill for Dodworth's Musical Festival at Metropolitan Hall, New York, 20 February 1852, with Harvey B. Dodworth as director and Allen Dodworth and the young Theodore Thomas among the soloists: from Thomas's "A Musical Autobiography" (Chicago, 1905)

See also BANDS, §3.

BIBLIOGRAPHY

P. S. Gilmore: "American Military Bands," *Music Trade Review*, viii/7 (1879), 6

"Band Music then and now: Reminiscences of the Veteran Leader, Harvey B. Dodworth," *American Art Journal*, xxxiii (1880), 177

Obituaries of Harvey B. Dodworth: *American Art Journal*, lvi (1890–91), 241; *New York Times* (25 Jan 1891)

H. Krehbiel: *The Philharmonic Society of New York: a Memorial* (New York, 1892/*R*1979)

Obituaries of Allen T. Dodworth: *Musical Age*, xiii/2 (1896), 8; *New York Times* (14 Feb 1896)

Obituary of Thomas J. Dodworth: *New York Times* (9 May 1896)

R. O'Neill: "The Dodworth Family and Ballroom Dancing in New York," *Dance Index*, ii (1943), 44; repr. in *Chronicles of the American Dance*, ed. P. Magriel (New York, 1948)

R. E. Eliason: *Brass Instrument Key and Valve Mechanisms made in America before 1875 with Special Emphasis to the D. S. Pillsbury Collection in Greenfield Village, Dearborn, Michigan* (diss., U. of Missouri, 1968)

FRANK J. CIPOLLA

Dohnányi, Christoph von (*b* Berlin, Germany, 8 Sept 1929). German conductor. He attended the Musikhochschule in Munich (1948–51) and came to the USA in 1952 to study with his grandfather, the composer Ernő Dohnányi; he also studied conducting at the Berkshire Music Center with Bernstein. His extensive European career, which included the directorships of the Frankfurt Opera (1968–75) and the Hamburg Staatsoper (1975–), has been augmented by numerous engagements in the USA. He made his American operatic début leading *Der fliegende Holländer* with the Lyric Opera of Chicago in October 1969; his Metropolitan Opera début was with *Falstaff* in 1972. He has also conducted the San Francisco Opera and the orchestras of Chicago, New York, Cleveland, Pittsburgh, and Detroit. His appointment as music director of the Cleveland Orchestra from 1984 was announced in 1982. Dohnányi can be considered one of the most successful German conductors in the post-1945 period, as much for his technical ability as for his qualities of orchestral leadership and the expressive, spontaneous personality often reflected in his performances. He is more successful in works requiring intricate conducting technique than in those calling for a purely musical approach; he has been responsible for widely praised productions of Schoenberg's *Moses und Aron* at Frankfurt and Vienna. A champion of the works of Henze, he conducted the premières of *Der junge Lord* (Berlin, 1965) and *Die Bassariden* (Salzburg Festival, 1966).

BIBLIOGRAPHY

P. Gorner: "D is for . . . Dohnanyi," *Opera News*, xxxv/4 (1970), 24

J. Badal: "Cleveland's Christoph von Dohnanyi," *Symphony Magazine*, xxxv/3 (1984), 49

HANSPETER KRELLMANN/R

Doktor, Paul (*b* Vienna, Austria, 28 March 1919). Violist. He studied the violin with his father, Karl Doktor, violist in the Busch Quartet, and graduated from the Vienna Academy of Music in 1938. He changed to the viola and in 1942 won the Geneva International Music Competition. His début (1938–9) was with the Busch Quartet in quintets in Zurich and London. Doktor left Vienna in 1938 and from 1939 to 1947 was a soloist with the Lucerne SO. His American début, at the Library of Congress in 1948, was followed by tours of the USA, Canada, and Europe. He became an American citizen in 1952. He joined the staff of Mannes College in 1953, the Philadelphia Academy in 1970, and the Juilliard School in 1971. From 1972 to 1975 he was a member of the New String Trio of New York.

Doktor's tone is warm and sweet, though light; he possesses a virtuoso technique and his large repertory is extended by his own transcriptions. He gave first performances of concertos by Quincy Porter and Walter Piston. He is a founder-member of the Rococo Ensemble, the New York String Sextet, and the Paul Doktor String Trio. His 17th-century viola is attributed to Pietro Guarneri of Mantua.

WATSON FORBES/R

Dolge, Alfred (*b* Leipzig, Germany, 22 Dec 1848; *d* Milan, Italy, 5 Jan 1922). Manufacturer of piano felts and soundboards, and dealer in piano supplies. He began his career as an apprentice in the piano factory of A. Dolge & Co. in Leipzig, and immigrated to the USA in 1866. From 1867 to 1869 he worked in New Haven in the shop of Frederick Mathushek (who had worked with Henri Pape in Paris). He then became an importer of piano supplies (skins for piano hammers and Poehlmann's music wire), and by 1871, in Brooklyn, he was manufacturing hammer felts, which in 1873 won a first prize at the Vienna Exhibition. The demand for felts of a high quality led him to establish, in 1874, a larger manufacturing concern in the Adirondack village of Brockett's Bridge, New York (renamed Dolgeville in 1887). The availability of ample water power and of timber for the making of soundboards enabled him to transform the town into a busy industrial community; the Zimmermann autoharp was later manufactured there. Dolge's felts and soundboards were used by most leading piano makers. Throughout his career he maintained a large piano supply business at 122 East 13th Street, New York.

After attempting to build a railway connection for the transport of his products, Dolge suffered financial disaster in 1898 and left Dolgeville for southern California, where he was first an orange rancher and wine producer, and later a felt maker at the Alfred Dolge Felt Co., in Dolgeville, California. His book *Pianos and their Makers* gives valuable information about early 20th-century developments in American piano making, including descriptions of his own improvements in the quality of felt, and in the machines used to apply the felt to hammers.

BIBLIOGRAPHY

D. Spillane: *History of the American Pianoforte* (New York, 1890/*R*1969), 316ff

A. Dolge: *Pianos and their Makers*, i (Covina, CA, 1911/*R*1972); ii (Covina, 1913)

J. C. Freund: "An Inspiring Memorial Tribute to Alfred Dolge," *Music Trades*, lxiii (11 Feb 1922), 15

CYNTHIA ADAMS HOOVER

Dolmetsch, (Eugène) Arnold (*b* Le Mans, France, 24 Feb 1858; *d* Haslemere, England, 28 Feb 1940). English instrument maker and pioneer in the revival of performances of early music on original instruments. Having learned piano- and organ-making in his youth from his father and maternal grandfather, he began to acquire and restore early instruments in 1889. He made his first lute in 1893, his first clavichord in 1894. Throughout the 1890s he gave concerts on period instruments in his home in England. His first American concert tour was in January and February, 1903; the performances, which were concentrated in and around New York and Boston, were greeted with enthusiasm. He returned to the USA in 1904 for an extended tour, playing in Baltimore, Pittsburgh, Indianapolis, Ann Arbor, and Chicago, on the West Coast, and in the Northeast. He also provided music for a Shakespeare festival, in collaboration with the Shakespearean actor and manager Ben Greet. The planned seven-week tour was extended several times, and the enthusiasm displayed by American audiences, much greater than that of the British, convinced Dolmetsch to stay in the USA. He settled his family in Chicago briefly, then in 1905 moved to Boston after signing a contract with Chickering & Sons to establish and run a department for the manufacture of early instruments. Working under what he termed "ideal conditions," Dolmetsch produced over 80 instruments for Chickering, including viols, lutes, virginals, harpsichords, clavichords, and his own type of piano. Some of his finest instruments date from this period, including a harpsichord for Busoni. While at Chickering he also made occasional East Coast concert tours. In 1910 a trade recession forced Chickering to close its early-instrument department, and Dolmetsch left the USA for Paris, bringing to a close his American career. He returned to England in 1914, moving to Haslemere in 1917, where he perfected the first modern recorders made to Baroque specifications and created an early-music center. In 1929 the Dolmetsch Foundation was established to further the study and performance of music according to Dolmetsch's principles: it provides apprenticeships and scholarships to students of all nationalities and produces an annual journal devoted to its aims, the *Consort* (first published in 1929, sporadically until 1948, and continuously from that date).

Dolmetsch's great gift was that, in a period when early music was virtually ignored except for academic study, he had both the imagination and the musicianship to take a musical work which had become a museum piece and make it speak to the people of his own time in a language intelligible to them. He wrote the book *The Interpretation of the Music of the XVII and XVIII Centuries* (London, 1915, 2/1946/*R*1969).

For illustration *see* EARLY-MUSIC REVIVAL, fig. 1.

BIBLIOGRAPHY

R. Donington: *The Work and Ideas of Arnold Dolmetsch* (Haslemere, 1932)

P. Grainger: "Arnold Dolmetsch: Musical Confucius," *MQ*, xix (1933), 187

Obituaries: *The Times* [of London] (1 March 1940) [funeral report, 4 March]; *MT*, lxxxi (1940), 137

W. McNaught: "Arnold Dolmetsch and his Work," *MT*, lxxxi (1940), 153

M. Dolmetsch: *Personal Recollections of Arnold Dolmetsch* (London, 1958)

S. Bloch: "Saga of a Twentieth-Century Lute Pioneer," *Journal of the Lute Society of America*, ii (1969), 37

M. Campbell: *Dolmetsch: the Man and his Work* (London, 1975)

MARGARET CAMPBELL/KATHERINE K. PRESTON

Dolphy, Eric (Allan) (*b* Los Angeles, CA, 20 June 1928; *d* Berlin, Germany, 29 June 1964). Jazz alto saxophonist, bass clarinetist, and flutist. He began playing clarinet at about the age of six, and while in junior high school played alto saxophone professionally at dances. After studying music at Los Angeles City College he played lead alto saxophone in the Roy Porter band (1948–50). He then served in the US Army for two years, after which he transferred to the US Naval School of Music (1952). He returned to Los Angeles the following year and played locally in various groups before joining Chico Hamilton's quintet early in 1958. Late in 1959 he settled in New York, where he joined Charles Mingus's group. During his time with Mingus (1959–60) he played freelance a great deal and recorded his first albums as a leader, but thereafter he ceased to work steadily, even as his fame grew. In mid-1961 he co-led a quintet with the trumpeter Booker Little. He played in Europe in August to September of that year, and again in November to December during a brief spell with John Coltrane (to March 1962). In March 1962 he formed a short-lived group which made few public appearances, and in November he joined John Lewis's Orchestra USA. He spent the rest of his short career working freelance with Mingus, Lewis, and Coltrane. He died after a heart attack occasioned by diabetes.

Dolphy was a highly versatile musician, playing jazz but also performing third stream music by Gunther Schuller and pieces such as Varèse's *Density 21.5* at the Ojai Festival in 1962. This close link to 20th-century art music influenced his fondness for dissonant harmonies in jazz. His startling intonation, especially on alto saxophone, reflected the acknowledged influence of Ornette Coleman, as well as Dolphy's love of African and Indian music; he also imitated bird calls. As a jazz improviser Dolphy was unrivaled in his ability to leap fluently between traditional and avant-garde idioms. His lyrical interpretation on flute of *You Don't Know What Love Is* (1964) epitomizes the conventional side of his art, while his radicalism is most apparent in his bass clarinet improvisations on Coleman's revolutionary *Free Jazz* album (1960) and his bass clarinet or alto saxophone "conversations" with Mingus on *What Love* (1960) and *Epitaph* (1962). An intense, passionate improviser, Dolphy constantly surprised his listeners with his rapid flow of ideas and his unexpected phrasing and intervals. Perhaps his greatest contribution was his exploration of the bass clarinet as a medium for jazz improvisation.

RECORDINGS

(selective list)

As leader: *Outward Bound* (1960, New Jazz 8236); *Live! at the Five Spot*, i (1961, New Jazz 8260), ii (1961, Prst. 7294); *The Eric Dolphy Memorial Album* (1961, Prst. 7334); *Eric Dolphy in Europe*, i (1961, Prst. 7304); *Conversations* (1963, FM 308); *Iron Man* (1963, Douglas 785); *Out to Lunch* (1964, BN 84163); *Last Date* (1964, Limelight 86013), incl. You Don't Know What Love Is

As sideman: C. Hamilton: *Gongs East* (1958, WB 1271); C. Mingus: *Presents Charles Mingus* (1960, Candid 8005), incl. What Love; *Mingus!* (1960, Candid 8021); G. Schuller: *Jazz Abstractions* (1960, Atl. 1365); O. Coleman: *Free Jazz* (1960, Atl. 1364); Spiritual, on J. Coltrane: *Live at the Village Vanguard* (1961, Imp. 10); India, on J. Coltrane: *Impressions* (1961, Imp. 42); C. Mingus: *Town Hall Concert* (1962, UA 15024), incl. Epitaph; *The Great Concert of Charles Mingus* (1964, America 003–5)

BIBLIOGRAPHY

V. Simosko and B. Tepperman: *Eric Dolphy: a Musical Biography and Discography* (Washington, DC, 1974/*R*1979)

R. Jannotta: "God Bless the Child: an Analysis of an Unaccompanied Bass Clarinet Solo," *Jazzforschung*, ix (1977), 37

A. White: *Dolphy Series Limited* (Washington, DC, n.d.) [transcriptions]

BARRY KERNFELD

Domingo, Placido (*b* Madrid, Spain, 21 Jan 1941). Spanish tenor. The son of two well-known zarzuela artists, Pepita Embil and Placido Domingo, he was taken by his parents to Mexico in 1950, where he studied piano and singing, and later observed a number of Igor Markevich's classes in conducting at the National Conservatory in Mexico City. Domingo made his début in 1957 as a baritone in the zarzuela *Gigantes y cabezudos* and continued to perform this repertory, often with his parents, during the next five years. In 1959 he was accepted by the Mexico National Opera as a tenor and, having made the vocal transition with the help of the respected singing teacher Carlo Morelli, sang his first major tenor role (Alfredo in *La traviata*) in Monterrey, Mexico, in May 1961. On 16 November of the same year he made his American début as Arturo in a production of *Lucia di Lammermoor* with Joan Sutherland at the Dallas Civic Opera, and a year later took the leading male role, Edgardo, in the same opera at Forth Worth, opposite Lily Pons. From 1962 to 1965 he was a member of the Israeli National Opera, where he sang some 300 performances of 12 operas, most of them in Hebrew.

Domingo made his New York début at the City Opera on 17 October 1965 in *Madama Butterfly*, covering for an indisposed Pinkerton. He sang Don José there four days later, and in the following February the title role in the North American première of Alberto Ginastera's *Don Rodrigo*. His long association with the Metropolitan Opera began in 1966 with a concert performance of *Cavalleria rusticana* at the Lewisohn Stadium (9 August). His first stage appearance with the company was as Maurizio in Francesco Cilea's *Adriana Lecouvreur* (28 September 1968), and his débuts at other leading houses have included Ernani (La Scala, 1969), Rodolfo (San Francisco, 1969), and Cavaradossi (Covent Garden, 1971). He scored great successes as Vasco da Gama in a revival of Meyerbeer's *L'africaine* at San Francisco in 1972, as Arrigo in Verdi's *Les vêpres siciliennes* in a production (in Italian) done at the Paris Opéra and at the Metropolitan in 1974, and as Othello in Hamburg and Paris (respectively 1975 and 1976). One of the busiest artists in the world, Domingo sang at the

Metropolitan in a single month (March 1982) the leading tenor roles in *Norma*, *Les contes d'Hoffmann*, and *La bohème*, as well as a joint recital with the mezzo-soprano Tatiana Troyanos. In the company's 1982–3 season he added to his repertory the roles of Paolo in Riccardo Zandonai's *Francesca da Rimini*, Aeneas in Berlioz's *Les troyens*, and Lohengrin.

Domingo's voice, though not highly individual, is always used with intelligence, musicianship, and taste, and his warm and outgoing stage personality, together with his vocal gifts, makes him one of the leading lyric-dramatic tenors since Jussi Björling. He intends to devote himself to conducting once he retires from the stage, having made his début in this capacity in New York, at the City Opera on 7 October 1973 (*La traviata*) and his Metropolitan Opera début in *La bohème* during the 1984–5 season. He has appeared in numerous television broadcasts of complete operas and his list of recordings is extensive, including a notable Othello and Rodolfo (in Verdi's *Luisa Miller*). In 1984 he appeared as Don José in a film version of *Carmen*.

BIBLIOGRAPHY

H. Rosenthal: "Placido Domingo," *Opera*, xxiii (1972), 18
G. Walker: " 'You're Singing too much'/'The more I Sing, the better I Sound,' " *New York Times Magazine* (27 Feb 1972), 18
"Domingo, Placido," *CBY 1972*
S. Jenkins: "¿Placido?," *Opera News*, xxxvii/19 (1973), 14
S. von Buchau: "Bel sogno," *Opera News*, xli/20 (1977), 25
R. Jacobson: "What Makes Placido Run," *Opera News*, xlvi/16 (1982), 10
A. Swan and A. Kuflik: "Bravissimo, Domingo!," *Newsweek*, xcix (8 March 1982), 56
P. Domingo: *My First Forty Years* (New York, 1983)
B. Holland: "The Well-Tempered Tenor," *New York Times Magazine* (30 Jan 1983), 28
D. Snowman: *The World of Placido Domingo* (New York, 1985)

HAROLD ROSENTHAL/R

Domino, Fats [Antoine] (*b* New Orleans, LA, 26 Feb 1928). Rock-and-roll singer and pianist. He studied the piano from the age of nine, and in his early teens developed a boogie-woogie technique derived from the playing styles of Kid Stormy Weather, Sullivan Rock, and Drive 'em Down (Willie Hall). His pleasant, nasal singing style was influenced by the singer and guitarist Smiley Lewis (Amos Overton Lemmon). By the time he was 21 Domino was house pianist at the Hideaway Club, where he was heard by the trumpeter and bandleader Dave Bartholomew; together they recorded *The Fat Man* (1950), a rhythm-and-blues hit that launched Domino's career. Domino's soft, understated singing was a perfect contrast to the powerful saxophone riffs of Bartholomew's band, whose rambling sound – midway, stylistically, between rhythm-and-blues and rock-and-roll – attracted both black and white listeners. In 1955 Domino's single *Ain't That a Shame* reached no.10 on the pop charts, which was highly unusual for a rhythm-and-blues song at that time. It was followed by a series of hits, a mixture of new tunes and retailored pop standards, including *I'm in Love Again*, *My Blue Heaven*, *When my Dreamboat Comes Home*, *Blueberry Hill*, and *Blue Monday* (all 1956). These placed Domino alongside Elvis Presley, Chuck Berry, Little Richard, and Jerry Lee Lewis as one of the founders of rock-and-roll, although he had none of their sexual or anti-authoritarian allure.

Fats Domino, c1956

Domino continued to write and record hit songs until the early 1960s, and for a brief period he and Bartholomew were the most successful songwriting team in pop history. But by 1964 their music had lost much of its original character and their audience had dwindled. After working for a time at gambling casinos in Las Vegas and Reno, Domino began recording again in 1968 with the Beatles' song *Lady Madonna* and an album, *Fats is Back*, produced in the big-band rock fashion of the period. These did not sell well enough to merit further recording, however, and Domino entered semiretirement in New Orleans. He resumed an active career in the late 1970s and early 1980s when he made several tours of Europe.

RECORDINGS

(selective list)

The Fat Man (1950, Imper. 5058); Ain't That a Shame (1955, Imper. 5348); I'm in Love Again/My Blue Heaven (1956, Imper. 5386); When my Dreamboat Comes Home (1956, Imper. 5396); Blueberry Hill (1956, Imper. 5407); Blue Monday (1956, Imper. 5417); *This is Fats* (1957, Imper. 12391); *Fats is Back* (1968, Rep. 6304); *Fats Domino: Legendary Masters* (1971, UA 9958); *Live in Europe* (1977, UA 30121)

BIBLIOGRAPHY

J. Broven: *Walking to New Orleans: the Story of New Orleans Rhythm and Blues* (Bexhill-on-Sea, England, 1974)
P. Guralnick: "Fats Domino," *The Rolling Stone Illustrated History of Rock and Roll*, ed. J. Miller (New York, 2/1980)

LANGDON WINNER

Donaldson, Walter (*b* Brooklyn, NY, 15 Feb 1893; *d* Santa Monica, CA, 15 July 1947). Songwriter, lyricist, and publisher. He was a pianist and song plugger in Tin Pan Alley before World War I and then became a staff composer for Irving Berlin's publishing company. His best-known songs include *My Mammy* (1918), *My Buddy* (1922), *Carolina in the Morning* (1922), *Yes, sir, that's my baby* (1925), *My Blue Heaven* (1927), *Makin' Whoopee* (1928), and *Little White Lies* (1930). In 1928 he helped found the music publishing company Donaldson, Douglas, and Gumble, and from 1929 he wrote for film musicals in Hollywood. Donaldson's melodies are characterized by repeated motifs and inventive harmonies and rhythms. Many of his tunes have been favorite material for jazz musicians.

BIBLIOGRAPHY

A. Wilder: *American Popular Song* (New York, 1972)

DEANE L. ROOT

Donath, Helen (*b* Corpus Christi, TX, 10 July 1940). Soprano. Educated at Del Mar College in Corpus Christi, she made her début in 1962 as Inez (*Il trovatore*) at Cologne, where she was a member of the opera studio, and performed with the Hanover Opera from 1963 to 1967. She sang Pamina at the 1970 Salzburg Festival and made her American début a year later with the San Francisco Opera as Sophie, a role she also sang at her Chicago début three years later. As Anne Trulove in *The Rake's Progress* she made her Covent Garden début in 1979, and has sung such roles as Susanna, Ilia (*Idomeneo*), Zerlina, Marzelline (*Fidelio*), Ännchen (*Der Freischütz*), Oscar, Micaela, Mélisande, Mimì, Liù (*Turandot*), and Martinů's Julietta in many of the leading European houses. A most sensitive singer, she has moved from soubrette to lyric roles without losing the inherent purity of her voice.

ELIZABETH FORBES

Donato, Anthony (*b* Prague, NE, 8 March 1909). Composer and violinist. At the Eastman School he studied composition with Rogers and Hanson, conducting with Goossens, and violin with Tinlot (BM 1931, MM 1937, PhD 1947). As a violinist he was a member of the Rochester PO (1927–31) and of the Hochstein Quartet (1929–31); he also made appearances as a soloist with various chamber music ensembles, and organized his own quartet for radio broadcasting. He was head of the violin departments of Drake University (1931–7), Iowa State Teachers College (Northern Iowa University, 1937–9), and the University of Texas (1939–46). From 1947 he taught composition and conducting at Northwestern University, becoming professor emeritus in 1976. He has received a Fulbright award to lecture on contemporary American music in England and Scotland (1951–2) and a number of commissions, including one from the Cincinnati SO for *Solitude in the City* (1954) and one from the Chicago Little SO for *Serenade* (1962). Donato shows dexterity in a variety of media, and his style combines practicality with a marked sensitivity to timbre. He is best known for his skillfully didactic piano pieces and choral works. His textbook, *Preparing Music Manuscript* (1963), is a vital contribution to the teaching of notational techniques.

WORKS

Opera: The Walker through Walls (after M. Aymé), 1964

Choral: March of the Hungry Mountains (Sandburg), T, SATB, small orch, 1949; The Sycophantic Fox and the Gullible Raven (R. W. Carryl), SATB/TTBB, pf, 1950; Last Supper (Bible), Bar, SSATBB, 1952; Thou Art my God (Ps. lxiii), S, SSA, pf, 1953; The Congo (V. Lindsay), S, SATB, large orch, 1957; Prelude and Choral Fantasy (Pss. xv, lxi, cl), TTBB, 2 tpt, 2 trbn, perc, org, 1961; Blessed is the Man (Ps. lxxxiv), SATB, brass qt, org, 1970; many other works

Orch: 2 sinfoniettas, 1936, 1959; Elegy, str, 1938; 2 syms., 1944, 1945; Mission San José de Aguaya, 1945; Prairie Schooner, ov., 1947; Suite, str, 1948; The Plains, 1953; Episode, 1954; Solitude in the City (after J. G. Fletcher), nar, orch, 1954; Serenade, small orch, 1962; Centennial Ode, 1967; Improvisation, 1968; Discourse, fl, str/pf, 1969; 4 other works

Inst: 2 vn sonatas, 1938, 1949; 4 str qts, 1941, 1947, 1951, 1975; Drag and Run, cl, 2 vn, vc, 1946; Precipitations, 1946; 2 Pastels, org, 1948; Sonatine, 3 tpt, 1949; Hn Sonata, 1950; Wind Qnt, 1955; Prelude and Allegro, tpt, pf, 1957; Pf Trio, 1959; Cl Sonata, 1966; Discourse II, sax, pf, 1974; many other works

Pf: African Dominoes, 1948; Recreations, 1948; 3 Preludes, 1948; Sonata, 1951; over 20 teaching pieces, 1948–50

Other: many songs, incl. 3 Romantic Songs (J. H. L. Hunt), 1954, 3 Poems from Shelley, T, str qt, 1971; 4 band works

Principal publishers: Boosey & Hawkes, Boston, E. B. Marks, Remick, Southern

BIBLIOGRAPHY

EwenD

DAVID COPE

Donner, Dave. Pseudonym of STUART HAMBLEN.

Donovan, Richard Frank (*b* New Haven, CT, 29 Nov 1891; *d* Middletown, CT, 22 Aug 1970). Composer, organist, and teacher. He studied at Yale University, at the Institute of Musical Art, New York (BMus 1922), and with Charles-Marie Widor in Paris. In 1923 he joined the faculty of Smith College; he was later appointed instructor (1928) and then Battell Professor of theory (1947) at Yale, remaining there until 1960. From 1936 to 1951 he was conductor of the New Haven SO. After an early post-impressionist phase Donovan's compositional style developed to a lucid polyphony, despite closely woven textures, with frequent use of modal themes, sometimes of folktunes. After 1950 his music became more astringent and chromatic, verging towards atonality but still characterized by dense polyphony and strong asymmetrical rhythms. His *Design for Radio* won the BMI Publication Award and his organ works have been often performed.

WORKS

Orch: Wood-notes, fl, str, harp, 1924–5; Smoke and Steel, sym. poem after Sandburg, 1932; Sym., chamber orch, 1936; Ricercare, ob, str, 1938; Suite, ob, str, 1944–5; Design for Radio, 1945; New England Chronicle, ov., 1947; Passacaglia on Vermont Folk Tunes, 1949; Sym., D, 1956; Epos, 1963

Chamber: Sextet, wind, pf, 1932; 2 pf suites, 1932, 1953; Cl Sonata, 1937; 2 pf trios, 1937, 1963; Serenade, ob, str trio, 1939; Terzetto, 2 vn, va, 1950; Soundings, bn, tpt, perc, 1953; Ww Qt, 1953; Music for 6, ob, cl, str qt, 1957; Fantasia, bn, 7 insts, 1960, rev. 1961; other pf pieces

Choral: How far is it to Bethlehem?, female vv, org, 1927; Chanson of the Bells of Oseney, female vv, pf, 1930; To all you ladies now at hand, male vv, pf/orch, 1932; Fantasy on American Folk Ballads, male vv, pf/orch, 1940; Hymn to the Night, female vv, 1947; 4 Songs of Nature, female vv, 1953; Mass, unison vv, org, 3 tpt, timp, 1955; Magnificat, male vv, org, 1961; 10 others

15 songs, incl. 5 Elizabethan Lyrics, S/T, str qt, 1963

Org: 2 Chorale Preludes on American Folk Hymns, 1947; Paignion, 1947; Antiphon and Chorale, 1955

Principal publishers: ACA, Boosey & Hawkes, Galaxy

BIBLIOGRAPHY

EwenD

A. Frankenstein: "Richard Donovan," *ACAB*, v/4 (1956), 2 [incl. list of works]

"Richard Donovan," *Compositores de América/Composers of the Americas*, ed. Pan American Union, xv (Washington, DC, 1969), 90 [incl. list of works]

H. WILEY HITCHCOCK

Doobie Brothers. Rock group. Formed in California in 1970, its original members were Tom Johnston, singer and guitarist; John Hartman, drummer; Patrick Simmons, singer and guitarist; and Dave Shogren, bass guitarist. During the early 1970s they played popular, but undistinguished, hard rock and blues. Their hit recordings in this period included *Listen to the music* (no. 11, 1972), *Long train runnin'* (no. 8, 1973), *Black Water* (no. 1, 1975), and *Take me in your arms* (no. 11, 1975). They were one of the first rock groups to forego the use of a lead singer and to give equal importance to two or more vocal lines; in *Listen to the music*, for example, three voices create a high, harsh harmony over a restful guitar figure. The Doobie Brothers' musical style underwent an important change when Michael McDonald joined the group in 1976 as its lead singer, keyboard player, and principal songwriter. Later recordings, including *What a Fool Believes* (no. 1, 1979), *Minute by Minute* (no. 14, 1979), and *Real Love* (no. 5, 1980), are characterized by complex cross-rhythms, jazz-inspired chord progressions, and McDonald's smooth, romantic singing. After the Doobie Brothers disbanded in 1982 McDonald pursued a solo career; his album *If that's What it Takes* was released in 1982.

RECORDINGS

(selective list; all recorded for Warner Bros.)

The Doobie Brothers (1919, 1971); *Toulouse Street* (2634, 1972), incl. Listen to the music; *The Captain and Me* (2694, 1973), incl. Long train runnin'; *What Were once Vices are now Habits* (2750, 1974), incl. Black Water; *Stampede* (2835, 1975), incl. Take me in your arms; *Takin' it to the Streets* (2899, 1976); *Livin' on the Fault Line* (3045, 1977); *Minute by Minute* (3193, 1978), incl. What a Fool Believes; *One Step Closer* (3452, 1980), incl. Real Love

KEN TUCKER

Doors. Rock group. Its members were Jim Morrison (*b* Melbourne, FL, 8 Dec 1943; *d* Paris, France, 3 July 1971), singer; Ray Manzarek (*b* Chicago, IL, 12 Feb 1935), keyboard player; Robby Krieger (*b* Los Angeles, CA, 8 Jan 1946), guitarist; and John Densmore (*b* Los Angeles, 1 Dec 1945), drummer. The group was formed in 1965 in Los Angeles, where Morrison and Manzarek (who had been trained as a classical pianist, attended the Chicago Conservatory College, and played in blues bands) were students at the UCLA Graduate School of Film. Krieger, who had played in folk and blues groups, and Densmore, who had a background as a jazz drummer, had both been members of the Psychedelic Rangers.

The Doors began performing in the Los Angeles area late in 1965. They were engaged by the Whisky-a-Go-Go nightclub as its regular opening act, but were dismissed after they performed their song *The End*, in which the instrumentalists vamped while Morrison recited violent lyrics. In 1966 they were signed to the Elektra recording label, for which they recorded *The Doors*, which included *Light my Fire*, a song by Krieger that reached no. 1 on the pop chart, and an 11-minute version of *The End*. During the next few years the group exemplified the darker side of psychedelic rock; among their successful songs were *People are Strange* (no. 12, 1967), *Hello, I love you* (no. 1, 1968), and *Touch me* (no. 3, 1969). At the same time they aroused controversy; their lyrics focused on sex and death, and Morrison, who had emerged as the group's leader and principal songwriter, was on several occasions arrested on charges of obscenity and disorderly conduct. By 1969 he was devoting considerable attention to extramusical pursuits; he wrote poetry (two collections, *An American Prayer* (1970) and *The Lords and the New Creatures* (1971), were published), directed a film called *A Feast of Friends*, and collaborated on a screenplay with Michael McClure, a playwright. After the release of *L. A. Woman* in 1971 he moved to Paris; his death there later that year was attributed to heart failure.

The Doors' remaining members recorded *Other Voices* (1971) and *Full Circle* (1972) as a trio. Densmore and Krieger then formed a short-lived blues-rock group, the Butts Band. An album entitled *An American Prayer*, on which the surviving Doors added music to tapes of Morrison reciting his poetry, was issued in 1978. The publication in 1980 of a biography of Morrison and the reissue of their greatest hits on an album revived the group's popularity for a time; in 1982 Krieger recorded an album of instrumental rock. Manzarek made solo recordings, led a short-lived group called Nite City, produced four albums by the group X, and recorded a rock version of Carl Orff's *Carmina Burana*, which was produced by Philip Glass.

The Doors' music was austere and atmospheric, with a distinctive jazz flavor; in some ways they perpetuated the beatnik idea of "poetry-and-jazz." Their use of minor keys and modal drones and Morrison's portentous singing gave the Doors' songs an air of high seriousness. Their spare music, despairing lyrics, and defiant image had a profound impact on the punk rock movement of the late 1970s, particularly on groups such as Joy Division.

See also Rock, §2.

RECORDINGS

(selective list; all recorded for Elektra)

The Doors (74007, 1967); People are Strange (45621, 1967); *Strange Days* (74014, 1967); Hello, I love you (45635, 1968); Touch me (45646, 1968); *Waiting for the Sun* (74024, 1968); *The Soft Parade* (75005, 1969); *Morrison Hotel* (75007, 1970); *L. A. Woman* (75011, 1971); Love her madly (45726, 1971); *Other Voices* (75017, 1971); Riders on the Storm (45738, 1971); *Full Circle* (75038, 1972); *An American Prayer* (502, 1978); *Alive, she Cried* (60269, 1983)

BIBLIOGRAPHY

J. Hopkins and D. Sugerman: *No one Here Gets Out Alive* (New York, 1980)

JON PARELES

The Doors: (from left to right) John Densmore, Ray Manzarek, Jim Morrison, and Robby Krieger

Doo-wop. A style of vocal rock-and-roll popular in the 1950s and early 1960s. It was essentially an unaccompanied type of close-harmony singing by groups of four or five members; if an accompaniment was added it functioned as a restrained background, largely obscured by the voices. The beginnings of the style can be detected in 19th-century barbershop singing and in the music of such black vocal groups as the Ink Spots in the 1930s and the Orioles in the late 1940s. The Orioles inspired a number of groups named for birds in the early and mid-1950s, among them the Larks and the Flamingos; other popular doo-wop groups included the Chords (*Sh-boom*), Frankie Lymon and the Teenagers (*Why do fools fall in love?*), the Moonglows, and the Nutmegs. The black groups were soon imitated by white ensembles, which often consisted of Italian-Americans from New York and Philadelphia; their style differed from that of the black groups in that their sound was closer to Tin Pan Alley and their lyrics correspondingly more escapist and less sexually suggestive. Such groups as the Capris (*There's a moon out again*), Danny and the Juniors (*At the Hop*), and Dion and the Belmonts (*A teenager in love*) enjoyed enormous popularity from 1961 to 1963, and many of them continued to perform in rock-and-roll revival shows. In the early 1980s there was renewed interest in doo-wop, and in 1982 several groups (including the Harptones, the Moonglows, and the Capris) made recordings on the Ambient Sound label.

JOHN ROCKWELL

Doran, Matt H(iggins) (*b* Covington, KY, 1 Sept 1921). Composer and flute teacher. He attended Los Angeles City College and the University of Southern California (BM 1947, DMA 1953), where he studied composition with Toch, Kubik, and Eisler. His principal flute teachers were Ary Van Leeuwen, Archie Wade, Jules Furman, and William Hullinger; early in his career he played with the Corpus Christi (Texas) and Muncie (Indiana) symphony orchestras and other ensembles. From 1953 to 1955 he taught at Del Mar College (Corpus Christi) and in 1957, after a year at Ball State University (Muncie), he joined the faculty of Mount St. Mary's College in Los Angeles, becoming professor in 1966. He has received a MacDowell Colony Fellowship (1954) and two Huntington Hartford Foundation awards (1956, 1964). His somewhat conservative style is characterized by great clarity and, in his own words, "contemporary practicality."

WORKS

Operas: 9 chamber operas, incl. The Committee (1, T. Lawrence), 1953, The Marriage Counselor (1, Doran), 1977, The Little Hand So Obstinate (grand opera, 3, S. Brown), 1969

Orch: 4 syms., 1946, 1959, 1977, 1979; Fl Conc., 1953; Hn Conc., 1954; Pf Conc., 1975; Vc Conc., 1975; Double Conc., fl, gui, str, 1976

Vocal: Eskaton, oratorio, solo vv, chorus, orch, 1976; songs, incl. 3 Sonnets (Shakespeare), S, fl, 1984

Inst: Four Short Pieces, fl, 1963; Pastorale, org, 1964; Poem, fl, pf, 1965; Cl Sonata, 1967; Sonatina, fl, vc, 1968; Qt, ob, cl, bn, va, 1970; Trio, fl, cl, pf, 1979–80; over 25 works with fl; sonatas; pf pieces

Principal publisher: Belwin-Mills

BIBLIOGRAPHY

EwenD

BARBARA A. PETERSEN

Dorati, Antal (*b* Budapest, Hungary, 9 April 1906). Conductor and composer. The son of professional musicians, he entered the Liszt Academy in Budapest at the age of 14. He studied there with Bartók, Kodály, and Leo Weiner, and attended courses in philosophy at Vienna University. After graduating at 18 he became a vocal coach at the Budapest Royal Opera, where he made his conducting début the same year (1924) and remained for four years.

In 1928 Dorati became assistant to Fritz Busch at the Dresden Opera, then music director at Münster, Germany (1929–33). He spent the next eight years as conductor with the Ballets Russes de Monte Carlo (successor to the Diaghilev company), taking musical charge of the De Basil wing after the 1938 split. He toured with the company in Europe, North America, Australia, and New Zealand; his numerous guest appearances with major orchestras included his American concert début with the National SO in 1937. In 1941 he became music director of the new American Ballet Theatre and for four years helped significantly to establish its professional basis. He became an American citizen in 1947.

From 1945 Dorati acquired a distinguished reputation as an orchestral trainer, beginning with his postwar reorganization of the Dallas SO (1945–9). He then spent 11 years as music director of the Minneapolis SO, making it internationally known through recordings. His European tours at this time included associations with the London SO and the Philharmonia Hungarica; he later became the latter's honorary president, and between 1970 and 1973 he recorded with the orchestra all Haydn's symphonies. He has received many honors and was made a Chevalier de l'Ordre des Arts et Lettres by the French government, a Knight of the Swedish Order of Vasa, and a KBE.

After periods as principal conductor of the BBC SO (1963–6) and the Stockholm PO (1966–70), Dorati became music director of the National SO, which he conducted at the inaugural concert of the Kennedy Center (9 September 1971). In 1975 he became senior conductor of the Royal PO, London (Conductor Laureate, 1978). He left the National SO in 1977 and was music director of the Detroit SO, 1977–81 (*see* DETROIT, §2). Throughout his career he has championed Bartók's music and given many first performances of contemporary works. He has been a frequent guest conductor of opera in Europe and North America, but his talents have usually benefited most from close and sustained contact with an orchestra. His conducting is distinguished by vigorous, direct rhythm and an acute ear for rich color.

Dorati has composed more than 40 works in an idiom he has described as "recognizably contemporary but not afraid of melody," all publicly performed, and has published numerous orchestral arrangements, including the Johann Strauss music for *Graduation Ball*, a widely successful ballet by David Lichine. His autobiography, *Notes of Seven Decades*, was published in 1979.

WORKS

The Way (Claudel), dramatic cantata, A, Bar, nar, chorus, orch, 1956; Sym., 1957; The Two Enchantments of Li-Tai-Pe (Dorati), Bar, chamber orch, 1958; Missa brevis, SSAATTB, perc, 1959; Magdalena (ballet, D. Lichine), 1960–61; Chamber Music (J. Joyce), S, 25 insts, 1967; Night Music, fl, orch, 1968; Pf Conc., 1975; Die Stimmen (Rilke), song cycle, B, pf, 1975, arr. B, orch, 1978; Vc Conc., 1977; Str Qt, 1980; Duo concertante, ob, pf, 1983; The Chosen, opera, 1984

25 other works incl. orch pieces, songs, choruses, inst works

Many transcrs., arrs. for orch, incl. J. Strauss: Graduation Ball (ballet, Lichine), 1939, works by Bartók

Principal publishers: Belwin-Mills, Chester, Leeds, Suvini Zerboni

BIBLIOGRAPHY

"Dorati, Antal," *CBY 1948*

H. Stoddard: *Symphony Conductors of the U.S.A.* (New York, 1957), 47

M. Rayment: "Antal Dorati," *Audio Record Review*, ii/4 (1962), 17 [with discography by F. F. Clough and G. J. Cuming]

G. Turner: "Antal Dorati Talks," *Records and Recording*, xviii/2 (1974), 12 [with discography by M. Ashman; suppl. to discography, xviii/5 (1975), 8]
L. M. Apcar: "Symphony Builder: Detroit's Antal Dorati, Master Merchandiser, Thrives on Promotion," *Wall Street Journal* (22 Jan 1980), 1
J. Rockwell: " 'Orchestras Play Better for Me,' " *New York Times* (11 May 1980)
A. Doráti: "Bartókiana (Some Recollections)," *Tempo*, no.136 (1981), 6
C. MacDonald: "Antal Doráti: Composer: a Catalogue of his Works," *Tempo*, no.143 (1982), 16

NOËL GOODWIN

Dorham, Kenny [McKinley Howard] (*b* nr Fairfield, TX, 30 Aug 1924; *d* New York, 5 Dec 1972). Jazz trumpeter. He played in swing orchestras and in the innovative, bop big bands of Dizzy Gillespie and Billy Eckstine (1945); while with Gillespie he also appeared as a blues singer. In 1948 he began an important association with Charlie Parker's quintet, with which he remained until 1949. He was a founding member of the Jazz Messengers in 1954, and briefly led a similar group called the Jazz Prophets. From 1956 to 1958 he played in Max Roach's quintet, replacing Clifford Brown. Later he taught at the Lenox School of Jazz in Massachusetts (1958–9), contributed to two Parisian films in 1959, and led a quintet with Joe Henderson in the mid-1960s. In his best recordings of the middle and late 1950s Dorham rivaled his greatest contemporaries in technical command, tunefulness, and beauty of timbre.

RECORDINGS
(selective list)

As leader: *Kenny Dorham and the Jazz Prophets* (1956, ABC-Para. 122); *Jazz Contrasts* (1957, Riv. 239); *Blue Spring* (1959, Riv. 297); *Quiet Kenny* (1959, New Jazz 8225); *Whistle Stop* (1961, BN 4063); *Trumpet Toccata* (1964, BN 84181)

As sideman: F. Navarro: Everything's Cool (1946, Savoy 586); J. J. Johnson: Opus V/Hilo (1949, New Jazz 806); S. Rollins: *Sonny Rollins Quintet* (1954, Prst. 186); A. Blakey: *The Jazz Messengers at the Cafe Bohemia*, i–ii (1955, BN 1507–8); M. Roach: *Jazz in 3/4 Time* (1957, EmArcy 36108); J. Henderson: *In 'n' Out* (1964, BN 84166)

BIBLIOGRAPHY

"Kenny Dorham's 3 Careers," *Down Beat*, xxvi/4 (1959), 20
G. Feehan: "Durable Dorham," *Down Beat*, xxix/25 (1962), 16
J. Binchet: "Kenny Dorham: l'éternel second," *Jazz magazine*, no.147 (1967), 16
M. Gardner: "Farewell Kenny Dorham," *Jazz Journal*, xxvi/3 (1973), 7
Obituary, *Down Beat*, xl/2 (1973), 10
B. Raftegard: *The Kenny Dorham Discography* (Karlstad, Sweden, 1982)

BARRY KERNFELD

Doria, Clara. Pseudonym of CLARA KATHLEEN ROGERS.

Dorian Wind Quintet. Wind quintet formed in the summer of 1961 at the Berkshire Music Festival through a program funded by the Fromm Foundation; its members are flutist Karl Kraber (who replaced John Perras), clarinetist Jerry Kirkdale (who was preceded by William Lewis and Arthur Bloom), oboist Gerard Reuter (preceded by Charles Kuskin and David Perkett), bassoonist Jane Taylor, and horn player David Jolley (preceded by Robin Graham, Barry Benjamin, and William G. Brown). The group made its New York recital début in October 1961 and toured Europe during the following season, giving part of a series of concerts sponsored by various American embassies. In addition to serving from 1963 to 1973 as ensemble-in-residence for the SUNY system, the quintet has also been a resident ensemble at Brooklyn and Hunter colleges, CUNY. It not only offers exemplary performances of the standard repertory for its instrumentation, but has also encouraged many leading composers of the late 20th century to write for the medium; among those who have produced works especially for the ensemble are Berio, Foss, Davidovsky, and Druckman.

JAMES WIERZBICKI

Doring, Ernest N(icholas) (*b* New York, 29 May 1877; *d* Chicago, IL, 9 May 1955). Writer, publisher, and expert on violins. He studied violin and viola as a boy, and from 1893 to 1926 worked for John Friedrich & Brother in New York as secretary, treasurer, purchaser, writer of catalogues, and publicity manager. From 1926 until 1937 he was with the Rudolph Wurlitzer Co., working first as assistant to the violin expert J. C. Freeman in New York and later as manager of the violin department in the Chicago store. He prepared catalogues for the company, including a famous one of 1931 that listed an enormous collection of violins and had a separate section devoted entirely to bows. In 1937 he opened his own shop in Evanston, Illinois, and began publishing a magazine, *Violins*. In 1941 his business was bought by William Lewis & Son of Chicago with whom he worked as salesman and magazine editor until his death.

Although well known and highly regarded as an expert on classical instruments and bows, Doring's reputation rests mainly on his publications. The first issue of *Violins* appeared in March 1938 and in October the name was changed to *Violins and Violinists*; it ceased publication in December 1960. In addition to information on violin performances and performers, the magazine carried detailed and informative essays on classic violin makers of the past; the best-known of these were Doring's long articles, which were published in book form as *How Many Strads?* (1945) and *The Guadagnini Family of Violin Makers* (1949).

PHILIP J. KASS

Dorsey, Jimmy [James] (*b* Shenandoah, PA, 29 Feb 1904; *d* New York, 12 June 1957). Jazz clarinetist, saxophonist, and dance-band leader. He began playing slide trumpet and cornet at the age of seven, but changed to reed instruments in 1915. With his brother Tommy he co-led Dorsey's Novelty Six and Dorsey's Wild Canaries, then joined the Scranton Sirens in the early 1920s. In September 1924 Jimmy joined the California Ramblers, a very popular East Coast dance band. Between 1925 and 1934 he worked freelance with leading New York bands such as those of Paul Whiteman, Jean Goldkette, and Vincent Lopez. More importantly, from 1926 he began recording extensively with leading midwestern white jazz pioneers, including Bix Beiderbecke and Red Nichols. He played in Nichols's popular Five Pennies group, a widely influential band not only in the USA but also in England; this established Dorsey as a leading jazz reed player.

In 1934 Dorsey founded with Tommy Dorsey the successful but short-lived Dorsey Brothers Orchestra. After a public argument in 1935 Jimmy took over the leadership of the group, building it into one of the leading dance bands of the late 1930s and early 1940s. He appeared with the group in several films, including *The Fabulous Dorseys* (1947), a fictionalized version of the brothers' careers. He continued to lead dance bands sporadically after World War II until his death, at one period joining Tommy to form a new Dorsey Brothers Orchestra (1953–6).

Because Dorsey led one of the most popular dance bands of the swing era and scored novelty hits such as *Oodles of Noodles* (1932), his importance as a jazz player has been neglected; yet in the 1920s he was a major model for other jazz musicians, both on clarinet and saxophone. Lester Young and Coleman Hawkins both acknowledged his influence. Like many of his contemporaries, Dorsey was attracted to jazz by the examples of the white New Orleans clarinetists Larry Shields and Leon Roppolo, but by the late 1920s he came under the influence of the black clarinetist Jimmie Noone. Dorsey had an excellent technique and played in a fluid, polished style which could be strongly rhythmic. He can safely be placed among the finest jazz players of reed instruments during the period 1925 to 1935.

For illustration *see* DORSEY, TOMMY.

RECORDINGS
(selective list)

As leader: St. Louis Blues (1930, Decca F6142); Oodles of Noodles (1932, Col. 36063); Amapola (1941, Decca 3629); Green Eyes (1941, Decca 3698)

As sideman: R. Nichols: Alabama Stomp/Hurricane (1927, Bruns. 3550)

BIBLIOGRAPHY

E. Edwards and others: *Jimmy Dorsey and his Orchestra: a Complete Discography* (Whittier, CA, 1966)

H. Sandford: *Tommy and Jimmy: the Dorsey Years* (New Rochelle, NY, 1972)

G. T. Simon: *The Big Bands* (New York, 1974)

C. Garrod: *Jimmy Dorsey and his Orchestra* (Zephyr Hills, FL, 1980)

JAMES LINCOLN COLLIER

Dorsey, Lee (*b* New Orleans, LA, 24 Dec 1924). Rhythm-and-blues singer and songwriter. He was a professional boxer when he wrote *Ya ya* with Bobby Robinson: this reached no.7 on the rhythm-and-blues chart in 1961. In the mid-1960s he began a long association with the producer and arranger Allen Toussaint, who worked with him on such songs as *Ride your pony* (no.28, 1965), *Working in the coal mine* (no.8, 1966), and *Holy Cow* (no.23, 1966). He was backed by the New Orleans rhythm-and-blues group the Meters, and these recordings helped to define the sound of New Orleans popular music in that period, with their ebullient brass arrangements and driving rhythms. The albums *Yes we Can* (1970) and *Night People* (1977) were not commercial successes, but they received much critical acclaim. In 1976 Dorsey made a guest appearance on the first album by Southside Johnny and the Asbury Jukes.

RECORDINGS
(selective list)

Ya ya (Fury 1053, 1961); Do-re-mi (Fury 1056, 1962); Ride your pony (Amy 927, 1965); Get out of my life, woman (Amy 945, 1966); Holy Cow (Amy 965, 1966); Working in the coal mine (Amy 958, 1966); *Yes we Can* (Pol. 2482280, 1970); *Night People* (ABC 1048, 1977)

Dorsey, Thomas A(ndrew) ["Georgia Tom"] (*b* Villa Rica, GA, 1899). Blues singer, gospel songwriter, and pianist. The son of a revivalist preacher, he moved to Atlanta in 1910 and came under the influence of local blues pianists. He left for Chicago during World War I and studied at the Chicago College of Composition and Arranging, also becoming an agent for Paramount records. Dorsey's compositions at the time included *Riverside Blues* (recorded by King Oliver's Creole Jazz Band, 1923, Para. 20292). His skill as a pianist, composer, and arranger gained him a job with Les Hite's Whispering Serenaders in 1923, and soon afterwards he formed his own Wildcats Jazz Band, with which Ma Rainey performed. As "Georgia Tom" he made several recordings with her, usually including the slide guitarist Tampa Red (Hudson Whittaker). In the late 1920s Dorsey formed a duo with Tampa Red; their blues recording *Tight like that* (1928, Voc. 1216) became a great hit and prompted further collaboration on works combining urban sophistication, rural humor, and often ribaldry, as in *Terrible Operation Blues* (1930, Champion 16171).

Thomas A. Dorsey, 1976

Dorsey's first gospel song, *Someday, Somewhere*, was published in the collection *Gospel Pearls* (1921), and in the early 1930s he turned exclusively to gospel music. In 1931 he organized the first gospel choir at the Ebenezer Baptist Church in Chicago; the following year, with Sallie Martin, he founded the National Convention of Gospel Choirs and Choruses, and also opened the Thomas A. Dorsey Gospel Songs Music Publishing Company, the first publishing house for the promotion of black American gospel music.

Dorsey was the most influential figure in the gospel song movement. His earliest gospel songs, including *Stand by me*, *If I don't get there*, and *We will meet him in the sweet by and by*, were strongly influenced by C. A. Tindley. They are based on church hymns and spirituals and lack the swing and open structure of his later songs. In the early 1930s he made a small number of gospel recordings, including *How about you* (1932, Voc. 1710) and *If you see my saviour* (1932), and the widely recorded song *If I could hear my mother pray* (1934, Voc. 02729). His light voice, suited to the earlier blues recordings, lacked conviction or excitement for gospel music and he made no further recordings, concentrating instead on writing songs that others would interpret. Of these his most successful was *Precious Lord, take my hand* (1932), written after his first wife's death. As he became known for his compositions, Dorsey toured with Mahalia Jackson and Roberta Martin, selling sheet music of his songs. Among the best known are *There'll be peace*, *I will put my trust in the Lord*, and *The Lord has laid His hands on me*.

See also GOSPEL MUSIC, §II; for further illustration *see* BLUES, fig. 1.

BIBLIOGRAPHY

A. Bontemps: "Rock Church Rock," *The Book of Negro Folklore* (New York, 1958), 313

T. Heilbut: *The Gospel Sound: Good News and Bad Times* (New York, 1971/*R*1975)

H. C. Boyer: "Analysis of his Contributions: Thomas A. Dorsey, 'Father of Gospel Music'," *Black World*, xxiii (1974), 20
J. O'Neal and A. O'Neal: "Georgia Tom Dorsey," *Living Blues*, xx (1975), 17 [interview]
S. Harris: *Blues Who's Who* (New Rochelle, NY, 1979)
I. V. Jackson: *Afro-American Religious Music: a Bibliography and Catalogue of Gospel Music* (Westport, CT, 1979)

PAUL OLIVER/R

Dorsey, Tommy [Thomas] (*b* Shenandoah, PA, 19 Nov 1905; *d* Greenwich, CT, 26 Nov 1956). Jazz trombonist and dance-band leader. He studied trumpet with his father, a part-time musician, and later changed to trombone. With his brother Jimmy he was co-leader of Dorsey's Novelty Six and Dorsey's Wild Canaries, then joined the Scranton Sirens in the early 1920s. Later in the decade Tommy worked with Jean Goldkette, Paul Whiteman, and other prominent dance orchestras of the time. He then moved to New York, where he was in demand as a player in studio and pit orchestras. In 1934 he founded with Jimmy the successful but short-lived Dorsey Brothers Orchestra. After a public argument in 1935 the two separated, and Tommy founded a dance orchestra of his own which quickly became one of the most popular of the swing era. The band's music was characterized by smooth, well-crafted arrangements played with great precision and, at times, with excellent jazz solos by Bunny Berigan, Yank Lawson, Buddy Rich, and others. One of its most successful recordings was *Boogie Woogie* (1938), an orchestral adaptation of a piano piece by Pine Top Smith; other hits included lively swing versions of *Marie* and *Song of India* (1937), both with brilliant solos by Berigan. However, Dorsey's orchestra was known primarily for its renderings of ballads at dance tempos, frequently with singers such as Jack Leonard and Frank Sinatra. After the collapse of the swing-band movement in the late 1940s Dorsey struggled to keep his band intact. Eventually he brought in his brother Jimmy to form another version of the Dorsey Brothers Orchestra (1953–6) which had some success, particularly in its television appearances.

Although Dorsey recorded, especially in the 1920s, with Bix Beiderbecke and other major jazz players, he was not a notable jazz soloist. He was vastly admired by other musicians, however, for his technical skill on his instrument. His tone was pure, his phrasing was elegant, and he was able to play an almost seamless legato line; as a player of ballads he has rarely been surpassed.

For further illustration, *see* WHITEMAN, PAUL.

RECORDINGS
(selective list)

As leader: I'm Getting Sentimental over You (1935, Vic. 25236); Marie/Song of India (1937, Vic. 25523); Boogie Woogie (1938, Vic. 26054); I'll Never Smile Again (1940, Vic. 26628); Opus One (1944, Vic. 20–1608)

As sideman: J. Bland: Who Stole the Lock (1932, Banner 32605); Jam Session at Victor: Honeysuckle Rose/Blues (1937, Vic. 25559)

BIBLIOGRAPHY

H. Sandford: *Tommy and Jimmy: the Dorsey Years* (New Rochelle, NY, 1972)
G. T. Simon: *The Big Bands* (New York, 1974)
C. Garrod: *Tommy Dorsey and his Orchestra* (Zephyr Hills, FL, 1980–82)
S. Voce: "Talking of Tommy," *Jazz Journal International*, xxxviii/2 (1985), 20

JAMES LINCOLN COLLIER

Dougherty, Celius (Hudson) (*b* Glenwood, MN, 27 May 1902). Pianist and composer. He studied piano and composition with Donald Ferguson at the University of Minnesota, performing his own piano concerto with the university orchestra in 1922. Two years later he was awarded scholarships to study composition and piano with Goldmark and Lhévinne at the Juilliard School. He gave the premières of his Piano Sonata no. 1 and Violin Sonata at Town Hall. His songs were introduced in New York by Gauthier and Teyte during the 1930s, and later by Anderson, Swarthout, Farrell, and Warfield, many of whom he has accompanied in recordings and recitals throughout the USA and abroad. With the pianist Vincent Ruzicka, he has toured North America and

The Dorsey brothers: Tommy (trombone) and Jimmy (clarinet)

Europe as a piano duo, giving world premières of works by Stravinsky, Hindemith, Schoenberg, Berg, Milhaud, and others. His own music is predominantly tonal and adheres to classical forms.

WORKS

Stage: Many Moons (opera, 1, after J. Thurber), 1962

Inst: Pf Conc., 1922; 2 pf sonatas, 1925, 1934; Vn Sonata, 1928; Str Qt, 1938; Music from Seas and Ships, sonata, 2 pf, 1942–3

Vocal: over 100 songs, incl. Pied Beauty (G. Hopkins), 1932; Song of the Jasmin (Arabian Nights), 1939; Primavera (A. Lowell), 1942; Hush'd be the Camps (W. Whitman), 1945; Everyone Sang (S. Sassoon), 1948; Love in the Dictionary (Funk and Wagnall's), 1948; Whispers of Heavenly Death (Whitman), 1966; Ballad of William Sycamore (S. Benét), 1970

Principal publishers: Boosey & Hawkes, C. Fischer, G. Schirmer

BIBLIOGRAPHY

"Celius Dougherty," *Compositores de América/Composers of the Americas*, ed. Pan American Union, ix (Washington, DC, 1963), 57

J. Bender: *The Songs of Celius Dougherty* (thesis, U. of Minnesota, 1981)

NADIA TURBIDE

Douglas, Isaac (*b* Philadelphia, PA, *c*1939). Gospel singer. He began singing as a youth with choirs in Philadelphia. In the early 1960s he appeared with Ruth Davis and the Davis Sisters in a series of concerts that introduced him to the gospel public. Later he moved to New York and sang for a while with the Raymond Rasberry Singers before organizing his own group, the Isaac Douglas Singers. In October 1970, with Benny Diggs, he formed the New York Community Choir, an ensemble of 65 voices. Douglas, who is known for his strained-sounding baritone voice and extremely wide range, made several successful recordings with this choir, including *Let the redeemed of the Lord say so* and *Until you come again* (Savoy 14426, 1976). In the early 1970s he began an association with James Cleveland and the Gospel Music Workshop of America as soloist and choir director, and conducted a series of concerts throughout the USA. He has appeared on national television and was nominated for a Grammy Award for his recording of *The Harvest Is Plentiful* (Creed 3056, 1974).

HORACE CLARENCE BOYER

Douglas, Lizzie [Minnie]. *See* MEMPHIS MINNIE.

Douglass, Joseph Henry (*b* Washington, DC, 3 July 1871; *d* Washington, 16 Dec 1935). Violinist and music administrator. His grandfather (the abolitionist Frederick Douglass) and father were both violinists. He studied at the New England Conservatory (1889–91) and later under Joseph Hasper in Washington, where he also conducted the American Orchestral Club (from 1892), and managed the Dumas Lyceum Bureau. He was the first violin teacher engaged by Howard University and he retained his position there until 1907, when he moved to New York. There he operated the Douglass Lyceum Bureau and taught violin, both privately and as head of the violin department at David Martin's Music School Settlement (1911–14). He returned to Washington in 1914, and became conductor of the orchestra at the New Republic Theater there in 1921. Among his solo performances was an appearance at the World's Columbian Exposition in Chicago (1893). His wife, the pianist Fannie Howard Douglass, often served as his accompanist on his many tours of the USA between 1900 and 1930.

BIBLIOGRAPHY

SouthernB

E. Southern: *The Music of Black Americans: a History* (New York, 1971, rev. 2/1983), 273, 305

DOMINIQUE-RENÉ DE LERMA

Dover. Firm of publishers. In 1941 Hayward Cirker established in New York a business as a dealer in academic remainders. He issued his first reprint in 1943 and Dover has since become known for its reissues of scholarly texts. Although it specialized initially in scientific literature, the firm soon extended its interests to other areas, including music. Notable among its reprints of music texts are the works on Bach by Albert Schweitzer and Philipp Spitta, and Rimsky-Korsakov's *Principles of Orchestration*. Dover began to publish musical scores in 1963, when it brought out a reprint of the Fitzwilliam Virginal Book. Since then the firm has issued classics of the vocal, piano, chamber, and orchestral repertory, as well as popular music of the past. Its publications, mostly in paperback, are distinguished by their high quality and low prices.

BIBLIOGRAPHY

J. Rockwell: "A Different Kind of Music Publishing," *New York Times* (6 Jan 1980), §II, 13

J. F. Baker: "What's Doing at Dover," *Publishers Weekly*, ccxx (14 Aug 1981), 21

FRANCES BARULICH

Dowd, William (Richmond) (*b* Newark, NJ, 28 Feb 1922). Harpsichord maker. He studied English at Harvard University (BA 1948). His interest in music began while he was at school, where he had piano lessons. At Harvard he and his friend Frank Hubbard became increasingly interested in early keyboard instruments, and built a clavichord. They decided not to follow their proposed careers as teachers of English, and instead founded a workshop for building harpsichords constructed on historical principles. In summer 1948, while Hubbard studied in Europe, Dowd served an apprenticeship in the Detroit workshop of John Challis, a disciple of Dolmetsch and the pioneer builder of harpsichords in the USA. In autumn 1949 Hubbard and Dowd established their workshop in Boston. By 1955, when Hubbard left for a research trip in Europe, the firm had constructed 13 harpsichords and four clavichords, and had restored several important antique instruments. Dowd continued the firm's production and restoration work during Hubbard's absence, and worked out an important design based on the two-manual harpsichords of Pascal Taskin. This French double harpsichord soon found wide favor with performers as a general-purpose concert instrument.

After the dissolution of the firm in late 1958 Dowd established his own workshop in Cambridge, Massachusetts, which continued production of harpsichords based on historical models, attaining an annual output of 20 to 22 instruments, a large number for instruments of the highest quality.

In 1971 Dowd established an additional workshop under his name in Paris in collaboration with Reinhard von Nagel that produces between 20 and 24 instruments annually. Both the Cambridge and Paris workshops are largely given over to the production of two-manual harpsichords based on the great French prototypes by the Blanchets, Hemsch, and Taskin, including Taskin's reconstructions *en grand ravalement* of Ruckers harpsichords. They also make a smaller double harpsichord of Flemish design and a French single-manual model, as well as specially commissioned instruments based on other models, and restorations of antique harpsichords. Dowd harpsichords are probably in wider use by leading professional performers in North America and Europe than those of any other maker.

BIBLIOGRAPHY

H. L. Haney: "Portrait of a Builder: William Dowd," *The Harpsichord*, iv/1 (1971), 8

HOWARD SCHOTT

Downes, Edward O(lin) D(avenport) (*b* Boston, MA, 12 Aug 1911). Musicologist, son of Olin Downes. He attended Columbia University, the Manhattan School of Music, and universities in Paris and Munich. From 1939 to 1941 he was music critic for the *Boston Transcript*. He taught at Wellesley College and the Longy School of Music (1948–9) and at the University of Minnesota (1950–55). He received a PhD in musicology from Harvard University in 1958 with a dissertation on J. C. Bach and *opera seria*. In 1966 he was appointed professor of music history at Queens College, CUNY, where he taught until his retirement in 1983. As a musicologist Downes has concentrated on opera of the early Classical period and the development of music criticism in the USA. He is also active outside the academic community: in 1958 he became quizmaster for the Metropolitan Opera radio broadcasts, and since 1960 has written program notes for the New York PO. He is author of numerous articles in journals such as *Opera News* and *High Fidelity*.

PAULA MORGAN

Downes, (Edwin) Olin (*b* Evanston, IL, 27 Jan 1886; *d* New York, 22 Aug 1955). Music critic, father of Edward O. D. Downes. He studied piano at the National Conservatory of Music, New York, and, in Boston, history and analysis with Louis Kelterborn, piano with Carl Baermann, theory with Homer Norris and Clifford Heilman, and music criticism with John P. Marshall. In addition to his career as music critic of the *Boston Post* (1906–24) and the *New York Times* (1924–55), he was also a guest lecturer at Boston University, Lowell Institute, Harvard University (1911), the Curtis Institute, and the Metropolitan Opera Guild, and a commentator for concerts at the Brooklyn Academy of Arts and Sciences (1932–4) and the Berkshire Music Festival (1937). He was particularly well known for his quiz program during the intermissions of the Metropolitan Opera's Saturday afternoon broadcasts.

Downes's reviews strongly influenced contemporary popular musical opinion in the USA. Though the taste defined in them has dated, he recognized the value of new works by Richard Strauss, Stravinsky, Prokofiev, and Shostakovich before their reputations were established in the USA. In particular he was a passionate advocate of Sibelius's music; he secured its American reputation, and in return Finland awarded him the order Commander of the White Rose (1937) and invited him to speak at Sibelius's 75th-birthday celebration (1940). Downes's papers, acquired by the University of Georgia, include about 50,000 letters to and from composers (Bloch, Prokofiev, Stravinsky, Varèse, Vaughan Williams), musicologists, performers, and critics. His writings include *The Lure of Music* (1918), *Symphonic Broadcasts* (1931), *Symphonic Masterpieces* (1935/*R*1972), and *Sibelius the Symphonist* (1956). (*See also* CRITICISM, §4.)

BIBLIOGRAPHY

I. Downes: "Dedication"; H. Taubman: "Preface: Olin Downes," *Olin Downes on Music*, ed. I. Downes (New York, 1957/*R*1968), p.v; p.vii

L. Weldy: *Music Criticism of Olin Downes and Howard Taubman in "The New York Times," Sunday Edition, 1924–29 and 1955–60* (diss., U. of Southern California, 1965)

J. Réti-Forbes: "The Olin Downes Papers," *Georgia Review*, xxi (1967), 165

F. R. Rossiter: "Downes, Edwin (Olin)," *DAB*

JON NEWSOM

Downey, John (Wilham) (*b* Chicago, IL, 5 Oct 1927). Composer. He attended DePaul University (BM 1949), studying piano with S. Tarnovsky and composition with Leonard Stein; at the Chicago Musical College he studied with Rudolph Ganz, Vittorio Rieti, Ernst Krenek, and Alexander Tcherepnin (MM 1951). He also studied in Paris at the Conservatoire (1952) with Milhaud, Boulanger, and Messiaen and at the Sorbonne with Jacques Chailley and Victor Janklevitch (docteur dès lettres 1957). He has taught at DePaul University, Chicago City College, and Roosevelt University, and became professor of composition and composer-in-residence at the University of Wisconsin, Milwaukee, in 1964. In 1970 he founded the Wisconsin Contemporary Music Forum for the performance of new works by composers associated with Wisconsin. He has been awarded Fulbright and Copley Foundation fellowships, among others, was a fellow at the Institute for Advanced Studies, Princeton (1959, 1960), and has received numerous commissions, including those from George Sopkin, the Milwaukee SO, the Ford Foundation, the Fine Arts Foundation, and the NEA. In 1980 the title Chevalier de l'Ordre des Arts et Lettres was bestowed on him by the French government.

Downey frequently uses modified serial procedures to achieve pitch coherence and large-scale harmonic relationships in his music; motivic development, sometimes polyphonically layered, in conjunction with timbral identities or timbral mixtures, further contribute to the overall structure. A number of compositions (for example the Cello Sonata and the String Quartet no.2) employ transformations of bell sonorities; he has also used electronic and computer-generated sounds. A number of his works have been recorded. Downey is the author of *La musique populaire dans l'oeuvre de Béla Bartók* (1966).

WORKS

Stage: Ageistics (ballet), 1967; Twelfth Night (incidental music, Shakespeare), 1971, Come away Death and Hey ho the Wind and the Rain arr. high v, pf

Orch: La joie de la paix, 1956; Chant to Michelangelo, 1958; Conc., harp, chamber orch, 1964; Jingalodeon, 1968; Prospectations III-II-I, 3 orch, 1970; Sym. Modules 5, 1972; Tooter's Suite, youth orch, 1973; The Edge of Space, fantasy, bn, orch, 1978, arr. bn, pf; Discourse, ob, hpd, str, 1984; Db Conc., 1985

Chamber: Adagio lyrico, 2 pf, 1953; Wind Octet, 1958; Eastlake Terrace, pf, 1959; Edges, pf, 1960; Pyramids, pf, 1961; 2 str qts, 1962, 1976; Vc Sonata, 1966; Agort, ww qnt, 1967; Almost 12, ww qnt, str qnt, perc, 1970; Lydian Suite, vc, 1975; Crescendo, perc ens, 1977; High Clouds and Soft Rain, 24 fl, 1977; Silhouette, db, 1980; Duo, ob, hpd, 1981; Portrait no.1, pf, 1981, no.2, bn, cl, 1983, no.3, fl, pf, 1984; Pf Trio, 1984; Prayer, str trio, 1984; various other chamber pieces

Vocal: Lake Isle of Innisfree (Yeats), high v, pf, 1963; What If? (Cummings), chorus, timp, 8 brass, 1973; A Dolphin (I. Downey), high v, a fl, va, pf, perc, 1974; Tangents (J. Downey), jazz oratorio, S, mixed chorus, str qnt, elec gui, perc, 1981, Life Flows By and Who are They arr. unacc. chorus; Qu'en avez-vous fait (M. Désbordes-Valmore), S, pf, 1982

Tape: Afternoon's Purple, 1971; Earthplace, 1971; Processions, 1979

Principal publishers: Editions Françaises, Heritage, Mentor, Plymouth, Presser

RICHARD SWIFT

Dozier, Lamont (*b* 1941). Songwriter and record producer, member of the HOLLAND-DOZIER-HOLLAND team.

Dragon, Carmen (*b* Antioch, CA, 28 July 1914; *d* Santa Monica, CA, 28 March 1984). Conductor and composer. After study at California State University, San Jose, he pursued a varied musical life. He directed and recorded light classics with an orchestra made up essentially of members of the Los Angeles PO; his later career as a conductor continued on similar lines, principally with the Glendale (California) SO, which he joined in 1963 and which under him gained national celebrity. He also made guest appearances in concert and on television with leading orchestras in the USA, South America, and Europe. Dragon had many years of experience as a speaker and conductor in radio and television, notably on the network for the armed forces and as music director for more than 25 years (from around 1950) of the Standard School Broadcast music appreciation program: his televised annual Christmas concert with the Glendale SO won an Emmy Award (1964). As a composer and arranger, he was responsible for more than 30 film scores (including *Cover Girl*, for which he won an Academy Award in 1944); he has also composed for television, variety shows, and musicals. A skillful performer in all the areas of his activity, Dragon was among the most successful and widely known figures in light classical music. His son Daryl Dragon (*b* Los Angeles, 27 Aug 1942) is a rock musician who has played with several groups including the Beach Boys.

BIBLIOGRAPHY

"Carmen Dragon [and] the Glendale Symphony," *International Musician*, lxxii/11 (1974), 4

Obituary, *New York Times* (29 March 1984)

KAREN MONSON

Drake, Earl R(oss) (*b* Aurora, IL, 26 Nov 1865; *d* Chicago, IL, 6 May 1916). Violinist and composer. He studied in Chicago and Cincinnati, graduating in 1885, and after further studies in New York went to the Berlin Hochschule für Musik as a pupil of Joachim. On his return to the USA he founded the Violinists' Guild, formed his own quartet, and toured widely. From 1893 to 1897 he was head of the string department of the Gottschalk Lyric School in Chicago; in 1900 he organized there the Drake School of Music. He composed the operas *The Blind Girl of Castel-Cuillé* (Jacques Jasmin, translated by Longfellow; performed in Chicago in 1914) and *The Mite and the Mighty* (performed in Chicago in 1915); the *Brownie Suite* (1905), a *Dramatic Prologue* (1915), and *Ballet* for orchestra; *Gypsy Scenes* for violin and orchestra; and a number of works for violin and piano. He also wrote articles on bowing, violin tone, and the "Joachim method."

BIBLIOGRAPHY

E. E. Hipsher: *American Opera and its Composers* (Philadelphia, 1934), 162

H. WILEY HITCHCOCK

Drake University. University founded in DES MOINES in 1881.

Dresel, Otto (*b* Geisenheim, Germany, 20 Dec 1826; *d* Beverly, MA, 26 July 1890). Pianist, teacher, writer, and composer. He studied with Moritz Hauptmann in Leipzig, where he also had guidance from Mendelssohn, and with Ferdinand Hiller in Cologne. In 1848 he settled in New York as a teacher and pianist, appearing as a soloist and in ensembles. He returned briefly to Germany, but from 1852 lived in Boston as a pianist and teacher. A conservative, cultivated musician, his repertory consisted principally of classical German works, and he exercised a strong influence on American audiences through his personal tastes and standards. He further publicized his views in the many articles he wrote for *Dwight's Journal of Music*. As an intimate friend of Robert Franz, he introduced the latter's songs in America, and at the time of his death was collaborating with Franz on a new edition of Bach's *Das wohltemperirte Clavier*. He was known to be a harsh critic of his own compositions, only a few of which were published. His works include songs, piano pieces, a quartet for piano and strings, a piano trio, *In memoriam* (1874) for soprano and orchestra (a setting of Longfellow's *The 50th Birthday of Agassiz*), and *Army Hymn* (1863) for soloists, chorus, and orchestra to words by Oliver Wendell Holmes; he also made a piano score (1885) of Franz's orchestration of *Messiah*, and arranged some of Mendelssohn's songs and Handel's arias.

BIBLIOGRAPHY

Obituaries, *Boston Daily Advertiser* (29 July 1890); *Folio*, xxxv (1890), 331

S. B. Schlesinger: "Otto Dresel," *American Art Journal*, lv (1890), 354

F. H. Martens: "Dresel, Otto," *DAB*

JOHN GILLESPIE

Dresher, Paul (Joseph) (*b* Los Angeles, CA, 8 Jan 1951). Composer-performer. He studied at the University of California, first at Berkeley (BA 1977), and then at San Diego with Robert Erickson, Reynolds, and Oliveros (MA 1979). He also worked with Terry Riley, Steve Reich, and Lou Harrison, and has studied non-Western instruments and music including north Indian sitar, Ghanaian drumming, and Javanese music. He has built several Javanese gamelans, in Berkeley and San Diego (for the University of California), and in Seattle, where he taught composition, theory, and percussion at the Cornish Institute (1980–82). His compositional and performance output falls into three categories: ensemble pieces; theater works, including the highly acclaimed *The Way of How*, created in collaboration with the experimental theater director George Coates; and live solo performances (generally entitled *Liquid and Stellar Music*), in which Dresher performs on the electric guitar or keyboard and interacts in real time with a tape-processing system he designed and built himself, resulting in music that is, as he has said, "multi-leveled in design, may have a lush hypnotic quality when perceived from a narrow time perspective but [is revealed] over larger time frames to be constantly developing via a multiplicity of simultaneous but discrete processes." Dresher received an NEA grant in 1979 and in 1979–80 traveled throughout India and southeast Asia. He received a commission from the Kronos Quartet in 1982 (for *Casa vecchia*), and in the same year was awarded the Goddard Lieberson Fellowship of the American Academy and Institute of Arts and Letters. *Re:act:ion* was commissioned by the San Francisco SO. In 1984 he formed his own ensemble, with which he tours regularly.

WORKS

This Same Temple, 2 pf, 1976–7; Z (American Indian texts), S, 6 perc, tape, 1977–9; Night Songs (American Indian texts), S, 2 T, fl, trbn, perc, 2 pf, db, 1979–81; Liquid and Stellar Music, elec gui, live elec, 1981; Study for Variations, fl, ob, cl, tpt, trbn, vn, pf, 1981; The Way of How, theater piece, 2 T, elec kbd, trbn, fl, elec gui, 1981, collab. G. Coates; Casa vecchia, str qt, 1982; Industrial Strength Music, elec gui, perc, live elec, 1982; Dark Blue Circumstance, elec gui, elec, 1982–3; Are are, opera, 1983; Re:act:ion, orch, 1984; Seehear, opera, 1984

PETER GARLAND

Dresser [Dreiser], **(John) Paul, (Jr.)** (*b* Terre Haute, IN, 22 April 1858; *d* New York, 30 Jan 1906). Songwriter, lyricist, publisher, and performer. He was the brother of the novelist Theodore Dreiser. He learned guitar and piano, and at the age of 16 joined a traveling show (adopting the pseudonym Dresser).

From 1885 he performed with the Billy Rose Minstrels, composed sentimental songs, and wrote and acted in five plays. After his first successful songs, *The letter that never came* (1886) and *The Outcast Unknown* (1887), he became one of the first American performers to enter the music publishing trade, as a staff composer for Willis Woodward Co. He continued to write songs (e.g., *The pardon came too late*, 1891), and about 1894 helped found the George T. Worth Co. (eventually Howley, Haviland & Dresser, 1901). The company thrived, mostly on Dresser's tragic and sentimental ballads (e.g., *On the banks of the Wabash*, 1897, the Indiana state song); some were prompted by his disintegrating marriage with the burlesque performer May Howard. According to the Tin Pan Alley publisher Edward B. Marks, "He usually wrote his songs on an organ at one of the Broadway hotels where he lived for the last fifteen years of his life." A protégée, Louise Kerlin, who took his surname for her stage name, introduced many of his works on the vaudeville stage. From 1902 his songs were less popular and his publishing company failed in 1905 despite the success of his last and best-known song *My gal Sal*.

Dresser was the leading American writer of sentimental ballads in the late 19th century, and he "inaugurated and sustained the new school of weeping balladry" in Tin Pan Alley popular song (Goldberg). Though much of his work is maudlin or cloying, the best songs have a sensitive poetic feeling; according to Theodore Dreiser they are "tender and illusioned," with a "wistful seeking" nature. Through them the popular sheet-music industry established a counterpart, readily accepted by the white, Christian middle and lower classes, to the more frolicsome styles of the "Gay Nineties." The songs have much the same melodic simplicity, nostalgic texts, and naive, direct appeal as the songs of Stephen Foster earlier in the 19th century, though the harmonic language is slightly more complex, particularly in some of the chromatic passages at phrase endings (*My gal Sal* has remained a favorite of barbershop quartets). A film biography of Dresser, *My Gal Sal* (1942), was written by Dreiser, with music composed and arranged by Ralph Rainger. Some of Dresser's letters and other papers are in the libraries of Indiana University and the University of Pennsylvania.

WORKS

Edition: *The Songs of Paul Dresser*, ed. T. Dreiser (New York, 1927)
(all lyrics by Dresser; all printed works published in New York)

*c*50 songs, incl. The letter that never came (1886); The Outcast Unknown (1887); The pardon came too late (1891); Take a seat, old lady (1894); Just tell them that you saw me (1895); On the banks of the Wabash (1897); Our country, may she always be right (1898); We are coming, Cuba, coming (1898); Come home, Dewey, we won't do a thing to you (1899); The Curse of the Dreamer (1899); The Blue and the Gray (1900); My heart still clings to the old first love (1901); The boys are coming home today (1903); My gal Sal (1905)

Principal publisher: Howley, Haviland & Dresser

BIBLIOGRAPHY

T. Dreiser: "My Brother Paul," *Twelve Men* (New York, 1919)
I. Goldberg: *Tin Pan Alley: a Chronicle of the American Popular Music Racket* (New York, 1930/*R*1961)
E. B. Marks: *They All Sang: from Tony Pastor to Rudy Vallée* (New York, 1934)
A. R. Markle: "Some Light on Paul Dresser," *Terre Haute Tribune and Terre Haute Star* (14 April 1940), 10
D. Ewen: *The Life and Death of Tin Pan Alley* (New York, 1964)
V. Dreiser: *My Uncle Theodore* (New York, 1976)
C. Hamm: *Yesterdays: Popular Song in America* (New York, 1979)

DEANE L. ROOT

Drew, James M(ulcro) (*b* St. Paul, MN, 9 Feb 1929). Composer. After attending the New York School of Music from 1954 to 1956, he studied privately with Varèse (1956) and Riegger (1956–9). In 1964 he received an MA from Tulane University, New Orleans, and then undertook a year of postgraduate work at Washington University, St. Louis. He has held positions as composer-in-residence or faculty member at several universities, including Northwestern (1965–7), Yale (1967–73), and UCLA (1977–8), as well as at the Berkshire Music Center (1973). In 1974 he became director of the American Music Theater, Studio City, California, and from 1980 was also director of the Mysterious Traveling Cabaret and the Contemporary Arts Center, both of New Orleans. His awards include a Guggenheim Fellowship (1972–3) and the Panamerica Prize (1974, for *West Indian Lights*). Drew's style, which frequently draws on principles of indeterminacy, is eclectic and dramatic, and exploits the Ivesian technique of presenting diverse musical materials simultaneously. He has often served as his own librettist and has contributed many articles to both English- and Spanish-language publications; he has also been active as a radio broadcaster.

WORKS

Stage: Toward Yellow (ballet), 1970; Mysterium (television opera, Drew), 1974–5; Crucifixus Domini Christi (ballet), 1975; Suspense Opera (Drew), 1975; Dr. Cincinnati (Drew), 1977; Five O'Clock Ladies (ballet), 1981

Orch: Passacaglia, 1957; 3 syms., 1968, 1971, 1977; 4 concs., violine grande, 1969, perc, 1972–3, va, 1973, 2 vc, 1981; October Lights, 1969; West Indian Lights, 1973; Sinfonia, str orch, 1980; Open/Closed Forms, chamber orch, 1982; Faustus, 2 pf, vc, orch, 1983; other works

Inst: Indigo Suite, pf, db, perc, 1959; Divisiones, 6 perc, 1962; Pf Trio, 1962; Polifonica I, fl, cl, ob, str qt, pf, 1963; 4 Pieces, str qt, 1964; Polifonica II, fl, perc, 1966; Primero libro de referencia laberinto, pf, 1969; The Maze Maker, vc, tape, 1970; Almost Stationary, pf trio, 1971; Gothic Lights, brass, 1972; 2 str qts, 1972–5, 1977; Chamber Sym., 1976; 3 sonatas, vc, pf, 1980, vn, pf, 1981, va, 1982; St. Mark Triple Conc., str trio, 1981; other works

Vocal: choral works, incl. The Fading of the Visible World (Drew), oratorio, S, T, B, 4vv, orch, 1976; 9 songs, incl. Orangethorpe Aria, S, cl, pf trio, 1978

Principal publisher: Presser

BIBLIOGRAPHY

J. Drew: "Sabe lo que estoy oyendo?," *Sonda*, ii (Feb 1968), 32
J. K. Cordes: *A New American Development in Music: Some Characteristic Features Extending from the Legacy of Charles Ives* (diss., Louisiana State U., 1976)
G. Clarke: *Essays on American Music* (Westport, CT, 1977)

MICHAEL MECKNA

Dreyfus. Max Dreyfus (1874–1964) and his brother Louis Dreyfus (1877–1967), music publishers, were directors of the firms of HARMS and CHAPPELL.

Drifters. Name used by two rhythm-and-blues vocal groups. The first of these was active from 1953 to 1958, the second from 1959. The first group's original members were Clyde McPhatter (*b* Durham, NC, 15 Nov 1933; *d* New York, 13 June 1972), lead singer, Billy Pinkney (*b* Sumter, SC, 15 Aug 1925), Andrew Thrasher (*b* Wetumpka, AL), and Gerhart Thrasher (*b* Wetumpka); their first successful recordings were *Money Honey* (1953), *White Christmas* (1954), and *Whatcha gonna do* (1955). At the end of 1954 McPhatter left the group on his induction into the US Army; he was succeeded by a number of lead singers, including Dave Baughn, Johnny Moore (*b* Selma, AL, 1934), and Bobby Hendricks (*b* Columbus, OH, 1937), before the group disbanded in 1958. The following year George Treadwell, who had been the Drifters' manager and retained the rights to their name, hired a group called the Five Crowns to fulfill their remaining tour obligations, and renamed them the Drifters. The new ensemble included Ben E. King (Benjamin Earl Nelson) (*b* Henderson,

NC, 28 Sept 1938), a baritone who was the lead singer; Charlie Thomas; and Elsbeary Hobbs. They soon achieved success with such songs as Leiber and Stoller's *There goes my baby* (no.2, 1959), *This magic moment* (no.15, 1960), and *Save the last dance for me* (no.1, 1960). King left the group in 1960 to pursue a career as a soloist and was replaced by Rudy Lewis, who was the lead singer on *Sweets for my sweet* (no.16, 1961), *Up on the roof* (no.5, 1962), and *On Broadway* (no.9, 1963). On Lewis's death in 1963, Johnny Moore, who had sung with the first Drifters group in the mid-1950s, joined the ensemble; he was the lead singer on *Under the Boardwalk* (no.4, 1964). The Drifters went to England in 1972 and had some success with *Like Sister and Brother* (1973), *Kissin' in the Back Row of the Movies* (1974), and *Down on the Beach Tonight* (1974).

Although the two groups known as the Drifters were distinct entities, records issued under that name have a peculiarly homogenous sound. This is because the singing of both groups remained rooted in the gospel and close-harmony traditions, and never quite broke free of those constraints. Whereas many black vocal groups of the early 1960s (such as the Temptations) quickly developed a sophisticated and individual sound, the Drifters' recordings often achieved their significance only because of the elaborate productions of Ahmet Ertegun and Jerry Wexler (until 1958) and the distinctive material of Leiber and Stoller (in the 1960s), rather than any intrinsic characteristics of the vocal parts.

RECORDINGS

(selective list; recorded for Atlantic unless otherwise stated)

Money Honey (1006, 1953); Honey Love (1029, 1954); Such a Night (1019, 1954); White Christmas (1048, 1954); Whatcha gonna do (1055, 1955); Dance with me (2040, 1959); There goes my baby (2025, 1959); Save the last dance for me (2071, 1960); This magic moment (2050, 1960); Sweets for my sweet (2117, 1961); Up on the roof (2162, 1962); On Broadway (2182, 1963); Under the Boardwalk (2237, 1964); *The Drifters Now* (Bell 219, 1973); *Love Games* (Bell 246, 1975); *Every Night is Saturday Night* (Ari. 4140, 1976)

BIBLIOGRAPHY

B. Millar: *The Drifters* (New York, 1971)

M. Goldberg and M. Redmond: "Drifters Discography," *Record Exchanger*, iv/2 (1974), 14

Drinker, Henry S(andwith) (*b* Philadelphia, PA, 15 Sept 1880; *d* Merion, PA, 9 March 1965). Music scholar. He was a lawyer by profession but devoted himself in his spare time to music. He held informal gatherings at his home and from these developed the Accademia dei Dilettanti di Musica, a mixed choir that met at the Drinkers' home from 1930 to 1960 to study and perform vocal music of the 17th to 20th centuries. Concerned that the words should be understood but also fit the music, Drinker began a series of translations remarkable for their consistent craftsmanship, faithful prosody, and sheer number; between 1941 and 1954 he translated the texts of nearly all Bach's vocal works and of numerous vocal compositions by Brahms, Mozart, Schumann, Schubert, Wolf, Mussorgsky, and Medtner.

His sister, Catherine Drinker Bowen (1897–1973), was a well-known biographer, whose works include *Beloved Friend: the Story of Tchaikovsky and Nadejda von Meck* (1937) and *Free Artist: the Story of Anton and Nicholas Rubinstein* (1939). His wife was the writer on music Sophie Drinker.

WRITINGS

The Chamber Music of Johannes Brahms (Philadelphia, 1932)

Bach's Use of Slurs in Recitativo Secco (Merion, PA, 1946)

Drinker Library of Choral Music: Catalogue (Philadelphia, 1957)

Accademia dei Dilettanti di Musica, 1930–1960 (Merion, PA, 1960)

BIBLIOGRAPHY

S. R. Rosenbaum: "Henry S. Drinker: 1880–1965," *American Choral Review*, vii/4 (1965), 4

C. D. Bowen: *Family Portrait* (Boston, 1970), 175

JON NEWSOM/R

Drinker [née Hutchinson], **Sophie (Lewis)** (*b* Philadelphia, PA, 24 Aug 1888; *d* Chestnut Hill, PA, 6 Sept 1967). Writer on music and champion of women in music, wife of Henry S. Drinker. With her husband she organized the Accademia dei Dilettanti di Musica, and in 1932 she initiated the Montgomery Singers, an amateur women's chorus over which she presided for at least ten years. It was conducted only by women and performed a wide range of contemporary and older repertory (including works by one of its conductors, Lela Vauclain), all selected and provided by Drinker. She also wrote articles in the 1930s on women's choruses and the music for them, and with this background embarked on research for her first book, *Music and Women* (1948), a study of women's activities in music from prehistoric times to the 20th century which became a landmark in the field. Her interest in choral literature led to a second book, *Brahms and his Women's Choruses* (1952). Drinker lectured widely about women in music and women's rights in general; though she was less well known than her husband during her lifetime, her importance in documenting and promoting the activities of women in music was acknowledged during the 1980s. Her papers are housed in the Sophia Smith Collection, Smith College, and the Radcliffe-Schlesinger Collection, Radcliffe College, Harvard University; her unpublished autobiography is in the Radcliffe-Schlesinger Collection.

BIBLIOGRAPHY

Obituary, *New York Times* (10 Sept 1967)

K. Geiringer: "Sophie H. Drinker (1888–1968 [sic])," *JAMS*, xi (1968), 409

LAURA KOPLEWITZ

Driscoll, Loren (*b* Midwest, WY, 14 April 1928). Tenor. He studied at Syracuse and Boston universities and sang frequently on American radio before making his New York City Opera début as the Emperor in *Turandot* (9 October 1957). In 1962 he became a member of the Deutsche Oper, Berlin, where he sang in the world premières of *Montezuma* by Roger Sessions (1964) and *Der junge Lord* by Hans Werner Henze (1965). He created the role of Dionysus in another of Henze's operas, *The Bassarids*, at the Salzburg Festival in 1966, and in the same year (on 23 December) made his début at the Metropolitan Opera, as David in *Die Meistersinger*. Driscoll's light, lyrical voice is always used with intelligence and a fine regard for the text, both in opera and in his wide concert repertory.

ALAN BLYTH/R

Drucker, Stanley (*b* Brooklyn, NY, 4 Feb 1929). Clarinetist. He started playing at the age of ten and became a pupil of Leon Russianoff. At 16 he was appointed first clarinet in the Indianapolis SO and at 19 joined the New York PO, becoming its principal clarinetist in 1960. As a soloist Drucker has performed with the Busch Chamber Players and the Juilliard Quartet. He has not followed the modern free style of playing but the classical, achieving impeccable control of tone and phrasing. In 1968 he joined the faculty of the Juilliard School. He has edited clarinet music and compiled an exhaustive series of orchestral studies.

He is the dedicatee of John Corigliano's Clarinet Concerto, of which he gave the première in 1977.

PAMELA WESTON/R

Druckman, Jacob (Raphael) (*b* Philadelphia, PA, 26 June 1928). Composer. As a youth he studied piano and violin, played trumpet in jazz ensembles, and was composing by the age of 15. He received a thorough training in solfège, harmony, and counterpoint with Longy and Louis Gesensway. In the summer of 1949 he was accepted by Copland into the composition class at the Berkshire Music Center and in the autumn of that year he entered the Juilliard School, where his teachers were Mennin, Persichetti, and Wagenaar. A Fulbright Fellowship (1954) took him to Paris for study at the Ecole Normale de Musique. After completing the master's degree (1956) he returned to teach at Juilliard and remained there until 1972. He also taught part time at Bard College (1961–7), was associated with the Columbia-Princeton Electronic Music Center (1967), and served for one year (1971–2) as director of the electronic music studio at Yale University. From 1972 to 1976 he was associate professor of composition at Brooklyn College, CUNY, and then was appointed chairman of the composition department and director of the electronic music studio at Yale.

Jacob Druckman

Druckman's awards include two Guggenheim Fellowships (1957, 1968) and a Brandeis University Creative Arts Award (1975). He has had works commissioned by many leading organizations including the St. Louis SO (*Mirage*, 1976), the Cleveland Orchestra (*Chiaroscuro*, 1977), IRCAM (*Animus IV*, 1977), the New York PO (Viola Concerto, 1978; *Aureole*, 1979), the Koussevitzky Foundation (String Quartet no.3, 1981), and the Metropolitan Opera (an opera provisionally entitled *Medea*, 1982–). Among his recorded works are *Lamia*, *Windows*, *Aureole*, and *Antiphonies*. In 1978 he was elected to the Institute of the American Academy and Institute of Arts and Letters; he became chairman of the Composer-Librettist Panel of the NEA in 1980 and in the same year was elected president of the Koussevitzky Foundation. In 1982 he was appointed composer-in-residence with the New York PO, under a program administered by the Meet the Composer organization and partially sponsored by the Rockefeller Foundation. In that capacity he was artistic director of the orchestra's series of new music concerts, Horizons, in 1983 and 1984.

Druckman's early works attest to the composer's interest in the musical world of Debussy and Stravinsky and the large orchestral works of Mahler, Ravel, and Schoenberg from the turn of the century. As he began to explore more advanced techniques he became interested in the possibilities of the tape medium. The year 1966 marked an important transition: with the String Quartet no.2 Druckman reached the limits of his adaptation of serialism, and with *Animus I* he began a series of works employing tape. Electronic music was a catalyst for discovering new ways of manipulating live sound as a plastic medium. At the same time Druckman began to incorporate elements of theater into his musical language, animating the central interplay between live performers and tape with dramatic, even ritualistic, scenarios. But it is a theater in which the protagonists are amalgams of sound, gesture, and persona.

In 1972 Druckman composed *Windows*, for which he won the Pulitzer Prize the same year. It was the first of a series of major works for full orchestra that contribute to the revival of the orchestra as a vehicle for new music. Druckman has successfully translated into the orchestral medium his delight in virtuosity and his ability to create brilliantly paced sequences of strongly colored images that have an earthy physicality and dramatic impact. *Windows* recalls music from the tonal past; the orchestral version of *Incenters* (1973) contains jazz elements and chords from the coronation scene of Mussorgsky's *Boris Godunov*, and *Lamia* (1974) has literal quotations from Wagner (text) and Francesco Cavalli (both text and music). This interplay of styles is more fully evolved in *Mirage* (which quotes Debussy), *Aureole* (with a melody from Bernstein's Third Symphony), and *Prism* (1980), a work in three movements each of which contains music from a different opera (by Marc-Antoine Charpentier, Cavalli, and Luigi Cherubini) based on the myth of Medea and Jason. In the so-called new romanticism of these works Druckman goes beyond the ethos of structuralism to a wide-ranging awareness of historical idioms that becomes an integral component of a new musical awareness.

WORKS

(pubd unless otherwise stated)

ORCHESTRAL

Windows, 1972; 16 March 1972, Chicago SO, cond. Maderna

Incenters, tpt, hn, trbn, orch [arr. of ens work], 1973; 23 Nov 1973, Minnesota Orchestra, cond. Skrowaczewski

Lamia (Ovid, Wagner, trad.), S, orch, 1974, rev. 1975; 20 April 1974, DeGaetani, Albany SO, cond. J. Hegyi, R. Kogan; rev. version 17 Oct 1975, DeGaetani, New York PO, cond. Boulez, D. Gilbert

Mirage, 1976; 4 March 1976, St. Louis SO, cond. Slatkin

Chiaroscuro, 1977; 14 March 1977, Cleveland Orchestra, cond. Maazel

Concerto for Viola and Orchestra, 1978; 2 Nov 1978, S. Greitzer, New York PO, cond. Levine

Aureole, 1979; 9 June 1979, New York PO, cond. Bernstein

Prism, 1980; 21 May 1980, Baltimore SO, cond. Comissiona

Unpubd: Music for the Dance, 1949; Conc., str, 1951; Suite (ballet), 1953; Volpone Ov., 1953; Conc., vn, small orch, 1956; Performance (ballet, J. Limón), 1960; Measure for Measure, incidental music, 1964; Odds and Evens: a Game, children's orch, 1966

VOCAL

Laude (medieval), Bar, fl, va, vc, 1952; The Simple Gifts (Shaker), SATB, pf, 1954; 4 Madrigals: Shake off your Heavy Trance (F. Beaumont), The Faery Beam upon you (Jonson), Death, Be not Proud (Donne), Corinna's going a'Maying (R. Herrick), SATB, 1958; Dark upon the Harp (Pss.), Mez, brass qnt, 2 perc, 1962; Antiphonies I, II, III (G. M. Hopkins), double chorus, 1963; The Sound of Time (Mailer), S, pf, 1964, arr. S, orch, 1965; Dance of the Maidens, SATB, org, perc, 1965, unpubd; Hymnus referamus (Ps.), SATB, org, perc, 1965, unpubd; Psalm lxxxix, SATB, org, perc, 1965, unpubd; Sabbath Eve Service, Shir Shel Yakov, T, SATB, org, 1967; Vox humana (Bible), S, Mez, T, Bar, SATB, orch, 1983

INSTRUMENTAL

Inst: Str Qt no.1, 1948, unpubd; Duo, vn, pf, 1949, unpubd; Divertimento, cl, hn, harp, vn, va, vc, 1950; Spell, ballet, 2 pf, 1951, unpubd; Interlude, ballet music, fl, cl, timp, 1953, unpubd; The Seven Deadly Sins, pf, 1955; Str Qt no.2, 1966; Incenters, 13 insts, 1968; Valentine, db, 1969; Other Voices, brass qnt, 1976; Bō (Chin.), b cl, 3 female vv, harp, mar, 1979; Str Qt no.3, 1981; Tromba marina, 4 db, 1981

With tape: Animus I, trbn, tape, 1966; Animus II, S/Mez, 2 perc, tape, 1968; Animus III, cl, tape, 1969; Look Park, film score, tape, 1970; Orison, org, tape, 1970; Traite du rossignol, film score, tape, 1970; Synapse, tape, 1971; Delizie contente che l'alme beate [after F. Cavalli], ww qnt, tape, 1973; Animus IV, T, vn, trbn, pf/elec pf, elec org, perc, tape, 1977

Principal publisher: Boosey & Hawkes

BIBLIOGRAPHY

EwenD

S. Fleming: "Jacob Druckman," *HiFi/MusAm*, xxii/8 (1972), 4

W. Wager: "Jacob Druckman: ASCAP '63 and Pulitzer '72," *ASCAP Today*, vi/2 (1974), 16

A. Porter: *Music of Three Seasons: 1974–77* (New York, 1978), 541

C. Gagne and T. Caras: "Jacob Druckman," *Soundpieces: Interviews with American Composers* (Metuchen, NJ, 1982), 153

J. Rockwell: "The Philharmonic Looks at Contemporary Music," *New York Times* (29 May 1983), §II, p.17

N. Uscher: "Two Contemporary Viola Concerti: a Comparative Study," *Tempo*, no.147 (1983), 23

AUSTIN CLARKSON

Druian, Rafael (*b* Vologda, Russia, 20 Jan 1922). Violinist. He studied at the Curtis Institute from 1933 to 1943 under Lea Luboshutz and Efrem Zimbalist. In 1947 he was named concertmaster of the Dallas SO and later served in the same capacity with the Minneapolis SO (1949–60), the Cleveland Orchestra (1960–69), and the New York PO (1970–73). He has taught at the University of Minnesota (1949–60), the Cleveland Institute (1964–9), the University of California, San Diego (1973–8), the Hartt School of Music (1979–81), and Boston University (from 1982). Though best known as a concertmaster of major American orchestras, Druian has also had a career as a soloist (he made his début in Town Hall, New York, in 1952); his important solo recordings include sonatas by Mozart (with Szell), Bloch, Bartók, and Ives.

KAREN MONSON

Dubensky, Arcady (*b* Viatka, Russia, 15 Oct 1890; *d* Tenafly, NJ, 14 Oct 1966). Composer and violinist. By the age of 13 he was playing violin in a local theater orchestra. A scholarship enabled him to enroll in the Moscow Conservatory in 1904, where he studied violin with Jan Hřímalý, counterpoint with Alexander Il'yinsky, and conducting with Arends (diploma 1909). From 1910 until 1919 he was first violinist in the Moscow Imperial Opera orchestra; he left revolutionary Russia in 1919, settled in New York in 1921, and the following year joined the New York SO (later New York PO), where he remained for 31 years.

Dubensky's works, many of which have unusual scorings, are diatonic and representative of the Russian Romantic School. They were played frequently in Boston, Philadelphia, New York, and other cities during Dubensky's active years with the New York PO but were very little heard after his retirement in 1953. His son, Leo Arcady Dubensky, born in Russia, is also a composer and a violinist with the New York PO.

WORKS

Operas (all unperf.): Romance with Double Bass (after Chekhov), 1916; Downtown, 1930; On the Highway, 1936; Two Yankees in Italy, 1944

Orch: Sym., g, 1916; Intermezzo and Complement, 1927; From Old Russia, 1927; 3 Compositions, 1928; Russian Bells, sym. poem, 1928; Caprice, pic, orch, 1930; The Raven (Poe), nar, orch, 1931; Prelude and Fugue, 1932; Tom Sawyer, ov., 1935; Serenade, 1936; Rondo and Gigue, str, 1937; Fantasy on a Negro Theme, tuba, orch, 1938; Stephen Foster: Theme, Variations, Finale, 1940; Orientale, song and dance, 1945; Fugue, 34 vn, 1948; Conc. grosso, 3 trbn, tuba, orch, 1949; Trbn Conc., 1953; 4 suites, str; 13 other works

Inst: Passacaglia, 1v, vc, 1931; 2 str qts, C, 1932, B♭, 1954; Fugue, 18 vn, 1932; Variations, 8 cl, 1932; Theme and Variations, 4 hn, 1932; Str Sextet, C, 1933; Prelude and Fugue, 4 db, 1934; 2 suites, 4 tpt, 1935, 9 fl, 1935; Song of November, ob, pf, 1950

Incidental music for Mowgli (B. Tarkington), 1940

BIBLIOGRAPHY

EwenD

STEPHEN W. ELLIS

Duble, Charles E(dward) (*b* Jeffersonville, IN, 13 Sept 1884; *d* Jeffersonville, 19 Aug 1960). Trombonist and composer. Little is known of his life, except that he played trombone in a number of circus bands, including those of the Sun Brothers, John Robinson, Hagenbeck-Wallace, Sells-Floto, Sparks, the Downie Brothers, the Gentry Brothers, and the combined Ringling Brothers and Barnum & Bailey Circus. During his many years on the road, Duble wrote more than 40 marches, almost all for the circus. The best-known of these is *Bravura*; others that remain popular include *The Circus King*, *Battle of the Winds*, and *Barnum & Bailey's Royal Pageant*. A number of his compositions are recorded in the Heritage of the March series (compiled by ROBERT HOE, JR.), subseries 11, B, EE, ZZ, and RRR.

BIBLIOGRAPHY

R. Hoe, Jr., ed.: "Brief Biographies of Famous March Composers," *Journal of Band Research*, xvi/1 (1980), 49

RAOUL CAMUS

Dubois, William (*d* ?1854). Music publisher. His name appears in New York City directories as piano manufacturer and music dealer from 1813. He purchased the plates of John Paff in 1817 and began to issue several of Paff's publications under his own name. In 1821 Dubois went into partnership with William Stodart, who had previously operated in Richmond; George Bacon replaced Stodart in 1835. Dubois ceased to publish in about 1841, but continued to sell music and pianos until 1854.

BARBARA TURCHIN

Duckles, Vincent H(arris) (*b* Boston, MA, 21 Sept 1913; *d* Berkeley, CA, 1 July 1985). Musicologist and librarian. He took the BA at the University of California, Berkeley, and the MA (1937) and the EdD (1944) at Columbia University. After teaching for a time he returned to Berkeley, and was awarded a degree in librarianship in 1950 and the doctorate in musicology (1953). He was appointed head of the music library at Berkeley in 1947 and remained on the faculty of the department of music until his retirement in 1981. He served as president of the Music Library Association (1960–62) and was active in both the American Musicological Society and the International Association of Music Libraries. Beginning with his dissertation on the Gamble Commonplace Book, Duckles made important contributions to the history of 17th-century English song. Later he turned his attention to the historiography of music and the history of musical scholarship; his bibliography *Music Reference and Research Materials* (1964, 3/1974) is an indispensable aid to every musical scholar. In some ways, however, his major achievement is the magnificent collection of books and music at Berkeley, which he was instrumental in building into one of the best libraries for musical research in the USA.

PHILIP BRETT/R

Duckworth, William (Ervin) (*b* Morganton, NC, 13 Jan 1943). Composer and educator. He studied composition with Martin Mailman at East Carolina University (BM 1965) and with Ben Johnston at the University of Illinois, where he also studied trombone with Robert Gray and education with Charles Leonhard (MS 1966, DMEd 1972). He founded and directed Media Press (1969–72), publishers of new music, and the Association of Independent Composers and Performers (1969–72), an international organization of musicians dedicated to the promotion of contemporary music. In 1973 he became associate professor of music at Bucknell University. He received NEA grants for *The Time Curve Preludes* for piano (1978), the book *The Language of Experimental Music* (1981), and *Songs of the Pale Horseman* (1983). With Edward Brown he wrote *Theoretical Foundations of Music* (1978), a widely used college text.

Duckworth has written a substantial number of works, among which *A Ballad in Time and Space* (1968) and *Seven Shades of Blue* (1974) are two of the most important chamber pieces. *Pitch City* (1969), an early work for any four wind players, exemplifies his use of indeterminate compositional techniques. His chief piano work, *The Time Curve Preludes* (recorded by Neely Bruce in 1983), uses rhythmic structures as a means of formal organization, an approach Duckworth has used in other works, among them *Southern Harmony* (1981); commissioned by the Wesleyan Singers, it employs material from the 1854 edition of William Walker's shape-note tunebook *The Southern Harmony*.

WORKS
(selective list)

Orch and vocal: A Mass for these Forgotten Times (Lat.), SATB, 1973; A Summer Madrigal (1960s rock lyrics), rock singer, fl, vn, pf, perc, 1976; Southern Harmony, Books 1–4, SSAATTBB, 1981; Marches and Flourishes for the Close of the World, orch, 1982; Simple Songs about Sex and War (H. Carruth), S, 1984

Chamber and inst: Str Qt, 1964; A Ballad in Time and Space, t sax, pf, 1968; Pitch City, any 4 wind, 1969; 7 Shades of Blue, fl, cl, vn, vc, pf, 1974; Trilogy, pf, 1974; A Book of Hours, fl, cl, vn, vc, pf, 1976; Binary Images, 2 pf, 1977; The Time Curve Preludes, Books 1 and 2, pf, 1978; Music in Seven Regions, pf, 1979; Tango Voices, pf, 1984; many others

Elec and mixed media: Gambit, solo perc, tape, 1967; Western Exit, chamber ens, nar, film, slides, 1969; Year, amp pf, slides, 1979; Songs of the Pale Horseman (Scott, Freud, Milton, Joyce, others), S, A, T, B, elec, 1983

Principal publishers: Peters, Seesaw

BIBLIOGRAPHY

B. Prentice: "Bruce: Duckworth's Premières," *HiFi/MusAm*, xxix/7 (1979), 32

T. Johnson: "New Music America Takes over a Town," *Village Voice* (25 June 1980), 64

STEPHEN RUPPENTHAL

Ducloux, Walter (Ernest) (*b* Lucerne, Switzerland, 17 April 1913). Conductor and opera director. He was educated at the University of Munich (PhD 1935) and the Vienna Academy, where he studied conducting with Felix Weingartner and Josef Krips. He was co-founder of the Lucerne International Music Festival and assisted Toscanini there in 1938–9 before coming to the USA. He became an American citizen in 1943 and served in the US Army during World War II. He gained experience in Europe and the USA as a conductor of opera and symphonic works and was appointed music director for opera for CBS Television and Voice of America in 1950. In 1953 he became director of opera at the University of Southern California, where he produced and conducted Verdi's *Don Carlos* (1958) and *Simon Boccanegra* (1961), Stravinsky's *The Rake's Progress* (1963), Hindemith's *Mathis der Maler* (1966), and the American premières of Strauss's *Die Liebe der Danae* and *Friedenstag* (1967). While on the West Coast he was also operatic adviser to the film industry and music director of the Los Angeles Orchestral Society. In 1968 Ducloux became professor of music and drama at the University of Texas, where he established an opera theater and developed academic courses in opera. From 1973 to 1975 he was artistic director of the Austin SO. He has translated several operas into English, being awarded a National Endowment grant in 1975 for his translation of Hindemith's *Die Harmonie der Welt*. He served on the panel of Texaco's Metropolitan Opera Quiz from 1949 to 1974.

FRANK MERKLING

Dueño Colón, Braulio (*b* San Juan, Puerto Rico, 26 March 1854; *d* San Juan, 4 April 1934). Composer. He studied with his father, a cellist, and with the Italian-born Rosario Aruti and the composer and church musician Felipe Gutiérrez Espinosa; as a composer he was self-taught. In 1880 he organized a municipal band in Bayamón, and that same year was named flutist for the chapel of San Juan Cathedral. He acquired local prominence as a composer as early as 1877, when he won first prize for his overture *La amistad* in a contest sponsored by the Ateneo Puertorriqueño. In 1901 he was awarded a silver medal at the Pan American Exposition in Buffalo for the first two series of *Canciones escolares*, a collection of original songs and arrangements for school children that was long popular in Puerto Rico. Although unsympathetic to the more modern currents of European music, Dueño Colón attempted to secure a wider appreciation of the "classical" masters, i.e., from Scarlatti to Chopin, in his native land. At the same time, he took interest in the *danza* and in 1914 wrote a serious study of it; his own examples of the genre are warmly expressive and strongly indigenous in flavor. His music in general does not venture much beyond the 19th-century traditions in which he was steeped.

WORKS

Stage: Los baños de coamo (zarzuela, J. Aranzamendi), 1879; El génesis de un nuevo sol (Alemania sometida) (operetta)

Orch: 4 ovs., incl. La amistad, 1877; Sinfonia dramática, 1878; Noche de otoño, sym., 1886; Ecos de mi tierra, sym., 1892; other orch works; danzas for band

Inst: 5 waltzes, nos. 1–3, pf, fl, no. 4, 2 fl, no. 5, pf; pf works

Vocal: many sacred choral works, incl. Ave Maria, SATB, orch, 1879, Salve regina, A, chorus, 1910, and 1 mass, D, vv, orch; songs, incl. 3 vols. of teaching pieces [Canciones escolares]

MSS in Archivo General de Puerto Rico, San Juan

BIBLIOGRAPHY

F. Callejo Ferrer: *Música y músicos puertorriqueños* (San Juan, 1915, 2/1971)

M. Dueño: *Braulio Dueño Colón estudio biográfico* (Bayamón, 1944, 2/1951)

H. Campos-Parsi: "Braulio Dueño Colón," *Le gran enciclopedia de Puerto Rico*, vii (San Juan, 1981), 203

C. Dower: *Puerto Rican Music Following the Spanish American War [to] 1898: the Aftermath of the Spanish American War and its Influence on the Musical Culture of Puerto Rico* (Lanham, MD, 1983), 141

GUSTAVO BATISTA

Duerksen, George L(ouis) (*b* St. Joseph, MO, 29 Oct 1934). Music educator. He studied at the University of Kansas (BME 1955, MME 1956, PhD 1967), and in 1956–7 at the University of Melbourne, Australia, on a Fulbright scholarship. Between 1955 and 1963 he taught music in various Kansas public schools, and from 1965 to 1969 was on the music faculty at Michigan State University, where he was also director of the laboratory for studies in music psychology. In 1969 he returned to the University of Kansas to chair the department of music education and music therapy. Duerksen has lectured widely in the USA, Great Britain, and Australia on music education, music therapy, and the psychology of music, and is perhaps best known for his often quoted monograph *Teaching Instrumental Music* (1972). He has been active in various professional bodies, including the National Association for Music Therapy and the Music Educators National Conference, and from 1980 to 1982 he was national chairman of the MENC Music Education Research Council.

GEORGE N. HELLER

Dufallo, Richard (John) (*b* East Chicago, IN, 30 Jan 1933). Conductor and clarinetist. After studying at the American Conservatory of Music, Chicago, and with Foss at UCLA, he gained valuable experience as a member of Foss's Improvisation Chamber Ensemble, and soon proved himself as a highly gifted clarinetist, and equal to the most demanding contemporary scores. He was associate conductor of the Buffalo PO (1962–7) and conductor for the Center of Creative and Performing Arts at SUNY, Buffalo (1964–7), where he also taught (1963–7). His studies with William Steinberg at the New York PO seminar for conductors led to invitations to conduct that orchestra, with which he toured the Far East in 1967, and also the Pittsburgh SO; he subsequently conducted the Chicago SO, Philadelphia Orchestra, Dallas SO, Louisville Orchestra, St. Paul Chamber Orchestra, and the Syracuse SO, among others. He studied with Boulez in Basle in 1969, and since his European début with the Paris RO in 1971 he has appeared as guest conductor of such orchestras as the Concertgebouw Orchestra (début 1975), Berlin PO (début 1976), London SO, BBC SO, and the National Orchestra of Spain. In 1969 he became director of the contemporary music conferences at the Aspen Music Festival, and from 1972 to 1979 he was music director of the Juilliard School's 20th-century music series. He became artistic director of the Gelders Orkest in Arnhem, the Netherlands, in 1980.

Although Dufallo has a wide repertory of 18th- and 19th-century music, he is principally known as an interpreter of new scores, a reputation he established as one of the conductors in performances of Stockhausen's *Carré* for four orchestras in The Hague, Paris, and London in 1972. He has conducted world premières of works by Iannis Xenakis, Richard Wernick, and Peter Maxwell Davies, American premières of works by Copland, Crumb, Penderecki, and Aribert Reimann, and first European performances of works by Ives, Varèse, Ruggles, and Druckman. Also active in opera, he was director of the "Mini-Met" series at the Metropolitan Opera (1972–4), and has worked for the Cincinnati Opera (*Boris Godunov*) and the New York City Opera (Puccini's *Il trittico* and Offenbach's *Les contes d'Hoffmann*). Dufallo's approach, unlike that of many new music specialists, is dramatic rather than structural. His experience as a clarinetist and ensemble player enables him to deal with instrumental problems in a practical way, and his projection of each score strives for the clearest emotional as well as musical impact.

For illustration *see* DEGAETANI, JAN.

RICHARD BERNAS/DENNIS K. McINTIRE

Duke, John (Woods) (*b* Cumberland, MD, 30 July 1899; *d* Northampton, MA, 26 Oct 1984). Composer and pianist. He studied piano and composition with Harold Randolph and Gustav Strube at the Peabody Conservatory (1915–18), and continued his studies with Franklin Cannon in New York and with Schnabel and Boulanger in Europe (1929–30). From 1923 to 1967 he taught at Smith College, from which he retired as professor of music. His most important contribution was in the field of song, in which his style became more conventional after experiments during the 1920s and 1930s. Two recordings devoted wholly to his songs have been issued: *Seventeen Songs by John Duke* (1977) and *Songs of John Duke* (1979); the latter received praise both for the quality of the songs and for the performance (by the soprano Carole Bogard and the composer).

WORKS

Stage, texts by D. Duke: The Cat that Walked by itself (children's musical), 1944; Captain Lovelock (chamber opera, 1), 1953; The Sire de Maletroit (chamber opera, 1), 1958; The Yankee Pedlar (operetta), 1962

Orch: Ov., d, 1928; Conc., A, pf, str, 1938; Carnival Ov., 1940

Chamber and inst: The Fairy Glen, pf, 1922; Suite, va, 1933; Suite, vc, 1934; Fantasy, a, vn, pf, 1936; Str Trio, 1937; 2 str qts, 1941, 1967; Narrative, va, pf, 1942; Pf Trio, D, 1943; Dialogue, vc, pf, 1943; Melody, vc/va, pf, 1946

Choral: Magnificat, unison vv, org, 1961; 3 River Songs (after Chin.), female vv, pf, 1963; O Sing unto the Lord a new song, female vv, str orch, 1965

*c*260 songs

Principal publishers: Boosey & Hawkes, C. Fischer, Mercury, G. Schirmer, Peer-Southern, Valley

BIBLIOGRAPHY

R. Friedberg: "The Songs of John Duke," *NATS Bulletin*, xix/4 (1963), 8

E. Compton: *A Singer's Guide to the Songs of John Duke* (diss., U. of Rochester, 1974)

R. Friedberg: "The Recent Songs of John Duke," *NATS Bulletin*, xxxvi/1 (1979), 31 [incl. complete list of songs to 1978]

P. Kresh: "Songs by John Duke," *Stereo Review*, xliv/4 (1980), 131 [review]

R. Friedberg: *American Art Song and American Poetry*, ii (Metuchen, NJ, 1984)

RUTH C. FRIEDBERG

Duke, Vernon [Dukelsky, Vladimir Alexandrovich] (*b* Parfianovka, nr Pskov, Russia, 10 Oct 1903; *d* Santa Monica, CA, 16 Jan 1969). Composer. He studied with Reinhold Glière (1916–19) and Marian Dombrovsky (1917–19) at the Kiev Conservatory and then fled the Revolution with his family, settling first in Constantinople (1920–21) and then in New York (1922). There he wrote a piano concerto for Artur Rubinstein. From 1924 he was in Paris and was commissioned by Sergei Diaghilev to write a ballet based on his concerto, which was performed by the Ballets Russes at Monte Carlo and Paris in 1925. In London he wrote music for the stage (*c*1926–9) before returning to New York, where he studied orchestration with Joseph Schillinger (1934–5). He became an American citizen in 1936. In 1948 he founded the Society for Forgotten Music. His first successful popular song, "I'm only human after all," was included in *The Garrick Gaieties of 1930*. At George Gershwin's suggestion he adopted the pseudonym Vernon Duke for his popular songs and light music, continuing to use his Russian name for his other works until 1955. Duke developed two styles, one for his choral works, operas, ballets, and orchestral and chamber compositions, which were championed in the USA and Europe by Koussevitzky, and another for his revues, musicals, and film scores, for which he was best known. His most successful work was the musical play *Cabin in the Sky* (1940), which was performed on Broadway by an all-black cast that included Ethel Waters and was choreographed by Balanchine. In many of his concert works Duke used a contrapuntal style; in his songs the melodic style is expansive, almost rhapsodic, and uses chromaticism and wide arpeggios. In addition to an autobiography, *Passport to Paris* (1955), he wrote *Listen Here!: a Critical Essay on Music Depreciation* (1963) and Russian poetry published under his original name.

WORKS

(only those composed in the USA)

STAGE

Unless otherwise stated, all are revues and dates are those of first New York performance; librettists and lyricists are listed in that order in parentheses.

Walk a Little Faster (E. Y. Harburg), 7 Dec 1932 [incl. April in Paris]

Ziegfeld Follies of 1934 (Harburg), 4 Jan 1934 [incl. Suddenly, I like the likes of you, What is there to say?]

Public Gardens (ballet, choreographed by L. Massin), Chicago, 8 March 1935

Ziegfeld Follies of 1936 (I. Gershwin), 30 Jan 1936 [incl. I can't get started, That moment of moments, An Island in the West Indies, Words without music]

The Show is On (T. Fetter), 25 Dec 1936 [incl. Now]

Cabin in the Sky (musical, L. Root; J. T. Latouche), 25 Oct 1940 [incl. Cabin in the Sky, Takin' a Chance on Love]; film, collab. H. Arlen, 1943

Banjo Eyes (musical, J. Quillan, I. Elinson, after J. C. Holm, G. Abbott: Three Men on a Horse; Latouche, H. Adamson), 25 Dec 1941 [incl. We're having a baby]

The Lady comes Across (musical, F. Thompson, D. Powell; Latouche), 9 Jan 1942

Dancing in the Streets (H. Dietz), Boston, 1943

Jackpot (musical, G. Bolton, S. Sheldon, B. Roberts; Dietz), 13 Jan 1944

Sadie Thompson (musical, Dietz, R. Mamoulian, after S. Maugham: Rain; Dietz), 16 Nov 1944 [incl. The love I long for]

Sweet Bye and Bye (O. Nash), New Haven, CT, 10 Oct 1946

Two's Company (P. de Vries, C. Sherman; Nash), 15 Dec 1952 [incl. Roundabout, Out of the clear blue sky]

Time Remembered (incidental music), 1957

Emperor Norton (ballet), San Francisco, 1957

Mistress into Maid (opera, Duke, after A. Pushkin), Santa Barbara, CA, 1958

Lady Blue (ballet), 1961

Zenda (opera, E. Freeman; L. Adelson, S. Kuller, M. Charnin), San Francisco, Aug 1963

FILMS

April in Paris (S. Cahn), 1952; She's Working her Way through College (Cahn), 1952; completed score for G. Gershwin: The Goldwyn Follies, 1938

VOCAL

Songs: I'm only human after all (I. Gershwin, Harburg), in Garrick Gaieties of 1930; Autumn in New York (Duke), in Thumbs Up, 1935; 3 Chinese Songs (M. Kuzmin), *c*1937; 5 Victorian Songs, 1942; 5 Victorian Street Ballads, 1944; Ogden Nash's Musical Zoo, 20 songs, *c*1947; La bohème et mon coeur (F. Carco), 7 songs, 1949; A Shropshire Lad (A. E. Housman), 6 songs, *c*1949; 4 Songs (W. Blake), 1955

Other: Epitaph (O. Mandelstamm), S, chorus, orch, 1932; Dédicaces (G. Apollinaire), S, pf, orch, 1934; The End of St. Petersburg (various authors), oratorio, 1937; Moulin-rouge (A. Symons), S, 6vv, pf, 1944; Paris aller et retour (P. Gilson), cantata, chorus, pf, 1948

INSTRUMENTAL

Orch: Pf Conc., 1924; 3 syms., 1927–8, 1928–30, 1947; Vn Conc., *c*1943; Ode to the Milky Way, 1946; Vc Conc., 1946; Variations on Old Russian Chant, ob, str orch, 1958

Chamber: Ballade, pf, chamber orch, 1931; Capriccio mexicano, vn, pf, 1939; Etude, vn, bn, 1939; 3 Pieces, fl, ob, cl, bn, pf, 1946; Nocturne, 6 wind insts, pf, 1947; Vn Sonata, 1948; Str Qt, *c*1956; Vn Sonata, 1960

Pf: Sonata, 1928; 2 pièces, 1930; Printemps, 1931; New York Nocturne, 1939; Surrealist Suite, 1940; Vieux carré, 1940; Homage to Boston, suite, 1943; 3 Caprices, 1944; Music for Moderns, 6 soloists, 1944; Parisian Suite, 1955; Souvenir de Venise, 1955; Serenade to San Francisco, 1956

Principal publisher: C. Fischer

BIBLIOGRAPHY

EwenD

N. Slonimsky: "Vladimir Dukelsky," *MM*, iv/3 (1927), 37

"Duke, Vernon," *CBY 1941*

D. Ewen: *Popular American Composers* (New York, 1962; suppl., 1972)

Obituary, *New York Times* (18 Jan 1969)

A. Wilder: *American Popular Song: the Great Innovators, 1900–1950* (New York, 1972)

RONALD BYRNSIDE/R

Dukelsky, Vladimir Alexandrovich. *See* DUKE, VERNON.

Duke University. A private university founded in 1838 in Durham, North Carolina. *See* CHAPEL HILL, RALEIGH, DURHAM; *see also* LIBRARIES AND COLLECTIONS, §3.

Dulcimer, Appalachian. *See* APPALACHIAN DULCIMER.

Dulcimer, hammered. *See* HAMMERED DULCIMER.

Dunbar, Paul Laurence (*b* Dayton, OH, 27 June 1872; *d* Dayton, 9 Feb 1906). Poet and lyricist. He was born into a family of former slaves, and although he had the opportunity to attend college through the generosity of several white patrons, he decided to pursue a career as a poet and writer. In little over a decade he produced six collections of poems, four collections of short stories, four novels, three plays, and the lyrics and librettos for several works written in collaboration with the composer Will Marion Cook, including *Clorindy, or The Origin of the Cakewalk* (1898), *Jes' Lak White Fo'ks* (1899), and *In Dahomey* (1902). Although Dunbar's fame rests mostly on his dialect poems, these comprise less than half his poetic output. Several composers, including Henry T. Burleigh, Cowell, Cadman, Swanson, J. Rosamond Johnson, Gilchrist, Ulysses Kay, Hadley, Carpenter, and Still, have set his works, the most popular being those from the collections *Majors and Minors* (1895) and *Lyrics of the Hearthside* (1899).

BIBLIOGRAPHY

SouthernB

B. Brawley: *Paul Laurence Dunbar, Poet of his People* (Chapel Hill, 1936)

A. Gayle, Jr.: *Oak and Ivy* (Garden City, NY, 1971)

R. Friedberg: *American Art Song and American Poetry*, i (Metuchen, NJ, 1981)

M. A. Hovland: *Musical Settings of American Poetry: a Bibliography* (Westport, CT, in preparation)

JOHN GRAZIANO

Dunbar, W. Rudolph (*b* Nabaclis [now in Guyana], 5 April 1907). Conductor. He played clarinet in the British Guiana Militia Band from 1916 to 1919, when he enrolled at the Institute of Musical Art as a student of clarinet, piano, and composition. While in New York he played in E. Gilbert Anderson's Harlem Orchestra and Will Vodery's Plantation Orchestra. After graduating in 1924 he went on tour to Europe with the revue *Dixie to Broadway*. He studied in Paris with Louis Cahuzac, Philippe Gaubert, and Paul Vidal, and also with Felix Weingartner in Vienna. In 1931 he moved to London, where his orchestra African Polyphony was recorded early in the 1930s; his band at the Cossack Restaurant became the first black ensemble to broadcast on the BBC (1934). He also conducted the stage show *Black Rhythm* (1934). Dunbar returned to New York in 1938, where he conducted a performance of his *Dance of the Twenty-first Century*. On 26 April 1942 he became the first black conductor to lead the London PO, when he appeared with the orchestra at the Royal Albert Hall; in March 1944 he made a guest appearance with the Liverpool PO in a program of American music. He then joined the Allied Forces in France as a newspaper correspondent, and appeared in Paris on 18 November 1944 with the Association des Concerts Pasdeloup. The following year he conducted the Berlin PO in its first postwar concert and organized a festival of American music in Paris. He made a tour of the Caribbean and his native country in 1948 with the Hollywood Bowl Orchestra. He became the first black musician to conduct concerts in Poland and the USSR in 1959 and 1964 respectively. His memorabilia are at Yale University.

BIBLIOGRAPHY

SouthernB
V. Arvey: "Britain Applauds Rudolph Dunbar," *Opportunity: Journal of Negro Life*, xx (1942), 330
R. Abdul: *Blacks in Classical Music* (New York, 1977), 241
D. de Lerma: "Rudolph Dunbar, Conductor," *Baltimore Afro-American*, lxxxvi (17 June 1978), 17
"In Retrospect: W. Rudolph Dunbar," *BPiM*, ix (1981), 193

DOMINIQUE-RENÉ DE LERMA

Duncan, Isadora [Angela I.] (*b* San Francisco, CA, 26 May 1877; *d* Nice, France, 14 Sept 1927). Dancer. She studied ballet as a child but abandoned classical ballet technique, which she regarded as artificial, to develop her own style of dancing based on the principles of natural movement. Early in her career she danced for the theatrical manager Augustin Daly in the USA and with Loïe Fuller's company in Europe, but she subsequently performed mainly as a solo recitalist. Although she gave an early performance (New York, 1898) to works by the American composer Ethelbert Nevin, she soon turned to the music of such composers as Beethoven, Schumann, Wagner, and Chopin. Duncan is chiefly significant as a liberator and she became a pioneer of modern dance: through her example she encouraged serious dancers (particularly in the USA and Germany) to develop new styles and techniques, and her innovations in music, costume, and scenery led other dancers and choreographers to experiment with those elements.

Isadora Duncan

See also DANCE, §III, 2.

WRITINGS

Der Tanz der Zukunft (Leipzig, 1903; Eng. trans. as *The Dance*, New York, 1909)
The Dance of the Future (New York, 1908)
The Art of the Dance (New York, 1928)

BIBLIOGRAPHY

Isadora Duncan: *My Life* (New York, 1927, 2/1933/*R*1955)
Irma Duncan and A. R. Macdougall: *Isadora Duncan's Russian Days and her Last Years in France* (New York, 1929)
P. Magriel, ed.: *Nijinsky, Pavlova, Duncan: Three Lives in Dance* (New York, 1946–7/*R*1977)
A. R. Macdougall: *Isadora: a Revolutionary in Art and Love* (New York, 1960)
Irma Duncan: *Duncan Dancer* (Middletown, CT, 1966)
I. I. Schneider: *Isadora Duncan: the Russian Years* (London, 1968)
V. Seroff: *The Real Isadora* (New York, 1971)
F. Steegmuller: *Your Isadora* (New York, 1974)
G. McVay: *Isadora and Esenin* (Ann Arbor, MI, 1980)
M. Niehaus: *Isadora Duncan: Leben, Werk, Wirkung* (Wilhelmshaven, Germany, 1981)
F. Rosemont, ed.: *Isadora Speaks* (San Francisco, 1981)

SUSAN AU

Duncan, (Robert) Todd (*b* Danville, KY, 12 Feb 1903). Baritone. After attending Butler University, Indianapolis (BA 1925), and Columbia University Teachers College (MA 1930), he joined the voice faculty of Howard University in Washington, DC, where he remained until 1945. He made his opera début on 10 July 1934 as Alfio in Mascagni's *Cavalleria rusticana* with the Aeolian Opera in New York, and later became the first black member of the New York City Opera, where he first appeared on 28 September 1945 as Tonio in Leoncavallo's *Pagliacci*. Also active in musical theater, he created the role of Porgy in Gershwin's *Porgy and Bess* at New York's Alvin Theatre (10 October 1935), and sang it again in the revivals of 1937 and 1942; he appeared in the London production of *The Sun Never Sets* (1938), as the Lord's General in Vernon Duke's *Cabin in the Sky* (New York, Martin Beck Theatre, 25 October 1940), and in *The Barrier* (1951); his performance as Stephen Kumalo in Kurt Weill's *Lost in the Stars*, which ran at New York's Music Box from 30 October 1949 to 3 April 1950, earned him the Donaldson and New York Drama Critics awards in 1950. Duncan made his recital début in 1944 at Town Hall, New York, and between then and the time he retired he gave more than 2000 recitals in 56 countries. He also made two films, *Syncopation* (1942) and *Unchained* (1955). In later years he was active as a singing teacher, in his own studio in Washington and at the Curtis Institute in Philadelphia. He received a number of honors, including a doctorate from Howard University (1938), a special tribute from the Washington Performing Arts Society (1978), and the George Peabody Medal (1984).

BIBLIOGRAPHY

SouthernB
R. Abdul: *Blacks in Classical Music* (New York, 1977), 15, 100, 136, 147, 150

P. Turner: *Afro-American Singers* (Minneapolis, 1977)

DOMINIQUE-RENÉ DE LERMA

Dunham, Henry M(orton) (*b* Brockton, MA, 27 July 1853; *d* Brookline, MA, 4 May 1929). Organist and composer. He studied organ with George E. Whiting at the New England Conservatory, graduating in 1873, and attended the Boston University College of Music. Most of his career was spent as an organ teacher at the New England Conservatory; he also taught at Boston University and at Lasell Seminary in suburban Auburndale, where he created an academic music course designed as a preparation for the junior-level curriculum at the New England Conservatory. He served as organist in several Boston churches and was active as a recitalist, presenting all the major works of Bach in concerts on the famous instrument in Boston Music Hall. As a composer, Dunham was best known for his works for organ and orchestra, among them *Cortège*, *Evening in Venice* (for strings, organ, harp, and timpani), and *Aurora* (1919), a symphonic poem that was performed by a number of leading American orchestras. He also composed chamber music, many works for organ (including four sonatas and three volumes of studies), and some choral pieces. Conservative in his musical outlook, he inveighed late in life against jazz and ragtime on the one hand and Schoenberg and Copland on the other as "the extremes of vulgarity in music of the present day."

BIBLIOGRAPHY

H. M. Dunham: *The Life of a Musician Woven into a Strand of History of the New England Conservatory of Music* (New York, 1931)

J. C. Gamble: *The Organ Sonatas of Henry Morton Dunham* (diss., Memphis State U., 1980)

WILLIAM OSBORNE

Dunn, Bob (*d* Houston, TX, 1972). Country-music steel guitarist. He made his professional début with the Panhandle Cowboys and Indians, an Oklahoma band, in 1927, but gradually developed a style that was heavily infused with jazz. In 1934 he became one of the first country musicians to play an electric steel guitar. He joined Milton Brown's Musical Brownies later that year and played on 84 of the sides recorded at the group's two Decca sessions. His staccato, trumpet-like style became characteristic not only of the Musical Brownies' sound, but of western-swing steel-guitar playing in general. After the Brownies disbanded, following Brown's death in April 1936, Dunn worked for a time with Major Kord's Hi Flyers. In 1939 he recorded for the first time with his own group, the Vagabonds. Dunn was the pioneer steel guitarist of western swing, creating a style that has influenced Leon MacAuliffe, Noel Boggs, and many other musicians.

BIBLIOGRAPHY

B. Pinson: "The Musical Brownies," *Country Directory*, iv (1962), 11

R. Sheets: "A History of Western Swing Steel," *Steel Guitarist* (May 1979), 22

RONNIE PUGH

Dunn, James Philip (*b* New York, 10 Jan 1884; *d* Jersey City, NJ, 24 July 1936). Organist and composer. After receiving the BA from City College of New York (1903) he studied at Columbia University with MacDowell, Leonard McWhood, and Cornelius Rybner. Upon being awarded the MA (1905) he began a lengthy career as organist at Catholic churches in the area: Holy Innocents', New York; St. Henry's, Bayonne; and St. Patrick's, Jersey City. He also taught piano, organ, and composition, coached singers, accompanied professional musicians, contributed articles to *Musical America*, *Musical Observer*, and *Music News*, and served as a contributing editor (1927–30) of *Singing* (later *Singing and Playing*). A member of the New York Tonkünstler Society and Musicians' Society of Jersey City (president, 1915–16), he also served on the board of directors of the Manuscript Society of New York in its later years and had 15 of his compositions performed from manuscript at five private meetings of the Society between December 1908 and May 1916.

Dunn's setting of Poe's *Annabel Lee* for voice and orchestra, performed at a People's SO Concert in New York during the 1913–14 season, brought him critical attention because of its innovations, and his episodic *Lyric Scenes* for the stage added to that reputation. A facile composer, he gained notice when his tone poem *We* was first performed by the New York PO in a Lewisohn Stadium concert on 27 August 1927; the work, commemorating Lindbergh's transatlantic flight of the previous May, had been composed in less than three weeks after the event.

WORKS

(selective list)

Stage: The Galleon (F. H. Martens), 1918; Lyric Scenes (after C. McMillan: The Fountain, and M. Lavelle: A Kiss in the Dark)

Orch: Annabel Lee (Poe), 1v, orch, 1913; Lovesight, sym. poem, perf. 1919; The Confessions of St. Augustine, 1925; Ov. on Negro Themes, 1925; We, tone poem, 1927; Sym., C, 1929; The Barber's 6 Brothers: Passacaglia and Theme Fugatum, 1930; Choral, a, 1930

Chamber and inst: Pf Qnt, g, 1910; Vn Sonata, g, 1912; Pf Trio, B♭, 1913; 2 str qts, 1913; Variations, vn, pf, 1915; Love's Benediction, 8 arrs. of an Irish folk tune; many pf and org works

Vocal: The Phantom Drum (Martens), cantata, S, Bar, SSA, orch, 1917, arr. mixed vv, 1918; It was a lover and his lass (Shakespeare), female chorus, orch, 1918, arr. mixed chorus; The Music of Spring, female vv, pf/orch, 1918, arr. SATB, 1923; Marquesan Isle (M. M. Smith), female vv, pf, 1923, arr. vv, orch/jazz band, 1924, arr. mixed vv, pf, 1926; Song of the Night, SSAATTBB, 1923; Salve Regina, female chorus, 1924; Missa choralis, SATB, org, 1925 [arr. of work by L. Refice]; *c*20 songs; part songs

Principal publisher: J. Fischer

BIBLIOGRAPHY

"James P. Dunn," *Fischer Edition News*, i/2 (1923), 4

J. T. Howard: *Studies of Contemporary American Composers: James P. Dunn* (New York, 1925) [incl. list of pubd works]

"About James P. Dunn," *Singing*, i/9 (1926), 30

C. Reis: *American Composers: a Record of Works Written between 1912 and 1932* (New York, 2/1932)

Obituary, *New York Times* (25 July 1936)

"The World of Music," *The Etude*, liv/11 (1936), 680 [obituary]

MARGERY MORGAN LOWENS

Dunn, Mignon (*b* Memphis, TN, 17 June 1931). Mezzo-soprano. With a scholarship she was awarded from the Metropolitan Opera, she studied singing in New York with Karin Branzell, and after a number of engagements with several small companies she made her New York City Opera début as Carmen in 1956. After her first performance at the Metropolitan two years later as the Nurse in *Boris Godunov* (she was later to sing the role of Marina in the new production of the opera in 1975), she became a mainstay of the company with more than 50 roles to her credit, including Wagner's Venus, Brangäne, and Fricka; Verdi's Amneris and Azucena; Giulietta (*Les contes d'Hoffmann*); Laura (in Ponchielli's *La Gioconda*); Saint-Saëns' Delilah; Carmen; Mascagni's Santuzza (*Cavalleria rusticana*); and Strauss's Nurse (*Die Frau ohne Schatten*), Herodias (*Salome*), and Adelaide (*Arabella*). She made her début at the San Francisco Opera as Brangäne in 1967, a role she repeated in a new production of *Tristan* at the Lyric Opera of Chicago in the 1979–80 season; she subsequently appeared in San Francisco as Baba the Turk (in Stravinsky's *The Rake's Progress*),

Ulrica (*Un ballo in maschera*), and Erda (*Das Rheingold*). Dunn has performed virtually every important mezzo role, and her extensive career has included engagements with most of the leading opera companies, musical festivals, and orchestras in the USA and abroad. She has performed and recorded Thomson's *The Mother of us all*. Her voice is a large, dramatic instrument, and as an artist she has an expressiveness that is best suited to the grand gesture. She is married to the conductor Kurt Klippstätter, with whom she performed for the first time as Tchaikovsky's Joan of Arc at the Michigan Opera Theater in 1979.

BIBLIOGRAPHY

R. Jacobson: "The Other Valkyrie," *Opera News*, xxxviii/20 (1974), 16
J. Heimenz: "Mignon Dunn," *HiFi/MusAm*, xxv/4 (1975), 18

RICHARD LESUEUR

Dunn, Thomas (Burt) (*b* Aberdeen, SD, 21 Dec 1925). Conductor. Brought up in Baltimore, he studied there at the Peabody Conservatory and Johns Hopkins University, and later at Harvard and the Amsterdam Conservatory. His teachers included Charles Courboin, Virgil Fox, E. Power Biggs, and Ernest White for organ; Robert Shaw, G. Wallace Woodworth, and Ifor Jones for choral conducting; Gustav Leonhardt for harpsichord; and Anton Van der Horst for orchestral conducting. He held church appointments in Baltimore and Philadelphia, and in 1957 became music director at the Church of the Incarnation, New York. His reputation spread, and in 1959 he was appointed music director of the Cantata Singers, impressing particularly with performances of Handel's *Belshazzar* and Rameau's *Les Indes galantes*, and expanding the group's repertory to include 19th- and 20th-century music. He founded the Festival Orchestra of New York (1959, disbanded in 1969). In 1961–2 he became known to a wider public through a series of Bach concerts in Carnegie Hall in which he conducted the B minor Mass with 25 singers and 26 players, forces approximately equal to Bach's; he gave four performances of *Messiah* in 1963, each in a different version. These ventures demonstrated his firm belief in scholarship as the basis of convincing performances using appropriate forces. In 1967 he became music director of the Handel and Haydn Society, Boston, which he converted from a conservative choral society to a forward-looking organization whose concerts are highly diversified. His performances are clean, transparent, rhythmic, and, in a broad repertory from Schütz to Dallapiccola and Stravinsky, he is particularly effective in works with chorus. He has taught at many universities and music schools in the USA.

MICHAEL STEINBERG

Duo-Art. Reproducing piano mechanism (*see* PLAYER PIANO) introduced by the AEOLIAN CO. in 1913.

Duo Geminiani. Early-music duo formed in 1974 by STANLEY RITCHIE and his wife Elizabeth Wright.

Duport, Pierre Landrin (*b* Paris, France, 1762 or 1763; *d* Washington, DC, 11 April 1841). Dancing master, violinist, teacher, and composer. His father, surnamed Landrin, was a dancing master and teacher to the royal family. In 1783 Duport went to Dublin to teach in the studio of Gordon McNeill, whose daughter, Charlotte, he married on 8 August 1783; in 1787 the two went to France, where he is said to have taught Queen Marie Antoinette's children. After Bastille Day they fled to the USA (17 July 1789), arriving in 1790. Duport produced ballets and taught in Philadelphia, New York, Boston, Baltimore, Georgetown, and Norfolk, then retired to Washington, DC. A holograph at the Library of Congress contains 104 of his dance tunes, many carefully dated between 1780 and 1834, including the genres cotillion, contredanse, march, quickstep, minuet, allemande, sarabande, gavotte, jig, waltz, and reel. Several of his works were published, including *Favorite Cotillions* (n.d.), *No.1 of a New Sett of Cotilions with Figures called after the American Navy* (before 1802), and *United States Country Dances* (1791). His daughter Anna married Alexander Reinagle.

Louis Duport, claimed as a son by P. L. Duport, made his dancing début in 1790 at the age of nine; he is not known to have been in the USA after 1796 and could have been the prominent French dancer Louis Antoine Duport (*d* 1853).

BIBLIOGRAPHY

O. G. T. Sonneck: *A Bibliography of Early Secular American Music* (Washington, DC, 1905, rev. and enlarged by W. T. Upton 2/1945/*R*1964)
L. Moore: "The Duport Mystery," *Dance Perspectives*, vii (1960) [special issue]
R. J. Wolfe: *Secular Music in America, 1801–1825: a Bibliography* (New York, 1964)

J. BUNKER CLARK

Durán, Narciso (1776–1846). Franciscan teacher and composer, founder of the San José Mission; *see* CALIFORNIA MISSION MUSIC, §§1 and 3, and HISPANIC-AMERICAN MUSIC, §1.

Durante, Jimmy [James Francis] (*b* New York, 10 Feb 1893; *d* Santa Monica, CA, 29 Jan 1980). Comedian and singer. He began playing piano in New York bars at the age of 17. Around 1916 he organized a five-piece jazz band in Harlem. With the singer Eddie Jackson and vaudeville actor Lou Clayton he opened the Club Durant in 1923 and perfected his inimitable blend of comedy, raspy-voiced singing, and honky-tonk piano playing which he used to great effect, often in his own songs. The club flourished until it was closed by Prohibition officials, whereupon the three worked in other clubs, appeared in vaudeville shows, made recordings and a motion picture, and performed on Broadway. From 1932 to 1941 Durante appeared in 21 films. These generally failed to capture his style and were less well-received than his Broadway shows of the period, such as *Jumbo* (1935). In the 1940s he was successful in nightclubs and on radio, leading to further film roles and, after 1950, to frequent appearances on television, including his own series.

BIBLIOGRAPHY

"Durante, Jimmy," *CBY 1946*
G. Fowler: *Schnozzola* (New York, 1951)
Obituary, *New York Times* (30 Jan 1980)
S. Green: *The Great Clowns of Broadway* (New York, 1984)

ROBERT SKINNER

Durham. City in North Carolina (pop. 100,831); *see* CHAPEL HILL, RALEIGH, DURHAM.

Dushkin, Samuel (*b* Suwalki [now in Poland], 13 Dec 1891; *d* New York, 24 June 1976). Violinist. He came to the USA as a child, and his talent was discovered at the Music School Settlement of New York; he became a protégé of the American composer Blair Fairchild, who brought about his studies with Rémy (violin) and Ganaye (composition) at the Paris Conservatoire, and with Auer and Kreisler in New York. Dushkin began to tour in Europe from 1918, and in the USA from 1924, when he first appeared with the New York SO. As well as making a number of successful transcriptions for his own use of works by other composers including Gershwin and Thomson, he became known as a persuasive advocate of contemporary music, a reputation consolidated by his friendship with Stravinsky, who composed for him his Violin Concerto (1931) and *Duo concertant* (1932). Stravinsky, in his autobiography, praised Dushkin for his "remarkable gifts as a violinist, a delicate understanding and, in the exercise of his profession, an abnegation that is very rare." With the composer's collaboration, Dushkin made several transcriptions from Stravinsky's stage works and, with these and the *Duo concertant*, undertook extensive European tours with Stravinsky as pianist between 1932 and 1934. They also recorded these works; Dushkin later described their collaboration (in *Igor Stravinsky*, ed. E. Corle, 1949). He also published teaching manuals for the violin and editions of Baroque and Classical violin works (some of them in fact his own compositions attributed to earlier composers, including Johann Benda and Boccherini).

BIBLIOGRAPHY

I. Stravinsky: *An Autobiography* (New York, 1936, 3/1962)
E. W. White: *Stravinsky: the Composer and his Works* (London, 1966)
J. Creighton: *Discopaedia of the Violin, 1889–1971* (Toronto, 1974)
B. Schwarz: *Great Masters of the Violin* (New York, 1983)

NOËL GOODWIN

Duss, John S. (*b* Zoar, OH, 22 Feb 1860; *d* Economy, PA, 1951). Cornetist, bandmaster, and composer. He studied the cornet and other band instruments under Jacob Rohr (1827–1906), a Pittsburgh bandmaster, but was largely self-taught. He was engaged as a schoolteacher by George Rapp's Harmony Society in 1888, and elected a senior trustee in 1892. This position gave him control of the Harmonists' wealth, which he used to organize bands and to pursue a career as a bandmaster. In 1902 he conducted band concerts at the Metropolitan Opera and at the St. Nicholas Rink on Columbus Avenue and 66th Street, New York. The following year, after a tour of 30 North American cities, he engaged the Metropolitan orchestra and the singers Lillian Nordica and Edouard de Reszke to give concerts at Madison Square Garden which, at a cost of more than $100,000, he transformed into a reproduction of the city of Venice. In spite of unfavorable reviews, Duss returned to New York for the summer season in 1904. His programs were eclectic, consisting of opera arias, overtures, and marches (the last largely of his own composition). In 1906 and 1907 he formed bands that included some of the finest performers in the country, and gave concerts at popular parks and resorts in the East, Midwest, and Canada. He retired to Economy after the 1907 season and devoted himself to composing religious music and writing an autobiography.

WORKS

(selective list; all printed works published in Pittsburgh)

Band, all marches unless otherwise stated: Liberty Chimes (1894); Life's Voyage, waltz (1894); The Limited Express (1894); March G.A.R. in Dixie (1895); The Brownies, dance characteristic (1895); Diana Polonaise, cornet solo (1895); The Great Northwest (1896); Pittsburgh Dispatch (1896); The Cross and Crown, march and two-step (1898); The Shot and Shell, march and two-step (1898); America up to Date (1899); The Fighting Tenth (1899); Jordan's Riffles, two-step (1899); Festival March (1900); The Trolley Song (1901); The Battle of Manila in a Nutshell (1902)

Vocal: Mass in Honor of St. Veronica (1929); O sacred book, anthem (1929); O salutaris, anthem (1929); Psalm of Psalms, anthem (1929); Florida, all hail, song (1935)

Principal publishers: Ott, Volkwein

BIBLIOGRAPHY

J. S. Duss: *The Harmonists: a Personal History* (Harrisburg, PA, 1943)
K. J. R. Arndt: *George Rapp's Successors and Material Heirs* (Cranbury, NJ, 1971)
R. D. Wetzel: *Frontier Musicians on the Connoquenessing, Wabash, and Ohio: a History of the Music and Musicians of George Rapp's Harmony Society, 1805–1906* (Athens, OH, 1976)

RICHARD D. WETZEL

Dutch Reformed Church, music of the. The Reformed Church in America (RCA) and the Christian Reformed Church of North America (CRC) are the two primary representatives of the Dutch Reformed tradition in the USA. Both denominations initially inherited Genevan Calvinist psalmody from their Dutch roots as their only form of music in worship. Founded early in the 17th century, the RCA had accepted organs and hymnody by the turn into the 18th century, and choirs by the later 18th century. A 19th-century wave of Dutch immigrants led to the CRC's accepting similar changes by the early 20th century. Today both denominations are thoroughly Americanized in their practices of worship music. This article gives an account of the development of congregational song in each of them.

1. The Reformed Church in America. 2. The Christian Reformed Church.

1. The Reformed Church in America. The Dutch merchants who landed in what is now New York in 1613 and set up the RCA brought with them Peter Datheen's Dutch translation (1566) of Calvin's Geneva psalter (1562). For more than 100 years these Dutch settlers sang their psalms in unison, *a cappella*, in slow tempo, and usually under the leadership of a *voorzanger* (precentor) until organs were introduced. Their first English psalter was *The Psalms of David* (1767), for which Francis Hopkinson adapted the psalm paraphrases of Tate and Brady (1696) to be sung to altered versions of the Genevan tunes.

After the RCA gained its independence from the Dutch Church in 1771, a new psalter was authorized with a supplement of "some well-composed spiritual hymns." *The Psalms of David, with Hymns and Spiritual Songs* (1789) featured the psalms in short, common, and long meters, with many texts by Isaac Watts. Most of its 135 hymns were designated for use with preaching based on the catechism and with the administration of the sacraments. This change in language, the adoption of Watts's texts and of hymnody, and the loss of virtually all Genevan tunes marked a clear break with the Dutch Reformed tradition. In each later edition of the book (1814, 1831, 1869) the number of hymns was increased. By 1890 the RCA had approved an altered version of Edwin Bedell's hymnal which appeared as *The Church Hymnary* (1891) with almost 1000 hymns. A *Sabbath School and Social Hymn Book* (1843) and *Hymns of Prayer and Praise* (1871) were published for use in RCA Sunday schools and informal services of worship. Other hymnals were also approved.

During the first half of the 20th century, the RCA participated in the preparation of two ecumenical hymnals. The *Hymnal of the Reformed Church* (1920) was prepared jointly by the RCA and the (German) Reformed Church in the USA; it contained a few psalm paraphrases interspersed with the hymns, an arrangement that contributed to the decline of psalm singing in the RCA. *The Hymnbook* (1955), containing almost 600 hymns, resulted from the cooperation of several Presbyterian denominations and the RCA. It and various other hymnals are currently in use by RCA congregations. The taste for congregational song in the RCA ranges from classic Christian hymnody to gospel songs, but includes few metrical psalms. *Rejoice in the Lord* (1985), edited by Erik Routley, is the most recent RCA hymnal; it contains many high-quality hymn texts and tunes from the late 20th century and more than 60 psalm paraphrases.

A comprehensive history of church music in the RCA has not yet been published; research materials are available in the RCA seminaries at New Brunswick, New Jersey, and Holland, Michigan.

2. THE CHRISTIAN REFORMED CHURCH. As a result of a secession in the Reformed Church of the Netherlands (1834), Dutch immigrants moved to Michigan and Iowa, and, after briefly uniting with the RCA, formed the CRC in 1857. Initially isolating themselves from American culture, these settlers sang exclusively Dutch psalms, using an edition of 1773 which featured tonal, isorhythmic versions of the Genevan tunes. Later in the 19th century, some German-speaking Reformed congregations in Iowa and some English-speaking Reformed congregations in New Jersey merged with the CRC. These unions brought some marginal use of hymns into the denomination, though the CRC largely remained committed to Dutch metrical psalmody until just before World War I. In 1914 it adopted the Presbyterian psalter (1912) as its first English-language worship book. This had 413 settings of British and American psalm and hymn tunes for the 150 psalms, and included in an appendix the texts for the catechism hymns from the RCA, but all of these could be sung only by the English-speaking CRC congregations in New Jersey. Only four (corrupt) Genevan tunes appear in this book. This psalter, similar to the RCA book of 1789, thus signaled for the CRC a significant break with its Dutch roots.

The inclusion of hymn tunes and hymn texts in the 1914 psalter, the popularity of hymn singing in singing-schools associated with the CRC and in church choirs, and the commercial promotion of American Sunday-school and gospel hymnody led to the "hymn question" in the CRC. After much debate, the battle was settled in favor of hymns, and the *Psalter Hymnal* of the CRC was published in 1934. This contained 327 psalm settings and 141 hymns, including 39 Genevan tunes with new English psalm paraphrases by Dewey Westra and some CRC clergy. Though metrical psalmody was to be maintained, members of the CRC could now sing a variety of English translations of Latin, Greek, and German hymns, and many 18th- and 19th-century hymns. Thus the *Psalter Hymnal* indicated a growing ecumenical awareness within the CRC, and in its eclectic selection of psalms and hymns reveals the Americanization that had broken the earlier isolation. Although the Genevan tunes were presented in rhythmic versions in the 1934 edition, later printings (1939, 1948) saw changes in the harmonizations and reverted to isorhythm.

To mark the denomination's centennial in 1957, a new edition of the *Psalter Hymnal* was published (1959). It has 310 items for the 150 psalms, and 183 hymns. A number of its 37 Genevan tunes now appear again in rhythmic settings. An experimental *Psalter Hymnal Supplement* (1974) features new hymns, some folk hymn tunes, and some settings of prose psalmody by Joseph Gelineau. Although the *Psalter Hymnal* is the CRC's official songbook, a survey in 1980 revealed that almost 80% of CRC congregations use other hymnals or their own compilations as supplementary books. And though psalmody is still used in the Canadian segment of the CRC (the result of Dutch emigration to Canada after World War II), it is in serious decline in the American part. Another revision of the *Psalter Hymnal* is now in progress.

Research materials on church music in the CRC are held at Heritage Hall Library, Calvin College, Grand Rapids, Michigan.

BIBLIOGRAPHY

REFORMED CHURCH IN AMERICA

D. D. Demarest: *History and Characteristics of the Reformed Protestant Dutch Church* (New York, 1856, rev. and enlarged 4/1889 as *The Reformed Church in America*)

V. L. Redway: "James Parker and the 'Dutch Church'," *MQ*, xxiv (1938), 481

C. S. Smith: "The 1774 Psalm Book of the Reformed Protestant Dutch Church in New York," *MQ*, xxxiv (1948), 84

J. P. Luidens: *The Americanization of the Dutch Reformed Church* (diss., U. of Oklahoma, 1969)

W. A. Weber: "The Hymnody of the Dutch Reformed Church in America, 1628–1953," *The Hymn*, xxvi (1975), 57

A. R. Brouwer: *Reformed Church Roots* (New York, 1977)

G. F. DeJong: *The Dutch Reformed Church in the American Colonies* (Grand Rapids, MI, 1978)

A. Christ-Janer, C. W. Hughes, and C. S. Smith: *American Hymns Old and New* (New York, 1980)

D. R. Steele: "Hymnody in the Reformed Church in America," *American Organist*, xv/9 (1981), 29

CHRISTIAN REFORMED CHURCH

J. H. Kromminga: *The Christian Reformed Church: a study in Orthodoxy* (Grand Rapids, 1949)

J. Oranje: *Calvinism and Music, Retrospect and Prospect* (diss., Northwestern U., 1951)

H. A. Bruinsma, ed.: *Accompanists of the Gospel* (Grand Rapids, 1954)

D. Westra: *150 Psalm Paraphrases for the Genevan Tunes* (MS, n.d., *MiGrC*)

S. Swets: *Fifty Years of Music at Calvin College* (Grand Rapids, 1973)

C. S. Sterrett: "The Use of the Psalms in the Christian Reformed Church," *The Biblical Doctrine of Worship* (Pittsburgh, 1974), 261

J. ten Hoor: *The Transition from Psalmody to Hymnody in the Christian Reformed Church* (thesis, Arizona State U., 1976)

Proceedings of a Conference on Liturgy & Music in Reformed Worship (Grand Rapids, 1979)

V. K. Folgers: "Hymnody in the Christian Reformed Church," *American Organist*, xv/1 (1981), 28

B. F. Polman: *Church Music & Liturgy in the Christian Reformed Church of North America* (diss., U. of Minnesota, 1981)

R. Zuiderveld: "Some Musical Traditions in Dutch Reformed Churches in America," *The Hymn*, xxxvi (1985), 23

BERT F. POLMAN

Dutrey, Honore (*b* New Orleans, LA, *c*1894; *d* Chicago, IL, 21 July 1935). Jazz trombonist. His brothers Sam (clarinet) and Peter (violin) were also highly proficient musicians. From 1910 to 1917 Honore worked in various New Orleans brass bands and in John Robichaux's orchestra. He left New Orleans to join the US Navy, and while in service suffered accidental damage to his lungs. He was eventually able to resume regular playing, however, and settled in Chicago, joining King Oliver's band, with which he worked from 1920 until 1924, taking part in many recordings. He briefly led his own band in 1924, and subsequently worked for various leaders including Carroll Dickerson, Louis Armstrong, and Johnny Dodds. He retired due to ill health in 1930. Although he was not an inventive improviser or the possessor of an exceptional sense of harmony, Dutrey had a sonorous tone and an effective way of playing long legato phrases in the lower register. His main gift was probably his power of understatement, an effective contrast to the volatile creativity of the musicians with whom he usually worked.

For illustration *see* OLIVER, KING.

RECORDINGS

(selective list; all with King Oliver)

Snake Rag (1923, OK 4933); Jazzin' Babies' Blues (1923, OK 4975); Tears (1923, OK 40000); Riverside Blues (1923, OK 40034); Mabel's Dreams (1923, OK 8235)

BIBLIOGRAPHY

S. B. Charters: *Jazz: New Orleans: 1885–1957* (Belleville, NJ, 1958, rev. 2/1963)

JOHN CHILTON

Dvořák, Antonín (Leopold) (*b* Nelahozeves, nr Kralupy [now in Czechoslovakia], 8 Sept 1841; *d* Prague, Czechoslovakia, 1 May 1904). Czech composer. With Bedřich Smetana and Leoš Janáček he is regarded as one of the greatest composers of the nationalist movement in what is now Czechoslovakia. From the autumn of 1892 to the spring of 1895 he served as director of the National Conservatory of Music in New York.

1. Life. 2. "American" works. 3. Influence in America.

1. Life. Dvořák was first taught music by the schoolmaster of his native village. In 1857 he entered the Prague Organ School, where he received the orthodox training of a church musician. He also became a capable viola player, and his first professional post was as a violist in a small band which played in restaurants and for balls; in 1862, during the great upsurge of national culture in Bohemia, it became the nucleus of the new Provisional Theater orchestra. For the next nine years Dvořák was principal violist in the orchestra (from 1866 under Smetana). His earliest serious compositions date from this period: some chamber music, two symphonies, a cello concerto, and a song cycle.

After relinquishing his position at the theater in 1871 Dvořák was able to devote more time to composition, relying (until at least 1878) on teaching as the main source of his income. He began to attract attention when he was 31; by July 1874 he had enough confidence and enough new works to enter the competition for the Austrian State Stipendium, which he won (as he did again in 1876 and 1877). Publication of his works, aided by Brahms's positive representation to the firm of Simrock, brought foreign performances – in Germany, France, England, and even the USA (the Slavonic Rhapsody no.1 was played in Baltimore on 21 February 1880; other works were given in Cincinnati and New York). By the early 1880s he was internationally recognized. He was received with particular warmth in 1884 in London, where he conducted outside Bohemia for the first time; he was immediately invited to conduct his *Stabat mater* and Sixth Symphony at the Three Choirs Festival in Worcester, and was commissioned to write new choral works for the Birmingham and Leeds festivals and a symphony for the Philharmonic Society.

The years 1884–92 were vintage ones for Dvořák. With several more visits to England he added to his reputation as one of the most important contemporary composers, having already won international fame with his orchestral, choral, and chamber compositions, if not with works for the theater. In 1889 he was invited to join the faculty of the Prague Conservatory but, unprepared to commit himself to teaching at the time, he deferred accepting until January 1891. Meanwhile other honors and triumphs accrued: in June 1889 the Order of the Iron Crown (from Austria); a few months later an audience granted by the emperor; then an invitation from Tchaikovsky to visit Russia (which he did, in March 1890); election to the Czech Academy of Sciences and Arts; successful reception in London of the Eighth Symphony (April 1890) and in Birmingham of the première of his Requiem Mass (October 1891).

In June 1891 Dvořák was invited by Jeannette Thurber, who had founded the National Conservatory of Music in New York in 1885, to assume its directorship, at a salary of $15,000 a year. After considerable negotiations Dvořák accepted, agreeing to take the post for two years from 1 October 1892 with the stipulation that he would be in New York for the eight months of each academic year. His arrival in the USA in late September 1892 was timed to coincide with the celebrations commemorating the fourth centenary of Columbus's discovery of America. Since Joseph Rodman Drake's poem *The American Flag* failed to reach him in time, he wrote instead, before leaving home, a *Te Deum* (and completed his setting of the poem, a cantata of the same title, in January 1893). Thurber's aim in inviting him was twofold: she expected him to found an American school of composition; and she wanted a figurehead, rather than an administrator, for her conservatory. She was also eager for Dvořák to write an opera based on Longfellow's *Song of Hiawatha*, but the project never advanced beyond a few preliminary sketches. Her conservatory was run on philanthropic lines, and she controlled the finances, having access to the fortune of her husband, a highly successful wholesale grocer. Dvořák was expected to teach composition and orchestration to the most talented students three mornings a week, and, on the other three mornings, to conduct the choir and orchestra and to be available for business consultations. During the first winter he conducted his *Te Deum*, Tragic Overture, Symphony no.6, and Hussite Overture in New York and the Requiem in Boston; between January and May 1893 he composed the Symphony no.9, *Z Nového světa* ("From the New World"). Being keenly interested in the music of black Americans, Dvořák seized the opportunity of inviting a gifted black singer to sing spirituals to him. This was Harry T. Burleigh, a student at the National Conservatory (though not a pupil of Dvořák).

Dvořák spent the summer vacation of 1893 with his family at Spillville, a Czech community in northeastern Iowa; during his stay there he composed his String Quartet in F and String Quintet in E♭, each known as the "American." He went to Chicago for the World's Columbian Exposition and on its "Czech Day," 12 August, he conducted the Symphony no.8, three Slavonic Dances from the op.72 set, and the overture *My Home*. He was invited to Omaha by Edward Rosewater, a Czech-American newspaper publisher, who arranged a banquet for him at the beginning of September. From there he went to St. Paul to see Pastor P. J. Rynda, a Moravian, and was given another banquet by the Czechs of that city. On the return trip to New York he stopped at Buffalo and Niagara Falls. A few days later he conducted his Hussite Overture and Psalm cxlix at the 36th Worcester Music Festival.

The Symphony "From the New World" was first presented (to an eager and very enthusiastic audience) by Dvořák's friend Anton Seidl, conducting the New York Philharmonic Society orchestra at Carnegie Hall, on 16 December 1893, and the Kneisel Quartet gave the premières of the Quartet in F at Boston on 1 January and the new Quintet in New York on 12 January.

For nearly a year Thurber had been urging Dvořák to sign a new contract to take effect when their first one expired in May 1894. He was in no hurry to do so; apart from having fits of nostalgia, he was seriously worried about the financial stability of the conservatory. As a result of the economic crisis of 1893 Thurber's husband was on the verge of bankruptcy, and consequently she was well in arrears with Dvořák's salary. However, after receiving a promissory note he signed a second two-year contract on 28 April 1894. He returned to Bohemia for the summer, and spent a quiet and happy time at his country retreat. Although Thurber did not fully honor her promise, he returned to America in time to resume his duties at the National Conservatory on 1 November.

For some time Dvořák had composed comparatively little, his two most significant works being the Violin Sonatina in G op.100 of 1893 and the *Biblical Songs* op.99 of 1894. On returning to the conservatory for his third year (which in the event lasted only six months) he settled down to writing the Cello Concerto in B minor. He finished it three months later (but its première did not take place until 1896, when Leo Stern played it in London with the Philharmonic Society).

Having returned to Europe following the official conclusion of the conservatory's 1894–5 academic year, Dvořák consulted with several of his more influential friends, including Dr. Tragy (who was also a lawyer), about his future. On 17 August he wrote to Thurber to say that he regretted it very much, but it was impossible to return to New York for the agreed eight months in 1895–6. He gave several family reasons for this decision. In November he returned to the Prague Conservatory to resume teaching as professor of composition, becoming director (without administrative duties) in July 1901. Except for one visit to Vienna to discuss a possible production of his opera *Rusalka* with Mahler, he remained in Bohemia for the rest of his life, continuing to reap international honors and recognition.

2. "AMERICAN" WORKS. Leaving aside his arrangement (for soprano, bass, chorus, and orchestra) of Foster's *Old Folks at Home* (1893–4), the principal works of Dvořák's American period are the Symphony no.9 in E minor ("From the New World") op.95 (first published as no.5); the Cello Concerto op.104; three chamber compositions: the "American" String Quartet no.12, op.96, the "American" String Quintet op.97, and the Violin Sonatina in G op.100; the *Biblical Songs* op.99; and, for piano, the Suite in A op.98 (orchestrated as op.98*b*) and eight Humoresques op.101. It is impossible to gauge precisely the extent of American influence on these works. Dvořák had written pentatonic themes and used flattened sevenths in minor keys before he came to the USA, and he was already familiar with the Scotch snap and similar types of rhythmic device found in the songs of black Americans, since they occur in Slovak and Hungarian folk music. He had partly foreshadowed the syncopated main theme of the "American" Quartet as early as 1886 in his Slavonic Dance no.9. Furthermore, the persistent dotted rhythms of the first movement of the String Quintet op.97 and the finale of the Violin Sonatina, which might be thought to have had an American Indian origin, occurred four years earlier in the Piano Quartet op.87. Yet pentatonic themes and flattened sevenths are indeed more common in the music Dvořák wrote during his first two years in the USA, and the thematic material is sometimes more "primitive" than in his earlier music.

While working on the Symphony "From the New World," Dvořák stated, "The influence of America can be felt by anyone who has a 'nose.' " In saying later that it was really "a study or sketch for a longer work," he had in mind his project on *The Song of Hiawatha*. The dance of Pau-Puk-Keewis lay behind the Scherzo, and Minnehaha's funeral in the forest may have inspired the Largo. But he explained that the title of the work simply signified "Impressions and greetings from the New World," and although some American influences are obvious, it is fundamentally Czech.

The first of the three chamber works Dvořák wrote in the USA, all of them in 1893, is the "American" Quartet in F. Although he modeled the opening bars on the beginning of Smetana's First Quartet, he created an entirely different mood. Several of the themes have pentatonic tendencies, but few are strictly pentatonic. The theme at bars 21–4 in the Scherzo is adapted from a birdsong that Dvořák heard in the Iowa woodlands. The String Quintet in E♭ op.97 also includes some "primitive" features; for example, the motif at bars 63–4 of the first movement is a transformed fragment – the melodic outline but not the rhythm – of Indian music, which Dvořák is known to have heard during his summer in Iowa through the songs and dances of a mixed group of Indians. The outstanding movement is the Larghetto, a set of variations that follows Haydn's example in having a double theme, in A♭ minor and major. Dvořák had originally drafted the second one as a tune for the American national song *My country, 'tis of thee*. The third American chamber work is the Violin Sonatina; its themes also tend to be "primitive." The Larghetto (the title "Indian Lament" is unauthorized) is especially appealing, and so is the E major melody in the Finale. (A fourth chamber work associated with the USA – the String Quartet in A♭, which received its première on 26 October 1896 in Boston at the hands of the Kneisel Quartet and in Halle, Germany, at the hands of the Gewandhaus Quartett of Leipzig – was composed mainly elsewhere, between 26 March and 30 December 1895.)

American influence is conspicuous in two piano works of 1894, the Suite in A op.98 (orchestrated in 1895) and the eight Humoresques op.101, for many of their themes are pentatonic. The seventh Humoresque (G♭) quickly became one of Dvořák's most internationally popular pieces, perhaps in some measure because of its piquant "blue-note" cadences vacillating between the major and minor third.

The set of *Biblical Songs* op.99, an intensely personal document, is an affirmation of faith on Dvořák's part after his friends Tchaikovsky and Hans von Bülow had died and while his own father was critically ill. All the songs are settings of verses from psalms taken from the Bible of Kralice. As with the Largo of the Ninth Symphony, Dvořák's recollection of spirituals seems to have affected these songs. But by the time he wrote the Cello Concerto (November 1894–February 1895) he appears to have tired of these exotic elements, which in any case were never more than tendencies. Much of what he wrote during his years in the USA is either marked by Czech influence or was inspired by events in his personal life, as is clearly exemplified by his own continuation of a fragment of *Swing low, sweet chariot* in the G major theme of the Ninth Symphony. Nevertheless he seems not to have dismissed American influence entirely after returning home; the element of pentatonicism and a cadence avoiding the leading tone which appear in the opera *Armida* (1902–3) may well owe something to it.

3. INFLUENCE IN AMERICA. Dvořák's arrival in the USA in autumn 1892 coincided with currents of reaction among some American composers against the predominantly Germanic cast of post-Civil War art music. Some turned with interest to the new musical styles emerging in Russia and France; others sought to find a national identity in American folk music. To the latter, Dvořák seemed to speak directly when he based the principal themes of his Symphony "From the New World" on pentatonic scales, having pointed to them as common to American Indian and black American melodies in an article in the *New York Herald* on 15 December 1893 (the day before the symphony's première). Both earlier and later, especially in a widely read and influential article (in *Harper's New Monthly Magazine* of February 1895), he seemed to be urging American composers to turn to such melodies for source material: "A while ago I suggested that inspiration for truly national music might be derived from the negro melodies

or Indian chants. . . . The so-called plantation songs are indeed the most striking and appealing melodies that have yet been found on this side of the water." Here was a world-famous composer who had not only demonstrated in his earlier works how absorption of his native land's traditional and popular music could assure him a unique personal and national voice, but had also suggested in both words and music how American composers could do the same.

Among the first to follow the suggestion were some of Dvořák's students at the National Conservatory: Goldmark, with works like the overture *Hiawatha*, *A Negro Rhapsody*, and *The Call of the Plains* (for violin and piano); Loomis, with many arrangements of Indian melodies as well as original compositions like *Lyrics of the Red Men* (for piano); and William Arms Fisher, with arrangements of spirituals (he also added the text "Goin' home" to the melody of the Largo of Dvořák's "New World" Symphony). Burleigh, the conservatory student whose singing had introduced Dvořák to black spirituals, based many works on black American melodies, among them the widely sung spirituals arranged by him in *Jubilee Songs of the United States of America* (1916). The most striking reflection of Dvořák's influence was the establishment in 1901, by Arthur Farwell, of the Wa-Wan Press. Named for an Omaha tribal ceremony, it was a vehicle for Farwell and eventually almost 40 other composers who aimed explicitly to "launch a progressive movement for American music, including a definite acceptance of Dvořák's challenge to go after our folk music." Ultimately, however, the "primitive" music of black and native Americans was found unsatisfactory – too restrictive and too artificial – as a direct source of musical raw materials (although in popular songs and dance music, and especially in jazz, the music of blacks was seminal), and by the 1920s the search in it for a national musical vocabulary was generally abandoned.

BIBLIOGRAPHY

A. Dvořák: "Real Value of Negro Melodies," *New York Herald* (21 May 1893)

——: "Antonín Dvořák on Negro Melodies," *New York Herald* (25 May 1893)

"How Dr. Dvořák gives a Lesson," *New York Herald* (14 Jan 1894), §3, p.5 [mostly interview]; repr., abridged, in *Musical Standard*, new ser., xxxii (17 Feb 1894), 147

A. Dvořák: "Music in America," *Harper's New Monthly Magazine*, xc (1895), 428; repr., abridged, in *Composers on Music*, ed. S. Morgenstern (New York, 1956)

J. M. Thurber: "Dvořák as I knew him," *Etude*, xxxvii (1919), 693

R. Evans: "Dvořák at Spillville," *The Palimpsest*, xi (Iowa City, 1930), 113

H. G. Kinscella: "Dvořák and Spillville, Forty Years After," *MusAm*, liii/10 (1933), 4

J. J. Kovařík: "Dr. Antonín Dvořák," *Kalendář Katolík*, xl (Chicago, 1934), 156

P. Stefan: "Why Dvořák would not return to America," *MusAm*, lviii/4 (1938), 34

A. Robertson: *Dvořák* (London, 1945, rev. 2/1974)

J. Clapham: "The Evolution of Dvořák's Symphony 'From the New World,'" *MQ*, xliv (1958), 167

J. Burghauser: *Antonín Dvořák* (Prague, 1966; Eng. trans., 1967)

J. Clapham: *Antonín Dvořák: Musician and Craftsman* (London, 1966)

——: "Dvořák and the American Indian," *MT*, cvii (1966), 863

——: "Dvořák's Musical Directorship in New York," *ML*, xlviii (1967), 40

——: "Indian Influence in Dvořák's American Chamber Music," *Musica cameralis: Brno VI 1971*, ed. R. Pečman (Brno, 1977), 174 [music exx., 525]

D. Beveridge: "Sophisticated Primitivism: the Significance of Pentatonicism in Dvořák's *American Quartet*," *CMc*, no.24 (1977), 25

J. Clapham: "Dvořák's Musical Directorship in New York: a Postscript," *ML*, lix (1978), 19

——: *Dvořák* (New York, 1979)

——: "Dvořák's Cello Concerto, a Masterpiece in the Making," *MR*, xl (1979), 123

——: "Dvořák on the American Scene," *19th Century Music*, v (1981–2), 16; rev. in *Journal of the Conductors' Guild*, vi/2 (1985), 45

——: "Dvořák's Visit to Worcester, Massachusetts," *Slavonic and Western Music: Essays for Gerald Abraham*, ed. M. H. Brown and R. J. Wiley (Ann Arbor, MI, 1985), 207

——: *Dvořák: Man and Artist* (in preparation)

JOHN CLAPHAM/H. WILEY HITCHCOCK

Dvorsky, Michel. Pseudonym of JOSEF HOFMANN.

Dwight, John Sullivan (*b* Boston, MA, 13 May 1813; *d* Boston, 5 Sept 1893). Writer on music. He began adult life as an intellectual of liberal views but modest capacities, graduating from Harvard College (1832) and Harvard Divinity School (1836). He was an early but largely passive member of the transcendentalist group led by Emerson, Alcott, and the Ripleys. After a brief, unhappy experience as a Unitarian minister, he joined the utopian Brook Farm community in 1841 and became a leading contributor to the Fourierist *Harbinger* (1845–8), where much of his early music criticism appeared.

John Sullivan Dwight: portrait by Caroline Cranch, 1884 (Harvard Musical Association)

He was sole editor of *Dwight's Journal of Music* (Boston, 1852–81), a primary source for the history of music in New England from the earliest orchestral concerts to the founding of the Boston SO. An influential music periodical with an eventual nationwide circulation of over 1500, it included reviews of concerts and new music; extended essays on music history, theory, and education; translations of important French and German works; and musical news and correspondence from across the country and abroad (for illustration of the title page of the first cumulative index *see* PERIODICALS, fig. 1). Among its contributors were William F. Apthorp, George W. Curtis, W. S. B. Mathews, Frédéric Ritter, and Alexander W. Thayer. By far the largest contributor was Dwight, who without formal training in music established his authority as a literary amateur, relying on enthusiasm and an uneven verbal facility. Much concert-going and a journey to Europe in 1860–61 enabled him to write like an informed and dedicated missionary in a field largely unoccupied. He became famous for his devotion to Beethoven, Mozart, and Handel, and for an ever-stiffening resistance to Wagner and other new music. In spite of his limitations, he must be regarded as a music critic of considerable historical importance.

A childless widower after the death of his wife Mary (Bullard) in 1860, Dwight spent his last 20 years as resident librarian and permanent president of the Harvard Musical Association, which sponsored an annual series of concerts, conducted by Carl Zerrahn, under Dwight's management (1865–82).

See also CRITICISM, §3.

WRITINGS

ed.: *Dwight's Journal of Music* (Boston, 1852–81/*R*1968)

"The History of Music in Boston," *The Memorial History of Boston*, iv (Boston, 1881), 415–64

BIBLIOGRAPHY

W. S. B. Mathews, ed.: *A Hundred Years of Music in America* (Chicago, 1889/*R*1970)

G. W. Cooke, ed.: *Early Letters of George William Curtis to John S. Dwight* (New York, 1898)

G. W. Cooke: *John Sullivan Dwight: Brook-Farmer, Editor, and Critic of Music* (Boston, 1898/*R*1969)

E. N. Waters: "John Sullivan Dwight, First American Critic of American Music," *MQ*, xxi (1935), 69

H. McCusker: "Fifty Years of Music in Boston," *More Books: the Bulletin of the Boston Public Library*, xii (1937), 341, 397, 451 [repr. as *Fifty Years of Music in Boston* (Boston, 1938)]

W. L. Fertig: *John Sullivan Dwight, Transcendentalist and Literary Amateur of Music* (diss., U. of Maryland, 1952)

I. Lowens: "A Check-list of Writings about Music in the Periodicals of American Transcendentalism (1835–50)," *Music and Musicians in Early America* (New York, 1964), 311

W. W. Lebow: *A Systematic Examination of the Journal of Music and Art Edited by John Sullivan Dwight* (diss., UCLA, 1969)

B. E. Chmaj: "Fry versus Dwight: American Music's Debate over Nationality," *American Music*, iii/1 (1985), 63

WALTER L. FERTIG

Dwight, Timothy (*b* Northampton, MA, 14 May 1752; *d* New Haven, CT, 11 Jan 1817). Poet and author of hymn texts. He graduated from Yale College in 1769, becoming a tutor there two years later. He served as a chaplain in the Continental Army during the Revolutionary War, and wrote the texts of several patriotic songs, of which *Columbia, Columbia, to glory arise* (1787) became widely popular. From 1783 to 1795 he was pastor of the Congregational Church in Greenfield Hill, Connecticut, where he rose to eminence as a preacher, educator, and poet. He was elected president of Yale College in 1795. In 1798, at the request of both Congregational and Presbyterian governing bodies, he prepared a new revised edition of Isaac Watts's *Psalms and Hymns*, published in Hartford in 1801 as *The Psalms of David*; it became widely known as "Dwight's Watts," and was used throughout New England over the next 30 years. With it Dwight included a selection of hymns, most of which were by Watts and his followers, though some were by Dwight himself. A number of his psalm versifications and hymns were widely circulated in the 19th century, the best-known being "I love thy kingdom, Lord," which is one of the earliest American hymns still in current use.

BIBLIOGRAPHY

F. M. Bird: "Dwight, Timothy," *A Dictionary of Hymnology*, ed. J. Julian (New York, 1892, 2/1907/*R*1957), i, 316

L. F. Benson: "The American Revisions of Watts' Psalms," *Journal of the Presbyterian Historical Society*, ii (1903), 18, 75

H. E. Starr: "Dwight, Timothy," *DAB*

K. Silverman: *Timothy Dwight* (New York, 1969)

PAUL C. ECHOLS

Dwyer, Doriot Anthony (*b* Streator, IL, 6 March 1922). Flutist. She studied privately with Georges Barrère and William Kincaid, and at the Eastman School under Joseph Mariano (1939–43). After graduating, she was second flutist of the National SO and then of the Los Angeles PO (1945–52); she also played first flute in radio studios and Hollywood Bowl concerts. In 1952 she became first flutist of the Boston SO; she was the first woman appointed to a principal position in a major American orchestra and was the Boston SO's only female principal until 1980. Dwyer has appeared as a soloist in the USA and Europe, and also plays with the Boston Symphony Chamber Players; she has given the first performances of works for flute by Piston, Bergsma, and Bernstein, and has made recordings of music by La Montaine, Pinkham, and Piston. She is adjunct professor of music at Boston University. She became the first orchestral player to receive the Sanford Fellowship from the Yale School of Music (1975) and an honorary doctorate from Harvard University (1982).

BIBLIOGRAPHY

P. Estevan: *Talking with Flutists* (n.p., 1976), 47

D. Rosenberg and B. Rosenberg: "Doriot Anthony Dwyer," *The Music Makers* (New York, 1979), 237

BARBARA JEPSON

Dyer, Richard (Morgan) (*b* Mineral Wells, TX, 29 Dec 1941). Music critic. He was educated at Hiram College (BA 1963) and studied English literature at Harvard (MA 1968). He joined the *Boston Globe* in 1973, and in 1976 succeeded Michael Steinberg as the paper's music critic. He won the Deems Taylor Award for music criticism in 1976 and again in 1977. Dyer possesses a felicitous style and responds enthusiastically to music; his chief areas of interest are opera, newer music, and new ideas about music. He has also been active as a teacher, of criticism and of English, the latter as Briggs-Copeland Lecturer at Harvard (1980–84).

PATRICK J. SMITH

Dyett, Walter Henri (*b* St. Joseph, MO, 1 Jan 1901; *d* Chicago, IL, 17 Nov 1969). Music teacher and bandmaster. He learned to play piano and violin as a child, and continued his instrumental studies while taking courses in medicine at UCLA. He began playing professionally in dance orchestras in 1918, and moved to Chicago in 1921, where he was active as a recitalist and chamber musician, and conductor of various ensembles. In 1925 he formed the Pickford Orchestra, which he conducted and for which he also arranged music. He received further musical training in Chicago at the Columbia School of Music, the VanderCook College of Music (BMus 1938), and the Musical College (MMus 1942). Dyett taught at various schools in the city: the Coleridge-Taylor School of Music (1927–31), the Wendell Phillips High School (1931–5), and the Du Sable High School (1935–69). At the last two he also served as bandmaster, in which capacity he influenced the musical education of a generation of black students; his pupils included Nat "King" Cole, Gene Ammons, and Richard Davis.

BIBLIOGRAPHY

SouthernB

DOMINIQUE-RENÉ DE LERMA

Dykema, Peter (William) (*b* Grand Rapids, MI, 25 Nov 1873; *d* Hastings-on-Hudson, NY, 13 May 1951). Music educator. He studied at the University of Michigan (BS 1895, Master of

Law 1896) and, after teaching in high schools in Illinois and Indiana, became music supervisor at the New York Ethical Culture School (1903–13). During his time in New York he studied singing and theory at the Institute of Musical Art (1903–5), and later (1911–12) he was a pupil of Edgar Stillman Kelley in Berlin. In 1913 he was appointed professor of music and chairman of the public school music department at the University of Wisconsin, and from 1924 to 1940 he was professor of music education at Teachers College, Columbia University. Dykema was the first editor of the *Music Supervisors Journal* (1914–21) and is well known for his *Twice 55 Community Song Book* (1919–27). He also produced classroom music series, music education textbooks, numerous articles, and a standardized test in music (with Jacob Kwalwasser). He was very active in the Music Supervisors National Conference and other professional organizations.

BIBLIOGRAPHY

J. W. Beattie: "The Unknown Peter Dykema," *MEJ*, xxxvii/6 (1951), 12
"The Journal's First Editor," *MEJ*, xxxvii (June–July 1951), 12
H. E. Eisenkramer: *Peter William Dykema: his Life and Contribution to Music Education* (EdD diss., U. of Michigan, 1963)

GEORGE N. HELLER

Dylan, Bob [Zimmerman, Robert Allen] (*b* Duluth, MN, 24 May 1941). Folk and rock singer and songwriter. He was the most influential figure in the urban folk-music revival of the 1960s and 1970s, and his lyrics, music, and performing style made an important impact on all types of rock music.

1. Early career: acoustic folk. 2. Later career: electric folk. 3. Influence.

1. EARLY CAREER: ACOUSTIC FOLK. He grew up in Duluth and in Hibbing, Minnesota, where his family moved when he was six years old; his father, Abraham, was an appliance dealer. He taught himself to play guitar, harmonica, and piano, and in high school performed with a rock-and-roll band, the Golden Chords. He attended the University of Minnesota for three semesters in 1959–60, when the folk-music revival was in its ascendancy; he heard recordings by the folksinger Odetta, abandoned the electric guitar in favor of an acoustic instrument, and began playing in coffeehouses as Bob Dylan (his pseudonym was taken from the name of the Welsh poet Dylan Thomas).

In 1961 Dylan went to New York, in part to meet Woody Guthrie – whose music had strongly influenced his own – during his last days. He started to perform in Greenwich Village, where he attracted attention for his versions of Guthrie's songs and for his own traditionalist songs; these were rendered in a "talking blues" style, characterized by spoken, irregular lines, accompanied by strummed guitar chords and interspersed with simple, keening harmonica solos (he supported the harmonica on a rack round his neck). He encouraged rumors that he was an orphan from the Southwest who was partly of American-Indian descent. By the end of 1961 he had received favorable reviews and had signed a recording contract with CBS Records through John Hammond, who had also signed Billie Holiday and Aretha Franklin. His first album, *Bob Dylan* (1962), contained only two of his own songs, one of them *Song to Woody*. His aggressive delivery showed Guthrie's influence, and that of the blues (Leadbelly, Blind Willie McTell, Big Joe Williams, Sonny Terry, Brownie McGhee), country music (Hank Williams, Jimmie Rodgers), and rock-and-roll (Buddy Holly, Chuck Berry, Bo Diddley, Elvis Presley).

The Freewheelin' Bob Dylan (1963) revealed his gift for oracular imagery in such songs as *A hard rain's a-gonna fall*, *Masters of War*, and *Blowin' in the wind*, and for surrealistic narrative in *I shall be free* and *Bob Dylan's Dream*. His harsh, nasal singing style was often criticized, but his songs were taken up by other musicians, such as Peter, Paul and Mary (whose version of *Blowin' in the wind* reached no. 1 in 1963), and Joan Baez, with whom he toured and had a widely publicized liaison. As his songs achieved popularity Dylan became the acknowledged leader of the protest-song movement of the early 1960s, and several of his works became associated with the civil rights cause. In 1963 he was scheduled to appear on Ed Sullivan's television program, but canceled the engagement when he was forbidden to sing his *Talking John Birch Society Blues*, which dealt with the far-right-wing organization. *The Times they Are a-Changin'* (1964) included a number of straightforward protest songs, but Dylan soon felt confined by the role of protest singer, and, with the pointedly titled *Another Side of Bob Dylan* (1964), he turned to more personal lyrics. At the same time his public pronouncements grew more cryptic; *Don't Look Back*, a documentary film (directed by D. A. Pennebaker) of his first British tour, shows a young man who is by turns playful, arrogant, and immersed in the frenzy that surrounds him.

2. LATER CAREER: ELECTRIC FOLK. *Bringing it All Back Home* (1965) represented a breakthrough in Dylan's recording career: one side consists of electric blues with fantastic lyrics (*Subterranean Homesick Blues*, *Bob Dylan's 115th Dream*), the other of visionary songs accompanied by acoustic guitar (*Mr. Tambourine Man*, *Gates of Eden*). On this album, and on *Highway 61 Revisited* (1965) and *Blonde on Blonde* (1966), he used blues and folk forms, but his lyrics and singing, and the intense performances of his backing group, belonged unmistakably to rock; indeed, these recordings represent one of the artistic peaks of rock music. Like all his albums until *Slow Train Coming* (1979), they were recorded live, without overdubbing (a studio technique that allows vocal parts and each instrument to be recorded separately). In 1965 the Byrds' arrangement of *Mr. Tambourine Man* with electric instruments became the first folk-rock hit single. On 25 July 1965 Dylan appeared at the Newport Folk Festival playing electric guitar and backed by members of the Paul Butterfield Blues Band; this angered many members of the audience, who felt he had abandoned folk music. At the same time his *Like a rolling stone* (from *Highway 61 Revisited*) reached no. 2 on the chart – his first single to get into the Top Ten – as did *Rainy Day Women no.12 & 35* in 1966. By this time he had married Sara Lowndes (Shirley Nozniski), who was later the subject of his song *Sara* (1975); during this period he also wrote a raving, epistolary novel, *Tarantula*, which was published in 1966.

On 29 July 1966 Dylan sustained a motorcycle accident that nearly cost him his life. He disappeared from public view, and while recuperating in Woodstock, New York, he wrote and, with his backing musicians, recorded a number of songs that were later issued on the album *The Basement Tapes* (1975); the backing group began performing and recording on its own as The Band. Dylan returned to the stage in 1968 at a concert in honor of Woody Guthrie. He also resumed his recording career in that year with *John Wesley Harding*, which was notable for the spareness of its arrangements and Dylan's understated delivery in such songs as *All Along the Watchtower*; the country style of *I'll be your baby tonight* was further explored on *Nashville Skyline* (1969), which consisted of songs to comparatively straightforward lyrics, sung in a deeper, more relaxed voice, and accompanied by session musicians who usually played for country-music singers. *Nashville Skyline*, one of the first country-rock albums, was the last of Dylan's recordings to have a strong impact on rock music; it included the hit single *Lay Lady Lay*. His later work was of a less consistently high quality than that of the 1960s, although it did have inspired moments.

For much of the 1970s Dylan seemed to be retracing his steps. He wrote a few songs with George Harrison of the Beatles (including *If not for you*) and sang to acoustic guitar accompaniment at Harrison's benefit concert for Bangladesh in 1970. *Self-portrait* (1970) was a collection of material by other songwriters; *New Morning* (1970), which used arrangements derived from gospel and focused on the piano, was vigorous but unexceptional. In 1971 he recorded a protest song, *George Jackson*, and in the early 1970s worked as a backing musician for Roger McGuinn of the Byrds, the singer Steve Goodman, and the country-rock performer Doug Sahm; he was also a co-producer of an album recorded in 1973 by the keyboard player Barry Goldberg. In 1972 he wrote the score for, and acted in, Sam Peckinpah's film *Pat Garrett and Billy the Kid*; the soundtrack included a hit single, *Knockin' on heaven's door*. He reunited with The Band in 1974 to record *Planet Waves*, and to make a successful tour that resulted in a live album, *Before the Flood* (1974). *Blood on the Tracks* (1974), an album of uneven quality, was a return to the sound of his bands of the mid-1960s. *Desire* (1975), for which he wrote some songs in collaboration with the dramatist Jacques Levy, showed the influence of the Egyptian singer Om Kalsoum.

In 1975 Dylan returned to the folk-music venues of Greenwich Village and began playing with Jack Elliott (a follower of Woody Guthrie), Joan Baez, and others. This group eventually became the Rolling Thunder Revue, a loosely organized, unpredictable touring ensemble. Originally planned as an unpretentious variety show with different performers for every engagement, the group's tour began with a concert before 200 listeners in Plymouth, Massachusetts, and culminated with performances in large arenas, one of which was broadcast as an NBC television program, "Hard Rain"; scenes from these concerts were later included in *Renaldo and Clara* (1978), a four-hour film directed by Dylan. The best-known song from the tour was *Hurricane*, a protest about the murder conviction of the boxer Rubin "Hurricane" Carter.

In 1977 Dylan's wife filed for divorce. The following year he recorded *Street Legal*, another muddled attempt to recapture the sound of his bands of the 1960s; he then embarked on a world tour, on which he performed rewritten, more relaxed versions of his songs and wore clothes that recalled the late appearances in Las Vegas of Elvis Presley. Dylan's most controversial change of direction since the 1960s came in 1979 when he announced that he had become a fundamentalist Christian. Although he had used religious images in his songs throughout his career, *Slow Train Coming* (1979), *Saved* (1980), and *Shot of Love* (1981) presented overt images of a wrathful, apocalyptic Jesus, as well as clichéd gospel-song lyrics. Dylan won his first Grammy Award for *You gotta serve somebody* from *Slow Train Coming*. His next album, *Infidels* (1983), contained no explicit religious message – in fact its lyrics are deliberately equivocal. Produced by the English songwriter Mark Knopfler, a member of the group Dire Straits, it featured a rhythm section of reggae musicians, Sly Dunbar playing drums and Robbie Shakespeare bass guitar. Dylan used a similar group on *Empire Burlesque* (1985), an album on which he sang more love-songs and made fewer pronouncements.

3. Influence. There has been more critical attention paid to Dylan's lyrics than to those of any other folk, rock, or pop singer; in them commentators have found autobiography, parables, prophecies, wordplay, and doggerel. Perhaps because of their elusive, abstract quality, they have proved lasting, and have been quoted in many contexts (a radical political group, the Weathermen, took its name from a phrase in *Subterranean Homesick Blues*, and an excerpt from one of Dylan's texts was used by President Jimmy Carter in his inaugural address). Dylan's literary gifts, which did much to raise the standard of rock lyrics, have tended to overshadow his music, which may prove to have the greater influence. Like Chuck Berry, Presley, and the Beatles, Dylan successfully integrated folk and popular elements from black and white musical traditions to create a sound that was distinctive and personal. Each of his stylistic changes in the 1960s gave rise to a new genre of popular music: first the confessional song, then folk-rock, and finally country-rock; his willingness to experiment

Bob Dylan

with different styles of singing and instrumentation encouraged other singers to do so as well. His grainy, unpolished voice and conversational delivery had a profound effect on popular music, and his phrasing, especially on his recordings from 1965–6, was spontaneous and unpredictable; in the song *Memphis Blues Again* (from the album *Blonde on Blonde*, 1966), for example, even a short phrase like "Oh mama" is never sung twice in the same way. Among the singers who have been influenced by Dylan are Lou Reed, Roger McGuinn, Bruce Springsteen, Elvis Costello, David Bowie, Tom Petty, and Rod Stewart. His songs were performed by Hendrix (*All Along the Watchtower*), Eric Clapton (*Knockin' on heaven's door*), Stevie Wonder (*Blowin' in the wind*), and Bryan Ferry (*A hard rain's a-gonna fall*), among others. As a public figure Dylan taught a generation of performers how to manipulate the mass media. Several collections of his songs, writings, and drawings have been published, including *Writings and Drawings by Bob Dylan* (1973) and *The Songs of Bob Dylan, 1966–1975* (1976).

See also POPULAR MUSIC, §IV, 3.

RECORDINGS

(selective list; all recorded for Columbia unless otherwise indicated)

Bob Dylan (PC8579, 1962); *The Freewheelin' Bob Dylan* (JC8786, 1963); *Another Side of Bob Dylan* (PC8993, 1964); *The Times they Are a-Changin'* (PC8905, 1964); *Bringing it All Back Home* (JC9128, 1965); *Highway 61 Revisited* (JC9189, 1965); *Blonde on Blonde* (C2S841, 1966); *John Wesley Harding* (JC9604, 1968); *Nashville Skyline* (JC9825, 1969); *New Morning* (PC30290, 1970); *Self-portrait* (P2X30050, 1970); George Jackson (45516, 1971); *Pat Garrett and Billy the Kid* (PC32460, 1974); *Planet Waves* (Asylum 7E-1003, 1974)

Before the Flood (Asylum AB-201, 1974); *Blood on the Tracks* (JC33235, 1974); *The Basement Tapes* (C2-33682, 1975); *Desire* (JC33893, 1975); *Hard Rain* (PC34349, 1976); *Street Legal* (JC35453, 1978); *Dylan Live at Budokan* (PC2-36067, 1979); *Slow Train Coming* (FC36120, 1979); *Saved* (FC36553, 1980); *Shot of Love* (TC37496, 1981); *Infidels* (QC38819, 1983); *Empire Burlesque* (FC40110, 1985)

BIBLIOGRAPHY

"Dylan, Bob," *CBY 1965*

A. Rémond: *Les chemins de Bob Dylan* (Paris, 1971)

M. Gray: *Song & Dance Man: the Art of Bob Dylan* (London, 1972)

C. McGregor, ed.: *Bob Dylan: a Retrospective* (London, 1972)

A. Scaduto: *Bob Dylan* (New York, 1972)

P. Marchbank, ed.: *Bob Dylan in his Own Words* (New York, 1978)

C. Summer: "The Ballad of Dylan and Bob," *Southwest Review*, lxvi/1 (1981), 41

E. Willis: *Beginning to See the Light* (New York, 1981), 3

B. Bowden: *Performed Literature: Words and Music by Bob Dylan* (Bloomington, IN, 1982)

J. Henderson: *Voice Without Restraint: a Study of Bob Dylan's Lyrics and their Background* (New York, 1982)

J. Cott: *Dylan* (Garden City, NY, 1984)

W. Mellers: *A Darker Shade of Pale* (New York, 1985)

JON PARELES

Illustration Acknowledgments

We are grateful to those listed below, who have supplied illustrative material, or given permission for it to be reproduced, or both: where two or more names are given, separated by a spaced slash (/), the name given first is usually that of the supplier of the illustration, who may or may not be the copyright holder; names of photographers are given wherever possible, preceded by "photo." Every effort has been made to contact copyright holders and we apologize to anyone whose name may have been omitted from this list. Where an illustration is taken from a book or article out of copyright, the title and place and date of publication are given here unless they appear in the caption to the illustration. The names of contributors (though they are not necessarily the contributors of the articles for which they have supplied illustrations) are preceded by a double dagger sign; their last known places of work or residence are given in the List of Contributors at the end of Volume 4.

Abravanel, Maurice Utah Symphony, Salt Lake City, UT

Adams, John ‡John Adams / photo Roy H. Williams, *Oakland Tribune*, Oakland, CA

Adler, Larry Popperfoto, London, England

Afro-American music *1* Abby Aldrich Rockefeller Folk Art Collection, Colonial Williamsburg Foundation, Williamsburg, VA; *2* Schomburg Center for Research in Black Culture, New York Public Library (Astor, Lenox and Tilden Foundations), New York; *3, 4* Music Division, Library of Congress (*4* National Negro Opera Company Collection), Washington, DC; *5* Wide World Photos, Inc., New York

Allen, Henry "Red" Jazz Music Books, Middleton-on-Sea, West Sussex, England

Allman Brothers Band photo David Redfern, London, England

Amirkhanian, Charles ‡Charles Amirkhanian / photo Carol Law, Arts Plural, El Cerrito, CA

Anderson, Laurie Warner Bros. Records, Inc., New York / photo Michael O'Brien

Anderson, Marian Metropolitan Opera Archives, New York / photo Sedge LeBlang, New York

Antheil, George *1, 2, 3* ‡Charles Amirkhanian / *(1)* Collection of Olga Rudge, *(2)* photo Karl Bauermann, *(3)* photo William Claxton

Apache Arizona State Museum, University of Arizona, Tucson, AZ / photo Helga Teiwes

Appalachian dulcimer University of Oregon Library (Doris Ulmann Collection), Eugene, OR

Arapaho National Anthropological Archives, Smithsonian Institution, Washington, DC / photo George A. Dorse

Arlen, Harold Theatre Collection, Museum of the City of New York, New York

Armstrong, Louis Camera Press Ltd., London, England

Ashley, Robert Performing Artservices, Inc., New York / photo Gwen Thomas

Asian-American music *1* photo ‡Nora Yeh; *2* photo ‡Amy Ruth Catlin; *3* ‡Ricardo D. Trimillos / Kalilang Ensemble, San Francisco, CA / photo Allen Nomura

Astaire, Fred Academy of Motion Picture Arts and Sciences, Beverly Hills, CA / copyright RKO Pictures, Inc., New York (© renewed 1963)

Autry, Gene Country Music Foundation, Inc., Nashville, TN

Ayler, Albert photo Hans Harzheim, Düsseldorf, Germany (BRD)

Babbitt, Milton *1* Camera Press Ltd., London, England / photo Vytas Valaitis; *2* Milton Babbitt and John Hollander, C. F. Peters Corporation, New York (© 1983), reproduced by permission of Peters Edition, London and New York

Baez, Joan photo David Redfern, London, England

Baker, Josephine Alexander Calder: *Josephine Baker* (iron-wire construction, 99 × 56.6 × 24.5 cm, 1927–9), Collection, Museum of Modern Art, New York, gift of the artist

Ballad opera American Antiquarian Society, Worcester, MA

Baltimore *1* Peale Museum, Baltimore, MD; *2* Baltimore Symphony Orchestra, Baltimore

Band, The Michael Ochs Archive, Venice, CA

Bands *2* Prints and Photographs Division, Library of Congress, Washington, DC; *3* Smithsonian Institution (photo no.74-3394), Washington; *4* University of Michigan Bands, Ann Arbor, MI

Banjo *1a, b* Smithsonian Institution (photo nos.76-13994, 76-13992), Washington, DC; *2* Bettmann Archive, Inc., New York

Barber, Samuel *1* World, Inc., New York / photo *Saturday Review*; *2* Music Division, Library of Congress, Washington, DC / G. Schirmer, Inc., New York

Bartók, Béla G. D. Hackett, New York

Basie, Count Jazz Music Books, Middleton-on-Sea, West Sussex, England

Battle music Boston Public Library, Boston, MA

Beach, Amy Marcy *1* Music Division, Library of Congress, Washington, DC; *2* Special Collections, University of New Hampshire Library, Durham, NH

Beach Boys Capitol Records, Inc., Hollywood, CA

Beardslee, Bethany Bethany Beardslee, New York / Sheldon Soffer Management, Inc., New York / photo James Graves

Beaux Arts Trio Columbia Artists Management, Inc., New York
Bechet, Sidney Max Jones, Middleton-on-Sea, West Sussex, England
Becker, John J. ‡Don C. Gillespie
Bellringing University of Kansas, Lawrence, KS
Berlin, Irving Stills Collection, National Film Archive, London, England / copyright 1948 Loew's Inc., renewed 1975 Metro-Goldwyn-Mayer Inc., Culver City, CA
Bernstein, Leonard *1* Music Division, Library of Congress, Washington, DC / Leonard Bernstein and Stephen Sondheim, G. Schirmer, Inc., and Chappell Music, New York; *2* Curtis Institute of Music, Philadelphia, PA
Berry, Chuck photo David Redfern, London, England
Bethune, Thomas Prints and Photographs Division, Library of Congress, Washington, DC
Biggs, E. Power Mrs. E. Power Biggs, Cambridge, MA
Billings, William William L. Clements Library, University of Michigan, Ann Arbor, MI
Bing, Rudolf *Opera News*, New York
Blackfoot (i) Minnesota Historical Society, St. Paul, MN / photo A. B. Coe, Kipp, MT
Blake, Eubie Eileen Southern Collection, Cambria Heights, NY
Blitzstein, Marc Mrs. Edward Davis, Philadelphia, PA / Estate of Marc Blitzstein
Bloch, Ernest G. Schirmer, Inc., New York
Bluegrass music Country Music Foundation, Inc., Nashville, TN
Blues *1–4* Paul Oliver Collection, Woodstock, England; *5* photo Paul Oliver, Woodstock
Boston (i) *1* Österreichische Nationalbibliothek, Vienna, Austria; *2, 5* Boston Symphony Orchestra, Inc., Boston, MA; *3* Handel and Haydn Society, Boston; *4* photo Peter Schweitzer, Cambridge, MA
Brant, Henry Henry Brant / photo Amy Snyder
Broadcasting *1* KDKA Radio 1020, Pittsburgh, PA; *2* Popperfoto, London, England
Brombaugh, John John Brombaugh & Associates, Inc., Eugene, OR
Broonzy, Big Bill *Jazz Journal*, London, England
Brown, Clifford *Jazz Journal*, London, England
Brown, Earle *1* Music Associates of Aspen, Inc., Aspen, CO, and New York / photo Charles Abbott, New York; *2* Earle Brown and Associated Music Publishers, Inc., New York
Brown, James Pop Record Research, Ossining, NY
Brubeck, Dave *Jazz Journal*, London, England / photo Marc Sharratt, London
Buchla, Donald Buchla Associates, Berkeley, CA
Buffalo Kleinhans Music Hall, Buffalo, NY

Cage, John *1* Peters Edition Ltd., London, England / photo James Klosty, Millbrook, NY; *2* Performing Artservices, Inc., New York; *3* Henmar Press, Inc., New York (© 1960), reproduced by permission of Peters Edition, London and New York
Caldwell, Sarah Metropolitan Opera Archives, New York
Callas, Maria Stuart-Liff Collection, Port Erin, Isle of Man / photo Foto-Semo, Mexico City, Mexico
Cannon, Gus Val Wilmer/Format, London, England
Carmichael, Hoagy John Edward Hasse Collection, Alexandria, VA / Mitchell Parish and Hoagy Carmichael / copyright Mills Music, Inc., (© 1929, renewed 1957)
Carter, Elliott *1* Associated Music Publishers, Inc., New York; *2* Music Division, Library of Congress, Washington, DC / Associated Music Publishers, Inc., New York
Carter Family Country Music Foundation, Inc., Nashville, TN
Caruso, Enrico *Opera News*, New York
Cash, Johnny Country Music Foundation, Inc., Nashville, TN
Castle, Vernon Brown Brothers, Sterling, PA
Chadwick, George Whitefield *1* ‡Victor Fell Yellin; *2* Music Division, Library of Congress, Washington, DC
Chamber music *2* Music Division, Library of Congress (Elizabeth Sprague Coolidge Foundation Collection), Washington, DC
Chamber Music Society of Lincoln Center Alix B. Williamson, New York / photo James Houghton
Charles, Ray Pop Record Research, Ossining, NY
Charleston (i) South Carolina Historical Society, Charleston, SC
Charleston (ii) Culver Pictures, Inc., New York
Chautauqua and lyceum ‡Frederick Crane
Cherry, Don photo Hans Harzheim, Düsseldorf, Germany (BRD)
Chicago (i) *1* Chicago Symphony Orchestra, Chicago, IL; *3* Max Jones, Middleton-on-Sea, West Sussex, England; *4* photo Paul Oliver, Woodstock, England
Chicken scratch ‡J. Richard Haefer / photo Jim Griffith, Tucson, AZ
Choral music *1* Connecticut Historical Society, Hartford, CT; *2* Eileen Southern Collection, Cambria Heights, NY
Christy, Edwin Pearce Music Division, Library of Congress, Washington, DC
Church of Jesus Christ of Latter-day Saints, music of the ‡Roger L. Miller / Corporation of the President of the Church of Jesus Christ of Latter-day Saints, Salt Lake City, UT
Cincinnati *1* Library of Congress, Washington, DC; *2* Cincinnati Symphony Orchestra, Cincinnati, OH
Circus music Circus World Museum, Baraboo, WI
Cleveland Cleveland Orchestra, Cleveland, OH
Cleveland, James L. Times Newspapers Ltd., London, England
Coci, Claire Phillip LaBerge, Concord, MA
Cohan, George M. ‡Stephen M. Fry / US Postal Service, Washington, DC
Coleman, Ornette photo David Redfern, London, England
Collins, Judy Boston Symphony Orchestra, Inc., Boston, MA
Computers and music Experimental Music Studio, Massachusetts Institute of Technology, Cambridge, MA / photo Jim Harrison, Charlestown, MA
Condon, Eddie David Redfern Photography, London, England / photo William Gottlieb
Confederate music Special Collections Department, Robert W. Woodruff Library, Emory University, Atlanta, GA
Cooke, Sam photo Lloyd Yearwood, New York
Coolidge, Elizabeth Sprague Library of Congress (Irving Lowens Collection), Washington, DC
Coon song John Edward Hasse Collection, Alexandria, VA
Copland, Aaron *1* CBS Records, London, England / photo Julian Hann; *2* Music Division, Library of Congress (Elizabeth Sprague Coolidge Foundation Collection), Washington, DC; *3* Aaron Copland and Boosey & Hawkes, Inc., New York
Country music Country Music Foundation, Inc., Nashville, TN
Courting flute *1* Museum of the American Indian (Heye Foundation), New York; *2* Brian and Constance Dear, after ‡Mary Riemer-Weller
Cowell, Henry *1* Associated Music Publishers, Inc., New York; *2* Music Division, Library of Congress, Washington, DC / Associated Music Publishers, Inc., New York
Crawford, Ruth ‡Matilda Gaume / Estate of Carl Crawford
Criticism Music Division, New York Public Library at Lincoln Center (Astor, Lenox and Tilden Foundations), New York
Crosby, Stills and Nash photo David Redfern, London, England
Crow Museum of the American Indian (Heye Foundation), New York / photo William Wildschut
Crumb, George C. F. Peters Corporation, New York, reproduced by permission of Peters Edition, London, England, and New York
Cunningham, Merce Cunningham Dance Foundation, Inc., New York / photo Jack Mitchell, New York

Dallas Dallas Opera, Dallas, TX
Dance *2* Mansell Collection, London, England; *3* photo Martha Swope, New York; *4* photo Barbara Morgan, Scarsdale, New York; *5* Nikolais Dance Theatre, New York / photo Susan Schiff Faludi; *6* Popperfoto, London, England

Davies, Dennis Russell St. Paul Chamber Orchestra, St. Paul, MN
Davis, Miles photo David Redfern, London, England
DeGaetani, Jan Music Associates of Aspen, Inc., Aspen, CO, and New York / photo Charles Abbott, New York
Del Tredici, David Boosey & Hawkes, Inc., New York (© 1979), reproduced by permission of Boosey & Hawkes Music Publishers Ltd., London, England
Denver *1* ‡Sanford A. Linscome / photo Mile-High Photo; *2* Denver Public Library, Western History Department, Denver, CO
Detroit Pop Record Research, Ossining, NY
Dett, R. Nathaniel Eileen Southern Collection, Cambria Heights, NY
Diamond, David David Diamond, Rochester, NY / photo J. Petticrew
Dixie Hummingbirds photo Lloyd Yearwood, New York
Dixon, Dean Music Division, Library of Congress, Washington, DC
Dlugoszewski, Lucia Center for Integrative Education, New Rochelle, NY, from *Main Currents in Modern Thought*, xxx/1 (Sept–Oct 1973)
Domino, Fats Pop Record Research, Ossining, NY
Doors WEA Records, London, England / photo Paul Ferrara
Dorsey, Thomas A. John Edward Hasse Collection, Alexandria, VA
Dorsey, Tommy *Jazz Journal*, London, England
Druckman, Jacob Boosey & Hawkes, Inc., New York
Duncan, Isadora Dance Collection, New York Public Library at Lincoln Center (Astor, Lenox and Tilden Foundations), New York
Dwight, John Sullivan Harvard Musical Association, Harvard University, Cambridge, MA
Dylan, Bob CBS Records, London, England

Music Example Acknowledgments

We are grateful to music publishers, and others, as listed below, for permission to reproduce copyrighted material. Every effort has been made to trace copyright holders and we apologize to anyone whose name may have been omitted from this list.

Armstrong, Louis *3* © 1928 Clarence Williams Music Pub. Co. Inc., USA, by permission of EMI Music Publishing Ltd., London, England
Babbitt, Milton *3, 4* © 1972 C. F. Peters Corporation, New York, by permission of Peters Edition Ltd., London, England; *5* Boelke-Bomart Publications, Hackensack, NJ; *6* Lawson-Gould Music Publishers, Inc., New York
Cherokee *1* Oklahoma Historical Society, Oklahoma City, OK
Coltrane, John *1, 2* Andrew's Musical Enterprises, Inc., Washington, DC, by permission of *Annual Review of Jazz Studies*, New Brunswick, NJ
Copland, Aaron Boosey & Hawkes Music Publishers Ltd., London, England